DAGESH

URDAN

URDAN Industries Ltd.

A MEMBER OF THE CAL GROUP

NOTION GNIHCNITION CONVERSION/BREECHING EQUIPMENT
BALLISTIC PROTECTION
BALLISTIC SUSPENSION CONVERSION & BREECHING EQUIPMENT
TANK ASSAULT SPARE PARTS

For additional info

NATANYA, Telex: UASF-341822

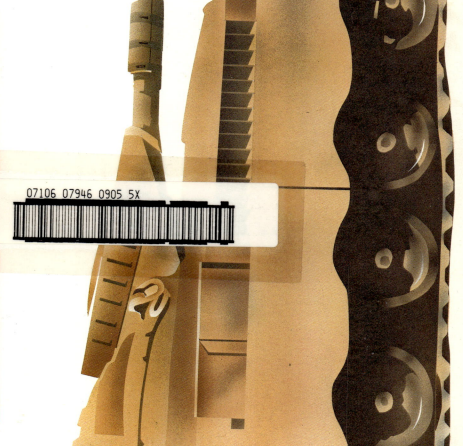

"TURN-KEY" SHELTER SYSTEMS

MEDICAL/SURGICAL CENTERS
TELECOMMUNICATION CENTERS
COMMAND POST
WORKSHOPS

SWISEL MILITARY APPLICATIONS

MECHANICS

POWER SUPPLY UNITS

SWISEL

SWISEL ITALIANA SPA
FIELD - ITALY

THE NEW LAND ROVER ONE TEN

Formed in 1925 to fulfil the increasing demand for emergency service vehicles, Pilcher-Greene pioneered the development of specialist mobiles. Today Pilcher-Greene continues this lead with the building and conversion of all types of vehicles from the smallest cross country ambulance or fire fighting appliance to the largest mobile operating theatre. Designed for use in the most demanding of situations throughout the world, Pilcher-Greene vehicles meet the needs of those whose work takes them into difficult terrain and varying climates.

Pilcher-Greene is first again in introducing a range of ambulances and fire appliances based on the new Land Rover One Ten. Features include coil spring suspension and wider track, giving greater ride comfort, plus additional width and 25% greater vision. All vehicles can be equipped with a wide range of equipment, and air conditioning is available as one of the many optional extras. Pilcher-Greene specialises in meeting the individual specifications of each customer.

Bodywork approved by Land Rover Limited.

PILCHER-GREENE LIMITED, Consort Way, Burgess Hill, West Sussex RH15 9NA.
Tel: Burgess Hill 5707/9. Telex: 877102 Cables: Ambulap Burgess Hill.

[3]

Alphabetical list of advertisers

ALPHABETICAL LIST OF ADVERTISERS

Classified list of advertisers

The companies advertising in this publication have informed us that they are involved in the fields of manufacture indicated below:

Air conditioning/ventilation/heating and refrigeration
Defense NBC

Ambulances
Pilcher-Greene

Ammunition (tank and artillery)
BMY

Amphibious armoured cars (air-droppable)
Creusot-Loire
Dowty Hydraulic Units
Emergency One
FIAT Veicoli

Amphibious armoured personnel cars
(air-droppable)
Creusot-Loire
Emergency One
FIAT Veicoli

Amphibious bridges
CNIM
Dowty Hydraulic Units
Laird (Anglesey)

Amphibious personnel cars
Dowty Hydraulic Units
Emergency One

Amphibious trucks
Dowty Hydraulic Units
ENASA Pegaso
FIAT Veicoli

Armoured bridgelayers
BMY
Creusot-Loire

Armoured fighting vehicles and personnel carriers
Creusot-Loire
Dowty Hydraulic Units
Emergency One
FIAT Veicoli
GKN Sankey
MAN
OTO Melara
Steyr-Daimler-Puch

Armoured recovery vehicles
BMY
Creusot-Loire
GKN Sankey
MAN
Napco Industries
Steyr-Daimler-Puch

Associated equipment including bridging boats
Dowty Hydraulic Units
Laird (Anglesey)

Atmosphere sampling systems
Defense NBC

Bonded rubber to metal articles
BMY

Brakes & braking systems
A P Precision Hydraulics

Bridge laying systems
A P Precision Hydraulics
BMY
Creusot-Loire
Dowty Hydraulic Units
Laird (Anglesey)

Bridging craft
Dowty Hydraulic Units
Laird (Anglesey)

Bridging systems
BMY
CNIM
Dowty Hydraulic Units
Laird (Anglesey)

Bulldozer power equipment
A P Precision Hydraulics

Bulldozers
J I Case
Napco Industries

Cable winches and lifting gear
Rotzler

Camouflage equipment
Defense NBC

Cargo handling equipment
LancerBoss Lift Trucks

Cargo trucks
ENASA Pegaso

Chemical detectors
Defense NBC

Construction equipment
J I Case
Napco Industries

Container handling equipment
J I Case
LancerBoss Lift Trucks

Cranes
Creusot-Loire
Napco Industries

Cranes—mounted on military vehicles
ISOLI

Decontamination containers
Alfred Kärcher

Decontamination trailers
Alfred Kärcher

Decontamination vehicles
Alfred Kärcher

Detection equipment
Defense NBC

Diesel engines
Bombardier
Land Rover

Diggers
J I Case
Napco Industries

Electrical systems for fighting vehicles
Bradley Electronics

Electronic detection devices
Electronique Serge Dassault

Electronic test equipment
Bradley Electronics

Engines
Land Rover

Escape hoods (fire protection equipment)
Sekur

Excavators
J I Case
Napco Industries

Filter units
Sekur

Fire appliances
Pilcher-Greene

Fork-lift trucks
J I Case
LancerBoss Lift Trucks
Napco Industries

Gearbox controllers
A P Precision Hydraulics

Gears and gearboxes
Land Rover

Generating equipment
Dale Electric of Great Britain

High mobility vehicles
Laird (Anglesey)
LancerBoss Lift Trucks
MAN

Hydraulic controls/systems
A P Precision Hydraulics

Intruder detection
Defense NBC

Jeeps and Land-Rover type vehicles
Bombardier
Napco Industries
Pilcher-Greene

Land-Rover type vehicles
Land Rover
Pilcher-Greene

Levelling/lifting jacks for use with bridges and pontoons
A P Precision Hydraulics

Light patrol boats
Dowty Hydraulic Units

Light transport vehicles
Bombardier
Land Rover
MAN
Napco Industries

Light utility vehicles
Bombardier
Land Rover

Liquid-logistic systems
Uniroyal

Loaders
J I Case
Napco Industries

Military trucks
Astra
Bombardier
Laird (Anglesey)
MAN

Mine detectors
Guartel

Minelayers (including helicopter mounted)
Creusot-Loire
Misar
Tecnovar

Mines
PRB
Tecnovar

[8]

CLASSIFIED LIST OF ADVERTISERS

Mine warfare equipment
Misar
PRB
Tecnovar

Mobile field hospitals
Laird (Anglesey)
Land Rover

Mobile kitchens
Alfred Kärcher

Mobile workshop units
Laird (Anglesey)
Land Rover
Steyr-Daimler-Puch
Swisel Italiana

Modular float
Laird (Anglesey)

Multi-purpose military vehicles
ISOLI

Munitions and ordnance
PRB
SMI

NBC decontamination equipment
Alfred Kärcher

NBC equipment
BMY
Defense NBC

NBC protective clothing
James North and Sons
Sekur

On/off highway vehicles
Bombardier
Emergency One
Laird (Anglesey)
MAN

Petrol engines
Land Rover

Pontoon bridges
CNIM
Dowty Hydraulic Units
Laird (Anglesey)

Portable roadways
Laird (Anglesey)

Power engineering units distribution systems
Swisel Italiana

Power packs for armoured fighting vehicles
A P Precision Hydraulics

Rapid runway repair equipment
Laird (Anglesey)

Recovery equipment
BMY
Creusot-Lore
Defense NBC
FARID
Napco Industries
Steyr-Daimler-Puch

Recovery equipment & controls
A P Precision Hydraulics

Respirators
Defense NBC

Respiratory protection
James North & Sons
Sekur

Road wheels
GKN Sankey

Rubber collapsible tanks
Sekur

Rubber safety fuel tanks
Sekur

Shelters and containers (fabric)
Defense NBC

Shelters and containers (including communication containers)
Defense NBC
Swisel Italiana

Specialist vehicle builders
Emergency One
Laird (Anglesey)
Pilcher-Greene

Steering controls
A P Precision Hydraulics

Storage shelters
Defense NBC
Modus Accommodation
Swisel Italiana

Support vehicles
Bombardier
GKN Sankey
Laird (Anglesey)
Land Rover
MAN

Tank fighters
Steyr-Daimler-Puch

Tanks
Creusot-Loire
Steyr-Daimler-Puch

Technical assistance (operational and maintenance: tank and artillery)
COFRAS

Telescopic all-terrain cranes
Creusot-Loire

Tracked cargo carriers
Bombardier
Laird (Anglesey)

Track links
Creusot-Loire

Track shoes
BMY
GKN Sankey

Tractors
J I Case
LancerBoss Lift Trucks
MAN

Trailers of all types
Alfred Kärcher
Cometto
Creusot-Loire
GKN Sankey
PRB

Training aids
COFRAS

Transporters/mobilisers for shelters, containers and pallets
MAN

Transport vehicles
Bombardier
Cometto
Land Rover
MAN

Truck-mounted bridges
CNIM

Trucks and variants
ASTRA
Bombardier
FIAT Veicoli
MAN
Napco Industries
Steyr-Daimler-Puch

Vehicles—military
Land Rover

Vehicles—military (track and wheel)
Bombardier
Creusot-Loire
Emergency One
GKN Sankey
Laird (Anglesey)
MAN
Pilcher-Greene
Steyr-Daimler-Puch

One step forward.

More than 10.000 of the new generation of tactical vehicles have proved themselves in the services. With outstanding performance and reliability. Day by day. In extreme environment.

Now there is an improved generation of M.A.N. vehicles. With increased performance and M.A.N. engines even more powerful and economical. From 177 KW (240 hp) to 268 KW (365 hp). With tilt cab. As 4 x 4, 6 x 6, or 8 x 8 versions. And in four models: as cargo truck, tractor, multi-purpose systems carrier, and as recovery vehicle. For rugged conditions.

The overall height has been reduced so that the vehicle is capable of being airlifted. And the larger tyres make for optimal mobility in rough terrain. Thus this new generation of tactical vehicles meets the demands of the services better than ever before.

So do the Category III high mobility trucks of M.A.N. And the cross-country vehicles from a joint M.A.N. and Volkswagen venture.

That is what M.A.N. understands as progress, which moves a step forward.

M.A.N.-Category III
Typ 20.280 DFAEG

M.A.N./Volkswagen
Typ 9.136 FAE

M·A·N

THE NAME FOR TRUCKS AND BUSES

TECNOVAR DAT SYSTEM IN ANY SKY FROM ANY KIND OF HELICOPTER

1 Rapid deployment of a minefield, when and where needed.

Capability to deploy minefields in enemy territory.

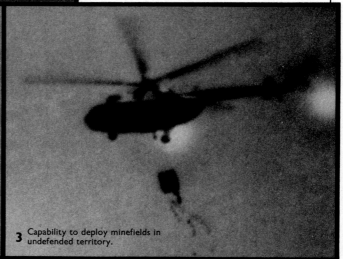

3 Capability to deploy minefields in undefended territory.

DISPENSER
homologated by standard NATO

Two standard models are currently in production: Model 'A' and model 'B'

MODEL 'A' can carry:
- n. 1.536 A.P. mines or
- n. 128 A.T. mines or
- n. 768 A.P. and n. 64 A.T.

MODEL 'B' can carry:
- n. 768 A.P. mines or
- n. 64 A.T. mines or
- n. 384 A.P. and n. 32 A.T.

The two models can be coupled once or more according the helicopter's transport capacity.

4 Capability to defend harbours and coastal installations against frogmen.

SCATTER MINES
homologated by standard NATO

A.P.
T.S./50
Total weight 210 gr.
Charge weight 50 gr.

A.T.
Mats /1,4
Total weight 3,5 kg.
Charge weight 1,4 kg. (C/B)

Mats /2,5
Total weight 4,5 kg.
Charge weight 2,5 kg.
(C/B or TNT)

TECNOVAR

GROUP HEADQUARTERS 95, via Argiro, 70121 Bari (Italy) Tel. (080) 237763 - 211661 - 211744 - TLX 810345

THE BOMBARDIER 2.5-TON

The 6×6 - 2.5-ton Truck
Designed by the Military for the Military

Featuring automatic transmission, a fuel-saving engine and independent suspension, this personnel and cargo carrier provides ideal strategic mobility. Currently in use with the Canadian Forces, it has passed with success the most rigorous RAMD tests, the international seal of approval in logistic vehicles. And thanks to Bombardier's engineering flexibility, it can be built to meet specific user needs and requirements.

Complete technical information available on request.

Bombardier Inc.
Logistic Equipment Division
Valcourt, Québec, Canada
J0E 2L0
Telephone: (514) 532-2211
Telex: 05-832504

Put us to the test on second-line support

Bradley Electronics announce a comprehensive second-line test facility.

This new system, known as 'CUED', is semi-automated and microprocessor controlled, and is designed to test electronic equipment to 'Centrem' or sub-assembly level to meet the requirements of the British Army.

Matrix selection and level settings of a variety of stimuli are achieved manually by means of cued instructions to the operator. These instructions are given by an alpha-numeric display and indicator lights associated with each control.

The Bradley CUED provides a total capability for diagnosis of faults on the following equipment used in Fighting Vehicles:–

★ ENGINE CONTROL ELECTRONICS ★ GEAR BOX CONTROL ELECTRONICS
★ GENERATOR REGULATOR ELECTRONICS ★ GUN CONTROL ELECTRONICS

The CUED system enables a semi-skilled operator to confirm serviceability of line replaceable units in minutes rather than hours. In the event of a failure being confirmed the unit under test may be stripped down and faulty 'centrems' identified. Typical test times for each 'centrem' vary from 2 to 10 minutes and thus a unit may be tested completely well within 2 hours. A valuable additional facility enables the operator to revert to a manual mode of operation.

Variants can readily be designed to meet individual customer requirements and the equipment is particularly suited for testing analogue systems. For further details please contact Brian Epton.

Bradley Electronics Ltd.,
Electral House.
Neasden Lane.
London. NW10 1RR.
Tel: 01-450 7811. Telex: 25583

Bradley Electronics

Increase mission capabilities with Uniroyal liquid-logistics.

Uniroyal portable fuel and water support systems are designed for maximum flexibility. Developed in actual military operations in every part of the world, they are providing the required logistical support for a wide range of

missions, large or small, in any environment or terrain.

Uniroyal liquid-logistic systems are based on lightweight elastomer-fabric collapsible containers that are rugged

enough for all military operations. They can be transported by a variety of equipment, and, when empty, collapse to a fraction of the fully loaded size.

Centralized tank farm and fuel dump facilities are provided by collapsible "static storage" tanks. These tanks range in size from 1,500 gallons to 50,000 gallons and are highly resistant to severe environmental conditions such as sunlight, ozone, mildew, salt, sand and temperatures from $-60°F$ to $160°F$. When empty they collapse to as little as 2% of filled size.

Vehicles and aircraft can be loaded directly from static storage tanks via manifold-pumping systems; or, liquids can be off-loaded for forward transport into Sealdtank® and Sealdrum® portable containers.

Sealdtanks are collapsible roll-up containers that convert any vehicle to a tanker truck. They are used primarily to establish fuel dumps in forward areas and are available in capacities from 1,500 to 4,570 gallons.

Sealdrum containers allow maximum system flexibility. They are lighter and stronger than steel drums and can be transported by trucks, helicopters, airplanes, boats, and can be parachuted into forward areas or

behind lines of operation. Sealdrums are available in capacities of from 55 to 500 gallons. When empty they collapse to less than 15% of filled size.

Complete liquid-logistics systems are available for every size unit and every type of mission. They include the collapsible containers, pumps, filters, manifolds, hoses, and all necessary hardware. Uniroyal containers meet applicable Mil-Spec requirements.

For information on either complete liquid-logistic systems, or separate storage tanks, Sealdtanks or Sealdrums, write or call Uniroyal World Headquarters

UNIROYAL Middlebury, CT 06749 USA
Phone 203-573-3685
Telex 962-435
UNIRoyal-MDDY

UN-C-6R

[15]

REPOWER

New trucks are expensive because of the high cost of new military standard 6 x 6's or the too short life cycle of commercial trucks in tough military service.

Old trucks are expensive because of high-cost gasoline, high-cost spares and overworked maintenance facilities filled with trucks that should be in the field.

Now those aging veterans can become their own replacements. Trucks too-long planned for retirement, can be brought to fully-operational status for a fraction of the cost of new vehicles.

The International Marketing Group of Napco Industries has designed, tested and built a complete line of Repower and Overhaul kits for the ¾-, 2½-, and 5-ton trucks of U.S. Military pattern. Repower kits contain all the parts necessary for a successful modernization program. New diesel engines mean lower fuel bills and plentiful, economical spare parts support. Overhaul kits for axles, transmissions, transfer cases, brakes and suspensions complete the modernization program.

For more information contact:
Marketing Manager
Repowered Vehicles

NAPCO INDUSTRIES, INC.
P.O. Box 570, Minneapolis, Minnesota 55440 U.S.A.
Telephone: (612) 931-2400 ● Telex: 29-0436 ● Cable: NORAUTO

Creusot-Loire
experience in the up to date armament

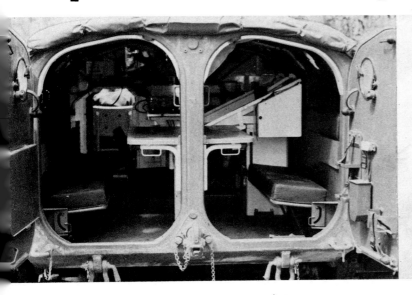

In the Schneider tradition, Creusot-Loire manufactures :

- tanks and armoured vehicles of the AMX 13 family
- turrets for AMX 30 tanks
- turrets and weapons supports for armoured vehicles
- armoured hulls (AML, Crotale...)

- body (and general assembly) of the V.A.B.
- rolled and cast armoured plates
- rough forgings, tracks elements, track rollers suspension arms track tensioning devices

- forgings and drop forgings
- mechanical components for any vehicle
- cranes for recovery AMX 30 tank
- handling hydraulic cranes "all terrain"
- T 40 Ampliroll tank-carrier

CREUSOT-LOIRE
DIVISION MÉCANIQUE SPÉCIALISÉE - 15, rue Pasquier, 75383 Paris Cedex 08. Tél. (1) 268.15.15. Télex : Motoy 650 309 F.

CRL 822

[17]

Dale Group: A comprehensive range of power units for military application.

Lightweight Generating Plant.

This Dale lightweight generating set, having an output of 40kVA, 36kW 415/250 volts 3 phase, 50Hz at site conditions varying from –30°C to +55°C ambient altitudes up to 8000 feet above sea level, forms part of a range which extends from 24kVA to 50kVA. The plant is completely self-contained and incorporates lifting facilities suitable for helicopter transportation.

The Dale lightweight set utilises a welded aluminium alloy skid baseplate and canopy, the engine and alternator being spigot located, flange mounted and supported on anti-vibration mountings.

High Speed Trailer Mounted Sets.

The 15kVA, 415/240 volts, 3 phase, 50Hz unit illustrated is built on a high speed two-wheel trailer, for use with mobile communications equipment. Other voltages are available. The range of highspeed two-wheeled trailers extends from 5 to 20kVA and is based on multi-cylinder, air-cooled diesel engines, close coupled to brushless, statically regulated alternators.

[18]

Containerised Generating Set.

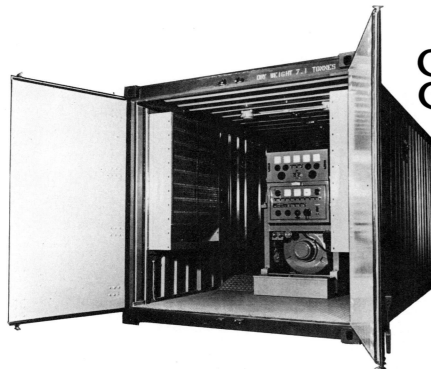

This Dale containerised generating set has an output of 187.5kVA, 150kW, 416/250 volts, 3 phase, 50Hz. It is part of a range of self-contained generating sets from 20kVA to 590kVA, completely housed within a standard walk-in-type ISO shipping container ensuring ease of transportation and site to site movement.

Four Wheel Trailer Mounted Sets.

The 27.5kVA set illustrated has a 415/240 volt, 3 phase, 50Hz output and is powered by a 6 cylinder water cooled engine. Other voltages are available. The generating set is removable from the 2 ton trailer, which can then be used for general purposes.

Portable Generators.

From Erskine (a member of the Dale Group) a range of petrol, diesel or gas dual voltage generating sets up to 15kVA.

**Dale is approved for building to
Defence Standards DEF 05.24.**

DALE

Dale Electric of Great Britain Ltd., Electricity Buildings, Filey, Yorks YO14 9PJ, UK.
Tel: 0723 514141, Telex: 52163.
Erskine Systems Ltd., Lee De Forest House, Eastfield Scarborough,
North Yorkshire YO11 3DU, UK. Tel: Scarborough (0723) 583511, Telex: 52562.

French industrial knowhow
for comprehensive NBC defence

"Défense NBC" is a French consortium*
of international standing to assure Nuclear, Biological and Chemical defence.
"Défense NBC" groups established
producers of NBC materials, adopted
by French Armed Forces, to further
this advanced technology.
"Défense NBC" delivers all complementary NBC products -detection-
protection-decontamination-
for both military and civil defence.

reliability - security - protection

Défense NBC 52 Avenue des Champs-Élysées 75008 PARIS

*BACHMANN-TMB/BEFIC/BONNA/PAUL BOYE/ETRI/GIAT/LACROIX/SEPPIC/SERAE/SOFILTRA-POELMAN/SUPCA/TECHNOFAN

Recovery vehicle F25 cross-country

Iveco technology – Farid reliability

The Iveco-Farid wrecker crane has been specially designed to perform in the easier and safest way all problems of lifting and recovery of heavy duty vehicles on and off-road. The technical solutions, the first class components, their careful processing and the safety devices make this vehicle a right combination of technology and reliability, putting it in a leader position in the field. The large range of accessories, the very easy use and the all driving wheels, make easy and safe also the most difficult works in environment particulary unfavourable for terrain and climat.

For more technical information see page number 51

IVECO FIAT
Fiat Veicoli industriali SpA
Via Puglia 35 - 10156 Torino, Italia - P.O. Box 1371
Telex 221660-221456-220485 Fiatvi

FARID
Farid SpA
C.so Savona 39 bis - 10024 Moncalieri (To), Italia
Telex 220348 Farid I

JANE'S YEARBOOKS

Jane's Yearbooks are regarded as the most accurate works of reference in their respective fields and are subscribed to and used by political, military and civilian strategic planners. They are referred to constantly by state and government procurement agencies, embassies and consulates throughout the world, industrialists involved in the manufacture and marketing of defence equipment and by civilian officials and military officers.

Publishing Programme 1984

April
Jane's Surface Skimmers 1984
Jane's Freight Containers 1984

May
Jane's Urban Transport Systems 1984
Jane's Military Vehicles and Ground Support
    Equipment 1984

June
Jane's Military Communications 1984

August
Jane's Fighting Ships 1984-85
Jane's Infantry Weapons 1984-85

September
Jane's Airport Equipment 1984-85
Jane's Avionics 1984-85
Jane's World Railways 1984-85

November
Jane's Armour and Artillery 1984-85
Jane's Weapon Systems 1984-85

December
Jane's All the World's Aircraft 1984-85

To ensure your copy is delivered on publication contact:
The Marketing Services Dept
Jane's Publishing Company
238 City Road London EC1V 2PU
Tel: 01-251 9281

Jane's Publishing Inc.
13th Floor 135 West 50th Street
New York 10020 USA
Tel: (212) 586 7745

Ⓢsèkur
PIRELLI
for protection

brand for 75 years of experience

sèkur is the trade mark which identifies the protective equipment developed for many years by Pirelli.
Pirelli started manufacturing products for human safety as from the first World War, and has continuously expanded and updated its range, to meet the rising needs created, over the years, by the growing threats of new technology.
sèkur is also the name of the Pirelli Group company to which the Group itself has assigned the activities related to Protection.
sèkur makes a broad range of products in the following fields:

Respiratory protection
- full face masks
- filters and cartridges
- s. c. breathing apparatus

Fire protection
- escape hoods

Body protection
- NBC sweat-free outfits
- NBC air-tight overalls
- NBC gloves and overshoes

Collective protection
- filter units for:
  shelters, caverns, casemates,
  armoured vehicles, ships, airplanes...

sèkur is also well known as a manufacturer of:

Rubber safety fuel tanks
- self-sealing
- crash resistant
- flexible
for armoured vehicles, airplanes, helicopters, light vessels...

Rubber collapsible tanks
for storage and transportation of fuel and water.

sèkur has acquired great expertise during the years and can grant the users a complete service, starting from the exact identification of the problem, to the choice of the right product, the development and engineering of tailor-made solutions, the training and supply of technical documentation, the spares and maintenance service.

sèkur: Quality and Service

sèkur S.p.A.
Via di Torrespaccata 140 - 00169 Rome - Italy
Telex 611084 - Tel. 06/260046.

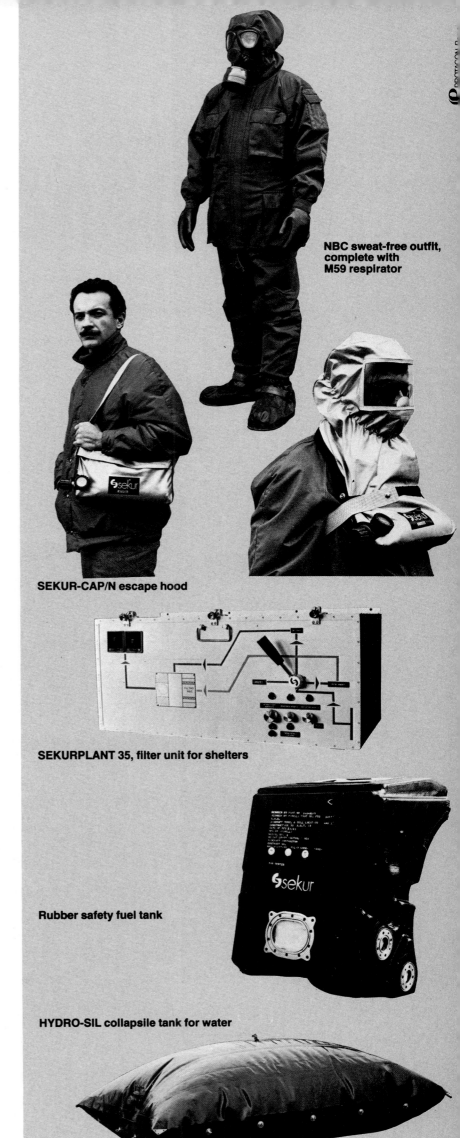

NBC sweat-free outfit, complete with M59 respirator

SEKUR-CAP/N escape hood

SEKURPLANT 35, filter unit for shelters

Rubber safety fuel tank

HYDRO-SIL collapsile tank for water

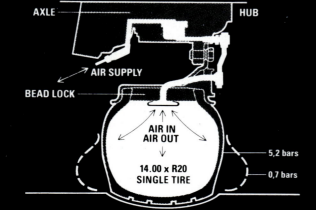

BILITY

M923 (Member of the M939 Series)
5-ton cargo/personnel truck, equipped with Enhanced Mobility System

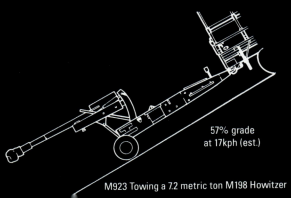

57% grade
at 17kph (est.)

M923 Towing a 7.2 metric ton M198 Howitzer

M939 SERIES 5-TON by

 Aerospace and Defense

AM General Division
World Leader in Military Trucks

[26]

TOUGH GOING?
Laird will keep you mobile

Centaur, the Multi-Role Military vehicle seen here in various configurations – Oerlikon 20 mm GAM BO1 cannon (above), Four stretcher ambulance (right) and as anti-tank mine layer (left).

Portable roadways (left) trucklaid and heavy duty types. Class 30, for wheeled and tracked vehicles with rubber pads and Class 60 for tracked vehicles and tanks. Their non-skid surfaces are designed for use on soft ground where conditions would become increasingly difficult. They can be taken up and relaid time and again with the absolute minimum use of manpower.

Runway repair system. Class 60 Trackway (below) can quickly mobilise any airfield put out of action by bomb damage. As supplied to the RAF and NATO.

For more detailed information on our products please contact

LAIRD (ANGLESEY) LIMITED

Beaumaris, Gwynedd,
Great Britain LL58 8HY.
Telephone: Beaumaris
810431 (STD 0248 810431)
Telex: 61295
Cables: Searoads Beaumaris

[27]

Transportable vhf radio relay equipment (Triffid)

Scimitar-V vehicle receiver

PRC420 Commander in manpack role

JANE'S MILITARY COMMUNICATIONS 1984

Edited by R J Raggett

This latest edition of Jane's Military Communications provides an extensive reference guide to the vast range of communications equipment in service with naval, military and air forces worldwide.

Presented by category of equipment, then alphabetically by country of manufacture, each item's development, specification, function and service is described and illustrated with accuracy and attention to detail.

Equipment
- Radio communications (tactical ground; ground-based; terrestrial microwave and tropospheric scatter; shipborne; airborne; satellite)
- Line communications
- Data transmission and reception, modems and terminals
- Message switching
- Encryption and security
- Electronic warfare (surveillance and signal analysis; direction finding; jamming and miscellaneous)
- Facsimile
- Audio ancillaries
- Antennas and masts
- Test and measurement
- Laser and optical
- Miscellaneous

Systems
- Major systems

- Appendices (acronyms and code names; glossary; AN numbered communications equipment; Directory of manufacturers)
- Fully indexed

The work gives detailed assessments of communications equipment and systems used by armed forces. This high technology industry is continuing to expand and the equipment of over 300 companies in the most significant manufacturing countries is described, accompanied by over 1900 photographs and line drawings. Jane's Military Communications is indeed a unique publication for it is the only single-volume reference source detailing all major communications equipment and systems in use with both NATO and Warsaw pact countries, from satellite to underwater systems; major networks to hand-held items.

An essential work of reference for anyone involved with communications and intelligence.

In the USA contact:

Jane's Publishing Inc.,
13th Floor,
135 West Fiftieth Street,
New York,
New York 10020
USA
or Telephone: (212) 586 7745

further information from:

Marketing Services Dept.
Jane's Publishing Company
238 City Road
London
EC1V 2PU
Telephone: 01 251 9281

COFRAS

an ally
for your defense

engineering

civil works

operational
& maintenance
training

data
processing systems
management

Compagnie Française d'Assistance Spécialisée
32, rue de Lisbonne 75008 Paris
Tél. : 561.99.33 - Télex : 660449 F.

CONTACT CASE

- **Innovator and producer of military engineer and material handling equipment**
- **Air mobility specialist**
- **Complete logistics support**

Case military equipment is designed specifically to meet the user's needs. Includes tractor loader/backhoes, crawler dozers and loaders, 4-wheel-drive loaders, 2- and 4-wheel drive tractors, crawler and 4-wheel-drive excavators, crawler and rubber-tired trenchers, soil compaction equipment, 4-wheel-drive rough terrain forklifts and container handling equipment. Before you finalize your specification, contact Case. Government Marketing Department, 700 State Street, Racine, WI 53404 U.S.A. Phone: (414)636-6561. Telex: 26448. TWX: 910-271-2609.

J I Case
A Tenneco Company

Iveco military vehicles are the result of successfully combining advanced technology and stringent military requirements. Requirements specified in over 90 countries where Iveco has supplied vehicles tailored to local clients, terrains and operating conditions. That is why Iveco military vehicles can meet every demand and challenge. Each and every model of Iveco's military range - with payloads from 0.75 to 60 t - is particularly outstanding. And together with the rest of the product lineup manufactured in France, Germany and Italy, Iveco can offer the most complete vehicle range in the world. And yet the real secret of Iveco's superiority may be due to the standardisation of its mechanical components. With only four engine sizes in the range, water or air cooled from 80 to 450 horsepower, it ensures simplicity and economy in purchase, training and operation. We'd like to tell you more about our products and services. Please contact us: Iveco - Defence Vehicles Division - 10156 Torino (Italy) - 35, Via Puglia - Telex: FIAT VI 221660.

FIAT

MAGIRUS

UNIC

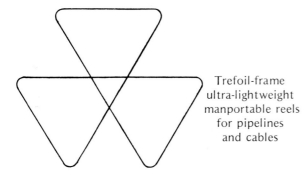

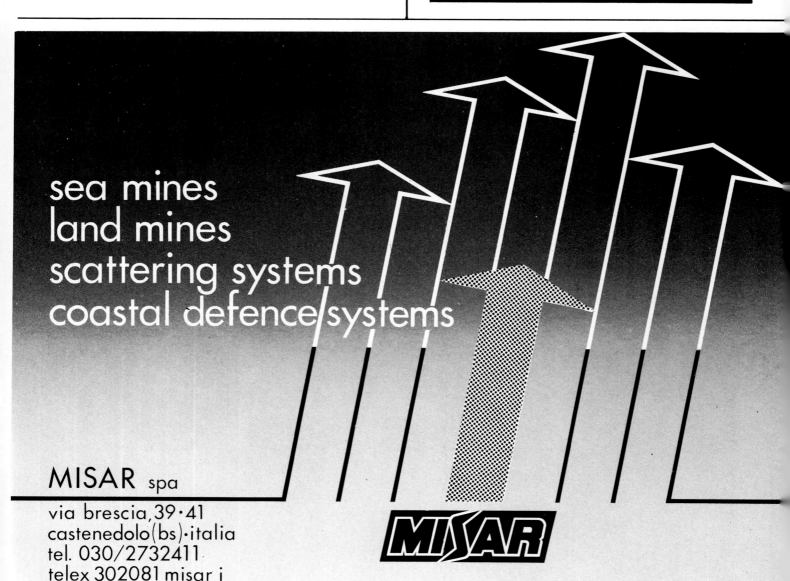

On land and sea, Dowty reliability and experience count.

For over 20 years Dowty has pioneered hydrojet propulsion, and has an international reputation for performance and reliability in amphibious vehicles and marine craft. Dowty hydrojets are in use worldwide with the U.S., British, French and Spanish Armies.

Dowty hydrojets produce high thrust, superior manoeuvrability and low vulnerability – vital requirements for amphibious fighting vehicles and bridging equipment.

Dowty Hydraulic Units Ltd
Arle Court, Cheltenham, Glos GL51 0TP, England.
Tel: (0242) 521411. Telex: 43176.

Overseas
Sterling, Virginia, U.S.A; Ajax, Ontario, Canada;
Darmstaedter Str 3A, 6101 Bickenbach/Bergstr, West Germany;
Madrid, Spain.

Dowty Industrial Division Companies.

Leaders in Hydrojet Technology

JANE'S DEFENCE WEEKLY

3 MARCH 1984

VOLUME 1 NUMBER 8

BRAZIL AIMS TO BUILD

NO ONE ELSE GIVES YOU THE IN·DEPTH FACTS FASTER

The internationally acknowledged authority of Jane's combined with the constant update of the very latest developments in defence matters worldwide—that's Jane's Defence Weekly.

No other defence journal has the pedigree of such objective reporting and now, no other journal can be so instantly responsive in its reporting—bringing you the news as it happens anywhere at any level, be it behind the scenes or in action.

For anyone concerned with defence matters it is indispensable reading.

IF IT'S NEWS YOU'LL FIND IT IN OUR WEEKLY

JANE'S
YEARBOOKS and DEFENCE WEEKLY
Where the facts are found!

JANE'S

Jane's Publishing
Co Limited
238 City Road
LONDON EC1V 2PU
Tel: 01-251 9281
Tlx: 894689

ASTRA VEHICLES FOR THE ARMY: LONG OPERATIONAL LIFE, RELIABILITY, PERFORMANCES.

The ASTRA military vehicles are looking for the future in the Armies and in the civilian Defense. Trucks series 300, for special military heavy equipment, trucks 201 series for engineers corps, amphibians, light high mobility trucks represent the highest technology of one industry born and growth at the service of his country.

ASTRA
Veicoli Industriali
Italy Defense Division

Left hand view of Ultimax 100 Mark III with interchangeable barrel.

JANE'S INFANTRY WEAPONS 1983-84

Ninth edition

Soviet AK-74 Rifle.

ISOLI

MILITARY CRANE TRUCK

ISOLI M180/3 CRANE TRUCK ON FIAT 260PM35 - 6x6 VEHICLE

ISOLI PICK-UP PLATFORM ON FIAT CHASSIS

ISOLI M140/C CRANE TRUCK ON FIAT 6605 - 6x6 VEHICLE

ISOLI M120/C CRANE TRUCK ON FIAT 260PM35 - 6x6 VEHICLE

MULTI-PURPOSE MILITARY CRAFTS

ISOLI 'MULTI-PURPOSE' ON FIAT 260PM35 - 6x6 VEHICLE TRANSPORT AND LOADING OF LARGE SIZE AGGREGATES

ISOLI 'MULTI-PURPOSE' ON FIAT 260PM35 - 6x6 VEHICLE PERSONNEL TRANSPORT

ISOLI 'MULTI-PURPOSE' ON FIAT 260PM35 - 6x6 VEHICLE RECOVERY AND TOWING OF TRUCK USING THE REAR BOOM

ISOLI 'MULTI-PURPOSE' ON FIAT 260PM35 - 6x6 VEHICLE LOADING-TRANSPORT-UNLOADING TRACK-LAYING TANKS

ISOLI 'MULTI-PURPOSE' ON FIAT 260PM35 - 6x6 VEHICLE LOADING-TRANSPORT-UNLOADING ARMOURED VEHICLES

ALLESTIMENTI ISOLI FONTANIVA

ISOLI S.p.A. INDUSTRIA COSTRUZIONI MECCANICHE
Via Boschi, 1/C - Tel. (049) 567600 Telex. 430496 ISOLI I
35014 FONTANIVA (PD) ITALY

In a year when the importance of land mine warfare has been re-emphasised the anti-tank British Ranger anti-personnel mine system and the Royal Ordnance Factories Bar Mine and minelayer are still among the most advanced land mine systems in service today. *(Royal Ordnance Factories)*

JANE'S
MILITARY VEHICLES AND
GROUND SUPPORT
EQUIPMENT

FIFTH EDITION

EDITED BY
CHRISTOPHER F FOSS AND TERRY J GANDER

1984

ISBN 0 7106-0794-6 ✓ 623 REF

JANE'S YEARBOOKS

"Jane's" is a registered trade mark

Copyright © 1984 by Jane's Publishing Company Limited, 238 City Road, London EC1V 2PU, England

In the USA and its dependencies and the Philippines
Jane's Publishing Inc, 13th Floor, 135 West 50th Street, New York, NY 10020, USA

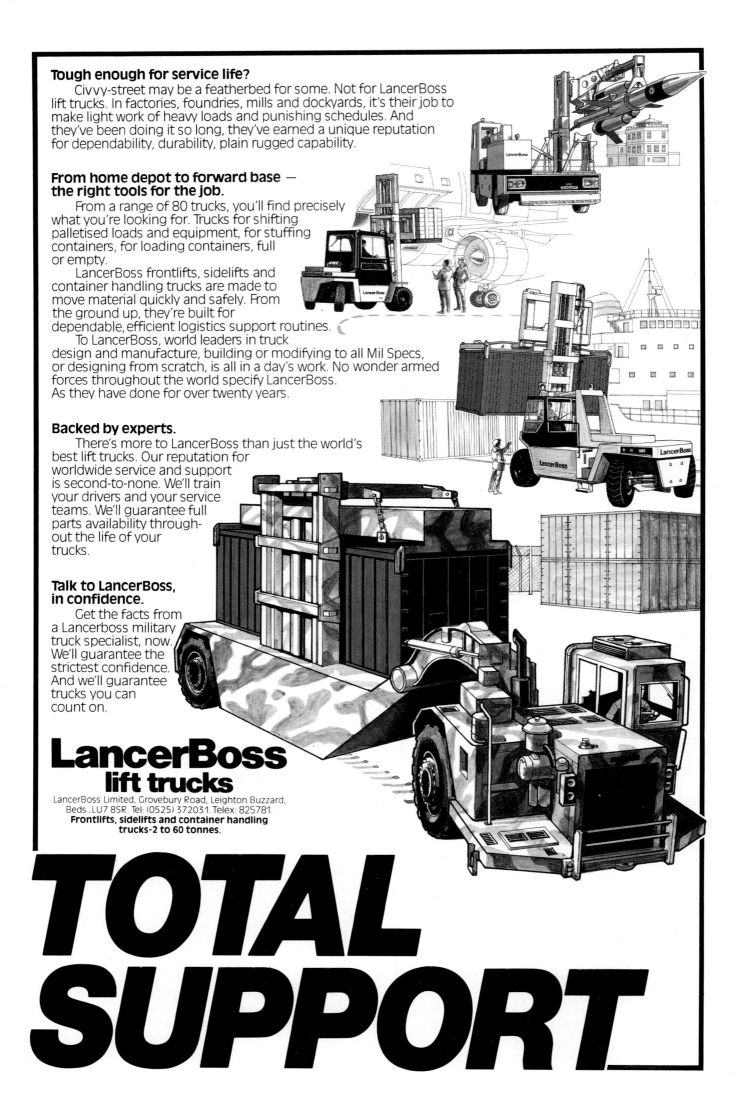

Tough enough for service life?

Civvy-street may be a featherbed for some. Not for LancerBoss lift trucks. In factories, foundries, mills and dockyards, it's their job to make light work of heavy loads and punishing schedules. And they've been doing it so long, they've earned a unique reputation for dependability, durability, plain rugged capability.

From home depot to forward base — the right tools for the job.

From a range of 80 trucks, you'll find precisely what you're looking for. Trucks for shifting palletised loads and equipment, for stuffing containers, for loading containers, full or empty.

LancerBoss frontlifts, sidelifts and container handling trucks are made to move material quickly and safely. From the ground up, they're built for dependable, efficient logistics support routines.

To LancerBoss, world leaders in truck design and manufacture, building or modifying to all Mil Specs, or designing from scratch, is all in a day's work. No wonder armed forces throughout the world specify LancerBoss. As they have done for over twenty years.

Backed by experts.

There's more to LancerBoss than just the world's best lift trucks. Our reputation for worldwide service and support is second-to-none. We'll train your drivers and your service teams. We'll guarantee full parts availability throughout the life of your trucks.

Talk to LancerBoss, in confidence.

Get the facts from a Lancerboss military truck specialist, now. We'll guarantee the strictest confidence. And we'll guarantee trucks you can count on.

LancerBoss lift trucks

LancerBoss Limited, Grovebury Road, Leighton Buzzard, Beds.,LU7 8SR. Tel: (0525) 372031. Telex: 825781. **Frontlifts, sidelifts and container handling trucks-2 to 60 tonnes.**

TOTAL SUPPORT

Contents

In military terms, both Land Rover and Range Rover have always been forces to reckon with.

Now, we've extended the range with a vehicle that combines the best features of both: the One Ten.

Like every Land Rover, the One Ten will admirably fulfill the role of a rugged all-terrain vehicle. Plus better visibility and a larger payload. Plus a more powerful $2\frac{1}{4}$ or $3\frac{1}{2}$ litre five main bearing engine.

Like the Range Rover, the One Ten will also serve as smooth and comfortable transport. Because it has the same chassis concept with coil

LAND ROVER'S NEW RECRUIT

springs and optional levelled suspension. Plus Range Rover high manoeuvrability type steering and front disc brakes. Plus an ergonomically designed interior.

Land Rover's new One Ten is now ready and waiting to contribute to the manoeuvres of any military unit.

Just issue the orders.

Technical Specifications
OVERALL LENGTH: 175″ (4444mm). WHEELBASE: 110″ (2794 mm) PAYLOAD: Up to 1.35 tonnes. MINIMUM TURNING RADIUS: 21ft (6.4m). TOWING WEIGHTS: Up to 4 tonnes with 4 wheel trailer with coupled brakes. ENGINES: $2\frac{1}{4}$ litre 4 cylinder petrol – 74bhp (55KW); $2\frac{1}{4}$ litre 4 cylinder diesel – 60bhp (45KW); $3\frac{1}{2}$ litre V8 petrol – 114bhp (85KW). TRANSMISSIONS: $2\frac{1}{4}$ litre – 5 speed main gearbox; 2 speed transfer box; $3\frac{1}{2}$ litre – 4 speed main gearbox; 2 speed transfer box. FUEL TANK CAPACITY: up to 32·5 gallons. CHASSIS: Rigid box section construction, long travel coil springs all round. PERMANENT 4 WHEEL DRIVE. CLUTCH: Single dry plate, hydraulic. BRAKES: Front-disc, rear-drum, servo assisted.

LAND ROVER

ONE TEN

Land Rover's new Land Rover.

Land Rover Limited, Lode Lane, Solihull, West Midlands B92 8NW, England. Telephone 021-743 4242. Telex Lan Rov G338641. Cables: Rover Solihull.
Land Rover Ltd; is approved to British Ministry of Defence 05.21 quality standard.

Foreword

1983 was a quietly significant year for students of military vehicles and ground support equipment. It was a period of introspection on several counts, not the least of which was the analysis of the Falklands Campaign of 1982. Although military vehicles were minimally involved, mainly due to the nature of the terrain, the logistic chain leading to the front line soldier has been reappraised in the light of experience there. The exact results of this analysis may not be seen for some time but already there are indications that consideration of support for the front-line soldier in both equipment and methods is now being afforded greater emphasis than in the past. This applies not only in the United Kingdom but in many other military establishments around the world. The United States is in the early stages of a massive re-equipment programme that will eventually lead to the replacement of its entire military vehicle fleet (see p 12), the world's largest. Various nations are now busy purchasing large fleets of new vehicles, the Egyptian order for large numbers of Spanish Pegaso trucks being only one example. 1983 also saw the selection of the AM General submission for the US Army's High Mobility Multi-purpose Wheeled Vehicle. This is the M998 HUMMER and the first increment in what is planned to be a massive purchase of no fewer than 54 973 vehicles was contracted during March 1983. Once in service the M998 will replace three types of vehicle already in service and supplement other fleets. This order, when fulfilled, will be one of the largest purchases of its kind for many years.

1983 was also a year of financial retrenchment in many aspects of ground support equipment. Due to escalating costs and the world recession, several promising programmes have either been terminated or shelved. These cut-backs have largely involved some of the less 'glamorous' aspects of what is in publicity and 'attraction' terms one of the least regarded sectors of the defence market, but none the less tactical bridging, mines and combat engineer equipments are nowadays as important to the soldier as the rifle and the artillery piece. He cannot do without them. In France, however, there have been some severe cut-backs in the procurement of modern assault bridging, the advanced American ERAM 'smart' land mine's development has been suspended and also in the United States only a token purchase of the M9 multi-purpose tractor is to be made in the near future and a decision to procure the required total of 1400 M9s has been delayed for two more years (although advanced funding plans have been made).

Despite these retrenchments there are over one hundred new entries in this year's edition of *Jane's Military Vehicles and Ground Support Equipment*. There has been some revision of the contents and a new section *Field fortifications and related emplacement equipment* has been incorporated. This section emphasises the importance that 'digging in' still has in modern warfare. The power and effectiveness of many modern weapons, including artillery, can still be partly off-set by providing adequate protection, often in the form of trenches or earthworks. Much of the equipment involved has been adapted from existing construction equipment but specialised items have appeared which deserve of their own mention. Despite the intended use of mobile warfare by all sides in any potential conflict there is certain to be an imbalance in the attackers' favour and only battlefield fortifications can hope to remedy any such disparity.

An outline commentary on each of the main sections follows. These indicate only the main trends and outstanding items of news and do not attempt to make predictions. It has already been mentioned that much of the equipment included in this Yearbook has a low priority in military budgets and many promising items never progress beyond the prototype stage.

However, before specific items are considered, it seems to us that a topic of over-riding importance which merits mention is that in too many aspects of military vehicle and ground support equipment development current technology, rather than users'

needs, is determining standards. The case of the M998 HUMMER is typical. This vehicle will be a world-beater as far as performance is concerned with a speed and cross country capability well beyond that of any comparable vehicle but these assets will be obtained at a hefty price. The first 2334 vehicles will cost no less than $59·8 million but with, we suspect, the final cost being much higher. The suspension system is such that it will call for an inordinate amount of maintenance and the supply of spare parts and their subsequent installation will no doubt be comparatively expensive. Also the actual term of in-service life remains to be seen. The M998 is not the only item in this category but it is an indication of how the adoption of modern technology, regardless of the apparent advantages on the drawing board, can be off-set once the item reaches the soldier. Other examples could be quoted of advanced components or design arrangements being incorporated into the next generation of vehicles (and other equipments mentioned in this Yearbook) that may well prove to be of doubtful worth once they reach the field.

What the soldier wants from a vehicle, or any other item of ground support equipment, is that it will be available when he wants to use it, and will continue to work for as long as he requires it to do so. This simple fact seems to be increasingly forgotten in the race to adopt more and more fancy (and expensive) innovations. More tried and tested designs and components will have to be readopted soon if the soldiers of tomorrow are to have the items of equipment that they need. Behind much terminated project equipment lies the simple fact that many nations can no longer afford the expense of modern military projects. Not all nations have the material wealth of the United States or the determined application of the Soviet Union but both these power blocs expect to supply the rest of the world with the output of their military programmes. It remains to be seen how many nations decide to adopt the M998 and its ilk. Instead the Third World is purchasing ACMAT, Pegaso, and DAF trucks. Few nations wish to purchase FASCAM-type mines (or, for that matter, would be allowed to do so) but Italy supports a thriving land mine industry that supplies the world and many nations continue to employ the same types of mine that were used during the Second World War. The reasons behind these trends in the Third World are few and simple; the products are basic, easy to maintain and the price is right. If any form of balance is to be maintained between the numerical might of the Warsaw Pact nations and the overall state of readiness of the rest of the world these basics should not be forgotten.

Armoured engineer vehicles

During 1983 two new armoured engineer vehicles were introduced, each at different ends of the development scale. At the top and most expensive end is the American Counter-Obstacle Vehicle or COV which was mentioned in the 1982 edition. Based on the hull and suspension of BMY's M88 armoured repair vehicle, the COV will also be built by BMY. The COV will have all manner of obstacle-clearing devices from the usual dozer blade to articulated arms carrying clearing claws. Prototypes are now under construction and it is interesting to note that one of these will be passed to Israel for their tests and comments.

Further down the development scale, an interesting programme is being undertaken in Spain. Spain already has an armoured fighting vehicle (AFV) industry involved in the licence production of French AMX-30 MBTs but the conversion of this vehicle is obviously too expensive as far as an armoured engineer vehicle is concerned. The French themselves have produced prototypes of their Engin Blindé de Génie (EBG) but the projects progress appears to be slow and the costs substantial. So the Spanish armed forces have instead made use of relatively cheap surplus M47 tanks to produce their M-47 E2I armoured engineer

Mercedes-Benz:
Equally Reliable in all Payload Classes.

When it is necessary to transport soldiers or material over treacherous terrain to their destination, Mercedes-Benz vehicles demonstrate their performance capabilities. All-wheel drive, differential locks and high torque engines ensure that sufficient driving power is always available. The comprehensive vehicle range includes the right Mercedes for every tactical or logistic application with payloads for off-road operation from 0.6 tons to a splendid 12 tons. Cross-country vehicles with 2 wheelbases and engines delivering from 53 kW to 115 kW (72 to 156 DIN/hp). Unimogs from 44 kW to 124 kW (60 to 168 DIN/hp). 2 and 3-axle trucks and tractors from 96 kW to 368 kW (130 to 500 DIN/hp).

Excellent services to match excellent engineering. For Mercedes-Benz this also means: 1. Worldwide service network with more than 5000 agencies. 2. Reliable spare parts supply worldwide. 3. Training for repair personnel and drivers. 4. Information and advisory service.

Leaders in technology and in service. Mercedes-Benz.

vehicle. By adapting the superstructure and equipment of the West German Leopard armoured engineer vehicle to suit the hull of the M47, a relatively inexpensive solution has been found to the Spanish Army's requirement. The conversion programme includes a new engine, the adoption of M48 MBT suspension components and some other changes. The result appears to be a thoroughly serviceable piece of kit. At the time of writing the M47 project is in the prototype stage but already the basic approach is being used to produce bridging and armoured recovery vehicles (these are included in the relevant sections).

Innovations in the armoured engineer vehicle have otherwise been few. It would appear that the US Army now has sufficient M728 Combat Engineer Vehicles to meet its immediate needs and in the United Kingdom the production line for the Combat Engineer Tractor (CET) has likewise been still for some time. However it now appears that the CET line may be reactivated to provide the hull and suspension for a proposed family of combat vehicles to meet an Egyptian requirement. It is also possible that a combat engineer version of the GKN MCV-80 APC will emerge.

Meanwhile the saga of the American M9 multi-purpose tractor drags on. The US Army has a definite requirement for at least 1400 of these versatile vehicles, development of which dates back to 1958. The M9 prototypes have now been developed to the point where they can meet all relevant requirements but production funding is not forthcoming. In many ways this M9 saga epitomises the difficulties under which the essential but 'unglamorous' equipments, so earnestly requested by the combat engineer, fail to attract the necessary high-level support. Despite hopes that funding for M9 production would, at long last, be provided during 1983 this has once more been delayed. Instead a batch of 15 equipments has been ordered for further product development and plans to procure more have been postponed until fiscal year 1985. In the meantime the American combat engineer is required to carry out front-line sapper tasks with conventional bulldozers.

Recovery vehicles and equipment

As far as armoured recovery vehicles are concerned 1983 was an uneventful year. The American M88A1 appears set for a long service life with the US Army and is capable of carrying out all foreseen repair and recovery tasks on main battle tanks (MBTs) up to the M1 Abrams until well into the 1990s. The Spanish adaptation of the basic M47 to the armoured recovery role, (the M-47 E2R) mentioned above, is still in the prototype stage.

Perhaps the most important news in this category comes from the United Kingdom with the conversion of the Chieftain ARV (armoured recovery vehicle) to the Chieftain ARRV (armoured recovery/repair vehicle). The ARRV now has a side-mounted hydraulic crane similar to that originally produced for export to Iran several years ago. The adoption of the Challenger MBT by the British Army, the new engine pack of which is too heavy for handling by the FV434 armoured repair vehicle, has led to the adoption of the Chieftain ARRV. The adoption of other new equipment has also led to new recovery vehicles for the British Army. Now that the AT105 Saxon APC has been ordered for one brigade of the British Army a special recovery variant will also be produced (this news arrived too late for inclusion in this edition but will be covered as comprehensively as possible in the 1985 edition). Special recovery variants of the MCV-80 APC are also envisaged.

Another vehicle innovation that arrived too late for this edition relates to the Tracked Rapier Forward Area Support Team (FAST), a maintenance support vehicle based on the M548 tracked cargo carrier and intended for direct front-line support of the British Army's new Tracked Rapier vehicles. This innovation has a small hydraulic crane over the cab and carries all the spares and test equipment required to keep the Tracked Rapier vehicles in action. Other new inclusions this year are the French Panhard VCR-AT (6 × 6) armoured recovery vehicle produced for export and the South African Ratel armoured repair vehicle which is a simple conversion of a normal Ratel APC for the recovery role. MOWAG has introduced a new configuration for its Piranha 8 × 8 armoured repair vehicle while numbers of its Canadian 6 × 6 counterparts, the Husky armoured repair vehicle, are now in service with Canadian forces serving in Europe as part of NATO.

With wheeled recovery vehicles there are some new items. In both France and the United Kingdom there are competitions under way to select a new wheeled heavy wrecker for army use. In France the Renault TRM 10000 has been selected as the carrier

vehicle but the top hamper competition is between PPM and Pinguely. In the United Kingdom the contest between the Foden 6 × 6 recovery vehicle and the Scammell S26 6 × 6 which uses an Eka Compact recovery top hamper seems to favour the Foden vehicle. Many other companies continue to produce wheeled recovery vehicles but a recent addition to the list is the Norwegian company Moelven. Its BV 730 is based on a Mercedes-Benz chassis and is just one in a series of recovery equipments that extend to a recovery crane mounted on an M548 tracked cargo carrier.

One unusual addition to the recovery vehicle section is the Brimont ETR 206 S Type 'Mase', a French prototype for recovering amphibious bridging units during river crossings. With large earth-anchoring spades, it is little more than a mobile winch but can obviously pull very heavy loads and could well have applications outside the amphibious bridging unit sphere.

Bridging systems

In the mechanised bridges field the main news of 1983 related to the awarding of contracts for the US Army's proposed Heavy Assault Bridge (HAB). Development contracts have been awarded to BMY which has called in Israel Military Industries to develop the bridge itself. The bridge will have a minimum gap-crossing capability of 30 metres and will be able to carry vehicles up to class 70 with current proposals suggesting a three-section folding-bridge. The prototype is not expected to appear before 1986 and the same time scale seems likely for a similar West German programme that could produce bridges up to 42 metres long. West Germany is also the base for another new project, the Krupp-MAN Iguana assault bridge to be carried on a heavy duty wheeled 8 × 8 chassis. At the time of writing, this project was in the model and design stages with hopes for its appearance in the near future. Like other West German mechanised bridging systems this bridge is moved into position horizontally and thus avoids indicating the presence of a bridging vehicle as with many other 'up and over' systems.

As already mentioned, Spain has plans to produce a mechanised bridging system based on the M47 MBT and from India come hints that a bridging system based on a heavy 10 × 10 wheeled chassis is being considered.

With floating bridges the main item of interest is that the French PFM Mle F1 is now in production for the French Army but in nothing like the quantity originally anticipated. Cut-backs in French defence expenditure have virtually ended any further development of the promising Matériel Amphibie de Franchissement (MAF 2). Although trials of the prototypes were successful further development was judged necessary and in the current financial climate it does not seem likely that funds will be made available for many years to come.

Military bridging is not an area of dramatic change and the market for assault bridging continues to be dominated by the Fairey Medium Girder Bridge (MGB) and the West German Krupp-Festbrücke. The Festbrücke has now demonstrated an ability to act as a floating bridge and continues to make inroads into the South American and Far East markets while the MGB has been provided with a welcome continuation of its production run by a large order from the Indian Army, news of which arrived as this foreword was being written.

Mine warfare equipment

One aspect of the Falkland Islands campaign that has attracted a great deal of attention has been mine warfare. For some time this Yearbook has been outlining the characteristics and potential of modern land mine warfare but it has taken a shooting campaign to concentrate minds on its actual effects. Despite the large scale scattering of mine fields of all types around the approaches to Port Stanley it now appears that the number of casualties due directly to mines detonating were, thankfully, relatively few. However the long-term effects of indiscriminate sowing of mines are much more severe. The nature of many modern anti-personnel mines is such that detection by most current methods is both lengthy and difficult. Given the extremely difficult nature of the Falklands terrain the clearing of many minefields will be virtually impossible and large tracts of land on East Falkland are as impassable as if contaminated by the effects of nuclear warfare.

It requires little imagination to transfer the after-effects of the Falklands campaign to Europe and it can then be appreciated that mine warfare has taken on a new and frightening aspect. Many modern land mines contain virtually no metal and unless special

measures are taken when the mines are laid to ensure that they can be re-located they are likely to remain buried and lethal for ever. Sophistication of many mines has been considerably increased by modern micro-electronics and slow-acting fuzes that are invulnerable to rapid build-ups in pressure such as produced by explosives or some other types of clearing device. For short-term military purposes such innovations are highly desirable but as demonstrated in the Falklands the long-term effects are not. Thus, as land mine design becomes more sophisticated new forms of detection device will have to be introduced accordingly. Devices such as rollers, flails and ploughs have all been reintroduced for the short term military objective but for complete clearance measures new forms of detection such as infra-red scanning, some form of chemical 'sniffer' and even irradiating the affected area with low-level nuclear radiation will have to be developed. Various projects along these lines are currently under way in several nations. One thing is certain, the use of dogs has not proved to be the hoped-for answer to the all-plastic mine.

Among the mines themselves, the Argentinian FMK-1 and FMK-3, which proved so troublesome in the Falklands, are included here for the first time. These two mines have no outstanding features and in these pages are included many with identical construction techniques, hence the same clearing problems can be anticipated. Even more troublesome in the Falklands than the little FMK-1 anti-personnel mine was the essentially similar Italian SB-33 which is of such a shape and size that it has blended in with the local soil to become proof against all tried detection methods. Also in the anti-personnel category are the unpleasant Claymore-type mines, several new varieties of which are mentioned for the first time. One is the British Padmine now being issued for service with the British Army.

British innovations also occur on the anti-tank mine front. The Bar Mine produced by the Royal Ordnance Factories is being converted, by modern fuzing systems, to the far more effective Full Width Attack Mine, or FWAM, while the elderly Mark 7 metal anti-tank mine has had its effective life extended with a new carbon tilt-rod fuze. In France several companies are competing for the contract to produce the next generation of HPD anti-tank mine and the outcome of this competition should be announced soon.

FWAM demonstrates that, for land mines, fuzes are becoming far more sophisticated than the mines themselves. Micro-electronics has raised the selection and detection capabilities of fuzes to a level of sophistication hitherto un-dreamed. So much so that they can now differentiate between various types of tracked target. This sophistication has been purchased at a high price, so high in fact that the development costs have frequently outstripped the ability of the customer to pay for them. Into this category come the American ERAM (Extended Range Anti-armor Munition) and the FASCAM Modular Pack Mine Laying System (MOPMS). Both these advanced systems were developed to a point where funds were no longer available for more work and both are now either in a state of limbo or low-level development. In both cases it is hoped to resume development once funds are procured.

As rapid sowing of mine fields is envisaged in any future conflict the methods of distributing anti-personnel and anti-tank mines are of prime importance. Although the term FASCAM should, strictly speaking, be applied to the American systems only, the term is now loosely applied to all rapid minelaying systems. In the United Kingdom a new FASCAM family is under development and when it is unveiled in the not too distant future it seems certain that some existing minelaying methods such as the THORN-EMI Ranger will still be included, along with the Bar Minelayer adapted to distribute FWAMS. Equipments such as the Ranger system do however require specialist carrying vehicles and in many armies such vehicles will not be available. Thus there has been a definite move towards easily adaptable distribution methods of which the helicopter mine dispenser is perhaps the best example. Any helicopter can carry a mine distributor such as the Italian Technovar DAT scatter-dropping system resulting in a minefield as randomly distributed as any area sown by specialist projectors. The West Germans are continuing with their MSM/W systems which are expected to see full-scale service during 1986, and the Americans are developing their Volcano helicopter-dispenser system for use in the 1990s.

Mine detection and clearing have already been mentioned above but, for the most part, current combat-clearing systems involve the mine roller or the plough. Both methods are being investigated with the general concensus that not only is the flail

method too uncertain but it creates an area of broken ground that is either impassable to other traffic or makes any subsequent clearance more difficult. Thus the roller and the plough prevail. The Soviet Union is still in the forefront of both methods to the extent that the Israeli RKM rollers and ploughs are virtual copies of the Soviet KMT ploughs and the PT-54/55 rollers. Both types are under consideration by the US Army so if the Israeli products are eventually taken into American service the same designs will be used by both major protagonists in any future conflict. The United Kingdom has also adopted a mine plough but the British design is original and has been under field trial for some years. Now in production, examples have already been fitted to some BAOR Centurion Mk 5 AVRES and to some Chieftain Bridgelayers.

Transport equipment

One of the most significant developments in light vehicles in recent years was the agreement between the American Motors Corporation and the Chinese Beijing Automotive Works to build a new Jeep production line in China. In time this joint venture will be funded with US $51 million and Jeeps will be produced for use within China and for Japan and the Far East market. The long-term results could be considerable for this will be the first Chinese vehicle production project with no Soviet involvement apart from the Franco-Chinese EQD 142 (4 × 2) truck with which Renault is involved.

In the United Kingdom the Land Rover One Ten with its Range Rover coil spring suspension, frame and other components, has made its market debut and the first military sales announcements can be expected in the very near future. The One Ten is an improvement on the basic Land Rover in nearly all respects and provides a much smoother ride over rough ground. In time it is expected that the British Army will replace all its existing Land Rovers with One Tens. Meanwhile production of the ordinary Land Rover continues at full steam and it will be some time before the last of the existing models leaves the line. In West Germany production of the VW Iltis ceased at the end of 1981, only to recommence across the Atlantic under the Bombardier nameplate when the Iltis was selected as the utility 4 × 4 vehicle for the Canadian Armed Forces. In France production of the Peugeot P4 is now well established with 100 vehicles a month rolling off the line.

With heavier trucks the field is dominated by happenings in the United States. The HMMWV contest resulted in the production contract going to AM General for their M998 HUMMER. Mention has already been made of this vehicle but it bears repeating that the US armed forces have a requirement for no fewer than 54 973 of these remarkable vehicles. The HUMMER is not the only vehicle that has made its mark on the American military scene for the entire American armed forces fleet of vehicles, the largest in the world, is now deemed due for replacement. The costs and resources involved are enormous but are partly due to previous neglect. For too many years the decision to implement one aspect or another of the eventual replacement of all manner of trucks has been postponed or has failed to attract the necessary funding. The defence establishment concerned seems prone to lavish the considerable funds available on 'shooting' materiel and has become oblivious to the fact that an AFV (armoured fighting vehicle) in the field is useless without a supply back-up which must be provided by trucks. The result is that a good proportion of the American truck fleet is over two decades old and becoming increasingly unreliable and expensive to maintain. Some inroads have already been made into dealing with this problem, for example, the introduction of the M939 5-ton family, but a full-scale programme is now sorely needed.

There are already signs that things are moving. The initial stages in a programme for a new Medium Tactical truck (MTT) were planned to be well under way by the end of 1983 and early indications are that the required vehicle will be a 4 × 4 truck with a forward control cab and a capacity of between 2500 kg and 3500 kg. The MTT may well be selected from an existing design. However it is to be hoped that the outcome of the MTT programme will be more fortunate than that of the Heavy Expanded Mobility Tactical Truck (HEMTT) project. It has been discovered that some components of the production versions of this large 8 × 8 truck are unsuitable for service and the vehicles are currently being stored when completed as there is no funding available at present for developing the required replacement components. This has not prevented the US Marine Corps from

placing a large order for the essentially similar Oshkosh MK48 series of 8 × 8 trucks. An initial order worth US $245 million has been placed and the final order may well be worth more than twice that sum.

Away from the United States, orders continue to flow in from the Third World and other areas for more and more military trucks. The inroads that the Soviet Union made into nearly every continent during the 1960s and 1970s now appear to be dwindling away as the recipient nations make long-term assessments on the effectiveness of Soviet equipment. Soviet trucks are still to be found in many quarters but tend to be acquired for their relative cheapness rather than for other considerations. In service Soviet trucks have generally proved to be relatively inefficient in fuel consumption and weight-to-payload factors compared with similar vehicles from the West. But these advantages have not been purchased at the cost of increased complexity in many cases. It is noticeable that the majority of the trucks purchased by many of the less technologically advanced nations tend to be equally non-technically advanced designs. Trucks such as those produced by ACMAT, Pegaso and DAF tend to be simple vehicles with no refinements such as turbo-superchargers, hydraulic systems or complex electrics. They are all orthodox trucks into which any driver can climb, start up and drive. They do not require large and expensive maintenance facilities and in many cases parts can be replaced without recourse to special tools.

It is also noticeable that Pegaso and DAF have pulled off two of the largest orders of the last year outside the major power blocs. The deal between Pegaso and the Egyptian Government has finally been sealed and DAF has managed to make a sizable sale to Portugal. The relatively small ACMAT company in France continues to sell its remarkable trucks throughout Africa and elsewhere and it is also in Africa that some of the most rugged of all military trucks are being built. These trucks are produced by the South African company SAMIL, part of the ARMSCOR concern, and the SAMIL trucks have been built to survive and function over some of the most rugged terrain anywhere. The capabilities of these vehicles to travel over the roughest terrain and survive handling by virtually untrained drivers have to be seen to be fully appreciated. As these vehicles are now being offered on the open market it will be surprising if their attributes are not demonstrated outside South Africa before very long. There are three basic trucks in the SAMIL range, the SAMIL 20, 50 and 100 with capacities of 2000, 4800 and 10 000 kg respectively. Onto these three basic chassis can be placed all manner of bodies to suit a variety of uses from wreckers to ambulances. SAMIL also produces a range of trailers to match.

Brazil continues to expand its truck industry and the ENGESA EE-50 (6 × 6) 5000 kg truck has attracted its first export order. In France the Renault TRM 2000 (4 × 4) 2000 kg truck was placed in production for the French Army and further up the Renault scale the TRM 10 000 (6 × 6) 10 000 kg truck seems set for a long service life with the French Army once production commences during 1985. Unimogs continue to pour off the Mercedes-Benz production lines in West Germany and also from licence production lines in many other countries. Also in West Germany, Magirus-Deutz has changed its name to Iveco Magirus but continues to produce many models of excellent diesel-powered trucks that have made this company's name throughout the world.

In the United Kingdom 1983 was relatively quiet. No large orders or new models have materialised but the TM 4-4 continues to roll off the Bedford assembly lines. The recession's effect in the United Kingdom is demonstrated by plans to extend the in-service life of the venerable Stalwart high mobility load carrier rather than replacing this invaluable vehicle with something similar, which would be far too costly an exercise.

With the rest of the Transport Equipment section there is little new to report. The Scammell Commander is in full production to meet the British Army's requirements for a combination to carry the new Challenger MBT and the first examples should be in service ready for 'Operation Lionheart' in Germany during September and October 1984. With amphibians the Pegaso VAP 3550 has reportedly been ordered by Egypt, and in the tracked prime mover field the American BMY M992 Field Artillery Ammunition Support Vehicle (FAASV) is to enter production in 1984. A new over-snow vehicle, the French SIGAL M25, has been introduced and in the same field the future of the Swedish Bandvagn Bv 206 looks optimistic: it has been adopted by the US Army as their M973 Small Unit Support Vehicle (SUSV) and seems almost certain to be procured as a standard NATO vehicle. The United

Kingdom is expected to order a large batch to replace their ageing Bv 202s.

The *Materials handling equipment* section does not normally attract the attention of the military world but 1984 will be different. 1984 will be the year in which the final development of the British DROPS (demountable rack off-loading and pick-up system) project will be unveiled. DROPS has consumed a great deal of time and resources within the United Kingdom defence establishment as its ramifications will have a considerable effect on the British Army logistic structure. DROPS had its origins in the French Ampliroll system of off-loading heavy goods such as ammunition or vehicles. Continued development within the United Kingdom over a period of years has reached the point where special racks for ammunition such as MLRS rocket pods are planned to be prepositioned throughout 1 (BR) Corps area in West Germany in an emergency. The racks will be carried from the stockpiles to the field in one operation with no off-loading or re-loading en route. At present several concerns are involved in the final competitive stage including Powell Dufferyn. The expected number of racks involved in the DROPS project is substantial but exact figures will probably not be given. The final contract will probably be announced during 'Operation Lionheart'.

Nuclear, biological and chemical warfare

There was a definite swing of interest towards the unpleasant subject of NBC warfare in 1983. The United States military establishment progressed towards a more advanced form of NBC defence and a resumption of the stockpiling of modern NBC munitions. Definite inroads have been made into the field of decontamination at all levels, an area which the United States has hitherto neglected. As a result this edition notes, for the first time, a series of decontamination equipments, however most are still in the development stage and may not reach the field for some years yet. The portable M13 DAP, intended for carriage on all American military vehicles and in all establishments is the only one of four types in the pipeline which will be ready for issue during 1985. Of the remainder the XM16 Jet Exhaust Decontamination Apparatus is little more than a direct copy of the Soviet TMS-65 (and the Czechoslovak TZ 74) but will not be ready for type classification until the second quarter of fiscal year 1986.

West Germany also consider decontamination equipment of prime importance. There Alfred Kärcher GmbH continues to develop its range of steam pressure equipments and is now offering its container-based Decocontain system for large scale employment. Perhaps the most interesting West German innovation is the OWR DEKON system. Based on heavy trucks carrying various bodies it deals with all aspects of NBC warfare effects.

NBC instruments came into the news during the past year and especially in the field of chemical vapour detection. It has been mentioned in the past that many in-service nerve gas detectors are highly efficient and effective but too heavy for extended use. The heavy power cells required were partly responsible but with micro-electronics such heavy cells are not always necessary as in the case of the little Bendix BxCAD miniature chemical agent detector. The BxCAD is small enough to be worn as a virtual individual alarm system but is as effective as larger and heavier equivalents. Thus the BxCAD must be regarded as one of the most significant NBC innovations in recent years. The other significant innovation is the British Chemical Agent Monitor (CAM), a light and portable 'sniffer' device that introduces a novel technique into the detection of chemical agents. CAM is being developed for the British armed forces and is currently undergoing trials with the US Army.

Acknowledgements
One of the more pleasant tasks afforded to the editors of this Yearbook is to thank the many people and organisations who have been instrumental in many ways in the preparation and production of the book. The completion of this Yearbook would not have been possible without the help of companies, governments, government agencies, establishments and individuals all over the world who have contributed material, information, advice and illustrations.

Individuals who have been foremost in contributing material include Simon Dunstan (UK), Kensuke Ebata (Japan), Paul Handel (Australia), Steve Kessler (INCO of USA), Franz Kosar (Austria), Robert W Forsyth (Vehicle Systems Development

OTO MELARA NEW VEHICLES CAPRAIA AND GORGONA

Both with armoured
alluminium hull (up to 7.62 NATO)
95HP supercharged Diesel engine
Range: 500 km Max gradient: over 75%
Aiming: panoramic sight by training optic (360°)

R3 CAPRAIA Special Task Scout and Carrier: Armament: 7.62 or 12.7 or 20 mm
Anti-tank (twin): TOW, Folgore, 106 r.g. Weight: 3 tons
Max speed: over 115 km/h Crew: 6
Amphibious (hydrojet propulsion)

R2.5 GORGONA Command: Reconnaissance Duty
Combat: Armament 7.62 or 12.7
Weight: 2.5 tons Max speed: over 120 km/h Crew: 4

OTO MELARA S.p.A., 15 Via Valdilocchi - 19100 La Spezia (Italy) - Tl. (0187) 530.111
TX. 270368 - 211101 OTO I

OTO MELARA

[52]

Corporation, USA), Frank Gaal (United States Army Tank Automotive Command), Ronaldo S Olive (Brazil), Gene Osolinsky (United States Army Mobility Equipment Research and Development Command), Keiichi Nogi (Japan), J I Taibo (Spain), Geoffrey Tillotson, Dr Arthur Voltz (USA) and C R Zwart. There are many other individuals to whom our thanks are due.

Paul Hocking supplied the 1/76th scale drawings and has often been called on to produce his excellent drawings at short notice while maintaining his high standard. The resultant drawings enhance this Yearbook.

On the publisher's sub-editing team Terri Doyle has assumed the sub-editing task from Frances Jary and has managed to smooth out the many difficulties that are bound to arise in the compilation of any work of this size with both cheerfulness and a commendable efficiency. Her part in this year's edition has been considerable, for she has not only had to cope with well over 100 additions to the text but the problems inherent with handling well over 500 new illustrations. Special thanks are also due to the production team, David Moyes and Alan Griggs.

Valerie Passmore, Editorial Director, has co-ordinated the efforts of the whole team. The editors would also like to express their thanks to Anne McKrill and Gillian Thompson for their efforts in obtaining material for use in this Yearbook from all around the world.

On behalf of the entire *Jane's Military Vehicles and Ground Support Equipment* team we would once again like to thank the hard-working typesetters, printers and binders for all the valuable work they have carried out in the production of the book.

March 1984

Christopher F Foss
Terry Gander

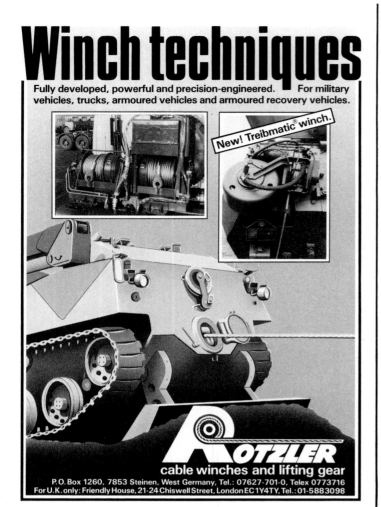

GLOSSARY

AAT all arms trencher
ABC All-purpose Ballastable Crawler; America, Britain and Canada
ACAS automatic chemical alarm system
ACPM Anti Char à Pose Mécanique
ACT airportable cargo trailer
ADAM Area Denial Artillery Munition
ADM atomic demolition munition
ADS ammunition delivery system
AEC Associated Equipment Company
AEV armoured engineer vehicle
AFARV Armored Forward-Area Rearm Vehicle
AFV armoured fighting vehicle
AHE ammunition handling equipment
Ah ampère hour
AMIDS Airborne Minefield Detection System
AMX Atelier de Construction d'Issy-les-Moulineaux
AOMC Aerojet Ordnance and Manufacturing Company
APC armoured personnel carrier
APFC air portable fuel container
APU auxiliary power unit
ARCE Amphibious River Crossing Equipment
ARE Atelier de Construction Roanne
ARS aerial radiac system
ARRV armoured recovery and repair vehicle
ARV armoured recovery vehicle
AT anti-tank
ATAC all terrain all climate
ATGW anti-tank guided weapon
ATMDS anti-tank mine-dispensing system
ATS Atelier de Construction de Tarbes
AVLB armoured vehicle-launched bridge
AVRE Assault Vehicle Royal Engineers

BAEE British Army Equipment Exhibition
BAOR British Army of the Rhine
BARC beach amphibious resupply cargo
BARV beach armoured recovery vehicle
BFTA bulk fuel tank assembly
bhp brake horse power
BLU bomb live unit

CAD combat assault dory
CAU central alarm unit
CBU cluster bomb unit
CCE commercial construction equipment
cd candelas
CDE Chemical Defence Establishment
CEE combat emplacement excavator
CET Combat Engineer Tractor
CFV Cavalry Fighting Vehicle
CLAMS Clear Lane Marking System
CLC charge linear cutting
CLD Camion Lourd de Dépannage
CLEWP cleared lane explosive widening path charge
CNIM Constructions Navales et Industrielles de la Méditerranée
COE cab over engine
COV Counter Obstacle Vehicle
CRS cable reinforcement kit
CSB Combat Support Boat
CUCV Commercial Utility Cargo Vehicle
CVR(T) Combat Vehicle Reconnaissance (Tracked)

DAP decontamination apparatus

db decibel
DCAN Direction des Constructions et Armes Navales
DEF.STAN Defence Standard
DIN Deutsche Industrie Normen
DROPS demountable rack off-loading and pick-up system
DU detector unit

EBG Engin Blindé de Génie (combat engineer tractor)
EMI electro-magnetic interference
EMP electro-magnetic pulse
EMS enhanced mobility system
EPO Evershed Power Optics
EPU electrical power unit
ETAS Etablissement Technique d'Angers
EWK Eisenwerke Kaiserslautern
EWT engineer wheeled tractor

FAASV Field Artillery Ammunition Support Vehicle
FAC forward air controller; fast attack craft
FAE fuel air explosive
FARE forward area refuelling equipment
FASCAM Family of Scatterable Mines
FAV fast attack vehicle
FAWPSS forward area water point supply system
FCS fire control system
FDC fire direction centre
FEBA forward edge of the battle area
FFR fitted for radio
FN Fabrique Nationale
FOM Forces d'Outre Mer
FV fighting vehicle
FVRDE Fighting Vehicles Research and Development Establishment
FVS fighting vehicle system
FWAM Full Width Attack Mine
FWD four-wheel-drive

GCW gross combination weight
GEMSS Ground-Emplaced Mine-Scattering System
GIAT Groupement Industriel des Armements Terrestres
GLCM Ground Launched Cruise Missile
GMC General Motors Corporation
GPM gallons per minute; Gepanzerte Pioniermaschine
GPMG general-purpose machine gun
grp glass-reinforced plastic
GSRS General Support Rocket System
GVW gross vehicle weight
GW guided weapon

HAB heavy assault bridge
HB heavy barrel
HDRV heavy duty recovery vehicle
HE high explosive
HEAT high explosive anti-tank
HEMTT Heavy Expanded Mobility Tactical Truck
HESH high explosive squash head
HET heavy equipment transporter
HGV heavy goods vehicle
HMD helicopter mine dispenser
HMMHE high mobility materiel handling equipment
HMMWV High-Mobility Multi-purpose Wheeled Vehicle
HMTT High Mobility Tactical Truck
hp horse power

HPD Haut Pouvoir de Destruction
HVSS horizontal volute spring suspension

IFV infantry fighting vehicle
IMP infantry mine project
IOC initial operational capability
IR infra-red
ISDS interior surface decontamination apparatus

JATO jet assisted take-off
JEDSS jet exhaust decontamination apparatus

KHD Klöckner-Humboldt-Deutz

LAB light assault bridge
LAD light aid detachment
LAF light assault ferry
LAR light artillery rocket
LARC lighter amphibious resupply cargo
LHD left-hand drive
LMG light machine gun
LOTS logistics over shore
LPC launch pod container
LVS Logistic Vehicle System
LVT landing vehicle tracked
LWB long wheelbase

MAB Mobile Assault Bridge
MACI military adaptation of commercial items; mine anti/char indetectable
MAF Matériel Amphibie de Franchissement
MARS Military Amphibious Reconnaissance System
MAV maintenance assist vehicle
MBB Messerschmitt-Bölkow-Blohm
MBT main battle tank
MDR Moyen de Déminage Rapide
MERADCOM Mobility Equipment Research and Development Command
METRRA metal re-radiation
MEV medical evacuation vehicle
MEXE Military Engineering Experimental Establishment
MHC material handling crane
MGB Medium Girder Bridge
MIACAH Mine Antichar d'Action Horizontale
MICLIC mine clearing line charge
MICV mechanised infantry combat vehicle
MIL military
MLC military load class
MLRS Multiple Launch Rocket System
MMW medium multi-purpose wheeled
MoD Ministry of Defence
MOLAR mortar/artillery locating radar
MOPMS Modular Pack Mine System
MoT Ministry of Transport
MOWAM mobile water mine
MRTFL medium rough terrain fork lift
MSG Minensuchgerät
MSM/W Minenstreumittel-Werfer
MTT medium tactical truck
MTU Motoren-und-Turbinen-Union
MVEE Military Vehicles and Engineering Establishment

NATO North Atlantic Treaty Organisation
NBC nuclear, biological, chemical

OFC overhead foxhole cover

OHC   overhead cam shaft
OHV   overhead valve
ORATMS   off-route anti-tank mine
system

PAA   Pont Automoteur
d'Accompagnement
PADS   Position Attack Defence System
PDRM   portable dose rate meter
PFC   parapet foxhole cover
PI   product improvement
PIP   product improvement programme
POL   petrol, oil and lubricants
POMINS   Portable Mine Neutralisation
System
POP   Pipeline Outfit, Petroleum
PTO   power take-off
PVC   polyvinyl chloride

RAC   Royal Armoured Corps
RAAC   Royal Australian Armoured
Corps
RAAMS   Remote Anti-Armor Mine
System
RAE   Royal Australian Engineers; Royal
Aircraft Establishment
RATS   Ranger anti-tank system
RBEB   ribbon bridge erection boat
RCT   Royal Corps of Transport
R & D   research and development
RDJTF   Rapid Deployment Joint Task
Force
RE   Royal Engineers
REME   Royal Electrical and Mechanical
Engineers
RFI   radio frequency interference

RFP   request for proposals
RHD   right-hand drive
RLT   rolling liquid transporter
RMID   road mine detector
ROF   Royal Ordnance Factory
ROPS   rollover protective structure
ROWPU   reverse osmosis water
purification unit
rpm   revolutions per minute
RPV   remotely piloted vehicle
RRR   Rapid Runway Repair
RTFL   rough terrain fork lift

SAE   Society of Automotive Engineers
SAM   surface-to-air missile
SAS   Schnellbrücke auf Stutzen
SCADS   Shipborne Containerised Air
Defence System
shp   shaft horse power
SLUFAE   Surface-Launched Unit, Fuel
Air Explosive
SLUMINE   Surface-Launched Unit, Mine
SMS   scatterable mine system
SPB   section personnel bridge
SPG   self-propelled gun
SRDE   Signals Research and
Development Establishment
SRDL   Saunders-Roe Developments
Limited
SS   surface-to-surface
SSM   surface-to-surface missile
STORMS   Sense, Tank Off-Route Mine
System
SUMB   Simca-Unic Marmon-Bocquet
SUMMADE   System Universal Modular
Mine and Demolition Explosives

SUSV   small unit support vehicle
SUU   suspended underwing unit
SWB   short wheelbase
SWG   standard wire gauge

TACOM   Tank-Automotive Command
TARADCOM   Tank-Automotive
Research and Development Command
TD   tank destroyer
TECOM   Test and Evaluation Command
TRM   Toutes Roues Motrices
TWDS   tactical water distribution system
TWMP   track width mine plough

UET   Universal Engineer Tractor
UMIDS   Universal Mine-Dispensing
System

VAB   Véhicule de l'Avant Blindé
VCG   Véhicule de Combat du Génie
VCI   véhicule de combat d'infanterie
VEMASID   Vehicle Magnetic Signature
Duplicator
VLRA   véhicule léger de reconnaissance et
d'appui
VLTT   véhicule de liaison tout terrain
VMRMDS   Vehicle-Mounted Road Mine
Detector System
vpm   vibrations per minute
VRDE   Vehicle Research and
Development Establishment
VVSS   vertical volute spring suspension

WOMBLE   Wire Operated Mobile Bomb
Lifting Equipment

Armoured engineer vehicles

AUSTRIA

Steyr Engineer Tank 4KH7FA–Pi

DEVELOPMENT
The Steyr Engineer Tank 4KH7FA–Pi is a further development of the Steyr 4KH7FA–B Greif ARV which is described and illustrated in the *Armoured recovery vehicles* section.

DESCRIPTION
The hull is made of all-welded steel with the fully enclosed crew compartment at the front. Normal means of entry to the crew compartment is by two doors in the left side of the hull but there are additional hatches in the roof. The engine and transmission are at the rear of the hull. The engine compartment is fitted with a fire extinguishing system that can be operated manually or automatically. Over the engine decking is a stowage platform.

The torsion bar suspension consists of five dual rubber-tyred road wheels with the drive sprocket at the rear and the idler at the front. There are three track return rollers and hydraulic shock absorbers are fitted at the first and fifth road wheel stations.

Mounted on the right side of the superstructure at the front is a hydraulically-operated excavation device, the boom of which can be traversed through 234 degrees. Earth drilling equipment with a 350 mm diameter auger can be mounted in place of the bucket, as can a crane hook.

A winch is situated in the lower part of the hull and leads out through the front part of the hull. It is provided with 57 metres of 16 mm diameter cable and has a maximum pulling capacity of 8000 kg.

Mounted at the front of the hull is a hydraulically-operated dozer blade 2·5 metres wide with a hoisting height of 900 mm.

A full range of engineer equipment is carried including cutting and welding equipment. The Engineer Tank does not have an NBC system but the crew compartment is provided with a ventilation and heating unit.

SPECIFICATIONS
Crew: 4
Weight: 22 000 kg approx
Length: 7·45 m
Width: 2·5 m
Height: 3·15 m
Height transported: 2·8 m

Steyr Engineer Tank 4KH7FA-Pi

Ground clearance: 0·4 m
Track: 2·12 m
Track width: 380 mm
Length of track on ground: 3·037 m
Ground pressure: 0·8 kg/cm²
Max speed: (road) 65·34 km/h
Range: (road) 600 km
Fuel capacity: 500 litres
Fording: 1 m
Gradient: 70%
Side slope: 40%
Trench: 2·1 m
Turning radius: 2·12 m
Engine: Steyr 7FA 6-cylinder liquid-cooled 4-stroke turbo-charged diesel developing 320 hp at 2400 rpm

Transmission: ZF type 6HP500 with 6 forward and 1 reverse gears
Electrical system: 24 V
Batteries: 2 × 12 V, 180 Ah
Armament:
  1 × 12·7 mm M2 HB
  4 smoke dischargers

STATUS
Prototype completed in 1981.

MANUFACTURER
Steyr-Daimler-Puch AG, Werke Vienna, Postfach 100, A1111 Vienna, Austria.

FRANCE

AMX-13 Engineer Combat Vehicle

DEVELOPMENT
The AMX-13 Engineer Combat Vehicle or Véhicule de Combat du Génie (VCG) is based on the chassis and hull of the AMX VCI MICV, which in turn is a development of the AMX-13 light tank chassis. The first prototype of the VCG was completed in 1961 and was simply an AMX VCI fitted with a hydraulically-operated dozer blade at the front of the hull and was limited to clearing operations. This was followed by a second prototype in 1964 and, after troop trials, series production began in 1969. The vehicle has been designed to undertake a wide variety of roles including clearing battlefield obstructions and preparing fire positions.

DESCRIPTION
The hull of the VCG is of all-welded steel construction. The driver is seated at the front of the hull on the left side, with a single-piece hatch cover and three periscopes for observation. The engine is mounted to the right of the driver. The commander and gunner are behind the driver. The armament consists of a standard 12·7 mm or 7·62 mm machine gun which can be traversed through a full 360 degrees, and can be aimed and fired from within the vehicle. A white light searchlight is mounted to the right of the machine gun. To the right of the gunner's position is another hatch, with four periscopes mounted to the front and right. The other seven members of the crew are seated in the rear of the vehicle and enter and leave by two doors, each with a single firing port, in the rear of the hull. On each side of the personnel compartment are two sets of hatches. Each hatch has an upper part which folds back onto the roof and a lower part which has two firing ports and folds down horizontally.

The suspension of the VCG is of the torsion bar type. There are five road wheels with the drive sprocket at the front and the idler at the rear, and four track return rollers. Shock absorbers are provided on the first and fifth road wheel stations. The manual gearbox has five forward gears (second, third, fourth and fifth have

Véhicule de Combat du Génie in travelling order with A-frame lowered and dozer blade raised, and towing trailer (ECP Armées)

synchromesh) and one reverse gear, and steering is through a Cleveland-type differential.

The VCG is provided with an NBC system and infrared driving lights are standard. It is air-portable in the Transall C160 transport aircraft.

EQUIPMENT
At the front of the vehicle is a hydraulically-operated dozer blade 2·85 metres wide and 0·7 metre high, oper-

ated by the driver, which can clear 45 cubic metres of soil an hour.

The sheer legs are mounted one each side of the hull and pivoted at the front; when not in use they lie horizontally along each side of the hull. When assembled, they can lift a maximum of 4500 kg. The winch is also hydraulically operated and the drum is mounted externally on the front of the superstructure, and is provided with 40 metres of cable.

Other equipment carried includes eight rifles, two sub-machine guns, one rocket launcher and six projectiles, one metallic mine detector, one non-metallic mine detector, one electric drill, one hammer drill, power saw and demolition equipment. An external electric socket is provided to operate the electric tools carried. The VCG can also tow a four-wheeled trailer which carries additional equipment and weighs 2500 kg unladen. The trailer can be detached from the VCG without the crew leaving the vehicle.

SPECIFICATIONS
Crew: 10 (commander, driver, gunner and 7 men)
Weight combat: 17 600 kg
Length: (dozer blade in travelling position) 6·05 m
Width: 2·895 m
Height:
  (sheer legs in working position) 3·66 m
  (sheer legs on tripod) 3·46 m
  (sheer legs disassembled and stowed) 2·41 m
Ground clearance: 0·58 m
Track: 2·16 m
Track width: 350 mm
Length of track on ground: 3·012 m
Ground pressure: 0·845 kg/cm²
Max speed: (road) 60 km/h
Range: (road) 350 km
Fuel capacity: 410 litres
Fording: 1 m
Gradient: 60%
Vertical obstacle:
  (forward) 0·65 m
  (reverse) 0·45 m
Trench: (straight sides) 1·6 m
Engine: SOFAM Model 8 GXb, 8-cylinder, water-cooled petrol developing 250 hp at 3200 rpm
Transmission: manual with 5 forward and 1 reverse gears (2nd, 3rd, 4th and 5th are synchromesh)
Electrical system: 24 V
Batteries: 4 × 12 V, 95 Ah
Generator: 4·5 kW

Véhicule de Combat du Génie with A-frame carrying fascine (ECP Armées)

Armament:
  1 × 0·50 (12·7 mm) MG
  3 smoke dischargers
Armour
crew compartment front: 30 mm
crew compartment side: 20 mm
crew compartment roof: 15 mm
hull rear: 15 mm
hull glacis: 15 mm
floor forward: 20 mm
floor rear: 10 mm

STATUS
In service only with the French Army. Production as required.

MANUFACTURER
Creusot-Loire at Châlon-sur-Saône.
  Enquiries to Creusot-Loire, 15 rue Pasquier, 75383 Paris Cedex 08, France.

AMX-30 Combat Engineer Tractor (EBG)

DEVELOPMENT
The AMX-30 Engin Blindé du Génie (EBG) has been developed by the ARE and GIAT to meet the requirements of the French Engineers and the prototype was shown for the first time at the 1981 Satory Exhibition of Military Equipment. From 1985 the French Army will receive 150 EBG vehicles to replace the AMX-13 Engineer Combat Vehicle described in the previous entry.

Typical roles envisaged for the EBG include clearing away battlefield obstacles, preparing obstacles, improving roads, destroying roads, clearing river banks and preparing crossing sites, preparing fire positions, and laying a small minefield quickly.

DESCRIPTION
The chassis of the EBG is almost identical to that of the AMX-30 ARV described in the following section but

uses automotive components of the more recent AMX-30 B2 MBT including the engine, transmission, torque converter and suspension. The three-man crew consists of the vehicle commander, sapper and driver.

Mounted at the front of the hull is a hydraulically-operated dozer blade with a capacity of 250 cubic metres per hour for transport and filling, or 120 cubic metres per hour for excavating. Mounted at the back of the lower part of the dozer blade are six scarifying teeth, these being used for ripping up the surface of roads to a depth of 200 mm when the vehicle is being driven in reverse. The dozer blade is 3·5 metres wide when fully extended and 1·1 metres high.

The hydraulic winch has a capacity of 15 000 to 20 000 kg and is provided with 80 metres of cable and has a winching speed of 0·2 to 0·35 metre per second irrespective of traction force. Automatic winding speed is from 0·2 to 1·4 metres per second with traction capability interlocked with the speed of the vehicle. The winch, which leads out through the front of the vehicle, can be used during amphibious operations.

Pivoted at the front of the hull on the right side is a hydraulic arm with a maximum lifting capacity of 15 000 kg; the two-part arm can be extended to 7·5 metres and traversed through a full 360 degrees. The arm is provided with a lifting hook and pincer type grab similar to that fitted to the Soviet IMR engineer

vehicle described elsewhere in this section. The arm can also be fitted with an auger which can drill 220 mm diameter holes in the ground to a depth of three metres. A 220 mm cutting saw is carried and a 50 kW hydraulic PTO is provided as standard.

Mounted in the centre of the hull, slightly offset to the right, is a two-tier turret. The upper part has a single-piece hatch cover that opens to the rear and is fitted with a 7·62 mm machine gun. To the rear of the turret on either side are two electrically-operated smoke dischargers.

Mounted on the forward part of the lower tier is a launching tube for demolition charges and either side of this are two mine launching tubes, each of which has a launching container of five mines.

The 142 mm calibre demolition charge is 800 mm long, weighs 17 kg and contains 10 kg of explosive. The charge is fin stabilised and fitted with a nose-mounted point detonating fuze; range is between 30 and 300 metres.

The mines are 139 mm in diameter, weigh 2·34 kg and contain 0·7 kg of explosive. The launcher discharges the mines to a distance of between 60 and 250 metres and the mines are then triggered by any vehicle weighing over 1500 kg. According to GIAT, the mines will penetrate a tank floor equivalent to 50 mm of armour plate at 500 mm stand-off distance and 60 degrees

142 mm demolition charge on left with mine dispensers on right with mine visible next to far mine dispenser (T J Gander)

AMX-30 combat engineer tractor (EBG) from left showing equipment stowage and arm extended (T J Gander)

incidence, or break up a tank's track if the mine is run over. Self-destruction of the mines is automatic after a pre-set time.

Standard equipment on the EBG includes provision for deep fording with the aid of a snorkel, passive night periscope for the driver, NBC system and a rangefinder telescope for the sapper.

STATUS
Prototype undergoing trials.

MANUFACTURER
Atelier de Construction Roanne (ARE).

Enquiries to Groupement Industriel des Armements Terrestres (GIAT), 10 place Georges Clémencau, 92211 Saint Cloud, France.

SPECIFICATIONS
Crew: 3
Weight combat: 38 000 kg
Length: (dozer blade up) 7·9 m
Width:
  (over tracks) 3·14 m
  (over hull) 3·5 m
Height: (overall) 2·94 m
Ground clearance: 0·45 m
Track: 2·52 m
Track width: 570 mm
Length of track on ground: 4·12 m
Ground pressure: 0·9 kg/cm²
Max speed: (road) 65 km/h
Fording:
  (without preparation) 2·5 m
  (with preparation) 4 m

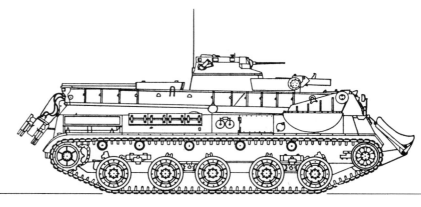

AMX-30 combat engineer tractor (EBG)

Gradient: 60%
Side slope: 30%
Vertical obstacle: 0·9 m
Trench: 2·9 m
Engine: Hispano-Suiza HS 110-2 12-cylinder, water-cooled super-charged multi-fuel developing 700 hp at 2000 rpm, or HS 110-S2 developing 800 hp
Transmission: 5 SD with 5 gears in both directions, or ENC 200 gearbox with lock-up torque converter with 5 forward and 1 reverse gears

Electrical system: 24 V
Armament:
  1 × 7·62 mm MG
  2 × 2 smoke dischargers
  1 × 142 mm demolition charge projector
  4 × mine projectors
Ammunition:
  (MG) 4000 rounds
  (demolition charges) 5
  (mines) 40 (8 containers each holding 5)

Panhard M3 VLA Engineer Vehicle

DESCRIPTION
The Panhard M3 VLA Engineer Vehicle is essentially the Panhard M3 APC fitted with a removable hydraulically-operated dozer blade at the front of the hull. Its six-man crew consists of commander/gunner, driver, pioneer section commander and three pioneers.

The hull is made of all-welded steel with the driver seated at the front in the centre. He has a single-piece hatch cover that opens to the right and has three integral periscopes for forward observation. There are three small hatch covers in each side of the hull which lift upwards and there is also a large door in each side of the hull that opens to the front. At the rear of the hull are two doors, each with a single firing port. There are two circular hatches in the roof, the forward one of which is fitted with a Creusot-Loire STB rotary support shield armed with a 7·62 mm machine gun.

The engine and transmission are immediately behind the driver. The transmission consists of two gearboxes in one, coupled on both sides of the bevel pinion. The low-range gearbox comprises two low gears, top gear, and one reverse, which are used in rough country. The high-range gearbox has three low gears and an over-drive. There is no clutch pedal, just a gear selection gate.

The suspension consists of coil springs and hydro-pneumatic shock absorbers acting on the suspension arms of the wheel mechanism. Brakes are hydraulic, with separate circuits for the front and rear wheels. The tyres have puncture-proof Hutchinson inner tubes.

The M3 VLA is fully amphibious, propelled in water by its wheels. Optional equipment includes a ventilation system and infra-red or passive night vision equipment.

Mounted at the front of the M3 VLA is a hydraulically-operated dozer blade which can be used to clear obstacles and fill in craters. The blade is 2·2 metres wide and can be raised a maximum of 0·4 metre.

The tools and equipment of the pioneer section are carried at the rear of the hull and include one set of trench crossing plates and two removable searchlights with magnetic attachments for night work.

SPECIFICATIONS
Crew: 6
Configuration: 4 × 4
Weight: 6215 kg
Length:
  (travelling) 4·75 m
  (working) 5·05 m
Width: 2·45 m
Height: (without armament) 2 m
Ground clearance: 0·35 m
Track: 2·054 m
Wheelbase: 2·7 m
Max speed:
  (road) 90 km/h
  (water) 4 km/h
Range: 600 km
Fuel: 165 litres
Fording: amphibious
Gradient: 60%
Side slope: 30%
Vertical obstacle: 0·3 m
Trench: (with 1 channel) 0·8 m

Panhard M3 VLA engineer vehicle with dozer blade lowered

Panhard M3 VLA engineer vehicle with dozer blade raised

Engine: Panhard Model 4 HD 4-cylinder, horizontally-opposed petrol developing 90 hp at 4300 rpm
Transmission: 6 forward and 1 reverse gears (see text)
Armament:
  1 × 7·62 mm MG
  4 smoke dischargers (optional)

STATUS
In production. In service with Bahrain.

MANUFACTURER
Société de Constructions Mécaniques Panhard et Levassor, 18 avenue d'Ivry, 75621 Paris, France.

GERMANY, FEDERAL REPUBLIC

Leopard Armoured Engineer Vehicle

DEVELOPMENT

The Leopard Armoured Engineer Vehicle is a direct development of the Leopard ARV and differs from it only in minor details. The first prototype, based on a design by Dr Ing hc P Porsche KG, was completed by MaK of Kiel in 1967, with the first production vehicles completed in 1968. Wherever possible standard Leopard MBT components have been used, for example the engine, transmission and suspension.

Typical roles carried out by the Leopard Armoured Engineer Vehicle are:

excavation work such as levelling and filling bomb craters, preparing river entries and estuaries, erecting soil obstacles and walls and scarifying solid and frozen ground.

removing barriers and obstacles.

drilling holes for the preparation of demolitions, for fox holes or for foundations.

recovering and lifting loads up to 20 000 kg by the 270 degree traversable crane.

dozing and recovery work with the main winch.

carrying loads on the rear platform; a powerpack can be carried in place of the earth auger.

supporting repair work on the battlefield and engineer operations of all kinds, including the use of demolition equipment.

DESCRIPTION

The hull is of all-welded construction with the crew compartment at the front and the engine and transmission at the rear. The driver is seated at the front of the vehicle to the left of the crane and is provided with a single-piece hatch cover and three periscopes for observation, one of which can be replaced by an infra-red periscope. The commander is seated to the rear of the driver and has a single-piece hatch cover and eight periscopes, one of which can be replaced by an infra-red periscope. There is another hatch to the rear of the commander's position, and three periscopes provide vision to the rear of the vehicle. Finally, there is a swivelling periscope in the roof of the superstructure. The crew of four, commander, driver and two mechanics, can enter the vehicle either through the roof hatches or through two doors in the left side of the hull. The suspension is of the torsion bar type and consists of seven road wheels with the drive sprocket at the rear and the idler at the front. There are four track return rollers. The first, second, third, sixth and seventh road wheel stations are fitted with hydraulic shock absorbers. The tracks are of the double-pin type and have rubber pads.

The AEV can carry out similar roles to the ARV including recovering disabled vehicles and changing vehicle components (although an auger is carried in place of the spare engine carried on the ARV).

The dozer blade is mounted at the front of the hull and operated by two hydraulic cylinders through two lever arms, and is mechanically locked when not in use. The dozer blade has a maximum capacity of 200 cubic metres an hour and the width of the blade can be extended to 3·75 metres by additional side attachments. It can be fitted with four scarifiers to rip up the surface of roads. The installation of a heat exchanger enables the vehicle to perform unlimited bulldozing activities even at high ambient temperatures. In addition to being used for dozing operations, the dozer blade is also used to stabilise the AEV when the crane is being used, or when vehicles are being recovered.

The main winch with its horizontal cable drum is in the centre of the crew compartment under the floor. This winch is provided with a total of 90 metres of 33 mm cable. The maximum tractive effort of the main winch in the lowest cable position is 35 000 kg, which can be increased to 70 000 kg when using an appropriately located guide pulley. The exit opening for the main winch is located at the nose of the vehicle. A hydraulically driven cable tensioning device is located immediately behind the opening and automatically extends or rewinds the cable.

The crane is mounted at the front of the hull on the right side and when in the travelling position lies horizontally along the right side of the hull. It has a maximum lifting capacity of 20 000 kg when being used with the dozer blade as a stabiliser. A scale on the side plate of the jib shows the allowed load: if it is exceeded the jib is automatically stopped. The two hydraulic cylinders for lifting the jib are arranged so that they are fully splinter proof in the travelling position and extensively splinter proof in the operating position. The jib is turned by the traversing gearbox directly underneath the console of the crane. If the hydraulics fail the traversing gear can be operated by hand. The ladder mounted on the jib assists in the assembly of the earth drilling equipment and can also be used for other work such as overhead lines. The auger is mounted when required at the end of

Leopard armoured engineer vehicle carrying out dozing operations

Leopard armoured engineer vehicle preparing to use auger to bore hole (Federal German Army)

the jib crane and can drill holes 700 mm in diameter to a maximum depth of 2 metres. The hydraulic oil is supplied to the radial piston motor of the earth drill through hoses which can be connected to the jib boom by means of quick-disconnect couplings.

The hoisting winch with a vertical cable drum is mounted on the right side of the crew compartment. It is provided with 100 metres of 13 mm diameter cable.

Equipment carried on the AEV includes a set of shackles, tow bar, electric impact wrench, guide pull, and electric welding and cutting equipment. For demolition work a total of 117 kg of explosives are carried. This consists of one igniter set B, 98 demolition blocks DM12, five demolition blocks DM19, six demolition blocks DM29, 12 demolition blocks DM51, conduit for detonation cord, three round heads for conduit for detonation cord DM51.

Armament consists of a 7·62 mm MG3 machine gun mounted in the bow of the tank on the left side; this has an elevation of +15 degrees, a depression of −15 degrees, and a traverse of 15 degrees left and right. A similar machine gun is mounted on the commander's hatch for anti-aircraft defence. Six smoke dischargers are mounted on the left side of the hull.

The AEV is also provided with an NBC system, crew heater, fire warning and extinguishing system and a hull escape hatch. The basic model can ford to a depth of 2·1 metres, but for deep fording operations a snorkel can be installed quickly.

SPECIFICATIONS

Crew: 4
Weight:
(empty) 40 200 kg
(loaded) 40 800 kg
Length: (with dozer blade raised) 7·98 m
Width:
(with side elements of blade fitted) 3·75 m
(hull) 3·25 m
Height: (with AA MG) 2·69 m
Ground clearance: 0·44 m
Track: 2·7 m
Track width: 550 mm
Length of track on ground: 4·236 m
Ground pressure: 0·86 kg/cm²

Max speed: (road) 65 km/h
Range:
(road) 850 km
(cross country) 500 km
Fuel capacity: 1410 litres
Fording: 2·1 m
(with snorkel) 4 m
Gradient: 60%
Side slope: 30%
Vertical obstacle: 1·15 m
Trench: 3 m
Engine: MTU MB 838 Ca.M500 10-cylinder multi-fuel developing 830 hp at 2200 rpm
Transmission: ZF 4 HP 250 4 forward and 2 reverse speeds
Electrical system: 24 V
Batteries: 6 with total capacity of 300 Ah, charged by 3-phase generator driven from main engine
Armament:
1 × 7·62 mm MG3 MG in bow
1 × 7·62 mm MG3 MG on commander's hatch
4250 rounds of 7·62 mm ammunition
6 smoke dischargers
Armour
nose: 40 mm at 60°
front: 40 mm at 45°
sides upper: 35 mm at 65°
sides lower: 25 mm at 90°
superstructure sides: 35 mm
superstructure front and rear: 25 mm
roof and decking: 10 mm
hull rear: 25 mm at 90°
hull floor: 15 mm

STATUS

Production complete. In service with Belgium (6), Federal Republic of Germany (37), Italy (12), Netherlands (25). If further orders are received the vehicle can be placed back in production. OTO Melara are now building 28 Leopard AEVs for the Italian Army with deliveries expected in 1984–85.

MANUFACTURER

Krupp MaK Maschinenbau GmbH, PO Box 9009, 23 Kiel 17, Federal Republic of Germany.

GPM Engineer Vehicle

Prototypes of the GPM (Gepanzerte Pioniermaschine), or Pionier Panzer 2, based on the chassis of a Leopard 1 MBT, were built by Krupp MaK and Eisenwerke Kaisers-lautern Göppner but owing to the present defence budgetary situation in West Germany no production contract has yet been awarded. Photographs and brief details on both of the prototypes of the GPM were given on page 5 of *Jane's Military Vehicles and Ground Support Equipment 1981/82.*

ISRAEL

RKM Bulldozer Attachment

DESCRIPTION

The RKM bulldozer attachment was developed jointly by Urdan RKM Limited and the Israeli Army to provide every main battle tank with the ability to act as an earth-moving vehicle.

The RKM bulldozer attachment has three main assemblies. The first is a standard bulldozer blade which has been modified slightly to improve its performance when working in sandy soils. The second part is the electro-hydraulic unit which is connected to the vehicle's electrical system to supply hydraulic power to the main cylinder. The electro-hydraulic system and the movements of the blade are controlled from a control box inside the driver's compartment. The third part of the RKM bulldozer attachment is the main structure which houses the electro-hydraulic unit and is attached to the tank. It carries the bulldozer blade and the activating cylinder. The attachment can be installed on a tank by the normal crew in about 30 minutes. Removing the system takes 15 minutes. If required the blade can be locked in its upper (travel) position manually even if the hydraulic system is damaged, and without any member of the crew leaving the tank.

The RKM bulldozer attachment has four operating modes. One is the travel position with the blade in the maximum up position. The bulldozer blade can also be made to 'float' so that the blade rests on the soil, but in the 'blade down' mode the hydraulic cylinder pushes the blade down into the soil for heavy earthmoving. In this 'blade down' position the blade routers can be extended for the fourth mode.

The Israeli Army has fitted the RKM to its Centurion and M60 tanks but the attachment can also be adapted for the Leopard 1 and 2, the AMX-30 and the Chieftain by adapting the mounting lugs.

RKM bulldozer attachment on Centurion MBT

STATUS
Production. In service with the Israeli Army.

MANUFACTURER
Urdan RKM Limited, Industrial Centre 42378, Natanya, Israel.

Israeli Armoured Engineer Vehicles

DESCRIPTION

The Israeli Army uses two modified Sherman tank chassis in the armoured engineer role. The first of these is a Sherman with a cast hull and horizontal volute suspension system, turret traversed to rear and armament removed, and an hydraulically-operated dozer blade fitted at the front of the hull. The bow machine gun has also been removed on this model.

The second vehicle is called the Trail Blazer by the Israeli Army and also uses a modified Sherman tank chassis with a cast hull and horizontal volute suspension system, and turret removed. Mounted at the front of the hull on the right side is a large hydraulically-operated crane similar to that installed on Leopard 1 and AMX-30 ARVs which is used for removing obstacles and changing powerpacks in the field. When not required this lies along the right side of the hull. Mounted at the front and rear are hydraulically-operated blades; the rear one is normally used when the Trail Blazer is employed in the recovery mode, while the front one can be used to clear obstacles as well. The winch compartment is in the

Sherman dozer tank with angled dozer blade lowered (Israeli Army)

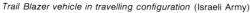

Trail Blazer vehicle in travelling configuration (Israeli Army)

Trail Blazer vehicle with crane deployed (Israeli Army)

centre of the hull where the turret was previously situated and stowage boxes are mounted along either side of the hull.

STATUS
In service with the Israeli Army.

MANUFACTURER
Chassis, United States. Conversion, Israeli Army facilities.

JAPAN

Type 67 Armoured Engineer Vehicle

DESCRIPTION
The Type 67 Armoured Engineer Vehicle is based on the chassis of the Type 61 MBT and was preceded by a trials vehicle which was based on the Sherman M4A3E8. This had a dozer blade at the front of the hull and a small crane. The Type 67 AEV has been designed to clear obstacles off the battlefield and for this purpose is provided with a dozer blade and crane.

SPECIFICATIONS
Crew: 4
Weight: 35 000 kg
Length: 7·46 m
Width: 3·21 m
Height: 2·23 m

Ground clearance: 0·4 m
Track: 2·45 m
Track width: 500 mm
Length of track on ground: 3·7 m
Ground pressure: 0·95 kg/cm²
Max speed: (road) 45 km/h
Range: 200 km
Fording: 0·99 m
Gradient: 60%
Vertical obstacle: 0·685 m
Trench: 2·489 m
Engine: Mitsubishi Type 12 HM 21 WT V-12 direct injection turbo-charged air-cooled diesel developing 600 hp at 2100 rpm
Transmission: mechanical with 5 forward and 1 reverse gears, with 2-speed auxiliary reduction unit
Electrical system: 24 V
Batteries: 4 × 12 V, 200 Ah

Armament:
 1 × 0·50 (12·7 mm) MG
 1 × 0·30 (7·62 mm) MG
Armour
hull front: 46 mm
hull sides: 25 mm
hull rear: 15 mm

STATUS
Production complete. In service only with the Japanese Ground Self-Defence Force.

MANUFACTURER
Production was undertaken at the Maruko, Tokyo, plant of Mitsubishi Heavy Industries, but AFV production is now at the Sagamihara plant near Tokyo. Mitsubishi Heavy Industries, 5-1, Marunouchi 2-chome, Chiyoda-ku, Tokyo, Japan.

Type 75 Armoured Dozer

DEVELOPMENT
Development of an armoured dozer began in 1964 and two prototypes were built in fiscal year 1972 by Komatsu, one with a straight dozer blade and another with an angled blade. After extensive trials the latter was standardised in 1975 and the dozer is now in service with the Japanese Ground Self-Defence Force.

The Type 75 armoured dozer can carry out over 90 per cent of the tasks of the D6 medium dozer but has a much higher road speed, which enables it to keep up with the leading elements of a convoy.

DESCRIPTION
When the vehicle is travelling the dozer blade is to the rear and the fully armoured crew compartment at the front. The two-man crew can enter either by a door in the right side of the hull or through two circular rear-opening roof hatches. The driver is seated on the left with a rectangular shutter hinged at the top immediately in front of him. This has an integral vision block and can be locked open. The commander is seated to the right of the driver and has a small square shutter hinged at the top, which also has a vision block and can be locked open. Vision blocks are provided in each side of this compartment and there is a shutter with an integral vision block in the rear of the crew compartment for forward vision during dozing operations. There is also a single vision block to the left of the shutter.

The engine and radiator are at the rear of the vehicle. In a combat area they are protected by armoured plates which are removed when the Type 75 is operating in a non-combat area.

The torsion bar suspension consists of five dual rubber-tyred road wheels with the drive sprocket at the front and the idler at the rear. There are also two track return rollers. Hydraulic shock absorbers are fitted at the first, second and fifth road wheel stations.

The hydraulically-operated dozer blade is controlled by the driver from inside the armoured cab. The dozer

Type 75 armoured dozer showing angled dozer blade. This vehicle is not fitted with armour plates for engine compartment

blade is hinged in the middle and a hydraulic winch can be fitted in front of the cab if required.

SPECIFICATIONS
Crew: 2
Weight: 19 200 kg
Length:
 (travelling) 6·84 m
 (working) 6·3 m
Width:
 (travelling) 2·7 m
 (working) 3·45 m
Height: 2·79 m
Max speed: 45 km/h

Fording: 1 m
Gradient: 60%
Engine: water-cooled diesel developing 345 hp at 2100 rpm on road and 160 hp at 1850 rpm when working
Armament: none

STATUS
In production. In service with the Japanese Ground Self-Defence Force.

MANUFACTURER
Komatsu Ltd., 2-3-6, Akasaka, Minato-ku, Tokyo, Japan.

SPAIN

M-47 E2I Combat Engineer Vehicle

DEVELOPMENT
In 1981 Spain purchased 100 M47 tanks from West German and Italian sources, half of which were modernised to become 105 mm gun-armed tanks for the Spanish Army. One vehicle, after conversion, was used as a prototype which could later be converted into either a combat engineer vehicle or an armoured recovery vehicle. The superstructure of the two conversions is very similar both having a front-mounted dozer blade and a swivelling jib crane. They differ in the type and scale of equipment carried. To date only a prototype has been constructed but it is anticipated that 19 will be converted to the combat engineer vehicle configuration and the final total may well be 25. Work is being undertaken by the Talbot Company, formerly Chrysler Hispania. Before the Chrysler take-over the company was known as Barreiros.

DESCRIPTION
On the M-47 E2I (I – Ingenieros) the basic hull and suspension of the American M47 is retained. The

transmission has also been retained but the main powerpack is now a Continental V-12 diesel. The main hull superstructure appears to be closely modelled on that of the Leopard 1 armoured engineer vehicle and armoured recovery vehicle as the shape and layout are very similar. The main box-shaped compartment is to the left of a 360-degree swivelling crane jib with the traversing platform mounted well forward. The box compartment houses the crew of four, a commander, driver and two mechanics. Mounted on the front hull is a dozer blade operated via two hydraulic cylinders.

The M-47 E2I is equipped with various items of special equipment. The large crane jib can be elevated to 65 degrees at which angle the jib hook will be 7·08 metres above the ground. At zero degrees and extended to the right-hand side of the hull the jib has an extension of 4·81 metres. The main item carried by the jib appears to be a large hook but the jib arm is provided with ladder rungs and a series of tubing side supports allows the top of the jib to be used as a form of working platform for overhead constructions. The main box compartment houses a winch equipped with 100 metres of cable. With

a single strand of this cable the winch can pull a load of 35 000 kg through the bottom front hull. If the cable is doubled the load can be up to 70 000 kg. The dozer blade is used during winching and loads can be pulled from an angle of 15 degrees either side of the hull centre line. Loads can also be pulled from 15 degrees above the horizontal and 40 degrees below. There is an electrical generator powered by an 8 hp air-cooled diesel engine which supplies 220/380 volts at 5·5 kVA. An air compressor supplying a 50-litre air tank is also carried. The crane jib has a maximum lift of 50 000 kg. The dozer blade is 3·65 metres wide and 0·88 metre high and is fitted with three scarifying teeth.

A 12·7 mm (0·50) Browning HB machine gun is mounted on a pintle over the commander's hatch with a 7·62 mm MG1-A3 machine gun to the left of the driver's position, firing through the front hull. Two sets of three-barrelled Wegmann smoke grenade launchers are carried, one on each side of the crew compartment.

Various types of specialised engineer equipment such as demolition materials, tools and shackles can be carried both internally and externally.

SPECIFICATIONS
Crew: 4
Weight: 47 100 kg
Length:
   (jib rear, dozer blade raised) 8·15 m
   (jib rear, dozer blade down) 8·17 m
Width:
   (overall) 3·65 m
   (over tracks) 3·415 m
   (inside tracks) 2·235 m
Height:
   (overall) 3·35 m
   (top of commander's cupola) 2·89 m
Ground clearance: 0·47 m
Track width: 590 mm
Length of track on ground: 3·91 m
Ground pressure: 1·02 kg/cm²
Max speed: 56 km/h
Range: 600 km
Fuel capacity: 1500 litres
Fording: 1·2 m
Gradient: 60%
Side slope: 30%
Vertical obstacle: 0·9 m
Trench: 2·6 m
Engine: Continental Model AVDS-1790-2D 29·316-litre V-12 air-cooled diesel developing 760 hp at 2400 rpm
Transmission: GMC-Allison CD-850-6A with 2 forward and 1 reverse ranges
Electrical system: 24 V
Number of batteries: 6 × 12 V, 300 Ah
Armament:
   1 × 12·7 mm (0·50) MG
   1 × 7·62 mm MG
   2 × 3-barrel smoke dischargers
Ammunition:
   (12·7 mm) 600 rounds
   (7·62 mm) 2000 rounds

STATUS
Prototype completed. Conversion of at least 19 vehicles planned. Final total may be 25.

MANUFACTURER/CONVERTOR
Talbot, Apartado 140, Madrid, Spain.

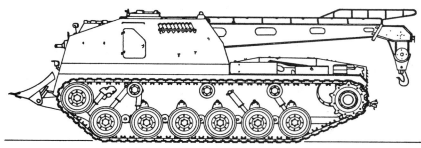

M-47 E21 combat engineer vehicle

UNION OF SOVIET SOCIALIST REPUBLICS

Combat Engineer Vehicle (IMR)

DESCRIPTION
The Soviet Combat Engineer Vehicle IMR (engineer vehicle for the removal of obstacles) (Inzhenernaia Mashina Razgrazhdeniia) was first seen in 1973 and is based on the T-55 MBT chassis. The turret has been removed and replaced by a hydraulically-operated crane which can be traversed through 360 degrees. The jib of this crane is telescopic and when in the travelling position rests on a cradle at the rear of the hull. The cradle folds down against the engine deck when the crane is being used. The crane is provided with a pair of pincer type grabs which are used to remove trees and

Soviet combat engineer vehicle (IMR) showing dozer blade, with crane traversed to rear

Soviet combat engineer vehicle (IMR) with dozer blade in V-configuration and using pincers to lift tree trunk

Soviet combat engineer vehicle (IMR) with crane traversed forward, showing bucket above 4th and 5th road wheels and unditching beam at rear of hull

other obstacles. The grab can be replaced by a small bucket which is normally carried above the left rear track when not required. The crane operator is provided with an armoured cupola which has observation windows. A searchlight is mounted on the crane for night operations. At the front of the hull is a hydraulically-operated dozer blade which can be used in the straight or V-configuration, but cannot angle doze. An unditching beam is carried at the rear of the hull.

SPECIFICATIONS (provisional)
Crew: 2
Weight: 34 000 kg
Length:
(dozer blade in operating position and crane stowed) 10·6 m
(hull) 6·45 m
Width:
(hull) 3·28 m
(over dozer blade) 3·48 m

Height:
(crane operator's cupola) 2·48 m
(crane in travelling position) 3·37 m
Ground clearance: 0·425 m
Track: 2·64 m
Track width: 580 mm
Length of track on ground: 3·84 m
Ground pressure: 0·76 kg/cm²
Max speed: (road) 48 km/h
Range: 400 km
Fuel capacity: 812 litres
Fording: 1·4 m
Gradient: 60%
Vertical obstacle: 0·8 m
Trench: 2·7 m
Engine: Model V-55 V-12 water-cooled diesel developing 580 hp at 2000 rpm
Transmission: manual with 5 forward and 1 reverse gears
Electrical system: 24 V

Batteries: 4 × 12 V, 280 Ah
Armament: nil
Armour
hull front: 100 mm at 60°
hull sides: 70 mm
hull rear: 60 mm
hull floor: 20 mm
hull roof: 30 mm

STATUS
In service with the Soviet Army, other members of the Warsaw Pact and Yugoslavia.

MANUFACTURER
Soviet state arsenals.

UNITED KINGDOM

Centurion Mk 5 Assault Vehicle Royal Engineer (AVRE)

DEVELOPMENT
The Centurion Mk 5 Assault Vehicle Royal Engineer (or AVRE) was developed by the Fighting Vehicles Research and Development Establishment (now the Military Vehicles and Engineering Establishment) to replace the Churchill AVRE which entered service shortly after the end of the Second World War. The first prototype of the Centurion AVRE was completed in 1957 with production being undertaken in the early 1960s. It is deployed with Armoured Engineer Squadrons in the British Army of the Rhine. Some of the roles performed by the Centurion AVRE, such as preparing fire positions and removing roadblocks, have been taken over by the new Combat Engineer Tractor, but the Centurion AVRE will remain in service for the foreseeable future.

DESCRIPTION
The Centurion AVRE (FV 4003) is based on a standard Centurion tank hull. The hull is of all-welded construction and the turret is cast with the roof welded in position. The driver is seated at the front of the hull on the right side and is provided with two hatch covers which open left and right, each hatch cover being provided with a periscope. The co-driver is seated to the left of the driver and is also provided with two hatch covers, but only one of these has a periscope. The other three crew members are in the turret, the commander and gunner being on the right and the loader on the left. The commander's cupola can be traversed through a full 360 degrees and has seven periscopes for observation plus a sight linked to the gunner's sight. The loader has a two piece hatch cover which opens fore and aft. In addition to the stowage boxes on either side of the turret a large wire stowage basket is mounted at the rear of the turret.

The engine and transmission are at the rear of the hull, as are the fuel tanks. The suspension is of the Horstmann type and consists of three units, each with two pairs of road wheels. The drive sprocket is at the rear and the idler is at the front. There are six track support rollers. Shock absorbers are provided for the first and last road wheel stations.

Main armament of the Centurion AVRE consists of a short barrelled 165 mm demolition gun with a fume extractor. This gun has been designed to destroy pillboxes and other battlefield targets. The 165 mm gun fires a HESH projectile weighing 29 kg to a maximum range of 2400 metres. However, its effective range is 1200 metres as it has a very low muzzle velocity. A 0·30 Browning machine gun is mounted to the left of the main armament and there is a similar weapon on the commander's cupola for anti-aircraft defence. Six smoke dischargers are mounted either side of the turret.

A hydraulically-operated dozer blade mounted at the front of the hull can move 229 cubic metres of soil an hour. A fascine cradle, which can also be used to carry a length of class 60 trackway, is also mounted at the front of the vehicle. Full details of this are given in the *Portable roadways* section. Centurion AVREs in West Germany are now being equipped with mine-clearing ploughs as an alternative to the dozer blade. Details can be found in the *Mine-clearing* section. The fascine is a 1·828 metre diameter bundle of wood or piping and is dropped into anti-tank ditches and other obstacles, either manually or by electrically fired blow-out pins. The fascine can also be split to provide 18 metres of trackway. A jib can be mounted at the front of the hull for lifting operations if required. At the rear of the hull is a rotatable

Centurion Mk 5 AVRE fitted with mine ploughs, shown raised (T J Gander)

Centurion Mk 5 AVRE carrying fascine assembled from plastic piping (T J Gander)

towing hook which can be electrically jettisoned if required. The Centurion can also tow a two-wheeled trailer carrying the Giant Viper mine clearance system, or a 7·5-ton four-wheeled trailer. The latter can carry a variety of equipment including 130 rounds of 165 mm HESH ammunition or 280 jerricans.

The Centurion AVRE is not provided with an NBC

system but can be fitted with infra-red night vision equipment. A deep fording kit was developed but was not issued.

STATUS
Production complete. In service only with the British Army.

SPECIFICATIONS
Crew: 5
Weight:
  (empty) 49 627 kg
  (loaded) 51 810 kg (without fascine)
Length: 8·686 m
Width:
  (over hull) 3·39 m
  (over dozer blade) 3·962 m
Height: 3·009 m
Ground clearance: 0·46 m
Track: 2·641 m
Track width: 610 mm
Length of track on ground: 4·572 m
Ground pressure: 0·95 kg/cm²

Max speed: (road) 34·6 km/h
Range:
  (road) 176 km
  (cross country) 113 km
Fuel capacity: 1037 litres
Fording: 1·45 m
Gradient: 60%
Vertical obstacle: 0·941 m
Trench: 3·352 m
Engine: Rolls-Royce Meteor Mk IVB 12-cylinder liquid-cooled petrol developing 650 bhp at 2550 rpm
Transmission: Merritt-Brown Z51R with 5 forward and 2 reverse gears
Electrical system: 24 V
Batteries: 4 × 6 V, 115 Ah

Armament:
1 × 165 mm demolition gun
1 × 0·30 (7·62 mm) Browning MG coaxial with main armament
1 × 0·30 (7·62 mm) Browning AA MG
6 smoke dischargers either side of turret
Armour
turret front: 152 mm
glacis: 118 mm
nose: 76 mm
hull sides: 51 mm
hull rear upper: 38 mm
hull rear lower: 20 mm
hull floor: 17 mm

Combat Engineer Tractor (FV180)

DEVELOPMENT
In 1962 a General Staff Target (GST 26) was issued for an engineer equipment which would combine the characteristics of an armoured vehicle and an earth mover. Existing commercial earthmoving equipment could not meet this requirement as it had poor mobility, lacked both armour protection and communications equipment and had no amphibious capability.

The following year, three companies, Caterpillar UK, GKN and Vickers, were invited to put forward their proposals for a vehicle to meet the General Staff Target. GKN and Vickers responded but their proposals were not taken up. In 1965 the Military Engineering Experimental Establishment at Christchurch (now part of the Military Vehicles and Engineering Establishment) prepared a design to meet GST 26. At the same time discussions took place between Britain, France and West Germany for the joint development of a Combat Engineer Tractor.

Subsequently, two prototypes were built by the Royal Ordnance Factory at Leeds, based on a design prepared by the Military Engineering Experimental Establishment. They were powered by a Cummins V8 diesel which developed 350 hp, were fully amphibious and incorporated some features of the American Universal Engineer Tractor. They were delivered in 1968 but France had meanwhile dropped out of the project as it required a vehicle with a higher water speed and only limited earthmoving capabilities.

In 1970, after trials with the two test rigs in both West Germany and the United Kingdom, the West Germans withdrew from the programme as they required a heavier vehicle without amphibious capability mainly for clearing river crossing points. One was eventually

developed as the GPM and prototypes have been built by both MaK and EWK using a Leopard 1 MBT chassis, but so far has not been placed in production.

Meanwhile a major redesign of the vehicle had been carried out with two major objectives: to use standard commercial components wherever possible (engine, transmission, steer unit and winch), and to make the vehicle amphibious with the minimum preparation. In 1969 a General Staff Requirement was issued and the following year Royal Ordnance Factory Leeds was nominated as the prime manufacturer with the Military Vehicles and Engineering Establishment responsible for design work. A contract was awarded to Leeds for seven prototypes, all of which were delivered between February 1973 and January 1974.

Extensive trials were carried out in both the United Kingdom and West Germany and in July 1975 the Combat Engineer Tractor was accepted for service with the British Army. As a result of trials modifications were incorporated in production vehicles, including improved track tension, replacing the steel-rimmed tyre with a rubber one at the front road wheel station and improvements to the buoyancy system.

Production of the Combat Engineer Tractor began at the Royal Ordnance Factory at Nottingham in 1977 and the first production vehicle was accepted in May 1978. The Combat Engineer Tractor was evaluated in 1978 by the United States Air Force for possible use in rapid runway repair. Production was completed in March 1981 after 141 had been built for the British Army.

DESCRIPTION
The CET has been designed to provide integral engineer support for the battle group and typical roles include excavating vehicle and gun pits for defensive purposes, repairing and maintaining roads, preparation

of river banks, recovering disabled vehicles, and preparing or clearing obstacles.

The hull of the CET is made of all-welded aluminium armour, which is supplied by Alcan. The vehicle is normally driven with its bucket to the rear, and in this position the crew are seated on the left side. The following description is for the vehicle in this condition.

The driver is seated at the front and also operates the winch, with the bucket operator to his rear. Both crew members can reverse their seats and essential controls are duplicated so that either crew member can operate the vehicle. The crew compartment is provided with two hatch covers which open to the right and a total of ten vision blocks.

The engine and transmission are mounted at the right side of the hull with the final drives being mounted at the front of the hull. From the engine, power is passed through two gear boxes to a steering unit and final drives. The first of these gear boxes, the transfer box, provides PTOs for the water propulsion units and hydraulic pumps. Controlled differential steering is used for road and cross country drive and skid steering is used for bulldozing operations, and an independent clutch/brake system is provided for this purpose.

The suspension is of the torsion bar type and consists of five road wheels with the fifth road wheel acting as the idler. The drive sprocket is at the front. The tracks are of cast steel with rubber bushes and rubber pads are provided to reduce damage when operating on roads. Hydraulic double acting ram type dampers are mounted on the front and rear wheel stations and can be locked from the crew compartment if required.

The CET can ford to a depth of 1·829 metres (without preparation), but with preparation the vehicle is fully amphibious. It is propelled in the water by two 330 mm Dowty water jets which are mounted one either side of

Combat Engineer Tractor afloat (T J Gander)

Combat Engineer Tractor showing rocket-propelled anchor and carrying class 30 trackway in bucket (Royal Ordnance Factories)

Combat Engineer Tractor with jib mounted in bucket and carrying bridging panels
(Royal Ordnance Factories)

Combat Engineer Tractor showing alternative trailing idler configuration
(T J Gander)

the hull. When in the water steering is accomplished by deflecting the thrust from the unit on the inside of the turn and deflecting both units gives reverse. The preparation required before entering the water is to unfold the trim board at the front of the hull and inflate two Hycafloat units to the rear of the trim board. The units were developed by FPT Industries of Portsmouth and replace the original bellows type units installed on the prototypes. Two plastic-cased polyurethane foam blocks are fitted into the bucket and held in place by retaining straps.

The bucket is of light alloy construction with steel cutting edges and tines, and has a maximum capacity of 1·72 cubic metres. Its maximum lift height is 1·829 metres and its minimum lift height is 102 mm below the track line. This can be used for both digging or bulldozing and can also be used as an earth anchor. Its maximum capacity is 300 cubic metres per hour over 100 metres hauling distance.

The two-speed winch has a maximum pull of 8000 kg and is provided with 107 metres of 16 mm diameter rope; maximum winching speed is 113 metres a minute. For self assistance, the winching speed is matched to the speed of the tractor. A high speed winching facility is available for ferrying work. The rope can be led to the front or rear of the vehicle by direction changing blocks.

A self-emplacing earth anchor is mounted on the top of the hull and this can be rocket-propelled to a maximum distance of 91·4 metres. The anchor is attached to the vehicle's winch rope and is used to assist the vehicle when leaving a river with a steep bank.

All CETs are provided with an NBC filtration pack which is installed at the front of the vehicle, providing clean air to the crew compartment. The filters are changed through an external hatch. If required a passive night vision device can be installed at either crew position.

The CET will also be used to tow the trailer mounted Giant Viper mine clearance system. The vehicle is airportable in the Lockheed C-130 Hercules aircraft.

The following ancillary equipment can be installed on the CET if required:
Pusher bar for launching bridging pontoons
Class 30 and class 60 trackway laying equipment
A jib crane attachment for handling palletised stores up to a maximum weight of 4000 kg can be installed in the bucket.

VARIANTS
In 1982 it was announced that the Royal Ordnance Factories were designing a new vehicle family based on the hull and running gear of the Combat Engineer Tractor. The bulk of the development is to be carried out under the aegis of ROF Leeds and the first vehicle will be a self-propelled gun, mounting the ordnance of the Soviet 122 mm D-30 gun, for Egypt. Following the self-propelled gun and using the same basic running gear and hull will be an ammunition tender, armoured personnel carrier, ambulance, armoured recovery vehicle and an air defence vehicle.

Combat Engineer Tractor showing earth-moving bucket (Royal Ordnance Factories)

SPECIFICATIONS
Crew: 2
Weight combat: 18 000 kg
Length:
  (overall) 7·544 m
  (hull) 5·334 m
Width:
  (bucket) 2·896 m
  (hull) 2·793 m
  (tracks) 2·769 m
Height:
  (overall) 2·667 m
  (top of hull) 2·286 m
Ground clearance: 0·457 m
Track width: 508 mm
Length of track on ground: 3·76 m
Ground pressure: 0·435 kg/cm^2
Max speed:
  (road) 56 km/h
  (water) 8 km/h
Range: 320 km
Fuel capacity: 430 litres
Fording: 1·829 m
  amphibious with preparation

Gradient: 60%
Vertical obstacle: 0·61 m
Trench: 2·06 m
Engine: turbo-charged Rolls-Royce C6TFR 6-cylinder in-line diesel developing 320 bhp at 2100 rpm
Transmission: TN26 manually controlled power shift with 4 gears in each direction coupled to Rolls-Royce CGS 312 steering system
Electrical system: 24 V
Batteries: 4 × 6TN rated at 100 Ah connected in series/parallel giving total capacity of 200 Ah
Armament:
  7·62 mm MG (optional)
  6 smoke dischargers
Armour: aluminium

STATUS
Production complete. In service with the British Army.

MANUFACTURER
Royal Ordnance Factory Nottingham.
Enquiries to Sales and Marketing Director, Royal Ordnance Factories, Ministry of Defence, St. Christopher House, Southwark Street, London SE1 0TD, England.

Chieftain Bulldozer Kit

DESCRIPTION
By fitting a special bulldozer kit any mark of Chieftain MBT can be used for basic tactical earth-moving tasks. The kit consists of a hydraulic powerpack with a joystick controller, main linkage assemblies, an aluminium bulldozer blade and protective ducting for the hydraulic linkages. The scale of issue of the kit is variable but is usually of the order of one or two to a troop.

To attach the kit the only part to be removed from the parent tank is the front right-hand trackguard stowage bin. This is replaced by the armoured steel powerpack

using the existing attachment points and plugging control and power cables into existing points. This powerpack is in two halves, one with the electrical assemblies and the other with the hydraulic components. The joystick unit for the pack is installed in the driver's compartment to the right of the driver's seat. The front towing eyes are used to mount the main linkage assemblies on the front of the hull and the bulldozer blade is secured to the linkages by its fulcrum pins. The kit can be exchanged from tank to tank with no loss of hydraulic fluid, and all hydraulic hoses are fitted with protective ducts and quick-release, self-sealing couplings.

In use the tank driver can use the joystick control unit to start and stop the hydraulic motor, raise and lower the

Self-contained hydraulic powerpack for Chieftain MBT

Chieftain bulldozer kit aluminium dozer blade

Chieftain bulldozer kit in use

blade, or allow the blade to 'float'. The unit has a 'pump-running' indicator lamp and a further indicator for when the fluid filter requires cleaning. Mechanical locks are provided for travelling, one in the highest position for daylight use, and one lower to allow the headlights to function at night.

The power unit operates off the vehicle 24 volt nominal supply which is used to power the hydraulic system 6·5 hp drive motor.

By altering four attachment links, the blade assembly can be fitted to the American M60 MBT attachment points.

STATUS
Production. In service with the British Army.

MANUFACTURER (hydraulics)
AP Precision Hydraulics, PO Box 1, Shaw Road, Speke, Liverpool L24 9JY, England.

UNITED STATES OF AMERICA

M728 Combat Engineer Vehicle

DEVELOPMENT
In the 1950s the United States Army developed a medium tank called the T95 which had a number of advanced features including a hydro-pneumatic suspension system. A Combat Engineer Vehicle, the T118, was also developed from the T95, but the M60 was subsequently chosen to become the standard MBT of the United States Army so all work on the T95 and T118 was stopped. Design work on a new CEV based on the M60/M60A1 was soon started and the first prototype was known as the T118E1. After trials this was type classified as the M728 in 1963 and it entered production in 1965, and entered Army inventory in 1968. It is issued to the Engineer Battalions of armoured, mechanised and infantry divisions. Engineer battalions in armoured and mechanised divisions have eight M728s. Infantry division engineer battalions have only three M728s, and separate engineer companies have two M728s each. No funds were requested for the procurement of the M728 in fiscal years 1976 and 1977. For fiscal year 1978, the Army requested five M728s at a cost of US $3·4 million, but this request was denied by Congress. In fiscal year 1979 the Army requested funds for 51 M728s at a cost of US $31·4 million, but this request was also denied by Congress. In July 1978 the Department of Defense notified congressional committees of its proposed letter of offer to sell the Saudi Arabian government 15 M728s with radios and two-years supply of spare parts at a total cost of $21 million. In fiscal year 1980 the Army requested funds for 56 M728s at a cost of US $51·5 million. These two orders have now been delivered. No funds were requested for M728 production in fiscal year 1981.

DESCRIPTION
The M728 is based on the M60A1 MBT. The hull is of cast sections welded together whilst the turret is cast in one piece. The driver is seated at the front of the hull and is provided with a single-piece hatch cover. He has three M27 periscopes for observation purposes, of which the centre one can be replaced by an M24 infra-red periscope on a separate mount for night operations. The other three crew members are in the turret, with the commander and gunner on the right and the loader on the left. The commander's cupola can be traversed through a full 360 degrees and he is provided with a total of eight vision blocks and an M34 periscope, which can be replaced by an M36 infra-red periscope for night observation. The gunner has an M105 telescope and an M32C periscope. The loader is seated on the left side of the turret and is provided with a single-piece hatch cover that opens towards the rear and an M37 periscope for observation purposes. The engine and transmission are at the rear of the hull as are the fuel tanks.

The suspension of the M728 is of the torsion bar type and consists of six road wheels with the drive sprocket at the rear and the idler at the front; there are three track support rollers. Hydraulic shock absorbers are provided at the first, second and sixth road wheel stations.

The M728 is designed to carry out numerous roles on the battlefield including the destruction of field fortifications and roadblocks, filling in gaps, craters and ditches, preparing fire positions and roadblocks.

Main armament of the M728 consists of an M135 165 mm demolition gun which has an elevation of +20 degrees and a depression of −10 degrees. Turret traverse is a full 360 degrees at 1·6 degrees per second; traverse and elevation are either powered or manual. A 7·62 mm M219 machine gun is mounted coaxially with the main armament (late production vehicles are equipped with an M240 coaxial machine gun) and a ·50 (12·7 mm) M85 machine gun is mounted in the commander's cupola; this has an elevation of +60 degrees and a depression of −15 degrees. A total of 30 rounds of 165 mm, 3600 rounds of 7·62 mm and 300 rounds of ·50 ammunition are carried.

The A-frame is mounted at the front of the hull and when not required lies back over the rear of the hull. This has a maximum lifting capacity of 15 876 kg; the two-speed winch, which is mounted at the rear of the turret, is provided with 61 metres of 19 mm thick rope and is controlled by the vehicle commander. The dozer blade is hydraulically operated and is mounted at the front of the hull. (Trials have been carried out using a two-part mine plough in place of the dozer blade.)

The M728 is provided with infra-red night driving equipment and most vehicles now have a Xenon infra-

M728 combat engineer vehicle from rear with A-frame in travelling position (US Army)

M728 combat engineer vehicle with dozer blade and A-frame in travelling position (Larry Provo)

red searchlight mounted over the top of the main armament. A central air filtration system pipes fresh air to each crew member.

SPECIFICATIONS
Crew: 4
Weight:
   (empty) 50 439 kg
   (loaded) 53 200 kg
Length:
   (with boom erected) 9·3 m
   (with blade and boom in travelling position)
   8·91 m
Width:
   (including blade) 3·7 m
   (hull) 3·631 m
Height:
   (travelling) 3·2 m
   (lowest operable) 3·257 m
Ground clearance: 0·381 m
Track: 2·921 m
Track width: 711 mm
Length of track on ground: 4·235 m
Ground pressure: 0·89 kg/cm²
Max speed: (road) 48·28 km/h
Range: 450 km
Fuel capacity: 1420 litres
Fording: 1·219 m
   (with kit) 2·438 m
Gradient: 60%
Vertical obstacle: 0·76 m

Trench: 2·51 m
Engine: Continental AVDS-1790-2A or -2D, 12-cylinder diesel developing 750 bhp at 2400 rpm
Transmission: General Motors Corporation (Allison Division) CD-850-6A with 3 ranges (low, high and reverse)
Electrical system: 24 V
Batteries: 6 × 6TN
Armament:
   1 × 165 mm demolition gun
   1 × 7·62 mm MG coaxial with main armament
   1 × 0·50 (12·7 mm) AA MG
Armour
turret front: 120 mm
turret sides: 76 mm
turret rear: 50 mm
turret top: 25 mm
hull front: 120 mm
hull sides, front: 76 mm
hull sides, rear: 51 mm
hull top: 57 mm
hull rear: 44 mm
hull floor: 13·63 mm

STATUS
In service with the United States Army and Saudi Arabia. Production as required.

MANUFACTURER
General Dynamics, Land Systems Division, PO Box 1901 Warren, Michigan 48090, USA.

M9, Tractor, Full Tracked, High Speed, Armored Dozer-Scraper Combination

Note: This has now been renamed the M9 High Speed Armored Combat Earth Mover

DEVELOPMENT
In 1958 the United States Army Mobility Equipment Research and Development Center at Fort Belvoir began work on a vehicle called the All-purpose Balastable Crawler (or the ABC). This eventually became known as the Universal Engineer Tractor (UET).

The first prototypes of the Universal Engineer Tractor were built by the Caterpillar Tractor Company and the International Harvester Company. In January 1975 the Pacific Car and Foundry Company completed a further four vehicles, two of which underwent field evaluation at Fort Hood. The result of these trials was considered satisfactory and indicated the vehicle's superiority over currently available equipment. TECOM testing was completed in August 1976 and type classification (Standard A) was approved in February 1977.

Trials of the M9 have subsequently been carried out in both Yuma and Alaska to test modifications made as a result of previous trials and new equipment, such as a winterisation kit. In fiscal year 1979 $21·1 million was requested for the production of 75 vehicles, but only $10·6 million was authorised for 29 vehicles. Since production of such a small number was not considered an economic proposition, production was delayed in the hope that the fiscal year 1980 request, for $40·5 million, plus the 1979 allocation, would allow the production of up to 155 vehicles. No M9 funding was made in either the 1980 or 1981 budgets. In November 1982 a revised contract worth $29 million was awarded for the purchase of 15 equipments of which $19·3 million was for the vehicle and the remainder for product improvements (the original contract was to have been $40·4 million for 36 vehicles). There will be no purchases in fiscal years 1983 and 1984 but there are plans to purchase 80 M9s worth $72·4 million in fiscal year 1985, 190 M9s worth $135·6 million in fiscal year 1986 and 300 M9s worth $217·8 million in fiscal year 1987 by which time the unit price should have been reduced to $600 000 in fiscal year 1982 terms. Ultimately the US Army plans to purchase 1400 M9s which will ensure that one M9 will be allocated to each combat engineer platoon.

DESCRIPTION
The M9 is intended to operate in forward areas and due to its high road speed can be placed up with the lead tanks in a convoy, closer to where it is needed, rather than at the back as is the case with vehicles (such as the D7 medium crawler) which the M9 is intended to replace.

The M9 is a general-purpose engineer vehicle and can carry out tasks in three critical areas, mobility, countermobility and survivability. Mobility tasks include filling craters and ditches, assisting fighting vehicles (winching or towing), removing road blocks, trees, rubble and other battlefield obstacles, preparing access/egress for fording sites and river crossings, preparing and maintaining combat routes and preparing and maintaining assault airfields. Countermobility tasks include the construction of anti-armour obstacles, demolishing fords and bridge by-passes, participating in the digging of tank ditches, destroying landing fields and airfields, participating in the preparation of strong points and hauling obstacle materials. Survivability tasks include the digging of hull defilade positions for armour, construction of defensive positions for command and control operations, construction of earth berms for protection, hauling material for protective shelters, clearing fields of fire and digging slots for vehicle mounted TOWs and other battlefield weapons.

The M9 is airportable in the C-130, C-141 and C-5A aircraft and the CH-54 helicopter. It is unarmed but has standard vision devices and an NBC system. Smoke obscurants are also carried. It has a limited amphibious capability and armour protection is provided for the engine, power train and the operator.

The hull of the M9 is made of all-welded aluminium. At the front of the vehicle is the scraper bowl (ballast compartment), hydraulically-operated apron and positive load ejector. The driver is seated at the rear of the vehicle on the left side and is provided with a cupola which swings upwards through 180 degrees when not required, to be stowed to his rear. The engine is on the right of the driver's compartment and the transmission is at the rear. On-vehicle equipment includes a bilge pump and a winch with a line pull of 11 340 kg. The M9 can also be used to tow trailers and other equipment as it has a maximum drawbar pull of 16 783 kg. It is fully amphibious being propelled in water by its tracks. The bucket bottom acts as a bow and aids in steering. The M9 is not suitable for operating in fast-flowing rivers.

The dozer blade is mounted on the apron and dozing and scraping are accomplished by raising and lowering the entire front of the vehicle by means of the hydro-pneumatic suspension. This consists of four 711 mm diameter forged aluminium road wheels with drive sprocket at the rear. The hydro-pneumatic suspension allows the tractor to be tilted to apply the dozing effort to one corner of the blade. The capability of the vehicle for such operations as dozing can be nearly doubled by loading the bowl with ballast.

The M9 self-loads to its working height by dumping to the rear over the back of the bucket. In the maximum dump position, the bucket has a dumping angle of 50 degrees. It normally takes four bucket loads to fill the bowl with 4·58 to 5·35 cubic metres of soil. Only three bucket loads are normally required to reach a ballasted weight of 18 144 kg. Unloading is accomplished with a bulldozer type ejector actuated by two double-acting hydraulic rams. The height of the bucket enables the M9 to unload straight into a 5-ton truck. Cargo loads can be lifted into the bowl using the lift arms and a hook-eye on the back of the bulldozer. A clamping force of 2800 kg between the near edge of the bucket and the bulldozer blade gives the tractor the ability to pick up tree stumps and similar objects.

STATUS
Development complete.

MANUFACTURER
Development under the direction of United States Army Tank-Automotive Command, Warren, Michigan 48090, USA.

Pacific Car and Foundry Company, 1400 North 4th Street, Renton, Washington 98055, USA.

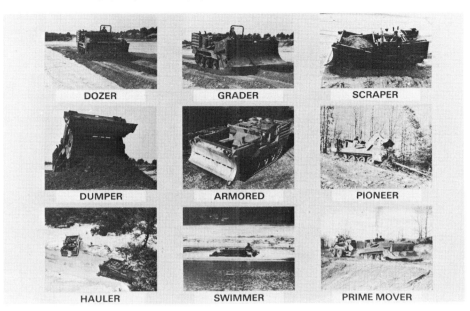

DOZER GRADER SCRAPER

DUMPER ARMORED PIONEER

HAULER SWIMMER PRIME MOVER

M9 can be used as dozer, grader, scraper, dumper, carrier, pioneer, hauler, swimmer and prime mover

M9 Tractor with operator's hatch closed and windscreen raised

SPECIFICATIONS
Crew: 1
Weight:
(empty) 15 800 kg
(loaded) 24 500 kg
Length: 6·248 m
Width:
(with dozer wings) 3·2 m
(without dozer wings) 2·79 m
(over tracks) 2·692 m
Height: 2·36 m
Ground clearance: 0·457 m
Track: 2·24 m
Track width: 457 mm
Length of track on ground: 2·641 m
Ground pressure: 0·64 kg/cm² (empty)
Max speed:
(road) 48·3 km/h
(water) 4·8 km/h
Range: 322 km
Fuel capacity: 507 litres
Fording: 1·83 m
amphibious with minimum preparation
Freeboard with load of 1814 kg: 0·28 m
Gradient: 60%
Side slope: 35%
Engine: Cummins V903 diesel developing 295 hp at 2600 rpm
Transmission: powershift planetary with 6 forward and 2 reverse gears. Geared system for high-speed road and cross country travel, and clutch and brake system for bulldozing operations
Armament: nil
Armour: aluminium

Counter-Obstacle Vehicle (COV)

DEVELOPMENT
During 1981 and 1982 the US Army Engineer School at Fort Belvoir, Virginia, produced conceptual studies for a new counter-obstacle vehicle (COV). The US Army Mobility and Equipment Research and Development Command (MERADCOM) is designing and fabricating a COV test bed using the M88 armoured recovery vehicle chassis as a basis. The BMY Corporation of York,

Pennsylvania is the prime contractor to manufacture two test beds, one for the US Army and one for Israel.

DESCRIPTION
The proposed COV will have an engine in the 900 to 1200 hp range and will function as a counter-mine and counter-obstacle vehicle using two large-capacity telescopic arms, combination dual-function bulldozer blade and a full-width mine-clearing plough. It is proposed that the COV will be issued on a scale of two per divisional

combat engineer company and one per corps engineer company.

STATUS
Development.

SPECIFICATIONS (test bed)
Length: 8·153 m
Width: 3·43 m
Height: 3·226 m
Weight: 48 806 kg

Recovery vehicles and equipment

ARMOURED RECOVERY VEHICLES

AUSTRIA

Bergepanzer 4KH7FA-SB 20 Greif Armoured Recovery Vehicle

DEVELOPMENT
The Greif armoured recovery vehicle is based on the chassis of the Panzerjäger Kürassier tank destroyer. The first prototype of the Greif was completed in 1974 with first production vehicles following in 1976/77.

DESCRIPTION
The hull is of all-welded construction with the winch and crew compartment at the front. Normal means of entry to the crew compartment is via two doors in the left side of the hull. In addition there are hatches in the roof. The engine and transmission are at the rear of the hull and there is a stowage platform over the engine decking, which is used to carry spare components. The torsion bar suspension consists of five road wheels with the drive sprocket at the rear and the idler at the front. There are three track return rollers. Hydraulic shock absorbers are provided at the first and fifth road wheel stations.

Mounted on the right side of the superstructure, at the front, is a hydraulic crane, which is traversed to the rear for travelling. This crane can be traversed through 234 degrees and its boom elevated from 0 to +60 degrees. The boom can be extended from its normal length of 3 metres to 3·9 metres, and has a maximum lifting capacity of 6000 kg. The crane is provided with 42 metres of cable and is capable of lifting the complete turret of the Kürassier tank destroyer.

The main winch is in the lower part of the hull and leads out through the front of the hull. This opening can be sealed for fording operations. The winch is provided with 95 metres of 24 mm diameter cable and has a maximum pull of 20 000 kg. This enables the Greif to recover both the Kürassier tank destroyer and the Saurer APC. A rake blade is mounted at the front of the hull and is used in conjunction with the main winch. A full range of tools is carried as is cutting and welding equipment. The Greif does not have an NBC system, but the crew compartment is provided with a ventilation and heating unit.

VARIANTS
Recently Steyr has developed a pioneer vehicle based on the chassis of the Greif ARV. Available details are given in the *Armoured engineer vehicles* section.

SPECIFICATIONS
Crew: 4
Weight: 19 800 kg
Length: 6·705 m
Width: 2·5 m
Height:
   (overall) 2·74 m
   (top of hull) 2·3 m
Ground clearance: 0·4 m
Track: 2·12 m
Track width: 380 mm
Length of track on ground: 3·04 m
Ground pressure: 0·75 kg/cm²
Max speed: (road) 67·5 km/h
Range: (road) 625 km
Fuel capacity: 500 litres
Fording: 1 m
Gradient: 70%
Side slope: 40%
Vertical obstacle: 0·8 m
Trench: 2·1 m
Engine: Steyr Type 7FA 6-cylinder turbo-charged diesel developing 320 hp at 2300 rpm

Greif ARV in travelling configuration with rake blade raised and crane retracted

Greif ARV with rake blade lowered and crane extended forward

Transmission: ZF manual with 6 forward and 1 reverse gears
Turning radius: 7·25 m
Electrical system: 24 V
Batteries: 2 × 12 V, 180 Ah
Armament:
   1 × 0·50 (12·7 mm) M2 HB MG
   4 smoke dischargers
Ammunition: (12·7 mm) 1500 rounds

STATUS
In production. In service with the Austrian Army. Argentina, Bolivia, Morocco and Tunisia have a number of Kürassier tank destroyers and may therefore have taken delivery of some Greif ARVs.

MANUFACTURER
Steyr-Daimler-Puch AG, Werke Vienna, Postfach 100, A1111 Vienna, Austria.

BELGIUM

SIBMAS 6 × 6 Armoured Recovery Vehicle

DEVELOPMENT
The SIBMAS 6 × 6 armoured recovery vehicle is a conversion of the basic SIBMAS 6 × 6 vehicle range and uses the same basic hull and drive train. No prototype vehicle is being produced as the first example, due to be produced in mid-1983 will retain much of its commonality with the rest of the SIBMAS 6 × 6 range. Full details of the SIBMAS 6 × 6 range can be found in *Jane's Armour and Artillery 1983–84*, pages 251–254.

DESCRIPTION
The hull is all-welded steel and is fully watertight. It provides the crew with full protection against 7·62 mm armour-piercing rounds. The driver is seated in the centre of the hull front behind three bullet-proof windscreens. Behind him there is a circular hatch for the commander. Mounted on the hatch rail is a 7·62 mm machine gun which can be elevated 65 degrees and depressed 10 degrees. On each side of the hull, midway between the first and second road wheels are two large hatches for the crew and there is another entry hatch on the right of the hull rear. Internally there is rearward-facing seating for three fitters, one each side of the commander's position and next to the side hatches, and one just inside the rear hatch. Each position has a roof escape hatch.

The engine arrangement, type, suspension and drive chain are all identical to the rest of the SIBMAS 6 × 6 range.

Specialist recovery equipment mounted externally consists of two hydraulically-operated spades, a hydraulic crane and two winches. The spades are mounted one at the front and the other at the rear and both are fully folding when required. The hydraulic crane is mounted centrally on the hull roof and can be telescopically extended. It has a 3000 kg capacity for lifting and has a limited traverse. When extended a crane jib support is used to secure heavy loads for towing. Of the two winches one is used as the main multi-purpose winch and is centrally mounted to enable guide pulleys for the cable to be extended front or rear. The hydraulically-operated main winch has a direct pull of 20 000 kg. The other winch is used as an auxiliary and is mounted behind the main winch. It has a 1500 kg capacity and is used to unwind the main winch cable.

Other external equipment includes towing eyes front and rear, a 360-degree rotating searchlight on the hull roof, an emergency rotating warning light, a tow rope, a lifting bar, vehicle tool kit and an axe, shovel and pick-axe, sand channels, stowage box, a hydraulic lifting jack with an 8000 kg capacity, fuel and water jerricans, first aid kit, compressor air outlet for tyre inflation, and four three-barrel 76 mm smoke launchers.

Internally, there is stowage capacity for a wide range of specialist equipment including a portable gas welding kit and a hydraulic lifting jack with a 10 000 kg capacity. There is also a VHF communications radio set and full internal communications loudspeakers, only the driver and commander have headsets. The driver has a passive periscope for night driving, and air conditioning is provided for the full crew.

SPECIFICATIONS
Crew: 2 + 3
Configuration: 6 × 6
Length overall: (travelling) 7·63 m
Width: 2·5 m
Height: (top of crane) 3·08 m
Ground clearance: 0·4 m
Track: 2·066 m
Wheelbase: 2·8 m + 1·4 m
Angle of approach/departure: 35°/35°
Max road speed: 80 km/h
Fuel capacity: 425 litres
Max range: (road) 1000 km
Fording: 1·5 m
Engine: MAN D 2566 MT 6-cylinder, in-line, water-cooled turbo-charged diesel developing 320 hp at 1900 rpm
Transmission: fully automatic power-shift gearbox with hydropneumatic torque converter type ZF 6 HP-500
Steering: power assisted
Tyres: 14.00 × 20
Electrical system: 24 V

STATUS
In production. In service with Malaysia.

MANUFACTURER
SIBMAS, Departement de BN-Constructions Ferrovaires et Metalliques SA, Rue de Bellecourt 46, B-6538 Manage, Belgium.

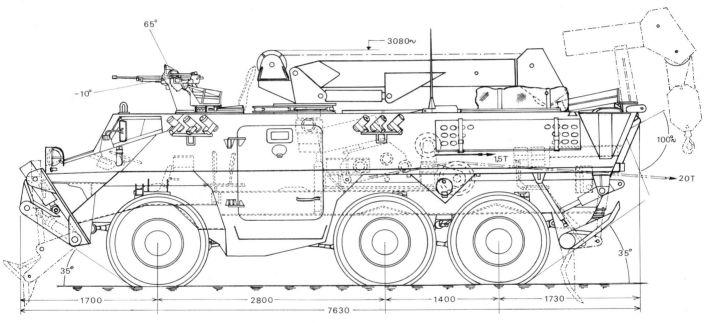

SIBMAS 6 × 6 armoured recovery vehicle (not to 1/76th scale)

CZECHOSLOVAKIA

WPT-TOPAS Armoured Recovery Vehicle

DEVELOPMENT
The WPT-TOPAS is a Polish modification of the Czechoslovak OT-62A APC which is used by the Polish Army under the name of the TOPAS (Transporter Obojzivelvý Pásový Stredni). The OT-62 is the Soviet BTR-50 series APC built in Czechoslovakia with many modifications and improvements. The Polish Army calls the WPT-TOPAS a technical support vehicle and East Germany calls it a recovery, maintenance and repair vehicle. It is used by units equipped with PT-76 amphibious tanks and TOPAS APCs.

DESCRIPTION
The hull is of all-welded steel armour with the crew compartment at the front and the engine and transmission at the rear. The driver is seated at the front of the hull in the centre and has a one-piece hatch cover that opens outwards with an integral viewing block. There are a further three viewing blocks below the hatch cover.

On the left and right sides of the hull at the front are semi-circular projecting bays, each with three observation blocks. The commander is normally seated in the left bay which has a single-piece hatch cover. Over the right projecting bay is a 7·62 mm machine gun in an armoured mounting, which can be traversed through 360 degrees. The machine gun can be elevated from −15 to +80 degrees. In addition the WPT-TOPAS carries an RPG-7 anti-tank grenade launcher, F-1 hand grenades and a signal pistol. Most vehicles have at least two roof hatches and a single door in each side of the hull.

The suspension is of the torsion bar type and consists of six road wheels with the drive sprocket at the front and the idler at the rear. There are no track return rollers. The first and sixth road wheel stations are provided with a hydraulic shock absorber.

The WPT-TOPAS is fully amphibious, propelled in water by two waterjets, one on each side of the hull.

Before entering the water a trim board is erected at the front of the hull and the bilge pumps are switched on.

It is believed that the vehicle has an NBC system as one is installed on the standard APC. Infra-red night vision equipment is provided.

The WPT-TOPAS is provided with a winch with a capacity of 2500 kg and 600 metres of cable, a hand-operated crane with a capacity of 1000 kg that can be mounted at various points on the vehicle, spare parts, welding equipment, tools and a four-man tent.

STATUS
Production complete. In service with East Germany and the Polish Army and Marines.

MANUFACTURER
Czechoslovak state arsenals with conversion work carried out by Poland.

SPECIFICATIONS
Crew: 5
Weight: 15 000 kg
Length: 7 m
Width: 3·14 m
Height: 2·72 m
Ground clearance: 0·41 m
Track: 2·74 m
Track width: 360 mm
Length of track on ground: 4·08 m
Ground pressure: 0·53 kg/cm²
Max speed:
  (road) 60 km/h
  (water) 10·8 km/h
Range: (road) 500 km
Fuel capacity: 417 litres
Fording: amphibious
Gradient: 55%
Vertical obstacle: 1·1 m
Trench: 2·3 m
Engine: PV-6, 6-cylinder in-line diesel developing 300 hp at 1800 rpm with pre-heater for cold starts
Transmission: manual with 5 forward and 1 reverse gears
Electrical system: 24 V
Armament: 1 × 7·62 mm PK MG
Armour
glacis: 11 mm at 80°
upper hull side: 14 mm at 0°
hull roof: 10 mm
hull rear: 10 mm
hull floor: 10 mm (max)

WPT-TOPAS armoured recovery vehicle with 1000 kg capacity hand-operated crane in position on left side of hull

T-55 Armoured Recovery Vehicle

DESCRIPTION
This ARV has been designed in Czechoslovakia and is based on the chassis of a T-55 MBT which has been manufactured in the country for both the home and export markets.

The hydraulic crane has a maximum lifting capacity of 1500 kg. On the roof of the ARV, towards the rear, is a platform 2 × 1·6 metres which can take a maximum load, such as an engine, of up to 3000 kg.

The ARV has two winches. The main winch is mechanically driven by the tank's engine and has a maximum capacity of 44 000 kg and is provided with 28 mm diameter cable. The hydraulically-operated aux-iliary winch has a capacity of 800 kg and is provided with 400 metres of 6·3 mm diameter cable. The seat of the winch operator rotates with a small turret.

All vehicles have several tow bars and a tow cable 4·2 metres long. Electric welding equipment, work-bench and a vice are mounted above one of the tracks and are pulled out when required. At the rear of the vehicle is a spade which can also be used as a dozer blade. If required mine-clearing rollers can be mounted at the front of the hull.

The machine gun turret can be traversed through 360 degrees and the 7·62 mm machine gun can be used against ground and aerial targets. The vehicle has a four-man crew and standard equipment includes a crew compartment heater, NBC system and infra-red night vision equipment. A snorkel can be fitted for deep fording.

STATUS
Production complete. In service with Czechoslovakia. Possibly exported.

MANUFACTURER
Martin State Arsenal, Czechoslovakia.

Czechoslovak T-55 ARV showing crane and 7·62 mm machine gun

FRANCE

AMX-13 Armoured Recovery Vehicle

DEVELOPMENT
The AMX-13 ARV (or Char de Dépannage AMX Model 55) is the standard light tracked ARV of the French Army and is based on the chassis of the AMX-13 light tank. Initial production of the AMX-13 ARV was undertaken at the Atelier de Construction Roanne (ARE), but once the ARE became involved in the AMX-30 MBT programme production was transferred to Creusot-Loire at Châlon sur Saône.

DESCRIPTION
The front of the ARV is cast and the remainder of the vehicle is of all-welded construction. The driver is seated at the front of the hull on the left side and is provided with a single-piece hatch cover and three peri-

scopes for observation. The engine is mounted to the right of the driver. The crew compartment is in the centre of the hull. At the front of the superstructure is a hatch cover which opens inwards and on either side of the hull is a single vision port which is covered by a simple swinging type cover when not required. At the rear are twin doors which open outwards. The commander is seated on the left side and is provided with a single-piece hatch cover and eight vision periscopes. To his right is the winch operator who has a single-piece hatch cover that opens to the rear and a single periscope.

The suspension is of the torsion bar type and consists of five road wheels with the drive sprocket at the front and the idler at the rear. There are four track return rollers. Hydraulic shock absorbers are provided for the first and fifth road wheel stations, and the front suspension can be locked when the jib crane is being used. The drive sprocket has been modified to assist the vehicle in unditching by winding onto an anchored cable.

At the rear of the hull are four spades which are lowered manually for recovery operations. The main winch is provided with 50 metres of 25 mm diameter cable and has a maximum capacity of 17 000 kg. A warning light comes on when a load of 14 000 kg has been reached and the winch automatically stops when 17 000 kg is reached. The secondary winch has a maximum capacity of 11 000 kg and is provided with 120 metres of 6 mm diameter cable. The A-frame is pivoted towards the front of the hull and has a maximum capacity of 5000 kg; it can lift components such as AMX-13 tank turrets to a maximum height of 3·4 metres. When travelling the A-frame rests over the rear of the hull.

A full range of tools is carried and other equipment includes tow bars, a 250-watt searchlight for night work and an 1800-watt power unit. The AMX-13 ARV is not provided with an NBC system and does not have any infra-red night vision equipment.

SPECIFICATIONS
Crew: 3
Weight in action: 15 300 kg
Length: (outrigger in rear position) 5·6 m
Width: 2·59 m
Height:
(jib stowed) 2·615 m
(jib in use) 4·65 m
Ground clearance: 0·44 m
Track: 2·16 m
Length of track on ground: 2·8 m
Ground pressure: 0·76 kg/cm²
Max speed: (road) 60 km/h
Range: (road) 400 km
Fuel capacity: 480 litres
Fording: 1 m
Gradient: 60%
Vertical obstacle:
(forwards) 0·65 m
(rear) 0·45 m
Trench: 1·6 m
Engine: SOFAM Model 8 GXb, 8-cylinder, water-cooled petrol developing 250 hp at 3200 rpm
Transmission: manual with 5 forward and 1 reverse gears (2nd, 3rd, 4th and 5th are synchromesh)
Electrical system: 24 V
Batteries: 4 × 12 V, 95 Ah
Armament:
1 × 7·5 or 7·62 mm MG 2000 rounds of ammunition
Dutch vehicles have 6 smoke dischargers mounted on top of crew compartment at front
Armour
crew compartment front: 30 mm
crew compartment sides: 20 mm
crew compartment roof: 10 mm
hull rear: 15 mm
hull glacis: 15 mm
floor forward: 20 mm
floor rear: 10 mm

STATUS
Production complete. Additional production can be undertaken if required. The AMX-13 light tank is used by Algeria, Argentina, Chile, the Dominican Republic, Ecuador, El Salvador, France, India, Indonesia, the Ivory Coast, Jibuti, Lebanon, Morocco, Nepal, the Netherlands, Peru, Singapore, Tunisia and Venezuela. Many of these countries also have the ARV.

MANUFACTURER
Creusot-Loire at Châlon-sur-Saône.
Enquiries to Creusot-Loire, 15 rue Pasquier, 75383 Paris Cedex 08, France.

AMX-13 armoured recovery vehicle on display at 1983 Satory exhibition (T J Gander)

AMX-13 armoured recovery vehicle

AMX-30D Armoured Recovery Vehicle

DEVELOPMENT
The AMX-30D has been designed to carry out three basic tasks: recovery of disabled and damaged AFVs, major field repairs such as changing engines, and engineer work.

DESCRIPTION
The chassis of the AMX-30D ARV (or Char AMX-30 Depanneur-Niveleur) is identical to that of the basic AMX-30 MBT, but the superstructure is new. Its crew of four consists of commander, driver and two mechanics.
The driver is seated at the front of the hull slightly to the left and is provided with three periscopes for observation. His single-piece hatch cover swings to the left. The commander is seated to his rear and is provided with a TOP 7 cupola. This is similar to that installed on the AMX-30 MBT but does not have the infra-red searchlight or the contra-rotating equipment. The cupola has ten periscopes for observation and a ×10 sight for the machine gun, which is mounted externally but aimed and fired from within the turret. To the rear of the commander's cupola is the entrance hatch for the engineers which opens to the right. There is a single M336 periscope fore and aft of this hatch cover.
The engine and transmission at the rear of the hull are separated from the crew compartment by a fireproof bulkhead. The suspension is of the torsion bar type and consists of five road wheels with the drive sprocket at the rear and the idler at the front. The first, second,

AMX-30D armoured recovery vehicle showing dozer blade, front winch and folded crane arm to right of commander's cupola (T J Gander)

fourth and fifth road wheels are mounted on bogies which are provided with hydraulic shock-absorbers. Five rollers support the inside of the track.

At the front of the hull is a dozer blade which is hydraulically operated by two cylinders. It is controlled by the driver and is used both for dozing operations and to stabilise the vehicle when the winch crane is being used.

The Griffet crane is mounted at the front right side of the ARV and can lift a load of 12 000 kg through 240 degrees, or 15 000 kg when the crane is towards the front and the dozer blade is in the support position. This crane is normally used for changing major AFV components such as engines and turrets. A spare engine is normally carried on the rear of the hull for the rapid replacement of an engine in the field.

The main winch is mounted in the centre of the hull and consists of three sub-assemblies, frame, transfer gearbox and winch drum with integral reduction gear. The winch cable is led out through the front of the hull. The winch is provided with 100 metres of 34 mm diameter cable and is also provided with a safety device which consists of two overload sensing cylinders operated by a pressure switch, which automatically stops the winch when the maximum load of 35 000 kg is reached. The winch has a maximum speed on external layer of 23 metres a minute and on internal layer of 18·8 metres a minute.

The auxiliary winch is a Retel TRA 251 mounted at the front of the hull. It is provided with 120 metres of 11·2 mm diameter cable and has a maximum capacity of 3500 kg.

The AMX-30D is provided with an NBC system and a crew heater. A snorkel can be installed over the mechanics' hatch enabling the tank to ford to a depth of four metres.

VARIANTS
The AMX-30D(S) is a special export model for operations in the Middle East, with sand shields over the top half of the tracks, and modified gearbox. The engine develops 620 hp at 2400 rpm.

The AMX-30DI has been developed by the Pinguely Division of Creusot Loire. The first prototype was completed in July 1974. This model has a boom which can lift a maximum load of 15 000 kg and slew it through 240 degrees.

SPECIFICATIONS
Crew: 4
Weight: (loaded) 38 000 kg

AMX-30D armoured recovery vehicle with dozer blade lowered and crane arm to rear in travelling position
(T J Gander)

Length: (dozer blade up, jib in travelling position) 7·53 m
Width: 3·15 m
Height: 2·65 m
(with jib at maximum extension) 6·15 m
Ground clearance: 0·45 m
Track: 2·53 m
Track width: 570 mm
Length of track on ground: 4·12 m
Ground pressure: 0·8 kg/cm²
Max speed: (road) 60 km/h
Range: 650 km
Fuel capacity: 1100 litres
Fording: 2 m
(with preparation which takes 5 minutes) 4 m
Gradient: 60%
Vertical obstacle: 0·93 m
Trench: 2·9 m
Engine: Hispano-Suiza HS-110, 12-cylinder, water-cooled, multi-fuel developing 700 hp at 2400 rpm

Transmission: automatic with 5 forward gears; reverse gear gives same speeds in reverse
Electrical system: 28 V
Batteries: 8 × 12 V, 100 Ah in 2 groups of 4
Armament:
1 × 7·62 mm MG
3 smoke dischargers

STATUS
In production. In service with the French Army (over 100) and probably in service with the other countries using the AMX-30 MBT, which include Chile, Greece, Iraq, Qatar, Saudi Arabia, Spain (confirmed) and Venezuela and UAE.

MANUFACTURER
Atelier de Construction Roanne (ARE).
Enquiries to Groupement Industriel des Armements Terrestres (GIAT), 10 place Georges Clémenceau, 92211 Saint-Cloud, France.

GERMANY, FEDERAL REPUBLIC

Leopard Armoured Recovery Vehicle

DEVELOPMENT
At an early stage in the development of the Leopard MBT the Germans decided to develop an ARV based on its components. Design work was carried out by Porsche with the first prototype being completed by Jung, Jungenthal in 1964. The first production ARV (the Germans call it the Bergepanzer, or BPZ) was completed in September 1966. Production of the ARV and other specialised members of the Leopard family was undertaken by MaK of Kiel, while production of the MBT was undertaken by Krauss-Maffei of Munich.

The ARV has been designed to undertake the following roles:
    recovering vehicles disabled through enemy action, mechanical failure or which have become bogged down.
    towing disabled vehicles.
    changing components such as engines and turrets. (A spare Leopard engine pack is carried on the rear decking and a complete engine change can be carried out in less than 30 minutes. The fastest engine change to date from the tank's stopping to moving off again is 8 minutes.)
    carrying out dozing operations.
    refuelling and defuelling other vehicles.

DESCRIPTION
The Leopard ARV is almost identical to the Leopard AEV, and the reader is referred to this entry for a detailed description of the vehicle. The main differences between the ARV and the AEV are:
    the ARV carries a spare powerpack and no auger.
    the ARV carries no explosives for demolition work.
    no heat exchanger is installed.
    the dozer blade is not provided with scarifiers to rip up the surface of roads.

In 1978 the Federal German Army took delivery of 100 product-improved Leopard ARVs from MaK. Main improvement is the installation of a hydraulically-operated rear support on the right side of the hull at the

Leopard ARV in travelling order and showing equipment stowage (T J Gander)

rear. This relieves the suspension on the crane side and enables the crane to lift a maximum load of 16 000 kg and traverse it through 270 degrees. In addition the main winch has a higher cable pay out speed (74 metres a minute) than the original vehicle's (22 metres a minute), which corresponds to that of the creeping speed of a Leopard 1 MBT.

The lifting capability of the Product-Improved Leopard ARV compared with the original ARV is as follows:

Basic ARV

max permissible load	working angle from centre slewing track	hook height	traversing range	dozer blade support
7000 kg	5 m	2·5 m	200°	without
13 000 kg	3·3 m	5·1 m	270°	with
20 000 kg	2 m (only to front)	5·85 m	0°	with

Product-Improved ARV

7000 kg	5·3 m	below 1 m	200°	with
16 000 kg	3·5 m/2·6 m	5 m/5·75 m	270°	with
20 000 kg	2·7 m (only to front)	5·65 m	0°	with

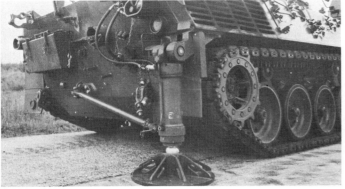

Close-up of hydraulically-operated rear support on product-improved Leopard ARV

Leopard ARV from left showing superstructure outline and equipment stowage
(T J Gander)

SPECIFICATIONS
(data in square brackets relate to product-improved Leopard ARV where different from basic vehicle)
Crew: 4
Weight: (with spare powerpack)
 (empty) 39 200 [39 980] kg
 (loaded) 39 800 [40 580] kg
Length: (spade raised) 7·57 [7·68] m
Width: 3·25 m
Height: (including MG) 2·7 m
Ground clearance: 0·44 m
Track: 2·7 m
Track width: 550 mm
Length of track on ground: 4·236 m
Ground pressure: 0·83 [0·85] kg/cm^2
Max speed: (road) 62 km/h
Range:
 (road) 850 km
 (cross country) 500 km
Fuel capacity: 1410 litres
Fording: 2·1 m
 (with snorkel) 3 m
Gradient: 60%
Side slope: 30%
Vertical obstacle: 1·15 [0·88] m
Trench: 3 m
Engine: MTU MB 838 Ca.M500 10-cylinder multi-fuel developing 830 hp at 2200 rpm
Transmission: ZF 250 with 4 forward and 2 reverse speeds
Electrical system: 24 V
Batteries: 6 with total capacity of 300 Ah, charged by 3-phase generator driven from main engine
Armament:
 1 × 7·62 mm MG3 MG in bow
 1 × 7·62 mm MG3 MG on commander's hatch
 4250 rounds of 7·62 mm ammunition
 6 smoke dischargers

Leopard ARV carrying Leopard MBT powerpack (T J Gander)

Armour
nose: 40 mm at 60°
front: 40 mm at 45°
side upper: 35 mm at 65°
side lower: 25 mm at 90°
superstructure side: 35 mm
superstructure front and rear: 25 mm
superstructure roof and decking: 10 mm
hull rear: 25 mm at 90°
hull floor: 15 mm

STATUS
Production. In service with Australia (6), Belgium (36), Canada (8) (called Taurus), West Germany (444 plus 100 product-improved versions), Greece (4), Italy (69), the Netherlands (51), Norway (6), and Turkey (4).

MANUFACTURER
Krupp MaK Maschinenbau GmbH, PO Box 9009, D-2300 Kiel 17, Federal Republic of Germany.

JAPAN

Type 78 Armoured Recovery Vehicle

DEVELOPMENT
The prototype of an ARV based on the chassis of the Type 74 MBT was completed in 1974 and subsequently standardised as the Type 78 ARV in 1978. At present production is running at one vehicle per year, but the fiscal year 1979 budget included funds for three vehicles at a total cost of 891 million yen.

DESCRIPTION
The layout of the Type 78 ARV is very similar to that of the West German Leopard 1 ARV and the French AMX-30D ARV. Mounted on the right side of the hull at the front is a hydraulically-operated crane which is 3·5 metres long and has a jib that can be extended a further 1·5 metres. The jib can be traversed through 270 degrees and lift a maximum load of 20 000 kg. Mounted at the front of the hull is a hydraulically-operated dozer blade that can be used both for dozing operations and

as a stabiliser when the winch is being used. The Type 78 retains the hydro-pneumatic suspension of the Type 74 MBT.

The winch has a maximum capacity of 38 000 kg, is provided with 60 metres of 32 mm diameter cable and has two speeds: 6 and 15 metres a minute. A hydraulic motor is used to extract the cable from the winch at a maximum speed of 30 metres a minute and there is also a system to apply tension to the cable for rewinding smoothly into the winch when there is no load.

Prototype of Type 78 ARV with dozer blade lowered and crane forward
(Kensuke Ebata)

Type 78 ARV with dozer blade raised and crane retracted (Kensuke Ebata)

Armament of the Type 78 ARV consists of a pintle-mounted 12·7 mm (0·50) M2 HB machine gun and six smoke dischargers.

SPECIFICATIONS
Crew: 4
Weight: 38 000 kg
Length: 7·95 m
Width: (overall) 3·38 m
Height: (to top of hull) 2·4 m
Ground clearance: 0·4 m
Max speed: 53 km/h

Gradient: 60%
Engine: Mitsubishi 10 ZF 2-cycle 10-cylinder air-cooled diesel, developing 720 hp at 2200 rpm
Transmission: Mitsubishi powershift with 6 forward and 1 reverse gears
Suspension: hydropneumatic with suspension lock at kneeled position
Crane capacity: 20 000 kg
Main winch capacity: 38 000 kg
Armament:
1 × 0·50 (12·7 mm) MG
6 × smoke dischargers

STATUS
In production. In service with the Japanese Ground Self-Defence Force.

MANUFACTURER
Mitsubishi Heavy Industries, Sagamihara. Mitsubishi Heavy Industries, 5-1, Marunouchi 2-chome, Chiyoda-ku, Tokyo, Japan.

Type 70 Armoured Recovery Vehicle

DESCRIPTION
The Type 70 armoured recovery vehicle is based on the chassis of the Type 61 MBT. Its turret has been replaced by a new superstructure which has a winch mounted in the bustle at the rear. The layout of the Type 70 is conventional, with the driver's compartment at the front, crew compartment in the centre and the engine and transmission at the rear. The suspension is of the torsion bar type and consists of six road wheels with the drive sprocket at the front and the idler at the rear. There are three track support rollers and shock absorbers are provided for the first, second, fifth and sixth road wheel stations.

A dozer blade is mounted at the front of the hull for clearing obstacles and for stabilising the vehicle when the A-frame is being used. The latter is pivoted either side of the hull superstructure and is used to change components. A full range of equipment is carried including tow bars, tools, cutting and welding gear.

A 0·50 (12·7 mm) Browning machine gun is mounted on top of the superstructure for anti-aircraft defence and an 81 mm mortar can be mounted on the front of the hull.

STATUS
Production complete. In service only with the Japanese Ground Self-Defence Force.

MANUFACTURER
Production was undertaken at the Maruko, Tokyo, plant of Mitsubishi Heavy Industries, but AFV production is now at the Sagamihara Plant, near Tokyo. Mitsubishi Heavy Industries, 5-1, Marunouchi 2-chome, Chiyoda-ku, Tokyo, Japan.

SPECIFICATIONS
Crew: 4
Weight: 35 000 kg
Length: 8·4 m
Width: 2·95 m
Height: 3·1 m
Ground clearance: 0·4 m
Track: 2·45 m
Track width: 500 mm
Length of track on ground: 3·7 m
Ground pressure: 0·95 kg/cm²
Max speed: (road) 45 km/h
Range: 200 km
Fording: 0·99 m
Gradient: 60%
Vertical obstacle: 0·685 m
Trench: 2·489 m
Engine: Mitsubishi Type 12 HM 21 WT V-12 diesel injection turbo-charged, air-cooled developing 600 hp at 2100 rpm
Transmission: mechanical with 5 forward and 1 reverse gears, with 2-speed auxiliary reduction unit
Electrical system: 24 V

Type 70 ARV showing dozer blade lowered and A-frame erected

Type 70 ARV in travelling order with A-frame to rear and dozer blade raised

Batteries: 4 × 12 V, 200 Ah
Armament:
1 × 0·50 (12·7 mm) Browning M2 HB MG
1 × 81 mm mortar

Armour
hull front: 46 mm
hull sides: 25 mm
hull rear: 15 mm

SPAIN

M-47 E2R Armoured Recovery Vehicle

DEVELOPMENT
In 198? Spain purchased 100 M47 tanks from West German and Italian sources, half of which were modernised to become 105 mm gun-armed tanks for the Spanish Army. One vehicle, after conversion, was used as a prototype which could later be converted into either a combat engineer vehicle or an armoured recovery vehicle. From this, a further prototype was developed into a full armoured recovery vehicle. The armoured recovery vehicle and the combat engineer vehicle are very similar both having a front-mounted dozer blade and a swivelling jib crane. To date only the prototypes have been converted from the basic M47 tank but it is anticipated that at least 29 conversions to the armoured recovery vehicle role will be made. Some reports mention even

more. The conversion work is being undertaken by the Talbot Company, formerly Chrysler Hispania. Before the Chrysler take-over the company was known as Barreiros.

DESCRIPTION
On the M-47 E2R the basic hull of the American M47 tank is retained but the running gear is replaced by M60 components. The transmission has been replaced by an automatic system and the main powerpack is now a Continental V-12 diesel. The main hull superstructure appears to be closely modelled on that of the Leopard 1 armoured engineer vehicle and armoured recovery vehicle as the shape and layout are very similar. The main box-shaped compartment is to the left of a 360-degree swivelling crane jib with the traversing platform mounted well forward, but on the M-47 E2R the crane is slightly shorter than the M-47 E2I's and lacks the rungs along the jib arm. The box compartment houses the crew of

four (commander, driver and two mechanics). Mounted on the front hull is a dozer blade operated via two hydraulic cylinders.

The crane jib of the M-47 E2R has a lift capacity of 50 000 kg and can be elevated to an angle of 61 degrees at which height the hook is 6·34 metres above the ground. When traversed directly to the right-hand side of the hull the jib has an extension of 4·12 metres. The main box compartment houses a winch equipped with 100 metres of cable. With a single core of this cable the winch can pull a 35 000 kg load through a port in the bottom front hull. If the cable is doubled using pulleys the load can be increased to 70 000 kg. The dozer blade is used during winching and loads can be pulled from an angle 15 degrees either side of the hull centre line. Loads can also be pulled from 15 degrees above the horizontal and 40 degrees below.

The M-47 E2R carries an electrical generator powered by an 8 hp air-cooled diesel engine and supplying

220/380 volts at 5·5 kVA. An air compressor is carried with various items of specialist recovery equipment such as shackles, joists, spare wheels and tracks, tools, and other such items.

A 12·7 mm (0·50) Browning HB machine gun is on a pintle over the commander's hatch with a 7·62 mm MG1-A3 machine gun to the left of the driver's position, firing through a port in the front hull. Two sets of three-barrelled Wegmann smoke grenade launchers are carried, one each side of the superstructure.

STATUS
Prototype completed. Conversion of at least 29 vehicles planned.

MANUFACTURER/CONVERTOR
Talbot, Apartado 140, Madrid, Spain.

SPECIFICATIONS
Crew: 4
Weight: 45 600 kg
Length:
  (jib rear, dozer blade raised) 7·53 m
  (jib rear, dozer blade down) 7·55 m
Width:
  (overall) 3·65 m
  (over tracks) 3·415 m
  (inside tracks) 2·235 m
Height:
  (overall) 3·35 m
  (top of commander's cupola) 2·89 m
Ground clearance: 0·47 m
Track width: 590 mm
Length of track on ground: 3·91 m
Ground pressure: 0·99 kg/cm²
Max speed: 56 km/h
Range: 600 km
Fuel capacity: 1500 litres
Fording: 1·2 m
Gradient: 60%
Side slope: 30%
Vertical obstacle: 0·9 m
Trench: 2·6 m

M-47 E2R armoured recovery vehicle

Engine: Continental Model AVDS-1790-2D 29·316-litre V-12 air-cooled diesel developing 760 hp at 2400 rpm
Transmission: GMC-Allison CD-850-6A with 2 forward and 1 reverse ranges
Electrical system: 24 V
Number of batteries: 6 × 12 V, 300 Ah

Armament:
  1 × 12·7 mm (0·50) MG
  1 × 7·62 mm MG
  2 × 3-barrel smoke dischargers
Ammunition:
  (12·7 mm) 600 rounds
  (7·62 mm) 2000 rounds

SWEDEN

Bärgningsbandvagn 82 Armoured Recovery Vehicle

DEVELOPMENT
The Bärgningsbandvagn 82 (or Bgbv 82 as it is usually known) was developed by Hägglund and Söner to meet a Swedish Army requirement for an ARV to recover the S tank and other AFVs. The first prototype was completed in July 1968, and as a result of user trials some modifications were requested by the Swedish Army. The Bgbv 82 was then accepted for service and 24 vehicles were completed between April and December 1973. The vehicle has an almost identical hull to the Brobandvagn 941 (bridgelayer) which was designed at the same time, and to keep costs to a minimum both vehicles share many common components with the Ikv 91 tank destroyer. In addition to being used as a recovery vehicle the Bgbv 82 can also be employed as an engineer vehicle, as for example in clearing river exit points.

DESCRIPTION
The hull of the Bgbv 82 is of all-welded steel construction with the crew compartment at the front and the recovery compartment at the rear. The front of the vehicle is immune to attack from projectiles up to and including 20 mm in calibre, while the sides of the hull, above the tracks, are of a double skinned construction which gives added protection against attack from HEAT projectiles.

The crew consists of four: commander, gunner, driver and winch operator. The gunner is seated in the turret (which is identical to that fitted on the Pbv 302 APC) on the left side of the hull. This is armed with a 20 mm Hispano 804 cannon which can be elevated from −10 to +50 degrees. Both elevation and traverse are manual. For engaging ground targets the gunner uses a sight with a magnification of ×8 while a special sight is provided for engaging aerial targets, but to use this the gunner has to open his hatch cover and is therefore exposed to small arms fire. A total of four M17 periscopes are provided in the turret, three to the front and one to the rear. Eight smoke dischargers are mounted on either side of the turret. The driver is seated in the centre of the hull and is provided with three periscopes to his front for observation, and a single-piece hatch cover which opens to the rear. The vehicle commander is seated to the right of the driver and is provided with six periscopes for all-round observation and a single-piece

Bgbv 82 ARV showing spades in travelling position, crane and recovery equipment

hatch cover. The winch operator is seated to the rear of the commander facing the rear, with his single-piece hatch cover opening to the rear. All the recovery equipment is hydraulically operated from the crew compartment.

The engine, torque converter, clutch, gearbox and steering gear box (including the bevel gear) can be removed from under the floor of the load/recovery compartment as a complete unit. The fuel tank is also under the floor.

The six road wheels on each side are supported by trailing arms individually suspended by transversal torsion bars. Shock absorbers are mounted on the first and last trailing arms. The idler is at the front and the drive sprocket is at the rear. The track tension is automatically adjusted by a hydraulic system.

The Hägglund HM 20 winch is mounted to the rear of the crew compartment and is provided with 145 metres of wire rope which leads out through the rear of the hull. Two ground anchor spades are mounted at the rear of the hull and are hydraulically positioned. When in position they can absorb a force of 60 000 kg, the maximum traction for a three-part pull.

The Hiab-Foco 9000 lifting crane is mounted on the right side of the hull and can lift 5500 kg with a jib length of 1·5 metres, 3500 kg with a jib length of 2·5 metres and 1500 kg with a jib length of 5·5 metres. At the front of the hull is a hydraulically-operated dozer blade which is normally positioned when the winch or lifting crane is being used.

The Bgbv 82 is fully amphibious being propelled in the water by its tracks. The only preparation required is to erect the trim vane at the front of the hull and switch on the bilge pumps. If the vehicle is carrying a heavy load, such as a complete powerpack for an S tank, a low flotation screen is erected.

The vehicle is not provided with an NBC pack although provision was made in the design for one to be installed at a later date. Infra-red driving lights are provided.

SPECIFICATIONS
Crew: 4
Weight:
(empty) 19 800 kg
(loaded) 26 300 kg (with S tank powerpack)
Length: 7·2 m
Width: 3·25 m
Height:
(top of turret) 2·45 m
(top of spades) 2·63 m
Ground clearance: 0·45 m (centre of hull)
Track width: 450 mm
Length of track on ground: 3·6 m
Ground pressure: 0·78 kg/cm²
Max speed:
(road) 56 km/h
(water) 8 km/h
Range: 400 km
Fuel capacity: 550 litres
Fuel consumption: (road) 1 litre/km
Fording: amphibious
Gradient: 60%
Vertical obstacle: 0·6 m

Bgbv 82 ARV showing dozer blade raised

Trench: 2·5 m
Engine: Volvo-Penta Model THD 100C turbo-charged 6-cylinder in-line diesel developing 310 bhp at 2200 rpm
Transmission: manual Volvo-Penta R61 with 8 forward and 2 reverse gears
Electrical system: 24 V
Armament:
1 × 20 mm cannon
505 rounds of ammunition
16 smoke dischargers

STATUS
Production complete. In service with the Swedish Army only. Can be placed back in production if required.

MANUFACTURER
AB Hägglund and Söner, Vehicle Division, S-891 01 Örnsköldsvik, Sweden.

SWITZERLAND

Entpannungspanzer 65 Armoured Recovery Vehicle

DEVELOPMENT
In 1961 the Swiss Federal Armament Factory at Thun started the development of an armoured recovery vehicle based on the chassis of the Pz 61 MBT. The first prototype was completed in 1967/68 and after trials a modified version, based on the chassis of the later Pz 68 MBT chassis, was placed in production. First production Entpannungspanzer 65s (or Entp Pz 65 for short) were completed in 1970 and these, together with a quantity of British supplied Centurion Mk 2 ARVs (called the Entp Pz 56 by the Swiss) are the standard ARVs of the Swiss Army. Each battalion of Pz 61/Pz 68 MBTs has two or three Entp Pz 65 ARVs in its service company.

DESCRIPTION
The hull of the Entp Pz 65 is of cast sections welded together, with the crew and winch compartment at the front and the engine and transmission at the rear. An entry door is provided in the left side of the hull towards the front. In the crew compartment roof on the left side are two periscopes which provide observation to the front of the vehicle. To the rear of this position is a cupola with a two-piece hatch cover, which is provided with vision blocks for observation purposes. A 7·5 mm machine gun is mounted externally on this cupola. The driver is seated at the front on the right side and is provided with a one-piece hatch cover which opens vertically to the rear. Three periscopes are mounted to the front of the hatch. To the rear of the driver is another cupola which has vision blocks, a two-piece hatch cover, and four smoke dischargers mounted on its front.

The suspension of the Entp Pz 65 is of the Belleville type which consists of six road wheels with the drive sprocket at the rear, the idler at the front, and three track return rollers. Each road wheel is independently sprung by layers of Belleville washers, or conical springs.

The main winch is provided with 120 metres of cable and has a maximum capacity of 12 500 kg at high speed, at a maximum speed of 0·4 metre a second, and a maximum capacity of 25 000 kg at low speed, at a maximum speed of 0·2 metre a second. The capacity at low speed can be increased to 75 000 kg with snatch blocks. The auxiliary winch, which is used to pull out the main cable, is provided with 240 metres of cable. Maximum speed on a full drum is 1·79 metres a second and on an empty drum is 1·22 metres a second. A hydraulically-operated dozer blade mounted at the front of the hull is used either to stabilise the vehicle when the A-frame is being used or to clear away obstacles. Maximum height of the cutting edge above surface level is 0·9 metre and below surface level 0·49 metre. The A-frame is pivoted at the front of the hull and when not required lies back in the horizontal position on the roof. It has a maximum lifting capacity of 15 000 kg which enables it to lift complete tank turrets. An unusual feature of the frame is that at the lower end of each arm is a hydraulic jack, which allows the operator to make minor adjustments when lifting loads such as tank powerpacks into position.

Entp Pz 65 in action showing winch cables and with dozer blade lowered

Entp Pz 65 from rear with A-frame raised

A full range of tools, cutting equipment and tow bars are carried and storage lockers are provided along each side of the hull. The Entp Pz 65 has an NBC system.

SPECIFICATIONS
Crew: 5
Weight: 38 000 kg
Length: 7·6 m
Width:
(hull) 3·15 m
(blade) 3·15 m
Height: (including MG) 3·25 m
Ground clearance: 0·45 m
Track: 2·59 m
Track width: 520 mm

Length of track on ground: 4·23 m
Ground pressure: 0·85 kg/cm²
Max speed: (road) 55 km/h
Range:
(road) 350 km
(cross country) 160 km
Fuel capacity: 905 litres
Fording: 1·1 m
Gradient: 60%
Vertical obstacle: 0·75 m
Trench: 2·6 m
Engine: German MTU MB 837 8-cylinder diesel developing 660 hp at 2200 rpm
Auxiliary engine: DM OM 836 4-cylinder diesel developing 35 hp at 2800 rpm

Transmission: Schweizerische Lokomotiv und Maschinenfabrik semi-automatic with 6 forward and 6 reverse gears
Electrical system: 24 V
Batteries: 4 × 6 V, 360 Ah
Armament:
1 × 7·5 mm Mg 51 MG
3200 rounds of ammunition
8 smoke dischargers

STATUS
Production complete. In service only with the Swiss Army.

MANUFACTURER
Federal Armament Factory, Thun, Switzerland.

UNION OF SOVIET SOCIALIST REPUBLICS

M1977 Armoured Recovery Vehicle

DEVELOPMENT/DESCRIPTION
In the 1950s the Soviet Union developed a tank destroyer based on the chassis of the T-55 MBT. It is believed to have been called the SU-130 and was probably armed with a modified version of the 130 mm M-46 field gun. In concept and appearance it was similar to the earlier SU-100 but was produced only in small numbers as was a similar vehicle based on the chassis of the T-62 MBT. As far as it is known none of these remain in service in their original roles although some have been converted into ARVs which are very similar in appearance to the earlier SU-85-T and SU-100-T ARVs. They are limited to towing operations and as far as it is known they are not fitted with winches or other specialised recovery equipment. The Soviet designation for the ARVs based on the T-55 and T-62 assault gun chassis is not known, although the United States calls the T-62 model the M1977 ARV, or the T-62-T ARV.

SPECIFICATIONS
(ARV based on SU-130 chassis)
Crew: 3–4
Weight: 36 000 kg
Length: 6·4 m
Width: 3·352 m
Height: 3·438 m
Ground clearance: 0·41 m
Track: 2·64 m
Track width: 580 mm
Length of track on ground: 3·84 m
Ground pressure: 0·81 kg/cm²
Max speed: (road) 50 km/h
Range: 500 km
Fuel capacity: 960 litres
Fording: 1·5 m

M1977 ARV clearly showing former space for 130 mm gun in glacis plate

Gradient: 60%
Vertical obstacle: 0·8 m
Trench: 2·7 m
Engine: Model V-55 V-12 water-cooled diesel developing 580 hp at 2000 rpm
Electrical system: 28 V

STATUS
Production complete. In service with the USSR.

MANUFACTURER
Soviet state arsenals.

T-54/T-55 Armoured Recovery Vehicles

DEVELOPMENT
The first ARV based on the chassis of the T-54 MBT appeared in the 1950s and was designated the T-54-T. Since then at least seven other T-54/T-55 ARVs have been developed. Most of them have very limited capabilities compared with ARVs which have been developed in the West, and few are equipped with a winch, limiting their capabilities to towing damaged vehicles off the battlefield. These vehicles are known as BTS (medium armoured towers) in the Soviet Army. The more recent T-55-TK is an improvement over the earlier models as it can lift vehicles up to 20 000 kg.

DESCRIPTION
All these ARVs use a T-54 or T-55 MBT chassis which has had its turret removed. The driver is seated at the front of the hull on the left side and is provided with two periscopes for observation and a single-piece hatch cover. The vehicle commander is normally seated to his right and is provided with a single-piece hatch cover which opens to the right. The other crew members normally sit in the cargo area, which is often very cramped as the snorkel and spare fuel drums are also usually carried there. An unditching beam is carried on the right side of the hull and tow bars of varying lengths are also carried.

The engine and transmission are at the rear of the hull but unlike the T-54/T-55 MBT there does not appear to be any provision for carrying additional fuel tanks on the rear of the hull. It is assumed that most of these ARVs are provided with an NBC system.

The suspension is of the torsion bar type and consists of five road wheels with the idler at the front and the drive sprocket at the rear. There are no track return rollers.

T-54 (A) ARV with snorkel mounted for deep fording operations

VARIANTS
T-54-T/T-55-T
This was the first model to enter service and performs a similar role to the T-34-T (B) ARV but is based on a more powerful chassis. A loading platform is mounted in the centre of the vehicle, with sides which can be folded down to facilitate the loading or unloading of spare components such as an engine or a transmission. A large spade is mounted at the rear of the hull and a large diameter snorkel can be installed to the rear of the driver's position for deep fording operations. A jib crane which can lift a maximum weight of 1000 kg is provided. There is no winch so the vehicle is limited to towing operations. The Finnish Army uses a version of the T-54-T called the BTS-2, which has a winch, spade and a small dismountable crane.

T-54 (A)
This is an East German development and can be fitted with a snorkel for deep fording operations. Standard equipment includes a push/pull bar, full range of tools including both welding and cutting equipment, dismountable crane with a lifting capacity of 1000 kg, radiation warning equipment and a chemical warfare agent detector. This model does not have a winch, nor a spade at the rear. If required PT-54 or PT-55 roller type mine-clearing equipment can be installed at the front.

T-54 (B)
This is also an East German development and is similar to the T-54 (A) but at the rear of the hull are brackets for securing tow ropes and on the glacis plate at the front of the hull is a protective plate. This model is not provided with a winch or a spade.

T-55-TK (previously known as T-54 (C))
This is another East German development and is provided with a stowage platform, snorkel, spade at the rear, dozer blade at the front and a heavy duty crane which is mounted on the right side of the hull. This has a telescopic jib and can lift a maximum weight of 20 000 kg. When not required the crane is traversed to the rear so that its jib rests along the left side of the hull.

Czechoslovak T-55 ARV
There is a separate entry for this vehicle in this section under Czechoslovakia.

Polish T-54/T-55 ARVs
Poland has developed at least two ARVs based on T-54 or T-55 MBT chassis, designated the WZT-1 and WZT-2. No further details are available.

SPECIFICATIONS
(T-54-T; data in square brackets refer to T-54 (B) and T-55-TK where different)
Crew: 3–5
Weight: (empty) 36 000 [32 000], [34 000] kg
Length: 7·12 [7·05], [9·74] m
Width: 3·23 m
Height: 1·89 [2·2], [2·65] m
Ground clearance: 0·425 m
Track: 2·64 m
Track width: 580 mm
Length of track on ground: 3·84 m
Ground pressure: 0·72 [0·72], [0·77] kg/cm²
Max speed: (road) 48 km/h
Range: 400 km
Fuel capacity: 812 litres

T-54-T ARV

T-54-T ARV from top showing spade raised and snorkel in travelling position

Fording: 1·4 m
Gradient: 60%
Vertical obstacle: 0·8 m
Trench: 2·7 m
Engine: Model V-54, V-12, water-cooled diesel developing 520 hp at 2000 rpm
Transmission: manual with 5 forward and 1 reverse gears
Electrical system: 24 V
Batteries: 4 with total capacity of 280 Ah
Armament: nil
Armour
glacis plate: 100 mm at 60°
upper hull sides: 70 mm at 0°
hull rear: 60 mm
hull floor: 20 mm
hull roof: 30 mm

Note: Models based on a T-55 chassis are powered by a V-55 engine that develops 580 hp at 2000 rpm.

STATUS
Production complete. The T-54 and T-55 are in service with the following countries so it can be assumed that most of these use the T-54/T-55 ARV: Afghanistan, Albania, Algeria, Angola, Bangladesh, Bulgaria, People's Republic of China, Congo, Cuba, Cyprus, Czechoslovakia, German Democratic Republic, Egypt, Equatorial Guinea, Ethiopia, Finland, Guinea, Guinea-Bissau, Hungary, India, Iraq, Israel, Libya, Mali, Mongolia, Morocco, Mozambique, Nicaragua, Nigeria, North Korea, Pakistan (both Chinese and Soviet models), Peru, Poland, Romania, Somalia, Sudan, Syria, the USSR, Viet-Nam, North and South Yemen, Yugoslavia, Zambia and Zimbabwe.

MANUFACTURERS
Czechoslovak, Polish and Soviet state arsenals. The basic T-54 was manufactured in China under the designation T-59, and it can be assumed that ARV models of this tank also exist.

ARVs based on T-34 and SU-85/SU-100 Chassis

DEVELOPMENT
All these ARVs are based on the chassis of the T-34 tank. In the case of the T-34 ARVs the chassis and hull are used and in the case of the SU-85/SU-100 ARVs, the chassis of the SU-85 and SU-100 assault guns are used. All ARVs based on T-34 chassis are now being replaced by vehicles using a more modern tank chassis. This applies especially to primitive towing vehicles such as the Soviet SU-85-T, SU-100-T and the T-34-T(A), and the Polish CW-34.

The T-34 has a hull of all-welded construction with the crew compartment at the front and the engine and transmission at the rear. The driver is seated at the front of the hull on the left side and is provided with a one-piece hatch cover that opens upwards on the outside of the glacis plate. The torsion bar suspension consists of five road wheels with the drive sprocket at the rear and the idler at the front. There are no track support rollers. None of these vehicles is known to be provided with an NBC system or infra-red night vision equipment. Most models can carry two, or, in some cases, three additional fuel tanks on either side of the hull towards the rear which increase its range of operation from 300 to about 360 km.

WPT-34 (Polish) armoured recovery vehicle

Czechoslovak T-34 with heavy crane being used to construct bridge

DESCRIPTION
T-34-T (Model A)
This was the first T-34 ARV to enter service and is simply a T-34 with its turret removed and is limited to towing operations. It does not have a winch, spade, stowage platform, snorkel or pushbar.

T-34-T (Model B)
This variant is provided with a stowage platform, winch, and a small crane which can lift components with a maximum weight of 3000 kg.

T-34-T (Model B, East German)
This is similar to the Soviet Model B but has a special pushbar on the front of the glacis plate which folds back when not required. A large cable drum is mounted on the forward part of the hull, to the rear of the driver's position.

SKP-5
This variant has a large crane mounted over the turret ring, which can be traversed through 360 degrees and can lift a maximum weight of 5000 kg. When travelling the crane is traversed to the rear so that its jib is over the rear of the vehicle. This model does not have a winch, spade or stowage platform.

T-34 ARV (Czechoslovakia)
This is provided with a winch and a crane which can be used to lift heavy components such as complete tank turrets. It is also used by engineer units, especially in the construction of bridges. A spade is mounted at the rear of the hull.

WPT-34 (Poland)
This Polish variant has a large superstructure mounted at the front of the hull, similar in appearance to the Soviet ISU-122/ISU-152 assault guns. The WPT-34 is provided with a 30 000 kg winch, stowage platform and two spades at the rear of the hull and a 1000 kg crane. A telescopic snorkel can be mounted on the top of the superstructure at the front right side. Some models mount a 12·7 mm DShKM anti-aircraft machine gun. The WPT-34 is now being replaced by the more recent WZT-1 and WZT-2, both of which are based on a T-55 tank chassis.

An older recovery vehicle is the CW-34, which has a winch only and no spade.

SU-85-T and SU-100-T ARVs
These are SU-100 (100 mm) and SU-85 (85 mm) assault guns with their guns removed and the gun position plated over. They have additional roof hatches not found in the basic vehicles. As they are not provided with a winch, crane, spade, stowage platform or pushbar, they are limited to towing operations. They are seldom seen today.

SPECIFICATIONS
(T-34-T; data in square brackets relate to SKP-5 and WPT-34 where different)
Crew: 3 [2], [5]
Weight: 29 000 [26 000], [31 000] kg
Length: 6·19 [8], [6·5] m
Width: 3·05 m
Height: 2·14 [2·6], [2·48] m
Ground clearance: 0·4 m
Track: 2·45 m
Track width: 500 mm
Length of track on ground: 3·85 m
Ground pressure: 0·75 [0·68], [0·86] kg/cm²
Max speed: (road) 55 km/h
Range: 300 km
Fuel capacity: 560 litres
Fording: 1·3 m
Gradient: 60%
Vertical obstacle: 0·73 m
Trench: 2·5 m
Engine: Model V-2-34 (or V-2-34 m), V-12, water-cooled diesel developing 500 hp at 1800 rpm
Transmission: manual with 4 (some have 5) forward and 1 reverse gears
Electrical system: 24 V
Batteries: 4
Armour
glacis plate: 45 mm at 60°
hull sides: 45 mm at 40° and 90°
hull rear: 45 mm at 50°
hull roof: 18–22 mm
floor: 18–22 mm

STATUS
Production complete. The SU-85-T and SU-100-T ARV are no longer in service in large numbers but may be encountered in some Warsaw Pact countries. The T-34/85 tank is in service with the following countries, so it can be assumed that some of these countries also use the T-34 ARV: Afghanistan, Albania, Angola, Bulgaria, China, Cuba, Cyprus, Czechoslovakia, Equatorial Guinea, Ethiopia, German Democratic Republic, Guinea, Guinea-Bissau, Hungary, Kampuchea, North Korea, Mali, Mongolia, Mozambique, Poland, Romania, Somalia, Syria, Viet-Nam, North Yemen, South Yemen, Yugoslavia and Zimbabwe.

T-34-T Model B armoured recovery vehicle showing stowage platform on rear hull top

SKP-5 armoured recovery vehicle with crane traversed to rear

ARVs based on IS Chassis

It is believed that most types of ARV based on the IS chassis have now been either withdrawn from use or that their use is confined to either training or the reserves. Details of these vehicles can be found on page 27 of *Jane's Military Vehicles and Ground Support Equipment 1983.*

BTR-50PK(B) Amphibious Armoured Recovery Vehicle

DESCRIPTION
The BTR-50PK(B) is a fully amphibious version of the BTR-50 armoured personnel carrier developed especially for the amphibious recovery of AFVs at water obstacles. It retains the basic layout and automotive components of the original vehicle together with the twin hydrojet propulsive units that provide enough thrust to maintain a speed on water of 10 km/h and sufficient power to tow an amphibious AFV.

For the recovery role the BTR-50PK(B) is equipped with R 123M and R 124 radio sets, a rear-mounted towing coupling, towing gear and hook and two extra towing cables, two special quick-release shackles, standard shackles and snap hooks, a searchlight, two lifebelts, life jackets and four fenders. Also carried is RG-UF life-saving equipment for use only in an emergency when no qualified divers are available. Other safety equipment includes two PG6Hi hand-held dry fire extinguishers. A set of mechanics tools is also carried.

The normal crew of the BTR-50PK(B) is a commander and driver but there are another four seats for auxiliary personnel. During recovery operations the vehicle can accommodate up to eight rescued personnel. Combat weight of the BTR-50PK(B) is 14 000 kg.

STATUS
Production. In service with various Warsaw Pact armed forces.

MANUFACTURER
Soviet state arsenals.

UNITED KINGDOM

Future British Armoured Recovery Vehicles

The United Kingdom Ministry of Defence is understood to have drawn up a General Staff Requirement for an armoured repair and recovery vehicle (ARRV) based on the suspension, chassis and hull of the Challenger MBT. This Challenger ARRV would use the same Rolls-Royce Condor powerpack as the Challenger and would be equipped to carry and handle this powerpack. At present Chieftain ARVs are being converted to the ARRV standard by the addition of a hydraulic crane to cope with the Challenger MBTs that are now entering service in West Germany as the existing FV 434 armoured repair vehicles cannot carry the Condor powerpack.

Now that the MCV80 MICV has been ordered for the British Army it is expected that between 100 and 200 recovery vehicles based on the MCV80 will be ordered at some future date.

Alvis Samson Armoured Recovery Vehicle

DEVELOPMENT

The Samson (FV106) is a member of the Scorpion range of light tracked vehicles developed by Alvis Limited and the Military Vehicles and Engineering Establishment. The first prototype (03SP38) was completed in the early 1970s, but as a result of trials some redesign work had to be carried out and the final design entered production in 1977/78.

DESCRIPTION

The hull of the Samson is similar to that of the Spartan APC, and is of all-welded aluminium construction. The driver is seated at the front of the hull on the left side and is provided with a single-piece hatch cover which opens to the front. To his front is a wide-angle periscope for driving in the closed down position. This can be replaced by a passive night periscope. The engine, which is mounted to the right of the driver, is the same as that used in the Fox (4 × 4) armoured car.

To the rear of the driver, in the centre of the roof, is a No 27 cupola, which has a single-piece hatch cover that opens to the left and can be traversed manually through 360 degrees. Mounted in the forward part of the cupola is a periscope with a magnification of ×1 which can be replaced by a passive night periscope. There are another five periscopes for all-round vision. Mounted externally on the right side of the cupola is a 7·62 mm GPMG.

The NBC unit, if carried, is on the right hand sponson plate with the radio in a corresponding position on the left side. Alternatively, an air cooling or through-flow air circulation system can be installed.

The winch compartment is at the rear of the hull and a small door is provided in the rear of the hull, which has a built-in vision block. Over the winch compartment is a roof hatch.

The suspension is of the torsion bar type and consists of five road wheels with the drive sprocket at the front and the idler at the rear. The first and fifth road wheel stations are provided with a hydraulic shock absorber.

The Samson can ford to a depth of 1·067 metres without preparation, but with the flotation screen erected it is fully amphibious, being propelled in the water by its tracks at a speed of 6·44 km/h. A propeller kit increases its water speed to 9·6 km/h.

The recovery winch is mounted in the rear of the hull and is driven from a PTO on the main engine. This winch is provided with 229 metres of rope and has a variable speed of up to 122 metres a minute. Maximum pull, with a 4:1 snatch block, is 12 000 kg and this enables the Samson to recover vehicles such as the FV432 APC. The cable leads out over the top of the hull at the rear. On prototypes this lead out was through an opening in the lower part of the hull. Two spades at the rear of the hull are released manually, an additional strengthening piece is then added and the Samson reversed on to the spades. An A-frame can be mounted at the rear of the vehicle to enable the Samson to change light components in the field. A full range of tools, tow bars and blocks is carried.

SPECIFICATIONS
Crew: 3
Weight: (loaded) 8738 kg
Length: 4·788 m
(including vice and bench) 5·004 m
Width: 2·43 m
Height:
(top of hull) 1·718 m
(including MG) 2·254 m
(including A-frame) 2·83 m
Ground clearance: 0·356 m

Rear view of Samson ARV with spades lowered (T J Gander)

Alvis Samson armoured recovery vehicle in travelling order (Ministry of Defence)

Track: 1·7 m
Track width: 432 mm
Length of track on ground: 2·74 m
Ground pressure: 0·358 kg/cm²
Max speed:
(road) 72·5 km/h
(water) 6·44 km/h
Range: 483 km
Fuel capacity: 404·51 litres
Fording: 1·067 m
Freeboard with screen raised:
(front) 0·965 m
(rear) 0·815 m
Gradient: 60%
Vertical obstacle: 0·5 m
Trench: 2·057 m
Engine: Jaguar OHC 4·2-litre petrol developing 190 bhp at 4750 rpm
Transmission: TN 15 cross drive, 7 speeds in each direction
Electrical system: 28 V

Batteries: 4 × 6TN, 100 Ah; generator has output of 140 A at 28 V
Armament:
1 × 7·62 mm MG
2000 rounds of ammunition
4 smoke dischargers on each side of hull front

STATUS

The following countries have ordered the Alvis Scorpion: Belgium, Brunei, Honduras, Iran, Ireland, Kuwait, Malaysia, New Zealand, Nigeria, Oman, Philippines, Tanzania, Thailand, United Arab Emirates and the United Kingdom. Of these, Belgium, Brunei, Thailand and the United Kingdom (Army and Air Force), are known to use the Samson ARV.

MANUFACTURER

Alvis Limited, Holyhead Road, Coventry, West Midlands CV5 8JH, England.

Enquiries to Alvis Limited, 10 Fitzroy Square, London W1P 6AB, England.

Vickers Armoured Recovery Vehicle

DEVELOPMENT

Early in 1977 Kenya placed an order with Vickers for 38 Vickers Mk 3 MBTs and three ARVs based on the same chassis. First production MBTs were delivered in 1979 and first production ARVs were delivered in 1981. Two of the ARVs have a crane. In 1978 Kenya placed an additional order for 38 MBTs plus four ARVs, two with a crane and two without. Late in 1981 Nigeria placed an order for 36 MBTs, six ARVs and two bridgelayers.

DESCRIPTION

The all-welded steel armour hull is divided into three main compartments: front, centre and rear. The front compartment is divided into two with the driver's compartment on the right and the winch compartment on the left. The driver has a single-piece hatch cover which can be locked open, forward of which is a single wide angle periscope.

The centre compartment accommodates the radio operator, commander and mechanic and also contains the radio sets, batteries, machine gun ammunition stowage and recovery kit. The commander's cupola can be traversed manually through 360 degrees and is provided with a single-piece hatch cover that opens to the rear, periscopes for all-round observation and an externally-mounted 7·62 mm MG which can be aimed and fired from inside the cupola and has an elevation of +90 degrees and a depression of −10 degrees.

The rear compartment houses the power and transmission units and panniers above each track contain two bag type fuel tanks. The V800 powerpack, which can be removed from the vehicle without disturbing the gearbox, consists of the General Motors Detroit Diesel engine, mounting frames, radiators, turbochargers, air filter, oil filter and other accessories. The engine is cooled by twin radiators mounted horizontally on either side of the engine compartment. The drive for the engine is transmitted by a resilient trailing link coupling, through a centrifugal clutch, into the gearbox and onto the final drives. The TN12 Mark V5 transmission combines the Wilson Epicyclic gear change principle with the Merritt steering system.

Suspension is the torsion bar type with each side consisting of six dual rubber-tyred road wheels with the drive sprocket at the rear, idler at the front and three track return rollers. All suspension stations mount a secondary torsion bar within the body of the axle and the first, second and sixth road wheel stations have a hydraulic shock absorber. The tracks are of manganese steel and when new each track comprises 96 links.

The main winch is operated by the driver and is mechanically driven through an input gearbox with hydraulically-operated selector box. The engine PTO, mounted on the rear bulkhead of the winch/crew compartment, must be engaged to provide a drive to the input gearbox and raise hydraulic pressure before the winch can be operated. The twin capstan winch is equipped with 122 metres of 28 mm diameter cable and has a nominal capacity of 25 000 kg when being used in conjunction with an earth anchor spade fitted to the front of the vehicle. The winch, when achieving 25 000 kg direct line pull, is capable of dealing with all normal recovery operations, but where necessary the line pull can be increased to a nominal figure of 65 000 kg by multi-reeving the cable using recovery equipment provided with the vehicle. The hydraulically-operated earth anchor enables the maximum pull to be achieved without moving the vehicle.

Optional equipment for the Vickers ARV includes passive night vision equipment for both the commander and driver, cradle for transporting a complete V800 powerpack and TN12 transmission, auxiliary winch with a capacity of 4060 kg and 250 metres of 11 mm diameter cable, hydraulic crane with a lifting capacity of 4000 kg, smoke grenade launchers, NBC system and a heater.

Vickers armoured recovery vehicle with hydraulic crane deployed

SPECIFICATIONS
Crew: 4
Weight: 36 800 kg
Length:
(vehicle) 7·56 m
(vehicle with spade) 8·38 m
Width: 3·16 m
Height: (top of commander's cupola) 2·28 m
Ground clearance: 0·432 m
Track: 2·52 m
Track width: 521 mm
Length of track on ground: 4·28 m
Ground pressure: 0·79 kg/cm²
Max speed: (road) 50 km/h
Range: (road, at 32·2 km/h) 483 km
Fuel: 1000 litres
Fording: 1·1 m
Gradient: 60%

Side slope: 30%
Vertical obstacle: 0·914 m
Trench: 3 m
Engine: Rolls-Royce TCE 12-cylinder developing 750 bhp at 2300 rpm
Transmission: TN12 Mark V5 automatic with 6 forward and 2 reverse gears
Electrical system: 24 V
Batteries: 2 × 12 V 6TN
Armament: 1 × 7·62 mm L37A1 MG

STATUS
In production. In service with Kenya and on order for Nigeria.

MANUFACTURER
Vickers Limited, Defence Systems Division, Scotswood Road, Newcastle-upon-Tyne NE99 1CP, England.

Chieftain Armoured Recovery Vehicle

DEVELOPMENT

The Chieftain armoured recovery vehicle (FV4204) was developed by the Military Vehicles and Engineering Establishment and the Royal Ordnance Factory at Leeds as the replacement for the Centurion armoured recovery vehicle (FV4006). The final requirement, issued late in 1964, called for a vehicle which could clear obstacles on the battlefield, tow an immobilised Chieftain both on roads and across country, and be fitted with a winch with a capacity of 90 000 kg.

The first of two prototypes (designated R1 and R2) was built and delivered to the School of Electrical and Mechanical Engineering at Bordon late in 1971. Trials with the first prototype resulted in a complete redesign of the hydraulic system of the vehicle, undertaken by Lockheed Precision Products. This redesign, with a few more modifications, was considered satisfactory and production was authorised. Production of the Chieftain armoured recovery vehicle was undertaken by Vickers at its Elswick facility and the vehicle entered service with the British Army in 1976.

Iran ordered 71 Chieftain ARVs, the last of which was completed early in 1980. About 40 vehicles had been delivered to Iran by the time of the revolution, and the remaining vehicles are in store in the United Kingdom. Jordan may also order a batch of Chieftain ARVs to support the 278 Khalid tanks ordered in 1979. Late in 1981 unconfirmed reports indicated that the UK had supplied a number of Chieftain ARVs to Iraq, these being ex-Iranian stocks.

DESCRIPTION

The Chieftain ARV is based on the chassis of the Chieftain Mk 5 MBT and has three main compartments. The winch compartment is at the front of the vehicle on the right side with the driver seated on the left. The driver is provided with a single-piece hatch cover hinged to his rear, with a single periscope. The other three crew members are seated in the centre of the vehicle. Provision is made for carrying a fifth man. The commander has a No 17 cupola which can be traversed through a full

Chieftain armoured recovery vehicle (T J Gander)

360 degrees. In the forward part of the cupola is a No 62 sight periscope with a magnification of ×1 and ×10 and seven No 40 periscopes give the commander vision to the sides and rear. An image intensification sight can be fitted if required and a white/infra-red spotlight is mounted externally. The 7·62 mm L37A1 machine gun can be aimed and fired from inside the cupola. There is a second hatch in the roof of the vehicle, to the rear of the commander's cupola.

The crew compartment has an NBC system and a heater. The engine and transmission at the rear of the hull are separated from the crew compartment by a

fireproof bulkhead. The crew consists of commander, driver/winch operator, radio operator and a recovery mechanic.

The suspension is of the Horstmann type and consists of three bogies per side, each bogie with two sets of road wheels and a set of three horizontal springs. The first road wheel station has a hydraulic shock absorber. The drive sprocket is at the rear and the idler at the front, with three track return rollers. The top half of the track is covered by armoured skirts which can be removed for maintenance.

Standard equipment includes a Graviner fire warning,

detection and extinguishing system, NBC system, heater and infra-red detection equipment.

The main winch is of the double capstan type with electro-hydraulic controls. It is provided with 122 metres of 28 mm diameter cable and has a maximum speed of 13·73 metres per minute. The auxiliary winch is also of the double capstan type and is hydraulically operated with 260 metres of 11 mm diameter cable and a maximum speed of 137 metres a minute. Power for both winches is taken from a PTO on the main engine.

The front-mounted dozer blade, which weighs 833 kg, is operated by two hydraulic arms. When lowered it allows the vehicle to exert a pull of up to 90 000 kg.

The vehicle is provided with a full range of recovery equipment including pulleys, cables and tow bars. Some of the Chieftain ARVs for Iran have been fitted with an Atlas AK 6000M crane which in this application can lift a maximum load of 5803 kg at a reach of 3·62 metres. Distance from the hook to the ground at a radius of 3·62 metres is 4·67 metres and minimum radius with boom extended is 1·445 metres. Maximum lifting speed is 4·3 metres a minute and maximum slewing speed is nine degrees a second.

Chieftain ARRV with Atlas hydraulic crane traversed to left and dozer blade raised

VARIANTS
Armoured Repair and Recovery Vehicle
Chieftain ARVs for the British Army fitted with hydraulic cranes to enable the vehicle to change the powerpack of the new Challenger MBT in the field. The current FV434 armoured repair vehicle cannot lift this.

SPECIFICATIONS
(Vehicle with crane)
Crew: 4
Weight: 56 000 kg
Length: 8·57 m
Width:
(including blade) 3·53 m
(tracks) 3·33 m
Height: 2·79 m
Ground clearance:
(front) 0·5 m
(rear) 0·58 m

Track: 2·718 m
Track width: 610 mm
Length of track on ground: 4·775 m
Ground pressure: 0·96 kg/cm²
Max speed: (road) 42·4 km/h
Range:
(road) 400–500 km
(cross country) 200–300 km
Fuel: 955 litres
Fording: 1·067 m
Gradient: 70 %
Vertical obstacle: 0·902 m
Trench: 3·15 m
Engine: Leyland L60 No 4 Mark 8A, 2-stroke, compression ignition, 6-cylinder (12 opposed pistons) vertically opposed multi-fuel developing 750 hp at 2250 rpm

Transmission: TN12 with 6 forward and 2 reverse gears plus emergency mechanical selector for second gear forward and low reverse
Electrical system: 28·5 V (24 V nominal) dc
Batteries: 4 × 12 V, 200 Ah
Armament:
1 × 7·62 mm MG and 1600 rounds
2 × 6 smoke dischargers (front)
2 × 4 smoke dischargers (rear)

STATUS
Production complete. In service with Iran, Iraq (unconfirmed) and United Kingdom.

MANUFACTURER
Vickers Limited, Defence Systems Division, Scotswood Road, Newcastle-upon-Tyne NE99 1CP, England.

Centurion Mk 2 Armoured Recovery Vehicle

DEVELOPMENT
The standard ARV of the British Army after the Second World War was the Churchill, but it could not handle the heavier Centurion tank. As an interim measure the Centurion Mk 1 ARV was produced, which was the gun tank with its turret removed and a winch with a capacity of 20/30 tons installed. The first prototype of the Centurion ARV Mk 2 (FV4006) was completed in 1952/53 and after user trials was adopted with the first production vehicles being completed by Vickers at Elswick in 1956/57. The Centurion ARV is normally issued on the scale of four per armoured regiment. The Mk 2 ARV was to have been followed by the Mk 3 ARV (FV4013) which would have been based on the Mk 7 MBT hull, but it did not enter service.

DESCRIPTION
The hull of the Centurion Mk 2 ARV is of all-welded construction with the driver at the front, crew and winch compartment in the centre and engine and transmission at the rear. The driver is seated at the front of the hull on the right side and is provided with a two-piece hatch cover that opens to the left and right, with each piece having an integral periscope. The other three crew members are seated in the crew compartment. The commander's cupola, on top of the crew compartment, can be traversed through 360 degrees, and is fitted with a 0·30 machine gun which can be elevated from −15 to +45 degrees and be aimed and fired from inside the vehicle. Two thousand rounds of machine gun ammunition are carried. The engine and transmission are at the rear of the hull.

The suspension is of the Horstmann type and consists of three units per side. Each unit carries two pairs of road wheels which are sprung by one set of concentric springs. The drive sprocket is mounted at the rear and the idler at the front, with six track return rollers. The top halves of the tracks are protected by track skirts which can be removed for maintenance.

The winch has a capacity of 31 000 kg which can be increased, with the aid of snatch blocks, to a maximum of 90 000 kg. A Rolls-Royce B80 petrol engine developing 160 hp at 3750 rpm drives an electric generator, which supplies current to a motor mounted below the winch, and this powers the winch via a chain drive. The winch is provided with 137 metres of 88·9 mm diameter rope. At the rear of the ARV are large spades as the vehicle normally recovers with the winch cable leading out to the rear. A jib crane capable of lifting a maximum load of 10 000 kg can be erected if required. The vehicle

British Army Centurion Mk 2 ARV with canvas tilt over vehicle rear (T J Gander)

was designed to be fitted with an A-frame but one is seldom used today.

The Centurion ARV does not have an NBC system and has no night-vision equipment.

SPECIFICATIONS
Crew: 4
Weight:
(empty) 47 247 kg
(loaded) 50 295 kg
Length: 8·966 m
Width: 3·39 m
Height: 2·895 m
Ground clearance: 0·45 m
Track: 2·641 m
Track width: 610 mm
Length of track on ground: 4·572 m
Ground pressure: 0·9 kg/cm²
Max speed: (road) 34·6 km/h
Range: 102 km
Fuel capacity: 1045 litres
Fording: 1·45 m

Gradient: 60%
Vertical obstacle: 0·914 m
Trench: 3·352 m
Engine: Rolls-Royce Meteor Mk IVB 12-cylinder liquid-cooled petrol developing 650 bhp at 2550 rpm
Auxiliary engine: Morris 4-cylinder petrol developing 20 bhp at 2500 rpm
Transmission: manual Merritt-Brown Z51R with 5 forward and 2 reverse gears
Electrical system: 24 V
Batteries: 4 × 6 V
Armament:
1 × 0·30 (7·62 mm) Browning MG
10 smoke dischargers in 2 groups of 5
Armour
glacis: 76 mm
nose: 76 mm
hull sides: 51 mm
hull rear upper: 38 mm
hull rear lower: 20 mm
hull floor: 17 mm
superstructure front, sides and rear: 30 mm

STATUS
Production complete. The ARV is known to be used by Denmark, India, Israel, the Netherlands, Sweden (called Bgbv 81), Switzerland (called Ent Pz 56) and the United Kingdom. It may be used by Jordan and South Africa.

MANUFACTURER
Vickers, Elswick, and Royal Ordnance Factory, Woolwich Arsenal, England.

Swiss Army Centurion Mk 2 ARV (Swiss Army)

Centurion Beach Armoured Recovery Vehicle

DEVELOPMENT
The Centurion Beach Armoured Recovery Vehicle FV4018 (BARV) was developed by the FVRDE from 1958 as the replacement for the Sherman BARV, which entered service during the Second World War. The first prototype Centurion BARV was completed in 1959 with the first production models following in 1961.

The Centurion BARV has two primary roles. First, to push into deeper water landing craft which have become stuck on the beach, for which purpose a push bar covered in rope is mounted at the front of the hull. Second, to pull any disabled vehicles out of deep water onto the beach. Only a small number of BARVs were built and these are used by the British Amphibious Forces on board Royal Naval Amphibious Assault Ships and in the BAOR where they are used during river crossings.

DESCRIPTION
The Centurion BARV is based on a Centurion MBT chassis with its turret removed and a new superstructure of all welded construction added which extends to the very rear of the hull. The driver is seated at the front of the hull on the right side and is provided with a reinforced observation window to his front. The crew entry hatch is in the roof of the superstructure at the front end and consists of a two-piece rectangular split hatch cover that opens left and right. The two exhaust pipes are mounted on top of the superstructure at the rear. One of the four crew members is a trained diver and his role is to connect tow cables to the damaged vehicle underwater. Automotive and suspension details are similar to the Centurion ARV/AVRE and the reader is referred to those entries for details. Unlike the Centurion ARV/AVRE, the BARV does not have any side skirts.

SPECIFICATIONS
Crew: 4
Weight:
(empty) 37 848 kg
(loaded) 40 643 kg
Length: 8·076 m
Width: 3·402 m
Height: 3·453 m
Ground clearance: 0·5 m
Track: 2·641 m

Centurion beach armoured recovery vehicle. Note push bar at front of hull (T J Gander)

Track width: 610 mm
Length of track on ground: 4·572 m
Ground pressure: 0·78 kg/cm²
Max speed: (road) 34·6 km/h
Range: 63 km
Fuel capacity: 550 litres
Fording: 2·895 m
Gradient: 60%
Vertical obstacle: 0·914 m
Trench: 3·352 m
Engine: Rolls-Royce Meteor Mk IVB 12-cylinder liquid-cooled petrol developing 650 bhp at 2550 rpm
Auxiliary engine: Morris 4-cylinder petrol developing 20 bhp at 2500 rpm
Transmission: manual Merritt-Brown Z51R with 5 forward and 2 reverse gears
Electrical system: 24 V

Batteries: 4 × 6 V
Armament: 1 × 7·62 mm Bren LMG
Armour
glacis: 76 mm
nose: 76 mm
hull sides: 51 mm
hull rear and upper: 38 mm
hull rear lower: 20 mm
hull floor: 17 mm
superstructure front, sides and rear: 20 mm

STATUS
Production complete. In service with the British Army and Royal Marines only.

MANUFACTURER
Royal Ordnance Factory, Leeds, England.

UNITED STATES OF AMERICA

V-150 Commando Recovery Vehicle

DEVELOPMENT
The Commando (4 × 4) vehicle was developed as a private venture by the Cadillac Gage Company with the first production models being completed in 1964. These were designated the V-100 and were followed a few years later by the larger V-200. Current production is based on the V-150 which has many improvements over the earlier V-100. Over 4000 Commando vehicles of all types have now been built and a similar vehicle called the Chaimite (V-200) is built in Portugal, but not under licence from Cadillac Gage.

DESCRIPTION
The hull of the Commando is of all-welded steel construction which provides the crew with protection from small arms fire. The driver is seated at the front of the hull on the left side with the co-driver to his right. Both are provided with vision blocks and a single-piece hatch cover that opens to the left or right. There is a further vision block on either side of their positions.

The remainder of the crew are seated to the rear of the driver's position. The gunner's hatch is in the centre of the roof and a 7·62 mm or 0·50 (12·7 mm) machine gun is mounted at this position.

There is a door in each side of the hull and a third door in the rear on the right side, all with a vision block and a firing port. These doors are in two parts, top and bottom, the bottom part opening downwards to form a step and the top half opening left or right. There is a further firing port and vision block in each side of the hull forward of the side doors. There is also a two-part roof hatch to the right of the engine compartment.

The engine and transmission are mounted at the rear of the hull on the left side with access hatches in the roof and side of the hull. The engine compartment is provided with a fire suppression system which is operated by the driver.

The suspension is of the solid axle type with semi-elliptical springs and heavy duty shock absorbers at each wheel station. The axles have automatic silent positive locking differentials. The steering is power-assisted and the tyres are of the run flat type and have a self-cleaning tread. The Commando is fully amphibious, propelled in the water by its wheels; two electric bilge pumps are provided.

The A-frame is supported when in operation by two cables attached to the rear of the vehicle. A hydraulically actuated spade is provided at the front of the hull and is operated through the same controls used for the winch and boom. The winch is mounted in the centre of the hull and leads out through an opening in the forward part of the commander's roof pod. The winch has a maximum capacity of 11 340 kg and has 60·9 metres of 19 mm

V-150 Commando recovery vehicle in travelling order

diameter cable. The boom has a maximum lifting capacity of 4536 kg with the two jack stands in position. When not in use this rests on the rear of the hull.

Equipment carried on board includes 15·24 metres of hose for the compressor, fuel transfer pump, jacks, gunner's platform/workbench, portable spotlight, slave cables, tools and tow bars.

SPECIFICATIONS
Crew: 5
Configuration: 4 × 4
Weight: (loaded) 9820 kg
Length: 5·689 m
Width: 2·26 m
Height: 2·311 m
Ground clearance: 0·647 m (under hull)
Track:
(front) 1·914 m
(rear) 1·943 m
Wheelbase: 2·667 m
Ground pressure: 1·5 kg/cm²
Max speed:
(road) 88 km/h
(water) 4·8 km/h
Range: 643 km

Fuel capacity: 303 litres
Fording: amphibious
Gradient: 60%
Side slope: 30%
Vertical obstacle: 0·609 m
Engine: V-8 diesel developing 202 bhp at 3300 rpm
Transmission: automatic with 3 forward and 1 reverse gears
Electrical system: 24 V
Batteries: 2 × 12 V, 100 Ah
Armament:
1 × 7·62 mm or 0·50 (12·7 mm) Browning MG
2200 rounds of ammunition

STATUS
In production. Users of the Commando include Bolivia, Cameroon, Ethiopia, Gabon, Guatemala, Haiti (ARV confirmed), Indonesia, Jamaica, Malaysia, Oman, Philippines, Saudi Arabia (ARV confirmed), Singapore, Somalia, Sudan, Thailand, Tunisia, Turkey, USA and Viet-Nam.

MANUFACTURER
Cadillac Gage Company, PO Box 1027, Warren, Michigan 48090, USA.

ARVs and Repair Vehicles based on M113 APC Chassis

DEVELOPMENT
The M113 is the most widely used APC in the world and in addition to being produced in the United States was also built in Italy by OTO Melara. The first M113s were completed in 1960, followed by the M113A1 which has a diesel engine. In the late 1960s a fitter's vehicle was developed and was limited to changing AFV components.

As a private venture, FMC developed a recovery vehicle which became known as the XM806 (gasoline), followed by the XM806E1 (diesel). The improved M113A1, the M113A2, is the current production model. It has an improved suspension and cooling system, and a new dual-air personnel heater compatible with NBC protective systems. As the US Army has never purchased the XM806 type recovery vehicle, FMC is calling the latest version the M113A1/A2 recovery vehicle. It is in service with several countries.

FMC has developed a new vehicle that combines the features of the current recovery vehicle with the fitter's vehicle, and for which the technical data package is complete. It is called the FMC maintenance-recovery vehicle (MRV). The most obvious external change is the larger hydraulically-operated crane that was on the fitter's vehicle. The first prototype was ready early in 1982; already several countries have shown interest and a few armies have placed advance orders.

The new MRV can swim without the need for a water barrier, and it has a buoyant trim vane. It has a heavier duty crane with a longer reach, and at a specified extension point can lift up to 3402 kg. The crane is hydraulically operated and has its own winch. The Royal Netherlands Army MRVs have an interior towing winch rated at a heavier capacity than the MRVs ordered by the Egyptian Army, which are fitted with the standard proven towing winch. The FMC MRV weighs approxi-

Australian Army M113 fitter's vehicle removing turret of M113 APC (Paul Handel)

mately 113 kg more than the M113A1 Recovery Vehicle, caused mainly by the heavier crane.

DESCRIPTION
M113A1/A2
The hull of the M113A1/A2 is made of all-welded aluminium. The driver is seated at the front of the hull on the left side and is provided with a single-piece hatch cover that opens to the rear. For observation purposes he has four M17 periscopes and an M19 periscope in his

roof hatch which can be replaced by an infra-red periscope for night driving. The engine is mounted to the right of the driver. The commander's cupola has five periscopes and a single-piece hatch cover that opens to the rear. A 0·50 Browning M2 machine gun is mounted on the commander's cupola with an elevation of +53 degrees and a depression of −21 degrees. To the immediate rear of the commander is a rectangular hatch which opens to the rear. Normal means of entry and exit is by a power-operated ramp in the rear of the hull.

FMC maintenance-recovery vehicle (MRV) with crane extended

FMC maintenance-recovery vehicle (MRV) with rear ramp lowered

The torsion bar suspension consists of five road wheels with the drive sprocket at the front and the idler at the rear. There are no track return rollers.

The vehicle is fully amphibious, propelled in water by its tracks. Before entering the water the trim vane is erected at the front of the hull and the bilge pumps are switched on. The basic vehicle does not have an NBC system, but this and a variety of other kits are available as optional extras.

The M113A1/A2 recovery vehicle has a P30 modified hydraulic winch which is provided with 91·4 metres of 16 mm diameter cable, with a capacity on a full drum of 5103 kg and on a bare drum of 9070 kg. A rotating fairlead that guides the cable at the rear of the vehicle allows pulling at an angle to the vehicle. A cable tensioner, built into the fairlead, allows free cable to be wound tightly. A level winder keeps the cable properly coiled on the winch drum and heavy shrouds over the winch assembly and a swing-up guard set into the ramp opening protect the operator during winching operations.

A single spade is mounted on each side of the hull at the rear and an additional spade unit can be mounted between the two outer ones for recovery in soft soil.

A Star Machine and Tool Company 300-H manually-operated hydraulic crane is mounted on the left side of the vehicle with an extensible arm with two positions for flexibility of use. This crane has a maximum lifting capacity of 1361 kg at 1·52 metre reach.

Fitter's Vehicle

This is often incorrectly called the M579, and has an almost identical hull to the M113A1/A2 but does not have the small crane or heavy winch. Mounted on the left side of the roof is a hydraulic crane which can lift a maximum of 1769 kg at a reach of 3·2 metres. The commander's cupola and the hatch to his rear are mounted on a large top hatch that opens to the right. This is 2·39 × 1·37 metres and enables a spare M113 engine to be carried inside the vehicle, and to be lifted out with the aid of the crane. The vehicle is also provided with a Gearmatic Model 6E (modified) winch which has a maximum capacity on a full drum of 1360 kg, or 1770 kg on a bare drum. 15·2 metres of 11 mm cable are provided for this winch.

STATUS

Production as required. Both the M113A1/A2 armoured recovery vehicle and the fitter's vehicle are known to be in service with the Australian Army.

In service with Israel and Lebanon.

Australian Army M113 fitter's vehicle with generator on end of hydraulic crane arm (Paul Handel)

MANUFACTURER
FMC Corporation, Ordnance Division, San Jose, California 95108, USA.

SPECIFICATIONS
(M113A1/A2; data in square brackets relate to fitter's vehicle where different)
Crew: 4
Weight:
(empty) 10 355 [9 829] kg
(loaded) 11 567 [11 703] kg
Length: 5·4 [4·86] m
Width: 2·69 m
Height: (with MG) 2·5 m
Ground clearance: 0·406 m
Track: 2·159 m
Track width: 381 mm
Length of track on ground: 2·667 m
Ground pressure: 0·57 [0·576] kg/cm²

Max speed:
(road) 67·57 [67·59] km/h
(water) 5·3 [5·8] km/h
Range: 483 km
Fuel capacity: 360 litres
Fording: amphibious
Gradient: 60%
Vertical obstacle: 0·62 m
Trench: 1·68 m
Engine: GMC Diesel Model 6V53, 6-cylinder, water-cooled developing 215 bhp at 2800 rpm
Transmission: Allison TX-100-1 with 3 forward and 1 reverse gears
Differential: FMC DS200
Electrical system: 24 V
Batteries: 2 × 12 V
Armament:
1 × 0·50 (12·7 mm) Browning M2 HB MG
2000 rounds of ammunition
Armour: 12–38 mm

Landing Vehicle, Tracked, Recovery, Model 7

DEVELOPMENT

The Landing Vehicle, Tracked, Recovery, Model 7 (or LVTR7) was developed by the FMC Corporation under contract to the Naval Sea Systems Command, to recover other members of the LVTP7 family. The first prototype, designated the LVTRX2, was completed in 1968 and after trials was standardised as the LVTR7.

DESCRIPTION

The hull, which is almost identical to that of the LVTP7, is made of all-welded aluminium. The engine and transmission are at the front of the vehicle and can be removed as a complete unit. The crew compartment and repair area are at the rear of the vehicle.

The driver is seated at the front of the hull on the left side and is provided with a single-piece hatch cover that opens to the rear. A total of seven vision blocks are provided for observation and for night driving an M24 periscope can be mounted in the hatch cover. The commander is seated to the rear of the driver and also

US Marines Corps LVTR7A1 operating in full amphibious mode (S Glen)

has a single-piece hatch cover that opens to the rear and seven direct vision blocks. For night observation he has an M17C infra-red periscope which extends vertically enabling him to see over the driver's position. The winch/crane operator is seated on the right side and has nine direct vision blocks, with his hatch cover opening to the rear; when operating the crane he uses a seat on the crane structure.

Over the top of the repair area is a large cargo hatch. Normal means of entry and exit are via the large power-operated ramp in the rear of the hull, which is provided with an integral door.

The torsion bar suspension consists of six road wheels with the idler at the rear and the drive sprocket at the front. The first and sixth road wheel stations are provided with a hydraulic shock absorber. The LVTR7 is fully amphibious being propelled in the water by two waterjets, one in each side of the hull at the rear. These waterjets are driven through right-angled gearboxes. Deflectors are used for steering and reverse. If these fail, the vehicle can be propelled in the water by its tracks at a slower speed.

Armament consists of a pintle-mounted 7·62 mm M60 machine gun. The LVTR7 is not provided with an NBC system but does have infra-red driving lights. Kits for the vehicle include a winterisation kit, visor kit for the driver and a navigation light kit for use when the vehicle is afloat at night.

On the right side of the hull is a hydraulic crane which can be elevated from 0 to +65 degrees. Its boom is telescopic and can lift 2722 kg at 6·552 metres reach. A two-speed winch with a maximum capacity of 13 605 kg on a bare drum at low speed and 1877 kg on a full drum at high speed is also installed. Equipment carried includes an air compressor, ac generator, auxiliary power unit, work benches, welding kit and a complete range of tools. If required a tent can be erected at the rear of the vehicle to enable repairs to be carried out in bad weather or under blackout.

LVTR7A1
FMC developed the LVTR7A1 under contract to the Naval Sea Systems Command. Improvements to the hull, suspension and power train, plus the fuel, hydraulic, electrical and auxiliary systems were incorporated. The recovery equipment underwent major modification. Following successful completion of US Marine Corps testing in 1981 a contract was awarded to industry to convert the present LVTR7 vehicles to the LVTR7A1 configuration.

SPECIFICATIONS
Crew: 5
Weight:
(empty) 22 580 kg
(loaded) 23 618 kg

LVTR7A1 with crane traversed to front and jib partly extended

Length: 8·14 m
Width: 3·27 m
Height: 3·2 m
Ground clearance: 0·406 m
Track: 2·609 m
Track width: 533 mm
Length of track on ground: 3·94 m
Ground pressure: 0·55 kg/cm²
Max speed:
(road) 72·4 km/h
(water) 10·94 km/h
Range:
(land) 482 km at 40 km/h
(water) 7 h at 2600 rpm
Fuel capacity: 647 litres
Fording: amphibious
Gradient: 60%
Vertical obstacle: 0·914 m
Trench: 2·438 m
Engine:
(LVTR7) Detroit Diesel Model 8V53T
(LVTR7A1) Cummins VT400
Both are 8-cylinder, water-cooled, turbo-charged diesels developing 400 hp at 2800 rpm
Transmission: FMC HS400-3A1 giving 4 forward and 2 reverse gears, manually operated but with power assistance

Electrical system: 24 V
Batteries: 4 × 12 V 6 TN
Armament:
1 × 7·62 mm M60 MG
1000 rounds of ammunition
Armour
ramp outer: 25·4 mm
ramp inner: 12·7 mm
hull sides: 31–44·5 mm
hull floor and roof: 30 mm
hull rear: 35 mm

STATUS
Production complete. The basic LVTP7 is in service with Argentina, Italy, South Korea, Spain, Thailand, USA and Venezuela.

The LVTR7 is in service with Argentina (1), South Korea (3), Spain (1), Thailand (1), USA (54) and Venezuela (1).

The LVTP7A1 has been ordered by Brazil, South Korea and the Philippines.

MANUFACTURER
FMC Corporation, Ordnance Division, San Jose, California 95108, USA.

M578 Light Armoured Recovery Vehicle

DEVELOPMENT
In 1956 the Pacific Car and Foundry Company of Renton, Washington, was awarded a contract to design a new range of self-propelled guns which would all use the same basic chassis. One of the main requirements was to reduce the overall weight of the chassis so that it could be carried by transport aircraft then in service. The following year the programme was expanded to include three armoured recovery vehicles, designated the T119, T120 and T121. The T119 and T121 both had their cranes in an unarmoured mounting, but were not developed beyond the prototype stage. Further development of the T120 (which had a petrol engine) resulted in the T120E1 which had a diesel engine, and was accepted for service as the M578. The first production contract was awarded to the FMC Corporation which produced the first production vehicle late in 1962. Production was originally completed in the late 1960s but in 1975 the M578 was placed back into production. For fiscal year 1975 the Army requested 178 vehicles at a cost of $27·6 million, for fiscal year 1976, 210 vehicles at a cost of $38·9 million, and for fiscal year 1977 the request was for 60 at a cost of $18·5 million. The fiscal year 1978 request was for 20 M578s at $7·7 million, subsequently cancelled by the Carter Administration. For fiscal year 1979 the Army requested a further 111 M578s at a total cost of $44·6 million but these were not produced. Since then there have been no orders for the US Army although production has continued for export.

DESCRIPTION
The hull of the M578 is similar to that of the 175 mm M107 and 203 mm (8 inch) M110 self-propelled guns. The driver is seated at the front of the hull on the left side and is provided with a single-piece hatch cover and three M17 periscopes for driving when closed down. The engine is to his right and the transmission is at the front of the hull.

At the rear of the hull are the turret and crane which

M578 light armoured recovery vehicle of Netherlands Army showing smoke dischargers on front and rear of turret (Royal Netherlands Army)

can be traversed through 360 degrees. The turret has a door in each side and double doors in the rear. Both the commander and operator are provided with a single-piece hatch cover which opens to the rear and six M17 periscopes for observation.

The torsion bar suspension consists of five road wheels with the drive sprocket at the front, the fifth road wheel acting as the idler. Four of the road wheels have a hydraulic bump-stop and during recovery operations the suspension can be locked to provide a more stable platform.

Armament consists of a single 0·50 (12·7 mm) Browning M2 HB machine gun mounted at the commander's position. The M578 is provided with infra-red driving lights and has an NBC filter kit option for the driver and cab crew. The vehicle does not have an amphibious capability.

Equipment carried includes tools, tow bars, hydraulic

impact wrench, acetylene welding and cutting equipment. A spade is mounted at the rear of the hull. The vehicle has two winches: a tow winch with a maximum capacity of 27 000 kg on a bare drum and a hoisting winch with a maximum capacity of 6750 kg. Details of these winches are given below:
Tow/winch cable; this has 70·1 metres of 25·4 mm diameter cable and has the following capacity:
 bare drum 27 000 kg at 7·3 m/minute, low gear
 bare drum 6713 kg at 28·59 m/minute, high gear
 full drum 19 051 kg at 10·45 m/minute, low gear
 full drum 4672 kg at 36·58 m/minute, high gear
Hoist/winch cable; this has 70·1 metres of 15·87 mm diameter cable and has the following capacity:
 bare drum 9299 kg at 10·45 m/minute, low gear
 bare drum 2041 kg at 45·72 m/minute, high gear
 full drum 6750 kg at 13·53 m/minute, low gear
 full drum 1497 kg at 52·24 m/minute, high gear
Hoisting capacity:
 13 620 kg at 3·58 m distance from the rear of the vehicle, with spade emplaced
 13 620 kg at 1·93 m distance from the rear of the vehicle, with spade retracted
 Maximum distance from ground to hook with boom at minimum reach is 5·63 m
 Maximum distance from ground to hook with boom at maximum reach is 1·67 m

STATUS
In production until end of 1981. In service with Bolivia, Brazil, Canada, Denmark, Egypt (43 ordered in 1980 at a cost of $25·3 million, including spares), Iran, Jordan, Morocco, the Netherlands, Norway, Philippines, Saudi Arabia, Spain, the United Kingdom and the USA.

MANUFACTURER
BMY Division of HARSCO, PO Box 1512, York, Pennsylvania 17405, USA.

SPECIFICATIONS
Crew: 3
Weight: 24 300 kg
 (air transport) 20 443 kg
Length:
 (overall) 6·426 m
 (hull) 5·588 m

M578 light armoured recovery vehicle in travelling order from rear (Simon Dunstan)

Width: 3·149 m
Height:
 (top of cupola) 2·921 m
 (including MG) 3·416 m
Ground clearance: 0·44 m
Track: 2·692 m
Track width: 457 mm
Length of track on ground: 3·758 m
Ground pressure: 0·7 kg/cm²
Max speed: (road) 54·71 km/h
Range: 725 km
Fuel capacity: 1135·5 litres
Fording: 1·066 m
Gradient: 60%
Vertical obstacle: 1·016 m

Trench: 2·362 m
Engine: General Motors Model 8V71T turbo-charged 8-cylinder liquid-cooled diesel developing 425 bhp at 2300 rpm
Transmission: Allison XTG-411-2A cross-drive with 4 forward and 2 reverse gears (automatic)
Electrical system: 24 V with 300 A generator
Batteries: 4 × 6 TN
Armament:
 1 × 0·50 (12·7 mm) Browning M2 HB MG and 500 rounds of ammunition
 Dutch vehicles have smoke dischargers installed (United Kingdom M578s mount a 7·62 mm Bren LMG with 1200 rounds)
Armour: steel

ARVs based on Sherman Chassis

DEVELOPMENT
The first medium ARV to see service with the United States Army in the Second World War was the M31. It was based on the chassis of the M3 Grant/Lee medium tank and entered service in 1942/3. Shortages of surplus M3 Grant/Lee chassis resulted in the development of a similar ARV based on the chassis of the M4 Sherman. The modifications were quite extensive and included the replacement of the turret by an armoured superstructure, the installation of a winch and an A-frame. This was standardised in September 1943 as the M32. The M32B1 used the M4A1 chassis, the M32B2 used the M4A2, the M32B3 used the M4A3, and finally the M32B4 used the chassis of the M4A4.
 The M74 (development designation T74) was a post-war development as the M32 could not handle the heavier tanks which entered service after the war. Conversion of M4A3 tanks (with the Horizontal Volute Spring Suspension) to M74 standard was carried out by Bowen-McLaughlin-York Incorporated from February 1954 to October 1955. In 1958 a further 60 M32B3s were brought up to M74 standard by Rock Island Arsenal, pending the introduction of the M88 ARV.

DESCRIPTION
M32
The M32 has a hull of either all-cast or all-welded construction. The driver is seated at the front on the left side with the bow machine gunner to his right. Both are provided with individual hatch covers. The crew compartment is in the centre of the hull and the engine and transmission are at the rear. Most of the early Shermans had the Vertical Volute Spring Suspension (VVSS) consisting of three bogies each side. Each bogie had two small road wheels pivoted on arms against a vertical spring, which was protected by the bogie carrying bracket. A return roller was mounted at the top of the bogie. The drive sprocket is at the front and the idler at the rear. From 1943 Shermans started to have the Horizontal Volute Spring Suspension (HVSS), which has three bogies either side, each of which has four bogie wheels with each pair sprung horizontally against the other on the bogie unit. A return roller is mounted at the top of the bogie. The HVSS gave a much smoother ride than the earlier VVSS and was also easier to repair.
 At the front of the hull is an A-frame, which is 5·486 metres long and when not required lies back over the rear of the hull. A winch with a capacity of 27 216 kg is mounted in the crew compartment to the rear of the driver, who also operates the winch.

M74 armoured recovery vehicle

M32 ARV of Japanese Ground Self-Defence Force (via T Bell)

M74

This is similar in layout to the M32 and also has an A-frame. At the front of the hull is a dozer blade. The main winch is provided with 60·9 metres of 32 mm diameter cable and has a maximum pull of 40 823 kg. The auxiliary winch has a capacity of 4536 kg and is provided with 122 metres of 12·7 mm diameter cable. The boom winch has 45·7 metres of 22 mm diameter cable and can lift 11 340 kg, or 22 680 kg with a two part pull.

For anti-aircraft defence, a 0·50 (12·7 mm) Browning M2 machine gun is mounted on top of the superstructure. Mounted in the bow is a 0·30 (7·62 mm) machine gun. This has a traverse of 24 degrees left and right and can be elevated from −10 to +24 degrees. Many countries have removed this weapon.

VARIANTS

NAPCO Industries of Hopkins, Minnesota, USA has developed a repower package for the Sherman tanks. This package can be utilised for repower of both the M74 and M32 ARV. This repower has been prototyped and tested and is ready for production. Details are given in the *Engines and powerpacks* section of *Jane's Armour and Artillery 1983–84*, page 962.

STATUS

M32: Production complete. In service with Austria, Brazil, Israel, Japan and Yugoslavia.

M74: Production complete. In service with Belgium, Portugal, Turkey and Yugoslavia.

MANUFACTURERS

Builders of the Sherman in the USA were the American Locomotive Company, Baldwin Locomotive Company, Detroit Tank Arsenal, Federal Machine and Welder Company, Ford Motor Company, Grand Blanc Tank Arsenal, Lima Locomotive Works, Pacific Car and Foundry, Pressed Steel Car Company and Pullman Standard Car Company.

SPECIFICATIONS

Model	M32	M74
Crew	4	4
Weight	28 123 kg	42 525 kg
Length	5·82 m	7·95 m
Width	2·616 m	3·095 m
Height	2·467 m	3·095 m
Ground clearance	0·434 m	0·394 m
Track	2·108 m	2·26 m
Track width	419 mm	584 mm
Length of track on ground	3·733 m	3·831 m
Ground pressure	0·935 kg/cm²	0·956 kg/cm²
Max speed (road)	42 km/h	34 km/h
Range	165 km	161 km
Fuel capacity	651 litres	636 litres
Fording	1·219 m	0·914 m
Gradient	60%	60%
Vertical obstacle	0·609 m	0·609 m
Trench	1·879 m	2·28 m
Engine	Continental R975-C1 9-cylinder petrol developing 350 hp at 2400 rpm	Ford GAA 8-cylinder petrol developing 450 bhp at 2600 rpm
Transmission	manual, 5 forward, 1 reverse	manual, 5 forward, 1 reverse
Electrical system	24 V	24 V
Armament bow	1 × 0·30 (7·62 mm) MG	1 × 0·30 (7·62 mm) MG
Armament anti-aircraft	1 × 0·50 (12·7 mm) MG	1 × 0·50 (12·7 mm) MG
Ammunition 0·30 (7·62 mm)	2000	2000
Ammunition 0·50 (12·7 mm)	300	1050
Armour	12 – 51 mm	12 – 51 mm

M88 and M88A1 Armoured Recovery Vehicles

DEVELOPMENT

The standard ARV in the United States Army immediately after the Second World War was the M74, designed by Bowen-McLaughlin-York, which produced over 1000 vehicles. Bowen-McLaughlin-York was awarded a contract to build three prototype vehicles under the designation of the T88, to use as many components as possible of the M48 tank. These prototypes were followed by ten pre-production vehicles for troop trials. The production contract was awarded to Bowen-McLaughlin-York in 1960 with the first production M88s being completed in February 1961. Final vehicles were completed in 1964, by which time 1075 had been built at a cost of $169 410 per vehicle. The M88 was powered by a Continental AVSI-1790-6A, 12-cylinder, air-cooled super-charged, fuel injection petrol engine.

In 1973 an M88 was fitted with the engine of the M60 MBT, an AVDS-1790-2DR 12-cylinder diesel which develops 750 bhp at 2400 rpm. This vehicle was designated the M88E1. Trials showed an increase in operating range from 360 km of the M88 to 450 km. In addition the M88E1 had a modified transmission, personnel heater and an auxiliary power unit was installed. In the 1970s the Army found itself short of M88 ARVs so the production line at Bowen-McLaughlin-York was reopened. In fiscal year 1975 the Army requested 115 M88s to the new standard (called the M88A1) at a total cost of $50·2 million, in fiscal year 1976 a further 159 vehicles at $72·2 million and in 1977 141 at $80·1 million. The fiscal year 1978 request was for 72 M88A1s at a cost of $42·6 million, subsequently cut by the Carter Administration to 29 vehicles at $17 million.

The 1979 fiscal year request was for 78 M88A1s at $48·6 million and the 1980 request was for 67 at $46·3 million. The 1981 request was for 166 M88A1s at $124·4 million. Up to fiscal year 1982 a total of 1706 vehicles had been procured at a cost of $588·8 million. In both fiscal year 1983 and 1984 180 vehicles a year are planned for procurement at a cost of $140·4 million in 1983 and $142·3 million in 1984. The planned fiscal year 1985 order will be for 199 M88A1s costing $166·5 million. Thus by then the total number of M88A1s will be 1083 at a cost of $1109·1 million. This will bring the entire cost of the M88 series programme, including conversions, to $2147·1 million, accounting for a total of 3348 vehicles.

Most of the earlier M88 ARVs were converted into M88A1s. In fiscal year 1976 the Army requested $29 million to convert 189 M88s to M88A1 standard and in fiscal year 1977 a further $27 million was requested for a conversion of another 240 vehicles. The conversion programme continued until April 1982 when the last of 866 M88 to M88A1 conversions was delivered to the US Army.

The M88A1 is type classified for use in the United States Army through the 1990s and is used to recover vehicles up to M48, M60 and M1 MBTs.

DESCRIPTION

The hull of the M88 and M88A1 is of cast armour and rolled armour welded together with the crew compartment at the front and the engine and transmission at the rear. The driver and mechanic are seated at the front of the hull, each with a single-piece hatch cover and periscopes. The commander was originally provided with a cupola with an internally mounted 0·50 (12·7 mm) machine gun but this was subsequently replaced by a

M88A1 armoured recovery vehicle from rear with A-frame raised (T J Gander)

M88A1 armoured recovery vehicle carrying M60 MBT engine cover (T J Gander)

simple cupola with a pintle-mounted 0·50 (12·7 mm) machine gun. There is also an entry door in each side of the hull.

The suspension is similar to that used on the M48 MBT and consists of six road wheels with the drive sprocket at the rear and the idler at the front. There are three track return rollers. Hydraulic shock absorbers are provided for the first, second and sixth road wheel stations.

At the front of the vehicle is a hydraulically-operated blade which stabilises the vehicle when the winch is being used and assists in bulldozing operations. An A-type boom pivoted at the front of the hull can lift a vehicle weighing up to 5443 kg without using the blade or suspension lockout at the front or 18 143 kg using lockout without using the blade. The vehicle can lift 22 680 kg when using the blade. The two winches are in the lower part of the hull and have the following capabilities:

Main winch is provided with 61 metres of 31·75 mm diameter cable, line pull and speed being:
bare drum 40 823 kg at 6 m/minute, low speed, 10·206 kg at 24 m/minute, high speed.
full drum 23 314 kg at 12·801 m/minute, low speed, 5829 kg at 51·2 m/minute, high speed.
The hoist winch is provided with 61 metres of 15·87 mm cable. Line and lifting speeds are:
bare drum – 4 part line: 22 680 kg at 2·7 m/minute, low speed, 5670 kg at 10·8 m/minute, high speed
full drum – 4 part line: 13 608 kg at 4 m/minute, low speed: 3402 kg at 16 m/minute, high speed.

The M88 is not provided with an NBC system and has no amphibious capability. The M88A1 can be provided with an optional NBC collective protection system in kit form. Also available is a fording kit for use in water up to 2·6 metres deep. Infra-red driving lights are provided and the driver can replace one of his day periscopes with an infra-red periscope. Standard equipment includes tools, tow bars, and an auxiliary fuel pump which allows the vehicle to transfer fuel to other AFVs at 95 litres per minute.

The M88A1 is also fitted with an auxiliary power unit (APU) powered by an Onan 10·8 hp (8·1 kW) diesel, 2-cylinder, 4-cycle engine. The APU powers an auxiliary hydraulic system that can be used to power the boom, spade and main winch and hoist cables if the main hydraulic system is inoperative. It also provides power for the refuelling and fuel transfer pump, which allows the M88A1 to act as a mobile filling station. The hydraulic system also provides power to operate a 19 mm drive hydraulic impact wrench used for track maintenance and other maintenance and recovery tasks.

VARIANTS
The chassis of the M88 is being considered as the basis for the proposed Counter Obstacle Vehicle (COV) (for full entry see Armoured engineer vehicles section). The COV will have a more powerful engine pack, specialised counter-obstacle equipment and a new suspension.

M88A1 from left with A-frame raised (T J Gander)

STATUS
In production. In service with Austria, Egypt (43 ordered in 1980 at a cost of $34·2 million), West Germany, Greece, Israel, Jordan (30 ordered in 1981 at a cost of $27 million), North Yemen (6), Norway, Oman, Pakistan, Portugal, Saudi Arabia, South Korea, Tunisia (2) and the USA (Army and Marines).

MANUFACTURER
BMY Division of HARSCO, PO Box 1512, York, Pennsylvania 17405, USA.

SPECIFICATIONS
(M88; data in square brackets relate to M88A1 where different)
Crew: 4
Weight combat: 50 400 [50 803] kg
Length: (dozer blade raised) 8·267 m
Width: 3·428 m
Height:
(with MG) 3·225 m
(top of commander's hatch) 2·921 m
Ground clearance: 0·43 m
Track: 2·717 m
Track width: 711 mm
Length of track on ground: 4·61 m
Ground pressure: 0·764 kg/cm²
Max speed: (road) 42 km/h
Range: 360 [450] km
Fuel capacity: 1514 litres
Fording: 1·42 m
Gradient: 60%
Vertical obstacle: 1·066 [1·7] m
Trench: 2·61 m
Engine: Continental AVSI-1790-6A, 12-cylinder, air-cooled, super-charged, fuel injection petrol developing 980 bhp at 2800 rpm [Continental AVDS-1790-2DR, 12-cylinder, air-cooled, super-charged fuel injection diesel developing 750 bhp at 2400 rpm]
Transmission: XT-1410-2 cross drive [XT-1410-4]
Electrical system: 24 V
Armament:
1 × 0·50 (12·7 mm) Browning M2 HB MG
1500 rounds of ammunition
2 × 6 smoke dischargers
Armour: 12·7–50 mm (estimate)

ARMOURED REPAIR VEHICLES

CANADA

Husky Armoured Repair Vehicle

DEVELOPMENT

In the early 1970s the Swiss MOWAG company developed a range of 4 × 4, 6 × 6 and 8 × 8 vehicles known as the Piranha. These all share many common components such as wheels, suspensions, steering system, hull front and rear, hatches, doors and propellers. In 1977 the Canadian Armed Forces placed an order with the Diesel Division of General Motors of Canada Limited for 350 of the 6 × 6 version. Total value of this order is £52 million ($88 million) and comprises 179 Grizzly APCs, 152 Cougar fire support vehicles (with British-supplied Scorpion turrets) and 19 Husky repair and recovery vehicles. The original order for 350 vehicles has now been increased to 491 vehicles and final deliveries were made in 1982.

The Canadian Armed Forces call the vehicle the Husky wheeled maintenance and recovery vehicle and a total of 26 are now in service.

DESCRIPTION

The hull of the vehicle is of all-welded steel armour; the driver is seated at the front of the hull on the left side and is provided with a single-piece hatch cover and three periscopes. The engine is mounted to the right of the driver and the personnel compartment is at the rear. Entry to this is via two doors in the rear of the hull, each with a MOWAG designed firing port. Hatches are provided in the roof.

The rear suspension is of the torsion bar type with coil springs and hydraulic shock absorbers at each wheel station. The front suspension is of the coil spring and wishbone type and each wheel station has a hydraulic shock absorber. The tyres have Hutchinson run-flat inner tubes. Brakes are hydraulic on all wheels.

The vehicle is fully amphibious, employing two propellers at the rear. Before entering the water a trim vane is erected at the front of the vehicle. Standard equipment on the Husky includes a HIAB 650 crane with a maximum capacity of 3250 kg.

VARIANTS

There is a separate entry for the 8 × 8 recovery vehicle under Switzerland.

STATUS

Production complete in Canada. In service with the Canadian Armed Forces. The MOWAG Piranha is also used by a number of other countries.

MANUFACTURER

Canada – General Motors of Canada Limited, Diesel Division, London, Ontario, Canada.

Switzerland – MOWAG Motorwagenfabrik AG, Kreuzlingen, Switzerland.

SPECIFICATIONS

Crew: 4
Configuration: 6 × 6
Weight: (loaded) 10 500 kg
Length: 5·97 m
Width: 2·5 m
Height: (hull top) 1·85 m
Ground clearance:
  (max under hull) 0·5 m
  (under differential) 0·39 m
Track:
  (front) 2·18 m
  (rear) 2·2 m
Tyres: 11.00 × 16
Wheelbase: 2·04 m + 1·04 m
Angle of approach/departure: 40°/45°
Max speed:
  (road) 100 km/h
  (water) 10 km/h
Range: (road) 600 km
Fuel: 210 litres
Fording: amphibious
Gradient: 70%
Side slope: 30%
Vertical obstacle: 0·5 m
Engine: turbo-charged Detroit Diesel model 6V53T developing 300 hp at 2800 rpm
Transmission: Allison MT 650 automatic with 5 forward and 1 reverse gears
Electrical system: 24 V
Armament: 1 × 7·62 mm MG

Canadian Armed Forces Husky armoured repair vehicle with crane retracted but with stabilisers extended (T J Gander)

Bow-mounted recovery winch on Husky armoured repair vehicle (T G Lynch)

Canadian Armed Forces Husky armoured repair vehicle from rear showing doors and crane remote control box on right-hand door (T J Gander)

FRANCE

AMX-10 ECH Repair Vehicle

DEVELOPMENT
The AMX-10 ECH is the repair vehicle member of the AMX-10P MICV family which entered service with the French Army in 1973. The vehicle was shown for the first time at the 1977 Satory Exhibition of Equipment for the Ground Forces. It has no recovery capability and is limited to changing components of other AFVs, for example, the engine of the AMX-10P.

DESCRIPTION
The hull of the AMX-10 ECH is almost identical to that of the AMX-10P and is of all-welded aluminium construction. The driver is seated at the front of the hull on the left side and is provided with a single-piece hatch cover and three periscopes for observation. The engine, which is made under licence by Renault, is mounted to his right. The crew compartment is at the rear of the hull and entrance to it is by the large power-operated ramp at the rear, which is provided with a door in case the ramp fails to open.

The suspension is of the torsion bar type and consists of five road wheels with the drive sprocket at the front and the idler at the rear. There are three track return rollers. Double-acting lever-type shock absorbers are provided for the first and fifth road wheel stations.

The crew of five consists of the driver, commander in the turret and three mechanics. The AMX-10 ECH is fully amphibious, propelled in water by either its tracks at a speed of 6 km/h, or by two waterjets, one in each side of the hull, giving a maximum water speed of 7·92 km/h. Before entering the water a trim board is erected at the front of the hull.

The vehicle has a Toucan I turret slightly offset to the left side of the hull fitted with a 20 mm cannon and a coaxial 7·62 mm machine gun. The turret can be traversed through 360 degrees and the armament elevated from −13 to +50 degrees. Elevation and traverse are manual, maximum elevation speed is 16 degrees per second and maximum traverse speed is 12 degrees per second. Optical equipment for the turret includes six periscopes, a sight with a magnification of ×6 for engaging ground targets and a separate sight for anti-aircraft fire. A total of 576 rounds of 20 mm and 2000 rounds of 7·62 mm ammunition are carried. The 20 mm cannon can fire a variety of ammunition including HE, HE-I and AP, with a maximum muzzle velocity of 1050 metres a second.

On the right side of the roof, at the rear, is the hydraulically-operated crane with an extensible jib, which can lift a maximum of 6000 kg. The operator is provided with a small roof hatch. When using this crane jacks are placed under the rear of the hull to support the vehicle. Other equipment carried includes tools, two sheer legs and two jacks, which are used to replace suspension components (for example torsion bars) on other AFVs including the AMX-30 MBT.

Optional kits for the AMX-10 ECH include an NBC system and passive night vision equipment.

STATUS
In production. In service with Saudi Arabia. The basic AMX-10P is also in service with France, Greece, Mexico, Qatar, Saudi Arabia and Sudan.

MANUFACTURER
Atelier de Construction Roanne (ARE).

Enquiries to Groupement Industriel des Armaments Terrestres (GIAT), 10 place Georges Clémenceau, 92211 Saint-Cloud, France.

AMX-10 ECH repair vehicle removing engine from AMX-10P MICV

AMX-10 ECH, a member of AMX-10P family of tracked combat vehicles

SPECIFICATIONS
Crew: 5
Weight:
(empty) 11 300 kg
(loaded) 13 800 kg
Length: 5·76 m
Width: 2·78 m
Height:
(top of hull) 1·92 m
(overall) 2·62 m
Ground clearance: 0·45 m
Ground pressure: 0·53 kg/cm²
Max speed: (road) 65 km/h
Range: (road) 600 km

Fording: amphibious
Gradient: 60%
Vertical obstacle: 0·7 m
Trench: 1·6 m
Engine: Hispano-Suiza HS 115-2, V-8, water-cooled super-charged diesel developing 280 hp at 3000 rpm
Transmission: preselective with 4 forward and 1 reverse gears
Electrical system: 24 V
Armament:
1 × 20 mm cannon
1 × 7·62 mm MG coaxial with main armament
2 smoke dischargers either side of turret

Renault VAB ECH Repair Vehicle

DEVELOPMENT
In 1969 the French Army issued a requirement for a new wheeled vehicle called the Véhicule de l'Avant Blindé (VAB) which would undertake a wide range of roles including use as an APC, load carrier, ambulance and anti-tank vehicle. Prototypes were built by Panhard and Saviem, and after comparative trials, the Saviem model was adopted by the French Army in 1974. The first production orders were placed the following year and first deliveries were made to the French Army late in 1976. The French Army uses the 4 × 4 version only at present, but during the 1980s 420 examples of the 6 × 6 version will have been procured. At least eight other countries have ordered the VAB and by late 1981 over 1500 VABs had been completed. The VAB ECH repair vehicle is one of the many variants being offered by Renault/Creusot-Loire.

DESCRIPTION
The hull of the VAB is of all-welded steel armour with the driver seated at the front of the vehicle on the left and the commander, who also operates the machine gun, to his right. Both the driver and commander have a bullet-proof windscreen in front which can be covered by an armoured plate if required, and a side door with a bullet-proof window. The driver has a single-piece hatch cover in the roof which opens to the rear. The armament installation is over the commander/gunner's position.

The engine and transmission are mounted to the rear of the driver's position and are removed as a complete unit through the roof. The engine compartment is provided with a fire-extinguishing system.

The crew compartment is at the rear of the vehicle and there is a connecting corridor between the driver's and commander's compartment at the front and the rear compartment on the vehicle's right hand side. At the rear of the vehicle are two doors which open outwards, each with a bullet-proof window with an armoured cover. There is no centre post so bulky equipment can be easily loaded. There are two large roof hatches over the rear compartment. In each side of the rear compartment are three bullet-proof windows covered by an armoured shutter.

The VAB ECH can be fitted with at least three different types of armament installation:

Creusot-Loire CB 52 ring mount with a 7·5 or 7·62 mm machine gun, which can be traversed by the gunner's shoulder through 360 degrees. Elevation is from −15 to +45 degrees, and 200 rounds of ready use ammunition are provided.

Creusot-Loire TLi 52A turret with a 7·5 or 7·62 mm machine gun. The turret can be traversed through 360 degrees, and the machine gun elevated from −12 to +45 degrees. The gunner is provided with a tilting-head prism periscope with a magnification of ×1, linked to a sight with a magnification of ×5. For observation purposes there are six periscopes. A white light searchlight is mounted externally on the turret and fumes from firing the MG are extracted by an electric fan system. A total of 200 rounds of ready use ammunition are provided.

Creusot-Loire CB127 gun ring shield with 12·7 mm machine gun which can be traversed through a full 360 degrees and elevated from −15 to +65 degrees. 100 rounds of ready use ammunition are provided.

The steering is power assisted on the front four wheels (in the case of the 6 × 6 model) and the suspension is of the torsion bar type with telescopic shock absorbers. The tyres are of the run flat type.

Power is transmitted from the engine to the wheels through a hydraulic torque converter and the gearbox. Gears are selected by means of a short pneumatically assisted lever which also operates the clutch.

The basic vehicle is fully amphibious, propelled in the water by its wheels, but if required the VAB can be delivered with two water-jets mounted in each side of the hull at the rear. Other optional equipment includes infra-red or passive night vision equipment, NBC system, heater and a front mounted winch with 60 metres of cable and a maximum capacity of 7000 kg.

The VAB ECH is provided with the following equipment: cylinders of oxygen and acetylene, generator, grinding machine, hand drill, hoist, searchlight, storage cabinets and drawers, water tank, workbench, vice and tool kit. To give the repair crew more head room a PVC roof extension can be quickly raised over the rear compartment.

STATUS
The VAB is in production and in service with the French Army and at least eight other countries including Ivory Coast, Mauritius, Morocco, Qatar and the United Arab Emirates.

MANUFACTURER
Renault Véhicules Industriels and Creusot-Loire.
Enquiries to Société des Matériels Spéciaux Renault V.I Creusot-Loire, 316 Bureaux de la Colline, 92213 Saint-Cloud, Cedex, France.

Renault VAB ECH repair vehicle with hatches and rear doors open

SPECIFICATIONS
Crew: 4
Configuration: 6 × 6
Weight:
  (empty) 12 000 kg
  (loaded) 14 000 kg
Length: 5·98 m
Width: 2·49 m
Height: (top of hull) 2·06 m
Ground clearance: (axles) 0·4 m
Track: 2·035 m
Angle of approach/departure: 45°/45°
Wheelbase: 1·5 m + 1·5 m
Tyres: 14.00 × 20

Max speed:
  (road) 92 km/h
  (water) 7·2 km/h (with wheels)
Range: (road) 1000 km
Fuel capacity: 300 litres
Fording: amphibious
Gradient: 60%
Side slope: 30%

Vertical obstacle: 0·6 m
Trench: 1 m (6 × 6 version only)
Engine: MAN D.2356 HM 72 6-cylinder diesel developing 235 hp at 2200 rpm
Transmission: semi-automatic with 5 forward and 1 reverse gears
Electrical system: 24 V
Armament: 1 × 7·62 mm MG (see text)

Panhard VCR-AT (6 × 6) Armoured Repair Vehicle

DEVELOPMENT
The Panhard VCR-AT (Véhicule de Combat à Roues – Atelier Technique) has been developed from the Panhard VCR (6 × 6) APC to carry out second and third line battlefield repairs on vehicles of the ERC and VCR types. It can also carry a stock of spare parts. Production so far has been for export.

DESCRIPTION
The VCR-AT follows the same general lines as the 6 × 6 version of the VCR armoured personnel carrier but the interior has been revised to provide a working area and stowage for the four-man crew. The crew consists of a driver, commander and two mechanics. Externally the main alteration is a steel beam protruding over the rear door for the suspension of a lifting device capable of carrying 500 kg.

The driver is seated centrally towards the front of the hull. Just in front of his vision hatch (which has a small winch mounted on the outside of the hull. Behind the driver is the commander's position underneath a roof-mounted hatch cover surrounded by vision periscopes. This hatch may have a 7·62 mm or 12·7 mm (0·50) machine on a ring mounting around its perimeter. The main working area is behind the commander's posi-

tion and has seating for the two mechanics, a work bench equipped with jaw vices, space for tool chests and stowage for spare parts including two complete wheel mechanisms, two transmissions, two transfer cases and universal joints. Normally the lifting device is stowed internally. There is also space for hf and vhf radio equipment. The front-mounted self-recovery winch is optional as is a full NBC protection system and a land navigation system. Other extras include a working spotlight at the rear, a hook and towing bar, smoke dischargers and extra recovery cables and equipment.

In water the VCR-AT is amphibious with primary propulsion from two hydrojets and secondary propulsion from the rotation of the road wheels. Steering is via two jet deflecters.

Panhard VCR-AT (6 × 6) armoured repair vehicle from rear

Panhard VCR-AT (6 × 6) armoured repair vehicle from rear

SPECIFICATIONS
Crew: 4
Configuration: 6 × 6
Weight:
(combat) 8200 kg
(empty) 7200 kg
Length:
(overall) 6·275 m
(hull) 4·875 m
Width: 2·478 m
Height:
(overall) 2·17 m
(top of hull) 2·13 m
Ground clearance: 0·315 m
Track: 2·16 m
Tyres: 11.00 × 16 run-flat
Wheelbase: 1·66 m + 1·425 m
Angle of approach/departure: 53°/45°
Front overhang: 1·045 m
Rear overhang: 0·745 m
Max speed:
(road) 100 km/h
(water) 3·6 km/h
Range: (road) 800 km/h
Fuel capacity: 242 litres
Fuel consumption: (road) 30 litres/100 km
Fording: amphibious
Gradient: 60%
Side slope: 30%
Vertical obstacle: 0·8 m
Trench: 1·1 m
Engine: Peugot PRV 6-cylinder, water-cooled V-6 petrol, 2·8-litre developing 145 hp at 5250 rpm
Transmission: Panhard mechanical, constant 6 × 6 drive
Suspension:
(extreme wheels) coil springs with oleopneumatic shock absorbers
(middle wheels) oleopneumatic jack for 4 wheels (road) or 6 wheels (cross-country)

Panhard VCR-AT (6 × 6) armoured repair vehicle (T J Gander)

Steering: hydraulic power on 2 front wheels
Brakes: hydraulic power discs
Armament: 7·62 mm or 12·7 mm (0·50) MG
2 × 2-barrel smoke dischargers (optional)

STATUS
Production for export.

MANUFACTURER
Société de Constructions Mecaniques Panhard & Levassor, 18 avenue d'Ivry, BP No 6-75621 Paris Cedex, France.

Panhard M3 VAT Repair Vehicle

DEVELOPMENT
The first prototype of the Panhard M3 APC was completed in 1969 with the first production vehicles following in 1971. The M3 uses 95 per cent of the mechanical components of the Panhard AML light armoured car which is used by many armies. The Panhard M3 VAT (or Véhicule Atelier) is basically the standard M3 APC modified to undertake repairs in the field. It has no recovery capability although it can tow other vehicles.

DESCRIPTION
The hull of the M3 is of all-welded steel construction with the driver seated at the front of the hull. He has a single-piece hatch cover that opens to the right and has three integral periscopes for observation. There are three small hatch covers in each side of the hull which lift upwards and there is a large door in each side of the hull. At the rear of the hull are two doors, each of which has a firing port. Future production vehicles are likely to have a single large door to enable wider components to be loaded through the rear of the vehicle. There are two circular hatches in the roof and the 7·62 mm machine gun is normally mounted on the forward hatch cover position.

The engine and transmission are to the rear of the driver. The transmission consists of two gearboxes in one, coupled on both sides of the bevel pinion. The low range box comprises two low gears, top gear, and one reverse, which are used in rough country. The high range box has three low gears and an overdrive. There is no clutch pedal, just a gear selection gate.

The suspension consists of coil springs and hydro-pneumatic shock-absorbers acting on suspension arms of the wheel mechanism. Brakes are hydraulic, with separate circuits for front and rear wheels. The tyres have puncture-proof Hutchinson inner tubes.

The M3 is fully amphibious, propelled in the water by its wheels. Optional equipment includes a ventilation system and night vision equipment of the infra-red or passive type.

Equipment installed includes a generator, tools, workbenches, inspection lamp, tow bars and tow cables. A penthouse can be erected at the rear to enable repairs to be carried out in bad weather. A block and tackle can be erected at the rear to enable the VAT to carry out engine and other component changes.

STATUS
In production. The M3 is in service with the following countries, some of which also have the VAT: Angola, Bahrain, Gabon, Iraq, Ireland, Ivory Coast, Kenya, Lebanon, Malaysia, Mauritania, Morocco, Niger, Portugal, Rwanda, Saudi Arabia, Senegal, Spain, Sudan, Togo, United Arab Emirates, Upper Volta and Zaïre.

Panhard M3 VAT repair vehicle showing unditching channels and bench vice at front of vehicle

Panhard M3 VAT repair vehicle from side in travelling order, showing hoist

MANUFACTURER
Société de Constructions Mécaniques Panhard et Levassor, 18 avenue D'Ivry, 75621 Paris, France.

SPECIFICATIONS
Crew: 5
Configuration: 4 × 4
Weight:
(empty) 5300 kg
(loaded) 6100 kg
Length: 4·45 m
Width: 2·4 m
Height: (without armament) 2 m
Ground clearance: 0·35 m

Track: 2·05 m
Wheelbase: 2·7 m
Max speed:
(road) 90 km/h
(water) 4 km/h
Range: (road) 600 km
Fuel: 165 litres
Fording: amphibious
Gradient: 60%
Side slope: 30%

Vertical obstacle: 0·3 m
Trench:
(with 1 channel) 0·8 m
(with 5 channels) 3·1 m
Engine: Panhard Model 4 HD 4-cylinder, horizontally opposed petrol developing 90 hp at 4700 rpm
Transmission: 6 forward and 1 reverse gears (see text)
Armament:
1 × 7·5 or 7·62 mm MG
4 smoke dischargers (optional)

SOUTH AFRICA

Ratel Armoured Repair Vehicle

DESCRIPTION
The Ratel armoured repair vehicle is a slight variation of the basic Ratel MICV and is a modification that can be carried out on virtually any Ratel MICV although the only examples seen to date have been made to the Ratel 20 version which is armed with a 20 mm cannon. The main armament and layout of the vehicle is retained but a fixed lifting jib made up from four tubular steel posts is mounted on the rear hull. A block and tackle arrangement is used on the jib to raise and carry damaged vehicles which would normally be of the Ratel type. The Ratel armoured repair vehicle carries various repair equipment both internally and in a wire mesh stowage basket mounted on the front hull. An air compressor is carried in a compartment in the hull rear and spare wheels may be carried on the roof. The vehicle retains its full combat capabilities.

Full details of the Ratel MICV can be found in *Jane's Armour and Artillery 1983–84*, page 333.

SPECIFICATIONS
Crew: (basic) 4
Configuration: 6 × 6
Combat weight: (approx) 18 000 kg
Length: 7·21 m
Width: 2·7 m
Height: (overall) 3·11 m
Track: 2·08 m
Wheelbase: 4·23 m
Max speed: 105 km/h
Range: (road) 1200 km
Fuel capacity: 480 litres
Fording: 1·5 m
Gradient: 70%
Side slope: 30%
Vertical obstacle: 0·35 m
Trench: 1·2 m
Turning radius: 8·5 m

Ratel armoured repair vehicle with jib on rear hull (T J Gander)

Steering: mechanical recirculating with hydraulic assistance
Engine: 6-cylinder, 4-stroke, water-cooled turbo-charged diesel developing 230 hp at 2350 rpm
Transmission: automatic with 6 forward and 1 reverse gears
Armament:
(main) 1 × 20 mm
(coaxial) 1 × 7·62 mm
(anti-aircraft) 1 × 7·62 mm

Ammunition:
(20 mm) 500 rounds
(7·62 mm) 900 rounds

STATUS
Production. In service with the South African Army.

MANUFACTURER
Sandrock-Austral Beperk Limited, PO Box 6390, West Street Industrial Sites, Boksburg, Transvaal, South Africa.

Lifting jib of Ratel armoured repair vehicle (T J Gander)

Stowage basket on front hull of Ratel armoured repair vehicle (T J Gander)

SWITZERLAND

MOWAG Piranha (8 × 8) Armoured Repair Vehicle

DEVELOPMENT
One of the Piranha series of vehicles developed by the Swiss MOWAG concern during the early 1970s is the 8 × 8 armoured repair vehicle, which may also be used if required as an armoured recovery vehicle. It follows the same general lines as the MOWAG Piranha 6 × 6 armoured repair vehicle built in Canada as the Husky.

DESCRIPTION
The hull of the vehicle is of all-welded steel armour with the front, sides and rear proof against NATO 7·62 mm ball-ammunition. The driver is seated at the front of the hull on the left side and is provided with a single-piece hatch cover and three periscopes. The engine is mounted to the right of the driver and the personnel compartment is at the rear. Entry to this compartment is via two doors at the rear of the hull, each with a firing port. Roof hatches are provided.

The rear suspension is of the torsion bar type, and the front suspension has coil springs and wishbone. All wheels are fitted with hydraulic shock absorbers. When the crane is in use, the vehicle is stabilised by hydraulic and mechanical ground-supports. All tyres have run flat cores, and the dual circuit brakes are hydraulic, assisted by compressed air.

The vehicle is fully amphibious, driven in the water by two propellers at the rear. Before entering the water a trim vane is erected at the front of the vehicle. The usual crane fitted to the Piranha 8 × 8 is the HIAB 650 with a maximum capacity of 3250 kg, although other cranes may be fitted.

A new version of the MOWAG Piranha is an 8 × 8 vehicle with a revised superstructure to mount a 7000 kg hydraulic crane centrally. This version has several layout changes from the original, one of which is the provision of stabiliser legs inset in the sides in a central position. The centrally-mounted crane position allows more internal storage space so that more tools and repair equipment can be carried.

STATUS
Production.

MOWAG Piranha (8 × 8) repair vehicle in travelling configuration

MANUFACTURER
MOWAG Motorwagenfabrik AG, Kreuzlingen, Switzerland.

SPECIFICATIONS
Crew: 4 plus
Configuration: 8 × 8
Weight:
(loaded) 12 300 kg
(empty) 8800 kg
Length: 6·365 m
Width: 2·5 m
Height:
(hull top, front) 1·85 m
(hull top, rear) 2·15 m
Ground clearance: (under hull) 0·5 m
Track:
(front) 2·18 m
(rear) 2·205 m

Tyres: 11.00 × 16
Wheelbase: 1·1 m + 1·335 m + 1·04 m
Angle of approach/departure: 40°/45°
Max speed:
(road) 100 km/h
(water) 10·5 km/h
Range: (road) 780 km
Fuel: 300 litres
Fording: amphibious
Gradient: 70%
Side slope: 35%
Vertical obstacle: 0·5 m
Engine: Detroit Diesel 6V53T developing 300 hp at 2800 rpm
Transmission: Allison MT-653 automatic with 5 forward and 1 reverse gears
Electrical system: 24 V
Armament: optional

New version of MOWAG Piranha (8 × 8) showing 7000 kg capacity hydraulic crane

MOWAG Piranha (8 × 8) armoured repair vehicle with 7000 kg hydraulic crane and array of tools and equipment carried

---

UNION OF SOVIET SOCIALIST REPUBLICS

Technical Support Vehicle MTP

DEVELOPMENT
This vehicle has been in service with the Soviet Army since the early 1970s and is used for recovery and repair of armoured personnel carriers and the BMP MICV. It is also used to deliver POL supplies to forward units which are difficult to reach with normal truck-mounted bowsers. Since the vehicle can be hermetically sealed for operation in contaminated terrain it can also be used for NBC reconnaissance.

DESCRIPTION
The MTP has the basic automotive characteristics of the BTR-50P tracked APC and has a maximum road speed of 45 km/h. It is fully amphibious, propelled in the water by its two hydrojets at a maximum speed of 10 km/h. Armour protection is probably similar to that of the BTR-50P.

Recovery equipment consists of anchoring equipment, pushing and towing equipment, tow cables and

Technical support vehicle MTP which is based on BTR-50P APC chassis

block and tackle. The drawbar pull of the MTP is 8000 kg which can be increased to 15 000 kg with the aid of block and tackle. The pushing equipment can adjust to the shocks generated by various changes in

speed. The crane has a maximum lifting capacity of 1500 kg and can be extended to 2·85 metres.

The POL pump, which is reported to be very compact, enables fuel to be transferred from barrels and containers into the fuel tanks of vehicles. Capacity with nozzle is 52 litres per minute and without nozzle 65 litres per minute. The pump can be connected to the on-board system of any vehicle with a direct current source of 24 volts.

The raised workshop compartment, which is the distinctive feature of the MTP, is high enough to allow the crew to stand while working. It also provides sleeping room for three crew members (two in hammocks and one on top of a stowage box). The compartment is heated and hermetically sealed and is also provided with firing ports for the crew's assault rifles and a machine gun which is part of the basic equipment of the MTP.

The repair and maintenance equipment includes a G-74 generator and four 12-volt starting batteries, a complete welding set for welding and cutting non-ferrous and ferrous metals, a 40-litre oxygen bottle, an acetylene generator, replacement compressed air bottles, hydraulic press and various other tools and equipment. The sensitive measuring instruments and electrician's tools are stored in a compact metal case which is protected from shock.

STATUS
Production complete. In service with the USSR.

MANUFACTURER
Soviet state arsenals.

Technical Support Vehicle MTP-LB

DEVELOPMENT
Several variations of the MT-LB multi-purpose tracked vehicle existed before the MTP-LB Technical Support Vehicle was issued to the Soviet Technical Emergency Service which has the responsibility of vehicle recovery and repair in the front line. In early 1982 it was announced by the Warsaw Pact press that the MTP-LB was already in service with both Soviet and Warsaw Pact forces.

DESCRIPTION
The basic form of the MT-LP vehicle remains unchanged but several alterations have been made to adapt it for recovering armoured fighting vehicles by direct tow or winch, and the recovery of amphibious vehicles from water obstacles. One of the main fitments is an A-frame crane mounted on the front of the vehicle. This has two working positions. One is with the crane jib length at 2·15 metres giving a lift height of 3·6 metres. The other, with the jib length at 1·35 metres gives a lift height of 4·2 metres. With the crane under load the vehicle can be driven at speeds up to 5 km/h and with a list of five degrees.

The vehicle is also provided with a cable winch, a jacking device, a towing attachment, chocks and other arresting devices, waterborne salvage equipment, and gas welding and oxyacetylene cutting equipment for both steel and aluminium. The hydraulic cable winch is driven by the auxiliary gearbox and drives a cable 85 metres long; winching capacity is 67 kN. The jacking device on the front of the vehicle acts not only as an anchor when the cable winch is in use, but also as a metalwork workbench. A hand winch is provided for moving the jacking device from its normal transport position on the vehicle front to the cargo platform when the MTP-LB is afloat. The towing attachment is used for towing armoured fighting vehicles whose steering is out of action.

Other specialised changes to the MTP-LB are the removal of the MT-LB turret and its replacement by an extra hatch and periscope over the commander's position for use when afloat. Extra frames and containers have been fitted to carry the extra equipment, and apart from the recovery role the MTP-LB carries the equipment required for observation, command, warning, reconnaissance, decontamination and camouflage. Interior lighting is also fitted. Illustrations seen so far show no armament.

SPECIFICATIONS
Crew: 2
Combat weight: 12 300 kg
Length: 6·8 m
Width: 2·85 m
Height: 2·3 m
Ground clearance: 0·4 m
Track width: 350 mm
Max speed:
  (land) 55 km/h
  (water) 6·5 km/h
Fording: amphibious
Engine: YaMZ 238 V, 8-cylinder diesel, developing 240 hp at 2100 rpm

STATUS
Production. In service with Soviet and Warsaw Pact forces.

MANUFACTURER
Soviet state arsenals.

MTP-LB in travelling configuration with driver's and commander's hatches open and jacking device raised

MTP-LB technical support vehicle with A-frame raised

MTP-LB technical support vehicle rear with access doors open

UNITED KINGDOM

FV434 Armoured Repair Vehicle

DEVELOPMENT
The FV434 (Carrier, Maintenance, Full Tracked) is a member of the FV432 family of APCs and is operated by the Royal Electrical and Mechanical Engineers (REME). Its primary role is to repair disabled and damaged vehicles, for example changing the complete powerpack of a Chieftain MBT, but it has no recovery capability.

DESCRIPTION
The hull of the FV434 is of all-welded steel construction. Its crew of four consists of commander, driver (who is also the crane operator) and two mechanics. The driver is seated at the front of the hull on the right side and is provided with a single-piece hatch cover that opens to his left and has an integral AFV No 33 Mk 1 periscope which can be replaced by an infra-red periscope for night driving. To his rear is the commander's cupola, which has a single-piece hatch cover, and three No 32 Mk 1 periscopes for observation. The FV434 is armed with either a 7·62 mm Bren LMG or a 7·62 mm GPMG. To the rear of the commander's position is another hatch which opens to the left. The engine is mounted at the front of the vehicle, to the left of the driver. The load area is at the rear of the hull and is normally covered by bows and a tarpaulin cover.

The suspension is of the torsion bar type and consists of five road wheels with the drive sprocket at the front and the idler at the rear. There are two track return rollers. The first and fifth road wheel stations are provided with hydraulic shock absorbers which are normally locked when the crane is being used.

A flotation screen is carried around the top of the hull and when erected the FV434 is fully amphibious, propelled in the water by its tracks. The vehicle is provided with a ventilation system and infra-red driving lights.

On the right side of the vehicle is a HIAB crane, which has a lifting capacity of 1250 kg at 3·96 metres radius to 3050 kg at 2·26 metres radius. A full range of tools is carried, as are a workbench, vice, and tow bars for towing disabled vehicles.

For the recovery of members of the FV432 family, an FV432 with a winch installed in its hull rear is used. This winch is of the double capstan type and is mechanically driven from the PTO on the engine transfer case, and has both high and low speed gears. This winch has a maximum pull, using a three part tackle, of 18 299 kg. Maximum speeds are 18·34 metres a minute at 6608 kg and 122·24 metres a minute at 3050 kg.

STATUS
Production complete. In service only with the British Army.

MANUFACTURER
GKN Sankey Limited Defence Operations, PO Box 20, Hadley Castle Works, Telford, Salop TF1 4RE, England.

FV434 with extra stowage boxes on front hull, roof, sides and crane jib (T J Gander)

FV434 showing extra stowage boxes on roof and crane jib (T J Gander)

SPECIFICATIONS
Crew: 4
Weight:
(empty) 15 040 kg
(loaded) 17 750 kg
Length: 5·72 m
Width: 2·84 m
(over tracks) 2·527 m
Height:
(roof) 1·891 m
(crane travelling) 2·794 m
Ground clearance: 0·35–0·46 m
Track: 2·184 m

Track width: 343 mm
Length of track on ground: 2·819 m
Ground pressure: 0·91 kg/cm²
Max speed:
(road) 47 km/h
(water) 6 km/h
Range: 480 km
Fuel capacity: 454 litres
Fording: 1·066 m (amphibious with preparation)
Gradient: 60%
Vertical obstacle: 0·609 m
Trench: 2·05 m

Engine: Rolls-Royce K60 No 4 Mk 4F, 2-stroke, 6-cylinder, twin-crankshaft, multi-fuel developing 240 bhp at 3750 rpm
Transmission: GM Allison TX-200-4A semi-automatic with 6 forward and 1 reverse gears
Electrical system: 24 V
Batteries: 6 × 12 V, 100 Ah
Armament:
1 × 7·62 mm GPMG with 1000 rounds or
1 × 7·62 mm Bren LMG with 336 rounds
2 × 3-barrelled smoke dischargers on hull front
Armour: 6–12 mm

RECOVERY VEHICLES

AUSTRALIA

Truck, Wrecker, Medium, 5-ton, (6 × 6) General Service

Information on this vehicle will be found under the entry for the Truck, Cargo (6 × 6) 5-ton General Service, in the *Trucks* section.

CZECHOSLOVAKIA

AD-090 Wheeled Recovery Vehicle (6 × 6)

DESCRIPTION
This is basically a Tatra 138 (6 × 6) truck chassis fitted with a rear-mounted hydraulically-operated crane with a capacity of 9000 kg and a winch with an 8000 kg capacity. It is normally used in conjunction with the PV-10 towing axle which has a capacity of 10 000 kg. An ear-

lier model of the AD-090 is believed to be designated the AV-8. Full details of the Tatra (6 × 6) chassis are given in the *Trucks* section.

STATUS
In service with Czechoslovak Army.

MANUFACTURER
(Tatra 138) Tatra, Národini Podnik, Kopřivnice, Czechoslovakia.

SPECIFICATIONS
Configuration: 6 × 6
Weight: 15 900 kg
Length: 9·25 m
Width: 2·45 m
Height: (travelling) 3·08 m
Max road speed:
 (without load) 60 km/h
 (with 4700 kg load) 40 km/h

FRANCE

ACMAT TPK 4·20 SL7 (4 × 4) Light Recovery Truck

DEVELOPMENT
The ACMAT TPK 4·20 SL7 is a development of the VLRA (4 × 4) long-range reconnaissance vehicle and the reader is referred to this entry in the *Trucks* section for both the development history and the technical description of the basic vehicle.

DESCRIPTION
The basic vehicle is identical to the standard VLRA except that in the rear of the cargo area a derrick and ratchet hoist has been installed, which can lift a maximum load of 3000 kg. A full range of tools is carried. The front-mounted winch has a maximum capacity of 3000 kg and is provided with 70 metres of cable. Two spare tyres are carried, one next to the driver's position and one in the rear of the truck.

ACMAT TPK 4·20 SL7 (4 × 4) light recovery truck

SPECIFICATIONS
Cab seating: 1 + 2
Configuration: 4 × 4
Towed load: 3000 kg
Weight:
 (empty) 4500 kg
 (loaded) 6750 kg
 (on front axle, loaded) 2900 kg
 (on rear axle, loaded) 3850 kg
Length: 5·705 m (excluding derrick overhang at rear)
Width: 2·066 m
Height: 2·621 m (with tarpaulin erected over rear of vehicle)
Ground clearance: 0·416 m (axle housing)
Track:
 (front) 1·76 m
 (rear) 1·66 m

Wheelbase: 3·6 m
Angle of approach/departure: 43°/41°
Max speed: (road) 95 km/h
Range: 1600 km
Fuel capacity: 360 litres (2 tanks each of 180 litres)
Max gradient: 60%
Max side slope: 30%
Fording: 0·8 m
Engine: Perkins 6-cylinder diesel type 6.354.4 developing 125 hp at 2800 rpm
Transmission: manual with 4 forward and 1 reverse gears, 2-speed transfer case
Turning radius:
 (left) 9·35 m
 (right) 6·1 m
Steering: worm and nut

Suspension: leaf springs and double acting hydraulic shock absorbers front and rear
Tyre size: 12.50 × 20
Brakes: air
Electrical system: 24 V
Batteries: 2 × 6 TN
Generator: BPG 24 V, 600 W
Derrick overhang: 1 m

STATUS
The basic vehicle is in production and in service with the French Army and more than 30 other armies.

MANUFACTURER
ACMAT (Ateliers de Constructions Mécaniques de L'Atlantique), Le Point du Jour, 44600 Saint-Nazaire, France.

ACMAT TPK 6·40 SWT 5-tonne (6 × 6) Recovery Truck

DEVELOPMENT
The ACMAT TPK 6·40 SWT is a development of the VLRA (6 × 6) long range reconnaissance vehicle. The reader is referred to this entry in the *Trucks* section for both the development history and the technical specifications of the basic vehicle.

DESCRIPTION
The vehicle is equipped with a 360-degree slewing two-piece telescopic jib crane Type H 1870 which is fixed rigidly over the rear of the vehicle and has a maximum lifting capacity of 5000 kg. A pair of heavy duty ratchet jacks are included as well as two double action hydraulic jacks. An 8-tonne winch is fitted as standard to the front of the vehicle and a comprehensive tool kit is supplied.

ACMAT Type TPK 6·40 SWT 5-tonne (6 × 6) recovery truck

SPECIFICATIONS
Cab seating: 1 + 2
Configuration: 6 × 6
Towed load: 5000 kg
Length: 7·91 m
Width: 2·46 m

Height: 2·65 m
Crane overhang: 0·93 m

STATUS
In production.

MANUFACTURER
ACMAT (Ateliers de Constructions Mécaniques de L'Atlantique), Le Point du Jour, 44600 Saint-Nazaire, France.

Renault TRM 9000 CLD (6 × 6) Wrecker

DEVELOPMENT
The Renault TRM 9000 CLD (6 × 6) wrecker is a member of the Renault TRM 9000 family of 9-ton trucks and is the replacement for the earlier Berliet TBC 8 KT (6 × 6) wrecker. There is also a similar wrecker based on the chassis of the more recent Renault TRM 10 000 (6 × 6) truck chassis which has been adopted by the French Army.

DESCRIPTION
The chassis and cab are identical to those of the TRM 9000 (6 × 6) truck and the reader is referred to this entry for a detailed description of the basic chassis.

The front-mounted winch has a maximum capacity of 3500 kg, or 4500 kg when using an earth anchor. The rear winch has a maximum capacity of 15 000 kg which can be increased to 18 000 kg with the use of an earth anchor. The crane can be slewed through 270 degrees and is provided with a telescopic jib, which has a maximum lifting capacity of 12 000 kg with the retracted boom supported by two arms resting on the frame of the truck, and the stabilisers in the lowered position. Two hydraulically-operated stabilisers are mounted on either side of the vehicle.

STATUS
In production. In service with a number of countries including Morocco.

MANUFACTURER
Renault Véhicules Industriels, 8 Quai Léon Blum, 92152 Suresnes, France.

SPECIFICATIONS
Cab seating: 1 + 5
Configuration: 6 × 6
Weight: (empty) 18 500 kg
Length: 7·865 m

Renault TRM 9000 CLD (6 × 6) wrecker

Width: 2·48 m
Height: 3·06 m
Ground clearance: 0·367 m
Track:
(front) 1·971 m
(rear) 1·886 m
Wheelbase: 3·8 m + 1·4 m
Angle of approach/departure: 43°/35°
Max speed: (road) 82 km/h
Range: 800 km
Fuel capacity: 400 litres (in 2 tanks each of 200 litres)
Max gradient: 45%
Max side slope: 22%
Fording: 1 m

Engine: Renault Type MIDS 0620.30 turbo-charged 6-cylinder diesel developing 228 hp at 2200 rpm
Transmission: BDSL 091 with 6 forward and 1 reverse gears and 2-speed transfer box
Turning radius: 11 m
Steering: power assisted
Suspension:
(front) leaf springs with telescopic hydraulic shock absorbers
(rear) leaf springs (steel equaliser beam rear bogie)
Tyre size: 14.00 × 20
Brakes: air with independent front and rear system
Electrical system: 24 V
Batteries: 4 × 12 V, 190 Ah

Renault TRM 10 000 CLD (6 × 6) Heavy Wrecker

DEVELOPMENT
The French Army currently has a requirement for a heavy wrecker truck capable of removing AMX-30 MBT turrets as well as performing the usual range of heavy duty recovery operations. Using the Renault TRM 10 000 as the basic chassis, trials are being carried out with two types of hydraulic crane, both with a 15 000 kg lifting capacity and almost identical in appearance. One crane is a PPM product, the other, the GIC 156, is a Pinguiely product.

DESCRIPTION
The layout of the Renault TRM 10 000 CLD is much the same for both types of hydraulic crane currently undergoing trials. For details of the basic vehicle refer to the entry in the *Trucks* section. The main difference in the layout of the two vehicles is that the PPM uses large hydraulic stabiliser legs mounted just behind the main cab and two further stabiliser spades at the rear while the Pinguely GIC 156 crane is stabilised by smaller legs mounted both at the rear and under the main crane platform, again just behind the cab.

Both vehicles are fitted with winches with a rearward pull of 15 000/18 000 kg. A forward-mounted winch has a pull of 6000/8000 kg. Both types of crane can be used

either for a direct lift or for use with the crane boom extended. As an example the PPM crane can lift a 12 000 kg tank turret to a hook height of six metres. Heavier loads can be lifted by placing support bars under the crane arm so that loads of up to 18 000 kg can be lifted. The normal towing capacity of the TRM 10 000 is 22 000 kg but on roads this can be increased for short distances to a load of 40 000 kg.

The TRM 10 000 chassis is used to carry an array of specialist recovery equipment and tools. Numerous optional accessories are available ranging from side-mounted capstans to a cable transfer winch.

SPECIFICATIONS (PPM crane version)
Cab seating: 1 + 3
Configuration: 6 × 6
Weight:
(complete) 22 530 kg
(front axle) 7400 kg
(rear axle) 15 130 kg
Length: (travelling) 9·72 m
Width:
(travelling) 2·48 m
(stabilisers extended) 3·23 m
Height: (overall) 3·33 m
Wheelbase: 4·1 m + 1·4 m
Max speed: 90 km/h
Range: 1000 km
Angle of approach/departure: 40°/40°
Engine: 6-cylinder diesel developing 260 hp at 1400 rpm
Transmission: automatic, 9 forward speeds (8 synchromesh plus 1 crawling)
Steering: hydraulic power assisted
Tyres: 14.00 × 20
Electrical system: 24 V

STATUS
Pre-production trials.

MANUFACTURERS
Vehicle: Renault Vehicles Industriels, 129 rue Servient, 'La Part Dieu', 69003 Lyon, France.
Cranes: Pinguiely, Creusot-Loire, BP 9, 42152 l'Horme, France.
PPM, 11 Villa de Saxe, 75007 Paris, France.

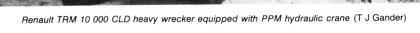

Renault TRM 10 000 CLD heavy wrecker equipped with PPM hydraulic crane (T J Gander)

Berliet TBC 8 KT (6 × 6) Wrecker

DEVELOPMENT
The Berliet TBC 8 KT (6 × 6) CLD (Camion Lourd de Dépannage) is a member of the Berliet GBC 8 KT (6 × 6) 4-ton truck family and the reader is referred to the entry on the latter vehicle for a detailed history of its development and a description of its technical characteristics.

DESCRIPTION
The rear winch is provided with 60 metres of cable and has a maximum capacity of 5000 kg which can be increased to 7000 kg with the aid of earth anchors. The crane mounted in the rear is hydraulically operated, slews through 270 degrees, and has the following capacity:

Berliet TBC 8 KT (6 × 6) wrecker recovering Jeep

	Jib retracted	Jib extended
With auxiliary conversion hoist on the ground and auxiliary conversion hoist on the platform	6000 kg	3000 kg
With auxiliary conversion hoist on the ground, and without auxiliary conversion hoist on the platform, arm at any position in azimuth	4500 kg	1800 kg
Without auxiliary conversion hoist on the ground, and with auxiliary hoist on the platform	4000 kg	1500 kg
Without auxiliary conversion hoist on the ground, and with auxiliary conversion hoist on the platform	1450 kg	500 kg

Two stabilisers on each side are lowered to the ground manually. Equipment carried includes two telescopic arm brackets to support the jib, two rear radius rods to support the jib on the ground, tow bars, two earth anchor spades, tackles, one acetylene bottle and hose, one oxygen bottle and hose and tools.

VARIANTS
A light recovery version of the GBC 8 KT (6 × 6) truck is also in service. This has drop sides and an overhead rail and is provided with a 2000 kg hoist which can be used

to lift light vehicles and change components. A winch with a capacity of 5000 kg (or 7000 kg with earth anchors in use) is fitted and can be led out through the front or rear. Loaded weight is 12 600 kg and empty weight is 9600 kg (eg 4400 kg on the front axles, and 2600 kg on each of the rear axles).

SPECIFICATIONS
Cab seating: 1 + 2
Configuration: 6 × 6
Weight: (empty) 13 650 kg

Length: 7·693 m
Width: 2·4 m
Height: 2·97 m
Ground clearance:
(max) 0·515 m
(axles) 0·28 m
Track: 1·86 m
Wheelbase: 3·31 m + 1·28 m
Angle of approach/departure: 45°/45°
Max speed: (road) 80 km/h
Range: 800 km
Fuel capacity: 200 litres
Max gradient: 50%
Side slope: 22%
Fording: 1·2 m
Engine: Berliet MK 520 5-cylinder multi-fuel developing 125 hp at 2100 rpm
Transmission: Berliet BDSL with 6 forward and 1 reverse gears, 2-speed transfer case
Turning radius: 10·5 m
Steering: worm gear and nut with servo assistance, turning circle indicator provided
Suspension:
(front) longitudinal leaf springs with hydraulic shock absorbers
(rear) leaf springs
Tyre size: 12.00 × 20
Brakes: air with 3 circuits (1 for front, 1 for rear and 1 for trailer) with exhaust retarder
Electrical system: 24 V
Batteries: 4 × 12 V

STATUS
Production complete. In service with the French Army. The cargo truck version is also used by Algeria, Austria, China, Iraq, Morocco and Portugal, some of which also use the recovery version.

MANUFACTURER
Automobiles M. Berliet, Bourg. Berliet is now part of the Renault group.

Berliet GBC 8 KT (6 × 6) light recovery vehicle showing overhead gantry with lifting equipment

Berliet TBU 15 CLD (6 × 6) Wrecker

DESCRIPTION
The TBU 15 CLD (Camion Lourd de Dépannage) is the recovery member of the GBU 15 (6 × 6) cargo truck family and uses the same basic chassis and cab. The basic truck model entered production in 1959/60 with the wrecker following in 1962.

Mounted at the rear is a hydraulic crane with a maximum lifting capacity of 10 000 kg, which can be swung through 278 degrees. Its telescopic jib has a maximum length when extended of 5·518 metres. Two stabilisers on each side of the hull are lowered manually when heavier loads are being lifted. The front-mounted winch has 60 metres of 15 mm diameter cable and a capacity of 5000 kg, which can be increased to 7000 kg with the aid of earth anchors. The rear-mounted winch has 60 metres of 20 mm diameter cable and a maximum capacity of 8000 kg which can be increased to 12 000 kg with earth anchors. A full range of tools and other equipment is carried including oxygen and acetylene cylinders. Its replacement is the Renault TRM 9000 CLD (6 × 6) wrecker.

STATUS
Production complete. In service with Belgian, French and other armed forces.

MANUFACTURER
Automobiles M. Berliet, Bourg. Berliet is now part of the Renault group.

Berliet TBU 15 CLD (6 × 6) wrecker (T J Gander)

SPECIFICATIONS
Cab seating: 1 + 3
Configuration: 6 × 6
Weight: 21 200 kg
Length: 8·88 m
Width: 2·5 m
Height: 3 m
Ground clearance: 0·6 m (max)
Track: 2·04 m
Wheelbase: 3·48 m + 1·45 m

Angle of approach/departure: 45°/45°
Max speed: (road) 68 km/h
Range: 800 km
Fuel capacity: 400 litres (2 tanks each of 200 litres)
Max gradient: 60%
Max side slope: 30%
Fording: 1 m
Engine: Berliet MK 640 6-cylinder, multi-fuel, water-cooled developing 214 hp at 1800 rpm

Transmission: manual with 5 forward and 1 reverse gears, 2-speed transfer box
Turning radius: 9·2 m
Steering: screw and nut with power assistance
Suspension: longitudinal leaf springs front and rear
Tyres: 14.00 × 20
Brakes: air
Electrical system: 24 V
Batteries: 4 × 6TN

Brimont ETR 206 S Type 'Mase' (4 × 4) Recovery Vehicle

DEVELOPMENT
The Brimont ETR 206 S is a specialist recovery vehicle intended for the recovery of amphibious bridging units rather than road vehicles. It is intended primarily for use by the French Army Gillois bridging units and should replace the CR8 bulldozers at present used by such units. Designed to operate from the banks of water obstacles the ETR 206 S is primarily a mobile winch with the necessary anchoring equipment and has only limited earth clearing capabilities using a small front-mounted dozer blade.

DESCRIPTION
The Brimont ETR 206 S is a 4 × 4 cross-country truck with an articulated frame fitted with a device that keeps all four wheels in constant contact with the terrain. It weighs approximately 10 000 kg and power is supplied by a Renault Véhicules Industriels MIDR 060212 6-cylinder air-cooled diesel developing 172 hp at 2900 rpm.

The main winch for the amphibious bridging recovery is a THB 300 unit mounted on the rear chassis with a maximum capability of 30 000 kg. When in use the winch and vehicle are securely anchored in place by a large hydraulic blade which is forced downwards into the ground, raising the rear wheels off the ground. Further stabilisation can be provided by using the front-mounted dozer blade, normally employed in the clearing of small earth obstacles and for clearing water entry and exit points. This dozer blade is hydraulically operated. There is an 8000 kg capacity winch at the front of the vehicle for self-recovery, and a trailer hook with a towing capacity of 13 000 kg is provided at the rear. This towing hook point also has a trailer air brake connection.

The vehicle has provision for steering on all four wheels.

SPECIFICATIONS
Cab seating: 1 + 1 or 2
Configuration: 4 × 4
Weight: (loaded) approx 11 000 kg
Ground clearance: 0·465 m

Max speed: (road) 70 km/h
Fuel capacity: 130 litres (200 or 350 litres optional)
Max gradient: 60%
Fording: 0·9 m
Engine: Renault VI MIDR 060212 6-cylinder air-cooled diesel developing 172 hp at 2900 rpm
Transmission: 12 speeds in two ranges
Transfer box: 2-speed
Turning radius:
(two wheel) 7·7 m
(four wheel) 4·8 m
Suspension: progressive flexibility leaf springs, shock absorbers front and rear
Tyres: 16.5 × 75 R20 BIB
Brakes: hydro-pneumatic
Electrical system: 24 V, 96 Ah

STATUS
Prototype.

MANUFACTURER
Brimont SA, BP 3 Sillery, 512500 Rilly-la-Montagne, France.

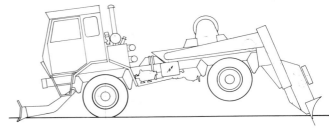

Drawing of Brimont ETR 206 S recovery vehicle for amphibious bridging units (not to 1/76th scale)

Brimont ETR 206 S recovery vehicle with rear hydraulic spade anchor dug in and rear wheels raised

GERMANY, DEMOCRATIC REPUBLIC

ADK 70 (4 × 4) Mobile Crane

DEVELOPMENT
The ADK 70 (4 × 4) crane entered production in the German Democratic Republic during late 1981. It is based on the chassis of the W50 (4 × 4) 3000 kg truck.

DESCRIPTION
The ADK 70 may be used for a variety of military purposes from removing and carrying tank engine packs to off-loading stores and for use in civil emergencies. The vehicle has a two-man enclosed cab behind which the open frame chassis has been adapted to carry a 7000 kg capacity crane. The crane can be extended to up to four jib extensions hydraulically with the maximum extension being 14·8 metres at 0 degrees elevation. Outriggers, four in all, are used to provide stability. The crane has a full 360-degree traverse and is normally carried with the jib facing forward. Loads can be towed suspended from the jib at speeds of up to 5 km/h when the load is less than 6000 kg, and 1·5 km/h when the load exceeds 6000 kg. When the crane cable is fully retracted three metres will still be left to carry the hook sheave which is normally secured to a clamp on the front fender.

STATUS
In production.

MANUFACTURERS
VEB Maschinenbau 'Karl Marx', Bablesberg, German Democratic Republic.
VEB IFA Automobilewerke, Ludwigsfelde, Bezirk Potsdam, German Democratic Republic.

ADK 70 (4 × 4) mobile crane

SPECIFICATIONS
Cab seating: 1 + 1
Configuration: 4 × 4
Weight: (complete) 11 400 kg
Length: 7·8 m
Width: 2·5 m
Height transported: 3·35 m
Ground clearance: 0·3 m
Wheelbase: 3·2 m

Max speed: (road) 70 km/h
Range: 550 km
Engine: 4-cylinder water-cooled diesel developing 125 hp at 2300 rpm
Gearbox: manual
Transfer box: 2-speed
Steering: power assisted
Electrical system: 24 V

GERMANY, FEDERAL REPUBLIC

Wheeled Recovery Vehicles

In addition to the Faun LK 1212/485 crane truck, the Federal German Army use the following wheeled recovery vehicles:

Mercedes-Benz LG 315/46 (4-tonne), details of which will be found under the entry for this vehicle in the *Trucks* section.

Magirus-Deutz (6 × 6) (7-tonne), details of which be found under this entry for the vehicle in the *Trucks* section.

MAN Type 27365 VFAE (8 × 8) Recovery Vehicle (M1002)

DEVELOPMENT
The MAN Type 27365 VFAE is a development from the main line of MAN 10-tonne trucks and was produced for use by the US Army in Europe. The first two examples of this recovery vehicle were delivered between July and September 1981 under the designation XM1002. They were later approved for service as the M1002 and production is now underway by MAN for the US Army.

DESCRIPTION
The main engine is situated just behind the tilt-forward cab which has air-assisted suspension seating for the driver and two passengers. The entire chassis frame is constructed from all-welded steel and is a torsion-free box structure. A spare wheel is located to the right of the engine and has to be removed for air transportation. Behind the engine is an open equipment-carrying box with drop sides 2·3 metres long. Behind the box is an Atlas crane with a capacity of 20 tonnes which is provided with a remote control unit and outriggers for stability. Directly over the third and fourth axles is a sub-structure which can either be used as a 'fifth wheel' load carrying surface or as the position for a recovery assembly capable of lifting up to 11 340 kg and towing 38 556 kg. The recovery assembly may be fitted with a towing bar or other recovery equipment. Other special equipment includes a heavy duty recovery winch with a 20 412 kg capacity, and a self-recovery winch with a 9072 kg capacity. Power take-offs for all these equipments can be selected from the main power train. Extra spare wheels can be carried over the main recovery assembly, and the complete vehicle is finished in an NBC decontaminant-resistant paint.

SPECIFICATIONS
Cab seating: 1 + 2
Configuration: 8 × 8
Length: 8·996 m
Width: 2·5 m
Height:
(spare wheel) 2·85 m
(top of cab, air transportable) 2·656 m
(operating) 2·921 m

MAN Type 27365 VFAE (8 × 8) recovery vehicle produced for US Army as M1002

Ground clearance: 0·457 m
Track:
(front) 2·066 m
(rear) 2·072 m
Wheelbase: 1·93 m + 3·2 m + 1·5 m
Angle of approach/departure: 42°30'/45°
Max speed: (approx) 90 km/h
Fuel capacity: 418 litres
Max gradient: (without trailer) 60%
Fording: 1·22 m
Engine: MAN D 2840 MFG V-10 water-cooled diesel developing 365 hp at 2300 rpm
Gearbox: ZF synchromesh 4S-150 8-speed
Clutch: ZF torque converter clutch 400
Transfer box: ZF-GPA
Steering: recirculatory ball hydro-steering

Suspension: coil springs and telescopic shock absorbers
Tyres: 16.00 × 20
Axle loadings:
(front) 2 × 7500 kg
(rear) 2 × 10 500 kg
Brakes: two circuit air and air over hydraulic
Electrical system: 24 V
Batteries: 4 × 12 V, 125 Ah
Alternator: 28 V, 95 A

STATUS
In production since 1982. In service with the US Army.

MANUFACTURER
MAN, Commercial Vehicle Division, Postfach 500620, D-8000 Munich, Federal Republic of Germany.

Faun LK 1212/485 (6 × 6) Crane Truck

DESCRIPTION
The Faun LK 1212/485 is called the Kranwagen 10-tonne (6 × 6) by the Federal German Army, but as it is widely used for recovery purposes it is included in this section rather than the crane section. The crane is mounted at the rear of the vehicle and can be traversed through a full 360 degrees. Two stabilisers are provided each side of the vehicle and these are lowered into position before the crane is used. The crane operator's cab is fully enclosed and the jib of the crane can be extended. The crane has a maximum lifting capacity of 10 000 kg.

VARIANTS
A more recent development is the MKF 33·35/485 which has a more powerful engine which develops 340 hp giving the vehicle a maximum road speed of 67·5 km/h.

STATUS
Production complete. In service with the Federal German Army.

MANUFACTURER
Faun-Werke Abteilung ZE, 8560 Lauf AD Pegn, Postfach 8, Federal Republic of Germany.

SPECIFICATIONS
Configuration: 6 × 6
Weight: (empty) 28 150 kg
Length: 9·14 m
Width: 2·5 m

Faun LK 1212/485 (6 × 6) crane truck in travelling order

Height: 3 m
Ground clearance: 0·42 m
Track:
(front) 1·98 m
(rear) 1·991 m
Wheelbase: 4·85 m + 1·7 m
Max speed: (road) 60 km/h
Range: 600 km
Fuel capacity: 300 litres
Max gradient: 41%

Fording: 0·9 m
Engine: Deutz 12-cylinder multi-fuel type F 12 L 714 A developing 265 hp at 2300 rpm
Transmission: ZF type AK 6-75 with 6 forward and 1 reverse gears and 2-speed transfer case
Turning radius: 15 m
Tyres: 16.00 × 25
Electrical system: 24 V
Batteries: 4 × 12 V
Generator: 600 W

ITALY

FIAT 6605 (6 × 6) AG Recovery Vehicle

DEVELOPMENT
The FIAT 6605 AG is the recovery member of the FIAT 6605 range of vehicles for which there is a separate entry in the *Trucks* section. The first prototype of the vehicle was completed in 1972 with first production models following in 1974. The Italian Army designation for the vehicle is the Autogru AG 70-5 ton (6 × 6).

DESCRIPTION
The chassis is the ladder type with two longitudinal pressed steel channels, to which are riveted the cross-members, brackets and spring supports. The forward control cab is all-steel and has a removable canvas top and side screens and a windscreen which can be folded flat against the bonnet. Standard equipment includes a cab heater and ventilator.

Mounted at the rear of the vehicle is a hydraulically-operated crane with an extensible jib which can lift a maximum load of 5000 kg. Before the crane is used two stabilisers are extended either side and lowered to the ground. The FIAT 6605 AG has two winches, one front mounted with a capacity of 9200 kg and one rear mounted winch with a capacity of 20 000 kg.

The transmission consists of a set of gears mounted on four shafts (input, primary, layshaft and reverse). Shifting from each gear is controlled by a lever through a pneumatic servo. Shifting from the high to the low range, or vice versa, is by electro-pneumatic control with a pre-selector switch, interlocked with the clutch pedal. The transfer box is mechanical and consists of helical constant mesh gears mounted on three shafts (input, intermediate and output) of which the input one carries the dog clutch with a lockable divider differential distributing power to the front and rear axles.

STATUS
In production. In service with the Italian Army.

MANUFACTURER
FIAT, Direzione Mezzi Speciali, Corso G Marconi 10/12, Turin, Italy.

FIAT 6605 AG (6 × 6) recovery vehicle showing front-mounted winch

SPECIFICATIONS
Cab seating: 1 + 1
Configuration: 6 × 6
Weight:
 (empty) 17 000 kg
 (loaded) 22 100 kg
Max load: 5000 kg
Towed load: 15 000 kg
Length: 8·627 m
Width: 2·455 m
Height:
 (cab) 2·74 m
 (top of crane in travelling position) 2·807 m
Ground clearance: 0·363 m
Track: 2·072 m
Wheelbase: 3·217 m + 1·365 m
Angle of approach/departure: 35°/40°
Max speed: (road) 91 km/h
Range: 700 km
Fuel capacity: 360 litres
Max gradient: 60%
Max side slope: 20%

Fording: 1·5 m
Engine: Model 8212.02 6-cylinder in-line water-cooled diesel developing 260 hp
Gearbox: manual with 8 forward and 1 reverse gears
Clutch: single dry plate
Transfer box: 2-speed
Steering: ZF hydraulic assisted
Turning radius: 8 m
Suspension:
 (front) 2 semi-elliptical constant rate leaf springs with double acting hydraulic shock absorbers
 (rear) rocker and torque arms with 2 constant rate leaf springs
Tyres: 14.00 × 20
Number of tyres: 6 + 1 spare
Brakes:
 (main) drum air-operated on all wheels, dual circuit with connections for trailer braking
 (parking) drum, hand-operated, mounted on transfer rear output shaft
Electrical system: 24 V
Batteries: 4 × 12 V, 90 Ah

FARID Recovery Equipment

DESCRIPTION
The Italian company of FARID has developed a new range of heavy duty recovery equipment which can be installed on a variety of tracked and wheeled chassis. The equipment can be divided into three families; slewing cranes, fixed turret cranes and pick-up platforms; all of these are hydraulic but have different applications.

Slewing Cranes
Model F 25 cross-country
This model can be installed on a 6 × 6 chassis that has a gross vehicle weight of not less than 26 000 kg. The hydraulic crane has a lifting capacity of 25 000 kg and can be slewed through 360 degrees; it is stopped in the desired position by an automatic belt braking device.

The telescopic boom is provided with two hydraulic plus one mechanical extensions and can reach a height of 17 metres, and horizontally 9 metres from the rear end and 11 metres from the side boards. Before operations four outriggers are lowered to the ground, two each side, by means of hydraulic and independent control.

Two auxiliary hydraulic winches are fitted, one on the rear having a capacity of 10 000 kg with 70 metres of 20 mm diameter steel cable, and one at the front with a capacity of 5000 kg and 75 metres of 16 mm steel cable. Both winches are controlled from the driver's cab.

Power is provided by two hydraulic piston pumps

driven by the vehicle's PTO which has an in-built strainer and return filter fitted. The crane is also provided with a pressure relief valve to prevent overloading of the various hydraulic systems, lock valves on the outrigger's cylinder, and a pressure gauge, showing the working pressure, in front of the operator's seat.

Standard equipment includes tow hitch, snatch block chains, tools, yellow flashes and rear spotlight for operations at night.

Fixed Turret Cranes
Model F 20 f
This wrecker crane consists of a fixed turret on which a telescopic boom is hinged. The boom is provided with hydraulic hoisting and two hydraulic extensions. This model can be installed on a chassis and cab that have a gross vehicle weight of not less than 19 000 kg. The two main hydraulic winches are fitted on the turret and are provided with independent control, 50 metres of 16 mm diameter steel cable and have a capacity of 10 000 kg each.

The two main steel cables, after passing through their independent control, end with a steel hook. These two winches can be used both together, having a total capacity of 20 000 kg, or separately. For lateral strength one winch anchors while the other provides pull.

Before the crane is used two rear stiff-legs are lowered to the ground by means of hydraulic and independent controls. A third hydraulic winch, having a capacity

of 15 000 kg and 100 metres of 20 mm diameter steel cable, is mounted on the rear part of the vehicle so that a total pulling capacity of 35 000 kg can be obtained.

The front-mounted winch has a capacity of 5000 kg and is provided with 75 metres of 16 mm steel cable and is controlled from the driver's cab.

The rear hydraulic lift-and-tow device is made by a foldable boom and has a variety of lifting and towing attachments to permit towing of disabled vehicles once they have been recovered.

All the control levers are fitted on the rear part of the vehicle and the boom and winch controls are duplicated on a remote control. Tow hitch, snatch block, chains, tools, yellow flashes and spotlights for night operations are fitted as standard.

Model F 12 f
This wrecker equipment has the same main features as the Model F 20 f but is a lighter version. It can be installed on a chassis/cab combination that has a gross vehicle weight of not less than 13 000 kg.

The two main hydraulic winches fitted on the turret have a capacity of 6000 kg each and are provided with 35 metres of 16 mm diameter steel cable. The third hydraulic winch has a capacity of 6000 kg and is provided with 75 metres of 16 mm diameter steel cable. It is mounted on the rear of the vehicle so that a total pulling capacity of 18 000 kg can be obtained.

The front-mounted hydraulic winch has a capacity of 4000 kg and is provided with 46 metres of 11 mm

FARID F 20 f recovery vehicle with anchors lowered at rear

FARID F 20 f recovery vehicle

FARID F 25 (6 × 6) cross-country recovery vehicle on FIAT chassis

FARID F 25 (6 × 6) cross-country recovery vehicle on FIAT chassis

FARID F 12 f recovery vehicle

FARID F 12 f recovery vehicle

FARID pick-up platform on FIAT chassis in travelling configuration

FARID pick-up platform on FIAT chassis in ready to load configuration

diameter steel cable and is controlled from the driver's cab. Standard equipment includes remote control, tow hitch, snatch block, chains, standard tools, yellow flashes and rear lights for night operations.

Pick-up Platform

This equipment is to be installed on a chassis/cab combination having a gross vehicle weight of not less than 7500 kg and has been designed for the recovery of light trucks and Land-Rover type vehicles. The pick-up platform truck is made up of three separate parts each of which has its own task: the boom crane is provided with hydraulic hoisting, hydraulic extension and a 3000 kg winch; it is for lifting or pulling broken down vehicles and after use it is stowed between the platform rails. The loading platform permits the transport of one vehicle which is loaded on it. It is hydraulically lifted and two rear loading ramps can be extended by means of a hydraulic and independent control. Before operations are carried out two rear-mounted hydraulic stiff-legs are lowered to the ground. The rear hydraulic "lift-and-tow" device is for towing a second vehicle, when the first one has already been loaded over the platform. Standard equipment includes front winch remote control, snatch block, chains, yellow flashes and rear lights for recovery operations at night.

SPECIFICATIONS

Model	F 25	F 20 f	F 12 f	Pick-up platform
Turret	360° slewing	fixed	fixed	none
Max lifting capacity	25 000 kg	20 000 kg	12 000 kg	2000 kg
(fully extended)	3000 kg	5000 kg	2700 kg	800 kg
Max pulling capacity	10 000 kg	35 000 kg	18 000 kg	3000 kg
Max boom height	17 m	12 m	10 m	5 m
Max horizontal extension				
(from rear end)	9 m	6 m	5 m	2 m
Main cable (diameter)	14 mm	16 mm	16 mm	12 mm
(length)	150 m	50 m	35 m	30 m
Max rear auxiliary winch capacity	10 000 kg	15 000 kg	6000 kg	n/app
Max front-mounted winch capacity	5000 kg	5000 kg	4000 kg	3000 kg
Rear auxiliary winch cable				
(diameter)	20 mm	20 mm	16 mm	n/app
(length)	70 m	100 m	75 m	n/app
Front auxiliary winch cable				
(diameter)	16 mm	16 mm	11 mm	12 mm
(length)	75 m	75 m	46 m	30 m

STATUS

In production. In service with many armed forces in Africa and the Middle East.

MANUFACTURER

FARID SpA, Corso Savona 39 bis, 10024 Moncalieri, Italy.

Astra BM 20MR1 (6 × 6) Recovery Vehicle

DESCRIPTION
The Astra BM 20MR1 (6 × 6) recovery vehicle uses the chassis of the Astra BM 20M series of vehicles which includes the Astra BM 20MT dump truck described in the *Construction equipment* section. The fully-enclosed forward cab, which is common to the BM 20M series, is made of fibreglass with a metallic frame. In addition to the driver and passenger seats, there are two folding seats in the rear of the cab for emergency use. The chassis is made of high-strength steel and the frame consists of two double C-shaped side members connected through rigid cross-members.

Mounted on the rear is a 7500 kg crane with a single boom extension. The crane is mounted on a 360-degree turntable and has a lifting capacity of 7500 kg at a distance of 2·5 metres; this decreases to 3600 kg at 5·7 metres, the maximum extension of the jib. Hydraulic power for the crane is also used to raise and lower the four outriggers which are connected directly to the platform. The crane operator's cab rotates with the crane and is open.

Mounted just behind the driver's cab is an auxiliary winch with a capacity of 15 000 kg. The winch is provided with 75 metres of cable.

VARIANTS
There are two further variants of the Astra BM 20MR1. One is the Astra BM 20MR2 which is equipped with a 16 000 kg extending jib crane which is intended for use with engineer equipments. Fully loaded this variant weighs 23 500 kg and is 10·12 metres long.

A further variant is the Astra BM 20NR2 with a 20 000 kg crane. For details of this see the entry in the *Construction equipment* section.

SPECIFICATIONS
Cab seating: 2 + 2
Configuration: 6 × 6
Weight:
  (chassis and accessories) 9700 kg
  (chassis, accessories and crane) 17 820 kg
Towed load: 28 000 kg
Length: (overall) 8·59 m
Width: 2·5 m
Height:
  (cab) 2·75 m
  (top of crane in travelling position) 3·3 m
Ground clearance: 0·365 m
Track:
  (front) 2 m
  (rear) 1·85 m
Wheelbase: 3·485 m + 1·3 m
Max speed: (road) 67·2 km/h

Astra BM 20MR1 (6 × 6) recovery vehicle

Range: 1000 km
Fuel capacity: 280 litres
Max gradient: 70%
Engine: FIAT Model 8210.02 6-cylinder in-line diesel developing 260 hp at 2200 rpm
Gearbox: ZF manual, 6 forward and 1 reverse gears
Clutch: single dry plate
Transfer box: 2-speed
Steering: hydraulic assisted
Suspension:
  (front) semi-elliptical springs with 4 rubber bumpers and hydraulic shock absorbers
  (rear) oscillating semi-elliptical type springs with rocker arm system

Tyres: 12.00 × 20
Number of tyres: 10 + 1 spare
Brakes:
  (main) air
  (parking) mechanical
Electrical system: 24 V
Batteries: 4 × 12 V

STATUS
Production.

MANUFACTURER
Astra Veicoli Industriali SpA, Via Caorsana 79, 29100 Piacenza, Italy.

JAPAN

Mitsubishi Model FW103MW (6 × 6) 7000 kg Recovery Vehicle

DESCRIPTION
This recovery vehicle uses the same chassis as the Type 74 (6 × 6) 10 000 kg cargo truck used by the Japanese Self-Defence Force. The two-door all-steel control cab can be tilted forward to allow access to the engine for maintenance.

Mounted to the rear of the cab is a hydraulically-operated crane with a telescopic jib. When the recovery equipment is being used, two stabilisers are lowered each side of the recovery equipment. Winches are provided front and rear and earth anchors can be fitted to the rear of the vehicle if required.

Details of other Japanese Army recovery vehicles are given in the *Trucks* section under their respective chassis.

STATUS
Production. In service with the Japanese Ground Self-Defence Force.

MANUFACTURER
Mitsubishi Motors Corporation, 33-8, Shiba 5-chome, Minato-ku, Tokyo, Japan.

SPECIFICATIONS
Cab seating: 1 + 2
Configuration: 6 × 6
Weight: 17 820 kg
Length: 9·325 m

Mitsubishi Model FW103MW (6 × 6) 7000 kg recovery vehicle (Kensuke Ebata)

Width: 2·49 m
Height: 3·048 m
Wheelbase: 5·45 m
Track:
  (front) 1·915 m
  (rear) 1·865 m

Max speed: (road) 100 km/h
Engine: 8-cylinder diesel developing 300 hp at 2500 rpm
Turning radius: 10·5 m
Tyres: 10.00 × 20
Number of tyres: 10 + 1 spare

KOREA, REPUBLIC

Kiamaster 3-ton Crane Truck

DESCRIPTION
The Kiamaster 3-ton crane truck uses the chassis of the Kiamaster 4-ton (4 × 2) Boxer Truck (for which there is a separate entry in the *Trucks* section), but the frame behind the enclosed cab is open. The turntable used is for the Model CH30-1 crane. The crane has a 3000 kg capacity at a radius of 4·2 metres and the boom length can be extended from 4·18 to 7·78 metres. Maximum working radius is from 0·82 to 7·38 metres. For extra stability four outrigger legs and jacks can be lowered from each corner of the rear frame. The crane operator is seated on an open seat at a level slightly higher than that of the cab roof and although the crane has a theoretical 360-degree traverse it is limited to an arc of about 240 degrees by the driver's cab. The crane is equipped with 48 metres of 10 mm cable which can move the hook at speeds up to 10 metres in one minute. The jib boom angle can vary between −7 and +80 degrees. The full elevation from minimum to maximum takes 27 seconds.

STATUS
In production.

MANUFACTURER
Kia Industrial Company Limited, 1, 1-Ka Euiju-Ro, Choong-Ku, Seoul, Republic of Korea.

NETHERLANDS

DAF YB 616 and YB 626 (6 × 6) Recovery Vehicles

DESCRIPTION
The YB 616 and the later YB 626 (6 × 6) recovery vehicles are both based on the chassis of the YA 616 (6 × 6) 6-ton cargo truck which was in production for the Netherlands Army from 1957 to 1958. Over 260 of these vehicles were supplied to the Netherlands Army and a smaller number to the Netherlands Air Force. The first model, the YB 616, had dual rear wheels while the later YB 626 has single rear wheels.

The cab is of all steel construction and if required the sides and roof can be removed and the windscreen folded down. Mounted at the rear is an Austin-Western hydraulically-operated crane built under licence in the Netherlands by DAF. The hydraulic system is powered by the truck engine through a transfer PTO to a hydraulic pump assembly mounted underneath the oil reservoir; this is located in the centre of the tool box.

Two stabiliser jacks each side of the vehicle are lowered when the crane is being used. The front-mounted winch has a capacity of 9072 kg and the rear winch has a capacity of 20 412 kg.

DAF YB 616 (6 × 6) recovery vehicle

SPECIFICATIONS
(YB 616; data in square brackets relate to YB 626 where different)
Cab seating: 1 + 1
Configuration: 6 × 6
Weight:
 (total) 15 670 [17 270] kg
 (on front axle) 4960 [6700] kg
 (on rear bogie) 10 710 [10 575] kg
Length: (overall) 8·85 m
Width: 2·5 m
Height: 3 m
Ground clearance: 0·31 m
Track:
 (front) 1·885 m
 (rear) 1·83 [1·828] m
Wheelbase: 3·475 m + 1·37 m
Angle of approach/departure: 28°/32°

Max speed: (road) 80 km/h
Range: 400 km
Fuel capacity: 400 litres
Gradient: 59%
Fording: 0·75 m
Engine: Continental R6602 6-cylinder water-cooled petrol developing 232 hp at 2800 rpm
Transmission: 5 forward and 1 reverse gears and 2-speed transfer case
Turning radius: 11 m
Tyre size: 14.00 × 20

Electrical system: 24 V
Batteries: 2 × 12 V
Generator: 900 W

STATUS
Production complete. In service with the Netherlands Army and Air Force.

MANUFACTURER
DAF Trucks, Geldropseweg 303, 5645 TK, Eindhoven, The Netherlands.

NORWAY

Mercedes/Moelven BV 730 Recovery Vehicle

DESCRIPTION
The Mercedes/Moelven BV 730 recovery vehicle is built for heavy recovery operations and can also be used for winching, towing and hoisting. Using a Mercedes-Benz 2628 A/38 (6 × 6) truck chassis, the BV 730 uses a hydraulic winch and a hydraulic telescopic crane mounted on a frame equipped with four hydraulically-operated outriggers.

These outriggers are controlled separately and when extended they lift the vehicle clear of the ground for crane stability and to provide anchors when using the recovery winch. The crane arm is elevated to a maximum angle of 70 degrees from the horizontal. It has a telescopic extension of 2·5 metres that can operate with a full load. The maximum lifting capacity of the crane with the extension retracted is 8400 kg, and with the extension in use, 4000 kg. When fully extended the crane arm is 6·1 metres long and the maximum height of the hook from the ground is eight metres. Normally the full traverse of the arm over the rear of the vehicle is 270 degrees but a full 360 degrees is possible if required.

The main recovery winch has a single pull capacity of 20 000 kg and is mounted in the traversing frame of the crane. The winch is provided with 85 metres of 22 mm diameter cable on a 418 mm diameter drum. A self-recovery winch with a capacity of 7000 to 10 000 kg

Mercedes/Moelven BV 730 recovery vehicle in travelling order

Mercedes/Moelven BV 730 recovery vehicle towing 6 × 6 truck

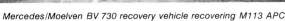

Mercedes/Moelven BV 730 recovery vehicle recovering M113 APC

Mercedes/Moelven BV 730 recovery vehicle in operation

may be fitted either on the front of the vehicle or on one side.

The outrigger arms are used as anchoring spades and each outrigger is capable of carrying the full pulling force of 40 000 kg. This pulling capacity can be utilised to the rear of the vehicle plus or minus 35 degrees from the centre line. The sideways pulling capacity is 15 000 kg.

A standard NATO towing hook is provided at the rear and there is also an adjustable triangle operated by the crane for towing wrecked vehicles. An alternative equipment is a telescopic lift recovery boom. Hydraulic power take-offs for various hydraulic tools are provided around the vehicle as are lockers for tools and accessories.

The crane may be operated either from a seat at the side of the crane or from a remote control unit.

The hydraulic system used on the BV 730 operates at a maximum hydraulic pressure of 210 bars and the hydraulic tank has a capacity of 160 litres.

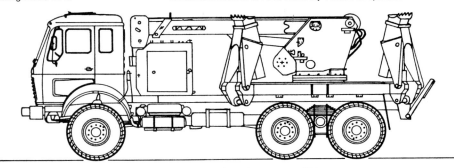

Mercedes/Moelven BV 730 recovery vehicle

SPECIFICATIONS
Cab seating: 1 + 2 or 3
Configuration: 6 × 6
Weight:
  (total) 18 500 kg
  (front axle) 7000 kg
  (bogie axle) 11 500 kg

Length:
  (travelling) 8·2 m
  (between lowered outriggers) 5·7 m
Width:
  (travelling) 2·5 m approx
  (between lowered outriggers) 4·2 m
Height: 3·15 m
Wheelbase:
  (12.00 × 20 tyres) 3·85 m + 1·35 m
  (14.00 × 20 tyres) 3·8 m + 1·45 m
Crane max lift capacity: 8400 kg

Max winch capacity, single cable: 20 000 kg
Max anchoring on outriggers: 40 000 kg
Max crane outreach: 6·1 m
Max lift height: 8 m
Tyres: 12.00 × 20 or 14.00 × 20

STATUS
Production.

MANUFACTURER (recovery equipment)
A/S Moelven Brug, N-2391 Moelv, Norway.

SOUTH AFRICA

SAMIL Recovery Vehicles

SAMIL produces two types of recovery vehicle, one based on the chassis of the SAMIL 50 and the other based on the chassis of the SAMIL 100. Full details of the SAMIL 50 and SAMIL 100 can be found under the SAMIL entry in the *Trucks* section but information relevant to the two recovery vehicles is provided below. Chassis specifications are given under the SAMIL trucks entries.

SAMIL 50 recovery vehicle
The SAMIL 50 recovery vehicle may be provided with a fully protected cab for use against land mine fragments or small arms fire. It has two winches driven by a power

take-off from the main gearbox with a combined pull of 20 000 kg and two booms which extend to the rear for a suspended tow. The combined lifting capacity of the booms is 7250 kg when retracted and 2500 kg when fully extended. The rear platform is used for recovery equipment stowage and self-recovery rollers are fitted to each corner of the superstructure. The protected cab, when fitted, has seating for four men.

SAMIL 100 recovery vehicle
The SAMIL 100 recovery vehicle is normally fitted with the standard cab of the SAMIL 100 truck and not with a mine-proof cab. However, the cab is enlarged to carry a

crew of five men. The recovery hamper is carried to the rear of the vehicle and consist of a twin jib structure on a flat-bed heavy-duty body. The main winch is mounted centrally and much of the space at the rear is taken up with recovery equipment stowage.

STATUS
Production probably complete. In service with South African Defence Forces.

MANUFACTURER
Enquiries to: Armscor, Private Bag X337, Pretoria 0001, South Africa.

SAMIL 100 (6 × 6) recovery vehicle

SAMIL 50 recovery vehicle with mine-proof cab (T J Gander)

SWEDEN

Volvo F10 (4 × 4) Recovery Vehicle

DESCRIPTION

The Volvo F10 (4 × 4) recovery vehicle is basically the 4 × 2 model with a slightly lower front axle capacity. The forward control cab is spring-mounted on the chassis and can be hydraulically tilted forward 60 degrees to give access to the engine for maintenance. The cab has a roof hatch and a heater/fresh-air system and can be fitted with an air-conditioning system if required. The F10 can also be supplied with a sleeper cab with single or twin bunks.

Mounted to the rear of the cab is the Bärgningsbilar EKÅ D2030 recovery equipment which can be used for three main roles: recovering disabled vehicles, towing disabled vehicles once they have been recovered and changing components in the field.

The lifting device centres around the main lift boom which is raised by a telescopic ram. The folding boom, which stems from the main boom, houses the hydraulically-operated extensible boom which is used for reaching under vehicles. A variety of lifting and towing attachments connect to the extensible boom for direct recovery. The main boom is positioned on the centre line of the vehicle and is extended and retracted by a hydraulic ram and can be mechanically locked in three different positions.

The folding boom houses the extensible boom vertically when not in use, and is locked in the stowed position by an automatic mechanical lock. Two extensible legs behind the rear axle provide anchorage and stability when winching or craning. The anchor legs are individually extended and retracted by hydraulic rams and each leg has a wide spade with profiled teeth.

A hydraulic winch on the top of the main boom has a hydraulically-released spring-loaded brake, free spool and reversing facilities. The cable runs through the main boom and out via guide rollers fitted in the end of the main boom. The cable tensioner provides tension when winding in without load on the cable. Power is provided by a hydraulic piston pump driven by the vehicle's PTO which has an in-built strainer and return filter fitted. The hydraulic oil reservoir is an integral part of the main boom and the direction control valve with six operating levers is on the offside rear locker. Pressure relief valves are fitted to prevent overloading of the various hydraulic systems and a pressure gauge shows the working pressure and how much lifting or pulling power is being used.

Optional equipment includes an auxiliary 10 000 kg capacity winch mounted on the main boom, 5000 or 7000 kg front winch with ballasted front bumper, second telescopic ram to increase lifting power, extra hydraulic pump for faster winching speed, various towing and lifting equipment, illuminated signs and flashing lights, side leg for extra stability when side winching, second set of operating levers in opposite compartment and a remote control unit which allows the operator to operate the controls of the recovery equipment from a distance of up to 100 metres.

SPECIFICATIONS
Configuration: 4 × 4
Length: 6·3 m
Width: 2·489 m
Height:
(cab roof) 2·911 m
(air intake) 3·244 m
Track:
(front) 1·945 m
(rear) 1·82 m
Wheelbase: 4·6 m
Fuel capacity: 300 litres

Engine: TD 100A diesel developing 250 hp at 2200 rpm
Gearbox: manual with 4 forward and 1 reverse gears, 2-speed transfer box
Clutch: twin dry plate
Steering: recirculating ball and nut with built-in servo unit
Turning radius: 7·6 m
Number of tyres: 6 + 1 spare
Brakes:
(main) dual circuit air
(parking) air-operated spring on rear wheels
exhaust brake
Electrical system: 24 V

Boom
Max lifting height: 4·5 m
Max lifting capacity:
(at horizontal level) 22 000 kg
(in crane position) 10 000 kg
Reach: 2·4 m

Winch
Max pulling power: (when stalling) 34 000 kg
Max rope speed:
(at low pulling power) approx 19 m/minute
(at high pulling power) approx 1 m/minute
Rope diameter: 26 mm
Rope length: 40 m

STATUS
In service with undisclosed countries including Malaysia.

MANUFACTURER
Volvo AB, Göteborg, Sweden.

Volvo F10 (4 × 4) recovery vehicle showing HIAB crane to cab rear

Volvo F10 (4 × 4) recovery vehicle from side

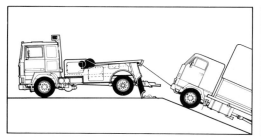

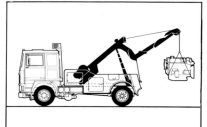

Volvo F10 (4 × 4) recovery vehicle, (left) recovering vehicle, (centre) towing recovered vehicle and (right) changing engine

SWITZERLAND

Holmes Recovery Vehicles

DESCRIPTION
Holmes AG is the Swiss distributor for the Ernest Holmes Corporation of the United States. The Swiss company offers a wide range of wheeled recovery vehicles based on the West German Mercedes-Benz chassis, although other types of chassis can also be fitted with the Holmes range of recovery equipment.

The latest models introduced by Holmes are the Lancer 1701 with a capacity of 35 tons, and the Victor 1801 with a capacity of 45 tons. Both are fully hydraulically-operated and are suitable for tasks such as AFV recovery.

STATUS
Ernest Holmes recovery equipment is used all over the world including Australia, Egypt, Jordan, India, Saudi Arabia and the USA. For additional information on the recovery equipment the reader is referred to the Ernest Holmes entry in the United States section.

MANUFACTURER
Holmes AG, Tödistrasse 42, CH-8002 Zürich, Switzerland.

Vehicle model	Wheelbase	Gross vehicle weight	Type of crane	Max crane load	Max crane load while driving
207 D/307 D	3·05 m	2550 kg	Holmes 220	3630 kg	approx 1400 kg
208/308	3·05 m	2800 kg	Holmes 220	3630 kg	approx 1400 kg
L 508 D	3·5 m	5000 kg	Holmes 440	3600 kg	1400 kg
L 608 D	3·5 m	5990 kg	Holmes 440	3600 kg	2000 kg
L 407 D/L 409	3·5 m	4000/4600 kg	Holmes Trooper 1100	4530 kg	approx 1800 kg
L 508 D	3·5 m	4000 kg	Holmes Trooper 1100	4530 kg	approx 1800 kg
L 608 D	3·5 m	5600 kg	Holmes Trooper 1100	4530 kg	approx 1800 kg
LPK 813	3·2 m	7490 kg	Holmes 440	3600 kg	2486 kg
LPK 709/LPK 809	3·2 m	5990/7490 kg	Holmes Commander 1200	6350 kg	approx 2400 kg
LPK 813/LPK 913	3·2 m	7490/9200 kg	Holmes Commander 1200	6350 kg	approx 2400 kg
LAK 911 B	3·6 m	8990 kg	Holmes 480	8000 kg	3008 kg*
LAK 911 B	3·6 m	8990 kg	Holmes 500	10 000 kg	3024 kg*
1013 K/AK 1017 A	3·2 m	10 300 kg	Holmes 480	8000 kg	3415 kg*
1213/1219 K/AK	3·2 m	11 800 kg	Holmes 500	10 000 kg	3990 kg
1619 K	3·2 m	16 000 kg	Holmes 600	16 000 kg	4775 kg
LK 1924/1928	4·2 m	19 000 kg	Holmes 600 (or Holmes 600 × 6H)	16 000 kg	6687 kg
1928 L/AK	3·8 m	19 000 kg	Holmes 600 (or Holmes 600 × 6H)	25 000 kg	4695 kg*
LK 2624/2628	3·6 m + 1·34 m	26 000 kg	Holmes 750, 1701 (or Holmes 750 × 7)	25 000 kg	6687 kg
2628 K/2632 K/AK	3·2 m + 1·35 m	26 000 kg	Holmes 750, 1701 (or Holmes 750 × 7)	25 000 kg	7210 kg*
2628/2632 K/AL	3·85 m + 1·4 m	38 000 kg	Holmes 850, 1801	36 290 kg	approx 5000 kg

* On request can be fitted with single tyres; permissible GVW and maximum crane load while driving will be reduced accordingly
Type 600 × 6 is a mechanical crane with telescoping booms
Type 750 × 7 is a mechanical crane with mechanically telescoping booms
Type 600 × 6 is also available as 600 × 6H unit

Mercedes-Benz Model 911 truck with Holmes Model 500 10 000 kg capacity recovery equipment

Mercedes-Benz Model 2632 with Holmes 850 36 290 kg capacity recovery equipment

UNITED KINGDOM

Recovery Vehicle, Wheeled Light, Bedford RL, (4 × 4)

DEVELOPMENT/DESCRIPTION
This is a standard Bedford 4 × 4 RL 4-ton chassis adapted for use in the light recovery role. The reader is referred to the entry for the Bedford RL in the *Trucks* section for the development history and detailed description of the vehicle. The vehicle (FV13115) can recover all vehicles up to and including the 3000 kg class. The jib can lift a maximum of 3000 kg at a radius of 2·438 metres, the hoist winch drive being taken from a PTO on the main gearbox. The main winch, which can be used to the front or the rear, is driven from a PTO on the transfer case and has a maximum first layer pull of 7000 kg. With the assistance of a special sprag type earth anchor and two part tackle, the winch can exert a maximum rear pull of 13 000 kg, or a side pull of 6000 kg.

These vehicles are due to be replaced in the near future by a new vehicle based on the Bedford MK (4 × 4) chassis. It will use a TK cab and will mount a new recovery hamper produced by Reynolds Boughton Limited (see separate entry).

Recovery Vehicle Wheeled Light, Bedford RL (4 × 4)
(T J Gander)

SPECIFICATIONS
Cab seating: 1 + 1
Configuration: 4 × 4
Weight: 8128 kg
Length: 7·98 m
Width: 2·32 m
Height: 2·71 m
Track:
  (front) 1·85 m
  (rear) 1·7 m
Wheelbase: 3·962 m
Max speed: (road) 80 km/h
Range: 400 km
Fuel capacity: 118 litres

Max gradient:
  (in bottom gear) 41%
  (for stop and restart solo) 16·7%
Side slope: 20%
Engine: Bedford 6-cylinder OHV, in-line, petrol developing 130 bhp at 3200 rpm (gross) (114 bhp at 3200 rpm net)
Transmission: manual with 4 forward and 1 reverse gears and 2-speed transfer case
Turning radius: 9·15 m
Steering: worm and sector
Suspension: semi-elliptical springs front and rear with double acting hydraulic shock absorbers front and rear
Tyre size: 9.00 × 20

Brakes: air/hydraulic drum on all wheels
Electrical system: 12 V
Batteries: 1 × 12 V, 80 Ah
Generator: 12 V, 297 W

STATUS
Production complete. In service with the British Army and other armed forces. An SWB (the RS) is used by the Royal Navy.

MANUFACTURER
Chassis – Vauxhall Motors Limited, Luton, Bedfordshire. Body – Marshall of Cambridge (Engineers) Limited or Reynolds Boughton Limited, Bell Lane, Amersham, Buckinghamshire, England.

Reynolds Boughton (4 × 4) 6000 kg Recovery Vehicle

DESCRIPTION
The Reynolds Boughton 4 × 4 6000 kg recovery vehicle has been developed as the replacement for the Recovery Vehicle, Wheeled Light, Bedford RL (4 × 4). It uses a Bedford M-type chassis with a 3·962 metres wheelbase and a Bedford TK style cab. The recovery unit is mounted on the rear and is constructed on load carrying longitudinal main channels with cross channel bearers gussetted at all intersections. Six stowage lockers with side-opening lids are fitted, three to each side. The floor has a non-slip metal covering. Access steps are at the front and rear.

The recovery jib is mounted on a main turret tower. The jib has inner and outer rectangular box sections and

a position stay is provided for use when carrying suspended loads. The winch is mounted on the hydraulically operated jib. The cable diameter is 14 mm, and the lifting capacity 6000 kg. Four hydraulically powered stabiliser legs are provided, one at each corner of the recovery unit, and each leg is independently operated for levelling. The hydraulic pump is driven from a power take-off on the vehicle gearbox. All crane operations are carried out from the crane turret platform while stabiliser levelling is from the side of the vehicle. Most of the hydraulic piping is carried in flexible two-wire hose.

A salvage winch is an optional extra, having a capacity of 6096 kg. The 14 mm cable for this winch is 65 metres long.

STATUS
In production for the British Army.

MANUFACTURER
Reynolds Boughton Limited, Bell Lane, Amersham, Bucks HP6 6PE, England.

SPECIFICATIONS
Cab seating: 1 + 2
Configuration: 4 × 4
Length: 6·452 m
Width: 2·438 m
Height: 2·591 m
Wheelbase: 3·962 m
Jib radius retracted: 3·327 m
Jib extension: 1·727 m
Max rear lift:
  (0·482 m jib overhand from body rear) 6000 kg
Crane slewing speed: 270° in 40 s
Jib extension from retract to extension: 16 s

Reynolds Boughton (4 × 4) 6000 kg recovery vehicle with crane jib at maximum 1·727 m extension

Reynolds Boughton (4 × 4) 6000 kg recovery vehicle (T J Gander)

Foden (6 × 6) Recovery Vehicle

DEVELOPMENT
The new Foden (6 × 6) recovery vehicle embodies the new Eka top hamper model AK6500 EA12 and supercedes the Swedish Eka type D2030B with a fixed boom which was originally adopted for evaluation by the British Army. (For details of the earlier vehicle refer to page 54 of *Jane's Military Vehicles and Ground Support Equipment 1983*).

DESCRIPTION
The Foden chassis retains many of the features and performance of the FH-70 gun tractor and limber medium mobility vehicles described in the *Trucks* section, but introduces the more modern Rolls-Royce Eagle 290L engine, Hudson Wharton HWD/10/C front mounted winch and a Fuller main gearbox. It has a four-man grp tilting cab fitted with impact resistant front panels and strengthened roof to support a machine-gun mounting and an observation hatch.

The recovery equipment retains the support tow feature of the original concept. This includes a hydraulically-operated folding boom with an extending boom and has maximum lift capacity of 11 000 kg. It is designed to recover all British Army in-service logistic support vehicles.

The main winch is the Rotzler type 25000 HS/390 mounted on the main towing boom. It has a single line pull capacity of 25 000 kg and is supplied with 80 metres of effective cable. Hydraulic and independently operated ground anchors are adequate for all rear winching operations.

A slewing crane with 220 degrees of slewing angle and a maximum lift capacity of 12 000 kg provides

Foden (6 × 6) recovery vehicle

optimum lifting facilities and for vehicle stability two extendible hydraulically-operated outriggers are fitted, one to each side of the vehicle. Detachable load-bearing feet are also provided for the rear ground anchors when these are used as stabilisers.

NATO pattern towing hooks are fitted front and rear together with recovery eye plates and a heavy duty protective steel front bumper. Stowage is provided for all the necessary supporting recovery equipment.

STATUS
Undergoing Ministry of Defence trials.

MANUFACTURER
Foden Trucks, a division of Paccar UK Limited, Elworth Works, Sandbach, Cheshire CW11 9HZ, England.

SPECIFICATIONS
Cab seating: 1 + 3
Configuration: 6 × 6
Weight: (loaded) 25 338 kg
Length: 9·055 m
Width: 2·492 m
Height: (cab) 3·55 m
Ground clearance: 0·375 m
Track:
(front) 2·029 m
(rear) 2·06 m
Wheelbase: 4·728 m + 1·516 m
Max gradient: 33%
Engine: Rolls-Royce Eagle 290L Mark 3
Clutch: Spicer twin plate hydraulically operated
Gearbox: Fuller RTO 11609B
Transfer box: Kirkstall 2-range with optional integral PTO
Axle:
(front) Kirkstall 10·1-tonne with differential lock
(rear) Kirkstall 20·3-tonne bogie with differential locks on both axles, 5·9/1 overall axle ratio. Third differential on foremost axle
Steering: recirculatory ball with integral power assistance
Suspension: semi-elliptical laminated springs front, two-spring fully articulated rear spring rated to match axle capacity
Brakes: air, split-circuit, trailer brake connection to front and rear of chassis
Fuel capacity: 360 litres
Wheels and tyres: 16.00 × 20 – 20-20 ply tyres, 11.25 rims
Electrical system: 24 V

Foden (6 × 6) recovery vehicle

Scammell S26 (6 × 6) Recovery Vehicle

DEVELOPMENT/DESCRIPTION
The Scammell S26 (6 × 6) recovery vehicle is a variant of the S26 truck and has been produced for evaluation trials to be conducted by the Ministry of Defence in connection with a possible order for the British Army. The recovery vehicle is a short wheelbase version of the S26 with an Eka Compact recovery top hamper at the rear. The top hamper is similar to that used on the Foden entry for the same evaluation trials.

The Eka Compact top hamper uses two Rotzler pulling winches and a Rotzler crane winch for the extending jib crane unit. Two hydraulically-operated stabiliser legs are extended, one from each side, for use when the crane is lifting heavy loads. Maximum lift capacity of the crane jib when fully retracted is 12 500 kg.

STATUS
Undergoing Ministry of Defence trials.

MANUFACTURER
Scammell Motors Limited, Tolpits Lane, Watford, Hertfordshire WD1 8QD, England.

Scammell S26 (6 × 6) recovery vehicle lifting Scorpion light reconnaissance vehicle

Scammell Crusader (6 × 4) Recovery Vehicle

DEVELOPMENT
In 1977 the British Army ordered 130 Scammell Crusader 6 × 4 recovery vehicles. They have the same chassis, cab, engine and transmission as the Scammell Crusader 35 000 kg tractors used by the Royal Engineers for hauling semi-trailers which are fully described in the *Trucks* section. The full designation of the vehicle is Recovery Vehicle, Wheeled, CL (Low Mobility Recovery Vehicle).

DESCRIPTION
The vehicle can provide recovery support for wheeled vehicles up to the 16-tonne range and can support or suspend tow laden 8-tonne or unladen 16-tonne vehicles and straight tow vehicles up to 30 tonnes gross weight on gradients not exceeding 1 in 5.

The main recovery equipment, of Swedish Eka design, consists of hydraulically-operated earth anchors, main-boom and a winch, which, together with stowage bins, are mounted on a sub-frame at the rear of the vehicle. The main boom is lifted by a hydraulic ram and incorporates a folding boom which houses an extending boom that carries a variety of attachments for support or suspend tow. When support or suspend towing a rear bogie blocking system maintains sufficient front axle loading for safe steering.

A winch with a maximum pulling capacity of 7 tonnes is mounted at the front behind the bumper. The main boom can lift 7·5 tonnes at a maximum distance of 2·6 metres from the rear bogie centre line and the main winch exerts a maximum pull of 20 tonnes. Both winches have fail-safe automatic brakes capable of holding the maximum winch loads. Using the main winch, with suitable attachments to the extending boom, there is a limited craning facility for loads up to 3 tonnes. Apart from main controls for the recovery equipment housed at the right hand rear side of the vehicle, a hand-held remote control unit, usable up to 30 metres away, can operate the main recovery functions.

STATUS
In production. In service with the British Army (130), and Royal Air Froce (2).

MANUFACTURER
Scammell Motors Limited, Tolpits Lane, Watford, Hertfordshire WD1 8QD, England.

SPECIFICATIONS
Cab seating: 1 + 3
Configuration: 6 × 4
Weight: 16 700 kg
Length: 8·37 m
Width: 2·98 m
Height: 3·28 m
Track:
   (front) 2·05 m
   (rear) 1·98 m
Wheelbase: (first axle to centre of rear bogie) 4·59 m
Max speed: 78 km/h
Range: 1150 km
Fuel capacity: 455 litres
Max gradient: 33%
Engine: Rolls-Royce Eagle 305 Mk 111 turbo-charged diesel developing 305 bhp at 2100 rpm
Transmission: manual with 15 forward and 3 reverse gears
Turning radius: 11 m
Steering: balland nut, power-assisted
Suspension:
   (front) longitudinal semi-elliptical springs pivoted front with slipper rear ends, and telescopic shock absorbers
   (rear) fully articulated, inverted longitudinal semi-elliptical springs, trunnion mounted at centre with slipper rear ends
Tyre size: 11.00 × 20
Number of tyres: 10
Brakes:
   (main) air
   (parking) hand on all wheels
Electrical system: 24 V
Batteries: 4 × 12 V, 100 Ah

Scammell Crusader (6 × 4) recovery vehicle (T J Gander)

Crane Fruehauf Recovery Vehicles

Crane Fruehauf is the United Kingdom distributor for the Ernest Holmes Corporation of the United States. The British company offers a wide range of wheeled recovery vehicles based on a variety of different chassis. A recent order was for the supply of ten wreckers to the Bangladesh Army. These were based on the Bedford MK (4 × 4) chassis with the Holmes twin-boom '655' equipment installed. Each boom has a 12·5-ton rating.

For details of the complete range of Ernest Holmes equipment the reader is referred to the Ernest Holmes entry in the United States section.

MANUFACTURER
Crane Fruehauf Limited, Toftwood, Dereham, Norfolk, England.

Twin-boom '750' wreckers on Bedford MK (4 × 4) chassis awaiting shipment for Bangladesh Army

AEC (6 × 6) Mk 3 Recovery Vehicle, Wheeled Medium

DEVELOPMENT
The AEC (6 × 6) Mk 3 Recovery Vehicle, Wheeled Medium (FV11044) was developed in the 1960s as the replacement for the older Scammell (6 × 6) recovery vehicle. The chassis was built by AEC of Southall, recovery equipment by Transport Equipment (Thorneycroft) Limited of Basingstoke, and the crane by Coles Cranes Limited of Sunderland.

DESCRIPTION
The vehicle is capable of recovering on suspended tow all wheeled vehicles up to and including the 10-ton class. The hydraulic crane mounted at the rear can slew through 240 degrees and its jib can be extended from 3·124 to 5·563 metres. This can lift and slew 1400 kg at 5·563 metres radius without outrigger jacks or 2600 kg at 5·563 metres with outrigger jacks. Maximum hook height is 6·706 metres and maximum lift of hoist cable is 3·048 metres. The winch is rated at 12 300 kg continuous line pull for the full effective length of the winch rope and 15 000 kg on the bottom layer. A hydraulically-operated spade is mounted at the rear of the vehicle and when in the lowered position pulls of up to 30 000 kg can be exerted. Towing hooks are provided front and rear, and two stabilisers can be lowered either side of the rear if required.

STATUS
Production complete. In service with the British Army.

MANUFACTURER
AEC Limited, Southall, Middlesex, England. (Now part of BL Limited.)

SPECIFICATIONS
Configuration: 6 × 6
Weight: 21 000 kg

AEC (6 × 6) Mk 3 Recovery Vehicle, Wheeled, Medium (T J Gander)

Length: 8·23 m
Width: 2·5 m
Height: 3·1 m
Track:
   (front) 2 m
   (rear) 1·99 m
Wheelbase: 3·238 m + 1·37 m
Max speed: (road) 78 km/h
Range: 483 km
Fuel capacity: 218 litres
Max gradient: 50%
   (for stop and re-start) 50%
Engine: AEC AV 760 6-cylinder diesel developing 226 bhp at 2200 rpm

Transmission: manual with 6 forward and 1 reverse gears and 2-speed transfer case
Turning radius: 11·88 m
Steering: worm and nut with hydraulic power assistance
Suspension:
   (front) semi-elliptical springs with hydraulic shock absorbers
   (rear) semi-elliptical springs
Tyre size: 16.00 × 20
Brakes: air
Electrical system: 24 V
Batteries: 24 V, 100 Ah
Generator: 28 V, 90 Ah

Leyland (6 × 6) Recovery Vehicle Wheeled, Heavy

DESCRIPTION

The Leyland (6 × 6) recovery vehicle wheeled, heavy (FV1119) is based on the chassis of the FV1103 cargo truck, and is capable of recovering on suspended tow all wheeled vehicles up to and including the 10-ton class. The hydraulic power-operated crane mounted at the rear of the vehicle can be slewed through 140 degrees. Its jib can be extended from 3·048 to 5·486 metres and with the jib stays in position the crane can lift 15 000 kg. At maximum radius without stays it can lift 1500 kg. The hydraulic winch has two speed ranges which give the following maximum rope pulls and speeds:

147 kN at 4·572 m/min (low range)
49 kN at 13·72 m/min (high range)

At the rear of the vehicle is a hydraulically mounted spade. When this is in the lowered position, pulls of 39 000 kg can be exerted.

SPECIFICATIONS

Cab seating: 1 + 2
Configuration: 6 × 6
Weight: 21 610 kg
Length: 8·89 m
Width: 2·591 m
Height: 3·1 m
Track:
(front) 2·089 m
(rear) 2·096 m
Wheelbase: 3·72 m + 1·397 m
Max speed: (road) 56·2 km/h
Range: 562 km
Fuel capacity: 446 litres
Max gradient for stop and restart: 20%
Engine: Rolls-Royce B81 Mk 5K 8-cylinder petrol developing 195 bhp at 3 750 rpm
Transmission: manual with 4 forward and 1 reverse gears and 3-speed transfer case
Turning radius: 10·67 m
Steering: cam and roller with hydraulic power assistance
Suspension:
(front) single transverse semi-elliptical springs
(rear) 2 semi-elliptical springs
Tyre size: 15.05 × 20
Brakes: air
Electrical system: 24 V
Batteries: 24 V, 60 Ah
Generator: 28 V, 12 A

STATUS

Production complete. In service with the British Army.

MANUFACTURER

Leyland Motors Limited, Leyland, Lancashire, England. (Now part of BL Limited.)

Leyland FV1119 heavy recovery vehicle towing Foden FH-70 limber vehicle (T J Gander)

Leyland (6 × 6) Recovery Vehicle, Wheeled, Heavy (T J Gander)

UNITED STATES OF AMERICA

Ernest Holmes Recovery Equipment

DEVELOPMENT

Ernest Holmes built its first recovery vehicle before the First World War but its first successful twin-boom vehicle was not completed until 1914. Since then the Ernest Holmes Company, now a division of the Dover Corporation, has developed a wide range of twin-boom equipment which can be mounted on a variety of wheeled and tracked chassis, including chassis available from International Harvester, Chevrolet, GMC, Ford, Dodge, Bedford, Foden and Mercedes-Benz.

In Switzerland sales are handled by Holmes AG of Zürich and in the United Kingdom by Crane Fruehauf of Hayes, Middlesex and readers are referred to the entries in this section for these two companies for details of chassis/recovery combinations available.

The main advantage of the twin-boom recovery equipment is that the vehicle can recover disabled vehicles from the side as well as the rear because the booms can be swung to the left and right of the vehicle. By securing the cable from one of the booms to a suitable anchorage point, the second boom can handle vehicles equalling the weight of the recovery vehicle itself.

DESCRIPTIONS

Model 1200 Wrecker
This is equipped with two hydraulic winches and service cables, independently controlled, and a single hydraulically-powered boom which has dual hydraulic cylinders attached to its lower side to raise and lower the boom while loaded or unloaded. The equipment can be

Holmes 750 equipment installed on International Harvester truck for US Marine Corps

installed on a two-axle truck with dual rear wheels with a gross vehicle weight of not less than 4536 kg.

Model 655 Wrecker
This equipment can be installed on a vehicle that has a gross vehicle weight of not less than 10 886 kg. Optional equipment includes booms that can be extended to 5·486 metres, a rapid reverse twin-worm power unit, two outboard legs, two 12·7 mm 61-metre load cables, two snatch blocks and nylon bushed dual controls.

Holmes 750 Wrecker
This equipment can be installed on a two- or three-axle chassis that has a gross vehicle weight of not less than 14 514 kg. Equipment which can be fitted (including optional equipment) includes two stiff legs and a bolster, chain and pinion guards, extensible or non-extensible booms, controls recessed into the body, towing chains, rear jacks to increase lifting stability, dual power unit with a gear reduction of 214 to 1, 14 anchor points, back-lash brakes, telescoping outboard legs, cable drums with guards, and two snatch blocks.

Holmes 850 Wrecker

On the Holmes 850 wrecker both booms are power-operated and may be raised and lowered when fully loaded. Central and ground controls are provided, the latter enabling the operator to control the operation from the best position. This equipment can be installed on a three-axle truck which has a gross vehicle weight of at least 20 865 kg.

Holmes Model 1701 Lancer Wrecker

The Holmes Model 1701 uses a single, non-traversable boom. The type is described as a 35-ton power wrecker and uses a system of stabilising jacks and stays for lifting heavy loads. The single boom has a single stage maximum extension of 2·438 metres and has a maximum lift of 31 750 kg retracted and 10 886 kg extended. The boom is located on a steel mast structure which also carries a single adjustable extending stabiliser leg on each side. The mast can also be used as the main load-carrying structure when side pulls are used as the Model 1701 uses a twin-winch system. The twin winches can be used either over twin cable pulleys at the end of the boom or over the sides of the central mast. Twin hydraulic cylinders raise and lower the boom. With side pulls it is possible to use one winch cable as an anchor for improved stability. The winches, which are the same as that used on the Model 750, are specially produced for wrecker use and have such features as manual rewind and nylon bearings. The winch gear reduction is 214 to 1.

Holmes Model 1801 Victor Wrecker

The Holmes Model 1801 Victor wrecker follows the same general lines as the Model 1701 but the lifting capacity is much greater. In time it will replace the Model 850 as the largest and heaviest wrecker in the Holmes range. The single non-traversable boom of the Model 1801 has a maximum extension of 2·54 metres. Retracted it has a maximum lift capacity of 40 823 kg and fully extended it can lift 13 608 kg. This lift capacity enables the vehicle to assist disabled AFVs using other vehicles as anchors to assist in side pulls. The Model 1801 boom has the lifting capacity to enable it to be used as a heavy repair vehicle, lifting tank turrets and engine packs when necessary. The Model 1801 has a three-stage hydraulic motor. One 321·7 litres/minute stage drives one winch and the boom extension cylinder. Another 321·7 litres/minute stage drives the other winch and the boom lift cylinders. A third 56·8 litres/minute stage drives the outboard legs and rear jacks. Each stage can be operated independently.

STATUS

In production. In service with many armed forces throughout the world.

MANUFACTURER

Ernest Holmes Division, Dover Corporation, 2505 East 43rd Street, Chattanooga, Tennessee 37407, USA.

SPECIFICATIONS

Model Type	1200	655	750	850
Rating (with both booms)	n/app	14 515 kg	22 680 kg	36 287 kg
(of each boom)	6350 kg	7257 kg	11 340 kg	18 144 kg
(of boom fully extended)	2268 kg	1814 kg	5443 kg	n/app
Drum rating, each drum	4536 kg	7257 kg	11 340 kg	n/app
Cable (diameter)	10 mm	15 mm	16 mm	19 mm
(length)	30·48 m	60·96 m	60·96 m	91·44 m
Load cable diameter	102 mm	305 mm	380 mm	560 mm
Recommended working limit of each cable	1587 kg	2077 kg	4309 kg	6169 kg
Boom (working length, 2-axle truck)	n/app	3·1 m *	3·44 m †	3·797 m
(working length, 3-axle truck)	n/app	n/app	3·949 m	4·255 m
(horizontal swing)	n/app	90°	90°	120°
(vertical swing)	60°	60°	60°	60°
Height of equipment above truck chassis	n/app	1·53 m	1·995 m	1·995 m

Working length boom fully extended * 5·371 m (X-7 boom)
† 6·388 m (X-7 boom)

Holmes 850 equipment on Kenworth truck in Middle East

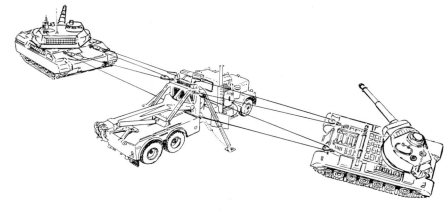

Holmes 1801 wrecker recovering tank using second tank as anchor

Holmes 1801 used as repair vehicle to lift tank turret

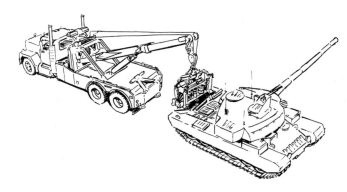

Holmes 1801 used as repair vehicle to lift tank engine

SPECIFICATIONS

Model	1701 Lancer	1801 Victor
Basic wrecker rating	31 750 kg	40 823 kg
Boom rating (retracted)	31 750 kg	40 823 kg
(fully extended)	10 886 kg	13 608 kg
Winch characteristics (each drum)		
(load rating, first cable layer)	18 144 kg	23 587 kg
(drum diameter)	381 mm	508 mm
(line speed)	5·79 m/min	6·096 m/min
(cable length, max)	86·87 m	94·5 m
(gear box/cable drum gear red)	214 to 1	485 to 1

Model	1701 Lancer	1801 Victor
Winch type	6 × 25, Dyform-6 IWRC	
Winch cable diameter	15·875 mm	19 mm
Cable length (each drum)	76·2 m	91·44 m
Working load limit (single line)	5883 kg	8373 kg
Breaking strength (single line)	20 593 kg	29 302 kg
Wrecker height above truck frame	1·963 m	2·083 m
Wrecker body width	2·438 m	2·438 m
Weight (wrecker with body approx)	5693 kg	7824·5 kg
(wrecker without body approx)	4241 kg	6373 kg

Holmes Model 1701 preparing for US Army trials

Holmes Model 1801 wrecker on AM General chassis preparing for US Army trials

FWD Wrecker (6 × 6) Model RB66-2144

DESCRIPTION

The FWD Wrecker (6 × 6) Model RB66-2144 may be fitted with either a 275 or 300 hp diesel engine. The enclosed all-steel cab has seating for the driver and a passenger and is equipped with all the normal instruments and accessories. The main frame is made from formed channel steel and measures 3143 × 889 × 95 mm. The rear-mounted boom is powered by a hydraulic winch and is supplied with 45·7 metres of 152·4 mm cable. There is also a main winch with a capacity of 13 605 kg and 76 metres of 191 mm cable. Power for both winches comes from a main transmission power take-off and is controlled from panels on each side of the body rear.

Extra equipment carried on the Model RB66-2144 includes a heavy duty tow bar, rear frame jacks, lengths of heavy duty safety chain 127 mm thick and 3·6 metres long, a rear throttle control, revolving lights and two rear working lights. Dual rear tyres may be fitted, and a variant exists with a 15 910 kg main winch.

SPECIFICATIONS
Crew: 1 + 1
Configuration: 6 × 6
Weight:
   (loaded) 25 500 kg
   (empty) 10 000 kg
   (on front axle, loaded) 8520 kg
   (on rear axle, loaded) 17 200 kg
Length: 8·92 m
Width: 2·55 m
Height: 3·05 m
Ground clearance: 0·3 m
Track: 2·11 m
Wheelbase: 4·72 m
Max speed: 70 km/h
Range: 485 km
Fuel capacity: 378 litres
Max gradient: 60%
Fording: 0·46 m
Engine: Detroit 6-71T diesel (turbo-charged) developing 275 hp at 2100 rpm or
Cummins NTC turbo-charged diesel developing 300 hp at 2100 rpm
Gearbox: 10-speed manual
Clutch: 2 plate
Transfer box: FWD 2-speed
Steering: power assisted
Turning radius: 12·8 m
Suspension: (front/rear) leaf/semi-elliptical
Tyres: 16.00 × 20 – single all round
Brakes: full air "S" cam
Electrical system: 12 V
Batteries: 2 × 12 V

STATUS
Production.

MANUFACTURER
FWD International Inc, 1020 West 31st Street, Downers Grove, Illinois 60515, USA.

FWD Wrecker (6 × 6) Model RB66-2144

FWD Wrecker (6 × 6) Model RB66-2144 from left rear

2½-ton (6 × 6) M60 and M108 Wreckers

DEVELOPMENT

The M60 and M108 wreckers, or to give them their official United States Army designations, Truck, Wrecker: Crane, 2½-ton, 6 × 6, M108 and Truck, Wrecker: Light, 2½-ton, 6 × 6, M60, are both members of the M35 series of 2½-ton (6 × 6) truck family and the reader is referred to this entry in the *Trucks* section for both the development history and technical description of the basic vehicle.

DESCRIPTION

The M60 uses the M45C chassis while the M108 uses the M45 chassis. The M45C chassis has a walking beam suspension on the rear axle. The crane on the rear of the M60 can be traversed through 270 degrees and has a maximum elevation angle of 45 degrees. Its jib can be extended from 2·438 metres to a maximum of 4·876 metres and can lift up to 3628 kg with the outriggers in position and the jib retracted, or 1814 kg with the jib fully extended and the outriggers in position. There are two outriggers mounted either side of the crane platform. A winch mounted at the front of the vehicle has a maximum capacity of 4536 kg.

The M108 also has a front-mounted winch with a maximum capacity of 4536 kg, two stabilisers either side, and a hydraulically-operated crane which has the following capabilities:

	With outriggers	Without outriggers
Single part line, maximum jib extension	1814 kg	907 kg
Single part line, minimum jib extension	2268 kg	1814 kg
Twin part line, maximum jib extension	1814 kg	907 kg
Twin part line, minimum jib extension	3629 kg	1814 kg

SPECIFICATIONS

(M60; data in square brackets relate to M108 where different)
Chassis designation: M45C [M45]
Configuration: 6 × 6
Weight: (empty) 10 900 [9000] kg
Length: 7·02 [7·7] m
Width: 2·36 [2·44] m
Height: 2·477 [2·515] m
Ground clearance: 0·33 m
Track:
  (front) 1·72 m
  (rear) 1·778 m
Wheelbase: 3·302 m + 1·219 m
Angle of approach/departure: 40°/40°
Max speed: (road) 93 km/h
Range: 480 km
Fuel capacity: 189 litres
Max gradient: 63%
Fording:
  (without preparation) 0·76 m
  (with preparation) 1·828 m
Engine: Reo model OA-331 or Continental COA-331 6-cylinder developing 146 hp at 3400 rpm
Transmission: 5 forward and 1 reverse gears and 2-speed transfer box
Turning radius: 11·429 m
Tyre size: 9.00 × 20
Brakes: air/hydraulic
Electrical system: 24 V
Batteries: 2 × 12 V

VARIANTS

NAPCO Industries, Hopkins, Minnesota, USA, has developed a complete repower package for these vehicles. Details are given in the *Trucks* section under NAPCO Industries Repower/Modernisation Packages.

STATUS

In service with the United States Army and many other armed forces, including Austria.

MANUFACTURER

The basic chassis has been manufactured by many companies including Curtiss Wright, Kaiser Jeep, Reo, Studebaker and White. Last manufacturer was the AM General Corporation, 14250 Plymouth Road, Detroit, Michigan 48232, USA.

M218, Truck, Light Wrecker, 2½-ton (6 × 6)

This vehicle is no longer in the United States Army inventory but may be found in other armed forces. The reader is referred to the entry on the M207 2½-ton (6 × 6) truck in the *Trucks* section for further details of this series.

M62, Truck, Wrecker: Medium, 5-ton, (6 × 6)
M246, Truck, Tractor, Wrecker: 5-ton, (6 × 6)
M543, Truck, Wrecker: Medium, 5-ton, (6 × 6)

DEVELOPMENT

These vehicles are all members of the M39 series of 5-ton (6 × 6) trucks which were developed after the end of the Second World War, and the reader is referred to this entry in the *Trucks* section for the development history and technical description of the basic vehicle.

DESCRIPTION

M62
This has a hydraulically-operated crane mounted at the rear which has a maximum lifting capacity of 9072 kg when used with the two stabilisers either side of the vehicle. A winch is mounted at the front with a maximum capacity of 9072 kg when being used to the front and 18 144 kg when being used to the rear. Later models of the M62 are the M62A1 and M62A2.

M246
This has been designed for use as both a recovery vehicle and for towing semi-trailers. The Austin-Western crane at the rear has a jib which can be extended from 3·504 to 7·924 metres. This crane can be slewed through 360 degrees and its jib elevated to a maximum of 45 degrees. Later models of the M246 are the M246A1 and the M246A2, which has a Continental LDS 465–1 or LDS 465–2 multi-fuel engine. The M246 was replaced in production by the similar M819 for which there is a separate entry.

M543
This has a Gar Wood hydraulically-operated crane at the rear which can lift a maximum of 4536 kg. Two stabilisers are provided each side and a winch is mounted at the front and rear. The M543A1 has a diesel engine. In 1963 the M543A2 was introduced. It has an LDS-465 multi-fuel engine which develops 180 hp at 2600 rpm and gives the vehicle a maximum road speed of 84 km/h and a range of 938 km. The M543A2 was replaced in production by the similar M816 for which there is a separate entry.

Truck, Tractor, Wrecker, 5-ton (6 × 6) M246 with front-mounted winch (US Army)

Truck, Wrecker, Medium, 5-ton (6 × 6) M543A2 with front-mounted winch (US Army)

VARIANTS
NAPCO Industries, Hopkins, Minnesota, USA, has developed a complete repower package for these vehicles. Details are given in the *Trucks* section under NAPCO Industries Repower/Modernisation Packages.

STATUS
Production complete. In service with United States Forces and many other armed forces including Australia (a few M543 and M543A1s are in service) and Spain (all re-engined with Spanish diesels).

MANUFACTURER
The basic chassis has been manufactured by various companies since the early 1950s including International Harvester, Kaiser Jeep (now AM General Corporation) and Mack Trucks. Last manufacturer was AM General Corporation, 14250 Plymouth Road, Detroit, Michigan 48232, USA.

Truck, Wrecker, Medium, 5-ton (6 × 6) M62 (US Army)

SPECIFICATIONS

Designation	M62	M246	M543
Chassis designation	M40C	M63C	M40C
Configuration	6 × 6	6 × 6	6 × 6
Towed load (road)	13 608 kg	20 865 kg	13 608 kg
(cross country)	9072 kg	17 010 kg	9072 kg
Weight (empty)	15 275 kg	14 829 kg	15 603 kg
Length	7·848 m	8·953 m	10·007 m
Width	2·463 m	2·489 m	2·444 m
Height	2·59 m	3·352 m	2·743 m
Ground clearance	0·279 m	0·279 m	0·279 m
Wheelbase	3·86 m + 1·371 m	4·775 m + 1·371 m	3·86 m + 1·371 m
Angle of approach/departure	37°/38°	35°/55°	37°/38°
Max speed (road)	84 km/h	84 km/h	84 km/h
Range	344 km	369 km	360 km
Fuel capacity	295 litres	295 litres	295 litres (some have 504 litres)
Max gradient	36%	47%	61·4%
Fording (without preparation)	0·762 m	0·762 m	0·762 m
(with preparation)	1·981 m	—	1·981 m
Engine	Continental 6-cylinder petrol developing 196 hp at 2800 rpm		
Transmission	5 forward and 1 reverse gears and 2-speed transfer case		
Turning radius	12·648 m	14·325 m	14·5 m
Tyre size	11.00 × 20	11.00 × 20	11.00 × 20
Brakes	all have hydraulic brakes, air-actuated		
Electrical system	24 V	24 V	24 V
Batteries	2 × 12 V	2 × 12 V	1 × 12 V

M816, Truck, Wrecker, 5-ton, (6 × 6)
M819, Tractor, Wrecker, 5-ton, (6 × 6)

DESCRIPTION
Both these vehicles are members of the M809 series of 5-ton (6 × 6) trucks and the reader is referred to this entry in the *Trucks* section for the development history of this vehicle.

The M816 is provided with a revolving hydraulic crane at the rear which has a self-supported extensible boom and boom to ground supports. Outriggers are provided to stabilise the vehicle when the crane is being used. Winches are supplied. The M819 also has a hydraulic crane mounted on the rear but has a longer wheelbase and can tow a trailer or vehicle weighing up to 13 608 kg on roads, or 9076 kg across country.

Optional kits for these vehicles include an air brake kit, closure hard top, deep water fording kit, slave receptacle, thermal barrier kit, winterisation personnel heater kit and a power plant kit.

M816 5-ton (6 × 6) wrecker showing front mounted winch

M816 5-ton (6 × 6) wrecker of Australian Army towing tilt bed trailer with M113 APC (Paul Handel)

SPECIFICATIONS

Designation	M816	M819
Chassis type	M809A1	M811A1
Cab seating	1 + 2	1 + 2
Configuration	6 × 6	6 × 6
Weight (unloaded)	16 403 kg	15 392 kg
(on front axle empty)	4966 kg	6304 kg
(on rear bogie empty)	11 418 kg	9251 kg
Length	9·049 m	9·124 m
Width	2·476 m	2·489 m
Height	2·896 m	3·352 m
Ground clearance	0·267 m	0·295 m
Track	1·88 m (front) and 1·829 m (rear)	
Wheelbase	4·547 m + 1·371 m	4·125 m + 1·371 m
Angle of approach/departure	34°/38°	36°/55°
Max speed (road)	84 km/h	83·6 km/h
Range	805 km	563 km
Fuel capacity	503 litres	295 litres
Max gradient	31%	31%
Fording (without preparation)	0·76 m	0·762 m
(with preparation)	1·98 m	1·879 m
Engine	Model NHC-250 6-cylinder in-line diesel developing 243 hp (gross) at 2100 rpm	
Transmission	5 forward and 1 reverse gears, 2-speed transfer box	
Tyre size	11.00 × 20	12.00 × 20
Electrical system	24 V	24 V

STATUS
M816 in production and in service with the US Forces, Australia, South Korea, Zaïre and many other forces. M819 production complete.

MANUFACTURER
AM General Corporation, 14250 Plymouth Road, Detroit, Michigan 48232, USA.

M816 5-ton (6 × 6) wrecker of Australian Army lifting LWB Land-Rover onto tilt bed trailer (Paul Handel)

M816 5-ton (6 × 6) wrecker

M553 10-ton (4 × 4) Wrecker

DEVELOPMENT
For a detailed history of the development of the GOER series, of which the M553 is a member, refer to the entry on the M520 (4 × 4) 8-ton cargo truck in the *Trucks* section. A total of 117 M553s were built by the Caterpillar Tractor Co, with final deliveries being made in June 1976.

DESCRIPTION
The layout and construction of the M553 are almost identical to those of the M520 (4 × 4) vehicle with the front section carrying the crew and engine and the rear section carrying the recovery equipment.

The crane has a maximum lifting capacity of 10 000 kg, depending on the operating radius. The boom is 5·409 metres long and has a 0·914 metre extension. The hoisting mechanism is operated by a hydraulic pump driven from the engine crank-shaft. Manually operated outriggers provide additional stability for crane operations. The front-mounted winch is provided with 45·72 metres of 12·7 mm diameter cable and has a maximum capacity of 4536 kg, while the rear-mounted winch is provided with 91·44 metres of 22 mm cable and has a capacity of 20 412 kg.

The following kits are available for the M553: arctic kit, arctic kit for crane cab, gun ring mount kit, infra-red filter kit and rear canopy kit.

M553 GOER 10-ton (4 × 4) wrecker with crane in travelling position

SPECIFICATIONS
Cab seating: 1 + 1
Configuration: 4 × 4
Towed load: 9027 kg
Weight:
(empty) 17 799 kg
(loaded with M60 powerpack) 21 110 kg
(on front axle loaded) 11 322 kg
(on rear axle loaded) 9788 kg
Length: 10·185 m
Width: 2·743 m
Height:
(reduced) 2·997 m
(top of exhaust pipe) 3·396 m

Ground clearance: (front and rear axle) 0·59 m
Track: 2·203 m
Wheelbase: 5·968 m
Angle of approach/departure: 35°/35°
Max speed:
(1st gear) 9·17 km/h
(2nd gear) 16·09 km/h
(3rd gear) 20·92 km/h
(4th gear) 27·84 km/h
(5th gear) 36·37 km/h
(6th gear) 48·28 km/h
(reverse gear) 11·59 km/h
(water) 5·108 km/h
Range: 540 km
Fuel capacity: 416 litres
Max gradient: 60%
Max side slope: 30%
Fording: amphibious

Engine: Caterpillar Type D333, 4-cycle, in-line, 6-cylinder turbo-charged diesel developing 213 hp at 2200 rpm
Transmission: power shift with 6 forward and 1 reverse gears, 1 speed transfer box
Turning radius: 8·3 m
Steering: worm and sector, power assisted
Tyre size: 18.00 × 33
Brakes: air
Electrical system: 24 V

STATUS
Production complete. In service only with the US Army.

MANUFACTURER
Defense Products Department, Caterpillar Tractor Co, Peoria, Illinois 61629, USA.

M984 Recovery Vehicle 10-ton (8 × 8)

DEVELOPMENT
The M984 Recovery Vehicle 10-ton (8 × 8) is the recovery component of the Oshkosh HEMTT range of vehicles; for full details refer to the entry in the *Trucks* section.

DESCRIPTION
The M984 follows the same general construction lines as the rest of the HEMTT range. While the basic configuration remains the same, some changes have been made to the cab area where a spare tyre is mounted on the cab right-hand rear. The tyre is removed when the vehicle is being prepared for air transport in the C-5A Galaxy cargo transport. Between the second and third axles is a flat bed steel cargo body 2·286 metres wide with fold down sides 3·048 metres long. The main recovery crane is mounted at the rear and can be folded down for transport to a height of 2·591 metres. The crane can lift up to 20 412 kg. A centrally-mounted recovery winch is standard and has a bare drum capacity of 9072 kg.

SPECIFICATIONS
Cab seating: 1 + 1
Configuration: 8 × 8
Weight:
  (chassis) 12 927 kg
  (curb) 18 733 kg
  (GCW) 45 359 kg
Length: 9·5631 m
Width: 2·4 m
Height:
  (travelling) 2·845 m
  (top of cab) 2·565 m
  (crane extended) 3·759 m
  (loading, flat bed) 1·6 m
Ground clearance: 0·625 m
Wheelbase: 5·334 m
Angle of approach/departure: 43°/45°
Max speed: 88 km/h

Range: 483 km
Fuel capacity: 587 litres
Fording: 1·17 m
Engine: Detroit Diesel 8V92TA V-8 developing 445 hp at 2100 rpm
Gearbox: Allison HT7400 with torque converter, 4 forward, 1 reverse
Transfer box: Oshkosh 55000 2-speed
Steering: integral hydraulic main and booster gears
Suspension:
  (front) Hendrikson RT340
  (rear) Hendrikson RT450
Tyres: 16.00R × 20
Electrical system: 24 V
Batteries: 4 × 12 V

STATUS
In production for the US Army.

MANUFACTURER
Oshkosh Truck Corporation, POB 2037, Oshkosh, Wisconsin 54903, USA.

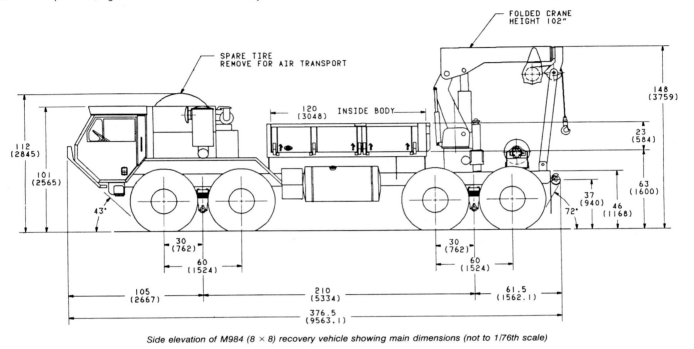

Side elevation of M984 (8 × 8) recovery vehicle showing main dimensions (not to 1/76th scale)

RECOVERY EQUIPMENT

FRANCE

Heavy Wrecking Truck Crane MH.45

DESCRIPTION

Intended for use on the Renault TRM 9000 or TRM 10 000, 6 × 6 or TBH 280, the MH.45 crane is designed for the heavy wrecker role. It is a single jib heavy duty crane mounted on a dummy frame situated on the rear of a heavy 6 × 6 chassis. The frame mounts not only the crane and its associated control and power equipment but also lockers and racks for other equipment. The telescopic crane boom is hydraulically controlled, and has an extension of 2·5 metres. For normal use the crane can be traversed through an angle of 135 degrees, but for maintenance this can be increased to 350 degrees. When fully raised the boom angle is 38 degrees, with hook clearance of 5·5 metres. For elevation the boom is raised by a hydraulic jack, while the crane itself rotates on a staggered roller-type bearing. The rotation is hydraulic by a motor/reduction unit with mechanical braking. Once in position, the crane and the truck chassis are further stabilised by four flipper-type outriggers, two on each side. A searchlight is mounted on the right of the jib.

The main crane hoist has a 4·5 tonne pull from a two-layer winding containing 40 metres of cable. There are also two winches, at the front and rear. The front winch has a 3·5/4·5 tonne line pull with a cable length of 70 metres. The rear winch has a 15/18 tonne line pull and a cable length of 90 metres, and is fitted with an unwinding winch. The power supply for the crane and the winches comes from a two-stage hydraulic pump driven by a power take-off from the main chassis transmission. A single control panel contains all the hydraulic controls with hand operated gradual action selector valves. The crane jib can cover a radius of 5·7 metres and has a maximum load of 13 tonnes. With a load of 4·5 tonnes on the hook at 1·3 metres from the chassis rear edge, the crane vehicle can travel at a speed of 40 km/h.

Mounted on the Renault TRM 9000 or TRM 10 000 6 × 6, the gross weight of the crane/vehicle combination is 18 500 kg, with a weight distribution of 6500 kg on the front axle and 12 000 kg on the rear axles.

SPECIFICATIONS
Gross weight: (vehicle crane) 18 500 kg
Crane operating radius:
(max) 5·775 m
(min) 2·23 m
Hook clearance: 5·5 m

Heavy wrecking truck crane MH.45 fitted to Renault TRM 10 000

Jib:
(elevation) 38°
(traverse) 135°
Crane hoist: 4·5 tonnes
Winch pull:
(rear) 15/18 tonnes
(front) 3·5/4·5 tonnes

STATUS
In production.

MANUFACTURER
Division Hydromécanique des Bennes Marrel SA (Marrel-Hydro), Saint-Étienne-Bouthéon, ZI, BP56, 42160 Andrézieux-Bouthéon, France.

GERMANY, DEMOCRATIC REPUBLIC

8-tonne Pneumatic Tyred Towing Axle

DESCRIPTION
This is used for recovering wheeled vehicles with a maximum weight of 8000 kg. The towing vehicle must be equipped with a winch to pull the disabled vehicle onto the towing axle. When this takes place the towing axle is coupled to the towing vehicle. It is often used to recover vehicles with damaged wheels and suspen-

sions. Average time for recovery is quoted as 60 minutes. This equipment fulfils a similar role to the British developed Trailer, Dummy Axles, also included in this section.

STATUS
In service with the East German Army.

MANUFACTURER
East German state factories.

SPECIFICATIONS
Weight: 1520 kg
Length: 3·942 m
Width: 2·49 m
Height: 1·216 m
Ground clearance: 0·31 m
Track: 2·3 m
Max towing speed: (with or without load) 40 km/h
Average towing speed: (across country) 15 km/h
Gradient: (with load) 25%

GERMANY, FEDERAL REPUBLIC

Rotzler Winches

The Rotzler company manufactures a wide range of hydraulic and mechanical winches for both civil and military applications. Brief specifications are given in the table below. In addition the company manufactures laterally mounted cable winches for Mercedes-Benz trucks and a complete range of lifting winches.

STATUS
In production. In service with the West German and other armed forces.

MANUFACTURER
Rotzler GmbH and Company, Postfach 1260, D-7853 Steinen, Federal Republic of Germany.

Model	Type	Pulling power[1]	Weight of load[2]	Diameter cable drum	Gear reduction	Average cable speed[3]	Average cable speed[4]	HP required[5]
3000h	hydraulic	3000 kg	9000 kg	130 mm	1:47	13 m/minute/ 50 l/minute	13 m/minute/ 50 l/minute	23
5000 mvh	hydraulic	5000 kg	15 000 kg	170 mm	1:144	7 m/minute/ 50 l/minute	17·5 m/minute/ 125 l/minute	23
5000H	hydraulic	5000 kg	15 000 kg	225 mm	1:96	13 m/minute/ 50 l/minute	35 m/minute/ 125 l/minute	23
5000 H/2-96	hydraulic	7000 kg	21 000 kg	225 mm	1:96	11 m/minute/ 50 l/minute	34 m/minute/ 159 l/minute	23
8000 H/2-96	hydraulic	8000 kg	24 000 kg	240 mm	1:96	11 m/minute/ 50 l/minute	35 m/minute/ 158 l/minute	23
10 000 H	hydraulic	10 000 kg	30 000 kg	280 mm	1:190	10 m/minute/ 90 l/minute	17·5 m/minute/ 159 l/minute	41
10 000 H/2-96	hydraulic	9000 kg	27 000 kg	280 mm	1:96	13 m/minute/ 60 l/minute	50 m/minute/ 193 l/minute	23
15 000 H/3-313	hydraulic	15 000 kg	45 000 kg	280 mm	1:313	9 m/minute/ 90 l/minute	12·5 m/minute/ 125 l/minute	41
20 000 H	hydraulic	20 000 kg	60 000 kg	390 mm	1:430	7 m/minute/ 90 l/minute	12·7 m/minute/ 159 l/minute	41
25 000 H	hydraulic	25 000 kg	75 000 kg	390 mm	1:430	6 m/minute/ 90 l/minute	13 m/minute/ 193 l/minute	41
30 000 H	hydraulic	30 000 kg	90 000 kg	390 mm	1:573	5 m/minute/ 90 l/minute	9 m/minute/ 159 l/minute	41
50 000 H	hydraulic	50 000 kg	150 000 kg	400 mm	1:800	5 m/minute/ 160 l/minute	6 m/minute/ 193 l/minute	75
7000 HS	hydraulic	7000 kg	21 000 kg	105 mm	1:68	12 m/minute/ 50 l/minute	38 m/minute/ 159 l/minute	23
DS 5000	hydraulic	6000 kg	18 000 kg	160 mm	1:116	15 m/minute/ 50 l/minute	15·5 m/minute/ 50 l/minute	32
1200 E	mechanical	1200 kg	3600 kg	110 mm	1:360	n/app	n/app	12 V or 24 V
3000 m	mechanical	3000 kg	9000 kg	130 mm	1:47	n/app	n/app	18
5000 m	mechanical	7000 kg	21 000 kg	170 mm	1:41	n/app	n/app	44
8000 MV	mechanical	10 000 kg	30 000 kg	170 mm	1:81	n/app	n/app	45
15 000 m	mechanical	15 000 kg	45 000 kg	200 mm	1:120	n/app	n/app	55
20 000 m	mechanical	20 000 kg	60 000 kg	200 mm	1:20	n/app	n/app	90
5000 ms	mechanical	7000 kg	21 000 kg	170 mm	1:41	n/app	n/app	44
8000 MVs	mechanical	8000 kg	24 000 kg	170 mm	1:81	n/app	n/app	45

[1] Pulling power on first cable position
[2] Weight of load can be pulled with pulling power on flat ground
[3] Average cable speed with hydraulic drive and usual quantity of oil in litres quoted
[4] Average cable speed with hydraulic drive and maximum quantity of oil in litres quoted
[5] Required driving power with mechanical drive at 1000 rpm, with hydraulic drive with usual quantity of oil

Rotzler Capstan Winch

Under contract to the West German Office for Defence Technology and Procurement, Koblenz, Krupp MaK has tested a constant tension capstan-type winch, developed by Rotzler, which is capable of lifting or pulling up to 35 000 kg.

This winch was successfully tested both in a Leopard 1 ARV and on a Krupp MaK crane and winch test bed, and has shown that there is a considerable improvement over current winches.

Rotzler capstan winch on Krupp MaK crane and winch test bench

Rotzler capstan winch being tested mounted in Leopard 1 ARV

Vetter Mini Lifting Bags

DESCRIPTION
The Vetter range of Mini Lifting Bags has been designed for a wide range of civilian and military applications including lifting vehicles, equipment and other objects such as trees and blocks of concrete, forcing apart the doors of crashed vehicles and withdrawing couplings.

The bags require an insertion space of only 25 cm and need no maintenance. They have no large metal surfaces liable to cause sparks and have a non-slip ribbed surface. They are inflated with compressed air from an air cylinder, mains compressed air installation, heavy goods vehicle tyre inflation compressor, HGV compressed air system (trailer connector) or by a hand or foot pump. In an emergency the spare tyre of an HGV can be used, or the bag can be filled with water.

The following equipment has been designed for use with the Vetter range of mini lifting bags:

Pressure Regulator 200 bar
Finger-tight connector for faster, simpler changing of

compressed air cylinders, self-sealing, non-icing, cylinder pressure indicator, outlet pressure indicator, adjustable up to ten bar to vary the speed of the mini lifting bag, safety valve, two pressure gauges with protective covers, shut-off valve, two metres of hose complete with brass quick-release connector.

Dual Control Safety Unit bar
For safe dual operation with separate control of two mini lifting bags (for lifting uneven or cylindrical loads etc) with quick release coupling, two shut-off valves, two pressure gauges with protective covers, two pressure relief valves preset at eight bar which allows precisely controlled bag deflation for lowering loads exactly to the position required.

Other accessories include braided transparent air hose, high pressure regulator, high pressure regulator with American type connector, single safety control unit bar, compressed air cylinders (four, six and ten litres capacity), dual connectors, HGV compressed air connector, HGV type inflation connector, HGV type valve, HGV filling station connector, compressed air main connector and various lengths of hoses.

Vetter mini lifting bags lifting Leopard 1 MBT

STATUS
Production.

MANUFACTURER
Manfred Vetter GmbH, 5352 Zülpich, Federal Republic of Germany.

SPECIFICATIONS

Type	V10	V12	V18	V24	V24L	V31	V40	V54	V68
Lifting capacity max KN	96	120	177	240	240	314	396	544	677
Max kgs	9600	12 000	17 700	24 000	24 000	31 400	39 600	54 400	67 700
Size cm	37 × 37	32 × 52	47 × 52	52 × 62	31 × 102	65 × 69	78 × 69	86 × 86	95 × 95
Lifting height max cm	20·3	20·0	27·0	30·6	20·1	37·0	40·2	47·8	52·0
Water requirement at 8 bar nominal content litres	8·4	10·5	21·5	33·0	24·0	57·0	75·0	124·5	161
Air requirement at 8 bar litres	75·6	95·0	194	297	216	511	675	1120	1451
Max working pressure bar	8	8	8	8	8	8	8	8	8
Inflation time secs	3·8	4·8	9·0	13·8	9·9	23·7	31·1	51·9	66·3
Test pressure bar	16	16	16	16	16	16	16	16	16
Bursting pressure bar	48·3	71·3	38·7	48·3	74·3	42·0	35·0	35·5	34·7
Height cm	2·5	2·5	2·5	2·5	2·5	2·5	2·5	2·5	3·0
Weight approx kgs	4·5	5·5	8·0	10·3	10·2	17	19·8	26	39

UNITED KINGDOM

Marlow Kinetic Energy Tow Rope

DESCRIPTION
The Marlow kinetic energy tow rope has been developed since 1971 by Marlow Ropes Limited and the British Army as the replacement for the steel wire cables at present used to recover light armoured vehicles. After trials using Ferret scout cars under different climatic and terrain conditions, the 'snatch' recovery method was proved possible.

The recovery method involves two stages employing the physical parameters of kinetic energy and force impulse respectively. The first stage is based on the conversion of the energy released during combustion of the towing Ferret's petrol into the kinetic energy of a moving mass making the energy to be used in the recovery attempt independent of the towing Ferret's wheel traction. So long as the traction is good enough for the towing Ferret to achieve some speed before the rope tightens, it does not matter whether the vehicle is on sand or rock when the nylon rope tightens to the potential energy stage whereby the kinetic energy of the moving Ferret is converted into the potential energy of the stretched nylon rope. At this point the second stage of recovery commences. The stretched nylon rope is pulling at both ends with a force of several tons so that obviously one of the vehicles is going to move. Since the deceleration and acceleration in the opposite direction take time, it will usually be the stuck vehicle that moves under the impulse of the considerable force applied to it.

A typical recovery would take place as follows. The recovery vehicle backs up to the ditched vehicle and shackles the snatch recovery tow rope on to the towing point. The rope lies coiled on the ground between the two vehicles. The driver of the recovery vehicle then accelerates as fast as possible, generally reaching a top speed of about 24 km/h. When the rope goes taut, the driver of the ditched vehicle revs his engine into gear. On the first pull, the vehicle moves only a few inches, in which case the procedure is repeated. Heavier vehicles can recover lighter vehicles, and vice versa (but it is important that the rope stipulated for the size of the vehicle to be recovered is used). It is recommended that both drivers wear safety belts, their hatches are closed, and that all other personnel stand well clear of the area in case there is a rope failure or towing eye failure. To ensure adequate rope life, the maximum load must be kept below 50 per cent of minimum breaking load, and heat build-up should be allowed to dissipate between successive loadings.

The rope has been approved for the following vehicles by the British Army:
Ferret and Fox scout cars: 32 mm diameter × 12·2 m long
Scorpion vehicles: 40 mm diameter × 13·7 m long
FV603 Saracen and FV432 series APC: 48 mm diameter × 13·7 m long

SPECIFICATIONS

Gross weight of vehicle	Rope size	Rope strength	Overall length of rope	Rope weight
Under 7000 kg	32 mm	20 000 kg	12·2 m	8·1 kg
7000 to 7900 kg	36 mm	24 800 kg	12·2 m	10·24 kg
8000 to 11 000 kg	40 mm	30 000 kg	13·7 m	13·5 kg
12 000 to 15 400 kg	48 mm	42 000 kg	13·7 m	20·5 kg
15 500 to 18 400 kg	52 mm	48 800 kg	13·7 m	24 kg
18 500 to 21 900 kg	56 mm	56 000 kg	13·7 m	27·8 kg
22 000 to 23 500 kg	60 mm	63 800 kg	13·7 m	32 kg
24 000 to 30 000 kg	64 mm	72 000 kg	15 m	40 kg
31 000 to 43 000 kg	68 mm	79 500 kg	15 m	44·25 kg
44 000 to 54 000 kg	72 mm	90 000 kg	15 m	50·4 kg

Other sizes are available for vehicles weighing up to 55 000 kg.

Marlow Ropes also manufactures a wide range of other ropes including Copper/Terylene Aerial Braid, three-strand stretched Terylene/Polyester rope, 16-plait Terylene/Polyester Land Rover winch rope, Scorpion Multiplait Terylene/Polyester road towing

strops (these are supplied for every member of the Alvis Scorpion family), Multiplait Polypropylene film bridging rope and a Multiplait Terylene/Polyester tank track removal rope.

STATUS
In production. In service with the British Army and other armed forces.

MANUFACTURER
Marlow Ropes Limited, South Road, Hailsham, East Sussex BN27 3JS, England.

Alvis Spartan APC recovering Alvis Samson ARV with aid of Marlow kinetic energy rope

Tirfor Recovery Equipment

DESCRIPTION
The Tirfor models T-7, TU-16 and T-35 are all portable hand-operated machines which can be used for a wide range of loading, lifting, hauling and lowering operations. They are reversible and are available with a range of accessories which includes slings, shackles, snatch blocks, ground anchors, automatic wire rope reeling devices, wire rope grips and girder clamps. The latest model is the TU-16H, which is a hydraulically-operated strengthened TU-16. Hydraulic pump units allow the operation of 1, 2 or 4 TU-16Hs and the system can work both forwards (pulling or lifting) or reverse (lowering). The hydraulic power system gives the TU-16H a normal capacity of 1600 kg. This model can be operated from a unit with the following capability:

    Flow: 8 – 13 litres per minute maximum
    Pressure: 120 – 140 bars
    Hydraulic oil: 2° to 5° Engler viscosity at 50° C
    Viscosity index: over 100
    Filter: 40 microns

For light recovery operations the company offers the Jockey, which weighs less than 1·8 kg and can lift 300 kg, and pull up to 500 kg. The handle has been designed to bend when the rated pulling capacity is exceeded by 50 per cent. Finally there is the Super-winch PM3000, which weighs 8·165 kg and is powered from any 12 volt source (eg from the vehicle's battery). It has a maximum lifting capacity of up to 363 kg and a continuous pulling load of 454 kg and is capable of pulling a vehicle weighing 1542 kg up a 20 per cent slope. This winch is provided with 7·62 metres of 4·7 mm diameter steel cable, and will automatically cut out and hold the load if an excess weight is applied.

Other hand-operated Tirfor machines

Model	J5 Junior	T508	T-30
Pulling capacity	800 kg	1200 kg	5000 kg
Lifting capacity	500 kg	800 kg	3000 kg
Weight	4 kg	6·6 kg	27 kg
Breaking strength	3000 kg	4800 kg	16 800 kg
Diameter of wire rope	6·5 mm	8·2 mm	16·3 mm

STATUS
All this equipment is in production. The T-7, TU-16 and T-35 are used by many armed forces around the world.

MANUFACTURER
Tirfor Limited, Halfway, Sheffield S19 5GZ, England.

Tirfor T-35 being used with Fairey Medium Girder Bridge

SPECIFICATIONS

Model	T-7	TU-16	T-35
Safe working load for lifting operations	750 kg	1600 kg	3000 kg
		2500 kg (pulling)	5000 kg (pulling)
Effort	27 kg	46 kg	43·2 kg (slow speed)
			68·1 kg (fast speed)
Distance of rope travel for one complete cycle of operating lever	64 mm	70 mm	38 mm (slow speed)
			48 mm (fast speed)
Mechanical advantage	28:1	38:1	70:1 (slow speed)
			45:1 (fast speed)
Weight of machine only	5·9 kg	18 kg	26·8 kg
Overall dimensions (without handle)	510×10×204 mm	660×356×152 mm	718×140×318 mm
Length of operating handle (fully extended)	0·731 m	1·13 m	1·157 m
Standard length of wire rope	9·15 m	18·3 m	9·15 m
Rope diameter	8·2 mm	11·3 mm	16·3 mm
Rope end fitting	safety hook	safety hook	shackle

Trailer, Dummy Axle, Recovery, 10/30 Ton (FV3561)

DEVELOPMENT
The dummy axle has been designed to provide a sus-pended tow capability of 10 000 kg and can be towed by a variety of vehicles. The basic idea is that a recovery vehicle is used to recover the disabled vehicle and once this is on firm ground the dummy axle is used to take the damaged vehicle away for repair. This allows the recovery vehicle to carry on with its primary task of recovering other disabled vehicles. The vehicle towing the dummy axle is normally in the same weight class as the casualty.

DESCRIPTION
The disabled vehicle is lifted by a jib pivoted on the axle, with the winch 4-fall reeving, and lifting bar. The casu-alty is further located by an A-frame which incorporates a pivoted towing eye with an automatic catch to facilitate coupling to the disabled vehicle.

The hydraulic system, which is powered by the 7·5 bhp diesel engine, operates the winch (which has a lifting capacity of 10 400 kg), moves the jib between lifting and travelling positions, and raises and lowers the dolly wheels. A hand winch with a capacity of 250 kg is provided for positioning the A-frame and towing beam.

The dummy axle has a three-line air-pressure braking system working in conjunction with drum brakes. A mechanical hand brake allows the dummy axle to be parked on slopes of 1 in 6 in either direction. To facilitate night operations, floodlights are provided and a lighting beam is carried for fastening to the rear of the disabled vehicle. A stowage locker, a spare wheel, safety links, lifting chains and a towing beam are provided.

SPECIFICATIONS
Weight: 3250 kg
Length: 3·682 m
Width: 2·667 m
Height in towed position: 3·25 m
Towing eye height:
    (normal) 0·92 m
    (max) 1·066 m

Trailer, Dummy Axle, Recovery, 10/30 ton (FV3561) (T J Gander)

Ground clearance under dolly wheel: 0·38 m
Track: 2·057 m
Angle of approach: 80°
Fording: 0·76 m
Engine: Hatz air-cooled diesel developing 7·5 bhp, with hand starting
Tyres:
    (rear, 4 off) 10.00 × 15
    (front, 2 off) 4.00 × 8

STATUS
In production. In service with the British Army.

MANUFACTURER
Royal Ordnance Factory, Nottingham.
    Enquiries to Ministry of Defence, ROF Marketing, St. Christopher House, Southwark Street, London SE1 0TD, England.

Trailer, Dummy Axle, Recovery, 1–5 Tonne (FV 2692)

DESCRIPTION
The trailer is capable of performing a suspended tow of wheeled armoured and unarmoured vehicle casualties up to a gross vehicle weight of 6·25 tonnes. The trailer has an unsprung twin-wheeled axle carrying the integrally constructed chassis frame and jib. The recovery is effected by means of a handwinch and four-fall pulley system. A system of spreader bars and chains allows the winch unit to be relieved of all load once the casualty is attached to the dummy axle. High- and low-level floodlights are fitted to facilitate night time operations. An emergency lighting kit is carried to fit the rear of the disabled vehicle.

SPECIFICATIONS
Weight: (unladen) 1183 kg
Length: 3·47 m
Width: 2·362 m
Height: 2·31 m
Wheelbase: (axle to towing eye) 2·746 m
Track: 1·816 m
Tyres: 8.25 × 15 (radial ply)
Wheels: 6.5 × 15, 8 stud × 275 mm pcd
Brakes: 312 × 190 mm S cam units, overrun operated when unladen and air operated when laden
Handbrake: mechanical operating via overrun system

STATUS
In production. In service with the British Army.

Trailer, Dummy Axle, Recovery, 1–5 Tonne

MANUFACTURER
Defence Equipment Division, Rubery Owen Group Services Limited, Darlaston PO Box 10, Wednesbury, West Midlands WS10 8JD, England.

Fairey 10-ton Winch FF 10/12

DESCRIPTION
When the new ranges of Foden Low and Medium Mobility vehicles were undergoing initial acceptance trials, the Ministry of Defence issued a specification for a forward-mounted hydraulic recovery winch, with a minimum line pull of 10 tons, to provide a bare drum capacity of 12·5 tons at 140·6 kg/cm² (2000 psi). Fairey Winches Limited was awarded the contract for its model FF 10/12 winch.

The FF 10/12 uses aluminium castings and has a drum capacity of 50 metres of 18 mm cable although it is recommended that only 40 metres should be used. In use the FF 10/12 has over-load protection provided by pressure relief through an adjustable valve. Free spool is obtained by a hand-operated involute splined clutch. The spiroid gear ratio is 1:25·33.

The FF 10/12 is now in British Army service on Foden Low Mobility 6 × 4 and 8 × 4 vehicles and on the Foden Medium Mobility 6 × 6 FH-70 Tractor and Limber vehicles. It is also fitted to the Foden (6 × 6) recovery vehicle.

STATUS
In production. In service with the British Army.

MANUFACTURER
Fairey Winches Limited, Whitchurch Road, Tavistock, Devon PL19 9DR, England.

SPECIFICATIONS
Line pull: 10·7 tons
Line speed: (2nd layer rope)
  (flow rate 60 litres/min) 4·9 m/min
  (flow rate 99 litres/min) 7·6 m/min
  (flow rate 150 litres/min) 11·6 m/min
Bare drum line pull: 12·5 tons
Capacity of 18 mm cable:
  (maximum) 50 m
  (recommended) 40 m

Fairey FF 10/12 winch fitted to Foden (6 × 6) recovery vehicle

Drum:
  (barrel diameter) 270 mm
  (flange diameter) 435 mm
  (width) 258 mm

Operating pressure: 140·6 kg/cm²
Height: 817 mm
Width: 946 mm
Depth: 670 mm

Fairey Light Recovery Equipment

DESCRIPTION
Fairey Winches Limited produces a range of recovery equipment suitable for fitting to light vehicles. This range includes capstan and drum winches, power take-offs and accessories.

There are two types of capstan winch; the Capstan 99 and the Capstan 199. The Capstan 99 is produced for use with all models of Land-Rover and is in service with the British Army. It is driven from the front of the crankshaft and has a recommended line pull of 1400 kg, although it is overload tested to 2500 kg. 58 mm rope is recommended. The winch is supplied in kit form and can be fitted in approximately three hours. Overload protection is provided by a shearpin in the driveline, a feature shared by all the light Fairey winches. The Capstan 199 is a version for the Range Rover or 6-cylinder Toyota Land Cruiser and is similar except for the weight which is 33 kg, 3 kg more than the Capstan 99.

The Fairey drum winch can be fitted to the Land-Rover, including the 1-tonne version. It has a line pull of 2270 kg and can be provided with 9 mm or 11 mm cable. Weight is 65·3 kg, less cable. It is provided in kit form and can be fitted by one man in eight to ten hours. Control can be from inside or outside the cab.

A new drum winch has been produced for use with the new Land-Rover 110 (One-Ten) and is suitable for fitting to the four-cylinder 110 models. It uses a mechanical drive from a power take-off fitted to the rear of the gearbox transfer case. It has an automatic overload protection adjustable to suit the maximum line pull permitted. To fit the winch to the 110 takes approximately six hours. In use it can be controlled from inside or outside the cab. 9 mm or 11 mm cable can be used, 77 metres of the 9 mm and 46 metres of the 11 mm. The maximum line speed in fifth gear is 11·73 metres a minute and the total weight of the winch and accessories (less cable) is 92·76 kg.

When using the Fairey winches on a Land-Rover it is recommended that a special heavy duty bumper is fitted to the vehicle. Other accessories include ground anchors which are provided with reversable plates to provide straight edges for use on hard ground and splines for use on earth surfaces. A chain secures the anchor to the bumper. When not in use the anchors fold flat measuring 610 × 311 × 76·2 mm. Weight per pair is 45 kg. A slightly larger version is available for use with the 1-tonne Land-Rover which weighs 54 kg per pair. Folded dimensions are 838 × 357 × 76·2 mm.

STATUS
In production. Capstan 99, heavy duty bumper and ground anchors in service with the British Army.

MANUFACTURER
Fairey Winches Limited, Whitchurch Road, Tavistock, Devon PL19 9DR, England.

Fairey drum winch for Land-Rover 110

Land-Rover fitted with Fairey drum winch and ground anchors

Rubery Owen Recovery Equipment

DESCRIPTION
A special range of lightweight recovery equipment has been designed using safety factors as low as one and a half times the working load limit. Meeting the needs of skilled recovery personnel, all of the equipment has been subjected to rigorous field and destruction test programmes.

A schedule of available recovery equipment has been prepared for the Military Vehicles and Engineering Establishment and covers the range of equipment used by the British Army. Further details available on request.

STATUS
Manufactured as required. In service with the British Army.

MANUFACTURER
Defence Equipment Division, Rubery Owen Group Services Limited, Darlaston, PO Box 10, Wednesbury, West Midlands WS10 8JD, England.

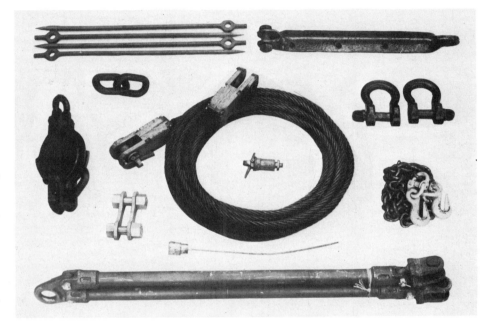

The selection illustrated is typical of recovery equipment supplied by Rubery Owen

UNITED STATES OF AMERICA

Holmes FW-35 Towing Unit

DESCRIPTION
The Holmes FW-35 towing unit is designed to be fitted over the 'fifth wheel' turntable unit of heavy tractors for extreme heavy-duty lift and towing of tactical vehicles, such as tank recovery vehicles and missile carriers. When fitted the FW-35 is capable of towing vehicles with a gross cargo weight of up to 38 555 kg, and it can lift up to 15 875 kg. Once lifted the towed vehicle travels on its rear axle(s).

STATUS
Production. In service with US Forces in Europe.

MANUFACTURER
Ernest Holmes Division, Dover Corporation, 2505 East 43rd Street, Chatanooga, Tennessee 37407, USA.

Holmes FW-35 towing unit

Bridging systems

MECHANISED BRIDGES

BRAZIL

XLP-10 Armoured Vehicle Launched Bridge

DEVELOPMENT/DESCRIPTION

The XLP-10 AVLB (or Carro de Combate Lancador de Ponte) has been developed by the Bernardini company to meet the requirements of the Brazilian Army and basically consists of an X1A chassis fitted with a bridge-launching mechanism and a single-span bridge.

The X1A chassis is an old American M3A1 Stuart light tank with the original engine replaced by a six-cylinder Saab-Scania diesel developing 280 bhp, new suspension designed by Novatracao company, new turret with 90 mm gun and a new fire-control system. Following trials with two prototype vehicles, 80 Stuarts were brought up to X1A standard and delivered to the Brazilian Army.

Trials with the prototype were completed in 1978 and the Brazilian Army then placed an order for about ten vehicles to be based on the X1A1's chassis rather than the X1A's. The X1A1 is essentially a stretched X1A with an additional suspension group and new track tension

wheel each side and the same engine as the X1A tank. The X1A2, the latest development, is a new tank, rather than a conversion of a Stuart, and is currently in production for the Brazilian Army.

The bridge itself is aluminium and steel, weighs 2750 kg, can span a gap of ten metres and takes a maximum load of 20 000 kg. On arrival at the river or ditch a stabiliser blade is lowered at the front of the hull, the bridge is extended across the gap on a cantilever arm and lowered in position. The cantilever arm is then withdrawn, the stabiliser blade raised and the vehicle withdraws. The bridge takes three minutes to lay in position and a similar time to be retrieved.

Bernardini is also converting 35 Brazilian Army Sherman tanks into bridgelayers with a single-span bridge with a capacity of 35 000 kg.

SPECIFICATIONS
(model based on X1A1 chassis)
Crew: 2
Length:
(chassis) 5·85 m
(chassis and bridge) 11·2 m

Width:
(chassis) 2·4 m
(chassis and bridge) 2·745 m
Height:
(chassis) 1·63 m
(chassis and bridge) 2·5 m
Ground clearance: 0·5 m
Max speed: 60 km/h
Range: 520 km
Fording: 1·3 m
Gradient: 60%
Vertical obstacle: 0·8 m
Engine: Saab-Scania diesel developing 280 bhp
Electrical system: 24 V

STATUS
In production. In service with the Brazilian Army.

MANUFACTURER
Bernardini S/A Indústria e Comércio, Rua Hipólito Soares No 79, 04201 São Paulo, SP, Brazil.

Prototype of XLP-10 AVLB laying bridge in position

Prototype of XLP-10 AVLB from rear in travelling order

CZECHOSLOVAKIA

MT-55 Armoured Bridgelayer

DEVELOPMENT/DESCRIPTION
The MT-55 is the replacement for the earlier MT-34 and has also been adopted by other countries including the Soviet Union. It is based on a T-55A tank chassis with the turret removed. The basic chassis is similar to that used for the T-54/T-55 ARVs and the reader is referred to this entry in the *Armoured recovery vehicles* section for a description of the chassis.

There are two types of scissors bridge. The first model has circular holes in the sides of the bridge, similar to those on the bridge carried by the MT-34 bridgelayer, while the more recent model has solid panels. It is easy to mistake the latter for the East German BLG-60 armoured bridgelayer. The main distinguishing feature between the two is that the bridge surface of the MT-55 has a pattern whereas the BLG-60's is smooth with a plastic covering.

The bridge is launched over the front of the vehicle hydraulically by an electro-hydraulic control system. In an emergency the hydraulic system can be operated with the aid of three mechanical levers and, if the engine fails, the tank's batteries can provide sufficient power to launch the bridge.

The launching procedure is as follows: the MT-55 stops short of the gap and raises the bridge slightly from its horizontal travelling position, the launching girder foot is lowered to the ground and the span is raised to the vertical and the bridge is then unfolded and lowered across the gap. The bridge takes between two and three minutes to lay in position and five to six minutes to retrieve. The bridge itself weighs 6500 kg and when opened out is 18 metres long, 3·34 metres wide and 0·9 metre high. It has a maximum clear span of 16 metres and a maximum capacity of 50 000 kg.

Standard equipment on the MT-55 includes an NBC system, snorkel, inclinometer and other equipment for determining the width of the gap before the bridge is laid in position.

MT-55 armoured bridgelayer laying bridge

STATUS
Production complete. In service with Czechoslovakia, the USSR and Yugoslavia, and some countries in the Middle East.

MANUFACTURER
Chassis: Czechoslovakia; conversion work and bridge: Czechoslovak state arsenals.

SPECIFICATIONS
Crew: 2
Weight: (with bridge) 36 000 kg
Length: (with bridge) 9·8 m
Width: (with bridge) 3·34 m
Height: (with bridge) 3·72 m
Ground clearance: 0·525 m
Track: 2·64 m
Track width: 580 mm
Length of track on ground: 3·84 m
Ground pressure: 0·81 kg/cm²
Max speed: (road) 48 km/h
Range: 500 km
Fuel capacity: 960 litres
Fording: 1·4 m
Gradient: 60%
Vertical obstacle: 0·8 m
Trench: 2·7 m
Engine: V-55, V-12, water-cooled diesel developing
580 hp at 2000 rpm
Transmission: manual with 5 forward and 1 reverse
gears
Electrical system: 24 V
Batteries: 4, 280 Ah
Armament: nil
Armour
glacis plate: 100 mm at 60°
upper hull side: 70 mm at 0°
hull rear: 60 mm
hull floor: 20 mm
hull roof: 30 mm

MT-55 armoured bridgelayer in travelling configuration (Israeli Army)

Czechoslovak Truck-mounted Scissors Bridge AM-50

DESCRIPTION
Czechoslovakia has developed a scissors bridge which is launched over the rear of a Tatra 813 (8 × 8) truck. It is launched in a similar fashion to the Soviet TMM treadway bridge but the Czechoslovak system has the added advantage that the trestle columns have hydraulic rather than manual adjustment. Another feature is that the bridge has a full width roadway rather than the two single tracks of the Soviet TMM system. The designation AM-50 probably refers to the 50 000 kg capacity of the bridge.

Full details of this system are not available but it is estimated that each span is approximately 14 metres long when opened out and 3·8 metres wide, and that three spans would enable a river 40 metres wide to be crossed. It is also estimated that a three-span bridge could be erected by a well-trained crew in under 20 minutes.

Czechoslovak scissors bridge AM-50 being launched from rear of Tatra 813 (8 × 8) truck

STATUS
In production. In service with the Czechoslovak Army.

MANUFACTURER
Czechoslovak state factories.

FRANCE

AMX-30 Armoured Bridgelayer

DEVELOPMENT
The prototype of the AMX-30 bridgelayer was built in 1966/67, but it was not until 1976/77 that the vehicle entered service with the French Army. There were initial technical problems and the original builder of the bridge, Société CODER, went into liquidation and the Titan company subsequently took over responsibility for the bridge.

DESCRIPTION
The class 50 bridge is composed of two hinged elements with removable widening panels and wheel guides. When opened out it is 22 metres long and will span a gap of up to 20 metres. The bridge is 3·1 metres wide without the widening panels and 3·92 metres wide with them. The bridge is launched hydraulically over the rear of the vehicle and takes about five minutes to lay into position. It can be recovered from either end. The bridge can be launched on relative slopes of ±30 per cent with a relative slant reaching 15 per cent.

The basic chassis is almost identical to that of the standard AMX-30 MBT. The hull provides the crew with protection against small arms fire and artillery splinters, and is fitted with the same NBC system as the MBT.

The driver is seated at the front of the vehicle on the left side and is provided with a single-piece hatch cover and three periscopes for observation. One of these can be replaced by a night periscope of the infra-red or image intensification type. The commander and bridge operator are seated to the rear of the driver. The engine and transmission are at the rear of the tank and are separated from the crew compartment by a fire-proof bulkhead.

The suspension is of the torsion bar type and consists of five road wheels with the drive sprocket at the rear

AMX-30 bridgelayer with bridge folded for travelling (ECP Armées)

and the idler at the front. There are five track support rollers which support the inside of the track only. The first two and last two road wheels are mounted on bogies and are provided with hydraulic shock absorbers.

A special version of the AMX-30 has been developed

for operation in hot climates with a derated engine which develops 620 hp at 2400 rpm, reduction in gearbox ratios and sand guards. Unconfirmed reports state that Saudi Arabia has ordered this version of the bridgelayer as it has already ordered a modified version of the AMX-30 MBT called the AMX-30S.

STATUS
Production as required. In service with the French Army.

MANUFACTURER
Bridge: Compagnie d'Exploitation Française CEF Titan, 69400 Villefranche-sur-Saône.
　Chassis: Atelier de Construction Roanne (ARE).
　Enquiries to Groupement Industriel des Armements Terrestres (GIAT), 10 place Georges-Clémenceau, 92211 Saint-Cloud, France.

SPECIFICATIONS
Crew: 3
Weight:
　(with bridge) 42 500 kg
　(without bridge) 34 000 kç
Length:
　(with bridge) 11·4 m
　(hull only) 6·7 m
Width:
　(with bridge) 3·95 m
　(without bridge) 3·15 m
Height: (with bridge) 4·29 m
Ground clearance: 0·4 m
Track: 2·53 m
Track width: 570 mm
Length of track on ground: 4·12 m
Ground pressure: (with bridge) 0·93 kg/cm²
Max road speed:
　(with bridge) 50 km/h
　(without bridge) 60 km/h

Range: 600 km
Fuel capacity: 1100 litres
Fording: 1 m
Gradient: 50%
Side slope: 25%
Vertical obstacle: 0·93 m
Trench: 2·9 m

Engine: Hispano-Suiza HS-110, 12-cylinder, water-cooled, multi-fuel diesel developing 700 hp at 2400 rpm
Transmission: automatic with 5 forward gears. A reverse gear gives the same speeds in reverse
Electrical system: 28 V
Batteries: 8 × 12 V, 100 Ah in 2 groups of 4
Armament: nil

AMX-30 bridgelayer shortly after laying bridge in position (GIAT)

AMX-13 Armoured Bridgelayer

DEVELOPMENT
The AMX-13 bridgelayer, or Char Poseur de Pont AMX-13, entered service with the French Army in the 1960s but was not produced in large numbers. The bridge was designed and built by Société Nouvelle de Gestion des Etablissements CODER.

DESCRIPTION
The basic chassis is similar to that of other members of the AMX-13 light tank family. The driver is seated at the front on the left side and is provided with three periscopes for observation and a single-piece hatch cover. The engine is to the right of the driver. The other two crew members, the commander and the operator, are seated in the crew compartment to the rear of the driver's position. The suspension is of the torsion bar type and consists of five road wheels with the drive sprocket at the front and the idler at the rear. There are four track return rollers. Hydraulic shock absorbers are provided for the first and fifth road wheel stations.
　The bridge is hydraulically laid over the rear of the vehicle and can be picked up again from either end. It is in two halves connected by a hinge. The bridge is 14·3 metres long when unfolded and 7·15 metres long folded. Overall width is 3·15 metres, height unfolded 1·12 metres and height folded 1·8 metres. The bridge is provided with widening panels and wheel guides. When the bridge has been laid in position, vehicles up to class 25 can cross. Two bridges laid side by side will take vehicles up to class 50.

SPECIFICATIONS
Crew: 3
Weight:
　(with bridge) 19 200 kg
　(without bridge) 15 100 kg
Length:
　(with bridge) 8·02 m
　(without bridge) 6·44 m
　(hull) 4·88 m
Width:
　(with bridge) 3·16 m
　(without bridge) 2·7 m
Height:
　(with bridge) 4·05 m
　(without bridge) 2·72 m
Ground clearance:
　(with bridge) front 0·43 m; rear 0·36 m
　(without bridge) 0·48 m
Track: 2·16 m
Track width: 350 mm
Length of track on ground: 2·8 m
Ground pressure:
　(with bridge) 0·905 kg/cm²
　(without bridge) 0·755 kg/cm²
Max road speed:
　(with bridge) 40 km/h
　(without bridge) 60 km/h
Range: (road) 350 km
Fuel capacity: 480 litres
Fording: 1 m
Gradient:
　(with bridge) 30%
　(without bridge) 60%

Side slope:
　(with bridge) 20%
　(without bridge) 50%
Vertical obstacle:
　(forward) 0·65 m
　(reverse) 0·45 m
Trench:
　(with bridge) 1·3 m
　(without bridge) 1·6 m
Engine: SOFAM Model 8 GXb 8-cylinder water-cooled petrol developing 250 hp at 3200 rpm

Transmission: manual with 5 forward and 1 reverse gears (2nd, 3rd, 4th and 5th gears synchromesh)
Electrical system: 24 V
Batteries: 4 × 12 V, 95 Ah
Armour
crew compartment front: 30 mm
crew compartment sides and rear: 20 mm
crew compartment roof: 10 mm
hull rear: 15 mm
hull glacis: 15 mm
floor forward: 20 mm
floor rear: 10 mm

AMX-13 bridgelayer raising folded bridge to vertical (ECP Armées)

STATUS
Production complete. In service with Argentina, France and Indonesia. Additional production can be undertaken if required.

MANUFACTURER
Creusot-Loire at Chalon-sur-Saône.
Enquiries to Creusot-Loire, 15 rue Pasquier, 75383 Paris Cedex 08, France.

AMX-13 bridgelayer opening out bridge. Note stabilisers at rear of hull (ECP Armées)

PAA Self-propelled Bridge System

DEVELOPMENT
The PAA (Pont Automoteur d'Accompagnement) has been developed as a follow-up vehicle to the AMX-30 AVLB and would be used to replace the AVLB bridges to the rear of assault units, pending the arrival of engineer units with permanent bridges. This allows the AVLBs to recover their bridges and continue the advance.

Development can be traced back to the late 1950s when the West German company Eisenwerke, under contract to the Service du Matériel du Genie, built three prototype vehicles. Between 1963 and 1968 the Direction des Constructions et Armes Navales (DCAN) at Lorient and the Etablissement d'Expériences Techniques d'Angers completely redesigned the vehicle. Two prototypes were built, the first of which was completed in 1968 and the second in 1970. After extensive trials, the PAA was adopted by the French Army in 1972 and

production began at Lorient in 1973. First production vehicles were delivered to the French Army in 1974 and by early 1980 51 had been received. Production was completed in 1978.

DESCRIPTION
The PAA consists of a rigid and watertight hull of light alloy (AZ5G) construction with a removable span in two sections on the front and an access ramp at the rear. The hull is divided into three compartments, front, centre and rear. The front section is the crew compartment with the driver seated on the left and the operator on the right. This compartment is provided with an NBC and air-conditioning system. The engine compartment is in the centre and is provided with an electric pump which automatically operates as soon as water reaches a certain level. The rear compartment contains the fuel tanks.

Power is transmitted by the engine to the four road wheels through a Guinard-Clark hydrokinetic torque converter, a power-assisted Clark-Genemat gearbox and a sliding joint transmission shaft. Steering is power assisted.

The hydraulic system operates the following: retraction and extension of the forward and rear sets of wheels, locking and unlocking the forward and rear sets of wheels, tilting of the prismatic boom supporting the span, opening and closing of the two access ramp hinged links, locking and unlocking of the span on the prismatic boom, and the hoisting and lowering of the span.

The PAA can be used in two basic roles: first by laying its bridge and then leaving the bridge in place and second by laying the span and remaining in position with the vehicle acting as the ramp of the bridge.

When deployed, the four wheels of the PAA are raised off the ground and the hull is supported on shoes. The bridge and ramp has a normal width of 3·05 metres

PAA in travelling configuration being marshalled into position

PAA with Berliet GBC 8KT truck on ramp as bridge unfolds

PAA bridge being laid across dry gap

AMX-30 MBT crossing PAA bridge

but this can be increased to 3·55 metres with widening panels. These are normally carried in a Berliet GBC 8 KT (6 × 6) truck which also carries the wheel guide sections, hand-rope posts and ropes. The widening panels can be left on the vehicle for travelling, but are normally removed to reduce the overall width of the vehicle.

The removable span has a total length of 21·72 metres and consists of two symmetrical sections coupled by a hinge. The access ramp also consists of two symmetrical hinge-coupled sections which permit the access ramp to be folded on the body of the bridge when not in use. The prismatic boom is hinged at the front part of the body by a rugged hinge, and houses the hydraulically-operated hoisting, gripping and locking devices.

With the vehicle remaining in position the PAA can be used to span a gap, with soft banks, up to 17·4 metres wide, or a gap of up to 22·4 metres with hard banks. The bridge itself can span a gap, with soft banks, of up to

15·63 metres, or, with hard banks, a span of up to 20·63 metres. This bridge can be used by vehicles up to class 40 or, with precautions, class 45. By using two PAA vehicles and a special jointing section, it is possible to bridge a gap of up to 40 metres. A triangular support boom has also been developed which has an adjustable leg and is used to span 40-metre gaps.

SPECIFICATIONS
Weight:
  (loaded) 34 500 kg
  (without span but including 18 widening panels) 25 620 kg
Length:
  (travelling) 13·15 m
  (bridge unfolded) 38·25 m
Width:
  (without widening panels) 3·05 m
  (with widening panels) 3·55 m
Height: 3·99 m

Max speed: (road) 60 km/h
Range: (road) 800 km
Fording: 1·5 m
Gradient: 50%
Side slope: 20%
Turning radius: 20·5 m
Engine: Deutz V12 diesel developing 300 hp
Brakes: air/oil, 2 independent front and rear systems, disc brakes on all axles
Electrical system: 24 V
Batteries: 4

STATUS
Production complete. In service with the French Army.

MANUFACTURER
DCAN Lorient. Enquiries to Direction Techniques des Constructions Navales, 2 rue Royale, BP 1, 75200 Paris Naval, France.

Gillois Series 2 Ferry System

DEVELOPMENT
The Gillois Series 2 is a development of the Gillois Bridge and Ferry System, details of which can be found in this section under International. The Gillois Series 2 is now intended primarily as a ferry system and differs from the original version mainly in having an increased load capacity (to 45 000 kg) and in being fully powered in all aspects so that preparation time for use is reduced to five minutes. One prototype has been produced to date and the French Army has ordered 60 units. Production was scheduled to commence in early 1984.

DESCRIPTION
The layout and general description of the Gillois Series 2 follows that of the ramp unit of the original Gillois system. When travelling the vehicle has a front-mounted cab for the crew of four. The main hull is steel but the top-mounted ramp and the side walls are aluminium. All the preparation stages are now powered, including raising the side walls for inflation of the main flotation cells. Raising and lowering the ramp is also powered. For use the ramp may be placed at an angle of up to 26·5 degrees above the horizontal or 15 degrees

below. This enables the ramp to be used at a height of 3·4 metres above the horizontal or 2 metres below. The ramp and main ferry vehicle now have a load capacity of up to 45 000 kg and as the 50 square metre loading area has a width of 3·3 metres it can now carry all French Army armoured vehicles such as the AMX-30 MBT or the 155 mm GCT self-propelled gun. In the water the Gillois Series 2 is propelled by propellers that can be swivelled through 360 degrees for manoeuvring.

Although the Gillois Series 2 has a normal crew of four, only two are needed to operate the sysem.

STATUS
Prototype. Ordered for French Army (60).

MANUFACTURER
Chaudronnerie et Forges d'Alsace, 67250 Soultz-sous-Forêts, BP 11, France.

SPECIFICATIONS
Crew: 4
Configuration: 4 × 4
Weight:
  (total) approx 28 300 kg
  (front axle) approx 13 600 kg
  (rear axle) approx 14 700 kg

Length:
  (travelling) 11·28 m
  (floating, ramp extended) 19·6 m
  (ramp section) 7·753 m
Width:
  (travelling) 3·7 m
  (floating) 6·94 m
  (load area) 3·3 m
Height: 3·59 m
Loading area: 50 m²
Wheelbase: 6·2 m
Track:
  (front) 1·79 m
  (rear) 2 m
Max speed:
  (road) 60 km/h
  (water, empty) approx 12 km/h
  (water, loaded) approx 11 km/h
Range:
  (road) approx 800 km
  (water) approx 12 h
Gradient: 50%
Engine: Deutz air-cooled diesel developing 250 hp at 2100 rpm
Tyres: 21 × 25 tubeless

Matériel Amphibie de Franchissement

DEVELOPMENT
The Matériel Amphibie de Franchissement (MAF) was under competitive development as the replacement for the Gillois system currently used by the French Army. The Etablissement Technique d'Angers was in charge of the study and evaluation of the two prototypes and overall project management was under the Direction Technique des Armements Terrestres. Two prototypes have been built and have been evaluated, the petrol-engined MAF 1 bis under direction of the Lorient Board for the Construction of Naval Weapons (Direction des Constructions et Armes Navales de Lorient) and MAF 2 under the direction of the Alsace Metals and Steel Company (Chaudronnerie et Forges d'Alsace) and Eisenwerke Kaiserslautern Göppner of West Germany.

The French Army decided to provide funds for further testing of the MAF 2 after the first prototype had been completed in 1976. These trials were completed in June 1983 and while they were largely successful it was decided that some further design alterations would be required. However a shortage of defence funding has postponed further development and/or trials until at least 1990.

DESCRIPTION
The hull of the MAF is made of welded light alloy. On the

top of the vehicle, at each end, is a 12-metre jointed ramp also of welded light alloy. Before the unit enters the water airbags are positioned under hinged flaps on either side of the hull and inflated. The unit has four large wheels with low-pressure tyres and is propelled in the water by two propellers, one each end of the hull, which can be rotated through 360 degrees.

The MAF can be used both as a bridge and a ferry. As a bridge it has a 24-metre span, can take loads of up to MLC 50 normally and MLC 60 with precautions, and be used in rivers flowing at up to 2·5 metres per second.

The main differences between the two prototypes are that the MAF 1 bis has a hydrostatic wheel and propeller transmission, oleo-pneumatic suspension and independent wheel system whereas MAF 2 has a manually-operated gearbox and oleo-pneumatic suspension on a fixed axle.

STATUS
Trials completed.

MANUFACTURERS
MAF 1 bis: DCAN Lorient, Direction Technique des Constructions Navales, 2 rue Royale, BP 1, 75200 Paris Naval, France.

MAF 2: Chaudronnerie et Forges d'Alsace, 67250 Soultz-sous-Forêts, France and Eisenwerke Kaiserslautern Göppner GmbH, Barbarossastrasse 30, D-6750 Kaiserslautern, Federal Republic of Germany.

SPECIFICATIONS
Both the MAF 1 bis and MAF 2 have similar physical characteristics but specifications below relate to the MAF 2.
Crew: 4
Weight: 39 000 kg
Length: (travelling) 12·35 m
Width: (travelling) 3·6 m
Height: (travelling) 3·8 m
Track: 2·17 m
Wheelbase: 3·6 m
Max speed:
  (road) 60 km/h
  (water, loaded) 9 km/h
  (water, empty) 12 km/h
Range: (road) 700 km
Fording: (without preparation) 0·8 m
Gradient: 50%
Side slope: 30%
Engine: Deutz air-cooled diesel developing 455 hp at 2500 rpm
Electrical system: 24 V
Ferry configuration:
  (length) 36 m
  (width) 8 m
  (loading platform size) 12 × 4 m
Bridge configuration:
  (length) 24 m
  (width) 4 m

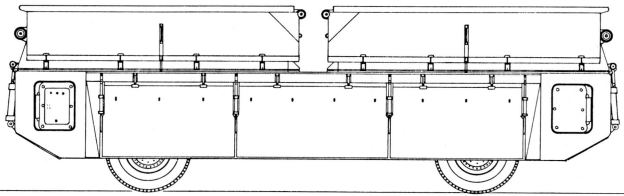

Matériel Amphibie de Franchissement 2 (MAF 2)

GERMANY, DEMOCRATIC REPUBLIC

BLG-60 Armoured Bridgelayer

DEVELOPMENT/DESCRIPTION
The BLG-60 is a joint development between East Germany and Poland and is used by their armies in place of the Czechoslovak MT-55 scissors bridgelayer. The bridge is launched in a similar fashion to the MT-55 and the reader is referred to this entry for the method of launching the bridge.

In position the bridge has a total length of 21·6 metres, a width of 3·2 metres and a height of 0·8 metre. It can span a maximum gap of 20 metres compared with the maximum span of 16 metres of the MT-55, and has a maximum capacity of 50 000 kg.

The main external differences between the MT-55 and the BLG-60 are that the surface of the BLG-60s bridge is smooth and covered in plastic (the MT-55 has a patterned surface), the bridge girder ends are closed (on the MT-55 they are open), and the pulley wheels for the scissors action operating gears are solid.

The BLG-60 is provided with an NBC system and a snorkel. Reference has also been made to a new model called the BLG-60(M), but no firm details are available at present.

SPECIFICATIONS
Crew: 2–3
Weight:
  (with bridge) 37 000 kg
  (without bridge) 31 000 kg
Length: (with bridge) 10·57 m
Width: (with bridge) 3·48 m
Height: (with bridge) 3·4 m
Ground clearance: 0·425 m
Track: 2·64 m
Track width: 580 mm
Length of track on ground: 3·84 m
Ground pressure: 0·83 kg/cm²
Max speed: (road) 50 km/h
Range: 500 km
Fuel capacity: 960 litres
Fording: 1·4 m
Gradient: 58%

BLG-60 armoured bridgelayer in travelling order

Vertical obstacle: 0·8 m
Trench: 2·7 m
Engine: V-55, V-12, water-cooled diesel developing 580 hp at 2000 rpm
Transmission: manual with 5 forward and 1 reverse gears
Electrical system: 24 V
Batteries: 4, 280 Ah
Armament: nil
Armour
glacis plate: 100 mm at 60°
upper hull side: 70 mm at 0°
hull rear: 60 mm
hull floor: 20 mm
hull roof: 30 mm

STATUS
Production complete. In service with East German and Polish armies. Bulgaria uses a version of the BLG-60 called the BLG-67, but no details of the differences, if any, are available.

MANUFACTURER
Chassis: Polish state arsenals; bridge and conversion work: East Germany.

BLG-60 armoured bridgelayer laying bridge into position

GERMANY, FEDERAL REPUBLIC

Future West German Bridging

Known future West German bridging projects include what is stated to be a novel form of rapidly-launched dry support bridge for the West German Army. As the result of some company-funded preliminary work carried out by Dornier Systems GmbH, the company has now been given an order for further definition studies regarding a folding-type bridge of variable lengths up to 42 metres.

Krupp-MAN Iguana Bridgelayer

DEVELOPMENT/DESCRIPTION
MAN Gustavsburg has recently completed the development of a new 26 metre light metal bridge which is carried and laid by a wheeled bridgelaying vehicle known as the Iguana. According to MAN, the Iguana will be able to bridge about 85 per cent of all likely obstacles and the heavy duty 8 × 8 wheeled vehicle can cross difficult terrain to reach the bridge site.

The vehicle involved is a Magirus Deutz design with a 400 hp engine and an 8 × 6 or 8 × 8 configuration. It has a crew of two, a road range of 600 to 700 km and the vehicle and bridge together weigh 33 000 kg. The bridge itself weighs 10 000 kg with an overall length of 26 metres and consists of four track girder elements each 13 metres long and 2 metres wide. Once laid, it has a carrying capacity in the MLC 60 class and is 4·01 metres wide. The laying system is designed to have a very low silhouette without the upright raised position that can advertise the presence of a bridgelaying operation and thus invite unwanted enemy attentions.

In use the vehicle is reversed into the laying position

and the stacked bridge halves are connected by automatic horizontal and vertical movements. The shifting frame, moving along the longitudinal plane and holding the bridge on rollers, is extended to the rear to rest on hydraulic jacks in the end position. A rack-and-pinion drive then engages the bridge and pushes it over the obstacle. Once extended, a hydraulically-driven arm lowers the far bridge end onto the far bank, and then the near end onto the near bank. The whole operation takes under four minutes, after which the vehicle can move away to pick up other bridges.

Preparation of banks is not normally necessary as the system can traverse and accommodate longitudinal inclinations of up to ten per cent. For transport by vehicle or air the elements of the system can be carried normally and connected to the cross-girder brackets to provide bridge halves just before use. If damaged only a single element normally needs to be changed. The bridge elements are of a commercially-available cold-hardened aluminium alloy which requires no special repair equipment.

Suitable vehicles, other than the Magirus Deutz vehicle proposed, may be used with the Iguana bridge-laying system.

STATUS
Development complete.

MANUFACTURER
Fried Krupp GmbH, Krupp Industrie-und Stahlbau, Franz-Schubert-Strasse 1–3, 4100 Duisburg-Rheinhausen, Federal Republic of Germany.

MAN Brückengeräte, D-6095 Ginsheim-Gustavsburg 1, Federal Republic of Germany.

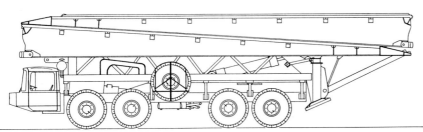
Iguana bridgelayer in travelling configuration (not to 1/76th scale)

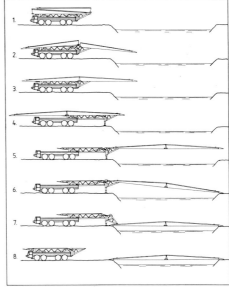
Laying phases of 26 m Iguana bridge

SPECIFICATIONS (provisional)
Bridge and Vehicle
Length: (overall) 13·4 m
Width: (overall) 4·01 m
Height: 3·922 m
Ground clearance: 0·4 m
Angle of approach/departure: 20°/25°
Total weight: 33 000 kg

Bridge
Class: MLC 60
Length: (extended) 26 m

Width: 4·01 m
Wheel tread girder width: 1·555 m
Bridge height: (at ramp tip) 0·075 m
Height: (at bridge centre) 1·1 m
Weight: 10 000 kg

Magirus Deutz vehicle
Crew: 2
Engine power: 400 hp
Max speed: (road) 70 km/h
Length: 13·4 m
Width: 2·6 m

Height: 2·73 m
(to cab roof) 2·1 m
Wheelbase: 1·5 m + 3·225 m + 1·45 m
Ground clearance: 0·4 m
Angle of approach/departure: 20°/25°
Front overhang: (from front axle) 2·5 m
Track: 2·044 m
Turning circle: 31 m
Gradient: 100%
Range: (road) 600–700 km
Weight: 23 000 kg

SAS Bridgelayer

DEVELOPMENT/DESCRIPTION
The SAS (Schnellbrücke auf Stützen) bridgelayer was developed by Magirus-Deutz with Porsche as the main sub-contractor. The development model of the SAS was manufactured, assembled and tested by the Helicopter and Communications Division of MBB and was handed over to the Federal Agency for Defence Technology and Procurement early in November 1979. It basically consists of the Biber chassis with a bridge which is 19 metres long when opened out. This bridge is composed of two parts, one 11 metres long and the other 8 metres long. The normal bridge of the Biber is 22 metres long, in two 11-metre halves. To build a bridge 85 metres long five segments are used. These are carried on two SAS units and three trucks. The segments may be removed from the trucks without using cranes. Maximum vehicle speed over the finished bridge is 15 km/h. Wheeled vehicles up to Class 50 and tracked vehicles to Class 60 can be carried.

The bridge of the SAS is operated in a similar manner to the Biber except that at the far end of the bridge are two legs which can be hydraulically extended to a maximum of 4·5 metres and unfold into the vertical position as the bridge is extended. At the end of each leg is a circular base pad which stops the leg sinking into the ground or river bed. Once the bridge has been laid in position, the bridgelayer withdraws to the rear and another SAS takes its place. Gaps of up to 85 metres can be crossed using this method. In concept the SAS is similar to the Soviet truck-mounted KMM bridgelayer, although the Germans had a similar concept based on a Panzer IV chassis as early as 1939.

SPECIFICATIONS
The basic chassis is identical to that of the Biber bridgelayer and the reader is referred to this entry for full specifications of the chassis.

STATUS
Development ceased Spring 1983.

MANUFACTURER
Chassis: Krupp MaK Maschinenbau, PO Box 9009, D-2300 Kiel 17, Federal Republic of Germany.

SAS bridge being loaded onto MAN (6 × 6) truck for transport with legs retracted

SAS bridging system extending legs into vertical position before extending them hydraulically to ground

Brückenlegepanzer Biber, Armoured Bridgelayer

DEVELOPMENT
In 1969 prototypes of two different types of bridgelayer based on the chassis of the Leopard MBT were built, known as Type A and Type B. The Type A had a telescopic beam which was extended to the far bank; the bridge was then slid across and the telescopic beam removed. Type B was of the cantilever type. The bridge was designed by Klöckner-Humboldt-Deutz, with Porsche in charge of overall development. After comparative trials, the Type B was selected for production by MaK of Kiel and the first production bridgelayers, which became known as the Biber, were completed in 1975. The official West German Army designation is the Brückenlegepanzer Biber or BRLPZ-1.

DESCRIPTION
The hull of the Biber (Beaver) is almost identical to that of the Leopard 1 MBT with the driver seated at the front of the hull on the right side and the commander in the centre, and the engine and transmission at the rear. The torsion bar suspension consists of seven road wheels with the drive sprocket at the rear and the idler at the front. There are four track return rollers. The first, second, third, sixth and seventh road wheel stations are provided with a hydraulic shock absorber. The tracks

Australian Army Biber bridgelayer in travelling order

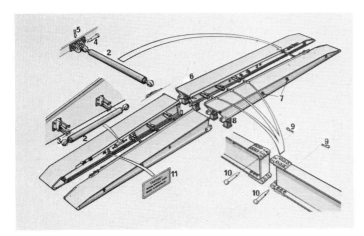

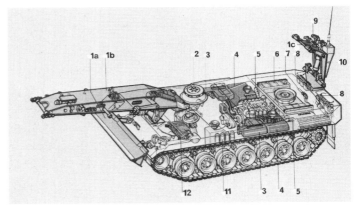

Main components of bridge carried by Biber (2) rod (3) bracket (4) connecting pin (5) lock (6) assembly (7) shackle with lock (8) support block (9) lock (10) connecting pin (11) instruction plate

Cutaway drawing of Biber chassis (1) bridge hydraulic system (a) support blade (b) main jib (c) rear jib (2) commander's cupola (3) air filter system (4) fuel tank (5) exhaust system (6) motor (7) brake valve block (8) battery (9) smoke grenade launcher system (10) antenna box with antenna (11) fire extinguisher system (12) ventilation and NBC system

are of the double pin type and have rubber pads. Standard equipment includes an NBC system.

The bridge is of aluminium construction and has a total span of 22 metres, which allows a gap of up to 20 metres to be breached. The main advantage of the Biber is that its bridge is extended horizontally rather than vertically as with the majority of bridgelayers. This means that it does not have the disadvantage of being seen from some distance away laying its bridge. The bridge may be taken up from either end and, according to MaK, allows some 60 per cent of all watercourses and most of the soil cuttings in West Germany to be crossed.

The bridge has been designed to take AFVs and other vehicles up to a maximum weight of 50 000 kg, but in an emergency it is able to take loads of up to 60 000 kg. The bridge is constructed for 49 000 crossings of MLC 16, 6800 crossings of MLC 30 and 5400 crossings of MLC 50. The bridge can be laid on longitudinal and lateral slopes of ten per cent: the opposite bank can be 2 metres higher or lower, or have a difference in inclination of ten per cent towards the bank on the laying vehicle's side.

When the Biber arrives at the ditch or river, the vehicle first lowers the support blade (which can also be used for dozing operations such as preparing a river bank) at the front of the hull, the lower half of the bridge slides forward until its end is lined up with the end of the upper half and the two sections are then locked together and extended over the gap. The bridge is lowered into position and the cantilever arm withdrawn. The Biber then raises the support blade and pulls away. The bridge can be retrieved from either end.

SPECIFICATIONS
Crew: 2
Weight:
(with bridge) 45 300 kg
(without bridge) 35 100 kg
Length:
(with bridge) 11·82 m
(without bridge) 10·56 m
Width:
(with bridge) 4 m
(without bridge) 3·3 m

Biber bridgelayer showing bridge being extended across gap

Height:
(with bridge) 3·57 m
(without bridge) 2·56 m
Ground clearance: 0·42 m
Track: 2·7 m
Track width: 550 mm
Length of track on ground: 4·236 m
Ground pressure: 0·97 kg/cm²
Max speed: (road) 62 km/h
Range:
(road) 550 km
(cross country) 400 km
Fuel capacity: 995 litres
Fording:
(without preparation) 1·2 m
(with preparation) 1·65 m
Gradient: 60%
Side slope: 30%
Vertical obstacle: 0·7 m
Trench: 2·5 m
Engine: MTU MB 838 Ca. M500 10-cylinder multi-fuel developing 830 hp at 2300 rpm
Transmission: ZF HP 250 with 4 forward and 2 reverse gears

Electrical system: 24 V
Batteries: 6, 300 Ah, charged by 3-phase generator driven from main engine
Armament: 8 smoke dischargers
Armour
nose: 70 mm at 55°
glacis: 70 mm at 60°
glacis top: 25 mm at 83°
sides upper: 35 mm at 50°
sides lower: 25 mm at 90°
hull rear: 25 mm at 88°
hull roof: 10 mm
hull floor: 15 mm

STATUS
Production complete. Production can be resumed if further orders are received. In service with Australia (5), Canada (6), West Germany (105) and the Netherlands (14). In production in Italy by OTO Melara for the Italian Army (64).

MANUFACTURER
Krupp MaK Maschinenbau, PO Box 9009, D-2300 Kiel 17, Federal Republic of Germany.

M2 Amphibious Bridging and Ferry System

DEVELOPMENT
The M2 amphibious bridging and ferry system was developed by Eisenwerke Kaiserslautern (EWK) and Klöckner-Humboldt-Deutz (KHD). First production units were delivered to the Federal German Army Pioneer battalions early in 1968.

DESCRIPTION
The M2 has a chassis of high alloy construction with the four-man crew seated in the cab at the front of the vehicle. All four wheels can be steered and the suspension is adjustable.

Before entering the water the hydraulically-operated hinged buoyancy tanks, which when travelling are on the top of the vehicle to reduce the overall width, are swung through 180 degrees into position. The decking is positioned in a few minutes by a light alloy crane which when travelling is on the centreline of the vehicle. When assembled the roadway is 7·62 metres long and 5·486 metres wide. When the roadway has been positioned the crane is traversed 90 degrees to the

Nine M2 units forming bridge across River Weser during Exercise Spearpoint (Ministry of Defence)

centre of the unit. Once in the water, the units are coupled together to form a class 50 bridge or ferry. For the latter, three M2s are required.

The M2 is fully amphibious: one of the main engines drives two 600 mm propellers for sideways propulsion while the second engine powers the 650 mm diameter steering propeller. One of the two side propellers can also be used for steering. When swimming, the cab of the M2 is to the rear and the wheels are raised to reduce drag.

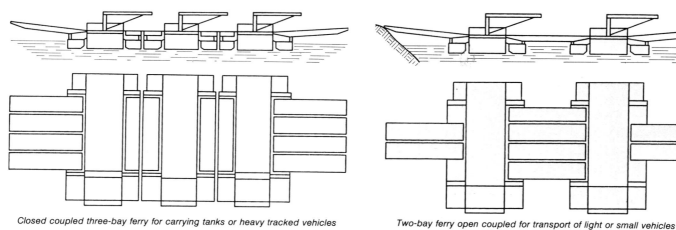

Closed coupled three-bay ferry for carrying tanks or heavy tracked vehicles   *Two-bay ferry open coupled for transport of light or small vehicles*

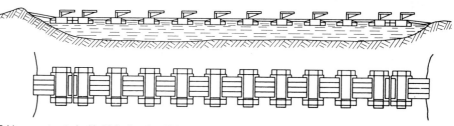

Bridge constructed with 12 ferries: 2 vehicles at each end are close coupled, remainder are open coupled

M2 used as single-bay ferry with two ramp panels on each side

British Army M2 units entering River Weser near Hameln (Ministry of Defence)

M2 of 28 Amphibious Engineer Regiment in travelling position crossing River Weser in West Germany on M2 bridge (Ministry of Defence)

SPECIFICATIONS
Crew: 4
Configuration: 4 × 4
Weight: 22 000 kg
Length: (travelling) 11·315 m
Width: (travelling) 3·579 m
Overall width: (with ramps and buoyancy tanks in position) 14·16 m
Height: (travelling) 3·579 m
Ground clearance: 0·6–0·84 m
Track:
  (front) 2·13 m
  (rear) 2·161 m
Wheelbase: 5·35 m
Max speed:
  (road) 60 km/h
  (water, single unit) 14 km/h
Range:
  (road) 1000 km
  (water) 6 h
Max gradient: 60%
Engines: Deutz Model F 8 L 714a V-8 diesels developing 178 hp at 2300 rpm each (Singapore vehicles have Deutz model F 8 L 413 F diesels developing 180 hp at 2300 rpm)
Turning circle: 25·4 m
Tyres: 16.00 × 20

STATUS
In production. In service with West Germany, Singapore and the United Kingdom. The British Army of the Rhine has one M2 Amphibious Engineer Regiment which has

two squadrons each with 30 M2 units. Each squadron has two troops each with 15 M2 units and each troop also holds four M2s that are not manned in peacetime, giving the regiment 76 M2 units in all.

MANUFACTURER
Eisenwerke Kaiserslautern Göppner GmbH, Barbarossastrasse 30, D-6750 Kaiserslautern, Federal Republic of Germany.

INDIA

Indian Bridging Vehicles

India is now known to be developing two types of wheeled bridging vehicle at the Vehicle Research and Development Establishment. The smaller of these is an 8 × 8 10 ton vehicle for general purpose bridging and the larger a special-purpose 10 × 10 25 ton vehicle. The larger vehicle will have a driver's cab at each end, 12·5 metres long and carrying a class 50 scissors-folding bridge weighing 25 tons. Power will be provided by a 12-cylinder turbo-charged diesel engine developing 700 hp at 2100 rpm, giving a maximum speed of 50 km/h. The turning circle is 25 metres.

Both vehicles are still under development and it is not yet known if a prototype of either has been constructed.

INTERNATIONAL

Gillois Bridge and Ferry System

DEVELOPMENT
The Gillois bridge and ferry system was designed by General J Gillois of the French Army with production being undertaken by the German company EWK. Further development by the company resulted in the M2 amphibious bridge and ferry system which was adopted by the British, West German and Singapore armies. The United States Army had a number of Gillois units which it called the Amphibious River Crossing Equipment (or ARCE). In the late 1950s the Americans developed their own amphibious bridge and ferry system called the Mobile Assault Bridge (MAB).

DESCRIPTION
The Gillois bridge and ferry system consists of two major units, the bridge unit and the ramp unit. Each unit has a hull of all welded construction with five compartments. The four-man crew compartment is at the front of the hull and is fully enclosed. Two compartments hold the wheels, which are retracted once the unit is afloat. The centre compartment houses the engine and air compressor units while the fifth compartment forms the bow of the unit when waterborne, or the rear of the unit when travelling on land.

Each unit has a pneumatic float on each side of the hull which is inflated before the vehicle enters the water. When inflated each float is 10·972 metres long and 1·371 metres in diameter. These floats provide stability and additional buoyancy when afloat. In daylight, with a well trained crew, it takes about 25 minutes to prepare the unit for use. When in the water the vehicle is propelled by a propeller unit at the front of the hull (crew compartment), which rests on the top of the hull when travelling on land.

Bridge unit
The bridge superstructure consists of two steel treadways with an aluminium filler panel, and has an effective length of eight metres. When travelling on land the superstructure is carried in the longitudinal position and on entering the water the superstructure is rotated through 90 degrees and widened to provide a roadway four metres wide. The filler panel is lowered hydraulically. Each treadway is equipped with a male plug at one end and a female receiver at the other end. When two superstructure units are brought together, a hydraulic lock pin cylinder mounted beneath the male plug is actuated and the pin connects the lower chord on the two adjacent treadways of the bridge units.

Ramp unit
The ramp superstructure consists of two treadway sections with an effective length of four metres. Each treadway section consists of four major components: a welded aluminium tapered ramp, a short steel deck section, two hydraulic articulator cylinders and hinged filler panels. The ramp superstructure is transported in a longitudinal position and on entering the water the ramp is rotated through 90 degrees and then widened to provide a roadway four metres wide. The ends of the short deck section are identical to the bridge unit superstructure and the two can be connected. The centre gap between the two aluminium ramp treadway sections is filled by a system of hinged panels connected to the upper chord of the short steel deck section and the aluminium ramp sections. Once the units have been joined up in the water, the hydraulic lines of the four hydraulic articulator cylinders are transferred from the ramp unit hydraulic system to the bridge unit. Once sufficient bridge units are connected to the ramp unit, the ramp is hydraulically raised and the ramp hull is removed from beneath the ramp superstructure.

When being used as a bridge, the Gillois bridge can take vehicles up to class 60 in currents of up to 2·98 metres per second. The following rafts can be constructed:

One-bay raft using the ramp unit which can carry two AMX-13 light tanks with care
Two-bay raft which can carry between 29 900 and 49 896 kg with care
Three-bay raft which can carry between 64 870 and 79 834 kg
Four-bay raft which can carry between 89 810 and 109 771 kg

Gillois vehicle entering water with roadway already through 90 degrees into position (ECP Armées)

Gillois vehicle with pneumatic floats inflated. This vehicle is a ramp unit (ECP Armées)

STATUS
Production complete. In service with the French Army.

MANUFACTURER
Eisenwerke Kaiserslautern Göppner GmbH, Barbarossastrasse 30, D-6750 Kaiserslautern, Federal Republic of Germany.

SPECIFICATIONS

	Bridge vehicle	Ramp vehicle
Crew	4	4
Configuration	4 × 4	4 × 4
Weight	26 950 kg	27 400 kg
Length (travelling)	11·861 m	11·861 m
Width (travelling)	3·2 m	3·2 m
Width (deployed)	5·994 m	5·994 m
Ground clearance	0·715 m	0·715 m
Height	3·991 m	3·991 m
Track (front)	1·79 m	1·79 m
(rear)	1·79 m	1·79 m
Wheelbase	6·197 m	6·197 m
Max speed (road)	64 km/h	64 km/h
(water)	12 km/h	12 km/h
Range	780 km	780 km
Fuel capacity	547 litres	547 litres
Gradient	50%	50%
Fording	amphibious	amphibious
Engine	Deutz, V-12, 4-cycle air-cooled diesel developing 220 hp at 2000 rpm	
Tyres	18 × 25	18 × 25
Electrical system	24 V	24 V

Gillois raft capacities
Current velocity m/s

Raft construction	0–1·463	1·524–2·012	2·04–2·49
2-bay	49 896 kg	44 900 kg	39 900 kg
3-bay	79 834 kg	72 850 kg	64 870 kg
4-bay	109 771 kg	99 800 kg	89 810 kg

ITALY

Astra Bridgelayer A26

DEVELOPMENT
In the late 1960s the Astra company of Piacenza developed a scissors bridge which could be mounted on MBT chassis such as the M47, M48, M60 or Centurion. A small number of these bridgelayers were subsequently built for the Italian (on M47 chassis) and Israeli (on Centurion chassis) armies. The M-47 E2 LP bridgelayer produced by Talbot of Spain also uses an Astra system.

DESCRIPTION
The scissors bridge is of aluminium and steel construction and is launched hydraulically over the front of the vehicle in three minutes, being launched and retrieved from either end. Launching or retrieving time inclusive of connecting and disconnecting operations is six minutes.

The bridge has an overall length of 21·4 metres and will span a clear gap of 20 metres. It is four metres wide and has a maximum capacity of 54 000 kg. Each end of the bridge is pivoted so that it can be used as a pile, which enables two bridges to be connected to span a clear gap of 36–38 metres. The bridge can be launched in the following conditions:

Max difference in level between ground under the bridge ends and ground under the vehicle during the launching and retrieving operation: 0·1 m to 0·5 m
Max difference in level between the two ends of the bridge launched: −2 m to +6 m
Max longitudinal angle between ground under the tracks and ground under the bridge during the launching and retrieving operation: ±20 per cent
Max transversal angle between the ground under the

M47 MBT chassis with Astra scissors type bridge, showing second span being used as conventional bridge

M47 MBT chassis with Astra scissors type bridge, showing end ramp being used as pile

vehicle and the ground under the bridge ends during the launching and retrieving operation: 6 per cent
Max side inclination of the vehicle during the launching and retrieving operation: 10 per cent
Max twist of the bridge loaded: 10 per cent
Inclination of end ramps: any angle up to 25 degrees plus fixed position at 85 degrees.

STATUS
Production complete. Small numbers delivered to the Israeli and Italian armies.

MANUFACTURER
Astra Veicoli Industriali SpA, Via Caorsana, 79-29100 Piacenza, Italy.

JAPAN

Type 67 Armoured Vehicle Launched Bridge

DEVELOPMENT/DESCRIPTION
The Type 67 AVLB is basically a Type 61 MBT with its turret removed and replaced by a scissors bridge. This AVLB was preceded by a trials vehicle based on a Sherman M4A3E8 tank with its turret removed and replaced by a scissors bridge.

The bridge is similar in design and construction to the American M48 AVLB bridge but is much shorter. When opened out it is 12 metres long, compared with the M48's bridge which is 19·202 metres long, and will span a gap of up to 10 metres. The bridge is opened out over the front of the Type 67 and can be picked up from either end. Launching time is between three and five minutes. The bridge has a maximum loading capacity of 40 000 kg.

The chassis is almost identical to that of the Type 61 with the driver seated at the front of the hull on the right side with three periscopes for observation and a single-piece hatch cover. The other two crew members are positioned in the centre of the hull with the engine and transmission at the rear. The suspension is of the torsion bar type and consists of six road wheels, with the drive sprocket at the front and the idler at the rear, and three track return rollers per side. Hydraulic shock absorbers are provided for the 1st, 2nd, 5th and 6th road wheel stations.

STATUS
Production complete. In service only with the Japanese Ground Self-Defence Force.

MANUFACTURER
Production was undertaken at the Maruko, Tokyo, plant of Mitsubishi Heavy Industries, but AFV production is now undertaken at the Sagamihara Plant, near Tokyo. Mitsubishi Heavy Industries, 5-1, Marunouchi 2-chome, Chiyoda-ku, Tokyo, Japan.

SPECIFICATIONS
Crew: 3
Weight: 36 700 kg
Length:
(with bridge) 7·4 m
(hull) 6·3 m
Width:
(with bridge) 3·5 m
(without bridge) 2·95 m
Height: (with bridge) 3·7 m
Ground clearance: 0·4 m
Track: 2·45 m
Track width: 500 mm
Length of track on ground: 3·7 m
Ground pressure: 0·95 kg/cm²

Type 67 AVLB in travelling order (front view)

Type 67 AVLB laying scissors bridge (Kensuke Ebata)

Max speed: (road) 45 km/h
Range: 200 km
Fording: 0·99 m
Gradient: 60%
Vertical obstacle: 0·685 m
Trench: 2·489 m
Engine: Mitsubishi Type 12 HM 21 WT V-12 turbocharged air-cooled diesel developing 600 hp at 2100 rpm

Transmission: mechanical with 5 forward and 1 reverse gears, with 2-speed auxiliary reduction unit
Electrical system: 24 V
Batteries: 4 × 12 V, 200 Ah
Armament: 1 × 7·62 mm MG
Armour
hull front: 46 mm
hull sides: 25 mm
hull rear: 15 mm

Type 70 Self-propelled Pontoon Bridge

DEVELOPMENT/DESCRIPTION

In the early 1960s the Japanese Ground Self-Defence Force issued a requirement for a self-propelled pontoon bridge system which could also be used as a ferry. Development by the Hitachi Manufacturing Company began in 1965 and the first prototype bridge was completed the following year. After further trials it was standardised as the Type 70 Self-propelled Pontoon Bridge. Most recent funding was for fiscal year 1979 when three sets were ordered.

In concept the Type 70 is similar to the West German M2. Before entering the water a hydraulic mechanism rotates the floats from the deck through 180 degrees so that they lie along the sides of the vehicle and act as floats. When afloat the wheels, which have large low-pressure tyres, are retracted into the hull to reduce water resistance. To provide additional buoyancy the wheel wells are pressurised. The vehicle is fitted with a central tyre-pressure regulation system which allows the tyre pressure to be adjusted to suit the type of ground being crossed.

Once afloat a built-in crane emplaces the three treadways and the units are joined to form a ferry bridge. The crane is also used to emplace drive-on ramps. Three Type 70 units coupled together have a capacity of 40 tonnes and a roadway width of 3·9 metres.

SPECIFICATIONS
Configuration: 4 × 4
Weight: 26 000 kg
Length: 11·4 m
Width:
  (without floats) 2·8 m
  (floats extended) 5·4 m
Height: 3·4 m

Superstructure length: 8·5 m
Superstructure width: 3·8 m
Engine: Nissan V-8 diesel developing 330 hp at 2200 rpm

Max speed:
  (road) 56 km/h
  (water)12 km/h
Gradient: 47%

Type 70 self-propelled pontoon bridge unit in travelling order (Kensuke Ebata)

Nine Type 70 units being used as bridge (MARU Magazine)

Three Type 70 units coupled together to form raft with 40-tonne capacity (MARU Magazine)

Type 81 Bridgelayer

DESCRIPTION

This is a Type 74 (6 × 6) 10 000 kg truck chassis with a hydraulically-launched bridge mounted to and laid from the rear of the cab.

To lay a bridge, which can take armoured vehicles weighing up to 40 000 kg, two vehicles are required. Each vehicle carries a bridge span in two halves with one also carrying two telescopic pier legs. The vehicle with the pier legs approaches the gap to be bridged tail first and the telescopic pier legs are attached to the end of the bottom pier half. The bottom pier half is then hydraulically driven by rams out across the gap. As the bridge half is driven across the gap the two pier legs fall downwards and when the full length of the first bridge half is reached, the top half is attached and the hydraulic rams then push the second half out to the full extent. When the full extent of the bridge half is reached the two are lowered with the telescopic pier legs resting on the ground. The legs can accommodate slight variations in level and the full weight of the two connected bridge halves is taken up by lowering the bridge to the ground at the truck end. The weight of the span in the centre is then taken onto foot pads, each about one metre square. A ramp is then fitted to the truck end ready for the second truck to approach backwards onto the bridge to lower the second half of the bridge span. This is carried out in exactly the same way as the first except that there are no pier legs. Once the second bridge section has been laid, a further drive-on ramp can be fitted to the far end and the bridge is ready for use. Some

additional levelling may be required before heavy vehicles use the bridge.

The above relates to a two-section bridge but extra sections along with extra pier legs may be employed to build longer bridges when necessary.

STATUS
In service with Japanese Ground Self-Defence Forces.

Type 81 mechanised bridge in travelling configuration (K Nogi)

SPECIFICATIONS
(chassis and bridge)
Configuration: 6 × 6
Weight: 21 800 kg
Length: 9·6 m
Width: 2·85 m
Height: 3·4 m
Max road speed: 85 km/h

NETHERLANDS

Netherlands Centurion Bridgelayer

DESCRIPTION
The Dutch Army has a number of Centurion
bridgelayers which have the American scissors bridge
as installed on the M48 and M60 bridgelayers. These
bridgelayers have an overall length of 11·2 metres (with
bridge), width of 4·02 metres (with bridge) and a height
of 3·99 metres (with bridge). The bridge itself is 19·202
metres long when opened out and will span a gap of up
to 18·288 metres.

*Centurion with scissors type bridge of Royal
Netherlands Army* (Royal Netherlands Army)

POLAND

SMT-1 Truck-mounted Treadway Bridge

DESCRIPTION
The SMT-1 consists of four 11-metre spans each of
which is carried on the rear of a Star 66 2½-ton (6 × 6)
truck (or the later Star 660 M1 or Star 660 M2). They are
launched over the front of the vehicle, unlike the Soviet
TMM and KMM treadway bridges which are launched
over the rear.

Unlike the Soviet TMM and KMM treadways, the
SMT-1 treadways do not have to be spread before
launching as they are fixed. Each treadway consists of
tubular steel trusses welded together by struts, cross-
pieces and diagonal stiffeners with steel mesh panels
mounted on the top of the trusses to form the treadway.
The Polish SMT-1 is much lighter than the Soviet TMM
treadway: the TMM weighs 666 kg and the SMT-1
210 kg per linear metre.

Each span is launched in three to five minutes with the
launching controlled from the cab. Individual spans of
the SMT are used for other purposes, for example as
ramps on pontoon bridges. The SMT-1 is often used as
a single-span bridge without the trestle legs. Additional
spans are carried on a single-axle trailer which has dual
tyres.

The SMT-1 truck-mounted treadway bridge is used in
conjunction with the PSMT-1 intermediate support
which is also used with other bridges such as the East
German BLG-60 AVLB. The PSMT-1 is positioned by
crane or floated into position. It consists of a platform
and four trestles which are adjustable in height. The
trestles are five metres long and can be folded for travel.
The PSMT-1 is capable of floating, primarily because of

the plastic foam material used in its construction. It is
transported on a single-axle trailer and can be floated
directly by reversing the prime mover into the water.

SPECIFICATIONS
Vehicle with bridge
(full technical characteristics of the Star 66 appear in the
Transport equipment section)
Cab seating: 1 + 2
Configuration: 6 × 6
Weight: 9600 kg
Length: 11·97 m
(pre-launch position) 11·67 m
Width: 3·3 m
Height: 3·15 m
Ground clearance: 0·27 m
Track: 1·804 m
Wheelbase: 2·858 m + 1·2 m
Max speed: (road) 50 km/h
Range: 500 km
Fuel capacity: 300 litres
Fording: 0·9 m
Engine: S-47, 6-cylinder water-cooled petrol develop-
ing 105 hp at 3000 rpm
Transmission: manual with 5 forward and 1 reverse
gears and 2-speed transfer case
Tyres: 11.00 × 20

Bridge
Weight: 2300 kg
Length: 11 m
Width: 3 m
Trestle leg height: adjustable to 3·5 m
Capacity: 40 000 kg

STATUS
Production complete. In service with the Polish Army.

MANUFACTURER
Polish state factories.

*SMT-1 truck-mounted treadway bridge being laid in
position*

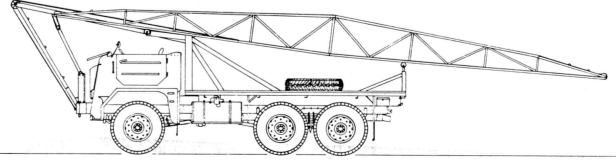

SMT-1 bridgelayer carried on Star 66 (6 × 6) truck chassis

SPAIN

M-47 E2 LP Armoured Bridgelayer

DEVELOPMENT
The M-47 E2 LP (LP – Lanzapuentes) is a prototype produced by the conversion of one of the batch of 100 M47 tanks purchased from West Germany and Italy in 1981. A single M47 has been converted to carry and launch an assault bridge design apparently based on a design produced by the Italian Astra concern. Only one prototype has been produced to date and plans to con- vert a further 25 vehicles appear to have been post- poned. The conversion was carried out by Talbot of Madrid. For details of the M-47 E2I armoured engineer vehicle and the M-47 E2R armoured recovery vehicle conversions carried out on M47 tanks by the same company see the appropriate sections in this issue.

DESCRIPTION
The M-47 E2 LP has a crew of two housed in the forward part of the hull. The main central crew compartment is now sealed off and carries part of the load of the hy- draulic ram system employed by the Astra bridgelaying mechanism. The suspension is now of the M60 type and the original engine has been replaced by a Teledyne- Continental AVDS-1790-2D diesel V-12. The trans- mission has been converted to an Allison CD-850-6A automatic.

The bridge is of the Astra A20 series type and if not actually an Italian product it has at least been inspired by Astra. It is a scissors bridge with a class 60 load classi- fication. The length is 21·4 metres and width 4 metres. Weight of the bridge is 9300 kg and it can carry a total weight of 54 000 kg. The bridge is triple hinged with one hinge in the centre for unfolding and the other two used for the ramps at either end.

No armament is carried.

STATUS
Prototype.

MANUFACTURER
Talbot, Apartado 140, Madrid, Spain.

SPECIFICATIONS
Crew: 2
Weight:
   (with bridge) 54 000 kg
   (without bridge) 44 700 kg
Length:
   (with bridge) 10·8 m
   (without bridge) 10·4 m
Width: (with bridge) 4 m
Height:
   (with bridge) 3·8 m
   (without bridge) 3·08 m
Ground clearance: 0·47 m
Track width: 0·58 m
Length of track on ground: 3·91 m
Ground pressure:
   (with bridge) 1·17 kg/cm²
   (without bridge) 0·97 kg/cm²

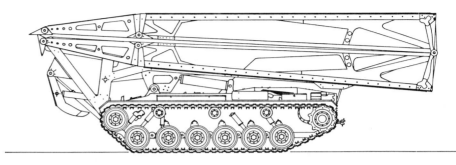

M-47 E2 LP armoured bridgelayer   *(not to 1/76th scale)*

Artist's impression of M-47 E2 LP armoured bridgelayer

Max speed: (with bridge) 43 km/h
Range: 600 km
Fuel capacity: 1500 litres
Fording: 1·2 m
Gradient: (with bridge) 45%
Vertical obstacle: 0·48 m

Trench: 2·45 m
Engine: Continental AVDS-1790-2D V-12 air-cooled 29·316 litre diesel developing 760 hp at 2400 rpm
Transmission: GMC-Allison CD-850-6A automatic
Electrical system: 24 V
Batteries: 6 × 12 V, 300 Ah

SWEDEN

Brobandvagn 941 Armoured Bridgelayer

DEVELOPMENT
The first prototype of the Brobandvagn 941 (or Brobv 941) was completed by Hägglund in 1968. It entered production late in 1972 and 17 vehicles were delivered to the Swedish Army the following year.

DESCRIPTION
The chassis and hull of the Brobv 941 are almost identi- cal to those of the Bgbv 82 armoured recovery vehicle, and the reader is referred to this entry in the *Armoured recovery vehicles* section for a full description of the chassis. The main difference between the two vehicles, apart from the bridge, is that the Brobv 941 does not have a 20 mm gun turret mounted on the left side of the crew compartment.

The gunner can fire his 7·62 mm machine gun from either his open hatch or from an alternative position on top of the bridgelaying mechanism when engaging air- craft. In addition, provision has been made for mounting a 7·62 mm machine gun in the loading platform at the rear, and on the commander's hatch. The crew of four consists of the commander, driver, gunner and operator, all seated in the front compartment.

At the front of the vehicle is a hydraulically-operated bulldozer blade, which can be used for levelling opera- tions as well as stabilising the vehicle when the bridge is

Brobv 941 in travelling order

being laid. On arriving at the river or ditch, the dozer blade is first lowered into position, a telescopic beam is extended until the point of the beam reaches the other bridge abutment, the aluminium bridge is slid across the beam which is then withdrawn so that the bridge is horizontal. The laying mechanism then returns to the travelling position, the dozer blade is raised, and the vehicle can cross the bridge. This complete operation takes less than five minutes with all the crew under

armour protection. If required, one of the crew can be outside the vehicle directing the laying of the bridge via a communications link with the vehicle. The bridge itself is 15 metres long and has a maximum load capacity of 50 000 kg.

The Brobv 941 is fully amphibious, being propelled in the water by its tracks. Before entering the water a trim vane is erected at the front of the vehicle and the electric bilge pumps switched on. When the Brobv 941 is afloat the bridge, which is buoyant, is towed behind the vehicle.

Infra-red night vision equipment is provided but the vehicle does not have an NBC system, although provision was made for one in the design of the vehicle.

STATUS
Production complete. In service only with the Swedish Army.

MANUFACTURER
AB Hägglund and Söner, Vehicle Division, S-891 01 Örnsköldsvik, Sweden.

SPECIFICATIONS
Crew: 4
Weight:
  (with bridge) 28 400 kg
  (without bridge) 21 400 kg
Length:
  (with bridge) 17 m
  (without bridge) 6·7 m
Width:
  (with bridge) 4 m
  (without bridge) 3·25 m
Height:
  (with bridge) 3·24 m
  (without bridge) 2·9 m
Ground clearance: 0·41 m
Track width: 450 mm
Length of track on ground: 3·6 m

Ground pressure: 0·84 kg/cm²
Max speed:
  (road) 56 km/h
  (water) 8 km/h
Range: 400 km
Fuel capacity: 550 litres
Fording: amphibious
Gradient: 60%
Side slope: 30%
Vertical obstacle: 0·6 m

Trench: 2·5 m
Engine: Volvo-Penta THD 100C 6-cylinder in-line turbo-charged diesel developing 310 bhp at 2200 rpm
Transmission: Volvo-Penta R61 with 8 forward and 2 reverse gears
Electrical system: 24 V
Batteries: 2 × 12 V, 152 Ah
Armament:
  1 × 7·62 mm MG
  12 smoke dischargers

Brobv 941 crossing bridge it has just laid

SWITZERLAND

Brückenlegepanzer 68

DEVELOPMENT
The first prototype of the Brückenlegepanzer 68 was based on the chassis of the Pz 61 MBT but production vehicles were based on the chassis of the later Pz 68 MBT. The prototype vehicles carried a steel bridge which was replaced on production vehicles by an aluminium bridge. Production was completed in June 1977.

DESCRIPTION
The hull of the Brückenlegepanzer 68 (Brü Pz 68) is almost identical to that of the MBT. The driver is seated at the front of the hull and is provided with three periscopes for observation and a single-piece hatch cover. The commander and the bridge operator are seated in the centre of the vehicle with the engine and transmission at the rear.

The suspension of the Brü Pz 68 is the Belleville type and consists of six road wheels with the drive sprocket at the rear and the idler at the front. There are three track return rollers. Each road wheel is independently sprung by layers of Belleville washers.

The bridge itself has an overall length of 18·23 metres and a width of 3·79 metres, maximum trackway width being 3·55 metres. Its maximum capacity is 60 000 kg but it is normally limited to a maximum load of 50 000 kg. The bridge is launched as follows: the bridgelayer approaches the obstacle and halts, the bridge is tilted forwards and a beam slid across to the far bank, the bridge is slid across the beam until it reaches the far bank and the beam is then withdrawn back into the horizontal position. The bridge takes between two and three minutes to lay and five minutes to recover.

SPECIFICATIONS
Crew: 3
Weight:
  (with bridge) 44 600 kg
  (without bridge) 38 000 kg
Length: (with bridge) 20·1 m
Width: (with bridge) 3·9 m
Height: (with bridge) 3·3 m

Ground clearance: 0·4 m
Track: 2·59 m
Track width: 520 mm
Length of track on ground: 4·22 m
Ground pressure: 0·98 kg/cm²
Max speed: (road) 55 km/h
Range:
  (road) 300 km
  (cross country) 160 km
Fuel capacity: 760 litres
Fording: 1·1 m
Gradient: 60%
Vertical obstacle: 0·75 m
Trench: 2·6 m

Engine: MTU MB 837 8-cylinder diesel developing 704 hp at 2200 rpm
Transmission: semi-automatic with 6 forward and 2 reverse gears
Electrical system: 24 V
Batteries: 4 × 6 V, 360 Ah
Armament: nil
Armour: 20–60 mm

STATUS
Production complete. In service with the Swiss Army.

MANUFACTURER
Swiss Federal Armament Factory, Thun, Switzerland.

Brü Pz 68 approaching water obstacle with bridge partially extended

Brü Pz 68 crossing its own newly-laid bridge

Brü Pz 68 completing bridge laying operation

UNION OF SOVIET SOCIALIST REPUBLICS

MTU-20 Armoured Bridgelayer

DEVELOPMENT/DESCRIPTION

The MTU-20 was introduced into the Soviet Army in the late 1960s as the replacement for the older MTU bridgelayer and is based on the T-55 tank chassis rather than the T-54 tank chassis used for the MTU.

The method of laying the bridge is almost identical to that of the MTU bridgelayer and the reader is referred to this entry for the method of launching and for a description of the chassis. Stabilisers at the nose of the tank are lowered into position before the bridge is launched.

The bridge weighs 7000 kg and is of the box construction type. It has a maximum length of 20 metres and can span a gap of up to 18 metres. It is 3·3 metres wide, 1 metre high and has a maximum capacity of 60 000 kg. When travelling the ends of the bridge are folded back through 180 degrees so that they lie on top of the bridge. They are lowered and locked in position before the bridge is launched. The bridge takes five minutes to lay in position and between five and seven minutes to recover.

As the MTU-20 is based on a T-55 chassis it is thought likely that an NBC system is installed.

SPECIFICATIONS
Crew: 2
Weight: (with bridge) 37 000 kg
Length: (with bridge) 11·64 m
Width: (with bridge) 3·3 m
Height: (with bridge) 3·4 m
Ground clearance: 0·425 m
Track: 2·64 m
Track width: 580 mm
Length of track on ground: 3·84 m
Ground pressure: 0·83 kg/cm²
Max speed: (road) 50 km/h
Range: 500 km
Fuel capacity: 960 litres
Fording: 1·4 m
Gradient: 40%
Vertical obstacle: 0·8 m
Trench: 2·7 m
Engine: V-55, V-12, water-cooled diesel developing 580 hp at 2000 rpm
Transmission: manual with 5 forward and 1 reverse gears
Electrical system: 24 V
Batteries: 4, 280 Ah

MTU-20 armoured bridgelayer opening out each end of bridge before launch

MTU-20 armoured bridgelayers in travelling position

Armament: nil
Armour
glacis plate: 100 mm at 60°
upper hull sides: 70 mm at 0°
hull rear: 60 mm
hull floor: 20 mm
hull roof: 30 mm

STATUS
Production complete. The MTU-20 is known to be in service with East Germany, Egypt, Finland, India, Israel, Syria and the Soviet Union.

MANUFACTURER
Soviet state arsenals.

MTU Armoured Bridgelayer

DEVELOPMENT
The MTU bridgelayer entered service with the Soviet Army in the late 1950s as the replacement for an older bridgelayer based on a T-34 chassis. In recent years the MTU has been replaced in many units by the MTU-20 which has the ability to span a gap of up to 18 metres compared with the 11 metres of the MTU. The MTU is also sometimes referred to as the MTU-1 and late production models use a T-55 chassis rather than the T-54 chassis.

DESCRIPTION
The MTU is based on the chassis of the T-54 MBT with its turret removed. The driver is seated at the front of the hull on the left side and is provided with two periscopes for observation and a single-piece hatch cover. The commander is seated in the crew compartment to the rear of the driver with the engine and transmission at the rear of the hull. The suspension is of the torsion bar type and consists of five road wheels with the idler at the front and the drive sprocket at the rear. There are no track return rollers.

A 12·7 mm DShKM machine gun mounted in the centre of the hull between the two treadways has to be removed before the bridge can be laid in position.

The MTU does not have an NBC system and has no deep fording capability. Auxiliary fuel drums and an unditching beam are often carried at the rear of the hull.

The bridge itself is 12·3 metres long, 3·27 metres wide and 1 metre high, and will span a gap of 11 metres. It has a maximum loading capacity of 50 000 kg.

It consists of four box-truss panels. The outer treadways are used by tracked vehicles and the inner treadways by smaller vehicles. When travelling the ramp sections of the inner treadways are folded on top of the main treadways.

The bridge is positioned as follows: a chain drive mechanism moves the bridge over the cantilever launching girder until the far bank is reached, the cantilever launching girder is depressed and lowers the span

MTU armoured bridgelayer launching its bridge across gap

onto the near bank. The bridge takes between three and five minutes to launch and can be retrieved from either end.

STATUS
Production complete. The T-54 is used by the following countries, some of which also use the MTU bridgelayer: Afghanistan, Albania, Algeria, Angola, Bangladesh, Bulgaria, China, Congo, Cuba, Cyprus, Czechoslovakia (does not use the MTU), Egypt (confirmed), Equatorial Guinea, Ethiopia, Finland (confirmed), East Germany (confirmed), Guinea, Guinea-Bissau, Hungary, India, Iraq, Israel (confirmed), North Korea, Libya, Mali, Mongolia, Morocco, Mozambique, Nigeria, Pakistan, Peru, Poland, Romania, Somalia, Sudan, Syria (confirmed), the USSR (confirmed), Viet-Nam, North and South Yemen, Yugoslavia and Zimbabwe.

MANUFACTURER
Soviet state arsenals.

SPECIFICATIONS
Crew: 2
Weight: (with bridge) 34 000 kg
Length: (with bridge) 12·3 m

Width: (with bridge) 3·27 m
Height: (with bridge) 2·87 m
Ground clearance: 0·425 m
Track: 2·64 m

Track width: 580 mm
Length of track on ground: 3·84 m
Ground pressure: 0·76 kg/cm²
Max speed: (road) 48 km/h
Range: 400 km
Fuel capacity: 812 litres
Fording: 1·4 m
Gradient: 60%
Vertical obstacle: 0·8 m
Trench: 2·7 m
Engine: V-54, V-12, water-cooled diesel developing 520 hp at 2000 rpm
Transmission: manual with 5 forward and 1 reverse gears
Electrical system: 24 V
Batteries: 4, 280 Ah
Armament: 1 × 12·7 mm DShKM MG
Armour
glacis plate: 100 mm at 60°
upper hull sides: 70 mm at 0°
hull rear: 60 mm
hull floor: 20 mm
hull roof: 30 mm

MTU armoured bridgelayer in travelling position

TMM Truck-mounted Treadway Bridge

DESCRIPTION

The TMM (heavy mechanised bridge) consists of four 10·5-metre spans each of which is carried and launched from the rear of a modified KrAZ-214 7-ton (6 × 6) or the more recent KrAZ-255B 7½-ton (6 × 6) truck. The latter model has improvements in the bridgelaying mechanism and is recognisable by the spare tyre, which is carried on the roof of the cab, rather than at the rear of the cab as on the KrAZ-214. The model carried on the KrAZ-255B (6 × 6) truck is designated the TMM-3. Three of the spans have integral mounted adjustable trestle legs; the fourth (or far-shore) span does not as it is the link between the third span and the far bank.

The system works as follows: before launching the treadway the trestle legs must be adjusted to the correct height, so the roadway is level when the bridge has been positioned. During transit they are folded and stored beneath the folded scissors span. The treadways are then spread to the full roadway width of 3·8 metres. The truck backs up to the river and the hydraulic launching girder raises the folded span to the vertical position, the span is straightened by a cable and winch system and then lowered. As it is lowered in position, the integral trestle legs swing into place. Once in position the cables are disconnected, the launching girder is brought back into the travelling position and the truck moves off. This procedure is repeated until the bridge is complete. If required the bridge can be extended past the basic four spans by further additions. The launched spans can be recovered from either end and recovery takes about the same time as launching.

A complete TMM with four spans can span a gap of up to 40 metres in 45 to 60 minutes in daylight or 60 to 80 minutes at night. These times are for an average crew and can be halved by a well-trained crew. To reduce the possibility of detection, the TMM can also be laid under

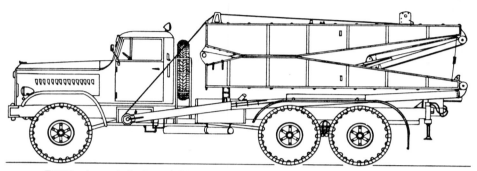

TMM truck-mounted scissors bridge in travelling position on rear of KrAZ-214 (6 × 6) truck

the surface of the water, which takes 50 per cent longer than the normal method.

SPECIFICATIONS

Vehicle with bridge
(full technical characteristics of the KrAZ-214 will be found in the *Transport equipment* section)
Cab seating: 1 + 2
Configuration: 6 × 6
Weight: 19 500 kg
Length: 9·3 m
Width: 3·2 m
Height: 3·15 m
Ground clearance: 0·36 m
Track: 2·03 m
Wheelbase: 4·6 m + 1·4 m
Max speed: (road) 55 km/h
Range: 530 km
Fuel capacity: 450 litres
Fording: 1 m
Engine: YaMZ M206B, 6-cylinder water-cooled diesel developing 205 bhp at 2000 rpm

Transmission: manual with 5 forward and 1 reverse gears and 2-speed transfer box
Tyres: 15.00 × 20

Bridge
Weight: 7000 kg
Length: 10·5 m
Width: 3·8 m
Trestle leg length: 3 m
Capacity: 60 000 kg

STATUS

Production complete. In service with members of the Warsaw Pact including Bulgaria, East Germany, Hungary, and other armed forces including China and Yugoslavia. The Bulgarian Army has developed a modified bridge using tubular section metal parts. It is not known if it has been adopted or produced in quantity.

MANUFACTURER

Soviet state factories.

TMM-3 truck-mounted scissors bridge being lowered into position, showing front wheels of KrAZ-255B (6 × 6) truck off ground as centre of gravity is well to rear when bridge is being lowered into position (TASS)

KMM Truck-mounted Treadway Bridge

DESCRIPTION

The KMM (mechanised treadway bridge) consists of five seven-metre spans each of which is carried and launched from the rear of a modified ZIL-157 2½-ton (6 × 6) truck. Four of these spans have integral mounted adjustable trestles while the fifth (or far-shore) span does not as it is the link between the fourth span and the far bank.

Each trestle has a pair of octagonal shoes with a tip that protrudes about 0·6 metre below the shoe. When buried in the soil the tip provides additional stabilising strength to the bridge support. When travelling the trestle shoes are detached from the trestle columns.

The system works as follows: before launching the treadway, the trestle legs must be adjusted to the correct height, so the treadway is level when the bridge has been positioned, and the treadway is spread to the full roadway width of 2·95 metres. Each clear span can bridge a gap of 6 metres and a set of five spans can bridge 34 metres. Bridge capacity is reported to be 12 000 kg. The truck then backs up to the river, and the span is raised hydraulically to the vertical with the launching girder. Once in this position, the launching girder serves as a brace for the cables which support the downward movement of the span. Once the launch has been completed, the launching girder is lowered back to the travel position. The procedure is repeated with more spans until the far bank has been reached. The launched spans can be recovered from either end with recovery taking about the same time as launching.

A single KMM can span a gap of up to 9·5 metres and can be launched in about 15 minutes. A complete five-span KMM bridge can span a gap of up to 35 metres in 45 to 60 minutes in daylight, or 60 to 80 minutes at night. These times are for an average crew and can be halved by a well-trained crew. If required the KMM can also be laid under water to reduce the possibility of detection, which takes approximately 50 per cent longer than the normal method.

SPECIFICATIONS

Vehicle with bridge
(full technical characteristics of the ZIL-157 will be found in the *Transport equipment* section)
Cab seating: 1 + 2
Configuration: 6 × 6
Weight: 8800 kg
Length: 8·3 m
Width: 3·15 m
Height: 3·36 m
Ground clearance: 0·31 m
Track:
(front) 1·755 m
(rear) 1·75 m
Wheelbase: 3·665 m + 1·12 m
Max speed: (road) 40 km/h
Range: 430 km

Fuel capacity: 215 litres
Max gradient: 28%
Fording: 0·8 m
Engine: ZIL-157K 6-cylinder water-cooled petrol engine developing 109 hp at 2800 rpm
Transmission: manual with 5 forward and 1 reverse gears and 2-speed transfer box
Tyres: 12.00 × 18

Bridge
Weight: 1420 kg
Length: 7 m
Width:
(without trestle leg) 2·95 m
(with trestle leg) 3·95 m

Trestle leg height: 1–3 m (adjustable)
Capacity: 15 000 kg
Crossing speed:
(tracked vehicles) 1 km/h
(wheeled vehicles) 15–20 km/h
Minimum distance between crossing vehicles: 15 m

STATUS

Production complete; replaced in many front-line units by the TMM truck-mounted treadway bridge. In service with members of the Warsaw Pact and other armed forces including China.

MANUFACTURER

Soviet state factories.

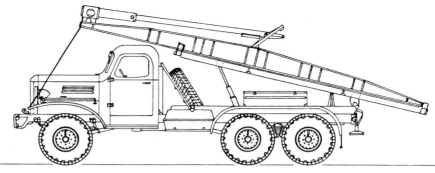

KMM truck-mounted treadway bridge on ZIL-157 (6 × 6) truck

KMM truck-mounted treadway bridge on ZIL-157 (6 × 6) truck with TMM truck-mounted treadway bridge on KrAZ-255B (6 × 6) truck behind (Egyptian Ministry of Defence)

UNITED KINGDOM

Chieftain Armoured Bridge Launcher

DEVELOPMENT

The Chieftain AVLB (FV4205) was developed as the replacement for the Centurion AVLB (FV4002) and the Centurion ARK (FV4016), both of which have been phased out of front-line British Army service. Development of the Chieftain bridgelayer began in 1962, but owing to some necessary redesign, the first production vehicles were not delivered to the army until 1974. Design work of the AVLB was carried out by the Military Vehicles and Engineering Establishment, AP Precision Products and the Hydraulic Controls Department of Tubes (Birmingham).

DESCRIPTION

The hull of the AVLB is similar to that of the basic MBT. The driver is seated at the front of the hull and is provided with a single-piece hatch cover and a periscope. The commander and radio operator are behind the driver. The engine and transmission are at the rear of the hull. The suspension is of the Horstmann type and consists of three bogies per side, each bogie with two sets of road wheels and a set of three horizontal springs. The first and last road wheel stations have a hydraulic shock absorber. The drive sprocket is at the rear and the idler at the front, with three track return rollers. The top half of the track is covered by armoured skirts which are removable for maintenance. The Chieftain AVLB has an NBC system.

The Chieftain AVLB can have either a No 8 or a No 9 Tank Bridge, the latter manufactured by Laird.

Chieftain AVLB laying No 8 tank bridge (T J Gander)

The No 8 bridge is carried folded and is launched over the front of the vehicle. The hull-mounted hydraulic pump, which is driven from a PTO on the main engine, operates five cylinders arranged to launch the bridge in three manually sequenced stages. Once the clamps have been removed the launching can begin. The Stage 1 cylinders pivot the folded bridge about the forward part of the glacis casting. This operation is continued until

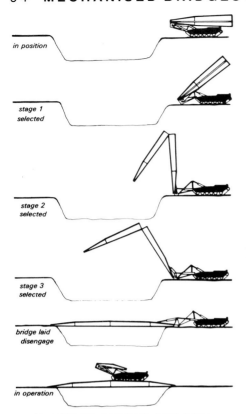

in position

stage 1
selected

stage 2
selected

stage 3
selected

bridge laid
disengage

in operation

Launching sequence for No 8 tank bridge

Chieftain AVLB with hydraulic rams extended after laying bridge and crossing Medium Girder Bridge (T J Gander)

Chieftain AVLB carrying No 9 tank bridge (Ministry of Defence)

Chieftain AVLB carrying No 8 tank bridge (T J Gander)

the launching pad meets the ground or Stage 1 cylinders reach the end of their stroke, when the folded bridge will be at an angle of about 30 degrees to the horizontal. The Stage 2 cylinders then tilt the launching pad on the ground until approximately level. At this point the bridge is partly scissored by the rods connecting the central quadrant to the launching frame and is approximately vertical. Once the Stage 2 cylinders have reached the end of their strokes, the single Stage 3 cylinder is actuated causing the bridge to scissor further until the far end reaches the required bank height. At this point the rods slacken and on further lowering the bridge becomes a rigid connection at its centre point. The rods are then free and can be detached using the remotely operated release mechanism, thus separating the rods from the launching structure. The tank then reverses and the launching structure is removed from the bridge. The tank retracts all its cylinders and then either moves to the rear to pick up another bridge or crosses the bridge and picks up the bridge from the other end. The launch normally takes between three and five minutes, with recovery of the bridge taking about ten minutes.

The bridge girders and launching structure are made of high-strength nickel-alloy maraging steel developed by the International Nickel Company. The deck and kerbing are of weldable aluminium alloy. The bridge is made up of two tracks, each 1·62 metres wide, with a 0·76-metre centre gap between. Each track is divided into four parts, two toe pieces each 4·55 metres long and two centre pieces each 7·6 metres long. A hinge is provided at each joint. The bridge has a maximum capacity of class 60 and Land-Rovers and similar small vehicles can cross on a single track, allowing two-way traffic with vehicles of this size. By hinging the 4·55-metre long toes of the bridge and dropping them at will, it is possible to cater for a range of bank conditions. A bank-sensing device is incorporated in the ramp sections, and a gap range finder is under development.

The No 9 bridge consists of two interconnected trackways 13·411 metres long and 1·62 metres wide, with a gap between them of 0·76 metres. Total effective roadway width is 4·01 metres. The bridge takes between three and five minutes to launch and can be recovered from either end. It is launched in three stages: Stage 1 raises the bridge from the horizontal to an angle of 45 degrees, Stage 2 raises it to the vertical and Stage 3 lowers it to the horizontal. The launching arm is then disengaged and the vehicle is reversed away and the launching structure retracted.

Each Chieftain bridgelayer normally has one No 8 and one No 9 tank bridge, one carried on the vehicle and the other on a specially adapted Scammell prime mover towing a semi-trailer.

Some Chieftain bridgelayers have been observed carrying the same type of mine plough as that fitted to the Centurion Mk 5 AVRE (see page 9).

STATUS
In service with the British Army and the Iranian Army. Production as required.

MANUFACTURER
Chassis: Royal Ordnance Factory, Leeds.
 Enquiries to Ministry of Defence, ROF Marketing, St. Christopher House, Southwark Street, London SE1 0TD, England.

SPECIFICATIONS
(with No 8 bridge)
Crew: 3
Weight: 53 300 kg
Length: 13·741 m
Width: 4·165 m
Height: 3·923 m
Ground clearance: 0·5 m

Track width: 610 mm
Length of track on ground: 4·8 m
Ground pressure: 0·9 kg/cm²
Max speed: (road) 48 km/h
Range: 400 km
Fuel capacity: 950 litres
Fording: 1·066 m
Gradient: 60%
Vertical obstacle: 0·9 m
Trench: 3 m
Engine: Leyland L60, 2-stroke, compression ignition, 12-cylinder vertically opposed multi-fuel developing 730 hp at 2100 rpm
Transmission: TN12 with 6 forward and 2 reverse gears, plus emergency mechanical selection for second gear forward and low reverse
Electrical system: 28·5 V (24 V nominal) dc
Batteries: 4 × 12 V, 200 Ah
Armament: 2 × 7·62 mm GPMGs

No 8 Tank Bridge
Overall length: 24·384 m
Centre section length: 7·62 m
Ramp end length: 4·572 m
Overall width: 4·165 m
Roadway width: 4·012 m
Centre gap: 0·762 m
Depth of centre section: 0·914 m
Max span:
 (good banks) 22·86 m
 (soft banks) 22·25 m
Weight: 12 200 kg

No 9 Tank Bridge
Overall length: 13·411 m
Overall depth: 0·914 m
Overall width: 4·165 m
Max clear span: (firm bank) 12·192 m
Weight: 9144 kg

Vickers Armoured Bridgelayer

DEVELOPMENT
Preliminary design work on the Vickers Armoured Bridgelayer (VAB) was started during the late 1970s to meet the requirement for a family of support vehicles for the Vickers main battle tank which was being ordered in increasing numbers. The first order for two VABs was placed by Nigeria in 1981.

DESCRIPTION
The hull, automotive and running gear components of the VAB are based on the Vickers MBT, with modifications where required to accommodate the changed role from tank to bridgelayer. The hull structure is divided into three main sections. The forward compartment houses the commander and driver. The centre section contains the radio operator, communications equipment and stowage for personal equipment. The power-pack and transmission are in the rear compartment.

The VAB is designed to transport, launch and recover a tank bridge, 13·41 metres long, with a military load bridge classification of 60/70. The bridge launching equipment is hydraulically operated with the power provided by a pump driven from a power take-off from the main engine. The launching operation is in four stages:
 bridge securing and clamping devices released
 bridge launched hydraulically
 release of bridge from launching structure
 vehicle reverses to withdraw clear of bridge.
To recover the bridge after use, the bridgelayer vehicle is aligned with the bridge so that the launching arm engages with the bridge lifting brackets. The hydraulic lifting mechanism then recovers the complete bridge onto the roof of the vehicle ready for re-use.

STATUS
Prototype under construction. On order for Nigeria (2).

MANUFACTURER
Vickers Limited, Defence Systems Division, Scotswood Road, Newcastle-upon-Tyne NE99 1CP, England.

SPECIFICATIONS
Crew: 3
Weight: (with bridge) 43 910 kg

Model of Vickers armoured bridgelayer (T J Gander)

Length: (with bridge) 13·7 m
Width: (with bridge) 4·16 m
Height: (with bridge) 3·26 m
Ground clearance: 0·432 m
Tracks:
 (distance between centres) 2·52 m
 (width) 521 mm
 (length on ground) 4·28 m
Ground pressure: 0·94 kg/cm²
Max speed: (road) 50 km/h
Range: (road at 32·2 km/h) 600 km
Fuel capacity: 1000 litres
Fording: 1·1 m
Gradient: 60%

Side slope: 30%
Vertical obstacle: 0·914 m
Trench: 3 m
Bridge:
 (overall length) 13·41 m
 (overall width) 4·16 m
 (weight) 8300 kg
 (classification) 60/70
Engine: Rolls Royce TCE 12-cylinder engine developing 750 bhp at 2300 rpm
Transmission: TN12 Mk V5 with 6 forward and 2 reverse gears
Electrical system: 24 V
Armament: 1 × 7·62 mm MG on commander's cupola

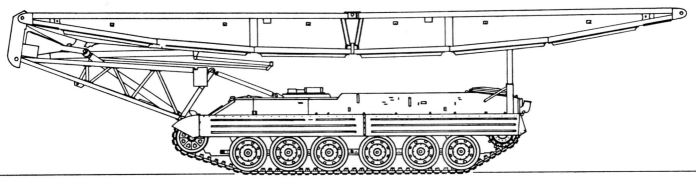

Side view of Vickers armoured bridgelayer (provisional drawing)

UNITED STATES OF AMERICA

M48 and M60 Armoured Vehicle Launched Bridges

DEVELOPMENT
In the 1950s the standard AVLB of the United States Army was the M48A2 AVLB. This was an M48 MBT chassis fitted with a scissors bridge designed by the United States Army Engineer Research and Development Laboratories (now the US Army Mobility Equipment Research and Development Center) at Fort Belvoir. Production of the M48 was completed in 1959 and from 1963 the chassis of the M60 MBT was used. The chassis of these two vehicles is almost identical, the major difference being the type of engine. The M48, M48A1 and M48A2 were all powered by a 12-cylinder petrol engine which developed between 810 and 825 hp at 2800 rpm, while the M48A3 was powered by a 12-cylinder diesel (AVDS-1790-2A) engine which developed 750 hp at 2400 rpm, giving the vehicle an increased operational range. In fiscal year 1978 the United States Army requested $20·9 million to convert 136 M48A1 and M48A2 tanks into M48A5 AVLBs (these vehicles now have M60 AVLB launcher components and the AVDS-1790-2D engine).

DESCRIPTION
The basic chassis of the M60 AVLB is almost identical to that of the M60 MBT with the crew compartment at the front (the original crew compartment has been sealed off and now supports the overhead cylinder) and the engine and transmission at the rear. Early M48 AVLBs had two turrets each with a 0·50 Browning M2 machine gun, but they were later removed and replaced by two conventional hatch covers. The crew of two consists of the driver and the commander.

The suspension is of the torsion bar type and consists of six road wheels with the idler at the front and the drive sprocket at the rear, with three track return rollers. Hydraulic shock absorbers are fitted at the first, second and sixth road wheel stations.

The bridge weighs 13 380 kg and is made of aluminium. It is carried folded and launched over the front of the vehicle hydraulically as follows: the AVLB is driven up to the obstacle and halted, the bridge is raised hydraulically into the vertical, unfolded and lowered into place and the launcher detached. The bridge takes three minutes to launch and can be recovered from either end. Recovery time is between 10 and 60 minutes depending on the ground conditions. The bridge has an overall length of 19·202 metres and can span a gap of up to 18·288 metres. Its maximum capacity is 54 431 kg.

VARIANTS
The US Army has advised *Jane's Military Vehicles and Ground Support Equipment* that the 18·288-metre and 27·43-metre M60 AVLBs are no longer being developed. Details of these were given in the 1981 edition on page 80/81.

As part of the International 'Bridging in the 1980s' programme carried out by the USA, West Germany and the United Kingdom, an M48 tank chassis was modified to carry a 31-metre bridge employing novel construction methods and materials. Although a prototype was produced this project was terminated with the International agreement in June 1981. For a photograph of this vehicle see page 69 of the 1982 edition of *Jane's Military Vehicles and Ground Support Equipment*.

M48 AVLB crossing part of Bridging System for 1980s dry bridge

M60 AVLB opening bridge (US Army)

SPECIFICATIONS
M60 AVLB
Crew: 2
Weight:
(with bridge) 55 205 kg
(without bridge) 41 730 kg
Length:
(with bridge) 11·28 m
(chassis) 8·648 m
Width:
(with bridge) 4·002 m
(chassis) 3·64 m
Height:
(with bridge) 3·9 m
(without bridge) 3·04 m
Ground clearance: 0·36 m
Track: 2·921 m
Track width: 711 mm
Length of track on ground: 4·235 m
Ground pressure: 0·92 kg/cm²
Max speed: (road) 48·28 km/h
Range: 500 km
Fuel capacity: 1420 litres
Fording: 1·219 m
Gradient: 30%

Vertical obstacle: 0·914 m
Trench: 2·59 m
Engine: Continental AVDS-1790-2A or AVDS-1790-2D 12-cylinder diesel developing 750 bhp at 2400 rpm
Transmission: Allison CD-850-6 with 2 forward and 1 reverse ranges
Electrical system: 24 V
Batteries: 6 × 12 V, 100 Ah
Armament: nil
Armour
hull front: 101–120 mm
hull sides front: 76 mm
hull sides and rear: 51 mm
hull top: 57 mm
hull floor: 12·7–63 mm
hull rear: 44 mm

STATUS
Production of the M60 AVLB is undertaken as required. Current users are known to include West Germany, Israel, Spain and the USA.

MANUFACTURER
M60 chassis: General Dynamics, Land Systems Division, PO Box 1901, Warren, Michigan 48090, USA.

Mobile Assault Bridge/Ferry

DEVELOPMENT
The Mobile Assault Bridge (MAB) was developed from 1959 by the United States Army Engineer Research and Development Laboratories at Fort Belvoir, Virginia (now the United States Army Mobility Equipment Research and Development Command). The first production batch had hulls of riveted construction. A total of 32 end bays and 66 interior bays were delivered to the Army between April 1963 and December 1967. The basic vehicle was manufactured by the FMC Corporation of San Jose, California, with the interior and end bridge bays being built by the Consolidated Diesel Electric Corporation of Schenectady, New York.

After the initial batch of MABs was built, a product improvement programme was initiated which was completed in September 1970. This version has an all-welded hull and an improved electrical and hydraulic system. A total of 220 MABs of the improved design were built for the United States Army between 1973 and 1976.

The MAB is issued on the scale of 24 units for each division and non-divisional bridge units. The total requirement, for 298 units to equip NATO earmarked

Six-bay MAB raft carrying two M113 APCs and one tank transporter carrying an M60 MBT (US Army)

units, was completed with fiscal 1974 funding. It was for 44 MAB end bays at a cost of $1·5 million, 88 interior bays at $1·6 million and 132 MAB transporters at $18·4 million.

DESCRIPTION
The MAB consists of a 4 × 4 transporter which is fitted with either an interior bay or an end bay superstructure. These two types of superstructure can be interchanged,

with the aid of a crane, in approximately 15 minutes. The hull is of all aluminium construction which is either welded or riveted together. The sides and deck are 3 mm thick while the bottom, bow and stern are 4·7 mm thick. Reinforcing ribs provide additional strength to the sides and bottom of the transporter.

The crew consists of three: a driver who is also the bridge crew chief, an assistant driver who is also the bridge pilot, and a crewman. The three-man watertight cab is mounted at the front of the hull and can be removed for transportation if required. Entrance to the cab is by two hatches in the roof and rear of the cab.

The air compressor provides power for the windscreen wiper, tyre inflation and brake system. The MAB has two hydraulic systems. The high pressure system provides power for positioning the superstructure, raising and lowering the wheels and operating the capstans. The low pressure system operates the power steering (all four wheels can be steered), marine drive functions and the air blower for the wheel-well pressurisation. Each MAB has four electrically-operated bilge pumps, which are located at the four corners of the engine compartment and have a combined capacity of 507 litres a minute.

Two hydraulically-operated capstans are provided, one on the forward and one on the aft deck, to pull units together for pinning during superstructure connection. The capstans have a capacity of 2268 kg at 15·24 metres per minute. An anchor with 60·96 metres of line is stowed on the top of the cab.

The MAB is propelled in water by a single 711 mm propeller which is mounted at the rear of the hull. This has a maximum thrust of 2268 kg and when in the travelling position is swung up horizontally. The propeller system can be rotated 360 degrees for steering and reversing. Once in the water, the wheels are raised and the propeller lowered into position. Draught when loaded is 1·066 metres.

The interior bay superstructure is constructed of welded steel girders and an extruded aluminium decking. It is carried parallel to the axis of the hull for road travel and is rotated 90 degrees for use during water operations. When extended it has an effective length of 7·924 metres and is 3·657 metres wide. After the 228 mm kerbs are raised, the bridge deck has an overall width of 4·224 metres.

The end bay superstructure is constructed of aluminium girders with aluminium decking and consists of two sections hinged together. The ramp section is 7·315 metres long and 3·657 metres wide with the kerbs down. The combined ramp and deck section is 10·972 metres long. The superstructure can be rigged before entering the water and can be rotated either to the left or the right. The ramp can be articulated to reach different bank heights down to and including 0·914 metre below water level.

The MAB can be used for two basic roles, either as a ferry unit, or as a floating bridge. Ferries and bridges are assembled by joining successive MAB units. In ferry assembly an end bay and an interior bay are jointed to form a double bay, two of which are then joined to form a four-unit ferry which can be used to carry a 60-ton load at 12·875 km/h.

Bridges are constructed by connecting units and then lowering the ramps from the end bays to the shore. The

Mobile Assault Bridge in travelling position

combined crews can assemble a four-unit ferry in about six minutes, and dismantle it in about four minutes.

In a stream, bridges can be assembled at the rate of 4·572 to 6·096 metres per minute and dismantled at the rate of 4·572 to 7·62 metres per minute. When assembled the bridge has a maximum capacity of 60 tons with a gap of at least 30·48 metres between MBTs and other heavy vehicles crossing.

SPECIFICATIONS
Crew: 3
Configuration: 4 × 4
Weight:
(basic vehicle) 15 386 kg
(vehicle with interior bay) 21 850 kg
(vehicle with end bay) 24 599 kg
Length: 13·029 m
Width:
(travelling) 3·657 m
(over wheels) 2·844 m
Height:
(travelling, interior bay) 3·327 m
(travelling, end bay) 3·529 m
Ground clearance: 0·457 m

Track: 2·336 m
Wheelbase: 5·943 m
Angle of approach/departure: 25°/25°
Max speed:
(road) 64·37 km/h
(water) 16·093 km/h
Range:
(land) 596 km
(water) 185 km
Fuel capacity: 378 litres
Gradient: 60%
Side slope: 20%
Fording: amphibious
Engine: 335 hp diesel
Electrical system: 24 V
Batteries: 4 × 12 V

STATUS
Production complete. In service with Belgium, Israel and the USA.

MANUFACTURER
ConDiesel Mobile Equipment Division, CONDEC Corporation, 84 Progress Lane, Waterbury, Connecticut 06705, USA.

Heavy Assault Bridge (HAB)

DEVELOPMENT
The Heavy Assault Bridge (HAB) is the outcome of concept evaluation work by the US Army that followed on from the cancellation of the 'Bridging in the 1980s' programme in 1981. The result of the evaluation was that a new heavy assault bridge with a class 70 load classification would be required. A minimum gap-crossing capability of 30 metres was specified. A request for quotations was issued to industry and from the resultant designs the US Army has selected the submission from BMY (Bowen-McLaughlin-York) with Israel Military Industries as a major subcontractor. BMY were awarded the contract in July 1983 and were given 35 months in which to develop a working prototype for delivery to the US Army. On delivery the Army will immediately commence a 12-month test period. The first prototype is expected to be ready in 1986 with a possible in-service date of 1994.

DESCRIPTION
The HAB will be based on the hull of a turretless M1 Abrams tank. A two-man crew is anticipated and they will not have to leave the vehicle for any part of the bridgelaying operation. The intended bridge will be a double-fold design from Israel Military Industries and will be some 32 metres long when extended, although a greater length, if possible, has been requested. The bridge construction will be high-strength aluminium and composite materials; the aluminium is field-weldable for repairs. To further simplify repairs in the field the bridge will be made from three basic components that will be interchangeable. The use of lightweight materials

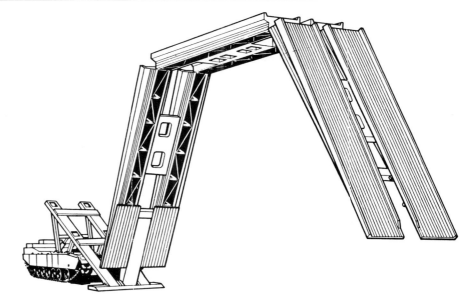

Artists impression of BMY submission for Heavy Assault Bridge (HAB)

means that the HAB will be some 4990 kg lighter than the M60 AVLB.

STATUS
Development. Prototype to be ready by early 1986.

CONTRACTORS
BMY, PO Box 1512, Pennsylvania 17405, USA.
Israel Military Industries, PO Box 7055, Tel Aviv, Israel.

Light Assault Bridge (LAB)

DEVELOPMENT/DESCRIPTION
In early 1983 the US Army Mobility Equipment Research and Development Command (MERADCOM) awarded Foster-Miller Associates of Waltham, Massachusetts, a contract for the design and production of three prototypes of a new assault bridge for the US Army's projected Light Infantry Division. The new bridge is known as the Light Assault Bridge (LAB). The contract

is worth $766,000 and is the first increment of a four-year $4·2 million contract. The first prototype is planned for completion in June 1984 with the other two to be delivered in January 1985.

The LAB will be 25 metres long and will be capable of carrying loads up to class 30. It will be of the double-fold scissors design and will be transported on and launched from a semi-trailer that can be towed by any vehicle capable of towing up to 6800 kg. The bridge construction will be from aluminium and the approximate weight

will be 4 US tons. Two men can set up the bridge in about five minutes. It will be air transportable in a C-141 Starlifter transport aircraft.

STATUS
Development. First prototype scheduled for June 1984.

CONTRACTOR
Foster-Miller Associates, Waltham, Massachusetts, USA.

YUGOSLAVIA

Truck-mounted Scissors Treadway Bridge

DESCRIPTION
The Yugoslav truck-mounted scissors bridge consists of three 13-metre spans carried and launched from the rear of a modified FAP 2220BDS (6 × 4) truck.

The system is laid in a similar manner to the Soviet TMM truck-mounted scissors treadway bridge and has similar capabilities. An advantage of the Yugoslav bridge is that its trestle legs can be extended to a maximum of four metres, whereas the TMM's trestle legs can be extended to only three metres, enabling the bridge to be used for deeper crossings.

The Yugoslav treadway bridge is laid as follows: before launching the treadway, the trestle legs are adjusted to the correct height so that the roadway is level when the bridge is in position; the truck then backs up to the river and the treadway is raised to the vertical position. The span is then straightened and lowered into position and at the same time the trestle legs swing into place. Once this is complete, the truck drives off and the procedure is repeated until the bridge is complete. Each individual span takes five to six minutes to lay in position and can be recovered from either end. Recovery takes about the same time as launching. A complete three-span bridge will span a river up to 36 metres wide.

SPECIFICATIONS
Vehicle with bridge
(full technical characteristics of the FAP 2220BDS will be found in the *Transport equipment* section)
Cab seating: 1 + 1
Configuration: 6 × 6
Weight: 20 000 kg
Length: 8·2 m
Width: 2·5 m

Yugoslav truck-mounted scissors treadway bridge in travelling position on rear of FAP 2220BDS (6 × 4) truck

Height: 2·56 m
Track:
(front) 1·97 m
(rear) 1·745 m
Wheelbase: 3·12 m + 1·2 m
Max road speed: 60 km/h
Range: 300 km (estimate)
Fuel capacity: 200 litres
Engine: Famos 2F/002A 6-cylinder water-cooled diesel developing 200 hp
Tyres: 11.00 × 20

Bridge
Length: 13 m
Width: 2·5 m
Trestle leg length: 4 m

STATUS
In service with the Yugoslav Army.

MANUFACTURER
Yugoslav state factories.

TACTICAL FLOATING BRIDGES AND FERRIES

AUSTRIA

Aluminium Footbridge

DESCRIPTION
This consists of a string of aluminium hollow-plate floats connected to form a flush deck walkway without any additional superstructure. Each float is reinforced internally with truss stiffeners and can support a load of 136 kg in the water. The deck surface is covered with a plastic material.

The footbridge is assembled by joining the floats end-to-end with a pot-shaped connecting device attached to the adjoining corners, which also float. In a strong current an additional float is added either side of the bridge at intervals. Guy ropes extending from the eyelets on the connectors to the shore anchor the bridge.

STATUS
Believed to be in service with the Austrian Army.

SPECIFICATIONS
Float
Weight: 81 kg
Length: 5 m
Width: 1·2 m
Depth: 0·13 m

CZECHOSLOVAKIA

LMS Light Pontoon Bridge

DESCRIPTION
The LMS light pontoon bridge is similar in design to the larger Czechoslovak SMS medium/heavy pontoon bridge. Both the centre and bow pontoons are of aluminium. The centre pontoon is fully enclosed while the bow pontoon has an open deck. Once the pontoons are in the water they are assembled, balks added and bolted together, and then the trackway is added, which can be of the full width roadway type, or a dual trackway, the latter being more common. The LMS can also be used as a raft with the following types being constructed: 10 ton, 15 ton, 20 ton and 24 ton. The rafts are propelled by a 22 hp outboard motor and can attain a maximum speed in the water of 11 km/h.

A complete LMS light pontoon bridge set consists of 48 bow and 24 centre sections, which are carried in Praga V3S (6 × 6) 3-ton trucks.

SPECIFICATIONS

	Bow pontoon	Centre pontoon
Weight	470 kg	450 kg
Length	5·43 m	4 m
Width	2·02 m	2·02 m
Depth	0·8 m	0.8 m

Bridge construction

Bridge type	15t	20t
Roadway width	3 m	3 m
Bridge length	92 m	92 m
Pontoon sections per support	3	3
Assembly time	40 minutes	n/a

STATUS
Production complete. In service with the Czechoslovak Army.

MANUFACTURER
Czechoslovak state factories.

SMS Heavy Pontoon Bridge

DESCRIPTION
The SMS pontoon bridge is classified as a medium bridge by the Czechoslovaks although by American standards it is a heavy pontoon bridge. It can also be used as a raft.

A Praga V3S (6 × 6) 3-ton truck can carry a pontoon unit. This is of all steel construction and is made up of two bow sections and one centre section. For travelling, the two bow units nest on top of each other. A Tatra 111 (6 × 6) 10-ton truck carries the deck and balk for three complete pontoon units.

The centre pontoon has a fixed deck while the bow pontoons have a removable deck, but this is not always fitted in place. The bow pontoon is also provided with a winch. The pontoons have to be unloaded from the truck by crane and the SMS bridge therefore has a slower rate of construction than other pontoon bridges. Once the pontoons have been assembled, the balk is added, then the chess and finally the curb. A complete SMS bridge set consists of 72 bow and 36 centre sections.

SPECIFICATIONS

	Bow pontoon	Centre pontoon
Weight	1000 kg	1090 kg
Length	6 m	5 m
Width	2·3 m	2·3 m
Depth	1·05 m	1·05 m

Bridge construction

Bridge type	20t	40t	60t
Roadway width	4·5 m	4·5 m	4·5 m
Bridge length	228 m	196 m	24 m
Pontoon sections per support	3	3	3
Working party (men)	120	120	120
Assembly time (minutes)	192	210	210

Raft construction

Raft type	20t	40t	60t
Rafts per set	12	12	9
Pontoon sections per raft	9	9	12
Assembly time (minutes)	30	35	40

STATUS
Probably held in reserve as it has been replaced in most front-line units by the Soviet PMP heavy folding pontoon bridge.

MANUFACTURER
Czechoslovak state factories.

T-34 tanks crossing SMS heavy pontoon bridge

FRANCE

Light Infantry Bridge Type 1949

DESCRIPTION
The light infantry bridge type 1949, introduced in 1949 and modified in 1962, can be used as either a footbridge or a light raft. In the former role, the pneumatic floats, which are also used for reconnaissance, are fixed under the spans of the bridge. A complete bridge set contains sufficient equipment to span a river up to 50 metres wide when the current is slower than 3 metres per second, or a maximum gap of 100 metres when the current is 1·5 metres per second or slower.

The bridge set can also be used for the assembly of two rafts, each of which can support a maximum load of 2 tons. When the current is up to 2·5 metres a second the raft can be pulled across the river by cables, but if the current is faster than 2·5 metres a second two pneumatic boats with outboard motors are used to push the raft across the river. The raft has two trackways and has two ramps at each end which are lowered manually for loading and unloading.

The complete bridge set weighs about 2800 kg, consists of 20 floats and 18 duckboards, and the individual components are light enough to be carried by hand.

STATUS
Production complete. In service with the French Army.

MANUFACTURER
Spans: Atelier de Construction de Tarbes, 2 rue Alsace-Lorraine, BP 313, 65013 Tarbes, France.

Floats: Société Industrielle Angevinière et Joué-les-Tours and the Société Zodiac.

Light infantry bridge type 1949 being used as footbridge

SPECIFICATIONS
Floats
Weight: 49 kg
Length: 3·7 m
Width: 1·4 m
Depth: 0·5 m

Duckboards
Weight: 38 kg
Length: 3 m
Width: 0·6 m

Depth: 0·1 m
Assembled bridge
Total length: 51 m
Width of walkway: 0·6 m

Assembly time:
  (day) 34 minutes
  (night) 51 minutes
Carrying capacity:
  (day) 75 men/minute
  (night) 40 men/minute

Light infantry bridge type 1949 being used as raft

Castor Light River Crossing Equipment

DEVELOPMENT

The Castor light river crossing equipment (Matériel Léger de Franchissement) was developed by the Etablissement Technique d'Angers and was adopted by the French Army in 1976. It is now in production at the Atelier de Construction de Tarbes.

DESCRIPTION

The Castor can be used as a floating bridge; a raft or an individual flotation unit can be used as an assault or river boat. When being used as the latter it can carry 32 men, and is propelled in the water by paddles or an outboard motor.

The flotation units, which are of fibreglass construction, are made up of two flat-bottom boats assembled stern to stern by pins, and have an assembled length of 9·8 metres. The gunwales are capped by stiffeners which are attached to the boat by four locking pins. Each unit is also provided with handrails, outboard motor attachment and a floor.

The bridge deck comprises two tracks made up of deck components, steel assemblies, articulation units and ramp units. The central deck units fill the space between the tracks and are of reinforced plastic. The bridge decks are secured to the flotation units by the sets of tiltable pegs on the gunwale stiffeners. The bridge deck components are made of light-alloy sections welded together and are provided with anti-skid strips. The deck bridge components are arranged in pairs, end to end, and spaced 0·7 metre apart.

The articulated joints provide the connection between the bridge deck components located on the floating support and those acting on the ramp. Each articulation joint weighs 165 kg and is adjusted manually. The ramp units are of welded light alloy construction and assembled by means of pins. Each ramp weighs 50 kg and is provided with a steel contact edge. Each bridge-deck unit can be fitted with a track guide in tubular light alloy, which is articulated on bosses welded to the outside of the bridge deck. The track guide can be retracted into a free space on the side of the bridge deck.

Rafts

Various types of raft of two, three, four, five or six flotation units can be assembled. A 4/3 type basic raft can be assembled by three teams of eight men in about 40 minutes. This raft can be carried on a Berliet GBC 8 KT (6 × 6) truck towing an SKD 3536 trailer carrying the eight flotation unit halves stacked one inside the other. The raft is either propelled in the water by outboard motors or pushed by a bridging boat. For example, a 4/3 raft would be propelled by two 40 hp outboard motors on the first and fourth flotation units.

Bridges

Two types of bridge can be built using the Castor system: the medium bridge composed of bridge-deck units with flotation units under them, and the heavy duty bridge with the flotation units positioned one alongside the other. The medium bridge (1/1) is 8·07 metres long and will span a river 7 metres wide, while the heavy duty bridge has an overall length of 16·13 metres and will span a river of 15 metres.

SPECIFICATIONS

Flotation unit (individual unit)
Length: 4·9 m
Width: 1·75 m
Height: 0·75 m

Castor 4/3 raft carrying Berliet GBC 8 KT (6 × 6) 4000 kg truck

Weight:
  (without equipment) 160 kg
  (with floor and superstructure) 245 kg
  (with floor, superstructure and gunwale stiffeners) 250 kg

Bridge decks
Length: 3·44 m
Width: 1 m
Depth: 0·26 m
Weight: 205 kg

Raft construction

Raft type	2/2	3/3	4/3 basic	5/3	5/4	6/4
Complete flotation units	2	3	4	5	5	6
Bridge deck units	4	6	6	6	8	8
Articulated joints	4	4	4	4	4	4
Bridge end units	4	4	4	4	4	4
Track guides	8	12	12	12	16	16
Central deck units	4	6	6	6	8	8
Total length	16·13 m	19·57 m	19·57 m	19·57 m	23·01 m	23·01 m
Useful length	7·58 m	11·02 m	11·02 m	11·02 m	14·46 m	14·46 m

Raft and bridge load capacities

Type of raft or bridge	Current speed		
	1·5 m/s	2 m/s	2·5 m/s
2/2 raft	6	–	–
3/3 raft	10	8	6
4/3 (basic) raft	16	13	10
6/4 raft	22	20	15
Medium duty bridge	15	13	8
Heavy duty bridge	22	20	16

STATUS

In production. In service with the French Army.

MANUFACTURER

Atelier de Construction de Tarbes, 2 rue Alsace-Lorraine, BP 313, 65013 Tarbes, France.
  Enquiries to Groupement Industriel des Armements Terrestres (GIAT), 10 place Georges Clémenceau, 92211 Saint Cloud, France.

Castor being used as floating bridge with AMX VCI crossing

Attaching gunwales to pontoons after they have been connected end to end

CNIM Pont Flottant Motorisé Mle F1

DEVELOPMENT

The Pont Flottant Motorisé Modèle F1 (PFM Mle F1) was developed by Constructions Navales et Industrielles de la Méditerranée (CNIM) under contract to the Direction Technique des Armements Terrestres. It was tested in competition with a similar system developed by Creusot-Loire (*Jane's Military Vehicles and Ground*

Support Equipment 1981, page 84) and compared to other equipment available in western nations during 1979–80. It was adopted by the French Army in early 1981. During the 1980s French Army engineer units will take delivery of 3600 metres of PFM bridging.
  Production of the French Army PFM units will commence during February 1984 with the first production prototype being scheduled for mid-1984. It is expected that the first operational unit will be fully equipped with

the PFM during 1985. The unit concerned will probably be part of the 1st Army Engineers based at Strasbourg. In service the PFM will supplement Gillois ferry units.

DESCRIPTION

The PFM Mle F1 may be employed as either a bridge or a raft, and can be used in rivers with a current of up to 3 metres a second and banks up to 2 metres high. Maximum load capacity is class 60 (class 70 with restric-

AMX-30 tanks crossing PFM Mle F1 floating bridge

AMX-30 tanks crossing PFM Mle F1 floating bridge

Deck-level view of AMX-30 tanks crossing PFM Mle F1 bridge

PFM Mle F1 ferry section being launched from TRM 10 000-towed trailer (T J Gander)

tions), and the roadway is 4 metres wide. The main advantages claimed for the PFM Mle F1 are that floating bridges and rafts can be assembled rapidly with minimum manpower, the main elements can be launched and recovered without cranes (even from 2-metre high river banks), no pontoon boats are required as each centre section has two outboard motors, and section assembly is eased by the use of pre-locking devices.

The PFM Mle F1 consists of two major components, the centre section and the approach ramp. The centre section has locking elements at both ends, two wing tanks and two ballast tanks. The centre and wing units are constructed from light alloy, the ballast tanks from laminated GRP. Included in the centre section is a light alloy framework which contains the outboard motor (55 hp or 75 hp). The approach ramps are also light alloy and their ends can be set hydraulically into various positions to suit the river bank height. The centre section and ramp are transported folded on a special semi-trailer towed by a Berliet GBC 8 KT (6 × 6) tractor or any tractor of the same capacity. The semi-trailer is provided with power for unfolding, launching, recovery and refolding the section. The components are launched as follows: the tractor reverses to the water's

edge and the section is unfolded, hydraulic rams push up the forward end of the tilting frame and the section slides down into the water. A number of 10-metre long sections are assembled in the water and the bridge is completed by adding the approach ramps. Each section of the bridge is propelled in the water by two outboard motors.

A team of 21 men can assemble a class 60 raft in 20 minutes. Each such raft would consist of three centre sections and two approach ramps. A team of 45 men can build a 100 metre bridge in 45 minutes.

SPECIFICATIONS
Main section
Weight: 10 500 kg
Length: 10 m
Width:
  (folded) 3·6 m
  (unfolded) 9·8 m
Track width: 4 m
Height:
  (folded) 2·1 m
  (unfolded) 0·73 m
Draught: (unloaded) 0·1 m
Positive buoyancy: 42 tons

Approach ramp
Weight: 5700 kg
Length: 12 m
Track width: 4 m

Berliet GBC 8 KT with trailer and section
Weight: 23 500 kg
Length: 16 m
Width: 3·5 m
Height: 4 m
Ground clearance: (min) 0·3 m
Max speed:
  (road) 60 km/h
  (off-road) 10 km/h
Fording: 1·2 m

STATUS
In production. Adopted by the French Army.

MANUFACTURER
Constructions Navales et Industrielles de la Méditerranée (CNIM), Chantiers et Ateliers, 83501 La-Seyne-sur-Mer, BP 208 France.
  Enquiries to CNIM Head Office, 35 rue de Bassano, 75008 Paris, France.

GERMANY, FEDERAL REPUBLIC

Infantry Bridge

This consists of small rubber dinghies, foot boards, hand-rails and ropes, and retaining ropes, and is used by infantry to cross rivers and streams.

STATUS
In service with the West German Army.

West German infantry crossing lightweight bridge of rubber dinghies and foot boards (Federal German Ministry of Defence)

Bridge, Pneumatic Float, Class 16/30/50

DESCRIPTION

This is called the Schlauchbootbrücke MLC 16/30/50 by the West German Army but is now being supplemented by the German version of the American-designed Ribbon Bridge.

It consists of an aluminium deck superstructure supported on pneumatic floats. The floats are made of rubberised fabric and are inflated by an air compressor. One end of each float is upturned and the other is fitted with a stern mount on which an outboard motor can be mounted.

The deck balk is made of aluminium alloy covered in non-skid plastic, the saddle beam assembly is also of aluminium alloy and the connectors are steel.

Unlike the American M4T6 bridge the deck balk is not laid in a staggered pattern, but in parallel rows with individual balk joined end-to-end by H-shaped balk connectors.

The roadway can be either a flush deck or a treadway

Bridge, pneumatic float, class 16/30/50 in position (Federal German Army)

type. The overall width of the flush deck roadway is 4·2 metres and the width of the treadway bridge can be varied from 3 to 4·9 metres, depending on the number of balks used in each treadway.

The last floating bay is provided with an articulated balk connector which allows the roadway of the shore span to fluctuate between ± 30 degrees.

A complete bridge set, which is carried on six 7-tonne trucks and three 1·5-tonne trailers, includes ten floats which is sufficient to make an MLC 16, 30 or 50 floating bridge, 16, 24, 30 or 50 class ferry or a short dry-gap bridge of MLC 24, 30 or 50.

SPECIFICATIONS

	Pneumatic float	Deck balk
Weight	329 kg	146 kg
Length	10·8 m	4·8 m
Width	2·3 m	0·34 m
Depth	0·8 m	0·27 m

Bridge assembled

Class	16	30	50
Length	86 m	43 m	28 m
Width of roadway	4·2 m	4·2 m	4·2 m
Centre-to-centre of floats	9·6 m	4·8 m	3·3 m

STATUS

Production complete. In service with the West German Army and Indonesia.

Floating Bridge Class 50/80

DESCRIPTION

This heavy floating bridge, called the Hohplattenbrücke MLC 50/80 by the West German Army, consists of hollow rectangular steel pontoon sections joined end to end and side by side to form a bridge. Two types of pontoon are used, bow and centre, connected by upper and lower coupling devices to form a bridge. The pontoon deck, which is covered with non-skid plastic, serves as a roadway. A complete bridge set consists of 60 bow and 40 centre pontoons.

A 10-tonne truck carries three pontoon sections and also tows a trailer carrying a further two pontoons. The pontoons are launched hydraulically by tilting the truck bed, or in the case of the trailer, by tilting manually, so that they slide into the water. They can also be lifted off the truck or trailer by a crane. Once in the water the pontoons are assembled into a bridge with the aid of bridging boats.

A class 50 bridge consists of two rows of pontoons and can be assembled by an engineer company in five hours. The completed bridge is 115 metres long, including ramps, and has a roadway width of 4·2 metres.

A class 80 bridge consists of three rows of pontoons and can be assembled by an engineer company in six hours. The completed bridge is 80 metres long, including ramps, and has a roadway width of 6·4 metres.

A class 50 ferry can also be constructed with 12 bow and 8 centre pontoons.

Mobile crane lowering bow section of floating bridge class 50/80 into position (Federal German Ministry of Defence)

SPECIFICATIONS

	Bow pontoon	Centre pontoon
Weight	1207 kg	1153 kg
Length	4·7 m	4·2 m
Width	2·1 m	2·1 m
Depth	0·8 m	0·8 m

STATUS

Production complete. In service with the West German Army and Iraq.

Krupp Festbrücke Floating Bridges

DESCRIPTION

The Krupp Festbrücke system can be adapted to become a floating bridge or ferry by the addition of extra modular components. Main components are still the twin-triangular, cross-section, wheel tread girders (see also entry on page 126) but to this are added a hydraulic ramp adjusting section, pontoons with load-bearing saddles and anchoring and drive units. These floating bridges and ferries can carry loads up to class 60.

The floating bridge can be adapted to almost all shore conditions by using the ramp adjusting section. One side of this section is joined to the floating bridge and the height and angle of the outer section can be raised or lowered 20 degrees by means of a hand-operated hydraulic pump acting on a pressure cylinder. This angle corresponds to a difference in height of approximately 7·6 metres with a ramp length of 19·3 metres. The time required for raising and lowering the ramp from the highest to the lowest point is five minutes. A special pressure compensating unit between pressure cylinders positioned close to each other in the bridge cross-section prevents tilting or jamming during raising or lowering. These adjusting sections can also be used as part of the floating bridge itself so that the bridge can be assembled from one shore and can assume angles to suit the required conditions.

The Festbrücke pontoons are light metal components each 8·8 metres long, 2·25 metres wide and 1·23 metres high. Each has a carrying capacity of 11 400 kg at which weight each will have a freeboard of 300 mm. For supporting a bridge two single pontoons are joined stern-to-stern using twin pins inserted vertically over the full height. Each pontoon has a foam-filled decking covered by metal plating and each weighs 830 kg. The pontoons can be powered by 115 hp outboard engines and various accessories are available including mooring posts, trimming tanks, an anchor, a winch with 100 metres of cable, etc. Normally these pontoons are carried on special trailers 9·4 metres long

Krupp Festbrücke in use as floating bridge

onto which the pontoons can be stacked five high to a height above the trailer carrying area of 2·43 metres.

The bridge and pontoon are connected by longitudinal saddle girders set on each pontoon wall and joined by cross beams. The lower chords of the Festbrücke are engaged by clamping jaws. For launching from a shore each pontoon is set afloat using at least three inflatable

load rollers each with a diameter of 0·5 metre and a length of 3 metres.

The floating Festbrücke is anchored with winches on each pontoon. If this system cannot be used each pontoon uses its outboard engine.

When used as a floating bridge the load capability can be altered by changing the pontoon spacing. Assuming the minimum interval between vehicles crossing the bridge is 30·5 metres, the intervals are as follows:

Class	Tracked vehicles	Wheeled vehicles
12	23·1 m	21 m
16	21 m	18·9 m
20	18·9 m	16·8 m
24	16·8 m	14·7 m
30	14·7 m	12·6 m
40	12·6 m	10·5 m

Class	Tracked vehicles	Wheeled vehicles
50	10·5 m	8·4 m
60	8·4 m	8·4 m

It is anticipated that most floating bridges will be between 60 and 200 metres long. These bridges can be used in water velocities of up to three metres a second. Normal crossing speeds should not exceed 10 km per hour.

When used as a ferry, the Festbrücke is powered by the pontoon outboard engines alone, and can reach speeds of up to 20 km an hour on smooth water.

STATUS
Production. In service with European and other armies.

MANUFACTURER
Krupp Industrietechnik GmbH, Franz-Schubert Strasse 1-3, Postfach 14 19 60, D-4100 Duisburg 14 (Rheinhausen), Federal Republic of Germany.

Bundeswehr Ribbon Bridge

DEVELOPMENT/DESCRIPTION
In 1976 the West German Army decided to participate in the United States Army's test and evaluation programme of the first production ribbon bridge which is fully described in the United States section. The trials were carried out in West Germany between September 1976 and March 1977. Early in 1977 the West German Army decided to adopt the Ribbon Bridge System and subsequently obtained a licence to undertake production in West Germany. Production by EWK began in 1978 with first deliveries being made to the West German Army in December 1978. Each of the West German Army's 12 Division Combat Engineer Companies now has one complete Ribbon Bridge set of 26 segments; 18 bridge segments and 8 ramp elements. To the West Germans the Ribbon Bridge system is known as the Faltschwimmbrücke.

The West German version of the Ribbon Bridge, unlike the American model, is built to metric standards as well as incorporating a number of improvements to suit West German requirements, none of which affect its compatibility with the original American version.

The hydraulic system for raising the ramp bay to adjust to varying bank conditions has been modified and non-polluting hydraulic fluid introduced; on the original model oil sometimes leaked out and water got in. Other improvements include winch-operated approach ramps, changes made to interior bays to prevent the cables from getting crushed as the section folds, non-skid coating on roadways and walkways and stops on the bridge sections to keep the bridging boats in place when the bridge is being used as a raft.

The German version of the Ribbon Bridge is carried on the rear of the MAN 7000 kg (6 × 6) new generation truck, designated the Lkw 7t gl Brückentransporter. Full specifications of this truck are given in the *Trucks* section.

EWK also produces an all-steel version of the Ribbon Bridge system which is compatible with the original Soviet PMP system. This version was originally developed for Egypt. The main differences between the steel and the aluminium versions are given in the specification tables below.

The all-steel version is in service with Egypt and one African country.

STATUS
In production. In service with the Belgian, Egyptian, West German and Swedish armies.

MANUFACTURER
Eisenwerke Kaiserslautern Göppner GmbH, Barbarossastrasse 30, D-6750 Kaiserslautern, Federal Republic of Germany.

SPECIFICATIONS
Vehicle with folded Ribbon Bridge unit
Cab seating: 1 + 2
Configuration: 6 × 6
Weight: (loaded) 18 800 kg
Length: (overall) 10·4 m

Bundeswehr Ribbon Bridge segment being launched by Swedish Army Scania-Vabis LA 82 (6 × 6) bridging vehicle; numbers of these specialised vehicles have been converted from artillery tractors

Bundeswehr Ribbon Bridge segment being assembled with one interior bay being positioned by bridging boat (Federal German Ministry of Defence)

Width: (overall) 3·31 m
Height: (overall) 3·93 m
Ground clearance: 0·415 m
Wheelbase: 5·4 m
Track:
(front) 2·066 m
(rear) 2·07 m
Angle of approach/departure: 45°/31°
Max speed: 90 km/h
Range: 700 km
Max gradient: 60%
Fording: 1·2 m

Bridge section	Aluminium	Steel
Weight	5400 kg	7700 kg
Length	6·7 m	6·7 m
Width unfolded	8·12 m	8·02 m
Road width	4·1 m	6·6 m
Ramp section		
Weight	5500 kg	7500 kg
Length	5·6 m	5·5 m
(with unfolded		
plate)	7·6 m	7·5 m
Road width	4·1 m	6·6 m

Heavy Ferry

DESCRIPTION
The Pionier Fahre, or heavy ferry, was designed and built by the Boden-Werft shipyards at Kressbronn. It consists of 12 pontoons, each of which weighs 10 300 kg and can be transported on a railway flatcar with a loading space of at least 8·8 metres, or on truck trailers. On arrival at the launch site the pontoons are joined side-by-side in three rows, with four pontoons in each row. When assembled the ferry is 36·6 metres long and 7·6 metres wide with the deck of the pontoons serving as the roadway, which has a usable width of 5·2 metres. The 120-tonne heavy ferry is powered by four 125 hp diesel engines, one at each corner pontoon, each of which powers a propeller which can be raised or lowered hydraulically and can be traversed through 360 degrees. Maximum water speed is 16 km/h.

A feature of the heavy ferry is that the bridge, on the right side, can be raised or lowered to permit the ferry to pass under bridges and other river obstacles. There are ramps fore and aft for loading and unloading and a

Heavy ferry carrying British soldiers and equipment across Rhine during exercise held in 1977 (Ministry of Defence)

20 mm Rheinmetall cannon is mounted on each side for anti-aircraft defence.

STATUS
Production complete. In service with the West German Army.

SPECIFICATIONS
Pontoons
Length: 9·1 m
Width: 2·59 m
Depth: 1·9 m

Assembled ferry
Length: 36·6 m
Width: 7·6 m
Capacity: 120 tonnes

GREECE

Aluminium Floating Footbridge

DESCRIPTION
The aluminium floating footbridge, as produced by the Greek EBEX SA, is a licence-produced version of the American Aluminium Floating Footbridge; for details and specifications see the relevant entry in the United States of America section.

STATUS
In production. In service with the Greek Army.

MANUFACTURER
EBEX SA, 2 Varnali Street, Nea Halkidon, Athens, Greece.

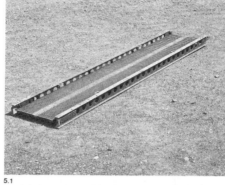

5.1

5.2

5.3

5.4

Main components of aluminium floating footbridge: 5·1 treadway, 5·2 pontoon, 5·3 handrail post and 5·4 method of assembly

Light Tactical Bridge and Raft

DESCRIPTION
This equipment is a license-built version of the American Bridge Floating: Raft Section, Light Tactical. For a full description and specifications see the relevant entry in the United States of America section.

STATUS
In production. In service with the Greek Army.

MANUFACTURER
EBEX SA, 2 Varnali Street, Nea Halkidon, Athens, Greece.

4.1

4.2

4.3

4.4

4.5

Main components of light tactical bridge and raft: 4·1 half pontoon, 4·2 deck panel, 4·3 deck filler panel, 4·4 ramp panel and 4·5 articulating assembly

ISRAEL

Two-Tank Ferry Raft (2TFR)

DESCRIPTION

The two-tank ferry raft (2TFR) is intended for use as a ferry raft carrying one or two main battle tanks or for connecting with one or more 2TFRs to form a floating bridge. On land the 2TFR is sufficiently mobile to allow it to be towed into position by the tanks that will use it to cross water obstacles, and on roads the 2TFR may be towed by heavy trucks. Each 2TFR is an independent unit handled by a crew of only three. A 33-man force with eleven 2TFRs can bridge 300 metres of water. Linking time for two 2TFR units is about five minutes.

The 2TFR consists of a floating loading platform, 21 metres long and 5 metres wide, with two side floats, each 21 metres long and 1·6 metres wide. The side floats are folded onto the loading platform during transit and are usually opened before reaching the operational area. At each end of the platform is a hinged loading ramp, 7·5 metres long and 5 metres wide, which is folded up onto the platform until the unit is launched. Both side floats and platform are filled with rigid polyurethane foam to ensure buoyancy in the event of battle damage.

The 2TFR is propelled by two identical power units which may be produced by Schottel (West Germany) or Stewart and Stevenson (USA). The two power units may be controlled from either of two control units, or from a remote control unit which may be mounted anywhere on the 2TFR. The power units propel the raft in the water and raise and lower the side floats and loading ramps. Each power unit is connected to the propulsion unit by a 270 degree pivot for steering. The propeller shaft can be raised and lowered to suit varying water depths and in transit the whole propulsion unit can be angled upward and over for road clearance. On land the raft travels on a wheeled undercarriage with four pairs of wheels, each pair with its own suspension. The wheels are low pressure and specially designed. Once water-borne the entire undercarriage can be uncoupled and dropped. A hydraulically-operated tow boom, powered by either of the power units, is located on the stern of the raft, and is self-uncoupling.

In use the 2TFR is towed by a heavy truck, semi-trailer or wheeled tractor to the nearest possible point by road. When the road is left the 2TFR is hitched to a tank by the hydraulic boom on the stern of the raft, and towed to the edge of the water obstacle. The tank then pulls the raft round and pushes it into the water. The tow boom is uncoupled from the raft and drops off the tank. The 2TFR can then proceed under its own power and the undercarriage can be separated from the raft. The loading ramps are extended and once lowered the raft can take on its load of two main battle tanks. The entire sequence, once the raft is in the water, takes under five minutes.

The wheels on the undercarriage may be fitted with high speed brakes, and for road towing the width of the 2TFR may be reduced to 4·25 metres. For water use the undercarriage can be supplied in a retractable form, in

Israel Military Industries 2TFR carrying Centurion and M48 tanks

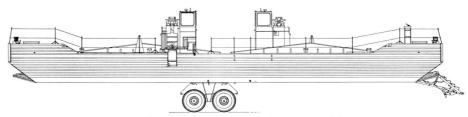

Israel Military Industries 2TFR (not to 1/76th scale)

which state the wheels will extend only 50 cm. Propulsion hydro-jets may be used in place of the normal propulsion units, and another option is that the 2TFR can be fitted with only one loading ramp allowing the raft to be used as a one-direction raft with both propulsion units at the rear. A smaller version of the 2TFR can be produced which will carry only one tank. This unit will have a transit length of 17 metres and a width of 4·45 metres.

For maintenance, the power units can be removed and stored separately from the rest of the raft. Tank drivers need no special training to tow the 2TFR.

STATUS
Production. In service with the Israeli Army.

MANUFACTURER
Israel Military Industries, POB 1044, Ramat Hasharon 47100, Israel.

SPECIFICATIONS
Crew: 3
Length:
(transit) 21 m
(water) 31 m
(bridging formation) 27·5 m
Width:
(road) 5·25 m
(water, side floats down) 8·25 m

Height:
(road) 5·1 m
(water) 3·5 m
Loading platform width: 5 m
Weight:
(transit, less power units) 46 000 kg
(ready for launch) 54 000 kg
(waterborne) 48 000 kg
Towing speed:
(road) 60 km/h
(tank-towed, off road) 25 km/h
Uphill inclination angle: (tank towed) 11°
Lateral inclination angle: (tank towed) 15°
Turn radius: 20 m
Speed in water:
(unloaded) 14 km/h
(one tank) 11 km/h
(two tanks) 9 km/h
Draught:
(unloaded) 0·35 m
(one tank) 0·71 m
(two tanks) 1·2 m
Manoeuvrability: 360°
Operational time before refuelling: 12 hours
Sea-going capability: to sea scale 3
Bridging capability:
(resistance to current) velocities up to 2·5 m/s
(length) unlimited

JAPAN

Aluminium Floating Footbridge

DESCRIPTION

The Japanese aluminium floating footbridge is very similar to the old American M1938 footbridge. Major differences are that aluminium alloy is used instead of white pine for the float body and the duckboard stringer and cedar wood is substituted for pine in the transverse slats of the duckboard. The floats are filled with foam rubber to give increased buoyancy.

A bridge set, which is carried on two 2½-ton trucks, consists of 21 duckboards and 42 floats which is sufficient to provide 76 metres of walkway 0·55 metre wide and has a carrying capacity of 75 men a minute in single column. It can be assembled in 11 minutes by a working party of 45 men. Alternatively, a reinforced footbridge 25·2 metres long and 1·65 metres wide with a capacity of 150 men a minute in two columns can be assembled by 45 men in 18 minutes.

SPECIFICATIONS	Floats	Duckboards
Weight	43 kg	37 kg
Length	3 m	3·6 m
Width	0·25 m	0·55 m
Depth	0·4 m	0·15 m

STATUS
Production complete. In service with the Japanese Ground Self-Defence Force.

Japanese floating bridge ready to receive vehicle (K Ebata)

Japanese floating bridge with Type 70 SPRR being carried (K Ebata)

Aluminium floating footbridge being built at night (K Ebata)

27 ft bridge erection boat used by JGSDF (K Ebata)

Light Tactical Raft

DESCRIPTION
This is similar to the American Bridge Floating: Raft Section, Light Tactical and is transported on 2½-ton 6 × 6 trucks. It consists of Japanese folding assault boats which are joined stern-to-stern to form a pontoon. Either two bow sections or one bow and one stern section may be joined. Attached to the gunwales of the pontoons are dual plywood treadways which form the raft deck. Side-rails are then placed along the inside edge of the treadways to stop vehicles being driven off.

Rafts of 9-, 10- and 13-tonne capacity can be assembled with three, four or five pontoons respectively. A

three-pontoon raft is normally propelled by one 25 hp outbcard motor and the four- and five-pontoon rafts are propelled by two outboard motors. Maximum speed of a loaded three-pontoon raft is 6·5 km/h.

STATUS
Production complete. In service with the Japanese Ground Self-Defence Force.

SPECIFICATIONS

	Pontoon	Treadway
Weight	269 kg	100 kg
Length	7·7 m	2·5 m
Width	1·5 m	0·9 m
Depth	0·65 m	0·18 m

Assembled raft

Raft class	9t	10t	13t
Number of pontoons	3	4	5
Number of treadways	8	10	12
Overall length of deck	9 m	12 m	15 m
Distance between pontoon centres	2·5 m	2·5 m	2·5 m

NETHERLANDS

DAF YGZ 2300 (6 × 6) 10 000 kg Ribbon Bridge Launcher

DESCRIPTION
The DAF YGZ 2300 is the version of the DAF YAZ 2300 developed for carrying and launching the Ribbon Bridge. The first prototype was produced in late 1982

and on 15 November 1982 the first launching of a Ribbon Bridge segment was made. The accompanying photographs show the vehicle and the launching sequence.

STATUS
Prototype.

MANUFACTURER (truck)
DAF Trucks, Geldropseweg 303, 5645 TK, Eindhoven, Netherlands.

DAF YGZ 2300 (6 × 6) 10 000 kg Ribbon Bridge launch vehicle

DAF YGZ 2300 from rear

DAF YGZ 2300 with hydraulic arm for launching Ribbon Bridge segment in raised position

DAF YGZ 2300 commencing Ribbon Bridge launch procedure

POLAND

PP-64 Heavy Folding Pontoon Bridge

DESCRIPTION
In 1964, following the success of the Soviet PMP heavy folding pontoon bridge, Poland started design work on a folding pontoon bridge. The initial prototype was finished in 1965 with first production units being completed the following year.

In design the PP-64 is quite different from the Soviet PMP and has a much faster construction rate. According to some sources this is over 25 metres a minute. The basic bridge has a capacity of 40 tons whereas the Soviet bridge has a capacity of 60 tons, which is not a great tactical disadvantage as the PP-64 can still handle the T-54/T-55 and T-62 MBTs. The PP-64 can probably handle recent Soviet tanks such as the T-64 and T-72.

A PP-64 set consists of 48 river pontoons carried on trucks, 6 shore pontoons carried on trucks, 12 ramps for ferries carried on trucks which also tow the KH-200 bridging boats, 6 KH-200 bridging boats and one special connecting piece for use in joining PP-64 with Soviet PMP bridges.

Three types of bridge can be built: 40-tonne (A), 40-tonne (B) and 80-tonne. The 40-tonne (A) is the single roadway type and is 186 metres long, 4·35 metres wide roadway width, can take a 12-tonne axle load and be constructed in rivers with a maximum velocity of 1·2 metres a second. Working party consists of 60 pontoon workers, 60 drivers, 6 powerboat operators and 10 NCOs. The 40-tonne (B) is also the single roadway type and is 145 metres long, 4·35 metres wide, can take a 12-tonne axle load and be constructed in rivers with a maximum velocity of 2 metres a second. Working party consists of 54 pontoon workers, 60 drivers, 6 powerboat operators and 10 NCOs. The 80-tonne bridge is double width, 97 metres long, has a roadway width of 8·7 metres, can take a 12-tonne axle load and be constructed in rivers with a maximum velocity of 3 metres a second. The working party consists of 54 pontoon workers, 60 drivers, 6 powerboat operators and 10 NCOs.

The following ferries can be constructed with the basic PP-64 set: six 40-tonne ferries 14·8 metres long and 12·8 metres wide each with eight river pontoons, one shore pontoon and two ramps, a working party of 20 pontoon workers and three NCOs, and two powerboats per ferry or two large ferries 37 metres long and 12·5 metres wide each with 20 river pontoons, two shore pontoons and four ramps, a working party of 30 pontoon workers and four NCOs and three powerboats per ferry.

The bridge is launched as follows: the truck backs up to the river and the pontoon, which is in two parts hinged in the middle, is unfolded and then launched. The pontoons are carried on the rear of a Polish Star 660 M2 (6 × 6) 2½-ton truck. The Soviet PMP pontoons are much heavier and therefore have to be carried on a 7- or 7½-ton (6 × 6) truck chassis. Bridging boats used with the PP-64 are the Soviet BMK-130 and the Polish KH-200.

SPECIFICATIONS
Pontoon
Weight: 1000 kg
Length: 3·7 m
Width: 6·2 m
Depth: 0·85 m

STATUS
In service with the Polish Army.

MANUFACTURER
Polish state factories.

PP-64 heavy folding pontoon bridge in travelling position on rear of Star 660 (6 × 6) 2½-ton truck

PP-64 heavy folding pontoon bridge in position showing hand-operated winch for adjusting ramp

PP-64 heavy folding pontoon bridge being launched from rear of Star 660 (6 × 6) 2½-ton truck

ROMANIA

PR-60 Heavy Pontoon Bridge

DESCRIPTION
The PR-60 was developed by the Romanians as the replacement for the Soviet-supplied TMP heavy pontoon bridge, and can be used both as a pontoon bridge and as a raft. The PR-60 is not of the folding type like the Soviet PMP and Polish PP-64, and is therefore slower to construct.

The PR-60 consists of enclosed shore and river pontoons, which are launched from the rear of the Bucegi SR-114 (4 × 4) 4-ton truck by gravity and are recovered by being lifted out of the water by a crane as the truck has no recovery capability. Once launched the pontoons are connected to form a continuous roadway. Both single- and double-lane bridges can be constructed, the latter with double pontoons.

A complete PR-60 pontoon set consists of 56 river pontoons and four shore pontoons. Each Bucegi SR-114 truck (4 × 4) carries either one shore pontoon or two river pontoons resting on top of each other.

SPECIFICATIONS

	River pontoon	Shore pontoon
Weight	1200 kg	1350 kg
Length	6 m	6·2 m
Width	2·4 m	4·2 m
Height/depth	0·7 m	0·7 m

Bridge construction

Bridge type	40t	60t
Roadway width	3·8 m	7·6 m
Bridge length	142·8 m	80·4 m
Assembly time	1 hour	1½ hours
Number of pontoons*	50	60

* Including shore pontoons

STATUS
In service with the Romanian Army.

MANUFACTURER
Romanian state factories.

SWITZERLAND

Bridge, Pneumatic Float, Model 1961

DESCRIPTION
This bridge, designated the Schlauchbootbrücke Model 1961, was designed by Krupp and MAN of West Germany to meet the requirements of the Swiss Army. It entered service in 1961 as the replacement for the Model 1935 pontoon bridge.

The Model 1961 uses the same aluminium deck balk as the West German class 16/30/50 pneumatic floating bridge, from which it differs in having turned ends. The floats each have 12 air compartments and can support a normal load even with four compartments punctured. It is claimed that even with one float destroyed the floating bridge will carry its normal load.

A class 50 bridge is 100 metres long with a distance between the floats of 4·8 metres, and can be assembled, in currents with a velocity of up to 3·5 metres a second, in three hours by a 132-man team. The bridge is assembled by the successive raft method with each raft being assembled along the river bank and then brought into the line of the bridge by two or three assault boats powered by an 85 hp outboard motor. The basic bridge has a roadway width of 4·2 metres, but a two-lane roadway, 5·6 metres wide, can also be constructed. The Model 1961 bridge can also be used to assemble ferries with capacities of 16, 30 and 50 tonnes.

Swiss bridge, pneumatic float, Model 1961 being assembled

SPECIFICATIONS
Pneumatic float
Weight: 45 kg

Deck balk
Weight: 146 kg
Length: 4·8 m
Width: 0·35 m
Depth: 0·25 m

Raft class	16t	30t	50t
Number of floats	2	3	4
Overall length of deck	9·6 m	14·4 m	19·1 m
Assembly time	1·5 hours	1·5 hours	2 hours
Working party	33 men	33 men	33 men

STATUS
Production complete. In service with the Swiss Army.

UNION OF SOVIET SOCIALIST REPUBLICS

GSP Heavy Amphibious Ferry

DESCRIPTION
The GSP, introduced in 1959, is the standard heavy amphibious ferry of the Warsaw Pact and was used by the Egyptian Army during the crossing of the Suez canal in October 1973.

A complete GSP ferry consists of two units, left and right, which are not interchangeable and which enter the water separately and are then linked up. Once linked together the pontoon, which when travelling on land is in the inverted position, is swung through 180 degrees into the floating position. Each unit carries retractable track-ways which enable vehicles to be loaded or unloaded either side. The GSP can carry a maximum load of 52 000 kg which enables it to carry the T-10 heavy tank. According to American reports, under favourable circumstances a tank is able to fire its main armament when loaded on the GSP.

The track suspension of the GSP is similar to that used on members of the PT-76 light amphibious tank family and consists of seven road wheels with the idler at the front and the drive sprocket at the rear. There are no track return rollers. The hull of the GSP is of light-weight welded steel filled with plastic foam, both to increase its buoyancy and to reduce its vulnerability to damage by enemy fire. Before entering the water a trim vane is erected at the front of the hull, although this was not fitted to early units. Each unit is propelled in the water by two propellers which are mounted in separate tunnels under the hull. As a direct result of user experience the GSP has been modified in recent years. These modifications include an improved suspension which has given the unit a higher ground clearance, a stronger hull and an improved cab for the crew at the front of the hull.

The GSP has two major disadvantages: GSPs cannot be joined together to form a floating bridge and the bank where the GSP unloads must be no higher than 0·5 metre and must have a minimum water depth of 1·2 metres, otherwise the GSP will be damaged.

GSP heavy amphibious ferry with T-54 MBT

Two GSP units unfolding their pontoons in water

SPECIFICATIONS
Half-ferry unit
Crew: 3
Weight: 17 000 kg
Length: 12 m
Width: 3·24 m
Height: 3·2 m
Ground clearance: 0·35 m
Track: 2·62 m
Track width: 360 mm
Length of track on ground: 4·83 m
Ground pressure: 0·52 kg/cm²
Max speed: (road) 40 km/h
Range: (road) 300 km (estimate)
Fuel capacity: 370 litres
Fording: amphibious
Gradient: 45%

Vertical obstacle: 0·8 m (estimate)
Trench: 3 m (estimate)
Engine: Model 8D6 6-cylinder water-cooled diesel developing 240 hp at 1800 rpm

Full-ferry
Weight: 34 000 kg
Length: 12 m
Width: 12·63 m

Draught:
(unloaded) 0·97 m
(loaded) 1·5 m
Max water speed:
(unloaded) 10·8 km/h
(loaded) 7·7 km/h
Roadway width: 3·54 m
Roadway track: 1·66 m
Max payload: 52 000 kg

STATUS
In production. In service with all members of the Warsaw Pact, Egypt, Iraq, Israel, Uganda and Yugoslavia. Known as the GSP-55 in East Germany.

MANUFACTURER
Soviet state arsenals.

Very early T-54 MBT being unloaded from GSP heavy amphibious ferry

TZI Footbridge

DESCRIPTION
The TZI floating footbridge was first employed by the Soviet Army during the Second World War, and can also be used as a raft for carrying light crew-served weapons such as mortars and light anti-tank guns.

The individual floats are of rubberised fabric filled with buoyant material such as straw or hay. Each float weighs between 30 and 40 kg when filled and has a safe capacity of 250 kg. These floats are very difficult to sink with small arms fire. The duckboards and saddles are of wood while the handrail posts are metal.

The primary use of the TZI is as a single span footbridge, but it can also be constructed as a half-length, double-lane footbridge so that crew-served weapons can cross. The complete bridge can be carried in two light trucks.

Assembly time with a 64-man working party is 14 to 22 minutes.

SPECIFICATIONS
Float
Length: 2·74 m
Width: 0·48 m
Depth: 0·7 m
Bridge assembly time:
  (single lane bridge) 10–18 min
  (double lane bridge) 14–22 min
Bridge length:
  (single lane) 56 m
  (double lane) 28 m
Capacity of 4-float raft: 1000 kg
Construction time:
  (4-float raft) 3–4 min
  (7-float raft) 8–10 min

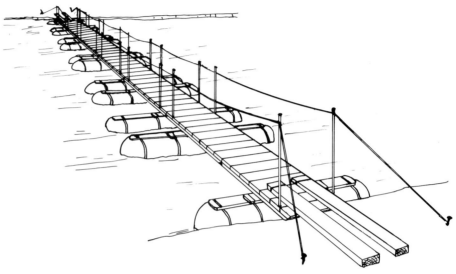

TZI single-lane footbridge

STATUS
Production complete. In service with members of the Warsaw Pact and other armies.

MANUFACTURER
Soviet state factories.

PVD-20 Airportable Bridge

DESCRIPTION
The PVD-20 has been designéd for use by the airborne units of the Warsaw Pact and if required can be dropped by parachute. On the ground the bridge is transported in ten GAZ-63 (4 × 4) 2-ton trucks or six ZIL-157 (6 × 6) 2½-ton trucks. The PVD-20 can be used as a bridge or as a raft.

The basic bridge consists of ten units, each unit with two NDL-20 pneumatic boats and treadways weighing 100 kg each and made of duralumin to save weight, plus ancillary equipment. A complete PVD-20 bridge system consists of 20 NDL-20 pneumatic boats and 60 treadways. Using one set ten 4-ton, six 6-ton or four 8-ton rafts can be assembled.

SPECIFICATIONS
NDL-20 pneumatic boat
Weight: 150 kg
Length: 6 m
Width: 2·2 m
Depth: 0·55 m

PVD-20 airportable bridge being used as ferry carrying Czechoslovak Praga V3S (6 × 6) 3-ton truck

Bridge construction

Type	4t	6t	8t
Length	88·2 m	88·2 m	64·6 m
Assembly time	50 mins	50 mins	50 mins

Raft construction

Type	4t	6t	8t
Length	5·85 m	8·8 m	11·75 m
Rafts per set	10	6	4
NDL-20s per raft	2	3	5
Assembly time	15 mins	20 mins	25 mins

STATUS
In service with members of the Warsaw Pact including Poland and the Soviet Union.

MANUFACTURER
Soviet state factories.

LPP Light Pontoon Bridge

DESCRIPTION
The LPP was developed after the end of the Second World War as the replacement for the war-time DLP wooden pontoon bridge. It is used both as a pontoon bridge and a raft.

The design of the LPP is similar to that of the heavier TPP pontoon bridge. Each pontoon is carried on the rear of a GAZ-63 (4 × 4) 2-ton truck and is launched by gravity. On the top of each pontoon is a turntable which carries all the necessary superstructure components. After being launched this is rotated through 90 degrees, balks connected up, chess laid and the roadway completed.

For 12-ton bridges, single pontoon sections are used, while the 24-ton bridge has two and three section pontoons as the floating supports. The carrying capacity is governed by the makeup of the pontoon elements rather than by the spacing of the supports. For load capacities of 12, 24 and 40 tons the distance between the centres of the floating supports remains the same. A complete LPP light pontoon bridge set consists of 24 bow and 12 centre pontoons.

SPECIFICATIONS

	Bow pontoon	Centre pontoon
Length	5 m	4·6 m
Width	2·2 m	2·2 m
Height	0·95 m	0·95 m

Bridge construction

Type	12t	24t	40t
Roadway width	3 m	3·67 m	3·85 m
Length	160 m	88 m	64 m
Pontoon sections per support	1	2	3
Working party	105 men	105 men	105 men
Assembly time	50/55 minutes	50/55 minutes	55/60 minutes

Raft construction

Type	24t	24t(large)	40t
Length	12 m	12 m	12 m
Rafts per set	6	6	4
Pontoon sections per raft	6	6	9
Assembly time	18 minutes	20 minutes	20 minutes

STATUS

Production complete. No longer in front-line service with members of the Warsaw Pact but still held in reserve. The LPP may be used by the People's Republic of China and is known to have been used in Viet-Nam.

MANUFACTURER

Soviet state factories.

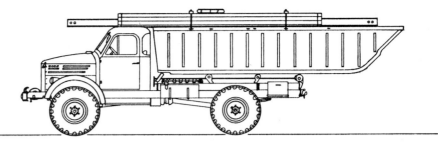

GAZ-63 (4 × 4) truck carrying bow pontoon for LPP pontoon bridge

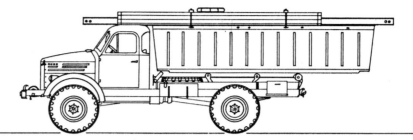

GAZ-63 (4 × 4) truck carrying centre pontoon for LPP pontoon bridge

PMP Heavy Folding Pontoon Bridge

DESCRIPTION

The PMP (or Ribbon Bridge as it is also known) is considered to be a major breakthrough in the design of floating bridges. It was used successfully by the Egyptian Forces during the crossing of the Suez canal in October 1973. Since the introduction of the PMP (Pomtommo Mostovoy Park, or pontoon bridge set) the USA has developed and put into production a similar bridge system called the Ribbon Bridge. The pontoons on the American bridge are made of aluminium rather than steel and are therefore much lighter: the American river pontoon weighs 5440 kg while the Soviet one weighs 6676 kg, and the American shore pontoon weighs 5310 kg while the Soviet one weighs 7252 kg.

Each pontoon of the PMP is constructed of SKhL-4 steel and is in four major sections which are hinged together. They are carried in the folded position on the rear of a 6 × 6 or 8 × 8 truck. Initially the Soviets used the KrAZ-214 (6 × 6) 7-ton truck chassis but this was later supplemented by the more powerful KrAZ-255B (6 × 6) 7½-ton truck.

The pontoon is launched as follows: the travel locks on the pontoon are disengaged and the truck backs to the edge of the water; it brakes sharply and the pontoon slides over a roller system into the water where it almost immediately unfolds; six locking devices are activated stiffening the pontoon, and the pontoons are then normally connected together on the near shore to form a continuous roadway which is swung into position by bridging boats. Once in position the bridge is ready for immediate use. The surface of the roadway is ribbed to prevent vehicles from skidding when they cross the bridge.

The pontoon is recovered as follows: the pontoon truck backs up to the water's edge and an integral jib is unfolded from the truck bed, two cables are strung from the winch, which is to the rear of the cab, through the jib pulley, around the pontoon retrieval guides, and secured to the pontoon retrieval studs. The winch then simultaneously folds and lifts the pontoon on to the truck bed. The jib is folded back into the truck bed, and the pontoon winched over the roller and secured.

The basic bridge has a capacity of 60 tons but it is also possible to build a half-width bridge of 20 tons capacity and of greater length. This is achieved by splitting the pontoons lengthwise once they are launched. Full length pontoons are placed at intervals to give greater stability.

The PMP can also be used to construct rafts of varying sizes, the maximum having a capacity of 170 tons.

The Czechoslovaks use a Tatra 813 (8 × 8) 8-ton roadway truck in conjunction with the PMP; details will be found in the *Portable roadway* section. They also have some of their Tatra 813 (8 × 8) 8-ton trucks fitted with a dozer blade, which are used to prepare river banks before launching the pontoons. The PMP has also been used by East German forces to assist in the unloading of landing ships.

A complete PMP pontoon set consists of 32 river pontoons, 4 shore pontoons and 12 BMK-T (or BMK-130/BMK-130M or BMK-150/BMK-150M) bridging boats. A half set has 16 river and 2 shore pontoons.

In West Germany, EWK produce an all-steel version of the American Ribbon Bridge which is very similar to the original PMP. See page 103 for details.

KrAZ-214 (6 × 6) truck carrying PMP shore pontoon

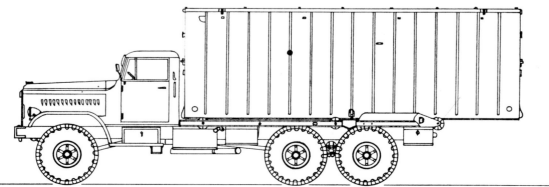

PMP river pontoon being carried on rear of KrAZ-214 (6 × 6) truck

SPECIFICATIONS

	River pontoon (open)	Shore pontoon (open)
Weight	6676 kg	7252 kg
Length	6·75 m	5·58 m
Width	7·1 m (3·21 m)*	7·02–7·32 m (3·3 m)*
Depth	0·915 m	0·73 m

* Folded dimensions are in brackets

Pontoon carriers
Bulgaria: KrAZ-214 (6 × 6) 7-ton truck
Czechoslovakia:
Tatra 813 (8 × 8) 8-ton truck or
Tatra 138 (6 × 6) 8-ton truck
East Germany:
KrAZ-214 (6 × 6) 7-ton truck or
KrAZ-255B (6 × 6) 7½-ton truck
Hungary: KrAZ-214 (6 × 6) 7-ton truck
Soviet Union:
KrAZ-214 (6 × 6) 7-ton truck or
KrAZ-255B (6 × 6) 7½-ton truck
Yugoslavia:
KrAZ-214 (6 × 6) 7½-ton truck or
FAP 2220BDS (6 × 4) 8-ton truck

Bridge construction

Type	20t	60t
Roadway width	3·27 m	6·5 m
Length of bridge		
(whole set)	389 m	227 m
(half set)	281 m	119 m
Working party	82 men*	82 men *
Assembly time	50 minutes*	30 minutes*
Number of whole pontoons including shore		
(whole set)	34†	34†
(half set)	18	18

* Data are for whole set
† Two additional shore pontoons are held in bridge set

Bridge can be constructed in streams with a maximum velocity of 2 metres per second

Raft construction

Type	40t	60t	80t	110t	150t	170t
Length	13·5 m	20·25 m	27 m	39·25 m	52·75 m	59·6 m
Rafts per set	16	10	8	4	4	4
Pontoons per raft	2	3	4	5 + 1 shore	7 + 1 shore	8 + 1 shore
Assembly time	8 minutes	10 minutes	12 minutes	15 minutes	20 minutes	20 minutes

T-54 tanks crossing PMP pontoon bridge held in position by BMK-150 bridging boats

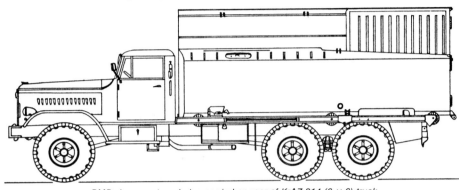

PMP shore pontoon being carried on rear of KrAZ-214 (6 × 6) truck

STATUS
In production. In service with members of the Warsaw Pact except Poland (which uses the Polish designed PP-64) and Romania (which uses the Romanian designed PR-60). It is also used by Egypt (some are now carried on West German Magirus-Deutz 6 × 6 chassis), Iraq, Israel and Yugoslavia.

The PMP is known as the PMS in Czechoslovakia.

MANUFACTURER
Soviet state factories.

PMP pontoons being carried on KrAZ-255B (6 × 6) trucks (Egyptian Army)

FAP 2220BDS (6 × 4) truck of Yugoslav Army recovering PMP pontoon

---

TPP Heavy Pontoon Bridge

DESCRIPTION
The TPP heavy pontoon bridge was developed after the Second World War as the replacement for the similar TMP heavy pontoon bridge. Like the TMP, the TPP can be used as a pontoon bridge or a raft.

The TPP is launched in a similar manner to the TMP but its main improvement is its faster construction. This is made possible by the use of a turntable on the deck of each individual steel pontoon section. This turntable carries all the necessary superstructure components and after launching is rotated through 90 degrees as the prepared superstructure elements are assembled.

Recognition features of the TPP are the turntable on the top of the pontoon, the crossbeams which extend from gunwale to gunwale, deck hatch cover on the port side of the bow section and in the corner of the centre pontoon section, and the indented ribs of the pontoon section sides.

A complete TPP set consists of 48 bow sections, 48 centre sections, 8 trestles, 4 flotation drums, 12 BMK-150 bridging boats (or similar boats) and a total of 116 vehicles of all types. The TPP was used by the Egyptian Army during the crossing of the Suez canal in October 1973.

STATUS
Production complete. In service with members of the Warsaw Pact including Bulgaria, East Germany and Hungary, China, Egypt and Yugoslavia.

MANUFACTURER
Soviet state factories.

SPECIFICATIONS

	Bow pontoon	Centre pontoon
Weight	1051 kg	988 kg
Length	5·97 m	4·94 m
Width	2·4 m	2·4 m
Depth	1·15 m	1·15 m

Pontoon carriers
Bulgaria: Praga V3S (6 × 6) 3-ton truck
East Germany: G5 (6 × 6) 3½-ton truck
Hungary: K300 (6 × 6) 2½-ton truck
Poland: Star 66 (6 × 6) 2½-ton truck
Soviet Union: ZIL-151 or ZIL-157 (6 × 6) 2½-ton truck

Bridge construction
(at a stream velocity of 1·5 metres per second)

Type	16t	50t	70t
Roadway width	3·2 m	4 m	4 m
Length of bridge			
(whole set)	335 m	265 m	205 m
(half set)	163 m	135 m	103 m
(quarter set)	77 m	73 m	58 m
Pontoon sections			
per support	2	2	2
Working party	384 men†	384 men†	384 men†
Assembly time	2½ hours‡	2 hours‡	3 hours‡

(at a stream velocity of over 1·5 metres per second, maximum velocity for using this bridge is 4 metres per second)

Type	16t*	50t	50/70t
Roadway width	3·2 m	4 m	4 m
Length of bridge			
(whole set)	333 m	265 m	185 m
(half set)	148 m	133 m	93 m
(quarter set)	77 m	73 m	52 m
Pontoon sections			
per support	2	2	2
Working party	384 men†	384 men†	384 men†
Assembly time	4 hours‡	2½ hours‡	3 hours‡

* This bridge can be increased in length by the addition of local materials. Maximum lengths are then 506 m, 258 m and 133 m for a whole set, half set, and quarter set respectively, at velocities up to 1·5 m per second. For higher velocities the lengths are 404 m, 203 m and 108 m respectively.

† This is the requirement for a whole set.

‡ The bridge can be constructed at night which takes between 50 per cent and 100 per cent longer.

TPP heavy pontoon bridge being constructed. Bridging boat is BMK-130

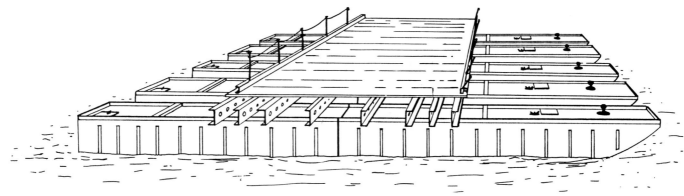

TPP heavy pontoon bridge

TMP Heavy Pontoon Bridge

As far as is known the TMP heavy pontoon bridge is no longer in service anywhere, with the possible exception of China. For details and specifications refer to page 95 of *Jane's Military Vehicles and Ground Support Equipment 1981*.

PPS Heavy Girder Floating Bridge

DESCRIPTION
The PPS heavy girder floating bridge, first observed in 1962, consists of large sectional pontoons, Warren-type truss girders with a full flushdeck roadway mounted on top. Each pontoon consists of a bow section, two centre sections and a stern power unit. Each section is carried on the rear of a ZIL-151 (6 × 6) 2½-ton truck. The pontoon is approximately 23 metres long when assembled. The deck is about 0·38 metres below the gunwales, which support six rows of truss girders, with the top chords carrying I-beam stringers. Decking is laid on these I-beams to form a roadway about six metres wide. The bridge has a maximum capacity of at least 60 000 kg.

STATUS
In service with the Soviet Army.

MANUFACTURER
Soviet state factories.

UNITED KINGDOM

Class 16 Air-Portable Bridge

DESCRIPTION

The class 16 air-portable bridge was designed by the Military Engineering Establishment at Christchurch (now part of the Military Vehicles and Engineering Establishment). Production and marketing of the bridge are undertaken by Laird of Anglesey.

The bridge is constructed of a high strength aluminium zinc-magnesium alloy and can be used either as a clear span bridge of up to 15·2 metres in length, as a floating bridge of any length or as a powered raft with a maximum speed of 6 knots. All have a non-skid roadway 3·3 metres wide when assembled.

The basic components of the class 16 bridge are the deck boxes, ramps, articulator boxes, floats and the sponsons. These components are normally carried by ¾-ton Land-Rovers which also tow a single-axle trailer. A Wessex helicopter can carry any component of the class 16 bridge and a Lockheed C-130 Hercules can carry all the components required to build a ferry.

The deck box combines the functions of bridge girders and cross girders, and contributes buoyancy in floating applications. The top of the box forms the deck of the bridge. At either end of the bridge tapered ramps provide access. When being used as a floating bridge or raft, hydraulically operated articulator boxes are fitted between the deck boxes and the ramps to allow adjustment for varying heights. For floating bridges and rafts, pneumatic floats are fitted to give additional buoyancy and stability. When being used as a floating raft for powered raft operations, sponsons with integral turntable brackets are fitted at each corner of the raft, each sponson having a 40 hp outboard motor.

Clearspan bridge

A 15·2-metre clearspan bridge is assembled from seven deck boxes and two pairs of ramps. Three ¾-ton Land-Rovers and trailers carry all the components for one 15·2-metre clearspan bridge. The bridge can be constructed and positioned by 16 men in approximately 20 minutes using a special launching nose and rollers. A launching nose and three pairs of rollers are used for building and launching the bridge. One pair of rollers is subsequently used as a landing roller on the far bank. The angle of the launching nose can be altered by means of its built-in jack to allow for varying heights of the far bank. The far end of the bridge is lowered to the ground by operating a jack.

Floating bridge

A floating bridge 58 metres long can be assembled from 40 deck boxes, two pairs of articulator boxes and two pairs of ramps and floats using a standard bridge set. Five ¾-ton Land-Rovers and trailers carry all the necessary components for a floating bridge. A team of 24 men takes 45 minutes to build the 58-metre bridge and there is no limit to the length of floating bridge that can be built. The floating bridge is assembled in the same manner as the raft but the sponsons are omitted and floats fitted in their place.

Powered raft

The standard raft has a 12·2-metre level deck and is 22 metres overall. It is assembled from 10 deck boxes, two pairs of articulator boxes, two pairs of ramps, floats and four sponsons with outboard motors. Twenty ¾-ton Land-Rovers and trailers carry all the components necessary to build one standard powered raft. Building time is approximately 40 minutes with 24 men. The raft is constructed as follows: the ramps and articulators are assembled and launched in the water, deck boxes added, then the rear articulator and finally the rear ramps, the sponsons and outboard motors are fitted to the raft and the floats are fitted to the boxes. The floats are inflated from the Land-Rovers' exhaust gases. Longer rafts may be built up to a maximum length of 28 metres overall, with an 18·3-metre level deck. These are powered by six outboard motors and have a total distributed load of 24 tons.

STATUS

In production. In service with Australia, Canada, Nigeria and the United Kingdom.

MANUFACTURER

Laird (Anglesey) Limited, Beaumaris, Gwynedd LL58 0HY, Wales.

SPECIFICATIONS

	Deck box	Ramp	Articulator box	Float and support frame	Sponson (with motor and accessories)
Length	3·6 m	3·6 m	1·8 m	2 m	2 m
Width	1·2 m	1·8 m	1·2 m	1·2 m	1·2 m
Height	0·38 m	0·38 m	0·38 m	0·75 m	0·75 m
Weight	305 kg	346 kg	279 kg	23 kg	281 kg

Assembly	Major components					
	Deck box	Ramp	Articulator	Float & support	Sponson & motor	Launching nose & roller set
1 × 15·2 m clear-span bridge	7	4	nil	nil	nil	1
1 powered raft	10	4	2 port 2 starboard	20	4	nil
1 × 58 m floating bridge	40	4	2 port 2 starboard	80	nil	nil
1 British Army bridge set						
Components	40	16	8 port 8 starboard	80	16	2
Assemblies	4 × 15·2 m clearspan bridges or 4 powered rafts or 1 × 58 m floating bridge					

Class 16 air-portable bridge being used as floating raft (T J Gander)

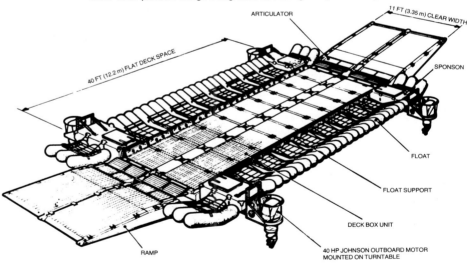

ARTICULATOR
11 FT (3.35 m) CLEAR WIDTH
40 FT (12.2 m) FLAT DECK SPACE
SPONSON
FLOAT
FLOAT SUPPORT
DECK BOX UNIT
RAMP
40 HP JOHNSON OUTBOARD MOTOR MOUNTED ON TURNTABLE

Class 16 air-portable bridge being used as raft

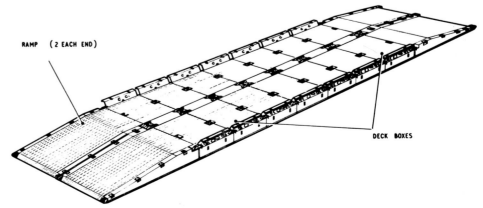

RAMP (2 EACH END)
DECK BOXES

Class 16 air-portable bridge being used as clearspan bridge

Class 80 Heavy Ferry

DESCRIPTION
The class 80 heavy ferry, introduced in the 1950s, is designed for rapid crossing of wide water obstacles by all tracked and wheeled vehicles up to class 80.

The ferry consists of four main pontoon sections, four bow pontoon sections, four buoyancy sections and four hydraulically-operated ramps. All pontoon sections and ramp sections are made of aluminium alloy.

The four main pontoon sections are in the centre with buoyancy sections on either side and the bow pontoon and ramps at either end. Loads are carried only on the four main pontoon sections.

Built into each bow pontoon section are four Gill hydrojet propulsion units, each powered by a 120 hp Rolls-Royce petrol engine. The powerpack, consisting of the engine, clutch and gearbox, is bolted onto the deck of each bow pontoon section. The Gill propulsion unit is basically an axial-flow pump that takes in and ejects water at the base of the pontoon. For steering the jet can be traversed through a full 360 degrees.

A complete class 80 heavy ferry is carried on four 10-tonne trucks, each of which tows a special four-wheeled trailer, and two 4-tonne trucks each towing a one-tonne trailer. Each 10-tonne truck carries one bow pontoon and one buoyancy section with the trailer carrying one main pontoon section and one ramp unit.

Class 80 heavy ferry carrying Chieftain MBT (Ministry of Defence)

For assembly, two cranes and two dozers are normally used: the cranes lift the pontoons from the truck and the dozers push them into the water. Once assembled the class 80 heavy ferry can carry one MBT, or three APCs or six wheeled vehicles. Maximum speed without a load is 14 km/h and with a load is 11 km/h.

STATUS
Production complete. In service with Australia and the British Army.

SPECIFICATIONS

	Main pontoon section	Bow pontoon section	Buoyancy section	Ramp
Weight	4830 kg	2030 kg	760 kg	1270 kg
Length	9·8 m	5·5 m	4·3 m	6·1 m
Width	2·3 m	2·1 m	2·1 m	2·1 m
Depth	1·2 m	1·2 m	1·2 m	n/app

Assembled class 80 Heavy Ferry
Assembled time with 30 man team: 30 minutes
Assembled length:
    (without ramps) 19·5 m
    (with ramps) 31·7 m
Width:
    (overall) 8·7 m
    (usable) 4·6 m

MEXEFLOTE – Multi-purpose Pontoon and Harbour Equipment

DESCRIPTION
MEXEFLOTE is a multi-purpose pontoon equipment which has been designed specifically for marine applications. It is of Military Load Class 60 and can be rapidly constructed as lighterage rafts, for use at sea and in harbours, and can also be assembled as causeways, jetties and other floating structures. The equipment can be used in the following wave conditions: pontoons connected into rafts, causeways and jetties in 0·61 metre waves; operation of rafts, causeways and jetties in 1·22- to 1·52-metre waves; survival of causeway, raft or jetty (unladen) at moorings in 2·74- to 3·05-metre waves; survival of causeways or rafts (unladen) in tow in 3·66 metre waves.

The system is based on the use of three steel pontoons: bow, centre and stern. These can be connected end to end and side to side to form rafts, causeways, jetties and floating platforms of any shape. The pontoons are of welded steel construction with flush sides. Built into the sides and ends of the pontoons are recessed slots into which the connectors are fitted. There is a 50 mm gap between pontoons.

The bow pontoon consists of a forward section, an aft section and a ramp. The forward section is hinged to the bottom edge of the box-shaped aft section and can articulate vertically to a maximum of 457 mm above the deck level and lowered to a maximum of 380 mm below the surface of the aft section. The manually operated, demountable articulator is mounted in a recess in the aft section and is connected to the forward section by an articulator ram. The articulator has a safe working load of 81 280 kg. The pontoon ramp is hinged to the forward section and slides over the forward end of the aft section to bridge the gap between the sections.

The centre pontoon is a box-shaped unit with an internal lateral bulkhead dividing the interior into two watertight compartments. Each compartment has a hatch cover, air-line connector and a bilge discharge outlet fitted with nylon plugs set flush with the deck surface.

The stern pontoon is also a box-shaped unit with an internal lateral bulkhead dividing the interior into two watertight compartments. Each compartment has a hatch cover, air-line connector and a bilge discharge outlet fitted with nylon plugs set flush with the deck surface. The bottom edge of the stern pontoon is chamfered to allow the propeller and skeg of the propelling unit to be rotated through 360 degrees when the unit is mounted at the stern of the pontoon.

The pontoon connector is a rectangular unit weighing 73·94 kg and fits into any full length connector slot of a pontoon and is used to join together pontoons side by

90-ton MEXEFLOTE being used as general lighterage raft at Army School of Transport's Marchwood Military Port (Ministry of Defence)

MEXEFLOTE during Exercise Forte '76 on Normandy beach of Merville-Franceville (Ministry of Defence)

side and end to end. Each connector has one fixed pin and one movable pin at the bottom which can be raised or lowered by a handle in the top of the connector to make the bottom connection of adjoining pontoons. The top connection is made by passing a short bolt of each adjoining pontoon through a hole in the connector.

The pontoon link is a triangular box-shaped unit which weighs 20·87 kg. This has short bolt holes through the top and a fixed pin at the bottom which fits through a hole in a jaw at the bottom of the short slot in the side of the bow pontoon forward section and in the end of the stern section.

Rafts

The most common types of raft are:
20·22 × 7·42 metres which can carry one class 60 tank or three 4-ton trucks.
38·4 × 7·42 metres which can carry two class 60 tanks or six 4-ton trucks.
38·4 × 12·9 metres (Maxi—MEXEFLOTE) which has a maximum capacity of 198 tonnes and can carry three class 60 tanks or equivalent vehicles.

A Landing Ship Logistic, or similar ship, is capable of carrying one 38·4 × 7·42 metre raft on each side or two 20·22 × 7·42 metre rafts on each side. When approaching the beach these are released and can be used as rafts (with the addition of propulsion units) or connected end to end to form a causeway to the beach.

The MEXEFLOTE pontoons can easily be handled as they are compatible with ISO container storage and handling systems: the centre and bow pontoons conform to the 6·1 × 2·4 metre container dimension.

STATUS

No longer in production. Production was originally undertaken by the Gloster Railway Carriage and Wagon Company (a member of the Wingate Group). Fairey Engineering Limited holds the licence for production. In service with the British Army and other armed forces.

MANUFACTURER

Fairey Engineering Limited, PO Box 41, Crossley Road, Heaton Chapel, Stockport, Cheshire SK4 5BD, England.

SPECIFICATIONS

MEXEFLOTE

	Bow pontoon	Centre pontoon	Stern pontoon
Weight	5909 kg	4654 kg	4418 kg
Length	7·92 m	6·1 m	6·1 m
Width	2·44 m	2·44 m	2·44 m
Depth	1·45 m	1·45 m	1·45 m

Typical raft

Length	Width	Number of strings per raft	Number of pontoons per raft			
			Bow	Centre	Stern	Total
20·22 m	7·42 m	3	3	3	3	9
26·37 m	7·42 m	3	3	6	3	12
32·51 m	7·42 m	3	3	9	3	15
38·66 m	7·42 m	3	3	12	3	18
38·66 m	12·39 m	5	5	20	5	30

Raft characteristics

Raft size	Displacement	Load capacity 0·61 m free board	Deck space	Speed unladen	Speed laden
20·22 × 7·42 m	48·77 tonnes	55·88 tonnes	125·4 m²	3·22 m/s	3·48 m/s
38·66 × 7·42 m	95·508 tonnes	111·76 tonnes	260·1 m²	3·09 m/s	2·83 m/s
38·66 × 12·39 m	142·25 tonnes	201·178 tonnes	456·9 m²	2·83 m/s	2·64 m/s

Typical causeway

Length	Width	Number of pontoons per causeway			
		Bow	Centre	Stern	Total
99·36 m	3 pontoons	3	30	15	48
99·36 m	5 pontoons	5	50	25	80
123·75 m	3 pontoons	3	36	21	60
123·75 m	5 pontoons	5	60	35	100

Acrow Uniflote System

DESCRIPTION

The Acrow Uniflote was conceived in the late 1950s as a flotation system based on unit construction principles in which identical flotation units can be assembled together to form rafts of various load-carrying capacities, as well as pontoon bridges.

It is used by military forces throughout the world for line of communication bridges, floating bridges, ship-to-shore causeways and as vehicle and personnel rafts. It is also widely used for civil purposes such as landing stages, roll-on and roll-off terminals, and temporary applications to carry land-based plant such as cranes, excavators and pile driving equipment for marine works.

All Uniflote equipment can be carried on standard commercial vehicles and if necessary can be skidded into the water. Assembly in the water is accomplished by a maximum of four men, and the units are held together by locking pins inserted in the couplers.

The standard Uniflote is 5·283 metres long, 2·438 metres wide and 1·219 metres deep. It is a structural steel-framed unit of all welded construction with 4 mm skin-plates welded to the frame. Two internal watertight bulkheads are incorporated to provide three watertight compartments, each with a watertight hatch. Individual compartments in the flotation units can be flooded or emptied by compressed air. Under a load of 10 000 kg, each Uniflote maintains a freeboard in the region of 0·23 metre. Couplers are placed so that Uniflotes can be joined end to end, side to side and end to side. Steel gunwales are provided along the side of the Uniflote and are drilled to allow simple saddles to be fitted. The couplers allow for the transmission of loads throughout a Uniflote raft. Concentrated loads can be applied to the gunwales through saddle attachments. Runners are attached to the bottom to assist in skidding operations on shore, and four lifting shackles are fitted. The Uniflote is also available in a 1·828-metre deep version.

The standard Uniflote has the deck approximately 0·08 metre below gunwale level so that a replaceable timber deck may be fitted if required. This is fitted in the form of three pre-assembled mats (one centre and two outer sections) to each Uniflote. Each mat is designed so that it is retained laterally by the gunwales and is of such a thickness that it stands 0·05 metre above the gunwale level. Side rings enable Uniflotes to be craned from the shore to the water. Cross junction and side junction mats are also available. The special military version has an integral steel deck set level with the top of the gunwales over which traffic may drive direct.

Scow ends are designed to be attached to either end or side of the Uniflote and have identical end sections. They also have short lengths of gunwale to correspond with the gunwales in the Uniflote. The bottom plate slopes up at an angle of 30 degrees and terminates in a reinforced nosing plate on which a bollard is mounted.

The ramp unit can be connected to the end or sides of the basic Uniflote by ramp connectors which allows the ramp to articulate and gives access for shore loading over a wide variation in bank heights.

The various Interflote connectors available allow Uniflotes to be spaced apart, giving greater stability to floating platforms where required without the need for additional buoyancy.

A range of saddles is available to allow the secure fixing of winches and propulsion units. These saddles can be fitted over a bow or stern unit, over the junction between a bow or stern unit and a Uniflote, over a Uniflote, over the junction between two Uniflotes, or an outrigger (fitted to the side of a Uniflote). Other saddles are available for fixing Acrow Panel or Bailey bridging, and other ancillary equipment.

Details of the Thos Storey Motorflote are given in the *Bridging boats* section.

Uniflote causeway carrying tank transporter loaded with Leopard 1 MBTs of Belgian Army (Photo Bureau de Presse 1 Belgian Corps)

Acrow Panel/Uniflote floating bridge

Standard Uniflote

SPECIFICATIONS
Standard Uniflote (U4/1A)
Weight: 2895 kg
Length: 5·283 m
(coupler to coupler) 5·41 m
Width: 2·438 m
Height: (without gunwale) 1·219 m
Gunwale size: 76·2 × 76·2 mm

Bow Unit (female U4/3A, male U4/2A)
Weight: 843 kg
Length: 1·82 m
Width: 2·438 m
Height: 1·219 m

Ramp Unit (U4/6A)
Weight: 1879 kg
Length: 3·658 m
Height: 1·219 m

50 ton Uniflote ferry carrying Coles 315M crane truck

STATUS
In production. In service with many armed forces all over the world including Belgium and Brazil.

MANUFACTURER
Thos Storey (Engineers) Limited, 8 South Wharf Road, London W2 1PB, England.

Mabey "Flatpack" Pontoons

DESCRIPTION
The Mabey "Flatpack" pontoon has been designed for high strength and buoyancy. This provides the advantages in floating bridge designs of long pontoon piers with high lateral stability and long floating spans which reduce the slopes under load. The equipment can deal with high banks and high rise and fall of water by using long landing bays. If required, the bridge deck can be raised by panel piers on the pontoons. Floating bridges can be built to all loading specifications with either Mabey Universal or Mabey Bailey bridge superstructure and can be provided with opening navigation spans if necessary.

The pontoons are designed to be suitable for supplying in kit form, hence the "Flatpack" designation. The resulting packages are very advantageous for shipping to remote sites. All jigs and detailed assembly instructions are supplied for rapid completion on site by local labour.

There are two types of pontoon, 1·3 metres deep with 10 tonnes buoyancy and 2·1 metres deep with 30 tonnes buoyancy. The centre pontoon is divided by a stiff bulkhead into two watertight compartments which may be flooded to provide trim or reduction of freeboard during erection manoeuvres. End to end connections are pinned using Bailey-type male and female eyes. The strength of these connecting eyes is a key feature of the design, permitting the building of long floating piers. Rails on the gunwales of the pontoon are drilled to accept a saddle which connects pontoon to bridge. This caters for all possible variations in layout of pontoon pier and bridge widths, both Mabey Bailey and Universal, and also spreads the load from the bridge into the pontoon. These holes also provide locations for lifting shackles. Runners on the bottom of the pontoon provide necessary strength when the unit is grounded and also act as rails on which the coupled units may be launched.

The bow unit is similar to the centre pontoon but incorporates a streamlined scow end. The 25-degree slope of the scow reduces the resistance of the pier to river and tidal currents, and therefore the drag on the anchorages. Like the centre pontoon, the bow pontoon is provided with two watertight compartments, access hatches, rails and runners. It also has jaws at the transom end so that it may be coupled to either centre or bow pontoons.

There are three ways in which a pier may be con-

Mabey pontoons being used with Mabey and Johnson Bailey bridge

structed: on shore to be launched as a complete unit from rollers; by coupling the individual pontoons in the water and trimming by crane; or by coupling the individual pontoons in the water and trimming by using a work party.

A coupling pin is used to connect the pontoons together. This incorporates a long taper to facilitate assembly and is secured by a spring steel safety pin. Pontoons are fitted with bollards to aid handling and anchoring.

Development of the Mabey pontoon began in 1974 and it entered service in 1977.

SPECIFICATIONS

	Centre pontoon	Bow pontoon
Weight	3824 kg	3300 kg
Length	6 m	6 m
Width	2·47 m	2·47 m
Height	1·3 m	1·3 m

STATUS
In production. In service.

MANUFACTURER
Mabey and Johnson Limited, Floral Mile, Twyford, Reading, Berkshire RG10 9SQ, England.

Mabey Ferries

DESCRIPTION
The Mabey "Flatpack" pontoon system has been developed and extended to give a range of ferries suitable for use in remote areas while having the same low shipping volume as the "Flatpack" design. The ferry pontoons are identical to the Mabey "Flatpack" bridging pontoons except that the side panels are equipped with two coupler sets. There is also a ramp unit, propulsion

platform, decking system and associated equipment. In use, ferries are built up by coupling the units together using a special connector unit for the side to side connection. Assembly can be carried out before or after launching. A balanced ramp arrangement is provided to allow loading from various shore slopes.

SPECIFICATIONS

Carrying capacity (tonnes)	Overall size (metres)	Number of units		
		Centre	Ramp	Bow
36	9·6 × 21	4	4	—
64	11·5 × 21	4	4	4
80	12·5 × 27	9	6	—
100	11·5 × 33	8	4	4

STATUS
In production.

MANUFACTURER
Mabey and Johnson Limited, Floral Mile, Twyford, Reading, Berkshire RG10 9SQ, England.

Mabey Ferry carrying Combat Engineer Tractor

UNITED STATES OF AMERICA

Aluminium Floating Footbridge

DESCRIPTION
The aluminium floating footbridge consists of treadways, pontoons, handrail posts, ropes, holdfasts and approach posts. One bridge set contains 144 metres of bridge in normal type of assembly and is allocated on the scale of one bridge set per corps/army engineer float bridge company. Half the bridge set is carried on a 2½-ton (6 × 6) truck which tows a 2½-ton utility pole type trailer. The complete bridge can be carried in a C-130 Hercules transport aircraft and one-half set of the footbridge can be delivered by parachute from a C-130 using two 2721 kg bearing platforms.

The treadways are made of aluminium and consist of two I-beams carrying traverse channels which support a corrugated aluminium sheet tread. The ends of the I-beam are fitted with spring-loaded connectors, male at one end and female at the other to provide connection between the treadways.

The pontoons are of sheet aluminium reinforced with light aluminium members. The pontoon has a false bottom 171 mm above its true bottom which provides a compartment that is filled with a light cellular plastic material. Each gunwale is fitted with two hooks which grip the outer bottom flanges of a treadway I-beam. Each pontoon has a hole 25 × 51 mm in the bow and stern just above the false bottom to make the pontoon self-bailing.

The handrail post is of aluminium 32 mm in diameter and is mounted on a base of aluminium bar. This is installed by inserting the base in a socket in the treadway and rotating the post 180 degrees to lock it in position. Each bridge set contains 12·7 mm diameter manila rope which is cut as required for handrail line, guy lines and bridle ties. Two 182·88-metre reels of 9·5 mm galvanised wire rope for use as anchor cables and guys for improvised cable towers are provided together with 20 wire rope clips, 4 holdfasts (each complete with 9 pickets) and 16 approach posts.

The bridge is normally assembled using the successive bay method but if the water is too deep for this method the bridge is assembled in sections, which takes twice as long. The bridge can also be assembled on the shore, which requires a shore assembly area as long as the bridge, straight, and cleared to a width of 6·096 metres. Finally the bridge can be assembled in the water or on steep banks. In this case two skids are set in the water and inclined against the bank. This allows the bays or bridge sections to be launched into the water. In currents up to 2·438 metres a second the number of troops who can cross single file at two-pace intervals is as follows:

Daylight: 75 men per minute, single file, double-time
Moonlight: 40 men per minute, single file, quick time
Blackout: 25 men per minute, single file, quick time

If current velocity is between 2·743 and 3·352 metres a second, the crossing rates should be reduced by 20 per cent.

If required the pontoons can also be used as rafts. An expedient two-pontoon raft is formed by lashing two pontoons side by side with one treadway across them. This will carry one wounded man and two paddle men, one in the bow and one in the stern. A three-pontoon expedient raft is formed by lashing three pontoons side by side with one treadway across them and an additional treadway along each side of the centre treadway. This can carry four wounded men and four paddle men, two in the bow and two in the stern.

An expedient bridge 30·48 metres long, which will take a Jeep and trailer, can be constructed from the components of the aluminium footbridge set. This may not be used where the current exceeds 1·524 metres a second.

SPECIFICATIONS
Assembly time
Daylight: 15 minutes plus 1 minute per 4·572 m of bridge
Night-time: (with illumination or moonlight) 20 minutes plus 1¼ minutes per 4·572 m of bridge
Blackout: 30 minutes plus 2 minutes per 4·572 m of bridge

Maximum safe allowable deflection

Number of bays	Effective length of bridge	Max allowable deflection
4	13·716 m	0·05 m
6	20·57 m	0·1 m
8	27·43 m	0·152 m
10	34·29 m	0·254 m
12	41·148 m	0·381 m
18	61·72 m	0·863 m
24	82·29 m	1·549 m
36	123·44 m	3·479 m

Treadway
Weight: 38·1 kg
Length:
(overall) 3·555 m
(effective) 3·428 m
Width:
(overall) 0·711 m
(walkway) 0·527 m
Depth: 0·133 m

Pontoon
Weight: 45·36 kg
Length: 4·267 m
Width: 0·609 m
Depth: 0·367 m (gunwale)

Post
Weight: 1·02 kg
Length: 1·092 m

Weight of complete bridge set: 4105 kg

STATUS
In service with the US Army and other countries including Australia and South Korea. License-produced in Greece.

Australian engineers erecting aluminium floating footbridge (Australian Army)

Bridge Floating: Raft Section, Light Tactical

DESCRIPTION
The bridge set has sufficient components for one four-pontoon reinforced raft, or 13·41 metres of normal bridge. The same set is used in assembling a combination of floating bridges or rafts of various classes. One bridge set is carried by two 2½-ton (6 × 6) trucks, one of which tows a 2½-ton pole type trailer which carries the eight half-pontoons stacked one on top of the other.

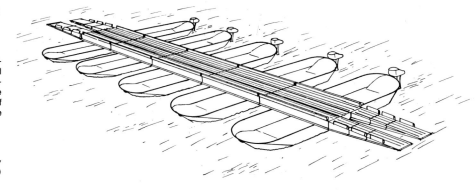

Bridge Floating: Raft Section, Light Tactical (five-bay normal raft)

Two aluminium half-pontoons are joined stern to stern to form a complete pontoon. The deck panel is positioned and retained laterally by four retainer lugs on the pontoons. One end of each deck panel is male and the other female. Two deck filler panels are used to fill the space between one set of deck panels. These are normally retained in position by pintles, but provision is made for bolting the filler panels to the deck panels. Two types of ramp panel are provided, one to mate with the male end of a deck section and one with the female end. The articulating assembly is provided to permit variations in the end span abutment elevations in bridges and rafts from 1·041 metres above the horizontal position of the deck to 0·482 metre below. It consists of male and female sections. A connecting pin and adjusting bar are used to join the two sections.

There are two sizes of kerb. The deck panel kerb is used on the normal bay of the superstructure and the short ramp kerb is used on the ramp and articulator panels. These are held in position by holding lugs that extend from the bottom of the kerb and bear directly on the underside of the top flange of the deck panel.

A raft normally consists of three bays of decking with ramps at each end on four complete pontoons. The loading space from kerb to kerb is 2·743 metres and loading length is 8·992 metres.

The bridge is rated as class 11 in a current of 2·438 metres per second and the four-pontoon three-bay raft as class 12 in a current of up to 2·438 metres per second. The light tactical bridge has loading space kerb to kerb of 2·743 metres with the pontoons normally being spaced at 3·352-metre centres. Reinforced bridges have the pontoons spaced at 2·438-metre centres.

Each pontoon is provided with a fluked marine anchor and each raft set is issued with four outboard motor brackets. The outboard motors normally used are rated at 25 hp.

A six-pontoon, four-bay reinforced raft has a length of 21·336 metres, a loading length of 12·192 metres and a roadway width (kerb to kerb) of 3·352 metres.

Ferry conversion set
Trail ferry method
A bicycle traveller allows the raft to move smoothly along a ferry cable. The ferry cable is stretched across the river and made fast. The bicycle traveller is attached to the cable so that its sheaves roll smoothly. The hauling line is attached to the grommet in the bicycle traveller and the manoeuvre lines to the snatch blocks which are attached to the sheave housings of the traveller. On the raft, the hauling line is attached to the upstream end of the centre pontoon. The manoeuvre lines are attached to the gunwales of the outside pontoons. The ferry is operated by adjusting the manoeuvre lines so that the raft is at an angle to the stream current. The upstream end of the pontoon inclines towards the opposite shore. The current pushes against the upstream side of the pontoon and forces the raft across the river. As the pontoons are pushed into the current, the speed of the raft increases. This method may be used when the current exceeds 0·914 metre a second.

The Flying Ferry works on a similar principle to the trail ferry except that the raft is held in the stream by an anchor well upstream from the crossing site. As the raft moves from shore to shore, it swings in an arc of a circle centred on the anchor. This ferry requires a maximum stream or river velocity of 1·219 metres a second.

SPECIFICATIONS
Half pontoon
Weight: 295 kg
Length: 5·638 m
Width: 2·044 m
Depth: 0·863 m

Deck panel
Weight: 256·28 kg
Length: 3·701 m
(effective) 3·352 m
Width: 1·066 m
Depth: 0·323 m

Deck filler panel
Weight: 43 kg
Length: 1·647 m
Width: 0·787 m
Height: 0·161 m

Ramp panel
Weight:
(male) 149·9 kg
(female) 181 kg

Length:
(male) 2·438 m
(female) 2·136 m
Width: 1·066 m
Height: 0·323 m

Articulating assembly
Weight: 290 kg
Length: 2·2 m
Width: 1·066 m
Height: 0·514 m

Kerb
Weight:
(normal) 49·9 kg
(short) 9·07 kg
Length:
(normal) 3·295 m
(short) 0·865 m

Construction time
4-pontoon, 3-bay raft: 30 minutes
5-pontoon, 5-bay raft: 35 minutes
6-pontoon, 4-bay raft: 45 minutes

Raft classes (normal)	Stream velocities in metres per second						
Type of assembly	0·914	1·524	2·133	2·438	2·743	3·048	3·352
4-pontoon, 3-bay without articulators	16a	16a	16b	12b	8c	4d	0d
4-pontoon, 3-bay with articulators	12a	12a	12b	12b	8c	4c	0d
4-pontoon, 4-bay with articulators	10a	10a	10b	10b	6c	2d	0d
5-pontoon, 5-bay without articulators	16a	16a	14b	11b	8c	5d	2
5-pontoon, 5-bay with articulators	9a	9a	9b	9b	8c	5d	2
6-pontoon, 5-bay without articulators	18a	18a	18b	18c	18d	12	6
6-pontoon, 4-bay with articulators	13a	13a	13b	13c	13d	12	5

No. of 25 hp outboard motors required to hold loaded raft in the maximum indicated stream velocity:
a: 1
b: 2
c: 3
d: 4

STATUS
In service with the US Army and other armed forces including South Korea. License-produced in Greece (q.v.).

Ribbon Bridge

DEVELOPMENT
The Ribbon Bridge was developed by Pacific Car and Foundry Company of Renton, Washington and the United States Army Mobility Equipment Research and Development (MERADCOM) Center at Fort Belvoir, Virginia, and is based on the design of the Soviet PMP Ribbon Bridge which was used by the Egyptian Army during the crossing of the Suez Canal in October 1973. The Ribbon Bridge has two main differences from the Soviet PMP: it is aluminium rather than steel and so weighs about a third less, and the PMP uses torsion bars to help unfold the pontoons, which is effective in

launching but means that the torsion force must be overcome during retrieval, which results in longer retrieval times. Development of the American bridge began in 1969 and the bridge was type classified as standard A in June 1972, less than three years after development started. The first production contract, worth $10 million, was awarded to the Consolidated Diesel Electric Division of the CONDEC Corporation at Old Greenwich, and was for 250 interior bays, 50 ramp bays and 300 transporter trucks. The Ribbon Bridge will augment and replace the mobile assault bridging emplaced by the forward elements. It can be placed in use ten times faster with a fifth of the personnel required to emplace standard floating bridges. The bridge can sup-

port 70-ton loads in currents of up to 2·438 metres per second and up to 80 tons when conditions are ideal.

The Ribbon Bridge system was first fielded by the United States Army in West Germany and South Korea in 1976. A normal United States bridge company has 30 interior bays and 12 ramps, sufficient for 212 metres of bridge or six rafts.

DESCRIPTION
The Ribbon Bridge consists of integral float-deck elements connected longitudinally to form a continuous floating roadway. There are two basic bridge elements, the interior and the ramp bays, both of which are of aluminium construction. The interior bay consists of two

M812 (6 × 6) truck carrying interior bay of Ribbon Bridge after retrieval

Interior bays of Ribbon Bridge being assembled to form bridge

Ribbon Bridge in position with M109 155 mm howitzer being driven across

Ribbon Bridge in position with M60A1 MBT being driven across

Interior bays of Ribbon Bridge at intermediate retrieval on back of M812 (6 × 6) truck with CSB in background

Interior bay of Ribbon Bridge being winched back into position on M812 (6 × 6) truck

roadway pontoons and two bow pontoons joined by hinges and pins. During deployment the bow and roadway pontoons are automatically latched at each end. The end bay has the same configuration as the interior bay except for an adjustable joint at the interior bay connection and the tapered end section. The joint is controlled by two hydraulic cylinders which adjust automatically to the condition of the river bank by providing a 0 to 20 degree range of angles between the ramp and the bank.

The bays are carried folded on the rear of M812 5-ton (6 × 6) trucks and are launched as follows: the two-man crew of the truck releases the travel latches, in three minutes, and the truck backs up to the edge of the water and brakes. The bay element then slides off the rear of the truck into the water and the bays automatically unfold by water buoyancy acting through tension cables and levers. Water must be at least 0·914 metre deep for launching which is accomplished from the driver's seat in a matter of seconds. The bays are joined by steel pins to form bridges or ferries. A T-wrench is used to drive the 67 mm diameter steel pins at the bottom ends of each of the two roadway pontoons. Spring-loaded 'dogbone' connectors secure the decks.

The bridge is normally assembled along the shore and the complete bridge is then swung across the river using bridge erection boats. Bridging boats are used to hold the bridge in position and in a current with a velocity of 2·5 metres a second are normally positioned every 20 metres. If the bridge is to remain in place for extended periods overhead anchor cables may be employed. It can also be constructed using the method of successive bays or rafts. If required, individual bays can be emplaced by helicopter. The Ribbon Bridge can be constructed at the rate of 6·705 metres per minute over rivers with a current of up to 2·438 metres per second. The roadway itself is 4·114 metres wide and there is a 1·219-metre walkway on either side.

To retrieve a bridge bay the transporter is backed into the water and the boom is raised to the vertical. The lifting cable runs from the winch over a sheave at the top of the boom and down to the bridge bay. The cable hook is attached to the roadway hinge pin and when the cable is reeled in, one end of the bay is lifted out of the water until water pressure acting on the other end causes the bay to fold up. At this time, a series of latches automatically lock the bay in the folded position. The bay is then lowered into the restraint hooks at the back of the transporter, the boom is lowered, and the bay is winched onto the transporter. The front restraint is engaged and the vehicle is ready to drive away. Bridge sections can be launched or retrieved by one man but each transporter carries an assistant to speed up operations, especially during retrieval, and to assist in assembling the bridge.

The bridge transporter was originally a dedicated vehicle with little use when not carrying bridge equipment. In order to overcome this shortcoming, a special pallet has been developed which permits the transporter to haul up to 9000 kg of cargo (4500 kg across country). The pallet can be self-loaded or off-loaded while carrying up to 4500 kg, a feature which lends itself to pre-palletised loads.

VARIANTS
Improved Ribbon Bridge
It has been proposed that an Improved Ribbon Bridge should be developed to provide the US Army with a floating bridge of class 70 capacity in a stream velocity of 2·5 metres per second. The floats will have positive flotation and the ramp length will be 7 metres. The basic composition will be an improved hydraulically-operated ramp, interior bays and end bays. It will be transported on a specially modified high-mobility truck.

The Improved Ribbon Bridge is still under development.

SPECIFICATIONS
Interior bay
Weight: 5440 kg
Length:
(folded) 6·9 m
(unfolded) 6·9 m
Width:
(folded) 3·2 m
(unfolded) 8·127 m
Height:
(folded) 2·311 m
(at bow, unfolded) 1·117 m
(at roadway, unfolded) 0·736 m

Ramp bay
Weight: 5310 kg
Length:
(folded) 5·8 m
(unfolded) 7·721 m
Width:
(folded) 3·175 m
(unfolded) 8·127 m
Height:
(folded) 2·311 m
(of roadway, unfolded) 0·736 m
(of shore end, unfolded) 0·381 m

Transporter loaded
Weight: 17 900 kg
Length: 10·7 m
Width: 3·43 m
Height: 3·91 m

STATUS
In production. In service with the US Army and some other armed forces. It has also been adopted by the West German Army for which model there is a separate entry.

The fiscal year 1981 request was for 150 interior bays at a total cost of $4·9 million, 42 ramps at $1·8 million and 347 transporters $19·6 million.

MANUFACTURER
ConDiesel Mobile Equipment Division, CONDEC Corporation, 84 Progress Lane, Waterbury, Connecticut 06705, USA.

Bridge, Floating Aluminium, Highway Type, Deck Balk Superstructure on Pneumatic Floats (M4T6)

DESCRIPTION
The M4T6 floating bridge combines the best features of the class 60 and M4 bridges. It consists of the substructure of the class 60 bridge (24-ton pneumatic float with saddle assembly) adapted to the superstructure

(aluminium balk) of the M4 bridge. It is hand-erectable and airportable, and like the class 60 bridge can carry all vehicles in the armoured and infantry division. The bridge is issued on the scale of division (armour, infantry and mechanised) engineer battalion: four sets, and corps/army float bridge company: five sets.

The M4T6 floating bridges, rafts and ferries consist of a deck built of square, hollow aluminium sections (balk), supported on pneumatic floats. The pneumatic float consists of two half floats assembled stern to stern. The saddle panels rest on the float and are attached to it with

straps through the D-rings. The saddle beams rest on the saddle panels with the carrying handles of the saddle beams in line with the D-rings on the saddle panels. The straps on the floats are run through the D-rings on the saddle panels, and then through the carrying handles of the beam. The spring-actuated catches of the saddle panels are then placed over the flanges of the saddle beams. The saddle adapters rest on the saddle beams and are connected using sliding retainer lugs. The balk-connecting stiffeners rest on the saddle adapters and are connected to them by four connecting pins. The balk-connecting stiffeners support the balk. Each of the latter has lugs which fit into recesses in the balk-connecting stiffener and are secured by balk-connecting pins. Kerb adapters inserted between the balk and the balk-connecting stiffener are used to raise the balk to form a kerb.

The M4T6 bridge is normally assembled using the successive bay or successive raft method. Reinforced floating sections are constructed by placing the floats closer together than normal. Minimum float spacing is 3·048 metres centre to centre. The bridge set can also be used to assemble bridges with a reduced capacity. A full width bridge with floats spaced at intervals of 9·144 metres, 13·716 metres or 18·288 metres can be constructed for light loads, and when heavier loads are required, the capacity of the bridge can be increased by adding floats and/or deck balk without the necessity of breaking the bridge. A half width bridge using the 12-ton half-float spaced on 4·572 centres can also be constructed, but its capacity cannot be increased without dismantling the bridge.

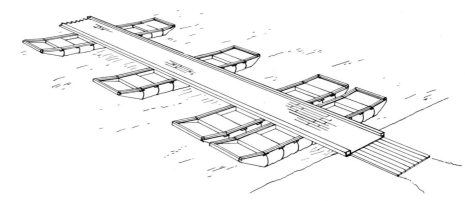

Bridge floating aluminium, highway type, deck balk superstructure on pneumatic floats (M4T6) 9·144 m spacing

SPECIFICATIONS
Pneumatic half-float
Weight: 340 kg
Length: 6·705 m
Width: 2·743 m

Float connections
Length of bar: 2·2 m

Saddle
Weight:
(interior saddle panel) 74·84 kg
(end panel) 81·64 kg
(centre beam) 211 kg
(end beam) 125·74 kg
(outriggers) 3 kg
(saddle adapter normal) 118 kg
(saddle adapter offset) 125 kg

Normal deck balk (22 per floating bay)
Weight: 102 kg
Length: 4·572 m
Width and height: 222 mm × 234 mm

Short deck balk
Weight: 55·33 kg
Length: 2·54 m
Width and height: 222 mm × 234 mm

Tapered deck balk
Weight: 453 kg

Kerb adapter
Weight: 6·804 kg

Abutment plates
Bearing plate
Weight: 74·84 kg
Length: 1·771 m
Width: 0·304 m
Height: 95 mm
Cover plate
Weight:
(short cover plate) 12·7 kg
(long cover plate) 43·99 kg
Length:
(short cover plate) 0·457 m
(long cover plate) 1·625 m

Ramps (4 required each end)
Weight: 107 kg

Other equipment includes universal trestle, trestle bracing and accessories, handrail posts and ropes, bicycle traveller, anchors and holdfasts. All components are normally carried in 5-ton (6 × 6) trucks.

GRADINGS
Normal: vehicle may travel anywhere on the bridge up to 40 km/h
Caution: vehicle restricted to within 0·304 m of the bridge centre line, maximum speed 12·8 km/h and a 46 m gap between vehicles

Risk: vehicle restricted to within 0·228 m of bridge centre line, maximum speed 4·8 km/h, only one vehicle on bridge at a time

Assembly time and supporting units for varying bridge lengths

Length (metres)	Recommended size unit for construction	Float bridge platoons required for support	No. of assembly sites*	Time (hours)†
45·72	1 company	2 bridge platoons	2	4
60·96	1 company	2 bridge platoons	2	5
76·2	1 company	3 bridge platoons	2	6
91·44	2 companies	3 bridge platoons	3	4
106·68	2 companies	4 bridge platoons	3	5
121·92	2 companies	5 bridge platoons	4	5½
152·4	2 companies	5 bridge platoons	5	6
182·88	1 engineer battalion	5 bridge platoons	6	4
213·36	1 engineer battalion	6 bridge platoons	6	5–7
243·84	1 engineer battalion	6 bridge platoons	6	6–8
304·84	1 engineer battalion	8 bridge platoons	6	7–10
365·8	1 engineer battalion	10 bridge platoons	6	8–12

* Each assembly site crew consists of 53 men, exclusive of centre-line crews.
† Assembly site output 18·288 m of bridge per hour with trained crews under ideal conditions.

Raft classes and propulsion requirements

Raft construction	Overall length	Normal crossing velocity (metres per second)				
		1·524	2·133	2·438	2·743	3·352
4-float normal	26·543 m	(50) 55/1	(45) 50/2*	(40) 45/2	(35) 40/3†	(30) 35/4
4-float reinforced	26·543 m	(50) 55/1	(50) 55/2*	(45) 50/2	(40) 45/3†	(35) 40/4
5-float normal	31·115 m	(55) 60/1	(50) 55/2*	(45) 50/3†	(40) 45/3	(35) 40/5
5-float reinforced	27·051 m	(60) 65/1	(60) 65/2*	(55) 60/3†	(55) 60/3	(45) 50/5
6-float reinforced	31·496 m	(65) 70/1	(65) 70/2*	(65) 70/3†	(60) 65/3	(45) 50/5

Upper figure in parentheses represents wheeled vehicle class, lower represents tracked vehicle class and the number of 27 ft (8·229 m) bridge erection boats required to hold the loaded raft in the maximum indicated stream velocity.
One 19 ft (5·791 m) bridge erection boat may be used in stream velocity up to 1·219 metres per section.

* Three 19 ft bridge erection boats may be used here in place of two 27 ft boats.
† One 19 ft and two 27 ft boats may be used in place of three 27 ft boats.

STATUS
In service with the US Army and other armed forces.

Floating bridge classes

Floating bridge classes	Stream velocity (metres per second)					
	0·914	1·524	2·133	2·438	2·743	3·352
Normal	(50) 55	(45) 55	(40) 50	(35) 45	(30) 40	(25) 30
Caution	(60) 61	(58) 59	(54) 55	(49) 51	(45) 47	(35) 37
Risk	(68) 69	(66) 67	(62) 63	(59) 60	(54) 56	(43) 45

Upper figure, in parentheses, represents wheeled vehicle class and the lower figure represents tracked vehicle class. Ratings are quoted for an 18-balk roadway and a 22-balk deck, with the end spans 6·603 m long and reinforced with 2 floats spaced close together.

Classes of reinforced bridge with floats spaced at 3·048 metres average spacing

Type of crossing	Stream velocity (metres per second)					
	0·914	1·524	2·133	2·438	2·743	3·352
Normal	(75) 75*	(75) 75*	(70) 75	(65) 70	(55) 60	(27) 30
Caution	(80) 80*	(80) 80*	(79) 79	(73) 73	(66) 67	(43) 45
Risk	(90) 90*	(90) 90*	(90) 90*	(87) 87	(81) 81	(59) 60

Upper figure, in parentheses, represents wheeled vehicle class, lower figure represents tracked vehicle class. Capacities are based on abutment elevation range from 0 to 0·762 m and 18-balk roadway used throughout. 22-balk deck used in bottom deck from shore abutments to 2 end bays beyond end of superimposed end span.

* Capacities limited by end spans.

Bridge, Floating, Pneumatic Float Class 60 Steel Superstructure

DESCRIPTION

The class 60 floating bridge has a deck of flush surfaced steel-grid panels 4·114 metres wide between kerbs, supported by 24-ton pneumatic floats spaced 4·572 metres centre to centre. The deck panels are pinned together end to end to provide rigid connections. The deck has the rigidity to transmit the load of class 65 to approximately ten floats.

The class 60 floating bridge is allocated on the scale of four sets per division (infantry, armoured, mechanised) engineer battalion and five sets per army/corps float bridge company.

One bridge set contains sufficient components for the assembly of one floating bridge 41·148 metres long, exclusive of the length of the 4·876-metre tapered ramps used at each shore connection and of the length of one short 1·524-metre bay of superstructure by which the length of the shore connection can be increased.

The pneumatic floats and saddle assembly are identical to those used for the Bridge Floating Aluminium Highway Type Deck Balk Supported on Pneumatic Floats (M4T6). One float normally carries one 1·524-metre bay of superstructure. This is assembled from two deck-tread panels, one deck filler panel and two kerbs.

One ramp bay is used in each shore connection; it is assembled from two ramp-tread panels, one ramp-filler panel, one short deck-filler panel and four short deck kerbs. One or more short bays, each consisting of two short deck-tread panels, one short deck-filler panel, and two short deck kerbs, normally form a part of each shore connector. Two cover plate treads and one cover plate filler are installed at each joint between bridge deck and ramp bay. Ramp stiffeners are issued as part of the bridge set.

Two methods of bridge construction are used: normal and expedient. In the latter method, bays are assembled on a trailer in a concealed position and are then taken to the bridge site for launching. The expedient methods are in four general categories:
Assembly using roller conveyors and expedient crane equipment
Assembly using roller conveyors and a truck-mounted crane
Launching completed ramp bays from trucks
Preinflating and transporting the floats to the bridge site on top of 5-ton (6 × 6) truck.

An assembly crew for a normal class 60 floating bridge is:
2 officers, 10 NCOs and 80 men when trestles are being used
2 officers, 9 NCOs and 72 men when trestles are not being used.

Class 60, Bridge, Floating, Pneumatic being positioned by Italian Army (Italian Army)

French Army 4-float raft carrying AMX-30 MBT being pushed by F1 pontoon boat

SPECIFICATIONS

Floating-section classes

Max stream velocity in m/s

Type of crossing	0·914	1·524	2·133	2·434	2·743	3·352
Normal (a)	60/65	55/65	45/55	40/50	35/45	22/25
Caution (b)	65/70	62/67	56/61	52/56	45/49	34/37
Risk (c)	75/79	72/77	67/72	62/67	57/62	45/50

First figure is for wheeled vehicle class and second for tracked vehicle class.
a: vehicle can go anywhere on bridge deck at a recommended speed of 24 km/h, max speed of 42 km/h. Vehicle spacing 27·43 m. Tanks weighing up to 60 tons and a width of up to 3·631 m can make normal crossings in stream velocities up to 2·133 m per second.
b: centre of the vehicle must be within 0·304 m of the bridge centre line, max speed 12·87 km/h.
c: centre of vehicle must be within 0·228 m of bridge, max speed 4·8 km/h. One vehicle at a time on bridge, no stopping, guide for vehicle.

Raft lengths and classes

Number of floats and type of raft	Number of normal bays of deck	Overall length of raft	Length available for loading	Current velocities in m/s					
				0·914	1·524	2·133	2·434	2·743	3·352
4-float normal	4	28·169 m	15·544 m	40	40	40	35	35	25
				451	451	452e	402	403	304
5-float normal	5	32·74 m	20·116 m	50	50	50	45	40	30
				551	551	552	503f	454	355
5-float reinforced	4	28·169 m	15·554 m	55	55	50	50	45	35
				601	601	552	553f	504	405
5-float reinforced (with 1 short deck bay)	3	25·323 m	13·334 m	60	60	55	55	50	45
				651	651	602	603f	554	505
6-float reinforced	4	28·169 m	16·469 m	65	65	65	60	60	50
				751	751	752	703	654	556

The top figure indicates the wheeled vehicle capacity and the lower figure indicates the tracked vehicle capacity.
Indices relate to the number of 27 ft (8·229 m) bridging boats required to propel the raft.
e   Three 19 ft (5·791 m) bridging boats may be used in lieu of two 27 ft bridging boats.
f   One 19 ft (5·791 m) and two 27 ft bridging boats may be used in lieu of three 27 ft boats.

STATUS

This is no longer in service with the US Army but may be in service with other countries.

Part of Bridge, Floating, Pneumatic Float Class 60 being pushed into position (US Army)

Bridge, Floating, M4

DESCRIPTION
The M4 floating bridge may be used to assemble floating bridges, fixed bridges and rafts. The bridge consists of an aluminium alloy flush deck supported by aluminium pontoons. The deck consists of aluminium balks that serve the purpose of stringers and tread. The bridge deck is 22 balks wide and has a roadway width of 4·228 metres inside to inside of kerb walk. The M4 is no longer standard issue for the United States Army.

The spans are supported on whole pontoons which are formed by fastening half-pontoons together stern to stern. The pontoons are normally spaced 4·572 metres apart centre to centre, except the end of the bridge where the pontoons are spaced 2·186 metres apart centre to centre. The basic bridge is reinforced to provide for vehicles that cannot cross on the bridge as

normally assembled. Only component parts of the basic bridge set are used as reinforcement. The methods of reinforcing the bridge are:
100% reinforcement with a whole pontoon every 2·286 metres
50% reinforcement with whole pontoons. In this case three whole pontoons are assembled on 2·286-metre centres and placed one pontoon (2·54 metres) apart. To reinforce normal assembly, add whole pontoons in alternate places.
100% reinforcement with pneumatic floats (18 ton). In this case the pneumatic floats are alternated with whole pontoons with the floats being on 2·286-metre centres.
The deck components of the M4 are identical to those used for the M4T6 bridge. Bridges of less than 91·44 metres are usually assembled by the successive pontoon method. When the river is wider than 91·44 metres, the raft method of assembly is used.

Rafts can be assembled using M4 components and operated as towed or flying ferries, propelled in the water either by outboard motors or bridging boats. The recommended types of raft are as follows:
4-pontoon raft with 4·572 metres spacing
Reinforced pontoon raft with 5, 6 or 7 pontoons
Shortened raft with 4 or 5 pontoons

SPECIFICATIONS
Half-pontoon
Weight: 793·8 kg
Length: 9·082 m
Width: 2·108 m
Depth: 1·028 m

STATUS
The M4 floating bridge is no longer standard issue for the US Army. It may still be found in service with other countries.

Capacities of floating bridge M4

	Stream velocities in m/s														
	Normal					Caution					Risk				
Type of Assembly	0·914	1·524	2·133	2·743	3·352	0·914	1·524	2·133	2·743	3·352	0·914	1·524	2·133	2·743	3·352
Normal[1]	60	60	50	35	20	65	65	55	45	30	70	70	60	50	40
Reinforced[2]	100	100	100	70	40	105	105	105	85	55	110	110	110	100	70

[1] Bridge assembled with 7 m end span with reinforcing pontoon. Deck consists of 22 balk with 18 balk roadway.
[2] Bridge 100% reinforced with full pontoons, with 7 m end span and a 11·582 m superimposed deck.

Load classes, M4 rafts (18-balk roadway)

	Stream velocities in m/s												
	Normal						Risk						
Type	0·914	1·524	2·133	2·438	2·743	3·352	0·914	1·524	2·133	2·438	2·743	3·352
4 pontoons load class	50/55	50/55	50/55	50/55	50/55	40/45	55/60	55/60	55/60	55/60	55/60	45/50
No. of bridge erection boats required	1	1	1	1	1	2	1	1	1	1	1	2
6 pontoons load class	70/75	70/75	70/75	65/70	65/70	50/55	75/80	75/80	75/80	75/80	75/80	55/60
No. of bridge erection boats required	1	1	1	2	2	2	1	1	1	1	2	2
7 pontoons load class	85/90	85/90	85/90	80/85	80/85	55/60	90/95	90/95	90/95	90/95	90/95	65/70
No. of bridge erection boats required	1	1	1	2	3	3	1	1	1	2	3	3

The first figure is wheeled vehicle class and second tracked vehicle class.

Light Assault Ferry (LAF)

DESCRIPTION
The Light Assault Ferry has been proposed as an item of engineering equipment for the new US Army Light Infantry Divisions. As yet it appears to be more of a development concept than an operational requirement. A sum of $750 000 per unit has been proposed for budgetary forecasts.

The Light Assault Ferry will be towed into action on

trailers by the vehicles that will use it to cross water obstacles. It may be used as a ferry or be built up to form a float bridge and in both cases it will be propelled or anchored by self-contained power units. Once the ferry has been placed in position by the water obstacle it will be assembled so that the central deck area is surrounded by hydraulically-operated ramps front and rear and two side floats. Power from the self-contained power units is used to drive the hydraulic system. Each

ferry will have a crew of two but a further two men will be required for assembly. A floating bridge 150 metres long can then be assembled in 40 minutes using 44 men. The time taken to assemble a ferry is about five minutes. The Light Assault Ferry will be capable of air transport in a C-130 Hercules transport aircraft.

STATUS
Development.

YUGOSLAVIA

M-70 Light Pontoon Bridge

DESCRIPTION
The M-70 is of Yugoslav design and construction and can be used both as a light pontoon bridge and as a raft. Each pontoon consists of two aluminium half-pontoons joined together. The balk and decking are also of aluminium construction. The load of the bridge depends on the velocity of the stream. For example a 12-ton bridge can be constructed in a stream with a maximum velocity of 2·5 metres a second, and a 16-ton bridge can be constructed in a stream with a maximum velocity of 2·1 metres a second.

A raft normally consists of four complete pontoons (eight half-pontoons) and the balk from three bridge bays, with or without articulators. Again, the load depends on the velocity of the stream. Twelve-ton rafts can be constructed for use in streams with a maximum velocity of 2·5 metres a second and 16-ton rafts can be

constructed for use in streams with a maximum velocity of 2·1 metres a second.

A complete M-70 light pontoon bridge set has a total of 60 half-pontoons plus deck balk and other ancillary equipment; the deck balk is carried in the rear of a TAM 4500 (4 × 4) truck, which also tows a single axle pole type trailer carrying six half-pontoons inverted on top of each other.

STATUS
Production probably complete. In service with the Yugoslav Army.

MANUFACTURER
Yugoslav state factories.

SPECIFICATIONS
Pontoon
Weight: 295 kg

Length: 5·64 m
Width: 2·04 m
Depth: 0·86 m

Bridge construction
Type	12t and 16t
Roadway width	2·8 m
Length	120 m
Half pontoons per support	2
Assembly time	45–60 minutes

Raft construction
Type	12t and 16t
Length	9 m
Rafts per set	7
Half pontoons per raft	8
Working party	30 men
Assembly time	15 minutes

TACTICAL (NON-FLOATING) AND
LINE OF COMMUNICATION BRIDGES

CZECHOSLOVAKIA

TMS Heavy Truss Panel Bridge

DESCRIPTION
The TMS heavy truss panel bridge is the largest
capacity bridge used by the Czechoslovak Army. It is of
the double-truss, single-storey through-type with a
capacity of 100 tons and a span of 45 metres.

STATUS
In service with the Czechoslovak Army.

MANUFACTURER
Czechoslovak state factories.

MS-1 (SM-60) Heavy Panel Bridge

DESCRIPTION
The MS-1 (SM-60) is a single-storey through-truss type
bridge which in some respects resembles the Bailey
bridge. The MS-1 however has truss members made of
triangles placed back to back to form verticals while the
Bailey bridges are of the diamond-shaped pattern.
  The bridge has a maximum capacity of 60 tons and
a maximum clear span of 21 metres. Its roadway is
4 metres wide. Multi-span bridges can be constructed
with the aid of trestles. These have circular base plates
and can be adjusted for heights of between 1·5 and
7 metres. The bridge is assembled with the aid of
cranes and is launched by the cantilever method. The
heaviest part of the bridge weighs 3150 kg. The bridge
components are carried on standard Tatra 111 (6 × 6)
10-ton trucks or similar vehicles.

STATUS
In service with the Czechoslovak Army.

MANUFACTURER
Czechoslovak state factories.

MS-1 (SM-60) heavy panel bridge showing trestles

*MS-1 (SM-60) heavy panel bridge components being
carried on Tatra 111 (6 × 6) 10-ton truck*

GERMANY, DEMOCRATIC REPUBLIC

Railway-Road Bridge
Set ESB-16

(Eisenbahn-Strassen-Brückengerät)

DESCRIPTION
This East German bridge was designed specifically for
civilian and military use within the Warsaw Pact. It has a
greater clear span and is more suitable for road traffic
than the previously employed Soviet-designed
REM-500. It can be built over both dry and wet gaps and
can take either European standard or Soviet wide
gauge track.
  The individual spans are made up of two hollow box-
girders and cross-pieces. In the ES bridge variants the
roadway is four metres wide and distance between
railings is five metres. The E bridge variant, which is
narrower and unsuitable for road traffic, is primarily
designed for civilian use.
  Individual spans are 16 metres long and have a construction height of 1·15 metres. Two different roadway
panels are available: Type FM which is used over the
cross-pieces, and FS panels which are used also for the
walkway and kerbing and can be employed as treadway

ESB-16 railway-road bridge equipment being used to span river

for the approaches. The rail carriers and roadway
panels are designed to float.
  There are nine supports (trestles) provided which can
be adjusted in height from 1·65 to 11·5 metres at 10 mm

intervals. They rest on footers 7 square metres in area.
The trestle legs can be made up of six different sections:
three sections 0·8, 2 and 3 metres high for rough
adjustment, one section 0·2 metre high for attaching the

traverse bracing, a telescopic section for finer adjustment of height and a sixth section which is the trestle cap.

Bridge abutments can be piles or ties, massive prefabricated parts or locally made concrete. Two anchor plates are provided.

Bridge components are fastened together by bolts or screws. The trestles are assembled on an assembly bench which is set up in the axis of the assembly track.

The most suitable crane is the railway console crane SRK-50, but smaller types can be used if it is not available. If short trestles are used the MDK-63 and MDK-204 mobile cranes are suitable, and for high supports the MDK-160 and MDK-404. In these cases the trestles and superstructure are built separately, not combined as is possible with the SRK-50. In case of

emergency other heavy lifting equipment and railway cranes can also be used. The SRK-50 requires a clear height of 8·6 metres in travel so electric powerlines must be removed.

The ESB-16 can be built in stream velocities up to 2 metres a second and in water up to 6 metres deep. The pressure on the footers on the stream bottom cannot exceed 2 kg/cm². The top of the rails can range from 2·8 to 12·6 metres above the terrain. If it must be less than 2·8 metres the trestles must be replaced by other supports such as piles or ties.

Bridge components are stored in the open in groupings not exceeding 10 tonnes. Small parts, tools, connectors are stored in containers. Everything can be transported in trucks or by rail.

In streams flowing faster than 0·5 metres a second

and deeper than 1·5 metres, the trestles must be anchored until they have been firmly placed. Normally this is done with a river tug boat, but recently a method has been developed where a PT-SM is used with a cable, "deadman" and a Ural-375D. This obviates finding a river tug boat in case of emergencies, and allows military organisations to build bridges with organic equipment.

STATUS
In service with the East German Army.

MANUFACTURER
East German state factories.

SBG-66 Bridging Equipment

DESCRIPTION
The SBG-66 (Schiffsbrückengerät, or Barge Bridge Equipment 66) has been designed for civil and military applications, and can be used both as a floating bridge or a bridge with fixed supports. As a floating bridge the following variations are possible: vehicle bridge, railway bridge, combined road and railway bridge and high capacity road bridge. As a bridge with fixed supports, the equipment can be used as a railway overpass bridge, jetty, bridge on fixed supports and support trestles for a roadway bridge. As a fixed bridge it can also be used as an approach to floating bridges, but not for rail traffic.

The length of the bridge can be varied as the components are in lengths of 6 and 8·5 metres. The two-lane bridge is 8 metres wide with a 7-metre wide carriageway. The single-lane bridge is 5-metres wide with 4-metre wide carriageway. The bridge is class 80. Vehicles can cross the bridge at speeds of up to 30 km/h provided that there is a gap between vehicles of at least 50 metres. Trains can cross the bridge at a maximum speed of 10 km/h.

The bridging equipment comprises the supports, superstructure and the pontoons. The supports include the pontoon trestles I and II, land trestle, bank support, support block and bearing flange for the bridge on fixed supports. The superstructure consists of roadway elements A (length 6 metres), B (length 8·5 metres) and C (length 2·5 metres). Roadway elements A and B exist in road and rail variants, element C is for road only. The

pontoons, which are 32·5 metres long and 8·2 metres wide, are positioned by riverboats and have a load capacity of 400 to 550 tonnes. The pontoon trestle I is a space frame with a triangular cross section, the struts of which are bolted to the sole plate of the truss and to the truss beam. The hinged joint of the superstructure is supported by pontoon trestle I. Pontoon trestle II is a truss construction of two vertical plane truss sections connected by horizontal K-bracing. The rigid joints are always supported on pontoon trestle II. The pontoon trestles are connected to the pontoons by connecting base plates.

The land trestle is a steel tubular framework corresponding to the width of the bridge, standing on two different heights (0·5 and 1 metre), with a vertically-adjustable support footing.

The bank trestle is a steel framework with adjustable frame members and has a vertically adjustable support footing. The support batten is divided into sections longitudinally.

The support blocks are built up out of the block supports of the bridging equipment, support being provided by the bearing flange on the bank trestle.

The superstructure consists of single 0·5 metre modules which are also referred to as roadway elements as they also serve as the roadway itself. On the front surface of the modules are holes which enable the roadway elements and the ridge tube of the trestle, or the support flange, to be connected together.

Ferries can also be built, for example high capacity versions with three parallel roadways suitable for 12 to 15 tanks.

Tatra 813 (8 × 8) truck towing 130 mm M-46 field gun crossing SBG-66 bridge

SBG-66 being used as bridge overpass

STATUS
In service with the East German Army.

MANUFACTURER
East German state factories.

Mobile Treadway Bridge 13 Mp

DESCRIPTION
The Mobile Treadway Bridge 13 Mp (Fahrbare Spurbahnbrücke) enables vehicles to overcome small ditches and other obstacles without the assistance of conventional bridging equipment. It is towed behind a truck and consists of a standard 1200 kg two-wheeled trailer on the top of which are mounted three aluminium treadway beams. The remaining treadway beams are lashed together and carried on top of the trailer. All the treadway beams have a non-skid coating.

The bridge is used as follows: on arrival at the ditch, the trailer is uncoupled and pushed into the obstacle, the four jacks are lowered to take the strain off the wheels, the remaining treadways are removed from the top of the trailer and attached to each end of the chassis and then staked to the ground. Vehicles can then cross the bridge.

SPECIFICATIONS
Weight: 1320 kg
Length:
(travelling) 4·38 m
(extended) 5·48 m
Width:
(travelling) 2·93 m
(position) 2·86 m
Height:
(travelling) 1·48 m
(in use) 1·56 m
Ground clearance: 0·52 m
Max capacity: 13 000 kg
Vehicle crossing speed: 5 km/h
Max towing speed: 80 km/h
Assembly time: 10 minutes
Disassembly time: 15 minutes

Mobile treadway bridge 13 Mp before attachment of end treadways and lowering of jacks

STATUS
In service with the East German Army.

MANUFACTURER
East German state factories.

Collapsible Loading Ramp ZLR 60/1

DESCRIPTION
The Collapsible Loading Ramp Type ZLR 60/1 (Zerlegbar Laderampe), which is used for loading and unloading railway flatcars, consists of girders, headpieces and footpieces of hollow box construction, with hollow tubing used for the crossbeam trestles. The equipment can be assembled for use as a side-loading ramp (three sets

Collapsible loading ramp ZLR 60/1

required) or an end-loading ramp (one set required). The former has a capacity of 60 000 kg for tracked vehicles and the latter has a 17 400 kg capacity for tracked vehicles and wheeled vehicles with a maximum of 9500 kg per axle.

One end-loading ramp can be assembled by a team of one NCO and ten men. The ZLR 60/1 has two other applications: as a repair ramp with one lower and three centre crossbeam trestles, 12 support girders, two outside foot-pieces and two end stops, and as a washdown and decontamination ramp with three lower crossbeam trestles, eight support girders and four outer footpieces.

SPECIFICATIONS
Assembled (one set)
Weight: 3500 kg
Length: 9·09 m
Width: 3·37 m
Height: 3·255 m

STATUS
In service with the East German Army.

MANUFACTURER
East German state factories.

Components

	No. in set	Weight (each)
Upper crossbeam trestle	1	330 kg
Supports	2	95 kg
Top piece	1	103 kg
Struts	2	12·5 kg
Chains	4	3 kg
Centre crossbeam trestle	1	283 kg
Supports	2	73 kg
Top piece	1	103 kg
Struts	2	11 kg
Chains	1	3 kg
Lower crossbeam trestle	1	112 kg
Support girder	20	110 kg
Headpieces		
(outer)	2	85 kg
(inner)	2	57 kg
Outer footpieces		
(left)	1	83 kg
(right)	1	83 kg
Inner footpieces	1	127 kg

LBü-60 Landing Ramp

DESCRIPTION
The LBü-60 landing ramp has been developed by the East Germans for use with the Soviet TPP heavy pontoon bridge. The ramp set is used in conjunction with TPP ferries to facilitate loading and unloading operations when either there is not enough time to prepare shore abutments or where no landing stages exist. It can be erected in the water if required and this allows vehicles to be unloaded from ferries up to their maximum fording capability.

One ramp can be constructed in between 10 and 15 minutes from one half-set. This is carried in a standard G5 (6 × 6) 3½-ton truck and consists of five ramp panels, one transom, two footers, two lifting winches, two cable supports and other miscellaneous equipment. The LBü-60 has a maximum capacity of 60 tons for tracked vehicles and 10 tons per axle for wheeled vehicles.

STATUS
In service with the East German Army.

MANUFACTURER
East German state factories.

SPECIFICATIONS
Weight of equipment: 4000 kg
Length of treadway element: 5 m
Width of treadway element: 0·45 m
Max width of roadway: 3·5 m
Angle of treadways from horizontal: 25°
Max adjustable height: 2·8 m
Minimum adjustable height: 1·8 m

Flushdeck Pushed Barge Bridging and Harbour Equipment

DEVELOPMENT/DESCRIPTION
With the development of new inland waterway barges which have both civilian and military application, East Germany has taken an important step toward perfecting line of communication bridges. Further modification into seagoing craft has made possible their employment as elements of artificial harbours on an open seacoast. East German military periodicals report that these new barges make possible a reduction of the construction time for bridges down to 10 per cent of that needed with modern open pushed barges (used for the SBG-66 bridge) and 3 per cent of that needed with older model towed barges.

GSP-54 Flushdeck Pushed Barge
The GSP-54 (Glattdeckschubprahm-54) is used as a heavy ferry to construct road or rail bridges of 60 t capacity. In the ferry role it is equipped with two ZAR-9 ramps, while in the bridging role these ramps are attached singly to the shore ends only. In unfavourable water conditions the GSP-54 is supplemented by the BFP-36 inland waterway barge as part of the bridge combination to give extra anchorage capability. The East German military press has discussed the employment of floating bridges using three GSP-54 (162-metre bridge) and two GSP-54 and one BFP-36 (144-metre bridge). Manoeuvring takes place by means of inland waterway pushships since neither the GSP-54 nor the BFP-36 have propulsion units.

The GSP-54 is constructed as a flushdeck full pontoon with a tapered bow end. All parts of the superstructure can be removed so that the barge may be used side-by-side as well as end-to-end. The equipment necessary to operate the barge is either under the deck or flush with it. The barge has six watertight compartments; the rear one can be flooded to compensate for bow heaviness as well as aid in coupling.

Each barge has a total of four cable couplings and eight cylinder lock couplings located on either side and at both ends. The cylinder lock couplings connect the barges with each other keeping the proper position of the roadway under load and give the bridge the necessary longitudinal stability. A single hand operated rudder at the bow enhances manoeuvrability. The two 495 kg anchors are operated from the pilot house of the pushship, either by hand or electrically. To increase usefulness the GSP-54 is strengthened against ice.

The ZAR-9 dismountable ramp, which can be employed at either end of the barge, is either hand or electrically operated and is fitted with wooden flooring to increase the traction and help distribute the load.

BFP-36 Inland Waterway Barge
The BFP-36 (Binnenfährprahm-36) is an anchored barge which is not used in ferrying operations. Normally it is joined end-to-end to form a ribbon bridge which can be used for either road or rail traffic. The barge can also be employed with the GSP-54 in a combined bridge when unfavourable water conditions require its additional anchorage capability. The BFP-36 is similarly equipped to the GSP-54, but is notable because of the set of twelve 495 kg anchors each with a 100 metre anchor chain. These anchors can be lowered or raised via winches which are either hand or electrically operated.

KamAZ trucks crossing combined bridge made up of BFP-36 barges and Soviet MARM

Road bridge made up to GSP-54 smooth deck push barges with ZAR-9 ramp

GSP-65 Flushdeck Pushed Barge
The GSP-65 (Glattdeckschubprahm-65) is similar in design to the GSP-54, but is modified for seagoing use, primarily as a roadstead lighter. It may also be employed as an element of a bridge, but is less suitable than the GSP-54 for this role. The watertight compartments of the GSP-65 can be flooded for trimming and/or adjustment of the barge to pier heights. Some of the compartments are also fitted for the transport of POL. For its seagoing role the forward end of the barge has been tapered and raised. Although the 7·2 metre wide roadway is basically the same width as that of other barges it narrows to 4 metres at the bow and stern exits. The ZAR-9·1 dismountable ramp which can be used on the bow is similar to the ZAR-9 of the GSP-54, but is operated mechanically rather than electrically. Trials have shown that the GSP-65 has good seagoing qualities and that it should be employed in tandem and propelling by pushships in exceptional cases. Towing should take place only in exceptional cases. With a loaded tandem lighter a top speed of 15 km/h was obtained along with a turning circle of 200 metres. Stopping distance was 150 metres. With only one barge the speed increased to 19 km/h and the turning circle and stopping distance went down to 100 metres. In future trials it is planned to test the suitability of the GSP-65 for unloading railway ferries and roll-on/roll-off ships.

FP-36 Barge
The FP-36 (Fährprahm-36) is very similar to the inland waterway BFP-36, but is suitably modified for its new role in coastal waters. As in the GSP-65, some of the watertight compartments have been fitted for the transport of POL. Additional changes include heavier anchors and the provision for the attachment of a hydraulically-operated treadway ramp on the stern. Like the BFP-36, the FP-36 has a skid-free deck coating and all of the equipment needed to operate the barge is either under the deck or is flush with it. The curbing for the 7-metre wide roadway is removable and for safety a 1·1-metre high hand rail is provided on both sides.

The FP-36 barges have many uses. They can be joined to form a helicopter platform, a floating road bridge, a roadstead lighter, or to build the SSB-60 floating causeway. Tests will also take place with railway ferries and roll-on/roll-off ships. To make up a floating helicopter platform several FP-36s are manoeuvred into position side-by-side, coupled and anchored. The construction of a floating road bridge takes place by the end-to-end method, similar to that used with the inland waterway BFP-36. The prefered configuration of the roadstead lighter is two FP-36s in tandem, with pushships or tugs being used for propulsion. In this role the treadway ramp can be mounted for unloading vehicles via the SSB-60 floating causeway. In harbours the bow barge can be flooded so the deck is level with the top of the pier, allowing direct unloading without a ramp. The employment of the FP-36 as a lighter is an exception since it will normally be used with the SSB-60 causeway.

SSB-60 Floating Causeway
The SSB-60 (Schwimmende Seebrücke-60) is constructed with varying numbers of FP-36 barges coupled

Truck column crossing GSP-54 bridge

Two pushboats moving BFP-36 bridge into place

together end-to-end and/or side-by-side in various configurations and lengths. The length is governed by the water depth necessary to tie up lighters or seagoing ships. The configuration depends on the specific needs. The elements are manoeuvred into position by tugs or pushships and use the extensive anchor systems to hold their position. The standard FP-36 connecting systems ensure positive coupling, leveling of the pontoons and longitudinal and lateral stability in the water.

SPECIFICATIONS
GSP-54
Length: 54 m
Width: 11 m
Height: 2·2 m
Maximum draught: 2 m
Draught empty: 0·38 m
Roadway width: 7 m
Payload: 1000 t
Deck loading: 9 t/m²
Individual load: 60 t
Anchors: (2) 495 kg

ZAR-9
Length of ramp elements: 9 m
Width of ramp: 7 m
Width of ramp elements: 0·5 m
Length of claw: 3 m
Load capacity: 60 t
Weight of individual elements: 1·5 to 2 t

BFP-36
Length: 36 m
Width: 9 m
Height: 2·5 m
Draught empty: 0·72 m
Roadway width: 7 m
Payload: 240 t
Deck loading: 9 t/m²
Individual load: 60 t
Anchors: (12) 495 kg

GSP-65
Length: 65 m
Width: 9·46 m
Height: 2·4 m
Draught empty: 0·47 m
Roadway width: 7·2 m
Payload: 824 t
Deck loading: 9 t/m²
Individual load: 60 t
POL capacity: 150 m³
Anchors: (2) 495 kg

ZAR-9·1
Length of ramp elements: 9 m
Width of ramp elements: 0·5 m
Width of ramp: 3·78 m
Length of claw: 3 m
Roadway width: 3·5 m
Load capacity: 60 t

FP-36
Length: 36 m
Width: 9 m
Height: 2·5 m
Draught empty: 0·72 m
Roadway width: 7 m
Payload: 240 t
Deck loading: 9 t/m²
Individual load: 60 t
POL capacity: 200 m³
Anchors:
(4) 1250 kg
(8) 525 kg

Treadway Ramp for FP-36

Type	long	short
Length of treadway elements	10 m	5 m
Width of treadway elements	1·5 m	1·5 m
Weight of treadway elements	3·21 t	2·01 t
Length of claws	1·5 m	1·5 m
Weight of claws	0·37 t	0·37 t
Total weight	7·16 t	4·76 t
Load capacity	60 t	60 t
Height adjustment	±15°	±15°

STATUS
In production.

MANUFACTURER
East German state factories.

Sectional Road and Railway Bridges

DESCRIPTION
The East German Army uses a wide range of sectional road and railway bridges, some of which date back to the First World War. The East German Army also uses the more recent Soviet REM-500 sectional road and railway bridge. Similar bridges are undoubtedly in service in other Warsaw Pact armies.

RW (Roth Wagner) Sectional Railway Bridge
This bridge is an Austrian design which dates back to the First World War. It can be built as a single-storey bridge using either rectangular or rhombic girders, or as a two- or three-storey bridge using rectangular girders.

The RW bridge can be built in either the deck-truss or through-truss manner. The normal-length bridge panels are 4 metres high and 3 metres long and the special end panel is 2·5 metres long. The clear spans can be adjusted at either 1·5-metre or 3-metre lengths with special intermediate panels. The bridge was designed for a 20-ton train axle load. The clear spans are as follows:
Deck truss
 single-storey, rectangular girders 25·5 to 36 m
 double-storey, semi-rhombic girder 45 to 54 m
 triple-storey, rhombic girder 27 to 42 m
 triple-storey, rectangular girder up to 87 m
Through-truss
 single-storey, rectangular girder 24 to 42 m
 double-storey, rectangular girder 43·5 to 63 m
 triple-storey, rectangular girder up to 87 m

MZ Medium Sectional Railway Bridge
This was developed by the Germans and used during the Second World War and is a single-storey bridge

which can be built either in the deck-truss or through-truss manner. Individual centre panels are 3·25 × 3·25 metres, while the end panels are 2 metres long. Special centre panels 2·75 metres long also exist. Maximum clear span is 45·5 metres for a 20-ton train axle load and 38 metres for a 25-ton train axle load.

R Type Sectional Road and Railway Bridge
This was designed by Krupp and can be used for the construction of both road and railway bridges. The bridge is constructed of individual panels which are 4 metres high and 3 metres in length. It can be built in either the deck-truss or through-truss manner and appears in single-storey (54-metre clear span), double-storey (84-metre clear span) or triple-storey (105-metre clear span).

SKR-6 Sectional Road and Railway Bridge
The SKR-6 (Schaper Krupp Reichsbahn) bridge can be used for both road or rail traffic. The bridge is normally built in the through-truss manner as a double-storey bridge but it can also be built as a single- or triple-storey bridge. Individual panels are 6 × 6 metres with the special panels being 5 metres long. The clear span of the bridge can be adjusted to within 0·4 metre with the use of special panels 1·6 metres in length used in conjunction with the 5- and 6-metre spans.
Maximum clear spans are:
 single-storey 72 m
 double-storey 120 m
 triple-storey 150 m

K Sectional Road and Railway Bridge
This bridge was developed from the SKR-6 and the panels are the same size as this bridge. Both single and double-storey bridges can be built. The clear span is 66 metres for the single-storey and 96 metres for the

double storey, and can be adjusted to 1-metre intervals. Distances between the main girders are either 5·5 metres or 8·25 metres.

45 m Sectional Railway Bridge
This single-storey bridge uses panels which are 3·75 × 3·75 metres in size and the bridge is capable of carrying a 20-ton train axle load.

ZM-16 Sectional Railway Bridge
This is the most recent East German railway bridge and can be built in single-, double- or triple-storey configurations, with either single or double trusses.

The panels for the bridge are 3·3 metres high and 3 metres long, and the maximum weight of any individual part is 1230 kg. Maximum clear spans are 72 metres for single-storey, 99 metres for a double-storey and 114 metres for a triple-storey bridge. All three bridges have a width of 4·8 metres.

Average construction times, including launching, are 12 metres an hour for a single-storey and 3·6 metres an hour for a double-storey bridge. Depending on the type of bridge, the ZM-16 has a capacity of either 18-ton train axle loads or 20-ton train axle loads. Maximum train speed is 50 km/h. By using parts of the bridge, and additional elements, piers with a maximum height of 80 metres can be built.

Span (metres)	42	63	84
Weight (tonnes/metre)	2·4	2·6	4·5
Assembly time (metres/hour)	6	3·6	1·5

STATUS
In service with the East German Army.

MANUFACTURER
Austrian or East German factories.

GERMANY, FEDERAL REPUBLIC

Krupp Festbrücke System

DESCRIPTION
The Krupp Festbrücke is a single-lane road bridge of wheel-tread girder design which can be used by tracked and wheeled vehicles of all types up to class 60 for normal loading and class 70 in special load cases.

The main load-bearing elements are the two triangular, torsion-resistant, wheel tread girders in between which are suspended intermediate plates. The roadway width is 4·026 metres and the structural height 1·5 metres with a ramp inclination of approximately 13 per cent. The commercially available construction material is weldable, cold-hardened aluminium alloy, Al Zn 4·5 Mg 1. Weight of the bridge is 435 kg per metre and the heaviest single component is the 260 kg wheel tread girder plate.

The bridge is assembled by hand and is pushed over an obstacle using a special erection platform. It is possible to assemble the bridge from a helicopter.

After training, a 34·4 metre bridge can be assembled in approximately 25 minutes, a 47 metre bridge in approximately 100 minutes and a 60 metre bridge in approximately two hours.

For obstacles of up to 60 metres the Festbrücke can be constructed as a single-field girder with or without a reinforcement kit or as a two-field girder with pendulum support. Obstacles over 60 metres in width can be crossed using the Festbrücke as a continuous girder bridge supported on trestles. Use of the Festbrücke as a floating bridge or ferry is covered in a separate section.

STATUS
In production. In service with European and other armies.

MANUFACTURER
Krupp Industrietechnik GmbH, Franz-Schubert Strasse 1-3, Postfach 14 19 60, D-4100 Duisburg 14 (Rheinhausen), Federal Republic of Germany.

SPECIFICATIONS
Bridge length, single-span girder: 17·6–59·6 m
Roadway width: 4·026 m
Height: 1·5 m
Ramp inclination: 13%
Bridge weight: 435 kg/m
Heaviest component: 260 kg

Krupp Festbrücke bridge with reinforcement kit

Krupp Festbrücke with pendulum support

SE Road and Railway Bridge

DESCRIPTION
The SE (Strassen und Eisenbahnbrücke) road and railway bridge is designed for use in rear areas. Components, which are bolted together, are carried in 5-tonne trucks.

The superstructure of the bridge consists of two main girders and carries a roadway of deck panels or railway ties and rails. The main girders are made of rhombic truss panels and chord members. Multi-storey girder bridges can be constructed on similar lines to Bailey type bridges.

Fixed or floating bridges with single or double lanes can be constructed with a maximum capacity of class 80. In the case of floating bridges sectional pontoons are used for floating supports. For rail traffic, through or deck type bridges can be built.

A single-lane class 80 road bridge is 86 metres long and has a roadway 4·3 metres wide. A double-lane class 80 road bridge is 84·1 metres long and has a roadway 6·1 metres wide. A through-type railway bridge is 61·6 metres long and 5·5 metres wide.

SPECIFICATIONS
Weight:
(truss panel) 220 kg
(chord panel) 485 kg
(deck panels) 142 kg
(transom) 570 kg

STATUS
Production complete. In service with the West German Army.

Mobile Railway Loading Ramp

DESCRIPTION
The mobile railway loading ramp enables tracked and wheeled military vehicles to be loaded or unloaded on the open track, making the rail transport of vehicles independent of stationary side or end ramps. The ramp can handle tracked vehicles up to 60 000 kg and wheeled vehicles up to 40 000 kg.

The ramp, which is aluminium, consists of three major components, a baseplate, two ramp sections and the tie rod. The wedge-shaped baseplate is positioned on the rails behind the last flatcar. The tie rod is bolted to the baseplate and its other end attached to the coupling hook of the flatcar. The two ramp sections are then placed with their beak-shaped ends on the flatcar and pushed back to the baseplates where they are bolted

into position. When in position the ramps are inclined 18 degrees and the gap between the two ramp ends is 0·7 metre, which enables them to be used by small wheeled vehicles such as Jeeps. The surface of the ramps is ribbed, ensuring a high degree of grip for both tracked and wheeled vehicles. The ramp can be positioned by eight men in 20 minutes, and has been approved for use by the Federal German Railways.

SPECIFICATIONS
Base plate
Weight: 320 kg
Width: 3·3 m

Ramp section
Weight: 320 kg
Width: 1·3 m

Tie rod
Weight: 35 kg
Length: 3·9 m

STATUS
In production. In service with the Dutch and French armies.

MANUFACTURER
Eisenwerke Kaiserslautern Göppner GmbH, Barbarossastrasse 30, D-6750 Kaiserslautern, Federal Republic of Germany.

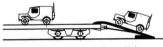

1 base plate (320 kgs) 2 two ramp sections (320 kgs each)
3 tie rod (35 kgs)

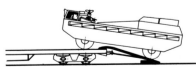

loading of smaller vehicles

loading M2 amphibious bridging vehicle

Top, plan view of mobile railway loading ramp
Below, method of using ramps and stowage of equipment when being carried on flatcar

M2 amphibious bridge and ferry unit being loaded onto railway flatcar using EWK mobile railway loading ramp

HUNGARY

Hungarian Barge Bridge

DESCRIPTION
Hungary has recently developed a standard nose-to-stern barge bridge using standard inland waterway barges. Each barge is 80·4 metres long and 10 metres wide and can be used for road or rail traffic, but not both together. Modified barges can be used normally in peacetime and then quickly converted when needed.

Each barge has a payload of 1600 tonnes, and the draught, depending on the weight carried, may be from 0·4 to 2·5 metres. Normal deck loading for an evenly distributed load is 3000 kg per square metre, but an individual can produce a deck loading as high as 10 000 kg per square metre.

STATUS
In service with Hungarian forces.

MANUFACTURER
Hungarian state factories.

Hungarian barge bridge in position and being used for railway traffic

Hungarian barge bridge for railway traffic being assembled

ISRAEL

IMI SPB24 Personnel Foot Bridge

DESCRIPTION
Intended for infantry use, the SPB24 sectional foot bridge is transported in six four-metre sections and assembled on site by three men in ten minutes. Each section weighs 30 kg and is carried by two men using its retractable handles. When assembled the bridge is 24 metres long and can be launched across a gap by one man who uses a roller mounted on a small frame. The bridge has a hand rail on each side and is only 0·378 metre wide. Stretchers can be carried across the bridge by placing them on a two-wheel bogie mounted on the hand rails; the stretcher can then be pushed across the bridge by one man. When launching the bridge across water obstacles a small pontoon can be fitted to the leading edge.

SPB24 stands for Sectioned Personnel Bridge 24 metres.

STATUS
Ready for production.

MANUFACTURER
Israel Military Industries, PO Box 1044, Ramat-Hasharon 47100, Israel.

JAPAN

Bridge, Panel, Class 30

DESCRIPTION
The Bridge, Panel, class 30, a modified version of the American M2 type Bailey bridge, was introduced in 1960. The main difference between the American and Japanese versions is that the Japanese components are smaller and lighter, facilitating and reducing transport requirements.

Typical examples are the truss of the Japanese model which is 2·5 metres long, 1·3 metres high and weighs 222 kg compared with the American model which is 3·3 metres long, 1·5 metres high and weighs 262 kg. The Japanese bridge does however have a narrower roadway (3·4 metres) and a smaller carrying capacity than the American M2 bridge. This is not a great disadvantage as Japanese AFVs tend to be somewhat smaller than their American counterparts. A class 30 bridge, which is assembled with a 40-man team, is 25 metres long and has a roadway width of 3·4 metres.

SPECIFICATIONS
Truss panel
Weight: 222 kg
Length: 2·5 m
Width: 0·2 m
Height: 1·3 m

Transoms
Weight: 241 kg
Length: 5 m

Width: 0·2 m
Height: 0·25 m

Stringers
Weight: 88 kg
Length: 2·5 m
Width: 0·6 m
Height: 0·1 m

STATUS
Production complete. In service with the Japanese Ground Self-Defence Force.

MANUFACTURER
Kisha Seizo Kaisha Limited, Tokyo, Japan.

NETHERLANDS

DAF Treadway Bridge Type YEE 2000 SB

DESCRIPTION
The DAF YEE 2000 SB treadway bridge consists of two separate two-wheeled trailers, each with one treadway. Each treadway is normally towed by a truck such as the DAF YA 314 (4 × 4) 3-ton. Investigation by the Dutch Army Engineers and DAF has shown that 80 per cent of gaps which will be encountered in action can be crossed using this treadway bridge.

The treadway consists of three main components, bridge body, sliding beam and the running gear. The sliding beam has a length of 11 metres and fits inside the bridge body and can be drawn out either end. It also acts as a drawbar and a rotatable lunette is provided at each end. The running gear can be moved along the body of the bridge and clamped in position. The treadways are constructed so that the front and rear are identical and can therefore be towed by either end.

On arriving near the ditch or river, the trailer is uncoupled and the traffic accessories removed. The locking device on the sliding beam is removed and the sliding beam and rollerguide clamps are slackened. The sliding bar is then pulled out towards the obstacle and the running gear is adjusted so that the ramp is

Sliding beam of treadway bridge in position

balanced. The running gear is clamped in position and the trailer pushed towards the obstacle. The beam support is then positioned and the trailer halted about 0·5 metre from the obstacle and the brakes applied. The beam is lowered on to the far bank and a man crosses the beam and anchors it to the ground by driving a pin through the towing eye. The rollerguide clamps are then slackened and the bridge is pushed over the beam. The second treadway is launched in a similar manner. The distance between the sliding beams must be at least 1·9 metres. The running gear on the second bridge is locked in the same position as the first bridge. The bridge body is then pushed down the slope while applying the handbrake from the bridge deck, enabling the bridge body to rest on both banks. This procedure is repeated for the second bridge. The beam support is retracted into the bridge body and the cover closed. Depending on the nature of the ground, ground pins or shore bars are provided. Application of the latter allows deviation in transversal direction of about 0·5 metre and in longitudinal direction of about 0·1 metre.

The YEE 2000 SB takes about six minutes to position and has a maximum load capacity of between 18 102 and 21 724 kg depending on the type of vehicle crossing the bridge. The bridge can be used to span a gap of up to 12 metres when the sloping bank is less than 45 degrees, or 10 metres when the sloping bank is more than 45 degrees.

SPECIFICATIONS
Weight: 2994 kg
Length travelling: 14·248 m
Length of bridge frame: 13·6 m
Max span of bridge: 12 m
Width: 1·879 m
Height: 1·339 m
Max capacity:
(tracked vehicles) 18 102 kg
(wheeled vehicles) 21 724 kg

STATUS
Production complete. In service with the Netherlands Army.

MANUFACTURER
DAF Trucks, Geldropseweg 303, 5645 TK, Eindhoven, The Netherlands.

Netherlands Army AMX VCI armoured personnel carrier crossing completed DAF treadway type bridge YEE 2000 SB

POLAND

DMS-65 Heavy Girder Bridge

DESCRIPTION
The DMS-65 is basically a modern development of the well-known Bailey panel bridge. It is normally built as a single-storey, through-truss road bridge, but can also be constructed as a deck-truss railway bridge. There are only five basic elements of the bridge which are carried in Star 66M (6 × 6) 2½-ton cargo trucks. The DMS-65 can be assembled by manpower or with the aid of cranes, and bridges of different lengths, with either single or multiple spans, can be built. The roadway consists of metal plates which are covered with crushed stone.

STATUS
In service with the Polish Army.

MANUFACTURER
Polish state factories.

Star 660 (6 × 6) truck carrying DMS-65 components

Bailey Type Panel Bridges

DESCRIPTION
The British designed Bailey bridge was also adopted by the United States Army during World War Two, and the Soviet Union obtained some of these under lend-lease. Even today, some of these bridges may still be in service with members of the Warsaw Pact, together with local copies of the bridge. Poland is one of the countries which copied the Bailey bridge with some minor modifications. This is distinguishable from the standard Bailey bridge by the increased number of holes in the transom.

There are separate entries in this section for the Czechoslovak MS-1 (SM-60) and the Polish DMS-65 panel bridges, both of which resemble the Bailey bridge in some respects.

STATUS
In service with the Polish Army.

MANUFACTURER
Polish state factories.

Polish Developments

Poland has recently developed a new footbridge; no further details are available.

Poland has developed a new ferry with a capacity of 2500 kg for transporting troops and other equipment.

Poland has developed a net for catching floating river mines or napalm. It consists of a 200-metre long steel cable fastened to floats 2 metres long, 300 mm in diameter and filled with Styropor. The floats are fitted with eyes for connecting to each other and for attaching the cable. They can be connected ashore and fastened to the cable or after the cable has been laid across the obstacle. The cable is anchored every 50 metres and a 1·2-metre deep Dederon net is fastened to the floats. The net is transported on a Star 660 truck with cable on a drum and the floats separate.

SWITZERLAND

Bridge, Steel Truss, Model 52

DESCRIPTION
This bridge was designed in the early 1950s to meet the requirements of the Swiss Army. It is a through deck-type Warren truss bridge that can be erected by the cantilever method using a crane and derrick, and can also be assembled on the river bank and pushed across the gap with the aid of a launching nose.

The truss members are square or rectangular, box-shaped and airtight. The hollow beams are made of either lightweight or heavyweight steel sections, light sections for the diagonals and heavy sections for the top and bottom chords. The truss members have the same external dimensions but not the same weight. Stringers are made of two I-beams welded together, similar to the Bailey stringers. The transoms, which carry the floor,

can be placed on either the top or the bottom of the trusses. The basic bridge is class 20, but a class 55 can be built by adding a second truss to the existing structure.

SPECIFICATIONS
Chord members (truss)
Weight: 117 kg
Length: 3 m
Width: 0·15 m
Depth: 0·15 m

Diagonals (truss)
Weight: 89 kg
Length: 3 m
Width: 0·15 m
Depth: 0·15 m

Transoms
Weight: 443 kg

Stringers
Weight: 112 kg
Length: 3 m
Depth: 0·15 m

Assembled Bridge

Class	20t	55t
Roadway width	4·2 m	4·2 m
Assembly time	5·5 to 6 hours	8 to 8·5 hours
Working party	77 men	77 men

STATUS
In service with the Swiss Army.

Universal Light Pier

DESCRIPTION
At the request of the Swiss Army the Swiss Federal Aircraft Factory has produced a form of Universal light pier for use with the Fairey Medium Girder Bridge. The piers are used to support lengths of MGB over wide dry or wet gaps and can be up to 20 metres high, capable of

carrying loads up to 120 000 kg. The piers are built in lattice form and 12 men can construct a 12-metre pier in one hour without using special tools or cranes.

The Universal light pier is now being marketed in the United Kingdom by Fairey Engineering Limited.

STATUS
In production. In service with the Swiss Army.

MANUFACTURER
Federal Aircraft Factory, Thun, Switzerland.

Marketed in United Kingdom by Fairey Engineering Limited, PO Box 41, Crossley Road, Heaton Chapel, Stockport, Cheshire SK4 5BD, England.

Universal light pier in use

Universal light pier in use

UNION OF SOVIET SOCIALIST REPUBLICS

PVM Foot Suspension Bridge
LVM Light Suspension Bridge
TVM Heavy Suspension Bridge

DESCRIPTION
These suspension bridges are designed primarily for use in mountainous country and are normally transported by pack animal, or if the terrain is suitable, by motor transport.

The PVM (pedestrian suspension footbridge) set contains sufficient components to construct either two bridges 60 metres long and 0·7 metre wide, or a single bridge 120 metres long and 0·7 metre wide. A team of 18 men can erect the former in two hours or the latter in three hours. The complete PVM bridge set weighs

4360 kg and can be transported by 46 pack animals.

The LVM (light suspension bridge) set contains sufficient components to construct either two bridges 40 metres long and 2 metres wide or a single bridge 80 metres long and 2 metres wide. With a team of 27 men, the former can be erected in four hours and the latter in two hours. The complete LVM bridge set weighs 13 500 kg and can be transported by 160 pack animals, maximum weight of each individual component not exceeding 50 kg. The LVM has a maximum rated capacity of 2000 kg but the maximum axle load of any vehicle must not exceed 635 kg.

The TVM (heavy suspension bridge) is 60 metres long and has a maximum rated capacity of 10 000 kg.

STATUS
In service with the Soviet Army.

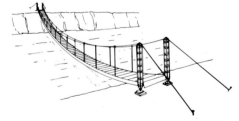

PVM foot suspension bridge

MANUFACTURER
Soviet state factories.

Underwater Bridge Set

DESCRIPTION
Although in the past the Soviet engineers have shown great skill in constructing underwater bridges, it is only recently that a special bridge set for this purpose has been noted. The set consists of hollow pontoons carried on specially modified ZIL-131 trucks. These pontoons are estimated to be 8 to 8·5 metres long and 3 to 3·5 metres wide, and are off-loaded from the trucks by gravity (similar to the TPP and PMP pontoons). They are then assembled on the shoreline to form a 'ribbon' bridge and brought into position by powerboats. Bridge piers or pilings are then placed, after which the bridge is sunk into position by flooding the pontoons. No further details are available.

STATUS
In service with the Soviet Army.

MANUFACTURER
Soviet state factories.

Underwater bridge set in use with ZIL-131 (6 × 6) truck crossing

MARM Sectional Arch Bridge

DESCRIPTION
The MARM is a sectional bridge which is used for bridging dry gaps, rivers and is often used as a road overpass. The spans are approximately six metres long and are supported by integral folding trestles which are adjustable in height. These trestles are normally assembled by a truck-mounted crane such as the K-162 and are laid side by side to permit wide vehicles, such as tanks, to use the bridge. Once the trestles are positioned, bracing is normally added. The bridge has a maximum capacity of 50 tons.

The spans are transported two at a time by ZIL-130V1 (4 × 2) 5-ton tractor trucks which tow a single-axle, four-wheeled, pole type trailer. The East German SBG-66 bridge set can be similarly used in addition to its other uses not shared by MARM.

STATUS
In service with members of the Warsaw Pact.

MANUFACTURER
Soviet state factories.

T-54 MBTs crossing MARM sectional arch bridge used as overpass

Construction of MARM bridge over waterway in combination with heavy barge bridge elements

Prefabricated Wooden Bridges

DESCRIPTION
Members of the Warsaw Pact still use wooden bridges assembled from prefabricated wooden deck sections which are supported on trestles of pile bents. To allow greater flexibility in their use, the trestle bents are often constructed of metal and are adjustable in height. Standard Soviet wooden fixed bridges have capacities of 12, 40 and 60 tons. Equipment required in the construction of these bridges includes truck-mounted cranes and, if required, pile driver rafts such as the KMS.

The East Germans also have a bridge which is constructed of prefabricated trestle bents and treadways. Each span is four metres long and consists of two treadway sections and one trestle bent; each of the latter has a wooden cap, six tubular metal columns, a wooden sill and two pieces of metal transverse bracing.

The columns consist of two pieces of pipe, one smaller in diameter than the other. The height of the bent is adjusted by raising or lowering the smaller pipe in the larger one. Once adjusted at the correct height, they are held in place by steel pins.

There are two treadways, each constructed from six wooden beams. Spacer blocks are used between the beams and wooden decking is laid on top of the perpendicular to the centre line of the bridge. Kerbing is then added to each roadway. The roadway has a width of five metres and a maximum capacity of 35 tons. One 2½-ton (6 × 6) truck can carry two treadways, one trestle bent and other miscellaneous components.

STATUS
Prefabricated wooden bridges are in service with members of the Warsaw Pact and other countries.

MANUFACTURER
East German and Soviet state factories.

RMM-4 Portable Steel Fixed Bridge

DESCRIPTION
The RMM-4 portable steel fixed bridge was developed in the 1940s but is no longer in front line use with the Soviet Army. It is most probably held in reserve. The bridge is used in forward areas to replace destroyed bridges, and in addition to being used as a clear-span bridge can, with the aid of intermediate supports, be used for the construction of longer bridges.

A complete RMM-4 bridge set consists of 24 intermediate and 8 end sections which are carried in 12 GAZ-63 (4 × 4) 2-ton trucks. The bridge consists of a timber deck which is supported by two to four deck-type steel trusses. These are assembled by bolting sections together. The number of trusses depends on the required capacity and the length of the bridge required. The assembled trusses form girders which are pushed across the gap manually or mechanically by using a launching nose and rollers, which are removed after the span is emplaced. The bridge is completed by adding the approach ramps.

STATUS
No longer in front line service with the Soviet Army but probably still held in reserve. May still be in service with other countries.

MANUFACTURER
Soviet state factories.

SPECIFICATIONS

	Intermediate truss section	End truss section
Weight	500 kg	500 kg
Length	3 m	3·5 m
Width	0·8 m	0·8 m
Height	1·85 m	1·85 m

Bridge construction Type	16t	30t	60t
Roadway width	3 m	4 m	4 m
Length	25 or 34 m	25 m	16 m
Number of trusses	2 or 3	4	4
Working party	n/a	40 men	40 men
Assembly time	n/a	150 minutes	120 minutes

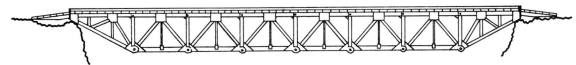
Side elevation of RMM-4 portable steel fixed bridge

SARM Sectional Deck Truss Bridge

DESCRIPTION
The SARM is a sectional deck-truss bridge made up of triangular and rectangular sections bolted together to support a roadway of steel deck panels. A single roadway is 4·2 metres wide and has a capacity of 40 tonnes and a dual roadway has a capacity of 60 tonnes and is 7·2 metres wide. The bridge is carried on one-axle semi-trailers which are towed by MAZ-504 or ZIL-130V (4 × 2) 5-ton tractor trucks.

Deck truss is made of welded steel sections, roadway panels with kerbing sections welded together. Clear spans of 18·6, 25·6 and 32·6 metres are feasible.

Where possible, existing piers are used in the construction of the SARM bridge, but where none is available, and the span required is greater than 32·6 metres, piers have to be provided. For low-level bridges, either pile bents or trestle bents are used while for high-level bridges panel-type crib piers are used. Steel towers can be used on existing bridge supports, piles or floating supports. Tower supports are adjustable at 2-metre intervals, maximum height being 8·8 metres.

The SARM takes a relatively long time to build compared with more recent tactical bridges. For example a 158-metre bridge takes about 24 hours to construct. As the maximum weight of any individual component is only 4400 kg, a 5000 kg capacity crane is sufficient in the construction of the SARM. Other elements in the SARM bridge system include pile drivers, crane trucks, gang saws and powerboats.

STATUS
In service with the Soviet Army and probably the East German Army.

MANUFACTURER
Soviet state factories.

REM-500 Railway and Road Section Bridge

DESCRIPTION
The Soviet REM-500 is a sectional railway bridge which can also be used as a road bridge with the addition of a wooden floor. It is employed over wide and shallow water barriers, closing breaches in railway lines, and as approaches for floating bridges.

The bridge is composed of individual steel spans 12·51 metres long and weighing 10 700 kg, which rest on trestles that can be adjusted in height from 3 to 12·7 metres and weigh between 5000 and 7000 kg. The trestles' feet are provided with large circular baseplates so that they will not sink into soft ground. The footers

REM-500 bridge complete with train carrying T-54 tanks and T-54 ARV on railway flat cars

have an area of 7 square metres and a ground pressure of 1·2 kg/cm² . Both longitudinal and transverse bracing is provided where necessary. The bridge can be built across rivers with maximum water depth of 7 metres and maximum water velocity of 1·2 metres per second.

The bridge can have a single track of either European (1·435 metres) or Soviet (1·524 metres) standard gauge. The speed of a train crossing the bridge must not exceed 30 km/h, with a maximum axle load of 20 tons. The REM-500 can also be used in combination with floating railway bridges which use river barges as their floating supports. The bridge is constructed a span at a time with each span and trestle being positioned at once by an overhead gantry (called the SRK-2D) which travels along the completed spans.

STATUS
In service with the East German, Polish and Soviet armies.

MANUFACTURER
Soviet state arsenals.

REM-500 section bridge being built

NZhM-56 Heavy Floating Railway and Road Bridge

DESCRIPTION
The NZhM-56 was developed after the Second World War as the replacement for the wartime SP-19 bridge which could be used as either a road bridge or railway bridge. The NZhM-56 bridge can carry road and rail traffic at the same time.

The pontoons which support the bridge are made up of three sections, bow (coded H), centre (coded C) and stern (coded K). Each of these sections is carried on the rear of a modified ZIL-131 (6 × 6) 3½-ton truck or a ZIL-157 (6 × 6) 2½-ton truck, which also tows a single axle four-wheeled trailer to support the end of the pontoons. Unloaded, these vehicles are very similar in appearance to a timber truck and trailer combination. Other equipment includes truck-mounted cranes, adjustable height piers for the construction of the shore connecting span, superstructure, and both conventional and special bridging boats. The latter are carried on special four-wheeled trailers and towed by KrAZ-214 (6 × 6) 7-ton trucks.

The pontoons are unloaded from the vehicles at the water's edge by truck-mounted cranes. They are then joined up into rafts, superstructure added and positioned by special powerboats. These are very short and have a square-cut bow which allows them to push the pontoons into position. When the bridge is in position, one of the special powerboats is normally positioned every second or third pontoon. A more recent modification to the pontoon trucks allows the pontoons to be launched by gravity, thus speeding up the construction of the rafts and reducing the reliance on truck-mounted cranes.

The superstructure carries both the road and railway

NZhM-56 heavy floating railway and road bridge with train carrying PT-76 and T-54 tanks on railway flat wagons

sections, with the latter being at the higher level. The railway section is made up of a large I-beam laid on its side carrying a steel deck with either the Soviet gauge (1·524 metre track) or the European gauge (1·435 metre track). This superstructure rests on a steel trestle which is fitted to the deck of the centre pontoon section. The roadway section is mounted across the centre and stern sections of the pontoon and consists of I-beam stringers supporting a wooden deck with a capacity of at least 40 tons.

STATUS
In service with members of the Warsaw Pact.

MANUFACTURER
Soviet state factories.

SPECIFICATIONS (estimated)
Pontoon (less power unit)
Length: (overall) 25·7 m
Width: (overall) 2·4 m
Height: (overall) 1·4 m

Sections

Type	H	C	K
Length	8·6 m	8·4 m	8·6 m
Width	2·4 m	2·4 m	2·4 m
Height	1·4 m	1·4 m	1·4 m

Power unit
Length: 5·2 m
Width: 2·4 m
Height: 1·5 m

SP-19 Self-propelled Pontoon Bridge

Details of the SP-19 self-propelled pontoon bridge can be found in *Jane's Military Vehicles and Ground Support Equipment 1983*, page 126.

Heavy Barge Bridges

DESCRIPTION
The Warsaw Pact armies widely use heavy floating road and railway bridges constructed from standard inland waterway barges of various capacities. The Soviets normally use the standard 600-ton and 1000-ton barges suitably modified. These can be used to bridge a river in three different ways. The most common method is by placing the barges end to end with the vehicles crossing from one barge to another over the bows of the barge. A river 400 metres wide would require seven 600-ton standard Soviet barges and would take about 24 hours to position. Equipment required to position this bridge would include truck-mounted cranes, bulldozers, brac-

ing equipment and three river tugboats, one with a 300 hp engine and two with 475 hp engines.

The second method is connecting the barges side by side with the barges resting in the direction of the current. Some of the barges used for this method have been provided with special supports which can carry an integral roadway. The third method, which is a recent development, is to connect the barges side by side, but aligning them on a slant towards the current, with the vehicles crossing from one barge to another via the sides of the barges. The main disadvantages of these bridges are the length of time required to position the barges and the delay to other river traffic when the barges are in position.

These barges are also used for railway bridges, where the barges are used as pontoons. Finally, river

barges have been used to construct heavy ferries which are pulled by tugboats.

Improved bridges are now available using either the open-type pushed barges (SBG-66) or the more modern flush-deck models such as the GSP-54, GSP-65, BFP-36 and FP-36. These are easier to build and have faster construction times.

STATUS
Barge bridges appear to be used in most Warsaw Pact countries using locally produced components. They are known to be used in East Germany, Hungary and the USSR.

MANUFACTURER
Warsaw Pact factories.

UNITED KINGDOM

Thos. Storey Bailey Bridge

DEVELOPMENT/DESCRIPTION

The Bailey bridge was originally developed by Sir Donald Bailey at the Military Engineering Experimental Establishment at Christchurch and was widely used during the Second World War. In 1948, Thos. Storey (Engineers) gained a licence from the National Research Development Corporation to manufacture and sell Bailey bridging components and equipment. In 1950 this licence was extended granting exclusive rights to the patent, production and selling of the Bailey bridge system. Since then the company has been continually improving the system which remains in production to meet a continuing demand.

The Bailey bridge was designed as a universal unit-construction military bridging system, with the Bailey panel as its basic component. The great advantage of the system lies in its use of these standard interchangeable components, which, combined with the simplicity of design, enables it to be erected by unskilled labour, under limited specialist supervision, in a short time.

The Bailey panel, the basic component, is made of high tensile steel. Panels can be connected together to form beams or columns. They are connected by panel pins and chord bolts to give a series of composite girders with varying strengths to meet loading conditions.

Using basic equipment, the maximum span is 61 metres and the maximum military load is class 80. The bridge can be constructed in three widths, 3·28, 3·81 and 4·19 metres. The bridge is normally constructed on rollers on one side of the gap and then launched into position using a skeleton, cantilever nose, which is detached after the bridge has crossed the gap.

Over the years, Thos. Storey has improved the original design. These improvements include a new steel decking which is quick and easy to erect, provides an anti-skid surface, and, unlike the wooden deck, has a long life. This can be used with the standard, standard widened, extra wide or double width Bailey bridges. Another development is the Thos. Storey Bailey panel, which provides an extra 40 per cent safe working shear load plus increased bending capacity and is completely interchangeable with the standard Bailey panel. Finally a double width Bailey 7·23 metres wide has been developed to permit two way traffic.

In addition to being used as a road bridge, the Bailey bridge has been widely used for other applications including rail and foot bridges, retractable lift bridges, derrick supports and mobile gantries. It can also be used in conjunction with the Acrow Uniflote for floating bridges.

STATUS

In production. In service with many armed forces all over the world.

MANUFACTURER

Thos. Storey (Engineers) Limited, 8 South Wharf Road, London W2 1PB, England.

Through-type Bailey bridge with decking system carried between two side girders formed from Bailey panels

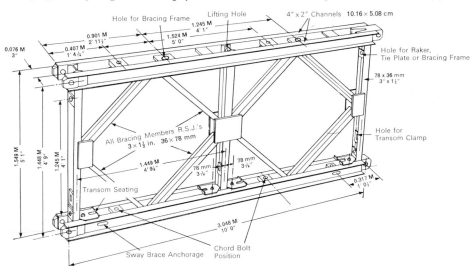

Bailey panel, major component of Bailey bridge system

Bailey bridge being constructed by Royal Engineers over River Ouse (Ministry of Defence)

Acrow Panel Bridge

DESCRIPTION

The Bailey bridge, which is some 40 years old, was designed to take military traffic up to class 80 standard and to cope with the maximum single-axle loadings of 20 tons, which were normal 30 years ago. Today a bridge may have to be class 150 and cope with single-axle loadings of 60 tons or more, particularly where heavy earth moving equipment is using the bridge. Such capacities could be achieved only by making extensive modifications to the standard Bailey design.

Thos. Storey decided that a new design was required, based on the Bailey system and principles, but taking advantage of modern developments in bridge design and steel technology. The result is the Acrow panel bridge which uses the Bailey unit construction system with its ease of assembly, but employs higher tensile steels and advanced design to give enhanced load-carrying capacity, and in particular, a fatigue life many times that of the Bailey system at less cost.

Like the Bailey bridge, the decking can be either steel or timber. Varying strengths of decking can be provided depending on the axle load the bridge is required to carry. The Acrow Panel Bridge can have roadway

Heavy earth-moving equipment crossing Ultra Wide Acrow Panel Bridge

widths of 3·43, 4·13, 4·84 and 7·23 metres to give two-lane traffic using standard equipment. Again, as with the Bailey, the Acrow panel bridge can be launched on rollers and constructed, without a crane if necessary, using unskilled labour.

Acrow panel equipment can be used even more successfully than Bailey to produce structures other than road bridges, for example rail bridges and gantries. All components of the bridge have been designed to be carried in standard military transport vehicles. Bridges can be installed either for permanent use, or subsequently dismantled and stored for re-use when required.

The major advantages of the Acrow panel bridge can be summarised as follows: improved bending moment capacity, improved shear capacity, improved stability against buckling under load, increased efficiency of stress transfer, greater rigidity and stability overall and a fatigue life approximately four times that of the standard Bailey bridge.

The Acrow panel bridge is constructed on rollers on one side of the gap to be bridged and an additional temporary structure, the launching nose, utilising standard components, is built on the leading end. The length of the nose is so judged that when the construction is moved across the gap, the nose tip engages on rollers on the opposite bank before the point of balance is reached. With the bridge positioned across the gap, the launching nose is removed and dismantled. The bridge is then jacked up off the rollers and lowered on to permanent bearings on the abutments on either bank.

BASIC COMPONENTS
The Acrow panel is the basic truss component. This has a shear capacity in a single storey of 25 tons, 67 per cent more than the standard Bailey panel, and a shear capacity in a double storey of 41 tons, again, 67 per cent more than the standard Bailey bridge.

Panel pins with circlips are used to connect panels end to end. These provide a locking feature which is also a useful precaution against thoughtless tampering.

Chord reinforcements can be bolted to top and bottom panels for additional bending movement capacity and are staggered over panel joints in the compression chord to provide greater stability under load. Four bolts are used to connect panels to chord reinforcements to increase the efficiency of stress transfer.

Chord bolts are used to connect panels one on top of another in the case of two or more panel heights or to connect chord reinforcements to panels.

Transoms of different lengths give four roadway widths; there are two basic profiles and light, heavy and super heavy versions. Transoms are located by dowels and bolted down to the transom seatings at intersections between diagonals and the bottom chord of panels at exactly 1·52-metre centres.

The steel decking is available in different versions for different load requirements. Deck units, consisting of chequer plate decking welded to the stringers, are clamped at each transom. Decking can terminate 0·762 metre inside the ends of the bridge or may be extended 0·762 metre onto abutments. Sloping ramps can be provided.

In the timber decking, deck chesses are held in position by steel kerb units which are bolted down to the outer stringers.

An Acrow four-panel type pier can be constructed for use as a supporting member for the bridge. This form of construction is very rigid and will carry an axial load of 400 tons on a pier as high as 41 metres. Two panel adjustable towers, capable of carrying axial loads of up to 200 tons (dependent on height) can also be provided.

The Acrow panel bridge can also be used in conjunction with the Acrow Uniflote system, for floating bridges, jetties and ro-ro terminals.

In mid-1978 Thos. Storey (Engineers) announced the development of the AB1X hybrid panel for use with either Bailey or Acrow panel bridging. It is manufactured from the same materials as the AB1 Acrow panel, which has better shear capacity, bending-movement capacity and fatigue life than the Bailey. Used one way up the hybrid panel accepts the Acrow Panel decking system at standard 5-foot centres in the normal way and the other way up reverts to a Bailey panel and can be used with standard Bailey decking and other components to form Bailey bridging, with the added advantage that the shear capacity is increased by the full 67 per cent of an Acrow Panel.

Bridge widths
Single Traffic Lane Bridges

Roadway width	Type of Bridge	Clearance between inner trusses
3·43 m	Standard Acrow Panel Bridge	3·76 m
4·13 m	Extra Wide Acrow Panel Bridge	4·78 m
4·85 m	Ultra Wide Acrow Panel Bridge	5·48 m

Two Traffic Lane Bridges

7·23 m	Double Width Acrow Panel Bridge	7·6 m

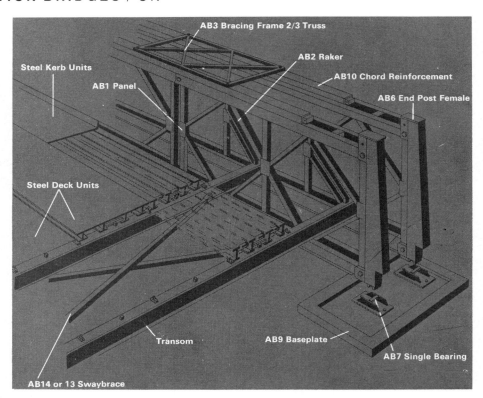

Main components of Acrow panel bridge

30·5-metre Acrow panel bridge for two-lane traffic

Acrow panel bridge with intermediate supports on Acrow panel square towers

STATUS
In production. In service with many armed forces around the world.

MANUFACTURER
Thos. Storey (Engineers) Limited, 8 South Wharf Road, London W2 1PB, England.

Acrow Heavy Bridge

DESCRIPTION
Acrow panel bridges, like the Bailey, are normally limited to a clear span of 61 metres. But there are occasions when a longer span is required and to meet this requirement Thos. Storey has developed the Acrow heavy bridge. The bridge is of the Warren Truss type and has all the advantages of unit construction based on the uniformity of similar components, produced by a strict jig control during the manufacturing process. The bridge has been designed for two-lane traffic on single spans of up to 100 metres in length, or for single line railway bridges. The maximum span depends on the loading required.

The Acrow heavy bridge has been designed to be launched, in the same way as the Bailey, with a cantilever nose on the front. Although it has been designed primarily for use as a permanent bridge, it is quick and easy to erect and can, if necessary, be dismantled and re-used elsewhere. The bridge requires a crane to assist its erection but because of the simplicity of the design and the method of assembly no skilled labour is required.

Alternative in-situ reinforced concrete, with or without asphalt wearing surface, steel, or timber decking systems are available. In each case the decking is rigidly connected to the bridge structure, forming an integral part of the bridge. Footwalks can be cantilevered on either side of the bridge structure outside the main trusses.

Each component of the bridge is an all-welded fabrication designed not only for its structural purpose but also for ease of handling, transportability and for rapid and simple construction on site.

82·3-metre Acrow heavy bridge for two-lane traffic

STATUS
In production. In service in many parts of the world.

MANUFACTURER
Thos. Storey (Engineers) Limited, 8 South Wharf Road, London W2 1PB, England.

Mabey Bailey Bridging

DEVELOPMENT
The Mabey Group has fabricated and erected bridges for over a century, and supplies a complete range of unit construction and modular bridges worldwide. Mabey and Johnson is a British Government authorised manufacturer of Bailey bridging, which it has supplied to the British Army and armies overseas. It is bridging consultant to NATO.

DESCRIPTION
Bailey is a through type bridge in which the roadway is carried between the main girders. It has been designed on the unit construction principle; the basic unit is a bay of 3·05 metres which means that bridges of varying spans and load capacities can be built from a stock of standard parts. The Bailey system has been devised for construction by unskilled labour under the supervision of an engineer. The heaviest component can be carried by six men and all components can be carried to the site in standard 3-tonne trucks.

Various decking systems have been developed to cater not only for the usual military loadings, but also for civilian loading and roadway width requirements. Decks can be supplied in timber or stiffened steel plate in 3·28-, 3·81- and 4·19-metre widths or combined in a three-truss dual carriageway configuration. Special timber decks are also available for abnormal heavy axled vehicles.

Mabey and Johnson Bailey bridging in position

The latest development, being marketed as "Mabey Compact Bailey", incorporates grade 55 steel and improvements to panel, bracing and deck system giving greater strength and enhanced fatigue life. It is the result of extensive research and development and has been proved in full scale tests at the Military Vehicles and Engineering Establishment, Christchurch.

All these equipments can be erected by launching from one side of the gap to be bridged, and equipment and detailed instructions for these operations are supplied.

STATUS
In production. In service.

MANUFACTURER
Mabey and Johnson Limited, Floral Mile, Twyford, Reading, Berkshire RG10 9SQ, England.

Mabey Universal Bridging

DESCRIPTION
Mabey and Johnson has used its wide experience of the Bailey bridge to develop the Universal bridge, which entered production and service in 1975.

The equipment extends the capability of speedily erected panel bridging as it is available in no fewer than six carriageway widths and for long spans up to 100 metres. The road widths are 3·28 metres (standard) and 4·19 metres (extra wide) for single-lane traffic, two-lane roadways of 6·1 and 7·5 metres, and three-lane of 9·1 and 10·9 metres. For special vehicles, decks to carry 40- and 60-tonne axles can be provided.

As in Bailey, the construction strength can be varied to suit the loading, and bridge construction is chosen by reference to load tables. The equipment is intended as a military line of communication bridge and for long-term and permanent civilian use. To this end, load factors are a minimum of 1·7 in accordance with British Standards, and low maintenance is a significant factor in the detailing of parts. If required, the bridges can be completely galvanised. The roadway comprises steel panel decking which will accept an asphalt wearing course if required, or can be supplied with an epoxy anti-skid wearing course.

The deeper Universal panel (4·5 × 2·36 metres) has more than twice the bending resistance of Bailey, result-

Mabey Universal Bridging in position

ing in simpler and lighter truss formations. The deeper panel also makes single-storey spans possible up to 54 metres, thus extending economical single-storey bridging through all the spans normally encountered in practice. With double-storey, spans up to 100 metres are possible.

The bridges can be launched by the standard cantilever method, thus combining most of the benefits of Bailey, including ease of erection, multiple use, and guaranteed load carrying capacities with permanent bridge capability.

STATUS
In production. In service.

MANUFACTURER
Mabey and Johnson Limited, Floral Mile, Twyford, Reading, Berkshire RG10 9SQ, England.

Fairey Medium Girder Bridge

DEVELOPMENT

The Medium Girder Bridge was designed and developed by the Military Vehicles and Engineering Establishment at Christchurch, formerly the Military Engineering Experimental Establishment, with production and marketing undertaken by Fairey Engineering Limited. The MGB entered service with the British Army in 1971 and since then has been adopted by over 30 countries in Africa, Europe, Middle and Far East, and North and South America.

Main advantages of the MGB can be summarised as follows: it is quickly and easily built by hand, little training is required, no site preparations or grillages are required, it is easily transported by road or air as palletised loads, is of light and sturdy construction, it has a multi-span capability with span junction set, a portable pier set is available, it can also be used as a ferry or floating bridge of unlimited length, it has loading capacity of up to class 60 and little or no maintenance is required.

DESCRIPTION

The MGB is a lightweight, easily transported bridging system which can be quickly erected by hand to provide a flexible and manoeuvrable bridging system covering the full range of military bridging requirements. The MGB has also been adopted by a number of governments for emergency bridging operations.

Much of the success of the MGB lies in the material from which the components are manufactured. The MVEE(C) developed a weldable alloy of aluminium, zinc and magnesium (DGFV 232A) necessary to ensure both the strength and the lightness of the bridge. Seven major components are used in the basic bridge construction, and all except two weigh under 200 kg, and can be easily handled by a team of four men. The two heavier components are handled by six-man teams.

The MGB is a two-girder deck bridge in which the longitudinal girders with the deck units between produce a four-metre wide roadway. Girders of the top panels joined at each end by a bankseat form a shallow single-storey construction for short spans and light loads. A double-storey configuration using deeper girders of top and bottom panels, together with additional end of bridge components, can be constructed for heavier loads over longer spans.

The MGB can be supported on unprepared and uneven ground without foundations and is constructed on one roller beam for single-storey construction and on two roller beams 4·6 metres apart in a building frame for double-storey construction. The ends of the roller beam can be adjusted in height within the building frame so that no levelling or other preparation of the ground is required.

All components of the MGB are transported in standard loads of up to 3500 kg on a special pallet. The British Army use the Bedford RL or MK (4 × 4) which also tows a Rubery Owen two-wheeled trailer which carries another pallet. There is a separate entry for the MGB trailer (FV2842) in the *Trailers* section. When the vehicle and trailer arrive at the bridge-building area the pallet is attached to a stationary vehicle, or an alternative anchorage point, and the towing vehicle is driven away pulling off the pallet, which falls onto the ground. Rubber buffers cushion the fall. A single nine-metre bridge is transported on two pallet loads while a 31-metre double-storey bridge is transported on ten pallet loads.

Single-span bridging

The MGB can be built either in the single- or double-storey configuration. Single-span single-storey bridges can be used by class 60 vehicles at a length of nine metres and by lighter vehicles up to a maximum length of 22 metres at class 16. Single-span double-storey bridges can be used by class 60 vehicles at lengths of up to 31 metres and at increasing lengths for lower load classes, to a maximum length of 49 metres at load class 16.

The single-storey bridge is constructed using top panels pinned together forming two girders and joined at each end by a bankseat beam. In the double-storey configuration, the girders consist of top and bottom panels with junction panels, and end taper panels forming the sloping end of the bridge. In both cases, ramp, deck and kerb units complete the construction.

Single-span bridges are launched using a centrally-mounted launching nose made up of three-metre sections. During launching, the bridge is supported on roller

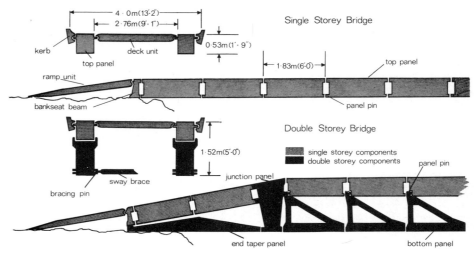

Main components of MGB

Loaded MGB pallet being off-loaded from MGB trailer

Three Alvis Scorpion CVR(T)s crossing single-span, double-storey MGB

Chieftain MBT crossing 9-metre single-span MGB

beams at the home bank and a roller at the far bank. Single-storey bridges are launched over one roller beam, supported on baseplates. Double-storey bridges are launched over two such roller beams supported 4·9 metres apart in a building frame. To adjust the height and levels of the roller beams, a hydraulic jack (with a lift of 300 mm) can be mounted at each corner of the building frame. These jacks are also used to lower the bridge on both banks after construction. Short single-storey bridges can be launched by simply pushing them off the home bank roller beam and letting them fall to the ground.

Reinforcement set
This extends the single-span capability of the MGB to 49·4 metres at load class 60. It complements the capability of the MGB pier and span junction equipment as it can be used in terrain where deep valleys make it impracticable to use piers. The kit contains all the additional components required for use with normal double-storey bridge sets to construct a length of reinforced class 60 MGB from 32·9 to 49·4 metres. The latest reinforcement sets provide a capability of load class 70 at a span of 45·8 metres. The kit consists of reinforced links 3·66 metres long (with one pair of links 1·83 metres long to provide the greatest range of spans), which are connected to form a pair of chains, one beneath each bridge girder. Links are connected to bottom panels at the ends of the bridge by a reinforcing anchorage. The links are positioned two metres below the bridge by reinforcing posts which enable the system to be tensioned towards a vertical position by Tirfor cable jacks (details of these will be found in the *Recovery equipment* section). The reinforcing is added by an extra party of eight men while the bridge is being constructed by the normal 24-man team. Further development is intended to achieve reinforced spans of over 50 metres.

In March 1983 the US Army Mobility Equipment Research and Development Command (MERADCOM) awarded a contract to Fairey Engineering worth $6·7 million for 19 Link Reinforcement Sets, seven sets for the US Army and 12 sets for the US Marine Corps.

With this order the MERADCOM project to produce their own cable reinforcement kit (CRS) was terminated.

Span junction set
The basic single span MGB can be given a multi-span capability by the use of the MGB span junction set. This equipment enables bridges of any length up to class 60 load capacity to be handbuilt over any fixed or floating supports, existing or improvised.

The span junction set consists of span junction posts which are pinned together at the top and connected towards the bottom by hydraulic articulators. A span junction link is fitted to join the bottom chords of the junction post to permit movement over rollers during launching. After launching the junction link is removed to allow articulation of the junction posts. The other main component is the capsill. This is a beam to which can be pinned rocking rollers which incorporate bridge bearings. The capsill fitted with rocking rollers can be used on top of a pier to carry the bridge during launching or when in use, or in the MGB adjustable roller beam support to form the heavy duty capsill roller beam (CRB) required when launching most multi-span bridges.

Portable pier set
The portable pier set provides the MGB with its own two-legged pier which can be assembled during the building of the bridge. Two legs pass through housing at each end of a pier beam. The legs are constructed in three-metre sections and piers up to 12 metres in height can be used in water gaps with current speeds of up to 5·5 metres a second. In dry gaps, legs up to 18 metres can be used.

The pier beam with housing, leg base section and one standard leg section at each end is pre-assembled and then pinned to the span junction post on the home bank and launched with the bridge. Once the bridge is in position, the adjustable braces are used to set the pier beam vertical before the legs are lowered and any additional leg sections are added. The pier components are also transportable on the standard MGB pallet and the heaviest component weighs 408 kg.

Multi-span
Using the MGB portable pier set for multi-span bridges, the piers can be launched with the bridge by temporarily placing the first pier in position as the next is brought up, then moving the piers successively by booming the bridge back and forward.

The span junction components allow double-storey floating bridges of any length to be constructed on virtually any type of floating support which has sufficient buoyancy.

The articulation provided by the span junction bay and the use of long landing bays means that the MGB is the only modern military bridge equipment which can be used in a situation where bank heights range from 0 to 5 metres. Even this range can be extended to 6 metres if the MGB portable pier is used to form trestle bays.

Close-up of MGB portable pier before leg is lowered to river bed

Chieftain MBT crossing single-span reinforced double-storey MGB. Reinforcement links can be seen under bridge

Chieftain MBT crossing multi-span, double-storey, 78-metre, class 60 MGB with portable piers

The MGB pontoon matches the ease of handling and transport of the MGB system. Made of aluminium, it is 8 metres long, 2·7 metres wide and 1·2 metres deep. It has plastic foam for buoyancy when the open section is flooded and is fitted with self-draining valves which operate when the load is released from the pontoon pier. Each pontoon weighs one tonne and a load of four with ancillaries is carried on a platform for launching each pontoon in rapid succession, and for recovery from the river. A DROPS for transport by prime mover is available. In the water two pontoons are coupled end-to-end to form piers, which are coupled side by side for landing bay rafts as required.

Floating bridges up to load class 60 can be constructed with single- or double-storey MGBs. Double-storey floating construction allows long landing bay spans up to 26·5 metres and so is suitable where there is a considerable rise and fall in the water level. The single-storey floating MGB is very quick to build and requires fewer bridge components for long spans though more pontoons are required than for double-storey construction. The single-storey arrangement will provide ferries for load classes up to MLC 90.

New developments
Universal Light Pier
Fairey Engineering is now marketing a Universal light pier on behalf of the Swiss Federal Aircraft Factory which originated the design for the Swiss Army. The light pier can be assembled without the use of cranes or special equipment in a lattice pier leg form. The pier legs can be up to 20 metres long and can take loads of up to 120 000 kg. A 12-metre pier can be assembled by 12 men in one hour. The Universal light pier is now in service with the Swiss Army. Illustrations of this are given in this section under Switzerland.

Ski jump for V/STOL
The components of the MGB readily adapt to the Ski jump profile when raised at one end. The ramp surface comprises three MGB single-storey girders supporting MGB deck units between them. Outrigger units provide a total ramp width of ten metres. A full description of the Ski jump is given in the *Rapid runway repair equipment/portable runway* section.

Container ship flight deck
The MGB will provide a rapid easily erected flight deck on a wide range of commercial container ships. An MGB deck structure is supported on beams mounted on ISO containers which creates a hangar space underneath and/or side dispersal.

ISO container floats
The MGB was designed to form easily into palletised loads. This concept is completely compatible with the stowing of a MGB within the 20 × 8 × 8 foot ISO container. Where logistic systems now require the widespread use of containers for transportability, this is of considerable importance.

The MGB has a float bridge capability and the idea of using the container as a float offers significant logistic advantages. Two four foot high container floats can be handled by the normal field logistic system equipment and, when placed on the ground, the upper part of the container is removed and inverted. The bridge parts are unloaded from the pallet base which is then replaced on top of the container. In the water the two containers are linked together and with the addition of bow sections form a float. These floats give the MGB the capability of forming a class 60 floating bridge of any length.

The US Marine Corps has awarded a series of contracts to Fairey Engineering for container float evaluation in the class 60 double-storey floating bridge requirement set out by the US Marine Corps.

The container floats are to be integrated into the Marine Corps Logistic Handling System and meet all the ISO container requirements.

Roll on-roll off shipping
Further uses of the MGB are its possible inclusion in an unloading ramp for ro-ro ships. This ramp can be used in conjunction with pontoons for expeditionary unloading.

SPECIFICATIONS

NATO stock code	Service designation	Unit weight
8714	Top panel	175 kg
8710	Bottom panel	197 kg
8713	Junction panel	182 kg
8611	End taper panel	272 kg
8687	Bankseat beam	258 kg
8723	Ramp unit	120 kg
8698	Deck unit	74 kg

Bridge lengths and load classification

Load class	Single-storey		Double-storey	
	Bays	Span	2 ends + bays	Span
60	5	9·8 m	12	31·1 m
50	5	9·8 m	14	34·8 m
40	6	11·6 m	16	38·5 m
30	8	15·2 m	18	42 m
24	9	17·1 m	20	45·8 m
20	10	19 m	21	47·6 m
16	12	22·5 m	22	49·4 m

The load class equates to a multi-axled wheeled vehicle of about the same weight in tonnes as the load class, and to a tracked vehicle of weight less than the load class (about 6 tonnes less for load class 60). The exact load class of a vehicle depends on axle space, wheel loadings and track length etc.

Single-storey bridge
Launching and completed bridge weight of single-storey MGB at various lengths (all bridges are launched undecked):

	Weights per given span				
	9·8 m 5 bays	11·6 m 6 bays	15·3 m 8 bays	19 m 10 bays	22·6 m 12 bays
Launching weight	2367 kg	2733 kg	3467 kg	4199 kg	4932 kg
Bridge weight	4166 kg	4892 kg	6344 kg	7797 kg	9249 kg

Weight of 14 ramps at ends of bridge is 1676 kg.

Weight of launching parts, including building aids for given length of single-storey MGB:

	Span in bridge bays			
	5	6, 7 & 8	9 & 10	11 & 12
Total weight	504 kg	524 kg	1679 kg	1857 kg

Double-storey bridge
Weight per bay double-storey MGB: 1156 kg
Weight per end of bridge: 2697 kg

	Weights per given span						
	19 m 10 bays	31·1 m 12 bays	34·8 m 14 bays	38·5 m 16 bays	42 m 18 bays	45·8 m 20 bays	49·4 m 22 bays
Launching weight	11 970 kg	13 562 kg	15 294 kg	16 888 kg	18 484 kg	20 079 kg	21 676 kg
Decked weight	17 301 kg	19 612 kg	22 081 kg	24 395 kg	26 711 kg	29 026 kg	32 341 kg

Class 60 single-storey MGB ferry with Chieftain MBT on board

Class 60 single-storey Medium Girder Bridge floating bridge

Foden 6 × 4 truck fitted with Boughton Swap-body system being used to unload Medium Girder Bridge pontoons

Class 60 double-storey Medium Girder Bridge floating bridge

Weight of 14 ramps at ends of bridge is an additional 1676 kg.

Weight of launching parts, including building aids for given length of double-storey MGB:

	Span in bridge bays				
	10	**12**	**14, 15 & 16**	**17 & 18**	**19, 20, 21 & 22**
Total weight	2530 kg	2705 kg	3364 kg	3539 kg	4239 kg

Span junction set

NATO stock number	Service designation	Unit weight
8159	Post span junction	260 kg
8157	Articulator, hydraulic	172 kg
8153	Capsill bridging	160 kg
8154	Roller assembly, rocker bearing	111 kg
8125	Beam, pier, half section	445 kg
8123	Housing, pier leg	272 kg
8122	Pier leg, base section	162 kg
8121	Pier leg, standard section	208 kg
8119	Beam, grillage, pier	82 kg
8118	Sleeper pier	64 kg

Approximate weight of portable pier in bridge with maximum leg length 12·2 metres is 4026 kg.

MGB configurations

Type	Length	Class	Building party	Building time	Transport in 4000 kg pallet loads
Single-storey	9 m	60	9	15 minutes	2
	22 m	16	17	30 minutes	5
Double-storey	30 m	60	25	45 minutes	10
	49 m	16	25	1 h 20 minutes	16
2-span + pier	51 m	60	40	3 h	20
3-span + piers	76 m	60	40	6 h	27
Reinforcing kit	49 m	60	32	2 h	18
Single-storey floating bridge	any	60	n/a	dependent on length	dependent on length
Double-storey floating bridge	any	60	40+	dependent on length	dependent on length

STATUS
In production. Up to July 1982, 32 countries had placed orders for the Medium Girder Bridge including Australia, Canada, Denmark, Federal Republic of Germany, Ghana, Ireland, Italy, Jordan, Kenya, Malaysia, the Netherlands, Pakistan, Philippines, Singapore, Switzerland (Feste Brücke 69), the United Kingdom and the USA.

In September 1982 the US Department of Defense ordered a further 36 lightweight bridging sets for the US Army (16) and the US Marine Corps (20). This will bring the number of MGBs in US service to 70.

MANUFACTURER
Fairey Engineering Limited, PO Box 41, Crossley Road, Heaton Chapel, Stockport, Cheshire SK4 5BD, England.

Various components and configurations of MGB ISO container float

UNITED STATES OF AMERICA

M2 Bailey Bridge

DEVELOPMENT
The Bailey bridge was developed by the United Kingdom before the Second World War and was adopted by the United States Army during the war. In 1958 the United States Army type classified it as Standard A. The bridge is used both as a tactical and a line of communication bridge to span either water obstacles or dry gaps and is capable of carrying all loads of traffic.

DESCRIPTION
The Bailey bridge is a fixed through-truss type bridge with the roadway carried between two main girders. The trusses in each girder are formed from 3·048-metre panels pinned end to end. Transverse floor beams, called transoms, are clamped to the bottom chords of the trusses, and support stringers and decking. Sway braces between the girders provide horizontal bracing and rakers between the trusses and transoms provide lateral bracing within each girder. The clear roadway between guardrails is 3·809 metres wide. The transom

supporting the roadway is normally set on the bottom chords of the trusses. Ramps are used at either end of the bridge but must not exceed a slope of 10:1 for loads up to and including 50 tons, and 20:1 for loads over 50 tons. Footwalks 0·762 metre wide can be carried on the transoms outside the main trusses on each side of the bridge. End posts pinned to the end of each truss sit on cylindrical bearings, which rest on a steel baseplate. On soft soil, timber grillage is used under the baseplates to distribute the load. The bridge can be assembled between banks of different elevations, but the slope should not exceed 30:1.

The bridge set contains 33 types of bridge part and 30 types of erection equipment. The decking is of wood while the panels, end posts, transoms and ramps are of a low-alloy, high tensile steel. All other parts are of carbon structural steel.

The two main girders can be assembled from a single truss or from two or three trusses side by side. A second or third storey of trusses can be added for greater strength. For stability, multi-storey bridges must have at least double trusses and all triple-storey bridges with the

deck at the bottom are braced at the top by transoms and sway braces.

Using auxiliary equipment the bridge can also be used to construct suspension, floating and railway bridges, crib-piers, towers and causeways.

SPECIFICATIONS
(full details of the Bailey bridge will be found in the United Kingdom section.)
Length of single span:
(minimum) 9·144 m
(max) 64 m
Width of roadway: 3·809 m
Vehicular interval: 27·43 m

STATUS
Production complete. In service with the US Army and other armed forces.

SUPPLIER
Bailey Bridges Inc, PO Box 1186, San Luis Obispo, California 93406, USA.

Expedient Methods of Bridging

Listed below is a résumé of the expedient methods of bridging using floating bridge equipment.

Light Tactical Raft
Superstructure components can be used to erect fixed bridges with a clear span of between 6·096 and 11·582 metres. The 6·096-metre bridge can take a class 21 wheeled vehicle or a class 17 tracked vehicle and the 11·582-metre bridge can take a class 7 wheeled or tracked vehicle.

M4 and M4T6 Fixed Spans
Short fixed spans can be erected with components of the M4 and M4T6. Aluminium deck-balk fixed spans from 4·572 to 13·716 metres can be assembled without intermediate support, but spans of over 13·716 metres require intermediate support.

Class 60 Fixed Spans
Components of the class 60 bridge set can be used to provide fixed bridges with a road width of 4·113 metres over short gaps of 7·315 to 18·288 metres.

Expedient Raft
Four 24-ton pneumatic floats are used as support for the bridge used on the M48 and M60 AVLBs. The floats are connected together with rope or turnbuckles with no gaps being left between the floats. The AVLB is then launched on to the floating supports and secured to the floats with four ratchet chain hoists attached to the D-rings of the deck and the carrying handles of the saddle beam. The raft has approximately the same capacity as a four-float reinforced raft assembled from M4T6 components, eg between class 50 and 35 for wheeled vehicles and class 55 and 40 for tracked vehicles, depending on the velocity of the current.

Light Vehicle Raft
A light vehicle raft can be assembled from 12-ton half-floats and light tactical raft deck. The floating supports for the raft consist of four half-floats each with four interior saddle panels and one outrigger panel, two saddle beams and two outrigger beams. The superstructure consists of deck components from the light tactical raft set. This raft can carry a Jeep and a trailer in a river with maximum current velocity of 1·524 metres a second.

Twelve-ton Half-float and M4 Balk Light Vehicle Raft
Four half-floats are used for floating supports and M4 balk is added for the deck. Capacity of this raft is limited to a Jeep and a trailer, or an equivalent load.

Line of Communication Bridges

Listed below is a résumé of the various types of line of communications bridging available to the US Army. All the types listed are standard but their scales of issue are not determined and thus they may be issued as required.

Bridge Fixed: Highway, 27- to 36-inch Beam, Wide Flange Stringers, 51-inch Plate
This type of beam and girder bridge may be used as a single span bridge or can be combined into a multiple span bridge with intermediate supports. The number and types of stringers are determined by span length. Three depths of stringer are available: 686 mm, 914 mm and 1295 mm. Using the basic components a two-way traffic bridge with a class 60 capacity, or a single track class 100 capacity bridge, with open lengths of up to 39 metres can be constructed. Standard components consist of abutments, bents, piers, towers and pier and tower foundations.

A double lane bridge 39 metres long with square ends weighs 194 tons when constructed. A double lane bridge 11·94 metres long with square ends will weigh 22 tons.

Bridge Fixed: Highway, Semi-permanent
Produced in lengths of 9·14, 18·29 and 27·43 metres this type of bridge can take loads up to class 50. The bridges are issued in sets of components including girders, bearing plates and assorted clips and bolts. The timber decking used for the roadway is not issued in the

set and has to be obtained locally. The sets are normally carried on rail cars but can be road transported on 8- or 16-ton flatbed trailers. When assembled the bridge is 4·724 metres wide. A 9·14-metre long bridge weighs 5860 kg; an 18·29 metre long bridge weighs 20 774 kg; and 27·43-metre long bridge weighs 27 941 kg.

Bridge Fixed: Railway, Through Truss, 70 ft Long Span
Although intended primarily for railway use, this type of bridge can also be used for road traffic when wide gaps must be bridged without intermediate piers. It can be erected in the field by unskilled labour under the direction of a skilled engineer. The bridge is composed of a launching nose, a tail frame, trolleys, receiving and lowering equipment, and erection gantries and travellers. This type of bridge is always constructed as a through-type structure. It uses a conventional floor system with ties fastened directly to the stringers by hook bolts.

When fully assembled this type of bridge is 21·34 metres long, 59·9 metres wide and 41·53 metres high. Weight is 44 162 kg.

Bridge Fixed: Railway, I-Beam
Intended primarily for railway use, this type of bridge is constructed in spans of 5·18, 6·4, 8·23 and 10·67 metres with the smallest three spans being the more usual. The bridge spans are issued as standard unit parts of rolled, wide-flange I-beams which can be assembled by unskilled labour. Intermediate piers and supports are constructed from standard parts. The two

smallest spans are 457 mm high; the two largest 610 mm high. A 5·18-metre span weighs 2315 kg; a 6·4-metre span weighs 3926 kg; and an 8·23-metre span weighs 5225 kg.

Bridge Fixed: Railway, 27- to 36-inch Beam, Wide Flange Stringers, 51-inch Plate G
This type of bridge follows the same general lines as the corresponding Highway bridge (see above) and uses the same sizes of stringers. As with the Highway bridge, the number and depth of stringers are determined by the span length. The shortest span that is normally constructed with the associated sub-structures of abutments, bents, piers, towers and pier and tower foundations is 6·1 metres; construction time is about 80 man-hours. The longest bridge length available is 30·5 metres for which the construction time is 1300 man-hours. The bridge can be built in varying widths to suit the rail gauge. A typical narrow gauge rail bridge would be 1·38 metres wide. A wide gauge bridge would be 1·84 metres wide. The weight of materials for the smallest type of bridge is about 3630 kg; for the largest 112 490 kg.

Bridge Fixed: Railway, Deck, 70 ft Long Span
Designed to take a single track railway, this truss girder, deck-type bridge is issued in crated form weighing 65 924 kg. Included in the kit are angle bracing, bedplates, chords, diagonal and vertical webs, splice plates and vertical end posts. When constructed the bridge is 21·34 metres long.

BRIDGING BOATS

CZECHOSLOVAKIA

Mo-108, Mo-111 and Mo-930 Bridging Boats

Mo-108
This is identical to the Mo-111 but is powered by a T-108, V-8 air-cooled diesel which develops 105 hp, giving the boat a lower performance than the Mo-111.

Mo-111
This is basically a modification of a Second World War German bridging boat and retains the German design of three rudders and a Kort nozzle, a metal ring-guard which houses the screw. The Mo-111 is transported on a large two-wheeled trailer called the MP-4. It is also known as the M-111 and the Tatra 111. The Mo-111 was introduced in the 1950s and built at the CXD plant at Decin.

Mo-930
This is the latest Czechoslovak bridging boat and uses the same engine as the Tatra 813 (8 × 8) truck to power a single screw. The Mo-930 is transported on a single-axle trailer weighing 2500 kg.

SPECIFICATIONS

Type	Mo-111	Mo-930
Crew	2	2
Weight	3200 kg	4000 kg
Length	7·5 m	7·68 m
Beam	2·2 m	2·2 m
Depth	1·2 m	n/a
Draught	0·85 m	0·85 m
Max speed	24 km/h	20 km/h
Fuel capacity	178 litres	n/a
Endurance	n/a	7 h

Type	Mo-111	Mo-930
Engine model	T-111A-4	T-930-53
Engine type	diesel	petrol
Cylinders	V-12	V-12
Hp	170	200
Cooling	air	air
Towing power		
(forward)	n/a	2275 kg
(reverse)	n/a	1200 kg

STATUS
Production complete. In service with the Czechoslovak Army.

MANUFACTURER
Czechoslovak state factories.

FRANCE

F1 Pontoon Boat

DEVELOPMENT
The F1 pontoon boat was designed to meet the requirements of the Corps of Engineers by the Etablissement Technique d'Angers (ETAS) with production being undertaken by the Atelier de Construction de Tarbes (ATS). The first prototype was built by the ETAS with the second being built with the assistance of the ATS. The two prototypes were followed by five pre-production boats which were completed in 1971. A total of 135 production model F1 pontoon boats were built for the French Army between 1972 and 1975.

The boat has been designed to undertake a wide range of roles including the pushing and pulling of pontoons, installation of protective nets, transport of personnel and cargo, a platform for drivers, and other bridging and mooring roles.

DESCRIPTION
The hull of the F1 pontoon boat is made of all-welded alloy (AG4MC) with 4·1 cubic metres of the boat filled with polyurethane foam to make it virtually unsinkable. The boat consists of two sections, fore and aft. The fore section contains the engine and crew compartment while the aft section contains the two propellers, their protective frames and steering motor. This is hinged to the main hull and can be swung upwards by two hydraulic joints to enable the boat to be operated very close inshore.

The engine is mounted forward of the crew compartment, and transmits power to a reduction gearbox with twin output shafts coupled via electromagnetic clutches to two variable displacement hydraulic pumps. Each pump feeds oil under pressure to a hydraulic motor mounted in a submerged nacelle directly behind the propeller. Each propeller has four blades and is 0·9 metre in diameter. The boat has no rudder as the propellers, which are pod-mounted, can be traversed through 360 degrees. The boat has exceptional acceleration and deceleration, as has been demonstrated at numerous Satory Exhibitions.

The boat is provided with three bilge pumps with a capacity of 1200 litres per hour each. Hand-operated capstan winches with a 3500 kg capacity are mounted on either side of the hull and there is a towing post at the front of the hull and a second towing post at the rear of the crew compartment. The height of the rubber clad bow fender post can be adjusted. Two white light searchlights (one movable and one fixed) with a range of 100 metres are provided together with two infra-red lights with a range of 50 metres (one fixed and one movable).

The F1 pontoon boat is normally carried in two sections, with the bow section being carried on the rear of a Berliet GBC 8 KT (6 × 6) truck, which also tows a single-pole 2½-ton trailer carrying the rear half of the boat. These are off-loaded by a crane and assembled in the water. It takes only three minutes to assemble the two units.

The basic boat was fitted with a 20 mm M621 cannon for trials. This could be elevated from −5 degrees to +50 degrees, but was not adopted. The boat was also offered on the civilian market. A single undivided boat was also offered, weighing 4600 kg and 8·3 metres long. As far as it is known it was not adopted by any country.

STATUS
Production complete. In service with the French Army.

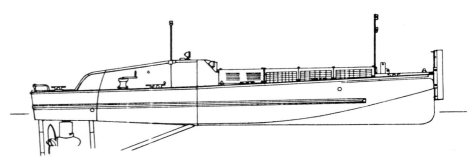
F1 pontoon boat

F1 pontoon boat (GIAT)

F1 pontoon boat showing stern with propellers raised (ECP Armées)

MANUFACTURER
Atelier de Construction de Tarbes, 2 rue Alsace-Lorraine, BP 313, 65013 Tarbes, France.
Enquiries to Groupement Industriel des Armements Terrestres (GIAT), 10 place Georges Clemenceau, 92211 Saint-Cloud, France.

SPECIFICATIONS
Crew: 2–3
Weight:
(forward section) 3000 kg
(aft section) 1800 kg
Length: 8·3 m

Beam: 2·49 m
Height above waterline, excluding lights: 1·3 m
Draught:
(max) 1·15 m
(minimum) 0·45 m
Max speed: 25 km/h
(carrying 3 men plus 400 kg of cargo) 24·4 km/h
(pushing 4-pontoon floating bridge with a 40-ton load) 9·36 km/h
Engine: Deutz F10 L413 V-10 air-cooled diesel developing 237 hp at 2400 rpm
Electrical system: 24 V
Batteries: 4 × 6 V

GERMANY, DEMOCRATIC REPUBLIC

BB-120 Bridging Boat

DESCRIPTION
The BB-120 is an East German version of the Soviet BMK-90 bridging boat but differs from it in having no hand rails on the sides. However, a spray rail is fitted at the rear. The BB-120 is propelled in the water by a three-bladed propeller and steered by a conventional rudder. It is transported on and launched from a four-wheeled flatbed type trailer.

SPECIFICATIONS
Crew: 2
Length: 7·85 m
Width: 2·1 m
Height: 1·5 m
Draught: 0·55 m
Weight: 3500 kg
Max speed: 22 km/h
Engine: G-5 6-cylinder diesel developing 120 hp at 2000 rpm

Towpower:
(forward) 1200 kg
(reverse) 700 kg

STATUS
Production complete. In service with the East German Army in limited numbers.

MANUFACTURER
East German state factories.

GERMANY, FEDERAL REPUBLIC

Bridging Boat

DESCRIPTION
This bridging boat is used in the construction of floating bridges (including the West German version of the American Ribbon Bridge) and ferries. It has two adjustable pushing knees at the front, a windscreen that can be fitted with a removable canvas cover to give some degree of protection to the crew and is propelled in water by two propellers. The hull is aluminium and the built-in air compartments make it very difficult to sink. The boat is carried on and launched from a two-wheeled single-axle trailer.

SPECIFICATIONS
Crew: 2
Weight: 4600 kg
Length: 7·45 m
Beam: 2·48 m
Depth: (overall) 1·85 m
Max speed: 22·5 km/h
Engine: air-cooled diesel developing 250 hp

Trailer plus boat
Weight: 8100 kg
Length: 9·75 m
Width: 2·48 m
Height: 3·36 m

STATUS
In service with the Belgian and West German armies.

West German bridging boat of Belgian Army on two-wheeled trailer (C R Zwart)

HUNGARY

Hungarian Bridging Boat

The Hungarian Army uses at least one bridging boat of local design which has two propellers. Full details of this boat are not available.

STATUS
In service with the Hungarian Army.

MANUFACTURER
Hungarian state factories.

ITALY

SAI Ambrosini Bridging Boat

DESCRIPTION
This bridging boat was designed by SAI Ambrosini to meet the requirements of the Italian Army and entered service in 1974. The stainless steel hull is divided into six watertight compartments to guarantee buoyancy. The inboard-mounted engine is towards the front and the semi-enclosed cabin towards the rear.

SPECIFICATIONS
Crew: 2–3
Weight: 3800 kg
Length: 7·5 m
Beam: 2·45 m
Height:
  (without cabin) 1·8 m
  (with cabin) 2·3 m
Draught: 0·7 m
Max speed:
  (pushing or towing half MLC 60 raft in 1·75 m/s current) 3 km/h
  (in calm water without load) 25 km/h
Endurance: 6 h
Turning radius: 8·5 m
Engine: Deutz model SF12L413 12-cylinder, 16·96-litre, air-cooled diesel developing 260 hp

STATUS
Production complete. In service with the Italian Army.

MANUFACTURER
SAI – Societa' Aeronautica Italiana SpA, Viale Roma 25, 06065 Passignano sul Trasimeno (PG), Italy.

SAI Ambrosini bridging boat being lowered into water by Astra BM 20MB1 crane truck, which was designed to carry this boat. Boat has cockpit/cabin housing removed (T J Gander)

SAI 121 Bridging Boat

DESCRIPTION
The SAI bridging boat has been designed to cope with loads involved in the assembly of class 60 floating bridges on rivers and inland water obstacles. It can be used with several types of floating bridge and can be used in the assembly of non-floating bridging such as the Bailey Bridge. The hull is constructed from stainless steel with light alloy components. The layout is conventional with the engine compartment at the rear, the main crew compartment amidships and a bluff bow. On the bow is an angled assembly for nudging bridging components into place and behind this there is a small working area for assemblers. The crew compartment can be covered with a canvas tilt for extra shelter.

SPECIFICATIONS
Weight: 4450 kg
Length: 7·5 m
Beam: 2·45 m
Draught: 0·8 m
Max speed: 25 km/h
Range: 4 h
Turning radius: 4 m
Engines: 2 × AIFO 8061 SM 5·5-litre 6-cylinder water cooled (closed circuit) developing 177 hp each

STATUS
Due to enter service with the Italian Army during 1984.

SAI 121 bridging boat

MANUFACTURER
SAI – Societa' Aeronautica Italiana SpA, Viale Roma 25, 06065 Passignano sul Trasimeno (PG), Italy.

POLAND

KH-200 Bridging Boat

DESCRIPTION
The KH-200 was developed in the late 1960s and after four years of trials was approved for production in 1971. It has a hull of all steel construction and a pusher knee mounted at the bow, similar to that mounted on the Soviet BMK-T bridging boat. The crew is seated in a cabin towards the bow which has an open back. The engine is mounted to the rear of the crew and drives a single propeller at the rear. The KH-200 is used with the Polish PP-64 heavy folding pontoon bridge and can also be used as a transporter carrying up to 15 troops. The boat is transported on a large two-axle trailer which weighs 2800 kg unladen.

SPECIFICATIONS
Crew: 2–3
Weight: 3865 kg
Length: 8·14 m
Beam: 2·3 m
Draught: 0·72 m
Max speed: 25 km/h
Endurance: 12·1 h
Towing power:
 (forward) 2500 kg
 (reverse) 1200 kg
Engine: Leyland UE 680 6-cylinder water-cooled diesel developing 169 hp

STATUS
In service with the Polish Army.

Polish KH-200 bridging boat

MANUFACTURER
Polish state arsenals.

UNION OF SOVIET SOCIALIST REPUBLICS

BMK-T Bridging Boat

DESCRIPTION
The BMK-T is the most powerful bridging boat in the Soviet inventory and is used with pontoon bridges such as the PMP. The boat is carried on the rear of a KrAZ-214 7-ton (6 × 6) or a KrAZ-255 7½-ton (6 × 6) truck chassis and is launched by gravity, often with its engine running ready for immediate use. The recovery technique is as follows: the truck is reversed into the water and a cable from the truck's winch is connected to the stern of the BMK-T and the boat is then pulled out of the water over runners at the rear of the truck until it is back in the travelling position.

The hull of the BMK-T is of the 'sled' design for greater stability and has four enclosed compartments. Even if two non-adjacent compartments are flooded, the boat will not sink. The crew cabin is towards the front of the boat and is fully enclosed. The engine compartment is to the rear of the crew cabin and is also fully enclosed, allowing the boat to operate in very rough water. It is propelled in the water by two propellers at the stern which have a maximum speed of 945 rpm. On encountering an obstacle during forward travel the two propellers are lifted out of the water automatically by hinges at the stern. When in the travelling position, the propellers

BMK-T bridging boat being carried on rear of KrAZ-255B 7½-ton (6 × 6) truck

are swung through 180 degrees so that they are on top of the boat. The BMK-T is highly manoeuvrable in the water and can be steered equally well in reverse. All controls are electrical and if required the boat can be remote-controlled by a cable from a maximum distance of 30 metres. A pusher knee is mounted at the bow, although the boat is also used for towing pontoons.

STATUS
In service with members of the Warsaw Pact including East Germany and the Soviet Union.

MANUFACTURER
Soviet state factories.

SPECIFICATIONS
Crew: 2
Weight: 6000 kg
Length: 8·6 m
Beam: 2·7 m
Depth: 2·2 m
Draught: 0·75 m
Max speed: 17 km/h
Fuel capacity: 300 litres
Fuel consumption: 20 litres/h
Endurance: 15–17 hours

BMK-T bridging boat in water

Towing power:
  (forward) 2000 kg
  (reverse) 750 kg
Engine: YaMZ-236, SP4 V-6, water-cooled diesel developing 180 hp at 2100 rpm

KrAZ-255B with BMK-T Boat
Weight: 19 100 kg
Length: 10·6 m
Width: 2·8 m
Height: 3·76 m

BMK-130 and BMK-150 Bridging Boats

DESCRIPTION
BMK-130/BMK-130M
The hull of the BMK-130 is of steel construction and is divided into individual watertight compartments. Mounted each side of the hull is a strut and a wheel which assist in the launching and recovery of the boat. Once afloat, the wheels are folded up alongside the hull. The BMK-130M, introduced in the mid-1960s, has a modified hull and when afloat the wheels are swung forward and stowed in wells on either side of the hull. This reduces not only drag but also the chances of damage to the wheels when afloat. The launching sequence is as follows: the bow attachment is connected to the front bumper of the truck, the boat is pushed into the water stern first and once the boat is afloat it is disconnected from the truck and the wheels of the boat are swung forward and stowed in the wells.

BMK-150/BMK-150M
Until the introduction of the BMK-T this was the most powerful bridging boat used in the Warsaw Pact. It has a hull of aluminium construction and is much lighter than the BMK-130, and has two engines with separately controlled twin screws. Unlike the BMK-130, this boat is provided with a windscreen and a cover that can be erected in bad weather. The basic BMK-150 has wheels which fold up on the outside of the hull, while the later BMK-150M has wheel wells like the BMK-130M.

SPECIFICATIONS

Type	BMK-130M	BMK-150
Crew	2	2
Weight	3450 kg	2500 kg
Length	7·85 m	8·2 m
Beam	2·1 m	2·55 m
Depth	1·5 m	2 m
Draught	0·622 m	0·66 m
Max speed	21 km/h	22 km/h
Fuel capacity	n/a	300 litres
Endurance	12 hours	7 hours
Engine model	YaAZ-M204VKr-2, 5	M51-SPE-3, 5(2)
Engine type	diesel	petrol
Number of cylinders	4	6
Hp	120	62 × 2
Cooling	water	water
Towing power		
(forwards)	1450 kg	1500 kg
(reverse)	800 kg	n/a

STATUS
Production probably complete. In service with members of the Warsaw Pact.

MANUFACTURER
Soviet state factories.

BMK-150 bridging boat

BMK-130M bridging boat being towed by Ural-375D (6 × 6) 4½-ton truck

BMK-130 bridging boat with wheels lowered

BMK-150M bridging boat in travelling order being towed by truck

BMK-70 and BMK-90 Bridging Boats

DESCRIPTION
BMK-70
The BMK-70 was widely used by the Soviet Army during the Second World War for a wide variety of roles including the assembly of pontoon bridges, towing of barges and rafts and for general ferrying work. It is no longer in front-line service but is probably held in reserve. The hull of the BMK-70 is of steel construction. It is normally carried on a trailer of the single-axle pole type or on a two-axle trailer.

BMK-90
This was developed in the 1950s and has a more powerful engine than the BMK-70. The BMK-90 has a hull of corrugated steel whereas the later BMK-90M has a hull of duralumin as well as a redesigned propeller shaft. The boat is provided with a wheel and strut on each side of the hull to assist in the launching and recovery of the boat. When waterborne these can be folded up alongside the boat or removed. This feature was subsequently adopted by the later BMK-130 and BMK-150 bridging boats. The BMK-90 is transported on the PBMK-90 single-axle trailer which weighs 2100 kg.

STATUS
Production complete. The BMK-70 is held in reserve while the BMK-90 and BMK-90M are still in service with some members of the Warsaw Pact.

MANUFACTURER
Soviet state factories.

BMK-90 bridging boat with wheels lowered

SPECIFICATIONS

Type	BMK-70	BMK-90	BMK-90M	Type	BMK-70	BMK-90	BMK-90M
				Fuel capacity			
Crew	2	2	2	(litres)	n/a	340	340
Weight				Endurance	n/a	14 h	14 h
(without fuel)	2450 kg	2450 kg	2200 kg	Engine model	ZIL-20S	ZIL-120	ZIL-120
Length	7·83 m	7·83 m	7·85 m	Engine type	petrol	petrol	petrol
Beam	2·1 m	2·1 m	2·1 m	Number of			
Depth	1·5 m	1·5 m	1·5 m	cylinders	6	6	6
Draught	0·64 m	0·53 m	0·52 m	Hp	75	90	90
Max speed				Cooling	water	water	water
(unloaded)	20·5 km/h	20·5 km/h	20·5 km/h	Towing power			
(loaded)	n/a	8 km/h	8 km/h	(forwards)	681 kg	1100 kg	1100 kg
				(reverse)	n/a	1400 kg	1400 kg

UNITED KINGDOM

Fairey Allday Marine Combat Support Boat

DEVELOPMENT
Based on a requirement issued by the United Kingdom Military Vehicles and Engineering Establishment at Christchurch, the company started development of the 8-metre Combat Support Boat in the autumn of 1975 with the first prototype being delivered to the British Army for trials early in 1977. As a result of extensive trials by the British Army both in the United Kingdom and on the Rhine in West Germany a pre-production boat was ordered by the British Army for further trials. It was delivered in May 1978. The boat was accepted for service with the British Army in February 1979, and an order placed for 56 boats the following year. In 1983 the Ministry of Defence ordered a further 12 CSBs for the British Army to replace those lost on the *Atlantic Conveyor* during the Falkland Islands campaign. After extensive evaluation by the US Army MERADCOM the CSB was accepted under NATO Standardisation and Rationalisation arrangements. To date 280 have been ordered. Several other countries are now evaluating the CSB.

DESCRIPTION
Based on the well proven Allday 8-metre hull, the boat features a pusher bow and an aft mounted capstan/tow hook. The mast and cabin top are both removable for low profile operations, and transport/stowage. The two self-draining cockpits are each designed to accommodate a standard one-tonne NATO pallet.

The Fairey Allday Marine Combat Support Boat is made of welded marine grade aluminium alloy for a lightweight, yet extremely strong boat. Based on a well-tried hull, the craft was designed to meet the requirements of the British Army for a boat to assist with bridging operations and other river and estuary support and assault duties. Waterjets enable the boat to be used in shallow water with twin 180 shp turbo-charged marine diesels providing the power. For transport, launching and recovery of the tug, a cross-country trailer is available.

Standard equipment includes navigation and towing lights and a searchlight, fire extinguishers, windscreen wipers, bilge pumping system, heavy duty fendering, Explosafe filled fuel tank and built-in buoyancy to float craft in an upright position.

The batch of 12 ordered by the Ministry of Defence during 1983 will all have 'winterisation' kits for operations at low temperatures. This includes extra cable insulation, more powerful screen wipers, pump and engine heaters, de-frosting equipment and personnel heaters.

Fairey Allday Marine Combat Support Boat of US Army where it is known as the Ribbon Bridge Erection Boat (RBEB)

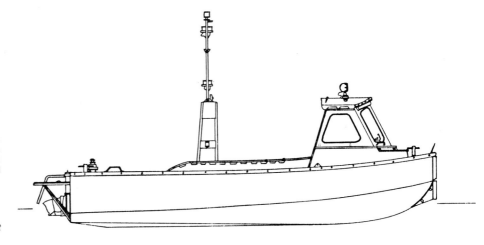
Fairey Allday Marine Combat Support Boat

US Army CSBs in action with Ribbon Bridge in West Germany

US Army CSB about to be retrieved onto trailer

SPECIFICATIONS
Length: 8·2 m
Beam over fenders: 2·5 m
Height:
  (without cab) 1·98 m
  (with cab) 2·79 m
Weight:
  (fully fitted out and fuelled) 4080 kg
Maximum payload: 2000 kg
Draught:
  (fully fitted out and fuelled) 0·56 m
  (fully laden) 0·66 m
Engines: twin Sabre 212 turbo-charged marine diesel continuously rated at 180 shp or 212 shp at 2450 rpm
Propulsion units: twin Dowty 300 mm two-stage water-jets coupled to engines through Borg Warner 72C hydraulic direct drive reverse gearbox
Maximum static forward thrust: 1·6 tonne
Maximum static reverse thrust: 1 tonne
Maximum speed:
  (unladen) 40 km/h
  (fully laden) 30 km/h
Fuel tank capacity: 227 litres

STATUS
In production. In service with Greece (18), United Kingdom and United States.

MANUFACTURER
Fairey Allday Marine Limited, Hamble, Southampton, Hampshire, England.

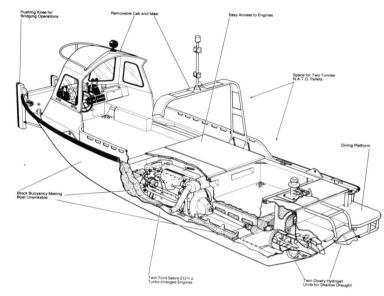

Cut-away drawing of Fairey Allday Marine Combat Support Boat. Hand rail over top of cockpit identifies it as US Army boat; British Army boats have inset hand grips

Rotork Combat Support Boat Type CSB 508

DESCRIPTION
The CSB 508 has been designed to undertake a wide range of duties including bridging, tug-boat, supply and diving. The boat is capable of static thrusts of up to 1700 kg for tugging purposes and can transport 3600 kg of cargo. The wide deck and bow ramp permit the loading of men and equipment from either beach or quay and with the jet propulsion system the boat has a draught of 0·42 metre, allowing the boat to operate in very shallow water.

The hull of the CSB 508 is made of glass-fibre reinforced plastic and has a built-in foam buoyancy in excess of the craft's gross displacement, making the boat unsinkable. The hull requires the minimum of maintenance and can easily be repaired in the field.

The deck has a non-slip bonded grit surface applied. The gunwales are of stainless steel rolled section and full peripheral fendering is provided at the gunwale with a solid nylon rubbing strake installed at the waterline. The winch-operated ramp is reinforced and has a non-slip surface. Scuppers for the removal of water from the deck are located at the transom.

Two pushing knees are mounted at the bow and a towing post is mounted aft of the helmsman's seat.

Standard equipment includes six warping bollards and four lifting points mounted on the gunwale rail, navigation lights, floodlight, klaxon and a rechargeable fire extinguisher.

Optional equipment includes an illuminated helmsman's compass, deck gear, cargo/vehicle lashing kit, demountable jib crane with a capacity of 500 kg and a four-wheel close coupled boat trailer.

STATUS
In production. In service with several countries.

MANUFACTURER
Rotork Marine Limited, Lake Road, Hamworthy, Poole, Dorset BH15 4NY, England.

Rotork combat support boat Type CSB 508

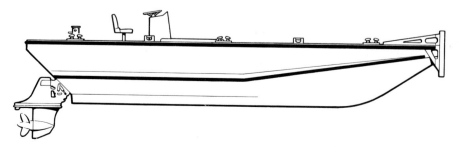

Rotork combat support boat Type CSB 508

SPECIFICATIONS
Length: (overall) 8·23 m
Beam: (overall) 3·05 m
Height:
(overall) 1·88 m
(of gunwales above deck) 0·75 m
Deck area: 15·1 m²
Fuel capacity: 2 × 200-litre pannier tanks

Propulsion systems

Engine type	Speed km/h light	Speed km/h 50%	Speed km/h laden	Performance cruise litres/h	Weight light kg	Max payload kg	Draught laden drive up cm	down cm
2 × 100 hp diesel/waterjet GM 3·53 MN (naturally aspirated) coupled to heavy duty high thrust waterjet	33·3	27·75	18·5	45·46	3800	2200	42	42
2 × 130 hp diesel/waterjet GM 3·53 MTI (turbo-charged and intercooled) coupled to heavy duty high thrust waterjet	38·85	31·45	25·9	54·55	3900	2100	42	42
2 × 130 hp diesel/outdrive Volvo AQD 40/280	44·4	37	29·6	50	3900	2100	42	95
2 × 75 hp diesel/waterjet GM 4·43 MTI (turbo-charged and intercooled) coupled to heavy duty waterjets	44·4	38·38	33·3	82	4250	1750	42	42
2 × 200 hp outboard motors OMC 200	70·3	59·2	38·85	136·3	2300	3700	42	83

All engine options include full instrumentation, steering and throttle controls. Power tilt is included as standard on all diesel units and power tilt and trim on all petrol engines.

Task Force General Purpose Q 26 Push/Pull Tug

DESCRIPTION
The Task Force Q 26 Push/Pull Tug is made of heavy duty glass-reinforced plastic and has been designed to undertake a wide range of roles including bridging. Standard equipment includes a pushing knee, samson post at quarter and amidships, towing hook with quick releases and a cabin. It is road transportable on a four-wheeled trailer which is also used for launching and recovery.

SPECIFICATIONS
Weight: 4500 kg
Length: (overall) 8 m
Beam: 2·85 m
Draught:
(lightly laden) 0·46 m
(fully laden) 0·64 m
Max speed: 42·55 km/h
Fuel capacity: 636 litres
Endurance: 5 hours at full thrust with an additional 3 hours at low output
Max thrust:
(forward) 1633 kg
(rear) 953 kg
Engines: 2 × 212 hp Sabre diesels coupled to Dowty waterjets

STATUS
Production.

MANUFACTURER
The Boat Showrooms of London Limited, 286–290 Kensington High Street, London W14 8PA, England.

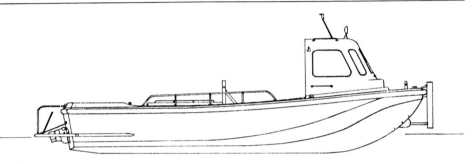

Task Force General Purpose Q 26 Push/Pull Tug

Task Force General Purpose Q 26 Push/Pull Tug from rear

Thos. Storey Motorflote

DESCRIPTION
The Thos. Storey Motorflote has been designed for use with the Thos. Storey Uniflote System and consists of a modified Uniflote box-section pontoon powered by an internal marine diesel engine. The engine drives a propeller situated in a protected area underneath the rear of the Motorflote. Steering is carried out by a rudder operated from a wheel in the control cabin in the centre of the Motorflote pontoon. Having a simple box section the Motorflote can be readily secured to any Uniflote pontoon combination such as a raft or ferry. The advantages of using the Motorflote in place of orthodox outboard engines on a Uniflote raft or float are said to be that the Motorflote can be easily connected and disconnected to any Uniflote System construction, the propel-

ler is less vulnerable to damage as it is contained within a protected area, as well as being quieter and cheaper.
The control cabin may be fully open or enclosed, and hand rails can be fitted if required. Two Motorflotes are operating in the Falkland Islands propelling a 12-Uniflote ferry with a capacity of over 100 tons.

STATUS
Production.

MANUFACTURER
Thos. Storey (Engineers) Limited, 8 South Wharf Road, London W2 1PB.

SPECIFICATIONS
Length: 3·05 m
Width: 2·44 m

Depth:
(deck to skids) 1·71 m
(deck to cabin top) 2·14 m
(total) 3·85 m
Draught: 1·1 m
Freeboard: 0·61 m
Weight: approx 4500 kg
Fuel capacity: 226 litres
Engine: Mermaid Mariner 6-cylinder 6·227-litre diesel developing 115 bhp at 2600 rpm continuous
Propeller diameter: (4 blades) 0·7 m
Static bollard pull: 13·9 kN
Speed in still water:
(unladen pushing) 2·4 m/s
(unladen towing) 1·8 m/s
(loaded pushing 150 tons) 1·7 m/s

Uniflote raft being propelled by Motorflote (T J Gander)

Motorflote with auxiliary bow fitted for use when not pushing Uniflote ferry (T J Gander)

UNITED STATES OF AMERICA

27 ft Bridge Erection Boat

DESCRIPTION
The 27 foot (8·24-metre) bridge erection boat is used for a variety of roles including pushing and towing floating bridge rafts, assisting in the erection of bridges and for general river work. If required, the boat can carry either nine fully equipped men or 1360 kg of cargo in its bow section.

The hull is of all aluminium construction. The stern section contains the two engines and the crew compartment, while the bow unit contains the cargo carrying compartment and the pusher knee. The two sections are quickly attached by connecting hooks and clamps.

The two separately controlled engines are mounted side by side forward of the crew compartment and each drives a single propeller. Both engines have a standard marine-type propeller drive with forward, reverse and neutral gears.

Standard equipment includes a built-in fire extinguisher system, bilge blower system (which blows out explosive gases from the engine compartment prior to starting the engine) and an automatic petrol cut-off valve.

The boat is normally carried in two sections, with the stern section carried in the rear of a 2½-ton truck (6 × 6) and the bow section on a single axle, two-wheeled pole type trailer. If required the bow unit can be launched by floating it off the submerged trailer. Until recently the boat was normally lifted into the water by a crane which is part of most bridging systems. The Mobility Equipment Research and Development Center at Fort Belvoir has developed a boat cradle assembly which is mounted on the rear of a 5-ton (6 × 6) truck chassis. This enables the whole boat to be launched directly into the water from the rear of the truck, which takes only two minutes compared with the previous crane method of 30 minutes. A total of 54 of these cradles have been built by the Pacific Car and Foundry Company of Renton, Washington.

SPECIFICATIONS
Crew: 2
Weight:
(complete boat with fuel) 3084 kg
(bow section) 522 kg
(stern section with fuel) 2562 kg
Length:
(overall) 8·241 m
(bow section without pusher knee) 3·352 m
(stern section) 4·775 m

27 ft bridge erection boat being launched from rear of 5-ton (6 × 6) truck for use with Ribbon Bridge

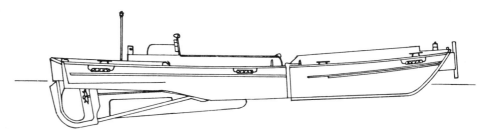

27ft bridge erection boat

Beam: 2·489 m
Depth: 1·981 m
Depth reduced for transport: 1·828 m
Draught:
(aft) 1·016 m
(forward) 0·127 m
Max speed
(unladen) 32 km/h
(with 1360 kg of cargo) 28 km/h
Fuel capacity: 340 litres
Fuel consumption: 30 litres/h at max speed
Endurance at max speed: 11 hours

Max thrust:
(forward) 1587 kg
(reverse) 1179 kg
Engines: 2 × M-251 6-cylinder, L-head, 4-cycle, petrol engines developing 90 hp each at 3200 rpm

STATUS
In service with the USA (Type B classified) and allied countries. Being replaced in US Army service by the Combat Support Boat.

MANUFACTURER
Highway Products Incorporated.

19 ft Bridge Erection Boat

DESCRIPTION
The 19 foot (5·854-metre) bridge erection boat is used for a variety of roles including the assembly of tactical floating bridges, propelling light tactical rafts, installation of anchorage systems, emplacing mine protection booms and for general utility work during river operations. If required the boat can carry 1360 kg of cargo, or nine fully equipped infantrymen. The boat's shallow draught allows it to undertake work that the larger 27 foot bridge erection boat with its greater draught cannot do.

Its two-man crew consists of the operator and the assistant operator. The hull is of all aluminium construction and the bow is full and rounded with flush sides

rounding into a V-shaped bottom. The engine has a standard marine type propeller drive with forward, reverse and neutral gears. The propeller is right hand with a diameter of 501 mm and a 584 mm pitch. Instead of a conventional rudder the boat has a Kort-nozzle steering mechanism, which is directly connected to the steering wheel through shafts and a reduction worm gear.

Standard equipment includes lifting attachments, pusher knee at the bow, haul chocks, cleats, towing bits, running lights, removable searchlight, floodlight, fire extinguisher and anchor.

The boat rests in a cradle which is normally carried on a 2½-ton utility trailer and launched by a truck-mounted crane. It can also be launched by skids running from the trailer into the water or directly by backing the trailer into the water.

SPECIFICATIONS
Crew: 2
Weight: (unloaded) 1724 kg
Length: 5·854 m
Beam: 2·444 m
Depth: 1·981 m
Draught: 0·762 m
Max speed: (unloaded) 34 km/h
Fuel capacity: 163 litres
Fuel consumption: 30 litres/h at max speed
Endurance: 5·4 hours at max speed
Max thrust:
(forward) 952 kg
(reverse) 385 kg
Engine: 6-cylinder petrol developing 90 hp at 3200 rpm

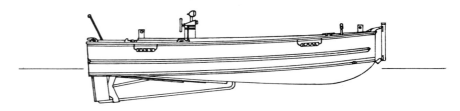

STATUS
This is no longer in service with the US Army but may be in service with other countries.

19ft bridge erection boat

YUGOSLAVIA

Yugoslav Bridging Boat

The Yugoslav Army uses at least two bridging boats of local design and construction, full details of which are not available.

STATUS
In service with the Yugoslav Army.

MANUFACTURER
Yugoslav state factories.

Mine warfare equipment

MINES

ARGENTINA

FMK-1 Non-metallic Anti-personnel Mine

DESCRIPTION

The FMK-1 is a small circular non-metallic anti-personnel mine 82 mm in diameter and 43 mm deep. In its storage and transport form it is carried with two safety and arming pins held in place by a length of yellow tape. The same tape also holds in place a steel washer and a small shaped collar. When the tape is removed the washer can fall away or be kept manually in place for later detection. In practice the washers are not retained. The shaped collar is placed in position in the pressure detonator train in such a way that the mine can be either used as an anti-personnel mine or as the igniter for the FMK-3 anti-tank mine (see below). These mines have been encountered in the Falkland Islands.

STATUS

In service with the Argentinian armed forces.

FMK-1 non-metallic anti-personnel mine (T J Gander)

MAPG Anti-personnel Mine

DESCRIPTION

This is a conventional cylindrical metallic anti-personnel mine fitted with a top-mounted fuze for either pressure or pull activation.

SPECIFICATIONS
Weight: 2·6 kg
Weight of main charge and booster: 0·4 kg
Type of main charge: TNT
Type of booster charge: RDX

Operating force:
(pressure) 9–12 kg
(pull) 1·8–3·5 kg
STATUS
In service with the Argentinian Army and Marine Corps.

MAPPG Anti-personnel Bounding Mine

DESCRIPTION

This is similar in appearance to the MAPG but is fitted with a propulsive charge to propel the mine body to a suitable height for detonation. Activation is either by pressure or pull on a tripwire.

SPECIFICATIONS
Weight: 2·6 kg
Weight of main charge and booster: 0·4 kg
Type of main charge: TNT

Type of booster charge: RDX
Operating force:
(pressure) 9–12 kg
(pull) 1·8–3·5 kg

STATUS
In service with the Argentinian Army and Marine Corps.

MAP I Anti-personnel Practice Mine

DESCRIPTION

This is a cylindrical mine weighing 2·2 kg fitted with an illumination smoke signal as the main charge for training purposes. A small explosive device is used to expel the charge from the mine when it is activated. This can either be by pressure or pull on a tripwire.

STATUS
In service with the Argentinian Army and Marine Corps.

FMK-3 Non-metallic Anti-tank Mine

DESCRIPTION

The FMK-3 non-metallic anti-tank mine is basically a block of explosive contained in a plastic coated case 240 mm square and 90 mm deep. A central well on the top of the explosive block will accommodate an FMK-1 anti-personnel mine with a shaped collar in the base arranged to suit the heavier pressures involved with a tank target. A rope handle is mounted on one side. These mines have been encountered in the Falkland Islands and as they contain virtually no metal components they are difficult to detect.

STATUS
In service with the Argentinian armed forces.

FMK-3 non-metallic anti-tank mine (T J Gander)

MAA-1 Anti-tank Mine

DESCRIPTION

This is a circular non-metallic anti-tank mine fitted with a top-mounted pressure plate. The body is cast TNT with an outer casing 5 to 10 mm thick made of TNT with seven to eight per cent cotton. The pressure plate is also made of TNT and seven to eight per cent cotton. The mine is resistant to blast type countermeasures and is activated by pressure of 150 kg plus. A practice concrete version designated MAAA-1 is available and is fitted with a white smoke and red signal main charge.

STATUS
MAA-1 and MAAA-I are in service with the Argentinian Army.

Anti-tank Mine 'Ministry of the Navy'

DESCRIPTION

This is a circular anti-tank mine with a top-mounted pressure plate and a main charge of 5·5 kg of cast TNT. The mine is activated by a pressure of 150 kg plus.

STATUS
In service with the Argentinian Marine Corps.

AUSTRIA

ARGES Anti-personnel Bounding Mine SpM75

DESCRIPTION
The SpM75 anti-personnel bounding mine consists of three main components: the body, guiding and bounding mechanism, and the fuze mechanism.

The body is plastic and contains 4600 spherical fragments. The thickness of the body and the number of fragments decline towards the lower half of the body. The body is closed at the top by a cover plate which has two holes, one for the rotary trip fuze and one for the electric fuze.

In the vertical axis of the body is a discharge tube which is firmly fixed to the body of the mine and is closed at the top by a receptacle for the fuzes. In the discharge tube is a guide tube anchored to a baseplate in the ground. The two tubes are connected by a thin wire about 1·5 metres long. The top of the wire is attached to a pin in the receptacle of the discharge tube. A second guide tube with a helical compression spring and firing pin passes vertically through the receptacle of the discharge tube. When the mine is propelled vertically into the air by the propulsive charge and reaches a height of 1·5 metres (the length of the wire), the pin is withdrawn from the anchor in the receptacle and releases the firing pin. This strikes a percussion cap which in turn ignites a detonator. The explosive charge between the discharge tube and the casing explodes and scatters the spherical fragments.

The mine is normally ignited by a rotary fuze which has three twisting arms, with a tripwire attached to each arm. When pressure is applied to the tripwire a pin is released and the three twisting arms with the tripwires fall away. The tensioned, spring-loaded firing pin lies safely with the free end (with rollers) of a cross pin on two narrow supports with semi-circular recesses. When the firing pin is twisted through half the width of the supports by one of the twisting arms, the mine is armed, it loses its support and strikes the percussion cap. The mine can also be triggered by an electric detonator.

A training model is also available with a replaceable smoke compound substituted for the jumping mechanism and propulsive compound.

STATUS
In production for the Austrian Army.

MANUFACTURER
Armaturen-Gesellschaft GmbH, A-4690 Schwanenstadt/Rüstorf, Austria.

SPECIFICATIONS
Weight: 6 kg
Diameter: 125 mm
Height:
  (with fuze) 255 mm
  (without fuze) 170 mm
Weight of main charge: 500 g
Number of spherical balls: 4600
Weight of individual balls: 0·7–0·85 g
Effective range: 20 m
Operating force: 5–10 kg

ARGES anti-personnel bounding mine SpM75

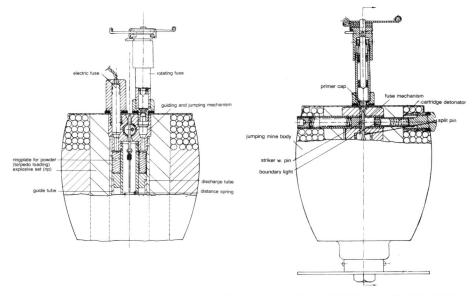

Side and front cutaway drawings of ARGES SpM75 anti-personnel bounding mine

ARGES M80 Horizontal Anti-personnel Mine

DESCRIPTION
The ARGES M80 (HzSM 80) is a revised version of an earlier model and consists of a plastic casing with a convex front face containing approximately 1250 anti-personnel fragments. A sight for alignment is fitted at the top of the mine body and sighting marks are also provided along the sides. Two sets of hinged legs are provided. In the bottom of the mine are two igniter ducts for use by a detonation fuze or by an electrical igniter. A firing device is provided with each mine and although this is intended to be disposable it will fire up to 20 times. The mine can also be fired by a trip-wire operated igniter.

The mines are delivered packed four to a wooden case containing four firing devices and 50 metres of firing cable.

STATUS
In production and service.

MANUFACTURER
Armaturen-Gesellschaft GmbH, A-4690 Schwanenstadt/Rüstorf, Austria.

SPECIFICATIONS
Weight: 3 kg
Length: 250 mm
Width: 75 mm
Height:
 (body) 130 mm
 (body with legs) 220 mm
Weight of main charge: 1·3 kg
Type of charge: PETN
Number of fragments: 1250 approx
Diameter of fragments: 6·5 ± 1·5 mm

ARGES M80 horizontal anti-personnel mine

SMI 17/4C Giant Shotgun

DESCRIPTION
The SMI 17/4C is a novel weapon concept in that it is intended for clearing barbed wire and similar obstacles, yet it has considerable potential as an anti-personnel or anti-vehicle mine. It consists of a dished plate some 300 mm across that is intended to fire a matrix of steel balls, each some 8 to 9 mm in diameter in a narrow-dispersion cone out to a range of 50 metres or more. At 50 metres the closely-controlled steel ball cone is powerful enough to clear a way through a five-coil barbed wire obstacle with three coils underneath and two on top. The steel ball cone diameter at 50 metres is only two metres across and at that range each ball can penetrate 8 mm of armour plating. It can also be used to clear dense jungle foliage. Before firing the SMI 17/4C Giant Shotgun is supported on a simple steel frame and

the dished plate can be swivelled vertically and locked in position by simple thumb-screws.

STATUS
Development complete.

MANUFACTURER
SMI, Military Defence Products, Südsteirische Metall-industrie GmbH, A-8430 Leibnitz, Austria.

SPECIFICATIONS
Weight: 8 kg
Diameter of mine face: 302 mm
Depth: 150 mm
Height to centre of face axis: 240 mm
Weight of charge: 5 kg
Type of charge: Composition B

SMI 17/4C Giant Shotgun (T J Gander)

SMI Directional Fragmentation Mines

DESCRIPTION
The SMI 20/1C is a fixed directional fragmentation mine for use against personnel, light skinned vehicles, helicopters and as a clearance device for objects such as barbed wire fences.

The mine body is made of reinforced plastic and uses a layer of Composition B for the fragment propellant. At a 60 degree spray angle about 80 per cent of the fragments produced are within the target area. The fragments also have a high penetration capability, for example at 50 metres at least 25 mm of pinewood will be pierced.

There are two fuze wells, one on top which is usually for an electric detonator and one at the bottom which can be used either to connect the mine to other mines by detonating cord or to fit an anti-lift device. Activation is by pull-wire, trip-wire or remote control.

The mine has either a conventional peep sight, or optionally it is fitted with an optical sight with a 60 degree opening angle that allows improved aiming. It has scissors type folding legs for use on uneven ground.

SMI 20/1C anti-personnel mine

STATUS
Production.

The SMI 21/3C is of similar design but of larger dimensions and heavier weight. The penetration capability allows the mine to be used against all types of light skinned vehicles.

SMI 21/3C anti-personnel mine

This mine is available with different fragment sizes according to required application and range.

STATUS
Development completed.

SMI 21/11C anti-personnel/vehicle mine

The SMI 21/11C is a heavy fixed directional fragmentation mine, mainly used for area defence against troops, light skinned vehicles and landing gunship helicopters at a range of about 150 metres.

It is also used in fixed installations like coastal defence, airports etc.

STATUS
Development completed.

MANUFACTURER
SMI, Military Defence Products, Südsteirische Metall-industrie GmbH, A-8430, Leibnitz, Austria.

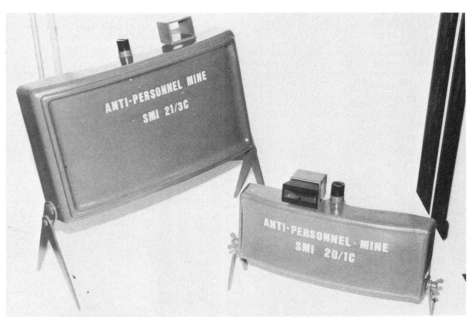

SMI 21/3C directional anti-personnel mine on left with SMI 20/1C direcitonal anti-personnel mine on right
(T J Gander)

SPECIFICATIONS

Model	SMI 20/1C	SMI 21/3C	SMI 21/11C	Model Fragments/m²	SMI 20/1C	SMI 21/3C	SMI 21/11C
Weight	1·9 kg	8·2 kg	20 kg	(30 m)	10–15		
Height	110 mm	180 mm	235 mm	(50 m)	5–8	6	
Width	260 mm	240 mm	560 mm	(100 m)		2	4
Weight of main charge	0·9 kg	4·2 kg	11·5 kg	(150 m)			2
Type of main charge	Comp B	Comp B	Comp B	Penetration			
Number of fragments	845	870	1180	(30 m)	3 mm steel		
Weight of fragments	0·5 g	3 g	4·5 g	(50 m)	25 mm pinewood	5 mm steel	
Spray angle	60°	60°	35°	(100 m)		2 mm steel	4 mm steel
				(150 m)			2 mm steel

SMI 22/7C Off-route Anti-tank Mine

DESCRIPTION
The SMI 22/7C off-route anti-tank mine supersedes the SMI 22/6 model described in *Jane's Military Vehicles and Ground Support Equipment 1983*, page 151. The mine is aimed by the integral sight along a pre-determined line across an important road or passage and the sensor is placed as required and then connected to the mine. The mine can be fitted with a self-neutralisation device if required.

The main charge when detonated forms a projectile with a very high penetrating power. The mine also has an integral electronics unit with two sensors that can differentiate between various types of vehicle. The maximum distance that the mine can be positioned off the route is 50 metres. It is also fitted with a self-deactivation device which operates after a pre-determined time.

Each mine is packed in a sealed plastic ammunition container together with accessories. Two ammunition containers are packed in a wooden case. Dummy training mines are also available.

SPECIFICATIONS
Weight: 13·5 kg
Length: 290 mm
Diameter: 180 mm
Weight of main charge: 7 kg
Type of main charge: Composition B
Maximum effective range: 50 m
Armour penetration:
(30 m) 80 mm steel
(50 m) 70 mm steel
Penetration diameter: 80 mm
Deviation from flight path: ±0·5°
Battery life-time: (operational) 3 months

STATUS
Trials.

MANUFACTURER
SMI, Military Defence Products, Südsteirische Metall-industrie GmbH, A-8430, Leibnitz, Austria.

SMI 22/7C off-route anti-tank mine can penetrate 80 mm of steel at 50-metre range

SMI 22/7C off-route anti-tank mine complete with stand

Panzermine 75 Anti-tank Mine

DESCRIPTION
The Panzermine 75 anti-tank mine is square and made from plastic. A carrying handle is attached to the main case and there is a three-pronged pressure plate unit on the centre part of the mine top. The fuze is in a fuze-well within this unit. The fuze may also be fitted with an anti-lift device. A secondary fuze can also be fitted into a mounting in the side of the mine for booby-trapping.

The fuzes and their housings are waterproof so the mine can be used under water. The mine is armed by pulling out a cotter pin and then swinging out and removing the safety lever and is activated by a load to one or all of the three pressure plate horns. Depression of the plate depresses the plastic springs that retain the striker which is released to fire the booster-charge that detonates the main charge.

STATUS
In production. In service with the Austrian Army.

MANUFACTURER
SMI, Military Defence Products, Südsteirische Metallindustrie GmbH, A-8430 Leibnitz, Austria.

SPECIFICATIONS
Weight: 8·2 kg
Length: 280 mm
Width: 280 mm
Height:
   (with fuze) 120 mm
   (explosive block) 70 mm
Weight of main charge: 7·4 kg
Type of main charge: HE

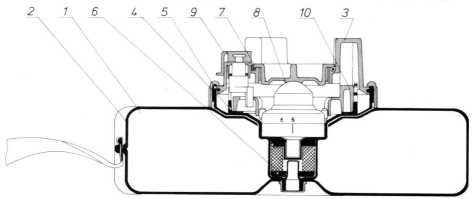

Panzermine 75 anti-tank mine showing (1) explosive (2) plastic housing (3) pressure plate (4) breaking ring (5) primer seating (6) booster (7) screw cap (8) fuze (9) transport safety mechanism

Panzermine 75 anti-tank mine (T J Gander)

Hirtenberger APM-3 Anti-personnel Mine

DESCRIPTION
Intended for use as a controlled fragmentation mine, the Hirtenberger APM-3 is a Claymore-type mine for use against personnel and light vehicles. It consists of a rectangular double-curved plastic fragmentation body set on a small tripod with one leg adjustable to compensate for irregularities in surface levels. Construction is nearly all plastic. The fragmentation face is formed horizontally convex and vertically concave to direct fragments in a 60 degree arc. There are about 1800 0·5-gram steel balls set into a plastic matrix in the body and behind the fragmentation face a 1·2 kg layer of explosive (Composition B) is used as the main propellant charge. The back of the fragmentation body has stiffening strips that also act as rear location guides for use in darkness.

The APM-3 has a detonator well on each side of the body which allows the mine to be fired from two locations or by either electrical or interconnection by detonating cord. A time fuze which can be set from one minute up to 24 hours is available for nuisance-type tactical applications. A small sight on top of the body provides not only the angle of sight but also an indication

of dispersion. A ball and socket head on the tripod assists in aiming. A safety area of about 80 metres must be provided behind the mine when fired. This can be reduced to 15 metres if a foxhole is used.

The APM-3 is packed five to a wooden case which also contains the ignition devices.

STATUS
Production.

MANUFACTURER
Hirtenberger Patronen-, Zündhütchen- und Metallwarenfabrik Aktiengesellschaft, A-2552 Hirtenberg, Austria.

SPECIFICATIONS
Weight: 3 kg
Length: (mine body) 280 mm
Height: (mine body) 140 mm
Depth: (mine body) 23 mm
Height: (with tripod) 400 mm
Weight of explosive charge: 1·2 kg
Number of fragments: 1800
Fragment:
   (weight) 0·5 g
   (diameter) 5 mm
   (velocity) approx 1220 m/s

Hirtenberger APM-3 anti-personnel mine (T J Gander)

BELGIUM

Anti-personnel Mine PRB M35

DESCRIPTION
The body of the M35 anti-personnel mine is cylindrical and is of a drab olive material. The top of the mine has a circular threaded recess into which the fuze is inserted.

The M5 fuze is the double percussion type. Two steel strikers are held apart by a cylindrical hollow bolt with two apertures. The bolt is connected to the pressure membrane of the fuze and moves freely along a slide in which there are two percussion caps pressed against each other. The bolt holds the two strikers apart and covers the percussion caps. When pressure is applied

to the fuze membrane the bolt is displaced and the apertures then uncover the percussion caps before the release of the strikers. The strikers then hit the percussion caps, the detonator fires and the mine explodes.

Both the fuze and the mine body are watertight. An inert training version of the M35 and a practice model which emits a puff of smoke are available.

Anti-personnel mine PRB M35 complete with fuze

Anti-personnel mine PRB M35 with fuze removed

SPECIFICATIONS
Weight: 158 g
Diameter: 65 mm
Height: 39 mm
Main charge type: TNT/KNO$_3$
Weight of explosive charge: 100 g
Operating force: 5–15 kg (1·5–3 mm depression of membrane pressure)

Operating temperature range: −30 to +60°C
Weight:
(wooden box containing 64 mines) 8·5 kg
(wooden box containing 128 fuzes) 9·7 kg
(wooden box containing 64 mines and 64 fuzes) 9·9 kg

STATUS
In production. In service with undisclosed countries.

MANUFACTURER
PRB SA, avenue de Tervueren 168, B-1150 Brussels, Belgium.

Anti-personnel Mine Type PRB M409

DESCRIPTION
The M409 is a circular anti-personnel mine with a drab olive plastic casing. The pressure membrane of the mine is protected by a safety plate which is held in position by a steel safety pin.

The fuze is of the double percussion type. Two steel spring strikers are held apart by a cylindrical bolt with two apertures. The bolt is connected to the pressure membrane of the fuze and moves freely along a slide in which there are two percussion caps pressed against each other. The bolt holds the two strikers apart and covers the percussion caps. When pressure is applied to the fuze membrane the bolt is displaced and the two apertures uncover the percussion caps before the release of the strikers. The strikers hit the percussion caps, the detonator fires and the mine explodes. The only metal components are the two steel strikers and the two aluminium primer-caps.

An inert training version and a practice model which emits a small puff of smoke when ignited are available.

SPECIFICATIONS
Weight: 183 g
Diameter: 82 mm
Height: 28 mm
Main charge type: cast Trialene
Weight of main charge: 80 g
Operating force: 8–30 kg
Weight: (wooden box containing 150 mines) 45 kg
Operating temperature range: −32 to +52°C

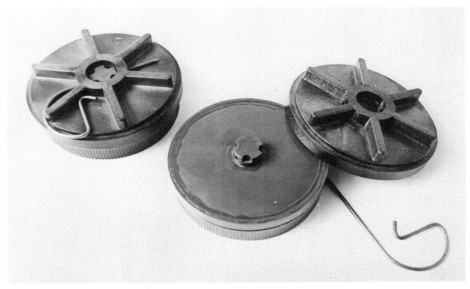

(Left) complete PRB M409 anti-personnel mine, (right) with safety plate removed

STATUS
In production. In service with undisclosed countries.

MANUFACTURER
PRB SA, avenue de Tervueren 168, B-1150 Brussels, Belgium.

Anti-personnel Fragmentation Mine PRB 413

DESCRIPTION
The PRB 413 anti-personnel mine has four major components: the mine body, firing device, steel picket and two 15-metre reels of tripwire. The firing device, the PRB 410, is also used in other mines for initiating trip flares and booby traps. It has four antennas, each with a ring at the end. As many wires as necessary can be attached to the same ring or to the other rings (eg eight wires at 45 degrees, two per ring, allow the installation of a ring covering 360 degrees).

The fragmentation sleeve is made of a spirally wound steel wire casing, pre-notched to ensure fragmentation into about 600 regular pieces.

The mine operates as follows: when one of the tripwires is pulled, the antenna lifts up both the slider and the striker, compressing the spring; the two balls of the striker are ejected laterally and release the striker head which is then pushed downward by the spring and causes the firing pin to strike the primer igniting the detonator, and the mine explodes before pressure on the wire causes the mine to tilt. The PRB 413 has a lethal radius of 14 metres and a safe radius of 30 metres.

STATUS
In production. In service with undisclosed countries.

MANUFACTURER
PRB SA, avenue de Tervueren 168, B-1150 Brussels, Belgium.

SPECIFICATIONS
Weight:
(complete mine) 640 g
(picket) 230 g
(fragmentation sleeve) 200 g
Diameter: (mine body) 46 mm
Height: (front top of mine to ground level when emplaced) 230 mm
Type of main charge: Composition B
Weight of main charge: 95 g
Operating temperature range: −32 to +52°C

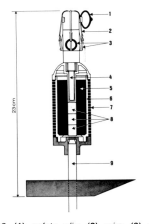

PRB 413 (1) safety clip (2) wire (3) pull ring (4) detonator (5) main charge (6) casing (7) fragmentation sleeve (8) booster (9) steel picket

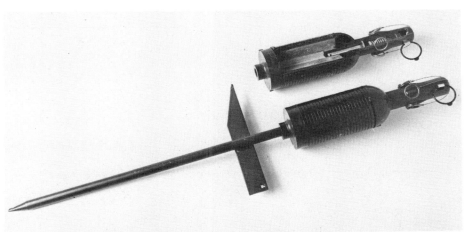

Anti-personnel fragmentation mine PRB 413 shown with and without stake

Anti-personnel Mine Model U/1

DESCRIPTION
This anti-tank mine is circular and consists of two plastic cases screwed together. The lower case contains the main charge, flash charge and detonator, and the upper contains the actuating mechanism. When pressure is applied to the top of the mine a spring is depressed. This is compressed against a shear wire which shears and pushes the plunger into a chemical flash compound, igniting the flash charge which sets off the detonator and explodes the mine.

STATUS
In service with the Belgian Army.

SPECIFICATIONS
Weight: 138 g
Diameter: 57 mm
Height: 65 mm
Main charge type: TNT
Weight of main charge: 60 g

Anti-tank Mine PRB M3

DESCRIPTION
The PRB M3 anti-tank mine consists of three major components: the mine body, M30 fuze and the pressure plate.

The mine body is of drab olive polyethylene and contains the main charge and the booster. A carrying handle is provided on the side of the mine. The top surface of the body is fitted with an ammonia-free bakelite seating on to which the pressure plate is screwed. The fuze-well is at the centre of the seating, and if required the mine can be fitted with a PRB M30 anti-lifting device, which detonates when the mine is lifted more than 30 mm.

The M30 fuze is of the double percussion type, is made of plastic and is waterproof. The only metal parts are the steel strikers and the aluminium primer caps. Two steel spring strikers are held apart by a cylindrical hollow bolt with two apertures. The bolt is connected to the pressure membrane of the fuze and moves freely along a slide in which two percussion-caps pressed against each other are placed. The bolt holds the strikers apart and covers the two percussion caps. When pressure is applied to the fuze membrane, the bolt is displaced and the two apertures uncover the percussion

caps before the release of the strikers. The strikers hit the percussion cap which fires the detonator and the mine explodes.

The pressure plate, which is also of drab olive plastic, consists of two plates, one movable and the other fixed. The former transmits the operating pressure from the armoured vehicle to the fuze, while the fixed plate ensures continuity between the pressure plate and the mine body. The two plates are joined by shear pins.

The fuze and pressure plate are both watertight, and the mine and body will not break when dropped from a height of two metres. Trials have shown that the mine cannot be set off by sympathetic detonation.

An inert training version and a practice model which emits a small puff of smoke when activated are available.

SPECIFICATIONS
Weight: 6·8 kg
Length: 230 mm
Width: 230 mm
Height: 130 mm
Main charge type: Trialene
Weight: (main charge) 6 kg
Type of booster: Hexolite
Operating force: 250 kg
Weight: (case of 6 mines and fuzes) 44·5 kg

Anti-tank mine PRB M3 with pressure plate and fuze removed

STATUS
In production. In service with undisclosed countries.

MANUFACTURER
PRB SA, avenue de Tervueren 168, B-1150 Brussels, Belgium.

SUMMADE System

DESCRIPTION
The SUMMADE (System Universal Modular Mine And Demolition Explosives) is composed of the demolition charge type PRB 416, standard initiator type PRB 407, tripwire initiator type PRB 410 and the anti-tank mine type PRB 408. These can be adapted for a wide range of uses including demolition work, and both anti-tank and anti-personnel mines.

The latter consists of a single watertight demolition charge type PRB 416 with the PRB 410 tripwire initiator, or the PRB 407 initiator (100-second delay), or the PRB 3 time fuze (4·5-second delay). The PRB 410 initiator is also used with the anti-personnel mine type PRB 413 and the reader is referred to this entry for a detailed description of the method of operation. The PRB 407 watertight initiator has a minimum delay of 100 seconds and a maximum delay of 125 seconds, with a 300 mm length of cord.

The anti-tank mine type PRB 408 consists of nine PRB 416 demolition charges in an olive drab watertight plastic envelope pierced laterally by three holes which go from one side to the other. This allows the installation of the tripwire fuze PRB 410, the PRB 407 or any other firing device with the European thread Sl/10 or American 9/16th inch or 12 UNC-1A thread. On top of the mine is a skirt which contains the anti-tilt pressure plate of the PRB M3 anti-tank mine and the anti-personnel mine type PRB 430.

SPECIFICATIONS
PRB 410 charge
Weight: 400 g

Left: PRB 416 demolition block cut away to show interior; right: complete PRB 416 demolition block

Length: 70 mm
Width: 70 mm
Height: 50 mm
Type of main charge: Brisance
Weight: (main charge) 355 g
Type of booster: Tetryl
Weight: (booster) 15 g

PRB 408 anti-tank mine
Weight: (complete) 4·13 kg
Length: 215 mm
Width: 215 mm
Height: (with pressure plate) 98 mm
Operating pressure: 250 kg

STATUS
In production. In service with undisclosed countries.

PRB 416 demolition block fitted with PRB 410 fuze and used as anti-personnel mine

MANUFACTURER
PRB SA, avenue de Tervueren 168, B-1150 Brussels, Belgium.

Other Belgian Mines

Type	ND/M1 ND/M2	PRB M4
Diameter	330 mm	229 mm
Height	175 mm	99 mm
Fuze	pressure	pressure
Actuating force	150–200 kg	250 kg approx
Remarks	circular, anti-tank	square, anti-tank

BRAZIL

Anti-personnel Mine Min AP NM AE T1

DESCRIPTION
The Min AP NM AE T1 (Mina Anti-Pessoal Não-Magnética Alto Explosiva modelo T1) is a non-metallic anti-personnel mine undetectable by conventional mine detectors. It has a main charge of Pentolite 50/50 and a secondary (booster) charge of Nitropenta.

SPECIFICATIONS
Weight of complete mine: 420 g
Diameter: 85 mm
Height: (including fuze) 95 mm
Activation pressure: 17 kg
Effective range: 0·5 m

STATUS
In production. In service.

MANUFACTURER
Quimica Tupan Ltda, Av. Erasmo Braga, 299 – 4° andar – 20000 Rio de Janeiro, RJ – Brazil.

Anti-personnel mine Min AP NM AE T1 sectioned to show main components (Ronaldo S Olive)

Anti-personnel mine Min AP NM AE T1 (Ronaldo S Olive)

Anti-tank Mine Min AC NM AE T1

DESCRIPTION
The Min AC NM AE T1 (Mina Anti-Carro Não-Magnética Alto Explosiva modelo T1) is an anti-tank mine of non-metallic construction that cannot be detected by conventional mine detectors, such as the SCR-625 and AN/PRS-5. It has a main charge of Trotil, a secondary (reinforcing) charge of Pentolite 50/50 and has been proved effective against different types of tracked and wheeled vehicles. A plastic carrying handle is incorporated.

STATUS
In production. In service.

MANUFACTURER
Quimica Tupan Ltda, Av. Erasmo Braga, 299 – 4° andar – 20000 Rio de Janeiro, RJ – Brazil.

SPECIFICATIONS
Weight of complete mine: 8 kg
Weight of Trotil charge: 7 kg
Length: 225 mm
Width: 255 mm
Height: 155 mm
Activation pressure:
  60 kg to 140 kg (T1 pressure plate)
  95 kg to 200 kg (T1A pressure plate)
Effective range: (max) 2 m

Anti-tank mine Min AC NM AE T1 cut away to show main components (Ronaldo S Olive)

Effect of anti-tank mine Min AC NM AE T1 on Stuart M3A1 light tank (Ronaldo S Olive)

CANADA

C3A1 Non-metallic Anti-personnel Mine (Elsie)

DESCRIPTION
This groundburst plastic anti-personnel mine was developed by the Canadian Army. It was accepted as standard by the ABC countries and was produced in Canada for the British Army. The C3A1 version has an aluminium shell 6 gram detonator while the M25 contains a gilding metal shell M46 detonator but otherwise they are identical.

The mine consists of two assemblies, a body and a charge. The body assembly is 50 mm in diameter, 75 mm long and weighs 57 grams. The charge assembly is 38 mm in diameter, 56 mm long and weighs 28 grams. Total weight of explosive is 9·45 grams. The mines are loaded by the Filling Division of Canadian Arsenals.

The body assembly has a transit plug which is removed after the body assembly has been emplaced and replaced by the charge assembly fitted with a safety clip. When the safety clip is removed the mine will operate when a force of 7·25 to 11·8 kg is applied.

The mine is olive-coloured and has been designed with integral camouflage material. It is undetectable with conventional electro-magnetic equipment but if required a detector ring can be fitted to enable the mine to be detected.

The practice version is designated the C4A1 and is emplaced in the same manner as the C3A1 and functions in the same way except that it produces a blue smoke charge when actuated. The C4A1 is reusable at least five times by the replacement of the spotting charge and re-cocking of the body assembly. Inert and dummy versions of the mine are also produced.

STATUS
Production.

MANUFACTURER
Canadian Arsenals Limited, 5 Montée des Arsenaux, Le Gardeur, Quebec, Canada J5Z 2P4.

C3A1 non-metallic anti-personnel mine complete with safety clip

Fuze assemblies and precision metal parts of C3A1 non-metallic anti-personnel mine

CHILE

Cardoen Anti-personnel Mine II

DESCRIPTION
This is a cylindrical anti-personnel mine that has a secondary role against light vehicles. The mine consists of two halves, the lower containing the explosive charge and inner cone for anti-vehicle use and with a central fuze-well, and the upper, which is ribbed, acting as a sleeve to the lower half, is kept in place by two holding pins and a spring. The mine is armed after burial by withdrawing an arming card attached to the fuze. A pressure of 10 to 14 kg applied to the top of the mine detonates the main charge.

SPECIFICATIONS
Weight: 770 g
Diameter: 113 mm
Height: 83 mm
Type of main charge: Mexatol C
Weight of main charge: 370 g
Operating force: 10–14 kg

STATUS
Production. In service with the Chilean armed forces.

MANUFACTURER
Industrias Cardoen SA, Avda. Providencia 2237, 6° Piso, Santiago, Chile.

Cardoen anti-personnel mine II with detonator inside tube taped to side of mine for safety during transport

Cardoen anti-personnel mine II disassembled with detonator

Cardoen Anti-personnel Mine

DESCRIPTION
The mine consists of a compartmented metal box with a hinged lid that overlaps the sides. Inside, in the smaller compartment, there is provision to carry the fuze and detonator for transport.

The fuze is inserted into its housing via a plastic seal on the front of the mine so that only an arming cord remains visible. The lid of the mine is then closed and the mine buried. A pull on the cord releases a pin in the fuze assembly to arm the mine.

Application of a minimum pressure of 5 kg to the top of the mine causes it to explode. The anti-personnel effect is enhanced by a shrapnel charge that forms part of the main charge. The effective radius against personnel is approximately 20 metres.

SPECIFICATIONS
Weight: 5·8 kg
Length: 240 mm
Width: 240 mm
Height: 80 mm
Weight of main charge: 2·6 kg
Weight of shrapnel charge: 1 kg

STATUS
Production complete. In service with the Chilean armed forces.

MANUFACTURER
Industrias Cardoen SA, Avda. Providencia 2237, 6° Piso, Santiago, Chile.

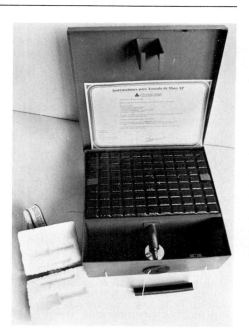

Cardoen anti-personnel mine with lid open to show position of detonator

Cardoen Directional Anti-personnel Mine

DESCRIPTION
This mine is used for defensive and ambush purposes. It consists of a curved rectangular main body that can be installed either on posts or trees, or on the ground on four metallic legs. It is normally carried in a canvas sack with a No. 8 blasting cap, nonel cable, a three-minute delay timer and a pull-type detonator.

The mode of operation is shown in the two accompanying diagrams. There is a slit type peep sight on top of the mine.

STATUS
Production. In service with the Chilean armed forces.

MANUFACTURER
Industrias Cardoen SA, Avda. Providencia 2237, 6° Piso, Santiago, Chile.

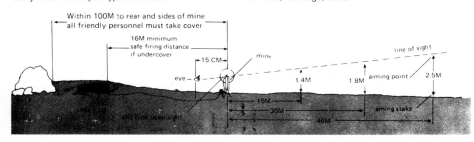

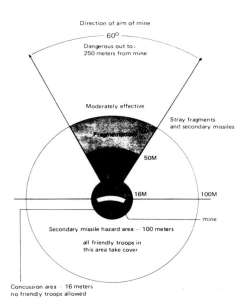

Deployment and operation of Cardoen directional anti-personnel mine

Effective range of Cardoen directional anti-personnel mine

Cardoen directional anti-personnel mine with detonators and nonel cables attached

Cardoen directional anti-personnel mine with haversack for accessories in foreground

Cardoen Anti-tank Mine

DESCRIPTION
This is a circular metallic anti-tank mine with a central fuze-well. There is a carrying handle on the side. The fuze is protected by a pressure plate housing that acts as the bottom of the mine when it is emplaced.

SPECIFICATIONS
Weight: 14 kg
Diameter: 380 mm
Height: 150 mm
Type of main charge: Pentolyte and Mexal 1500
Weight of main charge: 9·5 kg

STATUS
Production. In service with the Chilean armed forces.

MANUFACTURER
Industrias Cardoen SA, Avda. Providencia 2237, 6° Piso, Santiago, Chile.

Cardoen anti-tank mine with top removed to show position of detonator

Cardoen anti-tank mine with top removed and detonator disassembled

CHINA, PEOPLE'S REPUBLIC

No. 4 Dual-purpose Mine

DESCRIPTION
This cast-iron mine is used against both troops and armoured vehicles. The fuze is in the top centre of the mine which has a carrying handle on either side. On the top of the mine is a pressure spider which is supported on three legs. The mine operates as follows: pressure on the spider is transferred to the top of the fuze shearing the striker-retaining pin and releasing the spring loaded striker against the percussion cap, which fires and detonates the main charge.

STATUS
In service with the Chinese Army. It has also been seen in other South-east Asian countries.

MANUFACTURER
Chinese state arsenals.

SPECIFICATIONS
Weight: 5·17 kg
Diameter: 228 mm
Height: 100 mm
Main charge type: TNT
Weight: (main charge) 2·04 kg
Operating force:
(pressure) 136–226 kg
(pull) 4·536–22·68 kg

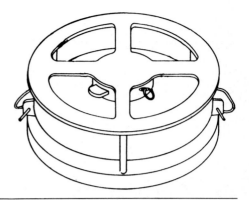

No. 4 dual-purpose mine

Anti-tank Mine M72

DESCRIPTION
Described in Chinese literature as an 'iron shell anti-tank mine', the M72 is a conventional circular mine with a sheet steel body. The centrally-placed pressure fuze operates at pressures between 180 and 400 kg and is stated to be able to operate when only half the fuze surface is depressed. A wire carrying handle is welded to one side of the body. There does not appear to be any provision for anti-handling devices and there is no provision for an anti-lift well in the base.

When laid in on normal surfaces the fuze upper edge should be 10 mm above the ground surface; on soft ground it can be buried below the surface. The M72 can be used under water at depths up to 1·2 metres. The explosive charge is a 50/50 mixture of RDX and TNT and the normal fuze is the M72, although a double-impulse pressure fuze is available.

The mines are issued two to a wooden box measuring 655 × 330 × 163 mm. Each box contains two mines, two fuzes and a cap spanner. The complete box weighs 21 kg.

STATUS
In production. In service with Chinese Army. Offered for export.

SPECIFICATIONS
Weight: 8 kg
Diameter: 279 mm
Height: 93 mm
Main change type: 50/50 RDX/TNT
Weight of main charge: 5 kg
Operating pressure: 180 to 400 kg

MANUFACTURER
China North Industry Company, People's Republic of China.

Anti-personnel Shrapnel Mine

DESCRIPTION
This is the Chinese version of the Soviet POMZ-2 anti-personnel mine but it is lighter and requires a greater operating force. The mine consists of a wooden stake, serrated cast-iron body, cylinder of cast TNT and a pull-actuated fuze. It has an effective radius of 20 metres. The mine operates as follows: a pull on the tripwire removes the pull pin in the fuze, which releases the striker which hits the percussion cap and detonates the mine.

SPECIFICATIONS
Weight: 1·4 kg
Diameter: 60 mm
Height: (without stake) 105 mm
Main charge type: TNT

Weight of main charge: 1·17 kg
Operating force: 9–18 kg
Fuze: MUV or UPF

STATUS
In service with the Chinese Army and probably supplied to countries which have received Chinese aid.

MANUFACTURER
Chinese state arsenals.

PMD-6 Anti-personnel Mine

DESCRIPTION
This is identical in design and construction to the Soviet PMD-6 anti-tank mine and the reader is referred to this entry in the Soviet section for full details and specification.

STATUS
In service with the Chinese Army.

MANUFACTURER
Chinese state arsenals.

Anti-tank Mine

DESCRIPTION
This anti-tank mine is identical to the Soviet TM-41 but is thought to have a universal type fuze which can be actuated either by pull or pressure action. The pressure fuze is also used in the No. 4 dual-purpose mine. Pressure on the top shears the retaining pin, or a pull on the striker pin releases the striker to fire the percussion cap which fires the detonator and explodes the mine.

STATUS
In service with the Chinese Army.

MANUFACTURER
Chinese state arsenals.

Other Chinese Mines

Type	Diameter	Height	Fuze	Remarks
No. 8	228 mm	100 mm	pressure or pull type	circular, anti-tank

More modern mines are believed to be under development and in production.

CZECHOSLOVAKIA

PP-Mi-Ba Anti-personnel Mine

DESCRIPTION
This is a circular anti-personnel plastic mine.

SPECIFICATIONS
Weight: 340 g

Diameter: 150 mm
Height: 60 mm
Main charge: TNT
Main charge weight: 200 g
Operating force: 0·5–1 kg

STATUS
In service with the Czechoslovak Army.

MANUFACTURER
Czechoslovak state arsenals.

PP-Mi-D Anti-personnel Mine

DESCRIPTION
The PP-Mi-D wooden anti-personnel mine is almost identical to the Soviet PMD-7 mine except that it uses the Ro-1 fuze.

SPECIFICATIONS
Weight: 0·5 kg

Length: 135 mm
Width: 105 mm
Height: 55 mm
Main charge: TNT
Weight of main charge: 200 g
Operating force: 4 kg

STATUS
In service with the Czechoslovak Army.

MANUFACTURER
Czechoslovak state arsenals.

PP-Mi-Sb and PP-Mi-Sk Anti-personnel Stake Mines

DESCRIPTION
The PP-Mi-Sb anti-personnel stake mine is very similar in appearance to the German Second World War concrete ball mine, and also has a body of concrete with steel scrap fragments. It uses the UPM-1 pull fuze. Its external recognition feature is its smooth surface. The mine can also be taken off the stake and buried. In this case an Ro-2 pressure fuze is used.

The PP-Mi-Sk is almost identical to the Soviet POMZ-2M stake mine but uses the Ro-2 pull fuze. This mine has six rows of fragments, the same as the Soviet POMZ-2.

These mines operate as follows: when the striker-retaining pin is removed, the spring-loaded striker falls on and fires the percussion cap and detonator that set off the main charge.

SPECIFICATIONS

Model	PP-Mi-Sk	PP-Mi-Sb
Weight	1·6 kg	2·1 kg
Diameter	60 mm	75 mm
Height (with fuze but excluding stake)	137 mm	140 mm
Main charge type	TNT	TNT
Weight of main charge	75 g	75 g
Operating force	n/a	1 kg

STATUS
In service with members of the Warsaw Pact.

MANUFACTURER
Czechoslovak state arsenals.

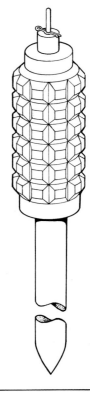

PP-Mi-Sk anti-personnel stake mine

PP-Mi-Sr Bounding Anti-personnel Mine

DESCRIPTION
The PP-Mi-Sr metallic bounding anti-personnel mine has a central fuze-well with a transit cap. On opposite sides of the fuze-well are the filler and the detonator well plugs. The body of the mine fits into an outer casing that also contains the propelling charge. The space between the inner and outer walls of the mine body is filled with shrapnel made of short pieces of steel rod. The mine has an effective fragmentation radius of 20 metres.

The mine can be fitted with the Ro-8 pressure fuze or the Ro-1 pull fuze: in both cases the fuze ignites a delay train. After three to five seconds the propellant charge ejects the body of the mine from the container taking with it the wire attached to the bottom of the container. When the wire becomes taut at a height of approximately one metre it activates the integral fuze, which fires the detonator and then the mine.

There are three other ways of employing this mine:
By inserting the Ro-1 pull fuze into the detonator well with the detonator upside down which converts the mine into a non-bounding anti-personnel mine.
Using the Ro-1 pull fuze in the normal fuze-well and retaining the bounding feature.
Using the P-1 or P-2 electric squibs for remote control.

SPECIFICATIONS
Weight: (without fuze) 3·2 kg
Diameter: 102 mm
Height: 152 mm

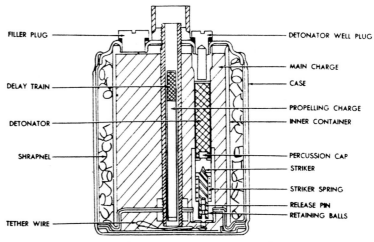

PP-Mi-Sr bounding anti-personnel mine (US Army)

Main charge: TNT
Weight of main charge: 325 g
Booster charge: black powder
Booster charge weight: 37 g
Operating force:
    3-6 kg with Ro-8 pressure fuze
    4-8 kg with Ro-1 pull fuze

STATUS
In service with the Czechoslovak Army and some Near East armies.

MANUFACTURER
Czechoslovak state arsenals.

PT-Mi-Ba Anti-tank Mine

DESCRIPTION
The PT-Mi-Ba circular non-metallic anti-tank mine was introduced into the Czechoslovak Army in the 1950s and is also known as the PT-Mi-Ba-53. It is similar in physical appearance to the German Second World War Tellermines 42 and 43. It consists of two bakelite mould-ings cemented together, and can be laid by hand or mechanically. The fuze-well is in the bottom of the mine and is closed by a threaded cover plate. The two filler holes are also in the bottom of the mine and are closed by lugs. These lugs also hold either end of the carrying handle. The mine operates as follows: force on the pressure plate ruptures the shear groove, puts pressure on the fuze, which activates the detonator and starts the firing chain. The fuze contains some metallic components. No provision is made for booby-trapping.

STATUS
In service with the Czechoslovak Army and some Middle Eastern armies.

MANUFACTURER
Czechoslovak state arsenals.

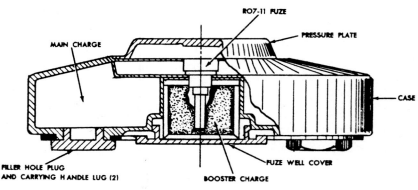

PT-Mi-Ba anti-tank mine

SPECIFICATIONS
Weight: 7·83 kg
Diameter: 324 mm
Height: 115 mm
Main charge: TNT
Weight of main charge: 6 kg
Booster charge: TNT
Weight of booster: 208 g
Operating force: 200–400 kg
Fuze model: Ro-7-11 (pressure)

PT-Mi-Ba-II Anti-tank Mine

DESCRIPTION
The PT-Mi-Ba-II plastic non-metallic anti-tank mine is rectangular and is not suitable for mechanical laying. It has two Ro-7-II pressure fuzes and operates as follows: force on the pressure plate ruptures the shear groove, puts pressure on the fuze, which activates the detonator and starts the firing chain. The fuze contains some metallic components. No provision is made for booby-trapping.

STATUS
In service with the Czechoslovak Army.

MANUFACTURER
Czechoslovak state arsenals.

SPECIFICATIONS
Weight: 9·6 kg
Length: 395 mm
Width: 230 mm
Height: 135 mm
Main charge: TNT
Weight of main charge: 6 kg
Operating force: 200–450 kg
Fuze model: Ro-7-II (pressure)

PT-Mi-Ba-III Anti-tank Mine

DESCRIPTION
The PT-Mi-Ba-III bakelite non-metallic anti-tank mine is circular and can be laid by hand or mechanically. A carrying handle slides into the mine for storage pur-poses. The mine operates as follows: force on the pres-sure plate ruptures the shear groove, puts pressure on the fuze, which activates the detonator and starts the firing chain. The fuze contains some metallic compo-nents. No provision is made for booby-trapping. This mine is resistant to short duration clearing methods. A training version is available.

SPECIFICATIONS
Weight: (without fuze) 9·9 kg
Diameter: 330 mm
Height: 108 mm
Main charge: TNT
Weight of main charge: 7·2 kg
Operating force: 200 kg
Fuze model: (pressure) Ro-7-II

STATUS
In service with the Czechoslovak Army.

MANUFACTURER
Czechoslovak state arsenals.

Czechoslovak PT-Mi-Ba-III anti-tank mine

PT-Mi-K Anti-tank Mine

DESCRIPTION
This metallic anti-tank mine can be laid mechanically or by hand. Before laying the cover is removed from the open type pressure plate on top of the mine. The pres-sure plate has four spikes which are held in place by shear pins which pass through the collar of the casing. An anti-lifting fuze-well is provided in the bottom of the mine. The mine functions as follows: force on top of the pressure plate ruptures the shear pin, which releases the fuze striker and detonates the mine. Provision has been made to prevent over-pressure from a nuclear burst activating the pressure plate and detonating the mine.

SPECIFICATIONS
Weight: 7·2 kg
Diameter: 300 mm
Height: 102 mm
Main charge: TNT
Main charge weight: 4·9 kg
Booster charge: 99 g
Operating force: 300-450 kg
Fuze model: Ro-5 or Ro-9

STATUS
In service with the Czechoslovak Army and some Middle Eastern armies.

MANUFACTURER
Czechoslovak state arsenals.

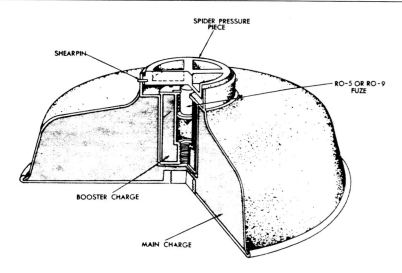

PT-Mi-D, PT-Mi-D-I and PT-Mi-D-II Anti-tank Mines

DESCRIPTION
The PT-Mi-D wooden anti-tank mine is similar to the Soviet TMD-B but is of a more complicated design. To increase or decrease activation pressure, wooden shear dowels are provided at each end of the mine. The mine has two Ro-1 pull fuzes and can be booby-trapped by passing an anchor wire from one of the fuzes through

one of the two holes in the bottom of the mine. The PT-Mi-D-I and PT-Mi-D-II are similar to the PT-Mi-D but have different dimensions and weights.

SPECIFICATIONS
PT-Mi-D
Weight: 9 kg
Length: 320 mm
Width: 230 mm
Height: 140 mm
Main charge: TNT

Weight of main charge: 6·2 kg
Booster charge: two TNT blocks
Weight of booster charge: 400 g
Operating force: 200–450 kg
Fuze model: Ro-1

STATUS
In service with the Czechoslovak Army.

MANUFACTURER
Czechoslovak state arsenals.

Plate-charge Anti-tank Mine

DESCRIPTION
This is the Czechoslovak equivalent of the Soviet TMK-2 anti-tank mine and is hemispherical in shape. The explosive charge is slightly concave at the top and a 5 mm thick steel plate with the same configuration is fitted on top. This gives the mine a shaped charge effect.

The mine is fitted with an adjustable length, tilt-rod fuze which is mounted on the side of the mine.

STATUS
In service with the Czechoslovak Army.

MANUFACTURER
Czechoslovak state arsenals.

SPECIFICATIONS
Weight: (without fuze) 9·5 kg
Diameter: 240 mm
Height: 230 mm
Main charge type: RDX/TNT
Operating force: 5·7 kg

Na-Mi-Ba Anti-tank Mine

DESCRIPTION
This is a non-metallic circular anti-tank mine which can be laid either mechanically or by hand. It is believed to have a mechanical chemical fuze rather than the Ro-7-II pressure fuze used on the other Czechoslovak non-metallic anti-tank mines.

SPECIFICATIONS
Diameter: 200 mm
Height: 250 mm
Main charge: Tritol
Weight of main charge: 2·4 kg
Operating force: 2·2 kg

STATUS
In service with the Czechoslovak Army.

MANUFACTURER
Czechoslovak state arsenals.

Anti-tank Mine TQ-Mi

DESCRIPTION
This circular anti-tank mine has a pressed cardboard case with a fuze body and glass cap. The fuze is of the pressure/chemical type.

SPECIFICATIONS
Weight: 10 kg

Diameter: 560 mm
Height: 150 mm
Main charge type: TNT
Weight of main charge: 5·21 kg
Booster type: Toul
Weight of booster: 100 g
Operating force: 320 kg

STATUS
In service with the Czechoslovak Army.

MANUFACTURER
Czechoslovak state arsenals.

M1 and M2 Limpet Mines

DESCRIPTION
These two magnetic shaped-charge limpet mines are intended for use against ships but can also be used against armoured vehicles. Both mines are electrically fuzed with a delay element which can be adjusted from one to eleven hours.

SPECIFICATIONS

Model	M1	M2
Weight	6·3 kg	14·3 kg
Diameter	90 mm	187 mm
Height	258 mm	483 mm
Weight of main charge	0·55 kg (est)	3·5 kg
Armour penetration	70 mm	150 mm

STATUS
In service with the Czechoslovak forces.

MANUFACTURER
Czechoslovak state arsenals.

Training Mines

DESCRIPTION
Czechoslovak training mines have the abbreviation Cv (training) before the model designation to distinguish them from the real mine; for example the Cv PT-Mi-Ba III is the anti-tank training version of the PT-Mi-Ba III mine.

STATUS
In service with the Czechoslovak Army.

MANUFACTURER
Czechoslovak state arsenals.

DENMARK

Danish Mines

The Danish Army has advised us that the following mines and other mine warfare equipment are currently in service:

	National Nomenclature	Origin
Anti-tank mine	Pansermine M/75	Bar mine (UK)
	Pansermine M/51	M2A3B2 (USA)
	Pansermine M/55	M16 (USA)
Anti-personnel mines	Fodfolksmine M/56	AIPD 51 (France)
	Fodfolksmine M/58	M14 (USA)
	Fodfolksmine M/51	M2A3B2 (USA)
	Fodfolksmine M/66	DM31, Splinter (FGR)
Mine-clearing equipment	Manual equipment only	
Mine detectors	Minesøger M/75	(USA)
Minelayers	Mineudlaegger M/75	Bar minelayer (UK)

EGYPT

Anti-tank Mine

DESCRIPTION
This circular anti-tank mine is a copy of the Italian SACI mine. It has a case of plastic with the three fuzes in the top of the mine. These are covered by a pressure plate 190 mm in diameter. The only metallic parts in the mine are the fuze striker and the detonator. The mine is detonated as follows: pressure on the top of the mine

crushes the pressure plate, which ruptures the shear mechanism and detonates the mine.

STATUS
In service with the Egyptian Army.
  Egypt also manufactures a copy of the Soviet MUV pull fuze, a copy of the British No. 6 Mk 1 pressure release switch, and a tilt-rod fuze for anti-personnel mines.

SPECIFICATIONS
Diameter: 280 mm
Height: 205 mm
Main charge type: TNT
Weight of main charge: 7 kg
Booster charge: 2 RDX pellets
Operating force: 63·5–362 kg

FRANCE

Anti-personnel Mine Model MAPED F1

DESCRIPTION
This anti-personnel mine is the French equivalent of the American M18 Claymore mine and can be detonated by a remote controlled electric igniter (Mk F1), wire-breaking electronic igniter (Mk F2) or a pressure igniter. The mine is normally mounted on two A-type legs. When detonated it projects 500 metallic splinters in an arc 60 degrees to the front to a maximum range of 40 metres. A smoke model is available for training.

SPECIFICATIONS
Weight: 1 kg
Length: 180 mm
Width: 60 mm
Height: (with legs) 220 mm
Main charge type: plastic explosive

STATUS
In production. In service with the French Army and other armies.

MANUFACTURER
Société d'Armement et d'Etudes Alsetex, 4 rue de Castellane, 75008 Paris, France.

Anti-personnel mine Model MAPED F1 from rear with legs in position

Anti-personnel Stake Mines Mk 61 and Mk 63

DESCRIPTION
These two anti-personnel mines are both staked to the ground with an integral stake. Both mines have sealed plastic cases and can be detonated by pressure or a tripwire. The Mk 63 has an anti-lifting device as a standard fitting. For handling, the cap, which contains the fuze, can be removed. When detonated these mines

project 225 metallic splinters through a radius of 360 degrees with a maximum effective range of ten metres. For training, a smoke model is available.

STATUS
In production. In service with the French Army and other armies.

MANUFACTURER
Société d'Armement et d'Etudes Alsetex, 4 rue de Castellane, 75008 Paris, France.

SPECIFICATIONS

Model	Mk 61	Mk 63
Weight	125 g	100 g
Diameter	35 mm	35 mm
Height	270 mm	270 mm
Main charge type	TNT	Tetryl
Weight of explosive	57 g	30 g

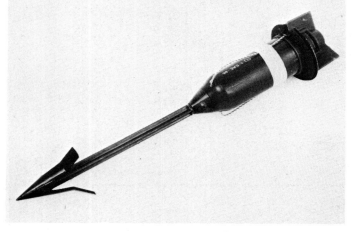

Anti-personnel stake mine Mk 63

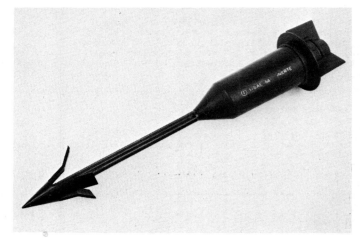

Anti-personnel stake mine Mk 61

Anti-personnel Mine Model 59 (MAPDV)

DESCRIPTION
The Model 59 MAPDV, or Inkstand mine as it is also known, was developed as the replacement for the Model 1951 anti-personnel mine. The case is made of plastic with the Model NM SAE 59 pressure friction fuze or Mle 1959 mechanical fuze, being inserted in the top of the mine. Attached to the mine is a metal detection plate which is removed before the mine is emplaced. A smoke model of this mine is available for training.

STATUS
In production. In service with the French Army and other armies.

MANUFACTURER
Société d'Armement et d'Etudes Alsetex, 4 rue de Castellane, 75008 Paris, France.

SPECIFICATIONS
Weight: 130 g
Diameter: 62 mm
Height: (with fuze) 55 mm
Main charge type: TNT
Weight of main charge: 56·7 g
Booster charge: Tetryl
Weight of booster charge: 17 g

Anti-personnel mine model 59 (MAPDV)

Anti-personnel Bounding Mine
Model 1951/1955

DESCRIPTION
This mine consists of a cylindrical metal case which acts as a mortar, and a canister which contains the main charge, integral fuze, steel shrapnel, and is closed by a cap which contains the main, central and self-destruction fuze-well plug.

The mine can be activated by a tilt of the rod or downward pressure on the rod when the mine is fitted with a tilt-rod fuze, or a pull on the tripwire when the mine is fitted with a pull fuze. This initiates the fuze and fires the delay train and the propelling charge. The expanding gases project the canister into the air. The canister has a cord attached to its lower end and when it reaches a height of 1.5 metres (the full length of the cord), it pulls out the retaining pin of the canister fuze. This releases the striker-retaining balls which escape and free the spring-driven striker. This initiates the firing chain which consists of a percussion cap, detonator and the main charge which hurls shrapnel in all directions up to a radius of 45 metres.

SPECIFICATIONS
Weight: 4·49 kg
Diameter: 97 mm
Height: 158 mm
Main charge type: picric acid
Weight of main charge: 408 g
Operating force: 3 kg
Fuze: Model 1952 tilt-rod

STATUS
In service with the French Army.

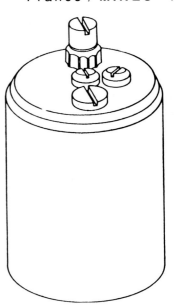

Anti-personnel bounding mine model 1951/1955

Anti-personnel Mine
Model 1951

DESCRIPTION
This non-metallic anti-personnel mine consists of a ribbed plastic case with an integral pressure-friction fuze mounted in the centre. The mine operates as follows: when pressure is applied to the top of the mine, the shear collar holding the firing pin fails. This pin is coated with a friction compound and when its tapered end slides against the mating sleeve, a flame is produced. This ignites the detonator which sets off the main charge.

SPECIFICATIONS
Weight: 85 g
Diameter: 69 mm
Height: 50 mm
Main charge type: PETN
Weight of main charge: 51 g
Operating force: 14–24 kg

STATUS
In service with the French Army.

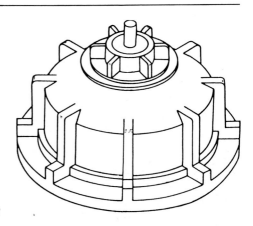

Anti-personnel mine model 1951

Horizontal Action Anti-tank
Mine Mle F1

DESCRIPTION
The Horizontal Action Anti-tank Mine (Mine Antichar à Action Horizontale: MIACAH) consists of a cylindrical drum pivot mounted on a circular frame. The drum, which has a carrying handle, contains a shaped charge which can penetrate 50 mm of armour at a range of 80 metres with an angle of impact of 0 degrees or at a range of 40 metres with a 30-degree angle of impact and can penetrate 70 mm of armour at a range of 40 metres, with an angle of impact of 0 degrees.

The mine is normally anchored to the ground, camouflaged and pointed across the tank's expected route. A wire is stretched out in line with the mine and when a tracked vehicle crosses this wire, the mine operates and the shaped charge penetrates the side armour of the tank.

One training model of the mine is available. It is called the MIACAH d'Exercice (MIACAH F1) and has the shaped charge replaced by an Alsetex MMI 30699 marking cartridge which has an effective range of 50 metres. This is positioned in a similar manner to the real mine and when the tracked vehicle crosses the wire the cartridge marks the point of impact on the tank by the use of a marking sponge.

SPECIFICATIONS
Weight: 12 kg
Length: 260 mm
Diameter: 200 mm

STATUS
In production. In service with the British (the British mines were filled in the United Kingdom), French and other armed forces. The training mine MIACAH d'Exercice is in service with the British and French armies.

MANUFACTURER
Atelier de Fabrication de Toulouse, 155 avenue de Grande-Bretagne, 31053 Toulouse, France.

Enquiries to Groupement Industriel des Armements Terrestres (GIAT), 10 place Georges Clémenceau, 92211 Saint-Cloud, France.

Horizontal action anti-tank mine Mk F1 (T J Gander)

MIACAH d'Exercice, training version of horizontal action anti-tank mine Mle F1

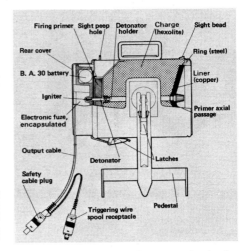

Cutaway drawing of horizontal action anti-tank mine Mle F1

Horizontal Action Anti-tank Mine F1 with infra-red radiation sensor CAPT BAR IR Mle F1

DESCRIPTION

Now in production for the French Army, this is a standard action anti-tank mine Mle F1 (MIACAH F1) fitted with an infra-red and acoustic sensor type CAPT BAR IR Mle F1 to improve the mine's performance in difficult terrain such as marsh, rocky ground and snow.

The sensor is attached to the main body of the mine and utilises the infra-red and acoustic emissions from the target vehicle to trigger the mine. It is capable of detecting targets up to 80 metres away when travelling at speeds of between 5 and 60 km/h. A built-in programmer enables the mine to engage either the first, second or third target detected. It also has built-in immunity to countermeasures.

SPECIFICATIONS
(IRMAH Type F 1 sensor unit)
Weight: 1·35 kg
Length: 250 mm
Diameter: 80 mm
Power supply: MIACAH mine's
Detection range: 0–80 m on target moving at 5–60 km/h

STATUS
Production. Adopted by the French Army.

MANUFACTURER
Atelier de Fabrication de Toulouse, 155 avenue de Grande-Bretagne, 31053 Toulouse, France.

Enquiries to Groupement Industriel des Armements Terrestres (GIAT), 10 place Georges Clémenceau, 92211 Saint-Cloud, France.

Horizontal action anti-tank mine Mle F1 with infra-red radiation sensor

Anti-tank Mine Type HPD1

DESCRIPTION

The HPD (Haut Pouvoir de Destruction) anti-tank mine was developed and adopted by the French Army in 1974. The mine is manufactured and marketed by Télécommunications Radioélectroniques et Téléphoniques. It can be laid by hand or mechanically by the ARE or Matenin minelayers, details of which will be found in the *Minelaying equipment* section.

The mine has a plastic case which contains the power supply (a battery), fuze and explosive charges. The double-influence (seismic and magnetic) igniter activates the fuze when the tank passes overhead, eg under the belly or under the tracks of the tank. During trials the mine perforated 70 mm belly armour and broke the tracks of a tank. The mine is normally buried in the ground; the first charge blows away the earth covering and the main second charge, which is of the shaped type, then ignites.

The HPD mine can be delivered with a self-destruction device, or a self-neutralising device. It is watertight to a depth of five metres. The mine conforms to the United States Specification Mil Std 331.

SPECIFICATIONS
Weight: 6 kg
Length: 280 mm
Width: 185 mm
Height: 105 mm

STATUS
In production. In service with the Dutch (45 360 ordered in 1981) and French armies.

MANUFACTURER
Télécommunications Radioélectroniques et Téléphoniques, Defence and Avionics Equipment Division, 88 rue Brillat-Savarin, 75640 Paris Cedex 13, France.

HPD anti-tank mine opened to show interior (T J Gander)

HPD anti-tank mines packed in pallet holding 112 mines (T J Gander)

HPD anti-tank mine

Anti-tank Mine Type HPD F2

DESCRIPTION

The HPD F2 anti-tank mine is also referred to as the HPD-2 and is a development of the original HPD. It is described as a second generation high-power mine that can penetrate tank belly armour 200 mm thick across a three metre width tank. Designed to be used with existing mine-laying systems the HPD F2 consists of two modular sub-assemblies. One is the fuze section that contains the influence sensors, laying safety, the self-neutralising system, the power supplies, a pyrotechnical safety and the arming devices. The other section contains the clearing charge to blow away any covering earth or snow and the main shaped charge. It can be laid in up to five metres of water. The self-neutralisation system is such that if the mine is not used during a pre-set length of time the mine can be lifted and re-used.

STATUS
Development. Production expected during 1985.

MANUFACTURER
Télécommunications Radioélectroniques et Téléphoniques (TRT), Defence and Avionics Equipment Division, 88 rue Brillat-Savarin, 75640 Paris Cedex 13, France.

SPECIFICATIONS
Weight: 6·5 kg
Length: 280 mm
Width: 185 mm
Height: 105 mm

HPD F2 anti-tank mine

Anti-tank Exercise Mine Type HPD-X F1A

DESCRIPTION

This simulates the HPD anti-tank mine and its setting up is identical to the real mine. The weight and centre of gravity are also identical. The explosive charge has been replaced by a red smoke cartridge that emits smoke for 30 seconds after activation by the igniter. The mine is self-defuzed after 24 hours.

STATUS
In production for the French Army.

MANUFACTURER
Atelier de Fabrication de Toulouse, 155 avenue de Grande-Bretagne, 31053 Toulouse, France.

Enquiries to Groupement Industriel des Armements Terrestres (GIAT), 10 place Georges Clémenceau, 92211 Saint-Cloud, France.

SPECIFICATIONS
Weight: 6 kg
Length: 280 mm
Width: 187 mm
Height: 103 mm
Power supply: BA58 battery
Operating temperature range: −31·5 to +51°C

HPD-X F1A anti-tank exercise mine

Anti-tank Mine HPD-1A

DESCRIPTION
This mine is designed to be laid or buried by the mechanical laying devices of the HPD family. It is fitted with an influence fuze capable of operating across the width of vehicles weighing 8 tons and above. When laid on the surface the mine is capable of penetrating 200 mm of armoured vehicle belly armour plate from a stand-off distance of 0·5 metre. If it is buried under 150 mm of earth it can penetrate 50 mm of belly armour from the same stand-off distance. It will also destroy tank tracks. Arming is initiated after a 10-minute delay and the mine can be set for self-neutralisation after one month.

SPECIFICATIONS
Weight: 7 kg
Length: 280 mm
Height: 103 mm
Width: 187 mm
Weight of main charge: 3·3 kg
Power supply: 2 rechargeable lithium batteries

STATUS
Development.

MANUFACTURER
Etablissements d'Etudes et de Fabrications d'Armement de Bourges.
   Enquiries to Groupement Industriel des Armements Terrestres (GIAT), 10 place Georges Clémenceau, 92211 Saint-Cloud, France.

Anti-tank mine HPD-1A

ACPM Anti-tank Mine

DESCRIPTION
Formerly known as the AC 1d RE Lacroix anti-tank mine (or Type LXT 542), the ACPM (anti-char a pose mecanique) anti-tank mine is designed to break the tracks or destroy the wheels of AFVs to obtain a mobility kill. The mine body is made from two resin-based half casings and is fitted with a pressure plate that detonates the mine only when a tank, APC or heavy wheeled combat vehicle passes over it. The mine can either be laid by a mine-layer or be buried manually. It is provided with a safety double fuze-train interrupter that remains active for 15 minutes after laying. It can be raised and re-used if necessary. A secondary fuze well is provided for an extra igniter or booby-trap system.

SPECIFICATIONS
Weight: 6·3 kg
Length: 280 mm
Height: 105 mm
Width: 185 mm
Weight of main charge: 4 kg

STATUS
Production for export.

MANUFACTURER
Société E Lacroix, route de Toulouse, 31600 Muret, France.

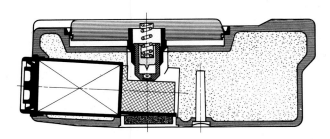

Cross section of ACPM anti-tank mine

ACPM anti-tank mine

Anti-tank Shaped Charge Mine Models 1953 and 1954

DESCRIPTION
Both these mines consist of a light alloy tube containing a modified 73 mm Strim shaped charge anti-tank grenade. The mines are normally buried in the ground with the aid of a special boring tool. When buried in a hole 330 mm deep, with the mine covered by 50 mm of earth, and the belly of the tank 600 mm above the ground, the mine will penetrate 100 mm armour.
   The Model 1953 consists of a pair of grenades joined by a detonating cord and is operated as follows: pressure on the trigger mine or offset fuzing device fires the fuze and the detonating cord continues the firing chain to the two shaped charge grenades.

Anti-tank shaped charge mine Model 1953 complete with detonating cord; anti-tank shaped charge mine model 1954

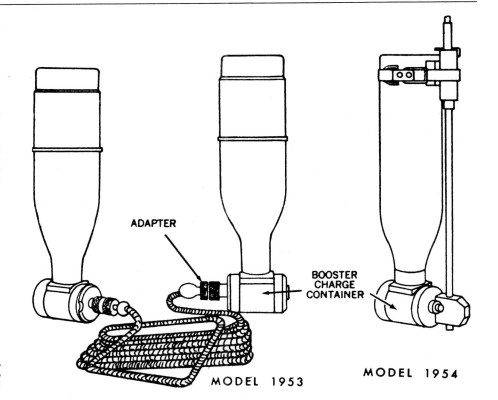

ADAPTER

BOOSTER CHARGE CONTAINER

MODEL 1953   MODEL 1954

The Model 1954 consists of a single grenade with the tilt-rod mounted alongside the mine. The mine operates as follows: lateral pressure on the tilt-rod actuates the fuze which detonates the mine. To ensure that the tank is completely over the mine before it detonates, a half-second delay is built into the firing chain.

SPECIFICATIONS

Model	1953	1954
Weight	1·9 kg	1·2 kg
Diameter of charge	73 mm	73 mm
Height	280 mm	280 mm
Weight of main charge	300 g	300 g

STATUS
Production complete. In service with the French Army.

MANUFACTURER
Luchaire SA, 180 boulevard Haussmann, Paris 75008, France.

Anti-tank Mine Model 1951 MACI

DESCRIPTION
The Model 1951 MACI (Mine Anti-Char Indetectable) consists of three sections of cast TNT reinforced with glass wool: the pressure-plate section, central core that holds the fuze and detonator, and an outer clamping ring which holds the first two sections together. The latter also contains the anti-lifting well and the carrying handle. There is a second anti-lifting well in the bottom of the mine.

The Model 1951 mine operates as follows when fitted with the Model 52 pressure-friction fuze: pressure on the top of the mine shears away the pressure plate and the plastic fuze collar fails, a plastic cone coated with a glass and phosphorus mixture is pressed into a plastic mating sleeve causing friction and flashes, initiating the firing chain which detonates the mine.

When fitted with the Model 1950 pressure chemical fuze the mine operates as follows: pressure on top of the mine pushes down onto the plunger, the shear pin fails and the plunger is forced downwards crushing the vial of acid, which mixes with the pallet of chemical and flashes. This initiates the firing sequence which sets off the mine.

For training purposes, a smoke model of this mine is available.

SPECIFICATIONS
Weight: 7 kg

Diameter: 300 mm
Height: 95 mm
Main charge type: cast TNT
Weight of main charge: 6·486 kg
Booster type charge: RDX
Weight of booster: 498 g
Operating force: 300 kg

STATUS
In production. In service with the French Army and other armies.

MANUFACTURER
Société d'Armement et d'Etudes Alsetex, 4 rue de Castellane, 75008 Paris, France.

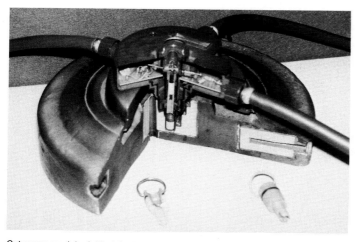

Cut-away model of Model 1951 anti-tank mine fitted with 'spider' type lateral pressure detonator (T J Gander)

Cut-away model of Model 1951 anti-tank mine (T J Gander)

Anti-tank Mine Model 1952 MACI

DESCRIPTION
The Model 1952 MACI (Mine Anti-Char Indetectable) consists of three sections of cast TNT reinforced with glass wool, with a carrying handle. The basic mine is similar in appearance to the Model 1951 MACI anti-tank mine but the Model 1952 has a tilt-rod fuze which is activated by vertical or lateral pressure. For training purposes, a smoke model of this mine is available.

STATUS
In service with the French Army and other armies.

MANUFACTURER
Société d'Armement et d'Etudes Alsetex, 4 rue de Castellane, 75008 Paris, France.

SPECIFICATIONS
Weight: 9 kg
Diameter: 300 mm
Height: (without tilt-rod fuze) 120 mm
Main charge type: cast TNT
Weight of main charge: 6·486 kg
Booster type charge: RDX
Weight of booster: 498 g

Model 1952 anti-tank mine with tilt-rod fuze installed

Anti-tank Track Mine ACPM

DESCRIPTION
The ACPM is a non-metallic thermoplastic anti-tank mine designed for mechanical laying. The mine is fitted with a safety arming timer which enables the mine to be laid or buried while it is inert. The device is two-way and allows the mine to be recovered for relaying if it is disarmed correctly. Detonation is by the application of pressure to the pressure plate on the upper face of the mine. This activates a percussion igniter which initiates the firing chain and detonates the main charge. A booby trap well is also fitted.

SPECIFICATIONS
Weight: 5 kg
Length: 280 mm
Width: 185 mm
Height: 105 mm
Weight of main charge: 3·5 kg

STATUS
Development/trials.

MANUFACTURER
Société d'Armement et d'Etudes Alsetex, 4 rue de Castellane, 75008 Paris, France.

Anti-tank track mine ACPM

SISMA Detector

DESCRIPTION
The SISMA (l'allumeur autonome à influences) is a self-contained proximity detector used for detonating hollow charges, mines, and adapted charges. The simultaneous presence of a seismic and magnetic influence causes the detonator to fire. It is effective against both tracked and wheeled vehicles weighing over 8000 kg and within a speed range of 2 to 90 km/h. The vehicle does not have to come into contact with the mine to ensure detonation.

A self-destruct device is fitted which is programmeable to 3, 8 or 15 days. When it is activated the pyrotechnic actuator, attached to the detonator body by a red and white cord, is ejected.

STATUS
Under evaluation.

MANUFACTURER
Atelier de Fabrication de Toulouse, 155 avenue de Grande-Bretagne, 31052 Toulouse Cédex, France.
Enquiries to Groupement Industriel des Armements Terrestres (GIAT), 10 place Georges Clémenceau, 92211 Saint-Cloud, France.

SISMA detector mounted on anti-tank mine
(Christopher F Foss)

SPECIFICATIONS
Weight: 350 g
Dimensions: 110 × 83 × 25 mm
Arming delay: 5 minutes

SISMA detector

GERMANY, DEMOCRATIC REPUBLIC

K-2 Anti-personnel Mine

DESCRIPTION
The K-2 anti-personnel mine was developed in 1958 as a bounding anti-personnel mine. It resembles a stick grenade and has a short cylindrical plastic body with a long fuze housing. A tripwire is attached to the fuze and a pull on the wire causes the fuze to activate a propellant

charge that fires the main mine body to a height of some 1·5 metres where it explodes. The filling consists of steel ball-bearings.

SPECIFICATIONS
Weight: 5 kg
Diameter: 100 mm
Height: 250 mm

Type of main charge: Nitro Penta
Weight of main charge: 3 kg

STATUS
In service with the East German Army.

MANUFACTURER
East German state arsenals.

PM-60 (or K-1) Anti-tank Mine

DESCRIPTION
Developed in 1958 the K-1 or PM-60 plastic anti-tank mine has a two-part circular body with two fuze-wells. The body contains the pressure plate (on top), filler shield, filler seal, spacer, booster assembly, detonator and fuze. The fuze is threaded into the booster assembly. The detonator is installed in the booster well cap, below the fuze, and is contained by a closing plug. Two models of the PM-60 are known to be in service, one with a mechanical fuze which has a small number of metal components, and a second with a chemical fuze. Both have a bottom fuze for booby-trapping and can be laid by hand or mechanically. The mine is operated as follows: pressure applied to the pressure plate is transmitted to the fuze, driving the firing pin into the primer

which initiates the detonator-booster main charge firing chain and ignites the mine. If required, a blasting cap and firing device may be installed in the booby-trap well in the base of the mine, which initiates the secondary booster and main charge.

SPECIFICATIONS
Weight: 11·35 kg
Diameter: 320 mm
Height: 117 mm
Main charge type: TNT
Weight of main charge: 7·5 kg
Booster charge: Tetrol
Weight of booster: 499 g
Operating charge: 200–500 kg

STATUS
In service with the East German Army.

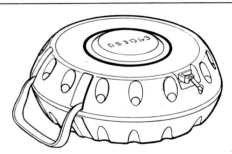

PM-60 anti-tank mine

MANUFACTURER
East German state arsenals.

SM-70 'Ratte' Directional Fragmentation Mine

DESCRIPTION
The SM-70 'Ratte' directional fragmentation mine was specially developed to be part of the anti-personnel obstacle belt that forms the physical border between East and West Germany. The first examples of this specialised mine were produced in 1968 and issued in 1970. It was 1971 before they were used in appreciable numbers and are now installed along approximately 480 kilometres of the border barriers. Recent reports have indicated that they are being replaced by the improved SM-701 or removed altogether.

SM-70s are installed along the border fences in clusters of three. Each SM-70 is usually painted white, is cone shaped and has a mouth diameter of 50·5 mm and a length of 83 mm. The mines are positioned to face along the border fence and may be fixed to the fence itself or on steel posts. The clusters of three are aimed to

fire at three levels. One of each cluster is at leg height, another at body height and the third at head height. Firing is effected by either attempting to climb a fence or by cutting through wires built into the fence structure. Some reports mention that merely touching a fence is enough to fire the devices. Each SM-70 has its own hollow charge lined at the mouth by a cone of 118 steel cubes and when fired these cubes have a lethal range of about 25 metres. They can cause serious injury beyond that range. The SM-70 is fired electrically, usually via a sensitive sprung micro-switch initiator and as the device is fired a secondary circuit actuates an alarm circuit in a local border guard post.

The SM-701 is understood to be a slightly larger device with an increased range.

STATUS
Production probably complete. In service with East German border guard units.

MANUFACTURER
East German state arsenals.

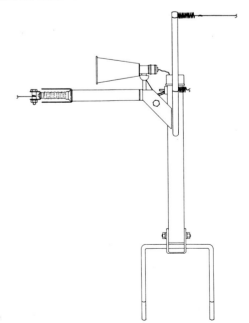

SM-70 'Ratte' directional fragmentation mine

GERMANY, FEDERAL REPUBLIC

Anti-personnel Mine No 11

DESCRIPTION
The only information available on this mine is that it is circular and has a pressure fuze. A practice version of the mine, designated anti-personnel No 18 practice mine, is also available.

SPECIFICATIONS
Weight: 200 g
Diameter: 85 mm
Height: 35 mm
Type of main charge: TNT/RDX

Weight of main charge: 120 g
Operating force: 5–10 kg

STATUS
In service with the West German Army.

MANUFACTURER
DIEHL Ordnance Division, Fischbachstrasse 20, 8505 Röthenbach, West Germany.

Anti-personnel mine No 11 with transport cover removed (West Germany Army)

Anti-personnel Bounding Mine No 31

DESCRIPTION
The No 31 anti-personnel mine has a cylindrical metal outer case with a centrally-mounted fuze assembly on its top. Two or three tripwires may be attached to the assembly. A pull on one or more of the tripwires releases the firing pin which then strikes the percussion cap and initiates the firing sequence. The propelling charge then projects the inner mine case to a certain height that is determined by the length of a tethering wire attached. The mine then explodes to produce a spherical fragmentation pattern of the metallic pellets that constitute the mine filling. A practice version of the mine, designated anti-personnel No 28 practice mine, is also available.

SPECIFICATIONS
Diameter: 100 mm
Height: (without fuze assembly) 135 mm

STATUS
Production. In service with Denmark and West Germany.

MANUFACTURER
DIEHL Ordnance Division, Fischbachstrasse 20, 8505 Röthenbach, West Germany.

Cutaway drawing of anti-personnel bounding mine No 31

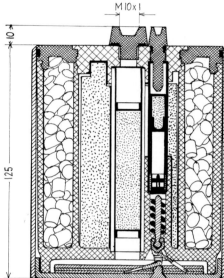

Anti-personnel bounding mine No 31 (West German Army)

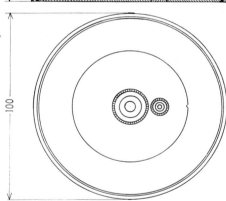

Top view of No 31 anti-personnel bounding mine

Anti-tank Mine Model DM-11

DESCRIPTION
This circular anti-tank mine is very similar in appearance to the French Model 1951 anti-tank mine and is made entirely of explosives mixed with five per cent polyester resin for added strength. The plastic fuze is in the centre of the mine and is of the pressure friction type. There is also an anti-lifting well in the side of the mine.

STATUS
Production complete. In service with the West German Army.

SPECIFICATIONS
Weight: 6·98 kg
Diameter: 300 mm
Height: 94 mm
Main charge type: TNT
Weight of main charge: 6·48 kg
Booster charge type: RDX
Booster charge weight: 500 g
Operating force: 150–400 kg

Anti-tank mine Model DM-11 (T J Gander)

Anti-tank Mine DM-24

DESCRIPTION
This circular anti-tank mine has a case of aluminium with the fuze-well in the centre of the mine. It has a carrying handle on the side. The DM-24 is normally buried or laid on the surface but can also be air-dropped

from a height of ten metres. The mine has a pressure fuze which can also be set to act when an attempt is made to remove the cover.

SPECIFICATIONS
Weight: 8·48 or 9·16 kg
Diameter: 305 mm

Height: 133 mm
Main charge type: RDX/TNT (50/50)
Weight of main charge: 4·49 or 5·17 kg
Operating force: 150–170 kg

STATUS
In service with the West German Army.

Other West German Mines

Anti-tank mine No.3
Plastic anti-tank mine fitted with clockwork safety device. Can be laid by hand or by minelayer. Diameter 240 mm, height 108 mm, with a 4 kg TNT/RDX main charge.

Anti-tank mine No.3
Plastic anti-tank mine. Can be laid by hand or by minelayer. Diameter 300 mm, height 80 mm, with a 5 kg TNT/RDX main charge.

DM39 anti-personnel mine which may be used as anti-handling device with DM-11 anti-tank mine

DM49 anti-personnel mine

DM18 anti-tank mine

DM21 anti-tank mine

DM30 anti-tank mine

Minenstreumittel-Werfer (MSM/W) Mine System

DESCRIPTION
The MSM/W mine system is due for entry into service in the mid-1980s. It is based on two minelayers, the MSM-Fz for motor vehicles and the MSM-Hs for helicopters.

MSM-Fz
The MSM-Fz is an FMC M548 derivative and carries six magazine launching units that are under the control of a central setting, testing and firing device (EPAG) which controls the laying density and fuzing options. The magazine launcher unit contains 20 mine ejection racks that each hold five AT-II (AT-2) anti-tank mines. During laying operations single racks are fired alternately by propelling charges to the right and left. The mines are fitted with self-destruct delay fuzes ranging from 6 to 96 hours and with arming times from 15 seconds to 5 minutes. The mine is actuated against the belly of a target by a vertical wire sensor. It can penetrate the belly plate of any known tank and destroy any type of track.

MSM-Hs
The MSM-Hs is usually carried by either a Bell/Dornier UH-1D or UH-1H helicopter, although other helicopters may also be used. Dornier has carried out successful trials of this system on a UH-1D helicopter. Emplacement of the mine barrage kit, which consists of the magazine launcher frame suspension, EPAG control unit and internal electrical fittings, needs no changes to the helicopter itself. Two magazines are carried, one on the port and one on the starboard side. Both can be adjusted in azimuth and elevation. The helicopter laying speed and altitude are approximately 50 knots and 5 to 15 metres.

STATUS
Development.

MANUFACTURERS
Dynamit-Nobel main contractor for MSM/W system. Dornier, sub-contractor for helicopter minelaying system MSM-Hs. Krauss-Maffei for vehicle minelaying system MSM-Fz.

MSM-Hs prototype magazine with 20 launch tubes each containing five AT-II anti-tank mines

UH-1D helicopter fitted with prototype MSM-Hs system showing mines being dispensed either side

*M548 fitted with MSM-Fz system, with six launching
magazines each containing 100 AT-II anti-tank mines*

West German Artillery and Rocket Delivered Mines

FH-70
At one time it was intended that the FH-70 (a joint
development by West Germany, Italy and the United
Kingdom) 155 mm weapon would fire a projectile containing six anti-tank stick type mines. As far as it is
known, this proposal has now been dropped. It is possible that one or more of these NATO nations may enter
into co-production with the United States of the RAAMS
and ADAMS 155 mm howitzer ammunition.

LARS
The 110 mm Light Artillery Rocket System, introduced
into the Federal German Army in 1970, launches a
rocket to a maximum range of 14 000 metres. This can
be fitted with a variety of warheads including one which
contains eight Pandora AT-1 anti-vehicle mines, or
another which contains five AT-2 Medusa hollow charge
anti-tank mines. In the 1980s it is planned to introduce a
LARS II rocket which will have a range of 20 000 metres.
The rocket will have five AT-2 mines as its payload. The
mines are ejected from a flight stabilised dispenser unit
and their passage to the ground is controlled by a parachute that is discarded on impact. A salvo of 36 rockets
can deliver 180 mines into the target area in approximately 18 seconds.

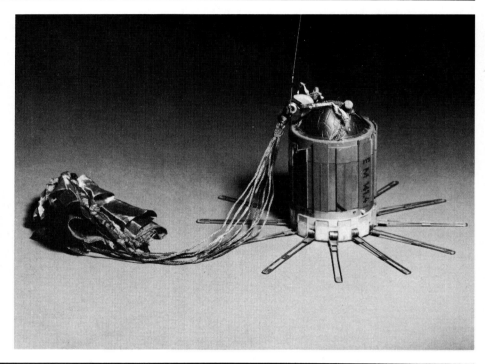

*AT-2 Medusa hollow charge mine as used in Light
Artillery Rocket System (LARS)*

HUNGARY

Gyata-64 Anti-personnel Mine

DESCRIPTION
The Gyata-64 is a small, non-metallic, anti-personnel
mine which uses approximately 0·4 kg of explosive
packed into a dark brown phenolic moulding covered
with a black rubber shroud. The main charge is two
blocks of cast TNT.

SPECIFICATIONS
Weight: 0·45 kg
Diameter: 106 mm
Height: 61 mm
Type of charge: cast TNT

STATUS
In service with the Hungarian Army.

MANUFACTURER
Hungarian state arsenals.

M62 Anti-personnel Mine

DESCRIPTION
The M62 plastic anti-personnel mine is similar in size to
the Hungarian M49 wooden anti-personnel mine and
has the same amount of explosive. The mine has the
following metal components: pivot pin, safety pin, fuze
and striker pin, striker spring and detent. The mine
operates as follows: when pressure is applied, the lid
pivots about the hinged end and the free end of the lid
pushes the winged pin down, out of the firing pin. When
the winged pin is removed, the firing pin is driven forwards, striking the primer and detonating the mine.

SPECIFICATIONS
Weight: 318 g
Length: 187 mm
Width: 50 mm
Height: 65 mm
Main charge type: TNT
Weight of main charge: 75 g
Operating force: 1·5–4·5 kg

STATUS
In service with the Hungarian Army.

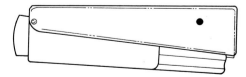

M62 plastic anti-personnel mine

MANUFACTURER
Hungarian state arsenals.

M49 Anti-personnel Mine

DESCRIPTION
The M49 wooden anti-personnel mine is similar to the
Soviet PMD-7ts anti-tank mine, but longer and made in
two halves with the top half fitting over the lower and the
fuze projecting through at one end. Activation is by a
tripwire that triggers a pull fuze. The pull required is only
one kg. A version with a plastic case is also in service.

SPECIFICATIONS
Weight: 0·33 kg
Length: 185 mm
Width: 50 mm
Height: 58 mm
Main charge type: TNT
Weight of main charge: 75 g
Operating force: 1 kg

STATUS
In service with the Hungarian Army.

MANUFACTURER
Hungarian state arsenals.

Bounding Anti-personnel Mine

DESCRIPTION
This cylindrical anti-personnel mine is staked to the ground and operates as follows: when the tripwire is pulled the striker-retaining pin is pulled out releasing the twin-pronged striker. This simultaneously hits the two percussion caps which ignite a short piece of time fuze and a longer piece of instantaneous fuze, which burns through first and sets off the black powder propellant. The mine is projected into the air about 0·5 metre above the ground where the main charge explodes, scattering the filling of steel balls in all directions.

SPECIFICATIONS
Weight: 3·629 kg
Diameter: 120 mm
Height: 300 mm
Main charge type: TRI-II
Weight of main charge: 770 g
Type of booster charge: black powder
Operating force: 4·5–9·1 kg

STATUS
Uncertain.

MANUFACTURER
Hungarian state arsenals.

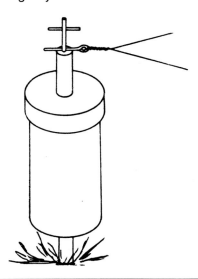

Bounding anti-personnel mine with tripwires attached

Anti-personnel Ramp Mine

DESCRIPTION
The Hungarian anti-personnel ramp mine consists of four blocks of explosive in an elongated sheet metal case. It has a mechanical fuze with a spring-loaded striker and a metal stand to hold it in the armed position. When pressure is applied to the elevated end of the mine, the tongue is pushed out of the hole in the striker, the striker is released and hits the percussion cap, which ignites the detonator and sets off the mine.

SPECIFICATIONS
Weight: 1·361 kg
Length: 475 mm
Width: 50 mm
Height: 30 mm
Main charge type: TNT
Weight of main charge: 0·816 kg
Operating force: 4·536 kg

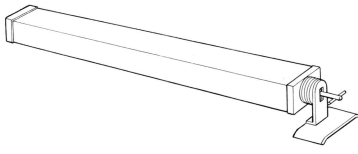

Anti-personnel ramp mine

STATUS
Uncertain.

MANUFACTURER
Hungarian state arsenals.

Universal Anti-tank Mine

DESCRIPTION
This new mine, which is based on the plate charge principle, can be used as a conventional track destruction mine, belly attack mine or off-road mine depending on the type of fuzing and method of emplacement. It has replaced the plate charge and shaped charge (*Jane's Combat Support Equipment 1979–80*, page 128) in the Hungarian Army inventory.

It may be laid by hand or mechanically, although probably not when used for belly attack or off-road mining. As an off-road mine it is emplaced some 30 to 50 metres in front of the target. Four fuzes are provided, including a tilt-rod type. The mine is resistant to shock waves and relatively insensitive to mechanical mine-clearing equipment. It is 300 mm in diameter and weighs 9 kg. A training version is also available.

STATUS
In service with the Hungarian Army.

MANUFACTURER
Hungarian state arsenals.

Training version of Universal anti-tank mine fitted with tilt rod fuze

INDIA

The Indian Army has introduced into service an indigenously designed non-metallic anti-tank mine that is laid mechanically. No other details are available.

ISRAEL

No. 4 Anti-personnel Mine

DESCRIPTION
This is a rectangular plastic anti-personnel mine fitted with a hinged cover. It is activated by an 8 kg force on a pressure-plate.

STATUS
In service with the Israeli Army and Argentina.

MANUFACTURER
Explosive Industries Ltd, 25 Nahmani Street, POB 1363, Tel Aviv, Israel.

SPECIFICATIONS
Weight: 350 g
Length:
(armed) 152 mm
(unarmed) 145 mm
Width: 65 mm
Height: 50 mm
Main charge type: TNT
Weight of main charge: 180 g
Weight of booster charge: 22 g
Operating force: 8 kg

No. 4 anti-personnel mine

No. 10 Anti-personnel Mine

DESCRIPTION
This is a circular plastic anti-personnel mine that can be laid on the ground or easily buried. It is armed by removing a safety cap and fitting a pressure fuze assembly, which is activated by a 15–35 kg force being applied to a pressure plate.

SPECIFICATIONS
Weight: 120 g
Diameter: 70 mm
Height: 75 mm
Main charge type: TNT
Weight of main charge: 50 g
Fuze type: pressure
Operating force: 15–35 kg

STATUS
Production complete. In service with the Israeli Army and Uganda.

MANUFACTURER
Israel Military Industries, Export Division, PO Box 1044, Ramat-Hasharon 47100, Israel.

No. 12 (or M12A1) Anti-personnel Mine

DESCRIPTION
This is a picket-mounted tripwire-actuated bounding anti-personnel mine made of metal. The ignition assembly is a three-anchor pull, pressure or push unit with a built-in 4·5 second delay. Once triggered a small propellant charge causes the main mine body to bound about one metre into the air where it explodes. The filling is 260 g of TNT and a number of cast-steel ball-bearings to cause fragmentation, the effective radius of which is about 40 metres.

SPECIFICATIONS
Weight: 3·5 kg
Diameter: 102 mm
Height:
(fuzed) 240 mm
(packed) 159 mm
Main charge type: TNT
Weight of main charge: 260 g

STATUS
In service with the Israeli Army, Argentina and Uganda.

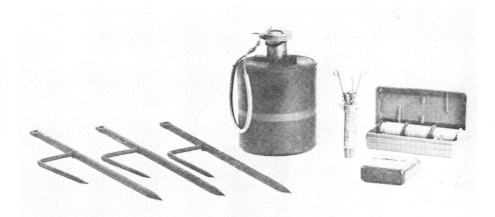

No. 12 (or M12A1) anti-personnel mine

MANUFACTURER
Israel Military Industries, Export Division, PO Box 1044, Ramat-Hasharon 47100, Israel.

No. 6 Anti-tank Mine

DESCRIPTION
During the various Middle East conflicts the Israeli armed forces captured so many Soviet TM-46 anti-tank mines that the type has been taken into Israeli service as standard. The TM-46 has also been copied direct to produce the Israeli No. 6 anti-tank mine and this No. 6 has also been exported. It was one of the anti-tank mines encountered by the British armed forces in the Falkland Islands.

SPECIFICATIONS
Weight: 9 kg
Diameter: 205 mm
Height: 110 mm
Main charge type: TNT
Weight of main charge: 6 kg
Weight of booster charge: 45 g
Fuze type: No. 61 (an optional fuze may be fitted)
Operating force: 260 kg

STATUS
In service with the Israeli Army and Argentina.

MANUFACTURER
Explosive Industries Ltd, 25 Nahmani Street, POB 1363, Tel Aviv, Israel.

No. 6 anti-tank mine (T J Gander)

Other Israeli Mines

Designation	Type	Weight	Main charge type and weight	Fuze type	Operating force	STATUS
No. 25	anti-tank	7·257 kg	cast TNT, 6·98 kg	friction	15–16 kg	In service with the Israeli Army.
No. 26	anti-tank	8·98 kg	TNT, 7 kg	pressure	79–120 kg	

ITALY

Valsella VS-50 Anti-personnel Scatter Drop Mine

DESCRIPTION
The VS-50 non-metallic mine has been designed for scatter laying from helicopters using the Valsella developed VS/MD helicopter-mounted mine-dropping system. The mines can also be scattered from vehicles or laid by hand to a maximum depth of 20 mm.

The VS-50 mine has a plastic case. It is available in various colours including khaki, marshy green and sand. It is waterproof and non-buoyant and is not affected by the explosion of another VS-50 mine more than 100 mm away.

A training model which gives off smoke when actuated is available. One plastic case containing 60 mines, with the detonators stowed separately in the same case, weighs 15 kg.

SPECIFICATIONS
Weight: 190 g
Diameter: 87 mm
Height: 45 mm
Main charge type: RDX/TNT
Weight of main charge: 42 g
Operating force: about 10 kg
Operating temperature range: −31·5 to +70°C

STATUS
In production. In service with undisclosed countries.

MANUFACTURER
Valsella Meccanotecnica SpA, 25018 Montichiari, Brescia, Italy.

Sales handled by Valtec Italiana, Via M Mercati 22, Rome, Italy.

Valsella VS-50 anti-personnel scatter mine without safety device

Valsella VS-50 anti-personnel scatter mine with safety device

Valsella VS-Mk 2 Anti-personnel Scatter Drop Mine

DESCRIPTION
The VS-Mk 2 non-metallic mine has been designed for scatter-laying from helicopters using the Valsella helicopter-mounted mine-dropping system. It can also be scattered from vehicles or by hand. It is fully waterproof.

The VS-Mk 2 has a disc-shaped resin-based plastic case available in various camouflage colours. It is activated by pressure applied to both the pressure plate on the mine's top face and on its bottom face. A model fitted with an electrical anti-lift device is known as the VS-Mk 2-E.

SPECIFICATIONS
Weight: 135 g
Diameter: 90 mm
Height: 32 mm
Main charge type: RDX
Main charge weight: 33 g (22 g for VS-Mk 2-E)
Operating force: 10 kg
Operating temperature range: −31·5 to +55°C

STATUS
In service with the Italian Army.

MANUFACTURER
Valsella Meccanotecnica SpA, 25018 Montichiari, Brescia, Italy.

Sales handled by Valtec Italiana, Via M Mercati 22, Rome, Italy.

Valsella VS-Mk 2 anti-personnel scatter drop mine with safety device

Valsella VS-Mk 2 anti-personnel scatter drop mine without safety device

Technovar TS-50 Anti-personnel Scatter Mine

DESCRIPTION
The TS-50 is a circular plastic anti-personnel mine which is fully waterproof and non-buoyant. It can be laid by hand, to a maximum depth of 30 mm, or by the Technovar DAT minelaying system for helicopters flying at a maximum speed of 200 km/h and at altitudes of up to 100 metres. Actuation is by application of a 12·5 kg force to a pressure plate. A training version is also available.

SPECIFICATIONS
Weight: 186 g
Diameter: 90 mm
Height: 45 mm
Main charge type: T4
Weight of main charge: 50 g
Operating force: 12·5 kg
Operating temperature range: −40° to +70°C

STATUS
In production. In service with the Italian Army.

MANUFACTURER
Technovar, 95 Via Argiro, 70121 Bari, Italy.

Technovar TS-50 anti-personnel scatter mine with safety device removed (Italian Army)

MISAR SB-33 Scatter-dropped Anti-personnel Mine

DESCRIPTION

The SB-33 scatter-dropped anti-personnel mine was developed from early 1977 and entered production in October 1977. Features of the mine can be summarised as follows: irregular shape and small size that make it difficult to locate on the ground; low weight which increases the quantity of mines that can be carried by a helicopter; wide pressure plate which allows the mine to function either upright or upside down; an anti-shock device which makes it insensitive to countermeasures such as fuel air explosives, and the mine can be scattered from helicopters with the MISAR SY-AT system, or laid by hand. It can also be buried just under the surface of the ground.

The mine is circular and has a plastic case which is available in any colour. If required it can also be delivered coated with a special paint that makes it undetectable by infra-red equipment.

When the mine is scattered with the SY-AT system its safety pin remains in position until the mine leaves the magazine. The mine is maintenance-free and has a shelf life of ten years, it is waterproof and will not float. It is available with an electronic anti-removal device and a training version is produced.

The magazine is used for carrying and storing the mines as well as being used in the SY-AT system. The detonator can be inserted into the mine when the mine is still in its magazine.

SPECIFICATIONS
Weight: 140 g
Diameter: 88 mm
Height: 32 mm
Main charge type: HE
Weight of main charge: 35 g
Operating force: 5 – 20 kg
Packaging: magazine of 78 mines weighs 15 kg

STATUS
In production. In service with some NATO and other countries including Spain and Argentina. The SB-33 is also produced in Spain.

MANUFACTURERS
MISAR SpA, Via Gavardo 6, 25016 Ghedi (Brescia), Italy.
Explosivos Alaveses, S.A., Vitoria, Spain.

MISAR SB-33 mine before detonation on 400 × 400 mm steel plate, 5 mm thick

MISAR SB-33 scatter-dropped anti-personnel mine

Magazines for SB-33 mines

Results of effectiveness test of SB-33 mine placed upright or upside down on 400 × 400 mm steel plate, 5 mm thick

Anti-personnel Mine, Air Droppable, Maus-1

DESCRIPTION

This circular anti-personnel mine has a resin-based plastic and metal case and is designed to be dropped from aircraft and helicopters at speeds up to 100 km/h and from a height of 100 metres. There is a safety pin in the side of the mine, which keeps open the valve connecting the space under the rubber diaphragm to the outside and allows air to enter and leave. The mine is operated as follows: when pressure is applied to the top of the mine, the rubber diaphragm is compressed, pushing down the integral igniter which triggers the M41 detonator that fires the mine.

SPECIFICATIONS
Weight: 267 g
Diameter: 89 mm
Height: 46 mm
Main charge type: T4

Maus anti-personnel air-droppable mine from above (Italian Army)

Weight of main charge: 15·5 g
Operating force: 8·9–11·8 kg

Maus anti-personnel air-droppable mine from below (Italian Army)

STATUS
In service with the Italian Army.

Anti-personnel Mine Model AUS 50/5

DESCRIPTION
The AUS 50/5 anti-personnel mine is shaped like a spinning top with the PS-51 pressure pull fuze on the top of the mine. The main case of the mine is plastic.

The mine functions as follows: pressure on the top of the mine or on a tripwire shears the safety pin, the striker hits the percussion cap, initiating the two delay trains. The first delay fires the black powder charge, hurling the complete mine into the air, and when the mine reaches a height of 0·5 metre, the second delay fires the main charge, which projects the shrapnel embedded in cement to a height of 1·8 metres and a radius of 15 metres.

SPECIFICATIONS
Weight: 1·4 kg
Diameter: 126 mm
Height: 98 mm
Main charge type: TNT or Compound B
Weight of main charge: 147 g
Booster type: black powder
Operating force:
(pressure) 13·6–22·6 kg
(pull) 0·454–7·2 kg

STATUS
Obsolete.

Anti-personnel mine Model AUS 50/5

Technovar VAR/40 Anti-personnel Mine

DESCRIPTION
The VAR/40 is a cylindrical button-head type of mine made of a resin-based plastic. It is a small and compact mine that can be carried by soldiers in pockets or knapsacks. The mine is buried so that only the button-head is jutting out of the ground and the safety cap is then removed from the head. A 12 to 13 kg load on the button-head activates the mine, which is capable of damaging light vehicles. The VAR/40 is fully waterproof and non-floating. A training version is also available.

SPECIFICATIONS
Weight: 105 g
Diameter: 78 mm
Height: 45 mm
Main charge type: T4 or Composition B
Weight of main charge: 40 g
Operating force: 12–13 kg
Operating temperature range: −41 to +70°C

STATUS
In production.

MANUFACTURER
Technovar, 95 Via Argiro, 70121 Bari, Italy.

Technovar VAR/40 anti-personnel mine (Italian Army)

Technovar VAR/100 Anti-personnel Mine

DESCRIPTION
The VAR/100 is a cylindrical button-head type of mine made of resin-based plastic. It is a small and compact anti-personnel and sabotage mine that is carried by soldiers in their pockets and knapsacks. It is fully waterproof and non-buoyant. The mine is buried with only the button-head jutting out of the ground, and the safety cap is then removed from the head. A 12 to 13 kg force on the button-head activates the mine, which is capable of severely damaging light vehicles. A training version is also available.

SPECIFICATIONS
Weight: 170 g
Diameter: 78 mm
Height: 57 mm
Main charge type: T4 or Composition B
Weight of main charge: 100 g
Operating force: 12–13 kg
Operating temperature range: −41 to +70°C

STATUS
In production.

MANUFACTURER
Technovar, 95 Via Argiro, 70121 Bari, Italy.

Technovar VAR/100 anti-personnel mine with safety cap in position

Technovar VAR/100/SP Anti-personnel Mine

DESCRIPTION
The VAR/100/SP is a cylindrical cast-iron button type mine fitted with a splinter casing and a three-prong actuator assembly. It is fully waterproof and non-buoyant. It can be buried, so that only the button-head with its three-pronged pressure actuator unit is jutting out of the ground, or mounted on a metal pile some 800 mm above ground. Actuation may be either by the application of a 12 to 13 kg force to the three prongs or by a pull from a 6 kg force on one or both tripwires that can be attached to the mine. The pull causes a jerk-igniter attached to the button-head to detonate the main charge which splinters the 1·6 kg cast iron casing into about 500 pieces, the lethal radius of which extends to some 25 metres from the point of detonation. The mine is also capable of damaging light vehicles. A training version is available.

SPECIFICATIONS
Weight: 1·77 kg
Diameter: 120 mm
Height: 138 mm
Main charge type: HE

Technovar VAR/100/SP anti-personnel mine with latch and wire spools for trap device

Weight of main charge: 100 g
Effective radius: 25 m
Operating force:
(pressure) 12–13 kg
(pull) 6 kg
Operating temperature range: −41 to +70°C

STATUS
In production.

MANUFACTURER
Technovar, 95 Via Argiro, 70121 Bari, Italy.

Valsella Anti-personnel Bounding Mine Valmara 69

DESCRIPTION
This cylindrical anti-personnel bounding mine has a plastic case with a removable fuze mounted on the top. To obtain a more effective fragmentation pattern the main charge, surrounded by more than 1000 metal splinters, is projected about 0·45 metre into the air by a propelling charge before detonation. The lethal casualty radius is at least 25 metres. The explosive train of the mine consists of a percussion igniter cap, a propelling charge, a percussion detonator, a booster detonating charge and a main explosive charge.

The mine is fitted with a tripwire fuze. The traction load on the tripwire required to activate the fuze is 6 to 8 kg. The fuze can also be activated by direct pressure on one or more of the fuze prongs. When activated the fuze primes the igniter cap which fires the propelling charge. The internal body of the mine, consisting of the main charge surrounded by the splinters, the booster, the detonator and a striker mechanism, is then projected into the air. A steel wire connected to the striker mechanism is extended to its maximum length causing the percussion of the detonator and the explosion of the mine. The striker mechanism cannot strike the detonator until the body is ejected. The mine is fully waterproofed.

A training version of the Valmara 69 is also available. This has a smoke charge and can be used at least ten times with only the smoke candle and fuze being replaced each time.

SPECIFICATIONS
Weight: 3·2 kg
Diameter: 130 mm

Anti-personnel bounding mine Valmara 69 (Italian Army)

Height: (with fuze) 205 mm
Main charge type: Composition B
Weight of main charge: 420 g
Type of booster charge: RDX
Weight of booster charge: 13 g
Operating force:
  (pressure) 10·8 kg
  (pull) about 6·5 kg
Operating temperature range: −31·5 to +55°C

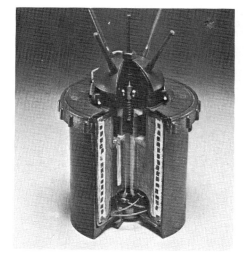

Cutaway anti-personnel bounding mine Valmara 69

STATUS
In production. In service with the Italian Army and other armies including Angola.

MANUFACTURER
Valsella Meccanotecnica SpA, 25018 Montichiari, Brescia, Italy.
Sales handled by Valtec Italiana, Via M Mercati 22, Rome, Italy.

MISAR P-25 Anti-personnel Mine

DESCRIPTION
The MISAR P-25 anti-personnel mine was developed from early 1977 and entered production in 1978. It consists of a cylindrical plastic casing which can be delivered in any colour, with the fuze mounted on top. The mine can be buried but for maximum effect should be staked to the ground. A slot for mounting a stake is provided on the side of the mine. It is activated by two tripwires which can extend up to 15 metres away from the mine. When activated the charge explodes and splinters are scattered in a radial path. Effective range of the P-25 mine is 15 metres.

The mine is waterproof, will not float and has a maintenance-free life of at least ten years. Smoke-producing and inert models are available for training.

SPECIFICATIONS
Weight: 0·63 kg
Diameter: 80 mm
Overall height: 180 mm
Main charge type: HE
Weight of main charge: 0·14 kg
Operating force: 2–10 kg
Packing: case of 15 mines weighs 14 kg

STATUS
In production.

MANUFACTURER
MISAR SpA, Via Gavardo 6, 25016 Ghedi (Brescia), Italy.

MISAR P-25 anti-personnel mine

MISAR P-40 Anti-personnel Jumping Mine

DESCRIPTION
The MISAR P-40 anti-personnel jumping mine was developed from early 1977 and entered production in 1978. It consists of a cylindrical plastic casing, which can be made in any colour, inside which is another container holding the high explosive and shrapnel. The mine is buried with just the fuze showing above the ground. The fuze is attached to the two tripwires which can be up to 15 metres from the mine. The mine operates as follows: when the tripwire is pulled the inside container is ejected into the air and when it reaches a pre-determined height it explodes and scatters the shrapnel in a radial path. Trials conducted by MISAR have shown that this mine will cause injury to at least 55 per cent of men standing within a radius of 15 metres of the mine when it is ignited.

The mine is waterproof, will not float and has a minimum maintenance-free life of ten years. Smoke-producing and inert training models are available.

SPECIFICATIONS
Weight: 1·5 kg
Diameter: 90 mm
Height with fuze: 200 mm
Height of casing: 120 mm
Main charge type: HE
Weight of main charge: 0·25 kg
Operating force: 2–10 kg
Packing: case of 8 mines weighs 16 kg

STATUS
In production.

MANUFACTURER
MISAR SpA, Via Gavardo 6, 25016 Ghedi (Brescia), Italy.

MISAR P-40 anti-personnel mine

Valsella VS-1.6 Anti-tank Scatter Mine

DESCRIPTION
The VS-1.6 plastic non-metallic anti-tank mine is circular and has been designed for rapid laying from helicopters by means of the Valsella developed VS/MD helicopter-mounted minelaying system. The mine can also be scattered from trucks or laid by hand. It is normally left on the surface but can also be buried to a maximum depth of 75 mm. The VS-1.6 is pressure-activated. A training version of this mine is also available.

STATUS
In production. In service with undisclosed countries. Under evaluation by the Italian Army.

MANUFACTURER
Valsella Meccanotecnica SpA, 25018 Montichiari, Brescia, Italy.
   Sales handled by Valtec Italiana, Via M Mercati 22, Rome, Italy.

SPECIFICATIONS
Weight: 3 kg
Diameter: 225 mm
Height: 93 mm
Main charge type: HE
Weight of main charge: 1·85 kg
Operating force: 190–220 kg

Valsella VS-1.6 anti-tank scatter mine

Valsella VS-1.6/AR/AN Electronic Anti-tank Scatter Mine

DESCRIPTION
The Valsella VS-1.6/AR/AN anti-tank scatter mine is physically identical to the VS-1.6 anti-tank scatter mine. It differs in being fitted with an electronic fuze, powered by long life batteries. The mine is pressure- and tilt-activated. It is fitted with an electrical delay arming device, is fully waterproof and provided with an electronic booby-trap against removal by mine-clearing parties. An automatic neutralisation device, which is preset before the mine is laid, is fitted and an optional self-destruct unit may be fitted.

STATUS
In production. Under evaluation by the Italian Army.

MANUFACTURER
Valsella Meccanotecnica SpA, 25018 Montichiari, Brescia, Italy.
   Sales handled by Valtec Italiana, Via M Mercati, 22, Rome, Italy.

Valsella VS-1.6/AR/AN electronic anti-tank scatter mine from above

Valsella VS-1.6/AR/AN electronic anti-tank scatter mine from below

SPECIFICATIONS
Weight: 3·1 kg
Diameter: 225 mm
Height: 93 mm
Main charge type: HE

Weight of main charge: 1·65 kg
Operating force: 190–220 kg
Arming delay: 15 minutes
Neutralisation delay: adjustable from 1–128 days

MISAR SB-81 Scatter-dropped Anti-tank Mine

DESCRIPTION
The MISAR SB-81 can be scattered from helicopters with the MISAR SY-AT system, or laid manually. It can be buried in the ground to a maximum depth of 100 mm. Air-dropping does not impede its ability to destroy tank tracks or irreparably damage tank running gear.

   The mine is circular and has a plastic case available in any colour. It is pressure-activated and will function whether it lands on its top or its bottom.

   The SB-81 is waterproof, will not float, is maintenance-free and has a shelf life of ten years. The explosive content of the mine can be removed and stored separately. The magazine is used for carrying and storing the mine as well as being used in conjunction with the SY-AT scattering system. The detonator can be inserted into the mine even when it is stored in the magazine.

   Other versions of the mine are available including a model with an electronic anti-removal and self-neutralising device, and another with an electronic anti-removal device and a self-destruction device, which both operate at pre-determined times. In appearance these are identical to the standard mines. Smoke and inert models are available for training purposes.

   The SB-81 is produced in Spain as the EXPAL SB-81.

SPECIFICATIONS
Weight: 3·2 kg
Diameter: 232 mm
Height: 90 mm
Main charge type: HE
Weight of main charge: 2 kg
Operating force: 150–310 kg
Packaging: magazine containing 5 rounds weighs 19·5 kg

STATUS
In production. In service in Argentina (Spanish production), Italy and Spain.

MANUFACTURERS
MISAR SpA, Via Gavardo 6, 25016 Ghedi (Brescia), Italy.
   Explosivos Alaveses, S.A., Vitoria, Spain.

MISAR SB-81 scatter-dropped anti-tank mine

Result of effectiveness test of MISAR SB-81 mine placed on 30 mm thick steel plate 400 × 400 mm

MISAR magazines for SB-81 anti-tank mine

Valsella VS-3.6 Anti-tank Mine

DESCRIPTION
This non-metallic anti-tank mine has a resin-based plastic case with an integral carrying handle. The VS-3.6 is waterproof, non-buoyant and shockproof. A VS-N pneumatic type fuze is fitted to the main body by a thread coupling. The mine is laid manually with the pressure plate placed to a maximum depth of 150 mm. An inert training version of the mine has been produced.

SPECIFICATIONS
Weight: 5 kg
Diameter: 250 mm
Height: 114 mm
Main charge type: Composition B or TNT
Weight of main charge: 3·75 kg
Booster charge type: RDX
Weight of booster charge: 280 g
Operating force: 180–220 kg
Operating temperature range: −31 to +55°C

Assembled Valsella ·VS-3.6 anti-tank mine

Disassembled Valsella VS-3.6 anti-tank mine (Italian Army)

STATUS
In production. Version with fuze VS-N in service with the Italian Army.

MANUFACTURER
Valsella Meccanotecnica SpA, 25018 Montichiari, Brescia, Italy.
  Sales handled by Valtec Italiana, Via M Mercati 22, Rome, Italy.

Valsella VS-2.2 Anti-tank Mine

DESCRIPTION
This non-metallic anti-tank mine has a resin-based plastic case with an integral carrying handle. The VS-2.2 is waterproof, non-buoyant and shockproof. A VS-N pneumatic type fuze is fitted to the main body by a thread coupling. The mine is laid manually with the pressure plate placed to a maximum depth of 150 mm. An inert training version of the mine is produced.
  Practice mines are available of the same size, shape and weight. They are of the smoke type and can be reused. A box containing four VS-2.2 mines, with the fuzes packed separately in the same box, weighs about 17 kg.

SPECIFICATIONS
Weight: 3·6 kg
Diameter: 246 mm
Height: 117 mm
Weight:
  (main charge) 1·85 kg
  (booster) 280 g
Charge type:
  (main) Composition B
  (booster) RDX
Operating force: 180–220 kg
Operating temperature range: −31·5 to +55°C

STATUS
In production. In service with undisclosed countries.

MANUFACTURER
Valsella Meccanotecnica SpA, 25018 Montichiari, Brescia, Italy.
  Sales handled by Valtec Italiana, Via M Mercati, 22, Rome, Italy.

Valsella VS-2.2 anti-tank mine (Italian Army)

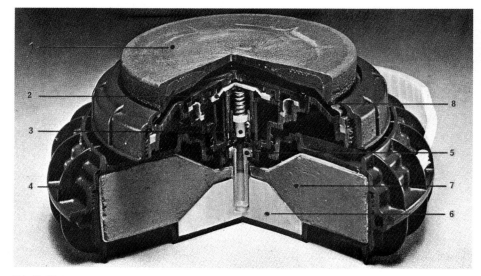

Valsella VS-2.2 anti-tank mine: **(1)** *pressure plate* **(2)** *pressure membrane* **(3)** *striker* **(4)** *plastic casing* **(5)** *detonator* **(6)** *booster* **(7)** *explosive charge* **(8)** *sealing membrane*

Valsella VS-HCT Anti-tank Mine

DESCRIPTION
The Valsella VS-HCT anti-tank mine is fitted with an electronic influence fuze that is effective against any type of MBT and tracked combat vehicle. It utilises a shaped-charge effect against the vehicle's belly armour and blast effects against the tracks and can penetrate more than 70 mm of armour.
  It may be laid on the surface or buried to a maximum depth of 150 mm. The mine is fitted with a mechanical and electrical delayed arming device and is fully waterproof and provided with an electronic booby-trap against removal. It is automatically neutralised after a preset time, and an optional self-destruct unit can be fitted.

SPECIFICATIONS
Weight: 4 kg
Diameter: 222 mm
Height: 104 mm
Main charge type: HE
Weight of main charge: 2·1 kg
Neutralisation delay: adjustable from 1–128 days

STATUS
In production. Under evaluation by the Italian Army.

MANUFACTURER
Valsella Meccanotecnica SpA, 25018 Montichiari, Brescia, Italy.
  Sales handled by Valtec Italiana, Via M Mercati 22, Rome, Italy.

Valsella VS-HCT anti-tank mine

Valsella FSA-ATM Hollow Charge Anti-tank Mine

DESCRIPTION
This mine was specifically developed for the 122 mm FIROS 25 rocket system as one of the payloads for the sub-munition warhead. The mine is electrically programmed via a cable for its operational life-time of from a minimum of two hours to a maximum of 48 hours, after which it self-destructs.

The mode of operation of the warhead and the mine is as follows: at the target zone the warhead splits into three sections which facilitates release of the seven mines. Each mine then deploys a parachute that slows the descent rate to about 15 metres a second and orientates it for landing. On impact with the ground the parachute is discarded and, after a short delay, flexible legs are deployed so that the mine assumes an upright position with the hollow charge facing upwards.

The arming of the mine is accomplished in three stages: the first is the fragmentation of the rocket warhead, second is the removal of the safety pin by traction caused by the parachute deploying and third is the shock produced by impact with the ground. A short electrical pulse is initiated after a delay following ground impact activating the mine's proximity fuze to detect the presence of suitable targets. The mine is also fitted with an anti-removal device.

SPECIFICATIONS
Weight: 1·3 kg
Diameter: 115 mm
Height: 97 mm
Operational lifetime: 2–48 h

STATUS
Under development.

MANUFACTURER
Valsella Meccanotecnica SpA, 25018 Montichiari, Brescia, Italy.
   Sales handled by Valtec Italiana, Via M Mercati 22, Rome, Italy.

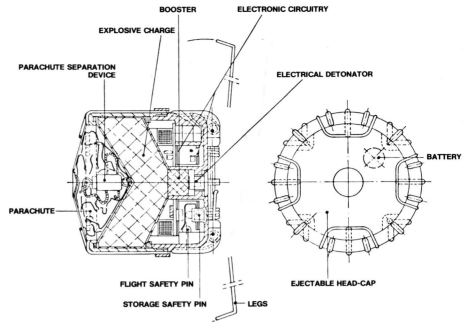

Valsella FSA-ATM hollow charge anti-tank mine

MISAR SB-MV/T Anti-tank Mine

DESCRIPTION
The SB-MV/T anti-tank mine entered series production in early 1979.

   It is circular and has a plastic casing which is available in a variety of colours. It is of the hollow charge type and has an influence fuze. MISAR claims that it is three times more effective than conventional anti-tank mines as it acts against the belly armour of the tank as well as its tracks. The mine will penetrate up to 100 mm of steel armour and cause serious damage to the interior of the tank, immobilising it.

   The mine can be laid by hand or mechanically and is normally buried to a maximum depth of 100 mm. If the arming lever is rotated and the detonator inserted after the lever has passed the arming delay, a safety circuit that stops the mine igniting comes into operation. When in its packing case, the mine cannot be activated as the arming lever cannot be moved from its safety position. A delayed mechanical arming is incorporated in the mine so that the mine does not become fully active until after the external arming lever has been operated.

   The mine operates as follows: the approach of a tank towards the mine is accompanied by vibrations in the ground which are detected by the seismic transducer and the electronic amplification and discrimination circuit of the fuzing system. This alerts the magnetic sensor part of the system which locates the tank by detecting the change in the magnetic field of the earth caused by the metallic mass of the tank and, when it is over the mine, transmits a signal to the firing circuit. This operates both the ignition cap of the uncovering charge – which blows off the upper part of the mine and any camouflage over it to leave the liner of the bursting charge unobstructed – and the detonator. The detonator has a time-lag built in to delay the firing of the booster charge and the main charge. The delay is determined by the uncovering time.

   Only two-thirds the number of SB-MVT anti-tank mines are needed to provide the same obstructive capability as Second World War type mines. They also require a third of the time and need fewer personnel to lay.

   The mines are packed in magazines of five, and the detonators can be inserted into the mines without removing the mines from the magazine. The mines can be quickly removed from the magazine for manual laying and the magazine is also used when the mines are being laid mechanically.

   There is a variant of the SB-MV/T known as the SB-MV/AR which has the same operational characteristics and is externally identical to it but is fitted with an anti-lifting device designed to operate the detonator if any change in trim of the mine is detected and a self-neutralisation device which is programmed to operate after a pre-set period.

STATUS
In production.

MISAR SB-MV/T anti-tank mine

MANUFACTURER
MISAR SpA, Via Gavardo 6, 25016 Ghedi (Brescia), Italy.

SPECIFICATIONS
Weight: 5 kg
Diameter: 236 mm
Height: 101 mm
Main charge type: melted CB
Weight of main charge: 2·6 kg
Booster charge type: compressed RDX
Uncovering charge type: propelling powder
Power supply: replaceable lithium batteries
Packing: magazine of 5 mines weighs 28 kg

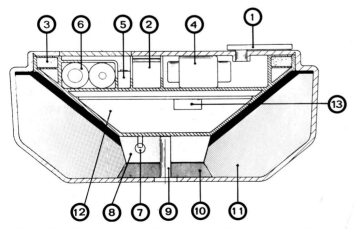

MISAR SB-MV/T anti-tank mine (1) arming lever (2) seismic sensor (3) magnetic sensor (4) activation delaying device (5) neutralisation programmer (6) battery (7) ignition cap (8) uncovering charge (9) detonator (10) booster (11) main charge (12) electronic assembly (13) active mine signaller

Result of effectiveness test of MISAR SB-MV/T anti-tank mine: three 50 mm thick steel plates were pierced at distance of 600 mm

Technovar MATS Anti-tank Scatter Drop Mine

DESCRIPTION
The Technovar MATS is a circular plastic anti-tank mine. It is fully waterproof and has been designed for rapid laying from helicopters flying at speeds of up to 200 km/h and altitudes up to 100 metres. The system used to dispense the mines is the Technovar DAT mine dispenser. The mine may also be laid by vehicles or buried by hand at depths down to 75 mm. The MATS is pressure activated and is capable of destroying any armoured vehicle tracks. Two versions of the mine are available together with inert training versions.

STATUS
In production. In service with the Italian Army.

MANUFACTURER
Technovar, 95 Via Argiro, 70121 Bari, Italy.

SPECIFICATIONS
Weight:
  (version 1) 3·6 kg
  (version 2) 5 kg
Diameter:
  (version 1) 220 mm
  (version 2) 260 mm
Height: 90 mm
Main charge type: T4 or Composition B
Weight of main charge:
  (version 1) 1·5 kg
  (version 2) 2·4 kg
Operating force:
  (average) 180 kg
  (max) 310 kg
Operating temperature range: −31 to +70°C

Technovar MATS anti-tank scatter mine (left) from top and (right) from bottom (Italian Army)

Technovar TC/3.6 Anti-tank Mine

DESCRIPTION
The TC/3.6 is a circular plastic anti-tank mine that is fully waterproof and non-buoyant. It can be laid by hand, to a depth of between 75 and 150 mm in soil and up to one metre in snow, or mechanically from a vehicle.
Actuation is by the application of a load of 180 kg to a pressure plate. The mine is capable of destroying the tracks and severely damaging the suspension of armoured vehicles. A training version is also available.

STATUS
In production.

MANUFACTURER
Technovar, 95 Via Argiro, 70121 Bari, Italy.

SPECIFICATIONS
Weight: 6·8 kg
Diameter: 270 mm
Height: 145 mm
Main charge type: Composition B
Weight of main charge: 3·6 kg
Operating force:
  (average) 180 kg
  (max) 310 kg
Operating temperature range: −31 to +70°C

Technovar TC/3.6 anti-tank mine

Technovar TCE/3.6 Electronic Anti-tank Mine

DESCRIPTION
The TCE/3.6 is physically similar to the TC/3.6 mine but is fitted with an electronic arming/disarming device that can be used to activate or deactivate a minefield sector composed of these mines on receipt of a command signal.
The mine may be laid by hand, to a depth of between 75 and 150 mm in soil, and in snow up to a depth of one metre, or mechanically from vehicles. A training version is also available. Actuation is by the application of a load to a pressure plate.

SPECIFICATIONS
Weight: 6·8 kg
Diameter: 270 mm
Height: 145 mm
Main charge type: Composition B
Weight of main charge: 3·6 kg
Operating force:
  (average) 180 kg
  (max) 310 kg
Operating temperature range: −31 to +70°C

STATUS
In production.

MANUFACTURER
Technovar, 95 Via Argiro, 70121 Bari, Italy.

Technovar TCE/3.6 electronic anti-tank mine

Technovar TC/6 Anti-tank Mine

DESCRIPTION
The Technovar TC/6 is a circular resin-based plastic anti-tank mine that is fully waterproof and non-buoyant. It can be laid by hand, to a depth of between 75 and 150 mm in soil and up to one metre in snow, or mechanically from a vehicle.
Actuation is by the application of force to a pressure plate. The mine is capable of destroying the tracks and severely damaging the suspension of armoured vehicles. A training version is available.

STATUS
In production.

MANUFACTURER
Technovar, 95 Via Argiro, 70121 Bari, Italy.

SPECIFICATIONS
Weight: 9·6 kg
Diameter: 270 mm
Height: 185 mm
Main charge type: Composition B
Weight of main charge: 6 kg
Operating force:
  (average) 180 kg
  (max) 310 kg
Operating temperature range: −31 to +70°C

Technovar TC/6 anti-tank mine

Technovar TCE/6 Electronic Anti-tank Mine

DESCRIPTION
The TCE/6 is physically similar to the TC/6 mine and is fitted with an electronic arming/disarming device that can be used to activate or deactivate a minefield or minefield sector composed of these mines on receipt of a command signal. The mine is fully waterproof and non-buoyant. It may be laid by hand, to a depth of between 75 and 150 mm in soil and up to one metre in snow, or mechanically from vehicles. A training version is available. The TCE/6 is actuated by the application of a load to a pressure plate.

STATUS
In production.

MANUFACTURER
Technovar, 95 Via Argiro, 70121 Bari, Italy.

SPECIFICATIONS
Weight: 9·6 kg
Diameter: 270 mm
Height: 185 mm
Main charge type: Composition B
Weight of main charge: 6 kg
Operating force:
  (average) 180 kg
  (max) 310 kg
Operating temperature range: −31 to +70°C

MISAR SBP-04 and SBP-07 Anti-tank Mines

DESCRIPTION
Both these mines have been designed for hand laying and are identical in design and operating characteristics, differing only in their dimensions and weight of high explosive. The mines have the same firing pressure type device which can easily be removed for arming. When activated the mines have sufficient explosive to break the tracks of a tank or damage its suspension.

The mines are non-magnetic and have a plastic case which is available in any colour. They are also waterproof, will not float, are maintenance-free and have a shelf life of ten years. A smoke-producing model of the mine is available for training.

The SBP-04 and SBP-07 mines can be fitted with a SAT igniter that has countermeasures against Fuel Air Explosive sweeping techniques. The SAT igniter fitted with anti-lift and self-neutralisation devices is designated SAT/AR; it is externally identical to the basic SAT model. A version fitted with an anti-lift and programmable self-neutralisation device is designated SAT/QZ. It is also physically identical to the basic SAT.

STATUS
In production. All three igniter types are in production.

MANUFACTURER
MISAR SpA, Via Gavardo 6, 25016 Ghedi (Brescia), Italy.

SPECIFICATIONS

Mines	SBP-04	SBP-07
Weight	5 kg	8·2 kg
Diameter	250 mm	300 mm
Height	110 mm	130 mm
Main charge type	HE	HE
Weight of main charge	4 kg	7 kg
Operating force	150–310 kg	150–310 kg
Packing	case of 4 mines weighs 24 kg	case of 3 mines weighs 28 kg

Igniters	SAT	SAT/AR	SAT/QZ
Weight	700 g	830 g	950 g
Diameter	182 mm	182 mm	182 mm
Height	76 mm	76 mm	76 mm

SAT/QZ igniter, top (left) and bottom (right)

Anti-tank Mine Saci 54/7

DESCRIPTION
There are two models of the circular Saci 54/7 anti-tank mine, a smaller version with a small amount of metal in the striker and a larger model with no metallic components.

The mine has three AC-52 pressure/mechanical fuzes in the top of the mine. When sufficient pressure is applied to the top of the fuze, the shear rings fracture and the plunger moves downwards. This action frees the striker-retaining balls and allows the spring-loaded striker to hit the percussion cap, which fires the detonator and the mine explodes. This fuze cannot be disarmed. There are two anti-lifting fuze-wells, one in the side and the other in the bottom of the mine.

STATUS
Obsolete.

SPECIFICATIONS

Model	Light version	Heavy version
Weight	6·21 kg	10·2 kg
Diameter	276 mm	276 mm
Height	154 mm	188 mm
Main charge type	TNT	TNT
Weight of main charge	5 kg	9 kg
Operating force	120–190 kg	n/a

Valsella Anti-tank Track Mine SH-55

DESCRIPTION
This circular anti-tank track mine has a plastic case and is fitted with a VS-N igniter. There are two wells for fitting anti-lifting fuzes, one in the bottom and the other in the side of the mine, opposite the carrying handle.

The fuze operates as follows: pressure on the top of the mine forces down the pressure plate which puts pressure on the striker, the striker retaining collar fails, and the striker hits the detonator and fires the main charge.

SPECIFICATIONS
Weight: 7·3 kg
Diameter: 280 mm
Height: 122 mm
Main charge type: Composition B
Weight of main charge: 5·5 kg

Booster charge type: T4
Weight of booster charge: 50 g
Operating force: 185 kg

STATUS
Production complete. In service with the Italian Army.

SH-55 anti-tank mine (Italian Army)

SH-55 anti-tank mine with pressure plate and fuze removed (Italian Army)

Italian Army Mines

The following mines are currently in service with the Italian Army:
Anti-personnel mine, air droppable, Maus-1 (see page 178)
Valsella anti-tank track mine SH-55 (see above)

Anti-personnel mine AUPS (*Jane's Combat Support Equipment 1978-79*, page 133)

The following mines are no longer in service:
Anti-personnel mine Model AUS 50/5 (see page 179)
Anti-personnel mine Minelba (*Jane's Combat Support Equipment 1978-79*, page 130)

Anti-personnel mine Lory (ibid, page 129)
Anti-personnel mine R (ibid, page 133)
Anti-tank mine Saci 54/7 (see above)
Anti-tank mine CS 42/2 (*Jane's Combat Support Equipment 1978-79*, page 133)
Anti-tank mine CS 42/3 (ibid, page 133)

JAPAN

Anti-tank Mine Type 63

DESCRIPTION
The Type 63 anti-tank mine is circular and non-metallic. It is waterproof and can therefore be used for under-water operations, eg buried in the beds of streams which may be forded by tanks and other vehicles. The mine is activated as follows: pressure is applied to the pressure plate and this compresses a hard rubber collar, the pressure forces the firing pin past steel balls to initiate the booster which sets off the main charge.

SPECIFICATIONS
Weight: 14·515 kg
Diameter: 305 mm
Height: 216 mm
Main charge type: Composition B
Weight of main charge: 11 kg
Operating force: 181 kg

STATUS
In service with the Japanese Ground Self-Defence Force.

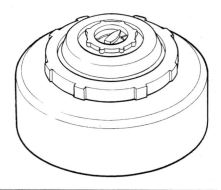

Anti-tank mine Type 63

KOREA, DEMOCRATIC PEOPLE'S REPUBLIC

Anti-personnel Mine Model 15

DESCRIPTION
This anti-personnel mine is an adaptation of the Soviet POMZ-2M mine. The cast-iron body has five rows of serrations with the fuze at the top. The fuze is a copy of the Soviet MUV pressure fuze or the UPF pull fuze. The

TNT charge is in the centre of the body which is closed at its lower end by the wooden picket which is used to emplace the mine in the ground.

STATUS
In service with the North Korean Army.

MANUFACTURER
North Korean state arsenals.

SPECIFICATIONS
Weight: (without stake) 2·6 kg
Length: (without stake) 107 mm
Diameter: 60 mm
Main charge type: TNT
Weight of main charge: 75 g
Operating force: 1 kg

KOREA, REPUBLIC

Anti-personnel Mine M18A1

DESCRIPTION
The South Korean anti-personnel mine M18A1 is a license-produced version of the American M18A1 for which there is an entry in this section. Data relating to the South Korean mine is the same as that for the

American M18A1 except for the South Korean M18A1s are packed six to a 24 kg wooden box measuring 341 × 260 × 345 mm.

STATUS
Production. In service with South Korean armed forces.

MANUFACTURER
Korea Explosives Company Limited, 34 Seosomoon-Dong, Chung-Ku, Seoul, Republic of Korea.

Korean-produced M18A1 anti-personnel mine showing fragment matrix

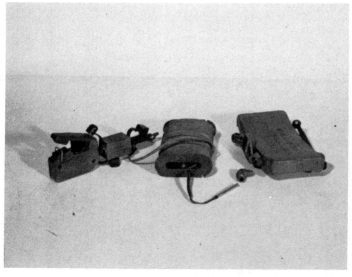

Complete Korean-produced M18A1 anti-personnel mine outfit

Anti-tank Mine M19

DESCRIPTION
The South Korean M19 anti-tank mine is a license-produced version of the American M19 anti-tank mine for which there is a separate entry in this section. Data relating to the South Korean M19 is exactly the same as for the American M19. South Korean M19s are packed two to a 34 kg wooden box which contains an M22 arming wrench.

STATUS
Production. In service with South Korean armed forces.

MANUFACTURER
Korea Explosives Company Limited, 34 Seosomoon-Dong, Chung-Ku, Seoul, Republic of Korea.

Korean-produced M19 anti-tank mine

NETHERLANDS

Anti-personnel Mine
Model 15

DESCRIPTION

The non-metallic anti-personnel mine Model 15 consists of a plastic box with a hinged lid with the fuze-well on the opposite side of the hinge. This mine has no safety device and is detonated as follows: pressure on the lid of the mine pushes down on top of the No. 15 pressure fuze, which crushes the ampoule. The acid and powder then ignite and in turn ignite the primer which detonates the mine.

SPECIFICATIONS
Weight: 0·79 kg
Length: 113 mm
Width: 100 mm
Height: 67 mm
Main charge type: TNT
Weight of main charge: 176 g
Operating force: 6–25 kg

STATUS
In service with the Netherlands Army.

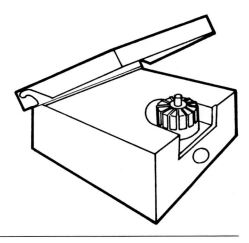

Anti-personnel mine Model 15

Anti-personnel Mine
Model 22

DESCRIPTION

This circular anti-personnel mine consists of four main components: plastic case, integral fuze, main charge and the detonator. The plastic case is provided with external strengthening ribs. The Model 22 pressure-friction fuze is in the centre of the mine with the striker showing above the top of the mine. The mine is detonated as follows: pressure on the striker causes the shear collar to fail, which fires the striker which is charged with a friction compound into a mating sleeve where abrasion causes the friction compound to flash, setting off the detonator and then the main charge.

STATUS
In service with the Netherlands Army.

SPECIFICATIONS
Weight: 85 g
Diameter: 72 mm
Height: 50 mm
Main charge type: TNT
Weight of main charge: 40 g
Operating force: 5–25 kg

AP 23 Anti-personnel Mine

DESCRIPTION

The AP 23 is a bounding anti-personnel mine with a steel case. It can be either buried just below the surface or mounted on a mine anchor picket driven into the ground.

The mine is activated either by a pull on a tripwire attached to the tilt-rod fuze fitted to the top of the mine or by direct contact with the tilt-rod itself. Both result in the movement of a pressure table that causes the firing pin body with firing pin and Belleville spring to be moved downwards. The spring inverts and the pin hits the percussion primer igniting the igniter charge that fires the expelling charge which propels the main fragmentation unit to a height of one metre where it detonates. Full safety devices are built into the mine to prevent premature detonation.

SPECIFICATIONS
Weight: 4·5 kg
Diameter: 100 mm
Height:
   (with tilt-rod) 252 mm
   (without tilt-rod) 185 mm
Main charge: Composition B
Weight of main charge: 500 g
Weight of booster charge: 24 g
Weight of expelling charge: 3 g

STATUS
Production complete.

MANUFACTURER
Eurometaal NV, Zaandam, Netherlands.

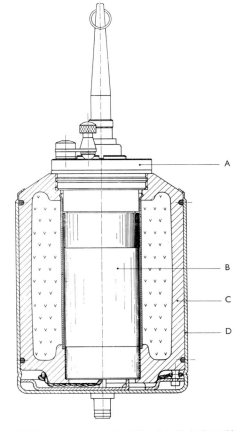

*AP 23 anti-personnel mine (**A**) pull-push igniter with detachable tilt-rod (**B**) expelling charges (**C**) fragmenting body with explosive train (**D**) outer jacket with anchor nipple*

AP 23 anti-personnel mine

Anti-tank Mine Type 2, T40

DESCRIPTION

This metallic anti-tank mine consists of two dished pressings joined by a watertight seal. A carrying handle is provided. The two filler plugs are on top of the mine, either side of the central socket, which contains the pressure fuze. The mine is waterproof and operates as follows: pressure applied to the top of the mine crushes the fuze cover, which depresses the plunger and plunger housing, and compresses the striker spring. The plunger has a recess which, when opposite the striker-release balls, lets them escape into it, releasing the spring-loaded striker. This fires the percussion cap which ignites the detonator, which in turn fires the booster which sets off the main charge.

STATUS
In service with the Netherlands Army.

SPECIFICATIONS
Weight: 6 kg
Diameter: 280 mm
Height: 90 mm
Main charge type: TNT
Weight of main charge: 4·08 kg
Operating force: 45 kg

Anti-tank Mine Model 25

DESCRIPTION
The Model 25 anti-tank mine is circular and has a steel case. There are two anti-lifting fuze-wells, one in the side and the other in the bottom of the mine. The mine has three booster charges, one surrounding the main fuze-well in the centre of the mine and the other two around each of the two anti-lifting fuze-wells.

The mine is detonated as follows: pressure on the top of the mine forces down the pressure plate onto the fuze (the Model 29). This shears the shear pin, releasing the spring-loaded striker, which hits the percussion cap, ignites the detonator and sets off the mine.

SPECIFICATIONS
Weight: 12·97 kg
Diameter: 305 mm
Height: 128 mm
Main charge type: TNT
Weight of main charge: 9 kg
Booster charges: 3
Operating force: 250–350 kg

STATUS
In service with the Netherlands Army as the nr. 25.

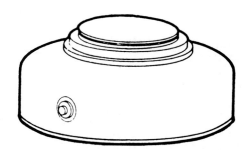

Anti-tank mine Model 25

Anti-tank Mine Model 26

DESCRIPTION
The Model 26 anti-tank mine is composed almost entirely of explosive reinforced with glass wool. The main charge is in three components which are the pressure plate section, central core and the clamping ring which holds the first two parts together. The mine has two booster charges, one on the central axis serving the main fuze-well and the bottom anti-lifting well, and another on a radial axis serving the second anti-lifting well.

The mine operates as follows: pressure applied to the top of the mine causes the pressure plate to separate along the shear groove and push down on the fuze, the shear collar on the fuze fails and the friction compound flashes and fires the detonator which in turn fires the booster charge and sets off the main charge.

STATUS
In service with the Netherlands Army.

SPECIFICATIONS
Weight: 9 kg
Diameter: 298 mm
Height: 113 mm
Main charge type: cast TNT
Weight of main charge: 4·536 kg
Operating force: 350 kg
Fuze type: Model 26 pressure friction

POLAND

Plastic Anti-personnel Mine

DESCRIPTION
Very little information on this plastic anti-personnel mine is available. It is rectangular and has a fuze-well at one end. The plastic case is very brittle which improves the effectiveness of the mine as it scatters into many fragments when detonated.

SPECIFICATIONS
Weight: 248 g
Length: 140 mm
Width: 70 mm
Height: 51 mm

STATUS
Uncertain.

MANUFACTURER
Polish state arsenals.

Plastic Anti-tank Mine

DESCRIPTION
This plastic mine is circular with the main fuze in the centre top of the body. The auxiliary fuze-well is in the side of the mine, below the cover. The body consists of three parts, the plate type base plate, a partitioned insert without a bottom and a cover which screws onto the base.

SPECIFICATIONS
Weight: 6 kg
Diameter: 315 mm
Height: 80 mm

STATUS
Uncertain.

MANUFACTURER
Polish state arsenals.

SINGAPORE

Anti-tank Mine STM-1

DESCRIPTION
Manufactured from non-magnetic materials, the STM-1 is waterproofed to a depth of about one metre. It is of a conventional design with a centrally-located detonator set to operate at pressures of between 225 to 550 kg. There is provision for anti-handling devices or booby traps and the normal production colour is a light brown. Designed for manual-laying only, the STM-1 has a simple carrying handle manufactured from light cord with a plastic sleeving grip.

The STM-1 is packed four to a wooden box which when loaded weighs 44 kg. The box is 415 mm high, 395 mm wide and 530 mm wide.

SPECIFICATIONS
Weight: 7 kg
Diameter: 300 mm
Height: 95 mm

STATUS
In production. In service with Singapore defence forces.

MANUFACTURER
Chartered Industries of Singapore (PTE) Limited, 249 Jalan Boon Lay, Singapore 2261.

Anti-tank mine STM-1

SOUTH AFRICA

High-explosive Anti-personnel Mine

DESCRIPTION
Known as the Mine A/P HE, this small anti-personnel mine has a circular moulded plastic body filled with 58 grams of RDX/WAX 88:12. It has an operating pressure of between 3 to 7 kg and it can be laid in streams and rivers up to a depth of one metre. Before use a water-proof booster is inserted into the waterproof detonator and the mine is armed by removing a cord attached to a safety pin and clip.

A practice mine is available which is coloured light blue instead of the normal brown. This practice mine fires a small smoke pellet in place of the operational charge but is otherwise identical. It weighs 126 grams.

Both types of mine are packed 40 to a plastic box which also holds eight containers each with five boosters.

STATUS
Production. In service with South African armed forces.

MANUFACTURER
Enquiries to: Armscor, Private Bag X337, Pretoria 0001, South Africa.

SPECIFICATIONS
Weight: 128 g
Weight of main charge: 58 g
Weight of firing mechanism: 6·5 g

Mine A/P HE

Shrapnel Mine No. 2

DESCRIPTION
The Shrapnel Mine No. 2 is an exact copy of the American M18A1 Claymore mine and differs from it in few details. The body is moulded polystyrene and contains 680 grams of plastic explosive which forms the main propellant charge for the matrix of steel fragments. Optimum range is given as 15 metres with the maximum of 50 metres. The mine can produce a fan-like pattern of projectiles 2 metres high and 50 metres wide at 50 metres. As with the M18A1, two detonator points are provided on top of the mine body, between which is a simple sight. Two pairs of folding legs support the mine in position.

The Shrapnel Mine No. 2 is packed four to a steel carrying box which also contains four sets of electric detonators, cable assemblies, exploders for electric current supply, test sets, carrier bags and rods.

Each mine weighs 1·58 kg.

STATUS
Production. In service with South African armed forces.

MANUFACTURER
Enquiries to: Armscor, Private Bag X337, Pretoria 0001, South Africa.

Shrapnel Mine No. 2

Anti-tank Mine No 8

DESCRIPTION
Known generally as the High Explosive Anti-tank Mine, the No. 8 has an injection-moulded thermoplastic body with a main charge of 7 kg RDX/TNT 60:40. The only metal used in construction is the striker mechanism of the initiator. During transit or storage, the mine is fitted with a transit plug which is not removed until the mine is being prepared for laying. A cord carrying handle is provided. An impact load of from 150 to 220 kg is required to detonate the mine and a two-position safety lever is provided. The top of the detonator plate is moulded in an irregular pattern to aid concealment and the normal body colour is neutria. No. 8 anti-tank mines are packed two to a plastic box.

STATUS
Production. In service with South African armed forces.

MANUFACTURER
Enquiries to: Armscor, Private Bag X337, Pretoria 0001, South Africa.

SPECIFICATIONS
Weight: 7·4 kg
Weight of main charge: 7 kg
Weight of firing mechanism:
(LZY waterproof detonator) 6·5 kg
(tetryl booster) 3 g
(RDX/WAX 88/12 charge) 58 g

Anti-tank mine No. 8 and plastic packing box

Anti-tank mine No. 8

SPAIN

Anti-personnel Mine Model FAMA

DESCRIPTION
This anti-personnel mine consists of an upper and lower case, both plastic, joined and sealed by a sealing ring. The fuze is in the top of the mine and is protected by a circular cover. The mine is detonated as follows: pressure is applied to the top of the mine, which causes the upper cover to break along the shear groove; the inner portion then moves downwards until it contacts the firing pin plunger, which shears at a shear collar and drives the firing pin into the primer, igniting the detonator which sets off the mine. A practice version has also been produced with slightly different dimensions (diameter: 73 mm, height: 33 mm).

SPECIFICATIONS
Weight: 86 g
Diameter: 71 mm
Height: 38 mm
Main charge type: TNT or Tetryl
Weight of main charge: 50 g
Operating force: 30 kg

STATUS
In service with the Spanish Army.

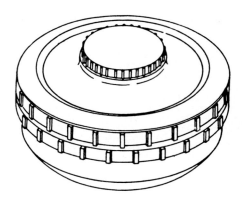

Anti-personnel mine model FAMA

Anti-personnel Mine P-S-1

DESCRIPTION
The P-S-1 is a cylindrical steel case anti-personnel bounding mine with a top-mounted fuze assembly. Actuation is by a pull on a tripwire connected to the fuze unit which fires the main body propelling charge to a height of approximately 1.2 metres where it explodes into small fragments. The effective radius against personnel is 20 metres. Instruction and practice versions are available.

STATUS
In production. In service with the Spanish Army.

MANUFACTURER
Explosivos Alaveses SA, Vitoria, Spain.

SPECIFICATIONS
Weight: 3·78 kg
Diameter: 98 mm
Height:
   (mine plus fuze) 189 mm
   (mine) 127 mm
Main charge type: TNT
Weight of main charge: 450 g
Weight of shrapnel: 2·6 kg
Effective radius: 20 m

P-S-1 anti-personnel mine complete with fuze and detonator

Anti-personnel Mine P-4-A

DESCRIPTION
The P-4-A is a circular anti-personnel mine consisting of a plastic main body and a plastic pressure-actuated centrally located fuze assembly which is normally removed for transport. Instruction, cross section teaching and practice versions are available.

STATUS
Production complete. In service with the Spanish Army and in Argentina.

MANUFACTURER
Explosivos Alaveses SA, Vitoria, Spain.

SPECIFICATIONS
Weight: 210 g
Diameter: 72 mm
Height: 55 mm
Main charge type: TNT
Weight of main charge: 100 g

P-4-A anti-personnel mine (top) body with transport cap and (below) fuze with safety device

Anti-tank Mine Type CETME

DESCRIPTION
This anti-tank mine is circular and has a bakelite case. It is activated by either a chemical or mechanical fuze. To make the mine resistant to mechanical and explosive mine-clearing equipment three hydraulic cylinders are fitted to retard the downward movement of the pressure plate. There is an anti-lift fuze-well in the base of the mine.

STATUS
In service with the Spanish Army.

MANUFACTURER
Centro de Estudios Tecnicos de Materiales Especiales, Madrid, Spain.

SPECIFICATIONS
Weight: 9·98 kg
Diameter: 460 mm
Height: 153 mm
Main charge type: TNT
Weight of main charge: 5·22 kg
Fuze: chemical or mechanical

Anti-tank Mine C-3-A

DESCRIPTION
The C-3-A is a circular anti-tank mine consisting of a plastic mine body and a central plastic fuze and pressure plate assembly. Actuation is by means of a heavy load to the top-mounted pressure plate.

Instruction, training and practice versions are available. A wooden box contains two mines and two fuzes

which are separated from the mines and screwed in the rings fitted on the inside part of the lid. Total weight of the box with two mines and two fuzes is 18 kg.

STATUS
In production. In service with the Spanish Army and in Argentina.

MANUFACTURER
Explosivos Alaveses SA, Vitoria, Spain.

SPECIFICATIONS
Weight: 5·9 kg
Diameter: 285 mm
Height: 115 mm
Type of main charge: TNT
Weight of main charge: 5 kg

C-3-A anti-tank mine (T J Gander)

C-3-A anti-tank mine fitted with travelling cap (T J Gander)

Other Spanish Mines

Designation	Type	Weight	Diameter	Height	Weight of main charge	Operating force	Comments	STATUS
								Believed to be in service with the Spanish Army.
CP – X.02	anti-personnel	58 g	72 mm	34 mm	40 g	13·6 kg (adjustable)	also known as the Cardona fuze is type EP-01(a)	
H-1	anti-personnel	n/a	188 mm	118 mm	n/a	n/a	pressure fuze	
M45B	anti-personnel	n/a	n/a	n/a	n/a	n/a	cylindrical	

SWEDEN

Anti-personnel Mine Type LI-11

DESCRIPTION
The anti-personnel mine LI-11 consists of a fixed lower part and a movable upper part, both made of rubber and held together by a moisture-proof rubber casing. The

mine incorporates a humidity shield allowing it to be used in marshy ground.

The mine has a pressure fuze and is detonated when pressure is applied to the centre or edge. It cannot be detonated by the shock waves from other detonating mines.

The LI-11 mine is normally packed in a wooden case

which holds 20 mines, 20 detonators and 20 safety rings, all weighing 7 kg. When being carried the safety ring is fitted in place of the detonator. A practice mine which emits orange smoke is also in service.

SPECIFICATIONS
Weight: 200 g
Diameter: 80 mm
Height: 35 mm
Main charge type: TNT
Weight of main charge: 110 g
Operating force: 5–10 kg
Operating temperature: −40 to +65°C

STATUS
Production complete. In service with the Swedish Army as Truppmina 10.

MANUFACTURER
Lindesbergs Industri AB, Box 154, S-711 00 Lindesberg, Sweden.

Cross-section of LI-11 anti-personnel mine

Cross-section of LI-11 anti-personnel mine showing method of operation when pressure is applied to edge of mine

Anti-personnel Mine FFV 013

DEVELOPMENT
Development of the FFV 013 anti-personnel mine began in the early 1970s. The Swedish Army carried out troop trials with the mine in 1978.

The mine is intended for use in tactical situations where quick reaction and instantaneous firepower are required, for example: defence against airborne and heliborne landings, airfield defence, defence of vulnerable points and ambushes.

DESCRIPTION
The mine consists of a prefragmented plate behind which an explosive charge is contained in a fibreglass housing. On detonation, the explosive charge accelerates the prefragmented plate to a high velocity. The plate, which consists of balls with a hexagonal cross section, will then disintegrate and the balls will continue in their trajectories in an unchanged pattern. At a range of 150 metres, the balls cover an area 100 metres wide and 4 metres high.

The mine is normally mounted on a tripod or on a

FFV 013 anti-personnel mine complete with carrying case and cable

permanent emplacement. The mine is ignited by a special shock tube system which is non-electric and is thus insensitive to electrical radiations or pulses from thunderstorms.

SPECIFICATIONS
Weight:
   (mine body) 20 kg
   (container with mine, tripod and firing device) 35 kg
Width: (mine body) 420 mm
Height: (mine body) 250 mm
Number of ball fragments: 1200
Fragment density: (within 150 metres) approx 2 fragments per m²
Weight of ball fragment: approx 6 g

STATUS
Production. Ordered for Swedish armed forces in September 1982.

MANUFACTURER
FFV Ordnance, S-631 87 Eskilstuna, Sweden.

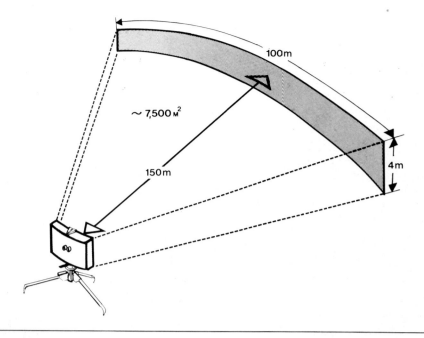

Effective area of FFV 013 anti-personnel mine when detonated

Anti-personnel Fragmentation Mine M/48

DESCRIPTION
The M/48 anti-personnel mine is basically a cut-off 75 mm cartridge case filled with TNT and scrap iron. For fixing, a metal strap with two holes is mounted on the side of the case towards the bottom. A hole on the top of the mine with the exit hole in the side of the mine near the top enables the mine to be hung in position.
   The mine is used with a tripwire and pull fuze and

operates as follows: pressure on the tripwire removes the striker-retaining pin, causing the striker to be released, the pin hits the percussion cap, fires the detonator and the mine explodes.

STATUS
In service with the Swedish Army.

SPECIFICATIONS
Weight: 2·9 kg
Diameter: 90 mm
Height: 180 mm
Main charge type: TNT
Weight of main charge: 226 g
Operating force: 2·5 kg

Anti-personnel Mine M41

DESCRIPTION
The Model 1941 anti-personnel mine consists of a wooden box with a hinged lid, containing the pull fuze, a block of explosive and a wooden spacer block. The mine is operated as follows: pressure on the lid of the mine forces the lid down, which removes the striker-retaining pin; the striker then hits and fires the

percussion cap, which fires the detonator and the mine explodes.

SPECIFICATIONS
Weight: 350 g
Length: 200 mm
Width: 80 mm

Height: 50 mm
Main charge type: TNT
Weight of main charge: 120 g
Operating force: 2 kg

STATUS
Probably no longer in service with the Swedish Army.

Anti-personnel Concrete Mines Model 43 and 43 (T)

DESCRIPTION
This anti-personnel mine consists of an explosive-filled glass bottle upside down in a concrete jacket. A 240-degree segment of the concrete jacket has steel shrapnel embedded in it, unlike the remainder of the jacket, marked by a depression on the top of the mine. The mouth of the glass bottle is fitted with a hollow cork

cylinder with a threaded nipple, into which the pull fuze and detonator are screwed. For fixing, two metal hoops are embedded in the top and bottom of the mine.
   The difference between the Model 43 and the Model 43 (T) is that the latter has a Trotyl instead of a Nitrolit charge. The mine is used with a tripwire and pull fuze and operates as follows: pressure on the tripwire removes the striker retaining pin, causing the striker to be released, the pin hits the percussion cap, fires the detonator and the mine explodes.

SPECIFICATIONS
Weight: 5·8 kg
Diameter: 106 mm
Height: 230 mm
Main charge type: Nitrolit or Trotyl
Weight of main charge: 590 g
Operating force: 1 kg or less

STATUS
In service with the Swedish Army.

Anti-personnel Mine Truppmina 9

DESCRIPTION
This anti-personnel mine consists of a piece of pipe threaded at one end to accept an M/48 fuze. The inside is filled with TNT and has a maximum fragmentation radius of less than ten metres. The mine is normally

used with a tripwire and operates as follows: pressure on the wire removes the striker retaining pin, the spring-driven striker then hits the percussion cap, which ignites the detonator and the mine explodes. Several sections can be screwed together to form a Bangalore torpedo.

STATUS
In service with the Swedish Army.

SPECIFICATIONS
Weight: 590 g
Diameter: 36 mm
Height: 190 mm
Weight of main charge: 122 g
Operating force: 1·8–5 kg

Anti-tank Mine Type FFV 028

DEVELOPMENT
In the second half of the 1960s studies were made in Sweden to find new and more effective anti-tank mines. Main requirements were the ability to kill the tank, rather than immobilise it temporarily, and that the mine should permit a reduction of the mine density in the minefield without reducing the probability of a mine's being activated. Full scale development of the mine began in the early 1970s and in early 1978 the mine was at the pre-production stage. The FFV 028 was ordered by the Swedish armed forces in 1982.

DESCRIPTION
The mine consists of two main components, the body and the fuze. The body contains the hollow charge with the liner and the battery housing. The battery is a standard single-cell type and maintains its performance even at low temperatures. It has a shelf life of more than ten years and can be replaced from the outside of the mine. The hollow charge of the mine is contained in a non-magnetic housing.
   The FFV 028 can be laid by hand or by the FFV mechanical minelayer which has been developed specifically for use with this mine. Details will be found in the *Minelaying equipment* section.

When laying the mine, the transport safety is removed and the arming lever is pressed down and turned 90 degrees. This connects the battery and the electric time circuit starts. The shutter is released and its time mechanism starts. When the time delay has expired, the shutter turns to the armed position, the explosive train is aligned and the electric detonator is connected to the electronic unit. At this time the electronic safety also ceases and the mine is armed.
   The mine is effective against the whole width of the tank and operates as follows: when a vehicle passes over the mine its fuze senses the disturbances in the terrestial magnetic field, the electronic unit processes

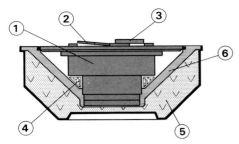

Main components of FFV 028 anti-tank mine (1) fuze
(2) transport safety (3) arming lever (4) uncovering
charge (5) bursting charge and (6) liner

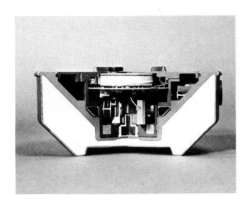

FFV 028 anti-tank mine sectioned to show main
components

Number of mines	Transport requirement	Personnel requirement	Time consumption [1]
Conventional mines, manual laying from vehicle on the ground 1000 mines approx. 10 kg/mine	10 tons	1 platoon (30 soldiers)	3 1/2 hours
Mine FFV 028, manual laying from vehicle on the ground 400 mines approx. 7.5 kg/mine.	3 tons	1 platoon (30 soldiers)	1 1/2 hour
Mine FFV 028 with mine-laying equipment, buried mines 400 mines approx. 7.5 kg/mine.	3 tons	4 soldiers	1 hour

1) For laying without vehicle: the times are twice as long.

Comparison between conventional mines and FFV 028 for 1000 m obstructive minefield (70% actuation
probability) in easily dug ground

the signal and, when the conditions for initiation have
been met, it emits an initiation pulse to the electronic
detonator. The uncovering charge blows off the upper
part of the fuze and any camouflage over the mine. Thus
the hollow charge jet is unobstructed when the bursting
charge detonates after a certain delay. The mine will
penetrate the belly armour of any tank and causes considerable damage by blast and fragments. As there is a
trend to stow all ammunition in a tank below the turret
ring, it is highly probable that the ammunition of the tank
will explode. The mine is insensitive to shock waves
caused by artillery fire or nuclear explosions.

The FFV 028 has a considerably higher probability of
being actuated than a conventional mine: 2·5 to 3 times
as many conventional mines as FFV 028 mines are
required to attain the same probability of a mine's being
actuated in a minefield.

Two versions of the mine are available: the reusable
FFV 028 RU with an operational life of 120 days, and the
FFV 028 SN which has a self-neutralisation mechanism
that operates after 30 days. The mine can also be
manufactured with an arming delay of up to 60 minutes.

SPECIFICATIONS

Model	FFV 028 RU	FFV 028 SN
Weight	7·5 kg	7·5 kg
Diameter	250 mm	250 mm
Height	110 mm	110 mm
Bursting charge type	RDX/TNT	RDX/TNT
Weight of bursting charge	3·5 kg	3·5 kg
Operation life of mine	180 days	30 days
Self-destruction/ neutralisation	no	yes
Booby trap	no	yes

STATUS
Production. Ordered by Swedish armed forces.

MANUFACTURER
FFV Ordnance, S-631 87 Eskilstuna, Sweden.

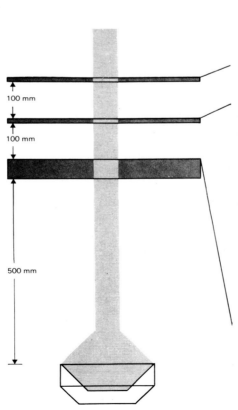

Penetration performance of FFV 028 anti-tank mine
in armour plate arrangement with mine placed half
metre below plates

Witness plate No. 1: 10 mm commercial iron. Exit
hole diameter approx. 150 mm

Witness plate No. 2: 10 mm commercial iron. Exit
hole diameter approx. 150 mm

50 mm armour plate: Exit hole diameter approx. 65 mm

FFV 028 anti-tank mine

Anti-tank Mines Model 52 and 52B

DESCRIPTION

This circular anti-tank mine has a moulded plywood case covered with waterproof fabric. A carrying handle is provided on the side of the mine. The single fuze-well is in the top of the mine and a Model 47 pressure fuze is installed. Three types of pressure piece may be used with the mine: a pentagonal spider, a small three-pronged pressure piece or a tilt-rod.

The mine operates as follows: pressure on the pres-sure piece crushes the head of the fuze, causing the shear pin to fail, the fuze plunger moves downward allowing the striker-retaining balls to escape, the striker then hits the percussion cap, which fires the detonator and the mine explodes.

There is also a Model 52B which may be fitted with either a three-pronged pressure sensor or a tilt-rod fitted to a pressure adaptor m/49. The mine operates when a pressure of 100 to 200 kg is applied to the three-pronged sensor or 15 kg to the tilt-rod. Both applications use a fuze model m/47. The Model 52B weighs 9·5 kg.

SPECIFICATIONS
Weight: 8·98 kg
Diameter: 345 mm
Height: 77 mm
Main charge type: TNT
Weight of main charge: 7·48 kg
Operating force: 250 g (with tilt-rod fuze) 14·5 kg

STATUS
In service with the Swedish Army.

Anti-tank Mines Model 41-47 and 47

DESCRIPTION

These anti-tank mines are circular and have a metal case and a carrying handle. They differ only in their size and weight. The five-armed pressure spider is sup-ported by a metallic band attached to a collar that screws into the fuze-well which is in the centre of the mine with the booster charge under the fuze. The mine functions as follows: pressure on the top of the spider forces this down until it pushes on the fuze, the shear pin of the fuze fails and the plunger moves downwards, compressing the striker spring and allowing the retain-ing balls to escape, the striker is driven downwards and hits the percussion cap, which fires the detonator, then the booster and the mine explodes.

There is also an anti-tank mine Model 47-52B. This is a Model 47 anti-tank mine body with the same pressure adaptor m/49 with optional three-pronged sensor or tilt-rod as that used on the anti-tank mine Model 52B. As with the Model 52B, the three-pronged sensor will oper-ate at a pressure of 100 to 200 kg or 15 kg applied to the tilt rod.

SPECIFICATIONS
Weight:
(Model 41-47) 8 kg
(Model 47) 9·5 kg
Diameter: 270 mm
Height with spider: 125 mm
Main charge type: TNT
Weight of main charge: 5 kg
Type of booster: pressed TNT
Operating force:
(centre of spider) 200 kg
(edge of spider) 400 kg

STATUS
In service with the Swedish Army.

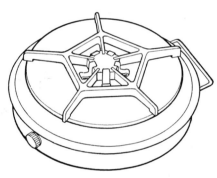

Anti-tank mine Model 41-47

SWITZERLAND

Anti-personnel Mine P59

DESCRIPTION

The P59 is circular and consists of a waterproof cover, plastic nylon body, firing mechanism and the explosive charge. When pressure is applied to the top of the mine, the striker is depressed, which breaks the glass, strikes the detonator and initiates the mine.

STATUS
In service with the Swiss Army.

SPECIFICATIONS
Diameter: 72 mm
Height: 54 mm
Main charge type: pressed TNT
Weight of main charge: 48–59 g
Operating force: 5 kg

Anti-personnel Mine Model 49

DESCRIPTION

This mine is cylindrical with a carrying handle and is normally staked to the ground. Its concrete fragmenta-tion jacket contains embedded steel shrapnel. This mine uses the Model ZDZ-49 combination fuze which can be activated by pull, tension-release or pressure. The fuze-well is in the top of the mine.

STATUS
In service with the Swiss Army.

SPECIFICATIONS
Weight: 8·618 kg
Diameter: 150 mm
Height: 224 mm
Main charge type: TNT
Weight of main charge: 0·49 kg
Operating force: 8 kg

Other Swiss Mine

This is the only other mine in Swiss Army service.

Designation	Type	Fuze designation	Type of fuze	Operating force
Model 49	anti-tank	DKZ.49	pressure	175 kg

TAIWAN

The Hsing Hua Company of Taiwan is producing a variety of anti-personnel, anti-tank and illuminating mine types under licence from the United States of America. These include the M6A1 anti-tank mine, the M2A4 anti-personnel bounding mine and the M48 trip-flare mine.

MANUFACTURER
Hsing Hua Company Ltd, PO Box 8746 Taipei, Taiwan.

TURKEY

Anti-tank Mine Model 4 Skg

DESCRIPTION
The circular anti-tank mine has a case with a zinc top and bottom, sheet metal surround, with the single fuze-well in the centre of the mine. The mine operates as follows: when sufficient pressure is applied to the spring-driven striker, the shear pin fails and is forced downwards to strike the percussion cap, igniting the detonator which sets off the mine.

SPECIFICATIONS
Weight: 6·48 kg
Diameter: 254 mm
Height: 78 mm
Main charge type: cast TNT
Weight of main charge: 4·49 kg
Booster type: TNT and Tetryl
Operating force: 75 kg

STATUS
In service with the Turkish Army.

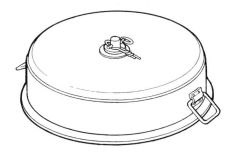

Anti-tank mine Model 4 Skg

UNION OF SOVIET SOCIALIST REPUBLICS

PMK-40 Anti-personnel Mine

DESCRIPTION
The PMK-40 anti-personnel mine is circular and has a waxed cardboard case. An earlier model had a metallic case. The detonator is inserted through a hole in the side of the mine which is then sealed by a plug. The mine operates as follows: when pressure is applied to the lid, the lever is depressed, releasing the spring-driven striker against the percussion cap, which ignites the detonator which sets off the mine.

STATUS
It is believed that this mine is no longer in the inventory of the Soviet Army, although it may still be held in reserve. In service with the Vietnamese Army.

MANUFACTURER
Soviet state arsenals.

SPECIFICATIONS
Weight: 90 g
Diameter: 70 mm
Height: 38 mm
Main charge type: TNT
Weight of main charge: 51 g
Operating force: 9–18 kg

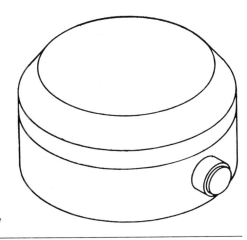

PMK-40 anti-personnel mine

PMN Anti-personnel Mine

DESCRIPTION
The PMN anti-personnel mine was developed after the end of the Second World War and has been deployed along the East German border, as well as in Viet-Nam. Another version of this mine is the PMN-6. Its case is made of duroplastic and has a side hole for the firing mechanism and primer charge, opposite which is the initiator adaptor plug. The top half of the mine has a rubber cover which covers the pressure plate, which is secured to the case by a thin metal band.

After the mine has been laid and the safety pin removed, there is a 15 to 20 minute delay in arming. This is because the firing pin moves forward under pressure of the firing pin spring until a wire in the after end of the firing pin spindle contacts a lead strip in the arming delay assembly. After the 15 to 20 minute period the wire cuts through the lead strip and releases the pin, which moves forward into a cavity of the pressure cylinder. This is held in place by a step in the cylinder and remains in this position until the mine is set off. When pressure is applied to the top of the case, the spring-loaded striker is released which in turn hits a percussion cap capsule, which sets off the main charge.

SPECIFICATIONS
Weight: 600 g
Diameter: 112 mm
Height: 56 mm
Main charge: TNT
Main charge weight: 240 g
Booster charge: Tetryl
Booster charge weight: 9 g
Operating force: 0·23 kg

STATUS
In service with members of the Warsaw Pact including East Germany. The mine has also been encountered in the Far East and Africa. In service with Viet-Nam and China.

MANUFACTURER
Soviet state arsenals.

PMN non-metallic anti-personnel mine (T J Gander)

POMZ-2 and POMZ-2M Anti-personnel Stake Mines

DESCRIPTION
The POMZ-2 anti-personnel stake mine was developed in the Second World War and consists of a wooden stake with cast iron fragmentation body with six rows of fragmentation, rather like that of a hand grenade, and a cylinder of cast TNT.

These mines are normally laid in clusters of four or more and are equipped with tripwires. When fitted with the MUV fuze, a pull on the tripwire removes the striker-retaining pin, which releases the spring-driven striker against the percussion cap and detonates the mine. If fitted with the VPF fuze, when the tripwire is pulled it removes the pullring from round the head of the striker bolt, releasing the spring-loaded striker against the per-cussion cap and detonating the mine. Late models are designated the POMZ-2M. These have a threaded fuze-well and five rows of fragmentation whereas the POMZ-2 has six.

SPECIFICATIONS

Model	POMZ-2	POMZ-2M
Weight	2 kg	1·7 kg
Diameter	64 mm	64 mm
Height (with fuze but without stake)	135 mm	111 mm
Main charge type	TNT	TNT
Weight of main charge	75 g	75 g
Operating pressure	1 kg	1 kg
Fuze	MUV or VPF	MUV or VPF

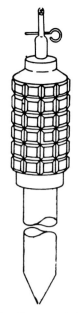

POMZ-2 anti-personnel stake mine

POMZ-2M anti-personnel stake mine (T J Gander)

STATUS
In service with members of the Warsaw Pact. A similar mine is made in China, which is lighter and requires a

greater operating force (9–18 kg). The North Koreans also make a mine similar to the POMZ-2. Also in service with Angola, Yugoslavia and Viet-Nam.

MANUFACTURER
Soviet state arsenals.

Wooden Anti-personnel Mine PMD-6, PMD-6M, PMD-7, PMD-7ts and PMD-57

DESCRIPTION
The PMD-6 wooden anti-personnel mine was developed before the Second World War and was first used operationally in the Soviet/Finnish Winter War of 1939/40. The mine consists of a wooden box with a

PMD-57 wooden anti-personnel mine

hinged lid that overlaps the sides. A deep groove is cut in the front end of the lid so that it may fit over the fuze and rest on the striker retaining pin. Some mines have a safety device which consists of a safety rod which prevents the lid from actuating the fuze prematurely. The mine operates as follows: pressure on the lid forces the winged retaining pin from the striker and this detonates the mine.

The PMD-6M is the post-war model of the PMD-6 and has the MUV-2 pull fuze.

The PMD-7 followed the PMD-6 and is a smaller mine and therefore has less explosive. The PMD-7ts has a mine body made of a single block of wood hollowed out for the charge. The PMD-57 is a post-war wooden anti-personnel mine.

SPECIFICATIONS

Model	PMD-6	PMD-7	PMD-7ts
Weight	0·4 kg	0·3 kg	0·3 kg
Length	200 mm	152 mm	152 mm
Width	89 mm	76 mm	76 mm
Height	64 mm	51 mm	51 mm
Main charge type	TNT	TNT	TNT
Weight of main charge	200 g	75 g	75 g
Operating force	1–9 kg	1–9 kg	1–9 kg
Fuze	MUV	MUV	MUV

STATUS
These mines are still held in the inventory of the Warsaw Pact. The PMD-6 is known to be manufactured in China and is in service with Viet-Nam and North Korea.

MANUFACTURER
Soviet state arsenals.

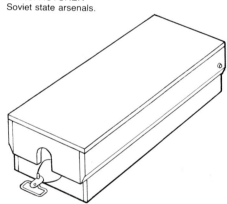

Wooden anti-personnel mine model PMD-6

MON-100 and MON-200 Direction Anti-personnel Mines

DESCRIPTION
The MON-100 and MON-200 direction anti-personnel mines are the current Soviet equivalent of the 'Claymore' fragmentation mines in service. They differ only in size and performance with the MON-200 being much larger than the MON-100. Similar in appearance, they

both use circular dished plates bearing numbers of steel fragments which are projected in a pattern once the mine is detonated by trip wire or remote control. The dish is carried on a flat steel frame that can act as a carrying handle when folded. Once in place the frame acts as a stabilising and aiming device.

STATUS
In service with Soviet armed forces.

MANUFACTURER
Soviet state arsenals.

SPECIFICATIONS

Model	MON-100	MON-200
Weight:	5 kg	25 kg
Diameter of plate:	220 mm	550 mm
Weight of explosive:	2 kg	12 kg

PFM-1 Anti-personnel Mine/Bomblet

DEVELOPMENT
The PFM-1 anti-personnel mine/bomblet was first used during the Israeli-Syrian conflict in October 1973 but has been employed in large numbers in Afghanistan ever since the Soviet forces took over the country. It has been marked as the PFM-1 (anti-personnel high explosive mine) or PMZ (area denial mine).

DESCRIPTION
The PFM-1 is a small air-delivered plastic weapon with a low metallic signature containing 35 to 40 grams of liquid explosive. It is designed to maim rather than kill and has no self-destruct or neutralising capability.

The PFM-1 has an irregularly shaped bulbous body containing the liquid explosive in its lower part which is flexible to a limited degree. In the firmer centre are the delayed arming and initiation systems. The rest of the

body is a flat section that acts as a form of stabiliser while the weapon is dropped from an aircraft. The material used for the body is very low density polythene, and may be coloured green, sand or white.

When released from fixed or aimable containers carried on fixed-wing aircraft or helicopters a safety/arming plug is released from one side of the central part of the body. As the mine falls to the ground a piston is then allowed to travel under spring pressure through a silicon-based viscous liquid. This provides an arming delay that does not arm the weapon until after it is on the ground. Thereafter any distortion of the plastic body will cause the striker to hit the detonator. This distortion may be from a single movement produced by stepping on or kicking the mine but may also be detonated by an accumulation of light pressures such as those produced by handling. The fuze employed is the VGM-6 although it is sometimes marked as the VGM-572.

The PFM-1 has been named the 'Green Parrot' by Afghan tribesmen and this name has been used in some Western references.

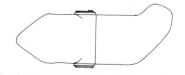

Soviet helicopter-dispensed PFM-1 anti-personnel mine

SPECIFICATIONS
Weight: 70 g
Width over wings: 112 mm
Height central body: 60 mm
Thickness of body: 15 mm
Weight of charge: 35–40 g
Type of charge: liquid explosive

STATUS
In service with Soviet forces.

MANUFACTURER
Soviet state arsenals.

OZM, OZM-3 and OZM-4 Bounding Anti-personnel Mines

DESCRIPTION
During the Second World War, the Soviets used the improvised OZM (fragmentation obstacle mines). These consisted of an artillery shell (122 or 152 mm) or a mortar (120 mm) shell buried in the ground, nose down. Under the nose was a UVK-1 propellant assembly and a flash tube running to the surface. These mines are detonated by either a remote electrical firing capability, pressure on a fuze or by pulling a wire attached to the fuze. This sets off the propellant which forces the mine out of the ground and ignites the delay element. The delay unit burns until it explodes the detonator. The mines explode 1·5 to 2·4 metres above the ground. Guidance of the mine upwards is achieved by earth piled around its body during emplacement. Although intended primarily for anti-personnel use, these mines were capable of disabling an armoured vehicle.

The cylindrical OZM-3 bounding anti-personnel mine was introduced post-war and can be set off by remote control, pull fuze, pressure fuze or a pull-tension fuze. When set off, the base of the mine blows through with the rest of the mine bounding. The height of the explosive (1·5 to 2·4 metres) is determined by a tethering wire. This mine has an effective radius of 25 metres.

No definite information on the OZM-4 mine is available.

SPECIFICATIONS (OZM-3)
Weight: 3 kg
Diameter: 75 mm
Height: 120 mm
Main charge type: TNT
Weight of main charge: 75 g

STATUS
The OZM-3 is in service with members of the Warsaw Pact.

MANUFACTURER
Soviet state arsenals (also field assembly for OZM mines).

OZM-3 bounding anti-personnel mine

KhF-1 and KhF-2 Bounding Anti-personnel Chemical Mines

DESCRIPTION
These two chemical mines were developed during the Second World War but not deployed. Both are cylindrical and differ only in their dimensions. The mine consists of a sheet metal container inside which is a sheet metal mine unit which contains the liquid contaminant. The mine is fired electrically by an observer who can be positioned up to 300 metres away. The detonator ignites the propellant and this hurls the mine out of the container and ignites the delay fuze. After a delay of 1 to 1·5 seconds, the delay fuze sets off the explosive charge, shattering the mine and spreading liquid contaminant. This covers an area of 250 to 300 square metres with an average concentration of 15 to 20 grams per square metre.

STATUS
Unknown; it is likely that they have been replaced by chemical mines of an improved type.

MANUFACTURER
Soviet state factories.

SPECIFICATIONS

Model	KhF-1	KhF-2
Weight	15 kg	15 kg
Diameter	150 mm	185 mm
Height	345 mm	280 mm
Main charge type	Toluol or Melinite	Toluol or Melinite
Weight of main charge	10 g	10 g
Propellant charge	black powder	black powder
Quantity of agent	4·5 litres	4·5 litres

TM-62 Anti-tank Mine

DESCRIPTION
In its metallic form the TM-62 anti-tank mine is a progressive development of the TM-57 but is also used as the 'family' name for a group of anti-tank mines that differ in their construction. These are as follows:
TM-62M metal casing
TM-62P plastic casing
TM-62D rectangular wooden case
TM-62B waterproof cardboard casing
These mines all appear to have a built-in firing delay of approximately two seconds to ensure that the tank is well over the mine before it detonates.

The TM-62M uses a sheet steel casing, is similar in appearance to the TM-57 and has provision for a tilt-rod detonator. The central fuze well of the TM-62 has a diameter of 125 mm and a depth of 80 mm.

STATUS
Production. In service with Warsaw Pact armed forces.

MANUFACTURER
Soviet state arsenals.

SPECIFICATIONS (TM-62M)
Weight: 9·65 kg
Diameter: 318 mm
Height: 112 mm
Main charge weight: approx 7 kg
Operating pressure: 175–600 kg

TM-62 anti-tank mine (T J Gander)

TM-57 Anti-tank Mine

DESCRIPTION
In appearance, the TM-57 metallic anti-tank mine is very similar to the TM-46 and TMN-46 anti-tank mine. The TM-57 has a larger charge and improved fuzing, and can be laid by hand or mechanically. It can be recognised as it has no well in the bottom for a booby trap (the TMN-46 has a well) and has seven ribs underneath (the TMN-46 has five ribs).

STATUS
In production. In service with members of the Warsaw Pact.

MANUFACTURER
Soviet state arsenals.

SPECIFICATIONS
Weight: 9·5 kg
Diameter: 299 mm
Height: 99 mm
Main charge type: TNT
Main charge weight: 7 kg
Operating force: 200–300 kg
Fuze model: MVZ-57
(hand laying) MVSh-57 tilt-rod

TM-57 anti-tank mine (T J Gander)

TM-46 Anti-tank Mine

DESCRIPTION
The TM-46 is metallic and can be laid either by hand or mechanically. The MVM pressure fuze is used for mechanical laying, or the MV-5 fuze for hand laying. The mine is detonated as follows (MV-5): pressure applied to the pressure plate compresses the striker spring in the fuze until the striker-retaining ball escapes into a recess in the pressure cap, releasing the spring-loaded striker which detonates the mine. In appearance the TM-46 is almost identical to the TMN-46, which however has a fuze-well in the bottom of the mine for booby-trapping.
   The Israeli No. 6 anti-tank mine is an exact copy of the TM-46. It has also been reported that the TM-46 is produced in China.

SPECIFICATIONS
Weight: 8·4 kg
Diameter: 304 mm
Height: 91 mm
Main charge type: TNT
Main charge weight: 5·3 kg
Booster charge: TNT
Booster charge weight: 198·45 g
Operating force: approx 210 kg
Fuze model: MV-5 or MVM (angled tilt-rod) MVSh-46

STATUS
In service with members of the Warsaw Pact and has been exported to the Middle and Far East and Africa.

MANUFACTURER
Soviet state arsenals.

TM-46 metallic anti-tank mine (T J Gander)

TMN-46 (Anti-lift) Anti-tank Mine

DESCRIPTION
The TMN-46 is metallic and can be laid either by hand or mechanically. The MVM pressure fuze is used for mechanical laying, or the MV-5 fuze for hand laying. There is a fuze-well in the bottom of the mine for booby-trapping. The mine is detonated as follows (MV-5 fuze): pressure forces the pressure cap down on the head of the fuze, depressing it and releasing the striker to detonate the mine. In appearance, the TMN-46 is almost identical to the TM-46, which does not have the fuze-well in the bottom of the mine for booby-trapping.

SPECIFICATIONS
Weight: 8·98 kg
Diameter: 304 mm
Height: 110 mm
Main charge type: TNT
Main charge weight: 5·95 kg
Booster charge: Tetryl
Booster charge weight: 76·54 g
Operating force: 210 kg
Fuze model: MV-5 or MVM (hand laying) MVSh-46 angled tilt-rod

STATUS
In service with members of the Warsaw Pact.

MANUFACTURER
Soviet state arsenals.

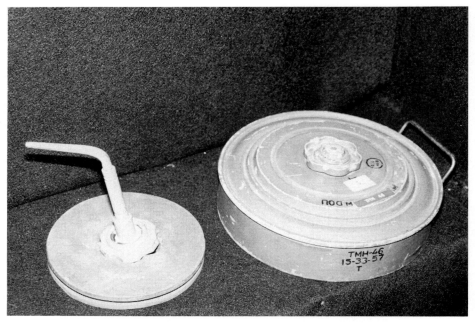

TMN-46 (anti-lift) anti-tank mine with presure/tilt plate on left (T J Gander)

TM-41 Anti-tank Mine

DESCRIPTION
The TM-41 metallic anti-tank mine consists of a cylindrical drum with a lid. In the centre of the lid is the pressure cap and under this are the fuze and fuze-well. The explosive filling plug is in the base of the mine. The mine is detonated as follows: pressure on the top of the mine crushes the corrugated sides, depressing the sliding head of the fuze until it functions and detonates the mine.

SPECIFICATIONS
Weight: 5·4 kg
Diameter: 252 mm
Height: 145 mm
Main charge type: Amatol 80/20 or flaked TNT
Weight of main charge: 3·8 kg
Booster type: picric acid
Weight of booster: 74 g
Operating pressure: 200 kg
Fuze type: MV-5 (pressure)

STATUS
The TM-41 is no longer in front-line use with the Soviet Army but is still probably held in reserve. It is still used by other countries, especially in the Far East. The Chinese manufacture a mine almost identical to the TM-41.

MANUFACTURER
Soviet state arsenals.

TM-38 Anti-tank Mine

DESCRIPTION
The TM-38 anti-tank mine was used initially during the Second World War and while no longer in Warsaw Pact armed forces service it does appear from time to time around the world. Sources for these appearances seem to be some form of Soviet Bloc long-term reserve storage. The TM-38 is contained in a thin sheet steel box that is in two horizontal halves. The bottom half contains the main TNT charge while the top, which has its sides sloped towards the centre, contains the main fuze elements. The mine operates at a pressure of around 200 kg.
   A version of this mine is known as the TM-39 and is identical in most respects to the original.

STATUS
No longer in Warsaw Pact service but some issued to Soviet-influenced states.

MANUFACTURER
Soviet state arsenals.

SPECIFICATIONS
Weight: 5·17 kg
Length: 250 mm
Width: 250 mm
Height: 80 mm
Weight of explosive: 3·6 kg
Type of explosive: TNT
Operating force: 200–700 kg

TM-38 anti-tank mine (T J Gander)

TMD-B and TMD-44 Anti-tank Mines

DESCRIPTION
The TMD-B wooden anti-tank mine entered service with the Soviet Army in 1943 and was also used in Korea. The wooden box is of simple construction with the boards being either nailed together or fastened by tongue-and-groove joints. On the top of the mine are three pressure boards. The centre board is hinged to allow the MV-5 fuze to be inserted. When armed, the pressure board is held in place by a wooden locking bar. The main charge normally consists of two waterproof paper-wrapped blocks of pressed amatol, ammonite or dynammon. The mine operates as follows: when weight is applied the top breaks down the cover at the sawn grooves and transmits pressure to the pressure block, which actuates the fuze and sets off the mine.
   The TMD-44 is similar to the TMD-B but has a centrally located plastic fuze-well cover and only two pressure boards. Like the TMD-B, it uses the MV-5 pressure fuze.

SPECIFICATIONS

Model	TMD-B	TMD-44
Weight	7·7 kg	10 kg
Length	318 mm	315 mm
Width	279 mm	280 mm
Height	140 mm	158 mm
Main charge type	varies	varies
Weight of main charge	5–6·8 kg	6 kg
Booster charge	TNT	n/a
Weight of booster charge	199 g	n/a
Operating force	200 kg	200 kg
Fuze model	MV-5 (pressure)	MV-5 (pressure)
Detonator	MD-2	MD-2

STATUS

The TMD-B is in service with members of the Warsaw Pact and is known to be used by North Korea and Viet-Nam.

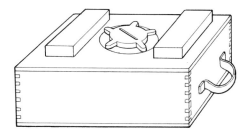

TMD-44 anti-tank wooden mine

The TMD-44 is not currently in service but is thought to be held in reserve with Soviet forces. Cuba produces a variant with a bakelite fuze-well, MV-5 fuze and MD-2 detonator.

The TMD-B is sometimes converted to anti-personnel

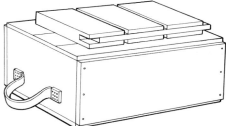

TMD-B anti-tank wooden mine

use. The Yugoslav version of the TMD-B is called the TMD-1.

MANUFACTURER

Soviet state arsenals.

TMB-1, TMB-2 and TMSB Anti-tank Mines

DESCRIPTION

These non-metallic anti-tank mines were developed during the Second World War. They have a two-piece, tar-impregnated cardboard body, with the join between the two halves being sealed with black tape and asphalt. The entire mine body is coated with a waterproof tar and in the case of the TMB-2 is brownish in colour. The fuze-well is in the top centre of the mine and is covered with a threaded glass plug and rubber washer. The mine operates as follows: the application of force on the glass pressure plug on top of the mine activates the fuze and detonates the mine. No provision is made for booby-trapping.

STATUS

Production complete. Probably held in reserve by members of the Warsaw Pact. These mines have been encountered in South-east Asia with Vietnamese armed forces.

MANUFACTURER

Soviet state arsenals.

SPECIFICATIONS

Model	TMB-2	TMSB
Weight	7 kg	8 kg
Diameter	273 mm	287 mm
Height	155 mm	168 mm
Main charge type	TNT or Amatol	Amatol
Weight of main charge	5 to 6·6 kg	5·9 kg
Booster charge	Tetryl or TNT	n/a
Weight of booster charge	113 g	n/a
Operating force	11·8 kg	11·8 kg
Fuze model	MV-5	MV-5
Detonator	MD-2	MD-2

YaM-5 and YaM-10 Anti-tank Mines

DESCRIPTION

The YaM-5 series of wooden anti-tank mines were widely used during the Second World War. The four models, which differ only in size, weight and size of the pressure board on the mine lid, are designated the YaM-5, YaM-5K, YaM-5M and the YaM-5U. They are

YaM-5 wooden anti-tank mine

easy to manufacture and when constructed without nails are difficult to detect.

The mine consists of a wooden box with a hinged lid lip which overlaps the box, recessed in the centre to fit over the protruding end of the fuze striker. A staple is placed at each end of the recess which accommodates the pin which passes through the eye of the striker retaining pin. The pull fuze is actuated by pressure. Inside the box are the two explosive charges, booster charge, fuze holder block and the fuze. The mine operates as follows: when pressure is applied to the lid it collapses forcing the overlapping edge down. The wooden peg passing through the eye of the striker-retaining pin is also pushed down. This removes the striker-retaining pin and activates the fuze. To reduce the operating pressure, the underside of the lid may have sawn grooves.

The YaM-10 is a post-war mine and is similar in construction to the YaM-5, but is larger and contains more explosive.

SPECIFICATIONS

Model	YaM-5	YaM-10
Weight	6·8–7·7 kg	11·8 kg
Length	474 mm	620 mm
Width	194 mm	216 mm
Height	93 mm	196 mm
Main charge type	TNT or amatol	TNT or amatol
Weight of main charge	3·6–5 kg	10 kg
Booster charge	TNT	TNT
Weight of booster charge	198 g	n/a
Operating force	136 kg	136 kg
Fuze model	MUV	MUV

STATUS

In service with members of the Warsaw Pact.

MANUFACTURER

Soviet state arsenals.

TMK-2 Anti-tank Mine

DESCRIPTION

The TMK-2 anti-tank mine is a relatively new post-war design and consists of a double-truncated, conical mine body with the shaped charge in the lower half. The mine is fitted with an adjustable-length, tilt-rod fuze which is fitted into a holder attached to the side of the mine at the point of its greatest diameter. The mine is normally buried in the ground with the tilt-rod fuze showing. The HEAT charge (similar to that used in recoilless rifle ammunition and anti-tank guided weapons) has sufficient power to penetrate the belly armour of a tank. The mine itself is 350 mm high, 300 mm in diameter and weighs 8·5 kg. Total weight of the assembly is 12·5 kg.

STATUS

In service with the Soviet Army.

MANUFACTURER

Soviet state arsenals.

Soviet troops receiving instruction in use of TMK-2 anti-tank mine

---

YaRM Anchored River Mine

DESCRIPTION

This is a spherical river mine which is anchored to the bed of the river. Maximum water velocity must not exceed one metre a second. The mine has a single tilt-rod fuze. A larger version with conventional horn contacts is also believed to be in service for coastal defence and the mining of rivers and lakes; the designation is thought to be YaM.

SPECIFICATIONS
Weight: 15 kg
Height: 900 mm
Diameter: 300 mm
Weight of main charge: 3 kg

STATUS

In service with Soviet forces.

MANUFACTURER

Soviet state arsenals.

PDM-1, PDM-1M, PDM-2 and PDM-6 River-bottom Mines

DESCRIPTION
The PDM anti-landing mines have been designed to disable and damage landing craft and amphibious vehicles and would be used in rivers or lakes with a maximum velocity of 1·5 metres per second. They can also be used on the sea shore in depths of water ranging from one to five metres.

PDM-1
This is similar to the PDM-1M but lacks the booster in the firing chain.

PDM-1M
This consists of a hemispherical case resting on a concrete base and is normally used in water one to two metres deep. The mine is detonated when the

VPDM-1M tilt-rod fuze is struck. Two men can lay and arm the mine in ten to twenty minutes.

PDM-2
This mine is also spherical and rests on a concrete base. It has a VPDM-2 tilt-rod fuze and is normally used in water from 2·4 to 3·8 metres deep.

PDM-6
This is similar to the PDM-1M but has four fuze-wells, one of which is in the bottom of the mine and is used as an anti-disturbance device. Each of the three fuze-wells in the top of the mine has a tilt-rod fuze which can be adjusted so that the mine will detonate immediately on contact, or adjusted so that a rod deflection will trigger the mine.

STATUS
In service with members of the Warsaw Pact.

MANUFACTURER
Soviet state arsenals.

SPECIFICATIONS

Model	PDM-1M	PDM-2	PDM-6
Weight	21 kg(1)	100 kg(2)	47·5 kg(4)
Height	1 m	1·4 m(3)	2·5 m(5)
Diameter	—	270 mm	500 mm
Base diameter	—	—	1 m
Main charge type	TNT	TNT or ammonite	TNT or PETN
Weight of main charge	10 kg	15 kg	28 kg
Operating force	18–26 kg	40–50 kg	n/a

(1) Without concrete base which weighs 24–29 kg
(2) On low stand, 135 kg on high stand
(3) Range from 1·1–2·7 m depending on type of stand
(4) With base plate
(5) Mine only, between 550–1050 mm with fuze

Limpet Mines

DESCRIPTION
Plastic Limpet Mine
This limpet mine is in moulded plastic and uses a mechanical time delay (metal fatigue) which can be set from 5 minutes to 8·32 hours by the use of six delay tabs. The mine has two fuze-wells and an arming device 180 degrees from the wells. The mine has two horse-shoe magnets on either end which provide a standoff of 160 mm from the ship. A cylindrical cavity charge is mounted on a bridge supported by the two magnets.

Turtle Metallic Limpet Mine
This is hemispherical and its flat bottom is magnetised with two rows of circular magnets which are mounted nearly flush with the surface. The mine has three fuzes, two main detonator fuzes and one anti-disturbance fuze. The two main fuzes are of the mechanical time delay type and can be set at five different time delays which range from 15 minutes to 12 hours. When the

safety pin is removed, the spring tension begins to exert a downward pull on a metal cutting surface and slowly cuts through a soft wire. When this wire is severed the firing pin is released and strikes the detonator cap. The time delay is dependent on the softness and thickness of the wire.

BPM-2 Limpet Mine
This mine is hemispherical and has an aluminium casing. It is attached to the ship's hull by four arcs of 11 small horseshoe magnets on its flat side. The mine is activated by two metal-fatigue time delay fuzes like those on the plastic limpet mine. There is an anti-disturbance fuze in the centre of the flat side of the mine.

STATUS
In service with members of the Warsaw Pact.

MANUFACTURER
Soviet state arsenals.

Plastic limpet mine

SPECIFICATIONS

Model	Plastic	Turtle	BPM-2
Weight	2·7 kg	6·8 kg	6·6 kg
Length/diameter	270 mm	300 mm	255 mm (305 mm overall)
Width/height	115 mm	180 mm	115 mm
Main charge weight	0·95 kg	3 kg	3 kg
Main charge type	Tritanol	TNT	Tritanol

Other Soviet Mines

Designation	
AKS	Second World War anti-clearance mine with 6·8 kg of TNT explosive and tilt-rod fuze.
APM	Under-ice mine in current use.
DM	Second World War vibration road mine

Designation	
MZD	with 1·2 kg of TNT explosive, used against soft-skinned vehicles. First used in the Second World War; delayed action mines of various types with between 400 grams and 10 kg of explosive. Various types of fuzes were used including electric, electro-chemical, vibration, electric delay or

Designation	
	combinations of these fuzes. They were often left behind when retreating and detonated from some distance. Current models include the MZD-5m and MZD-60.
PMP-71	A plastic anti-personnel mine, diameter 170–200 mm, height 115 mm and a 100 g TNT charge.

Soviet Training Mines

DESCRIPTION
The Soviet Union has a wide range of training mines in service. Some are of the inert type and simply give personnel training in laying a minefield, while others are fitted with a fuze which sets off a smoke charge.

A more specialised training mine is the UITM-60 training anti-tank mine. In appearance, this resembles the TM-46 mine and can be laid by hand or mechanically. The mine functions as follows: when the tank passes over the mine the lid is depressed until the bottom of the

lid comes into contact with the top of the fuze initiating the firing chain; after a delay of three to four seconds a signal cartridge is expelled, tossing two green and two red flares 10 to 40 metres into the air. This mine is reusable and can also be operated electrically with an electric blasting cap.

STATUS
In service with members of the Warsaw Pact.

MANUFACTURER
Soviet state arsenals.

SPECIFICATIONS
UITM-60
Weight: 8·7 kg
Diameter: 316 mm
Height: 125 mm
Operating force: 200–600 kg

UNITED KINGDOM

Scatterable Mine System (SMS)

In order to provide the armed forces with a viable mine system for the future, the United Kingdom at one point approached the USA with a view to taking out a licence to produce the FASCAM mine dispensing system. The costs involved were regarded as too high so it was decided to sponsor the development of a United Kingdom-based system to be known as the Scatterable Mine System (SMS). During 1982 two nine-month fixed price project definition contracts were issued, one to a consortium of Marconi Space and Defence Systems and the Royal Ordnance Factories, and the other to THORN EMI and Hunting Engineering. It is expected that the resultant system will be in service during the late 1980s.

SMS will be used in four modes: by hand, by a dispenser slung under a helicopter, by a 155 mm artillery cargo round (either the US M483A1 or a new all-British design), or a short-range scattering device along the lines of the THORN EMI Ranger.

At one point in the late development of the Ranger system it was proposed that a variant could be produced to project the US FASCAM BLU 91B scatter mine. Known as the Ranger Anti-Tank System (RATS) this was developed past the concept stage and may be used as part of the new SMS. The term RATS 2 has been applied to this part of the SMS programme.

The Technovar DAT scatter mine-dispensing system has been used in a concept study as part of the SMS programme. Hunting has developed a helicopter-borne scatter system in its Helicopter Mine Dispenser (HMD) which was originally designed for use with the US FASCAM BLU 91B scatter mine and incorporating a 24-mine module. The HMD experience may well be incorporated into SMS.

THORN EMI Ranger Anti-personnel Mine System

DESCRIPTION

The THORN EMI Ranger anti-personnel mine system has been developed by the Royal Armament Research and Development Establishment at Fort Halstead and THORN EMI Electronics Limited.

It has a variety of applications including covering rows of anti-tank mines as they are being laid, covering an existing anti-tank minefield by firing anti-personnel mines from outside the field, delaying the repair of demolitions, rapid infesting of woods, roadsides and tracks to impede and canalise enemy movement, infesting the far bank of a canal or river to impede enemy movement.

The system consists of 72 disposable tubes loaded in a discharger which can be mounted on any medium or heavy vehicle. The British Army use the FV432 armoured personnel carrier with the Ranger system mounted on the top of the hull and the vehicle towing the Bar minelaying system. Each tube contains 18 anti-personnel mines which are ejected by means of a cartridge. The firing is controlled manually and each tube can be fired independently. The mines disperse in flight and form a random pattern on the ground. This pattern can be varied by traversing, elevating and by selecting the number of tubes to be fired. The launcher can travel safely fully loaded, as the mines are not armed until 20 seconds after firing. Palletised resupply mines, already in tubes, enable the complete system of 1296 mines to be reloaded in under six minutes. The system comprises four main units, dischargers, filled magazine, firing control unit and the mine.

Discharger

The discharger is mounted on pivots and is adjustable in both elevation and azimuth. An adaptation frame can be designed and produced to enable the discharger to be installed on most vehicles. A power supply of 24 volts dc is required. The magazines are locked into position in the dischargers which incorporate a safety system making all mines inoperative until ready to be fired. This is the first of three safety devices to be operated before the mine is fuzed for operation.

Magazine

The magazine consists of an aluminium breech assembly attached to a disposable tube of paper/polythene/paper layered material. The cartridge fits into the breech assembly and makes contact with the electrical firing circuit when the magazine is loaded into the discharger. The 18 mines are held firmly in the tube by an end cap which prevents accidental ejection and also provides an environmental seal. The tubes are mounted in sets of four, with a suitable carrying handle, to enable rapid loading of the discharger. The electrically initiated cartridge propels the mines at distances of up to 100 metres, depending on group and wind conditions.

Firing control unit

The firing control unit produces firing impulses and is controlled by a hand-held unit on a wander-lead which incorporates a push-button. As one cartridge is fired, the unit sets the system so that the next cartridge is fired when the push button is pressed again. This sequence continues until all 72 tubes have been discharged.

The mine

The mine is cylindrical and measures 32 mm deep and 62 mm in diameter. It is moulded from polycarbonate plastic and is assembled on either side of a central bulkhead and includes a safety system, arming system and a main charge. The charge consists of approximately 10 g of RDX/Wax encased in a metal container with a CE pellet to ensure reliable take-over from the detonator. The mine is pressure actuated and has been designed to immobilise personnel without inflicting a fatal wound.

Three safety devices are incorporated into the mine to ensure that the mine does not arm until 20 seconds

THORN EMI Ranger anti-personnel mine system installed on FV432 armoured personnel carrier (T J Gander)

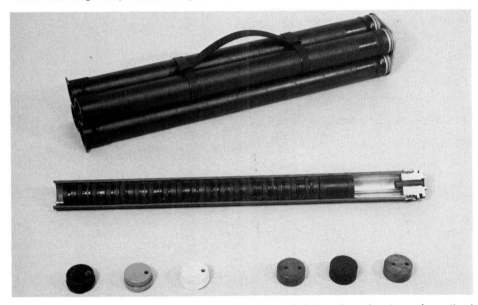

Top shows four-barrel magazine with cross-sectioned barrel beneath; bottom shows three types of operational mine on left with training mines (peat) on right

Inert Ranger practice mines, from left: underside primed and ready to fire; centre, top side; right after firing and cocked for use

Infantry Ranger launcher for full four-tube magazine with adaptor for 51 mm mortar baseplate at bottom; this version did not prove suitable for service use (T J Gander)

British Army Combat Support Boat being used to fire THORN EMI Ranger mines onto a river bank

after leaving the discharger. As the time of flight is less than five seconds, the mine can be on the ground, having come to rest, for some 15 seconds before automatic arming occurs. The mine is camouflaged green but can be provided in alternative colours. It is fully waterproof.

For training and drill purposes, a low-cost compressed peat drill mine can be supplied for use with a special drill magazine. This obviates the time-consuming clearance of the training area.

Infantry Ranger
In an attempt to provide a Ranger projector suitable for infantry use, a device capable of firing a normal Ranger magazine one tube at a time was produced for use with the base-plate of the new 51 mm lightweight mortar or

the older 2-inch mortar. The tubes were fired by percussion via an adaptor in the mortar base. This system was produced in prototype form but proved too heavy for infantry use and turning the magazines into line with the adaptor proved to be too difficult a task operationally. A new mini-discharger is now being developed which will use a 51 mm lightweight mortar base and firing mechanism to fire specially-produced individual tubes of 18 mines a distance of 60 metres. These tubes would be supplied separately to normal magazines. A soldier could fire and load the tubes from the prone position. Trials of this mini-discharger have taken place at the School of Infantry, Warminster and, if required, production could commence in about one year.

STATUS
In production. In service with the British Army.

MANUFACTURER
THORN EMI Electronics Limited, 135 Blyth Road, Hayes, Middlesex UB3 1BP, England.

SPECIFICATIONS
Payload: 1296 mines
Weight:
(of discharger fully loaded) 630 kg
(of operational magazine loaded) 14 kg
Azimuth: adjustable through 180°
Elevation: adjustable over +5° to +35°
Loading time: (with 2 men) under 6 minutes
Range: 100 m
Firing rate: 1 tube of 18 mines per second (max)
Height: (above vehicle platform) 1·3 m
Width: 2·2 m
Length: 1·5 m

Hunting Engineering IMP Lightweight Anti-tank Mine

Development of the Hunting Engineering IMP lightweight anti-tank mine has now been discontinued, although much of the technology involved will be updated and used in a new product. Details of the IMP can be found in *Jane's Military Vehicles and Ground Support Equipment 1983*, page 198.

PADMINE Anti-personnel Mine

DEVELOPMENT
The anti-personnel weapon now known as PADMINE was developed originally for local defensive use at fixed installations in Northern Ireland and was at one time known as the Position Attack Defence System or PADS; the name was changed to prevent confusion with the PADS vehicle navigation system. In time PADMINE will replace the American M18A1 in British Army service as it is a far more accurate weapon and less indiscriminate in its scattering of fragments.

DESCRIPTION
The PADMINE is carried in a small satchel with all associated accessories except the sight assembly which is carried separately. In use the mine is mounted on folding scissor legs with the front, which is marked in tactile lettering, towards the expected enemy approach. The sight assembly is then mounted on the mine using two lugs on top of the body and the accurate alignment is made using an optical prism which can rotate through 180 degrees to suit local conditions (ie the layer can either look downwards through the sight or rotate the prism to either side for use in the prone position). The prism of the sight is illuminated by a Trilux device for night use and the expense of this is such that the sight assembly is a separate device. If the device is not available a sight formed from the centre of the cable bobbin supplied with each mine can be used instead. Sighting can be fairly precise as the main arc of the 650 steel ball projectiles is limited to 800 mils with a less effective secondary arc reaching out to 1618 mils. The maximum lethal range is 160 metres.

PADMINE can be detonated by a conventional trip-wire or remotely using a Shrike exploder which is already in service for demolition purposes. Each Shrike can be used for up to four PADMINES. The detonator on the mine is on top of the mine body.

SPECIFICATIONS
Weight: 1·26 kg
Height: 120 mm
Width: 205 mm
Thickness at widest point: 55 mm
Range: up to 160 m
Number of steel projectiles: 650

STATUS
Production. Entering service with the British Army.

MANUFACTURER
Royal Ordnance Factories.
Enquiries to Ministry of Defence, ROF Marketing, St Christopher House, Southwark Street, London SE1 0TD, England.

PADMINE anti-personnel mine with mock-up of sight assembly fitted (T J Gander)

British Anti-personnel Mines

The British No. 5, No. 6, No. 7 and Doris anti-personnel mines are no longer produced or in British service, however some may still be used by other countries. For details of these anti-personnel mines refer to *Jane's Military Vehicles and Ground Support Equipment 1983*, pages 198 and 199.

Bar Mine System and FWAM

DESCRIPTION

The Bar mine system has been developed by the Royal Armament Research and Development Establishment at Fort Halstead, Kent, as the replacement for the Mark 7 anti-tank mine. The system consists of two major components, the mine and the minelayer.

The Bar mine is plastic with only a few metal components in the fuze and is difficult to detect using current electro-magnetic mine detectors. The mine is stored complete with its fuze, which saves time and manpower in fitting the fuze before the mine can be laid.

The long shape of the Bar mine doubles the chance of the mine's being actuated by a tank and dramatically reduces the number of mines required to lay a minefield. Trials have confirmed that the Bar mine is completely effective against any tank track when the tank has a part of the mine inboard of the tracks. The explosive effect is sufficient to break the tracks and damage the belly armour of the tank. The fuzes at present employed with the Bar mine are the single and double impulse pressure types that are sometimes susceptible to mine clearance techniques. To counter this, Marconi Space and Defence Systems has developed a series of fuze options to convert the Bar mine into the Full Width Attack Mine (FWAM). The first of these options is a single or double impulse fuze. There is also a mechanical fuze (L127) which is armed as the mine travels down the Bar minelayer. Once armed a spring-operated mast sensor is allowed to rise. The mast sensor is actuated by the belly of a tank travelling over the fuze, but the fuze delays detonation until under the most vulnerable part of the tank's armour. The fuze has a safety and arming unit which will not arm the fuze until a time delay has passed. Once the delay has passed the detonator is mechanically swung across in line with the firing train. To complete the FWAM fuzes there is an electronic fuze (L128) which is stimulated by a particular radiation signature produced by an approaching tank from within a defined distance. The thin film electronics of this fuze are powered by a lithium copper oxide battery with a laid life of six months and a shelf life of five years. The circuits have safety and arming units which incorporate an arming delay. Both the mechanical and the electronic FWAM fuzes are armed by pulling on wire lanyards which release switch arms to operate the fuze mechanisms and also provide clear indications of whether the mine is 'safe' or 'armed'. All three FWAM fuzes are in pro-duction and are in service with the British Army. To use the new fuzes a small modification has to be made to the standard Bar minelayer. It is intended that all three fuzes will be used in a 'mix' in minefields.

The Bar mine has been designed for use with the Bar minelayer but can also be laid by hand; a man-portable pack of four mines is available. The Bar mine is normally packed in pallets of 72 mines which can be handled by a fork lift truck such as the Eager Beaver. The pack of 72 mines weighs 855 kg of which 88 per cent is Bar mines and the remainder packing. Practice and drill versions of the Bar mine are also available.

The Bar minelayer is simple in design and has no complicated hydraulic or electrical components. The crew place the Bar mines on to the loading chute and they are automatically armed as they pass through the layer into the ground. The laying depth and mine spacing are adjustable, and wearing parts such as the plough point can be quickly and easily replaced. A chain towed behind the minelayer levels the earth again.

To provide additional stability for fast towing and very rough terrain, cage wheels can be attached either side of the layer. The British Army uses the FV432 APC to tow the Bar minelayer, but the equipment can also be towed by other vehicles such as the M113, Stalwart, 4-ton truck or the LWB Land-Rover. The tow bar and mine conveyor belt can be adjusted for height.

The Bar minelayer can lay between 600 and 700 mines an hour with one towing vehicle and a three-man crew. To maintain this high rate of laying over long periods additional crew and vehicles are required.

The main advantages of the Bar mine system can be summarised as follows: high rate of laying mines, simplicity of operation, reduced manpower requirements, reduced number of mines to cover a given area and simplified storage and logistics.

SPECIFICATIONS

Bar Mine
Weight: 11 kg
Length: 1·2 m
Width: 108 mm
Height: 81 mm
Weight of explosive: 8·4 kg

Bar Mine Pack
Weight: 855 kg
Length: 1·22 m
Width: 1·02 m
Height: 0·84 m

Mast sensor for Full Width Attack Mine (FWAM)

Bar Minelayer
Weight: 1240 kg
Length: 4·19 m
Width: (with wheel cages) 1·6 m
Height: 1·27 m

STATUS

In production. In service with the British Army, Danish Army (Pansermine M/75) and Egypt.

MANUFACTURER

Royal Ordnance Factories.

Enquiries to Ministry of Defence, ROF Marketing, St Christopher House, Southwark Street, London SE1 0TD, England.

2½-tonne truck towing Bar minelayer raised for travelling (T J Gander)

Laird Centaur multi-purpose military vehicle towing Bar minelayer

FV432 towing Bar minelayer being loaded with cardboard exercise mines (Ministry of Defence)

FV432 fitted with THORN EMI Ranger anti-personnel mine system and towing Bar minelayer (T J Gander)

Anti-tank Mine Mark 7

DESCRIPTION
The Mark 7 anti-tank mine was the replacement for the Mark 5 anti-tank mine and has been partially replaced in the British Army by the Bar mine.

The Mark 7 is circular with a carrying handle on the side of the mine. The waterproof pressure plate, which also contains the fuze-well cover, is in the centre of the top of the mine. There is a second anti-lifting fuze-well in the base of the mine.

The mine operates as follows: when sufficient pressure is applied to the top of the mine, the pressure plate is forced down on to the top of the pressure fuze, and the striker, which is held by a Belleville spring, is forced down until the spring returns, driving the striker against the percussion cap, firing the detonator, and the mine explodes. A detonator system using a frangible carbon tilt-rod is also in use.

SPECIFICATIONS
Weight: 13·6 kg
Diameter: 325 mm
Height: 130 mm
Main charge type: TNT
Weight of main charge: 8·89 kg
Booster type: Tetryl
Weight of booster: 850 g
Operating force: 275 kg

STATUS
Production complete. In service with the British Army and many other armed forces.

MANUFACTURER
Royal Ordnance Factories.

Mark 7 anti-tank mine with tilt-rod detonator (T J Gander)

Mine, Anti-tank, Non-metallic

DEVELOPMENT
The Mine, Anti-tank, Non-metallic was first placed in production in 1961 and since then has been used mainly for training and as a reserve item. It is not used as a front line anti-tank mine. The current designation is Mine, Anti-tank, L3A1 (Non-metallic).

DESCRIPTION
This anti-tank mine is constructed using two polythene mouldings joined together and filled with TNT. The pressure fuze on the top is armed by rotating a metal key through 180 degrees which is then removed; the key can be replaced and turned to render the mine safe if required. The mine is covered with a thin black rubber coating and a handle is provided for carrying.

These mines are normally carried on a pallet in packs of 48. When removed from the pallet they are carried in twos in a clip. The pressure fuze used is the L39.

STATUS
Reserve use with the British Army.

SPECIFICATIONS
Weight: 7·7 kg
Diameter: 266 mm
Height: 145 mm
Weight of explosive: 6 kg
Type of explosive: TNT
Operating pressure: 120–200 kg

Mine, Anti-tank, Non-metallic (T J Gander)

Other British Anti-tank Mine

DESCRIPTION
The Mark 5 heavy charge anti-tank mine is no longer in British Army service but may be encountered with some other nations such as India and Pakistan. For details of this mine refer to *Jane's Military Vehicles and Ground Support Equipment 1983*, page 200.

Other Mines

The following mines are no longer in service with the British Army but may still be in service in other countries.

Designation	Type	Weight	Diameter	Height	Main charge type	Main charge weight	Fuze type	Operating force
Mk.1	anti-tank	3·175 kg	190 mm	72 mm	baratol	1·814 kg	pressure	159 kg
Ointment box	anti-personnel	0·227 kg	n/a	n/a	TNT	85 g	pressure	13·6 kg
Mk.2 Bounding	anti-personnel	4·536 kg	89 mm	201 mm	amatol	0·454 kg	mechanical (tripwire)	1·814 kg

Miltra Training Mine Replicas

DESCRIPTION
In addition to their range of military models Miltra also produce a range of full-size replicas of Soviet mines in metal or plastic to exact weights. The mines have removeable fuzes and mechanisms to allow full discovery and disarming drills and procedures to be followed. At present the range includes the PMN anti-personnel mine, the OZM bounding anti-personnel mine and the TM-46 anti-tank mine but other types can be produced to order.

STATUS
Production. Under evaluation by the British Army and overseas governments.

MANUFACTURER
Miltra Division of Z. M. Iwaszko Limited, 357 Uxbridge Road, Rickmansworth, Hertfordshire WD3 2DT, England.

Miltra training mine replicas; from left PMN, OZM, TM-46

UNITED STATES OF AMERICA

Area Denial Artillery Munition (ADAM)

DESCRIPTION

The Area Denial Artillery Munition (ADAM) consists of a 155 mm projectile which is fired from an M109 or M109A1 self-propelled howitzer; it is a member of the Family of Scatterable Mines (FASCAM). There are two types of projectile: the M692 projectile carries 36 mines with a long (more than a day) self-destruct time and the M731 projectile carries 36 mines which have a factory-set short (less than a day) self-destruct time.

After ground impact the M74 wedge shaped mines expel seven tripwires and the detonator unit is armed so that if any disturbance is detected the mine will explode. It also detonates if the battery voltage drops to a level which impairs the mine's function or at the set self-destruct time. On detonation the wedge body breaks up and the fragmentation sphere unit, containing 21·25 g of Composition A5 explosive, is propelled upwards to a predetermined height by a liquid propellant surrounding the unit and explodes. A spherical fragmentation pattern is produced with hundreds of fragments moving at velocities in the order of 900 metres a second.

The projectile is of the separate-loading type and is handled in the same way as a conventional artillery projectile. It has an M557 fuze which is set to function at a pre-determined time in flight. This initiates the explosive charge which projects the mines from the rear of the projectile. Centrifugal force dispenses the mines radially from the projectile.

These mine projectiles can be fixed to a maximum range of 17 740 metres and would normally be used in conjunction with the RAAMS mines to provide a minefield with both anti-tank and anti-personnel mines.

STATUS

In production. In service with the US Army.

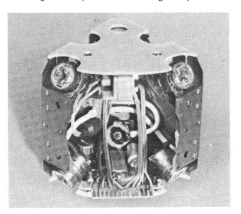

ADAM mine

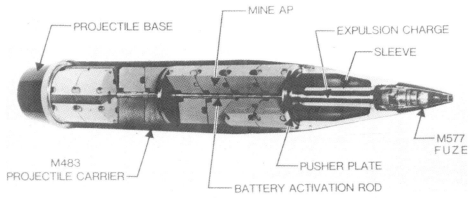

Projectile, 155 mm, HE, M692/M731 ADAM (Area Denial Artillery Munition) (US Army)

Anti-personnel Mine M18A1

DESCRIPTION

The M18A1, or Claymore as it is usually known, is a directional, fixed fragmentation mine which is used for defensive and ambush purposes. The original model was designated the M18 and was slightly lighter than the current model.

The M18A1 consists of a curved rectangular moulded case of fibreglass-filled polystyrene plastic. In the front part are 700 steel spheres embedded in a plastic matrix, with C-4 plastic explosive behind the spheres. The fragmentation face is convex horizontally to direct the fragments and concave vertically to control the vertical dispersion of the fragments. A moulded peepsight is provided on the top of the mine for sighting. The two detonator wells are in the top of the mine. The mine is mounted on two pairs of scissors type folding legs.

The mine is normally fired from a distance by an M57 firing device. This is a hand-held pulse generator which by a single actuation of the handle produces a double electrical pulse. The M57 is attached to 30 metres of wire which is connected to an M4 blasting cap in the mine. The Claymore can also be activated by a pull wire or a tripwire.

When detonated, a fan-shaped sheaf pattern of spherical steel fragments is projected in a 60 degree horizontal arc covering a casualty area of 50 metres to a height of one metre. There is a danger area of 16 metres to the rear of the mine.

The M7 bandolier contains the mine, firing device, M40 test set and electric blasting cap assembly M4.

There is a practice version of the M18A1 designated the M68.

The M18A1 is widely license-produced, for example in South Korea (qv). The design has also been copied direct as with the South African Shrapnel Mine No. 2 (qv).

SPECIFICATIONS
Weight: 1·58 kg
Length: 216 mm
Width: 35 mm
Height: 83 mm
Main charge type: Composition C-4
Weight of main charge: 682 g
Operating temperature range: −40 to +51·5°C

STATUS
In service with the US Army.

M18A1 anti-personnel mine in position (US Army)

Anti-personnel Mine M26

DESCRIPTION

The M26 is a small integrally fuzed anti-personnel bounding mine. The main body is made of die-cast aluminium and is cylindrical, tapering towards the bottom where there are four vertical ribs on the outside of the mine body. Inside the body is the fragmentation ball assembly which consists of a steel ball containing an explosive charge and a delay and booster unit recessed within the charge. At the base of the ball is the propelling charge.

Actuation may be either by directly applying a force to the mine top or by a pull on one or more of four 6·1-metre long tripwires that may be attached to the mine top via a trip lever. The propelling charge then ejects the fragmenting steel ball assembly to a height of about 2 metres where the delay and booster charge detonates the main charge to shatter the steel ball.

The training version of this mine is the M35 which is reloadable and uses a blank ·32 pistol cartridge to fire a capsule of blue dye.

STATUS
In service with the US Army.

SPECIFICATIONS
Weight: 1 kg
Diameter: 79 mm
Height: 145 mm
Main charge type: Composition B
Weight of main charge: 170 g
Booster charge type: Tetryl
Weight of booster charge: 1·5 g
Operating temperature range: −40 to +51·5°C
Operating force: 6·4–12·7 kg

Anti-personnel Bounding Mines, M16, M16A1 and M16A2

DESCRIPTION

The anti-personnel bounding mine M16A1 (an earlier model was the M16) consists of a sheet steel case which contains the projectile and the propelling charge, and an M605 combination fuze which is screwed into the top of the mine and extends through the centre of the projectile to the bottom of the case where the propelling charge is located.

The mine operates as follows: pressure applied to one of the three prongs or the fuze compresses the pressure spring and forces the trigger downwards, forcing the release pin outwards and the firing pin is released. This initiates the firing chain and the cast-iron projectile is propelled into the air. When this reaches a height of one metre the main charge detonates and metal fragments are scattered in all directions. The mine can also be fitted with a tripwire and in this case operates as follows: when a pull is applied to the trip-wire the release pin ring of the fuze pulls the release pin outwards to a position where the firing pin is released and the mine then operates as above. There is an inert training version of this mine. The M16A2 is an advanced version of the M16 series and incorporates only one booster detonator and delay instead of two of each. This allows for a greater explosive charge.

An inert version of the M16 series is known as the M16A1, inert with fuze, M605 inert.

SPECIFICATIONS

Model	M16	M16A1	M16A2
Weight	3·74 kg	3·74 kg	2·83 kg
Height	199 mm	199 mm	199 mm
Diameter	103 mm	103 mm	103 mm
Main charge type	TNT	TNT	TNT
Weight of main charge	521 g	513 g	590 g
Type of booster	Tetryl	Tetryl	Composition A5
Weight of booster	54 g	33 g	11 g
Weight of propelling charge	70 g	70 g	70 g
Type of propelling charge	black powder	black powder	black powder
Operating force			
(pressure)	3·6–20 kg	3·6–20 kg	3·6–20 kg
(tripwire)	1·6–3·8 kg	1·6–3·8 kg	1·6–3·8 kg
Operating temperature range	−40 to +51·5°C	−40 to +51·5°C	−40 to +51·5°C

STATUS
In service with the US Army and other countries.

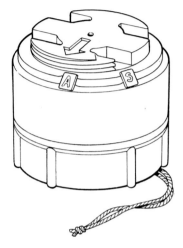

Anti-personnel bounding mine M16A1

Anti-personnel Mine M14

DESCRIPTION

This small circular blast type anti-personnel mine consists of an all plastic body with an integral plastic fuze which has a steel firing pin, and a main charge. The plug-type plastic detonator holder with the M46 detonator is packaged separately and is installed in the base of the mine when required.

The mine operates as follows: pressure applied to the top of the mine depresses the pressure plate and this depresses the lock key, forcing the lock ring to slide through notches in the inner ring of the spider and depress the Belleville spring. This snaps into reverse and drives the firing pin into the detonator and this explodes the main charge.

The pressure plate on the top of the mine has a yellow indicating arrow which points to the letter S for safe or A for armed. Slots are provided in the pressure plate for the insertion of a steel, U-shaped safety clip which is removed by pulling the pull cord.

There is also a training version called the Mine, Anti-Personnel Practice: NM, M17, which emits a smoke charge when activated.

SPECIFICATIONS
Weight: 99 g
Diameter: 56 mm
Height: 40 mm
Main charge type: Tetryl
Weight of main charge: 28·4 g
Operating force: 9–16 kg
Operating temperature range: −40 to +51·5°C

STATUS
In service with the US Army and the Danish Army. (Fodfolksmine M/56).

Anti-personnel mine M14

Anti-personnel Mine M3

DESCRIPTION
The M3 is a fragmentation type mine and consists of a rectangular case of cast iron fitted with an M7A1 combination fuze. The mine can be buried but is more effective when placed 0·5 metre above the ground. The M3 has three threaded fuze-wells, one in either side and one in the top. The M7A1 fuze consists of a three-pronged firing mechanism and a primed base coupled to which a non-electric blasting cap is crimped.

The mine functions as follows: pressure applied to one of the three prongs on the fuze, or a pull on the release pin, will release the firing pin. This strikes the primer and explodes the blasting cap which in turn explodes the bursting charge and scatters fragments in all directions.

An inert training version of this mine is available.

SPECIFICATIONS
Weight: 4·68 kg
Height:
(with fuze) 220 mm
(without fuze) 136 mm
Width: 89 mm
Main charge type: TNT (flaked)
Weight of main charge: 408 g
Operating force:
(on prongs) 3·6–9 kg
(pull) 1·36–4·56 kg
Operating temperature range: −40 to +51·5°C

STATUS
In service with the US Army. Classified obsolete.

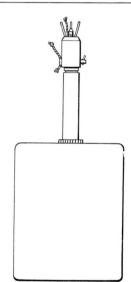

Anti-personnel mine M3 and fuze mine combination M7A1

Anti-personnel Bounding Mine M2A4

DESCRIPTION
The anti-personnel bounding mine M2A4 (earlier models were designated the M2, M2A1 and M2A3) consists of a baseplate on which is mounted the M16A1 combination fuze and a projector tube which contains the projectile and a propelling charge. The projectile is a modified 60 mm mortar bomb.

The mine is normally buried in the ground with the fuze prongs extending above the ground by 6 to 19 mm. No provision is made in the design of the mine for the installation of an anti-lifting device.

The mine is operated as follows: pressure on one or more of the three prongs or a pull on the tripwire attached to the release pin ring of the fuze releases the firing pin which strikes the percussion cap and initiates the firing chain. The propelling charge projects the shell from the mine and at a height of two to three metres it explodes.

An inert version of this mine is available for training and a practice version is designated the mine, anti-personnel practice M8 with fuze combination, practice M10 or M10A1. The M8 has the mortar bomb replaced by a cardboard tube that contains a spotting charge assembly, which gives off a bang. The M8A1 uses smoke pellets.

SPECIFICATIONS
Weight: 2·948 kg
Diameter: 104 mm
Height: (including fuze) 244 mm
Main charge type: TNT
Weight of main charge: 154 g
Booster type: Tetryl
Weight of booster charge: 16 g
Operating force:
(pressure) 3·6–9 kg
(pull) 1·36–4·5 kg
Operating temperature range: −40 to +51·5°C

STATUS
In service with the US Army and Danish Army (Fodfolksmine M/51).

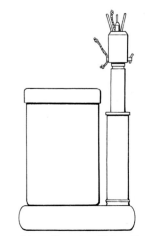

Anti-personnel bounding mine M2A4 with fuze mine combination M6A1

Extended Range Anti-armor Munition (ERAM)

DESCRIPTION
The Extended Range Anti-armor Munition (ERAM) is a member of the United States Air Force Wide Area Anti-armor Munitions (WAAM) programme. The ERAM submunition is engineered to fit into the USAF Tactical Munitions Dispenser (TMD) SUU-65/B. The TMD-Avco ERAM combination is designated CBU-92/B.

The CBU-92/B is capable of being delivered over a wide range of aircraft altitudes and speeds from 61 metres and 200 knots. Once released, the TMD splits open over the target area and ejects the ERAM sub-munitions. These deploy individual parachutes that are designed to disperse them randomly over a wide area with a ground impact velocity of 50 metres per second. Once on the ground three probes are extended and the two Avco Skeet self forging fragment (SFF) warheads armed. When a target is detected, classified and tracked by the probes, an on-board data processor calculates its future position and the upper launcher section is rotated to aim the first warhead. This is then launched at about 45 degrees on a target intercept trajectory. The seeker on the warhead then detects the target and fires the SFF to impact on the vehicle top. The ERAM launcher meanwhile rotates 180 degrees and prepares to launch the second Skeet at any following armoured vehicle.

STATUS
Development suspended.

MANUFACTURER
Avco Systems Division, 201 Lowell St, Wilmington, Maryland 01887, USA.

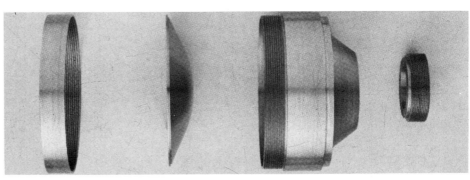

Components of Skeet sub-munition for Extended Range Anti-armor Munition

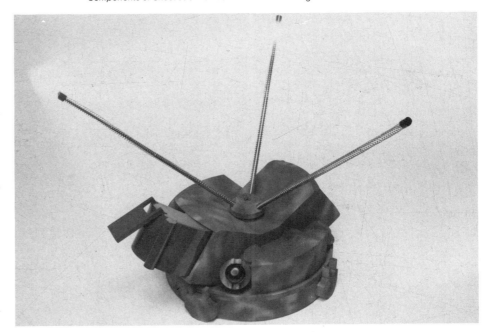

Avco Systems Division Extended Range Anti-armor Munition in deployed configuration

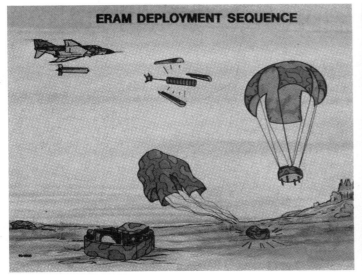

ERAM DEPLOYMENT SEQUENCE

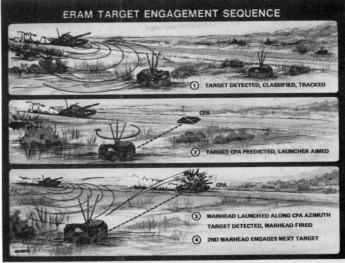

ERAM TARGET ENGAGEMENT SEQUENCE

GATOR Anti-armor System

DESCRIPTION
The GATOR anti-armor system was developed over several years. It has been designed for laying from high-speed aircraft of the US Air Force, US Navy and US Marine Corps for interdiction of second echelon enemy forces in assembly areas and on the march. The mines developed for the system are the Honeywell BLU-91/B anti-tank mine and the Aerojet BLU 92/B anti-personnel mine. They have three selectable self-destruct times which can be set at the dispenser. The minimum dispensing altitude is approximately 60 metres at speeds up to 700 to 800 knots. A single aircraft can deliver some 600 mines over an area of 200 × 300 metres by varying the number of dispensers dropped, the rate of release of the dispensers and the aircraft release parameters. The following cluster bomb units have so far been identified with the GATOR system:

CBU-78/B: SUU-58/B dispenser with BLU-91/B and BLU-92/B
CBU-82/B: SUU-58/B dispenser with BLU-91/B
CBU-83/B: SUU-58/B dispenser with BLU-92/B
CBU-84/B: SUU-54A/B dispenser with BLU-91/B and BLU-92/B
CBU-85/B: SUU-54A/B dispenser with BLU-91/B
CBU-86/B: SUU-54A/B dispenser with BLU-92/B

STATUS
Production. Standardisation was in late 1981.

GATOR anti-tank mine

Other Air-delivered Cluster Bomb Mine Systems

DESCRIPTION

As a direct result of the Viet-Nam war a number of air-delivered interdiction mine systems were developed. A summary of some of these is given below with brief data.

CBU-28: SUU-13 dispenser with 40 × CDU-2 clusters, each of 120 BLU-43 triangular shaped blast anti-personnel minelets known as 'Short Dragon Teeth'. Weight of minelet is 20 g.

CBU-33/A: Weight 350 kg, SUU-36/A dispenser with 30 × BLU-45 anti-tank optimised anti-vehicle mines. Weight 9·1 kg with a shaped charge and self-destruct timer.

CBU-34/A: SUU-38/A dispenser with 10 × CDU-18 or CDU-19 clusters, each of 52 BLU-42 minelets. The BLU-42 is a vaned surface spherical bounding anti-personnel minelet. It is fitted with an anti-disturbance unit, a short life self-destruct timer and tripwire sensors. It is filled with 120 g of Composition B explosive. Known as Wide Area Anti-Personnel Mine (WAAPM).

CBU-37/A: SUU-13/A dispenser with 40 CDU-3 clusters, each of 120 BLU-44 triangular shaped blast anti-personnel minelets, known as 'Long Dragon Teeth'. Weight of minelet 20 g.

CBU-42/A: SUU-38/A dispenser with 10 × CDU-20 or CDU-21 clusters each of 52 BLU-54 minelets. The BLU-54 minelet is identical to the BLU-42 but fitted with a longer self-destruct timer and filled with 134 g of Composition B. Also known as Wide Area Anti-personnel Mine (WAAPM).

CBU-45: TFD, multi-purpose minelet dispenser.

CBU-66/B: SUU-51/B dispenser with CDU-24/B clusters of BLU-81 anti-vehicle 'Grasshopper' mines. Both the CBU-66 and BLU-81 are now cancelled.

The SUU-13 is an external carriage downward ejection 40-bay dispenser. Each bay is some 280 mm long and 120 mm in diameter and is opened by an explosive cartridge. It can be used only at subsonic speeds. A typical impact pattern for the minelets dropped from this dispenser at 450 knots aircraft speed is 1110 metres long and 60 metres wide. The SUU-36 and the SUU-38 are ten-bay external carriage downward ejection dispensers that can function at supersonic speeds. As such they are known as Tactical Fighter Dispensers (TFD).

STATUS

In service with the United States Air Force and other unspecified countries. To be replaced by GATOR system.

United States Aerial Land Mines

DESCRIPTION

These were developed during the Viet-Nam war as a specialist family of munitions used for interdiction missions.

MLU 10/B 750 lb land mine
This is a cylindrical steel casing with a high explosive filling of Destex. The mine is fitted with a multi-influence detonator using seismic, magnetic and infra-red sensors to determine the presence of vehicles. The infra-red sensor was added after early versions in Viet-Nam were accidentally detonated by civilians carrying metallic objects. The total weight of the mine is 347 kg (766 lb).

BLU 31/B 750 lb demolition bomb
This is an MLU 10/B optimised to attack tanks. It is equipped with an improved seismic sensor to distinguish tanks from wheeled vehicles and an acoustic sensor tuned to the frequencies of tank engines.

Service Destructor Mines (DST)
These are modified general-purpose low drag bombs. The modification is accomplished by using a Mk 75 Mod 0 Destructor Modification Kit on the Mk 82 500 lb, Mk 83 1000 lb and Mk 84 2000 lb general purpose bombs. The bombs can also be fitted with Snakeye retarding units.

Once converted the bombs can be used as either land or water mines. The primary targets as water mines during the Viet-Nam war were sampans, junks and other coastal craft with low magnetic signatures. The Mk 36 was used extensively during Operation Igloo White to interrupt supplies transported by motor traffic along the Ho Chi Minh trail. A summary of available information on the Destructor family is given in the accompanying table.

STATUS

MLU 10/B in service with the US Air Force.
BLU 31/B in service with the US Air Force.
DST Mk 36, 40, 41 in service with the US Navy.

SPECIFICATIONS

Designation	DST Mk 36 Mod 0/Mod 3	DST Mk 36 Mod 4	DST Mk 36 Mod 5	DST Mk 40 Mod 0/Mod 3	DST Mk 40 Mod 4	DST Mk 40 Mod 5	DST Mk 41 Mod 0/Mod 3	DST Mk 41 Mod 4/Mod 5
Type	land and sea bottom influence	land and sea bottom influence	land and sea bottom influence	land and sea bottom influence	land and sea bottom influence	land and sea bottom influence	land and sea bottom influence	land and sea bottom influence
Actuation	thin film magnetometer	dual magnetic-seismic	dual magnetic-seismic	thin film magnetometer	dual magnetic-seismic	dual magnetic-seismic	thin film magnetometer	dual magnetic-seismic
Max length	2·25 m	2·25 m	2·25 m	2·86 m	2·86 m	2·86 m	3·83 m	3·83 m
Max diameter over fins	0·4 m	0·4 m	0·4 m	0·57 m	0·57 m	0·57 m	0·63 m probably	0·63 m probably
Max water depth	91·4 m	91·4 m	91·4 m	91·4 m	91·4 m	91·4 m	91·4 m	91·4 m
HE type*	H6	H6	H6	H6	H6	H6	H6	H6
HE weight	87·27 kg	87·27 kg	87·27 kg	202·27 kg	202·27 kg	202·27 kg	429·55 kg	429·55 kg
Assembly weight†	261·82 kg	261·82 kg	261·82 kg	482·27 kg	482·27 kg	482·27 kg	928·64 kg	923·18 kg
Remarks‡	conversion of Mk 82 LDGP bomb	conversion of Mk 82 LDGP bomb	conversion of Mk 82 LDGP bomb	conversion of Mk 83 LDGP bomb	conversion of Mk 83 LDGP bomb	conversion of Mk 83 LDGP bomb	conversion of Mk 84 LDGP bomb	conversion of Mk 84 LDGP bomb

* Alternative fillings Minol 2 or Tritonal.
† Weight of a TRD is 18·18 kg; this must be added to assembled weight to give total mine weight.
‡ All bombs have cast steel casings. They are also fitted with automatic neutralisation devices that are preset before use.

Mobile Water Mine (MOWAM)

DESCRIPTION

The Mobile Water Mine (MOWAM) is designed to prevent or deter enemy tanks and amphibious vehicles from crossing rivers and streams. It is a lightweight, torpedo-like vehicle approximately 203 mm in diameter, 808 mm long and weighing 19·7 kg. The weight includes the high explosive warhead and a small rocket motor. The main components of the mine are seismic, acoustic and magnetic sensor units, printed circuit board electronics, warhead, battery module and rocket motor. The secondary components include the anchor and parachute mechanisms, nose piece and shroud assemblies, a safety and arming device and guidance control valves.

Deployment is either by helicopter or boat, after which the mine anchors itself to the river bottom and then orientates itself by control fins to face either up- or downstream. The seismic sensor is contained in the anchor mechanism and the acoustic sensor is fitted in the forward face of the mine. Primary power is provided by a lithium cell battery which is activated on initial immersion. An embedded microprocessor classifies the seismic and acoustic data. Once a target is confirmed and is within engagement range the mine tether is severed and the rocket motor is ignited. The vehicle is steered underwater by two pairs of reaction jets powered by a small proportion of the main propellant gas. The terminal homing system utilises a directional high-frequency acoustic sonar for sound ranging, in combination with a magnetic proximity sensor, to achieve a target mobility kill.

STATUS
Development.

MANUFACTURER
EDO Corporation, Government Systems Division, 14-04 111th Street, College Point, New York 11356, USA.

SPECIFICATIONS
Weight: 19·7 kg
Length: 808 mm
Diameter: 203 mm

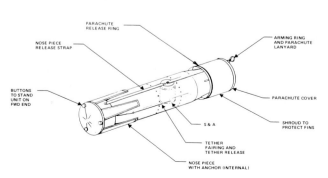

Component parts of Mobile Water Mine

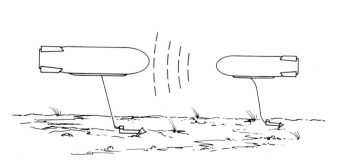

Artist's impression of two Mobile Water Mines in place awaiting targets

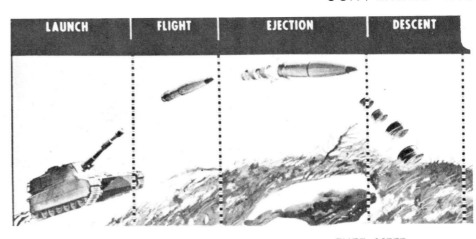

Remote Anti-Armor Mine System (RAAMS)

DESCRIPTION

The Remote Anti-Armor Mine System (RAAMS) consists of a 155 mm projectile carrying anti-armour mines which are fired from an M109 or M109A1 self-propelled howitzer. It is a member of the Family of Scatterable Mines (FASCAM).

There are two types of projectile: the M741 projectile carries nine mines with a factory-set short self-destruct time of under 24 hours and the M718 carries nine mines with a factory-set long self-destruct time of well over 24 hours.

Each circular M75 anti-tank mine weighs about 2·26 kg. Arming is automatic on landing. Actuation is by a Honeywell magnetic influence fuze that operates against the width of the tank. The detonation then occurs in two stages: the first when a clearing charge blows off the mine cover and removes any ground debris and the second 30 milliseconds later when the main charge, which consists of two plate charges so as to make the ground orientation of the mine non-critical, is detonated. The mine is capable of destroying any tank track or wheel passing over it and is said to cause a spalling effect when it penetrates tank belly armour. The projectile is fired to a maximum range of 17 000 metres and a single battery of six 155 mm weapons can lay a minefield 300 metres long and 250 metres deep with two volleys. The 12 projectiles fired provide a density of 0·001 mines per square metre for the minefield. The density can be changed to meet the tactical situation by varying the lay of the guns and the number of rounds fired.

The Modular Pack Mine System (MOPMS) is a man-pack mine system derived from the RAAMS system.

STATUS

RAAMS is in production for the US Army.

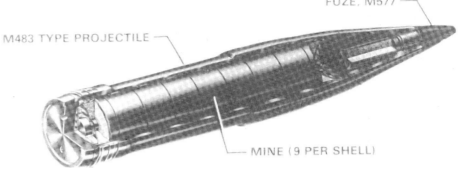

Projectile, 155 mm, Anti-tank, M718/M741 (RAAMS) (US Army)

M56 Helicopter-delivered Scatterable Mine System

DEVELOPMENT

The M56 offensive/defensive scatterable mine system is the first member of the Family of Scatterable Mines (FASCAM) to enter service with the United States Army. It originated in the early 1960s as a design concept that became a weapons requirement during the Viet-Nam war and was developed as the XM56 system by the United States Army's Picatinny Arsenal in the early 1970s under the direction of the Armament Research and Development Command. The system was type classified in fiscal year 1974 and was in production from 1975 to 1977. It entered service in the European theatre of operations in 1977.

DESCRIPTION

The system's basic components are two SUU-13/A bomb dispensers, a control panel inside the carrying aircraft, normally a Bell UH-1 helicopter, and an inter-connecting wiring harness. The dispenser holds 40 canisters each of which contains two mines. The dispensers are suspended on the standard weapons pylons of the carrier helicopter, on either side of the fuselage. The control panel for the system is in the cockpit and allows the pilot to control the modes, patterns and density of the minefield to be laid. It can also be used to drop the dispensers simultaneously if necessary. The wiring harness is removable, which eliminates any modification to the helicopter's electrical system and greatly simplifies the transference of the M56 system between aircraft.

The commander who issues the initial order for an aircraft emplacement of scatterable mines determines the location, length, width and mine density per square metre of the required minefield. One aircraft on a contour flight sortie can lay a minefield 100 metres long and 40 metres wide with a mine density of 0·04 mines per square metre, and 30 sorties can provide a field 2000 metres long and 40 metres wide with a density of 0·06 mines per square metre.

Number of sorties needed to emplace minefields of varying lengths and densities (one pass lays a 20-metre wide strip, two passes side by side are required to complete the minefield) are shown in the table below:

m²/density mines	·01	·02	·04	·06
100	1	1	1	2
200	1	1	2	3
300	1	2	3	5
400	1	2	4	6
500	2	3	5	8
600	2	3	6	9
700	2	4	7	11
800	2	4	8	12
900	3	5	9	14
1000	3	5	10	15
2000	5	10	20	30

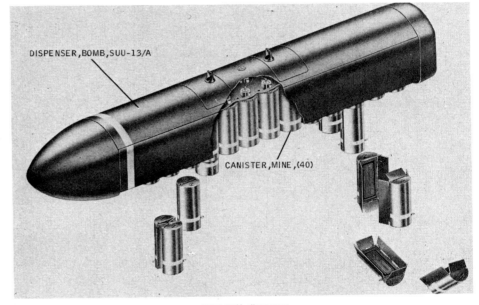

SUU-13/A dispenser

The M56 mine is 254 mm long with a 114 mm diameter half-round body and weighs approximately 2·7 kg. The explosive filling, Composition H-6, weighs 1·4 kg. Once the mine is launched by a small propellant cartridge downwards from the dispenser at 4·6 metres per second, the initial arming is achieved and four spring-folded fins open to increase the frictional drag of the mine and slow it down to minimise the impact force. They also orientate the mine in flight so that it strikes the ground with the flat face uppermost so as to activate the final arming device some one to two minutes after the impact. The dispenser contains a mixture of the three variants of the M56 mine, all superficially identical which prevents detection of the type or its capabilities by simple inspection. The basic version is the anti-tank/anti-vehicular mine that is activated when a pressure plate on the flat side of the mine is depressed and sends a firing signal to the electro-mechanical fuze. The anti-tank/anti-roller version is designed to defeat minefield roller-clearing operations by allowing the rollers to pass over the mine without detonation and then exploding on contact with the following tank tracks. The last version is the anti-disturbance mine which is designed to explode when it is picked up, jarred, rolled or tampered with by any physical means (including, under certain circumstances, the rotor wash of a helicopter) thus discouraging manual clearance parties. All three versions can also be used to mine shallow water fording areas as submergence does not decrease their capabilities or

UH-1H helicopter ejecting M56 mines from SUU-13/A dispensers mounted on either side of fuselage

operational efficiency. The variants are also fitted with factory-set (longer than one day) self-destruct timers.

The M56 system has two major disadvantages: the vulnerability of the carrier aircraft to groundfire, as the mines must be dropped from at least 30·5 metres above ground level to ensure correct orientation and arming on impact, and the total system weight of 580 kg which necessitates some external structural modifications to the aircraft.

The system is issued to assault helicopter companies and air cavalry troops on the scale of one system per three UH-1 helicopters. The complete system comprises one M56 dispenser fully loaded and four refill kits.

STATUS
Production complete. In service with the US Army.

SPECIFICATIONS
Mine
Weight: 2·7 kg
Length: 254 mm
Diameter: 114 mm
Main charge type: Composition H-6
Weight of main charge: 1·4 kg
Fuze type: electro-mechanical

M21 Heavy Anti-tank Mine

DESCRIPTION
The M21 metallic anti-tank mine is circular and has a sheet steel case. An adjustable carrying strap attached to the side of the mine can also be used for lifting the mine into position.

The top cover of the mine contains a charge cap assembly which has a threaded hole in the centre into which the fuze is screwed. For travelling this is covered by a plug assembly. Under the charge cap assembly is the black powder expelling charge and under this is the concave steel plate, beneath which is the HE charge.

The M21 mine has an M607 fuze which can be fitted with an extension rod adaptor and an extension rod which is actuated when it comes into contact with the tracks or belly of the tank. With the extension rod and adaptor removed, the fuze may be used as a pressure type fuze.

When fitted with the extension rod the mine is operated as follows: when the rod is tilted with a minimum horizontal force of 1·7 kg through an angle of 20 degrees or more the plastic collar in the fuze is broken. When used with the rod, a minimum force of 132 kg applied to the top of the mine will shatter or break the plastic collar. Once this plastic collar is shattered or

broken, the tilt-rod in the fuze presses against the bearing cap, forcing it downward causing the Belleville spring to snap into the reverse position, driving the firing pin assembly into the M46 detonator which fires the black powder charge. This blows off the top cover of the mine and the pressure created by this explosion drives a firing pin into the M42 primer, initiating the main firing chain. The main charge detonates and blows the body of the mine apart and causes the steel plate to be ejected upwards at a high velocity into the belly of the tank.

The M21 can also use the M612 pneumatic fuze and the M609 influence fuze.

SPECIFICATIONS
Weight: 7·9 kg
Diameter: 230 mm
Height:
  (with tilt-rod) 813 mm
  (with fuze) 206 mm
Main charge type: Composition H6
Weight of main charge: 4·9 kg
Type of booster: RDX
Weight of booster: 11 g
Operating force: 132 kg
Operating temperature range: −40 to +51·5°C

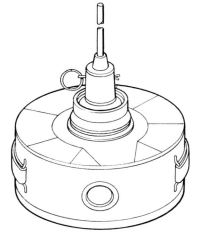

M21 heavy anti-tank mine

STATUS
In service with the US Army.

Off-route Anti-tank Mine System (ORATMS)

DESCRIPTION
This anti-tank mine system has been under development since 1979 to replace the existing M24 off-route anti-tank mine system (see next entry). It uses a self-

forging fragment warhead that will be effective at ranges up to 50 metres and will be capable of penetrating 80 mm of armour at an angle of incidence of 45 degrees. To fire the mine an acoustic sensor is employed along with an infra-red fuze.

A similar project developed by Motorola has now been terminated.

STATUS
Development.

DEVELOPMENT AGENCY
Hughes Aircraft Company.

M24 Off-route Anti-tank Mine

DEVELOPMENT
The M24 off-route (or off-the-road) anti-tank mine was developed from December 1961 by Picatinny Arsenal. Between September 1968 and November 1968 Picatinny delivered 50 000 of these mines to the US Army. It is issued on the scale of 15 per company in armour, airborne, infantry, mechanised and engineer combat battalions.

DESCRIPTION
The mine consists of a discriminating pressure-actuated vehicle detector tapeswitch (designated the M2), battery-powered M61 demolition firing device, and an M143 plastic dispenser tube for launching the M28 HEAT rocket. The latter is fin-stabilised and is the same as that used for the 3·5 inch M20 rocket launcher. The launcher is located up to 30 metres off-the-route and is sighted along the tapeswitch vehicle detector. When the target traverses the tapeswitch the circuit is completed and the rocket is launched. The HEAT warhead of the M28 rocket will penetrate all known conventional armour.

SPECIFICATIONS
Weight: (loaded) 8·164 kg
Length: 609 mm
Height: 89 mm
Main charge type: Composition B
Weight of main charge: 853 g
Weight of rocket: 4 kg
Operating temperature range: −40 to +51·5°C

STATUS
Production complete. In service with the US Army.

MANUFACTURER
Picatinny Arsenal, Dover, New Jersey, USA.

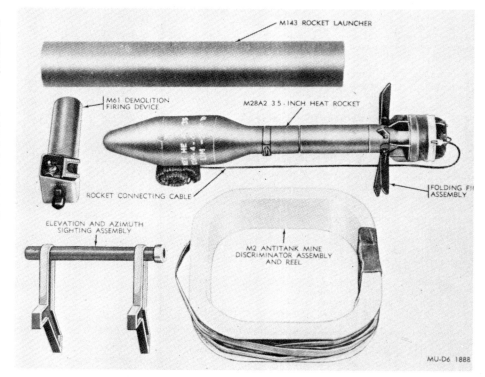

Main components of M24 off-route anti-tank mine (US Army)

M19 Anti-tank Mine

DESCRIPTION
The M19 non-metallic anti-tank mine is square and has an all-plastic case. A carrying handle is provided on one side of the mine. The main fuze-well is in the centre of

the mine and there are also two anti-lifting fuze-wells, one in the side of the mine and the second in its base.

The mine has an M606 fuze which is of the mechanical pressure type and is also plastic. The mine operates as follows: when sufficient pressure is applied to the top of the mine, the pressure plate is depressed and this depresses the Belleville spring of the fuze, which snaps

into reverse driving the firing pin into the detonator. This explodes and sets off the booster, which then sets off the main charge.

Sympathetic detonation can be avoided if the mine is buried 38 mm deep, with a 45-degree slope of holes and 5·5 metres centre-to-centre between adjacent mines. The M19 is waterproof and can be laid on riverbeds.

An inert training version of this mine is available, designated the mine, AT: training, M80.

SPECIFICATIONS
Weight: 12·56 kg
Length: 332 mm
Width: 332 mm
Height: 94 mm
Main charge type: Composition B
Weight of main charge: 9·53 kg
Type of booster: RDX
Weight of booster: 52 g
Operating force: 136–227 kg
Operating temperature range: −40 to +51·5°C

STATUS
In service with the US Army.

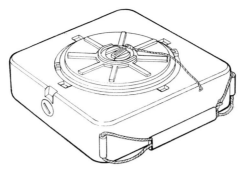

M19 anti-tank mine

Mine: AT: Training, M80, inert practice version of M19 anti-tank mine (T J Gander)

M15 Anti-tank Mine

DESCRIPTION
This heavy metallic anti-tank mine is circular and has a carrying handle. The main fuze-well is in the centre of the mine and there are also two anti-lifting fuze-wells, one in the side and the other in the bottom of the mine. The M15 is fitted with the M603 or M608 mechanical pressure fuze and operates as follows: when sufficient pressure is applied to the top of the mine the pressure plate is depressed, which depresses the Belleville spring which snaps into reverse, driving the firing pin into the detonator. This explodes the booster which in turn ignites the main charge.

A practice version of this mine is designated the M12 (or M12A1) and has the M604 fuze, with a smoke charge in the main fuze-well. Another practice mine is designated the M20. Canadian Arsenals Limited pro-

duces an anti-tank practice mine which closely resembles the M15. Designated the C9, it is coloured bright blue.

SPECIFICATIONS
Weight: 14·27 kg
Diameter: 337 mm
Height: 125 mm
Main charge type: Composition B
Weight of main charge: 10·33 kg
Type of booster: RDX
Weight of booster: 11 g
Operating force: 159 kg–340 kg
Operating temperature range: −40 to +51·5°C

STATUS
In service with the US Army.

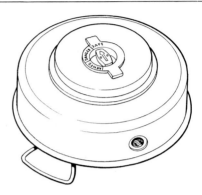

M15 anti-tank mine

One Gallon Chemical Mine

DESCRIPTION
The One Gallon (3·785 litres) Chemical Mine can be used to disperse distilled mustard (HD) or Levenstein mustard (H). It consists of an unpainted one gallon can with a carrying handle and a threaded cap. Two short copper wires are soldered to one side of the mine, to which is attached the bursting charge which consists of

detonating cord electrically or non-electrically detonated. When the bursting charge is detonated, the mine bursts and dispenses the chemical agent over a wide area. The mine is filled by use of an M2 land mine field filling apparatus that consists of a pipette assembly and a pedestal assembly.

STATUS
In service with the US Army.

SPECIFICATIONS
Weight: 4·99 kg
Width: 167 mm
Depth: 105 mm
Height: 270 mm
Type of filler: HD
Weight of filler: 4·49 kg

M23 Chemical Agent Mine

DESCRIPTION
The M23 chemical agent mine has the same metallic case as used for the M15 anti-tank mine and can be distinguished from the latter by the eight raised projections spaced in pairs around the top of the mine, and its grey colour with three 13 mm green bands and one 6 mm yellow band.

The mine can be used as an anti-tank or antipersonnel mine and can be fuzed for contact or remote detonation. The main fuze-well is in the centre of the

mine but there are also two secondary fuze-wells, one in the side and the other in the base of the mine. The mine operates as follows: when sufficient pressure is applied to the top of the mine the pressure plate is depressed. This depresses the Belleville spring which snaps into reverse, driving the firing pin into the detonator, which explodes the M120 booster and the contents of the mine are scattered. When buried under 77 to 127 mm of earth, the mine has an effective radius of four metres.

STATUS
In service with the US Army.

SPECIFICATIONS
Weight: 10·376 kg
Diameter: 330 mm
Height: 127 mm
Type of filler: VX agent
Weight of filler: 4·76 kg
Type of booster: RDX
Weight of booster: 11 g
Operating force: 256 kg ±79 kg
Operating temperature range: −40 to +51·5°C

M10 Anti-tank Practice Mine

DESCRIPTION
This inert mine is used for training personnel in the handling of mines. It was originally designed to simulate the M7 series of anti-tank mines which are no longer in service with the US Army.

The mine operates as follows: when sufficient pres-

sure is applied to the pressure plate it is depressed causing the Belleville spring of the fuze to snap into reverse, which drives the firing pin into the igniter which ignites the smoke charge which then emits a cloud of smoke.

STATUS
In service with the US Army.

SPECIFICATIONS
Weight: 3·72 kg
Length: 178 mm
Width: 127 mm
Height: 64 mm
Weight of smoke filler: 17 g
Operating force: 54–109 kg

VENEZUELA

Anti-personnel Mine M6

DESCRIPTION
The M6 anti-personnel mine is circular and is actuated by a pull-friction fuze connected to a tripwire.

STATUS
In service with the Venezuelan Army.

SPECIFICATIONS
Diameter:
(with cover) 152 mm
(case) 140 mm
Height: 79 mm

Anti-personnel mine M6

VIET-NAM

Vietnamese Mines

The status of many Vietnamese mines, especially those of an improvised nature is now very uncertain and impossible to verify. As it now seems certain that many types will no longer be encountered readers seeking information on these mines should refer to *Jane's Military Vehicles and Ground Support Equipment 1983*, page 209.

YUGOSLAVIA

PMA-3 Anti-personnel Mine

DESCRIPTION
The PMA-3 mine consists of two interlocking plastic circular sections held together by a rubber cap. The lower section has a centrally located fuze-well. A plastic spring-loaded safety band is attached about the mine to lock both parts together to prevent any premature detonation caused by movement of the two parts. The mine is armed by removing the fuze-well plug and inserting a chemically activated detonator into the hole. The plug is then replaced and the spring-loaded safety clip is removed by use of a one-metre long nylon cord. Application of a small force to the mine top pivots the two halves on each other causing the chemical detonator to shear through and the mine to explode.

SPECIFICATIONS
Weight: 185 g
Diameter: 100 mm
Height: 37 mm

Main charge type: Amatol
Weight of main charge: 150 g

STATUS
In service with the Yugoslav Army.

MANUFACTURER
Federal Directorate of Supply and Procurement (SDPR), PO Box 308, Knez Mihailova 6, Beograd, Yugoslavia.

PMA-2 Anti-personnel Mine

DESCRIPTION
The PMA-2 is a cylindrical anti-personnel mine with a ceramic body. The mechanical pressure fuze, which is operated by a pressure of 9 to 15 kg, is inserted into the fuze well on top of the mine.

A practice mine, the VPMA-2, is identical to the PMA-2 in all respects other than detonation produces a grey smoke cloud which lasts for a minimum of 5 seconds. The complete VPMA-2 can be used only once and only the body is reusable.

STATUS
In service with the Yugoslav Army.

MANUFACTURER
Federal Directorate of Supply and Procurement (SDPR), PO Box 308, Knez Mihailova 6, Beograd, Yugoslavia.

SPECIFICATIONS
Weight: 140 g
Diameter: 65 mm
Height: 62 mm
Main charge type: TNT
Main charge weight: 100 g

VPMA-2, training version of PMA-2 anti-personnel mine

PMA-1 Anti-personnel Mine

DESCRIPTION
This plastic non-metallic anti-personnel mine consists of a box with a hinged cover containing a fuze, detonator and the explosive charge. In the bottom of the mine case are two drain holes for use in wet terrain. The mine operates as follows: when pressure of 3 to 15 kg is applied to the lid, the projection on the lid crushes the capsule and ignites the contents, which actuates the No. 8 detonator and initiates the explosive charge.

There is a model PMA-1A which differs from the basic PMA-1 only in detail.

The practice version of the PMA-1A is the VPMA-1A made up of a mine body, mine cover, an explosive charge simulator, a practice fuze, a smoke container, a safety 'element' and a practice detonator. The smoke container, fuze and practice detonator can each be used only once and the entire practice mine has a minimum life of five actuations. Each actuation produces a five second grey smoke cloud.

SPECIFICATIONS
Weight: 280 g
Length: 140 mm
Width: 65 mm
Height: 40 mm
Main charge type: TNT
Weight of main charge: 200 g
Fuze: UPMAH-1 chemical pressure fuze

STATUS
In service with the Yugoslav Army.

MANUFACTURER
Federal Directorate of Supply and Procurement (SDPR), PO Box 308, Knez Mihailova 6, Beograd, Yugoslavia.

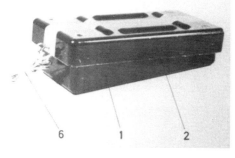

*VPMA-1A, training version of PMA-1A non-metallic anti-personnel mine with **1** mine body, **2** mine cover and **6** trip wire and safety element*

PMD-1 Anti-personnel Mine

DESCRIPTION
The PMD-1 wooden anti-personnel mine is very similar in design and construction to the Soviet PMD-6 mine except that it uses the UPMD-1 fuze.

STATUS
In service with the Yugoslav Army.

MANUFACTURER
Federal Directorate of Supply and Procurement (SDPR), PO Box 308, Knez Mihailova 6, Beograd, Yugoslavia.

SPECIFICATIONS
Weight: 0·5 kg

Length: 120 mm
Width: 100 mm
Height: 40 mm
Main charge type: TNT
Weight of main charge: 200 g
Operating force: 5 kg

PROM-1 Bouncing Anti-personnel Mine

DESCRIPTION
This cylindrical bouncing anti-personnel mine has an UPROM-1 fuze which can be activated by pressure or a pull release (ie attached to a tripwire). In the former case, the pressure pushes the cylinder down, freeing the retaining balls which allow the striker to hit the percussion cap which explodes igniting the bouncing charge, which ejects the mine 0·7 to 1·5 metres above the ground. The main charge then explodes and causes fragmentation which is lethal to a radius of 25 metres and dangerous to a radius of 100 metres. The training version is designated VPROM-1.

SPECIFICATIONS
Weight: 3 kg
Diameter: 75 mm
Height: (with fuze) 470 mm
Main charge type: TNT
Weight of main charge: 0·5 kg
Operating force:
  (pull) 3–5·5 kg
  (pressure) 9–16 kg

STATUS
In service with the Yugoslav Army.

MANUFACTURER
Federal Directorate of Supply and Procurement (SDPR), PO Box 308, Knez Mihailova 6, Beograd, Yugoslavia.

VPROM-1, training version of PROM-1 bouncing anti-personnel mine

PMR-1 and PMR-2 Anti-personnel Stake Mines

DESCRIPTION
The PMR-1 anti-personnel mine is very similar to the Soviet POMZ-2M mine but has nine instead of five rows of fragments. The PMR-2 mine has a concrete and scrap metal fragmentation body and is similar to the Czechoslovak PP-Mi-Sb. This mine uses the UPM-1 pull fuze. A training model is designated the VPMR-3.

STATUS
In service with the Yugoslav Army.

MANUFACTURER
Federal Directorate of Supply and Procurement (SDPR), PO Box 308, Knez Mihailova 6, Beograd, Yugoslavia.

SPECIFICATIONS

Model	PMR-1	PMR-2
Weight	2 kg	2·2 kg
Diameter	80 mm	80 mm
Height (with fuze)	120 mm*	120 mm*
Main charge type	TNT	TNT
Weight of main charge	75 g	75 g

* Excluding stake

*VPMR-3, training version of PMR-1 and PMR-2 anti-personnel stake mines with **1** mine body, **5** practice fuze, **6** stake/carrier and **8** trip wire on bobbin*

TMA-5 Anti-tank Mine

DESCRIPTION
The TMA-5 is a square plastic bodied anti-tank mine with a central fuze-well. The four corners of the plastic outer casing have been reinforced and elongated to allow several mines to be stacked on top of each other. A carrying handle is included as an integral part of the body. The mine may be laid in any type of ground within a 60 × 60 × 60 cm space which must be clear to ensure the correct functioning of the mine fuze which requires a pressure of 120 to 320 kg to operate.

The practice version of the TMA-5 is the VTMA-5 which has a hard rubber mine body. It consists of the hard rubber mine body, a cover with a fuze well, a protective cover for the smoke container, the smoke container, a practice fuze and a cover for the fuze well. The VTMA-5 may be used at least 30 times but for each detonation new covers, practice fuzes and smoke containers are required. When detonated the VTMA-5 produces yellow smoke for at least five seconds.

STATUS
In service with the Yugoslav Army.

MANUFACTURER
Federal Directorate of Supply and Procurement (SDPR), PO Box 308, Knez Mihailova 6, Beograd, Yugoslavia.

*VTMA-5, training version of TMA-5 anti-tank mine with **1** mine body, **2** mine cover with fuze well, **3** cover for smoke container and **6** fuze well cover*

TMA-4 Anti-tank Mine

DESCRIPTION
The TMA-4 is a circular plastic anti-tank mine which is larger than the TMA-3, and also has multiple fuze-wells. The top three wells take the UTMAH-1 fuze and the bottom well is used for the booby-trapping fuze. The mine is fitted with a canvas carrying handle on the side.

The practice version of this mine is the VTMA-4.

SPECIFICATIONS
Weight: 6 kg
Diameter: 285 mm
Height: 65 mm
Weight of explosive: 5·5 kg
Operating pressure: approx 200 kg

STATUS
In service with the Yugoslav Army.

MANUFACTURER
Federal Directorate of Supply and Procurement (SDPR), PO Box 308, Knez Mihailova 6, Beograd, Yugoslavia.

*VTMA-4, training version of TMA-4 anti-tank mine with **1** mine body and **3** practice fuzes*

TMA-3 Anti-tank Mine

DESCRIPTION
The TMA-3 circular plastic anti-tank mine is blast- and water-resistant. All parts of the mine are non-metallic. The three fuze-wells in the top of the mine casing each accept a UTMAH-1 fuze, which are left exposed after they have been screwed into position. The bottom fuze-well is used for the booby-trap fuze.

The practice version of this mine is the hard rubber VTMA-3.

SPECIFICATIONS
Weight: 6·6 kg
Diameter: 260 mm
Height: 82 mm
Main charge type: Trotyl or TNT
Weight of main charge: 6·5 kg
Operating force: 180–350 kg
Fuze model: UTMAH-1

STATUS
In service with the Yugoslav Army.

MANUFACTURER
Federal Directorate of Supply and Procurement (SDPR), PO Box 308, Knez Mihailova 6, Beograd, Yugoslavia.

TMA-3 anti-tank mine with fuze wells plugged (T J Gander)

*VTMA-3, training version of TMA-3 anti-tank mine with **1** mine body and **3** practice fuzes*

TMA-2A Anti-tank Mine

DESCRIPTION
This plastic anti-tank mine is rectangular and has two fuze-wells, one in the top centre of the pressure plate for the main fuze, and a second one in the bottom of the mine for booby-trapping. Its method of operation is identical to the circular TMA-1A anti-tank mine.
    The practice version of the TMA-2A is the VTMA-2A.

SPECIFICATIONS
Weight: 7·5 kg
Length: 260 mm
Width: 200 mm
Height: 140 mm

Main charge type: TNT
Weight of main charge: 6·5 kg
Operating force: 120–320 kg
Fuze model: UTMAH-1

STATUS
In service with the Yugoslav Army.

MANUFACTURER
Federal Directorate of Supply and Procurement (SDPR), PO Box 308, Knez Mihailova 6, Beograd, Yugoslavia.

VTMA-2A, training version of TMA-2A anti-tank mine with 1 mine body, 2 mine cover, 3 safety pins and 6 smoke container and fuze stoppers

TMA-1A Anti-tank Mine

DESCRIPTION
This plastic circular anti-tank mine has two fuze-wells, one in the top centre of the pressure plate for the main fuze, and a second in the bottom of the mine for booby-trapping. The TMA-1A has a very distinctive corrugated top pressure plate. Along the body circumference are four openings set crosswise for the insertion of joints which are designed to regulate the treading force. The downward pressure breaks the fuze cap, which causes friction to ignite the incendiary mixture which in turn ignites the No. 8 detonator. This initiates the primer and the main explosive charge.
    The practice version of this mine is the VTMA-1A.

SPECIFICATIONS
Weight: 5·5 kg
Diameter: 300 mm
Height: 105 mm
Main charge type: TNT
Weight of main charge: 5 kg
Operating force: 120–320 kg
Fuze model: UTMAH-1

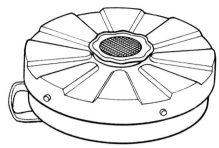

TMA-1A anti-tank mine

STATUS
In service with the Yugoslav Army. Being replaced by more modern TMA type mines.

MANUFACTURER
Federal Directorate of Supply and Procurement (SDPR), PO Box 308, Knez Mihailova 6, Beograd, Yugoslavia.

VTMA-1A, training version of TMA-1A anti-tank mine with 1 mine body, 2 mine cover, 4 smoke container and fuze stopper and 6 safety pins

TMD-1 Anti-tank Mine

DESCRIPTION
The TMD-1 wooden anti-tank mine is almost identical in design and construction to the Soviet TMD-B and has similar specifications.

STATUS
In limited service with the Yugoslav Army reserve units.

MANUFACTURER
Federal Directorate of Supply and Procurement (SDPR), PO Box 308, Knez Mihailova 6, Beograd, Yugoslavia.

TMM-1 Anti-tank Mine

DESCRIPTION
The Yugoslav TMM-1 metallic anti-tank mine is a copy of the German World War Two Tellermine 43 (also called the Mushroom mine). The mine can be laid by hand or mechanically, for example by a PMR-3 minelayer. The TMM-1 has two anti-lifting wells, one in the bottom and one in the side. The mine is operated as follows: downward pressure on the mushroom crushes the walls and forces the head of the striker down, igniting the mine.
    The practice version of the TMM-1 is the VTMM-1 which has a hard rubber body and a useful life of at least 30 operations. It is identical to the TMM-1 and uses the VUTMM-1 practice fuze which can be used at least ten times provided the practice detonator, percussion primer and element are replaced after every activation.

When activated the VTMM-1 produces a yellow smoke cloud that lasts at least five seconds.

SPECIFICATIONS
Weight: 8·6 kg
Diameter: 310 mm
Height: 100 mm
Main charge type: Trotyl
Weight of main charge: 5·6 kg
Operating force: 130–420 kg
Fuze model: UTMM (pressure)

STATUS
In limited service with the Yugoslav Army reserve units.

MANUFACTURER
Federal Directorate of Supply and Procurement (SDPR), PO Box 308, Knez Mihailova 6, Beograd, Yugoslavia.

VTMM-1, training version of TMM-1 anti-tank mine with 1 mine body and 2 mine cover

Pot Type Anti-tank Mine

DESCRIPTION
This circular pot shaped anti-tank mine consists of a sheet metal case with curved side walls and a handle. Over the top of this fits a convex pressure plate. The mine has a central fuze-well and is detonated as follows: when pressure is applied to the top of the mine, the

cover is forced down on to the top of the firing pin which has a spring held in position by a shear pin. Under pressure, this is sheared and the spring forces the firing pin downward, actuating the detonator. This fires the primer which in turn fires the main charge.

STATUS
Uncertain.

MANUFACTURER
Federal Directorate of Supply and Procurement (SDPR), PO Box 308, Knez Mihailova 6, Beograd, Yugoslavia.

SPECIFICATIONS
Weight of main charge: 2·5 kg
Operating force: 100 kg

PMRS Bounding Anti-personnel Flare Mine

DESCRIPTION
The PMRS anti-personnel bounding fragmentation mine is similar in appearance to the Soviet POMZ-2/POMZ-2M, Czechoslovak PP-Mi-Sb/PP-Mi-Sk, Yugoslav PMR-1/PMR-2, and the Chinese and North Korean versions of the original Soviet POMZ-2 anti-personnel mine.

The mine has a serrated case of steel, in the bottom of which is the opening for the charge and the stake. There are two holes for draining water. The mine has an effective fragmentation range of 100 metres and is operated by a pull fuze. When the tripwire is pulled, the double-ended safety element is extracted, releasing first the small and then the large firing pin. The small firing pin strikes the initiating primer of the flare cartridge, actuating it. The larger pin is then released, striking the initiating primer which ignites the detonator and in turn sets off the explosive charge.

SPECIFICATIONS
Main charge type: TNT
Weight of main charge: 200 g
Operating force: 2·7–16·7 kg

STATUS
In service with the Yugoslav Army.

MANUFACTURER
Federal Directorate of Supply and Procurement (SDPR), PO Box 308, Knez Mihailova 6, Beograd, Yugoslavia.

MINELAYING EQUIPMENT

AUSTRIA

Minelaying Chute

DESCRIPTION
The Austrian Army uses a vehicle-mounted minelaying chute to dispense Panzermine 75 anti-tank mines rapidly on the surface of the ground. The mines are fed onto the chute by hand and then slide to the ground by gravity. The system can lay 380 mines in 15 minutes over a distance of 1600 metres. Several vehicles operating in parallel can lay a minefield sufficiently dense to hinder or stop an armoured attack temporarily.

STATUS
In service with the Austrian Army.

Truck towing minelaying chute with Panzermine 75 anti-tank mines sliding to ground

FRANCE

ARE Type SOC Plough Type Minelayer

DESCRIPTION
The ARE plough type minelayer has been developed specifically for use with the HPD anti-tank mine which is in production for the French Army by TRT. The minelayer is towed behind a four-ton truck or tracked vehicle, which also carries the crew and mines. A crew of four is required to operate the complete system: commander, two loaders and the driver.

The minelayer opens up a furrow in the ground, lays the mines and then replaces the top soil. If required the mines can be laid on the surface. The HPD mines can be buried to a maximum depth of 150 mm and can be spaced 2·5, 3·3 or 5 metres apart. Maximum laying rate is between 900 and 1500 mines per hour.

SPECIFICATIONS
Weight: 2500 kg
Length:
   (travelling) 4·86 m
   (operating) 5·685 m
Width: 2·335 m
Height: 2·245 m
Max towing speed:
   (on roads) 80 km/h
   (operating) 4·5 km/h
Towing effort: 40 kN

STATUS
Development. Under evaluation by at least one army.

ARE Type SOC plough type minelayer (T J Gander)

MANUFACTURER
Atelier de Construction Roanne, BP 504, 42328 Roanne, France.

Enquiries to Groupement Industriel des Armements Terrestres (GIAT), 10 place Georges Clémenceau, 92211 Saint-Cloud, France.

Creusot-Loire Mine Distributor

The Creusot-Loire mine distributor competed in trials with the Matenin mine distributors for acceptance by the French Army. The Matenin mine distributor was chosen, so further development of the Creusot-Loire equipment was suspended. For details of this equipment refer to *Jane's Military Vehicles and Ground Support Equipment 1983*, page 213.

Matenin Mine Burier

DESCRIPTION
The Matenin mine burier is a self-propelled 4 × 4 vehicle based on components used in the Matenin trench digger. Development began in 1971. It is capable of cross-country operations and can lay or bury mines on any ground which can be negotiated by armoured fighting vehicles. It can also lay mines in river and stream beds not more than 1·2 metres deep.

The mines are buried by a hydro-mechanical push tool that enters and leaves the soil by the same route. There is no exterior change in vegetation as the entry point is automatically closed by a roller which stamps down the vegetation after the mine is buried. The stopping, deceleration and acceleration of the vehicle after each burial are fully automatic due to its hydrostatic transmission.

The vehicle carries four containers each loaded with 112 mines. The mines may be laid in straight lines, curves (with diameters under 20 metres) and zig zags.

Matenin minelayer in travelling order

The distance between mines can be varied between 2·5 and 10 metres during laying. The average burying speed is 400 mines an hour but with a 3-metre interval between mines this can be increased to 500. The vehicle is used by the French Army to lay HPD anti-tank mines.

SPECIFICATIONS
Crew: 1 + 2
Configuration: 4 × 4 or 4 × 2
Weight:
  (empty) 12 700 kg
  (loaded) 16 000 kg
Length: 7·3 m
Width: 2·5 m
Height: 2·8 m
Ground clearance: 0·5 m
Wheelbase: 3 m
Max speed: (road) 70 km/h
Average speed: (road) 50 km/h
Speed with hydrostatic transmission: 3·6 km/h
Range: (road) 600 km
Endurance while laying: 11 h
Max gradient: 50%
Max side slope: 25%
Vertical obstacle: 0·45 m
Trench: 0·65 m
Fording: 1·2 m
Engine: MAN type D2156 HM 6-cylinder water-cooled diesel developing 225 hp at 2400 rpm
Steering: power assisted
Turning circle radius: 11 m
Tyres: 16.00 × 25 low pressure

Matenin minelayer in operational mode

Gearbox: power shift hydro-mechanical unit with torque converter. 6 forward and 3 reverse gears
Brakes: air
Winch capacity: 5000 kg (10 000 kg when tackle is used)
Electrical system: 24 V

STATUS
In production. In service with the French Army.

MANUFACTURER
Etablissements Matenin, 34 avenue des Champs Elysées, 75008 Paris, France.

Matenin Mine Distributor

DESCRIPTION
To meet the French Army's requirement for at least 150 systems of this type and in competition with Creusot-Loire, Etablissement Matenin designed and built a mine distributor for the HPD anti-tank mine. Following trials held in 1982 the Matenin system was chosen as the model for the French Army and it is now in production.

Towed by a truck carrying the mines, the mines are manually placed into the layer to slide down the chute under gravity. They are automatically armed in the process. The laying distance between mines is adjustable. Weight of the minelayer is 150 kg and it can be broken down into three parts for transport purposes. The maximum laying speed is approximately 1800 mines per hour.

STATUS
In production. In service with the French Army.

MANUFACTURER
Etablissement Matenin, 34 avenue des Champs Elysées, 75008 Paris, France.

Operator's station on Matenin mine distributor showing control unit and HPD mines on chute (T J Gander)

Matenin mine distributor (T J Gander)

GERMANY, DEMOCRATIC REPUBLIC

MLG-60 Mechanical Minelayer

DESCRIPTION
In appearance the MLG-60 is very similar to the Soviet PMR-3, its main difference being the large twin follow-up scraper mounted high on the rear of the two-wheeled trailer and the absence of a seat for the operator as he is seated in the towing vehicle. The MLG-60 can lay the mines on the surface or bury them. Mine spacing is between four and six metres. The unit is normally towed by a 6 × 6 truck or a BTR-152 (6 × 6) armoured personnel carrier. A slightly improved model is the MLG-60M.

STATUS
In service with the East German Army.

MANUFACTURER
East German state arsenals.

SPECIFICATIONS
MLG-60M
Crew: 2
Weight: 800 kg
Length:
  (travelling order) 4·9 m
  (operating order) 5·9 m
Width: 1·87 m
Height:
  (travelling order) 1·95 m
  (operating order) 2·1 m
Operating speed: 3–5 km/h
Tyre size: 10–20 extra

MLG-60 minelayer being towed by BTR-152 (6 × 6) APC

ITALY

Valsella VS/MD Scatter-Dropping Mine System

DESCRIPTION
The VS/MD scatter-dropping mine system has been designed to allow the scatter-dropping of 2080 anti-personnel (Valsella VS-50 or VS-Mk 2) or 200 anti-tank mines (Valsella VS-1·6) in varying ratios. The complete system consists of two main components; the control panel in the helicopter and the mine dispensing system. This consists of a metal rack designed to accept 40 modular disposable magazines. On the bottom of each magazine is a stop which keeps the mines in place during storage, shipment and while inserting the magazines into the rack of the dispenser. Once in the dispenser the stop is removed.

The anti-personnel mines are dropped in groups of 52 and anti-tank mines in groups of five. They are dispensed through doors in the bottom of each magazine. The door-opening sequence has been designed to prevent any change in the centre of gravity of the dispenser. At the end of the scatter-dropping programme, a safety device actuated by a push button closes all the doors.

The dispenser is attached to the centre-of-gravity hook of the helicopter, usually a Bell UH-1, by strong webbing straps with forged-steel rings. The system's remote controls are connected to the control panel in the helicopter via a cable fitted with a multi-pole connector. This has been designed for quick release both on the ground and in the air in case of an emergency.

The compact control panel can be mounted on the console of the helicopter, or in any other suitable position. The system has been designed for both manual and automatic scatter dropping and consists of a transistorised electronic-control unit which can open the doors at intervals of 0·1 to 0·6 seconds. This, together with the speed of the helicopter, allows the mines to be dispersed according to the tactical requirement. The helicopter normally flies at a height of 200 metres and a speed of 100 km/h. A read-out on the control console indicates when each door of the dispenser is opened and the operator can also see at a glance how many

mines have been dispensed and how many are left. When operated manually one door opens every time the button is depressed. There is also an emergency device which, when operated, causes the complete dispenser to be emptied at once. The whole system requires a 28 volt dc electrical supply.

SPECIFICATIONS
Weight:
  (empty) 240 kg
  (loaded) 930 kg

Length: 1·7 m
Width: 1·6 m
Height: 1·7 m

STATUS
In production and service.

MANUFACTURER
Valsella SpA, 25018 Montichiari, Brescia, Italy.
  Sales handled by Valtec, Italiana Via M Mercati 22, Rome, Italy.

UH-1 helicopter fitted with Valsella VS/MD scatter-dropping mine system laying minefield

---

MISAR SY-AT Helicopter Anti-tank and Anti-personnel Mine-scattering System

DESCRIPTION
The MISAR SY-AT helicopter-carried scattering system has been designed for use with the MISAR SB-81 anti-tank and MISAR SB-33 anti-personnel mines which are already in production. The first production SY-AT system was completed in April 1978.

The system is composed of a basic distributor module and two ancillary modules. The former is connected to the baricentric hook of the helicopter by a special suspension sling and connector hook, which also contains the electrical connection. The unit can be carried slung under standard helicopter types.

The mines are dispensed through hatches in the bottom of the distributors. The hatches can be opened at a programmed frequency, or manually by pushing a button on the control console mounted in the helicopter. Safety blocks ensure that the hatches do not open until the scattering reaches the target area. The scattering ratio of anti-tank to anti-personnel mines is variable according to mission requirements and is controlled from the control panel. Indicators on the panel advise the operator when the magazines are empty as well as how many full magazines remain. Safety pins are removed from the mines as they leave the plastic

magazines. In an emergency it is possible to unload all the mines in the distributor simultaneously.

The basic module contains 32 magazines which contain 2496 anti-personnel or 160 anti-tank mines. The ancillary distributors are hooked on each side of the basic module, each with eight magazines for 624 anti-personnel or 40 anti-tank mines, or a combination. The complete system, basic module and two ancillary modules, has a total of 3744 anti-personnel mines or 240 anti-tank mines, or a combination of these mines.

STATUS
In production. In service with various countries.

MANUFACTURER
MISAR SpA, Via Gavardo 6, 25016 Ghedi (Brescia), Italy.

SPECIFICATIONS
Magazine of anti-tank mines
Weight:
  (empty) 3·5 kg
  (loaded) 19·5 kg
Number of SB-81 mines: 5
Dimensions: 246 × 110 × 1142 mm

Magazine of anti-personnel mines
Weight:
  (empty) 3·6 kg
  (loaded) 15 kg

Number of SB-33 mines: 78
Dimensions: 246 × 110 × 1142 mm

Basic distributor module
Empty weight: 150 kg
Loaded weight:
  (with anti-tank mines) 774 kg
  (with anti-personnel mines) 630 kg
Capacity: 32 magazines containing 5 anti-tank or 78 anti-personnel mines each
Dimensions: 1545 × 1320 × 1380 mm

Ancillary distributor module
Weight empty: 35 kg
Loaded weight:
  (with anti-tank mines) 191 kg
  (with anti-personnel mines) 155 kg
Capacity: 8 magazines containing 5 anti-tank or 78 anti-personnel mines each
Dimensions: 1545 × 399 mm

Complete unit
Weight: (empty) 220 kg
Weight loaded:
  (with anti-tank mines) 1156 kg
  (with anti-personnel mines) 940 kg
Capacity: 48 magazines each holding 5 anti-tank or 78 anti-personnel mines each
Dimensions: 1545 × 2119 × 1380 mm
Voltage requirements: 24–28 V dc

MISAR SY-AT helicopter anti-tank and anti-personnel mine scattering system slung under Lama helicopter; SB-81 and SB-33 mines being dispensed

MISAR SY-AT helicopter anti-tank and anti-personnel mine scattering system slung under Lama helicopter

MISAR SY-TT Anti-tank and Anti-personnel Mine-scattering System

Development of the MISAR SY-TT mine-scattering system has been suspended. For details of this system refer to *Jane's Military Vehicles and Ground Support Equipment 1983*, page 216.

Technovar DAT Scatter-dropping Mine System

DESCRIPTION

The DAT scatter-dropping mine system provides for automatic or manual dropping of loads of either TS-50 anti-personnel or MATS anti-tank mines, or a combination of both. The complete system consists of two main components, the electronic programmer fitted to the instrument panel of the carrier helicopter and the automatic dispenser system. There are two versions of the dispenser: model A, which can carry 128 anti-tank or 1280 anti-personnel mines, and model B, which can carry 64 anti-tank, 640 anti-personnel or 32 anti-tank and 320 anti-personnel. The mines are carried in preloaded magazines slotted into the dispenser. The anti-tank magazine carries 8 mines and the anti-personnel magazine 40 mines. The two models can be coupled together to form combinations, such as A + A, A + B and A + A + B. The type of combination used depends on the underslung cargo capacity of the helicopter and the type of minefield to be laid.

The dispenser system is attached to the helicopter on the end of a sling fitted with a rotary hook. The distributor doors are opened only after the correct signal is received from the electronic programmer unit, which controls the interval between door openings. The interval may be set between 0·1 and 9·9 seconds in increments of 0·1 second.

For an anti-personnel minefield the mines are dropped in groups of 80, for an anti-tank minefield in groups of 8 and for a mixed minefield in groups of 4 anti-tank mines and 40 anti-personnel mines. The typical flight altitude for laying is up to 100 metres at speed of up to 200 km/h.

SPECIFICATIONS

Anti-personnel mine magazine
Construction: steel
Length: 280 mm
Width: 145 mm
Height: 910 mm
Weight: (empty) 8 kg
Capacity: 40 TS-50 anti-personnel mines

Anti-tank mine magazine
Construction: steel
Length: 290 mm

Technovar DAT scatter-dropping mine system in use slung under Lynx helicopter

Width: 200 mm
Height: 910 mm
Weight: (empty) 11·5 kg
Capacity: 8 MATS anti-tank mines

Model A dispenser unit
Length: 1214 mm
Width: 1224 mm
Height: 1244 mm
Weight:
(empty, including sling, cables and hook) 170 kg
(filled with 128 anti-tank mines) 800 kg
(filled with 1280 anti-personnel mines) 740 kg

Model B dispenser unit
Length: 622 mm

Technovar DAT mine dispenser for Technovar MATS anti-tank scatter drop mine (T J Gander)

Width: 1224 mm
Height: 1244 mm
Weight:
(empty, including sling, cables and hook) 100 kg
(filled with 64 anti-tank mines) 425 kg
(filled with 640 anti-personnel mines) 355 kg
(filled with 32 anti-tank and 320 anti-personnel mines) 385 kg

Typical combinations of Models A and B dispenser units

	A + A	A + B	A + A + B
Length	2·428 m	1·836 m	3·050 m
Height	1·244 m	1·244 m	1·244 m
Width	1·224 m	1·224 m	1·224 m

Power requirement for electronic programmer:
28 V dc

STATUS
Models A and B in production and service.

MANUFACTURER
Technovar, 95 Via Argiro, 70121 Bari, Italy.

FIROS 25 Rocket-delivered Mine System

DESCRIPTION
The 122 mm calibre FIROS 25 rocket system is intended to act as a complementary system to the standard 155 mm NATO howitzer. As such, a wide variety of warheads has been developed for the rocket, including two carrying respectively anti-tank and anti-personnel mines as payloads.

The anti-tank mine warhead contains seven Valsella FSA-ATM hollow charge anti-tank mines that are being specially developed for the FIROS system. Details of this are given in the *Mines* section, page 179. The anti-personnel mine warhead contains 44 anti-personnel mines of an unspecified type. Maximum range with a sub-munition warhead is 25 000 metres with the warhead breaking into three sections over the target zone to allow the mines to be scattered. The launcher, which has 40 tubes, can be loaded with either single warhead type rockets or a variety of types allowing mixed minefields to be laid.

SPECIFICATIONS
Rocket motor
Calibre: 122 mm
Length: 2·005 m
Launch weight: 35·1 kg
Propellant weight: 22 kg
Max range with sub-munition warhead: 25 000 m

Sub-munition warhead
Calibre: 122 mm
Length: 1·186 m
Total weight: 17·5 kg
Weight of safety arming unit: 0·7 kg
Weight of timer and impact sensor: 0·2 kg
Number of sub-projectiles: 7 anti-tank or 44 anti-personnel mines

STATUS
Prototype. Full details of FIROS 25 are given in *Jane's Armour and Artillery 1983–84*, page 728.

MANUFACTURER
BPD DIFESA-SPAZIO, Defence and Aerospace Division, 00187 Rome, Via Sicillia 162, Italy.

SWEDEN

FFV Minelayer

DEVELOPMENT
This mechanical minelayer has been developed by FFV and is designed specifically for use with the FFV 028 anti-tank mine. Development began in 1976 and the equipment has been adopted by the Swedish Army. Series production began in 1982.

DESCRIPTION
The FFV minelayer can lay the mines either on the surface or buried to a depth of 0·25 metre. The distance between the mines can be varied between 4 and 99 metres and maximum laying capacity is 20 mines per minute at a speed of 7 km/h. All the crew has to do is remove the transport safety tab and place the mine on the chute. The minelayer then buries the mine and replaces the soil.

The system can be towed behind most types of vehicle. Sweden has used the Volvo BM 860 TC (6 × 6) vehicle as it combines a high loading capacity of 1000 mines with exceptional cross-country mobility, and gives the plough effective traction even on extremely hard soil. Information on the Volvo BM 860 TC can be found in the *Construction equipment* section.

SPECIFICATIONS
Crew: 2–4
Weight: 1700 kg
Length: 4·3 m
Width: 2·4 m

STATUS
In production.

MANUFACTURER
FFV Ordnance Division, S-631 87 Eskilstuna, Sweden.

FFV minelayer

FFV minelayer with FFV 028 anti-tank mines on loading chute

UNION OF SOVIET SOCIALIST REPUBLICS

GMZ Tracked Minelayer

DESCRIPTION
The GMZ (gusenichnyi mino-zagraditel) tracked minelayer is based on the chassis of the SA-4 (Ganef) surface-to-air missile system. The driver is seated at the front of the vehicle on the left side with the engine to his right. This leaves the rear of the vehicle clear for the mounting of the minelaying equipment and the stowage of mines. The suspension of the GMZ consists of seven road wheels with the drive sprocket mounted at the front and the idler at the rear. There are four track return rollers. The minelayer is of the plough type and resembles the Soviet PMR-3 and the East German MLG-60 mechanical minelaying systems. Like the latter systems, the GMZ can lay the mines on the surface or bury them.

Infra-red vision equipment enables the GMZ to carry out minelaying operations during darkness. Scale of issue is 3 per engineer company of a motorised rifle or tank regiment, replacing the PMR-3.

STATUS
In service with the Soviet Army.

MANUFACTURER
Soviet state arsenals.

GMZ tracked minelayer in travelling order

SPECIFICATIONS
(provisional)
Crew: 4
Weight: 25 000 kg
Length:
   (vehicle) 7·5 m
   (vehicle with plough lowered) 10·3 m
   (vehicle with plough in travelling position) 9·1 m
Width: 3·1 m
Height:
   (to top of plough in travelling position) 2·5 m
   (to top of searchlight) 2·7 m
Track: 2·66 m
Track width: 540 mm
Length of track on ground: 5 m
Max speed: (road) 50 km/h
Gradient: 60%
Vertical obstacle: 1 m

Trench: 3·2 m
Engine: water-cooled diesel developing 600 hp
Armament: 14·5 mm KPVT machine gun
Mine capacity: 208 (estimated)
Work speed:
   (surface laying) 4–10 km/h
   (burying) 2–3 km/h
Minelaying rate:
   (surface laying) 8 mines/minute
   (burying) 4 mines/minute
Mine spacing: 4–5·5 m apart
Reload time: 12–15 minutes

Rear view of GMZ tracked minelayer with minelaying equipment covered

PMR-2, PMR-3 and PMZ-4 Towed Minelayers

DESCRIPTION
The PMR-2 (pritsepnyi mino-zagraditel-2) is a two-wheeled trailer with two chutes. The upper part of the chute has a wide mouth into which the anti-tank mines are loaded. They then slide down a double roller conveyor into the distributing mechanism, which spaces them at intervals of two or four metres. The chain drive distribution mechanism is controlled by a three position lever mounted on the control box. The mines are laid on the surface and buried by a follow-up team if required. The trailer is normally towed by a 6 × 6 truck or a BTR-152 (6 × 6) armoured personnel carrier, with a crew of seven. The work speed of the PMR-2 is 3 to 5 km/h and mine load is 120 mines.

The PMR-3 (pritsepnyi mino-zagraditel'-3) has a single chute and the operator, who is seated on the two-wheeled trailer, can select either surface or buried laying, to 300 or 400 mm depth, and also controls the spacing of the mines. The PMR-3 is normally towed by a specially modified BTR-152 (6 × 6) armoured personnel carrier which carries 120 TM-46 or similar anti-tank mines. A fully loaded BTR-152, carrying 120 mines, can lay a minefield 500 metres long when the mines are spaced at 4-metre intervals in five minutes.

For both systems the capacity varies as follows if the tow vehicle is other than the BTR-152: ZIL-157 200, BTR-60 100–130, Ural-375 350. The PMZ-4 towed minelayer is the same as the PMR-3 but with a 200-mine capacity.

SPECIFICATIONS
PMR-3
Crew: 4 or 5
Length: 3 m
Width: 2 m
Height: 2·5 m

PMR-3 towed minelayer in travelling position

PMR-2 minelayer in travelling position

Tyre size: 7.50 × 20
Mine spacing: 4–5·5 m apart
Burial depth: (soft soil) 300–400 mm
Work speed:
   (surface laying) 4–10 km/h
   (burying) 2–3 km/h
Minelaying rate: 10–12 mines/minute
Reload time: 10–12 minutes

PMR-3 towed minelayer in operational use

STATUS
In service with members of the Warsaw Pact and other countries that have received Soviet aid.

MANUFACTURER
Soviet state arsenals.

Minelaying Chutes

DESCRIPTION
Before the introduction of mechanical minelaying equipment such as the PMR-2 and the PMR-3 the Warsaw Pact armies made wide use of simple minelaying chutes for laying anti-tank mines. They were attached to the sides or rear of 6 × 6 trucks or the BTR-152 (6 × 6) armoured personnel carrier. The mines were fed onto the chute by hand and then slid to the ground by gravity. They were normally left on the surface but were sometimes buried by follow-up teams.

This method of laying mines was normally used when a minefield had to be laid rapidly. Its major disadvantage was that the surface laid mines could be easily detected. The mine chute illustrated is a more modern system for laying anti-personnel mines of the stake type.

SPECIFICATIONS (Anti-tank chute)
Length: 4·8 m
Width: 0·406 m
Height: 1·27 m
Laying rate: 4 mines/minute

STATUS
Minelaying chutes are no longer used on a wide scale.

MANUFACTURER
Warsaw Pact state factories.

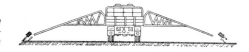

Drawing from Soviet source showing 6 × 6 truck with launching chutes rigged either side for POMZ-2 anti-personnel mines

Soviet Anti-tank Minelaying Helicopter

DESCRIPTION
Recent reports in Soviet military periodicals have indicated that they are using a helicopter-borne anti-tank minelaying system to protect the flanks of armoured spearhead units. The system is basically a chute (4·8 metres long, 0·406 metre wide and 0·127 metre high) attached to the side of the helicopter down which mines slide to the ground. Although this method has the disadvantage of the mines being conspicuous it does allow the tactical commander a quick reaction and long-range capability for laying anti-tank mines.

Helicopters seen with this system are the Mil Mi-4 Hound (estimated carrying capacity 200 metallic anti-tank mines such as the TM-46 with MVM fuze) and the Mil Mi-8 Hip C (estimated carrying capacity 400 metallic anti-tank mines).

STATUS
In service with the Soviet Army and other Warsaw Pact forces including Poland.

Mil Mi-8 Hip C laying anti-tank minefield

UNITED STATES OF AMERICA

Family of Scatterable Mines (FASCAM)

DEVELOPMENT
The Family of Scatterable Mines, developed by the United States Army Armament Research and Development Command (AARADCOM), under the direction of the Project Manager for Selected Ammunition, is a family of anti-personnel/anti-tank mines and mine launch systems designed specifically for emplacement flexibility, including quick airstrike capability and selected ground delivery.

This low-cost family of scatterable mines provides many ways to emplace a variety of minefields rapidly, the purpose being to block, delay, divert, interdict, or destroy the enemy.

It consists of the following systems, all of which are briefly mentioned in the *Mine warfare equipment* section:
Ground Emplaced Mine Scattering System (GEMSS); Gator mine system; Modular Pack Mine System (MOPMS); Universal Mine Dispensing System (UMIDS).

STATUS
In service with US armed forces.

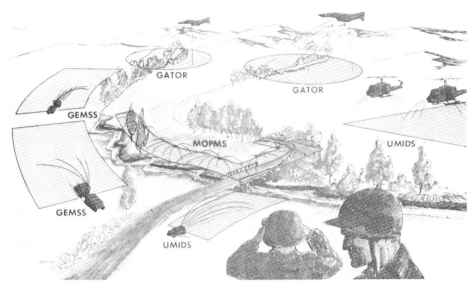

Roles of members of Family of Scatterable Mines

M128 Vehicle-towed Mine Dispenser

DESCRIPTION
The Ground Emplaced Mine Scattering System (GEMSS) M128 (or Frisbee Flinger as it is more popularly known) has been developed by Picatinny Arsenal and the Ordnance Division of the FMC Corporation of San Jose, California.

It is mounted on a modified M794 flatbed trailer and can be towed behind a truck or tracked vehicle such as an M113 APC, over both roads and cross country. Anti-tank and anti-personnel mines of the same dimensions are carried in the drum type magazine and can be dispensed concurrently or separately to preselected patterns and minefield densities. Weight of the M128 empty is 4773 kg and loaded 6364 kg.

The M128 feeds mines out of a hydraulic drum type magazine, flips them through a directional tunnel and sends them spinning to the ground. The mines are left on the surface and a percentage of mines in each batch is fitted with an anti-disturbance mechanism.

The system uses the M74 anti-personnel and M75 anti-tank mines. It can carry up to 800 mines in its storage drums and dispense two mines per second. The mines have a factory-set long (more than a day) self-destruct time, which can be changed to a still longer time by the M128 while the mines are being dispensed. The anti-personnel mine is tripwire-activated and has a blast kill mechanism. The anti-tank mine is very similar to the mine used in the Remote Anti-Armor Mine System. Both types of mine have anti-disturbance features fitted.

The M74 and M75 mines are shipped in special crates each holding 40 mines. A crate carrying M74 anti-personnel mines weighs 88·45 kg and a crate carrying M75 anti-tank mines weighs 97·5 kg. Inside the crate the mines are packed in tubular sleeves each carrying five mines. Loading the M128 dispenser takes from three to five men up to 20 minutes with the normal mine mix being five anti-tank to one anti-personnel.

STATUS
Type classified for Army service early in 1980. Fiscal year 1980/81 funding covered 41 units, fiscal year 1982 funding was $34·7 million for 70 units, with 37 units being requested for fiscal year 1983.

M128 vehicle-towed mine dispenser with jacks lowered (US Army)

M128 vehicle-towed mine dispenser being towed by M113 APC (US Army)

Volcano Universal Mine-dispensing System

DEVELOPMENT/DESCRIPTION
Volcano was originally an Aerojet Ordnance Company project but has now passed to Honeywell Inc who have been awarded a $10·5 million, 30-month contract for advanced development of the system. This is specifically for use by the new US Army Light Divisions and could be in service by 1990.

Volcano is a high-capacity mine dispenser and has been developed for the UH-60 helicopter but could be adapted for use with other helicopters or ground vehicles. On the UH-60, two dispensers with 40 mine canisters each are attached to the sides of the fuselage (160 canisters in all). In flight the load of 960 anti-tank and anti-personnel mines (six to each canister) are ejected in a sequence that covers an area about 100 metres wide. The resultant mine density can be as high as one mine to each square metre.

STATUS
Development.

Modular Pack Mine System (MOPMS)

DESCRIPTION

The Modular Pack Mine System (MOPMS) is a member of the Family of Scatterable Mines (FASCAM). It is a portable system for selective protection and small area coverage for withdrawing friendly forces.

The MOPMS modules, weighing 68 kg each, are taken to the operation site by truck and carried by two men to the required position. If unused they can be retrieved and reused. Firing of modules is by a coded remote control radio command or by a signal sent through a cable connected to a standard US Army blasting device on the dispenser module. Both XM131 anti-tank/anti-vehicle and XM132 anti-personnel mines are used.

The mines contain three Large Scale Integrated (LSI) microelectronic chips in the electronics package, which also includes a command destruct/recycle receiver and a sensor circuit. The package fits within 5·8 cubic inches. Ammonium/lithium batteries are fitted that remain passive until the command to scatter the mines is received. On landing the magnetic field sensor orien-

Module Pack Mine System dismantled to show major components and 21 mines carried

tates the anti-tank/anti-vehicle mine towards the target vehicle and enables the entire belly of the target vehicle to be attacked by the warhead, in addition to tank tracks or wheels.

The mines are supplied with preset self-destruction devices or can be detonated by remote control. The built-in timers can be recycled, extending the life of the minefield.

The anti-personnel mine is activated by four tripwires. These are automatically deployed on landing and, when disturbed, initiate a fragmenting kill mechanism.

STATUS

Under development.

MANUFACTURERS

Engineering development of the command destruct/recycle electronics is undertaken by Hughes Aircraft Company Ground Systems Group, Fullerton, California, USA.

Aerojet is responsible for the dispenser and Honeywell is systems integrator with responsibility for the mines.

Module Pack Mine System with anti-tank and anti-personnel mines displayed on top (Christopher F Foss)

Close up of anti-personnel mine used in Module Pack Mine System

Remote control unit developed by Hughes for Module Pack Mine System (Christopher F Foss)

Universal Mine Dispensing System

DESCRIPTION

The Universal Mine Dispensing System (UMIDS) is an expansion of the Modular Pack Mine System (MOPMS). It is in early development for an as yet undefined requirement as part of the Family of Scatterable Mines (FASCAM). It is based on a launcher module containing nine mines grouped in three sequentially launched sets. The modules are to be rack mounted for armoured vehicles, all types of soft-skinned vehicles and trailers, fixed wing aircraft, helicopters and bipod mounted, in a single tube configuration, for firing by a single soldier.

STATUS

Under development.

M57 Anti-tank Mine Dispensing System (ATMDS)

DESCRIPTION
The M57 Anti-tank Mine Dispensing System is a side-lift plough with a side-insertion mine chute mounted on a two-wheeled trailer towed by a 2½-ton (6 × 6) truck which carries the crew and supply of mines. The M57 can lay M15 anti-tank mines on the surface, or buried below the ground at a sustained rate of 375 mines per hour. The mines can be buried to a maximum depth of 152 mm. The system is not suited to use in very hard soil or on sideslopes. It is issued on the scale of one per combat engineer company in Europe.

STATUS
Production complete. In service with the US Army.

Complete M57 ATMDS from mine pallets on left to dispenser on right (US Army)   *Side-lift plough of M57 ATMDS with mine dispenser chute above* (US Army)

MINE DETECTION EQUIPMENT

BULGARIA

M62 Mine Detector

DESCRIPTION
This is the latest Bulgarian mine detector; it can detect metallic mines or plastic mines with some metallic components such as metallic fuzes.

The detector head assembly is rectangular and is mounted on a search handle which also contains the power source and operating controls. It is of the induction-coil low-frequency type and can detect a metallic object 300 mm in diameter at a range of 500 mm. Weight of the complete equipment is 2·5 kg.

STATUS
In service with the Bulgarian Army.

MANUFACTURER
Bulgarian state factories.

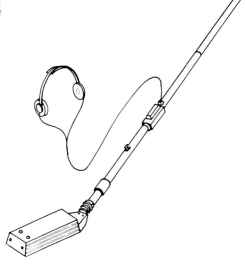

M62 metallic mine detector

CZECHOSLOVAKIA

M-10 and M-11 Metallic Mine Detectors

DESCRIPTION
Both these mine detectors operate on the beat-frequency oscillation principle, the only difference between the two models being the construction of their search head. The M-10's search head consists of two detachable plates 300 mm in diameter which overlap by 100 mm while the M-11 has a single plate of the same effective area.

The equipment consists of the search head assembly, search handle consisting of four jointed aluminium sections each 500 mm long, tuning box with tone regulator, power supply of three dry cells (25 volt), and the headphones. The tuning-box tone regulator and the three 25-volt dry batteries are carried in a canvas pack on the operator's back. The batteries, when not in use, are kept in a small pouch on the side of the pack.

SPECIFICATIONS
Weight of complete equipment: 12 kg

STATUS
In service with the Czechoslovak Army.

MANUFACTURER
Czechoslovak state factories.

M-10 and M-11 mine detectors showing different heads

FRANCE

Metallic Mine Detector Model F1

DESCRIPTION
The electromagnetic metallic mine detector Model F1 (Le Détecteur Electromagnétique de Mines) is designed for detecting anti-tank and anti-personnel mines that contain at least one metal part.

The complete detector is packed into a case 655 mm long, 320 mm wide and 160 mm high, which has two foam packing pieces to protect the equipment from vibration. The complete equipment can be assembled for use in less than five minutes.

The mine detector consists of five major components: the detecting head, telescopic handle, electronics box, connecting cable and a set of standard dry batteries. The batteries provide sufficient power for up to 30 hours of continuous use. The accessories are the flexible cover for the detection head and headset with cable and connector. The former is fitted to the detection head when the terrain has fluctuating temperatures, for example shade and sunshine areas.

There are two methods of using this mine detector, upright and prone. For the upright method, the telescopic handle is extended and the angle of the search head on the handle is adjusted to enable the operator to sweep the head in front of him from side to side as he proceeds forward. For the prone position, the sweep motion is similar but the operator lies on the ground with the handle and the head parallel to the ground.

SPECIFICATIONS
Weight ready for use: 3·5 kg
Dimensions: 650 × 300 × 155 mm
Operational life of batteries: 30 h (continuous operation)
Operating temperature range: −31·5 to +51°C

Detection capability	Detection range
1 g of steel	100 mm
20 g of aluminium	300 mm
100 g of aluminium	450 mm

STATUS
In production. In service with the French Army, under designation DHPM-1A.

MANUFACTURER
Atelier de Fabrication de Toulouse, 155 avenue de Grande-Bretagne, 31052 Toulouse, France.

Enquires to Groupement Industriel des Armements Terrestres (GIAT), 10 place Georges Clémenceau, 92211 Saint-Cloud, France.

Metallic mine detector Model F1

GERMANY, DEMOCRATIC REPUBLIC

MSG 64 Metallic Mine Detector

DESCRIPTION
The equipment consists of the oval head assembly which can be adjusted to various angles, three piece search handle, tuning box in the second handle, tone regulator on the lower portion of the second handle, power supply of four 1·2 volt dry batteries in the lower portion of the second handle and the headphones.

The detector head is waterproof and can detect metallic shaped objects 50 mm in diameter at a range of 180 mm. When disassembled the complete equipment is carried in a camouflaged water-repellent canvas case.

SPECIFICATIONS
Weight:
 (complete equipment) 4·4 kg
 (detector) 2·35 kg
Length of search handle: 2·4 m

STATUS
In service with the East German Army.

MANUFACTURER
East German state factories.

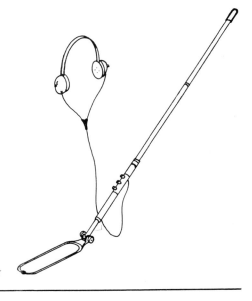

MSG 64 metallic mine detector

GERMANY, FEDERAL REPUBLIC

Mine Detector MSG1

DESCRIPTION
The Mine Detector MSG1 (Minensuchgerät) has been designed for installation on the front of lightweight cross-country vehicles such as the British Land-Rover or the German Auto-Union LKW (Munga). Eltro claims that the MSG1 will detect both metallic and non-metallic mines. The search antenna radiates microwave energy into the ground and the reflected signals are displayed on a monitor screen. No specification on the MSG1 has been released but the vehicle may incorporate a braking system which would bring the vehicle to a halt automatically once a mine was detected. Some form of remote control equipment may be installed to enable the vehicle to be operated from a safe distance.

STATUS
Prototype.

MANUFACTURER
Eltro GmbH, D-6900 Heidelberg 1, Federal Republic of Germany.

MSG1 mine detector installed on front of LKW (4 × 4) cross-country vehicle

---

Vallon Vehicle-mounted Metal Detector Model ML1750

DESCRIPTION
The integrated circuit Model ML1750 vehicle-mounted metal detector is non-metallic and is mounted on a frame about one metre in front of the vehicle. It is designed to detect mined areas and concealed metallic objects. An indicator meter, optical alarm signal, sensitivity switch and other systems are mounted in the vehicle. Zero compensation is by push button and the sensitivity switch allows one of twelve sensitivity detecting steps to be selected. The sensitivity can be adjusted during use. The vehicle speed during sweeping operations is limited to between 5 and 15 km per hour depending on the terrain.

STATUS
In production. In service with various countries.

MANUFACTURER
Vallon GmbH, Im Grund 3, D-7412 Eningen, West Germany.

SPECIFICATIONS
Weight of detecting coil: 43 kg
Width of locating area: 1·6 m
Power supply: 12 V battery
Current consumption: 3 A

Sensitivity Object	Metal type	Dimensions (length × diameter)	Detection depth
shell	iron	51 × 13 mm	400 mm
shell	iron	150 × 37 mm	600 mm
shell	iron	330 × 75 mm	900 mm
shell	iron	440 × 105 mm	1100 mm

Vallon vehicle-mounted metal detector Model ML1750 mounted on front of LKW (4 × 4) cross-country vehicle

Vallon Iron Detector Model EL1302

DESCRIPTION
The Model EL1302 iron detector was designed to locate ferromagnetic objects such as bombs, mines, shells and current carrying cables. The instrument monitors the earth's magnetic field and signifies any disturbance of the field by a buried object by both visual and acoustic methods. There are six steps of sensitivity and automatic zero compensation is used.

SPECIFICATIONS
Weight of instrument: 6 kg
Weight of instrument in case: 19·5 kg
Dimensions of case: 970 × 400 × 180 mm
Power supply: 10 × 1·5 V monocell type IEC R 20

STATUS
In production. In service with various countries.

MANUFACTURER
Vallon GmbH, Im Grund 3, D-7412 Eningen 1, West Germany.

Sensitivity

Object	Metal type	Dimensions (length × diameter)	Detection depth
shell	iron	51 × 13 mm	250 mm
shell	iron	150 × 37 mm	1000 mm
shell	iron	330 × 75 mm	1200 mm
shell	iron	440 × 105 mm	1800 mm
1000 kg bomb	iron	1750 × 510 mm	6000 mm

Vallon iron detector Model EL1302

Vallon Metal Detector Model ML1612

DESCRIPTION
The Vallon Metal Detector Model ML1612 has now replaced the Model ML1611 in production (for details of the Model ML1611 see entry on page 211 of *Jane's Military Vehicles and Ground Support Equipment 1982*). The ML1612 uses integrated circuits and is designed to detect all kinds of ferrous and non-ferrous metals buried underground. High search sensitivity, simple one-control operation and an automatic battery test facility are some of the more important features. The Model ML1612 is waterproof.

SPECIFICATIONS
Weight of set: 3 kg
Weight of set in case complete: 15·8 kg
Dimensions of case: 760 × 410 × 170 mm
Carrying bar length: 1030–2000 mm
Power supply: 4 × 1·5 V monocell type IEC R 20

STATUS
In production. In service with various countries.

MANUFACTURER
Vallon GmbH, Im Grund 3, D-7412 Eningen, West Germany.

Sensitivity

Object	Metal type	Dimensions (length × diameter)	Detection depth
projectile	lead	6·35 × 11·5 mm	190 mm
case	mild steel	8·5 × 17 mm	230 mm
projectile	iron	7·8 × 31 mm	280 mm
grenade case	iron	28·5 × 31 mm	570 mm
shell	iron	105 × 385 mm	800 mm
shell	iron	105 × 440 mm	900 mm

Vallon metal detector Model ML1612

Förster Metallic Detector Model FEREX 4.021

DESCRIPTION
The Förster Model 4.021 metallic detector was developed as a replacement for the earlier Model 4.015 and 4.016 detectors and the first production deliveries were made in 1976/77. The Model 4.021 has undergone some production alterations since the early models and it is now described in the manufacturer's literature as a search instrument for ferromagnetic objects. The FEREX Model 4.021 is the detector component of the AB Bofors system for the location and disposal of unexploded ordnance.
There are now three versions of the Model 4.021. They are as follows:
FEREX K 4.021.02. This is the universal version of the Model 4.021 as it can be used for land, water and borehole applications.
FEREX L 4.021.03. This version is intended for use over land only.
FEREX W 4.021.04. Intended for underwater search only this version lacks the carrying probe of the K and L versions. It can be either used by a diver, towed from a boat or towed to and fro across rivers and streams. A prototype of this W version has now been produced in which the entire equipment is enclosed within a streamlined housing for use by a swimming diver.
The K and L versions used over land have the

downward-pointing probe carried on a long handle supported by a carrying strap. Over the probe is the control unit which has touch-control buttons and an instrument scale as well as connections to the probe and the power unit which is at the opposite end of the carrying handle. There are three main search modes selectable with a fourth enabling the instrument to be used as a compass. The first mode is known as static difference which is the normal search mode when all ferrous objects will be detected. The second mode is static difference selective in which only large signals will be indicated. The third mode is dynamic difference when static signals are suppressed. All indications from the probe are shown directionally and quantitatively on the meter scale on the control unit and the scale also provides directional indication.
The control unit has a built-in loudspeaker for aural warnings and a functional test facility is incorporated.
The K version is normally carried in a specially-fitted transit case which includes extensions cables for the underwater search role and for use in boreholes. Headphones are an optional accessory as are rechargeable batteries and charging units. The L version is normally carried in a long canvas rucksack. The W version is not provided with a carrying handle but has extra connecting cable from the control unit to the probe and ropes for towing are normally carried. On the W version the control unit is carried on the power supply housing which are then both enclosed in a carrying case.
A switch on the control unit can be used to alter the

Prototype of version of Ferex Marine for use by swimming divers

sensitivity of the instrument. The Model 4.021 can detect an 88 mm projectile at depths up to three metres, a 100 mm projectile at depths up to four metres, and large objects such as 250 kg bombs will be detected at depths up to five metres.

SPECIFICATIONS
Weight of basic components: (all versions) 3·8 kg
Weight of probe: 1·2 kg
Weight of carrying handle: 0·7 kg
Power supply: (with batteries) 1·7 kg
Probe unit length: 600 mm
Probe unit diameter: 45 mm
Carrying handle length: 1055 mm
Dimensions:
   (power supply) 104 × 315 × 100 mm
   (control unit) 104 × 252 × 96 mm
   (transit case) 1120 × 310 × 175 mm
Operating voltage: 6–12 V
Batteries: 6 mono-cells each 1·5 V IEC R 20
Operating temperature range: −15 to +65°C

STATUS
In production. In service with the Swedish Air Force and
undisclosed countries.

MANUFACTURER
Institut Dr Förster GmbH and Co KG, In Laisen 70,
D-7410 Reutlinger 1, Postfach 925, West Germany.

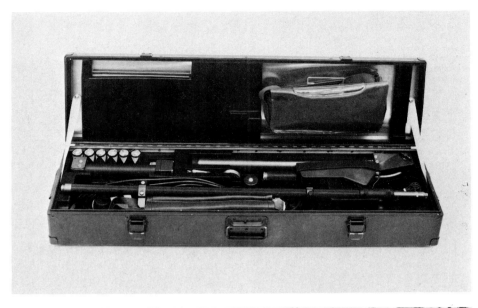

FEREX Model 4.021 K complete in transit case

FEREX Model L 4.021.03 being carried in rucksack

FEREX Model L 4.021.03 in use

Förster-METEX 4.125 Metal Detector

DESCRIPTION
The Förster METEX 4.125 has now replaced the earlier
METEX 4.122 (for details of METEX 4.122 see page
213 of *Jane's Military Vehicles and Ground Support
Equipment 1982*) and is intended for detecting metal
objects under ground, in walls or in shallow water. It is
sensitive enough to detect plastic mines with a small
metal content.
   The METEX 4.125 operates on the electromagnetic

alternating field principle and detects any radiation
reflected by metal objects.
   The METEX 4.125 has three main components. The
first is the probe assembly which consists of a waterproof circular search coil, a four part telescopic handle
and the associated cables and plugs. The handle can be
used from the conventional sweeping position standing
upright, or held on an arm clamp support for use when
prone. The second component is the control box with
only one switch control and the batteries. The third
component is the headphones. The whole equipment is
splashproof, and the search coil can be used in shallow
water.

The METEX 4.125 can be carried in a special
aluminium transit case which contains all the accessories and a spare set of batteries, but an alternative
carrier is a canvas rucksack. Other accessories include
a carrying bag, carrying strap, test pieces and a hand-
grip and arm-rest.

STATUS
Production.

MANUFACTURER
Institut Dr Förster GmbH and Co KG, In Laisen 70,
D-7410 Reutlingen 1, Postfach 925, West Germany.

SPECIFICATIONS
Weight of equipment: 3·5 kg approx
Weight of transit case: 11 kg approx
Search coil diameter: 260 mm
Length of search coil and handle:
(minimum) 940 mm
(maximum) 2000 mm
Dimensions
(control box) 177 × 122 × 77 mm
(transit case) 740 × 400 × 160 mm
Temperature operating range: −15 to +55°C
Battery voltage: 9 V
Battery power supply: 6 × 1·5 V mono-cells IEC R 14
Battery life: approx 60 h

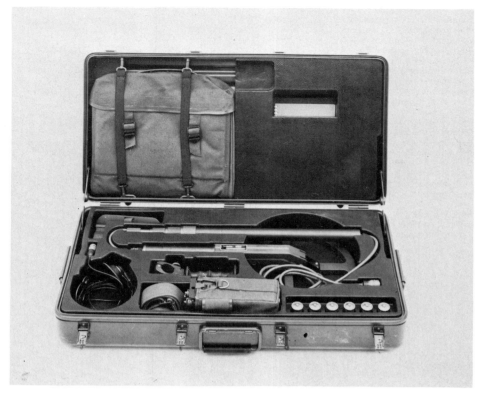

Transit case for METEX 4.125

Rucksack for METEX 4.125

METEX 4.125 in use

METEX 4.125 in use in prone position

INDIA

The Indian Army has introduced into service mine detection equipment capable of detecting non-metallic mines. No other details are available at present.

ISRAEL

BETA BMD-34 Metallic Mine Detector

DESCRIPTION
The BETA metallic solid state mine detector type BMD-34 is a sensitive, sophisticated, miniature detector which can be used to detect metallic anti-tank or anti-personnel mines in both magnetic or non-magnetic soils. The instrument detects any conductive material, ferrous or non-ferrous, in any type of soil.

The instrument comprises a search-head mounted on the end of a telescopic handle, a belt-carried electronic control unit, and a headset for the audible output signal. As an optional extra, a visual display can be clamped on the telescopic handle. The visual display consists of a 40 mm diameter meter with a central zero and a self-illuminated scale.

The controls consist of an on/off control, search-head balance knob and the battery check toggle switch. The mine detector is human-engineered for the minimum of adjustments during operation and features an auto-matic compensation for variables such as search-head characteristics, amount of magnetic material in the soil and temperature variations.

The mine detector has been designed for military use under severe environmental conditions. It is immersion proof in two metres of water, shock and vibration proof and has EMI protection.

SPECIFICATIONS
Weight of equipment ready for use: 2·9 kg
Detection capability: metallic anti-tank mine 300 mm deep
Operating temperature range: −15 to +72°C

STATUS
In production since 1976. In service with undisclosed countries.

MANUFACTURER
BETA Engineering and Development Limited, PO Box 98, Beer-Sheva, 84100 Israel.

BETA BMD-34 metallic mine detector in use

KOREA, REPUBLIC

NMD-9 Mine Detection Set

DESCRIPTION
Developed by the Agency for Defence Development of Korea, the NMD-9 is a rugged, solid-state portable device capable of detecting metallic and non-metallic mines. The search head generates and radiates a continuous wave RF signal and receives and demodulates the resultant signal for aural presentation in a headset. The search head is encased in a rubber cover and is mounted on the end of a long carrying handle which also mounts the control box. The control box contains the system electronics on a single board and the battery which has an operating life of 15 hours in continuous use. The control box also has a 'search' switch used to locate the general presence of a mine when a 'point' mode with three varying degrees of sensitivity may be selected.

STATUS
Production.

MANUFACTURER
Gold Star Electric Company Limited, 537 Namdaemun-ro 5ga, Jung-gu, Seoul 100, Republic of Korea.

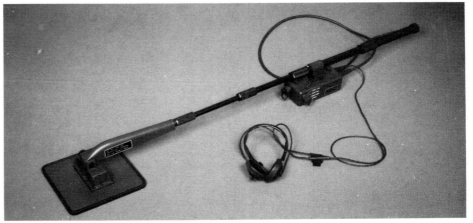

NMD-9 mine detection set

SPECIFICATIONS
Weight: (complete) 3·63 kg approx
Battery life: (continuous) 15 hours

UNION OF SOVIET SOCIALIST REPUBLICS

IMP Mine Detector

DESCRIPTION
This is the latest Soviet mine detector; it can detect metallic mines, or plastic mines which contain some metallic components, for example the fuze.

The IMP mine detector consists of the detector head assembly, a four-piece search handle, tuning box which is combined with the battery pack, power supply which consists of four 1·6-volt batteries and the headphones.

When dismantled all the components are carried in a lightweight rectangular metal box. The detector head assembly consists of two transmitting antennas and a receiving antenna, all encased in a bakelite cylinder (417 mm long × 38 mm diameter). The handle consists of four aluminium sections which when joined together are 1·58 metres long. One or more of these sections can be removed to reduce the length of the equipment for use in confined areas. The tuning box, or amplifier, consists of five transistors and associated components which are mounted in a lightweight metal box, with the tone regulator on top of the tuning box.

An added advantage of the IMP over earlier Soviet mine detectors is that the equipment can be used underwater to a maximum depth of one metre.

SPECIFICATIONS
Weight of complete equipment: 9·7 kg
Detection range: 300–460 mm

Detector head assembly
Weight: 7·2 kg
Length: 417 mm
Diameter: 38 mm

STATUS
In service with the Soviet Army.

MANUFACTURER
Soviet state factories.

IMP mine detector being used in snow

Helicopter-mounted Mine Detectors

DESCRIPTION
A number of Warsaw Pact countries, including Poland, have fitted helicopters such as the Mil Mi-1 Hare with a search head which is suspended from a cable under the helicopter. This flies over the suspected area and if a minefield is located the pilot radios the units on the ground and a more complete search using conventional mine detectors is carried out. This system allows a commander to carry out area searches ahead of the main units.

STATUS
Limited service.

MANUFACTURER
Warsaw Pact state factories.

DIM Vehicle-mounted Mine Detector

DESCRIPTION
The DIM vehicle-mounted mine detector consists of a UAZ-69 (4 × 4) light vehicle, or the more recent UAZ-469 (4 × 4) light vehicle, modified to carry a frame on which is mounted a non-magnetic sensing head. This is supported by a frame attached to the front bumper. When travelling the equipment is swung upwards through 180 degrees and rests on top of the cab. When required for use, the equipment is swung forward and rests on two rubber-tyred wheels which are in contact with the surface of the road. The sensing head is mounted in front of the two wheels and is provided with three sets of dual wheels.

The DIM system will detect mines to a maximum depth of 250 mm, or when fording to a depth of 700 mm with a sweep width of 2·2 metres. The vehicle is normally driven at a maximum speed of 10 km/h during mine detection operations and once a mine or metallic object has been detected an audio alarm sounds and the vehicle stops automatically. Once the vehicle comes to a halt its operator can adjust the search coils to pinpoint the exact location of the metal object. No provision is made for remote control of the vehicle.

As the equipment lacks mobility, it is normally used only for clearing roads and airfields. The system has been mounted on T-62 MBTs in Afghanistan.

STATUS
In service with members of the Warsaw Pact and some countries in the Middle East.

MANUFACTURER
Soviet state factories.

DIM mine detector in travelling position on GAZ-69 (4 × 4) light vehicle

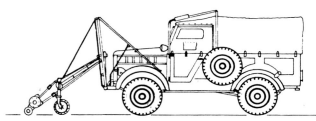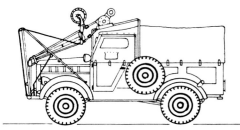

DIM mine detector mounted on front of UAZ-69 (4 × 4) vehicle. Left: equipment in operating position; right: in travelling position

Mine Probes

DESCRIPTION
During the Second World War the Soviet Army developed a selection of probes of varying shapes and sizes to locate mines. They were used simply to probe the earth to find any buried mines. It is thought likely that similar probes are in use today although the number of casualties among personnel detecting mines by this method is rather high.

Typical versions that may be met are as follows:

A simple metal probe with a pointed end.
A simple wooden pole with a metal rod projecting from one end.
A wooden or metal pole, with three or four detachable sections making up the shaft, and a metal rod projecting from one end.
A wooden or metal pole made up of three or four sections that fold together for carriage with a metal rod projecting from one end.
A wooden or metal pole with metal prongs at one end and a metal rod projecting from the other.
A short collapsible wood or metal probe.

A wooden or metal pole with several metal rods projecting from one end.
The Vladimarov probe which is equipped with a microphone to detect mines and bombs fitted with delayed action fuzes.

STATUS
In service with the Soviet Army and other Warsaw Pact forces.

MANUFACTURER
Soviet state arsenals.

UMIV-1 Metallic Mine Detector

DESCRIPTION
The UMIV-1 metallic mine detector was introduced into the Soviet Army in the post-Second World War period. The equipment consists of a rectangular search head assembly, four-piece search handle, two single-tube oscillators in the search handle, tone regulator on the upper search handle, powerpack carried in a haversack on the operator's back and the headphones. The powerpack contains a 3-volt filament supply and a 70-volt plate supply. The metal handle consists of four pieces, two detachable, with the upper part of the handle having a larger diameter than the lower part. The detector cannot function under water.

SPECIFICATIONS
Weight of complete unit: 6·6 kg
Detector head assembly size: 220 × 146 mm
Detection range: 450 mm
Length of search handle assembly:
 (2 piece) 660 mm
 (4 piece) 1·3 m

STATUS
In service with members of the Warsaw Pact and other countries.

MANUFACTURER
Soviet state factories.

UMIV-1 metallic mine detector

UNITED KINGDOM

Mine Detector No. 4C

DESCRIPTION

The United Scientific Instruments Mine Detector No. 4C (NATO Ref. No. 6665-99-900-9265) has been the standard mine detector of the British Army since 1968. Earlier models were the No. 4 and No. 4A. It comprises a search head mounted on a telescopic handle, an amplifier unit, headphones and connecting cables. For transport, the equipment is disassembled and carried in a wooden transport case which also contains the spare battery, test boxes, extension cables and other accessories.

The search head contains two mutually reacting inductance coils. Inductance is adjustable by means of a dust core trimmer assembly, and when adjusted the mutual inductance of the two coils is in balance. When any metal component is brought within the field of the coils, the balance is distorted, resulting in an oscillating difference potential. This is then amplified by the amplifier unit and fed to the earphone as a distinctly audible signal.

There are two modes of operation, normal and pavé. The former is used for detecting metallic mines in normal soil while the latter is used for detecting metallic mines in ferrite-bearing soil (pavé), or if there are likely to be any metallic splinters on the surface. The preferred mode of operation is selected by a selector switch on the amplifier unit.

For use, the telescopic pole is extended, one end strapped to the forearm and the other attached to the search head. The amplifier unit, which also contains the batteries, is clipped to the operator's belt and the cable from the search head is plugged into the unit. The lead of the earphones is connected to the amplifier unit and the equipment is then ready for immediate use.

There are two methods of searching for mines, upright and prone. For the upright method, the telescopic handle is extended and the angle of the search head on the handle is adjusted to enable the operator to sweep the head in front of him from side to side as he proceeds forward. For the prone position the sweep motion is similar but the operator lies on the ground, the handle is not extended and the head is parallel to the ground.

STATUS

In production. In service with the British Army and several overseas nations.

MANUFACTURER

United Scientific Instruments Limited, 10 Fitzroy Square, London W1P 6AB, England.

SPECIFICATIONS

Weight of detector in transit case: 14·4 kg

Transit case
Length: 533 mm
Width: 254 mm
Height: 203 mm

Search head
Weight: 1·8 kg
Length: 285 mm
Width: 185 mm
Height: 108 mm

Telescopic handle
Weight: 1·15 kg
Length:
(collapsed) 380 mm
(fully extended) 1·28 m

Amplifier unit
Weight with battery: 1·8 kg
Length: 216 mm
Width: 108 mm
Height: 108 mm

Battery type: 9 V dry cell PP6 or equivalent
Current consumption: 3·3 – 3·6 mA
Operational life of battery: 300 hours of intermittent use

Detection capacity	Detection range
British Mk. 7 anti-tank mine normal ground	510 mm
British Mk. 7 anti-tank mine pavé ground	320 mm

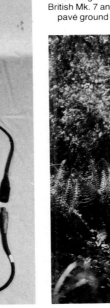

No. 4C mine detector in use

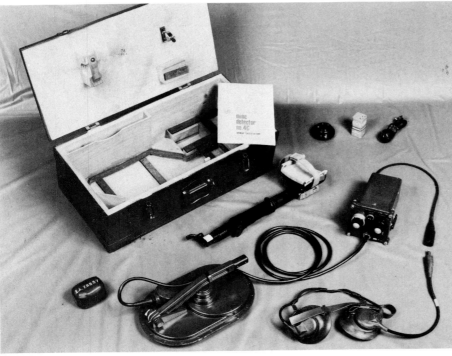

Component parts of Mine Detector No. 4C

Mine Detector 156 PMD

DESCRIPTION

The United Scientific Instruments Mine Detector 156 PMD (NATO Ref. No. 6665-01-079-9522) is suitable for use in detecting both non-metallic and metallic mines. It comprises a search head assembly, a handle assembly (either long or short), a control box assembly with processor module and headphones with connecting cable. For transport the equipment is dismantled and carried in a waterproof case.

The search head assembly consists of two transmitting antennas, a receiving antenna and transmission lines mounted on a laminated glass cloth plate. A transmitter and receiving assembly are mounted in a housing on the search head. This generates and radiates multiple chopped RF signals and receives and detects returned signals. There is a protective rubber bumper around the search head.

A short handle attached to the search head assembly by means of the transmitter-receiver housing can be

United Scientific Instruments 156 PMD mine detector being used in normal standing position

United Scientific Instruments 156 PMD mine detector being used in prone position

adjusted and held at the most favourable angle for use with a friction clutch arrangement. The long handle unit consists of four adjustable aluminium sections that fasten to the short handle by a bayonet coupling. The handle is normally used in the upright walking position and allows the operator to hold the search head approximately 1·2 metres away from his body.

The control box assembly contains the 16-bit microprocessor module with its associated electronics components, the system controls and a lithium battery for long-life operation. The housing for the control box is an aluminium watertight enclosure. A hook on the assembly allows it to be attached to the operator's belt when operating in the prone position.

The processor module converts the output of the search head to a signal which is heard in the headset which consists of two earphones joined by an adjustable stainless steel headband. Rubber ear cushions are fixed to the earphones to reduce extraneous noise.

STATUS
Production complete. In service with the British Army.

MANUFACTURER
United Scientific Instruments Limited, 10 Fitzroy Square, London W1P 6AB, England.

SPECIFICATIONS
Carrying case
Length: 600 mm
Width: 400 mm
Height: 190 mm
Weight:
  (empty) 6·2 kg
  (loaded) 10 kg

Search head assembly
Length: 221 mm
Width: 221 mm
Height: 56 mm
Weight: 770 g

Control box assembly
(without battery and processor module)
Length: 180 mm
Width: 64 mm
Height: 78 mm
Weight: 800 g

Processor module
Length: 122 mm
Width: 66 mm
Height: 10 mm
Weight: 57 g

Battery
Type: BA-5847/u lithium battery providing nominal +5·6 V for 20 h at ambient room temperature
Length: 95 mm
Width: 38 mm
Height: 64 mm
Weight: 250 g

Short handle
Length: 300 mm
Width: 30 mm
Height: 56 mm
Weight: 110 g

Long handle
Length:
  (nested) 480 mm
  (extended) 1·46 m
Diameter: 35 mm
Weight: 620 g
RF frequency range: 300–600 MHz
Audio frequency:
  (search mode) 1 click/2·5 s
  (point mode) 3–150 clicks/s
Operating temperature: −32 to +52° C

Mine Detector NMD-78

DESCRIPTION
The mine detecting set NMD-78 is a compact portable device which enables the operator to detect metallic and non-metallic mines buried in any type of soil.

The unit combines a new battery-powered solid state transmitter and receiver sweeping over selected bands of radio frequencies. This concept provides a significant increase in the search head response compared with the simplex operation of earlier types of magnetic/ non-magnetic mine detector.

During operation the NMD-78 automatically adapts its initial threshold sensitivity to the various soil conditions and thereafter continually updates the micro-

processor with the changing dielectric constant of the surrounding soil. The unit comprises a search head assembly, handle, control box and head set and is contained in a carrying case suitable for use in the field or for long term storage. The unit can be supplied with either long-life lithium or rechargeable nickel-cadmium batteries.

STATUS
Production.

MANUFACTURER
United Scientific Instruments Limited, 10 Fitzroy Square, London W1P 6AB, England.

United Scientific Instruments NMD-78 mine detector

MD 2000 Metallic Mine Detector

DESCRIPTION
The first prototype of the MD 2000 metallic mine detector was completed in June 1976, with the first production models following in November 1976.

The MD 2000 employs pulse induction technology rather than tuned oscillators as used in many other mine detectors. The manufacturer claims the advantages of the system are greater sensitivity, freedom from drift, ability to discriminate between small objects and minimal loss of sensitivity in conditions such as sea water, damp undergrowth or mineralised soil.

All the controls and batteries are in the electronics pack which has been designed for mounting on the operator's belt or shoulder. The pack has a cast and extruded aluminium casing and the electronics comprise six replaceable plug-in modules on one board. The electronics pack contains the following operating controls:
on/off switch: red light-emitting diode above the switch indicates that the unit is on. This flashes a warning to the operator when the batteries are approximately 75 per cent discharged.
sockets: the search coil lead plugs into the small socket and the headphones plug into the larger socket.
mode switch: there are two levels of response, normal and boost. For most situations normal response will be sufficient. The boosted response increases sensitivity but reduces the battery life. Within each level of response there are two sub-divisions, total and selec-

tive. In the total position the unit responds to metal objects of all sizes whereas in the selective position small objects are ignored.
fast/slow zero: the unit automatically and continuously adjusts to the optimum operating conditions, eg when operating over heavily mineralised soil, it will zero out responses from the soil and report only the metallic objects. The rate at which this compensation takes place can be varied by switching to fast or slow zero. The equipment is at its most sensitive when the mode switch is set to boosted response: total, with the zero switch set to slow zero.

The MD 2000 operates as follows: a continuous stream of electric pulses passes through the search coil and creates magnetic pulses which in turn penetrate the earth or surrounding environment. This pulsing magnetic field creates eddy currents in any metallic objects near by and the resulting echoes are received by the search coil in its receive mode. All these magnetic responses, when added together, produce an output signal which indicates whether metal is present.

Detection capability
  British 2p piece (cupro-nickel, 25 mm diameter and 2 mm thick)
  400 mm length of coaxial cable
  Mallory battery type R675H (11 mm diameter and 5 mm thick)
  Aluminium plate (250 × 250 × 1·17 mm)
  Steel plate (216 × 216 × 19 mm)

STATUS
In production. In service with at least 12 countries.

MANUFACTURER
Quartel Limited, 32 St Mary's Road, London W5 5EV, England.

Detection range

  400 mm
  190 mm

  175 mm
  847 mm
  876 mm

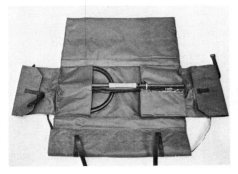

MD 2000 metallic mine detector in carrying case

SPECIFICATIONS
Headphone type: S G Brown model 3C 100
Headphone weight: 376 g
Weight of electronics/battery pack without batteries: 1·9 kg

Electronics/battery pack
Length: 252 mm
Width: 153 mm
Height: 43 mm

Power supply: 12 V 1·8 A power sealed rechargeable lead acid or 7 'C' cells in slide container
Weight of rechargeable unit: 400 g
Search coil diameter: 100 mm or 300 mm
Weight of 300 mm coil: 1 kg
Weight of 100 mm coil: 300 g
Search probe size: 400 or 1000 mm
Weight
  (400 mm probe): 400 g
  (1000 mm probe): 700 g

MD 2000 metallic mine detector in use

Plessey P6/2 Metal/Mine Detector

DEVELOPMENT
The Plessey P6/2 metal/mine detector is a military development of the commercial P6 equipment which was the product of four years' sponsored research in conjunction with the British Home Office. Development of the P6/2 began in 1974 and the equipment entered service with the British Army the following year. It is now in use with military and police forces in both the United Kingdom and overseas.

DESCRIPTION
The Plessey P6/2 is a rugged lightweight metal/mine detector for use in man-pack mobile or static roles. The detector consists of an electronic unit and a set of four operator-interchangeable search probes. It has been improved to operate between −40°C and +60°C. The electronic unit is sealed against water and the four probes are waterproof and can be used underwater down to 1·6 metres.

The electronic unit is carried in a haversack slung over the shoulder for man-pack operation. The probes are suitable for a wide range of military and counter-insurgency search operations, including detection of

mines and buried arms and searching of personnel for concealed weapons and ammunition.

The instrument uses pulsed induction techniques to produce sensitive responses in operation. Automatic balancing reduces the ground response signals to a very low level and eliminates the need for any manual compensation for drift. Dual mode sensitivity and response times are provided, with the lower sensitivity being suitable for searching cluttered environments. These features are achieved by use of a single switch control. Target location is indicated either by an inbuilt loudspeaker or by a plug-in earpiece headphone unit.

The detector has been designed for ease of maintenance with the aid of conventional workshop test equipment. All the parts, components and spares have been NATO codified.

SPECIFICATIONS
Weight: (complete system with electronic unit, haversack and search probe) 4·5 kg
Sensitivity: open loop probe, 400 mm pistol, 220 mm 2p coin
Power supply: self-contained standard HP 11, MN1400 or nickel-cadmium rechargeable batteries

STATUS
In production. In service with the British Army and in other undisclosed countries.

MANUFACTURER
Plessey Defence Systems, Exchange Works, 39 Cheapside, Liverpool L2 2EA, England.

Plessey P6/2 metal mine detector in use

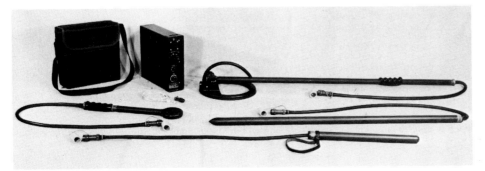

Plessey P6/2 metal mine detector showing carrying haversack, electronics pack, 4 search probes and ear set

MILDEC Metallic Mine Detectors

DESCRIPTION
MILDEC E1 and H4 incorporate a unique method of body-mounting the search probe which leaves the operator's hands free during the search and also enables him to carry an automatic weapon or radio. In an emergency the operator can quickly jettison the equipment by use of quick-release clasps built into the body harness.

The operational technique is based on the pulse induction principle and the detector may be used underwater as the handle and coil are waterproof. The power supply is provided by a separate box with rechargeable 4 Ah units. The basic search coil is 500 mm in diameter and is fitted with a three-section support stem with handle grip and arm support. The whole system is attached to the operator by a nylon body harness.

SPECIFICATIONS
Electronic unit
Weight: approx 3·8 kg
Dimensions: 250 × 225 × 70 mm
Output power: variable from 13 – 360 W peak, 100 – 1200 μ/s
Sensitivity: variable from 44 000 – 1 140 000 gain

Battery unit
Weight: approx 1·8 kg
Dimensions: 300 × 65 × 45 mm
Battery voltage: 12 and 18 V dc

Harness: nylon webbing with quick-release clasps
Handle: 3 glassfibre sections with adjustable and self-locking glassfibre stem
Basic search head: 500 mm diameter coil with angle adjusting knuckle
Detection capabilities:
(small objects) up to 1 m
(large objects) up to 5 m

STATUS
Production.

MANUFACTURER
Pulse Induction Ltd, Unit S11, Rectory Lane Industrial Estate, Kingston Bagpuize, Abingdon, Oxon OX13 5AS, England.

Sequence photographs showing speed at which equipment can be jettisoned **(1)** *operational position* **(2)** *0·6 seconds: operator brings weapon to bear and reaches for release harness* **(3)** *1·3 seconds: operator crouches and returns fire* **(4)** *3·5 seconds: operator has returned fire, pulled quick-release mechanism and starts to withdraw, jettisoning equipment as he goes* **(5)** *5 seconds: control unit now completely jettisoned and search probe falling clear, operator continuing to return fire* **(6)** *6 seconds: operator has jettisoned equipment completely and withdraws still returning fire*

HYPODEC Mk 4 Total Clearance Detector

DESCRIPTION
The HYPODEC Mk 4 total clearance detector has replaced the HYPODEC Mk 3 metallic mine detector (*Jane's Military Vehicles and Ground Support Equipment 1981*, page 207). The detector is fitted with a body mount handle and harness, which leaves the operator's hands free. The control box is fitted behind the hip and the lightweight telescopic glassfibre stem has been designed to collapse under pressure to enable the operator to kneel without removing his body harness. A quick release clip is fitted to the harness to allow the handle and stem to be removed individually. A 2 kg battery pack is fixed to the operator's belt via a special quick-release clip.

The detector works by the pulse technique and has a detection range of up to one metre for small objects and up to four metres for large objects. It can be used over any type of terrain including beaches and river banks. The search head and part of the stem can be immersed in sea or river water without affecting the sensitivity or balance. The system comprises an electronic unit, a 2·5 Ah battery pack, a 500 or 380 mm diameter search head, a 3-section stem arm and handle, a nylon body harness, headphones, a charger unit and a storage/shipping case.

SPECIFICATIONS
Weight of total system in shipping case: 15 kg
Dimensions of shipping case: 588 × 540 × 250 mm
Output gain: variable 13–360 W peak
Battery power: 18 V
Sensitivity: variable between 44 000 and 1 140 000 gain

STATUS
In production.

MANUFACTURER
Pulse Induction Ltd, Unit S11, Rectory Lane Industrial Estate, Kingston Bagpuize, Abingdon, Oxon OX13 5AS, England.

UNITED STATES OF AMERICA

Future Mine Detection Developments

The US Army Mobility Equipment Research and Development Command (MERADCOM) at Fort Belvoir, Virginia, is developing a wide range of new equipment for the detection and neutralisation of mines. As the US Army Material Readiness and Development Command's main laboratory for countermine technology, the command is also co-ordinating development efforts at the Land Warfare Laboratory, Picatinny Arsenal, Ballistics Research Laboratory, Tank Automotive Command, Missile Command and the National Bureau of Standards. Close liaison is also maintained with many other commands and establishments including Training and Doctrine Command, Force Command and Test and Evaluation Command.

AN/PRS-7 Non-metallic Mine Detector

DESCRIPTION

The AN/PRS-7 (company designation is the 4D6) was developed by the US Army with production being undertaken by Fourdee Incorporated. It is a simple, rugged solid state equipment capable of detecting non-metallic anti-tank and anti-personnel mines.

The AN/PRS-7 consists of four major components: search head, handle, control box and headset.

The mine is detected by the field of the square search head assembly, which consists of two transmitting antennas, one receiving antenna and transmission wires which run inside the handle to the control box. The search head generates and radiates a continuous wave RF signal and receives and demodulates this signal. A rubber bumper is mounted around the search head as a protective measure.

The telescopic handle, which is detachable from the search head, can be extended from 0·482 to 1·752 metres. The handle is normally used in the walking position with the search head about 1·219 metres away from the operator's body. The detector head can also be swivelled to allow the operator to use the equipment while prone.

The control box, which is mounted on the handle, consists of the signal processing board with its associated electronic components, the battery and the controls. The latter features a 'search' mode that is used to locate the presence and general position of the mine. The exact position of the mine is determined in the 'point' mode, using any of the sensitivity levels. By control sensitivity selection, the mine detector will discriminate and work effectively on both magnetic and non-magnetic soil, and terrain covered with other debris. The AN/PRS-7 performed well in the Far East, Europe and the United States but when confronted with non-metallic mines in desert soils, as found in the Middle East, the response was very poor.

The presence of a mine is indicated audibly to the operator through the headset assembly, which consists of two headphones which produce a 1000 Hz signal.

One complete AN/PRS-7 system comprises the mine detector, replacement mode, spare battery and bolt, arctic warming case for battery, carrying case, and operating and maintenance handbooks.

Left: AN/PSS-11 metallic mine detector; right: AN/PRS-7 non-metallic mine detector (US Army)

SPECIFICATIONS
Weight:
  (mine detector) 4·082 kg
  (complete equipment in case) 10·886 kg
Case:
  (length) 615 mm
  (width) 406 mm
  (height) 184 mm
Audio frequency of headset: 1000 Hz
Battery voltage: ±16·2 V
Battery type: mercury
Battery life: 28 h continuous operation
Battery capacity:
  + section 0·5 Ah
  − section 1·8 Ah

Operating temperature range: −31·7 to +51·7°C
Storage temperature range: −53·9 to +68·3°C
Relative humidity operational: 95%
Relative humidity storage: 100%

STATUS
In production. In service with the US Army and many other armed forces. By 1979, Fourdee had delivered over 30 000 mine detectors to various countries. The AN/PRS-7 is now being replaced by a product-improved version, the AN/PRS-8.

MANUFACTURER
Fourdee Incorporated, 440 Plumosa Avenue, Casselbury, Florida 32707, USA.

This company is now part of the Emerson Electric Company.

AN/PRS-8 Metallic and Non-metallic Mine Detector

DESCRIPTION
In fiscal year 1976 the US Army Mobility Equipment Research and Development Command (MERADCOM) initiated an AN/PRS-7 Product Improvement Programme (PIP) with the Cubic Corporation Defence Systems Division. Under this the detector was improved using new solid-state electronics and signal processing equipment for better mine detection in any type of soil, the designation AN/PRS-8 being assigned to the detector. The new solid-state transmitter and receiver sweeps over a wide radio frequency band instead of the single frequency of the earlier AN/PRS-7 and provides an order of magnitude increase in the search-head data gathered. This is then processed by a single board processor module fitted with a 16-bit microprocessor and memory on a single chip. The algorithm used is one developed from that used on the AN/VRS-5 vehicle-mounted road mine detector system and results in a vastly increased performance over the AN/PRS-7, specifically in a higher detection rate and lower false alarms.

The detector automatically adapts its threshold sensitivity to various soils. Handling characteristics have been improved with end-point blanking to eliminate false alarms produced by the operator's tendency to tilt the search head at the ends of the swing, a metronome pacing signal to set the optimum search sweep rate, and more distinctive audio signals. An automatic switch from 'search' to 'point' is also included.

In late 1981 a $7·3 million contract was placed for 1461 AN/PRS-8 detectors. This contract included retrofit kits to update the 9500 AN/PRS-7 detectors in service to AN/PRS-8 standard.

STATUS
In service with the US Army. A total of 9500 AN/PRS-7 detectors are undergoing product improvement.

MANUFACTURER (for Improvement Programme)
Cubic Defense Systems, 9333 Balboa Avenue, San Diego, California 92123, USA.

SPECIFICATIONS
Search head assembly
Weight: 0·77 kg
Length: 221 mm
Width: 221 mm
Height: 56 mm

Control box (without battery)
Weight: 0·857 kg
Length: 180 mm
Width: 64 mm
Height: 78 mm

Battery
Weight: 0·25 kg
Length: 95 mm
Width: 38 mm
Height: 65 mm

Long handle
Weight: 0·62 kg
Length: 0·48 m
Height:
  (nested) 35 mm
  (extended) 1·46 m

Short handle
Weight: 0·11 kg
Length: 0·3 m
Width: 30 mm
Height: 56 mm

Miscellaneous (headset, cables, straps, etc.)
Weight: 1·2 kg

Carrying case
Weight:
  (without unit) 6·2 kg
  (with unit) 10 kg

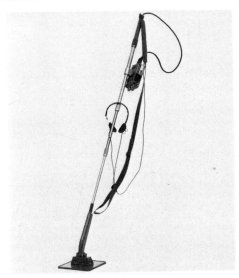
AN/PRS-8 handheld mine detector

Length: 0·6 m
Width: 0·4 m
Height: 0·19 m

RF frequency range: 300–600 MHz
Audio frequency:
  (search mode) 1 click per 2·5 s
  (point mode) 3–150 clicks per s
Temperature range:
  (operating) −32 to +52°C
  (storage) −55 to +70°C
Battery complement: Type BA-5847 (Lithium)/U
Battery voltage: +5·6 V nominal
Battery life: 20 hours (at ambient room temperatures)

AN/PSS-11 and AN/PSS-12 Metallic Mine Detectors

DESCRIPTION

The AN/PSS-11 was developed by the US Army with production now being undertaken by Cubic Corporation's Defense Systems Division. The AN/PSS-12 is a modernised version of the AN/PSS-11. The work involved was carried out by Cubic Corporation's Defense Systems Division under contract to the US Army Mobility Equipment Research and Development Command (MERADCOM).

It is a simple, rugged, solid state equipment which can detect metallic anti-tank and anti-personnel mines of ferrous and non-ferrous materials.

The equipment consists of five major components: detection head, telescopic handle, control box, receiver transmitter and headset.

The detection head is square and contains four coils which are electrically balanced. These transmitter coils send out electro-magnetic waves which set up a magnetic field with a radius of 0·914 to 1·219 metres. When a metallic object is encountered, the magnetic field is distorted, which results in an imbalance in the mutual inductance bridge.

The receiver/transmitter, which is carried in a pouch on the operator's belt, amplifies the imbalance and causes a signal increase in the headset, and indicates the presence of the metallic object. A phase discriminating circuit cancels false signals caused by salt water or magnetic soils and only signals caused by metallic objects are transmitted to the headset.

The control box is on the handle and nulls the signal to the headset to establish initial balance condition and has low, intermediate and high sensitivity selections to locate metallic objects and pinpoint their exact positions.

The telescopic handle, which is detachable from the detector head, can be extended from 0·482 to 1·752 metres. It is identical to the handle on the AN/PRS-8. The handle is normally used in the walking position with the search head about 1·219 metres from the body. The detector head can also swivel to allow the operator to use the equipment while prone.

The headset consists of two headphones which produce a 625 Hz audible sound.

A complete AN/PSS-11 set consists of a carrying case, mine detector, spare modules, spare batteries, arctic kit, and operations and maintenance handbook.

AN/PSS-12 improvements include: new solid state electronics; reduced weight; increased reliability (MTBF is over 1000 hours); improved maintainability; increased battery life; and improved magnetite rejection. The four modules employed by the original equipment have been replaced by one solid-state encapsulated electronic module. An automatic nulling feature has been incorporated to replace one of the the two manual nulling operating controls. The overall weight of the original system has been reduced by 25 per cent. Other improvements include a 70-hour battery (twice the life of the previous battery operation) and a lower false alarm rate.

AN/PSS-11 metallic mine detectors in service with Brazilian Marine Corps (Ronaldo S. Olive)

SPECIFICATIONS
Weight: 10 kg
Case:
(length) 600 mm
(width) 400 mm
(height) 180 mm
Audio frequency of headset: 625 Hz
Battery voltage: 10·7 to 14 V
Battery type: BA-1568/U
Battery life: 70 h continuous operation
Detection capability:
(small metal object) 304–355 mm
(large metal object) 1·219–1·828 m
Operating temperature range: −32 to +52°C
Storage temperature range: −55 to +70°C
Relative humidity operational: 100%
Relative humidity storage: 100%

STATUS
Production. $10 million contract placed for US Army use, April 1983. Also ordered by Egypt ($4·5 million contract 1983). Known to be in service in Brazil.

MANUFACTURER
Cubic Defense Systems, 9333 Balboa Avenue, San Diego, California 92123, USA.

AN/PSS-11 hand-held mine detector

AN/VRS-5 Vehicle-mounted Road Mine Detector System

DESCRIPTION

The AN/VRS-5 vehicle-mounted road mine detector system (VMRMDS) has been developed since 1974 by the Cubic Corporation under contract to the US Army Mobility Equipment Research and Development Command (MERADCOM), Fort Belvoir, Virginia, to meet a requirement for a road interdiction mine detector capable of finding metallic and non-metallic mines at rapid rate along unpaved roads and trails or on fairly flat and sparsely vegetated ground.

The system is designed to be fitted to the front of an armoured personnel carrier or any other standard army vehicle, such as a jeep or truck, and consists of a steerable search head (composed of an array of antenna modules) mounted on a boom assembly. When not in use the system is carried on its own two-wheeled trailer and needs two men to fit it to the designated carrying vehicle and connect it to the vehicle's 24-volt power supply. It has a high detection rate and a low false alarm rate. The system utilises sophisticated microwave and microprocessor techniques to differentiate between buried metallic and non-metallic anti-tank/anti-vehicle mines and normal soil. Because background response can vary considerably with different soil types and moisture content the VMRMDS has the inbuilt capability to adjust its threshold sensitivity automatically to match the terrain type, so no previous knowledge of soil type is

AN/VRS-5 vehicle-mounted road mine detector system mounted on front of M113 APC

needed. The presence and exact location of a mine are indicated on a visual display and by an audio alarm. The vehicle mounting the system is then stopped and a clearance team removes the mine. The path swept is some 3·35 metres wide and the maximum sweeping speed attainable by the carrier vehicle is 12·8 km/h.

STATUS
Undergoing final phase of development testing.

MANUFACTURER
Cubic Defense Systems, 9333 Balboa Avenue, San Diego, California 92123, USA.

SPECIFICATIONS
Receiver transmitter, radio (RT-1381/VRS-5)
Weight: 6·8 kg
Length: 360 mm
Width: 200 mm
Height: 150 mm
Power requirements: 24 V (+6 V, −2 V) 100 W max

Indicator unit (ID-2275/VRS-5)
Weight: 5·9 kg
Length: 360 mm
Width: 240 mm
Height: 130 mm

Antenna (AS-3501/VRS-5)
Weight: 103·5 kg
Length: 1·35 m
Width: 3·5 m
Height: 640 mm

Mount (MT-6190/VRS-5)
Weight: 38 kg
Length: 3 m
Width: 1·2 m
Height: 640 mm

Interface unit-position, vehicle (J-3755/VRS-5)
Weight: 58·2 kg
Length: 760 mm
Width: 510 mm
Height: 250 mm
Power requirements: 24 V dc (+6 V, −2 V) 65 A max

AN/VRS-5 vehicle-mounted road mine detector system mounted on front of M151A2 light vehicle

Trailer, mine detector set (V-525/VRS-5)
Weight: 225 kg
Length: 4·9 m

Width: 1·9 m
Height: 1·6 m
Operating temperature range: −32 to +52°C

Airborne Minefield Detection System (AMIDS)

DESCRIPTION
The Countermine Laboratory of the US Army Mobility Equipment Research and Development Command (MERADCOM) is currently working on a new method of detecting minefields, including surface-laid mines. Known as the Airborne Minefield Detection System or AMIDS, the system will employ a remotely-piloted airborne drone vehicle carrying electro-optical sensors to detect the minefields. Radar and electro-magnetic sensors will also be employed.

STATUS
Early development.

MINE-CLEARING EQUIPMENT

CHILE

Cardoen Bangalore Torpedo

DESCRIPTION
This is used for clearing minefields and obstacles such as barbed wire. It consists of 1·5-metre lengths of 65 mm diameter light aluminium or steel pipes filled with

high explosive. A complete issue unit consists of four main pipe charge sections, four sleeve connectors and two heads.

Each pipe charge weighs 7·5 kg and is filled with 5 kg of cast Pentolyte and Mexal 1500 explosive. The torpedo assembly is detonated by a standard No. 8 blast-

ing cap. Total assembled weight is approximately 31 kg and the torpedo is capable of clearing passages 4 to 5 metres wide.

STATUS
Production. In service with the Chilean armed forces.

MANUFACTURER
Cardoen Explosives, Carlos Antúnez, Of.102, Santiago, Chile.

Cardoen Bangalore torpedo

CHINA, PEOPLE'S REPUBLIC

Bangalore Torpedoes

DESCRIPTION
The armed forces of the People's Republic of China employ at least four types of Bangalore torpedo for clearing minefields and other obstacles. Three types use a heavy steel body and the other a lightweight metal body, but all four employ pull friction igniters that allow them to be used as extemporised land mines with trip wires if required. The torpedoes have conventional

rounded noses, although simple plugs may be fitted at both ends. Booster charges may be used but are not always fitted. As with other such devices, lengths of torpedo can be joined to make up any length as required.

SPECIFICATIONS

Type	Type 1	Type 2	Type 3	Lightweight
Length	0·998 m	0·99 m	1·187 m	0·99 m
Diameter	33 mm	45·7 mm	35·5 mm	54 mm

STATUS
In service with the Chinese Army and exported to some other countries.

MANUFACTURER
Chinese state arsenals.

CZECHOSLOVAKIA

Tank-mounted Mine-clearing Roller

Tank-mounted Mine-clearing Plough

DESCRIPTION
The Czechoslovak Army uses tank-mounted mine-clearing rollers and ploughs of its own design instead of the normal Soviet equipment of this type. The former consists of three to five rollers of varying thickness mounted on an arm in front of each track in a similar manner to the Soviet equipment. The Czechoslovak rollers are bigger than their Soviet counterparts and also have a different type of serrated edge. Between and in front of the two sets of rollers is a frame for detonating the tilt-rod fuzes of any mines before the tank passes over them.

The plough type equipment is similar in concept to the Soviet equipment but uses a larger plough and also has a frame for detonating mines with tilt-rod fuzes.

STATUS
In service with the Czechoslovak Army.

MANUFACTURER
Czechoslovak state factories.

T-55 MBT fitted with Czechoslovak mine-clearing rollers

Mine-clearing Charges

DESCRIPTION
The Czechoslovak Army has a two-wheeled trailer which is towed behind a T-54/T-55 MBT fitted with mine-clearing equipment of the roller or plough type. The trailer lays a series of explosive cords behind the

tank on those parts of the ground which have not been cleared by the mine-clearing equipment installed on the front of the tank. The cords are detonated from inside the tank and clear any remaining mines.

The Czechoslovak Army also has a trailer-mounted mine-clearance system. This is an armoured four-wheeled trailer that is towed behind an OT-64 (8 × 8) or similar vehicle, and contains rockets to which a number

of flexible mine-clearing explosive lines are attached. This is fired over the minefield and then detonated.

STATUS
In service with the Czechoslovak Army.

MANUFACTURER
Czechoslovak state factories.

GERMANY, FEDERAL REPUBLIC

Rapid Land Mine-clearance System

DEVELOPMENT/DESCRIPTION
In 1973 the Federal German Defence Ministry and the Procurement Office issued a request for proposals for a rapid land mine-clearance system (Landminen-Schnellräummittel). A number of companies, including AEG/Telefunken, Dynamit Nobel, Industriewerke Karlsruhe and Rheinstahl (now Thyssen-Henschel) submitted proposals for the system. As a number of NATO

countries have a requirement for a similar system, including France and Italy, this is likely to become a NATO project.

During 1982 it was revealed that the Federal Republic of Germany, in a co-operative venture with the French government, had produced a prototype of a flail tank based on the chassis of the M48. The vehicle has no turret but carries the mine flail rollers, which are together wider than the tank chassis, forward on a system of girders and gantries. There are two flail drums mounted on the same axis and supported by a central arm. Each

flail chain has its weighted end in the shape of an anchor spade which is designed to remove earth and spoil by digging it out to the left at a 20-degree angle thus exposing the mines which are then smashed or detonated by other flails.

The flail tank is reported to be able to clear a path 4·7 metres wide, 250 mm deep and 120 metres long in only 10 minutes.

STATUS
Development.

Comet No 3001 One-man Minesweeping Line Device

DESCRIPTION

The basic system consists of an 18 kg box containing an 80-metre long detonating cord with 73 × 100 g plastic explosive charges placed along it at one-metre intervals. A smokeless solid propellant rocket with a launching projector is fitted with a foot-plate and ground spike. The rocket is fitted with a DM47A1 propellant fuze that has a 6-second delay and the detonating cord has a DM4 fuze with an 8-second delay. The rocket's towing gear consists of two 2·6-metre long steel wire ropes fitted with thimbles.

The mode of operation is that the elements of the system are assembled by one man approximately 20 metres in front of the minefield to be breached. The rocket is fired using the DM47A1 fuze and the minesweeping line is extended to its full length. The line is then detonated either automatically by the DM4 fuze or electrically by hand. As detonation takes place all the mines lying under the explosives will be detonated as well. The consecutive craters thus created result in a narrow mine-free path approximately 72 metres long. If a longer path is required then the procedure is repeated with a second unit. A training system No 3002 is available and can be used for repeated firings.

STATUS

Development complete. Production on receipt of an order.

MANUFACTURER

Comet GmbH Pyrotechnik-Apparatebau, Postfach 10 02 67, 2850 Bremerhaven-1, Federal Republic of Germany.

Comet No 3001 one-man minesweeping line device with packing case

Comet No 3010 Two-man Ladder Type Minesweeping Device

DESCRIPTION

The basic system consists of a canvas storage bag containing a rope ladder minesweeping device with three synthetic fibre lines interconnected in parallel with each other by wooden slats to give a total length of 53 metres and width of 0·6 metre. Detonator cords with 600 × 50 g plastic explosive charges, at staggered intervals of 0·25 metre, are secured to the lines. A DM10 smokeless solid propellant rocket with a launcher is fitted with a base, ground spikes and adjustable guide bar. The rocket is fitted with a DM41 propellant fuze that has a 20-second delay and the sweeping device with a DM91 fuze lighter with a 2-second delay. The rocket's towing gear consists of two steel wire ropes and buffer springs attached to the front transverse spar of the ladder and there are two brake springs, fitted with earth drills, to absorb the rocket's pull attached to the rear transverse spar.

The mode of operation is that the elements of the system are towed on a skid in their storage bag by the two-man crew to a position in front of the minefield to be breached. The bag is opened out on all four sides and

Comet No 3010 two-man ladder type minesweeping device ready for action

the components are assembled. The rocket is fired and the ladder is extended to its full length. The detonator cords are then fired automatically by the DM91 fuze lighter. The resultant mine-free path is some 50 metres long and 0·8 metre wide. If the path needs to be extended the procedure is repeated with a second system. A training device No 3011 is available and can be used for repeated firings.

STATUS

Development complete. Production on receipt of an order.

MANUFACTURER

Comet GmbH Pyrotechnik-Apparatebau, Postfach 10 02 67, 2850 Bremerhaven-1, Federal Republic of Germany.

ISRAEL

Ramta Track Width Mine Plough (TWMP)

DESCRIPTION

The Ramta Track Width Mine Plough (TWMP) can be fitted to all types of modern main battle tank using a specially-designed kit. No alterations to the tank are needed as the plough is attached to the towing lugs on the tank front hull. Transferring the TWMP from one tank to another takes less than one hour using the tool kit supplied. It consists of two plough units with separate lifting mechanisms and depth control systems.

The TWMP is operated by the tank driver. When travelling the ploughs are raised and secured by a locking device. For operations the driver releases the locking devices and the ploughs drop freely for the plough teeth to dig into the ground and dislodge buried mines which are then pushed aside. Any tilt-rod mines in the central unploughed area between the ploughs will be detonated by a chain suspended between the ploughs. Each plough unit operates independently and follows the natural terrain contours, clearing a path 1·154 metres wide and 300 mm deep.

After use the TWMP can be lifted back to the travelling position by a mechanical device connected to the track tension wheel or by 24-volt dc electrical motors.

The TWMP has been fitted to Centurion, M48 and M60 tanks.

Ramta Track Width Mine Plough (TWMP) attached to M48 MBT

STATUS
Production. In service with Israeli armed forces.

MANUFACTURER
Ramta Structures and Systems, Israel Aircraft Industries Limited, PO Box 323, Beer Sheba 84 102, Israel.

SPECIFICATIONS
Max lifted height above ground: 1·6 m
Ploughing depth: 300 mm
Ploughed width each side: 1·154 m
Unploughed width between tracks: 1·612 m
Skidshoe track each side: 0·45 m

Chain track in centre: 0·712 m
Clearing speed:
  (loess) 6·5 km/h
  (sand and clay) 9·5 km/h
  (stony) 6·5 km/h

RKM Mine-clearing Rollers

DESCRIPTION
The RKM mine-clearing rollers are an Israeli adaptation of the Soviet KMT-5 mine-clearing rollers and differ only in details. The RKM rollers can be used on M47, M48, M60, M60A1, Centurion, Chieftain, AMX-30 and all types of Leopard MBTs.

The RKM mine-clearing rollers are track width rollers mounted in two banks in front of the carrier tank pushed and suspended from two pusher arms. The weight and suspension of the rollers is used to detonate any mine over which they travel and a weighted chain between the two roller banks is used to detonate any tilt-rod actuated mines that might explode under the tank's belly. As the rollers detonate a mine, the force of the explosion causes the roller to be lifted upwards on its suspension arm thus reducing the force of the blast which is distributed in the mass of the roller and arm and in the mass of the carrier vehicle attachment point.

The two sets of rollers can articulate independently with each set being able to move upwards 152 mm and downwards 254 mm to take account of ground surface irregularities. The entire roller banks can caster up to 30 degrees either side when the carrier tank makes a turn. Each push beam arm has a compartment containing a hand winch to connect or disconnect the RKM mine-clearing system to the carrier tank. Using the two winches, two men can fit the system in about 15 minutes, provided the tank is already fitted with the adaptor assembly coupled to the hull glacis lifting and towing eyes. In an emergency the system can be disconnected from the tank from within the carrier tank without the crew having to leave the interior. This manual release facility can be completed in 30 seconds.

RKM mine-clearing rollers fitted to Centurion tank

STATUS
In production. In service with Israeli armed forces and exported to several countries.

MANUFACTURERS
Urdan Industries Limited, Industrial centre, Natanya 42378, Israel.
  Metal Works Netzer-Sereni, Beer Yaacob 70395, Israel.

No 21 Demolition Bangalore Torpedo Charge

DESCRIPTION
Although this charge is used primarily to breach barbed wire fences it may also be employed against minefields. The assembly consists of four sections of aluminium pipe charge, four sleeve couplings and two head units. The charge is actuated by a No 41 firing device with an 18-second delay.

The 1·1-metre long charge sections are assembled into the charge unit and pushed into the minefield. Detonation is then accomplished by use of the No 41 firing unit and the resultant explosion clears a narrow path by detonating the mines underneath it.

SPECIFICATIONS
Total charge assembly weight: 19·35 kg

Single charge section
Length: 1·1 m
Diameter: 57 mm
Weight: 4 kg
Charge type: cast TNT
Charge weight: 3·3 kg

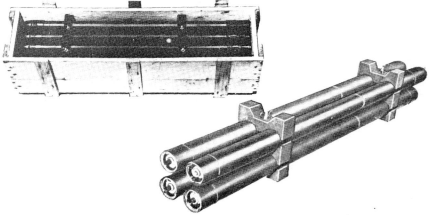
No 21 demolition Bangalore torpedo charge

STATUS
In service with the Israeli Army.

MANUFACTURER
Israel Military Industries, Export Division, PO Box 1044, Ramat-Hasharon 47100, Israel.

No 30 Demolition Pipe Charge

DESCRIPTION
The pipe charge assembly consists of 26 steel pipe charge sections, two front skids fitted with obstacle clearing wheels and four detonating units fitted with No 41 firing devices that have 18-second delays.

The pipe charge is used for breaching barbed wire fences and minefields. The 2·162-metre long sections are assembled into a unit of the required length and an obstacle-clearing skid unit is fixed to the front to facilitate pushing the charge into position. Detonation is accomplished by the 380 mm long detonating unit fitted with a No 41 firing device. The wide path cleared by the resulting explosion is some 50 metres long.

SPECIFICATIONS
Pipe charge section
Length: 2·162 m
Diameter: 55 mm
Weight: 8·5 kg
Charge type: Composition B
Charge weight: 3 kg

No 30 demolition charge

Pipe skid unit
Length: 2·7 m (with pipe section)
Weight: 17 kg

Detonating unit
Length: 380 mm (with No 41 firing device)
Weight: 1·5 kg (with No 41 firing device)
Charge type: Composition B
Charge weight: 0·5 kg

STATUS
In service with the Israeli Army.

MANUFACTURER
Israel Military Industries, PO Box 1044, Ramat Hasharon 47100, Israel.

ITALY

Italian Mine-clearing Charge

Italy is believed to have developed to the prototype stage a rocket-propelled explosive-filled mine-clearing charge. No further details of this equipment, or its current status, are available.

JAPAN

Japanese Mine-clearing Equipment

DESCRIPTION
Japan is known to have developed at least two items of mine-clearing equipment. The first is a tank-mounted mine-clearing roller system on which no information is available, and the second a rocket-propelled explosive-filled mine-clearing charge, known as the Type 70 flexible detonating cable, designed for clearing anti-personnel minefields. The equipment consists of a rocket launcher frame and a rocket with a wire rope attached to its end. The rope is attached to eight coils of flexible detonating cable. The end of this cable is attached to a nylon rope which is anchored to the ground. The rocket is fired across the minefield and brought to a halt by the anchored cable. It falls to the ground and the detonating cable is ignited, clearing a path about 130 metres long through the anti-personnel minefield.

STATUS
Type 70 flexible detonating cable is in service with the Japanese Self-Defence Force (Army).

MANUFACTURER
Type 70 flexible detonating cable: Aeronautical and Space Division, Nissan Motor Company Limited, 5-1 3-chome, Momoi, Suginami-ku, Tokyo, Japan.

Type 70 mine-clearing equipment being carried in rear of (4 × 4) 750 kg light vehicle (Kensuke Ebata)

Type 70 flexible detonating cable ready for launch. On left is anchor and nylon rope, in centre coil flexible detonating cable, and on right rocket launcher and rocket

---

SINGAPORE

CIS Bangalore Torpedo

DESCRIPTION
The Bangalore Torpedo produced by Chartered Industries of Singapore is virtually identical to the US M1A1. It is issued in four-section tubes made from aluminium and each section is loaded with 4·25 kg of cast TNT grade 1. Each tube has a diameter of 620 mm and the sections are joined by connecting sleeves. A compressed PETN/RDX booster is used. Standard non-electric detonators can be employed to detonate the charges.

The torpedoes are issued in wooden boxes each containing two sets. The gross weight of a box is 45 kg and the box dimensions are 1375 × 370 × 270 mm. A matt olive green finish is given to the tubes.

STATUS
Production.

CIS Bangalore torpedo

MANUFACTURER
Chartered Industries of Singapore (PTE) Limited, 249 Jalan Boon Lay, Singapore 2261.

SPAIN

EXPAL Bangalore Torpedo

DESCRIPTION
The EXPAL Bangalore Torpedo follows conventional lines and is issued in six units. The first unit is a sheet steel ogival head and the other five are steel tubes each filled with 2·7 kg of amatol 80/20. The units are joined together by sleeves and the weight of the complete torpedo is 28 kg.

The torpedoes are issued in wooden boxes, each containing two complete units ready to assemble. Detonation can be carried out by electrical means or by a blasting cap.

STATUS
Production.

MANUFACTURER
Explosivos Alaveses, SA, PO Box 198, Vitoria, Spain.

SWEDEN

Swedish Mine-clearing Equipment

DESCRIPTION
The Swedish Army uses at least one type of rocket-propelled mine-clearance equipment. This consists of seven manpacks each weighing 19 kg. When assembled this linear charge is 137 metres long and 34 mm in diameter. Every 915 mm of the charge is a block of thyelene-coated explosive weighing 453 grams. The linear charge is projected across the minefield by a 100 mm rocket at a speed of 46 metres per second. The rocket and linear charge then fall to the ground and the charge is detonated, clearing a path up to 137 metres long and 600 mm wide.

STATUS
In service with the Swedish Army.

UNION OF SOVIET SOCIALIST REPUBLICS

Tank-mounted Mine-clearing Rollers Types PT-54, PT-54M and PT-55

Tank-mounted Mine-clearing Plough Type KMT-4

Tank-mounted Mine-clearing Plough and Roller Type KMT-5

DESCRIPTION
PT-54
This was introduced into service in the 1950s as the replacement for the earlier PT-3 system. The equipment consists of two independent roller sets which are mounted on arms in front of each track. Each roller set has six rollers, and provision is made for clearing mines fitted with tilt-rod fuzes before they can detonate under the hull of the front. To enable following tanks to see which ground has been cleared the equipment leaves a furrow in the ground 80 mm deep and 100 mm wide. As the tank moves forward the rollers should detonate any mines in its path. The area between the tracks remains uncleared. To widen the lane, additional tanks fitted with mine-clearing rollers are used. Normally three tanks work in a wedge pattern to clear a minefield.

PT-54M
This is a modified PT-54 system.

PT-55
This is similar to the PT-54 but has four instead of six rollers in each section and clears a narrower path, but at a higher speed than the PT-54. The PT-54/55 series take three to five minutes to detach and can survive the explosions of ten swept anti-tank mines.

KMT-4
This was introduced into service in the 1960s and consists of a 600 mm wide cutting device with teeth mounted at an angle in front of each track. Each cutting device is lowered to the ground by a hydraulic ram. This equipment has a number of advantages over the roller type mine-clearing equipment which can be summarised as follows: reduced weight of equipment, retention of tank's cross-country mobility, and the removal of mines from a path instead of their detonation.

KMT-5
This was recently introduced into service to combine the plough and roller mine-clearing equipment. The plough system used is the KMT-4 but the roller design is new, lighter, and has only three rollers per section. Each KMT-5 roller sweeps approximately 80 centimetres. The KMT-5 also incorporates the lane marking plough and the PSK equipment, which marks the clear lane at night with a luminous substance. When not in use the system is carried on a KrAZ-214 truck fitted with a special KM-61 auxiliary crane.

The roller and plough cannot be used simultaneously. The choice of which to use depends on the type of terrain, soil or minefield to be breached. The system is fitted with a quick-release disconnect unit to allow the tank driver to release both systems rapidly. The system can survive eight to ten 5 to 6 kg explosions.

East German T-54 MBT fitted with PT-55 mine-clearing rollers passing over MTU bridge

T-55 MBT fitted with PT-55 mine-clearing rollers clearing minefield

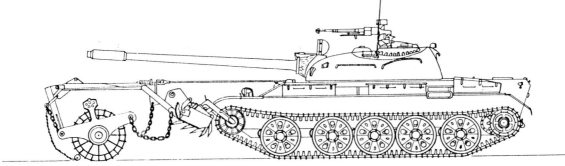

KMT-5 roller plough set mounted on front of T-54B tank

KMT-6
A KMT-6 mine-clearing plough has been reported but no details are available.

Associated equipment
The KM-61 crane on the KrAZ-214 (6 × 6) chassis has been designed specifically for use with the plough and roller type mine-clearing equipment and is used to position and remove the equipment. The crane has a maximum capacity of 3200 kg with boom at a reach of two metres. It can be rotated a maximum of 80 degrees from the forward axis of the truck and may be used on slopes up to a maximum of 4 degrees in any direction.

STATUS
In service with members of the Warsaw Pact. Tank-mounted mine-clearing rollers are also known to be in service with Yugoslavia and a number of countries in the Middle East including Egypt and Syria. The equipment is usually mounted on a T-54/T-55 MBT but some T-62s and the more recent T-72 MBT have provision for installing mine-clearing equipment of the roller or plough type.

MANUFACTURER
Soviet state factories.

SPECIFICATIONS

Type	PT-54	PT-54M	PT-55	KMT-5
Weight (equipment)	8808 kg	7000 kg	6700 kg	7500 kg
(section)	3752 kg	2700 kg	n/a	2265 kg
(roller)	500 kg	500 kg	500 kg	n/a
(plough)	—	—	—	420 kg
Assembly (length)	n/a	2·64 m	n/a	3·18 m
(width)	3·9 m	3·8 m	n/a	4 m
Lane swept (each)	1·3 m	0·89 m	0·83 m	0·73–0·81 m
Width unswept	1·2 m	n/a	1·7 m	2·1 m
Operating speed	6–10 km/h	n/a	8–12 km/h	n/a
Safe turning radius	40 m	n/a	85 m	65 m
Ditch crossing ability	3 m	n/a	n/a	2·5 m
Attachment time	10–15 min	10–25 min	10–15 min	n/a

KMT-4 tank-mounted mine-clearing plough mounted on T-62 MBT of East German Army

T-54 MBT with KMT-4 mine-clearing ploughs raised

Soviet Armoured Mine-clearing Vehicle

DESCRIPTION
This vehicle is based on the chassis of the amphibious M1974 122 mm self-propelled howitzer. It has a turret-like superstructure that contains three rockets on launch ramps. These, together with the upper part of the super-structure, are hydraulically elevated for firing. Range of the rockets is estimated to be 200 and 400 metres with each rocket connected, via a towing line, to 170 metres of mine clearance hose that is stowed folded in the uncovered base of the turret on the vehicle roof.

The hose is connected by a cable to the vehicle which allows the vehicle crew to position the hose in the optimum breaching position once the launching has been carried out. The hose is then command detonated.

The vehicle is capable of operating in an NBC environment and has a good cross-country performance. Details of the M1974 122 mm self-propelled howitzer are given in *Jane's Armour and Artillery 1983-84*, page 495.

STATUS
Trials with Soviet units 1979/80. Thought to have entered service in 1981/82.

ITB-2, SPZ-2 and SPZ-4 Mine-clearance Charges

DESCRIPTION
ITB-2

A rocket-launched anchor and cable is propelled across the minefield and then a winch, or another source of motive force, is used to draw more cable with explosive charges toward the anchor and onto the minefield. Once in position the charge is detonated.

SPZ-2

The SPZ-2 uses a metal-framed anchor guide, placed at the forward edge of the minefield, to draw by winch, at a rate of 200 metres per hour, a cable, with explosive charges attached, across the minefield. The charges may be either single, double or triple and, depending on type, may clear a path 300 to 500 metres long and up to 6 metres wide.

SPZ-4

This consists of a double or triple charge which can either be pushed into the minefield by the tank at a rate of 100 metres per hour, or, if the tank is equipped with roller or plough type mine clearing equipment, laid behind the tank in the gap between the cleared paths left across the minefield by the mine clearing equipment. In the former case, the charge is detonated after it has been positioned by the tank while in the latter case the charge is detonated by the tank crew.

STATUS
In service with the Soviet Army.

MANUFACTURER
Soviet state factories.

BDT Mine-clearing Charge

DESCRIPTION
The BDT mine-clearance charge consists of three separate linear charges which are connected in parallel to form a triple charge. The BDT can also be disassembled to form a single or double charge. Each charge consists of a light metal tube 50 mm in diameter filled with 8·62 kg of cast TNT per linear 305 mm. Lengths of charges can be coupled together to form any desired length. Maximum practical length is 500 metres

and a squad of men can assemble a 500 metre triple charge in between one and one and a half hours.

Once the charge has been assembled to the desired length, the nose and detonator are added, and a roller is fitted to the forward end of the charge with a shield mounted above to ensure that there is no premature detonation by enemy small arms fire. The BDT is normally assembled to the rear and towed by a tracked vehicle to the minefield at a maximum speed of 10 km/h. The tank then pushes the BDT into the minefield and it is then detonated by either an electric blasting cap which

is initiated by a firing cable connected to the batteries of the pushing tank or by the detonation box. This contains a number of percussion detonators connected by a booster charge, which are detonated by machine gun fire from the pushing tank. When detonated, a triple BDT line charge will clear a path six metres wide.

STATUS
In service with the Soviet Army and other armies.

MANUFACTURER
Soviet state factories.

Other Warsaw Pact Mine-clearing Equipment

Soviet UZR-3

This consists of a UZR-3 triple charge Bangalore torpedo with rockets attached, which is fired across the minefield and detonated.

Polish Tank-Mounted Rocket-propelled Equipment

This equipment consists of a rocket (probably an AT-1 Snapper ATGW) with a 170-metre explosive-filled hose attached and is mounted in a boat-shaped container on the left and/or right rear of a T-54 or T-55 MBT which is also fitted with the KMT-4 mine-clearing plough. This model is known to be in service with the Polish Army.

Soviet BTR-50PK with Rocket-propelled Equipment

Known by the Soviet designation MTK, this is a BTR-50PK tracked APC with a special launcher mounted on top of the hull to the rear of the troop compartment. This fires rockets to which are attached 170-metre long flexible tubes containing high explosive which fall on to the minefield and are then detonated from the vehicle.

Polish PTS with Rocket-propelled Equipment

This is a PTS tracked amphibian carrying a modified S-60 57 mm anti-aircraft gun carriage fitted with two launcher bins for the 170-metre long rocket-propelled explosive hose. The carriage allows 360-degree traverse and the system is used to clear gaps in mined coastal waters and rivers.

STATUS
In service with the Soviet Army and other Warsaw Pact armies.

MANUFACTURER
Soviet state factories.

Polish Army T-55 fitted with KMT-4 plough type mine-clearing equipment, provision for mounting roller type mine-clearing equipment, and launcher bins for rocket-propelled explosive hose for mine-clearing

Polish PTS tracked amphibian with rocket-propelled mine-clearing equipment

UZ-1 and UZ-2 Bangalore Torpedoes

DESCRIPTION
The UZ-1 and UZ-2 Bangalore torpedoes are used for clearing a path through minefields and barbed wire. Each section of a UZ-1 Bangalore torpedo consists of a metal tube 1 metre long and 53 mm in diameter containing 5·3 kg of explosive. Each section of a UZ-2 Bangal-ore torpedo is 2 metres long, 52 mm in diameter and contains 3 kg of explosive. Collars are provided for connecting sections together for the required length.

When assembled, the Bangalore torpedo is pushed across the minefield and detonated, which clears a path between 2·5 and 3 metres wide. If a wider path is required, double or triple charges may be assembled with special collars. These charges may also be placed on carts, sleds or rollers, not only for ease of movement and of employment but also for maintaining a more

favourable detonation height. A metal shield is sometimes positioned on the forward end of the torpedo to ensure that there is no premature detonation by enemy small arms fire.

STATUS
In service with members of the Warsaw Pact.

MANUFACTURER
Soviet state factories.

KR Minefield Reconnaissance and Clearing Kit

DESCRIPTION
The KR (komplekt razvedki i razminirovaniia) kit is issued to reconnaissance units of the Soviet Army and consists of a three-piece sectional probe, grapnel (with either two, three or four prongs) complete with approximately 50 metres of cord, wire cutters, reel of black and white engineer tape and a set of marking poles complete with flags.

STATUS
In service with the Soviet Army.

MANUFACTURER
Soviet state factories.

UNITED KINGDOM

Giant Viper Anti-tank Mine-clearing Equipment

DESCRIPTION
The Giant Viper (L1) mine-clearance system consists of a 229-metre long, 68-mm diameter hose filled with plastic explosive. This is packed coiled in a wooden box which is mounted on a two-wheeled trailer, which can be towed by a variety of tracked vehicles. The British Army use the Centurion AVRE, FV432 APC or the Combat Engineer Tractor to tow the trailer. The hose is fired across the minefield by a cluster of eight rocket motors. The tail end of the hose is fitted with arrester gear in the form of three parachutes which straighten the hose during flight and operate the striker mechanism, which detonates the charge after the hose has landed.

The equipment is used as follows: the Giant Viper is towed to the firing point approximately 45 metres from the edge of the minefield and the trailer, which remains attached to the towing vehicle during the operation, is lined up on the proposed line of flight, taking into account any factors which will alter the trajectory, for example wind and temperature of the rocket motors. Giant Viper is then fired electrically from the towing vehicle. Giant Viper has been designed to blast a passage for vehicles through a minefield up to 182 metres long and 7·28 metres wide. During trials, up to 90 per cent of anti-tank mines were cleared, provided that they were not blast-proofed or multi-impulse fuzed.

Each Giant Viper system requires the support of a 3-ton truck. The expendable stores are packed in containers which can be manhandled, except the box containing the hose which weighs 2136 kg and is handled by a fork-lift truck or crane. For training purposes, practice equipment is available.

STATUS
In production. In service with the British Army.

MANUFACTURER
Royal Ordnance Factories.
Enquiries to Ministry of Defence, ROF Marketing, St Christopher House, Southwark Street, London SE1 0TD, England.

Giant Viper projector base ready to fire (Royal Ordnance Factories)

Giant Viper being towed by Centurion Mk 5 AVRE (T J Gander)

Track Width Mine Plough

DESCRIPTION
Following trials in BAOR with a batch of six Track Width Mine Ploughs the British Army is fitting them to Centurion Mark 5 AVREs and to Chieftain bridgelayers. The ploughs can be fitted to almost any in-service British Army tank and are stated to be wider than any other in-service mine ploughs with the possible exception of the Soviet KMT-6. The plough units are mounted in two independent parts, one over each track and each one is directed by a bulls-horn guide on the inside of each plough half. The ploughs dig out any mines buried in their path and guide them outwards clear of the user vehicle.

STATUS
Production. In service with the British Army.

MANUFACTURER
T. B. Pearson and Sons Engineers Limited, Wincomblee Road, Walker, Newcastle-upon-Tyne, England.

Track width mine ploughs fitted to Centurion Mk 5 AVRE (T J Gander)

One half of track width mine plough (T J Gander)

Half of track width mine plough from above (T J Gander)

UNITED STATES OF AMERICA

Fuel Air Explosive for Mine-clearing Operations

DEVELOPMENT/DESCRIPTION
The US Navy detonated its first successful FAE (Fuel Air Explosive) in 1960. First operational use of FAE was in Viet-Nam, where the US Marine Corps employed canisters of ethylene oxide for clearing minefields. After trials in Viet-Nam in 1971, the US Navy adopted the 227 kg CBU-55B for a wide range of roles including clearing minefields and clearing areas of jungle for use as helicopter landing zones.

The CBU-55B cluster bomb is delivered by a helicopter such as the UH-1 or slow-flying aircraft such as the A-1 Skyraider, flying at a height of 600 metres. The UH-1 can carry one CBU-55B on each side of the fuselage. A fire control panel in the cockpit provides the pilot with the option of releasing either the right or the left weapon, or both simultaneously.

The cluster bomb contains three 45 kg unpressurised containers, each 530 mm long, 345 mm in diameter and filled with 32·6 kg of liquid ethylene oxide. Once the bomb has left the aircraft or helicopter, the three containers are ejected from the bomb casing and are slowed down by parachute. Each bomb has a 1·219 metre electronic probe. On impact with the ground, each container ruptures and the liquid ethylene oxide reacts to form a vapour cloud 15 metres in diameter and 2·5 metres high. This is then detonated by two delayed action igniters, which creates a surface overpressure of 22 kg/square cm over an area of 182 square metres. During trials, FAE was successful against conventional single impulse pressure and pull fuzed mines, more complex double fuzed mines and long impulse mines of both American and foreign manufacture.

The US Army started its own programme in 1972 when it acquired some CBU-55B cluster bombs from the Navy. The US Army Mobility Equipment Research and Development Command (MERADCOM) at Fort Belvoir, with the assistance of other establishments, carried out many improvements to the CBU-55B specifically for dealing with minefields. After extensive trials, the FAE system for delivery by helicopter (FAESHED) was not adopted for service.

In 1973, the US Army started development of the Surface Launched Unit, Fuel Air Explosive (SLUFAE) multiple rocket system for clearing pressure mines. This system consists of an FMC M548 tracked carrier on the rear of which is mounted a 30-barrel multiple rocket launcher. This fires a Zuni rocket weighing 59 kg to a maximum range of 1000 metres. The rocket has a warhead of liquid propylene oxide which weighs 38·5 kg. An FAU-83 mechanical detonator is used to preprogramme the rocket separation point for each round. The carrier would normally stop just under 1000 metres away from the minefield and the rockets would be ripple fired into the minefield at intervals of 10 metres. On impact, the probe detonates a burster charge to disperse the fuel into an aerosol cloud which is then detonated to produce a 300 millisecond overpressure of about 90 kg plus that clears single-impulse mines with 100 per cent effectiveness. In 1979 the SLUFAE system was tested on its effectiveness in clearing a minefield. The system failed for a number of reasons including the use of the M548 tracked vehicle, which was of marginal effectiveness in carrying the heavy and bulky weapons

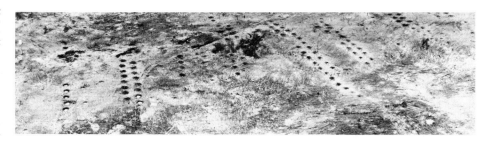

UH-1 dropping 2 FAEs, FAEs exploding and cleared path through minefield (US Army)

pod over different types of terrain, lack of confidence in the vehicle by its crew and a large number of human errors in range estimating, calculating necessary data and in setting up the firing programmes which resulted in a high miss rate for the rockets. Analysis of the trial results showed that apart from engineering problems there was a need to revaluate the operational doctrine of the system as what were thought to be relatively simple operating procedures turned out to produce a high probability of error. It was tested a second time in mid-1980 at Fort Benning after improvements had been made. The result was a resounding success. The system is still under development. Development has reached the stage where the rocket used is now the 345 mm XM130, with a practice rocket being the

XM131. A Resupply Vehicle Assembly (RSV) is now being considered for the SLUFAE system which could be based on either the 5-ton M812A2 or the 10-ton M985, the US Army prefers the latter. A Test Set Electronics XM138 has been produced for use by maintenance personnel. When fully developed it is intended to issue SLUFAE to combat engineer companies of separate armoured and infantry brigades, of divisions and of corps.

The SLUMINE (Surface Launched Unit, Mine) uses the same launcher as the SLUFAE but is designed to disperse air-scatterable belly-attack anti-tank mines over long ranges. It completed the demonstration of validation stage of the project but development was then suspended due to lack of funds.

FAE Helicopter: development complete, did not enter service.

    SLUFAE: development nearly complete.
    SLUMINE: development suspended.

MANUFACTURER

The US Army programme is directed by the US Army Material Development and Readiness Command. Many other establishments are involved in the programme. The US Air Force and Navy are also developing FAE for a wide range of air, land and sea applications.

FAE being used to clear minefield. (Inset) aerosol cloud shortly before detonation (US Army)

Surface-Launched Unit, Fuel-Air Explosive, based on modified FMC M548 tracked carrier, launching rocket with FAE warhead (US Army)

Vehicle Magnetic Signature Duplicator (VEMASID)

DESCRIPTION

The Vehicle Magnetic Signature Duplicator (VEMASID) is a system designed to detonate magnetically-fuzed mines before the carrier vehicle reaches them. The VEMASID system effectively reproduces the magnetic radiation signature of the carrier vehicle and projects this signature in front of the tank as it travels. Any magnetically-fuzed mines in the path of the carrier will then be detonated before the carrier reaches them. VEMASID is now in the advanced development stage.

VEMASID operates by using an electromagnetic coil mounted on the front of the carrier vehicle. Radiation from the coil produces the magnetically-fuzed mines to detonate. It can be fitted onto the M1 Abrams, the M2

and M3 Bradley Fighting Vehicles, the M60 tank series, the M113 APC, the M548 cargo carrier and the M728 CEV. On all these vehicles the coil is carried over the front hull of the vehicle but with the M113 APC it is carried in place of the trim vane. The coil is usually held in place by tie-down straps, and can be fitted in 15 minutes. Distribution to units is expected to be at the rate of one to each M728 CEV and one to a platoon for armour, armoured cavalry, engineer and mechanised infantry units. VEMASID is intended to be used in conjunction with other mine-clearing devices such as mine rollers or ploughs for absolute assurance.

The coil for the majority of vehicles weighs 115·6 kg and that for the M113 APC weighs 136 kg. The coil has a diameter of 152 mm and the larger version measures 3·25 × 0·99 metres. That for the M113 is 2·29 × 0·838 metres. The system operates off the vehicle's 24 volt

power supply and the weight of the electronics package carried either on the rear of the vehicle or internally when space is available (as on the M113) is about 38·5 kg. The full VEMASID kit consists of the coil, amplifier, capacitor bank, control panel (placed near tank commander or M113 driver), cables, instructions (also moulded into coil), and tools. No maintenance is required and a fault is cured only by changing the assembly.

STATUS
Development.

AGENCY
US Army Mobility Equipment Research and Development Command, Fort Belvoir, Virginia 22060, USA (DRDME-NNT).

Mine-clearing Roller

DESCRIPTION

The mine-clearing roller system has been developed by the United States Army Mobility Equipment Research and Development Command (MERADCOM) at Fort Belvoir, Virginia to meet a European theatre of operations requirement for an all-weather day and night mine-clearance system that is capable of rapidly breaching defended minefields. The complete system consists of the roller assemblies, a removable mounting kit and two manually operated winches. The entire kit weighs less than ten tons. Two different kits are required to fit the system to the M48 and the M60. The system has also been tested on the M1 Abrams.

M60A3 MBT fitted with mine-clearing roller system

The tank crew, by use of the winches, takes some 15 minutes to mount the roller system on hard points previously fitted to the front of the tank. The tank then pushes the roller through the minefield to be breached to detonate any buried or surface-laid single-pulse pressure actuated mines in its path. Once breaching has been completed the tank driver can disconnect the roller with an internally mounted hydraulic release system.

The US Army plans to order an intial 90 sets of rollers at an estimated $112 000 per set. They will be issued to units based in the USA and Europe only and will be organic to the tank battalion with one set to each tank company. When not in use the rollers will be carried on M172A1 trailers (one roller per trailer) and M818 tractors. The rollers will also be used by the projected Counter Obstacle Vehicle (COV) (see page 14).

STATUS
Production.

MANUFACTURER
General Dynamics, Land Systems Division, PO Box 1901, Warren, Michigan 48090, USA.

MERADCOM Remotely-Controlled Mine-clearing Vehicle

DESCRIPTION
The US Army's Mobility and Equipment Research and Development Command (MERADCOM) at Fort Belvoir, Virginia has successfully developed and tested a remotely-controlled mine-clearing vehicle based on a modified M60A2 MBT chassis. The tank has been fitted with a bow-mounted mine-clearing roller system, a US Marine Corps M58A1 rocket propelled mine-clearing line charge system (on top of the chassis in place of the turret) and a marking system for designating safe lanes mounted on the rear.

In the tests conducted so far at Fort Knox, Kentucky the vehicle has been successfully controlled from up to 1600 metres from the operator. The mode of operation is first to identify the minefield boundary by using the mine-clearing rollers to detonate one of the mines. The vehicle is then reversed to a position just in front of the minefield and the mine-clearance line charge laid by means of the rocket. The charge is detonated to breach the minefield and, after clearing a path through, the vehicle is commanded to move forward to mark a safe lane by means of the marking system.

STATUS
Development.

Robotic obstacle breaching assault tank demonstrated at Fort Knox, Kentucky, late in 1981 (US Army)

M173 Mine-clearing Equipment

DESCRIPTION
The M173 mine-clearing equipment was developed by Picatinny Arsenal and the Martin Company of Baltimore. The equipment consists of a boat-shaped glass-fibre sled which is divided up into three compartments. The front compartment contains an M95 JATO rocket attached to a 60·1-metre length of plastic explosive coiled in the centre compartment. The rear compart-

ment contains the accessories and towing cable when not being used.

The sled, which will float, can be towed behind a tracked vehicle such as an M113 APC or an M48 MBT. The sled is normally brought up to the edge of the minefield and the rocket is launched across the minefield trailing the explosive charge. The rocket is halted by an arresting wire attached to the sled. The line then falls onto the minefield and detonates, exploding any mines in its path.

SPECIFICATIONS
Weight: 1360 kg
Length: 3·657 m
Width: 1·524 m

STATUS
In service with the US Army.

Mine-clearing Line Charge M58A1

DESCRIPTION
The linear mine-clearing charge M58A1 is a rocket-pulled 795 kg charge of C4 explosive designed to rapidly clear a lane 107 metres long and 3·7 to 4·6 metres wide in a minefield. The charge can be fired from a truck or a ground position. A three charge system for amphibious vehicles is currently under development.

The mode of operation is to place the charge about 60 metres from the edge of the minefield, the firing angle of the rocket is then set to approximately the optimum angular setting and the unit firmly anchored to the ground. The rocket is fired and the fuze for the main charge activated whilst in flight. If this fails to fire then the charge has to be detonated by a hand emplaced explosive charge. After detonation the swept lane is then manually checked for unexploded mines. If the breach has to be extended then the procedure is repeated. An M68 inert linear charge is available for training purposes.

The M58A1, a US Marine Corps equipment, is now being used as an evaluation model for the Mine Clearing Line Charge (MICLIC) project. The in-service date is 1985 and it is intended that there will be two MICLIC trailers per engineer company in divisions, separate brigades, armoured cavalry regiments and corps.

STATUS
In service with the US Marine Corps.

Mine-clearing Line Charge M58A1 (MICLIC) mounted on trailer and showing rocket projector and coiled charges (US Army)

Anti-personnel Mine-clearance Device M1 and M1A1

DESCRIPTION
This kit, officially designated Cable, Detonating, Anti-Personnel, Mine-Clearing, M1, consists of a circular aluminium storage and carrying case, a 52-metre length of detonating cable, propulsion unit, launcher unit and the firing equipment.

The detonating cable consists of 19 strands of nylon-covered detonating cord, each of which contains 100 grams of oil-soaked PETN per 305 mm. The launcher unit consists of a folding stand constructed of aluminium angles with connected legs.

The propulsion unit consists of a rocket unit with a length of wire rope attached to the front of the detonating cable, length of time fuze and two M2 fuze lighters. To detonate the detonating cable, a 15-second delay detonator is used.

The equipment is used as follows: the complete equipment is positioned just outside the minefield and one end of the detonating cable is staked to the ground. The detonating cord is projected by the launcher across the minefield by the jet propulsion system, falls to the ground and is detonated.

The M1 is now being supplemented by the M1A1 (formerly the M1E1) which follows the same general lines. It is slightly larger and heavier (weight crated 64·4 kg with the explosive line weighing 28·5 kg). When detonated it can clear a path about 2·44 metres wide of anti-personnel mines.

SPECIFICATIONS
Weight of complete equipment: 42 kg
Diameter of storage case: 420 mm
Type of explosive: PETN
Weight of explosive: 21 kg

STATUS
In service with the US Army.

Projected Charge M3A1

DESCRIPTION
The Projected Charge M3A1 consists of two parallel, linear, corrugated-aluminium or steel plates bolted together to form a rigid assembly. This is flexible in the vertical plane to allow it to pass over rough ground and rigid in the horizontal plane to maintain as straight a course as possible when being pushed.

When assembled it is 360 mm wide, 130 mm high and 122 metres long. Aluminium models weigh 4082 kg and steel models between 5670 and 6800 kg. Both contain up to 2042 kg of high explosive. Once assembled, the charge is pushed by a tracked vehicle such as an M48 or M60 MBT across the minefield and then detonated by the action of rifle or machine gun fire. The complete charge then explodes along its entire length and the pressure waves created should detonate any mines in the immediate area.

STATUS
In service with the US Army.

Projected Charge M157

DESCRIPTION
The Projected Charge M157 is an updated version of the Projected Charge M3A1 and follows the same general lines. The M157 is issued in kit form and takes from six to eight man-hours to assemble. It is drawn from stocks only as and when required. Each M157 section is made up from 62 centre loading sections each 1·524 metres long and weighing 64·4 kg; 13 body sections which are inert, 1·524 metres long and weighing 35·8 kg; two impact fuze sections each 1·524 metres long and weighing 69·4 kg with a M603 fuze; a single tail section weighing 70·3 kg. Each centre loading section and impact fuze section contains 20·4 kg of Composition B and 2·268 kg of Composition B-4.

The M157 is assembled in a rear area and towed to the edge of the minefield where it is pushed across the area to be cleared. The M157 is detonated by firing at the impact plate on the impact fuze sections with either 0·30 or 0·50 ball ammunition. Once a hit is registered the charge explodes leaving a path 90 metres long, 4 to 5 metres wide and 1 to 1·5 metres deep.

STATUS
In service with the US Army.

SPECIFICATIONS
Length: 122·225 m
Width: 305 mm
Height: 178 mm
Weight: 4989 kg

Projected Charge: Mine/Wire Obstacle Breach, XM271

DESCRIPTION
This portable equipment started as part of the Portable Mine Neutralisation System (POMINS) and has now been developed to the stage where hardware in the form of the Projected Charge: Mine/Wire Obstacle Breach, XM271 is under development. The XM271 can be carried by a single man and it is intended that it will be issued to units that normally carry Bangalore torpedoes when two will be carried at platoon headquarters level.

The XM271 is composed of a line charge with wire-wound grenades spaced along a reinforced detonating cord. The cord is coiled within a canister and is rocket-projected across a minefield. When fully extended the cord impacts across the minefield when the cord is detonated by a fuze system. The resultant blast and fragments from the grenades can clear anti-personnel mines and booby traps and also clear wire obstacles. The XM271 also has a capability against dug-outs and concrete obstacles.

The XM271 consists of a combination launcher and backpack frame, a rocket motor with (very probably) a manually initiated time delay fuze, a base assembly with a delay fuze and a line charge coiled inside the container. The equipment takes only two minutes or less to set up and can clear a path 0·6 metre wide and 25 metres long.

STATUS
Development.

SPECIFICATIONS (provisional)
Weight: 26·3 kg
Length: 1·168 m
Width: 355 mm
Height: 457 mm

Torpedo, Bangalore M1A1 and M1A2

DESCRIPTION
This is used for clearing minefields and other obstacles such as barbed wire. It consists of 1·524 metre lengths of high-explosive steel tubes with connecting sleeves. A complete item of issue consists of ten loaded assemblies, ten connection sleeves and one nose sleeve. Each sleeve, which is 54 mm in diameter, is filled with Amatol, with 102 mm of TNT at each end. Total weight of explosive in each assembly is 4·09 kg.

Each end of the tube contains a threaded well to accommodate a firing device with a crimped-on non-electric blasting cap or a delay detonator. The firing device can consists of six turns of detonating cord wrapped around one end of a loading assembly, to which is attached an 8 to 15 second delay detonator. When one loading assembly is detonated, the entire series will be detonated. The connecting sleeve consists of a short tube into which the ends of the loading assemblies fit, held in position by spring clips. The nose sleeve has a round point to assist in pushing the torpedo through obstacles.

The lengths of tube are connected together for the required length and then pushed across the minefield and detonated. The shock waves created by the explosive should detonate any mines in its path, although many modern mines have been designed to resist detonation by this method.

The M1A1 is now being supplemented by the M1A2 which follows the same general lines but each loading charge weighs 6·8 kg and total weight is 89·8 kg.

STATUS
In service with the US Army.

Cleared Lane Explosive Widening and Proofing Charge (CLEWP)

DESCRIPTION
Developed originally by Israel but now under active development by the US Army Mobility Equipment Research and Development Command (MERADCOM), the Cleared Lane Explosive Widening and Proofing charge (CLEWP) is still in the development stage and is not expected to be issued to field units until 1986.

CLEWP is carried in a box on the back of a minefield breaching vehicle which is used to clear minefields using either the track-width plough or mine rollers. As the vehicle enters the minefield the CLEWP box lid is ejected and then acts as an anchor while a length of explosive line charge unravels behind the vehicle. Once the vehicle has reached the far side of the minefield the explosive line charge can be detonated which effectively widens the cleared lane and clears any mines left by the plough or rollers, thus proofing the lane for other units to use.

STATUS
Development.

MINEFIELD MARKING EQUIPMENT

FRANCE

Minefield Lane Marking Lamp F1

DESCRIPTION
This flashing lamp (French Army designation is Lampe Clignotante pour lot léger de balisage de champ de mines modèle D1F1) is used for marking cleared lanes through minefields, and can be seen from a distance of up to 1000 metres which can be reduced by a screen if neccesary.

The lamp can be mounted on a pole or left on the ground, and a green filter can be fitted over the lamp if required.

STATUS
In production. In service with the French Army.

MANUFACTURER
Atelier de Fabrication de Toulouse, 155 avenue de Grand-Bretagne, 31053 Toulouse, France.

Enquiries to Groupement Industriels des Armements Terrestres (GIAT), 10 place Georges Clémenceau, 92211 Saint-Cloud, France.

SPECIFICATIONS
Weight: (without battery) 185 g
Height: 170 mm
Diameter: 50 mm
Power supply: 1 BA 30 battery
Operating period: 100 h
Operating temperature range: −31·5 to +51°C

F1 minefield lane marking lamp

ISRAEL

Clear Lane Marking System (CLAMS)

DESCRIPTION
The Clear Lane Marking System (CLAMS) is a self-contained add-on system which can be mounted on the rear of an armoured vehicle (other types of vehicle can also use the system) to mark a cleared path through a minefield. Normally only one CLAMS dispenser is centrally-mounted to a vehicle to indicate the centre of a cleared path but if two CLAMS units are mounted one each side of a vehicle they can indicate the boundaries of a cleared path.

CLAMS has two main components, a dispenser and the markers. The dispenser is a sheet metal box with a cover into which 150 markers can be loaded. It also has a release mechanism and a light stick activator. There is also an accessory compartment for stowage of the control box, ground travel meter, electrical harness and the loading accessories when not in use. In use the dispenser may be fitted to the user vehicle by two men in about ten minutes. An adaptor is mounted on the vehicle, which may incorporate a heat shield if required, and a cable harness connects the dispenser to the control box mounted in the driver's compartment. The system may be operated manually or automatically. In the automatic mode the interval for release of the markers may be set at 6, 12, 18, 24, 36 or 48 metres with the intervals being measured by a ground travel meter attached to the vehicle's speedometer. Manual release is carried out by pressing a release button on the control unit.

The marker consists of a sheet metal base disc on which is mounted a light stick and a flag. The light stick is automatically activated as it is released from the dis-

penser and glows for approximately 12 hours. For marking by day the flag alone may be used. The base is so designed that it will ensure the light stick is erect once dropped and is base-heavy to remain upright even in high winds. After use the markers may be retrieved and re-used. Light sticks are available in green, blue and orange, the flags are red and the normal colour for the base is white, although other colours are available.

In addition to indicating cleared paths through minefields, CLAMS may be used to indicate passages through difficult terrain, indicate the periphery of chemical or nuclear fallout contamination, or marking emergency runways for aircraft. It is a candidate for the US Army CLAMS requirement.

STATUS
Production. In service with Israeli armed forces.

MANUFACTURER
Israel Military Industries, Export Division, POB 1044 Ramat Hasharon 47100, Israel.

SPECIFICATIONS
Markers
Light stick height: 127 mm
Base disc diameter: 155 mm
Weight: 300 g

Dispenser
Length: 860 mm
Width: 280 mm
Height: 970 mm
Weight:
  (empty) 165 kg
  (loaded) 210 kg
Operating voltage: 24 V dc (12 V optional)

Clear Lane Marking System (CLAMS) in use

UNITED KINGDOM

Hunting Engineering Lightweight Perimeter Marking System

DESCRIPTION

The Hunting Engineering Perimeter Marking System delineates minefields and other hazards, route and lane markings and similar operations. It comprises a lightweight picket post with one end slotted to hold tape, wire or light rope; a flanged interface unit secured by a steel pin which is hammered into the ground or tarmac surface; a reel of yellow or red tape 16 mm wide and 125 metres long and a simple hand-held dispenser. Minefield and other marking triangles and signs can be provided. Using this equipment a two-man team can mark areas faster than one kilometre an hour.

Packaging can be arranged to suit customer requirements and satchels are available to enable one man to carry equipment sufficient for 250 metres of fencing.

STATUS

Production.

MANUFACTURER

Hunting Engineering Limited, Reddings Wood, Ampthill, Bedford MK45 2HD, England.

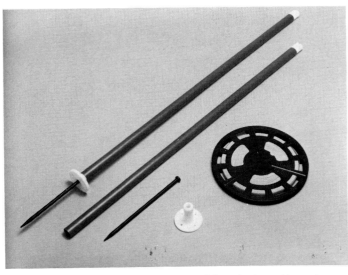

Components of Hunting Engineering lightweight perimeter marking system

Hunting Engineering lightweight perimeter marking system in use

Betalight Illuminated Defile Marker

DESCRIPTION

The Saunders-Roe Developments Limited Defile Marker was originally designed for use with the Medium Girder Bridge but has since undergone extensive trials by the British Army covering a wide range of other applications, including marking routes through minefields.

When being used for bridgemarking, two inward facing Defile Markers show the commencement of the defile, upward facing ones guide through the defile and two outward facing ones indicate the end of the defile.

The Defile Marker consists of a white arrow on a black background with a Betalight illuminated head, fitted in a tough plastic housing. The arrow can be rotated to one of eight fixed positions, allowing position or other information to be indicated.

Illumination is provided by SRDL Betalight self-powered light sources which are borosilicate glass capsules internally coated with phosphor and filled with tritium gas which activates the phosphor to emit light. The arrow is clearly visible in both day and night conditions. They are perfectly safe for the user and have a long maintenance-free life of between 15 and 20 years. The marker is small, compact and soldier-proof, and will withstand normal army mechanical environmental requirements, and can be used in all climatic conditions.

The marker can be attached to Military Police mounting poles, screwed or attached to mortar base plates or to the entry flag of a bridging layout, or even to a bayonet. The ring allows the marker to be attached to a nail, tree or other available support. Twelve Defile Markers can be carried in a standard 7·62 mm ammunition box.

SPECIFICATIONS

Weight: 170 g
Length: 130 mm
Width: 70 mm
Height: (including backplate) 27 mm

STATUS

In production. In service with the British Army and other armed forces.

MANUFACTURER

Saunders-Roe Developments Limited, Millington Road, Hayes, Middlesex UB3 4NB, England.

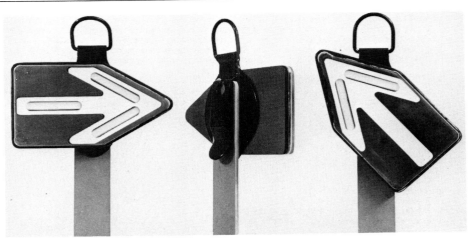

Saunders-Roe Developments Betalight illuminated defile marker in different positions

Saunders-Roe Developments Betalights being used to mark bridge laid by AVLB

Brandhurst Self-Illuminated Defile/Route Marker

DESCRIPTION
The Brandhurst Defile/Route Marker is a self-illuminated arrow on a metal disc that can be attached by a variety of means to any convenient point. The illumination can be green, yellow, blue, orange or white and is provided by a Brandhurst Microlight, a borosilicate glass capsule coated on the internal surface with a phosphor and filled with tritium gas. The gas activates the phosphor causing light to be emitted for periods longer than 15 years. The markers can be seen from as far as 750 metres. The arrow can be rotated in any direction and the colour of the backing face may be varied to suit customer requirements.

STATUS
Production.

MANUFACTURER
Brandhurst Company Limited, PO Box 70, Wellington Road, High Wycombe, Buckinghamshire HP12 3PS, England.

SPECIFICATIONS
Weight: 240 g
Length including ring: 130 mm
Diameter: 102 mm
Thickness including clip: 25 mm

Brandhurst route marker (three lights) on left and defile marker (two lights) on right

UNITED STATES OF AMERICA

Hand Emplaceable Minefield Marker Set M133

DESCRIPTION
The Hand Emplaceable Minefield Marker Set M133 has been developed by the US Army Mobility Equipment Research and Development Command (MERADCOM) at Fort Belvoir, Virginia, and is used for the temporary rapid marking of indefinite-life minefields by troops on foot. The major components of the equipment are a pole, orange fluorescent marking tape and an orange flashing light (152·4 mm long and 50·8 mm in diameter) which is mounted on top of the pole. The lamp is neon and initially flashes at about 82 times per minute. A shield inside the dome of the flasher prevents the light from being seen directly overhead. A reflector behind the neon lamp directs the light so that it can be seen from only one direction. The outside of the plastic case has a reflective surface to make it visible in light from vehicle headlights. Additional components are provided in the kit for emplacing and retrieving the poles. The poles are normally spaced at intervals of between 10 and 15 metres except for those adjacent to corner poles which are then spaced 4 metres from the corner pole; the marking tape is threaded through a holder on the side of the pole. The equipment has been designed to mark a 700 to 1000 metre perimeter minefield if the average pole spacing is not less than 10 metres, for 15 days under intermediate cold temperature conditions and be reusable between three and ten times.

STATUS
Production started late 1979. Entered service late 1980.

Soldier installing flashing light on top of pole (US Army)

Method of employing hand emplaceable minefield marker set M133 (US Army)

Clear Lane Marking System (CLAMS)

DESCRIPTION
Still under development by the US Army Mobility Equipment Research and Development Command, the Clear Lane Marking System will be used to mark cleared lanes through minefields in an assault breach. The system will be mounted on the lead vehicle which will mechanically emplace markers to denote either the centre of the cleared lane or its sides. It will be capable of being used in day or night conditions and the eventual system may include safety flares, fluorescent tape, black or white solvent paint, red flags or chemiluminescent light sticks.

The planned distribution is one set to a platoon for engineer, armour, armoured cavalry and mechanised infantry units.

The Israeli CLAMS is a candidate for this requirement (see page 250).

STATUS
Development.

Transport equipment

LIGHTWEIGHT VEHICLES

AUSTRIA

Steyr-Puch 700 AP (4 × 4) 555 kg Haflinger Light Vehicle

DESCRIPTION
The Haflinger all-terrain light vehicle was designed by Erich Ledwinka in the 1950s and entered production in 1959. Production was completed in 1974.

Its layout is unusual with the driver and one passenger at the front, two seats in the centre and the cargo area at the rear. The two rear seats can be folded flat to increase the load carrying area of the vehicle. The engine is mounted at the very rear, under the cargo area. The Haflinger has a windscreen that can be folded forward, and removable canvas top and sides. A wide range of optional equipment included a PTO, extra low gear (until the model with a five-speed gearbox was introduced), tropical kit, snow plough and a 1500 kg capacity winch.

The Austrian Army uses the vehicle as a cargo carrier, command vehicle and a radio vehicle and some have also been fitted with a 0·50 Browning machine gun or a 57 mm M18A1 American recoilless rifle. A number of specialised anti-tank models was also developed. These included one mounting the Swedish Bofors 90 mm PV 1110 recoilless rifle, another carrying four Mosquito wire guided anti-tank guided missiles with a further four missiles carried in reserve at the rear of the vehicle. The Swiss and Swedish armies use the vehicle fitted with the Bofors Bantam ATGW: six missiles are carried in the ready to launch position at the front of the vehicle on the right side with another eight missiles on the same side facing the rear.

In 1962 a long wheelbase model was introduced, which was available with the Haflinger type top or a fully enclosed cab. This model was 3·125 metres long, 1·4 metres wide, 1·74 metres high, with a wheelbase of 1·8 metres and unladen weight of 700 kg.

Steyr-Puch 700 AP (4 × 4) Haflinger with fully enclosed body

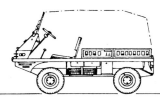

Steyr-Puch 700 AP (4 × 4) 555 kg Haflinger light vehicle

SPECIFICATIONS
Cab seating: 1 + 3
Configuration: 4 × 4
Weight:
(empty) 645 kg
(loaded) 1200 kg
Max load: 555 kg
Max weight:
(on front axle, loaded) 620 kg
(on rear axle, loaded) 700 kg
Load area: 1·54 × 1·275 m
Length: 2·85 m
Width: 1·4 m
Height:
(overall) 1·74 m
(reduced) 1·36 m
Ground clearance: 0·24 m
Track: 1·13 m
Wheelbase: 1·5 m
Max speed: 75 km/h
Range: 400 km
Fuel capacity: 31·5 litres

Steyr-Puch 700 AP (4 × 4) Haflingers, (left) armed with 0·50 Browning machine gun and (right) with 57 mm M18A1 recoilless rifle

Max gradient: 65%
Fording: 0·4 m
Engine: Model 700 AP 2-cylinder air-cooled petrol developing 24 hp at 4500 rpm. From 1967 production vehicles were fitted with engines that developed 27 hp at 4800 rpm
Gearbox: manual with 4 forward and 1 reverse gears. Vehicles produced after 1966 had 5 forward and 1 reverse gears
Clutch: single dry plate
Transfer box: none
Suspension: independent with coil/rubber springs
Turning radius: 3·8 m
Tyres: 165 × 12

Number of tyres: 4 + 1 spare
Brakes:
(main) hydraulic
(parking) mechanical
Electrical system: 12 V

STATUS
Production complete. In service with Austria, Indonesia, Italy, Nigeria, South Africa, Sweden and Switzerland.

MANUFACTURER
Steyr-Daimler-Puch AG, Werke Graz, Postfach 423, A-8011 Graz, Austria.

BELGIUM

FN AS 24 (3 × 2) 340 kg Lightweight Airborne Vehicle

DEVELOPMENT

The AS 24 (Véhicule Aéroporte) was designed by Nicholas Straussler and the first prototype was built in Germany. Production was undertaken by FN of Belgium which built about 300 vehicles, with final deliveries being made in 1966. FN is no longer involved in the design and manufacture of vehicles.

DESCRIPTION

The chassis of the FN is of all-welded tubular construction with the engine mounted over the rear axle. The side members are in two parts which slide together allowing the vehicle to be collapsed and extended. In both positions the tubes are locked together by assembly clamps. The four men are seated on a canvas bench type seat in the centre of the vehicle. The wheels are made of pressed aluminium alloy and are fitted with wide Lypsoid low pressure tyres to absorb any bumps as the vehicle is not provided with suspension.

The vehicle has been designed for parachuting on a standard platform measuring 1·8 × 1·2 metres. The platform can take a load of 500 kg, for example one collapsed AS 24 and eight cases of 7·62 mm ammunition. The drop platform has shock absorbers which consist of layers of honeycomb paper, separated by sheets of corrugated cardboard to cushion the honeycombs and prevent them from crushing together on impact with the ground. The vehicle can be ready for action within one minute of landing. A trailer with identical wheels and tyres has been developed for use with the AS 24 and can carry a maximum load of 250 kg. The basic vehicle has been designed to carry three men, plus the driver, or up to 250 kg of cargo such as ammunition and fuel.

VARIANTS

Many variants were designed by FN but few were put into production. Variants included ambulance, mortar carrying vehicle (one vehicle carrying the mortar and ammunition and the other the crew), mine carrying vehicle, telephone cable laying vehicle, anti-tank vehicle with ATGWs, fire fighting vehicle and an over-snow vehicle, the last with an additional small road wheel in front of each of the rear wheels, with a rubber band type track running round both wheels.

SPECIFICATIONS
(data in square brackets relate to vehicle when folded)
Seating: 1 + 3
Configuration: 3 × 2
Weight:
  (empty) 224 kg
  (loaded) 564 kg
Weight on front axle: (loaded) 205 kg
Weight on rear axle: (loaded) 359 kg
Max load: 340 kg
Towed load: 250 kg
Length: 1·89 [1·065] m
Width: 1·64 [1·64] m
Height: 0·89 [0·75] m
Track: (rear) 1·306 m
Wheelbase: 1·27 m
Max speed: 57·2 km/h
Range: 200 km
Fuel capacity: 10·5 litres
Max gradient: 60%
Engine: FN 24 2-cylinder, 2-stroke petrol developing 15 hp at 5300 rpm
Gearbox: FN 24 with 4 forward gears, no reverse
Clutch: FN 24, Ferodo multi-disc in oil bath
Transfer box: none
Steering: rack
Turning radius: 1·75 m
Tyres: 12.00 × 20
Brakes: mechanically operated on rear wheels
Electrical system: none

STATUS
Production complete. In service with the Belgian Army.

MANUFACTURER
FN, Herstal, Belgium.

FN AS 24 (3 × 2) lightweight airborne vehicle

FN AS 24 (3 × 2) lightweight airborne vehicle towing two trailers

FN AS 24 (3 × 2) lightweight airborne vehicle

BRAZIL

SAFO (4 × 4) 500 kg Light Vehicle

DEVELOPMENT

The SAFO (Sistema de Alta Flexibilidad Operacional, or High Operational Flexibility System) 500 kg light vehicle has been developed by the Jamy company in collaboration with the Brazilian Army Military Institute of Engineering (Instituto Militar de Engenharia) to meet a requirement for a light all-terrain vehicle that could be parachuted without any special preparation.

So far two prototypes have been built and trials carried out by the Brazilian Army have been successful. Once the 30 000 km endurance test has been completed series production vehicles could be finished within six months of certification and a unit price of about $22 000 is being quoted.

DESCRIPTION

The SAFO is an unusual design with the driver at the front on the left, the engine to his right recessed under the floor and a passenger seat on the far right. There is a flat corrugated load area to the rear. To reduce the overall length for air drop, or stowage in a transport aircraft, the rear half of the load surface folds up and through 180 degrees to rest on the top of the remaining cargo area and the rear suspension units are unlocked and swung forwards towards the front wheels through an arc of about 160 degrees. Lights are fitted as standard enabling the vehicle to be driven on normal roads.

VARIANTS

The vehicle can be adapted for a wide variety of roles including being armed with a pintle-mounted 7·62 mm or a 12·7 mm (0·50) M2 HB machine gun, or anti-tank weapons such as three Cobra ATGWs.

SAFO (4 × 4) 500 kg light vehicle in folded configuration (Ronaldo S Olive)

Front and side drawings of SAFO (4 × 4) 500 kg light vehicle (not to 1/76th scale as other drawings (Ronaldo S Olive)

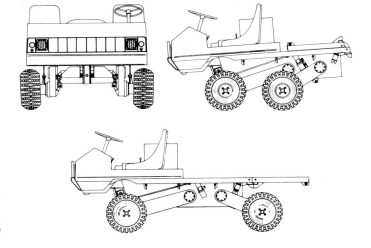

SAFO (4 × 4) 500 kg light vehicle in travelling configuration (Ronaldo S Olive)

SAFO (4 × 4) 500 kg light vehicle fitted with Cobra ATGWs (Ronaldo S Olive)

STATUS
Trials.

MANUFACTURER
Jamy, Sociedade Industrial de Equipamentos Especiais Ltda, Rua Miguel Angelo 276, 20781 Rio de Janeiro, RJ, Brazil.

SPECIFICATIONS
Seating: 1 + 1
Configuration: 4 × 4
Weight:
(empty) 600 kg
(loaded) 1100 kg
Weight on front axle: (empty) 320 kg
Weight on rear suspension units: (empty) 280 kg

Max load: 500 kg
Length:
(travelling) 3·24 m
(folded) 2·45 m
Width: 1·8 m
Height:
(overall) 1·46 m
(body) 1·18 m
(load area) 0·75 m
Track:
(front) 1·52 m
(rear) 1·57 m
Wheelbase:
(travelling): 1·85 m
(folded) 0·76 m

Angle of approach/departure: 50°/55°
Max speed: 87 km/h
Range: 150 km
Fuel capacity: 30 litres
Max gradient: 60%
Max side slope: 40%
Engine: Volkswagen 1300 4-stroke, 4-cylinder petrol developing 38 hp (DIN) at 4000 rpm
Steering: rack and pinion
Brakes:
(main) hydraulic
(parking) mechanical
Electrical system: 12 V

Ford U-50 (4 × 4) Light Vehicle

DESCRIPTION
The Ford U-50 (4 × 4) light vehicle is virtually identical to the M38 Jeep in appearance and general layout. Ford of Brazil produced the U-50 in both civil and military versions with the civil version being available in two wheelbase lengths, 2·057 and 2·565 metres. In both wheelbase lengths open, soft-top and hard-top versions were available.

For the military version of the U-50 only the short 2·057-metre wheelbase was produced. This has a canvas top and a windscreen that can hinge forward onto the bonnet. Bench seats are provided in the rear and a tow hook is fitted. The normal electrical circuit for the military version is 12 volts dc, but a version fitted for radio with a 24 volt dc system was available. Other military additions

such as special lighting, towing shackles on the front and rear bumpers, and electrical take-off point for trailer towing, racks for tools and fuel or water canisters, a transmission protection plate, and a completely screened electrical system are provided.

A special military version to carry a 106 mm recoilless rifle has an open tail-gate, a specially-strengthened rear axle and a split windscreen to accommodate the rifle barrel when travelling. The rear has squab seating on the sides for the gun crew and racks are provided in the floor to stow six rounds of ammunition.

STATUS
Production complete.

MANUFACTURER
Ford Brasil SA, Sao Paulo, Brazil.

Ford U-50 (4 × 4) light vehicle showing stowage of 106 mm recoilless rifle

Military version of Ford U-50 (4 × 4) light vehicle for carrying 106 mm recoilless rifle

Rear view of military version of Ford U-50 (4 × 4) light vehicle for carrying 106 mm recoilless rifle showing split windscreen, barrel clamp and ammunition stowage racks

Front view of basic military version of Ford U-50 (4 × 4) light vehicle

SPECIFICATIONS

Model	Military	Recoilless rifle
Seating	1 + 3	1 + 3
Configuration	4 × 4	4 × 4
Weight (empty)	1167 kg	1165 kg
(loaded)	1707 kg	1766 kg
Weight on front axle (empty)	568 kg	570 kg
Weight on rear axle (empty)	599 kg	595 kg
Length (overall)	3·509 m	3·509 m
Width	1·521 m	1·68 m
Height (overall)	1·82 m	1·682 m
Ground clearance	0·203 m	0·196 m
Track (front)	1·234 m	1·234 m
(rear)	1·232 m	1·232 m
Wheelbase	2·057 m	2·057 m
Angle of approach/departure	35°30'/29°20'	46°30'/28°
Max speed	125 km/h	125 km/h
Range	400 km	305 km
Fuel capacity	50 litres	50 litres
Max gradient	100% plus	100% plus
Fording	0·35 m	0·35 m
Engine	Ford I-4 OHC 2·3-litre 4-cylinder OHC petrol developing 91 hp at 5000 rpm	
Gearbox	manual synchromesh with 4 forward and 1 reverse gears	
Transfer box	2-speed	2-speed
Clutch	single disc dry plate HD type	
Steering	worm and roller	worm and roller
Turning radius	6 m	5·41 m
Suspension	semi-elliptical springs and shock absorbers	
Tyres	6.00 × 16	6.00 × 16
Brakes (main)	hydraulic	hydraulic
(parking)	mechanical	mechanical
Electrical system	12 or 24 V	12 or 24 V

Rear three-quarter view of military version of Ford U-50 (4 × 4) light vehicle

Comando (4 × 4) Command and Reconnaissance Vehicle

DEVELOPMENT
The Comando has been developed by the Jamy company in collaboration with the Brazilian Army Military Institute of Engineering (Instituto Militar de Engenharia) to meet a requirement for a reconnaissance/command vehicle capable of operating cross-country with both armoured and mechanised infantry units.

The prototype was completed early in 1980 and series production is expected to begin as soon as the army completes a final 30 000 km endurance test. When in production the Comando is expected to cost approximately $25 000.

DESCRIPTION
In many respects the layout of the Comando is similar to the now discontinued American XR311 with a well sloped front to give maximum forward visibility to the driver seated on the centre-line of the vehicle with a single seat each side and slightly to the rear for the commander and radio operator, and the engine at the rear.

The chassis is a tubular steel frame structure fitted with a light steel body. The windscreen can be folded towards the front and an anti-roll bar is mounted to the immediate rear of the crew area. Provision is made for the installation of various types of communication equipment and a winch is mounted internally at the front of the vehicle.

The prototype is fitted with an alcohol-powered Chevrolet engine but export vehicles may be fitted with a conventional diesel engine.

STATUS
Trials.

MANUFACTURER
Jamy, Sociedade Industrial de Equipamentos Especiais Ltda, Rua Miguel Angelo 276, 20781 Rio de Janeiro, RJ, Brazil.

Comando (4 × 4) command and reconnaissance vehicle showing central position of driver (Ronaldo S Olive)

SPECIFICATIONS
Cab seating: 1 + 2
Configuration: 4 × 4
Weight:
  (empty) 2200 kg
  (loaded) 2950 kg
Max load: 750 kg
Length: 4·27 m
Width: 1·7 m
Height: 1·6 m
Ground clearance: 0·3 m
Wheelbase: 2·9 m
Angle of approach/departure: 70°/50°
Max speed: 120 km/h
Range: 500 km

Max gradient: 83%
Engine: Chevrolet 250S 6-cylinder in-line alcohol developing 171 hp at 4800 rpm
Gearbox: Chevrolet automatic with 3 forward and 1 reverse gears
Transfer box: 2-speed with PTO for winch
Steering: hydraulic
Turning radius: 6·9 m
Suspension: independent
Tyres: 9.00 × 10
Number of tyres: 4
Brakes:
  (main) disc
  (parking) mechanical
Electrical system: 12 V (24 V in FFR model)

Gurgel X-12 and X-15 Light Vehicle Family

DESCRIPTION

The Gurgel X-12-RM light vehicle has been developed primarily for civil applications but does have a military use as, for instance, a command and reconnaissance vehicle.

The chassis of the Gurgel is all steel and the body is fibreglass. Many of the automotive components are from the Volkswagen range of vehicles that are produced in Brazil.

The layout of the Gurgel is unconventional with the stowage space under the bonnet at the front, driver and passenger in the centre with the small load area to the immediate rear, and the engine at the back. All vehicles are 4 × 2 with drive to the rear wheels and are fitted with a Selectraction device which allows selective locking of the rear wheels if one is slipping.

The X-12-RM is fitted with a fully enclosed two-man cab and can be fitted with a front-mounted winch. Other models, such as the X-12-M and X-12-L, have a windscreen that folds forwards, a canvas top that folds down to the rear, removable side doors and an anti-roll bar.

VARIANTS

X-12-L: Basic model with canvas top, removable doors and folding windscreen. All models have manual front-mounted winch with 25 metres of cable.
X-12-TR: Hard top (teto rigido) with two doors with windable windows and seating for four or five people.
X-12-RM: Hard top for two people (driver plus passenger) with load area at the rear.
X-12-M: Military version as used by the Brazilian armed forces.

X-12-Caride: Tourist model.
G-15-CS: Forward control type vehicle with fully enclosed three-man cab, longer wheelbase than the X-12 series and payload of 700 kg.
G-15-GD: Twin cabin (Carbine Duplex) of forward control type with seats for six people and payload of 500 kg.
C-15-L: Furgao, fully enclosed van-type vehicle, also a special military police model.
X-15-TR: Fully enclosed model with seating for eight people.

SPECIFICATIONS

Model	X-12-L X-12 Caride	X-12-TR X-12-RM	G-15-CD	G-15-CS
Configuration	4 × 2	4 × 2	4 × 2	4 × 2
Weight (empty)	770 kg	800 kg	1000 kg	950 kg
Length	3·31 m	3·31 m	3·74 m	3·74 m
Width	1·6 m	1·6 m	1·8 m	1·8 m
Height	1·55 m	1·595 m	1·88 m	1·88 m
Ground clearance	0·33 m	0·33 m	0·31 m	0·31 m
Track (front)	1·35 m	1·35 m	1·46 m	1·46 m
(rear)	1·405 m	1·405 m	1·42 m	1·42 m
Wheelbase	2·04 m	2·04 m	2·23 m	2·23 m
Range	600 km	600 km	800 km	800 km
Fuel capacity	37 litres	37 litres	80 litres	80 litres
Angle of approach/departure	63°/41°	63°/41°	55°/45°	55°/45°
Engine	1600 cc Volkswagen 4-cylinder petrol rear mounted, developing 65 hp (SAE) at 4600 rpm			
Gearbox	manual with 4 forward and 1 reverse gears			
Transfer box	2-speed	2-speed	2-speed	2-speed
Suspension	independent, front torsion bars and rear helical springs, shock absorbers at each wheel station			
Tyres	7.50 × 15	7.50 × 15	7.00 × 14	7.00 × 14
Brakes (main) (front)	hydraulic disc	hydraulic disc	hydraulic disc	hydraulic disc
(main) (rear)	hydraulic drum	hydraulic drum	hydraulic drum	hydraulic drum
Electrical system	12 V	12 V	12 V	12 V

STATUS

G-15 production complete. X-12 in production. In service with the Brazilian armed forces.

MANUFACTURER

Gurgel SA, Rodovia Washington Luiz, km 171, CEP 13500, Caixa Postal 98, Rio Claro, SP, Brazil.

Gurgel X-12-M (4 × 2) military vehicle with 12·7 mm (0·50) M2 MG

Service version of G-15 (4 × 2) with 106 mm recoilless rifle

ENGESA EE-34 (4 × 4) 750 kg Light Vehicles

DEVELOPMENT

The ENGESA EE-34 (4 × 4) 750 kg light vehicle was developed to the prototype stage as a command car by ENVEMO (Engenharia de Veiculos e Motores) but production was undertaken by ENGESA at its main facility at São Jose dos Campos. The first prototype was completed in 1980 and production began in 1982.

DESCRIPTION

The body of the command car version is made of pressed steel with the engine at the front, driver and passengers in the centre and a small cargo area at the rear. Standard equipment includes a windscreen that folds downwards onto the bonnet when not in use, four removable vinyl doors, removable vinyl top and a drop tailgate at the rear for loading stores. The maximum payload across country is 750 kg and on roads 1000 kg.

Optional equipment includes a Perkins model 4.236 diesel engine, Mercedes-Benz OM-314 diesel, automatic transmission, power steering, hard top and an electrically-operated front-mounted winch.

The basic vehicle can be used for a wide range of roles including radio vehicle, forward area ambulance and reconnaissance vehicle. Various radio installations can be fitted.

Variants announced to date include a light truck version with a longer wheelbase and a pick-up bodied version with the normal wheelbase. There is also an ambulance-bodied variant of all-pressed steel with internal fittings for two stretchers, one above the other,

EE-34 (4 × 4) 750 kg pick-up truck

EE-34 (4 × 4) ambulance

and seating for three personnel. The ambulance body is entered by two large rear doors.

STATUS
Production.

MANUFACTURER
ENGESA Engenheiros Especializados SA, Avenida das Nacões Unidas 22.833, Santo Amaro, 04697 São Paulo, Brazil.

SPECIFICATIONS
(command car; data in square brackets relate to truck version where different)
Configuration: 4 × 4
Weight:
(empty) 1895 [2250] kg
(loaded, road) 2895 [3250] kg
(loaded, cross country) 2645 [3000] kg

Max load:
(road) 1000 kg
(cross country) 750 kg
Length: 4·12 [5·055] m
Width: 1·89 m
Height:
(tarpaulin) n/app [2·115 m]
(cab top) 2·025 m
(windscreen down) 1·493 m
Ground clearance: 0·36 m
Track:
(front) 1·56 m
(rear) 1·55 m
Wheelbase: 2·4 [2·95] m
Angle of approach/departure: 37°/35° [37°/28°]
Max speed: (road) 120 km/h
Range: 640 [600] km
Max gradient: 60%
Max side slope: 30%

Engine: 6-cylinder water-cooled petrol
Gearbox: manual, 4 forward and 1 reverse gears
Clutch: single dry plate
Transfer box: mechanical, single speed [mechanical, 2-speed]
Steering: mechanical
Suspension: leaf springs and hydraulic shock absorbers
Tyres: 10.00 × 15
Number of tyres: 4 + 1 spare
Brakes:
(main) hydraulic, disc on front and drum on rear wheels
(parking) drum type, mechanical, operating on transmission output shaft
Electrical system: 12 V

ENGESA EE-34 (4 × 4) 750 kg command car

ENGESA EE-34 (4 × 4) 750 kg truck

CANADA

Canadian Light Vehicles

DEVELOPMENT
The standard light vehicle of the Canadian Armed Forces is the American M38, which was built in Canada as the M38CDN, and the M38A1, built as the M38A1CDN.

In October 1981 Volkswagen AG of West Germany agreed to cede and transfer to Bombardier Incorporated of Canada the design and manufacturing technology of its Iltis (4 × 4) 500 kg light vehicle as used by the West German Army. The agreement also granted to Bombardier the worldwide rights for the marketing, sale and distribution of the Iltis, as well as the rights to manufacture and market the civilian version of the vehicle. Bombardier also acquired the tooling equipment used in the manufacture of the Iltis.

Before this announcement the Canadian Department of National Defense asked the company to submit a proposal, based on the Iltis, for the replacement of the existing utility 4 × 4 vehicles of the Canadian Armed Forces. On November 1st 1983 it was announced that the Canadian government had awarded a contract for 1900 Iltis vehicles to the Logistic Equipment Division of Bombardier Inc. The contract includes the supply of spare parts, manuals and training programmes for operators and maintainers and is valued at C$68 million. Production is scheduled to begin by the end of summer 1984, and should be complete by the end of 1985.

For the specifications of the Iltis refer to the entry under Germany, Federal Republic in this section.

STATUS
Ordered for the Canadian armed forces (1900).

Bombardier-produced Iltis (T J Gander)

MANUFACTURER
Bombardier Incorporated, Logistic Equipment Division, Valcourt, Quebec J0E 2LO, Canada.

CHINA, PEOPLE'S REPUBLIC

BJ-212 (4 × 4) 425 kg Light Vehicle

DESCRIPTION
This light vehicle is very similar in appearance to the Soviet UAZ-469B and can carry a maximum load of 425 kg. Its unladen weight is 1530 kg and it has a maximum cruising range of 440 km. The layout of the vehicle is conventional with the engine at the front and the passenger/cargo area to the rear. The vehicle has two doors in each side, a removable canvas top which folds down at the rear when not required and a windscreen that folds flat against the bonnet.

SPECIFICATIONS
Configuration: 4 × 4
Weight:
  (empty) 1530 kg
  (loaded) 1955 kg
Weight on front axle:
  (loaded) 918 kg
Weight on rear axle:
  (loaded) 1112 kg
Max load: 425 kg
Length: 3·86 m
Width: 1·75 m
Height: 1·87 m
Wheelbase: 2·3 m
Max speed: 98 km/h
Range: (road) 440 km
Fuel capacity: 60 litres
Max gradient: 58%
Fording: 0·5 m
Engine: Model 492 4-cylinder petrol developing 75 hp at 3500 rpm
Gearbox: manual, 4 forward and 1 reverse gears
Clutch: single dry plate
Transfer box: 2-speed
Suspension: semi-elliptical springs and hydraulic shock absorbers
Tyres: 6.50 × 16

BJ-212 (4 × 4) 425 kg light vehicle (A. McKrill)

Number of tyres: 4 + 1 spare
Brakes:
  (main) hydraulic
  (parking) mechanical
Electrical system: 12 V

STATUS
In service with the Chinese Army and Chad.

MANUFACTURER
Pei-Ching Shih, China.

CZECHOSLOVAKIA

TAZ (4 × 4) 900 kg Truck

DESCRIPTION
In 1975 it was reported that the Trnava Motor Vehicle Plant was preparing for the production of a new 4 × 4 truck which would use many existing components and have a payload of 900 kg. This vehicle has a forward control cab and a rear cargo area with drop sides and a drop tailgate.

STATUS
Uncertain.

MANUFACTURER
Trnava Motor Vehicle Plant (TAZ), Slovakia, Czechoslovakia.

EGYPT

Egyptian Jeep Production

DEVELOPMENT
Egypt is currently manufacturing under licence from the American Motors Corporation the CJ6 (4 × 4) Jeep. This agreement was concluded as part of the Arab Organisation of Industrialisation plans but when the AOI folded the Egyptian government took a majority shareholding in the company.

First production Egyptian Jeeps were completed late in 1978 and 2500 vehicles were built in 1979, all of which were supplied to the Egyptian Army. In 1980 4500 vehicles were built, 3000 for the Egyptian Army, 1000 for commercial sales and 500 for export to Oman.

VARIANTS
The Egyptian Army has at least two variants of the CJ6 in service, one carrying Soviet SA-7 SAMs and the other carrying British Aerospace Dynamics Group Swingfire ATGWs which are also manufactured under licence in Egypt. The latter version has a Swingfire pallet mounted to the rear of the cab. When travelling the launcher is horizontal and is elevated at an angle of about 40 degrees when required for firing. The missiles, which have a range of 4000 metres, are launched away from the vehicle with a cable connected separation sight, or from within the cab, with the launcher vehicle being concealed behind natural cover.

STATUS
Production. In service with the Egyptian Army.

Egyptian-built Jeep with British Aerospace Dynamics Group Swingfire ATGW system mounted to rear of cab

FRANCE

LOHR Fardier FL 500 and FL 501 (4 × 4) 500 kg Light Vehicles

DEVELOPMENT

These light airportable vehicles were developed by SOFRAMAG (now LOHR) for the use of airborne troops and 300 have been ordered by the French Army. A C-130 Hercules or a C-160 Transall transport aircraft can carry six FL 500s ready for air dropping or 12 FL 500s for delivery as cargo. The SA 330 Puma helicopter can carry one FL 500 and one 120 mm mortar. The vehicle can carry a maximum load of 500 kg, including the driver, and tow a trailer or weapon such as a 120 mm Hotchkiss-Brandt mortar, weighing a maximum of 500 kg.

DESCRIPTION

The FL 500 has a chassis of tubular steel welded construction with the load area covered by aluminium sheeting. The driver is seated at the front of the vehicle on the left side and if required, an inverted U-shaped safety bar can be fitted to the rear of the driver's position.

The engine is mounted crosswise in the centre of the vehicle and connected to the front and rear axles by two cardan driven central transmission units with shock absorbing guides. The light alloy reinforced axles are mounted on cushioned rubber and the suspension arms consist of helicoidal springs placed horizontally on each side of the chassis, in two suspension boxes.

Brakes are hydraulic on all wheels, with an independent parking brake for each rear wheel. A complete lighting system is installed enabling the vehicle to be driven on roads.

VARIANTS

The latest production version is the FL 501 which has the optional 36 hp engine fitted as standard. This allows loads of up to 800 kg to be towed. The FL 501 is now in production, and has been demonstrated carrying two MATRA SATCP surface-to-air missiles.

The FL 500 has been used for trials with the MILAN ATGW system and has been equipped with light machine guns. Alternative loads could include radios and the FL 500 and FL 501 can be used to tow 120 mm mortars.

SPECIFICATIONS

Cab seating: 1
Configuration: 4 × 4
Weight:
  (empty) 680 kg
  (loaded) 1180 kg
Max load: 500 kg
Towed load:
  (FL 500) 500 kg
  (FL 501) 800 kg

LOHR Fardier FL 501 (4 × 4) 500 kg light vehicle (T J Gander)

Load area: 1·93 m²
Length: 2·375 m
Width: 1·5 m
Height:
  (steering wheel) 1·18 m
  (load area) 0·92 m
Ground clearance: 0·26 m
Track: 1·26 m
Wheelbase: 1·735 m
Angle of approach/departure: 90°/90°
Max speed: (road) 80 km/h
Range: (road) 200 km
Fuel capacity: 25 litres
Max gradient: 60%
Max side slope: 30%
Vertical obstacle: 0·2 m
Fording: 0·4 m
Engine: Citroën AK 2 flat twin petrol developing 29 hp (DIN) at 6750 rpm (or a 36 hp engine which gives a maximum road speed of 71 km/h)
Gearbox: Citroën, manual with 4 forward and 1 reverse gears
Steering: rack and pinion
Turning radius: 4·8 m

LOHR Fardier FL 500 (4 × 4) 500 kg light vehicle

Suspension: independent, with helical spring and hydraulic shock absorber at each wheel station
Brakes:
  (main) hydraulic disc
  (parking) hand-brake on each rear wheel
Electrical system: 12 V
Battery: 1 × 12 V, 30 Ah

STATUS

In production. In service with the French Army, Argentina and other undisclosed countries.

MANUFACTURER

LOHR SA, 67980 Hangenbieten, France.

Fardier FL 500 (4 × 4) light vehicle towing 120 mm Brandt mortar

Fardier FL 500 (4 × 4) light vehicle fitted with Euromissile MILAN ATGW system

SAMO (4 × 4) Light Vehicle

DEVELOPMENT

The 4 × 4 SAMO light vehicle was a joint development between SAMO and Gevelot and was first shown at the 1977 Satory Military Exhibition. It is manufactured by Société Internationale de Matériels Industriels (SIMI).

DESCRIPTION

The vehicle is available in standard and long wheelbase

versions. According to the manufacturers the standard version has a road carrying capacity of 1200 kg and the long wheelbase version a road carrying capacity of 1800 kg. Their cross country capacities have not been announced but have been estimated at 800 kg and 1200 kg respectively. The ladder-type chassis is made up of two rectangular box-section main members, 120 × 60 mm and 5 mm wall thickness, linked by six transverse cross-members, three welded and three bolted (two of which constitute the bumpers). The body

structure is 2 mm thick sheet steel welded onto the chassis giving exceptional rigidity overall.

The layout of both vehicles is similar with the engine at the front, driver and passenger seats in the centre and the cargo area at the rear with a bench seat down each side and a tailgate. The basic model is fitted with removable bows, canvas top and a windscreen that can be folded down onto the bonnet if required. A hard top model is also offered.

Optional equipment includes a 24-volt electrical sys-

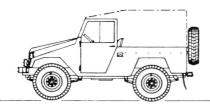

Standard version of SAMO (4 × 4) light vehicle

tem, different tyres (eg 9.00 × 16), 3500 kg capacity winch, PTO, cooling radiator for engine oil, water tank, power clutch, power brakes, searchlight, vertical exhaust, heater, right hand drive, special equipment for operations in the desert, long range fuel tanks, overdrive, power assisted steering, heavy duty axles (front with capacity of 1250 kg, rear 2500 kg), additional fuel tank, folding windscreen, gear box and axle protection plates and tropical ventilation.

VARIANTS
Both models can be modified for a wide range of roles including ambulance, command vehicle and radio vehicle. The standard model can be armed with a 0·50 calibre M2 HB machine gun or a 7·62 mm machine gun. The long wheelbase model can be armed with ATGWs, a 106 mm M40 type recoilless rifle or a 20 mm cannon.

STATUS
Production. In service with Burundi, Cameroon, Central African Republic, Chad, Congo, Ivory Coast, Madagascar, Upper Volta, Zaïre and other countries.

MANUFACTURER
Société Internationale de Matériels Industriels (SIMI), 42260 Saint-Germain-Laval, France.

SPECIFICATIONS

Model	Standard	LWB
Cab seating	2 + 4	2 + 8
Configuration	4 × 4	4 × 4
Weight (empty)	1400 kg	1600 kg
(loaded)	2600 kg	3400 kg
Max load	1200 kg	1800 kg
Towed load (road)	3000 kg	3000 kg
(cross country)	800 kg	800 kg
Load area	1·1 × 1·4 m	1·7 × 1·41 m
Length	3·6 m	4·23 m
Width	1·592 m	1·592 m
Height (overall)	1·9 m	1·9 m
(reduced)	1·3 m	1·3 m
(load area)	0·7 m	0·7 m
Ground clearance	0·216 m	0·216 m
Track	1·36 m	1·36 m
Wheelbase	2·04 m	2·54 m
Angle of approach/departure	42°/35°	42°/30°
Max speed (road)	115 km/h	115 km/h
Range	900 km	900 km
Fuel capacity	55 litres	55 litres
Max gradient	65%	65%
Max side slope	30%	30%
Fording	0·6 m	0·6 m
Engine	Peugeot 4-cylinder diesel developing 67·4 hp at 4000 rpm or Saviem 4-cylinder diesel developing 85 hp at 3000 rpm or Renault 4-cylinder petrol developing 80 hp at 5000 rpm	
Gearbox	manual with 4 forward and 1 reverse gears	
Clutch	single dry plate	single dry plate
Transfer box	2-speed	2-speed
Steering	recirculation and ball	recirculation and ball
Turning radius	5·3 m	6·4 m
Suspension	semi-elliptical springs and hydraulic shock absorbers	
Tyres	7.50 × 16	7.50 × 16
Number of tyres	4 + 1 spare	4 + 1 spare
Brakes (main)	hydraulic	hydraulic
Electrical system	12 V	12 V

LWB SAMO (4 × 4) light vehicle (T J Gander)

SAMO (4 × 4) light vehicle produced in Portugal by UMM, fitted with three SS-11 ATGWs for Portuguese Army trials

Citroën Méhari Armée

DEVELOPMENT
The Citroën Méhari Armée is a military version of the standard civilian Méhari vehicle. Its low weight enables it to be used for a variety of military applications such as traffic control, command/radio vehicle and light supplies carrier. Over 8000 of these vehicles have been delivered to the French armed forces and police.

DESCRIPTION
The vehicle has an all steel chassis with a plastic body which is available in montana green, TP orange, beige, kalahari and tibetan green. The engine is mounted at the front with the driver's and passenger's seats in the centre and the cargo area at the rear.
There are two basic models of the Méhari, two plus two and two-seat utility. The first has two seats at the front, removable or fold-away back seat, fold down windscreen, black cotton canopy, safety door chains and an anti-theft device. Optional equipment includes a complete hood with transparent side panels and doors. The two-seat utility model has the two seats at the front, flat load area at the rear, fold down windscreen, black cotton canopy, safety door chains and an anti-theft device. Optional equipment includes a hood without transparent side panels and doors.
Trials at the French Airborne Centre at Toulouse have confirmed that the Méhari Armée is suitable for dropping by parachute when strapped to a landing platform. The basic vehicle can be used for a variety of roles including ambulance, traffic control and radio vehicle (fitted with various communications equipment including TRVP 13, TMF 623B, TRVP 213 and ANVRC 10).

Citroën Méhari Armée used in communications role

SPECIFICATIONS
Cab seating: 1 + 1
Configuration: 4 × 2 (front wheel drive)
Weight:
 (empty) 570 kg
 (loaded) 955 kg
Max load: 385 kg
Load area: 1·34 × 1 m
Length: 3·52 m
Width: 1·53 m
Height:
 (overall) 1·635 m
 (load area) 0·65 m
Wheelbase: 2·37 m
Max speed: (road) 100 km/h
Range: 300 km
Fuel capacity: 25 litres

Max gradient: 40%
Engine: AK 2 2-cylinder petrol, air-cooled developing 29 hp at 5500 rpm
Gearbox: manual with 4 forward and 1 reverse gears
Clutch: single dry plate
Transfer box: none
Steering: rack and bar
Turning radius: 5·35 m
Suspension: both axles suspended by arms with lateral interplay on spiral springs. Hydraulic shock absorbers front and rear
Number of tyres: 4 + 1 spare
Brakes:
 (main) hydraulic
 (parking) mechanical
Electrical system: 12 V or 24 V
Batteries: 2 × 12 V

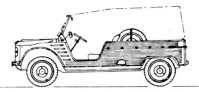

Citroën Méhari Armée (4 × 2) light vehicle

STATUS
In production. In service with the French Army, Air Force, Navy and Police, and Spain.

MANUFACTURER
S A Automobiles Citroën, 133 quai André Citroën, 75015 Paris, France.

Renault Rodeo (4 × 4) Light Vehicle

DEVELOPMENT/DESCRIPTION
The Renault Rodeo (4 × 4) light vehicle, also called the ACL 1100, is basically the standard civilian vehicle adapted to military requirements. It has not so far been adopted by the French armed forces. Its low weight makes it suitable for a variety of military uses including command/radio vehicle and light supplies carrier.

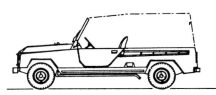

Renault Rodeo (4 × 4) light vehicle

Its layout is conventional with the engine at the front, driver and one passenger in the centre and the load area at the rear. Two basic models are offered: canvas top with seat for driver and one passenger, canvas top with seat for driver and three passengers and a fully-enclosed hard-top model. The canvas-topped models were known as the Artisane and the hard-top as the Chantier. The latest model is the Renault Rodeo 5 which is designed primarily for civil use.

SPECIFICATIONS
(data in square brackets relate to Rodeo 5 model where different)
Cab seating: 1 + 1 [1 + 3]
Configuration: 4 × 4
Max load: 300 [400] kg
Max towed load: 750 [720] kg
Length: 3·75 [3·56] m
Width: 1·54 [1·49] m
Height: 1·55 m
Wheelbase: 2·425 m

Angle of approach/departure: 40°/40°
Max speed: 115 km/h
Range: 400 km
Engine: 4-cylinder petrol developing 48 hp at 5300 rpm [32 hp]
Gearbox: manual, 4 forward and 1 reverse gears
Clutch: single dry plate
Transfer box: 2-speed
Steering: rack and pinion
Turning radius: 4·95 m
Brakes:
 (front) hydraulic, disc
 (rear) hydraulic, drum
Electrical system: 12 V

STATUS
Production.

MANUFACTURER
Renault, 8 avenue Emile Zola, 92109 Boulogne-Billancourt, France.

Citroën A FAF 400 kg (4 × 2) and 400 kg (4 × 4) Light Vehicles

DEVELOPMENT/DESCRIPTION
The Citroën A FAF is basically a standard civilian vehicle with the minimum of modifications for military use. Two models are currently in production, a 4 × 4 version with a payload of 400 kg and a 4 × 2 version also with a 400 kg payload. For ease of maintenance and obtaining spare parts, all the automotive components are from Citroën A type vehicles of which some 7 million have been built.

The chassis and body are all steel and the windscreen can be folded forward onto the bonnet. The layout is conventional with the engine at the front, passenger and driver seats in the centre and the load area at the rear. A model is also available with an additional two-man bench seat behind the driver's and front passenger's seats, which folds forward to increase the cargo area. In wet weather a cover can be erected over the top of the vehicle.

The Citroën A FAF is suitable for a number of roles including cargo carrier, command/radio and reconnaissance, and can be dropped by parachute. Optional equipment includes a 24-volt electrical system and hydraulic shock absorbers.

SPECIFICATIONS
(4 × 2 version; data in square brackets relate to 4 × 4 model where different)
Configuration: 4 × 2 [4 × 4]
Weight:
 (empty) 690 [850] kg
 (loaded) 1090 [1250] kg
Max payload: 400 kg
Length: 3·62 m
Width: 1·55 m
Height: 1·68 m
Wheelbase: 2·4 m
Track:
 (front) 1·26 m
 (rear) 1·28 m
Ground clearance: 0·238 m
Max speed: 100 [110] km/h
Gradient: 50%
Fuel capacity: 66 litres

Citroën A FAF (4 × 4) 400 kg light vehicle (T J Gander)

Fording: 0·35 m
Engine: air-cooled Citroën 4-stroke petrol developing 28·5 hp (DIN) at 6750 rpm [same engine or 4-cylinder petrol developing 34 hp (DIN) at 5500 rpm]
Gearbox: manual with 4 forward and 1 reverse gears (road, 4 forward and 1 reverse gears, cross-country, 3 forward and 1 reverse gears, rear differential)
Clutch: single dry plate
Steering: rack and pinion
Turning radius: 6 m
Brakes:
 (main) (front) disc on gearbox
 (main) (rear) disc on differential
 (parking) acts on front wheels

Suspension: arms with lateral interaction, working with helicoidal springs and inertia stabilisers
Tyres: 155.14 × CM
Number of tyres: 4 + 1 spare
Electrical system: 12 V, 48 Ah (24 V optional)

STATUS
Production. The 4 × 4 model is in service with Burundi and has been selected by the French Army (5000 requested in 1981). Produced in Greece as the Namco Pony (qv).

MANUFACTURER
S A Automobiles Citroën, 133 quai André Citroën, 75015 Paris, France.

Hotchkiss M 201 (4 × 4) 400 kg Light Vehicle

DEVELOPMENT
The M 201 (4 × 4) is the standard light vehicle of the French Army. It is almost identical to the Jeep used in the Second World War and over 40 000 M 201s were built in France under licence from Willys between 1953

and 1969. They were built by Hotchkiss-Brandt, which is no longer involved in the design and production of vehicles.

DESCRIPTION
The layout is conventional with the engine at the front and a cargo area at the rear which has a removable cover. The windscreen can be folded down onto the top of the bonnet. Special models were developed for use in

North Africa and those vehicles with anti-tank weapons have reinforced suspensions. The M 201 is known as the VLTT by the French Army (Véhicule de Liaison Tout Terrain).

VARIANTS
The basic vehicle is widely used as a radio/command vehicle by the French Army and a number have been fitted with surveillance radars.

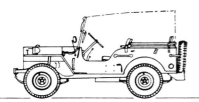

M 201 (4 × 4) 400 kg light vehicle

Anti-tank
The Belgian and French armies use the vehicle armed with the ENTAC ATGW system with two missiles being carried each side at the rear of the vehicle. When travelling they remain under cover but when required are swung through 180 degrees to face the front. A further three missiles are carried inside the vehicle. The French Army uses a number of M201s fitted with 106 mm M40 recoilless rifles.

Others
Hotchkiss built a number of vehicles known as the HWL which had a longer wheelbase (2·53 metres) and a gross vehicle weight of 1900 kg and were 3·89 metres long overall, 1·45 metres wide and 1·99 metres high. The company also built the Willys CJ3B, as the JH-101 (between 1955 and 1960) and the JH-102 (from 1961 onwards).

STATUS
Production complete. In service with Belgium, France and many armies in North Africa.

MANUFACTURER
Hotchkiss-Brandt, Paris, France.

SPECIFICATIONS
Cab seating: 1 + 3
Configuration: 4 × 4
Weight:
(empty) 1120 kg
(loaded) 1520 kg
Weight on front axle: (loaded) 684 kg
Weight on rear axle: (loaded) 836 kg
Max load: 400 kg

Basic M 201 (4 × 4) 400 kg light vehicle (T J Gander)

Towed load: 500 kg
Length: 3·36 m
Width: 1·58 m
Height:
(overall) 1·77 m
(reduced) 1·37 m
Ground clearance: 0·22 m
Track: 1·24 m
Wheelbase: 2·03 m
Range: 348 km
Fuel capacity: 49 litres
Gradient: 65%
Fording: 0·533 m

Max speed: 100 km/h
Engine: 4-cylinder in-line water-cooled petrol developing 61 hp at 3600 rpm
Gearbox: manual with 3 forward and 1 reverse gears
Clutch: single dry plate
Transfer box: 2-speed
Suspension: semi-elliptical springs and hydraulic shock absorbers
Tyres: 6.50 × 16
Brakes:
(main) hydraulic on all wheels
(parking) mechanical
Electrical system: 24 V

Peugeot P4 (4 × 4) 750 kg Light Vehicle

DEVELOPMENT
At present the standard light vehicle of the French Army is the Hotchkiss M 201 (4 × 4) 400 kg, production of which was completed in 1969. To replace this fleet three manufacturers each submitted 12 vehicles for extensive trials; these were the Renault TRM 500 (4 × 4) 500 kg based on the Italian FIAT 1107 AD, the Citroën C 44 based on the West German Iltis and the Peugeot P4 based on the Mercedes-Benz vehicle. Early in 1981 the French Army selected the Peugeot P4 and placed an order for 15 000 vehicles for delivery between 1983 and 1987. Mass production began in early 1983 and the current production rate is 100 a month. To date the French Army has ordered the short wheelbase model with a soft-top only. Later production may well involve the long wheelbase model. The P4 is often referred to as the VLTT (Véhicule de Liason Tout Terrain).

DESCRIPTION
The layout is conventional with the engine at the front, driver and passenger immediately behind the engine and the cargo area at the rear with a two-man bench seat down either side and an opening tailgate on which the spare wheel is mounted.

The front seats are adjustable and hinge forward to give access to the rear seats and the tool boxes beneath each of them. The driver and passengers are provided with seat belts with automatic rollers. The bench seats in the rear can be folded down to clear the load-carrying area.

The chassis is formed of two parallel longitudinal beams with rectangular sections connected by five round transverse members. The rear axle is fitted with a hydraulically-controlled differential lock.

The sheet metal body is connected to the chassis with eight flexible mounts and has a removable roll-over bar and a folding windscreen of bonded safety glass. Fixtures, bumpers, inner bumper liners and the front portion are mounted to the body structure. For ease of replacement these are bolted on. The two cloth doors have translucent window panels and are removable. The rear troop/cargo area is covered by a tarpaulin of plastic-coated cloth, with translucent sides and rear windows, which folds to the rear and is easily removable.

The fuel tank is below the floor of the vehicle between the chassis beams. A fuel can is carried externally at the rear of the vehicle on the left side. The P4 is fitted with a

Basic SWB versions of Peugeot P4 (4 × 4) 750 kg light vehicle showing anti-roll bar and fitted with Euromissile MILAN ATGW system (left) and F1 machine guns (right)

Variants of Peugeot P4 (4 × 4) 750 kg light vehicle, left to right: SWB, SWB with F1 machine gun, LWB van for command role, SWB with MILAN ATGW system, LWB troop carrier

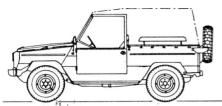

Peugeot P4 (4 × 4) 750 kg light vehicle

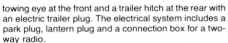

The Peugeot CBHcp, an armoured variant of the Peugeot P4, equipped with radar system (T J Gander)

Basic SWB version of Peugeot P4 (4 × 4) 750 kg light vehicle complete with doors and cover (Christopher F Foss)

towing eye at the front and a trailer hitch at the rear with an electric trailer plug. The electrical system includes a park plug, lantern plug and a connection box for a two-way radio.

Optional equipment includes power-assisted steering, front locking differential, PTO front and rear, front-mounted electric winch, 15-litre fuel can and various adapters for mounting machine guns and other weapons.

VARIANTS
The basic vehicle will be used by the French Army for a variety of roles, including one armed with twin F1 machine guns for use by scout teams and traffic control squads while another will be equipped with a MILAN ATGW launcher and four missiles and used by motor-

ised infantry. A LWB model is also available with a drop tailgate, bows, tarpaulin cover and back-to-back seating for eight fully equipped infantrymen at the rear. Both the SWB and LWB versions will be fitted with radios for use in the command role and fully enclosed van-type versions of both the LWB and SWB models are available.

A further variant of the Peugeot P4, first shown in mid-1983, is the CBHcp. This is a version of the 2·4-metre wheelbase P4 with an armoured rear body capable of withstanding the force of a 7·62 mm NATO projectile at five metres. It can be used either as a personnel carrier for up to six men or as a weapon tractor for loads up to 1750 kg. Alternative equipment could be 7·62 mm or 12·7 mm machine guns or the vehicle could be used as a launcher for MILAN or MATRA missiles. The prototype has been shown fitted with a small radar system

and the type could also be used as a communications vehicle. The CBHcp may be fitted with either the Peugeot petrol or diesel engine and with both the useful payload is 1100 kg. Length is 4·2 metres, width 1·7 metres and height 2·06 metres. Maximum all-up weight with either engine is 5000 kg but empty the diesel-engined version is 80 kg heavier than the petrol-engined version which weighs 3300 kg.

STATUS
In production for the French Army. First deliveries made in January 1983.

MANUFACTURER
Automobiles Peugeot, 75 Avenue de la Grande-Armée, 75016 Paris, France.

SPECIFICATIONS

Model	SWB	LWB
Configuration	4 × 4	4 × 4
Weight (empty) (petrol/diesel)	1815 kg/1895 kg	1985 kg/2065 kg
(loaded) (petrol/diesel)	2565 kg/2645 kg	2985 kg/3065 kg
Max load	750 kg	750 kg
Length	4·2 m	4·65 m
Width (with antenna mount)	1·83 m	1·83 m
(less antenna mount)	1·7 m	1·7 m
Height	1·9 m	1·9 m
Ground clearance	0·24 m	0·24 m
Track	1·4 m	1·4 m
Wheelbase	2·4 m	2·85 m
Angle of approach/departure	42°/37°	42°/37°
Fording	0·5 m	0·5 m
Gradient (loaded) (petrol/diesel)	73·5%/55%	73·5%/55%
Side slope (loaded)	30%	30%
Max speed (petrol/diesel)	118 km/h/108 km/h	118 km/h/108 km/h
Fuel capacity	75 litres	75 litres
Fuel consumption over 100 km		
(at 40 km/h) (petrol)	9·7 litres	9·7 litres
(diesel)	7·6 litres	7·6 litres
(at 90 km/h) (petrol)	15·25 litres	15·25 litres
(diesel)	14·5 litres	14·5 litres
(at 108 km/h) (petrol)	23·3 litres	23·3 litres
(diesel)	18 litres	18 litres

Model	SWB	LWB
Engine	Peugeot 1·971-litre 4-cylinder petrol developing 79 hp at 4750 rpm or Peugeot 2·498-litre 4-cylinder diesel developing 70·5 hp at 4500 rpm	
Gearbox	manual, 4 forward and 1 reverse gears	
Clutch	single dry disc with ball-bearing thrust mechanism	
Transfer box	2-speed	2-speed
Steering	rack and pinion with damper	
Turning radius	5·5 m	6·45 m
Suspension (front)	coil springs, anti-sway bar and double-acting telescopic hydraulic shock absorbers	
(rear)	coil springs and double-acting telescopic hydraulic shock absorbers	
Tyres	700 RC 16 × C type L	700 RC 16 × C type L
Number of tyres	4 + 1 spare	4 + 1 spare
Brakes	hydraulic dual circuit, discs front and drum rear	
Electrical system	24 V	24 V

Peugeot 504 Dangel (4 × 4) 1110 kg Light Vehicle

DESCRIPTION
The Peugeot 504 is basically a standard civilian 4 × 2 vehicle modified to 4 × 4 configuration and fitted with seats, bows and a tarpaulin cover in the rear cargo area.

The layout of the Peugeot 504 is conventional with the engine at the front, three-man fully enclosed cab in the centre and the load area at the rear. The load area has a drop tailgate, removable bows, tarpaulin cover and

bench seats running down the centre facing outwards. In addition to the driver and two passengers in the cab, ten fully equipped troops can be carried in the rear.

The front and rear axles have Peugeot limited slip differentials. The Dangel transfer case is mounted in the tunnel and is independent of the transmission due to a short universal joint shaft turning in a reaction tube. It gives four road and four cross-country gears. Shifting from road gears to all-terrain gears is fully synchronised and can be carried out while the vehicle is travelling.

Mounted at the front of the vehicle is a winch. Special protection is provided for the underside of the vehicle.

VARIANTS
In addition to the basic 4 × 2 version the following versions of the 4 × 4 model are available.

Ambulance
This can carry three stretcher patients in the fully enclosed rear body which is also provided with a two-man seat. A 4 × 2 version is also available.

Station wagon
This is the standard civilian vehicle converted to 4 × 4 configuration and can carry five people, two in front and three in the rear. Basic specifications are: length 4·8

metres, width 1·73 metres, height 1·74 metres, weight unloaded 1525 kg and maximum loaded weight 3270 kg.

SPECIFICATIONS
Cab seating: 1 + 2
Configuration: 4 × 4
Max load: 1110 kg
Load area: 2 × 1·5 m
Length: 4·8 m

Width: 1·73 m
Height: (cab) 1·74 m
Max road speed:
  (petrol model, no tarpaulin) 135 km/h
  (petrol model, with tarpaulin) 125 km/h
  (diesel model, no tarpaulin) 120 km/h
  (diesel model, with tarpaulin) 115 km/h
Engine: XN-1 4-cylinder petrol developing 96 hp at 5200 rpm or XN-2 4-cylinder diesel developing 70 hp at 4500 rpm

Gearbox: manual with 4 forward and 1 reverse gears
Clutch: single dry plate
Transfer box: 2-speed

STATUS
Production for the French Navy and Marines.

MANUFACTURER
Automobiles Peugeot, 75 Avenue de la Grande-Armée, 75016 Paris, France.

Peugeot 504 (4 × 4) pick-up truck from rear

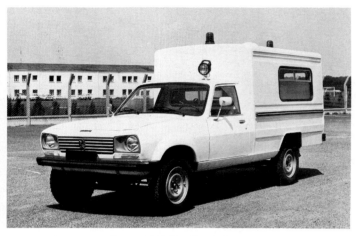

Peugeot 504 (4 × 4) ambulance

Peugeot 504 (4 × 4) station wagon

Peugeot 504 (4 × 2) ambulance

GERMANY, DEMOCRATIC REPUBLIC

P3 (4 × 4) 700 kg Light Vehicle

DESCRIPTION
The P3 entered production in 1962 as the replacement for the earlier P2M (4 × 4) vehicle which was not considered a successful design. The vehicle has been designed to carry 700 kg of cargo both on roads and across country and also tow a trailer weighing 700 kg. The P3 has a number of improvements in the engine, transmission, suspension and body of the earlier vehicle. The layout of the P3 is conventional with the engine at the front and the passenger/load carrying area at the rear. A single door is provided in each side of the body, and there is also a single door in the rear, hinged on the left side. The windscreen can be folded down if required and a canvas sheet can be erected over the top of the vehicle.

VARIANTS
An amphibious model of the P3 was to have been produced to replace the amphibious version of the P2M (the P2MS), but did not proceed past the design stage.

STATUS
In service with the East German Army. It has been replaced in many front-line units by the Soviet UAZ-469B (4 × 4) 600 kg light vehicle.

MANUFACTURER
VEB Sachsenring Automobilwerke, Zwickau, Bezirk Karl-Marx-Stadt, German Democratic Republic.

P3 (4 × 4) 700 kg light vehicle

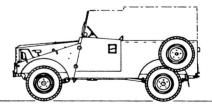

P3 (4 × 4) 700 kg light vehicle

SPECIFICATIONS
Seating: 1 + 1 (6 in rear)
Configuration: 4 × 4
Weight:
(empty) 1860 kg
(loaded) 2560 kg
Weight on front axle: (empty) 1004 kg
Weight on rear axle: (empty) 856 kg
Max load: 700 kg
Towed load: 700 kg
Length: 3·71 m
Width: 1·95 m

Height: 1·95 m
Ground clearance: 0·33 m
Track:
(front) 1·42 m
(rear) 1·4 m
Wheelbase: 2·4 m
Max speed: (road) 95 km/h
Range: 520 km
Fuel capacity: 104 litres
Fuel consumption: 24 litres/100 km
Max gradient: 60%
Fording: 0·6 m

Engine: OM 6/35L 6-cylinder water-cooled petrol
developing 75 hp at 3750 rpm
Gearbox: manual with 4 forward and 1 reverse gears
Transfer box: 2-speed
Suspension: torsion bar
Tyres: 7.50 × 16
Number of tyres: 4 + 1 spare
Brakes:
(main) hydraulic
(parking) mechanical
Electrical system: 12 V

P2M (4 × 4) 400 kg Light Vehicle

DESCRIPTION
The P2M was in production at Zwickau from 1955 to 1962 when it was replaced by the P3 (4 × 4) light vehicle. Most reports indicate that it was not a successful design as it rapidly became overheated and had a poor towing capability. The P2M has been replaced in most units by the later East German P3 as well as Soviet UAZ-69 and UAZ-469B (4 × 4) vehicles.

The vehicle has an all steel body with the engine at the front and the crew compartment at the rear with four doors, folding canvas top and a windscreen which can be folded forwards onto the bonnet when not required.

VARIANTS
The P2S was an amphibious version similar in concept to the Soviet MAV (4 × 4) vehicle, but was not produced in large numbers and is thought to have been phased out of service.

SPECIFICATIONS
Cab seating: 1 + 3
Configuration: 4 × 4
Weight:
(empty) 1770 kg
(loaded) 2170 kg
Max load: 400 kg
Towed load: 750 kg
Length: 3·755 m
Width: 1·685 m
Height: (canvas top in position) 1·835 m
Ground clearance: 0·3 m
Track: 1·4 m
Wheelbase:
(right) 2·215 m
(left) 2·285 m

P2M (4 × 4) 400 kg light vehicle

Max speed: 95 km/h
Range: 600 km
Fuel capacity: 100 litres
Fording: 0·55 m
Engine: OM 6/35 6-cylinder water-cooled petrol developing 65 hp at 3500 rpm
Gearbox: manual with 4 forward and 1 reverse gears
Transfer box: 2-speed
Suspension: torsion bar
Tyres: 6.50 × 16
Electrical system: 12 V

Brakes:
(main) hydraulic
(parking) mechanical

STATUS
Production complete. In limited service with the East German Army.

MANUFACTURER
VEB Sachsenring Automobilwerke, Zwickau, Bezirk Karl-Marx-Stadt, German Democratic Republic.

GERMANY, FEDERAL REPUBLIC

Kraka 640 (4 × 2) 870 kg Light Vehicle

DEVELOPMENT
The Faun Kraka (an abbreviation for Kraftkarren, or power cart) was originally designed by Nicholas Straussler with the prototype being completed in the 1960s by the German company Zweirad Union, which was subsequently taken over by Faun. The first production vehicles were officially handed over to the Federal German Army in June 1974, and 762 were built for the Federal German Army airborne units.

DESCRIPTION
The Kraka has been designed specifically for airborne and airmobile forces and can be transported by aircraft or helicopter. The CH-53 helicopter can carry five folded Krakas and the C-160 Transall aircraft can carry 16 folded or 10 in the normal position. The driver is seated at the front of the vehicle with the flat cargo area to his rear. The engine and gearbox are mounted at the rear, just in front of the rear axle. Power is transmitted from the engine to the clutch and gearbox, to the final drives and then by chains to the rear road wheels.

The Kraka is made up of five major sections: the front axle with the two wheels and steering system; the front bodywork, with two boxes for stowing tools and kit, instrument panel, electric circuitry, handbrake system and the two suspension springs; the fuel tank; the rear section with the engine, gearbox and rear axle and the front and rear platforms, with driver's seat, two retractable passenger seats and four side guard rails.

There are five different versions of the Kraka: the basic model 644, the 643, 642, 641 and finally the 640 which is the model used by the Federal German Army. The basic 644 model can carry a maximum payload of 1000 kg and has no passenger seats or rear platform. The 643 has a rear platform and side-flaps for load carrying. The 642 has additional front wheel covers, padded seats and foot rests for the passengers, and

Faun 640 Kraka (4 × 2) 870 kg light vehicle as used by West German Army (T J Gander)

Faun Kraka (4 × 2) 870 kg light vehicle in travelling and folded configurations

Faun Kraka (4 × 2) 870 kg light vehicle with launcher for Euromissile MILAN ATGW, and carrying 6 missiles

mud flaps. The 641 has additional stowage boxes on either side of the driver, large instrument panel and mudguards for the front wheels. The 640 is the 644 with all the optional accessories including 45 Ah battery in place of the standard 25 Ah battery.

VARIANTS
The Federal German Army has fitted many vehicles with the Euromissile MILAN ATGW system and six missiles, which have replaced the Krakas with the 106 mm M40 recoilless rifles. The vehicle can also be armed with a 20 mm Rheinmetall cannon and be adapted for a wide range of other applications including ambulance vehicle, cable layer, fire-fighting unit, generator, mortar carrying vehicle (carrying a 120 mm mortar and 20 rounds of ammunition), NBC decontamination vehicle, radio, starter vehicle, towing vehicle for aircraft and helicopters, warm air vehicle and fitted with water purification equipment.

SPECIFICATIONS
Seating: 1 + 2
Configuration: 4 × 2
Weight:
(loaded) 1610 kg
(empty) 740 kg
Max load: 870 kg
Weight on front axle: (loaded) 610 kg
Weight on rear axle: (loaded) 1000 kg
Towed load:
(trailer with brakes) 960 kg
(trailer without brakes) 350 kg
Load area: 1·4 × 1·4 m
Length: 2·78 m

Faun Kraka (4 × 2) 870 kg light vehicle carrying two stretchers

Width: 1·51 m
Height: 1·28 m
(load area) 0·755 m
Ground clearance: 0·25 m
Track:
(front) 1·138 m
(rear) 1·13 m
Wheelbase: 2·058 m
Max speed: 55 km/h
Fuel capacity: 24·5 litres
Max gradient: 55%
Fording: 0·5 m
Engine: BMW 427 2-cylinder 4-stroke petrol developing 26 hp at 4500 rpm
Gearbox: BMW 959 manual with 4 forward and 1 reverse gears
Clutch: single dry plate
Transfer box: 2-speed
Steering: rack and pinion
Turning radius: 4·375 m

Suspension:
(front) 2 semi-elliptical transverse springs with 1 parabolic spring with rubber hollow spring
(rear) engine suspension arm with rubber spring
Tyres: 22.00 × 12 (Lypsoid)
Brakes:
(main) hydraulic on all wheels
(parking) mechanical, rear wheels
Electrical system: 12 V
Battery: 1 × 12 V, 45 Ah
Generator: 130 W

STATUS
Production complete. In service with the West German Army. A few were also supplied to Italy and Spain for trials.

MANUFACTURER
Faun-Werke Nuernberg, POB 8, 8560 Lauf/Pegn, Federal Republic of Germany.

Auto-Union Lkw (4 × 4) 250 kg Light Vehicle

DEVELOPMENT
When the West German Army was re-formed in the 1950s one of its requirements was for a 4 × 4 250 kg light vehicle. To meet this requirement prototypes were built by Porsche, Goliath and Auto-Union. After comparative trials the Army selected the Auto-Union vehicle and 55 000 were built for both civil and military use between 1958 and 1968. The Federal German Army call the vehicle the Lkw 0.25t but it is also known as the Munga (Mehrzweck Universal Geländewagen mit Allrad Antrieb).

DESCRIPTION
The chassis consists of an anti-distortion box section frame with double side members. The body is of pressed steel and has a canvas top which can be folded back to the rear if required, removable side doors and a windscreen that folds forwards onto the bonnet. The Munga has permanent 4 × 4 drive. On some of the

early models the driver could select either 4 × 4 or 4 × 2 drive.
There are three basic models of the Munga: Munga 4, 6 and 8. The basic model is the Munga 4 with seats for the driver and three passengers or up to 375 kg of cargo. It can tow a trailer weighing up to 500 kg on roads. The Munga 6 has two seats at the front and a bench seat down either side of the rear of the vehicle and can carry six men or 690 kg of cargo. Towed load on roads is 750 kg (if the trailer has a braking system) or 500 kg (for a trailer without a braking system). This model has a tailgate for unloading. The Munga 8 has two seats at the front and a three-man bench seat down each side of the rear of the vehicle. When being used to carry cargo a total of 690 kg can be carried. A tailgate is provided for loading and unloading. It can also tow a trailer weighing up to 500 kg.

VARIANTS
The West German Army has a number of vehicles in service as ambulances, anti-tank vehicles (armed with the MBB Cobra ATGW system), and radio vehicles.

SPECIFICATIONS
Specifications relate to late production Munga 4; earlier models have 38 or 40 hp engines.
Cab seating: 1 + 3
Configuration: 4 × 4
Weight:
(empty) 1245 kg
(loaded) 1620 kg
Max load: 375 kg
Towed load: 500 kg
Length: 3·445 m
Width: 1·81 m
Height:
(overall) 1·735 m
(windscreen lowered) 1·33 m
Ground clearance: 0·24 m
Track: i·206 m
Wheelbase: 2 m
Angle of approach/departure: 43°/41°
Max speed: 93 km/h
Range:
(road) 350 km
(cross country) 260 km
Fuel capacity: 45 litres
Max gradient: 60%
Fording: 0·5 m
Engine: Auto-Union/DKW 3-cylinder petrol developing 44 hp at 4250 rpm
Gearbox: manual with 4 forward and 1 reverse gears
Clutch: single dry plate
Transfer box: 2-speed
Steering: rack and pinion
Turning radius: 6·25 m
Suspension: transverse springs and double acting telescopic shock absorbers
Tyres: 6.00 × 16
Brakes:
(main) hydraulic
(parking) mechanical
Electrical system: 24 V
Batteries: 2 × 12 V, 45 Ah
Generator: 600 W

Munga being used as ambulance (Christopher F Foss)

Lkw (4 × 4) 250 kg light vehicle

STATUS
Production complete. In service with West Germany, Indonesia and the Netherlands. Some have also been used by the British and French forces in West Berlin and West Germany.

MANUFACTURER
Auto-Union, 8070 Ingolstadt, Postfach 220, Federal Republic of Germany.

VW 181 (4 × 2) 400 kg Light Vehicle

DEVELOPMENT
The VW 181 is basically the standard civilian Volkswagen 181 slightly modified to meet military requirements. A total of 2000 were supplied to the Federal German Army between 1969 and 1970 under the designation Pkw 0.4t.

DESCRIPTION
The chassis consists of a central tubular frame with the floor welded into position. The sheet steel body has four doors each with a removable plastic window, folding windscreen and a folding pvc top. The engine is mounted at the rear. Stowage space is provided under the bonnet and to the rear of the two rear seats which fold down individually. The rear cargo area and the backs of the rear seats are provided with C-profile rails for securing equipment such as radios. When being used as a radio vehicle an additional dynamo is fitted.

Standard equipment on the military version includes an axe, headlamp blackout covers, map light, radio suppression, reclining front seats, four rifle mounts, spade, starting handle, towing eye, towing hook and a wheel chock.

SPECIFICATIONS
Cab seating: 1 + 3
Configuration: 4 × 2
Weight:
  (loaded) 1350 kg
  (empty) 900 kg
Max load: 450 kg
Weight on front axle: (loaded) 550 kg
Weight on rear axle: (loaded) 800 kg
Towed load: 650 kg
Length: 3·78 m
Width: 1·64 m
Height: 1·62 m
Ground clearance: 0·205 m
Track:
  (front) 1·354 m
  (rear) 1·446 m
Wheelbase: 2·4 m
Angle of approach/departure: 36°/31°
Max speed: (road) 113 km/h
Range:
  (road) 320 km
  (cross country) 260 km
Fuel capacity: 40 litres

VW 181 (4 × 2) 400 kg light vehicle with hood in position (Christopher F Foss)

Max gradient: 48% (road, low gear)
Fording: 0·396 m
Engine: 4-cylinder petrol developing 44 bhp at 4000 rpm
Gearbox: manual with 4 forward and 1 reverse gears
Clutch: single plate, dry
Transfer box: none
Steering: worm and roller with hydraulic damper
Turning radius: 5·48 m
Suspension: torsion bar with shock absorbers
Brakes:
  (main) hydraulic
  (parking) mechanical
Electrical system: 12 V
Battery: 1 × 12 V, 36 Ah (45 Ah also available)
Generator: 280 W

The above specifications relate to vehicles used by the West German Army. Current models offered by Volkswagen are powered by a petrol engine developing 48 bhp at 4000 rpm and have other detail differences.

VW 181 (4 × 2) 400 kg light vehicle with hood folded

STATUS
Production complete. The vehicle is used by Austria, Denmark, France and the Netherlands. It is still built in Mexico.

MANUFACTURER
Volkswagenwerk Aktiengesellschaft, 3180 Wolfsburg, Federal Republic of Germany.

VW Iltis (4 × 4) 500 kg Light Vehicle

DEVELOPMENT
In the 1960s France, West Germany and Italy started a joint project for a new 500 kg (4 × 4) amphibious vehicle which became known as the Europe Jeep. Prototypes were built by two consortia, FIAT/MAN/Saviem and Hotchkiss/Büssing/Lancia, but France subsequently withdrew and in 1976 the project was cancelled. Two German companies, MBB and Glas/BMW, have also built lightweight 4 × 4 amphibious vehicles but none has entered production.

The Federal German Army then issued a new requirement for a 4 × 4 vehicle which could carry 500 kg of cargo both on roads and cross country and this time the amphibious requirement was dropped. Both Daimler-Benz and Volkswagen built prototypes for trials and in 1977 the Volkswagen vehicle was selected for production. Production of the Iltis continued until December 1981 when the last of 8800 vehicles was handed over to the German armed forces. Of this total 8470 went to the Army, 310 to the Luftwaffe and the remaining 20 to the Navy.

DESCRIPTION
The Volkswagen Iltis is very similar in appearance to the current Lkw but uses components of the Volkswagen Polo and Audi vehicles. The body is all steel with the engine at the front and the crew and cargo area to the rear. The rear seat can be folded down to increase the

load carrying area and the vehicle is provided with a folding hood, removable side flaps and a folding windscreen. The driver can select either 4 × 4 drive for cross country, or 4 × 2 for road drive, in which case the front axle is disengaged.

The Volkswagen Iltis 4 × 4 light vehicle was entered

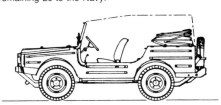

VW Iltis (4 × 4) 500 kg light vehicle

VW Iltis (4 × 4) 500 kg light vehicle in ambulance form (T J Gander)

by Citroën under the designation C44 in the French Army competition for a new light vehicle to replace the current Hotchkiss M 201, but this competition was won by Peugeot with its P4 based on the Mercedes-Benz vehicle described in the following entry.

VARIANTS
Variants include ambulance, anti-tank (with MILAN ATGWs), artillery survey, command/radio and field telephone line layer.

SPECIFICATIONS
Cab seating: 1 + 3
Configuration: 4 × 4
Weight:
  (empty) 1550 kg
  (loaded) 2050 kg
Max load: 500 kg
Max towed load:
  (with brakes) 2000 kg
  (without brakes) 750 kg

Length: 3·972 m
Width: 1·52 m
Height: 1·837 m
Ground clearance: 0·225 m
Track:
  (front) 1·23 m
  (rear) 1·26 m
Wheelbase: 2·017 m
Angle of approach/departure: 41°/32°
Max speed: 130 km/h
Fuel capacity: 86 litres
Max gradient: 77%
Fording: 0·6 m
Engine: 4-cylinder OHC petrol developing 75 hp at 5000 rpm
Gearbox: manual with 5 forward and 1 reverse gears
Clutch: single dry plate
Steering: rack and pinion
Turning radius: 5·5 m
Suspension: overhead semi-elliptical leaf springs and double acting shock absorbers

Transfer box: 2-speed
Tyres: 6.50 × R-16
Number of tyres: 4 + 1 spare
Brakes:
  (main) hydraulic, dual circuit, drum
  (parking) mechanical
Electrical system: 24 V
Batteries: 2 × 12 V, 45 Ah

STATUS
Production complete. In service with the West German Army. In October 1981 the Canadian company of Bombardier Incorporated obtained a licence to produce the Iltis vehicle. Further details are given in this section under Canada.

MANUFACTURER
Volkswagenwerk Aktiengesellschaft, 3180 Wolfsburg, Federal Republic of Germany. (Production undertaken at Volkswagen's Ingolstadt plant.)

Mercedes-Benz (4 × 4) 750 kg Light Vehicle

DEVELOPMENT
The Mercedes-Benz (4 × 4) 750 kg light vehicle was entered by Peugeot in the French Army competition for a new light vehicle to replace the current Hotchkiss M 201. After comparative trials between prototype vehicles submitted by Citroën (C44 based on the West German Iltis), Renault (TRM 500 based on the Italian FIAT 1107 AD) and Peugeot (P4 based on the Mercedes-Benz vehicle), the P4 was finally selected by the French Army and entered service in 1982. There is a separate entry in this section for the Peugeot P4 (4 × 4) light vehicle and its variants.

Mercedes-Benz is now offering it for civil and military use with a standard wheelbase of 2·4 metres or a long wheelbase of 2·85 metres. The main components of the vehicle, with the exception of the specially designed transfer case, are from the Mercedes-Benz passenger car and light truck series production. Four different engines and four different bodies are available: for example, a fully-enclosed four-door model is offered on the long wheelbase chassis.

Gelaendewagenfahrzeug Gesellschaft (GFG) began production in 1980 with an initial target of 9000 vehicles a year. In 1980 approximately 7500 vehicles were completed for the home and export markets. The Austrian-based GFG is owned jointly by Mercedes-Benz and Steyr-Daimler-Puch. Daimler-Benz will supply engines, transmissions and axles and Steyr-Daimler-Puch the chassis and body. In July 1981 it was announced that Steyr-Daimler-Puch was to buy out its West German partner, Daimler-Benz, in the GFG company. The Austrian group will continue to manufacture the vehicles on contract for Daimler-Benz at its works at Graz and will remain responsible for sales in Austria, Switzerland and Yugoslavia, and COMECON countries under the name Puch. Daimler-Benz will still hold the sales rights to all other markets under the Mercedes-Benz name.

DESCRIPTION
The layout of the vehicle is conventional with the engine at the front, driver and passenger immediately behind the engine, two passenger seats and a small cargo area at the back. The two passenger seats can be folded forward to give a load area of 1·23 × 1·52 metres. The floor of the load area is made of sheet steel and is fitted with C-type rails, which allows communications equipment to be installed quickly. The vehicle has a folding hood, removable side flaps and a folding windscreen. A front winch may be fitted.

VARIANTS
There are station vehicle and van variants of the basic vehicle and Binz GmbH has produced a special body to form the Binz 2000 GS forward-area ambulance. There is also a light cable-laying version with an open rear and a dash-mounted spare wheel on the right. Various seating arrangements are possible with the short wheelbase version having up to eight seats and the long wheelbase version up to ten. A radio/command variant and a variant carrying anti-tank missiles have been mentioned.

STATUS
Production. In service with Argentina, France (see separate entry), Norway (450 ordered for delivery between 1984/86) and United Kingdom (captured Argentine vehicles used in Falkland Islands).

Mercedes-Benz (4 × 4) 750 kg light vehicle with hood and windscreen raised

Mercedes-Benz (4 × 4) 750 kg light vehicle with hood lowered and carrying 0·50 machine gun

MANUFACTURER
Daimler-Benz AG, Stuttgart-Untertürkheim, Federal Republic of Germany, but production is undertaken in Austria by GFG.

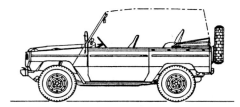

Mercedes-Benz (4 × 4) 750 kg light vehicle

SPECIFICATIONS
(Standard wheelbase version, data in square brackets relate to long wheelbase version)
Configuration: 4 × 4
Weight:
(empty, including driver) 1670 [1780] kg
(loaded) 2400 [2800] kg
Max load: 750 [1000] kg
Max towed load:
(braked) 2500 kg
(unbraked) 750 kg
Length: 4·145 [4·595] m
Width: 1·7 m
Height: (overall) 1·995 [1·975] m
Ground clearance: 0·24 m
Track: 1·425 m
Wheelbase: 2·4 [2·85] m
Angle of approach/departure: 39°/34°

Max road speed:
(OM616 engine) 117 km/h
(OM617 engine) 117 km/h
(M115 engine) 134 km/h
(M123 engine) 148 km/h
Fuel capacity: 70 litres
Max gradient: 80%
Fording: 0·6 m
Engine:
OM616 4-cylinder diesel, 2404 cc, 65 hp (DIN) at 4200 rpm
or OM617 5-cylinder diesel, 3005 cc, 80 hp (DIN) at 4200 rpm
or M115 4-cylinder petrol, 2307 cc, 90 hp (DIN) at 4800 rpm
or M123 6-cylinder petrol, 2525 cc, 115 hp (DIN) at 5500 rpm
Gearbox: manual, 4 forward and 1 reverse gears

Clutch: single dry plate
Transfer box: for mechanical front-axle engagement and synchronised cross-country gear
Steering: re-circulating ball, power assisted
Turning radius: 5·5 [6·2] m
Suspension: front and rear, coil springs and telescopic shock absorbers. Both front and rear axles are located by 1 transverse and 2 longitudinal control links
Tyres: 7.00 × 16
Number of tyres: 4 + 1 spare
Brakes: (main) hydraulic, dual circuit with vacuum booster, disc front, drum rear
Electrical system: 24 V

MBB Chico (4 × 2) 1000 kg Vehicle

DEVELOPMENT
The Chico cross-country vehicle has been developed by MBB and marketed by ATM. As an alternative to supplying the complete vehicle the Chico can be supplied in assemblies for final construction in the purchasing country's own facilities. The next stage would be to undertake the production of certain components and final assembly, with the manufacturer supplying the necessary training and tooling. In the final stage complete manufacture of the Chico would be undertaken in the user's country. This type of programme would offer an underdeveloped country a number of advantages, such as the transfer of expertise, creation of job opportunities and a valuable end product.

DESCRIPTION
The Chico has a simple design and an all-sheet steel body, with driver and one passenger in the front and six passengers or cargo area at the rear. It has good cross-country performance due to a high ground clearance, large angles of approach and departure both front and rear, low centre of gravity, good gear ratios, lockable differential, low pressure cross-country tyres and a joint in the centre of the vehicle that permits the front and rear bodies to roll in relation to each other.

It can ford to a depth of 0·7 metre and once in deeper water it begins to float, the rear wheels providing propulsion. If required the Chico can be fitted with a propeller which is driven by a gear-independent auxiliary drive shaft or hydraulic pump.

The basic version has a windscreen and open platform at the rear, but other body styles are available including front safety bar and rear platform with side boards, canvas hood for front section and fully enclosed rear body, canvas hood for front section and bows and tarpaulin cover at the rear, or fully enclosed front and rear body.

VARIANTS
A wide range of military uses are envisaged for this vehicle including ambulance, anti-tank (eg TOW), personnel carrier, radio/command vehicle and supply carrier (machine gun, cannon or mortar).

SPECIFICATIONS
Cab seating: 1 + 1
Configuration: 4 × 2
Weight: (empty) 1400 kg
Max load: 1000 kg
Length: 3·75 m
Width: 1·62 m

Chico (4 × 2) 1000 kg cross country vehicle

Height: 1·85 m
Ground clearance: 0·4 m
Wheelbase: 2·19 m
Angle of approach/departure: 40°/40°
Max speed: 65 km/h
Fuel capacity; 50 litres
Max gradient: 60%
Fording: 0·7 m then amphibious
Engine: air-cooled diesel
Clutch: hydraulic single dry disc
Transmission: 8 forward drives (two groups of four), one for road, one for off-road, plus eight reverse drives in same groupings

STATUS
Late in 1981 it was announced that production of the Chico would be undertaken in Ireland by ATW-Auto-Montan-Werke. It is anticipated that between 15 000 and 18 000 vehicles will be produced a year with a 1000 man work force at Buncrana, Co. Donegal.

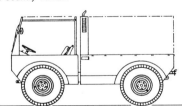

Chico (4 × 2) 1000 kg vehicle

MANUFACTURER
Messerschmitt-Bölkow-Blohm GmbH, Postfach 80 12 20, 800 Munich, Federal Republic of Germany.

Marketing undertaken by ATM Auto-Montan, Paul-Ehrlich-Haus, Westendstrasse 58–62, 6000 Frankfurt/Main, Federal Republic of Germany.

GREECE

NAMCO Pony (4 × 2) Light Vehicle

DESCRIPTION
NAMCO SA (National Motor Company) manufactures the Pony (4 × 2) light vehicle under licence from Citroën

of France. The vehicle is powered by a Citroën air-cooled engine with a fuel consumption of 6·5 litres/100 km. Full details of the vehicle are given in the entry for the Citroën A FAF 400 kg (4 × 2) and 400 kg (4 × 4) light vehicles under France.

STATUS
Production. In service with the Greek armed forces.

MANUFACTURER
NAMCO SA, Thessaloniki, Greece.

NAMCO Pony (4 × 2) light vehicle as used by the Greek Military Police (T J Gander)

NAMCO Pony (4 × 2) light vehicle

HUNGARY

Csepel 130 (4 × 4) 681 kg Truck

DESCRIPTION
The Csepel 130 is basically a copy of the Second World War American ¾-ton Beep vehicle. It was in production until 1956 and is still in service in small numbers. The engine is mounted at the front with the crew and cargo area at the rear with a hinged tailgate. If required the cargo area can be covered by bows and a tarpaulin cover.

VARIANTS
An ambulance version is in service.

STATUS
Production complete. In service in limited numbers with the Hungarian Army.

MANUFACTURER
Csepel, near Budapest, Hungary.

SPECIFICATIONS
Configuration: 4 × 4
Weight:
  (empty) 3178 kg
  (loaded, cross country) 3859 kg
Max load:
  (road) 1362 kg
  (cross country) 682 kg
Towed load: (road) 1362 kg
Length: 4·237 m
Width: 2·103 m

Height: (tarpaulin) 2·195 m
Ground clearance: 0·269 m
Track: 1·676 m
Wheelbase: 2·489 m
Max speed: (road) 80 km/h
Range: 386 km
Fuel capacity: 112 litres
Max gradient: 60%
Fording: 0·864 m
Engine: 4-cylinder water-cooled petrol developing 85 hp
Turning radius: 7·35 m
Tyres: 9.00 × 16
Number of tyres: 4 + 1 spare

INDIA

VV501 Toofan (4 × 4) 500 kg Light Vehicle

DEVELOPMENT/DESCRIPTION
The VV501 Toofan has been developed at the Indian Vehicle Research and Development Establishment (VRDE). Seven prototypes have been completed and used for Indian Army trials. A production contract is impending.

The VV501 is a Jeep-type light vehicle of conventional layout with the water-cooled petrol engine mounted forward under a prominent square bonnet. The radiator is large for a vehicle of its size and the

headlamps are set into large square mudguards. The cab has seating for the driver and one passenger and to the rear the cargo area may be adapted for up to four passengers. To date prototypes have been fitted with a canvas top and sides but it is expected that more specialised body types will be fitted on future production examples.

SPECIFICATIONS
Cab seating: 1 + 1
Configuration: 4 × 4
Weight: (gross) 2500 kg
Payload: 500 kg

Length: 4 m
Width: 1·72 m
Height: 1·95 m
Max speed: 120 km/h
Range: 500 km
Engine: 6-cylinder water-cooled 4-litre petrol developing 110 bhp at 3200 rpm
Gearbox: manual, 3 forward and 1 reverse gears
Transfer box: 2-speed
Number of tyres: 4 + 1 spare

STATUS
Prototypes. User trials completed.

Indian Light Vehicles with a capacity of up to 1000 kg

Indian-built Jeeps
Various types of American Jeep have been built under licence in India by Mahindra and Mahindra Limited of Bombay, including the CJ3A, CJ3B, CJ4 and later models in both 4 × 4 and 4 × 2 configurations. They are used for a variety of roles by the Indian Army including command and radio and some have also been fitted with 7·62 mm machine guns. In 1980 Mahindra jeep production amounted to some 15 000 vehicles. The same year the company supplied 4000 Jeeps in knock-down form for assembly in Iran.

Indian-built Jeep (Indian Army)

¾-ton (4 × 4) Truck
This is basically the Japanese Nissan D4W73 (4 × 4) truck built under licence in India. First production vehicles were completed at the Defence Unit (Ordnance Factory) at Jabalpur in 1961. The layout of the vehicle is conventional with the engine at the front, cab in the centre and the cargo area at the rear. The cab has a removable canvas top and a windscreen that can fold forward onto the bonnet. The rear cargo area is provided with seats, drop tailgate, removable bows and a canvas cover. Some vehicles have a front-mounted winch.

Indian Jonga (4 × 4) Light Vehicle
This is basically the Japanese Nissan Patrol (4 × 4) light vehicle built under licence at the Defence Unit (Ordnance Factory) at Jabalpur. It is used by the Indian Army and some have been fitted with SS-11 ATGWs for anti-tank use. In 1977 it was reported that the Indian Government had sold 200 to the Mozambique Army.

SPECIFICATIONS (Jonga 4 × 4)
Configuration: 4 × 4
Weight:
    (empty) 2730 kg
    (loaded) 4186 kg
Length: 4·952 m
Width: 2·004 m
Height: 2·362 m
Wheelbase: 2·8 m
Track: 1·6 m
Engine: 6-cylinder water-cooled petrol developing 125 bhp at 3800 rpm
Gearbox: manual with 4 forward and 1 reverse gears
Transfer box: 2-speed
Tyres: 7.50 × 20

STATUS
All the above vehicles are in service with the Indian Army.

Jonga (4 × 4) light vehicle (Indian Army)

Indian-built ¾-ton (4 × 4) vehicle with special tyres for desert operations (Indian Army)

INDONESIA

Banteng (4 × 4) Light Vehicle

DEVELOPMENT
Late in 1979 the Indonesian Security Ministry's Research and Development Centre completed the prototype of the Banteng (4 × 4) light vehicle. It is based on the British Land-Rover with half its components made in Indonesia. PT Java Motors is responsible for final assembly, assisted by PT Fabrik Mosin.

ISRAEL

AAI Lizard (4 × 4) 600 kg Light Vehicle

DESCRIPTION
The Lizard (4 × 4) light vehicle has been developed by Ashot Ashkelon Industries Limited, an affiliate of Israel Military Industries and was shown for the first time early in 1981. It was originally conceived as a vehicle for airborne operations and its low weight of 600 kg allows it to be easily transported by aircraft and helicopter. It can carry a maximum payload of 600 kg in addition to the driver and one passenger.

The Lizard is an unusual design consisting of two parts, both of which are rigid individual units, joined by a single bearing so permitting lateral pivoting in operation.

The forward section has a small load area at the front and a seat for the driver and passenger either side of the engine compartment. The rear part also acts as a load-carrying area.

There are no bumpers as the front and rear tyres

AAI Lizard (4 × 4) 600 kg light vehicle showing position of engine

Astra L1, the Italian version of AAI Lizard (4 × 4) 600 kg light vehicle (T J Gander)

AAI Lizard (4 × 4) 600 kg light vehicle

project beyond the body so permitting direct contact on approach and immediate climbing of obstacles up to one metre high.

The engine drives four hydraulic pumps, each of which powers a separate hydraulic motor which in turn drives one of the wheels. Each road wheel is individually suspended so that the Lizard has no front or rear axle. Since the system is entirely hydraulic, speeds ranging from 0 to 60 km/h are achieved without gear changes and without a clutch. A single hand-operated lever controls both forward and reverse speeds.

An agreement has been made with Astra Veicoli Industriali SpA of Italy to produce the AAI Lizard in Italy as the Astra L1. As such it was shown at the Passo Corese Exhibition 1982.

SPECIFICATIONS
Configuration: 4 × 4
Seating: 1 + 1
Weight:
(empty) 600 kg
(loaded) 1200 kg
Max load: 600 kg
Length: 2·33 m
Width: 1·32 m
Height:
(steering wheel) 1·4 m
(front loading area) 0·96 m
Ground clearance: 0·33 to 0·38 m
Wheelbase: 1·67 m

Track: 1·085 m
Max speed: (forward and reverse) 60 km/h
Fuel capacity: 40 litres
Gradient: 100%
Vertical obstacle: 1 m
Engine: 1600 cc air-cooled petrol developing 47 hp at 4000 rpm
Brakes:
(main) by hydrostatic transmission
(emergency) 4 disc brakes
(parking) hand brake attachment on 2 front brakes

MANUFACTURER
Ashot Ashkelon Industries Limited, PO Box 21, Ashkelon, Israel.
Also produced by Astra Veicoli Industriali SpA, Via Caorsana 79, 29100 Piacenza, Italy.

Matmar CJ-5 (691 kg) and CJ-6 (820 kg) (4 × 4) Light Vehicles

DESCRIPTION
Matmar Industries manufactured two Jeep type vehicles, the CJ-5 (691 kg) and the long wheelbase CJ-6 (820 kg), under licence from the United States.

The chassis consists of box channel side rails secured by six cross-members and additional reinforcing for heavy duty operations. The body panels are of 18 gauge steel.

The layout of both vehicles is conventional with the engine at the front, driver and passenger in the centre and the cargo area at the rear. The windscreen can be folded down onto the bonnet or removed and a roll-over-bar is fitted as standard. The cargo floor is ribbed for additional strength.

The basic model has a 12-volt electrical system and a 37-amp alternator (51-amp alternator is optional), but a 24-volt system with a 60-amp alternator is fitted when it is being used as a radio vehicle.

Optional equipment includes a front-mounted winch and heater. The vehicle can be quickly adapted to carry two stretchers.

VARIANTS
Tolar Anti-tank
This is fitted with a 106 mm M40 recoilless rifle, made in Israel by IMI, mounted at the rear of the vehicle which

when travelling is traversed to the front and the barrel held in position by a clamp. Ramps enable the weapon to be removed from the vehicle for use on the ground. Standard equipment includes ammunition containers, cleaning kit, camouflage net, digging tools, fire extinguisher, smoke torches, jerrican holders and rifle and SMG clamps.

Command
As a command vehicle the CJ-5 can have four seats and the CJ-6 has seating for eight men. A canvas body top complete with doors and zippered windows is provided. Other equipment includes radios and a map reading light.

Reconnaissance
This model can be fitted with machine guns front and rear and modifications include reinforcement for gun base, gun swivel supports, ammunition box mounts and accessories, reinforced anchorage for two radios and base for antenna.

SPECIFICATIONS
(data in square brackets relate to CJ-6 where different)
Configuration: 4 × 4
Weight:
(empty) 2041 [2200] kg
(loaded) 1350 [1380] kg
Max load: 691 [820] kg

Length: 3·65 [4·16] m
Width: 1·79 m
Height: 1·88 [1·91] m
Ground clearance: 0·2 m
Wheelbase: 2·13 [2·64] m
Angle of approach/departure: 30°/29°
Fuel capacity: 58 litres
Engine: American Motors Corporation 6-cylinder OHV in-line petrol developing 90 bhp at 3050 rpm
Gearbox: manual, 3 forward and 1 reverse gears
Clutch: single dry plate
Transfer box: 2-speed
Steering: recirculating ball
Turning radius: 5 [5·75] m
Suspension: semi-elliptical springs and hydraulic shock absorbers
Tyres: 7.60 × 15
Number of tyres: 4 + 1 spare
Brakes:
(main) hydraulic
(parking) mechanical
Electrical system: 12 V

STATUS
Production complete. In service with the Israeli Army.

MANUFACTURER
Matmar Industries Limited, POB 1007, Haifa, Israel.
This plant has now ceased operations.

ITALY

Mountain Power Truck

DEVELOPMENT
The Mountain Power Truck has been developed to meet the requirements of the Italian mountain troops for a vehicle which could be used to transport equipment over mountain roads and tracks. The first prototype was completed in 1974 and following extensive trials a pre-production batch was delivered for operational trials with Italian mountain units in June 1978.

DESCRIPTION
The Mountain Power Truck is a small all-wheel drive vehicle with a platform for carrying up to 200 kg of cargo. The vehicle can be steered by the operator when seated on the platform or when walking behind. The engine is mounted in the centre of the vehicle under the load area which has a folding handrail on the sides and rear.

SPECIFICATIONS
Configuration: 4 × 4
Weight:
(empty) 363 kg
(loaded) 563 kg
Max load: 200 kg
Length:
(overall) 1·98 m
(over wheels) 1·75 m
(over platform) 1·72 m
Width: 0·9 m
Height:
(over steering wheel) 1·01 m
(over platform) 0·84 m
Ground clearance: 0·2 m
Track: 0·7 m
Wheelbase: 1·07 m
Max speed: 8 km/h
Max gradient: 50%

Max side slope: 30%
Engine: 4-cylinder air-cooled petrol engine developing 10 hp at 3600 rpm
Gearbox: hydrostatic closed circuit with variable displacement radial piston primary pump and 2 fixed displacement orbital hydraulic motors
Steering: hydraulic, power-assisted on all 4 wheels
Turning radius: 3·6 m
Suspension: independent with transverse leaf springs for each axle and hydraulic shock absorbers
Brakes:
(main) operating on hydrostatic transmission
(parking) disc brakes on all 4 wheels

STATUS
In service with Italian Army mountain units.

MANUFACTURER
Fresia (Millessimo SV), Via Trento e Trieste 30, Italy.

Mountain Power Truck showing position of engine under centre of vehicle (Italian Army)

Mountain Power Truck showing adjustable steering wheel (Italian Army)

FIAT AR-59 (4 × 4) 500 kg Light Vehicle

DEVELOPMENT
After the end of the Second World War the FIAT company developed a 4 × 4 light vehicle called the Campagnola. This was adopted by the Italian Army in 1951 as the AR-51 (AR stands for Autovettura da Ricognizione, or reconnaissance car). The AR-51 was powered by a four-cylinder petrol engine developing 53 hp, which gave the vehicle a maximum road speed of 100 km/h. In 1955 it was replaced in production by the AR-55 which was powered by a 59 hp engine. In 1959 the AR-59 was introduced with the FIAT designation model 1101B and remained in production until replaced by the new FIAT lightweight vehicle, the 1107 AD which is fully described in the following entry.

DESCRIPTION
The AR-59 has been designed to carry 480 kg of cargo both on roads and cross country and tow a trailer weighing up to 500 kg. The Italian Army does however use the vehicle to tow the OTO Melara 105 mm pack howitzer which weighs 1290 kg.

The layout of the AR-59 is conventional with the engine at the front and the crew compartment at the rear. The canvas top can be folded down at the rear if not required. The windscreen can be folded flat against the bonnet and the tops of the doors removed. An unusual feature of the doors is that they can be swung back through 180 degrees and clipped to the side of the vehicle. The driver and co-driver have individual seats while the other four personnel have bench seats, two each side.

VARIANTS
The Italian Army has some vehicles fitted with

FIAT AR-59 (4 × 4) 500 kg light vehicle towing OTO Melara 105 mm pack howitzer (Christopher F Foss)

106 mm M40 type recoilless rifles and SS-11 anti-tank guided weapons. It is also used as a radio vehicle.

SPECIFICATIONS
Cab seating: 1 + 5
Configuration: 4 × 4
Weight:
(empty) 1440 kg
(loaded) 1920 kg
Weight on front axle: (loaded) 830 kg
Weight on rear axle: (loaded) 1090 kg
Max load: 480 kg
Towed load: 500 kg
Load area: 1 × 0·825 m
Length: 3·596 m
Width: 1·57 m
Height:
(overall) 1·8 m
(reduced) 1·4 m
Ground clearance: 0·203 m
Track:
(front) 1·254 m
(rear) 1·26 m
Wheelbase: 2·25 m
Angle of approach/departure: 60°/35°
Max speed: 110 km/h
Range: 450 km

Fuel capacity: 58 litres
Max gradient: 89%
Fording: 0·6 m
Engine: Model 105B.017 4-cylinder, OHV, liquid-cooled petrol developing 56 hp (DIN) at 4000 rpm (some vehicles have diesel engines)
Gearbox: manual with 4 forward and 1 reverse gears
Clutch: single dry plate
Transfer box: 2-speed
Tyres: 6.40 × 16
Turning radius: 5·4 m
Number of tyres: 4 + 1 spare
Brakes:
(main) hydraulic
(parking) mechanical
Electrical system: 24 V
Batteries: 2 × 12 V, 40 Ah
Generator: 600 W

STATUS
Production complete. In service with the Italian Army.

The vehicle was also manufactured under licence in Yugoslavia with the designation AR-51 Zastava.

MANUFACTURER
FIAT, Direzione Mezzi Speciali, Corso G Marconi 10/20, Turin, Italy.

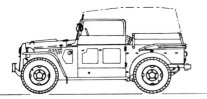

FIAT AR-59 (4 × 4) 500 kg light vehicle

FIAT 1107 AD (4 × 4) 750 kg Light Vehicle

DEVELOPMENT
The FIAT 1107 AD (4 × 4) light vehicle entered production in 1974 as the replacement for the older FIAT AR-59. Main improvements include a more powerful engine, increased load carrying capability and the option of a hard top. In 1980 production of the Campagnola for both civil and military applications amounted to 3900 vehicles.

DESCRIPTION
The vehicle is available in hard and soft top versions and there is also a longer model, with an overall length of 4·025 metres and with the same wheelbase, also in hard and soft top models. The longer model has three-man bench seats down either side behind the front seat rather than two as in the basic model. FIAT is now offering a model, the FIAT Campagnola 2500, powered by a four-cylinder diesel engine which develops 72 hp at 2400 rpm, which has a maximum road speed of 120 km/h and a fuel consumption of 12·6 litres per 100 km. Empty weight of the canvas top model is 1880 kg.

Special equipment for operation in dusty and tropical zones includes an air cleaner with centrifugal pre-cleaner, fuel filter between feed pump and carburettor, sealed type declutch thrust bearing, engine compartment front protection and a low octane number petrol engine with 7·5 compression ratio, which develops 75 hp.

The body is of all steel construction and has two side doors and a tailgate. Seating is provided for three including the driver at the front and four at the rear, two each side on bench type seats. The canvas top and side curtains can be removed and the windscreen folded forward flat against the bonnet.

Standard equipment includes a spare wheel, heater, ventilating and defrosting system, pintle towing hook at the rear, towing eyes at the front, fire extinguisher, pick and shovel and additional fuel cans.

VARIANTS
No variants have been announced although the vehicle can easily be adapted for a wide variety of other roles such as ambulance, command, radio and anti-tank armed with ATGWs or a recoilless rifle. The Italian company of Grazia offers an ambulance based on the chas-

FIAT 1107 AD (4 × 4) 750 kg light vehicle with canvas top raised

FIAT 1107 AD (4 × 4) 750 kg light vehicle with canvas top raised, from rear

sis of the FIAT 1107 AD. Brief details of the company's production range are given in the *Shelters, containers and vehicle bodies* section.

The FIAT 1107 chassis is used as the basis for the ASA Guardian armoured security vehicle, details of which can be found on page 321 of *Jane's Armour and Artillery 1983–84*.

Renault Véhicules Industriels entered a modified version of the FIAT 1107 AD in the French Army competition for a vehicle to replace the Hotchkiss M 201 under the designation of the TRM 500. This was not adopted and is no longer being offered; details were given in *Jane's Military Vehicles and Ground Support Equipment 1981*, page 232.

FIAT 1107 AD (4 × 4) 750 kg light vehicle

SPECIFICATIONS
(canvas top model; data in square brackets relate to hard top where different)
Cab seating: 3 + 4 [3 + 6, LWB version]
Configuration: 4 × 4
Weight:
  (empty) 1670 [1740] kg
  (loaded) 2420 [2490] kg
Max load: 750 kg
Towed load:
  (road) 1740 kg
  (off road) 900 kg
Length: 3·775 m
Width: 1·58 m
Height: 1·901 [1·945] m
Track:
  (front) 1·365 m
  (rear) 1·404 m
Wheelbase: 2·3 m
Angle of approach/departure: 44°/45°
Max speed: (road) 120 km/h
Range: 400 km
Fuel capacity: 57 litres
Max gradient: 100%
Max side slope: 40%
Fording: 0·7 m

Engine: 4-cylinder in-line petrol developing 80 hp (DIN) at 4600 rpm
Gearbox: manual with 5 forward and 1 reverse gears
Clutch: single plate dry
Transfer box: 2-speed
Steering: hourglass and roller
Turning radius: 5·4 m
Suspension: independent McPherson type with longitudinal torsion bar, single telescopic shock absorbers at front and twin at rear
Tyres: 7.00 × 16
Brakes:
  (main) drum, hydraulically operated on all 4 wheels, dual circuit
  (parking) operates on rear drums
Electrical system: 24 V
Batteries: 2 × 12 V, 45 Ah

STATUS
In production. In service with Italy and Tunisia (400). Now being built in Yugoslavia as the replacement for the AR-51 Zastava.

MANUFACTURER
FIAT, Direzione Mezzi Speciali, Corso G Marconi 10/20, Turin, Italy.

Lamborghini LM-002 and LM-004/7000 1000 kg (4 × 4) Light Vehicles

DESCRIPTION
The Lamborghini LM-002 is a militarised and enlarged version of the Lamborghini Cheetah dune buggy and has been produced for the command and control vehicle role. While retaining the general appearance of its civilian counterpart, the LM-002 is much bulkier and heavier, and has a larger engine. The LM-004/7000 has a 7-litre engine but is otherwise similar.

The cab has seating for two, although there is room at the rear for more seating. The rear space could be used for communications equipment, surveillance equipment or possibly weapons such as a TOW launcher, as the roof has a canvas tilt which can be folded back. There are four doors, two providing access to the rear, and the door frames and windscreen surround act as an anti-roll bar. The engine is mounted at the front with a steel tubular frame protecting the radiator grill. Sump protectors are provided under the engine. Behind the cab there is a small open cargo-carrying boot on the rear of which is space for a spare wheel and two fuel or water cans. A towing hook is provided at the rear.

In an all-passenger version there would be provision for the driver and up to ten passengers. There is space at the front of the vehicle for a small winch.

SPECIFICATIONS
(data in square brackets refers to LM-004/7000 where different from LM-002)
Cab seating:
  (basic) 1 + 1
  (all-passenger) 1 + 10
Configuration: 4 × 4
Weight:
  (loaded) 3600 [3700] kg
  (empty) 2600 [2700] kg
Max load: 1000 kg
Length: 4·79 [4·9] m
Width: 2 m
Height: 1·85 m
Ground clearance:
  (belly pan, centre) 0·425 m
  (differentials) 0·295 m
Track: 1·615 m
Wheelbase: 2·95 [3] m
Angle of approach/departure: 75°/45°
Max speed: 188 [206] km/h
Range: 900 km
Fuel capacity: 280 [320] litres

Fording: 0·82 m
Engine: Lamborghini L.503 4·754-litre petrol developing 332 hp at 6000 rpm or (LM-004/7000) Lamborghini 7000 7-litre petrol developing 420 hp at 5400 rpm
Gearbox: manual with 5 forward and 1 reverse gears
Transfer box: 2-speed
Transmission: ZF S5-24/3
Steering: variable ratio, linked, with hydraulic assistance
Turning radius: 12·2 m
Suspension: 4-wheel, independent double wishbones with helical springs and telescopic, oil, double acting shock absorbers with integral bump stop
Tyres: 14 × 16 LT
Brakes:
  (main) hydraulic dual power assist on all 4 wheels
  (parking) mechanical
Electrical system: 12 V
Battery: 1 × 12 V, 90 Ah

STATUS
Prototypes.

MANUFACTURER
Nuova Automobili Ferruccio Lamborghini SpA, 40019 S. Agata Bolognese (Bo), Italy.

Lamborghini LM-002 (T J Gander)

Lamborghini LM-004/7000

Leoncino (4 × 4) 1000 kg Truck

DEVELOPMENT
This vehicle, adopted as the standard 1000 kg truck of the Italian Army in the 1960s, is known as the Autocarro Leggero 1 Tonnellata, 4 × 4, Leoncino. Although nominally rated as a 1000 kg vehicle it has a payload of 1140 kg off the highway and 1497 kg on the highway.

Its layout is conventional with the engine at the front, driver and two passengers in the soft-top cab, which has a windscreen that folds forward onto the bonnet and removable side doors, and the cargo area at the rear with no drop sides or tailgate but with removable bows and a tarpaulin cover. Mounted at the front of the vehicle is a winch.

STATUS
Production complete. In service with the Italian Army.

MANUFACTURER
FIAT Azienda OM, Brescia, Italy.

SPECIFICATIONS
Cab seating: 1 + 2
Configuration: 4 × 4
Weight:
  (empty) 2860 kg
  (loaded, road) 4357 kg
  (loaded, cross-country) 4000 kg
Weight on front axle: (empty) 1670 kg
Weight on rear axle: (empty) 1190 kg
Max load:
  (road) 1497 kg
  (cross-country) 1140 kg
Towed load: (cross-country) 2000 kg
Length: 4·45 m
Width: 2 m
Height overall: 2·13 m
Ground clearance: 0·24 m
Track:
  (front) 1·63 m
  (rear) 1·67 m

Wheelbase: 2·5 m
Max speed: 76·6 km/h
Range: (road) 500 km
Fuel capacity: 90 litres
Max gradient: 60%
Engine: Model CO2D/12, 4-cylinder diesel developing 85 hp at 2400 rpm
Gearbox: manual, 5 forward and 1 reverse gears
Clutch: single dry plate
Transfer box: 2-speed
Turning radius: 5·2 m
Suspension: semi-elliptical springs and hydraulic shock absorbers
Tyres: 9.00 × 16
Brakes:
  (main) hydraulic, dual circuit
  (parking) mechanical
Electrical system: 24 V
Batteries: 2 × 12 V

JAPAN

Mitsubishi (4 × 4) Light Vehicles

DESCRIPTION

In 1953 Mitsubishi obtained a licence from the American Willys (later Kaiser Jeep) company to manufacture the Jeep in Japan for both civil and military use. The first model was the CJ3B-JB and was followed by many other models, all available with petrol or diesel engine, left or right hand drive, long or short wheelbase and with an open or enclosed passenger/cargo area.

Standard Mitsubishi (4 × 4) J24 light vehicle

Standard Mitsubishi (4 × 4) J56 light vehicle

For many years the standard ¼-ton vehicle of the Japanese Self-Defence Force was the Mitsubishi J54A, powered by a four-cylinder petrol engine which develops 75 hp at 3800 rpm, coupled to a manual gearbox with three forward and one reverse gears and a two-speed transfer case. Basic details of the J54A are: 3·33-metre length, 1·595-metre width, 1·85-metre height, 2·03-metre wheelbase, 92 km/h maximum road speed and 6.00 × 16 tyres. Variants in service include an ambulance, anti-tank armed with a 106 mm Type 60 recoilless rifle and anti-tank armed with two KAM-3D (Type 64) wire guided anti-tank missiles.

The J54A has been replaced by the J24A which is designated the Type 73 by the Japanese Ground Self-Defence Force (Army). Basic details of the military model are 1 + 5 seating, 4 × 4 configuration, 1900 kg loaded weight, 1420 kg empty weight, 480 kg maximum load, 3·75-metre length, 1·655-metre width, 1·95-metre height, 0·21-metre ground clearance, 1·296-metre track, 100 km/h maximum road speed, four-cylinder engine developing 80 hp at 3700 rpm, 5·8-metre turning radius and 7.00 × 15 tyres.

Mitsubishi currently manufactures the following Jeep type vehicles: J56 (4G53) powered by a four-cylinder petrol engine with a 2·03-metre wheelbase, J26 (4G53) powered by a four-cylinder petrol engine, 2·225-metre wheelbase, J24 (4DR5) powered by a four-cylinder diesel engine with a wheelbase of 2·225-metres, J38 (4G53) powered by a four-cylinder petrol engine with a wheelbase of 2·64 metres, J36 (4DR5) powered by a four-cylinder diesel engine with a wheelbase of 2·64 metres, J46 (4G53) powered by a four-cylinder petrol engine with a 2·64-metre wheelbase and J44 (4DR5) powered by a four-cylinder diesel engine with a wheelbase of 2·64 metres.

STATUS

Production. In service with the Japanese Self-Defence Force and other armed forces in the Far East.

MANUFACTURER

Mitsubishi Motors Corporation, 33-8, Shiba 5-chome, Minato-ku, Tokyo, Japan.

SPECIFICATIONS

Model	J56 (4G53)	J24-A
Configuration	4 × 4	4 × 4
Weight (empty)	1080 kg	1420 kg
(loaded)	1630 kg	1900 kg
Max load	550 kg	480 kg
Length	3·39 m	3·75 m
Width	1·665 m	1·655 m
Height	1·905 m	1·95 m
Ground clearance	0·21 m	0·21 m
Track	1·235 m	1·295 m
Wheelbase	2·03 m	2·225 m
Fuel capacity	120 litres	100 litres
Engine	4-cylinder petrol developing 110 bhp at 5000 rpm	4-cylinder diesel developing 80 bhp at 3700 rpm
Gearbox	manual with 4 forward and 1 reverse gears	
Clutch	single dry plate	single dry plate
Transfer box	2-speed	2-speed
Steering	recirculating ball	recirculating ball
Turning radius	5·9 m	5·8 m
Suspension	semi-elliptical leaf springs with hydraulic shock absorbers	
Tyres	6.00 × 16	7.00 × 15
Brakes (main)	hydraulic	hydraulic
(parking)	mechanical	mechanical
Electrical system	12 V	12 V

Mitsubishi (4 × 4) Jeep used by Japanese Ground Self-Defence Force and fitted with 106 mm recoilless rifle (K Nogi)

Mitsubishi (4 × 4) Jeep used by Japanese Ground Self-Defence Force and fitted with Type 64 (KAM-3D) ATGWs (Kensuke Ebata)

Mitsubishi (4 × 4) Jeep used by Japanese Ground Self-Defence Force (Kensuke Ebata)

Mitsubishi (4 × 4) Jeep used by Japanese Ground Self-Defence Force and fitted with Type 62 7·62 mm machine gun (Kensuke Ebata)

Nissan Patrol (4 × 4) Light Vehicles

DESCRIPTION
The first Nissan light vehicles were closely patterned on the American Jeep but in 1960 Nissan introduced the Patrol vehicle, which was designed primarily for the civilian market but has since been adopted by a number of armed forces.

The layout of the Nissan Patrol vehicle is conventional with the engine at the front and the passenger/cargo area at the rear. The basic model has a canvas top and is designated the L60. Variants include a hard top, the KL60, a deluxe hardtop with a 2·5-metre wheelbase, designated the KLG60V, and a pickup with a 2·8-metre wheelbase, designated the 62ZLG60H.

The L60 series of Nissan Patrol light vehicles has been discontinued but in 1980 production began of an updated series of vehicle also known as the Nissan Patrol but not aimed specifically at the military market. Models produced for the commercial market are known as the Nissan 'Safari' but are also marketed under the 'Patrol' name. This version is produced in several configurations varying from a station waggon to a heavy-duty, soft top waggon.

STATUS
L60 series no longer in production. In service with a number of armed forces. Also built under licence in India. Nissan 'Safari' Patrol now in production.

MANUFACTURER
Nissan Motor Company Limited, 17–1, Ginza 6-chome, Chuo-ku, Tokyo, Japan.

SPECIFICATIONS
(60 canvas top; data in square brackets relate to KLG 60V hard top model where different)
Cab seating: 1 + 5
Configuration: 4 × 4
Weight:
  (empty) 1620 [1720] kg
  (loaded) 2185 [2285] kg
Max load: 565 kg

Nissan Patrol known commercially as Nissan 'Safari'

Length: 3·77 [4·07] m
Width: 1·715 m
Height: 1·98 [1·945] m
Ground clearance: 0·22 [0·215] m
Track: (front/rear) 1·386/1·404 m
Wheelbase: 2·2 [2·5] m
Fuel capacity: 72 litres
Engine: 4-cylinder in-line water-cooled petrol developing 130 hp at 3600 rpm
Gearbox: manual with 3 forward and 1 reverse gears
Clutch: single dry plate

Transfer box: 2-speed
Steering: recirculating ball
Turning radius: 5·6 [6·2] m
Suspension: semi-elliptical leaf springs with hydraulic shock absorbers
Tyres: 6.50 × 16
Number of tyres: 4 + 1 spare
Brakes:
  (main) hydraulic
  (parking) mechanical
Electrical system: 12 V

Toyota Land Cruiser (4 × 4) Series Light Vehicle

DESCRIPTION
The Toyota Land Cruiser was developed in the 1950s primarily for the civilian market but has since been adopted by a number of armies in the Middle East and South America.

The basic model has a conventional layout with the engine at the front and the passenger and cargo areas at the rear. The windscreen can fold flat against the bonnet and the side doors and vinyl top are removable. Six basic models of the Toyota Land Cruiser are currently in production; these are hard top (regular wheelbase of 2·285 metres and super long wheelbase of 2·95 metres), vinyl-top series (regular wheelbase of 2·285 metres, long wheelbase of 2·43 metres and super long wheelbase of 2·95 metres) and pickup (super long wheelbase of 2·95 metres). In addition there is a four-door station wagon version of the Land Cruiser.

STATUS
In production. In service with armed forces in the Middle East, South Africa and South America. In 1982 Toyota built 129 620 Land Cruisers for the home and export markets.

MANUFACTURER
Toyota Motor Sales Co Limited, No 23–22, Izumi I-chome Higashi-ku, Nagoya, Japan. The vehicle is also built under licence in Brazil. Note: This vehicle has not been designed specifically for military application.

SPECIFICATIONS

Model	Regular wheelbase	Long wheelbase	Super long wheelbase
Configuration	4 × 4	4 × 4	4 × 4
Weight (empty)	1680 kg	1740 kg	1865 kg
(loaded)	2295 kg	2445 kg	3035 kg
Max load	615 kg	705 kg	1170 kg
Length	3·915 m	4·275 m	4·955 m
Width	1·665 m	1·665 m	1·665 m
Height	1·955 m	1·96 m	2·03 m
Ground clearance	0·21 m	0·21 m	0·225 m
Track (front)	1·415 m	1·415 m	1·415 m
(rear)	1·4 m	1·4 m	1·41 m
Wheelbase	2·285 m	2·43 m	2·95 m
Fuel capacity	85 litres	85 litres	85 litres
Engine	6-cylinder in-line OHV petrol developing 135 hp (DIN) at 3600 rpm		
	6-cylinder in-line OHV diesel developing 103 hp (DIN) at 3500 rpm		
	4-cylinder in-line OHV petrol developing 90 hp (DIN) at 3500 rpm		
	4-cylinder in-line OHV diesel developing 80 hp (DIN) at 3600 rpm		
Gearbox	all have manual, 4 forward and 1 reverse gears		
Clutch	single dry plate	single dry plate	single dry plate
Transfer box	2-speed	2-speed	2-speed
Steering	recirculating ball	recirculating ball	recirculating ball
Turning radius	5·3 m	5·5 m	6·5 m
Suspension (front and rear)	semi-elliptical springs with hydraulic double acting shock absorbers at each wheel station		
Tyres	7.00-15-6 PR	7.00-15-6 PR	7.50-16-8 PR
Number of tyres	4 + 1 spare	4 + 1 spare	4 + 1 spare
Brakes (main)	hydraulic, all wheels	hydraulic, all wheels	hydraulic, all wheels
(parking)	mechanical	mechanical	mechanical
Electrical system	12 V	12 V	12 V

Toyota Land Cruiser (4 × 4) light vehicle with fully enclosed cab and cargo area

Toyota Land Cruiser (4 × 4) light vehicle with removable top (extra long wheelbase model)

Toyota Land Cruiser (4 × 4) light vehicle in long wheelbase pick-up configuration

Diesel-engined Toyota Land Cruiser (4 × 4) light vehicle in service with South African Army (T J Gander)

Nissan Q4W73 (4 × 4) 750 kg Truck

DESCRIPTION
This was developed in the 1950s for the Japanese Self-Defence Force and is based on the Second World War American Dodge T214 ¾-ton (4 × 4) truck. Early production vehicles used the same engine as the early Nissan Patrol vehicle. This truck has also been built under licence in India at the Defence Unit (Ordnance Factory) at Jabalpur.

The layout of the vehicle is conventional with the engine at the front, two-man cab with removable top in the centre and the cargo area at the rear with a drop tailgate, removable bows and a tarpaulin cover. Variants in service include an ambulance and a fire-fighting vehicle.

STATUS
Production complete in Japan. Production continues in India. In service with the Japanese Self-Defence Force. Quantities were also supplied to South Korea and South Viet-Nam.

MANUFACTURER
Nissan Motor Company Limited, 17–1, Ginza 6-chome, Chuo-ku, Tokyo, Japan.

SPECIFICATIONS
Cab seating: 1 + 1
Configuration: 4 × 4
Weight:
  (empty) 2690 kg
  (loaded, road) 4190 kg
  (loaded, cross country) 3440 kg

Nissan Q4W73 (4 × 4) 750 kg truck (Japanese Ground Self-Defence Force)

Max load:
  (road) 1500 kg
  (cross country) 750 kg
Max towed load: 2000 kg
Length: 4·71 m
Width: 2·045 m
Height: 2·39 m
Wheelbase: 2·8 m
Max speed: 97 km/h
Max range: 319 km
Fuel capacity: 68 litres
Gradient: 60%
Fording: 0·51 m

Engine: 6-cylinder water-cooled petrol developing 145 hp at 4000 rpm
Gearbox: manual with 4 forward and 1 reverse gears
Clutch: single dry plate
Transfer box: 2-speed
Suspension: semi-elliptical springs and hydraulic shock absorbers
Tyres: 7.50 × 20
Number of tyres: 4 + 1 spare
Brakes:
  (main) hydraulic
  (parking) mechanical
Electrical system: 12 V

Toyota 2FQ15L (4 × 4) 750 kg Truck

DEVELOPMENT
This was developed in the 1950s for the Japanese Self-Defence Force and is a further development of the Second World War American T214(WC52) ¾-ton (4 × 4) truck. It is very similar in appearance to the Nissan Q4W73 (4 × 4) 750 kg truck which was developed at the same time. Other Toyota trucks of this type include the FQ10 and FQ15 which are almost identical in appearance to the T214(WC52).

DESCRIPTION
The layout of the Toyota 2FQ15L is conventional with the engine at the front, two-man cab with removable top in the centre and the cargo area at the rear with a drop tailgate, removable bows and a tarpaulin cover.

The ambulance model is designated the HQ15V, has a crew of two and can carry five stretcher patients or nine seated patients. Basic data are: loaded weight 4300 kg, length 5·165 metres, width 2·13 metres and height 2·815 metres.

STATUS
Production complete. In service with the Japanese Self-Defence Force. Also used by the US Army (in Far East only), South Korea and Viet-Nam.

MANUFACTURER
Toyota Motor Company Limited, 1 Toyota-cho, Toyotashi, Aichi-ken, Japan.

Toyota (4 × 4) 2FQ15L 750 kg truck (Kensuke Ebata)

Toyota (4 × 4) HQ15V ambulance (Kensuke Ebata)

SPECIFICATIONS
Cab seating: 1 + 1
Configuration: 4 × 4
Weight:
(empty) 2800 kg
(loaded, road) 3867 kg
(loaded, cross country) 3640 kg
Max load:
(road) 1067 kg
(cross country) 840 kg

Length: 5·08 m
Width: 2·02 m
Height: 2·32 m
Wheelbase: 3 m
Max speed: (road) 82 km/h
Engine: Toyota 6-cylinder water-cooled petrol
developing 105 bhp at 3200 rpm
Gearbox: manual with 4 forward and 1 reverse gears
Transfer box: none
Tyres: 7.50 × 20

Number of tyres: 4 + 1 spare
Brakes:
(main) hydraulic
(parking) mechanical

KENYA

Jeep Production

Late in 1981 it was announced that American Motors was to establish an assembly plant in Kenya at the

General Motors factory in Nairobi to produce the Jeep. It was expected that first production models will be completed in mid-1982 and that at least three versions will be produced, Cherokee (4 × 4) pick up,

Cherokee (4 × 4) station wagon and the CJ (4 × 4). In addition to sales within Kenya, exports will be to Burundi, Madagascar, Malawi, Mozambique, Rwanda, Seychelles, Tanzania, Uganda and Zambia.

NETHERLANDS

DAF 66 YA (4 × 2) 400 kg Utility Vehicle

DEVELOPMENT
This vehicle is based on commercial components and the first prototype, known as the DAF 55 YA, was completed in 1970. A total of 1200 vehicles were built for the Dutch Army between 1973 and mid-1977.

DESCRIPTION
The layout of the DAF 66 YA is conventional with the engine at the front and the passenger/cargo area at the rear. The body is an all welded unit with a chassis of box-section members. The two rear seats can be folded down to increase the cargo carrying area. The windscreen can be folded forward onto the bonnet if required and collapsible bows and a tarpaulin cover are provided at the rear of the cargo area. Both front and rear bumpers are interchangeable and are provided with towing eyes.
Power is transferred from the engine to the transmission via an automatic clutch and an aluminium propeller shaft. The transmission comprises an infinitely variable twin-belt Vario-matic, a differential unit and secondary drive shafts to the rear wheels. Cooling air for the transmission is obtained from the front of the vehicle and through longitudinal box-section girders. If required, the differential unit can be provided with a locking device.
Hydraulic brakes are provided for all wheels, with a separate circuit for front and rear wheels. The front brakes are of the disc type and the rear brakes are of the drum type. Division of braking effort between front and rear is 73/27. The parking brake, applied by a lever on the propeller shaft tunnel, operates mechanically on the rear wheels. A vacuum brake booster, power factor 2·12, can be fitted as an optional extra.
Standard equipment includes a spare wheel carried under the bonnet, windscreen washers, heater, transmission low-ratio hold control, hazard warning lights, inspection lamp socket, map reading light and cable connectors for radio operations.

VARIANTS
The basic vehicle can be adapted for a variety of different roles including use as a military police vehicle, radio vehicle (it has a 24 volt electrical system as standard),

DAF 66 YA (4 × 2) 400 kg utility vehicle

DAF 66 YA (4 × 2) 400 kg utility vehicle with bows and cover erected

and an ambulance carrying two stretcher patients plus the driver and attendant.

SPECIFICATIONS
Cab seating: 1 + 3
Weight:
(empty) 860 kg
(loaded) 1295 kg
Weight on front axle: (loaded) 560 kg
Weight on rear axle: (loaded) 735 kg
Max load: 435 kg
Load area: (with rear seats folded) 1·4 × 1·25 m
Length: 3·75 m
Width: 1·52 m
Height:
(with bows and tarpaulin cover raised) 1·59 m
(windscreen folded flat) 1·11 m
Ground clearance: 0·19 m
Track:
(front) 1·31 m
(rear) 1·24 m
Wheelbase: 2·255 m
Angle of approach/departure: 31°/37°
Max speed: (road) 115 km/h
Range: 500 km
Fuel capacity: 50 litres
Max gradient: 20%
Fording: 0·2 m

Engine: B 110E, water-cooled 4-cylinder in-line petrol developing 47 hp (DIN) at 5000 rpm
Gearbox: Vario-matic (3 positions: forward, neutral and reverse)
Clutch: single dry plate
Steering: rack and pinion
Turning radius: 4·77 m
Suspension:
(front) independent by means of longitudinal torsion bars with anti-roll bar and telescopic double-acting hydraulic shock absorbers
(rear) De Dion axle with semi-elliptical leaf springs and telescopic double acting hydraulic shock absorbers
Tyres: 14.5 × 14
Number of tyres: 4 + 1 spare
Brakes:
(main) hydraulic
(parking) mechanical
Electrical system: 24 V
Batteries: 2 × 12 V

STATUS
Production as required. In service with the Dutch Army. Gradually being replaced in service by the Land-Rover (4 × 4) vehicle.

MANUFACTURER
DAF Trucks, Eindhoven, Netherlands.

DAF YA 126 (4 × 4) 1000 kg Weapon Carrier

DEVELOPMENT
The prototype of the YA 126 (4 × 4) truck was completed in 1950 and the vehicle was in production for the Dutch Army from 1952 to 1960. The YA 126 can carry 1000 kg of cargo or eight men, and tow a maximum load of 2500 kg.

DESCRIPTION
The engine is mounted at the front with the two-man cab in the centre. The cab has a removable canvas roof,

removable sidescreens and a windscreen which can be folded forward onto the bonnet. The rear cargo area has removable bows, tarpaulin cover and a rear dropdown tailgate. Freewheeling spare wheels on each side of the cab assist the vehicle in overcoming obstacles as well as protecting the drive line. Some vehicles are fitted with a 2500 kg capacity winch.
The four wheels are driven by short axle shafts connected with a bevel gear and pinion housed in a final drive unit. These units are hinged on the end of the longitudinal trailing arms and are driven via propeller shafts from bevel drive boxes on each side of the chassis which are connected to the central differential in the transfer case by short axle shafts.

VARIANTS
Variants in service with the Dutch Army include a fully enclosed van type ambulance which can carry four stretcher patients, an open command/radio vehicle and a workshop vehicle.

STATUS
Production complete. In service with the Dutch Army. Gradually being replaced by the DAF YA 4440 (4 × 4) 4000 kg truck.

MANUFACTURER
DAF Trucks, Geldropseweg 303, 5645 TK, Eindhoven, Netherlands.

DAF YA 126 (4 × 4) 1000 kg truck being used for personnel transport with bows and tarpaulin cover removed

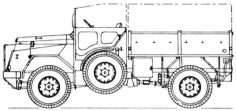

DAF YA 126 (4 × 4) 1000 kg weapon carrier

SPECIFICATIONS
Cab seating: 1 + 1
Configuration: 4 × 4
Weight:
(empty) 3230 kg
(loaded) 4230 kg
Weight on front axle: (empty) 1995 kg
Weight on rear axle: (empty) 1235 kg
Max load: 1000 kg
Towed load: 2500 kg
Load area: 2·006 × 1·905 m
Length: 4·55 m

Width: 2·1 m
Height:
(tarpaulin) 2·22 m
(reduced) 1·828 m
Ground clearance: 0·35 m
Track: 1·72 m
Wheelbase: 2·83 m
Angle of approach/departure: 45°/45°
Max speed: (road) 84 km/h
Range: 330 km
Fuel capacity: 110 litres
Max gradient: 65%
Fording: 0·76 m
Engine: Hercules JXC 6-cylinder in-line petrol developing 102 hp at 3200 rpm
Gearbox: manual with 4 forward and 1 reverse gears
Transfer box: 2-speed
Turning radius: 7 m
Suspension: both front and rear wheels suspended on two longitudinal trailing arms connected at front with transversely mounted tubular beams containing torsion bars. Auxiliary rubber springs are mounted between upper trailing arms and chassis. Hydraulic shock absorbers for all wheels.
Tyres: 9·00 × 16
Number of tyres: 4 + 2 spare
Brakes:
(main) air/hydraulic
(parking) mechanical
Electrical system: 24 V
Batteries: 2 × 12 V
Generator: 900 W

PAKISTAN

Nispak (4 × 4) 400 kg Light Vehicle

DEVELOPMENT/DESCRIPTION
The Nispak has been designed under the direction of the Inspector of Vehicles and Engineering Equipment, Pakistan Army, and is patterned on the Japanese Nissan (4 × 4) light vehicle. At least 90 per cent of the components of the Nispak, including the engine, transmission, chassis and body, are manufactured in Pakistan.

The layout of the Nispak is conventional with the engine at the front, driver and passenger in the centre and the cargo area at the rear. The single-piece windscreen folds forward onto the bonnet and the canvas cover folds down to the rear.

SPECIFICATIONS
Configuration: 4 × 4
Weight:
(empty) 1580 kg
(loaded, road) 2180 kg
(loaded, cross-country) 1980 kg

Weight on front axle: (empty) 853 kg
Weight on rear axle: (empty) 727 kg
Max load:
(road) 600 kg
(cross-country) 400 kg
Towed load:
(road) 907 kg
(cross-country) 680 kg
Length: 3·772 m
Width: 1·689 m
Height: 1·981 m
Ground clearance: 0·235 m
Track:
(front) 1·382 m
(rear) 1·4 m
Wheelbase: 2·2 m
Max speed: 125 km/h
Range: 290 km
Fuel capacity: 50 litres

Gradient: 65%
Fording: 1·88 m
Engine: 6-cylinder petrol developing 145 hp at 3800 rpm
Gearbox: manual, 3 forward and 1 reverse gears
Clutch: single dry plate
Transfer box: 2-speed
Turning radius: 5·69 m
Suspension: semi-elliptical springs and hydraulic shock absorbers
Tyres: 7·00 × 16
Number of tyres: 4 + 1 spare
Brakes:
(main) hydraulic
(parking) mechanical
Electrical system: 24 V

MANUFACTURER
Facility at Chaklala, Pakistan.

PHILIPPINES

Delta Explorer (4 × 4) Light Vehicle

DEVELOPMENT
The Delta Explorer (4 × 4) light vehicle, originally known as the Delta Mini-Cruiser, was developed from 1972 by the Delta Motor Corporation with the assistance of the Research and Development Centre of the Philippines Armed Forces. It is the country's first major project called for by the Self-Reliance Defence Posture Program initiated by President Marcos.

Following trials with 40 pre-production models, the Philippine armed forces placed an order for an initial batch of 500 vehicles under the designation RJ-2.

The left-hand drive model is designated the RJ-2BL, and the right-hand drive version the RJ-2BR. The more recent diesel model, the DJ-2, is powered by an Isuzu C-190 4-stroke vertical in-line OHV diesel developing 55 bhp at 4400 rpm.

The vehicle entered service with the Philippine Army in 1975 and all foreign made light utility vehicles will now be phased out of service. The export of the vehicle to any friendly foreign country was approved in principle by the Ministry of National Defence in February 1980.

The Explorer is powered by the same 12 RM OHV petrol engine as in the Toyota Corona car, also manufactured in the Philippines, where practically all the components of the vehicle are manufactured, and the remaining imported components, about 10 per cent, are limited to the relatively unimportant parts which will eventually be made by Delta Motor Corporation. At present the company can produce about 300 Explorer vehicles a month for export.

Military version of Delta Explorer (4 × 4) light vehicle with soft top

DESCRIPTION
The chassis is the channel section girder type with five cross-members. The main panels are made of 1·6 mm thick steel and other panels of steel 1·2 mm thick. The layout is conventional with the engine at the front, driver and passenger in the centre and two two-man seats down each side at the rear. The crew compartment is covered by a tarpaulin cover which folds down at the back and the windscreen can be folded forward onto the bonnet. Apart from the basic military model there are two other canvas-topped versions, one with canvas doors and the other with steel doors.

VARIANTS
The basic vehicle can also be used as a command vehicle and weapons carrier. More specialised variants are the ambulance and police versions.

STATUS
In production. In service with Philippines, Qatar and UAE. Sold to Australia, Columbia, Italy, Pakistan and Thailand.

MANUFACTURER
Delta Motor Corporation, PO Box 305, MCC, Makati, Metro Manila 3117, Philippines.

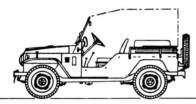

Delta Explorer (4 × 4) light vehicle

SPECIFICATIONS

Model	RJ-2B	DJ-2B
Cab seating	1 + 5	1 + 5
Configuration	4 × 4	4 × 4
Weight (empty)	1070 kg	1220 kg
(loaded)	1740 kg	1740 kg
Weight on front axle (empty)	600 kg	670 kg
Weight on rear axle (empty)	470 kg	550 kg
Length	3·575 m	3·575 m
Width	1·595 m	1·595 m
Height (overall)	1·925 m	1·925 m
(reduced)	1·505 m	1·505 m
Ground clearance	0·215 m	0·215 m
Track (front)	1·3155 m	1·3155 m
(rear)	1·2693 m	1·2693 m
Wheelbase	2·185 m	2·185 m
Angle of approach/departure	52°/39°	52°/39°
Fuel capacity	45 litres	45 litres
Engine	Toyota 12RM, 1·587-litre 4-cylinder OHV petrol developing 90 bhp at 5400 rpm	Isuzu C-190 4-stroke vertical in-line OHV diesel developing 55 bhp at 4000 rpm
Gearbox	manual, 4 forward and 1 reverse gears	
Clutch	single dry plate	single dry plate
Transfer box	2-speed	2-speed
Steering	2-shaft with worm and recirculating ball sector	
Turning radius	4·75 m	4·75 m
Suspension	front and rear, semi-elliptical leaf springs front and rear with hydraulic telescopic shock absorbers	
Axles (front)	full-floating with steering knuckles and hub locks	
(rear)	semi-floating hypoid type	
Tyres	6.00 × 16	6.00 × 16
Number of tyres	4 + 1 spare	4 + 1 spare
Brakes (main)	dual system hydraulic drum type	
(parking)	mechanical	mechanical
Electrical system	12 V	12 V
Battery	1 × 12 V	1 × 12 V

Ambulance (military) version of Delta Explorer (4 × 4) light vehicle

Integrated National Police (INP) model of Delta Explorer (4 × 4) light vehicle

Military version of Delta Explorer (4 × 4) light vehicle being used as carrier for 0·30 machine gun

Military version of Delta Explorer (4 × 4) light vehicle being used as carrier for 106 mm recoilless rifle

PORTUGAL

Bravia Comando Mk II (4 × 4) 605 kg Light Vehicle

DESCRIPTION
This vehicle is manufactured in Portugal under licence from the Jeep Corporation of the USA. Its layout is similar to that of other Jeep-type vehicles with the engine at the front and the cargo area at the rear. The Comando is equipped with a windscreen that can be folded forward onto the bonnet and removable doors, sides and top. The basic vehicle can be adapted for a wide variety of roles.

SPECIFICATIONS
Cab seating: 1 + 1 (plus 4 in the rear)
Configuration: 4 × 4
Weight:
  (empty) 1096 kg
  (loaded) 1701 kg
Max load: 605 kg
Length: 3·444 m
Width: 1·699 m
Height: 1·733 m
Ground clearance: 0·204 m
Track:
  (front) 1·234 m
  (rear) 1·232 m
Wheelbase: 2·057 m
Fuel capacity: 40 litres
Engine: Model 104 HC 4-cylinder in-line petrol developing 91 hp at 5000 rpm
or Perkins 4.154 4-cylinder diesel developing 70 bhp at 3600 rpm
Gearbox: manual with 4 forward and 1 reverse gears
Clutch: single dry plate
Transfer box: 2-speed
Steering: worm and sector
Suspension: semi-elliptical springs and hydraulic shock absorbers

LWB Bravia Comando Mk II (4 × 4) 605 kg light vehicle armed with 106 mm M40A1 rifle

Tyres: 6.00 × 16
Number of tyres: 4 + 1 spare
Brakes:
  (main) hydraulic
  (parking) mechanical
Electrical system: 12 V
Battery: 1 × 12 V

STATUS
Production.

MANUFACTURER
Bravia, Sociedade Luso-Brazileira de Viaturas E Equipamentos, SARL, Avenue Duarte Pacheco, 21-5°, Lisbon, Portugal.

Bravia Gazela (4 × 4) 1000 kg Truck

DESCRIPTION
The Bravia Gazela truck has a conventional layout with the engine at the front, cab in the centre and the cargo area at the rear. The standard cab, which has a windscreen that can be folded forward onto the bonnet and a canvas top, can be replaced by a fully enclosed cab similar to the one on the Bravia Leopardo Mark III 3000 kg (6 × 6) truck.

The cargo area has drop sides and a drop tailgate which can be removed. Fold up troop seats which are an integral part of the sides can be fitted back-to-back along the centre-line of the cargo area so that the troops are facing outwards. Bows and a tarpaulin cover are fitted as standard.

The chassis weighs 3100 kg and the maximum gross vehicle weight is 5300 kg, allowing 2200 kg for the body and cargo. Optional equipment includes a Bredem winch with a capacity of 4536 kg.

SPECIFICATIONS
Configuration: 4 × 4
Weight:
  (empty) 4300 kg
  (loaded) 5300 kg
Max load: 1000 kg
Length: 5·78 m
Width: 2·165 m
Height: (cab) 2·46 m
Ground clearance: 0·25 m
Track:
  (front) 1·72 m
  (rear) 1·665 m
Wheelbase: 3·365 m
Fuel capacity: 150 litres
Engine: Dodge H-225 6-cylinder in-line petrol developing 150 hp at 4000 rpm
or Perkins P.4-236 4-cylinder in-line diesel developing 81 hp at 2800 rpm
Gearbox: manual, 4 forward and 1 reverse gears
Clutch: single dry plate
Transfer box: 2-speed
Suspension: semi-elliptical springs and hydraulic double action shock absorbers
Tyres: 9.00 × 16 or 10.50 × 16
Brakes:
  (main) hydraulic
  (parking) mechanical on rear wheels
Electrical system: 12 V

STATUS
Production. In service in Portugal.

Bravia Gazela (4 × 4) 1000 kg truck with front-mounted winch

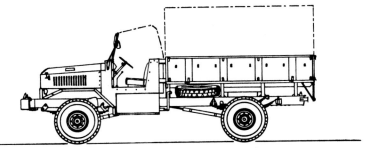

Bravia Gazela (4 × 4) 1000 kg truck

MANUFACTURER
Bravia, Sociedade Luso-Brazileira de Viaturas E Equipamentos, SARL, Avenue Duarte Pacheco, 21–5°, Lisbon, Portugal.

ROMANIA

ARO 240 (4 × 4) 700 kg Light Vehicle

DESCRIPTION
The ARO 240 has been developed as the replacement for the M-461 (4 × 4) vehicle which is the Soviet UAZ-69 but with a more powerful 70 hp engine. Production of the ARO 240 began in 1970. The engine, which is mounted at the front, is one bank of the SR-211 engine installed in the SR-113 (4 × 2) truck. The body of the vehicle is of all-steel construction and has two side doors, tailgate and removable canvas roof.

VARIANTS
Other variants are the ARO 241, ARO 243 and the ARO 244, a fully enclosed station wagon type vehicle with four doors.

STATUS
In production. It is assumed that this vehicle is in service with the Romanian Army as it is also available for civil applications and has been exported since 1972. The ARO is also produced in Portugal as the Portaro and in 1980 Tudo Imports Limited of the United Kingdom announced that it would be importing it into the UK. At that time the company said that the range consisted of five 1·25-tonne commercial type vehicles and three cross-country vehicles suitable for farming and military uses: the Ranger 240 canvas top pick-up, 242 pick-up with all-steel hard-top cab, and the 243 with full length steel bodywork and higher roof to enable it to be used in a troop transport role. Optional equipment includes bench seats down either side at the rear, freewheel hubs and a Peugeot XDP diesel engine in place of the standard petrol engine.

MANUFACTURER
Romanian state factories.

SPECIFICATIONS
Cab seating: 1 + 1
Configuration: 4 × 4
Weight:
  (empty) 1500 kg
  (loaded) 2200 kg
Weight on front axle: (loaded) 900 kg
Weight on rear axle: (loaded) 1300 kg
Max load: 700 kg
Max towed load: 1000 kg
Length: 3·974 m
Width: 1·784 m
Height: 1·936 m
Ground clearance: 0·25 m

ARO Ranger 243 (4 × 4) light vehicle

Track:
  (front) 1·445 m
  (rear) 1·467 m
Wheelbase: 2·35 m
Max speed: 100 km/h
Range: 500 km
Fuel capacity: 95 litres
Max gradient: 60%
Fording: 0·6 m
Engine: L 25 4-cylinder water-cooled petrol developing 80 hp (DIN) at 4200 rpm (some sources state 75 hp at 4000 rpm)
Tyres: 6.50 × 16
Brakes:
  (main) hydraulic
  (parking) mechanical
Electrical system: 12 V
Battery: 1 × 12 V, 56 Ah
Generator: 500 W

ARO 240 (4 × 4) 700 kg light vehicle

SPAIN

Santana Land-Rover Model 88 Militar (4 × 4) 500 kg Light Vehicle

DEVELOPMENT
Until 1956 a production agreement between Land-Rover and Metalurgica de Santa Ana established Land-Rover production in Spain but since then Land-Rover have retained only a 49 per cent share holding in this production facility. Since 1956 therefore Metalurgica de Santa Ana have marketed their Land-Rovers under the Santana name and now produce 88-inch/2·23 metre wheelbase and 109-inch/2·768 metre wheelbase models (see also following entry).

DESCRIPTION
The Santana Land-Rover Model 88 Militar (4 × 4) 500 kg light vehicle closely resembles the British air-portable 500 kg Land-Rover. The Model 88 Militar has a welded chassis, sheet aluminium body and steel bumpers front and rear. The layout is conventional with the engine at the front, driver and two passengers in the centre and a loading area with bench seating on each side at the rear. It is produced in an open form only, with removable side doors and stowage for a spare wheel on the bonnet. A version for operations in shallow water is produced with the exhaust pipe routed upwards to the left of the windscreen.

The six-cylinder engine may be petrol or diesel, both models having a capacity of 2·286 litres, with the petrol version being the usual model fitted. The suspension uses semi-elliptical leaf springs with non-adjustable shock absorbers.

Various versions of the Model 88 Militar have been produced. A variety of weapons can be carried including a 12·7 mm machine gun, a MILAN anti-tank missile launcher and a 106 mm recoilless rifle (this version has a split windscreen to accommodate the barrel). A command/communication post version has also been produced.

STATUS
Production. In service with the Spanish armed forces and some other nations, including Morocco.

MANUFACTURER
Santana, Avenida Manoteras 12, Madrid 34, Spain.

Santana Land-Rover Model 88 Militar ambulance equipped for wading

Santana Land-Rover Model 88 Militar (4 × 4) 500 kg light vehicle equipped for wading

SPECIFICATIONS
Cab seating: 1 + 2 (up to 4 in rear)
Configuration: 4 × 4
Weight:
(empty) 1660 kg
(loaded) 2160 kg
Max load: 500 kg
Length: 3·725 m
Width: 1·574 m
Height: 2 m
Ground clearance: 0·21 m

Wheelbase: 2·23 m
Track: 1·33 m
Max speed: 105 km/h
Range: (road) 560 km
Fuel capacity: 100 litres
Fording: 0·5 m
Engine: 6-cylinder, in-line, 2·286 litre petrol developing 68 hp at 4000 rpm or
6-cylinder, in-line, 2·286 litre diesel developing 60 hp at 4000 rpm
Gearbox: manual with 4 forward and 1 reverse gears

Clutch: diaphragm
Transfer box: 2-speed
Steering: geared
Turning radius: 5·8 m
Suspension: leaf springs and shock absorbers
Number of tyres: 4 + 1 spare
Brakes: dual circuit hydraulic, servo-assisted
Electrical system: 24 V

Santana Land-Rover Model 109 Militar (4 × 4) 1000 kg Light Vehicle

DESCRIPTION
In appearance the Santana Land-Rover Model 109 Militar (4 × 4) 1000 kg light vehicle is very similar to its British counterpart but the main changes are to the engine fitted. On the Santana model the engine is either a petrol or diesel six-cylinder in-line model with a capacity of 3·429 litres. Versions are produced in both open and box-body form with the box-body having a tropical roof if required. Versions intended for wading in shallow water may be fitted with the exhaust pipe routed upwards alongside the windscreen.

The Model 109 Militar is produced in various forms which include a command post, radio vehicle, 81 mm mortar carrier, light howitzer tractor, ambulance verison and a personnel carrier with seating for up to six men in the rear.

SPECIFICATIONS
Cab seating: 1 + 2 (up to 6 in rear)
Configuration: 4 × 4
Weight: (empty) 2040 kg
Max load: 1100 kg
Length: 4·545 m
Width: 1·574 m
Height: (less top) 1·7 m
Ground clearance: 0·22 m
Wheelbase: 2·768 m
Track: 1·31 m
Range: (road) 600 km

Santana Land-Rover Model 109 Militar 1000 kg (4 × 4) light vehicle

Fuel capacity: 115 litres
Engine: 6-cylinder, in-line, 3·429 litre petrol developing 140 hp at 4000 rpm or
6-cylinder, in-line, 3·429 litre diesel developing 126 hp at 4000 rpm
Gearbox: manual with 4 forward and 1 reverse gears
Clutch: hydraulic diaphragm
Transfer box: 2-speed
Turning radius: 6·85 m

Number of tyres: 4 + 1 spare
Brakes: dual circuit servo-assisted
Electrical system: 24 V

STATUS
Production. In service with the Spanish armed forces and some other nations, including Morocco.

MANUFACTURER
Santana, Avenida Manoteras 12, Madrid 34, Spain.

SWEDEN

Volvo L3304 (4 × 4) Reconnaissance Vehicle

DESCRIPTION
The Volvo L3304 was developed specifically to meet the requirements of the Swedish Army and was not available on the civilian market. The first prototype was completed in 1962 with production being undertaken from 1963 to 1965. The vehicle uses many components of the Volvo L3314 (4 × 4) Laplander truck which is also used by the Swedish Army.

The vehicle is designated the Pvpjtgbil 9031 by the Swedish Army and is used for both reconnaissance and anti-tank roles, when it is armed with a Bofors PV-1110 90 mm recoilless rifle. A travelling lock for the weapon is provided at the left front of the vehicle.

The engine is in the forward part of the vehicle with the crew compartment at the rear with an open top and usually an anti-roll bar. The spare wheel is at the front of the vehicle.

SPECIFICATIONS
Configuration: 4 × 4
Weight:
(empty) 1570 kg
(loaded) 2200 kg
Weight on front axle: (loaded) 820 kg
Weight on rear axle: (loaded) 750 kg
Max load: 630 kg
Length: 4·4 m
Width: 1·7 m
Height: (without armament) 1·5 m
Ground clearance: 0·285 m
Track: 1·34 m
Wheelbase: 2·1 m
Angle of approach/departure: 35°/32°
Max speed: (road) 90 km/h
Range: 330 km
Fuel capacity: 46 litres
Max gradient: 60%
Max side slope: 30%
Fording: 0·8 m

Volvo L3304 (4 × 4) reconnaissance vehicle showing universal-jointed steering column on left side

Engine: Volvo B18A 4-cylinder OHV petrol developing 68 bhp
Gearbox: Volvo M40 manual with 4 forward and 1 reverse gears
Clutch: single dry plate
Transfer box: 2-speed
Steering: ZF cam and roller
Turning radius: 5·7 m
Suspension: semi-elliptical leaf springs, progressive auxiliary rubber springs and double-acting hydraulic telescopic shock absorbers at each wheel station

Tyres: 8.90 × 16
Number of tyres: 4 + 1 spare
Brakes:
(main) hydraulic
(parking) mechanical
Electrical system: 12 V

STATUS
Production complete. In service with the Swedish Army.

MANUFACTURER
AB Volvo, Göteborg, Sweden.

Volvo L3314 (4 × 4) Laplander and Volvo C202 (4 × 4) Cross Country Vehicles

DEVELOPMENT
The first prototype of the Volvo Laplander L3314 vehicle was completed in 1961 with production beginning the following year. Over 10 000 Laplanders were built for delivery to some 40 countries before production was completed. Two basic versions of the Laplander were built, a pick-up (designated PU) and a hard-top (designated HT). Both are used by the Swedish Army, the PU being known as the Pltgbil 903 and the hard-top as the Pltgbil 903B. Further development of the Laplander resulted in the C202.

DESCRIPTION
Volvo L3314 (4 × 4) Laplander
The chassis of the Laplander consists of an all-welded box section frame of pressed and welded 3 mm sheet steel, two tubular cross-members, one box-section cross-member and one U-section cross-member.

Both models have an all-welded steel body with a forward control two-door fully enclosed cab with a heater and defroster. The hard top model has the same body as the pick-up but in addition has a fully enclosed hard top steel body built integrally with the cab containing six removable folding seats and a heater.

The vehicle is powered by a Volvo B18A four-cylinder petrol engine which develops 75 bhp (SAE) at 4500 rpm and is coupled to an M40 four-speed gearbox with four forward and one reverse gears. The transfer box has four gear positions: four-wheel drive in low ratio, neutral, four-wheel drive in high ratio and reverse drive in high ratio.

The suspension consists of semi-elliptical springs which have progressive springing with rubber bush type helper springs and double-acting telescopic hydraulic shock absorbers at each wheel station. Brakes are hydraulic with the parking brake operating on the propeller shaft.

Optional fittings include Rockinger type towing hook, hitch plate, PTO (centre and rear), speed governor for PTO and side-mounted winch with a capacity of 2100 kg which can be used to the front or rear of the vehicle. Variants in use with the Swedish Army include an ambulance, fire-fighting and radio vehicles.

Volvo C202 (4 × 4)
The C202 was also manufactured in Hungary by Csepel. The vehicle was offered in three basic versions, a pick-up, a fully enclosed hard top model and a canvas top model. The pick-up model has a fully enclosed two-door all steel cab and a single tailgate at the rear. The hard top model has five doors, two each side and one at the rear. At the rear are two foldable seats, and two foldable bench seats. All versions have a heater and defroster for the front cab and the hard top model also has a heater for the rear compartment. A wide range of specialised variants have been developed by Volvo including fire-fighting, ambulance, repair and rescue versions.

The C202 is powered by a Volvo B20A four-cylinder petrol engine which develops 82 bhp at 4700 rpm and is coupled to a manual Volvo M45 gearbox with four forward and one reverse gears. The transfer gearbox is a Volvo FD51 with high and low ratios. All wheel drive is engaged in the high range and automatically when low range is engaged.

Brakes are of the vacuum-hydraulic drum type. The parking brake is mechanical and operates off the propeller shaft. Suspension consists of semi-elliptical leaf springs, telescopic double acting shock absorbers, and hollow-rubber springs to soften bottoming from extreme spring deflection. Optional equipment included an air-conditioning system, canvas top, electric engine heater, fire extinguisher, PTO, sand tyres, snow tyres, spotlight, tyre inflation pump, tropical radiator and a winch with a capacity of 2000 kg.

Volvo Laplander (4 × 4) pick-up model with canvas top and side doors

Volvo C202 (4 × 4) canvas top model

Volvo C202 (4 × 4) with ambulance body

STATUS
The Volvo Laplander is no longer in production but remains in service with the Swedish Army. The Volvo C202 was manufactured in Hungary by Csepel.

MANUFACTURERS
AB Volvo, Göteborg, Sweden.
Csepel, Hungary.

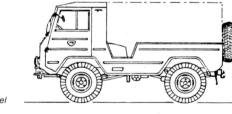
Volvo L3114 Laplander (4 × 4) pick-up model

SPECIFICATIONS
Model	Laplander PU	C202 Hard top	C202 PU
Cab seating	1 + 1	1 + 7	1 + 1
Configuration	4 × 4	4 × 4	4 × 4
Weight (empty)	1520 kg	1795 kg	1600 kg
(loaded)	2450 kg	2525 kg	2525 kg
Weight on front axle (empty)	935 kg	1020 kg	990 kg
Weight on rear axle (empty)	585 kg	775 kg	610 kg
Max load	900 kg	730 kg	925 kg
Towed load	1000 kg	1500 kg	1500 kg
Load area	2·3 × 1·535 m	2·27 × 1·4 m	2·27 × 1·53 m
Length	3·985 m	4·015 m	4·015 m
Width	1·66 m	1·68 m	1·68 m
Height	2·09 m	2·09 m	2·09 m
(load area)	0·665 m	0·665 m	0·665 m
Ground clearance	0·285 m	0·285 m	0·285 m
Track (front/rear)	1·338/1·338 m	1·348/1·338 m	1·348/1·338 m
Wheelbase	2·1 m	2·1 m	2·1 m
Angle of approach/departure	40°/40°	39°/48°	39°/48°
Max speed (road)	90 km/h	115 km/h	115 km/h
Range	330 km	330 km	330 km
Fuel capacity	46 litres	51 litres	51 litres
Max gradient	60%	65%	65%
Max side slope	40%	40%	40%
Fording	0·8 m	0·45 m	0·45 m
Steering	cam and roller	cam and roller	cam and roller
Turning radius	5·4 m	5·4 m	5·4 m
Tyres	8.90 × 16	8.90 × 16	8.90 × 16
Number of tyres	4 + 1 spare	4 + 1 spare	4 + 1 spare
Brakes (main)	hydraulic	hydraulic	hydraulic
(parking)	mechanical	mechanical	mechanical
Electrical system	12 V	12 V	12 V

SWITZERLAND

CROCO (4 × 4) 500 kg Light Vehicle

DESCRIPTION
The CROCO (cross-country) 500 kg light vehicle has been designed as a private venture by CROCO Limited and is suitable for a wide range of civil and military applications.

The vehicle consists of two units of tubular steel construction covered in 2 mm thick sheet steel and connected by a pivoting joint. Both units are rust-proofed and sealed for amphibious operations.

The front unit has seats for the driver and one passenger at the front and the engine compartment is at the rear. The cabin has a split windscreen, upper half hinged, roll-over bar and three-point safety belts, roll-back top, two seats with spring suspension, anti-theft lock blocking the transmission, toolbox integral with the instrument panel and full instrumentation. The steering wheel is detachable to reduce the overall height of the vehicle when being carried in an aircraft. The fuel system consists of three standard 20-litre metal containers, one of which is always engaged.

The rear half has a flat grooved floor panel with two integral luggage boxes each with a capacity of 22 litres. Its tube-like configuration allows it to carry up to 600 kg of cargo or four men on individual bucket type seats. Attachment points are provided for special superstructures to be fitted to the vehicle.

The vehicle is fitted with four low-pressure tyres with self-cleaning treads that have been specially designed for the vehicle. The basic CROCO is fully amphibious being propelled in the water by its wheels at a speed of 4 km/h; as an option a three-bladed propeller can be fitted at the rear driven by a PTO, in which case water speed is 8 km/h.

A feature of the CROCO is that it has been designed for ease of handling and once the appropriate gear is engaged all the driver has to do is to steer and operate the brake and accelerator pedals. The modular construction of the CROCO enables major components of the vehicle such as the engine, transmission, electrical system and even one half of the vehicle to be changed in the field in two hours.

Optional equipment includes propeller drive or outboard engine for amphibious operations, seats for rear unit, frame with folding top for rear section and remote radio control system to various standards.

VARIANTS
In addition to its being used as a personnel carrier, the manufacturers have suggested that the CROCO can be used for the following roles: ambulance, anti-tank vehicle with TOW ATGW system, communications/radio vehicle, fuel carrier, repair vehicle and weapons carrier. Bullet proof versions are available.

SPECIFICATIONS
Cab seating: 1 + 1 (front unit)
Configuration: 4 × 4
Weight:
  (empty) 900 kg
  (loaded) 1400 kg
Max load: 500 kg
Length: 2·7 m
Width: 2 m
Height:
  (hood) 1·95 m
  (roll-over bar) 1·5 m
  (load area) 0·95 m
Ground clearance: 0·28 m
Track: 1·65 m
Wheelbase: 1·62 m
Max speed:
  (1st gear) 25 km/h
  (2nd gear) 50 km/h
  (water, wheels) 4 km/h
  (water, propeller) 8 km/h
Range: 500 km
Fuel capacity: 60 litres
Max gradient: 100%
Fording: amphibious
Engine: CROCO single rotary (produced under licence from NSU-Wankel), single rotor, developing 32 bhp at 5500 rpm
Gearbox: belt driven torque converter, CROCO gearbox with 2 forward and 1 reverse gears. Worm gear differential trans axles with automatic locking device
Steering: rack and pinion with ball-jointed rods to all wheels
Turning radius: 4·6 m
Tyres: 31.00 × 15.50
Number of tyres: 4
Brakes:
  (main) mechanical, dual circuit, all wheels
  (parking) handbreak on gearbox

CROCO (4 × 4) 500 kg light vehicle

CROCO (4 × 4) 500 kg light vehicle

STATUS
In production at Karlsruhe, Federal Republic of Germany. License production planned in Malaysia.

MANUFACTURER
CROCO Limited, CH-8001 Zürich, Lowenstrasse 61 (Bahnhofplatz), Switzerland.

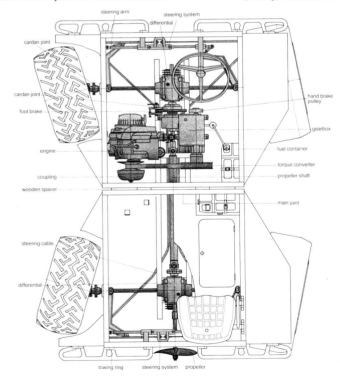

CROCO (4 × 4) 500 kg light vehicle

Main components of CROCO (4 × 4) 500 kg light vehicle

Saurer 232 M (4 × 4) 800 kg Light Vehicle Family

DEVELOPMENT
Saurer started the development of a new light vehicle family in the late 1970s with the first prototypes being completed in 1979. At the Geneva Commercial Vehicle Exhibition, held in January 1980, the F006 (4 × 4) 800 kg vehicle made its first public appearance (*Jane's Military Vehicles and Ground Support Equipment 1981*, page 658). Further development of the F006 resulted in the new family of vehicles which comprises the 232 M (canvas top), 260 M LWB (canvas top) and the 288 M LWB (pick-up), all of which share the same basic automotive components. This range of vehicles was evaluated by the Swiss Army.

DESCRIPTION
The basic 232 M is of conventional layout with the engine at the front, seats for the driver and one passenger in the centre and the load area at the rear. The load area is provided with a door that opens to the right on which the spare wheel is mounted. If required the load area can be fitted with bench seats down either side. Standard 80 × 120 cm pallets can be carried in the

rear. The windscreen does not fold down onto the bonnet. The one-piece side doors are provided with sliding windows. The top, sides and rear of the cargo area are supplied with a tarpaulin cover which has transparent panels in the sides and rear.

The body of the 232 M series is of glass fibre reinforced polyester which, as well as being corrosion resistant, can be built at low cost. The bonnet folds forward to give access to the engine, steering and front suspension for maintenance.

VARIANTS
No variants have been announced although the vehicles can be adapted for a wide range of roles such as ambulance, anti-tank vehicle with ATGW, command/radio vehicle, to name but a few.

STATUS
Development complete.

MANUFACTURER
Adolph Saurer Limited, 9320 Arbon, Switzerland.

Load compartment of Saurer 232 M (4 × 4) 800 kg light vehicle

SPECIFICATIONS

Model	232 M	260 M	288 M
Cab seating	1 + 1	1 + 1	1 + 1
Configuration	4 × 4	4 × 4	4 × 4
Weight (empty)	1600 kg	1630 kg	1720 kg
(loaded)	2400 kg	2500 kg	2650 kg
Max load	800 kg	870 kg	900 kg
Length	3·893 m	4·173 m	4·453 m
Width	1·748 m	1·748 m	1·748 m
Height	1·9 m	1·9 m	1·9 m
Overhang (front/rear)	739 mm/834 mm	739 mm/834 mm	739 mm/834 mm
Ground clearance	0·2 m	0·185 m	0·185 m
Wheelbase	2·32 m	2·6 m	2·88 m
Fuel capacity	70 litres	70 litres	70 litres
Engine	B 23 A, 4-cylinder 2·315 litre petrol developing 95 hp at 4700 rpm		
Gearbox	M45 manual, 4 forward and 1 reverse gears		
Clutch	single dry plate, mechanically operated		
Transfer box	FD 51, 2-speed	FD 51, 2-speed	FD 51, 2-speed
Turning radius	5 m	5·5 m	6 m
Tyres	20.5 × 16	20.5 × 16	20.5 × 16
Number of tyres	4 + 1 spare	4 + 1 spare	4 + 1 spare
Brakes (main, front)	disc	disc	disc
(main, rear)	drum	drum	drum
Electrical system	12 V	12 V	12 V

Saurer 232 M (4 × 4) 800 kg light vehicle from front

Saurer 232 M (4 × 4) 800 kg light vehicle from rear

UNION OF SOVIET SOCIALIST REPUBLICS

VAZ-2121 (4 × 4) 400 kg Light Vehicle

DESCRIPTION

The VAZ-2121 (4 × 4) 400 kg light vehicle is known on the civilian market as the Lada Niva and also has a military application. It has a fully enclosed all-steel body with the engine at the front, driver and passenger in the centre, each with a forward-opening side door and to the rear a bench seat which folds forward to provide cargo space.

In 1980 production of the Niva was running at some 25 000 vehicles a year.

SPECIFICATIONS
Cab seating: 1 + 1 (2 in rear)
Configuration: 4 × 4
Weight:
  (empty) 1150 kg
  (loaded) 1550 kg
Towed load:
  (with brakes) 1500 kg
  (without brakes) 300 kg

Max load: 400 kg
Length: 3·72 m
Width: 1·68 m
Height: 1·64 m
Ground clearance: 0·22 m
Track:
  (front) 1·43 m
  (rear) 1·44 m
Wheelbase: 2·2 m
Max road speed: 132 km/h
Acceleration:
  (0–60 km/h) 7·5 s
  (0–100 km/h) 23 s
Fuel capacity: 45 litres
Max range: 280 km
Gradient: 58%
Engine: 4-cylinder petrol developing 75 hp at 5400 rpm
Gearbox: manual, 4 forward and 1 reverse gears
Clutch: single dry plate
Transfer box: 2-speed
Turning radius: 5·8 m
Electrical system: 12 V

VAZ-2121 (4 × 4) 400 kg light vehicle

STATUS
Production.

MANUFACTURER
Volga Motor Vehicle Plant, Tolyatti, USSR.

LuAZ-967M Amphibious Battlefield Medical Evacuation Vehicle

DESCRIPTION

This vehicle was developed in the 1960s and was first seen during trials with Soviet troops based in East Germany in the late 1960s. The LuAZ-967M uses some components of the LuAZ-969 (4 × 4) light vehicle described in the following entry.

The body of the LuAZ-967M is made of all-welded steel with the engine at the front. The driver sits immediately behind the windscreen which folds forward to reduce the overall height. His seat is on the centre line of the vehicle and can be folded down so that he can drive lying flat. The steering column and steering wheel can also be lowered.

The LuAZ-967M has two folding seats for walking wounded as well as two stretchers, but its normal load is two patients plus the driver. It is fully amphibious being propelled in the water by its wheels. A treadway is carried on each side of the vehicle to help in crossing trenches and other obstacles. There is a winch with a capacity of 200 kg and 100 metres of cable mounted at the front of the vehicle.

SPECIFICATIONS
Seating: 1 + 2
Configuration: 4 × 4
Weight:
  (empty) 930 kg
  (loaded) 1350 kg
Max load: 420 kg
Max towed load: 300 kg
Length: 3·682 m
Width: 1·712 m

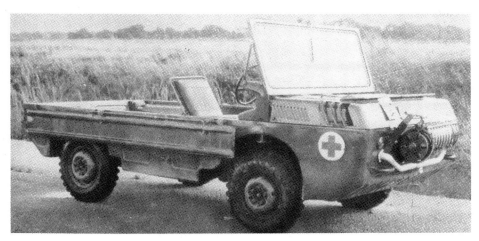

LuAZ-967M amphibious battlefield medical evacuation vehicle

Height: (including windscreen) 1·55 m
Ground clearance: 0·285 m
Angle of approach/departure: 34°/36°
Max road speed: 75 km/h
Max water speed: 5–6 km/h
Range: 411 km
Fuel capacity: 37 litres
Fuel consumption: 9 litres/100 km at 40 km/h
Gradient: 58%
Fording: amphibious
Engine: MeMZ-967A 4-cylinder air-cooled petrol developing 37 hp at 4200 rpm

Gearbox: manual, 4 forward and 1 reverse gears, plus cross-country gear
Turning radius: 5·8 m
Suspension: individual torsion bar
Electrical system: 12 V

STATUS
In service with East Germany and the Soviet Union. Production probably complete.

MANUFACTURER
Lutsk Motor Vehicle Plant, USSR.

LuAZ-969 (4 × 4) Light Vehicle

DEVELOPMENT/DESCRIPTION

In 1965 the Zaporozhe Motor Vehicle Plant developed a 250 kg vehicle, based on the ZAZ-966 passenger car, called the ZAZ-969, but it was not placed in production. In the late 1960s the project was transferred to the Lutsk Machine Building Plant and the designation was changed from the ZAZ-969 to the LuMZ-969. Production finally began in 1972 under the designation LuAZ-969 as the plant name was changed from the Lutsk Machine Building Plant to the Lutsk Motor Vehicle Plant. The vehicle is intended primarily for civilian use although it has an obvious military application.

The chassis of the LuAZ-969 light vehicle is also used as the basis for the LuAZ-967M amphibious battlefield medical evacuation vehicle described in the previous entry.

The vehicle has an all-steel body with the engine at the front and the crew compartment at the rear with two side doors, a windscreen which can be folded forward onto the bonnet and a removable canvas top. The driver can select either 4 × 4 or 4 × 2 drive, in which case the rear instead of the front axle is disengaged. A winch with a capacity of 200 kg and 100 metres of cable can be fitted.

The latest model is the LuAZ-969M. This is powered by an engine which develops 40 hp at 4200 rpm giving the vehicle a maximum road speed of 85 km/h. Empty weight is 970 kg, overall length is 3·37 metres and width is 1·64 metres.

STATUS
Production.

MANUFACTURER
Lutsk Motor Vehicle Plant, Ukraine, USSR.

SPECIFICATIONS
(LuAZ-969)
Cab seating: 1 + 1
Configuration: 4 × 4
Weight:
  (empty) 820 kg
  (loaded) 1200 kg
Weight on front axle: (empty) 510 kg
Weight on rear axle: (empty) 310 kg
Towed load: 300 kg
Length: 3·2 m
Width: 1·6 m
Height: 1·77 m
Ground clearance: 0·3 m
Track: 1·32 m
Wheelbase: 1·8 m
Max speed: 75 km/h
Range: 400 km
Fuel capacity: 32 litres
Fuel consumption: 8 litres/100 km
Gradient: 58%
Turning radius: 3 m
Fording: 0·45 m

LuAZ-969M (4 × 4) light vehicle

Engine: MeMZ-946 V-4 air-cooled petrol developing 27 hp at 4000 rpm
Gearbox: manual with 4 forward and 1 reverse gears
Transfer box: 2-speed
Suspension: torsion bar
Tyres: 5.90 × 13
Brakes:
  (main) hydraulic
  (parking) mechanical
Electrical system: 12 V

UAZ-469B (4 × 4) 600 kg Light Vehicle

DEVELOPMENT
For many years the standard Jeep-type vehicle of the Soviet Army had been the UAZ-69 (or GAZ-69), but for a number of reasons it has never been considered a satisfactory design. In 1960 a new 4 × 4 light vehicle called the UAZ-460B was tested. This used many components of the UAZ-450 truck, but was not placed in production. Further development of this vehicle resulted in the UAZ-469B which began production late in 1972 and entered service with the Soviet Army the following year. The UAZ-469B uses many components, including the axles, brakes, engine, transmission and parts of the chassis of the UAZ-452 series of 4 × 4 light vehicles.

DESCRIPTION
The basic vehicle has an all-steel body with the engine at the front and the four door crew compartment towards the rear, with a removable canvas top, and windscreen that can be folded down flat against the bonnet. The tops of the doors can also be removed. There are two individual seats at the front, a three-man seat in the centre and two men can sit facing each other at the rear. Normal load is two men plus 600 kg of cargo or seven men and 100 kg of cargo. A hard top can be fitted if required.

In 1973 the UAZ-469 was shown. This has a number of improvements including a portal axle which gives the vehicle both a higher ground clearance (300 mm) and improved cross-country capability, but the engine is identical to that in the standard UAZ-469B.

The vehicle is sold in the West as the Tundra.

VARIANTS
Variants include the UAZ-469BG ambulance which can carry a driver and four patients, van type vehicles and a special version for dispensing lane marking pennants into the ground (see *NBC Detection* section).

SPECIFICATIONS
Cab seating: 1 + 6
Configuration: 4 × 4
Weight:
  (empty) 1540 kg
  (loaded) 2290 kg
Weight on front axle: (loaded) 1000 kg
Weight on rear axle: (loaded) 1400 kg
Max load: 600 kg
Max towed load:
  (unbraked) 600 kg
  (braked) 2000 kg
Length: 4·025 m
Width: 1·785 m
Height: 2·015 m
Ground clearance: 0·22 m
Track: 1·422 m
Wheelbase: 2·38 m
Angle of approach/departure: 52°/42°
Max speed: 100 km/h
Range: 750 km
Fuel capacity: 78 litres
Fuel consumption:
  (road) 10·6 litres/100 km
  (dirt road) 28 litres/100 km
  (cross country) 39 litres/100 km
Max gradient: 62%
  (towing trailer) 40%
Vertical obstacle: 0·45 m
Fording: 0·7 m
Engine: ZMZ-451M 4-cylinder water-cooled petrol developing 75 hp at 4000 rpm
Gearbox: manual with 4 forward and 1 reverse gears
Transfer box: 2-speed
Turning radius: 6·5 m
Tyres: 8.40 × 15
Number of tyres: 4 + 1 spare

Brakes:
  (main) hydraulic
  (parking) mechanical
Electrical system: 12 V

STATUS
In production. In service with members of the Warsaw Pact including East Germany, Hungary, Poland and the Soviet Union. Also exported to other countries including Iran, Iraq and Syria.

MANUFACTURER
Ul'yanovsk Motor Vehicle Plant, Ul'yanovsk, USSR.

UAZ-469B (4 × 4) 600 kg light vehicle with hood raised

UAZ-469B (4 × 4) 600 kg light vehicles of Hungarian Army

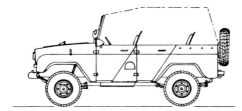

UAZ-469B (4 × 4) 600 kg light vehicle

GAZ-69 and GAZ-69A (4 × 4) Light Vehicles

DESCRIPTION
The GAZ-69 series of light 4 × 4 vehicles entered production at the Gor'kiy Plant in 1952 and continued in production at this plant until 1956 when production was transferred to the Ul'yanovsk Plant. They were then also known as the UAZ-69 and UAZ-69A and production continued until the UAZ-469B was introduced. These vehicles use many components of the UAZ-450 range of civilian vehicles.

There are two basic models in service, the GAZ-69 and the GAZ-69A. The former has two doors and has been designed to carry 500 kg of cargo. Bench seats down each side in the rear seat two men on each side facing each other. The spare wheel is mounted externally on the left side of the body. This model is widely used as a command/radio vehicle and for towing recoilless rifles and light anti-aircraft guns such as the 23 mm ZU-23. The second model is the GAZ-69A, which has four doors and can carry five men plus 100 kg of cargo. The spare wheel is carried under the rear of the vehicle. Both models have a removable top, windscreen that can be folded forward onto the bonnet and removable door tops.

Late production models of the UAZ-69 are the UAZ-69M which has a 65 hp M-21 engine, and the UAZ-69-68. Late production models of the UAZ-69A are the UAZ-69AM which also has a 65 hp engine and the UAZ-69A-68.

VARIANTS
Anti-tank (missile)
This is armed with four Snapper anti-tank missiles mounted at the back facing the rear. When travelling they are covered by a tarpaulin cover, which is folded downwards when they are deployed. These missiles can be launched from within the vehicle, an observation window being provided on the right side of the cab rear for this purpose, or away from the vehicle with the aid of a separation sight and controller. This version is no longer widely deployed by the Warsaw Pact but is still used by countries in the Middle East and Yugoslavia.

Anti-tank (recoilless rifle)
Some countries in the Middle East have mounted a recoilless rifle in the rear of the vehicle.

Aircraft starter
This is the GAZ-69 with a modified rear on which is mounted an aircraft starting unit.

Amphibious vehicle
This is designated the MAV or GAZ-46 and there is a separate entry for it in the *Amphibians* section.

Mine detector vehicle
The GAZ-69 is widely used fitted with the DIM mine detection system and there is a separate entry for it in the *Mine detection equipment* section.

Democratic People's Republic of Korea
North Korea has built a version of the GAZ-69A (4 × 4) vehicle with a new front.

Romania
Romania has built this vehicle under the designation M-461. This is almost identical to the Soviet model but has a four-speed gearbox.

UAZ-456
This is a tractor version for towing semi-trailers.

SPECIFICATIONS

Model	GAZ-69	GAZ-69A
Configuration	4 × 4	4 × 4
Weight (empty)	1525 kg	1535 kg
(loaded)	2175 kg	1960 kg
Weight on front axle		
(loaded)	940 kg	935 kg
Weight on rear axle		
(loaded)	1235 kg	1035 kg
Max load	500 kg	5 men
		+ 100 kg
Towed load	850 kg	850 kg
Length	3·85 m	3·85 m
Width	1·85 m	1·75 m
Height	2·03 m	1·92 m
Ground clearance	0·21 m	0·21 m
Track	1·44 m	1·44 m
Wheelbase	2·3 m	2·3 m
Angle of approach/		
departure	45°/35°	45°/35°
Max speed	90 km/h	90 km/h
Range	530 km	420 km
Fuel capacity	75 litres	60 litres
Fuel consumption	14 litres/100 km at 40 km/h	
Max gradient	60%	60%
Fording	0·55 m	0·55 m
Engine	M-20 4-cylinder water-cooled petrol developing 52 hp at 3600 rpm	
Gearbox	manual with 3 forward and 1 reverse gears	
Clutch	single disc, dry	single disc, dry
Transfer box	2-speed	2-speed
Steering	globoid worm with double collared cone	
Turning radius	6 m	6·5 m
Suspension	longitudinal semi-elliptical springs with double acting hydraulic shock absorbers front and rear	
Tyres	6.50 × 16	6.50 × 16
Number of tyres	4 + 1 spare	4 + 1 spare
Brakes (main)	hydraulic on all wheels	
(parking)	on transmission	
Electrical system	12 V	12 V
Battery	1 × 6 V	1 × 6 V
	ST 54	ST 54
Generator	250 W	250 W

STATUS
Production complete. In service with members of the Warsaw Pact and most countries that have received Soviet aid: for example Cuba, Egypt, Finland, Syria and Viet-Nam.

GAZ-69 armed with Snapper ATGWs

GAZ-69 armed with Snapper ATGWs

MANUFACTURER
Gor'kiy Motor Vehicle Plant, Gor'kiy, USSR (1952 to 1956) and Ul'yanovsk Motor Vehicle Plant, Ul'yanovsk (from 1956 onwards).

GAZ-69 (4 × 4) 500 kg light vehicle

GAZ-69 (4 × 4) 500 kg light vehicle

GAZ-69 (4 × 4) 500 kg light vehicle

UAZ-452D (4 × 4) 800 kg Light Vehicle

DESCRIPTION
The UAZ-452D (4 × 4) light vehicle entered production at the Ul'yanovsk Motor Vehicle Plant in 1966. Although used primarily for civilian applications, the vehicle and its variants are used in some numbers by the Soviet forces, especially the ambulance models.

The UAZ-452D has a two door all steel forward control type cab. The rear cargo area has drop sides and a drop tailgate.

VARIANTS
Variants of the vehicle are the UAZ-452 (van), UAZ-452A (ambulance carrying three seated patients plus three stretcher patients), UAZ-452P (tractor truck), UAZ-452E (with shielded electrical system), UAZ-452DE (with shielded electrical system) and the UAZ-452V (ten seater bus).

The vehicle was preceded by the UAZ-450 series of 4 × 4 vehicles which were in production from 1958 to 1966 and included the UAZ-450 (van), UAZ-450A (ambulance), UAZ-450B (bus) and the UAZ-450D (cargo truck). These were all powered by a 65 hp four-cylinder petrol engine and had a gearbox with three forward and one reverse gears and a two-speed transfer case.

In 1962 a series of similar 4 × 2 vehicles, the UAZ-451 (van) and the UAZ-451D (cargo), entered production. These were replaced by the improved UAZ-451M in 1966. The UAZ-451DM is also a 4 × 2 vehicle which can carry 1000 kg of cargo.

UAZ-450 (4 × 4) van which preceded the UAZ-452 series

SPECIFICATIONS
(UAZ-452D cargo truck)
Cab seating: 1 + 1
Weight:
  (empty) 1670 kg
  (loaded) 2620 kg
Weight on front axle: (loaded) 1190 kg
Weight on rear axle: (loaded) 1143 kg
Max load: 800 kg
Towed load: 850 kg
Load area: 2·6 × 1·87 m
Length: 4·46 m
Width: 2·004 m
Height:
  (cab) 2·07 m
  (load area) 1·04 m
Ground clearance: 0·22 m

Track: 1·442 m
Wheelbase: 2·3 m
Angle of approach/departure: 34°/33°
Max speed: 95 km/h
Range: 430 km
Fuel capacity: 56 litres
Fuel consumption: 13 litres/100 km
Gradient: 58%
Fording: 0·7 m
Engine: ZMZ-451E 4-cylinder water-cooled petrol developing 72 hp at 4000 rpm
Gearbox: manual with 4 forward and 1 reverse gears
Clutch: single dry disc
Transfer box: 2-speed
Turning radius: 6 m

Suspension: longitudinal semi-elliptical springs with hydraulic double acting shock absorbers on both axles
Tyres: 8.40 × 15
Brakes:
  (main) hydraulic
  (parking) mechanical
Electrical system: 12 V
Battery: 1 × STE-54EM
Generator: 250 W

STATUS
In production. In service with members of the Warsaw Pact.

MANUFACTURER
Ul'yanovsk Motor Vehicle Plant, Ul'yanovsk, USSR.

UNITED KINGDOM

Crayford Cargocat (8 × 8) Light Vehicle

DEVELOPMENT
The Cargocat was developed by Crayford in the late 1960s and has since been adopted for a wide variety of civil and military applications. It is available in both 8 × 8 and 6 × 6 configurations and under development is a 4 × 4 model with conventional front wheel steering rather than the skid steering used on the earlier vehicles.

DESCRIPTION
The chassis consists of welded steel channels with the body itself in two halves (upper and lower) riveted

together on a central steel surround with four steel handles for the manual movement of the vehicle.

The engine is mounted at the front with the commander and driver seated on a two-man bench seat in the centre. The cargo area is at the rear with a bench type seat down each side of the hull. Suspension is provided by the balloon type tyres. Engine power is delivered by a torque converter similar to the DAF type, with two variable drive pulleys and a transmission belt. Drive is then taken through a gearbox with two forward and one reverse speeds to a differential assembly with two output shafts, one to the left and one to the right of the vehicle. These output shafts have disc brakes fitted to them. When the right lever is pulled back the calliper operates on the right disc slowing it down, leaving a differential drive through on the left, enabling the

machine to turn right on a skid-steer system similar to that used on armoured vehicles.

Vehicles being used in the desert are equipped with a special bonnet with additional air cooling ducts on the right-hand side of the vehicle and an electric extractor fan can also be installed if required.

A wide range of optional equipment is available for the vehicle including hand swivel spot lamp, hood with frame, fire extinguisher, front-mounted electric winch, road trailer, snow tracks, spare wheel, sump shield, outboard motor (15 hp), and a windscreen wiper.

VARIANTS
The basic vehicle can be adapted to mount a variety of military equipment including radars, radios, recoilless rifles and light machine guns. British Aerospace Dynam-

Crayford Cargocat (8 × 8) fitted with front-mounted winch

Crayford Cargocat (8 × 8) showing bench seats to rear

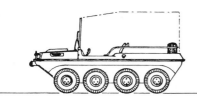

Crayford Cargocat (8 × 8) light vehicle

ics has mounted a pallet with four Swingfire ATGWs on the rear of the Cargocat. The missiles are launched away from the vehicle with the aid of a separate sight and cable. Firing trials with this installation have already been carried out.

Marconi Space and Defence Systems Limited have used the Cargocat as the basis for the Remotely-Controlled Agile Target (or RECAT), used for gunnery and guided missile training. It can have manual, on-board, pre-programming, ground wire following or long-range radio control.

A special model called the Long Range Desert Patrol has also been developed, which normally has a more powerful engine, winch and long-range 60- or 90-litre capacity fuel tanks.

SPECIFICATIONS
Seating: 1 + 1
Configuration: 8 × 8
Length: 3·05 m
Width: 1·475 m
Height:
(without hood) 0·965 m
(with hood) 1·73 m
Track: 1·1 m
Wheelbase: 0·61 m + 0·61 m + 0·61 m

Max speed:
(road) 25 km/h
(water) 5 km/h
Range: 8 h
Fuel capacity: 32 litres
Max gradient: 100%
Engine: air-cooled twin-cylinder 4-stroke or single cylinder 4-stroke with 17 and 16 bhp respectively
Gearbox: planetary differential gear system (high, low, neutral and reverse) with a differential transmission
Battery: 40 or 80 Ah according to mission requirements

STATUS
Production. In service with undisclosed armed forces, particularly in the Middle East.

MANUFACTURER
Crayford Special Equipment Company Limited, High Street, Westerham, Kent, England.

Saboteur Trooper (8 × 8) Light Vehicle

DEVELOPMENT
In February 1977 the British Aircraft Corporation (now British Aerospace), awarded a contract to Somerton Rayner Vehicles (subsequently renamed the Saboteur Vehicle Company Limited) for the development of an all-terrain mobile platform light enough to be carried under a Lynx or Bell UH-1D series helicopter. The vehicle was required to carry a launcher with four Swingfire ATGWs and a crew of two, be capable of a maximum road speed of 56 km/h, have good cross-country mobility and be amphibious.

The first two prototypes were completed late in 1977 and delivered to British Aerospace Dynamics for the installation of a launcher with four missiles in the ready-to-launch position in the centre of the vehicle with the missiles being launched away from the vehicle with the aid of a separation sight and controller.

Early in 1978 a further two vehicles were built, one for evaluation at the Military Vehicles and Engineering Establishment and the second for the Marconi Company for use as a Radio-Controlled Agile Target (RECAT). The latter system was fully described in *Jane's Armour and Artillery 1979–80*, page 617. Further development of this concept has now been taken over by Flight Refuelling Limited.

By January 1980 over 40 vehicles had been produced for Middle East, European and British customers, both civilian and military, with production continuing at the rate of two vehicles a week to meet a 100-vehicle contract for a United Kingdom civilian order.

The initial vehicle was followed by the Terranger and, in 1981, the redesigned Trooper replaced the earlier vehicles in production and has been evaluated by a number of military authorities in various parts of the world. Two vehicles have been on trials in the Falkland Islands, and a version with larger tyres to decrease ground pressure is under construction.

The Trooper can be used for a variety of roles including ambulance, reconnaissance, command, radio and logistic support with the military as well as various civilian applications.

DESCRIPTION
The driver and two passengers are seated at the very front of the vehicle with the troop/cargo area in the centre and the engine at the rear. The chassis consists of two fabricated box sections in N8 marine grade aluminium 6 mm gauge plate welded to two cross-members of identical construction. The side members carry the stub axles and enclose the drive system in an oil bath. Welded to the rear of the side members are the drop gear boxes which also form an oil bath. Onto the cross-members are welded the engine support plates, seat, controls, other fittings and the lifting lugs.

The body is constructed of marine quality aluminium to NS8 and is of various gauges ranging from 12 to 20 depending on the position with strengthening being added in critical areas.

Heavy duty ball bearings are used for the axles and are common throughout and are carried in bearing housings bolted to the chassis for ease of replacement and general maintenance.

The engine driven hydraulic swash plate pumps drive two bent axis motors, one to each side of the vehicle, which in turn drive the master axle via drop gears. The master axle drives the three slave axles (eg first, second and third) via a Triplex roller chain stressed to 6804 kg.

Steering is controlled by a patent "Bell" system of twist grips controlling the speed and torque output of the hydraulic pumps. This varies the speed differentially to

Saboteur Trooper (8 × 8) light vehicle with Euromissile MILAN ATGW mounting (T J Gander)

the drive on each side of the vehicle. With the length/width ratio of 1 to 4 a well trained driver can carry out turns within the flexible limit of the tyre side wall and avoid scuffing the tyre. Emergency neutral turns are possible with the system but with increased tyre wear.

The Trooper is fully amphibious being propelled in the water by a single three bladed 330 mm propeller under the rear of the hull. It has hydraulic gear pumps drive and a hydraulic motor with a 1·8/1 reduction to the propeller shaft. Speed when afloat is controlled by engine speed. Only engage and disengage control is fitted with no reverse, the latter being achieved by disengaging the propeller and rotating the road wheels in reverse. Steering in water is by a rudder controlled by a tiller mounted to the side of the driver.

Optional equipment includes a fully enclosed cab, tracks for improved traction across snow, Volkswagen six-cylinder diesel engine developing 77 hp, 24-volt electrical system and a 109-litre long range fuel tank. Design studies have also been carried out to incorporate Ford and other engines in the 65 to 78 hp ranges.

VARIANTS
Anti-tank
The Trooper can be fitted with a Hughes TOW ATGW system and four missiles or a Euromissile MILAN ATGW system and nine missiles, each of these would have a three man crew and the MILAN version has been tested by the British Army.

SPECIFICATIONS
Seating: 3 + 6
Configuration: 8 × 8
Weight:
(empty) 900 kg
(loaded) 1807 kg
Max load: 907 kg
Load area: 1·12 × 1·17 m
Length: 4 m
Width: 1·18 m
Height: (overall) 1·15 m
Ground clearance: 0·36 m
Track: 1·7 m
Wheelbase: 2·64 m

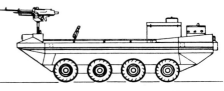

Saboteur Trooper (8 × 8) light vehicle with 7·62 mm GPMG mounting

Angle of approach/departure: 45°/45°
Max speed:
(road) 56 km/h
(water) 6·4 km/h
Range: 241 km
Fuel capacity: 55 litres
Max gradient: 60%
Max side slope: 60%
Fording: amphibious
Engine: Volkswagen 127 air-cooled petrol developing 73 hp at 3600 rpm
Gearbox: chain drive on all eight wheels, Linde hydraulic motor driving number 4 axle
Suspension: none, tyres absorb shock
Ground pressure: 0·206 bar/0·344 bar
Tyres: 21.00 × 11.00 × 8 NHS
Number of tyres: 8
Brakes/steering: by levers varying position of swash plate in hydraulic pumps
Electrical system: 12 V
Battery: 1 × 12 V
Temperature range: −15° to +35° C in standard configuration

STATUS
In production. Ordered by Nigeria (100). In service in Iraq.

MANUFACTURER
Saboteur Vehicle Company Limited, Quarley, Near Andover, Hamphire, England.

Transcraft Model 1600PL Privateer Light Vehicle

DEVELOPMENT
The first Transcraft Privateer 6 × 6 light vehicle was produced in 1972 and gradual development led to the evolution of an 8 × 8 vehicle. The first Model 1600PL was produced during late 1980 but since then this model has undergone continuous testing and modification until it is now in production. It has been sold to the Ministry of Defence.

DESCRIPTION
The main body assembly is made in two sections with the lower section housing the chassis and the upper section comprising the engine, bonnet and the flat sides for load carrying. Front and rear wells protect the chassis and moving parts and the bonnet cover can be removed for access to the engine. The body is made from colour-impregnated reinforced glass fibre. The chassis is steel and carries the engine, transmission, transmission drives, axles and axle drives. The engine is mounted forward on a four-point suspension on rubber mountings. A belt couples the engine to the hydrostat drive and there are two hydrostats, one to each side. From the hydrostats drive to the axles is through a series of chains and sprockets to provide a full 8 × 8 drive. All axles are sealed for amphibious operations. The hydrostat drive is also used for braking and the vehicle can turn around in its own length. Only one seat is normally fitted. Extras include a windscreen, cabin, roll bar a passenger seat and a towing hitch.

SPECIFICATIONS
Seating: 1 + 1 (passenger seat optional)
Configuration: 8 × 8
Weight:
(empty) 680 kg
(loaded) 1361 kg
Max load: 725 kg
Length: 2·743 m
Width: 1·753 m

Transcraft Model 1600PL Privateer light vehicle

Height:
(without cab) 1·041 m
(with cab) 1·83 m
Ground clearance: 0·203 m
Max speed: (land) 26 km/h
Fuel capacity: 18·9 litres
Gradient: 40%
Engine: Reliant 848 cc water-cooled 4-cylinder petrol developing 40 bhp at 4000 rpm
Transmission: hydrostat
Braking: hydrostatic controlled

Tyres: 21 × 10 ATV
Electrical system: 12 V

STATUS
Production.

MANUFACTURER
Transcraft Limited, Unit 10, Holton Heath Trading Park, Poole, Dorset BH16 6LG, England.
Sales Office: Transcraft Limited, Telford Way, Thetford, Norfolk, England.

Land-Rover (4 × 4) 564 kg Airportable Light Vehicle

DEVELOPMENT
This vehicle was designed and developed by Rover in conjunction with the Military Vehicles and Engineering Establishment to meet the special airportable requirements of the British Army, Royal Air Force and Royal Marines. It was shown for the first time at the Commercial Motor Show at Earls Court in September 1968. The vehicle is now the standard 4 × 4 in its class in the British forces. The engine, transmission, axles, suspension and brakes are from the commercial 88-inch Land-Rover modified for military use.

DESCRIPTION
The layout of the vehicle is similar to other Land-Rovers with the engine at the front, driver and two passengers in the centre and cargo area at the rear with a drop tailgate and a bench seat down either side.

The main feature of this vehicle is that the hood, body sides, doors, windscreen, bumpers and spare wheel can easily be removed to facilitate transport by aircraft or helicopter.

The basic model has a 12-volt electrical system but a 24-volt fitted-for-radio version is available with the two batteries installed between the front seats in place of the third seat in the 12-volt model. This model features a unitary radio kit containing radio, batteries, operator's

Netherlands Army airportable (4 × 4) 564 kg Land-Rover (T J Gander)

Airportable (4 × 4) 564 kg Land-Rover towing ¼-ton trailer (T J Gander)

Airportable (4 × 4) 564 kg Land-Rover fitted with radio as Royal Artillery battery command vehicle (T J Gander)

seat and radio mounting equipment installed in the rear of the vehicle.

VARIANTS
Land-Rover has developed special models of the ½-ton Land-Rover to meet specific overseas requirements, a vehicle developed for the Netherlands Army with a diesel engine (56 bhp at 4000 rpm) and 24-volt 60-amp electrical system, being typical.
Ambulance: can carry two stretchers in an emergency.
Anti-tank: to meet the requirements of a foreign army, in November 1976 Marshall of Cambridge designed a 106 mm Land-Rover gun vehicle which entered service the following year. This is the standard vehicle modified to mount a 106 mm M40 recoilless rifle in the rear of the vehicle. The design permits an arc of fire of 180 degrees forwards. Seats for the crew of the weapon and stowage of 106 mm and 0·50 ranging machine gun ammunition are provided. A blast shield is fitted to the bonnet and a barrel clamp is fitted to the dashboard. Known users of this model include Saudi Arabia and Sudan. A prototype of the airportable Land-Rover with a 120 mm Wombat recoilless anti-tank weapon was built.

SPECIFICATIONS
Cab seating: 1 + 2
Configuration: 4 × 4
Weight:
(empty) 1386 kg
(stripped down) 1206 kg
(loaded) 2020 kg
Max load: 564 kg
Towed load: 1130 kg
Load area: 1·14 × 1·4 m
Length: 3·65 m
Width: 1·52 m
Height:
(overall) 1·95 m
(reduced) 1·47 m
(load area) 0·71 m
Ground clearance: 0·21 m

Land-Rover (4 × 4) 564 kg airportable light vehicle

Track: 1·31 m
Wheelbase: 2·23 m
Angle of approach/departure: 49°/36° (58°/38° in stripped down form)
Max speed: (road) 105 km/h
Range: 600 km
Fuel capacity: 90 litres
Max gradient:
(high) 39%
(low) 115%
Fording: 0·5 m (with preparation)
Engine: 4-cylinder 2·286-litre in-line OHV petrol developing 70 bhp at 4000 rpm or 4-cylinder 2·286-litre in-line diesel developing 60 bhp at 4000 rpm
Gearbox: manual with 4 forward and 1 reverse gears
Clutch: single dry plate
Transfer box: 2-speed
Steering: recirculating ball
Turning radius: 6·4 m
Suspension: semi-elliptical springs with hydraulic shock absorbers
Tyres: 6.50 × 16 or 7.50 × 16
Number of tyres: 4 + 1 spare
Brakes:
(main) drum, hydraulic oval line, servo assisted
(parking) drum, mechanical on transmission
Electrical system: 12 V (24 V optional)
Battery: 1 × 12 V

Belgian Army airportable (4 × 4) 564 kg Land-Rovers
(R Zwart)

STATUS
In production. In service with Belgium, Brunei, Guyana, Hong Kong, Jamaica, Libya, the Netherlands (24 V and a diesel engine), Saudi Arabia, Sudan and the United Kingdom.

MANUFACTURER
Land-Rover Limited, Military Products, Lode Lane, Solihull, West Midlands B92 8NW, England.

Land-Rover (4 × 4) Vehicles

DEVELOPMENT
After the end of the Second World War the British Government was compelled to ration steel to the motor industry in proportion to the value of its exports. This created serious difficulties for the Rover company since its luxury cars were not proving to be exportable. It became obvious that the company would have to produce something which would have a world appeal and be outside the luxury class, a working vehicle which would attract buyers from agricultural and industrial markets of the world.
Early in 1947 a decision was made to build a new all purpose cross country vehicle and by late 1947 prototypes of a 4 × 4 vehicle suitable for both agricultural and industrial applications had been built. Trials proved the concept and Rover first introduced the Land-Rover at the Amsterdam Motor Show in April 1948. Quantity production began at Solihull in July 1948. The first model had an 80-inch (2·032 m) wheelbase and was powered by a 1·6-litre petrol engine, which used many components, including the engine, of the Rover P3 '60' car. The basic model was fitted with a canvas hood and was followed late in 1948 by a fully enclosed estate model which could seat six plus the driver. The British Government placed its first order for the Land-Rover in 1949.
By 1950 over 24 000 Land-Rovers had been built and in 1952 the 1·6-litre petrol engine was replaced by a 2-litre petrol engine. In 1954 the original 80-inch

(2·032 m) wheelbase model was replaced in production by an 86-inch (2·184 m) model. In the same year the first long wheelbase model with a wheelbase of 107 inches (2·717 m) and which could carry 750 kg of cargo, was introduced.
In 1956 the 86-inch (2·184 m) model gave way to the 88-inch (2·23 m) and the 107-inch (2·717 m) was replaced by the 109-inch (2·768 m) model. The same year the British Army adopted the Land-Rover as its standard ¼-ton (4 × 4) vehicle. In 1957 Land-Rover offered a diesel engine in place of the standard petrol engine.
In February 1958 the Series II Land-Rover was introduced in both 88-inch (2·23 m) and 107-inch (2·717 m) configurations with a 2¼-litre petrol engine. Late in 1958 production of the 107-inch (2·717 m) was discontinued.
In 1959 the Land-Rover was adopted by the Australian Army followed by the Swiss Army the next year.
In September 1961 the Series IIA was introduced and the 2¼-litre engine replaced the 2-litre engine and in 1962 the 109-inch (2·768 m) 12-seater station wagon and a new 1000 kg forward control Land-Rover were introduced.
By April 1966 half a million Land-Rovers had been completed and late in 1966 a 110-inch (2·794 m) model of the forward control Land-Rover was introduced, powered by a six-cylinder petrol engine and capable of carrying 1500 kg of cargo.
From early 1967 a 2·6-litre six-cylinder petrol engine was offered for the 109-inch (2·768 m) Land-Rover.

This was subsequently deleted in 1980 with the introduction of the 3·5 litre V-8 version.
Early in 1968, to comply with new legal requirements governing vehicle lighting in the Netherlands, Belgium and Luxembourg, a new headlight modification was made and for the first time the headlights were incorporated in the wings instead of the grille panel.
In September 1968 two new Land-Rovers specifically for military use were introduced, the ½-ton and 1000 kg, for which there are separate entries in this section. In 1970 the Range Rover, for which there is a separate entry in this section, was introduced.
By July 1971 half a million Land-Rovers for export had been completed. The following year production of the forward control model ceased.
In October 1971 the Series III Land-Rover was introduced with a restyled grille, redesigned safety facia, improved gearbox and other detailed modifications.
The millionth Land-Rover was completed in June 1976 and in early 1979 production of the standard Land-Rover was running at 1600 units a week, increased to 2700 units a week by 1981. Further expansion is expected to increase production to 3200 units a week. About 70 per cent of Land-Rovers are exported and according to Land-Rover, Viet-Nam is the only country not to have ordered the vehicle.
In 1979 Land-Rover Limited, a new and autonomous company was formed to manufacture, develop and market Land-Rovers and Range Rovers.
In March 1982, a 'High Capacity' version of the 109-inch long wheelbase vehicle was introduced which

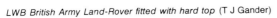

LWB British Army Land-Rover fitted with hard top (T J Gander)

Belgian-built Minerva Land-Rover (T J Gander)

LWB British Army Land-Rover with Decca Radar No. 17 Mark 1 (Mobile)

Land-Rover with Bofors RBS 70 anti-aircraft missile. This combination is known as the RBS 70 VLM system

Long wheelbase Land-Rover with V-8 engine for New Zealand Army

Standard long wheelbase Land-Rover FFR of British Army (T J Gander)

Belgian Army Land-Rover (T J Gander)

Australian Army Land-Rover fitted for radio (FFR) (P Handel)

is available in both full length hood and pick-up forms and in both cases provides greater passenger or cargo carrying ability than the standard body and is available in both 12-volt and 24-volt configurations. In its standard form the High Capacity 109-inch has a gross vehicle weight of 3020 kg and a payload of up to 1450 kg, or seating for up to 13 including the driver.

In July 1982 it was announced that Land-Rover Limited and Perkins Engines were jointly developing a diesel engine version of the 3·5-litre V-8 petrol engine used in Land-Rovers and Range Rovers.

DESCRIPTION
88-inch (2·23 m)
No 88-inch military model is now offered as it was replaced by the ½-ton airportable vehicle, but quantities of the civilian version are still sold for a military application.

The Land-Rover has an all-welded box section ladder type chassis. The body is of aluminium panels with the

steel bumpers, cappings and other vital components galvanised. The layout is conventional with the engine at the front, driver and two passengers in the centre and the cargo area at the rear with a drop tailgate. The basic model has a galvanised steel hood frame and a full length hood.

Optional equipment for the standard and the long wheelbase model includes a front-mounted 2270 kg capacity mechanical drum winch controlled from the driver's seat, capstan winch with a 1360 kg capacity, overdrive, rubber helper springs, lamp guards and a fire extinguisher.

Land-Rover has developed special models of the 88-inch (2·23 m) Land-Rover to meet special overseas requirements. The Danish Army in 1977 ordered a version based on the commercial model with a 2¼-litre diesel engine, and a 12-volt and supplementary 24-volt electrical system which entered service in 1978. Many armies have adapted the vehicle to their own specific requirements, for example the Australians had some

armed with a 106 mm M40 series recoilless rifle. A conversion to adapt the vehicle to this role is available through Marshall of Cambridge (Engineering) Limited.

109-inch (2·768 m)
This has a similar layout to the 88-inch (2·23 m) model and is the standard vehicle in its load class in the British Army and many other armed forces. Standard equipment on the military version includes an FV design towing hook, twin fuel tanks, vehicle lashing eyes at front and rear, freight lashing points in the rear, oil cooler, FV pattern lights, stowage for shovel, pick and axe on tailboard, water jerrican at the bulkhead and provision for stowing a rifle on the dashboard. The fitted-for-radio version has a 90-amp rectified electrical system with provision for charging radio batteries, full suppression of electrical equipment, radio table battery carrier, two 100-amp batteries, coaxial leads and operator's seat.

There are many variants of the long wheelbase

Long wheelbase Land-Rover equipped for telephone cable laying (T J Gander)

Land-Rover conversion to FV 18067 ambulance 2/4 stretcher (T J Gander)

Land-Rover in service including an anti-tank version armed with 120 mm Wombat recoilless rifle or American 106 mm M40 recoilless rifle, ambulance (details of which appear in the entry for Marshall of Cambridge in the *Shelters, containers and vehicle bodies* section), command, fire control and numerous other roles. It is also used for towing artillery such as the 105 mm Italian pack howitzer, missiles such as the Tigercat, Bofors RBS 70 or Rapier and radars such as the EMI Cymbeline. The chassis is also used as a basis for the Shorland armoured patrol vehicle and the SB.401 armoured personnel carrier.

As with the standard version, Land-Rover has built modified versions of the long wheelbase model to meet specific overseas countries' requirements. In 1973 the Norwegian Army ordered the vehicle with a 24-volt electrical system and fitted with lifting and towing facilities, petrol-burning heater, radio and aerial mountings and inter-vehicle starting capability. In 1976 the Dutch Army ordered a version based on the commercial long wheelbase Land-Rover with a four-cylinder OHV diesel engine, 24-volt electrical system, fresh air heater, sun visors, shovel and axe stowage, radio and aerial mountings and radio battery stowage.

In February 1979 Land-Rover launched the 3·5-litre V-8 Land-Rover which is now available worldwide and is currently in service with the Iraqi Army. The vehicle has been developed for FFR and as a half-track (by Laird for which there is a separate entry in the following section) and a 6 × 6 version has been developed in conjunction with Hotspur Limited (details of which are given in the following section). This model is available in 3·175-metre (standard body and armoured versions) and 3·529-metre (standard) wheelbase.

The Range Rover's well-proved 3·5-litre engine has been modified to give maximum torque for the Land-Rover V-8 at a lower engine speed. Maximum 166 lb/ft at 2000 rpm compares with the Range Rover figure of 186 lb/ft at 2500 rpm and the 122 lb/ft at 2000 rpm produced by the six-cylinder engined Land-Rover, which considerably improves the new vehicles' off-road performance.

The Land-Rover V-8 has permanent four-wheel-drive, with high and low ratio gears and a differential lock, as on the Range Rover. Modification of the body-work in the engine compartment provides plenty of room for the larger engine and allows easy access for servicing.

Military equipment available on the V-8 Land-Rover includes fighting vehicle design towing hook, twin fuel tanks, front and rear lifting and towing rings, stowage for shovel, pick and axe on rear tailboard, rifle clips, bumperettes, wire lamp guard, oil cooler, split charge facility, hand throttle, bonnet-mounted spare wheel and raised air intake. 24-volt electrics have been developed to meet military requirements and are in service with Middle East defence forces.

The Italian company Grazia offers an ambulance based on the chassis of the long wheelbase Land-Rover. Brief details of the company's production range are given in the *Shelters, containers and vehicle bodies* section. Details of the British Carawagon command

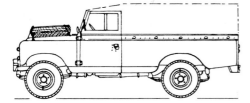

109-inch (2·768 m) long wheelbase Land-Rover

post version of the long wheelbase Land-Rover are also given in the same section. Herbert Lomas Limited and Pilcher-Greene Limited also manufacture ambulance bodies for the Land-Rover.

The High Capacity Pick-Up which was introduced during 1982 has since been developed as a full length hood derivative and was first shown at the British Army Equipment Exhibition at Aldershot, England during June 1982. This vehicle is now offered with a 12/24 volt, 60 amp fully suppressed FFR electrical system and can also be supplied as a field ambulance by Pilcher Greene Limited in both fully assembled or KD forms.

SPECIFICATIONS
88-inch (2·23 m)
Cab seating: 1 + 2 in front (4 in rear)
Configuration: 4 × 4
Weight:
(empty) 1430 kg
(loaded) 2120 kg
Weight on front axle: (loaded) 930 kg
Weight on rear axle: (loaded) 1190 kg
Max load: 690 kg
Length: 3·65 m
Width: 1·68 m
Height: 1·97 m
Ground clearance: 0·2 m
Track: 1·33 m
Wheelbase: 2·23 m
Angle of approach/departure: 46°/30°
Max speed: (road) 105 km/h
Range: 560 km
Fuel capacity: 45 litres
Max gradient:
(high) 39%
(low) 115%
Fording: 0·5 m
Engine: 4-cylinder OHV diesel developing 51 bhp at 4000 rpm or 4-cylinder OHV petrol engine developing 69 bhp at 4000 rpm
Gearbox: manual with 4 forward and 1 reverse gears
Clutch: single dry plate
Transfer box: 2-speed
Steering: recirculating ball
Turning radius: 5·79 m
Suspension: semi-elliptical springs front and rear with double acting telescopic shock absorbers
Tyres: 7.50 × 16
Number of tyres: 4 + 1 spare
Brakes:
(main) drum, hydraulic, tandem braking system
(parking) drum, mechanical on transmission
Electrical system: 12 V (24 V optional)

109-inch (2·768 m) LWB
Cab seating: 1 + 2 in front (optional seating for 8 in rear)
Configuration: 4 × 4
Weight:
(empty) 1750 kg
(loaded) 2600 kg
Max load: 850 kg
Load area: 1·85 × 1·619 m
Length: 4·56 m
Width: 1·68 m
Height:
(overall) 1·98 m
(reduced) 1·52 m
Ground clearance: 0·2 m
Track: 1·33 m
Wheelbase: 2·768 m
Angle of approach/departure: 45°/29°
Max speed: 90 km/h
Range: 600 km
Fuel capacity: 90 litres

Gradient:
(high) 25%
(low) 58%
Fording: 0·7 m
Engine: 4-cylinder in-line OHV petrol developing 69 bhp at 4000 rpm
Gearbox: manual with 4 forward and 1 reverse gears
Clutch: single dry plate
Transfer box: 2-speed
Steering: recirculating ball
Turning radius: 7·5 m
Suspension: semi-elliptical springs front and rear with hydraulic double acting shock absorbers
Tyres: 7.50 × 16
Number of tyres: 4 + 1 spare
Brakes:
(main) hydraulic, tandem braking system, servo assisted
(parking) drum, mechanical on transmission
Electrical system: 12 V (24 V optional)

110-inch (2·8 m) with V-8 petrol engine

Model	Standard 110-inch	High Capacity Pick-Up
Cab seating	1 + 2 front (9 in rear)	1 + 2 front (10 in rear)
Configuration	4 × 4	4 × 4
Weight (unladen)	1587 kg	1600 kg
(laden)	3050 kg	3050 kg
Max load	1463 kg	1440 kg
Load area	2·7 m²	3·2 m²
Length	4·39 m	4·39 m
Width	1·79 m	1·79 m
Height	1·98 m	1·98 m
Ground clearance	0·21 m	0·21 m
Track	1·49 m	1·49 m
Wheelbase	2·794 m	2·794 m
Angle of approach/ departure	54°/33°	54°/33°
Max speed	120–144 km/h	120–144 km/h
Range	900 km	900 km
Fuel capacity	150 litres	150 litres
Gradient	up to 45°	up to 45°
Fording depth	0·7 m	0·7 m
Engines	2·5-litre petrol/2·5-litre diesel/3·5-litre V-8 petrol	
Gearbox	5 forward 1 reverse (2·5-litre) 4 forward 1 reverse (V-8)	
Clutch	single dry plate	
Transfer box	2-speed	2-speed
Steering	ball, worm and nut type	
Turning radius	6·9 m	6·9 m
Suspension	coil springs	coil springs
Tyres	7.50 × 16	7.50 × 16
Number of tyres	4 + 1 spare	4 + 1 spare
Brakes	disc front, drum rear	
Electrical system	12 V (24 V option)	

STATUS
In production. In service with over 140 armed forces.

MANUFACTURER
Land-Rover Limited, Military Products, Lode Lane, Solihull, West Midlands B92 8NW, England.

Land-Rovers are also assembled or manufactured in plants, in all of which British Leyland have an interest, in Algeria, Australia, Kenya, New Zealand, Nigeria, Portugal, South Africa (66% local content), Spain (100% local content), Turkey, Zaïre, Zambia and Zimbabwe.

There are distributor-owned Land-Rover plants in Angola, Costa Rica, Ethiopia, Ghana, Indonesia, Iran, Madagascar, Malaysia, Morocco, Mozambique, Nigeria, Sudan, Tanzania, Thailand, Trinidad and Venezuela.

Land-Rover One Ten (4 × 4) Light Vehicle

DEVELOPMENT
First shown publicly in early 1983 the Land-Rover One Ten has a 110-inch/2·794-metre wheelbase and is an amalgam of the usual Land-Rover body with the Range Rover suspension and chassis. Early production has been mainly for the commercial market but the Land-Rover Stage 2, powered by a 2¼-litre diesel engine, is being developed for the British Army where it will eventually replace all existing Land-Rover models (other than the Airportable and 1000 kg versions).

DESCRIPTION
In appearance the Land-Rover One Ten is similar to existing Land-Rover models but can be identified by the new moulded injection grille and one-piece windscreen. The increased track has involved the introduction of grp deformable 'eye-brows' over the wheels which are held in place by frangible pins.

The One Ten is based on a box-section steel chassis used on the Range Rover but considerably strengthened. The chassis is robot welded and the centre section is over 190 mm deep. The overall strength is said to withstand the most demanding off-road conditions. Detail design of the chassis is such that the fuel tank has added protection: a cross member is bolted into place for working on the engine, gearbox and transfer box, and wiring looms are routed along the insides of the box sections. Four new jacking points are provided on the frame.

The One Ten uses Range Rover coil springs in place of the earlier leaf springs. The coil springs have been reinforced and provide 180 mm of wheel travel at the front and 210 mm at the rear. Minimum ground clearance is now 0·21 metre. Suspension movement at the front and rear is controlled by long-stroke hydraulic dampers. A Boge Hydromat ride-levelling unit is optional on all models but fitted to the station waggon variant as standard. The Land-Rover beam front axle is located by radius arms with a Panhard rod providing lateral location. A Salisbury axle is used on the rear. 300 mm disc brakes are fitted on the front wheels with drum brakes fitted to the rear.

The increased track of the One Ten has led to a redesigned steering linkage that provides a turning radius of 6·4 metres. Factory-fitted power-assisted steering is optional.

Three engines are available for the One Ten. The largest is the 3·528-litre V-8 equipped with twin Zenith Stromberg CD carburettors. This overhead valve V-8 develops 114 bhp at 4000 rpm. Also available is the four-cylinder 2·286-litre five bearing engine fitted with a revised camshaft and a twin-choke 32/34DMTL Weber carburettor. This develops 74 bhp at 4000 rpm. A 2·286-litre diesel counterpart to the petrol engine develops 60 bhp at 4000 rpm. This has a 23:1 compression ratio and CAV Pintaux injectors. Changes have been made to the inlet manifold and a solenoid-operated cut-out on the injector pump provides the convenience of a car-type ignition key. The One Ten has two power take-offs.

To take advantage of the extra power provided by the

Land-Rover One Ten (4 × 4) light vehicle with hard top

four-cylinder engines, a strengthened version of the five-speed LT77 gearbox has been fitted. Matched with the LT230R transfer box used on the automatic version of the Range Rover, the LT77 can provide ten forward and two reverse ratios and the transmission has been 'tuned' to make use of this. The V-8 engine uses the four-speed LT95 integral gearbox and transfer box of the Range Rover and Series 111 V-8 Land-Rover.

The One Ten has permanent four-wheel drive with front and rear axle differentials as well as a lockable centre unit. A selectable two- or four-wheel drive is available on the four-cylinder five-speed models.

One Ten production has not yet been ostensibly for military use, however this is anticipated. Specialist constructors such as Pilcher-Greene have already produced ambulance bodies specifically for the One Ten.

STATUS
Production.

MANUFACTURER
Land-Rover Limited, Lode Lane, Solihull, West Midlands B92 8NW, England.

SPECIFICATIONS
(Data refers to High Capacity Pick-up version of One Ten)
Cab seating: 1 + 2 in front (4 to 8 in rear)
Configuration: 4 × 4
Weight:
(standard suspension) 3050 kg
(levelled suspension) 2950 kg
Max load: 1162 kg

Towed load:
(braked) 1000 kg
(unbraked) 500 kg
Length: 4·669 m
Width: 1·79 m
Height: 2·035 m
Cargo bed length: 2·01 m
Ground clearance: 0·216 m
Track: 1·486 m
Wheelbase: 2·794 m
Angle of approach/departure: 50°/35°
Fuel capacity: 79·5 litres
Engine: 3·528-litre V-8 water-cooled petrol developing 114 bhp at 4000 rpm or
2·286-litre 4-cylinder water-cooled in-line petrol developing 74 bhp at 4000 rpm or
2·286-litre 4-cylinder water-cooled diesel developing 60 bhp at 4000 rpm
Gearbox:
(4-cylinder) manual with 5 forward and 1 reverse gears
(V-8) manual with 4 forward and 1 reverse gears
Clutch: Borg and Beck diaphragm spring
Transfer box: 2-speed
Steering: manual, recirculating ball (power assist optional)
Turning radius: 6·4 m
Suspension: beam axles front and rear with coil springs controlled by hydraulic telescopic dampers
Tyres: 7.50 × 16
Number of tyres: 4 + 1 spare
Brakes: dual servo-assisted, discs front, drums rear
Electrical system: 12 V

New 110-inch wheelbase version of military Land-Rover

New model of 110-inch wheelbase Land-Rover station wagon to civilian specifications

Range Rover (4 × 4) 748 kg Vehicle

DEVELOPMENT
The Range Rover, first announced in June 1970, combines a formidable cross-country capability with the comfort and road performance of a high-speed saloon car and is ideally suited to a variety of military applica-

tions including use as an ambulance, command/radio vehicle, fire tender, personnel carrier and border patrol vehicle. A number of factory approved conversions are available including 6 × 4 configurations equipped for use as fast response emergency units. The recent introduction of a four-door variant extends the vehicle's versatility still further, particularly for personnel carrier

or security duties where ease of access for all passengers is important.

DESCRIPTION
The Range Rover is based on a rigid box-section steel chassis. The rubber mounted steel body frame is clad in separate body panels, most of which are formed in

Range Rover (4 × 4) 748 kg vehicle (four door)

Carmichael (6 × 4) Commando Rapid Intervention vehicle showing front-mounted pump

Range Rover (4 × 4) 748 kg vehicle (two door)

lightweight, corrosion resistant aluminium alloy. Power is provided by a 3·5-litre light alloy engine driving through a five speed plus reverse gearbox coupled to a two-speed transfer box, providing ten forward and two reverse gears in total. The vehicle features permanent four-wheel drive with a lockable centre differential. The long travel coil spring suspension is fitted with a rear ride levelling device and disc brakes are fitted at all four-wheel stations.

Accommodation is provided for five persons, access being gained through two or four doors. The load area may be extended by folding the rear seat. The tailgate is of a split two-piece design.

A wide range of optional equipment includes heavy-duty suspension, split charge system and various types of towing equipment.

The Italian company Grazia offers an ambulance based on the chassis of the Range Rover. Brief details of the company's production range are given in the *Shelters, containers and vehicle bodies* section.

SPECIFICATIONS
Cab seating: 1 + 4
Configuration: 4 × 4
Weight: (2-door/4-door)
(empty) 1762 kg/1793 kg
(loaded) 2510 kg/2510 kg
Weight on front axle: (loaded) 1000 kg
Weight on rear axle: (loaded) 1510 kg
Max load: 748 kg
Length: 4·47 m
Width: 1·78 m
Height: 1·8 m
Ground clearance: 0·19 m
Track: 1·49 m

Range Rover (4 × 4) 748 kg vehicle (two door)

Wheelbase: 2·54 m
Angle of approach/departure: 45°/30°
Max speed: 154·5 km/h
Fuel capacity: 82 litres
Engine: Rover V-8 3·528-litre petrol
high compression (9·35:1) max power 125 hp at 4000 rpm
low compression (8·13:1) max power 130 hp at 5000 rpm
Gearbox:
(manual) 5 forward and 1 reverse gears
(automatic) 3 forward and 1 reverse gears
Clutch: (manual) single dry plate
Transfer box: 2-speed incorporating lockable third differential
Steering: recirculating ball with steering damper and power assistance (optional manual)

Turning radius: 5·65 m
Suspension: coil springs, long-stroke hydraulic telescopic dampers, axles located by radius arms, self-energising ride-level unit on rear suspension
Brakes:
(main) hydraulic disc on all wheels, dual circuit
(parking) mechanical on transmission
Electrical system: 12 V

STATUS
In production. In service with the Royal Air Force (6 × 4), and many other armed forces.

MANUFACTURER
Land-Rover Limited, Lode Lane, Solihull, West Midlands B92 8NW, England.

Scottorn Range Rover (6 × 6) Vehicle

DESCRIPTION
The Scottorn 6 × 6 all-wheel-drive Range Rover has been designed and developed to meet an increasing requirement for a high-performance, cross-country vehicle with large passenger and cargo-carrying capacity. There is a 935 mm extension behind the second axle to accommodate a third, driven, axle.

In both low and high ranges 6 × 6 drive is engaged with the option of paired differential locks in both ranges.

The body incorporates modified Rover parts providing five doors: four forward and one, horizontally split, at the rear. The extension for the third axle lengthens the cargo area or provides a large area to the rear for fitting any specialised equipment or extras.

The main feature of this Range Rover is increased load-carrying area and capacity, and the third driven axle which uprates the cross-country ability accordingly to accommodate the increases.

Body design, interior and equipment can be modified to suit customers specifications. Standard equipment includes air-conditioning, bush bar, lamp guards, roof rack and a front-mounted winch.

Scottorn Range Rover (6 × 6) vehicle

SPECIFICATIONS
Cab seating: 1 + 4
Configuration: 6 × 6
Length: 5·36 m
Width: 1·78 m
Height: 1·83 m
Track: 1·49 m
Wheelbase: 2·544 m + 0·935 m
Fuel capacity: 86 litres
Engine: Rover V-8 petrol developing 130 hp (DIN) at 5000 rpm

Gearbox: manual with 4 forward and 1 reverse gears
Clutch: single dry plate
Transfer box: 2-speed
Steering: recirculating ball with steering damper and power assistance
Suspension:
  (front) coil springs, long-stroke hydraulic telescopic dampers, axle located by radius arms
  (rear) coil springs, radius arms, A-frame location arms and Boge Hydromat self-energising levelling device

Brakes:
  (main) hydraulic disc on all wheels, dual circuit
  (parking) duo-servo drum brake on rear of transfer box
Electrical system: 12 V

STATUS
Production.

MANUFACTURER
Scottorn Trailers Limited, Chartridge, Chesham, Buckinghamshire, England.

SMC Sahara Six (6 × 6) or (6 × 4) Vehicle

DEVELOPMENT
The Sahara Six has been developed as a private venture by SMC Engineering Limited which previously designed the Sandringham 6 (6 × 6) 2000 kg vehicle, based on a modified LWB Land-Rover chassis, which is covered in the following section.

DESCRIPTION
The Sahara Six is based on the Range Rover (4 × 4) chassis but with an additional axle at the rear which can be powered (6 × 6 configuration) or unpowered (6 × 4 configuration). A smooth ride is maintained by the normal usage, on the additional axle, of coil springs and hydraulic dampers. Location of the axle is by means of radius arms and wishbone assembly.

Access to the pick up area at the rear of the Sahara Six is via the normal tailgate; the bed is 2·286 metres long and 1·574 metres wide. The Sahara Six has a payload, including crew and personnel equipment, of 1500 kg.

The Sahara Six is available in three standard body styles including an ambulance. Special bodies can be produced to order.

Standard equipment includes power assisted steering, inertia reel seat belts, cloth seats and tinted glass.

SPECIFICATIONS (passenger body)
Seating: 1 + 5 plus
Configuration: 6 × 6 (6 × 4 option)
Weight:
  (empty) 2250 kg
  (loaded) 3500 kg
Length: 5·36 m
Width: 1·78 m
Height: 1·83 m
Track: 1·49 m

SMC Engineering Sahara Six vehicle based on Range Rover with additional powered or unpowered axle

Wheelbase: 2·544 m + 0·935 m
Fuel capacity: 86 litres
Engine: V-8 3·528-litre OHV water-cooled petrol developing 130 hp at 5000 rpm
Gearbox: manual, 4 forward and 1 reverse gears
Transfer box: 2-speed
Suspension:
  (front) live axle with coil springs, radius arms and panhard rod
  (rear) live axle with coil springs, radius arms, A-frame location arms and Boge Hydromat levelling device

Tyres: 20.5 × 16
Brakes: servo assisted, dual operation discs
Electrical system: 12 V

STATUS
Production. Vehicles have been provided to a number of military forces in the Middle and Far East and Europe.

MANUFACTURER
SMC Engineering (Bristol) Limited, Simmonds Buildings, Hambrook, Bristol BS16 1RY, England.

SMC Sahara Six (6 × 6) vehicle

SMC Sahara Six (6 × 6) vehicle

Land-Rover (4 × 4) 1000 kg Truck

DEVELOPMENT
The 101-inch wheelbase forward control Land-Rover was developed by the Rover Company in co-operation with the Military Vehicles and Engineering Establishment to meet a British Army requirement for a 1000 kg payload 4 × 4 vehicle with the added capacity of towing a 1500 kg powered axle trailer. The vehicle was first shown to the public at the Commercial Vehicle Show at Earls Court, London, in September 1968. A pre-production run of vehicles was completed in 1972 and the vehicle entered service with the British Army in 1975. Production has now been completed.

DESCRIPTION
The vehicle is of the forward control type with the engine at the front and the cargo area at the rear. The chassis is of steel frame construction with two U-sections over-

lapped and welded on the vertical faces full length flat topped side-members and intermediate support bearing for rear PTO on bolt on cross-members between the third and fourth cross-members.

The 1000 kg Land-Rover is powered by a military version of the successful lightweight aluminium Rover 3·5-litre V-8 engine, which is basically the same as the car engine but with a reduced compression ratio of 8·5 to 1 to enable it to operate on low octane fuels.

The four-speed all-synchromesh Range Rover type transmission with a high and low transfer box provides eight forward and two reverse gears. A third differential between the front and rear axles obviates transmission wind-up associated with four-wheel drive transmission. This differential can be locked by a vacuum-actuated control to provide maximum traction through both axles. The front axle drive provides a 35-degree steering lock through constant velocity joints.

The complete hood, body sides, windscreen, bumpers, and spare wheel can be removed from the

vehicle for air transport. The vehicle can be lifted by medium lift helicopters such as the Wessex and Puma.

Tool lockers are provided in the rear body behind the wheel arches. As a result of trials with the pre-production run, production vehicles have an anti-roll bar at the front, mud flaps and a folding rear entry step.

Standard equipment includes rear bumperettes, helicopter lifting rings front and rear, rotating towing hooks front and rear, trailer brakes operated from the towing vehicle using single line vacuum system on foot and hand brake.

The British Army uses this vehicle for a wide range of roles including towing the British 105 mm Light Gun and for carrying 81 mm mortars. The Royal Air Force and the Australian and British armies use the vehicle to tow the Rapier SAM system.

In 1975 the Royal Luxembourg Army ordered a number of vehicles with a 24-volt electrical system (FFR), cable drum winch with front or rear pull and a fresh air heater to cab and rear body.

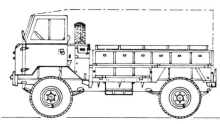

Land-Rover (4 × 4) 1000 kg truck

VARIANTS

Ambulance

In July 1976 Marshall of Cambridge (Engineering) Limited received a contract from the Ministry of Defence for a two- to four-stretcher ambulance version of the Land-Rover. This has now been built and has been designed to meet an MoD requirement for an improved pattern lightweight ambulance for casualty evacuation from forward areas to carry four stretcher or six sitting patients. The aluminium alloy thermally insulated body provides a high standard of patient comfort while a new pattern stretcher gear simplifies loading and unloading in the upper position. Additional equipment which may be fitted includes an Eberspacher heater, an air-conditioner, and automatic resuscitation equipment. This model is now in service with the British Army.

MILAN Carrier

The British Army uses this vehicle to carry MILAN ATGW teams. Each vehicle carries 6 men, 2 MILAN firing posts plus 14 missiles.

Anti-tank

The Egyptian Army uses this vehicle fitted with the British Aerospace Swingfire ATGW system. Four missiles carried in the rear of the vehicle can be launched away from the vehicle with the aid of a separation sight and controller.

SPECIFICATIONS

Cab seating: 1 + 1 (8 men can be carried in the rear)
Configuration: 4 × 4
Weight:
  (empty) 1924 kg
  (loaded) 3120 kg
  (stripped) 1580 kg
Weight on front axle: (loaded) 1608 kg
Weight on rear axle: (loaded) 1512 kg
Max load: 1000 kg
Load area: 2·49 × 1·727 m
Length: 4·127 m
Width: 1·842 m
Height: 2·138 m
Ground clearance: 0·254 m
Track:
  (front) 1·524 m
  (rear) 1·549 m
Wheelbase: 2·565 m
Angle of approach/departure: 50°/46°
Max speed: 120 km/h
Range: 560 km
Fuel capacity: 109 litres
Max gradient: 60%
Engine: Rover V-8 petrol developing 128 bhp at 5000 rpm
Gearbox: manual with 4 forward and 1 reverse gears
Clutch: single dry plate
Transfer box: 2-speed with permanent 4-wheel drive
Steering: recirculating ball with steering damper

Land-Rover (4 × 4) 1000 kg truck towing 105 mm Light Gun (T J Gander)

Land-Rover (4 × 4) 1000 kg truck in service with Australian Army (P Handel)

Turning radius: 5·14 m
Suspension: semi-elliptical taper leaf springs with telescopic hydraulic dampers, anti-roll bar at front
Tyres: 9.00 × 16
Number of tyres: 4 + 1 spare
Brakes:
  (main) hydraulic, split system, servo assisted
  (parking) drum, mechanical on transmission
Electrical system: 12 V (24 V optional)

STATUS
Production complete. In service with Australia, British Army (2500), Royal Air Force, Egypt and Luxembourg (57).

MANUFACTURER
Land-Rover Limited, Military Products, Lode Lane, Solihull, West Midlands B92 8NW, England.

Tuareg Mark II Remote Area Patrol Vehicle

DESCRIPTION

The Tuareg remote area patrol vehicle has been designed specifically for long-range operations in desert and other remote areas. The vehicle has left-hand drive. The commander sits on the right with the crew members to the rear. The body of the Tuareg is steel with limited armour protection available. The rear body area can be adapted to meet customers' requirements for communications, ammunition or additional crew space.

Standard equipment includes two 113-litre water tanks, a 3000 kg winch, two spare wheels and digging and vehicle tools. Other items include a magnetic compass, night driving facility, bivouac, camouflage net and multi-barrelled smoke dischargers at each corner of the vehicle.

Fuel capacity of up to 560 litres is carried in three separate tanks which are filled with 'Explosafe'.

The basic vehicle is fitted with pillars front and rear on which customers can fit their own machine gun mountings; space can be made available for carrying a portable anti-tank weapon such as the 84 mm Carl Gustaf.

Tuareg remote area patrol vehicle (4 × 4)

Optional equipment available includes radio equipment and navigational aids such as satellite or Decca systems. A telescopic radio antenna mast and a portable 12- or 24-volt dc generator can be supplied.

Provision can be made to supply a machine gun mounting suitable for the 7·62 mm NATO GPMG and also for the 12·7 mm (0·50) Browning.

SPECIFICATIONS
Configuration: 4 × 4
Weight: 7300 kg
Length: 5·45 m
Width: 2·34 m

Height: 2·68 m
Ground clearance: (axles) 0·319 m
Wheelbase: 2·8 m
Angle of approach/departure: 36°/35° laden
Fuel capacity: up to 560 litres
Engine: Mercedes-Benz OM352A diesel developing 168 bhp at 2800 rpm
Gearbox: manual with 6 forward and 1 reverse gears
Transfer box: 2-speed
Differential locks: inter-axle and rear axle cross-lock differential
Turning radius: 8 m
Tyres: 13.00 × 20

Number of tyres: 4 + 2 spare
Brakes: air-assisted hydraulic with drum brakes on all wheels
Winch: nominal 3000 kg capacity with approximately 90 m of wire rope

STATUS
In service.

MANUFACTURER
Glover Webb and Liversidge Limited, Hamble Lane, Hamble, Hampshire SO3 5NY, England.

UNITED STATES OF AMERICA

Fast Attack Vehicle (FAV)

DEVELOPMENT
The Fast Attack Vehicle (FAV) is based on the design of the Chenowth off-road racing vehicle (dune buggy) and developed for its military role by Emerson Electric. In October 1982 Emerson Electric was awarded a contract worth nearly $2 million for the production of 80 FAV prototypes. The first examples were delivered to the US Army 9th Infantry Division's High Technology Test Bed at Fort Lewis, Washington for extensive testing, prior to possible use by the Rapid Deployment Force. The first 25 FAVs were delivered in October 1982 and the remaining 55 were all delivered by 15 December 1982. The contract was awarded by the US Army Tank-Automotive Command (TACOM) at Warren, Michigan.

DESCRIPTION
The FAV is virtually an armed off-road racer with a combination of light weight and a good cross-country performance. The chassis is largely an open high strength tubular frame with an integral roll cage. The engine, a 94 hp STD petrol unit, is air-cooled and mounted at the rear. Just forward of the engine the driver is seated on the left (looking forward) with the passenger/gunner to his right. Weapons may be mounted forward on a mounting bar or mounted on the integral roll bar. Weapon choices proposed include a 30 mm Chain Gun, a 12·7 mm (0·50) machine gun, a 40 mm grenade launcher or a TOW 2 anti-tank missile launcher.

Various options include the use of either a 90 or 100 hp water-cooled diesel. Possible uses include operation as an unmanned reconnaissance or electronic warfare vehicle, and a version carrying three or four men is projected

Overall the FAV is fast and light, but added to the vehicle's low centre of gravity is the rapid response rear-wheel drive providing a high cross-country speed.

STATUS
In production for the US Army.

MANUFACTURER
Chenowth Racing Products Inc, El Cajon, San Diego, California, USA.

Enquiries to Emerson Electric Company, Government and Defence Group, 8100 West Florissant Avenue, St Louis, Missouri 63136, USA.

Fast Attack Vehicle armed with 30 mm Chain Gun

SPECIFICATIONS
Cab seating: 1 + 1
Configuration: 4 × 2
Weight: (curb) 698·5 kg
Length: 3·81 m

Height: 1·524 m
Wheelbase: 2·54 m
Max speed: 128 km/h plus
Engine: STD air-cooled petrol developing 94 hp at 4400 rpm

Gearbox: manual, 4 forward and 1 reverse gears
Suspension: 2 high performance shock absorbers on each front wheel, 3 on each rear wheel
Steering: rack and pinion
Electrical system: 12 V

Warrior NMC-40 Long Range Fast Attack Vehicle

DEVELOPMENT
The Warrior NMC-40 fast attack vehicle was designed and developed as part of the Fast Attack Vehicle (FAV) programme initiated by the US Army Tank-Automotive Command (TACOM). It was first shown publicly in July 1983 and is now being offered for sale and export.

DESCRIPTION
The Warrior NMC-40 is a four-wheeled light vehicle with a high strength tubular steel roll-cage frame. Seating is provided for three men, two facing forward and one facing the rear. The air-cooled engine, which is described as 'German', appears to be a 80 hp four-

cylinder type with dual air filters at the rear. Provision has been made for mounting two weapons, usually two M60 machine guns or one M60 and an automatic 40 mm grenade launcher, one at the front and the other at the rear.

The Warrior NMC-40 is supplied complete with equipment ranging from personal body armour to radios and special tools. Also included are map cases, grenades in racks and a neoprene vehicle cover.

STATUS
Prototype. Ready for production.

MANUFACTURER
Nordac Manufacturing Corporation, Route 12, Box 124, Fredericksburg, Virginia 22405, USA.

SPECIFICATIONS
Cab seating: 1 + 2
Configuration: 4 × 2
Weight: (less crew and armament) 748 kg
Ground clearance: 0·355 m
Range: (cross-country) 483–644 km
Gradient: 75%
Side slope: 40%
Max speed: 153–161 km/h
Engine: air-cooled 4-cylinder petrol developing 80 hp
Gearbox: manual with 4 forward and 1 reverse gears
Suspension: torsion bars and shock absorbers providing 0·355 m wheel travel front and rear
Steering: rack and pinion with dampers
Brakes: drums front and discs rear with hydraulic steering brake
Electrical system: dual 12 V, 100 A

Warrior NMC-40 fast attack vehicle with open roll-cage frame and rear-mounted M60 machine gun

Warrior NMC-40 fast attack vehicle with equipment in foreground

M274 (4 × 4) Lightweight Vehicle (Mechanical Mule)

DESCRIPTION

The M274 is officially known as the Truck, Platform, Utility: ½-Ton, 4 × 4, M274, but is normally referred to as the Mechanical Mule. It was adopted for service with the US Army and Marine Corps in 1956 and is widely used by infantry, airborne and marine units. It has been designed to carry a maximum of 454 kg of cargo but has no towing capability.

The M274 consists of a platform mounted on two axles with four wheels. The engine is under the platform at the rear. It has no suspension system as shock is absorbed by the low pressure tyres. The vehicle has permanent 4 × 4 drive.

The driver is seated at the front of the flat platform, which has a handrail that can be raised to accommodate the payload or lowered for shipping and storage. The seat (which can be adjusted to two positions) and the foot rest can be detached and stowed underneath the platform for air transport. If required, the driver can disconnect the telescopic brace holding the steering column in its upright position and reposition the column forward in front of the vehicle from where he can retain control while walking or crouching in front of the vehicle.

The first models, the M274 and M274A1, had a Willys engine while the later models, the M274A2, M274A3, M274A4 and M274A5 have a Continental Hercules engine. The latter model also has a magnesium instead of an aluminium chassis.

VARIANTS

Some models have been fitted with the 106 mm M40 series recoilless rifle. This has now been replaced by the Hughes TOW ATGW.

SPECIFICATIONS

Seating: 1
Configuration: 4 × 4
Weight:
(empty) 376 kg
(loaded) 830 kg
Load area: 2·413 × 1·168 m
Length: 2·98 m
Width: 1·78 m
Height:
(steering wheel) 1·193 m
(load area) 0·685 m

M274 (4 × 4) lightweight vehicle (Mechanical Mule) in travelling configuration (US Army)

Ground clearance: 0·292 m
Track: 0·95 m
Wheelbase: 1·447 m
Angle of approach/departure: 41°/36°
Max speed: 40 km/h
Range: 180 km
Fuel capacity: 30·3 litres
Max gradient: 60%
Max side slope: 40%
Fording: 0·2 m
Engine:
M274, Willys A053 4-cylinder air-cooled horizontally opposed petrol developing 17 bhp at 3200 rpm
M274A1, Willys A0531 4-cylinder air-cooled horizontally opposed petrol developing 17 bhp at 3200 rpm
M274A2 to M274A5, Continental Hercules A042 2-cylinder air-cooled horizontally opposed petrol developing 13·6 bhp at 3000 rpm
Gearbox: manual with 3 forward and 1 reverse gears
Clutch: single dry plate
Transfer box: 2-speed
Steering: a quick change mechanism allows the driver to select 2- or 4-wheel steer

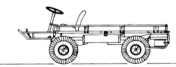

M274 (4 × 4) lightweight vehicle (Mechanical Mule)

Suspension: none; tyres absorb shock
Tyres: 7.50 × 10
Brakes:
(main) mechanical
(parking) mechanical
Electrical system: none

STATUS

Production complete. In service with the US Army and Marines. To be replaced by the High Mobility Multipurpose Wheeled Vehicle in the mid-1980s. A few M274s are used by the Spanish Marines.

MANUFACTURER

Willys, Baifield Industries, Carrollton, Texas (from 1965), Brunswick Corporation (from 1970).

DJ-5 (4 × 2) Dispatcher 499 kg Light Vehicle

DESCRIPTION

The AM General Dispatcher is designed for use in rear areas where little or no cross-country capability is required. Typical roles include staff communications, military police, carrying light supplies, light maintenance and logistical support.

The engine is mounted at the front with the all-steel fully enclosed passenger/cargo area at the rear with a single seat for the driver with the option of a passenger seat which can be installed facing the rear when the vehicle is being used as a command vehicle. The two doors, one either side, slide to the rear and can be latched open to the rear if required. The full width door at the rear opens to the left. If required, the vehicle can tow an M416 ¼-ton trailer.

The latest model is the DJ-5L which is powered by a model 4-151 four-cylinder petrol engine developing 90 hp at 4000 rpm. Empty weight is 1020 kg and gross vehicle weight is 1520 kg.

STATUS

Production. In service with the US Army, Navy and Air Force.

MANUFACTURER

AM General Corporation, 14250 Plymouth Road, Detroit, Michigan 48232, USA.

AM General DJ-5 (4 × 2) Dispatcher 499 kg light vehicle

SPECIFICATIONS
Cab seating: 1 (in basic version)
Configuration: 4 × 2
Weight:
  (empty) 1020 kg
  (loaded) 1520 kg
Weight on front axle: (loaded) 540 kg
Weight on rear axle: (loaded) 980 kg
Max load: 499 kg
Length: 3·378 m
Width: 1·612 m
Height: 1·765 m
  (load area) 0·622 m
Ground clearance: 0·165 m
Track:
  (front) 1·308 m
  (rear) 1·27 m
Wheelbase: 2·057 m
Angle of approach/departure: 43°/25°
Max range: (road) 370 km
Max speed: 120 km/h
Fuel capacity: 38 litres
Max gradient: 20%
Engine: Model 4-151 4-cylinder water-cooled petrol developing 90 hp at 4000 rpm
Gearbox: automatic with 3 forward and 1 reverse gears
Steering: recirculating ball
Turning radius: 5·486 m
Suspension: leaf springs with direct double action shock absorbers
Brakes:
  (main) hydraulic
  (parking) mechanical
Electrical system: 12 V
Battery: 1 × 12 V, 505 A cold crank current

AM General DJ-5 (4 × 2) Dispatcher 499 kg light vehicle

M151 (4 × 4) 362 kg Light Vehicle and Variants

DEVELOPMENT
In 1950 the Continental Army Command placed a requirement with the Ordnance Corps for a new ¼-ton vehicle. Research and development began that year at the Ordnance Tank-Automotive Command. In 1951 the Ford Motor Company was awarded a development contract for the new vehicle and the first prototypes were completed in 1952. A further batch was completed in 1954 under the designation XM151 and in 1956 the XM151E1 (of conventional steel construction) and the XM151E2 (of aluminium construction) were built and tested. The former was selected for production in 1959; Ford was awarded the first production contract and first production vehicles were completed in 1960 at Ford's Highland Park Plant. The M151 has replaced the M38 (4 × 4) ¼-ton vehicle in the United States' forces. Later production contracts were awarded to the AM General Corporation. The fiscal year 1978 request was for only 3880 vehicles at a cost of $29·1 million. It was then stated that the engine of the vehicle no longer met emission standards and that this procurement would be the last for several years. At one time production was running at as many as 18 000 vehicles a year.

DESCRIPTION
The body and chassis of the M151 are integral and are of all-welded construction. The layout of the vehicle is conventional with the engine at the front and the crew area at the rear with a removable canvas top and side curtains, and a windscreen that can be folded forward flat on the bonnet.

M151A2 (4 × 4) ¼-ton light vehicle

M718A1 (4 × 4) ambulance

M825 (4 × 4) weapons carried armed with 106 mm recoilless rifle

M151A2 (4 × 4) ¼-ton light vehicle carrying TOW anti-tank missile launcher

M151A2 (4 × 4) ¼-ton light vehicle carrying TOW anti-tank missiles

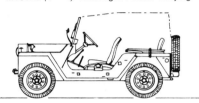

M151A2 (4 × 4) ¼-ton light vehicle

M718A1 (4 × 4) ¼-ton ambulance

In 1964 the M151 was replaced in production by the M151A1 which had improved suspension as the earlier model had a tendency to oversteer. The M151A2 followed in 1970 with modifications to the rear suspension, dual brake system, collapsible steering wheel, two-speed wipers and modified lighting. The M151A2LC has a gearbox with three forward and one reverse gears (other vehicles have four forward and one reverse gears) and two-speed transfer case (other vehicles have a single-speed transfer case). The vehicle also has a different suspension which consists of semi-elliptical springs and shock absorbers instead of the coil springs and telescopic shock absorbers fitted to other versions.

The basic vehicle can also be armed with a pintle-mounted 7·62 mm M60 or a 12·7 mm (0·50) Browning machine gun and many have been fitted with the Hughes TOW ATGW system which has replaced the 106 mm recoilless rifle in many units.

Many kits are available including a front-mounted winch, heater, hard top, 100 amp alternator and a Xenon searchlight. The vehicle can ford to a depth of 0·533 metres without preparation and 1·524 metres with the aid of a kit.

VARIANTS
M107 and M108 are communications vehicles with the radios installed in the rear of the vehicle. The passenger seat faces the rear to enable the radio operator to work his equipment.

M718 and M718A1 are ambulance versions and have a crew of two, a driver and a medical attendant. This version can carry a stretcher and three seated patients, two stretchers and two seated patients or three stretcher patients.

SPECIFICATIONS

Model	M151	M151A1	M151A2	M718A1	M825
Cab seating	1 + 3	1 + 3	1 + 3	1 + 1	1 + 3
Configuration	4 × 4	4 × 4	4 × 4	4 × 4	4 × 4
Weight (empty)	1012 kg	1088 kg	1107 kg	1247 kg	1174 kg
(loaded)	1575 kg	1633 kg	1652 kg	1656 kg	1959 kg
Weight on front axle (empty)	574 kg	607 kg	618 kg	620 kg	655 kg
Weight on rear axle (loaded)	448 kg	481 kg	490 kg	626 kg	519 kg
Max load (road)	554 kg	544 kg	545 kg	409 kg	785 kg
(cross country)	362 kg	362 kg	363 kg	409 kg	785 kg
Towed load (road)	970 kg	970 kg	970 kg	not authorised	not authorised
(cross country)	680 kg	680 kg	680 kg	not authorised	not authorised
Length	3·352 m	3·371 m	3·371 m	3·631 m	3·645 m
Width	1·58 m	1·634 m	1·633 m	1·819 m	1·943 m
Height (overall)	1·803 m	1·803 m	1·803 m	1·94 m	1·621 m
(reduced)	1·332 m	1·332 m	1·333 m	1·313 m	1·346 m
Ground clearance	0·26 m	0·24 m	0·24 m	0·23 m	0·21 m
Track	1·346 m	1·346 m	1·346 m	1·346 m	1·346 m
Wheelbase	2·159 m	2·159 m	2·159 m	2·159 m	2·159 m
Angle of approach/departure	66°/37°	65°/37°	66°/37°	67°/36°	62°/33°
Max speed	106 km/h	104 km/h	90 km/h	90 km/h	80 km/h
Range	482 km	482 km	482 km	442 km	483 km
Fuel capacity	56 litres	56 litres	59·8 litres	59·8 litres	59·8 litres
Max gradient	60%	60%	60%	60%	50%
Max side slope	40%	40%	40%	40%	30%
Fording (without preparation)	0·533 m	0·533 m	0·533 m	0·533 m	0·533 m
(with preparation)	1·524 m	1·524 m	1·524 m	1·524 m	1·524 m
Engine	L-142 4-cylinder liquid-cooled OHV petrol developing 72 hp at 4000 rpm				
Gearbox	manual with 4 forward and 1 reverse gears				
Clutch	single dry disc				
Transfer box	single-speed, integral with transmission. Driver can select either 4 × 4 or 4 × 2 drive				
Steering	worm and double roller				
Turning radius	5·486 m	5·638 m	5·638 m	5·638 m	5·638 m
Suspension	coil springs with hydraulic shock absorbers				
Tyres	7.00 × 16	7.00 × 16	7.00 × 16	7.00 × 16	7.00 × 16
Brakes: (main)	hydraulic	hydraulic	hydraulic	hydraulic	hydraulic
(parking)	mechanical	mechanical	mechanical	mechanical	mechanical
Electrical system	24 V	24 V	24 V	24 V	24 V
Battery	1 × 2 HN	1 × 2 HN	1 × 2 HN	1 × 2 HN	1 × 2 HN

M825 is fitted with the M40 106 mm recoilless rifle mounted in the rear. This model is rapidly being replaced in United States' services by the Hughes TOW ATGW.

There have been many trial versions of the vehicle including a fully amphibious vehicle which was propelled in the water by special attachments to its wheels. The XM384 was a 6 × 6 vehicle and the XM408 an 8 × 8 vehicle.

STATUS
In production. In service with the US Army, Air Force and Marines, and over 100 other countries including Ecuador (including M825), Greece, Indonesia, Netherlands, Peru, Portugal, Saudi Arabia, Senegal, Spain (marines only), Thailand, Venezuela (including M835) and Zaïre. By early 1980 AMG had built 95 000 M151 series. The company holds the current production contract to supply M151A2 series vehicles on a 'requirement' basis.

MANUFACTURER
AM General Corporation, 14250 Plymouth Road, Detroit, Michigan 48232, USA.

Jeep (4 × 4) Light Vehicle

DEVELOPMENT
In 1963 Willys-Overland became Kaiser Jeep which became the Jeep Corporation in 1970, a subsidiary of American Motors Corporation. In 1950 Willys developed the M38 (4 × 4) vehicle for the US Army, followed by the M38A1 in 1952. (There is a separate entry for the M38 in this section.) Today Jeep Corporation manufactures three basic models of CJ line vehicles for the US market, the CJ-5, CJ-7 and Scrambler (CJ-8); the CJ-6 is no longer in production but is still in widespread use. The company has supplied a military version of the CJ-5 for export under the Military Assistance Program. The basic model for the CJ range was the M606 followed by the M606A1, M606A2 (CJ-5) and the M606A3 (CJ-5 fitted for radio). In addition to the CJ-5 and CJ-7 special configurations of the CJ-8 with a full soft-top, full hard-top wagon or a panel van are available for international markets. The latest model is the CJ-10, a heavy-duty utility pick-up truck which has greater cargo and payload capabilities than other CJ versions released in the USA to date. Militarised versions of the CJ range are available on vehicles classified as the AM7, AM8, AM10 and AM720, all for use outside the USA.

Jeep Corporation also has manufacturing and assembly plants and licensees in Australia, Bangladesh, Egypt, India (by Mahindra and Mahindra, for which there is a separate entry), Indonesia, Israel, Japan (by Mitsubishi, for which there is a separate entry), Kenya, South Korea (Asia Motors Company), Mexico, Morocco, Pakistan, Phillipines, Portugal (by Bravia, covered in a separate entry), Spain (VIASA), Sri Lanka, Taiwan, Thailand and Venezuela. They were also assembled in the Netherlands at Rotterdam by NEKAF and Van Twist in Dordrecht. Ebro of Spain manufactured the CJ-3B for the Spanish Army under the designation of CJ-3B-14 between 1975 and 1980.

AM8 version of Jeep (4 × 4) light vehilcle

AM10 pick-up version of Jeep (4 × 4) light vehilcle

In May 1983 it was announced that a production agreement between the American Motors Corporation (AMC) and the Chinese Beijing Automotive Works had been signed. The agreement established a new company, the Beijing Jeep Corporation, to produce Jeeps on a new production line to be established in China. The agreement has been backed by a $16 million investment by the American company. Production in China will be for the home market and also for export to Japan and the Far East. The joint venture will eventually be worth $51 million.

The Jeep plant in Pakistan, the Karachi-based Pakistan Automobile Corporation, has entered into an agreement with the Saudi Arabian government to establish a Jeep production plant in Saudi Arabia. The initial output of the new plant is planned to be 5000 vehicles.

DESCRIPTION
The layout of the Jeep is conventional with the engine at the front, individual seats for the driver and one passenger in the centre, bench seat to the rear, a small cargo area behind the bench seat and a tailgate at the very rear.

Both four- and five-speed gearboxes are available and the CJ-7, CJ-8 and CJ-10 can be fitted with an automatic transmission and a part-time four-wheel drive system. A four-cylinder petrol engine is standard with a six-cylinder petrol and four-cylinder diesel available as options. A wide range of optional equipment is available including: air conditioning system for the CJ-7 and CJ-8; soft-tops; removable plastic hard-top for the CJ-7; full metal hard-tops for the CJ-7 and CJ-8; various seating arrangements; different tyres; heavy-duty suspension; battery and alternator and special equipment for use in hot or cold climates.

The militarised versions of the CJ contain more heavy-duty equipment than that available on the commercial units. Items included are a heavy-duty air cleaner, severe use frame reinforcement package, shock absorbers and a battery clamp. All units are fitted with lift eyes and two hooks plus a complete black-out light system.

STATUS
Production.

MANUFACTURER
Jeep Corporation, International Operations, 27777 Franklin Road, Southfield, Michigan 48034, USA.

SPECIFICATIONS

Model	CJ-5	CJ-6	CJ-7
Configuration	4 × 4	4 × 4	4 × 4
Cab seating	1 + 5	1 + 7	1 + 5
Weight (empty)	1460 kg	1420 kg	1400 kg
(loaded)	2200 kg	2200 kg	2200 kg
Max load	740 kg	780 kg	800 kg
Length	3·67 m	4·08 m	3·89 m
Width	1·52 m	1·6 m	1·52 m
Height	1·72 m	1·91 m	1·72 m
Ground clearance	0·21 m	0·2 m	0·175 m
Track (front/rear)	1·33 m/1·28 m	1·31 m/1·27 m	1·42 m/1·4 m
Wheelbase	2·12 m	2·64 m	2·37 m
Fuel capacity	57 litres	58 litres	57 litres
Engine	Model 6-238 6-cylinder OHV petrol developing 110 hp at 3400 rpm		
Gearbox	manual 4 forward and 1 reverse	manual 4 forward and 1 reverse	manual 4 forward and 1 reverse
Transfer box	2-speed	2-speed	2-speed
Steering	recirculating ball	recirculating ball	recirculating ball
Turning radius	5 m	5·85 m	5·45 m
Suspension	semi-elliptical leaf springs and hydraulic shock absorbers		
Electrical system	12 V	12 V	12 V
Battery	1 × 12 V, 50 Ah	1 × 12 V, 50 Ah	1 × 12 V, 50 Ah

Model	AM7	AM8	AM10
Configuration	4 × 4	4 × 4	4 × 4
Cab seating	1 + 5	1 + 7	1 + 1
Weight (empty)	1275 kg	1328 kg	1718 kg
(loaded)	2200 kg	2200 kg	3035 kg
Max load	925 kg	872 kg	1317 kg
Length	3·89 m	4·5 m	4·85 m
Width	1·66 m	1·66 m	1·73 m
Height	1·83 m	1·98 m	1·83 m
Wheelbase	2·37 m	2·63 m	3·04 m
Ground clearance	0·21 m	0·21 m	0·23 m
Track (front/rear)	1·42 m/1·4 m	1·42 m/1·4 m	1·54 m/1·48 m
Fuel capacity	57 litres	57 litres	77 litres
Engine	Model 258 C1D 6-cylinder OHV developing 112 hp at 3000 rpm		
Gearbox	manual 4 forward and 1 reverse gears		
Transfer box	2-speed	2-speed	2-speed
Steering	recirculating ball	recirculating ball	recirculating ball
Turning radius	5·36 m	5·73 m	6·55 m
Brakes	manual, front disc, rear drum		power, front disc, rear drum
Suspension	semi-elliptical leaf springs and hydraulic shock absorbers		
Electrical system	12 V	12 V	12 V

AM-7 version of Jeep (4 × 4) light vehicle

M38 Series (4 × 4) 363 kg Light Vehicle

DEVELOPMENT

The M38 was developed by Willys from 1950 to meet an urgent US Army requirement for a light 4 × 4 vehicle to replace the large number of Second World War Jeeps still in service. The M38 was basically the standard CJ3A civilian vehicle with a deep fording kit, 24-volt electrical system and a semi-floating rear axle, and in appearance was similar to the wartime vehicle. The M38 was in production from 1950 to 1952 when it was replaced by the M38A1. The M38A1 is different in appearance from the M38 and has a more powerful engine and a slightly longer wheelbase. From the early 1960s the M38 and M38A1 were replaced in the US Army by the M151 (4 × 4) series of light vehicles.

DESCRIPTION

M38

The layout of the M38 is conventional with the engine at the front and the passenger/cargo area at the rear. Individual seats are provided for the driver and one passenger at the front with a bench seat for two passengers at the rear. The top of the vehicle can be covered by a canvas cover and when not in use the bows fold down at the rear of the vehicle. Both the M38 and M38A1 can be fitted with a front-mounted winch.

M38A1

The layout of the M38A1 is identical to the M38. The front axle is a full-floating, single reduction type fitted with a conventional differential with hypoid drive gears. The rear axle is a semi-floating single reduction type equipped with a conventional differential with hypoid drive gears. The M38A1C has a split windscreen to provide stowage space for the barrel when the vehicle is fitted with a 105 mm recoilless rifle. The vehicle also has its rear bench seat removed to make space for the mount. Racks for ammunition under the mount are reached by a rear tailgate. The spare wheel on the M38 is mounted at the rear and on the M38A1C on the right side of the vehicle.

M170 Ambulance

The full designation of the vehicle is Truck, Ambulance: ¼-ton, 4 × 4, M170, Front Line. It is a long wheelbase version of the M38A1 and can carry three patients on stretchers or six seated. The spare wheel is carried inside at the right of the front passenger seat and the handbrake has been modified to avoid interference with the left lower stretcher. Additional facilities include crash pads and an interior emergency light.

M38A1 (4 × 4) 363 kg light vehicle

M38A1 of Netherlands Army (T J Gander)

SPECIFICATIONS

Model	M38	M38A1	M170
Cab seating	1 + 3	1 + 3	1 + 1
Configuration	4 × 4	4 × 4	4 × 4
Weight (empty)	1247 kg	1209 kg	1344 kg
(loaded road)	1791 kg	1753 kg	1706 kg
Max load (road)	544 kg	544 kg	n/app
(cross country)	363 kg	363 kg	n/app
Towed load (road)	907 kg	907 kg	n/app
(cross country)	680 kg	680 kg	n/app
Length	3·377 m	3·517 m	3·936 m
Width	1·574 m	1·539 m	1·536 m
Height	1·879 m	1·85 m	2·032 m
(reduced)	1·379 m	1·428 m	n/app
Ground clearance	0·234 m	0·234 m	0·23 m
Track	1·247 m	1·247 m	1·247 m
Wheelbase	2·032 m	2·057 m	2·565 m
Angle of approach/departure	55°/35°	55°/35°	46°/34°
Max speed (road)	88·5 km/h	88·5 km/h	88·5 km/h
Range	362 km	450 km	482 km
Fuel capacity	49 litres	64·3 litres	75·7 litres
Max gradient	65%	69%	71%
Fording (without preparation)	0·939 m	0·939 m	0·381 m
(with preparation)	1·879 m	1·778 m	n/app
Engine model	Willys MC	Willys	Willys MD
Engine type	4-cylinder petrol	4-cylinder petrol	4-cylinder petrol
Output	60 bhp at 4000 rpm	72 bhp at 4000 rpm	68 bhp at 4000 rpm
Gearbox	manual with 4 forward and 1 reverse gears		
Clutch	single dry plate	single dry plate	single dry plate
Transfer box	2-speed	2-speed	2-speed
Turning radius	6·096 m	5·892 m	7·467 m
Suspension	semi-elliptical springs front and rear with hydraulic telescopic shock absorbers		
Tyres	7.00 × 16	7.00 × 16	7.00 × 16
Number of tyres	4 + 1 spare	4 + 1 spare	4 + 1 spare
Brakes (main)	hydraulic	hydraulic	hydraulic
(parking)	mechanical	mechanical	mechanical
Electrical system	24 V	24 V	24 V
Batteries	2 × 12 V	2 × 12 V	2 × 12 V

M170 (4 × 4) front line ambulance (US Army)

M38 (4 × 4) 363 kg light vehicle (US Army)

MANUFACTURER
AM General Corporation, 14250 Plymouth Road,
Detroit, Michigan 48232, USA.

*M38A1 of Spanish Marines fitted with radio
equipment (J I Taibo)*

M37 (4 × 4) 680 kg Cargo Truck and Variants M42, M43 and M201

DEVELOPMENT
Immediately after the Second World War the standard
680 kg vehicle in the US Army was the wartime T214 (or
Beep as it was more commonly known), which was
placed back in production during the early 1950s. This
was replaced by another Dodge called the M37
(development designation T245). More than 136 000
M37 trucks were built between 1950 and 1970. From the
late 1960s the M37 series was supplemented by the
M715 series of 1¼-ton trucks, but many M37s still
remain in service with the US Army.

DESCRIPTION
The basic cargo truck is designated the M37 (official
designation Truck, Cargo: ¾-Ton, 4 × 4, M37) and can
carry 907 kg of cargo on roads or 680 kg of cargo across
country. Towed allowance is 2722 kg on roads and
1815 kg across country.
  The engine is mounted at the front of the vehicle with
the three-man cab in the centre and the cargo area at
the rear. The cab has a windscreen which can be folded
forward onto the bonnet, removable canvas roof and a
door either side. The tops of the doors can be removed.
The rear all steel cargo area has a drop tailgate, removable bows and a tarpaulin cover, folding troop seats,
removable front rack, seat backs and supports.
  Power is taken from the engine through the clutch to
the transmission; a short propeller shaft connects the
transmission to the two-stage transfer case and power
is then transmitted to the front and rear axles by a
propeller shaft.
  The basic chassis is designated the M56 (with or
without a front-mounted winch with a capacity of
3402 kg) and other chassis are the M56C which has an
improved rear suspension and the M56B1 which has a
greater interchangeability of components with other
vehicles.

VARIANTS
Many countries have adopted the vehicle to mount light
weapons such as machine guns. The vehicle was also
built in Canada in the 1950s.

M42 Command Post
This differs from the cargo model in that it has side
curtains with windows and a split-type rear curtain, map
light, folding table and provision for the installation of
communications equipment.

M43 Ambulance
This model has a fully enclosed steel body consisting of
driver's and patients' compartments with a connecting
door. It can carry four stretcher patients plus an attendant or eight seated patients and an attendant. A winch
with a capacity of 3500 kg is mounted at the front of the
vehicle. The M43B1 has an aluminium rather than a
steel body and does not have the winch. An adjustable
spotlight is mounted on top of the cab and this can be
controlled from within the cab. A personnel heater and
surgical light are provided for the rear compartment.

M201 Maintenance Truck
This has an all-steel body with compartments for
stowing tools and supplies. It is used for telephone
installation and maintenance.

NAPCO Repowering Unit
NAPCO Industries of Hopkins, Minnesota, USA has
developed a repower package for this series of vehicle.

SPECIFICATIONS

Model	M37	M43	M201
Cab seating	1 + 2	1 + 2	1 + 2
Configuration	4 × 4	4 × 4	4 × 4
Weight (empty)	2585 kg	3952 kg	4218 kg
(loaded)	3493 kg	4617 kg	4218 kg
Length	4·81 m	5·004 m	5·174 m
Width	1·784 m	1·866 m	2·235 m
Height	2·279 m	2·333 m	2·323 m
Track	1·574 m	1·574 m	1·574 m
Wheelbase	2·844 m	3·2 m	3·2 m
Angle of approach/departure	38°/32°	32°/47°	44°/32°
Max speed	88·5 km/h	88·5 km/h	88·5 km/h
Range	362 km	362 km	362 km
Fuel capacity	91 litres	91 litres	91 litres
Max gradient	68%	68%	68%
Fording (without preparation)	1·066 m	1·066 m	1·066 m
(with preparation)	2·133 m	2·082 m	2·082 m
Engine	Dodge T245 6-cylinder in-line petrol developing 78 bhp at 2300 rpm		
Gearbox	manual with 4 forward and 1 reverse gears		
Clutch	single dry plate	single dry plate	single dry plate
Transfer box	2-speed	2-speed	2-speed
Steering	worm and sector	worm and sector	worm and sector
Turning radius	7·01 m	7·62 m	8·229 m
Suspension	semi-elliptical springs with hydraulic shock absorbers front and rear		
Tyres	9.00 × 16	9.00 × 16	9.00 × 16
Number of tyres	4 + 1 spare	4 + 1 spare	4 + 1 spare
Brakes (main)	hydraulic	hydraulic	hydraulic
(parking)	mechanical	mechanical	mechanical
Electrical system	24 V	24 V	24 V
Batteries	2 × 12 V	2 × 12 V	2 × 12 V

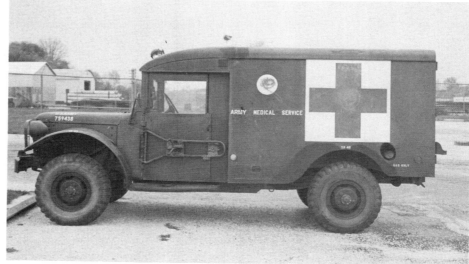

M43 (4 × 4) ambulance (Larry Provo)

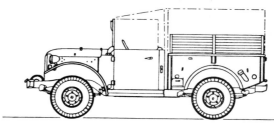

M37 (4 × 4) 680 kg cargo truck

Details of this are given under the entry for NAPCO Industries Repower/Modernisation Packages in the *Trucks* section.

STATUS
Production complete. In service with the US Army and many other armed forces including Canada, Greece, Spain, Thailand and Turkey. Dodge has also exported large numbers of its Power Wagon vehicles for military use including the M611 (cargo) and M615 (ambulance).

MANUFACTURER
Dodge Division of Chrysler Corporation, Detroit, Michigan, USA.

M37 (4 × 4) without front-mounted winch and with tarpaulin cover removed (Michael Ledford)

YUGOSLAVIA

Zastava (4 × 4) AR-51 Light Vehicle

DESCRIPTION
The Zastava AR-51 is the Italian FIAT AR-59 Campagnola 4 × 4 vehicle built under licence in Yugoslavia and is almost identical to the Italian vehicle. The engine is at the front of the vehicle with the crew compartment at the rear with a tailgate, two seats at the front and two bench seats down either side. The crew compartment can be covered with bows and a tarpaulin cover and side screens. When not required the bows are attached to the rear of the body. The AR-51 is used to tow mortars such as the 120 mm UB M52 and the 20 mm (triple) M55 anti-aircraft gun.

VARIANTS
An ambulance version is in service.

SPECIFICATIONS
Cab seating: 1 + 1 (4 in rear)
Configuration: 4 × 4
Weight:
  (empty) 1320 kg
  (loaded) 1800 kg
Max load: 480 kg
Towed load: 500 kg
Length: 3·565 m
Width: 1·545 m
Height: (cover up) 1·8 m
Ground clearance: 0·2 m
Track:
  (front) 1·254 m
  (rear) 1·26 m
Wheelbase: 2·25 m

Max speed: (road) 100 km/h
Range: 470 km
Fuel capacity: 58 litres
Fuel consumption: 16·6 litres/100 km
Fording: 0·6 m
Engine: 4-cylinder water-cooled petrol developing 48 hp
Tyres: 6.40 × 16

STATUS
Production complete. In service with the Yugoslav Army. Replaced in production by the FIAT 1107 (4 × 4).

MANUFACTURER
Red Flag Factory, Kragujevac, Serbia, Yugoslavia.

Zastava (4 × 4) AR-51 light vehicle towing 120 mm mortar

Zastava (4 × 4) AR-51 light vehicle towing 76 mm M48 gun

TRUCKS (over 1000 kg)

AUSTRALIA

Australian Army Truck Programme

DEVELOPMENT
In 1977 the Australian Army invited tenders for evaluation vehicles to replace its present fleet of International (4 × 4) 2500 kg and (6 × 6) 5000 kg series of trucks. The former is to be replaced by a 4000 kg truck and the latter by an 8000 kg truck.

In September 1978 contracts were awarded to General Motors-Holden and Mercedes-Benz (Australia) for three 4000 kg prototypes each, and to Leyland Motor Corporation of Australia, Mack Trucks of Australia and Thiess-Toyota for three 8000 kg prototypes each. All the vehicles were completed the following year and subsequently tested by the Medium Truck Trial Team of the Australian Army which was formed in February 1979 and disbanded in May 1980.

For the 4000 kg requirement Mercedes-Benz entered the West German UL 1700 L (4 × 4) Unimog truck and General Motors-Holden the Bedford MKP (4 × 4) which is powered by an 8·2-litre Bedford diesel engine and is similar to the Bedford MK series of 4 × 4 trucks used by the British and many other armies.

4-tonne (4 × 4) truck
In October 1981 the Australian Ministry of Defence announced that the Australian Army was to order 1295 Unimog (4 × 4) 4-tonne trucks from Mercedes-Benz (Australia) Pty Limited at a cost of $67 million. The vehicles will be assembled in Australia in conjunction with normal production at the Mercedes-Benz plant in Mulgrave, Victoria. Deliveries began in 1982 and are expected to be completed by 1987.

Australian content, valued at some $25 million, will be used in the vehicles, including locally produced components such as generators, fuel tanks, tyres and inner tubes and exhaust pipes, as well as the assembly of the cab and chassis. Mercedes-Benz (Australia) will purchase from specialist Australian manufacturers cargo and dump bodies, cranes and earth augers for fitting to the trucks.

In addition, the Australian automotive component industry will participate in offset orders worth at least $33 million for automotive-related goods and service to be placed by Daimler-Benz of the Federal German Republic.

Out of the planned total of 1295 vehicles 858 will be cargo trucks, 287 cargo trucks with winches, 76 cargo trucks with cranes, 69 dump trucks (with winches) and five will be fitted with earth augers/pole erectors.

The first of the Australian Unimogs entered service in November 1982.

For full details of the Mercedes-Benz U 1700 L see the separate entry in this section.

8-tonne (6 × 6) truck
In June 1981 Mack Trucks of Australia was awarded a contract for 940 8-tonne (6 × 6) trucks. At the same time Ford of Australia was awarded a contract for 170 light trucks based on its F-250 range of vehicles.

First deliveries of the Mack R (6 × 6) trucks were made in 1982 and final deliveries are expected to be

Prototype of Mercedes-Benz 4000 kg (4 × 4) truck (Australian Army)

made in 1987. Each vehicle will be able to carry ten 1-tonne pallets on roads or eight 1-tonne pallets across country.

Some 75 per cent of the Mack R truck will be built in Australia and this will boost the Australian vehicle industry with local expenditure of $73 million.

Variants of the Mack R series, using the same commercial cab and chassis, include a cargo vehicle with hydraulic crane mounted to the cab rear, 8 cubic-metre dump truck, water tanker, fuel tanker, bitumen distributer, wrecker, transit cement mixer, gun tractor and ammunition carrier. The gun tractor and ammunition carrier are to be used with the new American 155 mm M198 towed howitzers recently introduced into service with the Australian Army.

Ford Cargo 0913 truck
In early 1982 the Australian Army made an extra purchase of 372 Ford Cargo 0913 trucks to bring the number of Ford trucks it has in service to 715. The order was worth US$8 million and the first examples were delivered in March 1982 with the last being delivered by the end of July the same year.

The Ford Cargo 0913 trucks are powered by Ford 6·2-litre six-cylinder diesel engines. They are fitted with alumiunium bodies and are used for carrying troops or supplies, and some are fitted with cranes for material handling in the field. Some of the earlier Ford trucks purchased were of the Ford D-series type.

SPECIFICATIONS (Mack R)
Configuration: 6 × 6
Max load:
(road) 10 000 kg
(cross country) 8000 kg
Length: 9·68 m
Width: 2·516 m
Height: 3·285 m
Engine: Mack Maxidyne turbo-charged diesel developing 284 hp
Gearbox: manual, 5 forward and 1 reverse gears
Transfer box: 2-speed
Steering: Sheppard power-assisted
Suspension:
(front) semi-elliptical leaf springs
(rear) camel leaf springs
Number of tyres: 6 + 1 spare

STATUS
Both the 4-tonne (4 × 4) and 8-tonne (6 × 6) are in production and entering service with the Australian Army.

MANUFACTURERS
4-tonne (4 × 4) Mercedes-Benz (Australia) Pty Limited, Mulgrave, Victoria, Australia.

8-tonne (6 × 6) Mack Trucks (Australia) Pty Limited, 1728 Ipswich Road, Rocklea, Queensland 4106, Australia.

Mercedes-Benz Unimog (4 × 4) 4000 kg truck (Paul Handel)

Mack RM 6866 RS (6 × 6) 8000 kg truck (Paul Handel)

International (4 × 4) 2500 kg Truck

DEVELOPMENT
The International (4 × 4) 2500 kg truck was developed in the early 1950s by the International Harvester Company of Australia. The first three prototypes were completed in 1955. Production began in 1959 and continued

until 1971; by then 2363 had been completed. There have been four basic marks, 1, 2, 3 and 4. The official Australian Army designation for the vehicle is Truck, Cargo, 2½-ton, 4 × 4, General Service.

DESCRIPTION
The chassis consists of pressed steel channel side

members and cross-members riveted together. The cab is of the forward control type and is identical to that on the International 5-ton (6 × 6) truck.

The rear cargo body is of all steel construction and has a drop tailgate, bows and a tarpaulin cover. Swing-up seats along each side of the body can be refitted along the centre of the body, back to back, in which case the canopy cannot be fitted. The canopy, bows, seats, sides, and tailboard can be removed to leave a flat cargo bed.

The two-speed transfer case is mounted behind the gearbox and drive is transmitted to the front and rear axles by propeller shafts of equal lengths. The transfer case lever has four positions: low four-wheel drive, neutral, high rear wheel drive and high four-wheel drive. Drive to the front road wheels is transmitted through the hypoid gear of the front axle differential to the inner drive shafts which are connected to the outer drive shafts by 'tracta' constant velocity joints. The rear axle drive is also transmitted through the hypoid gears, and the drive to the road wheels is transmitted by fully floating axle shafts. The same types of stub axle and hub assembly are used on both front and rear axles.

The vehicle can be prepared for deep fording. A 5000 kg capacity Olding 20L winch is mounted in the centre of the vehicle under the chassis and is provided with 61 metres of cable.

VARIANTS
Variants in service with the Australian Army include fire-fighting, machinery, office, portable roadway laying vehicle with the British Laird class 30 trackway system, stores (with air conditioner) and an 1818-litre water tanker.

SPECIFICATIONS (Mark 3)
Cab seating: 1 + 1
Configuration: 4 × 4
Weight:
(empty) 5537 kg
(loaded, cross country) 8032 kg
Weight on front axle: (loaded, cross country) 3747 kg
Weight on rear axle: (loaded, cross country) 4285 kg
Max load: (cross country) 2495 kg
Towed load:
(road) 4536 kg
(cross country) 2722 kg
Load area: 4·367 × 2·438 m
Length: 6·375 m
Width: 2·438 m
Height:
(cab) 2·616 m
(tarpaulin) 2·896 m
(load area) 1·295 m
Ground clearance: 0·343 m
Track: 1·854 m
Wheelbase: 3·683 m
Angle of approach/departure: 44°/37°
Max speed:
(road) 80·4 km/h
(road, towing trailer) 64·4 km/h
Range: (road) 483 km
Fuel capacity: 200 litres
Max gradient: 60%
Fording:
(without preparation) 1·092 m
(with preparation) 1·981 m
Engine: International AGD-282 6-cylinder in-line water-cooled petrol developing 148 bhp (gross) at 3800 rpm
Gearbox: manual with 5 forward and 1 reverse gears (2nd to 5th synchromesh)
Clutch: single plate, dry
Transfer box: 2-speed
Steering: semi-reversible cam and twin lever
Turning radius: 9·14 m
Suspension: semi-elliptical springs with heavy duty double acting shock absorbers front and rear
Tyres: 12.00 × 20
Number of tyres: 4 + 1 spare
Brakes:
(main) hydraulic air-actuated
(parking) handbrake operates on rear axle
Electrical system: 12 V
Battery: 1 × 12 V, 60 Ah

Truck, Cargo, 2500 kg, GS (S Glen)

Truck, Cargo, 2500 kg, GS (Paul Handel)

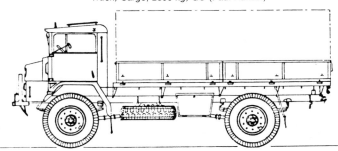
Truck, Cargo, 2500 kg, GS

STATUS
Production complete. In service only with the Australian Army.

MANUFACTURER
International Harvester Company of Australia, 211 Sturt Street, South Melbourne, Victoria 3205, Australia.

International (6 × 6) 5000 kg Truck

DEVELOPMENT
The International (6 × 6) 5000 kg truck was developed in the late 1950s by the International Harvester Company of Australia and the Army Design Department of the Department of the Army. The first two prototypes were completed in 1960 with the second series of prototypes following in 1964 (two cargo trucks and two dump trucks). The first production truck was handed over to the Australian Army in November 1966 and production continued until 1974, by which time 1410 had been completed. The correct Army designations of the vehicles are Truck, Cargo, 5-ton, General Service, F1 and Truck, Dump, 5 cubic yard, General Service, F2. Many of the components of this vehicle are identical to those used in the 2500 kg (4 × 4) truck which was also developed by International Harvester.

DESCRIPTION
The chassis consists of two parallel steel channels with six cross-members. The all-steel forward control cab is identical to that used for the 2500 kg truck and has a two-piece opening windscreen and a circular observation hatch in the right side of the roof.

The cargo body is of steel construction and has drop sides and a drop tailgate, all of which can be removed to enable the vehicle to carry pallets, removable bench seats and removable bows and a tarpaulin cover. The floor is steel with a wood lining.

The two-speed transfer case is mounted behind the gearbox and provides drive to the front wheels and rear bogie. Drive to the intermediate and rear axles is through power dividers attached to the forward face of each axle housing. Drive to the wheels is transmitted through the two-power divider differentials and axle shafts.

Two air-take-off valves are fitted, one for inflating the tyres and the other for deep wading and for pressurising

the transmission. A winch at the rear of the cab can be used to the front or rear of the vehicle. The engine automatically shuts off when overloading occurs.

Some cargo trucks have an Abbey hydraulic crane mounted between the cab and the body for unloading.

VARIANTS
Dump truck
This has a capacity of five cubic metres and a body of all welded aluminium sections which is tipped by a three-stage front-mounted hydraulic hoist. The tailgate is secured by an air-controlled latch mechanism. If required, the rear dump body can be fitted with bench seats down either side and provided with bows and a tarpaulin cover to enable the vehicle to be used for carrying passengers.

Other variants include a bitumen spreader, fire-fighting truck, van type stores vehicle, water tanker and a twin boom recovery vehicle designated the Truck, Wrecker, Medium, 5-ton General Service (6 × 6) (F5).

There is also a 4 × 2·5-ton tractor truck which has a similar chassis to the 5-ton cargo truck.

SPECIFICATIONS
(data in square brackets relate to dump truck where different from cargo truck)
Cab seating: 1 + 1
Configuration: 6 × 6
Weight:
  (empty) 6780 [7007] kg
  (loaded road) 13 584 [13 811] kg
  (loaded cross country) 11 316 [11 543] kg
Max load:
  (road) 6804 kg
  (cross country) 4536 kg
Towed load:
  (road) 8165 kg
  (cross country) 5900 kg
Load area: 4·267 [3·657] × 2·133 m
Length: 6·908 [6·527] m
Width: 2·438 m
Height:
  (cab) 2·616 m
  (tarpaulin) 3·022 m
Ground clearance: 0·33 m
Track: 1·85 m
Wheelbase: (1st axle to centre of rear bogie) 3·784 m
Angle of approach/departure: 44°/40° [44°/56°]
Max speed: (road) 77 km/h
Range: 483 km
Fuel capacity: 191 litres
Max gradient: 60%
Fording:
  (without preparation) 0·914 m
  (with preparation) 1·981 m
Engine: International AGD-283, 6-cylinder in-line water-cooled petrol developing 150 bhp (gross) at 3400 rpm
Gearbox: manual T-54 with 5 forward and 1 reverse gears
Clutch: single plate dry
Transfer box: 2-speed
Steering: semi-reversible cam and twin lever
Suspension:
  (front) semi-elliptical springs with double acting hydraulic shock absorbers
  (rear) multi-leaf 6-rod tandem
Tyres: 12.00 × 20
Number of tyres: 6 + 1 spare
Brakes:
  (main) hydraulic, 2 circuits, 1 for the 1st and 3rd axles and 1 for the 2nd axle
  (parking) handbrake on rear wheels
Electrical system: 12 V
Battery: 1 × 12 V, 76 Ah

STATUS
Production complete. In service with the Australian Army.

MANUFACTURER
International Harvester Company of Australia, 211 Sturt Street, South Melbourne, Victoria 3205, Australia.

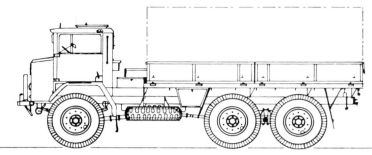

Truck, Cargo, 5-ton, General Service (6 × 6) (F5)

International Truck, Cargo, 5-ton, GS (6 × 6) (F5) (Paul Handel)

International F5 (6 × 6) truck with earth auger (Paul Handel)

International F5 (6 × 6) GS truck with Abbey loading crane (Paul Handel)

AUSTRIA

Steyr-Daimler-Puch Pinzgauer (4 × 4) 1000 kg and (6 × 6) 1500 kg Vehicles

DEVELOPMENT
The Pinzgauer range of all-terrain vehicles was developed by Steyr-Daimler-Puch as the successor to the highly successful 700 AP Haflinger range of 4 × 4 vehicles. The first prototype of the 4 × 4 Pinzgauer was completed in 1965 with first production models being completed in 1971. The vehicle was adopted by the Austrian Army in 1973. The 6 × 6 model was first shown in 1968 and entered production in 1971–72. The company is currently building about 2500 Pinzgauer 4 × 4 and 6 × 6 vehicles a year.

DESCRIPTION
Both the 4 × 4 and 6 × 6 models are available with two basic types of body, fully enclosed or with a military type cargo body. The former has an all-steel fully enclosed body with two doors in each side and a single door at the rear and the military type body has a single door each side for the driver and one passenger. The tops of the doors are removable and the windscreen can be folded forward onto the bonnet. The rear cargo area has removable bows and a tarpaulin cover and there are bench seats down each side of the rear body for eight men in the 4 × 4 model and twelve in the 6 × 6 model.

The chassis consists of a torsion resistant central tube with independent swing axles incorporating the transfer case and axle drive. The engine is mounted towards the front of the vehicle and is coupled to a ZF manual gearbox which transmits power via a propeller shaft to the transfer case, which also supports the hydraulically operated shifting clutch for the power transmission to the front axle. The drive shaft is to the front and rear differentials are within the central tube chassis. The differentials have a hydraulically operated mechanical lock.

Optional equipment for the Pinzgauer includes antenna holder (middle and side), camouflage net holders, convoy lights, blackout blinds, divided windscreen, foldable table, jerrican holders, rear mounting trays, rifle holders, mounting points for shovels, split battery system, rear tow hook and a 125-litre petrol tank.

VARIANTS
Ambulance
Versions of both the 4 × 4 and 6 × 6 Pinzgauer are available with a fully enclosed rear body which can be fitted with air-conditioning.

The basic military type vehicles with cargo type body are designated the 710 M (4 × 4) and 712 M (6 × 6), the radio vehicles the 710 K (4 × 4) and 712 K (6 × 6), the 6 × 6 fire-fighting vehicle the 712 FW, the 6 × 6 workshop vehicle the 712 W and the flatbed version, used to carry the 20 mm cannon is designated the 712 T.

In 1981 the 712 DK (6 × 6) was introduced, this has an enlarged four-door cab which extends to just over the second axle but still has a payload of 1500 kg.

Anti-aircraft
The Austrian Army has fitted a number of 6 × 6 Pinzgauers with 20 mm Oerlikon anti-aircraft cannon at the rear, with spare drum type magazines stowed to the immediate rear of the driver's position.

The Swiss Army has ordered 310 Austrian Steyr-Daimler-Puch Pinzgauer 6 × 6 ambulances in addition to the 1000-plus 4 × 4 and 6 × 6 cargo versions in service. As well as the driver and one medical assistant, the vehicle can carry four stretcher patients, or two stretcher and four seated patients, or six seated patients.

The chassis will be supplied dismantled by Steyr-Daimler-Puch with final assembly being undertaken in Switzerland by the Saurer company in Arbon. The additional cost entailed because of final assembly in Switzerland will be about ten per cent of the overall cost.

The body, interior fittings and tyres will all be made in Switzerland. Total cost of the 310 ambulances will be 32 million francs.

STATUS
In production. In service with Austria, Ghana, Nigeria, Sudan, Switzerland, Tunisia and Yugoslavia. Syria is reported to have purchased 2000.

MANUFACTURER
Steyr-Daimler-Puch AG, POB 823, A-8011 Graz, Austria.

SPECIFICATIONS

	4 × 4	6 × 6
Configuration		
Weight (empty, soft top/hardtop)	1950/2100 kg	2350/2600 kg
(loaded, soft top/hardtop)	3050/3100 kg	3900/4100 kg
Max weight on front axle (loaded)	1550 kg	1500 kg
Max weight on rear axle (loaded)	1550 kg	2600 kg (axles)
Max load	1000 kg	1500 kg
Towed load (road)	5000 kg	5000 kg
(cross country)	1500 kg	1800 kg
Load area	2·25 × 1·592 m	3·03 × 1·592 m
Length	4·175 m	4·955 m
Width	1·76 m	1·76 m
Height	2·045 m	2·045 m
(load area)	0·94 m	0·94 m
Ground clearance	0·335 m	0·335 m
Track	1·44 m	1·44 m
Wheelbase	2·2 m	2 m + 0·98 m
Max speed	110 km/h	100 km/h
Fuel capacity	75 litres	75 litres
	(125 litres optional)	(125 litres optional)
Fuel consumption (road)	17 litres/100 km	19 litres/100 km
(cross country)	6–10 litres/h	7–11 litres/h
Gradient	100%	100%
Side slope	40%	40%
Fording	0·7 m	0·7 m
Engine	Steyr 4-cylinder in-line air-cooled petrol developing 87 hp at 4000 rpm (92 hp at 4000 rpm optional)	
Gearbox	manual with 5 forward and 1 reverse gears	
Clutch	single dry plate	single dry plate
Transfer box	2-speed	2-speed
Steering	worm with roller	worm with roller
Turning radius	5·18 m	6·14 m
Suspension	independent. 4 × 4: coil springs at all wheel stations. 6 × 6: coil springs at front wheel stations; leaf springs and hydraulic shock absorbers rear suspension	
Tyres	7.50 × 16	7.50 × 16
Number of tyres	4 + 1 spare	6 + 1 spare
Brakes	hydraulic drum	hydraulic drum
Electrical system	24 V	24 V
Batteries	2 × 12 V, 66 Ah	2 × 12 V, 66 Ah

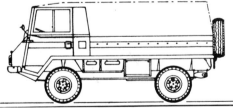

Steyr-Daimler-Puch Pinzgauer (4 × 4) 1000 kg vehicle

Steyr-Daimler-Puch Pinzgauer (6 × 6) 1500 kg vehicle

Steyr-Daimler-Puch Pinzgauer (4 × 4) 1000 kg vehicle with fully enclosed body

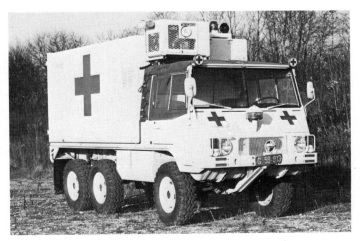

Steyr-Daimler-Puch Pinzgauer (6 × 6) fitted with ambulance body

Steyr-Daimler-Puch Pinzgauer (4 × 4) 1000 kg vehicle　　　*Steyr-Daimler-Puch Pinzgauer (6 × 6) 1500 kg vehicle*

Husar HA 2–90 (4 × 4) 1500 kg Truck

DESCRIPTION
The Husar (Herreslastkraftwagen) was developed by
ÖAF and the Austrian Army specifically for military use.
The first prototype was completed in 1966 with production beginning in 1968. Only 100 of these vehicles were
built. The layout of the Husar is conventional with the
engine at the front, all steel two-door fully enclosed cab
in the centre and the cargo area at the rear with dropsides and a tailgate, removable bows and a tarpaulin
cover and a removable bench seat down each side.
Some vehicles have been fitted with a 3500 kg capacity
winch.

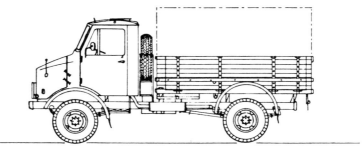

Husar HA 2–90 (4 × 4) 1500 kg truck

SPECIFICATIONS
Cab seating: 1 + 1
Configuration: 4 × 4
Weight:
(empty) 3750 kg
(loaded, road) 6750 kg
Max load:
(road) 3000 kg
(cross country) 1500 kg
Length: 5·65 m
Width: 2·13 m
Height: 2·84 m

Track:
(front) 1·78 m
(rear) 1·71 m
Wheelbase: 3·4 m
Max speed: 85 km/h
Range: 500 km
Max gradient: 60%
Fording: 0·8 m
Engine: ÖAF model D-0834 M8 4-cylinder diesel
developing 90 bhp at 2500 rpm
Gearbox: manual with 5 forward and 1 reverse gears
Clutch: single dry plate

Transfer box: 2-speed
Tyres: 9.00 × 20
Number of tyres: 4 + 1 spare
Brakes: hydraulic, air-assisted

STATUS
In service with the Austrian Army. Production
complete.

MANUFACTURER
Österreichische Automobilfabrik ÖAF, Gräf und Stift
AG, Brünner Strasse 72, A-1211 Vienna, Austria.

Steyr 680 M (4 × 4) 4500 kg Truck

DESCRIPTION
The Steyr 680 M is a 4 × 4 cargo truck designed to carry
a maximum of 4170 kg of cargo (when fitted with a
winch) across country, although for practical purposes it
is normally kept to 4570 kg, or 6570 kg on roads.

The all-steel cab is of the forward type and has two
doors, observation hatch in the roof, heater and fresh air
ventilator. The rear cargo area is provided with removable bows, tarpaulin cover, collapsible seats for up to 20
men and a drop tailgate. A winch with 90 metres of
13 mm diameter cable is fitted as standard.

This vehicle is now produced by Steyr Hellas in
Greece as the 680 MH. It is produced for use by the
Greek armed forces and for export.

NOTE
In previous editions of this yearbook this vehicle was
rated at 2500 kg payload for cross country operations,
but late in 1981 the manufacturers advised *Jane's Military Vehicles and Ground Support Equipment* that its
maximum cross country payload was 4500 kg.

Steyr 680 M (4 × 4) 4500 kg truck

VARIANTS
A fuel tanker is in service. The Steyr 680 M3 (6 × 6)
3500 kg truck is a development of the Steyr 680 M
(4 × 4) truck.

SPECIFICATIONS
Cab seating: 1 + 1
Configuration: 4 × 4
Weight:
(empty, with winch) 5830 kg
(road, loaded) 12 000 kg
(cross country, loaded) 10 000 kg
Weight on front axle: (empty) 3260 kg
Weight on rear axle: (empty) 2570 kg
Max load:
(road) 6500 kg
(cross country) 4500 kg
Towed load:
(road) 8000 kg
(cross country) 4000 kg
Load area: 4·06 × 2·2 m

Length: 6·57 m
Width: 2·4 m
Height:
(cab) 2·63 m
(tarpaulin) 2·85 m
(load area) 1·16 m
Ground clearance: 0·3 m
Track:
(front) 1·81 m
(rear) 1·67 m
Wheelbase: 3·7 m
Angle of approach/departure: 28°/28°
Max speed: (road) 80 km/h
Range: 450 km
Fuel capacity: 160 litres
Max gradient: (in low range at weight of 10 000 kg)
62%

Fording: 0·8 m
Engine: Steyr WD 610·23 6-cylinder direct injection
water-cooled diesel developing 132 hp (SAE) at
2800 rpm
Gearbox: manual with 5 forward and 1 reverse gears
Clutch: single dry plate
Transfer box: 2-speed
Steering: ZF hydraulic
Turning radius: 7·25 m
Suspension: semi-elliptical springs front and rear
Tyres: 9.00 × 20
Number of tyres: 6 + 1 spare
Brakes:
(main) hydraulic, air assisted
(parking) mechanical
Electrical system: 24 V
Batteries: 2 × 12 V, 110 Ah

STATUS
Placed back in production. In service with Austria, Greece, Nigeria and Switzerland.

MANUFACTURERS
Steyr-Daimler-Puch AG, Werke Steyr, A-4400 Steyr, Austria.
 Steyr Hellas SA, Industrial Area, PO Box 239, Sindos, Thessaloniki, Greece.

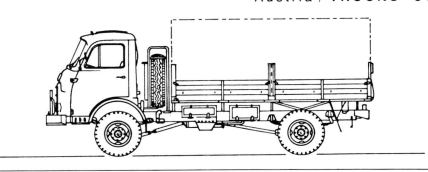

Steyr 680 M (4 × 4) 4500 kg truck

Steyr 680 M3 (6 × 6) 3500 kg Truck

DESCRIPTION
The Steyr 680 M3 is a 6 × 6 cargo truck designed to carry a maximum of 3500 kg of cargo cross country or 6500 kg of cargo on roads. It is a direct development of the Steyr 680 M (4 × 4) 4500 kg truck and shares many common components with this vehicle.

The all steel cab is of the forward control type and has two doors, observation hatch in the roof, heater and fresh air ventilator. The rear cargo area is provided with removable bows, tarpaulin cover, drop tailgate and

Top view of Steyr 680 M3 (6 × 6) cargo truck showing rectangular observation hatch in cab roof

collapsible seats down the centre. Most models have a 4500 kg capacity winch with 90 metres of 13 mm diameter cable. Some vehicles have a hydraulic crane for unloading mounted to the rear of the cab.

VARIANTS
Dump Truck
This is known as the Dreiseitenkipper and can tip to either side or the rear. Its loaded weight for road use is 13 000 kg and for cross country use is 10 000 kg.

Rocket Launcher
In the 1960s the Austrian Army received a number of Czechoslovak 130 mm (32 round) M-51 multiple rocket launchers mounted on the Czechoslovak Praga V3S (6 × 6) truck. They have now been mounted on a Steyr 680 M3 truck which has a larger four-door cab than the normal version. Full details of this version are given in *Jane's Armour and Artillery 1983–84*, page 720.

Tanker
This is known as the Einheitstankwagen (or ETW for short) and carries 8000 litres of fuel.

680 MH 3
The 680 MH 3 is a license-built version produced by Steyr Hellas in Greece for the Greek Army. It is also being offered for export. 55 per cent of this vehicle is now produced in Greece.

SPECIFICATIONS
Cab seating: 1 + 1
Configuration: 6 × 6
Weight:
 (empty) 6500 kg
 (loaded, road) 13 000 kg
 (loaded, cross country) 10 000 kg
Weight on front axle: (empty) 3200 kg
Weight on rear bogie: (empty) 3300 kg
Towed load:
 (road) 8000 kg
 (cross country) 4000 kg
Load area: 4·06 × 2·198 m
Length: 6·73 m
Width: 2·4 m

Height:
 (cab) 2·63 m
 (tarpaulin) 2·85 m
 (load area) 1·21 m
Ground clearance: 0·3 m
Track:
 (front) 1·81 m
 (rear) 1·72 m
Wheelbase: 2·76 m + 1·2 m
Angle of approach/departure: 28°/32°
Max speed: (road) 79·7 km/h
Range: 500 km
Fuel capacity: 180 litres
Max gradient: (low range at weight of 10 500 kg) 99%
Fording: 0·8 m
Engine: Steyr model WD 610·71 6-cylinder direct injection supercharged diesel developing 165 hp (SAE) at 2800 rpm
Gearbox: manual with 5 forward and 1 reverse gears
Clutch: single dry plate
Transfer box: 2-speed
Steering: ZF hydraulic
Turning radius: 7·25 m
Suspension:
 (front) semi-elliptical springs with telescopic shock absorbers
 (rear) semi-elliptical springs, reverse mounted with reversible spring hangers positioned in middle of rear axles
Tyres: 9.00 × 20
Number of tyres: 10 + 1 spare
Brakes:
 (main) hydraulic, air assisted
 (parking) mechanical
Electrical system: 24 V
Batteries: 2 × 12 V, 110 Ah

STATUS
Back in production. In service with the Austrian Army. It is now being built by Steyr Hellas in Greece for the Greek Army.

MANUFACTURERS
Steyr-Daimler-Puch AG, Werke Steyr, A-4400 Steyr, Austria.
 Steyr Hellas SA, Industrial Area, PO Box 239, Sindos, Thessaloniki, Greece.

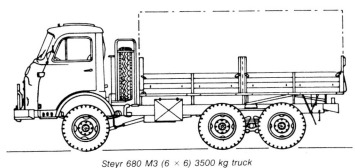

Steyr 680 M3 (6 × 6) 3500 kg truck

Steyr Hellas 680 MH 3 (6 × 6) 3500 kg truck (T J Gander)

Steyr 480 (4 × 2) 4000 kg Truck

DESCRIPTION
The Steyr 480 (4 × 2) truck is a standard commercial vehicle used for carrying a maximum load on roads of up to 4000 kg. The layout of the vehicle is conventional with the engine at the front, all steel two-door cab in the centre and the cargo area at the rear with drop sides, drop tailgate, removable bows and a tarpaulin cover. With a bench seat fitted down each side it can carry 20 fully-equipped men and 28 with the addition of a centre bench seat.

VARIANTS
A 4 × 4 model called the Steyr 580g can carry 3000 kg of cargo across country or 5000 kg on roads. Maximum towed load on roads is 8000 kg. Two basic models of the Steyr 580g are in service, one with a fully enclosed all-steel cab and the other with a cab with a removable soft top and a windscreen that can be folded forward onto the bonnet. A driver training version of the 580g with a large cab is also in service. The Steyr 586g (4 × 4) truck is powered by a 120 hp six-cylinder diesel engine.

STATUS
Production complete. In service with the Austrian Army.

MANUFACTURER
Steyr-Daimler-Puch AG, Werke Steyr, A-4400 Steyr, Austria.

SPECIFICATIONS
(data in square brackets relate to the Steyr 580g where it differs from the Steyr 480)
Cab seating: 1 + 1
Configuration: 4 × 2 [4 × 4]
Weight:
 (empty) 3850 [4250] kg
 (loaded, road) 7850 [9250] kg
Max load:
 (road) 4000 [5000] kg
 (cross country) n/a [3000 kg]
Length: 6·84 m
Width: 2·4 m
Height: 2·8 [3·3] m
Wheelbase: 3·71 m
Max speed: (road) 78 [69] km/h
Range: 300 [480] km
Max gradient: 30 [60]%
Fording: 0·9 m
Engine: Steyr model WD 413c 4-cylinder diesel developing 95 hp
Gearbox: manual with 5 forward and 1 reverse gears
Transfer box: none [2-speed]

Steyr 480 (4 × 2) 4000 kg truck (Austrian Army)

Gräf and Stift LAVT-9F/2H and ZAVT-9F/1 (4 × 4) 6000 kg Trucks

DESCRIPTION
The LAVT-9F/2H has a two-door all-steel fully enclosed forward control cab with the cargo area at the rear with a drop tailgate, removable bows and a tarpaulin cover. Some vehicles have been fitted with a HIAB crane to the rear of the cab for unloading. Flatbed versions of this truck also in service are used for a variety of roles including carrying pontoon boats and bridging components.

The ZAVT-9F/1 has an extended four-door cab, which is also fitted to the Gräf and Stift ZA-200/1 truck, and is often used as a prime mover for artillery. A 4500 kg capacity winch is fitted.

SPECIFICATIONS
(data in square brackets relate to ZAVT-9F/1 where different from LAVT- 9F/2H)
Configuration: 4 × 4
Weight:
 (empty) 8300 [7200] kg
 (loaded) 14 300 [13 200] kg
Max load: 6000 kg
Length: 6·35 [6·8] m
Width: 2·4 m
Height: 2·9 [3] m
Wheelbase: 3·86 m
Max speed: (road) 75 km/h
Range: 500 [400] km

Max gradient: 60%
Fording: 0·8 m
Engine: Gräf and Stift model 6 VT-145 6-cylinder diesel developing 145 hp
Gearbox: manual with 5 forward and 1 reverse gears
Transfer box: 2-speed
Tyres: 11.00 × 20

STATUS
Production complete. In service with the Austrian Army.

MANUFACTURER
Gräf und Stift AG, Brünner Strasse 72, A-1211 Vienna, Austria.

Gräf and Stift LAVT-9F/2H (4 × 4) 6000 kg truck (Austrian Army)

Gräf and Stift ZAVT-9F/1 (4 × 4) 6000 kg truck with extended cab (Austrian Army)

Steyr 1291.280/4 × 4 M 6000 kg Truck

DESCRIPTION
The Steyr 1291.280/4 × 4 M is a 4 × 4 cargo truck designed to carry a maximum load of 6000 kg on both roads and cross country, and to share many common components with the Steyr 1491 M3 (6 × 6) 10 000 kg truck.

The chassis consists of a low distortion parallel ladder frame with bolted tubular cross-members. The forward control cab is of all-steel construction and can be tilted forwards at an angle of 70 degrees to allow access to the engine and transmission for maintenance purposes. The driver's suspension seat is adjustable and the cab can be fitted with a single or twin passenger seat. The cab has two doors, observation/machine gun hatch in the roof, heater and a fresh air ventilator.

The rear cargo area is provided with removable bows, tarpaulin cover, drop tailgate and, down the centre, collapsible seats for 20 fully-equipped troops. Seat benches, bows and the tarpaulin cover can be stowed behind the head board.

Optional equipment includes a winch with a capacity

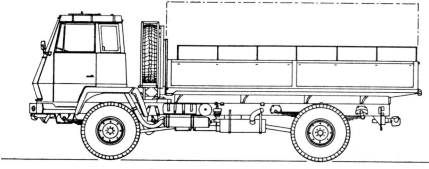

Steyr 1291.280/4 × 4 M 6000 kg truck

of 10 000 kg and 60 metres of cable; alternative engines and transmission are also available.

VARIANTS
No variants have been announced although the vehicle can be adopted for a wide variety of military applications.

STATUS
Production.

MANUFACTURER
Steyr-Daimler-Puch AG, Werke Steyr, A-4400 Steyr, Austria.

Steyr 1291.280/4 × 4 M 6000 kg truck showing spare wheel to cab rear

Steyr 1291.280/4 × 4 M 6000 kg truck with bows and tarpaulin cover

SPECIFICATIONS
Cab seating: 1 + 1 (or 1 + 2)
Configuration: 4 × 4
Weight:
(empty) 9500 kg
(loaded) 15 500 kg
Weight on front axle: (loaded) 6500 kg
Weight on rear axle: (loaded) 9000 kg
Max load: (road and cross country) 6000 kg
Towed load: (road and cross country) 10 000 kg
Load area: 5·5 × 2·43 m
Length: 7·189 m
Width: 2·5 m
Height: (cab) 3·025 m
Ground clearance: 0·38 m
Track:
(front) 2·072 m
(rear) 2·072 m

Wheelbase: 4·2 m
Angle of approach/departure: 35°/40°
Max speed: (road) 79·3 km/h
Range: 900 km (with 300 hp engine, 800 km)
Fuel capacity: 400 litres
Gradient: 100% (low range)
Fording: 0·8 m (1 m optional)
Engine: Steyr model WD 615.77, 6-cylinder, direct injection, water-cooled diesel, developing 293 hp (SAE) at 2400 rpm
Gearbox: ZF 5 S 111 GP manual with 9 forward and 1 reverse gears
Clutch: single dry plate (or ZF hydraulic torque converter in combination with 6 forward and 2 reverse synchromesh gears, or Allison automatic with 5 forward and 1 reverse gears)
Transfer box: Steyr VG 1200 2-speed
Steering: ZF hydraulic

Turning radius: 8·25 m
Suspension:
(front) semi-elliptical springs with telescopic shock absorbers
(rear) semi-elliptical springs with telescopic shock absorbers
Tyres: 14.00 × 20
Number of tyres: 4 + 1 spare
Brakes:
(main) two circuit compressed air brake
(parking) spring energy, air operated
Electrical system: 24 V
Batteries: 2 × 12 V, 135 Ah

Gräf and Stift ZA-200/1 A (6 × 6) 10 000 kg Truck

DESCRIPTION
The Gräf and Stift ZA-200/1 (6 × 6) was, until the introduction of the new ÖAF Type 20.320 (6 × 6), the standard 10 000 kg truck of the Austrian Army. The two-door all-steel forward control cab has a circular observation hatch in the right side of the roof. The rear cargo area has drop sides and a drop tailgate. Many vehicles have been fitted with a HIAB crane to the rear of the cab for unloading. A 4500 kg capacity winch leads out through the front of the vehicle.

VARIANTS
The Austrian Army engineers use a model with a large four-door all-steel cab and thus a shorter cargo area, which can carry 8000 kg of cargo.
The ZAFD-210/36 is basically the engineers' version with a KS-45M revolving crane mounted on the rear. Stabilisers are lowered to the ground before the crane is used. The jib of the crane can be disassembled to reduce the overall length of the vehicle for travelling.
The ZAFD-240/36 is used for towing semi-trailers carrying MBTs of the Austrian Army (M60A1s and M47s) and has the same chassis as the engineers' model and an unladen weight of 10 650 kg. Immediately behind the cab is a hydraulic crane and two winches with a capacity of 20 000 kg each.
LAFD-145/42 and LAFD-210/46 are both aircraft refuellers used by the Austrian forces.

SPECIFICATIONS
Cab seating: 1 + 1
Configuration: 6 × 6

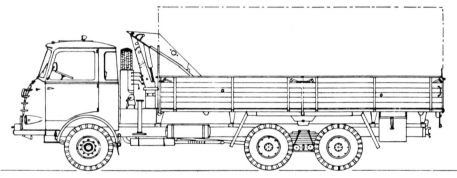

Gräf and Stift ZA-200/1 A (6 × 6) 10 000 kg truck with HIAB crane to cab rear

Weight:
(empty) 10 630 kg
(loaded, cross country) 20 630 kg
Max load:
(road) 15 000 kg
(cross country) 10 000 kg
Length: 8·6 m
Width: 2·4 m
Height: 2·9 m
Track:
(front) 1·91 m
(rear) 1·73 m
Wheelbase: 3·62 m + 1·4 m
Max speed: (road) 70 km/h
Range: 350 km
Max gradient: 72%

Fording: 0·6 m
Engine: Gräf and Stift model 6 VT-200 6-cylinder diesel developing 200 hp at 2200 rpm
Transfer box: 2-speed
Tyres: 11.00 × 20
Number of tyres: 10 + 1 spare
Brakes:
(main) air
(parking) mechanical

STATUS
Production complete. In service with the Austrian Army.

MANUFACTURER
Gräf und Stift AG, Brünner Strasse 72, A-1211 Vienna, Austria.

ÖAF Type 20.320 (6 × 6) 10 000 kg Truck

DEVELOPMENT
The ÖAF Type 20.320 (6 × 6) 10 000 kg truck is essentially a modified version of the West German Army MAN 7000 kg truck built in Austria. Modifications have included the replacement of the Klockner-Humbolt-Deutz engine by a MAN, installation of a hydraulic crane and provision for mounting a machine gun on the roof of the cab. The initial order was for 350 trucks, the first of which was handed over in 1975.

DESCRIPTION
The chassis is constructed from welded box-section longitudinal girders strengthened by tubular cross-members. An auxiliary frame to the rear of the cab carries the loading crane.
The cab is made of welded sheet steel and is mounted on rubber supports on the chassis. It is divided into two compartments, crew at the front and engine at the rear. Forward opening doors are fitted left and right and there are seats for three people which can be arranged to provide two couchettes. The centre seat has a 180-degree vertical movement and serves as a step for the machine gun slewing ring mounted on the

roof. The roof has a sliding hatch. The spare wheel is housed in the upper part of the engine compartment and there is a small hoist provided to raise and lower it. The battery box is on the right side of the engine compartment.
The base for the body comprises seven sheet steel cross-members bolted firmly to the chassis, the floor of which is 40 mm tongue-and-groove pine. The side- and tailboards consist of 25 mm hollow-section aluminium. The front is 1·5 metres high and the sides and rear boards 700 mm high. The sideboards are divided and removable seats for eight men are fitted to the floor either to the front or rear. If required a second similar

seat-group can be fitted. With only one eight-seater in place there is a load area for 72 ammunition boxes on the floor. The three adjustable bows support the canvas tarpaulin which has windows towards the top.

The vehicle is radio suppressed and a junction for an external current supply is provided. An Eberspacher independent diesel-driven warm air heating unit is fitted as standard. Mounted to the rear of the cab is a Palfinger PK 7500 loading crane with a capacity of 7000 kg.

The latest production version is the Type 20.320 G2 which has a centrally-mounted winch with a 7500 kg capacity front and rear.

STATUS
Production. In service with the Austrian Army.

MANUFACTURER
Österreichische Automobilfabrik ÖAF-Gräf und Stift AG, Brünner Strasse 72, A-1211 Vienna, Austria.

SPECIFICATIONS
Cab seating: 1 + 2
Configuration: 6 × 6
Weight:
(empty) 12 500 kg
(loaded, cross country) 22 000 kg
Max load: (cross country) 10 000 kg
Length: 8·85 m
Width: 2·5 m
Height:
(tarpaulin cover) 3·34 m
(cab) 3 m
Ground clearance: 0·415 m
Track: 2·07 m
Wheelbase: 3·8 m + 1·4 m
Angle of approach/departure: 42°/38°
Max road speed: 84 km/h
Max range: 700 km
Fuel capacity: 500 litres
Gradient: 60%
Fording: 0·8 m

ÖAF Type 20.320 (6 × 6) 10 000 kg truck

Engine: MAN D 2538 MT V-8 diesel developing 320 bhp at 2500 rpm
Gearbox: hydraulic torque converter with lock-up clutch (foot operated), 6-speed gearbox (6 forward and 1 reverse gears) and 3 axle transfer case with differential lock between front and rear axle drive
Steering: recirculating ball with hydraulic assistance
Turning radius: 9·75 m

Suspension: progressively acting helical springs and hydraulic shock absorbers
Tyres: 14.00 × 20
Number of tyres: 6 + 1 spare
Brakes:
(main) air/hydraulic
(parking) mechanical
Electrical system: 24 V

Steyr 1491 M3 (6 × 6) 10 000 kg Truck

DESCRIPTION
The Steyr 1491 M3 is a 6 × 6 cargo truck designed to carry a maximum load of 10 600 kg on both roads and cross country, and to share many common components with the Steyr 1291 M (4 × 4) 6000 kg truck.

The chassis consists of a low distortion parallel ladder frame with bolted tubular cross-members. The forward control cab is of all-steel construction and can be tilted forwards at an angle of 70 degrees to allow access to the engine and transmission for maintenance purposes. The driver's suspension seat is adjustable and the cab can be fitted with a single or twin passenger seat. The fully enclosed cab has two doors, observation/machine gun hatch in the roof, heater and a fresh air ventilator.

There is a lockable differential lock between the two rear axles and a lockable differential on each of the rear two axles.

The rear cargo area is provided with removable bows, tarpaulin cover, drop tailgate and collapsible seats for troops down the centre. Seat benches, bows and the tarpaulin cover can be stowed behind the head board.

Optional equipment includes a winch with a capacity of 10 000 kg and 60 metres of cable.

VARIANTS
Two versions of the Steyr 1491 have been announced to date, with main differences being in engine power. They are the 1491.280/6 × 6 M and the 1491.330/6 × 6 M. The 1491 can be adapted for a wide variety of military applications.

STATUS
Production.

MANUFACTURER
Steyr-Daimler-Puch AG, Werke Steyr, A-4400 Steyr, Austria.

Steyr 1491 M3 (6 × 6) 10 000 kg truck

Steyr 1491 M3 (6 × 6) 10 000 kg truck

SPECIFICATIONS
Cab seating: 1 + 1 (or 1 + 2)
Configuration: 6 × 6
Weight:
 (empty) 12 400 kg
 (loaded) 22 000 kg
Weight on front axle: (loaded) 6500 kg
Weight on each rear axle: (loaded) 8000 kg
Max load: 10 600 kg
Towed load:
 (cross country) 15 000 kg
 (road, up to) 40 000 kg
Load area: 6·2 × 2·408 m
Length: 8·389 m
Width: 2·5 m
Height: (cab) 3·025 m
Ground clearance: 0·38 m
Track:
 (front) 2·072 m
 (rear) 2·072 m
Wheelbase: 4 m + 1·4 m
Angle of approach/departure: 35°/40°
Max speed: (road) 79·3 km/h (85·2 km/h for V-8)
Range: (approx) 800 km
Fuel capacity: 400 litres
Max gradient: 100% (low range at weight of 22 500 kg)
Fording: 0·8 m (1 m optional)
Engine: Steyr model WD 615.7, 6-cylinder, direct injection, turbo-charged, water-cooled diesel, developing 293 hp (SAE) at 2400 rpm or Steyr model WD 815.74, V-8, direct injection, turbo-charged diesel developing 340 hp (SAE) at 2200 rpm

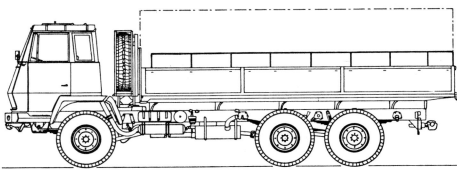

Steyr 1491 M3 (6 × 6) 10 000 kg truck

Gearbox: ZF 5 S 111 GP manual with 9 forward and 1 reverse gears
Clutch: single dry plate (mechanically operated with assistance of compressed air)
Transfer box: Steyr VG 1200 2-speed
Steering: ZF hydraulic
Turning radius: 10·45 m
Suspension:
 (front) semi-elliptical springs with telescopic shock absorbers
 (rear) individual semi-elliptical springs with telescopic shock absorbers

Tyres: 14.00 × 20
Number of tyres: 6 + 1 spare
Brakes:
 (main) dual circuit compressed air
 (parking) spring energy, air operated
Electrical system: 24 V
Batteries: 2 × 12 V, 135 Ah (165 Ah for V-8)

BELGIUM

FN 4RM/62 Ardennes (4 × 4) 1500 kg Truck

For details of this truck see *Jane's Military Vehicles and Ground Support Equipment 1983*, page 313.

FN 4RM/62C (4 × 4) 3000 kg Truck

DESCRIPTION
The FN 4RM/62C (4 × 4) 3000 kg truck was designed in the late 1940s to meet the requirements of the Belgium Army. Production was initially by FN but due to an increase in orders a co-production agreement was concluded with Brossel and Miesse. By the time production was completed in 1954 4150 trucks had been built.

 The all-steel forward control cab has a circular observation hatch in the roof. The all-steel rear cargo area has a drop tailgate, removable bows and a tarpaulin cover.

VARIANTS
A tipper model is in service in small numbers.

SPECIFICATIONS
Cab seating: 1 + 1
Configuration: 4 × 4
Weight:
 (empty) 5000 kg
 (loaded, road) 9500 kg
 (loaded, cross country) 8000 kg
Max load:
 (road) 4500 kg
 (cross country) 3000 kg
Max towed load: 3000 kg
Length: 5·66 m
Width: 2·24 m
Height:
 (cab) 2·5 m
 (tarpaulin) 2·85 m
Track:
 (front) 1·605 m
 (rear) 1·65 m
Ground clearance: 0·26 m
Wheelbase: 2·85 m
Max road speed: 75·6 km/h
Max range: 500 km
Fuel capacity: 105 litres
Gradient: 40%
Fording: 1 m

FN 4RM/62C (4 × 4) 3000 kg truck (C R Zwart)

Engine: FN 64E 6-cylinder petrol developing 92 hp at 3000 rpm
Gearbox: manual, 4 forward and 1 reverse gears
Clutch: single dry plate
Transfer box: 2-speed
Steering: semi-irreversible cam and sector
Turning radius: 7·04 m
Suspension: (front and rear) semi-elliptical leaf springs and hydraulic shock absorbers
Tyres: 8.50 × 20
Number of tyres: 6 + 1 spare

Brakes:
 (main) hydraulic
 (parking) mechanical
Electrical system: 12 V

STATUS
Production complete. In service only with the Belgian Army.

MANUFACTURER
FN, Brossel and Miesse, Belgium.

BRAZIL

ENGESA EE-15 (4 × 4) 1500 kg Truck

DESCRIPTION
The EE-15 (4 × 4) truck has been designed by ENGESA for both civil and military use. Its chassis is of high tensile steel with cross members riveted into position. A rear towing hook and four lifting eyes are fitted. The cab has a vinyl top and doors, folding down windscreen with wipers, adjustable seat for the driver and a seat for the two passengers. The standard all steel cargo body has a tailgate, bows and a tarpaulin cover.

A wide range of optional equipment is available including a body with tilting troop seats, hydraulic loader with a maximum capacity of 3000 kg, front-mounted 3000 kg capacity winch with 50 metres of 12·7 mm steel cable, centre or rear 7500 kg capacity winch with two drums each with 80 metres of 16 mm diameter steel cable, power take off, fire extinguisher and detection system and engine starting pilot for cold areas.

VARIANTS
ENGESA can also supply the EE-15 with other types of body including ambulance, crash tender and van.

STATUS
In production. In service with Brazil, Chile, Columbia, Gabon and undisclosed countries.

MANUFACTURER
ENGESA Engenheiros Especializados SA, Avenida das Nacoes Unidas 22.833, Santo Amaro, 04795 São Paulo, Brazil.

SPECIFICATIONS
Cab seating: 1 + 2
Configuration: 4 × 4
Weight:
 (empty) 4200 kg
 (loaded, road) 7200 kg
 (loaded, cross country) 5700 kg
Max load:
 (road) 3000 kg
 (cross country) 1500 kg

Max towed load: 1500 kg
Length: 5·65 m
Width: 2·25 m
Height:
 (cab) 2·5 m
 (tarpaulin) 2·8 m
Ground clearance: 0·35 m
Track: 1·71 m
Wheelbase: 3·3 m
Angle of approach/departure: 42°/35°
Max speed: (road) 90 km/h
Range: 600 km
Fuel capacity: 120 litres
Max gradient: (loaded, cross country) 60%
Max side slope: 30%
Fording: 0·9 m
Vertical obstacle: 0·4 m
Engine: Mercedes-Benz OM-352 6-cylinder in-line water-cooled diesel developing 149 hp (gross) at 2800 rpm

Gearbox: Mercedes-Benz G-3/40 manual with 5 forward and 1 reverse gears
Clutch: dry, single disc
Transfer box: mechanical ENGESA, double speed with constant mesh helical gears, optional front or rear left side PTO
Suspension:
 (front) semi-elliptical springs and double acting hydraulic shock absorbers
 (rear) 2 semi-elliptical springs and double acting hydraulic shock absorbers
Steering: mechanical
Turning radius: 6·6 m
Tyres: 9.00 × 20-12 PR
Number of tyres: 4 + 1 spare
Brakes:
 (main) drum type, air/hydraulic
 (parking) mechanical acting on transfer case
Electrical system: 12 V
Battery: 1 × 12 V, 140 Ah

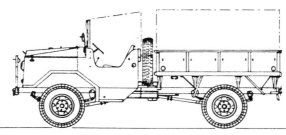

ENGESA EE-15 (4 × 4) 1500 kg truck

ENGESA EE-15 (4 × 4) 1500 kg truck fitted with van type body

ENGESA EE-15 (4 × 4) 1500 kg truck

ENGESA EE-25 (6 × 6) 2500 kg Truck

DESCRIPTION
The EE-25 (6 × 6) truck has been developed by ENGESA for both civil and military applications. Its chassis is of high tensile steel with cross-members riveted into position. A rear tow hook is provided. The layout of the vehicle is conventional with the engine at the front, cab in the centre and the cargo area at the rear. The cab has a vinyl top and doors, folding down windscreen with wipers, adjustable seat for the driver, and a single seat for the two passengers. The all-steel body has a tailgate, bows and a tarpaulin cover.

Optional equipment includes a 5000 kg capacity hydraulic crane, front-mounted 3000 kg capacity winch with 50 metres of 13 mm diameter cable, centre or rear winch with a 7500 kg capacity and two drums of 80 metres of 16 mm diameter cable, power take off, fire extinguisher and detection system, engine start pilot for cold areas. A 4 × 4 model of the EE-25 is also available and both models can have either single or dual rear wheels.

VARIANTS
The basic chassis can be used for a variety of other roles including ambulance, crash tender, dump truck (4 × 4), recovery, tanker (fuel or water), lubrication vehicle and van (eg command or workshop).

ENGESA EE-25 (6 × 6) 2500 kg truck showing Boomerang rear suspension in operation

SPECIFICATIONS (6 × 6 model)
Cab seating: 1 + 2
Configuration: 6 × 6
Weight:
  (empty) 6800 kg
  (loaded, road) 11 800 kg
  (loaded, cross country) 9300 kg
Max load:
  (road) 5000 kg
  (cross country) 2500 kg
Length: 6·82 m
Width: 2·25 m
Height:
  (cab) 2·5 m
  (tarpaulin) 3·1 m
Ground clearance: (axles) 0·35 m
Track: 1·8 m
Wheelbase: (front axle to centre of rear bogie) 4·2 m
Angle of approach/departure: 52°/52°
Max speed: (road) 90 km/h
Range: 600 km
Fuel capacity: 200 litres
Max gradient: 60%
Max side slope: 30%
Fording: 0·9 m
Vertical obstacle: 0·4 m
Engine: Mercedes-Benz OM-352A 6-cylinder in-line diesel developing 174 hp at 2800 rpm

Gearbox: manual with 5 forward and 1 reverse gears
Clutch: single disc, dry
Transfer box: ENGESA 2-speed
Steering: power assisted
Turning radius: 9·9 m
Suspension:
  (front) semi-elliptical springs with double acting hydraulic shock absorbers
  (rear) semi-elliptical springs. Rear axle is ENGESA Boomerang type with walking beams
Tyres: 11.00 × 20-14 PR
Number of tyres: 6 + 1 spare

Brakes:
  (main) air/hydraulic
  (parking) mechanical acting on transfer case
Electrical system: 12 V

STATUS
In production. In service with Bolivia, Brazil, Chile, Columbia, Gabon and undisclosed countries.

MANUFACTURER
ENGESA Engenheiros Especializados SA, Avenida das Nacoes Unidas 22.833, Santo Amaro. 04795 São Paulo, Brazil.

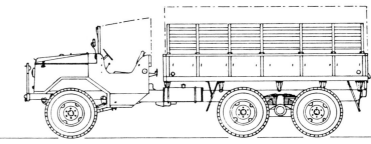

ENGESA EE-25 (6 × 6) 2500 kg truck

ENGESA EE-25 (4 × 4) 2500 kg truck with basic cargo/troop body

ENGESA EE-25 (4 × 4) 2500 kg truck with tanker body

ENGESA EE-50 (6 × 6) 5000 kg Truck

DEVELOPMENT
The ENGESA EE-50 (6 × 6) 5000 kg truck has been designed to meet the requirements of the Brazilian Army. Following trials with prototypes it has been selected to become the standard 5000 kg truck of the Brazilian Army in the 1980s. First production vehicles were completed late in 1980.

DESCRIPTION
The EE-50 chassis is made of riveted steel rails and cross-members. The all-steel forward control cab can be tilted forward to allow access to the engine. The windscreen is in two parts, left and right, both hinged at the top and with a windscreen wiper.
  The all-steel rear cargo area is provided with lateral tilting troop seats, drop tailgate, removable bows and a tarpaulin cover. Optional equipment includes an engine-starting pilot for cold weather and a fire detection and extinguishing system.

VARIANTS
The EE-50 can be supplied with a number of types of body including an ambulance, van, fuel tanker, light recovery, water tanker, fire tender and mobile workshop.

STATUS
Production. In service with the Brazilian Army and on order for at least one other country.

MANUFACTURER
ENGESA Engenheiros Especializados SA, Avenida das Nacoes Unidas 22.833, Santo Amaro, 04795 São Paulo, Brazil.

ENGESA EE-50 (6 × 6) 5000 kg truck

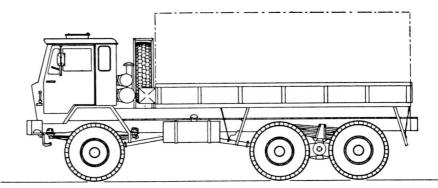

ENGESA EE-50 (6 × 6) 5000 kg truck

SPECIFICATIONS
Cab seating: 1 + 1
Configuration: 6 × 6
Weight:
(empty) 12 000 kg
(loaded, road) 22 000 kg
(loaded, cross country) 17 000 kg
Max load:
(road) 10 000 kg
(cross country) 5000 kg
Max towed load: 6000 kg
Length: 7·85 m
Width: 2·6 m
Height:
(cab hatch) 3·025 m
(tarpaulin cover) 3·5 m

Ground clearance: 0·35 m
Track: 2·1 m
Wheelbase: (first axle to centre of rear bogie) 4·5 m
Angle of approach/departure: 40°/50°
Max speed: 85 km/h
Range: 700 km
Fuel capacity: 300 litres
Max gradient: 60%
Max side slope: 30%
Fording: 1·4 m
Vertical obstacle: 0·6 m
Engine: Scania D11 6-cylinder water-cooled diesel developing 215 hp (SAE) at 2200 rpm
Gearbox: manual, 5 forward and 1 reverse gears
Clutch: single dry plate
Transfer box: mechanical, 2-speed

Suspension:
(front) leaf springs, front wheels driven by hypoid angular transmission and bevel differential gears
(rear) leaf springs, ENGESA Boomerang articulated axle with hypoid angular transmission, bevel differential gears and side walking beams with helical gears
Steering: integral hydraulic
Tyres: 14.00 × 20-18 PR
Number of tyres: 6 + 1 spare
Brakes:
(main) air
(parking) air, on transfer case output shaft
Electrical system: 24 V

ENGESA Total Traction Line

In addition to producing the EE-15, EE-25 and EE-50 series of cross-country military vehicles, ENGESA offers a Total Traction Line of transmission and suspension parts suitable for pickups and trucks.

4 × 4

Through the use of the combination of front-driven axle, transfer case, levers, connections and other parts, 4 × 2 vehicles can be converted into 4 × 4 configuration for off-the-road operation. On roads the front axle is disengaged.

6 × 4

This is primarily for civilian application. A rear bogie-type suspension, plus transfer and reduction case, with lockable inter-differential, plus reinforced front axle, will increase the cargo capacity of a standard 6 × 4 cargo truck for operations in snow and on dirt tracks. For even

Mercedes Benz LG-1213 (4 × 4) truck of Brazilian Army (Rinaldo S Olive)

Mercedes Benz LG-1819 truck of Brazilian Army (Rinaldo S Olive)

Chevrolet truck of Brazilian Army carrying pallet with 105 mm OTO-Melara Pack Howitzer (Rinaldo S Olive)

Mercedes Benz LG-1519 (6 × 6) truck of Brazilian Army with ENGESA Boomerang rear suspension (Rinaldo S Olive)

Chevrolet truck of Brazilian Army (Rinaldo S Olive)

Mercedes Benz LG-1819 truck, of Brazilian Army, as workshop (Rinaldo S Olive)

greater improvement in cross-country capability the rear bogie can be replaced by the ENGESA Boomerang rear independent suspension.

6 × 6
With the same parts of the 6 × 4 model, plus a front driving axle, a medium or heavy truck can be transformed into a 6 × 6 model with a high off-the-road potential.

Boomerang
This is fitted as standard on all ENGESA 6 × 6 military vehicles (EE-25 and EE-50) as well as the EE-9 and EE-11 (6 × 6) armoured vehicles. It consists of four driving wheels mounted on walking beams with gears inside, which are fixed onto a single rear axle. The wheels have independent vertical travel up to one metre and as an option a differential locking system can be installed.

STATUS
Production.

MANUFACTURER
ENGESA Engenheiros Especializados SA, Avenida das Nacoes Unidas 22.833, Santo Amaro, 04795 São Paulo, Brazil.

BULGARIA

Madra (4 × 2) 3500 kg Truck

DEVELOPMENT
One of the many products of the Shumen Assembly Plant is the Madra (4 × 2) 3500 kg truck which is essentially a copy of the Soviet GAZ-53A (4 × 2) truck but with its original GAZ-53 water-cooled V-8 engine developing 115 hp at 3200 rpm replaced by a British Perkins diesel developing 115 hp at 3200 rpm.

DESCRIPTION
The layout of the Madra is conventional with the engine at the front, two-door all-steel fully enclosed cab in the centre and the cargo area at the rear with drop sides and a drop tailgate. It can be fitted with bows and a tarpaulin cover.

SPECIFICATIONS
Cab seating: 1 + 1
Configuration: 4 × 2

Weight:
(empty) 3250 kg
(loaded) 7250 kg
(on front axle, empty) 1460 kg
(on rear axle, empty) 1790 kg
Max load:
(road) 4000 kg
(cross country) 3500 kg
Towed load: (road) 4000 kg
Load area: 3·74 × 2·17 m
Length: 6·395 m
Width: 2·38 m
Height: (cab) 2·22 m
Ground clearance: 0·265 m
Track:
(front) 1·63 m
(rear) 1·69 m
Wheelbase: 3·7 m
Angle of approach/departure: 40°/25°
Max speed: 80 km/h

Fuel capacity: 90 litres
Engine: Perkins diesel developing 115 hp at 3200 rpm
Gearbox: manual, 4 forward and 1 reverse gears
Turning radius: 8 m
Suspension:
(front) semi-elliptical springs
(rear) semi-elliptical springs with overload springs
Tyres: 8.25 × 20
Number of tyres: 6 + 1 spare
Brakes:
(main) vacuum/hydraulic
(parking) mechanical
Electrical system: 12 V

STATUS
Production.

MANUFACTURER
Shumen Assembly Plant, Bulgaria.

CANADA

Chevrolet 1¼-ton (4 × 4) Series

DESCRIPTION
In 1976 the Canadian Armed Forces selected a Chevrolet (4 × 4) 1¼-ton vehicle to replace the M37CDN (4 × 4) ¾-ton vehicle which entered service in the early 1950s. The first order was for 600 vehicles, followed later in 1976 by a second order for 2848 vehicles at a total cost of $20·8 million.

The Chevrolet is a standard commercial vehicle with the minimum of modifications to suit it for military use. It has a 150 hp engine, automatic transmission, power steering and power brakes.

The layout of the vehicle is conventional with the engine at the front, two-door fully enclosed cab in the centre and the cargo area at the rear with a drop tailgate, troop seats, removable bows and a tarpaulin cover.

Variants include an ambulance, cable-layer, communications vehicle and a light repair vehicle.

STATUS
In service with the Canadian Armed Forces.

MANUFACTURER
Chevrolet Division, General Motors Corporation, Oshawa, Ontario, Canada.

Canadian Armed Forces Chevrolet 1¼-ton (4 × 4) truck equipped for cable laying
(T J Gander)

Chevrolet 1¼-ton (4 × 4) with fully enclosed rear body

Bombardier M35 CDN (6 × 6) 2½-ton Truck

DEVELOPMENT/DESCRIPTION
The Canadian Armed Forces' (CAF) tactical truck fleet consists of several thousand M135 CDN (single rear wheels, cargo), M211 (dual rear wheels, cargo), M216 CDN (single rear wheels, dump), M220 (shop/van) and M222 CDN (water tanker) 6 × 6 vehicles assembled in Canada in the early 1950s by General Motors, Ontario. They were based on the American M211 series which has been phased out of front line US Army service.

In 1977 the Department of National Defense announced its intention to re-equip the CAF truck fleet and Canadian commercial truck manufacturers were invited to supply prototypes which were tested over a 12 month period. The results of the test proposed by the commercial manufacturers proved to be unsatisfactory

and the vehicles did not meet the specific needs of the CAF.

Bombardier Inc. then proposed the proven American AM General Corporation M35 (6 × 6) 2½-ton truck, which is the standard vehicle of its class in the US Army and is also used by many other countries, and obtained a licence to manufacture them in Canada. As well as meeting the CAF specifications the Bombardier proposal was competitive in relation to the other vehicles proposed and guaranteed maximum Canadian content.

In the spring of 1980 the Canadian government invited Bombardier to submit a production proposal to manufacture 2762 trucks. As a result of negotiations the company was awarded a $150 million contract early in 1981 to supply 2762 (6 × 6) trucks.

According to the Canadian Ministry of Supply and Services, the licensing agreement promised to be the first of a series with AM General Corporation. The contract price will be subject to adjustment for inflation,

which will be calculated in accordance with specific indices for the American and Canadian automotive industries. The contractor will also be protected against variations in the rate of exchange between the Canadian and US dollar.

The order for 2762 trucks comprises 2450 M35 CDN trucks, 137 M36 CDN long wheelbase cargo trucks and 175 M36C CDN long wheelbase cargo trucks with hydraulic cranes for loading and unloading cargo and other material. At least 485 will be issued in Europe in support of infantry battalions, artillery and armoured regiments and the tactical helicopter squadron. Another 1400 are destined for Canada to support the three Brigade Groups and for the training organisation, and 621 will go to the Militia and the Communications Reserve. The first ten were delivered in December 1981 and production should continue until May 1984. By the end of 1983 2767 trucks had been delivered.

The Canadian model has a number of significant

improvements over the basic version used by the American Army, including a more fuel-efficient commercial diesel engine, fully automatic transmission and power-assisted steering. The cab is sound-proofed, has better heating, and the driver has a four-way adjustable seat. All versions will have removable drop sides with integral folding seats and it is anticipated that a wide range of pods will be carried, including communications, fuel, office and workshop. With the pod removed the trucks will be airportable in the Lockheed C-130 Hercules operated by the CAF.

STATUS
In production for the Canadian Armed Forces.

MANUFACTURER
Bombardier Inc, Logistic Equipment Division, Valcourt, Quebec J0E 2L0, Canada.

M35 CDN (6 × 6) 2½-ton truck prototype built by Bombardier Incorporated for the Canadian Armed Forces

SPECIFICATIONS
In general, the Canadian vehicles are similar to the American M35 series described in the American section of *Jane's Military Vehicles and Ground Support Equipment*, with the exception of the following:

Type	M35 CDN	M36 CDN	M36C CDN
Weight (empty with winch)	6523 kg	6622 kg	7756 kg
Max load (road)	4545 kg	4536 kg	3402 kg
(cross country)	2272 kg	2268 kg	1134 kg
Gross vehicle weight	11 022 kg	11 340 kg	11 340 kg
Range	500 km	500 km	500 km
Fuel capacity	177 litres	200 litres	200 litres
Wheelbase	3·9 m	4·82 m	4·82 m
Engine	V-8 Detroit Diesel Fuel Pincher, 8·2 litres, 165 bhp at 3000 rpm		
Transmission	Detroit Diesel Allison MT-643 with TC-370 torque converter giving 4 forward and 1 reverse gears		
Transfer box	Rockwell T-136, 2-speed		
Steering	power assisted		
Suspension (front)	semi-elliptical leaf springs		
(rear)	semi-elliptical leaf springs, inverted		
Tyres	11.00 × 20	11.00 × 20	11.00 × 20
Brakes	drum, power assisted, air over hydraulic		
Electrical system	24 V	24 V	24 V
Batteries	4	4	4

CHINA, PEOPLE'S REPUBLIC

CA-30 (6 × 6) 2500 kg Truck

DEVELOPMENT
The CA-30 (6 × 6) 2500 kg truck entered production at the Yueh-Yeh (Cross-Country) Motor Vehicle Sub-Plant of the Ch'ang-Ch'un Number 1 Motor Vehicle Manufacturing Plant in 1959 and it is the standard vehicle in its class in the Chinese Army.

It is very similar to the Soviet ZIL-157 (6 × 6) 2500 kg truck but has a different cab with the headlamps in the mudguards rather than mounted externally as on the ZIL-157.

DESCRIPTION
The layout of the vehicle is conventional with the engine at the front, two-door fully-enclosed cab in the centre and at the rear the cargo area which consists of a wooden platform with sides, bench seats down each side which can be folded up when the vehicle is carrying cargo, and a drop tailgate. If required, the vehicle can be fitted with bows and a tarpaulin cover.

STATUS
Production. In service with the Chinese Army, also exported.

MANUFACTURER
Yueh-Yeh (Cross-Country) Motor Vehicle Sub-Plant of the Ch'ang-Ch'un Number 1 Motor Vehicle Manufacturing Plant, China.

SPECIFICATIONS
Cab seating: 1 + 2
Configuration: 6 × 6
Weight:
(empty) 5450 kg
(loaded, road) 9950 kg
(loaded, cross country) 7950 kg
(on front axle, empty) 2360 kg
(on rear bogie, empty) 3090 kg
Max load:
(road) 4500 kg
(cross country) 2500 kg
Towed load: (cross country) 3600 kg
Load area: 3·57 × 1·8 m
Length: 6·684 m
Width: 2·315 m
Height: (cab) 2·36 m
Ground clearance: 0·305 m
Track: (front and rear) 1·752 m
Wheelbase: (first axle to centre of rear bogie) 4·785 m

Max speed: (road) 65 km/h
Range: 680 km
Fuel capacity: 150 litres
Max gradient: 30%
Fording: 0·85 m
Engine: Chieh'Fang 120 6-cylinder liquid-cooled petrol developing 95 hp at 2800 rpm
Gearbox: manual, 5 forward and 1 reverse gears
Clutch: single dry plate
Transfer box: 2-speed
Turning radius: 12·1 m
Suspension: (front and rear) semi-elliptical leaf springs
Tyres: 12.00 × 18
Number of tyres: 6 + 1 spare
Brakes:
(main) air
(parking) mechanical
Electrical system: 12 V

CA-10 (4 × 2) Liberation 3540 kg Truck

DEVELOPMENT
The CA-10 (4 × 2) Liberation 3540 kg truck entered production at the Ch'ang-Ch'un Motor Vehicle Plant Number 1 in July 1956. It is a slightly modified Soviet ZIL-150 (4 × 2) 3500 kg truck. Although it has a very limited cross-country capability, it is used in some numbers as a cargo carrier and as a prime mover for light artillery. Compared with the original Soviet model it has an inferior engine and a lack of climbing power.

DESCRIPTION
The layout of the vehicle is conventional with the engine at the front, two-door fully enclosed cab in the centre and the cargo area at the rear with drop sides and a drop tailgate. Both left- and right-hand drive models are in service.

VARIANTS
These are known to include a dump truck and a tractor truck.

SPECIFICATIONS
Cab seating: 1 + 1
Configuration: 4 × 2
Weight:
(empty) 3840 kg
(loaded, road) 7375 kg
(on front axle, empty) 1735 kg
(on rear axle, empty) 2100 kg
Max load: (road) 3540 kg
Load area: 3·54 × 2·26 m
Length: 6·502 m
Width: 2·29 m
Height: 3·98 m
Ground clearance: 0·27 m
Track:
(front) 1·69 m
(rear) 1·74 m
Wheelbase: 3·98 m
Angle of approach/departure: 40°/24°
Max speed: 82 km/h
Range: 415 km
Fuel capacity: 158 litres
Max gradient: 37%

Engine: CA-10 6-cylinder in-line liquid-cooled petrol developing 95 hp at 2800 rpm
Gearbox: manual, 5 forward and 1 reverse gears
Clutch: single dry plate
Turning radius: 9 m
Suspension:
(front) semi-elliptical leaf springs and hydraulic shock absorbers
(rear) semi-elliptical springs with overload springs
Tyres: 9.00 × 20
Number of tyres: 6 + 1 spare
Brakes:
(main) air
(parking) mechanical
Electrical system: 12 V
Batteries: 2 × 6 V

STATUS
Production. In service with the Chinese Army.

MANUFACTURER
Ch'ang-Ch'un Motor Vehicle Plant Number 1, China.

EQD 142 (4 × 2) Truck

DEVELOPMENT
The Chinese No 2 Factory at Shiyan in Hubei Province manufactures 50 000 medium weight trucks annually. These trucks use a petrol engine. As a result of an agreement signed between the Chinese Government and Renault Vehicles Industriels in 1980, 100 examples of these Chinese trucks are to be fitted with 133 hp Renault diesel engines for test marketing in Cameroon. The vehicle/engine combination is known as the EQD 142 and examples have been tested in France and China. The first production examples were expected in September 1983.

DESCRIPTION
The EQD 142 is a conventional design in the 11-tonne gross weight class. Configuration is 4 × 2 with the engine at the front, and a conventional steel cab. Prototypes have a steel GS cargo body with a raised 'ladder' grill for the protection of the cab rear. Twin tyres are fitted on the rear axle.

STATUS
Pre-production testing. Production was expected to commence in September 1983.

MANUFACTURER
Vehicle: No 2 Truck Factory, Shiyan, Hubei Province, China.

EQD 142 (4 × 2) truck

Chiao-T-'ung (4 × 2) 3500 kg Truck

DEVELOPMENT
This entered production in 1961 at the Shanghai Communications and Transport Bureau Goods Vehicle Repair Factory. Although designed primarily as a civilian truck it is used in some numbers by the Chinese Army for carrying cargo and troops and as a prime mover for light artillery.

DESCRIPTION
The cab is of the fully enclosed forward control type and the rear cargo area has drop sides and a drop tailgate.

The propeller shaft and front and rear axles are from the CA-10 (4 × 2) 3540 kg truck, engine and transmission are based on the International K7 truck's, steering on the GMC CCKW truck's and the brakes on the M-541-6 truck's.

STATUS
Production. In service with the Chinese Army.

MANUFACTURER
Shanghai Communications and Transport Bureau, Goods Vehicle Repair Factory, China.

SPECIFICATIONS
Cab seating: 1 + 4
Configuration: 4 × 2
Weight:
  (empty) 4225 kg
  (loaded, road) 8225 kg
  (on front axle, empty) 1910 kg
  (on rear axle, empty) 2315 kg
Max load:
  (road) 4000 kg
  (cross country) 3500 kg
Towed load: 4500 kg
Load area: 3·6 × 2·26 m
Length: 6·435 m
Width: 2·4 m

Height: 2·2 m
Ground clearance: 0·28 m
Wheelbase: 4 m
Max speed: 70 km/h
Range: 428 km
Fuel capacity: 120 litres
Max gradient: 24%
Engine: Chiao-T'ung petrol developing 88 hp at 3000 rpm
Gearbox: manual, 5 forward and 1 reverse gears
Clutch: single dry plate
Turning radius: 8·02 m
Suspension:
  (front) semi-elliptical springs
  (rear) semi-elliptical springs with overload springs
Tyres: 9.00 × 20
Brakes:
  (main) air
  (parking) mechanical
Electrical system: 12 V

Chinese Military Vehicles

The Chinese Army still uses large numbers of vehicles supplied by the USSR in the 1950s including the GAZ-63 (Chinese model known as the NJ-230), GAZ-51, ZIL-150 (Chinese model CA-10), ZIL-164, ZIL-151 and the ZIL-157 (Chinese model the CA-30), Chinese-designed vehicles include the 7000 kg capacity JN-150 Huang Ho dump truck and the CN-130 truck for towing semi-trailers.

In the 1950s vehicles were also obtained from other Eastern bloc countries including East Germany and Hungary. In recent years China has obtained vehicles from a number of Western countries including France (Berliet trucks) and Sweden (Volvo trucks). The Berliet trucks were the 6 × 6 GBC 8MT and the heavier GBU (Chinese model is known as the GCH).

MANUFACTURER
Chinese state factories.

SPECIFICATIONS
NJ-230 (or NS-230) 1½-ton
Configuration: 4 × 4
Weight: (empty) 3440 kg
Payload: (road) 2100 kg
Towed load: (road) 2100 kg
Range: 500 km

CZECHOSLOVAKIA

Tatra 805 (4 × 4) 1500 kg Truck

DESCRIPTION
The Tatra 805 was introduced in 1953 as the replacement for the earlier Praga A150 (4 × 2) truck. It is used for a variety of roles by the Czechoslovak Army including towing light anti-tank weapons and is also used for civil roles. The Tatra 805 has exceptional cross country mobility, especially in mountainous terrain, but it appears that it had a number of weaknesses and so was phased out of production.

The two-door all steel cab is of the forward control type and has a circular observation hatch in the right side of the roof. The rear cargo area is provided with drop sides and a drop tailgate and can be fitted with removable bows and a tarpaulin cover.

VARIANTS
A van type model is in service in both ambulance and repair roles.

Tatra 805 (4 × 4) 1500 kg truck

STATUS
Production complete. In service with the Czechoslovak
Army.

MANUFACTURER
Tatra, Národni Podnik, Kopřivnice, Czechoslovakia.

SPECIFICATIONS
Cab seating: 1 + 1
Configuration: 4 × 4
Weight:
(empty) 2750 kg
(loaded, cross country) 4250 kg
(loaded, road) 5000 kg
Max load:
(road) 2250 kg
(cross country) 1500 kg
Towed load:
(road) 2250 kg
(dirt road) 1600 kg
Length: 4·72 m
Width: 2·04 m
Height:
(cab) 2·42 m
(tarpaulin) 2·92 m
Ground clearance: 0·4 m

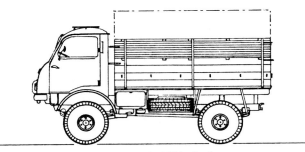

Tatra 805 (4 × 4) 1500 kg truck

Track: 1·6 m
Wheelbase: 2·7 m
Max speed: 77·5 km/h
Range: 600 km
Fuel capacity: 120 litres
Max gradient: 60%
Fording: 0·65 m
Engine: Tatra 603A V-8 air-cooled petrol developing
75 hp at 4200 rpm
Gearbox: manual with 4 forward and 1 reverse gears

Clutch: single dry plate
Transfer box: 2-speed
Turning radius: 4·11 m
Suspension: torsion bar
Tyres: 10.50 × 16
Number of tyres: 4 + 1 spare
Brakes:
(main) hydraulic
(parking) mechanical
Electrical system: 12 V

Praga V3S (6 × 6) 3000 kg Truck

DEVELOPMENT
The V3S was developed in the early 1950s. Initial production was undertaken by Praga but in 1964 it was
transferred to Avia as Praga began to concentrate on
automotive components. It is being replaced in many
Czechoslovak units by the Soviet ZIL-131 (6 × 6)
3500 kg truck.
A 4 × 2 model of the Praga V3S was built under the
designation S5T.

DESCRIPTION
The layout of the Praga V3S is conventional with the
engine at the front, cab in the centre and cargo area at
the rear. The two-door cab is of all steel construction.
There is a circular observation hatch in the right side of
the roof. The windscreen is of the split type and both
parts can be opened horizontally for increased vision.
The rear cargo area has a tarpaulin cover and removable bows which can be stowed to the rear of the cab
when not required. Some V3S trucks have a winch with
a 3500 kg capacity.

VARIANTS
Crane truck, hopper type dump truck (V3S-K, described
in *Construction equipment* section), shop/van (including some with an A-frame mounted at the front of the
vehicle), tanker (special), 3000-litre capacity tanker
(V3S-C) and tractor truck (V3S-A). The chassis is also
used to mount the 130 mm (32 round) M51 multiple
rocket system (*Jane's Armour and Artillery 1983–84*,
page 720) and is used as a basis for the M53/59 twin
30 mm self-propelled anti-aircraft gun system. (*Jane's
Armour and Artillery 1983–84*, page 527).

SPECIFICATIONS
Cab seating: 1 + 1
Configuration: 6 × 6
Weight:
(empty) 5350 kg
(loaded, road) 10 650 kg
(loaded, dirt road) 8650 kg
(loaded, cross country) 8350 kg
Max load:
(road) 5300 kg
(dirt road) 3300 kg
(cross country) 3000 kg

Towed load:
(road) 5500 kg
(cross country) 3100 kg
Length: 6·91 m
Width: 2·31 m
Height:
(cab) 2·51 m
(tarpaulin) 2·92 m
Ground clearance: 0·4 m
Track:
(front) 1·87 m
(rear) 1·755 m
Wheelbase: 3·58 m + 1·12 m
Angle of approach/departure: 72°/32°
Max speed: 62 km/h
Range: 500 km
Fuel capacity: 120 litres
Fuel consumption: 27 litres/100 km
Max gradient: 60%
Fording: 0·8 m
Engine: T-912 in-line air-cooled diesel developing
98 hp at 2100 rpm (late production vehicles have
T-912-2 developing 110 hp at 2200 rpm, which is also
installed in the Praga S5T2 truck)
Gearbox: manual with 4 forward and 2 reverse gears
Clutch: single dry plate
Transfer box: 2-speed
Turning radius: 10·5 m
Suspension: (front and rear) semi-elliptical springs
Tyres: 8.25 × 20
Number of tyres: 10 + 1 spare
Brakes:
(main) hydraulic, air assisted
(parking) mechanical
Electrical system: 12 V

STATUS
Production complete. In service with members of the
Warsaw Pact as well as some countries in the Middle
East.

MANUFACTURER
Avia Závody NP, Letňany, Czechoslovakia.

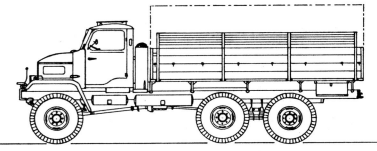

Praga V3S (6 × 6) 3000 kg truck

Praga V3S (6 × 6) 3000 kg truck

Praga V3S (6 × 6) 3000 kg van

Tatra 813 (4 × 4, 6 × 6 and 8 × 8) Trucks

DESCRIPTION

The Tatra 813 series of trucks, which are also known as the Kolos series, were developed in Czechoslovakia in the early 1960s with the first production vehicles (8 × 8s) being completed in 1968. The vehicle is related to the OT-64 (8 × 8) amphibious armoured personnel carrier.

The standard cargo truck version has an all steel forward control type cab which usually has one or two circular observation hatches in the roof. The cab is pressurised and is provided with an effective ventilation system and individual masks for each member of the crew. The engine is in the centre of the cab at the front, with the transmission to the rear of the cab, under the cargo area. The rear cargo area has all steel drop sides and a drop tailgate, removable seats, and can be equipped with bows and a tarpaulin cover if required. All military versions are fitted with a central tyre pressure regulation system and a 22 000 kg capacity winch. The vehicle is sometimes fitted with the BZ-T hydraulically operated dozer blade at the front; a snow plough can also be fitted.

The Tatra 813 (8 × 8) is widely used by both Czechoslovakia and East Germany as a cargo/personnel carrier and for towing heavy artillery up to 152 mm in calibre, and for towing trailers carrying engineer equipment and MBTs.

A more recent model is the Tatra 813-12, which is powered by a 310 hp multi-fuel engine.

VARIANTS

The basic chassis (8 × 8) is used for a variety of roles including carrying and launching PMP heavy floating pontoon bridge units (these vehicles are often fitted with the BZ-T hydraulically operated dozer blade) for carrying and laying the Czechoslovak truck-mounted AM-50 scissors bridge, described in the *Mechanised bridges* section. There is also a special roadway laying version which is used with the PMP system, details of which will be found in the *Portable roadways* section.

The Tatra 813 (road prime mover) is the basic truck with the rear cargo area replaced with ballast. There is also a 6 × 6 cargo truck version with a multi-fuel engine, designated the Tatra 813-8.

The Tatra 813 (8 × 8) chassis is also used as the basis for the M1972 122 mm (40 round) multiple rocket system with a fully armoured cab with 40 rockets in the ready-to-launch position and another 40 rockets ready to reload the launcher. Details of this model are given in *Jane's Armour and Artillery 1983-84*, page 721. These are often fitted with the BZ-T hydraulically operated dozer blade for clearing obstacles and preparing fire positions.

There are two prime movers for civil use, the Tatra 4-813 T-3 (6 × 6) and the Tatra 4-813 T-2 (4 × 4), which can tow a trailer weighing up to 65 000 kg. These do not have the central tyre pressure regulation system as fitted to the military versions. There are at least three dump truck models in service, the Tatra 813 S1 (6 × 6), Tatra 813 S3 (6 × 6) and the Tatra 813 S1 (8 × 8), which also do not have the central tyre pressure regulation system. Crane versions are also in service for both civil and military use; details of the Tatra ZA-T813 Kolos 20-ton mobile crane are given in the *Construction equipment* section.

STATUS

In production. In service with Czechoslovak and East German forces.

MANUFACTURER

Tatra, Národni Podnik, Kopřivnice, Czechoslovakia.

SPECIFICATIONS

Model	Tatra 813	Tatra T-3
Type	Truck	Tractor truck
Cab seating	1 + 6	1 + 2
Configuration	8 × 8	6 × 6
Weight (empty)	14 100 kg	21 050 kg*
(loaded)	22 000 kg	22 000 kg
Max load	7900 kg	950 kg
Towed load (road)	100 000 kg	100 000 kg
Length	8·75 m	7·76 m†
Width	2·5 m	2·5 m
Height (cab)	2·69 m	2·78 m
(tarpaulin)	3·34 m	n/app
Ground clearance	0·4 m	0·33 m
Track (front/rear)	2·03 m/2·03 m	1·986 m/1·946 m
Wheelbase	1·65 m + 2·2 m + 1·45 m	1·65 m + 2·7 m
Max speed (road)	80 km/h	70 km/h‡
Range (road)	1000 km	n/a
Fuel capacity	520 litres	380 litres
Fuel consumption	48 litres/100 km	50 litres/100 km
Max gradient	100%	8·9°‡
Trench	1·6 m	n/a
Vertical obstacle	0·6 m	0·6 m
Fording	1·4 m	n/a
Engine	Tatra T-930-3 12-cylinder air-cooled diesel developing 250 hp at 2000 rpm	Tatra T-930-31 12-cylinder air-cooled diesel developing 250 hp at 2000 rpm
Gearbox	dual range 5-speed plus overdrive providing a total of 20 forward and 4 reverse gears	
Steering	power-assisted	power-assisted
Tyres	15.00 × 21	18.00 × 22.5
Brakes (main)	air	air
(parking)	mechanical	mechanical
Electrical system	24 V	24 V

* With a ballast 8800 kg
† With towing hook
‡ Without load

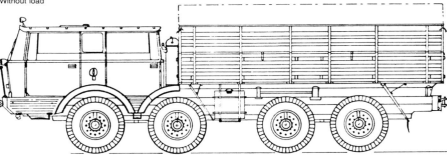

Tatra 813 (8 × 8) truck

Tatra 813 (8 × 8) truck fitted with bows and tarpaulin cover

Tatra 813 (8 × 8) truck towing 152 mm D-20 gun/howitzer

Tatra 815 VT (8 × 8) 10 000 kg Truck

DESCRIPTION
The Tatra 813 (see above) has been joined in service by the Tatra 815 VT, both known as Kolos. The basic construction of the Tatra 813 has been retained, as has the layout, but a new engine has been introduced to provide more power and greater all-round performance and load carrying capabilities. A new hydraulic power assisted single disc dry clutch has been introduced but the pneumatic power assisted gearbox is that of the Tatra 813. The Tatra 815 VT's all-metal four-door cab is similar to that of the Tatra 813 and can be tipped forward for access to the engine and gearbox. Inside are six seats and provision for two make-shift beds. The ventilation system is served by an independent multi-fuel heating system.

The side and rear walls of the loading platform swing on torsion bars. The loading platform is 5·335 metres long and 2·42 metres wide. Other Tatra 813 features carried over include the central-tube frame, the jointed cross-shaft axle and the tyre pressure regulating system. The winch traction power has been increased but the cable used is now 85 metres long.

VARIANTS
The Tatra 815 VT chassis is used as the basis for the 152 mm Dana self-propelled howitzer. For details of this equipment see *Jane's Armour and Artillery 1983–84*, page 467.

SPECIFICATIONS
Cab seating: 1 + 6
Configuration: 8 × 8
Weight: (loaded) 25 400 kg
Max load: 10 000 kg
Towed load:
(road) 70 000 kg
(cross country) 15 000 kg
Length: 9·4 m
Width: 2·5 m
Height:
(cab) 2·98 m
(side wall) 2·055 m
(load surface) 1·5 m
Ground clearance: 0·41 m
Track:
(front) 2·034 m
(rear) 1·994 m

Tatra 815 VT (8 × 8) trucks towing 152 mm D-20 gun-howitzers

Wheelbase: 1·65 m + 2·97 m + 1·45 m
Max speed: (road) 80 km/h
Range: (road) 1000 km
Fuel capacity: 540 litres
Fuel consumption: 45 litres/100 km
Angle of approach/departure: 33°/37°
Max climb: 30°
Trench: 2 m
Vertical obstacle: 0·6 m
Fording: 1·4 m
Engine: Tatra T3-930-51 diesel/multi-fuel developing 254 kW at 2200 rpm
Gearbox: dual-range 5-speed plus overdrive providing 20 forward and 4 reverse gears
Steering: power-assisted

Turning circle: 24 m
Clutch: single disc, hydraulic power assisted
Tyres: 15.00 × 21 TO
Brakes:
(main) air
(parking) mechanical
Electrical system: 24 V
Batteries: 175 Ah
Generator: 28/60 V/A

STATUS
Production. In service with Czechoslovak armed forces.

MANUFACTURER
Tatra, Národni Podnik, Kopřivnice, Czechoslovakia.

Tatra 111 Series (6 × 6) 10 000 kg Trucks

DESCRIPTION
For many years the Tatra 111 series trucks were the most powerful in service with the Czechoslovak Army, and were also used for a variety of civil roles. The layout of the Tatra 111 is conventional with the engine at the front, fully enclosed cab in the centre and the cargo area at the rear.

The basic model has a drop tailgate but there are also models with dropsides (Tatra 111N), and with dropsides and a winch with a capacity of 6000 kg (Tatra 111 NR). The military version is designated the Tatra 111P. The rear cargo area can be covered by a tarpaulin and bows which are stowed to the rear of the cab when not required.

The Tatra 141 and Tatra 141 B are heavy duty prime movers and are used for towing trailers such as the P-32, P-46, P-50 or P-80. These have a larger four-door cab which seats eight men and a winch with an 8000 kg capacity.

The Tatra 111 was replaced in production by the Tatra 138 (6 × 6) truck from 1963.

VARIANTS
Crane-shovel: Models D-030, D-030A and D-031.

Crane trucks (including HSC 4, HSC 5, AJ6 and AV8, described in *Construction equipment* section), 7000-litre fuel tanker (Tatra 111 C), hopper dump truck (Tatra 111 DC5, described in *Construction equipment* section), tractor truck (Tatra 111 A) and a side dump truck (Tatra 111S and Tatra 111S-2, described in *Construction equipment* section). A 4 × 4 model called the T-128 was built in the late 1950s.

STATUS
Production complete. Still used in some numbers by the Czechoslovak Army, also exported to Viet-Nam and the Middle East.

MANUFACTURER
Tatra, Národni Podnik, Kopřivnice, Czechoslovakia.

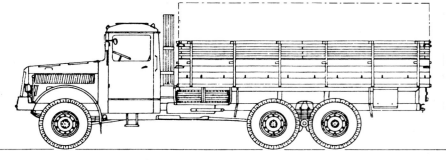

Tatra 111 NR (6 × 6) 10 000 kg truck

SPECIFICATIONS

Model	Tatra 111 NR	Tatra 141
Configuration	6 × 6	6 × 6
Weight (empty)	8600 kg	12 140 kg
(loaded, road)	18 840 kg	18 140 kg
(loaded, dirt road)	16 600 kg	18 140 kg
Max load (road)	10 240 kg	6000 kg
(dirt road)	8000 kg	6000 kg
Towed load (road)	8000 kg	100 000 kg
(dirt road)	22 000 kg	12 000 kg
Length	8·3 m	7·45 m
Width	2·5 m	2·85 m
Height (cab)	2·64 m	2·8 m
(tarpaulin)	3·05 m	n/app
Ground clearance	0·29 m	0·29 m
Track (front/rear)	2·08 m/1·8 m	2·08 m/1·8 m
Wheelbase	4·175 m + 1·22 m	3·5 m + 1·22 m
Max speed road	61·5 km/h	38 km/h
Range	400 km	560 km (estimate)
Fuel capacity	135 litres	420 litres
Fuel consumption	34 litres/100 km	75 litres/100 km
Max gradient	27·5°	31°
Fording	0·8 m	0·8 m
Engine	T-111A	T-111A-5
	12-cylinder air-cooled diesel developing 180 hp at 1800 rpm	
Gearbox	manual with 4 forward and 1 reverse gears	
Transfer box	2-speed	2-speed
Tyres	11.00 × 20	11.00 × 20

Tatra 148 (4 × 4 and 6 × 6) Trucks

DESCRIPTION
The Tatra 148 range of trucks was introduced in 1972 as the replacement for the older Tatra 138 series. They are very similar in appearance to the earlier vehicles but have more powerful engines and increased payload. A further development of the Tatra 148, the Tatra 157, has been built.

The basic cargo model is designated the Tatra 148. This has a conventional layout with the engine at the front, all steel two-door cab and the cargo area at the rear with a drop tailgate, bows and a tarpaulin cover. Vehicles fitted with a winch have the suffix N, eg Tatra 148 N.

VARIANTS
The TZ 74 decontamination vehicle is based on the chassis of the Tatra 148 (6 × 6) truck chassis. Details of this vehicle are given in the *NBC equipment* section.

Dump trucks: Tatra 148 S1 (6 × 6), Tatra 148 S3 (6 × 6), Tatra 148 S3 CH-HMH (6 × 6), Tatra JMH (6 × 6, single-seater cab on left side), Tatra TMCH (forward control type cab, 6 × 6) and the Tatra 148 S3 CH-JMH (4 × 4). Details of the T148 S-1 and T-148 S-3 are given in the *Construction equipment* section.

Tractor trucks: Tatra 148 NTt (6 × 6), Tatra 148 NTPt (6 × 6), Tatra NTPst (6 × 6), Tatra NTt (4 × 4) and Tatra TTt (4 × 4).

SPECIFICATIONS

Model	Tatra 148	Tatra 148 NTt
Type	Truck	Tractor truck
Cab seating	1 + 2	1 + 2
Configuration	6 × 6	6 × 6
Weight (empty)	11 060 kg	8500 kg
(loaded)	25 640 kg	n/app
Max load (road)	14 580 kg	n/app
Towed load (road)	13 580 kg	28 500 kg
Length	9 m	6·5 m
Width	2·5 m	2·5 m
Height	2·44 m	2·44 m
Ground clearance	0·29 m	0·29 m
Track (front/rear)	1·966 m/1·77 m	1·93 m/1·764 m
Wheelbase	4·8 m + 1·32 m	3·69 m + 1·32 m
Max speed	71 km/h	n/app
Fuel capacity	n/app	200 litres
Fording	1·4 m	1·4 m
Engine	T 2-928-1 V-8 air-cooled diesel developing 212 hp* at 2000 rpm	T 2-928-19 V-8 air-cooled diesel developing 232 hp at 2000 rpm
Tyres	11.00 × 20	11.00 × 20
Number of tyres	10 + 1 spare	10 + 1 spare

* If required, the vehicle can be supplied with the same engine as the Tatra 148 NTt.

STATUS
In production. It is believed that this vehicle is used by the Czechoslovak Army as the previous Tatra 138 has been used for a variety of roles. Also in service with the East German Army.

MANUFACTURER
Tatra, Národni Podnik, Kopřivnice, Czechoslovakia.

Tatra 138 (6 × 6) Trucks

DESCRIPTION
The Tatra 138 series entered production in 1963 as the replacement for the earlier Tatra 111 (6 × 6) series and from 1972 was in turn replaced by the Tatra 148 range which is a direct development of the earlier vehicle.

The layout of the vehicle is conventional with the engine at the front, two-door all steel cab in the centre and the cargo area at the rear with drop sides and a drop tailgate. The military model, designated the Tatra 138 VN, also has higher hinged sideboards, removable bows, tarpaulin cover and a winch.

VARIANTS
Crane trucks (including the AJ-6, AV-8 and the ADK-160 which is fully described in the *Construction equipment* section), crane/shovel truck (D-031A), tanker (T-138 C12 and T-138C, both 12 000 litres), tractor truck (Tatra 138 NT) in service in both 4 × 4, also known as the Tatra 137, and 6 × 6 configurations, dump trucks (Tatra 138 S1 and 138 S3 which are fully described in the *Construction equipment* section), and airfield lighting truck. The Czechoslovaks have also used the Tatra 138 to carry and launch the PMP pontoon bridge system, but the more powerful Tatra 813 has taken over this role.

SPECIFICATIONS
(138; data in square brackets relate to 138 NT where different)
Cab seating: 1 + 2
Configuration: 6 × 6
Weight:
(empty) 8740 [8000] kg
(loaded, road) 20 590 kg [n/app]
Max load:
(road) 11 850 kg [n/app]
(dirt road) 8000 kg [n/app]
Towed load:
(road) 22 000 kg [n/a]
(dirt road) 10 800 [28 000] kg
Length: 8·565 [6·665] m
Width: 2·45 m
Height:
(cab) 2·44 [2·485] m
(tarpaulin) 3·2 m
Ground clearance: 0·29 m
Track: (front/rear) 1·93 m/1·764 m
Wheelbase: 4·26 m + 1·32 m [3·69 m + 1·32 m]
Max speed: 71 km/h
Range: 540 [700 (estimate)] km

Tatra 138 (6 × 6) truck complete with bows and tarpaulin cover

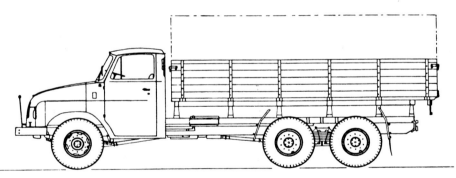

Tatra 138 VN (6 × 6) truck

Fuel capacity: 150 [300] litres
Fuel consumption: 38 litres/100 km [42 litres/100 km]
Max gradient: 35 [25]%
Fording: 1 m
Engine: T-928-12, V-8 air-cooled diesel developing 180 hp at 2000 rpm
Gearbox: manual with 5 forward and 1 reverse gears
Transfer box: 2-speed
Suspension: (front and rear) torsion bars
Tyres: 11.00 × 20

(The vehicle was also available with a 928K supercharged diesel developing 220 hp)

STATUS
Production complete. In service with the Czechoslovak and East German armies, also exported to the Middle East.

MANUFACTURER
Tatra, Národni Podnik, Kopřivnice, Czechoslovakia.

FINLAND

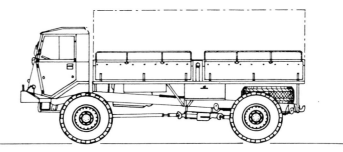

SISU A-45 (4 × 4) 3000 kg truck

SISU A-45 (4 × 4) 3000 kg Truck

DESCRIPTION
The SISU A-45 (4 × 4) truck has been designed to carry 3050 kg of cargo across country and 4050 kg of cargo on roads. Maximum towed load is 2000 kg cross country and 4000 kg on roads. The vehicle is used by the Finnish Army both in Finland and overseas as part of the United Nations Forces. The vehicle is also used for a variety of civil applications.

The cab has a steel lower half with a door in each side, with a detachable glassfibre upper half. The driver's seat is adjustable and the cab has a heater as a standard feature. The engine is mounted to the immediate rear of the cab and projects into the load area of the vehicle. The rear platform is of steel construction and attached to the chassis by rubber mountings. The sideboards and tailgate can be folded down. The tailgate has access steps. The load area can be fitted with bows and a tarpaulin cover if required. A tow hook is mounted at the rear of the vehicle and a pulling jaw is mounted in the centre of the front bumper.

Optional equipment includes a hydraulic mechanism for the operation of SISU hydraulic motors in the trailer (for example when a two-wheel trailer is being towed the wheels of the trailer are powered giving the truck/trailer combination full 6 × 6 drive), trailer air pressure brake system, cold starting equipment, blowlamp operated coolant and oil sump heater and a SISU 6500 kg capacity hydraulic winch, with 60 metres of cable which can be used to the front or rear of the truck.

SPECIFICATIONS
Cab seating: 1 + 2
Configuration: 4 × 4
Weight:
 (empty) 5950 kg
 (loaded, road) 10 000 kg
 (loaded, cross country) 9000 kg

Max load:
 (road) 4050 kg
 (cross country) 3050 kg
Towed load: 9000 kg
Load area: 4·28 × 2·16 m
Length: 6 m
Width: 2·3 m
Height:
 (cab) 2·6 m
 (tarpaulin) 2·8 m
 (load area) 1·29 m
Ground clearance: (axles) 0·4 m
Track: 1·89 m
Wheelbase: 3·7 m
Angle of approach/departure: 38°/38°
Max speed: (road) 100 km/h
Range: 700 km
Fuel capacity: 210 litres
Max gradient: 60%
Fording: 1 m
Engine: 6-cylinder direct injection diesel developing 130 hp (DIN) at 2600 rpm or turbo-charged diesel developing 160 hp (DIN) at 2600 rpm

Gearbox: manual with 5 forward and 1 reverse gears
Transfer box: 2-speed (front and rear axles have differential lock, planetary gears in wheel hubs)
Steering: hydraulic assisted
Turning radius: 8·2 m
Suspension: leaf springs front and rear with shock absorbers on front axle only
Tyres: 14.00 × R 20
Number of tyres: 4 + 1 spare
Brakes:
 (main) air
 (parking) mechanical
Electrical system: 24 V
Batteries: 2 × 12 V, 145 Ah

VARIANTS
Ambulance, fire, radio, command and workshop.

STATUS
Production. In service with the Finnish Army.

MANUFACTURER
SISU-Auto Ab, PO Box 307, 00101 Helsinki 10, Finland.

SISU A-45 (4 × 4) 3000 kg truck

SISU A-45 (4 × 4) 3000 kg truck

SISU SA-150 VK (4 × 4) 6500 kg Truck

DEVELOPMENT
Design of the SA-150 VK (4 × 4) 6500 kg truck began in the second half of 1978 with the first prototype being completed in February 1980. Following successful trials the vehicle was adopted by the Finnish Army and first production vehicles were completed in October 1980. Although the vehicle has been designed primarily to tow artillery it is suitable for a wide range of civilian and military applications.

DESCRIPTION
The SA-150 has a well balanced load distribution and a twisting chassis which ensures that all four wheels are in contact with the ground at all times. The cab and cargo body are attached to the chassis with elastic pads which prevent the frames from twisting.

The all-steel forward control cab has seats for the driver and two passengers with the driver's seat being adjustable for length and height. Standard equipment in the cab includes a heater with two speed fan, roof hatch, washers and a camouflage net support frame.

The rear cargo area has a steel frame construction with removable sides. Standard equipment includes an 8000 kg winch with 50 metres of cable that can be used to the front or rear of the vehicle.

VARIANTS
Projected variants include a crane carrier, light recovery vehicle and a fire-fighting vehicle.

SISU SA-150 VK (4 × 4) 6500 kg truck

SISU SA-150 VK (4 × 4) 6500 kg truck

SISU SA-150 VK (4 × 4) 6500 kg truck

STATUS
Production. In service with the Finnish Army.

MANUFACTURER
SISU-Auto Ab, PO Box 307, 00101 Helsinki 10, Finland.

SPECIFICATIONS
Cab seating: 1 + 2
Configuration: 4 × 4
Weight:
(empty) 7600 kg
(loaded) 14 000 kg
Weight on front axle: (loaded) 7000 kg
Weight on rear axle: (loaded) 8000 kg
Max load: 6400 kg
Length: 6·76 m
Width: 2·48 m
Height:
(cab) 2·9 m
(tarpaulin) 3·1 m
(load area) 1·5 m
Ground clearance: (axles) 0·4 m
Wheelbase: 3·85 m
Track: 2 m
Angle of approach/departure: 42°/39°
Max speed: 100 km/h
Range: 800 km

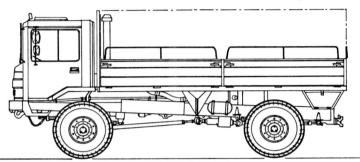

SISU SA-150 VK (4 × 4) 6500 kg truck

Fuel capacity: 225 litres
Fording: 1 m
Engine: Valmet 611 6-cylinder (in-line), water-cooled turbo-charged developing 150 hp at 2500 rpm
Gearbox: ZF manual with 6 forward and 1 reverse gears
Clutch: single dry plate
Transfer box: 2-speed
Steering: power assisted
Turning radius: 8·2 m

Suspension:
(front) leaf springs and hydraulic shock absorbers
(rear) leaf springs
Tyres: 14.00 × 20
Brakes:
(main) dual-circuit air-operated
(parking) spring-operated, controlled by compressed air operating on rear wheels
Electrical system: 24 V
Batteries: 2 × 12 V, 150 Ah

FRANCE

Renault B70 (4 × 4) Ambulance

DESCRIPTION
The Renault B70 (4 × 4) ambulance is a development of a commercial vehicle with the bodywork alterations made by Sanicar Ambulances. The ambulance can carry six stretcher or 12 seated patients in a steel-bodied rear area. Entrance is normally via two large rear doors but there is also a side door on the right-hand side of the body. Standard equipment includes a double jerrican holder, retractable footboard at the rear, infra-red green paint, front and rear blackout lighting, internal lighting, 12-volt light socket, static blower, extractor fan, pioneer tools mounted on a rack on the sloping front bonnet, two-tone horn, self-contained diesel heater, internal insulation, NBC decontamination equipment and the usual stretchers and other medical equipment.

STATUS
Prototype.

MANUFACTURERS
Vehicle: Renault Vehicles Industriels, 129 rue Servient, La Part Dieu, 69003 Lyon, France.
    Body: Sanicar Ambulances, Zone Industrielle, Colombe 38690, Le Grand Lemps, France.

SPECIFICATIONS
Cab seating: 1 + 1
Configuration: 4 × 4
Length: 5·67 m
Width: 2·06 m
Height: 2·83 m
Wheelbase: 3·2 m
Front overhang: 0·887 m
Rear overhang: 1·583 m

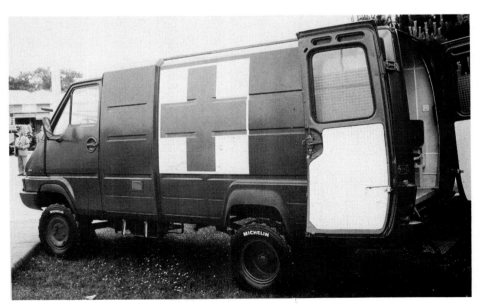

Renault B70 (4 × 4) ambulance (T J Gander)

Max speed: 90 km/h
Range: 400 km
Angle of approach/departure: 38°/20°
Engine: RVI 4-cylinder diesel developing 72 hp (DIN) at 4200 rpm
Gearbox: 4 forward and 1 reverse gears
Transfer box: 2-speed
Turning radius: 16·5 m

Tyres: 9.00 × 16
Brakes: dual-circuit air
Electrical system: 24 V

Ambulance body interior:
Length: 3·6 m
Width: 1·78 m
Height: 1·65 m

Renault TRM 1200 (4 × 4) 1200 kg Truck

DEVELOPMENT
The Renault TRM 1200 was previously known as the Saviem TP3 and was in production at Renault's Blainville factory from 1969; by mid-1981 some 9200 had been produced, of which 4000 were for the French Army and 4000 for overseas military sales.

DESCRIPTION
The Renault TRM 1200 is based on standard commercial components and can carry 12 fully-equipped men or 1200 kg of cargo.

The chassis consists of cold-drawn steel side members with the cross-members welded into position. The vehicle can be delivered with a two-door all steel fully enclosed cab, or a cab with a tarpaulin roof, removable door tops and a windscreen which folds forward onto the bonnet when not required. The rear cargo area is provided with removable drop sides, drop tailgate, removable bows and a tarpaulin cover. Removable seats can be installed down the centre of the vehicle (eg back to back) or along each side of the vehicle.

Optional equipment includes a 72 hp petrol engine, a winch with a capacity of 2000 kg, 120-litre fuel tank in place of the standard 70-litre fuel tank, 7- and 12-pin outlet sockets, 10.50 × 20 tyres and a fire extinguisher.

VARIANTS
These include an ambulance capable of carrying six stretcher patients or twelve seated patients which is in service with the French Army, command post (in service with the French police), dump truck, fire-fighting vehicle, and a light recovery vehicle.

The Italian company of Grazia offers an ambulance based on the chassis of the Renault TRM 1200 truck. Brief details of this company's production range are given in the *Shelters, containers and vehicle bodies* section.

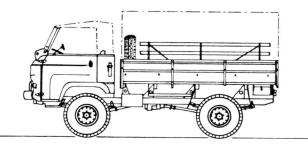

Renault TRM 1200 (4 × 4) 1200 kg truck with tarpaulin roof for cab

STATUS
Production complete. In service with the French Army, Algeria, Morocco and undisclosed countries.

MANUFACTURER
Enquiries to Renault Véhicules Industriels, 8 quai Léon Blum, 92152 Suresnes, France.

SPECIFICATIONS
Cab seating: 1 + 1
Configuration: 4 × 4
Weight:
  (empty) 2620 kg
  (loaded) 3950 kg
Max load: (cross country) 1330 kg
Load area: 3·025 × 1·85 m
Max towed load: 1000 kg
Length: 5·005 m
Width: 1·996 m
Height:
  (cab) 2·4 m
  (tarpaulin) 2·594 m
  (load area) 1·094 m
Ground clearance: 0·27 m

Track: 1·641 m
Wheelbase: 2·64 m
Angle of approach/departure: 31°/40°
Max speed: 95·5 km/h
Range: 600 km
Fuel capacity: 70 litres
Max gradient: 58·9%
Fording: 0·5 m
Engine: Renault 712 4-cylinder diesel developing 72 hp at 3200 rpm
Gearbox: Renault 321-4 manual with 4 forward and 1 reverse gears
Clutch: single dry disc
Transfer box: Renault 433 2-speed
Steering: cam and roller
Turning radius: 8·25 m
Suspension: leaf springs with Evidgom pads and hydraulic shock absorbers
Tyres: 9.00 × 16
Number of tyres: 4 + 1 spare
Brakes:
  (main) hydraulic
  (parking) mechanical
Electrical system: 24 V
Batteries: 2 × 12 V, 96 Ah

Renault TRM 1200 (4 × 4) 1200 kg truck with fully enclosed cab

Renault TRM 1200 (4 × 4) ambulance

Renault TRM 1200 (4 × 4) 1200 kg truck with soft top cab, bows and tarpaulin cover

Renault TRM 1200 (4 × 4) command vehicle

SUMB (4 × 4) 1500 kg MH 600 BS and SUMB (4 × 4) 3000 kg Trucks

DEVELOPMENT

The SUMB (Simca-Unic Marmon-Bocquet) 1500 kg model MH 600 BS truck was developed in the late 1950s by M Bocquet, who was president of Marmon-Herrington which subsequently became Marmon-Bocquet. Series production was undertaken from 1964 and although production has been completed, it remains the standard 1500 kg truck of the French Army.

The engine and cab are at the front with the cargo area at the rear. The cab has two doors and a canvas top mounted on an articulated frame, which enables the top to be folded to the rear to reduce the vehicle's overall height. The windscreen can be folded forward onto the bonnet. The rear cargo area has a drop tailgate, bows and a removable tarpaulin cover. A bench seat can be fitted down the centre of the rear cargo area when the truck is carrying passengers. A locking differential is fitted to the rear axle. Some versions have a front-mounted winch with 60 metres of cable.

A long wheelbase model of this truck, known as the SUMB (4 × 4) 3000 kg truck, was produced from 1971 with the same engine, transmission and cab as the 1500 kg version, but a longer wheelbase and cargo area.

VARIANTS

Variants include a fuel servicing vehicle and a light digger with a Poclain light shovel mounted to the rear of the cab.

SPECIFICATIONS

(data in square brackets apply to the 3000 kg truck where it differs from the 1500 kg model)
Cab seating: 1 + 1
Configuration: 4 × 4
Weight:
  (empty) 3670 [4220] kg
  (loaded) 5300 [7420] kg
Max load: 1500 [3000] kg
Towed load: 2000 kg
Load area: 2·95 × 1·97 [4·4 × 2·29] m
Length: 5·195 [6·55] m
Width: 2·305 [2·41] m
Height:
  (cab) 2·27 m
  (tarpaulin) 2·88 [2·97] m
Ground clearance: 0·33 [0·38] m
Track: 1·704 m
Wheelbase: 2·9 [4·1] m
Angle of approach/departure: 43°/42°
Max speed: (road) 85 [82] km/h

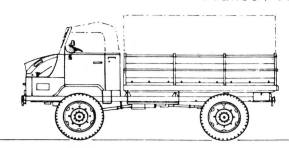

SUMB (4 × 4) 1500 kg MH 600 BS truck

SUMB (4 × 4) 1500 kg MH 600 BS truck (Christopher F Foss)

Range: 550 km
Fuel capacity: 130 litres
Fuel consumption: 30–32 litres/100 km
Max gradient: 60 [50]%
Max side slope: 30%
Fording:
  (without preparation) 0·8 m
  (with preparation) 1·2 m
Engine: 8-cylinder petrol developing 100 bhp at 3000 rpm or 6-cylinder diesel developing 100 bhp at 3000 rpm [6-cylinder diesel developing 100 bhp at 3000 rpm]
Gearbox: manual with 4 forward and 1 reverse gears
Clutch: single dry plate
Transfer box: 2-speed
Turning radius: 7·5 [11·5] m

Suspension: coil springs and hydraulic shock absorbers
Tyres: 10.00 × 20 [12.50 × 20]
Number of tyres: 4 + 1 spare
Brakes:
  (main) hydraulic
  (parking) mechanical
Electrical system: 24 V
Batteries: 2 × 12 V

STATUS
Production complete. In service with the French Army.

MANUFACTURER
FFSA, 3 bis rue Salomon de Rothschild 92, Suresnes, France.

Renault TRM 2000 (4 × 4) 2000 kg Truck

DEVELOPMENT

Following a competition for a new 2000 kg truck in which five European vehicles were tested by the French Army, it was announced in March 1981 that the high mobility version of the Renault TRM 2000 (4 × 4) 2000 kg truck had been selected. The French Army has a requirement for some 12 000 vehicles with first production vehicles completed at Renault's Blainville facility during 1983, with final deliveries being made in 1990. The first 2000 examples will be delivered to signal units in the three French Army corps and will be used to carry RITA communications equipment. At the time the order was placed it was stated that total value of the contract was two billion French francs.

DESCRIPTION

The Renault TRM 2000 was initially produced in two versions, Standard and High Mobility. The main difference between the two was that the Standard had a ground clearance under the axle of 0·305 metre as opposed to the High Mobility's 0·425 metre. The Standard version has now been dropped and only the High Mobility version was placed in production in early 1983.

The chassis consists of U-beam side members (180 mm × 70 mm × 4 mm) with the cross members riveted and bolted together. A towing bracket and a protective skid pad are provided at the front with a five ton towing hook at the rear.

The forward control cab is of all-steel construction and is mounted onto the chassis at three points with elastic pads and two shock absorbers at the rear. The cab tilts forward and is provided with a torsion bar tilting mechanism with double lock and warning indicator lamp, toughened glass windscreen, fully wind down door windows, rear quarter lights, two-man passenger seat and an adjustable driver's seat. To the rear of the cab on the cab roof a Creusot-Loire STR TA rail-mounted rotary support is fitted to a hatch. This mounting can accommodate a

Renault TRM 2000 (4 × 4) 2000 kg truck adopted by French Army in 1981

7·5 mm or 7·62 mm machine gun and is a standard fitting.

The cargo area is provided with drop sides and rear, bows and a tarpaulin cover. If required seats can be fitted down the centre of the vehicle to carry 12 fully equipped troops (eg six down each side facing outwards).

Optional equipment includes a front-mounted winch with a capacity of 2500 kg and a pioneer tool holder.

VARIANTS

Projected variants include a fully-enclosed ambulance, command post with shelter mounted RITA system, forward air control, 2000-litre fuel tanker, missile carrier, prime mover for heavy mortars and the GIAT 20 mm Tarasque 53 T2 anti-aircraft cannon, recovery vehicle, water tanker and a workshop vehicle.

SPECIFICATIONS
Cab seating: 1 + 2
Configuration: 4 × 4
Weight:
(empty) 4300 kg
(loaded) 6300 kg
Max load: 2615 kg
Towed load: 2000 kg
Length: 5·02 m
Width: 2·14 m
Height: (cab) 2·713 m
Ground clearance:
(axles) 0·425 m
(centre of vehicle) 0·484 m
Track: (front and rear) 1·8 m
Wheelbase: 2·7 m
Angle of approach/departure: 42°/48°
Maximum road speed: 89 km/h
Range: 1000 km
Fuel capacity: 130 litres
Max gradient:
(1st gear, high range) 30%
(1st gear, low range) 50%
Max side slope: 30%
Fording: 0·9 m
Engine: Type 720S 4-stroke 4-cylinder in-line turbo-compressor supercharged diesel developing 115 hp at 3000 rpm
Gearbox: S 5-24/3, 5 forward and 1 reverse gears
Clutch: single dry plate
Transfer box: 2-speed
Axles:
(front) axle nose with single, non-locking differential
(rear) axle nose with single reduction differential lock, total reduction 6·39. Electro pneumatic rear axle differential lock control
Steering: ball race, hydraulic
Turning radius: 7·25 m
Suspension: semi-elliptical leaf springs front and rear, with Evidgom pads, hydraulic telescopic shock absorbers, anti-roll bar on rear axle
Tyres: 12.50 × 20
Number of tyres: 4 + 1 spare
Brakes:
(main) air, dual circuit with load equaliser on rear circuit
(parking) mechanical
Electrical system: 24 V
Batteries: 2 × 12 V, 6TN, 95 Ah

STATUS
Production commenced in early 1983 at Blainville, Normandy, for the French Army.

MANUFACTURER
Enquiries to Renault Véhicules Industriels, 8 quai Léon Blum, 92152 Suresnes, France.

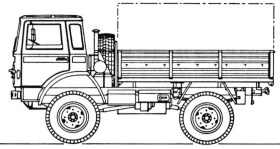

Renault TRM 2000 (4 × 4) 2000 kg truck

Renault TRM 2000 (4 × 4) 2000 kg truck carrying GIAT 20 mm Tarasque 53 T2 anti-aircraft cannon on rear (T J Gander)

ACMAT/ALM VLRA 1500 kg and 2500 kg (4 × 4) and 4300 kg (6 × 6) Vehicles

DESCRIPTION
The VLRA (Véhicule de Liaison, de Reconnaissance et d'Appui) was developed in the late 1950s specifically for operations in the Sahara. Since then it has been adopted by the French Army and many other countries throughout the world and is also used for a variety of civil applications, for example by oil companies.

The layout of the vehicle is conventional with the engine at the front, cab in the centre and cargo area at the rear. The cab has a windscreen which can be folded forward onto the bonnet and a removable nylon canvas roof and side doors. The spare wheel is mounted to the left of the driver's position, or following the customer's requirements. The cargo area at the rear has a drop tailgate, removable bows and nylon canvas covers. Seats can be fitted down the sides or centre of the cargo area when the vehicle is carrying passengers.

Special equipment fitted as standard includes long range fuel tanks, giving an autonomy of 1600 km or 34 hours cross-country operation, and a 200-litre water tank. These figures are reduced to 900 km and 100 litres for the TPK 4.15 SM2. Standard equipment also includes four jerricans, two sand channels, heavy duty air filtration equipment, a six-bladed 500 mm fan driven by twin fan belts as well as a specially-designed water radiator. A heavy duty chassis, gearbox and suspension are also employed. The reduction box and axles are of ACMAT design.

All vehicles are suppressed to second degree (NATO

standard) and a 3000 kg winch can be fitted to the front of the vehicle, if required. A 6000 kg towing hook is standard and a multi-position version is also available for artillery-towing duties. Full EEC lighting equipment is available if required as is power assisted steering. Finally, all VLRA vehicles can be produced in left or right hand drive form.

The basic vehicle can be armed with a 7·5 mm or 7·62 mm machine gun, which is pedestal mounted, and a 12·7 mm machine gun incorporated above the passenger's seat if required. Brandt 60 mm or 81 mm mortars can be mounted in the cargo space over the rear axle. For anti-tank use the VLRA can be armed with a launcher for the SS 11 or SS 12 ATGW, or a Euromissile MILAN ATGW system.

It is important to note the high degree of commonality of wearing parts throughout the entire range of ACMAT

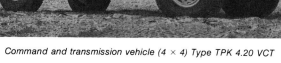

Command and transmission vehicle (4 × 4) Type TPK 4.20 VCT

VLRA (4 × 4) TPK 4.20 SM2 (4 × 4) troop carrier

vehicles. Not only is the same engine used in every ACMAT vehicle, but all front axles, tyres, wheels and reduction boxes are identical. Wearing parts such as roller bearings, oil seals, bushes and so on are standardised to a very high degree.

While detailed items are the subject of continued research and development, the overall dimensions of the major components do not change, thus ACMAT are able to guarantee the availability of exchange components for the life of the vehicle.

VARIANTS
Troop/Cargo Carrier – TPK 4.15 SM2
This parachutable, air-portable 4 × 4 troop/cargo carrier is a new addition to the ACMAT range. It has a carrying capacity of 15 fully-equipped soldiers or 1500 kg of cargo. An operating range of 900 km is available, and a 100-litre drinking water tank is standard. Virtually all wearing parts are identical to the 4.20 SM2 and the 4.15 SM2 uses the same chassis.
Dimensions are:
Length: (overall) 5·28 m
Width:
(overall) 2·07 m
(internal) 1·94 m
Height:
(overall) 2·38 m
(internal) 1·44 m
Wheelbase: 3·3 m
Track: 1·66 m

Command and Transmission Vehicle – TPK 4.20 VCT
This parachutable, airportable command vehicle has nine seats of which two are folding and used by the radio operators. Other equipment fitted as standard includes five stowage compartments, folding table, antenna mounting, two supports for identification flag on front wings, hand rail on commander's position for use during parades and a fold-down hood. Basic specifications are overall length 5·035 metres, overall width 2·07 metres, height with windscreen and hood lowered 1·331 metres, wheelbase 3·3 metres and track 1·66 metres.

Troop Carrier – TPK 4.20 SM2
This parachutable, airportable 4 × 4 troop carrying vehicle has the capacity for 17 fully equipped soldiers. It can be adapted to carry a wide range of weapons, as noted in "Description". It is the basic vehicle of the ACMAT range.

Other adaptations on the identical chassis include:
Ambulance Vehicle – TPK 4.20 SAM
An airportable vehicle with a fully enclosed rear body with lateral windows, two large rear access doors, four stretchers with swivelling frames for ease of access, a folding seat, wash basin, hand pump, 200-litre water tank, first aid kit and cabinet.
Dimensions are:
Length: (overall) 5·8 m
Width:
(overall) 2·04 m
(internal) 1·95 m
Height:
(overall) 2·52 m
(internal) 1·58 m
Wheelbase: 3·6 m
Track: 1·66 m

Radio Command Post – TPK 4.20 PCR
An airportable vehicle designed for command and listening-in duties. The internal design, which includes wiring for wireless transmitters, two desks to carry equipment, two cupboards, chairs, etc, can be completed to customer's individual requirements.
Leading dimensions are identical to those given above, including the internal dimensions.

Also available are:
TPK 4.20 SL7 – Light Recovery Duty Vehicle (see *Recovery vehicles* section)
TPK 4.20 SC – 2500-litre Bowser Vehicle (water, oil, petrol, etc.)
TPK 4.20 VPL2 – Scout Car
TPK 4.20 VBL – 10 Men Light Armoured Personnel Carrier
TPK 4.20 SM 2000 kg Shelter Carrier (2·96 × 2·07 metre platform)
TPK 4.20 FFM Fire-fighting Vehicle

Troop Carrier – TPK 4.35 SM
This airportable 4 × 4 vehicle has a troop carrying capacity of 21 fully equipped soldiers or 2500 kg of cargo.
Other adaptations on the same chassis, a "stretched" version of the TPK 4.20 SM2 above, include:

Workshop Vehicle – TPK 4.30 FAM
This vehicle is supplied as a fully equipped workshop vehicle and the following items are included: 28 KVA generating set, engine and transmission oil tanks, large working surfaces, lubricating etc, oil-lines, air compressor, battery charging equipment, portable welder, seven power points for hand tools, column drill, two tool cabinets (1 with 14, 1 with 28 drawers) and tyre galvanising equipment.
Dimensions are:
Length: (overall) 6·9 m
Width:
(overall) 2·22 m
(internal) 2·14 m
Height:
(overall) 2·79 m
(internal) 1·8 m
Wheelbase: 4·3 m
Track: 1·66 m

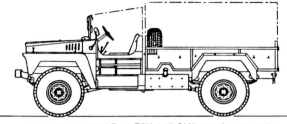

VLRA (4 × 4) ALM Type TPK 4.15 SM2 troop/cargo carrier

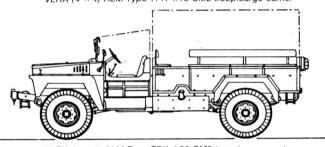

VLRA (4 × 4) ALM Type TPK 4.20 SM2 troop/cargo carrier

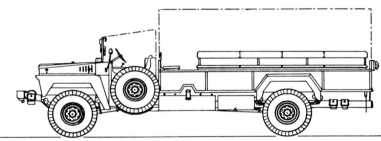

VLRA (4 × 4) ALM Type TPK 4.35 SM 21-seat troop carrier

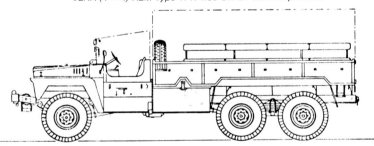

VLRA Type 6.40 SM2 heavy reconnaissance and support vehicle (6 × 6)

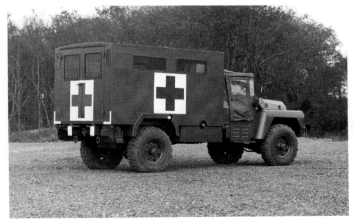

VLRA (4 × 4) TPK 4.20 SAM ambulance

VLRA (6 × 6) TPK 6.40 SM2 truck carrying twin 20 mm 53T4 anti-aircraft gun (T J Gander)

VLRA (6 × 6) TPK 6.40 SM2 troop carrier with ring mount for 7·62 mm or 12·7 mm MG (T J Gander)

VLRA (4 × 4) TPK 4.15 SM2 light truck

Off-Highway Bus – TPK 4.30 BUS
This airportable, rough terrain bus can carry 28 passengers with their luggage in comfort. Pneumatic doors are fitted front and rear. Air conditioning can be supplied, if required.
Dimensions are:
Length:
(overall) 7·12 m
(internal) 4·3 m (driver excluded)
Width:
(overall) 2·2 m
(internal) 2·12 m
Height: 2·6 m
Wheelbase: 4·3 m
Track: 1·66 m

Other adaptations on the identical chassis include:
TPK 4.35 SCM – Mechanical Handling Vehicle, fitted with flat cargo area and telescopic crane.
TPK 4.35 VPC – Convoy Protection Vehicle, fitted with 20 mm M693 GIAT cannon.
TPK 4.30 FAE/FME, FMA1, FMA2 and FRA range of electrical and armament workshop vehicles.

Troop Carrier – TPK 6.40 SM2
This airportable 6 × 6 vehicle has a troop carrying capacity of 21 fully equipped soldiers or 4300 kg of cargo.
Other adaptations on the same chassis, a 6 × 6 version of the TPK 4.20 SM2 above, include:
Shelter Carriers – TPK 6.40/50/60 SH
This vehicle is capable of carrying standard width and height shelters, up to a maximum length of 5·2 m. Corresponding sizes of refrigerating or plain shelters are available.
Dimensions are:
Length: (overall) 7·23 m–8·13 m
Width: (overall) 2·4 m
Height: (overall) 3·46 m
Wheelbase: 4·1 m–4·8 m
Track: 1·8 m

Bowser Vehicle – TPK 6.40 SC
An airportable 4000-litre bowser that is available for carrying water, oil, or petrol.
Dimensions are:
Length: (overall) 6·94 m
Width: (overall) 2·25 m
Height: (overall) 2·13 m
Wheelbase: 4·1 m
Track: 1·8 m

SPECIFICATIONS

Model	TPK 4.15 SM2 truck	TPK 4.20 SM2 truck	TPK 4.35 SM2 LWB truck	TPK 6.40 SM2 truck
Cab seating	1 + 2	1 + 2	1 + 2	1 + 2
Configuration	4 × 4	4 × 4	4 × 4	6 × 6
Weight (empty)	4150 kg	4300 kg	4830 kg	5700 kg
(loaded)	5650 kg	6800 kg	7300 kg	10 000 kg
Max load	1500 kg	2500 kg	2470 kg	4300 kg
Max towed load	3000 kg	3000 kg	3000 kg	6000 kg
Load area	2·6 × 1·94 m	2·8 × 1·94 m	4 × 1·94 m	3·9 × 2·15 m
Length	5·28 m	6 m	7·25 m	6·94 m
Width	2·07 m	2·07 m	2·07 m	2·25 m
Height (cab roof)	1·83 m	1·83 m	1·83 m	1·83 m
(tarpaulin)	2·838 m	2·62 m	2·62 m	2·62 m
(load area)	0·92 m	1·273 m	1·273 m	1·5 m
Ground clearance	0·271 m	0·273 m	0·273 m	0·48 m
Track (front)	1·66 m	1·8 m	1·8 m	1·8 m
(rear)	1·66 m	1·66 m	1·66 m	1·66 m
Wheelbase	3·3 m	3·6 m	4·3 m	4·3 m
Angle of approach/departure	51°/41°	43°/41°	43°/41°	43°/41°
Max road speed	100 km/h	100 km/h	100 km/h	85 km/h
Range	900 km	1600 km	1600 km	1600 km
Fuel capacity	2 × 120 litres	2 × 180 litres	2 × 180 litres	2 × 210 litres
Max gradient	60%	60%	60%	50%
Fording	0·8 m	0·9 m	0·9 m	0·9 m
Engine (Perkins 6.354.4)	120 hp at 2800 rpm	120 hp at 2800 rpm	120 hp at 2800 rpm	138 hp at 2800 rpm
Gearbox (manual)	4 + 1 speed	4 + 1 speed	4 + 1 speed	5 + 1 speed
Clutch	single dry plate	single dry plate	single dry plate	single dry plate
Transfer box	2-speed	2-speed	2-speed	2-speed
Steering	worm and nut	worm and nut	worm and nut	worm and nut
Turning radius	8·4 m	9·25 m	11 m	10·35 m
Suspension	leaf springs and double action hydraulic shock absorbers			
Tyres	11.00 × 16 XL	12.5 × 20 XL	12.5 × 20 XL	12.5 × 20 XL
Number of tyres	5	5	5	7
Brakes (main)	air	air	air	air
(parking)	hydraulic	hydraulic	hydraulic	hydraulic
Electrical system	24 V	24 V	24 V	24 V
Batteries	2 × 12 V, 100 Ah	2 × 12 V, 100 Ah	2 × 12 V, 100 Ah	2 × 12 V, 100 Ah

Also available are the TPK 6.40 SG – Tar Spreader and TPK 6.40 SB – 6000 kg Tipper (details of which appear in the *Construction equipment* section), the TPK 6.40 SWT – 5000 kg Recovery Vehicle (see *Recovery vehicles* section) and the TPK 6.40 SPP – Temporary Track Layer (see *Portable roadways* section).

STATUS
Production. In service with French forces and many other countries including Benin, Cameroon, Chad, Gabon, Ireland, Ivory Coast, Morocco, Senegal, Somalia, Togo, Upper Volta and Zaïre. ACMAT vehicles are in service in 30 countries throughout the world.

MANUFACTURER
ACMAT (Ateliers de Construction Mécanique de l'Atlantique), Le Point du Jour, 44600 Saint-Nazaire, France.

Citroën FOM (4 × 4) 3000 kg and 5000 kg Trucks

DESCRIPTION
The FOM (Forces d'Outre Mer: overseas forces) truck was developed in the 1950s by Citroën specifically to meet French Army requirements for a vehicle with exceptional cross country mobility for use in Africa. The FOM was in production from 1964 to 1968.
The layout of the FOM is conventional with the engine at the front and the two-door cab in the centre with a windscreen which can be folded forward onto the bonnet and a removable canvas top. The rear cargo area has a drop tailgate, removable bows and a tarpaulin cover. A 5000 kg capacity winch with 60 metres of cable is mounted at the front of the vehicle.
The 3000 kg model has single rear wheels with 12.00 × 20 tyres all round and the 5000 kg model has dual rear wheels with 11.00 × 20 tyres all round. For long-range operations in the Sahara a 1500 km range model with 500-litre fuel tanks was built.

VARIANTS
The following variants were proposed, and small numbers of some were built: flatbed truck for carrying containers, 3500-litre fuel carrier, recovery vehicle, van for use as a command or radio vehicle, 3000-litre water carrier and a refrigerator van.

SPECIFICATIONS (3000 kg model)
Cab seating: 1 + 1
Weight: (loaded) 12 500 kg
Max load: 3000 kg
Towed load: (road) 5000 kg
Load area: 3·5 × 2·21 m
Length: 7·01 m
Width: 2·48 m
Height:
(cab) 2·77 m
(tarpaulin) 3·09 m
Wheelbase: 4·6 m

Angle of approach/departure: 57°/36°
Max speed: (road) 100 km/h
Range: 800 km
Fuel capacity: 150 litres plus 120 litres in jerricans; long range model has 250-litre tank
Fording: 0·5 m
Engine: 6-cylinder petrol developing 140 hp at 2800 rpm, or 97 hp petrol, or 6-cylinder diesel developing 85 hp at 2600 rpm
Gearbox: manual with 5 forward and 1 reverse gears
Transfer box: 2-speed
Steering: power-assisted
Turning radius: 5 m
Suspension: leaf springs and hydraulic shock absorbers
Tyres: 12.00 × 20
Number of tyres: 4 + 1 spare
Brakes: air
Electrical system: 24 V
Batteries: 2 × 12 V, 90 Ah

MANUFACTURER
Citroën, France.

*Citroën FOM (4 × 4) 3000 kg truck with single rear
wheels and front-mounted winch (ECP Armées)*

Simca-Unic F 594 WML (4 × 4) 3000 kg Truck

DESCRIPTION
This vehicle was designed in the 1950s for the French
Army and production continued until the 1960s. It is
basically a standard commercial vehicle adapted to
meet military requirements. The forward control cab has
a removable canvas top and a windscreen which can be
folded forward onto the bonnet. The rear cargo area has
removable bows, tarpaulin cover and a drop tailgate.
Some vehicles have a front-mounted winch with 60
metres of cable which unwinds to the front. The standard model, called the WML (long wheelbase), has a
3·655-metre wheelbase and the short wheelbase
model, the WMC, has a 3·04-metre wheelbase.

VARIANTS
Variants of the WML include a mobile compressor and a
van type model which is used for a variety of roles
including command vehicle, office or workshop. The
WMC is used as a dump truck, recovery vehicle and
water tanker.

SPECIFICATIONS (WML)
Cab seating: 1 + 1
Configuration: 4 × 4
Weight:
  (empty) 4800 kg
  (loaded, road) 9800 kg
  (loaded, cross country) 7800 kg
Max load:
  (road) 5000 kg
  (cross country) 3000 kg
Towed load:
  (road) 4000 kg
  (cross country) 2000 kg
Length: 6·806 m
Width: 2·286 m
Height:
  (cab) 2·55 m
  (tarpaulin) 3·2 m
Track:
  (front) 1·7 m
  (rear) 1·75 m
Wheelbase: 3·655 m
Angle of approach/departure: 33°/25°

Simca-Unic F 594 WML (4 × 4) 3000 kg truck fitted with van type body (ECP Armées)

Max speed: (road) 80 km/h
Range: 500 km
Fuel capacity: 120 litres
Max gradient: 40%
Fording: 0·8 m
Engine: Simca F6 CWM 8-cylinder petrol developing
85 bhp at 2900 rpm
Gearbox: manual with 4 forward and 1 reverse gears
Transfer box: 2-speed
Suspension: semi-elliptical springs with hydraulic
shock absorbers
Tyres: 9.00 × 20 or 10.00 × 20

Brakes:
  (main) hydraulic
  (parking) mechanical
Electrical system: 24 V
Batteries: 2 × 12 V

STATUS
Production complete. In service with the French Army.

MANUFACTURER
FFSA, 3 bis rue Salomon de Rothschild, 92
Suresnes, France.

Renault TRM 4000 (4 × 4) 4000 kg Truck

DEVELOPMENT
The Renault TRM 4000 (4 × 4) 4000 kg truck was
selected to be the standard vehicle in its class in the
French Army who, in the early 1970s, stated that it had a
requirement for 15 000 vehicles of this type. Production
commenced at Renault's Blainville facility in 1973, since
when over 3700 vehicles have been produced.
    The vehicle is essentially a commercial vehicle (the
Saviem SM8) modified to meet the requirements of the
French Army and uses proven commercial components, including cab, engine, transmission, chassis and
axles.

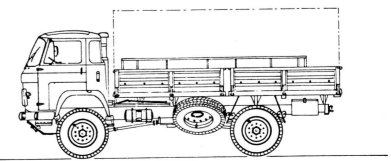

Renault TRM 4000 (4 × 4) 4000 kg truck

Renault TRM 4000 (4 × 4) 4000 kg trucks being built at Renault's Blainville facility

DESCRIPTION

The basic model has single rear wheels and a payload of 4000 kg but there is also a model with dual rear wheels and a payload of 5800 kg. The chassis consists of longitudinal side members with the cross-members welded into position. The two-door cab (type 812) is of all-steel construction and is of the forward control type. It can be tilted forward to an angle of 50 degrees to allow access to the engine and can also be delivered with an observation hatch in the roof. The rear cargo area has drop sides, drop tailgate, removable bows and a tarpaulin cover, and removable seats can be installed down the centre or sides of the vehicle if required.

Optional equipment includes long range fuel tanks, different tyres, 4500 kg capacity winch, twin rear wheels, differential lock, additional seat in the cab, exhaust retarder, 24 volt electrical system, blackout lights, 12-pin current outlet inspection socket on dashboard and a cab which can be split at door level to reduce overall height for air transport.

VARIANTS

Models announced so far include a Crotale missile carrying vehicle complete with hydraulic crane, crane truck, dump truck, fire-fighting vehicle, recovery vehicle, 5000-litre tanker/refueller (Decauville), van/command vehicle and a water tanker.

SPECIFICATIONS

Cab seating: 1 + 1
Configuration: 4 × 4

Renault TRM 4000 (4 × 4) 4000 kg truck (Christopher F Foss)

Weight:
(empty) 5680 kg
(loaded, road) 11 200 kg
(loaded, cross country) 10 000 kg
Weight on front axle: (loaded, cross country) 3190 kg
Weight on rear axle: (loaded, cross country) 2490 kg
Max load:
(road) 5340 kg
(cross country) 4320 kg
Towed load: 6000 kg
Load area: 4·48 × 2·296 m
Length: 6·538 m
Width: 2·47 m
Height:
(cab) 2·75 m
(tarpaulin) 3·26 m
(load area) 1·26 m
Ground clearance: 0·3 m
Track:
(front) 1·836 m
(rear) 2·018 m
Wheelbase: 3·85 m
Angle of approach/departure: 37°/39°
Max speed: (road) 87 km/h
Range: 700 km
Fuel capacity: 150 litres
Max gradient: 50%

Max side slope: 30%
Fording: 0·9 m
Engine: Renault model 797 6-cylinder diesel developing 133 hp at 2900 rpm
Gearbox: ET 301 manual with 5 forward and 1 reverse gears
Clutch: single dry plate
Transfer box: 2-speed
Steering: cam and roller with hydraulic power assistance
Turning radius: 10 m
Suspension: leaf springs with Evidgom pads, hydraulic shock absorbers
Tyres: 12.00 × 20
Number of tyres: 4 + 1 spare
Brakes:
(main) air, dual circuit
(parking) mechanical
Electrical system: 24 V
Batteries: 2 × 12 V, 95 Ah

STATUS

In production. In service with the French Army and undisclosed countries.

MANUFACTURER

Enquiries to Renault Véhicules Industriels, 8 quai Léon Blum, 92152 Suresnes, France.

Berliet GBC 8 KT (6 × 6) 4000 kg Truck

DEVELOPMENT

In the 1950s Berliet developed a 6 × 6 truck for use in North Africa called the Gazelle. With modifications it was subsequently adopted by the French Army in the late 1950s and by the time production had been completed over 18 000 trucks had been built.

DESCRIPTION

The layout of the vehicle is conventional with the engine at the front, cab in the centre and cargo area at the rear. The two-door cab has a removable top, removable door tops and the windscreen can be folded forward onto the bonnet. The rear cargo area is provided with a drop tailgate with an integral step, removable side boards, bows and a tarpaulin cover. The height of the bows can be adjusted for road or rail transport and bench type seats can be fitted down the centre of the vehicle if required. Optional equipment includes a Pan-Bonnier winch with a capacity of between 5000 and 7000 kg and drop sides for the rear cargo area. The KT series is powered by a multi-fuel engine while the MT series is powered by a diesel which develops 150 hp at 2100 rpm.

VARIANTS

Long wheelbase
This is 8·32 metres long, 2·4 metres wide and 3·23 metres high unladen; the wheelbase is 3·71 metres + 1·28 metres and empty weight of the vehicle is 9400 kg.

4 × 4 version
Small quantities of 4 × 4 versions were built for the Portuguese Army under the designation of GBC 8 (4 × 4).

Berliet GBC 8 KT (6 × 6) 4000 kg truck of French Army (T J Gander)

Light recovery
Details of this will be found in the entry for the Berliet TBC 8 KT (6 × 6) wrecker in the *Recovery vehicles* section.

Medium recovery vehicle
Details of this version, designated the Berliet TBC 8 KT (6 × 6) CLC, will be found in the *Recovery vehicles* section.

Tanker
This can carry 5000 litres of fuel.

Tipper
This can carry 4 cubic metres of soil. Unladen weight is 12 500 kg and principal dimensions are: length 7·175 metres, width 2·4 metres, height 2·845 metres, length inside tipper body 3·8 metres and width inside tipper body 2·3 metres.

Tractor truck
This has an overall length of 6·521 metres, width of 2·4 metres and a height (reduced) of 2 metres.

Other variants include a fire-fighting vehicle, bowser and a mobile compressor.

SPECIFICATIONS
Cab seating: 1 + 2
Configuration: 6 × 6
Weight:
  (empty) 8370 kg
  (loaded) 12 370 kg
Weight on front axle: (empty) 4180 kg
Weight on rear bogie: (empty) 4190 kg
Max load: (cross country) 4000 kg
Load area: 4·36 × 2·35 m
Length: 7·28 m
Width: 2·4 m
Height:
  (cab) 2·7 m
  (tarpaulin) 3·3 m
Ground clearance: (axles) 0·28 m
Track: 1·86 m
Wheelbase: 3·31 m + 1·28 m
Angle of approach/departure: 45°/45°
Max speed: 80 km/h
Range: 800 km
Fuel capacity: 200 litres
Max gradient: 50%
Fording: 1·2 m
Engine: Berliet MK 520 5-cylinder OHV water-cooled multi-fuel developing 125 hp at 2100 rpm
Gearbox: Berliet BDSL 13 manual with 6 forward and 1 reverse gears
Clutch: single dry plate
Transfer box: 2-speed
Steering: worm gear and nut, servo assisted
Turning radius: 10·5 m
Suspension:
  (front) semi-elliptical springs and hydraulic shock absorbers
  (rear) leaf springs on oscillating pivot
Tyres: 12.00 × 20
Number of tyres: 6 + 1 spare
Brakes:
  (main) air
  (parking) mechanical
Electrical system: 24 V
Batteries: 4 × 12 V, 100 Ah

Berliet GBC 8 KT (6 × 6) 4000 kg truck chassis fitted with Trailor designed system for refuelling vehicles in the field

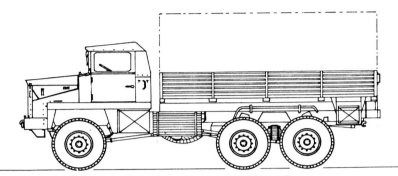
Berliet GBC 8 KT (6 × 6) 4000 kg truck

STATUS
Production complete. In service with Algeria, Austria, China, France, Iraq, Morocco and Portugal.

MANUFACTURER
Berliet, 160 boulevard de Verdun, 92402 Courbevoie, France. Berliet is now part of Renault Véhicules Industriels.

Brimont (4 × 4) 5000 kg Truck

DEVELOPMENT
Based on the company's experience in the development and production of agricultural tractors, forestry tractors and other cross-country vehicles, the Brimont group, which took over the activities of Latil in 1974, has designed a new 4 × 4 all-terrain vehicle called the ETR.

This is suitable for a wide range of civil and military applications and has already been adopted by the French Air Force.

DESCRIPTION
The ETR (Engineered to Reliance) has a well-balanced load distribution and uses an articulating chassis with an oscillating device that ensures that all four wheels are in contact with the ground at all times. The arch type axles with final planetary reduction in each wheel give a high ground clearance.

The all-steel forward control cab can be hinged forward to give access to the engine for maintenance. It is mounted on the chassis at three points with shock absorbers and variable suspension units. A special water-cooled system is fitted for the air-conditioning, heating and defrosting system.

Power is transmitted from the engine via the clutch to the hydro-mechanical reduction box and then by a short propeller shaft to a gear range multiplier which is coupled to the gearbox and transfer box. Power is then taken to the front and rear axles via propeller shafts.

The power train is a modular design and can be coupled with transfer boxes to give a wide range of speeds:

ETR-106, single ratio transfer box, 6 forward speeds (1·7 to 25 km/h) and 1 reverse speed, 3 km/h.
ETR-112, single ratio transfer box plus double range, 12 forward speeds (1·4 to 25 km/h) and 2 reverse speeds (2·6 and 3 km/h).
ETR-206, double ratio transfer box, 6 road speeds (5·5 to 85 km/h), 6 working speeds (1·7 to 25 km/h) and 2 reverse speeds (1·5 to 10 km/h).
ETR-212, double ratio transfer box plus double range, 12 road speeds (4·8 to 85 km/h), 12 working speeds (1·4 to 25 km/h) and 4 reverse speeds (1·5 to 10 km/h).
ETR-406, double ratio transfer box plus hydro-mechanical reduction, 6 road speeds (5·5 to 85 km/h), 6 working speeds (1·7 to 25 km/h), 6 slow speeds (1 to 7·3 km/h), 6 extra-slow speeds (0·1 to 2·2 km/h) and 4 reverse speeds (0·1 to 10 km/h).
ETR-412, double ratio transfer box plus double range plus hydro-mechanical reduction, 12 road speeds (4·5 to 85 km/h), 12 working speeds (1·4 to 25 km/h), 12 slow speeds (0·9 to 7·3 km/h), 12 extra-slow speeds (0·1 to 2·2 km/h) and 8 reverse speeds (0·1 to 10 km/h).

A typical cargo model would have an all-steel rear cargo body with drop tailgate, troop seats, removable bows and a tarpaulin cover.

The ETR can be delivered with a rear steering axle driven by two double-acting hydraulic cylinders actuated by a hydraulic distributor or by a steering wheel in symmetrical or asymmetrical co-ordination. A combination of both front and rear steering allows crab type driving. Turning radius with the front wheels only is 6·9 metres and with the rear wheels as well 4·37 metres. The rear steering cannot be used at speeds of over 25 km/h and is automatically switched off when driving at over this speed.

Optional equipment includes a military type cab with windscreen that folds forward and tarpaulin top, turbocharged Renault 798 engine developing 155 hp at 2900 rpm, different tyres, braking of the trailer with an electrical switch and a front-mounted winch with a capacity of 4500 kg.

VARIANTS
Typical roles of the Brimont (4 × 4) include use as an artillery (105 mm) or mortar (120 mm) prime mover, cargo carrier with or without a hydraulic crane, dump truck (side or rear tipping), engineer vehicles (those delivered to the French Air Force (designated the ETR 4 × 4 206 type VCUM) have a four-man cab, front loader, rear-mounted hydraulically-operated shovel and rear cargo area with drop sides and four-man bench seat), fire-fighting fitted with 2500-litre water tank, 300-litre foam tank, 1000-litre/minute pump which can simultaneously project water and foam (used by the French Air Force under the designation of the ETR 4 × 4 206 S type VIFF), recovery vehicle (two-man cab, winch with a capacity of 4500 kg, chain pulley block moving on mobile gantry with a capacity of 2000 kg), shelter (for use in roles such as ambulance, command post and workshop), snow plough and tanker.

To operate with the MAF amphibious bridging equipment, Brimont has developed a specialised version of the vehicle called the ETR 4 × 4 206 S type MASE. For details see page 49.

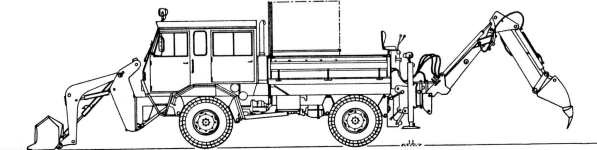
Brimont (4 × 4) Type 206 VCUM truck as used by French Air Force

Brimont (4 × 4) dump truck

Brimont (4 × 4) 5000 kg truck with hydraulic crane

Brimont (4 × 4) 5000 kg truck with front loader

Brimont (4 ×4) 5000 kg truck with hydraulically-operated shovel at rear

SPECIFICATIONS
Cab seating: 1 + 3
Configuration: 4 × 4
Weight empty: (average) 5400 kg
Weight on front axle: (empty) 3800 kg
Weight on rear axle: (empty) 1600 kg
Max load: (average) 5600 kg
Towed load: 8400 kg
Length: 4·965 m
Width: 2·27 m
Height: (cab) 2·66 m
Ground clearance: 0·465 m
Track: 1·8 m
Wheelbase: 2·955 m

Max road speed: 85 km/h (see text)
Range: 600 km
Fuel capacity: 200 litres
Gradient: 70–100% depending on tyres and type of surface
Engine: Renault 797 6-cylinder diesel developing 132 hp at 2900 rpm
Gearbox: ZF, 6 forward and 1 reverse gears
Steering: power assisted
Turning radius:
 (front wheels) 6·9 m
 (front and rear wheels) 4·37 m
Suspension: leaf springs with progressive flexible springs and hydraulic shock absorbers

Tyres: 14.5 × 20 E6
Brakes:
 (main) hydro-pneumatic
 (parking) disc brake on rear transmission
Electrical system: 24 V
Batteries: 2 × 12 V

STATUS
Production. In service with the French Air Force.

MANUFACTURER
Brimont SA, BP 3 Sillery, 51500 Rill-la-Montagne, France.

Renault TRM 6000 (4 × 4) 6000 kg Truck

DEVELOPMENT
The Renault TRM 6000 (formerly known as the Berliet GBD) (4 × 4) truck uses many components of the TRM 9000 (6 × 6) including the same engine but without the turbo-charger. Production of the TRM 6000 is undertaken at Bourg-en-Bresse which was previously the Berliet military truck plant.

DESCRIPTION
The chassis consists of two U-shaped side members with five cross-members riveted and welded into position. The two-door cab is of the forward control type and has a removable top and a windscreen which can be folded forward if not required. The rear cargo area is provided with drop sides, drop tailgate, removable bows and a tarpaulin cover, and bench seats which can be folded up to allow cargo to be carried.
    Optional equipment includes a hard top cab which can be tilted forward to an angle of 65 degrees to allow access to the engine for maintenance, differential lock, exhaust brake, additional 200-litre fuel tank, hydraulic front winch with a capacity of 3500/4500 kg and 60 metres of cable, single or twin 12.00 × 20 tyres or single 14.00 × 20 or 19.5 × 20 tyres, tow hook and connections for trailer brakes.

VARIANTS
Projected variants include light recovery vehicle, refueller, tractor truck for towing semi-trailers, tipper, Crotale SAM resupply vehicle and tanker.

Renault TRM 6000 (4 × 4) 6000 kg truck with bows and tarpaulin cover erected

STATUS
Production complete. This vehicle is not used by the French Army.

MANUFACTURER
Enquiries to Renault Véhicules Industriels, 8 quai Léon Blum, 92152 Suresnes, France.

SPECIFICATIONS
Cab seating: 1 + 1
Configuration: 4 × 4
Weight:
  (empty) 6400 kg
  (loaded) 12 400 kg
Max load:
  (road) 7000 kg
  (cross country) 6000 kg
Towed load: 6000 kg
Load area: 4·625 × 2·47 m
Length: 6·67 m
Width: 2·48 m
Height:
  (cab) 2·847 m
  (tarpaulin) 2·94 m
  (load area) 1·12 m
Ground clearance: 0·35 m
Track:
  (front) 1·94 m
  (rear) 1·938 m
Wheelbase: 3·8 m
Angle of approach/departure: 45°/33°
Max speed: 84 km/h
Range: 800 km
Fuel capacity: 200 litres
Max gradient: 60%

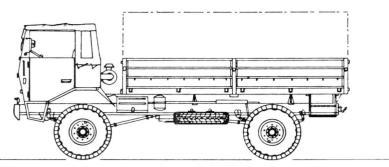

Renault TRM 6000 (4 × 4) 6000 kg truck

Max side slope: 30%
Fording: 1 m
Engine: Renault MID 06.20.30 6-cylinder in-line water cooled diesel developing 185 hp at 2400 rpm
Gearbox: Renault BDSL 021 manual with 6 forward and 1 reverse gears
Clutch: hydromechanic with pneumatic assistance
Transfer box: Renault BT 20 2-speed
Turning radius: 9·5 m

Suspension: leaf springs with auxiliary springs and telescopic shock absorbers
Tyres: 13.00 × 20
Number of tyres: 4 + 1 spare
Brakes:
  (main) air, dual circuit
  (parking) mechanical
Electrical system: 24 V
Batteries: 4 × 12 V type 6TN, 190 Ah

Renault TRM 9000 (6 × 6) 9000 kg Truck

DEVELOPMENT
Further development of the TRM 9000 resulted in the TRM 10 000 6 × 6 truck which has been adopted by the French Army and for which there is a separate entry in this section.

Production is undertaken in Vénissieux. First production vehicles were completed in 1975. By mid-1981, 2700 vehicles had been ordered for export of which 2100 units had been delivered. Largest orders have come from Algeria (500) and Morocco (1500).

The Renault TRM 9000 (formerly known as the Berliet GBD) (6 × 6) truck uses many components, such as the cab, gearbox, transfer case and steering, of the TRM 6000 (4 × 4) 6000 kg truck.

DESCRIPTION
The two-door forward control cab has a removable canvas roof, removable side screens and a windscreen that can be folded forward against the bonnet if required. The rear cargo area is fitted with drop sides and a drop tailgate, removable bows and a canvas cover. If required seats can be fitted in the rear. Optional equipment includes a four-door 6/7 seater cab, fully enclosed two- or four-door cab, winch with a capacity of 3500/4500 kg and 60 metres of cable, different tyres, dual wheels on the rear axles, additional 200-litre fuel tank, and an exhaust brake.

VARIANTS
Artillery tractor
Able to tow 155 mm artillery weapons as well as crew and ammunition.
Command/radio vehicle
Fitted with a container on the rear which would be fitted with communications equipment. Other types of equipment carried in containers can also be mounted for example, used as a workshop.
Tanker
Water or fuel vehicle (6000-litre).
Tipper
Two-man cab with hydraulically-operated tipping equipment to rear of cab.
Missile vehicle
This chassis can be used to mount Exocet or Otomat anti-shipping missiles, the Rafale multiple rocket system, RPV launching vehicle, and for mounting anti-aircraft systems such as the Euromissile Roland.
Recovery
This is known as the TRM 9000 CLD and is fitted with a four-door cab. Mounted at the rear is a hydraulically-operated crane that can be traversed through a full 360 degrees and can lift a maximum load of 12 000 kg at a radius of 1·8 metres with the four stabiliser legs (two each side) in position. The front-mounted winch has a 4500 kg capacity and 60 metres of cable and the rear winch has an 18 000 kg capacity and 90 metres of cable. Maximum weight is 18 500 kg. Overall length of the vehicle is 7·865 metres (crane in travelling position) and width is 2·4 metres. (Full details are given in the *Recovery vehicles* section.)
Tractor
This can tow a semi-trailer weighing a maximum of 27 000 kg. Unladen weight is 15 000 kg, length 7·566 metres and width 2·48 metres. For recovery purposes a winch with a capacity of 15 000 kg and 90 metres of cable is fitted as standard.

Renault TRM 9000 (6 × 6) 9000 kg truck

Renault TRM 9000 (6 × 6) 9000 kg truck

STATUS
In production. In service with armed forces including Algeria, Egypt and Morocco. This vehicle is not used by the French Army.

MANUFACTURER
Enquiries to Renault Véhicules Industriels, 8 quai Léon Blum, 92152 Suresnes, France.

SPECIFICATIONS
Cab seating: 1 + 1
Configuration: 6 × 6
Weight:
  (empty) 11 000 kg
  (loaded) 20 000 kg
Max load: (cross country) 9000 kg
Max towed load: 10 000 kg

Length: 9·87 m
Width: 2·48 m
Height: (cab) 3·066 m
Ground clearance: 0·382 m
Track:
  (front) 1·971 m
  (rear) 1·886 m
Wheelbase: 3·8 m + 1·4 m

Angle of approach/departure: 45°/50°
Max speed: 82 km/h
Range: 800 km
Fuel capacity: 200 litres
Max gradient: 45%
Max side slope: 30%
Fording: 1 m
Engine: MIDS 06.20.30 6-cylinder turbo-charged diesel developing 228 hp at 2200 rpm
Gearbox: BDS manual with 6 forward and 1 reverse gears
Clutch: air power assistance
Transfer box: BT 20 2-speed
Steering: power assisted
Turning radius: 11 m
Suspension:
  (front) leaf springs with auxiliary springs and 2 mechanical buffer stops, telescopic shock absorbers
  (rear) balancer by leaf springs and 4 mechanical buffer stops
Tyres: 14.00 × 20
Number of tyres: 6 + 1 spare
Brakes:
  (main) air
  (parking) mechanical
Electrical system: 24 V
Batteries: 4 × 6 TN 190 Ah

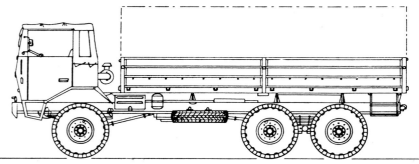

Renault TRM 9000 (6 × 6) 9000 kg truck

Berliet GBU 15 (6 × 6) 6000 kg Truck

DEVELOPMENT
In the 1950s the Rochet-Schneider company developed a 6 × 6 truck called the T-6. This company was subsequently taken over by the Berliet Company and production of the vehicle, now called the GBU 15, began in 1959. Production has been completed and its replacement in the French Army will be the new Renault TRM 10 000 (6 × 6) 10 000 kg truck.

DESCRIPTION
The forward control cab has four doors, removable canvas top and side screens, and a windscreen can be folded down onto the front of the cab if not required. The rear cargo area is provided with a drop tailgate, removable sides, removable bows and a canvas cover.

    Mounted at the rear of the vehicle is a winch with a capacity of 8000 kg. The engine is the multi-fuel type and will run on a variety of fuels including petrol, paraffin, JP4, gas-oil, light fuel and mineral or vegetable oils in the lower power ranges. The rear wheel train consists of two tandem axles operating with a flexible progressive air-driven differential device. This ensures power even when two wheels on one side of the vehicle are not in contact with the ground.

VARIANTS
Artillery tractor
This is a slightly modified GBU 15 and has ammunition storage racks and is used to tow the 155 mm Model 1950 howitzers of the French Army.
Tanker
Tipper
Tractor
This is designated the TBU 15 and has an unladen weight of 13 500 kg. It can tow a semi-trailer carrying a light tank such as the AMX-13 to a maximum weight of 22 000 kg.
Wrecker
This is called the TBU 15 CLD and full details are given in the *Recovery vehicles* section.

SPECIFICATIONS
Cab seating: 1 + 3
Configuration: 6 × 6
Weight:
  (empty) 14 500 kg
  (loaded, road) 24 500 kg
  (loaded, cross country) 20 500 kg
Max load:
  (road) 10 000 kg
  (cross country) 6000 kg
Max towed load: 15 000 kg
Length: 7·974 m
Width: 2·5 m
Height:
  (cab) 3 m
  (tarpaulin) 3·25 m
Track: 2·04 m
Wheelbase: 3·48 m + 1·45 m
Angle of approach/departure: 45°/45°

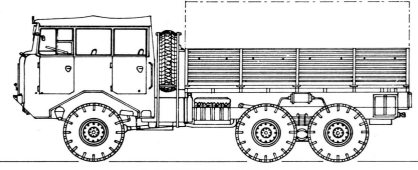

Berliet GBU 15 (6 × 6) 6000 kg truck

Berliet GBU 15 (6 × 6) 6000 kg truck

Max speed: 75 km/h
Range: 800 km
Fuel capacity: 400 litres
Max gradient: 60%
Fording: 1 m
Engine: Berliet 6-cylinder multi-fuel, water-cooled developing 214 hp at 1800 rpm
Gearbox: manual with 5 forward and 1 reverse gears
Clutch: dry
Transfer box: 2-speed
Steering: screw and nut, power assisted
Turning radius: 9·2 m
Suspension: longitudinal springs
Tyres: 14.00 × 20
Number of tyres: 6 + 2 spare

Brakes:
  (main) air, 3 circuits, front, rear and trailer
  (parking) operates on rear wheels only
  (emergency) pneumatic handbrake operates on rear wheels
Electrical system: 24 V

STATUS
Production complete. In service with Belgium, China, France and United Arab Emirates.

MANUFACTURER
Berliet, 160 boulevard de Verdun, 92402 Courbevoie, France. Berliet is now part of Renault Véhicules Industriels.

Renault TRM 10 000 (6 × 6) 10 000 kg Truck

DEVELOPMENT
The Renault TRM 10 000 (6 × 6) 10 000 kg truck has been developed from the Renault TRM 9000 (6 × 6) 9000 kg truck which has been in production at Renault's Bourg-en-Bresse facility since 1975. The main difference between the TRM 9000 and the TRM 10 000 is that the latter has a longer wheelbase, more powerful engine and a different transmission.

The TRM 10 000 (6 × 6) 10 000 kg truck has been selected by the French Army to be its standard truck in this class and has a requirement for 5000 vehicles. Production is scheduled to commence at Renault's Blainville factory in 1984 and is expected to continue until at least 1994.

DESCRIPTION
The chassis of the Renault TRM 10 000 consists of two U-shaped side members (302 mm × 85 mm × 8 mm) with cross members bolted and riveted into position. The front bumper is provided with a front towing shackle and impact buffers and shackles are provided front and rear.

The front axle is a type PA 721 double reduction with bevel gear and reducers in the hubs. The rear tandem is a Type PMR 2021 with double reduction (taper gear and reducers in hubs) and inter-wheel and inter-differential locking.

The basic version has a forward control cab which can be tilted forwards for maintenance purposes and is provided with two doors, tarpaulin cover over removable roof bows, suspended adjustable driver's seat, adjustable passenger's seat, fold down windscreen, heating, defrosting and ventilation equipment as standard.

The rear cargo area is provided with removable sides and tailgate, bows and a tarpaulin cover, and can be fitted with removable seats for 24 fully equipped troops. With the sides and rear removed the TRM 10 000 can carry standard 20 feet ISO containers.

Optional equipment includes an 8000 kg automatic winch which can be used to the front or rear, 10/40 tonne pivoting hook, rear impact buffers, fully enclosed four door cab, hard top on two door cab, four seats in the two door cab, one bunk in two door cab, 12·7 mm anti-aircraft machine gun mount on top of two or four door cab, PTO on gearbox, automatic gearbox model 6 HP 500 with two gear VG 500 transfer box and torque distributer, trailer braking device, ISO coupling plugs (two circuits) and ISO front coupling plugs, class A anti-interference with 50 A alternator, 7 or 12 pin trailer plug, additional 250-litre fuel tank on left hand side of chassis, tool box and boxes for wheel chains.

VARIANTS
Artillery prime mover for 155 mm TR howitzer with four door cab (adopted by the French Army), dump truck, fuel or water tanker, fitted with hydraulic crane of various types, mine carrying vehicle, carrying multiple rocket launcher or various types of surface-to-surface missile, missile resupply vehicle (eg Crotale or SA-10), lubrication vehicle, recovery truck or a tractor truck (4 × 4).

SPECIFICATIONS
Cab seating: 1 + 1
Configuration: 6 × 6
Weight:
(empty) 12 000 kg
(loaded) 22 000 kg
Max load: 12 480 kg
Max towed load: 10 000 kg
Length: (without body) 9·046 m

Width: (without body) 2·48 m
Height: (cab roof) 3·06 m
Ground clearance: 0·382 m
Track:
(front) 1·971 m
(rear) 1·886 m
Wheelbase: 4·1 m + 1·4 m
Angle of approach/departure: 45°/30°
Max speed: (road) 89 km/h
Range: 1200 km
Fuel capacity: 250 litres
Max gradient: 60%
Max side slope: 30%
Fording: 1 m
Engine: Renault MIDS 06.20-45 6-cylinder, supercharged exhaust, diesel developing 260 hp at 2200 rpm
Gearbox: Model B.9.150,9 forward and 1 reverse gears
Clutch: hydropneumatic control
Transfer box: A 800 3D
Steering: Type 8043, hydraulic

Turning radius: 11 m
Suspension:
(front) semi-elliptical leaf springs (auxiliary and main springs), mechanical stops and telescopic shock absorbers
(rear) semi-elliptical leaf springs, mechanical stops
Tyres: 14.00 × 20
Number of tyres: 6 + 1 spare
Brakes:
(main) air, dual circuit
(parking) locking on rear wheels
Electrical system: 24 V
Batteries: 4 × 12 V, 6TN, 190 Ah

STATUS
Selected by the French Army. Production commences 1985.

MANUFACTURER
Enquiries to Renault Véhicules Industriels, 8 quai Léon Blum, 92152 Suresnes, France.

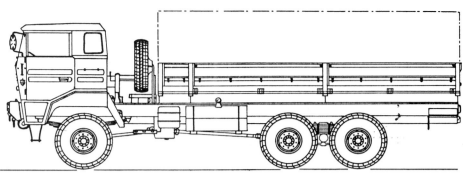

Renault TRM 10 000 (6 × 6) 10 000 kg truck with two door cab

Renault TRM 10 000 (6 × 6) 10 000 kg truck

Renault TRM 10 000 (6 × 6) 10 000 kg truck with four door cab for towing new French 155 mm TR towed gun (T J Gander)

Renault TRM 10 000 (4 × 4) 10 000 kg truck (T J Gander)

Renault TRM 12 000 (6 × 6) 12 000 kg Truck

DEVELOPMENT
The Renault TRM 12 000 (previously known as the Berliet GBH 280) (6 × 6) truck has been designed for towing heavy artillery or trailers up to a maximum gross combination weight of 36 000 kg, ie truck, cargo and artillery piece. This vehicle is a member of a wide range of 4 × 4 and 6 × 6 vehicles which have been adopted for a variety of military and civil applications. The vehicle has been in production at Bourg-en-Bresse since 1971 with orders being received for 2000 vehicles which had been completed by mid-1982.

DESCRIPTION
The chassis consists of two U-shaped longitudinal side members with the five cross-members bolted into position. The layout of the vehicle is conventional with the engine at the front, cab in the centre and cargo area at the rear. The two-door cab is fully enclosed, sound-proofed and ventilated. The rear cargo area has drop sides, drop tailgate, removable bows and a tarpaulin cover. The rear bogie has both inter-wheel and inter-axle differential locks. A winch with a 10 000 kg capacity can be used to the front or rear of the vehicle. Optional equipment includes exhaust retarder, radio suppression, 12-pin current outlet, different tyres and a 250-litre fuel tank.

VARIANTS
These include a dump truck, tipper truck (10·5 cubic metres) and a tractor truck for towing semi-trailers for which there is a separate entry in the *Tank transporters* section.

SPECIFICATIONS
Cab seating: 1 + 2
Configuration: 6 × 6
Weight:
   (empty) 12 000 kg
   (loaded) 24 000 kg
Max load: 12 000 kg
Towed load: 12 000 kg
Length: 7·925 m
Width: 2·5 m
Height:
   (cab) 2·85 m
   (tarpaulin) 3·3 m
Ground clearance: 0·275 m
Track:
   (front) 1·997 m
   (rear) 1·825 m
Wheelbase: 3·975 m + 1·35 m
Angle of approach/departure: 25°/42°
Max speed: (road) 80 km/h
Range: 550 km
Fuel capacity: 250 litres
Max gradient: 48%
Max side slope: 30%
Fording: 0·85 m
Engine: Renault model MIDS 06.35.40 6-cylinder diesel developing 280 hp at 1900 rpm
Gearbox: ZF 5S110 with 9 forward and 1 reverse gears
Clutch: Type 430 DB 1900, pneumatic control and servo
Transfer box: GA 800/3D 2-speed
Steering: hydraulic
Turning radius: 12 m
Suspension:
   (front) leaf springs, lever shock absorbers and buffer stops.
   (rear) leaf springs oscillating on a pivot
Tyres: 12.00 × 20X
Number of tyres: 10 + 1 spare
Brakes:
   (main) air
   (parking) mechanical
Electrical system: 24 V
Batteries: 4 × 6 V

STATUS
In production. In service with the French Army and other forces outside France.

MANUFACTURER
Enquiries to Renault Véhicules Industriels, 8 quai Léon Blum, 92152 Suresnes, France.

Renault TRM 12 000 (6 × 6) 12 000 kg truck

Renault TRM 12 000 (6 × 6) chassis fitted as recovery vehicle

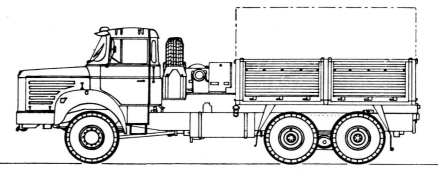

Renault TRM 12 000 (6 × 6) 12 000 kg truck

GERMANY, DEMOCRATIC REPUBLIC

Robur Garant 30K (4 × 4) Truck

DESCRIPTION/VARIANTS.
Between 1950 and 1953 the Phönomen Granit 27 (4 × 2) truck was produced, to be replaced in production in 1953 by the Garant 30K (petrol) and Garant 32 (diesel) trucks. Production of these vehicles continued until 1961 when the LO/LD 1800A/2500 entered production. There were many versions of these trucks including 4 × 4 (with single rear wheels) and 4 × 2 (with dual rear wheels), fully enclosed all-steel cabs and open-top cabs. The rear cargo area has a drop tailgate, removable bows and a tarpaulin cover. An ambulance version is in service in limited numbers.

The LWB chassis is used as the basis for the SK-1 armoured car, details of which are given in *Jane's Armour and Artillery 1983–84*, page 187.

SPECIFICATIONS (Robur Garant 30K)
Configuration: 4 × 4
Weight:
   (loaded, dirt road) 3250 kg
   (empty) 2250 kg
Max load:
   (road) 1950 kg
   (dirt road) 1000 kg
Towed load:
   (road) 2500 kg
   (dirt road) 1200 kg
Length: 5·3 m
Width: 2·1 m
Height:
   (cab) 2·06 m
   (tarpaulin) 2·575 m
Ground clearance: 0·245 m
Track:
   (front) 1·5 m
   (rear) 1·618 m
Wheelbase: 3·27 m
   (LWB) 3·77 m
Max speed: 80 km/h
Range: 450 km
Fuel capacity: 72 litres
Fuel consumption: 16 litres/100 km
Fording: 0·54 m
Engine: Model 30K 4-cylinder air-cooled diesel developing 60 hp at 2800 rpm
Gearbox: manual with 4 forward and 1 reverse gears
Transfer box: 2-speed
Suspension:
   (front) semi-elliptical springs
   (rear) semi-elliptical springs with overload springs
Brakes:
   (main) hydraulic
   (parking) mechanical
Tyres: 7.50 × 20
Number of tyres: 6 + 1 spare
Electrical system: 12 V

STATUS
Production complete. No longer used by the East German Army but still used by East German Workers' Militia.

MANUFACTURER
VEB Robur-Werke, Zittau, Bezirk Dresden, German Democratic Republic.

Robur Garant 30K (4 × 4) open topped truck towing 120 mm M1938 mortar

Robur LO 1800 A (4 × 4) 1800 kg Truck

DESCRIPTION

The Robur LO 1800 A (4 × 4) truck entered production in 1961 as the replacement for the older Robur Garant 30K (4 × 4) truck and has been produced for both civil and military use. The vehicle has an all-steel forward control type cab with an observation hatch in the right side of the roof. The rear cargo area has removable bows, tarpaulin cover and a drop tailgate.

In 1968 the LO 1800 A was replaced in production by the LO 1801 A, which has a slightly different engine and cab and is equipped with a 5000 kg winch. In 1972 the LO 2002 A was introduced. This has a more powerful 75 hp engine and can carry 2100 kg of cargo across country.

VARIANTS

Ambulance
The ambulance model has a fully enclosed rear van type body. A removable stretcher assembly is mounted in the rear for six stretchers.

Civil versions
The civilian versions are the LO 2500 (4 × 2), LO 2500 A (4 × 4), LO 2501 (4 × 2), LO 2501 A (4 × 4), LO 3000 (4 × 2), LD 2500 (4 × 2) and the LD 2501 (4 × 2), the last two models with diesel engines rather than the petrol engines used in the earlier models.

Decontamination
The East German Army has a number of these trucks fitted with the DA-66 decontamination shower system. This consists of a heating unit, pumps and a shower tent. The heating units and the pumps are carried in the rear of the truck with the tent, which is divided into sections for undressing, showering, and dressing, carried in a single axle trailer towed by the truck. The vehicle is also used to carry various types of clothing decontamination equipment including the BU-2, BU-3, BU-4 and BU-4M.

Tractor truck
This was developed to the prototype stage but did not enter production.

Van
Various van models are in service for command and repair roles.

Water purification
A version with a water purification system mounted in the rear is in service.

STATUS

In production. In service with the East German, Hungarian and Polish armies.

MANUFACTURER

VEB Robur-Werke, Zittau, Bezirk Dresden, German Democratic Republic.

SPECIFICATIONS

Model	LO 1800 A	LO 1801 A	LO 2002 A
Configuration	4 × 4	4 × 4	4 × 4
Weight (empty)	3200 kg	3375 kg	3340 kg
(loaded cross country)	5000 kg	5875 kg	6240 kg
Max load (road)	2500 kg	2500 kg	2900 kg
(cross country)	1800 kg	1875 kg	2100 kg
Towed load (road)	3000 kg	3000 kg	3000 kg
(cross country)	2100 kg	2100 kg	2100 kg
Length	5·38 m	5·4 m	5·4 m
Width	2·365 m	2·37 m	2·37 m
Height (cab)	2·365 m	2·37 m	2·37 m
Ground clearance	0·265 m	0·265 m	0·265 m
Track (front/rear)	1·636 m/1·664 m	1·636 m/1·664 m	1·636 m/1·664 m
Wheelbase	3·025 m	3·025 m	3·025 m
Max speed	80 km/h	80 km/h	80 km/h
Range	590 km	590 km	n/a
Fuel capacity	160 litres	160 litres	n/a
Max gradient	55%	55%	45%
Fording	0·8 m	0·8 m	0·8 m
Engine model	LO 4	LO 4/1	LO 4/2
Type	all 4-cylinder air-cooled petrol		
Hp/rpm	70/2800	70/2800	75/2800
Gearbox	all have a manual gearbox with 5 forward and 1 reverse gears		
Transfer box	all have a 2-speed transfer box		
Suspension	all have front, semi-elliptical springs, rear, semi-elliptical springs with helpers		
Brakes (main)	hydraulic	hydraulic	hydraulic
(parking)	mechanical	mechanical	mechanical
Tyres	10.00 × 20	10.00 × 20	10.00 × 20
Number of tyres	4 + 1 spare	4 + 1 spare	4 + 1 spare

Robur LO 1800 A (4 × 4) 1800 kg truck of East German Army

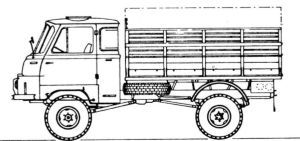

Robur LO 1800 A (4 × 4) 1800 kg truck

W 50 LA/A (4 × 4) 3000 kg Truck

DESCRIPTION

The W 50 L series of trucks entered production in 1965 as the replacement for the S 4000-1 series of 4 × 2 trucks, and have since been built in large numbers for both civil and military applications. While under development the vehicle was variously known as the S 4500 and the W45.

The basic civilian models are designated the W 50 L (4 × 2) and the W 50 L (4 × 4). The military version, which has larger tyres and a central tyre pressure regulation system, is known as the W 50 LA/A. This has an all-steel forward control cab with a circular observation hatch in the roof and a rear cargo area with removable bows, a tarpaulin cover and a drop tailgate. A winch with a capacity of 4500 kg is provided and can be used to the front or rear of the vehicle.

The letter L after the 50 indicates a 4 × 2 vehicle and the letters LA a 4 × 4 vehicle. After these letters is a stroke followed by another letter: A for military versions,

K for dump truck, L for truck with loading crane, S for tractor truck, and Z for prime mover. There are also combinations of these letters, for example the MK is a hopper dump truck and the 3 SK 5 is a three-sided dump truck with a capacity of 5000 kg.

VARIANTS (Army)
Recovery
The East German Army uses a number of recovery vehicles under the designation W 50 LA/AB. These have a loaded weight of 11 500 kg and can lift a maximum load of 6300 kg. A winch with 60 metres of cable and a capacity of 4500 kg is also provided.

Mobile blood station
This is called the Mobil Blutstation and is the W 50 L/A (4 × 4 truck with 8·25 × 20 tyres) with a container mounted on the rear. This is removed from the vehicle as follows: the truck is halted and legs are extended at each corner of the container on outriggers and the container is lowered to the ground. The sides of the container are unfolded to form the floors of the extensions and the sides and roof, which are of waterproof canvas, are then erected.

Shop/van
Various versions of the W 50 LA/A exist with van type bodies.

NBC laboratory
The W50 is used for carrying a special box-bodied NBC laboratory known as the RChLab-11. For details of this body see entry in *NBC Detection* section.

ECM
A special version of the W50, the WKCA (Werkstatt für KC-Aufklärungsgeräte) carries a box body with sloping sides at the top. Weight of this version is 8525 kg. If required the box body can be replaced by a standard ISO container.

Gas cylinder carrier
This is a version of the W50 known as the AZS-EA 12 which is equipped with special racks covered by a canvas tilt and used to carry large gas cylinders.

STATUS
In production. In service with the East German Army. Exported to countries including Egypt and Iraq.

MANUFACTURER
VEB IFA Automobile Works, Ludwigsfelde, Bezirk Potsdam, German Democratic Republic.

SPECIFICATIONS
Configuration: 4 × 4
Weight:
(empty) 5080 kg
(loaded, cross country) 8080 kg
(loaded, dirt road) 9800 kg
(loaded, roads) 10 380 kg
Max load:
(roads) 5300 kg
(dirt road) 4720 kg
(cross country) 3000 kg
Length: 6·53 m
Width: 2·5 m
Height:
(cab) 2·6 m
(tarpaulin) 3·2 m
Ground clearance: 0·3 m
Track:
(front) 1·7 m
(rear) 1·78 m
Wheelbase: 3·2 m
Max speed: (road) 83 km/h
Range: 720 km
Fuel capacity: 100 litres
Max gradient: 50%
Vertical obstacle: 0·4 m
Fording: 1 m
Engine: Model 4 VD 14·5/12 SRN-1 4-cylinder water-cooled diesel developing 125 hp at 2200 rpm (later models have 150 hp engines)
Gearbox: manual, 5 forward and 2 reverse gears
Transfer box: 2-speed
Steering: power-assisted

Mobile bloodstation based on W 50 L/A (4 × 4) chassis

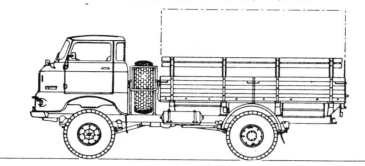

W 50 LA/A (4 × 4) 3000 kg truck

W50 truck carrying WKCA ECM and Communications body

Turning radius: 15·2 m
Suspension:
(front) semi-elliptical springs
(rear) semi-elliptical springs with helpers
Tyres: 16.00 × 20

Number of tyres: 4 + 1 spare
Brakes:
(main) air/hydraulic
(parking) mechanical
Electrical system: 24 V

G 5 Series of (6 × 6) 3500 kg Trucks

DESCRIPTION
This range of trucks entered production in 1952 and for many years was the standard cargo truck of the East German Army, but has been replaced in many units by the Soviet ZIL-131 (6 × 6) and Ural-375D (6 × 6) and the East German W 50 LA/A (4 × 4) trucks.

The layout of the G 5 is conventional with the engine at the front, cab in the centre and the cargo area at the rear with removable bows, tarpaulin cover and a drop tailgate. There are at least three different types of cab: all steel without observation hatch in the roof, all steel with observation hatch in the roof and an open type with a folding windscreen and a removable canvas top.

The first models of the G 5 were powered by a 120 hp diesel engine but the G 5/2 has a 150 hp diesel engine. The G 5/3 had many improvements including a more powerful V-8 air cooled diesel engine, central tyre pressure regulation system and an all-steel cab, but was not placed in production as it was decided to use the Soviet Ural-375D (6 × 6) truck instead and many of these were subsequently assembled in East Germany.

VARIANTS
Crane
There are various crane models of the G 5 in service for both civil and military applications.

Decontamination trucks
There are five known decontamination trucks, designated GEW-1, GEW-2, GEW-3, DA-2S and MOE. The GEW-1 truck is used to decontaminate vehicles, weapons, equipment, building and terrain and can also be used for fire-fighting if required. It consists of a 4500-litre tank, a pump which is driven by a PTO for the

main engine, hoses and nozzles. To decontaminate vehicles and equipment various sizes of hose are used and for decontaminating terrain spray nozzles can be mounted at the front and rear of the vehicle. The GEW-2 is used to decontaminate roads and terrain with dry, solid decontaminants. A hopper mounted at the rear of the body holds 3000 kg of decontaminant and a centrifugal dispenser which can be adjusted for spreading decontaminant over a width of three or six metres. The GEW-2 can also be used for sanding or salting roads. The GEW-3 is used to decontaminate vehicles, weapons, equipment, terrain and buildings, and consists of a 3100 litre tank with a separate diesel driven pump, hoses and nozzles. The DA-2S is a truck-mounted decontamination shower system. The MOE is used to decontaminate roads, airfields and terrain and consists of a centrifugal pump, spray booms (which spray an area 7·3 metres wide when opened out) and accessories. Dispensing speed is 600 litres per minute.

Dump trucks
Rear and three-way hydraulically operated dump trucks are in service.

Fire-fighting
Various fire-fighting versions of the G 5 are in service, one called the TLF15, which has a longer wheelbase and a larger cab.

Riot control
The G 5 chassis is used as the basis for the SK-2 armoured water cannon used for crowd control in East Germany.

Tanker
The tanker model is known as the TG 5 and can carry 4000 litres of fuel. It often tows a trailer carrying another 4500 litres of fuel.

Van and workshop
The G 5 is used as the basis for a variety of different types of van which are used as command posts and workshop vehicles. Some of the workshop vehicles have an A-frame at the front for removing vehicle components.

SPECIFICATIONS
Cab seating: 1 + 1
Configuration: 6 × 6
Weight:
  (empty) 8000 kg
  (loaded, cross country) 11 500 kg
  (loaded, roads) 13 000 kg
Max load:
  (road) 5000 kg
  (cross country) 3500 kg
Towed load:
  (road) 8000 kg
  (cross country) 3500 kg
Length: 7·3 m
Width: 2·5 m
Height:
  (cab) 2·6 m
  (tarpaulin) 3 m
Ground clearance: 0·255 m
Track:
  (front) 1·8 m
  (rear) 1·75 m
Wheelbase: 3·8 m + 1·25 m
Max speed: (road) 60 km/h
Range: 585 km
Fuel capacity: 150 litres
Fuel consumption: 361 litres/100 km
Max gradient: 42%
Vertical obstacle: 0·5 m
Fording: 1·05 m
Engine: EM 6 6-cylinder water-cooled petrol developing 120 hp at 2000 rpm. Late production models have 150 hp engines
Gearbox: manual with 5 forward and 2 reverse gears
Transfer box: 2-speed
Turning radius: 14 m
Suspension:
  (front) semi-elliptical springs
  (rear) semi-elliptical springs and overload springs

G 5 (6 × 6) 3500 kg truck with soft top cab and tarpaulin sides rolled up

G 5 (6 × 6) 3500 kg truck being used to assist in repairing 122-mm M-1938 (M-30) field howitzer

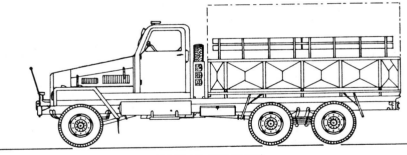

G 5 (6 × 6) 3500 kg truck

Tyres: 8.25 × 20
Number of tyres: 10 + 1 spare
Brakes:
  (main) hydraulic, air assisted
  (parking) mechanical
Electrical system: 12 V

STATUS
Production complete. In service with the East German Army.

MANUFACTURER
VEB, Kraftfahrzeugwerk Ernst Grube, Werdau, Bezirk Karl-Marx-Stadt, German Democratic Republic.

S 4000-1 (4 × 2) 4000 kg Truck

DEVELOPMENT
After the end of the Second World War East Germany manufactured a 4 × 2 truck known as the H3. In 1953 a new model called the H3A was introduced, powered by an 80 hp diesel engine and capable of carrying a maximum load of 3500 kg on roads. Production was completed in 1955 and in 1958 a new model known as the S 4000-1 entered production to continue until 1965 when the W 50 L entered production. The S 4000-1 is primarily a civilian vehicle but is used in some numbers by the East German Army.

DESCRIPTION
The layout of the vehicle is conventional with the engine at the front, two-door fully enclosed cab in the centre and the cargo area at the rear with drop sides and a drop tailgate and, optionally, bows and a tarpaulin cover.

VARIANTS
A prime mover is designated the S 4000-1Z. There are also a tractor truck, a dump truck, and a crane truck.

Between 1952 and 1958 a larger truck called the H6 was built in small numbers, similar in appearance to the H3A and S 4000-1. This was powered by a 120 or

150 hp diesel and had a payload of 6500 kg on roads and could tow a trailer weighing up to 6500 kg. Two dump truck models of this were also developed.

STATUS
Production complete. In service with the East German Army. Also supplied to China and Viet-Nam.

MANUFACTURER
VEB, Kraftfahrzeugwerk Ernst Grube, Werdau, Bezirk Karl-Marx-Stadt, German Democratic Republic.

SPECIFICATIONS
Cab seating: 1 + 2
Configuration: 4 × 4
Weight:
  (empty) 4100 kg
  (loaded, road) 8100 kg
Max load: (road) 4000 kg
Towed load: (road) 4500 kg
Length: 6·491 m
Width: 2·37 m

Height: (cab) 2·344 m
Ground clearance: 0·24 m
Track:
  (front) 1·652 m
  (rear) 1·633 m
Wheelbase: 3·55 m
Max speed: 74 km/h
Range: 500 km
Fuel capacity: 100 litres
Fuel consumption: 20 litres/100 km

Max gradient: 19°
Fording: 0·85 m
Engine: Model EM 4/22-90 4-cylinder water-cooled diesel developing 90 hp at 2200 rpm
Gearbox: manual with 5 forward and 1 reverse gears
Transfer box: none
Tyres: 8.25 × 20
Number of tyres: 6 + 1 spare

GERMANY, FEDERAL REPUBLIC

Mercedes-Benz Unimog (4 × 4) Series

DEVELOPMENT
The Unimog (Universal Motor Gerät, or universal power plant) was designed by Herr Friedrich in 1946 primarily for industrial and agricultural use. It was first shown in 1948 and initial production was undertaken by Gebr Boeringer at Goppingen in 1949. Two years later production was transferred back to Goppingen and since then large numbers of Unimogs have been manufactured for both civilian and military use, in many different models.

DESCRIPTION
The layout of all vehicles in the series is basically the same with the engine and cab at the front and the cargo area at the rear. Most military models have a two-door cab with a soft top and a windscreen which folds forward onto the bonnet, and a rear cargo area with a drop tailgate, drop sides, removable bows and a tarpaulin cover.

The Unimog vehicle is well known for its excellent cross-country capabilities and all vehicles are fitted with a differential lock on both the front and rear axles. For normal road use the vehicle is driven with only the rear wheels engaged while for cross-country use the front wheels are also engaged with the differential locks being used in very rough terrain.

A wide range of optional equipment is available for the vehicle including a fully enclosed two- or four-door cab, generator, front-mounted pump, snow plough and a winch.

VARIANTS
The Unimog is used for a variety of roles including use as an ambulance, command vehicle, fire-fighting vehicle, radio vehicle, workshop and as a prime mover for light artillery such as the 105 mm Italian pack howitzer.

The basic production models are listed below.
Model 406
This has a 2·38-metre wheelbase and can carry 2000 kg of cargo. Basic specifications are weight (loaded) 5000 kg, weight (empty) 3000 kg, length 4·55 metres, width 2 metres, height 2·25 metres, wheelbase 2·38 metres and track 1·536 metres.
Model 411
This has a 1·72-metre wheelbase and can carry 1100 kg of cargo. Basic specifications are length 3·46 metres, width 1·63 metres and height 2·05 metres.

Model 416
This is widely used by the military and carries a maximum load of 2500 kg, with a NATO-rated capacity of 2000 kg. The chassis of the 416 is also used as the basis for the Thyssen Maschinenbau UR-416 (4 × 4) armoured internal security vehicle. (*Jane's Armour and Artillery 1983-84*, page 308.) Full specifications are given in the table below.
Model 421
This has the same wheelbase as the 416 but is powered by a four-cylinder diesel which develops 66 hp whereas the 416 has a six-cylinder diesel which develops 110 hp.
Model S 404
This has the same wheelbase as the 416 but is powered by a six-cylinder engine which develops 118 hp at 4800 rpm and can carry a maximum load of 2650 kg. Basic specifications are length 5·03 metres, width 2·14 metres and height 2·63 metres.
Model S4 (or Type 404)
This also has the same wheelbase as the 416 and is powered by a four-cylinder engine which develops 90 hp at 4800 rpm. Basic specifications are length 4·925 metres, width 2·14 metres, cab height 2·19 metres and overall height 2·54 metres. Maximum payload is 1800 kg.

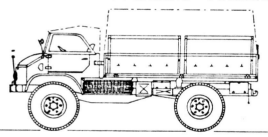

Unimog (4 × 4) Model 421

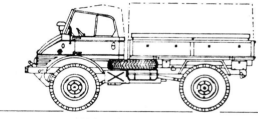

Unimog (4 × 4) Model S 421

Unimog (4 × 4) converted by AB Bofors to carry elements of RBS 70 low level air defence missile

Unimog (4 × 4) in use as helicopter forward base control post (T J Gander)

Unimog (4 × 4) light truck in use by West German Army (T J Gander)

Unimog (4 × 4) being used as radio vehicle by Belgian Army (C R Zwart)

SPECIFICATIONS
(421; data in square brackets relate to 416 where different)
Cab seating: 1 + 1
Configuration: 4 × 4
Weight:
  (empty) 2500 [3600] kg
  (loaded) 4000 [6000] kg
Max load: 1500 [2400] kg
Max towed load: 1500 [2500] kg
Length: 5·1 m
Width: 2·14 m
Height:
  (cab) 2·325 m
  (overall) 2·67 m

Ground clearance: 0·44 m
Track: (front and rear) 1·616 m
Wheelbase: 2·9 m
Angle of approach/departure: 45°/46°
Max speed: (road) 80 [85] km/h
Range: 500 [600] km
Fuel capacity: 90 litres
Gradient: 70%
Fording: 1 m
Engine: OM 616 [352] 4-cylinder 66 [110] hp diesel
Gearbox: manual with 6 forward and 1 reverse gears
Tyres: 10.50 × 18 [12.50 × 20]
Number of tyres: 4 + 1 spare
Electrical system: 12 [24] V
Batteries: 1 [2] × 12 V

STATUS
In production. Unimogs are in service with many armed forces including those of Argentina, Austria, Belgium, Finland, France, West Germany, Greece, India, Jordan, Netherlands, Norway, Senegal, Switzerland, Turkey and United Kingdom.

MANUFACTURER
Daimler-Benz AG, Stuttgart-Untertürkheim, Federal Republic of Germany.

Mercedes-Benz Unimog Export Models

DESCRIPTION
This section is a summary of the range of export models produced by Mercedes-Benz specifically for the export market. Some of the vehicles mentioned in the following table have their own separate entries (see the U 1300 L and the U 1700 L) but are included here to provide a complete survey of the models available.

Only the basic models are included in the specifications table. Variants such as vans, fire tenders, tractor units, snow ploughs and specialist airfield vehicles may be encountered. Many of them are also produced for civilian use, including agriculture.

STATUS
Production. In widespread service.

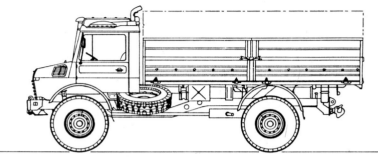
Unimog U 1700 L with 3·85-metre wheelbase

MANUFACTURER
Daimler-Benz AG, Gaggenau Plant, Federal Republic of Germany.

Enquiries to Daimler-Benz AG, Stuttgart-Untertürkheim, Federal Republic of Germany.

SPECIFICATIONS (all 4 × 4)

Model	U 600 L	U 800 L	U 1100 L (2·9 m WB)	U 1100 L (3·4 m WB)	U 1300 L	U 1700 L (3·25 m WB)	U 1700 L (3·85 m WB)
Cab seating	1 + 1	1 + 1	1 + 1	1 + 1	1 + 1	1 + 1	1 + 1
Weight (empty)	2250 kg	2860 kg	2860 kg	2980 kg	5250 kg	4900 kg	6900 kg
(loaded)	4200 kg	6000 kg	6000 kg	6000 kg	7500 kg	9000 kg	12 200 kg
(axle load, front/rear)	2600 kg	3600 kg	3700 kg	3700 kg	4000 kg	5300 kg	6500 kg
Max load	1250 kg	2500 kg	2800 kg	3000 kg	2250 kg	4000 kg	5000 kg
Load area	2·5 × 1·6 m	3 × 2 m	3 × 2 m	3·6 × 2 m	3·15 × 2·2 m	3·15 × 2·2 m	4·25 × 2·35 m
Length	4·74 m	5·1 m	5·1 m	5·7 m	5·54 m	5·58 m	6·7 m
Width	1·825 m	2·15 m	2·15 m	2·15 m	2·3 m	2·32 m	2·465 m
Height (cab)[1]	2·25 m	2·34 m	2·375 m	2·375 m	2·63 m	2·72 m	2·78 m
(canvas cover)[1]	2·365 m	2·665 m	2·7 m	2·7 m	2·83 m	3·02 m	3·14 m
Ground clearance[1]	0·39 m	0·405 m	0·44 m	0·44 m	0·44 m	0·5 m	0·5 m
Track	1·396 m	1·62 m	1·555 m	1·62 m	1·86 m	1·84 m	1·84 m
Wheelbase	2·605 m	2·9 m	2·9 m	3·4 m	3·25 m	3·25 m	3·85 m
Angle of approach/departure	45°/45°	45°/46°	45°/46°	45°/40°	46°/51°	48°/54°	45°/36°
Max speed	73 km/h	73 km/h	82 km/h	82 km/h	82 km/h	97 km/h	71·3 km/h
Fuel capacity	90 litres	120 litres	120 litres	120 litres	160 litres	160 litres	160 litres
Gradient	70%	70%	70%	70%	70%	70%	70%
Max side slope	40°	40°	40°	40°	40°	40°	40°
Fording	0·8 m	0·8 m	0·8 m	0·8 m	0·8 m	0·8 m	0·8 m
Engine type	OM 616	OM 314	OM 352	OM 352	OM 352	OM 352 A	OM 352 A
Number of cylinders	4	4	6	6	6	6	6
Capacity	2·404 litres	3·78 litres	5·675 litres	5·675 litres	5·675 litres	5·675 litres	5·675 litres
HP/rpm	60/3500	75/2600	110/2800	110/2800	130/2800	168/2800	168/2800
Gears[2]	4 forward, 1 reverse	4 forward, 1 reverse	4 forward, 1 reverse	4 forward, 2 reverse	4 forward, 4 reverse	4 forward, 4 reverse	4 forward, 4 reverse
Clutch	single dry disc	single dry disc	single dry disc	single dry disc	single dry disc	single dry disc	single dry disc
Turning radius	5·6 m	6·25 m	6·25 m	6·9 m	6·9 m	7 m	7·9 m
Tyres	10.5 × 18	10.5 × 20	11.0 × 20	11.0 × 20	11.0 × 20	11.0 × 24	13.0 × 20
Electrical system	12 V	12 V	12 V	12 V	12 V or 24 V	12 V	12 V or 24 V

[1] Unloaded   [2] Transfer box fitted

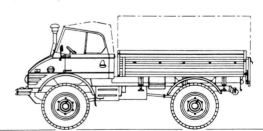
Unimog U 600 L

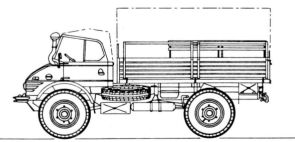
Unimog U 800 L

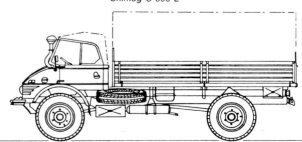
Unimog U 1100 L with 2·9-metre wheelbase

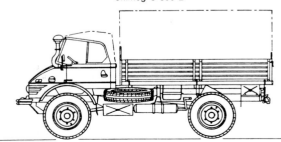
Unimog U 1100 L with 3·4-metre wheelbase

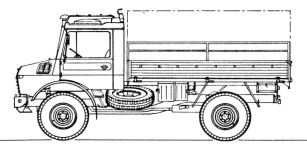

Unimog U 1300 L

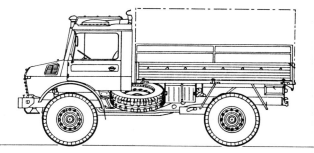

Unimog U 1700 L with 3·25-metre wheelbase

Mercedes-Benz Model U 1300 L (4 × 4) 2250 kg Unimog Truck

DEVELOPMENT

The Mercedes-Benz Model U 1300 L (4 × 4) 2250 kg truck was selected late in 1977 to become the standard truck in its class in the West German Army and an order for 17 000 vehicles was placed with Mercedes-Benz. First production vehicles were delivered in 1978 and production is expected to continue until 1987.

In September 1981 it was announced that the New Zealand Army was to purchase 210 Unimog U 1300 L trucks, following trials that had been held since 1978. These vehicles will be delivered gradually until 1989 and will be produced by Mills Tui Limited in Rotorua, New Zealand.

The Model U 1300 L is a standard production model with a number of alterations to suit it for military use, including a modified electrical system, use of a torsion-free platform with stowage boxes and mounting points for centre seat bench and tarpaulin frame as well as anchoring and lashing points for van bodies, supports and attachments in the cab for military equipment such as small arms and the addition of an observation hatch in the roof.

DESCRIPTION

The enclosed all-steel cab is noise and temperature insulated and can be tilted forward and locked in position for engine maintenance. The cab is designed to comply with the OECD specifications on roll-over stability and has passed the OECD test.

The cab is fitted with a ventilation system that incorporates a blower. Automatic circuit breakers for the electrical units are centrally located and accessible on the driver's side above the instrument panel.

The axles are connected to the transmission by means of torque tubes and to the chassis by control arms, coil springs and shock absorbers. A torsion bar stabiliser has been installed on the front axle to improve handling characteristics when the vehicle is fitted with a van type body with a higher centre of gravity.

The ladder arrangement of the side- and cross-members of the chassis gives good rigidity on the road and a high degree of elasticity in difficult terrain. The underslung U-shaped side-members are connected by welded-in tubular cross-members and the rear cross-member is screwed to the side-members.

The platform floor is provided with anchoring and lashing points for van bodies or shelters as well as eyelets for lashing pallets and supplies. The side walls (500 mm high) can be folded down even with the tarpaulin still in place. Side racks up to 900 mm high and a safety belt above the platform rear wall are available for the transport of troops. The tarpaulin has a frame plus mountings which is independent of the side walls and can be stowed away.

For special applications the vehicle can be equipped with a front cable winch.

VARIANTS

The chassis can be used for a wide number of roles but the only variant in service at present with the West German Army is an ambulance model with a fully enclosed rear body.

SPECIFICATIONS
Cab seating: 1 + 2
Configuration: 4 × 4
Weight:
(empty) 5250 kg
(loaded) 7500 kg
Max load: 2250 kg (inc 250 kg for crew)
Max towed load: 8500 kg
Length: 5·54 m
Width: 2·3 m
Height:
(tarpaulin, unloaded) 2·83 m
(tarpaulin, loaded) 2·71 m

Mercedes-Benz Model U 1300 L (4 × 4) 2250 kg Unimog truck complete with frame and tarpaulin cover (T J Gander)

West German Army Unimog U 1300 L (4 × 4) truck towing trailer (T J Gander)

Ground clearance: 0·44 m
Track: 1·86 m
Wheelbase: 3·25 m
Angle of approach/departure: 46°/51°
Max speed: 80 km/h
Range: 900 km
Fuel capacity: 160 litres
Gradient: 70%
Fording: 1·2 m
Engine: OM 352 6-cylinder diesel developing 96 hp at 2800 rpm
Transmission: Cascade gearbox with planetary gear group and flanged on transfer case giving 8 forward and 4 reverse gears
Steering: power assisted
Turning radius: 6·9 m

Suspension: coil springs and hydraulic shock absorbers
Tyres: 12.5 R 20 MPT/11 × 20
Number of tyres: 4 + 1 spare
Brakes:
(main) hydraulically operated disc
(parking) mechanical
Electrical system: 24 V
Batteries: 2 × 12 V

STATUS
Production. In service with New Zealand and the West German Army.

MANUFACTURER
Daimler-Benz Aktiengesellschaft, Stuttgart-Untertürkheim, Federal Republic of Germany.

Mercedes-Benz Model U 1300 L (4 × 4) 2250 kg Unimog truck

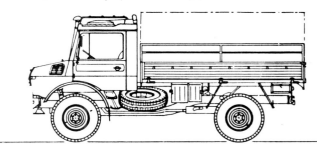

Mercedes-Benz Model U 1300 L (4 × 4) 2250 kg Unimog truck

Mercedes-Benz L 508 DG MA (4 × 2) 2105 kg Truck

DESCRIPTION

The Mercedes-Benz L 508 DG MA (4 × 2) 2105 kg truck is used for transporting men and cargo in rear areas and has little cross-country mobility. It is a standard commercial vehicle with a minimum of modifications to suit it for military use. Final deliveries will be made to the West German Army in 1985.

The chassis is a bend-resistant parallel ladder frame with tubular cross-members, except for the one at the rear. A coupling member is incorporated in the front cross-member suitable for a tow bar as used by the German Federal armed forces.

The all-steel forward control cab is noise and temperature insulated. A heater is fitted as standard on all models and the L 508 D/35 van type model, used as a command vehicle, has a heat exchanger and a special vent in the front part of the cab roof.

The rear cargo platform has a plywood floor with hinged steel side- and tail-boards, stowage boxes and support points for the centre bench, tarpaulin frame as well as locating and lashing points for fitting a shelter or transporting pallets.

VARIANTS

L 508 D/35
Box van with a wheelbase of 3·5 metres, which can be used for a number of roles including command.
L 508 D/35
This is the standard pick-up model with a wheelbase of 3·5 metres, cargo area 4·06 metres long and 2·26 metres wide and maximum cargo capacity of 2460 kg.
L 608 D/41
This is a pick-up with a wheelbase of 4·1 metres, cargo area 5·06 metres long and 2·26 metres wide and maximum cargo capacity of 3500 kg.

SPECIFICATIONS (L 508 DG MA)
Cab seating: 1 + 2
Configuration: 4 × 2
Weight:
 (empty) 3495 kg
 (loaded) 5600 kg
Max load: 2105 kg
Load area: 3·15 × 2·2 m
Max towed load: 1150 kg
Length: 5·325 m
Width: 2·32 m

Mercedes-Benz L 508 DG MA (4 × 2) 2105 kg truck (T J Gander)

Height:
 (cab, unloaded) 2·345 m
 (cab, loaded) 2·3 m
 (tarpaulin, unloaded) 2·68 m
 (tarpaulin, loaded) 2·535 m
Track:
 (front) 1·76 m
 (rear) 1·54 m
Wheelbase: 2·95 m
Max speed: 98 km/h
Range: 750 km
Fuel consumption: 11·2 litres/100 km
Gradient: 27%
Engine: OM 314 4-cylinder diesel developing 85 hp at 1800 rpm
Transmission: manual, 5 forward and 1 reverse gears
Clutch: single dry plate
Steering: recirculating ball

Turning radius: 5·7 m
Suspension: semi-elliptical leaf springs, hydraulic shock absorbers with both axles fitted with torsion bar stabilisers
Tyres: 7.00 R 16 C 10 PR
Number of tyres: 6 + 1 spare
Brakes:
 (main) air/hydraulic
 (parking) mechanical
Electrical system: 24 V
Batteries: 2 × 12 V

STATUS
In production. In service with the West German Army.

MANUFACTURER
Daimler-Benz Aktiengesellschaft, Stuttgart-Untertürkheim, Federal Republic of Germany.

Iveco Magirus Military Vehicles

Iveco Magirus (formerly Magirus-Deutz) is a member of the Industrial Vehicles Corporation (IVECO) and manufactures a wide range of vehicles suitable for military applications. The West German Army has placed an order for 7000 Iveco Magirus 168 M 11 FL (4 × 2) 5000 kg trucks for delivery by 1987 and 900 various trucks/tractor trucks of the following types: 320 D 20 FAT (6 × 6) 8000-litre tanker, 320 D 22 FS (6 × 4) tractor truck towing semi-trailer for carrying vehicles and 24 000- or 30 000-litre tanker semi-trailers, 320 D 26 FT (6 × 4) 15 000- and 18 000-litre tankers and 310 D 26 FAK (6 × 6) tipper truck.

VARIANTS
Iveco Magirus offers a wide range of bodies including cargo, recovery, crash rescue, fire-fighting, and van types for command, communications and other roles.

Iveco Magirus 232 D 16 AL (6 × 6) recovery truck

Iveco Magirus 130 series (4 × 4) tanker truck

SPECIFICATIONS
310 D 20 FAT 8000-litre tanker
Configuration: 6 × 6
Weight:
  (empty) 12 200 kg
  (loaded) 19 050 kg
  (max weight) 19 500 kg
Length: 7·7 m
Width: 2·5 m
Height: 2·93 m
Ground clearance: 0·31 m
Track:
  (front) 1·99 m
  (rear) 2·07 m
Wheelbase: 2·5 m + 1·38 m

Angle of approach/departure: 25°/30°
Max speed: 95 km/h
Fuel capacity: 400 litres
Engine: F10L 413 F 10-cylinder diesel developing
315 hp at 2500 rpm

168 M 11 FL 5000 kg truck
Configuration: 4 × 2
Weight:
  (empty) 6050 kg
  (loaded) 11 200 kg
Weight on front axle: (loaded) 3700 kg
Weight on rear axle: (loaded) 7700 kg
Max load: 5150 kg

Load area: 5 × 2·37 m
Length: 7·02 m
Width: 2·49 m
Height: 3·18 m
Ground clearance: 0·27/0·24 m
Track:
  (front) 1·8 m
  (rear) 1·72 m
Wheelbase: 3·6 m
Angle of approach/departure: 28°/17°
Max speed: 85·5 km/h
Fuel capacity: 130 litres
Engine: BF6L 913 6-cylinder diesel developing 166 hp
at 2650 rpm
Gradient: 45·3%

Model	Configuration	Wheelbase	Engine	Gearbox	Tyres	GVW	Approx payload	Approx platform size
Troop carriers								
90 M 6 FL	4 × 2	3 m	F4L 913	S 5-24	12.5 × 20	6000 kg	2500 kg	n/a
130 M 7 FAL	4 × 4	2·85 m	F6L 913	AK 5-35	12.5 × 20	7500 kg	2000/2500 kg	3·1 × 2·3 m
130 D 9 L	4 × 2	4·2 m	F6L 913	AK 5-35	13.00 × 20	10 500 kg	4000/5000 kg	4·2 × 2·3 m
130 D 9 AL	4 × 4	4·2 m	F6L 913	AK 5-35	13.00 × 20	10 500 kg	4000/5000 kg	4·2 × 2·3 m
168 M 11 FL	4 × 2	3·6 m	BF6L 913	S 6-65	9R 22.5	11 200 kg	4000/5000 kg	4·2 × 2·3 m
192 D 12 AL	4 × 4	4·2 m	F6L 413 F	S 6-65	13.00 × 20	12 700 kg	5000/7000 kg	4·2 × 2·3 m
130 D 13 L	4 × 2	4·2 m	F6L 913	AK 5-35	10.00 × 20	12 700 kg	5000/7000 kg	4·2 × 2·3 m
130 D 13 AL	4 × 4	4·2 m	F6L 913	AK 5-35	13.00 × 20	12 700 kg	5000/7000 kg	4·2 × 2·3 m
168 M 13 FL	4 × 2	4 m	BF6L 913	S 6-65	9.00 × 20	13 200 kg	5000/7000 kg	4·6 × 2·3 m
232 D 16 AL	6 × 6	4·2 m/1·38 m	F8L 413	AK 6-80	14.00 × 20	16 500 kg	7000 kg	5·6 × 2·4 m
256 D 18 AL	6 × 6	4·2 m/1·38 m	F8L 413 F	AK 6-90	14.00 × 20	18 000 kg	10 000 kg	5·6 × 2·4 m
320 D 18 FAL	6 × 6	3·5 m/1·38 m	F10L 413 F	AK 6-90	14.00 × 20	18 000 kg	10 000 kg	5·6 × 2·4 m
256 D 18 FAL	6 × 6	3·5 m/1·38 m	F8L 413 F	AK 6-90	14.00 × 20	18 000 kg	10 000 kg	5·6 × 2·4 m
168 M 11 FAL	4 × 4	4·2 m	BF6L 913	S 6-36	12.00 × 20PR18	11 800 kg	5000 kg	2 × 2·37 m
Tankers								
130 D 9 L	4 × 2	4·2 m	F6L 913	AK 5-35	13.00 × 20	10 500 kg	4000/5000 kg	n/app
130 D 9 AL	4 × 4	4·2 m	F6L 913	AK 5-35	13.00 × 20	10 500 kg	4000/5000 kg	n/app
130 D 13 K	4 × 2	4·2 m	F6L 913	AK 5-35	13.00 × 20	13 000 kg	5000/7000 kg	n/app
130 D 13 AK	4 × 4	4·2 m	F6L 913	AK 5-35	13.00 × 20	13 000 kg	5000/7000 kg	n/app
192 D 12 AL	4 × 4	4·2 m	F6L 413 F	S 6-65	13.00 × 20	12 700 kg	5000/7000 kg	n/app
232 D 16 AL	6 × 6	4·2 m/1·38 m	F8L 413	AK 6-80	14.00 × 20	16 500 kg	7000 kg	n/app
256 D 18 AL	6 × 6	4·2 m/1·38 m	F8L 413 F	AK 6-90	14.00 × 20	18 000 kg	10 000 kg	n/app
232 D 20 AL	6 × 6	3·9 m/1·38 m	F8L 413	AK 6-80	14.00 × 20	20 000 kg	10 000 kg	n/app
232 D 26 K	6 × 4	3·9 m/1·38 m	F8L 413	AK 6-80	12.00 × 20	26 000 kg	depends on application	n/app
232 D 26 AK	6 × 6	3·9 m/1·38 m	F8L 413	AK 6-80	12.00 × 20	26 000 kg	depends on application	n/app
310 D 34 AK	6 × 6	4 m/1·38 m	F10L 413	5 S 110 GP	14.00 × 20	34 000 kg	20 000/25 000 kg	n/app
320 D 34 AK	6 × 6	4 m/1·38 m	F10L 413 F	5 S 110 GP	14.00 × 20	34 000 kg	20 000/25 000 kg	n/app
Tractor Trucks								
192 D 12 AS	4 × 4	4·2 m	F6L 413 F	S 6-65	12.00 × 20	12 000 kg	depends on application	n/app
256 D 20 AS	6 × 6	3·9 m/1·32 m	F8L 413 F	6-90	12.00 × 20	20 000 kg	depends on application	n/app
232 D 20 AS	6 × 6	3·9 m/1·38 m	F8L 413 F	6-80	12.00 × 20	20 000 kg	depends on application	n/app
320 D 22 FS	6 × 4	2·85 m/1·32 m	F10L 413 F	5 S-110 GP	12.00 × R20	22 000 kg	depends on application	n/app
310 D 20 AS	6 × 6	3·9 m/1·38 m	F10L 413 L	AK 6-90	14.00 × 20	20 000 kg	depends on application	n/app
232 D 26 S	6 × 4	3·9 m/1·38 m	F8L 413	AK 6-80	12.00 × 20	26 000 kg	depends on application	n/app
232 D 26 AS	6 × 6	3·9 m/1·38 m	F8L 413	AK 6-90	12.00 × 20	26 000 kg	depends on application	n/app
310 D 34 AS	6 × 6	4 m/1·45 m	F10L 413 L	WSK 45-150	14.00 × 20	34 000 kg	depends on application	n/app
320 D 34 AS	6 × 6	4 m/1·45 m	F10L 413 F	WSK 45-150	14.00 × 20	34 000 kg	depends on application	n/app
400 D 34 AS	6 × 6	4 m/1·45 m	BF10L 413 F	WSK 45-150	14.00 × 20	34 000 kg	depends on application	n/app

Other variants produced by Iveco Magirus include tipper trucks, crane trucks, ambulance and other specialised chassis

Iveco Magirus 130 M 7 FAL 2500 kg (4 × 4) truck

Iveco Magirus 192 series (4 × 4) cargo truck

Iveco Magirus 168 M 11 FL 5000 kg (4 × 2) truck used by West German Army

Iveco Magirus 232 series (6 × 6) cargo truck

STATUS
In production. Known military users of Iveco Magirus trucks include Algeria, Belgium, Denmark, Egypt, West Germany, Iraq, Portugal, South Africa and Sudan.

MANUFACTURER
Iveco Magirus AG, Postfach 2740, 7900 Ulm, Federal Republic of Germany.

Iveco Magirus 320 D 22 FS (6 × 4) tractor towing 30 000-litre tanker semi-trailer

Ford G 398 SAM (4 × 4) 3000 kg Truck

DESCRIPTION
This truck was developed by Ford of Germany from a commercial vehicle and was in production for the West German Army from 1957 to 1961. In appearance it is very similar to the MAN 630 (4 × 4) 5000 kg truck, which has a wheelbase of 4·6 metres compared with the Ford's 4·013-metre wheelbase.

The layout of the vehicle is conventional with the engine and cab at the front and the cargo area at the rear. The cab has a removable canvas top, a windscreen which can be folded forward onto the bonnet and a single door on each side, the tops of which can be removed. A hardtop model with a circular observation hatch in the right side of the roof is also in service. The all-steel cargo area has drop sides, drop tailgate, removable bows which are stowed to the rear of the cab when not required and a tarpaulin cover. Some vehicles have a front-mounted winch.

VARIANTS
These include an ambulance, radar (AN/TPS-1D air defence) and a workshop vehicle.

STATUS
Production complete. In service with West Germany, Israel and Turkey.

MANUFACTURER
Ford-Werke AG, 5 Köln 21, Postfach 21 03 69, Federal Republic of Germany.

SPECIFICATIONS
Cab seating: 1 + 2
Configuration: 4 × 4
Weight:
  (empty) 4400 kg
  (loaded cross country) 7840 kg
Max load:
  (road) 5000 kg
  (cross country) 3440 kg
Load area: 4·25 × 2·25 m
Length: 7·25 m
Width: 2·445 m
Height:
  (tarpaulin) 2·94 m
  (reduced) 2·135 m
Ground clearance: 0·32 m
Track: 1·7 m
Wheelbase: 4·013 m
Max speed: 80 km/h

Ford G 398 SAM (4 × 4) 3000 kg truck with windscreen folded forward, cab roof, bows and tarpaulin cover removed and front-mounted winch

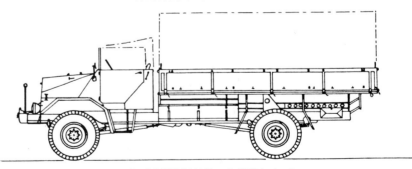

Ford G 398 SAM (4 × 4) 3000 kg truck

Range: 300 km
Fuel capacity: 110 litres
Max gradient: 60%
Fording: 1·1 m
Engine: Ford model G29T V-8 petrol developing 92 bhp at 3500 rpm
Gearbox: manual with 4 forward and 1 reverse gears
Transfer box: 2-speed
Turning radius: 10 m

Suspension: semi-elliptical springs with hydraulic shock absorbers
Tyres: 11.00 × 20
Number of tyres: 4 + 1 spare
Brakes:
  (main) hydraulic
  (parking) mechanical
Electrical system: 24 V
Batteries: 2 × 12 V, 100 Ah

Mercedes-Benz Unimog U 1700 L (4 × 4) 5000 kg Truck

DESCRIPTION
The largest of the Mercedes-Benz Unimog series, the U 1700 L, is intended primarily for the export market. It follows the same general lines as the smaller (4 × 4) Unimogs and is produced in two versions, the 3·25-metre wheelbase version and the more common 3·85-metre wheelbase version. Both have full cross-country capability and may be produced with a variety of special-purpose bodies.

Of the two versions, the 3·85-metre wheelbase version is the most favoured for military applications and has been sold to the Australian and New Zealand armies. This version has a two-man cab with a roof hatch behind which is the main cargo-carrying area. This area is steel with a drop tailgate and sides. There is provision for a canvas tilt and lash-down points are provided. If required, the load-carrying area can be fitted with seating for up to 20 men. There is provision for towing a trailer or the U 1700 L may be used as an artillery tractor.

Numerous accessories or equipment options are available. These include a trailer brake system, front and rear axle stabiliser, engine brake, a twin passenger seat, swivelling roof hatch, small arms racks, additional canister and other equipment stowage, provision for fording up to 1·2 metres, a front or central power take-off, a 24-volt electrical system, interference suppression for radio operation, blackout lighting system, trailer socket, tow bar and cross-country chains. Standard military equipment includes pallet tie-down points, lateral or cross-bench seating, air intake pipe, protected headlamps, canvas tilt frame points, reinforced suspension, military-pattern tyres and spare wheel, and equipment stowage.

The Australian Army has ordered 1295 U 1700 Ls at a cost of $67 million. They are being produced at the Mercedes-Benz plant in Mulgrave, Victoria. The New Zealand Army has ordered 412 and they will be produced by Mills Tui Limited in Rotorua. The New Zealand Army version is known as the UL 17000 L.

STATUS
Production. Ordered by the Australian and the New Zealand armies. In service with other armed forces.

MANUFACTURER
Daimler-Benz AG, Stuttgart-Untertürkheim, Federal Republic of Germany.

SPECIFICATIONS
(3·85 m wheelbase version only, 3·25 m wheelbase version details provided in entry on Unimog export models, in this section.)
Cab seating: 1 + 1 or 1 + 2
Configuration: 4 × 4
Weight:
  (empty) 6900 kg
  (loaded) 12 200 kg
  (axle loading, front/rear) 6500 kg
Max load: 5000 kg
Max towed load: 12 500 kg
Length: 6·7 m
Width: 2·465 m
Height:
  (cab) 2·78 m
  (canvas cover) 3·14 m
Ground clearance: 0·5 m
Track: 1·84 m
Wheelbase: 3·85 m

Angle of approach/departure: 45°/36°
Max speed: 71·3 km/h
Range: 600 km
Fuel capacity: 160 litres
Gradient: 70%
Fording: 0·8 m (1·2 m option)
Engine: Mercedes-Benz OM 352 A 6-cylinder, in-line, water-cooled, 5·675-litre diesel developing 168 hp at 2800 rpm
Gearbox: fully synchronised with 4 forward and 4 reverse gears
Transfer box: 2-speed
Steering: hydraulic power
Turning radius: 7·9 m
Suspension: (front and rear) coil springs with additional springs, telescopic shock absorbers
Tyres: 13.00 × 20
Brakes: dual circuit hydraulic with compressed air booster
Electrical system: 12 or 24 V

Mercedes-Benz Model 1017 (4 × 2) and Model 1017 A (4 × 4) 5000 kg Trucks

DEVELOPMENT
These two vehicles have been developed by Mercedes-Benz to meet the requirements of the West German Army and are essentially standard commercial vehicles with the minimum of modifications to suit them for military use. Adaptations include a modified electrical system, use of low-torsion platform with stowage boxes and adequate structure plus mounting points for van bodies, additional stowage space on the rear wall of the cab for military equipment and installation of an observation hatch in the roof of the cab. The major differences between the 1017 and the 1017 A are that the latter has 4 × 4 drive and larger tyres. Final deliveries will be made in 1987. It will be replaced in production by the Model 1217A export model.

DESCRIPTION
The layout of both vehicles is identical with the forward control cab at the front and the cargo area at the rear.

The parallel ladder chassis is bend resistant but flexible, the side members are the fish belly type in that the height of the web is tailored to the load acting on the chassis at the respective point. Open hat section cross-members, cold riveted to the frame, provide the desired torsional elasticity. With this design the chassis adapts to the surface of the road or track and imposes little stress on the material.

The all-steel forward control cab is noise and temperature insulated and the front rests on two rubber-bushed pivot bearings and its rear end on two vibration-damped spring struts.

The heating system keeps the inside temperature at between 25 and 77°F and the cab has a ventilation system incorporating a blower. Adjustable air inlets ensure well-balanced air distribution and window defrosting.

The platform has a wooden bed with sectional steel seam and is provided with lashing eyelets for pallets and supplies, plus countersunk anchors for the centre seat benches for the transport of troops. The top edges of the drop type wooden sideboards are covered by U-sections and side racks are installed for troop transport. The tarpaulin can be removed and the bows, which are adjustable for height, can be removed and stowed away. The truck can be loaded from the sides, even with the bows installed.

SPECIFICATIONS

Model	1017	1017 A
Cab seating	1 + 1	1 + 1
Configuration	4 × 2	4 × 4
Weight (empty)	6250 kg	6800 kg
(loaded)	11 700 kg	12 200 kg
Max load	5450 kg	5400 kg
Max towed load	12 800 kg	12 300 kg
Length	7·19 m	7·19 m
Width	2·47 m	2·47 m
Height (cab, unloaded)	2·7 m	2·88 m
(cab, loaded)	2·665 m	2·843 m
(load area, unloaded)	1·425 m	1·525 m
Load area	5 × 2·38 m	5 × 2·38 m
Ground clearance	0·263 m	0·288 m
Track (front)	1·954 m	2·067 m
Wheelbase	3·6 m	3·6 m
Angle of approach/departure	23°/20°	30°/23°
Max speed	87 km/h	81 km/h
Range	730 km	695 km
Fuel capacity	135 litres	135 litres
Fuel consumption	18·5 litres/100 km	19·4 litres/100 km
Gradient (road)	45%	46%
(cross country)	n/app	80%
Fording	0·5 m	0·5 m
Engine	OM 352 A 6-cylinder turbo-charged diesel developing 172 hp at 2800 rpm	
Clutch	hydraulically operated	hydraulically operated
Transfer box	nil	2-speed
Steering	hydraulic	hydraulic
Turning radius	7·4 m	8·75 m
Suspension (front and rear)	leaf springs, telescopic shock absorbers and torsion bar stabilisers, rear axle has secondary leaf spring	
Tyres	22.50/6.00 × 25	22.50/7.50 × 22.50
Number of tyres	6 + 1 spare	6 + 1 spare
Brakes (main)	hydraulic, dual circuit	hydraulic, dual circuit
(parking)	mechanical	mechanical
(exhaust brake)	standard	standard
Electrical system	24 V	24 V
Batteries	2 × 12 V	2 × 12 V

STATUS
Production. In service with the West German Army.

MANUFACTURER
Daimler-Benz Aktiengesellschaft, Stuttgart-Untertürkheim, Federal Republic of Germany.

Mercedes-Benz 1017 A (4 ×4) 5450 kg truck complete with bows and tarpaulin cover

Mercedes-Benz 1017 A (4 × 4) 5450 kg truck with bows stowed and tarpaulin cover removed

MAN Type 9136 FAE (4 × 4) 2500 kg Truck

DEVELOPMENT
The Type 9136 FAE is a 2500 kg cross-country cargo truck based on the design of a commercial 6000 to 9000 kg truck range. The design has been produced in co-operation with Volkswagen.

DESCRIPTION
The Type 9136 FAE is a 4 × 4 vehicle of conventional truck design with a steel cab situated forward. Head-lamps are recessed behind a heavy duty bumper and there is seating inside the cab for the driver and one passenger. Behind the cab lockers are provided for the spare wheel and tool stowage, and the load area may be covered by a canvas tilt. The axles have a limited degree of articulation and only single tyres are provided front and rear. A winch is situated just behind the rear axle with the cable leading forward through rollers mounted on the front bumper. A roof hatch is mounted just to the right of centre on the driver's cab.

SPECIFICATIONS
Cab seating: 1 + 1 or 2
Configuration: 4 × 4
Weight:
 (empty) 4725 kg
 (loaded) 9000 kg
 (weight on front axle, loaded) 3200 kg
 (weight on rear axle, loaded) 5800 kg

Length: 6·19 m
Height: (cab) 2·73 m
Width: 2·054 m
Ground clearance: 0·35 m
Wheelbase: 3·5 m
Track: 1·8 m
Angle of approach/departure: 31°/24°
Max speed: 90 km/h
Fuel capacity: 100 litres
Gradient: 58%
Engine: D 0226 MFA 5·687-litre, water-cooled, 6-cylinder diesel
Gearbox: type ZF S 5-35/2 with 5 forward and 1 reverse gears

Transfer box: 2-speed
Clutch: single dry disc
Tyres: 10.00 × 20XL
Suspension: semi-elliptical springs with telescopic shock absorbers, front and rear
Brakes: hydraulically-assisted
Electrical system: 24 V

STATUS
Production.

MANUFACTURER
MAN, Commercial Vehicle Division, Postfach 500620, D 8000, Munich, Federal Republic of Germany.

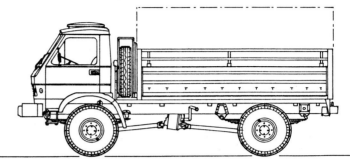

MAN Type 9136 FAE (4 × 4) 2500 kg truck

MAN Type 9136 FAE (4 × 4) 2500 kg truck

MAN Type 9136 FAE (4 × 4) 2500 kg truck

MAN 11.136 HA (4 × 4) 5000 kg Truck

DEVELOPMENT
The MAN 11.136 HA (4 × 4) 5000 kg truck is based on standard commercial components with suitable modifications for military use. MAN has delivered 3000 of these vehicles to the Belgian Army which already uses the older MAN 630 L2AE-B series of 5000 kg (4 × 4) trucks.

DESCRIPTION
The chassis consists of U-frame longitudinal members with riveted and bolted cross-members with four rein-forced couplings at the front and trailer coupling, type RU, size K3D, at the rear.
 The layout of the vehicle is conventional with the engine at the front, two-door fully enclosed cab in the centre and cargo area at the rear. The cab has a re-inforced bonnet, hydraulically cushioned seat for the driver and a buzzer connected to the differential lock that informs the driver when the differential is engaged. The rear cargo body has a steel frame, sheet steel drop sides and tailgate, pinewood floor, removable bows and a tarpaulin cover.

VARIANTS
A 4 × 2 model is also available under the designation 11.136 H.

STATUS
Production complete. In service with the Belgian Army.

MANUFACTURER
MAN, Commercial Vehicle Division, Postfach 500620, D 8000, Munich, Federal Republic of Germany.

MAN 11.136 HA (4 × 4) 5000 kg truck as used by Belgian Army (T J Gander)

Belgian Army MAN 11.136 HA (4 × 4) truck equipped with refrigerated box body (T J Gander)

SPECIFICATIONS
Cab seating: 1 + 2
Configuration: 4 × 4
Weight:
  (empty) 6000 kg
  (loaded) 11 000 kg
Max load: 5000 kg
Load area: 4·6 × 2·35 m
Length: 7·305 m
Width: 2·3 m
Height:
  (cab) 2·605 m
  (load area) 1 m
Ground clearance:
  (front) 0·33 m
  (rear) 0·334 m

Track:
  (front) 1·82 m
  (rear) 1·664 m
Wheelbase: 4·4 m
Max speed: 83·9 km/h
Range: 720 km
Fuel capacity: 200 litres
Max gradient: 60%
Fording: 0·75 m
Engine: MAN/Renault model 797/06 6-cylinder water-cooled diesel developing 150 hp (SAE) at 3000 rpm
Gearbox: ZF synchromesh model S 5-35 with 5 forward and 1 reverse gears
Clutch: single dry plate
Transfer box: G 300, 2-speed

Steering: ZF Gemmer worm and roller
Turning radius: 9·65 m
Suspension:
  (front) semi-elliptical leaf springs with progressively working hollow rubber springs
  (rear) leaf springs with progressively working stepped springs
Tyres: 9.00 × 20
Number of tyres: 6 + 1 spare
Brakes:
  (front) air/hydraulic
  (rear) air
  (parking) spring loaded on rear wheels
  (engine brake) exhaust
Electrical system: 24 V
Batteries: 2 × 12 V, 100 Ah

MAN Model 15.240 FA (4 × 4) Tractor Truck

DESCRIPTION
This tractor truck is basically a standard commercial vehicle modified to meet the requirements of the West German Army. The chassis is of the ladder-type with the main members being open-U-section. The two-door fully enclosed all-steel cab is provided with a roof rack. One of three fifth wheel couplings can be fitted; Jost JSK 36 AV, Rocklinger Type 64 F or Fischer SK-S36, all have a king pin distance of 200 mm.

SPECIFICATIONS
Configuration: 4 × 4
Weight:
  (unladen) 6970 kg
  (weight on front axle unladen) 4695 kg
  (weight on rear axle unladen) 2275 kg
  (fifth wheel load) 8030 kg
  (permissible GVW) 15 000 kg
  (permissible GTW) 29 200 kg
Length: 5·9 m
Width: 2·43 m
Height:
  (cab) 2·955 m
  (fifth wheel) 1·365 m
Wheelbase: 3·5 m
Angle of approach: 28°
Max speed: 84 km/h
Fuel capacity: 220 litres
Max gradient: 42%
Fording: 0·695 m
Engine: MAN series D 2566 MF 6-cylinder in-line diesel developing 240 hp at 2200 rpm
Gearbox: ZF S 6-80, manual, 6 forward and 1 reverse gears
Clutch: GF 380 single dry plate
Transfer box: MAN G 801 with differential lock

MAN Model 15.240 FA (4 × 4) tractor truck towing semi-trailer

Steering: ZF 8065 recirculating ball, hydraulic
Suspension:
  (front) leaf spring
  (rear) leaf spring with stepped springs
Tyres: 10.00 × 20
Brakes:
  (front) pneumatic diaphragm cylinder
  (rear) air brake with spring loaded parking brake
  (sustained action brake) exhaust throttle valve, pneumatically operated

Electrical system: 24 V
Batteries: 2 × 12 V, 125 Ah

STATUS
Production. In service with the West German Army.

MANUFACTURER
MAN, Commercial Vehicle Division, Postfach 500620, D 8000, Munich, Federal Republic of Germany.

Medium Range of Vehicles without Cross-country Capability (Category IV)

DEVELOPMENT
To meet the requirements of the Federal German Army for a range of vehicles without cross-country capability in the 5000 kg, 7000 kg and 10 000 kg classes, three German manufacturers built prototype vehicles for comparative trials. All were basically standard commercial vehicles with the minimum of modifications to suit them for military use, for example, military type bodies, rifle racks and a circular observation hatch in the cab roof for the installation of an anti-aircraft machine gun. These vehicles are designed to operate in the rear areas.

Daimler-Benz submitted three vehicles; the 5000 kg model 1017 A, the 7000 kg model 1419 and the 10 000 kg model 2024; Magirus-Deutz submitted the 5000 kg model 168 M 11 FL, the 7000 kg 192 D 14 FL and the 10 000 kg model 256 D 19 FL, and MAN submitted the 5000 kg model 13 192 FA, the 7000 kg 15 192 F and the 10 000 kg model 22 240 DF.

In June 1976 a decision was taken to order 22 000 Daimler-Benz 5000 kg trucks, 1500 MAN 7000 kg trucks and 2500 MAN 10 000 kg trucks. The MAN contract was worth DM300 million. In 1977 it was decided not to proceed with the Daimler-Benz truck and instead an order was placed with Magirus-Deutz of Ulm for 7000 5000 kg trucks, worth DM410 million, for delivery from 1978 onwards. Daimler-Benz was however awarded a contract for 17 000 (4 × 4) 2000 kg Unimog trucks worth DM740 million.

DESCRIPTION
All these vehicles are based on a standard commercial design and have a similar layout. The two-door fully enclosed forward control cab has a circular observation hatch in the roof on which a 7·62 mm MG3 machine gun can be installed. The rear cargo area has drop sides, drop tailgate, removable bows and a tarpaulin cover.

Iveco Magirus model 168 M 11 FL (4 × 2) 5000 kg truck

MAN model 15 192 F (4 × 2) 7000 kg truck

STATUS
In service with the West German Army.

MANUFACTURERS
5000 kg: Iveco Magirus AG, D 7900 Ulm/Donau, Federal Republic of Germany.

7000 and 10 000 kg: MAN, Commercial Vehicle Division, Postfach 500620, D 8000, Munich, Federal Republic of Germany.

SPECIFICATIONS

Manufacturer	Iveco Magirus	MAN	MAN
Designation	168 M 11 FL	15 192 F	22 240 DF
Configuration	4 × 2	4 × 2	6 × 4
Weight (empty)	6050 kg	7050 kg	9140 kg
(loaded)	11 200 kg	15 000 kg	20 000 kg
Max load	5150 kg	7000 kg	10 000 kg
Load area	5 × 2·37 m	5·6 × 2·44 m	7·1 × 2·44 m
Length	7·02 m	7·65 m	9·155 m
Width	2·49 m	2·49 m	2·49 m
Height	3·18 m	2·85 m	2·846 m
Wheelbase	3·6 m	4·1 m	3·85 m + 1·35 m
Engine (all diesel)	BF6L 913 6-cylinder	D 2565 MF 6-cylinder	D 2566 MXF 6-cylinder
Hp/rpm	166/2650	192/2200	240/2200

Mercedes-Benz 1628 A (4 × 4) 7000 kg Truck and 2028 A (6 × 6) 9000 kg Truck

DEVELOPMENT
These two Mercedes-Benz cross-country trucks have been produced for the export market and have many common components. Some civilian model design experience has been incorporated but the design is basically new.

DESCRIPTION
Both vehicles use the same design of cab with seating for the driver and two passengers. The centre seat has a folding back-rest to allow clear access to the roof-mounted hatch which is provided with a rail grip. There is a medium-length cab available which has extra space for crew equipment. Both cab types can be tilted forward for engine access to an angle of 65 degrees. For normal day-to-day maintenance access flaps are provided. Behind the cab there is spare wheel stowage, and in front of the cab the headlights and radiator grill are protected by heavy-duty tubular guards.

All the undersides and major drive components are fully waterproofed for a fording depth of one metre without preparation and the exhaust pipe is routed upwards to vent over the cab roof side. The load area has 500 mm high drop sides and tailgate, and is provided with lash-down points and a canvas tilt. A towing hook for trailers or artillery towing is provided at the rear. Optional equipment includes a hydraulic 10 000 kg winch with cable control to the front or rear. Various box and cab bodies may be provided, and both models may be produced as tankers, fire tenders or command and communication vehicles.

STATUS
Production.

MANUFACTURER
Daimler-Benz AG, Stuttgart-Untertürkheim, Federal Republic of Germany.

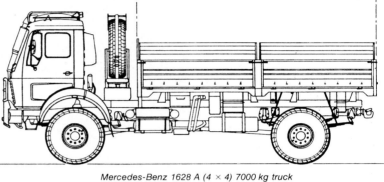
Mercedes-Benz 1628 A (4 × 4) 7000 kg truck

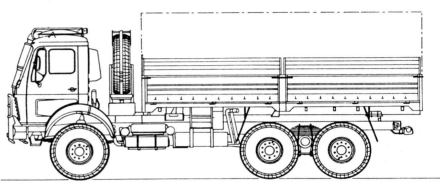
Mercedes-Benz 2028 A (6 × 6) 9000 kg truck

SPECIFICATIONS

Model	1628 A	2028 A	Model	1628 A	2028 A
Configuration	4 × 4	6 × 6	Max speed	91 km/h	91 km/h
Cab seating	1 + 2	1 + 2	Fuel capacity	300 litres	300 litres
Weight (empty)	9000 kg	11 200 kg	Gradient	80%	80%
(loaded)	16 000 kg	20 000 kg	Fording	1 m	1 m
(front axle load)	7300 kg	6700 kg	Engine	Mercedes-Benz OM 422 V-8 water-cooled diesel, 14·618 litres, developing 106 bhp at 1200 rpm	
(rear axle load)	9000 kg	2 × 6900 kg			
Max load	7000 kg	9000 kg	Transmission	ZF 5 S – 111 GP fully synchronised with 9 forward and 1 reverse gears	
Length	7·43 m	8·3 m			
Width	2·5 m	2·5 m	Turning radius	10·15 m	10·15 m
Height (cab)	3·08 m	3·04 m	Tyres	14.00 × 20 XL	14.00 × 20 XL
(canvas cover)	3·485 m	3·5 m	Brakes	dual circuit compressed air	dual circuit compressed air
Load area	4·6 × 2·35 m	5·5 × 2·35 m			
Ground clearance	0·435 m	0·435 m	Electrical system	24 V	24 V
Track	2·07 m	2·07 m	Batteries	2 × 12 V	2 × 12 V
Wheelbase	4·5 m	3·8 m + 1·45 m			
Angle of approach/departure	32°/42°	32°/46°			

MAN 14.240 FAEG (4 × 4) 6000 kg and 20.280 DFAEG (6 × 6) 10 000 kg Trucks

DEVELOPMENT
MAN has developed the Category III vehicles based on the Category I vehicles that it has developed for the West German Army and which are fully described in the following entry. They use the same suspension and drive train technology as the Category I vehicles, for example torsionally stiff chassis, coil springs, axles with planetary gear hub reduction but use MAN engines, commercial tilt cabs and allow a higher payload, 6000 kg for the 14.240 FAEG (4 × 4) and 10 000 kg for the 20.280 DFAEG (6 × 6).

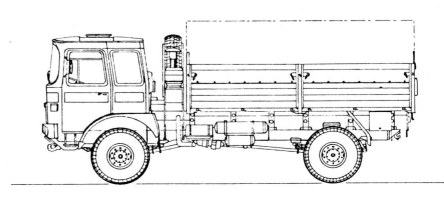
MAN 14.240 FAEG (4 × 4) 6000 kg truck

DESCRIPTION
The chassis consists of hollow section longitudinal members welded with tubular cross-members. The cab is a MAN two-door all-steel forward control type which can be tilted forward to allow access to the engine for maintenance purposes. The rear cargo area has a steel sub-frame, aluminium dropsides with two side walls and one tailgate, fixed corner stakes in the front, insertable in the middle and rear, pinewood floor, removable bows and a tarpaulin cover.

STATUS
Production. In service with Algeria, Ireland, Peru, Singapore and Venezuela.

MANUFACTURER
MAN, Commercial Vehicle Division, Postfach 500620, D 8000, Munich, Federal Republic of Germany.

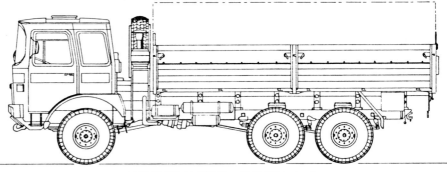

MAN 20.280 DFAEG (6 × 6) 10 000 kg truck

MAN 20.280 DFAEG (6 × 6) 10 000 kg truck

SPECIFICATIONS

Model	14.240 FAEG	20.280 DFAEG
Configuration	4 × 4	6 × 6
Weight (empty)	8350 kg	10 300 kg
(loaded)	14 350 kg	20 300 kg
Max load	6000 kg	10 000 kg
Load area	5 × 2·44 m	6·1 × 2·44 m
Length	7·85 m	8·95 m
Width	2·49 m	2·49 m
Height (cab)	3·01 m	3·01 m
Wheelbase	4·5 m	4 m + 1·4 m
Angle of approach/departure	40°/43°	40°/40°
Max road speed	80 km/h	80 km/h
Range	1000 km	1000 km
Fuel capacity	310 litres	310 litres
Max gradient	limit of adhesion	limit of adhesion
Fording	1 m	1 m
Engine (all diesel)	MAN D 2566 MFG 6-cylinder in-line water-cooled diesel developing 240 hp at 2200 rpm	MAN D 2566 MTFG 6-cylinder in-line water-cooled diesel developing 280 hp at 2200 rpm
Gearbox	manual, 6 forward and 1 reverse gears	manual, 6 forward and 1 reverse gears
Clutch	torque converter	torque converter
Transfer box	ZF A 600 with differential lock	ZF A 600 with differential lock
Tyres	14.00 × 20	14.00 × 20
Number of tyres	4 + 1 spare	6 + 1 spare
Brakes	air over hydraulic dual circuit with spring loaded auxiliary brake and starting auxiliary brake (climbing brake), exhaust brake	
Steering	ZF recirculating ball hydro-steering	ZF recirculating ball hydro-steering
Suspension	progressive coil springs, hydraulic telescopic shock absorbers	
Electrical system	24 V	24 V
Batteries	2 × 12 V, 110 Ah	2 × 12 V, 110 Ah

MAN 14.240 FAEG (4 × 4) 6000 kg truck

MAN 20.280 DFAEG (6 × 6) 10 000 kg truck

MAN 5000 kg (4 × 4), 7000 kg (6 × 6) and 10 000 kg (8 × 8) High Mobility Tactical Trucks

DEVELOPMENT
In the late 1950s and early 1960s the Federal German Technical Office for Armament and Military Purchases drew up requirements for a new range (or second generation) of tactical trucks for the West German Army.

This range was to have consisted of 4-tonne (4 × 4), 7-tonne (6 × 6) and 10-tonne (8 × 8) vehicles, 4 × 4 and 6 × 6 armoured amphibious load carriers and an 8 × 8 amphibious reconnaissance vehicle.

In 1964 a number of West German vehicle manufacturers were approached to build prototypes of this new range of vehicles and the following year a Joint Project Office was established with Büssing, Krupp, Rheinstahl/Henschel, Klöckner-Humbolt-Deutz and MAN undertaking development work. In addition the

Daimler-Benz company also developed some vehicles. After the first batch of prototypes had been completed it was decided in 1970 that the Joint Project Office would concentrate on the tactical trucks while Daimler-Benz concentrated on the armoured vehicles.

The first vehicle to enter production was the 8 × 8 amphibious armoured reconnaissance vehicle of which 408 had been built by Thyssen-Henschel (formerly the Rheinstahl company) with final deliveries being made in 1977. This vehicle is called the Luchs (*Jane's Armour* and Artillery 1983–84, pages 189–192) and is the replacement for the Hotchkiss reconnaissance vehicles which entered service in the late 1950s. Thyssen-Henschel is also building 996 of the 6 × 6 armoured load carriers for the West German Army (Jane's Armour and Artillery 1983–84, page 298) and it was expected that the 4 × 4 armoured vehicle would have entered production in a few years' time to meet a West German Army requirement for an Amphibious Engineer Reconnaissance Vehicle (or APE) (Jane's Armour and Artillery 1983–84, page 188) but budgetary problems have delayed this.

Since development of these new trucks began in the 1960s there have been some changes in the requirements of the army and in 1972 the amphibious specification and the requirement that the vehicles should be powered by a multi-fuel engine were dropped. In 1975 the 4-tonner was uprated to 5 tonnes and at the same time its rear cargo platform was lengthened and its wheelbase was increased from 4·3 to 4·5 metres.

In December 1975 MAN was awarded a contract to build 8385 4 × 4, 6 × 6 and 8 × 8 vehicles at a cost of DM1400 million. The 8 × 8 version was the first model to enter production and first deliveries were made in 1976. Deliveries of the 6 × 6 tipper and the 4 × 4 cargo truck began in 1977. Deliveries of the 6 × 6 cargo truck began in January 1979 and final deliveries were made in 1981.

This range of vehicles, which is produced at MAN's Watenstedt plant, is known as the category 1 and has been designed specifically for cross-country operations and can keep up with mechanised forces operating across country.

Many components of this range, such as axles, engines and gearboxes, are standard commercial components and spare parts can easily be obtained.

DESCRIPTION
The layout of the three basic vehicles is almost identical: the two-door fully enclosed forward control cab has an observation hatch in the roof and the rear cargo area has removable drop sides and a drop tailgate, removable bows and a tarpaulin cover. About 6000 of the 8385 vehicles will be fitted with a Rotzler winch.

VARIANTS
5-tonne (4 × 4) cargo truck
This has been designed to carry 5000 kg of cargo and will also be able to carry the new Dornier military container which is now in production for the West German Army.

7-tonne (6 × 6) cargo truck
This has been designed to carry 7000 kg of cargo and is also used to tow the 155 mm FH-70s used by the West German Army. Specialised versions include a bridging

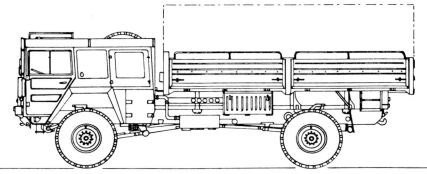

MAN (4 × 4) 5000 kg cargo truck

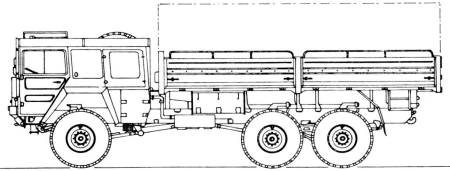

MAN (6 × 6) 7000 kg cargo truck

MAN (6 × 6) 7000 kg truck carrying section of German-built US-designed Ribbon Bridge

MAN (4 × 4) 5000 kg cargo truck (T J Gander)

MAN (6 × 6) 7000 kg three-way tipper truck (West German Army)

MAN (6 × 6) 7000 kg cargo truck

MAN (4 × 4) 5000 kg truck fitted with shelter-mounted Contraves Fieldguard artillery fire-control system (C R Zwart)

truck which transports and launches the West German version of the Ribbon Bridge (this has a longer wheelbase), CL 289 drone carrier while the 110 mm Light Artillery Rocket Systems, previously mounted on the older Magirus-Deutz chassis, have been installed on the MAN (6 × 6) 7000 kg truck chassis. Full details of the 110 mm Light Artillery Rocket System are given on pages 724 of *Jane's Armour and Artillery 1983–84*. The Austrian company Gräf and Stift was building 350 6 × 6 versions rated at 10 tonnes for the Austrian Army with a slightly different cab with a hydraulic crane mounted to the rear of the cab. Details of this version are given in this section under Austria.

7-tonne (6 × 6) tipper
This has the same chassis as the 7-tonne cargo model but is fitted with a three-way tipper body. It has an unladen weight of 11 500 kg and a laden weight of 18 500 kg.

10-tonne (8 × 8) truck
This has been designed to carry 10 000 kg of cargo and 1924 have been delivered to the Federal German Army, many fitted with a 1000 kg Atlas hydraulic crane for loading and unloading. The 8 × 8 chassis is also used to carry the West German AEG-Telefunken TRMS radar, has been proposed to carry and launch the Dornier Keibitz RPV, and has been tested carrying the shelter mounted version of the Roland 2 SAM system. The range has now been increased by the addition of a 10 000 kg truck with a hydraulic crane mounted at the rear. This version has the cargo area reduced to 5·5 × 2·5 metres.

10-tonne (8 × 8) trucks for US Army
On 31 October 1980 MAN was awarded a contract by the US Army for the supply of 13 (8 × 8) tractors designated XM1001 and two (8 × 8) recovery vehicles designated XM1002. These were delivered between July and September 1981. In December 1981 an order was placed by the US Army for 251 (8 × 8) vehicles for use with the Pershing II SSM and 214 (8 × 8) vehicles for use with the GLCM. The MAN (8 × 8) 10 000 kg truck was also tested by the US Army to meet its requirement for a Heavy Expanded Mobility Tactical Truck, but this contract was subsequently awarded to Oshkosh.

The M1001 (8 × 8) tractor has an Atlas hydraulic crane over the second and third axles with a capacity of 20 tonnes, 2-inch kingpin, 9072 kg self-recovery winch, tools and a tool box.

The M1002 (8 × 8) recovery vehicle has an Atlas hydraulic crane over the second and third axles with a capacity of 20 tonnes, recovery assembly with a tow bar and 11 340 kg lift and 38 556 kg pull, 9072 kg self-recovery winch and a 20 412 kg heavy recovery winch. For details see the entry in the *Recovery vehicles* section.

A 10 000 kg cargo truck using the same basic chassis as the 27 365 VFAE vehicles produced for the US Army is now available. The cab is the same as that used on the US Army vehicles and the load area is 6·71 × 2·5 metres. A curved canvas tilt may be fitted. Overall length is 9·72 metres.

MAN has proposed that this chassis, for missile and other tactical applications, could be fitted with four (two each side) hydraulic extended outriggers, combat tyres with an emergency run flat capability, coil spring suspension system with lock out capability, EMP hardening and an on board camouflage system. Other applications proposed by MAN include radar control centre, fuel resupply vehicle and Patriot SAM launcher.

Cargo truck version of MAN (8 × 8) 27 365 VFAE produced to be compatible with vehicles produced for US army

STATUS
In production. In service with the West German Army. Ordered by the US Army (8 × 8 model).

MANUFACTURER
MAN, Commercial Vehicle Division, Postfach 500620, D 8000, Munich, Federal Republic of Germany.

SPECIFICATIONS

Model	5000 kg	7000 kg	10 000 kg
Cab seating	1 + 2	1 + 2	1 + 2
Configuration	4 × 4	6 × 6	8 × 8
Weight (empty)	9700 kg	11 400 kg	15 040 kg
(loaded)	14 300 kg	18 700 kg	25 400 kg
Max load (across country)	5000 kg	7000 kg	10 000 kg
Load area	5 × 2.35 m	5.6 × 2.35 m	7.1 × 2.35 m
Length	8·02 m	8·62 m	10·12 m
Width	2·5 m	2·5 m	2·5 m
Height (cab)	2·86 m	2·86 m	2·86 m
(load area)	1·65 m	1·65 m	1·65 m
Ground clearance	0·415 m	0·415 m	0·415 m
Track	2·07 m	2·07 m	2·07 m
Wheelbase	4·5 m	3.8 m + 1.4 m	1·93 m + 3·67 m + 1·4 m
Angle of approach/departure	45°/40°	45°/42°	45°/45°
Max cruising speed (road)	90 km/h	90 km/h	90 km/h
Range	700 km	700 km	600 km
Fuel capacity	270 litres	270 litres	270 litres
Max gradient	limit of adhesion	limit of adhesion	limit of adhesion
Fording	1·2 m	1·2 m	1·2 m
Engine	V-8 diesel	V-8 diesel turbo-charged	V-8 diesel turbo-charged
Engine hp/SAE	256	320	320
Gearbox	ZF S 6-65	ZF S 6-90	ZF S 6-90
	with torque converter clutch and two-speed transfer case		
Steering	recirculating ball hydro-steering type ZF 8070		
Turning radius	9·45 m	9·75 m	13·2 m
Suspension	progressively acting helical springs		
Tyres	14.00 × 20	14.00 × 20	14.00 × 20
Number of tyres	4 + 1 spare	6 + 1 spare	8 + 1 spare
Brakes	air/hydraulic 2 circuit/2 lines	air/hydraulic 2 circuit/2 lines	air/hydraulic 2 circuit/2 lines
Electrical system	24 V	24 V	24 V
Batteries	4 × 12 V, 125 Ah	4 × 12 V, 125 Ah	4 × 12 V, 125 Ah

NOTE: Specification for 8 × 8 model relates to vehicle fitted with crane.

SPECIFICATIONS

Model	M1001	M1002
Cab seating	1 + 2	1 + 2
Configuration	8 × 8	8 × 8
Length	8·556 m	8·996 m
Width	2·5 m	2·5 m
Height (spare wheel)	2·852 m	2·85 m
(cab top)	2·656 m	2·656 m
Track (front)	2·066 m	2·066 m
(rear)	2·072 m	2·072 m
Wheelbase	1·93 m + 2·77 m + 1·5 m	1·93 m + 3·2 m + 1·5 m
Angle of approach	42°	42°
Max speed	90 km/h	90 km/h
Fuel capacity	418 litres	418 litres
Max gradient	limit of adhesion	limit of adhesion
Fording	1·22 m	1·22 m
Engine	MAN D 2840 MFG V-10 water-cooled diesel developing 365 hp (DIN)	
Gearbox	ZF synchromesh 4S-150 8-speed	
Clutch	ZF torque converter clutch 400	
Transfer box	ZF GPA	ZF GPA
Steering	recirculatory ball, hydraulic	
Suspension	coil springs and hydraulic telescopic shock absorbers	
Tyres	16.00 × 20	16.00 × 20
Brakes	dual circuit, air and air over hydraulic	

MAN (8 × 8) M1014 tractor unit for US Army

MAN (8 × 8) M1001 tractor delivered to US Army

MAN (8 × 8) M1013 tractor unit for US Army fitted with recovery kit and hydraulic crane

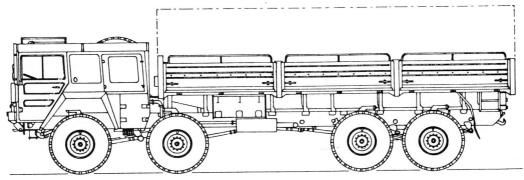

MAN (8 × 8) 10 000 kg cargo truck

MAN 630 Series of (4 × 4) 5000 kg Trucks

DESCRIPTION
The MAN 630 together with the MB LG 315/46 was the standard 5000 kg truck of the West German Army until the introduction of the new generation of tactical trucks. It is in service in two basic models, the MAN 630 L2A with dual rear wheels and the MAN 630 L2AE with single rear wheels.

The layout of the vehicle is conventional with the engine and cab at the front and the cargo area at the rear. The cab has a removable canvas top, windscreen which can be folded forward onto the bonnet and a single door on each side, the tops of which can be removed. The all-steel rear cargo area has a drop tailgate, removable bows and a tarpaulin cover. Some vehicles have been fitted with a winch at the front.

An earlier MAN truck was the 3000 kg MAN 400 L1AE which had an unladen weight of 4480 kg. This was followed by the MAN 415 series of (4 × 4) 4000 kg trucks powered by six-cylinder multi-fuel engines developing 100 bhp and with 4·2-metre wheelbases. The MAN 415 is produced in India with a number of modifications (including right-hand drive and dual rear wheels) as the Shaktiman, a photograph of which appears in the Indian section.

VARIANTS
Ambulance which can carry up to four stretcher patients, decontamination vehicle called the TER-Kfz, drone carrier for the Canadian AN/USD-501 reconnaissance system, field kitchen, radar vehicle for AN/TPS-1E system, tanker with two fuel tanks in the rear and dispensing equipment, tipper with a short wheelbase with either single or dual wheels at the rear, tractor with a wheelbase of 4·1 metres and dual rear wheels, and van.

STATUS
Production complete. In service in Belgium (assembled in Belgium by Ets Hocké and known as the L2AE-B), West Germany and India.

MANUFACTURER
MAN, Commercial Vehicle Division, Postfach 500620, D 8000, Munich, Federal Republic of Germany.

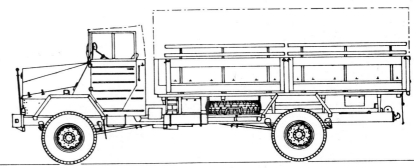

MAN 630 L2A (4 × 4) 5000 kg truck

West German Army MAN 630 L2A 5000 kg truck (T J Gander)

MAN 630 L2A 5000 kg truck fitted with office body (T J Gander)

SPECIFICATIONS
(data in square brackets relate to L2AE where different from the L2A)
Cab seating: 1 + 1
Configuration: 4 × 4
Weight:
  (empty) 7515 [7980] kg
  (loaded) 13 000 [13 200] kg
Load area: 5 × 2·35 m
Length: 7·9 [7·73] m
Width: 2·5 m
Height: (tarpaulin) 2·845 [2·98] m

Ground clearance: 0·35 [0·4] m
Track: (front/rear) 1·922 m/1·763 m [2·506 m/2·506 m]
Wheelbase: 4·6 m
Angle of approach/departure: 32°/45°
Max speed: (road) 66 km/h
Range: 440 km
Fuel capacity: 110 litres
Fuel consumption: 25 litres/100 km
Max gradient: 60%
Fording: 0·85 m
Engine: MAN Model D 1246 MV3A/W 6-cylinder multi-fuel developing 130 hp at 2000 rpm

Gearbox: manual with 6 forward and 1 reverse gears
Transfer box: 2-speed
Turning radius: 9·75 m
Suspension: semi-elliptical springs with hydraulic shock absorbers
Tyres: 11.00 × 20 [14.00 × 20]
Number of tyres: 6 + 1 spare [4 + 1 spare]
Brakes:
  (main) air
  (parking) mechanical
Electrical system: 24 V
Batteries: 2 × 12 V, 100 Ah

Mercedes-Benz LG 315/46 (4 × 4) 5000 kg Truck

DESCRIPTION
This was developed from the LG 6600 to meet the requirements of the West German Army and was in production at Mercedes-Benz Gaggenau plant from 1958 to 1964. The layout of the vehicle is conventional with the engine at the front, cab in the centre and the cargo area at the rear. The cab has a single door each side, windscreen which can be folded forward onto the bonnet and a removable canvas roof. The rear cargo area has drop sides and a drop tailgate, removable bows which are stowed to the rear of the cab when not in use and a tarpaulin cover. A hardtop model is also in service.

VARIANTS
Observation vehicle
This has a hydraulically operated observation mast and is known as the Beobachtungsmast.
Tanker
With two 2100-litre capacity fuel tanks. Basic specifications are weight unladen 7330 kg, length 8·12 metres, width 2·5 metres and height 3·2 metres.
Wrecker
Fitted with a 4000 kg capacity crane at the rear. Basic specifications are length 9·3 metres, width 2·5 metres and height 3 metres.

STATUS
Production complete. In service with the Federal German Army. A quantity were delivered to Chile in 1980.

MANUFACTURER
Mercedes-Benz AG, Gaggenau, Federal Republic of Germany.

SPECIFICATIONS
Cab seating: 1 + 1
Configuration: 4 × 4
Weight:
  (empty) 7600 kg
  (loaded) 12 850 kg
Max load: 5000 kg
Load area: 5 × 2·35 m
Length: 8·14 m
Width: 2·5 m
Height:
  (tarpaulin) 3·1 m
  (reduced) 2·68 m
Ground clearance: 0·408 m
Track:
  (front) 2·002 m
  (rear) 2·005 m
Wheelbase: 4·597 m
Max speed: (road) 70 km/h
Range: 510 km
Fuel capacity: 140 litres
Fuel consumption: 27 litres/100 km
Max gradient: 60%
Fording: 0·85 m
Engine: Daimler-Benz model OM 315 V 6-cylinder multi-fuel developing 145 hp at 2100 rpm
Gearbox: manual with 6 forward and 1 reverse gears
Transfer box: 2-speed
Turning radius: 10·7 m
Suspension: semi-elliptical springs with hydraulic shock absorbers
Tyres: 14.00 × 20
Number of tyres: 4 + 1 spare
Brakes:
  (main) hydraulic
  (parking) mechanical
Electrical system: 24 V
Batteries: 2 × 12 V, 100 Ah

Mercedes-Benz LG 315/46 (4 × 4) 5000 kg truck with bows stowed to rear of cab

Iveco Magirus (6 × 6) 7000 kg and earlier (4 × 4) Trucks

DESCRIPTION
Until the introduction of the new generation of tactical trucks the Magirus Lkw 7000 kg gl Winde (or Jupiter) was the standard truck in its class of the West German Army. Its company designation is model 178 D 15 A.

The layout of the vehicle is conventional with the engine at the front, cab in the centre and the cargo area at the rear. The cab has a door each side with a removable top, windscreen which can be folded forward onto the bonnet and a removable canvas top. The all-steel rear cargo area has four drop sides (two each side), drop tailgate and a removable tarpaulin cover. Many

Jupiters have a front-mounted winch. Late production models called the model 178 D 15 AL were powered by a model F 8L 413 180 hp engine.

VARIANTS
Tipper
This has a hydraulically operated three-way tipper body mounted at the rear. Basic specifications are unladen weight 8600 kg, length 8 metres, width 2·5 metres and height 2·55 metres.
Tractor truck model (4 × 4)
This has a wheelbase of 4·41 metres. Basic specifications are weight (unladen) 7200 kg, length 7·16 metres, width 2·15 metres and height 2·6 metres.
Wrecker
This has a rear-mounted crane which can be traversed

through a full 360 degrees and lift maximum load of 4000 kg. Basic specifications are length 9·4 metres, width 2·5 metres and height 3·15 metres.
Aircraft refueller
Decontamination truck (E-Kfz)
Fire-fighting truck
Between 1955 and 1957 Magirus-Deutz (now Iveco Magirus) built a number of (4 × 4) 7000 kg trucks for the West German Army under the designation of the A 6500. Basic specifications are unladen weight 7000 kg, length 8 metres, width 2·5 metres, height 2·95 metres, load area 5 × 2·35 metres, wheelbase 4·815 metres, powered by a Deutz F 8 L 614 eight-cylinder engine developing 170 hp at 2300 rpm, maximum road speed 73·6 km/h, range 500 km, gearbox manual with six forward and one reverse gears and a two-speed trans-

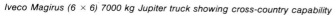

Iveco Magirus (6 × 6) 7000 kg Jupiter truck showing cross-country capability

Three-way tipper version of Iveco Magirus (6 × 6) 7000 kg Jupiter truck

Iveco Magirus (4 × 4) being used as prime mover by Belgian Army (T J Gander)

Iveco Magirus (6 × 6) wrecker used by Luftwaffe (T J Gander)

fer box. This was followed by the A 7000 which was in production for the army from 1958 to 1962. Basic specifications of this model are unladen weight 7500 kg, length 7·35 metres, width 2·5 metres, height 2·9 metres, load area 3·2 metres long and 2·35 metres wide, wheelbase 3·615 metres, powered by a Deutz F 8 L 714a eight-cylinder engine developing 178 hp at 2300 rpm, gearbox manual with six forward and one reverse gears and a two-speed transfer box. Maximum road speed 73·6 km/h and range 500 km. In addition Iveco Magirus has built a variety of 4 × 4 and 6 × 6 military trucks for export to such countries as Belgium, Denmark, India, Indonesia and Turkey.

Iveco Magirus (6 × 6) 7000 kg Jupiter truck

SPECIFICATIONS
Cab seating: 1 + 2
Configuration: 6 × 6
Weight:
  (empty) 7450 kg
  (loaded) 15 250 kg
Max load: 7000 kg
Load area: 5 × 2·35 m
Length: 8 m
Width: 2·5 m
Height: 2·95 m
Ground clearance: 0·315 m
Track:
  (front) 1·927 m
  (rear) 1·915 m
Wheelbase: 4·16 m + 1·28 m
Max speed: (road) 73·6 km/h

Max range: 500 km
Fuel capacity: 150 litres
Fuel consumption: (diesel) 30 litres/100 km
Fording: 0·85 m
Engine: Deutz model F 8 L 714a 8-cylinder multi-fuel developing 178 hp at 2300 rpm
Gearbox: manual with 6 forward and 1 reverse gears
Transfer box: 2-speed
Turning radius: 10·5 m
Suspension: semi-elliptical springs with hydraulic shock absorbers
Tyres: 11.00 × 20
Number of tyres: 6 + 1 spare

Brakes:
  (main) air/hydraulic
  (parking) mechanical
Electrical system: 24 V
Batteries: 2 × 12 V, 100 Ah

STATUS
Production complete. In service with the West German Army.

MANUFACTURER
Iveco Magirus AG, Postfach 2740, 7900 Ulm, Federal Republic of Germany.

Faun L 912/45A (6 × 6) 10 000 kg Truck

DESCRIPTION
The Faun L 912/45A (6 × 6) truck was designed to meet a West German Army requirement for a vehicle capable of carrying 10 000 kg of cargo across country or 15 000 kg of cargo on roads. It entered service in 1958 and is now being replaced by the new (8 × 8) 10 000 kg MAN truck.

The layout of the vehicle is conventional with the engine at the front, cab in the centre and the cargo area at the rear. The cab has a door each side with a removable top, a windscreen which can be folded forward onto the bonnet and a removable canvas top. The all-steel rear cargo area has a drop tailgate, removable bows and a tarpaulin cover. A winch with an 8000 kg capacity is mounted at the front of the vehicle.

VARIANTS
L 912/SA tractor truck
This is called the Sattelzugmaschine by the West German Army and can tow a trailer weighing a maximum of 60 000 kg. Basic specifications are unladen weight 12 500 kg, laden weight 27 000 kg, length 7·61 metres, width 2·5 metres, height 2·82 metres, wheelbase 3·77 m + 1·46 m and engine and transmission as for L 912/45A (6 × 6) truck. A later model was the L 912/VSA which could tow a semi-trailer weighing up to 80 000 kg.
L 908/ATW tanker
There are two 6 × 6 tanker versions in service; a 12 000-litre model for aircraft refuelling and a 15 000-litre vehicle refuelling model. They are powered by a Deutz model F 8 L 714 A multi-fuel engine which develops 178 hp at 2300 rpm, coupled to a manual

gearbox with six forward and one reverse gears. Empty weight is 13 050 kg and maximum gross vehicle weight is 25 400 kg.
L 912/5050A tipping truck with sliding platform
This vehicle, known as the Gleitkipper, is fitted with a special platform for carrying engineer plant such as bulldozers. When travelling the platform is horizontal and to load a vehicle it is extended to the rear and tilted until the far end is in contact with the ground. The bulldozer is driven up the platform which is then returned to the horizontal for transport. Basic specifications are unladen weight 12 500 kg, laden weight 25 200 kg, length 9·1 metres, width 2·5 metres, height 2·9 metres, wheelbase 4·3 + 1·5 metres, front track 2·028 metres, rear track 1·954 metres, engine and transmission as in the L 912/45A truck.

Faun L 912/45A (6 × 6) 10 000 kg truck

Faun L 912/SA (6 × 6) tractor truck (T J Gander)

STATUS
Production complete. In service with the West German Army.

MANUFACTURER
Faun-Werke Nuernberg, POB 8, 8560 Lauf/Pegn, Federal Republic of Germany.

SPECIFICATIONS (L 912/45A)
Cab seating: 1 + 2
Configuration: 6 × 6
Weight:
(empty) 12 000 kg
(loaded, road) 27 000 kg
(loaded, cross country) 22 000 kg

Max load:
(road) 15 000 kg
(cross country) 10 000 kg
Load area: 3·55 × 2·35 m
Length: 7·65 m
Width: 2·5 m
Height: 3·44 m
Ground clearance: 0·37 m
Track:
(front) 2·055 m
(rear) 1·81 m
Wheelbase: 3·77 m + 1·46 m
Max speed: (road) 76 km/h
Range: 660 km

Fuel capacity: 300 litres
Fuel consumption: 45 litres/100 km
Max gradient: 40%
Fording: 0·9 m
Engine: Deutz model F 12 L 714A 12-cylinder multi-fuel developing 265 hp at 2300 rpm
Gearbox: Model AK 6-75-3 manual with 6 forward and 1 reverse gears
Transfer box: 2-speed
Tyres: 12.00 × 24
Number of tyres: 10 + 1 spare
Brakes: air with exhaust retarder
Electrical system: 24 V
Batteries: 2 × 12 V, 100 Ah

Faun L 908/54 VA (6 × 6) 10 000 kg Cargo Truck

DESCRIPTION
The Faun L 908/54 VA (6 × 6) truck was designed in the 1950s to carry 10 000 kg of cargo on both roads and across country. It is now being replaced by the new MAN 10-ton (8 × 8) truck. The cab is of the forward control type and has a removable tarpaulin type cover and a windscreen which can be folded forward if required. The rear cargo area has drop sides and tailgate, and some models have removable bows and a tarpaulin cover. A winch with 10 000 kg capacity is fitted as standard. Some models have a TEHA model 1000/4.6 crane mounted in the cargo area which can lift a maximum of 1000 kg. When in use two stabilisers are lowered either side of the body, just in front of the second axles.

Faun L 908/54 VA (6 × 6) 10 000 kg cargo truck

SPECIFICATIONS
Cab seating: 1 + 2
Configuration: 6 × 6
Weight:
(empty) 11 500 kg
(loaded) 21 500 kg
Weight on front axle: (empty) 5500 kg
Weight on centre axle: (empty) 3000 kg
Weight on rear axle: (empty) 3000 kg
Max load: 10 000 kg
Load area: 6·7 × 2·35 m
Length: 9·75 m
Width: 2·5 m
Height: 3·35 m
Ground clearance: 0·37 m
Track:
(front) 2·046 m
(rear 2 axles) 1·944 m

Wheelbase: 4·7 m + 1·4 m
Max speed: 72 km/h
Range: 520 km
Fuel capacity: 200 litres
Fuel consumption: 38 litres/100 km (diesel)
Max gradient: 40%
Fording: 1 m
Engine: Deutz model F 8 L 714A 8-cylinder air-cooled multi-fuel developing 178 hp at 2300 rpm
Gearbox: ZF model AK 6-55 with 6 forward and 1 reverse gears
Clutch: F & S type LA 380
Transfer box: 2-speed ZF type VG 500
Steering: ZF hydraulic
Turning radius: 12 m
Suspension: semi-elliptical springs and hydraulic shock absorbers

Tyres: 14.00 × 20
Number of tyres: 6 + 1 spare
Brakes:
(main) hydraulic, air assisted
(parking) mechanical
Electrical system: 24 V
Batteries: 4 × 12 V, 100 Ah
Generator: 600 W

STATUS
Production complete. In service with the West German and the Turkish armies.

MANUFACTURER
Faun-Werke Nuernberg, POB 8,8560 Lauf/Pegn, Federal Republic of Germany.

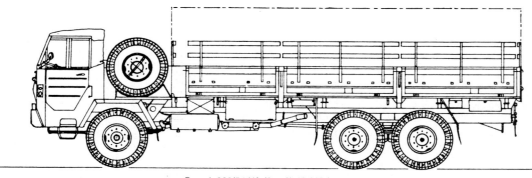
Faun L 908/54 VA (6 × 6) 10 000 kg cargo truck

GREECE

The Greek military vehicle industry consists of two major concerns; one of which is Steyr Hella SA, a subsidiary of the Austrian Steyr-Daimler-Puch. The Steyr Hellas plant is at Salonika and covers an area of 37 000 square metres. Annual output is now approximately 1500 military vehicles a year in addition to civil vehicle output. The military trucks involved are the Steyr 680 MH (4 × 4) and the Steyr 680 MH 3 (6 × 6), both of which are covered under *Austria* in this section.

The second Greek military vehicle producer is the National Motor Company (NAMCO) also based at Salonika. This company financed a consultant engineer bureau in Switzerland at one time and now has associations with the French Citroën company and the West German KHD Deutz. Using its patented Powermaster suspension and chassis, NAMCO produces two types of Milicar military truck in addition to its Agricar and Pyrocar range of vehicles.

NAMCO Milicar (4 × 4) and (6 × 6) Trucks

DEVELOPMENT

For five years NAMCO financed an independent design bureau in Switzerland to work on new vehicle designs, the outcome of which was the Powermaster design, the patents for which are now invested in NAMCO International, a subsidiary of NAMCO. Using the Powermaster basis, NAMCO now produces a range of civil and military vehicles, one of which, the Milicar (4 × 4) is now in production for the Greek Army. In 1979 the Army ordered 72 Milicar (4 × 4) trucks for use as artillery tractors, followed by an order for another 72 in 1982. A further 18 will be ordered for use as coastal-defence missile carriers.

DESCRIPTION

The Milicar 4 × 4 and 6 × 6 share many basic components but the 4 × 4 has a 4000 kg payload and the 6 × 6 a 6500 kg payload. The cabins used by both versions have single, double or triple capacity (the 4 × 4 version used as an artillery tractor by the Greek Army has a double capacity cabin). The payload area behind the cabin is open. On the 4 × 4 version the load area is equipped with cross-benches for six men and is 2·15 metres long. Steel sides are provided and there is limited stowage under the seats. The payload area of the 6 × 6 version is 4·1 metres long.

The engines used are air-cooled diesels manufactured by the KHD Deutz group. Power steering is provided. The suspension used the Powermaster patented principles which, among other items, uses double shock absorbers and rubber bump stops. Special axles and differentials combine to give the Milicar a good cross-country performance that is stated to match that of AFVs.

One example of a Milicar (4 × 4) has been converted to become a containerised fire control centre for the Artemis 30 low level air defence system. Very similar to the Milicar range is the civil Agricar range which is produced in several different versions including a trench digger. Agricar (4 × 4) versions are produced with wheelbases of 2·35, 2·9 and 3·3 metres. The 6 × 6 version of the Agricar has a wheelbase of 2·7 + 1·25 metres. The Pyrocar range uses the Powermaster chassis and suspension for fire engines and tenders.

SPECIFICATIONS

Configuration	4 × 4	6 × 6
Seating	see text	see text
Max weight	8500 kg	12 000 kg
Max load	4000 kg	6500 kg
Towed load	42 000 kg	60 000 kg
Length	4·5 m	6·3 m
Width	2·14 m	2·14 m
Height (top of cab)	2·43 m	2·43 m
(load area)	1·2 m	1·2 m
Ground clearance	0·45 m	0·45 m
Wheelbase	2·35 m	2·7 m + 1·25 m
Max speed	100 km/h	100 km/h
Fuel capacity	91 or 127 litres	127 litres
Max gradient	80%	80%
Engine	F4L 912 3·77-litre 4-cylinder air-cooled diesel developing 80 hp at 2800 rpm	F6L 912 5·665-litre 6-cylinder air-cooled diesel developing 120 hp at 2800 rpm

Configuration	4 × 4	6 × 6
Gearbox	ZF with 5 forward and 1 reverse, synchromesh on 2nd-5th	
Transfer box	2-speed	2-speed
Clutch	single dry disc	single dry disc
Steering	hydraulically assisted recirculating ball	
Suspension	semi-elliptical springs with double shock absorbers and rubber bumper stops	
Axles	portal type, Powermaster design modified by NAMCO	
Brakes	hydraulically assisted discs	
Electrical system	12 V	12 V

STATUS

Production. In service with the Greek Army.

MANUFACTURER

NAMCO SA, Nea Redestos/Industrial Zone, Thessaloniki, Greece.

2·35-metre wheelbase of civil Agricar (4 × 4) carrying trench digging equipment

Close-up of part of NAMCO Powermaster suspension used on Milicar range

Greek Army Milicar (4 × 4) being used as tractor for 155 mm howitzer

Milicar (4 × 4) converted for use as fire control centre for Artemis 30 low level air defence system (T J Gander)

HUNGARY

Csepel D-344 (4 × 4) 3000 kg Truck

DEVELOPMENT

The first Csepel truck was the D-350 which was introduced in 1950. In the early 1950s a 6 × 6 version was produced called the K-300, using the engine of the K-800 light tracked artillery tractor. It was used for a variety of roles including towing artillery and carrying bridging equipment.

In 1961 a 4 × 4 truck based on the Csepel D-450

(4 × 2) truck was introduced for military use under the designation D-344. This was followed by an improved model, the D-344.01, in 1966 and a civilian model, the D-344.02/2, in early 1969. The D-344 vehicles are unusual in that they have dual rear tyres. In the early 1970s a new 4 × 4 vehicle was developed from the D-344, called the D-346. Versions include a cargo truck and a 4000-litre tanker. There is a decontamination version of the D-344 used to decontaminate vehicles and equipment.

DESCRIPTION

The layout of the D-344 is conventional with the engine at the front, fully enclosed two-door cab in the centre and the cargo area at the rear with drop sides and a drop tailgate. If required bows and a tarpaulin cover can be fitted.

SPECIFICATIONS

Cab seating: 1 + 2
Configuration: 4 × 4
Weight:
  (empty) 5400 kg
  (loaded, cross country) 8400 kg
Max load:
  (road) 3500 kg
  (cross country) 3000 kg
Towed load: 2000 kg
Length: 6·716 m
Width: 2·56 m
Height:
  (cab) 2·43 m
  (tarpaulin) 2·775 m
Ground clearance: 0·27 m
Track:
  (front) 1·78 m
  (rear) 1·72 m
Wheelbase: 3·75 m
Max speed: 82 km/h
Range: 530 km
Fuel capacity: 145 litres
Fuel consumption: 27 litres/100 km
Engine: D-414h, 4-cylinder water-cooled diesel developing 100 hp at 2300 rpm
Gearbox: manual with 4 forward and 1 reverse gears
Clutch: single dry plate
Transfer box: 2-speed
Turning radius: 17·7 m
Suspension:
  (front) semi-elliptical springs
  (rear) semi-elliptical springs with overload springs
Tyres: 9.00 × 20
Number of tyres: 6 + 1 spare
Brakes:
  (main) air/hydraulic
  (parking) mechanical
Electrical system: 12 V

STATUS

Production complete. In service with the Hungarian Army.

MANUFACTURER

Csepel, near Budapest, Hungary.

Other Csepel 4 × 2 trucks (which are not thought to be in military service) include the D-350 (in production from 1950 to 1955), D-352 (in production from 1955 to 1956), D-420 (in production from 1956 to 1960), D-450 (in production from 1960 to 1970), D-450.1 (from 1970), D-450N (tractor truck), D-350B (dump), D-352B (dump) D-420B (dump), D-450B (dump), D-455B (dump), D-450.05 (dump), D-452 (replaced the D-450 from 1971), D-465, D-453 (three-way dump truck), D-705 (tractor truck), D-707, D-710, D-730 and D-740 (tractor truck). Hungary is also producing trucks under licence from MAN of Germany and engines for these vehicles are exported from Hungary to Romania for use in the Romanian DAC and ROMAN vehicles.

Csepel D-344 (4 × 4) 3000 kg truck

Romanian Army motor vehicle park with ZIL-131 (6 × 6) 3500 kg trucks and various Csepel D-420 (4 × 4 and 4 × 2) 4000 kg trucks

---

Csepel D-562 (4 × 2), D-564 (4 × 4), D-566 (6 × 6), D-566.02 (6 × 6) and D-588 (8 × 8) Trucks

DESCRIPTION

The D-566 (6 × 6) cargo truck appeared in 1970 and entered production the following year. It has a two-door all steel forward control cab with the cargo area at the rear with a drop tailgate, bows and a tarpaulin cover. A central tyre-pressure regulation system is fitted as standard. The D-566.02 is identical to the D-566 but has a 7000 kg capacity winch with 60 metres of cable.

The D-562 (4 × 2) and D-564 (4 × 4) vehicles were introduced in 1972 with first production vehicles being completed in 1974. These also have a two-door all-steel forward control cab with the cargo area at the rear with a drop tailgate, drop sides, a tarpaulin cover and bows. Both are provided with a central tyre-pressure regulation system. A dump truck model has been built.

The D-588 is an 8 × 8 truck with a forward control cab and a central tyre-pressure regulation system. It is not known if this version is in production.

Csepel D-566 (6 × 6) 5000 kg truck with central tyre-pressure regulation system

Csepel D-566 (6 × 6) recovery vehicle

Csepel D-566 (6 × 6) shop/van

VARIANTS (D-566)
These include a recovery vehicle and a shop/van.

STATUS
In production. The D-566 is in service with the Hungarian Army.

MANUFACTURER
Csepel Motor Vehicle Plant, Szigethzlem, Hungary.

SPECIFICATIONS

Model	D-562	D-564	D-566
Configuration	4 × 2	4 × 4	6 × 6
Weight (empty)	5200 kg	5400 kg	9000 kg
(loaded, cross country)	9200 kg	9400 kg	14 000 kg
Load (road)	5000 kg	5000 kg	8000 kg
(cross country)	4000 kg	4000 kg	5000 kg
Towed load (road)	n/a	n/a	10 000 kg
(cross country)	n/a	n/a	5000 kg
Length	6·43 m	6·43 m	7·18 m
Width	2·5 m	2·5 m	2·5 m
Height	2·67 m	2·67 m	2·74 m
Ground clearance	n/a	n/a	0·575 m
Track	2 m	2 m	2·05 m
Wheelbase	3·7 m	3·7 m	2·9 m + 1·4 m
Max speed	87·9 km/h	87·9 km/h	80 km/h
Range	n/a	n/a	700 km
Fording	n/a	n/a	1·2 m
Engine model	D-614.33	D-614.33	Raba-MAN
Engine type	6-cylinder water-cooled diesel	6-cylinder water-cooled diesel	6-cylinder water-cooled diesel
Hp	145/2300 rpm	145/2300 rpm	200/2200 rpm
Gearbox	n/a	n/a	manual, 5 forward and 1 reverse gears
Transfer box	none	n/a	2-speed
Tyres	16.5 × 19.5	16.5 × 19.5	14.00 × 20
Electrical system	24 V	24 V	24 V
Batteries	n/a	n/a	2 × 120 Ah
Generator	n/a	n/a	750 W

INDIA

Azad (4 × 4) 2500 kg Truck

DESCRIPTION
To date four prototypes of the Azad (4 × 4) 2500 kg truck have been produced. The truck has a forward-mounted steel cab with seating for a driver and at least one passenger and it would appear that the cab can be tilted forward for access to the engine and gearbox. The cab roof appears to have hatches for access to a machine gun roof mounting and the radiator grille is protected by a steel guard mounted on the front bumper; this guard also protects the headlights. The cargo area to the rear can be covered by a canvas tilt and the side and rear flaps either fold downwards or can be removed to enable the Azad to carry a variety of loads, including

container bodies. Apart from use as a cargo truck the Azad can be used as a personnel carrier, a tractor for light artillery field pieces, a tanker (fuel or water) or a missile launcher vehicle.

STATUS
Prototypes.

SPECIFICATIONS
Cab seating: 1 + 1 or 2
Configuration: 4 × 4
Weight: (loaded, max) 7500 kg
Max load: 2500 kg
Length: 5·4 m

Width: 2·25 m
Height: (cab roof) 2·45 m
Ground clearance: 0·32 m
Max speed: 84 km/h
Range: 800 km
Gradient: 60%
Fording: 0·8 m
Engine: Perkins P6-354 water-cooled diesel developing 120 hp at 2800 rpm
Gearbox: ZFAK-5-35 with 5 forward and 1 reverse gears
Transfer box: 2-speed
Steering: power-assisted

Shaktiman (4 × 4) 5000 kg Truck

DESCRIPTION
The Shaktiman 5000 kg (4 × 4) truck is basically the West German MAN 415 L1AR 4000 kg truck built under licence in India. Main differences between the German and Indian vehicle is that the latter has dual rather than single rear wheels. The vehicle entered production at Jabalpur in 1958 and was initially assembled from components supplied by West Germany, but as production built up an increasing number of the components were supplied by Indian companies. In the early 1970s the Jabalpur plant built a new 6 × 6 truck in the 5000 kg class and it is reported that this has now entered production for both military and civilian applications.

VARIANTS
An amphibious vehicle, the Rampar, has been developed from the Shaktiman. See entry in *Amphibians* section for available details.

STATUS
In service with the Indian Army.

MANUFACTURER
Heavy Vehicles Factory, Jabalpur, India.

Shaktiman (4 × 4) 5000 kg truck (Indian Army)

(8 × 8) 5000 kg Truck

DESCRIPTION
The Indian Vehicle Research and Development Establishment is known to have produced a test chassis of a new (8 × 8) 5000 kg payload truck. Gross weight of the proposed vehicle is 13 500 kg and the engine is a license-produced Leyland supercharged model which develops 225 hp. The eventual vehicle will be capable of high mobility duties but no other details are yet available.

ISRAEL

M-325 (4 × 4) 1800 kg Truck

DESCRIPTION
The M-325 (4 × 4) truck has been developed by Automotive Industries Limited specifically for military use and wherever possible standard commercial components have been used. Typical uses include personnel carrier (2 + 12), command vehicle, reconnaissance carrier and prime mover for mortars.

The engine is mounted at the front of the vehicle and the closed circuit cooling system is equipped with a heavy duty radiator. The system is designed to prevent overheating of the engine in ambient temperatures of up to 50°C (122°F). The large Donaldson Cyclopac air cleaner extends the engine's life during operations in the desert. An indicator on the dashboard warns when the filter element needs servicing.

The open cab is provided with two adjustable bucket type seats and a folding windscreen. The spare wheel is to the immediate left of the driver and under each seat is a tool compartment.

The all-steel cargo body has a longitudinal bench seat down each side, both with two closed compartments for personal equipment. The two sidewall battery compartments are equipped with sliding trays for ease of maintenance. The truck has two heavy-duty batteries each with a 12-volt, 150 Ah capacity. The non-inflammable tarpaulin top, which includes front and rear curtains, is supported by removable bows.

The benches are fitted for the installation of two radios, one on each bench, and the front wall is equipped with two terminal boards for 12 or 24-volt power supply. The standard electrical system of the M-325 provides sufficient power to supply the radios and there is no need for additional batteries or a battery charger.

Heavy duty steering is provided and the dual hydraulic system includes dual booster brakes. An indicating light on the dashboard warns if one of the systems fails.

The M-325 can tow a maximum load of 1800 kg across country and is fitted with a rear pintle hook with two safety eye bolts and front towing shackles. As an option it can be fitted with a mechanical winch rated at 4500 kg.

VARIANTS
Ambulance
A one-unit body contains the rear ambulance section and the driver's section with a passage between them. The driver's section has a door each side, two bucket seats, sun visors and ventilation louvres above the windscreen.

The rear ambulance section has a folding seat for a medical attendant, four stretcher support brackets, and two longitudinal cushioned benches with compartments for the stowage of stretchers and blankets.

There are two hooks for hanging bottles of plasma and an electric fan in the ceiling. The two rear doors open either side and a rear step folds down onto the bumper.

A 24-volt socket is incorporated for providing a power supply from the ambulance's electrical system and if required a radio can be installed behind the driver's seat.

Standard equipment includes lights, siren and supports for water containers.

SPECIFICATIONS
Cab seating: 1 + 2
Configuration: 4 × 4
Weight:
  (empty) 2520 kg
  (loaded, cross country) 4320 kg
Load: (cross country) 1800 kg
Length: 5·03 m
Width: 2·08 m
Height: (tarpaulin) 2·35 m
Track: 1·93 m
Wheelbase: 3·2 m
Max speed: 88 km/h
Range: 540 km
Gradient: 85%
Angle of approach/departure: 25°/34°
Engine: Chrysler 226 6-cylinder developing 105 hp at 3000 rpm
Gearbox: manual, 4 forward and 1 reverse gears
Transfer box: 2-speed
Tyres: 9.00 × 16
Electrical system: 24 V
Batteries: 2 × 12 V, 150 Ah

STATUS
Production. In service with the Israeli armed forces.

MANUFACTURER
Automotive Industries Limited, POB 535, Nazareth Illit, Israel.

M-325 (4 × 4) 1800 kg truck with tarpaulin top removed

ITALY

CL 51 (4 × 4) 1800 kg Truck

DESCRIPTION
The CL 51 (Light Truck 51) was built by three Italian companies (Autobianchi, Lancia and OM) in the early 1950s and remained in production until 1970. Although built to the same specification there were considerable differences between the three basic models. The fully enclosed two-door forward control cab has a circular observation hatch in the roof on the left side. The rear cargo area has a drop tailgate, removable bows and a tarpaulin cover. The Lancia model was known as the Z20 and a later model fitted with a winch was known as the Z30.

SPECIFICATIONS
Cab seating: 1 + 1
Configuration: 4 × 4
Weight:
  (empty) 2830 kg
  (loaded) 4630 kg
Length: 4·48 m
Width: 2 m
Height:
  (cab) 2·26 m
  (tarpaulin cover) 2·67 m
Wheelbase: 2·55 m
Engine: 4-cylinder developing 62·5 bhp
Gearbox: manual with 5 forward and 1 reverse gears
Clutch: single dry plate
Transfer box: 2-speed

STATUS
Production complete. In service with the Italian Army.

MANUFACTURERS
Autobianchi (Bianchi), Lancia (Turin) and OM (Brescia).

CL 51 (4 × 4) 1800 kg truck (Christopher F Foss)

FIAT 40 PM (4 × 4) 1500 kg Light Truck

DEVELOPMENT/DESCRIPTION
The FIAT 40 PM (4 × 4) 1500 kg light truck is a military derivative of the commercial FIAT Daily model and has been produced in prototype form at FIAT's Brescia factory. Intended for use by airborne troops the FIAT 40 PM has a useful payload of 1500 kg or ten fully-equipped men in the rear load area. The two-man cabin is protected by a removable canvas top and the windscreen folds down onto the bonnet. A canvas tilt can be erected over the rear.

An ambulance version of this light vehicle is planned along with a command post, and weapons such as machine guns or missiles may be mounted.

STATUS
Prototypes.

MANUFACTURER
FIAT, Direzione Mezzi Speciale, Corso G Marconi 10/20, Turin, Italy.

SPECIFICATIONS
Cab seating: 1 + 1 (10 in rear)
Configuration: 4 × 4
Max weight: 4000 kg
Max load: 1500 kg
Towed load: 1500 kg
Max speed: 100 km/h
Range: 500 km
Fuel capacity: 70 litres
Gradient: 60%
Side slope: 30%
Engine: FIAT 8140 turbocharged 4-cylinder, water-cooled 2·5-litre diesel developing 100 hp at 3800 rpm
Gearbox: 5 forward and 1 reverse gears
Transfer box: 2-speed
Turning radius: 6 m

FIAT 75 PM (4 × 4) 2500 kg Cargo Truck

DEVELOPMENT
This vehicle has been developed for both civil and military use and entered production in 1975. Production is undertaken at the Lancia plant at Bolzano. The FIAT 75 PM is a member of a family of vehicles which also includes the 65 P (4 × 4) and the 90 PM/16 (4 × 4). The 65 is the approximate gross vehicle weight (eg 6500 kg), P is Pesante (heavy duty service) and M is for Military. Initial Italian Army order was for 3800 vehicles.

DESCRIPTION
The chassis consists of longitudinal members to which the cross-members are cold riveted. The cab is all steel and is of the forward control type. It can be tilted forwards 55 degrees to allow access to the engine. A circular observation hatch is provided in the roof of the cab on the passenger side. The rear cargo area has drop sides and a drop tailgate and if required bows and a tarpaulin cover can be installed.

Optional equipment includes a front- or rear-mounted winch with a capacity of 4000 kg and an air-operated lockable front differential.

VARIANTS
The vehicle can be fitted with a wide range of different bodies and various other types of specialised equipment including aerial cage, bus body, crane, digger, enlarged cab, fire appliance, mobile lubrication and greasing unit and a three-way tipper body.

SPECIFICATIONS
Cab seating: 1 + 1
Configuration: 4 × 4
Weight:
  (curb) 4925 kg
  (loaded) 7425 kg
Weight on front axle: (loaded) 3200 kg
Weight on rear axle: (empty) 4225 kg
Max load: 2500 kg

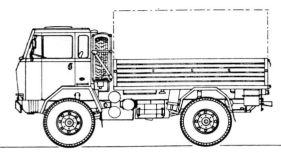

FIAT 75 PM (4 × 4) 2500 kg truck

Towed load: 4000 kg
Load area: 3 × 2·2 m
Length: 5·131 m
Width: 2·3 m
Height:
  (cab) 2·54 m
  (tarpaulin) 2·83 m
  (load area) 1·265 m
Ground clearance: 0·448 m
Track:
  (front) 1·85 m
  (rear) 1·85 m
Wheelbase: 2·75 m
Angle of approach/departure: 45°/42°
Max speed: 80 km/h
Range: 800 km
Fuel capacity: 145 litres
Max gradient: 60%
Max side slope: 30%
Fording: 0·85 m
Engine: Model 8062.02 6-cylinder direct injection water-cooled diesel developing 130 bhp (DIN) at 3200 rpm
Gearbox: manual with 5 forward and 1 reverse gears
Clutch: single dry plate
Transfer box: 2-speed

Steering: recirculating ball with hydraulic servo
Turning radius: 6 m
Suspension: leaf springs (dual at rear) with hydraulic telescopic shock absorbers
Tyres: 12.50 × 20
Number of tyres: 4 + 1 spare
Brakes:
  (main) air-hydraulic on all wheels with separate circuits
  (parking and emergency) single acting cylinder
Electrical system: 24 V
Batteries: 2 × 12 V

STATUS
In production. In service with the Italian Army as the ACL 75. In 1979 ten vehicles were being tested by the French Army under the designation Camion Militaire (4 × 4) 2·5-tonne UNIC 75 PM. The cab and engine were supplied from Italy and the remainder from French production facilities, but in 1981 the French Army selected the Renault TRM 2000 (4 × 4) 2000 kg truck to meet its requirements. Somalia (120).

MANUFACTURER
FIAT, Direzione Mezzi Speciali, Corso G Marconi 10/20, Turin, Italy.

FIAT 75 PM (4 × 4) 2500 kg truck

FIAT 75 PM (4 × 4) 2500 kg truck towing 105 mm Pack Howitzer

FIAT 90 PM 16 (4 × 4) 4000 kg Cargo Truck

DEVELOPMENT
This vehicle has been developed for both civil and military use and entered production in 1975 at the Lancia plant at Bolzano. It is a member of a family of vehicles which also includes the 65 P and the 75 PM. The 90 is the approximate gross vehicle weight (eg 9500 kg), P is for Pesante (heavy duty service) and M is for Military.

DESCRIPTION
The chassis consists of longitudinal members to which the cross-members are cold riveted. The cab is all steel and is of the forward control type. It can be tilted forwards to an angle of 55 degrees to allow access to the engine. There is a circular observation hatch in the roof of the cab on the right side. The rear cargo area has drop sides and a drop tailgate and if required bows and a tarpaulin cover can be installed.

Optional equipment includes a front- or rear-mounted winch with a capacity of 4000 kg and air-operated lockable front differential.

VARIANTS
60 examples of a wrecker on the 90 PM 16 chassis mounting a 5000 kg crane have been produced for Venezuela. For details see *Addenda*.

FIAT also built a half track version of the 90 PM under

the designation HT 90. Details of this vehicle were given on page 532 of the first edition of *Jane's Combat Support Equipment*; all work on it has now stopped.

SPECIFICATIONS
Cab seating: 1 + 1
Configuration: 4 × 4
Weight:
(curb) 5750 kg
(loaded) 9750 kg
Max load: 4000 kg
Towed load: 4000 kg
Load area: 4·21 × 2·15 m
Length: 6·352 m
Width: 2·3 m
Height:
(cab) 2·627 m
(tarpaulin) 2·935 m
(load area) 1·37 m
Ground clearance: 0·445 m
Track: 1·852 m
Wheelbase: 3·7 m
Angle of approach/departure: 45°/35°
Max speed: 80 km/h
Range: 700 km
Fuel capacity: 145 litres
Max gradient: 60%
Max side slope: 30%
Fording: 0·85 m
Engine: Model 8062.24 6-cylinder supercharged direct injection water-cooled diesel developing 160 hp (DIN) at 3200 rpm
Gearbox: manual with 5 forward and 1 reverse gears
Clutch: single dry plate
Transfer box: 2-speed
Steering: recirculating ball with hydraulic servo
Suspension: leaf springs (dual at rear) with hydraulic telescopic shock absorbers
Tyres: 12.5 R20 PR22
Number of tyres: 4 + 1 spare
Brakes:
(main) air-hydraulic on all wheels with separate circuits
(parking and emergency) single acting cylinder
Electrical system: 24 V
Batteries: 2 × 12 V

FIAT 90 PM 16 (4 × 4) 4000 kg cargo truck

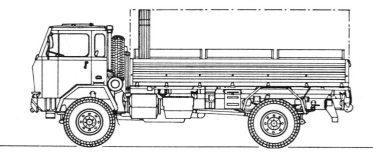

FIAT 90 PM 16 (4 × 4) 4000 kg cargo truck

STATUS
In production. In service with Somalia (100).

MANUFACTURER
FIAT, Direzione Mezzi Speciali, Corso G Marconi 10/20, Turin, Italy.

Astra BM 201 MC1 (4 × 4) 4000 kg Medium Mobility Truck

DESCRIPTION
The two-door fibreglass cab with a metal frame can be tilted forwards 48 degrees to allow access to the engine for maintenance. The chassis is made of high elastic steel and consists of two double C-shaped side-members connected through rigid cross-members. The two powered axles have double reduction centre bevel gears and planetary final drives.

The rear cargo area has drop sides, drop tailgate, removable bows and a tarpaulin cover. There is also a six cubic metre dump truck model which has 12.00 × 20 tyres, dual at the rear.

VARIANTS
Details of the dump truck model are given in the *Construction equipment* section.

SPECIFICATIONS
Cab seating: 1 + 1
Configuration: 4 × 4
Weight:
(empty) 7120 kg
(loaded, cross country) 11 120 kg
Max load: (cross country) 4000 kg
Towed load: 2500 kg
Length: 6·6 m
Width: 2·5 m
Height: (cab) 2·85 m
Ground clearance: 0·285 m
Track:
(front) 2 m
(rear) 1·85 m
Wheelbase: 3·45 m
Max road speed: 86·5 km/h
Fuel capacity: 180 litres
Max gradient: 60%
Fording: 1·2 m

Astra BM 201 MC1 (4 × 4) 4000 kg medium mobility truck

Engine: FIAT Model 8360 6-cylinder in-line diesel developing 169 hp at 2600 rpm
Gearbox: ZF manual, 6 forward and 1 reverse gears
Clutch: single dry plate
Transfer box: 2-speed
Steering: hydraulic
Turning radius: 8 m
Suspension:
(front) parabolic springs with hydraulic shock absorbers
(rear) semi-elliptical springs with double flexible auxiliary springs
Tyres: 14.00 × 20

Number of tyres: 4 + 1 spare
Brakes:
(main) air, dual circuit
(parking) mechanical
Electrical system: 24 V
Batteries: 2 × 12 V

STATUS
Production.

MANUFACTURER
Astra Veicoli Industriali SpA, Via Caorsana 79, 29100 Piacenza, Italy.

FIAT 6601 (4 × 4) 4000 kg Cargo Truck

DESCRIPTION
The FIAT 6601 (4 × 4) can carry 4150 kg of cargo on roads and 3152 kg of cargo across country. Although designated a 4000 kg vehicle by FIAT by most armies' standards the vehicle is rated at 3000 kg. The vehicle is designated the Autocarro Medio CM.52 by the Italian Army and replaced an earlier vehicle called the CM.50, which was almost identical but had a petrol instead of a diesel engine.

The cab is of the forward control type and is of all-steel construction with a heater and a circular observation hatch above the co-driver's seat. The cargo area is of all-steel construction with the floor lined with wood. The front and sides are fixed and the tailgate is of the drop down type. The tailgate is removable and has swing out steps. Tiltable seats are incorporated in the sides. The cargo area is normally provided with bows and a tarpaulin cover. When the bows are not required they are clipped together to the rear of the cab.

The chassis consists of pressed steel channels spot welded to cross-members with cross bracing and bolted spring supports. The electrical system is radio suppressed.

STATUS
Production complete. In service with the Italian armed forces. The earlier model was exported to Africa and South America.

MANUFACTURER
FIAT, Direzione Mezzi Speciali, Corso G Marconi 10/20, Turin, Italy.

SPECIFICATIONS
Cab seating: 1 + 1
Configuration: 4 × 4
Weight:
  (empty) 5216 kg
  (loaded) 9366 kg
Weight on front axle: (loaded) 3588 kg
Weight on rear axle: (loaded) 5778 kg
Max load:
  (road) 4150 kg
  (cross country) 3152 kg
Towed load:
  (road) 6490 kg
  (cross country) 3000 kg
Load area: 3·95 × 2·23 m
Length: 6·191 m
Width: 2·368 m
Height:
  (cab) 2·857 m
  (tarpaulin) 2·952 m
Ground clearance: 0·265 m
Track:
  (front) 1·88 m
  (rear) 1·727 m
Wheelbase: 3·27 m
Angle of approach/departure: 35°/25°
Max speed: (road) 58·5 km/h
Range: 450 km
Fuel capacity: 91 litres
Max gradient: 40%
Fording: 0·609 m
Engine: 6-cylinder liquid-cooled diesel developing 89 hp (DIN) at 2000 rpm
Gearbox: manual with 4 forward and 1 reverse gears (high and low ranges)
Clutch: single dry plate
Transfer box: single-speed; front axle can be disengaged if required
Steering: worm and sector
Turning radius: 7·32 m
Tyres: 10.00 × 20
Number of tyres: 6 + 1 spare

FIAT 6601 (4 × 4) 4000 kg cargo truck complete with bows and tarpaulin cover (Italian Army)

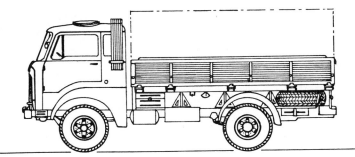

FIAT 6601 (4 × 4) 4000 kg cargo truck

Brakes:
  (main) drum, air over hydraulic acting on all wheels
  (parking) drum type on transmission output shaft

Electrical system: 24 V
Batteries: 2 × 12 V, 90 Ah
Generator: 600 W

FIAT 6602 CM (4 × 4) 5000 kg Cargo Truck

DEVELOPMENT
The FIAT 6602 CM (4 × 4) truck has been designed to carry 5000 kg of cargo on both roads and across country and is designated the Autocarro Pesante CP.70 by the Italian Army. Many of the components of the 6602 CM are also used in the 6607 CM (6 × 6) 5000 kg cargo truck, described in the following entry.

DESCRIPTION
The chassis is of the ladder type with two longitudinal steel channels to which the cross-members, brackets and spring supports are riveted. The cab is of the forward control type and is of all-steel construction with removable canvas top and side curtains. The windscreen can be folded flat against the front of the cab if not required. The cab is equipped with a heater.

The rear cargo area is of all-steel construction with a wood-lined floor. The drop tailgate has swing out steps and is removable. Along each side of the cargo area are seats which are folded flat against the sides when not required. The cargo area is covered by removable bows and a tarpaulin cover.

The 9200 kg capacity winch is mounted at the rear and is provided with 60 metres of 16 mm diameter cable. The electrical system is waterproof and radio suppressed.

VARIANTS
A fuel tank version is in service.

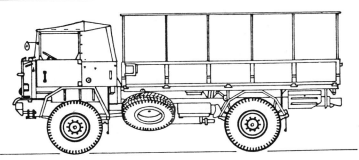

FIAT 6602 CM (4 × 4) 5000 kg cargo truck

FIAT 6602 CM (4 × 4) 5000 kg cargo truck complete with bows and tarpaulin cover

STATUS
Production complete. In service with the Italian Army.

MANUFACTURER
FIAT, Direzione Mezzi Speciali, Corso G Marconi 10/20, Turin, Italy.

SPECIFICATIONS
Configuration: 4 × 4
Weight:
(empty) 7500 kg
(loaded) 12 640 kg
Weight on front axle: (loaded) 4700 kg
Weight on rear axle: (loaded) 7940 kg
Max load: 5000 kg
Towed load:
(road) 10 000 kg
(cross country) 4000 kg

Load area: 4·28 × 2·23 m
Length: 6·55 m
Width: 2·46 m
Height:
(cab) 2·7 m
(tarpaulin) 2·974 m
(load area) 1·417 m
Ground clearance: 0·271 m
Track:
(front) 1·873 m
(rear) 1·785 m
Wheelbase: 3·57 m
Angle of approach/departure: 45°/35°
Max speed: (road) 74 km/h
Range: 700 km
Fuel capacity: 230 litres
Max gradient: 60%
Max side slope: 30%

Fording: 0·85 m
Engine: Model 8202.02 6-cylinder in-line liquid-cooled diesel developing 193 hp (DIN) at 2500 rpm
Gearbox: manual with 5 forward and 1 reverse gears
Clutch: single dry plate
Transfer box: 2-speed
Steering: worm and sector, power assisted
Turning radius: 8·1 m
Suspension: semi-elliptical springs front and rear with double acting hydraulic shock absorbers on the front axle only
Tyres: 11.00 × 20
Number of tyres: 6 + 1 spare
Brakes:
(main) air
(parking) mechanical
Electrical system: 24 V
Batteries: 2 × 12 V, 90 Ah

FIAT 6607 CM (6 × 6) 5000 kg Truck

DEVELOPMENT
The FIAT 6607 CM (6 × 6) truck has been designed to carry 5000 kg of cargo on both roads and across country. It is designated the Autocarro Pesante CP 70 by the Italian Army and entered service in December 1973. The vehicle is a further development of the FIAT 6602 CM (4 × 4) truck and uses many components of this model.

DESCRIPTION
The ladder-type chassis has longitudinal steel channels to which cross-member brackets and spring supports are riveted. The forward control cab is all-steel with a removable canvas top and side curtains. If required the windscreen can be folded forward flat against the front of the cab. The cab is provided with a heater.
The rear cargo area is all-steel with a wood-lined floor and has drop sides and a removable drop tailgate. The worm gear type winch mounted at the rear of the vehicle has a capacity of 9200 kg (first layer) and is provided with 60 metres of 16 mm diameter cable. The winch is fitted with an automatic safety brake. The electrical system is waterproof and radio suppressed.

SPECIFICATIONS
Cab seating: 1 + 1
Configuration: 6 × 6
Weight:
(empty) 8860 kg
(loaded) 14 000 kg
Weight on front axle: (loaded) 4520 kg
Weight on rear bogie: (loaded) 9480 kg
Max load: (road) 5140 kg
Towed load:
(road) 10 000 kg
(cross country) 4000 kg
Load area: 5·545 × 2·265 m

FIAT 6607 CM (6 × 6) 5000 kg truck (Italian Army)

Length: 7·824 m
Width: 2·43 m
Height:
(cab) 2·699 m
(reduced, top of steering wheel) 2·135 m
(load area) 1·392 m
Ground clearance: (axles) 0·244 m
Track:
(front) 1·873 m
(rear) 1·872 m
Wheelbase: 3·567 m + 1·25 m
Angle of approach/departure: 45°/29°
Max speed: (road) 74 km/h
Range: 750 km
Fuel capacity: 230 litres
Max gradient: 60%
Max side slope: 30%
Fording: 0·85 m
Engine: Model 8202.02 6-cylinder in-line liquid-cooled diesel developing 193 hp (DIN) at 2500 rpm
Gearbox: manual with 5 forward and 1 reverse gears
Clutch: single dry plate

Transfer box: 2-speed
Steering: power-assisted, worm and sector
Turning radius: 8·96 m
Suspension:
(front) semi-elliptical leaf springs and double acting shock absorbers
(rear) parallelogram torque arm with 2 constant rate leaf springs
Tyres: 11.00 × 20
Number of tyres: 6 + 1 spare
Brakes:
(main) drum, air-operated, dual circuit
(parking) drum on transfer rear output shaft
Electrical system: 24 V
Batteries: 2 × 12 V, 90 Ah

STATUS
Production complete. In service with the Italian Army.

MANUFACTURER
FIAT, Direzione Mezzi Speciali, Corso G Marconi 10/20, Turin, Italy.

FIAT 6605 (6 × 6) Series

DEVELOPMENT
In the 1960s FIAT built a light artillery tractor (6 × 6) called the Model 6606 (TL65) and a medium artillery tractor (6 × 6) called the Model 6605 (TM65). The TM65 (TM standing for Trattore Medio) was powered by a petrol engine and further development resulted in the diesel-engined TM69 which was adopted by the Italian Army. The range now consists of the 6605 TM which is used for towing medium artillery such as the 155 mm FH-70, the 6605 FH which is used for carrying ammunition, the 6605 AG recovery vehicle and the 6605 A cargo truck.

DESCRIPTION
6605 TM
The chassis is of the ladder type with two longitudinal pressed steel channels, to which are riveted the cross-members, brackets and spring supports. The forward control cab is all-steel and has a removable canvas top and side screens and a windscreen which can be folded flat against the bonnet. A cab heater and ventilator are standard on all versions. The gap to the rear of the cab and body houses the spare wheel, two water and two fuel containers, tyre chain locker and the exhaust pipe.
The rear cargo area is all-steel with a wood-lined floor. The sides consist of two boards, the front a drop

type and the rear fixed. The drop tailgate is fitted with integral steps and is removable. The rear cargo area is covered by removable bows and a tarpaulin cover. When not required the bows can be stowed under the central area of the body. The cargo space is divided into three compartments by removable partitions: the first is used for stowing the charges, the second for the projectiles and the rear for stores and the tarpaulin cover.
The transmission consists of a set of gears mounted on four shafts (input, primary, layshaft and reverse). Shifting from each gear is controlled by a lever through a pneumatic servo. Shifting from the high to the low range, or vice-versa, is by an electropneumatic control with a pre-selector switch, interlocked with the clutch pedal.

FIAT 6605 TM69 (6 × 6) artillery tractor fitted with removable cab roof, bows and tarpaulin cover

FIAT 6605 FH (6 × 6) with hydraulically-operated crane mounted to rear of cab

The transfer box is mechanical and consists of helical constant mesh gears mounted on three shafts (input, intermediate and output) of which the input one carries the dog clutch with a lockable divider differential distributing power to front and rear axles.

Mounted at the rear of the vehicle is a worm type winch with a capacity of 10 000 kg which can be used to the front or rear of the truck and has 60 metres of 18 mm diameter cable.

VARIANTS
FIAT 6605 FH
This is almost identical to the 6605 TM but has a shorter rear cargo area as a hydraulic crane is mounted between the cab and the cargo area for unloading the pallets of ammunition. The prototype was completed in 1974 with first production vehicles being completed in 1976.
FIAT 6605 AG
This is a recovery vehicle and has a hydraulically operated crane with a telescopic jib mounted at the rear. This has a maximum lifting capacity of 7500 kg. When the crane is being used stabilisers are lowered each side of the vehicle. The front-mounted winch has a 9200 kg capacity and the rear winch a capacity of 20 000 kg. This vehicle is called the Autogru AG 70 5-ton by the Italian Army. The first prototype was completed in 1972 with the first production vehicles following in 1974. Full details of this model are given in the *Recovery vehicles* section.
FIAT 6605 A
This is the truck version and has a two-man cab with the cargo area at the rear with tiltable troop seats down each side, drop tailgate with integral steps, removable bows and a tarpaulin cover. The prototype was completed in 1974 with first production vehicles following in 1976.

STATUS
In production. In service with the Italian Army, Libya and Somalia. Somalia has 10 6605 TM, 200 6605 A, 12 10 500-litre fuel tankers, 10 recovery vehicles, 4 command posts, 5 aircraft refuellers and 50 8000-litre water tankers.

MANUFACTURER
FIAT, Direzione Mezzi Speciali, Corso G Marconi 10/20, Turin, Italy.

SPECIFICATIONS

Model	6605 TM	6605 FH	6605 A
Cab seating	1 + 11	1 + 11	1 + 1
Configuration	6 × 6	6 × 6	6 × 6
Weight (empty)	11 860 kg	12 600 kg	11 220 kg
(loaded)	17 000 kg	17 600 kg	18 820 kg
Max load	5000 kg	5000 kg	7600 kg
Towed load	15 000 kg	15 000 kg	15 000 kg
Length	7·33 m	7·33 m	7·33 m
Width	2·5 m	2·5 m	2·5 m
Height (cab)	2·92 m	2·92 m	2·74 m
(tarpaulin)	2·85 m	2·78 m	3·08 m
(load area)	1·533 m	1·533 m	1·522 m
Ground clearance	0·363 m	0·363 m	0·363 m
Track	2·072 m	2·072 m	2·072 m
Wheelbase	3·217 m + 1·365 m	3·217 m + 1·365 m	3·217 m + 1·365 m
Angle of approach/departure	45°/40°	45°/40°	45°/40°
Max speed (road)	78 km/h	78 km/h	78 km/h
Range	700 km	700 km	700 km
Fuel capacity	360 litres	360 litres	360 litres
Max gradient	60%	60%	60%
Max side slope	20%	20%	20%
Fording	1·5 m	1·5 m	1·5 m
Engine	Model 8212.02.500 6-cylinder in-line water-cooled diesel developing 219 hp		
Gearbox	manual with 8 forward and 1 reverse gears		
Clutch	dry, dual plate	dry, dual plate	dry, dual plate
Transfer box	2-speed	2-speed	2-speed
Steering	ZF hydraulic assisted	ZF hydraulic assisted	ZF hydraulic assisted
Turning radius	8 m	8 m	8 m
Suspension (front)	2 semi-elliptical constant rate leaf springs with double-acting hydraulic shock absorbers		
(rear)	rocker and torque arms with 2 constant rate leaf springs		
Tyres	14.00 × 20	14.00 × 20	14.00 × 20
Number of tyres	6 + 1 spare	6 + 1 spare	6 + 1 spare
Brakes (main)	drum air-operated on all wheels, dual circuit with connections for trailer braking		
(parking)	drum, hand-operated, mounted on transfer rear output shaft		
Electrical system	24 V	24 V	24 V
Batteries	4 × 12 V, 90 Ah	4 × 12 V, 90 Ah	4 × 12 V, 90 Ah

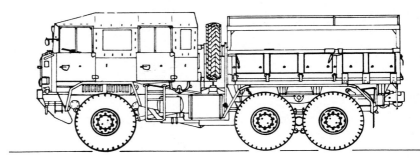

FIAT 6605 TM69 (6 × 6) artillery tractor

Astra BM 309 (6 × 6) Truck

DESCRIPTION
In 1983 Astra Veicoli introduced a new range of 6 × 6 trucks known as the 'Series 300' which are to be produced in a variety of wheelbases, engine fits, cabs and configurations. One of these is the BM 309 which is undergoing evaluation trials for the Italian Army.

The 'Series 300' are to be produced with two wheelbase lengths, 3·3 m + 1·4 m for tractor trucks and 3·5 m + 1·4 m for cargo and other chassis. Four different engine fits will be available (the BM 309 currently has a choice of two types, a FIAT and a Mercedes), and both 6 × 6 and 6 × 4 configurations will be available. Double and single cabs will be available. Numerous other options such as tyre sizes, power take-offs, etc, will be available. The current military version is the BM 309, details of which are provided in the specifications.

SPECIFICATIONS
Cab seating: 1 + 1
Configuration: 6 × 6
Weight:
(curb with FIAT engine) 10 180 kg
(curb with Mercedes engine) 9980 kg
Gross vehicle weight: 33 000 kg
Length: 7·06 m
Width: 2·5 m
Height: (overall) 3·06 m
Ground clearance: 0·385 m
Track:
(front) 2·047 m
(rear) 1·829 m
Wheelbase: 3·5 m + 1·4 m
Max speed: 80 km/h
Fuel capacity: 300 litres
Max gradient: 40%
Engine: FIAT 8280.02 diesel developing 352 hp at 2400 rpm or Mercedes OM423 diesel developing 355 hp at 2300 rpm

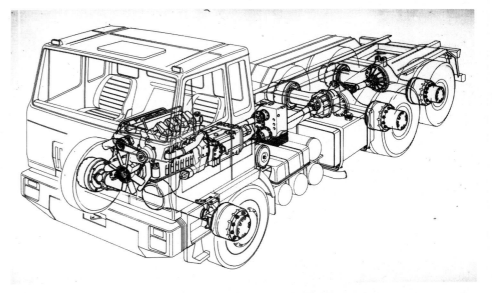

Drive layout of Astra BM 309 (6 × 6) truck

Gearbox: ZF 16-S-160 ECOSPLIT, mechanical synchronised, with 16 forward and 2 reverse gears
Steering: hydraulic servo
Turning radius: 9·75 m
Suspension:
(front) 4-leaf parabolic springs with hydraulic shock absorbers and torsion bar
(rear) 12-leaf semi-elliptical spring oscillating by pivot system; tandem axle is connected to the main frame by radius rod with rubber silent block
Brakes: dual circuit air

Tyres: 12.00 × 24
Number of tyres: 10 + 1 spare
Electrical system: 24 V

STATUS
Production commenced late 1983.

MANUFACTURER
Astra Veicoli Industriali SpA, Via Caorsana 79, 29100 Piacenza, Italy.

Chassis of Astra BM 309 (6 × 6) truck

Astra BM 20 Series (6 × 6) 10 000 kg Truck

DESCRIPTION
The two-door fibreglass cab with metal frame can be tilted forwards to 48 degrees allowing access to the engine for maintenance. The cab has seats for the driver and one passenger plus two emergency folding seats. The chassis is made of high elastic steel and consists of two double C-shaped side-members connected through rigid cross-members. The rear cargo area has drop sides, drop tailgate, removable bows and a tarpaulin cover.

VARIANTS
Dump truck
Full details of this are given in the *Construction equipment* section.
Recovery vehicle
Full details of this are given in the *Recovery vehicles* section.
Bridging Boat Carrier BM 20 NB1
This vehicle has the same chassis as the BM 20 N series but with provision for carrying, launching and recovery of a bridging boat. The bridging boat is carried on a platform to the rear of the cab which can be tilted through 45 degrees by means of a hydraulic multi-stage cylinder actuated by a hydraulic pump. The platform enables the launching and loading of the boat without any assistance apart from the driver in the cab.

This vehicle is now being evaluated by the Italian Army. Total weight loaded is 20 300 kg and the length with boat is 10·67 metres.
Truck Tractor for Engineer Corps Trailer Workshop BM 20 NC2
This vehicle, which is in service with the Italian Army, has the same chassis as the BM 20 N series but is equipped with a light body with drop sides and a drop tailgate. To the rear of the cab is a hydraulic crane which can lift 2500 kg to a height of 2·1 metres.
BM 20 NP1 Mobile Drilling Equipment
Details of this equipment are given in the *Construction equipment* section.

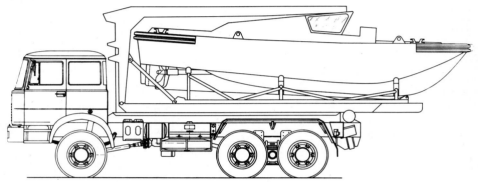

BM 20 NB1 (6 × 6) bridging boat carrier (not to 1/76th scale)

SPECIFICATIONS (BM 20 NC2)
Cab seating: 1 + 3
Configuration: 6 × 6
Weight:
  (empty) 11 550 kg
  (loaded, cross country) 22 100 kg
Max load:
  (road) 15 000 kg
  (cross country) 10 000 kg
Towed load: (road) 28 000 kg
Length: 7·51 m
Width: 2·5 m
Height: 2·75 m
Ground clearance: 0·265 m
Track:
  (front) 2 m
  (rear) 1·85 m
Wheelbase: 3·485 m + 1·3 m
Max speed: 67·2 km/h
Range: 1000 km
Fuel capacity: 280 litres
Max gradient: 60%
Fording: 1·2 m
Engine: FIAT 8210 6-cylinder in-line diesel developing 260 hp at 2200 rpm

Gearbox: ZF manual with 6 forward and 1 reverse gears
Clutch: single dry plate
Transfer box: 2-speed
Steering: hydraulic assisted
Turning radius: 11 m
Suspension:
  (front) semi-elliptical springs with four rubber bumpers and hydraulic shock absorbers
  (rear) oscillating semi-elliptical type springs with rocker arm system
Tyres: 12.00 × 20
Number of tyres: 10 + 1 spare
Brakes:
  (main) air
  (parking) mechanical
Electrical system: 24 V
Batteries: 4 × 12 V

STATUS
Production. The BM 20 NC2 tractor truck for engineer corps trailer workshop is in service with the Italian Army.

MANUFACTURER
Astra Veicoli Industriali SpA, Via Caorsana 79, 29100 Piacenza, Italy.

BM 20 NC2 (6 × 6) tractor truck for Engineer Corps trailer workshop as used by Italian Army (T J Gander)

Astra BM 20 NB1 (6 × 6) bridging boat carrier (T J Gander)

CP 56 (6 × 6) 10 000 kg Bridging Truck

DESCRIPTION

The CP 56 bridging truck (Autocarro de Ponte), also known as the FIAT/OM 6600, was developed in the 1950s by OM and was in production from 1956 to 1964. It is similar in appearance to the American 5-ton (6 × 6) M139 chassis which is used for a number of applications including carrying bridging equipment and is a member of the M54 series of 5-ton (6 × 6) trucks.

The layout of the CP 56 is conventional with the engine at the front, cab in the centre and the cargo area at the rear. The two-door cab has a removable canvas roof and a windscreen which can be folded forward onto the bonnet. The rear cargo area is all steel and is used for carrying bridging equipment.

SPECIFICATIONS
Cab seating: 1 + 2
Configuration: 6 × 6
Weight:
　(empty) 12 650 kg
　(loaded) 20 158 kg
Max load:
　(road) 9010 kg
　(cross country) 7508 kg
Towed load: 9000 kg
Length: 9·55 m
Width: 2·92 m
Height: 2·93 m
Wheelbase: 4·75 m + 1·42 m

CP 56 (6 × 6) 10 000 kg bridging trucks of Italian Army

Engine: FIAT 203B 6-cylinder in-line petrol developing 196 hp at 2000 rpm
Gearbox: manual, dual range with 4 forward and 1 reverse gears
Transfer box: 2-speed
Tyres: 14.00 × 20
Number of tyres: 10 + 1 spare

STATUS
Production complete. In service with Italy, Netherlands and Venezuela.

MANUFACTURER
FIAT Azienda OM, Brescia, Italy.

FIAT 260 PM 35 (6 × 4 and 6 × 6) 10 000 kg Trucks

DESCRIPTION

The FIAT 260 PM 35 series of 6 × 4 and 6 × 6 10 000 kg trucks has been developed by the company from standard commercial vehicles. The chassis consists of section side-members connected by cross-members with sheet steel bumper at the front and towing hook and bumper at the rear.

The all-steel two-door fully enclosed cab is of the forward control type and can be tilted forward by one man to give access to the engine for maintenance. The steering wheel and both seats are adjustable and a two-speed electrical ventilating system, combined with a water heater and defroster, is fitted as standard.

The rear cargo body is of sheet steel with wood-lined platform, fixed headboard, tiltable side boards with folding benches (22 troop seats), tiltable and removable tailgate with tiltable ladders for access to the platform. The body is attached to the chassis by means of elastic brackets with the spare wheel between the cab and the cargo body. Standard equipment includes removable bows and tarpaulin cover, black out lights, transceiver power input radio suppressed, auxiliary receptacle and master switch, NATO standard 12-point socket for trailer and tyre inflation system.

The 6 × 6 model has a combined gearbox and transfer box split from the engine and converter. The transfer box allows the torque distribution between front axle and rear bogie through a central differential, electro-pneumatically lockable.

The 6 × 4 model has a steering dead front axle with the 6 × 6 model having steer drive axle with epicyclic hub reduction. Both models have the same high articulation bogie for on/off highway use composed of two drive axles with hub reductions and pneumatically lockable differentials.

Optional equipment includes an OM DF 0·9 torque converter and a 1000 kg jib crane mounted to the cab rear.

VARIANTS
The chassis can be used for a variety of other applica-

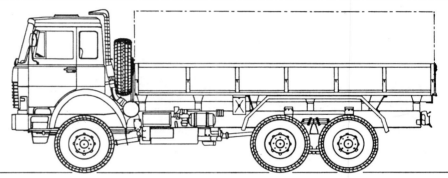

FIAT 260 PM 35 (6 × 6) 10 000 kg truck

FIAT 260 PM 35 (6 × 6) 10 000 kg truck

tions including a tractor truck for semi-trailers weighing up to 24 000 kg with load, mobile workshop, water or fuel tanker and a recovery vehicle. The latter would be fitted with a hydraulically operated crane with a capacity of 12 000 kg and a jib extendable from 4·4 to 7·4 metres and an auxiliary recovery winch.

STATUS
Production.

MANUFACTURER
FIAT, Direzione Mezzi Speciali, Corso G Marconi 10/20, Turin, Italy.

SPECIFICATIONS

	6 × 4	6 × 6
Configuration	6 × 4	6 × 6
Weight (loaded)	20 900 kg	24 000 kg
Max load	10 000 kg	14 000 kg
Towed load	20 000 kg	20 000 kg
Length (excluding body)	7·8 m	7·8 m
Width	2·5 m	2·5 m
Height (cab, unloaded)	3·125 m	3·26 m
Ground clearance	0·316 m	0·312 m
Track (front)	2·069 m	1·927 m
(rear)	1·809 m	1·809 m
Wheelbase	3·85 m + 1·38 m	3·85 m + 1·38 m
Angle of approach/departure	28°/22°	33°/27°
Max speed	96 km/h	94 km/h
Range	600 km	600 km
Fuel capacity	300 litres	300 litres
Max gradient	60%	60%
Side slope	30%	30%
Fording	0·65 m	0·65 m
Engine	FIAT 8280.02 V-8 liquid-cooled diesel developing 352 hp at 2400 rpm	

	6 × 4	6 × 6
Configuration		
Gearbox	FIAT 12802, 8 forward and 2 reverse gears	ZF 4S-150 GPA combined gearbox and transfer box, 8 forward and 1 reverse gears
Steering	ZF recirculating ball with integral power assistance	
Turning radius	9·75 m	9·75 m
Suspension (front)	single flexible leaf springs and hydraulic shock absorbers	
(rear)	single flexible leaf springs reversed and hydraulic telescopic shock absorbers	
Tyres	12.00 R 20 PR 18	12.00 R 20 PR 18
Number of tyres	10 + 1 spare	10 + 1 spare
Brakes (main)	air	air
(parking)	spring loaded acting on rear axle	
(exhaust)	pneumatic, controlled by separate foot control	
Electrical system	24 V	24 V
Batteries	12 V, 143 Ah	12 V, 143 Ah

JAPAN

Type 73 (4 × 4) 2000 kg Truck

DEVELOPMENT
The Type 73 (4 × 4) 2000 kg truck was standardised in 1973 as the successor to the Nissan and Toyota (4 × 4) 750 kg trucks that had been in service since the 1950s. The Type 73 is a full military version of the Hino WB500 (4 × 4) truck which was developed specifically for the military market.

DESCRIPTION
The Type 73 has an over-engine cab with a steel back and sides up to seat-top height and steel doors with glass windows. The single-piece windscreen can be folded forwards. The roof is a single-piece waterproof tarpaulin that can be fixed in place by removable braces. With the tarpaulin in place a high-capacity heater-blower-defroster system can be used. Seats for the driver and one passenger are provided, each with space for kit stowage behind.

The cargo body is all steel but has wooden side stakes and rails that are held in place by latches and unfold to serve as benches. The tail-gate has a built-in step that will unfold when a ring on each side is pulled. A heavy canvas tilt and braces can be used to cover the area which is three metres long and 1·95 metres wide.

Standard equipment includes a rear fender, tool box, canvas tilt and spare tyre and carrier. Optional equipment includes a winch (front-mounted), power take-off, and tropical cooling system.

VARIANTS
The only known variant is an ambulance with a fully enclosed cab and rear body.

SPECIFICATIONS
Cab seating: 1 + 1
Configuration: 4 × 4
Weight:
(empty) 3195 kg
(gross weight, on road) 5355 kg
(gross weight, off road) 4855 kg
Max load:
(on road) 2000 kg
(off road) 1500 kg
Front axle load: (on road, loaded) 2325 kg
Rear axle load: (on road, loaded) 3030 kg
Length: 5·36 m
Width: 2·09 m

Type 73 (4 × 4) 2000 kg truck (Kensuke Ebata)

Height: 2·49 m
Ground clearance: 0·28 m
Wheelbase: 2·9 m
Track:
(front) 1·61 m
(rear) 1·635 m
Angle of approach/departure: 37°/32°
Max speed: 87 km/h
Fuel capacity: 115 litres
Max gradient: 60%
Fording: 0·8 m
Engine: Hino DQ100 diesel developing 95 hp at 3000 rpm
Gearbox: 5 forward and 1 reverse gears
Transfer box: 2-speed
Clutch: single dry disc
Steering: recirculating ball

Turning radius: 6·4 m
Suspension: semi-elliptic leaf springs with shock absorbers
Tyres: 8.25 × 20
Number of tyres: 4 + 1 spare
Brakes: hydraulic with vacuum servo
Electrical system: 24 V
Batteries: 2 × 12 V, 100 Ah
Generator: 400 W

STATUS
Production. In service with the Japanese Ground Self-Defence Force.

MANUFACTURER
Hino Motors Limited, 1-1 Hinodai 3-chome, Hino-shi, Tokyo, Japan.

Isuzu (4 × 4) 2500 kg Trucks

DESCRIPTION
There are two basic production versions of the Isuzu (4 × 4) truck, the TSD45 and the TSD55 with a longer wheelbase. Both may be produced in a variety of forms which include numerous commercial configurations. The military versions are usually confined to cargo bodies or flat-bed types.

Layout and configuration of the Isuzu trucks are con-ventional with the engine at the front, the all-steel cab placed centrally and the cargo or payload area at the rear. Cargo bodies may be covered with a tarpaulin. Various standard fittings may be found on nearly all models; military options include power take-offs, towing hooks, radio fixtures, and a tyre inflation device.

One service version has an open flat-bed rear with a hydraulic crane that is extended forward over the cab for travelling. Two outriggers on each side of the crane provide stabilisation when the crane is in use. This crane version has the spare tyre stowed under the body rear while the cargo version has it behind the cab.

STATUS
Production. In service with the Japanese Ground Self-Defence Force.

MANUFACTURER
Isuzu Motors Limited, 22-10, Minami-oi, 6-chome, Shinagawa-ku, Tokyo, Japan.

SPECIFICATIONS

Model	TSD45	TSD55
Cab seating	1 + 1	1 + 1
Configuration	4 × 4	4 × 4
Weight (empty, cab and chassis)	3825 kg	3880 kg
(max permissible)	12 500 kg	12 500 kg
Length	6·465 m	6·91 m
Width	2·2 m	2·2 m
Height (top of cab)	2·43 m	2·445 m
(load area)	1·03 m	1·045 m
Ground clearance	0·23 m	0·23 m
Track (front)	1·68 m	1·68 m
(rear)	1·74 m	1·74 m
Wheelbase	4 m	4·445 m
Max speed	88 km/h	88 km/h
Fuel capacity	100 or 200 litres	100 or 200 litres

Model	TSD45	TSD55
Engine	6BD1 6-cylinder, in-line, 5·784-litre water-cooled diesel developing 160 hp at 3200 rpm	
Gearbox	Isuzu manual with 5 forward and 1 reverse gears	
Transfer box	2-speed	2-speed
Clutch	single dry plate	single dry plate
Steering	recirculating ball	recirculating ball
Turning radius	8·7 m	9·4 m
Suspension	semi-elliptical alloy springs, lever type shock absorbers	
Tyres	8.25 × 20	8.25 × 20
Brakes (standard)	hydraulic with vacuum or optional air assistance	
(braking)	mechanical	mechanical
Electrical system	24 V	24 V
Batteries	2 × 12 V, 65 Ah	2 × 12 V, 65 Ah

Isuzu (4 × 4) 2500 kg cargo truck with crane

Isuzu (4 × 4) 2500 kg cargo truck from side

Isuzu (4 × 4) 2500 kg cargo truck with crane

Isuzu (4 × 4) 2500 kg cargo truck

Isuzu (6 × 6) 2500 kg Trucks

DEVELOPMENT
The first Isuzu 6 × 6 truck completed in 1953 was called the TW and was almost identical in appearance to the American GMC 2½-ton truck of the Second World War. It was subsequently tested in the USA and in 1957 was adopted by the US Army for use in Japan. It was also adopted by the Japanese Self-Defence Forces and other countries in the Far East including South Korea, South Viet-Nam and the Philippines. First production vehicles were completed in 1957 and since then many versions have been built, including the TWD20 (1963) and the more recent TWD25, in both single and dual rear wheel configurations. They can carry 5000 kg of cargo on roads or 2500 kg of cargo across country.

DESCRIPTION
The layout of the vehicle is conventional with the engine at the front, two-door cab in the centre and the cargo area at the rear with fixed sides, drop tailgate, removable bows and a tarpaulin cover. The cab has a canvas top and a windscreen which folds forward onto the bonnet. Some versions, for example the tankers, have a fully enclosed cab. Many vehicles have a winch mounted at the front.

VARIANTS
Air compressor
Mounted on the rear is a compressor unit which is used to power a jack-hammer, concrete breaker and other air-driven tools and also for inflating and deflating inflatable craft. Basic specifications are length 6·595 metres, width 2·25 metres, height 2·595 metres and weight 8070 kg.
Dump truck
Two models are in service, one with a dump body that tips to the rear and the other with a dump body that tips to the sides or rear. Both single- and dual-rear wheel models are in service and all can be used for carrying troops as removable seats can be fitted down either side. Basic specifications are (with data in square brackets relating to the model with dual rear wheels) length: 6·3 [6·4] metres, width 2·22 metres, height 2·92 [3·02] metres and empty weight 6430 [6390] kg.
Cargo (long wheelbase)
Specifications are length 8·69 metres, width 2·4 metres, height 2·92 metres and empty weight 6860 kg.
Shop/van
There are many variants of this model including engineering (general), engineering (artillery), engineering (small arms), maintenance (general), maintenance (electric), and maintenance (communications). Basic specifications are length 6·91 metres, width 2·44 metres, height 3·19 metres and empty weight 6500 kg.
Tanker (fuel)
This carries 5000 or 2800 litres.
Tanker (water)
This carries 2800 litres and is fitted with a filtration system. Its basic specifications are length 6·7 metres, width 2·3 metres, height 2·68 metres and empty weight 6320 kg.
Wrecker (light)
This has a hydraulically-operated crane at the rear.
122 mm multiple rocket launcher
During the 1982 invasion of Lebanon, Israeli troops captured examples of Isuzu (6 × 6) 2500 kg trucks carrying two banks of 15 122 mm rocket launching tubes. For an illustration of this vehicle/rocket combination see *Jane's Armour and Artillery 1983–84*, page 743.

STATUS
Production complete. In service with the Japanese Ground Self-Defence Force and other armed forces.

MANUFACTURER
Isuzu Motors Limited, 22-10, Minami-oi, 6-chome, Shinagawa-ku, Tokyo, Japan.

Isuzu (6 × 6) 2500 kg trucks with air compressor (Kensuke Ebata)

Isuzu (6 × 6) 2500 kg truck with water tanker body (Kensuke Ebata)

Isuzu (6 × 6) 2500 kg truck towing 105 mm M101 howitzer (Kensuke Ebata)

Isuzu (6 × 6) 2500 kg dump truck (rear tipping model) being used as troop transporter (Kensuke Ebata)

SPECIFICATIONS (TWD 20)
Configuration: 6 × 6
Cab seating: 1 + 2
Weight:
(empty) 5695 kg
(loaded, road) 10 695 kg
(loaded, cross country) 8195 kg
Max load:
(road) 5000 kg
(cross country) 2500 kg
Length: 7·09 m
Width: 2·283 m

Height:
(cab) 2·41 m
(tarpaulin) 2·995 m
Ground clearance: 0·23 m
Track:
(front) 1·585 m
(rear) 1·744 m
Wheelbase: 4 m (first axle to centre of rear bogie)
Max road speed: 85 km/h
Fuel capacity: 100 litres
Engine: DA120 6-cylinder water-cooled diesel developing 125 hp at 2600 rpm
Gearbox: manual, 4 forward and 1 reverse gears

Clutch: single dry plate
Transfer box: 2-speed
Turning radius: 9 m
Suspension:
(front) semi-elliptical leaf springs and hydraulic shock absorbers
(rear) semi-elliptical leaf springs and torque rods
Tyres: 7.50 × 20
Number of tyres: 10 + 1 spare (or 6 + 1 spare)
Brakes:
(main) hydraulic
(parking) mechanical
Electrical system: 24 V

Toyota (6 × 6) 2500 kg Trucks

DESCRIPTION
The first model, the FQS, was introduced in 1955 for both civilian and military use and was adopted by the Japanese Self-Defence Force, US Army in Japan and other armies in the Far East. The layout of the vehicle is similar to the Isuzu vehicles in this class and it can carry 5000 kg of cargo on roads or 2500 kg of cargo across country. The six-cylinder diesel engine is coupled to a manual gearbox with four forward and one reverse

gears and a two-speed transfer box. Variants include compressor, dump truck, fire-fighting vehicle, shop/van, water tanker and a wrecker.

SPECIFICATIONS
Weight: (empty) 5235 kg
Length: 6·85 m
Width: 2·26 m
Height: 2·79 m
Wheelbase: 3·492 m (first axle to centre of rear bogie)
Tyres: 7.50 × 20

STATUS
Production complete. In service with the Japanese Self-Defence Force and other armed forces in Southeast Asia.

MANUFACTURER
Toyota Motor Company Limited, 1 Toyota-cho, Toyota-shi, Aichi-ken, Japan.

Type 73 (6 × 6) 3500 kg Truck

DEVELOPMENT
This has been developed by Isuzu from the late 1960s to replace the current range of 2500 kg (6 × 6) trucks used by the Japanese Self-Defence Force. After trials and modifications it was standardised in 1973 as the Type 73 large truck series; its company designation is SKW 440M. In addition to its specialised roles it is widely used to tow artillery such as 40 mm anti-aircraft guns and 105 mm M101 howitzers as well as trailers carrying the HAWK SAM.

DESCRIPTION
The forward control cab has a windscreen that can be folded forward onto the bonnet and a removable canvas top. The rear cargo body is all steel and has a drop tailgate, bench troop seats down either side, removable bows and a tarpaulin cover. All models have single rear wheels.

VARIANTS
Cargo with hydraulic crane
This is the basic model with a hydraulic crane mounted to the rear of the cab. Basic specifications are length 7·13 metres, width 2·41 metres, height 3·5 metres and empty weight 7500 kg.
Dump truck (utility)
This has a rear tipper. Basic specifications are length 6·89 metres, width 2·43 metres, height 3·17 metres and empty weight 7670 kg.
Tanker (aviation fuel)
This has a filtration system to the rear of the cab and a fuel tank at very back. Specifications are length 7·3 metres, width 2·45 metres, height 2·71 metres, empty weight 8220 kg and loaded weight 12 220 kg.
Tanker (utility)
Specifications are length 7·01 metres, width 2·45 metres, height 2·71 metres, empty weight 7515 kg, and payload 5100 kg of paraffin or 4800 kg of petrol.

Anti-aircraft control
This is a flatbed model with shelter-mounted Type 71 early warning radar (J/TPS-P5). Specifications are length 7·26 metres, width 2·49 metres, height 2·71 metres and weight (without shelter) 6620 kg.
Light wrecker
This has a hydraulically-operated crane mounted at the rear with a maximum lifting capacity of 4800 kg. Basic specifications are length 7·505 metres, width 2·43 metres, height 2·88 metres and weight 12 300 kg.
Shop/van
This is the basic model with a fully enclosed rear body that is used for a variety of roles such as forward maintenance. Basic specifications are length 6·67 metres, width 2·47 metres, height 2·765 metres and empty weight 6490 kg.
Tan-SAM carriers
This is used as the carrier for two components of the Tan-SAM surface-to-air missile system. One is the fire-

Type 73 (6 × 6) 3500 kg truck carrying shelter-mounted early warning radar (Kensuke Ebata)

Type 73 (6 × 6) 3500 kg fuel tanker (aviation) (Kensuke Ebata)

Type 73 (6 × 6) 3500 kg truck (Kensuke Ebata)

Type 73 (6 × 6) 3500 kg truck towing trailer carrying HAWK SAMs (Kensuke Ebata)

control system (FCS) vehicle which carries a control module housing a radar system and aerial at the rear. A 30 kW generator is placed just behind the cab. Three hydraulic outriggers provide stabilisation. The Type 73 is also used as the carrier for the Tan-SAM launcher with the actual launcher having two arms each holding two missiles. Normally the launcher receives fire-control information from the FCS but each launcher vehicle carries a demountable optical guidance system for the missiles. The Type 73 launcher vehicle is stabilised by four outrigger legs when in action.

SPECIFICATIONS (basic cargo truck)
Cab seating: 1 + 1
Configuration: 6 × 6
Weight:
(empty) 6640 kg
(loaded, road) 12 640 kg
(loaded, cross country) 10 140 kg

Max load:
(road) 6000 kg
(cross country) 3500 kg
Length: 6·67 m
Width: 2·41 m
Height: 3·02 m
Track:
(front) 1·8 m
(rear) 1·82 m
Wheelbase: 3·85 m
Angle of approach/departure: 45°/40°
Max road speed: 90 km/h
Gradient: 60%
Fording: 0·8 m
Engine: Model 8PA1 V-8 liquid-cooled diesel developing 175 hp at 2800 rpm
Gearbox: manual, 5 forward and 1 reverse gears
Clutch: single dry plate
Transfer box: 2-speed

Turning radius: 9·2 m
Suspension:
(front) semi-elliptical springs and hydraulic shock absorbers
(rear) inverted semi-elliptical springs and hydraulic shock absorbers
Tyres: 9.00 × 20
Number of tyres: 6 + 1 spare
Brakes:
(main) air/hydraulic
(parking) mechanical
Electrical system: 24 V

STATUS
In production. In service with the Japanese Ground Self-Defence Force.

MANUFACTURER
Isuzu Motors Limited, 22-10, Minami-oi, 6-chome, Shinagawa-ku, Tokyo, Japan.

Hino (6 × 6) 4000 kg Truck

DESCRIPTION
Hino has developed a series of 6 × 6 trucks which can carry 4000 kg of cargo across country or 8000 kg of cargo on roads, and are also available for civilian applications such as tractor trucks. The basic cargo model has a conventional layout with the engine at the front, two-door cab in the centre with a windscreen which folds forward onto the bonnet and a removable canvas top and the cargo area at the rear with fixed sides, drop tailgate, removable bows and a tarpaulin cover.

VARIANTS
Dump truck
Two models are in service, one that tips to the rear only and a second which tips to both sides and the rear. Basic specifications are length 6·75 metres, width 2·41 metres, height 2·66 metres, empty weight 8710 kg, maximum payload across country 4000 kg and maximum payload on roads 7000 kg.
Water sprinkler
This has a water tank behind the cab fitted with a sprinkler system.

Wrecker
Two models are in service, one with a hydraulically-operated and the other with a mechanically-operated crane, both with a maximum lifting capacity in the static configuration of 6700 kg and a suspended tow capacity of 4000 kg. Both are fitted with front- and rear-mounted winches. Basic specifications are as follows (those in square brackets relate to the model with a hydraulic crane) overall length 8·37 [9·3] metres, width 2·45 [2·45] metres, height 3·02 [2·88] metres, maximum road speed 65 [78] km/h and powered by a six-cylinder water-cooled diesel engine developing 125 [160] hp.
Tractor truck
This is used to tow 6000 kg and 10 000 kg trailers and its basic specifications are length 5·22 metres, width 2·37 metres, height 2·83 metres, empty weight 5460 kg, maximum speed 65 km/h and engine six-cylinder water-cooled diesel developing 140 hp.
Type 67 Model 30 Rocket Launcher
The chassis is used as the launcher for the 307 mm Type 67 Model 30 rocket, details of which are given in *Jane's Armour and Artillery, 1983–84*, page 729. A 4000 kg truck is also used as a missile resupply vehicle; it carries four Type 67 Model 30 rockets and has a hydraulic crane for loading.

SPECIFICATIONS
Cab seating: 1 + 2
Configuration: 6 × 6
Weight:
(empty) 8040 kg
(loaded, road) 16 040 kg
(loaded, cross country) 12 040 kg
Max load:
(road) 8000 kg
(cross country) 4000 kg
Length: 7·69 m
Width: 2·44 m
Height: 2·92 m
Max road speed: 78 km/h
Engine: 6-cylinder water-cooled diesel developing 160 hp at 2400 rpm

STATUS
Production complete. In service with the Japanese Ground Self-Defence Force.

MANUFACTURER
Hino Motors Limited, 1-1 Hinodai 3-chome, Hino-shi, Tokyo, Japan.

Hino (6 × 6) 4000 kg truck complete with bows and tarpaulin cover (Kensuke Ebata)

Hino (6 × 6) 4000 kg truck towing trailer carrying Nike-Hercules SAM (Kensuke Ebata)

Hino (6 × 6) 4000 kg truck rocket resupply vehicle with four Type 67 Model 30 rockets (Kensuke Ebata)

Hino (6 × 6) 4000 kg hydraulically-operated wrecker (K Nogi)

Mitsubishi W121P (6 × 6) 6000 kg Truck

DEVELOPMENT
In the 1950s Mitsubishi introduced the Fuso range of 6 × 6 trucks which were based on American Second World War type trucks. In the early 1960s these were replaced in production by the improved 6W series which had a redesigned cab as well as numerous other improvements. Production was completed in 1973.

DESCRIPTION
The layout of all models is similar with the engine at the front and cab in the centre. The cab has a removable canvas top and a windscreen that folds forward onto the bonnet. The rear cargo area has troop seats, drop tailgate, removable bows and a tarpaulin cover. Behind the cab, on the right side, is a winch that can be used to the front or rear.

VARIANTS
Tractor truck
The 6000 kg model is used to tow semi-trailers weighing up to 20 tonnes and the 10 000 kg model for semi-trailers up to 25 tonnes. The 6000 kg model is used by JGSDF Engineer Units and the 10 000 kg by construction battalions and engineer equipment companies. Basic specifications are length 7·57 metres, width 2·48 metres, height 3 metres, weight unloaded 9860 kg, maximum road speed 70 km/h and engine six-cylinder water-cooled diesel developing 200 hp.
Wrecker
Two models are in service, one with a mechanical and the other with a hydraulic crane and both with front- and rear-mounted winches. Basic specifications are as follows (those in square brackets relate to the model with a hydraulic crane): length overall 9·9 [9·32] metres, width 2·48 [2·48] metres, height 3·14 [3·01] metres, empty weight 13 400 [16 570] kg and maximum road speed 72 km/h.

SPECIFICATIONS
Configuration: 6 × 6
Weight:
  (empty) 9700 kg
  (loaded, road) 21 700 kg
  (loaded, cross country) 15 700 kg
Max load:
  (road) 12 000 kg
  (cross country) 6000 kg
Length: 7·42 m
Width: 2·48 m
Height: 3 m
Max road speed: 72 km/h
Engine: 6-cylinder water-cooled diesel developing 200 hp

STATUS
Production complete. In service with the Japanese Ground Self-Defence Force.

MANUFACTURER
Mitsubishi Motors Company, 33-8 Shiba 5-chome, Minato-ku, Tokyo, Japan.

Early model of (6 × 6) 6000 kg truck showing winch to rear of cab (Kensuke Ebata)

Late production model (6 × 6) 6000 kg truck towing twin 35 mm Oerlikon AA gun (Kensuke Ebata)

Late production model (6 × 6) tractor truck towing semi-trailer (K Nogi)

Mitsubishi FW115 (6 × 6) Trucks

DEVELOPMENT
The Mitsubishi FW115 series of trucks was introduced in 1979 when it replaced the FW105 series in production. The FW105 series, in its turn, had replaced the earlier W121P trucks which went out of production in 1973.

DESCRIPTION
The basic FW115 (6 × 6) truck is a forward-control design with an all-steel cab with seats for the driver and two passengers. The doors have extra vision panels for the driver and warning lights are set forward on the roof. The area immediately behind the cab is used for tool and spare wheel stowage on most models, and a heavy-duty fender extends behind the front wheel to just forward of the second wheel to protect the fuel tanks, transmission and other engine extensions. A towing hook is usually provided at the rear. The front headlights are set into the heavy-duty bumpers.

VARIANTS
FW115 L1 heavy duty truck
This is the base model of the FW115 series and has a

Mitsubishi FW115 M2 (6 × 6) long-bodied floating bridge carrier

Mitsubishi FW115 M4 (6 × 6) drop side truck

Mitsubishi FW115 L1 (6 × 6) heavy duty truck

Mitsubishi FW115 LD1 (6 × 6) heavy duty truck with winch

conventional heavy duty rear cargo area with provision for a canvas tilt, when not in use the folded tilt supports are stowed forward. The cargo area has a tailgate at the rear and a spare wheel is stowed in the space between the cab rear and the front of the cargo area. The FW115 L1 can be used as an artillery tractor for calibres up to 155 mm.

FW115 LD1 heavy duty truck
The FW115 LD1 heavy duty truck has an all-steel heavy duty cargo body with a protective steel bulkhead protecting the rear of the cab. It is provided with a centrally-mounted winch with the controls on each side of the cargo area between the body and the cab rear.

FM115 M1 recovery vehicle
This variant of the FW115 has the rear occupied by a large telescopic crane with a limited provision for traverse. The crane has a large cable-actuated pulley and is secured when travelling. The crane is controlled from the left-hand side and a spare wheel is stowed on the right. A high-capacity winch is located centrally and the cable pays out to the rear. A smaller self-recovery winch is situated under the front bumper on the right-hand side. There are four stabiliser legs for the crane which are located one leg fore and aft of each of the four rear wheels. Their stabilising feet can be lowered directly to the ground in use. Various tool and equipment lockers are provided.

FW115 M2
The FW115 M2 has a lengthened wheelbase and cargo body to carry floating bridge components. The cargo body extends forward to just behind the cab.
FW115 M4
The FW115 M4 has the same lengthened wheelbase and body as the FW115 M2 but is used as a conventional heavy duty cargo truck and is equipped with drop sides. There is provision for a canvas tilt.

STATUS
In production. In service with the Japanese Ground Self-Defence Force.

MANUFACTURER
Mitsubishi Motors Corporation, 33-8 Shiba 5-chome, Minato-ku, Tokyo, Japan.

Mitsubishi FW115 M1 (6 × 6) recovery vehicle

SPECIFICATIONS

Model	FW115 L1	FW115 LD1	FW115 M1	FW115 M2	FW115 M4
Configuration	6 × 6	6 × 6	6 × 6	6 × 6	6 × 6
Weight (empty)	9660 kg	11 300 kg	18 290 kg	11 480 kg	10 130 kg
(loaded)	19 160 kg	19 800 kg	18 530 kg	18 970 kg	19 870 kg
Length	8·39 m	8·135 m	9·32 m	9·205 m	9·285 m
Width	2·49 m	2·49 m	2·49 m	2·49 m	2·49 m
Height	3·05 m	3·1 m	3·23 m	3·05 m	3·09 m
Max road speed	95 km/h	95 km/h	95 km/h	95 km/h	95 km/h

Type 74 (6 × 6) 10 000 kg Truck

DESCRIPTION
This is a standard commercial truck modified to meet the requirements of the Japanese Ground Self-Defence Force for a 6 × 6 vehicle with a payload of 10 000 kg. It was standardised in 1974 as the Type 74 special large truck.

The all-steel cab is the forward control type and the rear cargo area has drop sides, drop tailgate, removable bows and a tarpaulin cover. The short model of the Type 74 does not have drop sides. A model of the Type 74 is also used to carry bridging equipment for which special unloading equipment is fitted.

SPECIFICATIONS
(data in square brackets relate to short model)
Configuration: 6 × 6
Weight:
(empty) 9850 [9600] kg
(loaded) 19 850 [19 100] kg
Max load: 10 000 [9500] kg

Length: 9·22 [8·3] m
Width: 2·49 [2·49] m
Height: 3·055 [3] m
Max road speed: 100 km/h
Engine: 300 hp diesel

Type 74 (6 × 6) 10 000 kg truck for transporting bridging equipment (K Nogi)

STATUS
In service with the Japanese Ground Self-Defence Force.

KOREA, DEMOCRATIC PEOPLE'S REPUBLIC

Victory-58 (4 × 2) 2000 kg Truck

DEVELOPMENT
The Victory-58 (4 × 2) 2000 kg truck entered production in 1958 and is basically a copy of the Soviet GAZ-51 (4 × 2) vehicle built to a much lower standard, including weaker springs and an engine that develops less than its stated 70 hp and has a much higher fuel consumption.

Civilian-built models have dual rear wheels and the military model single rear wheels.

DESCRIPTION
The Victory-58 has an all-steel two-seat cab with the cargo area at the rear. The cargo area is a wooden platform with three hinged side benches along both sides of the vehicle that can be folded up for carrying cargo. The rear tailgate drops down and bows and a tarpaulin cover can be fitted if required.

SPECIFICATIONS
Cab seating: 1 + 1
Configuration: 4 × 2

Weight:
(empty) 2710 kg
(loaded, road) 5360 kg
(loaded, cross country) 4710 kg
Max load:
(road) 2650 kg
(cross country) 2000 kg
Towed load: (road) 3500 kg
Load area: 2·94 × 1·99 m
Length: 5·525 m
Width: 2·2 m
Height: 2·13 m
Ground clearance: 0·244 m
Track:
(front) 1·585 m
(rear) 1·65 m
Wheelbase: 3·3 m
Angle of approach/departure: 40°/32°
Max speed: 70 km/h
Range: 344 km
Fuel capacity: 90 litres

Gradient: 26%
Fording: 0·64 m
Engine: Victory-58, 6-cylinder water-cooled petrol developing 70 hp at 2800 rpm
Gearbox: manual, 4 forward and 1 reverse gears
Clutch: single dry plate
Transfer box: none
Turning radius: 7·62 m
Suspension: (front and rear) semi-elliptical leaf springs
Tyres: 7.50 × 20
Brakes:
(main) hydraulic
(parking) mechanical
Electrical system: 12 V

STATUS
In production. In service with the North Korean Army.

MANUFACTURER
Tokch'on Plant, P'Yongan-Namde, Democratic People's Republic of Korea.

KOREA, REPUBLIC

Kiamaster (4 × 4) 1250 kg Truck

DESCRIPTION
The Kiamaster (4 × 4) 1250 kg truck has a conventional forward control cab constructed from steel. The cargo area at the rear is normally open but there is provision for a canvas tilt, and slatted sides are normally fitted. Internally the cargo area may be left open for general cargo or fitted with seats or benches for troop transport. Dual tyres are fitted on the rear axle. The cargo area is 3·5 metres long, 2 metres wide and 0·39 metre high. A rear tailgate is provided.

SPECIFICATIONS
Cab seating: 1 + 2
Configuration: 4 × 4
Weight:
(empty) 3950 kg
(loaded) 5365 kg

Max load: (cross country) 1250 kg
Load area: 3·5 × 2 m
Length: 5·92 m
Width: 2·15 m
Height: 2·39 m
Ground clearance: 0·25 m
Track:
(front) 1·7 m
(rear) 1·62 m
Wheelbase: 3·2 m
Max speed: 100 km/h
Fuel capacity: 140·2 litres
Gradient: 60%
Engine: 6-cylinder, in-line, 4·052-litre, water-cooled diesel developing 115 hp at 3600 rpm
Gearbox: manual, with 5 forward and 1 reverse gears
Transfer box: 2-speed
Turning radius: 8·5 m

Clutch: hydraulic, single dry plate
Steering: ball and nut
Suspension: semi-elliptical springs, double-action shock absorbers
Tyres: 7·50 × 20
Brakes:
(main) vacuum, hydraulic drum
(parking) mechanical plus prop shaft brake
Electrical system: 24 V

STATUS
Production. May be in service with the South Korean armed forces.

MANUFACTURER
Kia Industrial Company Limited, 1 1-ka Euiju-Ro, Choong-ku, Seoul, Republic of Korea.

KM25 (6 × 6) 2500 kg Truck Series

DESCRIPTION
The KM25 series of 2500 kg (6 × 6) trucks is based on the license-built chassis of the US M44A2 truck chassis, details of which are contained in the entry on the M35 (6 × 6) 2½-ton cargo truck series in this section. The

Korean trucks closely follow the American original in appearance and detail. They are produced in four basic versions:
KM250 cargo truck
KM255 fuel tanker
KM256 water tanker
KM258 shop-body van

STATUS
Production. In service with the South Korean armed forces.

MANUFACTURER
Asia Motors Company, Inc, 1-60, Yoido-dong, Yungdeungpo-ku, Seoul, Republic of Korea.

Kiamaster (4 × 2) 4000 kg Boxer Truck

DESCRIPTION
The Kiamaster (4 × 2) 4000 kg Boxer Truck uses the same cab as the Kiamaster (4 × 4) 1250 kg truck and is intended for general use in rear areas. It also uses the same engine and general automotive components of the 1250 kg truck but it has only a very limited cross-country capability. The wheelbase and cargo area are longer than those of the 1250 kg truck and the cargo area has bench seating along the sides. A canvas tilt may be fitted and when not in use the supports are stowed forward of the cargo area. A rear tail gate is provided. Dual tyres are fitted to the rear axle.

VARIANTS
A 3-ton crane truck has been produced. For details see page 54 of the *Recovery vehicles* section.

STATUS
Production. In service with the South Korean armed forces.

MANUFACTURER
Kia Industrial Company Limited, 1 1-ka Euiju-Ro, Choong-ku, Seoul, Republic of Korea.

SPECIFICATIONS
Cab seating: 1 + 2
Configuration: 4 × 2
Weight:
(empty) 3600 kg
(loaded) 7745 kg
Max load: 4000 kg
Load area: 4·27 × 2 m
Length: 6·505 m
Width: 2·14 m
Height: 2·18 m
Ground clearance: 0·195 m

Track:
(front) 1·69 m
(rear) 1·57 m
Wheelbase: 3·535 m
Max speed: 90 km/h
Fuel capacity: 150·2 litres
Gradient: 34·5%
Engine: 6-cylinder, in-line, 4·052-litre, water-cooled diesel developing 115 hp at 3600 rpm
Gearbox: manual, with 5 forward and 1 reverse gears
Steering: ball and nut
Turning radius: 8·5 m
Clutch: hydraulic, single dry plate
Suspension: semi-elliptical springs, double-action shock absorbers
Tyres: 7·50 × 16
Brakes:
(main) vacuum, hydraulic drum
(parking) mechanical plus prop shaft brake
Electrical system: 24 V
Batteries: 2 × 12 V, 100 Ah

KM50 (6 × 6) 5-ton Truck Series

DESCRIPTION
The KM50 series of 5-ton (6 × 6) trucks is based on the license-built chassis of the US M809 truck chassis, details of which are contained in the M809 entry in this

section. The Korean trucks follow the M809 design very closely and may differ from the original only in detail. The KM50 series is produced in four basic versions:
KM500 cargo truck
KM501 dump truck
KM502 wrecker
KM503 tractor

STATUS
Production. In service with the South Korean armed forces.

MANUFACTURER
Asia Motors Company, Inc, 1-60, Yoido-dong, Yungdeungpo-ku, Seoul, Republic of Korea.

NETHERLANDS

DAF YA 314 (4 × 4) 3000 kg Truck

DESCRIPTION
The DAF YA 314 (4 × 4) 3000 kg cargo truck was developed in the early 1950s and was in production for the Dutch Army from 1955 to 1965. It has an all-steel forward control type cab with a tarpaulin roof that can be folded backwards and a windscreen that can be folded forward of the radiator if required. The doors are removable. The rear cargo body is all-steel and has a drop tailgate, five bows and a tarpaulin cover. The wheel arches extend along the length of the cargo body on each side and provide seating when necessary. To enable wider cargo to be carried wooden panels can be inserted between the two wheel arches. Some vehicles are provided with a winch with a capacity of 4000 kg mounted at the front.

VARIANTS
Late production models of the YA 314 are designated the YA 324. Variants of this series included a truck-mounted air compressor, bomb carrier for the air force, office/command vehicle, radar towing vehicle, 3000-litre aircraft tanker, three-way tipper, water tanker and a workshop vehicle. The Spanish company of Pegaso has built a modified version of this vehicle called the Pegaso 3045D, details of which will be found in the Spanish section.

Basic DAF YA 314 (4 × 4) 3000 kg cargo truck complete with bows and tarpaulin cover

STATUS
Production complete. In service with the Dutch Army. Gradually being replaced by the DAF YA 4440 (4 × 4) 4000 kg truck.

MANUFACTURER
DAF Trucks, Geldropseweg 303, 5645 TK Eindhoven, Netherlands.

SPECIFICATIONS
Cab seating: 1 + 1
Configuration: 4 × 4
Weight:
  (empty) 4500 kg
  (loaded) 7500 kg
Weight on front axle: (empty) 2570 kg
Weight on rear axle: (empty) 1930 kg
Max load: 3000 kg
Towed load: 3000 kg
Load area: 4·2 × 2·15 m
Length: 6·09 m
Width: 2·425 m
Height:
  (tarpaulin) 2·785 m
  (without windscreen) 2·108 m
  (load area) 1·035 m
Ground clearance: 0·36 m
Track: 1·905 m
Wheelbase: 3·6 m
Angle of approach/departure: 40°/35°
Max speed: (road) 76 km/h
Range: 630 km
Fuel capacity: 210 litres
Gradient: 40%

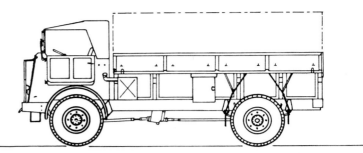

DAF YA 314 (4 × 4) 3000 kg cargo truck

Fording: 0·76 m
Engine: Hercules JXC 6-cylinder in-line water-cooled petrol developing 102 bhp (SAE) at 3200 rpm
Gearbox: manual with 4 forward and 1 reverse gears
Transfer box: 2-speed
Turning radius: 9 m
Suspension: semi-elliptical springs with double acting hydraulic shock absorbers
Tyres: 11.00 × 20

Number of tyres: 4 + 1 spare
Brakes:
  (main) air/hydraulic
  (parking) mechanical
Electrical system: 24 V
Generator: 900 W

DAF YA 328 (6 × 6) 3000 kg Truck/Prime Mover

DEVELOPMENT
In 1950 DAF built the prototype of a 6 × 6 vehicle called the YA 318. Only a few were built and further development resulted in the YA 328 which was in production for the Dutch Army from 1957 to 1959 and was built in two versions, artillery tractor and general purpose.

DESCRIPTION
The cab at the front of the vehicle is provided with a removable tarpaulin cover, removable side curtains and a windscreen which can be folded forward if required. The engine is mounted at the very front of the vehicle and projects into the cab. The complete assembly, which consists of the engine, transmission and radiator, can be removed as an integral unit.

The all-steel cargo area at the rear has a tarpaulin cover, removable bows and a drop tailgate. The wheel arches extend the entire length of the body and can be used as seats. They are covered with removable wooden panels and by placing the panels between the arches, the inside of the body can be converted to a flat loading platform.

With a special ring mount frame each YA 328 could be equipped with a 12·7 mm (0·50) Browning M2 HB MG for anti-aircraft defence.

Externally the vehicle has the appearance of being an 8 × 8 type but the second set of road wheels to the rear of the cab are spare wheels, which are however freewheeling and assist the vehicle in overcoming obstacles as well as protecting the drive line. A number of YA 328s have a winch with a capacity of 4500 kg and 50 metres of cable.

VARIANTS
There are a number of variants of this vehicle including a tractor truck, YA 328 fire truck, YC 328 crash tender, YF 328 oil refuelling truck and a standard cargo truck, which is identical to the truck/prime mover but has an overall length of 6·19 metres and an inside body length of 4·2 metres.

SPECIFICATIONS
Cab seating: 1 + 1
Configuration: 6 × 6
Weight:
  (loaded) 9000 kg
  (empty) 6000 kg
Max load: 3000 kg
Towed load: 4000 kg
Load area: 3·75 × 2·15 m
Length: 6·13 m
Width: 2·4 m
Height:
  (tarpaulin) 2·65 m
  (reduced) 1·905 m
  (load area) 1·003 m
Ground clearance: 0·42 m
Track: 2·08 m

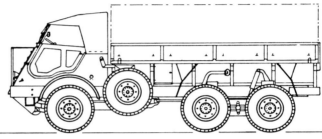

DAF YA 328 (6 × 6) 3000 kg truck

DAF YA 328 (6 × 6) 3000 kg truck/prime mover showing cross country capabilities

Wheelbase: (front axle to centre of rear bogie) 3·4 m
Angle of approach/departure: 40°/40°
Max speed: (road) 80 km/h
Range: 315 km
Fuel capacity: 210 litres
Max gradient: 50%
Fording: 0·76 m
Engine: Hercules JXLD 6-cylinder in-line water-cooled petrol developing 131 bhp at 3200 rpm
Transfer box: 2-speed
Suspension:
  (front) independent, each wheel supported by trailing arms and sprung by 2 cross-mounted torsion bars
  (rear) horizontal beams mounted on cross axle connected to frame by leaf springs.
  Hydraulic double acting telescopic shock-absorbers front and rear.

Turning radius: 8 m
Tyres: 9.00 × 20
Brakes:
  (main) air/hydraulic
  (parking) mechanical
Electrical system: 24 V
Batteries: 2 × 12 V
Generator: 900 W

STATUS
Production complete. In service with the Dutch Army. Gradually being replaced by the DAF YA 4440 (4 × 4) 4000 kg truck.

MANUFACTURER
DAF Trucks, Geldropseweg 303, 5645 TK Eindhoven, Netherlands.

DAF YA 4440 (4 × 4) 4000 kg Truck

DEVELOPMENT
The YA 4440 (4 × 4) 4000 kg medium mobility vehicle has been developed by DAF to meet the requirements of the Dutch Army. The first five prototypes were handed over to the Army for trials late in 1974 and late in 1976 the Dutch Army placed an order for 4000 for delivery

between 1977 and 1980. Late in 1977 a further order for 2500 was placed, with final deliveries made in mid-1983. The truck is based on proven commercial components and shares many common components with the DAF YA 2442 (4 × 4) 2-ton truck (this was developed to prototype stage but not placed in production), including the cab, engine, transfer case and transmission. It has been designed to carry 4000 kg of

cargo on both roads and across country and tow a trailer with a maximum weight of 4000 kg.

DESCRIPTION
The all-steel cab is of the forward control type and can be tilted forwards to allow access to the engine for maintenance. The engine is mounted at the front of the chassis and power is transmitted to the two-speed

transfer box via the five-speed synchromesh transmission. From the transfer case power is taken to the front and rear axles.

The reinforced cab roof allows the installation of a ring mounting for a light machine gun. The frame which supports this ring is bolted directly to the cab roof over the manhole cover. The rear cargo platform has bows, tarpaulin cover, sideboards and a tailgate which can be quickly removed to enable the truck to carry containers or pallets.

The truck is fitted with air brakes, with the parking brake acting on the front axle, an exhaust brake and a trailer brake. The electrical system is waterproof and radio suppressed.

Optional equipment includes a hydraulic crane to the rear of the cab with a capacity of 7000 kg, stabilisers on each side of the chassis for when the hydraulic crane is being used, automatic transmission, two-man passenger seat in place of the standard one-man seat, and a manually-operated crane with a 1000 kg capacity.

VARIANTS

The basic vehicle is suitable for adaptation for a wide variety of roles but the only variant announced so far is the YAL 4440. This is used for training drivers and has a four-man tilt cab with seats for the driver under instruction, instructor and two student drivers. A total of 375 of these vehicles have been built for the Dutch Army.

DAF delivered for trials 17 models of the YA 4440 fitted with a hydraulic crane for rapid unloading of ammunition and cargo. They have the same chassis as the YA 4440 but a shorter cargo body with no bows or tarpaulin cover. Immediately behind the cab is a hydraulic crane and stabilisers, either side of the cab rear, are lowered to the ground before the crane is used. Of the 17 versions 8 had a PESCI (P445G) crane and 9 an HIAB (850S) crane. Following trials with these prototype vehicles the Dutch Army placed an order for 200 units fitted with the HIAB hydraulic crane.

SPECIFICATIONS
Cab seating: 1 + 1
Configuration: 4 × 4
Weight:
　(empty) 6900 kg
　(loaded) 10 900 kg
Max load: 4000 kg
Towed load: 4000 kg
Length: 7·19 m
Width: 2·44 m
Height:
　(tarpaulin) 3·42 m
　(load area) 1·43 m
Ground clearance: 0·3 m
Track: 1·91 m
Wheelbase: 4·05 m
Angle of approach/departure: 36°/30°
Max speed: (road) 80 km/h
Range: 500 km
Max gradient: 50%
Max side slope: 30%
Fording: 0·9 m

Production version of DAF YA 4440 (4 × 4) 4000 kg truck (T J Gander)

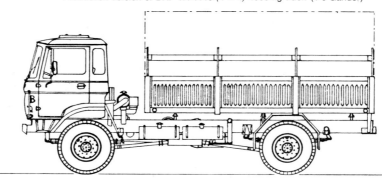

DAF YA 4440 (4 × 4) 4000 kg truck

Engine: DAF DT 615 liquid-cooled 6-cylinder in-line turbo-charged diesel developing 153 hp (DIN) at 2400 rpm
Gearbox: ZF S5-35/2 with 5 forward and 1 reverse gears
Clutch: hydraulic, single plate, dry
Transfer box: ZF VG 250/2
Steering: ZF hydraulic
Turning radius: 9 m
Suspension: semi-elliptical springs with double acting hydraulic shock absorbers on both axles
Tyres: 12.00 × 20 (radial)
Number of tyres: 4 + 1 spare

Brakes:
　(main) air, dual circuit (plus exhaust brake)
　(parking) mechanical, also holding brake
Electrical system: 24 V
Batteries: 2 × 12 V, 100 Ah

STATUS
In production. In service with the Dutch Army and Navy.

MANUFACTURER
DAF Trucks, Geldropseweg 303, 5645 TK Eindhoven, Netherlands.

DAF YA 4440 (4 × 4) 4000 kg truck with side- and tail-boards removed to carry specialised container

DAF YA 4440 (4 × 4) 4000 kg truck fitted with HIAB hydraulic crane and stabilisers lowered

DAF YA 5441 and YA 5442 (4 × 4) 5000 kg Trucks

DEVELOPMENT
The DAF YA 5441 (4 × 4) 5000 kg truck has been designed to carry 5000 kg of cargo on both roads and across country. It has been developed from a standard commercial design and uses many components of the YA 4440 (4 × 4) 4000 kg truck which is in service with the Dutch Army and Navy. A second production series with slight modifications from the YA 5441 is known as the YA 5442.

DESCRIPTION
The cab is of all-steel type and has a circular observation hatch in the roof. The cab can be tilted forward to allow access to the engine for maintenance. The rear cargo area is of all-steel construction and has drop sides and a drop tailgate with integral steps. Removable bows and a tarpaulin cover are fitted as standard.

The engine is mounted at the front of the vehicle with power being transmitted to the two-speed transfer box via the five-speed (plus one reverse) synchromesh gearbox. From the transfer case power is transmitted to the front and rear axles.

Standard equipment includes a front bumper with a built-in push/pull pin, rear towing hook, exhaust brake retarder and connections for the brakes on the trailer.

VARIANTS
None announced. The basic chassis can be adopted for other specific roles such as water tanker, fuel carrier and radio vehicle. DAF has also delivered to the Dutch Air Force a number of 4 × 2 tractor trucks based on the commercial FT 1600 series chassis.

STATUS
Production complete. In service with the Dutch Army and Navy and some NATO forces.

MANUFACTURER
DAF Trucks, Geldropseweg 303, 5645 TK Eindhoven, Netherlands.

DAF YA 5441 (4 × 4) 5000 kg truck complete with bows and tarpaulin cover (T J Gander)

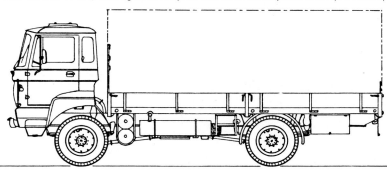

DAF YA 5441 (4 × 4) 5000 kg truck

SPECIFICATIONS

Model	YA 5441	YA 5442
Cab seating	1 + 1 or 2	1 + 1 or 2
Configuration	4 × 4	4 × 4
Weight (empty)	7290 kg	7300 kg
(loaded)	12 290 kg	12 600 kg
Weight on front axle (max load)	4900 kg	4800 kg
Weight on rear axle (max load)	8100 kg	8100 kg
Max load	5000 kg	5000 kg
Towed load	4000 kg	4000 kg
Length	7·54 m	7·54 m
Width	2·47 m	2·44 m
Height (overall)	2·96 m	2·96 m
(load area)	1·3 m	1·28 m
Ground clearance (axle)	0·27 m	0·265 m
(chassis)	0·45 m	0·45 m
Track (front)	1·938 m	1·93 m
(rear)	1·729 m	1·8 m
Wheelbase	3·85 m	3·85 m
Angle of approach/departure	32°/23°	32°/24°
Max speed	80 km/h	80 km/h
Range	500 km	500 km
Fuel capacity	200 litres	200 litres
Max gradient (without trailer)	59%	60%
(with trailer)	38%	40%

Model	YA 5441	YA 5442
Side slope	30%	30%
Fording	0·6 m	0·6 m
Engine	DAF model DT 615 6-cylinder in-line 6·17-litre liquid-cooled turbo-charged diesel developing 153 hp at 2400 rpm	
Gearbox	ZF S5-35/2 manual with 5 forward and 1 reverse gears	
Clutch	single dry plate	single dry plate
Transfer box	ZF VG250/2 2-speed	ZF VG250/2 2-speed
Steering	ZF 8065 power-assisted	ZF 8065 power-assisted
Suspension	semi-elliptical springs front and rear with double acting telescopic shock absorbers front and rear	
Tyres	10.00 × 20	10.00 × 20
Number of tyres	6 + 1 spare	6 + 1 spare
Brakes (main)	air, 2-line, dual circuit	air, 2-line, dual circuit
(parking)	spring-brake cylinders on rear axle	
Electrical system	24 V	24 V
Batteries	2 × 12 V, 100 Ah	2 × 12 V, 100 Ah

DAF YA 616 (6 × 6) 6000 kg Truck

DEVELOPMENT
Until the introduction of the new YAZ 2300 (6 × 6) 10 000 kg truck, the YA 616 (6 × 6) was the heaviest cargo truck that DAF had built for the Dutch Army. The first prototype was completed in 1956 and the vehicle was in production from the following year until 1968. The truck can carry 6000 kg of cargo across country and 10 000 kg on roads. It can also tow a trailer or artillery piece weighing a maximum of 14 500 kg.

DESCRIPTION
The cab is of the forward control type and is all steel with a tarpaulin type roof that can be folded back, and a windscreen that can be folded forward. The rear cargo area is of all-steel construction and has a drop down rear tailgate, removable bows and a tarpaulin cover. A winch with a 9000 kg capacity mounted to the rear of the cab can be used to the front or rear of the truck.

VARIANTS
YA 616 VL
This has a front-mounted winch, drop down sides and a tailgate that can be removed allowing the vehicle to carry containers.

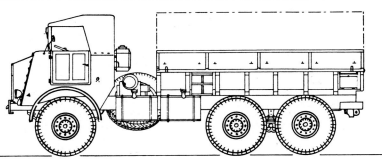

DAF YA 616 (6 × 6) 6000 kg truck

YB 616
This is a recovery vehicle with dual rear wheels, details of which will be found in the *Recovery vehicles* section.
YF 616
This is a 7000-litre capacity tanker vehicle. It has been designed for refuelling vehicles in the forward battle area. The tank consists of three compartments which can be filled and emptied by a pump driven by a two-stroke auxiliary engine or through a PTO. Four vehicles can be refuelled simultaneously at a rate of 91 litres per

minute by four hoses with nozzles. The YF 616 has an overall length of 8·35 metres, overall width of 2·45 metres and an overall height of 2·45 metres; unladen weight is 11 680 kg.
YK 616
This is a three-way tipper and has an unladen weight of 11 350 kg and can carry 5000 kg of soil across country or 9000 kg of soil on roads. Overall length is 7·3 metres, width 2·45 metres and height 3·12 metres. A winch with 80 metres of cable is mounted at the front

of the vehicle. There is also a model of the tipper with a hydraulic crane mounted to the rear of the cab.

YT 616
This is a tractor for hauling semi-trailers up to a maximum weight of 20 000 kg.

YB 626
This is a recovery vehicle with single rear wheels, details of which will be found in the *Recovery vehicles* section.

SPECIFICATIONS
Cab seating: 1 + 1
Configuration: 6 × 6
Weight:
 (empty) 10 850 kg
 (loaded, cross country) 17 000 kg
 (loaded, roads) 21 000 kg
Max load:
 (road) 10 000 kg
 (cross country) 6000 kg
Towed load: 14 500 kg

Load area: 4·19 × 2·159 m
Length: 7·27 m
Width: 2·45 m
Height:
 (tarpaulin) 3·32 m
 (tarpaulin removed and windscreen lowered) 2·49 m
 (load area) 1·397 m
Ground clearance: 0·36 m
Track:
 (front) 1·95 m
 (rear) 1·86 m
Wheelbase: 3·475 m + 1·37 m
Angle of approach/departure: 45°/40°
Max speed: 80 km/h
Range: 400 km
Fuel capacity: 400 litres
Max gradient: 59%
Fording: 0·75 m
Engine: Continental Model R 6602 6-cylinder water-cooled petrol developing 232 hp at 2800 rpm
Gearbox: manual with 5 forward and 1 reverse gears

Transfer box: 2-speed
Steering: hydraulic
Turning radius: 11 m
Suspension:
 (front) semi-elliptical springs with hydraulic shock absorbers
 (rear) leaf springs and hydraulic shock absorbers
Tyres: 14.00 × 20
Number of tyres: 6 + 1 spare
Brakes:
 (main) air/hydraulic
 (parking) mechanical acting on transmission
Electrical system: 24 V
Batteries: 2 × 12 V
Generator: 900 W

STATUS
Production complete. In service with the Dutch Army.

MANUFACTURER
DAF Trucks, Geldropseweg 303, 5645 TK Eindhoven, Netherlands.

DAF YA 616 VL (6 × 6) truck towing 155 mm artillery piece

DAF YF 616 (6 × 6) 7000-litre capacity tanker

DAF YK 616 (6 × 6) three-way tipper truck

DAF YT 616 (6 × 6) tractor truck

DAF YAZ 2300 (6 × 6) 10 000 kg Truck

DEVELOPMENT
In mid-1981, following trials with a number of prototypes submitted by several manufacturers, the Dutch Ministry of Defence placed an order with DAF Trucks worth Hfl 236·5 million for a family of new 10 000 kg (6 × 6) trucks to replace the current DAF YA 616 6000 kg (6 × 6) trucks. The new series is based on the commercial 2300 range and is powered by a DAF 245 hp diesel.

Delivery of the first batch commenced in mid-1983 and should be completed by 1985. Between 1985 and 1987 the Army expects to acquire 200 recovery vehicles to replace the YB 616 and YB 626 (6 × 6) recovery vehicles with a further 200 recovery vehicles and 580 trucks and tractors around 1990.

DESCRIPTION
The chassis is designed as a common ladder type platform and comprises two U-type and Omega-type cross-members. The longitudinal members are strengthened over their full length.

The fully enclosed two-door all-steel cab has been developed from the civilian F 220 type and can be tilted forward to an angle of 60 degrees allowing access to the engine for maintenance. The cab has a large capacity heating and ventilation system and thermal and sound insulation. The driver's and co-driver's seats are adjustable, with the third seat with foot rest being mounted

DAF YAZ 2300 (6 × 6) 10 000 kg truck fitted with hydraulic crane to cab rear (C R Zwart)

against the cab rear wall. The cab roof, in the cargo model only, is fitted with an observation hatch on which can be mounted a light machine gun.

The rear cargo area is of aluminium construction and is provided with removable drop sides and a drop tail-gate. To the rear of the cab is a hydraulic crane for unloading cargo, but before this is used, stabilisers are lowered to the ground either side of the vehicle to the rear of the cab.

The front axle is a Kirkstall DS 65 and is fitted with stabilisers. The rear bogie is a DAF 2699 T with lockable differentials and a lockable inter-axle differential.

Standard equipment includes a 7 and 12 pole trailer connector, slave connector, trouble light connector at front and rear, standard commercial traffic lighting and blackout lighting according to NATO specifications. At the front is a push/pull NATO-pin and at the rear is a 24 000 kg towing hook. Optional equipment includes a ZF automatic transmission and a larger four-man fully enclosed cab, when the latter is fitted however the crane is not mounted to the rear of the cab.

VARIANTS
YKZ 2300 Tipper (6 × 6)
This is being developed as the replacement for the current DAF YK 616 three way tipper and will be produced with and without a winch.
YTV 2300 Truck Tractor (4 × 4)
This is being developed to replace the YT 616 tractor and will have a DAF 2699 rear axle with lockable differential with the rear suspension consisting of main spring plus auxiliary spring with hydraulic telescopic double acting adjustable shock absorbers.
YBZ 2300 Wrecker (6 × 6)
This is being developed as the replacement for the YB 616 and YB 626 (6 × 6) wreckers but the type of wrecker equipment to be installed has yet to be decided.
YGZ 2300 Engineering Equipment Transport (6 × 6)
This is under trials to carry and launch the Ribbon Bridge (see separate entry under *Floating Bridges and Ferries* section).

STATUS
On order for the Dutch Army. Entered service in 1983.

MANUFACTURER
DAF Trucks, Geldropseweg 303, 5645 TK Eindhoven, Netherlands.

DAF YAZ 2300 (6 × 6) 10 000 kg truck (C R Zwart)

SPECIFICATIONS

Model	Truck	Tipper	Tractor	Wrecker	Engineer
Cab seating	1 + 2	1 + 2	1 + 2	1 + 2	1 + 2
Configuration	6 × 6	6 × 6	4 × 4	6 × 6	6 × 6
Weight (empty)	13 000 kg	12 500 kg	7200 kg	not released	not released
(loaded)	23 000 kg	22 500 kg	n/app	not released	not released
(max permissable)	25 500 kg	25 500 kg	17 500 kg	not released	not released
Max load	10 000 kg	10 000 kg	n/app	not released	not released
Max weight on 5th wheel	n/app	n/app	9500 kg	n/app	n/app
Max gross combination weight	40 000 kg	40 000 kg	40 000 kg	40 000 kg	40 000 kg
Load area	6·3 × 2·42 m	5 × 2·42 m	n/app	n/app	not released
Length	9·58 m	8·03 m	6·06 m	not released	not released
Width	2·49 m	2·49 m	2·49 m	2·49 m	3·25 m
Height (overall)	3·59 m	3·54 m	3 m	3 m	not released
(load area)	1·5 m	1·5 m	n/app	n/app	1·55 m
Ground clearance	0·32 m	0·32 m	0·32 m	0·32 m	0·32 m
Track (front)	1·99 m	1·99 m	1·99 m	1·99 m	1·99 m
(rear)	1·82 m	1·82 m	1·82 m	1·82 m	1·82 m
Wheelbase	4·85 m	4·45 m	3·6 m	4·85 m	5·35 m
Angle of approach/departure	30°/20°	30°/30°	30°/n/app	30°/30°	30°/30°
Max speed	80 km/h	80 km/h	80 km/h	80 km/h	80 km/h
Range	600 km	600 km	600 km	600 km	600 km
Fuel capacity	200 litres	200 litres	200 litres	200 litres	200 litres
Gradient	50%	50%	not released	50%	50%
Side slope	30%	30%	30%	30%	30%
Fording	0·75 m	0·75 m	0·75 m	0·75 m	0·75 m
Engine	DAF DHS 825, 4-stroke, 6-cylinder in-line direct injection, turbo-charged liquid-cooled diesel developing 245 hp at 2400 rpm				
Torque converter	ZF WSK 400/1	ZF WSK 400/1	ZF WSK 400/1	ZF WSK 400/1	ZF WSK 400/1
Gearbox	ZF 5S-110 GPA with 8 forward and 1 reverse gears. Transfer box is a ZF A 600/3D with lockable differential and is an integral part of the gearbox				
Steering	ZF, hydraulic power assisted				
Turning radius	6 m	not released	not released	not released	not released
Suspension (front)	semi-elliptical springs and hydraulic telescopic double action shock absorbers				
(rear)	semi-elliptical springs				
Tyres	12.00 × 20	12.00 × 20	12.00 × 20	12.00 × 20	12.00 × 20
Brakes (main)	air, mechanical, 2-line, dual circuit				
(parking)	spring brake	spring brake	spring brake	spring brake	spring brake
(retarder)	exhaust brake	exhaust brake	exhaust brake	exhaust brake	exhaust brake
Electrical system	24 V	24 V	24 V	24 V	24 V
Batteries	4 × 12 V, 100 Ah	4 × 12 V, 100 Ah	4 × 12 V, 100 Ah	4 × 12 V, 100 Ah	4 × 12 V, 100 Ah

DAF YKZ 2300 (6 × 6) 10 000 kg tipper truck (C R Zwart)

DAF YKZ 2300 (6 × 6) 10 000 kg tipper truck (C R Zwart)

Truck, Tractor COE, YT 1500L (4 × 2) 5000 kg

DEVELOPMENT
This truck tractor entered production for the Dutch Army in 1955 and uses many components of the DAF YA 314 (4 × 4) 3000 kg cargo truck. It has been designed to tow semi-trailers up to a maximum weight of 10 000 kg, for example the DAF YAA 602 (6/8000 kg) van type semi-trailer.

DESCRIPTION
The cab is of the forward control type. The windscreen can be folded forward and the canvas tarpaulin type cover is removable.

The front and rear axles are suspended by semi-elliptical leaf-springs of the sliding end type. The rear axle has dual tyres and two speeds, high and low. Brakes are Lockheed air/hydraulic with the parking brake operating on the rear axle. A stowage box is provided on the left side of the chassis and the spare wheel is carried on the right side of the chassis.

VARIANTS
The only variant is the YT 514 (4 × 4) tractor truck, which has a six-cylinder diesel engine.

SPECIFICATIONS
Cab seating: 1 + 1
Configuration: 4 × 2
Weight:
 (empty) 3700 kg
 (loaded) 5300 kg
Weight on front axle: (loaded) 2600 kg
Weight on rear axle: (loaded) 6400 kg
Length: 5·05 m
Width: 2·3 m
Height:
 (cab) 2·46 m
 (without windscreen) 1·96 m
 (to fifth wheel) 1·32 m
Ground clearance: 0·36 m
Track: 1·752 m
Wheelbase: 3·11 m
Angle of approach/departure: 35°/50°
Max speed: (road) 80 km/h
Range: 500 km
Fuel capacity: 210 litres
Max gradient: 24%
Fording: 0·76 m
Engine: Hercules JXLD 6-cylinder petrol developing 131 bhp (SAE) at 3200 rpm

Truck, Tractor YT 1500L (4 × 4) 5000 kg towing YTT 1004 10-tonne semi-trailer (C R Zwart)

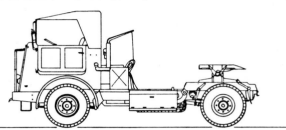

Truck, Tractor COE, YT 1500L (4 × 2) 5000 kg

Gearbox: manual with 5 forward and 1 reverse gears
Suspension: semi-elliptical springs with double acting hydraulic shock absorbers
Tyres: 9.00 × 20
Number of tyres: 6 + 1 spare
Brakes:
 (main) air/hydraulic
 (parking) mechanical
Electrical system: 24 V

Batteries: 2 × 12 V
Generator: 900 W

STATUS
Production complete. In service with the Dutch Army.

MANUFACTURER
DAF Trucks, Geldropseweg 303, 5645 TK Eindhoven, Netherlands.

NEW ZEALAND

New Zealand Army Truck Programme

DEVELOPMENT
In 1976 the New Zealand Army recognised a need to replace its fleet of 1586 Bedford trucks and Land-Rovers which were nearing the end of their economic service lives. A two-year study followed which resulted in the decision to acquire a total of 1307 vehicles based on the use of containerisation. The new vehicles were to be wheeled non-armoured types for use as personnel and weapon carriers, radio, command and liaison vehicles and cargo and general support vehicles. They had to be capable of towing trailers and moving across country. A total of 363 New Zealand-built ISO containers would also be required.

In late 1978 the New Zealand Army carried out a series of vehicle trials at its testing centre at Waiouru. In October 1980 tenders were called to supply the 1307 vehicles of the 750 kg, 1500 kg, 4000 kg and 8000 kg classes. Tenders were received from 12 companies for a total of 33 vehicle types.

In September 1981 it was announced that the New Zealand government had approved the purchase of the following vehicle types:
 567 750 kg V-8 Land-Rovers
 210 1500 kg Unimog U1300Ls
 412 4000 kg Unimog UL1700Ls
 118 8000 kg Mercedes-Benz 2228/41s
The Land-Rovers are produced in Nelson, New Zealand, and the Unimogs and the Mercedes trucks in Rotorua. Total cost of the programme is $NZ 73·931 million and the last production vehicle will be produced by 1989. Deliveries in the 1982–83 financial year comprised 175 Land-Rovers, 33 Unimog U1300Ls, 37 Unimog UL1700Ls and one Mercedes 2228/41.

SPECIFICATIONS (Mercedes-Benz 2228/41)
Cab seating: 1 + 2
Configuration: 6 × 4
Weight:
 (empty) 10 470 kg
 (loaded) 22 000 kg

Mercedes-Benz 2228/41 8000 kg (6 × 4) truck (New Zealand Army)

Max load: 10 000 kg
Max towed load: 16 000 kg
Range: 600 km
Fuel capacity: 300 litres
Engine: Mercedes-Benz OM 422 V-8 direct injection 14·616-litre diesel developing 280 hp at 2300 rpm

Transmission: Eaton Fuller constant mesh with 9 forward and 1 reverse gears
Steering: power
Turning radius: 20 m
Brakes: dual circuit air
Electrical system: 24 V, 85 Ah

PHILIPPINES

CM-125 (4 × 4) 1110 kg Truck

DEVELOPMENT

The CM-125 (4 × 4) 1110 kg truck was designed specifically for military use by the Canlubang Automotive Resources Corporation. Development started in March 1979 and the first prototype was completed in October 1979. The CM-125 has already completed trials with the Philippines armed forces and production was scheduled to start in early 1983.

The vehicle can be used in four configurations: as a troop carrier either with ten passengers seated five down each side facing inwards with entry and exit through the doors at the rear or with ten passengers seated five down each side back-to-back to enable them to leave the vehicle quickly by jumping over the side; as a cargo carrier with the seats folded to the sides for more cargo space and the rear opened completely for easier loading and unloading; and as an ambulance/rescue vehicle with the seats folded down flat to serve as a bed.

The axles, transmission, chassis and body are all produced in the Philippines and it is anticipated that the engine will also be manufactured locally. The major vehicle components, engine, axles, transmission and transfer case have been selected from existing product lines of Mitsubishi, Perkins, Isuzu and Dana-Spicer, thus making spare parts easily available worldwide.

DESCRIPTION

The layout of the CM-125 is conventional with the engine at the front, driver and passenger in the centre and the cargo/troop carrying area at the rear. The chassis is of ladder-type carbon steel welded construction with cross-members and box type side rails.

The cab is all welded and the windscreen can be folded down onto the bonnet. The canvas roof, which covers both the crew and the passengers, is supported by a 25 mm diameter pipe frame. Covers are provided for both the sides and rear and the complete roof and supports can be quickly removed.

The rear cargo/troop carrying area has a corrugated steel-plate floor with a steel partition separating it from the crew area. In the rear are two removable bench seats, each two metres long and able to seat five fully equipped men. They can be changed from inside to outside facing and can be made into a bed using the seat and seat back.

Normal entry to the cargo/troop area is through two doors in the rear, on each of which is mounted a jerrican. The left door is a one-piece unit and the right door is in two pieces with a hinge in the centre vertically.

Standard equipment includes front and rear tow hooks and a seven-pole trailer electric socket at the rear. If required the vehicle can be fitted with a front-mounted electrically-operated winch with a capacity of 3600 kg.

SPECIFICATIONS
Cab seating: 1 + 1
Configuration: 4 × 4
Weight:
  (empty) 2073 kg
  (loaded) 3323 kg
Weight on front axle: (loaded) 1368 kg
Front axle capacity: 1590 kg
Weight on rear axle: (loaded) 1955 kg
Rear axle capacity: 2500 kg
Max load recommended: 1250 kg
Load area: 2·05 × 1·6 m

Length: 4·55 m
Width: 1·7 m
Height: 2·26 m
Ground clearance: 0·274 m
Track: 1·4 m
Wheelbase: 2·77 m
Angle of approach/departure: 45°/35°
Max speed: 100 km/h
Range: 400 km
Fuel capacity: 70 litres
Max gradient: 70%
Fording: 0·5 m
Engine: Mitsubishi 4 D30 4-cylinder diesel developing 87·5 hp at 3500 rpm
Gearbox: Mitsubishi, manual, 5 forward and 1 reverse gears
Clutch: single dry plate
Transfer box: 2-speed
Steering system: two joint shaft with worm recirculating ball sector
Turning radius: 7 m
Suspension: (front and rear) semi-elliptical laminated leaf springs with hydraulic shock absorbers
Tyres: 9.00 × 16
Number of tyres: 4 + 1 spare
Brakes:
  (main) hydraulic
  (parking) mechanical
Electrical system: 24 V, 12 V optional

STATUS
Production for Philippines armed forces.

MANUFACTURER
Canlubang Automotive Resources Corporation, PO Box 4592, Manila, Philippines.

CM-125 (4 × 4) 1110 kg truck in cargo carrier configuration with roof removed

CM-125 (4 × 4) 1110 kg truck in troop carrier configuration

POLAND

Star 66 (6 × 6) 2500 kg Truck

DEVELOPMENT

In the 1950s Poland built a 4 × 4 (Star 44) and a 6 × 6 (Star 66) cargo truck to meet the requirements of the Polish Army. As a result of trials the Star 66 (6 × 6) was placed in production and the first pre-production trucks were completed in 1958 with full scale production beginning in 1960.

The first model was the Star 66 which was followed in the early 1960s by the improved Star 660 M1 which had larger tyres than the earlier vehicle. In the early 1970s the Star 660 M2 was introduced with a number of improvements including the ability to ford to a depth of 1·8 metres with preparation and a light sheet metal roof replacing the canvas roof of the earlier models. The roof is removable and is available with or without a circular observation hatch. The Star 660D was a diesel-powered version of the Star 660 M2, which was powered by a six-cylinder water-cooled S-530A1 diesel which developed 100 hp. The Star 66 range of vehicles has been replaced in production by the more powerful Star 266 vehicle.

Star 66 (6 × 6) 2500 kg truck

DESCRIPTION

The two-door cab is of the forward control type and has a removable canvas top and a windscreen that can be folded forward onto the bonnet. The rear cargo area has a drop tailgate, seats which can be folded up along either side when not in use, removable bows and a tarpaulin cover. Most vehicles have a 6000 kg capacity winch installed.

VARIANTS

Crane truck (ZSH-6), crane/shovel truck (KS-251), dump truck (prototypes only, not in production), pontoon carrying truck (for TPP and PP-64 pontoons), tanker (T-586), tractor truck (prototypes only, no production), water tanker (CW-66) and various shop/van type models for repair, command and communications role. One repair model is the T-574, with an A-frame mounted at the front of the vehicle. The vehicle is also used to carry and launch the SMT-1 truck-mounted treadway bridge; and details of which will be found in the *Mechanised bridges* section. The decontamination vehicle is known as the IRS and is used to decontaminate vehicles, weapons, equipment and terrain, refill portable decontamination apparatus and carry water and other liquids. Details of this model are given in the *Decontamination* section.

STATUS

Production of the Star 66 vehicle has now been completed. It is used by both the Czechoslovak and Vietnamese armed forces and is also used for a variety of civil roles.

MANUFACTURER

Starzchowice Motor Vehicle Plant, Poland.

SPECIFICATIONS

Model	Star 66	Star 660 M1	Star 660 M2
Cab seating	1 + 2	1 + 2	1 + 2
Configuration	6 × 6	6 × 6	6 × 6
Weight (empty)	5700 kg	5700 kg	5700 kg
(loaded, cross country)	8200 kg	8200 kg	8200 kg
Max load (road)	4000 kg	4000 kg	4000 kg
(cross country)	2500 kg	2500 kg	2500 kg
Towed load (road)	4400 kg	4400 kg	4400 kg
(cross country)	3500 kg	3500 kg	3500 kg
Length	6·527 m	6·527 m	6·58 m
Width	2·4 m	2·4 m	2·4 m
Height (cab)	2·485 m	2·485 m	2·485 m
(tarpaulin)	2·875 m	2·875 m	2·875 m
Ground clearance	0·285 m	0·285 m	0·285 m
Track (front/rear)	1·804 m/1·804 m	1·86 m/1·855 m	1·86 m/1·855 m
Wheelbase	2·858 m + 1·2 m	2·858 m + 1·2 m	2·858 m + 1·2 m
Max speed	73·4 km/h	73·4 km/h	73·4 km/h
Range	650 km	650 km	800 km
Fuel capacity	300 litres	300 litres	300 litres
Fuel consumption (road)	38 litres/100 km	38 litres/100 km	38 litres/100 km
Gradient	50%	50%	50%
Vertical obstacle	0·5 m	0·5 m	0·5 m
Fording (without preparation)	0·5 m	0·5 m	0·5 m
(with preparation)	n/app	n/app	0·9 m
Engine model	S-47	S-47E3W	S-47A or S-47E3W
Engine type	6-cylinder water-cooled petrol developing 105 hp at 3000 rpm		
Gearbox	manual with 5 forward and 1 reverse gears		
Transfer box	2-speed	2-speed	2-speed
Tyres	11.00 × 20	12.00 × 18	12.00 × 18
Number of tyres	6 + 1 spare	6 + 1 spare	6 + 1 spare
Brakes (main)	hydraulic	hydraulic	hydraulic
(parking)	mechanical	mechanical	mechanical
Electrical system	24 V	24 V	24 V

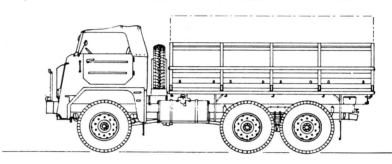

Star 66 (6 × 6) 2500 kg truck

Star 266 (6 × 6) 3500 kg Truck

DESCRIPTION

The Star 266 3500 kg truck is the replacement for the older Star 66 2500 kg range of 6 × 6 trucks. The first prototype was completed in 1976 and production began in 1976. Major improvements over the earlier vehicle are its increased load carrying capability, more powerful engine, all-steel fully enclosed cab and larger tyres. The cab is of the forward control type and the rear cargo area has removable bows, tarpaulin cover and drop tailgate. A winch with a capacity of 6000 kg is fitted.

Star 266 (6 × 6) 3500 kg truck

VARIANTS

A shop/van is known to be in service.

SPECIFICATIONS

Cab seating: 1 + 2
Configuration: 6 × 6
Weight:
(empty) 7200 kg
(loaded) 12 200 kg
Max load: 3500 kg
Towed load: 4000 kg
Length: 6·8 m
Width: 2·5 m

Height:
(cab) 2·64 m
(tarpaulin) 2·885 m
Ground clearance: 0·325 m
Track: 1·97 m
Wheelbase: 2·97 m + 1·25 m
Angle of approach/departure: 37°/47°
Max speed: (road) 86 km/h
Fuel capacity: 300 litres
Fuel consumption: 30 litres/100 km
Range: 800 km
Max gradient: 76%
Fording: 1·8 m
Engine: S-359 6-cylinder water-cooled diesel developing 150 hp at 2800 rpm. A petrol engined model is also available
Gearbox: manual, 5 forward and 1 reverse gears
Turning radius: 8·5 m
Tyres: 12.00 × 20
Number of tyres: 6 + 1 spare
Brakes:
(main) hydraulic
(parking) mechanical
Electrical system: 24 V

NOTE

A more recent vehicle is the Star 244 (4 × 4) cross country truck with a payload of 5000 kg which has a cab developed in association with Chausson of France. Another new vehicle is the Tropik 80 (4 × 4) which is powered by a multi-fuel engine and can ford water obstacles to a maximum depth of 1·8 metres. The manual gearbox has five forward and one reverse gears and a two-speed transfer box is fitted as standard. When being driven on roads the front axle is disengaged.

STATUS

In production. In service with the Polish Army.

MANUFACTURER

Starzchowice Motor Vehicle Plant, Poland.

Star 25 (4 × 2) 3500 kg Truck

DESCRIPTION

The Star 20 range of 4 × 2 trucks was in production from the late 1940s until phased out of production in 1968 in favour of the Star 28/29 series. The vehicles have been widely used by the Polish Army. The two-door fully enclosed cab is of the forward control type with the cargo area at the rear with drop sides and a drop tailgate. Some vehicles are fitted with removable bows and a tarpaulin cover.

The first model to enter production in 1948 was the Star 20 with an S-42 engine and a maximum road speed of 75 km/h, followed by the Star 21 in 1958 with the same engine as the Star 20, Star 25 and finally the Star 27. The Star 27 was powered by an S-53 six-cylinder water-cooled petrol engine which gave the vehicle a maximum road speed of 94 km/h. Long wheelbase and diesel-engined models of the Star 27 were also built.

There were many variants of this range of vehicles including crane trucks (Z prefix), tractor trucks (C-25 and C-60), dump trucks (W-14, W-25 and W-27) and tankers (25-C).

SPECIFICATIONS (Star 25 truck)
Cab seating: 1 + 1
Configuration: 4 × 2
Weight:
(empty) 3600 kg
(loaded, road) 7600 kg
Max load:
(road) 4000 kg
(dirt road) 3500 kg
Towed load: 4000 kg

Length: 5·9 m
Width: 2·2 m
Height:
(cab) 2·2 m
(tarpaulin) 2·8 m
Ground clearance: 0·255 m
Track: 1·6 m
Wheelbase: 3 m
Max speed: 98 km/h
Fuel capacity: 105 litres

Engine: S-472 6-cylinder liquid-cooled petrol developing 95 hp at 3000 rpm
Gearbox: manual with 5 forward and 1 reverse gears
Tyres: 8.25 × 20
Number of tyres: 6 + 1 spare

STATUS
Production complete. In service with the Polish Forces.

MANUFACTURER
Starzchowice Motor Vehicle Plant, Poland.

Star 28 and Star 200 Series (4 × 2) Trucks

DESCRIPTION
In 1968 the Star 28 and Star 29 entered production as the replacement for the Star 25 and Star 27. The Star 28 is powered by an S-530A1 six-cylinder diesel which develops 100 hp at 2600 rpm and gives the vehicle a maximum road speed of 81 km/h. Payload on roads is 5000 kg. The Star 29 is powered by an S-474 six-cylinder water-cooled petrol engine, which develops 105 hp at 3000 rpm and gives the vehicle a maximum road speed of 81 km/h. Payload on roads is 5000 kg and towed load is 5250 kg.

The Star 28 will be replaced by the Star 200 and Star 244. The Star 200 is powered by an S-533 (90 hp) or an S-534 (150 hp) engine and can carry a maximum payload of 5000 kg on roads; towed load is 6000 kg. The Star 244 is a 4 × 4 truck and has a military potential. It has a forward control, two-door all-steel cab with the cargo area at the rear with drop sides and a drop tailgate, removable bows and a tarpaulin cover.

The Star 200 is powered by an S-359 engine which develops 150 hp at 2800 rpm and is coupled to a manual gearbox with five forward and one reverse gears. Brief specifications are length 6·51 metres, width 2·37 metres, payload 6000 kg, towed load 8500 kg and maximum road speed 90 km/h. Variants include the L200(LWB), C200(tractor truck), Z200(crane chassis) and A200(box body).

VARIANTS
There are many variants of the Star 28 and Star 200 series including tankers (eg Star 20C, 21C (3500 litres), A3-573 and C-28), tipper (eg W-28) and crane truck (eg Z-28).

SPECIFICATIONS (Star 244 truck)
Configuration: 4 × 4
Weight:
(empty) 4275 kg
(loaded road) 9775 kg
Max load:
(road) 5500 kg
(cross country) 4500 kg

Length: 6·43 m
Width: 2·38 m
Height:
(cab) 2·325 m
(tarpaulin) 3 m
Ground clearance: 0·245 m
Track:
(front) 1·9 m
(rear) 1·75 m
Wheelbase: 3·4 m
Engine: S-533 6-cylinder water-cooled diesel developing 135 hp at 2800 rpm or S-534 diesel developing 150 hp at 2800 rpm
Tyres: 8.25 × 20
Number of tyres: 6 + 1 spare

STATUS
In production.

MANUFACTURER
Starzchowice Motor Vehicle Plant, Poland.

Jelcz Trucks

DESCRIPTION
From 1968 the Zubr (A-80) 4 × 2 trucks were replaced in production by the Jelcz series. This basic model is designated the Jelcz 315, and is powered by an SW 680/49 six-cylinder water-cooled diesel engine which develops 200 hp and gives a maximum road speed of 85 km/h. Payload on roads is 8000 kg and maximum towed load is 14 000 kg. The Jelcz 315M is almost identical and the 315A is the military version with the same payload as the civilian vehicles. The 315MB is the 315M but fitted with a hydraulic crane for loading purposes. The fuel tanker is designated the A3-591 and can carry 8000 litres of fuel.

The 315 has a two-door fully enclosed forward control type cab with the cargo area at the rear with drop sides, drop tailgate, removable bows and a canvas cover.

In 1970 the Jelcz 316 (6 × 2) truck entered production. It is powered by an SW 680/49 six-cylinder diesel which develops 200 hp and has a maximum payload of 10 000 kg and towed load of 14 000 kg. The following year the 316E appeared with a 240 hp diesel. The 317 is a 4 × 2 tractor truck and later versions include the 317D with the same engine as the 316 and the 317MD which can tow a semi-trailer weighing up to 22 500 kg.

Jelcz dump trucks include the 3W317-821 (4 × 2) and the 640 (6 × 4). Latest Jelcz are the 420 and the 620, the latter with a 240 hp diesel and a maximum payload of 14 000 kg.

New Jelcz trucks have been developed in conjunction with Austria, for example the Jelcz 640 (6 × 4) truck which is powered by a Steyr V-8 diesel developing 320 hp at 2600 rpm. Variants of this model include a dump truck (W-640) and a three-sided dump truck (W-640-S).

SPECIFICATIONS (Jelcz 315A)
Configuration: 4 × 2
Weight:
(empty) 6975 kg
(loaded) 14 975 kg
Max load: (road) 8000 kg
Towed load: (road) 14 000 kg
Length: 7·345 m
Width: 2·5 m
Height:
(cab) 2·64 m
(tarpaulin) 3·17 m
Ground clearance: 0·375 m
Track:
(front) 2·088 m
(rear) 1·8 m
Wheelbase: 4·1 m

Standard Jelcz 315 (4 × 2) 8000 kg truck with early cab

Max speed: (road) 90 km/h
Range: 500 km
Fuel capacity: 150 litres
Fuel consumption: 30 litres/100 km
Engine: SW 680/49 6-cylinder water-cooled diesel developing 200 hp at 2200 rpm
Tyres: 11.00 × 20
Number of tyres: 6 + 1

(Jelcz 315 MA)
Configuration: 4 × 2
Weight:
(empty) 7400 kg
(loaded) 15 400 kg
Max load: (road) 8000 kg
Towed load: (road) 14 000 kg
Length: 7·053 m
Width: 2·5 m
Height: 3·52 m
Ground clearance: 0·272 m

Track:
(front) 2·08 m
(rear) 1·8 m
Wheelbase: 4·1 m
Max speed: (road) 85 km/h
Range: 500 km
Fuel consumption:
(with trailer) 38 litres/100 km
(without trailer) 30 litres/100 km
Engine: SW 680 6-cylinder diesel developing 200 hp at 2200 rpm
Gearbox: manual with 5 forward and 1 reverse gears
Tyres: 11.00 × 20
Electrical system: 24 V

STATUS
In production. The Jelcz 315A is known to be in service with the Polish Army.

MANUFACTURER
Jelcz Motor Vehicle Plant, Poland.

PORTUGAL

Bravia Leopardo Mk III (6 × 6) 3000 kg Truck

DESCRIPTION
The Leopardo Mk III has been designed to carry 3000 kg of cargo across country or up to 6000 kg on roads. Its layout is conventional with the engine at the front, cab in the centre with a windscreen that folds forward onto the bonnet and a removable canvas top, and the cargo area at the rear with hinged seats, drop tailgate, removable bows and a tarpaulin cover. It is available with single- or dual-rear wheels and tracks can be fitted to the dual-rear wheel version to increase cross country mobility. The vehicle can be delivered with one of three types of engine, model V-8 318-3 petrol developing 202 hp at 2400 rpm, a V-8 361-3 petrol developing 210 hp at 4000 rpm or a British Perkins diesel type 6-354-2D. Optional equipment includes a fully enclosed cab, Braden model MU2-3 winch with a capacity of 4536 kg, 24-volt electrical system, power steering and an additional 250-litre fuel tank.

The Leopardo Mk I is a 4 × 2 truck with a 4·179-metre wheelbase, gross vehicle weight of 8845 kg and a 10 206 kg gross combination weight. The Leopardo Mk II is also a 4 × 2 truck and has a 4·444-metre wheelbase, gross vehicle weight of 10 206 kg and a gross combination weight of 16 330 kg.

VARIANTS
A dump truck model is in service.

SPECIFICATIONS
Cab seating: 1 + 2
Configuration: 6 × 6
Weight:
(empty) 5793 kg
(loaded, road) 11 793 kg
(loaded, cross country) 8793 kg
Max load:
(road) 6000 kg
(cross country) 3000 kg
Length: 6·832 m
Width: 2·159 m
Height: (cab) 2·5 m
Ground clearance: 0·292 m
Track: 1·72 m
Wheelbase: (from 1st axle to centre of rear bogie) 4·179 m

Fuel capacity: 150 litres
Engine: see text
Gearbox: manual, 5 forward and 1 reverse gears
Clutch: single dry plate
Transfer box: 2-speed
Steering: manual
Suspension:
(front) semi-elliptical springs and hydraulic double acting shock absorbers
(rear) Hendrickson type with semi-elliptical springs
Tyres: 9.00 × 20
Number of tyres: 10 + 1 spare
Brakes:
(main) hydraulic
(parking) mechanical
Electrical system: 12 V (24 V optional)

STATUS
Production. In service with Portuguese armed forces.

MANUFACTURER
Bravia, Sociedade Luso-Brazileira de Viaturas E Equipamentos, SARL, Avenue Eng. Duarte Pacheco 21-5°, Lisbon, Portugal.

Bravia Leopardo III (6 × 6) 3000 kg truck with single rear wheels

Bravia Leopardo III (6 × 6) 3000 kg truck with tracks fitted to rear wheels to increase traction in soft soil

Bravia Pantera (6 × 6) 6000 kg Truck

DESCRIPTION
The Pantera has been designed to carry 9000 kg of cargo on roads or 6000 kg of cargo across country. Its layout and appearance are almost identical to the Leopardo Mk III and it has the same wheelbase. It can be delivered with one of four types of engine, Perkins V-8-510 diesel developing 170 hp at 2800 rpm, Perkins V-8-540 diesel developing 180 hp at 2600 rpm, Cummins 378C diesel or a 361-4 petrol engine. Optional equipment is the same as the Leopardo except that the winch installed is an MU12 rated at 9072 kg. Tracks may be fitted to the dual rear wheels to increase mobility.

SPECIFICATIONS
Cab seating: 1 + 2
Configuration: 6 × 6
Weight:
(empty) 8236 kg
(loaded, road) 17 236 kg
(loaded, cross country) 11 236 kg
Max load:
(road) 9000 kg
(cross country) 6000 kg
Length: 7·289 m
Width: 2·4 m
Height: 2·5 m
Ground clearance: (axles) 0·292 m
Wheelbase: (1st axle to centre of rear bogie) 4·179 m
Fuel capacity: 150 litres
Engine: see text
Gearbox: manual, with 5 forward and 1 reverse gears
Clutch: single dry plate
Transfer box: 2-speed

Bravia Pantera (6 × 6) 6000 kg truck with front-mounted winch, bows and tarpaulin cover

Tyres: 11.00 × 20
Number of tyres: 10 + 1 spare
Brakes:
(main) hydraulic
(parking) mechanical
Electrical system: 12 V (24 V optional)
Batteries: 1 × 12 V, 48 Ah

STATUS
Production. In service with Portuguese armed forces.

MANUFACTURER
Bravia, Sociedade Luso-Brazileira de Viaturas E Equipamentos, SARL, Avenue Eng. Duarte Pacheco, 21-5°, Lisbon, Portugal.

ROMANIA

SR-132 Bucegi (4 × 4) truck

SR-131 Trucks and Variants

DESCRIPTION
The SR-131 Bucegi (4 × 2) truck replaced the SR-101 vehicle in production. It is powered by an SR-211 eight-cylinder diesel engine which develops 140 hp and gives the vehicle a maximum speed of 90 km/h. Payload on roads is 3000 kg. The 4 × 4 model, designated the SR-132 Bucegi, is almost identical and is powered by the same engine. The layout of both vehicles is identical, with the engine at the front, two-door all-steel cab in the centre and the cargo area at the rear with drop sides and a drop tailgate.

Further development of the SR-131/SR-132 vehicles resulted in the SR-113 (4 × 2) and SR-114 (4 × 4) Carpati trucks powered by the same engine as the earlier vehicles but with a wheelbase of 4 metres compared with the earlier vehicle's wheelbase of 3·4 metres. The SR-113's payload on roads is 5000 kg and the SR-114's is 4000 kg. Both vehicles are fitted with 9.00 × 20 tyres. The SR-114 is used as a carrier for Romanian Army 21-round BM-21 multiple rocket systems (for details of the BM-21 see *Jane's Armour and Artillery 1983–84*, page 742).

VARIANTS
Tractor truck models (4 × 2) are designated the SR-116 while dump trucks (4 × 2) include the 1 ABS-116 and AB45-116. Ambulance and van type versions are also in service. Other Bucegi vehicles include the 7-BA-1 L (4 × 2) 7000 kg truck, 7-BA-1 N (4 × 2) 6000 kg truck and the 18-BTA-1 (4 × 2) tractor truck which can pull a semi-trailer weighing up to 18 000 kg. The AC-302 is a 4000-litre tanker based on the SR-113 chassis. As far as it is known these are not used by the Romanian Army.

SPECIFICATIONS (SR-132 (4 × 4) truck)
Cab seating: 1 + 2
Configuration: 4 × 4
Weight:
(empty) 3750 kg
(loaded, road) 6750 kg
(loaded, dirt road) 5750 kg
Max load:
(road) 3000 kg
(dirt road) 2000 kg
Towed load:
(road) 3000 kg
(dirt road) 2000 kg
Length: 5·78 m
Width: 2·263 m
Height: (cab) 2·1 m
Ground clearance: 0·27 m
Track: 1·75 m
Wheelbase: 3·4 m
Max speed: (road) 95 km/h

Engine: SR-211 V-8 water-cooled petrol developing 140 hp at 3600 rpm
Gearbox: manual with 4 forward and 1 reverse gears
Transfer box: 2-speed
Tyres: 9.75 × 18
Number of tyres: 4 + 1 spare

STATUS
In production. In service with the Romanian Army.

MANUFACTURER
Red Star Motor Vehicle Plant, Brasov, Romania.

SR-101 (4 × 2) 3500 kg Truck

DESCRIPTION
The SR-101 is a copy of the Soviet ZIL-150 (4 × 2) truck and can be distinguished from the Soviet vehicle by the different shape of the top of the cab. The layout of the vehicle is conventional with the engine at the front, all-steel fully enclosed cab in the centre and the cargo area at the rear with a drop tailgate. This vehicle has been replaced in production by the SR-131 (4 × 2) Bucegi truck.

VARIANT
A dump truck model known as the SR-109 is a copy of the Soviet ZIL-585 (4 × 2) dump truck.

SPECIFICATIONS
Configuration: 4 × 2
Weight:
(empty) 3500 kg
(loaded) 7900 kg
Towed load:
(road) 4500 kg
(dirt road) 3500 kg
Length: 6·72 m
Width: 2·47 m
Height: (cab) 2·18 m
Ground clearance: 0·265 m
Track:
(front) 1·7 m
(rear) 1·74 m
Wheelbase: 4 m

Max speed: (road) 65 km/h
Range: 405 km
Fuel capacity: 150 litres
Fuel consumption: 38 litres/100 km
Fording: 0·8 m
Engine: SR-101 6-cylinder in-line water-cooled petrol developing 90 hp at 2400 rpm
Tyres: 9.00 × 20
Number of tyres: 6 + 1 spare

STATUS
Production complete. In service with the Romanian Army.

MANUFACTURER
Red Star Motor Vehicle Plant, Brasov, Romania.

DAC 665 T (6 × 6) 5000 kg Truck

DESCRIPTION
The DAC 665 T (6 × 6) 5000 kg truck will become the standard truck in its class in the Romanian Army. In apearance it is very similar to the Hungarian D-566 (6 × 6) 5000 kg truck.

The forward control all-steel cab hinges forward to allow access to the engine for maintenance and there is an observation hatch in the roof on the right side. The spare wheel is mounted to the rear of the cab on the right side.

The rear cargo area has a drop tailgate, removable bows and a tarpaulin cover. Bench seats can be fitted. Standard equipment includes a winch and a central tyre-pressure regulation system.

VARIANTS
There are no known variants, although some undoubtedly exist.

SPECIFICATIONS
Cab seating: 1 + 2
Configuration: 6 × 6
Max load:
(road) 10 000 kg
(cross country) 5000 kg
Length: 7·57 m
Width: 2·5 m
Height: 2·85 m
Ground clearance: 0·39 m
Track: 2 m
Wheelbase: 3·095 m + 1·31 m
Range: 450 km
Fuel capacity: 220 litres
Gradient: 60%
Fording: 0·65 m
Engine: 6-cylinder, 10·39-litre diesel developing 215 hp at 2200 rpm
Gearbox: 10 forward and 2 reverse gears
Tyres: 14.00 × 20
Number of tyres: 6 + 1 spare

STATUS
In production. In service with the Romanian Army.

MANUFACTURER
Red Star Motor Vehicle Plant, Brasov, Romania.

DAC 665 T (6 × 6) 5000 kg trucks

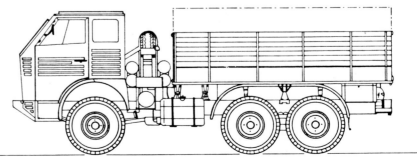

Provisional drawing of DAC 665 T (6 × 6) 5000 kg truck

ROMAN 12135 DFAE (6 × 6) 10 000 kg Truck

DESCRIPTION
Romania has a licence from the West German company MAN to build a wide range of 4 × 2, 6 × 2, 6 × 4 and 6 × 6 trucks, which are marketed under the name of the ROMAN (RO: Romania, MAN: MAN) series. ROMAN also supplies cabs to Hungary for its Raba series of trucks.

At least one of these vehicles, the ROMAN 12135 DFAE, is used by the Romanian Army. This has a two-door all-steel cab of the forward control type with the cargo area at the rear. The cargo area has a drop tailgate and can be fitted with seats. The civilian model is designated the ROMAN 12135 DF.

VARIANTS
Other variants of the ROMAN 12135 DFAE probably exist.

SPECIFICATIONS
Configuration: 6 × 6
Weight:
 (empty) 5755 kg
 (loaded) 15 755 kg
Max load: (road) 10 000 kg
Towed load: (road) 4000 kg
Length: 7·005 m
Width: 2·49 m
Height: (cab) 2·91 m
Ground clearance: 0·3 m
Track: 1·912 m
Max speed: (road) 90 km/h
Fuel capacity: 220 litres
Engine: Type 797-05 6-cylinder water-cooled diesel developing 135 hp
Tyres: 9.00 × 20
Number of tyres: 6 + 1 spare

STATUS
In production. In service with the Romanian Army.

MANUFACTURER
Red Star Motor Vehicle Plant, Brasov, Romania.

SOUTH AFRICA

SAMIL 20 (4 × 4) 2000 kg Trucks

DESCRIPTION
The SAMIL 20 (4 × 4) chassis provides the basis for a wide range of cross-country vehicles. The basic model is a 2200 kg cargo truck. This has a forward-control half cab with a canvas roof and removable side windows. The cargo area has pressed steel sides and may be covered with a canvas tilt over a steel framework. A removable bank of wooden seats may be fitted along the centre of the body for ten fully-equipped soldiers. These seats can be stored at the sides when the truck is required to carry cargo. Container lash-down points are provided on the body floor and two fork lift pockets are in the body frame bottom for lifting purposes. A spare wheel is mounted between the cab and the cargo area, and a light crane arrangement is provided to allow the wheel to be handled by one man.

VARIANTS
Protected transport
This version has the driver's cab protected against mine blast and small arms fire by a shaped arrangement of armoured plates around the cab and engine. The normal cargo area is retained.
Bulldog
This is a completely armoured personnel and load carrier based on the SAMIL 20. There is a centrally-placed cab for the driver. The rear carrying area is enclosed by folding armour plates round the sides. The open top may be covered by a canvas top.
Protected troop carrier (Rhino)
This version of the SAMIL 20 has a fully-armoured body with a two-man front cab and protection for ten men in the rear. Access to the rear is by two outward-opening armoured doors at the rear and 13 firing ports are provided along the sides and rear. Armoured glass windows and vision ports are provided. The rear passengers normally face inwards.
Valkiri rocket launcher
The SAMIL 20 will be used for the vehicle component of the full production version of the Valkiri multiple artillery rocket system. In this form the SAMIL 20 can be used as the launcher vehicle as well as the meteorological vehicle associated with the system (early versions of the Valkiri system used Unimog light trucks). When in use as the launch vehicle the SAMIL 20 carries 24 launching tubes and when covered with a canvas tilt it is virtually identical to the standard SAMIL 20 (4 × 4) truck. The Valkiri rocket has a body diameter of 127 mm and a potential range of 22 000 metres. Full details of the system can be found in *Jane's Armour and Artillery 1983–84*, pages 733 and 734.
Light repair workshop
On this version of the SAMIL 20 the rear area is occupied by a cabin constructed from fibreglass panels reinforced by steel strips and brackets. The rear and sides are flaps that fold upwards for access to the body interior and when raised act as partial weather protection. The interior contains racks for repair equipment.
Container body carrier
When the SAMIL 20 is used as a container body carrier, the container is fixed directly onto the chassis frame and can then carry a payload of up to 2200 kg. The containers may also be used as mobile offices, control or command posts and for radio and other equipment.

SPECIFICATIONS (basic SAMIL 20 truck)
Cab seating: 1 + 1
Configuration: 4 × 4
Weight:
 (chassis/cab) 4580 kg
 (loaded) 7700 kg
Front axle load: 3700 kg
Rear axle load: 4000 kg
Payload: 2200 kg
Towed load: 6300 kg
Length: 5·34 m
Width: 2·3 m
Height: 2·69 m
Ground clearance: 0·46 m
Track: 1·852 m
Wheelbase: 2·9 m
Angle of approach/departure: 40°/40°
Max speed: (road) 90 km/h
Range: 800 km
Fuel capacity: 200 litres
Max gradient: 87%
Side slope: 18°
Fording: 1·2 m at 5 km/h
Engine: 6-cylinder air-cooled diesel developing 106 hp at 2650 rpm
Gearbox: manual, 5 forward and 1 reverse gears
Transfer box: 2-speed
Clutch: self-adjusting, hydraulic
Steering: ball and nut, power assisted
Turning radius: 6 m
Suspension: telescopic hydraulic shock absorbers, leaf springs
Tyres: 14.5 × 20 PR 12
Number of tyres: 4 + 1 spare
Brakes: dual circuit, air/hydraulic
Electrical system: 24 V
Batteries: 2 × 12 V, 120 Ah

STATUS
Production. In service with the South African Defence Forces.

MANUFACTURER
Enquiries to Armscor, Private Bag X337, Pretoria 0001, South Africa.

SAMIL 20 (4 × 4) truck with mine-proof cab (T J Gander)

SAMIL 20 (4 × 4) truck with container body, artillery fire control equipment, and generator behind cab (T J Gander)

SAMIL 20 (4 × 4) truck (T J Gander)

SAMIL 20 (4 × 4) truck (T J Gander)

SAMIL 50 (4 × 4) 4800 kg Trucks

DESCRIPTION
The SAMIL 50 (4 × 4) 4800 kg truck forms the basis for a range of different types of vehicle all using the same chassis. The SAMIL 50 chassis frame is a single-piece channel section with parallel side members and bolted-in cross members and brackets. The engine is mounted at the front with the two-man all-steel cab mounted just to the rear. The cargo area may be covered by a canvas tilt and four removable wooden bench seats may be fitted along the sides and along the centre. When in use these seats can accommodate 40 fully equipped men. All the body panels are hinged and removable. A spare wheel is mounted between the cab and the body area and is provided with a small crane to handle the wheel. A towing hook is provided at the rear.

VARIANTS
Recovery vehicle
For details of this variant see separate entry under *Recovery vehicles* page 55.
Telecommunications workshop
This version of the SAMIL 50 has a mild steel section superstructure to house work tables, shelves and lockers together with telecommunications equipment repair requirements. Small windows are provided in the sides and ventilation louvres are provided. Access to the rear door is via a ladder which extends to the roof.
Battery charging vehicle
This version of the SAMIL 50 has a box-type body with side and rear panels hinging upwards if required. Inside there are two sets of battery charging equipment each capable of charging 18 batteries arranged on a bench.
Mobile welding workshop
This follows the same general lines as the battery charging vehicle but a fully-equipped welding workshop is enclosed.
Water tanker
The superstructure of this variant of the SAMIL 50 consists of a 4750-litre water tank fitted with a tropical roof. Each side of the tank there are five taps from which water can be drawn. At the rear is a single draw-off point and a spray bar for sprinkling. Two sections of armoured hose 75 mm in diameter and 4 metres long are stored in boxes alongside the tank. These hoses can be quickly coupled to the rear draw-off point. A water pump capable of passing 500 litres a minute for filling or disposal purposes is driven by a power take-off from the gear box.
Fuel tanker
This variant has an oval-shaped mild steel fuel tanker

SAMIL 50 (4 × 4) 4800 kg truck with box body (T J Gander)

body with a capacity of 6000 litres. The tank has a tropical roof cover and three manholes on the top. A 400 litres a minute fuel pump is provided and a meter and control platform is situated at the tank rear. Four delivery lines for can filling are provided.
Mine resistant ambulance (Kwëvoël)
This is a SAMIL 50 chassis fitted with a full armoured body and cab to carry four stretcher cases and six sitting wounded in the rear. The body interior is fully provided with fittings for medical equipment and a stowable ramp is provided under the body for access to the interior. The two outward-opening rear doors are pneumatically-operated from within the driver's cab or from ouside.

Two escape hatches that double as ventilators are provided in the roof. An intercom between the driver's cab and the body is provided. Normally the ambulance carries two medical attendants.
Mobile pantry
On this SAMIL 50 variant the superstructure box body is formed from rigid sandwich sections of foamed polyurethane contained in seamless glass fibre skins with reinforcing members. Internally there are two compartments with the forward section refrigerated and the rear for the stowage of canned and non-perishable goods. Each section has shelves and baskets for handling and stowage purposes.

SAMIL 50 (4 × 4) fuel tanker (T J Gander)

SAMIL 50 (4 × 4) truck fitted with workshop body

SAMIL 50 (4 × 4) mine resistant ambulance

SAMIL 50 (4 × 4) 4800 kg truck with standard cargo/personnel body (T J Gander)

STATUS
Production. In service with the South African Defence Forces.

MANUFACTURER
Enquiries to Armscor, Private Bag X337, Pretoria 0001, South Africa.

SPECIFICATIONS (basic SAMIL 50 truck)
Cab seating: 1 + 2
Configuration: 4 × 4
Weight:
(chassis/cab) 6340 kg
(loaded) 12 400 kg
Front axle load: 5500 kg

Rear axle load: 7700 kg
Payload: 4800 kg
Towed load: 6000 kg
Length: 7·78 m
Width: 2·5 m
Height: 3·1 m
Ground clearance: 0·355 m
Track:
(front) 1·985 m
(rear) 2·03 m
Wheelbase: 4·9 m
Angle of approach/departure: 35°/35°
Max speed: (road) 88 km/h
Range: 1000 km
Fuel capacity: 400 litres
Max gradient: 83%

Side slope: 18°
Fording: 1·2 m at 5 km/h
Engine: V-6 air-cooled diesel developing 161 hp at 2650 rpm
Gearbox: manual, 6 forward and 1 reverse gears
Transfer box: 2-speed
Clutch: self-adjusting, hydraulic
Steering: ball and nut, power assisted
Turning radius: 11·5 m
Suspension: telescopic hydraulic shock absorbers, leaf springs
Tyres: 14.00 × 20 PR 18
Number of tyres: 4 + 1 spare
Brakes: duplex compressed air
Electrical system: 24 V
Batteries: 2 × 12 V, 120 Ah

SAKOM 50 (4 × 2) 5000 kg Truck

DESCRIPTION
The SAKOM 50 is derived from the SAMIL range but is intended for rear-area and road use only. Many SAMIL components are used in its construction and it has the same cab as the SAMIL 20 but with a fixed roof and opening glass side screens. The basic version is a cargo truck with four drop side sections and a tailgate. Various other body forms exist.

SPECIFICATIONS
Cab seating: 1 + 1
Configuration: 4 × 2
Weight:
(empty) 4426 kg
(loaded) 11 000 kg
Weight on front axle: 3700 kg
Weight on rear axle: 7300 kg
Max load: 5000 kg
Length: 7·2 m
Width: 2·3 m
Ground clearance: 0·263 m
Track:
(front) 1·89 m
(rear) 1·7045 m
Wheelbase: 4 m
Engine: 6-cylinder air-cooled diesel developing 106 hp at 2650 rpm
Gearbox: 5 forward and 1 reverse gears
Clutch: self-adjusting hydraulic
Steering: manual, worm and roller
Tyres: 9.00 × 20 PR 18
Brakes: air/hydraulic dual circuit

SAKOM 50 (4 × 2) 5000 kg truck

STATUS
Production. In service with the South African Defence Forces.

MANUFACTURER
Enquiries to Armscor, Private Bag X337, Pretoria 0001, South Africa.

SAMIL 100 (6 × 6) 10 000 kg Trucks

DESCRIPTION
The SAMIL 100 (6 × 6) 10 000 kg truck shares many components with the SAMIL 50, including the cab, and like other vehicles in the SAMIL range is used as the basis for a wide range of bodies. The basic SAMIL 100 is a cargo truck with the rear body manufactured from pressed steel and fixed to the trapezoidal floor with supporting members. The basic SAMIL 100 chassis has a single-piece channel section frame with side members and bolted-in cross members with welded brackets to mount the body.
The cargo body sides have three dropsides on each side and a tailgate. A power-controlled crane is provided to handle the cargo and can lift 1000 kg at a jib extension of five metres.

VARIANTS
Protected transport
This is the same vehicle as the basic SAMIL 100 but is fitted with an armoured cab and engine cover.
Armoured personnel carrier
This version of the SAMIL 100 has a fully protected cab and engine cover and the rear is fully enclosed in an armoured box. Seating is provided internally and there are five armoured vision windows on each side.
Tipper
This is a conventional tipper truck with a 7·5 cubic metre capacity body.
Water tanker
This follows the same general lines as the SAMIL 50 water tanker but the tank capacity on the SAMIL 100 is 9100 litres. A water pump with a rate of 910 litres is provided. The oval-shaped stainless steel tank has a manhole on the top and is fitted with internal baffles. Spray devices are fitted at the rear and all controls are situated between the cab and the tank.
Fuel tanker
The tank for this variant is sub-divided into four baffled compartments and has a capacity of 13 000 litres. Each compartment has its own sump drain and manhole on

SAMIL 100 (6 × 6) gun tractor towing 155 mm G5 howitzer (T J Gander)

the top. A 64 mm diameter hose is used to fill containers directly from the tank, and three smaller hoses can be used to fill cans. All controls are on the left hand side of the tank.
Recovery vehicle
See separate entry under *Recovery vehicles* page 55.
Artillery tractor
Developed mainly to tow the 155 mm G5 howitzer, the SAMIL 100 artillery tractor has a crew compartment for the eight-man gun crew behind the driver's cab. This crew cab has a machine gun cupola hatch in the roof. Behind the crew cab is a cargo area for propellant charges stowed in compartments behind drop-sides.

On top of the compartments is stowage space for 15 projectile pallets, each weighing 189 kg. A canvas cover encloses the cargo area. At the rear is an extending hydraulic crane capable of traversing through 360 degrees and lifting 800 kg at a jib length of 3·5 metres.

STATUS
Production. In service with the South African Defence Forces.

MANUFACTURER
Enquiries to Armscor, Private Bag X337, Pretoria 0001, South Africa.

SPECIFICATIONS
(basic SAMIL 100 truck)
Cab seating: 1 + 2
Configuration: 6 × 6
Weight:
  (chassis/cab) 9135 kg
  (loaded) 21 000 kg
Front axle load: 6500 kg
Rear axle load: 15 400 kg
Payload: 10 000 kg
Towed load: 10 000 kg
Length: 10·27 m
Width: 2·5 m
Height: 3·35 m

Ground clearance:
  (front axle) 0·355 m
  (rear axles) 0·359 m
Track:
  (front) 2·002 m
  (rear) 2·048 m
Wheelbase: 5·25 m − 1·38 m
Angle of approach/departure: 30°/30°
Max speed: (road) 88 km/h
Range: 800 km
Fuel capacity: 400 litres
Max gradient: 70%
Side slope: 18°
Fording: 1·2 m at 5 km/h

Engine: V-10 air-cooled diesel developing 268 hp at 2650 rpm
Gearbox: manual, 6 forward and 1 reverse gears
Transfer box: 2-speed
Clutch: self-adjusting, hydraulic
Steering: power-assisted, ball and nut
Turning radius: 11·9 m
Suspension: telescopic hydraulic shock absorbers, leaf springs
Tyres: 14.00 × 20 PR 18
Number of tyres; 6 + 1 spare
Brakes: duplex, compressed air
Electrical system: 24 V
Batteries: 2 × 12 V, 120 Ah

SAMIL 100 (6 × 6) 10 000 kg truck with standard cargo/personnel body
(T J Gander)

SAMIL 100 (6 × 6) 10 000 kg truck with cargo body and mine resistant cab
(T J Gander)

SAMIL 100 (6 × 6) truck with box body (T J Gander)

SAMIL 100 (6 × 6) tipper truck (T J Gander)

SPAIN

Santana Land-Rover Model 2000 (4 × 4) Light Truck

DESCRIPTION
The Santana Land-Rover Model 2000 (4 × 4) light truck is manufactured mainly from Land-Rover components which have been revised to produce a multi-purpose vehicle with good cross-country performance. The Model 2000 has a spacious forward control cab which may be produced in either hard-top or soft-top versions. The soft-top version uses a canvas roof which can be removed, as can the side windows. The windscreen may be folded forward over the bonnet. The rear cargo area may be produced in several versions, one of which is with a canvas tilt and outward-facing bench seats for up to 12 men. This version has downward-folding sides and a tailgate. Another version has no cab roof or side windows and has the open rear flat-bed area clear to

accommodate a 20 mm anti-aircraft cannon. Versions with hard-tops to the cab may be used as the basis for mobile workshops, fire tenders and similar special-purpose vehicles.
The Model 2000 may be fitted with either petrol or diesel engines, both of 3·429 litres.

STATUS
Production. In service with the Spanish armed forces.

MANUFACTURER
Santana, Avenida Manoteras 12, Madrid 34, Spain.

SPECIFICATIONS
Cab seating: 1 + 1 or 2
Configuration: 4 × 4
Weight: (empty) 2360 kg
Weight on front axle: 1440 kg
Weight on rear axle: 920 kg

Load area: 2·85 × 1·77 m
Length: 4·94 m
Width: 1·96 m
Height: (hard top) 2·28 m
Ground clearance: 0·27 m
Track:
  (front) 1·46 m
  (rear) 1·48 m
Wheelbase: 2·56 m
Engine: 3·429-litre diesel developing 94 hp at 4000 rpm or 3·429-litre petrol developing 104 hp at 4000 rpm
Gearbox: 4 forward and 1 reverse gears
Clutch: hydraulic diaphragm
Transfer box: 2-speed
Turning radius: 7 m
Tyres: 9.00 × 16
Brakes: dual circuit hydraulic
Electrical system: 24 V

Pegaso 3046 (4 × 4) Cargo Trucks

DEVELOPMENT
The Pegaso 3046 trucks have been developed primarily as an export/commercial model. The first widely available model was the Pegaso 3046/50 which had a nominal payload of 3000 kg. This has now been replaced by the Pegaso 3046/10 with a nominal payload of 5000 kg

and it is this model which has been sold to Egypt. The first contract to export 2650 Pegaso 3046/10 trucks to Egypt was signed in November 1980. In July 1981 a contract was signed for a further 5000 trucks, and a contract for another 5000 trucks may be forthcoming.

DESCRIPTION
The Pegaso 3046/50 and 3046/10 are fundamentally

identical. The two-man cab is situated well forward over the engine and has a soft top which can be removed if required. The two-piece windscreen can be folded forwards over the short bonnet to reduce the vehicle height. In front of the bonnet a large steel frame provides protection for the radiator grill and headlamps which are set into the body work. At the rear the normal load-carrying body is an open cargo/personnel area that can be used to carry 5000 kg of stores or 23 men on bench seats situated along each side. Off-road the maximum load is 3000 kg. For protection against the weather a canvas tilt can be fitted. A spare wheel is carried under the load area on the left-hand side; the corresponding area on the right is occupied by the fuel tank. On some versions the spare wheel is carried behind the cab.

Optional equipment for the 3046/10 includes a metal roof for the cab, a fording kit, a power take-off on the gearbox and a 4500 kg capacity winch. Versions other than the cargo/personnel type include a tanker, a recovery vehicle with a swivelling crane, an ambulance, a communications post vehicle, a refrigerated cold storage vehicle and a command post. Various weapons can be fitted.

SPECIFICATIONS
Cab seating: 1 + 1 (23 in rear)
Configuration: 4 × 4
Weight:
    (empty) 7200 kg
    (loaded, on road) 12 200 kg
    (loaded, off road) 10 200 kg
Front axle load: (loaded, on road) 5475 kg
Rear axle load: (loaded, on road) 6725 kg
Max payload:
    (on road) 5000 kg
    (off road) 3000 kg
Towed load:
    (on road) 7500 kg
    (off road) 4500 kg
Length: 6·085 m
Width:
    (cab) 2·4 m
    (over rear axle) 2·406 m
Height: (cab) 2·765 m
Ground clearance: 0·34 m
Track: 1·96 m
Wheelbase: 3·7 m
Angle of approach/departure: 49°/49°
Max speed: 89 km/h
Range: 900 km
Fuel capacity: 350 litres
Max gradient: 87%
Side slope: 30%
Engine: Pegaso Model 9100/42, 6-cylinder, in-line, 10·17-litre four-stroke diesel developing 170 hp at 2100 rpm
Gearbox: Pegaso Model 8256.10 manual with 6 forward and 1 reverse gears
Clutch: Model 8500.01 single dry disc
Transfer box: Pegaso pneumatic 2-speed
Steering: block servo-hydraulic
Turning radius: 9·5 m
Suspension: semi-elliptical leaf springs and telescopic shock absorbers, front and rear

Tyres: 13.00 × 20 or 14.00 × 20
Number of tyres: 4 + 1 spare
Brakes: dual circuit air
Electrical system: 24 V
Batteries: 2 × 12 V, 110 Ah
Alternator: 840 W

STATUS
Production. Ordered by Egypt (7650).

MANUFACTURER
Pegaso, Empresa Nacional de Autocamiones SA, Military Division, José Abascal 2, Madrid 3, Spain.

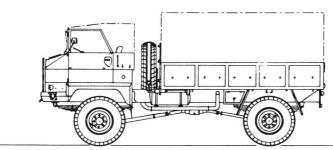

Pegaso 3046/50 (4 × 4) 3000 kg truck

Pegaso 3046/50 (4 × 4) 3000 kg cargo truck

Pegaso 3046 (4 × 4) fuel tanker

Pegaso 3046/10 (4 × 4) 5000 kg truck

Pegaso 3045 (4 × 4) 3000 kg Cargo Truck

DEVELOPMENT
The Pegaso 3045 (4 × 4) truck was designed by the DAF Company of the Netherlands to meet the requirements of the Spanish Army. While under development it had the DAF designation YA 414, and is basically an improved model of the DAF YA 314 (4 × 4) 3000 kg truck used by the Dutch forces (see page 382).

The Pegaso 3045 entered service in 1970 and initial production vehicles used many DAF components but as production increased more components of Spanish manufacture were used and eventually almost all of the truck was built in Spain.

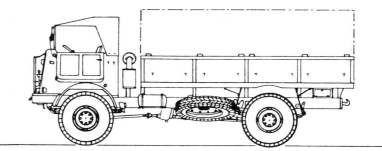

Pegaso 3045D (4 × 4) 3000 kg cargo truck

Pegaso 3045D (4 × 4) 3000 kg cargo truck

Pegaso 3045DV (4 × 4) 3000 kg truck fitted with deep wading equipment

Pegaso 3045DV (4 × 4) fuel tanker fitted with deep wading equipment

Pegaso 3045DV (4 × 4) dump truck

First production models were powered by a petrol engine coupled to a manual gearbox with five forward and one reverse gears, and had single rear wheels. This was soon replaced in production by the Pegaso 3045D powered by a Pegaso diesel engine built under licence in Spain from British Leyland, a gearbox with six forward and one reverse gears and dual rear wheels. To meet the requirements of the Spanish Marines a special model has been developed known as the Pegaso 3045DV which can ford to a maximum depth of two metres.

DESCRIPTION
The two-door forward control cab is made of steel and has a tarpaulin roof that can be folded backward and a windscreen that can be folded forward onto the radiator. The rear cargo body is all steel and has a drop tailgate, five removable bows and a tarpaulin cover. The wheel arches extend all the way along the cargo body on either side and provide seats when the vehicle is carrying passengers. Wooden panels can be inserted between the wheel arches to enable the vehicle to carry wider loads. A winch with a 4000 kg capacity can be installed.

VARIANTS
The Spanish Army has a number of vehicles fitted in the rear with the American M45 anti-aircraft gun system

which consists of four M2 12·7 mm/0·50 Browning HB machine guns, each with 200 rounds of ready-use ammunition. Other variants include a crane truck (Marines use one version and Army use at least two different versions), dump truck, refueller, water carrier and workshop.

SPECIFICATIONS (Pegaso 3045D)
Cab seating: 1 + 1
Configuration: 4 × 4
Weight:
 (empty) 6750 kg
 (loaded, cross country) 9750 kg
Max load:
 (road) 6000 kg
 (cross country) 3000 kg
Towed load: 4500 kg
Load area: 4·2 × 2·15 m
Length: 6·47 m
Width: 2·48 m
Height: (cab) 2·617 m
Ground clearance: 0·32 m
Track: 1·9 m
Wheelbase: 3·7 m
Angle of approach/departure: 48°/34°
Max speed: 72 km/h (3045 90 km/h)
Range: 650 km

Fuel capacity: 260 litres
Max gradient: 60%
Fording: 1 m
 (3045) 0·7 m
 (3045DV) 2 m
Engine: Pegaso Model 9026/13 6-cylinder diesel developing 125 hp at 2400 rpm (3045 DAF 6-cylinder petrol developing 134 hp at 3500 rpm)
Gearbox: manual with 6 forward and 1 reverse gears (3045, manual with 5 forward and 1 reverse gears)
Transfer box: 2-speed
Turning radius: 6·96 m
Suspension: semi-elliptical springs with double acting hydraulic shock absorbers
Tyres: 11.00 × 20 (3045, 12.00 × 20)
Number of tyres: 6 + 1 spare (3045, 4 + 1 spare)
Brakes:
 (main) air/hydraulic
 (parking) mechanical
Electrical system: 24 V

STATUS
Production complete. In service with the Spanish armed forces. Also used by Upper Volta (33) and Nicaragua.

MANUFACTURER
Pegaso, Empresa Nacional de Autocamiones SA, Military Division, José Abascal 2, Madrid 3, Spain.

Pegaso 3050 (6 × 6) 6000 kg Cargo Truck

DESCRIPTION
The Pegaso 3050 (6 × 6) cargo truck has been developed from the earlier Pegaso 3040 (4 × 4) 4000 kg truck and uses the same cab as the Pegaso 3045 (4 × 4) 3000 kg truck. The two-door forward control cab is of steel construction with a tarpaulin roof that can fold backward and a windscreen which folds forward onto the radiator. The rear cargo area is all steel and has a drop tailgate, seven removable bows and a tarpaulin cover. Most vehicles have a 6000 kg capacity winch.

VARIANTS
These include a bridging vehicle (for carrying components of the MAN bridge), dump truck, two recovery vehicles (one with a Bazán Onara crane, one with an IASA crane), shop/van and tractor truck. A Pegaso 3050 has been used as a prototype launcher for the artillery T-rocket. 40 rockets are carried and the vehicle has an enlarged armoured cab with two rows of seats for the crew.

Pegaso 3050 (6 × 6) tractor truck

Pegaso 3050 (6 × 6) 6000 kg cargo truck

Pegaso 3050 (6 × 6) recovery vehicle

Basic specifications of the Pegaso 3040 are: weight loaded, road 12 000 kg, weight loaded, cross country 9000 kg, unladen weight 5000 kg, length 6·78 metres, width 2·45 metres, height overall 3·2 metres and powered by a six-cylinder diesel engine developing 125 bhp. The Pegaso 3040 is used in small numbers by the Spanish Army and some have been sold to the Nigerian Army. The 3040 has a hardtop cab and the earlier 3020 is similar but with a soft top cab.

NOTE
The Spanish Army also uses the Barreiros Talbot R-3464 (6 × 4) as a tractor truck for hauling semi-trailers.

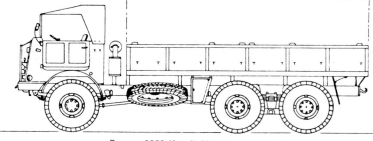

Pegaso 3050 (6 × 6) 6000 kg cargo truck

SPECIFICATIONS
Cab seating: 1 + 1
Configuration: 6 × 6
Weight:
  (empty) 8500 kg
  (loaded, cross country) 14 500 kg
Max load:
  (road) 10 000 kg
  (cross country) 6000 kg
Towed load:
  (road) 14 500 kg
  (cross country) 7500 kg
Length: 7·2 m
Width: 2·5 m
Height: (cab) 2·62 m
Ground clearance: 0·32 m
Track: 1·9 m
Wheelbase: 3·987 m + 1·426 m

Angle of approach/departure: 48°/44°
Max speed: (road) 68 km/h
Range: 500 km
Fuel capacity: 250 litres
Max gradient: 89% (low range, bottom gear)
Fording: 1 m
Engine: Pegaso model 910/40 6-cylinder in-line diesel developing 170 hp at 2000 rpm
Gearbox: manual with 6 forward and 1 reverse gears
Transfer box: 2-speed
Steering: power-assisted
Suspension:
  (front) semi-elliptical springs and hydraulic shock absorbers
  (rear) oscillating arms and spring common to both axles. Rear axles joined to chassis frame by torsion bars

Tyres: 13.00 × 20
Number of tyres: 6 + 1 spare
Brakes:
  (main) air/hydraulic
  (parking) mechanical
Electrical system: 24 V
Batteries: 2 × 12 V, 175 Ah

STATUS
Production. In service with Spanish forces and Nicaragua.

MANUFACTURER
Pegaso, Empresa Nacional de Autocamiones SA, Military Division, José Abascal 2, Madrid 3, Spain.

Pegaso 3055 (6 × 6) 6000 kg Truck

DEVELOPMENT
The Pegaso 3055 is a 6 × 6 derivative of the Pegaso 3046 (4 × 4) truck. In March 1982 it was announced that the Pegaso 3055 was to be the standard 6000 kg off-road truck chassis for all three Spanish armed services and is now in production in a range of variants.

DESCRIPTION
The cab of the Pegaso 3055 is the same as that used on the Pegaso 3046. It has a canvas hood as standard with an optional metal top. The cab has seating for the driver and one passenger and if required the hood can be removed and the windscreen folded forward over the short bonnet. The main load carrying area is at the rear and on the standard cargo/personnel body there is bench seating for 30 men. The engine fitted may have either a 200 hp or 220 hp output but the latter has been selected for use with the Spanish armed forces.
  The Pegaso 3055 is now being produced in the following versions: medium truck, medium fuel tanker, medium water tanker, heavy crane, medium tipper truck, fire-fighting vehicle, tractor, van body for workshops, stores, refrigerated bodies etc.
  The Pegaso 3055 can be used as an artillery tractor or missile launcher tractor and may be used to carry engineering stores such as bridging components. A 6000 kg winch may be fitted.

Pegaso 3055 (6 × 6) 6000 kg truck in use as tractor for 155 mm M114 howitzer

SPECIFICATIONS
Cab seating: 1 + 1 (30 in rear)
Configuration: 6 × 6
Weight:
  (empty) 9000 kg
  (loaded, on road) 19 000 kg
  (loaded, off road) 15 000 kg
Front axle load: (loaded, on road) 5800 kg
Rear axle load: (loaded, on road) 13 200 kg

Max payload:
  (on road) 10 000 kg
  (off road) 6000 kg
Towed load:
  (on road) 14 500 kg
  (off road) 7500 kg
Length: (cab and chassis) 6·956 m
Width:
  (cab) 2·4 m
  (rear wheels) 2·406 m
Height: (cab) 2·765 m
Ground clearance: 0·34 m
Track: 1·96 m
Wheelbase: 3·245 m + 1·484 m
Angle of approach/departure: 47°/50°
Max speed: 80 km/h
Range: 550 km
Fuel capacity: 350 litres
Max gradient: 51%
Side slope: 30%
Engine: Pegaso model 9220/10 6-cylinder, in-line, 10·518-litre 4-stroke, turbocharged diesel developing 200 or 220 hp at 2000 rpm

Gearbox: Pegaso Model 8256.10.09 manual with 6 forward and 1 reverse gears
Transfer box: Pegaso pneumatic 2-speed
Clutch: Model 8500.01 single dry disc
Steering: block servo-hydraulic
Turning radius: 10·2 m
Suspension:
  (front) semi-elliptical leaf springs and telescopic shock absorbers
  (rear) semi-elliptical leaf springs
Tyres: 13.00 × 20 or 14.00 × 20
Number of tyres: 6 + 1 spare
Brakes: dual circuit air
Electrical system: 24 V
Batteries: 2 × 12 V, 110 Ah
Alternator: 840 W

STATUS
In production for the Spanish armed forces.

MANUFACTURER
Pegaso, Empresa Nacional de Autocamiones SA, Military Division, José Abascal 2, Madrid 3, Spain.

Pegaso 3055 (6 × 6) 6000 kg truck

Pegaso 3055 (6 × 6) 6000 kg truck

SWEDEN

Volvo 4140 Series of 4 × 4 and 6 × 6 Cross Country Vehicles

DEVELOPMENT
In the early 1960s the Swedish Army Material Department drew up its requirements for a new generation of tactical vehicles for the 1970s and 1980s. In 1966 Volvo was awarded the development contract for the Class 1 and 2 vehicles in the 1000 to 2500 kg range and Saab-Scania the contract for the heavier Class 3 and 4 vehicles, subsequently known as the SBA (4 × 4) and SBAT (6 × 6).

Primary requirements were a high power-to-weight ratio, forward control cab, good angle of approach and departure, high ground clearance, tough suspension, chassis which could be adapted to accept a wide variety of bodies, commercial components to be used wherever possible, ease of repair and maintenance, low training requirement and a minimum total service life cost.

During the development stage it was decided to increase the payload of the 4 × 4 version to 2000 kg and of the 6 × 6 model to 2500 kg. An 8 × 8 version was built to the prototype stage but was not placed in production.

DESCRIPTION
4 × 4 4140/4141 (or C303)
The first prototypes completed in 1966 were powered by a B-20 (94 hp) engine which was subsequently replaced by the more powerful B-30 (145 hp) engine. First deliveries were made to the Swedish Army in 1974. First civilian vehicles were completed in 1976.

Two basic models were built, the 4140 cargo and the 4141 fully enclosed, or hardtop. Both have a two-door fully enclosed cab which can be split above the waist line. The cargo model has an all-steel rear cargo area with a drop tailgate, removable bows and a tarpaulin cover. The hardtop model has a fully enclosed steel rear body with an aluminium roof, and a large door at the rear and a door in each side.

All-wheel drive is engaged by a press-button in the high range and automatically when low range is engaged. Both front and rear axles have vacuum-operated mechanical differential locks which can be engaged separately or together. The chassis consists of box side members with tubular cross-members welded into position. The chassis is torsionally stiff to avoid stressing the superstructure.

The front suspension consists of underslung semi-elliptical leaf springs carried in rubber mountings, hollow-rubber springs and double-acting telescopic shock absorbers. The rear suspension consists of overslung semi-elliptical leaf springs carried in rubber mountings, hollow-rubber springs and double-acting telescopic shock absorbers. The main brakes are vacuum-hydraulic drum type, dual circuit, with one vacuum cylinder per circuit.

The handbrake is mechanical and acts on the propeller shaft. Optional equipment includes an air-conditioning system, electric engine heater, electric compressor with ten metres of hose for pumping tyres, PTO, protective wooden floor ribs, roof ventilator, tow hook, trailer electrical socket, Webasto engine and passenger area heater and a 2200/3000 kg capacity winch.

Volvo 4141 (4 × 4) fully-enclosed version

Malaysian Army Volvo 4143 (6 × 6) cargo truck (Simon Glen)

Interior view of Volvo 4141 (4 × 4) vehicle

Volvo 4140 (4 × 4) cargo truck

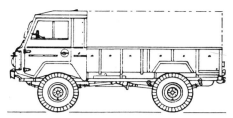

Volvo 4140 (4 × 4) cargo truck

The basic model is fitted with a thermostatically controlled heater, defroster system and a two-speed blower in the cab with a heater and two-speed blower for the rear compartment.

The C304 (4 × 4) version is almost identical to the C303 but has a wheelbase of 2·53 metres.

6 × 6 4143 (or C306)
The 6 × 6 model is based on the 4 × 4 model and has the same engine, gearbox, transfer box and cab. The vehicle can be fitted with a variety of bodies including cargo, fully enclosed and ambulance. The cargo model has drop sides, drop tailgate, removable bows and a tarpaulin cover. The fully enclosed body version has a large door in the rear and a door in each side, and can be used for a variety of roles including radio/command.

The front suspension consists of underslung semi-elliptical leaf springs, hollow-rubber springs and double acting telescopic shock absorbers. The rear suspension is of the double cantilever type with parabolic springs with progressively acting hollow-rubber springs and double-acting telescopic shock absorbers. The main brakes are vacuum-hydraulic drum type, with the mechanical parking brake operating on the transfer box output shaft. Optional equipment is similar to that available for the 4 × 4 version.

A 6 × 6 amphibious model with a payload of 1000 kg has been developed to the prototype stage but has not been placed in production.

SPECIFICATIONS

Model	C303 hardtop	C304 chassis and cab	C306 chassis and cab
Cab seating	1 + 6	1 + 1	1 + 1
Configuration	4 × 4	4 × 4	6 × 6
Weight (empty)	2250 kg	1940 kg	2400 kg
(loaded)	3450 kg	3900 kg	5500 kg
Weight on front axle (loaded)	1650 kg	1800 kg	1000 kg
Weight on rear axles (loaded)	1800 kg	2100 kg	1800 kg
Max load	1200 kg	1960 kg (inc body)	3100 kg (inc body)
Towed load	2500 kg	2500 kg	2500 kg
Load area	2·25 × 1·8 m	n/app	n/app
Length	4·25 m	4·28 m	5·735 m
Width	1·9 m	1·87 m	1·88 m
Height (cab)	2·13 m	2·13 m	2·13 m
(load area)	0·83 m	n/app	n/app
Ground clearance	0·386 m	0·386 m	0·386 m
Track	1·54 m	1·54 m	1·54 m
Wheelbase	2·3 m	2·53 m	2·72 m + 1·05 m
Angle of approach/departure	45°/45°	45°/45°	45°/40°
Max speed (road)	120 km/h	100 km/h	90 km/h
Fuel capacity	83 litres	125 litres	150 litres
Max gradient	100%	100%	100%
Max side slope	40%	40%	40%
Fording (without preparation)	0·7 m	0·7 m	0·7 m
Engine	Volvo B-30 in-line 6-cylinder OHV petrol developing 125 hp at 4250 rpm		
Gearbox	all have manual gearbox with 4 forward and 1 reverse gears		
Clutch	single dry plate	single dry plate	single dry plate
Transfer box	2-speed	2-speed	2-speed
Steering	all cam and roller type		
Turning radius	5·77 m	5·73 m	8·25 m
Tyres	8.90 × 16	8.90 × 16	8.90 × 16
Number of tyres	4 + 1 spare	4 + 1 spare	6 + 1 spare
Electrical system	12 V	12 V	12 V
Batteries	1 × 12 V, 60 Ah	1 × 12 V, 60 Ah	1 × 12 V, 60 Ah

STATUS
Production complete in Sweden. In service with the Swedish Army and Malaysia (4 × 4 and 6 × 6).

MANUFACTURER
Volvo AB, Göteborg, Sweden.

Volvo 4151 (4 × 4) Anti-tank Vehicle

DESCRIPTION
The Volvo 4151 was primarily designed to succeed the Volvo L3304 as an anti-tank and reconnaissance vehicle for the Swedish Army. It was not available on the civilian market.

The vehicle shares the mechanical components with the Volvo C303 (4 × 4) cross-country vehicle with a special superstructure supplied by Hägglund in northern Sweden. This superstructure consists of a metal bodywork up to waist level, and an upper part made from canvas, which can be easily folded down when the Bofors 1110 90 mm recoilless rifle is used. When travelling the gun is lowered, but it can easily be raised for use.

The engine is mounted in the forward part of the vehicle and while travelling the crew is protected by an anti-roll bar.

SPECIFICATIONS
In most respects, these are similar to the C303's.

STATUS
Production complete. In service with the Swedish Army.

MANUFACTURER
Volvo AB, Gotëborg, Sweden.

Volvo 4151 (4 × 4) anti-tank vehicle with canvas top in position

Volvo L 2204 (6 × 6) 1500 kg Truck

DEVELOPMENT
The L 2204 was developed for the Swedish Army in the late 1940s with the first prototype, the TL-21, being completed in 1950. The vehicle is known as the Lastterrängbil 912 (cross country truck) by the Swedish Army and was in production from 1955 to 1959.

DESCRIPTION
The layout of the L 2204 is conventional with the engine at the front, cab in the centre and the cargo area at the rear. The two-door all-steel cab has a hinged windscreen that can be lowered forward to increase visibility. The rear cargo area is all-steel with an opening tailgate, removable sides, removable bench troop seats, bows and a tarpaulin cover.

Vacuum-operated differential locks fitted on the front and rear axles can be engaged individually. The gearbox is fitted with a PTO for the worm-gear winch which is mounted on the right side of the chassis. It is fitted with an automatic check brake and can be used to the front or rear of the vehicle. The winch has a capacity of 4000 kg and 75 metres of 12 mm diameter cable.

Volvo L 2204 (6 × 6) 1500 kg truck with winch mounted just under forward part of cargo body

VARIANTS

There are two basic variants in service, a fire-fighting truck and a shop/van which is in service as a signals vehicle and as a mobile workshop.

SPECIFICATIONS

Cab seating: 1 + 2
Configuration: 6 × 6
Weight:
(empty) 4200 kg
(loaded, cross country) 5700 kg
Max load:
(road) 2250 kg
(cross country) 1500 kg
Load area: 2·7 × 1·82 m
Length: 5·86 m
Width: 1·9 m

Height:
(cab) 2·14 m
(tarpaulin) 2·56 m
Ground clearance: 0·27 m
Track:
(front) 1·55 m
(rear) 1·6 m
Wheelbase: 2·65 m − 1·06 m
Angle of approach/departure: 42°/40°
Max speed: (road) 80 km/h
Range: 300 km
Fuel capacity: 90 litres
Engine: Volvo model A6 6-cylinder OHV petrol developing 115 bhp at 3000 rpm
Gearbox: manual with 4 forward and 1 reverse gears
Clutch: single dry plate
Transfer box: 2-speed

Steering: twin-lever Ross type
Turning radius: 8·16 m
Suspension:
(front) semi-elliptical springs with double-acting hydraulic shock absorbers
(rear) double cantilever springs
Tyres: 11.00 × 20
Brakes:
(main) hydraulic
(parking) mechanical
Electrical system: 12 V
Battery: 1 × 12 V, 95 Ah

STATUS
Production complete. In service with the Swedish Army.

MANUFACTURER
Volvo AB, Göteborg, Sweden.

Volvo L 3154 (6 × 6) 3000 kg Truck

DEVELOPMENT

The L 3154 (6 × 6) truck was developed by Volvo specifically to meet the requirements of the Swedish Army. The first prototype, the TL-31, was completed in 1954 and the vehicle was in production between 1956 and 1962. The Swedish Army designation for the L 3154 is the Lastterrängbil 934 (cross country truck), or L 934 for short.

DESCRIPTION

The layout of the L 3154 is conventional with the engine at the front, two-door all-steel fully enclosed cab in the centre and the cargo area at the rear with dropsides, side-hinged rear door, bows and a tarpaulin cover. A winch with a capacity of 8000 kg is fitted as standard on all vehicles. The L 3154 is used both as a cargo truck and as a prime mover for heavy artillery.

VARIANTS

A recovery version is in service under the army designation of the Bargningsterrängbil 965 (Volvo 3164), and there is also a crash and rescue vehicle called the 3154S.

SPECIFICATIONS

Cab seating: 1 + 2
Configuration: 6 × 6
Weight:
(empty) 7320 kg
(loaded) 10 320 kg
Max load: 3000 kg
Length: 7·25 m
Width: 2·15 m

Volvo L 3154 (6 × 6) 3000 kg truck towing 150 mm m/39 field howitzer

Height:
(cab) 2·7 m
(overall) 2·95 m
Ground clearance: 0·37 m
Track: 1·72 m
Wheelbase: 3·3 m + 1·25 m
Angle of approach/departure: 40°/42°
Max speed: (road) 75 km/h
Range: 300 km
Fuel capacity: 120 litres
Engine: Volvo D 96 AS 6-cylinder OHV diesel developing 150 hp at 2200 rpm
Gearbox: manual Volvo K12 with 5 forward and 1 reverse gears

Transfer box: 2-speed
Turning radius: 9 m
Suspension:
(front) semi-elliptical springs
(rear) double cantilever spring
Tyres: 11.00 × 20
Brakes:
(main) hydraulic, air-assisted
(parking) mechanical

STATUS
Production complete. In service with the Swedish Army.

MANUFACTURER
Volvo AB, Göteborg, Sweden.

Saab-Scania SBA 111 4500 kg (4 × 4) and SBAT 111S 6000 kg (6 × 6) Trucks

DEVELOPMENT

In the early 1960s the Swedish Army Material Department drew up its requirements for a new generation of tactical vehicles for the 1970s and 1980s. Volvo was awarded the contract for the lighter Class 1 and 2 vehicles and Saab-Scania the contracts for the heavier Class 3 (4 × 4) and Class 4 (6 × 6) vehicles.

Saab-Scania started design work in 1966 and received its first development contract in 1968. Primary requirements of the Swedish Army were for a vehicle which would be easy to handle and maintain, use proved and standardised commercial components wherever possible, be reliable and have a low repair cost and finally have a low total service life cost. The first prototypes were completed early in 1971 with the second series of prototypes being completed late in 1972. The Swedish Army placed its first production order in 1974, for 2000 vehicles (both 4 × 4 and 6 × 6) at a total cost of SKr 225 million for delivery between 1976 and 1979. In 1977 a further 258 vehicles were ordered for the Swedish Air Force and Navy. A total of 2500 vehicles were delivered to the Swedish Army.

Production was completed in February 1982.

DESCRIPTION

The layout of both vehicles is almost identical, the only major differences being in their engines and configurations. Ninety per cent of the components of both vehicles are interchangeable.

The chassis consists of two longitudinal U-shaped members with the cross-members riveted into position. The two-door forward control cab is all steel and has a hatch in the right side of the roof. The driver's windscreen is hinged at the top and can be opened upward for improved visibility. The cab can be tilted forward to an angle of 55 degrees with the aid of a

Left: Saab-Scania SBA (4 × 4) truck; right: SBAT (6 × 6) truck

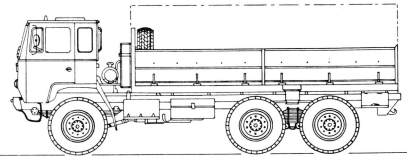

Saab-Scania SBAT 111S 6000 kg (6 × 6) truck

SBAT (6 × 6) chassis carrying Giraffe radar system

Crash rescue vehicle on SBAT (6 × 6) chassis as used by Swedish Air Force

SBAT (6 × 6) as used to tow Bofors 155 mm FH-77A weapon with gun crew in fully enclosed cabin behind cab

double-acting hydraulic pump. The grille on the front of the cab opens upwards to allow access to the oil dipstick, oil filter and oil tank for daily checks.

The engines of the two vehicles differ only in that the SBAT (6 × 6) has a turbocharger. The engine is fitted with a special fuel pump which allows the engine to continue running when inclined at an angle of 35 degrees.

The gearbox is of the automatic split type in which two-thirds of the power is always transmitted mechanically. The gearbox consists of the automatic gearbox, distributor gearbox and a torque converter. The main gearbox has six speeds, three hydraulic and three mechanical. The transfer box has one ratio for cross country operations and another for road operations. Changing up or down to the gear that corresponds to the engine speed and torque requirements is automatic.

All axles on both trucks are identical and each axle has a central bevel-gear, hub reduction gears and a differential lock.

The rear platform is torsionally rigid and the basic cargo models have removable drop sides and a drop tailgate.

Both vehicles have an 8000 kg capacity winch mounted on the right side of the chassis, driven by a PTO on the transfer box and operated by a switch on the dashboard and a winch brake control in front of the steering wheel. The winch can be used to the front or rear of the vehicle.

Cold weather equipment includes an engine heater, battery heater, fuel pre-heater, starting pilot and connections for starting cables.

VARIANTS

SBA (4 × 4)
This basic model has been designed for carrying cargo but some have been delivered to the Swedish Army with a 1500 kg hydraulic crane at the rear for unloading and some have been fitted for carrying passengers, with bows, canvas cover and bench seats down each side.

SBAT (6 × 6)
The basic model has been designed for carrying cargo but other variants include a version with a 5500 kg hydraulic crane mounted to the rear of the cab, which will be used for ammunition resupply for the Bofors 155 mm FH-77A weapon. The FH-77A is towed by an SBAT truck fitted with a fully enclosed cabin for the ten-man crew to the forward end of the platform. Mounted at the rear of the vehicle is a 1500 kg hydraulic crane. A 6 × 6 recovery vehicle has been built to the prototype stage but has not yet been ordered by the Swedish Army. The 6 × 6 version is also used to carry the Giraffe radar system which is used in conjunction with the Bofors RBS-70 SAM system.

Crash rescue vehicles
Following trials with two prototype bodies the Swedish armed forces ordered 47 crash rescue vehicles for delivery in 1979. They have a loaded weight of 16 000 kg and are fitted with both fire-fighting and crash rescue equipment.

Snow-clearing vehicle
This version is based on the chassis of the SBA (4 × 4) truck and is used by the Royal Swedish Air Force for clearing airfield runways of snow. A total of 45 of these vehicles has been ordered at a cost of SKr 12 million. When being driven forward on the road the vehicle is driven from the normal driver's position but when clear-

ing snow it is driven in reverse from the second cab which faces the rear. Maximum speed when clearing snow is 30 km/h. Steering during snow-clearing operations is by a duplicated hydrostatic steering system which acts on the ordinary steering mechanism of the vehicle. The snow-clearing equipment fitted is a ROLBA 1500S, which is of the cut and sling type and has a capacity of 30 to 35 000 kg of snow a minute.

SPECIFICATIONS

Model	SBA 111	SBAT 111S
Cab seating	1 + 2	1 + 2
Configuration	4 × 4	6 × 6
Weight (empty)	9150 kg	11 650 kg
(loaded, cross country)	13 700 kg	20 650 kg
Max load (cross country)	4500 kg	6000 kg
(road)	6000 kg	9000 kg
Towed load	6000 kg	12 000 kg
Load area	4·2 × 2·35 m	4·75 × 2·35 m
Length	6·75 m	7·78 m
Width	2·49 m	2·49 m
Height (cab)	2·9 m	2·88 m
(load area)	1·472 m	1·472 m
Ground clearance	0·4 m	0·4 m
Track	2·02 m	2·02 m
Wheelbase	4 m	3·55 m + 1·48 m
Angle of approach/departure	45°/40°	45°/40°
Max speed	90 km/h	90 km/h
Range	600 km	550 km
Fuel capacity	167 litres	167 litres
Max gradient	60%	60%
Max side slope	40%	40%
Fording	0·8 m	0·8 m
Engine	D11 6-cylinder diesel developing 202 hp at 2200 rpm	DS11 (supercharged) 6-cylinder diesel developing 296 hp at 2200 rpm
Steering	hydraulic	hydraulic
Turning radius	9 m	9·5 m
Suspension	semi-elliptical springs with double acting hydraulic shock absorbers	
Tyres	14.00 × 20	14.00 × 20
Brakes	air, dual circuit. Hand, spring type operating on front and rear wheels	
Electrical system	24 V	24 V

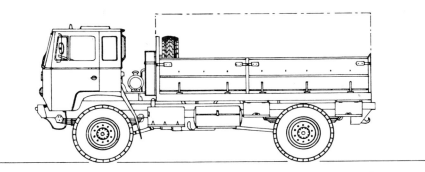

Saab-Scania SBA 111 4500 kg (4 × 4) truck

Volvo L 4854 (4 × 4) Truck

DEVELOPMENT
The Volvo L 4854 (4 × 4) truck is basically a standard
production vehicle modified to meet the requirements of
the Swedish Army. The first prototype was completed in
1960 and the vehicle was in production for the Army
between 1961 and 1963. The L 4854 is known as the
Lastterrängbil 939 (cross country truck) by the Army and
is in service in three basic models, the 939 BF with a
5·2 metre wheelbase, the 939 AF with a 4·4 metre
wheelbase and the 939 E with a 4·4 metre wheelbase
and a longer cab.

DESCRIPTION
The layout of the vehicle is conventional with the engine
at the front, cab in the centre and the cargo area at the
rear. The two-door all-steel cab has an observation
hatch in the roof, over which anti-aircraft machine guns
can be mounted. The rear cargo area has drop sides
and a drop tailgate. A winch with a capacity of 5000 kg
mounted under the right side of the chassis can be used
to the front or rear. Both front and rear axles have a
hand-operated differential lock. Some L 4854s have
been fitted with an HIAB crane to the rear of the cab for
unloading.

Volvo L 4854 (4 × 4) truck fitted with twin 7·5 mm machine guns over cab roof

SPECIFICATIONS
Cab seating: 1 + 2
Configuration: 4 × 4
Weight:
  (empty) 6720 kg
  (loaded, cross country) 9720 kg
Weight on front axle: (empty) 3630 kg
Weight on rear axle: (empty) 3090 kg
Max load:
  (road) 4500 kg
  (cross country) 3000 kg

Length: 7·5 m
Width: 2·28 m
Height: 2·82 m
Ground clearance: 0·25 m
Track:
  (front) 1·83 m
  (rear) 1·74 m
Wheelbase: 4·4 m
Angle of approach/departure: 38°/25°
Max speed: (road) 77 km/h
Range: 300 km
Fuel capacity: 120 litres
Engine: Volvo D67C 6-cylinder diesel developing
125 hp at 2400 rpm

Gearbox: manual Volvo K17 with 5 forward and
1 reverse gears
Clutch: single dry plate
Transfer box: 2-speed
Steering: ZF power-assisted
Turning radius: 10 m
Tyres: 10.00 × 20

STATUS
Production complete. In service with the Swedish Army.

MANUFACTURER
Volvo AB, Göteborg, Sweden.

Volvo F613 (4 × 2) Maintenance Supply Vehicle

DESCRIPTION
In 1979–80 Volvo delivered a quantity of maintenance
supply vehicles based on its commercial F613 chassis
to the Swedish Army under the designation model 112.
These have a forward control cab with a fully enclosed
body at the rear 6·5 metres long and 2·1 metres high
inside. Standard equipment includes a work bench,
wardrobe, hot water supply, 100-litre water tank and a
vertical exhaust pipe. Optional equipment includes a
toilet, cooking facilities and a refrigerator.

SPECIFICATIONS
Cab seating: 1 + 2
Configuration: 4 × 2
Weight:
  (empty) 8000 kg
  (loaded) 13 000 kg
Max load: 5000 kg
Length: 8·55 m
Width: 2·5 m
Height: 3·6 m
Fuel capacity: 130 litres
Engine: TD60B 6-cylinder 4-stroke, direct-injection
diesel with turbo-charging, developing 180 hp (metric)
at 2800 rpm
Gearbox: manual with 5 forward and 1 reverse gears or
automatic with 4 forward and 1 reverse gears
Steering: cam and roller, power-assisted
Suspension:
  (front) semi-elliptical springs and hydraulic double
acting telescopic shock absorbers
  (rear) semi-elliptical springs and integral mounted
helper springs

Volvo F613 (4 × 2) maintenance supply vehicle as used by Swedish Army

Tyres: 10.00 × 25
Number of tyres: 6 – 1 spare
Brakes:
  (main) air/hydraulic (dual circuit)
  (parking) mechanical
Electrical system: 12 V

STATUS
Production as required. In service with the Swedish
Army.

MANUFACTURER
Volvo AB, Göteborg, Sweden.

Other Volvo Vehicles

In addition to the Volvo vehicles fully described in this section, there are five other Volvo trucks in service with the Swedish Armed Forces which are all based on a standard civilian chassis with the minimum of modifications for military use.

STATUS
In production. In service with the Swedish Armed Forces.

MANUFACTURER
Volvo AB, Göteborg, Sweden.

Volvo F 407 (4 × 2) cargo truck with drop sides and tailgate

Volvo N 1025 (6 × 2) tanker truck towing tanker trailer (S Bengtson)

Volvo F 611 (4 × 2) cargo truck with drop sides, tailgate, bows and tarpaulin cover (S Bengtson)

Volvo F 10 (6 × 2) cargo truck towing trailer (Christer Olsson)

Volvo N 1020 (4 × 2) cargo truck towing radar trailer

SPECIFICATIONS

Model	F 407	F 611	F 10	N 1020	N 1025
Type	platform	platform	platform	platform	tanker
Cab seating	3	3	2	2	2
Configuration	4 × 2	4 × 2	6 × 2	4 × 2	6 × 2
Weight (loaded)	7000 kg	11 000 kg	24 500 kg	17 000 kg	25 000 kg
Weight on front axle (loaded)	2500 kg	3800 kg	6500 kg	6500 kg	7000 kg
Weight on rear axle/ axles (loaded)	4800 kg	7500 kg	18 000 kg	10 500 kg	18 000 kg
Length	5·9 m	7·3/7·45 m	n/a	7·35 m	n/a
Width	2·28 m	2·49/2·48 m	n/a	2·5 m	2·5 m
Height	2·45 m	2·55 m	n/a	3 m	3 m
Ground clearance	0·23 m	0·23 m	0·24 m	0·25 m	0·25 m
Track (front)	1·692 m	1·795 m	1·995 m	1·995 m	1·945 m
(rear)	1·594 m	1·671 m	1·82 m	1·82 m	1·82 m
Wheelbase	3·24 m	4 m	4·6 m	4·6 m	5 m
Fuel capacity	80 dm³	130 dm³	400 dm³	300 dm³	300 dm³
Engine type	D39C	Volvo D60A	Volvo TD100B	Volvo TD100A	Volvo TD100A
Engine hp	180	120	300	250	250
Clutch	KB 111	KB 113 B single dry plate in all vehicles	KF 214	KF 214 B	KF 116
Gearbox	ZF S 24-3	ZF S 5-35/2	SR 62	MR 61	R 61
Rear axle	RA EV 21	RA EV 41	RA N 181	RA N 181	RADR 80
Steering	ZF 7340	Burman	ZF 8045	ZF 8045	ZF 8045
Turning radius	6·24 m	7·74 m	8·9 m	8·68 m	10·28 m
Tyres	8R 17.5 × 5/10	9 – 22.5	12 × 22	11.00 R20/16	11.00/20

Scania-Vabis (4 × 2) L-36A 5920 kg Truck

DESCRIPTION

The Scania-Vabis L-36A is the standard civilian model L 3642 (4 × 2) truck with a minimum of modifications to suit it for military use. A total of 800 were built for the Swedish Army between 1964 and 1967.

The layout of the L-36A is conventional with the engine at the front, all-steel fully enclosed cab in the centre and the cargo area at the rear with drop sides and a drop tailgate. Some vehicles have been fitted with an HIAB crane mounted to the rear of the cab for loading.

VARIANTS

A fully enclosed mobile workshop version is in service under the designation of the Materielvardsbil 111. Scania-Vabis also delivered 1500 L-50 series 4 × 2 vehicles to the Swedish Army with various bodies. The L-50 is based on the civilian L-5042 (4 × 2) truck and has a wheelbase of 4·2 metres. Basic specifications are: length 6·5 metres, width 2·206 metres, height (cab) 2·538 metres, powered by a four-cylinder diesel developing 110 hp at 2400 rpm, and tyres 9.00 × 20.

SPECIFICATIONS

Cab seating: 1 + 2
Configuration: 4 × 2
Weight:
(empty) 4580 kg
(loaded) 10 500 kg
Weight on front axle: (loaded) 3500 kg
Weight on rear axle: (loaded) 7000 kg
Max load: 5920 kg
Length: (chassis) 6·59 m
Width: 2·19 m
Height: (cab) 2·76 m
Ground clearance: 0·355 m
Track: 1·85 m
Wheelbase: 4·2 m
Angle of approach/departure: 36°/30°
Max speed: (road) 77 km/h
Range: 450 km
Fuel capacity: 100 litres
Engine: Model D5 4-cylinder diesel developing 102 bhp at 2400 rpm
Gearbox: manual model S-5-35 with 5 forward and 1 reverse gears

Clutch: single dry plate
Transfer box: none
Steering: cam and triple roller
Turning radius: 7·3 m
Suspension:
(front) semi-elliptical springs and double acting hydraulic shock absorbers
(rear) semi-elliptical springs
Tyres: 8.25 × 20
Number of tyres: 6 +1 spare
Brakes:
(main) air
(parking) mechanical
Electrical system: 24 V
Batteries: 2 × 12 V

STATUS

Production complete. In service with the Swedish Army.

MANUFACTURER

Scania-Vabis, now Saab-Scania, Scania Division, Söndertälje, Sweden.

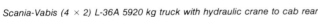

Scania-Vabis (4 × 2) L-36A 5920 kg truck with hydraulic crane to cab rear

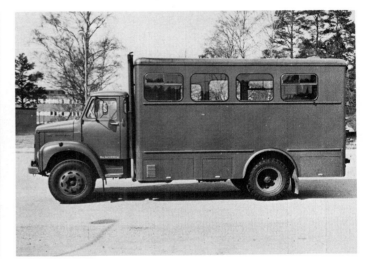

Scania-Vabis (4 × 2) L-36A mobile workshop

Other Scania-Vabis Vehicles

LT 110S (6 × 4) Tractor

This is a standard commercial vehicle (in production from 1968 to 1974) and is used to tow the Dutch DAF YTS 10050 semi-trailer carrying MBTs. The LTS 110S is powered by a DS11 four-stroke direct injection diesel with an exhaust turbo-charger, which develops 285 hp at 2200 rpm coupled to a manual GR 860 five speed (five forward and one reverse) gearbox combined with a two-speed pneumatically operated transfer box. Each axle has a differential lock and the brakes are air-operated, dual circuit, with an exhaust brake fitted as standard. Mounted to the rear of the cab are two Hägglund winches with a capacity of 20 000 kg each. The Royal Swedish Air Force uses the LS 110 as a fuel tanker.

L 75 (4 × 2) 7000 kg Truck

This is a standard commercial truck (in production from 1958 to 1963) modified for use by the Swedish Army Engineers. Provision is made at the front of the vehicle for fitting a snow plough and mounted to the rear of the cab is a HIAB crane. The L 75 also tows a trailer carrying engineer plant. It is powered by a D10 six-cylinder diesel developing 165 hp at 2200 rpm coupled to a manual gearbox with five forward and one reverse gears and a two-speed transfer box.

LT 76 (6 × 4) Tractor

This is used by the Swedish Army for towing the YTS 10050 semi-trailer carrying MBTs.

STATUS

Production complete. In service with the Swedish armed forces.

MANUFACTURER

Scania-Vabis, now Saab-Scania, Scania Division, Söntertälje, Sweden.

Scania-Vabis LS 110S (6 × 4) tanker of Royal Swedish Air Force towing tanker trailer

Scania-Vabis LT 110 (6 × 4) tractor towing YTS 10050 semi-trailer carrying Centurion MBT

SWITZERLAND

MOWAG (4 × 4) 1500 kg Truck

DESCRIPTION
Between 1951 and 1962 the MOWAG Company delivered 1688 of these 4 × 4 vehicles to the Swiss Army. They used many Dodge components and early models were powered by a 94 hp engine which was later replaced by a 103 hp engine. The two-door cab is of the forward control type with the engine mounted at the front of the vehicle. The cargo area at the rear has a drop tailgate, bench seat down each side, removable bows and a tarpaulin cover. Many vehicles have a front-mounted winch.

VARIANTS
Ambulance
This has a fully enclosed rear body which can accommodate five stretcher patients or eight to ten seated patients.
Radio/command vehicle
This has a fully-enclosed rear body.

STATUS
Production complete. In service with the Swiss Army.

MANUFACTURER
MOWAG Motorwagenfabrik AG, Kreuzlingen, Switzerland.

SPECIFICATIONS
Configuration: 4 × 4
Weight:
(empty) 2600 kg
(loaded) 4100 kg
Length: 4·64 m

MOWAG (4 × 4) 1500 kg truck

Width: 2 m
Height: 2·3 m
Wheelbase: 2·6 m
Speed: 89 km/h

Engine: Dodge 6-cylinder petrol developing 103 bhp
Gearbox: manual with 4 forward and 1 reverse gears
Transfer box: 2-speed
Tyres: 9.00 × 16

Saurer M4 (4 × 4) Artillery Tractor

DEVELOPMENT
The M4 (4 × 4) artillery tractor was developed to meet the requirements of the Swiss Army in the 1940s and is a member of a family of cross-country vehicles that also included the M6 (6 × 6) and M8 (8 × 8), the latter two having been phased out of service some years ago.

DESCRIPTION
The layout of the M4 is unconventional with the driver and one passenger seated at the front, ammunition and gun crew in the centre and engine at the rear. Hinged side doors fold down to allow the gun crew to unload ammunition. The upper part of the vehicle is covered by a tarpaulin cover with roll down sides. The windscreen can be folded forward and at the front of the vehicle is a winch with a capacity of 2500 kg and 50 metres of cable.

SPECIFICATIONS
Cab seating: 2 + 8
Configuration: 4 × 4
Weight:
(empty) 4250 kg
(loaded) 6500 kg
Payload: 2250 kg
Length: 5·2 m
Width: 2 m
Height: 2·32 m
Ground clearance: 0·56 m
Wheelbase: 2·9 m
Maximum road speed: 58 km/h
Range: 330 km

Saurer M4 (4 × 4) artillery tractor showing front mounted winch

Fuel capacity: 100 litres
Engine: 4-cylinder diesel developing 75 hp at 5820 rpm
Gearbox: manual, 5 forward and 1 reverse gears
Transfer box: 2-speed
Electrical system: 24 V

STATUS
Production complete. In service with the Swiss Army.

MANUFACTURER
Adolph Saurer Limited, Arbon, Switzerland.

Saurer 2CM and Berna 2UM (4 × 4) 3500 kg Trucks

DESCRIPTION
These vehicles were in production for the Swiss Army from 1950 to 1957 and are identical apart from their name-plates. The fully enclosed two-door forward control cab has a circular observation hatch in the left side of the roof. The rear cargo area, which can accommodate up to 28 fully equipped troops, has drop sides, drop tailgate, removable bows and a tarpaulin cover. Standard equipment includes a 6000 kg capacity winch with 55 metres of cable.

STATUS
Production complete. In service with the Swiss Army.

MANUFACTURERS
Adolph Saurer Limited, Arbon, Switzerland.
Berna AG, Olten, Switzerland.

Saurer 2CM (4 × 4) 3500 kg truck

SPECIFICATIONS
Cab seating: 1 + 1
Configuration: 4 × 4
Weight:
(empty) 5500 kg
(loaded, cross country) 9000 kg
Max load: (cross country) 3500 kg
Load area: 4 × 2·04 m
Length: 5·9 m
Width: 2·21 m
Height: 3·14 m

Ground clearance: 0·25 m
Track:
(front) 1·775 m
(rear) 1·655 m
Wheelbase: 3·4 m
Max speed: (road) 57 km/h
Fuel capacity: 100 litres
Fuel consumption: 27 litres/100 km
Engine: Model CR2D 4-cylinder diesel developing 75 hp
Gearbox: manual with 5 forward and 1 reverse gears

Transfer box: 2-speed
Suspension: (front and rear) semi-elliptical springs
Tyres: 8.25 × 20
Number of tyres: 6 + 1 spare
Brakes:
(main) air/hydraulic
(parking) mechanical
Electrical system: 24 V
Batteries: 2 × 12 V, 105 Ah

Saurer 2DM and Berna 2VM (4 × 4) 4500 kg Trucks

DESCRIPTION
These vehicles were in production for the Swiss Army from 1964 to 1973 and are identical apart from their name-plates. The layout of the vehicles is conventional with the engine at the front, two-door fully enclosed cab in the centre, with a circular observation hatch in the left side of the roof, and the cargo area at the rear with drop sides, drop tailgate, removable bows and a tarpaulin cover. Standard equipment includes a 6000 kg capacity winch with 55 metres of cable.

VARIANTS
There are two basic variants in service, two types of tipper truck and a tractor truck for hauling semi-trailers.

Further development by Saurer has resulted in the D180N (4 × 4) truck which can carry 9000 kg of cargo on roads or 5000 kg of cargo across country and is powered by a 180 hp diesel with the option of installing a 230 or 250 hp diesel. Deliveries of the D180N have already been made to the Middle East and South America.

Saurer 2DM (4 × 4) 4500 kg truck

SPECIFICATIONS
Cab seating: 1 + 2
Configuration: 4 × 4
Weight:
(empty) 6900 kg
(loaded) 12 000 kg
Weight on front axle: (empty) 3200 kg
Weight on rear axle: (empty) 3700 kg
Max load: 4900 kg
Load area: 4·1 × 2·18 m
Length: 7·37 m
Width: 2·3 m
Height: 3·2 m
Ground clearance: 0·27 m

Track:
(front) 1·898 m
(rear) 1·711 m
Wheelbase: 4·2 m
Angle of approach/departure: 34°/30°
Max speed: (road) 75 km/h
Fuel capacity: 160 litres
Fuel consumption: 35 litres/100 km
Engine: Saurer CT3D (or Berna T3) 6-cylinder diesel developing 135 hp at 2200 rpm
Gearbox: manual with 8 forward and 2 reverse gears
Transfer box: 2-speed
Turning radius: 8·51 m

Tyres: 9.00 × 20
Number of tyres: 6 + 1 spare
Brakes: air + exhaust retarder
Electrical system: 24 V
Batteries: 2 × 12 V

STATUS
Production complete. In service with the Swiss Army.

MANUFACTURERS
Adolph Saurer Limited, Arbon, Switzerland.
Berna AG, Olten, Bern, Switzerland.

Saurer 4CM and Berna 4UM (4 × 4) 5000 kg Trucks

DESCRIPTION
These vehicles were in production for the Swiss Army from 1949 to 1957 and are identical apart from their name-plates. They share many common components with the Saurer 2CM and Berna 2UM (4 × 4) 3500 kg trucks.

The fully enclosed two-door forward control cab has a circular observation hatch in the left side of the roof. The rear cargo area, which can accommodate up to 32 fully equipped troops, has drop sides, drop tailgate, removable bows and a tarpaulin cover. Standard equipment includes a 7000 kg capacity winch with 50 metres of cable.

VARIANTS
A tipper truck based on the Saurer 4CM is in service, with the same carrying capacity as the cargo truck but 6·41 metres long, 2·23 metres wide and 2·75 metres high. A bolster version is also in service. There is also a tipper version of the Saurer 5CM weighing 7900 kg empty and capable of carrying up to 6000 kg of rock or soil.

Saurer 4CM (4 × 4) 5000 kg truck

SPECIFICATIONS
Cab seating: 1 + 1
Configuration: 4 × 4
Weight:
(empty) 7000 kg
(loaded, cross country) 12 000 kg
Max load: (cross country) 5000 kg
Max towed load:
(road) 12 000 kg
(cross country) 8000 kg
Load area: 4·27 × 2·06 m
Length: 6·39 m
Width: 2·2 m
Height: (tarpaulin) 3·14 m
Ground clearance: 0·28 m

Track:
(front) 1·835 m
(rear) 1·65 m
Wheelbase: 3·4 m
Angle of approach/departure: 28°/24°
Max speed: 58 km/h
Max range: 600 km
Fuel capacity: 160 litres
Fuel consumption: 38 litres/100 km
Max gradient: 74·5%
Engine: Model CT2D 6-cylinder diesel developing 120 hp
Gearbox: manual with 5 forward and 1 reverse gears
Transfer box: 2-speed
Turning radius: 7·6 m

Suspension: (front and rear) semi-elliptical springs
Tyres: 10.00 × 20
Number of tyres: 6 + 1 spare
Brakes:
(main) air/hydraulic
(parking) mechanical
Electrical system: 24 V
Batteries: 2 × 12 V, 105 Ah

STATUS
Production complete. In service with the Swiss Army.

MANUFACTURERS
Adolph Saurer Limited, Arbon, Switzerland.
Berna AG, Olten, Switzerland.

Saurer 6 DM (4 × 4) 6000 kg and 10 DM (6 × 6) 10 000 kg Trucks

DEVELOPMENT
In the late 1970s Adolph Saurer started development of a new family of 6000 kg (4 × 4) and 10 000 kg (6 × 6) trucks to meet the requirements of the Swiss Army. The first prototypes, called the D250MF (4 × 4) and D300MF (6 × 6) were completed in 1978 and shown for the first time in public at the January 1980 Geneva Commercial Vehicle Exhibition.

They were subsequently redesignated the 6 DM (4 × 4) and 10 DM (6 × 6). By late 1981 the vehicles had been tested by the Swiss Army although no production order had been placed.

DESCRIPTION
Both vehicles share many common components. Both have a two-door fully enclosed all-steel forward control cab with a circular observation hatch in the roof on the right side. The rear cargo area is provided with removable drop sides and drop tailgate, removable bows and a tarpaulin cover. As an option a hydraulic winch with a capacity of 10 000 kg can be fitted.

The chassis is semi-flexible with independent leaf spring suspension with telescopic dampers, with all axles being fitted with differential locks. On both vehicles the front and rear axles are interchangeable.

VARIANTS
None has been announced although the chassis is suitable for a wide range of applications.

STATUS
Development complete. Ready for production.

MANUFACTURER
Adolph Saurer Limited, 9320 Arbon, Switzerland.

Saurer 10 DM (6 × 6) 10 000 kg truck

Saurer 6 DM (4 × 4) 6000 kg truck

SPECIFICATIONS

Model	6 DM	10 DM	Model	6 DM	10 DM
Configuration	4 × 4	6 × 6	Engine	Saurer D4KT, 6-cylinder in-line, 4-stroke diesel turbo-charged, developing 250 hp at 2200 rpm	Saurer D4KT, 6-cylinder in-line, 4-stroke diesel turbo-charged, developing 320 hp at 2200 rpm
Weight (empty)	10 000 kg	12 000 kg			
(loaded)	16 000 kg	22 000 kg			
Max load	6000 kg	10 000 kg			
Length	7·705 m	8·905 m			
Width	2·5 m	2·5 m	Gearbox	ZF S-6 90 with torque converter, retarder and splinter group (other types can also be fitted)	
Height (cab)	3·335 m	3·46 m			
Ground clearance	0·38 m	0·38 m	Transfer box	ZF A 800 3 D electro-pneumatically lockable	
Wheelbase	4·35 m	4 m + 1·4 m	Turning radius	8·75 m	9·75 m
Track	2·1 m	2·1 m	Axles	Saurer with lockable bevel gear differential	
Angle of approach/			Tyres	14.00 × 20	14.00 × 20
departure	40°/40°	40°/40°	Number of tyres	4 + 1 spare	6 + 1 spare
Fuel capacity	300 litres	300 litres	Brakes (main)	air, dual circuit	air, dual circuit
Fording	1·15 m	1·15 m	Electrical system	24 V	24 V

UNION OF SOVIET SOCIALIST REPUBLICS

Soviet Truck Designation Systems

Until 1966 Soviet vehicle designation followed a relatively straightforward system that relied upon an indication of the plant where the vehicle concerned originated and its design number in a numerical sequence which was set in an allotted batch of numbers to provide further identification. These numbers were in groups of two or three (even the two-figure numbers were actually three-figure numbers as the prefix 0 given to the Gor'kiy plant is usually omitted), with the first figure providing an extra origin indication over and above the simple name-place plant origin which is usually abbreviated to three or four letters. An example of this abbreviation is that the Minsk Motor Vehicle Plant is referred to as MAZ and the designs from this plant are in the 500 to 599 band only, eg MAZ-500 or MAZ-543. The numbers are allotted in a design sequence so that early designs can be differentiated from later designs.

The designation sequences allotted were as follows:

Motor Plant Location	Name	Digit band
Gor'kiy	GAZ	000 to 099 (1st zero omitted)
Moscow	ZIL	100 to 199
Yaroslavl, Kremenchug	YaAZ, later later KrAZ	200 to 299
Miass	Ural	300 to 399
Ul'Yanovsk	UAZ	400 to 499
Minsk	MAZ	500 to 599
Kutaisi	KAZ	600 to 699
Zaporozh'ye, Lutsk, Riga		900 to 1000

As in any designation system there were anomalies. For instance the AZLK abbreviation may be found allot-

ted to civil models in the 400 to 499 band and some bands were limited to 50 numbers or less with some held in reserve and not actually allotted. The 700 to 899 band was allotted to trailers.

On 1 August 1966, a new designation system came into use. It did not affect the designations given to models already in use but from that date new models were to be provided with an entirely new system that gives information on vehicle weight, type, design number, modification state and export status. The only part retained from the previous system was the continuing use of the plant abbreviation. It should be stressed that models in use before this date still retain their old-style designation.

The new system consists of up to six digits following the abbreviation of the manufacturing plant. The number of digits involved may vary from four to six with four being the more usual (eg Ural-4320).

The first digit of the sequence indicates the gross

weight band into which the vehicle falls. For trucks they are as follows:

1	below 1200 kg	5	14 000 to 20 000 kg
2	1200 to 2000 kg	6	20 000 to 40 000 kg
3	2000 to 8000 kg	7	over 40 000 kg
4	8000 to 14 000 kg		

This simple weight allocation designation is complicated by the fact that the same digit has another meaning when applied to light vehicles and cars. For these types the numbers refer to engine size:

1	less than 1.2 litres
2	1.2 to 2 litres
3	2 to 4 litres
4	over 4 litres

Leaving this anomaly aside, the second digit of the sequence denotes the vehicle type, as follows:

1	passenger cars
2	buses
3	trucks with sides
4	tractors
5	dump trucks
6	tanker trucks
7	vans
8	not alloted, in reserve
9	special vehicles

The third and fourth digits refer to the design sequence, usually starting with 01. There are special sequences relating to ambulances, high mobility vehicles and specially-heightened models.

The fifth digit, if used, is used to identify modifications to the basic design or product-improvements.

The sixth digit, if used at all, will apply to export models. There are only two of these digits in use, 6 and 7. Standard export models are denoted by the application of 6 at the end of the sequence, while 7 denotes export models for use in the tropics. Two other numbers, 8 and 9, are held in reserve for possible future applications.

To add one further complication to this sequence system, experimental models are indicated by the use of the letter E following the design sequence. This E is dropped once the design reaches production or acceptance.

For an example of the new sequence in use, the KamAZ-5320 might be considered. KamAZ denotes that the vehicle was produced at the Kama Motor Vehicle Plant at Naberezhyne Chelny. The first digit (5) shows that the vehicle has a gross weight of between 14 000 and 20 000 kg. The second digit (3) shows that

the model type is that of a truck with sides. The 20 denotes the design sequence. Although it is not used in this example the theoretical designation of KamAZ-532017 would show that the final two digits provide the presence of a major modification and that the vehicle is an export model for use in the tropics.

Trailers have their own designation system which follows the same general principles and is given in the *Trailers* section.

Automotive engines are also provided with a designation system along the same general lines but with only three or four digits. The first digit indicates the engine displacement and type, while the third and fourth are the model numbers which can also be used to denote the type of engine involved, ie 0 to 39 denote petrol engines and 40 to 99 denote diesels. If used, the fourth digit denotes the modification status. The first digit classification is as follows:

1	less than 0·75 litres
2	0·75 to 1·2 litres
3	1·2 to 2 litres
4	2 to 4 litres
5	4 to 7 litres
6	7 to 10 litres
7	10 to 15 litres
8	above 15 litres
9	gas turbine engines

GAZ-51 (4 × 2), GAZ-63 (4 × 4) Trucks

DEVELOPMENT/DESCRIPTION
The GAZ-51 (4 × 2) truck entered production at the Gor'kiy plant in 1946 and production continued until 1955 when it was replaced by the slightly modified GAZ-51A. The vehicle has now been replaced in production by the GAZ-52/GAZ-53.

The GAZ-63 is the 4 × 4 model of the GAZ-51 and has single rear tyres instead of the dual rear tyres of the GAZ-51. It was in production from 1946 until 1963 when the improved GAZ-63A was introduced, which continued in production until 1968. The chassis of the GAZ-63 was used as the basis for the BTR-40 (4 × 4) armoured personnel carrier. The replacement for this vehicle is the GAZ-66 which has increased load carrying capability.

These vehicles both have an all-steel two-seat cab with the cargo area at the rear. The cargo body of the GAZ-51 consists of a wooden platform with three hinged sideboards whereas the cargo body of the GAZ-63 consists of a wooden platform with high grilled sideboards. Benches along both sides of the vehicles can be folded upwards when carrying cargo. The rear tailgate is of the drop down type and bows and a tarpaulin cover can be fitted if required. Both versions can be fitted with a winch.

VARIANTS
GAZ-51
GAZ-51AS: GAZ-51A with two fuel tanks, for agricultural use
GAZ-51DU: with GAZ-93 dump truck body, export only
GAZ-51D: with GAZ-93 dump truck body
GAZ-51DYu: with GAZ-93 dump truck body, tropical climate export model
GAZ-51AU: export model of GAZ-51A
GAZ-51I: with KaVZ bus body
GAZ-51IU: with KaVZ bus body, export model
GAZ-51IYu: with KaVZ bus body, tropical climate export model
GAZ-51M: tank truck
GAZ-51N: GAZ-51A with two fuel tanks and lengthwise seats along side, GAZ-63 cab and truck bed
GAZ-51NU: export model of GAZ-51N
GAZ-51R: cargo/passenger taxi
GAZ-51T: cargo taxi
GAZ-51RU: export model of cargo/passenger taxi
GAZ-51S: GAZ-51A with auxiliary fuel tank
GAZ-51SE: GAZ-51S with shielded electrical system
GAZ-51P: truck tractor (from 1956)
GAZ-51Yu: GAZ-51A export model for tropical climates
GAZ-51Zh: bottled gas carrier
GAZ-51ZhU: bottled gas carrier, export model
GAZ-93A: dump truck
AS-3: ambulance carrying seven stretcher and two seated patients, or four stretcher and six seated patients, or fourteen seated patients, plus driver and medical orderly
PAZ-653: ambulance carrying four stretcher patients or thirteen seated patients, plus driver
NZ-51M: mobile oil supply vehicle
ATs 1,9-51A: 1900-litre tanker
ATs 2-51A: 2000-litre tanker
MZ-51M: 920-litre oil servicing truck
MZ-3904: 2160-litre oil servicing truck
Shop/van for various applications

GAZ-63
GAZ-63A: GAZ-63 with winch
GAZ-63AE: GAZ-63A with shielded electrical system
GAZ-63AYu: GAZ-63A truck, tropical climate export model
GAZ-63D: truck tractor with self-unloading semi-trailer
GAZ-63EU: GAZ-63E truck, export model
GAZ-63E: GAZ-63 with shielded electrical system
GAZ-63AU: export model of GAZ-63A
GAZ-63P: truck tractor based on GAZ-63
GAZ-63PU: GAZ-63P truck tractor export model
GAZ-63Ye: GAZ-63 chassis for bus body
GAZ-63YeYu: GAZ-63Ye chassis, tropical-climate export model
GAZ-63YeU: GAZ-63Ye chassis export model

GAZ-63U: GAZ-63 truck, export model
GAZ-63EYu: GAZ-63E truck, tropical climate export model
PSG-65/130: POL transfer pump station
AS-3: ambulance which can carry seven stretcher and two seated patients, or four stretcher and six seated patients, or fourteen seated patients, plus driver and medical orderly
ATs 2-63: 2000-litre tank truck
ATs 18-63: 1800-litre water tank truck
TZ-63 1965-litre POL truck
Shop/van for various applications
Multiple Rocket Launcher: the GAZ-63A chassis is also used to mount the 140 mm (17-round) BM-14-17 multiple rocket system. Details of this model are given in *Jane's Armour and Artillery 1983–84*, page 740.

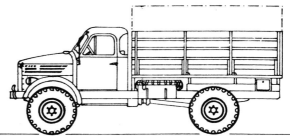

GAZ-63 (4 × 4) 1500 kg cargo truck

GAZ-63A (4 × 4) 1500 kg cargo truck

NBC Decontamination Vehicles

Both the GAZ-51 and the GAZ-63 are widely used for mounting the following NBC decontamination equipment:

DDA-53A truck-mounted decontamination apparatus
ADM-48D truck-mounted decontamination apparatus
BU-2, BU-3, BU-4 and BU-4M truck-mounted clothing decontamination apparatus
PDP-53 and PDM truck-mounted dry-contaminant spreader
Note: Additional details are given in the *Decontamination kits and equipment* section.

STATUS

Production complete. In service with most members of the Warsaw Pact as well as countries in the Middle East, Africa and the Far East. The GAZ-51 was built in Poland under the designation Lublin-51. China has received quantities of both the GAZ-51 and GAZ-63 and has produced a model similar to the GAZ-63 called the NJ-230. The vehicle has also been produced in North Korea under the designation Victory-58 truck. It has weaker springs and a less efficient engine.

MANUFACTURER

Gor'kiy Motor Vehicle Plant, Gor'kiy, USSR.

SPECIFICATIONS

Model	GAZ-51A	GAZ-63A
Cab seating	1 + 1	1 + 1
Configuration	4 × 2	4 × 4
Weight (empty)	2710 kg (road)	3490 kg (cross country)
(loaded)	5220 kg	4990 kg
Max load (road)	2500 kg	2000 kg
(dirt road)	2000 kg	n/app
(cross country)	n/app	1500 kg
Towed load (road)	3500 kg	2000 kg
(dirt road)	1200 kg	n/app
(cross country)	n/app	2000 kg
Load area	3·07 × 2·07 m	2·94 × 1·99 m
Length	5·715 m	5·8 m
Width	2·28 m	2·2 m
Height (cab)	2·28 m	2·245 m
(tarpaulin cover)	2·13 m	2·245 m
Ground clearance	0·245 m	0·27 m
Track (front/rear)	1·589 m/1·65 m	1·588 m/1·6 m
Wheelbase	3·3 m	3·3 m
Angle of approach/departure	40°/32°	28°/28°
Max speed	70 km/h	65 km/h
Range	450 km	650 km
Fuel capacity	90 litres	195 litres
Fording	0·64 m	0·8 m
Engine	GAZ-51A 6-cylinder in-line petrol developing 70 hp at 2800 rpm	
Gearbox	manual with 4 forward and 1 reverse gears	
Clutch	single dry disc	single dry disc
Transfer box	nil	2-speed
Steering	cone worm and dual ridge roller	cone worm and dual ridge roller
Turning radius	7·6 m	7·6 m
Suspension (front)	longitudinal semi-elliptical springs with hydraulic 2-way telescopic shock absorbers (GAZ-63 has articulated instead of telescopic shock absorbers)	
(rear)	longitudinal semi-elliptical springs with check springs	
Tyres	7.50 × 20	10.00 × 18
Brakes (main)	hydraulic	hydraulic
(parking)	mechanical	mechanical
Electrical system	12 V	12 V
Batteries	2 × ST-70	2 × ST-70
Generator	250 W	250 W

GAZ-66 (4 × 4) 2000 kg Truck

DEVELOPMENT

The GAZ-66 (4 × 4) 2000 kg truck is the replacement for the GAZ-63 and entered production at the Gor'kiy Automobile Plant in 1964. All vehicles built since 1968 have a central tyre pressure regulation system fitted as standard. The GAZ-66 is widely used by the Soviet armed forces and is also used for a variety of civilian roles.

DESCRIPTION

The two-door all-steel forward control cab hinges forward to allow access to the engine for maintenance. The all-steel rear cargo body has fixed sides and a drop tailgate. The vehicle can be fitted with five bows and a tarpaulin cover if required. Standard equipment includes a cab heater and an engine pre-heater and many vehicles have a winch.

VARIANTS

GAZ-66-02: with crane
GAZ-66-04: with shielded electrical system
GAZ-66-05: with shielded electrical system and crane
GAZ-66-01: with tyre pressure regulation system (also known as GAZ-66-51)
GAZ-66-02: with tyre pressure regulation system and winch

GAZ-66B (4 × 4) as used by Soviet airborne units

Czechoslovak Army GAZ-66 (4 × 4) 2000 kg truck

GAZ-66 (4 × 4) with van type body

GAZ-66 (4 × 4) 2000 kg truck with winch and tyre pressure regulation system

GAZ-66-03: with shielded electrical system
GAZ-66-04: with shielded electrical system and tyre pressure regulation system
GAZ-66-05: with shielded electrical system, tyre pressure regulation system and winch
GAZ-66-51: with tyre pressure regulation system and tropical equipment
GAZ-66-52: with winch and tropical equipment
GAZ-66-54: with shielded electrical system and tropical equipment
GAZ-66-55: with shielded electrical system, winch and tropical equipment
GAZ-66A: with tyre pressure regulation system and winch
GAZ-66E: with shielded electrical system
GAZ-66P: tractor truck, not placed in production
GAZ-66B: for airborne forces with collapsible canvas cab, removable doors and windscreen, telescopic steering wheel and tiedown points for parachute dropping
DDA-53C: NBC decontamination vehicle
AVTs-1.7: 1700-litre water tanker, built at Dalmatovo Molmashstroy plant
MZ-66: motor oil supply vehicle (820 litres)
Shop/van for command, communications and other roles

SPECIFICATIONS (GAZ-66)
Cab seating: 1 + 1
Configuration: 4 × 4
Weight:
  (empty) 3470 kg
  (loaded) 5800 kg
Weight on front axle: (loaded) 2730 kg
Weight on rear axle: (loaded) 3070 kg
Max load: 2000 kg
Towed load: 2000 kg
Load area: 3·33 × 2·05 m

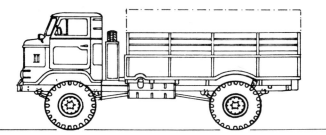

GAZ-66 (4 × 4) 2000 kg truck

Length: 5·655 m
Width: 2·322 m
Height:
  (cab) 2·44 m
  (load area) 1·11 m
Ground clearance: (axles) 0·315 m
Track:
  (front) 1·8 m
  (rear) 1·75 m
Wheelbase: 3·3 m
Angle of approach/departure: 42°/32°
Max speed: (road) 95 km/h
Range: 525 km
Fuel capacity: 210 litres (2 tanks each holding 105 litres)
Max gradient: 60%
Fording: 0·8 m
Engine: ZMZ-66 V-8 water-cooled petrol developing 115 hp at 3200 rpm
Gearbox: manual with 4 forward and 1 reverse gears
Clutch: single dry plate

Transfer box: 2-speed
Steering: globoid worm with 3 collar roller and hydraulic booster
Turning radius: 10 m
Suspension: longitudinal semi-elliptical springs and hydraulic double acting shock absorbers
Tyres: 12.00 × 18
Number of tyres: 4 + 1 spare
Brakes:
  (main) hydraulic
  (parking) mechanical operating on transmission
Electrical system: 12 V
Batteries: 1 × 6-ST-68

STATUS
In production. In service with members of the Warsaw Pact. Also exported to other countries such as Egypt, Finland and Iran.

MANUFACTURER
Gor'kiy Motor Vehicle Plant, Gor'kiy, USSR.

ZIL-157 (6 × 6) 2500 kg Truck

DEVELOPMENT
The ZIL-157 (6 × 6) truck replaced the ZIL-151 (6 × 6) truck in production from 1958 and in 1961 the improved ZIL-157K entered production to be replaced in 1966 by the more powerful ZIL-131 (6 × 6) 3500 kg truck. In appearance the ZIL-157 is very similar to the ZIL-151 but has a slightly different cab (which was also fitted to late production ZIL-151s), and single instead of dual rear wheels.

DESCRIPTION
The layout of the vehicle is conventional with the engine at the front, two-door fully enclosed cab in the centre, and the cargo area at the rear which consists of a wooden platform with sides, bench seats down each side which can be folded up when the vehicle is carrying cargo, and a drop tailgate. If required the vehicle can be fitted with bows and a tarpaulin cover. Standard equipment includes a cab heater and an engine pre-heater and many vehicles also have a winch.

VARIANTS
ZIL-157V and ZIL-157KV: tractor trucks for towing

semi-trailers (eg carrying SA-2, FROG-3, FROG-4 or FROG-5 missiles)
ZIL-157KG: with shielded electrical system
ZIL-157KE: temperate climate export model of ZIL-157K
ZIL-157KYu: tropical climate export model of ZIL-157K
ZIL-157GT: tropical climate export model of ZIL-157K with shielded electrical system
ZIL-157KYe: ZIL-157K chassis for special bodies
ZIL-157KYel: ZIL-157KYe chassis with high output generator
ZIL-157KYeG: ZIL-157KG chassis with shielded electrical system
ZIL-157YeT: ZIL-157KYe chassis, tropical climate export model
ZIL-157YeGT: ZIL-157KYeG chassis, tropical climate export model
ZIL-157KYeGT: ZIL-157KYeG chassis, tropical climate export model (chassis has features of the ZIL-157KYu)
ZIL-157YeT: ZIL-157KYe chassis, tropical climate export model (chassis contains features of ZIL-157KYu)
ARS-12U: decontamination vehicle for decontaminating vehicles, weapons, equipment, terrain, refilling portable decontamination equipment and fighting fires
AGV-3M and AGW-3M: decontamination stations

ATsM-4-157K: 4000-litre fuel truck (also on ZIL-157 chassis)
ATZ-3-157K and ATZ-3, 8-157K: fuel service trucks
ATsMM-4-157K: 4000-litre oil tank truck
AVTs 28-157: 2800-litre water tanker
Carrying pontoons and other bridging equipment
Crane truck
Carrying KMM treadway bridge system (details of this version are given in the *Mechanised bridges* section)
Multiple rocket system: 130 mm M51 (32-round) used only by the Romanian Army (*Jane's Armour and Artillery 1983–84* page 732), 200 mm BMD-20 (4-round) (*ibid* page 739), 240 mm BM-24T (12-round) (*ibid* page 739) and 140 mm (16-round) BM-14-16 (*ibid* page 740)
VMZ-ZIL-157K: water and oil service truck which carries 1400 litres of water and 700 litres of oil and is equipped with a heater system which maintains the temperature of the water at between 15 and 90°C and the oil at 80°C.

STATUS
Production complete. In service in declining numbers with members of the Warsaw Pact and other armed forces.

MANUFACTURER
Likhachev Motor Vehicle Plant, Moscow, USSR.

ZIL-157 (6 × 6) 2500 kg truck

ZIL-157 (6 × 6) 2500 kg with box body

SPECIFICATIONS
Configuration: 6 × 6
Weight:
(empty, with winch) 5800 kg
(loaded, with winch) 8450 kg
Weight on front axle: (loaded) 2930 kg
Weight on rear bogie: (loaded) 5520 kg
Max load: (road) 4500 kg
Max load: (cross country) 2500 kg
Towed load:
(dirt road) 3600 kg
(cross country) 2500 kg
(roads) 3600 kg
Load area: 3·57 × 2·09 m
Length: 6·922 m (with winch)
Width: 2·315 m
Height:
(cab) 2·36 m
(tarpaulin) 2·915 m
(load area) 1·388 m
Ground clearance: 0·31 m
Track:
(front) 1·755 m
(rear) 1·75 m
Wheelbase: 3·655 m + 1·12 m
Angle of approach/departure: 35°/43°
Max speed: (road) 65 km/h

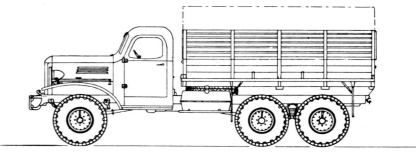

ZIL-157 (6 × 6) 2500 kg truck

Range: 430 km
Fuel capacity: 215 litres
Max gradient: 53%
Fording: 0·85 m
Engine: ZIL-157K 6-cylinder water-cooled petrol developing 109 hp at 2800 rpm
Gearbox: manual with 5 forward and 1 reverse gears
Clutch: single dry plate
Transfer box: 2-speed
Steering: cone worm with 3-ridge roller
Turning radius: 11·2 m

Suspension:
(front) longitudinal semi-elliptical springs with hydraulic double acting shock absorbers
(rear) bogie with semi-elliptical springs
Tyres: 12.00 × 18
Number of tyres: 6 + 1 spare
Brakes:
(main) air
(parking) mechanical
Electrical system: 12 V
Batteries: 2 × ST-84

ZIL-151 (6 × 6) 2500 kg Truck

DEVELOPMENT
The ZIL-151 was originally known as the ZIS-151 and was in production from 1947 until 1958. Late production vehicles had the bonnet and radiator of the ZIL-157 (6 × 6) truck which replaced the ZIL-151 in production. The ZIL-151 uses many automotive components of the ZIL-150 (4 × 2) truck and its chassis was used as the basis for the BTR-152 (6 × 6) armoured personnel carrier. The vehicle is no longer in large scale use with the Warsaw Pact countries.

DESCRIPTION
The layout of the vehicle is conventional, with the engine at the front, all-steel two-door cab in the centre and the cargo area at the rear with a drop tailboard, removable bows and a tarpaulin cover.

VARIANTS
ATs 4-151: 4000-litre fuel tank truck
ATZ 3-151: 3500-litre fuel service truck
AVTs 28-151: water tanker
VMZ-ZIL-151: water and oil service truck which can carry 1400 litres of water and 700 litres of oil and has heaters to maintain water temperature between 15° and 95° C and oil up to 80° C
ARS-12: decontamination vehicle used to decontaminate vehicles, weapons, and equipment, refill portable decontamination equipment; can also be used for fire duties
AGV-3M and AGW-3M: decontamination vehicles
Crane truck
Multiple Rocket Launcher: the ZIL-151 chassis is used for the BM-14-16 140 mm (16-round) (*Jane's Armour and Artillery 1983–84*, page 740), BM-24 240 mm (12-round) (*ibid*, page 739) and BMD-20 200 mm (4-round) (*ibid*, page 739)
Pontoon carrier: the ZIL-151 is used to carry and launch pontoons, eg the TPP
Shop/van: The basic chassis can be fitted with a variety of shop/van bodies for command, radio, medical and other purposes
ZIL-121D: tractor truck
ZIL-151D: tractor truck

SPECIFICATIONS
Cab seating: 1 + 2
Configuration: 6 × 6
Weight:
(empty) 5580 kg
(loaded, cross country) 8080 kg
Max load:
(road) 4500 kg
(cross country) 2500 kg
Towed load:
(road) 3600 kg
(cross country) 3600 kg

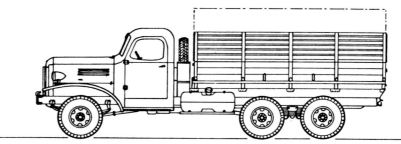

ZIL-151 (6 × 6) 2500 kg truck

ZIL-151 (6 × 6) 2500 kg truck with van body

Length: 6·93 m
Width: 2·32 m
Height:
(cab) 2·32 m
(tarpaulin) 2·74 m
Ground clearance: 0·265 m
Track: (front/rear) 1·59 m/1·72 m
Wheelbase: 3·665 m + 1·22 m
Max speed: (road) 60 km/h
Range: 600 km
Fuel capacity: 300 litres
Fuel consumption: 46 litres/100 km
Vertical obstacle: 0·46 m
Gradient: 55°
Fording: 0·8 m
Engine: ZIL-121 6-cylinder water-cooled petrol developing 92 hp at 2600 rpm
Gearbox: manual with 5 forward and 1 reverse gears
Transfer box: 2-speed

Tyres: 8.25 × 20
Steering: globoid worm with 3 collar roller
Turning radius: 12 m
Suspension:
(front) longitudinal semi-elliptical springs with hydraulic double-acting shock absorbers
(rear) two longitudinal springs
Tyres: 8.25 × 20
Brakes:
(main) air
(parking) mechanical
Electrical system: 12 V

STATUS
Production complete. In limited use with members of the Warsaw Pact. Also used by China and Viet-Nam.

MANUFACTURER
Likhachev Motor Vehicle Plant, Moscow, USSR.

GAZ-53 (4 × 2) 3000 kg Truck

DEVELOPMENT
The GAZ-53 (4 × 2) is the replacement for the older GAZ-51 series. While under development the vehicle was known as the GAZ-52 and was followed by the GAZ-52A which had an increased payload. From 1961 to early in 1967 the GAZ-53F was in production, powered by an improved version of the engine used in the older GAZ-51 truck, which developed 75 hp and gave

the vehicle a maximum road speed of 75 km/h. The GAZ-53F could carry 3000 kg of cargo on roads, 2500 kg on dirt roads and tow a trailer on roads weighing up to 4000 kg. In 1964 the GAZ-53 entered production and was followed in 1965 by the GAZ-53A.

DESCRIPTION
The layout of the GAZ-53 is conventional with the engine at the front, two-door all-steel fully enclosed cab in the centre and the cargo area at the rear with a

wooden platform with drop sides and a drop tailgate. It can be fitted with bows and a tarpaulin cover. Standard equipment includes a cab heater and an engine pre-heater.

VARIANTS
ATs-4, 2-53A: 4200-litre tanker
ATs 2, 6-53A: 2600-litre tanker
ATs 2, 9-53F: 2900-litre tanker
ATZ 3, 8-53A: 3800-litre fuel servicing truck

GAZ-53A (4 × 2) 3000 kg truck

GAZ-SAZ-53B: agricultural dump truck produced at the Saransk Plant and also known as the SAZ-53. The chassis is designated the GAZ-53-02 and the vehicle can carry 3500 kg of soil
GAZ-53P: tractor truck, developed but not placed in production
GAZ-33: 6 × 4 cargo truck, developed but not placed in production
GAZ-52-03: with a payload of 2500 kg, powered by a 6-cylinder in-line engine developing 75 hp at 2800 rpm
Crane truck

SPECIFICATIONS (GAZ-53A)
Cab seating: 1 + 1
Configuration: 4 × 2
Weight:
  (empty) 3250 kg
  (loaded) 7400 kg
Weight on front axle: (loaded) 1810 kg
Weight on rear axle: (loaded) 5590 kg
Max load:
  (road) 4000 kg
  (dirt road) 3000 kg

Towed load: (road) 4000 kg
Load area: 3·75 × 2·17 m
Length: 6·395 m
Width: 2·38 m
Height:
  (cab) 2·2 m
  (load area) 1·35 m
Ground clearance: 0·265 m
Track:
  (front) 1·63 m
  (rear) 1·69 m
Wheelbase: 3·7 m
Angle of approach/departure: 41°/25°
Max speed: (road) 80 km/h
Range: 375 km
Fuel capacity: 90 litres (additional 150-litre tank can be fitted)
Fuel consumption: 24 litres/100 km
Fording: 0·6 m
Engine: GAZ-53 V-8 water-cooled petrol developing 115 hp at 3200 rpm
Gearbox: manual with 4 forward and 1 reverse gears
Clutch: single dry plate
Steering: cone worm with 3-ridge roller
Turning radius: 8 m
Suspension:
  (front) longitudinal semi-elliptical springs and hydraulic shock absorbers
  (rear) longitudinal semi-elliptical springs with helper springs
Tyres: 8.25 × 20
Number of tyres: 6 + 1 spare
Brakes:
  (main) hydraulic
  (parking) handbrake operates on transmission
Electrical system: 12 V
Battery: 1 × 6-ST-68EM2

STATUS
In production. In service with members of the Warsaw Pact for second line roles.

MANUFACTURER
Gor'kiy Motor Vehicle Plant, Gor'kiy, USSR.

ZIL-131 (6 × 6) 3500 kg Truck

DEVELOPMENT
The ZIL-131 (6 × 6) truck entered production in December 1966 and is the replacement for the earlier ZIL-157 (6 × 6) 2500 kg truck and uses many components of the ZIL-133 (6 × 4) truck. Main improvements over the ZIL-157 can be summarised as increased load-carrying capacity, more powerful engine, power steering, shorter wheelbase, waterproof ignition and the central tyre-pressure regulation system. The front axle is engaged automatically when the driver selects first gear and the driver can also engage the front axle manually when in second gear. The vehicle is used for transporting cargo, personnel and as a prime mover for towing artillery such as the 122 mm D-30 howitzer.

DESCRIPTION
The layout of the vehicle is conventional with the engine at the front, fully enclosed two-door all-steel cab in the centre and the cargo area at the rear, consisting of a wooden platform with metal fittings and a hinged tailgate. The platform has recesses for the bows and hinged bench seats are provided down either side of the platform.
  The ZIL-131 has a central tyre pressure regulation

system and a 4500 kg capacity winch. Standard equipment includes a cab heater and an engine pre-heater.

VARIANTS
ZIL-131A: this is a truck with a standard ignition system rather than the shielded ignition system as fitted on the standard ZIL-131
ZIL-131D: dump truck
ZIL-131V: for towing semi-trailers
ZIL-137: tractor truck for towing a two-axle powered trailer (the complete unit then becomes a 10 × 10)
ARS-14: decontamination vehicle used to decontaminate vehicles, weapons, equipment, refill portable decontamination equipment and fight fires
ATs 4, 2-131: 4200-litre fuel tank truck
ATs 4, 2-131: 4100-litre fuel tank truck
ATs 4, 3-131: 4400-litre fuel tank truck
ATZ 3, 8-131: 4300-litre fuel service truck
ATZ 4, 3-131: 4300-litre fuel service truck
AVTs 28-131: 2800-litre water tanker
Shop/van
Various models are in service including bakery, maintenance and a field kitchen
MA-41
This is a combined fuel, lubricant and water service vehicle. It carries 1700 litres of diesel, 340 litres of

ZIL-137 tractor truck towing powered trailer

petrol, two 170-litre tanks of oil and 700 litres of water. Both the diesel and water tanks are heated as this unit is used in very cold climates
SA-6 Gainful SAM Resupply Vehicle
Three missiles are carried in a triangular formation with the warhead sections projecting over the roof of the cab. A foldable crane is mounted at the rear of the truck to facilitate reloading of the SA-6 tracked launcher vehicle
SA-3 Goa SAM Resupply Vehicle
Two missiles are carried adjacent to each other on a rail system with the warhead sections projecting over the

ZIL-131 (6 × 6) 3500 kg truck

ZIL-131 (6 × 6) 3500 kg truck

roof of the cab. The SA-3 launcher is reloaded by backing the vehicle in line with the twin launcher rails, connecting up the resupply rails and then winching the missiles onto the launcher rails

Multiple Rocket Launcher

A number of ZIL-131 trucks have recently been fitted with the 140 mm BM-14-16 multiple rocket system which is normally carried on the rear of a ZIL-151 (6 × 6) truck chassis (*Jane's Armour and Artillery*

1983–84, page 740) and the 122 mm BM-21 multiple rocket system (*ibid* page 742).

SPECIFICATIONS
Cab seating: 1 + 2
Configuration: 6 × 6
Weight:
(empty, with winch) 6700 kg
(loaded, cross country) 10 425 kg

ZIL-131 (6 × 6) 3500 kg truck

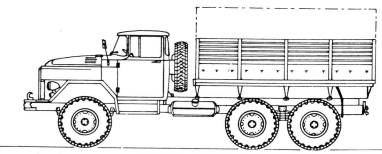

ZIL-131 (6 × 6) 3500 kg truck

Weight on front axle: (loaded) 3360 kg
Weight on rear bogie: (loaded) 7065 kg
Max load:
(road) 5000 kg
(cross country) 3500 kg
Towed load:
(road) 6500 kg
(dirt road) 4000 kg
Load area: 3·6 × 2·32 m
Length:
(without winch) 6·9 m
(with winch) 7·04 m
Width: 2·5 m
Height:
(cab) 2·48 m
(tarpaulin) 2·975 m
(load area) 1·43 m
Ground clearance: 0·33 m
Track: 1·82 m
Wheelbase: 3·35 m + 1·25 m
Angle of approach/departure: 36°/40°
Max speed: (road) 80 km/h
Range: 525 km
Fuel capacity: 340 litres
Max gradient: 60%
Fording: 1·4 m
Engine: ZIL-131 V-8 water-cooled petrol developing 150 hp at 3200 rpm
Gearbox: manual with 5 forward and 1 reverse gears
Clutch: single dry plate
Transfer box: 2-speed
Steering: screw and nut with hydraulic booster
Turning radius: 10·2 m
Suspension:
(front) longitudinal semi-elliptical springs with telescopic double acting hydraulic shock absorbers
(rear) equaliser arm on longitudinal semi-elliptical springs
Tyres: 12.00 × 20
Number of tyres: 6 + 1 spare
Brakes:
(main) air
(parking) mechanical
Electrical system: 12 V
Batteries: 1 × 6 ST 78

STATUS
In production. In service with the Soviet Union and other armed forces.

MANUFACTURER
Likhachev Motor Vehicle Plant, Moscow, USSR.

Ural-355M (4 × 2) 3500 kg Truck

DESCRIPTION
The Ural-355M was in production at Miass from 1958 to 1965 for both civil and military use. The vehicle is a modernised version of the Ural-355 which in turn was a copy of the ZIS-150 (4 × 2) truck. Many of the components of the vehicle are also used in the ZIL-150 (4 × 2) truck.

The layout of the vehicle is conventional with the engine at the front, fully enclosed two-door cab in the centre and the cargo area at the rear with drop sides and a drop tailgate.

VARIANTS
The only known variant is the ATsM 2,6-355M 2600-litre fuel tanker.

SPECIFICATIONS
Cab seating: 1 + 1
Configuration: 4 × 2
Weight:
(empty) 3400 kg
(loaded) 6400 kg
Max load:
(road) 3500 kg
(dirt road) 3000 kg
Towed load: (road) 5000 kg
Length: 6·29 m
Width: 2·28 m
Height: (cab) 2·095 m
Ground clearance: 0·262 m

Track:
(front) 1·611 m
(rear) 1·675 m
Wheelbase: 3·824 m
Max speed: 75 km/h
Range: 450 km
Fuel capacity: 110 litres
Fuel consumption: 24 litres/100 km
Max gradient: 15°
Fording: 0·8 m

Ural-355M (4 × 2) 3500 kg truck

Engine: Ural-353A 6-cylinder water-cooled petrol developing 95 hp at 2600 rpm
Tyres: 8.25 × 20
Number of tyres: 6 + 1 spare

STATUS
Production complete. In limited use with the Soviet Army.

MANUFACTURER
Ural Motor Vehicle Plant, Miass, USSR.

ZIL-164 (4 × 2) 3500 kg Truck

DESCRIPTION
The ZIL-164 was the replacement for the ZIL-150 (4 × 2) truck and was in production from October 1957 to late in 1961 when the improved ZIL-164A was placed in production. Production was finally completed in 1964. The vehicle uses many components of the ZIL-157 and its transmission is also used in the ZIL-130 truck. The vehicle has now been replaced in many Soviet units by the ZIL-130 truck.

The layout of the vehicle is conventional with the engine at the front, two-door fully enclosed cab in the centre and the cargo area at the rear with hinged sideboards and a hinged tailgate.

VARIANTS
AVTs 28-164: 2800-litre water tank truck
ATZ-164: 4000-litre fuel service truck
ATs 4-164: 4100-litre fuel tanker
Crane truck
Fire-fighting truck

ZIL-164AR: basic vehicle with 109 hp engine fitted with winch and air line connection for towing trailers
ZIL-164D: ZIL-164 with shielded electrical system
ZIL-164AD: ZIL-164A with shielded electrical system
ZIL-164R: truck/chassis
ZIL-164E: truck/chassis with cab for export
ZIL-164Ye: truck/chassis with cab for export (tropical climate model)
ZIL-164G: dump truck
ZIL-164AG: dump truck using ZIL-164A chassis
ZIL-164N: tractor truck

ZIL-164AN: tractor truck using ZIL-164A chassis
ZIL-166: truck/chassis with cab operating on compressed gas or petrol
ZIL-166A: truck/chassis with cab operating on liquefied gas or petrol
ZIL-MMZ-164N: tractor truck
ZIL-MMZ-585K: agricultural dump truck
ZIL-MMZ-585M: agricultural dump truck
ZIL-MMZ-585I: construction dump truck
ZIL-MMZ-585L: construction dump truck
Shop/van: various shop/van models are used for a variety of roles

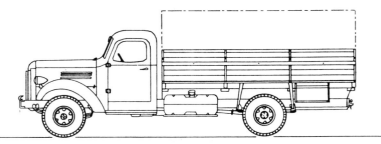

ZIL-164 (4 × 2) 3500 kg truck

SPECIFICATIONS
Cab seating: 1 + 2
Configuration: 4 × 2
Weight:
  (empty) 4100 kg
  (loaded) 8250 kg
Weight on front axle: (loaded) 2100 kg
Weight on rear axle: (loaded) 6150 kg
Max load:
  (road) 4000 kg
  (dirt road) 3500 kg
Towed load: (road) 4500 kg
Load area: 3·54 × 2·25 m
Length: 6·7 m
Width: 2·47 m
Height:
  (cab) 2·18 m
  (load area) 1·32 m
Ground clearance: 0·265 m
Track: (front/rear) 1·7 m/1·74 m
Wheelbase: 4 m
Angle of approach/departure: 40°/24°
Max speed: (road) 75 km/h
Range: 550 km
Fuel capacity: 150 litres
Max gradient: 15°
Engine: ZIL-164 6-cylinder water-cooled petrol developing 100 hp at 2800 rpm
Gearbox: manual with 5 forward and 1 reverse gears
Clutch: single disc
Steering: cone with 3-ridge roller
Suspension:
  (front) semi-elliptical springs with hydraulic shock absorbers
  (rear) semi-elliptical springs with check springs

ZIL-164 (4 × 2) 3500 kg truck

Tyres: 9.00 × 20
Brakes:
  (main) air
  (parking) mechanical
Electrical system: 12 V
Batteries: 2 × 3-ST-84PD or 2 × 3-ST-84PDS
Generator: G-108-V (250 W)

STATUS
Production complete. In limited use with members of the Warsaw Pact.

MANUFACTURER
Likhachev Motor Vehicle Plant, Moscow, USSR.

ZIL-150 (4 × 2) 3500 kg Truck

DESCRIPTION
The ZIL-150 (4 × 2) 3500 kg truck, also known as the ZIS-150, was in production from 1946 to 1957 when it was replaced by the similar ZIL-164. The ZIL-150 shares many components with the ZIL-151 (6 × 6) truck of the same period.
The layout of the vehicle is conventional with the engine at the front, two-door fully enclosed cab in the centre and the cargo area at the rear with drop sides and a drop tailgate.

VARIANTS
AVTs 28-150: 2800-litre water tanker
ATZ 4-150: 4000-litre fuel servicing truck
ATs 4-150: 4120-litre fuel tanker
Crane truck with K-32 crane
Dry decontaminant spreader: truck-mounted PDP-53 and PDM
ZIL-120N: tractor truck (from 1956 to 1957)
ZIL-585: dump truck (from 1949 to 1955)
ZIL-585K: agricultural dump truck (from 1955 to 1957)
ZIL-585V: construction dump truck
Shop/van version for various roles

SPECIFICATIONS
Configuration: 4 × 2
Weight:
  (empty) 3900 kg
  (loaded) 7400 kg

ZIL-150 (4 × 2) 3500 kg truck towing trailer

Max load:
  (road) 4000 kg
  (dirt road) 3500 kg
Towed load:
  (road) 4500 kg
  (dirt road) 3000 kg
Length: 6·72 m
Width: 2·47 m
Height: (cab) 2·18 m
Ground clearance: 0·265 m
Track: (front/rear) 1·7 m/1·74 m
Wheelbase: 4 m
Max speed: (road) 65 km/h
Range: 405 km

Fuel capacity: 150 litres
Fording: 0·8 m
Engine: ZIL-120 6-cylinder water-cooled petrol developing 90 hp at 2400 rpm
Gearbox: manual with 5 forward and 1 reverse gears
Tyres: 9.00 × 20

STATUS
Production complete. In limited service with members of the Warsaw Pact. It is also produced in China as the CA-10 (4 × 2) Liberation truck.

MANUFACTURER
Likhachev Motor Vehicle Plant, Moscow, USSR.

Ural-375 (6 × 6) 4000 kg Truck

DEVELOPMENT
The first model of the Ural-375 entered production in 1961. It had an open cab with a canvas top and a stake type rear cargo body. The second model was the Ural-375A, which had a number of automotive improvements as well as a fully enclosed all-steel cab. The Ural-375A was standardised as the Ural-375D; those with a winch (capacity of 7000 kg) are designated Ural-375T. The vehicle is fitted with a central tyre-pressure regulation system. The Ural-377 (6 × 4) truck uses many components of the Ural-375 truck.

DESCRIPTION
The layout of the vehicle is conventional with the engine at the front, fully enclosed two-door all-steel cab in the centre and the cargo area at the rear with hinged bench type seats, removable bows and a tarpaulin cover, and a drop tailgate. Standard equipment includes a cab heater and an engine pre-heater.
In 1973 a Ural-375D was being tested with a YaMZ-740 V-8 water-cooled diesel engine, which develops 210 hp and is used in the KamAZ range of 6 × 4 trucks. It has now entered production as the Ural-4320 (6 × 6) 4500 kg truck for which there is a separate entry in this section.

VARIANTS
Ural-375DK-1: Ural-375 adapted for operations in northern USSR
Ural-375K: Ural-375 adapted for operations in northern USSR
Ural-375L: timber truck
Ural-375N: cargo truck with drop sides
Ural-375S: tractor truck for towing semi-trailers
Ural-375Yu: designed for use in the tropics
ATs 5-375: 5000-litre fuel tank truck
ATsM 4-375: fuel tank truck
TZ 5-375: 5000-litre fuel service truck which also tows PTs 4,754 trailer with another 4200 litres of fuel. This

unit is provided with three 3-metre hoses, a 15-metre dispensing hose and a 9-metre pressure hose
TMS-65: truck-mounted decontamination apparatus used for the rapid decontamination of vehicles and equipment consisting of a Ural-375E truck chassis with a modified model VK-1F jet aircraft engine mounted on a turntable at the rear of the vehicle. Between the turntable and the truck cab is a 1500-litre tank for fuel and a similar tank for the decontamination solution. The truck also tows a trailer with another 4000 litres of decontaminant. The operator, who is seated in a cabin on the turntable, directs the engine towards the equipment to be decontaminated and water decontamination solution is then ejected into the hot gas stream. Details of this model are given in the *NBC equipment* section
ATsG-5-375: 5000-litre fuel tanker, equipped with four SRGS-70 3-metre and four SRGS-32 3-metre metal hoses
ATMZ-4.5-375: fuel lubricant truck (4500 litres), equipped with six dispensing hoses
Crane truck: the crane model is fitted with an 8 T 210 crane on the rear
Shop/van: the basic chassis is used to mount a wide range of van type bodies for command, communications and other roles
Recovery vehicle: designated the KET-L
Multiple Rocket Launcher: the Ural-375D is used to mount the BM-21 (40 round) 122 mm multiple rocket system (*Jane's Armour and Artillery 1983–84*, page 742)
Pontoon carrying vehicle: this vehicle is used for carrying pontoon sections.

SPECIFICATIONS
Cab seating: 1 + 2
Configuration: 6 × 6
Weight:
(empty, with winch) 8400 kg
(loaded, road) 13 300 kg
Weight on front axle: (loaded) 3910 kg
Weight on rear axle: (loaded) 9390 kg
Max load:
(road) 4500 kg
(cross country) 4000 kg
Towed load:
(road) 10 000 kg
(dirt road) 5000 kg
Load area: 3·9 × 2·43 m
Length: 7·35 m
Width: 2·69 m
Height:
(cab) 2·68 m
(tarpaulin) 2·98 m
(load area) 1·42 m
Ground clearance: 0·41 m
Track: 2 m
Wheelbase: 3·5 m + 1·4 m
Angle of approach/departure: 44°/40°
Max speed: (road) 75 km/h
Range: 650 km
Fuel capacity: 360 litres
Max gradient: 60%
Vertical obstacle: 0·8 m
Fording:
(without preparation) 1 m
(with preparation) 1·5 m
Engine: ZIL-375 V-8 water-cooled petrol developing 180 hp at 3200 rpm
Gearbox: manual with 5 forward and 1 reverse gears
Clutch: twin disc dry
Transfer box: 2-speed
Steering: double thread worm, hydraulic booster
Turning radius: 10·5 m
Suspension:
(front) longitudinal semi-elliptical springs (interchangeable with those of the MAZ-500) with hydraulic shock absorbers (also interchangeable with those of the MAZ-500)
(rear) bogie with longitudinal semi-elliptical springs
Tyres: 14.00 × 20
Brakes:
(main) air/hydraulic
(parking) mechanical
Electrical system: 12 V
Battery: 1 × 6-STEN-140M
Generator: G51

STATUS
In production. In service with the Soviet Army and other members of the Warsaw Pact. Also used outside the Warsaw Pact, including the Middle East.

MANUFACTURER
Ural Motor Vehicle Plant, Miass, USSR.

Ural-375D (6 × 6) truck fitted with van type body and A-frame at front for light repair work

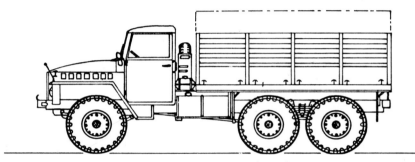
Ural-375D (6 × 6) 4000 kg truck

Ural-375D (6 × 6) 4000 kg truck

Ural-375 (6 × 6) fuel tanker

ZIL-130 (4 × 2) 4000 kg Truck

DESCRIPTION
The ZIL-130 entered production late in 1964 as the replacement for the older ZIL-164 (4 × 2) truck. The vehicle also forms the basis for the ZIL-131 series of 6 × 6 trucks, the ZIL-133 (6 × 4) trucks, and its engine is used on the KAZ-608 tractor truck.
  The layout of the vehicle is conventional with the engine at the front, two-door fully enclosed all-steel cab in the centre and the cargo area at the rear with drop sides and a drop tailgate.

VARIANTS
ZIL-130A1: cargo truck for towing trailers
ZIL-130D1: chassis for ZIL-MMZ-555 dump truck, 3·3 m wheelbase
ZIL-130D2: dump truck chassis
ZIL-130D1E: ZIL-MMZ-555 dump truck chassis, temperature climate export model
ZIL-130D1T: ZIL-130D1 dump truck chassis, tropical climate export model
ZIL-130E: temperate climate export model of ZIL-130
ZIL-130G: long cargo bed, length 4·686 metres, 4·5 metre wheelbase, from 1964
ZIL-130GE: temperate-climate export model of ZIL-130G
ZIL-130GT: tropical-climate export model of ZIL-130G
ZIL-130S: for use in the northern USSR
ZIL-130T: tropical climate export model of ZIL-130
ZIL-136I: export model of ZIL-130 with Perkins diesel engine
ZIL-136IG: export model of ZIL-130G with Perkins diesel engine
ZIL-136IDI: dump truck chassis with Perkins diesel engine
ZIL-130V1: truck tractor with 3.3 m wheelbase
ZIL-130V1T: tropical climate export model of ZIL-130V1
ZIL-130Ye: ZIL-130 with shielded electrical system
ZIL-130YeE: ZIL-130Ye temperate climate export model
ZIL-130YeT: tropical climate export model of ZIL-130Ye
ZIL-MMZ-554: dump truck for agricultural use
ZIL-MMZ-555: dump truck for agricultural use
ATs 4,2-130: 4200-litre fuel tank truck

ATZ 3,8-130: 3800-litre fuel servicing truck
AVTs 28-130: 2800-litre water tank truck
Crane truck
DDA-53B: decontamination vehicle
PAZS-3152: mobile fuelling unit
PSG-160 POL transfer-pump station
Shop/van: for various applications

SPECIFICATIONS
Cab seating: 1 + 2
Configuration: 4 × 2
Weight: (loaded) 9525 kg
Weight on front axle: (loaded) 2575 kg
Weight on rear axle: (loaded) 6950 kg
Max load:
  (road) 5500 kg
  (dirt road) 4000 kg
Towed load: (road) 6400 kg
Load area: 3·75 × 2·325 m
Length: 6·675 m
Width: 2·5 m
Height:
  (cab) 2·35 m
  (load area) 1·43 m
Ground clearance: 0·275 m
Track: (front/rear) 1·8 m/1·79 m
Wheelbase: 3·8 m
Angle of approach/departure: 38°/28°
Max speed: (road) 90 km/h
Range: 475 km
Fuel capacity: 170 litres
Max gradient: 21°
Fording: 0·7 m
Engine: ZIL-130 V-8 water-cooled petrol developing 150 hp at 3100 rpm

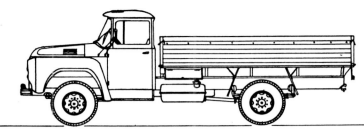

ZIL-130 (4 × 2) 4000 kg truck

ZIL-130 (4 × 2) 4000 kg truck

Gearbox: manual with 5 forward and 1 reverse gears
Clutch: single dry disc
Transfer box: none
Steering: screw and nut, hydraulic assisted
Turning radius: 8 m
Suspension:
  (front) longitudinal semi-elliptical springs with hydraulic telescopic 2-way shock absorbers
  (rear) semi-elliptical springs and check springs
Tyres: 9.00 × 20
Brakes:
  (main) air
  (parking) mechanical
Electrical system: 12 V
Battery: 1 × 6-ST-78EMSZ
Generator: 350 W

STATUS
In production. In service with members of the Warsaw Pact.

MANUFACTURER
Likhachev Motor Vehicle Plant, Moscow, USSR.

MAZ-502 (4 × 4) 4000 kg Truck

DESCRIPTION
The MAZ-502 was in production at the Minsk Plant from 1957 to 1966 and is based on the MAZ-501 (4 × 4) timber truck which in turn was based on the MAZ-200V tractor truck, a member of the MAZ-200 series of 4 × 2 vehicles.
  The layout of the MAZ-502 is conventional with the engine at the front, fully enclosed two-door cab in the centre and the cargo area at the rear with a drop tailgate, hinged seats for carrying personnel, removable bows and a tarpaulin cover. The MAZ-502A has a front-mounted winch.

VARIANTS
The MAZ-501V is a tractor truck used to tow semi-trailers, including missile resupply trailers, and can tow a trailer weighing a total of 12 000 kg.

SPECIFICATIONS
Cab seating: 1 + 2
Configuration: 4 × 4
Weight:
  (empty) 7700 kg
  (loaded) 11 925 kg
Weight on front axle: (loaded) 4475 kg
Weight on rear axle: (loaded) 7450 kg
Max load: 4000 kg
Towed load: 9500 kg
Load area: 3·5 × 2·03 m
Length: 7·15 m
Width: 2·7 m
Height:
  (cab) 2·725 m
  (tarpaulin) 3·025 m
  (load area) 1·48 m
Ground clearance: 0·35 m
Track: 2·03 m
Wheelbase: 4·52 m
Angle of approach/departure: 52°/30°
Max speed: 50 km/h
Range: 590 km
Fuel capacity: 450 litres
Fuel consumption: 45 litres/100 km
Max gradient: 20%
Fording: 0·8 m
Engine: YaAZ-M204V 4-cylinder in-line water-cooled diesel developing 135 hp at 2000 rpm

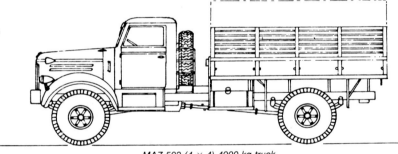

MAZ-502 (4 × 4) 4000 kg truck

MAZ-502A (4 × 4) 4000 kg truck with front-mounted winch

Gearbox: manual with 5 forward and 1 reverse gears
Clutch: single disc dry
Transfer box: 2-speed
Steering: worm and sector
Turning radius: 12·5 m
Suspension:
  (front) longitudinal semi-elliptical springs with double action hydraulic shock absorbers
  (rear) longitudinal semi-elliptical springs with helper springs
Tyres: 15.00 × 20
Number of tyres: 4 + 1 spare

Brakes:
  (main) air
  (parking) mechanical
Electrical system: 24 V
Batteries: 2 × ST 128
Generator: 250 W

STATUS
Production complete. In limited service with members of the Warsaw Pact.

MANUFACTURER
Minsk Motor Vehicle Plant, Minsk, Belorussia, USSR.

Ural-4320 (6 × 6) 4500 kg Trucks

DEVELOPMENT
The Ural-4320 (6 × 6) 4500 kg truck is a diesel-engined development of the Ural-375D truck produced by the Ural Motor Vehicle Plant, Miass. Development of the Ural-375D with a new diesel engine started in 1972 and the first production examples were produced in 1978.

DESCRIPTION
The diesel engine is the KamAZ-740, produced at the Kama Motor Vehicle Plant, Naberezhnye Chelny. It is a 10.85-litre, eight cylinder engine developing 210 hp at 2600 rpm. Fitting the new engine enabled the payload to be increased by 500 kg to 4500 kg, and the maximum speed is increased to 85 km/h. Fuel consumption is decreased by 30 per cent and maintenance by 10.8 per cent. Using typical Soviet figures the engine produced 16 per cent more power at 19 per cent fewer rpm. To use this extra power the transmission and rear-axle gear ratios have been reduced from 8:9 to 7:32 and numerous other small changes have been made.

The main outward appearance is that the radiator shell has been lengthened in front to accommodate the longer diesel engine which is also some 280 kg heavier than the earlier ZIL-375 petrol engine, which has led to some revision of the axle loading. The front axle now assumes 4350 kg of the total weight instead of 3865 kg; the rear axle assumes 9075 kg instead of 9335 kg. This revision improves the traction of the Ural-4320 over soft ground.

Other improvements on the Ural-4320 relate to the fuel, cooling, exhaust and electrical systems which have all been redesigned. Modifications have been made to the frame, clutch, front suspension and other assemblies. Safety alterations have been made including individual brake control links, an auxiliary motor brake and some warning devices. Inside the cab alterations have been made to the instrument layout and to the driver's seat which is now fully adjustable. A more powerful heater is now installed and changes have been made to the layout of the steering wheel and other controls. The batteries have also been removed from the driving cab.

There are four main versions of the Ural-4320: the basic model, the Ural-4420 and Ural-4202 tractors and the Ural-43202 truck. Differences occur in tyre size and the fact that the Ural-4320 and Ural-44202 have tyre pressure regulation systems while the other two do not. In addition, chassis without loading platforms, stretched chassis for box bodies and some other models are produced.

A winch with 65 metres of 17·5 mm cable is an option on all versions.

STATUS
In production. In service with the Soviet armed forces.

MANUFACTURER
Ural Motor Vehicle Plant, Miass, USSR.

SPECIFICATIONS

Model	Ural-4320	Ural-4420	Ural-43202	Ural-44202
Use	truck	tractor	truck	tractor
Cab seating	1 + 2	1 + 2	1 + 2	1 + 2
Configuration	6 × 6	6 × 6	6 × 6	6 × 6
Weight (empty)	8020 kg	7900 kg	7800 kg	7390 kg
Front axle loading (empty)	4020 kg	3830 kg	4040 kg	3950 kg
Rear axle loading (empty)	4000 kg	4070 kg	3760 kg	3440 kg
Payload/semi-trailer capacity				
(on road)	5000 kg	7000 kg	5500 kg	7500 kg
(off road)	—	5000 kg	—	5500 kg
Towed load/semi-trailer weight				
(on road)	7000 kg	11 500 kg	15 000 kg	18 500 kg
(off road)	—	7000 kg	—	12 500 kg
Length	7·366 m	7·611 m	7·1 m	6·836 m
Width	2·5 m	2·5 m	2·5 m	2·475 m
Height	2·87 m	2·6 m	2·68 m	2·6 m
Ground clearance	0·4 m	0·345 m	0·4 m	0·345 m
Track				
(front)	2 m	2·02 m	2 m	2·02 m
(rear)	2 m	2·02 m	2 m	2·02 m
Wheelbase	3·525 m + 1·4 m	3·525 m + 1·4 m	3·525 m + 1·4 m	3·525 m + 1·4 m
Max speed	85 km/h	80 km/h	72 km/h	72 km/h
Fuel capacity				
(main tank)	210 litres	210 litres	300 litres	300 litres
(auxiliary)	60 litres	none	60 litres	none
Gradient	58%	50%	28%	28%
Angle of approach/departure	45°/40°	42°/38°	44°/45°	42°/70°
Fording	1·5 m	0·8 m	1·5 m	0·8 m
Engine	KamAZ-740 V-8 10·85-litre, 4-stroke diesel developing 210 hp at 2600 rpm			
Gearbox	manual with 5 forward and 1 reverse gears			
Clutch	single dry disc			
Steering	worm with gear quadrant			
Turning circle	22·8 m	22·8 m	22·8 m	22·8 m
Suspension				
(front)	longitudinal semi-elliptical springs with hydraulic shock absorbers			
(rear)	longitudinal semi-elliptical springs with check springs			
Tyres	14.00 × 20	1.110 × 400.533	14.00 × 20	1.110 × 400.533
Brakes	dual circuit air plus auxiliary engine brake			
Electrical system	24 V	24 V	24 V	24 V
Trailer/semi-trailer coupling				
(height)	0·75 m	0·81 m	1·67 m	1·39 m

Ural-4320 (6 × 6) 4500 kg truck

MAZ-200 (4 × 2) 5000 kg Truck

DESCRIPTION
The MAZ-200 (4 × 2) truck was in production from 1947 to 1965 and was originally known as the YaAZ-200. The military version, the MAZ-200G, entered production in 1951. Its rear cargo area is provided with foldable seats, removable bows and a tarpaulin cover. Between 1963 and 1964 the MAZ-200P was built with the same V-6 engine as the MAZ-500, which develops 180 hp. The MAZ-200 was replaced in production by the MAZ-500 (4 × 2) truck.

Between 1955 and 1966 a 4 × 4 logging truck based on the MAZ-200V tractor truck and a 4 × 4 cargo version called the M-502 were built. The M-502N, for which there is a separate entry, is used by the Soviet Army.

The layout of the MAZ-200 is conventional with the engine at the front, two-door fully enclosed cab of wood with a metal covering in the centre and the cargo area at the rear with drop sides and a drop tailgate. Standard equipment includes a heater and an engine pre-heater.

MAZ-200 (4 × 2) 5000 kg truck

VARIANTS
ATs 8-200: 8000-litre fuel tank truck
ATZ 8-200 or TZ-200: 7000-litre fuel service truck
Crane truck
MAZ-200V tractor truck: powered by a YaMZ-M204V four-cylinder water-cooled diesel engine which develops 135 hp. Maximum towed load on roads is 16 500 kg.
MAZ-200M tractor truck: powered by a YaMZ-236 V-6 water-cooled diesel, which develops 180 hp. Maximum towed load on roads is 16 500 kg.
MAZ-205 dump truck

STATUS
Production complete. In limited service with the Soviet Army.

MANUFACTURER
Minsk Motor Vehicle Plant, Minsk, USSR.

SPECIFICATIONS
Cab seating: 1 + 2
Configuration: 4 × 2
Weight:
 (empty) 6750 kg
 (loaded) 13 625 kg
Weight on front axle: (loaded) 3565 kg
Weight on rear axle: (loaded) 10 060 kg
Max load:
 (road) 7000 kg
 (dirt road) 5000 kg
Towed load: (road) 9500 kg
Load area: 4·5 × 2·48 m

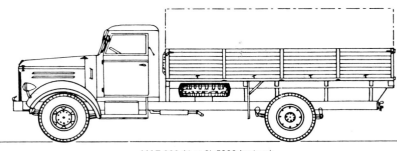

MAZ-200 (4 × 2) 5000 kg truck

Length: 7·62 m
Width: 2·65 m
Height:
 (cab) 2·46 m
 (tarpaulin) 2·935 m
 (load area) 1·39 m
Ground clearance: (axles) 0·29 m
Track:
 (front) 1·95 m
 (rear) 1·92 m
Wheelbase: 4·52 m
Angle of approach/departure: 43°/26°
Max speed: (road) 65 km/h
Range: 500 km
Fuel capacity: 225 litres
Fuel consumption: 46 litres/100 km
Max gradient: (loaded) 11°
Fording: 0·8 m

Engine: YaMZ-M204A 4-cylinder water-cooled diesel developing 120 hp at 2000 rpm
Gearbox: manual with 5 forward and 1 reverse gears
Clutch: single dry disc
Steering: worm with gear quadrant
Turning radius: 9·5 m
Suspension:
 (front) longitudinal semi-elliptical springs with hydraulic shock absorbers
 (rear) longitudinal semi-elliptical springs with check springs
Tyres: 12.00 × 20
Brakes:
 (main) air
 (parking) mechanical
Electrical system: 12 V
Batteries: 2 × 6-STM-128
Generator: G25-B,250 W

MAZ-500 (4 × 2) 7500 kg Cargo Truck

DEVELOPMENT
The MAZ-500 entered production at the Minsk Automobile Plant in 1965 and is the replacement for the earlier MAZ-200 series. It is primarily a civilian vehicle but is used in some numbers by the Soviet Army for general stores carrying, towing trailers carrying bridging equipment (for example the SARM) and with a fully enclosed body in the command role.

DESCRIPTION
The two-door all-steel forward control cab hinges forward to allow access to the engine for maintenance. The rear cargo area has a wooden floor with drop sides and a drop tailgate. If required bows and a tarpaulin cover can be fitted. Standard equipment includes a cab heater, engine pre-heater and a bunk for the driver. Late production models (including variants) have an A suffix, eg MAZ-500A and MAZ-503A.
 A 4 × 4 version was developed under the designation of MAZ-505, but as far as is known it was not placed in production.

VARIANTS
MAZ-500G: with a long wheelbase
MAZ-500S: for use in cold climates
MAZ-503: dump truck with back-tilting metal dump body
MAZ-503B: dump truck, as MAZ-503 except that the dump body has an automatically opening and closing tailgate
MAZ-504: tractor for towing semi-trailers up to 17 500 kg
MAZ-504B: tractor for towing automatic dump trailer
MAZ-509 and MAZ-509P: timber carriers (4 × 4) with two-axle pole carrier carried on rear when not in use
MAZ-511: side dump truck
ATs 8-500: 8000-litre fuel tanker
ATZ 8-500: 7000-litre fuel servicing truck
TZA 7, 5-500A: 7500-litre fuel service truck
Shop/van
Crane trucks

 The MAZ-514 series based on the MAZ-500 series is not used by the Soviet forces. The range includes the MAZ-514 (6 × 4), MAZ-516 (6 × 2), MAZ-516B (6 × 6) and MAZ-515 (6 × 4) tractor truck.

STATUS
Production. In service with the Soviet armed forces.

MANUFACTURER
Minsk Motor Vehicle Plant, Minsk, Belorussia, USSR.

MAZ-500 (4 × 2) 7500 kg cargo truck

MAZ-504 (4 × 2) tractor truck

SPECIFICATIONS
Cab seating: 1 + 2
Configuration: 4 × 2
Weight:
  (empty) 6500 kg
  (loaded) 14 225 kg
Weight on front axle: (loaded) 4225 kg
Weight on rear axle: (loaded) 10 000 kg
Max load: (road) 7500 kg
Towed load: (road) 12 000 kg
Load area: 4·86 × 2·325 m
Length: 7·33 m
Width:
  (11.00 × 20 tyres) 2·5 m
  (12.00 × 20 tyres) 2·65 m

Height: (cab) 2·64 m
Ground clearance: 0·27 m
Track:
  (front) 1·95 m
  (rear) 1·9 m
Wheelbase: 3·85 m
Angle of approach/departure: 30°/28°
Max speed: (road) 75 km/h
Range: 900 km
Fuel capacity: 200 litres
Max gradient: 30%
Engine: YaMZ-236 V-6 OHV diesel developing 180 hp at 2100 rpm
Gearbox: manual with 5 forward and 1 reverse gears
Clutch: single dry plate

Transfer box: none
Steering: screw, nut-rack with rolling balls, hydraulic booster
Turning radius: 8·5 m
Suspension:
  (front) longitudinal semi-elliptical springs with hydraulic telescopic shock absorbers
  (rear) longitudinal semi-elliptical springs with check springs
Tyres: 11.00 × 20 or 12.00 × 20
Brakes:
  (main) air
  (parking) mechanical
Electrical system: 24 V
Batteries: 2 × 6-TST-165EMS

Ural-377 (6 × 4) 7500 kg Truck

DESCRIPTION
The Ural-377 is a 6 × 4 version of the Ural-375 (6 × 6) truck and entered production in 1965. The layout of the vehicle is conventional with the engine at the front, fully enclosed all-steel two-door cab in the centre and the cargo area at the rear. It has a longer cargo area than the Ural-375D as the spare wheel is stowed on the right side of the chassis instead of to the rear of the cab as in the case of the Ural-375D. The rear cargo area has a wooden platform with drop sides and a drop tailgate. Standard equipment includes a cab heater and an engine pre-heater.

VARIANTS
Ural-377D: adapted for use in northern USSR with an insulated cab, cold weather tyres, central tyre pressure regulation system and windows with double glass
Ural-377M: the military version of the basic vehicle with a central tyre pressure regulation system not found on the basic vehicle
Ural-377S: the tractor truck version for towing semi-trailers
Ural-377V: side dump truck version

STATUS
In production. In service with members of the Warsaw Pact and also exported for military use.

MANUFACTURER
Ural Motor Vehicle Plant, Miass, USSR.

SPECIFICATIONS

Model	Ural-377	Ural-377M	Ural-377S
Cab seating	1 + 2	1 + 2	1 + 2
Configuration	6 × 4	6 × 4	6 × 4
Weight (empty)	7275 kg	6635 kg	6970 kg
(dirt road)	15 000 kg	14 635 kg	n/app
Weight on front axle (loaded)	4000 kg	n/app	n/app
Weight on rear bogie (loaded)	11 000 kg	n/app	n/app
Towed load (road)	10 500 kg	n/app	19 000 kg
(dirt road)	5600 kg	n/app	n/app
Load area	4·5 × 2·326 m	4·5 × 2·326 m	n/app
Length	7·6 m	7·86 m	6·9 m
Width	2·5 m	2·5 m	2·5 m
Height (cab)	2·62 m	2·535 m	2·62 m
(load area)	1·6 m	1·6 m	n/app
Ground clearance	0·4 m	0·4 m	0·32 m
Track	2 m	2 m	2 m
Wheelbase	3·5 m + 1·4 m	3·5 m + 1·4 m	3·5 m + 1·4 m
Angle of approach/departure	44°/42°	44°/42°	44°/65°
Max speed (road)	75 km/h	70 km/h (est)	65 km/h
Range	550 km	500 km	740 km
Fuel capacity	300 litres	300 litres	300 litres
Fording	0·8 m	0·8 m	0·8 m
Engine	ZIL-375Ya V-8 petrol developing 175 hp at 3000 rpm		
Gearbox	manual with 5 forward and 1 reverse gears		
Clutch	twin dry disc	twin dry disc	twin dry disc
Transfer box	2-speed	2-speed	2-speed
Steering	double-thread worm with hydraulic booster		
Turning radius	10·5 m	10·5 m	10·5 m
Suspension (front)	semi-elliptical springs with hydraulic shock absorbers (interchangeable with MAZ-500)		
(rear)	bogie with semi-elliptical springs		
Tyres	14.00 × 20	14.00 × 20	14.00 × 20
Brakes	air/hydraulic	air/hydraulic	air/hydraulic
Electrical system	12 V	12 V	12 V
Battery	1 × 6-STEN-140M	1 × 6-STEN-140M	1 × 6-STEN-140M
Generator	G130	G130	G130

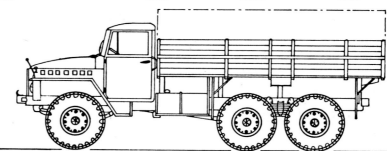

Ural-377 (6 × 4) 7500 kg truck

Ural-377 (6 × 4) 7500 kg truck

Ural-377S (6 × 4) tractor truck (A. McKrill)

ZIL-133 (6 × 4) 8000 kg Truck

DESCRIPTION
The ZIL-133 is the 6 × 4 version of the ZIL-130 (4 × 2) truck and also incorporates components of the ZIL-131 (6 × 6) truck. The prototypes had a 220 hp engine but production versions of the truck use a 150 hp engine as used in the ZIL-130. The layout of the vehicle is conventional with the engine at the front, two-door fully enclosed cab in the centre and the cargo area at the rear with drop sides and a drop tailgate.

VARIANTS
ZIL-133G1: long wheelbase truck, production
ZIL-133G: long wheelbase truck, not in production
ZIL-133B: agricultural dump truck, not in production
ZIL-133D: construction dump truck, not in production
ZIL-133V: tractor truck, not in production

STATUS
The ZIL-133G1 is reported to be the only model in production at present.

MANUFACTURER
Likhachev Motor Vehicle Plant, Moscow, USSR.

SPECIFICATIONS

Model	ZIL-133	ZIL-133G1	ZIL-133V
Cab seating	1 + 2	1 + 2	1 + 2
Configuration	6 × 4	6 × 4	6 × 4
Weight (empty)	6200 kg	6875 kg	6350 kg
(loaded)	14 200 kg	14 875 kg	n/app
Max load (road)	8000 kg	8000 kg	n/app
Towed load (road)	9500 kg	n/app	19 000 kg
Length	8·07 m	9 m	6·325 m
Width	2·5 m	2·5 m	2·48 m
Height (cab)	2·41 m	2·395 m	2·41 m
Ground clearance	0·275 m	0·25 m	0·275 m
Track (front/rear)	1·8 m/1·79 m	1·835 m/1·85 m	1·8 m/1·79 m
Wheelbase	4·02 m + 1·36 m	4·6 m + 1·4 m	3·42 m + 1·36 m
Max speed (road)	97·5 km/h	80 km/h	86 km/h
Fuel capacity	170 litres	170 litres	250 litres
Vertical obstacle	0·32 m	0·32 m	0·32 m
Engine	ZIL-133 V-8 water-cooled petrol developing 220 hp at 3600 rpm	ZIL-133 V-8 water-cooled petrol developing 150 hp at 3100 rpm	ZIL-133 V-8 water-cooled petrol developing 220 hp at 3600 rpm
Tyres	9.00 × 20	9.00 × 20	9.00 × 20

ZIL-133G (6 × 4) 8000 kg truck

YaAZ-214 and KrAZ-214 (6 × 6) 7000 kg Trucks

DEVELOPMENT/DESCRIPTION
Until the introduction of the ZIL-135 (8 × 8) and the MAZ-535/MAZ-537 (8 × 8) trucks, the KrAZ-214 was the largest all-wheel drive truck in service with the Soviet Army. The YaAZ-214 was produced at the Yaroslavl Plant from 1956 to 1959 when production was transferred to the Kremenchug Plant and the vehicle was renamed the KrAZ-214. Production continued until 1967 when it was replaced by the much improved KrAZ-255B. Early models were known as the YaAZ-214A and had a 12-volt electrical system; later production models are known as the YaAZ-214B. These vehicles are closely related to the KrAZ-219 and YaAZ-210 trucks.

The layout of the vehicle is conventional with the engine at the front, fully enclosed cab in the centre and cargo area at the rear with a hinged tailgate, removable bows and a tarpaulin cover. The vehicle is fitted with a tyre pressure regulation system and standard equipment on all vehicles includes an 8000 kg capacity winch, cab heater and engine pre-heater.

VARIANTS
Crane/shovel (E-305V), BM-25 250 mm (six-barrelled) Multiple Rocket System (*Jane's Armour and Artillery 1983–84*, page 738), timber truck, tractor truck, and for carrying bridging equipment such as the PMP heavy floating pontoon bridge and the TMM treadway bridge. The KrAZ-255B is now carrying out most of these roles.

SPECIFICATIONS
Cab seating: 1 + 2
Configuration: 6 × 6
Weight:
  (empty) 12 300 kg
  (loaded) 19 300 kg
Weight on front axle: (empty) 5370 kg
Weight on rear bogie: (loaded) 6930 kg
Max load: (road) 7000 kg
Towed load:
  (road) 50 000 kg
  (cross country) 10 000 kg
Load area: 4·565 × 2·5 m
Length: 8·53 m
Width: 2·7 m
Height:
  (cab) 2·88 m
  (tarpaulin) 3·17 m
  (load area) 1·65 m
Ground clearance: 0·36 m

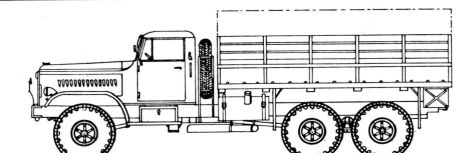

KrAZ-214 (6 × 6) 7000 kg truck

KrAZ-214 (6 × 6) 7000 kg truck

Track: 2·03 m
Wheelbase: 4·6 m + 1·4 m
Angle of approach/departure: 48°/32°
Max speed: 55 km/h
Range: 530 km
Fuel capacity: 450 litres
Fuel consumption: 70 litres/100 km
Max gradient: 30°
Fording: 1 m
Engine: YaMZ-M206B 6-cylinder water-cooled diesel developing 205 hp at 2000 rpm
Gearbox: manual with 5 forward and 1 reverse gears
Clutch: single dry disc
Transfer box: 2-stage, transfer case with interaxle differential and drive line to front axle

Steering: worm with lateral quadrant with pneumatic booster
Turning radius: 13 m
Suspension:
  (front) longitudinal semi-elliptical springs with hydraulic shock absorbers
  (rear) bogie, longitudinal semi-elliptical springs
Tyres: 15.00 × 20
Brakes:
  (main) air
  (parking) mechanical
Electrical system: 24 V (early vehicles had 12 V system)
Batteries: 4 × 6-STM-128
Generator: 400 W

STATUS
Production complete. In service with members of the Warsaw Pact.

MANUFACTURER
Yaroslavl Motor Vehicle Plant, Yaroslavl, and Kremenchug Motor Vehicle Plant, Kremenchug, Ukraine, USSR.

KrAZ-214 (6 × 6) truck being used to carry PMP pontoon

KrAZ-255B (6 × 6) 7500 kg Truck

DESCRIPTION
The KrAZ-255B replaced the KrAZ-214 (6 × 6) truck in production from 1967. It is very similar to the earlier vehicle but has a more powerful engine and a central tyre pressure regulation system.

The layout of the vehicle is conventional with the engine at the front, fully enclosed two-door cab in the centre and cargo area at the rear with a hinged tailgate, removable bows and a tarpaulin cover. Standard equipment on all vehicles includes a cab heater, engine pre-heater, winch with 12 000 kg capacity and suspension locking mechanism.

VARIANTS
There are at least three variants of the KrAZ-255B, the KrAZ-255L timber truck and the KrAZ-255V tractor truck. The latter weighs 10 600 kg and can tow a semi-trailer weighing 26 000 kg on roads or 18 000 kg across country. Principal dimensions are length 7·685 metres, width 2·75 metres and height 2·94 metres. The fuel service truck is designated the TZ 8-255B and carries 8000 litres of fuel.

Many roles previously undertaken by the KrAZ-214 are now being carried out by the KrAZ-255B including carrying and laying the TMM treadway bridge, carrying and launching the PMP heavy floating pontoon bridge, carrying and launching the BMK-T bridging boat, crane truck, E-305 BV crane shovel, excavator EDV-4421, ATsM 7-255B 7000-litre fuel tanker towing the PTsM 8925 5800-litre trailer and USM pile driving set.

For an illustration of the BMK-T the reader is referred to the entry for the BMK-T bridging boat in the *Bridging systems* section (page 143).

STATUS
In production. In service with the Soviet Army and other members of the Warsaw Pact.

MANUFACTURER
Kremenchug Motor Vehicle Plant, Kremenchug, Ukraine, USSR.

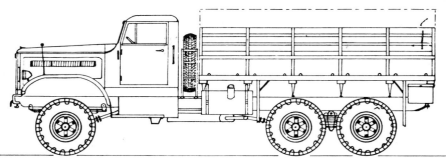

KrAZ-255B (6 × 6) 7500 kg truck

KrAZ-255B (6 × 6) 7500 kg truck

SPECIFICATIONS
Cab seating: 1 + 2
Configuration: 6 × 6
Weight:
(empty) 11 950 kg
(loaded, cross country) 19 450 kg
Weight on front axle: (empty) 5220 kg
Weight on rear bogie: (empty) 6730 kg
Max load: 7500 kg
Towed load:
(road) 30 000 kg
(cross country) 10 000 kg
Load area: 4·56 × 2·5 m
Length: 8·645 m

Width: 2·75 m
Height:
(cab) 2·94 m
(tarpaulin) 3·17 m
(load area) 1·65 m
Ground clearance: 0·36 m
Track: 2·16 m
Wheelbase: 4·6 m + 1·6 m
Angle of approach/departure: 48°/32°
Max speed: 71 km/h
Range: 650 km
Fuel capacity: 450 litres
Fuel consumption: 38 litres/100 km
Max gradient: 60%
Fording: 0·85 m
Engine: YaMZ-238 V-8 water-cooled diesel developing 2100 rpm
Gearbox: manual with 5 forward and 1 reverse gears

Clutch: dual dry disc
Transfer box: 2-speed with differential between axles
Steering: screw and nut with rolling ball, hydraulic booster
Turning radius: 13 m
Suspension:
(front) longitudinal semi-elliptical springs with telescopic double acting shock absorbers
(rear) equaliser type on 2 longitudinal semi-elliptical springs
Tyres: 15.00 × 20
Number of tyres: 6 + 1 spare
Brakes:
(main) air
(parking) mechanical
Electrical system: 24 V
Batteries: 2 × 6-TST-165EMS
Generator: 500 W

ZIL-133 (6 × 4) 8000 kg Trucks

DESCRIPTION
The ZIL-133 (6 × 4) 8000 kg series of trucks was developed using the ZIL-130 series as a basis, to the extent that 70 per cent of the basic parts are shared by the ZIL-130 and the truck version of the ZIL-133 series, the ZIL-133G. The ZIL-133G entered production in 1975.

The ZIL-133G is a conventional design powered by the same ZIL-130 61 V-8 150 hp petrol engine as used

on the ZIL-130 but by now will probably use the newer KamAZ 210 hp diesel engine. Payload is 8000 kg, which car be increased by the use of a two-axled trailer with a 6500 kg capacity. The vehicle is equipped with a five-speed gearbox driving the two rear axles through hypoid differentials equipped with locks. Steering is power-assisted and the suspension is conventional having rigid axles equipped with leaf springs and hydraulic shock absorbers. Overall length of the ZIL-133G is about nine metres. Useful life of the ZIL-133 between major overhauls is claimed to be 300 000 km. The

ZIL-133G has a very limited performance across country and is limited to road usage.

There is a tractor version of the ZIL-133 known as the ZIL-133V which can tow articulated trailers with capacities of up to 16 000 kg on roads. It has a more powerful engine than the ZIL-133G.

STATUS
In production. In service with the Soviet armed forces.

MANUFACTURER
Likhachev Motor Vehicle Plant, Moscow, USSR.

KamAZ-5320 (6 × 4) 8000 kg Truck

DEVELOPMENT
This is the basic member of a complete family of trucks which is available in both 6 × 4 and 6 × 6 configurations. All are powered by a V-type water-cooled diesel engine with the same bore and stroke (120 × 120 mm). Brief specifications of the various engines are:

Model	YaMZ-7401	YaMZ-740§	YaMZ-741
Type	V-8	V-8	V-10
Capacity	10·85 litres	10·85 litres	13·58 litres
Output	180 hp	210 hp	260 hp

§ The YaMZ-740 engine is also used in the new version of the Ural-375D truck, known as the Ural-4320, described earlier in this section.

It has been reported that the KamAZ-5510 dump truck is available fitted with the West German KHD 413 four-stroke air-cooled eight-cylinder diesel developing 256 hp at 2650 rpm, but it is probably for export only.

DESCRIPTION
The basic KamAZ-5320 (6 × 4) 8000 kg truck has a forward control cab and the rear cargo area has drop

KamAZ-5510 (6 × 4) 8000 kg dump truck

KamAZ-5410 (6 × 4) 8000 kg tractor truck

KamAZ-5320 (6 × 4) 8000 kg truck

KamAZ-5320 (6 × 4) 8000 kg truck towing trailer

KamAZ-5410 (6 × 4) 8000 kg tractor truck

SPECIFICATIONS

Model	KamAZ-5320	KamAZ-53202	KamAZ-5410	KamAZ-54102	KamAZ-4310
Type	cargo truck	cargo truck	tractor truck	tractor truck	cargo truck
Configuration	6 × 4	6 × 4	6 × 4	6 × 4	6 × 6
Weight (empty)	6800 kg	7240 kg	6445 kg	n/a	n/a
Max load	8000 kg	8000 kg	n/a	n/a	5000 kg*
Max towed load	11 500 kg	11 500 kg	19 000 kg	n/a	7000 kg*
Length	8·295 m	8·295 m	6·14 m	6·43 m	7·61 m
Width	2·496 m	2·496 m	2·48 m	n/a	n/a
Height (cab)	2·63 m	2·63 m	2·63 m	2·63 m	2·8 m
Ground clearance	0·285 m	0·285 m	0·285 m	n/a	n/a
Track (front)	2 m	2 m	2·01 m	n/a	n/a
(rear)	1·85 m	1·85 m	1·85 m	n/a	n/a
Wheelbase	3·69 m + 1·32 m	3·69 m + 1·32 m	2·84 m + 1·32 m	3·14 m + 1·32 m†	3·34 m + 1·32 m‡
Max speed (road)	85 km/h	85 km/h	85 km/h	85 km/h	80 km/h
Engine	YaMZ-740	YaMZ-740	YaMZ-740	YaMZ-741	YaMZ-740

* cross-country
† also quoted as 3·04 m + 1·32 m
‡ also quoted as 3·39 m + 1·32 m

sides, drop tailgate, removable bows and a tarpaulin cover.

VARIANTS
(6 × 4)
KamAZ-53201: chassis based on KamAZ-5320, 180 hp engine
KamAZ-53202: long wheelbase cargo truck
KamAZ-53203: chassis based on KamAZ-53202, 180 hp engine

KamAZ-5410: tractor truck
KamAZ-54101: tractor truck for dump semi-trailers
KamAZ-54102: tractor truck for heavier loads, 260 hp engine
KamAZ-5510: dump truck, 180 hp engine
KamAZ-55102: agricultural dump truck with trailer
(6 × 6)
KamAZ-4310: cargo truck with fixed sideboards
KamAZ-43101: cargo truck with drop sides
KamAZ-43102: same as KamAZ-43101 with bunk in

cab
KamAZ-43103: same as KamAZ-4310 with bunk in cab
KamAZ-4410 tractor truck

STATUS
Production.

MANUFACTURER
Kama Motor Vehicle Plant, Naberezhnye Chelny, USSR.

YaAZ-219 and KrAZ-219 (6 × 4) 10 000 kg Trucks

DESCRIPTION
The YaAZ-219 was the replacement for the earlier YaAZ-210 truck and was initially produced at the Yaroslavl plant between 1958 and 1959. In 1959 production was transferred to the Kremenchug plant and the vehicle was renamed the KrAZ-219. In 1963 the KrAZ-219A was introduced followed by the KrAZ-219B. Late production models of the latter were powered by a YaMZ-238N engine which developed 215 hp compared with the 180 hp of the earlier vehicles. In 1965-66 the KrAZ-219 was replaced in production by the KrAZ-257. The KrAZ-219 is related to the KrAZ-214 (6 × 6) truck.

The layout of the vehicle is conventional with the engine at the front, two-door fully enclosed cab in the centre and the cargo area at the rear with two drop sides either side and a drop tailgate. Standard equipment includes a cab heater and an engine pre-heater.

KrAZ-221 (6 × 4) tractor truck

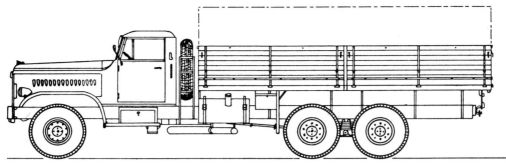

KrAZ-219 (6 × 4) 10 000 kg truck

VARIANTS
Crane truck: KrAZ-219 with K-104 crane mounted on rear
Dump truck: KrAZ-222 and KrAZ-222B each with a capacity of 10 000 kg
Tractor truck: KrAZ-221 and KrAZ-221B

STATUS
Production complete. In service with members of the Warsaw Pact.

MANUFACTURER
Kremenchug Motor Vehicle Plant, Kremenchug, Ukraine, USSR.

SPECIFICATIONS
Cab seating: 1 + 2
Configuration: 6 × 4
Weight:
  (empty) 11 300 kg
  (loaded) 23 530 kg
Weight on front axle: (loaded) 4670 kg
Weight on rear bogie: (loaded) 18 860 kg
Max load:
  (road) 12 000 kg
  (dirt road) 10 000 kg
Towed load: (road) 15 000 kg
Load area: 5·77 × 2·49 m
Length: 9·66 m
Width: 2·65 m
Height:
  (cab) 2·62 m
  (load area) 1·52 m
Ground clearance: 0·29 m
Track: (front/rear) 1·95 m/1·92 m

KrAZ-219 (6 × 4) 10 000 kg truck

Wheelbase: 5·05 m + 1·4 m
Angle of approach/departure: 42°/18°
Max speed: (road) 55 km/h
Range: 750 km
Fuel capacity: 450 litres
Fuel consumption: 55 litres/100 km
Engine: YaMZ-M206I 6-cylinder water-cooled diesel developing 180 hp at 2000 rpm
Gearbox: manual with 5 forward and 1 reverse gears
Clutch: single disc
Steering: worm with lateral quadrant, pneumatic booster

Turning radius: 12·5 m
Suspension:
  (front) longitudinal semi-elliptical springs with hydraulic shock absorbers
  (rear) bogie with longitudinal semi-elliptical springs
Tyres: 12.00 × 20
Brakes:
  (main) air
  (parking) mechanical
Electrical system: 24 V
Batteries: 4 × 6-STM-128
Generator: 400 W

YaAZ-210 (6 × 4) 10 000 kg Truck

DESCRIPTION
The YaAZ-210 series of 6 × 4 trucks was in production at the Yaroslavl plant between 1951 and 1959 when it was replaced by the very similar KrAZ-219 series of 6 × 4 trucks.
  The basic cargo model is designated the YaAZ-210 while the YaAZ-210A has a winch. The layout of the vehicle is conventional with the engine at the front, two-door fully enclosed cab in the centre and the cargo area at the rear.

VARIANTS
YaAZ-210D: tractor truck with a shorter wheelbase
YaAZ-210E: hopper type dump truck
YaAZ-210G: ballast truck, which has a shorter wheelbase and was built in two versions, one with a conventional stake type ballast area and the other with a metal ballast compartment
Crane truck: some vehicles were fitted with the K-104 crane

SPECIFICATIONS
Cab seating: 1 + 2
Configuration: 6 × 4
Weight:
  (empty) 11 300 kg
  (loaded, dirt road) 21 300 kg

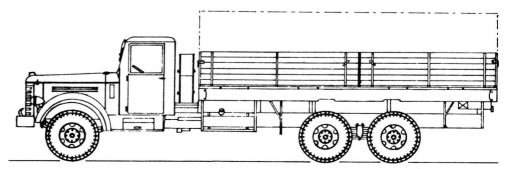

YaAZ-210G (6 × 4) ballast tractor towing trailer

Max load:
  (road) 12 000 kg
  (dirt road) 10 000 kg
Towed load: (road) 15 000 kg
Length: 9·66 m
Width: 2·65 m
Height: (cab) 2·575 m
Ground clearance: 0·29 m
Track: (front/rear) 1·95 m/1·92 m
Wheelbase: 5·05 m + 1·4 m
Max speed: 55 km/h
Range: 820 km

Fuel capacity: 450 litres
Max gradient: 10°
Fording: 1 m
Engine: YaAZ-M206A 6-cylinder water-cooled diesel developing 165 hp
Tyres: 12.00 × 20

STATUS
Production complete. In service with members of the Warsaw Pact.

MANUFACTURER
Yaroslavl Motor Vehicle Plant, Yaroslavl, USSR.

YaAZ-210 (6 × 4) 10 000 kg truck

YaAZ-210 (6 × 4) 10 000 kg truck

YaAZ-210G (6 × 4) 10 000 kg ballast truck

ZIL-169 12 000 kg Truck

DESCRIPTION
Few details are available regarding the ZIL-169 tractor truck which is understood to have entered service in 1978–79. It has a towing capacity of about 12 000 kg and is a two-axled tractor unit with a forward-tilting cab. The power unit is thought to be a 160 hp diesel.

STATUS
Production.

MANUFACTURER
Likhachev Motor Vehicle Plant, Moscow, USSR.

KrAZ-257 (6 × 4) 12 000 kg Truck

DESCRIPTION
The KrAZ-257 (6 × 4) truck replaced the KrAZ-219 in production at Kremenchug in 1965-66. In appearance they are almost identical to the earlier vehicles but have many detailed changes as well as a more powerful V-8 engine.

The layout of the vehicle is conventional with the engine at the front, fully enclosed two-door cab in the centre and the cargo area at the rear with a wooden platform with drop sides and a drop tailgate. Standard equipment includes a cab heater and an engine pre-heater.

VARIANTS
KrAZ-254: dump truck, developed to prototype stage but not placed in production
KrAZ-256: hopper type dump truck
KrAZ-256B: strengthened hopper dump truck
KrAZ-256BS: strengthened hopper type dump truck for use in cold climates
KrAZ-258: tractor truck for towing semi-trailers
Various crane trucks

SPECIFICATIONS
Cab seating: 1 + 2
Configuration: 6 × 4
Weight:
 (empty) 11 130 kg
 (loaded) 23 385 kg
Weight on front axle: (loaded) 4585 kg
Weight on rear bogie: (loaded) 18 800 kg
Max load: (road) 12 000 kg
Towed load: (road) 16 600 kg
Load area: 5·77 × 2·48 m
Length: 9·66 m
Width: 2·65 m
Height:
 (cab) 2·62 m
 (load area) 1·52 m
Ground clearance: 0·29 m
Track: (front/rear) 1·95 m/1·92 m
Wheelbase: 5·05 m + 1·4 m
Angle of approach/departure: 42°/18°
Max speed: (road) 60 km/h

KrAZ-258 (6 × 4) tractor truck towing van semi-trailer

Range: 1000 km
Fuel capacity: 450 litres
Max gradient: (loaded) 18°
Engine: YaMZ-238 V-8 water-cooled diesel developing 240 hp at 2100 rpm
Gearbox: manual with 5 forward and 1 reverse gears
Clutch: twin dry disc
Transfer box: 2-speed
Steering: worm with lateral gear quadrant, pneumatic booster
Suspension:
 (front) longitudinal semi-elliptical springs with hydraulic shock absorbers
 (rear) equalising, on longitudinal semi-elliptical springs
Tyres: 12.00 × 20

Brakes:
 (main) air
 (parking) mechanical
Electrical system: 24 V
Batteries: 2 × 6-STM-128 or 6-TST-165 EMS
Generator: G270 (500 W)

(Some early vehicles were powered by a YaAZ-238A engine which developed 215 hp)

STATUS
In production. In service with members of the Warsaw Pact.

MANUFACTURER
Kremenchug Motor Vehicle Plant, Kremenchug, Ukraine, USSR.

ZIL-135 Series (8 × 8) Trucks

DEVELOPMENT/DESCRIPTION
The ZIL-135 series of 8 × 8 trucks was introduced during the 1960s. The original design and development was carried out at the Likhachev Motor Vehicle Plant near Moscow, but production is carried out at the Bryansk Motor Vehicle Plant for which reason the range is sometimes known as the BAZ-135L4 (the cargo truck version is also known as the ZIL-135L4). These trucks are now widely used by members of the Warsaw Pact for both military and civil applications.

The vehicle is powered by two petrol engines, each of which drives the four wheels on one side of the vehicle. Steering is by the front and rear wheels only and these wheels are carried on axles with a torsion bar suspension. The two central axles are fixed and a central tyre

pressure regulation system is fitted. The fully enclosed forward control cab has two doors, one on each side. When being used for missile launching roles the windscreen is fitted with covers to protect it from blast when the missile is launched.

VARIANTS
FROG-7 Transporter/Launcher Vehicle
This carries and launches the FROG-7 surface-to-surface tactical missile system. Mounted on the right side of the vehicle is a hydraulic crane for reloading purposes. Stabiliser jacks are lowered to the ground before the missile is launched to provide a more stable firing platform.
FROG-7 Resupply Vehicle
This carries three FROG-7 missiles.

Sepal Transporter/Launcher Vehicle
This has a large cylindrical container which acts as the launcher for the Sepal cruise missile. This version has a different cab from the other members of this series and two stabiliser jacks are lowered to the ground either side before the missile is launched.
BM-27 Multiple Rocket System
The ZIL-135 series chassis is also used for the new Soviet BM-27 multiple rocket launcher and its associated resupply vehicle. For details see *Jane's Armour and Artillery 1983–84*, page 738.
ZIL-135 Convoy Escort Vehicle
Reports from Afghanistan have mentioned the use of an improvised convoy escort vehicle formed by mounting a ZU-23/2 twin 23 mm cannon on the rear of a ZIL-135 truck. Some form of armour is provided for the gun crew.

ZIL-135 (8 × 8) chassis being used as transporter/launcher for FROG-7 surface-to-surface tactical missile

ZIL-135 (8 × 8) chassis being used as transporter/launcher for Sepal cruise missile

BAZ-135L4 Cargo Truck
This is produced at the Bryansk Plant and is used for carrying cargo. The rear cargo area is provided with a drop tailgate. Also referred to as ZIL-135L4.

ZIL-135 Tractor Truck
As far as is known, this is only used for civilian roles, primarily for carrying long lengths of pipe used in constructing pipelines.

ZIL-E-167
This is an experimental 6 × 6 vehicle based on the chassis of the ZIL-135, designed specifically for operations in the desert and snow. Basic specifications are: unladen weight 7000 kg, payload 5000 kg, length 9·268 metres, width 3·13 metres, height 3·06 metres and maximum road speed 65 km/h. It has the same engines as the ZIL-135.

BAZ-135L4 (8 × 8) cargo truck

SPECIFICATIONS (BAZ-135L4 cargo truck)
Cab seating: 1 + 2
Configuration: 8 × 8
Weight:
  (loaded) 19 000 kg
  (empty) 9000 kg
Max load: 10 000 kg
Towed load:
  (road) 20 000 kg
  (cross country) 18 000 kg
Load area: (estimated) 4·57 × 2·65 m
Length: 9·27 m
Width: 2·8 m
Height: 2·53 m
Ground clearance: (axles) 0·58 m
Track: 2·3 m
Wheelbase: 2·415 m + 1·5 m + 2·415 m
Max speed: 65 km/h
Range: 500 km
Fuel capacity: 768 litres

Fuel consumption: 160 litres/100 km
Max gradient: 57%
Vertical obstacle: 0·685 m
Trench: 2·63 m
Fording: 0·58 m
Engines: 2 × ZIL-375 V-8 water-cooled petrol developing 180 hp (each) at 3200 rpm
Gearbox: hydro-mechanical
Steering: power assisted, 1st and 4th axles
Turning radius: 12·5 m
Suspension: 1st and 4th axles have torsion bars, 2nd and 3rd axles are fixed to chassis and have no suspension

Tyres: 16.00 × 20
Number of tyres: 8
Brakes:
  (main) hydraulic, air-assisted
Electrical system: 24 V

STATUS
In production. In service with members of the Warsaw Pact.

MANUFACTURER
Bryansk Motor Vehicle Plant, Bryansk, USSR.

MAZ-543 (8 × 8) Truck

DESCRIPTION
The MAZ-543 (8 × 8) truck uses many automotive components of the MAZ-537 (8 × 8) truck including the same engine. It was seen in public for the first time in November 1965. The engine is mounted at the front of the vehicle with a two-man cab on each side which hinge forward to allow access to the engine. Standard equipment includes a heater, engine pre-heater, central tyre pressure regulation system and power steering on the front four wheels.

VARIANTS
The MAZ-543 is used to carry and launch the SCUD-B (SS-1C) and Scaleboard (SS-12) surface-to-surface missile.

Other variants include an aircraft crash tender, tractor truck and a cargo truck with a drop tailgate and stake type sides.

MAZ-543 (8 × 8) chassis being used to carry and launch SCUD-B surface-to-surface missile

MAZ-543 (8 × 8) cargo truck with ZIL-135 (8 × 8) cargo truck in foreground

SPECIFICATIONS
Cab seating: 1 + 3
Configuration: 8 × 8
Weight: (chassis only) 17 300 kg
Max load: 15 170 kg
Length: 11·7 m
Width: 3·02 m
Height: 2·65 m
Ground clearance: 0·45 m
Track: (front and rear) 2·375 m
Wheelbase: 2·2 m + 3·3 m + 2·2 m
Max speed: 70 km/h
Range: 500 km
Max gradient: 57%
Vertical obstacle: 0·78 m
Trench: 3·38 m
Fording: 1 m
Engine: D12A-525 V-12 water-cooled diesel developing 525 hp at 2100 rpm
Tyres: 15.00 × 25
Electrical system: 24 V
Batteries: 4 × 6 V

STATUS
In production. In service with members of the Warsaw Pact.

MANUFACTURER
Minsk Motor Vehicle Plant, Minsk, USSR.

MAZ-543 (8 × 8) chassis being used to carry and launch SS-12 Scaleboard battlefield support missile

UNITED KINGDOM

Laird Centaur Multi-role Military Vehicle System

DEVELOPMENT
The Centaur Multi-role Military Vehicle System has been designed by Laird (Anglesey) Limited as a private venture with the assistance of Land-Rover. Design work began in 1977 with the first prototype being completed in April 1978.

In July 1978 a decision was taken to build, with company funds, a pre-production batch of six vehicles, five with a general service body and one with a fully enclosed body. The first was completed in mid-1979 and the last in December 1979. Since then the Centaur has been evaluated by many armies and one has been bought by Oman. The latter has a general service body with mounts for three 7·62 mm GPMGs, one each side and another at the front.

In August 1979 it was announced that the Centaur was to be evaluated by the British Army for a number of roles, both in the BAOR and with the Allied Mobile Force. These roles include towing the 105 mm Light Gun and British Aerospace Rapier SAM launcher, carrying an 81 mm mortar plus its crew and ammunition, towing the Bar minelayer and mounting the Ranger anti-personnel minelaying system.

The concept of the Centaur is to combine the road performance and ease of operation of a wheeled vehicle with the excellent traction, off-road capability and carrying capability of a tracked vehicle.

The Centaur consists of two main components, both of which have been proved in all parts of the world. The first is the chassis and cab of the long wheelbase Land-Rover with the standard engine replaced by a V-8 engine, and second the track of the Alvis Scorpion CVR(T) range of vehicles. The result is a multi-purpose vehicle with a low initial cost, low maintenance requirement and little or no driver training requirement as the controls are identical to the standard Land-Rover. Many of the components of the vehicle are already in many armies' inventories as both the Land-Rover and the Scorpion are in widespread use.

DESCRIPTION
The basic layout is similar to the Land-Rover with the engine at the front, driver and commander in the centre and the personnel/cargo area at the rear.

The bonnet, radiator, windscreen and doors are identical to those on the Land-Rover. The doors are angled outwards as the rear of the vehicle is wider (2 metres) than the front (1·63 metres). The vehicle is powered by a Rover V-8 3·5-litre petrol engine which drives both the front wheels and the tracks through a manually-operated gearbox with four forward and one reverse gears and a two-speed transfer box. Simultaneous track and front-wheel drive is arranged through a lockable differential unit built into the gearbox which transmits equal power to the track and road wheels. The differential can be locked when required.

The chassis to the rear of the cab has been replaced by a rigid steel platform to which the track and wheel suspension units are mounted. The rear track system consists of three road wheels with the drive sprocket at

Laird Centaur multi-role military vehicle fitted for radio

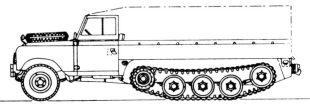

Laird Centaur multi-role military vehicle system

the front and the idler at the rear. A hydraulic ram is fitted on the rear idler wheel for track tensioning. The road and sprocket wheels are rubber tyred. The lightweight tracks incorporate bonded rubber road pads and maintenance free link joints.

The basic general service model has a drop tailgate, removable hoops, canvas tilt and a tow hook. This model has a crew of two (commander and driver) and can carry ten fully equipped men and a machine gunner. The machine gunner is stationed in the forward part of the personnel area and the machine gun is mounted on a ring mount to the rear of the cab. The infantry are seated five either side down the personnel area.

VARIANTS
Ambulance (crew of three plus four stretcher patients),

ammunition vehicle carrying two pallets of ammunition each weighing 1350 kg (unloaded with the aid of an on-board hydraulic system), anti-tank armed with Swingfire or TOW system, anti-tank team carrier which can carry two MILAN launchers, 27 MILAN missiles, two missile teams of two men each plus the driver and unit commander, gun tractor towing a 105 mm Light Gun or a similar weapon, missile tractor towing the Rapier system, fire support armed with a 60 mm breech-loaded mortar, long range reconnaissance armed with 7·62 mm machine guns, mine layer (Centaur has been tested by the British Army towing the Bar minelayer and has also been fitted with the EMI Ranger anti-personnel mine laying system), mortar carrier, radio vehicle, recovery vehicle fitted with a winch and a water/fuel carrier.

SPECIFICATIONS
Cab seating: 1 + 1 (plus 11 in rear)
Weight:
(empty) 3880 kg
(loaded) 6970 kg
Max load: 3090 kg
Load area: 3·28 × 1·78 m
(inside well) 2·6 × 1·05 m
Length: 5·8 m
Width:
(overall) 2 m
(front) 1·63 m
Height:
(windscreen up) 1·71 m
(top of rear body) 1·19 m
Ground clearance: 0·325 m

Track:
(front wheels) 1·33 m
(rear track) 1·56 m
Track width: 432 mm
Length of track on ground: 1·152 m
Ground pressure:
(empty) 0·22 kg/cm²
(loaded) 0·45 kg/cm²
Max speed: (road) 100 km/h
Fuel capacity: 218 litres
Max gradient: 75%
Engine: Rover V-8 petrol developing 132 bhp at 5000 rpm
Gearbox: manual with 4 forward and 1 reverse gears
Clutch: single dry plate
Transfer box: 2-speed

Steering type: Burman recirculating ball
Suspension:
(front) semi-elliptical springs with double acting hydraulic shock absorbers
(rear) independent torsion bar
Brakes:
(front) hydraulic drum
(rear) inboard disc each with twin callipers
(hand) mechanical on transmission
Electrical system: 12 V (24 V FFR)

STATUS
Development complete. Ready for production.

MANUFACTURER
Laird (Anglesey) Limited, Beaumaris, Gwynedd LL58 8HY, Wales.

SMC FC 82 (6 × 6) 2000 kg Light Truck

DEVELOPMENT
Development of the SMC FC 82 (Forward Control designed 1982) began in late 1981 with the detail design and prototype construction taking place in 1982. The FC 82 uses a large percentage of Land-Rover components and has been developed with the co-operation of Land-Rover Limited.

DESCRIPTION
The FC 82 is a 6 × 6 forward-control cab vehicle with the Land-Rover engine mounted forward and to the rear of the two-man cab. The engine is raised on A-frames and at the rear the lengthened Land-Rover chassis has an extra driven axle added. The transmission to the rear axles is so arranged that the raised load area is completely clear. The 6 × 6 FC 82 may be used in a number of ways either as a personnel carrier or a tractor for light artillery or guided missile systems. In production is a personnel carrier, with the load area having drop sides and a canvas tilt. There is cross-bench seating for 24 men plus their equipment and lockers between the cab

and load area. Panels to the rear of the cab provide more stowage space. Lockers are also provided under the load area. Panels to the rear of the cab provide access to the engine. Land-Rover components are used throughout the vehicle including the cab instrument panels and controls. A pick-up truck configuration with drop sides is also produced.

VARIANTS
A 4 × 4 version of the FC 82 was first shown at BAEE at Aldershot in 1982. This prototype closely followed the same general lines as the 6 × 6 FC 82 with a load area measuring 2·54 metres by 1·778 metres. The 4 × 4 FC 82 is based on the 109-inch wheelbase Land-Rover and has a possible payload of 1300 kg or 16 men and their equipment. In its basic form the 4 × 4 FC 82 is produced as an all-aluminium drop side flatbed truck but the basic chassis may be converted to numerous specialist body forms.

An armoured personnel carrier based on the 4 × 4 FC 82 is being developed.

SPECIFICATIONS ((4 × 4) in square brackets)
Cab seating: 1 + 1

Configuration: 6 × 6 [4 × 4]
Payload: 2000 [1300] kg
Load area: 3·998 × 1·778 [2·54 × 1·778] m
Length: 5·753 m [n/a]
Width: 1·842 m
Wheelbase: (front to rear axle) 3·531 [2·77] m
Fuel capacity: 66·6 litres
Engine: Rover V-8 3·5-litre diesel developing 96 hp
Gearbox: 4 forward and 1 reverse gears
Transfer box: 2-speed
Suspension: semi-elliptical leaf springs assisted by convoluted rubber springing on rear axles, telescopic hydraulic dampers

STATUS
6 × 6 in production for a Far Eastern customer.
4 × 4 under development. Being made ready for production.

MANUFACTURERS
SMC Engineering (Bristol) Limited, SMC House, Bristol Road, Hambrook, Bristol BS16 1RY, England.
Bodywork: Longwell Green Coachworks Limited, Longwell Green, Bristol BS15 6DN, England.

SMC FC 82 (6 × 6) truck in personnel carrier form

SMC FC 82 (6 × 6) truck in pick-up configuration

Gomba Stonefield Range of 4 × 4 and 6 × 4 Cross Country Vehicles

DEVELOPMENT
Stonefield Vehicles was formed in 1974 to investigate the design of military and commercial cross country vehicles. Its studies covered four main areas: chassis, transmission, suspension and brakes.

A flexible yet torsionally rigid chassis was regarded as a prime requirement to replace the conventional ladder frame which Stonefield considered weak and dependent on the vehicle's body structure to increase its strength and control movement. Constant four-wheel drive with a fully automatic transmission was preferred to manual gearboxes, with their inherent problems in driver training and their tendency to be subjected to driver abuse.

The need was established for a simple system of multi-leaf springing with maintenance-free attachments for minimum maintenance.

The major problem with braking systems in current four-wheel drive cross-country vehicles is rear wheel lock-up and loss of stability due to skidding caused by the transfer of weight from the rear to the front axle. Stonefield set out to overcome this problem by transferring unwanted braking torque from one axle to the other via the transmission.

These four considerations formed the basis of design work by Stonefield which, in turn, led to the building of experimental vehicles in 1975 and 1976 to evaluate the

Gomba Stonefield 4 × 4 truck carrying THORN-EMI Ranger minelayer

new design concepts and components. A market evaluation was also carried out concurrently from which Stonefield established its manufacturing objectives: as a new chassis built for left or right hand control, modern but well proved transmission, improved suspension and braking systems, sufficient construction flexibility to allow a wide range of bodies to be built on the basic vehicle and a choice of power units to give operational flexibility.

The prototypes were followed by ten pre-production vehicles which were tested both in the United Kingdom and overseas. One of the vehicles successfully completed a 24 000 km validation trial under the control of the Military Vehicles Engineering Establishment covering all aspects of performance. As a result, the Ministry of Defence, Defence Sales Organisation has recommended the Stonefield P 5000 4 × 4 all-terrain truck as suitable for general service medium mobility use and especially as a towing vehicle for the ROF 105 mm Light Gun now in service with the British Army and overseas countries.

First production 4 × 4 Stonefield vehicles were completed in mid-1978 since which time the Stonefield has entered service with a wide range of public authorities and industries for a variety of uses.

At the end of 1979 Stonefield Vehicles received its first military order, initially two vehicles for use as ambulances by the Royal Air Force. The vehicles were evaluated by the Royal Air Force for use in mountain and crash rescue operations.

In December 1982 it was announced that Malaysia had placed a contract worth £14 million for Gomba Stonefield vehicles.

In addition to the existing applications for the Stonefield, the vehicle has been evaluated in conjunction with the British Aerospace Rapier SAM system, THORN-EMI's Ranger minelayer, and Cymbeline mortar-locating radar, Ferranti vehicle range-finding equipment and a Racal-equipped 24-volt FFR communications centre.

DESCRIPTION
There are two basic versions of the Stonefield range, a 4 × 4 and a 6 × 4, both with the same basic components such as engine and transmission.

The chassis is an all-welded structure of rectangular tubing of varying sizes, the side frame of which extends up to waist rail height. The wheel arches and engine compartment are integral within the structure. All mountings for the road springs and other components are jig welded to the chassis. Two types of cab are available: a standard fully enclosed two-door cab constructed from square tubing and clad with aluminium panels and an alternative utility waist level version with tubular steel hoods to take a canvas roof with detachable side windows and a fold-flat windscreen. The rear cargo area in the pick up version has a drop tailgate and can be fitted with bows and a tarpaulin cover if required. Fully enclosed and specialised versions of the Stonefield are available.

The engine is beneath and to the rear of the cab. The transfer box has two speeds and three output shafts, one for each axle and one for a power take-off. The Chrysler engine is a Type 318-1 V-8 four-stroke petrol developing 150 bhp at 4000 rpm, coupled to a Chrysler A 727 automatic transmission (three forward and one reverse gears) and a model A 777 torque converter.

The third epicyclic differential gives a third of the power to the front wheels and two-thirds to the rear wheels. This has two major advantages: it allows the transfer from hard to soft terrain without stopping to engage all-wheel drive and it has an automatic lock-up device which passes power to all wheels when one loses surface adhesion.

Optional equipment includes an air-conditioning system, auxiliary fuel tanks, centrifuge and paper element air filter, external sun visor, flotation tyres, map light, radio, spot lights and directional beam lamps.

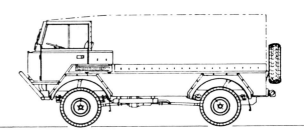

Gomba Stonefield 4 × 4 cargo vehicle

Gomba Stonefield 4 × 4 truck towing Royal Ordnance Factories 105 mm Light Gun

SPECIFICATIONS

Type	Pick up	Waist line	Pick up	Waist line
Configuration	4 × 4	4 × 4	6 × 4	6 × 4
Weight (empty)	2250 kg	2200 kg	2450 kg	2400 kg
(loaded)	4390 kg	4340 kg	5590 kg	5540 kg
(on front axle, loaded)	1990 kg	1940 kg	1990 kg	1940 kg
(on second axle, loaded)	2400 kg	2400 kg	1800 kg	1800 kg
(on third axle, loaded)	n/app	n/app	1880 kg	1880 kg
Max load	2140 kg	2140 kg	3140 kg	3041 kg
Load area	3·047 × 1·64 m	3·047 × 1·64 m	3·551 × 1·64 m	3·551 × 1·64 m
Length	4·94 m	4·94 m	5·445 m	5·445 m
Width	1·9 m	1·9 m	1·9 m	1·9 m
Height	2·4 m	1·795 m	2·36 m	1·77 m
(cargo area)	0·668 m	0·668 m	0·638 m	0·638 m
Track	1·644 m	1·644 m	1·644 m	1·644 m
Wheelbase	2·8 m	2·8 m	2·575 m + 0·95 m	2·575 m + 0·95 m
Angle of approach/departure	50°/45°	50°/45°	50°/50°	50°/50°
Fuel capacity (litres)	109	109	109	109
Fording	0·75 m	0·75 m	0·75 m	0·75 m
Engine	Chrysler	Chrysler	Chrysler	Chrysler
Steering	all re-circulating ball and nut			
Suspension	front, leaf springs, located at the front with rubber bushes, at rear with slippers. Hydraulic shock absorbers are fitted to all axles together with rubber bump stops and check straps			
Tyres	9.00 × 16	9.00 × 16	7.50 × 16	7.50 × 16
Number of tyres	4 + 1 spare	4 + 1 spare	6 + 1 spare	6 + 1 spare
Brakes	all have vacuum assisted hydraulic twin circuit system			
Electrical system (optional 24 V)	12 V	12 V	12 V	12 V
Battery (68 Ah)	1 × 12 V	1 × 12 V	1 × 12 V	1 × 12 V

STATUS
Production. Ordered by Malaysia. (Late in 1980 Stonefield Vehicles went into liquidation but was subsequently taken over and is now known as Gomba Stonefield.)

MANUFACTURER
Gomba Stonefield Limited, Cumnock, Ayrshire KA18 1SH, Scotland.

Gomba Stonefield 4 × 4 truck with ambulance body similar to those ordered by Royal Air Force

Gomba Stonefield 6 × 4 truck with Perren Fire Protection Limited equipment

Dosco HS 100-4 (4 × 4) 2070 kg and HS 100-6 (6 × 6) Trucks

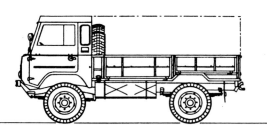

Dosco HS 100-4 (4 × 4) 2070 kg truck

DEVELOPMENT

The HS 100-4 (4 × 4) and HS 100-6 (6 × 6) vehicles have been developed as a private venture by Dosco Vehicles Limited, part of the Hawker Siddeley Group, and are based on the Volvo 4140 series of 4 × 4 and 6 × 6 vehicles of which some 9000 were built for civil and military applications between 1974 and 1980. Dosco Vehicles is now the sole licensee worldwide for this range of vehicles.

The Dosco HS 100-4 (4 × 4) vehicle has already been subjected to full cycle reliability trials at the Military Vehicles and Engineering Establishment and performance testing has indicated that the vehicle is fully compatible for use by British and overseas armed forces in all roles undertaken by this class of vehicle.

DESCRIPTION

The chassis of the HS 100-4 has box-type side-members with tubular cross-members welded to the sides: the chassis is torsionally stiff to avoid straining the superstructure.

The all-steel cab has adjustable seats for the driver and one passenger with folding backrests and is of pressed and formed panels, spot welded. The part above the waist line is detachable.

The rear cargo area is of aluminium construction with detachable canvas tilt, drop sides and rear door panels.

Four wheel drive is automatically engaged when low range is selected and by means of a push button operated vacuum in high range. Provision for fitting a full range torque PTO for winch drive or powered trailer is provided. The winch adds 110 kg to the vehicle's overall weight and the FFR kit adds 55 kg.

The front axle is rigid with a banjo of pressed steel and drive by centre-mounted spiral bevel gears through full floating shafts to constant velocity universal joints of the Rzeppa type. Drop gear hub reduction at each gear. The rear axle is identical to the front but without universal joints and steering knuckles. Both have vacuum-operated mechanical differential locks, standard on rear axle and optional on front axle, which can be engaged separately or together.

The basic model has a thermostatically-controlled heating and defroster system with a two-speed 40 W blower, in the rear area of the hard top version is a two-speed 30 W blower.

Dosco HS 100-4 (4 × 4) 2070 kg truck

Optional equipment, in addition to the FFR kit and 3000 kg winch, includes a PTO and an electric heater.

VARIANTS

A wide range of body options are available for both 4 × 4 and 6 × 6 models including ambulance, cargo (with seats for ten men on the 4 × 4 model), radio and command post.

STATUS

Development complete. Ready for production.

MANUFACTURER

Dosco Vehicles Limited, British Fields, Ollerton Road, Tuxford, Near Newark, Nottinghamshire NG22 0PQ, England.

SPECIFICATIONS

Model	HS 100-4	HS 100-6	Model	HS 100-4	HS 100-6
Configuration	4 × 4	6 × 6	Transfer box	Volvo FD51	Volvo FD51
Weight (empty)	1930 kg	2400 kg	Steering	mechanical, worm and roller	mechanical, worm and roller
(loaded)	4000 kg	5700 kg			
Max weight on front axle			Turning radius	6·4 m	8·25 m
(loaded)	1900 kg	1900 kg	Suspension (front)	underslung semi-elliptical leaf springs carried in rubber mountings, hollow rubber springs, double action telescopic shock absorbers	underslung semi-elliptical leaf springs carried in rubber mountings, hollow rubber springs, double action telescopic shock absorbers
Max weight on rear axle/					
axles (loaded)	2100 kg	3800 kg (1900 kg × 2)			
Max load	2070 kg	3300 kg			
Towed load	2500 kg	2500 kg			
Load area	2·91 m × 1·74 m	depends on body			
Length	4·485 m	5·725 m			
Width	1·87 m	1·88 m	(rear)	overslung semi-elliptical leaf springs carried in rubber mountings, hollow rubber springs, double action telescopic shock absorbers	double cantilever parabolic springs, hollow rubber springs, double action hydraulic shock absorbers
Height (overall)	2·13 m	2·13 m			
Ground clearance	0·386 m	0·386 m			
Track (front and rear)	1·54 m	1·54 m			
Wheelbase	2·53 m	2·72 m + 1·05 m			
Angle of approach/departure	45°/45°	45°/45°			
Max speed	110 km/h	100 km/h			
Max gradient	60%	60%			
Max side slope	40%	40%			
Fording	0·75 m	0·75 m	Tyres	9.00 × 16	9.00 × 16
Engine	Rover V-8 ohv petrol developing 130·2 bhp at 5000 rpm		Number of tyres	4 + 1 spare	6 + 1 spare
			Brakes (main)	vacuum/hydraulic	vacuum/hydraulic
Gearbox	ZF S5/18-3	ZF S5/18-3	(parking)	mechanical	mechanical
	5 forward, 1 reverse	5 forward, 1 reverse	Electrical system	12 V (24 V optional)	12 V (24 V optional)
Clutch	single dry plate	single dry plate	Battery	60 Ah	60 Ah

Hotspur Sandringham 6 (6 × 6) 2000 kg Vehicle

DESCRIPTION

The Hotspur Sandringham 6 (6 × 6) 2000 kg vehicle have been formed by converting a long-wheelbased Land-Rover to a 6 × 6 configuration. Using a 3·5-litre Rover V-8 petrol engine and placing the twin rear axles directly under the load area, the Sandringham 6 can carry a 2000 kg payload across country and in soft and difficult terrain. The Sandringham 6 has a large number of components common to the established Land-Rover line.

The Sandringham S6 is now produced in three basic versions, the S6 with a 125-inch/3·175-metre wheelbase, the S6E with a 139-inch/3·53-metre wheelbase, and an armoured personnel carrier. The S6 and S6E are produced in several forms ranging from personnel carriers to long-range patrol vehicles and, after trials at the Royal School of Artillery at Larkhill, have been selected for use as artillery tractors by several armed forces. The S6E is suitable as a light weapons platform and has been approved in that role for the Bofors RBS-70 anti-aircraft missile system and the THORN-EMI Ranger anti-personnel minelayer. A recent addition to the range is the Hiline communications/command vehicle which has already entered service in the Middle East. The S6 and S6E may be procured in both armoured and unar-moured versions (for the armoured version see *Jane's Armour and Artillery 1983–84*, pages 396–397).

Optional equipment for the S6 range includes full air conditioning, a shock-absorbing driver's seat, an auxiliary 50-litre fuel tank, CS gas or smoke dischargers, a driving siren, self-sealing fuel tanks, two-way intercom, heavy duty alternator, a barricade ram, a high power solvent screen wash, full seat belt harnesses in the rear, an automatic fire extinguishing system, a hostile fire indicator, military radio equipment, helicopter lifting lugs, a front-mounted winch, power take-off units, a public address system, twin driving spotlamps, a roof-mounted spotlamp, de-luxe seating, an undershield, spare wheel carriers and brackets for fuel or water cans.

SPECIFICATIONS

Model	S6 125-inch wheelbase	S6E 139-inch wheelbase
Cab seating	1 + 1	1 + 1
Configuration	6 × 6	6 × 6
Weight (empty)	1618 kg	1673 kg
(loaded)	3700 kg	3700 kg
Max load	2000 kg	2000 kg
Max towed load (on road)	4000 kg	4000 kg
(off road)	1000 kg	1000 kg
Load area	1·85 × 1·46 m	2·54 × 1·644 m
Length	4·445 m	5·156 m
Width	1·69 m	1·69 m
Height (top of body)	2·032 m	2·184 m
Ground clearance	0·209 m	0·209 m
Track	1·334 m	1·334 m
Wheelbase (front to rear axle)	3·175 m	3·53 m
Engine	Rover V-8 petrol engine developing 92 bhp (DIN) at 2000 rpm or 4-cylinder 2·25-litre diesel develoing 60 bhp (DIN) at 4000 rpm	
Transmission	manual, 4 forward and 1 reverse gears	
Transfer box	2-speed with permanent 6-wheel drive, lockable central differential	
Suspension	semi-elliptical leaf road springs assisted by convoluted rubber springs on rear axles, telescopic hydraulic dampers	
Electrical system	12 V	12 V

STATUS
Production. In service with various undisclosed countries.

MANUFACTURER
Hotspur Armoured Products Limited, Aberdulais, Neath, West Glamorgan, Wales SA10 8HH, United Kingdom.

Hotspur Sandringham S6E (6 × 6) with twin 20 mm Rheinmetall cannon

Hotspur Sandringham S6E (6 × 6) long range desert patrol vehicle

Hotspur Sandringham S6E (6 × 6) towing 105 mm Light Gun (T J Gander)

Hotspur Sandringham S6E (6 × 6) towing 105 mm Light Gun

Hotspur S6E with 'Hiline' body on 139-inch/3·53 m wheelbase

Reynolds Boughton RB-44 (4 × 4) Truck

DEVELOPMENT

The RB-44 has been developed as a private venture by the Boughton Group and was originally called the RB-510 (*Jane's Combat Support Equipment 1978–79*, page 532). In 1979 the vehicle successfully completed an 8047 km cyclic reliability trial at the Military Vehicles and Engineering Establishment.

In addition to its use as a cargo-troop carrier, it can be used for a variety of other roles such as towing a 105 mm artillery piece, the British Aerospace Dynamics Rapier SAM system or the Marconi Space and Defence Systems Blindfire radar, or mounting the Swingfire ATGW system.

It is offered with a range of engines and a choice of automatic or manual transmission and is available in three wheelbases, 3·3, 3·68 and 3·96 metres.

DESCRIPTION

It has a flat top and a ladder type riveted chassis which can be fitted with various types of body. A three-seat walk-through cab is standard, but an extended crew cab conversion is available for carrying extra personnel and/or equipment.

Details of some popular engine and transmission options are given below. Other fits are possible and details are available from the manufacturer on request.

A Boughton designed and manufactured two-speed transfer box with permanent four-wheel drive through a POWR-LOK differential is also a standard fitment. This box incorporates an eight-stud SAE aperture on the top (for full engine torque PTO) and a six-stud SAE PTO on the right hand side, capable of up to 30 bhp.

Suspension is by conventional semi-elliptical springs, fitted with double-acting telescopic shock absorbers. 320 mm diameter hydraulic brakes, with a duo-servo split system, are fitted both front and rear. The front and rear axles have hypo gearing with a ratio of 5·87 to 1. The front axle's plated capacity is 2032 kg and the rear axle's 3800 kg.

VARIANTS

In 1981 Scottorn Trailers, a member of the Boughton Group, announced the Scottorn RB-44 Lube body which enables the vehicle to carry out major servicing and minor repair work in the field. The electrically-welded body consists of a pressed steel channel sub-frame bolted to the vehicle chassis and incorporating a hardwood packing between the vehicle and the main body members. The canopy consists of a rolled hollow section structure with a one-piece fibreglass roof. Roll-up canvas curtains are provided all round. Standard equipment includes hot and cold high-pressure washer, electric start generator, air compressor, battery charger/engine starter, spark plug cleaner, penetrating oil dispenser and hose reel, air hose reel, oil pumps and hose reels, transfer pump, clamps for four 205-litre drums, hand grinder, hand drill and drill stand, hand lamp, extension lead, vice, flood lamp and tool box.

STATUS
Production.

MANUFACTURER
Reynolds Boughton Limited, Amersham, Buckinghamshire, England.

SPECIFICATIONS

Configuration	4 × 4	4 × 4	4 × 4
Length	5·27 m	5·652 m	5·931 m
Width	2·121 m	2·121 m	2·121 m
Height (cab top)	2·311 m	2·311 m	2·311 m
(top of chassis, laden)	0·838 m	0·838 m	0·838 m
Wheelbase	3·3 m	3·68 m	3·96 m
Track (front)	1·79 m	1·79 m	1·79 m
(rear)	1·753 m	1·753 m	1·753 m
Angle of approach/departure	45°/40°	45°/40°	45°/40°

Engine and transmission options

(a)	Rover V-8 petrol engine developing 130 bhp at 5000 rpm coupled to a ZF 25/4 manual gearbox with 5 forward and 1 reverse gears. Or a Chrysler A 727 Torqueflite automatic transmission with 3 forward and 1 reverse gears
(b)	Bedford 214 OHV petrol developing 100 bhp at 3600 rpm coupled to a B close ratio manual gearbox with 4 forward and 1 reverse gears
(c)	Perkins 6.247 naturally aspirated diesel developing 101 bhp at 3500 rpm coupled to a Chrysler F N 3 close ratio manual gearbox with 4 forward and 1 reverse gears or a Chrysler A 727 Torqueflite automatic transmission with 3 forward and 1 reverse gears

Transfer case	Boughton 2-speed
Suspension (front and rear)	heavy duty leaf springs with AEON rubber assisters and double acting telescopic shock absorbers
Tyres	9.00 × 16
Number of tyres	4 + 1 spare
Brakes	hydraulic, servo assisted, dual line system

Weights: (basic chassis, 3·3-metre wheelbase)

(unloaded)	2049 kg
(loaded)	5000 kg
Payload, including body	2951 kg

Reynolds Boughton RB-44 (4 × 4) truck towing Marconi Space and Defence Systems Blindfire radar (Christopher F Foss)

Reynolds Boughton RB-44 (4 × 4) truck fitted with British Aerospace Swingfire ATGW system

Bedford MK (4 × 4) 4000 kg Truck

DEVELOPMENT

In the early 1960s the British Army issued a requirement for a 4 × 4 4000 kg truck to replace the then current Bedford RL. To meet this requirement Austin submitted the FJ (FV 13701), Commer the CB (FV 13901) and Vauxhall the RK (FV 13801). After comparative trials the Vauxhall model, based on their civilian TK (4 × 2) truck, was selected and standardised as the Truck Cargo (Bedford MK 4 tonne 4 × 4). This is now the standard 4000 kg truck of the British Army although large numbers of the earlier Bedford RLs remain in service.

As from April 1981 Bedford changed the designation of the MK to MJ as the K multi-fuel engine has been superseded by the J diesel engine. The designation MK is an abbreviated form of the alpha designation MKP2BMO, MJ being MJP2BMO. B becomes W for winch variants.

In mid-1982 a £6 million order was announced for new MJP trucks fitted with a new 5·4-litre turbo-charged diesel engine designated the 5,4/105TD. This new series of trucks incorporated many minor modifications to take advantage of the new engine's power, and pro-

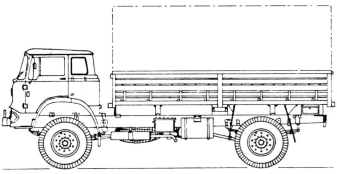

Bedford MK (4 × 4) 4000 kg truck

Bedford MK (4 × 4) 4000 kg tipper truck (T J Gander)

Bedford MK (4 × 4) 4000 kg truck with snow plough blade during exercise Hard Fall 1980 in Northern Norway (Ministry of Defence)

Bedford MK (4 × 4) truck chassis in use as carrier for pile driving rig used by Royal Engineer bomb disposal teams (T J Gander)

Bedford MK (4 × 4) 4000 kg in flatbed configuration carrying communications shelter and generator (United Kingdom Land Forces)

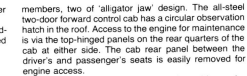

Bedford TK (4 × 2) truck with Marshall of Cambridge (Engineering) Limited body for use in rear areas

Bedford MK (4 × 4) 4000 kg truck with drop sides, tailgate, bows and tarpaulin cover removed and Atlas hydraulic crane fitted to rear of cab (T J Gander)

duction of the new model commenced in September 1982.

Production totals for the M-series of vehicles, including both military and civilian models, now exceed 36 000.

DESCRIPTION
The chassis is of the ladder type with six cross-members, two of 'alligator jaw' design. The all-steel two-door forward control cab has a circular observation hatch in the roof. Access to the engine for maintenance is via the top-hinged panels on the rear quarters of the cab at either side. The cab rear panel between the driver's and passenger's seats is easily removed for engine access.

The all-steel rear cargo area has drop sides and a drop tailgate, which can be removed quickly to provide a platform for the carriage of containers, pallets or the Gloster Saro demountable fuel pod. Removable bows and a tarpaulin cover are fitted as standard. A hydraulic crane can be fitted for unloading. Detachable outward-facing seats can be fitted in the centre of the cargo area for carrying passengers. The body of the MJP is manufactured by Marshall of Cambridge (Engineers) and a

Bedford MK (4 × 4) 4000 kg truck fitted with bows and tarpaulin cover (T J Gander)

Bedford MK (4 × 4) 4000 kg truck with flat bed being used to carry engineer equipment in crates (T J Gander)

full description of it, and of the CB 300 series of transportable containers developed by the company, will be found in the *Shelters, containers and vehicle bodies* section.

The MJP2 has a 3·962-metre wheelbase but a model with a wheelbase of 3·505 metres is also available (MOR1). Engines available are a six-cylinder petrol (4·927 litres), and six-cylinder diesels, a naturally aspirated (5·42 litres and 8·198 litres) and turbo-charged (5·42 litres).

The basic models of the M-type are designated the FV 13801/FV 13802 or when fitted with a winch the FV 13803/FV 13804. The winch has a capacity of 3500 kg and 76 metres of cable. Provision is made for a PTO to be driven from either the front or rear of the transfer box casing. In addition a standard six-stud SAE PTO facing is fitted to the side of the gearbox. The MJP has single rear wheels with 12.00 × 20 tyres but dual rear wheels with 9.00 × 20 tyres can be fitted. Standard equipment includes a heater and defroster and optional equipment includes stowage racks for small arms, heat insulation, protection for the radiator, power-assisted steering, and a five-speed gearbox.

VARIANTS

Drone carrier (for the Canadian Midge AN/USD-501 reconnaissance drone), dump truck, refueller, mineproof cab (conversion work carried out by Reynolds Boughton), portable roadway laying vehicle (a photograph of which appears under the Laird entry in the *Portable roadways* section), and with special bodies. The Royal Air Force uses the M-type for carrying bombs and other munitions to support the Harrier VTOL aircraft. Bedford TK trucks (4 × 2) are used for a wide variety of roles by all three British services including driver training vehicles, stores carriers and aircraft refuellers.

SPECIFICATIONS

Cab seating: 1 + 1
Configuration: 4 × 4
Weight:
  (empty, single rear wheels) 5120 kg
  (loaded, single rear wheels) 9650 kg
  (loaded, double rear wheels) 11 180 kg
Weight on front axle: (max loaded, single rear wheels) 4060 kg
Weight on rear axle: (max loaded, single rear wheels) 6100 kg
Max load: (single rear wheels) 4530 kg
Towed load: 5080 kg
Load area: 4·28 × 2·01 m
Length: 6·579 m
Width: 2·489 m
Height:
  (cab) 2·501 m
  (tarpaulin) 3·404 m
Ground clearance: 0·343 m
Track:
  (front) 2·05 m
  (rear) 2·03 m
Wheelbase: 3·962 m
Angle of approach/departure: 41°/38°
Max speed: (road) 77 km/h
Range: 560 km
Fuel capacity: 156 litres
Max gradient: 49%
Fording: 0·762 m
Engine: Bedford 6-cylinder diesel developing 103 bhp (gross) at 2600 rpm

Gearbox: manual with 4 forward and 1 reverse gears
Clutch: single dry plate
Transfer box: 2-speed
Steering: semi-irreversible worm and sector
Turning radius: 9 m
Suspension: semi-elliptical springs with telescopic hydraulic double action shock absorbers
Tyres: 12.00 × 20
Number of tyres: 4 + 1 spare
Brakes:
  (main) air/hydraulic
  (parking) mechanical
Electrical system: 24 V
Batteries: 2 × 12 V, 6 TN

Note: With the introduction of the new 5·4-litre turbocharged diesel engine, the following engine choices are now available with Bedford M-type (4 × 4) military vehicles:

Standard: 5·4 litres/105 turbocharged diesel
Optional: 4·9 litres/115 petrol
  5·4 litres/100 diesel
Special order: 8·2 litres/130 diesel
The 5·4 litres/93 multi-fuel engine has been discontinued.

STATUS

In production. In service with Bangladesh, Belgium, Ireland, Kenya, Netherlands, South Africa, Uganda, the United Kingdom and many other countries.

MANUFACTURER

Bedford Commercial Vehicle division of General Motors Overseas Commercial Vehicle Corporation, PO Box 3, Luton, Bedfordshire LU2 0SY, England.

Bedford RL (4 × 4) 4000 kg Truck

DEVELOPMENT

To replace Second World War trucks three new 3000 kg (4 × 4) trucks were introduced into the British Army in 1952. These were built by Bedford (the RL), Commer (the Q4) and Ford, and were all based on a civilian chassis.

The Bedford RL was based on the civilian 7-ton SLC chassis and the 4 × 4 version was in production from 1952 to 1969 by which time 73 135 had been built for both civil and military use. By the 1960s most of the Commer and Ford trucks had been phased out of service (although a few remain for specialised roles), but the RL remained the standard truck of the British Army in the 3000 kg class until the introduction of the Bedford MK in the late 1960s. In 1968 the RL's capacity was uprated from 3000 to 4000 kg and there are still many in service with the British Army and Royal Air Force.

DESCRIPTION

The basic RL (L for long) has a wheelbase of 3·962 metres and the short wheelbase RS (S for short) has a wheelbase of 3·35 metres.

The chassis consists of two deep channel section side members, tapered towards the front, riveted to five cross-members. The two-door all-steel forward control cab has an observation hatch in the roof. The rear cargo body is also of steel and has drop sides, a drop tailgate, removable bows and a tarpaulin cover. The following cargo models were built: FV 13101 (not dropside), FV 13105 (dropside), FV 13109 (not dropside), FV 13112 (dropside) and FV 13143 (left hand drive, not dropside). Many RLs are fitted with a 5000 kg capacity winch.

The engine is mounted between and below the driver's and passenger's seats and is removed through

Belgian Army Bedford S (4 × 2) 4000 kg truck (T J Gander)

the front of the vehicle after detaching the grille and engine cross bearer. Power is taken from the engine to the gearbox and then via propeller shafts to the transfer box which is under the chassis in the centre of the vehicle. Power is then taken from the transfer box to the front and rear axles by a propeller shaft. The differential

and hypoid gear assembly of both the front and rear axles are interchangeable.

VARIANTS

There are many variants of the RL, not all of which are still in service: charging vehicle (FV 13104), 3636-litre

Bedford RL (4 × 4) 4000 kg dump truck (FV 13111) (T J Gander)

Bedford RL (4 × 4) 4000 kg truck carrying office/workshop container body (T J Gander)

fuel tanker (FV 13106), signals vehicle (FV 13110), short wheelbase tipper (FV 13111), motor transport repair vehicle (FV 13113), light recovery vehicle (FV 13115) details of which will be found in the *Recovery vehicles* section (pages 57 and 58), 1728-litre tanker (FV 13120), flatbed for carrying containers (FV 13136), airportable cargo truck with removable cab top (FV 13142), container truck (FV 13152), dental surgery (FV 13165), and a 4 × 2 aircraft water refueller (FV 13197). The vehicle was also used for carrying the Canadian Midge reconnaissance drone (now mounted on the Bedford MK), the MGB (now also mounted on the Bedford MK), the Laird portable roadway (now carried on the Bedford MK), and as a fire engine.

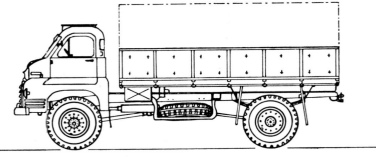

Bedford RL (4 × 4) 4000 kg truck

SPECIFICATIONS
Cab seating: 1 + 1
Configuration: 4 × 4
Weight:
  (empty) 4400 kg
  (loaded) 8800 kg
Max load: 4000 kg
Load area: 4·267 × 2·178 m
Length: 6·36 m
Width: 2·39 m
Height:
  (cab) 2·602 m
  (tarpaulin) 3·11 m
Track: 1·854 m
Wheelbase: 3·962 m
Angle of approach/departure: 36°/30°
Max speed: (road) 75 km/h
Range: 400 km

Fuel capacity: 118 litres
Max gradient: 33%
Engine: Bedford 6-cylinder ohv petrol developing 130 bhp (gross) at 3200 rpm. (Early models had 110 bhp. Others including 107 bhp 6-cylinder diesel available)
Gearbox: manual with 4 forward and 1 reverse gears
Clutch: single dry plate
Transfer box: 2-speed
Steering: semi-irreversible worm and sector
Turning radius: 9·13 m
Suspension: (front and rear) semi-elliptical springs with hydraulic double acting shock absorbers
Tyres: 11.00 × 20
Number of tyres: 4 + 1 spare

Brakes:
  (main) hydraulic
  (parking) mechanical
Electrical system: 12 V
Batteries: 1 × 12 V, 80 Ah
Generator: 230 W

STATUS
Production complete. In service with Belgium, Ireland, Malaysia, the Netherlands, Pakistan, South Africa and the United Kingdom.

MANUFACTURER
Vauxhall Motors Limited, PO Box 3, Luton, Bedfordshire LU2 0SY, England.

Alvis Stalwart (6 × 6) 5000 kg High Mobility Load Carrier

DEVELOPMENT
The first Stalwart, called the PV 1, was built as a private venture by Alvis Limited in 1959. It was based on the chassis of the FV 652 Salamander (6 × 6) fire/crash tender used by the Royal Air Force which in turn used many components of the FV 601 Saladin and FV 603 Saracen armoured vehicles. The PV 1 had a flatbed cargo area at the rear and was not amphibious. In 1961 a second, fully amphibious, prototype called the PV 2 was built with drop sides and a drop tailgate to the rear cargo area. Over 140 vehicles of this configuration were subsequently produced, being known as the Stalwart Mk 1, FV 620. As a result of trials with the British Army a number of modifications were carried out including the installation of a front-mounted winch and more powerful waterjets, improvement in cab layout and visibility, reduction in maintenance and improvement in reliability.

Production vehicles were known as the Alvis Stalwart Mk 2, FV 622 and were produced from 1966. Production continued until 1971.

Over 1400 Stalwarts were produced and a number are still in service with the British Army. A product improvement study is currently being carried out with a view to revising the payload capacity to over 7000 kg and updating the drive line elements.

DESCRIPTION
The fully enclosed cab is at the front of the vehicle and access is via two circular hatches in the roof which open forward. The driver is seated in the centre of the cab with a single passenger seat either side. The load area is at the rear and has drop sides and a drop tailgate. A tarpaulin cover can be fitted over the load area if required. The Stalwart can carry 5000 kg of cargo or 38 fully equipped troops. The engine is under the cargo area and engine drive is taken through a twin dry plate clutch and five-speed gearbox to the transfer box with a no-spin differential which transfers drive direct to each

centre bevel box, and then via transmission shafts to the front and rear bevel boxes. Each wheel houses epicyclic reduction gears and is connected to its appropriate bevel box by a transmission shaft and two universal joints.

The hydraulically-operated winch mounted at the front of the vehicle has a 4990 kg capacity.

The Stalwart is fully amphibious and is propelled in the water by two Dowty marine jets driven by a PTO from the gearbox. Steering is by two levers controlling vanes on the jet units which can be turned 180 degrees for reverse thrust. Before entering the water a trim vane is erected at the front of the vehicle.

VARIANTS
FV 623
This is basically the FV 622 fitted with an Atlas 3001/66 hydraulic crane to the cab rear for unloading pallets of ammunition, and is used by the Royal Artillery to supply self-propelled artillery regiments with ammunition.

Alvis Stalwart Mk 2 (6 × 6) high mobility load carrier (FV 623) fitted with Atlas 3001/66 hydraulic crane for unloading pallets of ammunition (T J Gander)

Alvis Stalwart Mk 2 (6 × 6) high mobility load carriers (T J Gander)

FV 624

This is a fitter's vehicle for the Royal Electrical and Mechanical Engineers.

The Stalwart is also in service fitted with the Gloster Saro refuelling pack and has been fitted with the THORN-EMI Ranger anti-personnel mine system.

SPECIFICATIONS
Cab seating: 1 + 2
Configuration: 6 × 6
Weight:
(empty) 8970 kg
(loaded) 14 480 kg
Max load: 5000 kg
Towed load: 10 000 kg
Load area: 3·6 × 2·4 m
Length: 6·356 m
Width: 2·616 m
Height:
(cab) 2·312 m
(tarpaulin) 2·64 m
(load area) 1·5 m
Ground clearance: 0·42 m
Track: 2·04 m
Wheelbase: 1·524 m + 1·524 m
Angle of approach/departure: 44°/40°
Max speed:
(road) 63 km/h
(water, empty) 10·2 km/h
(water, loaded) 9·6 km/h
Range: 515 km
Fuel consumption: 71 litres/100 km

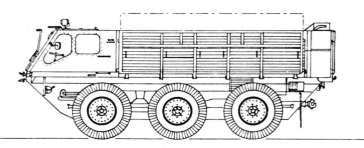

Alvis Stalwart Mk 2 (6 × 6) 5000 kg high mobility load carrier

Max gradient: 60%
Vertical obstacle: 0·46 m
Trench: 1·52 m
Fording: amphibious
Engine: Rolls-Royce B-81 Mk. 8B 8-cylinder water-cooled petrol developing 220 bhp at 3750 rpm
Gearbox: 5 forward and 5 reverse gears
Clutch: twin plate friction
Transfer box: bevel and helical gear incorporating reverse and no-spin differential
Steering: recirculating ball, hydraulic assisted on front 4 wheels
Turning radius: 8·38 m
Suspension: independent all wheels by double wishbone and torsion bars. Hydraulic telescopic double acting shock absorbers

Tyres: 14.00 × 20
Number of tyres: 6
Brakes:
(main) air over hydraulic on all wheels
(parking) contracting bands on drums on front bevel boxes
Electrical system: 24 V
Batteries: 2 × 12 V 6 TN, 100 Ah

STATUS
Production complete. In service with Austria, Sweden and the United Kingdom.

MANUFACTURER
Alvis Limited, Holyhead Road, Coventry, West Midlands CV5 8JH, England.

Shelvoke SPV (4 × 4) and (6 × 6) Heavy Duty Trucks

DEVELOPMENT
At the BAEE held at Aldershot in 1982, the long-established specialist vehicle company of Shelvoke and Drewry presented for the first time a new 4 × 4 military 8000 kg heavy duty truck. The new truck was presented as a relatively low cost cross-country vehicle capable of being produced in several versions such as a tanker, dump truck and recovery vehicle in addition to the standard cargo truck.

There is also a 6 × 6 24 000 kg GVW truck chassis based on a commercial design available which could be used as the basis for a heavy artillery tractor or a heavy recovery vehicle.

DESCRIPTION
Both vehicles have a large forward control cab on an all-bolted steel chassis frame. The cabs may be fitted with sleeping space and the engine is mounted under the cab. On the 4 × 4 version the load area is high enough to allow stowage underneath for the spare wheel and lockers. The 4 × 4 version uses a Leyland 411E turbo-charged 6·54-litre engine, and the 6 × 6 version a Rolls Royce 305 Eagle Mark 111 engine.

STATUS
Ready for production.

MANUFACTURER
Shelvoke and Drewry Limited, Military Projects and Sales, Letchworth, Hertfordshire SG6 1EN, England.

SPECIFICATIONS (6 × 6 version)
Cab seating: 1 + 2
Configuration: 6 × 6
Weight:
(empty) 10 960 kg
(loaded) 26 424 kg
Max load: 15 450 kg
Max towed load: 16 260 kg
Length: 9·38 m
Width: 2·48 m

Shelvoke SPV (4 × 4) 8000 kg truck

Height: (top of cab) 3·22 m
Wheelbase: 5·4 m
Max speed: 97 km/h
Fuel capacity: 205 litres
Engine: Rolls Royce 305 Eagle Mark 111 diesel developing 305 bhp at 2100 rpm
Gearbox: Eaton RTO 11609B with 9 forward and 2 reverse gears

Clutch: Lip Rollway 14-2LP twin plate
Transfer box: ZF A800/3D 2-speed
Steering: ZF model 8046 integral gear
Turning radius: 12·375 m
Tyres: 16.00 × 20
Brakes: Westinghouse dual circuit air
Electrical system: 24 V
Batteries: 2 × 12 V, 135 Ah

Bedford TM 4-4 (4 × 4) 8000 kg Truck

DEVELOPMENT
In the early 1970s the British Army issued a requirement for a new 4 × 4 8000 kg cargo truck as a part of its Medium Mobility Vehicle Programme. To meet this requirement prototypes were built by Foden, Leyland and Bedford and, after comparative trials, in September 1977 Vauxhall was awarded a contract worth almost £40 million for 2099 of its model TM 4-4. Production began in 1980 and first vehicles were delivered to the British Army in April 1981. The first unit to operate the vehicle was 7 Squadron of 27 Logistic Support Group, Royal Corps of Transport.

DESCRIPTION
The basic cargo model, of which 1330 have been ordered by the British Army, is designated the WNV3NPO by Bedford and has a GVW of 16 260 kg and a GTW of 24 300 kg. The vehicle uses many components of the civilian TM (4 × 2) range of commercial vehicles.

The TM 4-4 has a ladder type chassis with 450 N/mm² yield structural steel channel section side-members and constant depth and section throughout with special rear cross-members for drawbar trailer operations. The full width heavy-duty front bumper is bolted to the first chassis cross-member. Front towing pintle and brake pipeline couplings for trailer brake operations and vehicle recovery are incorporated.

The front axle is a Kirkstall fully-floating, single speed,

spiral bevel with 3·857 to 1 hub reduction with overall axle ratio of 5·887 to 1. The rear axle is a Kirkstall fully-floating, single speed, spiral bevel with 3·857 to 1 hub reduction and air actuated differential lock. Overall axle ratio is 5·887 to 1.

The all-steel two-door forward control cab has an observation hatch in the roof. The cab can be tilted forwards hydraulically through 60 degrees locking in a number of intermediate positions. The hinged front grille provides access to the engine for checking oil and other services such as heater and steering systems. The water level can be checked in the expansion tank at the rear of the cab and fuses can be changed from inside. Standard equipment includes an inter-vehicle starting system, heater and ventilation system and a spare wheel carrier and spare wheel.

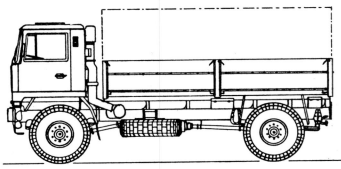

Bedford TM 4-4 (4 × 4) 8000 kg truck

Bedford TM 4-4 (4 × 4) 8000 kg truck with mid-mounted 8000 kg winch

Bedford TM 4-4 (4 × 4) 8000 kg truck with Atlas AK 3500 hydraulic crane to rear of cab and drop sides, tailgate, bows and tarpaulin cover removed (T J Gander)

Bedford TM 4-4 (4 × 4) SWB (3·883 m) tipper

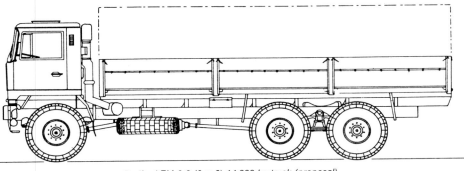

Bedford TM 6-6 (6 × 6) 14 000 kg truck (proposal)

The cargo body is built and mounted onto the chassis by Marshall of Cambridge and is fully described in the *Shelters, containers and vehicle bodies* section. It is steel with a wooden floor, removable drop sideboards and tailboard, lashing shackles for NATO pallets and longitudinal folding bench seats for personnel. An alternative platform body is available with headboard only. Twist-lock attachments or lashing hooks for securing containers are also fitted.

The central roof-mounted hip ring has a glass-fibre reinforced cover which is stowed on the rear of the cab when removed. The gunner's platform is centrally mounted in the cab, for use with the hip ring. The roof is reinforced to withstand the load of a light machine gun and two men.

The standard vehicle is equipped with a 24-volt electrical system, an exhaust system and fire screening which comply with United Kingdom petroleum-carrying regulations.

Power is transmitted from the engine to the gearbox and then to the transfer case which provides drive to the front and rear hub reduction axles.

The following optional equipment is available for the Bedford TM 4-4: exhaust brake, cab painted in NATO IRR green, ringfeeder drawbar coupling, flitch plates, NATO batteries, cab roof front marker lights, dry charged batteries (for CKD purposes), reverse lamps, rear fog guard lamps, tachograph, steering column lock and electric stop control, mid-mounted winch (see below), Atlas hydraulic crane (see below), inertia reel seat belts for driver and passenger, multi-leaf springs, transfer box differential, transfer box with PTO adaptor, transfer box with differential and PTO adaptor and military type cargo body.

VARIANTS
TM 4-4 with tipper body
A total of 169 of these has been ordered by the British Army and have the Bedford designation of WNV6NPO, wheelbase of 3·883 metres, GVW of 16 300 kg and GTW of 24 300 kg. The Edbro RPO 585 military tipper body has a capacity of 6·5 cubic metres. The body can be tipped to an angle of 54 degrees and is of all-steel construction with a three-stage front end ram. The tailgate is hinged at the top and bottom with hydraulic drive via the main gearbox PTO.

TM 4-4 with Atlas self-loading crane
A total of 300 of these has been ordered by the British Army and have the Bedford designation of WNV3NPO + RPO 355. Mounted to the cab rear is an Atlas self-loading crane controlled by the operator standing at the hip ring position. The hydraulic crane is driven via the main gearbox PTO and has a slew angle of 193 degrees and the following capabilities: 3650 kg lift at 2·02 metres reach, 2140 kg lift at 3·46 metres reach and 1700 kg lift at 4·32 metres reach.

TM 4-4 with winch
A total of 300 of these has been ordered by the British Army and are fitted with a mid-mounted RPO 414 winch with a capacity of 8000 kg powered from a transfer box from a PTO. The cable is 75 metres long and has a minimum speed of 4·5 metres per minute and a maximum speed of 23 metres per minute. The controls are air operated with fairleads and pulleys for front and rear winching capability, band type winch brake and safety overload cutout. Bedford designation for this model is WNV3NPO + RPO 414.

OTHER VARIANTS
Bedford have proposed the following variants of the TM 4-4: tanker, fuel carrier, airportable cargo with special cab, cargo towing single axle eight-tonne trailer and cargo towing two axle eight-tonne trailer.

Two other forms of Bedford TM 4–4 have been proposed. One is a 14 000 kg capacity version which will be produced by adding an extra axle at the rear to convert the 4 × 4 version into a 6 × 6 to be known as the TM 6–6. This new vehicle, a prototype of which has already been produced, will have a lengthened cargo area to carry ten standard NATO pallets. A General Staff Requirement for some 1500 14 000 kg 6 × 6 trucks is known to exist and the in-service date is 1986.

The other TM 4–4 proposal is to mount a central axle to convert the TM 4–4 into a 6 × 6 Stalwart amphibious vehicle replacement. The future of this proposal is not yet known.

In connection with the DROPS programme, one possible interim vehicle to carry MLRS 227 mm rocket containers/launchers would be a tractor version of the dump truck version of the TM 4–4 with a turntable to carry articulated trailers. This project is still at an early stage and may not be continued.

STATUS
Entered production in September 1980. In service with Abu Dhabi, Bahrain, Oman and the United Kingdom (Army and Royal Air Force Regiment).

MANUFACTURER
Bedford Commercial Vehicles division of General Motors Overseas Commercial Vehicle Corporation, PO Box 3, Luton, Bedfordshire LU2 0SY, England.

SPECIFICATIONS
Cab seating: 1 + 1
Configuration: 4 × 4
Weight:
 (empty) 8300 kg
 (loaded) 16 300 kg
Max load: 8000 kg
Towed load: 10 000 kg
Length: 6·623 m
Width: 2·476 m
Height:
 (cab) 2·997 m
 (tarpaulin) 3·454 m
Ground clearance: (axles) 0·352 m

Track:
 (front) 2·024 m
 (rear) 2·078 m
Wheelbase: 4·325 m
Angle of approach/departure: 41°/38°
Max road speed: 93 km/h
Max range: 500 km
Fuel capacity: 154 litres
Gradient: 55%
Fording: 0·762 m
Engine: Bedford 8·2-litre water-cooled direct injection turbo-charged diesel developing 206 bhp at 2500 rpm
Gearbox: Turner M6-47026 manual with 6 forward and 1 reverse gears

Clutch: twin dry plate
Transfer box: Rockwell T-226-133
Steering: recirculating ball with integral power assistance
Suspension: (front and rear) semi-elliptical taper leaf springs with hydraulic double acting telescopic shock absorbers
Tyres: 15.50/80 × 20 radial
Number of tyres: 4 + 1 spare
Brakes:
 (main) air
 (parking) air released spring brakes
Electrical system: 24 V

AEC Militant Mk 3 (6 × 6) 10 000 kg Cargo Truck

DEVELOPMENT
The Militant Mk 3 (6 × 6) 10 000 kg cargo truck was designed in the 1960s by AEC to meet a requirement for a 10 000 kg general service truck. The basic chassis is designated the FV 11046 and the truck the FV 11047. Its full designation is Truck, Cargo with Winch AEC 10-ton Mk 3 (6 × 6). The short wheelbase version is used as the basis for the AEC medium recovery vehicle (FV 11044) details of which will be found in the *Recovery vehicles* section (page 60).

DESCRIPTION
The two-door all-steel cab, designed and built by Park Royal Vehicles Limited, has a circular observation hatch in the roof and is resiliently mounted to the chassis. Standard equipment includes a fresh air heater, demister and de-froster with recirculatory provision, and for air transport the cab can be split at the waist rail.
 The rear cargo body, built by Marshall of Cambridge (Engineering) Limited has drop sides and a drop tailgate which can be removed to facilitate the carriage of containers, and removable bows and a tarpaulin cover. The winch has a 7000 kg capacity and 76·3 metres of cable.

SPECIFICATIONS
Cab seating: 1 + 1
Configuration: 6 × 6
Weight:
 (empty) 11 850 kg
 (loaded) 22 000 kg
Max load: 10 000 kg
Load area: 6·25 × 2·34 m
Length: 9·08 m
Width: 2·49 m
Height: (tarpaulin) 3·5 m
Track:
 (front) 2 m
 (rear) 2·06 m
Wheelbase: (front axle to centre of rear bogie) 4·877 m
Max speed: (road) 53 km/h
Range: 483 km
Fuel capacity: 218 litres
Max gradient: 33%
Engine: AEC AV 760 6-cylinder diesel developing 226 bhp at 2200 rpm

AEC Militant Mk 3 (6 × 6) 10 000 kg cargo truck

Gearbox: manual with 6 forward and 1 reverse gears
Clutch: power-assisted, hydraulically operated, single dry plate
Transfer box: 2-speed
Steering: worm and nut, hydraulic power-assisted
Turning radius: 11·4 m
Suspension:
 (front) leaf springs with double acting telescopic shock absorbers
 (rear) fully articulated rear bogie has inverted springs pivoted on cross-tube mounted in cast brackets
Tyres: 15.00 × 20
Number of tyres: 6 + 1 spare

Brakes:
 (main) air, all wheels
 (parking) air-assisted mechanical on rear bogie
Electrical system: 24 V
Batteries: 2 × 12 V, 100 Ah

STATUS
Production complete. In service with the British Army.

MANUFACTURER
AEC Limited, Southall, Middlesex, England. (AEC was taken over by British Leyland but was recently closed as part of company restructuring.)

AEC Militant Mk 1 (6 × 6) 10 000 kg Cargo Truck (FV 11008)

DEVELOPMENT
The AEC Militant Mk 1 (FV 11000) series of vehicles was developed for the British Army from the civilian model 0860 (6 × 6) and the model 0859 (6 × 4) trucks and was built in three wheelbases, 3·92, 4·49 and 4·887

metres. They have been widely used for a variety of roles but will be phased out of service in the next few years.

DESCRIPTION
The two-door forward control cab has a circular observation hatch in the roof. The all-steel rear cargo body, built by Marshall of Cambridge Limited or Strachans (Successors) of Acton, London, has drop sides and a drop tailgate which can be removed to facilitate the

loading of the vehicle by fork lift trucks. The cargo area is also provided with removable bows and a tarpaulin cover. Most vehicles have a 7000 kg capacity winch with 76·2 metres of cable. Over 300 of the cargo model have had their sides and tailgates removed and been fitted with a HIAB crane to the rear of the cab. These are used for carrying pallets of stores and ammunition.

VARIANTS
Variants of the Militant Mk 1 include the following, not all

AEC Militant Mk 1 (6 × 6) 10 000 kg truck with drop sides (T J Gander)

AEC Militant Mk 1 (6 × 6) 10 000 kg truck (T J Gander)

of which are still in service: FV 11001 6 × 4 artillery tractor with a 3·92-metre wheelbase, FV 11002 6 × 6 LAA tractor for towing Bofors 40 mm LAAG with a 3·92-metre wheelbase (no longer in service), FV 11003 bridging crane with a 4·49-metre wheelbase, FV 11005 6 × 4 three-way tipper with a 3·92-metre wheelbase, FV 11007 6 × 4 cargo, FV 11008 6 × 4 cargo with a 4·87-metre wheelbase (the description above relates to this truck), FV 11009 6 × 4 tanker with a 4·87-metre wheelbase, FV 11010 6 × 6 tractor truck for towing semi-trailers with a 3·92-metre wheelbase, FV 11013 6 × 4 crane truck with a 3·92-metre wheelbase, FV 11014 6 × 6 excavator with a 3·92-metre wheelbase, and the FV 11041 6 × 6 Mk 2 which did not progress beyond the prototype state. The Militant Mk 1 was followed by the Mk 3 which is still used by the British Army and for which there is a separate entry.

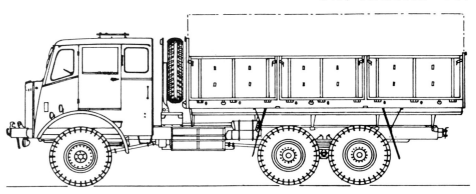

AEC Militant Mk 1 (6 × 6) 10 000 kg cargo truck (FV 11018)

SPECIFICATIONS (FV 11008)
Cab seating: 1 + 1
Configuration: 6 × 4
Weight:
   (empty) 11 100 kg
   (loaded) 21 200 kg
Max load: 10 160 kg
Load area: 5·486 × 2·324 m
Length: 8·58 m
Width: 2·49 m
Height: 3·606 m
Ground clearance: 0·34 m
Track:
   (front) 1·99 m
   (rear) 1·91 m
Wheelbase: (front axle to centre of rear bogie) 4·877 m
Angle of approach/departure: 45°/42°

Max speed: (road) 51·5 km/h
Range: 480 km
Fuel capacity: 218 litres
Engine: AEC 6-cylinder diesel developing 150 bhp at 1800 rpm
Gearbox: manual with 5 forward and 1 reverse gears
Clutch: single dry plate
Transfer box: 2-speed
Steering: worm and nut
Turning radius: 10·82 m
Suspension:
   (front) semi-elliptical springs with hydraulic shock absorbers
   (rear) inverted semi-elliptical springs with shock absorbers

Tyres: 14.00 × 20
Number of tyres: 6 + 1 spare
Brakes:
   (main) air, two line
   (parking) hand, mechanical on 4 rear wheels
Electrical system: 24 V

STATUS
Production complete. In service with the British Army.

MANUFACTURER
AEC Limited, Southall, Middlesex, England. (AEC was taken over by British Leyland but was recently closed as part of the company restructuring.)

Foden Medium Mobility (6 × 6) Range of Vehicles

DEVELOPMENT
The Foden Medium Mobility range of vehicles has been developed for use with the FH-70 155 mm howitzer in production for the British, West German and Italian armies. After trials with the 23 prototype vehicles the British Army placed a production order for 116 tractors and limbers, with the bodies built by Marshall of Cambridge (Engineering) Limited. Final deliveries to the British Army were made late in 1979.

The Medium Mobility range has been designed for both on- and off-road conditions and shares many common components with the Foden Low Mobility range.

DESCRIPTION
The chassis is of bolted construction with a flitch plate

and the full width front bumper has a towing jaw. Mounted at the rear is a rigid rear-pulling jaw and lift and recovery lugs front and rear.

The forward control cab is identical to that used for the Low Mobility range and the reader is referred to this entry for a description.

The Rolls-Royce engine is coupled to a Fuller gearbox with eight forward and one reverse gears. This has a single control stick and range change with overdrive.

The front axle is a Kirkstall SD.65-11-1 rated at 10 000 kg and fitted with a differential lock. The foremost tandem axle is a Kirkstall D65-111-1AF with an air-operated differential and the rearmost tandem axle is a Kirkstall D65-11-1 with a differential driving head. A cross axle differential lock is fitted to each of the rear axles and is air-operated with an electrical warning switch which indicates when the lock is engaged. The rear bogie has high articulation for cross-country operations.

The transfer (or auxiliary) gearbox is a Kirkstall

A6B7000 which comprises a two-speed, three-shaft, constant mesh helical gearbox with disengageable front-wheel drive. Engagement is pneumatically actuated via spur dogs designed to prevent any possibility of clutch throw out. Provision for optional high or low ratio live PTO is provided by utilising a duplicate front drive cartridge mounted at the rear of the input shaft.

VARIANTS
Gun tractor
This is used to tow the 155 mm FH-70. The platform comprises two sections of underframe with hardwood boarded floors, mounted fore and aft of the Atlas hydraulic crane. Mounted to the rear of the cab is a removable cabin which provides heated accommodation for eight men. Two NATO ammunition pallets are carried fore and aft of the crane. Stowage for the spare wheel and other gun equipment is provided at the rear of the vehicle. Spare wheels for the gun are stowed on the roof of the cabin.

Foden (6 × 6) medium mobility vehicle used as gun tractor for FH-70

Foden (6 × 6) medium mobility vehicle being used as FH-70 tractor with cab tipped forward for engine access (T J Gander)

Foden (6 × 6) medium mobility vehicle as gun tractor for FH-70 with hydraulic crane in use (T J Gander)

Foden (6 × 6) medium mobility vehicle being used as FH-70 limber vehicle (T J Gander)

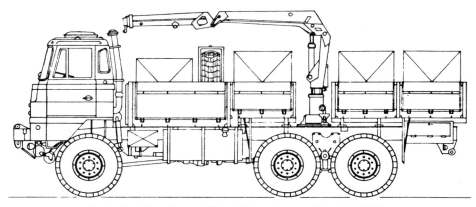

Foden (6 × 6) medium mobility vehicle used as gun limber for FH-70

Gun limber

This is used to carry eight NATO pallets containing 155 mm ammunition for the FH-70. The platform comprises two sections of underframe with hardwood boarded floor, mounted fore and aft of the crane.

16 000 kg truck

This is basically the 6 × 6 chassis and cab fitted with a new platform of welded steel with hardwood boarded floor and steel wearing strips. This body is mounted between the spare wheel and the forward end and the rear-mounted loading crane. The body is manufactured from mild steel sections and sheet and is of welded and bolted construction. A fixed bulkhead is fitted at the front end of the body and a detachable bulkhead at the rear. Hinged dropside panels and detachable intermediate pillars are fitted and can be removed to convert the truck body to a platform. This variant has not been adopted by the British Army.

Recovery vehicle

This is the 6 × 6 chassis and cab fitted with the EKA recovery equipment. Full details of this vehicle are given in the *Recovery vehicles* section (pages 58 and 59).

SPECIFICATIONS
Cab seating: 1 + 2
Configuration: 6 × 6
Weight:
  (loaded) 27 440 kg
  (chassis and cab) 10 990 kg
Max towed load: 9300 kg
Length: 9·16 m
Width: 2·5 m

Height: 3·75 m
Track:
  (front) 2·029 m
  (rear) 2·032 m
Wheelbase: 3·97 m + 1·516 m
Angle of approach/departure: 40°/29°
Max speed: (road) 104 km/h (tyre limitation 80 km/h)
Fuel capacity: 409 litres
Max gradient: 33%
Engine: turbocharged Rolls-Royce 305 Mk 111 6-cylinder liquid-cooled diesel developing 305 bhp at 2100 rpm
Gearbox: Fuller with 8 forward and 1 reverse gears
Transfer box: 2-speed
Steering: re-circulatory ball with integral power-assistance
Turning radius: 12 m
Suspension:
  (front) semi-elliptical springs
  (rear) 2 springs fully articulated
Tyres: 16.00 × 20
Number of tyres: 6 + 1 spare
Brakes:
  (main) air
  (parking) mechanical
Electrical system: 24 V
Batteries: 2 × 12 V

STATUS
Production complete but can be resumed if further orders are received. In service with the British Army.

MANUFACTURER
Foden Trucks, A division of Paccar UK Ltd, Elworth Works, Sandbach, Cheshire CW11 9HZ, England.

Foden Low Mobility (8 × 4) and (6 × 4) Range of Vehicles

DEVELOPMENT
The Foden Low Mobility range of vehicles has been developed to meet a British Army requirement for a vehicle that will operate satisfactorily when laden to its gross vehicle weight on both roads and unsurfaced tracks. The range is based on standard commercial components with emphasis on ease of maintenance. Deliveries to the British Army have amounted to 1275 units, of which over 60 per cent were delivered with left hand drive for use in the British Army of the Rhine.

DESCRIPTION
The two-door all-steel forward control S90 cab can be split at the waist rail for air transport. The vehicles are provided with a circular observation hatch in the centre of the roof. Standard cab equipment includes suspension seats, twin heaters/demisters, sun visors and visible warning system for air pressure, water temperature level, and oil pressure.

The cab has two stages of access for maintenance. The first, for daily and weekly servicing, involves lifting the front grille panel to gain access to power steer and clutch reservoirs, engine oil filter and dipstick, windscreen washer bottle, wiper motor and linkage, cab heater system, air auxiliary feed connections and wiring harness etc. The second stage involves using a hand-operated pump and ram assembly to tilt the cab forward to an angle of 65 degrees to enable the engine to be removed without removing the cab. The cab can be removed as a complete unit if required, as quick detachable, multi-point electrical connections are provided.

The front axles on the 8 × 4 versions are both Foden and rated at 6604 kg. The rear axles are also Foden with a capacity of 10 160 kg with single reduction hubs. A third differential is fitted to the foremost differential housing. There is provision for a differential lock on both rear axles.

The rear bogie is designed to a rating of 19 500 kg. A single spring is carried on each side of the vehicle in trunnion boxes of spheroidal graphite cast iron, and is free to pivot on pre-loaded rubber-bonded conical bushes fixed to a substantial centrally-mounted frame bracket. Axle location is by centrally-mounted torque rods connecting the worm gear housing to the frame, and also four torque rods mounted beneath and parallel to the springs.

Standard equipment on all models includes full width front bumper with central towing eye, rigid rear pulling jaw and lift and recovery lugs front and rear.

Foden (8 × 4) 16 000 kg low mobility cargo truck (Ministry of Defence)

Foden (8 × 4) low mobility tanker (T J Gander)

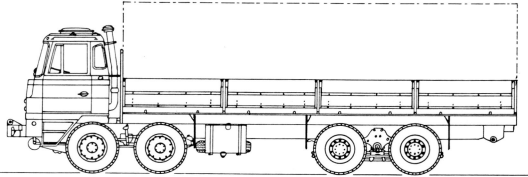

Foden (8 × 4) low mobility cargo truck

Foden (8 × 4) low mobility tipper with dump body in tipping position

Foden (6 × 4) low mobility tanker (T J Gander)

Foden (8 × 4) 16 000 kg low mobility truck with larger cab for driver training (T J Gander)

Foden (8 × 4) chassis fitted with Ampliroll system (T J Gander)

VARIANTS

8 × 4 Cargo
A total of 800 have been delivered. They can carry a maximum of 20 000 kg of cargo. The rear cargo body has drop sides, drop tailgate, removable bows and a canvas cover. Full details of the body are given in the *Shelters, containers and vehicle bodies* section under the entry for Marshall of Cambridge (Engineering). 120 are fitted with an S85 fibreglass cab and another 20 have a larger cab for driver training. In British Army use they are normally limited to carrying 16 000 kg, giving a gross vehicle weight of 27 000 kg, and unloaded weight (chassis, cab and cargo body) of 11 000 kg.

8 × 4 Tanker
A total of 218 has been delivered. The chassis is fitted

with a 22 500-litre tank body which has five compartments each of which holds 4500 litres of fuel. The tank is manufactured by Thompson Tankers of Bilston, Staffordshire.

8 × 4 Tipper
A total of 70 has been delivered. They have a shorter wheelbase than the other two 8 × 4 vehicles and are fitted with an Edbro 11 cubic metre all-steel end tipping body and an Edbro 6 NC single ram tip gear.

6 × 4 Tanker
A total of 199 has been delivered; the tank has a capacity of 12 000 litres. Tank body is by Charles Roberts (Engineering) Limited of Wakefield, West Yorkshire.

8 × 4 Ampliroll
Several 8 × 4 chassis have been fitted with the French designed Bennes Marrel Ampliroll system, details of which are given in the *Tank transporters* section.

STATUS
Production complete, but can be resumed if further orders are received. In service with the British Army.

MANUFACTURER
Foden Trucks, A division of Paccar UK Ltd, Elworth Works, Sandbach, Cheshire CW11 9HZ, England.

SPECIFICATIONS

Type	Cargo	Tanker	Tipper	Tanker
Cab seating	1 + 2	1 + 2	1 + 2	1 + 2
Configuration	8 × 4	8 × 4	8 × 4	6 × 4
Weight (loaded)	29 553 kg	28 888 kg	29 705 kg	22 786 kg
(chassis and cab)	9553 kg	9553 kg	9770 kg	9030 kg
Weight on front axle (loaded)	10 000 kg	11 570 kg	10 659 kg	5532 kg
Weight on rear axles (loaded)	19 553 kg	17 318 kg	19 046 kg	17 254 kg
Length	10·278 m	10·27 m	8·69 m	8·75 m
Width	2·497 m	2·502 m	2·497 m	2·497 m
Height	3·317 m	3·25 m	3·319 m	3·214 m
Wheelbase	1·372 m + 3·614 m + 1·516 m	1·372 m + 3·614 m + 1·516 m	1·372 m + 2·522 m + 1·516 m	3·97 m + 1·516 m
Angle of approach/departure	23°/23°	23°/23°	23°/23°	36°/28°
Max speed (road)	76 km/h	76 km/h	76 km/h	87 km/h
Fuel capacity	227 litres	227 litres	227 litres	227 litres
Max gradient	31·64%*	31·64%*	31·3%	28·6%
Engine	Rolls-Royce 220 Mk 111 6-cylinder liquid diesel developing 220 bhp at 2100 rpm			
Gearbox	Fuller with 9 forward and 1 reverse gears			
Steering	re-circulatory ball with integral power assistance			
Turning radius	12·25 m	12·25 m	10·35 m	11·4 m
Suspension (front)	semi-elliptical springs with telescopic hydraulic dampers			
(rear)	semi-elliptical, 2-spring fully articulated			
Tyres	11.00 × 20	11.00 × 20	11.00 × 20	12.00 × 20 (front) 14.00 × 20 (rear)
Number of tyres	12 + 1 spare	12 + 1 spare	12 + 1 spare	6 + 2 spare
Brakes (main)	2-line air, dual circuit			
(parking)	spring brake chambers on rear axles only. Air brake couplings front and rear for recovery			
Electrical system	24 V	24 V	24 V	24 V
Batteries	2 × 12 V	2 × 12 V	2 × 12 V	2 × 12 V

* At GVW of 24 000 kg

Scammell Crusader (6 × 4) Tractors

DESCRIPTION
The Scammell Crusader (6 × 4) tractor is basically a standard civilian vehicle adapted to meet military requirements. Two basic military models are available, both of which are in service with the British Army. The first, known as the 20-tonne payload tractor, has a two-man cab and the second, the 35-tonne tractor, has a three-man cab with provision for two bunks.

20 000 kg (6 × 4) tractor
The two-door forward control pressed steel cab is mounted on the chassis by two rubber bushed trunnion mountings at the front and two coil springs with integral telescopic dampers at the rear. The military version is powered by a Rolls-Royce Eagle 305 Mk 111 turbocharged diesel which develops 305 bhp at 2100 rpm coupled to a manual transmission with nine forward and two reverse gears.

35 000 kg (6 × 4) tractor
The two-door forward control pressed steel cab has two individual seats at the front (one for the driver and one for a passenger) and two seats at the rear. The rear seats convert to bunks. The cab is mounted on the chassis by two rubber bushed trunnion mountings at the front and two coil springs with integral telescopic dampers at the rear. The engine is the same as in the 20 000 kg model but is coupled to an RTO 915 manual gearbox with 15 forward and three reverse gears. Mounted to the rear of the cab is a Plummett capstan model CA80 winch with 120 metres of 16 mm cable which has a maximum capacity of 8000 kg at a speed of 27.5 metres a minute. The winch can be used either to the front or rear and is fitted with an overload warning bell.

VARIANTS
Late in 1977 the British Army ordered 130 Scammell Crusader (6 × 4) recovery vehicles. For details see *Recovery vehicles* section (pages 59 and 60).

STATUS
In production. In service with the British Army.

MANUFACTURER
Scammell Motors, Leyland Vehicles Limited, Tolpits Lane, Watford, Hertfordshire WD1 8QD, England.

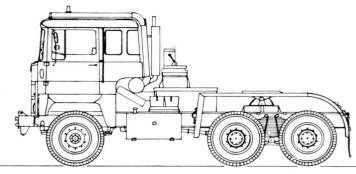

Scammell Crusader (6 × 4) 35 000 kg tractor

SPECIFICATIONS

Type	20 000 kg	35 000 kg
Cab seating	1 + 1	1 + 3
Configuration	6 × 4	6 × 4
Weight (empty)	9200 kg	11 095 kg
Towed load	20 000 kg	35 000 kg
Length	6·66 m	6·66 m
Width	2·502 m	2·502 m
Height (overall)	3·3 m	3·3 m
(5th wheel)	1·412 m	1·549 m
Track (front)	2·05 m	2·05 m
(rear)	1·845 m	1·845 m
Wheelbase (1st axle to centre of rear bogie)	3·962 m	3·962 m
Max speed (road)	85 km/h	65 km/h
Range	500 km	500 km
Fuel capacity	318 litres	455 litres
Max gradient (stop and restart)	24%	20·9%
Engine	Rolls-Royce Eagle 305 Mk 111 turbocharged diesel developing 305 bhp at 2100 rpm	
Gearbox	manual with 9 forward and 1 reverse gears	manual with 15 forward and 3 reverse gears
Clutch	twin dry plate	twin dry plate
Steering	ball and nut, power-assisted	
Turning radius	9·5 m	9·5 m
Suspension (front)	longitudinal semi-elliptical springs pivoted front with slipper rear ends, and telescopic shock absorbers	
(rear)	fully articulated, inverted longitudinal semi-elliptical springs, trunnion-mounted at centre with slipper rear ends	
Tyres	11.00 × 20	11.00 × 20
Number of tyres	10 + 2 spare	10 + 2 spare
Brakes	air on all axles incorporating 3-line brake system	
Electrical system	24 V	24 V
Batteries	4 × 12 V, 100 Ah	4 × 12 V, 100 Ah

Scammell Crusader (6 × 4) 35 000 kg tractor towing RE semi-trailer

Scammell Crusader (6 × 4) tractor of British Army carrying Lance vehicle of West German Army (T J Gander)

UNITED STATES OF AMERICA

West German Vehicles for US Army

In 1978 the United States Army awarded its first contracts in a seven-year programme to buy more than 10 000 vehicles from West Germany and other European manufacturers for use by United States forces in Europe.

The first contracts, worth a total of $2·2 million, were placed with five West German companies, Daimler-Benz, MAN, Magirus-Deutz, Still and Volkswagen, and covered 225 vehicles including 77 nine-passenger vans, 60 ½-ton pick-up trucks, 23 panel delivery trucks, as well as tractors, dump trucks and forklifts.

The seven-year plan called for the purchase of 10 820 administrative vehicles, of which 7000 will be used by the Army and the remainder by the Air Force. Total procurement cost was estimated to be $100 million in 1978, with spare parts and other support costs adding a further $10 to 20 million to this figure.

Commercial Utility Cargo Vehicles (CUCV)

DEVELOPMENT
Starting in 1981 a 14-month programme known as the 'Special Analysis of Wheeled Requirements' (usually abbreviated to just 'Wheels') was carried out by the US Army Tank Automotive Command. Its objective was to

find a commercial vehicle that could be easily procured for US Army use in areas where extreme environmental conditions would not be met and where expensive vehicles were not necessary. The objective was to replace 20 per cent of the M151 Jeeps in use and the bulk of the M880 series of pick-up trucks. The vehicle types chosen would also be used by the US Air Force and Marine Corps.

During the programme the US Army purchased 26

commercial vehicles and subjected them to exhaustive tests at the Aberdeen Proving Grounds, Maryland. The final choice was a General Motors design, the Model K which is one of the GM C/K series, 9 million of which have been produced.

In July 1982, a contract was awarded to General Motors worth $689 million, for a total of 53 248 vehicles to be known as the Commercial Utility Cargo Vehicles (CUCV). The first deliveries were made in August 1983

Truck Cargo, Tactical 1¼-ton, (4 × 4), M1008

Truck, Cargo, Shelter Carrier, Tactical 1¼-ton, (4 × 4), M1028

Truck Utility, Tactical ¾-ton, (4 × 4), M1009

Truck, Ambulance, Tactical 1¼-ton, (4 × 4), M1010

and the production programme should last three years.
Projected procurement is for 57 349 CUCVs for all the armed services with 54 087 for the US Army.

DESCRIPTION

The CUCV fleet is comprised of five types of vehicle, as follows:

Type A, Truck Utility, Tactical ¾-ton, 4 × 4, M1009
Type B, Truck Cargo, Tactical 1¼-ton, 4 × 4, M1008
Type C, Truck Ambulance, Tactical 1¼-ton, 4 × 4, M1010
Type D, Truck Chassis, Tactical 1¼-ton, 4 × 4, M1031
Type E, Truck Cargo Shelter Carrier, Tactical 1¼-ton, 4 × 4, M1028

All five types are based on a common power train but having different body and/or chassis variations to fulfil a variety of purposes and having varying payloads to suit their role. All five types have the 6·2-litre diesel engine, automatic transmission and two-speed transfer box. The rear and front axles are the same in all types other than the Type A. The 28 V electrical system in all types is the same apart from the Type C ambulance which has a system with doubled power.

The five types are all commercial models with the following alterations incorporated:

Blackout lights
Camouflage paint (three colour, NATO)
Engine diagnostic connector assembly
Military markings, including a removable red cross for the Type C ambulance
NBC warfare protection
NBC kit provisions
Position and Azimuth Determining System (PADS)
Rear pintle hook
Slave-start capability

Towing capability
Weapon holders
Winterisation kit to allow operations down to −46°C.
The Type C ambulance version has provision for four stretcher patients or eight seated wounded. An air filter system is also provided along with air conditioning and extra lighting, including spot lights. The Type E cargo shelter carrier is equipped with shelter tie-down brackets.
All five types are air-transportable.

STATUS

First production units delivered August 1983. In service with the US Army.

MANUFACTURER

General Motors Truck and Bus Group, Flint, Michigan, USA.

Enquiries to Truck and Bus International Staff, General Motors Corporation, GM Technical Centre, Warren, Michigan, USA.

SPECIFICATIONS

Type	A	B	C	D	E
Function	utility	cargo	ambulance	truck	cargo shelter carrier
Model	M1009	M1008	M1010	M1031	M1028
GM model number	K10516	K30903	K30903	K30903	K30903
	Blazer	Pickup	Chassis/cab	Chassis/cab	Pickup
Cab seating	1 + 1 + 3	3	1 + 1	3	3
Configuration	4 × 4	4 × 4	4 × 4	4 × 4	4 × 4
Weight (loaded)	2903 kg	3992 kg	4287 kg	4334 kg	4264 kg
Max payload	544 kg	1315 kg	943 kg	1792 kg	1633 kg
Length	4·873 m	5·607 m	5·784 m	5·408 m	5·607 m
Width	2·022 m	2·062 m	2·062 m	2·062 m	2·062 m
Height (overall)	1·905 m	1·915 m	2·581 m	1·938 m	1·92 m
Track (front)	1·485 m	1·488 m	1·488 m	1·488 m	1·488 m
Track (rear)	1·382 m	1·438 m	1·438 m	1·438 m	1·438 m
Wheelbase	2·705 m	3·34 m	3·34 m	3·34 m	3·34 m
Fording	0·508 m	0·508 m	0·508 m	0·508 m	0·508 m
Engine	General Motors 6·2-litre V-8 diesel developing 135 hp at 3600 rpm				
Gearbox	General Motors THM-400 3-speed automatic with 1 reverse				
Transfer box	2-speed	2-speed	2-speed	2-speed	2-speed
Suspension (front)	tapered leaf springs with 1021 kg capacity				
(rear)	semi-elliptical multi-leaf springs with 850, 1588, 1588, 1701, 1701 kg respectively				
Tyres	10.00 × 15	9.50 × 16.5	9.50 × 16.5	9.50 × 16.5	9.50 × 16.5
Electrical system	28 V, 100 Ah	28 V, 100 Ah	28 V, 200 Ah	28 V, 100 Ah	28 V, 100 Ah

M561 (6 × 6) 1¼-ton Truck

DEVELOPMENT

In the late 1950s a 6 × 6 high mobility vehicle was designed by Roger L Gamaunt and prototypes were built by the Ling-Tempo-Vought (LTV) Aerospace Corporation. The vehicle was subsequently entered, along with seven other entries from other companies, in a competition for a 1¼-ton vehicle for the US Army. The LTV entry, commonly known as the Gama Goat, won the competition and LTV was awarded a contract for two test rigs which were completed in January 1964. In July 1964 LTV was awarded a contract for 12 prototypes designated XM561. After trials the XM561 was accepted for service with the Army in June 1966 and the production contract, like most other American contracts of this type, was put out to competitive tender. Six firms bid for the contract: Consolidated Diesel Electric bid $132·1 million, Ford $153·4 million, LTV Aerospace/Kaiser Jeep $160 million, Baifield Industries $168·5 million, Chrysler $184·3 million and Bowen-McLaughlin-York bid $184·5 million.

In June 1968 a three-year production contract was awarded to Consolidated Diesel Electric. First production vehicles were completed late in 1969 and the vehicle entered service with the Army the following year. A House Armed Services Committee report of July 1972 recommended cancellation if the design could not meet Army requirements for cost effectiveness, durability, reliability and maintainability. The same month the Army cancelled the final 1000 of the M561 production contract and at that time the company still had over 4000 M561s to complete under the previously funded contract which called for 14 275 vehicles. Production was completed in 1973.

In 1981 the US Army had about 11 000 M561 series Gama Goats in service although its requirement was for about 32 000 vehicles of this type. It will be replaced in the mid-1980s by the High Mobility Multi-purpose Wheeled Vehicle (HMMWV).

DESCRIPTION
The M561 consists of two aluminium units, front and rear. The front (4 × 4) unit contains the two-man crew and the engine, and the rear (2 × 2) unit carries the cargo. Its two bodies are connected by an articulating assembly permitting them to arch vertically (pitch) and rotate (roll) with respect to each other, so that the two bodies always conform independently to all types of terrain. Co-ordinated four-wheel steering of front and rear wheels is provided and the driver can select either two or six wheel drive according to the type of terrain.

The front unit has a canvas hood and a windscreen and the rear unit has removable bows and a tarpaulin cover. Most vehicles have a Ramsey model CVD 200R front-mounted winch with a capacity of 3628 kg. The M561 is fully amphibious being propelled in the water by its wheels at a speed of 4 km/h.

A complete range of kits was developed for the vehicle, not all of which have been adopted. These kits include a heater, 7·62 mm M60 machine gun mounting, 100 amp power source, mortar carrier, and a mounting for a 106 mm recoilless rifle or a Hughes TOW ATGW system.

VARIANTS
An ambulance model is designated the M792. The M561 is also used to carry a standard shelter in the rear for use as command, radio and communications centres, as well as for mounting radars such as the Saunders Associates Forward Area Alerting Radar which is used in conjunction with the Chaparral and Vulcan air defence systems.

STATUS
Production complete. In service only with the US Army and Marine Corps.

MANUFACTURER
Condiesel Mobile Equipment Division, CONDEC Corporation, 1700 Post Road, Old Greenwich, Connecticut 06870, USA.

SPECIFICATIONS
Cab seating: 1 + 1
Configuration: 6 × 6
Roll at centre axle: ±15°
Roll at rear axle: ±30°
Pitch at rear axle: ±40°
Weight:
 (empty) 3311 kg
 (loaded) 4626 kg
Weight on first axle: (loaded) 1245 kg
Weight on second axle: (loaded) 1769 kg
Weight on third axle: (loaded) 1612 kg
Max load: 1315 kg
Towed load: 2812 kg
Load area: 2·26 × 1·89 m
Length: 5·76 m
Width: 2·13 m
Height:
 (tarpaulin) 2·31 m
 (reduced) 1·65 m
Ground clearance: 0·38 m
Track: 1·83 m

M561 (6 × 6) 1¼-ton truck, commonly known as Gama Goat with fully enclosed cab (Simon Dunstan)

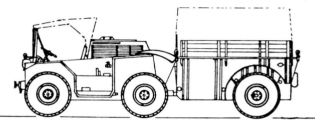

M561 (6 × 6) 1¼-ton truck

M561 (6 × 6) 1¼-ton truck

Wheelbase: 2·05 m + 2·16 m
Angle of approach/departure: 62°/45°
Max speed: 88 km/h
Range: 840 km
Fuel capacity: 151 litres
Max gradient: 60%
Vertical obstacle: 0·457 m
Fording: amphibious
Engine: GM 3-53, 3-cylinder in-line liquid-cooled diesel developing 103 hp at 2800 rpm

Gearbox: manual with 4 forward and 1 reverse gears
Transfer box: 2-speed
Steering: mechanical forward and rear wheels
Turning radius: 9 m
Suspension: independent coil spring at front and rear, single-leaf springs and swing axle at centre wheels
Tyres: 11.00 × 18
Brakes: hydraulic, internal expanding, sealed on all wheels
Electrical system: 24 V

M715 (4 × 4) 1¼-ton Truck

DEVELOPMENT
The M715 was developed in the 1960s as an interim replacement vehicle for the M37 (4 × 4) ¾-ton truck. The vehicle was developed by the Kaiser Jeep Corporation from its commercial Gladiator (4 × 4) vehicle and after trials with prototypes the company received its first production contract in March 1966. This was for 20 680 vehicles to be delivered over two years at a cost of $90.9 million. First deliveries were made in January 1967 and production continued until 1970 by which time 30 510 had been built. Late in 1969 the company received a contract to build 43 improved vehicles to be tested in

competition with the General Motors developed XM705. The company is currently offering an improved model under the designation AM 715, for which there is a separate entry. This series will be replaced in the mid-1980s by the High Mobility Multi-purpose Wheeled Vehicle (HMMWV).

DESCRIPTION
The layout of the vehicle is conventional with the engine at the front, cab in the centre and cargo/personnel area at the rear. The chassis of the M715 is designated the M724. The cab has a windscreen which can be folded forward onto the bonnet and removable canvas top. The rear cargo area has a drop tailgate, removable bows, a

tarpaulin cover and longitudinal folding seats on each side which can seat four men. Many vehicles have a front-mounted winch with a capacity of 3402 kg. Kits available for the M715 include deep fording kit, cargo and crew compartment enclosure kit, engine heater kit, and heaters for both the crew and cargo areas.

VARIANTS
M725 ambulance
This was the replacement for the M43 ambulance and has a fully enclosed rear van type body and can carry eight seated patients plus the driver and medical orderly or five stretcher patients plus the driver and medical orderly.

M726 telephone line maintenance vehicle
This was the replacement for the M201 ¾-ton mainten-
ance truck and its rear all-steel body has compartments
for stowing tools and spare parts.
M142
This is simply the standard M715 with the S-250 com-
munications shelter installed in the rear, used for a
variety of roles by the US Army and Marine Corps.
Repower package
  NAPCO Industries of Hopkins, Minnesota, has
developed a repower package for this series of vehicles.
Full details are given later in this section under NAPCO
Industries Repower/Modernisation Packages.

SPECIFICATIONS
Cab seating: 1 + 1
Configuration: 4 × 4
Weight:
  (empty without winch) 2494 kg
  (empty with winch) 2721 kg
  (loaded, cross country without winch) 3854 kg
  (loaded, cross country with winch) 4081 kg
Weight on front axle: (loaded, without winch) 1360 kg
Weight on rear axle: (loaded, without winch) 2450 kg
Max load:
  (road) 1360 kg
  (cross country) 1134 kg
Towed load:
  (road) 1628 kg
  (cross country) 1288 kg
Length: 5·327 m
Width: 2·159 m
Height:
  (overall) 2·413 m
  (reduced) 1·498 m
Ground clearance: 0·254 m
Track: 1·71 m
Wheelbase: 3·2 m
Angle of approach/departure: 45°/25°
Max speed: 96·6 km/h
Range: 362 km
Fuel capacity: 106 litres
Gradient: 58%
Fording:
  (without preparation) 0·914 m
  (with preparation) 1·524 m
Engine: Model OHC 6-230 6-cylinder in-line water-
cooled petrol developing 132·5 bhp at 4000 rpm
Gearbox: manual with 4 forward and 1 reverse gears
Transfer box: 2-speed
Steering: recirculating ball
Turning radius: 8·384 m
Suspension: horizontal semi-elliptical springs and
direct acting shock absorbers, with hydraulic dampers
Tyres: 9.00 × 10
Number of tyres: 4 + 1 spare
Brakes:
  (main) hydraulic
  (parking) mechanical
Electrical system: 24 V

STATUS
Production complete. In service with the US forces and
Israel.

MANUFACTURER
AM General Corporation, 14250 Plymouth Road,
Detroit, Michigan 48232, USA.

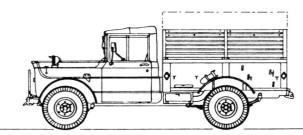

M715 (4 × 4) 1¼-ton truck (Michael Ledford)

M715 (4 × 4) 1¼-ton truck

M142 (4 × 4) 1¼-ton truck carrying S-250 communications shelter (R Young)

AM 715 Series (4 × 4) 1¼-ton Trucks

DESCRIPTION
When production of the M715 (4 × 4) 1¼-ton truck was
completed for the US Army in 1969 AM General
developed another version for export called the AM 715.
In appearance this is almost identical to the M715 but
has a more powerful engine and other small modifications. The chassis is designated the AM 724.
  The layout of the AM 715 is conventional with the
engine at the front, two-door cab with a removable
canvas top, windscreen which folds forward onto the
bonnet and side windows which can be wound down in
the centre and the cargo area at the rear with a drop
tailgate, stake type sides, removable bows and a tarpaulin cover. A fold-up bench seat, capable of seating
five fully-equipped men, is provided down each side of
the cargo area. The AM 715 can also carry a standard
S-250 military shelter and be used as a command or
communications vehicle.

VARIANTS
  AM 725: ambulance which can carry five stretcher
patients plus an attendant.
  AM 715C: weapon carrier, for example TOW.
  AM 715S: field service vehicle, similar to M726 tele-
phone line maintenance truck.

AM General AM 715 (4 × 4) 1¼-ton cargo truck

SPECIFICATIONS
(AM 715; data in square brackets relate to AM 725
where different)
Type: truck [ambulance]
Cab seating: 1 + 2
Configuration: 4 × 4
Weight:
(empty) 2132 [2676] kg
(loaded) 3537 [3583] kg
Weight on front axle: (loaded) 1361 [1383] kg
Weight on rear axle: (loaded) 2177 [2200] kg
Max load: 1134 [726] kg
Towed load: 1288 kg [n/app]
Load area: 2·355 × 1·626 m [n/app]
Length: 5·321 [5·359] m
Width: 2·032 [2·134] m
Height:
(reduced) 1·36 m [n/app]
(overall) 2·286 [2·451] m
(load area) 0·838 m [n/app]
Ground clearance: (axles) 0·22 [0·21] m
Track:
(front) 1·641 [1·626] m
(rear) 1·674 [1·661] m
Wheelbase: 3·327 [3·319] m
Angle of approach/departure: 41°[32°]/25°
Max speed: (road) 97 km/h
Range: 322 km
Fuel capacity: 72 litres
Max gradient: 60%
Fording: 0·457 m
Engine: Model 6-258 6-cylinder in-line ohv petrol
developing 150 hp at 3800 rpm
Gearbox: manual, with 4 forward and 1 reverse gears
Clutch: single plate
Transfer box: 2-speed
Steering: re-circulating ball
Turning radius: 7·11 [7·32] m

AM General AM 725 (4 × 4) 1¼-ton ambulance

Suspension: horizontal semi-elliptical springs with
hydraulic shock absorbers
Tyres: 7.50 × 16
Number of tyres: 4 + 1 spare
Brakes: front, power and rear, drum (vacuum assisted)
Electrical system: 12 V
Battery: 1 × 12 V, 63 Ah

STATUS
Production complete.

MANUFACTURER
AM General Corporation, 14250 Plymouth Road,
Detroit, Michigan 48232, USA.

M880 (4 × 4) and (4 × 2) 1133 kg Range

DEVELOPMENT
In February 1972 the WHEELS (Special Analysis of
Wheeled Vehicles) study was established under the
chairmanship of the Assistant Vice Chief of Staff, Army.
Its object was to conduct a comprehensive analysis of
the Army's wheeled vehicle needs, fleet management
and utilisation. The study was undertaken in three
phases, the last of which was completed in April 1973.
The study made many recommendations, most of which
have now been implemented. One of the recommendations was that standard commercial vehicles could be
used for many of the roles previously undertaken by
specialised vehicles. The US Army has a fleet of
600 000 vehicles and it is expected that 400 000 of
these will be replaced by commercial vehicles with little,
if any, modifications for Army use.

The first requirement was for a new 1¼-ton 4 × 4 and
4 × 2 series of vehicles. The Army issued a requirement for 33 759 vehicles and received bids from AM
General ($170·5 million), Chevrolet Division of General
Motors Corporation ($150·5 million), Ford Motor Corpo-
ration ($188·7 million) and the Chrysler Corporation,
Dodge Division ($145·7 million). In March 1975 the
latter bid was accepted and the contract was awarded to
Chrysler. First production vehicles were delivered to the
Army in May 1975 and final deliveries were made late in
1978. The range comprises both 4 × 4 (Dodge W200)
and 4 × 2 (Dodge D200) vehicles in both pick-up and
ambulance versions (about 4000). The pick-up contract
price was $3825·16 (retail price in 1975 was about
$5200), which included steel-belted radial tyres,
maintenance-free battery, rustproofing and lustreless
forest green paint. The vehicles were covered by the
standard new truck warranty of 19 312 km or 12 months,
and repairs were carried out by local Dodge dealers.

Approximately 44 000 M880 series trucks were built
between 1975 and 1977. This series will be replaced in
the mid-1980s by the High Mobility Multi-purpose
Wheeled Vehicle (HMMWV).

DESCRIPTION
The 4 × 4 cargo model is designated the M880 (Dodge
W200 chassis) and the 4 × 2 cargo model is designated
the M890 (Dodge D200 chassis). Both are identical in
appearance with the engine at the front, fully enclosed
two-door all-steel cab in the centre and the cargo area at
the rear with a drop tailgate. A bench-type seat for four
fully-equipped men can be fitted down either side.
Mounted at the rear is a swivel tow pintle and a trailer
lighting receptacle.

The 4 × 4 ambulance model is designated the M886
(Dodge W200 chassis) and the 4 × 2 ambulance model
the M893 (Dodge D200 chassis). They are identical in

M880 (4 × 4) 1¼-ton truck carrying S-250 shelter with roof-mounted Tactical Radar Threat Generator (TRTG)

appearance and the fully enclosed rear body can accommodate four to five stretcher patients and a medical attendant on a jump seat.

VARIANTS
Including the basic vehicle, there are 13 members in the family:
M880, Truck Cargo: 1¼ ton (4 × 4)
M881, Truck Cargo: 1¼ ton (4 × 4) with 60 A kit
M882, Truck Cargo: 1¼ ton (4 × 4) with 60 A kit and communication kit
M883, Truck Cargo: 1¼-ton (4 × 4) with 60 A and communications shelter tiedown kit
M884, Truck Cargo: 1¼-ton (4 × 4) with 100 A and communications shelter tiedown kit
M885, Truck Cargo: 1¼-ton (4 × 4) with communications shelter tiedown kit
M890, Truck Cargo: 1¼-ton (4 × 2)
M891, Truck Cargo: 1¼-ton (4 × 2) with 60 A kit
M892, Truck Cargo: 1¼-ton (4 × 2) with 60 A kit and communications kit
M886, Truck Ambulance: 1¼-ton (4 × 4)
M893, Truck Ambulance: 1¼-ton (4 × 2)
M887, Truck Contact Maintenance: 1¼-ton (4 × 4)
M888, Truck Telephone Maintenance: 1¼-ton (4 × 4)

STATUS
Production complete. In service with the US Army and Pakistan.

MANUFACTURER
Dodge Division of Chrysler Corporation, 7900 Jos Campau Avenue (Hamtramck), Detroit, Michigan 48211, USA.

SPECIFICATIONS

Designation (US Army)	M880	M886	M890	M893
(Dodge)	W200	W200	D200	D200
Type	cargo	ambulance	cargo	ambulance
Cab seating	1 + 2	1 + 2	1 + 2	1 + 2
Configuration	4 × 4	4 × 4	4 × 2	4 × 2
Weight (empty)	2108 kg	2774 kg	1913 kg	2578 kg
(loaded)	3629 kg	3629 kg	3402 kg	3402 kg
Max load	1133 kg	n/app	1133 kg	n/app
Towed load	1360 kg	n/app	1360 kg	n/app
Length	5·56 m	5·46 m	5·56 m	5·46 m
Width	2·02 m	2·02 m	2·02 m	2·02 m
Height	1·87 m	2·57 m	1·8 m	2·49 m
Wheelbase	3·33 m	3·33 m	3·33 m	3·33 m
Track	1·625 m	1·625 m	1·625 m	1·625 m
Fuel capacity	76 litres	76 litres	76 litres	76 litres
Engine	Chrysler V-8 OHV petrol developing 150 hp at 4000 rpm			
Transmission	Loadflite automatic with 3 speeds forward and a torque converter			
Transfer box (4 × 4 model only)	New Process model 203 with 2-speed full-time 4 × 4 drive with locking interaxle differential			
Steering	mechanical, recirculating ball			
Turning circle	14·63 m	14·63 m	14·63 m	14·63 m
Suspension	semi-elliptical springs with hydraulic double acting shock absorbers			
Brakes	power (vacuum/hydraulic); front disc, rear drum			
Electrical system	12 V	12 V	12 V	12 V
Battery	1 × 12 V	1 × 12 V	1 × 12 V	1 × 12 V

M880 series (4 × 4) 1¼-ton cargo truck carrying shelter and towing trailer in Norway (Ministry of Defence)

AM General HUMMER M998 Series Multi-Purpose Wheeled Vehicles

DEVELOPMENT
Based on the draft specification for the High Mobility Multi-purpose Wheeled Vehicle (HMMWV) issued by the US Army in mid-1979, AM General used its own company funds to design and build a prototype in the weapons carrier configuration.

The first prototype was completed in August 1980 and was sent to the Nevada Automotive Test Centre for extensive trials and by February 1981 the prototype had accumulated 21 000 km of instrumented and dynamic testing.

AM General became one of three contenders awarded a US Army contract for the design and construction of 11 prototype HMMWVs (six weapon carriers and five utility) which were delivered in May 1982. On March 22, 1983 AM General were awarded a $59·8 million contract by the US Army Tank Automotive Command (TACOM) for 2334 HMMWVs, which were then designated the M998 Series HUMMER. This was the first increment in a five-year contract for 54 973 vehicles worth approximately $1·2 billion. Of these some 39 000 are for the US Army and the remainder will be divided between the US Air Force and the US Marine Corps. Production will commence at Mishawaka, Indiana early in 1984.

Once in service the M998 Series HUMMERs will be used to replace some M151 Jeeps, the M274 Mule (830 in service), the M561/M792 Gama Goat (11 000 in service) and the M880 series (40 000 in service). It is expected that 20 per cent of the current fleet of M151s and many of the M880s will be replaced by the Commercial Utility Cargo Vehicle or CUCV.

DESCRIPTION
The AM General HUMMER has 2 × 2 seating on each side of the drive train which is in a midship position allowing the front differential to be raised. This, together

AM General HUMMER weapon carrier

with the geared hubs, provides a ground clearance of 0·4 metre. The location of the crew on each side of the drive train also allows a low centre of gravity. The windshield frame is strong enough to serve as a roll bar and support for various equipment kits. Other pillars also make the ballistically-protected weapon station inher-

ently strong and a steady location on which to mount a variety of weapons such as TOW, 7·62 mm and 12·7 mm machine guns and the MK19 40 mm grenade launcher. At the rear the cargo bed is large enough to accommodate an S-250 shelter without overhang.

Production versions of the HUMMER can be converted into 16 variants by changing the body configuration. These configurations are:

Basic vehicle
S-250 shelter carrier
TOW anti-tank missile launcher carrier
Cargo truck with tilt
Maxi-ambulance with space for four stretchers
Mini-ambulance with space for two stretchers
MK19 40 mm grenade launcher carrier
Pick-up truck with open rear and soft top over two-man cab
12·7 mm (0·50) M2 machine gun carrier
Four-man soft top personnel carrier
Basic two-stretcher ambulance
7·62 mm M60 machine gun carrier
Stinger anti-aircraft missile carrier
25 mm Bushmaster cannon carrier
C³I radio equipment carrier using Maxi-ambulance body
Squad carrier

To reduce life cycle and initial procurement costs, standard automotive components are used wherever possible, as in the engine, transmission, transfer case, brakes and steering.

The independent suspension, front and rear, gives good manoeuvrability, ease of handling and part commonality. The geared hubs give 0·406-metre all-round ground clearance incorporating raised axles for high speed operations on road and across country. They also provide a 1·92 to 1 torque output multiplication at the ground.

The suspended carrier front and rear axles are identical, have differentials and are mounted high directly in the chassis frame. The front propeller shaft has double cardan joints and the rear propeller shaft has single cardan joints which, according to AM General, give minimal motion, improved torque characteristics and higher reliability with resultant lower support costs. Vehicle handling is enhanced by the front stabiliser bar being attached to the lower control arms and pivot bracket reducing shock from the lower A-frame member to the chassis.

Acceleration of the HUMMER is such that it can move from a standstill to 48 km/h in seven seconds and from a standstill to 80 km/h in 20 seconds.

Three HUMMERS can be carried in a C-130 Hercules transport aircraft, six in a C-141B and 15 in a C-5A Galaxy.

SPECIFICATIONS
Cab seating: 1 + 3
Configuration: 4 × 4
Weight:
  (empty) 2254 kg
  (loaded) 3870 kg
Max load: 1134 kg
Towed load: 1542 kg
Length: 4·57 m
Height: 1·75 m
Width: 2·15 m
Ground clearance: 0·4 m

Track: 1·81 m
Wheelbase: 3·3 m
Angle of approach/departure: 69°/45°
Max speed: 105 km/h
Range: 563 km
Fuel capacity: 94 litres
Max gradient: 60%
Side slope: 40%
Vertical obstacle: 0·56 m
Fording: 0·76 m
  (with preparation) 1·52 m
Engine: V-8 6·2-litre, air-cooled diesel
Transmission: automatic with 3 forward and 1 reverse gears
Transfer box: 2-speed, full-time 4-wheel drive
Suspension: (front and rear) independent, double A-arm, coil spring
Steering: power-assisted
Turning circle: 14·63 m
Brakes: hydraulic disc front and rear
Tyres: 36 × 12.5–16.5
Electrical system: 24 V

STATUS
Production due to commence in early 1984 for the US Army.

MANUFACTURER
AM General Corporation, 14250 Plymouth Road, Detroit, Michigan 48232, USA.

AM General HUMMER weapon carrier with TOW anti-tank missile launcher

AM General HUMMER weapon carrier with 12·7 mm (0·50) M2 machine gun

General Dynamics High Mobility Multi-purpose Wheeled Vehicle TCM/GPD (4 × 4) High Mobility Multi-purpose Wheeled Vehicle

With the acceptance of the AM General entry for the High Mobility Multi-purpose Wheeled Vehicle (HMMWV) competition (see previous entry) the General Dynamics and Teledyne entries have been discontinued. For details of these two vehicles see *Jane's Military Vehicles and Ground Support Equipment 1983*, pages 441 and 442.

Medium Tactical Truck (MTT) Program

The US Army has a requirement for the long-term replacement of the M35/M44 2½-ton trucks currently in service. Although there are over 66 000 of these trucks presently in service many are now reaching the end of their useful service lives. To replace them a proposal for a new Medium Multi-purpose Wheeled Vehicle (MMW) has been made but during mid-1983 the name of this project was changed to Medium Tactical Truck (MTT).

The MTT will be a vehicle with a cross-country load capacity of between 2500 kg and 3500 kg with the current approach suggesting the higher figure. It would appear that the current requirement is for the MTT to be a 4 × 4 rather than a 6 × 6 vehicle and a forward control cab for carriage in transport aircraft is indicated. The MTT will be expected to carry shelters/containers as well as personnel and stores. As funds for the MTT project are understood to be 'strictly limited' it is likely that an existing design or a modification of an existing model will be selected.

Draft required operational capability (ROC) responses from the US Army commands were expected by the end of 1983. The defence budget for fiscal year

1984 contained a request for $4·1 million for research, development, test and evaluation in connection with the MTT project and the US Army Tank-Automotive Command (TACOM) at Warren, Michigan, was expected to issue a draft specification to industry by early 1984. Prototype design and construction contracts could be placed by mid-1984 with testing and evaluation to commence by mid-1985. First production deliveries could commence by the end of 1987.

Provisional forecasts are for 767 MTTs being procured during funded delivery period (FDP) 1986 (which extends into calendar year 1988). Figures for FDP 1987 are 1972, for FDP 1988 6072 and for FDP 1989 8444.

M35/M44A2 (6 × 6) 2½-ton Cargo Truck Series

DEVELOPMENT

In the late 1940s Reo and the Truck and Bus Division of General Motors Corporation each developed a new 2½-ton (6 × 6) truck for the US Army to replace wartime vehicles. Reo was awarded the initial production con-

tract for 5000 vehicles and delivered the first vehicle in 1950. Originally it was to have been only an interim solution pending large-scale production of the General Motors design, but as soon as the Korean War broke out it was apparent that Reo alone could not meet the requirements of the Army so the General Motors models were placed in immediate production. They were the M135 with single rear wheels and the M211 with dual rear wheels, but they were phased out of production

after the end of the Korean War in favour of the Reo design which was also built by Studebaker and was commonly known as the Eager Beaver.

The first vehicles were powered by a Reo (model OA-331) or Continental (COA-331) petrol engine which developed 146 bhp at 3400 rpm but later models with the suffix A1 (eg M35A1) were powered by a Continental LDS 427-2 multi-fuel engine. Current models (eg M35A2) have the Continental LD 465-1 multi-fuel

M35A2 2½-ton (6 × 6) cargo/personnel truck

M35A2 2½-ton (6 × 6) cargo/personnel truck with machine gun mounting over cab (T J Gander)

M35A2 cargo/personnel 2½-ton (6 × 6) truck fording a water course

M35A2 cargo 2½-ton (6 × 6) truck converted to generator truck and towing special equipment trailer for M1 Abrams MBT unit (T J Gander)

engine which develops 140 bhp (gross) at 2600 rpm.

In 1964 the Kaiser Jeep Corporation bought the Studebaker facilities in South Bend, Indiana and were awarded contracts to build both 2½-ton (6 × 6) and 5-ton (6 × 6) trucks for the US Army.

In 1967 Kaiser Jeep formed the Defense and Government Products Division to handle its government contracts but in 1970 Kaiser Jeep was acquired by American Motors and the Defense and Government Products Division of the Jeep Corporation was named the General Products Division of the Jeep Corporation. In 1971 it was renamed the AM General Corporation, a wholly-owned subsidiary of American Motors Corporation.

By early 1980 AM General had produced over 150 000 M35/M44 series 6 × 6 trucks. A product-improved prototype designated the M963 series is currently being developed by the company under contract to the US Army.

In early 1981 the US Army had 62 975 2½-ton (6 × 6) trucks of which 10 993 were over 15 years old. Total requirement is 101 489 vehicles.

The M963 series is powered by a Caterpillar Model 3208 V-8 diesel developing 210 hp and is coupled to an Allison MT643 four-speed automatic transmission. New axles give the vehicle a wider track and larger tyres improve soft soil mobility, allowing single instead of the usual dual rear wheels to be fitted. Other improvements include redesigned suspension, brakes and steering, a forward-tilting bonnet for easier maintenance and a wider three-man cab with a spring-mounted seat for the driver.

With these improvements it is expected that the vehicle will have a higher speed and a much reduced maintenance load.

DESCRIPTION

In the 1950s there were two basic models in this series, the M34 with single rear wheels and the M35 with dual rear wheels. Today the former is no longer in production although it still remains in service, especially with countries in Europe, the Far East and South America.

The layout of the basic cargo model is conventional with the engine at the front, two-door cab in the centre with a windscreen which can be folded forward onto the bonnet and a removable canvas top and the cargo area at the rear with a drop tailgate, removable bows, tarpaulin cover and troop seats down either side.

A wide range of kits is available including A-frame, alcohol evaporator, arctic, cargo body closure (arctic), central troop seats, electric brakes, fording, hardtop for cab, hoist and rail for installation in rear of vehicle for

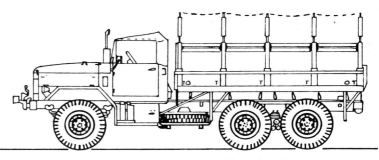

M35 (6 × 6) 2½-ton cargo truck with bows in position

carrying out minor repair work, ring mount for machine gun over cab, hot water personnel heater, fuel-burning personnel heater, power plant heater, slave cable and a thermal barrier. Many vehicles are fitted with a 4536 kg capacity winch which can be used to the front or rear of the vehicle, and has 61 metres of 13 mm diameter cable and two speeds forward and one speed in reverse.

VARIANTS

Repower package

NAPCO Industries Incorporated of Hopkins, Minnesota, has produced a repower package for this range of trucks, full details of which are given in the following entry.

Models with single rear wheels (no longer in production)

M34: cargo truck with an unladen weight of 5332 kg, chassis designated M44

M47: dump truck with an unladen weight of 6100 kg, chassis designated M57

Truck, maintenance: earth boring machine and pole setter V18A/MTQ, chassis M44

Truck, maintenance: telephone construction and maintenance V17A/MTQ, chassis M44

Models with dual rear wheels

M35: this is the basic member of the family and is based on the M45 chassis; current production model is designated the M35A2. The M35A2C (chassis M46A2C) is almost identical but has drop sides. Both drop sides and tailgate of this model are interchangeable with those of the M54A2C (5-ton) truck.

M36: this cargo truck is the long wheelbase version of

the M35 and its chassis is designated the M36. Current production model is the M36A2.

M48: tractor truck for towing semi-trailers, chassis designation M45, and is no longer in production.

M49: fuel tanker, current model the M49A2C (chassis M45A2), has an all-steel tank which holds 4542 litres of fuel for road travel or 2271 litres of fuel for cross-country travel. Fuel can be dispensed by gravity or pumped under pressure at a maximum rate of 303 litres per minute and the pump can also be used to refill the tank. The tanker can be fitted with bows and a tarpaulin cover to make detection more difficult.

M50: water tanker, current model the M50A3, has an aluminium tank which holds 3785 litres of water for road travel or 1893 litres of water for cross-country travel. Water can be dispensed by gravity or pumped under pressure at a maximum rate of 303 litres per minute and the pump can also be used to refill the tank. The tanker can be fitted with bows and a tarpaulin cover to make detection more difficult.

M59: dump truck, chassis designation M58, no longer in production.

M60: light wrecker, details of which will be found in the *Recovery vehicles* section (page 64).

M108: wrecker, details of which will be found in the *Recovery vehicles* section (page 64).

M109: shop van, chassis designated M45, current production model the M109A3, has a fully enclosed rear body and is used for a variety of roles such as workshop and maintenance.

M132: medical van, no longer in production.

M185: repair van, M45 chassis, no longer in production; late models were M185A3.

M275: tractor truck for towing semi-trailers on roads

M35A2 2½-ton (6 × 6) cargo truck (T J Gander)

M109A3 2½-ton (6 × 6) shop van (T J Gander)

weighing up to 16 329 kg and across country up to 7712 kg. Current production model is M275A2.

M292: shop van with extensible sides, no longer in production.

M342: dump truck, current production model is the M342A2 (chassis M45A2G) which can carry 1.9 cubic metres of soil.

M756A2: pipeline maintenance truck (chassis M45A2), fitted with rear winch, PTO and rear- or side-mounted A frame, removable cargo rack and sides.

M763: telephone maintenance truck.

M764: truck, maintenance, earth boring machine and pole setter, equipped with rear winch, PTO, boring machine. Pole setting is accomplished using derrick tube of boring machine and rear winch.

SPECIFICATIONS

Model	M35A2	M36A2	M49A2C	M50A3	M109A3	M342A2
Type	cargo	cargo	fuel	water	van	dump
Cab seating	1 + 2	1 + 2	1 + 2	1 + 2	1 + 2	1 + 2
Configuration	6 × 6	6 × 6	6 × 6	6 × 6	6 × 6	6 × 6
Weight (empty)	5900 kg	6900 kg	6500 kg	6644 kg	6800 kg	6800 kg
(loaded, road)	10 400 kg	11 500 kg	10 100 kg	10 408 kg	10 200 kg	11 300 kg
Weight on front axle (loaded)	2700 kg	3200 kg	2700 kg	2880 kg	3000 kg	3100 kg
Weight on rear axle (loaded)	7700 kg	8300 kg	7400 kg	7528 kg	7100 kg	8300 kg
Max load (road)	4535 kg	4535 kg	4542 (litres)	3785 (litres)	3401 kg	4535 kg
(cross country)	2268 kg	2268 kg	2271 (litres)	1893 (litres)	2268 kg	2268 kg
Towed load (road)	4535 kg	4535 kg	4535 kg	4535 kg	3628 kg	4535 kg
(cross country)	2721 kg	7721 kg	7721 kg	7721 kg	7721 kg	7721 kg
Load area	3·7 × 2·2 m	5·3 × 2·2 m	n/app	n/app	n/app	3·3 × 1·9 m
Length (without winch)	6·7 m	8·4 m	6·7 m	6·7 m	6·8 m	6·6 m
Width	2·4 m	2·4 m	2·4 m	2·4 m	2·4 m	2·4 m
Height (reduced)	2·1 m	2·1 m	2·3 m	2·4 m	3·3 m	2·1 m
(overall)	2·9 m	3·2 m	2·6 m	2·6 m	3·3 m	2·7 m
(load area)	1·32 m	1·4 m	n/app	n/app	1·3 m	1·3 m
Ground clearance (axles)	0·28 m	0·28 m	0·28 m	0·28 m	0·28 m	0·28 m
Track (front/rear)	1·721/1·778 m	1·721/1·778 m	1·721/1·778 m	1·721/1·778 m	1·721/1·778 m	1·721/1·778 m
Wheelbase	3·912 m	4·826 m	3·912 m	3·912 m	3·912 m	3·912 m
Angle of approach/departure	47°/40°	47°/24°	47°/40°	47°/40°	47°/40°	47°/70°
Max speed (road)	90 km/h	90 km/h	90 km/h	90 km/h	90 km/h	90 km/h
Range	480 km	480 km	480 km	480 km	480 km	480 km
Fuel capacity	189 litres	189 litres	189 litres	189 litres	189 litres	189 litres
Max gradient	60%	60%	60%	60%	60%	60%
Fording (without preparation)	0·76 m	0·76 m	0·76 m	0·76 m	0·76 m	0·76 m
(with preparation)	1·98 m	1·98 m	1·98 m	1·98 m	1·52 m	1·83 m
Engine	LDT-465-1C 6-cylinder in-line multi-fuel diesel developing 140 net hp at 2600 rpm					
Gearbox	all have a manual gearbox with 5 forward and 1 reverse gears					
Clutch	single dry plate is fitted to all models					
Transfer box	2-speed	2-speed	2-speed	2-speed	2-speed	2-speed
Steering	all have cam and twin lever type					
Turning radius	11 m	13·7 m	11 m	11 m	11 m	11 m
Suspension (front/rear)	semi-elliptical springs/semi-elliptical springs inverted					
Tyres	9.00 × 20	9.00 × 20	9.00 × 20	9.00 × 20	9.00 × 20	9.00 × 20
Brakes (main)	air over hydraulic	air over hydraulic	air over hydraulic	air over hydraulic	air over hydraulic	air over hydraulic
(parking)	internal/external	internal/external	internal/external	internal/external	internal/external	internal/external
Electrical system	24 V	24 V	24 V	24 V	24 V	24 V
Batteries	2	2	2	2	2	2

STATUS

Production. In service with USA and many other armed forces including Bolivia, Israel, South Korea, Lebanon, Morocco, Philippines, Saudi Arabia, Somalia, Spain (over 2000 of which have been re-engined), Thailand, Turkey and Zaïre.

MANUFACTURER

AM General Corporation, 14250 Plymouth Road, Detroit, Michigan 48232, USA.

NAPCO Industries Repower/Modernisation Packages

NAPCO offers repower/modernisation packages for many trucks of US military origin. This includes ¾-, 1-, 1¼- and 5-ton trucks. Versions of NAPCO truck repowering packages have been bought by countries on every continent and have been used to repower the complete vehicle fleets of several countries. In all cases the installations have been reviewed, tested and approved by NAPCO's own staff of repower engineers as well as the engine manufacturers.

NAPCO believes that repowering is a cost effective alternative to replacing a current inventory of 4 × 4 or 6 × 6 tactical trucks. Cross-country mobility is retained and the investment in existing trucks, spares inventories and maintenance facilities will not be lost. Logistic problems will not be compounded by the necessity of stocking and training to meet the new needs of a completely different vehicle. NAPCO also offers overhaul packages

for the vehicle drive train that matches the vehicle's power transmission system performance and reliability to that established by the new diesel engine.

M37 Truck, Cargo ¾-ton (4 × 4)

NAPCO Industries has designed and built a complete diesel conversion package for the M37 cargo truck and its derivative vehicles including the M42 command post, the M43 ambulance and the M201 maintenance truck. Replacing the original Dodge T245 six-cylinder petrol engine which developed 94 bhp at 3400 rpm with a NAPCO modified Mitsubishi six-cylinder diesel developing 100 bhp at 3700 rpm coupled to a Chrysler automatic transmission or a new four-speed manual transmission as part of a fully engineered repower package, returns the vehicle's systems to a like-new condition with all the added advantages of diesel power. This means lower fuel costs and reduced fuel consumption, reduced maintenance and an abundant supply of readily available spares. The automatic transmission reduces driver training and eliminates maintenance

problems caused by burned-out clutches and manual gear boxes. Complete overhaul packages have been developed for drive line items which are not replaced. Vehicle performance will be equal to or better than that of the original.

The NAPCO repower package kits contain everything for a complete installation including the new diesel engine, automatic transmission, radiators, air cleaner, instrument panel with new fuel gauge, engine temperature gauge, volt meter, speedometer and tachometer. Also included is an all-new, 12-volt electrical system including harnesses, driving lights and turn signals. All brackets, mounts, nuts, bolts and screws are provided.

Rebuild and overhaul kits have been developed to provide the parts to rebuild completely and overhaul the existing axles, transfer case, brakes, propeller shafts and suspension. Complete replacement sets for parts such as bearings, seals and gaskets, are supplied. Gears and shafts are supplied in proportions based on NAPCO's wide experience with vehicle repower and rebuild of the major item.

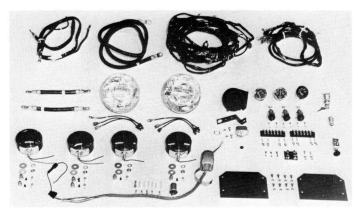

Electrical system kit for NAPCO M35 repowering package

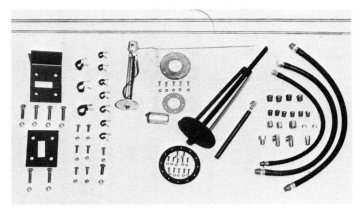

Fuel system kit for NAPCO M35 repowering package

M37 ¾-ton (4 × 4) cargo truck with NAPCO diesel conversion package

M715 1¼-ton (4 × 4) cargo truck showing NAPCO diesel conversion package

All parts of the repowered vehicle can be supported by NAPCO with new production parts identical or equivalent to the originals. It is possible using the NAPCO repower package and rebuild and overhaul kits to return deadlined or retired vehicles to active service with frontline units. Installation of the NAPCO package can be made using basic shop tools.

M601 Truck, Cargo 1-ton (4 × 4)
NAPCO has recently added a repower package for the M601 cargo truck. The package uses most of the same components as the M715 described below.

M715 Truck, Cargo 1¼-ton (4 × 4)
NAPCO has designed a repower package for the M715 cargo truck and its derivative vehicle, the M725 ambulance. The repower package for this truck is very similar to that used for the M37 except that the engine is turbocharged for a higher horsepower output. The new automatic transmission, air cleaner, radiator and electrical system guarantee long trouble-free service from the repowered truck.

M34, M35, M35A1, M35A2 and M602 Trucks, Cargo 2½-ton (6 × 6)
NAPCO's basic kit for the 2½-ton trucks listed above encompasses over 30 different truck types including dump, pole setting and instrument trucks and van bodies. This package is based on the NAPCO modified Detroit Diesel 4-53N. The basic engine model is currently in large-scale commercial production and is offered as original equipment by many US truck manufacturers. They are widely used by the US military forces in a variety of equipment. The 4-53N is a heavy duty diesel rated for a long trouble-free life. NAPCO's modification adapts this commercial engine for tactical use. It features replaceable cylinder liners, valve guides, seats and bearings throughout the basic engine. The NAPCO 2½-ton truck kits can be ordered in numerous optional configurations, including 12- or 24-volt electrical systems, manual or automatic transmissions, horizontal or vertical exhausts and turbocharged or naturally aspirated engines.

M211/M135 Truck, Cargo 2½-ton (6 × 6)
In addition to the widely known M34/35 series of 2½-ton trucks, NAPCO has engineered a conversion kit for this vehicle, utilising the 4-53N engine and a powershift transmission. It results in a vehicle with better performance and increased reliability especially off the road.

M52 Truck, Tractor, 5-ton (6 × 6)
NAPCO has developed a repower pack for the M52 (M61 chassis) 5-ton, 6 × 6 tractor truck which is also applicable to other members of the family including the M51 dump truck, the M54 cargo, the M55 long wheelbase cargo models, and the M62 and M543 wreckers.

The repowering package replaces the existing six-cylinder petrol engine with a Detroit Diesel 6V-53N two-cycle six-cylinder engine. The drive train package consists of all the parts necessary for the complete overhaul of the power train and brake system based on average mortality rates experienced by the US Army for this type of vehicle. When fitted with the Detroit Diesel 6V-53N the M52 has a maximum cruising range of 725 km compared to the 483 km of the original petrol-engined model.

DESCRIPTION
Included in the NAPCO repowering packages are all the conversion requirements for modifying or replacing the fuel, exhaust, cooling and electrical systems and other associated items. The various kits involved are as follows.

Engine kit
As well as the engine the kit includes a complete air cleaner assembly, modified flywheel, rocker cover vent assembly, engine mounts, throttle linkage assembly, new clutch, pressure plate, disc and all fittings, hoses, adaptors and gaskets. All the kits that use Detroit Diesel 53N series engines have a high commonality to other 53N series engines in military use such as the 6V53 in the M113A1.

Fuel system kit
The kit includes new fuel pump and lines to handle the diesel fuel for the compression-ignition type of engine, all filters, brackets, mounting hardware, gaskets and fuel lines necessary for conversion. This complete replacement is necessary not only because of the change in fuel, but also because of the different physical configuration of the new engine.

Exhaust system kit (standard)
The new exhaust system includes all clamps, flanges, tubing, mounting hardware, and muffler required. At the user's option the standard exhaust system kit can be replaced by a kit providing vertical exhaust. Both include all tubes, clamps, mounting hardware and silencer required for the installation.

Cooling system kit
A new radiator is included with shrouding, cap, tubing, hoses, clamps and mounting equipment necessary to accommodate the radiator assembly.

Electrical system kit
Converting to diesel power requires new gauges. This kit includes oil pressure, temperature, voltmeter, fuel level and air pressure gauges, as well as the necessary sending units. It also includes lights, horn, flashers, starter button and wiring harness.

Bonnet, bumpers and running board kit
This requires the modification of engine compartment side panel and bumpers. Parts and hardware required for the conversion are supplied.

Frame and brackets kit
The frame and brackets kit for mounting the new engine includes a front channel, clip front mounts, and new left rear engine frame bracket.

Body and cab kit
Included is the firewall modification, complete with hardware; the floorboard modifications and hardware, instrument panel and hardware, firewall modifications, emergency and engine stop cables.

Spring and shock absorber kit
This kit contains the U-bolts and spacers necessary to modify spring travel, and to prevent the front axle from coming into contact with the oil pan of the diesel engine.

Brakes kit
This kit provides parts to connect the new air compressor to the air intake system and the air lines of the truck.

For total conversion, NAPCO makes available a complete overhaul of the drive train and its component parts. To ensure complete performance reliability, all repair and overhaul requirements and parts for the front axle assembly, transmission assembly, transfer case assembly, rear axle assembly, suspension and drive shafts and service brakes are included.

SUMMARY
The original petrol engines of these vehicles were not designed for acceptable fuel economy, and even the more recent multi-fuel engines cannot match the life and reliability of modern diesel engines. Replacement with a

Detroit Diesel 4-53N engine will provide the following advantages, according to NAPCO:

decreased fuel consumption, featuring the unit injector type fuel system for economy, ease of service and an ability to use a wide range of diesel fuels without harmful effects;

greater productivity due to two-cycle design, and faster acceleration, which picks up the load more quickly and offers smoother engine performance;

the simplicity and decreased maintenance requirements of the Detroit Diesel 4-53N significantly increase reliability and assure less down time;

the quick availability of both maintenance parts and trained diesel mechanics assures continued operation and years of service life;

the diesel engine is easily serviced with simple hand tools for most repairs.

STATUS
Production.

MANUFACTURER
NAPCO Industries Incorporated, 1600 Second Street S, Hopkins, Minnesota 55343, USA.

Detroit Diesel 4-53N engine for NAPCO repowering package

M211 (6 × 6) 2½-ton Cargo Truck

DESCRIPTION
The M211 series of 6 × 6 2½-ton vehicles was developed in the late 1940s by the Truck and Bus Division of the General Motors Corporation at the same time as Reo developed the M34/M35 series of trucks in the same class. The M211 series is no longer in large scale use with the United States Army although it remains in service with other armies including Canada. The Canadian vehicles were assembled in Canada by General Motors at Oshawa, Ontario.

The chassis of the M211 is designated the M207 and the layout of the vehicle is conventional with the engine at the front, two-door cab in the centre with a windscreen which folds forward onto the bonnet and a removable canvas top and the cargo area at the rear with removable wooden sides, drop tailgate, removable bows and a tarpaulin cover. A winch with a capacity of 4536 kg can be mounted at the front of the vehicle and the M211 can also be fitted with a deep fording kit and a winterisation kit.

VARIANTS
Repower package
NAPCO Industries Incorporated of Hopkins, Minnesota, have developed repower packages to fit all the variants of this truck. Full details were given in the previous entry.
M214
Crane, chassis designated M207C as it has walking beam rear suspension.
M215
The official designation is Truck, Dump: 2½-ton, 6 × 6, M215. It is similar to M211 but has a wheelbase of 3·048 m + 1·219 m and a 303M hydromatic transmission. The M215 can carry 4083 kg of soil on roads or 1700 kg across country.
M217
Its official designation is Truck, Tank: Fuel Servicing: 2½-ton, 6 × 6, 1200-gallon, M217. The M217 has a capacity of 4542 litres and is used to refuel vehicles in the field. The M217C is fitted with a separator kit and is used to refuel aircraft and helicopters.
M218
This is a light wrecker based on the M207C chassis, used to tow and recover damaged and disabled vehicles.
M220
The official designation is Truck, Van: Shop, 2½-ton, 6 × 6, M220. It has a two-man fully enclosed cab with a fixed roof and a fully enclosed body at the rear which has twin doors at the back and three windows in each side, with sliding blackout panels. Basic specifications are loaded weight 10 450 kg, empty weight 6842 kg, towed load on roads 3629 kg and towed load across country 2772 kg.
M221
Its official designation is Truck, Tractor: 2½-ton, 6 × 6, M221. It is used to tow semi-trailers weighing up to 16 330 kg or up to 7711 kg across country. It has the same engine as the M211 but the chassis of the M215. Unladen weight is 4895 kg.
M222
The official designation is Truck, Tank: Water, 2½-ton, 6 × 6, 1000-gallon, M222. The tanker consists of two

M211 (6 × 6) 2½-ton cargo truck (US Army)

M135CDN (6 × 6) 2½-ton truck (T J Gander)

compartments and is aluminium with steel skirting. The 3785-litre water tank is insulated with fibreglass and has a built-in heating chamber. There are manhole openings for an immersion heater. Mounted at the rear of the vehicle is a pump with a capacity of 265 litres per minute.
M135
This is a cargo truck, similar to the M211 but with single

instead of dual rear wheels; the chassis is designated the M133. It can carry the same load as the M211 but has an unladen weight of 5778 kg.

Canadian trucks have a CDN suffix, for example cargo truck M135CDN, cargo truck M211CDN, dump truck M216CDN (with single instead of the dual rear wheels of the American M215), shop/van M220CDN and water tanker M222CDN. The Canadians have some vehicles fitted with a hydraulic crane for loading and have adapted the vehicle to carry special equipment, for example the Canadair AN/USD-501 reconnaissance drone. The Canadians also have a tractor truck model designated the M135CDN with single rear wheels.

SPECIFICATIONS (M221 Truck)
Cab seating: 1 + 1
Configuration: 6 × 6
Weight:
  (empty) 5974 kg
  (loaded, cross-country) 8242 kg
Max load:
  (road) 4536 kg
  (cross country) 2268 kg
Max towed load:
  (road) 4536 kg
  (cross country) 2722 kg
Load area: 3·733 × 2·38 m

Length: 6·527 m
Width: 2·438 m
Height:
  (cab) 2·438 m
  (tarpaulin) 2·847 m
Track:
  (front) 1·755 m
  (rear) 1·854 m
Wheelbase: 3·352 m + 1·219 m
Angle of approach/departure: 42°/37°
Max speed: (road) 88·5 km/h
Range: 483 km
Fuel capacity: 212 litres
Max gradient: 60%
Fording:
  (without preparation) 0·762 m
  (with preparation) 1·981 m
Engine: General Motors model 302 6-cylinder petrol developing 130 hp at 3200 rpm
Gearbox: hydromatic with 4 forward and 1 reverse gears in both high and low ranges

Transfer box: single speed
Steering: cam and twin lever
Turning radius: 10·515 m
Suspension:
  (front) semi-elliptical springs
  (rear) semi-elliptical springs, inverted
Tyres: 9.00 × 20
Number of tyres: 10 + 1 spare
Brakes:
  (main) air/hydraulic
  (parking) mechanical
Electrical system: 24 V
Batteries: 2 × 12 V

STATUS
Production complete. In limited service with the US Army, still in service with Canada and other armed forces.

MANUFACTURER
Truck and Bus Division of General Motors Corporation.

M656 (8 × 8) 5-ton Truck

DEVELOPMENT
The M656 was developed in the early 1960s by the Special Military Vehicles Operations of the Ford Motor Company as a result of the MOVER study of military vehicle requirements. Specific major requirements in order of priority were performance, durability, reliability, minimal and easy maintenance, configuration, transportability and kit requirements. Prototypes were known as the XM656 and were classified as standard A in April 1966. In January 1968 Ford received a contract for 500 vehicles at a cost of $26·5 million and first production vehicles were completed late in 1968. Final deliveries were made in October 1969. The M656 is used almost exclusively for the Martin Marietta Aerospace Pershing 1A battlefield support missile.

DESCRIPTION
The aluminium forward control cab has a windscreen which can be folded forward onto the front of the vehicle and a removable canvas top. The rear cargo area is also aluminium and has drop sides and a drop tailgate. The drop sides have integral troop seats which fold down flush with the sides when not required and can also be used as steps to assist in loading the vehicle with small items of cargo. The rear tailgate has integral steps. Typical loads include 77 rounds of 155 mm ammunition, 42 rounds of 8 inch ammunition, 38 rounds of 175 mm ammunition, three type 1 CONEX containers or one type 2 CONEX container. If required, bows and a tarpaulin cover can be fitted over the rear cargo area.

The M656 is fully amphibious being propelled in the water by its wheels. Before entering the water seals are inflated around the cab and cargo openings. A 9072 kg capacity winch with 60·9 metres of cable can be mounted at the front of the vehicle for recovery operations.

A variety of kits were developed for the M656 including arctic, air brake hand control, cargo box height extensions, machine-gun ring mount, slinging kit, windscreen demisting kit and a 100 amp alternator.

VARIANTS
M656
This is fitted with programmer-test station/power station for use with the Pershing 1A system.
M656
Fitted with radio terminal and inflatable antenna for use with Pershing 1A system.
M757
(Development designation XM757) tractor for towing semi-trailer with Pershing 1A missile. The trailer acts also as an erector/launcher for the missile.
M791
(Development designation XM791) battery control centre (with expanding sides) for use with Pershing 1A system.
  Projected variants included a dump truck and a wrecker.

SPECIFICATIONS (M656 truck)
Cab seating: 1 + 1
Configuration: 8 × 8

Weight:
  (empty, with winch) 7847 kg
  (loaded, cross country) 12 564 kg
Max load:
  (road) 10 160 kg
  (cross country) 4536 kg
Towed load: 5897 kg
Load area: 4·572 × 2·235 m
Length: (without winch) 7·06 m
Width: 2·438 m
Height:
  (cab) 2·704 m
  (tarpaulin) 2·946 m
  (reduced) 1·981 m
  (load area) 1·346 m
Ground clearance: 0·304 m
Track: 1·961 m
Wheelbase: 1·473 m + 2·286 m + 1·473 m
Angle of approach/departure: (without winch) 55°/64°
Max speed: (road) 80·46 km/h
Range: 515 km
Fuel capacity: 303 litres
Max gradient: 60%
Max side slope: 40%
Fording: amphibious
Engine: Model LDS-465-2 6-cylinder liquid-cooled turbo-charged multi-fuel diesel developing 200 bhp at 2800 rpm
Gearbox: TX-200-6 fully automatic with 6 forward and 1 reverse gears
Transfer box: single speed
Steering: worm and roller, power-assisted
Turning radius: 12·2 m
Suspension: bogie type with parallelogram torque arms and tapered 3-leaf springs
Tyres: 16.00 × 20
Number of tyres: 8 + 1 spare
Brakes:
  (main) air
  (parking) mechanical
Electrical system: 24 V
Batteries: 2 × 6 TN

STATUS
Production complete. In service only with the US Army.

MANUFACTURER
Ford Motor Company, Special Military Vehicles Operations, PO Box 2053, Dearborn, Michigan 48121, USA.

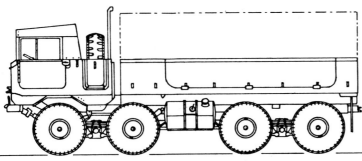

M656 (8 × 8) 5-ton truck

XM757 (8 × 8) tractor towing semi-trailer carrying Pershing 1A missile

XM791 (8 × 8) battery control centre in travelling order

M54 (6 × 6) 5-ton Cargo Truck Series

DEVELOPMENT

The M54 series of 6 × 6 5-ton trucks was developed in the immediate post-Second World War period to replace vehicles in the 4-, 5-, 6- and 7½-ton class. First production models were completed by Diamond T and International Harvester in 1950 with later production being undertaken by Kaiser Jeep (now AM General) and Mack. The first vehicles were powered by a six-cylinder petrol engine, which was replaced by a six-cylinder diesel engine in 1962, in turn replaced by a six-cylinder multi-fuel engine the following year. The multi-fuel engine was a super-charged version of the LD465 as used in the 2½-ton truck, which developed 230 hp but was not successful as it became known as The AM General Corporation replaced this with a commercial engine and the series then became known as the M809 range, for which there is a separate entry.

A wide range of kits was developed for the M54 series including A-frame, air brake, electric brake, engine heater, deep fording, hardtop, machine-gun mount, personnel heater, thermal barrier and a front-mounted winch with a capacity of 9072 kg.

DESCRIPTION

The layout of the basic cargo version is conventional with the engine at the front, two-door cab in the centre with a windscreen which can be folded forward onto the bonnet, a removable canvas top and the welded steel cargo area at the rear, with fixed sides, removable side racks, troop seats, removable bows and a tarpaulin cover.

VARIANTS

Repower package
NAPCO Industries Incorporated of Hopkins, Minnesota, have developed a repower package for the truck series. Full details were given earlier in this section.

AM General Retrofit Package
AM General has designed a retrofit kit which will upgrade M54 Series vehicles to an M809 Series configuration. These kits, now in production for the US Marine Corps, include a power pack, frame, steering system, brake system, fuel and exhaust system, and electrical and sheet metal components to achieve the M809 configuration.

The power pack includes a Cummins NHC 250 diesel engine, radiator and cooling lines, a 24 volt alternator and starter, clutch, flywheel, five-speed transmission and an air cleaner assembly. The frame includes rails and crossmembers for the new power pack while the steering includes steering gear, a power steering pump, power assist cylinder and hoses. The brake system includes air reservoir tanks, air and hydraulic lines and couplings, adaptors and mounting hardware. Included in the fuel system are a 295-litre tank, a cold start primer, filters, fuel lines and a new accelerator linkage. Exhaust pipes, a muffler exhaust stack, heat shield, gaskets and other hardware make up the exhaust system and the new electrical system contains wiring harnesses, bulbs and dials, batteries and cables and a new battery box. The kit is complete with a new hood, fenders, instrument panel and other items.

All items in the kit have been fitted to US military vehicles and tested at the Aberdeen Proving Grounds, Maryland.

Truck, Cargo, 5-ton, M41 (6 × 6)
This has single instead of dual rear wheels and can carry 6804 kg of cargo and tow a 13 608 kg trailer on roads or 6804 kg across country. It is powered by a Continental R6602 six-cylinder OHV petrol engine which develops 196 bhp at 2800 rpm, coupled to a five-speed gearbox and a two-speed transfer box.

Truck, Dump, 5-ton, M51 (6 × 6)
This has a rear tipping all-steel dump body and is based on the M61 chassis, and can also be used to carry cargo. The engine is the same as in the M41 and is coupled to a Spicer Model 6352 gearbox, Timken Model T-138 two-speed transfer box and a Spicer WND-61 PTO mounted on the transmission and powers the front-mounted winch (when fitted) and the hydraulic dump body mechanism. The equivalent vehicle in the M809 series is the M817. The M51A1 has a Mack model ENDT-673 six-cylinder diesel which develops 211 bhp at 2100 rpm and the M51A2 has an LD465 six-cylinder turbocharged multi-fuel which develops 230 hp.

Truck, Tractor, 5-ton, M52 (6 × 6)
The chassis is designated the M61 and is powered by the same engine as the M41. Later models were the M52A1 and M52A2 with diesel and multi-fuel engines respectively. The M52 can tow a semi-trailer on roads weighing up to 11 340 kg or across country up to 6804 kg. The equivalent vehicle in the M809 series is the M818.

Truck, Cargo, 5-ton, M54 (6 × 6)
This is the basic cargo model and its chassis is designated the M40. It has the same engine as the M41 with later models being the M54A1 (diesel) and M54A2 (multi-fuel). The equivalent in the M809 series is the M813.

Truck, Cargo, 5-ton, M55 (6 × 6)
This is the long wheelbase cargo model of the M54 and is based on the M63 chassis. It has the same engine as the M41 with later models being the M55A1 (diesel) and M55A2 (multi-fuel). The equivalent vehicle in M809 series is the M814.

Truck, Wrecker, Medium, 5-ton, M62 (6 × 6)
This is based on the M40C chassis with a walking beam rear suspension and details will be found in the *Recovery vehicles* section (pages 64 and 65).

Truck, Cargo, Van, 5-ton, M64 (6 × 6)
This has a fully enclosed rear body.

Truck, Tractor, Wrecker, 5-ton, M246 (6 × 6)
This is based on the M63C chassis and can be used for recovery operations as well as towing trailers. Details will be found in the *Recovery vehicles* section (pages 64 and 65).

Truck, Van, Expansible, 5-ton, M291 (6 × 6)
This is fitted with a fully enclosed rear van body with sides which are extended when the vehicle is stationary. Later models were the M291A1 (diesel) and M291A2 (multi-fuel). The equivalent vehicle in the M809 series is the M820.

Truck, Stake, Bridging, 5-ton, M328 (6 × 6)
This is used to carry bridge components. Later models were the M328A1 (diesel) and M328A2 (multi-fuel). The equivalent vehicle in the M809 series is the M821.

Truck, Wrecker, Medium, 5-ton, M543 (6 × 6)
This is based on the M40C chassis with walking beam rear suspension. Later models were the M543A1 (diesel) and M543A2 (multi-fuel). The equivalent vehicle in the M809 series is the M816, details of which will be found in the *Recovery vehicles* section (pages 65 and 66).

Truck, Bolster, 5-ton, M748 (6 × 6)
Later models were designated the M748A1 (diesel) and M748A2 (multi-fuel). The equivalent vehicle in the M809 series is the M815.

Chassis, Truck, 5-ton, M139 (6 × 6)
This chassis has been used for a variety of applications. The basic M139 is used for carrying bridging equipment and the M139C has been designed to carry the Honest John surface-to-surface rocket. The M139D has a different rear axle and jack bracket supports and both the M139C and M139D are equipped with high reduction axles to increase tractive power and a modified front cross-member. The Honest John has been replaced in most countries by the Lance but it remains in service

M51 (6 × 6) 5-ton dump truck (Larry Provo)

Re-engined M41 5-ton truck (6 × 6) of Israeli Army (Kensuke Ebata)

M54A2 (6 × 6) 5-ton cargo truck with bows stowed to rear of cab

M52 (6 × 6) 5-ton tractor truck (T J Gander)

with a few countries including Greece, South Korea and Turkey. There are two types of Honest John launcher. The M289 (M139D chassis) launcher has a long launcher rail which extends over the cab and is supported by an A-type frame while the M386 launcher has a short launcher rail and no frame.

STATUS
Production complete. In service with the US Army and most other armies that have received American aid including Spain (many of which have been re-engined), Turkey and South Korea.

MANUFACTURER
Last manufacturer of the M54 series was AM General Corporation, 14250 Plymouth Road, Detroit, Michigan 48232, USA.

Similar vehicles have been manufactured in Italy (as the CP 56) and Spain.

SPECIFICATIONS

Designation	M51	M52	M54	M55
Type	dump	tractor	cargo	cargo (LWB)
Cab seating	1 + 2	1 + 2	1 + 2	1 + 2
Configuration	6 × 6	6 × 6	6 × 6	6 × 6
Weight (empty)	9970 kg	8616 kg	8732 kg	10 915 kg
(loaded, road)	19 042 kg	19 956 kg	18 119 kg	20 146 kg
Weight on front axle (loaded, road)	4112 kg	—	4347 kg	—
Weight on rear axles (loaded, road)	15 088 kg	—	13 807 kg	—
Max load (road)	9072 kg	n/app	9072 kg	9072 kg
(cross country)	4536 kg	n/app	4536 kg	4536 kg
Towed load (road)	13 608 kg	24 948 kg	13 608 kg	13 608 kg
(cross country)	6804 kg	13 608 kg	6804 kg	6804 kg
Load area	3·175 × 2·082 m	n/app	4·267 × 2·235 m	6·15 × 2·235 m
Length	7·146 m	6·933 m	7·974 m	9·797 m
Width	2·463 m	2·463 m	2·463 m	2·463 m
Height (overall)	2·809 m	2·638 m	2·946 m	2·946 m
Ground clearance	0·267 m	0·267 m	0·267 m	0·267 m
Track (front/rear)	1·869/1·828 m	1·869/1·828 m	1·869/1·828 m	1·869/1·828 m
Wheelbase	3·555 m + 1·371 m	3·555 m + 1·371 m	3·86 m + 1·371 m	4·775 m + 1·371 m
Angle of approach/departure	52·5°/69°	52·5°/69°	37°/38°	37°/23°
Max speed (road)	84 km/h	84 km/h	84 km/h	84 km/h
Range	785 km	483 km	344 km	344 km
Fuel capacity	416 litres	416 litres	295 litres	295 litres
Max gradient	70%	77%	50%	65%
Fording (without preparation)	0·762 m	0·762 m	0·762 m	0·762 m
(with preparation)	1·981 m	n/app	1·981 m	1·981 m
Gearbox	manual with 5 forward and 1 reverse gears			
Clutch	single dry plate	single dry plate	single dry plate	single dry plate
Transfer box	2-speed	2-speed	2-speed	2-speed
Steering	cam and lever	cam and lever	cam and lever	cam and lever
Tyres	11.00 × 20	11.00 × 20	11.00 × 20	11.00 × 20
Brakes	all have hydraulic brakes, air actuated and mechanical parking brakes			
Electrical system	24 V	24 V	24 V	24 V
Batteries	2	2	2	2

M809 (6 × 6) 5-ton Cargo Truck Series

DEVELOPMENT
The M809 series of 6 × 6 5-ton cargo trucks is similar to the older M54 series fitted with a diesel engine in place of the multi-fuel engine by the AM General Corporation under a product engineering development and test programme.

AM General Corporation started production of the M809 series in 1970 and by the middle of 1980 had completed some 38 000 vehicles.

Further development of the M809 series by AM General, under engineering contract with the US Army, has resulted in the much improved M939 series for which there is a separate entry.

DESCRIPTION
The chassis of the vehicle consists of two rail type beams with six reinforced cross-members. Both front and rear axles are of the hypoid, single-speed, double-reduction type. The layout is conventional with the engine at the front, two-door cab in the centre with a windscreen which can be folded flat against the bonnet and a removable canvas top, and the cargo area at the rear. The basic cargo model has an all-steel rear cargo body with drop sides, removable bows, tarpaulin cover and troop seats down either side which enable 18 fully equipped troops to be carried.

There are three basic chassis in the series, the M809 (used for the M813, M813A1, M816 and M815), the M810 (used for the M817 and M818) and the M811/M812 (used for the M814, M819, M820 and M821). A variety of kits is available for the range including A-frame, air brake, closure hard top, deep water fording, level wind device, slave receptacle, thermal barrier, water personnel heater, winterisation personnel heater kit and a winterisation power plant kit. All models except the M820 can be fitted with a winch at the front.

M809 series vehicles can be fitted with the Enhanced Mobility System (EMS) for increased mobility over sand, mud and snow. See separate entry for details.

VARIANTS
M813 (Cargo Truck, 5-ton, 6 × 6)
This is the basic cargo model as described above and can carry 4535 kg of cargo across country and 9070 kg of cargo on roads. The foldable seats enable 26 fully equipped troops to be carried.

M813A1 (Dropside, Cargo Truck, 5-ton, 6 × 6)
This is similar to the M813 but has drop sides as well as a drop tailgate.

M814 (Long Cargo Truck, 5-ton, 6 × 6)
This is the long wheelbase model and can be delivered with removable bows and a tarpaulin cover.

M815 (Bolster Truck, 5-ton, 6 × 6)
This has the M809 chassis and can carry a maximum load of 4536 kg across country or 9072 kg on roads. Towed load is identical to the M813 cargo truck.

M816 (Wrecker, Truck, 5-ton, 6 × 6)
Details of this vehicle are given in the Recovery vehicles section (pages 65 and 66).

M817 (Dump Truck, 5-ton, 6 × 6)
This has an all-steel 3·8 cubic metre capacity rear dump body which can be fitted with bows and a tarpaulin cover.

M818 (Tractor, Truck, 5-ton, 6 × 6)
This has both a fifth wheel and a pintle tow hook and can tow semi-trailers weighing up to 24 970 kg on roads or 17 025 kg across country.

M819 (Tractor, Wrecker, 5-ton, 6 × 6)
Details of this vehicle are given in the Recovery vehicles section (pages 65 and 66).

M820 (Van, Expansible, Truck, 5-ton, 6 × 6)
This is provided with a fully enclosed body at the rear which is 2·1 metres wide and 1·9 metres high in its normal position. When static the sides of the van are extended either side and the interior is then 4·2 metres wide. Access to the body is via steps at the rear.

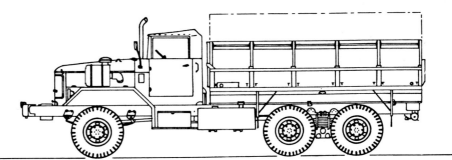

M813 (6 × 6) 5-ton cargo truck with winch

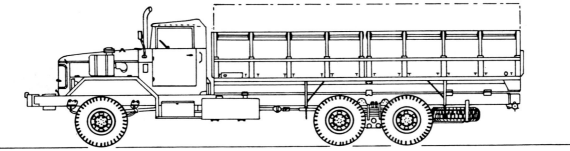

M814 (6 × 6) 5-ton cargo truck, long wheelbase, with winch

M821 (Bridge Transport, 5-ton, 6 × 6)
This is used to carry bridging components and is based
on the M812 chassis.

Ribbon Bridge Carrier and Launching Vehicle
An M809 chassis is also used to carry and launch the
Ribbon Bridge system as well as carrying and launching
the 27 ft bridge erection boat. Illustrations of both of
these vehicles will be found in the *Bridging systems*
section (pages 118 and 119).

STATUS
In production. In service with the US Army and other
armed forces including South Korea, Lebanon, Philippines, Saudi Arabia, Somalia, Spain, Thailand and
Zaïre.

MANUFACTURER
AM General Corporation, 14250 Plymouth Road,
Detroit, Michigan 48232, USA.

*M813 (6 × 6) 5-ton cargo truck fitted with refuelling
equipment (T J Gander)*

M817 (6 × 6) 5-ton dump truck

M820 (6 × 6) van, expansible (Larry Provo)

M820A1 5-ton (6 × 6) expansible van without windows

M809 5-ton (6 × 6) water tanker

M813A1 cargo/dropside 5-ton (6 × 6) truck

M809 5-ton (6 × 6) truck fitted with platform body for air compressor

SPECIFICATIONS

Specifications relate to a vehicle without winch, with the exception of the M817 which is fitted with a winch as standard equipment. All other vehicles, except M820, can be fitted with a front-mounted winch. When fitted with a front-mounted winch the vehicles have an angle of approach of 34 degrees.

Designation	M813	M813A1	M814	M817	M818	M820
Type	cargo	cargo	cargo (LWB)	dump	tractor	van
Cab seating	1 + 2	1 + 2	1 + 2	1 + 2	1 + 2	1 + 2
Configuration	6 × 6	6 × 6	6 × 6	6 × 6	6 × 6	6 × 6
Weight (empty)	9733 kg	10 043 kg	11 297 kg	10 776 kg	9 202 kg	12 474 kg
(loaded, road)	18 985 kg	18 993 kg	20 549 kg	20 028 kg	20 349 kg	29 459 kg
Weight on front axle (loaded)	5015 kg	5016 kg	5326 kg	4981 kg	4950 kg	4936 kg
Weight on rear axles (loaded)	13 969 kg	13 976 kg	15 223 kg	15 047 kg	15 399 kg	14 523 kg
Max load (road)	9070 kg	9070 kg	9070 kg	9070 kg	n/app	6803 kg
(cross country)	4535 kg	4535 kg	4535 kg	4535 kg	n/app	2268 kg
Towed load (road)	13 620 kg	13 620 kg	13 620 kg	13 620 kg	24 943 kg	13 620 kg
(cross country)	6802 kg	6802 kg	6802 kg	6802 kg	17 007 kg	6802 kg
Load area	4·3 × 2·2 m	4·3 × 2·2 m	6·2 × 2·2 m	3·2 × 2·1 m	n/app	5·2 × 2·1 m
Length	7·652 m	7·652 m	9·609 m	6·86 m	6·71 m	9·144 m
Width	2·464 m	2·464 m	2·464 m	2·464 m	2·464 m	2·483 m
Height (overall)	2·946 m	2·946 m	2·946 m	2·946 m	2·946 m	3·467 m
(reduced)	2·172 m	2·172 m	2·172 m	2·832 m	2·172 m	3·467 m
(load area)	1·4 m	1·4 m	1·4 m	n/app	n/app	n/app
Ground clearance (axles)	0·295 m	0·295 m	0·295 m	0·295 m	0·295 m	0·295 m
Track (front/rear)	1·88/1·829 m	1·88/1·829 m	1·88/1·829 m	1·9/1·829 m	1·9/1·829 m	1·9/1·829 m
Wheelbase	3·86 m + 1·371 m	3·86 m + 1·371 m	4·775 m+ 1·371 m	3·55 m + 1·371 m	3·55 m+ 1·371 m	4·775 m+ 1·371 m
Angle of approach/departure	46°/35°	46°/35°	46°/23.5°	34°/69°	45°/69°	46°/24°
Max speed (road)	84 km/h	84 km/h	84 km/h	84 km/h	84 km/h	84 km/h
Range	563 km	563 km	563 km	772 km	563 km	563 km
Fuel capacity	295 litres	295 litres	295 litres	295 litres	295 litres	295 litres
Max gradient (without towed load)	67%	67%	61%	61%	60%	65%
Max gradient (with towed load)	42%	42%	38%	31%	42%	41%
Max side slope (cross country)	20%	20%	20%	20%	20%	20%
Fording (without preparation)	0·76 m	0·76 m	0·76 m	0·76 m	0·76 m	0·76 m
(with preparation)	1·98 m	1·98 m	1·98 m	1·98 m	1·98 m	1·98 m
Engine	all powered by a NHC-250 6-cylinder in-line diesel developing 240 hp at 2100 rpm					
Gearbox	all have manual gearbox with 5 forward and 1 reverse gears					
Clutch	single dry plate	single dry plate	single dry plate	single dry plate	single dry plate	single dry plate
Transfer box	2-speed	2-speed	2-speed	2-speed	2-speed	2-speed
Steering	power-assisted	power-assisted	power-assisted	power-assisted	power-assisted	power-assisted
Turning radius	12·75 m	12·75 m	14·3 m	12·75 m	12·75 m	14·53 m
Suspension (front/rear)	semi-elliptical springs/semi-elliptical springs, inverted					
Tyres	11.00 × 20	11.00 × 20	11.00 × 20	11.00 × 20	11.00 × 20	11.00 × 20
Number of tyres	10 + 1 spare	10 + 1 spare	10 + 1 spare	10 + 1 spare	10 + 1 spare	10 + 1 spare
Brakes	main, air over hydraulic. Parking, dual grip on transfer case					
Electrical system	24 V	24 V	24 V	24 V	24 V	24 V
Batteries	4	4	4	4	4	4

M939 (6 × 6) 5-ton Cargo Truck

DEVELOPMENT

When the M809 was type classified it was intended that a product-improvement programme would be carried out in the areas of transmission, transfer case and brakes. Extensive testing of the M809 series in 1970 had shown that product improvements in these three aeas would be most beneficial. The programme however was shelved when the US Army withdrew from Viet-Nam but was reinstituted in 1975.

The M939 series have now completed more than 230 000 km of testing, which has shown that although initially more expensive than the current M809 series, cost (lifecycle) will be the same as that for existing vehicles.

In October 1979 the M939 (6 × 6) 5-ton cargo truck was type classified for inclusion in Army field units. In April 1981 AM General Corporation was awarded a contract for 11 394 M939 (6 × 6) 5-ton trucks by the US Army Tank Automotive Command. The total value of the five-year contract is $628·5 million. In addition the Army has a 100 per cent option which would increase its value to well over $1000 million. Production began in the first half of 1982 at AM General's plant at South Bend, Indiana. The M939 series became available for export during late 1983.

As of early 1981 the US Army owned 33 648 5-ton

(6 × 6) trucks of which 1915 were over 15 years old. Total requirement is for 58 594 vehicles.

DESCRIPTION

The M939 is essentially the existing M809 series improved in three major areas, transmission, transfer case and brake system. The existing M809's transmission and transfer case are under capacity and mismatched to the engine/axle ratio and performance requirements. There is no way to prevent the engine from overspeeding (rpm too high) or labouring in many gear ratio selections. The M939 has a fully automatic transmission that eliminates these problems, and it also requires less driver training, cuts fuel, is more reliable/ durable, lessens driver fatigue and improves safety.

The new transfer case is pressure- rather than splash-lubricated. The driver controls the engagement of the front wheels for 6 × 6 drive with an air system, eliminating a mechanical sprague clutch which frequently failed. The transfer case on the M939 can be shifted from either range while the vehicle is moving.

Tests have shown that the full air brakes on the M939 have four times the brakeshoe life of the air-over-hydraulic brakes on the current M809. The air brakes are self-adjusting and are backed by fail-safe mechanical spring brakes.

The M939 is the first tactical truck to meet Surgeon General standards for noise in the cab even with the windows open, which was achieved by relocating intake/exhaust ports to behind the cab.

The front-mounted winch is hydraulically driven and stops when overloaded and restarts when the overload is removed. The older mechanically-driven winches used on the current M809 require shear-pin replacement when similarly overloaded.

The bonnet and bumpers tilt forward so maintenance can be carried out from the ground, whereas even opening the M809's bonnet necessitates climbing onto the bumpers.

Flat tyres are replaced using a boom just behind the cab. The cab now holds three people, the current M809 only two.

The M939 is the first truck built with special connectors for use with the Army's new diagnostic equipment (STE/ICE). This will encourage the use of test equipment, cut maintenance time and eliminate incorrect replacements based on poor diagnosis.

The M939 Series will be manufactured for international use with AM General's Enhanced Mobility System (EMS) which is a central tyre inflation/deflation system that provides trucks with greater mobility in mud, sand and snow (see following entry).

M929 (6 × 6) 5-ton dump truck

M934 (6 × 6) Expansible Van with windows

VARIANTS

The complete listing of variants of the basic M939 is as follows:

M923: dropside cargo
M924: cargo; equivalent to M814

M925: dropside cargo with winch
M926: cargo with winch
M927: long wheelbase cargo
M928: long wheelbase cargo with winch
M929: dump truck; equivalent to M817

M930: dump truck with winch
M931: tractor
M932: tractor with winch
M933: tractor wrecker with winch
M934: expansible body
M935: expansible van body
M936: wrecker with winch
M939: chassis with or without winch
M939: chassis with winch
M940: chassis with winch
M941: chassis without winch
M941: chassis with winch
M942: long wheelbase chassis with or without winch
M943: long wheelbase chassis with winch
M944: long wheelbase chassis
M945: long wheelbase chassis with winch

The following kits will be available for the M939 series of truck: air brake, automatic chemical alarm, deep water fording, bow and tarpaulin cover, electric brake, engine coolant heater, front and rear lifting points, fuel burning heater, hard top closure, machine gun mount, radiator cover, hood and rifle mounting.

STATUS

In production for the US Army.

MANUFACTURER

AM General Corporation, 14250 Plymouth Road, Detroit, Michigan 48232, USA.

M923 (6 × 6) dropside cargo truck, part of M939 range

SPECIFICATIONS

Model	M923	M924	M925	M926	M927	M928	M929
Body	dropside	cargo	dropside	cargo	LWB cargo	LWB cargo	dump
Winch	no	no	yes	yes	no	yes	no
Cab seating	1 + 2	1 + 2	1 + 2	1 + 2	1 + 2	1 + 2	1 + 2
Configuration	6 × 6	6 × 6	6 × 6	6 × 6	6 × 6	6 × 6	6 × 6
Weight (empty)	9797 kg	10 156 kg	10 142 kg	10 433 kg	11 022 kg	11 526 kg	10 809 kg
Payload	4540 kg	4540 kg	4540 kg	4540 kg	4540 kg	4540 kg	4540 kg
Towed load	6810 kg	6810 kg	6810 kg	6810 kg	6810 kg	6810 kg	6810 kg
Length	7·741 m	7·741 m	8·293 m	8·293 m	9·672 m	10·218 m	6·934 m
Width	2·476 m	2·476 m	2·476 m	2·476 m	2·476 m	2·476 m	2·476 m
Height	2·946 m	2·946 m	2·946 m	2·946 m	2·946 m	2·946 m	3·05 m
Track (front)	1·905 m	1·905 m	1·905 m	1·905 m	1·905 m	1·905 m	1·905 m
(rear)	1·829 m	1·829 m	1·829 m	1·829 m	1·829 m	1·829 m	1·829 m
Wheelbase	4·547 m	4·547 m	4·547 m	4·547 m	5·461 m	5·461 m	4·242 m
Angle of approach/departure	46°/37°	46°/37°	31°/37°	31°/37°	46°/22·5°	31°/22·5°	46°/70·5°
Ground clearance	0·27 m	0·27 m	0·27 m	0·27 m	0·27 m	0·27 m	0·27 m
Gradient	60%	60%	60%	60%	60%	60%	60%
Side slope	20%	20%	20%	20%	20%	20%	20%
Max speed	84 km/h	84 km/h	84 km/h	84 km/h	84 km/h	84 km/h	84 km/h
Range (cruising)	563 km	563 km	563 km	563 km	563 km	563 km	772 km
(cruising, towed load)	483 km	483 km	483 km	483 km	483 km	483 km	644 km
Fording	0·76 m	0·76 m	0·76 m	0·76 m	0·76 m	0·76 m	0·76 m
Fording with kit	1·98 m	1·98 m	1·98 m	1·98 m	1·98 m	1·98 m	1·98 m
Engine	Cummins NHC 250 6-cylinder 4-cycle 14-litre diesel developing 240 hp at 2100 rpm						
Gearbox	Detroit Diesel Allison MT654CR 5-speed automatic						
Transfer box	2-speed with ratios 732:1/1·79:1						
Steering	Ross HFB 64 power-assisted with belt driven Eaton pump						
Turning radius	12·75 m	12·75 m	12·9 m	12·9 m	14·3 m	14·53 m	12·75 m
Suspension	Rockwell standard leaf springs front and rear						
Tyres	11.00 × 20 12-ply non-directional cross-country						
Brakes (main)	Rockwell Stopmaster air actuated						
Electrical system	24 V	24 V	24 V	24 V	24 V	24 V	24 V
Alternator	60 A	60 A	60 A	60 A	60 A	60 A	60 A

Model	M930	M931	M932	M933	M934	M935	M936
Body	dump	tractor	tractor	wrecker	expansible	expansible	wrecker
Winch	yes	no	yes	yes	no	no	yes
Cab seating	1 + 2	1 + 2	1 + 2	1 + 2	1 + 2	1 + 2	1 + 2
Configuration	6 × 6	6 × 6	6 × 6	6 × 6	6 × 6	6 × 6	6 × 6
Weight (empty)	11 086 kg	9303 kg	9721 kg	15 402 kg	12 483 kg	13 277 kg	n/av
Payload	4540 kg	6805 kg	6805 kg	5445 kg	2270 kg	2270 kg	3175 kg
Towed load	6810 kg	6810 kg[1]	6810 kg[1]	6810 kg[1]	6810 kg	6180 kg	9080 kg
Length	7·48 m	6·924 m	7·264 m	9·277 m	9·144 m	9·423 m	8·198 m
Width	2·476 m	2·476 m	2·476 m	2·476 m	2·476 m	2·476 m	2·476 m
Height	3·05 m	2·842 m	2·842 m	3·353 m	3·467 m	3·467 m	2·842 m
Track (front)	1·905 m	1·905 m	1·905 m	1·905 m	1·905 m	1·905 m	1·905 m
(rear)	1·829 m	1·829 m	1·829 m	1·829 m	1·829 m	1·829 m	1·829 m
Wheelbase	4·242 m	4·242 m	4·242 m	5·461 m	5·461 m	5·461 m	4·547 m
Angle of approach/departure	31°/70·5°	46°/60°	31°/60°	31°/55°	46°/24°	46°/24°	31°/37°
Ground clearance	0·27 m	0·27 m	0·27 m	0·27 m	0·27 m	0·27 m	0·27 m
Gradient	60%	60%	60%	60%	60%	60%	60%
Side slope	20%	20%	20%	20%	20%	20%	20%
Max speed	84 km/h	84 km/h	84 km/h	84 km/h	84 km/h	84 km/h	84 km/h
Range (cruising)	772 km	772 km	772 km	563 km	563 km	563 km	805 km
(cruising, towed load)	644 km	644 km	644 km	483 km	483 km	483 km	644 km
Fording	0·76 m	0·76 m	0·76 m	0·76 m	0·76 m	0·76 m	0·76 m
Fording with kit	1·98 m	1·98 m	1·98 m	1·98 m	1·98 m	1·98 m	1·98 m
Engine	Cummins NHC 250 6-cylinder 4-cycle 14-litre diesel developing 240 hp at 2100 rpm						
Gearbox	Detroit Diesel Allison MT654CR 5-speed automatic						
Transfer box	2-speed with ratios 732:1/1·79:1						
Steering	Ross HFB 64 power-assisted with belt driven Eaton pump						
Turning radius	12·9 m	12·75 m	12·9 m	14·53 m	14·3 m	14·3 m	12·9 m
Suspension	Rockwell standard leaf springs front and rear						
Tyres	11.00 × 20 12-ply non-directional cross-country						
Brakes (main)	Rockwell Stopmaster air actuated						
Electrical system	24 V	24 V	24 V	24 V	24 V	24 V	24 V
Alternator	60 A	60 A	60 A	60 A	60 A	60 A	60 A

1 5th wheel load 17 010 kg

AM General Enhanced Mobility System

DESCRIPTION

As a private venture AM General has developed the Enhanced Mobility System (EMS) to enable 5-ton (6 × 6) M809 and M939 series to travel over deep sand, mud or snow with relative ease. The Enhanced Mobility System is also known as the All-Terrain All-Climate System (ATAC).

The main part of the EMS is a pneumatically-controlled central tyre inflation/deflation system designed to adjust tyre pressure according to the terrain being crossed. The driver can select the tyre pressures from inside the cab as the truck moves from hard surfaces such as roads onto sand or mud. The driver has a single four-position switch mounted on the dashboard which allows him to select from the following tyre conditions:

Highway (HWY), pressure 5·2 bars, max speed 80 km/h
Cross country (C/C), pressure 2·1 bars, max speed 50 km/h
Mud, sand, snow, pressure 1·4 bars, max speed 15 km/h
Emergency, pressure 0·7 bars, max speed 10 km/h
By lowering the tyre pressure the mobility of the vehicle is increased as the tyres have greater contact area with the ground surface. Using the EMS a M939 (6 × 6) 5-ton truck could be used to tow a M198 155 mm howitzer across mud, sand and snow.

The system is engineered so that the brake mechanism is isolated. As a result a major failure in the tyre unit will not affect the brakes. It is possible to change a tyre without bleeding the entire air system. Other parts of the EMS include high flotation tubeless radial tyres, beadlocks, special wheels, non-slip differentials, an air-actuated transfer case and shielded air lines. The system automatically maintains the selected tyre pressure which can be monitored using a dashboard-mounted air pressure gauge. In the event of a leaking tyre the pressure is maintained up to the full capacity of the vehicle's air compressor.

AM General offers the EMS as a factory-installed item. The first production M809 vehicles with EMS were completed in early 1982 and the first M939s with EMS were due to be offered internationally in late 1983. The US Army Tank Automotive Command (TACOM) has evaluated EMS for production on the M939 Series 5-ton (6 × 6) trucks currently in production by AM General.

STATUS

Production. In service with undisclosed countries in the Middle East, North Africa and South America with M809 Series vehicles. M939 Series vehicles with EMS offered from end of 1983.

MANUFACTURER

AM General Corporation, 14350 Plymouth Road, Detroit, Michigan 48232, USA.

SPECIFICATIONS (for M939 Series)

Tyres: 14.00 × 20 tubeless, high flotation
Beadlocks: hard rubber reinforced with Kevlar; 7·9% bead compression
Wheels: 10-hole bolt circle, 254 mm rims; 3-piece take-apart design with bolt on lock ring for easy beadlock installation
Tyre pressure settings:
  highway (HWY), 5·2 bars (75 psi)
  cross country (C/C) 2·1 bars (30 psi)
  mud, sand, 1·4 bars (20 psi)
  emergency 0·7 bars (10 psi)
Tyre deflation times
  5·2 bars to 2·1 bars –2 min 36 s
  2·1 bars to 1·4 bars – 54 s
  1·4 bars to 0·7 bars – 1 min 42 s
Tyre inflation times
  0·7 bars to 1·4 bars – 55 s
  1·4 bars to 2·1 bars – 2 min 10 s
  2·1 bars to 5·2 bars – 10 min 30 s
Max vehicle speeds
  HWY – 80 km/h
  C/C – 50 km/h
  mud, sand, snow – 15 km/h
  emergency – 10 km/h
Air compressor: 0·46 m³/min, 2-cylinder water cooled
Differentials: fully automatic locking differentials on all axles
Transfer box: air actuated locking

M818 Tractor, one of the M809 5-ton (6 × 6) series, equipped with EMS

M809 5-ton (6 × 6) truck equipped with Enhanced Mobility System (EMS)

M923 cargo truck, part of the M939 5-ton (6 × 6) series equipped with EMS and towing 155 mm M198 howitzer

M923 cargo truck, part of the M939 5-ton (6 × 6) series

M520 (4 × 4) 8000 kg Cargo Vehicle

DEVELOPMENT

In 1956 the United States Armor Board studied current large rubber-tyred earth moving equipment and came to the conclusion that this type of vehicle could be further developed to meet a requirement for a high mobility vehicle capable of supporting mechanised units in the field. The following year trials were conducted with a number of commercial vehicles, all of which featured articulated steering. A number of companies were then awarded development contracts for 4 × 4 all-terrain vehicles including Clark Equipment, Le Tourneau-Westinghouse and Caterpillar. The Clark vehicle was

rated at 5 tons but only one prototype was built. Le Tourneau-Westinghouse built a number of 15-ton class vehicles including cargo (XM437), tanker (XM438) and wrecker (XM554), but none entered production as it was decided to concentrate on the Caterpillar 8-ton class range.

In 1960 Caterpillar was awarded a contract worth $14·5 million to design, develop and build eight 8-ton cargo trucks. These were delivered between 1961 and 1962 for trials at Fort Knox, Aberdeen Proving Ground and environmental testing in Alaska, Arizona and Panama. In June 1962 the contract was extended to include two 10-ton wreckers and two 2500-gallon tankers.

In May 1963 another contract was awarded to Caterpillar for the construction of 13 cargo vehicles, eight tankers and two wreckers. These were completed the following year and were subsequently delivered to Germany for extensive troop trials. At the end of these trials they were placed in store until 1966 when they were sent to Viet-Nam to form the Provisional Goer Transportation Company. These were based at Pleiku and supported the 4th Infantry Division.

In Viet-Nam they established a reputation for dependability and operated where no other vehicle could go. They achieved an availability rate (with no float inventory) of almost 90 per cent, even though the spare parts were not in the inventory at that time.

In May 1971 Caterpillar Tractor Co was awarded a production contract which covered the supply of 812 M520 cargo vehicles, 117 M553 wreckers and 371 M559 tankers. Final deliveries were made in June 1976.

DESCRIPTION

The Goer consists of two units, front and rear, connected by an articulated joint that permits lateral oscillation of 20 degrees and a steering angle of 60 degrees. The front section has seats for the driver on the left and the vehicle commander on the right. The vehicle has a windscreen and a removable canvas top with removable side curtains. The engine is at the rear of the front unit.

Power is transmitted from the engine to the transmission to a drop box and short propeller shaft to the front differential and out to the planetary drives in the front wheels. Power to the rear wheels is carried from the front differential through a disconnect clutch, then through propeller shafts and universals to the rear differential. The final drives in the rear wheels are also planetary.

The rear-wheel drive can be utilised in first and second gears at speeds of up to 17 km/h. The rear wheels are automatically disconnected on the shift from second to third gear. A manual override is provided so that the operator can engage the rear wheels at any speed from 17 to 48 km/h.

The cargo area is of high strength corrugated construction with side and rear doors, all of which are watertight. The cargo area can accommodate six standard military pallets, or one CONEX container and two pallets or 25 55-gallon drums.

Mounted on the front of the vehicle is a hydraulic 4536 kg capacity winch with 61 metres of 13 mm diameter cable.

When fitted with a crane for loading and unloading the M520 is designated the M877.

All vehicles are fully amphibious being propelled in the water by their wheels at a speed of 5.3 km/h. Special kits developed for the vehicle include arctic kit, infra-red driving light kit, wheel chain kit, machine gun kit, and a trailer brake kit.

VARIANTS

M553 10-ton Wrecker
Full details of this are given in the *Recovery vehicles* section (page 66).

M559 2500-gallon fuel tanker
This has a 9463-litre stainless steel tank, pump, military aircraft fuel filter, four pressure discharge outlets, two 189-litre per minute hoses, one 375-litre per minute hose and a 1135-litre per minute bulk outlet. It can discharge the first three hoses simultaneously at 757 litres per minute. The tanker also has a gravity discharge outlet for handling bulk fuel at storage sites. Basic specifications of this model are laden weight 20 797 kg, unladen weight 12 859 kg, length 9·931 metres, width 2·743 metres and height 2·514 metres.

Flatbed
A flatbed version towing a two-axle trailer developed to the prototype stage by Caterpillar can carry a maximum load of 20 400 kg but has no amphibious capability. The Goer was also proposed for a wide variety of other roles including towing dump units, surface-to-air missile systems and use as a command post.

SPECIFICATIONS (M520 Cargo)
Cab seating: 1 + 1
Configuration: 4 × 4
Weight:
(empty) 10 240 kg
(loaded) 18 500 kg
Max load: 8260 kg
Towed load: 9070 kg

Load area: 4·977 × 2·482 m
Length: 9·753 m
Width: 2·743 m
Height:
(overall) 3·396 m
(reduced) 2·438 m
Ground clearance: 0·59 m
Track: 2·203 m
Wheelbase: 5·968 m
Angle of approach/departure: 51°/41°
Max speed:
(road) 48·28 km/h
(water) 5·3 km/h
Freeboard forward: (loaded) 0·584 m
Freeboard rear: (loaded) 0·533 m
Range: 650 km
Fuel capacity: 416 litres
Max gradient: 60%
Max side slope: 30%
Fording: amphibious
Engine: Caterpillar model D333 4-cycle, 6-cylinder turbocharged diesel developing 213 hp at 2200 rpm
Transmission: Caterpillar powershift (with integral torque converter) with 6 forward and 1 reverse gears
Steering: articulated hydraulic
Turning radius: 8·3 m
Suspension: none, tyres absorb shock
Tyres: 18.00 × 33
Brakes:
(main) air
(parking) hydraulic
Electrical system: 24 V

STATUS
Production complete. In service with the US Army.

MANUFACTURER
Caterpillar Tractor Co, Defense Products Department, Peoria, Illinois 61629, USA.

M520 (4 × 4) 8000 kg cargo vehicle with cab and cargo covers in position (US Army)

M559 (4 × 4) tanker for refuelling vehicles and aircraft in the field (US Army)

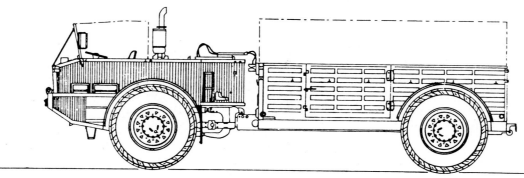

M520 (4 × 4) 8000 kg cargo vehicle

FWD Tractioneer (4 × 4) Truck

DESCRIPTION
The Tractioneer (4 × 4) truck has been developed as a private venture by FWD International and its company designation is Model RB441617NH230.

The layout of the vehicle is conventional with the engine at the front, two-door, fully-enclosed cab in the centre and the cargo area at the rear. The cargo area latter has a drop tailgate, removable bows and a tarpaulin cover. The cab is mounted on the subframe at three points and is fully insulated with reverse slope windscreen, curb visibility window, two cowl vents plus two wing window vents and seating for the driver and two passengers. Accessories include adjustable steering column, 35 000 BTU air heater and defroster, seat belts, dual-padded sun visors, dome lights and grab handles.

The chassis is of straight channel R7 alloy steel, heat treated, 11 000 psi grade eight bolted construction with cross-members designed to resist cornerwise shock loading are standard. The Tractioneer has a gross vehicle weight of 15 196 kg, gross chassis weight of 7711 kg and a wheelbase of 4·267 metres.

The vehicle was powered by a Cummins six-cylinder NH230 diesel developing 230 hp at 2100 rpm coupled to a manual gearbox with five forward and one reverse gears. The transfer assembly was a FWD dual range, constant mesh high range, sliding gear low shift with full-time power to both front and rear axles. Straight tooth bevel gear type centre differential compensates for unequal travel of front and rear axles and proportions

torque in relation to lead ratings of front and rear axles. FWD multiple disc, power actuated "Tractionlock" is manually controlled from the instrument panel to lock out centre differential for maximum traction.

Cummins Diesel have now discontinued their Cummins NH-230 diesel so FWD have now changed to a Cummins PT-240 diesel which has resulted in the change to a 10-speed transmission and a single speed transfer box. Tests have shown that this combination provides increased traction in sand. The specification relates to this version.

The front and rear axles are FWD one piece housing with removable carrier assembly, single reduction gearing, full floating axle shafts and multiple disc "Tractionlock" manually controlled from the instrument panel. The front steering and driving axle shafts have cardan joints completely enclosed in ball sockets with individual king pins. The parking brakes are spring actuated, air released, piggy back mounted at the rear service brake air chambers, with dashboard control. The service brakes are full air S cam type with 12 CFM compressor and three reservoirs having a total capacity of 3750 cubic inches.

Steering is twin cam and lever type with an adjustable steering column, hydraulic power assistance is standard. Tyres are Michelin 14.00 × 20 SS sand type, high flotation with a spare wheel being carried on the left side of the chassis. The fuel tank has a capacity of 190 litres.

Standard equipment includes heavy duty radiator with automatic shutters, heavy duty steel cargo body, rear pintle hook attached to reinforced frame crossmember, 4536 kg power-take-off winch with 39 metres of wire rope and hook, a heavy duty bumper, tow eye and grill guard.

VARIANTS

In 1983 FWD introduced a 6 × 6 version of the Tractioneer known as the Model RB66-2182D. Powered by the same engine as the 4 × 4 model, the 6 × 6 has a maximum gross vehicle weight rating of 22 000 kg on roads, 15 195 kg on tracks and 12 930 kg across sand. The approximate chassis weight is 7620 kg. Apart from the 6 × 6 feature this new model is otherwise identical in most respects, other than dimensions, to the 4 × 4 model.

SPECIFICATIONS

Cab seating: 1 + 2
Configuration: 4 × 4
Weight:
  (empty) 7711 kg
  (gross vehicle weight) 15 196 kg
Length: 7·24 m

Width: 2·49 m
Height: 3·05 m
Wheelbase: 4·267 m
Fuel capacity: 190 litres + 150 litres
Engine: Cummins PT-240, 240 hp at 2100 rpm
Gearbox: manual 10-speed
Transfer case: FWD 1640 single speed
Steering: Ross TE-70 twin cam and lever
Tyres: 14.00 × 20 sand, single front and rear
Number of tyres: 4 + 1 spare
Batteries: 2 × 12 V

STATUS

Ready for production.

MANUFACTURER

FWD International Incorporated, 1020 West 31st Street, Downers Grove, Illinois 60515, USA.

FWD International Tractioneer (4 × 4) vehicle showing rear cargo area

FWD International Tractioneer (4 × 4) vehicle showing fully enclosed cab

Oshkosh MK48 Series Articulated (8 × 8) Vehicle

DEVELOPMENT

During the 1960s Lockheed developed a vehicle known as the Twister which following US Army trials, evolved into a commercial model known as the Dragon Wagon. The Dragon Wagon is still a Lockheed commercial product but under a joint agreement with the Oshkosh Truck Corporation a small production batch was jointly produced by Oshkosh. Oshkosh continued development of the basic design into their DA Series and four prototypes were delivered to the US Marine Corps during 1981 and 1982.

As a result of extended user trials by the US Marine Corps an order was placed in September 1983 for 1433 vehicles to be known as the MK48 but based on the DA Series. The order for the Marine Corps is worth $245 million and the contract contains an option to double the quantity of vehicles.

DESCRIPTION

The MK48 Series consists of a front and rear body that are connected by a centre articulation joint that provides 64 degrees of powered steering motion coordinated with steering of the front axle. Articulated steering provides 30 per cent shorter turning radius than a conventional truck of the same wheelbase. The articulated joint also provides 12 degrees of roll capability between the front and rear modules. Roll capability and a new six-rod suspension with taper leaf springs provides superior wheel-to-ground contact for improved off-road capability. The rear body/module can be disconnected and another body/module of a different type quickly connected.

The rear body/module is available with axle capacities of 38 000 lb (17 236 kg), or 58 000 lb (26 038 kg).

The two-man enclosed cab mounted at the front of the vehicle has two optional roof hatches. The engine is mounted beneath the cab and is coupled to an automatic gearbox and a two-speed transfer case which provides full time all-wheel drive and has driver controlled lockout. The hydraulic boosted power steering for the front axle co-ordinates with twin hydraulic cylinders astride the articulated joint to induce rear-body yaw and assure a tight turning circle.

Optional equipment includes ammeter, exhaust temperature gauge, diagnostic connector assembly for STE/ICE, blackout lights, suspension passenger seat, winch, material handling crane, 24.00 × 21 radial sand tyres, arctic kit to −65 degrees, towing provision with air and electrical connections, traction control axle differentials, Jacobs engine brake, air conditioning, various axle and transfer ratios, strobe beacon, spare tyre and

Oshkosh MK48/17 (8 × 8) vehicle with cargo type rear module

Oshkosh MK48/14 (8 × 8) vehicle with flatbed rear module carrying container

wheel, spotlight, off-road on-board equipment, off-road cab and glass protection kit, various rear modules and other special military options.

The MK48 series will initially be produced as part of the US Marine Corps' Logistic Vehicle System (LVS) and will include four models, as follows:
MK48/14: logistics platform truck
MK48/15: recovery vehicle

MK48/16: truck tractor
MK48/17: cargo truck with material handling crane (MHC)

The MK48/14 logistics platform truck uses an aluminium flat deck with standard container lashing points to carry either one 20 foot/6·096 metre container, two 10 foot/3·048 metre containers or six 6·66 foot/2·03 metre containers. The platform length is 6·058 metres and loading height is 1·213 metres.

The MK48/15 recovery vehicle uses a steel cargo body with fold-down sides. At the rear is a hydraulic crane with a capacity of 18 700 kg and a recovery winch with a pull capacity of 27 216 kg.

The MK48/16 truck tractor has a fully oscillating fifth wheel for a 3·5-inch/88·9 mm kingpin mounted 1·6 metres above ground level. Full trailer air and electrical connections are provided as is a 27 216 kg recovery winch.

The MK48/17 cargo truck has a steel cargo body with fold-down sides and a 18 650-kg capacity hydraulic material handling crane at the rear.

The MK48 LVS range is designed to be air transportable in a C-130 Hercules aircraft.

STATUS
Ordered for US Marine Corps (1433)

MANUFACTURER
Oshkosh Truck Corporation, PO Box 2566, Oshkosh, Wisconsin 54903, USA.

SPECIFICATIONS

Model	MK48/14	MK48/15	MK48/16	MK48/17
Purpose	logistics platform truck	recovery	truck tractor	cargo truck
Cab seating	1 + 1	1 + 1	1 + 1	1 + 1
Configuration	8 × 8	8 × 8	8 × 8	8 × 8
Weight (empty)	18 370 kg	23 015 kg	18 477 kg	21 487 kg
Gross vehicle combination weight				
(on road)	68 040 kg	68 040 kg	85 277 kg	68 040 kg
(off road)	47 628 kg	47 628 kg	47 628 kg	47 628 kg
Payload				
(on road)	20 412 kg	9072 kg[1]	20 866 kg[2]	18 144 kg
(off road)	11 340 kg			9072 kg
Length	11·582 m	11·184 m	9·63 m	11·48 m
Width	2·438 m	2·438 m	2·438 m	2·438 m
Height (cab)	2·591 m	2·591 m	2·591 m	2·591 m
Track	2·007 m	2·007 m	2·007 m	2·007 m
Wheelbase	1·524 m + 6·579 m +1·524 m	1·524 m + 6·579 m +1·524 m	1·524 m + 5·615 m +1·524 m	1·524 m + 6·579 m +1·524 m
Angle of approach/departure	45°/45°	45°/48°	45°/85°[3]	45°/40°
Max speed (road)	84 km/h	84 km/h	84 km/h	84 km/h
Range (cruising)	483 km	483 km	483 km	483 km
Fuel capacity	2 × 284 litres	2 × 284 litres	2 × 284 litres	2 × 284 litres
Gradient	60%	60%	60%	60%
Side slope	40%	40%	40%	40%
Fording	1·524 m	1·524 m	1·524 m	1·524 m
Engine	Detroit Diesel 8V92TA V-8 2-cycle water-cooled 12·06 litre diesel developing 445 hp at 2100 rpm			
Gearbox	Allison HT740D 4-speed automatic with torque converter			
Transfer box	Oshkosh 2-speed			
Steering	hydraulic powered yaw steering with power-assist on No 1 axle			
Turning radius	11·7 m	11·7 m	11·7 m	11·7 m
Suspension	leaf springs with steel saddle and 6 torque rods front and rear giving 356 mm wheel travel			
Tyres	16.00 × 21	16.00 × 21	16.00 × 21	16.00 × 21
Electrical system	24 V	24 V	24 V	24 V
Batteries	4 × 12 V	4 × 12 V	4 × 12 V	4 × 12 V
Alternator	24 V, 62 A	24 V, 62 A	24 V, 62 A	24 V, 62 A

[1] towed load 14 515 kg
[2] load on 5th wheel
[3] tractor unit only

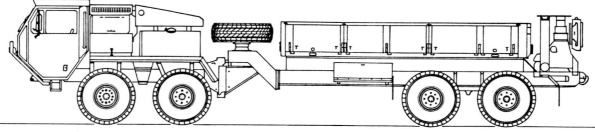

Oshkosh MK48/17 (8 × 8) articulated logistics platform truck

Oshkosh Heavy Expanded Mobility Tactical Truck (8 × 8) 9979 kg

DEVELOPMENT
The largest cargo truck in the US Army fleet today is the Caterpillar M520 (4 × 4) Goer 8000 kg vehicle, production of which was completed in 1976. The Goer has excellent cross-country mobility but is unsuitable for use on roads.

After evaluating a number of proposals and testing vehicles submitted by MAN (8 × 8) and Pacific Car and Foundry (8 × 8), in May 1981 the US Army Tank Automotive Command awarded a $251·13 million five-year

Oshkosh M977 Heavy Expanded Mobility Tactical Truck (8 × 8)

contract to the Oshkosh Truck Corporation for production of the 10-ton (US) Heavy Expanded Mobility Tactical Truck (HEMTT). Under the terms of this contract, the Army will receive 250 vehicles during the first year at a cost of $31·73 million and a total of 2140 vehicles over a five-year period. The contract also contains production options that will allow the Army to buy an additional 5350 vehicles making a total of 7490 units. The first prototype was completed in December 1981 with first production vehicles delivered in September 1982.

To reduce procurement and life cycle costs, the HEMTT features extensive use of commercial automotive components including an Oshkosh truck cab, standard eight-cylinder diesel engine and a standard four-speed automatic transmission. Some of the components used in this vehicle are also found in the LVS (8 × 8) vehicles used by the US Marine Corps.

DESCRIPTION
The chassis is of formed channel bolted construction with grade eight bolts, with heat-treated carbon manganese steel being used throughout. The chassis is provided with heavy duty front bumper and skid plate, external hydraulic connection, service and emergency air brake connection, slave start connection and trailer electrical connector.

The two-man two-door forward control cab is of heavy duty welded steel construction with corrosion resistant skins. Standard equipment includes suspension seats for the driver and passenger, seat belts, heater and defroster, dual sun visors, interior lights, variable speed air windscreen wipers, windscreen washers and electric air horns.

The spare wheel is mounted to the rear of the cab and is provided with a davit to assist in lowering it to the ground.

All models have Oshkosh 46K front tandem axles which are used for steering, single reduction, 30-degree front turning angle, single cardan joint, closed type steering ends with an inter-axle driver controlled differential.

The rear axles, except for the M984, are Eaton DS-480 single reduction type with driver controlled differential. The M984 has Eaton DS-580 axles with single reduction and driver controlled differential.

VARIANTS
M977 Cargo Truck
This is the basic member of the family with light duty material handling crane at the very rear, produced with and without a self-recovery winch which can be used to the front or rear of the vehicle. The cargo area is 5·4 metres long and is provided with drop sides.

M978 Tanker
9500-litre capacity tanker, produced with and without a self-recovery winch.

M983 Tractor Truck
Tractor truck with material handling crane and fifth wheel, produced either with a self-recovery winch, or without, in which case the crane is not fitted.

M984 Wrecker
Fitted with recovery winch as standard and flatbed cargo area three metres long between second and third axles, recovery equipment is at very rear. See *Recovery vehicles* section (page 67).

M985 Cargo Truck
Similar to M977 but with heavy-duty material handling crane at rear, will be produced with and without a self-recovery winch. Will, with two-axle trailer, be used to support the Multiple Launch Rocket System (MLRS).

STATUS
In production for US Army. Full production began in September 1982 at the rate of 36 units a month, which should have increased to 180 units a month by August 1983.

MANUFACTURER
Oshkosh Truck Corporation, POB 2566, Oshkosh, Wisconsin 54903 USA.

SPECIFICATIONS

Designation	M977	M978	M983	M985
Type	cargo	tanker	tractor	cargo
Cab seating	1 + 1	1 + 1	1 + 1	1 + 1
Configuration	8 × 8	8 × 8	8 × 8	8 × 8
Weight (empty)	15 825 kg	15 874 kg	12 440 kg	16 869 kg
(loaded)	28 123 kg	28 123 kg	28 123 kg	30 844 kg
Weight on front axles	13 608 kg	13 608 kg	13 608 kg	13 608 kg
Weight on rear axles	14 515 kg	14 515 kg	14 515 kg	17 237 kg
Length	10·1727 m	10·172 m	8·9027 m	10·1727 m
Width	2·4 m	2·4 m	2·4 m	2·4 m
Height (cab)	2·565 m	2·565 m	2·591 m	2·565 m
Wheelbase	5·334 m	5·334 m	4·597 m	5·334 m
Angle of approach/departure	43°/45°	43°/45°	43°/66°	43°/45°
Max speed	88 km/h	88 km/h	88 km/h	88 km/h
Gradient	60%	60%	60%	60%
Range	483 km	483 km	483 km	483 km
Fuel capacity	587 litres	587 litres	587 litres	587 litres
Engine	Detroit Diesel 8V92TA, V-8 2-stroke 12·06-litre diesel developing 445 hp at 2100 rpm			
Gearbox	Allison HT740D automatic with torque converter, 4 forward and 1 reverse gears			
Transfer box	Oshkosh 55000, 2-speed			
Steering	integral hydraulic, main and booster gears			
Suspension	Hendrickson RT340 spring with steel saddle and equalising beams, 250 mm vertical axle travel. M985 rear axle has Hendrickson RT380			
Tyres	16.00 × 20	16.00 × 20	16.00 × 20	16.00 × 20
Brakes (main)	air operated, dual system, internal shoe			
(parking)	spring brakes mounted on Nos 3 and 4 axles			
Electrical system	24 V	24 V	24 V	24 V
Batteries	4 × 12 V	4 × 12 V	4 × 12 V	4 × 12 V

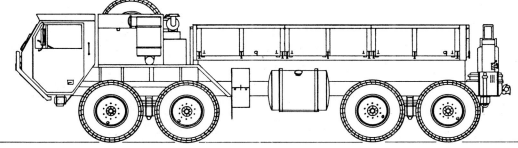

Provisional drawing of Oshkosh M977 Heavy Expanded Mobility Tactical Truck (8 × 8)

M125 (6 × 6) 10-ton Truck

DEVELOPMENT
The M125 was developed as the XM125 in the early 1950s by Mack. Initial production was by Mack but was subsequently taken over by the Consolidated Diesel Electric Company. The correct US Army designation of the vehicle is Truck, Cargo: 10-ton, 6 × 6, M125, with winch. The M125 was designed to carry 15 876 kg of cargo, or tow a 155 mm gun or an 8-inch (203 mm) howitzer. Its chassis is designated the M121 and is also used as the basis for the M123 tractor truck (6 × 6) which was manufactured by the Condiesel Mobile Equipment Division, details of which will be found in the *Tank transporters* section.

DESCRIPTION
The layout of the M125 is conventional with the engine at the front, two-door cab in the centre with a windscreen which can fold forward onto the bonnet and a removable canvas top and the cargo area at the rear with fixed sides, drop tailgate, bows, tarpaulin cover and a crane for handling ammunition. A 20 412 kg capacity winch is mounted at the front of the vehicle. Late production models have a diesel engine instead of a petrol engine and are designated the M125A1.

VARIANTS
M122: dump truck, developed to prototype stage but not placed in production.
XM124: long wheelbase version, development only.

SPECIFICATIONS
Cab seating: 1 + 1
Configuration: 6 × 6
Weight:
  (empty) 13 608 kg
  (loaded) 29 484 kg
Max load: 15 876 kg
Load area: 4·267 × 2·438 m

Length: 8·089 m
Width: 2·895 m
Height:
  (cab) 2·819 m
  (tarpaulin) 3·282 m
  (load area) 1·689 m
Ground clearance: 0·523 m
Track: (front) 2·006 m
Wheelbase: 3·847 m + 1·524 m
Angle of approach/departure: 30°/45°
Max speed: (road) 69 km/h
Range: 531 km
Fuel capacity: 736 litres
Max gradient: 60%
Fording:
  (without preparation) 0·76 m
  (with preparation) 1·981 m
Engine: Le Roi model T-H844 8-cylinder petrol developing 297 bhp at 2600 rpm
Gearbox: manual with 5 forward and 1 reverse gears
Transfer box: 2-speed
Steering: hydraulic
Turning radius: 10·97 m
Suspension:
  (front) semi-elliptical springs and hydraulic double acting shock absorbers
  (rear) pair of inverted semi-elliptical springs mounted longitudinally at centre to trunnion arrangement attached to chassis
Tyres: 14.00 × 24
Brakes:
  (main) air
  (parking) mechanical
Electrical system: 24 V
Batteries: 2 × 12 V

STATUS
Production complete. In service with the US Army and other armed forces.

MANUFACTURER
Mack Trucks Incorporated, Allentown, Pennsylvania 18105, USA. Later, Condiesel Mobile Equipment Division, CONDEC Corporation, 1700 Post Road, Old Greenwich, Connecticut 06870, USA.

M125 (6 × 6) 10-ton truck (US Army)

M915 Series of Trucks

DEVELOPMENT
One of the recommendations of the WHEELS study was that the Army should use commercial trucks wherever practicable. In January 1977 the United States Army Automotive Material Readiness Command (TARCOM) issued a request for technical proposals for a series of heavy trucks ranging from 22 680 to 34 019 kg gross vehicle weights. The Army subsequently received technical proposals from six truck manufacturers, AM General Corporation, FWD (Four Wheel Drive) Corporation, General Motors Truck and Coach, International Harvester Corporation, Kenworth Truck Corporation and White Autocar Corporation.

All six manufacturers who responded to the original request qualified to offer priced bids under the second step of the procurement. Bids were opened in June 1977 with AM General Corporation the lowest at $252·8 million for the requirement of 5507 trucks. In June 1977 a contract was awarded to AM General for 5507 trucks and in addition the Government had the right to exercise options on an additional 5507 trucks, giving a potential of 11 014 units. The contract was for four years with the first test vehicles (M915 Line Haul Tractor) being delivered early in 1978.

The US Government did not exercise its option on the additional 5507 trucks but in September 1981 awarded AM General a contract for 2511 M915A1 (6 × 4) tractor trucks.

The AM General series is based on the Centaur series of trucks built by the Crane Carrier Company of Tulsa, Oklahoma. A licence agreement between AM General and Crane Carriers gives rights to AM General to manufacture and sell vehicles to the United States Government.

The contract also requires complete after-market support of the M915 including spare part provisioning and a full complement of maintenance and service publications, as well as the training of Army instructors. The Army receives warranty covering defects in design, materials and workmanship for a period of 15 months or for 19 312 km. In addition, the Army receives "free time" up to six months, for new vehicles stored in depots.

DESCRIPTION
The series is based on a commercial vehicle with the minimum of modifications to suit them for military use, such as forest green paint, rear-mounted pintle hooks, front and rear tow hooks and blackout lights. There are three basic chassis, 6 × 4 for road use and 6 × 6 and 8 × 6 for both road and cross country use.

The layout of all vehicles is similar with the engine at the front, two-door all-steel fully enclosed cab in the centre and the fifth wheel or body at the rear.

M915, Tractor, Truck, 14-ton, 6 × 4
This is powered by a Cummins model NTC 400 6-cylinder diesel which develops 400 hp (gross) at 2100 rpm, coupled to a Caterpillar semi-automatic gearbox with 16 forward and 2 reverse gears. The suspension consists of front, Rockwell-Asymmetrical leaf pin and shackle and rear, Hendrickson RTE 380 walking beam.

The M915 will be used primarily for the long distance movement of containers and will normally tow the 34-ton (US) XM872 semi-trailer. It will replace the 5-ton military series tractors and certain commercial tractors used in moving cargo from the port of embarkation to the division rear boundary. The M52 and M818 truck-tractors will continue to operate from within the division and brigade areas, performing the same types of mission as currently assigned.

M915A1, Tractor Truck, 14-ton, 6 × 4
In September 1981 AM General Corporation was awarded a contract by the US Army Tank Automotive

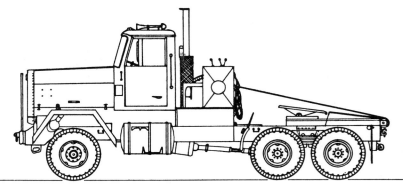

M916 (6 × 6) 20-ton tractor, truck

M915 14-ton line haul tractor towing semi-trailer

Command for 2511 M915A1 (6 × 4) tractor trucks. This contract is worth $130 million with a 100 per cent option for an additional 2511 units. Production began at the company's South Bend plant in January 1983 and continued for 18 months.

The M915A1 is similar to the earlier M915 except that it has a Detroit Diesel Allison HT 754 CR automatic transmission with five forward and one reverse gears.

SPECIFICATIONS (similar to the M915 except for the following details)
Length: 6·489 m
Width: 2·438 m
Height: 2·984 m
Fording: 0·616 m
Max road speed: 91·7 km/h
Speed on 3% slope: 45 km/h
Max gradient: 18·4%
Fuel capacity: 446 litres

M916, Tractor, Truck, 20-ton, 6 × 6
This is to replace the M123 (6 × 6) tractor and has the same engine and transmission as the M915 but also has an Oshkosh F-U29 transfer case. Suspension is the same as in the M915 and differential lock ups on front axle and rear bogie. Mounted to the rear of the cab is a hydraulic winch with a capacity of 20 250 kg.

The M916 will be used by units throughout the world as the prime mover for the M172A1 low-bed trailer to transport heavy construction equipment within the theatre of operations. It will also operate efficiently hauling the M870 40-ton low-bed semi-trailer when fully loaded; however a 6-inch fifth-wheel spacer must be used for compatibility with the M870 kingpin height.

M917, Dump Truck, 20-ton, 8 × 6
This has a rear tipping dump body by Fruehauf which has a heaped capacity of 10·7 cubic metres, and the same engine, gearbox, transfer box and suspension as the M916.

The M917 will be used for earthmoving and construction projects and will augment the current fleet of 20-ton dump trucks, and in some selected units will replace the 5-ton dump trucks.

M915 (6 × 4) 14-ton tractor, truck (US Army)

M916 (6 × 6) 20-ton tractor, truck (US Army)

M917 (8 × 6), 20-ton dump truck (US Army)

M918 (6 × 6) 1500-gallon bituminous distributor, (US Army)

M919 (8 × 6) 8-cubic yard, concrete mobile (US Army)

M920 (8 × 6) 20-ton tractor, truck (US Army)

M918, Bituminous Distributor, 1500 gallons, 6 × 6
This has a 56 775-litre bituminous spreader on the rear manufactured by E D Etnyre and Company of Oregon. Engine, transmission, transfer box and suspension are the same as for the M916.

The M918 will be used for distributing liquid bitumen for road and airfield construction and is provided with a hydrostatically driven bituminous pump.

M919, Concrete Mobile, 8 cubic yards, 8 × 6
This has a concrete mixer to the rear manufactured by the National Concrete Machinery Company of Lancaster, Pennsylvania. The engine, transmission, transfer box and suspension are the same as in the M916. It can transport dry concrete ingredients and water, mix the ingredients in various increments and proportions, and pour the mixed concrete. The M919 will be charged with dry ingredients by aggregate bins or scoop loaders and will discharge into mixed concrete handling equipment. This vehicle can also be used as a central mix plant where large amounts of concrete are required at a single location.

M920, Tractor, Truck, 20-ton, 8 × 6
This has a fifth wheel at the rear and will be used to haul semi-trailers. Mounted to the rear of the cab is a hyd-raulic winch with a capacity of 20 250 kg. The engine, transmission, transfer box and suspension are the same as in the M916.

The M920 will, together with the M916, replace the M123, and be used to haul the M870 semi-trailer.

STATUS
Production. In service with the US Army.

MANUFACTURER
AM General Corporation, 14250 Plymouth Road, Detroit, Michigan 48232, USA.

SPECIFICATIONS

Designation	M915	M916	M917	M918	M919	M920
Type	tractor	tractor	dump truck	bituminous	concrete	tractor
Cab seating	1 + 2	1 + 2	1 + 2	1 + 2	1 + 2	1 + 2
Configuration	6 × 4	6 × 6	8 × 6	6 × 6	8 × 6	8 × 6
Weight (empty)	8446 kg	11 327 kg	14 768 kg	13 535 kg	15 791 kg	12 414 kg
(loaded)	22 213 kg	29 629 kg	33 070 kg	19 789 kg	32 056 kg	30 716 kg
Weight on front axle (loaded)	5443 kg	6543 kg	3775 kg	5600 kg	4511 kg	3864 kg
Weight on rear axles (loaded)	17 236 kg	23 036 kg	33 070 kg	14 210 kg	32 506 kg	30 716 kg
Gross combination weight	47 627 kg	57 153 kg	n/app	n/app	n/app	61 235 kg
Length	6·49 m	7·48 m	8·9 m	8·9 m	9·5 m	8·11 m
Width	2·49 m	2·49 m	2·49 m	2·49 m	2·49 m	2·49 m
Height (cab)	2·93 m	3·25 m	3·25 m	3·25 m	3·25 m	3·25 m
(overall)	3·61 m	3·61 m	3·61 m	3·61 m	3·61 m	3·61 m
Ground clearance	0·254 m	0·305 m	0·305 m	0·295 m	0·305 m	0·295 m
Track (front/rear)	1·99/1·82 m	1·98/1·85 m	1·98/1·85 m	1·98/1·85 m	1·98/1·85 m	1·98/1·85 m
Wheelbase (excluding pusher axle)	4·24 m +	4·72 m +	4·876 m +	4·72 m +	4·876 m +	4·876 m +
	1·32 m	1·42 m	1·42 m	1·42 m	1·42 m	1·46 m
Angle of approach	38°	42°	41°	42°	42°	42°
Max speed (road)	107 km/h	103 km/h	107 km/h	103 km/h	107 km/h	103 km/h
(3.9% gradient)	40·2 km/h	40·2 km/h	40·2 km/h	40·2 km/h	40·2 km/h	40·2 km/h
Fuel capacity	416 litres	416 litres	416 litres	416 litres	416 litres	416 litres
Fording	0·51 m	0·73 m	0·61 m	0·61 m	0·61 m	0·61 m
Steering	all have Ross integral power system					
Turning radius	8·15 m	12·2 m	13·65 m	12·2 m	13·65 m	13·65 m
Tyres	10.00 × 20	11.00 × 24	11.00 × 24	11.00 × 24	11.00 × 24	11.00 × 24
Number of tyres	10 + 1 spare	10 + 1 spare	14	10 + 1 spare	14	14
Electrical system (24 V optional)	12 V	12 V	12 V	12 V	12 V	12 V
Batteries	4 × 12 V	4 × 12 V	4 × 12 V	4 × 12 V	4 × 12 V	4 × 12 V

Note: On the 8 × 6 model the second axle is of the pusher type and can be raised if required.

YUGOSLAVIA

TAM 110 T7 BV (4 × 4) 1500/2500 kg Truck

DEVELOPMENT

The TAM T7 BV has been referred to as the TAM 1500 in the past and was developed specifically to meet the requirements of the Yugoslav Army. It is the 4 × 4 component of two basically similar vehicles, the other being the TAM 150 T11 BV which is a 6 × 6 vehicle. Both vehicles use versions of the TAM L413 engine which is produced in Yugoslavia under license from the West German company Klockner-Humboldt-Deutz.

DESCRIPTION

The two-door all-steel frontal control cab has a reinforced PVC material roof which can be removed, as can the side windows. The cab has seating for two and can be tipped forward to an angle of 55 degrees of engine access. The windscreen can be tipped forward over the bonnet if required. Two forms of cab heating are available. The cargo body is of all-steel contruction and has two collapsible benches fitted one to each side to seat 12 soldiers. The cargo area has a capacity of 3·31 cubic metres and is 3·02 metres long, 2·12 metres wide and the sides are 0·64 metres high. A canvas tilt may be fitted.

The engine is mounted forward under the cab as is a 2500 kg capacity winch which can be used to the front or rear. A towing hook is provided at the rear under the downward-opening tailgate. Special equipment carried on the vehicle includes pioneer tools, equipment for the winch and an anti-biological and chemical kit. The ve-

hicle is fitted with radio interference protection and space is provided for the fitment of an infra-red device. There is provision for changing the tyre pressures in the range 0·7 to 3·5 atm while the vehicle is being driven.

VARIANTS

An ambulance version is known to exist and no doubt other hard-bodied variants have been produced.

STATUS

In production. In service with the Yugoslav Army. Has been offered for export.

MANUFACTURER

Tovama Avtomobilov Motorjev, Maribor, Slovenia, Yugoslavia.

SPECIFICATIONS
Cab seating: 1 + 1
Configuration: 4 × 4
Weight:
 (empty) 4500 kg
 (loaded, road) 7000 kg
 (loaded, off road) 6000 kg
Max load:
 (road) 2500 kg
 (off-road) 1500 kg
Towed load: 1800 kg
Load area: 3·02 × 2·12 m
Length: 4·85 m
Width: 2·27 m
Height (top of cab) 2·47 m
Ground clearance: 0·3 m

Wheelbase 2·85 m
Angle of approach/departure: 49°/45°
Max speed:
 (road) 90 km/h
 (off-road) 45 km/h
Fuel capacity: 100 litres
Fuel consumption: 16–21 litres/100 km
Max gradient:
 (less trailer) 67%
 (with trailer) 44·5%
Fording: 1 m
Engine: TAM F4 L413 R 4-cylinder 5·88 litre air-cooled diesel developing 115 hp at 2650 rpm
Gearbox: Z5-35S with 5 forward and 1 reverse gears
Clutch: GF 310K hydraulic with single dry plate
Transfer box: R 28 NP 2-speed
Steering: ZF 8038 988 110 servo-hydraulic
Turning radius: 6·5 m
Suspension: leaf-type springs with rubber buffers and telescopic shock absorbers
Tyres: 12.00 × 18 PR 8
Number of tyres: 4 + 1 spare
Brakes:
 (main) 2-circuit air-hydraulic on all wheels
 (parking) mechanical with air-servo assist on rear wheels
Electrical system: 24 V
Batteries: 2 × 12 V, 110 Ah

TAM 110 T7BV (4 × 4) 1500/2500 kg truck

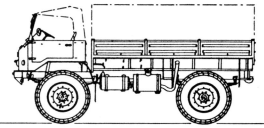

TAM 110 T7BV (4 × 4) 1500/2500 kg truck

Yugoslav (4 × 4) ambulance

TAM 110 T7BV (4 × 4) 1500/2500 kg truck

TAM 150 T11 BV (6 × 6) 3000/5000 kg Truck

DESCRIPTION

The TAM 150 T11 BV (6 × 6) truck may be regarded as an enlarged version of the TAM 110 T7 BV (4 × 4). It uses the same cab and general layout but the TAM 150 is larger and uses a 6-cylinder version of the TAM L413 in a 'V' configuration. This engine is built in Yugoslavia under license from the West German company Klockner-Humboldt-Deutz.

The TAM 150 T11 BV has a reinforced PVC cab roof which can be removed as can the side windows. The cab has seating for two and if required the windscreen may be folded forward over the bonnet. The cargo body is all-steel and has collapsible benches along each side to seat 18 men. A downward-opening tailgate is provided. A canvas tilt may be fitted. There is a 5000 kg capacity winch fitted under the cargo body rear which may be used forwards for self-recovery or to the rear.

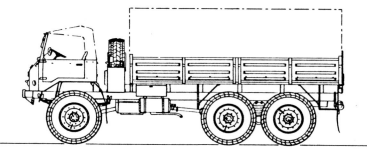

TAM 150 T11 BV (6 × 6) 3000/5000 kg truck

Power for the winch is taken from a reduction gear and a power take-off for tools may be fitted.

Tyre pressures may be altered while the TAM 150

T11 BV is being driven and a rear-mounted hook may be used to tow either a trailer or light artillery such as anti-tank guns.

STATUS
In production. In service with the Yugoslav Army. Has been offered for export.

MANUFACTURER
Tovama Avtomobilov Motorjev, Maribor, Slovenia, Yugoslavia.

SPECIFICATIONS
Cab seating: 1 + 1
Configuration: 6 × 6
Weight:
  (empty) 6400 kg
  (loaded, road) 11 400 kg
  (loaded, off-road) 9400 kg
Max load:
  (road) 5000 kg
  (off-road) 3000 kg

Towed load: 3600 kg
Load area: 4·17 × 2·12 m
Length: 6·55 m
Width: 2·275 m
Height:
  (max) 2·82 m
  (cab) 2·42 m
Ground clearance: 0·305 m
Wheelbase: 3·1 m + 1·2 m
Track: 1·86 m
Angle of approach/departure: 48°/40°
Max speed:
  (road) 85.3 km/h
  (off-road) 39 km/h
Fuel capacity: 150 litres
Fuel consumption: 14–21 litres/100 km
Max gradient:
  (less trailer) 71%
  (with trailer) 42·8%

Fording: 1 m
Engine: TAM F6 L413V 6-cylinder 8·48 litre V-6 air-cooled diesel developing 150 hp at 2650 rpm
Gearbox: Z5-35S with 5 forward and 1 reverse gears
Clutch: single dry plate
Transfer box: 2-speed
Steering: ZF 8038 spindle-type hydrosteering
Turning radius: 7·6 m
Suspension: leaf-type springs with rubber buffers and telescopic shock absorbers, additional front rubber springs
Tyres: 12.00 × 18 PR 10
Number of tyres: 6 + 1 spare
Brakes:
  (main) 2-circuit air-hydraulic on all wheels
  (parking) mechanical with air-servo assist on rear wheels
Electrical system: 24 V
Batteries: 2 × 12 V, 110 Ah

TAM 150 T11 BV (6 × 6) 3000/5000 kg truck

Yugoslav TAM 150 T 11 BV (6 × 6) 3000/5000 kg trucks used to tow anti-tank guns

TAM 4500/5000/5500/6500 Trucks

DESCRIPTION
The TAM 4500 series of trucks is manufactured in Yugoslavia under licence from the West German company of Magirus-Deutz. The 4500 is powered by an F4L 514 four-cylinder air-cooled diesel which develops 85 hp giving the vehicle a maximum road speed of 75 km/h. Payload on roads is 4500 kg. The layout of the vehicle is conventional with the engine at the front, fully enclosed two-door all-steel cab in the centre and the cargo area at the rear with drop sides and a drop tailgate. Suffixes are used to designate different versions: B for forward control, D for 4 × 4 drive and K for dump truck. The 4500D is the 4 × 4 model used by the Yugoslav Army and is similar in layout to the civil version but has a different rear cargo area with a drop tailgate. Seats can be installed if required. The forward control version is the TAM 4500B and the dump truck version is the 4500K.
  The TAM 5000 is powered by the same engine as the TAM 4500 and is available in two versions 4 × 2 (TAM 5000) and 4 × 4 (TAM 5000 DV). The DV version was developed specifically for the Yugoslav Army and has a central tyre pressure regulation system. The dump truck model is designated the TAM 5000K (4 × 2).
  The TAM 5500 is powered by a V-6 F41 614 air-cooled diesel engine, which develops 85 hp and gives the vehicle a maximum road speed of 85 km/h. Payload is 5000 kg. The dump truck model is the TAM 5500DK (4 × 4) and there is also a tractor truck model. The largest model in the range is the TAM 6500, which can carry 6500 kg and there is also a dump truck model.

SPECIFICATIONS (TAM 5000DV)
Configuration: 4 × 4
Weight:
  (empty) 4500 kg
  (loaded road) 9500 kg
Max load: (road) 5000 kg
Length: 6·75 m
Width: 2·19 m
Height: (cab) 2·75 m
Wheelbase: 4·2 m
Engine: F4 4-cylinder air-cooled diesel developing 85 hp at 2300 rpm
Tyres: 12.00 × 18

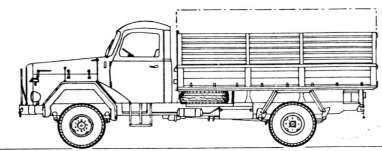

TAM 4500D (4 × 4) 4500 kg truck

TAM 4500D truck towing 128 mm M-63 Plaman multiple rocket system launcher

STATUS
In production. In service with the Yugoslav Army.

MANUFACTURER
Tovama Avtomobilov Motorjev, Maribor, Slovenia, Yugoslavia.

FAP 2220BDS (6 × 4) and FAP 2026BS (6 × 6) Trucks

DESCRIPTION

The FAP 2220BDS (6 × 4) truck is used for carrying and launching the Yugoslav truck-mounted scissors bridge and the reader is referred to this entry in the *Mechanised bridges* section for a photograph of the vehicle with the bridge (page 98). This vehicle can be distinguished from the FAP 2026BS which has a central tyre-pressure regulation system and single rear wheels.

The FAP 2026 BS/AV (6 × 6) is the latest FAP 6 × 6 truck; it has been developed specifically for the Yugoslav Army and features a central tyre-pressure regulation system. The two-door all-steel cab is of the forward control type with the cargo area at the rear with a drop tailgate, removable bows and a tarpaulin cover. The engine for these vehicles is built under licence from British Leyland.

VARIANTS

The FAB 2220BDS and FAP 2026BS (6 × 6) are also used as the chassis for the Yugoslav 128 mm (32 round) multiple rocket system. Details of these versions are given in *Jane's Armour and Artillery 1983–84*, page 748.

SPECIFICATIONS (FAP 2026BS/AV (6 × 6))

Cab seating: 1 + 1 (20 in cargo area)
Configuration: 6 × 6
Weight:
 (empty) 11 000 kg
 (loaded) 21 000 kg
Weight on front axle: (loaded) 6000 kg
Weight on rear axle: (loaded) 15 000 kg
Max load: 10 000 kg
Max towed load: 7200 kg
Max winch capacity: 10 000 kg
Load area: 4·53 × 2·342 m
Length: 7·72 m
Width: 2·49 m
Height: (top of cab) 3·1 m
Wheelbase: 3·4 m + 1·4 m
Track: 2·02 m
Angle of approach/departure: 40°/40°
Max speed: 80 km/h
Fuel consumption: 33 litres/100 km
Range: 600 km
Max gradient:
 (less trailer) 60%
 (with trailer) 40%
Fording: 0·3 m
Engine: V-8 direct injection water-cooled diesel developing 256 hp at 2500 rpm
Gearbox: 6MS-80 with 6 forward and 1 reverse gears
Clutch: single dry plate
Transfer box: 2-speed
Steering: hydraulic ball with bolt

FAP 2026BS (6 × 6) truck

FAP 2026BS (6 × 6) truck. Note tyre pressure regulation system on wheels

Turning radius: 11 m
Suspension: leaf springs with additional rubber springs and telescopic shock absorbers
Tyres: 15.00 × 21
Number of tyres: 6 + 1 spare
Brakes:
 (main) 2-circuit air drum type
 (parking) mechanical, air actuated

Electrical system: 24 V
Number of batteries: 2 × 12 V, 143 Ah

STATUS
In production. In service with the Yugoslav Army.

MANUFACTURER
Yugoslav Motor Vehicle Plant, Pribos, Yugoslavia.

FAP 2026BS carrying 128 mm 32-round multiple rocket system under canvas cover

FAP 2026BS (6 × 6) truck

Other Yugoslav Trucks

TAM trucks known to have been produced include the TAM 1500 (4 × 4) 1500 kg truck that was introduced in 1951. In the 2000 kg class there is the TAM 2000 (4 × 2), the TAM 2001 (4 × 2) and the TAM 2001K (4 × 2) 2000 kg dump truck. The first TAM vehicles were the TAM Pi 561 (4 × 2) cargo truck and the TAM Pi 563 (4 × 2) dump truck, both manufactured under license from Czechoslovakia.

FAP vehicles include the FAP 4 series (payload 5000 kg in 4 × 2 and 4 × 4 configurations built under license from Sauer of Austria), the FAP 6 series (payload 7000 kg in 4 × 2 and 4 × 4 configurations built under licence from Sauer of Austria), FAP 10 (payload 6350 kg, 4 × 2), FAP 13 (payload 8000 kg in 4 × 2 and 4 × 4 configurations built under license from Sauer of Austria), FAP 15B (payload 9300 kg, 4 × 2), and FAP 18B (payload 11 000 kg in 4 × 2 and 4 × 4 configurations).

TANK TRANSPORTERS

This section covers prime movers which are used principally for towing semi-trailers carrying main battle tanks. Many military trucks also exist as tractor trucks, these being used for towing semi-trailers carrying cargo or light armoured vehicles. For example the Berliet TBU-15 is the tractor truck version of the GBU-15 truck and is often used to tow a semi-trailer carrying an AMX-13 light tank. The reader is referred to the *Trucks* section for vehicles of this type. Details of the tank semi-trailers will be found in the *Trailers* section.

BELGIUM

MAN (6 × 4) Tractor Truck

The Belgian Army uses a modified West German commercial MAN (6 × 4) tractor truck to tow the Dutch DAF YTS 10050 semi-trailer of which 29 are in service.

MAN (6 × 4) tractor truck towing YTS 10050 semi-trailer carrying Leopard 1 MBT (C R Zwart)

MAN (6 × 4) tractor truck towing YTS 10050 semi-trailer carrying 105 mm M108 SPH (C R Zwart)

BRAZIL

Mercedes Benz 1924/42 (6 × 4) Tractor Truck

DESCRIPTION
The standard tractor truck of the Brazilian Army is the Mercedes Benz 1924/42 (6 × 4) truck fitted with a winch with a maximum capacity of 20 000 kg. It is manufactured under licence in Brazil and is used to tow a Biselli semi-trailer which can carry one X1A2 tank or two M113 series APCs.

STATUS
In production. In service with the Brazilian Army and Marines.

MANUFACTURER (trailer)
Biselli Viaturas e Equipamentos Industriais Ltda, Av Presidente Wilson 4930, 04220 São Paulo, SP, Brazil.

Mercedes Benz 1924/42 (6 × 4) tractor truck towing Biselli semi-trailer (Ronaldo S Olive)

FRANCE

Nicolas Tractomas (6 × 6) and (8 × 8) Tank Transporter Tractor Trucks

DESCRIPTION
The Nicolas Tractomas tractor trucks are designed to be used primarily as tank transporter tractor units for the Nicolas power-axle tank transporter trailers (see entry in the *Trailers* section). There are four models in the basic range, each of which may be equipped with a civil cab or a military cab with increased capacity and seating. All models are equipped with Mercedes OM 404 A diesel engines developing 520 hp at 2300 rpm. The gearboxes used are the Transmatic ZF type. Few details are available on the range but the performance outlines are provided below.

PERFORMANCE

Military Model	TA 66 OZ	TA 88 OZ	TATT 66 OZ	TATT 88 OZ
Max load 5th wheel	27 500 kg	33 000 kg	21 000 kg	33 500 kg
Max speed	86 km/h	86 km/h	66·5 km/h	66·5 km/h
(with 60 t trailer load)	67·5 km/h	67·5 km/h	65 km/h	65 km/h
Max gradient				
(at 2300 rpm with locking)	11·8%	11·8%	15·5%	15%
(at 1500 rpm with locking)	14%	14%	18·5%	17·8%
(at 1500 rpm with converter)	32·5%	32·5%	42%	40%
Speed on 10% with 60 t payload	12 km/h	12 km/h	10·2 km/h	10·2 km/h

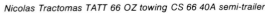

Nicolas Tractomas TATT 66 OZ towing CS 66 40A semi-trailer

Nicolas Tractomas TATT 66 OZ towing CS 66 40A semi-trailer

STATUS
Production.

MANUFACTURER
Nicolas Industri SA, 89290 Champs sur Yonne, France.

SPECIFICATIONS (TATT 66 OZ)
Cab seating: 1 + 4 or 5
Configuration: 6 × 6
Weight:
    (empty) 23 500 kg
    (loaded) 44 500 kg
Length: 8·065 m
Width: 3·3 m
Height:
    (cab, loaded) 3·72 m
    (5th wheel, loaded) 1·82 m
Wheelbase: 3·79 m × 1·65 m
Track: 2·65 m
Angle of approach: 30°
Max speed: 62 km/h
Gradient: 30%
Fuel capacity: 900 litres
Engine: Mercedes OM 404 A V-12, 4-cycle, water-cooled, supercharged diesel developing 520 hp at 2300 rpm
Gearbox: ZF 4S.150.GPA with 8 forward and 1 reverse gears
Converter: ZF WSK 400.59
Steering: hydraulic power-assisted
Turning radius: 10·5 m
Suspension:
    (front) leaf springs
    (rear) leaf springs, cantilever mounting
Tyres: 18.00 × 25 XS
Brakes: air
Electrical system: 24 V
Batteries: 4 × 6 V, 192 Ah
Alternator: 60 A

TYPE	(A) Civil cab	(B) Military cab
(A) TRB 66 OZ		
(B) TA 66 OZ		
(A) TR 88 OZ		
(B) TA 88 OZ		
(A) TRTT 66 OZ		
(B) TATT 66 OZ		
(A) TRTT 88 OZ		
(B) TATT 88 OZ		

Basic outline of Nicolas Tractomas range

Renault TRH 350 and R 360 (6 × 4) Tractor Truck

DEVELOPMENT
The TRH 350 (6 × 4) tractor truck is a standard commercial vehicle adapted to meet military requirements. It has been adopted by the French Army for road use and will be used in conjunction with the Nicholas STA 43 semi-trailer. The vehicle can be used with other semi-trailers carrying MBTs up to a maximum weight of 55 000 kg.

The TRH 350 has now been replaced by the R 360.33T (6 × 4) in production at Bourg en Bresse. It has a type KB 2480 cab but the same engine as the earlier model.

DESCRIPTION
The chassis consists of two U-shaped side-members with five cross-members welded and riveted into position. The vehicle is fitted with a model KB 2400 cab which is of the two-door forward control type and has seats for the driver, two passengers and two bunks at the rear of the cab. The cab is heated and soundproofed and can be tilted forward to an angle of 70 degrees to allow maintenance work on the engine. Optional equipment includes a hydraulic winch with a capacity of 15 000 kg and 90 metres of cable, dividing curtain, third central seat, elbow rests, heating system, fog lamps, tachograph, radio equipment, blackout lights, searchlight, flashing light, combined air/electric cables and an anti-freeze device for the brake circuit.

VARIANTS
The French Army uses a similar version of the Renault TRH 350 (6 × 4) tractor truck for towing semi-trailers carrying fuel and other supplies, designated the R 360.33T.

The French Army also uses the Berliet TR 260 (4 × 2) tractor truck for hauling a variety of semi-trailers.

Renault TRH 350 (6 × 4) tractor truck towing Nicolas semi-trailer carrying AMX-30 MBT (J B Boniface)

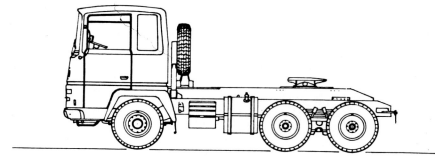

Renault TRH 350 (6 × 4) tractor truck

SPECIFICATIONS (data in square brackets relate to the R 360.33T where this differs from the TRH 350)
Cab seating: 1 + 2
Configuration: 6 × 4
Weight:
(empty) 10 300 kg
(loaded) 34 500 kg
Weight on front axle:
(empty) 5300 kg
(loaded) 6500 kg
Weight on rear bogie:
(empty) 5000 [6500] kg
(loaded) 28 000 kg
Max weight on 5th wheel: 24 000 kg
Length: 6·53 [6·445] m
Width: 2·49 m
Height: 3 [3·135] m

Ground clearance: 0·303 m
Track:
(front) 2·028 m
(rear) 1·825 m
Wheelbase: 2·95 m + 1·35 m
Angle of approach/departure: 22°/45°
Max speed: 66 km/h
Range: 800 km
Fuel capacity: 650 litres
Max gradient: (laden with 70 600 kg gross weight) 15%
Fording: 0·7 m
Engine: Renault model MIVS 08.35.30 8-cylinder water-cooled supercharged diesel developing 356 hp at 2000 rpm
Gearbox: Renault RTO 12 513 with 13 forward and 2 reverse gears
Steering: 8065 hydraulic power-assisted

Turning radius: 8·5 m
Suspension:
(front) leaf springs and shock absorbers
(rear) torsion bar stabiliser; rear wheels have reduction gears in the wheel hubs, differential locking system between axles and wheels
Tyres: 8.50 × 20 [13 × 22.5]
Brakes: pneumatic
Electrical system: 24 V
Batteries: 4 × 12 V, 200 Ah [2 × 12 V, 143 Ah]

STATUS
TRH 350 production complete. R 360.33T in production. Both in service with the French and other armies.

MANUFACTURER
Enquiries to Renault Véhicules Industriels, 33 quai Léon Blum, 92153 Suresnes, France.

Renault TBH 280 (6 × 6) Truck Tractor

DEVELOPMENT
The Renault (formerly Berliet) TBH 280 (6 × 6) truck tractor has been designed for towing semi-trailers both on roads and across country up to a maximum weight of 53 000 kg (eg trailer weighing 12 000 kg and tank weighing 41 000 kg). Renault built over 18 000 chassis of this type (in 6 × 6, 6 × 4, and 4 × 4 configurations) for a variety of civil and military applications (there is a separate entry in the *Trucks* section for the Berliet GBH 280, now known as the Renault TRM 12 000, 6 × 6 truck).

DESCRIPTION
The chassis consists of U-shaped side-members with the cross-members bolted into position. The layout of the vehicle is conventional with the engine at the front, cab in the centre and fifth wheel at the rear. The rear bogie has both inter-wheel and inter-axle differential locks. Optional equipment includes one piece laminated windscreen, two piece windscreen, air intake at cab roof level, sand filter, jerrican holder, tool box, weapon supports in cab, radio suppression, blackout equipment, exterior current outlet socket, spotlight, and either a 15 000 kg or twin 15 000 kg winches each with 90 metres of cable.

VARIANTS
The basic chassis can also be fitted with the Ampliroll equipment for which there is a separate entry in this section.

SPECIFICATIONS
Cab seating: 1 + 2
Configuration: 6 × 6
Weight:
(empty) 11 310 kg
(loaded) 28 350 kg
(max GCW) 75 000 kg
Weight on front axle:
(empty) 5590 kg
(loaded) 7350 kg
Weight on rear bogie:
(empty) 5720 kg
(loaded) 21 000 kg
Max weight on 5th wheel: 14 500 kg
Length: 7·675 m
Width: 2·48 m
Height:
(cab) 2·85 m
(5th wheel) 1·55 m
Ground clearance: 0·275 m

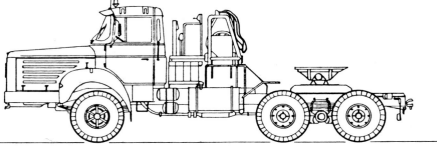
Renault TBH 280 (6 × 6) truck tractor

Renault TBH 280 (6 × 6) truck tractor towing semi-trailer carrying AMX-30 MBT

Track:
(front) 1·997 m
(rear) 1·825 m
Wheelbase: 3·975 m + 1·35 m
Angle of approach: 28°
Max speed: 80 km/h
Range: 700 km
Fuel capacity: 450 litres (200 + 250 litres)
Max gradient: (towing fully laden semi-trailer) 25%
Max side slope: 30%
Fording: 0·85 m
Engine: Renault MDS 0635.40 6-cylinder supercharged water-cooled diesel developing 280 hp at 1900 rpm
Gearbox: 5 S 110 GP with 9 forward and 1 reverse gears with pneumatic assistance
Clutch: 430 DB 1900 with pneumatic assistance
Transfer box: GA 800/3D 2-speed

Steering: 7438 power-assisted
Turning radius: 12 m
Suspension:
(front) leaf springs with 2 mechanical stops and shock absorbers
(rear) leaf springs with 4 mechanical stops
Tyres: 12.00 × 20
Brakes: pneumatic
Electrical system: 24 V
Batteries: 4 × 6 V

STATUS
In production. In service with a number of countries including Morocco, Qatar and the United Arab Emirates.

MANUFACTURER
Enquiries to Renault Véhicules Industriels, 8 quai Léon Blum, 92152 Suresnes, France.

Berliet TBO 15 M3 (6 × 4) Tractor

DEVELOPMENT
The Berliet TBO 15 M3 (6 × 4) tractor is a standard commercial model adapted to meet the requirements of the French Army. The first prototype was completed in 1959 with first production vehicles following in 1961. Production has now been completed. The vehicle was designed for towing semi-trailers up to a maximum weight of 60 000 kg.

DESCRIPTION
The engine is at the front, two-door all steel cab in the centre and the fifth wheel at the rear. The cab is provided with a heater and racks for stowing the crew's small arms.

Mounted to the rear of the cab are two Bonnier double-drum 15 000 kg capacity winches, each with 90 metres of cable. The winches are provided with a brake and holding system and can be used for recovering disabled vehicles or for self-recovery if the tractor becomes stuck. Two towing eyes are provided front

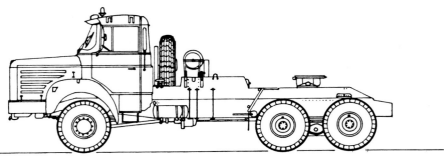
Berliet TBO 15 M3 (6 × 4) tractor

and rear and an inter-vehicle starting socket is also provided.

VARIANTS
Between 1973 and 1974 Berliet built an improved model

called the TBO 310 powered by a Berliet MIS 645 six-cylinder diesel developing 289 hp at 2100 rpm. Unladen weight was 19 000 kg. This was followed by the TBO 15 A (6 × 6) vehicle which did not however enter production.

SPECIFICATIONS
Cab seating: 1 + 2
Configuration: 6 × 4
Weight: (empty) 18 450 kg
Towed load: 60 000 kg
King-pin diameter: 89 mm
Length: 8·23 m
Width: 3·07 m
Height:
(cab) 2·95 m
(5th wheel) 1·65 m
Ground clearance: 0·5 m
Track:
(front) 2·1 m
(rear) 2·19 m
Wheelbase: 3·74 m + 1·52 m
Angle of approach/departure: 23°/45°
Max speed: 53 km/h
Range: 800 km
Fuel capacity: 500 litres
Gradient: 15%
Fording: 0·5 m
Engine: Berliet MS 640 A 6-cylinder in-line diesel developing 255 bhp at 1800 rpm
Gearbox: Berliet FBO 41 RA manual with 5 forward and 1 reverse gears and an integral reducer
Clutch: twin plate, air assisted
Steering: recirculating ball, hydraulic assisted
Turning radius: 10·5 m
Suspension: semi-elliptical springs with hydraulic shock-absorbers on front axle
Tyres: 16.00 × 20
Number of tyres: 10 + 1 spare
Brakes:
(main) air
(handbrake) mechanical
Electrical system: 24 V
Batteries: 4 Type 6 TN (12 V), 100 Ah
Generator: 600 W

Rear view of Berliet TBO 15 M3 (6 × 4) tractor showing position of two winches to rear of cab

STATUS
Production complete. In service with the French Army.

MANUFACTURER
Berliet, 160 boulevard de Verdun, 92402 Courbevoie, France. (Berliet is now part of Renault Véhicules Industriels.)

Lohr DMC Tank Transporter System

DESCRIPTION
The Lohr DMC tank transporter system is described by the manufacturer as a combined tank transporter and recovery vehicle system. It consists of a hydraulically-powered moving platform carried on the rear of a 6 × 6 open-framed truck chassis and operating along the same general lines as the Bennes Marrel Ampliroll system. The DMC system can off-load and recover the platform by the combined use of a hydraulic ram and for recovery a heavy duty hydraulic winch (on the platform) is provided. The platform may be traversed to one side or the other for off-loading or recovery. The forward part of the platform has a raised guard frame to protect the carrier cab and this frame is also used as the carrier for the vehicle spare wheel. The Lohr DMC system has a payload of 18 000 to 20 000 kg. Locking devices at the front and back of the platform anchor the load when transported.

Illustrations released to date show the DMC system fitted on a FIAT 260 PM 35 (6 × 6) 10 000 kg truck chassis.

STATUS
Development.

MANUFACTURER
Lohr, Hangenbieten, Strasbourg 67980, France.

Lohr DMC system carrying AMX VCI APC on FIAT 260 PM 35 (6 × 6) 10 000 kg truck

Lohr DMC system being used to carry AMX-10P APC on FIAT 260 PM 35 (6 × 6) 10 000 kg truck

Bennes Marrel Ampliroll System

DESCRIPTION
The Ampliroll system consists of a flatbed platform mounted on the rear of a Renault GBH 260 (6 × 4) or similar truck. The platform is lowered to the ground hydraulically, the AFV (eg AMX-10P MICV or AMX-13 tank or similar vehicle weighing up to 20 000 kg) is driven onto the platform and secured in position and the platform is then raised back onto the chassis of the truck over the rear roller. The complete operation takes a maximum of three minutes.

The tipping unit is of all-alloy construction and consists of a chassis reinforcing sub-frame, central beam to which the tipping rams are hinged, short hinged connecting arm framework which controls the extent of rearward movement, telescopic jib sliding in front of the central beams and carrying at its upper end the unit

Bennes Marrel Ampliroll system carrying AMX-10P MICV and towing trailer with demountable container

Bennes Marrel Ampliroll system carrying AMX-10P MICV on flatbed

lifting hook and rear hinges incorporating flanged rollers on bronze bushes to centralise the unit. The hydraulic system contains a pump complete with safety valve and transmission, two main arms providing both normal tipping action and lowering of platform, double acting ram to actuate the sliding jib beam and the direction and braking valve block actuated from the vehicle cab by a remote servo-control.

The deck of the platform has adjustable track guides and the vehicle is fitted with a stabilising device which locks the rear suspension (eg last axle) during loading and unloading. The Ampliroll system can also be used to carry containers, dump bodies, fuel and water tanks. There is a separate entry in this section for the Tidelium 40 Ampliroll system which has been designed to carry an MBT weighing up to 40 000 kg.

VARIANTS
There is a separate entry under United Kingdom for the Boughton Ampliroll Swap Body system which has been evaluated by the British Army.

STATUS
Production. Quantities of this system have been sold for military applications in Europe and Africa.

MANUFACTURER
Bennes Marrel SA, ZI St Etienne Boutheon, BP 56 42160 Andrezieux-Boutheon, France.

Tidelium 40 Ampliroll T 40 A (8 × 6) Tank Carrier

DESCRIPTION
This consists of a four-axle (8 × 6) truck chassis on the rear of which is mounted a Bennes Marrel Ampliroll system consisting of a hydraulically operated platform which is launched to the rear of the vehicle. The tank, which can weigh up to 40 000 kg, is recovered onto the platform, shackled firmly into position and the platform is then returned to the rear of the vehicle. This takes between two and three minutes to accomplish. The crew of the vehicle being carried is seated in the fully enclosed forward control cab. When the system is being used on roads the vehicle can tow a trailer carrying another MBT.

The system can be adapted to carry and lay in position containers for a wide variety of roles (eg command, radio, medical), platforms carrying ammunition and supplies, water and fuel tanks, and can also be modified to accept a dump truck body.

VARIANTS
A 60 000 kg payload version is now being developed.

SPECIFICATIONS
Cab seating: 1 + 5
Configuration: 8 × 6
Weight: 34 500 kg
Payload: 40 000 kg
Length: 11·6 m
Width: 3·62 m
Height:
(loaded with AMX-30 tank) 4·8 m
(carrier bed) 3·35 m
Max speed:
(road) 65 km/h
(cross country) 55 km/h
Max gradient: 30%
Engine: diesel developing 430 hp at 2500 rpm
Gearbox: 8 forward and 1 reverse gears
Tyres: 18.00 × 25
Flat bed length: 6 m
Flat bed height: 3·1 m

Sequence showing Tidelium 40 laying platform with AMX-30 MBT onto ground

STATUS
Development complete. Ready for production.

MANUFACTURER
Creusot-Loire, Division de la Mécanique Spécialisée, 15 rue Pasquier, 75008 Paris, France.

GERMANY, FEDERAL REPUBLIC

MAN (6 × 6) Tractor Trucks

DESCRIPTION
There are three MAN 6 × 6 tractor trucks which all use the same basic chassis, cab and equipment. They are the 32.320 DFAT with a maximum possible towed weight of 85 000 kg; the 32.365 DFAT with a maximum possible towed weight of 105 000 kg; and the 40400 DFAT with a maximum possible towed weight of 130 000 kg. Differences are found mainly in engine capacity and power (see Specifications table).

All three models have forward-control, all-steel cabs that can be tilted forward for engine access. The chassis frames have longitudinal members constructed from pressed U-sections with cross members both riveted and bolted in place. The front bumper is reinforced for winch operations. A sub-frame carries the fifth wheel.

All three models can be fitted with ZF gearboxes but the 32.320 and the 32.365 may be fitted with optional Fuller RTO 9513, Fuller, WSK or Allison gearboxes, the latter providing automatic transmission (the Specification tables provide the standard gearboxes). All gearboxes are provided with a power take-off.

This power take-off is used to power a Rotzler 25 000 kg hydraulic winch or a 25 000 kg winch. Both are equipped with 50 metres of 24 mm diameter cable. A mechanical winch is also provided. This may be an Itag-Celle M 240 or M 180, the former with a 24 000 kg capacity and the latter with 18 000 kg capacity. Both have 60 metres of 26 mm cable. Power for both is taken from the vehicle's main engine. The 40400 has only the mechanical M 240 winch with a 24 000 kg capacity.

Optional extra equipment for all models includes a variable speed governor for the fuel injection pump, a tropical radiator (which raises the cab height by 80 mm), a manual engine throttle, a reinforced transmission, reinforced exhaust and tank brackets, roof air induction inlet, an upswept exhaust stack, an alternative Jost fifth-wheel coupling, a raised axle bleed system, a spare wheel on the winch guard, a working platform behind the cab, a towing coupling, a battery charging socket and two 60-litre fibreglass water tanks.

STATUS
Production.

MANUFACTURER
MAN, Commercial Vehicle Division, Postfach 50060, D 8000 Munich, Federal Republic of Germany.

MAN 40400 (6 × 6) tractor truck carrying Leopard 1 MBT

MAN 40400 (6 × 6) tractor truck carrying Leopard 1 MBT

SPECIFICATIONS

Model	32.320 DFAT	32.365 DFAT	40400 DFAT
Cab seating	1 + 2	1 + 2	1 + 2
Configuration	6 × 6	6 × 6	6 × 6
Weight (loaded)	32 000 kg	32 000 kg	40 000 kg
Weight on front axle (loaded)	7500 kg	7500 kg	8500 kg
Weight on rear axle (loaded)	13 000 kg	13 000 kg	16 000 kg
Permissible towed load	80 000 kg	80 000 kg	100 000 kg
Max towed load	85 000 kg	105 000 kg	130 000 kg
Length	8·295 m	8·295 m	8·295 m
Width (cab)	2·49 m	2·49 m	2·49 m
(rear wheels)	2·721 m	2·721 m	2·721 m
Height (cab, loaded)	3·115 m	3·115 m	3·115 m
(5th wheel base plate)	1·28 m	1·28 m	1·353 m
Track (front)	2·034 m	2·034 m	2·034 m
(rear)	1·924 m	1·924 m	1·924 m
Wheelbase	3·825 m + 1·4 m	3·825 m + 1·4 m	3·825 m + 1·4 m
Max speed (road)	67 km/h	65 km/h	70 km/h
(cross-country)	45 km/h	43 km/h	47 km/h
Fuel capacity (total)	630 litres	630 litres	630 litres
Max gradient (permissible load)	26%	30%	18·5%
Engine	MAN type D 2530 MXF V-10 15·953-litre diesel developing 320 hp (DIN) at 2500 rpm	MAN type D 2840 MF V-10 18·272-litre diesel developing 365 hp (DIN) at 2500 rpm	MAN type D 2540 MTF V-10 15·953-litre diesel developing 440 hp (DIN) at 2300 rpm
Gearbox	ZF 5 K-110 GP, 9 forward and 1 reverse gears	ZF Synchroma type 4 S-150, 8 forward and 1 reverse gears	ZF Synchroma type 4 S-150, 8 forward and 1 reverse gears
Transfer case	MAN type G 801 2-speed	MAN type G 801 2-speed	MAN type G 801 2-speed
Clutch	2-plate hydraulic	2-plate hydraulic	hydrodynamic torque converter
Steering	ZF hydro-steer type 8065	ZF hydro-steer type 8065	ZF hydro-steer type 8065
Suspension (front)	semi-elliptic leaf springs with hollow rubber springs and telescopic shock absorbers	semi-elliptic leaf springs with hollow rubber springs and telescopic shock absorbers	semi-elliptic leaf springs with hollow rubber springs and telescopic shock absorbers
(rear)	semi-elliptic leaf springs	semi-elliptic leaf springs	semi-elliptic leaf springs
Tyres	14.00 × 20 X	14.00 × 20 X	14.00 × 20 X
Number of tyres	10 + 1 spare	10 + 1 spare	10 + 1 spare
Brakes	air, 2-circuit	air, 2-circuit	air, 2-circuit
Electrical system	24 V	24 V	24 V
Batteries	2 × 12 V, 143 Ah	2 × 12 V, 143 Ah	2 × 12 V, 143 Ah

Iveco Magirus Tractor Trucks

DESCRIPTION
Based on its extensive range of cross-country vehicles, some of which are described in the *Trucks* section, Iveco Magirus offers an extensive range of 6 × 6 tractor trucks, four of which are detailed below. All vehicles have the engine at the front, fully enclosed all-steel two-door cab in the centre and the fifth wheel at the rear. In each case a wide range of options is offered, for example, in the case of the 310/320 D 34 AS, auxiliary 5th wheel coupling, 2 × 20 000 kg or 1 × 30 000 kg hydraulic winch and a 60-litre water reservoir.

Iveco Magirus 400 M 34 AS (6 × 6) tractor truck towing semi-trailer carrying Leopard ARV

Iveco Magirus 310 (320) D 34 AS (6 × 6) tractor truck

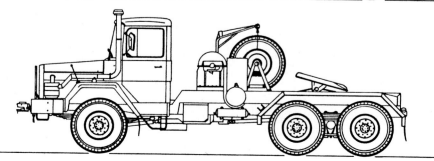

Iveco Magirus 360 D 34 AS (6 × 6) tractor truck

SPECIFICATIONS

Designation	310 D 34 AS	320 D 34 AS	360 D 34 AS	400 M 34 AS
Cab seating	1 + 2	1 + 2	1 + 2	1 + 2
Configuration	6 × 6	6 × 6	6 × 6	6 × 6
Weight (empty)	13 020 kg	13 750 kg	13 300 kg	13 150 kg
(on 5th wheel, loaded)	21 000 kg	21 000 kg	21 000 kg	21 000 kg
(gross combination weight)	76 000 kg	62 150 kg	69 150 kg	87 150 kg
Length	7·715 m	7·52 m	7·005 m	8·005 m
Width	2·5 m	2·832 m	2·58 m	2·5 m
Height (cab)	2·97 m	2·97 m	2·97 m	2·97 m
(5th wheel)	1·84 m	1·78 m	1·84 m	1·84 m
Ground clearance (front axle)	0·36 m	0·36 m	0·36 m	0·36 m
(rear axle)	0·42 m	0·36 m	0·39 m	0·391 m
Track (front)	1·982 m	1·982 m	2·002 m	2·002 m
(rear)	1·924 m	1·97 m	1·924 m	1·97 m
Wheelbase	4 m + 1·45 m	4 m + 1·39 m	4 m + 1·45 m	4 m + 1·45 m
Max speed (on road, high range)	57 km/h	64·3 km/h .	58·5 km/h	63 km/h
(cross country, low range)	36·4 km/h	41 km/h	32·4 km/h	39 km/h
Max gradient (high range)	14·6%	19·5%	20·4%	18·2%
(low range)	23·6%	32%	35%	30%
Engine model	F 10L 413 L	F 10L 413 F	BF 10L 413 F	BF 10L 413 F
(all are Iveco Magirus)	10-cylinder	10-cylinder	10-cylinder	(turbo-charged)
	air-cooled	air-cooled	air-cooled	10-cylinder
				air-cooled
Engine output	325 bhp/2650 rpm	342 bhp/2500 rpm	360 bhp/2500 rpm	400 bhp/2500 rpm
Gearbox type	4S-150 GP	RT 9509	4S-150 GP	4S-150 GP
Number of gears	8 forward, 1 reverse	8 forward, 1 reverse	8 forward, 1 reverse	8 forward, 1 reverse
Transfer box	2-speed	2-speed	2-speed	2-speed
Brakes (main)	air (dual circuit)	air (dual circuit)	air (dual circuit)	air (dual circuit)
(parking)	mechanical on rear wheels, actuated by spring energy brake cylinder			
Electrical system	24 V	24 V	24 V	24 V
Batteries	2 × 12 V	2 × 12 V	2 × 12 V	2 × 12 V

STATUS
Production. In service outside West Germany.

MANUFACTURER
Iveco Magirus AG, Postfach 2740, 7900 Ulm, Federal
Republic of Germany.

Iveco Magirus 310 D 34 AS (6 × 6) tractor truck

Faun FS 42.75/42 (8 × 6) Tractor Truck

DEVELOPMENT/DESCRIPTION
This 8 × 6 tractor truck is almost identical to the Faun
SLT 50-2 (8 × 8) fully described in the following entry
but has a less powerful engine and different transmission. It tows a Kässbohrer 12-wheeled trailer weighing
18 500 kg unladen and 56 000 kg laden.

STATUS
Production complete. In service with the West German
Army.

MANUFACTURER
Faun-Werke Nuernberg, POB 8, 8560 Lauf/Pegn,
Federal Republic of Germany.

SPECIFICATIONS
Cab seating: 1 + 3
Configuration: 8 × 6
Weight:
  (empty) 19 700 kg
  (on 5th wheel, loaded) 39 700 kg
  (gross combination weight) 95 000 kg
Length: 8·83 m
Width: 3·07 m
Height:
  (laden) 2·98 m
  (unladen) 3·02 m
Ground clearance: 0·33 m
Track:
  (front) 2·59 m
  (rear) 2·61 m
Wheelbase: 1·5 m + 2·7 m + 1·5 m
Angle of approach/departure: 30°/46°
Max speed: 67 km/h
Fuel capacity: 800 litres
Max gradient: 45%
Fording: 0·8 m

Faun FS 42.75/42 (8 × 6) tractor truck

Engine: Deutz Model BF 12 L 413 FC 12-cylinder air-
cooled diesel developing 518 bhp at 1750 rpm
Gearbox: manual ZF 4S-150 GPA with torque converter drive clutch ZF WSK 400, 8 forward and 1 reverse
gears
Steering: ZF hydraulic, dual circuit

Turning radius: (without trailer) 11·2 m
Tyres: 18-22.5 XS PR 20
Number of tyres: 8 + 1 spare
Brakes: air, dual circuit
Electrical system: 24 V

Faun SLT 50-2 (8 × 8) Tractor Truck

DEVELOPMENT

The development of the SLT 50-2, or Elephant as it is more commonly known, can be traced back to 1965 when West Germany and the USA decided to design a tank transporter known as the Heavy Equipment Transporter (HET) to carry the MBT-70 then under development by both countries. In the USA the Chrysler Corporation was the prime contractor for the tractor while in Germany Faun was responsible for the tractor and Krupp for the trailer. In 1970 the MBT-70 and the HET were cancelled. Further development in the USA resulted in the XM746, which was standardised as the M746 and production was undertaken by Ward La France. Development continued in Germany and the Federal German Army placed an order with Faun for 328 Elephants, the last of which were delivered in 1980. The SLT 50-2 and its semi-trailer can carry any of the AFVs in service with the Federal German Army including the Leopard 2 MBT.

DESCRIPTION

The SLT 50-2 is an 8 × 8 vehicle with powered steering on the front two axles. The fully enclosed cab is of steel and glassfibre construction and has seats for the driver and three passengers.

The drive train consists of a V-8 diesel engine coupled to a hot-shift transmission and a two-speed transfer case. The front and rear bogies are fitted with a lockable inter-axle differential and each axle has a lockable differential. The front and rear bogies are suspended by torque rods and taper leaf springs arranged in parallel with progressive springing.

Air brakes are provided for both the tractor and semi-trailer and an automatic load-sensitive brake valve ensures equal braking under all load conditions. The parking brake consists of spring-loaded cylinders mounted to the rear wheel brakes. A retarder is connected directly to the gearbox and is also connected via an electric control line to the service brakes of the semi-trailer.

Mounted to the rear of the cab is a dual winch unit, each winch with a capacity of 17 000 kg. Both winches have a winch up mechanism and the right winch can also be used to the front of the vehicle for self-recovery operations. Each winch is provided with 43 metres of 28 mm diameter rope; maximum winding speed is 24 metres a minute at a capacity of 8500 kg or 12 metres a minute at a capacity of 17 000 kg.

The spare wheel is mounted on the right side of the tractor and a small winch is provided to facilitate handling of the wheel.

SPECIFICATIONS
Cab seating: 1 + 3
Configuration: 8 × 8
Weight:
 (empty) 23 000 kg
 (on 5th wheel loaded) 18 300 kg
 (gross combination weight) 92 000 kg
Length: 8·85 m
 (with trailer) 18·82 m
Width: 3·07 m
Height: 3 m
 (to 5th wheel) 1·55 m

Faun SLT 50-2 (8 × 8) Elephant tractor truck

Faun SLT 50-2 (8 × 8) Elephant tractor truck towing trailer carrying Leopard ARV (T J Gander)

Ground clearance: 0·303 m
Track:
 (front) 2·535 m
 (rear) 2·593 m
Wheelbase: 1·5 m + 2·7 m + 1·5 m
Angle of approach/departure: 30°/50°
Max speed:
 (road, without semi-trailer) 65 km/h
 (road, with loaded semi-trailer) 40 km/h
 (15% gradient with loaded semi-trailer) 9 km/h
Range: 500 km
Fuel capacity: 800 litres
Max gradient: 30% (87 500 kg gross combination weight)
Fording: 0·8 m
Engine: MTU MB 837 Ea-500 V-8 diesel developing 730 hp at 2100 rpm

Gearbox: ZF 4 PW 200H2 with 4 forward and 2 reverse gears
Torque converter: ZF 500–10
Transfer box: 2-speed
Steering: power-assisted
Turning radius: (without trailer) 12 m
Tyres: 18.00 × 22.5
Number of tyres: 8 + 1 spare
Brakes: air
Electrical system: 24 V

STATUS
Production complete. In service with the West German Army.

MANUFACTURER
Faun-Werke Nuernberg, POB 8,8560 Lauf/Pegn, Federal Republic of Germany.

ITALY

Astra BM 20 NF1 (6 × 6) M113 Carrier

DESCRIPTION

The full Italian designation for this vehicle/platform combination is Astra BM 20 NF1 con attrezzatura per transporto M113 e derivati. It is a conversion of the Astra BM 20 (6 × 6) truck chassis to accommodate an Amplicar T25 loading platform to carry an M113 armoured personnel carrier and its various derivatives. The Amplicar T25 platform follows the same general lines as the Bennes Marrel Ampliroll system and is on and off-loaded by a combination of twin hydraulic jacks and a lifting arm acting on a carrier lug mounted on the front of the platform. Once on the platform the M113 is held secure by a combination of chains and chocks.

The Amplicar T25 has a payload of 13 000 kg and when being loaded and unloaded is stabilised by a roller (stabilizzatore) arm which extends downwards onto the ground as the platform rolls forwards or to the rear. Power for the system is from a hydraulic pump powered

Astra BM 20 NF1 (6 × 6) off-loading M113 APC (T J Gander)

Astra BM 20 NF1 (6 × 6) carrying M113 APC (T J Gander)

by the vehicle's main engine.

The full weight of a BM 20 NF1 loaded with an M113 is 28 000 kg.

STATUS
Prototype.

MANUFACTURER
Astra Veicoli Industriali SpA, Via Caorsana 79, 29100 Piacenza, Italy.

Astra BM 305 (6 × 6) Tractor Truck

DESCRIPTION
The Astra BM 305 (6 × 6) tractor truck is a militarised version of the BM 305 range of heavy construction vehicles. In its tank transporter form the Astra BM 305 can tow a variety of semi-trailers, one of the most common being the Cometto MPS 50 semi-trailer with a payload capacity of up to 60 000 kg.

In its tank transporter form the BM 305 has a forward control cab with an all-steel construction and seating for the driver and two passengers. There is a choice of two engines, the FIAT type 8280.02 or the Mercedes model OM 423, both diesels. There is also a choice of tyre size.

SPECIFICATIONS (FIAT engine version)
Cab seating: 1 + 2
Configuration: 6 × 6
Weight: (empty) 10 400 kg
Max towed load: 60 000 kg
Length: 7·06 m
Width: 2·5 m
Height:
(cab) 3·01 m
(turntable) 1·49 m
Ground clearance: 0·335 m
Track:
(front) 2·045 m
(rear) 1·825 m
Wheelbase: 3·3 m + 1·4 m
Max speed:
(unloaded) 78·6 km/h
(loaded) 67·1 km/h

Astra BM 305 (6 × 6) tractor truck towing Cometto MPS 50 semi-trailer carrying M60A1 tank (T J Gander)

Fuel capacity: 300 litres
Max gradient: 40%
Engine: FIAT type 8280.02 8-cylinder 17·173-litre diesel developing 352 hp
option
Mercedes model OM 423 10-cylinder 18·27-litre diesel developing 352 hp
Gearbox: 8 forward and 1 reverse gears
Transfer box: 2-speed
Steering: Calzoni HDA 45.13 servo-assisted
Turning radius: 16·8 m

Tyres: 12.00 × 20 (optional 12.00 × 24)
Brakes: air
Electrical system: 24 V
Number of batteries: 2 × 12 V, 143 Ah

STATUS
Production.

MANUFACTURER
Astra Veicoli Industriali SpA, Via Caorsana 79, 29100 Piacenza, Italy.

FIAT 320 PTM 45 (6 × 6) Tractor Truck

DEVELOPMENT
The FIAT 320 PTM 45 (6 × 6) tractor truck has been designed to meet an Italian Army requirement for a vehicle capable of towing a semi-trailer carrying a Leopard 1 MBT both on and off the road as well as having the capability to recover damaged and disabled vehicles. The first prototype was completed in 1978. Following successful trials the Italian Army placed an order for 70 vehicles.

The FIAT 320 PTM 45 (6 × 6) tractor tows an OTO Melara designed, Bartoletti-manufactured trailer, designated the Mod TCS 50 BO.

DESCRIPTION
The forward control six-man cab can be tilted forward to give access to the engine for maintenance. Two types of cab are available, one with a fully enclosed hard top and the other with a windscreen that can be folded forward through 180 degrees, removable door tops and side screens and a canvas roof that folds to the rear.

To the rear of the cab are two winches, each rated at 20 000 kg. The standard 89 mm diameter king-pin is positioned over the two rear axles. The vehicle can be delivered with either single or dual rear wheels.

SPECIFICATIONS
Cab seating: 1 + 5
Configuration: 6 × 6
Weight:
(curb) 14 900 kg
(max load on 5th wheel) 20 000 kg
(gross combination weight) 79 200 kg
Length: 7·42 m
Width: 2·545 m
Height:
(overall) 2·946 m
(5th wheel) 1·641 m
Ground clearance: 0·4 m
Track:
(front) 1·985 m
(rear) 1·97 m
Wheelbase: 3·6 m + 1·38 m
Angle of approach/departure: 43°/60°
Max speed: over 60 km/h
Range: 600 km
Fuel capacity: 500 litres
Gradient: 30%
Side slope: 20%
Fording: 1·2 m
Engine: FIAT 8280.22 V-8 water-cooled turbo-charged diesel developing 450 hp (DIN) at 2400 rpm

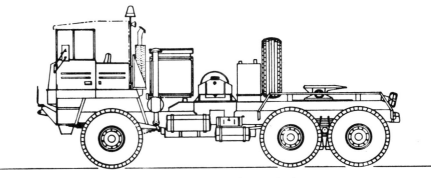

FIAT 320 PTM 45 (6 × 6) tractor truck

FIAT 320 PTM 45 (6 × 6) tractor truck with dual rear wheels

Gearbox: 8 forward and 1 reverse gears, torque converter, transfer box with lockable torque divider, lockable differential at rear axles
Steering: powered

Turning radius: 9·5 m
Suspension: leaf springs
Tyres: 14.00 × 20
Number of tyres: 10 + 1 spare

STATUS
Production. In service with the Italian Army.

MANUFACTURER
FIAT, Direzione Mezzi Speciali, Corso G Marconi 10/20, Turin, Italy.

FIAT 320 PTM 45 (6 × 6) tractor truck towing four-axle semi-trailer carrying Italian-built Leopard 1 MBT

JAPAN

Mitsubishi Model NW204JR (6 × 6) Truck Tractor

DESCRIPTION
The Mitsubishi Model NW204JR (6 × 6) truck tractor has been designed for towing a three-axle semi-trailer carrying an MBT with a maximum weight of 40 000 kg. The vehicle is designated the Type 73 truck tractor by the Japanese Self-Defence Force. The layout of the vehicle is conventional, with the engine at the front, two-door fully enclosed cab in the centre and the fifth wheel at the rear.

Mitsubishi Model NW204JR (6 × 6) truck tractor towing semi-trailer carrying Type 61 MBT

SPECIFICATIONS
Cab seating: 1 + 2
Configuration: 6 × 6
Weight:
  (empty) 9500 kg
  (loaded) 26 240 kg
  (on 5th wheel) 16 500 kg
Length:
  (tractor) 6·835 m
  (tractor and trailer) 16·255 m
Width: 3·29 m

Height:
  (cab) 2·92 m
  (5th wheel) 1·47 m
Track:
  (front) 1·915 m
  (rear) 1·865 m
Wheelbase: 4·65 m
Max speed: 60 km/h
Engine: Model DED 10-cylinder diesel developing 375 hp at 2500 rpm

Turning radius: 8·9 m
Tyres: 10.00 × 20

STATUS
In production. In service with the Japanese Ground Self-Defence Force.

MANUFACTURER
Mitsubishi Heavy Industries, 5-1, Marunouchi 2-chome, Chiyoda-ku, Tokyo, Japan.

NETHERLANDS

FTF MS 4050 (6 × 4) Tractor Truck

DEVELOPMENT
Floor's Handel en Industrie BV (FTF) is a license constructor of Mack trucks for the European market and when it was decided to replace the Dutch Army's Thornycroft Antars, FTF was requested to submit a design for a new tank transporter. The result was the FTF MS 4050 which, after comparison tests with Faun and MAN prototypes, was approved for Dutch Army service. Thirty-nine were purchased by the Dutch Army in December 1972.

DESCRIPTION
The FTF MS 4050 is a 6 × 4 tractor truck which is normally used to tow the FTF FLO 25-520 semi-trailer tank transporter. It has a forward control cab with two hydraulic suspension seats. The chassis is constructed from high-strength steel-manganese alloys with the

engine protruding to the rear of the cab. Various types of winches can be fitted, one being the Tulsa Model 80 with a capacity of 45 359 kg. As an alternative, two Rotzler 20 000 kg winches can be mounted. A spare wheel is carried under the chassis frame.

SPECIFICATIONS
Cab seating: 1 + 1
Configuration: 6 × 4
Weight:
  (empty) 15 500 kg
  (full load with semi-trailer) 110 000 kg
Length: 7·52 m
  (with trailer) 16·33 m
Width: 2·82 m
Height:
  (top of exhaust) 3·39 m
  (5th wheel) 1·68 m
Track: 2·16 m

Wheelbase: 4·2 m
Distance between 2nd and 3rd axle: 1·58 m
Fuel capacity: 450 litres
Range: (loaded) 650 km
Engine: Detroit Diesel type 12V7N (N65) V-12 water-cooled diesel developing 475 hp at 2100 rpm
Gearbox: Allison CLBT 5960 with 6 forward and 1 reverse gears
Steering: ZF 8072
Brakes: air

STATUS
Production complete. In service with the Netherlands Army.

MANUFACTURER
FTF, Floor's Handel en Industrie NV, Larenseweg 32, Hilversum, Netherlands.

FTF MS 4050 (6 × 4) tractor truck towing DAF YTS 10050 semi-trailer (C R Zwart)

FTF MS 4050 (6 × 4) tractor with forward control cab (C R Zwart)

SPAIN

Spanish Tank Transporters

In addition to the American M123 (6 × 6) 10-ton tractor truck, the Spanish Army also uses a Talbot/Barreiros R-3464 tractor truck and a Pegaso 2040 tractor truck with Spanish built DAF and Freuhauf semi-trailers.

SWEDEN

Volvo N12 (6 × 4) Tractor Truck

DEVELOPMENT
The Volvo N12 (6 × 4) tractor truck has been developed from a commercial vehicle to meet a Swedish Army requirement for a vehicle capable of carrying a Centurion or S-tank and having a large enough cab to accommodate the tank crew of three or four in addition to the crew of the truck.

The prototype was delivered to the Swedish Army in October 1975 for field trials and first production tractor trucks were delivered in April 1977. In the Swedish Army the N12 tows the DAF YTS 10050 semi-trailer although it can also tow other semi-trailers such as the Swedish HAFO H50-3-RLS or the H50-4-RLS, both of which have a maximum payload of 50 tonnes.

Volvo N12 (6 × 4) tractor truck towing DAF YTS 10050 semi-trailer carrying Centurion MBT

DESCRIPTION
The layout of the N12 is conventional with the engine at the front, fully enclosed four-door all-steel cab in the centre and the fifth wheel at the rear. The vehicle is not fitted with a winch and so cannot recover disabled and damaged vehicles.

The chassis sides are of rolled U-profile and reinforced. The rear axle is a tandem bogie, single reduction with hub reduction, differential lock for wheels and shafts are pneumatically controlled from the cab. The fifth wheel is a Jost JSK 25 pivoting type.

SPECIFICATIONS
Configuration: 6 × 4
Max weight on front axle: 6500 kg
Max weight on rear axle: 26 000 kg
Length: 7·56 m
Width: 2·5 m
Height: (overall) 3·1 m
Track:
(front) 1·945 m
(rear) 1·82 m
Wheelbase: 4·2 m + 1·37 m
Fuel capacity: 300 litres
Engine: 120 E 6-cylinder turbo-charged OHV diesel developing 326 hp at 2200 rpm
Gearbox: manual 8-speed range, supplemented with splinter section which provides 16 forward speeds
Clutch: twin dry plate
Steering: recirculating ball and nut with built-in servo
Tyres: 12.00 × 20

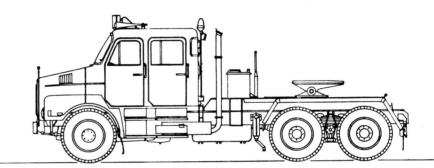

Volvo N12 (6 × 4) tractor truck

Brakes:
(main) air, dual circuit
(parking) air operated spring brakes operating directly on front and rear wheels
Suspension:
(front) semi-elliptical leaf springs with threaded spring bolt in front mounting and slipper type anchorage at rear. Shock absorbers and hollow rubber springs
(rear) multi-leaf springs with rubber springs at both ends

STATUS
Production. In service with the Swedish Army.

MANUFACTURER
Volvo AB, Göteborg, Sweden.

UNION OF SOVIET SOCIALIST REPUBLICS

MAZ-535 and MAZ-537 (8 × 8) Series

DESCRIPTION
These 8 × 8 vehicles were seen for the first time in public during a parade held in Moscow in November 1964, and are used for a wide variety of roles by the Soviet armed forces and for a variety of civil roles. They are closely related to the MAZ-543 (8 × 8) series of truck.

They all have full 8 × 8 drive with powered steering on the front two pairs of wheels, central tyre pressure regulation system, cab heater and an engine pre-heater. They are all powered by the same V-12 diesel used in Soviet tanks. In the case of the MAZ-535 the engine has been derated to deliver 375 hp instead of 525 hp as in the MAZ-537.

The MAZ-535A, MAZ-537A and MAZ-537K (which has a small crane) are cargo trucks but are also used to tow trailers or heavy artillery. The other models are used to tow semi-trailers carrying missiles or armoured fighting vehicles. The tractor trucks are normally used in conjunction with the ChMZAP-5247 and ChMZAP-5247G semi-trailers.

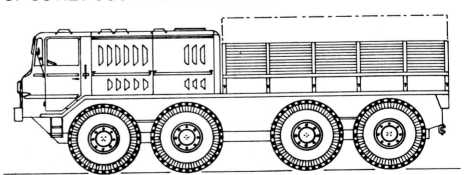

MAZ-535A (8 × 8) truck

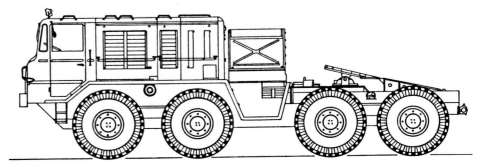

MAZ-537D (8 × 8) tractor truck with generator mounted over space between 2nd and 3rd axles

MAZ-535A (8 × 8) truck

MAZ-537 (8 × 8) tractor truck

VARIANTS
MAZ-535A: cargo truck
MAZ-537A: cargo truck
MAZ-537K: cargo truck
MAZ-537: tractor truck
MAZ-537D: tractor truck with additional generator to rear of engine compartment
MAZ-537E: tractor truck with generator, winch, can also be used with powered semi-trailer
MAZ-537G: tractor truck with winch

STATUS
In production. In service with members of the Warsaw Pact as well as Egypt, Finland, Iran, Syria and Yugoslavia.

MANUFACTURER
Minsk Motor Vehicle Plant, Minsk, Belorussia, USSR.

MAZ-535A (8 × 8) truck tows semi-trailers up to 50 000 kg

SPECIFICATIONS

Designation	MAZ-535A	MAZ-537A	MAZ-537
Type	Truck	Truck	Tractor Truck
Configuration	8 × 8	8 × 8	8 × 8
Weight (empty)	18 975 kg	22 500 kg	21 600 kg
(loaded)	25 975 kg	37 500 kg	n/app
Weight on front axles (loaded)	n/a	14 890 kg	n/a
Weight on rear axles (loaded)	n/a	22 610 kg	n/a
Max load (road and cross country)	6000 kg	15 000 kg	n/app
Towed load (road)	50 000 kg	75 000 kg	65 000 kg
(dirt road)	15 000 kg	30 000 kg	25 000 kg
Load area	4·5 × 2·595 m	4·562 × 2·53 m	n/app
Length	8·78 m	9·13 m	8·96 m
Width	2·805 m	2·885 m	2·885 m
Height (cab)	2·915 m	2·8 m	2·88 m
(load area)	1·4 m	1·875 m	n/app
Ground clearance	0·475 m	0·5 m	0·55 m
Track	2·15 m	2·2 m	2·2 m
Wheelbase	1·7 m + 2·35 m + 1·7 m	1·7 m + 2·65 m + 1·7 m	1·8 m + 2·65 m + 1·7 m
Angle of approach/departure	38°/60°	38°/52°	38°/52°
Max speed (road)	60 km/h	60 km/h	55–60 km/h
Range	650 km	650 km	650 km
Fuel capacity	760 litres	840 litres	840 litres
Fuel consumption	110 litres/100 km	125 litres/100 km	125 litres/100 km
Max gradient	30°	8° (laden)	8° (laden)
Fording	1·3 m	1·3 m	1·3 m
Engine model	D12A-375	D12A-525	D12A-525
Engine type	V-12 water-cooled diesel developing 375 hp at 1650 rpm	V-12 water-cooled diesel developing 525 hp at 2100 rpm	V-12 water-cooled diesel developing 525 hp at 2100 rpm
Gearbox	planetary, 3 speeds forward and 1 speed reverse, with smooth start device on low gear and reverse		
Transfer case	manual, 2-speed, with direct drive and reduction gears, pneumatic and manual backup control		
Auxiliary reduction gear transmission	manual, with inter-axle self-locking differential, consisting of spur gear pair		
Torque converter	single stage	single stage	single stage
Overdrive	single-row 3-shaft reduction gear with spur skew gears		
Steering	hydraulic, screw with nut on moving balls and rack engaged with gear quadrant		
Suspension	MAZ-535A, independent, individual, lever torsion bar (rear suspension equaliser, springless on MAZ-535V and MAZ-537), with hydraulic shock absorbers on all wheels. MAZ-537A, independent, individual, lever torsion bar, with hydraulic shock absorbers on both sides of front axle; rear: springless equaliser		
Tyres	18.00 × 24	18.00 × 24	18.00 × 24
Brakes	air/hydraulic	air/hydraulic	air/hydraulic
Electrical system	24 V	24 V	24 V
Batteries	4 × 12-ST-70	4 × 12-ST-70	4 × 12-ST-70
Generator	1500 W	1500 W	1500 W

UNITED KINGDOM

Scammell Contractor (6 × 4) Tractor Truck

DEVELOPMENT
The Scammell Contractor (6 × 4) vehicle was introduced by Scammell in 1964 and has since been used for a variety of civil and military applications. It is used by the military for hauling semi-trailers carrying MBTs such as the Centurion and M48/M60, and large numbers have been exported, especially to the Middle East and Africa.

DESCRIPTION
The layout of the vehicle is conventional with the engine at the front, two-door fully enclosed all-steel cab in the centre and the fifth wheel at the rear. A wide range of different engines and transmissions is available, according to the role for which the vehicle is required.

Optional equipment includes a larger four-door cab, three-line brake system (standard on British vehicles), engine brake, air-conditioning system, canopy over roof, cab heater and demister, searchlights, seven-pin plug at mid-chassis for semi-trailer, seven-pin plug and socket at front and rear of frame for full trailer, tow hitches front and rear, Scammell winch with a capacity of 15 240 kg or Darlington winch with a capacity of 22 680 kg, and a gearbox oil cooler. The Scammell winch has 131 metres of cable and an interlock is provided to ensure that a winch brake and cut-out device operate continuously during loading so that overloading is prevented and run-back cannot occur should the engine stop. A maximum pull of 50 800 kg is available by means of suitable sheaving; pull on first layer is 15 240 kg.

VARIANTS
The series comprises seven basic models. Gross weights covered are 86 300 kg, 101 600 kg, 111 700 kg, 122 000 kg, 152 400 kg and 182 800 kg for articulated operation, or 111 700 kg, 162 500 kg, 193 000 kg, and 244 000 kg respectively as ballasted tractors for specialised heavy duty haulage. The latest model has a maximum train weight of 244 000 kg. Standard models are 6 × 4 but 6 × 6 models are also available. Civilian applications include use as dump trucks and for logging.

CT15 C33F47: used for towing semi-trailers with a gross train weight of 152 450 kg while the CT19 C33X47 is used for towing drawbar trailers with a gross train weight of 193 100 kg. Both are powered by an NTC335 diesel engine and have an RV30 semi-automatic gearbox with eight forward and two reverse gears.

CT11 C33F48HD: used for towing semi-trailers with a gross train weight of 116 840 kg while the C11 C33X48HD is used for towing drawbar trailers with a gross train weight of 116 840 kg. Both are powered by a Cummins NTC 335 six-cylinder four-stroke diesel which develops 335 bhp (gross) at 2100 rpm. Transmission is an RTO 12515 with fifteen forward and three reverse speeds.

CT24 C42X52: used for pulling drawbar trailers with a gross train weight of 243 900 kg. It is powered by a Cummins KT450 six-cylinder, four-stroke, in-line turbocharged diesel which develops 425 bhp (gross) at 2100 rpm. Transmission is a CLBT750 fully automatic with five forward speeds, torque converter, lock up clutch and hydraulic retarder.

CT24 C33X52: used for pulling drawbar trailers with a gross train weight of 243 900 kg. It is powered by Cummins NTC 335 six-cylinder, four-stroke, in-line diesel, which develops 335 bhp (gross) at 2100 rpm. Transmission is an RV30 semi-automatic with eight forward and two reverse gears.

SPECIFICATIONS
Cab seating: 1 + 2
Configuration: 6 × 4
Weight: (gross combination)
  [CT11 C33F48] 116 840 kg
  [CT10 C33F48] 101 600 kg
  [CT85 C33F48] 86 360 kg
  (loaded, tractor truck) 38 530 kg
  (empty, tractor truck) 12 567 kg
Weight on front axle: (loaded) 8130 kg
Weight on rear bogie: (loaded) 30 490 kg
Length: 7·773 m
Width: 2·489 m
Height: 2·955 m
Height: (5th wheel) 1·622 m
Track:
  (front) 1·991 m
  (rear) 1·845 m

Wheelbase: 4·748 m
Max speed:
  (loaded) 77·14 km/h [CT85 C33F48] 86 360 kg GCW
  (loaded) 68·08 km/h [CT10 C33F48] 101 600 kg GCW
  (loaded) 61·87 km/h [CT11 C33F48] 116 840 kg GCW
Fuel capacity: 636 litres
Max gradient:
  [GCW 116 840 kg] (loaded) 16·67%
  [GCW 101 600 kg] 17·48%
  [GCW 86 360 kg] 18·18%
Engine: Cummins NTC 6-cylinder 4-stroke in-line diesel developing 335 bhp (gross) at 2100 rpm
Gearbox: RTO 12515 15 speed forward, 3 reverse, twin countershaft
Clutch: twin dry plate
Steering: power-assisted

Suspension:
  (front) longitudinal semi-elliptical leaf springs with telescopic hydraulic dampers
  (rear) fully articulated, inverted longitudinal springs, trunnion mounted at centre
Brakes: air
Electrical system: 24 V
Batteries: 4 × 6 V, 195 Ah

STATUS
In production. The Contractor is known to be in service in Australia, Jordan, Kenya and Libya.

MANUFACTURER
Scammell Motors, Leyland Vehicles Limited, Tolpits Lane, Watford, Hertfordshire WD1 8QB, England.

Late production Scammell Contractor (6 × 4) tractor truck towing semi-trailer carrying Chieftain MBT (T J Gander)

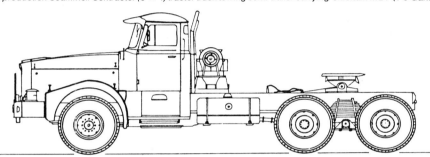

Scammell Contractor (6 × 4) tractor truck

Scammell Contractor (6 × 4) tractor truck of Australian Army with semi-trailer (Paul Handel)

Thornycroft Antar (6 × 4) Tractor

DEVELOPMENT/DESCRIPTION

The Antar range of 6 × 4 tractors was originally developed in the late 1940s for civilian applications by Transport Equipment (Thornycroft) Limited. It was subsequently adopted by the British Army as its main tractor for towing trailers or semi-trailers carrying MBTs including the Centurion and Chieftain.

The first model, the Mk 1, was designated FV 12001 and was fitted with a permanent steel ballast body at the rear and a 20 000 kg capacity winch. This was soon followed by the Mk 2 Antar, the FV 12002, which is powered by an eight-cylinder petrol engine which develops 285 bhp (gross) at 2000 rpm and is coupled to a manual, air-assisted four-speed gearbox and a two-speed transfer box. This is used to tow the 60 000 kg FV 3001 and 50 000 kg FV 3011 semi-trailers. Basic specifications of this model are unladen weight 19 630 kg, length 8·166 metres, width 3·124 metres, height 3·25 metres, front track 2·254 metres and rear track 2·292 metres and maximum road speed 45·2 km/h.

The next model was the FV 12003, which is almost identical to the FV 12002 but has a ballast body at the rear as it is used for towing conventional rather than semi-trailers. Basic specifications for this vehicle are unladen weight 20 080 kg, laden weight 35 590 kg, length 8·458 metres, width 3·2 metres, height 3·15 metres, front track 2·254 metres, rear track 2·292 metres and maximum road speed 44·8 km/h.

The last model was the Antar Mk 3, the FV 12004, which has a redesigned cab, new engine and transmission and many other improvements. It can also be fitted with a temporary ballast body for towing the FV 3601 trailer. A 20 000 kg capacity winch is mounted at the rear.

The layout of all Antars is similar with the engine at the front, fully enclosed two-door cab in the centre and the fifth wheel at the rear.

SPECIFICATIONS (Mk 3)

Cab seating: 1 + 2
Configuration: 6 × 4
Weight: (empty) 21 896 kg
Length: 8·7 m
Width: 3·2 m
Height: 3·15 m
Track:
   (front) 2·254 m
   (rear) 2·292 m
Max average speed: 32·18 km/h
Range at max average speed: 702 km
Fuel capacity: 910 litres
Engine: Rolls-Royce C8SFL-843 8-cylinder supercharged diesel developing 333 bhp at 2100 rpm
Gearbox: manual with 6 forward and 1 reverse gears
Clutch: twin plate, air-assisted
Transfer box: 6 forward and 1 reverse
Steering: cam and double roller, hydraulic assisted
Turning radius: 20·12 m
Suspension: semi-elliptical springs
Tyres: 14.00 × 24

Brakes: air, mechanical, air-assisted on rear wheels
Electrical system: 24 V
Batteries: 24 V, 300 Ah

STATUS

Production complete. In service with India, Netherlands, Pakistan, South Africa, Turkey and the United Kingdom.

All Thornycroft Antars are being overhauled and refurbished over three years by Fazakerley Engineering.

MANUFACTURER

Transport Equipment (Thornycroft) Limited, Basingstoke, Hampshire, England.

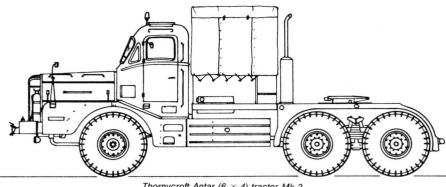

Thornycroft Antar (6 × 4) tractor Mk 3

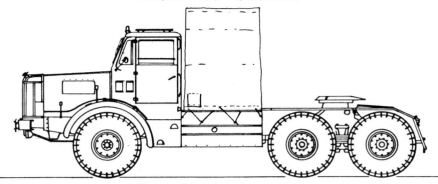

Thornycroft Antar (6 × 4) tractor Mk 2

Thornycroft Antar (6 × 4) Mk 3 towing trailer carrying BTR-60PB APC (T J Gander)

Thornycroft Antar (6 × 4) Mk 3 tractor (T J Gander)

Thornycroft Antar (6 × 4) Mk 3 towing semi-trailer (T J Gander)

Thornycroft Antar (6 × 4) Mk 3 (T J Gander)

Thornycroft Antar (6 × 4) Mk 3 from right rear (T J Gander)

Scammell Commander (6 × 4) Tractor Truck

DEVELOPMENT

The Scammell Commander Tractor Truck has been developed to meet the requirements of the British Army for a new tractor truck to replace its ageing Thornycroft Antars in the mid-1980s and to carry the Challenger MBT.

Design work on the Scammell Commander began in 1976 with the first three prototypes being completed in 1978. Two of them were powered by the Rolls-Royce CV12 TCE diesel and the third by an American Cummins KTA 600 diesel.

In 1981 there was a General Staff Requirement for a vehicle similar to the Commander but as a result of defence spending cuts the GSR was not endorsed at the time. However in late 1982 an order for 125 Commanders for the British Army was placed. The first examples were delivered in late 1983 and early 1984 and production will continue into 1985.

Although designed for towing semi-trailers carrying AFVs weighing up to 65 000 kg, the Commander can also be used for high-speed haulage of heavy indivisible loads.

DESCRIPTION

The engine is at the front, all-steel cab in the centre, winch to rear of the cab and the fifth wheel over the bogie at the rear.

The cab is arranged for left-hand drive and incorporates noise insulating material. A two-piece flat glass windscreen with an electric heating element is provided on the driver's side. For crew access large steps are fitted and full interior heating and ventilating equipment is standard. Air conditioning equipment is optional as are various radio installations. The cab has individual seats for the commander and driver behind which is a bench seat for two men which can be positioned to form two individual bunks, one above the other.

The chassis is of steel channel side-members with bolted-in fabricated and tubular cross-members. There are heavy duty members at the front and rear for towing, lifting and recovery.

The front axle is a Scammell 12 200 kg capacity steer. Forty-degree lock angles give high manoeuvrability. The rear axle is a Scammell 40 700 kg capability double drive bogie comprising two hub reduction axles linked by a lockable third differential for increased traction on poor surfaces. The fully articulated fifth wheel has an imposed load capacity of 34 600 kg.

A heavy duty Rotzler winch is standard for the Commander for self loading dead loads and the tractor is fully equipped with recovery fittings. The 20 300 kg line pull horizontal winch has 110 metres of 26 mm diameter rope. The winch is fitted with an automatic pay-on gear and has a fail-safe brake. A high rope warning and an automatic overload cut-out is provided. The rope can be led out over the neck of the semi-trailer or through fairleads at the rear of the chassis. Winch controls are mounted behind the cab in a weatherproof enclosure.

SPECIFICATIONS

Cab seating: 2 + 2
Configuration: 6 × 4
Weight: (empty) 19 920 kg
Weight on front axle: (empty) 9680 kg
Weight on rear bogie: (empty) 10 240 kg
Gross combination weight: 104 000 kg
Length: 9·01 m
Width: 3·25 m

Scammell Commander (6 × 4) tractor truck at speed on MVEE test track

Scammell Commander (6 × 4) tractor truck

Height: 3·5 m
Wheelbase: 5·03 m
Max speed: (with semi-trailer and 65 tonne MBT) 61 km/h
Fuel capacity: 817 litres
Engine: Rolls-Royce CV12 TCE turbo-charged 60° V-12 diesel developing 625 bhp at 2100 rpm
Gearbox: Allison CLBT 6061 6-speed epicyclic with torque converter permitting gear changes to be made under power. Hydraulic retarder for speed control on hills to supplement wheel brakes
Steering: hydraulic assisted
Suspension: leaf springs front and rear with telescopic dampers to front; 2-spring high-articulation rear bogie suspension ensures equal wheel loads

Tyres: 14.00 × 24
Brakes: twin leading show wedge brakes with automatic adjustment on all wheels, operated by 2 air circuits; 2-line couplings for trailer connections and additional couplings for double heading
Electrical system: 24 V
Batteries: 8

STATUS

125 ordered for the British Army. First deliveries expected late 1983 and early 1984.

MANUFACTURER

Scammell Motors, Leyland Vehicles Limited, Tolpits Lane, Watford, Hertfordshire WD1 8QD, England.

UNITED STATES OF AMERICA

FWD Model RB 662158 (6 × 6) Truck Tractor

DESCRIPTION

The RB 662158 (6 × 6) truck tractor has been developed as a private venture by FWD International and is used in conjunction with the FWD International Model 3ST50 semi-trailer low bed for carrying MBTs such as the M60A1.

The layout of the vehicle is conventional with the engine at the front, two-door fully enclosed cab in the centre and the fifth wheel at the rear.

The chassis is of 3143 × 890 × 95 mm straight channel bar with full frame innerliner.

The cab is a FWD "R" series all-steel reverse slope type with Bostrom Viking T-bar driver's seat, two-man passenger seat, dual west coast mirrors, fresh air heater and defroster, windshield wiper and washers, dual air horns and grab handles.

The front axle is FWD DR-2-21 rated at 9525 kg with S cam brakes; the rear axle is a Rockwell standard SUDD rated at 26 365 kg with spring loaded parking brakes on both rear axles and S cam brakes. Rear

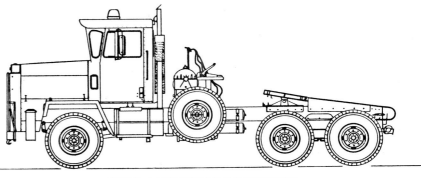

FWD Model RB 662158 (6 × 6) truck tractor

suspension is a Timken leaf spring SUD series rated at 26 365 kg.

Standard equipment includes front two hooks, rear window screen, tyre inflation kit with 7·5-metre hose, fire extinguisher, 20-ton hydraulic jack, wheel wrench and handle.

The trailer package includes hose tenna, break away valve, trailer connecting hoses and electric cable connections. Optional equipment includes 45 360 kg capacity winch with a 76-metre wire rope cable, Michelin 14.00 × 20 XS sand tyres and automatic radiator shutters.

FWD RB 662158 (6 × 6) truck tractor

FWD RB 662158 (6 × 6) truck tractor

SPECIFICATIONS
Cab seating: 1 + 2
Configuration: 6 × 6
Weight:
(empty) 12 000 kg
(loaded) 35 100 kg
Weight on front axle: 8735 kg
Weight on rear axle: 26 365 kg
Towed load:
(road) 63 900 kg
(cross country) 38 340 kg
Length: 7·85 m
Width: (over dual tyres) 3·125 m
Height: (loaded) 2·9 m
Ground clearance: (loaded) 0·292 m
Track: 2·03 m
Wheelbase: 5 m
Angle of approach/departure: 30°/30°

Max speed:
(loaded) 59 km/h
(empty) 70 km/h
Range: 300 km
Fuel capacity: 2 × 190 litres
Max gradient: (loaded) 24%
Fording: 0·46 m
Engine: Cummins NTC-350 turbo-charged diesel developing 350 hp at 2100 rpm
Gearbox: Fuller 10-speed
Clutch: 2-plate pull-type
Transfer box: FWD model 653 two-speed with FWD traction lock
Steering: gear with hydraulic frame mounted power steer
Turning radius: 14 m
Suspension: leaf spring
Tyres: 14.00 × 20, single front, dual rear

Brakes:
(main) air
(parking) spring loaded on both rear axles
Electrical system: 12 V
Batteries: 2 × 12 V, 225 Ah
Winch: 45 360 kg capacity with 76 m of 25 mm diameter cable and hook, one 2-part snatch-pulley block 355 mm diameter
Pintle hook capacity: 27 300 kg

STATUS
Production. 200 of these vehicles, plus the Model 3ST50 semi-trailer, have been supplied to an undisclosed country for a military application.

MANUFACTURER
FWD International Inc., 1020 West 31st Street, Downers Grove, Illinois 60515, USA.

M123 (6 × 6) 10-ton Tractor Truck

DEVELOPMENT
The M123 truck was manufactured in the early 1950s by the Mack Truck Corporation and is closely related to the M125 (6 × 6) 10-ton cargo truck. The last manufacturer of the M123 was the Consolidated Diesel Electric Corporation. It has been designed for towing semi-trailers carrying MBTs and engineering equipment on roads and across country. It is being replaced in many US units by the M911 (6 × 6) truck tractor.

DESCRIPTION
The layout of the vehicle is conventional with the engine at the front, cab in the centre, and winches and fifth wheel at the rear. The cab has two doors, removable canvas top and its windscreen can be folded down onto the bonnet if required.

The winch has a capacity of 20 412 kg. Power is derived from the PTO shaft of the transfer case. A remote throttle is mounted in the winch platform to control the vehicle engine speed from the platform. A safety brake automatically holds the drum when the hauling operation is stopped. When the winch power is reversed the brake releases to allow the drum to turn.

The drive axles consist of one front and two tandem axles. Universal-jointed propeller shafts transmit power from the transfer to the drive axles. The front axle is steerable with single reduction differential in the housing and dual reduction in the wheel assemblies. Rear axle drive is through a tandem axle arrangement. Each rear axle has dual reduction differential carriers mounted on top of the axle housing.

A differential braking system arrangement on the rear wheels assists in making tight turns. A towing pintle, towing shackles, air brake and electrical connections are provided at the rear of the vehicle. The M123 incorporates a tractor protection valve system for manual or automatic application of the trailer brake system.

The fuel system contains an intake manifold heater which is used to warm induction air for cold weather starting and to assist engine warm up when the air temperature is below 50°F. Kits available for the vehicle include a cold weather kit, deep fording kit, and a kit for towing trailers fitted with electric instead of air brakes.

VARIANTS
M123: dual winches and high mounted fifth wheel
M123C: single winch and low mounted fifth wheel
M123D: dual winches and low mounted fifth wheel
M123A1: single rear winch and a V-8 diesel engine developing 300 bhp. Cruising range 570 km.

M123A1C (6 × 6) 10-ton tractor truck

M123A1C (6 × 6) 10-ton tractor truck towing semi-trailer for carrying engineer plant (Larry Provo)

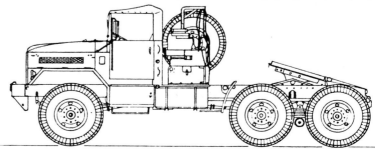

M123A1C (6 × 6) 10-ton tractor truck

STATUS
Production complete. In service with the US Army and other countries including Spain (Army and Marines).

MANUFACTURER
Condiesel Mobile Equipment Division, CONDEC Corporation, 1700 Post Road, Old Greenwich, Connecticut 06870, USA. (The vehicle was manufactured at CONDEC's Schenectady, New York, facility.)

SPECIFICATIONS
Cab seating: 1 + 2
Configuration: 6 × 6
Weight:
  (empty, early models) 14 628 kg
  (empty, late production models) 15 876 kg
  (loaded, road) 30 504 kg
  (loaded, cross country) 28 237 kg
Weight on front axle: (loaded, road) 6867 kg

Weight on rear axles: (loaded, road) 23 637 kg
Towed load:
  (road) 61 236 kg
  (cross country) 36 288 kg
Length: 7·315 m
Width: 2·315 m
Height: 2·87 m
  (reduced) 2·336 m
Ground clearance: 0·403 m
Track: (front) 2·006 m
Wheelbase: 3·847 m + 1·524 m
Angle of approach: 52°
Max speed: (road) 67 km/h
Range: (petrol model) 486 km
Fuel capacity: 563 litres
Max gradient: 60%
Fording:
  (without preparation) 0·762 m
  (with preparation) 1·981 m

Engine: Le Roi Model T-H844 8-cylinder petrol developing 286 hp at 2600 rpm (late models have 300 bhp diesel)
Gearbox: manual with 5 forward and 1 reverse gears
Clutch: 2-plate dry
Transfer box: 2-speed
Steering: hydraulic
Suspension:
  (front) semi-elliptical springs with hydraulic shock absorbers
  (rear) pair of inverted semi-elliptical springs mounted longitudinally at centre to trunnion arrangement attached to chassis
Tyres: 14.00 × 24
Number of tyres: 10 + 1 spare
Brakes: air
Electrical system: 24 V
Batteries: 4

M911 (8 × 6) Truck Tractor

DEVELOPMENT
Early in 1976 the US Army issued a requirement for a truck tractor which would operate at 71 km/h at 86 183 kg, at 22·5 km/h at 86 183 kg on a 3 per cent grade, start and operate at 86 183 kg on a 20 per cent grade, operate in ambient air temperatures of 52°C maximum to −32°C minimum without kits and to −46°C with arctic kits, provide reliability, long service life, and use components with adequate manufacturing life to provide parts backup for the anticipated life cycle of the truck and provide minimum weight, size and cost consistent with other criteria.

Another requirement was that the basic unit must have been in production as a standard model for at least one year. In September 1976 Oshkosh was awarded an initial contract for 747 vehicles designated the M911, based on the commercial Oshkosh F2365 truck. The US Army did not take up its option to order an additional 445

M911 (8 × 6) truck tractors. Twelve M911s were ordered by Thailand in 1980 and these have now been delivered.

DESCRIPTION
The layout of the vehicle is conventional with the engine at the front, all steel two-door cab in the centre and the fifth wheel at the rear. Standard equipment for the cab includes an adjustable seat for the driver, air-operated variable speed wipers, 22 000 BTU per hour hot water heater and defroster.

The brakes have a dual air supply system, one for the front and one for the rear axles. If the air system that supplies the front brakes fails the rear brakes can be operated normally. If the rear system fails, the front system as well as the rear spring chamber will still remain pressurised. A hydraulic retarder operated with a foot control in the transmission can absorb up to 70 per cent of the engine horsepower.

The main transmission is fully automatic and will

automatically upshift or downshift in all ranges above second gear, with a hold in each range. Built-in inhibitors prevent downshift or reverse shift at excessive speeds.

The Oshkosh pusher axle is rated at 9072 kg and is air-suspended. When in position it decreases the load on the rear tandem to about 11 340 kg per tandem axle with a 20 805 kg fifth wheel load.

Standard equipment includes two Branden winches with a capacity of 20 412 kg each, rear deck lights, spare tyre carrier with lift, rear pintle hook, trailer air and electric connections, spotlights, foglights, inspection light with 15·24 metre cable, tachograph, hydraulic jack, tyre inflation hose, oscillating fifth wheel, splash guards, radiator and headlight guard and towing eyes.

SPECIFICATIONS
Cab seating: 1 + 2
Configuration: 8 × 6
Weight:
  (empty) 13 573 kg
  (loaded) 39 917 kg
Length: 9·373 m
Width:
  (over bumpers) 2·438 m
  (rear duals) 2·896 m
Height:
  (top of exhaust) 3·658 m
  (cab) 3·175 m
  (5th wheel, no load) 1·626 m
Track: 2·06 m
Wheelbase: (excluding pusher axle) 5·207 m + 1·524 m
Max speed:
  (road, with gross combination weight of 86 183 kg) 71 km/h
  (3% gradient, fully loaded) 23 km/h
Range:
  (no payload, maximum speed) 1344 km
  (at 86 183 kg gross combination weight, economical speed) 990 km
Fuel capacity: 568 litres
Fuel consumption:
  (max speed, no payload on trailer) 2·5 km/litre
  (max speed, gross combination weight of 86 183 kg) 1·05 km/litre
  (at 1600 rpm, best economic speed, gross combination weight of 86 183 kg) 1·84 km/litre
Max gradient: 20%
Fording: 1·0711 m
Engine: Detroit Diesel model 8V-92TA-90 V-8 developing 435 hp at 2100 rpm
Gearbox: Allison CLBT-750 automatic with 5 forward and 1 reverse gears
Transfer case: single speed
Auxiliary transmission: Fuller AT 1202 2-speed
Steering: hydraulic
Turning radius: 14·72 m
Suspension:
  (front) Hotchkiss type with semi-elliptical main springs with Berlin eye and semi-elliptical auxiliary spring
  (rear) Hendrickson RT-500, steel spring, equalising beam design with 1·524-metre spread
Tyres: 14.00 × 24
Number of tyres: 12 + 1 spare
Brakes: dual system air
Electrical system: 24 V
Batteries: 4 × 12 V, 100 Ah
Alternator: 65 A

STATUS
Production complete but can be resumed if further orders are received. In service with the US Army (747) and Thailand (12).

MANUFACTURER
Oshkosh Truck Corporation, PO Box 2566, Oshkosh, Wisconsin 54901, USA.

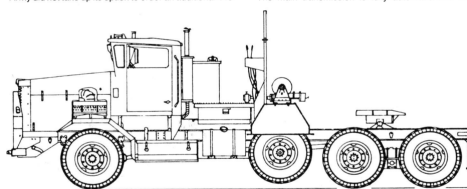

Oshkosh M911 (8 × 6) truck tractor with pusher axle raised

Oshkosh M911 (8 × 6) truck tractor with pusher axle raised

Oshkosh M911 (8 × 6) truck tractor towing M747 semi-trailer carrying M1 Abrams MBT (US Army)

M746 (8 × 8) 22½-ton Tractor Truck (Heavy Equipment Transporter)

DEVELOPMENT
The development of the Heavy Equipment Transporter (HET) can be traced back to 1965 when a contract was issued to the Chrysler Corporation for a joint study, with the West German companies of Faun and Krupp, for an HET which could carry the MBT-70 tank then under development by both the United States and West Germany. The first two American prototypes were completed by Chrysler in 1966 with a German supplied chassis and cab. The following year they were tested alongside German prototype vehicles. In 1970 the MBT-70 programme was cancelled. The Germans continued development of their vehicle which was standardised as the SLT-50. Production was undertaken by Faun. The Americans built a further three prototypes for additional testing under the designation XM746 which was subsequently standardised as the M746. The production contract was awarded to the Ward LaFrance company and first production vehicles were completed in 1975. Production for the United States Army continued until 1977.

DESCRIPTION
The fully enclosed all steel cab is of the forward control type and its overall height can be reduced for air transport. A circular observation hatch is provided in the right side of the roof. Mounted to the rear of the cab are two Pacific Car and Foundry P-60 hydraulic winches, each with a capacity of 27 216 kg and 45·72 metres of 25 mm diameter cable, which enable the M746 to recover disabled vehicles without additional assistance.

The power steering operates on the front four wheels. Power is transmitted to all four axles by a five-speed power shift transmission. The rear axles have no spin differentials. The brakes are automatically adjusted with a fail-safe and anti-skid braking system.

The HET is designed for use with the M747 semi-trailer, which is manufactured by the CONDEC Corporation. Full details will be found in the *Trailers* section.

SPECIFICATIONS
Cab seating: 1 + 2
Configuration: 8 × 8
Weight:
(empty) 20 412 kg
(loaded) 39 010 kg
Weight on front axles: (loaded) 8460 kg
Weight on rear axles: (loaded) 11 045 kg
Weight on 5th wheel: 20 412 kg
Towed load: 62 143 kg
Length: 8·229 m
Width: 3·048 m
Height:
(cab) 3·048 m
(reduced) 2·514 m
(5th wheel) 1·6 m
Ground clearance: 0·33 m
Track: 2·546 m
Wheelbase: 1·498 m + 1·27 m + 1·498 m
Angle of approach: 30°
Max speed: 62 km/h
(15% gradient) 8 km/h
Range: 322 km
Fuel capacity: 530 litres
Fording: 1·219 m
Engine: Detroit Diesel model 12V-71(T) 12-cylinder liquid-cooled diesel developing 600 hp at 2500 rpm
Gearbox: Twin Disc model TADC-51-2012 powershift with converter, 5 speeds forward and 1 reverse
Transfer box: one-speed drop box

Steering: powered
Suspension: taper leaf bogies with hydraulic shock absorbers
Tyres: 18.00 × 25
Brakes: air
Electrical system: 24 V
Batteries: 6, total capacity 300 Ah

STATUS
Production complete. In service with the USA (125) and Morocco (68).

MANUFACTURER
Ward LaFrance Truck Corporation, Elmira Heights, New York 14903, USA.

Ward LaFrance M746 (8 × 8) 22½-ton tractor truck from front

Rear view of Ward LaFrance M746 (8 × 8) 22½-ton tractor truck showing position of fifth wheel and two winches

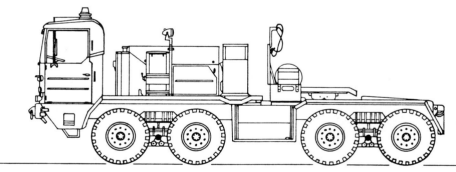

Ward LaFrance M746 (8 × 8) 22½-ton truck tractor

AMPHIBIANS

This section covers vehicles designed specifically for amphibious operations, such as crossing inland waterways or carrying cargo from ships off-shore on to the beach, or inland. It does not include vehicles which require preparation to make them amphibious such as the American M656 (8 × 8) cargo truck, nor does it include amphibious over-snow vehicles or tracked prime movers, details of which will be found in their respective sections.

BRAZIL

CAMANF (6 × 6) 2500 kg Amphibious Truck

DEVELOPMENT
The CAMANF (Caminhão Anfíbio, or amphibious truck) has been developed by Biselli Viaturas e Equipamentos Industriais to replace the old American supplied DUKWs currently in service with the Brazilian Marine Corps.

Development work began in 1975 and trials with prototype vehicles were completed in 1978. An initial batch of 15 vehicles has now been built for the Brazilian Marine Corps.

The CAMANF is based on a 6 × 6 Ford F-7000 chassis and has a number of significant improvements over the original American vehicles including a diesel engine for greater operational range and a strengthened bow to enable the vehicle to push barges and free smaller craft that often get stuck on beaches and river banks during amphibious operations.

DESCRIPTION
The layout of the CAMANF is similar to that of the American DUKW with the engine at the front, seats for the driver and two passengers immediately behind the windscreen and the cargo area at the rear. The cargo area has removable bows and a tarpaulin cover. A ring-mounted 12·7 mm (0·50) M2 HB machine gun can be positioned above and to the right side of the driver's seat.

A central tyre-pressure regulation system enables the driver to adjust to the type of ground being crossed. Before entering the water a trim board, which folds back onto the engine compartment when not in use, is erected at the front of the vehicle, and the bilge pumps switched on. The CAMANF is driven in the water by a propeller mounted at the rear of the hull.

STATUS
In production. In service with the Brazilian Marine Corps.

MANUFACTURER
Biselli Viaturas e Equipamentos Industriais Ltda, Av Presidente Wilson 4930, 04220 São Paulo, SP Brazil.

CAMANF (6 × 6) 2500 kg amphibious truck with 12·7 mm (0·50) M2 HB machine gun fitted (Ronaldo S Olive)

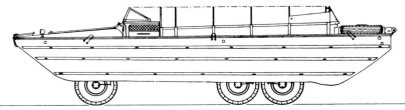

CAMANF (6 × 6) 2500 kg amphibious truck with dotted line showing position of tarpaulin cover when used

SPECIFICATIONS
Configuration: 6 × 6
Weight: (loaded) 13 500 kg
Max load:
(land and calm water) 5000 kg
(rough water) 2500 kg
Max towed load: 2500 kg
Length: 9·5 m
Width: 2·5 m
Height: 2·65 m

Max speed:
(road) 72 km/h
(water) 14 km/h
Range:
(land) 430 km
(water endurance) 18 h
Max gradient: 60%
Engine: Detroit Diesel model 40-54N
Tyres: 9.00 × 20
Number of tyres: 6 + 1 spare

GERMANY, FEDERAL REPUBLIC

Trippel (4 × 4) 550 kg Amphibious Vehicle

Trippel (4 × 4) 550 kg amphibious vehicle

DEVELOPMENT
The Trippel (4 × 4) 550 kg amphibious vehicle has been designed and developed by Hans Trippel who has been engaged in the design and development of amphibious vehicles since the 1930s. Two versions have so far been developed to the prototype stage; a universal version which is propelled in water by its wheels, with the option of being fitted with an outboard motor for higher water speeds, and a military version which is propelled in water by two three-bladed propellers mounted at the rear of the hull.

DESCRIPTION
The layout of the Trippel amphibious vehicle is conventional with the engine and transmission at the front, driver and passenger in the centre and the cargo area at the rear. The latter has an area of 3·22 square metres and a maximum capacity of 550 kg.

The chassis of the vehicle is of welded steel monocoque construction with longitudinal beams on which the main components are mounted. The upper-body is of pressed aluminium plate 1·5 mm thick and can be supplied in a variety of body styles in addition to the basic pick-up module. The lower part of the hull is made of 2 mm steel plate, reinforced along the bottom by two longitudinal beams on which major components such as

the engine, transmission, transfer box, forced-draught water cooler, differentials for both axles, suspension, springs and shock absorbers are mounted.

The prototypes are powered by Ford engines but other engines can be fitted and the vehicle has been designed for production with the minimum of expensive tooling.

A bilge pump is fitted as standard with the suction intake being positioned at the lowest point in the floor of the vehicle. This is switched on automatically as soon as the vehicle enters water.

The military version is propelled in water by twin three-bladed propellers mounted on a transverse horizontal shaft around which they can be swung through 360 degrees. The two propellers can be rotated independently of each other allowing a variety of manoeuvres to be carried out when afloat. Steering afloat is by turn-

ing the front wheels. Unlike other amphibious vehicles, no trim vane is required at the front of the vehicle.

In addition to various body styles, such as fully enclosed and open top, a wide range of optional equipment can be fitted to the Trippel amphibious vehicle including anti-mine protection, battery condition indicator, branch deflector on windscreen, communications equipment, electric winch, fire extinguisher, fuel/water cans, ground anchor, gradient/tilt indicator, heater, larger propeller, larger capacity bilge pump, larger wheels and tyres, locking differential front and rear, protective grills for all lights, roof rack, starting handle, trailer (both land and amphibious) and a 24 volt electrical system.

STATUS
Prototypes.

SPECIFICATIONS
Cab seating: 1 + 2 (plus 6 in rear)
Configuration: 4 × 4
Weight:
  (empty) 1450 kg
  (loaded) 2000 kg
Weight on front axle: (loaded) 1000 kg
Weight on rear axle: (loaded) 1000 kg
Max load: 500 kg
Max towed load: 1800 kg
Load area: 1·85 × 1·74 m
Length: 4·71 m
Width: 1·8 m
Height: 1·85 m
Ground clearance: 0·278 m

Track: 1·516 m
Wheelbase: 2·5 m
Angle of approach/departure: 36°/36°
Max speed:
  (road) 130 km/h
  (water) 20 km/h
Range: (road) 400 km
Fuel capacity: 60 litres
Max gradient: 85%
Max side slope: 40%
Fording: amphibious
Engine: Ford V-6 petrol developing 88 hp at 5100 rpm
or Ford 4-cylinder in-line developing 98 hp at 5200 rpm.
Diesel option
Gearbox: manual, 4 forward and 1 reverse gears

Clutch: single dry plate
Transfer box: 2-speed
Suspension: dual parallel link, independent. Super-progressive "mini-block" helical springs with double acting telescopic shock absorbers
Tyres: 6.00 × 15 or 6.50 × 15 or 7.00 × 15
Number of tyres: 4 + 1 spare
Brakes:
  (front) disc
  (rear) drum
  (parking) disc
Electrical system: 12 V
Battery: 1 × 12 V

EWK Bison (4 × 4) 5000/7000 kg Amphibious Truck

DEVELOPMENT
Developed primarily for civilian use in underdeveloped areas, the Bison (4 × 4) 5000/7000 kg amphibious truck was first shown in public at the 1982 Hanover Air Show. Despite its intended civilian use it has obvious military applications.

DESCRIPTION
The general layout of the Bison is that of a high-bodied 4 × 4 truck with the two- or three-man forward control cab having an anti-splash vane mounted on its front surface. Behind the cab, which has two roof hatches, is the auxiliary power unit/hydraulic pump compartment with folding access walkways on each side. The main load area, which can be covered by a canvas tilt, is conventionally placed at the rear. For float stabilisation purposes two large heavy-duty inflatable bags are situated, one each side, between the main driving wheels. When not in use these bags are folded down behind one-piece cover plates, and when the bags are inflated by air from a pump driven by the auxiliary power unit, the covers act as working platforms. In the water, propulsion is provided by two rear-mounted propellers situated behind tubular guards. Power for these propellers is taken from an auxiliary power unit and the propellers can be turned through 360 degrees for steering purposes.

The Bison can carry 5000 kg of cargo. The main power unit is an air-cooled Klöckner-Humbold-Deutz V-8 diesel with an exhaust-driven supercharger. Power is distributed through an automatic ZF-6 HP 500 gear-box with six forward and one reverse gears. There is a three-shaft A 6003 D distributor gear flange-connected to the automatic gears with a switchable differential lock. The exterior epicyclic axles have hydraulically retractable Koni-Lift shock absorbers, and the brake system is a dual-circuit system with hydraulic braking on the front axle and pneumatic on the rear. Tyre pressures can be adjusted while on the move.

VARIANTS
ALF-2 amphibious fire tender.
The ALF-2 uses the same basic layout as the Bison amphibious truck but the load area is replaced by an open platform and two fire hydrants with fire-fighting attachments. The inflatable bags of the Bison are replaced by fixed flotation boxes which are permanently attached to provide extra platform space. The fire-fighting pumps can deliver 4000 litres of water a minute. All up weight of the ALF-2 is 17 000 kg.

STATUS
Development complete. Ready for production.

MANUFACTURER
Eisenwerke Kaiserslautern Göppner GmbH, Barbarossastrasse 30, D-6750 Kaiserslautern, Federal Republic of Germany.

SPECIFICATIONS
Cab seating: 1 + 1 or 2
Configuration: 4 × 4
Weight:
  (empty) 11 000 kg
  (loaded) 16 000 kg

Max load:
  (normal) 5000 kg
  (permissible) 7000 kg
Load area: 6·03 × 2·33 × 1·54 m
Length: 9·34 m
Width:
  (on road) 2·5 m
  (inflatable bags extended) 4·46 m
Height:
  (cab) 2·96 m
  (tilt) 3·4 m
Ground clearance: 0·5 m
Track:
  (front) 2·02 m
  (rear) 2·05 m
Wheelbase: 5·1 m
Angle of approach/departure: 39°/28°
Max speed:
  (road) 80 km/h
  (water) 12 km/h
Range:
  (land) 900 km
  (water) 7 h
Engine: Klöckner-Humbold-Deutz V-8 air-cooled diesel developing 320 hp at 2500 rpm
Gearbox: ZF-6 HP 500 automatic with 6 forward and 1 reverse gears
Transfer box: A 6003 D 3-shaft with switchable differential lock
Steering:
  (land) ZF hydro ball and nut
  (water) Schottel steering propellers
Turning radius: 24 m
Tyres: 20.5 × 25 XL
Brakes: air 2-system

EWK Bison (4 × 4) 5000/7000 kg amphibious truck with flotation bags retracted (T J Gander)

EWK Bison (4 × 4) 5000/7000 kg amphibious truck with flotation bags extended (T J Gander)

INDIA

Rampar (4 × 4) 3000 kg Amphibious Vehicle

DEVELOPMENT/DESCRIPTION
The Rampar (4 × 4) 300 kg amphibious vehicle has been developed at the Indian Vehicle Research and Development Establishment and is a conversion of the Shaktiman (4 × 4) 5000 kg truck (see separate entry in *Trucks* section). It has been developed following experiences in the eastern sector during the 1971 Indo-Pakistan War when numerous river crossings were made necessary.

The Rampar can carry up to 22 men or 3000 kg of cargo. The basic Shaktiman is converted by adding a mild steel hull and providing two steering rudders at the rear. Speed in calm water is 10 km/hour. The boat hull is conventional with a prominent bow, a cabin for the driver and at least one passenger, and a cargo-carrying/passenger area at the rear. The load area can be covered by a canvas tilt as can the driver's cabin. A trim vane is fitted over the bow. A 4000-kg capacity winch is carried in the bow and a fribreglass trackway may be carried at the rear for use when crossing boggy ground. There is provision for a 7·62 mm machine gun pintle above the passengers' position on the cab. Light armour protection for the hull could be provided.

STATUS
Prototype.

SPECIFICATIONS
Cab seating: 1 + 1 (22 men in rear)

Configuration: 4 × 4
Weight:
  (empty) 6500 kg
  (loaded) 9500 kg
Length: 8·1 m
Width: 2·3 m
Height: 3 m
Ground clearance: 0·5 m
Max speed:
  (road) 74 km/h
  (water) 10 km/h
Angle of approach/departure: 38°/32°
Engine: 6-cylinder turbocharged diesel developing 125 hp at 2500 rpm
Gearbox: 5 forward and 1 reverse gears
Transfer box: 2-speed

ITALY

FIAT Model 6640 G (4 × 4) 2000 kg Amphibious Cargo Carrier

DEVELOPMENT
This vehicle, announced in 1980, is very similar to the FIAT Model 6640 A (4 × 4) amphibious cargo carrier described and illustrated in the following entry. The 6640 G has a much greater weight due to stronger construction and a slightly longer wheelbase; it has a more powerful diesel engine coupled to automatic transmission and is propelled in the water by a waterjet rather than a propeller as the earlier vehicle.

DESCRIPTION
The hull of the vehicle is of all-welded aluminium construction with a maximum thickness of 4 mm. The engine compartment is at the front of the hull and is separated from the crew compartment by a fireproof bulkhead. The two-man fully-enclosed cab is heated and ventilated. The cargo area is to the rear of the cab and is provided with removable bows and a tarpaulin cover. Folding bench seats run along both sides of the cargo area.

The vehicle is propelled in water by its wheels or the waterjet mounted under the hull at the rear, steering in the water is by a rear-mounted rudder linked to the steering wheel. In an emergency the rudder can be operated by hand. Three bilge pumps, one in the bottom of the engine compartment and two below the cargo area, are provided.

As an option, a winch with a capacity of 4500 kg on the first layer can be mounted at the front of the vehicle. A material handling crane with a capacity of 700 kg can be fitted if required.

SPECIFICATIONS
Cab seating: 1 + 1
Configuration: 4 × 4
Weight:
 (curb) 6100 kg
 (loaded) 8450 kg
 (on front axle, loaded) 3450 kg
 (on rear axle, loaded) 4650 kg
 (payload) 2000 kg
Load area: 3·21 × 1·95 m
Length: 8·2 m
Width: 2·5 m
Height:
 (cab) 2·7 m (approx)
 (tarpaulin) 3·05 m
 (load area) 1·72 m
Ground clearance: 0·43 m
Track: 1·96 m
Wheelbase: 3·1 m
Angle of approach/departure: 30°/25°
Max speed:
 (road) over 100 km/h
 (water, waterjet) 11 km/h
Range:
 (road) over 600 km
 (water, propelled by waterjet) 55 km (approx)
Fuel capacity: 180 litres
Max gradient: 60%
Max side slope: 30%
Fording: amphibious
Engine: Model 8062 6-cylinder 4-stroke liquid-cooled turbo-charged diesel developing 195 hp at 3200 rpm

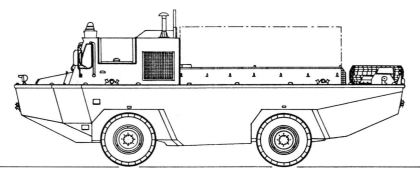

FIAT Model 6640 G (4 × 4) 2000 kg amphibious cargo carrier

FIAT Model 6640 G (4 × 4) 2000 kg amphibious cargo carrier with tarpaulin cover

Gearbox: automatic, 3 forward and 1 reverse gears with torque converter
Axle differential carriers: single reduction, spiral bevel drive. Air operated differential lock at front and rear
Planetary drives: (front and rear) epicyclic gear train in wheel hubs
Steering: power-assisted
Turning radius: (land) 7·5 m
Suspension: (front and rear) independent strut and link type with helical spring and rubber bump stop. Hydraulic shock absorber at each wheel station
Tyres: 14.5 × 20 PS 12 (combat)
Number of tyres: 4 + 1 spare

Brakes:
 (main) disc, air over hydraulic, dual circuit
 (parking) drum type, mounted on transfer rear output shaft
Electrical system: 24 V
Batteries: 2 × 12 V, 100 Ah

STATUS
Production.

MANUFACTURER
FIAT Direzione Mezzi Speciali, Corso G Marconi 10/20, Turin, Italy.

FIAT Model 6640A (4 × 4) 2140 kg Amphibious Cargo Carrier

DESCRIPTION
The FIAT Model 6640A (4 × 4) 2140 kg amphibious cargo carrier has been designed to meet the requirements of the Italian Home Office Civil Protection and Fire Fighting Department, but also has a number of military applications.

The hull of the vehicle is of all-welded aluminium construction with a maximum thickness of 4 mm. The engine compartment is at the front of the hull and separated from the driver's compartment by a fireproof bulkhead. The cab is fully enclosed and is heated and ventilated. The cargo area is to the rear of the cab and has removable bows and a tarpaulin cover. Hatches at the hull rear give access to tool and storage holds.

The vehicle is propelled in the water by its wheels or the four-bladed screw with a Kort nozzle. Steering in the water is by a rear-mounted rudder linked to the steering wheel. In an emergency the rudder can be operated by hand. Three bilge pumps, one in the bottom of the engine compartment and two below the cargo area, are provided. Mounted at the front of the vehicle is a winch with a capacity of 3000 kg on the first layer. The winch is provided with an automatic safety brake and has 30 metres of 11 mm diameter cable.

FIAT Model 6640A (4 × 4) 2140 kg amphibious cargo carrier (Italian Army)

SPECIFICATIONS
Cab seating: 1 + 1
Configuration: 4 × 4
Weight:
   (empty) 4810 kg
   (loaded) 6950 kg
Weight on front axle: (loaded) 2865 kg
Weight on rear axle: (loaded) 4085 kg
Max load: 2140 kg
Load area: 3·21 × 1·95 m
Length: 7·3 m
Width: 2·5 m
Height:
   (cab) 2·27 m
   (tarpaulin) 2·715 m
   (load area) 1·076 m
Ground clearance: (axles) 0·375 m
Track: 1·977 m
Wheelbase: 2·7 m
Angle of approach/departure: 30°/25°
Max speed:
   (road) 90 km/h
   (water, propelled by screw) 11 km/h
   (water, propelled by wheels) 5 km/h
Range:
   (road) 750 km
   (water, propelled by screw) 60 km
   (water, propelled by wheels) 30 km
Fuel capacity: 140 litres
Max gradient: 50%
Max side slope: 30%
Vertical obstacle: 0·43 m
Fording: amphibious
Engine: Model 8060.02 6-cylinder 4-stroke liquid-cooled diesel developing 117 hp at 3200 rpm

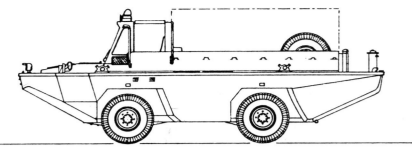

FIAT Model 6640A (4 × 4) 2140 kg amphibious cargo carrier

Gearbox: manual with 5 forward and 1 reverse gears with PTO for winch
Clutch: single dry type, hydraulically operated
Transfer box: 2-speed with PTO for screw
Axle differential carriers: single reduction, spiral bevel drive. Air-operated differential lock at front and limited slip differential at rear
Planetary final drives: (front and rear) epicyclic gear train in wheel hubs
Steering: power-assisted
Turning radius:
   (land) 6·8 m
   (water) 6 m
Suspension: (front and rear) independent strut and link type with helical spring and coaxial rubber bump-stop, hydraulic shock absorber at each wheel station

Tyres: 16.00 × 20
Number of tyres: 4 + 1 spare
Brakes:
   (main) air over hydraulic, dual circuit
   (parking) drum type mounted on transfer rear output shaft
Electrical system: 24 V
Batteries: 2 × 12 V, 100 Ah

STATUS
Production complete. In service with the Italian Home Office.

MANUFACTURER
FIAT, Direzione Mezzi Speciali, Corso G Marconi 10/20, Turin, Italy.

SPAIN

VAP 3550/1 (4 × 4) 3000 kg Amphibious Vehicle

DEVELOPMENT
The VAP 3550/1 (4 × 4) 3000 kg amphibious vehicle has been developed by ENASA to meet Spanish Navy requirements for a vehicle which can be launched from LSTs and other amphibious craft off-shore, reach the coast under its own power and then travel inland over rough country. VAP is the export name of this vehicle, within Spain it is known as the Pegaso 3550 with the first production batch being known as the 3550/1.

The vehicle uses many automotive components of the ENASA (Pegaso) range of 3045 (4 × 4) 3000 kg and 3050 (6 × 6) 6000 kg trucks of which over 6000 have now been supplied to the Spanish Army.

The Italian Astra company has obtained a licence to undertake production of the VAP in Italy.

DESCRIPTION
The boat-shaped hull of the VAP 3550/1 is made of all-welded 6 mm thick steel and is divided into watertight compartments. The driver sits in the semi-enclosed cab which has an open back, towards the front with two passengers seated on his right. A searchlight that can be operated from within the cab is mounted over the top of the cab. Immediately behind the cab is a hydraulic crane with a maximum lifting capacity of 350 kg.

The cargo area in the centre of the vehicle can be covered with removable bows and a tarpaulin cover. Removable benches for troops can be fitted down either side of the cargo compartment.

The engine compartment is at the rear with the air-outlet, air-inlet louvres and exhaust pipe mounted in the top.

The VAP is fully amphibious, propelled in the water by two waterjets at the rear of the hull immediately behind the second axle. The two single waterjets are driven by a hydraulic system composed of a pump directly connected to the vehicle's engine and two hydraulic motors acting directly on the hydrojets. It features a pressurising system for the mechanical units in contact with the water which operates as soon as the VAP enters the water. When afloat, pivot turns can be accomplished.

The load compartment is equipped with two pumps with a maximum capacity of 6000 litres an hour and there are two automatic bilge pumps in the hull with a maximum capacity of 3600 litres an hour. Mounted at the front is a winch with a maximum capacity of 4500 kg.

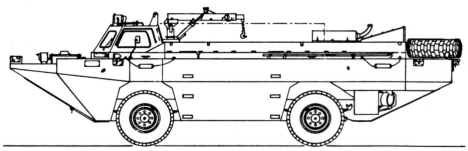

VAP 3550/1 (4 × 4) 3000 kg amphibious vehicle

VAP 3550/1 (4 × 4) 3000 kg amphibious vehicle

Front view of VAP 3550/1 (4 × 4) 3000 kg amphibious vehicle

VAP 3550/1 (4 × 4) 3000 kg amphibious vehicles

SPECIFICATIONS
Cab seating: 1 + 2 (rear, 24 men)
Configuration: 4 × 4
Weight:
(empty) 9500 kg
(loaded) 12 500 kg
Max load: 3000 kg
Load area: 3.2 × 2.05 m
Length: 9.058 m
Width: 2.5 m
Height:
(cab) 2.5 m
(crane) 2.83 m
Ground clearance: 0.32 m
Track: 1.927 m
Wheelbase: 3.45 m
Angle of approach/departure: 33°/27°
Max speed:
(road) 87 km/h
(water) 5·5 knots
Range:
(road) 800 km
(water) 80 km
Fuel capacity: 250 litres
Fuel consumption: (land) 30 litres/100 km
Max gradient: 60%

Max side slope: 30%
Fording: amphibious
Engine: Pegaso 9135/5 diesel developing 190 hp at 2600 rpm
Gearbox: manual, 6 forward and 1 reverse gears
Transfer box: 2-speed
Steering: power-assisted
Turning radius: 9 m
Suspension: semi-elliptical springs and hydraulic double acting shock absorbers, both axles have a self-locking differential case
Tyres: 13.00 × 20
Number of tyres: 4 + 1 spare
Brakes: dual circuit, air
Electrical system: 24 V
Batteries: 2 × 12 V, 99 Ah

STATUS
Production. Reported ordered by Egypt. Seven delivered to Mexico in 1982.

MANUFACTURER
Pegaso SA, ENASA, Military Division, Av Aragon, 402, Madrid-22, Spain.
    License production: Astra Veicoli Industriali SpA, Via Caorsana 79, 29100 Piacenza, Italy.

Bow of VAP 3550/1 (4 × 4) 3000 kg amphibious vehicle

UNION OF SOVIET SOCIALIST REPUBLICS

GAZ-46 MAV (4 × 4) 500 kg Amphibious Vehicle

DEVELOPMENT
During the Second World War the Soviet Union received many wheeled vehicles under the lend-lease programme including some American DUKW (6 × 6) and Ford GPA (4 × 4) amphibians. After the end of the war the Soviets designed, built and placed in production similar vehicles but based on Soviet chassis. The 6 × 6 model was called the BAV and the 4 × 4 model the MAV. The MAV was initially based on the GAZ-67B (4 × 4) chassis but from the early 1950s it was replaced by a version based on the UAZ-69 chassis. The earlier version was slightly smaller, powered by a 55 hp engine and had 7.50 × 16 tyres.

DESCRIPTION
The MAV has a watertight hull with the engine at the front and the passenger compartment towards the rear. Before entering the water a trim vane is erected at the front of the hull to prevent the vehicle being flooded by freak waves. It is propelled in the water by a three-bladed propeller under the rear of the hull. If required the passenger compartment can be covered by a canvas top which is kept folded at the rear of the crew compartment. The windscreen can be folded forward if required.
    The GAZ-46 MAV is still used by the Soviets for reconnaissance of river crossing points, but has been replaced in many units by the BRDM-1 and BRDM-2 (4 × 4) armoured vehicles.

SPECIFICATIONS (vehicle based on UAZ-69 chassis)
Cab seating: 1 + 4
Configuration: 4 × 4
Weight:
(empty) 1980 kg
(loaded) 2480 kg
Max load: 500 kg
Towed load: 500 kg
Length: 5·06 m
Width: 1·735 m
Height: (with hood erected) 2·04 m
Ground clearance: 0·24 m
Track: 1·44 m
Wheelbase: 2·3 m
Max speed:
(road) 90 km/h
(water) 9 km/h
Range: 500 km
Fuel capacity: 90 litres

GAZ-46 MAV (4 × 4) 500 kg amphibious vehicle

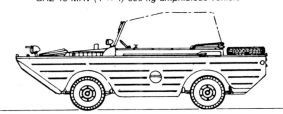

GAZ-46 MAV (4 × 4) 500 kg amphibious vehicle

Fuel consumption: 17·7 litres/100 km
Fording: amphibious
Engine: M-20 4-cylinder petrol developing 55 hp at 3600 rpm
Gearbox: manual, 3 forward and 1 reverse gears
Clutch: single dry disc
Transfer box: 2-speed
Suspension: (front and rear) longitudinal semi-elliptical springs with double acting hydraulic shock absorbers
Tyres: 6.50 × 16
Number of tyres: 4 + 1 spare

Brakes:
(main) hydraulic
(parking) mechanical
Electrical system: 12 V

STATUS
In service with the Soviet Army.

MANUFACTURER
(Chassis) Gor'kiy Automobile Plant (1952–56), then Ul'yanovsk Automobile Plant, USSR.

BAV 485 (6 × 6) 2500 kg Amphibious Vehicle

DEVELOPMENT
During the Second World War the Soviets received a number of American DUKW (6 × 6) amphibians under the lend-lease programme. After the war they designed a similar vehicle called the BAV 485 which first appeared in 1952. This was based on the ZIL-151 (6 × 6) truck chassis and was also known as the ZIL-485. A later model, the BAV 485A, was based on the ZIL-157 (6 × 6) truck chassis which was also used for the BTR-152 (6 × 6) armoured personnel carrier.

DESCRIPTION
The major improvement over the American DUKW was the provision of a drop tailgate at the rear of the cargo compartment. With the aid of ramps, artillery and small vehicles such as the UAZ-69 can be loaded in the rear cargo area. The first model had external air lines for the central tyre-pressure regulation system but the BAV 485A has an internal air line system. The layout of the vehicle is conventional with the engine at the front and the cargo area, which can be covered by bows and a tarpaulin when required, at the rear. In the water the vehicle is driven by a three-bladed propeller mounted under the rear of the hull. The basic vehicle is normally

unarmed although some have been seen fitted with a 12·7 mm DShKM machine gun behind the driver's position.

STATUS
Production complete. In service with members of the Warsaw Pact. Usually replaced in front-line units by the K-61 or PTS.

MANUFACTURER
(Chassis) Likhachev Motor Vehicle Plant, Moscow, USSR.

Rear view of BAV 485 (6 × 6) 2500 kg amphibious vehicle

BAV 485 (6 × 6) 2500 kg amphibious vehicle

SPECIFICATIONS
(data in square brackets relate to the BAV 485A where different from standard model)
Cab seating: 1 + 1 (25 troops can be carried in cargo area)
Configuration: 6 × 6
Weight:
　(empty) 7150 kg
　(loaded) 9650 kg
Max load: (land and water) 2500 kg
Length: 9·54 m
Width: 2·845 m
Height: (tarpaulin in position) 2·66 m
Ground clearance: 0·28 m
Track: 1·62 m
Wheelbase: 3·668 m + 1·12 m
Max speed:
　(road) 60 km/h
　(water) 10 km/h

Range: 480 km
Fuel capacity: 240 litres
Fuel consumption: 47 litres/100 km
Gradient: 60%
Vertical obstacle: 0·4 [0·6] m
Fording: amphibious
Engine: ZIL-123 6-cylinder in-line water-cooled petrol developing 110 hp at 2900 rpm [ZIL-157K developing 109 hp at 2800 rpm]

Gearbox: manual with 5 forward and 1 reverse gears
Clutch: single dry disc
Transfer box: 2-speed
Tyres: 11.00 × 18 [12.00 × 18]
Brakes:
　(main) air
　(parking) mechanical
Electrical system: 12 V

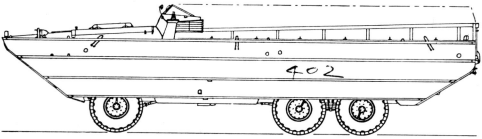

BAV 485A (6 × 6) 2500 kg amphibious vehicle with internal airlines for tyre pressure regulation system

6 × 6 Amphibious Vehicle

DESCRIPTION
The designation of this Soviet 6 × 6 amphibious vehicle is not known and no details are available other than illustrations that were released during the Soyuz T-2 space programme trials that took place during 1980. At least two versions of this vehicle exist, one carrying a crane jib and the other having a personnel carrier con-figuration. Both have a forward-mounted crew cabin that appears to have enough space for at least three crew. The area behind the cab may be either open for general cargo carrying purposes or for mounting special equipment such as the crane jib. In its personnel carrier form the load area is fully enclosed and some windows are provided. A rear tailgate is provided and the rear bulkhead has provision for towing attachments. Propulsion in water appears to be by the wheel treads alone although there may be a single water propulsion unit venting to the rear.

STATUS
Uncertain.

Soviet 6 × 6 amphibious vehicle equipped with crane jib to carry Soyuz T-2 descent module

Personnel carrier version of 6 × 6 amphibious vehicle seen over crane jib carried on another vehicle

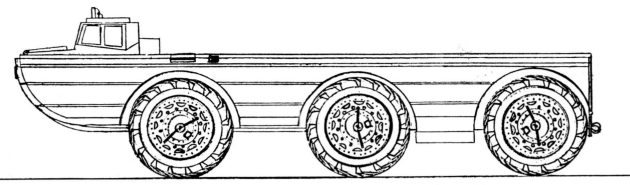

Provisional side-view drawing of 6 × 6 amphibious vehicle (not to 1/76th scale)

K-61 5000 kg Tracked Amphibious Cargo Carrier

DEVELOPMENT
The K-61 tracked amphibian was first seen in 1950 and is sometimes referred to as the GPT. The vehicle is intended primarily for carrying troops and cargo across rivers and other inland water barriers, although it can also be used for ship-to-shore transport. The K-61 is being replaced by the more recent PTS tracked amphibian which has almost twice the load carrying capability of the K-61.

DESCRIPTION
The hull of the K-61 is all steel with the crew compartment at the front and the cargo compartment at the rear. The commander and driver are both provided with a windscreen hinged at the top which can be opened horizontally. At the rear of the hull is a large tailgate which also acts as a loading ramp. If required, bows and a tarpaulin cover can be fitted over the crew and cargo compartment. The K-61 can carry a maximum load of 3000 kg on land and 5000 kg on water. Typical loads include a GAZ-63 truck, 120 mm mortar, 76 mm or 85 mm anti-tank guns, 14·5 mm ZPU-2 or ZPU-4 anti-aircraft guns, 122 mm M1938 (M30) howitzer. The suspension each side consists of seven small road wheels with the drive sprocket at the front and the idler at the rear. There are no return rollers as such but seven slides are provided to support the tracks. The K-61 is fully amphibious being propelled in the water by two three-bladed propellers at the rear of the hull, under the loading ramp.

The Polish Army is reported to have used K-61s as a floating bridge using superstructure of the LLP light or TPP heavy pontoon bridges.

SPECIFICATIONS
Cab seating: 1 + 1 (60 troops can be carried in rear)
Weight:
  (empty) 9550 kg
  (loaded, water) 14 550 kg
  (loaded, land) 12 550 kg
Length: 9·15 m
Width: 3·15 m
Height: 2·15 m
Ground clearance:
  (empty) 0·4 m
  (loaded) 0·36 m
Track: 2·6 m
Track width: 300 mm
Length of track on ground: 4·56 m
Ground pressure:
  (empty) 0·35 kg/cm²
  (loaded) 0·46 kg/cm²

Max speed:
  (road) 36 km/h
  (water) 10 km/h
Range: 260 km
Fuel capacity: 260 litres
Fuel consumption: 95 litres/100 km
Max gradient:
  (empty) 42°
  (loaded) 15°
Vertical obstacle: 0·65 m
Trench: 3 m
Engine: YaAZ-M204VKr 4-cylinder water-cooled diesel developing 135 hp at 2000 rpm

STATUS
Production complete. In service with members of the Warsaw Pact, Egypt and Viet-Nam.

MANUFACTURER
Soviet state factories.

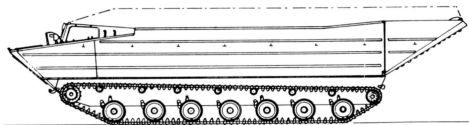

K-61 5000 kg tracked amphibious cargo carrier

K-61 5000 kg tracked amphibious cargo carrier

K-61 5000 kg tracked amphibious cargo carrier from above showing rear tailgate incorporating loading ramps

Egyptian Army K-61s carrying Mercedes-Benz Unimog (4 × 4) trucks (Egyptian Ministry of Defence)

PTS and PTS-M Tracked Amphibious Vehicle

DEVELOPMENT
The PTS tracked amphibious vehicle entered service in the mid-1960s as the replacement for the earlier K-61 (GPT) vehicle. Main improvements over the K-61 are its higher water-speed and its ability to transport 10 000 kg on land for 3 km in order to reach the water.

DESCRIPTION
The crew compartment is at the front of the vehicle and is fully sealed against NBC attack. The crew enter the cab via two circular hatches in the roof. The cargo area

PTS-M towing PKP trailer

is at the rear of the vehicle and vehicles are loaded via the hinged tailgate which also has integral loading ramps. Tie down points are fitted for securing the vehicle. The engine is under the centre of the cargo compartment with the exhaust exits just above the top of the cargo compartment on each side. The PTS is propelled in the water by two propellers in tunnels under the rear of the hull and steering is by two rudders at the rear of the hull.

The suspension is of the torsion bar type and consists of six road wheels with the idler at the rear and the drive sprocket at the front.

A winch is mounted at the front of the vehicle and before entering the water a trim vane is erected at the front and the bilge pumps are switched on. The cargo area can be covered by bows and a tarpaulin cover and is sometimes used as an ambulance vehicle. Standard equipment includes infra-red night vision equipment, intercom, radios and a searchlight mounted on the top of the crew compartment.

The PTS has been designed to carry 5000 kg on land or 10 000 kg on water, or up to 70 men.

A more recent development is the PKP trailer which has been designed specifically for use with the PTS. Basic specifications are: unladen weight 3600 kg, overall length 10·3 metres, width (travelling) 2·82 m, height 1·98 metres, ground clearance 0·4 metre and track 1·89 metres. This is a boat-shaped trailer and has two small pontoons pivoted either side which rest on top of the trailer when it is travelling and are swung through 180 degrees and locked in position before entering the water. Loading ramps are provided for loading the trailer. The trailer is normally used to carry 122 mm howitzers while the PTS carries the prime mover, for example the Ural-375D. The trailer can be towed at a speed of between 20 and 25 km/h laden or 25 to 30 km/h unladen.

The latest version is the PTS-M: exact differences from the original model are not known, but it could have an additional 705 or 750 litres of fuel. According to American reports the Group of Soviet Forces in East Germany has six river crossing battalions, each with 30 K-61s and 20 PTS-Ms, and 24 GSP ferry units.

VARIANTS
The Polish Army uses a number of PTS tracked amphibious vehicles fitted with rocket-propelled mine-clearing equipment in the rear. A photograph of this model appears in the *Mine-clearing equipment* section.

SPECIFICATIONS
Cab seating: 1 + 1
Weight:
  (empty) 17 700 kg
  (loaded, land) 22 700 kg
  (loaded, water) 27 700 kg
Max load:
  (land) 5000 kg
  (water) 10 000 kg
Load area: 7·9 × 2·6 m
Length: 11·5 m
Width: 3·3 m
Height: 2·65 m
Ground clearance: (loaded) 0·4 m
Track: 2·8 m
Track width: 480 mm

Length of track on ground: 5·63 m
Ground pressure:
  (empty) 0·382 kg/cm^2
  (with 5000 kg load) 0·483 kg/cm^2
  (with 10 000 kg load) 0·582 kg/cm^2
Max speed:
  (land with 5000 kg load) 42 km/h
  (water with 10 000 kg load) 10·6 km/h
Range: 300 km
Fuel capacity: 705 litres

Max gradient:
  (empty) 60%
  (loaded) 20%
Vertical obstacle: 0·65 m
Trench: 2·5 m
Engine: V-54P diesel developing 350 hp at 1800 rpm

STATUS
Probably still in production. In service with members of the Warsaw Pact as well as Egypt, Iraq and Yugoslavia.

Ural-375D being loaded into PTS-M tracked amphibious vehicle

Egyptian Army PTSs carrying artillery pieces during parade in Cairo (Egyptian Ministry of Defence)

PTS-M vehicle afloat

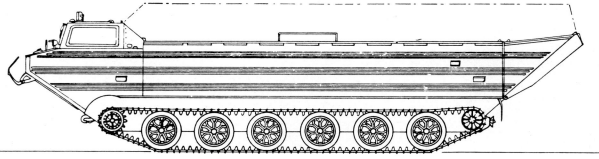
PTS-M tracked amphibious vehicle

UNITED STATES OF AMERICA

LARC-5 (4 × 4) 4536 kg Amphibious Cargo Carrier

DEVELOPMENT

The LARC-5 (Lighter, Amphibious, Resupply Cargo, 5-ton) (4 × 4) was developed by the Borg Warner Corporation from 1958 under the direction of the United States Transportation Engineering Command at Fort Eustis, Virginia. The first production contract was awarded to the Adams Division of Le Tourneau Westinghouse in June 1961 and between 1962 and 1968 950 LARC-5s were built. The last manufacturer was the Condiesel Mobile Equipment Division of Old Greenwich, Connecticut. The vehicle has been designed to carry 4536 kg of cargo, or 15 to 20 fully equipped troops from ships off-shore to the beach, or if required, farther inland, and is issued on the scale of 34 per Army light amphibious company.

DESCRIPTION

The hull of the LARC-5 is of all-welded aluminium construction with reinforced aluminium frames. The cab is at the front of the vehicle and contains, in addition to the operating controls, heater and windscreen defroster, portable lamp and cable, fire extinguisher, fabric cover for the back of the cab, radio, adjustable seat for the driver, two fixed seats for the other crew members and a magnetic compass. The cargo area is in the centre of the vehicle. Fabric curtains reinforced with stranded wire rope can be installed on each side of the cargo deck to protect the cargo.

The transfer transmission compartment is below the cargo deck and contains the transfer transmission, front wheel disconnects, drive shafts and service brakes.

The engine compartment is at the rear and is covered by two watertight hatches. Air is blown out of the compartment through a small grille between the two hatch covers. A fixed fire extinguisher is installed in the engine compartment and is controlled by a pull of a handle on the cargo deck rear bulkhead. Two manual bilge pumps are installed for use if the main hydraulic pump fails. The vehicle is propelled in the water by a three-bladed propeller under the rear of the hull.

Power is transmitted from the engine to a torque converter and hydraulic retarder installed on the flywheel end of the engine. The driver selects either forward or reverse by shifting the forward/reverse transmission lever. The main drive shaft connects the output of the forward/reverse transmission to the transfer transmission. This transmission has two gear ratios (high and low) for land operations and one gear ratio (marine) for water operations. The differential transmission transmits power to the four wheels. With the transmission in low or high range, power is always transmitted to the wheels. A mechanical disconnect can be used to apply power to the rear wheels only for two-wheel drive. Four drive shafts connect the differential transmission to the wheels. A right angle drive assembly is installed at each wheel to apply the driving power to the

Australian Army LARC-5 (4 × 4) amphibious cargo carrier (P Handel)

wheels. This is a gearbox used to apply the rotation of the four-drive shaft to the axle ends of the wheels.

VARIANTS

Some vehicles have been fitted with a hydraulically operated boom designed by the Condiesel Mobile Equipment Division. The boom is 4·51 metres long and can lift a maximum load of 2495 kg.

SPECIFICATIONS

Cab seating: 1 + 2
Configuration: 4 × 4
Weight:
  (empty) 9502 kg
  (loaded) 14 038 kg
Max load: 4536 kg
Load area: 4·876 × 2·971 m
Length: 10·668 m
Width: 3·149 m
Height:
  (overall) 3·034 m
  (reduced) 2·374 m
Ground clearance: 0·609 m
Track: 2·565 m
Wheelbase: 4·876 m
Angle of approach/departure: 28·5°/26·5°
Max speed:
  (road) 48·2 km/h
  (water) 16 km/h

Range:
  (land, empty) 400 km
  (land, loaded) 322 km
  (water, empty) 65 km
  (water, loaded) 56 km
Fuel capacity: 545 litres
Max gradient: 60%
Max side slope: 25%
Fording: amphibious
Engine:
  (early vehicles) 8-cylinder petrol developing 300 hp at 3000 rpm
  (late production vehicles) Cummins 4-cycle V-8 diesel developing 300 hp
Turning radius: 11·124 m
Suspension: rigid
Tyres: 18.00 × 25

STATUS

Production complete. In service with Argentina, Australia (87), Federal Republic of Germany and the USA.

MANUFACTURER

Condiesel Mobile Equipment Division, CONDEC Corporation, 1700 Post Road, Old Greenwich, Connecticut 06870, USA.

LARC-5 (4 × 4) 4536 kg amphibious cargo carrier operating in water

LARC-5 (4 × 4) 4536 kg amphibious cargo carrier loading cargo with hydraulically-operated boom

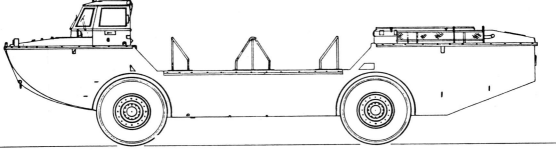

LARC-5 (4 × 4) 4536 kg amphibious cargo carrier

LARC-15 (4 × 4) 13 608 kg Amphibious Cargo Carrier

DEVELOPMENT

The LARC-15 (Lighter, Amphibious, Resupply, Cargo, 15-ton) (4 × 4) was developed by the Ingersoll-Kalamazoo Division of the Borg Warner Corporation. Three prototypes were built and further development resulted in the vehicle being classified as Standard A. First production contracts were awarded to the Military Products Division of the Fruehauf Corporation in 1963. The vehicle is issued on the scale of 24 per Army medium amphibian company. It has been designed to carry 13 608 kg of cargo from ships off-shore onto the beach, or if required, farther inland. A typical load could be a 155 mm M114 howitzer, together with its crew and ammunition or a 2½-ton (6 × 6) cargo truck.

DESCRIPTION

The hull of the LARC-15 consists of an aluminium frame covered by aluminium plates 5 mm thick. The rear-mounted cab is constructed of aluminium plate and is bolted into position over the engine room at the stern. The transmission is mounted forward of the engine room, below the cargo area. The cargo area has a flush deck and a hydraulically operated bow ramp also made of aluminium which presents a prow-like configuration when raised. Centring devices are provided on the cargo deck for quick loading and spotting of CONEX containers and the flush cargo deck permits unloading from the sides with conventional forklift equipment.

A closed-centre, demand type hydraulic system is used to power the steering system, bilge pump and ramp installation.

Forward/neutral/reverse transmissions control forward and reverse motions. A transfer transmission provides high, neutral and low range gearing to a differential transmission for four-wheel land drive and engagement of the propeller shaft for marine operation. In the water the vehicle is propelled by a single four-bladed propeller mounted under the stern of the vehicle. The LARC-15 is capable of operations in surf up to 3·048 metres high.

The driver can select one of three steer modes: two-wheel, four-wheel and oblique or crab steer. For marine operations, mechanical steering is provided and the marine steering wheel is mechanically linked to the rudder. When afloat, the wheels and the rudder are

LARC-15 (4 × 4) 13 608 kg amphibious cargo carrier with ramp lowered and M56 self-propelled anti-tank gun ready to be driven off (US Army)

used for steering. Transition from marine to land drive is made without loss of momentum.

STATUS

Production complete. In service with the Federal Republic of Germany and the USA.

MANUFACTURER

Military Products Division, Fruehauf Corporation, 601 So Placentia Avenue, Fullerton, California 92631, USA.

SPECIFICATIONS

Cab seating: 1 + 1
Configuration: 4 × 4
Weight:
(empty) 20 500 kg
(loaded) 34 100 kg
Max load: 13 608 kg
Load area: 7·315 × 4·114 m
Length: 13·716 m
Width: 4·419 m
Height:
(cab) 4·724 m
(reduced) 4·165 m
Ground clearance:
(hull) 0·74 m
(propeller shroud to ground) 0·42 m

Wheelbase: 6·362 m
Angle of approach/departure: 33°/22°
Max speed:
(road) 50 km/h
(water) 15 km/h
Range:
(road, empty) 482 km
(road, loaded) 418 km
(water, empty) 142 km
(water, loaded) 120 km
Fuel capacity: 1363 litres
Fuel consumption:
(road) 61 litres/h
(water) 105 litres/h
Max gradient: 40%
Max side slope: 25%
Fording: amphibious
Engines: 2 × 4-cycle, V-8 Cummins diesel developing 300 hp each at 3000 rpm
Steering: hydraulic
Turning radius: 13·716 m
Suspension: rigid
Tyres: 24.00 × 29
Brakes: hydraulic
Electrical system: 24 V
Batteries: 4 × 12 V

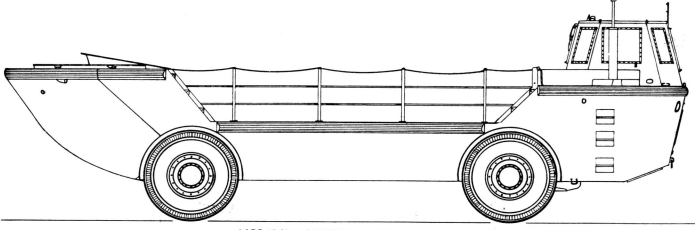

LARC-15 (4 × 4) 13 608 kg amphibious cargo carrier

LARC-60 (4 × 4) 60 000 kg Amphibious Cargo Carrier

DESCRIPTION

The development contract for the LARC-60 (Lighter, Amphibious, Resupply, Cargo, 60-ton) was awarded by the Transportation Corps to the Pacific Car and Foundry Company of Renton, Washington in 1951. It was originally known as the BARC (Beach, Amphibious, Resupply, Cargo), and is designed to transport men, cargo and vehicles from ships offshore onto the beach, or, if required, farther inland. It is issued on the scale of 15 per heavy amphibian company. The vehicle can carry 60 000 kg of cargo on both land and water, or 200 fully equipped men. In an emergency the vehicle can carry up to 100 000 kg of cargo. When alongside ships, the cargo is loaded overhead and unloaded onto the beach via the hydraulically operated bow ramp.

On land each of the four engines powers one of the four road wheels and when afloat the two port engines power the port propeller via a propeller shaft and the two starboard engines power the starboard propeller via a propeller shaft. The two propellers are in tunnels under

LARC-60 (4 × 4) 60 000 kg amphibious cargo carrier with bow ramp lowered

the stern of the vehicle. Power is transmitted from the engine to the four wheels via Allison torque converters and torqmatic transmissions. The tyres have a central tyre-pressure regulation system.

SPECIFICATIONS
Configuration: 4 × 4
Weight:
 (empty) 37 000 kg
 (loaded) 97 000 kg
Max load:
 (normal) 60 000 kg
 (emergency) 100 000 kg
Load area: 12·75 × 4·165 m

Length: 19·024 m
Width: 8·111 m
Height: 6·07 m
Ground clearance: 0·711 m
Max speed:
 (road, empty) 33 km/h
 (road, loaded) 27·35 km/h
 (water, empty) 12 km/h
 (water, loaded) 11 km/h
Range:
 (road, empty) 980 km
 (road, loaded) 835 km
 (water, empty) 241 km
 (water, loaded) 225 km

Fuel capacity: 2271 litres
Fording: amphibious
Engines: 4 × 6-cylinder General Motors diesels developing 165 hp each
Turning radius: 24·774 m
Tyres: 36.00 × 41

STATUS
Production complete. In service with the US Army.

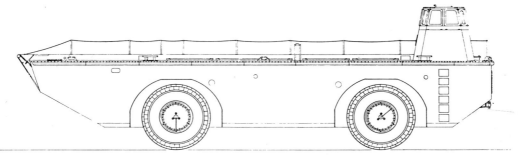

LARC-60 (4 × 4) 60 000 kg amphibious cargo carrier (Scale 1/152nd not 1/76th as all other drawings)

TRACKED PRIME MOVERS AND CARGO CARRIERS

This section excludes tracked vehicles which have been designed specifically for amphibious use (ie the Soviet K-61 and PTS-M) or for over-snow use (ie the American M116, Soviet GT series, and the Swedish Bv 202 and Bv 206), details of which will be found in their respective sections.

CHINA, PEOPLE'S REPUBLIC

Type 59 Artillery Tractor

DESCRIPTION
This has been designed to tow artillery such as the 122 mm Type 54 howitzer, which is a copy of the Soviet M1938 howitzer, or the 122 mm Type 60 gun, a copy of the Soviet D-74 gun. The fully enclosed cab at the front of the vehicle has sufficient seats for most of the crew of the gun and has a circular observation hatch in the left side of the roof. The rear cargo area has a stake type body and a drop tailgate, removable bows and a tarpaulin cover. The suspension is believed to be of the torsion bar type and consists of five road wheels with the drive sprocket at the front and the idler at the rear. The Type 59 may be powered by a V-12 truck diesel.

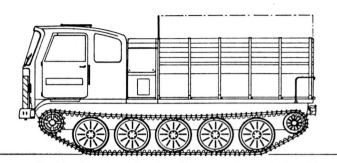

Provisional drawing of Type 59 artillery tractor (not to 1/76th scale)

STATUS
In service with China and Viet-Nam.

MANUFACTURER
Chinese state factories.

HUNGARY

K-800 Light Tracked Artillery Tractor

DEVELOPMENT
The K-800 is the Hungarian version of the Soviet M-2 light tracked artillery tractor and entered service with the Hungarian Army in the 1950s. It is no longer in large-scale use but is probably held in reserve. The K-800 is lighter than the Soviet M-2 and has a more powerful engine.

DESCRIPTION
Its layout is identical to the M-2 with the engine at the front, two-seat cab in the centre with a circular roof hatch which the M-2 does not have, and the cargo/personnel compartment at the rear. The suspension is similar to that of the SU-76 self-propelled gun and consists of five road wheels with the idler at the front, drive sprocket at the rear and three track return rollers.

The K-800 has also been built in Yugoslavia as the GJ-800. It differs from the Hungarian vehicle in that it is powered by a 6-cylinder water-cooled diesel engine developing 120 hp and has the cab of the FAP truck.

SPECIFICATIONS
Cab seating: 1 + 1
Weight:
  (empty) 6400 kg
  (loaded) 8200 kg
Max load: 1800 kg
Towed load: 8000 kg
Length: 5 m
Width: 2·4 m
Height: (cab) 2·2 m
Ground clearance: 0·3 m
Track: 2·1 m
Track width: 300 mm
Length of track on ground: 2·75 m

K-800 light tracked artillery tractor

Ground pressure: 0·45 kg/cm²
Max speed: (road) 35 km/h
Range: 300 km
Fuel capacity: 280 litres
Max gradient:
  (empty) 60%
  (towing) 36%
Vertical obstacle: 0·5 m
Trench: 1·5 m
Fording: 0·6 m

Engine: Csepel D613 6-cylinder water-cooled diesel developing 130 hp
Gearbox: manual with 5 forward and 1 reverse gears

STATUS
Production complete. Held in reserve in Hungary. Some were also exported to China.

MANUFACTURER
Hungarian state factories.

JAPAN

Type 73 Tracked Artillery Tractor

DEVELOPMENT
The Type 73 tracked artillery tractor was developed from 1969 as the replacement for the M4 and M8 high-speed tractors used by the Japanese Ground Self-Defence Force. Trials with prototype vehicles were successfully completed in 1972 and the following year it was standardised as the Type 73 tracked artillery tractor, or tractor (prime mover). Production began in 1974 but only a small number were built owing to restrictions in the defence budget.

DESCRIPTION
The Type 73 has a fully enclosed four-door cab at the front with the engine in the centre and the ammunition stowage area at the rear. The suspension is believed to be of the torsion bar type and consists of six road wheels with the drive sprocket at the front, the sixth road wheel acting as the idler. A 12·7 mm (Browning 0·50 M2 HB) machine gun is mounted on the roof for anti-aircraft defence. Some Type 73s have been fitted with a hydraulically operated dozer blade at the front of the hull for clearing obstacles and preparing fire positions. The tractor is used to tow artillery pieces such as the 155 mm M59 (Long Tom) and 8-inch (203 mm) M115.

SPECIFICATIONS
Crew: 1 + 11
Weight: 19 800 kg
Max towed load: 16 000 kg
Length: 6·13 m
Width: 2·95 m
Height: 2·3 m
Max speed: (road) 45 km/h
Range: 300 km
Gradient: 60%
Engine: Mitsubishi ZF6 6-cylinder air-cooled diesel developing 400 hp at 2200 rpm

STATUS
Production complete. In service with the Japanese Ground Self-Defence Force.

MANUFACTURER
Hitachi Manufacturing Co, Japan.

Type 73 tracked artillery tractor towing 155 mm M59 (Long Tom) (Kensuke Ebata)

Type 73 tracked artillery tractor showing position of roof-mounted 12·7 mm AA MG (K Nogi)

POLAND

Mazur D-350 Medium Tracked Artillery Tractor

DEVELOPMENT
The Mazur was developed in the 1950s and to some extent is based on the Soviet AT-S medium tracked artillery tractor. The first prototypes were known as the Mazur D-300; production versions have a more powerful engine and are known as the D-350, although sometimes referred to as the ACS. The Mazur D-350 is used for towing anti-tank guns and heavy artillery up to 152 mm in calibre.

DESCRIPTION
The engine is at the front with the cab in the centre and the cargo area at the rear. The cab has two doors in either side, one at each end of the cab, front windscreens that can be opened horizontally for improved vision and a square hatch in the forward part of the roof. The rear cargo area has a tailgate, removable bows and a tarpaulin cover. The suspension consists of five road wheels with the drive sprocket at the front and the idler at the rear. There are four track return rollers. A 17 000 kg capacity winch and 80 metres of cable are fitted as standard.

SPECIFICATIONS
Cab seating: 1 + 8
Weight:
(loaded road) 18 560 kg
(loaded cross country) 17 060 kg
Towed load:
(road) 15 000 kg
(cross country) 10 000 kg
Length: 5·81 m
Width: 2·89 m
Height: (cab) 2·6 m
Ground clearance: 0·465 m
Track: 2·448 m
Max speed: 53 km/h
Range: 490 km
Gradient: 50%
Vertical obstacle: 0·6 m
Trench: 1·45 m
Fording: 0·8 m
Engine: D-350 V-12 water-cooled diesel developing 350 hp at 1800 rpm
Gearbox: manual with 5 forward and 1 reverse gears

Mazur D-350 medium tracked artillery tractor towing 100 mm field gun M53

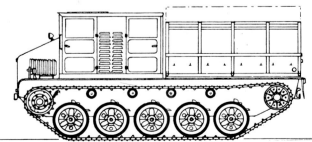

Mazur D-350 medium tracked artillery tractor

STATUS
Production complete, replaced in production in Poland by the ATS-59. In service only with Czechoslovakia and Poland.

MANUFACTURER
Heavy Machinery Plant, Labedy, Poland.

UNION OF SOVIET SOCIALIST REPUBLICS

AT-L and AT-LM Light Tracked Artillery Tractors

DEVELOPMENT
The AT-L first appeared in 1953 as the replacement for the M-2 light tracked artillery tractor. When first introduced the vehicle was widely used for towing artillery and mortars including 160 mm and 240 mm mortars, 122 mm and 152 mm howitzers and 57 mm anti-aircraft guns. These roles have now been mainly taken over by 6 × 6 trucks and although some artillery units still use the vehicles as prime movers they are mainly used for other specialised roles.

DESCRIPTION
The engine of the AT-L is at the front with the three-man cab in the centre and the cargo area at the rear with removable bows, tarpaulin cover and a drop tailgate. The fully enclosed all-steel cab has a three part windscreen with the two outer windscreens being hinged at the top. A circular observation hatch is provided in the right side of the cab roof. Seats can be provided for up to 12 men. The suspension is of the torsion bar type and consists of six road wheels with the idler at the rear, the drive sprocket at the front, and three return rollers. In 1956 the AT-LM was introduced. It has five large road wheels, with the drive sprocket at the front, idler at the rear but no track return rollers.

VARIANTS
Electronic versions
The AT-L and AT-LM are widely used for mounting electronic equipment including the Pork Trough (SNAR-2) and Small Yawn (ARSOM-2) radars.
Dozer
The AT-L and AT-LM can both be fitted with the OLT dozer blade on the front of the hull for general clearing work; when being used on soft soil at a speed of 4 km/h it can clear between 80 and 90 cubic metres an hour. Details of this are given in the *Construction equipment* section.

SPECIFICATIONS
Cab seating: 1 + 2
Weight:
  (empty) 6300 kg
  (loaded) 8300 kg
Max load: 2000 kg
Towed load: 6000 kg
Length: 5·313 m
Width: 2·214 m
Height: (cab) 2·18 m
Ground clearance: 0·35 m
Track: 1·9 m
Track width: 300 mm
Length of track on ground: 3·005 m
Ground pressure: 0·45 kg/cm²
Max speed: (road) 42 km/h
Range: 300 km
Fuel capacity: 300 litres
Vertical obstacle: 0·6 m
Trench: 1 m
Fording: 0·6 m (some can ford to 1 m)
Engine: YaMZ-204VKr 4-cylinder water-cooled diesel developing 130 or 135 hp at 2000 rpm

STATUS
Production complete. In service with members of the Warsaw Pact and countries in the Middle East and North Africa.

MANUFACTURER
Soviet state factories.

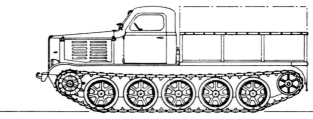

AT-LM light tracked artillery tractor

AT-LM light tracked artillery tractor with Pork Trough (SNAR-2) radar

AT-L light tracked artillery tractor

M-2 Light Tracked Artillery Tractor Ya-12 and Ya-13F Light Tracked Artillery Tractor

These light tracked artillery tractors are no longer in service but details can be found in the 1983 edition of *Jane's Military Vehicles and Ground Support Equipment*, pages 494 and 495.

ATS-59G Medium Tracked Artillery Tractor

DESCRIPTION
This was first seen during the parade in Moscow in November 1972, towing a 130 mm M-46 field gun. Until its correct designation became known the vehicle was called the M1972. It is essentially an ATS-59 with a redesigned cab. The new tractor has a much larger forward control type cab with the cargo area at the rear. The suspension consists of five large road wheels with the drive sprocket at the front and the idler at the rear. There are no track return rollers.

SPECIFICATIONS
Weight:
(empty) 13 750 kg
(loaded) 16 750 kg
Max load: 3000 kg
Max towed load: 14 000 kg
Fuel capacity: 580 litres
Ground pressure: 0·55 kg/cm²
Fording: 1·5 m

STATUS
Production probably complete. In service with Egypt, Yugoslavia and members of the Warsaw Pact including the Soviet Union.

ATS-59G medium tracked artillery tractor towing 130 mm M-46 field gun

MANUFACTURER
Soviet state factories.

ATS-59 Medium Tracked Artillery Tractor

DEVELOPMENT
The ATS-59 medium tracked artillery tractor appeared in the late 1950s as the replacement for the AT-S tractor, and uses a number of components of the T-54 MBT.

DESCRIPTION
The layout of the vehicle is unusual, with the engine behind the cab, preventing the full length of the cargo area being used as the engine compartment projects into it. The steel cab has a door in each side and there is a circular hatch in the right side of the roof. The rear cargo area has a tailgate, removable bows and a tarpaulin cover. The suspension consists of five large road wheels with the drive sprocket at the front and the idler at the rear. There are no return rollers.
The ATS-59 is used for towing artillery such as the 130 mm M-46 field gun.

VARIANTS
ATS-59 Tractor
Some ATS-59s have had the rear cargo area removed and a fifth wheel mounted on the top of the rear chassis for towing semi-trailers carrying the SA-2 missile.
ATS-59 Dozer
The vehicle has also been seen in service fitted with a hydraulically operated dozer blade on the front of the hull. Details of this model are given in the *Construction equipment* section.

STATUS
Replaced in production in the Soviet Union by the ATS-59G. Poland produced the ATS-59 after production of the Polish designed Mazur D-350 medium tracked artillery tractor had been completed. In service with members of the Warsaw Pact including Romania, and countries in the Middle East and North Africa.

MANUFACTURERS
Soviet state factories.
Heavy Machinery Plant, Labedy, Poland.

SPECIFICATIONS
Cab seating: 1 + 1
Weight:
(empty) 13 000 kg
(loaded) 16 000 kg
Max load: 3000 kg
Towed load: 14 000 kg
Length: 6·28 m
Width: 2·78 m
Height:
(cab) 2·3 m
(tarpaulin) 2·5 m
Ground clearance: 0·425 m

ATS-59 medium tracked artillery tractor towing 130 mm M-46 field gun

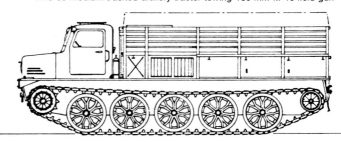
ATS-59 medium tracked artillery tractor

Track: 2·25 m
Track width: 525 mm
Ground pressure: 0·52 kg/cm²
Max speed: 39 km/h
Range: 350 km (500 km with long range tanks)
Vertical obstacle: 1·1 m
Trench: 2·5 m
Max gradient: 50%
Max side slope: 20%
Fording: 1·5 m
Engine: A-650 V-12 water-cooled diesel developing 300 hp at 1700 rpm

AT-S Medium Tracked Artillery Tractor

DEVELOPMENT
The AT-S medium tracked artillery tractor was introduced into service in the early 1950s to tow medium and heavy artillery such as 152 mm howitzers and 100 mm anti-aircraft guns. In recent years it has been sup-

plemented in this role by cross country trucks, but is still used for a variety of more specialised roles.

DESCRIPTION
The engine is mounted at the front, with the cab in the centre. The cab has a circular hatch on the right side of the roof, and two doors on either side. The cargo area at the rear has a tailgate, removable bows and a tarpaulin cover. The suspension either side consists of eight

small road wheels on four bogies, with the drive sprocket at the rear and the idler at the front. There are four track return rollers.

VARIANTS
BM-24T
This is the AT-S with a 12-round tube type 240 mm multiple system mounted at the rear. It is not in use today. An illustration of the BM-24T will be found in

Jane's Armour and Artillery 1982–83, pages 681–682.

Electronics
The AT-S is used to mount a variety of electronic equipment including radars.

OST
This is the basic AT-S with the OST dozer blade mounted at the front of the hull for general clearing work. When used on soft soil at a speed of 4 km/h it can clear between 80 and 90 cubic metres an hour. Details of this model are given in the *Construction equipment* section.

SBKh
This is an over-snow vehicle and has its tracks and suspension replaced by a very wide track with pneumatic road wheels. The SBKh has a maximum speed of 35 km/h, a loaded weight of 13 500 kg and a maximum carrying capacity of 7000 kg.

Uragan
This 8 × 8 over-snow vehicle uses the cab of the AT-S tractor.

STATUS
Production complete. In service with members of the Warsaw Pact (excluding Czechoslovakia), China, Finland, Yugoslavia and countries in the Middle East and North Africa.

MANUFACTURER
Soviet state factories.

SPECIFICATIONS
Cab seating: 1 + 6
Weight:
  (empty) 12 000 kg
  (loaded) 15 000 kg
Max load: 3000 kg
Towed load: 16 000 kg
Length: 5·87 m
Width: 2·57 m
Height:
  (cab) 2·535 m
  (tarpaulin) 2·85 m
Ground clearance: 0·4 m
Track: 1·9 m
Track width: 425 mm
Length of track on ground: 3·07 m

AT-S medium tracked artillery tractors towing 100 mm KS-19 anti-aircraft guns

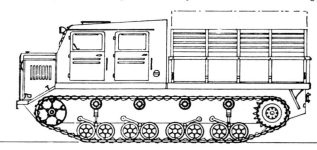

AT-S medium tracked artillery tractor

Ground pressure: 0·58 kg/cm²
Max speed: 35 km/h
Range: 380 km
Fuel capacity: 420 litres
Fuel consumption: 110 litres/100 km
Gradient: 50%

Vertical obstacle: 0·6 m
Trench: 1·45 m
Fording: 1 m
Engine: V-54-T V-12 water-cooled diesel developing 250 hp at 1500 rpm
Suspension: torsion bar

AT-T Heavy Tracked Artillery Tractor

DEVELOPMENT
The AT-T heavy tracked artillery tractor appeared in 1950 and is the heaviest vehicle of its type used by members of the Warsaw Pact. The tractor is used to tow heavy artillery such as the 180 mm S-23 gun/howitzer, 130 mm KS-30 anti-aircraft gun and the 130 mm SM-4-1 mobile coastal gun.

DESCRIPTION
The engine is under the floor of the four-man cab, which is of all steel construction and has a door either side. The cargo compartment is at the rear and is provided with a drop tailgate, removable bows and a tarpaulin cover. The fuel tanks are under the rear behind the engine and the winch is mounted at the very back.
The suspension of the torsion bar type and consists of five large road wheels with the drive sprocket at the front and the idler at the rear. There are no track return rollers.

VARIANTS
BTM Ditching Machine
MDK-2 Ditching Machine
BAT and BAT-M Dozers
Details of these will be found in the *Construction equipment* section.
Radar
The AT-T with a fully enclosed van type body is used to mount the Track Dish (ARSOM-1) radar system. A lengthened version of the AT-T with seven road wheels mounts the Long Track radar.

SPECIFICATIONS
Cab seating: 1 + 3
Weight:
  (empty) 20 000 kg
  (loaded) 25 000 kg
Max load: 5000 kg
Towed load: 25 000 kg
Length: 6·99 m
Width: 3·17 m
Height: (cab) 2·58 m
Ground clearance: 0·425 m
Track: 2·64 m
Track width: 508 mm
Length of track on ground: 3·836 m
Ground pressure:
  (empty) 0·52 kg/cm²
  (loaded) 0·68 kg/cm²

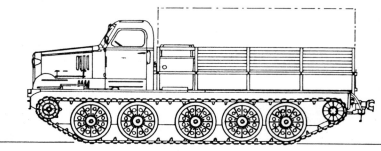

AT-T heavy tracked artillery tractor

AT-T heavy tracked artillery tractor

Max speed: 35 km/h
Range: 700 km
Fuel: 1415 litres
Fuel consumption:
  (not towing) 140 litres/100 km
  (towing) 190 litres/100 km
Max gradient: 60%
Vertical obstacle: 1 m
Trench: 2·1 m
Fording: 0·75 m (some can ford to 1 m)

Engine: V-401 V-12 water-cooled diesel developing 415 hp at 1500 rpm

STATUS
Production complete. In service with members of the Warsaw Pact, Yugoslavia and countries in the Middle East and North Africa.

MANUFACTURER
Mzlyshev Transport Machine Plant, Khar'kov, USSR.

UNITED KINGDOM

Streaker High Mobility Load Carrier

DEVELOPMENT
Streaker was developed during 1982 as an addition to the Scorpion/Spartan family of tracked vehicles (for details of these vehicles see *Jane's Armour and Artillery 1983–84*, pages 220 to 227), in order to provide a tracked cargo carrier with a good cross-country performance. It was developed as a result of experience gained in the Falkland Islands campaign as well as a British Army requirement for a vehicle to tow the Bar minelayer. A prototype was built at the end of 1982.

DESCRIPTION
The Streaker is based on the same hull as the Spartan light reconnaissance/armoured personnel carrier and the Samson armoured recovery vehicle (see entry on page 28). It has the same automotive layout with the main power plant to the right of the driver and the transmission forward of the driver's position. The engine can be either a Jaguar 4·2-litre petrol engine or a Perkins T6.3544 turbo-charged diesel. The transmission is a seven-speed hot shift unit with integral steering. Suspension is through transverse torsion bars and lever arm dampers. The track is of the single pin, active rubber-bush type, with integral rubber pad and a central horn. The vehicle is fully armoured forward of the load deck, so that the driver has a 'head down' position with an armoured periscope and an optional night driving sight. Alternatively the hatch can be opened and the seat raised into a 'head out' driving position. A door at the back of the driver's compartment provides emergency egress to the load deck.

The main load area is a completely flat bed, 2·75 metres long and 2·1 metres wide. At each end panels can be hinged out to reveal sponson seating and footwells, and stowage access. Recessed tie-down points are fitted in the decking and along the sides. The drop sides and the tailgate are removable. Maximum payload (including fuel and the deck crew) is 3600 kg. Loading is assisted by an electric winch and by deploying the drop sides as loading ramps. Lights, a towing pintle etc, are recessed under the decking to allow the vehicle to be reversed right back to a loading platform.

As well as a general cargo carrier, the vehicle is configured for rapid conversion into a variety of specialised roles by the fitting of palletised kits. In a few minutes the vehicle can be adapted for laying anti-tank mines (Bar Mines) or dispensing anti-personnel mines (Ranger) or refuelling other vehicles with a 2271-litre bowser.

Streaker high mobility load carrier

SPECIFICATIONS
Seating: driver under armour, up to 3 deck crew
Weight: (empty) 5354 kg
Max load: 3630 kg
Load area: (flat bed) 2·75 × 2·1 m
Length: 4·878 m
Width: 2·21 m
Height:
   (cab) 1·83 m
   (load area) 0·91 m
Ground clearance: 0·356 m (approx)
Length of track on ground: 2·74 m
Max speed: 80·5 km/h
Range: (road) 483 km plus
Fuel capacity: 320 litres
Fuel consumption: 1·6 km/litre at 48·3 km/h
Gradient: 45%
Vertical obstacle: 0·5 m
Fording: (unprepared) 1·067 m
Angle of approach/departure: 45°/45°

Engine: Jaguar J60 No 1 Mark 100B 4·2-litre, 6-cylinder, in-line petrol developing 190 hp at 4750 rpm
or
Perkins T6.3544 5·8-litre, 6-cylinder, in-line diesel developing 200 hp at 2600 rpm
Gearbox: TN15 manual foot-operated with 7 forward and 1 reverse gears
Steering: Merrit system incorporated in gearbox
Suspension: transverse torsion bar, 5 units per side; shock absorbers on front and rear stations
Electrical system: 28 V

STATUS
Ready for production.

MANUFACTURER
Alvis Limited, Holyhead Road, Coventry, West Midlands CV5 8JH, England.
   Enquiries to Alvis Limited, 10 Fitzroy Square, London W1P 6AB, England.

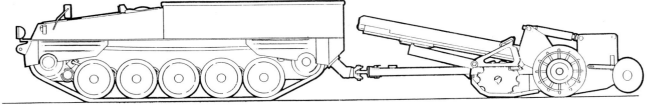
Streaker high mobility load carrier towing Bar minelayer (not to 1/76th scale)

UNITED STATES OF AMERICA

M5 Series Tracked High Speed Tractors

DEVELOPMENT
Late in 1941 development began on two medium tractors designated T20 and T21, the latter using the tracks and suspension of the M3 light tank. In 1942 development of the T20 was stopped and the T21 was standardised as the M5 medium tractor in October, 1942. In August 1943 its designation was changed to high speed tractor, 13-ton, M5. Production of the M5 was undertaken by International Harvester. These tractors, which all differ in, for example, their tracks, transmissions and crew compartments, are designed to tow artillery such as 105 mm and 155 mm howitzers up to a maximum weight of 9072 kg. Provision is made for carrying the crew of the weapons as well as ammunition: for example, if a 105 mm howitzer is being towed 56 rounds of ammunition can be carried.

VARIANTS
M5
This has an open top body which can be enclosed by a canvas top and side curtains. The vehicle has a front-mounted 6804 kg capacity winch. There are two small

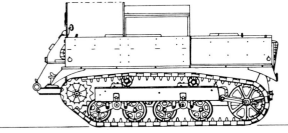
M5 high speed tractor

doors in the front of the body. The suspension consists of two bogies, each with two road wheels, drive sprocket at the front, large idler at the rear and two track return rollers. Track width is 295 mm.
M5A1
This has a wide covered cab, side doors and a double windscreen. The front-mounted winch assembly is under the floor of the cab, and the bumper is equipped with a pintle hook and two tow hooks. A ring mount for a 12·7 mm/0·50 Browning machine gun is provided on

top of the cab and 525 rounds of ammunition are carried for this weapon. Suspension is similar to the M5's with a 295 mm wide track.
M5A2
This differs from the M5 only in the track and suspension. Its suspension is of the horizontal volute spring type and the track is 533 mm wide.
M5A3
This is a modified M5A1 and its suspension system has been modified to provide for a wider track (533 mm) by

the addition of spacers between the tractor hull and the suspension brackets.

M5A4
This model is equipped with a mechanically operated clutch and has only one air reservoir. The clutch gear reduction unit is replaced by a two-speed auxiliary transmission. The tracks are equipped with welded extenders to improve flotation and increase traction (tracks are 435 mm wide). The vehicle is also wider to provide seating for additional crew members.

SPECIFICATIONS (M5A1)
Cab seating: 1 + 10
Weight: (loaded) 13 792 kg
Towed load: 9072 kg
Length: 4·987 m
Width: 2·54 m
Height: 2·68 m
Ground clearance: 0·5 m
Track: 2·108 m
Track width: 295 mm
Length of track on ground: 2·75 m
Ground pressure: 0·85 kg/cm²
Max speed: 48 km/h
Range: 242 km
Fuel capacity: 378·5 litres
Max gradient: 50%
Vertical obstacle: 0·457 m
Trench: 1·676 m
Fording: 1·326 m
Engine: Continental R6572 6-cylinder petrol developing 207 bhp at 2900 rpm
Electrical system: 12 V

M5 high speed tractor of Japanese Ground Self-Defence Force towing 155 mm M114 howitzer (Kensuke Ebata)

STATUS
Production complete. M5s are known to be in service with Austria, Japan and Yugoslavia.

MANUFACTURER
International Harvester Corporation, 2827 Ruck Drive, Fort Wayne, Indiana 46805, USA.

M8A1 and M8A2 Full Tracked High Speed Tractors

DEVELOPMENT
During the Second World War a cargo carrier called the T33 was developed, based on the chassis of the M24 light tank (the Chaffee), but was found to be underpowered and development of another vehicle, the T42, began. This was standardised after the war as the M8. The M8 was powered by a 475 hp radial engine and had a torqmatic transmission and controlled differential. Further development of the M8 under the designation M8E1 resulted in the M8A1 which used many components of the M41 light tank. This was subsequently standardised as the M8A1. The M8A2 is identical to the M8A1 but has a fuel injection system. The M8A1 and M8A2 were in production by Allis-Chalmers from 1950 to 1955, 480 of each being built.

The hull of the tractor is of all-welded steel construction with the engine at the very front of the vehicle. The driver is seated at the front on the left side with the commander seated on the right side, each with a fully enclosed cab. Over the roof of the commander's cab is a circular mount for a 12·7 mm/0·50 Browning machine gun for which 525 rounds of ammunition are carried.

The load area is at the rear and is normally provided with bows and a tarpaulin cover. Many vehicles have a hydraulic operated tailgate for unloading the ammunition, and a dozer blade is usually mounted at the front of the hull.

The suspension is of the torsion bar type and consists of six road wheels with the drive sprocket at the front and the idler at the rear. There are four return rollers. A winch with a capacity of 20 412 kg is fitted as standard.

VARIANTS
A recovery model with twin booms at the rear was developed but is no longer in service.

STATUS
Production complete. In service with the Japanese Ground Self-Defence Force and possibly other countries.

MANUFACTURER
Allis-Chalmers Corporation, PO Box 512, Milwaukee, Wisconsin 53201, USA.

SPECIFICATIONS
Cab seating: 1 + 1
Weight:
  (empty) 17 009 kg
  (loaded) 24 948 kg
Max load: 7939 kg
Towed load: 17 690 kg
Load area: 3·987 × 2·907 m
Length: 6·733 m
Width: 3·314 m
Height: 3·048 m

M8 series full tracked high speed tractor towing rolling liquid transporters (RLTs) (US Army)

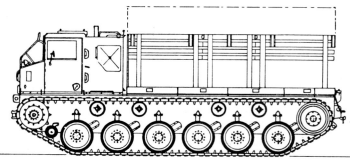

Full tracked high speed tractor M8A1

Ground clearance: 0·488 m
Track: 2·596 m
Track width: 533 mm
Length of track on ground: 3·965 m
Ground pressure: 0·53 kg/cm²
Speed: 64·4 km/h
Range: 290 km
Fuel capacity: 852 litres
Max gradient: 60%
Vertical obstacle: 0·762 m

Trench: 2·133 m
Fording: 1·06 m
Engine: Continental AOS-895-3 6-cylinder air-cooled petrol developing 863 bhp at 2800 rpm (M8A2 has AOS-895-5 with fuel injection)
Transmission: General Motors Corporation (Allison Division) CD 500-3 cross drive with 2 forward and 1 reverse gears
Electrical system: 24 V
Batteries: 2 × 12 V

M4 High Speed Tractor

DEVELOPMENT
In 1941 development began of a new medium tractor using components of the M2A1 medium tank. It was designed to tow a 90 mm anti-aircraft gun as well as carry the crew of the weapon and a quantity of ready-use ammunition. Following trials with the prototype of the T9 a further model known as the T9E1 was built and was standardised as the M4 medium tractor in 1942. In August 1943 its designation was changed to High Speed Tractor, 18-ton, M4. Two models were produced by Allis-Chalmers, one for towing the 90 mm anti-aircraft gun and the other for towing the 155 mm gun, 8-inch howitzer or 240 mm howitzer. A special swing crane was provided for loading ammunition into the tractor.

DESCRIPTION
The cab at the front of the M4 is divided into two compartments, with seats for the driver and two men at the front, and double seats for eight men at the rear. The suspension is of the horizontal volute type and consists of two bogies each with two wheels, with the drive sprocket at the front and the idler at the rear. There are two track return rollers. Mounted on the roof of the tractor is a 12·7 mm/0·50 Browning M2 machine gun with an elevation of +80 degrees and a depression of −20 degrees. A 13 608 kg capacity winch is provided on all M4s with 91·44 metres of 19 mm cable.

STATUS
Production complete. In service with Japan and Yugoslavia. They have recently been phased out of service with the Spanish Army.

MANUFACTURER
Allis-Chalmers Corporation, PO Box 512, Milwaukee, Wisconsin 53201, USA.

SPECIFICATIONS
Cab seating: 1 + 11
Weight: 14 288 kg
Towed load: 16 608 kg
Length: 5·231 m
Width: 2·463 m
Height: 2·514 m (including anti-aircraft mount)
Ground clearance: 0·508 m
Track: 2·032 m
Track width: 421 mm
Length of track on ground: 3·149 m

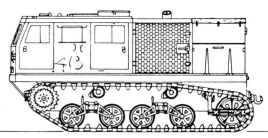

M4 high speed tractor

M4 high speed tractor of Brazilian Army (Ronaldo S Olive)

Ground pressure: 0·53 kg/cm²
Max speed: 53 km/h
Range: 290 km
Fuel capacity: 473 litres
Max gradient: 60%
Vertical obstacle: 0·736 m
Trench: 1·524 m

Fording: 1·041 m
Engine: Waukesha 145GZ 6-cylinder in-line petrol developing 210 hp at 2100 rpm
Gearbox: manual with 3 forward and 1 reverse gears
Clutch: spring loaded dry disc
Brakes: mechanical on controlled differential
Electrical system: 12 V

M992 Field Artillery Ammunition Support Vehicle

DEVELOPMENT
In 1979 prototypes of three armoured artillery resupply vehicles were tested during HELBAT (Human Engineering Laboratory, Battalion Artillery Test) trials. The Bowen-McLaughlin-York (BMY) vehicle was based on the chassis of the proven M109 155 mm self-propelled howitzer chassis, as was the HEL/AAI vehicle, and was named the M109 Ammunition Delivery System by the company. The FMC Corporation provided a stretched (eg additional road wheel on either side) and armoured M548 tracked vehicle.

Following completion of the initial trials and the Concept Evaluation Test, it was decided that the M109 chassis was most suitable for the Field Artillery Ammunition Support Vehicle, and in August 1980 Tank Automotive Command issued a request for proposals for the design, construction, test and integrated logistics support for the FAASV and in March 1981 Bowen-McLaughlin-York was awarded a contract by Tank-Automotive Command for the supply of five prototype FAASVs under the designation of XM992. These were delivered during November and December 1981 and underwent DT/OT II trials at Yuma Proving Ground and at Fort Sill during March 1982. Following these trials the XM992 was type classified as the M992 FAASV in the autumn of 1982. It is anticipated that 1464 vehicles will be built for the US Army between 1983 and 1987, with first production vehicles being delivered in July 1984.

Research, development, test and evaluation costs for the FAASV up to fiscal year 1982 amounted to $5·6 million and in fiscal year 1983 procurement costs totalled $30·7 million for 54 vehicles. Planned fiscal year 1984 procurement costs are $104·7 million for 217 vehicles, and fiscal year 1985 costs are planned as $144·2 million for a further 274 vehicles. This will leave outstanding 919 vehicles required at a total cost of $533·3 million. Thus the overall cost for the planned 1464 vehicles will be $812·9 million.

The following components are common to the M992 FAASV and the standard M109: hull structure, engine and auxiliary equipment, transmission and drive, complete suspension, driver's hatch and controls, heating and ventilation system, electrical components, communications equipment and lifting and towing provisions.

DESCRIPTION
The hull is made of all-aluminium armour with the driver at the front of the hull on the left, the engine to his right and ammunition stowage at the rear.

The driver has a hinged hatch cover that opens to the left, in front of which are three M45 periscopes which can be covered by small metal flaps to prevent damage.

The engine is coupled to the General Motors Allison Division XTG-411-2A cross-drive transmission which is at the front of the hull. The engine and transmission of the M109 are the same as in the M108 (105 mm), M107 (175 mm) and M110 (203 mm) self-propelled weapons.

The torsion bar suspension consists of seven dual rubber-tyred road wheels with the drive sprocket at the front and the idler at the rear. There are no track return rollers. The tracks are of the single pin, centre guide type with replaceable rubber pads.

In the forward part of the roof there is a three part ammunition resupply hatch and behind it is the commander's cupola. This can be traversed through 360 degrees and has a single piece hatch cover. A 12·7 mm (0·50) M2 HB anti-aircraft machine gun can be mounted at this station.

Prototype FAASVs had a 680 kg capacity crane mounted at the front of the hull but this crane will not be fitted to full production vehicles for the US Army. 155 mm projectiles are handled in racks of 10 projectiles, for example two horizontal layers of five projectiles each. If required projectiles can also be loaded individually using the powered conveyor to feed the empty racks.

The charges are located in their containers in either side of the FAASV at the rear with fuzes being stowed in the left side of the hull. Ammunition is transferred to the M109 through its lower rear door by a power-operated slat conveyor at a maximum rate of six rounds a minute, which is higher than the M109s rate of fire. Overhead protection is provided by the large upward opening powered door of the vehicle. The slat conveyor has lateral protection from the M109 and M992 lower rear doors. When not in use the conveyor folds up and is stowed inside the vehicle, this takes one man only 15 seconds to accomplish.

The projectiles are transferred from their stowed position in the forward part of the vehicle to the conveyor belt by the optional X-Y stacker which is part of the ammunition handling system and can be moved vertically and horizontally.

The upward-swinging rear door is hydraulically powered with the smaller lower door opening manually to the right. The commander's adjustable seat is over the rear part of the conveyor belt.

The US Army FAASVs are configured to carry 90 (nine honeycomb) storage racks each holding ten 155 mm projectiles plus charges, fuzes and other cargo. For export the following maximum quantities can be carried, according to Bowen-McLaughlin-York:

Calibre	155 mm	175 mm	203 mm
Projectiles	109	86	71
Propelling charges	109	87	78
Fuzes	136	104	104

In the US Army FAASV space has been allocated for special projectiles such as the Martin-Marietta Copperhead cannon-launched guided projectile, the Remote Anti-Armor Mine System (M718/M741) and the Area Denial Artillery Munition (M692/M731). Nuclear projectiles would be carried in special versions of the FAASV.

The auxiliary power unit is located in the forward part of the FAASV's superstructure and supplies hydraulic and electrical power to the vehicle systems as well as charging the batteries. In addition, it can also provide power to the self-propelled howitzer being serviced.

The FAASV also incorporates a number of improvements which may be included in future M109s as part of a product improvement programme. These include an automatic fire suppression system, NBC VFP protection system, simplified test equipment-ICE as fitted to more recent AFVs such as the M1 MBT, M2 IFV and M3 CFV, AN/VIC-1 intercom and an AN/PRC-68 small unit radio. Also fitted are chemical detection and alarm units and chemical decontamination units.

VARIANTS
In addition to the variants listed below the FAASV is now being developed as the basis for a complete family of vehicles, all using the same basic chassis. A command post vehicle, medical aid vehicle and a radar vehicle have been proposed.

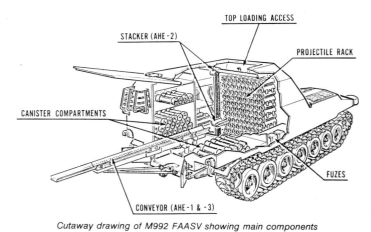

Cutaway drawing of M992 FAASV showing main components

Conveyor on FAASV deployed for transfer to 155 mm M109 SPH

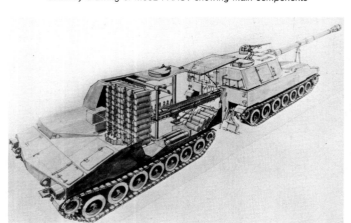

Cutaway drawing of M992 FAASV loading 155 mm M109A2 self-propelled howitze

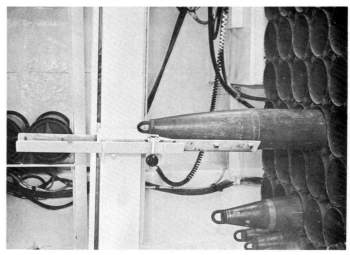

Transfer of 155 mm projectile from pallets to optional stacker

XM992 FAASV resupplying 155 mm M109 self-propelled howitzer during US Army trials

XM1050

The XM1050 is a version of the FAASV for use with 8-inch/203 mm howitzer ammunition which will be fitted with a stacker device. It is under development for the US Army.

Maintenance Assist Vehicle (MAV)

This would have a 4536 kg capacity boom crane, on-board replacement powerpack, welding capability, suspension lockout and an onboard auxiliary power unit.

Armoured Forward Area Rearm Vehicle (AFARV)

This would carry 6804 kg of ammunition in high density stowage with material handling equipment giving rapid rearm times.

Medical Evacuation Vehicle (MEV)

This variant would be configured as a medical evacuation vehicle carrying a minimum of eight litter patients plus a medical aid team and has a potential for carrying 12 litter patients.

Fire Direction Centre (FDC)

The company has already delivered a fire direction centre vehicle based on the chassis of the FAASV to the US Army for trials. This model is fitted with the following equipment: complete hybrid NBC protection system,

APU, Magnavox graphic display, Litton TACFIRE digital display terminal, PDP computer, Battery Computer System printer, power distribution system, pocket radio and a PRC-68 radio. This vehicle was completed in time to take part in the HELBAT 8 (October 1981) exercises.

SPECIFICATIONS
Crew: 2 (+ 6 passengers)
Weight:
  (empty) 20 000 kg
  (loaded) 26 136 kg
Max load: 6109 kg
Load area: 3·38 × 3·05 × 2·21 m
Length: 6·78 m
Width: 3·149 m
Height: 3·2 m
Ground clearance: 0·36 m
Track width: 381 mm
Length of track on ground: 3·962 m
Max speed: (combat loaded)
  (road) 57·5 km/h
  (10% slope) 20 km/h
Acceleration: (0–48 km/h) 19 s

Range: (at 40 km/h) 360 km
Fuel capacity: 506 litres
Max gradient: 60%
Max side slope: 40%
Fording: 1·066 m
Vertical obstacle: 0·533 m
Trench: 1·828 m
Engine: Detroit Diesel Model 8V71T turbo-charged, 2-stroke, liquid-cooled 8-cylinder diesel developing 405 bhp at 2350 rpm
Transmission: General Motors, Allison Division, XTG-411-2A cross-drive with 4 forward and 2 reverse gears
Suspension: torsion bar
Electrical system: 24 V
Batteries: 4 × 12 V GTN

STATUS
Development complete. Type classified in 1983. Expected to enter service in 1984. Ordered by Egypt.

MANUFACTURER
BMY Division of HARSCO, P O Box 1512, York, Pennsylvania 17405, USA.

Fighting Vehicle Systems Carrier

DEVELOPMENT

The Fighting Vehicle Systems Carrier (XM987) is part of the Fighting Vehicle Systems family which also includes the M2 Infantry Fighting Vehicle, the M3 Cavalry Fighting Vehicle, and the M993 MLRS carrier, all of which have been developed by the FMC Corporation under

contract to the United States Army. Details of these vehicles are given in *Jane's Armour and Artillery 1983–84*, pages 399–403.

The vehicle is a highly mobile armoured carrier for a wide range of requirements. Major features of the vehicle are its component commonality with the IFV and CFV, over-pressure ventilation system, nuclear hardened electrical system, built-in diagnostic test

equipment, air transportability in the Lockheed C-141 transport aircraft, tilt cab to facilitate maintenance and a maximum payload of 10 886 kg.

Prototypes of the Fighting Vehicle Systems Carrier were originally built by FMC specifically for use with the General Support Rocket System (now known as the Multiple Launch Rocket System), and the first prototype vehicles, under the designation XM993, were delivered

Fighting Vehicle Systems Carrier without body as used for MLRS

Fighting Vehicle Systems Carrier without body as used for MLRS

Field Artillery Ammunition Support Vehicle concept (FAASV)

Assault Breaker vehicle concept

Armoured command, communications and intelligence vehicle concept

Prototype of AFARV using conveyor to resupply M60A1 MBT with 105 mm ammunition

Prototype of AFARV using hydraulic crane to lift ammunition pallet into vehicle

to the two competing contractors late in 1978. After trials the Vought system was selected and in June 1980 the company was awarded a $26·9 million contract for 1374 missiles packed in launch containers and 16 self-propelled launcher loaders, to be built by FMC. Now designated M993, this vehicle is in its third year of production. Some 100 M993 carriers have been built out of an anticipated total of 342 to be built by October 1987.

DESCRIPTION

The basic FVS Carrier has a cab-over-powerpack arrangement with the cargo area at the rear.

The aluminium armour plate cab is fitted with noise attenuation materials and large ballistic windows to provide forward and side vision. When used with the MLRS the front windows are fitted with exterior louvres to provide protection during rocket firing and for nuclear survivability. The louvres can be opened or closed with levers inside the cab. All three sets of louvres operate individually and in a tactical situation the louvres may be rotated to a stowed position.

The cab has accommodation for the three-man crew, over-pressure ventilation system, space for radios and provisions and an instrument panel for operating the vehicle. Sufficient space is provided to add a second control panel for weapon system operation.

An overhead hatch above the right hand seat can be fully opened for use as an airguard, or fixed partially opened for additional ventilation. As an option the cab roof can be fitted with a NATO mount for a 7·62 mm M240 machine gun.

The engine compartment is behind and below the cab and encloses the powerpack. The powerpack is centred

in the vehicle with drive shafts and U-joints connected to both final drives. The complete powerpack, which is interchangeable with the one in the IFV and CFV, consists of a Cummins diesel engine coupled to a General Electric cross-drive transmission. The powerpack can be removed or installed without breaking cooling or hydraulic lines and this arrangement enables the powerpack to be operated on the ground outside the vehicle. Using the quick disconnects the powerpack can be removed and installed in 30 minutes.

The powerpack is wired to accommodate built-in test equipment for rapid fault isolation using RCA's STE/FVS (Simplified Test Equipment/Fighting Vehicle System), the same test equipment as used in the M1 MBT.

The powerpack has a negative pressure system where cooling air is drawn through the radiator and is discharged through the exhaust grille above the right sponson. The fuel is carried in two integral tanks under the floor plates at the rear of the vehicle.

The suspension is an elongated version of the IFV/CFV system and each side consists of six dual rubber roadwheels, two dual support rollers, two single support rollers, front drive sprocket, raised rear idler and a high return track.

The track is a single-pin design with forged steel blocks, rubber bushings and detachable rubber pads. Track tension is adjusted by a grease-filled cylinder mounted between the hull and idler wheel. Vertical road wheel travel is controlled by high strength steel torsion bars splined to trailing road arms forming a fully independent suspension. Linear hydraulic shock absorbers at the first, second and sixth road wheels stabilise the vehicle on rough terrain.

A suspension lockout system is provided for the MLRS application of the carrier. The lockout is a hydraulically actuated, multidisc brake mounted concentric with the torsion bar. Lockout units can be installed at some or all the torsion bar stations depending on the degree of suspension stiffness required. The lockouts provide platform stability during both launching and loading operations.

In the left rear corner of the cab is the over-pressure ventilation system. It consists of a 5-micron dust filter, 3-micron particulate filter, charcoal filter, bypass valve, and an axial-flow fan. Dual positioning of the bypass valve permits air to pass through all three filters or just through the dust filter, depending on the mission. As an option this system can be converted to a hybrid system. The present design has an M13A1 CBR unit in the cab. This secondary system provides for the crew's safety if the cabin air inadvertently becomes contaminated during the course of a mission.

VARIANTS

MLRS Carrier

This was the first application for the FVS Carrier, the chassis being designated the M993 for this purpose. Details of the MLRS are given in *Jane's Armour and Artillery, 1983–84*, page 744.

Cargo Carrier

This is designated the XM987 but is not yet in production.

Armoured, Forward-Area, Rearm Vehicle (AFARV)

The United States Army has tested the prototype of an Armoured, Forward-Area, Rearm Vehicle (AFARV) and is known to have a requirement for 700 vehicles of this

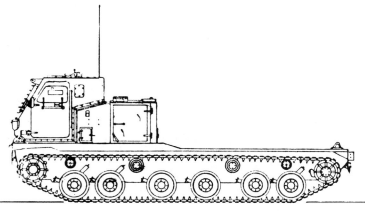

Fighting Vehicle Systems Carrier without body

SLUFAE/SLUMINE vehicle concept

type to resupply armoured and infantry units in the forward battefield area. Scale of issue is expected to be eight per mechanised infantry battalion and cavalry squadron and seven per tank battalion.

The vehicle is fitted with a 1½-ton hydraulic crane to lift pallets of ammunition from trucks to the internal stowage compartment. The crane can also be used to unload pallets. A conveyor system enables the vehicle to off-load single rounds of tank ammunition into the tank while the crew remains under the armour protection of the ammunition resupply module. Test reports have indicated that the AFARV can resupply an M60A1 MBT with 105 mm of ammunition in about 15 minutes. The AFARV can be used to carry 105 mm and 120 mm tank ammunition as well as TOW and Dragon ATGWs, LAWs and small arms ammunition.

PROPOSED VARIANTS
Field artillery ammunition support vehicle
Maintenance assist vehicle with hydraulic crane
Medical evacuation vehicle
SLUMINE vehicle (at present the prototype uses the M548 chassis)
Command post vehicle
Roland vehicle (at present the system is based on a modified M109 chassis)
Assault Breaker vehicle (with three missiles)

Armoured command, communications and intelligence vehicle
Recovery vehicle
Tactical operations centre
MLRS resupply vehicle carrying four pods of rockets and crane for self-loading and unloading
Fuel resupply vehicle: can deliver 9054 litres of fuel in one mission, sufficient to supply six M60A1 or five M1 MBTs.
Firefinder vehicle
For trial purposes a FVS carrier has been fitted with the Hughes AN/TPQ-37 Firefinder artillery locating radar. This trials vehicle is now being re-configured.

STATUS
In production for the US Army in MLRS role. Ordered for the British Army (48 for MLRS).

MANUFACTURER
FMC Corporation, Ordnance Division, 1105 Coleman Avenue, San Jose, California 95108, USA.

SPECIFICATIONS
Cab seating: 1 + 2
Weight:
  (empty) 14 514 kg
  (loaded) 25 400 kg
Max load: 10 886 kg

Load area:
  (cargo bed between sponsons) 3·96 × 1·78 m
  (above sponsons) 3·96 × 2·97 m
Length: 6·97 m
Width: 2·97 m
Height:
  (cab) 2·59 m
  (chassis) 1·206 m
  (top of load area) 1·09 m
Ground clearance: 0·43 m
Track width: 533 mm
Length of track on ground: 4·33 m
Max speed:
  (road) 61 km/h
  (10% gradient) 26 km/h
Acceleration: (0–48 km/h) 21 s
Range: (at 40 km/h) 483 km
Fuel capacity: 617 litres
Max gradient: 60%
Max side slope: 40%
Fording: 1·02 m
Vertical obstacle: 0·91 m
Trench: 2·29 m
Engine: Cummins VTA-903 turbo-charged 8-cylinder diesel developing 500 hp at 2400 rpm
Transmission: General Electric HMPT-500 hydromechanical
Steering: hydrostatic
Suspension: torsion-bar
Electrical system: 28 V
Batteries: 4 × 12 V 6TN, 100 Ah

M548 Tracked Cargo Carrier

DEVELOPMENT
The XM548 cargo carrier was designed for the United States Army Signal Corps in 1960 using the basic automotive components of the M113 tracked armoured personnel carrier. At that time its primary purpose was to serve as a highly mobile transport carrier for the AN/MPQ-32 Hostile Artillery Radar System. This application did not reach production and a modified version with a diesel engine, designated the XM548E1, was designed using the powerpack and automotive components common to the M113A1 APC. Engineer and service tests on three prototype vehicles were completed late in 1964 and the vehicle was type classified the following year. First production vehicles were completed early in 1966 by the FMC Corporation.

The vehicle is used in the United States Army for a wide variety of roles including use as an ammunition resupply vehicle with self-propelled artillery units equipped with the M109 and M110 weapons.

The United States Army did not procure any vehicles in fiscal years 1976 to 1978 but 193 vehicles were bought with fiscal year 1979 funding of $15·6 million and 242 with 1980 funding of $30 million. The fiscal year 1982 request was for a further 160 vehicles at $20·9 million.

DESCRIPTION
The engine and crew compartment are at the front of the vehicle and the cab roof, sides, front and rear can be removed for air transport. The cargo compartment has a rear opening that can be secured by two watertight doors. Six hollow aluminium extruded plates bolted in place in either an upper or lower position form the cargo deck. The lower position allows more cargo to be carried or provides leg room for seated passengers. Tie-downs are available for both cargo deck positions. The cargo area can be enclosed using a standard vinyl-coated nylon cover supported by bows.

If required an M66 ring mount for an anti-aircraft machine gun can be mounted over the top of the cab. If this is fitted with a 7·62 mm machine gun, 660 rounds of ammunition are carried, or if fitted with a 12·7 mm/0·50 machine gun, 300 rounds of ammunition are carried.

The suspension is of the torsion bar type and consists of five road wheels with the drive sprocket at the front and the idler at the rear. There are no return rollers. The

XM1015 tracked cargo carrier with AN/MSQ-103A TEAMPACK radar monitoring system

West German Army M668 Lance SSM supply vehicle on left and M752 Lance launch vehicle on right (C R Zwart)

M548 tracked cargo carrier of Israeli Army (Israeli Army)

M752 Lance launch vehicle of British Army (Ministry of Defence)

M548 tracked cargo carrier of Australian Army armed with 12·7 mm machine gun

first and last road wheel stations are provided with a hydraulic shock absorber and the tops of the tracks are covered by a rubber skirt.

The vehicle has the same wheels, sprocket, sprocket carrier, track adjuster, idler, idler wheel, shock absorber and mount, wheels and track as the M113A1 but has a larger diameter torsion bar and the final drive assembly has a different gear ratio.

The M548 is fully amphibious and is propelled in the water by its tracks. On US Army vehicles, however, the amphibious capability is being eliminated. A winch with a 9072 kg capacity is mounted at the front of the vehicle. Optional equipment includes a heater (personnel and cargo areas), heater (engine coolant and battery), and an air brake kit to actuate brakes on the towed trailer, and material handling hoist.

VARIANTS
XM1015
First shown in 1982 this is a modified version of the M548 intended to carry equipment containers or containerised shelters for electronic systems. It has been used to carry the first production units of the Emerson Electric Company's AN/MSQ-103A TEAMPACK radar monitoring system developed for the US Army under a contract from the US Army Electronics Warfare Laboratories at Fort Monmouth, New Jersey. TEAM-PACK is used to monitor ground-based radar systems on the battlefield which include mortar locating, surveillance and air defence radars. The equipment is contained in a shelter carried on the XM1015. The XM1015 has no provision for a tilt and carrying the TEAMPACK the vehicle has no provision for a machine gun mounting ring. A telescopic aerial is carried on the vehicle right front. The TEAMPACK containerised shelter has ballistic protection for its contents and crew. The XM1015 has now been standardised as the M1015 and also carries the AN/TSQ-114A communications intercept and direction-finding system.
Stretched M548A1E1
In 1977 the FMC Corporation completed the prototype of a stretched M548A1E1, which is about 0·66 metre longer than the basic model and has an additional set of road wheels. The standard 210 hp engine has been replaced by a turbo-charged model which develops 300 hp. Other improvements include a

transmission that features hydrostatic steering and a modified cooling system.
M667
This is the basic vehicle for the Lance tactical missile system. The loader transporter is called the M688 and the launch vehicle is the M752. Net weight of the M667 is 6455 kg. The suspension on the M667 can be locked to provide a more stable firing platform.
M730
This has four Chaparral SAMs on a launcher at the rear of the cab. Full details of this system are given in *Jane's Armour and Artillery 1983–84*, page 548.
Recovery vehicle
This version, known as the XM696, was developed only to the prototype stage.

The Norwegian firm of A/S Moelven Brug have fitted

M548 tracked cargo carrier of British Army used as re-supply vehicle for Rapier SAM batteries (T J Gander)

one of their NM84 wrecker cranes onto a M548 for the Norwegian Army. This crane has a maximum lift capacity of 5000 kg at 3·5 metres and a maximum winch pulling capacity of 18 000 kg. Maximum outreach is 5·3 metres at which 3400 kg can be lifted.
Rapier SAM system
This was developed by British Aerospace for the Iranian Army, but was adopted by the British Army and consists of a modified M548 with a fully armoured cab. On the rear are eight Rapier SAMs ready to launch. Full details of this system are given in *Jane's Armour and Artillery 1983–84*, page 571. A standard M548 will be used as a missile re-supply vehicle and will also carry battery logistic loads.
Radar vehicles
Many countries use the M548 for carrying radars: for

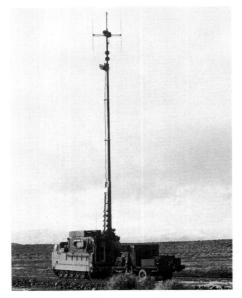

M548 carrying AN/TSQ-114A Trailblazer communications intercept and direction finding system

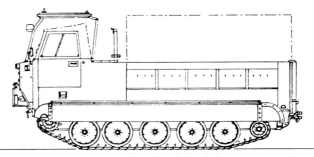

M548 tracked cargo carrier with anti-aircraft ring mount over cab

example, Contraves of Switzerland has fitted its Skyguard anti-aircraft radar in the rear of the vehicle for trials.

M45
This is used to support the M132A1 flamethrower version of the M113A1 APC; it is not currently in service with the US Army but is held in reserve.

M548A1
This is currently in production and has improved suspension and cooling systems.

M548/OE
This is a stretched version of the M548 that mounts a twin 35 mm rapid fire system developed by Oerlikon-Bührle of Switzerland and is at present undergoing trials. Full details of this system are given in *Jane's Armour and Artillery 1983–84*, page 559.

M548/G
This is a low side vehicle that mounts a platform for the West German MSM-Fz mine dispensing system, for details of which the reader is referred to the *Mines* section.

Eagle twin 35 mm SPAAG
Details of this system, which is based on an M548 chassis are given in *Jane's Armour and Artillery 1983–84*, page 577.

M548 SLUMINE
A M548 chassis has also been used to mount the

SLUMINE system, details and photographs of which are given in the *Mines* section.

M548/S
This has been developed to the prototype stage and is essentially an M548A1E1 stretched carrier with an armoured cab and armoured cargo area at the rear. Combat weight with a 5443 kg payload is 15 100 kg. Cargo can be loaded through twin doors at the rear.

Lightweight MLRS
A lightweight version of the Multiple Launch Missile System (MLRS) with a six-rocket launch pallet carrier has been proposed using the M667 Lance supply vehicle as a basis. The project is for the Rapid Deployment Force.

LAR 160
AAI Inc of the United States are acting as overall systems integrator to adapt the Israeli IMI LAR 160 light artillery rocket system to the M548. Also involved are Thiokol (Wasatch Division), Avco Systems Division and Westinghouse, with the intention of providing Rapid Deployment Force units with a long range artillery rocket system. The LAR 160, which is mentioned in *Jane's Armour and Artillery 1983–84*, page 727, has a body diameter of 160 mm, is 3·311 metres long and weighs 110 kg at launch. As the body diameter is very similar the LAR 160 can use 155 mm projectile warheads with both HE, bomblet and other loads. On the M548 the LAR 160 will be packed and fired from 18-rocket launch pod containers (LPCs), two of which can be carried on one vehicle. The LPCs act as transport containers and are discarded once the rockets have been fired. Each LPC weighs 2522 kg and the range is 30 000 metres. The weight of a M548 loaded with two LAR 160 pod rockets, each containing 13 rockets, would be approximately 12 800 kg.

SPECIFICATIONS (M548A1)
Cab seating: 1 + 3
Weight:
(empty) 7439 kg
(loaded) 12 882 kg
Max load: 5443 kg

Towed load: 6350 kg
Load area: 3·32 × 2·45 m
Length: 5·892 m
Width: 2·69 m
Width: (over tracks) 2·54 m
Height:
(excluding MG) 2·81 m
(reduced) 1·94 m
(load area) 1·21 m
Ground clearance: 0·6 m
Track: 2·159 m
Track width: 381 mm
Length of track on ground: 2·82 m
Ground pressure: 0·6 kg/cm^2
Angle of approach/departure: 57°/35°
Max speed:
(road) 64 km/h
(10% gradient) 18·2 km/h
Acceleration: (0–48 km/h) 34·5 s
Range: 483 km
Fuel capacity: 397 litres
Max gradient: 60%
Max side slope: 30%
Fording: 1 m
Vertical obstacle: 0·609 m
Trench: 1·68 m
Engine: GMC Model 6V53T 6-cylinder liquid-cooled diesel developing 215 hp at 2800 rpm
Gearbox: Allison TX-100 3-speed. A torque converter gives 6 forward and 2 reverse speeds
Suspension: torsion bar
Electrical system: 24 V
Batteries: 2 × 12 V, 6TN, 100 Ah

STATUS
In production. In service with Australia, Canada, Egypt, West Germany, Greece, Israel, Italy, Norway, Spain, Switzerland, Tunisia, United Kingdom and the USA.

MANUFACTURER
FMC Corporation, Ordnance Division, San Jose, California 95108, USA.

YUGOSLAVIA

GJ-800 Light Tracked Artillery Tractor

DESCRIPTION
This is the Yugoslav-built version of the Hungarian K-800 light tracked artillery tractor. It differs from the K-800 in that it has a FAMOS 120 hp 6-cylinder water-

cooled diesel engine and has the cab of the FAP truck. The reader is referred to the K-800 entry for full details of this vehicle (page 500).

STATUS
Production complete. In service with the Yugoslav Army.

MANUFACTURER
Yugoslav state factories.

OVER-SNOW VEHICLES

CANADA

Bombardier Ski Doo Elite Snowmobile Over-Snow Vehicle

DESCRIPTION
The Ski Doo Elite Snowmobile is powered by a two-cycle, liquid-cooled engine capable of propelling the 359 kg twin tracked vehicle at speeds of up to 75 km/h.

Fully loaded with two passengers, their equipment and 288 litres of petrol, the Elite can travel more than 200 km before refuelling.

The Snowmobile is being tested by the United States Marine Corps for possible use as a reconnaissance and command vehicle in ground combat.

STATUS
Evaluation by US Marine Corps.

MANUFACTURER
Bombardier Limited, Industrial Division, Valcourt, Quebec J0E 2LO, Canada.

Ski Doo Elite Snowmobile (US Marine Corps)

Bombardier Bombi Over-snow Vehicle

DEVELOPMENT
The Bombardier Bombi vehicle has been designed specifically for use in marginal terrain such as snow, swamplands and desert. The Canadian Armed Forces have used it when operating as part of United Nations Forces in the Sinai Desert.

DESCRIPTION
The chassis is the toboggan type with the fully-enclosed three-man safety cab in the centre and the engine at the rear. Entry to the cab is by a forward-opening door in either side. The Bombi can be delivered with a fully-enclosed four-door cab that extends to the very rear of the chassis and totally encloses the engine compartment.

The torsion bar suspension consists of four pneumatic tyres (4.60 × 10) either side with the drive sprocket at the front. There are no track return rollers. Two types of track can be fitted: the summer tracks are 457 mm wide and consist of rubber belts with steel crosslinks and the wider (584 mm) winter tracks consist of rubber belts with aluminium crosslinks.

Standard equipment includes a dry type air cleaner with added pre-cleaner, pusher fan, full instrumentation, differential oil cooler, shoulder and lap seat belts for all three occupants and a lighting system.

Optional equipment includes a spare wheel, tyre and inner tube mounted at the rear of the vehicle, 600-watt engine block heater, heater and defroster, brush guard, front- or rear-mounted electric winch, high altitude carburettor jets, 60 amp alternator, pintle hook, hydraulic system, front blade and all steel 453 kg payload trailer with dumping mechanism and hinged tailgate.

Bombardier Bombi over-snow vehicle with four-door fully enclosed cab

SPECIFICATIONS
Crew: 1 + 2
Weight:
(empty) 1075 kg
(loaded) 1525 kg
Max load: 450 kg
Length: 2·68 m
Width:
(with summer tracks) 1·52 m
(with winter tracks) 1·78 m
Height:
(with summer tracks) 1·87 m
(with winter tracks) 1·9 m
Ground clearance: 0·32 m
Track width:
(winter tracks) 584 mm
(summer tracks) 457 mm
Ground pressure:
(summer tracks) 0·1 kg/cm²
(winter tracks) 0·08 kg/cm²
Max speed: 33 km/h

Fuel capacity: 43 litres
Gradient: 60%
Engine: Ford 1600 cc 4-cylinder petrol developing 57 hp at 4000 rpm
Gearbox: manual, 4 forward and 1 reverse gears
Clutch: single dry plate
Differential: planetary controlled
Steering: manual, through controlled differential
Turning radius: 1·22 m
Suspension: torsion bar
Brakes:
(main) disc brake on drive line
(parking) locking device on brake disc
Electrical system: 12 V

STATUS
Production. In service with the Canadian Armed Forces.

MANUFACTURER
Bombardier Limited, Industrial Division, Valcourt, Quebec JOE 2LO, Canada.

Bombardier Bombi over-snow vehicle operated by Canadian Armed Forces as part of UN Forces in Sinai Desert

Bombardier Snowmobile Over-snow Vehicle

DEVELOPMENT
The Bombardier Snowmobile over-snow vehicle was originally developed for civilian uses but was subsequently bought by the Canadian Armed Forces for use in Northern Canada.

DESCRIPTION
The chassis is the toboggan type on which is mounted a fully insulated cab with seating for 12 people including the driver. The cab has a door in either side and a larger loading door on the right side towards the back. There is an escape hatch in the roof and the engine is at the rear.

Steering is by a conventional steering wheel. The front wheels can be replaced by skis if required. The track consists of rubber belts with steel crosslinks with the rear suspension each side having four road wheels, one rear trailing wheel with a solid rubber tyre and the drive sprocket at the front.

Standard equipment includes dual front and rear lighting system, safety belts for the front seats, dry type paper air filter, heater and defroster, block heater, two fuel tanks, full range of instruments and front skis/wheels. It takes only a few minutes to change from wheels to skis and vice versa.

Optional equipment includes non-slip differential, additional escape hatch and an additional rear heater for the passenger/cargo compartment.

Bombardier Snowmobile over-snow vehicle with wheels on front axle

SPECIFICATIONS
Cab seating: 1 + 11
Weight: (empty) 2337 kg
Length: 5·38 m
Width: 1·95 m
Height: 2·06 m
Track width: 420 mm
Length of track on ground: 2·2 m
Ground pressure: 0·09 kg/cm²
Max speed: 64 km/h
Range: 320 km
Gradient: 50%

Engine: Chrysler V-8 model 318 petrol developing 187 hp at 4000 rpm
Gearbox: Loadflite automatic with 3 forward and 1 reverse gears
Differential: hypoid truck type
Steering: rack and pinion, power-assisted
Turning radius: 10·66 m
Suspension:
  (front) skis or wheels on coil springs with hydraulic shock absorbers
  (rear) 8 independent wheels on trailing arms

Brakes: drum brake on drive line, pedal operated emergency brakes
Electrical system: 12 V

STATUS
In production. In service with the Canadian Armed Forces.

MANUFACTURER
Bombardier Limited, Industrial Division, Valcourt, Quebec J0E 2L0, Canada.

Bombardier Skidozer Over-snow Vehicle

DESCRIPTION
Like other members of the Bombardier range, the Skidozer has been designed specifically for use in marginal terrain such as snow, swamplands and desert. There are three basic models in the series, 252G (petrol), 252D (diesel) and 302HD (diesel with blade).

The chassis of the Skidozer is formed of steel on a tubular sub-frame. The two-man fully enclosed cab at the front of the vehicle has two adjustable seats with safety belts, heater, defroster, two front windscreen wipers and thermal windscreens. Entry to the cab is through a large door in either side that opens to the rear.

The Skidozer can carry a maximum payload of 907 kg and is also available with a four-door six-man fully-enclosed cab that extends to the rear of the vehicle. On the latter model, in addition to the two normal doors, there are two large doors in the rear of the cargo/personnel compartment.

The torsion bar suspension consists of five pneumatic tyres (5.30 × 12) each side and a drive sprocket at the

rear. There are no return rollers. Two types of track can be fitted, both of the rubber belt type with steel or aluminium crosslinks and with a width of 740 or 1040 mm.

Standard equipment includes a dry air cleaner, suction type fan, full instrumentation, differential oil cooler and a lighting system. Optional equipment includes six-way straight blade/six-way U-blade, power steering, two-speed gearbox, hydraulic systems, solid rubber tyres, rotating beacon, block heater and mirrors.

STATUS
Production. In service with Argentina, Greece and Italy.

MANUFACTURER
Bombardier Limited, Industrial Division, Valcourt, Quebec J0E 2L0, Canada.

SPECIFICATIONS (252D with 740 mm steel tracks)
Crew: 1 + 1
Weight:
  (empty) 3050 kg
  (loaded) 3957 kg
Max load: 907 kg

Length: 4·04 m
Width: 2·34 m
Height: 2·35 m
Ground clearance: 0·3 m
Track width: 740 mm
Ground pressure:
  (empty) 0·84 kg/cm²
  (loaded) 1·13 kg/cm²
Max speed: 23·8 km/h
Fuel capacity: 83 litres
Gradient: 60%
Side slope: 35%
Engine: Perkins model 4.236 4-cylinder diesel developing 78 hp at 2400 rpm
Gearbox: New Process, 4 forward and 1 reverse gears
Clutch: single dry plate
Differential: planetary controlled
Steering: manual, through controlled differential (optional, hydraulic power-assisted)
Suspension: torsion bar
Brakes:
  (main) disc brake on drive line
  (parking) mechanical device on drive line
Electrical system: 12 V

Bombardier 252 series Skidozer with 12-man fully enclosed cab

Bombardier 252 series Skidozer with 12-man fully enclosed cab showing two doors in hull rear

FRANCE

SIGAL M25 Over-snow Vehicle

DEVELOPMENT
Development of the M25 over-snow vehicle began in 1975 and was undertaken by Cabinet d'études Réné Martin (CERM) in an attempt to produce a vehicle more suited, for military purposes, to the lightly compacted snow of the French alpine regions than existing vehicles. Following development, the M25 was passed to the SIGAL Corporation, a subsidiary of CERM. Production will be carried out by the YUMBO Corporation. Twelve M25s have already been sold to the French Army and Air Force and the basic design is now being developed to produce versions for use over swamps and another for use over soft terrain in tropical regions.

DESCRIPTION
The M25 has a forward-mounted cab constructed from light alloy which is also used for the rest of the body construction. The engine is also mounted well forward and provides power for a 8 m³ pump to power the front and rear hydraulic power take-offs for the accessory systems. The main transmission is hydrostatic and is coupled to the main engine. Power is from two variable flow pumps and two hydraulic motors. The motors are operated at high or low gear and two epicycloidal reducers are standard. The hydrostatic oil system has its own radiator linked to that of the main engine.

The M25's tracks are rubber traction belts equipped with light alloy bars, ice spikes and anti-tilt fittings. Each track is 895 mm wide to provide a low ground pressure.

The main-frame with the cab can be tilted backwards for engine maintenance. Inside the cab are two seats, one for the driver and the other for a passenger, with space in the rear body for up to another eight personnel. Entrances are provided for the front cab on each side of the vehicle and there is a single rear door. A heating system is provided for the cab and the windscreens. There is an escape hatch in the roof. A rear-mounted towing pintle is provided and a winch may be fitted. An optional extra is a front-mounted snow-clearing blade. Two electrical systems are provided (24 volts dc and 220 volts ac).

The current production version of the M25 is a personnel/load carrier. Projected versions include a fire-fighting model, an ambulance, a missile launcher/carrier, a flatbed cargo carrier, a command and control post and a lightly-armoured version mounting light

SIGAL M25 over-snow vehicle (T J Gander)

weapons, possibly in a roof-mounted turret. A special fire-fighting version for use in the swamps around the French Naval Air Base at Hyeres has been developed. Versions with narrower tracks for desert areas are projected.

SPECIFICATIONS
Cab seating: 1 + 1 (plus 8 in rear)
Weight: (basic) 2750 kg
Max load: 998 kg
Ground pressure: (unloaded) 58 grams/cm²
Length:
(with front-mounted blade) 4·85 m
(without front-mounted blade) 3·81 m
Width: (with tracks) 2·49 m
Height: 2·25 m
Ground clearance: (unloaded) 0·375 m

Track width: 895 mm
Max speed: 30 km/h
Fuel capacity: 90 litres
Gradient: 100%
Side slope: 25%
Engine: VM turbo-charged 692 HT 3.589-litre, six-cylinder, in-line, water-cooled diesel developing 150 hp at 4200 rpm
Transmission: hydrostatic
Electrical system: 24 V dc and 220 V ac

STATUS
Production. In service with the French Army and Air Force (12).

MANUFACTURER
SIGAL, 12 rue Lecointre, 92310 Sevres, France.

ITALY

Prinoth All Track Over-snow Vehicle

DEVELOPMENT
Prinoth has been involved in the design and manufacture of small over-snow vehicles for many years, mainly for commercial purposes and such specialised roles as ski slope preparation. This experience was developed into the Prinoth 'All' series from which the All Track with military capabilities has been evolved.

DESCRIPTION
The All Track is a small fully-enclosed tracked vehicle with pneumatic road wheels and a hydrostatic transmission. The tractor alone has seating for the driver and five passengers and a further ten men can be accommodated in a trailer unit towed behind the vehicle. Access to the tractor unit is via side doors and a rear hatch. Bolt-on components are used throughout for easy maintenance and part replacement. Two types of track are available, winter and summer. The winter tracks are

made from a woven rubber belting reinforced with a copper/aluminium alloy and have stabilising lugs and steel-studded plates for use on ice. The summer track also has woven rubber belting with a tread and steel lugs. The summer track may be used over rough ground, grass and sand.

Two basic types of engine may be fitted, a 1700 cc diesel, as used in the FIAT Strada, or a 2-litre petrol engine. A mechanical governor is used on the smaller unit and an electronic governor on the larger. Both govern the amount of engine power that is taken by the hydrostatic transmission to reduce the driver's work load. Hydraulic lines take power to the trailer unit.

Two types of trailer unit are available, depending on the payload size, the P 1200/A and the P 2000/A. The All Track tractor unit can also tow a variety of loads

ranging from a flat-bed trailer to light artillery and mortars. The All Track can also be used as a troop transport, ammunition carrier, command or radio vehicle or as a general flat-bed carrier. There is also an ambulance version known as the Life All fitted with medical equipment by Saccab of Milan. The All Track has a fording capability but a fully amphibious version is projected as is a lightly armoured version for reconnaissance purposes.

STATUS
Production.

MANUFACTURER
Prinoth Snowmobiles, Via Purger 181, I-39046 Ortisei, Italy.

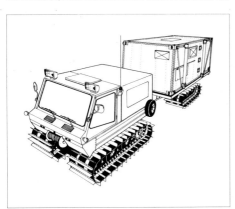

Prinoth All Track over-snow vehicle towing trailer with ISO container/shelter

Prinoth All Track over-snow vehicle

SPECIFICATIONS
Crew: 1 + 5
Trailer seating: 10
Weight: (empty) 1440 kg
Max load:
(tractor) 600 kg
(trailer) 1000 kg
Towed load: 3200 kg
Length:
(tractor) 2·7 m
(trailer) 2·49 m
(combination on tow) 6·62 m

Width:
(summer tracks) 1·9 m
(winter tracks) 2·1 m
Height:
(overall) 2·1 m
(cab roof) 1·895 m
(floor) 0·925 m
Ground clearance: 0·295 m
Max speed: 25 km/h
Fuel capacity: 36 litres
Fuel consumption: 7 litres/h
Gradient: 120%

Fording: 0·7 m
Trench crossing: 0·8 m
Engine: 1700 cc diesel developing 55 or 60 hp or 2-litre petrol developing 115 hp
Transmission: hydrostatic
Steering: hydrostatic
Turning radius: (combination) 3·7 m
Electrical system: 12 V

JAPAN

Type 60 Over-snow Vehicle

DEVELOPMENT
In 1952 the Komatsu Manufacturing Co Limited developed the KC-20 over-snow vehicle primarily for civilian use. Further development resulted in the KC-20-35 which entered production in 1960 and is widely used in Japan for civil applications.

The KC-20-35 was followed by the KC-20-3 which, with modifications, was adopted by the Japanese Ground Self-Defence Force in 1960 as the Type 60 Snow Mobile, or Medium Snow Mobile as it is sometimes called. It is widely used in the northern main Japanese island of Hokkaido.

DESCRIPTION
The engine is at the front of the vehicle with the crew and passenger/cargo area at the rear. The windscreen can be folded forwards onto the bonnet and the cargo area has bows, a tarpaulin-type cover with side windows and a drop tailgate at the rear.

The suspension is the bogie/torsion bar type with each side having eight dual road wheels, drive sprocket, idler and two track return rollers.

SPECIFICATIONS
Crew: 1 + 9
Weight:
(empty) 2870 kg
(loaded) 3770 kg
Max load: 900 kg
Max towed load: 1500 kg
Length: 4·07 m
Width: 1·98 m
Height: 2·05 m
Ground clearance: 0·3 m
Track: 1·34 m
Ground pressure: 0·105 km/cm²
Trench: 1·006 m
Max speed: 36 km/h
Range: 135 km

Type 60 over-snow vehicle (Kensuke Ebata)

Fuel capacity: 90 litres
Max gradient: 60%
Engine: Toyota 6-cylinder water-cooled petrol developing 105 hp at 3400 rpm
Gearbox: manual, 4 forward and 1 reverse gears
Suspension: bogie/torsion bar
Electrical system: 12 V

STATUS
Production complete. In service with the Japanese Ground Self-Defence Force.

MANUFACTURERS
Komatsu Manufacturing Co and Ohara Ironworks.

Type 61 Over-snow Vehicle

DEVELOPMENT
To meet the requirements of the Japanese Ground Self-Defence Force the Komatsu company and the Ohara Ironworks built a full tracked over-snow vehicle designated the KC-50-2. The prototype was completed in 1955 and after modification was adopted as the Type 61 Large Snow Mobile in 1961. In addition to being used as a cargo/troop carrier it is also used to tow 105 and 155 mm artillery weapons mounted on skis.

DESCRIPTION
The engine is at the front of the vehicle with the crew and passenger/cargo area at the rear. The engine is fitted with a turbo-charger for high altitude operations and aluminium is used wherever possible to save weight. The windscreen can be folded forwards onto the bonnet and the cargo area has a drop tailgate, bows and a tarpaulin cover with side windows.

The suspension is the bogie/torsion bar type with each side having eight dual road wheels, drive sprocket, idler and three track return rollers.

The Type 61 is distinguishable from the Type 60 by its larger size and much deeper engine compartment.

SPECIFICATIONS
Crew: 1 + 10
Weight:
(empty) 5220 kg
(loaded) 6500 kg
Max load: 1280 kg
Max towed load: 3200 kg
Length: 5·34 m
Width: 2·5 m
Ground clearance: 0·34 m
Track: 1·71 m
Track width: 790 mm

Length of track on ground: 3 m
Ground pressure: 0·135 kg/cm²
Trench: 1·5 m
Max speed: 35 km/h
Range: 166 km
Fuel capacity: 160 litres
Max gradient: 60%
Engine: Isuzu DA-120T 6-cylinder water-cooled diesel developing 155 hp at 2600 rpm
Gearbox: manual, 5 forward and 1 reverse gears
Suspension: bogie/torsion bar

STATUS
Production complete. In service with the Japanese Ground Self-Defence Force.

MANUFACTURERS
Komatsu Manufacturing Co and Ohara Ironworks, Japan.

SWEDEN

Aktiv Sno-Tric and Snow-Trac Over-snow Vehicles

These vehicles are no longer in service and for details of both vehicles see *Jane's Military Vehicles and Ground Support Equipment 1983*, pages 509 and 510.

Bandvagn Bv 202 Tracked Over-snow Vehicle

Bv 202 tracked over-snow vehicle

DEVELOPMENT

After the Second World War the Swedish Army bought a number of war surplus Studebaker Weasel over-snow vehicles but by the early 1950s they were becoming expensive to maintain. Between 1954 and 1956 the Swedish Ordnance Department evaluated a number of vehicles as possible replacements for the Weasel but none of the vehicles offered met its requirements. In 1956 a number of Swedish companies were approached and asked if they could design an over-snow vehicle, but none showed any interest in the project. In 1957 the Swedish Army started its own project and following trials with some test rigs, two prototypes were completed in 1958. These were followed by another batch of ten vehicles in 1960. In 1960 the completed design was sent out to Swedish companies for competitive bidding and late in 1961 Volvo was awarded a contract to prepare the design for production. First production vehicles were completed by Bolinder-Munktell in 1962-63.

By early 1980 some 5000 Bv 202s had been delivered, with final deliveries being made in 1981. In the Swedish Army it is now being supplemented by the Bv 206 all-terrain carrier.

DESCRIPTION

The Bv 202 consists of two tracked units joined by a universal coupling. The front and rear units have identical sub frames and their bodies are of all-welded construction. The front unit contains the engine and transmission at the front and the fully enclosed cab at the rear. The driver is seated on the left with the vehicle commander to his right. The cab is insulated from the engine compartment by aluminium sheets covering a 25 mm compressed layer of mineral wool – rockwool. The cab has a heater as a standard fitting. The rear unit, which can be fitted with a heater as an optional extra, is provided with a drop tailgate and a tarpaulin cover. A maximum load of 800 to 1000 kg can be carried in the rear unit.

Power from the engine is transmitted to a main gearbox which is combined with a transfer box. Power is transmitted from the transfer box to the drive axles at the front end of both units via propeller shafts.

The suspension system consists of torsion bars with pivoting and bogie arms, and rubber helper springs. The torsion bars are attached to the bottom of the front and rear of each units, eg two torsion bars per unit. This means that each torsion bar carries four wheels, two on each side. The fifth and rear wheel on each side serves as a track tensioning wheel and therefore has an individual rubber suspension system. The five road wheels each side all have pneumatic tyres. The drive sprocket is at the front of each unit and there is a single track

return roller. The tracks consist of endless rubber bands reinforced with stainless steel wire. They are moulded in one piece and have embedded steel plates which not only provide a meshing surface for the teeth of the drive sprocket, but also serve as retainers for the track guide tongues which are made of light alloy.

The steering system is mounted in the front unit and is of the hydrostatic type. It consists of a hydraulic pump, steering valve, steering wheel and steering cylinder. If the pump pressure should fail for any reason the vehicle can still be steered. The steering cylinder is double acting and actuates the steering joint in such a way that the two vehicle units are deflected in relation to each other. Apart from lateral steering deflection, the two vehicle units are able to move horizontally in relation to each other by up to 40 degrees. They can also move up to 34 degrees vertically and if necessary can be lifted or lowered in relation to each other by a maximum of 180 mm. The steering joint has two damping units with strong rubber springs, one on the front unit and the other on the rear.

The basic vehicle is fully amphibious, being propelled in the water by its tracks. Standard equipment includes two bilge pumps, jack, tools, towing cable, axe, crowbar, spade and two jerricans. Optional equipment includes a heater for the rear unit, tropical kit, fully enclosed rear unit, cold starting device, torque converter and stowage bin on the roof of the rear unit.

VARIANTS

The latest model is the Bv 202 Mk 2 which has a more powerful engine and a different transmission. The Bv 203 has a 24-volt electrical system, hard top for rear unit and is radio-suppressed.

The British Army uses the vehicle as an artillery prime mover towing the 105 mm Light Gun, ambulance, command, mortar carrier (81 mm), radio, repair vehicle, and for towing the Bar minelaying system many vehicles have a 7·62 mm GPMG machine gun installed over the commander's hatch.

STATUS

Production complete. In service with Finland (including Mk 2 version), the Netherlands (Marines, 60), Norway,

Sweden, Turkey and the United Kingdom. It has also been evaluated by other armies including Yugoslavia and the USA.

MANUFACTURER

Volvo BM, S-631 85 Eskilstuna, Sweden.

SPECIFICATIONS

(Bv 202 Mk 1; data in square brackets relate to Bv 202 Mk 2 where different)
Seating:
  (front) 1 + 1
  (rear) 8–10
Weight:
  (empty) 2900 kg
  (loaded) 4200 [4400] kg
Max load:
  (road) 1000 [1200] kg
  (cross country) 800 [1000] kg
Load area: (rear) 2·3 × 1·56 m
Length: 6·172 [6·175] m
Width: 1·759 m
Height: 2·21 m
Ground clearance: 0·3 [0·28] m
Track: 1·118 m
Ground pressure: 0·85 [0·9] kg/cm²
Max speed:
  (road) 39 km/h
  (water) 3·3 [3] km/h
Range: 400 km
Fuel capacity: 156 litres
Max gradient: 60%
Vertical obstacle: 0·5 m
Engine: Volvo B18 [Volvo B20B]
Engine type: 4-cylinder petrol
Engine hp: 91 [97] bhp at 5300 rpm
Gearbox: manual with 4 forward and 1 reverse gears
Clutch: single dry disc
Transfer box: 2-speed
Steering: power-assisted
Turning radius: 6·8 m
Brakes: hydraulic
Electrical system: 24 V
Batteries: 72 Ah

Bv 202 tracked over-snow vehicle showing climbing capabilities (Simon Dunstan)

Bv 202 tracked over-snow vehicle in typical operating environment

Bandvagn Bv 206 All-terrain Carrier

DEVELOPMENT
In 1974 the Swedish Defence Materiel Administration awarded Hägglund and Söner a contract worth S.Kr 13 million for the development of a new over-snow/all-terrain vehicle to succeed the Volvo Bv 202 in the Swedish Army. Three batches of vehicles were delivered to the Swedish Army for trials in 1976, 1977 and 1978. Hägglunds was awarded a first production contract in June 1979 from the Swedish Defence Administration. Under this S.Kr 800 million contract the company delivered pre-production vehicles late in 1980 and began full-scale production in early 1981. Full rate deliveries will run from the middle of 1981 until 1986–87. The initial batch of 350 was completed and delivered by mid-April 1982 and production is continuing at the rate of 100 per month.

In September 1981 the British Army purchased four Bv 206s for trials in a variety of forms and it is expected that a further number will be purchased to replace the Bv 202 vehicles in service with the Army and Royal Marines starting in 1984. In 1983 the US Army ordered 268 Bv 206s for service in Alaska as the M973 Small Unit Support Vehicle (SUSV). These were expected to enter service in 1983–84.

DESCRIPTION
The Bv 206 consists of two tracked units which are linked together with a steering unit, each unit consisting of a chassis with the body mounted on four rubber elements.

Each chassis consists of a central beam, a final drive assembly and two track assemblies. The chassis of the front and rear units are identical except that a two step drop-down gearbox is mounted in the rear end of the front chassis. The track assemblies are mounted to the central beam by two transversal leaf springs. Each track assembly is built up around a tubular bar which carries the sprocket assembly, road wheels and idler. In each track assembly there are four pairs of road wheels on trailing arms springed by rubber tension springs. The idler at the rear with a tensioning device is also supported by a rubber spring. All four track assemblies of the vehicle are identical and interchangeable. The tracks are rubber with longitudinal textile cord and integral steel profile reinforcements.

Steering is accomplished by changing the direction between the front and rear unit by two hydraulic cylinders, servo controlled from a conventional steering wheel. The hydraulic system is built up of commercially available components. The steering unit is designed to permit a large freedom of movement between the two bodies.

The engine and transmission are mounted in the front unit. A shaft connects the gearbox with the drop-down gearbox. A disc brake is mounted on this shaft in front of the drop-down gearbox inside the body. Cardan shafts transmit power to the final drives on the front end of both chassis.

The bodies are made of glassfibre reinforced plastic (GRP) which is fire-resistant. Each body is built like a closed box with integrated roll-over protection. Heating of the units is by heat exchangers and the de-icing capacity in the front unit is sufficient to keep the windscreen clear down to a temperature of −40° C. The bodies have holders for lashing cargo in the rear unit and also in the rear part of the front unit. The rear unit is also provided with brackets for carrying four stretchers.

The Bv 206 is fully amphibious being propelled in the water by its tracks.

VARIANTS
Anti-tank (Pvbv 2062)
This is armed with a Bofors 90 mm recoilless rifle or Hughes TOW ATGW on a pivot mount which can be hydraulically raised to the required level. The open front body is provided with roll-bars which can be quickly lowered. The low profile rear body is designed to withstand the back-blast of the weapon when it is fired and is used for storing ammunition. In time the 90 mm recoilless rifles will be withdrawn and replaced by the TOW version. The Bv 206 has been trialled as a possible carrier for the Bofors BILL anti-tank missile.
Command post/radio vehicle (Rabv 2061)
This accommodates six operators in the rear body and driver plus four men in the front body. Door arrangements are identical to the standard carrier version. The vehicle has vhf transceivers in the rear body and all the radios can be operated from the front unit.
Radar vehicle (projected)
The high payload of the Bv 206 permits the installation of a very wide range of specialist equipment including a self-contained radar unit inclusive of the operator's cab and power supply. For example, the Giraffe radar with the Bofors RBS-70 SAM used by the Swedish Army.

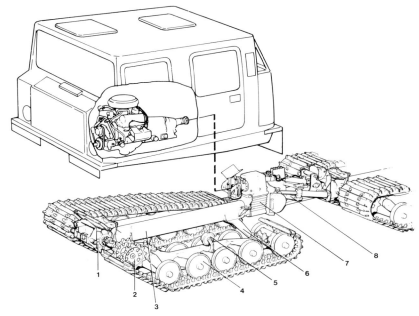

Major design features of Bv 206 all-terrain vehicle (1) *primal drive* (2) *drive sprocket* (3) *central beam* (4) *bogie* (5) *track return roller* (6) *transversal leaf spring* (7) *gearbox* (8) *steering unit*

Pvbv 2062 as anti-tank vehicle with Hughes TOW ATGW system in firing position

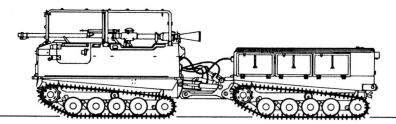

Pvbv 2062 all-terrain vehicle armed with 90 mm Bofors anti-tank recoilless rifle

SPECIFICATIONS
Cab seating:
  (front unit) 5–6
  (rear unit) 11
Weight:
  (empty) 4340 kg
  (loaded) 6340 kg
Weight of front unit: (empty) 2670 kg
Weight of rear unit: (empty) 1670 kg
Max load: 2000 kg
  (front unit) 600 kg
  (rear unit) 1400 kg
Load area:
  (front unit) 0·81 × 1·4 m
  (rear unit) 2·5 × 1·4 m
Length: 6·86 m
Width: 1·85 m
Height: 2·4 m
Ground clearance: 0·35 m
Track width: 620 mm

Max speed:
  (road) 55 km/h
  (water) 3 km/h
Max gradient:
  (hard surface) 60%
  (snow) 30%
Max side slope: 90%
Fording: amphibious
Range: 330 km
Engine: Ford model 2658 E V-6 water-cooled petrol developing 136 bhp at 5200 rpm (can also be fitted with Mercedes 5-cylinder in-line turbo-charged diesel engine developing 125 bhp at 4500 rpm)
Gearbox: fully automatic with torque converter, Daimler-Benz W4A-018 with 4 forward and 1 reverse gears
Turning radius: 8 m
Electrical system: 24 V
Batteries: 2 × 12 V, 58 Ah

Pvbv 2062 all-terrain vehicle with 90 mm Bofors anti-tank recoilless rifle in travelling position with rear unit carrying ammunition

Bv 206 all-terrain vehicle with fully enclosed bodies

STATUS
Production. In service with Finland, Norway (200) and Sweden (4000). Ordered by the US Army as M973 SUSV. Trial batches ordered by Canada, Italy and the United Kingdom.

MANUFACTURER
AB Hägglund and Söner, Vehicle Division, S-891 01 Örnsköldsvik, Sweden.

Bv 206 all-terrain vehicle with fully enclosed bodies

UNION OF SOVIET SOCIALIST REPUBLICS

GT-S Tracked Amphibious Over-snow Vehicle

DEVELOPMENT
The GT-S (or GAZ-47 as it is sometimes referred to) was the first of the tracked amphibious over-snow vehicles to enter service with the Soviet Army. It was in production from 1955 to 1970. It can carry 1000 kg of cargo and tow a trailer or light weapon such as a 57 mm anti-tank gun or a 120 mm mortar weighing up to 2000 kg. The vehicle has been used by the Soviet Army for a variety of roles on marshy and snow-covered terrain, and has also been used for civilian roles.

DESCRIPTION
The engine is mounted at the front of the vehicle and projects into the crew compartment. The driver is seated on the left and the commander on the right; both have a side door. The GT-S has an open roof which is normally covered by a tarpaulin extending to the rear of the hull, which has integral windows in the side and rear.

The suspension is of the torsion bar type and consists of five large road wheels with the last road wheel acting as the idler. The drive sprocket is at the front but there are no track return rollers. The GT-S is fully amphibious being propelled in the water by its tracks.

VARIANTS
The LFM-RVD-GPI-66 is a GT-S with its tracks removed and replaced by cylindrical screw pontoons. Unladen weight is 3600 kg and loaded weight is 4800 kg. Main improvements are a much higher water speed of 20 km/h and a higher speed across snow. The present status of this model is not known, although some reports have indicated that it has been placed in production. Further development of the GT-S resulted in the GT-SM for which there is a separate entry.

SPECIFICATIONS
Cab seating: 1 + 1
Weight:
(empty) 3600 kg
(loaded) 4600 kg
Max load: 1000 kg
Towed load: 2000 kg
Length: 4·9 m

GT-S with cover over crew and cargo compartment

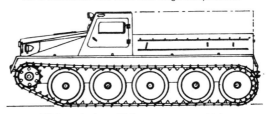

GT-S tracked amphibious over-snow vehicle

Width: 2·435 m
Height: 1·96 m
Ground clearance: 0·4 m
Track: 2·05 m
Track width: 300 mm
Length of track on ground: 3·35 m
Ground pressure: (loaded) 0·24 kg/cm^2
Max speed:
(road) 35–39 km/h
(water) 4 km/h
Range: 725 km
Fuel capacity: 208 litres
Max gradient: 60%

Vertical obstacle: 0·6 m
Trench: 1·3 m
Engine: GAZ-61 (or GAZ-47) 6-cylinder water-cooled petrol developing 85 hp (or 74 hp if GAZ-47 engine is installed)
Gearbox: manual, 4 forward and 1 reverse gears
Electrical system: 12 V

STATUS
Production complete. In service with the Soviet Army.

MANUFACTURER
Gor'kiy Motor Vehicle Plant, Gor'kiy, USSR.

GT-SM Tracked Amphibious Over-snow Vehicle

DEVELOPMENT
The GT-SM, or GAZ-71 as it is also known, is the replacement for the earlier GT-S tracked vehicle. It is widely used in marshy and snow-covered areas as it has a very low ground pressure and is used for both civil and military roles. The GT-SM has the same load carrying capability as the earlier vehicle but has a more powerful engine.

DESCRIPTION
The GT-SM is fully amphibious, propelled in the water by its tracks. The engine and cab are at the front of the vehicle, which is enclosed and has a door in either side and two roof hatches. The load area is normally covered by a tarpaulin cover with integral side and rear windows. Entry to the rear is by twin doors in the rear of the hull. The suspension is of the torsion bar type and consists of six large road wheels with the last road wheel acting as

the idler, with the drive sprocket at the front. There are no track return rollers.

STATUS
Production of the GT-SM is believed to have been completed. In service with the Soviet Army.

MANUFACTURER
Gor'kiy Motor Vehicle Plant, Gor'kiy, USSR.

SPECIFICATIONS
Crew: 1 + 1 (and up to 10 in rear)
Weight:
 (empty) 3750 kg
 (loaded) 4750 kg
Max load: 1000 kg
Towed load: 2000 kg
Length: 5·365 m
Width: 2·582 m
Height: 1·74 m
Ground clearance: 0·38 m
Track: 2·8 m
Track width: 390 mm
Length of track on ground: 3·63 m
Ground pressure: 0·17 kg/cm²
Max speed:
 (road) 50 km/h
 (water) 5–6 km/h
Range: 500 km (estimate)
Fuel capacity: 300 litres
Engine: GAZ-71 V-8 water-cooled petrol developing 115 hp

GT-SM tracked amphibious over-snow vehicle

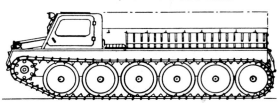

GT-SM tracked amphibious over-snow vehicle

GT-T Tracked Amphibious Over-snow Vehicle

DEVELOPMENT
The GT-T is the latest and largest in the GT range of tracked amphibious over-snow vehicles. It can carry a maximum of 2000 kg of cargo and tow a trailer weighing up to 4000 kg.

DESCRIPTION
The engine is at the front of the hull and extends rearwards into the crew compartment. The driver is seated on the left side and the vehicle commander on the right, both with a side door, and the commander has a circular hatch in the roof. The load area is at the rear and is usually covered by a tarpaulin cover. Up to ten men can be seated in the rear. An unusual feature of the GT-SM is that the fuel tanks are positioned externally above the tracks on each side at the rear.

The torsion bar suspension consists of six road wheels with the idler at the rear and the drive sprocket at the front. The road wheels are similar to those used on the PT-76 light amphibious tank family, and are also used as the basis for the more recent MT-LB multi-purpose tracked vehicle (*Jane's Armour and Artillery 1983–84*, page 363).

The GT-T is fully amphibious. Most sources state that it is propelled in the water by its tracks at a speed of between 5 and 6 km/h.

VARIANTS
A number of GT-Ts have had a fifth wheel mounted to the rear of the cab for towing semi-trailers, carrying missiles such as the SA-2. They are designated the GT-TS.

A number of specialised civilian models have been developed with a fully enclosed cabin at the rear. In 1965 the GT-T maintenance vehicle entered service with the Soviet Army with the designation MTO-SG. Mounted at the front of the vehicle is an A-frame for changing components and inside the hull rear is a workshop with a petrol-driven power generator, electric drill, electric grinder, arc welding equipment, compression pressure meter and a full set of tools. The A-frame can lift a maximum load of 1500 kg and radios are fitted as standard on all repair vehicles.

STATUS
Believed to be still in production. In service with the Soviet Army.

Soviet troops boarding GT-T tracked amphibious over-snow vehicles during winter exercises

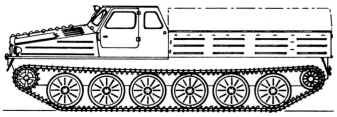

GT-T tracked amphibious over-snow vehicle

MANUFACTURER
Soviet state factories.

SPECIFICATIONS
Crew: 3 + 10
Weight:
 (empty) 8000 kg
 (loaded) 10 000 kg
Max load: 2000 kg
Towed load: 4000 kg
Length: 6·5 m
Width: 3·14 m

Height: 2·16 m
Ground clearance: 0·45 m
Track width: 540 mm
Ground pressure: (loaded) 0·24 kg/cm²
Max speed:
 (road) 45 km/h
 (water) 6 km/h
Range: 500 km
Max gradient: 60%
Engine: 1Z-6 6-cylinder water-cooled diesel developing 200 hp

MT-L Tracked Amphibious Over-snow Vehicle

DEVELOPMENT
The MT-L is thought to have been developed at the same time as the GT-T vehicle which is specifically an over-snow vehicle and is also used in swampy areas, whereas the MT-L is not strictly an over-snow vehicle as its ground pressure is 0·42 kg/cm² compared with the 0·24 kg/cm² of the GT-T.

A special variant of the MT-L, the MT-LV, has a ground pressure of 0·27 kg/cm², which puts it in almost the same class as the GT-T. Its major difference from the MT-L is probably wider tracks and hence a lower ground pressure.

The MT-L is the basis for a complete family of full tracked vehicles which replaces unarmoured over-snow vehicles, unarmoured artillery tractors, armoured artillery tractors and even APCs.

The MT-LB multi-purpose tracked vehicle, fully

described and illustrated in *Jane's Armour and Artillery 1983–84*, page 363, is a member of the family.

DESCRIPTION
The fully-enclosed cab is at the front of the hull and can seat eight men including the vehicle commander and the driver. The engine of the MT-L is in the rear part of the cab. Normal means of entry is through the door in either side of the hull, but there is also a roof hatch.

The load area is at the back and is provided with drop

tailgate, bows and a tarpaulin cover. The torsion bar suspension consists of six road wheels with the drive sprocket at the front and the idler at the rear. The MT-L can be fitted with extra-wide 565 mm tracks and with an aggressive grouser to facilitate over-snow and soft vehicle operations. This model is designated the MT-LV and has a ground pressure of 0·27 kg/cm². There are no track return rollers. The road wheels are similar to those used on members of the PT-76 light amphibious tank family and are also used on the MT-LB with a hydraulic

shock absorber being mounted at the first and last road wheel stations.

The MT-L is fully amphibious without preparation, being propelled in the water by its tracks at a maximum speed of 6 km/h. A bilge pump is fitted as standard.

STATUS
In production. In service with the Soviet Army.

MANUFACTURER
Soviet state factories.

SPECIFICATIONS
Crew: 2 + 11
Weight:
(empty) 8500 kg
(loaded, without trailer) 13 000 kg
(loaded, with trailer) 11 000 kg
Max load:
(without trailer) 4500 kg
(loaded, with trailer) 2500 kg
Towed load: 7000 kg
Length: 6·364 m
Width: 2·85 m
Height: 2·013 m
Ground clearance: 0·4 m
Track width: 350 mm
Track: 2·5 m
Ground pressure: 0·42 kg/cm²
Max speed:
(road, without trailer) 61·5 km/h
(road, with trailer) 46·8 km/h
(water) 5–6 km/h
Range: 500 km
Max gradient:
(without trailer) 60%
(with trailer) 40%
Side slope: 40%
Engine: YaMZ-238V V-6 diesel developing 240 hp at 2100 rpm
Transmission: manual with 6 forward and 1 reverse gears
Steering: clutch and brake
Suspension: torsion bar
Electrical system: 24 V

MT-L tracked amphibious over-snow vehicle

UNITED KINGDOM

Hytracker All-terrain Vehicle

DEVELOPMENT
The Hytracker all-terrain vehicle has been designed as a private venture by Craig Caledonia Company Limited and was shown in public for the first time in July 1981.

Although designed primarily for civil applications such as forestry and crop spraying, it has military potential as a troop, cargo and weapons carrier. It has been designed to transport a payload of 3750 kg over a wide range of terrain including rocks, swamp and deep snow.

DESCRIPTION
The fully enclosed and insulated two-man cab is at the front of the vehicle and has two large windscreens each of which has an electric wiper, wide windows and side opening doors with sliding windows.

The cargo area is at the rear and is fitted with bows, tarpaulin cover with integral transparent side windows, roll up rear and a single piece door that opens to the left. As an option a fully enclosed passenger/cargo body can be fitted at the rear. For military applications a fully enclosed GRP body and buoyant hull have been proposed.

The engine is mounted under the cab which drives two Rexroth pumps which in turn provide the hydraulic pressure to Renold motors located inside the rear sprockets.

The driver, seated on the right side of the cab, controls the vehicle with two small levers which give full control for forward to reverse, left and right, smooth variation in speed and braking with infinitely variable ratio change. Maintenance problems are reduced by the elimination of the clutch, gearbox, propeller shaft, differential, foot brake and conventional steering mechanism.

The suspension either side consists of two rubber damped articulating double-wheel bogies with the idler at the front and the drive sprocket at the rear; there are no track return rollers. The drive sprocket incorporates the parking brake and the track tensioner acts on the front sprockets.

The rubber track has detachable high tensile steel grousers, and two rows of guide horns which also transmit the drive from the sprocket to the track.

Hytracker all-terrain vehicle with fully enclosed two-man cab

SPECIFICATIONS
Cab seating: 2 + 10/12
Weight: (empty) 3400–4000 kg
Load: up to 3750 kg
Load area: 2·489 × 1·651 m
Length: 3·912 m
Width: 2·21 m
Height: 2·438 m
Ground clearance: 0·406 m
Ground pressure: 0·13 to 0·16 kg/cm²
Max speed: 19·3 km/h (higher speeds optional)
Max gradient: 100%

Vertical obstacle: 0·609 m
Engine: Perkins 4.236 diesel developing 78 hp at 2400 rpm
Transmission: hydrostatic drive to rear sprockets

STATUS
Production.

MANUFACTURER
Craig Caledonia Company Limited, Gartinstarry, Buchlyvie, Stirlingshire FK8 3PD, Scotland.

UNITED STATES OF AMERICA

General Dynamics Sno-Runner Over-snow Vehicle

DESCRIPTION
The Chrysler (now General Dynamics) Sno-Runner is a single-seat vehicle powered by an air-cooled engine. It is capable of reaching speeds of up to 60 km/h and has a cruising range of about 165 km on 4·7 litres of petrol. The single tracked vehicle has been tested by the United States Marine Corps for possible use as a reconnaissance, messenger and command vehicle in ground combat situations.

STATUS
Evaluation.

MANUFACTURER
Chrysler Marine and Industrial Division.

General Dynamics Sno-Runners (US Marine Corps)

DMC 1450 Over-snow Vehicle

DEVELOPMENT
Although designed primarily for over-snow operation, the DMC 1450 can also be used over other types of marginal terrain such as swamps. Five vehicles with a fully-enclosed six-man cab were delivered to the United States Marine Corps in 1979–80.

DESCRIPTION
The basic vehicle has a two-man fully-enclosed cab towards the front of the vehicle and behind the cab 2·41 square metres of uncovered cargo area. The cab is constructed to withstand two times the weight of the vehicle but roll bars are available as an option. The DMC 1450 is also available with a larger fully-enclosed cab which has 2·41 square metres of covered cargo area which can be used to seat an additional four people.

In the two-man cab the driver and passenger each have a bucket seat with a seat belt and in the six-man model there are in addition four padded fold-up passenger seats each with a seat belt.

In both versions the driver and one passenger have individual doors that open to the rear and the six-seater model also has a single rear door for loading and unloading cargo and personnel.

The engine is in the forward part of the vehicle and projects into the cab, which is insulated to decrease both noise and heat transfer.

The suspension each side consists of five rubber-tyred road wheels with the idler at the front and the drive sprocket at the rear. There are no track return rollers. The road wheels and idler are supported on semi-elliptical leaf springs. The track grousers are of steel alloy and the basic model has 644 mm wide tracks. The DMC 1450 can be delivered with 793 mm wide tracks. Steering controls consist of two levers which activate the hydraulic master cylinder which in turn activates slave master cylinders connected by linkage to each steering band. The steering levers are also used for normal braking.

STATUS
In production. In service with the US Marine Corps.

DMC 1450 over-snow vehicle for US Marine Corps with six-man cab and front-mounted winch

MANUFACTURER
DMC, Logan Division, PO Box 407, Logan, Utah 84321, USA.

SPECIFICATIONS (DMC 1450 with standard 644 mm wide tracks)
Crew: 1 + 1
Weight: (empty) 1586 kg
Max load: 1088 kg
Normal load: 453 kg
Load area: 1·524 × 1·574 m
Length: 3·479 m
Width: 1·778 m
Height: 1·905 m
Ground clearance: 0·228 m
Track width: 644 mm

Ground pressure:
(empty) 0·07 kg/cm²
(with 1088 kg of cargo) 0·1 kg/cm²
Max speed: 29 km/h
Fuel capacity: 91 litres
Gradient:
(dirt) 80%
(snow) 60%
Vertical obstacle: 0·355 m
Engine: Ford 6-cylinder petrol developing 104 hp at 4000 rpm
Gearbox: Ford C-4 automatic with 3 forward and 1 reverse gears
Steering: planetary differential on oil bath
Turning radius: 3·048 m
Suspension: semi-elliptical springs
Electrical system: 12 V

DMC 1200 Over-snow Vehicle

DEVELOPMENT
Although designed primarily for over-snow operation, the DMC 1200 can also be used over other types of marginal terrain such as swamps.

DESCRIPTION
The basic vehicle has a two-man fully-enclosed cab at the front of the vehicle and optional roll bars can be fitted to enable it to withstand two times its weight. Entry to the cab is by a door in each side that opens to the front. There is a combined heater and windscreen defroster unit and an optional second heater can be fitted into the cab. In all models seat belts are standard equipment for each crew member and passenger.

Fitted with the standard two-man cab the DMC 1200 has 4·08 square metres of uncovered cargo area behind the cab, with a five-man cab it has 2·6 square metres of uncovered cargo area and with the fully-enclosed ten-man cab, with the bench seats folded, it has 3·9 square metres.

The engine is in the forward part of the cab which is

DMC 1200 over-snow vehicle with ten-man fully enclosed body

insulated to decrease noise level. Steering is by a planetary steering differential providing drive to both track systems. The driver has two levers which actuate the hydraulic master cylinder, which in turn actuates the slave cylinders connected by linkage to each steering band.

The suspension each side consists of five rubber-tyred road wheels with the drive sprocket at the rear. There are no track return rollers and the track grousers are of steel alloy. The standard track is 0·914 metre wide but the DMC 1200 is also available with 1·152-metre tracks.

STATUS
Production. In service with the US Navy (3).

MANUFACTURER
DMC, Logan Division, PO Box 407, Logan, Utah 84321, USA.

SPECIFICATIONS (DMC 1200 with 914 mm wide tracks)
Crew: 1 + 1
Weight: (empty) 2803 kg
Max load: 1361 kg
Normal load: 453–907 kg
Length: 4·114 m
Width: 2·526 m
Height: 2·108 m
Ground clearance: 0·317 m

Track width: 914 mm
Ground pressure: 0·07 kg/cm²
Max speed: (with outboard reduction gearing) 27 km/h
Fuel capacity: 159 litres
Gradient:
  (dirt) 80%
  (snow) 60%
Engine: Ford 6-cylinder petrol developing 132 hp
Gearbox: Ford C-6 automatic, 3 forward and 1 reverse gears
Differential steering: planetary controlled
Turning radius: 4·572 m
Suspension: trailing arms in rubber
Brakes: (parking) double caliper disc
Electrical system: 12 V

DMC 3700 Over-snow Vehicle

DESCRIPTION
The DMC 3700 is primarily used as a snow-clearing vehicle pushing and towing a variety of snow-clearing implements but it has a limited capability as a personnel and cargo carrier according to the type of body fitted. The DMC 3700 layout has a one-man centrally located enclosed cab provided with vision areas all round. The engine is mounted forward with the exhaust stack venting upwards and the front of the engine cover being reinforced to accommodate a variety of snow clearing ploughs or other equipment. The tracks on both sides are completely open and may be of two widths, 1·448 metres or 1·651 metres. Power for the snow-clearing devices is hydraulic. One of the snow-clearing devices is a ten-way front dozer blade which may be controlled from within the cab by a joystick control holding extra push-button actuators. There are five road wheels and one drive wheel.

The engine protrudes from the rear of the cab but leaving a 1·117-metre long area for load carrying. Alternatively a small enclosed personnel or cargo shelter may be fitted. This shelter may overhang the tracks. A towing pintle is fitted as standard as are a wide variety of special fittings to enable the DMC 3700 to be operated in low temperatures. These include a cold-start facility, engine block heater and special cab heating.

DMC 3700 over-snow vehicle fitted with ten-way snow plough blade and personnel shelter behind cab

SPECIFICATIONS
Cab seating: 1
Weight: (empty) 4536 kg
Length: 4·547 m
Width:
  (body) 1·117 m
  (over 1·448 m tracks) 3·785 m
Height: (cab) 2·54 m
Track width: 1·448 m or 1·651 m
Ground clearance: 0·406 m

Track centres: (1·448 m track) 2·337 m
Fuel capacity: 162·7 litres
Gradient:
  (firm snow) 100%
  (soft snow) 60%
Engine: Allis Chalmers 6701 turbo-charged diesel developing 220 hp at 2400 rpm
Transmission: Sundstrand pumps and two-speed motors
Steering: hydrostatic, independent to each track

Turning radius: on own axis
Brakes: hydrostatic with emergency and parking multi-disc fail-safe

STATUS
Production. In service with the US Air Force (4).

MANUFACTURER
DMC, Logan Division, PO Box 407, Logan, Utah 84321, USA.

M973 Small Unit Support Vehicle (SUSV)

DEVELOPMENT/DESCRIPTION
During 1983 the US Army Tank-Automotive Command (TACOM) awarded a $24·2 million contract for 268 Bv 206 all-terrain carriers to be known as the Small Unit Supply Vehicle (SUSV). The contract followed a period of extensive trials carried out using a small trial batch of vehicles at the Cold Regions Test Centre at Fort Greely, Alaska. Most of the vehicles involved in the contract, delivered from Sweden in 1983 and 1984, were issued to the US Army's 172nd Infantry Brigade in Alaska. The M973 SUSVs will be powered by 3-litre four-stroke, five-cylinder in-line diesel engines developing 125 hp at 4500 rpm.

For details of the Bv 206 see separate entry in this section.

Bv 206 all-terrain carrier used for trials concerned with M973 Small Unit Support Vehicle (SUSV) (T J Gander)

M116 Tracked Over-snow Vehicle

DEVELOPMENT
By the early 1950s the M29C (Weasel) tracked over-snow vehicle, which was developed during the Second World War, was becoming expensive to maintain and operate. In 1952 a contract was awarded to the Studebaker Corporation, the original designer and manufacturer of the non-amphibious M29 and amphibious M29C vehicles, to design and build six prototypes of

a new amphibious cargo carrier, called the T107. Trials with the prototypes showed that a major redesign was necessary to overcome the many reported deficiencies. Concept studies of a new vehicle called the T116 began in September 1956 and were completed in December the same year. In May 1957 a contract was awarded to the Pacific Car and Foundry Company of Renton, Washington, for the design and construction of four prototype vehicles under the designation T116. These prototypes were powered by an air-cooled Continental

8AO-198 engine coupled to a Hydra-Matic model 198-M torque converter. As a result of trials two of the prototypes were rebuilt with a commercial powerpack consisting of a Chevrolet V-8 heavy duty truck engine coupled to a military standard Hydra-Matic transmission. Trials with these proved that the load-carrying and cross-country capabilities of the vehicle were a considerable improvement over the earlier vehicles. It was then decided to retrofit and update all the T116 vehicles, except the very first prototype, and at the same time

M116 showing amphibious capabilities (US Army)

M116 from above with top removed to show vehicle layout (US Army)

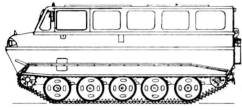

M116 tracked over-snow vehicle

correct all reported deficiencies and relocate and strengthen the suspension system to the more compatible design of a later companion vehicle, the XM476 missile servicing carrier. These three prototypes, when rebuilt, were redesignated the T116E1. In 1960 a further T116E1 was built for a special overseas requirement.

In June 1960 the Pacific Car and Foundry Company was awarded a contract for conversion of T116E1 R&D drawings, including incorporation of necessary product improvement, into a competitive ordnance procurement package, and the construction of three pre-production vehicles.

In December 1960 the T116E1 was type classified as Carrier, Cargo, Amphibious: M116, and the nickname Husky was adopted. At the same time the proposed uprating of the payload from ½ to 1½ tons was approved. The first production contract, for 197 vehicles, was awarded in December 1961.

DESCRIPTION
The M116 has been designed to carry cargo and/or passengers over roads, across country, sand, snow, ice, unfrozen tundra, muskeg, soft marsh, rock strewn areas and inland waterways, under all climatic conditions.

The hull is of all welded aluminium construction, reinforced with forged aluminium plates at critical areas. The driver is seated at the front of the vehicle on the left side with the engine mounted to his immediate rear. The passenger/cargo area is at the rear and has a single tailgate that unfolds downwards. Bench type seats can be fitted in the rear when it is being used to carry passengers. The vehicle can carry 11 men in winter gear or 13 in summer gear. The vehicle is normally fitted with a fully enclosed hard top which can be removed for air transport if required.

The suspension is of the torsion bar type and consists of five road wheels with the drive sprocket at the front and the idler at the rear. There are no track return rollers. A 2268 kg capacity winch is mounted at the front of the vehicle. The M116 is fully amphibious and is propelled in

M116 with fully enclosed cab (US Army)

the water by its tracks. It can be fitted with a winterisation kit, enabling it to operate in temperatures as low as minus 65°F.

VARIANTS
The M116 was modified to carry the Davy Crockett tactical nuclear system, which has now been withdrawn from service. For use in Viet-Nam a series of armoured vehicles was built under the Remote Area Mobility Study, including the XM729 and XM733, none of which was adopted for service.

SPECIFICATIONS
Cab seating: 1 + 11 (or 13)
Weight:
(empty) 3574 kg
(loaded) 5942 kg
Max load: 1360 kg
Towed load: 1088 kg
Length: 4·778 m
Width: 2·085 m
(over tracks) 1·993 m
Height:
(cab) 2·01 m
(reduced) 1·625 m
Ground clearance: 0·355 m

Track: 1·485 m
Track width: 508 mm
Length of track on ground: 2·616 m
Ground pressure: 0·22 kg/cm^2
Max speed:
(road) 59·5 km/h
(water) 6·43 km/h
Range: 480 km
Fuel capacity: 246 litres
Max gradient: 60%
Vertical obstacle: 0·457 m
Trench: 1·473 m
Fording: amphibious
Engine: Chevrolet 283 V-8 liquid-cooled petrol developing 160 hp at 4600 rpm
Gearbox: Detroit Transmission Division model 305 MC with 3 forward and reverse ranges
Electrical system: 24 V
Batteries: 4 × 12 V model 2HN

STATUS
Production complete. In service with the US Army.

MANUFACTURER
Pacific Car and Foundry Company, Renton, Washington, USA.

TRAILERS

Within each country, trailers appear in the following order:

general cargo trailers
tank-carrying trailers and flatbed type trailers used for
carrying engineer plant and armoured vehicles
tanker trailers
specialised trailers including those used for carrying
missiles, pontoons and radars

AUSTRALIA

Trailer, Cargo, 1-tonne, GS 2-wheel

DESCRIPTION
The Australian Army 1-tonne cargo trailer was developed concurrently with the Trailer, Chassis, Light MC2 (see following entry) to replace existing equipments in service. It is used for the carriage of general cargo, packaged POL, ammunition or missiles and stores. The box-body, with a hinged tail gate, is manufactured from aluminium and is demountable from the trailer chassis.

SPECIFICATIONS
Weight:
(loaded) 1510 kg
(empty) 510 kg

Max load: 1000 kg
Length:
(overall) 3·33 m
(body internal) 2·18 m
Width:
(overall) 2·06 m
(body internal) 1·95 m
Height:
(overall, loaded) 1·2 m
(overall, empty) 1·6 m
(body internal) 0·43 m
(lunette, loaded) 0·76 m
(lunette, empty) 0·87 m
(floor, loaded) 0·72 m
(floor, empty) 0·83 m

Track: 2 m
Suspension: semi-elliptic leaf springs with telescopic dampers and rubber bump stops
Brakes: hydraulic override
Tyres: 7.50 × 16
Electrical system: 12 V

STATUS
Production. In service with the Australian Army.

AGENCY
Department of Defence (Army Office), Engineering Development Establishment, Materiel Branch, PO Box E33, Queen Victoria Terrace, Canberra ACT 2600, Australia.

Trailer, cargo, 1-tonne, GS 2-wheel

Trailer, cargo, 1-tonne, GS 2-wheel

Trailer, Chassis, Light MC2 (1-tonne)

DEVELOPMENT
The Australian Army 1-tonne trailer chassis was developed to meet a requirement for the deployment of 10, 15 and 30 kVA generator sets in the field. Initially two variants were considered, a powered version and an unpowered version. After pilot model trials held in 1972–73 further development of the powered version was discontinued. Procurement detailing for the unpowered trailer began in 1976 and actual procurement was recommended in October 1980. Quantity production commenced in November 1980 and is still continuing.

DESCRIPTION
This trailer chassis is used for the carriage of twin-mounted 10 or 15 kVA generators, a single-mounted 30 kVA generator or the British-built hydrogen generator. It complies with all NATO standards and may be towed behind all wheeled vehicles from 1500 kg to 8000 kg capacity. The braking system is a mechanical/electrical override hydraulic system modified to operate with either 12 or 24 volt vehicle electrical systems. The trailer meets the requirements of Specification Army (Aust) 5798.

SPECIFICATIONS
Weight:
(loaded) 1500 kg
(empty) 500 kg

Length: 3·33 m
Width: 2·06 m
Height:
(loaded) 0·72 m
(empty) 0·83 m
Track: 2 m
Tyres: 7.50 × 16
Electrical system: 12 V or 24 V

STATUS
Production. In service with the Australian Army.

AGENCY
Department of Defence (Army Office), Engineering Development Establishment, Materiel Branch, PO Box E33, Queen Victoria Terrace, Canberra ACT 2600, Australia.

AUSTRIA

Goldhofer 25 000 kg Low Bed Trailer

DESCRIPTION
The Austrian Army uses this 3-axle, 12-wheel full trailer for the transportation of light AFVs of the Saurer 4K-7F and 4K-4F families and nearly all the engineer material used by the Austrian Army. The trailer is towed by the ÖAF 10-tonne 6 × 6 truck.

STATUS
Thirty trailers were supplied to the Austrian Army.

MANUFACTURER
Goldhofer, Austria.

CZECHOSLOVAKIA

Czechoslovak Heavy Transport Trailers
P-32, P-46, P-50 and P-80

These trailers are used for moving construction equipment and armoured vehicles and have unloading ramps at the rear of the trailer.

SPECIFICATIONS

Model		P-32	P-46	P-50	P-80
Weight	(empty)	10 600 kg	10 600 kg	16 200 kg	16 200 kg
	(loaded)	50 600 kg	56 600 kg	66 200 kg	79 200 kg
Payload		40 000 kg	46 000 kg	50 000 kg*	63 000 kg†
Length		9·474 m	9·5 m	10·715 m	10·7 m
	(of platform)	4·9 m	4·9 m	6·2 m	6·2 m
Width		3·1 m	3·1 m	3·1 m	3·1 m
Height		1·42 m	1·42 m	1·54 m	1·42 m
	(of platform)	1 m	1 m	1 m	1 m
Tyres		8.25 × 15	8.25 × 15	8.25 × 15	8.25 × 15
Number of axles		3	4	5	5
Towing speed		40 km/h	40 km/h	40 km/h	40 km/h

* Can be increased to 63 000 kg if towing speed is reduced to 10 km/h
† Can be increased to 80 000 kg if towing speed is reduced to 10 km/h

STATUS
In service with the Czechoslovak Army. The P-50 is also in service with the East German Army.

MANUFACTURER
Czechoslovak state factories.

Tatra 141 (6 × 6) prime mover towing P-32 trailer

FRANCE

Trailor 1100 kg Cross-country Cargo Trailer

DESCRIPTION
The Trailor 1100 kg cross-country cargo trailer is sometimes referred to as the Africa-type trailer and is intended for off-road use in remote areas. The frame of the trailer is constructed from two channel-shaped variable section high tensile steel beams on which a steel-bodied cargo carrier is placed, supported on one-piece cross-members. The body has steel sides 0·46 metre high that can be swung downwards for loading or may be removed altogether. The floor is also steel. To extend the height of the sides expanded metal extensions can be fitted to the sides and a tarpaulin cover may be fitted on bows. The axle is a 90 mm square beam and EEC-approved dual air brakes are fitted. Each trailer is equipped with a wheel nut wrench, a spare wheel carrier on the front panel, a tool box, a drinking water tank, a jerrican carrier and a rear stabilising strut. The trailer can be fitted with a fuel bowser or generating plant.

SPECIFICATIONS
Weight:
  (empty) 1400 kg
  (loaded) 2500 kg
Max load: 1100 kg
Length: 4·05 m
Width: 2·2 m
Height:
  (tarpaulin cover) 2·4 m
  (load area) 1 m
  (trail eye) 0·765 m
Load area: 2·71 × 2·06 m
Track: 1·953 m

Trailor 1100 kg cross-country cargo trailer

Suspension: Trailor single axle type SMU 7 SE with rubber-bushed radius rods, leaf springs and shock absorbers
Brakes: dual circuit air
Tyres: 8.25 × 20
Electrical system: 24 V

STATUS
Production. In service with several armed forces.

MANUFACTURER
Trailor SA, 5 route Nationale 10, Coignières 78311 Maurepas Cedex, France.

ACMAT RM 215S 1500 kg Cargo Trailer

DESCRIPTION
The ACMAT RM 215 series of trailers has been designed for maximum compatibility with the ACMAT range of vehicles. Each trailer has an integral 200-litre water tank and the standard specification includes eight jerricans and two sections of PSP-type sand channel. The RM 215S trailer is provided with canopy rails.

STATUS
In production.

MANUFACTURER
ACMAT, Ateliers de Construction Mécanique de l'Atlantique, Le Point du Jour, 44600 Saint-Nazaire, France.

ACMAT RM 215S 1500 kg cargo trailer

SPECIFICATIONS
Weight:
  (loaded) 2700 kg
  (empty) 1200 kg
Payload: 1500 kg
Length: (overall) 4·125 m

Width: 2·07 m
Height:
  (top of canopy rails) 2·4 m
  (load area) 1 m
Lunette height: 0·765 m
Internal clearance: (inside canopy) 1·4 m

Track: 1·74 m
Load area: 2·69 × 1·94 m
Suspension: semi-elliptical springs
Tyres: 12.50 × 20
Number of tyres: 2 + 1 spare

Titan T6 R2 3800 kg Trailer

DESCRIPTION
This two-axle trailer has been designed to carry a maximum load of 3800 kg or six standard pallets. The chassis is of all-steel construction. The floor is of light alloy sheet and has an anti-skid surface and tie down points. The ribbed sheet steel sides are of the drop down type and can be removed. The tailgate is similar and has an integral step. The front gate can be removed if required. Standard equipment includes air-line connection, parking brake on the rear axle, 12-pin (24 volt) socket, tool box, spare wheel and wheel chocks.

SPECIFICATIONS
Weight:
  (empty) 2200 kg
  (loaded) 6000 kg
Max load: 3800 kg
Length:
  (including tow bar) 6·3 m
  (excluding tow bar) 4·3 m
Width: 2·44 m
Height: 1·73 m
  (loading platform) 1·23 m

Titan T6 R2 3800 kg trailer

Ground clearance: 0·4 m
Load area: 4·26 × 2·4 m
Tyres: 10.50 × 20
Track: 1·86 m
Suspension: semi-elliptical springs

STATUS
Production.
MANUFACTURER
Titan SA, BP 407, 69400 Villefranche-sur-Saône, France.

Lohr RM16 16 000 kg Trailer

DESCRIPTION
This two-axle trailer, known as the Remorque Grande Capacité de 16 T PTC, has been designed specifically to meet the requirements of the Logistic Transport Squadrons of the French Army. The trailer has drop sides and a drop tailgate which can be quickly removed, bows that can be adjusted to any one of three heights and a quick banche system for the rapid uncovering of the load.

SPECIFICATIONS
Weight:
  (empty) 4280 kg
  (loaded) 16 000 kg
Max load: 11 720 kg
Length of platform: 6·3 m
Width of platform: 2·38 m

Lohr 16 000 kg trailer with sides and tailgate lowered

Tyres: 9.00 × 20
Number of tyres: 8

STATUS
In production. In service with the French Army.

Lohr 16 000 kg trailer complete with bows and cover

MANUFACTURER
Lohr SA, 67980 Hangenbieten, France.

Trailor 17 500 kg Semi-trailer

DESCRIPTION
This semi-trailer has been designed specifically to meet the requirements of the French Army and also meets current TIR requirements. The cargo area has eight drop sides (four each side), doors at the rear, bows and a tarpaulin cover. The floor is of wood and has retractable rings for securing cargo. The trailer is fitted with

dual air brakes, one line acting on each of the rear axles and a mechanical parking brake.

STATUS
In production. In service with the French Army.

MANUFACTURER
Trailor SA, 5 Route Nationale 10, Coignières, 78311 Maurepas, France.

SPECIFICATIONS
Weight:
  (empty) 5500 kg
  (loaded) 23 000 kg
Max load: 17 500 kg
Load area: 11·31 × 2·5 m
Tyres: 8 + 1 spare

Decauville SRPC 36/46-tonne Tank Transporter Semi-trailer

DESCRIPTION
This semi-trailer has been designed for transporting MBTs such as the AMX-30, Leopard 1, M47, T-54/T-55, T-62 and similar tanks. Its chassis consists of two longitudinal girders connected by crossbars and gussets, with a serrated steel sheet covering. Two loading ramps are provided at the rear of the trailer.

The suspension consists of four axles on oscillating balance bars. Air brakes are fitted on all wheels and a mechanical parking brake is provided. Shoe type stabilisers are provided at the front of the trailer.

Standard equipment includes stowage boxes, front roller, adjustable blocks and a jack. Optional equipment includes hydraulically-operated rear loading ramps, rear rollers, shrouded pulley wheels, drinking water tank, jerrican support racks and a camouflage net.

STATUS
In production. Has been exported to a number of countries in the Middle East.

MANUFACTURER
Decauville SA, BP38, 91102 Corbeil-Essonnes, France.

Decauville SRPC 36/46-tonne tank transporter semi-trailer carrying AMX-30 MBT

SPECIFICATIONS
Weight:
    (empty) 12 900 kg
    (loaded) 58 900 kg
Max load: 46 000 kg
Length:
    (overall) 12·05 m
    (of platform) 7·35 m

Width:
    (overall) 3·65 m
    (of loading ramps) 0·62 m
Height: (over loading ramps in vertical position) 2·6 m
Ground clearance:
    (under axles) 0·35 m
    (under front of semi-trailer) 1·65 m
Wheelbase: (from king-pin to centre of rear bogie) 9 m

Max towing speed: 60 km/h
Tyres: 9.00 × 20 or 12.00 × 20
Number of tyres: 16 + 2 spare

Decauville SRPC 48/54-tonne Tank Transporter Semi-trailer

DESCRIPTION
This semi-trailer has been designed for transporting MBTs such as the Chieftain, Centurion and M60. Its chassis consists of two longitudinal girders connected by crossbars and gussets, with a serrated sheet steel covering. Two loading ramps are provided at the rear of the trailer.

The suspension consists of four axles on oscillating balance bars. Air brakes are fitted on all wheels and a parking brake is provided. Shoe type stabilisers are provided under the front of the trailer. Standard equipment includes stowage boxes, shackles, front rollers, adjustable blocks and a jack. Optional equipment includes hydraulically-operated rear loading ramps, rear rollers, shrouded pulley wheels, drinking water tank, jerrican support racks and a camouflage net.

SPECIFICATIONS
Weight:
    (empty) 14 000 kg
    (loaded) 68 000 kg
Max load: 54 000 kg
Length:
    (overall) 12·05 m
    (of platform) 7·35 m
Width:
    (trailer) 3·65 m
    (of loading ramps) 0·62 m
Height: (over loading ramps in vertical position) 2·6 m

Decauville SRPC 48/54-tonne tank transporter semi-trailer with M47 MBT

Ground clearance:
    (under axles) 0·35 m
    (under front of semi-trailer) 1·65 m
Wheelbase: (from king-pin to centre of rear bogie) 9 m
Max towing speed: 60 km/h
Tyres: 11.00 × 20 or 12.00 × 20
Number of tyres: 16 + 2 spare

STATUS
Prototype completed. Ready for production.

MANUFACTURER
Decauville SA, BP38, 91102 Corbeil-Essonnes, France.

Other Decauville Trailers

In addition to manufacturing tank semi-trailers, Decauville manufactures a variety of other trailers, some of which are suitable for military use, including the following:

Truck bed semi-trailers with removable sides and tailgate with capacities ranging from 8000 to 52 000 kg.
Truck bed trailers with capacities ranging from 8000 to 30 000 kg.

STATUS
Production.

MANUFACTURER
Decauville SA, BP38, 91102 Corbeil-Essonnes, France.

Fruehauf Medium Tank Transporter Semi-trailer

DESCRIPTION
This semi-trailer has been designed for long distance transportation of tanks weighing up to 45 000 kg. The trailer has manually-operated 0·6-metre wide rear loading ramps, removable track guides and heavy duty manually-operated stabilisers mounted towards the

front. It can be towed on roads at a maximum speed of 80 km/h.

STATUS
In production. In service with at least one army outside France.

MANUFACTURER
Fruehauf France, 2 avenue de l'Aunette, 91130 Ris-Orangis, France.

SPECIFICATIONS
Max load: 45 000 kg
Length:
    (overall) 11·75 m
    (of loading platform) 7·92 m
Width: 3·1 m
King-pin size: 89 mm
Tyres: 8.25 × 15
Number of tyres: 16

Fruehauf medium tank transporter semi-trailer

Fruehauf medium tank transporter semi-trailer

Fruehauf Heavy Tank Transporter Semi-trailer

DESCRIPTION
This semi-trailer has been designed for carrying tanks weighing up to 60 000 kg. The trailer has manually operated 0·6-metre wide rear loading ramps, removable track guides, and heavy duty manually-operated stabilisers mounted towards the front of the trailer.

SPECIFICATIONS
Max load: 60 000 kg
Length:
    (overall) 12·5 m
    (of loading platform) 7 m
Width: 3·6 m
King-pin size: 89 mm
Tyres: 12.00 × 20
Number of tyres: 16

STATUS
In production. In service with at least one country outside France.

MANUFACTURER
Fruehauf France, 2 avenue de l'Aunette, 91130 Ris-Orangis, France.

Fruehauf heavy tank transport semi-trailer

Lohr SMC Tank Transporter Semi-trailers

DESCRIPTION
There are three semi-trailers in the Lohr SMC range, the SMC 60 DT, the SMC 60 RD and the SMC 40 PL. The SMC 60 DT has a maximum load of 60 000 kg and uses a hydraulically-operated rear ramp. The SMC 60 RD also has a maximum load of 60 000 kg but uses manually-lifted ramps. The SMC 40 PL has a maximum load of 44 000 kg and uses manually-lifted ramps.

On all three models the chassis and deck are made of all-welded steel and the suspension consists of twin unsprung walking beams on which are mounted the eight tyres. Winch cable guides and rollers are fitted and there are also guide blocks for the tracks of the vehicles being loaded. Spare wheels are carried under the loading deck.

STATUS
In production.

MANUFACTURER
Lohr SA, 67980 Hangenbieten, France.

SPECIFICATIONS

Model	SMC 60 DT	SMC 60 RD	SMC 40 PL
Weight (loaded)	78 500 kg	77 000 kg	60 000 kg
Maximum load	60 000 kg	60 000 kg	44 000 kg
Length	13·05 m	12·05 m	12·93 m
Length of load on deck	7·215 m	6·6 m	7·76 m
Length of overhang at rear	1·9 m	1·75 m	1·52 m
Height of load deck	1·54 m	1·38 m	1·35 m
Width	4·13 m	3·4 m	3·3 m
Tyres	24.00 × 20.5 sand	18.00 × 22.5 sand	13.00 × 20 P
Electrical system	24 V	24 V	24 V

Lohr SMC 60 tank transporter semi-trailer with ramps raised

Nicolas Tank Transporter Semi-trailers

DESCRIPTION
Nicolas Industrie SA manufactures a wide range of semi-trailers for military and commercial use and it recently expanded its military range by the introduction of a wide range of tank transporter trailers. The new range includes 14 separate models in place of the six previously offered and vary in payload from 16 500 kg up to 95 000 kg. The various semi-trailers differ not only in size but also in the number of short axles used, the tyre sizes and the number of tanks that can be carried. Two of the smaller models (the STAD 30.15 and the STAL 30.20) can each carry two light tanks of the AMX-13 type, while the STA 100 can carry two AMX-30 tanks using eight axle units and 32 tyres. The full range of models and their main characteristics can be seen on the Model table.

A typical example from the range is the STA S 60.20.5. This model can be used to carry most models of main battle tank in service and is mainly constructed from high tensile steel. The loading deck has two central main beams and two side rails connected by welded beams of 'I' section high tensile steel. The steel decking is 2 mm thick apart from the main channels which are 6 to 8 mm thick. Panels over the twin axles can be removed for access. A 250 mm adjustment for width is possible on the loading ramps which fold upwards for travelling and an optional hydraulic lift mechanism is available. The axles have a 10 degree oscillation and air brakes are used. One spare wheel is provided with an optional rack for another and a small crane is provided for handling the spare wheel. Optional equipment includes a tool box, cable guides on the goose-neck, lashing chains, blocks, track guides, black-out lighting and fuel and water tanks.

VARIANTS
Nicolas Industries SA has introduced a type of tank transporter semi-trailer with powered rear axles for use with its Tractomas tractor trucks. By varying the type of Tractomas tractor and the type of powered semi-trailer, loads of 40 000, 50 000 or 60 000 kg can be carried.

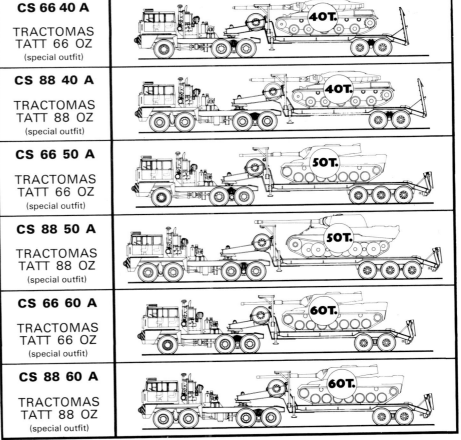

CS 66 40 A	
TRACTOMAS TATT 66 OZ (special outfit)	
CS 88 40 A	
TRACTOMAS TATT 88 OZ (special outfit)	
CS 66 50 A	
TRACTOMAS TATT 66 OZ (special outfit)	
CS 88 50 A	
TRACTOMAS TATT 88 OZ (special outfit)	
CS 66 60 A	
TRACTOMAS TATT 66 OZ (special outfit)	
CS 88 60 A	
TRACTOMAS TATT 88 OZ (special outfit)	

Range of powered axle semi-trailers used with Nicolas Industrie SA Tractomas truck tractors

Renault TRH 350 (6 × 4) tractor towing Nicolas STA 43 semi-trailer

The hydraulically-powered axles provide extra traction and power when travelling with loads across country and across soft terrain such as sand. All types can travel at 7 km/h with the power-assist facility selected. All the semi-trailers use 24 × 20.5 tyres and the number of axles used may be two or three per side.

The hydraulic system used to power the wheels of the semi-trailer is based on the use of a three-part motor produced by Poclain. One part is the cylinder block which supports the hydraulic cylinders and the associated rollers. The rollers controlled by the hydraulic cylinders press on cams on the second part which is the motor casing fastened onto the hub. Pressure on the cam makes the hub and wheel turn. When not in use the rollers are retracted and held away from the cams by springs. The third section of the motor is the timing section. The entire motor can be removed without removal of the wheel or any part of the axle. Power for the motor comes from a multi-cylinder pump on a declutchable power take-off on the gear box. Each cylinder of the pump feeds one axle motor. The system is operated from a remote control box carried in the vehicle cab.

SPECIFICATIONS (STA S 60.20.5 only)
Weight:
(empty) 17 000 kg
(on fifth wheel) 21 000 kg
(on axles) 56 000 kg
Max load: 60 000 kg
Max gross weight: 77 000 kg
Length:
(ramp folded) 13·1 m
(loading deck) 7·2 m
(loading ramp) 2·875 m
Width:
(overall) 4·195 m
(goose-neck) 2·5 m
(loading ramps) 0·8 m
Height:
(loading deck) 1·6 m
(fifth wheel) 1·8 m
Wheelbase: (5th wheel to centre of axle unit) 9·12 m
Tyres: 24 × 20.5
Number of tyres: 8 + 1 spare
Electrical system: 24 V

STATUS
The company is currently building several hundred STA 45.15 semi-trailers for the French Army.

MANUFACTURER
Nicolas Industrie SA, 89290 Champs-sur-Yonne, France.

LIST OF MODELS

Model	Weight* (empty)	Length*	Height (platform)	Payload*	Load* (5th wheel)	Load* (rear axle)	Axles (pairs)	Tyres (number)
STA 18.15	6000 kg	9·815 m	0·89 m	17 500 kg	7800 kg	15 700 kg	2	8.25 × 15 (8)
STA 18.20	6300 kg	9·815 m	1·1 m	17 500 kg	7800 kg	16 000 kg	2	9.00 × 20 (8)
STA D 30.15	12 000 kg	14·515 m	1·17 m	30 000 kg	15 000 kg	30 000 kg	3	10.00 × 15 (12)
STA L 30.20	10 500 kg	14·615 m	1·29 m	33 000 kg	15 500 kg	28 000 kg	2	12.00 × 20 (8)
STA 45.15	10 600 kg	10·815 m	0·998 m	45 000 kg	19 600 kg	36 000 kg	2	8.25 × 15 (16)
STA 40.20	10 800 kg	10·815 m	1·29 m	38 000 kg	15 800 kg	33 000 kg	2	12.00 × 20 (8)
STA 3 35.15	10 400 kg	11·115 m	0·83 m	40 400 kg	14 000 kg	31 500 kg	3	8.25 × 15 (12)
STA 3 45.22.5	11 200 kg	11·115 m	1·27 m	43 000 kg	17 200 kg	37 000 kg	3	18 × 22.5 (6)
STA 40.24	11 600 kg	11·915 m	1·38 m	40 000 kg	19 600 kg	32 000 kg	2	12.00 × 24 (8)
STA 50.20	12 600 kg	1·915 m	1·39 m	50 600 kg	21 600 kg	42 000 kg	3	12.00 × 20 (12)
STA 3 45.15	11 500 kg	11·115 m	1·17 m	44 500 kg	17 000 kg	39 000 kg	3	10.00 × 15 (12)
STA S 60.20.5	17 000 kg	12·62 m	1·6 m	60 000 kg	21 000 kg	56 000 kg	2	24 × 20.55 (8)
STA 60.20	16 500 kg	11·5 m	1·36 m	58 000 kg	22 500 kg	52 000 kg	2	12.00 × 20 (16)
STA 100	20 000 kg	18·215 m	1·15 m	95 000 kg	27 000 kg	88 000 kg	4	8.25 × 15 (32)

* approximate figures

Titan Tank Transporter Semi-trailers

DESCRIPTION
Titan offers two tank-carrying semi-trailers. The smaller has a capacity of 45 000 kg and has been designed for carrying tanks such as the AMX-30 and Leopard, and the larger has a capacity of 55 000 kg and has been designed for carrying tanks such as the British Chieftain.

The chassis consists of two laminated steel main bearers with the cross-members welded into position. The platform consists of full width steel section cross-members and side rails covered in chequered steel flooring. Traps give access to the axles. Two doors in the gooseneck give access to the tool box. The rear loading ramps are in two articulated parts, and a balance spring is fitted to assist in raising the ramps. The ramps are locked once raised.

Standard equipment includes air brake connection, parking brakes on each of the axles, spare wheel holder and tool box in the gooseneck, lashing rings, adjustable track guides and blocks, guide cables, tool kit, 12-pin (24 volt) socket, and telescopic, two-speed landing system with separate crank handle controls.

STATUS
Production.

MANUFACTURER
Titan SA, BP 407, 69400 Villefranche-sur-Saône, France.

Titan tank transporter semi-trailer with one rear loading ramp lowered

SPECIFICATIONS

Model	45	55
Weight (empty)	14 000 kg	17 000 kg
(loaded)	59 000 kg	72 000 kg
Max load	45 000 kg	55 000 kg
Length (overall)	12·61 m	13·6 m
(of platform)	7·9 m	8·64 m
Width	3·15 m	3·65 m
Height of platform (loaded)	1·15 m	1·32 m
King-pin size	89 mm	89 mm
Tyres	9.00 × 20	12.00 × 20
Number of tyres	16	16

Trailor Tank Transporter Semi-trailers

DESCRIPTION
There are three Trailor tank transporters and all are similar, differing only in load capacities and tyre sizes. All are of conventional two-axle configuration, with all-steel frames and decks. Three-line air braking and 3½-inch (89 mm) king-pins are standard and each trailer also has adequate track guides, chocks and winch cable rollers. The rear loading ramps are spring-balanced and mechanically operated.

STATUS
Production complete.

MANUFACTURER
Trailor SA, 5 Route Nationale 10, B P 49, 78311 Maurepas, France.

SPECIFICATIONS

Model	54T	62T	74T
Length	12·96 m	11·95 m	12·97 m
Width	3·1 m	–	–
Deck length	6·6 m	5·18 m	6·15 m
Capacity	38 000 kg	45 000 kg	55 000 kg
Tyres	7.50 × 15	E20 size	12.00 × 20
Number of tyres	16	16	16

Trailor 54T tank transporter semi-trailer

Trailor 62T tank transporter semi-trailer

ACMAT ALM Saharian Trailer Model RM 215 SC 1250-litre Tanker

DESCRIPTION

This trailer may be used to carry water, petrol or oil in a 1250-litre steel-plated tank. The tank, together with its associated stowage boxes, is carried in a 2 mm thick steel body on the standard ACMAT ALM Saharian trailer chassis. A Japy manual pump is fitted as standard but for the petrol version a reel with piping and connection pipes are carried. For the water tanker version a filter system is supplied. A 4-litre fire extinguisher is also carried with the petrol tanker version.

Standard fittings carried on all types of trailer include one spare wheel, stowage for eight jerricans, a tool set (in two boxes) and sand channels. Oil and air brakes are standard and a mechanical hand brake is also fitted for parking. A jockey wheel with a diameter of 0·4 metre is fitted.

SPECIFICATIONS
Weight:
  (loaded) 2850 kg
  (empty) 1600 kg
Max load: 1250 kg
Capacity of tank: 1250 litres
Length: 4·125 m
Width: 2·07 m
Height:
  (overall) 1·915 m
  (lunette) 0·765 m
Track: 1·71 m
Tyres: 12.00 × 16 TGS or 12.5 × 20 XL

ACMAT ALM Saharian trailer Model RM 215 SC

STATUS
In production.

MANUFACTURER
ACMAT, Ateliers de Construction Mécanique de l'Atlantique, Le Point du Jour, 44600 Saint-Nazaire, France.

Fruehauf 20 000-litre Tanker Semi-trailer

DESCRIPTION

This semi-trailer has been designed for transporting various fuels including petrol and has remote controlled drainage pipes with safety valves, pump operated by auxiliary engine, shielded electrical system, manually operated stabilisers mounted towards the front of the trailer and external fully enclosed containers on either side of the tank for stowage of fuel pipes.

SPECIFICATIONS
Capacity: 20 000 litres
Length: 9·92 m
Width: 2·5 m
King-pin size: 89 mm
Tyres: 12.00 × 20

STATUS
In production. In service with the French Army.

MANUFACTURER
Fruehauf France, 2 avenue de l'Aunette, 91130 Ris-Orangis, France.

Fruehauf 20 000-litre tanker semi-trailer

Trailor Tanker Semi-trailers

DESCRIPTION
The 30 000-litre tank is of all aluminium construction and has two compartments, upper and lower. The top of the tank is provided with a non-skid walkway and hand rails. The trailer has two-speed manually-operated telescopic stabilisers, hoses, hose racks and hose winder, air brakes (one line acting on each axle) and a shielded electrical system.

The 37 500-litre tank is of all aluminium construction and has five compartments. Other equipment is similar to that fitted to the 30 000-litre tanker.

SPECIFICATIONS

	30 000 litres	37 500 litres
Capacity	30 000 litres	37 500 litres
Length	10·36 m	12·36 m
Width	2·5 m	2·5 m
Tyres	18.00 × 22.5	18.00 × 22.5

STATUS
In production. In service with the French Army.

MANUFACTURER
Trailor SA, 5 Route Nationale 10, Coignières, 78311 Maurepas, France.

ACMAT RM 215 GCR Trailer-mounted Field Kitchen

DESCRIPTION
The RM 215 GCR is an airportable, trailer-mounted field kitchen capable of serving 350 meals in two hours. The kitchen equipment is mounted on a standard ACMAT trailer chassis, as described previously in this section.

The kitchen is equipped with four 100-litre cooking containers and may be fired by wood or diesel fuel, depending upon availability. Ovens or heating plates can be substituted for cooking containers. The equipment can also be butane-fired.

In the working position, the kitchen is surrounded by folding walkways and protected by a canvas/nylon canopy. A 400-litre water tank is incorporated in the trailer chassis and four jerricans are also carried. A fuel tank is incorporated and this allows over three hours continuous cooking on all burners. Two utensil cupboards and two working surfaces are also included and a jib and block are provided for handling cooking pots.

STATUS
In production.

MANUFACTURER
ACMAT, Ateliers de Construction Mécanique de l'Atlantique, Le Point du Jour, 44600 Saint-Nazaire, France.

SPECIFICATIONS
On tow
Weight: (laden) 2870 kg
Length: (overall) 4·225 m
Body length: 2·8 m
Height: (overall) 2·4 m
Width: (overall) 2·07 m
Track: 1·71 m
Lunette height: 0·765 m
Working position
Cooking area: 1·7 × 1·25 m
Walking area: 4·12 × 3·45 m
Height above ground: 1 m
Height: (overall) 4·3 m

ACMAT RM 215 GCR trailer-mounted field kitchen in working configuration

ACMAT RM 215 GCR trailer-mounted field kitchen in travelling order

ARE 2-tonne F2 Ammunition Trailer

DESCRIPTION
The F2 trailer has been designed to fill the need for additional ammunition to accompany the 155-mm self-propelled gun. It is specifically designed to be towed by the AMX-13 VCA which normally transports the gun detachment and some ammunition. The body is steel and is open at the top, although the sides provide a slight measure of ballistic protection to the contents. Removable racks and cases provide stowage for 30 155-mm projectiles and charges and six hinged cases for storing warhead fuze containers. The rear door is hinged along its base, forming a working platform when open and a water-tight seal when closed, allowing the trailer to ford to a depth of about one metre. The wheels are fitted with bullet-proof tyres and are mounted on torsion bars. By removing the ammunition racks the trailer may be used for general cargo.

SPECIFICATIONS
Length: 4·8 m
Width: 2·5 m
Height: 1·465 m
Weight:
(empty) 2500 kg
(loaded) 4400 kg
Capacity: 2·9 m³
Ground clearance: 0·48 m

STATUS
In service with the French Army.

MANUFACTURER
Creusot-Loire, 15 rue Pasquier, 75383 Paris Cedex 08, France.

ARE 2-tonne F2 ammunition trailer (ECPA)

GERMANY, DEMOCRATIC REPUBLIC

East German Heavy Transport Trailers TL-20, SL-40 and SL-60

DESCRIPTION

These trailers are used for moving construction equipment and armoured vehicles. The smallest trailer, the TL-20, has no ramps at the rear and the four-wheeled axle has to be removed before loading can begin. The SL-60 is normally towed by a KrAZ-214 6 × 6 truck.

STATUS

In service with the East German Army.

MANUFACTURER

East German state factories.

SPECIFICATIONS

Model	TL-20	SL-40	SL-60
Weight			
(empty)	8660 kg	11 000 kg	16 900 kg
(loaded)	28 660 kg	51 000 kg	74 400 kg
Max load	20 000 kg	40 000 kg*	57 500 kg
Length	10·9 m	n/a	11·73 m
(of platform)	5·2 m	5·8 m	5·65 m
Model	TL-20	SL-40	SL-60
Width	2·82 m	2·9 m	3·27 m
Height			
(of platform)	0·85 m	1·05 m	1·2 m
Tyres	11.00 × 20	8.25 × 15	8.25 × 15
Number of axles	2	3	3
Towing speed	20 km/h	32 km/h	8 km/h

* If speed is kept to 20 km/h max load can be increased to 45 000 kg

GERMANY, FEDERAL REPUBLIC

West German Military Trailers

Little information is available on the new range of trailers which forms part of the West German military transport programme. The information available is summarised below.

Description	Designation	Length	Width	Height	Weight	Payload	Prime mover	Manufacturer	Notes
–	–	–	–	–	–	1-6 tonnes	–	Kässbohrer	range of 2- and 4-wheel trailers for general cargo, bridge and assault boat transport
Trailer, cargo, 1·5-tonne, 2-wheel	–	4·11 m	2·09 m	1·07 m	0·98 tonnes	1·72 tonnes	3-7 tonne trucks	–	earlier range
Trailer, cargo, 6-tonne, 4-wheel	–	6·96 m	2·5 m	1·27 m	3·51 tonnes	6·19 tonnes	3-7 tonne trucks	–	earlier range
Semi-trailer, platform, 15-tonne, 2-axle	SAL 31.16/ 119.4z	–	–	–	–	15 tonnes	MAN 4 × 4 15.240 FAS	Blumhardt	
Semi-trailer, low bed, 25-tonne 3-axle	TL-SAL 38.22/109z	–	–	–	–	25 tonnes	Magirus-Deutz 320 D22 FS 6 × 4	Blumhardt	
Semi-trailer, low bed, 25-tonne 2-axle	–	13·72 m	2·9 m	–	12·1 tonnes	25 tonnes	Faun 25 tonnes	–	earlier range
Trailer, low bed, 25-tonne 16-wheel	–	14·75 m	2·5 m	2 m	15·2 tonnes	25 tonnes	Faun 12 tonnes	–	earlier range 4-axle full trailer
Semi-trailer, tank transporter, 50-tonne, 2-axle	–	14·75 m	2·5 m	–	15·2 tonnes	50 tonnes	Faun 25 tonnes	–	earlier range
Semi-trailer, low bed, 56-tonne, 6-axle	–	–	–	–	–	56 tonnes	Faun MFS 42 75/42, 8 × 6	Kässbohrer	low mobility
Semi-trailer, tank, fuel 24 000-litre	–	–	–	–	–	–	Magirus-Deutz 320 D22 FS	Kroll	for airfield use replaces earlier 18 000-litre model
Semi-trailer, tank, fuel 30 000-litre	–	–	–	–	–	–	Magirus-Deutz 320 D22 FS	Kroll	for road use

SLT 50-2 Tank Transporter Semi-trailer

DEVELOPMENT

In 1965 West Germany and the United States agreed on the joint development of a tank transporter for the MBT-70. The firm of Krupp was responsible for the design of the trailer. Even before the cancellation of the MBT-70 project each country had decided to go its own way on the design of the tank transporter, although in major design features the versions of both looked very similar. The SLT 50-2 semi-trailer (Schwerlast-transporter, or heavy load carrier) was adopted by the Federal German Army and 328 were ordered. The US Army version was standardised as the M747 (qv).

DESCRIPTION

The semi-trailer has four axles, each with two single-tyred steerable wheels. Steering of the wheels is hydraulically controlled and depends on the angle between the tractor and semi-trailer. Each axle is independently suspended on semi-leaf springs which also locate the axles. Swing arms and a connecting linkage provide for load equalisation and an additional mechanism allows the load platform to be lowered by about 0·1 metre to the required underpass height of 3·9 metres when loaded. All four axles are equipped with air brakes and parking brakes are fitted to two axles.

The load platform has a frame of box construction to resist longitudinal flexing and a bearing surface of sandwich construction. Folding, spring-balanced ramps are fitted and make an angle of only 14 degrees for loading, yet may be lifted by only two men. Cable guides are provided on the trailer gooseneck to assist in winching loads on and off the trailer.

STATUS

Production complete. In service with the West German Army.

MANUFACTURER

Karl Kässbohrer Fahrzeugwerke GmbH, Postfach 2660, 7900 Ulm/Donau, West Germany.

SPECIFICATIONS

Length: (overall) 13·1 m
Width: 3·15 m
Track: 2·65 m
Height: (to top of raised ramps) 3·15 m
Fifth wheel height: (loaded) 1·55 m
Loading platform
Length: 8 m
Height:
(unloaded) 1·37 m
(loaded) 1·28 m
(loaded, lowered) 1·16 m
Ground clearance: 0·31 m
Departure angle: 35°
Weight: 16 600 kg
Max load: 52 000 kg
Axle loadings:
(loaded) 13 000 kg
(unloaded) 3478 kg
Turning circle radius: (with SLT 50-2 tractor) 9 m
Tyres: 18.00 × 22.5, 20 PR
Ramps:
(length) 4·18 m
(width) 0·75 m each
King-pin: 89 mm

ITALY

Bartoletti One-axle 1000 kg Cargo Trailer Type B.10

DESCRIPTION
This single-axle trailer has an all steel body with drop tailgate, canvas supports and canvas cover, leaf spring suspension, 510 mm disc wheels, hydraulic overrun brakes, 12 pole 24 volt electric system, standard and blackout lights and a retractable dolly wheel.

SPECIFICATIONS
Weight:
(empty) 750 kg
(loaded) 1750 kg
Max load: 1000 kg
Inside length of body: 2·445 m
Inside width of body: 1·165 m
Height of side boards: 0·46 m
Length: 3·72 m
Width: 1·81 m,
Height: 1·8 m
Track: 1·51 m
Tyres: 8.25 × 20
Number of tyres: 2 + 1 spare

Bartoletti one-axle 1000 kg cargo trailer type B.10 with canvas cover

STATUS
Production.

MANUFACTURER
E Bartoletti, Via Leonardo Da Vinci 4, 47100 Forli, Italy.

Bartoletti One-axle 2000 kg Cargo Trailer

DESCRIPTION
This single-axle trailer can be fitted with a variety of different bodies and used for specialised applications such as carrying radar. The trailer has semi-elliptic simple flexible leaf spring suspension with hydraulic dampers, 510 mm disc wheels, compressed air two-line (automatically adjustable) brake booster, 12 pole 24 volt electric system, standard and blackout lights, removable screw type dolly wheel and two stabilisers that can be lowered at the rear.

SPECIFICATIONS
Weight:
(empty) 1000 kg
(loaded) 3000 kg
Payload: 2000 kg
Length:
(including towbar) 4·19 m
(excluding towbar) 2·3 m
Width: 2·07 m
Chassis width: 1·35 m
Height to upper edge of chassis: 1 m
Track: 1·77 m
Tyres: 11.00 × 20
Number of tyres: 2 + 1 spare

STATUS
Production.

Bartoletti one-axle 2000 kg cargo trailer

MANUFACTURER
E Bartoletti, Via Leonardo Da Vinci 4, 47100 Forli, Italy.

Bartoletti 3000 kg Light Cargo Trailer Type 2L-30 M

DESCRIPTION
This all steel trailer has drop sides and a drop tailgate with the front axle mounted on a ball type turntable, simple flexible semi-elliptic leaf spring suspension, 380 mm spoke wheels, 12 pole 24 volt electric system, standard and blackout lights, and a compressed air two-line (automatically adjustable) brake booster.

SPECIFICATIONS
Weight:
(empty) 1300 kg
(loaded) 4300 kg
Payload: 3000 kg
Length:
(including towbar) 4·325 m
(excluding towbar) 3 m
Width: 1·56 m
Height of deck from ground: (loaded) 0·92 m
Height of side boards: 0·4 m
Track: 1·295 m
Tyres: 7.50 × 15
Number of tyres: 4 + 1 spare

Bartoletti 3000 kg light cargo trailer type 2L-30 M

STATUS
Production.

MANUFACTURER
E Bartoletti, Via Leonardo Da Vinci 4, 47100 Forli, Italy.

Bartoletti One-axle Flat Bed Trailer Type B.40 MGB

DESCRIPTION
This single-axle trailer has been designed for the transportation of components of the British Fairey Medium Girder Bridge. The trailer has semi-elliptic flexible leaf spring suspension, 510 mm disc wheels, compressed air two-line (automatically adjustable) brake booster, 12 pole 24 volt electric system, standard and blackout lights and a removable screw type loading gear. Stabilisers are mounted at the rear of the trailer.

STATUS
Production. In service with the Italian Army.

MANUFACTURER
E Bartoletti, Via Leonardo Da Vinci 4, 47100 Forli, Italy.

SPECIFICATIONS
Weight:
  (empty) 1600 kg
  (loaded) 5700 kg

Bartoletti one-axle flat bed trailer type B.40 MGB

Max load: 4100 kg
Length:
  (with towbar) 5·5 m
  (without towbar) 3·6 m
Width: 2·5 m

Deck width: 2·31 m
Deck height from ground: (loaded) 1·145 m
Track: 2·05 m
Tyres: 11.00 × R20
Number of tyres: 2 + 1 spare

Bartoletti 24 000 kg Container Transport Trailer Type 24 RD

DESCRIPTION
This two-axle trailer has a flat deck designed for the transportation of standard 20 ft ISO containers, or general cargo. The trailer has semi-elliptic double flexible leaf springs on silent blocks with stabilisers, 510 mm disc wheels, 12 pole 24 volt electric system, standard and blackout lights and compressed air two-line (automatically adjustable) brake booster.

SPECIFICATIONS
Weight:
  (empty) 4750 kg
  (loaded) 24 000 kg
Payload: 19 250 kg
Length:
  (deck) 6·5 m
  (including towbar) 8·505 m
Width:
  (overall) 2·5 m
  (deck) 2·4 m
Height of deck from ground level: 1·29 m
Tyres: 12.00 × 20 PR 18
Number of tyres: 8 + 1 spare

Bartoletti 24 000 kg container transport trailer type 24 RD

STATUS
Production.

MANUFACTURER
E Bartoletti, Via Leonardo Da Vinci 4, 47100 Forli, Italy.

Bartoletti 1800-litre Water Tanker Type B.10

DESCRIPTION
This single axle trailer has an 1800-litre capacity drinkable water tank, 500 mm diameter safety manhole, gravity outlet through a 65 mm gate valve and 26 mm faucets, leaf spring suspension, 510 mm disc wheels, hydraulic overrun brake, 12 pole 24 volt electric system with standard blackout lights and a retractable dolly wheel.

SPECIFICATIONS
Weight:
  (empty) 1000 kg
  (loaded) 2800 kg
Max load: 1800 kg
Length: (including towbar) 3·72 m
Width: 1·81 m
Track: 1·51 m
Tyres: 8.25 × 20
Number of tyres: 2 + 1 spare
Maximum diameter of tank: 1·46 m
Minimum diameter of tank: 0·86 m
Height of tank: 2 m

STATUS
Production.

Bartoletti 1800-litre water tanker type B.10

MANUFACTURER
E Bartoletti, Via Leonardo Da Vinci 4, 47100 Forli, Italy.

Bartoletti 8000-litre Fuel Tanker Trailer Type 2M-55

DESCRIPTION
The front axle of this two-axle trailer is mounted on a turntable. The oval section tank is of all-steel construction and is provided with a single 255 mm loading mouth, metric rod and fuel level indicator, remote controlled foot valve, 80 mm gate valves with quick coupling mouth and standard accessories.

SPECIFICATIONS
Weight:
  (empty) 4200 kg
  (loaded) 11 000 kg
Max load: 6800 kg

Length:
  (including towbar) 7·32 m
  (trailer only) 5·75 m
Width: 2·47 m
Height: 2·84 m
Track: 1·727 m
Tyres: 12.00 × 20 PR 18
Number of tyres: 8 + 1 spare

STATUS
Production.

MANUFACTURER
E Bartoletti, Via Leonardo Da Vinci 4, 47100 Forli, Italy.

Bartoletti 8000-litre fuel tanker trailer type 2M-55

Bartoletti 2PX Trailer

DESCRIPTION
The trailer has been designed for the transportation of tracked vehicles such as armoured fighting vehicles and engineering equipment. The trailer has aligned axles on independent dollies, low bed, steering by means of equaliser and guide arms, sliding rear dollies with jacks, simple flexible semi-elliptical oscillating leaf spring suspension, 510 mm spoke wheels, 12 pole 24 volt electric system, standard and blackout lights, compressed air two-line (automatically adjustable) brake booster and rear loading ramps.

SPECIFICATIONS
Weight:
(empty) 7350 kg
(loaded) 27 350 kg
Payload: 20 000 kg
Length:
(including towbar) 9·56 m
(trailer only) 8·3 m
(bed) 4·7 m
Width:
(overall) 2·5 m
(bed) 2·5 m
Height of low bed: (loaded) 0·63 m
Tyres: 11.00 × 20 PR 16
Number of tyres: 8 + 1 spare

Bartoletti 2PX trailer in travelling configuration

STATUS
Production.

MANUFACTURER
E Bartoletti, Via Leonardo Da Vinci 4, 47100 Forli, Italy.

Bartoletti Tank Semi-trailer Type TCS 60 BO

DESCRIPTION
The TCS 60 BO semi-trailer has been designed for carrying MBTs weighing up to 60 000 kg and can be towed by tractor trucks such as the FIAT 320 PTM 45 (6 × 6).

The trailer has three axles each with four tyres, lowered chassis with double hydraulically-retractable loading ramps at the rear, balanced suspension with semi-elliptical leaf springs and reaction arms, pneumatic retractable forward landing gear and adjustable track guides to suit different types of tracked vehicles. The semi-trailer also has a system of rollers and pulleys for easy loading and unloading of vehicles.

Standard equipment includes 12 pole 24 volt electric system with standard and blackout lights, compressed air (two-line), automatically adjustable service brake and parking brake.

SPECIFICATIONS
Weight:
(empty) 20 000 kg
(loaded) 80 000 kg
Payload: 60 000 kg
Length: 11·95 m
Width: 4 m

Platform height from ground: (loaded) 1·42 m
Length of platform: 7·08 m + 0·95 m
Track: 2·6 m
Tyres: 16.00 × 20 XS
Number of tyres: 12 + 2 spare

STATUS
Production.

MANUFACTURER
E Bartoletti, Via Leonardo Da Vinci 4, 47100 Forli, Italy.

Bartoletti tank semi-trailer type TCS 60 BO towed by FIAT 320 PTM 45 (6 × 6) tractor truck

Bartoletti TCS 50 BO Tank Transporter Semi-trailer

DESCRIPTION
In the same way as the German SLT 50-2 and US M747 semi-trailers, the Bartoletti TCS 50 BO semi-trailer owes its origins to the US/FRG HET-70 programme and is in fact based on the design of the SLT 50-2. It is intended for the transportation of MBTs of up to 50 000 kg, such as the M60 series, without exceeding a height of 4·5 metres from ground level to permit transit through road tunnels. The Bartoletti TCS 50 BO is a four-axle semi-trailer with a lowered chassis and retractable loading ramps. The suspension is a combination of semi-elliptical springs and air springs, and the outer axles can be lifted to reduce tyre wear during unloaded running and to improve manoeuvrability at low speed. Rollers and pulleys are provided to facilitate the loading and unloading of damaged vehicles.

STATUS
In production. Under licence from OTO Melara.

MANUFACTURER
E. Bartoletti, Via Leonardo Da Vinci 4, 47100 Forli, Italy.

SPECIFICATIONS
Weight: (unladen) 14 000 kg
Payload: 50 000 kg
Maximum fifth wheel load: 20 000 kg
Length: 12·42 m
Width: 3·15 m
Track: 2·7 m
Load deck length: 7·67 m
Platform height: (loaded) 1·23 m
Height:
(over folded ramps) 2·93 m
(over spare wheel) 3·12 m
King-pin:
(height) 1·64 m
(diameter) 89 mm
Distance between axle centres: 1·25 m

Tyres: 18 × 22.5 XS
Number of tyres: 8 + 2 spare
Brakes: dual air

Electrical system: 24 V, with standard and blackout lights
Towing vehicle: FIAT 320 PTM 45 tractor

Bartoletti TCS 50 BO tank transporter semi-trailer

Cometto Military Trailers

The firm of Cometto Industriale manufactures a wide range of specialist military trailers and semi-trailers, including tank transporter trailers such as the S53 described over, water and fuel tank trailers, helicopter transport, missile launch pad and missile radar control trailers.

Brief details of some of these trailers are summarised below.

MANUFACTURER
Cometto Industriale Srl, via Cuneo 38, 12011 Borgo S Dalmazzo (Cuneo), Italy.

Cometto SA-38 fuel tank semi-trailer

Role	Model	Length overall	Width overall	Platform height	Weight	Payload	Load on fifth wheel	Number of axles	Tyre size	Notes
Missile radar control radar	TS 5	9·66 m	2·3 m	0·5 m	2000 kg	5500 kg	n/a	2	9.00 × 20 (4)	Parachutable sheltered trailer
Tank transporter semi-trailers	S 45A	9·68 m	2·5 m	0·95 m	10 000 kg	54 000 kg	20 000 kg	2	7.50 × 15 (16)	
	S 45B	11·2 m	3·1 m	1 m	11 000 kg	61 000 kg	20 000 kg	2	8.25 × 15 (16)	
	SB 2	12·64 m	2·5 m	1·18 m	10 000 kg	45 000 kg	24 000 kg	2	11.00 × 20 (8)	
	SB 3	12·54 m	2·5 m	1·18 m	11 300 kg	57 700 kg	26 000 kg	3	11.00 × 20 (12)	
	S 64M/2	12·6 m	2·5 m	1·18 m	20 300 kg	85 700 kg	24 000 kg	6	8.25 × 15 (24)	Extensible to 14·37 m
Launch pad transport trailers	T 98R	18·7 m	3·25 m	1·3 m	36 000 kg	120 000 kg	n/a	6	8.25 × 15 (48)	For use at −50 to +50°C
	T 68R	10 m	3·2 m	1·08 m	15 000 kg	60 000 kg	n/a	3	Front axle G20 (4) Rear axles 8.25 × 15 (16)	
Cargo semi-trailers	FB 2	12·2 m	2·5 m	1·6 m	7500 kg	40 500 kg	22 000 kg	2	11.00 × 20 (8)	Flatbed
	FB 3	12·2 m	2·5 m	1·6 m	8500 kg	50 000 kg	22 000 kg	3	11.00 × 20 (12)	Flatbed
	FBT 3	14 m	3 m	1·6 m	16 000 kg	60 000 kg	21 000 kg	3	14.00 × 20 (12)	Flatbed extensible to 16·4 m
Helicopter transport trailer	TE 13	8·25 m	3 m	0·89 m	6000 kg	13 000 kg	n/a	2	7.50 × 15 (4)	

Cometto MPS50 Tank Transporter Semi-trailer

DESCRIPTION
The MPS50 is the newest in the line of Cometto tank transporter semi-trailers. The twin axle rows may be fitted with either four or eight tyres to assist in weight distribution to suit the payload. An extra pair of tyres may be carried under the loading platform for use as spares; these two spare tyre carriers have lifting devices to assist stowage. The MPS50 is fitted with a five-speed roller and pulley system for loading disabled vehicles and when not on the tractor truck a folding stand is situated to the front of the trailer. The two loading ramps are spring-loaded to provide quick and easy loading and for extra stability two foldable rear stabiliser legs on the ramp hinges may be used. The loading ramps measure 1·7 × 0·75 metres. Sliding track guides are fitted as standard as are load fastening hooks and chains. Accessories include a tool kit and box and a 150-litre water tank.

Cometto MPS50 tank transporter semi-trailer carrying M60A1 tank

STATUS
Production.

MANUFACTURER
Cometto Industriale, PO Box 129, Corso Nizza N 90, 12100 Cuneo, Italy.

SPECIFICATIONS

Number of tyres per axle row	4	8
Weight (empty)	16 000 kg	16 600 kg
(loaded)	66 000 kg	76 600 kg
Max load	50 000 kg	60 000 kg
Length (overall)	12·3 m	12·3 m
(loading platform)	8·5 m	8·5 m

Number of tyres per axle row	4	8
Width	3·6 m	3·6 m
Height (loading platform)	1·25–1·3 m	1·25–1·3 m
(5th wheel, approx)	1·5 m	1·5 m
Axle wheelbase	1·5 m	1·5 m
King-pin	89 mm	89 mm
Tyre size	18.00 × 22.5	12.00 × 20

Cometto S53 Tank Transporter Semi-trailer

DESCRIPTION
The S53 is a heavy duty semi-trailer for the transportation of tanks and heavy equipment. Its running gear has 20 wheels, suspended independently in five pairs on each side. It is thought that there is provision for raising and/or steering at least some of the wheels hydraulically to assist manoeuvrability as an auxiliary power unit is mounted on the gooseneck. The operation and stabilisation of the rear loading ramps are also hydraulic.

STATUS
In production.

MANUFACTURER
Cometto Industriale Srl, via Cuneo 38, 12011 Borgo S Dalmazzo (Cuneo), Italy.

Cometto S53 tank transporter semi-trailer

SPECIFICATIONS
Weight: 27 000 kg
Payload: 51 000 kg
Load on fifth wheel: 21 500 kg
Length: (overall) 14·77 m

Width: 3·4 m
Load deck height: 1·4 m (can be adjusted by 0·28 m up or down)
Tyres: 18–19.5 × 5
Number of tyres: 20 + 1 spare

De Filippi Trailers

De Filippi manufactures a wide range of trailers and semi-trailers, many of which are suited for military use. Brief specifications are given below:

Model	Type	Payload	Empty weight	Length	Length of platform	Width	Tyres	Number of tyres	Axles	Notes
R-10	full trailer	8000 kg	3000 kg	5·8 m	5·6 m	2·4 m	7.50 × 15	8	2	Can be fitted with side panels
20/R	full trailer	13 400 kg	4500 kg	n/a	5·2 m	2·5 m	8.25 × 15	8	2	Fitted with hydraulic loading ramps
25/R	full trailer	19 000 kg	6000 kg	n/a	5·2 m	2·5 m	8.25 × 15	12	3	Fitted with hydraulic loading ramps
S-30/R	semi-trailer	23 900 kg	7200 kg	9·6 m	n/a	2·5 m	8.25 × 15	8	2	
S-36/3	semi-trailer	30 000 kg	6000 kg	12·5 m	n/a	2·5 m	16.5 × 22.5	12	3	Can be fitted with side panels
S-38	semi-trailer	30 000 kg	n/a	n/a	6·2 m	2·5 m	8.25 × 15	12	3	
40/R	full trailer	28 500 kg	8100 kg	n/a	5·1 m	2·5 m	8.25 × 15	16	3	Fitted with hydraulic loading ramps
S-40	semi-trailer	40 000 kg	10 000 kg	11 m	6·5 m	2·5 m	12.00 × 20	8	2	
S-50	semi-trailer	40 000/ 50 000 kg	n/a	n/a	6 m	2·5/3 m	8.25 × 15 or 7.50 × 15	16	2 3	Fitted with hydraulic loading ramps
55	full trailer	44 000 kg	10 000 kg	n/a	5·3 m	2·5 m	8.25 × 15	24	3	Fitted with hydraulic loading ramps
55/S	full trailer	50 000/ 60 000 kg	12 000/ 25 000 kg	8·65 m	6 m	2·5/4 m	8.25 × 15 or 7.50 × 15	24	3	Fitted with hydraulic loading ramps
SR-60	semi-trailer	50 000 kg	15 000 kg	13·7 m	9·5 m	3 m	12.00 × 20	12	3	
S-75	semi-trailer	70 000 kg	15 000 kg	11·3 m	6·8 m	3·5 m	12.00 × 20	16	2	

De Filippi SR-60 semi-trailer

De Filippi S-50 semi-trailer

STATUS
Production.

MANUFACTURER
Costruzioni Meccaniche A De Filippi SAS, Via Garibaldi 83, 12061 Carru' (CN), Italy.

De Filippi S-75 semi-trailer

KOREA, REPUBLIC

Dong-A Light Trailers

DESCRIPTION
The Dong-A Motor Company produces five types of light trailer in the ¼-ton to 1·5 ton payload range, including a water tank trailer. All five types are license-produced versions of American service trailers and the American designation is retained in the Korean designations, prefixed by the letters DA. In nearly every respect the Korean trailers are the same as the American originals but the data quoted by the Korean manufacturer differs from the American specifications and is thus shown here.

STATUS
Production. In service with South Korean armed forces.

SPECIFICATIONS

Model	DA-M100	DA-M101	DA-M105	DA-M332	DA-M106
Type	cargo	cargo	cargo	cargo	water tank
Max load	250 kg	750 kg	1500 kg	1500 kg	1520 litres
Length	2·755 m	3·78 m	4·23 m	3·76 m	4·22 m
Width	1·535 m	1·87 m	2·105 m	2·413 m	2·06 m
Height	1·07 m	2·1 m	2·43 m	1·352 m	2·26 m
Ground clearance	0·2 m	0·315 m	0·458 m	0·27 m	0·45 m
Track	1·35 m	1·575 m	1·714 m	2·032 m	1·714 m
Tyres	6.00 × 16	7.50 × 20	9.00 × 20	9.00 × 20	9.00 × 20
Electrical system	24 V	24 V	24 V	24 V	24 V

MANUFACTURER
Dong-A Motor Company Limited, 47-2, 2-Ka, Jeo-dong, Jung-ku, Seoul, Republic of Korea.

Dong-A Cargo Trailers

DESCRIPTION
The Dong-A Motor Company produces three types of military cargo trailer, a 10 000 kg capacity trailer, a 35 000 kg container trailer and a 35 000 kg platform trailer. It also produces a range of commercial trailers with capacities from 10 000 kg to 60 000 kg. The three military trailers are of conventional construction.

SPECIFICATIONS

Type	10 000 kg trailer	35 000 kg container	35 000 kg platform
Weight (empty)	3390 kg	5590 kg	5910 kg
Max load	10 000 kg	35 000 kg	35 000 kg
Length	7·42 m	12·34 m	12·335 m
Width	2·48 m	2·46 m	2·46 m
Height	2·32 m	1·39 m	1·42 m
Wheelbase	4·11 m	9·24 m	8·92 m
Tyres	10.00 × 20	11.00 × 20	11.00 × 20

STATUS
Production.

MANUFACTURER
Dong-A Motor Company Limited, 47-2, 2-Ka, Jeo-dong, Jung-ku, Seoul, Republic of Korea.

Dong-A Low Bed Semi-trailers

DESCRIPTION
The Dong-A Motor Company produces four types of low-bed semi-trailer with capacities of 25 000 kg, 35 000 kg, 40 000 kg and 60 000 kg. All may be used to carry a wide range of military vehicles and equipment ranging from construction equipment to self-propelled artillery and armoured fighting vehicles. All four types have rear-mounted loading ramps with the largest size at least using hydraulic power to lift the ramps after use.

STATUS
Production.

MANUFACTURER
Dong-A Motor Company Limited, 47-2, 2-Ka, Jeo-dong, Jung-ku, Seoul, Republic of Korea.

SPECIFICATIONS

Capacity	25 000 kg	35 000 kg	40 000 kg	60 000 kg
Weight (empty)	7200 kg	9900 kg	12 600 kg	14 000 kg
Length	10·75 m	10·25 m	10·79 m	11·91 m
Width	2·98 m	3 m	3·2 m	3·35 m
Height	1·65 m	1·6 m	1·7 m	1·8 m
Offset	3·63 m	3·36 m	3·7 m	4·35 m
Wheelbase	8·73 m	8·26 m	8·78 m	9·93 m
Tyres	9.00 × 20	7.50 × 16	9.00 × 20	11.00 × 20

NETHERLANDS

DAF 6-tonne Van Semi-trailer Type YAA 602

DESCRIPTION
This single-axle 6-tonne van type semi-trailer has a twin mechanically-operated front support and a 51 mm king-pin. Brakes are of the air/hydraulic type. Its body consists of a wooden floor structure with detachable steel plated wooden side panels. The rear of the body comprises two doors and a hinged type stake. This trailer is normally towed by a DAF tractor truck Type YT 1500L (4 × 2).

SPECIFICATIONS
Weight:
 (empty) 3670 kg
 (loaded) 9670 kg
Max load: 6000 kg
Length: (overall) 6·41 m
Width:
 (overall) 2·4 m
 (over wheels) 2·04 m
Height: (overall) 3·28 m
Coupling height: 1·65 m
Ground clearance: 0·28 m
Track: 1·75 m
Wheelbase: (king-pin to centre of rear axle) 4·9 m
Tyres: 9.00 × 20

STATUS
Production complete. In service with the Dutch Army.

DAF 6-tonne van semi-trailer type YAA 602

MANUFACTURER
DAF Trucks, Geldropseweg 303, 5645 TK Eindhoven, Netherlands.

DAF 6-tonne Semi-trailer Type YAA 612

DESCRIPTION
This single-axle 6-tonne semi-trailer has been designed for transporting both animals and general cargo. Its body consists of a wooden floor structure with wooden sides. There are doors in each side of the body and a ramp at the rear. The trailer has a twin mechan- ically-operated front support and a 51 mm (2-inch) king-pin; brakes are of the air/hydraulic type.
(**Note:** 3½- and 2-inch king-pins are standard world- wide)

SPECIFICATIONS
Weight:
 (empty) 3730 kg
 (loaded) 9730 kg
Max load: 6000 kg
Length: (overall) 7·38 m
Width:
 (overall) 2·4 m
 (over wheels) 2·04 m
Height: (overall) 3·35 m
Coupling height: 1·35 m
Ground clearance: 0·28 m
Track: 1·75 m
Wheelbase: (king-pin to centre of rear axle) 5·72 m
Tyres: 9.00 × 20

STATUS
Production complete. In service with the Dutch Army.

MANUFACTURER
DAF Trucks, Geldropseweg 303, 5645 TK Eindhoven, Netherlands.

DAF 6-tonne semi-trailer type YAA 612

DAF Flatbed Trailer Type YVW 1214

DESCRIPTION
This flatbed trailer is a standard commercial type adapted to meet military requirements. It has a wooden floor and tiedown points are provided for securing the load to the trailer. One hundred of these were supplied to the Dutch Army for the transport of bridge sections, bulldozers and other engineering equipment.

SPECIFICATIONS
Weight:
  (empty) 3910 kg
  (loaded) 11 884 kg
  (on front axle empty) 1930 kg
  (on rear axle empty) 1980 kg
Max load: 7974 kg
Length:
  (overall) 9·7 m
  (of flatbed) 8 m
Width:
  (overall) 2·45 m
  (over wheels) 2·28 m
Height: (to top of flatbed) 1·3 m
Ground clearance: 0·23 m
Track: 1·75 m
Wheelbase: 5·5 m
Tyres: 6.00 × 20
Number of wheels: 8

DAF flatbed trailer type YVW 1214

STATUS
Production complete. In service with the Dutch Army.

MANUFACTURER
DAF Trucks, Geldropseweg 303, 5645 TK Eindhoven, Netherlands.

DAF 10-tonne Cargo Semi-trailer Type YTT 1004

DESCRIPTION
This 10-tonne cargo body semi-trailer is equipped with tandem axle running gear, two mechanically operated front supports and a 51 mm (2-inch) king-pin. Brakes are of the air-hydraulic type.
  The frame of the trailer is of the flat deck type and the body consists of a wooden floor with detachable stake racks. A tarpaulin covers the body and is held in place by roof slats.
  The YTT 1004 trailer is normally towed by the DAF tractor truck type YT 1500L (4 × 2).

SPECIFICATIONS
Weight:
  (empty) 4740 kg
  (loaded) 14 740 kg
Max load: 10 000 kg
Length: (overall) 7·75 m
Width:
  (overall) 2·45 m
  (over wheels) 2·39 m
Height: (overall) 3·28 m
Coupling height: 1·65 m
Ground clearance: 0·45 m
Track: 1·75 m
Wheelbase:
  (from king-pin to centre of rear bogie) 4·64 m
  (rear bogie) 1·2 m
Tyres: 9.00 × 20
Number of tyres: 8 + 1 spare

DAF 10-tonne semi-trailer type YTT 1004

STATUS
Production complete. In service with the Dutch Army.

MANUFACTURER
DAF Trucks, Geldropseweg 303, 5645 TK Eindhoven, Netherlands.

DAF Tank Transporter Semi-trailer Type YTS 10050

DESCRIPTION
The DAF tank transporter semi-trailer Type YTS 10050 has been designed to carry all MBTs currently in service including the Chieftain. Provision has been made in the design of the semi-trailer to winch disabled tracked vehicles on to and off the trailer with the aid of the winch on the tractor.

The chassis frame consists of two steel box section girders which form a single welded unit together with the cross-pulley members, outriggers, outer rails, floor plates, fifth-wheel support frame, toolboxes, pulley housing and other components. The king-pin is a standard 89 mm (3½-inch) size.

The platform bed is provided with track guides to prevent sideways movement of the tank and these track guides can be adjusted laterally to suit different types of tracked vehicle.

The running gear comprises two separate and identical independently oscillating tandem axle units next to each other, each axle with four sets of twin wheels and tyres. The front and rear axles can oscillate 7 degrees longitudinally in relation to the rocker beam brackets. The transverse oscillation of the wheel axles in relation to the rocker beam is also 7 degrees.

Two ramps at the rear of the trailer can be raised and lowered by two men. Two mechanically operated, pivot-mounted front supports are raised and locked to the main girder at the gooseneck when travelling. As an optional extra, the semi-trailer can be equipped with two hydraulic front supports.

The trailer is fitted with a two-line brake system. Four of the eight diaphragm-type brake chambers are safety actuators with a locking mechanism functioning as a parking brake as well as a service brake. Standard equipment includes chains and two hydraulic jacks each with a capacity of 25 000 kg. Sweden uses the Scania-Vabis LT 110S or L76 (6 × 4) tractor truck to tow

DAF tank transporter semi-trailer Type YTS 10050

this semi-trailer. The YTS 10060 semi-trailer is similar to the YTS 10050.

SPECIFICATIONS
Weight:
  (empty) 15 000 kg
  (loaded) 70 000 kg
Max load: 55 000 kg
Length: (overall) 11·72 m
Width:
  (overall) 3·4 m
  (of platform) 3·04 m
Height:
  (top of platform) 1·27 m
  (over loading ramps) 1·81 m

Ground clearance: (under chassis) 0·61 m
Track: 1·78 m
Wheelbase: (king-pin to centre of rear bogie) 8·7 m
Max towing speed: 50 km/h
Tyres: 11.00 × 20
Number of tyres: 16 + 1 spare

STATUS
Production complete. In service with Belgium (29), Denmark (14), Netherlands (36), Spain (made under licence) and Sweden (91).

MANUFACTURER
DAF Trucks, Geldropseweg 303, 5645 TK Eindhoven, Netherlands.

FTF FLO 25-520 Tank Transport Semi-trailer

DESCRIPTION
The FTF FLO 25-520 is used in conjunction with the FTF 4050 tractor truck for carrying Dutch Army Leopard 1 tanks. A total of 39 trailers was purchased by the Dutch Army in 1972. The FLO 25-520 semi-trailer has two axles and a manually-lifted pair of loading ramps. To a large extent the FLO 25-520 has now been supplemented in service by the DAF type YTS 10050 tank transporter semi-trailer.

SPECIFICATIONS
Weight:
  (empty) 15 000 kg
  (loaded) 70 000 kg
Max load: 55 000 kg
Length:
  (overall) 11·4 m
  (platform) 7·76 m
Height:
  (loading ramp) 0·56 m
  (platform) 1·1 m

Width: (maximum) 3·4 m
Ground clearance: (max load) 0·63 m
Axle wheelbase: 1·48 m

STATUS
Production complete. In service with the Dutch Army.

MANUFACTURER
Floor's Handel en Industrie BV, Larensweg 32, Hilversum, Netherlands.

DAF Tanker Trailer, 2-wheel, 900-litre Type YEW 400

DESCRIPTION
This single-axle two-wheeled trailer has been designed for transporting drinking water and has a double acting hand pump with suction hose, one 26 mm and four 12·7 mm taps and four supporting legs.

SPECIFICATIONS
Weight:
  (empty) 670 kg
  (loaded) 1620 kg
Capacity: 900 litres
Length:
  (overall) 3·61 m
  (of tank) 1·55 m
Width:
  (overall) 1·55 m
  (of tank) 1·65 m
Height:
  (overall) 1·6 m
  (to towing eye) 0·89 m
Ground clearance: 0·4 m
Track: 1·5 m
Tyres: 9.00 × 16

STATUS
Production as required. In service with the Dutch Army.

MANUFACTURER
DAF Trucks, Geldropseweg 303, 5645 TK Eindhoven, Netherlands.

DAF tanker trailer, two-wheel, 900-litre type YEW 400

DAF Petrol Trailer 5000-litre Type YFW 610

DESCRIPTION
This two-axle trailer has been designed to carry 5000 litres of petrol. Two filler caps are provided in the top of the tank and the fuel is unloaded by gravity via two stopcocks at the rear of the tank. Fuel pipes are carried in external stowage containers mounted on either side of the tank. A stowage area 1·79 metres long is provided to the front of the tank. Brakes are of the air/hydraulic type.

DAF petrol trailer 5000-litre type YFW 610

SPECIFICATIONS
Weight:
(empty) 3780 kg
(on front axle empty) 1440 kg
(on rear axle empty) 2340 kg
Max load: 5000 litres
Length:
(overall) 7·45 m
(of tank) 3·11 m
Width:
(overall) 2·43 m
(over wheels) 2·4 m
(over tank) 1·81 m

Height: 2·7 m
Ground clearance: 0·37 m
Track: 1·81 m
Wheelbase: 4 m
Tyres: 9.00 × 20
Number of tyres: 6 + 1 spare

STATUS
Production complete. In service with the Dutch Army.

MANUFACTURER
DAF Trucks, Geldropseweg 303, 5645 TK Eindhoven, Netherlands.

DAF 10 000-litre Tanker Semi-trailer Type YAF 1014

DESCRIPTION
This 10 000-litre single-axle semi-trailer tanker has mechanically-operated twin leg front supports and a 51 mm king-pin. Brakes are of the air/hydraulic type.

The frameless tank consists of four compartments for the transport of fuel such as petrol, paraffin or diesel oil. The fuel is delivered from taps by gravity with or without the meter installed at the rear of the trailer.

The YA 1024 10 000-litre tanker semi-trailer is similar but has a pump with a discharge rate of 348 litres per minute. Four vehicles can be refuelled simultaneously at the rate of 91 litres per minute. The pump is powered by a two-stroke auxiliary engine.

STATUS
Production complete. A total of 80 was delivered to the Service Corps of the Dutch Army.

MANUFACTURER
DAF Trucks, Geldropseweg 303, 5646 TK Eindhoven, Netherlands.

DAF 10 000-litre tanker semi-trailer type YAF 1014 with twin leg front supports lowered

SPECIFICATIONS
Weight:
(empty) 4450 kg
(loaded) 11 426 kg
Fifth wheel load: 4440 kg
Max capacity: 10 000 litres

Length:
(overall) 7·7 m
(of tank) 6·6 m
Width:
(overall) 2·42 m
(over wheels) 2·29 m
(over tank) 2 m

Height: (overall) 2·49 m
Ground clearance: 0·37 m
Track: 1·75 m
Wheelbase: (king-pin to centre of rear axle) 5·35 m
Tyres: 9.00 × 20
Number of tyres: 4 + 1 spare

DAF 2-tonne Ammunition Trailer Type YEM 900

DESCRIPTION
This single-axle ammunition trailer has been designed to carry 2000 kg of ammunition. A single front support is mounted to the rear of the towing eye.

SPECIFICATIONS
Weight:
(empty) 1040 kg
(loaded) 3040 kg
Max load: 2000 kg
Length:
(overall) 3·78 m
(of body) 1·6 m
Width:
(over wheels) 2·2 m
(of body) 1·42 m
Height: (overall) 1·46 m
Depth: (of body) 0·56 m
Ground clearance: 0·41 m
Track: 1·96 m
Tyres: 9.00 × 20

STATUS
Production complete. In service with the Dutch Army.

MANUFACTURER
DAF Trucks, Geldropseweg 303, 5645 TK Eindhoven, Netherlands.

DAF 2-tonne ammunition trailer type YEM 900 with front support lowered

DAF 2000 kg 2-wheel Chassis Trailers Models M 390-17 and M 390-17C (Common)

DESCRIPTION
Over 1000 of these single-axle trailers were built by DAF for the European HAWK surface-to-air missile system. Each trailer consists of a frame, suspension system, two wheels, air-over-hydraulic service brakes, individually operated handbrakes, 24-volt electrical system, retractable support, levelling support jacks and a towing lunette. The trailers delivered to the Dutch Army were designated the M 390-17D and the ones delivered to the Bundeswehr the M 390-17G. The trailers are used to carry three HAWK surface-to-air missiles.

SPECIFICATIONS (Trailer only)
Weight: 1960 kg
Length: 4·8 m
Width: 2·469 m
Height: 1·13 m
Height of towing eye: 0·88 m
Tyres: 9.00 × 20
Number of tyres: 2

STATUS
Production complete. In service with members of NATO including Belgium, France, West Germany, Italy and the Netherlands.

DAF two-wheel chassis trailer model M 390-17 carrying 3 dummy HAWK missiles on loading pallet

MANUFACTURER
DAF Trucks, Geldropseweg 303, 5645 TK Eindhoven, Netherlands.

DAF 2500 kg Trailer Type M53 (YEP 600)

DESCRIPTION
This trailer has been designed for carrying pontoons for the Engineer Corps of the Netherlands Army. It has mechanical brakes and a single front support mounted to the rear of the towing lunette. The DAF trailer type YRE 600 and YRI 600 are similar to the YEP 600 but have torsion bar suspension and are used to transport radar and other electronic equipment.

SPECIFICATIONS
Weight:
  (empty) 1280 kg
  (loaded) 3780 kg
Max load: 2500 kg
Length:
  (overall) 4·59 m
  (of mounting) 2·2 m
Width:
  (over wheels) 2·23 m
  (over mounting) 2·08 m
Height: (to top of mounting) 1·2 m
Ground clearance: 0·45 m
Track: 1·97 m
Wheelbase: (towing eye to centre of axle) 3·34 m
Tyres: 9.00 × 20

STATUS
Production complete. In service with the Dutch Army.

DAF 2500 kg trailer type YEP 600

MANUFACTURER
DAF Trucks, Geldropseweg 303, 5645 TK Eindhoven, Netherlands.

DAF Bridging Boat Trailer Type YVW 1414B

DESCRIPTION
The YVW 1414B has been designed for transporting, launching and recovering from the water a pusher boat for use in bridge construction. Launching and recovery are effected by an extensible pivotally-mounted track. The boat is mounted on this track and has a number of air-cushioned rollers on each side. For launching, the track can be raised by a hydraulic jack. The shore configuration allowing a successful launching to be made is governed by the difference in height between the water and ground levels of a steep shore which may amount to 1·5 metres and a slope of 10 degrees.

The trailer is normally towed by a DAF YK-616 (6 × 6) truck with an 8000 kg capacity winch and 80 metres of cable.

The boat is launched as follows: after arriving at the river, the trailer is uncoupled and positioned near the river bank with its rear towards the river, the towing vehicle turns round and the tow bar of the trailer is coupled to the front of the truck; the trailer is pushed to the edge of the river bank, the track is extended to the water and the boat slides down into the river backwards. The boat is recovered in a similar manner.

SPECIFICATIONS
Weight:
  (with boat) 11 675 kg
  (without boat) 7264 kg

DAF bridging boat trailer type YVW 1414B at river bank with track and boat sliding towards river

Length:
  (overall) 10·77 m
  (without towbar) 8·4 m
Width:
  (overall) 2·8 m
  (over trailer) 2·42 m
Height: (overall) 3·36 m
Ground clearance: 0·24 m
Track: 1·95 m

Wheelbase: 5·8 m
Tyres: 9.00 × 20

STATUS
Production complete. In service with the Dutch Army.

MANUFACTURER
DAF Trucks, Geldropseweg 303, 5645 TK Eindhoven, Netherlands.

POLAND

Polish Heavy Transport Trailers and Semi-trailers
P-40, NP-40 and PN-600

DESCRIPTION
The P-40 and P-50 are conventional three-axle trailers with folding ramps at the rear of the trailer bed. The NP-40 is a semi-trailer and is towed by the single axle Zg-201A tractor. The PN-600 is a four-axle full trailer with a single-axle dolly and three axles under the loading platform. There are folding ramps at the rear of the platform.

SPECIFICATIONS

Model	P-40	NP-40	PN-600
Weight			
(empty)	13 575 kg	14 000 kg	13 500 kg
(loaded)	53 575 kg	54 000 kg	73 500 kg
Max load	40 000 kg	40 000 kg	60 000 kg
Length			
(overall)	11·2 m	n/a	11·75 m
(trailer only)	n/a	n/a	9·88 m
Length of			
platform	5·1 m	8·5 m	6·5 m
Width	2·9 m	3·15 m	3·1 m
Height	2 m	n/a	n/a
(to platform)	1 m	n/a	1·1 m

Model	P-40	NP-40	PN-600
Towing speed			
(empty)	15 km/h	40 km/h	80 km/h
(loaded)	–	–	60 km/h
Tyres	–	–	8.25 × 15 (32)

STATUS
The P-40 and P-50 are known to be in service with the Polish Army. The NP-40 and the PN-600 both have military applications.

MANUFACTURER (PN-600)
ZREMB Factory, Wroclaw, Poland.

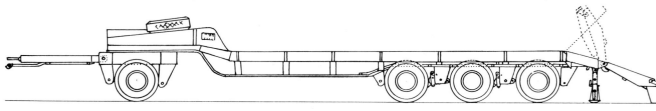

Polish PN-600 60 000 kg trailer

SOUTH AFRICA

SAMIL 10-ton Cargo Trailer

DESCRIPTION
This general purpose cargo trailer is the standard South African Defence Force load carrying trailer and can be towed by the SAMIL 50 and 100 trucks. The trailer is a twin-axled design with 800 kPa air brakes and an all-steel body. There are four downward-opening side panels, two to each side, and steel wire mesh panel extensions are permanently fitted for oversize loads. A spare wheel is carried under the cargo body, and a full set of rear lights is provided.

SPECIFICATIONS
Weight:
(empty) 4200 kg
(fully loaded) 14 200 kg
Payload: 10 000 kg
Length:
(inc towbar) 6·66 m
(body internal) 4·85 m
Height:
(inc cant rails) 2·85 m
(towing eye, coupling) 1 m
(body internal) 0·46 m
Width: (body internal) 2·335 m
Wheelbase: 3·2 m
Track: 2·03 m
Tyres: 12.00 × 20 × 14 ply

STATUS
Production. In service with the South African Defence Forces.

MANUFACTURER
Truckmakers (Pty) Limited, PO Box 362, Rosslyn 0200, South Africa.
Enquiries to Armscor, Private Bag X337, Pretoria 0001, South Africa.

SAMIL 10-ton cargo trailer (T J Gander)

SAMIL 3-ton 4-wheel Workshop Trailers

DESCRIPTION
There are a number of these workshop trailers, all basically the same in layout and appearance but differing in equipment and internal layout. A general repair trailer is one of the more numerous types but there is also an armourer's workshop trailer. Each trailer has a fully-enclosed body when being towed but once in position, side and rear-mounted flaps are opened upwards to reveal the interior. Once emplaced each trailer is usually covered by a canvas tent with the trailer roof and side flaps supporting the tent roof. The tent, when erected, is 8·5 metres long, 5·7 metres wide and 2·5 metres high. Each trailer has its own 10 kVA 380-volt three-phase 50 Hertz generator with a convertor supplying 265 volts at 200 Hertz. A 220-volt supply is used for internal lighting and two fans in the trailer roof. The general chassis voltage supply is 24 volts from batteries. Air brakes are fitted. The trailers are supplied complete with all the necessary machine and other tools.

SAMIL 3-ton 4-wheel workshop trailer (T J Gander)

STATUS
Production. In service with the South African Defence Forces.

MANUFACTURER
Truckmakers (Pty) Limited, PO Box 362, Rosslyn 0200, South Africa.
Enquiries to Armscor, Private Bag X337, Pretoria 0001, South Africa.

SPECIFICATIONS
Weight:
(empty) 3780 kg
(equipped) 5500 kg
Length:
(inc drawbar) 7·765 m
(interior) 5·6 m

Height:
(total) 2·49 m
(interior) 1·28 m
(interior, over goose-neck) 1·06 m
(tow eye) 0·9 m
Width: (total) 2·3 m
Track: 2·03 m
Tyres: 9.00 × 16 × 12 ply
Electrical system: 24 V

SAMIL 2-ton 4-wheel Office Trailer

DESCRIPTION
Intended for command and general administration purposes, this box-body trailer is suppled complete with an air conditioner, desk, two steel filing cabinets, a drawing table, a downwards folding table and two chairs. The box body is equipped with windows and a two panel outwards-opening door with steps over which a canvas penthouse can be erected on three poles. When erected this penthouse is 5·4 metres long, 1·9 metres wide and 2·6 metres high. An internal mesh door is provided. Air brakes are fitted.

SPECIFICATIONS
Weight:
(empty) 3545 kg
(loaded) 4700 kg
Length:
(inc towing bar) 7·1 m
(internal) 5·075 m
Width: (internal) 2·335 m
Height:
(total) 3·005 m
(internal) 2·125 m
Track: 2·03 m
Tyres: 9.00 × 16 × 10 ply

STATUS
Production. In service with the South African Defence Forces.

MANUFACTURER
Truckmakers (Pty) Limited, PO Box 362, Rosslyn 0200, South Africa.
Enquiries to Armscor, Private Bag X337, Pretoria 0001, South Africa.

SAMIL office trailer with penthouse erected

SAMIL 2-ton 4-wheel office trailer

SAMIL 2-ton 4-wheel Shower Unit Trailer

DESCRIPTION
This trailer body is basically the same as that used on the Office Trailer but is fitted with shower facilities for up to eight men at one session. Each shower head can be operated individually but normally an operator controls the shower cycle. Water is pumped from an outside source through a filter unit to three Junkers gas heaters, although any one or two of these heaters can be eliminated if required. Internal lighting is supplied from a 12-volt battery and a tunnel tent can be provided for

connection from the rear-situated access door to a standard military tent nearby. Air brakes are fitted. The water pump is powered by a petrol/gas operated engine carried behind an access flap.

STATUS
Production. In service with the South African Defence Forces.

MANUFACTURER
Truckmakers (Pty) Limited, PO Box 362, Rosslyn 0200, South Africa.
Enquiries to Armscor, Private Bag X337, Pretoria 0001, South Africa.

SPECIFICATIONS
Weight:
(empty) 3000 kg
(equipped) 4000 kg
Length:
(inc drawbar) 6·65 m
(internal) 4·79 m
Width: (internal) 2·21 m
Height:
(total) 3·075 m
(internal) 2·1 m
Track: 2·03 m
Tyres: 7.50 × 16 × 10 ply
Electrical system: 24 V

SAMIL 1-ton 2-wheel Dog Transporter Trailer

DESCRIPTION
The South African Defence Forces make extensive use of war dogs for border and internal security purposes and this trailer is used to carry the dogs over long distances. Each trailer can carry up to 10 dogs in cages, four to each side and two at the rear. A stowage box at the front carries food and other equipment for the dogs. Each cage is 0·78 metre long, 0·65 metre wide and 0·85 metre high, and has a wire mesh front that is covered by a canvas flap while on the move. The cage doors open downwards. A fire extinguisher is carried in the stowage box and a dolly wheel is provided.

SPECIFICATIONS
Weight:
(empty) 1380 kg
(loaded) 1780 kg
Length:
(body) 2·99 m
(drawbar) 1·5 m
Width: (body) 2·44 m
Height:
(body) 2·5 m
(towing eye) 1·08 m
Track: 2·03 m
Tyres: 7.50 × 16 × 8 ply

SAMIL 1-ton 2-wheel dog transporter trailer

STATUS
Production. In service with the South African Defence Forces.

MANUFACTURER
Truckmakers (Pty) Limited, PO Box 362, Rosslyn 0200, South Africa.
Enquiries to Armscor, Private Bag X337, Pretoria 0001, South Africa.

SAMIL 1-ton 2-wheel Medical Post Trailer

DESCRIPTION
This two-wheeled trailer has a steel body and contains all the necessary equipment to provide a forward area medical post. The box body of the trailer is provided with a number of doors and flaps; the two side flaps can be removed to be used as tables. Internally there are cupboards and drawers along each side and the centre of the trailer is used for stowage of a tent which is erected over the trailer with a frame support erected on the body roof. The tent has a groundsheet and a shade net in addition to the main tent body which is 10·5 metres long, 4·7 metres wide and 3·1 metres high. Other equipment carried includes two 18 kg liquid petroleum gas bottles each feeding a two-burner low pressure stove for sterilising equipment in pressure vessels. Also carried are two 15 kg oxygen bottles, two 90-litre refrigerators, a 90-litre water tank and 12-volt batteries for lighting purposes. The cupboards and drawers carry various medical equipment and supplies. A fire extinguisher is provided and the towing bar has a dolly wheel.

SPECIFICATIONS
Weight:
(empty) 1780 kg
(loaded) 2500 kg
Length:
(body) 2·7 m
(drawbar) 1·5 m
Width: (body) 2·4 m
Height:
(body) 2·7 m
(towing eye) 1·08 m
Track: 2·03 m
Tyres: 9.00 × 16 × 8 ply

STATUS
Production. In service with the Surgeon-General's arm of South African Defence Forces.

MANUFACTURER
Truckmakers (Pty) Limited, PO Box 362, Rosslyn 0200, South Africa.
Enquiries to Armscor, Private Bag X337, Pretoria 0001, South Africa.

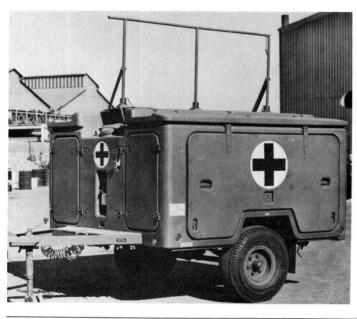

SAMIL medical post trailer tent erected

SAMIL 1-ton 2-wheel medical post trailer

SAMIL ¾-ton 2-wheel Training Media Trailer

DESCRIPTION
This specialised trailer is intended for troop training in remote areas and contains all the equipment necessary for the task. The trailer has a steel chassis and frame covered by a glass fibre body shell on which the top can be raised to expose a viewing screen and an area for blackboards, etc. To power the necessary electrical equipment the trailer has its own small 1·5 kVA generator carried internally. The trailer also carries its own classroom in the form of a canvas tent that covers the entire unit. This tent is 11·5 metres long, 5·3 metres wide and 2·68 metres high. Training equipment carried includes a white roll-down screen, a 16 mm film projector, a 35 mm slide projector, an overhead projector and screen, a tape recorder with a synchroniser, amplifier and two loudspeakers, a rear projection screen and mirror, a blackboard, magnetic board and flannel board and two lapel microphones. The trailer also carries a fire extinguisher and a spare wheel. A dolly wheel is provided under the drawbar. Over-run brakes are fitted.

SPECIFICATIONS
Weight:
(empty) 650 kg
(loaded) 1000 kg
Length:
(with drawbar) 3·6 m
(body internal) 2 m
Width: (body internal) 1·4 m
Height: (sides) 0·5 m
Track: 1·865 m
Tyres: 7.50 × 16 × 6 ply (sand type)

STATUS
Production. In service with the South African Defence Forces.

MANUFACTURER
Truckmakers (Pty) Limited, PO Box 362, Rosslyn 0200, South Africa.
Enquiries to Armscor, Private Bag X337, Pretoria 0001, South Africa.

Training media trailer closed

Training media trailer opened showing screens

250-man Mobile Field Kitchen Trailer

DESCRIPTION
This mobile kitchen unit is mounted on a heavy duty two-wheeled trailer fitted with air brakes. The cooking range, three pressure cookers, griddle plates, oven and hot water tank are enclosed by side flaps which can open upwards to the equipment and provide shelter for the operator. The cooking equipment is heated by gas supplied by low pressure gas cylinders through a vapouriser unit. All the control valves are fitted with flame failure devices and the oven is thermostatically controlled.

The full equipment carried on the trailer includes three pressure cookers, three pans, three gas lights, a poker lighter, four 14 kg liquid withdrawal gas cylinders, two fire extinguishers, a spare wheel and heavy duty jockey wheel, canvas sides and a canvas roof cover, a handbrake, four adjustable corner jacks with levellers and a removeable stainless steel worktop with a chopping board on the reverse side. The canvas sides are provided for black-out use at night and for protection in bad weather.

STATUS
Production. In service with the South African Defence Forces.

MANUFACTURERS
Basquin. Rowan Engineering.
Enquiries to Armscor, Private Bag X337, Pretoria 0001, South Africa.

250-man field kitchen trailer

Other SAMIL Trailers

DESCRIPTION
SAMIL produces in all some 80 types of trailer and semi-trailer. Trailers are produced with capacities from 1000 kg to 30 000 kg and semi-trailers (of which there are nearly 40 types) with capacities from 7000 kg to 60 000 kg. Most of these are produced to match the standard South African Defence Force truck capacities of 1-tonne, 2-tonne, 5-tonne and 10-tonne, but many

are specially produced for specific roles, some of which have been described in the preceding entries. Apart from specialist roles such as medical post, training media and office trailers, SAMIL also produces trailers for such roles as mobile blood banks, mobile food pantries and corpse embalming.

STATUS
Most types are in production. In service with the South African Defence Forces.

MANUFACTURER
Truckmakers (Pty) Limited, PO Box 362, Rosslyn 0200, South Africa.
Enquiries to Armscor, Private Bag X337, Pretoria 0001, South Africa.

UNION OF SOVIET SOCIALIST REPUBLICS

Soviet Trailer Designation Systems

The designation system applied before 1966 to Soviet-designed trailers followed the general lines applied to Soviet trucks (see *Trucks* section) in that bands of numbers in the sequence 700 to 899 followed an abbreviation of the plant of origin. Designations applied before 1 August 1966 are still used today but after that date a new system was brought into use.

When applied to the trailer designation alone, the new system commences with the plant abbreviation followed by four digits. The first digit may be 8 or 9 with 8 denoting a full trailer and 9 a semi-trailer or logging trailer.

The second digit denotes the type of vehicle with

which the trailer can be used. They are used as follows:
1 light motor vehicles
2 buses
3 trucks with sides
4 not used, in reserve
5 dump trucks
6 tanker trucks
7 vans
8 not used, in reserve
9 special vehicles
The third and fourth digits have two uses. One of these uses is as a product index but the main purpose is to denote the weight capacity. Log trailers have their

own weight capacity ratings which are outside the scope of this work and are thus not included.
01–24   below 4000 kg
25–49   4000 to 10 000 kg
50–69   10 000 to 16 000 kg
70–84   16 000 to 24 000 kg
85–90   over 24 000 kg
This four-digit designation may be used with the truck or tractor vehicle that is used to tow the trailer, eg MAZ-7310–8385. In this case the MAZ-7310 truck is used to tow the full trailer MAZ-8385. This designation combination can be used to discover the total weight and capacity of the truck and trailer combination.

GAZ-704 500 kg Trailer

DESCRIPTION
The trailer entered production at the UAZ plant in 1953 and was designed for use with the GAZ-69 and GAZ-69A (4 × 4) vehicles. The trailer has a single axle with 6.50 × 16 tyres. No brakes are provided. The body is of all steel construction and has a hinged tailgate.

SPECIFICATIONS
Weight:
(loaded) 840 kg
(empty) 340 kg

Max load: 500 kg
Length:
(overall) 2·7 m
(of body) 1·66 m
Width:
(overall) 1·645 m
(of body) 1·07 m
Height:
(overall) 1·15 m
(loading) 0·7 m
Depth: (of body) 0·45 m
Height of drawbar: 0·5 m
Track: 1·44 m

STATUS
In service with the Soviet Army and other armed forces.

MANUFACTURER
Ul'yanovsk Automobile Plant, Ul'yanovsk, USSR.

ChMZAP-2303V 20-tonne Heavy Load Trailer

DESCRIPTION
This three-axle heavy load trailer is normally towed by a KrAZ-255B (6 × 6) truck. If required the four-wheeled dolly can be removed and the trailer is then used as a semi-trailer and can be towed by a KrAZ-221 or similar vehicle. The suspension of the dolly consists of semi-elliptical springs with check springs while the rear suspension consists of semi-elliptical springs. The trailer is provided with drum type air-operated brakes on the rear axle, with a mechanical parking brake operating on one

rear axle. Standard equipment includes loading ramps, guide bars and guide rollers for the tractor winch cable.

STATUS
In service with the Soviet Army and other armed forces.

MANUFACTURER
Chelyabinsk Machine Building Plant for Motor Vehicle and Tractor Trailers, Chelyabinsk, RSFSR, USSR.

SPECIFICATIONS
Weight: (empty) 9750 kg
Max load:
(as trailer) 20 500 kg
(as semi-trailer) 22 000 kg

Length:
(overall) 12·95 m
(of platform) 6·59 m
Width: 3 m
Height:
(overall) 2·09 m
(loading) 1·35 m
Ground clearance: 0·28 m
Track: 1·92 m
Max towing speed:
(road) 50 km/h
(dirt road) 25 km/h
Tyres: 12.00 × 20
Number of wheels: 12 + 2 spare

ChMZAP-5523 Heavy Flatbed Trailer

DESCRIPTION
This has been designed for hauling heavy equipment on both hard surface and dirt roads. The front dolly can be removed enabling the trailer to be used as a semi-trailer. Two hydraulically-operated folding ramps are provided at the rear of the hull.

The suspension consists of longitudinal semi-elliptical springs with check springs while the rear bogie is provided with semi-elliptical springs. Drum type brakes are provided on all eight wheels of the rear axle and a parking brake operates on one of the rear axles.

SPECIFICATIONS
(with front dolly)
Weight:
(loaded) 31 000 kg
(empty) 9750 kg
(on front dolly unladen) 3750 kg
(on rear bogie unladen) 6000 kg
Max load: 21 250 kg
Length:
(overall) 12·95 m
(of platform) 6·43 m
Width:
(overall) 3 m
(of platform) 3 m

Height:
(overall) 2·08 m
(of platform) 1·35 m
Ground clearance: (under axle of rear suspension equaliser arm) 0·28 m
Max towing speed: 50 km/h
Tyres: 12.00 × 20
Number of wheels: 12 + 2 spare

STATUS
In service with the Soviet Army and other armed forces.

MANUFACTURER
Chelyabinsk Machine Building Plant for Motor Vehicle and Tractor Trailers, Chelyabinsk, RSFSR, USSR.

ChMZAP-5524 23-tonne Heavy Load Trailer

DESCRIPTION
The ChMZAP-5524 can be used either as a conventional trailer, or as a semi-trailer with its single-axle four-wheeled bogie removed. Its front suspension consists of semi-elliptical springs with check springs while its rear suspension consists of a bogie with semi-elliptical springs. The trailer is normally towed by a KrAZ-255B (6 × 6) 7½-ton truck or a tractor truck such as the KrAZ-255V (6 × 6) when being used as a semi-trailer.

VARIANTS
The ChMZAP-5524A is a similar trailer but has been extended by one metre.

SPECIFICATIONS
Weight:
(loaded) 30 000 kg
(empty) 6300 kg
Max load:
(as trailer) 23 700 kg
(as semi-trailer) 25 500 kg
Length: (overall) 11·36 m
Width: (overall) 2·64 m
Height:
(overall) 1·6 m
(loading) 1·09 m
Ground clearance: 0·28 m

Track: 1·92 m
Max towing speed:
(road) 50 km/h
(dirt road) 20 km/h
Tyres: 12.00 × 20
Number of wheels: 12 + 2 spare

STATUS
In service with the Soviet Army and other armed forces.

MANUFACTURER
Chelyabinsk Machine Building Plant for Motor Vehicle and Tractor Trailers, Chelyabinsk, RSFSR, USSR.

ChMZAP-5208 40-tonne Heavy Flatbed Trailer

DESCRIPTION
This trailer entered production at the Chelyabinsk plant in 1957 and has been designed for hauling heavy cargo on hard surfaced roads. The trailer has drum type air operated brakes on all wheels, with a hydraulic operated parking brake on the rear axle. Loading ramps, guide bars and load securing gear are also fitted. The ChMZAP-5208 is normally towed by the MAZ-537A (8 × 8) truck.

STATUS
In service with the Soviet Army and other armed forces.

MANUFACTURER
Chelyabinsk Machine Building Plant for Motor Vehicle and Tractor Trailers, Chelyabinsk, RSFSR, USSR.

SPECIFICATIONS
Weight:
(loaded) 51 000 kg
(empty) 11 000 kg
(on front dolly unloaded) 3900 kg
(on rear bogie unloaded) 7100 kg
Max load: 40 000 kg
Length:
(overall) 9·33 m
(of platform) 4·88 m

Width:
(overall) 3·2 m
(of platform) 3·2 m
Height:
(overall) 1·94 m
(of platform) 1·44 m
Ground clearance: (loaded under front suspension cross member) 0·35 m
Track: (centre of outer wheels) 2·41 m
Wheelbase:
(centre of front dolly to centre of rear bogie) 4·75 m
(rear bogie) 1·19 m
Max towing speed: 40 km/h
Tyres: 8.25 × 20
Number of wheels: 24 + 2 spare

ChMZAP-5247G 50-tonne Heavy Load Semi-trailer

DESCRIPTION
The ChMZAP-5247G 50-tonne semi-trailer is widely used for transporting MBTs such as the T-62 and is towed by the MAZ-537 (8 × 8) tractor truck. All eight wheels have air operated drum brakes with a mechanical parking brake. Standard equipment includes powered loading ramps, guide bars and load securing gear.

VARIANTS
The ChMZAP-5247B is a 45-tonne semi-trailer 14·68 metres long and 2·64 metres wide. The rear section is not provided with loading ramps and has no incline.

SPECIFICATIONS
Weight:
(loaded) 68 000 kg
(empty) 18 000 kg
Max load: 50 000 kg
Length:
(overall) 15·23 m
(of platform) 5·69 m
Width:
(overall) 3·38 m
(of platform) 3·23 m

ChMZAP-5247G 50-tonne heavy load semi-trailer carrying T-55 MBT, towed by MAZ-537 (8 × 8) tractor truck

Height:
(overall) 2·78 m
(of platform) 1·16 m
Ground clearance: 0·35 m
Track: 2·09 m
Max towing speed: 50 km/h
Tyre size: 15.00 × 20
Number of wheels: 8 + 1 spare

STATUS
In service with members of the Warsaw Pact and with countries in Africa and the Middle East.

MANUFACTURER
Chelyabinsk Machine Building Plant for Motor Vehicle and Tractor Trailers, Chelyabinsk, RSFSR, USSR.

ChMZAP-5212 60-tonne Heavy Flatbed Trailer

DESCRIPTION
This four-axle heavy flatbed trailer has been designed for carrying heavy loads on highways, and is normally towed by the MAZ-537A (8 × 8) truck. The trailer is provided with drum brakes, air operated on all wheels, loading ramps, guide bars and load securing gear.

STATUS
In service with the Soviet Army and other armed forces.

MANUFACTURER
Chelyabinsk Machine Building Plant for Motor Vehicle and Tractor Trailers, Chelyabinsk, RSFSR, USSR.

SPECIFICATIONS
Weight:
(loaded) 74 500 kg
(empty) 14 500 kg
(on front dolly empty) 7340 kg
(on rear bogie empty) 7160 kg
Max load: 60 000 kg

Length:
(overall) 11·37 m
(of load platform) 5·5 m
Width: (overall) 3·3 m
Height:
(overall) 2·07 m
(of load platform) 1·14 m
Ground clearance: (at full load under suspension equalisers) 0·19 m
Track: (on centres of external dual wheels) 2·48 m
Wheelbase: 1·2 m + 4 m + 1·2 m
Max towing speed: 32 km/h
Tyres: 9.00 × 15
Number of wheels: 32 + 4 spare

Soviet Trailers

Designation	Type	Unladen weight	Payload	Max tow speed	Length overall	Height overall	Width	Wheel-base	Track	Ground clearance	Load area (l × w)	No of tyres	Electrical system	Towing vehicle(s)
GAZ-704	cargo	340 kg	500 kg	75 km/h	2·5 m	1·15 m	1·645 m	–	1·44 m	0·28 m	1·66 × 1·07 m	2	12 V	GAZ-69, GAZ-69A
UAZ-8109	cargo	350 kg	500 kg	75 km/h	2·785 m	1·19 m	1·72 m	–	1·44 m	0·29 m	1·66 × 1·07 m	2	12 V	UAZ-469, UAZ-469B
TAPZ-755, TAPZ-755A	special	470 kg	1500 kg	80 km/h	3·025 m	0·8 m	2·07 m	–	1·77 m	0·375 m	1·73 × 0·936 m	2 + 1 spare	12 V	GAZ-66
GKB-8302	cargo	950 kg	1200 kg	90 km/h	3·82 m	2·52 m	2·24 m	–	1·82 m	0·35 m	2·153 × 1·82 m	2 + 1 spare	12 V	GAZ-66
GKB-83021	special	650 kg	1500 kg	90 km/h	3·25 m	1·115 m	2·2 m	–	1·82 m	0·35 m	1·685 × 1·56 m	2 + 1 spare	12 V	GAZ-66
IAZP-738	special	570 kg	1500/ 1800 kg	80 km/h	3·85 m	1·65 m	2·1 m	–	1·77 m	0·378 m	2·285 × 1·87 m	2 + 1 spare	12 V	GAZ-66
IAZP-739	special	470 kg	1000 kg	80 km/h	3·85 m	1·65 m	2·1 m	–	1·77 m	0·355 m	2·285 × 1·87 m	2 + 1 spare	12 V	GAZ-66
GKB-8301	cargo	1610 kg	2500 kg	80 km/h	4·825 m	2·9 m	2·5 m	–	1·89 m	0·36 m	3·225 × 2·325 m	2 + 1 spare	12 V	ZIL-131
GKB-83011	special	1110 kg	3000 kg	80 km/h	4·055 m	1·16 m	2·73 m	–	1·88 m	0·36 m	no platform	2 + 1 spare	12 V	ZIL-131
SMZ-710V	cargo	1500 kg	2000 kg	60 km/h	5·64 m	2·715 m	2·32 m	3·7 m	1·59 m	0·305 m	5·3 × 2·11 m	4 + 1 spare	12 V	ZIL-157K, ZIL-131
SMZ-710B	special	1250 kg	2500 kg	60 km/h	5·64 m	1·13 m	1·89 m	2·4 m	1·59 m	0·305 m	3·95 × 1·89 m	4 + 1 spare	12 V	ZIL-157K, ZIL-131
SMZ-8325	cargo	2030 kg	2100 kg	80 km/h	6·22 m	2·78 m	2·48 m	2·5 m	1·82 m	0·42 m	4·22 × 2·25 m	4 + 1 spare	12 V	ZIL-131
SMZ-8326	special	1650 kg	2500 kg	80 km/h	6·2 m	1·2 m	2·23 m	2·5 m	1·82 m	0·42 m	4·535 × 0·925 m	4 + 1 spare	12 V	ZIL-131
SMZ-810	cargo	2400 kg	4000 kg	50 km/h	6·24 m	2·315 m	2·35 m	2·95 m	1·97 m	0·3 m	4·21 × 2·185 m	4 + 1 spare	12 V	Ural-375D
SMZ-810A	special	1900 kg	4500 kg	50 km/h	6·34 m	1·275 m	2·35 m	2·95 m	1·97 m	0·3 m	4·5 × 1·8 m	4 + 1 spare	12 V	Ural-375D
782V	cargo	3030 kg	4000 kg	75 km/h	6·875 m	2·9 m	2·455 m	2·95 m	2 m	0·35 m	4·87 × 2·3 m	4 + 1 spare	12 V	Ural-4320, Ural-375N
782B	special	2320 kg	4680 kg	75 km/h	6·8 m	1·34 m	2·34 m	2·95 m	2 m	0·35 m	4·93 × 1·8 m	4 + 1 spare	12 V	Ural-4320, Ural-375N
GKB-817	cargo	2540 kg	5500 kg	80 km/h	6·68 m	1·87 m	2·5 m	3 m	1·8 m	0·37 m	4·95 × 2·35 m	4 + 1 spare	12 V	ZIL-130, ZIL-130G
GKB-817A	cargo	2450 kg	5500 kg	80 km/h	6·68 m	1·87 m	2·5 m	3 m	1·8 m	0·37 m	4·95 × 2·35 m	4 + 1 spare	12 V	ZIL-130, ZIL-130G
GKB-817V	special	2640 kg	5400 kg	80 km/h	n/a	n/a	n/a	n/a	1·8 m	0·37 m	n/a	4 + 1 spare	12 V	ZIL-130, ZIL-130G
MAZ-5207VSh	special	2450 kg	6750 kg	50 km/h	6·55 m	1·14 m	2·405 m	3 m	1·97 m	0·31 m	4·91 × 2·405 m	4 + 1 spare	24 V	KrAZ-255B
MAZ-8925	special	3000 kg	7000 kg	85 km/h	7·785 m	1·14 m	2·5 m	3·7 m	1·97 m	0·43 m	5·56 × 1·7 m	4 + 1 spare	24 V	KrAZ-255B
MAZ-8926	cargo	4000 kg	6000/ 8000 kg	85 km/h	7·71 m	2·79 m	2·5 m	3·7 m	1·97 m	0·43 m	5·5 × 2·365 m	4 + 1 spare	24 V	KrAZ-255B
GKB-8350	cargo	3500 kg	8000 kg	80 km/h	8·29 m	1·81 m	2·5 m	4·34 m	2·315 m	0·38 m	6·1 × 2·315 m	8 + 1 spare	24 V	KamAZ-5320
MAZ-5224V	special	4000 kg	10 500 kg	50 km/h	8·355 m	1·06 m	2·87 m	3·7 m	2·15 m	0·38 m	6·46 × 2·8 m	8 + 2 spare	24 V	KrAZ-255B
MAZ-8950	special	4500 kg	10 500 kg	70 km/h	8·92 m	1·2 m	2·82 m	4·1 m	2·16 m	0·4 m	6·78 × 2·8 m	4 + 1 spare	24 V	KrAZ-255B
MAZ-8378	cargo	5500 kg	14 500 kg	85 km/h	11·57 m	3·735 m	2·5 m	7·375 m	2·365 m	0·43 m	9·67 × 2·365 m	8 + 1 spare	24 V	MAZ-5335, MAZ-5336
ChMZAP-5208	transporter	10 900 kg	40 000 kg	40 km/h	9·33 m	1·74 m	3·2 m	4·13 m	2·55 m	0·26 m	7·43 × 3·2 m	24 + 2 spare	24 V	MAZ-537P
ChMZAP-8386	transporter	13 170 kg	40 000 kg	60 km/h	11·23 m	1·63 m	3·15 m	3·85 + 1·3 m	–	0·25 m	8·2 × 3·15 m	12 + 2 spare	24 V	MAZ-537P

Soviet Semi-trailers

Designation	Type	Weight	Payload	Max tow speed	Length overall	Height overall	Width	Coupling to Wheel-base	Track	Ground clearance	Load area (l × w)	No of tyres	Electrical system	Towing vehicle(s)
OdAZ-885	cargo	2850 kg	7500 kg	80 km/h	6·385 m	2·03 m	2·455 m	4·43 m	1·79 m	0·315 m	6·08 × 2·22 m	4 + 1 spare	12 V	ZIL-130V1, ZIL-MMZ-164N, KAZ-608, KAZ-606, KAZ-606A
MAZ-5245	cargo	3800 kg	13 500 kg	75 km/h	8·12 m	2·355 m	2·5 m	5·18 m	1·866 m	0·38 m	7·875 × 2·32 m	4	24 V	MAZ-504A
MAZ-93801	cargo	4100 kg	13 500 kg	85 km/h	8·745 m	2·035 m	2·5 m	5·75 m	1·86 m	0·43 m	8·535 × 2·365 m	4 + 1 spare	24 V	MAZ-504A, MAZ-5429
OdAZ-9350	cargo	5500 kg	9500 kg	75 km/h	10·57 m	3·49 m	2·5 m	4·545 + 1·42 m	2 m	0·4 m	10 × 2·335 m	4 + 1 spare	12 V	Ural-4420, Ural-375S
MAZ-938	special	7500 kg	13 000 kg	70 km/h	13·05 m	2·23 m	2·5 m	8·46 + 1·4 m	2·16 m	0·36 m	9·16 × 2·8 m	4	24 V	KrAZ-255V
MAZ-938B	special	7000 kg	13 500 kg	70 km/h	13·05 m	2·23 m	2·5 m	8·46 + 1·4 m	2·16 m	0·36 m	9·16 × 2·8 m	4	24 V	KrAZ-255V
OdAZ-9370	cargo	3700 kg	15 400 kg	80 km/h	9·64 m	2·03 m	2·5 m	6·14 + 1·32 m	1·85 m	0·26 m	9·18 × 2·32 m	8 + 1 spare	24 V	KamAZ-5410
MAZ-5205A	cargo	5700 kg	20 000 kg	80 km/h	10·18 m	3·615 m	2·5 m	5·53 + 1·54 m	1·9 m	0·34 m	9·965 × 2·32 m	8 + 1 spare	24 V	MAZ-504V
OdAZ-9385	cargo	4100 kg	21 000 kg	80 km/h	10·67 m	1·98 m	2·5 m	6·19 + 1·32 m	1·85 m	0·285 m	10·17 × 2·32 m	8 + 1 spare	24 V	KamAZ-54112
MAZ-9397	cargo	6000 kg	21 000 kg	85 km/h	11·465 m	3·715 m	2·5 m	6·5 + 1·54 m	1·79 m	0·35 m	11·24 × 2·4 m	8 + 1 spare	24 V	MAZ-5432
MAZ-941	cargo	6700 kg	25 000 kg	80 km/h	13·22 m	3·755 m	2·5 m	8·85 + 1·54 m	1·86 m	0·42 m	12·795 × 2·365 m	8 + 1 spare	24 V	MAZ-515B
ChMZAP-5524P	special	4400 kg	25 600 kg	68 km/h	9·8 m	1·6 m	2·638 m	4·52 + 1·4 m	1·92 m	0·24 m	n/a	8 + 2 spare	24 V	KrAZ-258
MAZ-9398	cargo	6500 kg	26 500 kg	85 km/h	12·325 m	3·715 m	2·5 m	6·485 + 1·5 + 1·5 m	1·97 m	0·42 m	12·12 × 2·4 m	6 + 1 spare	24 V	MAZ-6422
ChMZAP-5523A	transporter	7000 kg	25 000 kg	70 km/h	12·83 m	n/a	3 m	6·83 + 1·4 m	n/a	0·24 m	6·765 × 3 m	8 + 1 spare	24 V	KrAZ-258
MAZ-5247/ ChMZAP-5247G	transporter	18 000 kg	50 000 kg	50 km/h	15·355 m	2·73 m	3·395 m	10·84 + 1·58 m	3·5 m	0·35 m	n/a	8 + 1 spare	24 V	MAZ-537G
ChMZAP-9990	transporter	18 000 kg	52 000 kg	60 km/h	14·42 m	3·19 m	3·15 m	8·4 + 1·3 + 1·3 m	n/a	0·25 m	8·96 × 3·15 m	12 + 2 spare	24 V	MAZ-537G

Other Soviet trailers, some of which are in service with the Soviet Army:

Designation	Type	Manufacturer	Capacity	Unladen weight	Length	Width	Height	Notes
2-ASP-4.5	dump	Nal'chik	4500 kg	2190 kg	5·02 m	2·26 m	2·25 m	Side dump trailer
2-PN-2 (SMZ-710V)	low-bed, 2-axle		2000 kg	1500 kg	5·75 m	2·32 m	1·75 m	Towed by ZIL-157K or ZIL-131[1]
2-PN-4 (SMZ-810)	low-bed, 2-axle		4000 kg	2400 kg	6·24 m	2·35 m	1·45 m	Towed by Ural-375D[2]
2-PN-6 (MAZ-520)	low-bed, 2-axle		6000 kg	3200 kg	6·58 m	2·5 m	1·52 m	Towed by MAZ or KrAZ[3]
GKB-817 (2-P-5)	2-axle	Lugansk, 1967 Petropavlovsk, 1968	5000 kg	2540 kg	6·6 m	2·5 m	2·22 m	Wooden platform with hinged sides towed by Ural-375
GKB-816	2-axle		3000 kg	1500 kg	5·73 m	2·25 m	1·73 m	Towed by ZIL-131
KAZ-717	semi-trailer	Kutaisi, 1965	11 500 kg	4000 kg	7·69 m	2·48 m	1·98 m	Wooden platform, 3 hinged sides
MAZ-524Z	2-axle	Minsk, 1960	6800 kg	3200 kg	6·97 m	2·5 m	2·05 m	MAZ-524ZB has canopy

Designation	Type	Manufacturer	Capacity	Unladen weight	Length	Width	Height	Notes
MAZ-584B	semi-trailer	Mytishchi, 1956 Saransk, 1961	7000 kg	2525 kg	6·3 m	2·46 m	2 m	Hinged side boards and tailgate, towed by ZIL-164A
MAZ-886 (2-P-8)	2-axle	Minsk, 1968	8500 kg	3500 kg	7·12 m	2·5 m	3·31 m	Hinged on 3 sides, fitted canopy and bows, towed by MAZ-500 or KrAZ-255B
MAZ-938	semi-trailer	Minsk	15 000 kg	7500 kg	12·2 m	2·8 m	2·33 m	Towed by KrAZ-255
MAZ-941	semi-trailer	Minsk	24 700 kg	13 700 kg	10·67 m	2·5 m	2·3 m	Towed by MAZ-525
MAZ-5206	flatbed, 2-axle	Minsk	10 000 kg	5400 kg	9·23 m	2·53 m	1·53 m	Towed by wheeled or tracked vehicle
MAZ-5224	low-bed, 2-axle	Minsk	10 000 kg	5000 kg	8·04 m	2·68 m	1·77 m	Towed by KrAZ-255B[4]
MAZ-5243	2-axle	Minsk	6800 kg	3200 kg	6·97 m	2·5 m	2·05 m	Towed by MAZ-500 truck
MAZ-5245	semi-trailer	Minsk, 1961	14 000 kg	3800 kg	8·12 m	2·5 m	2·33 m	Towed by MAZ-504[5]
OdAZ-740	semi-trailer	Odessa	23 000 kg	7000 kg	11·33 m	2·5 m	3·45 m	Van type, towed by KrAZ-221B
OdAZ-760	semi-trailer	Odessa	14 000 kg	4800 kg	8·84 m	2·5 m	2·27 m	Towed by Ural-377
OdAZ-784	semi-trailer	Odessa, 1959	7000 kg	2950 kg	8 m	2·57 m	3·3 m	Van type, towed by Kaz-606
OdAZ-794	semi-trailer	Odessa, 1966	7500 kg	3000 kg	6·93 m	2·5 m	3·22 m	Van type
OdAZ-795	semi-trailer	Odessa, 1965	13 250 kg	4200 kg	9·38 m	2·5 m	3·32 m	Van type, towed by MAZ-504
OdAZ-832	semi-trailer	Odessa, 1965	12 000 kg	4000 kg	9·5 m	2·5 m	3·5 m	Van type, towed by MAZ-200V
OdAZ-828	semi-trailer	Odessa	5500 kg	5800 kg	8·46 m	2·37 m	1·97 m	Van type, towed by ZIL-157KV
OdAZ-935	semi-trailer	Odessa, 1965	13 500 kg	4800 kg	9·38 m	2·5 m	3·32 m	Van type, towed by Ural-377S
PAZS-3137	mobile fuelling unit trailer		4200 litres	2806 kg	5·99 m	2·31 m	2·84 m	Fitted with pumps and hoses
TAPZ-738 (1-P-1.5)	trailer chassis	Irbitsk	1800 kg	600 kg	3·94 m	2·07 m	1·77 m	Towed by GAZ-53A, GAZ-63, and GAZ-66
TAPZ-739 (1-P-1)	trailer chassis	Irbitsk	1000 kg	500 kg	3·55 m	1·81 m	0·92 m	Towed by GAZ-53A, GAZ-63,[6] and GAZ-66
TAPZ-754 V	2-axle	Irbitsk, 1958	4000 kg	1900 kg	6·05 m	2·39 m	2·13 m	Wooden platform, 3 hinged sides, towed by ZIL-164
TAPZ-755 A	trailer chassis	Irbitsk	1500 kg	470 kg	3·03 m	1·82 m	0·93 m	Towed by GAZ-51A, GAZ-53A and GAZ-66[7]
TsV-50	single-axle trailer	Biysk	1000 litres	910 kg	3·92 m	1·66 m	2·08 m	Drinking water trailer
PTs-4.2-754V	tanker-trailer	Grabovskiy, 1966	4200 litres	2268 kg	6 m	2·28 m	2·75 m	Fitted with dispensing equipment
PTs-6	tanker-trailer	Grabovskiy	6700 litres	3700 kg	5·06 m	2·4 m	2·55 m	Fitted with dispensing equipment
VMG-40-51	tanker-trailer		950 litres (water) 300 litres (oil)		4·2 m	2·13 m	2·28 m	Water and oil, heater fitted
PKhZ	semi-trailer, 2-axle	–	–	–	–	–	–	Field bakery
SP-32	4-axle	–	–	–	–	–	–	Dining hall

[1] SMZ-710B trailer chassis is modified version of 2-PN-2 with 2500 kg load capacity. The 2-PN-2M (SMZ-8325) trailer is used for the PPK material preservation trailer
[2] Modified versions of 2-PN-4 are SMZ-810A trailer chassis with 4500 kg load capacity and SMZ-810PA trailer chassis for special bodies
[3] Modified version of 2-PN-6 is MAZ-5207VSh trailer chassis with 6750 kg capacity, which is fitted with various types of body, and MAZ-847 dump trailer with 6000 kg capacity
[4] Modified version of MAZ-5224 is MAZ-5224V chassis for van bodies
[5] MAZ-5245B is provided with canopy. Between 1956 and 1961 plant produced MAZ-5215B semi-trailer with 12 500 kg capacity
[6] This chassis is used for 1-P-1 1000 kg cargo trailer. TAPZ-739K chassis is used for KP-125M field kitchen
[7] MNUM-50M trailer-mounted pump comprises 3V 40/25 pump on TAPZ-755A chassis

MANUFACTURERS
Biysk Molmashstroy Plant
Irbitsk Motor Vehicle Trailer Plant, Irbit
Grabovskiy Specialised Automobile Plant
Kutaisi Motor Vehicle Plant, Kutaisi, Georgia
Lugansk Motor Vehicle Assembly Plant

Minsk Motor Vehicle Plant, Minsk, Belorussia
Mytishchi Machine Building Plant, Mytishchi
Nal'chik Machinery Construction Plant
Odessa Motor Vehicle Assembly Vehicle Plant, Odessa, Ukraine

Petropavlovsk Machine Construction Plant
Saransk Dump Truck Plant, Saranski
Zelenokumsk Plant

UNITED KINGDOM

Scottorn 750 kg Trailers

DESCRIPTION
The firm of Scottorn Trailers Limited produces many military pattern trailers in various weight capacities. There are two 0·75-tonne trailers: the Bushranger trailer is lighter and simpler than the Military L model, and has a hinged removable tailboard.

SPECIFICATIONS

Model	Bushranger	Military L(510/760 kg)
Weight	279 kg	355 kg
Length		
(overall)	2·695 m	2·795 m
(of cargo area)	1·754 m	1·83 m
Width		
(overall)	1·587 m	1·475 m
(of cargo area)	1·015 m	1·475 m
Height		
(without canopy)	1·015 m	1·015 m
(of towing eye)	0·56 m	0·535 m
Track	1·333 m	1·335 m
Tyres	6.00 × 16	6.00 × 16 (Land-Rover wheels)
Suspension	6-leaf semi-elliptic leaf springs	

STATUS
Production.

MANUFACTURER
Scottorn Trailers Limited, Chartridge, Chesham, Buckinghamshire HP5 2SH, England.

Scottorn Military L(510/760 kg) cargo trailer

Scottorn Bushranger 750 kg cargo trailer

GKN Sankey 750 kg Cargo Trailers

DESCRIPTION

These two-wheeled trailers both have a capacity of 750 kg and are made of all-welded steel. The trailers are provided with stabilising jacks, one at the front and two at the rear and lashing points for securing the load and for a canvas canopy. Service braking is by means of an over-run unit which operates hydraulic brakes and there is also a mechanical parking brake. A hydraulic damper isolates the trailers from shock transmitted from the prime mover, prolonging the operational life of the trailers.

As cargo carriers these trailers meet the NATO requirement of fording to a depth of 0·76 metres in fresh or sea water without preparation. The limit for the protection of cargo while wading is 0·61 metres. When fully loaded the trailers will normally be towed by any suitable vehicle of up to 1-tonne capacity, and a NATO standard inter-vehicle connector is fitted.

The FV2360 0·75-tonne trailer chassis is identical to the above but without the cargo body. This chassis can be adapted to take a variety of equipment such as water tanks and generators.

The FV2361 trailer is the standard trailer of FV Specification 9307 and uses the FV2360 0·75-tonne trailer chassis. The FV2381 trailer is similar to the FV2361 trailer, but has a wider axle and a removable slatted wood floor. The basic FV2360 chassis is used for a number of other specialist trailers including the FV2365 (welding set, lightweight, trailer-mounted), the FV2362 (trailer, tanker, water, 0·75-tonne, 455 litre) and the FV2368 (trailer, 10 kW 400 Hz generator, 0·75-tonne).

The FV2362 water trailer has been largely supplanted by the introduction of water carriage packs, polythene containers which can be carried in several general service trucks and trailers. Further details may be found in the entry for the Stellar Water Carriage Pack in the *Water supplies* section.

GKN Sankey 750 kg cargo trailer

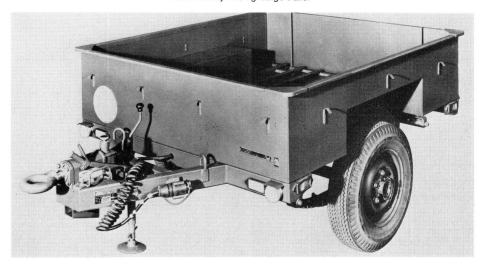

GKN Sankey 750 kg cargo trailer (wide-axle)

SPECIFICATIONS

Model	FV2361	FV2381
Weight (empty)	404 kg	408 kg
Length	2·92 m	2·85 m
Width	1·43 m	1·68 m
Track	1·2 m	1·42 m
Tyres	6.50 × 16	6.50 × 16
Max towing speed		
(road)	72 km/h	72 km/h
(cross country)	24 km/h	24 km/h

STATUS

The FV 2361 and FV 2381 trailers are in production and are in service with British armed forces.

MANUFACTURER

GKN Sankey Limited, Defence Operations, PO Box 20, Hadley Castle Works, Telford, Shropshire TF1 4RE, England.

Scottorn Bushmaster Powered Trailer

DESCRIPTION

The only Scottorn Bushmaster powered trailer in production is the single-axle version for use with the V-8 Land-Rover (4 × 4) light vehicle. The trailer chassis has two main members and four cross-members of 112 × 50 mm cold pressed steel channel with a 'V'-shaped drawbar and a 75 mm diameter swivel eye. The box body is all steel and may be extended for specialist bodies. It is bolted to the chassis. For the transmission system the Land-Rover is fitted with a 'bolt-in' drive unit coupled to the main transfer box. The drive to the trailer is by two propeller shafts which are connected to a rear bearing passing through the rear cross-member and terminating in a standard six-spline shaft. Power to the trailer is via a short intermediate shaft having a universal joint with a quick release coupling at each end, one mating to the main telescopic propeller shaft to the trailer axles, which is supported by a swinging arm adjacent to the coupling. A hand control is fitted in the driver's compartment to engage or disengage the trailer drive. The trailer may articulate 60 degrees either side of the vertical or horizontal planes.

The trailer axle uses the same differential, bearings, half-shafts, hubs and other components as the towing Land-Rover and has Land-Rover wheels with 7.50 × 16 tyres although 9.00 × 16 tyres may be used if they are also fitted to the towing Land-Rover. A dual brake system may be used, one system by vacuum and the other by inertia, depending on the system fitted to the towing vehicle. A hand brake is also provided.

Scottorn Bushmaster power trailer on tow by Land-Rover

Optional extras include a 946-litre tank and a canvas cover. A tubular tilt and cover can be provided.

The Scottorn Bushmaster powered trailer for use with the 1-tonne Land-Rover (4 × 4) is no longer a stock item but may be produced to order. Versions are now available for all four-cylinder and V-8 long wheel-base Land-Rovers including the One Ten models.

STATUS

Production as required.

MANUFACTURER

Scottorn Trailers Limited, Chartridge, Chesham, Buckinghamshire HP5 2SH, England.

Scottorn 1-tonne Trailers

DESCRIPTION
Four 1-tonne trailers are produced by Scottorn Trailers Limited for the military market. They differ in details of construction and in their intended roles. The Bush-ranger trailer has a hinged tailboard and angular mud-guards and uses Land-Rover wheels and independent suspension units. Of the 1-tonne general-purpose (GP) trailers, the first model is the simplest, with a one-piece body with the minimum of fittings. The next model has a hinged tailboard and cleats for securing a tarpaulin. The last model is heavier and is intended for use with larger trucks, such as the Bedford 4-tonne or the Mercedes Benz LA 911 and 1130 models. It has a canopy and a spare wheel.

Scottorn 1-tonne general purpose trailer (1st model) *Scottorn 1-tonne general purpose trailer (2nd model)*

SPECIFICATIONS

Model	Bushranger	GP (Model 1)	GP (Model 2)	GP (Model 3)
Length (overall)	2·87 m	2·79 m	2·79 m	n/a
Width	1·71 m	1·86 m	1·86 m	n/a
Height	1·15 m	1·25 m	1·25 m	n/a
Body (length)	1·86 m	1·83 m	1·83 m	n/a
(height)	0·46 m	0·54 m	0·54 m	n/a
(width)	1·12 m	1·22 m	1·22 m	n/a
Weight	n/a	540 kg	550 kg	n/a
Wheels	5-stud	5-stud	5-stud	6-stud; can be made interchangeable with towing vehicle
Tyres	7.50 × 16 (8 ply)	7.50 × 16	7.50 × 16	7.50 × 20, 12 ply rating
Suspension	rubber	8-leaf semi-elliptical	8-leaf semi-elliptical	n/a single line air
Brakes	mechanical over-run and parking brakes			

Scottorn 1-tonne general purpose trailer (3rd model)

STATUS
In production.

MANUFACTURER
Scottorn Trailers Limited, Chartridge, Chesham, Buckinghamshire HP5 2SH, England.

Scottorn Military 1000 kg/1250 kg General-purpose Trailer

DESCRIPTION
This trailer is designed for towing by vehicles of the Land-Rover class and, as with many other Scottorn trailers, the wheels are interchangeable with the Land-Rover. The trailer body is welded and has a removable hinged tailboard. Stoplights, tail lights and direction indicators and an electrical plug are provided to suit the towing vehicle. The square section beam axle is fitted with 9.00 × 16 tyres on Land-Rover wheels and is suspended on semi-elliptical leaf springs with shock absorbers and Aeon rubber helper springs. Mechanical over-run and parking brakes are fitted.

STATUS
Production.

MANUFACTURER
Scottorn Trailers Limited, Chartridge, Chesham, Buckinghamshire HP5 2SH, England.

Scottorn Military 1000 kg/1250 kg general-purpose cargo trailer with optional canopy supports

Scottorn Military 1500/2000 kg Cargo Trailer

DESCRIPTION
The chassis consists of main-members and two cross-members of 100 × 50 mm rolled steel channel with an additional three cross-members of 75 × 40 mm rolled steel channel. The drawbar is V-shaped and fabricated from 150 × 75 mm tapering to 75 × 75 mm pressed steel channel, strengthened at salient points. Mounted on the drawbar is a 75 mm tow eye. A solid or cushion tyre jockey wheel is fitted, screw adjustable to allow easy hitching and unhitching.

The body is constructed of heavy gauge sheet steel, with formed, integral cappings and vertical and diagonal strengthening pieces. A hinged full width drop tailboard with retaining chains is provided.

The trailer has a 100 mm diameter tubular beam axle and is fitted with cast steel hubs and drums. Six-, eight- or ten-stud fittings on 205, 275 and 335 pcd enable wheel interchangeability with such vehicles as the Mercedes Benz LA 911 and 1130 models, the Bedford RL and the Bedford MK trucks. The brakes are for the six-stud hub 310 × 90 mm and for the eight-stud hub 310 × 125 mm, operated by a single-line air system, or inertia braking. Suspension is provided by semi-

Scottorn 1500 kg general-purpose cargo trailer with mechanical brakes

elliptical springs, with double taper leaves and assisted by Aeon rubbers, shock absorbers and check straps. The trailer is normally supplied with 9.00 × 20 tyres.

Optional equipment includes 5-, 7- or 12-pin (NATO) pattern) electrical connector with lead and dummy socket, canvas tilt and tilt irons, 10.00, 11.00 or 12.00 × 20 tyres, 10.50 × 16 tyres with different axle specifications and other types of hubs.

SPECIFICATIONS
Weight: 850 kg
Length:
   (overall) 3·404 m
   (of cargo area) 2·235 m
Width:
   (overall) 2·108 m
   (of cargo area) 1·245 m
Height:
   (overall) 1·321 m
   (to towing eye) 0·99 m
Track: 1·79 m

STATUS
Production.

Scottorn Military 1500/2000 kg cargo trailer

MANUFACTURER
Scottorn Trailers Limited, Chartridge, Chesham, Buckinghamshire HP5 2SH, England.

Rubery Owen 2500 kg Trailers

DESCRIPTION
This series of trailers has been designed to meet the requirements of the British Ministry of Defence (Army Department) for a general-purpose two-wheeled cargo trailer capable of carrying a 2500 kg payload. The chassis is of rectangular hollow section and pressed steel. Wooden decking and pressed steel body side panels can also be supplied. The axle is a commercially-developed unit manufactured by Rubery Owen (Warrington) Limited. The suspension consists of two independent laminated square section torsion bars, integral with the axle tube, with rubber springs acting at the end of the trailing arms. A hydraulically damped over-run unit ensures that towing shock loads are minimised, and movement of the draught eye hydraulically operates the internally-expanding brakes. Three versions of these trailers have been developed; the chassis (FV2405), flat platform (FV2406) and cargo (FV2407) versions. The flat platform trailer is suitable for carrying generators and similar equipment and the cargo trailer can carry two of the 150-gallon (680-litre) water carriage packs manufactured by PD Technical Mouldings Limited.

See also the entry on Rubery Owen Close Coupled Trailer in this section.

SPECIFICATIONS
Length:
   (overall) 3·679 m
   (FV2406) 4·25 m
Width: (overall) 2·489 m

Rubery Owen FV2407 cargo trailer with water carriage packs

Height: (overall, loaded, to top of mudguards) 1·002 m
Track: 2·246 m
Towing speed:
   (road) 72 km/h
   (cross country) 24 km/h
Estimated unloaded weight:
   (FV2405 chassis) 905 kg
   (FV2406 flat platform) 990 kg
   (FV2407 cargo) 1080 kg

STATUS
Production. The cargo trailer with water carriage packs has been offered for sale to several countries including Pakistan.

MANUFACTURER
Defence Equipment Division, Rubery Owen Group Services Limited, Darlaston PO Box 10, Wednesbury, West Midlands WS10 8JD, England.

GKN Sankey 2500 kg Trailers

DESCRIPTION
There are three trailers in the GKN Sankey 2500 kg special purpose trailer range. The base element is the FV2405 Mark 11 Trailer Chassis (2·5 tonne). Then comes the FV2406 Mark 11 Flat Platform Trailer (2·5 tonne) and the FV2406 Mark 11 Trailer Cargo (2·5 tonne).

The FV2406 Mark 11 Flat Platform Trailer (2·5 tonne) was designed primarily for the carriage of a specialist 24/16 kW generator but the trailer is suitable for a wide range of equipment including water tanks, weapon systems, air conditioning units, etc. Welded steel construction is used for the chassis with uprated trailing arm suspension using rubber springs. The platform is constructed of exterior grade plywood and incorporates load lashing loops and wear strips. Three stabilising jacks are fitted as is a jockey wheel. Service braking is by means of an over-run unit operating hydraulic brakes through a hydraulic damper linkage to the master cylinder; a mechanical handbrake is fitted for parking. A spare wheel and carrier are fitted to the underside at the rear.

The normal tractor will be a 4 × 4, 4000 kg truck. Electrical equipment conforms to EEC regulations, and a NATO inter-vehicle connector is fitted.

STATUS
Production. In service with the British Army.

MANUFACTURER
GKN Sankey Limited, Military Contracts Department, Automotive Operations, PO Box 20, Hadley Castle Works, Telford, Shropshire TF1 4RE, England.

GKN Sankey FV2406 Mark 11 flat platform trailer (2·5 tonne)

SPECIFICATIONS (FV2406)
Weight: (empty) 1089 kg
Max load: 2500 kg
Length: 4·25 m
Width: 2·489 m

Height: (top of mudguard) 1·002 m
Track: 2·242 m
Max towing speed:
   (roads) 72 km/h
   (rough roads) 24 km/h

Scottorn 3000 kg Flatbed Cargo Trailer

DESCRIPTION
The trailer consists of a heavy gauge sheet steel decking mounted on a rolled steel channel chassis. The drawbar is provided with a 75 mm towing eye. Various wheels can be fitted to make the trailer compatible with its towing vehicle, which could be the Mercedes Benz LA 911 or 1130, or the Bedford R or M models, for example. A single-line air pressure brake system or inertia brake may be fitted.

SPECIFICATIONS
Weight: 750 kg
Length: (overall) 3·41 m
Height: (overall) 1·22 m
Width: (overall) 1·81 m
Deck:
(length) 2·24 m
(height) 0·87 m
(width) 1·25 m
Track: 1·79 m
Tyres: 9.00 × 20

STATUS
In production.

MANUFACTURER
Scottorn Trailers Limited, Chartridge, Chesham, Buckinghamshire HP5 2SH, England.

Scottorn 3000 kg flatbed cargo trailer

Trailer, Flat Platform, Air-portable, 5000 kg, 4-wheeled ACT 5

DESCRIPTION
This is a flat platform, four-wheeled trailer designed to carry 5 tonnes or six standard NATO pallets (1·02 × 1·22 metres) and is normally towed by the Eager Beaver rough terrain fork lift tractor. For air transport the trailer breaks down into packaged loads which can be reassembled by four men in 10 minutes. The trailer is air portable in medium and short range tactical aircraft.

STATUS
In service with British forces.

SPECIFICATIONS
Weight: (unloaded) 1300 kg
Length: (overall) 5·53 m
Width: 2·49 m
Height: 1·07 m
Wheelbase: 2·95 m
Track: (front) 2·13 m

10-tonne Tilt Bed Trailers

DESCRIPTION
These trailers have been designed to transport wheeled or tracked vehicles up to 10 tonnes in weight. The main bed platform tilts rearwards for loading and unloading and is controlled by a hydraulic hand pump on the drawbar extension with a single hydraulic ram in the main frame and beneath the main bed. Short ramps are provided which hinge on to the main bed platform when travelling. A 4-tonne hand-operated winch on the drawbar extension permits the vehicle to be used as a recovery unit. The towing extension incorporates a screw-down support leg and a swivel towing eye. The suspension is two-spring with one spring between the tandem axles on each side pivoting from central cross shafts. Eight twin 7.50 × 15-16 ply tyres are fitted. A spare wheel is mounted under the chassis on the left side of the trailer. Braking hoses and a lifting cable are provided for connecting the trailer to the towing vehicle. When loaded, the platform is held horizontal by spring-loaded pins at the front of the vehicle.

SPECIFICATIONS
Length:
(overall centre line towing eye to rear) 8·535 m
(tilt bed platform) 6·401 m
(centre line towing eye to front of tilt bed platform) 2·13 m
(centre line platform pivot to rear) 3·2 m
Width: (overall) 2·44 m
Height: (of tilt bed, empty and horizontal) 1·118 m
Track: 1·82 m
Wheelbase: 1·245 m

STATUS
Production.

MANUFACTURERS
Weeks Trailers Limited, Ferry Road, Hessle, North Humberside HU13 0DZ, England.
Crane Fruehauf, Toftwood, Dereham, Norfolk NR19 1JF, England.

Weeks 10-tonne tilt bed trailer in travelling position carrying Saladin armoured car

Crane Fruehauf 10-tonne tilt bed trailer tilted to rear

Dyson Trailers

For details of the Dyson 20-tonne cargo semi-trailer see *Jane's Military Vehicles and Ground Support Equipment 1983*, page 542.
Details of the Dyson 50-ton 16TW/4LB Transporter No 1 Mk 3 (FV3601) and the Dyson 55-ton tank transporting semi-trailer can be found in *Jane's Military Vehicles and Ground Support Equipment 1983*, page 544.

Crane Fruehauf 35-tonne Engineer Plant Semi-trailer (FV3541A)

DESCRIPTION
This is a cranked framed trailer with the vehicle being loaded over the rear suspension. The foredeck is narrow and fitted with tool lockers between the beams. The main frame is of high-tensile steel universal beam 406 × 178 mm on the maindeck with 356 × 171 mm on the foredeck. Frame-cross members are 152 × 89 mm rolled steel joists with a steel box section member of 203 × 152 mm at the extreme rear. Suspension is of the unsprung beam type with oscillating axles mounted at the ends of each beam to give full compensation between all wheels. Axles are constructed in solid form and oscillate on the rocker beams on plain bushes. The rear loading ramps are made from steel channel section with 34·9 mm finished hardwood boards, plus auxiliary ramps. The landing gear is screw operated with feet fitted at the crank. Rear support jacks are mounted under the tail of the frame to give support while loading.

Crane Fruehauf 35-tonne commercial type semi-trailer being towed by Scammell Constructor 20-tonne (6 × 6) tractor (FV12102)

SPECIFICATIONS
Length:
(overall) 13·98 m
(main deck from base of crank to start of suspension area) 5·51 m
(drop deck, including area over suspension and beavertail) 9·7 m
Width: (overall) 3·2 m

Height: (of platform) 1 m
Ground clearance: (minimum empty) 0·51 m
Slope of ramp: 1 in 5
Bogie wheeltrack: 0·84 m
Wheelbase: (king-pin to centre line of rear bogie) 10·08 m

STATUS
Production. In service with the British Army.

MANUFACTURER
Crane Fruehauf, Toftwood, Dereham, Norfolk NR19 1JF, England.

Craven Tasker 37-tonne RE Plant-carrying Semi-trailer

DESCRIPTION
This semi-trailer was supplied to the British Army Royal Mechanical and Electrical Engineers in 1982 and is one of eight special semi-trailers designated F6 47 LB. It is a low loading model designed to carry various items of Royal Engineer plant such as motor scrapers, bulldozers, etc, and uses a low profile Tasklift neck which is simple and rapid to detach and re-connect. The main

deck is 10·3 metres long and is supported on three axles. There is a 'beavertail' at the rear and 'cheese wedge' ramps for loading crawler and tyred equipment. Additional equipment includes a power pack to drive the hydraulic neck, spare wheel carriers, winch guides, stowage within the deck, heavy duty sunken rings and side extensions for wide loads.

SPECIFICATIONS
Weight: 12 000 kg
Load on towing unit laden: 17 000 kg
Deck length: 10·3 m

Width: 2·896 m
Height:
(main deck) 0·9 m
(rear) 1 m
Tyres: 8.25 × 15

STATUS
In service with the British Army.

MANUFACTURER
Craven Tasker (Andover) Limited, Anna Valley, Andover, Hampshire SP11 7NF, England.

Loading a Craven Tasker 37-tonne RE Plant semi-trailer with neck lowered

Craven Tasker 37-tonne RE Plant semi-trailer about to be raised

---

Crane Fruehauf Tank Transporter Semi-trailer Mk 1B

DESCRIPTION
This semi-trailer has been designed to carry MBTs weighing up to 60 000 kg. This chassis is all welded with a mild steel decking welded into position. The suspension consists of heavy duty unsprung rocker beam design with phosphor-bronze bushes on the pivot. The suspension is fitted with bump stops to limit fore and aft oscillation. The semi-trailer has four short axles mounted in two lines of two axles. Each axle is fitted with a taper roller bearing. Brakes are air-operated and a screw type handbrake operates on one row of axles only. Standard fittings include manually-operated rear loading gear, track guides, stowage boxes and tie-down points.

SPECIFICATIONS
Max load: 60 000 kg
Length: 11·87 m
Platform length: 6·7 m
King-pin to centre of rear bogie: 8·91 m
Width: 3·7 m
Height of bed: (loaded) 1·3 m
Ground clearance: 0·71 m

Crane Fruehauf tank transporter semi-trailer Mk 1 being towed by Scammel Super Constructor

STATUS
Production as required. In service with several armies including those of Jordan, Kenya, Kuwait and Libya.

MANUFACTURER
Crane Fruehauf, Toftwood, Dereham, Norfolk NR19 1JF, England.

Craven Tasker 20-tonne Flat Platform Recovery Trailer

DESCRIPTION
The Craven Tasker recovery trailer has been designed and developed to meet a British Ministry of Defence requirement for a trailer to carry a range of 'live' or 'dead' (disabled) wheeled or tracked military vehicles up to a weight of 20 tonnes, both on and off roads. It is a three-axle trailer with turntable steering.

The trailer has a sloping platform, terminating in a straked beavertail with spring-assisted ramps for rear loading, and the main frame is of ladder construction. The trailer is supplied with side extensions to increase the trailer loading width, and the ramps can be adjusted in position across the trailer to suit the width of the trailer. Winch rope rollers, recovery lugs and 5-ton shackles are supplied with the trailer, and stowage is provided for extension timbers, spare wheels, fire extinguishers, tools, winches and chains.

SPECIFICATIONS
Weight: (unloaded) 7000 kg
Length overall: (including drawbar) 11·78 m
Length of platform: 9·5 m

Craven Tasker 20-tonne flat platform recovery trailer

Wheelbase: (bogie centre-line to turntable centre) 7·12 m
Width: 2·5 m (extensible to 2·9 m)
Deck height: 1·07 m
Bogie suspension centres: 1·35 m
Fording depth: 0·76 m

STATUS
In production. In service with the British Army.

MANUFACTURER
Craven Tasker (Andover) Limited, Anna Valley, Andover, Hampshire SP11 7NF, England.

Crane Fruehauf 60 000 kg Tank Transporter Semi-trailer

DESCRIPTION
Shown publicly for the first time at the 1982 BAEE, the Crane Fruehauf 60 000 kg tank transporter semi-trailer can carry all existing in-service main battle tanks. It uses four short axles each carrying a heavy duty ten-stud disc wheel on a suspension of unsprung rocker beam design with heavy duty plastic bushes on all pivots to ensure an equal load distribution. All pivots are sealed. The main frame members are of 'I' section rolled steel channel joist angle and plate, with mild steel decking electrically welded to the frame members. Retractable landing legs with hydraulic fine adjustment support the front of the semi-trailer when uncoupled and the loading ramps are hydraulically operated. The hydraulic system is normally powered by a power take-off on the tractor truck but a hand pump system is also provided. A dual circuit air brake is used for normal use with a screw-type hand brake for parking. The rear lights are all guarded and operate from a 24 volt system. Accessories include three stowage lockers, racks for jerricans and a 60-litre drinking water container.

STATUS
Under evaluation by the British Army.

MANUFACTURER
Crane Fruehauf, Toftwood, Dereham, Norfolk NR19 1JF, England.

Crane Fruehauf 60 000 kg tank transporter trailer

SPECIFICATIONS
Max load: 60 000 kg
Length:
 (overall) 11·23 m
 (platform) 6·39 m
Width: 3·66 m
Ground clearance: 0·62 m
Brakes: dual air
Electrical system: 24 V

Craven Tasker 60-ton Tank Transporter Trailer

DESCRIPTION
Late in 1980 Craven Tasker (Andover) Limited completed a 60-ton tank transporter trailer for the British Army. This semi-trailer has hydraulically-operated ramps and forward leg gear, both of which are powered by an independent Lister engine on the top deck.

STATUS
Prototype in use with the British Army.

MANUFACTURER
Craven Tasker (Andover) Limited, Anna Valley, Andover, Hampshire SP11 7NF, England.

Tasker 60-ton tank transporter trailer being towed by Scammell (6 × 4) tractor truck

Ramps of Tasker 60-ton tank transporter trailer fold automatically when raised

Craven Tasker 110-tonne Modular Transporter Trailer

DESCRIPTION
This trailer has fully hydraulic steering and raising facilities powered by an electric start power pack. The height can be adjusted by 0·61 metre enabling the trailer to pick up loads by sliding between concrete supports. The tyres are 7.50 × 15 twin radials on five lines of oscillating axles, making a total of 40 tyres. The wheels can be steered hydraulically or mechanically by the drawbar. This trailer is in use with the Ministry of Defence at Rosyth, Scotland.

SPECIFICATIONS
Max load: 110 000 kg
Length: 7·95 m
Width: 2·98 m
Height: (mean) 1·1 m ± 0·3 m
Turning circle: 14·63 m
Tyres: 7.50 × 15
Number of tyres: 40

STATUS
In service with the British Ministry of Defence.

MANUFACTURER
Craven Tasker (Andover) Limited, Anna Valley, Andover, Hampshire SP11 7NF, England.

Craven Tasker 110-tonne modular transporter trailer

Scottorn Tanker Trailers

DESCRIPTION
Scottorn makes a range of tanker trailers of various capacities, of which three are described here. The smallest is a 680-litre (150-gallon) tanker which can be towed by any ¾-ton vehicle such as a Land-Rover. The other trailers differ in dimensions, capacities and fittings. All models have 3·2 mm welded steel plate tanks with 4·8 mm welded steel plate ends. Transverse baffles are incorporated in the tanks to prevent the liquid from surging. The tanks are filled through a 406 mm manhole with a 254 mm filling aperture, which is fitted with a lockable quick release cover with a pressure/vacuum valve. On the 680- and 1140-litre tankers a drainage pump, fitted with a 40 mm bsp gate valve, is provided at the rear of the tank. The 1350-litre tanker trailer is fitted with a water purification filter. The filtered liquid can be discharged either by gravity feed to four 12·5 mm bibcocks and one 25 mm bibcock, or pumped out by a 25 mm semi-rotary pump with 15 metres of 25 mm delivery hose. Similar filtering and pumping arrangements are also available as optional extras for the other trailers.

STATUS
Production.

MANUFACTURER
Scottorn Trailers Limited, Chartridge, Chesham, Buckinghamshire HP5 2SH, England.

Scottorn Military 1350-litre tanker trailer

Scottorn 680-litre tanker trailer

Scottorn 1140-litre tanker trailer with hand pump and meter

SPECIFICATIONS

Type	680-litre	1140-litre	1350-litre
Weight (empty)	350 kg	582 kg	860 kg
Length (overall)	2·49 m	2·794 m	3·404 m
(of tank)	–	1·524 m	1·829 m
Width (overall)	1·65 m	1·85 m	2·11 m
(of tank)	–	1·22 m	1·219 m
Height (overall)	1·12 m	1·473 m	1·524 m
(of towing eye)	–	0·66 m	0·99 m
Track	1·33 m	1·6 m	1·79 m
Tyres	6.00 × 16	7.50 × 16	10.00, 11.00 or 12.00 × 20 or 10.50 × 16

Type	680-litre	1140-litre	1350-litre
Wheels	5-stud	5-stud	6- or 8-stud to suit towing vehicle
Brakes	mechanical over-run and parking	mechanical over-run and parking	service brake: mechanical over-run or single-line air brake
Suspension	6-leaf, semi-elliptical	8-leaf, semi-elliptical	semi-elliptical springs with Aeon rubber assists

Scottorn 'Flat-Top' Tanker Trailers

DESCRIPTION
The Scottorn 'Flat-Top' tanker trailer range extends from tankers with capacities of 2280 to 10 000 litres. All the tankers have flat tops for carrying special equipment and the cross-section of the tank is 'D'-shaped. Most tankers have four wheels with the larger sizes having eight as an option. Typical of the range is the 4560-litre tanker which has a tank constructed from 5 mm mild steel plate, electrically welded. Internally there are two longitudinal and three transverse baffles. On the tank top are four 460 mm square manholes, one of which has a 406 mm cover and a 254 mm filling aperture, including a lockable quick release cover with a pressure/vacuum valve. A 50 mm outlet is fitted to the sump.

There is no chassis as such as it is replaced by a rear and front sub-frame integral with the tank. There are two square beam axles fitted with 305-mm diameter hubs. A 'V'-shaped drawbar with a 75-mm swivel is connected to the front carriage. The service brakes are single line vacuum with a hand parking brake. Optional extras include pumping and metering equipment, filtration equipment, body sides to convert the tank top into a cargo area and air brakes.

Scottorn 'Flat-Top' tanker trailer

SPECIFICATIONS (4560-litre)
Weight: 2250 kg
Capacity: 4560 litres
Length:
(overall) 5·182 m
(tank) 3·658 m
Width: 1·829 m

Height:
(overall) 1·753 m
(towing eye) 0·787 m
Wheelbase: 2·692 m
Track: 1·664 m
Tyres: 8.25 × 16

STATUS
Production.

MANUFACTURER
Scottorn Trailers Limited, Chartridge, Chesham, Buckinghamshire HP5 2SH, England.

Scottorn Mobile Servicing 510 kg Lubrication Trailer and Scottorn LAD 510 kg Workshop Trailer

DESCRIPTION
Both trailers are constructed on a chassis fabricated from rolled steel channel. Four retractable snapjack supports are fitted, one at each corner of the body, for added stability when the unit is in use. A tubular support frame is provided for a canvas tilt, which is raised when the unit is in use and lowered for travelling.

The lubrication trailer is fitted with a petrol engined compressor, grease pump, two oil pumps, grease reel, two oil reels, air reel, tyre inflator, penetrating oil reel, static sprayer and a spark plug cleaner. Optional extras include an all steel canopy and hubs and brakes fully interchangeable with the standard Land-Rover. A simi-

lar installation is now available mounted on a ¾-tonne (109-inch wheelbase) Land-Rover.

The LAD workshop trailer is provided with a 6 kVA, single-phase, 250-volt, 50-cycles alternator set with direct coupled air-cooled diesel engine complete with starter, starter battery and starter battery dynamo, totally enclosed sheet steel switch board mounted on the alternator and also fitted with a distribution panel incorporating one 30 amp fused isolator, one 25 amp Nipham output socket and seven output sockets. Equipment includes heavy duty drill, heavy duty grinder, bench grinder and polisher, pillar drill stand, portable air-cooled arc-welding set, portable air compressor, battery charger, two vices and a 9·14-metre extension cable.

SPECIFICATIONS

Type	Mobile servicing	LAD workshop
Weight	825 kg	1029 kg
Length (overall)	2·794 m	2·794 m
(of body)	1·829 m	1·829 m
Width	1·525 m	1·624 m
Height (overall)	1·955 m	2·134 m
(over equipment)	1·65 m	n/a
(to towing eye)	0·56 m	0·584 m
Track	1·333 m	1·333 m

STATUS
Production.

MANUFACTURER
Scottorn Trailers Limited, Chartridge, Chesham, Buckinghamshire HP5 2SH, England.

Scottorn mobile servicing 510 kg lubrication trailer

GKN Sankey 1-tonne Special Purpose Trailers

DESCRIPTION
This range of trailers shares the same basic suspension. Welded steel construction is used for the chassis, while the suspension is of the trailing arm type using rubber springs. Service braking is by means of an over-run unit operating hydraulic brakes through a hydraulic damper linkage to the master cylinder, and a mechanical handbrake is fitted for parking.

The trailers are normally towed by vehicles of ¼- to 1-tonne capacity, except in the case of the FV2415, which is described below.

The electrical equipment and inter-vehicle connector comply with NATO requirements. Optional fitments for the FV2411, FV2412, FV2413 and FV2415 include suspension retraction for airportability, front jockey wheels and support legs.

The trailer, missile resupply, 1-tonne FV2411, has been designed to carry spare missiles in their containers for the Rapier SAM system, while the trailer, cargo,

1-tonne FV2412, has been designed for the carriage of general cargo and specialist equipment for the Rapier system.

The 1-tonne flat platform trailers FV2413 and FV2415 have been designed for the carriage of specialist equipment such as generators for use in conjunction with weapon systems. The two trailers differ from each other in that the FV2415 has a raised and lengthened drawbar to permit towing by a 3- or 4-tonne vehicle, while the FV2413 is normally towed by vehicles of ¼- to 1-tonne capacity.

The 1-tonne airportable bridge trailer FV2420 has been designed to carry sections of the Laird Class 16 airportable bridge. Each trailing suspension arm is retractable to assist in loading and offloading the bridge sections and to reduce the overall height when the trailer is transported by air. The electrical system is mounted on a quickly detachable bar and extension cable enabling it to be mounted either on the rear cross-member of the trailer or on the bottom of the box on the bridge load. The side lamps are mounted on hinged bars to facilitate stacking of trailers. Turnbuckle-type lashing screws are provided for securing the bot-

GKN Sankey 1-tonne flat platform specialist trailer

tom box of the bridge to the chassis. These are also used for lashing stacked trailers together for transport by air.

The flat platform generator trailer FV2421, rated at

1·5 tonnes, has been designed primarily for the carriage of a specialist 24/16 kW generator used in conjunction with Electronic Repair Vehicles (ERVs), but is also suitable for a wide range of equipment such as air conditioning systems and water tanks. Its chassis is fitted with uprated suspension units, and three stabilising jacks and a jockey wheel.

The FV2425 trailer has been designed for the carriage of the EMI Cymbeline mortar locating radar (Radar FA No 15). Four steadying legs are fitted and the suspension may be retracted hydraulically to assist the functioning of the radar.

STATUS
FV2411/2412: In production. In service with countries using the Rapier SAM system: Australia, Iran, Oman, Singapore, United Arab Emirates, UK (Army and RAF Regiment) and Zambia.

FV2413/2415: In production. In service with the British Army and other armed forces.

FV2420: In production. In service with Australia, Canada, Nigeria and the UK.

FV2421: Production complete. In service with the British Army.

FV2425: In production. In service with the British Army and other armed forces.

MANUFACTURER
GKN Sankey Limited, Defence Operations, PO Box 20, Hadley Castle Works, Telford, Shropshire TF1 4RE, England.

SPECIFICATIONS

Model	FV2411	FV2412	FV2413	FV2415	FV2420	FV2421	FV2425
Weight	534 kg	534 kg	533 kg	533 kg	340 kg	533 kg	447 kg
Length	3·63 m	3·63 m	3·63 m	3·95 m	3·81 m	4·15 m	3·35 m
Width	1·75 m	1·75 m	1·75 m	1·75 m	2·01 m	2·02 m	1·78 m
Height	1·75 m	1·35 m	1·07 m	1·07 m	0·71 m	0·83 m	0·71 m
Track	1·5 m	1·5 m	1·5 m	1·5 m	1·75 m	1·77 m	1·5 m
Towing speed (good roads)	88 km/h	88 km/h	88 km/h	88 km/h	72 km/h	72 km/h	72 km/h
(rough roads)	40 km/h	40 km/h	40 km/h	40 km/h	24 km/h	24 km/h	24 km/h

GKN Sankey 1-tonne lightweight field artillery radar trailer No 2 (Cymbeline) (FV2425) showing levers for manually raising and lowering suspension

GKN Sankey 1·5-tonne flat platform generator trailer (FV2421)

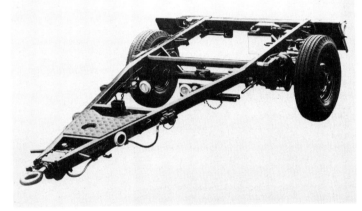

GKN Sankey 1-tonne class 16 airportable bridge trailer (FV2420)

GKN Sankey 1-tonne missile resupply trailer (FV2411)

GKN Sankey 1-tonne cargo trailer (specialist) (FV2412) of Australian Army (P Handel)

Rubery Owen Medium Girder Bridge Trailer (FV2842)

DESCRIPTION
This trailer has been designed to carry palletised loads of the Fairey Medium Girder Bridge (MGB), with a secondary role as a general purpose flat trailer. The trailer is the single-axle type fitted with semi-elliptical suspension springs with rubber bump stops with wire rope rebound slings. The chassis is constructed of rectangular tubular members on to which an aluminium corrugated decking is fitted. There is a three-line air pressure braking system and a mechanical parking brake. The trailer has been designed to be towed on roads at a maximum speed of 56 km/h and across country at a maximum speed of 24 km/h.

Some of these trailers have been converted to carry Giant Viper mine clearing equipment (see *Mine Clearing* section for details). These modified trailers have two wheels on each side of a walking beam suspension.

SPECIFICATIONS
Weight:
  (empty) 1461 kg
  (loaded) 4939 kg
Length: (overall) 5·867 m
Width: (overall) 2·565 m
Height:
  (overall, loaded) 2·62 m
  (overall, empty) 1·02 m
Track: 2·261 m
Tyres: 10.00 × 15, 14 ply rating

STATUS
In production. In service with most countries that use the Fairey Medium Girder Bridge.

MANUFACTURER
Defence Equipment Division, Rubery Owen Group Services Limited, Darlaston PO Box 10, Wednesbury, West Midlands WS10 8JD, England.

Medium Girder Bridge trailer with load of MGB sections

Rubery Owen Close Coupled Trailer

DESCRIPTION
Rubery Owen has been developing, in conjunction with the Military Vehicles and Engineering Establishment, an engineering research model trailer designed to investigate some of the problems of transporting heavy loads with a high centre of gravity (such as generator sets) on single-axle trailers. Even on trailers of 1·5-tonne capacity there are limitations in manoeuvrability. Jockey wheels and steady legs have been found to be of limited worth, chiefly on hard standing, and trailers of more than 1-tonne capacity cannot be satisfactorily manhandled off the road. The experimental trailer has been designed to meet six aims:
  to provide a rigid drawbar trailer capable of replacing existing steerable axle trailers of 2 to 6 tonnes capacity;
  to provide a suspension system of higher capabilities than hitherto, suitable for towing without any loss of performance, behind armoured fighting vehicles;
  to achieve tilt angles of 33 to 35 degrees with high centre of gravity loads;
  to provide a free-standing trailer capable of being loaded without the use of jockey wheels or steady legs;
  to provide a braking system for use with or without air pressure by both wheeled and tracked prime movers;
  to provide a load capacity of 4 × 1·5-tonne pallets.
The first version developed was a close coupled type with a capacity of 4 tonnes and was based on the axles used on the FV2406 2·5-tonne trailer. Because of the experimental nature of the trailer, provision was made for the two axles to be spaced at different centres and in reversible positions. The shock absorbers on the leading axle were replaced by dual shock absorber/jacking system manufactured by Sacol Powerline Limited. In this way the jockey wheel and steady legs were eliminated, and by means of a hand pump and change-over valve the system could be used as a variable damper or as a jack. When used as a jack, the drawbar could be raised or lowered to facilitate coupling to the prime mover, or locked to provide a stable platform when loading.
As a result of the success of the first development, the high mobility trailer of 8 tonnes gross vehicle weight was designed. The existing beam axles were divided and

mounted separately on widespread walking beams, increasing the available wheel movement from 0·165 to 0·37 metre and ensuring that all four wheels remained equally loaded under all conditions. The Sacol shock absorber/jacking units were lengthened and converted to double action, providing power jacking in both directions and allowing the whole suspension to be locked. In this way a stable platform was provided when loading and unloading the free-standing trailer. Trials with the 8-tonne trailer with both wheeled and tracked prime movers have highlighted the need for skid plates on the walking beams for operation in the more extreme conditions expected of a high mobility vehicle. A self-aligning drawbar was also fitted to overcome the need for accurate positioning of the prime mover when coupling up, which can now be accomplished by one man.
It has been proposed that there is considerable conversion potential for existing 2500 kg single-axle trailers carrying loads with a high centre of gravity and some investigation has been carried out on such trailers. It has also been suggested that there is considerable potential

for converting 1000 kg single-axle trailers that require a stable platform when deployed.

SPECIFICATIONS

Type	Medium mobility	High mobility
Platform length	2·44 m	2·44 m
Platform width	1·88 m	2·56 m
Platform height		
(laden)	0·76 m	1·04 m
Capacity	4000–5000 kg	6000 kg
Brakes	Lockheed hydraulic with	
	mechanical pull off for handbrake	
Tyres	8.25 × 16 radial, 14 ply rating	

STATUS
Development.

MANUFACTURER
Defence Equipment Division, Rubery Owen Group Services Limited, Darlaston PO Box 10, Wednesbury, West Midlands WS10 8JD, England.

Rubery Owen 6-tonne close coupled trailer test rig

1000 kg close-coupled trailer with all four jacks extended

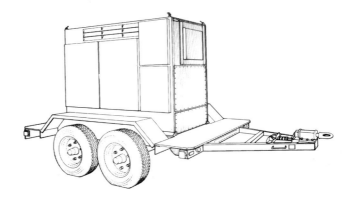

Suggested conversion of FV2406 single-axle trailer

Trailer, Mine Clearing Equipment, Giant Viper, No 2 Mk 3 (FV3705)

DESCRIPTION
This trailer has been developed specifically as the transportation and launch platform for the Giant Viper mine clearance device. It provides a cross-country capability for a payload of some 3 tonnes comprising explosive hose and launching rocket. It can be towed by wheeled or tracked vehicles. The chassis is of all steel welded construction, supported by semi-elliptical leaf springs on the single beam axle.

SPECIFICATIONS
Length: (overall) 5·867 m
Width: (overall) 2·477 m
Height:
(overall) 2·218 m
(platform) 1·089 m
Track: 2·134 m
Wheelbase: (axle to towing eye) 3·569 m
Gross vehicle weight: 4250 kg
Brakes: 3-line air system operation 394 mm diameter × 76 mm wide 'S' cam brakes
Tyres: 12.00 × 20 with run flat capability

STATUS
In production and in service with the British Army.

MANUFACTURER
Defence Equipment Division, Rubery Owen Group Services Limited, Darlaston PO Box 10, Wednesbury, West Midlands WS10 8JD, England.

Rubery Owen FV3705 Giant Viper trailer

Eezion SMT 800 Ground Level Loading Trailer

DESCRIPTION
The Eezion SMT 800 ground level loading trailer has a maximum payload of 5796 kg and can be towed by military vehicles such as the Bedford 4 × 4 four-ton trucks. Its chassis is of all welded steel construction. The wheel suspension is of a patented design which allows it to be pivoted, thus lowering the load platform to ground level for loading. Once loaded the platform is returned to the horizontal and locked. The tow coupling is a standard 76 mm eye mounted on a fully adjustable spring tow suspension giving a height variation of 0·609 to 0·914 metre from ground level by means of a hand wheel and screw complete with position lock. Three-line air-operated brakes and an independent hand parking brake are fitted as standard.

SPECIFICATIONS
Weight:
(empty) 2337 kg
(loaded) 8128 kg
Max load: 5796 kg
Length: 5·92 m
Platform length: 4·12 m
Width: 2·5 m
Platform width: 1·72 m
Tyres: 8.25 × 20

SMT 800 ground level loading articulated trailer immediately after being loaded

STATUS
In production. In service w th the British Army and Royal Air Force.

MANUFACTURER
Eezion Limited, Stanley Works, Ampthill Road, Kempston Hardwick, Bedfordshire MK40 3JD, England.

Dyson 12-Ton Airfield Runway Repair Strip Transporter

DESCRIPTION
This special-purpose drawbar trailer has been designed for transporting a roll of aluminium alloy extruded section for rapid runway repair, the approximate size of roll being 15·85 metres long and 1·52 metres in diameter. Development began in September 1973 and first production trailers were completed in January 1975.

The trailer consists of a twin-axle forecarriage with a single-axle rear carriage, both detachable from the main centre beam. The centre beam is in two pieces for ease of transport, and accommodates four detachable bolster units for roll location. Axle stands and canvas wheel covers are provided for use when parked for ready use by the runway.

SPECIFICATIONS
Weight:
(trailer) 4065 kg
(trailer and load) 15 755 kg
Length:
(overall excluding drawbar) 13·64 m
(centre line front bogie to centre line rear bogie) 10·98 m
Width: (overall) 2·32 m
Height: (to top of bolsters) 1·32 m

Dyson 12-ton airfield runway repair strip transporter with wheel covers for storage

STATUS
Production complete. In service with the British Army and other armed forces.

MANUFACTURER
R A Dyson and Company Limited, Grafton Street, Liverpool L8 6RH, England.

For a full description of the British Laird Rapid Runway Repair Kit the reader is referred to the Rapid runway repair equipment sub-section of the *Miscellaneous equipment* section.

Scottorn LUBE/LAD Servicing/ Workshop Trailer

DESCRIPTION

The Scottorn LUBE/LAD is a compact four-wheeled trailer on which is fitted lubrication and light workshop equipment for servicing and repairing vehicles and other equipment. The chassis is all welded and there are five cross-members to give additional support to the

equipment carried. The front axle is mounted on a ball-bearing turntable, and the drawbar is fitted with a tow box and 75 mm NATO eye, incorporating inertia and hand parking brake. There are two adjustable screw jacks, one on each side of the chassis.

The trailer floor is made of heavy gauge sheet steel, stressed at relevant points by the chassis cross-members. The equipment is enclosed by a canopy, the roof of which is steel, with roll-up vinyl sides and ends. A hinged dropdown workbench supported by retaining

chains and two removable props is fitted at the rear. There is an equipment locker which houses most of the electrical tools below the workbench.

Equipment fitted to the trailer includes a petrol-engined air compressor, a grease pump, three oil pumps, a transfer pump, a static sprayer, three oil hose reels, a penetrating hose reel, an air hose reel, a tyre inflator, a davit for loading and unloading oil drums, a spark plug cleaner, 1·5-kVa petrol generator, engine starter and charger, electric drill, drill stand, bench vice, flood lamp, hand lamp and lead and extension lead. Optional extras include hinged steel side and end panels, power brakes, waste oil tank and additional workbenches.

SPECIFICATIONS
Weight: 1497 kg
Length:
(overall) 5·34 m
(body) 3·91 m
Width:
(overall) 1·57 m
(body) 1·57 m
Height:
(overall) 2·19 m
(bench) 0·92 m
(tow) 0·65 m
Track: 1·34 m
Wheelbase: 3·05 m
Tyres: 6.00 × 16, 6 ply rating, on Land-Rover wheels
Suspension: semi-elliptical leaf springs front and rear

STATUS
Production.

MANUFACTURER
Scottorn Trailers Limited, Chartridge, Chesham, Buckinghamshire HP5 2SH, England.

Scottorn LUBE/LAD servicing/workshop trailer with side covers rolled up

Scottorn Mobile Workshop Unit

DESCRIPTION

The Scottorn Mobile Workshop Unit (MWU) is a conventional four-wheeled trailer fitted with a comprehensive range of equipment and workshop facilities for maintaining plant, equipment and vehicles in the field. The trailer is all steel and the side panels open to form working platforms and canopies. A generator normally carried internally can be removed and placed outside the trailer when operating. Equipment provided in the trailer includes blacksmiths', engineers', pipe fitters', electricians' and carpenters' tool kits and a range of specialist automotive maintenance equipment, jacks, grinders, welding and cutting equipment, and servicing equipment. The standard fit for the trailer includes three-line air brakes, but single-line air braking can be fitted as an alternative. Other options include air-conditioning, a translucent roof, and vacuum braking.

The trailer is fitted with two tubular beam axles with a wheel track of 2·43 metres, and 6-stud hubs of 205 mm pcd are fitted as standard. 14-ply radial tyres, of 8.25 × 16 size, are standard. The front axle is mounted on a ballbearing turntable and the drawbar is fitted with a 75 mm tow eye. Both axles are mounted to the body on heavy-duty semi-elliptical leaf springs.

STATUS
Production.

Scottorn mobile workshop unit ready for use

MANUFACTURER
Scottorn Trailers Limited, Chartridge, Chesham, Buckinghamshire HP5 2SH, England.

Miscellaneous British Military Trailers

The trailers listed below are believed to be in British military service and may also be in service with other armies.

DESIGNATION
Trailer, cargo, 1-tonne, FV2401(A).[1]
Trailer, cipher office, light, FV2401(E).
Trailer, water tank, 200 gallon, Mk 2, FV2401(B2).
Trailer, generating set, diesel engine, 10 kVA, FV2401(R).
Air conditioner, trailer-mounted, No 54 Mk 2, 1-tonne, FV2401(T).
Trailer, cargo, high loading, 2-ton, 4-wheel, FV2501.
Trailer, 2-ton, 4-wheel, FV2502 series, including generator, MT servicing, airfield construction laboratory, woodworking, and many other versions.
Trailers, flat platform, 2-ton, FV2505.[2]
Trailer, cargo, 5-ton, FV2601.
Trailer, AVRE, 7·5-ton, FV2721.[3]
Trailer, 4-tonne, motor tug, Mk 7, FV2823.[4]
Semi-trailer, 60-tonne, tank transporter, FV3005.
Semi-trailer, 50-tonne, tank transporter, FV3011.
Trailer, recovery, 10-tonne, FV3221.
Semi-trailer, 30-tonne, AVLB transporter, FV3542.[5]

FV2401(B2) water trailer (Soldier)

[1] Standard cargo trailer (Rubery Owen).
[2] FV2508 trailer, low platform, earthmoving ancillaries is similar.
[3] Used with AVRE to carry stores.

[4] Transports and launches motor tug used in bridging.
[5] Part of armoured vehicle launched bridge set; carries and can also lay No 9 (12 m) tank bridge for overbridging tasks.

FV3005 60-tonne tank transporter semi-trailer, with Antar Mk 2 tractor (Ministry of Defence)

FV3011 50-tonne tank transporter semi-trailer, with Antar Mk 2 tractor (Ministry of Defence)

UNITED STATES OF AMERICA

Trailer, Cargo: ¼-ton, 2-wheel, M416

DESCRIPTION
The M416 single-axle trailer is the replacement for the earlier ¼-ton M100 trailer and is towed by the M151 (4 × 4) light vehicle. The all welded body, bolted to the M569 chassis, is watertight and will float with a load of 226·8 kg. Two drain holes are provided in the floor of the trailer, which has a support leg and a tarpaulin cover. Its suspension consists of semi-elliptical springs. A mechanical parking brake is fitted as standard.

SPECIFICATIONS
Weight:
  (empty) 258 kg
  (loaded road) 599 kg
  (loaded cross country) 485 kg
Max load:
  (road) 340 kg
  (cross country) 227 kg
Length:
  (overall) 2·75 m
  (inside body) 2·44 m
Width: 1·54 m
  (inside body) 1·04 m
Height: 1·07 m
Depth: (inside body) 0·28 m
Coupling height: 0·58 or 0·66 m
Track: 1·44 m
Wheelbase: 1·87 m
Tyres: 7.00 × 16

Trailer, cargo: ¼-ton, 2-wheel, M416 with non-standard top (Michael Ledford)

STATUS
In service with the US Army and other armed forces.

Trailer, Amphibious: Cargo, ¼-ton, 2-wheel, M100

DESCRIPTION
The M100 single-axle trailer has been designed to carry cargo on both roads and cross country, or water, and is normally towed by an M151 light vehicle. The body and frame of the trailer are of all welded construction and are mounted on the trailer chassis M115. Two drain valves are provided in the floor of the trailer. The support leg at the front of the trailer is movable and a mechanical parking brake is provided, the hand lever for operating this being mounted on the right-front body panel. A canvas cover is provided to cover the cargo area and when not required this is stowed in a metal box mounted on the left front body panel.

STATUS
In service with the US Army. Being replaced by M416.

SPECIFICATIONS
Weight:
  (empty) 256 kg
  (loaded road) 596 kg
  (loaded cross country) 483 kg
Max load:
  (road) 340 kg
  (cross country) 227 kg
Length:
  (overall) 2·68 m
  (inside body) 1·83 m
Width:
  (overall) 1·47 m
  (inside body) 0·97 m

Height: 1·07 m
  (to towing eye) 0·69 m
Depth: (inside body) 0·46 m

Ground clearance: 0·35 m
Wheelbase: (towing eye to centre of axle) 1·77 m
Tyres: 7.00 × 16

Trailer, Amphibious: Cargo, ¼-ton, 2-wheel, M100

Trailer, Cargo: ¾-ton, 2-wheel
M101 Series
M101, M101A1

DESCRIPTION
This trailer has been designed to transport cargo both on roads and across country. Its body is all steel and is provided with a hinged tailgate, bows and a tarpaulin cover. The drawbar assembly is attached to the front of the chassis and a retractable pivoted front support is attached to the drawbar bracket. The chassis of the M101 trailer is designated the M116.

SPECIFICATIONS
Weight:
    (empty) 608 kg
    (loaded road) 1588 kg
    (loaded cross country) 1288 kg
Max load:
    (road) 1020 kg
    (cross country) 680 kg
Length:
    (overall) 3·73 m
    (inside body) 2·44 m
Width:
    (overall) 1·87 m
    (over wheels) 1·83 m
Height: (over tarpaulin) 2·11 m
Ground clearance: 0·36 m
Track: 1·57 m
Wheelbase: (towing eye to centre of axle) 2·54 m
Tyres: 9.00 × 16

Trailer, cargo, ¾-ton, 2-wheel, M101

STATUS
In service with the US Army, and many other armed forces.

Trailer, Cargo: 1½-ton, 2-wheel,
M105 Series
M105, M105A1, M105A2

DESCRIPTION
The M105 single-axle cargo trailer has been designed to transport cargo both on roads and across country and is normally towed by a 2½-ton (6 × 6) truck. The body of the trailer is of the box type and is provided with lattice type side extensions, tailgate, bows and a tarpaulin cover (optional). The brakes of the trailer are air-over-hydraulic with a mechanical parking brake.

The M105A1 and M105A2 are slightly smaller than the M105. The body of the M105A2 is wood and steel where the others are steel, and the M105A2 has an optional support leg.

SPECIFICATIONS
Weight: (empty) 1202 kg
Max load: 1361 kg
Length:
    (overall) 4·2 m
    (inside body) 2·79 m
Width:
    (overall) 2·11 m
    (inside body) 1·88 m
Height:
    (overall) 2·49 m
    (to towing eye) 0·87 m
Ground clearance: 0·42 m
Track: 1·71 m
Wheelbase: (towing eye to centre of axle) 2·79 m
Tyres: 9.00 × 20

Trailer, cargo: 1½-ton, 2-wheel, M105 complete with side extensions (R Young)

STATUS
In service with the US Army and other armed forces.

Trailer, Cargo: 1½-ton, 2-wheel,
M104 Series
M104, M104A1, M104A2

DESCRIPTION
The M104 trailer has been designed for general cargo work and is normally towed by a 2½-ton (6 × 6) truck. The trailer has a body of welded plate construction with the wheel housing integral with the body. The body has front and rear tailgates, hinged at the floor line and latched in the closed position by hooks. The chassis is designated the M102 (for the M104), M102A1 (for the M104A1) and M102A3 (for the M104A2). The M104A2 is identical to the M104 except that it does not have a hinged tailgate.

STATUS
In service with the US Army and other armed forces. The M104 trailers have been replaced in most units by the M105 series.

SPECIFICATIONS
(M104; data in square brackets relate to M104A1 where different)
Weight:
    (empty) 1089 [1238] kg
    (loaded road) 3583 [3733] kg
    (loaded cross country) 2449 [2599] kg
Max load:
    (road) 2495 kg
    (cross country) 1360 kg

Length:
    (overall) 4·2 m
    (cargo area) 2·79 m
Width:
    (overall) 2·11 m
    (over wheels) 2·06 m
    (inside body) 1·88 m
Height: 2·52 m
Ground clearance: 0·49 m
Track: 1·77 m
Wheelbase: (towing eye to axle centre) 1·77 m
Tyres: 11.00 × 20
Towing speed:
    (road) 80 km/h
    (cross country) 56 km/h

Semi-trailer, Stake: 6-ton, 2-wheel,
M118 Series
M118, M118A1

DESCRIPTION
The M118 semi-trailer, stake, consists of a stake type body mounted on an M117 chassis. Mounted towards the front of the trailer is the landing gear assembly. On the left side of the chassis is a box for storing the tarpaulin when not in use. The M118 has commercial type axles and air-brakes but the M118A1 has air-over-hydraulic brakes. For air transport, the suspension assembly of the M118A1 can be removed. These trailers are towed by 2½-ton (6 × 6) trucks.

STATUS
In service with the US Army and other armed forces.

SPECIFICATIONS
Weight: (empty) 3239 kg
Max load:
  (road) 7348 kg
  (cross country) 5443 kg
Length:
  (overall) 7 m
  (inside body) 6·7 m
Width:
  (overall) 2·41 m
  (over wheels) 2·35 m
Height: 3·37 m
  (to coupling) 1·19 m
Ground clearance: 0·49 m
Track: 1·52 m
Wheelbase: (king-pin to centre of rear axle) 5·18 m
Max towing speed:
  (road) 80 km/h
  (cross country) 48 km/h
Tyres: 9.00 × 20
Number of tyres: 4 + 1 spare

Semi-trailer, stake, 6-ton, 2-wheel, M118 (US Army)

Semi-trailer, Van: Cargo, 6-ton, 2-wheel, M119 Series
M119, M119A1

DESCRIPTION
The M119 semi-trailer van is used for carrying cargo both by road and across country and is normally towed by a 2½-ton 6 × 6 truck. The semi-trailer consists of a van body mounted on an M117 chassis. The body of the trailer consists of an angle iron framework covered on the outside with sheet metal and on the inside with plywood panels. The chassis consists of the frame, semi-elliptical springs mounted on an axle which is supported by dual wheels. The M119 has air-operated brakes while the later M119A1 has air-over-hydraulic brakes. Dual mechanically operated landing gear is mounted under the forward part of the chassis.

SPECIFICATIONS
Weight:
  (empty) 3257 kg
  (loaded road) 10 605 kg
  (loaded cross country) 8700 kg
Max load:
  (road) 7348 kg
  (cross country) 5443 kg
Length:
  (overall) 6·97 m
  (inside body) 6·78 m
Width:
  (overall) 2·53 m
  (inside body) 2·23 m
Height:
  (overall) 3·37 m
  (coupling) 1·19 m
Ground clearance: 0·49 m
Track: 1·78 m

Semi-trailer, van: cargo, 6-ton, 2-wheel, M119 (US Army)

Wheelbase: (king-pin to centre of rear axle) 5·18 m
Tyres: 9.00 × 20
Number of tyres: 4 + 1 spare

STATUS
In service with the US Army and other armed forces.

Semi-trailer, Stake: 12-ton, 4-wheel
M127 Series
M127, M127A1, M127A1C, M127A2C

DESCRIPTION
This trailer is used to transport general cargo and is towed by a 5-ton (6 × 6) tractor truck. The body frame consists of pressed steel side rails, cross-member, and short cross-members welded together forming one integral unit. The chassis consists of two drop-frame I-section longitudinal frame rails and intermediate cross-members with an upper fifth wheel plate, king-pin, two axles mounted on a leaf spring suspension and two foot-type landing legs.

    The basic M127 has air brakes but all later models have air-over-hydraulic brakes. The M127A1 is provided with chains which support the panels and also lifting rings for hoisting the semi-trailer. The M127A1C has a voltage control box mounted on the underside of the body and the M127A2C has improved landing legs.

SPECIFICATIONS
Weight:
  (empty) 6123 kg [M127]
         6531 kg [M127A1, M127A1C]
Max load:
  (road) 16 329 kg
  (cross country) 10 886 kg

Semi-trailer, stake: 12-ton, 4-wheel, M127 (US Army)

Length:
  (overall) 8·75 m
  (inside body) 8·53 m
Width:
  (overall) 2·46 m
  (inside body) 2·26 m
Height: (overall) 2·76 m
Ground clearance: 0·3 m
Track: 1·83 m

Wheelbase: (king-pin to centre of rear bogie) 6·12 m
Max towing speed:
  (road) 80 km/h
  (cross country) 48 km/h
Tyres: 11.00 × 20
Number of tyres: 8 + 1 spare

STATUS
In service with the US Army and other armed forces.

Trailer, Flatbed: 10-ton, 4-wheel M345

DESCRIPTION
The M345 flatbed trailer is used for carrying equipment both by road and across country and can be towed by a 5-ton 6 × 6 truck provided that it has an air supply.

The trailer is constructed of structural and pressed steel with the two axles forming a bogie unit. The trailer has an air-over-hydraulic brake system that is controlled from the towing vehicle. As the trailer has no parking brakes, chocks are provided to stop the trailer rolling when parked. Swing mounted landing gear is provided under the front and rear of the trailer.

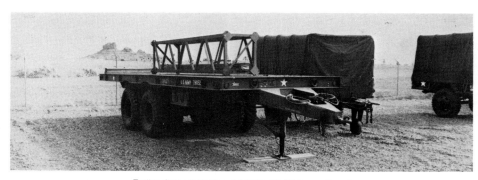

Trailer, flatbed: 10-ton, 4-wheel, M345 (Larry Provo)

SPECIFICATIONS
Weight:
(empty) 5107 kg
(loaded road) 16 901 kg
(loaded cross country) 14 179 kg
Max load:
(road) 11 793 kg
(cross country) 9072 kg

Length:
(overall) 8·38 m
(platform) 7·01 m
Width: 1·93 m
Height: 1·38 m
Track: 1·83 m

Tyres: 11.00 × 20
Number of tyres: 8

STATUS
In service with the US Army. A new 12-ton flatbed trailer is under development.

Semi-trailer, Low-bed: Wrecker, 12-ton, 4-wheel, M270 Series M270, M270A1

DESCRIPTION
The M270 semi-trailer is used for general haulage work and is normally towed by an M818 (6 × 6) 5-ton tractor truck. The semi-trailer has two axles at the rear mounted on a leaf-spring suspension. Mounted under the front of the trailer is a foot type landing gear, which supports the front of the trailer when not coupled to the towing vehicle.

The M270 is fitted with commercial axles and air brakes while the M270A1 has Ordnance-designed axles and air-over-hydraulic brakes.

SPECIFICATIONS
(M270; data in square brackets relate to M270A1 where different)
Weight:
(empty) 7938 [10 886] kg
(loaded road) 26 082 [29 030] kg
(loaded cross country) 18 824 [21 773] kg
Max load:
(road) 18 144 kg
(dirt roads and cross country) 10 886 kg
Length: (overall) 15 [15·17] m
Length of platform: 12·19 m
Width:
(overall) 2·46 m
(over platform) 2·44 m

Height:
(overall) 3·07 m
(over platform) 1·24 m
(to coupling) 1·37 m
Ground clearance: 0·46 m
Track: 1·83 m
Wheelbase: (king-pin to centre of rear bogie) 12·34 m
Tyres: 11.00 × 12
Number of tyres: 8 + 1 spare
Max towing speed:
(road) 80 km/h
(cross country) 48 km/h

STATUS
In service with the US Army.

Semi-trailer, Low-bed: 15-ton, 4-wheel M172
Semi-trailer, Low-bed: 25-ton, 4-wheel M172A1

DESCRIPTION
The M172 and M172A1 low bed semi-trailers are used to transport cargo including vehicles. The two tubular axles, mounted at the rear, are of the walking beam suspension type. Two mechanically actuated retractable, shoe type landing gears are provided to support the front end of the trailer when not coupled to the tractor truck. The two-speed landing gears are operated by a ratchet type handcrank on the right side of the gooseneck structure. The frame, which is the low bed of the semi-trailer, is of all welded steel. The M172 has commercial axles and air brakes while the M172A1 has Ordnance-designed axles, air-over-hydraulic brakes and a modified king pin arrangement. These trailers are normally towed by an M52 (6 × 6) 5-ton tractor truck; the 10-ton M123A1 (6 × 6) tractor truck; and the M816 20-ton (6 × 6) tractor truck.

M172 series trailer being towed by M123 (6 × 6) tractor truck (Larry Provo)

STATUS
In service with the US Army and other armed forces. The M172 is now being phased out of US service.

SPECIFICATIONS
(M172; data in square brackets relate to M172A1 where different)
Weight: (empty) 7030 [6740] kg
Max load: 13 608 [22 680] kg
Length: (overall) 10·31 [10·51] m

Width: 2·92 m
Height: 1·61 [1·73] m
(to coupling) 1·36 m
Ground clearance: 0·33 [0·38] m
Track: 2·08 [2·09] m
Wheelbase: (king-pin to centre of rear bogie) 8·33 m
Tyres: 10.00 × 15 [11.00 × 15]
Number of tyres: 8 + 1 spare
Max towing speed:
(road) 48 km/h
(cross country) 16 km/h

Semi-trailer, Tank Transporter: 45-ton, 8-wheel M15A1 and 50-ton, 8-wheel, M15A2

DESCRIPTION
These trailers are designed to transport tanks and other armoured vehicles and are normally towed by a 10-ton tractor truck such as the M123. The trailer consists of a low drop frame with a low bed-type platform, with two axles each of which has four wheels. The brakes on the semi-trailer are actuated by compressed air supplied by the tractor truck. The M15A2 has a reinforced frame, wider body to accept wider tanks, installation of track guides and the removal of the storage compartments at the forward end of the trailer. Two foot-type landing legs are provided under the forward end of the trailer.

Semi-trailer, tank transporter, 45-ton, 8-wheel M15A1

SPECIFICATIONS
(M15A1; data in square brackets relate to M15A2 where different)
Weight:
(empty) 19 219 [19 323] kg
(loaded) 60 043 [64 683] kg
Max load: 40 824 [45 360] kg
Length: 11·69 m
Width: 3·81 m
Coupling height: 1·72 m
Ground clearance: 0·33 m

Wheelbase: 9·5 m
Max towing speed: 41 km/h
Tyres: 14.00 × 20 [14.00 × 24]
Number of tyres: 8 + 1 spare

STATUS
In service with the US Army and other armed forces. Is being replaced by the M747 for which there is a separate entry. The M15A1 is now obsolete in the US Army.

Semi-trailer, Low Bed, 60-ton, M747 (Condec C2288)

DESCRIPTION

The M747 semi-trailer was originally designed as part of the HET-70 (Heavy Equipment Transporter for the 1970s) project. This was a joint development by Chrysler (USA) and Krupp and Faun of the Federal Republic of Germany, and was to have transported the MBT-70 tank which was cancelled in January 1970. The M747 is designed for use with the M746 (8 × 8) 22½-ton tractor manufactured by the Ward LaFrance Truck Corporation of New York.

The semi-trailer is equipped with four axles, dual wheels, and high flotation duplex tyres. The suspension for the two front axles is a walking beam type and the two rear axles are fitted with an adjustable air ride system which permits equalisation of loading among all four axles under a wide range of payloads. The air lift system, used with the two rearmost axles, raises these axles off the road surface when the vehicle is not loaded or is carrying a light load. Raising the rearmost axles also provides improved manoeuvrability when turning corners and reduces tyre wear. The West German version (SLT 50-2, qv) achieves this manoeuvrability with steered axles.

The semi-trailer is equipped with heavy duty, militarised, air-operated service brakes at all wheel positions. Each wheel is fitted with fail-safe provisions which require an initial build-up to a pre-set, continuous air supply pressure before normal operations begin. Emergency service provisions have been incorporated to provide for all wheel lock-up in the event of a sudden loss of air pressure. The brake system incorporates manual release to override both fail-safe and emergency service conditions facilitating subsequent movement of the vehicle.

Two removable aluminium loading ramps permit backloading operations without disconnecting the

M747 heavy equipment transporter

tractor/trailer. Four cable roller assemblies and a snatch block preclude the need of special rigging when winching operations are required to load disabled or trackless vehicles. Twenty-eight tiedowns are provided to secure the load.

SPECIFICATIONS
Weight:
(empty) 14 515 kg
(loaded) 69 015 kg
Max load: 54 500 kg
Length:
(overall) 13·06 m
(of platform) 8·05 m
Width:
(overall) 3·48 m
(of platform) 3·05 m

Height:
(overall) 2·71 m
(to platform) 1·12 m
Ground clearance: (under chassis) 0·69 m
Track: 2·59 m
Wheelbase: (king-pin to centre of first bogie) 8·07 m
Tyres: 15.00 × 19.5
Number of tyres: 16 + 1 spare
Fording: 1·22 m

STATUS
Production complete. In service with the US Army and Morocco.

MANUFACTURER
CONDIESEL Mobile Equipment, 1700 East Putnam Avenue, Old Greenwich, Connecticut 06870, USA.

FWD International Model 3ST50 50-tonne Heavy Equipment Transporter Semi-trailer

DESCRIPTION

The FWD International Model 3ST50 is a heavy duty semi-trailer for use on and off roads and is capable of carrying wheeled or tracked loads. The main platform deck may be steel or wood and the semi-trailer has three axles. When not on a tractor two front legs may be used; they are mechanically operated at two speeds. The loading ramps are steel (or aluminium) and the loading width is adjustable. Loads may be hand-winched on or off and once on the platform are held in place by eight removable curbs and four steel chocks. Legs under the loading ramps assist in stabilisation when loading or un-loading. The suspension uses torque rods and each system has nine heavy-duty leaf springs. A large stowage box is located on top of the trailer gooseneck to hold the trailer tool-kit and spares. Two spare tyres may be carried on the gooseneck. Air brakes are provided and the electrical system may be altered to suit customer requirements although the normal system is 12 volts.

SPECIFICATIONS
Weight: (empty) 15 585 kg
Max payload: 49 895 kg
Load on each axle: 13 608 kg
Length:
(overall) 14·681 m
(platform) 12·268 m

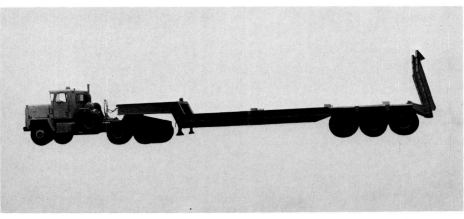

FWD International Model 3ST50 50-tonne heavy equipment transporter semi-trailer

Width: 3·6068 m
Height:
(overall) 2·057 m
(king-pin) 1·5113 m
(platform, unloaded) 1·397 m
(platform, loaded) 1·372 m
Ground clearance: 0·686 m
Axle wheelbase: 1·2934 m + 1·2934 m
Angle of departure: 40°
Electrical system: (standard) 12 V

Tyres: 14.00 × 20
Number of tyres: 12 + 2 spare (optional)

STATUS
Production. Believed to be in service with several armed forces.

MANUFACTURER
FWD International Inc, 1020 West 31st Street, Downers Grove, Illinois 60515, USA.

Semi-trailer, Flatbed, 22½-ton, Break Bulk/Container, Transporter, M871 and Semi-trailer, Flatbed, 34-ton, Break Bulk/Container, Transporter, M872

DESCRIPTION

The M871 and M872 semi-trailers have been procured to carry containers and other military freight in rear areas, and are intended for operation at sustained high speeds on main roads. The M872 will normally be operated from a port area as far forward as the Corps General Support Supply Activity (GSSA), while the M871 will be used for the transport of containers, shelters and cargo forward from the Corps GSSA to the Division Support Command (DISCOM) or even to user units.

The M871 semi-trailer is designed to carry containers and shelters of up to 6·1 metres in length, while the M872 is designed for the carriage of containers up to 12·2 metres long. Both can also carry break bulk (loose)

items of cargo. The two semi-trailers use many identical components and differ only in length and running gear. Each has a main frame on which the load bed and a headboard are fitted. The M871 is a 2-axle semi-trailer, while the M872 has a 3-axle bogie. Two landing jacks are provided and there are two storage lockers below the load deck. A yard kit is supplied with removable guide assemblies to aid positioning of containers before being secured with twistlock devices. Side racks are also provided with removable side and rear panels and cover plates. The side panels are hinged to allow for the carriage of loose break bulk cargo without spillage.

STATUS
In production. The US Army has a requirement for a total of 3982 M871 and 11 488 M872 semi-trailers.

MANUFACTURERS
M871: Southwest Truck Body Corporation.
M872: Heller Truck Body Company, Southwest Truck Body Corporation and Thurer-Greenville Corporation.

SPECIFICATIONS

Type	M871	M872
Weight	n/a	7893 kg
Payload	20 320 kg	30 481 kg
Length	9·1 m	12·45 m
Width	2·44 m	2·44 m
Deck (length)	9·1 m	12·44 m
(width)	2·44 m	2·44 m
(height)	1·4 m	1·5 m
King-pin height	1·27 m	1·27 m
Track	1·82 m	1·82 m
Ground clearance (min)	0·27 m	0·27 m
Tyres (commercial highway tread)	11.00 × 20, 12 PR	10.00 × 20, 12 PR
Number of tyres	8 + 1 spare	12 + 1 spare
Towing vehicle		
(primary)		M915 line haul tractor
(secondary)		M818 5-ton 6 × 6 tractor
(terminal)		M878 yard tractor

Semi-trailer, Flatbed, 22½-ton, Break Bulk/Container, Transporter M871

Semi-trailer, Flatbed, 34-ton, Break Bulk/Container, Transporter M872

Trailer, Tank: Water, 1½-ton, 2-wheel, 400-gallon, M106 Series M106, M106A1, M106A2

DESCRIPTION
The M106 single-axle trailer is used to transport, store and distribute drinking water. The aluminium tank has a capacity of 1514 litres and has an elliptical cross section. The trailer is provided with a hand water pump and a 7·62-metre suction hose for filling.

The trailer has been designed for fording where the trailer will be completely submerged and is normally towed by a 2½-ton (6 × 6) truck provided the towing vehicle has an air supply.

The M106A1 has a cover plate over the piping between the two welded metal tap boxes at the front of the tank. The M106A2 employs two hydraulic wheel cylinders for each wheel service brake. The M106A1 and M106A2 do not have a support leg, which is fitted only on the M106 trailer.

SPECIFICATIONS
(M106; data in square brackets relate to M106A1 where different)
Weight:
  (empty) 1034 [1070] kg
  (loaded) 2547 [2583] kg
Max load: 1514 litres
Length: 4·23 m
Width: 2·36 m
  (over tyres) 2·06 m
Height: 2·03 m
Ground clearance: 0·5 m
Track: 1·77 m
Wheelbase: 2·88 m
Tyres: 11.00 × 20
Max towing speed:
  (road) 80 km/h
  (cross country) 48 km/h
Fording: complete submergence

Trailer, Tank: Water, 1½-ton, 2-wheel, 400-gallon, M106

STATUS
In service with the US Army.

Trailer, Tank: Water, 1½-ton, 2-wheel, 400-gallon, M107 Series M107, M107A1, M107A2

DESCRIPTION
The M107 tanker trailer has been designed to transport, store and dispense drinking water, and is normally towed by a 2½-ton (6 × 6) truck, provided the truck has an air supply.

The trailer has a 1514-litre aluminium water tank with an elliptical cross section and is fitted with a hand water pump and a 7·62-metre suction hose for filling. Brakes on the trailer are of the air-over-hydraulic type, with a mechanical parking brake. The basic M107 is provided with a support leg, which is not fitted to the M107A1 and M107A2.

On the M107A1 and M107A2 there is a cover plate over the piping between the two welded metal tap boxes at the front of the tank, and the castor is raised and locked in a mounting bracket welded to the nose of the chassis frame. The M107A2 also employs two hydraulic wheel cylinders for each wheel service brake.

SPECIFICATIONS
(M107; data in square brackets relate to M107A1 where different)
Weight:
  (empty) 1034 kg
  (loaded) 2546 kg
Max load: 1512 litres
Length: (overall) 4·32 [4·14] m
Width: (overall) 2·27 [2·08] m
Height: 1·91 [1·96] m

Trailer, tank: water, 1½-ton, 2-wheel, 400-gallon, M107A1 of Spanish Army

Ground clearance: 0·41 m
Track: 1·72 m
Max towing speed:
  (road) 88 km/h
  (cross country) 24 km/h

Tyres: 9.00 × 20
Fording: complete submergence

STATUS
In service with the US Army and other armed forces.

Trailer, Tank: Water, 1½-ton, 2-wheel, 400-gallon, M149 Series M149, M149A1, M149A2 and M625

DESCRIPTION
This single-axle two-wheeled trailer is used to transport, store and dispense drinking water, and is normally towed by a 2½-ton (6 × 6) truck. The trailer has a filling cap on top of the tank and two dispensing taps in boxes in front of the tank. The main brakes are air-over-hydraulic, with a mechanical parking brake also provided. The M149A1 has an improved lighting system. The M149A2 has a stainless steel tank, while the other types all have fibreglass ones.

STATUS
Production. In service with the US Army. The M625 requires a towing vehicle equipped with a vacuum booster, and has been provided to other countries under the Military Aid Programme.

Trailer, tank: water, 1½-ton, 2-wheel, 400-gallon, M149

SPECIFICATIONS
Weight: 1288 kg
Max load: 1514 litres
Length: 4·09 m
Width: 2·09 m
Height: 1·94 m
  (towing eye) 0·76 to 1·04 m
Ground clearance: 0·43 m
Track: 1·71 m
Wheelbase: (towing eye to centre of axle) 2·87 m
Tyres: 9.00 × 20

Semi-trailer, Tank, Fuel, 5000-gallon, 4-wheel, M131 Series M131, M131A1, M131A1C, M131A2, M131A2C, M131A3, M131A3C, M131A4 (XM664), M131A4C (XM664C), M131A5, M131A5C, M131A5D, M131E6, M308.

DESCRIPTION
The M131 semi-trailer is designed to transport and dispense 18 927 litres of fuel. A cabinet mounted at the rear of the trailer houses the air-cooled auxiliary engine, pump and control equipment. A fire extinguisher is carried on each side of the trailer and there are two landing legs at the front. The M131 series semi-trailers are towed by a 5-ton (6 × 6) truck.

The M131 and M131A1 each have three compartments and the other models all have four. The coating of the tanks of the M131 to M131A3C is not corrosion-resistant. The M131A4 (known during development as the XM664) has a corrosion-resistant tank and can carry gasoline, diesel, JP4 and JP5. The M131A4C is similar to the M131A4 but has a complete servicing capability,

being provided with a filtration unit, hosereel and meter. The M131E6 (a development model) was configured as an aircraft refueller. The M308 is similar to the M131 series but is designed to carry 4000 gallons (15 140 litres) of water. The M857 series (qv) is the replacement for the M131 series of fuel semi-trailers.

STATUS
Most of the later models are still in service with the US Army.

SPECIFICATIONS
Type	M131A1	M131A2	M131A3C	M131A4C	M131A5	M131A5C
Weight						
(empty)	6770 kg	5610 kg	6680 kg	7020 kg	5660 kg	7020 kg
(loaded, cross country)	15 670 kg	14 510 kg	15 580 kg	15 920 kg	14 560 kg	15 920 kg
(loaded, road)	20 620 kg	19 460 kg	20 530 kg	20 870 kg	19 510 kg	20 870 kg
Max load						
(cross country)	8900 kg	8900 kg	8900 kg	8900 kg	8900 kg	8900 kg
(road)	13 850 kg	13 850 kg	13 850 kg	13 850 kg	13 850 kg	13 850 kg
Length	8·94 m	9·65 m	9·77 m	9·49 m	9·49 m	9·56 m
Width	2·48 m	2·48 m	2·49 m	2·48 m	2·48 m	2·45 m
Height	3·34 m	2·72 m	2·68 m	2·76 m	2·72 m	2·76 m
Coupling height	1·42 m	1·42 m	1·42 m	1·42 m	1·42 m	1·42 m
Ground clearance	0·3 m	0·3 m	0·3 m	0·3 m	0·3 m	0·3 m
Tyres	11.00 × 20	11.00 × 20	11.00 × 20	11.00 × 20	11.00 × 20	11.00 × 20
Number of tyres	8 + 1 spare	8 + 1 spare	8 + 1 spare	8 + 1 spare	8 + 1 spare	8 + 1 spare
Max towing speed						
(cross country)	32 km/h	32 km/h	32 km/h	32 km/h	32 km/h	32 km/h
(road)	84 km/h	84 km/h	84 km/h	84 km/h	84 km/h	84 km/h

Semi-trailer, Tank, Fuel, 5000-gallon, 4-wheel, M900 Series, M967, M969, M970

DESCRIPTION
The M900 series of fuel semi-trailers is the replacement for the earlier M131 series. It consists of the M967 bulk haul refueller, the M969 automotive refueller and the M970 aircraft refueller.

STATUS
In service with the US Army and (M970) US Marine Corps. The initial order was for approximately 850 semi-trailers of the M900 series. The fiscal year 1982 budget included a request for funds for 703 fuel semi-trailers. M900 series semi-trailers have been supplied to Portugal.

Trailer, Ammunition: 1½-ton, 2-wheel, M332

DESCRIPTION
The M332 ammunition trailer consists of a frame supported by an axle assembly with leaf spring suspension. A retractable support is provided at the front end of the trailer. Brakes are air-over-hydraulic and there is also a mechanical parking brake. If required, the top of the trailer can be covered by a tarpaulin which is stowed in a box on the forward part of the trailer when not in use.

SPECIFICATIONS
Weight:
  (empty) 1270 kg
  (loaded) 2630 kg
Max load: 1360 kg
Length: (overall) 3·76 m
Width: (overall) 2·48 m
Height: 1·35 m
  (to towing eye) 0·85 m
Track: 2·03 m
Towing speed:
  (road) 80 km/h
  (cross country) 40 km/h
Tyres: 9.00 × 20

STATUS
In service with the US Army.

Trailer, ammunition: 1½-ton, 2-wheel, M332

Chassis, Trailer: 2-ton, 2-wheel, M390 and M390C

DESCRIPTION
These chassis trailers are used in the Raytheon HAWK surface-to-air missile system. The M390 is used to transport electronic equipment while the M390C carries three missiles. Each trailer consists of a chassis, deck plate (not on the M390), suspension system, two wheels, air-over-hydraulic brakes, individual hand-brakes for each wheel, retractable landing gear, levelling support jacks and a towing eye.

These trailers have also been built in the Netherlands by the DAF company under the designation M390-17 and M390-17C, for which there is a separate entry in the Netherlands section.

STATUS
In production. In service with countries using the HAWK surface-to-air missile system including Belgium, Denmark, France, West Germany, Greece, Iran, Israel, Italy, Japan, Jordan, South Korea, Kuwait, the Netherlands, Saudi Arabia, Spain, Sweden, Taiwan, Thailand and the USA. Most trailers for the European countries were supplied by DAF.

SPECIFICATIONS
(M390; data in square brackets relate to M390C where different)
Weight:
  (empty) 1711 [1656] kg
  (loaded) 3525 [3470] kg

M390C trailer of Japanese Self-Defence Force with 3-round pallet of HAWK SAMs

Length: 4·77 m
Width:
  (travelling) 2·47 m
  (emplaced) 2·82 m
Height: (without equipment) 0·93 m
Ground clearance: 0·43 m
Track: 2·03 m

Wheelbase: (towing eye to centre of axle) 3·23 m
Tyres: 9.00 × 20
Number of tyres: 2
Towing speed:
  (road) 80 km/h
  (cross country) 40 km/h

Chassis, Trailer: 1-ton, 2-wheel, M514

DESCRIPTION
The M514 trailer consists of a heavy-duty frame supported by an independent trailing arm suspension. Mounted at the front of the chassis is an A-shaped extension on which the retractable swivel castor and towing eye are mounted. The chassis has three levelling jacks, one at the rear and one either side. The brakes are the air-over-hydraulic type with two mechanical hand brakes for parking. This trailer is used with the Raytheon HAWK SAM system and is used to mount the Radar Set, CW, Acquisition, AN/MPQ-34 and the Radar Set, CW, Illuminator, AN/MPQ-33.

STATUS
In service with countries using the HAWK SAM system including Belgium, Denmark, France, Germany (Federal Republic), Greece, Iran, Israel, Italy, Japan, Jordan, South Korea, Kuwait, the Netherlands, Saudi Arabia, Spain, Sweden, Taiwan, Thailand and the USA.

SPECIFICATIONS
Weight:
  (empty) 1034 kg
  (loaded) 2150 kg
Max load: 1116 kg
Length: (without radar) 4·35 m
Width: (without radar) 2·39 m
Height: (without radar) 1·67 m
Ground clearance: 0·36 m

Radar set, CW illuminator, AN/MPQ-33 mounted on M514 1-ton trailer chassis of Spanish Army (J I Taibo)

Towing eye height: adjustable from 0·56 to 0·86 m
Track: 2·03 m
Wheelbase: 2·69 m
Tyres: 9.00 × 20

Number of tyres: 2
Towing speed:
  (road) 80 km/h
  (cross country) 40 km/h

Chassis, Trailer: 3½-ton, 2-wheel, M353

DESCRIPTION
The M353 chassis has been designed to mount various types of bodies and other equipment such as generators. It consists of a heavy duty frame supported by an offset axle assembly with leaf spring suspension and has two retractable swivel castors mounted at the front. The trailer has air-over-hydraulic brakes operated from the towing vehicle and a mechanical parking brake. The castors are secured in the raised or lowered positions by gravity pin and chain assembly. The fuel tank for the PATRIOT system generator is mounted on the M353 trailer.

STATUS
In service with the US Army.

SPECIFICATIONS
Weight: (empty) 1202 kg
Max load:
  (road) 3629 kg
  (cross country) 3175 kg
Length: 4·58 m
Width: 2·43 m

Chassis, trailer: 3½-ton, 2-wheel, M353 fitted with generator (Michael Ledford)

Height:
  (overall) 1·23 m
  (to platform) 0·69 m
  (to towing eye) 0·86 or 0·96 m
Track: 2·07 m
Wheelbase: 3·36 m

Tyres: 11.00 × 20
Number of tyres: 2
Max towing speed:
  (road) 80 km/h
  (cross country) 40 km/h

Trailer, Low-bed: Guided Missile, 7-ton, 4-wheel M529

DESCRIPTION
This trailer has been designed to load, unload and transport the Nike-Hercules SAM. The trailer has a welded steel-box type chassis mounted on a front and rear dolly with the front dolly being steerable. Both dollies are fitted with a spring compressing system and the chassis is provided with special equipment for handling the missiles. Stabilising jacks are provided either side of the trailer. The trailer is normally towed by a 6 × 6 truck that has connections for the draw bar, electrical system and the air-over-hydraulic brake system.

SPECIFICATIONS
Weight:
  (empty) 6576 kg
  (loaded) 12 701 kg
Max load: 6125 kg
Length: 14 m
Width: 2·62 m
Height: (without missiles) 1·43 m
Ground clearance: 0·3 m
Wheelbase: 8·02 m

Nike-Hercules SAM on its trailer, low-bed: guided missile, 7-ton, 4-wheel M529

Tyres: 10.00 × 15
Number of tyres: 8
Max towing speed:
  (roads) 80 km/h
  (cross country) 8 km/h

STATUS
Production complete. In service with countries using the Nike-Hercules SAM system including Belgium, Denmark, West Germany, Greece, Italy, Japan, South Korea, Norway, Spain, Taiwan and the USA.

Semi-trailer, Transporter/Erector-launcher (GLCM) XM976

DESCRIPTION
The GLCM launcher trailer has been designed by the Design and Fabrication Divisions of TACOM's Engineering Support Directorate and can carry either the missile erector-launcher or the launch control centre. It was originally intended to modify the existing M270A1 semi-trailer, but US Air Force nuclear safety regulations require the trailer to be strong enough to handle a load twice its 17·24-tonne rated load capacity. The XM976 GLCM semi-trailer consists of two main I-beams connected by a series of crossbeams, and is constructed from T-I steel in order to obtain the required structural strength.

SPECIFICATIONS
Length: (overall) 10·87 m
Width: 2·44 m
Length of trailer bed: 7·62 m
Weight: 5190 kg
Load capacity: 17 240 kg
Tyres: 11.00 × 20 (total 8)

STATUS
The US Air Force requested the development of the GLCM semi-trailer in October 1977 and six prototypes were ordered. The first was delivered to General Dynamics Convair Division, the prime contractor for the GLCM, in the summer of 1979 and all six prototypes were completed by June 1980.

First prototype GLCM trailer

MANUFACTURER
Fabrication Division, US Army TACOM, Warren, Michigan, USA.

Semi-trailer, Van, Electronic, 4·5-ton, 4-wheel, XM1006

DESCRIPTION
The XM1006 van is designed to house and transport electronic diagnostic test equipment for the Pershing II missile system, forming part of the System Components Test Station (SCTS). It is the US Army's first NBC-hardened tactical wheeled vehicle and is designed to function after exposure to nuclear and chemical environments. The structure of the chassis and body has been reinforced to withstand the effects of nuclear weapon blast, and protection against electromagnetic pulse (EMP) has been built in. The body is constructed of 3 × 6 inch steel tubing with a steel skin welded in place. The suspension, axles and landing gear have also been reinforced to support the body, which is three times heavier than the standard body. The semi-trailer is towed by a standard 5-ton truck tractor.

In September 1981 one prototype was subjected to a simulated nuclear blast equivalent to the effects of a 1kT weapon in an experiment named MILL RACE. The XM1006 van was undamaged, while a standard van was severely damaged.

STATUS
Five prototypes were ordered and the first was delivered in May 1981.

MANUFACTURER
Miller Trailers Inc, Bradenton, Florida, USA.

Chassis, Semi-trailer, Coupleable, MILVAN Container Transporter

DESCRIPTION
The MILVAN chassis forms the basis of a military-owned fleet for the movement of military containers over primary roads in the Continental United States but appears to be used primarily to transport refrigerated containers within US Army Europe (USAREUR). It consists of a 20-foot (6·1-metre) frame, landing gear and a single-axle bogie, which can be moved along the length of the frame. Two chassis can be coupled together with the bogies under the rear frame to form a tandem-axle 40-foot semi-trailer. ISO twistlocks are provided.

SPECIFICATIONS

Type	20ft unit	20ft unit, tandem axle	40ft unit, tandem axle
Weight	1814 kg	2654 kg	3629 kg
Length	6·25 m	6·15 m	12·29 m
Width	2·44 m	2·44 m	2·44 m
Height (on landing legs with deck level)	1·36 m	1·36 m	1·36 m

STATUS
Production complete. 5106 chassis are in service with the US Army.

MANUFACTURER
Trailmobile.

Other United States Trailers

Many other trailers are in service, or have been in service, with the United States Army. Those listed below include some which have been declared obsolete, but which may still be found in other armies' inventories.

Designation	Notes
Trailer, mount, 20-mm automatic gun, 2-wheel, M42	For M167 towed Vulcan Air Defense System
Chassis, trailer: 1½-ton, 2-wheel, M102	For M104 and M106 trailers
Chassis, trailer: 1½-ton, 2-wheel, M103	For M105 and M107 trailers
Trailer, low bed, 3½-ton, 4-wheel, M114	M113 chassis
Chassis, trailer: ¼-ton, 2-wheel, M115	For M100 and M367 trailers
Chassis, trailer: ¾-ton, 2-wheel, M116	For M101 trailer
Chassis, semi-trailer: 6-ton, 2-wheel, M117	For M118, M119 and M508 semi-trailers
Chassis, semi-trailer: 12-ton, 4-wheel, M126	For M127, M128 and M129 semi-trailers
Semi-trailer, van, cargo, 12-ton, 4-wheel, M128 series	Production of 44 M128A2C semi-trailers at a cost of $1·4 m was included in FY82 budget request
Semi-trailer, van, supply, 12-ton, 4-wheel, M129 series	Similar to M128 series but with interior fittings
Trailer, bomb, 2-ton, 4-wheel, M143	M143A1 is shorter
Semi-trailer, van, shop, 6-ton, 2-wheel, M146	M146C has windows
Semi-trailer, low bed, 60-ton, 8-wheel, M162	
Semi-trailer, van, office, 6-ton, 2-wheel, M164	
Dolly, trailer converter, 4-ton, 2-wheel, M196	Converts 3- and 4-ton semi-trailers to full trailers
Dolly, trailer converter: 6-ton, 2-wheel, M197	For 6-ton semi-trailers
Dolly, trailer converter: 8-ton, 4-wheel, M198	For 12-ton semi-trailers
Dolly, trailer converter: 18-ton, 4-wheel, M199	For larger semi-trailers
Chassis, trailer, generator, 2½-ton, 2-wheel, M200	Production of 1704 M200A1 chassis at a cost of $7·5 m was included in FY82 budget request
Trailer, van, fire-control mount, 3-ton, 4-wheel, M242	
Trailer, flatbed: fire-control/acquisition radar, 2-ton, 4-wheel, M243	
Trailer, van, fire-control, 2-ton, 4-wheel, M244	
Tracking station, guided missile, trailer-mounted, M248	
Trailer, van, radar tracking control, M258	Used with Nike-Hercules system
Trailer, van, director station, M259	
Trailer, low bed, antenna mount, M260	
Trailer, flatbed, guided missile, M261	
Trailer, van, launching control, M262	
Chassis, trailer, generator, 2½-ton, 2-wheel, M267	
Trailer, bolster, pole handing, 3½-ton, 2-wheel, M271	M271A1 is later model
Chassis, semi-trailers, 6-ton, 4-wheel, M295	
Trailer, basic utility, 2½-ton, 2-wheel, M296	
Electrical shop, trailer-mounted, M304	
Semi-trailer, tank, water, 4000 gallon, 4-wheel, M308	Similar to M131 series of fuel semi-trailers
Trailer, cable reel, 3½-ton, 2-wheel, M310	Signal Corps designation was K37-B
Semi-trailer, van, expansible, 6-ton, 4-wheel, M313	
Semi-trailer, refrigerator, 15-ton, 4-wheel, M347	
Semi-trailer van, electronic, 3-ton, 2-wheel, M348	M348A1 and M348A2 are also 3-ton but M348A2C, -D, -F and -G models are 6-ton
Semi-trailer, van, refrigerator, 7½-ton, 2-wheel, M349 series	M349A1 is later model
Dolly, trailer converter, 18-ton, 4-wheel, M354	
Trailer, van, electronic shop, 2½-ton, 4-wheel, M359	
Dolly, trailer converter, 3-ton, 2-wheel, M363	
Dolly, trailer converter, 6-ton, 2-wheel, M364	
Dolly, trailer converter, 10-ton, 2-wheel, M365	
Trailer, maintenance, cable splicer, ¼-ton, 2-wheel, M367	Based on M100 trailer
Semi-trailer, van, electronic, 3-ton, 2-wheel, M373	Production of 235 M373A2 semi-trailers at a cost of $7·5 m was included in FY82 budget request
Trailer, van, electronic shop, 6-ton, 4-wheel, M382	
Trailer, van, electronic shop, 5-ton, 4-wheel, M383	
Semi-trailer, van, dental clinic, 3-ton, 2-wheel, M393	M393A1 is electronic shop
Semi-trailer, van, medical, 3-ton, 2-wheel, M394	
Semi-trailer, van, medical, 6-ton, 2-wheel, M395	
Trailer, antenna, 2-ton, 4-wheel, M406	For Nike-Hercules system
Trailer, guided missile director, M424	For Nike-Hercules system
Trailer, guided missile, tracking station, M428	
Dolly, trailer, front, M429 series	Used on M242, M244, M248, M258, M259, M260, M261, M262, and M359 trailers
Dolly, trailer, rear, M430 series	
Dolly, trailer, front, M431	Single-wheel dollies with electric brakes
Dolly, trailer, rear, M432	
Semi-trailer, van, shop, folding sides, 6-ton, 4-wheel, M447	
Trailer, van, shop, folding side, 1½-ton, 2-wheel, M448	
Chassis, trailer, 2½-ton, 2-wheel, M454	Mounts AN/MPQ-4 mortar locating radar
Semi-trailer, maintenance, weapon, mechanical unit, M457	Based on M508 semi-trailer
Semi-trailer, maintenance, weapon, electric unit, M458	Based on M508 semi-trailer
Semi-trailer, maintenance, weapon, connecting unit, M459	Based on M508C semi-trailer
Trailer, air-conditioner, 1½-ton, 2-wheel, M463	
Semi-trailer, van, shop, 6-ton, 2-wheel, M508	On M119 chassis; basis of M457 and M458
Semi-trailer, van, electrical, 6-ton, 2-wheel, M513	
Semi-trailer, low bed, 6-ton, 4-wheel, M527 series	For transport of Sergeant missile sections
Laundry unit, trailer-mounted, 80-lb capacity, M532	On M536 chassis
Bakery oven, trailer-mounted, M533	On M537 chassis
Chassis, trailer, laundry, 3½-ton, 2-wheel, M536	
Chassis, trailer, bakery oven, 2½-ton, 2-wheel, M537	
Chassis, trailer, bakery, dough mixing, 1½-ton, 2-wheel, M538	

Designation	Notes
Trailer, van, electronic, 10-ton, 4-wheel, M564	
Dolly, trailer, front, electronic shop, M565	
Dolly, trailer, rear, electronic shop, M566	
Chassis, trailer, ¼-ton, 2-wheel, M569	For M416 and M716 trailers
Chassis, trailer, 1½-ton, 2-wheel, M580	
Trailer, van, electronic, 1½-ton, 2-wheel, M581	
Trailer, van, electronic, 2-ton, 4-wheel, M582	
Trailer, van, electronic, 2-ton, 4-wheel, M583	
Dolly, trailer, front, M584	
Dolly, trailer, front, electronic shop, M589	
Dolly, trailer, rear, electronic shop, M590	
Semi-trailer, tank transporter, jointed, 52½-ton, 16-wheel, M627 ('Trackporter')	Previously designated XM793; believed to be for foreign military sales only
Semi-trailer, low bed, 15-ton, 4-wheel, M674	For transport of Nike-Hercules missile
Semi-trailer, van, 15-ton, 4-wheel, M681	
Semi-trailer, van, 15-ton, 4-wheel, M682	
Semi-trailer, van, 15-ton, 4-wheel, M683	
Dolly set, lifting, transportable shelter, M689	Comprises M690 and M691 dollies
Dolly, front, M690	
Dolly, rear, M691	Together form M689 dolly set
Dolly set, lift, M707	
Trailer, stake and platform, utility, ¾-ton, M709	
Trailer, cable splicer, ¼-ton, 2-wheel, M716	Based on M416 trailer
Dolly set, lifting, transportable shelter, M720	Comprises M721 and M722 dollies; for shelters
Dolly, front, M721	
Dolly, rear, M722	S-141/G, S-280/G, S-285/G
Semi-trailer, van, repair parts storage, 6-ton, 4-wheel, M749	
Semi-trailer, van, repair, shop, 6-ton, 4-wheel, M750	
Trailer, platform, ¾-ton, 2-wheel, M762	
Erector-launcher, guided missile, semi-trailer-mounted, M790	For Pershing 1A missile
Chassis, trailer, field laundry, 4-ton, 4-wheel, M794	
Chassis, trailer, dough mixer, 4-ton, 4-wheel, M795	
Trailer, utility, 2½-ton, 2-wheel, M796	
Radar course directing central, electronic shop, trailer-mounted, M802	
Dolly set, M805	Used with Pershing 1A missile system
Dolly set, lift, MUST, M840	Used with MUST hospital
Semi-trailer, low bed, construction equipment transporter, 40-ton, M870	Manufactured by Load King

Recent development model trailers

Designation	Notes
Shop equipment, nuclear projectile, semi-trailer mounted, XM21	
Trailer, aircraft cargo loading, 3½-ton, 4-wheel, XM712	
Trailer, flatbed, tilt loading, 6-ton, 4-wheel, XM714	
Semi-trailer, van, telephone, 10-ton, 4-wheel, XM738	
Semi-trailer, van, switchboard, 10-ton, 4-wheel, XM739	
Trailer, flatbed, tilt loading, ¾-ton, 2-wheel, XM789	
Semi-trailer, van, electronic, 10-ton, 4-wheel, XM823	
Semi-trailer, van, electronic, 10-ton, 4-wheel, XM824	
Dolly set, lift, transportable shelter, general support, XM832	
Chassis, semi-trailer, guided missile launching station, 4-wheel, XM869 (for XM901)	
Launching station, guided missile, semi-trailer mounted, XM901 (Patriot)	
Semi-trailer, tank, potable water, 5000-gallon, 4-wheel, XM972	
Semi-trailer, flatbed, 4-wheel, XM974	
Semi-trailer, guided missile transport, 4-wheel, XM976 (Patriot)	
Semi-trailer, van, 6-ton, 2-wheel, XM990	
Semi-trailer, low bed, 70-ton	
Semi-trailer, van, repair parts storage, 12-ton, 4-wheel	
Trailer, 11-ton, heavy, expanded mobility, ammunition, XM989 (HEMAT)	Production of 66 of these trailers for the MLRS rocket system at a cost of $1·3 m was requested in the FY82 budget estimate

YUGOSLAVIA

Yugoslav Heavy Equipment Semi-trailers NPP-32 and NPP-50

DESCRIPTION
The NPP-32 semi-trailer is towed by the Yugoslav-built FAP 1820 BST/A truck, the complete truck and trailer combination being known as the M-70. The NPP-50 is towed by the Soviet supplied MAZ-537G (8 × 8) tractor truck, and this combination is called the M-60.

SPECIFICATIONS

Type	NPP-32	NPP-50
Weight (empty)	8500 kg	13 700 kg
(loaded)	40 500 kg	63 700 kg
Max load	32 000 kg	50 000 kg*
Length (overall)	10·48 m	11·44 m
(of platform)	4·1 m	6·84 m

* Normal payload is 50 000 kg but the trailer can carry 64 000 kg at very low speeds.

Type	NPP-32	NPP-50
Width	3·3 m	3·4 m
Height	2·15 m	2·5 m
Tyres	8.50 × 15	7.50 × 15

STATUS
In service with the Yugoslav Army.

MANUFACTURER
Yugoslav state factories.

MATERIALS HANDLING EQUIPMENT

FRANCE

ACMAT TPK 4.35 SCM

DESCRIPTION
This 4 × 4 specialist mechanical handling vehicle is a development of the VLRA long range reconnaissance vehicle, and the reader is referred to this entry in the Transport equipment section for both the development history and the technical description of the basic vehicle (see pages 334 to 336).

This specialist mechanical handling vehicle has a flat cargo deck of 3·13 × 2·2 metres with the fully slewing type H 650 A hydraulic operated crane situated behind the driver's cab, complete with outriggers, and operated from beside the vehicle. Weight unloaded is 5670 kg.

SPECIFICATIONS
Capacities:
3500 kg at 1·7 metres
2500 kg at 2·4 metres
2000 kg at 3 metres
1700 kg at 3·5 metres
1200 kg at 5 metres
(using extension jib)

STATUS
In production.

MANUFACTURER
ACMAT, Ateliers de Construction Mécanique de l'Atlantique, Le Point du Jour, 44600 St Nazaire, France.

ACMAT TPK 4.35 SCM in travelling position

ACMAT TPK 4.35 SCM ready for use

GERMANY, FEDERAL REPUBLIC

Hanomag 220 Rough Terrain Fork Lift Truck

DESCRIPTION
The British firm of Massey-Ferguson sold its range of larger wheeled tractors to the West German firm of Hanomag in 1979. Several of the range can be fitted with a fork carriage in place of earthmoving attachments.

STATUS
The Hanomag 220 fork lift tractor is used by the British Army in Berlin.

MANUFACTURER
IBH Holding AG, Erthalstrasse 1, Hochhaus B, D-6500 Mainz, Federal Republic of Germany.

Hanomag (formerly Massey-Ferguson) 220 fork lift loading ammunition in Berlin (Berlin Field Force)

UNITED KINGDOM

Boughton Swap-body System

DEVELOPMENT
The Boughton Swap-body system has been evolved from the original Ampliroll system developed by Bennes Marrel of France. Using the Ampliroll system as a basis Boughton has gradually developed its own Swap-body system which incorporates features and ideas from several commercial equipments and Boughton's own experience. Boughton has developed its Swap-body system in conjunction with the British Ministry of Defence which has been using the Boughton design as part of a programme to develop an on- and off-loadable cargo platform concept for ammunition, fuel and other logistic loads which is currently known as the Demountable Rack Off-loading and Pick-up System, or DROPS.

DROPS is still in the concept and trials stage as the British Army current requirement is for the DROPS to be used on a 6 × 6 medium mobility chassis capable of carrying a 14 000 kg payload. Boughton is therefore developing its own chassis to have a full DROPS capability and the new design has been developed to the

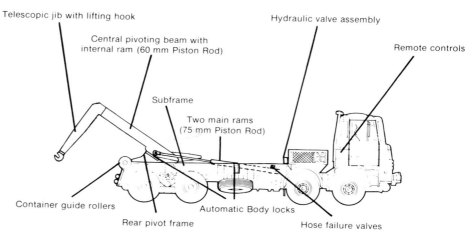

Mechanical and hydraulic features of Boughton Swap-body

Boughton Swap-body system carrying four dummy MLRS crates being unloaded from Foden (8 × 4) low mobility truck (T J Gander)

Three-quarter front view of 15 910-litre tanker body used with Boughton Swap-body (Ministry of Defence)

pre-production stage. Full production models of the new Boughton chassis were to be available in early 1984.

DESCRIPTION
The Boughton Swap-body is a hydraulically operated self-loading cargo system designed to improve the productivity of a chassis by speeding up turn-round times and freeing the chassis from dedicated roles. Thus, it is claimed, not only can a Swap-body equipped vehicle carry more than a conventional vehicle, but an army can increase its total logistic capability by switching chassis from secondary roles to meet peak requirements.

Roles envisaged for the Boughton Swap-body include a flat-rack cargo vehicle (especially for carrying pallets of ammunition), a recovery vehicle, a fuel or water tanker, a box bodied vehicle (for such bodies as command posts, ambulances, operating theatres, workshops and senior officers' accommodation) and for specialist engineer uses such as carrying, launching and recovering bridging pontoons, carrying palletised loads of bridging components, and for carrying and laying portable roadway.

The Boughton Swap-body can be fitted to any chassis and enables one man, the driver, to pick up a pre-loaded body in approximately 45 seconds.

Boughton has supplied six Swap-body 160 units fitted to Foden 8 × 4 chassis to the British Army to date. The company has also supplied two Swap-body units on Foden 6 × 4 chassis to Tanzania which uses them to carry Alvis Scorpion CVR (T) vehicles.

STATUS
Production. In service with British, Irish and Tanzanian armed forces.

MANUFACTURER
Hearncrest Boughton Engineering Limited, Bell Lane, Amersham, Buckinghamshire HP6 6PE, England.

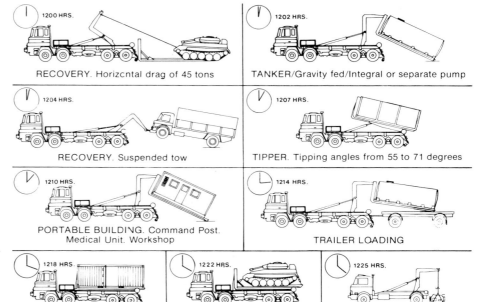

RECOVERY. Horizontal drag of 45 tons — 1200 HRS.

TANKER/Gravity fed/Integral or separate pump — 1202 HRS.

RECOVERY. Suspended tow — 1204 HRS.

TIPPER. Tipping angles from 55 to 71 degrees — 1207 HRS.

PORTABLE BUILDING. Command Post. Medical Unit. Workshop — 1210 HRS.

TRAILER LOADING — 1214 HRS.

CONTAINERS. I.S.O. or flat rack — 1218 HRS.

TRANSPORTER. Tracked vehicles or plant — 1222 HRS.

CRANE. Lift 6 tons — 1225 HRS.

Typical roles for Boughton Swap-body mounted on Foden (8 × 4) chassis

Eager Beaver Rough Terrain Fork Lift Tractor

DESCRIPTION
The Eager Beaver rough terrain fork lift tractor has been designed specifically for handling military loads in difficult terrain, including soft sand, deep mud and uneven surfaces.

The combination of the single beam mast and the driver's seat location at the left side of the vehicle gives the operator a full view of the load and forks. The Eager Beaver can lift a maximum load of 1814 kg at a load centre of 0·61 metre, maximum fork height being 2·74 metres. The mast can be tilted forward to a maximum angle of 13 degrees and backward to a maximum angle of 20 degrees. The forks can be adjusted from 0·533 to 0·787 metre apart and the mast has a side shift of 0·152 metre. A tow hook is provided at the rear and this enables the Eager Beaver to tow the ACT 5 airportable cargo trailer singly or in pairs.

The vehicle is airportable and for air transport the mast can be folded back to an angle of 60 degrees.

A crane attachment is carried on the vehicle as an alternative lift device. The axles are the same as those of the Bedford RL truck, the wheels are those used on the FV600 series of vehicles and many other components are common to other British Army vehicles. Standard equipment on all vehicles includes a windscreen, camouflage net and inter-vehicle starting equipment. Several Eager Beavers have been modified with a fully enclosed cab for use in Norway by the British Army component of the ACE Mobile Force (Land).

Eager Beaver rough terrain fork lift tractor (T J Gander)

Eager Beaver fork lift tractor unloading ammunition from Bedford TM 4-4 truck (T J Gander)

Eager Beaver fork lift tractor with fully enclosed cab for use in Norway (Ministry of Defence)

The current model is the Mk 2, but although a valuable addition to the logistic support of the Army, it does have some shortcomings. The operator is not protected from the weather; the vehicle cannot maintain a high convoy speed, and it cannot reach across a vehicle loadbed. Plans for a Mk 3 version were abandoned in favour of a vehicle which could be obtained on the commercial market, and an interim buy of the Liner Giraffe was made. The British Army still has a requirement for approximately 1000 rough terrain material handling equipments. A Mk 4 version has been developed for explosive ordnance disposal to carry the Wheelbarrow remote handling equipment to locations which would otherwise be inaccessible, enabling the Wheelbarrow to deal with devices in rough terrain or on the upper decks of buses, for example. The operator's position is armoured to protect the driver when the vehicle is in transit. In operation the vehicle is remotely controlled by means of a cable and electrically-operated controls acting on the steering column, a hydraulic drive with Moog valve for control of vehicle speed, and electro-hydraulic valves for the fork functions. The normal Eager Beaver function is retained.

SPECIFICATIONS
Cab seating: 1
Configuration: 4 × 4 or 4 × 2
Weight:
(operating) 2961 kg
(empty, airportable) 2838 kg
Weight on front axle: (empty, airportable) 1308 kg
Weight on rear axle: (empty, airportable) 1530 kg
Length: 5·499 m
Width: 1·854 m
Height:
(fork raised to max height) 3·708 m
(fork lowered, mast vertical) 2·387 m
(airportable) 1·828 m
Ground clearance: 0·3 m
Track: 1·55 m
Wheelbase: 2·54 m
Max speed:
(road) 56 km/h
(cross country) 24 km/h
Gradient: (with max load) 50%
Fording: 0·76 m
Engine: Perkins model 4.236 4-cylinder diesel developing 78 bhp at 2500 rpm

Gearbox: manual Bedford RL with 4 forward and 1 reverse gears
Clutch: single dry plate
Transfer box: British Leyland combined speed-change and 2/4 wheel drive
Steering: hydraulic power-steering on 2 or 4 wheels with Orbitrol control valve
Turning radius:
(2 wheels) 15·17 m
(4 wheels) 9·19 m
Tyres: 11.00 × 20
Brakes: hydraulic
Electrical system: 24 V
Batteries: 2 × 12 V, 100 Ah

STATUS
Production complete. In widespread service with the British Army and Royal Air Force.

MANUFACTURER
Royal Ordnance Factory, Nottingham.
Enquiries to Ministry of Defence, ROF Marketing, St Christopher House, Southwark Street, London SE1 0TD, England.

TEREX 72-25 Military General Purpose Tractor

DEVELOPMENT
The TEREX 72-25 Military General Purpose Tractor has been developed to be the base vehicle for three military roles as a Rough Terrain Fork Lift (RTFL), an Engineer Wheeled Tractor (EWT) and an All Arms Trencher

(AAT). The latter versions are covered in the *Construction equipment* section.
The current TEREX 72-25 was developed from a commercial design that was originally a West German product, the Zettelmeyer ZL 1700. This was marketed by TEREX Limited as the TEREX 72-25 wheeled loader and in turn is now being developed as the TEREX 72-25 Military General Purpose Tractor.

DESCRIPTION
This entry will deal with the Rough Terrain Fork Lift (RTFL) only.
Using hydrostatic transmission the 75-25 RTFL can be fitted with either a fork lift or a further attachment to add a crane accessory to the fork lift. Numerous optional fittings may be made to the RTFL including an armoured cab produced by Glover, Webb and Liversidge Limited

TEREX 72-25 RTFL with crane accessory carrying 2100 kg load

TEREX 72-25 military general purpose tractor in RTFL configuration

and weighing approximately 1240 kg. This cab can have air conditioning, a NBC facility and a manpack radio mounting. Other extras include a rear-mounted winch, a NATO towing hook, a starting socket and lifting eyes.

The fork lift can carry MLRS crates and standard NATO pallets and the TEREX 75-25 RTFL meets the US Army requirement for a 2722 kg RTFL. The fork lift and its crane accessory both weigh 2500 kg. Wide base or low profile radial tyres may be fitted.

STATUS
Development.

MANUFACTURER
TEREX Limited, Newhouse Industrial Estate, Motherwell, Scotland ML1 5RY.

SPECIFICATIONS (75–25 RTFL version)
Cab seating: 1
Configuration: 4 × 4
Weight: 11 320 kg
Weight on front axle: 5070 kg
Weight on rear axle: 6250 kg
Max load: 2722 kg
Length: (with forks) 7·57 m
Wheelbase: 2·55 m
Max speed: 40 km/h
Engine: Deutz F6L 4-stroke air cooled diesel developing 119 hp at 2800 rpm
Transmission: hydrostatic with two-speed gear box for working or travelling
Steering: centre pivot articulation, servo-assisted
Brakes: hydrostatic
Tyres: 20.5 R-25 or 25/65 R-25
Electrical system: 24 V

TEREX 72-25 military general purpose tractor in RTFL configuration

Hyster Fork Lift Trucks

DESCRIPTION
Diesel, petrol, LP gas and electric trucks with pneumatic tyres or cushion tyres are currently being manufactured at Hyster plants in Britain, Belgium and the Netherlands.

Trucks in the Challenger range have pneumatic tyres and are designed for both in-plant handling and outdoor handling such as lifting containers. The Challenger range extends from the H40J, lifting 2000 kg at 0·5 metre, to the H800A, which lifts 37 000 kg at 1·2 metres.

The Pioneer range of rough terrain fork lift trucks have extra-rugged steering assemblies and a high ground clearance, and are used for a variety of construction and other outdoor tasks. The range extends from the P40A, lifting 2000 kg at 0·5 metre, to the P200B, lifting 9000 kg at 0·6 metre.

STATUS
In production. Various models in the Challenger range are used by the British Army, Royal Navy and Royal Air Force and many other defence forces.

MANUFACTURER
Hyster Europe Limited, P O Box 54, Berk House, Basing View, Basingstoke, Hampshire RG21 2HQ, England.

SPECIFICATIONS

Model	H40J	H50J	H60JS
Capacity	2000 kg	2500 kg	3000 kg
Weight	3670 kg	3985 kg	4565 kg
Length (to face of forks)	2·51 m	2·61 m	2·73 m
Width	1·15 m	1·15 m	1·205 m
Height (upright lowered)	2·16 m	2·16 m	2·16 m
(upright extended)	3·93 m	3·93 m	3·84 m
Ground clearance	0·13 m	0·13 m	0·125 m
Track (front/rear)	0·955/0·955 m	0·955/0·955 m	0·97/0·955 m
Wheelbase	1·605 m	1·605 m	1·73 m
Fuel capacity	39 litres	39 litres	39 litres
Engine	Perkins Model 4.2032 4-cycle 4-cylinder 3·33-litre diesel or		
	GM Model 4.181 4-cycle 4-cylinder 2·965-litre petrol		
Turning radius	2·145 m	2·23 m	2·34 m

Model	H60E	H70E	H80E
Capacity	3000 kg	3500 kg	4000 kg
Weight	5140 kg	5420 kg	5730 kg
Length (to face of forks)	2·93 m	2·99 m	3·06 m
Width	1·375 m	1·375 m	1·375 m
Height (upright lowered)	2·16 m	2·16 m	2·16 m
(upright extended)	3·88 m	3·88 m	3·88 m
Ground clearance	0·12 m	0·12 m	0·12 m
Track (front/rear)	1·125/1·08 m	1·125/1·08 m	1·125/1·08 m
Wheelbase	1·905 m	1·905 m	1·905 m
Fuel capacity	60 litres	60 litres	60 litres
Engine	Perkins Model 4.2482 4-cycle 4-cylinder 4·067-litre diesel or		
	GM Model 6-250 4-cycle 6-cylinder 4·097-litre petrol		
Turning radius	2·5 m	2·58 m	2·65 m

Hyster Challenger H40J unloading ammunition boxes from railway van

Hyster Challenger H40J loading ammunition boxes in ship's hold

Coventry Climax Fork Lift Trucks

DESCRIPTION
Coventry Climax Limited manufactures over 80 models of fork lift truck, both electric- and engine-powered, with lifting capacities from 800 to 25 400 kg. They also produce moving mast and pantograph reach trucks, sideloaders, narrow aisle pallet placers, and pedestrian controlled trucks. A two-wheel drive Tough Terrain series of rough terrain fork lift trucks, one of which is understood to be a candidate for the British Army's requirement for some 1000 rough terrain material handling equipments, is also produced.

STATUS
In production. Several models are in service with the armed forces of Canada, Denmark, Egypt, Norway and the United Kingdom.

MANUFACTURER
Coventry Climax Limited, Sandy Lane, Coventry, West Midlands CV1 4DX, England.

JCB 520 Telescopic Handler

DESCRIPTION
The JCB 520 Telescopic Handler was the first of a new type of materials handling equipments. Development began in 1973 and production in 1977. With front wheel drive and rear wheel steer, the 520 has all the features of conventional rough terrain fork lift trucks, and the telescopic boom gives considerable forward reach, enabling it to place and lift a load over ditches, under low structures and through openings where the conventional vehicle cannot reach. It can also load and unload both trucks and rail vans from one side, and stand back from hazardous areas and soft ground.

The 520 is built around a rigid chassis and has an all-weather cab, which is also a safety cab meeting FOPS requirements. It has protection bars and a spill guard on the fork carriage. The 525 is a larger but otherwise similar version. Both models can be specified with 2- or 4-wheel drive.

SPECIFICATIONS (520-4)
Weight: 5840 kg
Length: (rear of forks) 4·06 m
Wheelbase: 2·25 m
Height: (to top of cab) 2·58 m
Width: 2·41 m
Track: (front) 1·77 m
Ground clearance: (minimum) 0·3 m
Engine: 4-cylinder water-cooled 3·86-litre diesel developing 71 hp
Transmission: full power-shift torque converter with 4 forward and reverse ranges
Steering: hydrostatic, on rear axle
Tyres:
  (front) 14.9/80-24, 12PR, traction
  (rear) 10.5/80-18, 8PR, traction
Road speed: 28 km/h
Turning radius: 4·83 m
Capacity at 0·5 m load centres: 2250 kg at 1·83 m radius to max height of approx 5·5 m, 900 kg at max radius of 3·65 m to max height of 6·4 m

STATUS
The JCB 520 has been evaluated by the British Army and four have been supplied to the Royal Navy.

MANUFACTURER
JCB Sales Limited, Rocester, Staffordshire ST14 5JP, England.

JCB 520 Mark 1 Telescopic Handler lifting fuel pod onto 4-tonne truck during British Army evaluation (Ministry of Defence)

LancerBoss 700 Series Sideloader

DESCRIPTION
The LancerBoss range of sideloaders comprises nine models with capacities between 1600 and 45 000 kg. The Royal Air Force uses LancerBoss 700 series sideloaders with the Bloodhound SAM at missile bases in the United Kingdom. Some of the vehicles are equipped with a missile handling attachment made by British Aerospace and all are electrically protected to the relevant explosives safety standard. Similar sideloaders are used by the British Army for depot handling of the Lance missile.

SPECIFICATIONS (700 series sideloader)
Cab seating: 1
Configuration: 4 × 2
Weight: 9625 kg
Length: 5·44 m
Height: 2·92 m
Width: 2·62 m
Ground clearance: 0·23 m
Wheelbase: 3·13 m
Track: 2·25 m
Max road speed: (unladen) 56 km/h
Engine: Ford 2714E diesel
Transmission: torque converter with 3 forward and reverse ratios
Steering: hydrostatic on front axles
Turning radius: 5·5 m
Tyres: 9.00 × 20
Lift height: 3·66 m
Free lift: 0·28 m
Lowered height: 2·92 m
Extended height: 5·03 m
Capacity: (stabilising jacks extended, typical) 6000 kg to 3·66 m lift height

Standard LancerBoss 700 series sideloader (foreground) and sideloader with BAe-designed attachment for Bloodhound SAM

STATUS
Production. In service with the British Army and Royal Air Force, Singapore armed forces, Swiss Air Force and US Army.

MANUFACTURER
LancerBoss Group Limited, Grovebury Road, Leighton Buzzard, Bedfordshire LU7 8SR, England.

Lansing Fork Lift Trucks

DESCRIPTION
Lansing Limited is a part of the Kaye Organisation and produces a range of mechanical handling equipment which includes both electric and engine-powered trucks ranging in capacity from 1000 kg to 40 000 kg. The electric trucks are made by Lansing Bagnall and the engine-powered machines are made in Blackwood, South Wales by Lansing Henley. In addition, rough terrain fork lift trucks are made by Bonser Engineering Limited in Nottingham, a subsidiary of the Kaye Organisation. The association between Lansing Limited and the British Ministry of Defence extends over many years, with technical appraisal covering design, manufacture and ease of maintenance being applied to many models, and Lansing Bagnall has been assessed by the Ministry of Defence to Quality Assurance standard 05-21. Many trucks have been developed to meet stringent military safety requirements, such as those for use on board ship and in hazardous areas. Fork lift trucks may also be electrically protected to conform to fire safety and radiation hazard requirements for use in ammunition depots.

Lansing Henley produces a range of over 50 models including front-loading trucks, sideloaders and container handlers. The Hercules range has capacities from 6800 kg to 11 800 kg. The Hermes range has capacities from 20 400 kg to 40 800 kg at 1·22 metre load centres, and some Hermes models are designed specifically for container handling. Lansing Henley also produces the 25TR truck designed for ro-ro operations.

STATUS
The Hercules fork lift truck is used by the Royal Air Force.

MANUFACTURER
Lansing Limited, Basingstoke, Hampshire, England.

Specially adapted Hercules fork lift truck being used to load Hercules aircraft of Royal Air Force

Fairey Engineering 6000 MRTFL 2722 kg Rough Terrain Fork Lift Tractor

DESCRIPTION

In 1981 the Fairey Engineering Company obtained the rights to manufacture the American Pettibone 6000 RTL 2722-kg capacity rough terrain fork lift truck. A development programme was instituted in the United Kingdom with a view to customising the machine to meet a Ministry of Defence requirement for the medium capacity replacement for the Eager Beaver. The result, now known as the Fairey Engineering 6000 MRTFL (military rough terrain fork lift – 6000 lbs/2722 kg capacity), is intended for handling the battlefield combat support requirements of the new weapon systems entering service over the next few years including the Multiple Launch Rocket System (MLRS) rocket transporter/launch pallets.

The Fairey Engineering 6000 MRTFL is capable of handling and placing loads of up to 2722 kg. An inching control and specific controls for tilt and side slope conditions, combined with a long outreach, mean that the 6000 MRTFL is able to load and unload vehicles or rail vans from one side only. The hydraulic oscillation cylinder enables the vehicle to rotate up to 10 degrees from the vertical to each side, keeping the load level and improving stability on side slopes. The ability to accept a wide front carriage means that exceptional fork adjustment is possible. This ensures that pallets, bulky items and stores possessing unusual centres of gravity can be handled by the one vehicle. Two- or four-wheel, crab and cramp steering may be selected while on the move.

The original Pettibone vehicle uses the detroit Diesel 4.53 engine but the 6000 MRTFL uses a Perkins 6.354.4. Optional extras include a weatherproof cab (with tropical roof if required), a digging bucket, crane boom or a snow blower attachment. A special beaching version capable of fording up to 1·5 metres is available.

The 6000 MRTFL is now being marketed both inside and outside Europe.

SPECIFICATIONS
Cab seating: 1
Configuration: 4 × 4
Weight: (cab version) 10 400 kg
Max load: (cross country) 2722 kg at 0·61 m load centre in all modes
Length: (forks open on ground) 6 m
Width:
(forks folded on ground) 5·4 m
(over tyres) 2·31 m
Height:
(with cab or ROPS cage) 3 m
(stripped) 2·35 m

Fairey Engineering 6000 MRTFL forklift tractor

Ground clearance: 0·35 m
Track: 1·805 m
Wheelbase: 2·286 m
Angle of approach/departure: 31°/32°
Max speed: 44 km/h
Range: 13 h without refuelling
Fuel capacity: 230 litres
Max gradient: 45%
Fording:
(standard version) 0·75 m
(beaching version) 1·5 m
Engine: Perkins 6.354.4 6-cylinder liquid-cooled normally aspirated diesel developing 116 bhp at 2600 rpm
Gearbox: Clark 18000 series powershift with 3 forward and 3 reverse gears
Transfer box: integral with main gearbox
Steering: full hydraulic 'orbital' with 3 modes selectable on the move from driver's seat providing front wheels only, all wheel or crab steer; ground drive pump for emergencies
Turning radius: 4·4 m
Suspension: axles bolted to bushed frame cradles providing up to ±10° of wheel movement on rear axle
Chassis oscillation: up to 10° either side of vertical possible for stability on side slopes and load levelling capability
Tyres: 14.00 × 24

Number of tyres: 4
Brakes: disc type dual circuit air over hydraulic service system plus transmission handbrake
Electrical system: 24 V
Batteries: 2 × 6 TN
Alternator: 40 A
Reach capability: 1·7 m
Side shift: (left and right) 0·35 m
Fork rotation: ±10° from vertical
Fork adjustment: 0·05 m increments
Fork length: 1·12 m
Spread of forks:
(max) 1·5 m
(min) 0·6 m
Fork tilt:
(forward) 45°
(rear) 30°
Max lift height: 4·1 m
Max fork depression: (below ground) 0·5 m

STATUS
Production.

MANUFACTURER
Military and Special Products Division, Fairey Engineering Limited, PO Box 41, Crossley Road, Heaton Chapel, Stockport SK4 5BD, England.

6000 MRTFL showing chassis tilt and fork rotation to its left

6000 MRTFL in normal upright position

6000 MRTFL showing chassis tilt and fork rotation to its right

Mark Giraffe 342 Rough Terrain Materials Handler

DESCRIPTION

In 1974 the Liner Giraffe 225 site placing vehicle was introduced to the construction industry, and it was subsequently evaluated by the British Army in trials in Germany and the United Kingdom. It is a telescopic handler; that is, unlike the conventional fork lift, it has no fork mast. Instead the fork carriage is mounted on a pivoted telescopic boom which gives a much improved

placing capability as well as clear unobstructed vision for the operator.

The Giraffe 225 is a two-wheel drive vehicle with a lifting capacity of 2000 kg which led to the development of the Giraffe 342 which is now in service with the British Armed Forces. The Giraffe 342 has a lifting capacity of 2870 kg when off-loading, and can lift and place a fully laden fuel pod which weighs 2360 kg. It has ample capacity for loading and unloading standard NATO palletised ammunition loads from one side of a flatbed truck, and the telescopic boom allows the vehicle to be used for container stuffing. The Giraffe 342 has four-

wheel drive and steer, although two-wheel steering can be selected for road work.

Remote control versions of the Giraffe equipped with television and handling devices are available for internal security and EOD operations.

STATUS
Production complete. In service with the British Army and Royal Air Force.

MANUFACTURER
Mark (UK) Limited, Park Road, Gateshead, Tyne & Wear NE8 3HR, England.

Giraffe 342 rough terrain materials handler (T J Gander)

Giraffe 342 rough terrain handler

SPECIFICATIONS
Cab seating: 1
Configuration: 4 × 4
Weight: (empty) 5488 kg
Length:
  (without forks) 4·5 m
  (with forks) 5·67 m
Height: 2·44 m
Width: 2·26 m
Ground clearance: 0·33 m
Wheelbase: 2·46 m
Track: 1·89 m

Max speed: (road) 30·4 km/h
Engine: Perkins D3-152 3-cylinder, water-cooled diesel developing 49 hp at 2500 rpm
Transmission: constant mesh, change-on-the-move gearbox; 3 speeds forward, 1 reverse – with high/low ratio selector
Steering: hydraulic; selector switch converts to 4- or 2-wheel or crab steer
Turning radius: 3·8 m
Tyres: 12.5 × 20 12-ply military tread, high flotation tyres

Reach and lift performance:
2359 kg at max clear forward reach of 1·7 m**
1814 kg at max clear forward reach of 2·23 m*
1134 kg at max clear forward reach of 3·23 m*
862 kg at max clear forward reach of 3·7 m*
Maximum placing height 5·64 m
Fork rotation: 24°
Sideshift: 0·15 m

** 1·2 m load centres   * 0·61 m load centres

Mark Markhandler Giraffe-type Rough Terrain Materials Handler

DEVELOPMENT/DESCRIPTION

By re-designing and improving the original Giraffe design, Mark (UK) Ltd has now produced a range of rough terrain materiel handlers known commercially as Markhandlers. The 400 series and 800 series have been available since 1979 and the latest 600 series since 1982.

The largest machine in the range, the 843 model (8 series, 4-wheel drive, 3 stage beam) has been undergoing evaluation by the US Army. The smaller 641 and 642 models have been offered to the British Armed Forces as a possible replacement for the Eager Beaver.

SPECIFICATIONS (Markhandler 843)
Cab seating: 1
Configuration: 4 × 4
Weight: (empty) 9216 kg
Length:
  (with forks) 6·42 m
  (without forks) 5·2 m
Height: 2·4 m
Width: 2·44 m
Ground clearance: 0·28 m
Wheelbase: 2·74 m
Track: 2 m
Max speed: (road) 29 km/h

Engine: Perkins A.236 industrial 4-cylinder water-cooled diesel developing 80 hp at 2500 rpm
Transmission: heavy duty Clark torque converter with 3 speed range and 'soft' powershift facility connected to transfer box
Steering: hydraulic; switch on instrument panel to select 2-wheel, 4-wheel or crab steer options
Outer turning circle: 9·1 m
Fork rotation: 24°
Fork side shift: 0·305 m
Reach and lift performance

Payload	Max forward reach	Lift height at max forward reach
3630 kg	2·31 m	6·85 m
2722 kg	2·8 m	8·38 m
1815 kg	3·63 m	9·4 m
907 kg	4·78 m	8·38 m
454 kg	5·59 m	7·47 m
Max lift height: 10·5 m		

SPECIFICATIONS (Markhandler 642)
Cab seating: 1
Configuration: 4 × 4
Weight: (empty) 6090 kg
Length:
  (with forks) 6·096 m
  (without forks) 4·877 m
Height: 2·515 m
Width: 2·464 m
Ground clearance: 0·343 m

Track: 2·032 m
Wheelbase: 2·845 m
Max speed:
  (standard) 30·4 km/h
  (optional) 45 km/h
Engine: Perkins 4.236 diesel developing 70 bhp at 2500 rpm
Transmission: Clark 18000 series torque converter with soft powershift
Steering: hydraulic; switch on instrument panel to select 2-wheel, 4-wheel or crab steer options
Outer turning circle: 8·23 m
Fork rotation: 24°
Fork side shift: 0·305 m
Reach and lift performance

Payload	Max forward reach	Lift height at max forward reach
2722 kg	1·83 m	7·09 m
1815 kg	2·44 m	6·48 m
1362 kg	2·97 m	5·82 m
907 kg	3·71 m	4·5 m
568 kg	4·34 m	–

STATUS
Evaluation by the US Army and British Ministry of Defence.

MANUFACTURER
Mark (UK) Limited, Park Road, Gateshead, Tyne & Wear NE8 3HR, England.

UNITED STATES OF AMERICA

Case Rough Terrain Fork Lift Trucks M4K, MC4000 and MW20BFL

DESCRIPTION

The Case M4K rough terrain fork lift truck is designed to load and unload containerised material and is compatible with ISO containers. The fork free lift, sideshift and the vehicle dimensions allow the equipment to enter a container to place or pick up loads. It is towable and has a tow bar and safety chains as standard equipment. The Roll Over Protective Structure (ROPS) also meets the Falling Object Protection (FOPS) requirements, and the canopy can be removed. Both lifting and tiedown facilities are to military specification. The M4K is equipped with high flotation tyres and driving, blackout and flood lights. In addition, it is capable of fording, the forks can be rotated, and the rear axle may be disconnected.

The Case MW20BFL articulated rough terrain fork lift truck is compatible with the C-130 Hercules cargo aircraft and the forks are fitted with conveyor ramps which are matched to the cargo hold of the aircraft. The all-weather cab can be removed to reduce the height and weight of the vehicle to allow transport in the same aircraft.

Both the M4K and the MW20BFL are air transportable and the M4K is also helicopter transportable and air droppable.

Case MW20BFL fork lift truck of US Air Force

Case M4K rough terrain fork lift truck

Case MC4000 rough terrain fork lift truck of US Marine Corps

SPECIFICATIONS

Type	M4K	MW20BFL	MC4000
Cab seating	1	1	1
Configuration	4 × 4	4 × 4	4 × 4
Weight (without load)	4411 kg	10 433 kg	3629 kg
(front axle)	2125 kg	4264 kg	1769 kg
(rear axle)	2286 kg	6169 kg	1860 kg
Length (with forks)	5·21 m	7·92 m	5·04 m
Height (over canopy/cab)	2·03 m	3·12 m	2·18 m
(cab/canopy removed)	1·8 m	2·46 m	1·97 m
Max lift height	2·54 m	1·98 m	1·73 m
Max free lift	1·22 m	n/a	0·91 m
Sideshift (right and left)	0·56 m	none	0·15 m
Fork rotation	22°	none	20°
Fork spacing (centre/centre)	0·2–0·76 m	0·36–1·3 m	0·41–1·14 m
Manual/power	manual	power	manual
Lift capacity (load centre)	1814 kg (0·61 m)	4536 kg (1·39 m)	1814 kg (0·61 m)
Tilt (backwards/forwards)	22°/11°	16·5°/10°	21°/10°
Ground clearance	0·34 m	0·43 m	0·32 m
Wheelbase	2·34 m	2·74 m	2·34 m
Track (tread)	1·6 m	1·85 m	1·68 m
Width (over tyres)	2·01 m	2·31 m	2·09 m
Steering	hydrostatic	hydrostatic	hydrostatic
Articulation (total)	86°	80°	86°
Max rear axle oscillation	25°	24°	25°
Towable	yes	no	yes
Engine	Case G207D 4-cylinder diesel	Case A401BD 6-cylinder diesel	Detroit Diesel 3-53N 3-cylinder
Hp/rpm (SAE net)	55/2200	103/2200	60/2200
Gearbox (forward/reverse)	3/3	4/2	4/2
Transmission	full powershift	full powershift	full powershift
Torque converter ratio	2·6:1	6·97:1	4·52:1
Max speed (road)	32 km/h	37 km/h	48 km/h
Tyres (standard)	15 × 19.5	17.5 × 25	15 × 19.5
Electrical system	24 V	24 V	24 V
Brakes	hydraulic	air/hydraulic	hydraulic

STATUS
The MC4000 fork lift truck has been adopted as a military standard item. The M4K improved model entered production at the Case plant in Terre Haute, Indiana at the beginning of 1981 for the US Army.

MANUFACTURER
J I Case Company, Government Marketing, 700 State Street, Racine, Wisconsin 53404, USA.

Mark Rough Terrain Fork Lift Trucks

DESCRIPTION
There are two versions of Mark rough terrain fork lift trucks. The Mark ML40 has a lifting capability of 1814 kg while the Mark ML60 has a capability of 2722 kg. Both are commercial models which can be easily adapted for military use and both have front-mounted lifting masts with a side-shift option. The mast is mounted almost directly over the front drive axle to improve traction and the rear steering axle is able to provide stability on uneven terrain by the use of an oscillating trunnion type suspension. The fork lifts are mounted on a parallel double steel frame to overcome torsional side-stress. The driver can see the forks without having to look round the mast; special attentions have been made in the design to provide good visibility from the cab and also to provide easy access to all parts of the vehicle for maintenance. The driver is seated in an open cab surrounded by a steel roll-bar frame. Mark trucks are designed for towing up to any legal speeds and various kits can be provided to suit the vehicles involved.

STATUS
Production.

MANUFACTURER
Mark Industries, Material Handler Division, PO Box 11276, Fresno, California 93772, USA.

Marketed in United Kingdom by Mark (UK) Limited, Park Road, Gateshead, Tyne and Wear NE8 3HR, England.

Mark ML60 rough terrain fork lift truck (T J Gander)

SPECIFICATIONS

Model	ML40	ML60
Cab seating	1	1
Configuration	4 × 2	4 × 2
Weight (approx)	4082 kg	5443 kg
Max load (at 0·61 m load centres)	1814 kg	2722 kg
Length (overall)	4·068 m	4·632 m
(less forks)	3·13 m	3·683 m
Width	1·854 m	2·108 m
Height (top of frame)	2·39 m	2·44 m
Mast heights	3·048, 3·657 or 6·401 m	3·048, 3·657, 6·401, or 9·144 m
Mast tilt (forward/backward)	5°/9°	47°/9°
Wheelbase	1·78 m	2·24 m
Max speed	43·4 km/h	43·4 km/h

Model	ML40	ML60
Fuel capacity	70 litres	70 litres
Engine	Ford 300 6-cylinder petrol	
Transmission	Borg-Warner, with 4 forward and 1 reverse gears	
Clutch	single dry plate	single dry plate
Suspension	twin heavy-duty leaf springs attached to three-point oscillating trunnion	
Steering	hydrostatic	hydrostatic
Turn radius (outside)	3·962 m	4·573 m
Tyres (front)	14.00 × 17.5	15.00 × 19.5
(rear)	12.00 × 16.5	12.00 × 16.5
Electrical system	12 V	12 V
Brakes	hydraulic	hydraulic

TEREX 72-31 Rough Terrain Fork Lift Trucks

DESCRIPTION

TEREX produced two main types of military fork lift truck for the US armed forces, both derived from the commercial TEREX 72-31 articulated front end loader. One was the TEREX 72-31MP2U/R for the US Marine Corps which was first produced in 1967; production continued until 1972. These were produced as scoop loaders but once in service trials demonstrated that the vehicle was capable of acting as a 4545 kg fork lift vehicle after it was fitted with rear-mounted counterweights and a modified US Air Force 463L fork carriage. The vehicle was then re-classified as a Tractor, Wheeled, Industrial with the capability of use as a fork lift truck or a loader with a bucket attachment. The US Marine Corps had 418 units.

In 1977 it was decided to rebuild these machines to new condition at the TEREX factory. During the rebuild a Rollover Protective Structure (ROPS), water compatible disc brakes, larger tyres, heavier counterweights and a side-shift fork carriage were fitted as part of a general up-grade package which took place from 1978 to 1981. A total of 369 vehicles was involved.

Another military version of the TEREX 72-31 was the TEREX 72-31F Adverse Terrain Forklift Truck (US Air Force Type A/S32 H-15) produced for the US Air Force to use as part of its 463L Material Handling System. As such it has an aluminium half-cab that can be easily removed by two men without tools, and a segmented counterweight system to allow the machine to be air-lifted in either a C-130 or C-141 aircraft. The TEREX 72-31F is widely used as the loader for the C-130 transport aircraft and the US Air Force alone has over 300. As with the 72-31M the vehicle is rated as a 4545 kg payload vehicle but the US Air Force uses the 72-31F at a rating of 6136 kg for short periods.

STATUS

Both versions are now out of production. 72-31M is in service with US Marine Corps. 72-31F is in service with the Argentinian, Belgian, Israeli and US air forces.

MANUFACTURER

TEREX Corporation, 5405 Darrow Road, Hudson, Ohio 44236, USA.

SPECIFICATIONS

Model	72-31M	72-31F
Used by	USMC	USAF
Cab seating	1	1
Configuration	4 × 4	4 × 4
Weight	15 727 kg	11 766 kg
Operating load	4545 kg	4545 kg
Length	7·2 m	7·2 m
Width	2·624 m	2·489 m
Height	3·086 m	3·01 m
Wheelbase	2·515 m	2·5 m
Ground clearance	0·343 m	0·343 m
Max speed	41·9 km/h	32·9 km/h
Fording	1·524 m	n/a

Model	72-31M	72-31F
Engine	Detroit Diesel Allison 2-cycle Model 4-71N developing 140 hp at 2300 rpm	Detroit Diesel Model 4-53N 2-cycle diesel developing 129 hp at 2800 rpm
Transmission	Detroit Diesel Allison Powershift CRT 3331-1 with 3 forward and reverse gears	Allison Twin Turbine Powershift Model TRT2220-1 with 4 forward and reverse gears
Brakes	air over hydraulic	air over hydraulic
Tyres	20.5 × 25 16PR	17.5 × 25 12PR
Electrical system	24 V	24 V

TEREX 72-31MP2U/R industrial wheeled tractor as used by US Marine Corps

TEREX 72-31F rough terrain fork lift truck as used by US Air Force

Military Fork Lift Trucks

Listed below is a résumé of the main types of rough terrain fork lift truck currently in production in the USA or in service with the Armed Forces. In most cases both diesel- and petrol-engined versions are in use.

Truck, fork lift, 2722 kg capacity:
Anthony MLT 6 (MHE-200)
Athey ARTFT-6 (MHE-222)
Chrysler MLT-6CH (MHE-202)
Baker RJF-060-M02 (MHE-164)
Truck, fork lift, 4536 kg capacity:
Pettibone-Mulliken RTL 10 (MHE-199)
RTL 10-1 (MHE-215)

Clark MR-100 (MHE-165, MHE-173)
MR-100B (MHE-179)
Truck, fork lift, 1360 kg capacity:
Clark ART-30
IHC Model M10A (MHE 236)
Case Model M4K (MHE 237)
The Clark CR40B rough terrain fork lift is also in US Army service.

Clark ART-30 fork lift truck of US Marine Corps showing integral towbar at rear

IHC Model M10A which is now replacing the RTL-10 in US Army service. Weight is 16 783 kg

Chrysler MLT-6CH 2·7-tonne fork lift truck of US Army

Clark 35 AWS (all-wheel steer) fork lift truck of Australian Army (P Handel)

High Mobility Materiel Handling Equipment (HMMHE)

DEVELOPMENT/DESCRIPTION

The High Mobility Materiel Handling Equipment (HMMHE) is a development of the Small Emplacement Excavator (SEE) project (see entry in *Field Fortifications* section) now being carried out by the US Army 9th Infantry Division to test potential equipment for the Rapid Deployment Joint Task Force. The SEE is based on the Euclid Military Tractor, a modified Unimog 800 series vehicle and this was taken as the basis for the HMMHE. In June 1982 two Military Tractors were equipped with front-mounted 4000 lb/1814 kg capacity fork lifts on the front- and rear-mounted 8700 lb/3946 kg capacity cranes. The HMMHEs were then tested and evaluated under service conditions.

The front-mounted fork lift has a maximum lift height of three metres. When the fork lift is in use the front suspension is mechanically locked. Telescopic stabilisers are used when the rear-mounted hydraulic folding crane is in use. The vehicle retains its normal towing hook.

STATUS
Under evaluation by the US Army.

MANUFACTURER
Euclid Inc (a subsidiary of Daimler-Benz AG), 22221 St Clair Avenue, Cleveland, Ohio 4417, USA.

SPECIFICATIONS
Cab seating: 1 + 1
Configuration: 4 × 4
Length: 4·88 m
Width: 2·36 m
Height: 2·6 m
Ground clearance: 0·43 m
Track: 1·62 m
Wheelbase: 2·38 m
Angle of approach/departure: 25°/55°
Max speed: (road) 74 km/h
Max gradient: 60%
Side slope: 30%
Fording: 0·76 m
Engine: OM 352 4-stroke direct injection diesel developing 110 hp at 2800 rpm
Transmission: main gearing fully synchromesh, 6 forward and 2 reverse gears with cascade gearing, fully synchromesh adding up to 14 forward and 6 reverse gears

Clutch: single dry plate
Steering: hydraulic power-assisted
Turning circle diameter: 10·9 m
Suspension:
   (front) coil springs, telescopic shock absorbers
   (rear) coil springs with helper springs, telescopic shock absorbers and stabiliser
Tyres: 14.5 × 20 × 10 PR
Brakes: hydraulic dual-circuit disc
Electrical system: 24 V
Batteries: 2 × 12 V, 125 Ah

Fork lift
Lifting capacity: 1800 kg
Lifting height: 3 m
Tilt angle: 11°
Fork rotation: 20°/20°

Crane
Lifting capacity: 3946 kg
Max reach: 7·67 m
Lifting height: 10·8 m
Outrigger span: 3·3 m

Caterpillar 988 50 000 lb (22 680 kg) Rough Terrain Container Handler

DESCRIPTION

The Rough Terrain Container Handler (RTCH) is a Military Adapted Commercial Item (MACI), consisting of an AH-60 lift mast and carriage mounted on the basic chassis of the Caterpillar 988B Wheeled Loader. It is designed to lift, carry and load containers 20 feet (6·1 metres), 35 feet (10·67 metres) and 40 feet (12·19 metres) long, up to 9 feet (2·74 metres) high and up to 50 000 lb (22 680 kg) in weight, and can stack them two high or place them on railway wagons or flatbed trucks. The RTCH is equipped with carriage sideshift as well as mast tilt to allow easy positioning of the container and lifting pins are locked in place when the container is being lifted.

Because the RTCH may have to operate at beachheads, it is capable of wading in seawater up to 5 feet (1·52 m) deep. Special radial tyres provide flotation on sand and traction in mud and the rear axle oscillates to maintain ground contact on all types of terrain.

In competition with three other major manufacturers Caterpillar was awarded a $61 million contract from the US Army Mobility Equipment Research and Development Command (MERADCOM) in September 1978 for the initial production of 177 units, with an option for a further 177.

STATUS
Production. The authorised acquisition objective is 444 with a further 35 for depot use.

MANUFACTURER
Caterpillar Tractor Company, Defense Products Department, Peoria, Illinois 61629, USA.

RTCH stacking composite container made from two standard US Army 20 ft MILVANS (US Army MERADCOM)

SPECIFICATIONS
Cab seating: 1
Weight: 46 866 kg
Length: 10·731 m
Width: (over tyres) 3·505 m
Height: (top of cab) 4·115 m
Ground clearance: 0·406 m

Fuel capacity: 624·5 litres
Fuel consumption: 23 litres/h
Engine: Caterpillar 3408 developing 393 hp at 2100 rpm
Tyres: 35/65–R33
Brakes: hydraulic

Truck, Tractor, Yard Type, 4 × 2, M878 and M878A1

DEVELOPMENT/DESCRIPTION
The original M878 was a commercially available vehicle primarily used to shuttle semi-trailers within permanent port installations or rail transfer areas. Twenty-eight were ordered for the US Army in 1976 and an additional 16 in 1977. In 1981 175 examples of a revised model, the M878A1, were procured bringing the number of Yard Tractors in service up to 219. The M878A1 differs from the original version by having a turbocharged 6V53T Detroit Diesel Engine in place of the original model 6V53. No additional requirements are anticipated.

The M878 and M878A1 tractors are high manoeuvrable vehicles with an automatic locking, hydraulic-lift fifth wheel which facilitates semi-trailer coupling and disengagement and allows movement of the semi-trailer or chassis without the need to retract landing legs.

SPECIFICATIONS (M878A1)
Cab seating: 1
Configuration: 4 × 2
Weight: 7384 kg
Length: 4·64 m
Width: 2·49 m
Height: 2·89 m
Wheelbase: 2·94 m
5th wheel height: 1·21 to 1·63 m
Engine: Detroit Diesel turbocharged 6V53T

STATUS
Production complete. In service with the US Army.

MANUFACTURER
Ottawa Truck Division, Gulf and Western.

Truck, Tractor, Yard Type (4 × 2) M878

140-ton (127-tonne) Mobile Container Handling Crane

DESCRIPTION
The 140-ton mobile crane has been procured to give a limited capability to discharge non-self-sustaining container ships during Logistics-over-the-Shore (LOTS) operations. It is also used to handle containers in permanent port installations, marshalling areas and terminal transfer sites. The crane is a commercially available item.

STATUS
In production. Two cranes were acquired from the Harnischfeger Corporation in 1976, followed by 2 more in 1979. In 1980 the crane was type classified and FMC Corporation was awarded a contract for an additional 28 cranes. The authorised acquisition objective is 86 cranes.

MANUFACTURERS
Harnischfeger Corporation.
  FMC Corporation.

SPECIFICATIONS
Weight: (with 120 ft (36·58 m) boom) 88 450 kg
Length: (with 50 ft (15·24 m) boom) 22·17 m
Width: 3·37 m
Height: 4·27 m
Capacity: 127 000 kg at 3·66 m radius

250-ton (227-tonne) Mobile Container Handling Crane

DESCRIPTION
The 250-ton mobile crane is used to discharge non-self-sustaining container ships and lighters in LOTS operations. It is a commercially available item and is mounted on a 6-axle carrier.

SPECIFICATIONS
Weight: (with 160 ft (48·77 m) boom) 167 830 kg
Length: 14·48 m
Width: 3·66 m
Height: 4·06 m
Capacity: 227 000 kg at 5·49 m radius

STATUS
In production. Two cranes were procured from the Harnischfeger Corporation in 1976. A further 2 cranes were ordered after type classification by the US Army in 1980, with preproduction testing scheduled for August 1981. The authorised acquisition objective is 13 cranes.

MANUFACTURER
Harnischfeger Corporation.

250-ton mobile container handling crane

Lightweight Amphibious Container Handler (LACH)

DESCRIPTION
The LACH is a straddle-lift type, towed, 2-wheel container handler. It is capable of lifting and carrying 20 ft (6·1 metres) containers through surf into and out of landing craft (LCU or LCM-8) and loading and unloading containers to and from trailers during amphibious/LOTS operations. The US Marine Corps developed the LACH to eliminate the need for shore-based cranes for unloading landing craft. It is propelled by a medium bulldozer, but power for container hoisting is provided by a separate engine.

SPECIFICATIONS
Weight: 18 144 kg
Length: 10·62 m
Width: 4·01 m
Height: 5·79 m
Capacity: 22 680 kg
Prime mover: medium bulldozer (Terex 82-32 in USMC use)

STATUS
USMC Developmental and Operational Testing is complete and funding for 56 equipments was provided in fiscal year 1981. The US Army has a possible requirement for 12 container handlers, but at present the Transportation Corps units with this mission are not issued with a suitable tractor.

Ramp, Loading, Mobile

Ramp, Loading, Mobile in use

DESCRIPTION
The mobile loading ramp is a commercial item produced for the loading ('stuffing') and unloading ('stripping') of standard eight foot containers when mounted on semi-trailers or MILVAN chassis. It is constructed of light alloy and has a capacity of 7257 kg, which allows fully laden fork lift trucks such as the Case M4K to use the ramp.

SPECIFICATIONS
Weight: 2722 kg
Length: 10·97 m including 1·83 m level section at container level
Width: approximately 2·44 m
Height: adjustable from 1·17 to 1·65 m
Capacity: 7257 kg

STATUS
In production. 775 ramps have been procured and additional orders were placed in late 1981. Acquisition of a total of 1426 ramps has been authorised.

MANUFACTURERS
Magline, Inc.
    Brooks and Perkins, Inc.

Construction equipment

AUSTRALIA

Engineer Equipment

The following equipments are known to be in service:
Wheel-mounted cranes
Mobilift Model BHB TC 23 (180 degree slewing, 2700 kg capacity)
Austin-Western Model 220 (360 degree slewing, 6350 kg capacity)
Austin-Western Model 410 Senior (360 degree slewing, 9070 kg capacity)

Crane shovels
Hy-Mac 580C and 610C (see separate entry under United Kingdom)
P & H Model 155 ATC, 0·38 cubic metres, truck-mounted
Ruston-Bucyrus 22 RB, 0·57 cubic metres, crawler-mounted

Bulldozers
Case 310G   replaced in June 1980 by
Caterpillar D4D   John Deere 450C

Caterpillar D6C   replaced in June 1980
International TD 15B   by International TD 15C
Caterpillar 955K (with multi-purpose bucket and backhoe)
Caterpillar D8H
Caterpillar D9G

Dump truck
White-Autocar 15-ton dump truck Model 7366 and Highgate 15-ton dump trailer. The trailer body is identical to the truck's and has a 12-cubic yard (11·5 cubic metre) capacity. Several of these combinations were supplied to the Royal Australian Air Force in the mid-1960s.

Graders
Caterpillar Models 12E and
12F (3·66-metre blade)   replaced in
Clyde Galion Model 118C   March 1979 by
(3·66-metre blade)   Caterpillar 130G

Scrapers
Euclid B8UOT (motorised)
Hancock 1262E (motorised)
International E211 (motorised, 10–12 cubic yard)
Wabco BT-2 (towed, 27 cubic yard)

Wheeled tractors and loaders
Case W10B and W10C; to be replaced by Clark 35 AWS
Caterpillar 966B and 966C; to be replaced by 64 Case W36M
Chamberlain Champion Mk 2
Pettibone 6000-RTL Rough Terrain Fork Lift Truck

STATUS
New equipment has been, or will be, introduced in the following quantities:
International TD15C tracked dozer: 54 (30 as bulldozer and ripper, 24 as angle dozer and winch); John Deere 450C: 59 (29 as multi-purpose bucket and backhoe, 30 as bulldozer and ripper); Caterpillar 130G grader: 42.

John Deere JD 450C light duty tracked tractor in bulldozer and ripper version (Australian Army)

John Deere JD 450C light duty tracked tractor with multi-purpose bucket and backhoe fitted (Australian Army)

International TD 15C medium duty tracked tractor in bulldozer and ripper version (P Handel)

Caterpillar 130G motor grader (Australian Army)

AUSTRIA

Voest-Alpine TROSS 130 Military Multi-purpose Vehicle

DESCRIPTION
The TROSS 130 is the result of a joint development between the Austrian Army and Voest-Alpine (TROSS stands for Technical and Rear Operation Support System). This military multi-purpose equipment is a four-wheeled, all-wheel steering vehicle with a swivel mount on which the various hydraulically-operated attachments, such as a front-loading bucket, lifting forks and a crane, can be fitted using a rapid-change device.

The TROSS 130 has been designed specifically for earth-moving and recovery operations as well as for handling military loads under difficult conditions. All the necessary auxiliary equipment, including a spare wheel and tools, can be carried with the TROSS 130, and with the vehicle's high cruising speed of 62 km/h it is able to travel in convoy with other military vehicles.

The TROSS 130 has an automatic differential lock

and a dual circuit brake system. Standard equipment includes an emergency steering system that allows towing of the vehicle after break-down, a cold starting device, a three phase dynamo and special military-proof indicator and control instruments. The driver's steel safety cabin is sound insulated and has two adjustable seats, a heater, de-froster, and stowage for weapons and a full pack. Optional equipment includes air conditioning, cab ventilation, a tropical roof, a tyre inflation system, black-out lights and an anti infra-red colour scheme.

SPECIFICATIONS
Cab seating: 1 + 1
Weight: 15 950 kg
Length: 8·3 m
Width: 2·65 m
Height: 3·13 m
Ground clearance: 0·435 m
Fording depth: 1 m
Turning radius: 5·35 m

Fuel capacity: 250 litres
Max speed: 62 km/h
Max gradient: 70%
Engine: MAN Type D 2565 ME water-cooled diesel developing 160 hp at 2100 rpm
Tyres: 20.5 × 25 EM 16 PR
Electrical system: 24 V
Max load:
  (front) 6000 kg
  (turning) 4000 kg
Bucket capacity: 1·8 m³
Winch capacity: 8000 kg
Winch cable length: 55 m

STATUS
Production. In service with the Austrian Army.

MANUFACTURER
Voest-Alpine AG, A-4010 Linz, Austria.
  Marketing and sales enquiries to NORICUM, Maschinenbau und Handel GmbH, PO Box 3, A-4010 Linz, Austria.

TROSS 130 with crane attachment

TROSS 130 with bucket attachment

TROSS 130 with bucket attachment fitted and on the road

TROSS 130 with fork lift attachment

CZECHOSLOVAKIA

Tatra ZA-T813 Kolos 20-ton Mobile Crane

DEVELOPMENT
The ZA-T813 crane has been developed from the basic T813 truck (see page 327). Apart from stabilisers and the addition of a bulldozer blade, the chassis is unchanged. Another crane, the AD 350.1, also uses the T813 chassis but is larger.

DESCRIPTION
In addition to normal engineering operations, the ZA-T813 was designed to assist in demolition and the construction of obstacles and is suitable for tasks when the combination of crane and bulldozer blade might be useful. The chassis gives the equipment a cross-country capability, and the arrangement of cabs and lights allows for night operation. Both the driver's cab and the crane operator's cab have NBC protection.

SPECIFICATIONS
Crew: 1 + 2 (can be operated by 1 man)
Chassis: see Tatra T813 truck entry (page 327)
Weight:
　(chassis) 12 550 kg
　(crane) 9000 kg
　(bulldozer blade) 1100 kg
　(all up, combat loaded) 23 130 kg

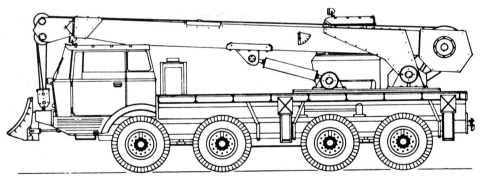

Tatra ZA-T813 Kolos mobile crane

Crane: hydraulically driven from chassis engine, telescopic jib
Capacities:
　(minimum radius, with supports) 2500 kg at 12·4 m
　(max radius, basic jib) 4500 kg at 6·6 m
　(max load, basic jib) 20 250 kg at 3·7 m
　(max height of lift, basic jib) 8·4 m
　(max radius, 1 section extended) 4 m
　(capacity, 1 section extended) 20 250 kg at 4 m
　(max height, 1 section extended) 11·5 m
　(max load, 2 sections extended) 14 000 kg at 5·2 m
　(max height, 2 sections extended) 13·6 m

STATUS
Believed to be in service with the Czechoslovak Army.

MANUFACTURER
Tatra, Národni Podnik, Kopřivinice, Czechoslovakia.

Czechoslovak Truck-mounted Cranes

Apart from the ADK-160 and ZA-T813 cranes, described in separate entries, two other cranes are believed to be in Czechoslovak service, the HSC 5 and AJ 6.

STATUS
It is believed that production of both models has ceased, as both chassis are obsolete.

SPECIFICATIONS

Model	HSC 5	AJ 6	Model	HSC 5	AJ 6
Operation	hydraulic	hydraulic	Length	7·8 m	8·25 m
Traverse	360°	360°	Width	2·5 m	2·44 m
Chassis	Tatra 111	Tatra 138	Height	3·45 m	3·35 m
Capacity (at minimum radius)	5000 kg/ 4·8 m	6000 kg/ 2·9 m	Weight	13 740 kg	14 430 kg
(at max radius)	—	2500 kg/ 8·5 m	Max speed	37 km/h	72 km/h

DOK Wheeled Engineer Tractor

DESCRIPTION
The Czechoslovak DOK (Dozer on Wheels) is a wheeled engineer tractor that has been designed specifically for military applications. The DOK has an articulated chassis and a rear-mounted diesel engine; drive is electric. An electrically-driven winch is located at the rear of the cab. In addition to the normal multi-purpose bucket a snowplough attachment is also available. The cab is hermetically sealed and has a filtered ventilation system, which enables the vehicle to operate in an NBC environment.

There are three variants of the DOK: the DOK-L, DOK-M and DOK-R; the DOK-L has a universal shovel and the DOK-M, a modified DOK-L, has the universal shovel with the addition of a sawtooth edge and a central ridge. The DOK-M also has hydraulic steering, improved brakes and an improved hydraulic system. The DOK-R has a vee-shaped blade that can be adjusted to form a straight blade for dozing.

STATUS
In service with Czechoslovak and East German armed forces. The DOK-M appears to be used only by East Germany.

MANUFACTURER
Czechoslovak state factories.

DOK-L wheeled engineer tractor

SPECIFICATIONS
Cab seating: 1
Configuration: 4 × 4
Weight: 28 000 kg
Towed load: 65 000 kg
Length: 10·53 m
Width: 3·15 m
Height: 3·15 m
Ground clearance: 0·45 m

Track: 2·45 m
Wheelbase: 5 m
Max speed: (road) 50 km/h
Range: (cross country) 250 km
Fuel capacity: 500 litres
Engine: T-930-42 V-12 diesel developing 255 hp at 1800 rpm
Tyres: 21 × 28

Tatra Dump Trucks

DESCRIPTION
Several dump trucks have been developed using the Tatra T111, T138 and T148 chassis. Details of the two- or three-side dump and rear dump only versions are given for each chassis. The T111 chassis dates from the mid-1950s, the T138 series appeared in 1963 and the T148 series in 1972. All three chassis are described here in 6 × 6 configuration.

STATUS
Believed to be in service with the Czechoslovak Army and other Warsaw Pact forces.

MANUFACTURER
Tatra, Národni Podnik, Kopřivinice, Czechoslovakia.

Tatra 111 DC5 dump truck

Tatra 138 S-1 dump truck

Tatra T148 S-3 dump truck

SPECIFICATIONS

Model	T111 S-2	T111 DC5	T138 S-3	T138 S-1	T148 S-3	T148 S-1
Type	2-side dump	rear dump	3-side dump	rear dump	3-side dump	rear dump
Weight	9640 kg	10 000 kg	10 000 kg	9400 kg	10 800 kg	10 660 kg
Length	7·43 m	6·13 m	7·43 m	7·14 m	7·285 m	7·185 m
Width	2·5 m	2·53 m	2·44 m	2·44 m	2·5 m	2·5 m
Height	2·57 m	2·6 m	2·57 m	2·59 m	2·61 m	2·645 m
Wheelbase	3·83 m +	2·9 m +	3·69 m +	3·69 m +	3·69 m +	3·69 m +
	1·22 m	1·22 m	1·32 m	1·32 m	1·32 m	1·32 m
Track (front)	2·08 m	2·08 m	1·93 m	1·93 m	1·97 m	1·97 m
(rear)	1·8 m	1·8 m	1·76 m	1·76 m	1·77 m	1·77 m
Engine (diesel)	T111A, 180 hp		T 928-12, 180 hp		T928-19, 200 hp	
Max speed (road)	62 km/h	60 km/h	71 km/h	71 km/h	71 km/h	71 km/h
Payload (road)	10 000 kg	10 200 kg	9500 kg	12 000 kg	15 200 kg	15 340 kg
Capacity	4·3 m³	5 m³	5·4 m³	5·2 m³	8 m³	9 m³

Praga V3S-K Dump Truck

DESCRIPTION
The Praga V3S-K is a conventional 6 × 6 rear-dumping truck. It is based on a fairly old chassis, the Praga V3S series, which dates from the early 1950s. It has a normal-control cab and is fitted with an all-steel dump body with a capacity of 2·5 cubic metres.

SPECIFICATIONS
Weight: 5780 kg
Length: 6·35 m
Width: 2·24 m
Height: 2·35 m
Wheelbase: 3·58 m + 1·12 m
Track:
 (front) 1·87 m
 (rear) 1·76 m (twin rear tyres)
Ground clearance: 0·4 m
Engine: T-912 6-cylinder air-cooled diesel developing 98 hp
Max speed: (road) 62 km/h
Payload: (road) 4650 kg
Tyres: 8.25 × 20

STATUS
Believed to be in service with the Czechoslovak Army and other Warsaw Pact forces.

MANUFACTURER
Avia Závody NP. Letňany, Czechoslovakia.

Praga V3S-K dump truck, showing method of lowering spare wheel

T-180 Series of Wheeled Tractor
T-180, T-180A and T-200

DESCRIPTION
The T-180 is a single-axle prime mover which has been designed to tow the 12-metre TV-10 side dump semi-trailer, 10-metre D-10 rear dumping semi-trailer or the 10-metre S-10 motorised scraper. All the attachments are hydraulically operated and the S-10 motorised scraper has a 160 hp engine mounted on the rear which is synchronised to work in unison with the prime mover.

The T-180 has a fully enclosed cab offset to the left, five-speed, dual-range and pneumatically synchronised transmission. The tractor can turn 90 degrees in either direction and is steered by two hydraulic ram cylinders or by braking each wheel independently. The latest model, the T-200, has a more powerful engine (180 hp) and different styling.

T-200 tractor with D-10 dump trailer

SPECIFICATIONS
Weight: 9000 kg
Drawbar pull: 11 600 kg
Length: 4·83 m
Width: 2·78 m
Height: 2·8 m

Track: 2·11 m
Max speed: (road) 40 km/h
Engine: T928-2 V-8 air-cooled diesel developing 160 hp at 1950 rpm
Tyres: 21 × 20

STATUS
Production.

MANUFACTURER
Czechoslovak state factories.

Earlier version of T-180 tractor with D-10 dump trailer

Newer T-200 tractor towing TV-10 dump truck

Czechoslovak Excavators

The D-030 and D-031 series of excavators are mounted on the Tatra 111, 138 and 148 truck chassis as follows:

Model	Chassis	Lifting capacity	Shovel capacity
D-030	Tatra 111 (obsolete)	–	–
D-030A	Tatra 111 (obsolescent)	4000 kg	0·35 m³
D-031	Tatra 111	4500 kg	0·4 m³
D-031A	Tatra 138	4500 kg	0·4 m³
D-031K	special purpose wheeled chassis	4500 kg	0·4 m³
D-031A	Tatra 148 (probable)	4500 kg	0·4 m³

D-031 excavator mounted on Tatra 111 chassis

D-030A excavator mounted on Tatra 111 chassis

D-031A excavator mounted on Tatra 138 chassis

FRANCE

ACMAT TPK 6.40 BS Dump Truck

DESCRIPTION

The ACMAT TPK 6.40 BS is an airportable rear tipping vehicle based on the standard 6 × 6 VLRA long range reconnaissance vehicle chassis. Details of the development history and the technical characteristics of the basic vehicle are given in the *Transport equipment* section.

The effective load of the tipper is 5050 kg and its angle of discharge is 50 degrees. When the vehicle is required to be transported by air, the spare wheel is placed in the cargo space and the cabin protective guard is hinged backwards into the tipper body. The overall height is then reduced to 1·9 metres.

A power-operated gravel spreader can be attached to the standard tipping body.

STATUS
Production.

MANUFACTURER
ACMAT, Ateliers de Constructions Mécaniques de l'Atlantique, Le Point du Jour, 44600 Saint-Nazaire, France.

SPECIFICATIONS
Cab seating: 1 + 2
Configuration: 6 × 6
Weight:
  (empty) 5950 kg
  (loaded) 11 000 kg
Weight on front axle: (loaded) 3030 kg
Weight on 2nd axle: (loaded) 11 000 kg
Weight on 3rd axle: (loaded) 7970 kg
Max load: 5050 kg
Load area: 3·35 × 1·9 m
Length: 6·77 m
Width: 2·22 m
Height:
  (operating) 2·4 m
  (air transport) 1·9 m
Ground clearance: 0·425 m
Track: 1·8 m
Wheelbase: (to centre of rear axles) 4·1 m

Angle of approach: 43°
Max road speed: 85 km/h
Fuel capacity: 410 litres + 40 litres
Range: 1600 km
Max gradient: 55%
Side slope: 30%
Fording: 0·9 m
Engine: Perkins 6-cylinder diesel developing 138 hp (SAE) at 2800 pm
Gearbox: Type TR 540 manual with 5 forward and 1 reverse gears
Clutch: single dry plate
Transfer box: ALM ACMAT type AL 660 2-speed
Steering: worm and nut
Turning radius: 10·35 m
Suspension: leaf springs and double action hydraulic shock absorbers
Tyres: 12.5 × 20 XL
Number of tyres: 6 + 1 spare
Brakes: (main) oil and air
Electrical system: 24 V
Batteries: 2 × 12 V, 100 Ah

ACMAT TPK 6.40 BS dump truck in air transport configuration

ACMAT TPK 6.40 BS dump truck fitted with gravel spreader

ACMAT TPK 6.40 SWT Truck-mounted Crane

DESCRIPTION
This equipment, intended primarily for the handling of logistic material rather than for construction tasks, is a development of the VLRA 6 × 6 long range reconnaissance vehicle, which is described separately in the *Transport equipment* section. The crane can be readily converted into a recovery vehicle by the addition of an A-frame between the bottom of the inner jib and the rear of the chassis.

The basic vehicle is identical to the standard 6 × 6 VLRA except that a fully slewing two-piece telescopic jib crane has been fitted. The four outriggers are controlled independently from their point of retraction into the chassis to ensure correct placing of the feet. The crane operator's position is beside the inner jib section to allow an unobstructed view of the load.

SPECIFICATIONS
Crane capacity:
5000 kg at 3·6 m (minimum) radius
3800 kg at 4·6 m (fully extended) radius
500 kg at 8·8 m (with extension jib) radius

STATUS
Production.

MANUFACTURER
ACMAT, Ateliers de Constructions Mécaniques de l'Atlantique, Le Point du Jour, 44600 Saint-Nazaire, France.

ACMAT TPK 6.40 SWT crane

ACMAT TPK 6.40 SG Bitumen Distributor

DESCRIPTION
The standard 6 × 6 VLRA vehicle chassis is used for this airportable tar spreader, which is intended for road and airfield construction tasks in air-landed operations. The basic vehicle is described in the *Transport equipment* section.

The welded steel bitumen tank carries 3000 litres of bitumen and the maximum effective load is 4050 kg. The tank is 3·1 metres long, 1·6 metres wide and 1·9 metres high. The tank alone, with heat lagging, weighs 900 kg and the end-wall diameter is 1·3 metres. The tank is equipped with all the necessary spraying and heating equipment and an auxilliary diesel engine supplies the power for a single-cylinder compressor unit. Unloaded the TPK 6.40 SG weighs 6450 kg and when fully loaded the weight is 10 500 kg. Height of the vehicle with the tank is 2·83 metres.

STATUS
Production.

MANUFACTURER
ACMAT, Ateliers de Constructions Mécaniques de l'Atlantique, Le Point du Jour, 44600 Saint-Nazaire, France.

ACMAT TPK 6.40 SG bitumen distributor

Creusot-Loire HA12 12-tonne Rough Terrain Crane

DESCRIPTION
The HA12 rough terrain crane uses the same basic 4 × 4 chassis as the RTC10 rough terrain carrier used on the MFRD/F1 drilling machine (see separate entry) but mounts instead a hydraulically-controlled crane with a maximum hoisting capacity of 15 000 kg. This will be limited to 12 000 kg for most practical purposes. The operator controls the crane from the forward control cab which has two control positions. The crane has a single element telescopic boom which, when retracted, has a total length of 8·09 metres. A spare wheel is normally carried under the boom. The crane can be operated on slopes as great as 15 degrees but loads are reduced when this is necessary. If required the crane can be operated without the stabilisers extended but the maximum lift capability is then reduced to 10 000 kg. If required a hydraulic joint device can be used by two vehicles to manoeuvre a broken-down vehicle between them.

SPECIFICATIONS
Cab seating: 1 + 2
Configuration: 4 × 4
Weight: (travelling) 22 000 kg
Length: (chassis) 7·665 m
Width:
(over wheels) 2·48 m
(stabilisers extended) 4·76 m

Creusot-Loire HA12 Haulotte 12-tonne rough terrain crane

Height:
(cab) 2·698 m
(top of boom, travelling) 3·425 m
Wheelbase: 4·1 m
Track:
(front) 1·987 m
(rear) 2·05 m
Angle of approach/departure: 42°/35°
Fording: 1 m
Vertical obstacle: 0·5 m
Max speed: 80 km/h

Engine: V-8 diesel developing 256 hp at 2500 rpm
Transmission: electro-hydraulically controlled torque converter kinematic system with automatic locking for moving to mechanical control of last 4 gears
Tyres: 16.00 × 25

STATUS
Series production.

MANUFACTURER
Creusot-Loire – Pinguelly, 15 avenue Jean-Jaurés, 94200 Ivry-sur-Seine, France.

Poclain Tracked and Wheeled Hydraulic Excavators

DESCRIPTION
Poclain is one of the world's leading specialists in hydraulic excavators and many of their products, both wheeled and tracked, are in service with the French Army and many other armed forces. The full range includes several models but in 1983 Poclain introduced their new B range of which four are wheeled and six tracked. The changes introduced in the B range relate mainly to a new delta shape design of chassis and to the method of manufacture which involves automatic welding. The hydraulics have been simplified but the main ram has been increased in size and the component layout has been revised to improve accessibility. A new heavier counterweight has been fitted to improve stability. The cab layout has been improved for both comfort and safety. All the models can accept a wide range of accessories including rock breakers, electro-magnets, ripper teeth, special buckets, etc.

STATUS
In production. In service with the French Army and many other armed forces.

MANUFACTURER
Poclain SA, 60330 Le Plessis-Belleville, France.

Poclain 75 P B wheeled hydraulic excavator

SPECIFICATIONS

Model	Poclain 75 P B	Poclain 75 CK B	Model	Poclain 75 P B	Poclain 75 CK B
Configuration	wheeled	tracked	Length of tracks on ground	n/a	3·03 m
Weight (stand, backhoe)	14 400 kg	16 200 kg	Engine hp (SAE)	86·8	86·8
Length (chassis)	4·86 m	3·81 m	Backhoe depth	6·8 m	7·05 m
Width (normal)	2·49 m	2·75 m	Loader reach	6·55 m	6·55 m
(over stabilisers)	3·2 m	n/a	Backhoe bucket capacity	0·85 m³	0·85 m³
Height (cab)	3·2 m	3·07 m	Clamshell bucket capacity	0·55 m³	0·55 m³
Ground clearance	0·28 m	0·42 m	Rock loader bucket capacity	0·95 m³	0·95 m³
Height over tracks	n/a	0·92 m	Rehandling loader	0·95 m³	0·95 m³

MFRD/F1 Mobile Drilling Machine

DESCRIPTION
The MFRD/F1 is a highly mobile drilling machine mounted on a Pinguely rough terrain carrier known as the RTC10. The drilling equipment can be used for a variety of field engineering purposes but the primary role is that of drilling holes into which demolition charges can be placed (MFRD – moyen de forage rapide de destruction). The French Army have ordered 122 examples of this equipment.

The drilling machine can be used at any angle from the vertical to the horizontal at 7½ degree intervals. The drill uses an auger for drilling in soft soils but in rock a bottom hammer is employed. Both have a working diameter of 220 mm. Maximum drilling depth is six metres. When drilling through rock the following drilling speeds can be attained:

Limestone	12 m/h
Granite	17 m/h
Schist	32 m/h

The RCT10 rough terrain carrier has a 4 × 4 configuration with a forward drive cab and seating for a driver/operator and one passenger. The drilling rig is carried on the area behind the cab with the gantry pivot overhanging the rear of the vehicle. An air compressor driven from a power take-off on the gearbox delivers 19 cubic metres a minute at 7 bars. A 6000–8000 kg winch can be fitted.

SPECIFICATIONS
Cab seating: 1 + 1
Configuration: 4 × 4
Weight:
(total) 16 800 kg
(front axle) 8300 kg
(rear axle) 8500 kg
Length:
(overall, travelling) 9·75 m
(chassis) 7·565 m
Width: 2·49 m
Height:
(overall) 2·384 m
(cab) 2·68 m
Ground clearance: 0·52 m
Wheelbase: 4·1 m
Track:
(front) 1·971 m
(rear) 2·038 m
Angle of approach/departure: 42°40'/35°
Fording: 1 m
Vertical obstacle: 0·5 m
Gradient: 50%
Max speed: (road) 70–75 km/h
Range: (road) 600 km
Engine: turbocharged diesel developing 260 hp at 2200 rpm
Transmission: torque converter semi-automatic hydro-mechanical gearbox with 3 forward and reverse gears
Suspension: double-action leaf springs and hydraulic shock absorbers
Turning radius: 11 m
Tyres: 16.00 × 25

STATUS
Ordered by the French Army (122).

MANUFACTURERS
Carrier: Creusot-Loire – Pinguelly, 15 avenue Jean-Jaurés, 94200 Ivry-sur-Seine, France.
Drilling equipment: Constructions Industrielles d'Anjou, Z.I. Ecouflant, 49000 Angers, France.

MFRD/F1 mobile drilling machine (T J Gander)

GERMANY, DEMOCRATIC REPUBLIC

KS-30 and KT-50 Crawler Tractors

DESCRIPTION
These two crawler tractors are very similar and were developed from the earlier KS-07. They have the same engine but different suspensions. The KS-30 is used for agricultural purposes and has four track rollers and an open cab while the KT-50 has been designed primarily for construction use and has five rigidly mounted track rollers and an open sided cab. The KT-50 is used by the East German Army as a dozer (KT-50P1) or as a front loader (KT-50Uk).

STATUS
Production. Although the KT-50 is in service with the East German Army, it is probably no longer used by front-line units.

MANUFACTURER
East German state factories.

SPECIFICATIONS

Model	KS-30	KT-50Uk
Weight	5200 kg	7900 kg
Drawbar pull	4730 kg	4250 kg
Towed load	n/a	9000 kg
Length	3·98 m	4·45 m
Width	1·61 m	1·95 m
Height	2·28 m	2·45 m
Model	KS-30	KT-50Uk
Ground clearance	0·28 m	0·28 m
Track	1·24 m	1·24 m
Track width	360 or 420 mm	420 mm
Length of track on ground	1·67 m	1·67 m
Ground pressure	0·46 kg/cm²	0·54 kg/cm²
Max speed (road)	8 km/h	8 km/h
Fuel capacity	180 litres	90 litres
Engine	4F175D2 4-cylinder diesel developing 63 hp at 1150 rpm	
Bulldozer blade	n/a	2·7 × 0·8 m (hydraulic)

G5 3·5-tonne Dump Truck

DESCRIPTION
The G5 dump truck is based on the standard G5 3·5-tonne 6 × 6 truck chassis and is a rear dumping truck with an all-steel body. The steel cab is protected by a rock shield on the dump body.

SPECIFICATIONS
Weight: 8000 kg
Length: 7·2 m
Width: 2·5 m
Height: 2·9 m
Wheelbase: 3·8 m + 1·25 m
Track:
(front) 1·7 m
(rear) 1·75 m
Ground clearance: 0·26 m
Engine: EM 6 6-cylinder air-cooled diesel developing 120 hp
Max speed: 60 km/h
Cruising speed: 585 km
Payload:
(dirt road) 3500 kg
(paved road) 5000 kg
Tyres: 8.25 × 20

STATUS
In service with the East German Army.

G5 3·5-tonne dump truck

MANUFACTURER
VEB Kraftfahrzeugwerk Ernst Grube, Werdau, Bezirk Karl-Marx-Stadt, German Democratic Republic.

W 50 LA/K Dump Trucks

DESCRIPTION
There are several versions of the W 50 series of dump trucks, which are based on the 4 × 2 and 4 × 4 chassis: L/K 3SK5 4 × 2 three-side dump, L/K 3SK5 4 × 4 three-side dump and LA/K-MK 5/6 4 × 4 rear dump.
Some of these may be on the LA/AK version which is the military model with larger tyres.

SPECIFICATIONS
(4 × 4, rear dump model)
Weight: 5080 kg
Length: 6·53 m
Width: 2·5 m
Height: 2·6 m
Ground clearance: 0·3 m
Wheelbase: 3·2 m
Track:
(front) 1·7 m
(rear) 1·78 m
Engine: 4 VD 4-cylinder water-cooled diesel developing 125 hp
Fuel capacity: 100 litres
Payload: (road) 5000 kg
Tyres: 8.25 × 20 (9.00 × 20, 14-ply rating for military versions)

STATUS
The military versions are believed to be in service with the East German Army.

MANUFACTURER
VEB IFA Automobile Works, Ludwigsfelde, Bezirk Potsdam, German Democratic Republic.

W 50 LA/K dump truck

AG-120 Motor Grader

The AG-120 motor grader is known commercially as the SHM-4E 'Elch'.

STATUS
The AG-120 is known to be in military use within the Warsaw Pact.

SPECIFICATIONS
Weight: 12 700 kg
Length: 7·7 m
Width: 2·5 m
Height: 3·3 m
(driver's platform) 1·83 m
Track:
(front) 2·14 m
(rear) 2·16 m
Wheelbase: 5·72 m

Ground clearance: 0·37 m
Engine: 6 KVD-14.55 RL 6-cylinder, 9·84-litre, air-cooled diesel developing 120 hp at 1750 rpm
Blade:
(length) 3·8 m
(height) 0·6 m
(rotation) 360°
(tilt) 0–70°
(adjustment left/right) 1·57 m/0·62 m
Max speed: (road) 40 km/h

GMG 2-7 Multi-purpose Wheeled Cross-country Vehicle

DESCRIPTION

The GMG 2-7 multi-purpose vehicle was developed in the 1960s for both civil and military purposes and is also known as the Combiquick. A wide range of attachments can be fitted to the vehicle including a clamshell, crane, dozer blade, forklift, shovel and winch.

SPECIFICATIONS

Configuration: 4 × 4
Weight: 3300 kg
Length: 3·75 m
Width: 2·1 m
Height: 2·4 m
Ground clearance: 0·28 m

Track:
 (front) 1·64 m
 (rear) 1·66 m
Wheelbase: 1·8 m
Max speed: (road) 57 km/h (diesel), 61 km/h (petrol)
Engine: Model 4 KVD 12, 5 SRL 4-cylinder air-cooled diesel developing 70 hp at 2600 rpm or LO 4 air-cooled petrol developing 70 hp at 2800 rpm
Fording: 0·9 m
Winch capacity: (when fitted) 2500 kg
Crane capacity: (when fitted) 1700 kg

STATUS

In service with the East German Army.

MANUFACTURER

East German state factories.

GMG 2-7 multi-purpose wheeled cross-country vehicle with dozer blade

East German Truck-mounted Cranes

The following truck-mounted cranes are known to be in service with the East German Army.

Model	ADK III/3	ADK v/5	ADK 63-2	ADK 70	ADK 100	ADK 125	MDK 12.5	MDK-160	MDK-63	MDK-404
Operation	hydraulic	hydraulic	hydraulic	hydraulic	hydraulic	hydraulic	hydraulic	hydraulic	hydraulic	mechanical
Chassis	G5	special	special	W50 LA/ADK	special (4 × 4)	special (4 × 4)	special (4 × 4)	special (4 × 4)	special (4 × 4)	special (8 × 8)
Capacity										
(max load/radius)	3000 kg/ 0·76 m	5000 kg/–	6300 kg/–	7000 kg/–	10 000 kg/ 3 m	12 500 kg/ 3 m	7500 kg/–	40 000 kg/–	20 000 kg/–	40 000 kg/–
(load at max radius)	1000 kg/ 4·56 m	n/a	n/a	n/a	20 000 kg/ 9·5 m	5000 kg/ 13·55 m	n/a	n/a	n/a	n/a
Weight	11 750 kg	12 700 kg	13 300 kg	11 400 kg	16 000 kg	19 500 kg	10 740 kg	39 000 kg	25 000 kg	40 500 kg
Length	6·81 m	8·18 m	8·17 m (7·35 m)	7·8 m	7·73 m	8·45 m	6·8 m	6·9 m	5·7 m	8·8 m
Width	2·5 m	2·57 m	2·56 m	3·1 m	2·45 m	2·5 m	2·5 m	3 m	3 m	3 m
Height	3·07 m	3·15 m	3·15 m (3·3 m)	3·31 m	3·48 m	3·4 m	3·55 m	3·85 m	3·6 m	3·99 m
Speed	60 km/h	42 km/h	55 km/h	70 km/h	71 km/h	70 km/h	40 km/h	22·5 km/h	40 km/h	48 km/h
Remarks	same crane also used on special 2-axle chassis known as 'Puma'		ADK 3-2 is lighter			improved version of ADK 100 also ADK 125A	also MDK 12·5/20 (improved version)	also MDK-160/1 (improved version)	MDK-63/1 is improved version	

All models have full 360° traverse. A 20-tonne mobile crane designated the ADK 200T is also in production.

ADK 100 truck-mounted crane

ADK III/3 crane on G5 truck chassis

ADK 125 12·5-tonne truck-mounted crane

ADK 160 16-ton Mobile Crane

DESCRIPTION

AD 160 or ADK 160 (for Autodrehkran 160) is the East German designation of a 16-ton hydraulic crane mounted on the Czechoslovak Tatra T138 6 × 6 chassis. The chassis differs from the standard truck chassis only in the addition of four stabilising jacks. The crane, made by CKD, is separately powered and has a two-section telescopic jib.

SPECIFICATIONS

Chassis: see under Czechoslovakia *except* max speed: 71 km/h
Weight: (in running order) 24 600 kg
Length: 9·85 m
Width: 2·5 m
 (over extended stabilisers) 4·5 m
Height: 3·4 m
Crane capacity: max 16 000 kg at 3·8 m radius
Traverse: 360°

STATUS

Believed to be in service with several Warsaw Pact armies.

MANUFACTURERS

Chassis: Tatra, Národni Podnik, Kopřivinice, Czechoslovakia.
 Crane: CKD, German Democratic Republic.

Tatra ADK 160 mobile crane on Tatra 138 chassis

ZT Wheeled Tractors
ZT-300, ZT-301, ZT-303 and ZT-304

DESCRIPTION
East Germany manufactures a number of farm tractors but the ZT range are the only models that have any military potential. All these tractors have the engine at the front and the fully enclosed cab at the rear. The ZT-300 is the basic farm model while the ZT-301 is primarily for construction use. The latter is powered by a three-cylinder model 3 VD 14 5/12 SRW water-cooled diesel which develops 60 hp giving the tractor a maximum road speed of 18·7 km/h. The ZT-303 has the

same engine as the ZT-301 but has 4 × 4 drive. The ZT-304 weighs 5200 kg and is reported to be a transport tractor.

SPECIFICATIONS (ZT-300)
Configuration: 4 × 2
Weight: 4950 kg
Length: 4·69 m
Width: 2·02 m
Height: (with cab) 2·59 m
Ground clearance: 0·46 m
Track: (front) 1·625, 1·75 or 1·87 m; (rear) 2 m
Wheelbase: 2·8 m
Max speed: (road) 30 km/h

Fuel capacity: 130 litres
Engine: Model 4 VD 14, 5/12 4-cylinder water-cooled diesel developing 90 hp
Tyres: 7.50 × 20 or 15.00 × 30

STATUS
Production. The ZT-303 is used by Road Construction Units of the East German Army, and the ZT-300 is also believed to be in use.

MANUFACTURER
Schönebeck Tractor Plant, German Democratic Republic.

GERMANY, FEDERAL REPUBLIC

Ahlmann AS 12B Wheeled Loader

DESCRIPTION
The AS 12B wheeled loader, known in the Federal German armed forces as Schwenklader, or swivel-loader, is a four-wheeled, rear-steering loader with a swivelling mounting on which the hydraulically-operated arms are fitted. It can be fitted with a variety of

attachments including a conventional front-loading bucket, an excavator, a crane jib, and forks. The AS 12B weighs 13 000 kg and has a 148 hp engine.

With the front bucket the loader can dig a position 5 metres long, 3 metres wide and 1·5 metres deep in 30 minutes. The excavator mounted on the lifting arm can dig a trench 0·6 metre wide and 1·5 metres deep at the rate of 40 metres per hour and the grab can load

3·5 cubic metres of gravel in four minutes. The front-mounted forks have a capacity of 2·5 tonnes.

STATUS
The AS 12B replaced various tracked loaders, excavators and the 2·5-tonne Feldarbeitsgerät wheeled tractor. Since 1976 it has been in service with the army, navy and air force of the Federal Republic of Germany.

AS 12B wheeled loader in travelling order, equipped with grab, excavator, forks, and crane attachment (Federal German Ministry of Defence)

Atlas 1702D Wheeled Excavator

DESCRIPTION
The Atlas AB 1702D is one of a large range of tracked and wheeled excavators, the smallest designated the AB 1202D and the largest the AB 2505D. The 1702 series models can be mounted on a standard, long or heavy duty tracked undercarriage or on a pneumatic-tyred undercarriage with either four stabilisers or two stabilisers and a bulldozer blade. The AB 1702D supplied to the British Army has four stabilisers on the four-wheeled undercarriage and is equipped with a backacting bucket on a standard three-piece boom. The axles are of 30-ton capacity and the steering axle has an automatic oscillating lock. The undercarriage is hydraulically driven by a variable speed motor acting as a hydrostatic torque converter.

STATUS
The AB 1702D wheeled excavator is in service with the British Army.

MANUFACTURER
Maschinenfabrik H Weyhausen KG, Stedingerstrasse 24, P O Box 207, 2870 Delmenhorst, Federal Republic of Germany.

Atlas AB 1702D wheeled excavator in use with British Army (MoD)

SPECIFICATIONS (AB 1702D)
Weight: 21 000 kg approx
Length: (travelling) 7 m
Width:
　(travelling) 2·55 m
　(operating, with stabilisers) 3·2 m
Wheelbase: 2·7 m

Track: 1·86 m
Engine: Deutz F6L912 air-cooled diesel developing 96 hp
Fuel capacity: 250 litres
Fuel consumption: 12·5 litres/h approx
Bucket capacity: 0·5–0·9 m³
Reach height: 7·8–9 m depending on boom type

Max reach: (radius) 7·4–9·9 m
Max digging depth: 5·5–8·05 m
Breakout force: 15 200 kg
Lifting capacity: 6900 kg at 5 m radius
Tyres: 10.00 × 20
Number of tyres: 8
Max speed: (road) 18 km/h

Hanomag Crawler Dozers

DESCRIPTION
The Hanomag D400D bulldozer has a full powershift transmission with three forward and three reverse speeds, selected by a single control. The blade pitch is adjustable by 10 degrees in two directions to suit ground conditions and can cut to a maximum depth of 0·41 metre. Its lift height is 1·1 metres. A version with a mechanically-adjusted angledozer is also available, and a heavy-duty ripper can be mounted at the rear.

The D600D bulldozer has a fully enclosed ROPS cab and a modulated full powershift transmission giving three forward and reverse speeds. A 16 000 kg hydrostatic winch may be fitted at the rear or alternatively a mechanical winch can be driven from the tractor PTO. A variety of straight dozer blades is available, as well as a wider blade for the LGP undercarriage and angledozer blade.

The D700D turbo bull- or angle-dozer has a push frame mounting, a long track and wide gauge giving good dozing and steering qualities. The multiple disc steering brake/clutch units are pedal controlled. Equipments that can be fitted to the rear of the cab include a one-tooth or three-tooth ripper and a 23 000 kg winch.

SPECIFICATIONS

Model	D400D	D600D	D700D turbo
Cab seating	1	1	1
Weight	10 750–11 600 kg	15 600–17 120 kg	20 520–21 960 kg
Length (with blade)	4·5–4·65 m	4·87–5·24 m	5·56–5·93 m
Width (over blade)	2·6–3·25 m	3·2–3·8 m	3·49–4·28 m
Height	2·93 m	3·11 m	3·23 m
Track width	0·51–0·77 m	0·59–0·91 m	0·51–0·91 m
Track centre distance	1·53 m	1·87 m	2 m
Ground contact length	2·43 m	2·47–2·75 m	3·14 m
Engine	Perkins 6-cylinder diesel developing 67 kW (90 hp) net at 2200 rpm	Hanomag 6-cylinder diesel developing 107 kW (144 hp) net at 2200 rpm	Hanomag 6-cylinder turbo-charged diesel developing 201 hp at 2300 rpm
Fuel capacity	220 litres	240 litres	400 litres
Max forward speed	10 km/h	11 km/h	12 km/h

STATUS
All three models in production. The D400D is in service with New Zealand.

The D600D is in service with Austria, Belgium, West Germany, the Netherlands and the United Kingdom.

The D700D is in service with the Canadian Army.

MANUFACTURER
Hanomag GmbH (a company of IBH Holding AG), Hanomagstr 9, 3000 Hannover 91, Federal Republic of Germany.

Hanomag D600D crawler dozer

Hanomag D700D turbo crawler dozer

Hanomag Wheeled Loaders

DESCRIPTION
Hanomag is well known for its complete range of wheeled loaders from 33 to 258 hp SAE net. One of these, the 33C, has recently been adopted by the Norwegian Army. The 33C is powered by a 94 hp Perkins diesel and has all-wheel drive through torque self-locking which ensures that traction is maintained in snow or on very soft ground.

SPECIFICATIONS (Hanomag 33C)
Cab seating: 1
Configuration: 4 × 4
Weight: (operating, approx) 9000 kg
Payload: 2600 kg
Length: 6·245 m
Width:
(overall) 2·44 m
(less bucket) 2·245 m
Height:
(top of cab) 3·085 m
(top of exhaust stack) 3·055 m
Ground clearance: 0·365 m
Track: 1·8 m
Wheelbase: 2·51 m
Fuel capacity: 180 litres
Engine: Perkins Model 6.354.4 5·8-litre 6-cylinder liquid-cooled diesel developing 94 hp (SAE) at 2250 rpm
Transmission: Hanomag G 412 full power shift with 3 forward and 3 reverse gears
Max speed: 32 km/h
Steering: articulated frame, 40° left and right

Hanomag 33C wheeled loader

Turning radius: (tyres) 4·77 m
Tyres: (standard) 15.5–25EM
Brakes: air over hydraulic, dual circuit
Electrical system: 24 V
Batteries: 2 × 12 V, 88 Ah

STATUS
The Norwegian Army has ten HN 33C loaders, which are fitted with a parallel-lift mechanism for the front loader and quick-attach plate for other front-mounted

attachments. Two 33B loaders were evaluated before the 33C was finally selected. The 33C is used for front-line support, such as the preparation of defences, clearing of obstacles and road improvements.

MANUFACTURER
Hanomag GmbH, Hanomagstr 9, 3000 Hannover 91 (a company of IBH Holding AG), Erthalstrasse 1, Hochhaus B, D-6500 Mainz, Federal Republic of Germany.

Hanomag D66C Wheeled Bulldozer

DESCRIPTION
The D66C is the only wheeled bulldozer in the Hanomag range and has a rear-mounted engine. The fully-enclosed cab, which has two doors and an adjustable seat, is at the front of the tractor. The front axle is rigid and incorporates planetary reduction gears and a differential lock, while the rear axle is similar but can oscillate through 14 degrees. The D66C bulldozer is very similar to the 66C loader and shares many features and mechanical components.

SPECIFICATIONS
Cab seating: 1

Configuration: 4 × 4
Weight: 18 300 kg (with front wheel ballast: 19 800 kg)
Length: 6·3 m
Width: (over blade) 3·55 m
Height: 3·43 m
Ground clearance: 0·44 m
Track: 2 m
Wheelbase: 3 m
Engine: Hanomag D 963 A1 6-cylinder turbo-charged diesel developing 211 hp at 2200 rpm
Transmission: power shift with 4 forward and 4 reverse gears
Max speed: (road) 50 km/h
Fuel capacity: 375 litres

Steering: full power, articulated, 40° left and right
Turning radius: 5·5 m
Tyres: 26.5 × 25
Brakes: air over hydraulic, dual circuit

STATUS
In production. In service with the armies of Belgium, the Netherlands and Kenya.

MANUFACTURER
Hanomag GmbH, Hanomagstr 9, 3000 Hannover 91 (a company of IBH Holding AG), Erthalstrasse 1, Hochhaus B, D-6500 Mainz, Federal Republic of Germany.

Hanomag D66C wheeled bulldozer of Belgian Army (C R Zwart)

Rear of Hanomag D66C wheeled bulldozer of Belgian Army (C R Zwart)

Kaelble PR660 Bulldozer

DESCRIPTION
Designated Planierraupe 160 PS, Schwenkschild (bulldozer, 160 hp, angled blade), the PR660 was introduced between 1958 and 1962 and was the standard medium dozer of the Federal German armed forces until recently. It may be fitted with a rear-mounted ripper or 15-tonne winch, and is normally transported on the 25-tonne low-loader trailer.

STATUS
Production has ceased but the PR660 may still be found in service. Its replacement is the Zettelmeyer ZD 3000 wheeled dozer, for which there is a separate entry.

SPECIFICATIONS
Weight: 20 500 kg (21 540 kg when fitted with ripper)
Length: 5·97 m
Width:
(tractor only) 2·56 m
(over blade) 4·1 m
Height: 3·2 m
Engine: 14·33-litre, 6-cylinder water-cooled diesel developing 160 hp
Max speed: 8 km/h
Endurance: 14 h
Blade:
(width) 4·1 m
(angles) 25° left and right
(operation) hydraulic
Work capacity: (medium soil, 50 m transport) 64 m³/h

Kaelble PR660 bulldozer (Federal German Ministry of Defence)

Kaelble SL 25 Wheeled Loader (Knicklader)

SPECIFICATIONS
Configuration: 4 × 4
Weight: 23 100 kg approx

Engine: Mercedes-Benz OM 403 water-cooled diesel developing 270 hp
Turning circle diameter: 15·4 m
Shovel capacity: 5 m³
Max speed: (road) 50 km/h

STATUS
The SL 25 is in service with the West German forces for rapid runway repair.

Hatra SL125 Wheeled Loader

DESCRIPTION
The Hatra SL125, also known as the Feldarbeitsgerät (FAG) or Feldumschlaggerät, was introduced in the mid-1960s. It may be fitted with several attachments in addition to the standard bucket, including a crane, forks and a grab. The SL125, with a road speed of 55 km/h, may be driven in convoy.

STATUS
Production of the SL125 has ceased. It has been largely replaced by the AS12B and the Erdarbeitsgerät, for which there are separate entries in this section. A similar model was produced by Wilhag. The Hatra SL125 is also used by the Austrian Army.

SPECIFICATIONS
Configuration: 4 × 4
Weight: 13 636 kg
Length: 7·9 m
Width: 2·52 m
Height: 3·13 m

Wheelbase: 2·6 m
Engine: Deutz F6L 714A 6-cylinder multi-fuel developing 125 hp
Transmission: 4-speed torque converter
Steering: 4-wheel
Speed: 55 km/h
Tyres: low pressure
Bucket capacity: (struck) 1·5 m³
Lifting capacity: 3125 kg
Endurance: 12 h
Range: 460 km

West German Truck-mounted Cranes

DESCRIPTION
In 1977 a new range of military truck-mounted cranes was announced. The existing range of 4-, 5·5-, 13- and 20-tonne truck cranes was to be replaced by two new models designated FKL and FKM (Fahrzeugkran, Leucht und Mittel, or light and medium vehicle cranes). The firm of Krupp in Wilhelmshaven was selected as prime contractor for the development of the FKL and FKM, and prototypes were produced by the end of 1976. The FKL was produced in both two- and three-axled versions, and the FKM was a three-axled vehicle. These second-generation truck cranes are very sophisticated vehicles, featuring all-wheel steering and high cross-country mobility. Few other details have been released on the FKL and FKM, but the table below gives a comparison with the first-generation vehicles which the FKL and FKM are intended to replace.

West German 4-tonne truck-mounted crane (Federal German Ministry of Defence)

Generation	First				Second		
	Autokran 4 t	Autokran 13 t	Autokran 20 t	FKL	FKL	FKM	
Chassis	Magirus-Deutz 7t, 6 × 6	Faun LK 1212/ 485 11, 6 × 6	6 × 6	4 × 4	6 × 6	6 × 6	
Crane	Wilhag	Wilhag (*)	O & K	Krupp	Krupp	Krupp	
Length	9·39 m	10·08 m	9·31 m	8·9 m	10·34 m	10·34 m	
Width	2·5 m	2·5 m	2·68 m	2·75 m	2·75 m	2·75 m	
Height	3·15 m	3·38 m	3·7 m	3 m	3·02 m	3·02 m	
Weight	14·5 tonnes	32 tonnes	34 tonnes	20 tonnes	24 tonnes	30 tonnes	
Crew	2	2	2	1	1	1	
Crane capacity	4 tonnes	13 tonnes	20 tonnes	10 tonnes	10 tonnes	20 tonnes	
Axle loading (1st axle)	5 tonnes	11·1 tonnes	8·8 tonnes	10·4 tonnes	7·5 tonnes	10 tonnes	
(2nd axle)	4·75 tonnes	11·1 tonnes	12·6 tonnes	10·4 tonnes	7·5 tonnes	10 tonnes	
(3rd axle)	4·75 tonnes	11·1 tonnes	12·6 tonnes	n/app	9 tonnes	10 tonnes	
Bridge load classification (MLC)	16	35	47	21	24	30	
Turning radius (front wheels only)	19 m	26 m	27·5 m	20·5 m	23·4 m	23·4 m	
(all-wheel steer)	n/app	n/app	n/app	13 m	17 m	23·4 m	
Engine	175 hp	265 hp	178 hp	320 hp	320 hp	320 hp	
Power-to-weight ratio	12 hp/t	8·2 hp/t	5·2 hp/t	16 hp/t	13·3 hp/t	10·7 hp/t	
Max speed	72 km/h	60 km/h	61·3 km/h	80 km/h	80 km/h	80 km/h	
Suspension (front)	leaf spring	leaf spring	leaf spring	hydro-pneumatic; each axle can be			
(rear)	can be blocked	walking beam	walking beam	individually blocked			
Angle of approach/ departure	30°/50°	30°/30°	very shallow	30°/30°			
Crane drive	hydraulic, from vehicle engine	hydraulic, from vehicle engine	separate engine	hydraulic, from vehicle engine			
Boom	hydraulic, telescopic	telescopic, hydraulic	lattice boom	telescopic, fully hydraulic			
Recovery winch	8 t, mechanical	8–10t	none	driven by vehicle hydraulics; hydraulic winch at front or rear			

STATUS
Production.

MANUFACTURER
Krupp, Wilhelmshaven, Federal Republic of Germany.

(*) A similar crane was manufactured by Orenstein & Koppel (O & K). Both cranes can be fitted with a grab.

West German 13-tonne truck-mounted crane (older O & K cable-operated boom) (Federal German Ministry of Defence)

West German 13-tonne truck-mounted crane (Wilhag crane) (Federal German Ministry of Defence)

Zettelmeyer ZL 1700 Articulated Loader

DESCRIPTION

Zettelmeyer produces a wide range of loaders in various load sizes. The ZL 1700 is produced in a military version and in various modes that can include a multi-purpose bucket, a fork lift device and a small crane. It can also act as a carrier for trench-digging devices. The ZL 1700 has an automatic hydrostatic drive with a single pedal control and a creep gear is also provided. Both axles have self-locking differentials and the articulated steering allows 40 degrees of turn in either direction. Maximum load height with the standard bucket is 4·6 metres and a further seven types of bucket are available. The cab is of the ROPS type.

The Zettelmeyer ZL 1700 is marketed in the United Kingdom as the TEREX 72-25 Military General Purpose Wheeled Tractor and for details of this development see the separate entries in this and the *Materials handling* section.

STATUS

Production.

MANUFACTURER

Zettelmeyer Maschinenfabrik GmbH, PO Box 1340, D-5503 Konz/Trier, Federal Republic of Germany.

SPECIFICATIONS
Cab seating: 1
Configuration: 4 × 4
Weight: (operating) 9500 kg
Lifting capacity: (max) 8000 kg
Length: 6·41 m
Width: 2·5 m

Height: (top of cab) 3·05 m
Ground clearance: 0·45 m
Wheelbase: 2·55 m
Max speed: 37 km/h
Engine: Deutz or Mercedes diesel developing 133 hp (SAE) at 2500 rpm
Transmission: hydrostatic, 2-speed power drive

Steering: central articulated joint with damped oscillation
Turning radius: 5·15 m
Brakes: hydrostatic
Tyres: (standard) 20–24 EM
Electrical system: 24 V
Batteries: 2 × 12 V, 135 Ah

Zettelmeyer ZL 1700 articulated loader

Zettelmeyer ZD 3000 Wheeled Tractor

DESCRIPTION

Known in the West German armed forces as 'Planier, Rad, mit Winde', the ZD 3000 has been introduced to replace the commercial 44 kW (60 hp) and 118 kW (160 hp) tracked bulldozers which were taken into service between 1958 and 1962. It was selected after a competition among nine German and foreign equipments, and was developed from the earlier KL-30-S tractor. As a wheeled bulldozer the ZD 3000 does not require the low-loaders and trucks needed to transport tracked equipments, and the Gleitkipper sliding bed truck and other low-loaders are being phased out of engineer units as they are re-equipped with the ZD 3000.

The ZD 3000 can excavate a heavy weapon emplacement at 20 cubic metres per hour, including a 30-metre transport distance, and scarifier teeth on the blade enable it to dig to a depth of 0·45 metre. Other applications for the vehicle include route improvement, obstacle clearance, assistance at river entry and egress

Zettelmeyer ZD 3000 wheeled dozer (C R Zwart)

Zettelmeyer ZD 3000-F wheeled loader

Zettelmeyer ZD 3001 wheel dozer with side-mounted crane

points, snow clearance and vehicle recovery (using the front-mounted winch).

A chassis with a total articulation of 76 degrees gives good manoeuvrability, while the hydropneumatic suspension allows the tractor to move on roads at convoy speeds. The two-man cab provides rollover protection and has many ergonomic features.

The ZD 3000 may be transported by rail without the need for dismantling.

This vehicle is built in the USA by the TEREX Corporation as the WD 3000 and is marketed in France by DPH SA as the MPG (matériel polyvalent du génie).

VARIANTS
ZL 3000-F articulated loader. This variant of the ZL 3000 is equipped with a front-mounted loading bucket. The 4-in-1 bucket has a capacity of 2·5 cubic metres and has a lifting capacity of 15 500 kg. The engine used on the ZL 3000-F is a Deutz V-10 air-cooled diesel developing 255 hp at 2300 rpm. Operating weight of the ZL 3000-F is 21 600 kg.

ZD 3001 SK wheel dozer. The ZD 3001 SK can be fitted with a side-mounted hydraulically-operated crane jib. This variant has a 260 hp (DIN) engine.

SPECIFICATIONS
Cab seating: 1 + 1
Configuration: 4 × 4

Weight: 23 000 kg
Length: 8·2 m
Width:
(over blade) 3·5 m
(in travelling order) 2·75 m
Height: 3·12 m
Wheelbase: 3·46 m
Ground clearance: 0·46 m
Track: 1·98 m
Engine: 10-cylinder in-line direct injection air-cooled diesel developing 280 hp at 2300 rpm
Transmission: torque converter powershift transmission with 4 forward and reverse ratios
Steering: frame articulation (total of 76°), hydraulically actuated
Turning circle diameter: 13·6 m
Road speed: 62 km/h
Fuel capacity: 500 litres
Suspension: hydropneumatic (blocked during earthmoving or winching operations). Axles have locking differentials and planetary hub reduction gearing
Brakes:
(service) air over hydraulic disc brakes on all wheels
(parking) mechanical disc brake on transmission output shaft
(retarder) on torque converter
Tyres: 30/65 × 25 earthmover, 20 PR

Electrical system: 24 V
Batteries: 2 × 12 V, 135 Ah
Winch: front-mounted, hydraulically-driven, of 20 000 kg capacity, with 90 m of 24 mm cable.
Pushing power: 20 000 kg

Blade
Width: 3·5 m (can be reduced to 2·75 m for transport)
Height: 1·35 m
Lift height: 1·4 m
Digging depth: 0·4 m (0·45 m with scarifier teeth)
Tilt: (forward/back) ±5°
Swivelling: (side to side) ±16°
Rotation: ±18°
Work capacity: 270 m³/h at 30 m transport distance and soil density of 2·25

STATUS
In production. In service with West German armed forces. The ZD 3000 and the TEREX-built version, the WD-3000, are now in service in Algeria, Bangladesh, France, Indonesia, Israel, Malaysia, Pakistan and South Africa.

MANUFACTURER
Zettelmeyer Maschinenfabrik GmbH (a company of IBH Holding AG), PO Box 1340, D 5503 Konz/Trier, Federal Republic of Germany.

Hamm DV8 Road Roller

DESCRIPTION
In 1982 the British Ministry of Defence ordered a total of 32 Hamm DV8 road rollers as part of a five-year contract. A further order for an extra four DV8 units was also made and of this order three were sent to the Falkland Islands.

The DV8 is an eight-tonne unit with drive and vibration to both roller drums and features off-set steering and split drums. The DV8 can handle all types of material on wearing courses, base courses and sub-base work.

STATUS
Production. In service with the British Army.

MANUFACTURER
Maschinenfabrik Hamm AG, 8593 Tirschenreuth, Federal Republic of Germany.

Enquiries to IBH Holding AG, Ersthalstrasse 1, 6500 Mainz, Federal Republic of Germany.

Hamm DV8 road roller

HUNGARY

Hungarian Dump Trucks

DESCRIPTION
Although a wide variety of dump trucks is produced, it is not known which models if any are used by the Hungarian armed forces. Among earlier Hungarian vehicles the D-350B, D-352B, D-420B, D-455B and D-450.05 dump trucks are known to exist. The D-453 is the direct

replacement for the D-455B. The Csepel D-564 military truck was produced in its prototype version as a dump truck, but no further details have been made available. A Csepel D-711 and D-717 dump truck have been announced but are not believed to be in normal military use. The Raba 836.00 is thought to be in the same category. On the other hand the Raba 106, Gödöllö 116, and the older DR-50D dump trucks are well suited for

military construction work, the Raba 106 and Gödöllö 116 having a 4 × 4 wheel arrangement while the DR-50D is a 4 × 2 vehicle.

Csepel D-455B dump truck

Gödöllö 116 dump truck

Csepel D-564 dump truck

SPECIFICATIONS

Model	Csepel D-455B (rear dump)	Csepel D-453 (3-side dump)	Gödöllö 116 (rear dump)
Weight	4700 kg	4380 kg*	9550 kg
Length	5·59 m	6 m*	5·13 m
Width	2·3 m	2·65 m*	2·5 m
Height	2·4 m	2·4 m*	3 m
Ground clearance	0·24 m	0·25 m	0·36 m
Wheelbase	3·3 m	3·2 m*	2·6 m
Track (front)	1·74 m	1·74 m	2·02 m
(rear)	1·72 m	1·72 m	2·04 m
Engine	D-414C 4-cylinder water-cooled diesel developing 100 hp	D-414.62 4-cylinder water-cooled diesel developing 95 hp	D-614.10 6-cylinder water-cooled diesel developing 125 hp
Fuel capacity	130 litres	140 litres*	n/a
Speed	78 km/h	—	45 km/h
Payload (road)	5000 kg	4800 kg	10 000 kg
Capacity	n/a	n/a	6 m³
Tyres	8.25 × 20 or 9.00 × 20	8.25 × 20	14.00 × 24

* Estimated on basis of D-452 truck.

STATUS
The D-455B is believed to be in military use.

MANUFACTURER
Csepel, near Budapest, Hungary.

Dutra Wheeled Tractors D4K, D4K-B, Dutra-Steyr 110

DESCRIPTION
These tractors have been designed for civil use but have a military potential. They all feature all-wheel drive,

D4K wheeled tractor with additional weights on wheels

long sloping bonnet with the driver seated at the rear (some have a fully enclosed cab) and an independent power take off. If additional ballast is required, weights can be added to the wheels and the tyres can be filled with water. The Dutra-Steyr 110 is produced in Hungary under licence from the Austrian firm of Steyr.

SPECIFICATIONS

Model	D4K	D4K-B	Dutra-Steyr 110
Weight	4328 kg	5100 kg	5100 kg
Length	4·6 m	4·92 m	5·02 m
Width	1·88 m	2·1 m	2·2 m
Height	2·26 m	2·56 m	2·53 m
Ground clearance	0·3 m	0·5 m	0·51 m
Wheelbase	1·85 m	1·95 m	1·95 m
Track	1·55 m	1·73 m	1·73 m
Max speed (road)	n/a	21·5 km/h	24·5 km/h
Engine	DT-414 diesel	D-613-15 diesel	Steyr WD diesel
Number of cylinders	4	6	6
Hp	65	90 at 1850 rpm	105 at 2300 rpm
Tyres	13.00 × 30	15.00 × 30	15.00 × 30

STATUS
Production. Military use of these tractors has not been confirmed.

MANUFACTURER
Hungarian state factories.

ITALY

Astra BM 201 MT Dump Truck

DESCRIPTION
This vehicle is essentially a 2-axle version of the earlier BM 20 NT 6 × 6 dump truck, for which there is a separate entry in this section. The cab is of fibreglass construction on a metal frame and can be tilted 48 degrees forward to allow access to the engine for maintenance.

SPECIFICATIONS
Cab seating: 1 + 1
Configuration: 4 × 4
Weight:
  (empty) 9300 kg
  (loaded) 20 000 kg
Capacity: (struck) 6 m³
Length: 6·1 m
Width: 2·49 m
Height: 2·88 m
Ground clearance: 0·83 m
Track:
  (front) 2 m
  (rear) 1·85 m
Wheelbase: 3·45 m
Max speed: (road) 77 km/h
Max slope: 24° (45%)
Fuel capacity: 180 litres
Engine: FIAT 8360 6-cylinder direct injection water-cooled in-line diesel of 8·1 litres displacement developing 124 kW (169 hp) at 2600 rpm
Transmission: single dry plate clutch: ZF mechanical constant-mesh gearbox with 6 forward and 1 reverse gears; 2-speed transfer case
Steering: hydraulically assisted
Turning circle diameter: 16 m
Suspension:
  (front) semi-elliptical springs
  (rear) semi-elliptical springs with double flex auxiliary springs
Tyres: 12 × 20 (18 PR)
Number of tyres: 6 + 1 spare
Brakes:
  (primary) air over hydraulic
  (parking) mechanical
Electrical system: 24 V
Batteries: 2 × 12 V

Astra BM 201 MT 4 × 4 dump truck (T J Gander)

STATUS
In production.In service with the Italian Army Engineer Corps.

MANUFACTURER
Astra Veicoli Industriali SpA, Via Caorsana 79, 29100 Piacenza, Italy.

Astra BM 20 MT Dump Truck

DESCRIPTION
The first production Astra BM 20 MT dump truck was completed in 1976. Its chassis is made of high strength steel and comprises two double C-shaped side members connected by rigid cross-members. The dump body is constructed of 6 mm T1A improved steel and is mounted on rubber-bushed pivots. In addition to seats for the driver and a passenger, the fibreglass cab is also fitted with two emergency folding seats.

STATUS
In production since 1976. In service with the Italian Army.

MANUFACTURER
Astra Veicoli Industriali SpA, Via Caorsana 79, 29100 Piacenza, Italy.

SPECIFICATIONS
Cab seating: 2 (+2 emergency folding seats)
Configuration: 6 × 6
Weight:
(empty) 13 300 kg
(loaded) 30 000 kg
Capacity: (struck) 8·5 m³
Towed load: 28 000 kg
Length: 7·765 m
Width: 2·5 m
Height:
(over dump body) 2·96 m
(over cab) 2·75 m

Ground clearance: 0·27 m
Track:
(front) 2 m
(rear) 1·85 m
Wheelbase: 3·49 + 1·3 m
Max speed: (road) 67 km/h
Max slope: 22° (40%) (fully loaded)
Fuel capacity: 280 litres
Engine: FIAT 8210 6-cylinder in-line diesel developing 191 kW (260 hp) at 2200 rpm
Transmission: single dry plate clutch; ZF mechanical constant-mesh gearbox with 6 forward and 1 reverse gears; 2-speed transfer case

Steering: hydraulic assisted
Turning circle diameter: 22 m
Suspension:
(front) semi-elliptical springs
(rear) oscillating semi-elliptical springs with rocker arm system
Tyres: 12 × 20 (18 PR)
Number of tyres: 10 + 1 spare
Brakes:
(primary) air over hydraulic
(parking) mechanical
Electrical system: 24 V
Batteries: 4 × 12 V

Astra BM 20 MT 6 × 6 dump truck of Italian Army

Astra BM 20 MT 6 × 6 dump truck of Italian Army

Astra BM 20 MP1 Mobile Drilling Equipment

DESCRIPTION
This vehicle uses the same chassis as the Astra BM 20 M 6 × 6 series of trucks. The Geo-Astra drilling rig Model G21 is driven by the vehicle engine and is capable of mud rotary, air rotary and rotary air percussion drilling. As with other mobile drilling equipments described in this section, this vehicle has applications both in the supply of fresh water and in the preparation of demolitions.

SPECIFICATIONS
Details of the chassis are the same as those of the BM 20 MT 6 × 6 dump truck, described previously in this section.
Weight:
(chassis) 9900 kg
(complete) 23 000 kg
Length: 9·3 m
Height: 3·8 m

Geo-Astra G21 drilling rig
Weight: 13 100 kg
Rating air drilling system: 200 m

Hole diameter: 200 mm
Drilling pressure: 12 000 kg

STATUS
In production.

MANUFACTURER
Astra Veicoli Industriali SpA, Via Caorsana 79, 29100 Piacenza, Italy.

Astra BM 20 MP1 mobile drilling equipment

Astra BM 20 MP1 mobile drilling equipment deployed

Astra BM20 NR2 (6 × 6) Crane Truck

DESCRIPTION
This vehicle uses the same chassis as the Astra BM20 MR1 (6 × 6) recovery vehicle (see page 53) and has been in production since 1983 for the Italian Army Engineer Corps. The vehicle carries a 20-ton crane on the rear which can be traversed through a full 360

degrees. The extending crane boom has a maximum length of 16 metres. When the crane is in use four stabilisers are lowered, two on each side, under hydraulic power. All the crane controls are inside the operator's cab which rotates with the boom. As well as the usual crane functions the winch and boom can be fitted with an oscillating hammer under hydraulic control for the demolition of structures such as walls.

STATUS
Production. In service with the Italian Army.

MANUFACTURER
Astra Veicoli Industriali SpA, Via Caorsana 79, 29100 Piacenza, Italy.

SPECIFICATIONS
Cab seating: 2 + 2
Configuration: 6 × 6
Weight:
    (chassis and accessories) 9700 kg
    (chassis, accessories and crane) 26 980 kg
Towed load: 28 000 kg
Length: (overall) 10·13 m
Width: 2·5 m
Height:
    (cab) 2·75 m
    (top of crane travelling) 3·06 m

Ground clearance: 0·265 m
Track:
    (front) 2 m
    (rear) 1·85 m
Wheelbase: 3·485 m + 1·3 m
Max speed: (road) 67·2 km/h
Fuel capacity: 280 litres
Max gradient: 40%
Engine: FIAT Model 8210.02 6-cylinder in-line diesel developing 260 hp at 2200 rpm
Gearbox: ZF manual, 6 forward and 1 reverse gears
Clutch: single dry plate

Transfer box: 2-speed
Steering: hydraulic assisted
Suspension:
    (front) semi-elliptical springs with 4 rubber bumpers and hydraulic shock absorbers
    (rear) oscillating semi-elliptical type springs with rocker arm suspension
Tyres: 12.00 × 20
Number of tyres: 10 + 1 spare
Electrical system: 24 V
Batteries: 4 × 12 V

Astra BM20 NR2 (6 × 6) crane truck

Astra BM20 NR2 (6 × 6) crane truck

Benati 610 HDB Hydraulic Excavator

SPECIFICATIONS
Weight: 68 000 kg
Height: (top of cab) 3·775 m
Width: 3·95 m
Ground contact length: 4·387 m
Track width: 0·7 m (0·9 m optional)
Track centre distance: 2·6 m
Engine: FIAT 828 V-8 direct injection water-cooled diesel of 17·2 litres displacement developing 340 hp at 2400 rpm
Transmission: hydrostatic, with 2 independent hydraulic motors
Max speed: (road) 2·05 km/h
Max slope: 79%
Bucket capacity: 0·95-3·85 m³
Reach: (with standard 2·5 m dipperstick) 11·9 m
Digging depth: 7·1 m
Dump height: 7 m
Breakout force: 26 100 kg
Electrical system: 24 V
Batteries: 2 × 12 V, 143 Ah each

STATUS
Understood to be in service with the Italian Army. The firm of Benati SpA also produces the BEN 150PS tracked loader which is also in military service.

MANUACTURER
Benati SpA, SS 610 Selice, 43/a, PO Box 83, 40026 Imola (Bo), Italy.

Benati 610 HDB hydraulic excavator

Benati 150PS tracked loader with backhoe

Cantatore APR 180/ES Wheeled Bulldozer

DESCRIPTION
The APR 180 is equipped with a front-mounted, hydraulically-operated bulldozer blade and a rear-mounted ripper with three teeth. The tractor is of rigid frame construction and is steered by means of the rear wheels. Standard military lighting is provided and the ends of the bulldozer blade can be folded inwards to reduce the overall width for road movement.

SPECIFICATIONS
Weight: (in working order) 18 050 kg
Length: 7 m
Width: 2·5 m
Height: 3·03 m
Engine: Deutz F8L413 V-8 air-cooled diesel of 11·31 litres displacement developing 180 hp
Max speed: (road) 42 km/h
Max gradient: 50%
Endurance: 15 h
Bulldozer:
  (blade width) 3·5 m
  (capacity) 1·9 m³
  (work rate) 56 m³/h (moved 50 m)
Ripper work rate: 1000 m²/h

STATUS
The APR 180/ES entered Italian Army service in 1972.

MANUFACTURER
Cantatore, Modigliana (Forli), Italy.

Cantatore APR 180/ES wheeled bulldozer (Italian Army)

Cantatore TC 135/ES Wheeled Tractor

DESCRIPTION
The Cantatore TC 135/ES is a rigid-framed tractor with rear-wheel steering. The specially-designed bowl is mounted on conventional linkage arms and is hydraulically-operated, but the bowl can be angled to displace soil to either side in the manner of an angle-dozer, and its parabolic shape and pointed cutting edge give the tractor a useful bulldozing capability. A rear-mounted hydraulic excavator is also provided.

SPECIFICATIONS
Weight: (in working order) 12 000 kg
Length: 8·15 m
Width: 2·5 m
Height: 3·66 m
Engine: Perkins T6-334 6-cylinder 135 hp 5·8-litre water-cooled diesel
Max speed: (road) 31 km/h
Max gradient: 40%
Bowl width: 2·5 m
Bowl capacity: 1·25 m³
Work rate: 85 m³/h at 16 h endurance
Excavator capacity: 0·31 m³
Excavation: (depth) down to 4 m
Excavator: (work rate) 30 m³/h

STATUS
The TC 135/ES is modified for military use and entered service with the Italian Army in 1970.

MANUFACTURER
Cantatore, Modigliana (Forli), Italy.

Cantatore TC 135/ES wheeled tractor (Italian Army)

FIAT AD 14 Bulldozer

DESCRIPTION
The FIAT AD 14 bulldozer is conventionally configured with a hydraulically-operated blade at the front. The blade can also be angled and tilted. A three-toothed ripper is fitted at the back.

SPECIFICATIONS
Weight: (in working order) 17 000 kg
Length: 7·25 m
Width: 2·89 m
Height: 3·87 m
Blade:
  (length) 3·87 m
  (height) 0·98 m
  (capacity) 2·5 m³
Engine: FIAT 620 A005 6-cylinder diesel, water-cooled, 9·82 litres, developing 140 hp
Max speed: (sustained) 10 km/h
Work rate: 100 m³/h, moved 50 m, for 16 h
Ripper work rate: 1200 m²/h to a depth of 0·4–0·6 m

STATUS
The FIAT AD 14 entered Italian Army service in 1972.

MANUFACTURER
FIATALLIS SpA, Lecce-Surbo, Zone Industriale, Italy.

FIATALLIS AD 14-F bulldozer (Italian Army)

FIATALLIS FL 14-C Tracked Loader

DESCRIPTION
Of a similar size to the AD-14F bulldozer, the FL 14-C loader is in the 150 hp class and is equipped as standard with a two cubic metres bucket. It features an in-line bucket linkage, one-piece loader frame, sealed hydraulic system, automatic bucket controls, a 13·75 second hydraulic cycle time, 360 degrees visibility and easy access for maintenance and service. The FL 14-C may be fitted with a backhoe equipment.

SPECIFICATIONS
Cab seating: 1
Weight: (operating, including ROPS canopy) 17 300 kg
Length: (bucket on ground) 5·38 m
Width: 2·3 m
Height: (over cab) 2·97 m
Ground contact length: 2·6 m
Track centre distance: 1·87 m
Ground pressure: 0·78 kg/cm²
Ground clearance: 0·43 m
Engine: FIAT 8205 6-cylinder naturally aspirated direct injection diesel of 9·82 litres displacement developing 112 kW (150 hp) at 2000 rpm
Transmission: torque converter and 3 × 3 full powershift transmission
Fuel capacity: 350 litres
Maximum speed: 9 km/h forwards; 11 km/h reverse
Breakout force: 12 620 kg
Static tipping load: 11 330 kg
Overall height: (with bucket raised) 4·76 m
Dump clearance at 45°: 3 m
Rated bucket capacity: 2 m³
Struck bucket capacity: 1·69 m³
Bucket:
   (width) 2·44 m
   (weight) 1230 kg
   (teeth) 9

STATUS
In production. In service with the Italian Army.

MANUFACTURER
FIATALLIS Europe SpA, Viale Torino 0/2, 10040 Stupinigi, Torino, Italy.

FIATALLIS FL 14-C crawler loaders fitted with backhoe equipment for military use

---

FIATALLIS FG 85 Motor Grader

SPECIFICATIONS
Configuration: 6 × 4
Weight: 12 578 kg
Length: 8·28 m
Width: 2·31 m
Height: 3·27 m
Track:
   (front) 1·95 m
   (rear) 2·3 m
Engine: FIAT 8365 6-cylinder in-line direct injection turbo-charged diesel of 8·1 litres displacement developing 108 net kW (145 hp) at 2200 rpm
Transmission: single stage torque converter with powershift and lockup clutch; 2·13 multiplication ratio; 4 forward and reverse ratios

Fuel: 231 litres
Speed:
   (forward) 33 km/h
   (reverse) 20 km/h
Steering: hydrostatic, with gear pump (wheels can lean ±17·5°)
Turning circle diameter: 20 m
Brakes:
   (service) hydraulic drum brakes on rear wheels
   (parking) drum brake on transmission

Mouldboard (standard)
Length: 3·65 m
Height: 0·61 m
Lift: 0·44 m

Sideshift:
   (left) 0·53 m
   (right) 0·68 m
Blade pressure: 6443 kg
Tyres: (standard) 13.00 × 24, 10 PR
Electrical system: 24 V; 45 A alternator, 165 Ah battery

STATUS
In production.

MANUFACTURERS
FIATALLIS Europe SpA, Viale Torino 0/2, 10040 Stupinigi, Torino, Italy.
   Produced in Brazil by FIATALLIS Latono Americana SA, Rue Gois Raposo, 1550 (Via Anchieta, km 12·5), Brazil.

Ursus Peroni 120 motor grader also in military service (Italian Army)

FIATALLIS FG 85 motor grader with front-mounted scarifier

Marchetti MG 102 TEL 20-tonne Crane

DESCRIPTION
Designed specifically for demolition and recovery purposes the Marchetti MG 102 TEL 20-tonne crane is mounted on an Astra BM 20 (6 × 6) chassis. The hydraulically-extended crane boom has a maximum length of 14 metres with a maximum lifting height of 18 metres. The operator's cab is on the left of the boom and four telescopic jacks are situated at each corner of the rear hamper for stabilisation when working. The main demolition attachment is a 1000 kg clapper weight which may be dropped vertically or swung for effect. Also provided is a 15 000 kg winch which may be operated to the front or sides.

SPECIFICATIONS
Cab seating: 1 + 2
Configuration: 6 × 6
Weight: 26 550 kg
Length: 9·27 m
Width: 2·5 m
Height: 3·65 m
Engine power: 260 hp
Transmission: 6 forward and reverse ranges; reducer for 2-speed
Suspension: leaf spring and shock absorbers
Steering: front axle, power-assisted
Lifting capacity: (outriggers extended)

at 3 m radius	20 000 kg
at 7 m radius	7200 kg
at 10 m radius	4500 kg
at 14 m radius	2200 kg

STATUS
Production. Under evaluation by the Italian Army.

MANUFACTURER
Marchetti Autogru SpA, Via Caorsana 49, 29100 Piacenza, Italy.

Marchetti MG 102 TEL 20-tonne crane on Astra BM20 (6 × 6) chassis

Marchetti MG 102 TEL 20-tonne crane on Astra BM20 (6 × 6) chassis

Marchetti MG 244 TEL 30-tonne Rough Terrain Crane

DESCRIPTION
The firm of Marchetti Autogru SpA manufactures a range of mobile cranes of capacities from 16 to 110 tonnes. The MG 244 TEL is mounted on a 4 × 4 carrier with high flotation tyres and is of 30-tonne capacity. Driving and crane operations are controlled from a single cab which rotates with the superstructure.

STATUS
Production.

MANUFACTURER
Marchetti Autogru SpA, Via Caorsana 49, 29100 Piacenza, Italy.

SPECIFICATIONS
Cab seating: 1
Configuration: 4 × 4
Length: 9·27 m
Width: 2·5 m
Height: 3·3 m
Ground clearance: 0·4 m
Track: 2·04 m
Wheelbase: 3·4 m
Engine: FIAT 8360 6-cylinder in-line water-cooled direct injection diesel of 8·1 litres displacement developing 165 hp at 2600 rpm
Transmission: powershift torque converter transmission with 6 forward and reverse ranges. Drive to front axle may be disengaged
Axles: rigid, with ZF planetary reduction gearing. Rear axle oscillates but is automatically locked on the side supporting the load during crane operations
Tyres: 16.00 × 25, 36 PR earthmover, tubeless
Steering: front axle controlled by steering wheel. Rear axle may be independently controlled, permitting 2-, 4-wheel or crab steering
Fuel: 260 litres
Electrical system: 24 V

Marchetti MG 244 TEL rough terrain crane

Crane
Capacity:

	outriggers extended		on tyres
(at minimum radius) (3 m)	30 000 kg at 3 m radius	(over front)	15 000 kg at 3 m
	30 000 kg	(360°)	13 500 kg
(at maximum radius) (20 m)	1700 kg	(over front)	1200 kg at 14 m radius
	1500 kg	(360°)	1600 kg at 7 m radius

Boom: 4 section, hydraulically extended
Length:
(retracted) 8·85 m
(fully extended) 26·85 m
Maximum lifting height: 29·8 m
Outriggers: hydraulically operated from cab
Main winch cable: 150 m, 15 mm diameter
Line pull: 3500 kg
Maximum single line speed: 80 m/minute

Italgru 12-ton Mobile Crane (Autogru OM/1 12 t)

DESCRIPTION
The OM/1 12-ton mobile crane consists of a T 12 conventional hoist-type crane mounted on the OM 6600 truck chassis. The chassis was modified into a crane carrier by the addition of four stabilising jacks and is very similar to the US M139 5-ton chassis used for the Honest John rocket launcher.

STATUS
The Autogru OM/1 12 t was approved for service in 1963 and is still in service with the Italian Army.

MANUFACTURER
Italgru, Lecco, Italy.

SPECIFICATIONS
Length: 8·91 m
Width: 2·92 m
Height: 3·83 m
Max speed: (road) 60 km/h
Max gradient: 39% (21·5°)

Crane
Capacity: 12 000 kg at 3·2 m radius (with stabilisers)
Boom length: minimum 7·8 m, extensible
Engine: V-4 diesel of 62 hp
Traverse: 360°
Endurance: 5 h approx
Winch: (mounted at front of truck chassis) 9100 kg
capacity

Autogru OM/1 12 t (Italian Army)

JAPAN

Komatsu PC200-2 Hydraulic Excavator

DESCRIPTION
The Komatsu PC200-2 hydraulic excavator is a
conventionally-configured excavator with a choice of
two working arm lengths plus an extension arm. For
heavy work the working arm is 2·44 metres long and for
all-round work 2·955 metres long. An extension arm
1·13 metres long is also available. Equipment for use on
the arms includes a narrow or normal width backhoe
bucket, a trapezoidal bucket, a slope finishing bucket
and a clamshell bucket. Single or three-shank rippers
can also be used. Two controls inside the operator's cab
are used for normal working operations and a further
two levers are used for travelling and steering. The cab
is mounted on rubber pads to reduce internal noise
levels and all windows are fitted with safety glass.

STATUS
Production. In service with the Japanese Ground Self-
Defence Force.

MANUFACTURER
Komatsu Limited, No 3–6, Akasaka 2-chome, Minato-
ku, Tokyo 107, Japan.

SPECIFICATIONS
Weight: (approx) 18 800 kg
Length: (arm down and folded) 9·25 m

Komatsu PC200-2 hydraulic excavator

Width: (over tracks) 2·79 m
Height: 2·935 m
Ground clearance: 0·455 m
Track: 2·18 m
Width of tracks: 610 mm
Fuel capacity: 260 litres

Engine: Komatsu 6D105 4-cycle 6-cylinder water-
cooled diesel developing 105 hp at 2150 rpm
Bucket capacity: 0·45 to 1 m³
Max digging height: 9 m
Max dumping height: 6·3 m
Max digging depth: 6·47 m

Hitachi UHO7 and Sumitomo LS2800AJ Hydraulic Excavators

SPECIFICATIONS
Length: (overall) 9·1 m
Width: (overall) 2·77 m
Height: (overall) 2·82 m

Weight: (loaded) 18 800 kg
Speed: over 2·4 km/h
Ground pressure: 0·41 kg/cm²
Gradient: 55%
Engine: Isuzu DA640, 85 hp
Bucket volume: (full) 0·7 m³

STATUS
The Hitachi UHO7 and Sumitomo LS2800AJ loaders
are in service with the Japanese Ground Self-Defence
Force.

MANUFACTURERS
Hitachi Construction Machinery Co, Sumitomo Heavy
Machinery Co, Japan.

10-tonne and 20-tonne Mobile Cranes

DESCRIPTION
There are two types of crane in service with the
Japanese Ground Self-Defence Force, tracked and
wheeled, with 10 000 and 20 000 kg models of each.
The former is issued to construction battalions and the
latter to engineering units.

MANUFACTURERS
(crane) Sumitomo Heavy Machinery Co, Hitachi Manufacturing Co, Japan.
(chassis) Mitsubishi Heavy Industries, Japan.

*20 000 kg truck-mounted crane used by Japanese
Ground Self-Defence Force (K Ebata)*

SPECIFICATIONS
(20 000 kg wheeled type)
Types:
Sumitomo HC68AJ
Hitachi F55S
Length: (travelling) 11·45 m
Width: (overall) 2·7 m
Height: (travelling) 3·5 m
Weight: 20 000 kg

Max road speed: 50 km/h
Range: over 300 km
Gradient: 30%
Fording: 0·6 m
Engine:
(chassis) Mitsubishi 6DB10W diesel developing
158 hp
(crane) Isuzu DA120P developing 67 hp

Crane capacity:
(hoisting weight) 15 000 kg
(hoisting height) 6·6 m
Attachments: (crane)
drag line (capacity 0·6 m³)
clamshell (capacity 0·6 m³)
back hoe (capacity 0·6 m³)
piledriver (weight 1360 kg)
shovel (capacity 0·6 m³)

Komatsu D20A-5 Light Bulldozer

DESCRIPTION
The Komatsu D20A-5 light bulldozer is orthodox in lay-out and can be equipped with various accessories including a power-angle tiltdozer, an angledozer and a trimmingdozer. As an alternative the D20A-5 can be used as a crawler tractor. Other optional equipment includes a ROPS cab, a backhoe and a towing winch. The latter has a bare drum line pull capacity of 5400 kg and has a 14 mm diameter cable 40 metres long. The diesel engine used on the D20A-5 develops 39 hp at 2450 rpm.

SPECIFICATIONS
Weight:
(tractor) 2960 kg
(power-angle tiltdozer) 3520 kg
(angledozer) 3542 kg
(with backhoe) 4622 kg
Length:
(angledozer) 3·36 m
(angledozer with backhoe) 4·2 m
Width: 2·41 m
Height: 2·16 m
(with backhoe) 3·03 m
Ground clearance: 0·31 m
Ground pressure:
(angledozer) 0·34 kg/cm²
(angledozer with backhoe) 0·46 kg/cm²
Max towing capacity: 4220 kg
Fuel capacity: 60 litres
Engine: Komatsu 4D94-2N 4-cycle 4-cylinder water-cooled diesel developing 39 hp at 2450 rpm
Max speed:
(forward) 7·4 km/h
(reverse) 6·5 km/h

Komatsu D20A-5 light bulldozer

Electrical system: 24 V
Batteries: 2 × 12 V, 60 Ah

STATUS
Production. In service with the Japanese Ground Self-Defence Force.

The Japanese Ground Self-Defence Force also has a number of Mitsubishi BD2D light bulldozers in service.

MANUFACTURER
Komatsu Limited, No 3–6, Akasaka 2-chome, Minato-ku, Tokyo 107, Japan.

Komatsu D50A-16 Bulldozer

DESCRIPTION
The Komatsu D50A-16 bulldozer is orthodox in layout and is capable of operating at altitudes of up to 2500 metres without recourse to fuel injection adjustment. It can be operated without accessories as a towing tractor

and options that can be fitted include a ROPS canopy, an angledozer, a special strengthened angledozer, a straight tiltdozer, an angle rakedozer, a multi-shank ripper, a trimmingdozer, a backhoe and a towing winch. The winch has a bare drum line pull capacity of 17 900 kg and a 22·4 mm cable 65 metres long.
The D50A-16 travels and works on a five-roller track

frame. The normal track shoes fitted are 460 mm wide and have single grousers. Wet-type clutches are used for steering and also for the brakes. The tracks are lubricated to extend their life.

SPECIFICATIONS
Weight:
(tractor) 10 000 kg
(angledozer) 11 890 kg
Length: (angledozer) 4·555 m
Width:
(over tracks) 2·34 m
(over angledozer blade) 3·72 m
Height: 2·86 m
Ground clearance: 0·325 m
Track: 1·88 m
Length of track on ground: 2·2 m
Ground pressure: (angledozer) 0·59 kg/cm²
Fuel capacity: 240 litres
Max speed:
(forward) 9·1 km/h
(reverse) 7·9 km/h
Engine: Komatsu 4D130-1 4-cycle, 4-cylinder water-cooled diesel developing 110 hp at 1900 rpm
Electrical system: 24 V
Batteries: 2 × 12 V, 150 Ah

STATUS
Production. In service with the Japanese Ground Self-Defence Force.

MANUFACTURER
Komatsu Limited, No 3–6, Akasaka 2-chome, Minato-ku, Tokyo 107, Japan.

Komatsu D50A-16 bulldozer

Komatsu D60A-7 Bulldozer and D60P-7 Swamp Bulldozer

DESCRIPTION
These two bulldozers use the same basic tractor unit and accessories but the D60P-7 has a special leng-thened track and suspension allied with extra-wide tracks and fitted with wide circular-arc swamp shoes.

The two models differ slightly in the accessories they can use as the D60A-7 can accept an angledozer, a mechanical angle-powerdozer, a straightdozer, and a straight tilt dozer. The D60P-7 does not use the mechanical angle-power dozer. Other accessories are a ROPS cab, an angle rakedozer and a multi-shank ripper. Both models can also use a 23 600 kg capacity towing winch fitted with 65 metres of 26 mm diameter

cable. Both models have manual transmission using a gear box with five forward and four reverse gears.

VARIANTS
The Komatsu D65A-7 is basically the same model as the D60A-7 but is equipped with the Komatsu TORQ-FLOW transmission consisting of a water-cooled, four element, single-stage, three-phase torque converter

and planetary gear, multiple-disc transmission. This gives a maximum forward speed of 10·6 km/h and maximum reverse speed of 13·6 km/h.

SPECIFICATIONS

Model	D60A-7	D60P-7
Weight (tractor)	12 960 kg	14 790 kg
(straight tiltdozer)	16 070 kg	17 550 kg
Length (straight tiltdozer)	5·025 m	5·585 m
Width (over tracks)	2·39 m	3 m
(over dozer blade)	3·415 m	3·97 m
Height	3·015 m	3·055 m
Ground clearance	0·4 m	0·51 m
Track	1·88 m	2·05 m
Track width	510 mm	950 mm

STATUS
All the above models are in production. All are in service with the Japanese Ground Self-Defence Force.

MANUFACTURER
Komatsu Limited, No 3–6, Akasaka 2-chome, Minato-ku, Tokyo 107, Japan.

Model	D60A-7	D60P-7
Ground pressure	0·52 kg/cm²	0·25 kg/cm²
Max towing capacity	17 580 kg	18 320 kg
Max speed (forward)	11·1 km/h	11·1 km/h
(reverse)	9·8 km/h	9·8 km/h
Fuel capacity	320 litres	320 litres
Engine	Komatsu-Cummins NH-220-C1 4-cycle, water-cooled diesel developing 155 hp at 1850 rpm	
Electrical system	24 V	24 V

Komatsu D60A-7 bulldozer

Komatsu D60P-7 swamp bulldozer

Caterpillar Mitsubishi D7F and Komatsu D80A-18 Heavy Bulldozers

DESCRIPTION
These are used by engineering groups and regional engineering units of the Japanese Ground Self-Defence Force.

SPECIFICATIONS (D80A-18)
Length: 5·77 m
 (with ripper) 7·1 m
 (with winch) 6·405 m
Width: 4·365 m
Height: 3·395 m
Weight: 23 270 kg
 (with ripper) 26 070 kg
 (with winch) 24 850 kg
Ground pressure: 0·75 kg/cm²
 (with ripper) 0·85 kg/cm²
 (with winch) 0·81 kg/cm²
Max towing capacity: 24 000 kg
Engine: NT855 4-cycle 6-cylinder water-cooled turbo-charged diesel developing 220 hp at 1800 rpm
Max speed: 9·9 km/h

Komatsu D80A-18 bulldozer of Japanese Ground Self-Defence Force (K Ebata)

MANUFACTURERS
Komatsu Ltd, Caterpillar Mitsubishi Co, Japan.

D-8 Motorised Scraper

SPECIFICATIONS
Length: 9·84 m
Width: 3·8 m
Height: 2·87 m
Weight: 15 700 kg
Bowl capacity:
 (max) 10·3 m³
 (normal) 8·4 m³
Engine: 6-cylinder water-cooled diesel developing 210 hp

STATUS
In service with the Japanese Ground Self-Defence Force. The D-7 towed scraper is also in service.

D-8 motorised scraper used by Japanese Ground Self-Defence Force (K Ebata)

Komatsu GD500R-2 Motor Grader

DESCRIPTION
The Komatsu GD500R-2 motor grader is conventional in layout and can be fitted, if required, with a fully-enclosed steel-framed cab. The normal grader blade is hydraulically controlled but may be replaced by a scarifier with either nine or eleven teeth. As a further alternative a front-mounted dozer blade can be mounted.

SPECIFICATIONS
Weight:
(total) 10 500 kg
(front wheels) 2935 kg
(rear wheels) 7565 kg
Length: 7·92 m
Width:
(over blade) 3·71 m
(over wheels) 2·335 m
Height: 2·975 m
Wheelbase: (front axle to centre rear axles) 5·78 m
Track:
(front) 1·92 m
(rear) 1·96 m
Max towing capacity: 6340 kg
Fuel capacity: 227 litres
Max speed: 41·2 km/h

Komatsu GD500R-2 motor grader

Engine: Komatsu S6D105 water-cooled 4-cycle ohv direct-injection turbocharged diesel developing 130 hp at 2400 rpm
Transmission: manual with 8 forward and 4 reverse gears
Tyres: 13.00 × 24
Electrical system: 24 V
Batteries: 2 × 12 V, 120 Ah

STATUS
Production. In service with the Japanese Ground Self-Defence Force.

MANUFACTURER
Komatsu Limited, No 3–6, Akasaka 2-chome, Minato-ku, Tokyo 107, Japan.

KLD6A Wheeled Loader

SPECIFICATIONS
Length: (bucket on ground) 6·43 m
Width: (chassis) 2·1 m
Height: (bucket up) 4·77 m
Weight: 10 650 kg
Bucket volume: 1·2–1·5 m³
Max speed: 37 km/h
Minimum turning radius: 5·85 m
Engine: Isuzu DA640 6-cylinder water-cooled diesel developing 103 hp

STATUS
Loaders, both wheeled and tracked, are used by infantry regiments, divisional engineer battalions, engineer groups and regional engineer units.

MANUFACTURER
Kawasaki Heavy Industries, Japan.

KLD6A wheeled loader of Japanese Ground Self-Defence Force (K Ebata)

Mitsubishi LG2-H Motor Grader

DESCRIPTION
The LG2-H is the standard grader of the divisional construction battalions, construction groups and regional construction units of the Japanese Ground Self-Defence Force.

SPECIFICATIONS
Length: (overall) 7·97 m
Width: 2·34 m
Height: 3·49 m
Weight: (loaded) 11 715 kg
Width of blade: 3·71 m
Minimum forward speed: 4 km/h
Max forward speed: 35 km/h
Minimum reverse speed: 7 km/h
Max reverse speed: 10·7 km/h
Engine: Mitsubishi 6DBD10C 6-cylinder water-cooled diesel developing 115 hp at 1800 rpm

MANUFACTURER
Mitsubishi Heavy Industries, Japan.

Mitsubishi LG2-H grader as used by Japanese Ground Self-Defence Force

Tadano TR-151 Rough Terrain Crane

SPECIFICATIONS
Cab seating: 1
Configuration: 4 × 4
Weight: 19 800 kg
Length: (travelling order) 9·63 m
Width: 2·49 m
Height: 3·4 m
Engine: Nissan ND-6 diesel developing 96 kW (130 hp) at 2800 rpm
Maximum speed: 40 km/h
Range: 250 km (4 h working time)
Fording depth: 0·8 m
Gradient: 53%

STATUS
In service.

Rear view of Tadano TR-151 rough terrain crane of Japanese Ground Self-Defence Force in travelling order (K Nogi)

POLAND

SL-34 Wheeled Loader

DESCRIPTION
This wheeled loader is a recent development and is used for a variety of tasks by Polish Army engineers. Its hydraulically-operated articulated steering gives the vehicle a small turning radius, and the versatility of the machine may be increased by replacing the standard loading shovel with a dozer blade or with lifting forks. The winch of the SL-34 may also be used in recovery operations.

STATUS
In service.

MANUFACTURER
Huta Stalowa Wola, Poland.

SPECIFICATIONS
Weight: 19 560 kg
Length: 8·1 m
Width: 3 m
Height: 3·67 m
Engine: SW 680/59/1 6-cylinder water-cooled turbocharged diesel developing 162 kW (220 hp) at 2200 rpm
Transmission: SP165 mechanical gearbox with ZM151N stepless torque converter; 4 forward and reverse ratios; torque multiplication 1–2·25
Shovel capacity: 3·4 m³
Lifting capacity: 7138 kg
Breakout force at bucket teeth: 14 276 kg
Earthmoving capability:
  (clay soil) 65 m³/h
  (sand/gravel) 145 m³/h

Max road speed: 39 km/h
Average convoy speed: 20–25 km/h
Endurance: (fuel) 20 h
Axles:
  (front) rigid
  (rear) oscillating
Tyres: 23.5 × 25, EM
Steering: hydraulic, articulating
Turning circle diameter: less than 6 m
Brakes: air-over-hydraulic
Electrical system: 24 V
Winch:
  (capacity) 1020 kg
  (rope) 65 m
  (winding rate) 12–18 m/min

Polish Dump Trucks

DESCRIPTION
The earlier Polish dump trucks, such as the Star W-14, W-25 and W-27 models, were produced in several versions. More recent models include the W-28 and W-244. Of these only the W-244 is a 4 × 4 model; the others are all 4 × 2. A Star WB-66 (6 × 6) dump truck with a 4-tonne payload, and newer Zubr (8-tonne) and Jelcz (7·5-tonne) vehicles are also reported. The W-28 truck has a 4·5-tonne payload.

SPECIFICATIONS
(W-25 3·5-tonne, 4 × 2)
Weight: 3800 kg
Payload: (road) 3500 kg
Length: 4·95 m
Width: 2·27 m
Height: 2·2 m
Wheelbase: 2·5 m
Track: (front and rear) 1·6 m

Engine: S-472 6-cylinder water-cooled petrol developing 95 hp
Max speed: 84 km/h
Capacity: 2·2 m³
Ground clearance: 0·25 m
Tyres: 8.25 × 20

MANUFACTURER
Polish state factories.

Star W-25 3·5-tonne dump truck

Star W-28/800 4·5-tonne dump truck

KS-251 Excavator

The KS-251 excavator is mounted on a 6 × 6 version of the Polish Star 66 chassis. Its status is uncertain.

Polish KS-251 excavator

Polish Truck-mounted Cranes

The following truck-mounted cranes are thought to be in service with the Polish Army:

Model	ZS-4	ZSH-6	ZS-25
Chassis	Star 27	Star 66 or 660	special 6 × 6
Capacity (max load)	4000 kg	6300 kg	25 000 kg
(load at max radius)	n/a	1000 kg/3 m	16 000 kg
Weight	7500 kg	10 500 kg	32 000 kg
Length	8·7 m	n/a	n/a
Height	3·02 m	n/a	n/a
Max speed	40 km/h	40 km/h	n/a
Remarks	—	also ZSH-6P	military use not confirmed

All models have 360° traverse.

Polish ZSH-6 6·3-tonne mobile crane

ROMANIA

1 ABS-116 5-tonne Dump Truck

Romanian 1 ABS-116 5-tonne dump truck

DESCRIPTION
The original Romanian dump truck was the SR-109, a licensed copy of the ZIL-150 chassis dump truck. It was replaced by the Bucegi SR-116 4 × 2 vehicles designated 1 ABS-116 and AB45-116. The latest MAN-based line of heavy trucks also includes the DAC 27.215 DFK 6 × 4 dump truck and it is possible that a 6 × 6 version exists.

SPECIFICATIONS
Weight: 3670 kg
Length: 6·73 m
Width: 2·5 m
Height: 2·2 m
Ground clearance: 0·27 m
Wheelbase: 4 m
Track: (front and rear) 1·75 m
Engine: SR-211 V-8 water-cooled petrol developing 140 hp
Max speed: 80 km/h
Payload: (road) 5000 kg
Tyres: 9.00 × 20

STATUS
It is probable that some of the vehicles mentioned are in military service but it has not been confirmed.

MANUFACTURER
Romanian state factories.

SWEDEN

Volvo BM 860 Dump Truck

Volvo BM 860 dumper in Swedish Army service

DESCRIPTION
The Volvo BM 860 dumper consists of a front unit, with the engine, cab and two powered wheels, and the rear unit with four wheels of which two are powered. The all steel dump body is mounted on the rear unit. The front axle has integral reduction gearing and a differential lock and the rear axle has hub reduction and a differential lock, four-wheel drive being engaged pneumatically. Each wheel of the rear bogie can move independently to enable the vehicle to traverse rough terrain. The BM 860 is hydraulically steered and the front unit can articulate 45 degrees to either side, relative to the rear unit.

Under the designation ATS, or Allround Transport System, the basic BM 860 TC chassis may be used for a variety of other applications. Most are associated with the construction industry, but the chassis has also been adapted to act as a minelayer for the FFV 028 anti-tank mine. The Swedish Army has also adapted the BM 860 dumper as a personnel carrier.

SPECIFICATIONS
Cab seating: 1
Configuration: 6 × 4
Weight:
  (empty) 12 800 kg
  (loaded) 31 300 kg
Weight on front axle: (loaded) 10 500 kg
Weight on rear bogie: (loaded) 20 800 kg
Max load: 18 500 kg
Dump body capacity:
  (level with tailgate) 8·3 m³
  (heaped) 11 m³
Length: 9·29 m
Width: 2·48 m
Height: (cab) 2·8 m
Wheelbase: 4·05 m + 1·54 m
Max speed: (road) 30 km/h
Fuel capacity: 225 litres
Engine: Volvo TD 60A 6-cylinder direct injection diesel developing 170 hp (SAE) at 2500 rpm
Gearbox: powershift with 4 forward and 4 reverse gears
Torque converter: single stage with freewheeling stator and automatic lock up clutch
Steering: full hydraulic articulated with mechanical follow up
Turning radius: 7·5 m
Tyres:
  (front) 18.00 × 25
  (rear) 16.00 × 24
Brakes: air on all wheels, mechanical parking on 4 wheels

Volvo BM 860 dumper modified as personnel carrier

Electrical system: 24 V
Battery: 152 Ah

STATUS
The BM 860 dumper is in service with the Swedish Army. The status of the personnel carrier version is unknown. The later BM 861 model is now in production.

MANUFACTURER
Volvo BM AB, S-632 Eskilstuna, Sweden.

Volvo 642 Wheeled Loader

DESCRIPTION
The Volvo 642 wheeled loader is a four-wheel drive loader fitted with a one cubic metre bucket, and is the smallest wheeled loader in the Volvo range. It is developed from the earlier 641 model and differs mainly in the provision of a heavier, hydraulically-operated attachment bracket. Noise insulation in the cabin is improved and the fuel filler opening has been made more accessible.

SPECIFICATIONS
Weight: 7900 kg
Length: (bucket on ground) 5·5 m
Width: 2·25 m
Height: (to top of cab) 2·64 m
Track:
  (front) 1·82 m
  (rear) 1·85 m
Wheelbase: 2·38 m
Engine: Volvo BM D42 4-cylinder 4·2-litre diesel developing 80 hp at 2300 rpm
Bucket capacity: 1–3 m³
Max dumping height: 2·9 m
Breakout force: 9440 kg
Tyres:
  (front) 16.9 × 30, 14-ply rating
  (rear) 12.4 × 24, 10-ply rating
Steering radius: 5·65 m (3·3 m with steering brake)
Max speed: (road) 30 km/h

Volvo 642 loader of Netherlands Army (Netherlands Army)

STATUS
The Volvo 642 loader is in service with the Netherlands and Swedish armies.

MANUFACTURER
Volvo BM AB, S-632 Eskilstuna, Sweden.

Volvo 642 loader of Swedish Army preparing defence position　　　*Volvo 642 loader used for resupply of emplaced FH-77A howitzer*

Volvo BM 846 Wheeled Loader

DESCRIPTION
The Volvo BM 846 is the smallest member of the Volvo heavy range of wheeled loaders and is available with a variety of buckets with capacities from 1·7 to 5 cubic metres.

The fully enclosed impact tested steel safety cab is sound insulated and provided with an adjustable driver's seat, heater and defroster. Standard equipment includes dual circuit air over hydraulic brakes with air pressure gauge and warning light for both circuits, electric socket for lead light, electric socket for trailer, and bucket indicator. Optional equipment includes an air-conditioner, cab ventilator, engine heater, tropical roof, tyre pumping hose, manual or hydraulic locking attachment and a heavy duty air filter. The BM 846 can be delivered with an attachment bracket that permits a wide range of attachments to be snapped in position quickly, including various buckets, forks and cranes.

The Swedish state-controlled defence equipment manufacturer FFV has developed a remotely-controlled version of the Volvo 846 loader, designated the Minotaur, which is designed for the investigation of dangerous materials such as chemical waste, nuclear contamination and unexploded ordnance. It could also be used for urban EOD tasks.

SPECIFICATIONS
Cab seating: 1
Configuration: 4 × 4
Weight: (empty) 10 250 kg
Length: (bucket on ground) 6·5 m
Width:
　(wheels) 2·49 m
　(bucket) 2·5 m
Height:
　(cab) 2·95 m
　(bucket in travelling position) 4·76 m

Ground clearance: 0·48 m
Track: 1·96 m
Wheelbase: 2·86 m
Max speed: (road) 30 km/h
Fuel capacity: 195 litres
Engine: Volvo D 60 A 6-cylinder in-line direct injection diesel developing 125 hp (SAE) at 2400 rpm
Gearbox: powershift with 4 forward and 4 reverse gears
Steering: hydraulic, front axle articulates 40° left and right

Tyres: 20.5 × 25 or 16.00 × 24
Brakes: air over hydraulic, dual circuits
Electrical system: 24 V
Battery: 96 Ah

STATUS
In production. In service with the Swedish Army.

MANUFACTURER
Volvo BM AB, S-632 Eskilstuna, Sweden.

Volvo BM 846 wheeled loader

Volvo BM 846 wheeled loader in Swedish Army service

FFV Minotaur remotely-controlled vehicle

Volvo BM 1240 Wheeled Loader

DESCRIPTION
The Volvo BM 1240 is the medium member of the Volvo heavy range of wheeled loaders and is available with a variety of buckets with capacities ranging from two to five cubic metres.

The fully enclosed impact tested cab is sound insulated and has an adjustable driver's seat, heater and defroster, and can be fitted with a high-efficiency cab ventilator with a capacity of 15·3 cubic metres a minute.

The vehicle has four-wheel drive, articulated steering, and is fitted with a lock-up differential on the front axle which, if one of the wheels loses its grip on the slippery ground, increases the tractive force on the other wheel automatically. When the brakes are applied a cut-out valve automatically disengages the engine from the

Swedish Army Volvo BM 1240 wheeled loader launching pontoon

transmission so that engine power is transmitted to the hydraulic pump.

Maximum outreach at two metres height and tipped bucket is 1·8 metres and lift height under level bucket is nearly 3·8 metres. The BM 1240 can be delivered with an attachment bracket that permits a wide range of attachments to be snapped quickly into position including various buckets, log grapples and cranes.

STATUS
In production. In service with the Swedish Army.

MANUFACTURER
Volvo BM AB, S-632 Eskilstuna, Sweden.

SPECIFICATIONS
Cab seating: 1
Configuration: 4 × 4
Weight: (empty) 12 374 kg
Length: (with bucket on ground) 6·81 m
Width: 2·49 m
Height:
(cab) 3·05 m
(bucket raised) 5·21 m

Ground clearance: 0·45 m
Track: 1·956 m
Wheelbase: 2·9 m
Max speed: (road) 42 km/h
Fuel capacity: 250 litres
Engine: Volvo D 70 8-cylinder direct injection diesel developing 160 hp at 2500 rpm
Gearbox: powershift with 4 forward and 4 reverse gears
Steering: power-assisted
Tyres: 23.5 × 25
Brakes: air, dual circuit
Electrical system: 24 V

Volvo BM 1641 Wheeled Loader

DESCRIPTION
The Volvo BM 1641 is the largest member of the Volvo range of heavy wheeled loaders and is available with a variety of buckets with capacities ranging from three to eleven cubic metres. The standard bucket has a 3·4 cubic metre capacity.

The fully enclosed impact tested cab is sound insulated and has an adjustable driver's seat, heater and defroster, and can be fitted with a high efficiency cab ventilator with a capacity of 15·3 cubic metres a minute.

The powershift gearbox has a planetary gear unit for each speed range. The final drive units are of the planetary type and are in the wheel hubs to isolate the drive shaft from stress. The front axle is fixed rigidly to the front framework while the rear axle oscillates on the rear frame section. The angle of oscillation (±17 degrees) permits the wheels to pass over vertical obstacles 0·61 to 0·76 metre high without losing ground contact. A disengagement system automatically disengages the engine from the transmission, permitting the entire output of the engine to be utilised to drive the hydraulic pump. Automatic bucket re-set is standard, with the driver merely setting the bucket angle and the tipping height.

The BM 1641 can be delivered with a bracket that permits a wide range of attachments to be snapped quickly into position, including various buckets, log grapples and cranes. Optional equipment includes an extra fuel filter, engine heater, a tyre inflation hose and a hydraulic locking attachment.

SPECIFICATIONS
Cab seating: 1
Configuration: 4 × 4
Weight: (empty) 17 000 kg

Volvo BM 1641 wheeled loader with crane attachment launching bridging boat

Static tipping load:
(straight) 11 700 kg
(full turn) 10 700 kg
Dump height: (at 45°) 2·91 m
Reach: (at 2 m height) 1·76 m
Length: (with bucket on ground) 7·89 m
Width:
(over wheels) 2·91 m
(over bucket) 3·1 m
Height:
(cab) 3·2 m
(bucket raised) 5·3 m
Ground clearance: 0·4 m
Track: 2·31 m
Wheelbase: 3·47 m
Max speed: (road) 42 km/h
Fuel capacity: 245 litres

Engine: Volvo TD 100 A 6-cylinder in-line direct injection diesel, turbo-charged developing 240 bhp (SAE) at 2200 rpm
Gearbox: powershift with 4 forward and 4 reverse gears
Torque converter: single speed
Steering: hydraulic, front axle articulates 37·5° left and right
Turning radius: 6·3 m
Tyres: 23.5 × 25 or 26.5 × 25 (16 ply rating)
Brakes: air, dual circuit
Electrical system: 24 V
Battery: 135 Ah

STATUS
In production. In service with the Swedish Army.

MANUFACTURER
Volvo BM AB, S-632 Eskilstuna, Sweden.

SWITZERLAND

Saurer D330N (6 × 4) 11-tonne Dump Truck

DESCRIPTION
The Swiss Armament Programme for 1978 included the procurement of 70 heavy-duty dump trucks for delivery between 1979 and 1980. The Swiss Army had dump trucks with a capacity of only 4·5 tonnes and constant overloading led to very high repair costs.

The Saurer D330N dump truck is derived from a commercial model. It is powered by a Saurer D2KT diesel engine developing 330 hp, which is coupled to an Allison HT 750 automatic gearbox, with a torque converter and retarder. The layout of the vehicle is conventional with a 6 × 4 chassis, three-man fully enclosed cab and dump body at the rear. The dump body is manufactured by Rochat and has a capacity of 7 cubic metres. If required, the Saurer D330N can tow a low loader trailer with a maximum load of 40 tonnes, suitable for carrying construction equipment or AFVs, for example. A 10-tonne winch is mounted behind the cab and is provided with 100 metres of cable.

With a payload of 11·6 tonnes, the loaded vehicle weighs 25 tonnes.

Saurer D330N dump truck (Swiss Army)

STATUS
In service with the Swiss Army.

MANUFACTURER
Aktiengesellschaft Adolph Saurer, 9320 Arbon, Switzerland.

UNION OF SOVIET SOCIALIST REPUBLICS

BelAZ-531 Wheeled Tractor

DESCRIPTION
The BelAZ-531 is a single-axle prime mover which can be coupled to a variety of semi-trailer equipment including dumpers and scrapers. The recent BelAZ-531T has a more powerful engine and a greater drawbar pull.

STATUS
Production.

MANUFACTURER
Belorussian Motor Vehicle Plant, Zhodino, USSR.

SPECIFICATIONS

Model	BelAZ-531	BelAZ-531T
Weight	14 000 kg	14 000 kg
Drawbar pull	15 000 kg	21 000 kg
Towed load	44 000 kg	40 000 kg
Length	4·88 m	4·95 m
Width	3·29 m	3·38 m
Height	3·23 m	3·35 m
Ground clearance	0·67 m	0·67 m
Track	2·53 m	2·49 m
Max speed (road)	55 km/h	60 km/h
Engine	M3 diesel	D-12A450 diesel
Number of cylinders	12	12
Output	n/a	450 hp at 1800 rpm
Tyres	27.00 × 33	27.00 × 33

BGM-1 Holeboring Machine

DESCRIPTION
This equipment, mounted on the ZIL-131 6 × 6 truck, can bore horizontal, vertical or slanting holes in most soils. It can bore a hole 150 mm in diameter to a depth of 30 metres, or a 300 mm hole to a depth of 20 metres. In frozen soil cutter heads are used. The accessories for the BGM-1 include special equipment with which pipes, flexible pipelines and cables can be pulled through holes bored in earth embankments and similar obstacles.

The crew comprises three men, including the driver. Although the auger itself is mechanically driven, other functions, such as moving the equipment in and out of action, are hydraulically operated. The BGM-1 would appear to be used primarily for construction and light well drilling tasks rather than for the preparation of demolitions, although it probably has a limited capability in this respect. Other truck-mounted earth augers or holeboring machines in Soviet service include the BKGM-AN-63, BKGM-63-2, BKGM-63-3, BKGM-66-2 and PZV models.

Soviet High Speed Tractor-mounted Bulldozers
BAT-1, BAT-M, OLT, OST, OTT

DESCRIPTION
Most of the Soviet full-tracked artillery tractors described in the *Tracked prime movers* section can be fitted with bulldozer blades. One vehicle, the BAT, has been specially modified as a bulldozer.

The BAT tractor dozer consists of the AT-T heavy tractor with a large dozer blade mounted at the front of the hull. It is designed for hasty building of roads and approaches to bridges and crossing sites, and for filling in ditches and similar obstacles. It can also fell trees, root out stumps and boulders and dig emplacements. The basic demolition blade can be fitted with attachments to form a V-blade, bulldozer and angledozer, and is provided with routers and a float.

The more recent BAT-M is an improved model and is electro-hydraulically operated, whereas the BAT (also known as the BAT-1) is electro-pneumatically operated. The BAT-M also has a hydraulic crane, and the dozer blade can be swung rearwards to improve the vehicle's load distribution when in travelling order.

The BAT tractor dozers should not be confused with the OTT dozer blade mounted on the AT-T tractor, for which data is also given here. Details of the basic tractor chassis are given in the *Tracked prime movers* section.

STATUS
All the tractor-mounted dozers are in service with armed forces of the Warsaw Pact. The BAT tractor dozer is also in service with some North African and Middle Eastern countries.

BAT-M tractor dozer with extra grouting tongue fitted to blade

BAT tractor dozer

BAT-M tractor dozer with dozer blade raised

Polish hydraulically-operated dozer (not OST) on ATS-59 tractor

BAT-M tractor dozer, showing hydraulic crane

SPECIFICATIONS

Model	BAT (BAT-1)	BAT-M	OLT	OST	OTT
Tractor	(integral)	(integral)	AT-L, AT-LM	AT-S*, ATS-59	AT-T
Weight (with blade)	25 300 kg	27 500 kg	7000 kg	13 392 kg	22 000 kg
Length (with blade)	10 m	7 m (travelling)	n/a	n/a	n/a
Width (with blade)	4·78 m	4·85 m	2·5 m	2·8 m	3·5 m
Height (travelling)	2·95 m	–	2·18 m	2·54 m	2·58 m
Max speed	35 km/h	35 km/h	42 km/h	35 km/h	35 km/h
Cruising range	700 km	550 km	300 km	380 km	700 km
Fuel consumption	140–190 litres/100 km	140–190 litres/100 km	140–190 litres/100 km	140–190 litres/100 km	140–190 litres/100 km
Trench	1·58 m	2·1 m	1 m	1·45 m	2·1 m
Max vertical obstacle	1 m	1 m	0·6 m	0·6 m	1 m
Max gradient	45%	n/a	60°	53°	60°
Fording depth	0·75 m	0·75 m	0·6 m	1 m	0·75 m
Ground pressure	0·65 kg/cm²	0·71 kg/cm²	0·45 kg/cm²	0·58 kg/cm²	0·68 kg/cm²
Working speed	1·5–10 km/h (moderate terrain)	1·5–10 km/h	4–6 km/h (moderate terrain)	4 km/h	n/a
Working capacity (depends on soil conditions)	120–140 m³/h	max 150 m³/h (excavation) max 200 m³/h (dozing)	40 m³/h	80–90 m³/h (light soil) 40–50 m³/h (medium soil)	100 m³/h
Crane capacity	n/app	2000 kg	n/app	n/app	n/app
Winch capacity	n/app	25 000 kg (100 m cable)	n/app	n/app	n/app
Blade control	electro-pneumatic	electro-hydraulic	n/a	cable-operated	n/a
Blade angle	n/a	straight (5 m wide) 55° (4 m wide) 110° (4·5 m wide)	n/a	n/a	n/a
Tractive effort	n/a	16 300 kg	n/a	n/a	n/a

* Data refers to OST dozer on AT-S tractor.

OST dozer on AT-S tractor

Soviet Tank-mounted Bulldozers BTU and BTU-55

DESCRIPTION
The BTU and BTU-55 tank-mounted bulldozers can both be fitted to either the T-54 or T-55 series of main battle tanks. The BTU-55 is the more recent version and is an improvement in all aspects. There does not appear to be a bulldozer for the T-62, but the latest T-64 and

T-72 main battle tanks each incorporate a form of dozer blade for self-emplacement.

STATUS
Production probably complete. In widespread service.

SPECIFICATIONS

Model	BTU	BTU-55
Weight	2300 kg	1400 kg
Width	3·4 m	3·8 m
Clearing speed	1·5–5 km/h	5–7 km/h
(in snow)	4–6 km/h	4–6 km/h
Digging performance	100–200 m³/h	130–250 m³/h
Pushing performance	350 m³/h	–
Mounting time	80–90 minutes	60 minutes
Dismounting time	30–60 minutes	45 minutes

MAZ-503B (4 × 2) Dump Truck

DESCRIPTION
The MAZ-503B (4 × 2) dump truck is based on the chassis of the MAZ-500 (4 × 2) truck and has been in production at the Minsk Automobile Plant since 1965. The all metal cab is of the forward control type and can be swung forward to give access to the engine. The cab

MAZ-503B (4 × 2) dump truck

is provided with a sleeping space for the driver. The rear body can carry 7000 kg or 3·8 cubic metres of soil.

SPECIFICATIONS
Cab seating: 1 + 1
Configuration: 4 × 2
Weight:
  (empty) 6750 kg
  (loaded) 13 900 kg
Weight on front axle: (loaded) 4540 kg
Weight on rear axle: (loaded) 9360 kg
Max load: 7000 kg
Load area: 3·28 × 2·28 m
Length: 5·97 m
Width: 2·6 m
Height: 2·7 m
Ground clearance: (axles)
  (front) 0·29 m
  (rear) 0·3 m
Track:
  (front) 1·95 m
  (rear) 1·9 m
Wheelbase: 3·2 m
Angle of approach/departure: 30°/50°

Max speed: (road) 75 km/h
Fuel capacity: 100 litres
Engine: YaMZ-236 6-cylinder diesel developing 180 hp at 2100 rpm
Gearbox: manual with 5 forward and 1 reverse gears
Clutch: single dry disc
Steering: screw and nut with hydraulic booster
Suspension:
  (front) longitudinal semi-elliptical springs and double acting hydraulic shock absorbers
  (rear) longitudinal semi-elliptical springs with helper springs
Tyres: 12.00 × 20
Brakes: air
Electrical system: 24 V
Batteries: 2 × 6 ST-165
Generator: G105G, 400 W, 16 A

STATUS
Production.

MANUFACTURER
Minsk Motor Vehicle Plant, Minsk, Belorussia, USSR.

Other Soviet Dump Trucks

The following dump truck versions of standard Soviet military chassis are known to exist and may be in military service.
  GAZ-53B 4-tonne dump truck on the GAZ-53A-02 4 × 2 chassis
  GAZ-93A 2·5-tonne dump truck on the GAZ-51 4 × 2 truck chassis
  ZIL-MMZ-585L dump truck
  ZIL-MMZ-555 5-tonne dump truck on the ZIL-130D1 4 × 2 chassis
  ZIL-130 5-tonne dump truck version of basic ZIL-130 vehicle

GAZ-53B 4-tonne dump truck

KrAZ-256B 7·5-tonne dump truck

ZIL-MMZ-585L dump truck

MAZ-205 5-tonne dump truck

GAZ-93A 2·5-tonne dump truck

ZIL-131D 3·5-tonne dump truck on the ZIL-131 6 × 6 chassis
ZIL-133D 3·5-tonne dump truck on the ZIL-133 6 × 4 chassis
MAZ-205 5-tonne dump truck
YaAZ-201Ye 10-tonne dump truck and YaAZ-218 side dump truck on the YaAZ-210 6 × 4 chassis
KrAZ-222B 7-tonne dump truck on the KrAZ-214 6 × 6 chassis
KrAZ-256B 7·5-tonne 3-way dump truck and KrAZ-256B dump truck on the KrAZ-255 6 × 6 chassis.

MANUFACTURER
Soviet state factories.

ZIL-MMZ-555 5-tonne dump truck

D-144 Motor Grader

SPECIFICATIONS
Weight: 13 400 kg
Length: 8·2 m
Width: 2·46 m
Height: (overall) 3·14 m
Ground clearance: 0·2 m
Wheelbase: 5·8 m
Track: 2 m
Max speed: 26·7 km/h
Engine: 100 hp 4-cylinder diesel model KDM-100
Mouldboard length: 3·7 m
Cutting depth: 200 mm

(all adjustments are mechanical)

STATUS
The D-144 is known to be in military use in the Soviet Union.

Soviet D-144 motor grader

E-305 Series Truck-mounted Excavators

DESCRIPTION
The E-305 series excavators are cable-operated and have a separate turntable engine. They are mounted on 7-ton, 6 × 6 trucks as follows:

Excavator	Chassis	Remarks
E-305V	KrAZ-214	basic model
E-305AV	KrAZ-214	improved model
E-305BV	KrAZ-255B	improved model, new chassis

SPECIFICATIONS (E-305V, typical)
Crew: 2
Weight: 17 500 kg
Length: (travelling) 8·98 m (10·25 m with shovel reversed)
Width: 2·68 m
Height: (travelling) 4·1 m (4·23 m with shovel reversed)
Engine: (excavator) D-48, 4-stroke diesel developing 48 hp
Excavator operation: pneumatic-mechanical
Max speed: (road) 55 km/h
Shovel capacity: 0·3 m³
Crane capacity: 5000 kg

Max reach: (shovel in normal position) 6·5 m
Work capacity:
(excavator) 45 m³/h
(face shovel) 40 m³/h

Details of the two chassis may be found in a separate entry in the *Trucks* section of the book.

STATUS
The E-305 series excavators are believed to be in service with the Soviet Army. The E-302B self-propelled wheeled excavator is known to exist, and may be in military service. It weighs 11·7 tonnes and has a bucket capacity of 0·4 m³.

E-305BV excavator

E-305BV excavator in face shovel configuration

EOV-4421 Truck-mounted Excavator

DESCRIPTION
The replacement for the E-305 series of truck-mounted excavators (for which there is a separate entry in this section), the EOV-4421 excavator is also mounted on the chassis of the KrAZ-255B 6 × 6 truck. The major

improvements over the E-305 include a much larger shovel capacity and hydraulic operation. The chassis now incorporates outriggers to stabilize the excavator when operating, and this has more than doubled the work capacity of the equipment.

STATUS
In service.

SPECIFICATIONS
Crew: 2
Max road speed: 75 km/h
Max speed on dirt road: 45 km/h
Shovel capacity: 0·63 m³
Trench:
(depth) 3·25 m
(width) 3 m
Work capacity: (medium soil) 100 m³/h

MAZ-529 Series of Wheeled Tractors
MAZ-529, MAZ-529E and MAZ-529V

DESCRIPTION
The MAZ-529 is a single-axle prime mover which can be coupled to a variety of semi-trailer equipment including rollers and scrapers. The MAZ-529 can also be used with the attachments of the more recent MoAZ-546, the replacement for the MAZ-529. Although developed primarily for civil use, the MAZ-529 is used by the Soviet Army. Late production models of the vehicle are the MAZ-529E and the MAZ-529V, which have different cabs and a more powerful engine.

SPECIFICATIONS

Model	MAZ-529	MAZ-529V
Weight	8500 kg	5500 kg
Length	4·15 m	3·5 m
Width	2·95 m	3·14 m
Height	2·92 m	3·39 m
Ground clearance	0·57 m	0·65 m
Track	2·3 m	2·3 m

Model	MAZ-529	MAZ-529V
Max speed (road)	40 km/h	40 km/h
Engine	YaAZ-204 diesel	YaAZ-M206 diesel
Number of cylinders	4	6
Hp/rpm	120/2000	180/2000
Tyres	24 × 28	21 × 28

STATUS
Production complete. In service with the Soviet Army.

MANUFACTURER
Minsk Motor Vehicle Plant, Minsk, Belorussia, USSR.

MAZ-538 Wheeled Tractor (BKT and PKT)

DESCRIPTION
The MAZ-538 wheeled tractor entered service with the Soviet Army in the early 1970s. There are at least two variants of the MAZ-538, the BKT (bulldozer) and the PKT (road machine).

SPECIFICATIONS
(Data in square brackets relate to PKT where different from BKT)
Weight: (approx) 20 000 [21 000] kg
Length:
  (over blade) [7·9 m]
  (tractor only) 5·03 m
Width: (without blade) 3·23 m
Height: 3·08 m
Track: (front and rear) 2·63 m
Wheelbase: 2·96 m
Ground clearance: 0·44 m
Engine: water-cooled diesel developing 375 hp
Max speed: (road) [45 km/h]
Cruising range: [500 km]
Blade width: 3·33 [3·3, 3·8, 4·2] m
Working speed: 2–3 km/h
  (in 0·8 m snow) 3–6 [4–6] km/h
Digging performance: 80–100 m³/h

STATUS
The MAZ-538 is in service with the Soviet Army in both BKT and PKT versions, and is also in service with the East German Army.

MANUFACTURER
Minsk Motor Vehicle Plant, Minsk, Belorussia, USSR.

MAZ-538 (BKT) with bulldozer blade installed at front

MAZ-538 (PKT)

MoAZ-542 Wheeled Tractor

DESCRIPTION
The MoAZ-542 wheeled tractor is the replacement for the older MAZ-528 and is closely related in design to the MoAZ-546 single-axle tractor-prime mover and the MoAZ-522 dump truck. The fully enclosed cab is in the centre of the chassis with the engine at the rear. In addition to being used as a prime mover the MoAZ-542 can be fitted with a range of attachments including backhoe, brush blade, brush cutter, bulldozer, drill rig, fork lift, front loader, snow blade, rotary snowplough and timber grab.

SPECIFICATIONS
Configuration: 4 × 4
Weight: 12 500 kg
Drawbar pull: 10 500 kg
Length: 5·9 m
Width: 3·15 m
Height: 3·25 m
Track: 2·4 m
Wheelbase: 2·7 m
Max speed: (road) 50 km/h
Engine: YaMZ-238 V-8 water-cooled diesel developing 240 hp at 2100 rpm
Tyres: 20.50 × 25 (or 21.00 × 18)

STATUS
Production.

MANUFACTURER
Mogilev Lift and Hoist Plant, Mogilev, Belorussia, USSR.

MoAZ-542 wheeled tractor with front loader attachment

MoAZ-546 Wheeled Tractor

DESCRIPTION
The MoAZ-546 is the replacement for the older MAZ-529 and is related to the MoAZ-542 (4 × 4) wheeled tractor, and the MoAZ-522 dump truck. It is a single-axle prime mover and can be attached to a wide range of semi-trailers including back dump, box trailer, engineer equipment transporter, elevating grader, forestry trailer, liquid transporter, pneumatic tyred roller, scraper, timber transporter and wheeled crane.

SPECIFICATIONS
Weight: 10 000 kg
Drawbar pull: 12 000 kg
Length: 4·4 m
Width: 3·15 m
Height: 2·99 m
Track: 2·4 m
Max speed: (road) 40 km/h
Engine: YaMZ0238 V-8 water-cooled diesel developing 240 hp at 2100 rpm

STATUS
Production.

MANUFACTURER
Mogilev Lift and Hoist Plant, Mogilev, Belorussia, USSR.

S-80 Series of Crawler Tractors
S-60, S-65, S-80, S-100, S-100B, S-100GP, S-100GS, T-100M, T-100MB, T-100MGP, T-100MGS

DEVELOPMENT/DESCRIPTION

The first tractor in this series, the S-60, entered production in 1933 and was followed by the improved S-65. In 1946 the S-80 was introduced and continued in production at the Chelyabinsk Tractor Plant (ChTZ) until 1958. The S-80 was replaced in production by the S-100, which had a number of improvements including a more powerful engine and an all metal cab. The KG-65 trenching machine was mounted on the S-80 tractor.

The S-100B has much wider tracks for operation in swampy areas, but these can be replaced by standard 500 mm wide tracks if required. The S-100GP has a hydraulic powerlift with a remote jack and front-mounted implement control linkage. This model is used by the Soviet forces on a wide scale. The S-100GS has a universal hydraulic system and is mainly for agricultural use.

The T-100M (originally called the T-108) has an all metal cab and variants of this model include the T-100MB swamp tractor, T-100MGP construction tractor which can have a dozer blade and the T-100MGS for agricultural use.

This series of tractors is being replaced by the T-130 series, also produced at the Chelyabinsk Tractor Plant.

The S-80, S-100 and T-100 series are all used as a basis for the D-271 bulldozer, a common equipment in the Warsaw Pact.

D-271 bulldozer on S-80 tractor

STATUS
In service with the Soviet Army and other armed forces.

MANUFACTURER
Chelyabinsk Tractor Plant, Chelyabinsk, USSR.

SPECIFICATIONS

Model	S-80	S-100	S-100B	S-100GP	T-100M	T-100MB	T-100MGP	T-100MGS
Weight	11 930 kg	11 400 kg	13 300 kg	12 100 kg	11 400 kg	13 300 kg	11 800 kg	12 400 kg
Drawbar pull	8800 kg	9000 kg	9000 kg	9000 kg	9500 kg	9500 kg	9500 kg	9500 kg
Length	4·22 m	4·25 m	4·72 m	4·25 m	4·25 m	4·72 m	4·3 m	5·34 m
Width	2·46 m	2·46 m	3·28 m	2·46 m	2·46 m	3·25 m	2·46 m	2·46 m
Height	2·77 m*	3·06 m	2·76 m	3·06 m	3·04 m	2·74 m	3·04 m	3·04 m
Ground clearance	0·33 m	0·39 m	0·33 m	0·33 m	0·39 m	0·39 m	0·39 m	0·39 m
Track	1·88 m	1·88 m	2·88 m	1·88 m	1·88 m	2·28 m	1·88 m	1·88 m
Track width	500 mm	500 mm	1000 mm	500 mm	500 mm	970 mm	500 mm	500 mm
Length of track on ground	2·37 m	2·37 m	n/a	n/a	2·37 m	n/a	n/a	n/a
Ground pressure (kg/cm²)	0·48	0·48	0·28	0·5	0·48	0·27	0·48	0·48
Max speed (road)	9·65 km/h	7·61 km/h	10·13 km/h	10·15 km/h	10·13 km/h	5·4 km/h	10·13 km/h	10·12 km/h
Fuel capacity (litres)	235	235	n/a	n/a	235	235	235	235
Engine	KDM-46 diesel	KDM-100 diesel	KDM-100B diesel	KDM-100 diesel	D-108 diesel	D-108 diesel	D-108 diesel	D-108 diesel
Number of cylinders	4	4	4	4	4	4	4	4
Hp/rpm	80	90	100	100	108/1070	108/1070	108/1070	108/1070

* To radiator

Soviet Tank-mounted Snow Ploughs STU and STU-2M

DESCRIPTION
There are two models of snow plough in service with the Soviet Army, both of which can be fitted to the T-54 and T-55 tanks.

SPECIFICATIONS

Model	STU	STU-2M
Weight	3100 kg	2500 kg
Width	3·6 m	3·6 m
Clearing speed	5–8 km/h	n/a
Mounting time	30–45 minutes	15–25 minutes
Dismounting time	10–15 minutes	15–25 minutes

T-4 Series Crawler Tractors

DESCRIPTION
The T-4 series of crawler tractor entered production at the Altay Tractor Plant in 1965. They all feature eight-speed transmissions, double plate synchromesh clutches, flexible propeller shafts and an independent PTO with a separate clutch on the rear axle housing. All models have hermetically sealed cabs which can be heated and ventilated.

The basic model is designated the T-4. The T-4M has a more powerful 120/130 hp diesel, which also powers the BT-4. The BT-4 has been designed specifically for operations in swamps and has a ground pressure of only 0·2 kg/cm². The T-4P model is for operations in hot climates. The TT-4 has a different suspension and a more forward mounted cab compared with the normal T-4M and has been designed for logging operations.

SPECIFICATIONS

Model	T-4	TT-4
Weight	7800 kg	11 300 kg
Drawbar pull	5000 kg	8880 kg
Length	4·47 m	5·91 m
Width	1·95 m	2·46 m
Height	2·61 m	2·66 m
Ground clearance	0·36 m	0·5 m
Track	1·38 m	2 m
Length of track on ground	2·46 m	n/a
Ground pressure	n/a	0·44 kg/cm²
Max speed (road)	9·17 km/h	10·16 km/h
Fuel capacity	300 litres	180 litres
Engine	AM-01 6-cylinder water-cooled diesel developing 110 hp at 1600 rpm	

TT-4A tractor

STATUS
Not in use by the Soviet Army, although the TT-4A appears to be the basis of the mechanical pipelaying equipment (TUM-150) of the Soviet Army.

MANUFACTURER
Altay Tractor Plant, Rubtsovsk, USSR.

T-125 and T-150K Series of Wheeled Tractors
T-125, T-127, T-128, T-150K, T-155 and T-158

DESCRIPTION
This range of wheeled tractors was developed from the T-90 tractor which originated in the early 1960s. The tractors are designed primarily for agricultural use but have been modified for other uses such as construction work and logging, as well as in a military role. All the tractors in the series have a front-mounted engine and a fully enclosed cab in the centre of the chassis.

The T-125 is the basic model of the series. It was followed by the T-127 with a more powerful engine, the 160 hp AM-03, giving a road speed of 34 km/h, and also has a front-mounted dozer blade. The T-128 has an even more powerful engine. The T-150K is based on the T-150 crawler tractor and uses 70 per cent of the components of the tracked tractor. It weighs 7442 kg and is powered by the SMD-60 engine which develops 160 hp,

giving the vehicle a maximum road speed of 29 km/h. The T-155 and T-158 both have more powerful engines than the earlier models.

SPECIFICATIONS (T-125)
Configuration: 4 × 4
Weight: 7800 kg
Drawbar pull: 3500 kg
Towed load: 12 000 kg
Length: 5·83 m
Width: 2·07 m
Height: 2·6 m
Ground clearance: 0·4 m
Track:
(front) 1·63 m
(rear) 1·91 m
Wheelbase: 2·86 m
Max speed: (road) 29 km/h
Fuel capacity: 330 litres
Max vertical obstacle: 0·6 m
Engine: SMD-462 6-cylinder water-cooled diesel developing 130 hp
Tyres: 18.00 × 24 or 18.4 × 15

T-125 wheeled tractor

STATUS
In production. The T-150K is used as the basis for the PZM regimental digger, and the PZM-2 digger is based on the T-155 tractor.

MANUFACTURER
Soviet state factories. The T-150K is manufactured at the Khar'kov tractor plant.

T-130 and T-170 Series of Crawler Tractors
T-130, T-130A, T-130B, T-130GP, T-130P and T-170

DESCRIPTION
The T-130 series of crawler tractors is the replacement for the earlier S-80 and S-100 series of crawler tractors and is also produced at the Chelyabinsk Tractor Plant. Many of the components of the T-130 are interchangeable with the earlier models. Production of the T-130 began in 1973–74.

The T-130A has been modified for use in cold climates, the T-130B is a swamp tractor with wider tracks and the T-130P is for use in the tropics. The T-130GP is for construction use and can be fitted with a number of different attachments including a dozer blade. The T-170 is similar to the T-130 but has a 175 hp engine.

STATUS
In production. The Soviet Army probably uses these tractors.

MANUFACTURER
Chelyabinsk Tractor Plant, Chelyabinsk, USSR.

SPECIFICATIONS

Model	T-130	T-130GP
Weight	11 500 kg	12 500 kg
Drawbar pull	9000 kg	9500 kg
Length	4·33 m	4·43 m
Width	2·47 m	2·47 m
Height	2·85 m	3·14 m
Ground clearance	0·42 m	n/a
Track	1·88 m	n/a
Ground pressure	0·48 kg/cm²	0·48 kg/cm²
Max speed (road)	10·5 km/h	10·4 km/h
Engine	D-130 diesel	D-130 diesel
Number of cylinders	4	4
Hp	135	135

T-140 and T-180 Series of Crawler Tractors

DESCRIPTION
Until the introduction of the DET-250, the T-140 was the most powerful tractor in the Soviet inventory. The engine is mounted at the front of the tractor with the hexagonal cab to the rear, extending over the tracks. The running gear consists of six road wheels with the drive sprocket at the rear and the idler at the front. There are three track return rollers.

The T-140D is the basic vehicle for the D-543 universal single bucket loader.

The T-180 series is an improved model of the T-140 with a more powerful engine.

SPECIFICATIONS

Model	T-140	T-180GP
Weight	15 150 kg	15 000 kg
Drawbar pull	13 300 kg	15 150 kg
Length	5·3 m	5·42 m
Width	2·74 m	2·74 m
Height	2·9 m	n/a
Ground clearance	0·48 m	n/a
Track	2·04 m	n/a
Track width	700 mm	n/a

Model	T-140	T-180GP
Length of track on ground	2·31 m	n/a
Ground pressure	0·5 kg/cm²	0·42 kg/cm²
Max speed (road)	10·9 km/h	11·9 km/h
Fuel capacity	420 litres	n/a
Engine	6 KMD-50T diesel	D-180 diesel
Number of cylinders	6	6
Hp/rpm	140/1000	180/1200

STATUS
Production.

T-150 Series of Crawler Tractors

DESCRIPTION
The T-150 series of crawler tractors has been developed by the Kharkov Tractor Plant (KhTZ) as the replacement for the older DT-54 series which entered production at the Volgograd Tractor Works in June 1944. The T-150 weighs 7200 kg and has a more powerful V-6 diesel engine of 150 hp, which gives a maximum speed of 16 km/h and a greater drawbar pull of 4250 kg. Other improvements include simplified steering and a quieter running gear. The engine is at the front of the tractor with the fully enclosed cab at the rear. The run-

ning gear consists of four road wheels with the drive sprocket at the rear and the idler at the front, with two return rollers. There is also a wheeled version of the T-150, the T-150K, for which there is a separate entry in this section. The T-250 tractor, with a 250 hp engine, is the planned replacement for the T-150 series.

STATUS
In production.

MANUFACTURER
Khar'kov Tractor Plant, Khar'kov, Ukraine, USSR.

T-150 crawler tractor

Soviet Truck-mounted Cranes

DESCRIPTION
Some of the more recent Soviet truck-mounted cranes are described briefly below. Many of these are in service with the Soviet and other Warsaw Pact armed forces, but the exact status of many is uncertain.

K-104 10-tonne crane

MKP-30 crane mounted on MAZ-529V chassis

K-67 6·3-tonne crane

K-162 16-tonne crane

K-61 6-tonne crane

8T210 6·3-tonne crane

AK-75 7·5-tonne crane

9T31M1 crane on Ural-375D (6 × 6) truck chassis

Model	Operation	Traverse	Chassis*	Capacity Max load /radius	Load at max radius	Length	Width	Height	Speed	Remarks
LAZ-690	mechanical	360°	(ZIL-150) ZIL-164A (ZIL-130)	3 t/2·5 m	1 t/5·5 m	8·88 m	2·4 m	3·45 m	45 km/h	Obsolescent
KS-1571	hydraulic	360°	GAZ-53A	4 t/3·3 m	–/9·35 m	–	–	–	–	Military use not confirmed
K-67	electric	360°	MAZ-500 (MAZ-200)	6·3 t/3·5 m	2 t/7·5 m	8·2 m	2·6 m	3·35 m	40 km/h	180 hp engine
K-68	electric	360°	MAZ-200 (MAZ-500)	6·3 t/5·5 m	2 t/7·5 m	8·9 m	2·71 m	3·3 m	40 km/h	Also K-68A
KS-2571	hydraulic	360°	ZIL-130	6·3 t/3·3 m	–/9·8 m	–	–	–	–	Military use not confirmed
8T210	hydraulic	360°	Ural-375D	6·3 t/3·5 m	1·8 t/7·5 m	8·3 m	2·45 m	–	70 km/h	Special military crane originally for missile units
9T31M1	–	360°	Ural-375D							Special military crane for missile units
AK-75	mechanical	360°	ZIL-164A (ZIL-130)	7·5 t/2·8 m	1·65 t/7 m	10·1 m	2·5 m	3·56 m	40 km/h	97 hp engine
KS-3562A	electric	360°	MAZ-500A	10 t/4 m	–	–	–	–	60 km/h	
KS-3571	hydraulic	360°	MAZ-500A	10 t/4 m	–/13·2 m	–	–	5 m	75 km/h	Military use not confirmed
KS-3572	hydraulic	360°	KrAZ-255B	10 t/4 m	–/9·1 m	–	–	–	70 km/h	
K-162	electric	360°	KrAZ-219 KrAZ-257	16 t/3·9 m	2·35 t/10 m	14 m	2·75 m	3·96 m	30 km/h	Also K-162M
KS-4571	hydraulic	360°	KrAZ-257	16 t/3·8 m	–/20·25 m	–	–	–	70 km/h	Military use not confirmed
MPK-30	electric	360°	MAZ-529V	30 t/3·7 m	6 t/27 m	12·8 m	4 m	4·2 m	25 km/h	Articulated, with 2-wheel tractor
8T26	–	–	–	10 t/4·5 m	2 t/9·5 m	–	–	–	40 km/h	Special military crane for missile units
KM-61	mechanical	80°	KrAZ-214 KrAZ-255B	3·2 t/2 m	2 t/2·8 m	–	–	–	–	Used with KMT-5 Mineclearing apparatus
KS-2561D	–	360°	–	6·3 t/–	1·5 t/–	–	–	–	–	150 hp engine

* Chassis designation in brackets are older or less common variants

UNITED KINGDOM

Aveling-Barford Motor Graders

DEVELOPMENT/DESCRIPTION

Two Aveling-Barford motor graders are in military service, the ASG 013 and the TG 011. The ASG 013 is the latest in a line of development which began with the Super MG motor grader in the early 1950s. The first production ASG 013 machines were completed in 1977. The TG 011 was introduced in 1968 as a successor to the earlier LG series.

Both models are in the process of being updated with many detailled product improvements and an increased range of options. The new models carry the designation ASG 113 and TG 012.

STATUS

Production. The ASG 013 is in service with the British and Nigerian armies. The Super MG was supplied to the armed forces of Egypt, Iran, Jordan, Libya, Malaysia, New Zealand, Yugoslavia and Zaïre. The TG 011 is in service with the Australian, Greek, Iranian, Kenyan, Nigerian and Pakistan armies. The earlier LG model is also in service with the Greek Army.

MANUFACTURER

Aveling-Barford International, Invicta Works, Grantham, Lincolnshire NG31 6JE, England.

Aveling-Barford Super MGH 12 ft motorised grader
(T J Gander)

Aveling-Barford ASG 113 motor grader

SPECIFICATIONS

Model	ASG 113	TG 012
Configuration	6 × 6	6 × 4
Weight	13 381 kg	12 020 kg
Length	8·29 m	7·79 m
Width	2·49 m	2·43 m
Height	3·29 m	3·3 m
Track (front)	2·02 m	2·01 m
(rear)	2·12 m	2·12 m
Engine (ASG 113)	General Motors 4-71n 4-cylinder water-cooled diesel developing 155 hp at 2200 rpm or Perkins V-8 540 8-cylinder diesel developing 167 hp at 2200 rpm	
(TG 012)	Leyland Model 402 6-cylinder water-cooled diesel developing 135 hp at 2400 rpm	
Transmission (ASG 113)	Clark model 13.5 HR 28450 full powershift with 2-speed transfer case giving 4 forward and reverse speeds in work and travel ranges	
(TG 012)	manual transmission providing 3 forward and reverse speeds in both work and travel ranges, or ZF 6WG181 powershift automatic transmission providing 6 forward and 3 reverse speeds through single speed transfer case	

Model	ASG 113	TG 012
Brakes (ASG 113)	air-over-hydraulic disc operating on all 4 rear wheels; hand-operated drum brake operating on transmission acts as parking brake on all wheels	
(TG 012)	air-over-hydraulic disc operating on rear 2 wheels; hand-operated transmission brake	
Steering (ASG 113)	hydraulic, with separate controls for front axle and rear bogie	
Turning circle diameter	23·8 m	23·8 m
Tyres	14.00 × 24	13.00 × 24
Max road speed	42·8 km/h	36 km/h (manual) 49 km/h (automatic)
Fuel capacity	259 litres	150 litres
Mouldboard length	3·66 m	3·66 m
Blade height	0·61 m	0·57 m
Lift height	0·34 m	0·34 m
Blade rotation	29°, 8 positions	
Bank cutting angle	90°	90°
Scarifier width	1·17 m (rear-mounted, 11 teeth)	1·17 m

Coles Mobile Cranes

DESCRIPTION
Coles Cranes Limited is a well established supplier of cranes and lifting equipment for military purposes, and over 40 types of Coles cranes are at present in military use throughout the world. Coles produces the widest range of mobile cranes in the world including industrial, port, all terrain, rough terrain and truck mounted, all of which can be used for military purposes, plus specialised military cranes, with lifting capacities from 6 to 250 tonnes.

Coles Supertruck 840

Hydra Truck, Supertruck and Octag
These ranges of truck-mounted telescopic boom cranes have lifting capacities from 12 to 135 tonnes and have limited off road capabilities and are therefore more suited to use in rear areas.

The Hydra Truck 12/14T general duties crane can be made on a special variant for use aboard aircraft carriers.

Hydra Speedcranes
The Speedcrane range consists of conventional truck-mounted telescopic hydraulically-operated cranes with lifting capacities from six to nine tonnes. The 4 × 2 chassis makes the Speedcrane range suitable for use in permanent installations.

The Speedcrane 8/9T Mk II, is the standard RAF seven tonne crane and is in use for general stores handling and aircraft maintenance work in the RAF and with the Fleet Air Arm both ashore and aboard.

Hydra Husky, Transit and Ranger
The Husky series of cranes is specifically designed for use on rough terrain and therefore has clear military applications. The Hydra Husky 150T has been the standard Medium Field Support Crane in the British Army for the past decade and is ideally suited to military applications.

The 6/8TCC Air Portable Husky, suitable for transportation in the C-130 Hercules transport aircraft, is used in quantity by the Yugoslav Army.

The Model 315M is the new generation of 'Cranes Field Medium' for use with the Royal Engineers for bridge building and general stores handling from base

to forward areas, with the REME for major unit changes on AFVs in the field and for workshop use, and with the RCT and RAOC in their general stores and overall support role in the whole length of the British Army's line of communication.

The Transit 517 Lightweight is a specially developed version of the 517 for use both on flight deck and in hangar operations on modern aircraft carriers.

The Ranger series of all terrain cranes has the on road performance of a truck crane and the off road capabilities of a rough terrain crane with lifting capacities from 15 to 30 tonnes and again is suited for military purposes.

Starlift
The Starlift range of self-propelled, telescopic aerial work platforms can place men and their equipment to working heights from 17 to 27·5 metres and at maximum outreach from 13·5 to 24 metres. Typical military applications include the maintenance and repair of buildings and aircraft. The standard versions are self-propelled, but truck-mounted variants are available on such chassis as the military version of the Bedford TK 4 × 2 truck or on the specialised Coles 315M crane chassis.

STATUS
Various models of Coles Cranes are in service with the British armed forces, the Belgian Air Force, the Yugoslav Army and numerous other armed forces.

MANUFACTURER
Coles Cranes Limited, Harefield, Uxbridge, Middlesex UB9 6QG, England.

SPECIFICATIONS

Model	Hydra Speedcrane 8/9T Mk II	Husky 6/8TCC	Model 315M	Hydra Truck 12/14T	Ranger (Transit) 517	Model 335M	Ranger 520	Ranger 530	Husky 680
Configuration	4 × 2	4 × 4	4 × 4	4 × 2	4 × 4	4 × 2	4 × 4	4 × 4	4 × 4
Traverse	360°	360°	360°	360°	360°	360°	360°	360°	360°
Lifting capacity									
(minimum radius)	8130 kg/2·45 m	7320 kg/2·8 m	15 000 kg/3 m	12 200 kg/3 m	18 000 kg/3 m	40 800 kg/3·5 m	20 000 kg/3 m	30 000 kg/3 m	75 000 kg/3 m
(max radius)	710 kg/11 m	1650 kg/25 m	2050 kg/10 m	820 kg/15 m	1400 kg/16·5 m	1150 kg/36 m	900 kg/24 m	600 kg/28 m	2560 kg/30 m
Length	6·55 m	7·27 m	9·14 m	8·6 m	8·71 m	15 m	10·7 m	11·08 m	14·63 m
Width	2·44 m	2.5 m	2·5 m	2·5 m	2·5 m	2·9 m	2·5 m	2·75 m	3·65 m
Height	2·82 m	2·67 m	3·6 m	3·26 m	3·62 m	3·9 m	3·4 m	3·66 m	4 m
Weight	13 590 kg	14 860 kg	21 130 kg	16 642 kg	18 430 kg	36 240 kg	21 250 kg	23 970 kg	50 460 kg
Engine	100 hp	158 hp	196 hp	146 hp	160 hp	165 hp	150 hp	240 hp	210 hp
Gears	5 forward, 1 reverse	4 forward, 4 reverse	6 forward, 3 reverse	6 forward, 1 reverse	6 forward, 1 reverse	4 forward, 4 reverse	6 forward, 3 reverse	5 forward, 1 reverse	6 forward, 6 reverse
Max speed	–	–	75 km/h	–	65 km/h	16 km/h	70 km/h	61 km/h	30 km/h

Coles Hydra Husky 6/8TCC being loaded onto RAF C-130 Hercules

Coles 315M, 27 were ordered in 1982 to be British Army's new Crane, Field, Medium

Coles Ranger 520 20-tonne mobile crane

Coles Starlift 728 mobile working platform

Coles Hydra Truck 12/14T operational with Sea Harrier on board HMS Hermes

Coles Hydra Husky 150T of British Army

Coles 335M Dynamic Compactor

DESCRIPTION
The Coles Model 335M Dynamic Compactor is designed for the consolidation of the sub base on crater damaged runways and aircraft working surfaces. Using the ejected spoil from any craters a surface can be formed of similar or even greater strength than the original sub base. On this consolidated base the final surface can be laid using a number of different materials or methods.

Compaction is accomplished with a special 5000 kg compaction weight designed by the MVEE(C). The weight is free-fall dropped from a height of around ten metres and the final suspension chain has a 'run-on' to enable the full force of the weight to be absorbed. A special 'over run' brake checks over run before the rope becomes loose on the barrel, thus preventing any damage to the rope or hoist unit and to facilitate rapid cycle speeds. With hydrostatic transmission and 'orbital' type hydraulic-assisted steering controlled from the cab,

instant mobility is available, enabling the unit to be quickly moved from one operation to another.

The superstructure has a fabricated steel bed. Primary and secondary transmission drives, hoisting and slewing gears, and all horizontal bedplate gearing are totally enclosed and are automatically pump lubricated. All the main shafts are mounted on anti-friction bearings and transmit power through involute spines. The 18·2-metre jib is the heavy duty lattice type and can be folded to ease movement and stowage. When fully folded forward for stowage the overall height of the unit is 3·9 metres and length overall is approximately 15 metres. The enclosed cab has a full 360 degree traverse, and telescopic jacks are fitted for extra stability when working.

SPECIFICATIONS
Cab seating: 1
Configuration: 4 × 2
Weight: 36 240 kg
Length: (travelling) 15 m

Width: 2·9 m
Height:
(cab, travelling) 3·84 m
(travelling, overall) 3·9 m
Angle of approach/departure: 11°/11°
Max speed: (road) 16 km/h
Engine: Caterpillar Model 3304T developing 165 hp at 2200 rpm
Tyres: 14.00 × 20 × 22PR
Number of tyres: 8
Electrical system: 24 V
Jib length: 18·28 m
Traverse: 360°
Hoist speed: 41·8 m/min

STATUS
Production.

MANUFACTURER
Coles Cranes Limited, Harefield, Uxbridge, Middlesex UB9 6QC, England.

Coles Model 335M dynamic compactor

Coles Model 335M dynamic compactor

FIATALLIS Wheeled Loaders

DESCRIPTION

The firm of FIATALLIS Great Britain Limited market the Italian FIATALLIS range of wheeled loaders in the United Kingdom. All are of conventional articulated frame design with drive to all wheels. Each is available with a range of bucket capacities and standard equipment includes an air cleaner and air cleaner service indicator, bucket level indicator, torque proportioning differentials, rear floodlights and adjustable seat.

Optional equipment includes various types of cab and tyres, air conditioning, automatic lift kickout, automatic bucket positioner, rear axle disconnect, brake moisture indicator, bucket teeth, cold weather equipment, non-slip diffentials, drawbar, engine oil by-pass filter, single lever hydraulic control, snow plough attachment and a sound suppression kit. In addition the FR15 may be fitted with a 50 amp alternator in place of the standard 30 amp alternator.

STATUS

In production. The 545-B is in service with the armies of Iraq and Portugal; the 605-B is in service with the Swedish and the Swiss armed forces, and the 645-B is in service with the British Army as its standard Medium Wheeled Tractor, although it is now being replaced by the TEREX 72-51 tractor, for which there is a separate entry in this section. Some of these have been fitted with a fork-lift attachment in place of the bucket and a Volvo snow blower can also be fitted.

MANUFACTURER

FIATALLIS Great Britain Limited, 24 Ivatt Way, Westwood, Peterborough, Cambridgeshire PE3 7PG, England.

(FIATALLIS Europe SpA, Viale Torino 0/2, 10040 Stupinigi, Torino, Italy.)

Model	FR 10	FR 12	FR 15
Cab seating	1	1	1
Configuration	4 × 4	4 × 4	4 × 4
Weight	8623 kg	9444 kg	11 639 kg
Length	6·01 m	6·27 m	6·32 m
Width	2·34 m	2·34 m	2·61 m
Height (bucket raised)	4·35 m	4·42 m	4·64 m
(over cab)	3·28 m	3·28 m	3·3 m
Ground clearance	0·38 m	0·38 m	0·47 m
Track	1·84 m	1·84 m	2 m
Wheelbase	2·795 m	2·795 m	2·945 m
Towing hook height	0·91 m	0·91 m	1·02 m
Max speed (road)	35 km/h	35 km/h	37 km/h
(reverse)	37 km/h	37 km/h	38 km/h
Fuel capacity	163 litres	163 litres	208 litres
Engine	FIAT 8065T	FIAT 8065T	FIAT 8365T
(hp)	105	120	155
Torque converter	twin turbine	twin turbine	twin turbine
Torque multiplication	5·1:1	5·1:1	5·05:1
Transmission	powershift planetary transmission with 4 forward and reverse ratios		
Turning circle diameter	4·52 m	4·52 m	4·85 m
Tyre size	14.00 × 24	14.00 × 24	17.5 × 25 or 20.5 × 25
Electrical system	12 V	12 V	24 V
Batteries	2 × 190 Ah	2 × 190 Ah	180 Ah
Rated bucket			
Capacity	1·34 m³	1·53 m³	1·91 m³
Struck capacity	1·09 m³	1·25 m³	1·58 m³
Bucket (weight)	593 kg	650 kg	793 kg
(width)	2·42 m	2·42 m	2·67 m
Dump height at 45°	2·82 m	2·75 m	2·85 m
Reach at 45°	0·78 m	0·85 m	0·84 m
Breakout force	10 750 kg	9721 kg	13 966 kg

FIATALLIS FR15 wheeled loader of 39 Engineer Regiment (Airfields) loading dump truck (Ministry of Defence)

FIATALLIS FR10 wheeled loader

FIATALLIS FR12 wheeled loader

FIATALLIS FR15 wheeled loader (Ministry of Defence)

British Army Medium Wheeled Tractor with appliqué armour for use in Northern Ireland (T J Gander)

Other Engineer Plant

Apart from those described in this section, the following equipments are also in service with the British armed forces:
Barker-Greene 44C Bucket Trencher

Chaseside Hi-Lift 11/2 cubic yard shovel
Coles 10-ton Truck-mounted Bridging Crane
Jones 565C and 971C 30- and 40-ton fully-slewing crawler-mounted cranes

NCK 304 3/4 cubic yard Crawler Excavator
Ruston-Bucyrus 19 RB and 33 RB Excavators
Thwaites All-drive 5000 and Giant Dumpers

Hymac Excavators

DESCRIPTION
Hymac hydraulic excavators are mounted on both tracked and wheeled undercarriages, and the product range consists of ten models.

SPECIFICATIONS

Model	580D	590C
Weight	12 000 kg	16 050 kg
Dipper length (monobloc, typical)	2·44 m	2·3 m
Bucket capacity (typical)	0·6 m³	0·76 m³
Max digging depth	5·4 m	4·98 m
Max reach	7·94 m	8·08 m
Max dump height	5·72 m	5·03 m
Engine	110 hp	101 or 100 hp

STATUS
The British Army originally bought 64 580BT tracked excavators, followed by a quantity of 590C excavators. The Australian Army operates both the tracked 580C and the wheeled 610C excavators. The Hymac 590CT excavator forms the basis of the 'WOMBLE' EOD vehicle. See next entry.

MANUFACTURER
Hymac Ltd, 2 Bath Road, Newbury, Berkshire RG13 1JJ, England.

Hymac 610C wheeled excavator of Australian Army (P Handel)

Hymac 'WOMBLE' Remote-controlled Excavator

DESCRIPTION
'WOMBLE' is an acronym for Wire Operated Mobile Bomb Lifting Equipment. The Hymac WOMBLE is a highly specialised conversion of the Hymac 590CT crawler excavator which enables the vehicle to carry out all its various functions in a hazardous environment while under the remote control of an operator positioned at a safe distance. It can quickly revert to normal manual control when not required for its specialist role.

The WOMBLE comprises a modified 590CT excavator, a control box, a 200-metre interconnecting cable and a closed circuit TV system. Radio control can also be provided either additionally or as an alternative to cable control allowing operation at extended distances of up to 500 metres. Cable control is preferred where there is any possibility of radio frequency interference or screening.

The unit can be fitted with any of the normal excavator attachments, such as bucket, concrete breaker, grab or ripper tooth.

It was originally developed to meet an MoD(Air) requirement for a remotely-controlled excavator for bombing range clearance. A tracked machine was specified in order to be able to negotiate rough terrain. The WOMBLE is capable of digging for buried munitions

Remote control Hymac 590CT working with hydraulic hammer

TV monitor and control panel for Hymac WOMBLE

or scooping up items lying on the surface. The remote control requirement was specified by the MoD to ensure operator safety. Polycarbonate windows and protective steel plate reinforcements protect the machine against the effects of explosions, and tests have indicated that if a medium-sized bomb or shell were to explode in the

grab bucket, the equipment would not be totally destroyed, while the safety of the operator, in his protected location, would be greatly enhanced.

STATUS
Production.

MANUFACTURER
Hymac Ltd, Sales Division, 2 Bath Road, Newbury, Berkshire RG13 1JJ, England.

International Harvester 100B Crawler Loader

DESCRIPTION
The International 100B Series 2 loader is in the one cubic metre range of loaders. In its design, attention has been paid to operator comfort and safety, visibility, simple controls and bucket design, among many other factors. The hydraulics are all protected and are fast-operating; the four-in-one bucket is lifted fully loaded in 6·7 seconds, dumped in 2·3 seconds and returned to ground line in 4·6 seconds.

SPECIFICATIONS
Cab seating: 1
Weight: (4-in-1 bucket, operating condition) 8074 kg
Length: (4-in-1 bucket on ground) 4·31 m
Width: 1·8 m
Height: (to top of cab) 2·26 m
Ground contact length: 1·85 m
Track width: 0·33 m
Ground pressure: 0·66 kg/cm²
Engine: International Diesel D-206 4-cylinder 3·38-litre developing 56 hp at 2500 rpm
Fuel capacity: 116 litres
Max speed: (road) 7·4 km/h

4-in-1 bucket
Max operating lift capacity: 2359 kg
Breakout force: 8981 kg
Capacity: 0·76 m³
Width: 1·8 m
Teeth: 6

International 100B Series 2 crawler loader with backhoe as supplied to British Army

STATUS
Production ceased in 1982. The International 100B is in service with the British Army.

MANUFACTURER
International Harvester Overseas Services Company, Pay Line Marketing, 730 London Road, Hounslow, Middlesex TW3 1PH, England.

International Harvester 630W Excavator

DESCRIPTION
The International Harvester range includes several wheeled excavators, of which the 630W was selected for adoption by the British Army. The excavator is hydraulically operated, and the forward-mounted operator's cab gives good all-round visibility. The four-wheel undercarriage has two rigid axles, the front axle being steerable and also capable of oscillation. The rear axle is rigidly mounted. Both two- and four-wheel drive are available, four-wheel drive being selected by means of an air-actuated dog clutch. Two hydraulically-operated outriggers mounted on the undercarriage directly in front of the rear axle are controlled from the cab.

Several modifications were required to adapt the 630W to military use. It was necessary to provide a hydraulic power take-off for the operation of road drills and other power tools; the machine was required to be capable of wading through 0·75 metre of water; it was to be capable of an output of 170 cubic metres an hour, and a special high speed transmission was needed to give the excavator the required convoy speed. In addition, military lighting, rifle clips, seat belts, a speedometer and stowage for a spare wheel were also specified.

STATUS
The 630W is now in service with the British and Kenyan armies. The earlier 3965 model was supplied to the Dutch Army, and the New Zealand Army uses several 640HD excavators.

MANUFACTURER
International Harvester Overseas Services Company, Pay Line Marketing, 730 London Road, Hounslow, Middlesex TW3 1PH, England.

SPECIFICATIONS
Weight: 13 200 kg (approx)
Length: (travelling) 8·6 m (with 2·6 m dipperstick)
Width:
(travelling) 2·5 m (approx)
(outriggers extended) 4·78 m
Height: (travelling) 3·35 m (approx)
Wheelbase: 2·95 m
Track:
(front) 1·94 m
(rear) 1·81 m
Engine: International D358 6-cylinder water-cooled diesel developing 75 net hp at 2500 rpm
Transmission: manual, 5 forward and 1 reverse speeds

International Harvester 630W excavator demonstrating maximum reach

International Harvester 630W excavator in travelling order (T J Gander)

Turning radius: 7 m
Tyres: 18 × 19.5 high flotation (4)
Bucket capacity: 0·8 m³
Max reach: (2·6 m dipperstick) 8·5 m

Max digging depth: (2·6 m dipperstick) 5·5 m
Work rate: 100 m³ per half hour recorded
Fording depth: 1 m
Road speed: 40 km/h

JCB Excavator Loaders

DESCRIPTION

JCB excavator loaders were first introduced in 1964. The basic design, using a one piece chassis to take all digging and loading stresses is still retained. The chassis is made of welded steel box sections, and provides high capacity tanks for hydraulic oils and fuel. Deep hardened pivot pins, stress relieved excavator components and rolled steel front axle also contribute to the strength and toughness of this type of machine. All three models in this range use the same proven 72 hp engine and modular transmission. The all-weather safety cab has ergonomically-placed controls. A wide range of options and attachments, including a full selection of excavator and loader buckets, a telescopic dipper providing an extra one metre of dig depth, hydraulic roadbreakers, loader-mounted forks and a dipper-mounted hydraulic breaker, is available.

SPECIFICATIONS

Model	3C	3CX	3D
Excavator			
(dig depth)	4·28 m	4·28 m	4·74 m
(reach)	6·25 m	6·25 m	6·72 m
(load height)	3·83 m	3·83 m	4·12 m
Loader capacity	0·8 m³	0·8 m³	0·9 m³

STATUS

JCB excavator loaders are in service with a number of armies including the British armed forces.

MANUFACTURER

JCB Excavators Limited, Rocester, Staffordshire ST14 5JP, England.

JCB Model 3CX hydraulic excavator loader

JCB Wheeled Loaders

DESCRIPTION

There are four basic models of JCB wheeled loader all of which have established a good reputation for reliability and performance. Smaller machines can be adapted to suit many different requirements from conventional loading duties to site preparation and even snow clearing. The optional Quick-hitch attachment allows immediate interchangeability of a wide range of buckets, forks and grapples, etc, to ensure maximum machine utilisation.

The operator's cab is mounted on the front module. The driving position makes loader alignment simple and improves all round visibility. Front mounting also isolates the operator from engine noise and vibration and, together with full sound-proofing provides him with a comfortable working environment. All models have full powershift three- or four-speed transmission, four-wheel drive, medium pressure gear pump hydraulics and visual engine/transmission fault warning with audible back-up.

For motive power all models have six-cylinder diesel engines, apart from the 410 which uses a four-cylinder unit.

JCB 410 with Quick-hitch unit and bucket attachment

SPECIFICATIONS

Model	410	420	423	428
Weight	6060 kg	7910 kg	14 280 kg	16 370 kg
Max load	1845 kg	2400 kg	4000 kg	5000 kg
Max bucket capacity	1·3 m³	4·5 m³	4·6 m³	4·6 m³
Max lift height				
(bucket pivot)	3·45 m	3·54 m	3·99 m	4·005 m
Turning circle	4·96 m	5·28 m	5·965 m	6·188 m
Standard bucket				
capacity	1 m³	1·3 m³	2·3 m³	2·9 m³

STATUS

Production.

MANUFACTURER

JCB Excavators Limited, Rocester, Staffordshire ST14 5JB, England.

JCB Hydraulic Excavators

DESCRIPTION

The range of JCB crawler excavators offers a variety of applications from conventional digging to specialised duties including demolition, waterway maintenance and rehandling. Three models in the range feature the JCB Powerslide Beam which can increase productivity by allowing the operator to instantly switch from maximum reach to maximum lift capacity without leaving his cab seat. Other advantages include faster work cycles, easier slewing and manouvring in confined spaces, safer dumping of excavated material and more compact transport dimensions.

The 805B Turbo and 806C use medium pressure gear pump hydraulic systems while the 807C uses a high pressure piston pump system with piston motors for tracking. Excavator controls are to ISO pattern with the boom/bucket on the right-hand lever and dipperstick/slewing on the left.

The 802 Mini Excavator is designed for small projects in confined locations, close-in to buildings and inside tunnels, shafts and caissons. A boom offset facility allows working close to walls or similar obstructions. A dozer blade for backfilling is standard equipment.

JCB 805B Turbo hydraulic excavator

SPECIFICATIONS

Model	805B Turbo	806C	807C
Weight	12 450 kg	13 230 kg	17 800 kg
Dig depth	5·73 m	5·78 m	6·28 m
Reach	8·5 m	8·5 m	9·18 m

Model	805B Turbo	806C	807C
Loadover height	5·44 m	5·44 m	5·77 m
Max bucket capacity	0·5 m³	0·6 m³	0·9 m³

STATUS
Production.

MANUFACTURER
JCB Excavators Limited, Rocester, Staffordshire ST14 5JP, England.

Muir-Hill A5000 Bucket Loader

DESCRIPTION
The Muir-Hill A5000 bucket loader is an all-wheel drive, all-wheel steer multi-purpose loading shovel, specially prepared for military applications. A major factor in its selection by the Royal Engineers was its versatility and its outstanding performance in conditions where speed, turning circle, reach and lift are essential.

It has a multi-purpose bucket for dozing, clam-shelling, scraping and loading which can be inter-changed with a side shift fork-lift attachment with a crane hook. In addition, a rear mounted backhoe for trenching can be interchanged with a hydraulically-operated winch. All these attachments can be interchanged rapidly and the complete machine is air transportable, and can be dropped by parachute.

SPECIFICATIONS
Cab seating: 1
Configuration: 4 × 4
Weight: (with fuel, cab, bucket and winch) 8695 kg
Front axle load: 3819 kg
Rear axle load: 4876 kg
Length:
  (with bucket on ground) 6·3 m
  (with bucket at carry) 6·3 m
Width:
  (over bucket) 2·29 m
  (over tyres) 2·16 m
Height:
  (with cab) 2·87 m
  (without cab) 2·3 m
Ground clearance: 0·42 m
Track: 1·77 m
Wheelbase: 2·29 m
Angle of approach/departure: 90°/25° (with winch)
Height of tow hooks: 0·71 m (with winch)
Fuel capacity: 182 litres
Engine: Perkins 4-stroke, water-cooled diesel developing 104 hp at 2500 rpm
Transmission: Allison Torqmatic powershift TT2221-1 incorporating soft shift system mounted direct to engine with flexiplate coupling

Gears	forward	reverse
Working range	0–6	0–8
Travelling range	0–22	—

Turning radius: 4·72 m
Tyres: 15.5 × 25
Tyre pressure:
  (front) 2·5 kg/cm²
  (rear) 1·8 kg/cm²
Electrical system: 24 V

Winch
Model: TT Boughton type 1NH

Muir-Hill A5000 of Royal Engineers fitted with armoured cab and fork lift attachment (T J Gander)

Bare drum line pull: 6123 kg
Rope:
  (length) 80 m
  (diameter) 14 mm
Winch weight: 689 kg

Bucket
Type: Rubery Owen multi-purpose
SAE capacity:
  (struck) 0·75 m³
  (heaped) 1 m³
Lifting capacity: (rated) 2268 kg
Max lifting capacity to full height of lift: 4082 kg
Max breakout force boom lift: 4899 kg
Max breakout force crowd: 5897 kg
Width outside: 2·29 m
Max dumping height: 3 m
Max load-over height: 3·57 m
Angle of dump: 45°
Raising time to max height with rated load: 6 s
Weight of bucket: 771 kg

Fork lift equipment
Type: Boughton
Size of forks: 127 mm wide
Max height of lift: 2·85 m
Full tilt range: (forwards to backwards) 110°
Side shift: (each side of central position) 229 mm

Capacity at 610 mm load centre: 1814 kg
Weight: 590 kg

Back acter
Type: Massey Ferguson MF220
Size of bucket: 610 mm
Capacity of bucket: 0·12 m³
Depth of dig: 3·66 m
Outreach: 4·27 m
Loading height: 3·48 m
Slew and digging arc: 193°
Max offset of king post from centre: 711 mm
Width of stabiliser base: 1·63 m
Weight: 1293 kg

Crane hook attachment
(used in conjunction with fork lift equipment)
Capacity:
  (at 610 mm outreach) 1814 kg
  (at 914 mm outreach) 1588 kg

STATUS
In production. A total of 400 A-5000s has been supplied to the British Army since 1969.

MANUFACTURER
Muir-Hill Tractors, Wiban, Winget Limited, Bristol Road, Gloucester GL1 5RX, England.

Muir-Hill A5000s fitted with fork lift attachments (T J Gander)

Muir-Hill A5000 fitted with fork lift attachment and backhoe (T J Gander)

Rapier HK17 Mobile Crane

DESCRIPTION
The Rapier HK17 is one of a range of Rapier hydraulic mobile cranes with capacities of up to 28 450 kg. The HK17 itself has 4 × 4 drive and four-wheel steering and is designed for use on rough terrain where good, even tractive effort is required. The chassis and superstruc-ture are of heavy steel fabrication. The top decking is suitably reinforced for load carrying. A three-part tele-scopic jib is mounted on the superstructure and has a full 360 degree traverse.

STATUS
The HK17 is in production and has been supplied to the British Army.

MANUFACTURER
Ransomes and Rapier plc, PO Box 1, Waterside Works, Ipswich, Suffolk IP2 8HL, England.

SPECIFICATIONS
Configuration: 4 × 4
Weight: (with 4-part jib) 22 100 kg
Length: (travelling order with 4-part jib) 8·05 m
Width: 2·5 m
Height: (travelling order) 3·24 m
Max speed: (road) 35 km/h
Wheelbase: 2·44 m
Engine: Perkins V8-540 diesel developing 140 hp at 2400 rpm
Transmission: twin disc torque converter and high/low transfer box, giving 4 forward and reverse speeds
Tyres: 14.00 × 24, 24 PR, earthmover tread
Steering: 2-, 4-wheel or crab
Turning radius:
(2-wheel steer) 7·01 m
(4-wheel steer) 4·34 m
Range: (at average road speed) 320 km
Lifting capacity:
(with stabilisers) 1930 kg at 12·3 m; 15 240 kg at 3 m
(free on wheels) 810 kg at 12·3 m; 10 870 kg at 2·4 m

Rapier HK17 mobile crane of British Army lifting Eager Beaver fork lift truck onto 4-ton truck

NCK-Rapier 406 Crawler-mounted Dragline

DESCRIPTION
The NCK-Rapier 406 is one of a wide range of diesel-powered, crawler-mounted draglines of rugged construction which are suitable for use on military engineering projects. With bucket sizes from 0·38 to 3·83 cubic metres, these machines can be easily converted to shovel, grab, lifting and piling operation, and lifting capacities range from 20 to 300 tonnes.

SPECIFICATIONS (406)
Weight: 31 900 kg (with 12·2 m boom)
Undercarriage length: 4·34 m
Width: 3·43 m
Height: (boom lowered) 3·4 m
Ground clearance: 0·32 m
Engine: water-cooled diesel developing 100 hp
Fuel capacity: 208 litres
Max boom length: 21·34 m
Max bucket capacity: 1·5 m³
Drag rope speed pull: 45·7 m/minute/9340 kg
Hoist rope speed pull: 51·8 m/minute/8250 kg
Dumping radius: (21·3 m boom) 19·82 m
Max dumping height: (21·3 m boom) 7·77 m
Max gradient: 25% (14°)
Max speed: 1·24 km/h

STATUS
In service with the British Army and other overseas forces engineering, construction and airfield construction units. The NCK-Rapier 406 has replaced the earlier NCK 304 series equipments.

NCK-Rapier 406 crawler-mounted dragline

MANUFACTURER
Ransomes & Rapier plc, PO Box 1, Waterside Works, Ipswich, Suffolk IP2 8HL, England.

Scammell LD55 Dump Truck

DESCRIPTION
The Scammell LD55 (previously known as the Aveling-Barford 690) has a conventional layout with the engine at the front, fully enclosed cab in the centre and dump body at the rear. The front end of the vehicle is protected by a sump guard and a safety frame is fitted forward of the radiator. The cab is mounted on four Metalastic rubber mounts and standard equipment includes an adjustable driver's seat and a heating and demister unit. The cab front has a reverse rake to reduce loss of visibility. The standard all steel rear dump body has a struck capacity of 7·6 cubic metres or a heaped capacity of 9·1 cubic metres. A heavy duty body with similar capacities is available. Optional equipment includes a six-speed gearbox and front and rear mounted tow hooks.

STATUS
Production complete. In service with the British Army.

MANUFACTURER
Scammell Motors, Leyland Vehicles Limited, Tolpits Lane, Watford, Hertfordshire WD1 3QB, England.

SPECIFICATIONS
Cab seating: 1 + 2
Configuration: 6 × 4
Weight:
(empty, chassis and cab only) 8016 kg
(max loaded weight) 25 610 kg
Weight on front axle: (empty, chassis and cab only)
3973 kg
Weight on rear bogie: (empty, chassis and cab only)
4043 kg
Length: 7·31 m
Width: 2·41 m
Height: (overall) 3·12 m
Track:
(front) 1·91 m
(rear) 1·9 m
Wheelbase: 3·86 m
Max speed: 55 km/h
Fuel capacity: 182 litres
Max gradient: 27·8%
Engine: AEC AV760 6-cylinder in-line 4-stroke diesel
developing 205 bhp at 2200 rpm
Gearbox: D443 manual with 5 forward and 1 reverse
gears
Clutch: single plate
Steering: cam and double roller, hydraulic assisted
Suspension:
(front) longitudinal semi-elliptical springs with
telescopic hydraulic shock absorbers
(rear) inverted longitudinal semi-elliptical leaf springs,
trunnion mounted at centre with slipper ends
Tyres:
(front) 11.00 × 22
(rear) 15.00 × 20
Brakes: air
Electrical system: 24 V
Batteries: 4 × 6 V, 121 Ah

Scammell LD55 dump truck (T J Gander)

Clyde Booth Cranes

DESCRIPTION
Clyde Booth (incorporating Thomas Smith), a trading
unit of NEI Cranes Ltd, produces three mobile cranes at
present in service with British forces. Two are for general use and the third is a specialised rough terrain
crane.

Smith Truck-mounted Cranes
The 10-tonne mobile crane has a two-piece telescopic
boom and is hydraulically operated. Its carrier has high
ground clearance and high approach angles for off-road
use, and is fitted with hydraulically-extended outriggers.
The suspension allows the crane bed to be lowered onto
the carrier axles to reduce the loading and manoeuvring
height. The 25-tonne mobile crane has a cable-
operated lattice boom and is powered separately from
its carrier. Attention has been paid to crew comfort in the
design of the cab which is used by both models, and the
same cab is used for both driving and operating the
crane.

Clyde Booth (Smith) L2825 25-tonne crane

SPECIFICATIONS

Model	10-tonne crane	L2825 (T25R) 25-tonne crane
Length	8·72 m	–
Width	2·5 m	–
Width (outriggers extended)	4·67 m	4·88 m
Height	3·47 m	–
Crane		
Capacity on wheels		
(minimum radius)	6700 kg at 3·05 m	10 160 kg at 3·05 m
(max radius)	1170 kg at 9·15 m	1020 kg at 24·4 m
Capacity on jacks/outriggers		
(minimum radius)	10 470 kg at 3·05 m	25 400 kg at 3·05 m
(max radius)	1830 kg at 9·15 m	1120 kg at 12·2 m
Boom length	7·8–12 m	10·67 m extensible
Traverse	360°	360°
Chassis		
Configuration	4 × 4	6 × 6
Max speed (road)	82 km/h	–
Angle of approach/departure	–	30°
Fording depth	–	0·76 m

Smith Rough Terrain Crane
The 10-tonne Rough Terrain Crane was developed for
use in the combat zone and has an excellent performance in all types of terrain, from water obstacles and
beaches to normal road use. It has a two-section
hydraulically-operated telescopic crane with 360
degree traverse and the driver's cab is double-ended to
allow the crane to be driven normally on roads. A single
engine on the carrier provides power for both the carrier
and the crane. Both axles are of the beam type, with the
front axle rigidly mounted to the chassis and the rear
axle locked in position when the crane traverses. No
outriggers are provided. The crane is waterproofed for
wading in sea water to a depth of 1·98 metres and can

Clyde Booth (Smith) 10-tonne telescopic crane

Clyde Booth (Smith) Rough Terrain Crane

operate in temperatures from −32 to +52°C and at altitudes up to 1500 metres.

STATUS
53 of the 10-tonne cranes were ordered by the British Ministry of Defence, and the L2825 crane has also been supplied to the British Army. Both are in production. The Rough Terrain Crane is in service with the British Army, but production has now ended.

MANUFACTURER
Clyde Booth (incorporating Thomas Smith), Union Crane Works, Rodley, Leeds LS13 2TG, England.

SPECIFICATIONS
Length: (travelling) 8·59 m
Width: 3·2 m
Height: (travelling) 3·63 m
Wheelbase: 4·42 m
Engine: Rolls-Royce C8NFL diesel developing 280 bhp at 2100 rpm
Transmission: Clark C606-2 torque converter single stage, 3:1 multiplication ratio Clark Power-shift R-66-FS gearbox (providing power take-off of 150 hp for crane superstructure)
Tyres: 24.00 × 29, tubeless, 24-ply rating
Steering: 2- or 4-wheel

Crane
Boom length: 6·93–10·52 m
Capacities:
(at 3·43 m radius) 10 160 kg
(at 4·27 m radius) 7110 kg
(at 5·87 m radius) 4060 kg
(at 9·53 m radius) 1525 kg
Max speed:
(road) 56 km/h
(with 7110 kg suspended load) 8 km/h
Max gradient: 40% (21°)

TEREX 32-04 (6 × 4) 23 000 kg Articulated Dump Truck

DESCRIPTION
The TEREX 32-04 23 000 kg articulated dump truck was announced in early 1983, although a variant of the vehicle using a different carrier chassis was shown publicly at the BAEE in 1982 (see *Variants* below). The 32-04 consists of an articulated vehicle with the forward unit housing the engine and cab and the rear unit the load-carrying dumper. The 32-04 has a 6 × 4 drive configuration.

Both front and rear frames are constructed from steel rectangular box sections and welded steel components. The coupling between the front and rear sections provides both articulation and oscillation with the articulation provided by widely spaced pivot points. A 267 mm diameter sealed bush provides the oscillation. The body has a maximum capacity of 16 cubic metres and top extensions are available for light materials. For raising the load-carrying body a gear pump mounted on the rear of the transmission supplies two single-stage double-acting rams. The hoist pump has a capacity of 5·08 litres per second at 2300 rpm and can raise the body in eleven seconds and lower it in six seconds.

The front cab, which is situated behind and over the engine, is centrally-located. The cab may be of the ROPS type and air conditioning is an optional extra.

Numerous standard features include a seat belt, torsion spring seat for the operator, tinted safety glass, a radio and sound insulation. Optional extras include a body tailgate, body wear plates, an exhaust-heated body, high flotation tyres and a reverse hoist interlock. Full hydrostatic power steering is fitted.

VARIANTS
A version with the body frame extended by 0·9 metre and carrying a Boughton Swap-body carrier has been demonstrated. This vehicle has been used as a concept evaluation vehicle for the British Army DROPS programme (see *Materials handling* section).

SPECIFICATIONS
Cab seating: 1
Configuration: 6 × 4
Weight:
(empty) 15 500 kg
(loaded) 38 500 kg
Weight on front axle: (loaded) 11 950 kg
Weight on rear axle: (loaded) 38 500 kg
Max payload: 23 000 kg
Length: 9·36 m
Width: 2·5 m
Height:
(top of cab) 3·19 m
(exhaust stack) 3·48 m
(body top) 2·615 m

Load area: 5·195 × 2·31 m
Ground clearance: 0·44 m
Track: (front and rear) 1·98 m
Wheelbase: 4·1 m + 1·6 m
Max speed: 53·3 km/h
Fuel capacity: 276 litres
Engine: Deutz BF 6L 413FR turbo-charged, air-cooled, 6-cylinder, 9·572-litre 4-stroke diesel developing 227 bhp at 2300 rpm
Transmission: ZF WG 180 with integral hydromatic torque converter providing 6 forward and 3 reverse gears
Steering: full hydrostatic power
Turning radius: 7·6 m
Suspension:
(front) leading arm with self-levelling air suspension and hydraulic dampers, 127 mm vertical travel
(rear) both axles mounted through rubber units on spaced longitudinal rocking beams, restraint by A-frames and panhard rods; 230 mm vertical travel
Brakes: air/hydraulic
Tyres: 20.5 × 25

STATUS
Development.

MANUFACTURER
TEREX Limited, Newhouse Industrial Estate, Motherwell, Lanarkshire ML1 5RY, Scotland.

TEREX 32-04 with Boughton Swap-body pallet carrying Scorpion reconnaissance vehicle (T J Gander)

TEREX 32-04 articulated dump truck prototype

TEREX 32-04 with extended frame unloading Boughton Swap-body pallet loaded with ammunition (T J Gander)

TEREX 32-04 articulated dump truck prototype

TEREX 72-25 Military General Purpose Wheeled Tractor

DESCRIPTION

For full technical details of the TEREX 72-25 Military General Purpose Wheeled Tractor please refer to the entry in the *Materials handling* section where full specifications will also be found.

In its construction mode the TEREX 72-25 can be operated in two forms; as an Engineer Wheeled Tractor (EWT) or as an All Arms Trencher (AAT). In the EWT form the 72-25 may be fitted with a 1·7 cubic metre bucket or a multi-purpose bucket with a maximum lift height of 3·515 metres. Optional extras include an armoured cab and a front-mounted winch. The armoured cab weighs approximately 1240 kg. For air transport the cab can be easily removed as can the normal ROPS cab. Other attachments are a fork lift, crane, scarifier or a quick-change plate. Mine clearing flails have been proposed for the EWT version.

The All Arms Trencher (AAT) version of the 72-25 includes a power take-off to power a Light Diggerhead carried forward on the lifting arms. Using the Diggerhead, trenches up to 1·5 metres deep can be produced.

STATUS

Development.

MANUFACTURER

TEREX Limited, Newhouse Industrial Estate, Motherwell, Lanarkshire ML1 5RY, Scotland.

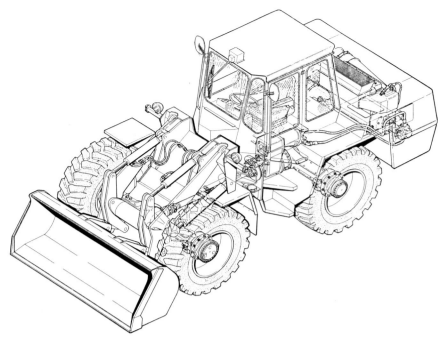

TEREX 72-25 wheeled tractor in Engineer Wheeled Tractor configuration

TEREX 72-25 GPWT with cab removed for air transport

TEREX 72-25 AAT with Light Mobile Diggerhead

TEREX 72-51 Medium Wheeled Tractor

DESCRIPTION

The TEREX Medium Wheeled Tractor was developed from the TEREX 72-51 commercial wheeled loader to meet the requirements of the British Army. After trials the tractor was selected as the standard Medium Wheeled Tractor for the British Army and an order for 70 machines was placed for delivery in 1977. The TEREX 72-51 is the largest loader which can be carried in the standard Lockheed C-130 Hercules transport aircraft stripped but mobile.

The loader can be used for a wide range of roles including preparation of field defences and weapon pits, vehicle recovery, road and airfield construction, bridge erection, loading vehicles and cable laying. It can also be modified for use as a rough terrain fork lift truck.

The military version is fitted with a four-in-one bucket, a front-mounted 11 340 kg winch, a rear-mounted ripper and a roll-over cab as standard. The cab is provided with a heater and defroster, and the rear axle is fitted with a no-spin differential. Optional equipment for the TEREX 72-51 Medium Wheeled Tractor includes different buckets, a snow plough and a quick coupling system.

SPECIFICATIONS

Cab seating: 1
Weight: 18 420 kg
Weight distribution:
  (front axle) 8012 kg
  (rear axle) 10 408 kg
Length: (bucket on ground) 7·32 m
Width: 2·87 m
Height: (over cab) 3·28 m
Ground clearance: 0·36 m
Track: 2·19 m
Wheelbase: 2·74 m
Engine: Detroit Diesel 6-71N 6-cylinder developing 194 hp at 2100 rpm
Transmission: Allison TRT-4280 automatic torque converter with 4 forward and reverse speeds in 2 ranges
Steering: full power articulation of frame through 60°
Brakes:
  (main) air over hydraulic discs with separate circuits for front and rear axles
  (parking) mechanical on transmission
Static tipping load:
  (straight) 11 925 kg
  (full turn) 10 525 kg
Capacity:
  (heaped) 2·7 m³
  (struck) 2·3 m³
Dump clearance at 45° at max lift: 3·05 m

STATUS

In production. The initial batch of 70 tractors ordered in early 1975 was delivered in 1977 and a further contract for 53 tractors was awarded in November 1979, for delivery in September 1980. The 5-year contract was completed in 1983 with a final order for 30 tractors.

MANUFACTURER

TEREX Limited, Newhouse Industrial Estate, Motherwell, Lanarkshire ML1 5RY, Scotland.

TEREX 72-51 Medium Wheeled Tractor (T J Gander)

TEREX TS-14B (4 × 4) Motor Scraper

DESCRIPTION
The TS-14B twin-power motor scraper was supplied to the British Army as a heavy motor scraper. It features a roll-over protected cab and a roller push-block. It can normally travel unladen on roads but when local regulations prevent this it can be carried on a 25-tonne long-bed transporter.

The four-section cutting edge allows straight or variable length drop centre and all sections are interchangeable and reversible. The bowl operation is by two interchangeable single-acting cylinders and linkage. The full floating apron has a large opening for easy ejection. Positive roll-out type ejection is actuated by a single hydraulic cylinder and the apron and ejector cylinders are interchangeable.

SPECIFICATIONS
Cab seating: 1
Weight:
 (empty) 23 950 kg
 (loaded) 45 270 kg
 (payload) 21 320 kg
Length: 12·06 m
Width: 3·06 m
Height: 3·4 m
Ground clearance: 0·58 m
Track: 2·27 m
Wheelbase: 7·06 m
Max road speed: 37 km/h
Fuel capacity:
 (tractor) 360 litres
 (scraper) 303 litres
Engines: (2) Detroit Diesel model 4-71N 4-cylinder diesels developing 160 hp at 2100 rpm (each)
Transmissions: (2) Allison CLT 3461 full powershift with 6 forward and 1 reverse speeds
Torque converter: Allison TC-420 integral with transmissions
Steering: full hydraulic, full 90° swing left and right

TEREX TS-14B (4 × 4) motor scraper (Ministry of Defence)

Brakes:
 (main) full air-operated drum brakes with automatic emergency application
 (parking) mechanical locking of service brakes
Tyres: 29.5 × 25
Electrical system: 12 V
Battery: 1 × 12 V, 135 Ah
Struck capacity: (SAE) 10·8 m³
Heaped capacity:
 (3:1 slope, SAE) 12·2 m³
 (1:1 slope, SAE) 15·3 m³

STATUS
In production. The initial batch of five machines was delivered to the British Army in March 1976 and another five were delivered in 1978.

MANUFACTURER
TEREX Limited, Newhouse Industrial Estate, Motherwell, Lanarkshire ML1 5RY, Scotland.

TEREX TS-8 (4 × 4) Motor Scraper

DESCRIPTION
This has been developed from the civilian scraper to meet a British Army requirement for a medium motor scraper, and is airportable in a Lockheed C-130 Hercules aircraft. The TS-8 can be used for a variety of roles including cut and fill to formation levels in road, track and airfield construction as well as level, spread, grade and compact road and airfield construction materials. It can also be used to excavate field defences and weapon pits.

Preparation for loading into the aircraft is limited to bolting two small load-spreading wheels to the cutting edge and reversal of the exhaust pipes to prevent contamination of the aircraft roof lining. The load-spreading wheels have a secondary function in enabling the vertical articulation of the machine to follow the aircraft ramp contours without risk of damaging the tail section. The scraper can also be sectionalised for carrying by helicopter.

The four-section cutting edge has a variable length drop centre and all blades are interchangeable and reversible. Two identical and interchangeable single-acting hydraulic cylinders connected directly to the bowl are used to operate the scraper bowl. The apron is operated by two double-acting, interchangeable cylinders acting directly on apron arms. Positive roll-out type ejection is actuated by a single-acting hydraulic cylinder.

SPECIFICATIONS
Weight:
 (empty) 15 740 kg
 (loaded) 26 630 kg
 (payload) 10 890 kg
Length: 10·67 m
Width: 2·745 m
Height: 2·895 m
Ground clearance: 0·46 m

Track: 2·08 m
Wheelbase: 6·35 m
Max speed: (road) 47 km/h
Fuel capacity: 318 litres
Engines: (2) Bedford 330 4-cycle 6-cylinder diesels developing 100 hp at 2600 rpm (each)
Transmissions: (2) Allison automatic MT-653 with 5 forward and 1 reverse ranges
Torque converter: Allison TC-570 integral with transmissions
Steering: full hydraulic, full 90° swing left and right
Brakes:
 (main) double calliper and disc
 (parking) calliper disc on transmission output
Tyres: 23.5 × 25
Electrical system: 24 V
Batteries: 2 × 12 V, 100 Ah
Struck capacity: 6·1 m³

TEREX TS-8 motor scraper being loaded into C-130 Hercules transport

TEREX TS-8 motor scraper being loaded in C-130 Hercules transport and showing load-spreading wheels fitted for this method of transport

STATUS
In production. 23 vehicles were delivered to the British Army in February 1980. An order for a further 12 was completed in early 1983.

MANUFACTURER
TEREX Limited, Newhouse Industrial Estate, Motherwell, Lanarkshire ML1 5RY, Scotland.

TEREX TS-8 motor scraper

Jones 15/18RT Crane

DESCRIPTION
Jones Cranes Limited makes the chassis for the Smith 10-tonne mobile crane described in a separate entry in this section. The same chassis is also used for the military Jones 15/18 RT crane. It differs from the standard commercial vehicle in that the military requirements call for the ability to operate the outriggers and to drive the whole machine from the top cab as well as from the chassis. A rear-mounted winch is fitted, and can be operated from the rear of the vehicle or from the cab, and fairleads allow the rope to be led out to the front or rear of the vehicle.

SPECIFICATIONS
Weight: 22 068 kg
Length: (travelling) 8·07 m

Width: 2·5 m
(outriggers extended) 3·99 m
Height: 3·63 m

Crane
Capacity on wheels:
(max radius) 500 kg at 10·7 m through 360°
(minimum radius) 7900 kg at 3 m through 360°;
9500 kg at 3 m over rear
Capacity with outriggers extended:
(max radius) 600 kg at 23·5 m through 360°
(minimum radius) 15 240 kg at 3 m through 360°
Boom length: (including fly jib) 7–24·7 m
Traverse: 360°

Chassis
Configuration: 4 × 4
Engine: GM Bedford 500 Phase 1 diesel developing 167 bhp at 2800 rpm

Transmission: Eaton 542 SMA and British Twin-Disc auxiliary gearbox of 15/18RT replaced in military version by Allison gearbox
Max speed: (road) 64·3 km/h
Gradient: 36% (approx)
Ground clearance: 0·39 m
Angle of approach: 25°
Turning radius: 7·85 m
Tyres: 16.00 × 20, 24 ply rating, non-directional cross-country

STATUS
The modified Jones 15/18RT crane is used in workshops to remove and carry tank powerpacks, and also for bridging.

MANUFACTURER
Jones Cranes Limited, PO Box 13, Letchworth, Hertfordshire SG6 1LU, England.

Military version of Jones 15/18RT mobile crane

Rubery Owen (Warrington) Double-4 Bucket

DESCRIPTION
Designed to be produced in various capacities and for attachment to both wheeled and tracked loaders, the Rubery Owen Double-4 bucket can carry out a variety of functions. It can be used as a scraper, bottom-dumper, grab, loader, bulldozer, digger, clam or backfiller. Produced in varying capacities ranging from 478 to 2773 nominal heaped litres, the Double-4 is manufactured from high yield stress structural steel and construction is all-welded. The Double-4 has replaceable bucket teeth, clam hinges with hardened and ground pivot pins, reversible mouldboard and clam rear cutting edges, twin hydraulic cylinders for clamping, cast clam corners, a reinforced double plate clam bottom and hard rod faced side plate lead edges.

STATUS
Production.

MANUFACTURER
Rubery Owen (Warrington) Limited.
 Enquiries to Rubery Owen Group Services Limited, Defence Equipment Division, Darlaston, PO Box 10, Wednesbury, West Midlands WS10 8JD, England.

Rubery Owen (Warrington) Double-4 bucket on Muir-Hill A5000 bucket loader

UNITED STATES OF AMERICA

Commercial Construction Equipment (CCE) Program

DESCRIPTION

The US Army's construction mission is similar to that undertaken by commercial concerns except in forward areas, where tactical mobility is an over-riding consideration. Its requirements for construction equipment are met by Commercial Construction Equipment (CCE), Military Adaptation of Commercial Items (MACI) and Military Designs.

Since the construction equipment industry in the United States is highly competitive and devotes a great deal of effort to research and development, the US Army is able to meet many of its requirements with commercially-developed items. The US Army Mobility Equipment Research and Development Command (MERADCOM) has procured more than 30 different items for rear area construction since the inception of the CCE program in 1969.

The essential elements of the CCE program are:

A requirements document which describes the user's need.

A commercial user survey to determine if industry has a product which may fulfill the needs of the Army and which has been fielded in significant numbers for over one year without untoward maintenance or durability characteristics.

The writing of a performance specification which expresses the needs of the Army and the equipment commercially available in a form familiar to commercial equipment manufacturers.

Five-year contracts for construction equipment using the 2-step formally-advertised method of procurement.

The elimination of government testing by the substitution of commercial user survey data and a short quality assurance-type demonstration to prove the effectiveness and durability of the product.

The use of contractor training, logistics support, warranty and manuals to the maximum extent practicable.

Several of the major items procured under the CCE program are described in this section.

US Army Bulldozers

DESCRIPTION

The US Army uses a wide variety of bulldozers, most of which are commercial models. They are classified into Light, Medium and Heavy Drawbar Pull (DBP) tractors as shown below. The Caterpillar D7E and D8K are typical of the Medium and Heavy DBP classes respectively and are described separately in this section.

STATUS

Most of these tractors are still in production in an improved form and are in service with the US Army. Some are also used by Construction Battalions of the US Navy. The Caterpillar D6C is also used by Australia, Denmark and the United Kingdom and the D9 has been adopted by Australia and Denmark.

SPECIFICATIONS

Manufacturer and model	Caterpillar D4*	Caterpillar D5A†	Allis-Chalmers HD6M	Caterpillar D6B‡	Case M-450	Allis-Chalmers HD16M	International Harvester TD-18-182	International Harvester TD-20-201	International Harvester TD-24-241
Class	Light	Light	Light	Light	Light	Medium	Medium	Medium	Heavy
Weight	–	7258 kg	7258 kg	7258 kg	n/a	21 873 kg	21 873 kg	21 873 kg	25 098 kg
DBP, 1st gear	–	8074 kg	5733 kg	11 295 kg	3400 kg	16 876 kg	13 608 kg	13 608 kg	18 656 kg
Length	–	3·78 m	3·78 m	3·78 m	–	5·84 m	5·84 m	5·84 m	6·35 m
Width	–	2·44 m	2·44 m	2·44 m	–	3·38 m	3·38 m	3·38 m	3·4 m
Height	–	2·18 m	2·18 m	2·18 m	–	2·15 m	2·15 m	2·15 m	2·74 m
Operation	hydraulic	hydraulic	hydraulic	hydraulic	–	hydraulic	–	hydraulic	cable

Notes:
* Air-droppable; width can be reduced to 1·52 m.

† Can be segmented into 2 modules each weighing less than 6800 kg; width can be reduced to 1·52 m.

‡ Air-transportable in Phase 1 operations.

Caterpillar D6C used as Heavy Crawler Tractor by Royal Engineers (T J Gander)

Allis-Chalmers HD16M medium dozer of US Army (Larry Provo)

Case Crawler Tractors

DESCRIPTION

Case has specialised in air-transportable crawler tractors. The 350, 450 and 850 models can be transported by helicopter and, with the addition of the 1150, are air droppable. All models have torque converter transmissions, and other standard equipment includes permanently lubricated track rollers, sealed tracks and hydraulic track adjusters. Several types of bucket, dozer blade, winch, ripper and brush rake are available and an excavator attachment can be fitted to the 450 and 850 models. ROPS cabs and canopies can be provided for all models and specific military modifications, including tiedowns, are also available.

STATUS

All models are in production and are used by the US Army, Air Force, Navy and Marine Corps.

MANUFACTURER

J I Case Company, Government Marketing, 700 State Street, Racine, Wisconsin 53404, USA.

Preparing Case 1150C with dozer blade for lift by CH-53E helicopter. This example is a US Marine Corps 1150C

SPECIFICATIONS

Model	350	450*†‡	850§	1150r	1450
Cab seating	1	1	1	1	1
Weight (with dozer)	3517 kg	5171 kg*	7348 kg	10 401 kg	13 505 kg
Types of dozer available (number)	1	2	2	2	3
Length (with dozer on ground)	3·26 m	3·7 m	4 m	4·57 m	5·05 m
Width of dozer blade	2·03 m	2·24 m	2·59 m	3·23 m	3·86 m
Height of dozer blade	610 mm	711 mm	914 mm	965 mm	914 mm
Track gauge (track)	1·22 m	1·32 m	1·52 m	1·57 m	1·88 m
Track width (range)	305 and 356 mm	356 and 406 mm	406–508 mm	406–559 mm	406–610 mm
Length of track on ground	1·6 m	1·73 m	1·99 m	2·2 m	2·34 m
Max speed (forward)	7·7 km/h	10 km/h	10 km/h	10 km/h	9 km/h
Transmission	spur gear	powershift	powershift	full powershift	full powershift
Number ranges forward/reverse	3/3	4/4	4/4	4/4	4/4
Torque converter ratio	2·23:1	2·10:1	2·92:1	2·35:1	2·32:1
Engine (diesel)	Case G188D	Case G207D	Case A336BDT	Case A451BD	Case A504BDT
Number of cylinders	4	4	4	6	6
Hp/rpm (SAE net)	39/2000	53/2000	75/2000	102/2100	130/2100
Steering	planetary	hydraulic clutch/brake	hydraulic clutch/brake	hydraulic clutch/brake	hydraulic clutch/brake
Weight loader	4495 kg	6589 kg	8977 kg	11 645 kg	15 277 kg
Bucket capacity (standard)	0·57 m³	0·76 m³	1·15 m³	1·33 m³	1·72 m³
Dump clearance (at 45° dump)	2·47 m	2·49 m	2·62 m	2·64 m	2·92 m
Max lift capacity	1996 kg	2359 kg	3402 kg	4173 kg	5216 kg
Length (with bucket on ground)	3·96 m	4·01 m	4·32 m	4·8 m	5·25 m
Width (over bucket)	1·6 m	1·72 m	2·01 m	2·06 m	2·24 m

* Can also pull 6·1 m³ scraper.
† Used by Army, Navy and Marine Corps.
‡ Army model has straight blade and is helicopter-transportable
and air-droppable. Weight 4539 kg. Army also uses 4-in-1 loader with weight of 7000 kg.
§ USMC.
r Loader version is transportable by CH-53E helicopter. Weight (including tractor, loader, winch, canopy and 4-in-1 bucket) is 13154 kg. 200 ordered by USMC.

450 loader in air-droppable configuration for US Army

450 dozer with helicopter transport options as supplied to USMC

Case Four-wheel Drive Loaders

DESCRIPTION

The J I Case Company manufactures a range of wheeled loaders, all of which have centre pivot articulation, full powershift with torque converter, and dual lift and dump cylinders as standard. With the exception of the W36, all the Case wheeled loaders are air transportable, and the W11 can also be carried by helicopter. A range of options and attachments is available, including the following:

Multi-purpose buckets and other front attachments
Operator-actuated quick disconnect system for front attachments can be fitted with pallet forks and crane jib or excavator
Rear-mounted excavator attachment available for W14, W18 and W24 models
ROPS canopy or cab
Various tyre sizes and patterns

STATUS

All models are in production and various models are in service with the US Army, Air Force and Navy. The earlier W10B and W10C, equipped with forks or buckets, are in service with the Australian Army as is the W36M (64).

A US Army contract for a further 1900 W24s has been placed, with delivery planned between 1984 and 1987.

MANUFACTURER

J I Case Company, Government Marketing, 700 State Street, Racine, Wisconsin 53404, USA.

SPECIFICATIONS

Model	W11	W14*†	W18	W24‡	W36
Cab seating	1	1	1	1	1
Configuration	4 × 4	4 × 4	4 × 4	4 × 4	4 × 4
Weight (SAE operating)	4699 kg	6688 kg	9018 kg	10 671 kg	15 050 kg
Tipping load (SAE straight)	3316 kg	4788 kg	6172 kg	8836 kg	11 532 kg
(SAE full turn)	2833 kg	4228 kg	5500 kg	7802 kg	9852 kg
Breakout force (SAE)	4631 kg	5607 kg	10 179 kg	9616 kg	13 756 kg
Bucket capacity (standard)	0·76 m³	1·15 m³	1·34 m³	1·91 m³	2·68 m³
Dump clearance (45° dump)	2·59 m	2·7 m	2·79 m	2·82 m	2·95 m
Length (bucket on ground)	5·18 m	5·59 m	6·07 m	6·74 m	7·39 m
Width (without bucket)	1·93 m	2·13 m	2·31 m	2·44 m	2·82 m
Height (cab/canopy)	2·39 m	3·05 m	3·12 m	3·53 m	3·2 m
Track width	254 mm	406 mm	432 mm	445 mm	406 mm
Wheelbase	2·34 m	2·54 m	2·74 m	3·09 m	3·23 m
Engine (diesel)	Case G207D	Case A336BD	Case A401BD	Case A504BD	Case A504BDTI
Cylinders	4	4	6	6	6
Hp/rpm (SAE net)	55/2100	83/2200	103/2200	132/2200	185/2200
Gearbox (forward/reverse)	3/3	4/2	4/2	4/2	4/4
Max speed (road)	36·3 km/h	40·2 km/h	37 km/h	35·5 km/h	32·7 km/h
Steering	hydrostatic	hydrostatic	hydrostatic	hydrostatic	hydrostatic
Turning radius	8·96 m	9·96 m	10·77 m	12·01 m	12·73 m
Articulation (total)	80°	80°	80°	80°	80°
Max rear axle oscillation	24°	24°	24°	24°	24°
Tyres (standard)	15.00 × 19.5	15.5 × 25	17.5 × 25	20.5 × 25	23.5 × 25
Electrical system	12 V	24 V	24 V	24 V	24 V

* Modified Commercial type for USN, USAF (100) and USMC.
† Some USN models have Model 26 backhoe.
‡ Modified electrical system. Over 500 in Army service with 4-in-1 buckets.

Case W24C loader fitted with excavator on front-mounted rapid attachment unit

Case W36M wheeled loader of Australian Army (P Handel)

Case/Drott Four-wheel Drive Excavators

DESCRIPTION
The Case/Drott 40 and 45 excavators have a single Detroit Diesel engine to power both the chassis and excavator. The chassis gives good mobility across rough terrain as well as high speed travel. From his position in the cab the operator can operate the excavator and drive the vehicle. A front-loading bucket is available for truck loading, and other military modifications can be included.

STATUS
Both the 40 and 45 models have been tested by the US Army, US Air Force and US Marine Corps and are in quantity production. In service with Canada and US Marine Corps.

MANUFACTURER
J I Case Company, Government Marketing, 700 State Street, Racine, Wisconsin 53404, USA.

Model 40 Case/Drott four-wheel drive excavator of US Marine Corps with various sizes of bucket

SPECIFICATIONS

Model	40EYR	45EYR	Model	40EYR	45EYR
Cab seating	1	1	Hp/rpm (SAE net)	113/2400	141/2300
Configuration	4 × 4	4 × 4	Gearbox (forward/reverse)	6/6	4/4
Weight	16 148 kg	19 096 kg	Transmission	full powershift	full powershift
Length (transport)	8·48 m	9·8 m	Max speed (road)	48·3 km/h	40·2 km/h
Height (transport)	3·96 m	4·1 m	Steering (front wheels)	hydrostatic	hydrostatic
Width (transport)	2·44 m	2·7 m	Brakes	air/hydraulic	air/hydraulic
Ground clearance	0·356 m	0·356 m	Tyres	17.5 × 25	20.0 × 21
Wheelbase	2·77 m	2·9 m	Max reach (at grade level)	8·83 m	9·9 m
Engine	Detroit Diesel 4-53N	Detroit Diesel 4-71N	Max digging depth	5·2 m	6·4 m
Cylinders	4	4	Lift capacity (rear at 4·6 m)	3869 kg	4695 kg

Case MC2500 30-ton Rough Terrain Crane

DESCRIPTION
The MC2500 crane is produced by the Drott Division of the J I Case Company. The hydraulic winching equipment includes a main and auxiliary winch, and the crane can be used for pile driving and clamshell operations as well as lifting duties. The boom can be lowered below the horizontal to assist in changing attachments. It is mounted on a 4 × 4 carrier which is driven from the crane operator's cab, and steering of both axles is hydraulic with two-wheel, four-wheel or crab steering possible. Four hydraulic outriggers are provided to stabilise the crane when operating.

SPECIFICATIONS
Weight: 32 790 kg
Length: (travelling) 13·29 m
Width:
(travelling) 2·92 m
(over outriggers) 5·39 m
Height: (travelling) 3·86 m
Wheelbase: 3·68 m

Crane
Max capacity: 27 200 kg at 3·05 m radius at 10 m boom extension
Boom length: 10 m, 3-section power extension to 24·3 m
Traverse: 360°

Carrier
Engine: Detroit Diesel 6V53N, with full powershift transmission giving 6 forward and 6 reverse speeds
Tyres: 26.5 × 25, 20-ply rating
Max speed: (road) 38·6 km/h
Fording depth: 1·52 m
Ground clearance: 0·55 m

STATUS
Production complete. 210 are in service with the US Marine Corps for use in construction, container handling, bridging and recovery of aircraft up to F-4 size.

MANUFACTURER
J I Case Company, Drott Division, Government Marketing, 700 State Street, Racine, Wisconsin 53404, USA.

Case MC2500 crane lifting US Army MILVAN container

Case Two-wheel Drive Loaders

DESCRIPTION
Case two-wheel drive tractor-loader/excavator equipments are built on a unitised chassis into which the power train is mounted. A torque converter is standard and on the largest models, the 680 and 780, a powershift gearbox is also provided. The loader is integral to

the tractor frame but the excavator attachments can be removed from the 480 and 580 tractors, and the dig depth and reach of the excavator can be extended on all models. The 480 and 580 tractors can be transported by helicopter and all models are air transportable. Variations and optional equipment include the following:
  Loader buckets

Excavator buckets of various widths
ROPS canopies and cabs
Three point hitch systems for 480 and 580 models
Horn and light fittings, backup alarm
Spark-arresting exhaust
Cold-starting assistance
Various tyre sizes and patterns

Case 580 loader/excavator

Case 680 loader/excavator

SPECIFICATIONS

Model	480D	580D*	680H†	780B
Cab seating	1	1	1	1
Configuration	4 × 2	4 × 2 (4 × 4 optional)	4 × 2	4 × 2
Weight	4250 kg	5200 kg	7670 kg	9600 kg
Loader (lift capacity to full height)	1361 kg	2338 kg	2631 kg	2801 kg
(breakout force)	2585 kg	3266 kg	46 706 N	45 556 N
(dump height)	3·24 m	3·29 m	3·56 m	3·51 m
Excavator (dig depth)	3·67 m	4·32 m	5·03 m	5·56 m
(reach from swing pivot)	4·79 m	5·39 m	6·04 m	6·68 m
(load height)	2·57 m	3·39 m	3·42 m	3·35 m
Length (travelling)	6·41 m	6·81 m	6·93 m	7·52 m
Width (travelling)	2·11 m	2·05 m	2·3 m	2·51 m
Height (to cab/canopy)	2·55 m	2·63 m	2·92 m	2·92 m
(excavator, travelling)	3·08 m	3·43 m	3·81 m	4·01 m
Wheelbase	2·3 m	3·4 m	2·21 m	2·21 m
Max speed (road)	33·7 km/h	33·8 km/h	31 km/h	32·2 km/h
Engine (diesel)	Case G188D	Case G207D	Case A336BD	Case A336BDT
Cylinders	4	4	4	4
Hp/rpm (SAE net)	47/2100	55/2100	80/2200	111/2200
Gearbox (forward/reverse standard)	4/4-manual	4/4-manual	3/3 powershift	3/3 powershift
Torque converter	standard	standard	standard	standard
Steering	hydrostatic	hydrostatic	hydrostatic	hydrostatic
Turning radius	7·14 m	7·34 m	10·9 m	12·4 m
Tyres (front/rear)	7.50 × 16–14.9 × 24	7.50 × 16–14.9 × 24	11.00 × 16–16.9 × 24	9.00 × 20–18.4 × 24
Electrical system	12 V	12 V	24 V	24 V

* Used by USMC.
† Modified commercial type; used by USAF and Canadian Forces (Army) with ROPS canopy.

STATUS
All models are in production and a total of 275 are in service with all the US services.

MANUFACTURER
J I Case Company, Government Marketing, 700 State Street, Racine, Wisconsin 53404, USA.

Caterpillar D8K (T-11) Heavy Tractor

DESCRIPTION
As procured under the CCE program, the D8K is equipped with either a winch and an angledozer blade or a hydraulic ripper and semi-U blade.

SPECIFICATIONS
Weight: 38 100 kg approx
Length: 5·26 m
Width: 3·05 m
Height: 2·44 m
Engine: Caterpillar D342 turbo-charged diesel developing 300 hp
Transmission: powershift, 3-speed
Operation: hydraulic

STATUS
In service with the US Army. Procured under the CCE program.

MANUFACTURER
Caterpillar Tractor Company, Defense Products Department, Peoria, Illinois 61629, USA.

Caterpillar D8K (T-11) tractor (US Army)

Caterpillar D7E Track-type Tractor

DESCRIPTION
Designated Tractor, Full-Tracked, Low Speed, Diesel Engine Driven, Medium Drawbar Pull; Oscillating Track, 78 in Gauge, the Caterpillar D7E is typical of the US Army's Medium Drawbar Pull class of bulldozers. There are slight modifications for military use, such as rear floodlights, and a powershift transmission with torque converter drive is standard on military models. The D7E is used for building roads and airfields, for quarry work, and many other construction projects. It can perform general bulldozing, scraper towing and pushing, tree dozing, angle dozing and snow clearance. The blade is hydraulically operated and can also be tilted and angled. A winch or ripper may be fitted at the rear.

SPECIFICATIONS
Weight: 14 456 kg
Length: 4·47 m
Width: 3·39 m
Height: 2·44 m
Engine: Caterpillar 4-cylinder turbo-charged diesel developing 200 hp
Fuel capacity: 439 litres
Max speed: 9·6 km/h
Max gradient: 60%

Winch capacity:
(deadman) 27 215 kg
(drag load) 22 680 kg
Fording depth: (unprepared) 0·76 m

STATUS
In production. The Caterpillar D7E is in service with the US Army, Navy and Air Force and the armed forces of many other countries, including Denmark.

MANUFACTURER
Caterpillar Tractor Company, Defense Products Department, Peoria, Illinois 61629, USA.

Caterpillar D5B Track-type Tractor

DESCRIPTION
The Caterpillar D5B track-type tractor is a commercial design that has been adapted for military purposes. A conventional tractor in appearance and layout, it can be fitted with the usual dozer blades and may be equipped with a ROPS cab.

The basic model, the Type 1, is in production while the Type 2, under advanced development, can be broken down into two loads for air transport and paradropping. Of the two loads the first includes track and suspension together with the dozer blade and arms, while the other includes the main engine, chassis and the driver's position. The latter load also carries the main hydraulic rams for the dozer blade. The track and suspension can be towed as one section but the chassis and engine are carried on a special dolly wheel arrangement with two of the wheels on one axle at the rear. Under the front of the chassis a single steerable dolly wheel is secured. It may be possible that the rear track driving wheel provides the basis for the rear dolly wheel attachment.

Both types of D5B can be equipped with a hydraulically-controlled winch having a maximum bare drum pull of 22 770 kg using a 19-mm diameter cable. This winch is removed on the Type 2 when it is prepared for paradropping.

STATUS
Type 1, production. Type 2, advanced development.

MANUFACTURER
Caterpillar Tractor Company, Defense Products Department, Peoria, Illinois 61629, USA.

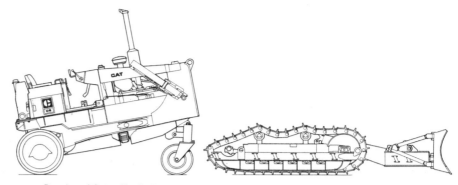

Drawing of Caterpillar D5B track-type tractor prepared for paradropping (not to 1/76 scale)

SPECIFICATIONS (Type 2)
Weight:
  (normal operating) 15 173 kg
  (air transport) 12 882 kg
  (air drop) 13 508 kg
  (chassis section) 7030 kg
  (suspension and dozer) 5851 kg
Length: (with blade and winch) 5·26 m
Width:
  (with blade) 2·809 m
  (without blade) 2·433 m
Height: (reduced) 2·197 m
Ground clearance: 0·277 m
Track width: 406 mm

Track: 2·286 m
Length of track on ground: 2·22 m
Max speed: (forward) 10·1 km/h
Engine: 3306 4-stroke diesel developing 105 fhp at 1750 rpm
Transmission: planetary powershift with 3 forward and 3 reverse gears
Torque converter: single stage type 6-1300-335 MS
Electrical system: 24 V

Caterpillar 621 Motorised Scraper

SPECIFICATIONS
Weight: (empty) 28 640 kg
Length: 12·68 m
Width: 3·18 m
Height: 3·65 m

Payload: 21 800 kg
Engine: Caterpillar 3406 diesel engine developing 330 hp
Bowl capacity:
  (heaped) 15·3 m³
  (struck) 10·7 m³

STATUS
In service with the British Army.

MANUFACTURER
Caterpillar Tractor Company, Defense Products Department, Peoria, Illinois 61629, USA.

Caterpillar 627 Motorised Scraper

SPECIFICATIONS
Weight: 32 380 kg
Length: 13·33 m
Width: 3·18 m
Height: 3·64 m
Payload: 21 800 kg

Engines: (2) Caterpillar 3306 diesel developing 225 hp each
Bowl capacity: 15·3 m³

STATUS
Both the Caterpillar 627 and the 22·9 m³ capacity

Caterpillar 637 are used by Construction Battalions of the US Navy.

MANUFACTURER
Caterpillar Tractor Company, Defense Products Department, Peoria, Illinois 61629, USA.

TEREX 82-30 Crawler Tractor

DESCRIPTION
The TEREX 82-30 crawler tractor is a commercial design that has been used as the basis for a military crawler tractor, the first of which was the TEREX 82-30 FAM for the US Marine Corps. The first deliveres to the US Marine Corps were made in 1967 and the last in 1972 by which time 255 had been delivered and the type remains the standard US Marine Corps heavy tractor-dozer with Active and Reserve Engineer forces. The 82-30 has a hydraulically-operated semi-U bulldozer blade with a hydraulic tilt strut. Extra equipment includes a winch, a three-tooth ripper and a double drum cable control.

The current production model of the TEREX 82-30 is the 82-30B which has been selected by the British Army as the Royal Engineer's Heavy Crawler Tractor. An initial batch of 23 machines was delivered to the British

Army in 1979 and a second batch in August 1981. This version has a hydraulically-operated straight tiltdozer blade, a low-bridge-height cab with full roll-over and noise protection. The cab is fully air-conditioned, the first British Army construction equipment to be so equipped. Other equipment includes a Ripco 3-tine ripper on a parallelogram mounting and a Hyster model 12E winch.

SPECIFICATIONS (TEREX 82-30 FAM)
Weight: (with blade) 25 227 kg
Length: 6·274 m
Width: 3·376 m
Height: (less exhaust stack) 2·432 m
Ground clearance: (minimum) 0·4445 m
Fording: 1·524 m
Track centre distance: 1·981 m
Track width: 559 mm
Length of track on ground: 2·924 m

Engine: Detroit Diesel 2-cycle diesel developing 225 hp at 2100 rpm
Transmission: Allison full powershift CRT 5534 with 3 forward and 3 reverse speeds
Torque converter: Allison single stage integral with transmission
Steering: clutch and brake, single lever per track

STATUS
TEREX 82-30 production complete. In service with the US Marine Corps.
  TEREX 82-30B in production. In service with the British Army.

MANUFACTURERS
TEREX Corporation, 5405 Darrow Road, Hudson, Ohio 44236, USA.
  TEREX Limited, PO Box 27, Newhouse Industrial Estate, Motherwell, Lanarkshire ML1 5RY, Scotland.

TEREX 82-30B Heavy Crawler Tractor of Royal Engineers (T J Gander)

TEREX 82-30 FAM crawler tractor of US Marine Corps

TEREX 82-20/D700 Crawler Tractor

DESCRIPTION
The official designation for this crawler tractor is 'Tractor, Full-Tracked, Low Speed (Diesel-Engine-Driven) Size T9'. It is a commercial model that was procured during 1983 by the US Air Force with deliveries proceeding into 1984. All the machines are equipped with semi-U blades, reversible fans, cold-start equipment and 20-inch/508-mm track shoes. Attachments include winches and single-shank rippers, and some of the machines delivered are fitted with 22-inch/559-mm 'snow shoes' on the tracks.

The TEREX 82-20/D700 can be used for all general bulldozing tasks including road building, land clearance, push loading and snow ploughing.

SPECIFICATIONS
Weight: (with blade) 19 733 kg
Length: 5·612 m
Width: 3·645 m
Height: 3·327 m
Ground clearance: 0·432 m
Fording: (unprepared) 0·61 m
Track: 1·981 m
Length of track of ground: 2·718 m
Track width: (standard shoe) 508 mm
Engine: Detroit Diesel 2-cycle developing 205 fhp at 2100 rpm
Transmission: Allison full powershift CRT 5434 with 3 forward and 3 reverse gears

TEREX 82-20/D700 crawler tractor

STATUS
Production. In service with the US Air Force.

MANUFACTURER
TEREX Corporation, 5405 Darrow Road, Hudson, Ohio 44236, USA.

Clark Wheeled Loaders 175 Series

DESCRIPTION
The full designation of the latest Clark loader to enter US Army service is Loader, Scoop Type, Diesel Engine Driven (4 × 4), Articulated Frame Steer, 4½- to 5-cubic yard capacity 175B. Its 4½-cubic yard (3·44-cubic metre) bucket is used for rock and the 5-cubic yard (3·82-cubic metres) bucket for general purpose work. This loader is primarily used in excavating, digging, loading and stockpiling and for the transfer of a wide variety of material such as rock and earth used in the construction of roads, airfields and ports.

STATUS
A total of 240 loaders were procured, at a unit cost of $56 568 in fiscal year 1974 (115 loaders) and fiscal year 1975 (125). The US Army has also been supplied with the earlier 85A series and 175A series loaders. Other users of Clark wheeled loaders include the British Army (75DS, 175DS and 285B), the Danish Army (65AWS), the French Army (model 125), and the Spanish Army (model 75).

MANUFACTURER
Clark Equipment Company, PO Box 547, Benton Harbor, Michigan 49022, USA.

Clark 175A-M25 wheeled loader (Larry Provo)

Clark 175B wheeled loader (US Army)

SPECIFICATIONS

Model	175B	175A-M (1·91 m³)	Model	175B	175A-M (1·91 m³)
Configuration	4 × 4	4 × 4	Engine	GM 8V-71N diesel developing 304 hp at 2100 rpm	Cummins JT-6-B1 diesel
Weight	21 233 kg (5 yd³ bucket)	12 587 kg	Transmission	Countershaft type power-shift with 4 forward and reverse speeds	Rockwell
Length	7·92 m	6·48 m			
Height	3·55 m	2·36 m			
Width	2·97 m	2·56 m	Max speed (road)	35 km/h	n/a
Ground clearance	0·51 m	n/a	Tyres	26.5 × 25	16.00 × 24
Breakout force	15 422 kg	n/a			

Crane, Truck-mounted, Hydraulic, 25-ton (CCE) (Grove TMS 300-5)

DESCRIPTION

The Grove TMS 300-5 25-ton crane is a commercial truck-mounted crane. It consists of a hydraulically-operated telescopic crane with a full 360 degree traverse mounted on an eight-wheeled carrier. The operator controls the crane from an electric control panel in the superstructure cab. Four outriggers are used to stabilise the crane in operation. The crane is used by Engineer units in the construction and repair of roads, airfields, pipelines and bridges, and can also be used for port, marine and beach facilities. In addition to lifting, it can also be used for pile-driving and clamshell operation.

SPECIFICATIONS

Weight: 28 250 kg
Length: (travelling) 12·8 m
Width: (travelling) 2·44 m

Crane

Boom length: 2-section hydraulically-extended boom with third lattice section, giving total length of 24·4 m
Counterweight: 4310 kg
Capacity: (max) 25 400 kg

Carrier

Configuration: 8 × 4, front 2 axles steering
Engine: GM 6-71N diesel, developing 203 net hp at 2100 rpm
Transmission: Fuller Roadranger RTO 613, providing 13 forward and 3 reverse gears
Tyres:
  (front) 11.00 × 14-ply
  (rear) 11.00 × 12-ply

STATUS

133 in service with the United States Army under the Commercial Construction Equipment (CCE) program. In production.

Grove TMS 300-5 crane in US Army service, showing lattice extension being swung into position

MANUFACTURER

Grove International Corporation, Box 21, Shady Grove, Pennsylvania 17256, USA.

Model M315T 15-ton capacity truck-mounted crane (US Marine Corps)

Harnischfeger MT-250 25-ton truck-mounted hydraulic crane (US Army)

Grove Mobile Hydraulic Cranes

DESCRIPTION

The Grove International Corporation produces a wide range of mobile hydraulic cranes for military and commercial purposes. Most of the military models are basically commercial ones converted for military use. The largest model in the range is the massive TM2500 with a 250-ton capacity but, even though this model is the world's largest mobile hydraulic crane, it is not yet produced for a military customer. The largest military model produced by Grove is the TM1400 with a 140-ton capacity, and the range of military mobile cranes extends down to a 7½-ton industrial crane. All the models are wheeled and use hydraulic extending booms, some with swingaway extensions.

STATUS

Not all the models quoted remain in production but all are in service with the US forces (as quoted) and with other armed forces.

MANUFACTURER

Grove International Corporation, Box 21, Shady Grove, Pennsylvania 17256, USA.

Groves RT41AA 4-ton rough terrain crane used by US Army for helicopter maintenance

Groves TM1400 140-ton mobile hydraulic crane

Groves RT980 80-ton rough terrain crane

Groves RT518 18-ton rough terrain crane

Groves RT58B 15-ton rough terrain crane as produced for Egyptian Air Force

SPECIFICATIONS

Model	Capacity	Jib length	Number of jib sections	Extension length	Engine	Tyres	Number of tyres	Users
TM1400	140 tons	13·71–52·73 m	4	9·754 m	GM 8V-92T diesel	14.00 × 20	18	US Army corps of Engineers (2)
RT980	80 tons	10·97–44·5 m	4	9·754 m	GM 6-71T diesel	33.25 × 35-32	4	US Air Force (2) US Army Engineers (2)
TM875	80 tons	10·97–44·5 m	4	9·754 m	Cat 3406T diesel	14.00 × 20	12	US Navy (5)
TM865	65 tons	10·97–44·5 m	4	9·754 m	GM 6-71T diesel	18.00 × 22.5	8	US Navy (3)
RT755	55 tons	10·36–35·357 m	3	9·754 m	GM 6V-53N diesel	29.5 × 25-22 PR	4	US Air Force (6)
TMS300-5	25 tons	10·06–34·14 m	3	9·754 m	GM 6-71N diesel	11.00 × 20	12	US Army (133)
TMS300	35 tons	10·06–34·14 m	3	9·754 m	GM 6-71N diesel	12.00 × 20	12	US Navy (10)
TMS250A	25 tons	9·754–32·3 m	4	7·925 m	Cummins VT225 diesel	9.00 × 20	10	US Marine Corps (2)
RT625	25 tons	9·754–32·3 m	3	7·925 m	GM 4-53T diesel	23.5 × 25	4	US Army Engineers (10)
RT518	18 tons	7·62–18·23 m	3	–	GM 4-53N diesel	16.00 × 25-20 PR	4	US Army Engineers (1)
RT515	15 tons	7·315–12·8 m	2	–	GM 4-53N diesel	14.00 × 24-20 PR	4	US Army (2)
RT58B	15 tons	7·315–12·8 m	2	–	Deutz F6L912 diesel	14.00 × 24-20 PR	4	Egyptian Air Force (16)
RT48MC	7·5 tons	6·7–12·192 m	2	–	GM 4-53N diesel	n/a	4	US Marine Corps (200)
IND.36	7·5 tons	4·267–19·144 m	3	–	GM 3-53N diesel	10.00 × 20-12 PR	6	US Navy (4)
IND.36	7·5 tons	5·49–12·8 m	3	–	GM 3-53N diesel	10.00 × 20-12 PR	6	US Army Engineers (12)
RT41AA	4 tons	5·8–10·1 m	2	–	D3400 diesel	9.00 × 20-8 PR	4	US Army (174)

Distributor, Bituminous, Truck-mounted 1500-gallon (CCE)

DESCRIPTION
This distributor is used to transport and spread bituminous materials in the construction and repair of roads, airfields, ports and marine POL facilities. The tank has a capacity of 5677 litres and the 750 000 BTU heater will run on fuel oil, paraffin or diesel fuel. The complete system is mounted on a standard M809 series (6 × 6) truck chassis manufactured by the AM General Corporation.

SPECIFICATIONS
Weight: (shipping) 11 022 kg
Length: 8·58 m
Width: 2·49 m
Height: 2·9 m
(other specification is same as for M809 series 6 × 6 truck)

STATUS
A total of 150 units (at a unit cost of $41 700) were procured between fiscal year 1972 and 1976 (30 per year).

1500-gallon bituminous distributor, mounted on M809 (6 × 6) truck chassis (US Army)

MANUFACTURER
E D Etnyre and Company, 200 Jefferson Street, Oregon, Illinois 61061, USA.

Caterpillar Model 130G Motor Grader

DESCRIPTION
This motor grader is a commercial design that has been modified to meet US Army requirements and is now capable of being sectionalised for helicopter transport or even for dropping by parachute from transport aircraft. The rear engine unit and the two main drive axles with their wheels form one main section while the other includes the forward section containing the blade frame and the forward axle. The ROPS can be removed. This sectional version is known as the Type 2 but there is also a version that cannot be sectionalised known as the Model 130G Type 1. When assembled the two versions are identical but the Type 2 is slightly heavier.

STATUS
Production. In service with Australia (42) and the US Army.

MANUFACTURER
Caterpillar Tractor Company, Defense Products Department, Peoria, Illinois 61629, USA.

SPECIFICATIONS (Type 2)
Weight:
(normal operating) 14 456 kg
(air transport w/o ROPS) 13 710 kg
(airdrop) 13 810 kg
(front section) 7248 kg
(rear section) 6538·5 kg

Length: 8·412 m
Height: (reduced) 2·31 m
Width: 2·426 m
Ground clearance: 0·33 m
Wheelbase: 5·918 m
Track: 2·013 m
Max speed: 39 km/h
Engine: Model 3304 T 4-stroke 4-cylinder diesel developing 135 hp at 2200 rpm
Transmission: direct drive powershift with 6 forward and 6 reverse gears
Steering: hydraulic power-assisted
Turning radius: 7·315 m
Tyres: 13.00 × 24, 10 PR
Electrical system: 24 V

Earth-moving Scraper

DESCRIPTION

This hydraulic all steel scraper is used for a variety of levelling purposes in the construction of airfields, roads and other projects. The scraper was developed from 1963 and manufactured by LeTourneau-Westinghouse and the Euclid Division of the General Motors Corporation. It is towed by Caterpillar 830M and Clark 290M wheeled tractors and Caterpillar D-7 and D-8, Allis-Chalmers HD-16 tracked tractors.

The scraper is also towed by the Westinghouse CT-4 (4 × 4) tractor, the complete unit being known as the M280.

SPECIFICATIONS

Weight: 14 062 kg
Length: 9·35 m
Width: 3·12 m
Height: (blade down) 2·66 m
Capacity:
   (struck) 14·45 m³
   (heaped) 18·35 m³
Bowl:
   (length) 3·81 m
   (width) 3·05 m
   (height) 2·44 m
Cutting edge width: 3·05 m
Digging depth: 0·38 m
Max depth of spread: 0·41 m

STATUS

In service with the US Army.

Earth-moving scraper being transported on railway flatcar (US Army)

MANUFACTURERS

LeTourneau-Westinghouse, Peoria, Illinois, USA.
  TEREX Corporation, 5405 Darrow Road, Hudson, Ohio 44236, USA.

Grader, Road, Motorised, Diesel Driven, Heavy

DESCRIPTION

The United States Army uses three main heavy motorised graders: the Caterpillar model 12, Huber-Warco model 4D and the LeTourneau-Westinghouse model 440HA.

SPECIFICATIONS

Weight: 11 794 kg
Length: 8·152 m
Length of mouldboard: 3·657 m
Width: 2·387 m
Height: 2·321 m
Fuel capacity: 227 litres
Fuel consumption: 21 litres/h
Tyres: 13.00 × 24
Brakes: hydraulic

STATUS

In service with the US Army. Other graders in US Army service include the Austin-Western 99-H, Caterpillar DV28, 112, 120, Galion 118, GM 4057, Huber F1500M, Huber-Warco DW, LeTourneau-Westinghouse 220 and

Grader, Road, Motorised, Diesel Driven, Heavy (US Army)

WABCO 330HAD and 440HA. Over 130 Caterpillar 130G motor graders have been supplied to the US Marine Corps.

Roller, Pneumatic-tyred, Hyster C530A

DESCRIPTION

The full designation of this equipment is Roller, Pneumatic-tyred, Variable Pressure, Self-propelled. It is used for compacting macadam, black base, soil stabilisation, asphaltic concrete and base course during the construction of roads, airfields and ports.

This equipment is issued to Engineer Combat Support Equipment Companies of Construction Support battalions and to Engineer Companies of Heavy Engineer Combat Battalions.

SPECIFICATIONS

Weight:
   (shipping without ballast) 3629 kg
   (with ballast) 11 431 kg
Length: 4·445 m
Width: 1·73 m
Height: 1·98 m
Wheelbase: 2·235 m
Max speed: 27 km/h
Engine: GM250 petrol developing 83 hp at 2500 rpm
Transmission: forward/reverse powershift with 3-speed manual transmission for range selection
Turning circle radius: 4·51 m
Tyre size: 7.50 × 15
Number of tyres:
   (front) 4
   (rear) 5
   (tyre pressures can be adjusted while vehicle is moving or when stationary)
Electrical system: 12 V

Hyster pneumatic compactor C530A

STATUS

A total of 193 units were procured at a unit cost of $31 067, 103 in fiscal year 1975 and 90 in fiscal year 1977.

MANUFACTURER

Hyster Company, Construction Equipment Division, PO Box 289, Kewanee, Illinois 61443, USA.

John Deere 410 Backhoe Loader

DESCRIPTION

The John Deere 410 tractor loader, procured for the US Army under the CCE program as the Tractor, Wheeled, Diesel Engine Driven, Loader/Backhoe, is a commercial utility machine. Fitted with a hydraulic impact tool and a hydraulic earth auger attachment, it is capable of excavation, stockpiling, loading, backfilling, rock and concrete breaking, asphalt cutting, earth boring and post driving.

The normal scale of issue of the John Deere 410 is one to each company in division, corps and Heavy Engineer Battalions. In Europe this has been increased to two per company in some cases.

SPECIFICATIONS

Cab seating: 1
Configuration: 4 × 2
Weight: 6446 kg
Length: 7·25 m
Width: (without bucket) 2·14 m
Height: (to top of cab) 2·56 m
Ground clearance: 0·33 m
Wheelbase: 2·08 m
Max speed: (road) 26 km/h
Engine: John Deere 4-cylinder water-cooled 2·589-litre diesel developing 62 hp at 2500 rpm
Transmission: constant mesh, 8 forward and reverse speeds
Tyres:
(front) 11L × 16 or 7.50/8.00 × 16
(rear) 16.9/18.4/19.5/21L × 24

Loader:
General purpose bucket: 0·96 m³
Width: 2·27 m
Dump height: 3·28 m
Breakout force: 3402 kg
Lifting capacity to full height: 2268 kg

Backhoe:
Segmented: (2-in-1) jaw
Opening width: 1·07 m
Clamping force: 2087 kg
Capacity: 0·21 m³
Auger capacity: 250 mm hole to depth of 1·83 m

STATUS

Production complete. A total of 589 loaders has been supplied to the US Army.

MANUFACTURER

Deere & Company, John Deere Road, Moline, Illinois 61265, USA.

John Deere 410 backhoe loader (US Army)

John Deere Motor Graders

DESCRIPTION

Several models of John Deere grader are in military service but most are unmodified commercial models. They feature articulated frame steering, powershift transmission, all-hydraulic control, leaning front wheels and cab incorporating roll-over protective structure (ROPS).

SPECIFICATIONS (JD 570A, typical)
Weight: 9174 kg
(on front axle) 2597 kg
(on rear bogie) 6577 kg
Length: (without scarifier) 7·43 m
Height: (with cab) 3·2 m
Width: (depending on tyre size) 2·39–2·53 m

Wheelbase: (front axle to bogie centre; bogie 1·44 m) 5·28 m
Track:
(front) 2 m (13.00 × 24 tyres); 2·07 m (15.1 × 25 tyres)
(rear) 2·06 m (13.00 × 24 tyres); 2·13 m (15.5 × 25 tyres)
Engine: John Deere 6-cylinder water-cooled turbo-charged diesel developing 85 net hp at 2300 rpm
Transmission: powershift, 8 forward and 4 reverse speeds
Fuel capacity: 189 litres
Tyres: 13.00 × 24; 8 or 10 PR, or 15.5 × 25, 8 PR
Turning radius: 5·49 m
Blade:
(length) 3·66 m
(height) 0·56 m

Scarifier: front-mounted, V-type cut to 1·17 m
Number of teeth: 5–9
Max speed: (road) 35 km/h

STATUS

The John Deere 570 and 570A are in service with the US Air Force and Navy.

The John Deere 670A motor grader is in service with the US Navy and Air Force.

The John Deere 770A is in service with the US Army and Marine Corps.

MANUFACTURER

Deere & Company, John Deere Road, Moline, Illinois 61265, USA.

John Deere 570 motor grader in US Navy service

John Deere 670A motor grader in service with the US Navy and Air Force

John Deere 450C Tractor Series

DESCRIPTION

The 450C series of tractors can be fitted with a variety of front- and rear-mounted attachments, including a bulldozer blade, four-in-one bucket, loader bucket, winch and scarifier. It features a single lever control for loader and bulldozer functions, hydraulic track adjustment, sealed track rollers, idlers and links, and self-adjusting, oil-cooled steering clutches and brakes.

STATUS

In production. The 450C is in service with the Australian Army (59) in both bulldozer and loader versions. The bulldozer is in service with the US Navy and Air Force.

MANUFACTURER

Deere & Company, John Deere Road, Moline, Illinois 61265, USA.

SPECIFICATIONS

(For bulldozer; data in square brackets relate to loader where different)
Weight: 6455 [7582] kg
Length: 3·61 [4·17] m
Width: (approx) 2·1 m
Height: (over ROPS canopy) 2·43 m
Ground contact length: 1·85 m
Track width: 400 [360] mm
Ground pressure: 0·43 [0·55] kg/cm²
Engine: John Deere 4-cylinder turbo-charged water-cooled diesel developing 65 net hp at 2500 rpm
Transmission: powershift, hi-lo-reverse, with 4 speed ranges
Fuel capacity: 117 litres

Australian Army John Deere 450C bulldozer (P Handel)

Max speed: (road) 10 km/h
Max drawbar pull: 8188 kg
Breakout force: [6513 kg]

Blade:
(width) 2·29 m
(height) 0·95 m

M-R-S 8 Cubic Yard Towed Scraper

DESCRIPTION

The M-R-S MS100 (M-64) earthmoving scraper is a hydraulically-operated, four-wheel, towed unit capable of loading, hauling, dumping and spreading up to 10·5 cubic yards (8 cubic metres) of earth. It consists essentially of a body with apron and ejector, a frame, a rear bogie and a front axle and tongue assembly. It is equipped with a traction mast so that it may be used to advantage with the weight transfer device incorporated on M-R-S tractors such as the Model 100, with which this scraper is intended to be used. The Model MS100 scraper can be sectionalised for air transport. It is similar to the Scraper, Earthmoving, Towed, Model H-82 (M-62).

SPECIFICATIONS

Weight: 7484 kg
Length: 9·6 m
Width: 2·79 m
Height: 2·67 m
Wheelbase: 5·59 m
Track:
(front) 1·75 m
(rear) 2·13 m
Capacity:
(struck) 6·1 m³
(heaped) 8 m³

M-R-S MS100 (M-64) towed scraper

Cutting width: 2·67 m
Ground clearance: 0·33 m
Max depth of cut: 0·25 m
Max depth of spread: 0·33 m
Apron opening: 1·52 m
Type of ejection: forced roll-out
Tyres: 20.5 × 25, 12 PR, low pressure
Brakes: air actuated, controlled from towing tractor

STATUS

The Model MS100 (M-64) Scraper was adopted by the US Marine Corps as standard for use with the Model 100 (4 × 4) MC tractor in March 1965.

MANUFACTURER

M-R-S Manufacturing Company, PO Box 199, Flora, Mississippi 39071, USA.

Murray AR-775 Series Earthmoving Scraper

DESCRIPTION

This scraper, designated Scraper, Earthmoving, Towed, was manufactured by Murray and is in service in two versions. The model AR-775 is of the trailer type and has four wheels while the AR-775M is of the semi-trailer type and has two wheels. They are both towed by light wheeled or crawler tractors, and are hydraulically operated. Both are airportable.

SPECIFICATIONS

Weight: (empty) 5307 kg
Length: 8·48 m
Width: 2·84 m
Height: 2·06 m

Tyres: 16.00 × 21
Brakes: air
Capacity:
(struck) 5·73 m³
(heaped) 6·88 m³
Cutting edge width: 2·11 m

STATUS

In service with the US Army.

Roller, Vibratory, Self-propelled (Tampo RS28)

DESCRIPTION

The self-propelled vibratory roller is designed to compact granular soils, base course material and, with required options, asphaltic material.

The unit is a single smooth vibrating drum roller propelled by a pneumatic-tyred diesel engined hydrostatically driven tractor. The roller can compact in both directions at speeds of up to 24 km/h.

The drum vibrator hydrostatic drive produces a frequency range from 1100 to 1800 vibrations per minute, independent of engine speed. Hydrodynamic braking enables the operator to stop the drum vibrations immediately.

STATUS

In service. Procured by the US Army for rear area operations under MERADCOM's CCE program.

MANUFACTURERS

Initial procurement – Tampo Manufacturing Co Inc, PO Box 7248, San Antonio, Texas 78285, USA.
Second procurement – Rexnord, Inc.

Roller, Vibratory, Self-propelled (Tampo RS28)
(US Army)

Rough Terrain Crane (4 × 4) 5-ton Hanson H-446A

DESCRIPTION
This rough terrain crane was developed to meet the requirements of the US Army by the Hanson Company of Tiffin, Ohio. The telescopic jib has a maximum reach of 7·62 metres and can be rotated through a full 360 degrees. A folding stabiliser leg is provided at each corner of the vehicle and most models have a bulldozer blade mounted at the front of the hull. The fully enclosed cab is at the front of the vehicle with the engine at the rear. Gross vehicle weight is 16 647 kg.

STATUS
In service with the US Army.

MANUFACTURER
Hanson Machinery Company, Tiffin, Ohio, USA.

Hanson rough terrain crane (4 × 4) 5-ton (Larry Provo)

Rough Terrain Crane, 20-ton, Air-transportable, American Hoist and Derrick 2380, 2385

DEVELOPMENT
The rough terrain crane was developed in 1965 by the United States Army Mobility Command Engineer Research and Development Laboratories at Fort Belvoir and production was undertaken by the American Hoist and Derrick Company, P & H and Harnischfeger.

DESCRIPTION
The crane is designed for dragline and clamshell operations, bridge assembly, pile driving, limited bulldozing and other duties, and is capable of operating in water up to 1·22 metres deep.

The crane has a boom 9·14 metres long which can lift a maximum load of 18 144 kg at 3·05 metres radius. If required the boom can be extended to 18·29 metres. A bulldozer blade is mounted at the front of the vehicle and two stabilisers can be lowered either side of the vehicle if required.

The vehicle has both four-wheel drive and four-wheeled powered steering. The driver can select one of three modes of steering: two-wheel (front) for normal road travel, four-wheel (cramp) for close manoeuvring or four-wheel (oblique) for moving close to the sides of walls, landing craft etc.

SPECIFICATIONS
Cab seating: 1
Configuration: 4 × 4
Weight:
(with boom) 27 896 kg
(without boom) 25 642 kg
Length:
(with boom) 13·21 m
(without boom) 8·43 m

Rough terrain crane with boom split in half to reduce overall length for road transport (Larry Provo)

Width: 3·23 m
Height: 3·86 m
Max speed: (road) 50 km/h
Fuel capacity:
(for vehicle) 416 litres
(for crane) 189 litres
Fording: 1·22 m
Engine:
(vehicle) Cummins V8-265 8-cylinder diesel developing 265 hp
(crane) Cummins JN6 6-cylinder diesel developing 98 hp at 3400 rpm

Tyres: 26.5 × 25
Brakes: air

STATUS
Production complete. In service with the US Army.

MANUFACTURERS
American Hoist and Derrick Company, 63 South Robert Street, St Paul, Minnesota 55107, USA.
Harnischfeger Corporation, P & H, Milwaukee, USA.

Scraper, Earth-moving, Towed, Hydraulic, 18 Cubic Yard Euclid 58SH-G; LeTourneau-Westinghouse (Wabco) CT-4

DESCRIPTION
This two-wheeled scraper was designed by the US Army in 1963 and built to its specifications by two manufacturers. It is used for a variety of levelling purposes in such tasks as the construction of airfields and roads. The scraper may be towed by wheeled tractors, such as the Caterpillar 830MB (see following entry) and the Clark 290M, with which it is designated the M280. When towed by tracked tractors such as the Caterpillar D-7, D-8 and Allis-Chalmers HD-16, the Euclid 9DY-G two-wheeled dolly is used.

SPECIFICATIONS
Weight: 14 062 kg
Length: 9·35 m
Width: 3·14 m
Height: (blade down) 2·66 m
Capacity:
(stuck) 14·45 m³
(heaped) 19·11 m³

M280 scraper with Clark 290M tractor (US Army)

Bowl:
(length) 3·81 m
(width) 3·05 m
(height) 2·44 m
Cutting edge width: 3·05 m
Digging depth: 0·38 m
Max depth of spread: 0·41 m
Tyres: 29.5 × 29 (2)

STATUS
In service with the US Army.

MANUFACTURERS
TEREX Corporation, 5405 Darrow Road, Hudson, Ohio 44236, USA.
LeTourneau-Westinghouse, Peoria, Illinois, USA.

Tractor, Wheeled, Industrial, Diesel Engine Driven, Medium Drawbar Pull

DESCRIPTION
The medium drawbar wheeled tractor was manufactured by both Caterpillar (model 830MB) and Clark (model 290M) and was introduced in 1962. Both have identical characteristics and configuration. The engine is mounted at the front with the fully enclosed cab in the centre. The chassis articulates in the centre for steering and also has a frame oscillation of 20 degrees to allow for operation on uneven ground. A hydraulically-operated bulldozer blade is mounted at the front of the vehicle. These tractors are used for a wide variety of roles including towing an 18 cubic yard (13·7 cubic metre) scraper and other engineer plant.

SPECIFICATIONS (Caterpillar 830MB)
Configuration: 4 × 4
Weight: 24 040 kg
Drawbar pull: 17 690 kg
Length: 7·37 m
Width: 3·17 m
Height: 3·47 m
Wheelbase: 3·56 m
Engine: Caterpillar D343 6-cylinder turbo-charged water-cooled diesel developing 357 hp at 2000 rpm
Fuel capacity: 643 litres
Fuel consumption: 61 litres/100 km
Road speed:
  (max) 50 km/h
  (laden, in convoy) 40 km/h
Tyres: 29.5 × 29, 28 PR

Caterpillar 830MB wheeled tractor (US Army)

Steering: full articulating, 45° left and right, hydraulically powered
Turning radius: 6·1 m
Brakes: air over hydraulic
Fording depth: 0·92 m

STATUS
Both the Caterpillar 830MB and the Clark 290M are believed to be still in service with the US Army. The Caterpillar 830M was an earlier model with a slightly less powerful engine.

MANUFACTURER
Caterpillar Tractor Company, Defense Products Department, Peoria, Illinois 61629, USA.

Tractor, Wheeled, Industrial, Diesel Engine Driven (M-R-S Model 100 MC)

DESCRIPTION
The M-R-S Model 100 (4 × 4) MC was designed for general purpose use as a prime mover, for light dozing, winching, towing and in combination with a four-wheeled hydraulically-operated scraper of approximately 8 cubic yard (6·1 cubic metre) capacity. It has a rigid chassis with two- or four-wheel steering. A weight transfer device is incorporated to improve the steering performance of a towed scraper or trailer. The M-R-S MS100 M-64 8 cubic yard scraper was used with this tractor and has a separate entry in this section. The Model 100 can be sectionalised for transport by helicopter or small aircraft, but the otherwise similar Model 200 cannot.

STATUS
The Model 100 (4 × 4) MC was adopted as standard by the US Marine Corps in July 1964. A similar model was also used by the US Army.

MANUFACTURER
M-R-S Manufacturing Company, PO Box 199, Flora, Mississippi 39071, USA.

SPECIFICATIONS
Configuration: 4 × 4
Weight: 10 886 kg
Max tractive effort: 10 886 kg
Length: 5·69 m
Width: (over dozer blade) 2·74 m
Height: 3·12 m, reducible to 2·48 m
Wheelbase: 2·84 m

M-R-S Model 100 (4 × 4) MC tractor showing weight transfer mast at rear

Track: (front and rear) 2·23 m
Ground clearance: 0·42 m
Engine: Detroit Diesel Series 4.71 Model 4914 4-cylinder water-cooled 4·65-litre developing 143 hp at 2440 rpm
Transmission: Allison Torqmatic CRT-3331-1, 3 forward and reverse ranges
Fuel capacity: 242 litres

Max speed: (road) 46 km/h
Steering: hydraulic, 2- or 4-wheel
Turning radius: 5·49 m
Tyres: 20.5 × 25, 12 PR, low pressure
Winch:
  (model) Pacific Car & Foundry E-24
  (capacity) 8165–9072 kg
  (cable) 78 m of 19 mm cable

Truck, Dump, 20-ton (8 × 6) M917 (AM General Corporation)

Details of this vehicle, procured under the MACI program, may be found in the *Trucks* section under the M915 Series of Trucks entry.

Truck, Dump, 20-ton, Off-highway, 71 000 lb GVWR (International Harvester (F5070))

DESCRIPTION
While the M917 20-ton dump truck has been procured for use by Engineer units in forward areas, there is still a requirement for a less specialised vehicle of this capacity for rear areas. The International Harvester F5070 dump truck, procured under the CCE program is an off-highway type. It is used to transport materials used in the construction and repair of airfields, roads, ports, beach and marine POL facilities. It has a struck capacity of 9·18 cubic metres.

STATUS
A total of 889 of these vehicles has been procured at a unit cost of $17 000.

MANUFACTURER
International Harvester, Truck Division, 2827 Rupp Drive, Fort Wayne, Indiana 46805, USA.

SPECIFICATIONS
Configuration: 6 × 4
Weight:
  (shipping) 10 445 kg
  (laden) 32 200 kg
Length: 8·1 m
Width: 2·57 m
Height: 3·18 m
Wheelbase: 4·67 m
Max speed: 62 km/h
Max gradient: 40%
Engine: Cummins NTC 290 6-cylinder diesel
developing 285 hp at 2100 rpm
Transmission: Allison HT 750 CRD 5-speed automatic
transmission
Transfer box: 3-speed
Tyres:
  (front) 16.5 × 22.5
  (rear) 12.00 × 20
Electrical system: 12 V
Steering: power, hydraulic
Brakes: air
Payload: 18 144 kg
Capacity: (struck) 9·18 m³

International Harvester F5070 18-tonne dump truck
(US Army)

YUGOSLAVIA

Yugoslav Dump Trucks

DESCRIPTION
A wide variety of dump trucks based on standard
military cargo trucks is in use by the Yugoslav forces.
It is likely that newer models based on the new line of
trucks recently introduced will also have been adopted.
Details are given below of two typical dump trucks with
all-wheel drive.

STATUS
Believed to be in service. Other known all-wheel drive
models are the FAP 6 GAF-K, FAP 1313 SK, FAP 1314
SK, and TAM 5500 DK, all of which are 4 × 4.

MANUFACTURER
Yugoslav state factories.

Yugoslav FAP 6 GAF-KL 6·5-tonne (4 × 4) dump truck

SPECIFICATIONS

Model	FAP 4 GAE-K	FAP 6 GAF-KL	Model	FAP 4 GAE-K	FAP 6 GAF-KL
Configuration	4 × 4	4 × 4	Engine	FAP-E 4-cylinder water-cooled diesel developing 90 hp	FAP-F 6-cylinder water-cooled diesel developing 130 hp
Weight	5800 kg	6350 kg			
Length	6·77 m	7·54 m			
Width	2·2 m	2·35 m	Max speed	71 km/h	62 km/h
Height	2·55 m	2·63 m	Payload (road)	4500 kg	6500 kg
Wheelbase	4·2 m	4·6 m	Tyres	9.00 × 20	11.00 × 20
Track (front)	1·75 m	1·9 m			
(rear)	1·65 m	1·72 m			

T-100 and T-120S Wheeled Tractors

DESCRIPTION
The T-100 (Tagar) wheeled tractor has been designed
primarily for construction work while the more recent
T-120S is a universal tractor for military use. Both have
an engine at the front which overhangs the front wheels,
with the driver seated at the rear.

STATUS
Production. The T-120S is in service with the Yugoslav
Army.

MANUFACTURER
Yugoslav state factories.

SPECIFICATIONS (T-100)
Weight: 9700 kg
Length: 3·73 m
Width: 2·64 m
Height: 2·6 m
Max speed: (road) 23·6 km/h
Engine: Famos FA-100 6-cylinder water-cooled diesel
developing 100 hp

T-100 wheeled tractor

Demolition equipment

AUSTRIA

SMI Rapid Cratering Kits

DESCRIPTION

The SMI Rapid Cratering Kits are formed from a series of four types of hollow charge and three types of crater charge. To form a crater, in a road or runway, the hollow charges are stood on their legs over the spot to be cratered. The hollow charge is fired which blasts a small diameter but deep hole into the surface. Into this hole is placed the crater charge which, when fired, creates the full crater. The size of crater produced can be enlarged by increasing the number of crater charges fired.

The four hollow charges in the SMI range, the SMI 01/11C, 02/4C, 03/2C and the 08/1C all stand on detachable steel legs, with the three largest having three legs and the smallest, the SMI 08/1C, having four. The SMI 08/1C may be regarded as being a fox-hole charge only. The two largest crater charges, the SMI 12/20T and the SMI 11/14CA are cylindrical charges in plastic casings. In practice, the results achieved by the SMI 12/20T and the SMI 11/14CA are identical as the lighter SMI 11/14CA uses a more powerful explosive than the SMI 12/20T. The crater charge used with the fox-hole producing SMI 08/1C hollow charge is the crater charge SMI 13/28CA. This charge is placed in transparent plastic bags each weighing 14 kg. The charge itself is made up from small, egg-shaped pieces of explosive which are emptied from their plastic bag into the cavity produced by the explosive of the hollow charge. The ovoid shapes can then spread themselves into virtually every part of the cavity in a concentration dense enough to attain the maximum explosive effect. The crater charge SMI 13/28CA is completed by a tubular primary charge.

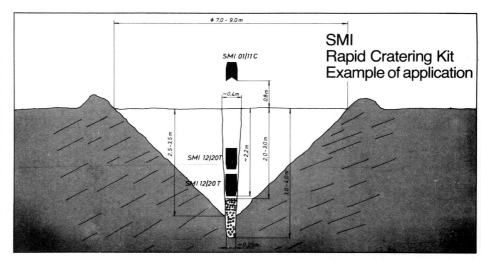

SMI Rapid Cratering Kit Example of application

Indication of effects of SMI 01/11C hollow charge and two SMI 12/20T crater charges

All SMI crater charges are provided with two firing circuits, one electrical and the other using conventional detonating cord.

Each hollow charge or crater charge is packed in a sealed PVC bag and packed in an olive drab seaworthy wooden case provided with carrying handles.

All the SMI cratering kits can also be used for the demolition of bunkers and building destruction, including bridges.

STATUS

All kits are in production.

MANUFACTURER

Südsteirische Metallindustrie GmbH, A-8430 Leibnitz, Austria.

SMI hollow charges, from left: 01/11C, 02/4C, 03/2C, 08/1C

SMI crater charges, from left: 12/20T 11/14CA 13/28CA

SPECIFICATIONS

Hollow charges

Model	01/11C	02/4C	03/2C	08/1C
Height	400 mm	300 mm	250 mm	190 mm
Diameter	215 mm	150 mm	110 mm	80 mm
Weight	16 kg	7 kg	3·5 kg	2 kg
Weight of explosive	11 kg	4·5 kg	2·3 kg	1 kg
Optimum charge distance	800 mm	600 mm	360 mm	200 mm

Crater charges

Model	11/14CA	12/20T	13/28CA
Height	450 mm	450 mm	–
Diameter	180 mm	215 mm	–
Weight	15 kg	21·5 kg	28 kg
Weight of explosive	14 kg	20 kg	28 kg

Penetration (all figures approximate)
Hollow charges

Model	01/11C	02/4C	03/2C	08/1C
Arable soil	3·5 m	3 m	2·5 m	1·8 m
Gravelly soil	3 m	2·5 m	2 m	1·5 m
Clay	3 m	2·5 m	2 m	1·5 m
Concrete	2 m	1·5 m	1·2 m	0·7 m
Steel	1 m	0·6 m	0·4 m	0·3 m

Blast hole diameter

Model	01/11C	02/4C	03/2C	08/1C
Soil	400 mm	300 mm	200 mm	150 mm
Concrete	200 mm	150 mm	100 mm	50 mm

Crater charges
Blasting steel-reinforced concrete road surface at a depth of 2·2 metres (figures approx)

Number of charges	2	1
SMI 11/14CA	28 kg	14 kg
SMI 12/20T	40 kg	20 kg
SMI 13/28CA	2 × 14 kg	14 kg
Crater diameter	8 m	6·5 m
Crater depth	3·5 m	2·5 m

Packing details
Hollow charges

Model	Number in case	Weight of case (approx)
SMI 01/11C	2	41 kg
SMI 02/4C	3	30 kg
SMI 03/2C	6	35 kg
SMI 08/1C	12	29 kg

Crater charges

Model	Number in case	Weight of case (approx)
SMI 11/14CA	2	40 kg
SMI 12/20T	2	51 kg
SMI 13/28CA	2 × bags	40 kg

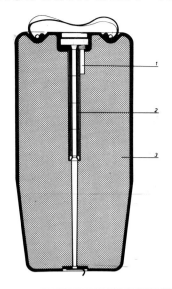

SMI Cratering Charge

DESCRIPTION

The SMI Crater charge is intended for the production of 'instant' tank traps or tank obstacles and will not normally be detonated until the approach of enemy armour. The charge consists of a cylinder of waterproof explosive enclosed in a plastic casing with a carrying strap at the top. The top has a central well for a detonating cord but if required there is provision for a secondary well to accommodate a detonator or an electrical fuze.

An earth drill with a diameter of 230 to 250 mm is used to bury the charge to an optimum depth of 1·5 metres. At this depth an exploded charge will form a crater 10 metres in diameter and 2·5 metres deep. As the charge is water-resistant it can be used underwater to form obstacles at fords or the approaches to streams and rivers.

The SMI crater charges are packed two to a wooden crate with six crates combined on a standard pallet.

STATUS
Production. In service with the Austrian Army.

MANUFACTURER
Südsteirische Metallidustrie GmbH, A-8430 Leibnitz, Austria.

SPECIFICATIONS
Weight: 21·5 kg
Weight of explosive: 20 kg
Length: 450 mm
Diameter: 215 mm

SMI crater charge: **(1)** *detonator well* **(2)** *main detonator charge* **(3)** *waterproof explosive charge*

SMI Cutting Charges

DESCRIPTION
SMI produces three special charges suitable for cutting pipes and other such structures. They are designated SMI 100, SMI 60 and SMI 45 with the numbers denoting the cutting capability in millimetres of the respective charge in steel. The largest charge rests on folding frame legs while the two smaller are fitted with side plate spacers.

STATUS
Production.

MANUFACTURER
Südsteirische Metallindustrie GmbH, A-8430 Leibnitz, Austria.

SMI 100 cutting charge

SMI 60 cutting charge

SMI 45 cutting charge

SMI Underwater Hollow Charges 09/2C and 10/4C

DESCRIPTION
The SMI Underwater Hollow Charges 09/2C and 10/4C may be used underwater to depths of up to 40 metres and charges for use at greater depths are available if required. The charges may be used on steel, concrete and other materials and are filled with what is described by SMI as a 'special explosive'. Both charges consist of a metal housing with a precision copper cone warhead placed at the correct working distance. The housing also has fittings for securing the charge to the target and an adaptor for the SMI time fuze. The time fuze may be set before diving and activated once the charge has been placed on the target. Ten time fuze settings are available with the lowest (0) being 7·5 minutes. Each setting doubles the previous time setting so that the highest (9) provides a time delay of 64 hours. The charges and fuzes are completely waterproof, and the charges can be supplied with either positive or negative buoyancy.

STATUS
Production.

MANUFACTURER
Südsteirische Metallindustrie GmbH, A-8430 Leibnitz, Austria.

SPECIFICATIONS

Model	09/2C	10/4C
Weight	5 kg	9 kg
Weight of explosive	2·3 kg	4·5 kg
Height	470 mm	640 mm
Diameter	110 mm	150 mm
Penetration depth		
(concrete)	1 m	1·3 m
(steel)	0·5 m	0·8 m

SMI underwater hollow charge 10/4C

Hirtenberger Hollow Charge HL-16/03

DESCRIPTION
The Hollow Charge HL-16/03 may be used for a number of demolition purposes ranging from the destruction of concrete structures to the preparation of road or runway surfaces for crater charges (e.g. the TL-30/02). The charge is held above its target by three folding legs that can be adjusted for height and levelling. The charge may be primed electrically or by a time delay detonating cord but in both cases the detonator is held in place above the charge by a rubber support.

An inert training version of the HL-16/03 is available.

SPECIFICATIONS
Weight: (complete) 16 kg
Weight of explosive: 12·3 kg
Charge:
　(height) 400 mm
　(diameter) 220 mm
Optimum charge distance: 800 mm
Diameter of crater: 200–300 mm

Penetration:
　(arable soil) 3–4 m
　(gravelly soil) 2–3 m
　(clay) 2·5–3·5 m
　(concrete) 2 m
　(steel) 1 m

STATUS
Production.

MANUFACTURER
Hirtenberger Patronen-, Zündhütchen-, und Metallwarenfabrik AG, A-2552 Hirtenberg, Austria.

Hirtenberger Crater Charge TL-30/02

DESCRIPTION
The Hirtenberger Crater Charge TL-30/02 may be used for creating craters as obstacles for vehicles or to rapidly produce weapon pits or foxholes. The full charge consists of a main charge comprising one or more bags of explosive pieces suspended from a wire, cord or chain that also carries the primary charge suspended underneath. The full charge is lowered into a hole formed by the detonation of a hollow charge (such as the HL-16/03) with the primary charge situated beneath the main charge. If the main charge is detonated 2·5 metres beneath a concrete roadway the resultant crater will have a diameter of approximately 8 metres and a depth of 3·5 metres. For maximum effect the charge should be stamped into place. A dual firing circuit is normally employed.

For training purposes, inert versions of the TL-30/02 are available. Two crater charges are packed in a waterproof wooden box weighing approximately 60 kg for storage and transport.

STATUS
Production.

MANUFACTURER
Hirtenberger Patronen-, Zündhütchen- und Metallwarenfabrik AG, A-2552 Hirtenberg, Austria.

SPECIFICATIONS
Charge weight: 27 kg
Primary charge weight: 1·5 kg
Charge length: 180 mm
Charge diameter: 80 mm

Hirtenberger Cutting Charge SL-12/01

DESCRIPTION
Intended for the demolition of large structures such as bridge pillars, the Hirtenberger SL-12/01 uses the hollow charge effect to produce results. Numbers of SL-12/01 may be combined to enhance their destructive effects and clamps on the main charge body enable charges to be closely linked together. Distance pieces below the charge are folded down into place before firing and numerous fixing devices such as wire, rails, plugs and power-driven studs can be employed to hold the charge in virtually any position; they can also be simply placed in position. Each charge is fitted with a priming channel cut through the main charge for linking with other charges, and detonation may be electrical or by using a detonating tape.

For storage and transport the SL-12/01 charges are packed two to a waterproof wooden case with a metal lining, each case weighing approximately 40 kg. Training versions of the SL-12/01 are available.

SPECIFICATIONS
Weight: 16 kg
Weight of charge: 10 kg
Charge length: 200 mm

Charge base width: 180 mm
Charge height: 260 mm
Optimum charge distance: 250 mm
Penetration: (approximate figures)
(steel) 200 mm
(concrete) 500 mm
Length of cut: 200 mm

STATUS
Production.

MANUFACTURER
Hirtenberger Patronen-, Zündhütchen-, und Metallwarenfabrik AG, A-2552 Hirtenberg, Austria.

Hirtenberger Explosive Device Demolition Charge ZL-100/01

DESCRIPTION
The Hirtenberger ZL-100/01 charge is intended for the demolition of unexploded ordnance devices such as mortar bombs or shells that are concealed underground or in inaccessible positions. The charge consists of a cylindrical explosive charge held on a flexible rod by a metal clip. In use the charge is pushed into a position near the device to be destroyed by using the rod to push or manoeuvre the charge into place. Ideally the charge should be placed near the unexploded device end on, and if the device is above ground tripods or base-plates may be used to ensure the charge is in the optimum position. If necessary the rod alone may be used to hold the charge in position.

ZL-100/01 charges are packed in 36 kg cases each holding 100 charges. Training versions are available.

STATUS
Production.

MANUFACTURER
Hirtenberger Patronen-, Zündhütchen- und Metallwarenfabrik AG, A-2552 Hirtenberg, Austria.

SPECIFICATIONS
Weight of charge: 180 g
Weight of explosive: 100 g
Length: 155 mm
Diameter: 40 mm
Penetration in steel: 120 mm approx
Diameter of channel hole: 5–10 mm

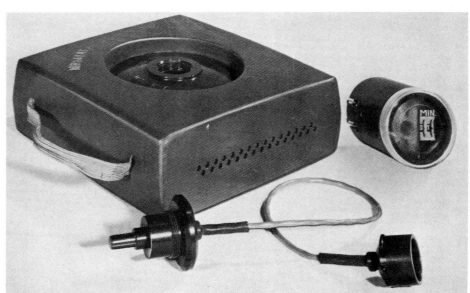

Hirtenberger ZL-100/01 charge in use on mortar bomb

BELGIUM

PRB Electronic Time-controlled Demolition Equipment

DESCRIPTION
The basis for the PRB range of electronically time-controlled demolition equipment is the PRB electronic firing device. This is a battery-powered device that can be connected to a number of demolition charges by various adapters and connectors. There are three versions of the timing device. One is the Type NR 2438 which is calibrated in minutes and can be preset for delays of from 1 to 99 minutes. The Type NR 2121 is pre-programmable in hours with steps of from 1 to 99 hours. The Type NR 2122 is programmable in one-day steps from 1 to 99 days.

The timing device is contained in a cylindrical plastic container with a clear plastic cover at one end and the connector plug at the other. Under the clear cover is a double tumbler switch, one switch showing units and the other the tens, both with the numbers luminescent for use in low-light conditions. Two lamps, one green and the other red, can be used to check the functioning of the device and the clear plastic cover also encloses the battery compartment snap-fit cover. In a body recess the device has a U-shaped locking key connected to a mechanical switch. This key is only removed when the device is in place and when lifted it removes the device's transport safety; when turned it initiates the timer. A variable extra safety delay may be incorporated to suit the user's needs; the delay may be 60, 120 or 180 seconds in addition to the pre-set timer delay. The timer is powered by two 3 volt lithium batteries with a shelf life of five years. When not in use they are removed from the timer.

The two indicator lamps act as operator assurance signals and come on only after the safety key has been turned. The green light will indicate that the timer is operating correctly and will remain lit as long as the safety delay lasts. The red lamp will only light when the timer has a fault, in which case it is preferable that the safety key is replaced. The red lamp can also be used to check the safety delay when the timer is being programmed.

The electronic delay timer is used with two types of demolition charge. The smallest is the PRB NR 416, a 360 gram block of trialene of which 15 grams constitutes the relay. The NR 416 is connected to the timer by an NR 2126 connector which is a lead 500 mm long. If required the timer may be connected directly to the NR 416 block by an NR 2124 electric activator. When using the connector an NR 2123 electric activator must be screwed into the NR 416 block. By connecting together extra NR 416 blocks by detonating tape virtually any size or form of demolition or 'necklace' charge can be formed.

The electronic timer can also be used with the PRB NR 141 or NR 141A1 mine to form a demolition charge or timed booby trap. In this case the timer is connected to the mine's centre well by an NR 2125 connector lead 500 mm long and an NR 2123 electric activator.

PRB electronic timer (right) with PRB NR 141 mine; NR 2125 connector in foreground

STATUS
Production.

MANUFACTURER
PRB SA, Departement Defense, avenue de Tervueren 168, B-1150 Brussels, Belgium.

SPECIFICATIONS (timer)
Weight:
  (with batteries) 245 g
  (without batteries) 225 g
Length: 102 mm
Diameter: 67 mm

CHILE

Cardoen Demolition Charges

DESCRIPTION
The Cardoen demolition charges are produced in three sizes, all of them square-section blocks of varying lengths. The No. 1 weighs 0·5 kg, the No. 2 1 kg and the No. 3, 1·5 kg. All three charges are Pentolyte blocks threaded at one end to take a standard cap or detonating cord. The thread can also accommodate a variety of push or pull detonating mechanisms (see following entry). Adhesive tape is supplied with the charges to secure them to their target or for coupling numbers of blocks together for greater effect.

STATUS
Production. In service with the Chilean armed forces.

MANUFACTURER
Industrias Cardoen S.A., Av. Providencia 2237, 6° Piso, Santiago, Chile.

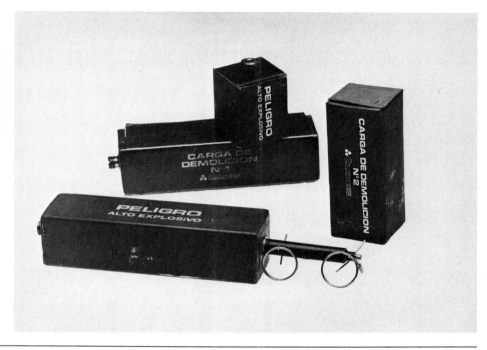

Cardoen demolition charges

Cardoen Pull and Pressure Firing Devices

DESCRIPTION
Cardoen produces two types of charge firing device to detonate demolition blocks or charges. One is a pull-type device that operates when a force of 4 to 6 kg is applied to a ring at one end of a cylinder containing a cocked spring. If a pull is applied the cocked spring is released allowing a hammer onto a pressure detonator. For safety purposes a spring clip is used to hold the cocked spring in place. The pressure device operates on the same principle but is operated by a pressure of between 5 and 10 kg. The pressure actuator may be held secure by a safety clip when required. Both types of firing device may be screwed directly into a demolition charge block if necessary.

The firing devices are packed in boxes of six with 36 boxes packed into a travelling crate weighing 26·2 kg.

STATUS
Production. In service with the Chilean armed forces.

MANUFACTURER
Industrias Cardoen S.A., Av. Providencia 2237, 6° Piso, Santiago, Chile.

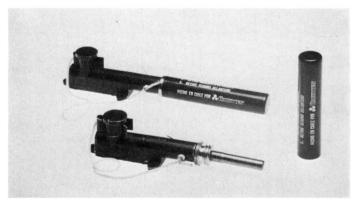

Cardoen pull-type firing device

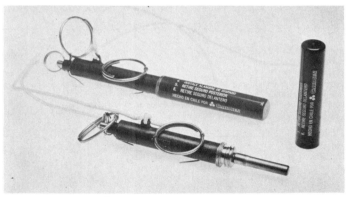

Cardoen pressure-type firing device

Cardoen/ERC 835 Encoder Unit

DESCRIPTION
The Cardoen/ERC 835 encoder unit is a device that allows demolition or other explosive charges to be detonated over long ranges. The encoder unit may be plugged into a standard infantry ERC 310/320 manpack radio using a flying 8-pin audio connector that also supplies dc voltage from the radio's internal batteries. Using the encoder, the radio operator can transmit a coded message to a small receiver connected to the demolition or explosive charge where the radio signal is de-coded to activate the charge detonator. Up to nine charges or channels can be handled by the encoder.

STATUS
Production complete. In service with the Chilean armed forces.

MANUFACTURER
Industrias Cardoen S.A., Av. Providencia 2237, 6° Piso, Santiago, Chile.

CZECHOSLOVAKIA

PN-4 and PN-14 Shaped Charges

DESCRIPTION
These two shaped charges are virtually identical in appearance but differ in weight and dimensions. Both are contained in metal housings and are equipped with tripod legs that fold for transport. A carrying handle is also fitted. The main charge is a 50/50 mixture of Tritol and Hexogen which is detonated by electrical or blasting cap means through a well at the top of the charge.

STATUS
Production status uncertain. In service with Czechoslovak armed forces and some other nations.

MANUFACTURER
Czechoslovak state arsenals.

SPECIFICATIONS

Model	PN-4	PN-14
Weight	6·4 kg	22 kg
Weight of explosive	4·8 kg	17 kg
Height (with tripod)	460 mm	750 mm
(without tripod)	340 mm	500 mm
Diameter	205 mm	320 mm
Penetration (armour)	500 mm	500 mm
(reinforced concrete)	1000 mm	1500 mm

PN-14 shaped charge

UTN-2 and UTN-600 Linear Shaped Charges

DESCRIPTION
These two shaped cutting charges are intended to create extended cuts in steel or concrete structures and although they differ in size and weight their appearance is similar. Both have a main charge formed from a 50/50 mixture of TNT and Hexogen with the fuze well located in the top centre with a built-in booster charge. Extra charges may be used in line to create longer cuts. The charge bodies have various built-in wire loops to assist in the securing of the charges to their targets.

SPECIFICATIONS

Model	UTN-2	UTN-600
Weight	2·8 kg	1·45 kg
Weight of explosive	1·96 kg	0·54 kg
Length	200 mm	100 mm
Width	110 mm	80 mm
Height	120 mm	95 mm
Penetration (steel)	75 mm	50 mm

STATUS
Production status uncertain. In service with Czechoslovak armed forces and some other nations.

MANUFACTURER
Czechoslovak state arsenals.

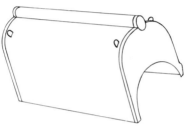

UTN-600 linear shaped cutting charge

WP4 Detonating Cord

DESCRIPTION
Although this detonating cord was first produced for commercial purposes, WP4 was adopted by the Czechoslovak Army and has since been exported to several other armed forces. It was considered, when first introduced, to be of an advanced form and still has some attractive properties in a field where few innovations occur. WP4 uses a core of Pentrite covered by several layers of woven fabric with an outer cover of thermoplastic that is both elastic and waterproof. The coverings for the core ensure that the cord remains water resistant for up to 48 hours and the cord has high tensile strength and is resistant to mechanical damage. The normal colour of WP4 is olive green and it is issued in 50-metre rolls. It has a diameter of 5·3 mm and an explosive weight of 12 grams per metre. The detonating velocity is 6700 metres/second.

STATUS
Production. In service with the Czechoslovak Army and some other armed forces.

MANUFACTURER
Czechoslovak state arsenals.

No.8 Blasting Caps

DESCRIPTION
Czechoslovak blasting caps are produced and used in both electrical and non-electric form. There are three types of non-electric cap still in service, all of which have a Tetryl charge but differ in body material which may be copper, aluminium or steel. These caps are 42 mm long and have a diameter of 7 mm. The electrical caps are 66 mm long with a diameter of 7 mm and also have a filling of Tetryl. They have connector leads 1·5 metres long.

Both types are issued in various quantities from cartons of 10 000 down to 100.

STATUS
Production. In service with Czechoslovak armed forces and probably other armed forces.

MANUFACTURER
Czechoslovak state arsenals.

DEOS 25 and DEOS 50 Blasting Machines

DESCRIPTION
These two blasting machines are hand-operated, low-tension electric generators. Both are contained in oval cases which house a steel magnet, an armature and a gear assembly. A shaft projecting from the gear assembly is rotated by a T-shaped wooden handle which acts as a hand crank and is inserted through a hexagonal nut in the top cover. Internally there are two terminals opposite the nut which when connected provide the machine power output. The DEOS 25, which weighs 3·18 kg, can fire up to 25 electrical caps wired in series while the DEOS 50, which weighs 5·2 kg, can fire up to 50.

STATUS
Production status uncertain. In service with the Czechoslovak Army.

MANUFACTURER
Czechoslovak state factories.

FRANCE

SAE Alsetex Cutting Charges

DESCRIPTION
The SAE Alsetex cutting charges are a new range designed to replace existing equivalents in French Army service. There are three versions, known for general reference purposes as Models 1, 2 and 3. Model 1 is a triangular shaped charge on a metal frame. A cap well at one end protrudes as at the other side the cap well is a hole into which the next charge can be connected. If required the extra charges can be connected by detonator cord in lengths of up to 20 metres.

Model 2 resembles a small bar charge but is a shaped charge 300 mm long held at its optimum working distance by four spiked feet. These legs fold for transport and are clicked down into place prior to use.

Model 3 is an extended bar charge which is intended to be used as one of an extended line of charges. At each end clip and spring attachment points are situated to enable the charges to be connected rapidly. Pressed flat metal feet act as working distance spacers and stabilisers. A channel through each charge connects the firing train to the next charge.

All three charges can cut through up to 250 mm of concrete. Against steel they can penetrate up to 70 mm of a welded steel structure. Against armoured steel the cutting depth is about 40 mm. All three charges produce only localised cutting effects with a minimum of other local damage.

Alsetex cutting charges: top left Model 1, top right Model 2 and below model 3

SPECIFICATIONS

Model	Model 1	Model 2	Model 3
Weight	1 kg	1·2 kg	1·3 kg
Weight of explosive	0·5 kg	0·6 kg	0·6 kg
Length	260 mm	300 mm	600 mm
Width	120 mm	50 mm	120 mm
Height	150 mm	120 mm	70 mm

STATUS
Model 1 undergoing pre-production testing. Models 2 and 3 still under development.

MANUFACTURER
Société d'Armament et d'Etudes Alsetex (SAE Alsetex), 4 rue de Castellane, 75008 Paris, France.

Alsetex Model F1 Heavy and Medium Shaped Charges

DESCRIPTION
These two shaped charges are virtually identical in general appearance but differ in size and weight. They both have their main charge housed in a light metal casing with the charge being Hexolite in both cases. Both have metal tripods to provide some form of stability with spiked feet. The intended firing method is by electrical detonator but forms of delayed action device may be used.

Smoke-emitting training versions are available.

STATUS
Production. In service with the French Army.

MANUFACTURER
Société d'Armement et d'Etudes Alsetex (SAE Alsetex), 4 rue de Castellane, 75008 Paris, France.

SPECIFICATIONS

Type	Heavy	Medium
Weight (approx)	13 kg	2·5 kg
Weight of explosive (approx)	8 kg	1·4 kg
Height with base	620 mm	385 mm
Diameter (max)	220 mm	150 mm

Performance		
Steel penetration	500 mm	300 mm
Steel penetration hole diameter	30 mm	10 mm
Concrete	2·5 m	1·5 m

Alsetex Model F1 Heavy (A) and Medium (B) shaped charges

Alsetex Crater Charge

DESCRIPTION
Intended to be fired singly or in groups, the Alsetex crater charge is used for the rapid production of tank traps and ditches. As with other such crater charges it consists of a shaped hole-cutting charge and a quantity of crater-producing explosive. The shaped charge for the Alsetex system is held suspended from the head of an adjustable tripod. This tripod uses telescopic metal tube legs which can be adjusted to produce the correct angle and optimum working height. Once fired the resultant hole has a diameter of between 200 and 250 mm and a depth of from 2·5 to 3 metres. Into this hole is poured the cratering charge which is made up from Hexal explosive pieces, each some 30 mm in diameter and encased in thin aluminium foil. This cratering charge is issued in plastic bags each containing 5, 10 or 20 kg of explosive and a single bore hole can be packed with up to 50 kg of explosive pieces. Alternatively the explosive may be supplied in waterproof plastic containers each holding 12·5 kg of HEXAL. Four such containers are used to form a full-size crater. Three such craters, by firing three shaped charges at intervals of 2·5 metres, will produce a final anti-tank ditch 15 metres long, 10 metres across and 3 metres deep.

Alsetex crater charge system with shaped charge on tripod (centre) and crater-producing main charges in plastic cases

SPECIFICATIONS
Shaped charge
Weight: 11 kg
Weight of explosive: 6·9 kg
Charge height: 490 mm
Charge diameter: 175 mm

Tripod
Height limits: 0·6 to 1 m
Maximum charge angle limits: 30°

STATUS
Pre-production development.

MANUFACTURER
Societe d'Armement et d'Etudes Alsetex (SAE Alsetex),
4 rue de Castellane, 75008 Paris, France.

Alsetex Demolition Charges

DESCRIPTION
Alsetex produces a range of demolition blocks ranging from 250 grams up to a massive 50 kg cylinder. These blocks may be produced with or without a coating of glass-fibre and may be fitted with one, two or three cap wells according to size. A 5 kg block can be used as an improvised land mine while the 50 kg block can be used in groups of up to ten for large-scale demolitions.

SPECIFICATIONS

Weight	250 g	500 g	1 kg	5 kg
Length	152 mm	115 mm	230 mm	245 mm
Width	47 mm	70 mm	70 mm	170 mm
Thickness	37 mm	45 mm	45 mm	85 mm

50 kg block

Weight	50 kg
Diameter	460 mm
Height	300 mm

STATUS
Production. In service with the French Army.

MANUFACTURER
Societe d'Armement et d'Etudes Alsetex (SAE Alsetex),
4 rue de Castellane, 75008 Paris, France.

Alsetex demolition charges

GIAT Model ASS 1 kg Demolition Block

DESCRIPTION
The Model ASS demolition block (*petard*) is designed to replace the Mod 1950 block in French Army service. It is a 980 gram charge of cyclotol wrapped in a protective insulating case, rectangular in shape and with an angled filling port bung at one corner. The insulating case is stated to be proof against fire, corrosive agents, ageing, drop shock and vibration.

SPECIFICATIONS
Weight: 1·1 kg
Weight of explosive: 0·98 kg
Length: 230 mm
Width: 70 mm
Thickness: 45 mm

STATUS
Under trial by the French Army.

MANUFACTURER
Atelier de Chargement de Salbris.

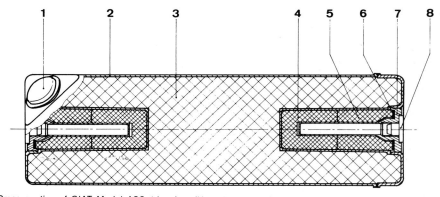

Cross section of GIAT Model ASS 1 kg demolition charge: (1) *filling port bung* (2) *insulating plastic coating* (3) *cyclotol charge* (4) *lower detonator booster* (5) *upper detonator booster* (6) *seating washer* (7) *priming cell* (8) *primer cap*

Enquiries to Groupement Industriel des Armements Terrestres (GIAT), 10 place Georges Clémenceau, 92211 Saint-Cloud, France.

Alsetex Tank Track Cutting Charge

DESCRIPTION
Although not strictly a demolition equipment, the Alsetex tank track cutting charge is an adaptation of demolition principles and doubtless could be used as such in an emergency. The track cutting charge is a shaped bar charge some 600 mm long which can be used to cut through a tank track in a combat emergency in order to change a mine-damaged track rapidly or to effect other repairs to a tank that may require the rapid removal of the track (tanks usually carry some spare track links for replacement). The charge is held at the optimum cutting distance by a hollow block of polystyrene or some similar material and is simply laid on the track link to be severed and fired by electrical or blasting cap means; it is possible that some form of manual delay setting device could be employed.

STATUS
Production.

MANUFACTURER
Société d'Armement et d'Etudes Alsetex (SAE Alsetex),
4 rue de Castellane, 75008 Paris, France.

Alsetex tank track cutting charge in position ready for firing

Lacroix Mark F2 Pull-type Igniter

DESCRIPTION
There are two types of Lacroix pull-type igniters, metallic and non-metallic. Both operate on the same principle and are primarily intended for use with mines and booby traps but they are also used for demolition purposes. On both, rotary igniter heads are used to allow a percussion primer to fire the igniter. Two safety measures are employed for transport and storage, one a cord wrapped around the device's body and the other a screw-off cap.

SPECIFICATIONS

Type	Metallic	Non-metallic
Weight	48 g	30 g
Height	63·5 mm	68 mm
Diameter (less safety cap)	26·6 mm	30·5 mm
(with safety cap)	–	34 mm

STATUS
Metallic type in production and in service with the French Army. Non-metallic type ready for production.

MANUFACTURER
Sté. E. Lacroix, Route de Toulouse, 31600, Muret, France.

Lacroix Mark F2 pull-type igniter, metallic version

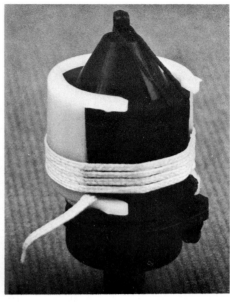

Lacroix Mark F2 pull-type igniter, non-metallic type

GIAT Mark F1 Cutting Charge

DESCRIPTION
Described by GIAT as a lightweight cutting charge, the Mark F1 is intended primarily for cutting through steel sheets up to 80 mm thick. The charge is a conventional shaped bar charge held at the optimum cutting distance by metal legs at each end. At each end there are also simple connecting devices (metal loops and a pin) for attaching other charges to increase the length of a cut.

Firing is carried out by electrical means or detonating cord and charges spaced apart from one another can be joined by a continuous detonating cord fitting with a special booster.

The Mark F1 charge can cut through a steel plate 80 mm thick or through three plates placed together, two 20 mm and one 30 mm thick.

STATUS
Production. In service with the French Army.

MANUFACTURER
Groupement Industriel des Armements Terrestres (GIAT), 10 place Georges Clémenceau, 92211 Saint-Cloud, France.

SPECIFICATIONS
Weight: 6·8 kg
Length: 500 mm
Length of cut: 500 mm
Depth of cut: (steel plate) 80 mm

GIAT Mark F1 Medium Cutting Charge

DESCRIPTION
Intended primarily for use against reinforced concrete structures, the GIAT Mark F1 medium cutting charge is of the 'hayrick' variety and is designed to be used in connected lengths rather than as an individual item. For this reason each charge is fitted with connecting clips in channels on the main body of the charge. At the top centre of each charge is a cap well under a metal cover

and along the top of each charge is a flat shelf that doubles as a storage support and cover for the detonating cord train. The charge support legs are rectangles of thick steel wire that can be raised and lowered along each side to vary the optimum stand-off distance to suit the material being cut. The charges are sealed for underwater use. A training device that emits smoke when fired is available.

This medium Mark F1 charge can cut through 300 mm of armoured steel from a working distance of 140 mm. From the same distance it can cut through ten 20 mm plates. When the working distance is increased

to 500 mm the cutting depth through armoured steel drops to 100 mm. Against reinforced concrete, a working distance of 400 mm creates a cut 400 mm deep.

The charge weighs 7·25 kg and is 194 mm wide.

STATUS
In service with the French Army.

MANUFACTURER
Groupement Industriel des Armements Terrestres (GIAT), 10 place Georges Clémenceau, 92211 Saint-Cloud, France.

Model 1962 Heavy Cutting Charge

DESCRIPTION
The Model 1962 heavy cutting charge is made up from sub-assemblies that are put together when required. In cross-section the Model 1962 resembles an inverted V-shape, and at each lower end of the V there are steel wire legs that fold outwards and down for support and act as distance spacers. Two handles are fixed to the upper body. At the top centre of the body is a cap well

under a plug and there are two further wells for various adaptors. A special booster is used when numbers of charges are fired by a single length of detonating cord. The body is sealed for underwater use, and a special smoke-emitting version is available for training purposes.

The Model 1962 heavy cutting charge can cut through reinforced concrete beams and pre-stressed concrete beams up to one metre thick. It can also cut through 300 mm thicknesses of armour plate.

The basic charge is 145·6 mm wide and weighs 14·85 kg.

STATUS
In service with the French Army.

MANUFACTURER
Groupement Industriel des Armements Terrestres (GIAT), 10 place Georges Clémenceau, 92211 Saint-Cloud, France.

GERMANY, DEMOCRATIC REPUBLIC

East German Blasting Machines

DESCRIPTION
There are two basic series of East German blasting machines, the A series and the M series. Each model in both series has a small crank, an indicator lamp and two connector terminals. Both series are contained in rectangular bodies with carrying handles and the main difference between the two is that the A series has the terminals under a hinged cover while the M series lacks this cover. Both are operated in the same manner, in

that the hand crank is turned until the indicator lamp glows to indicate that the firing charge voltage level has been reached and the circuit is complete. A few more turns fire the charges.

STATUS
In service with East German forces.

MANUFACTURER
East German state factories.

SPECIFICATIONS

Model	A 5105	A 5106W	M 504 K	M 524	M 514
Length	130 mm	130 mm	115 mm	115 mm	115 mm
Width	130 mm	130 mm	90 mm	90 mm	90 mm
Height	200 mm	200 mm	145 mm	145 mm	145 mm
Circuit resistance	260 ohms	520 ohms	260 ohms	510 ohms	1020 ohms

Demolition Tool Kit

DESCRIPTION
All East German Army engineers who are called upon to carry out demolition tasks are issued with a standard demolition tool kit containing virtually every item they are likely to require. The kit is carried over the shoulder in a canvas bag which contains a small hammer, a

socket spanner, crimping pliers, insulation stripping pliers, two screwdrivers, a metal ruler, a knife, scissors, a tube of sealing compound, adhesive tape, a small cutting board and a quantity of various types of fuze and detonator adaptors.

STATUS
In service with the East German Army.

MANUFACTURER
East German state factories.

GERMANY, FEDERAL REPUBLIC

West German Army Demolition Equipment

DESCRIPTION
The following items are basic standard issue demolition equipments supplied to all arms of the West German Army for their own demolition purposes. Other and more specialised equipment is held at combat engineer level.

Demolition Blocks
There are three standard issue demolition blocks with weights of 100, 200 and 1000 grams. The 100 gram block is a cylinder with a fuze well in one end. The 200 gram block has the fuze well in one side face while the 1000 gram (1 kg) has three cap or fuze wells. All three blocks are wrapped in yellow waxed paper. The 100 gram charge is 180 mm long. The 200 gram block is 70 mm long and has a 50 × 50 mm cross-section. The 1000 gram block is 180 mm long. There is a training version of the 200 gram block.

Tube charges are a standard issue which may be used individually or connected to form Bangalore torpedoes. These tubes are 550 mm long and weigh 1·5 kg. They are packed in olive-green metal tubes.

For specialised demolition purposes a small shaped charge is issued wrapped in brown oiled paper. It weighs 500 grams.

Detonator cord is issued in 25-metre rolls. Coloured green, the standard cord has a detonating velocity of 8000 metres/second.

STATUS
The above are in service with the West German Army.

MBB Thermic Charges

DESCRIPTION
The MBB thermal charges can be used for the destruction of metallic structures and even for the disablement of items such as gun barrels for the charges burn with an intense heat that can melt and re-weld metal. The charges, which burn at a temperature of 2400°C, can function under-water or in oxygen-free areas and are produced in three forms. The lightest is the NovaCo 1, a flat strip with the edges grooved in such a way that similar charges can be joined together to provide a larger burning area. The NovaCo 2 and NovaCo 3 are both produced in tubular forms. In each case an igniter is inserted into one end of the charge and then activated. After six seconds the charge will start to burn without exploding or fragmentation. Once the charges are burning they cannot be extinguished.

STATUS
Production.

MANUFACTURER
Messerschmitt-Bölkow-Blohm GmbH, Dynamics Division, Dept. AM03, PO Box 801149, 8000 Munich 80, Federal Republic of Germany.

SPECIFICATIONS
Model	NovaCo 1	NovaCo 2	NovaCo 3
Length	280 mm	378 mm	278 mm
Width/diameter	100 mm	70 mm	100 mm
Height	32 mm	–	–
Weight (approx)	1·3 kg	3·6 kg	7·5 kg

ISRAEL

IMI Demolition Blocks

DESCRIPTION
There are two main types of demolition block produced by Israel Military Industries (IMI), the No. 3 and the No. 4. They differ only in size and weight; both are rectangular blocks of cast TNT wrapped in impregnated paper and dipped in paraffin. Each block has a standard 9/16th threaded hole in one side that is normally closed by a threaded plug and which is capable of taking any standard firing device or detonator. Both blocks use a PETN booster charge that weighs between 30 and 35 grams.

The blocks may be used separately or combined for greater effect. The blocks are transported in standard wooden boxes each containing 20 No. 3 blocks or 40 No. 4 blocks. The weight in both instances is 13 kg, and each box has the facility to be used as a single combined charge. Each case has four corks in the lid which can be removed for detonators to be connected directly to the charges inside the case. The cases are fitted with carrying handles.

STATUS
Production. In service with the Israeli armed forces.

MANUFACTURER
Israel Military Industries, PO Box 1044, Ramat Hasharon 47100, Israel.

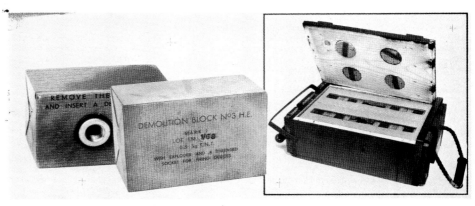

IMI No. 3 demolition blocks with carrying case, showing corks in lid

SPECIFICATIONS
Type	No. 3	No. 4	Carrying case	
Weight	470 g	220 g	Weight	13 kg
Weight of booster	30–35 g	30–35 g	Length	410 mm
Length	104 mm	67 mm	Width	255 mm
Width	67 mm	52 mm	Height	165 mm
Height	52 mm	52 mm	Volume	0·018 m³
Main charge type	TNT	TNT		

IMI No. 19 Shaped Demolition Charge

DESCRIPTION
The No. 19 demolition charge consists of a shaped charge held above its target by three rod supports that can be adjusted by wing nuts to accommodate slight changes in level. The shaped charge is held in a metal casing with a bee-hive shape. At the top of the casing is a canvas carrying handle and a well to take a standard detonator. When not required for use the well is covered by a plug. The main charge is 4·1 kg of Hexolite 50/50 and the face of the shaped charge is copper or copper alloy.

The No. 19 charges are packed two to a wooden box which weighs 20·5 kg.

STATUS
Production. In service with the Israeli armed forces.

MANUFACTURER
Israel Military Industries, PO Box 1044, Ramat Hasharon 47100, Israel.

SPECIFICATIONS
Weight: 7·18 kg
Weight of charge: 4·1 kg
Casing diameter: 280 mm
Charge diameter: 225 mm
Height: 350 mm

NATO

Standard NATO Blasting Caps

DESCRIPTION
Although most NATO forces maintain their own types and forms of demolition equipment, the relatively set state of the demolition art means that most equipment can be inter-changed. The main NATO-standard demolition item is the No. 8 blasting cap, and the following types are all accepted as standard throughout NATO. It should be noted that the term 'detonator' is used throughout NATO instead of the time-honoured term 'blasting cap'.

Detonator	Country of origin
Cap, blasting, electric, M6	USA
Cap, blasting, non-electric, M7	USA
Electric detonator	Italy
Non-electric detonator ET4	Italy
Detonator No. 1	Netherlands
PRB detonator	Belgium
BRISKA detonator	France
DM 11	West Germany

STATUS
All the above are in NATO use.

SINGAPORE

CIS Demolition Blocks

DESCRIPTION
Chartered Industries of Singapore (CIS) produces two standard demolition blocks, one weighing 250 grams and the other 500 grams. Both are standard rectangular blocks with a threaded 9/16th hole in one side to take standard detonators. The explosive used is TNT with PETN boosters and each block is wrapped in wax paper. The blocks are packed in wooden boxes, 40 to a box for the 250 grams size and 20 to a box for the 500 grams size. In both instances the box weighs 16 kg.

SPECIFICATIONS

Size	250 g	500 g
Weight	250 g	500 g
Length	54 mm	108 mm
Width	54 mm	54 mm
Height	70 mm	70 mm

STATUS
Production.

MANUFACTURER
Chartered Industries of Singapore (PTE) Limited, 249 Jalan Boon Lay, Singapore 2261.

CIS demolition blocks

SOUTH AFRICA

Charge Demolition, S.C. 450 grams

DESCRIPTION
The basic unit for this charge block is a high impact polystyrene injection-moulded block having a square cross-section with a central hole which forms a neck and accommodates the detonator tube. Three centrally perforated CE pellets are fitted around the detonator tube which can be supplied with a watertight mouthpiece on top of the block with provision for lead connections for electrical detonation. The main filling is 450 grams of RDX/TNT.

An alternative use for this block is as a form of anti-underwater personnel device for use against frogmen around harbour facilities or ships. In this form the central well is occupied by a zinc-based cast alloy adaptor with a striker mechanism and a fly-off lever with a delay element of nine seconds. When a safety pin is removed from the lever, the device may be used in the same manner as a conventional hand grenade and can be dropped into the water where it will detonate to provide a harmful shock wave after a delay of nine seconds.

The blocks are packed in moulded polystyrene trays each holding 14 units. Three of these loaded trays are packed into a steel box which weighs 23 kg and is 480 mm long, 350 mm wide and 220 mm high.

SPECIFICATIONS
Weight:
(complete) 0·52 kg
(charge) 0·45 kg
Height: 134 mm
Width:
(block only) 54 mm
(with striker mechanism) 75 mm

STATUS
Production. In service with the South African Defence Forces.

MANUFACTURER
Swartklip Products (Pty) Limited, PO Box 977, Cape Town 8000, South Africa.

Enquiries to Armscor, Private Bag X337, Pretoria 0001, South Africa.

Charge Demolition, S.C. 450 grams on right with anti-frogmen version (fitted with striker mechanism and fly-off lever) on left

Charge Demolition Clam HE 450 grams

DESCRIPTION
This device, often referred to as a clam bomb, uses the same basic block charge as the Charge Demolition, S.C. 450 grams but is fitted with a light sheet metal body with an adhesive strip along one face. This strip can be used to hold the clam charge against the surface of a target once the protective covering has been peeled off but if the charge cannot be secured by this method it is provided with a length of rubber cord coiled around the body in plastic clips from which it can be easily and rapidly uncoiled for use.

The clam charge can be detonated by a number of methods including a striker mechanism similar to that used on the anti-frogmen version of the Charge Demolition, S.C. 450 grams but using a delay element of 15 seconds. Other detonating methods include time pencils, a variety of snout detonators with a diameter of 10·5 mm, or conventional detonators. Other possible detonation methods include various firing devices including pull, pressure, release or combination pull/release units.

The clam charges are packed five to a moulded polystyrene tray with two such trays packed in a steel box weighing 11 kg. The box is 410 mm long, 190 mm high and 280 mm wide.

SPECIFICATIONS
Weight:
(complete) 0·59 kg
(charge) 0·45 kg
Height: 134 mm
Width:
(block only) 54 mm
(with striker mechanism) 75 mm

STATUS
Production. In service with the South African Defence Forces.

MANUFACTURER
Swartklip Products (Pty) Limited, PO Box 977, Cape Town 8000, South Africa.

Enquiries to Armscor, Private Bag X337, Pretoria 0001, South Africa.

Clam charge on right with block only, with snout detonator on left

IMP Exploder

DESCRIPTION
The IMP Exploder is a multi-channel electronic device which is small enough to fit into a pocket and rugged enough for field conditions when demolition or excavations using electrical detonators are required. IMP is used to control up to four independent channels and can transmit detonation pulses over ranges of up to 3 km. Any combination of detonators and cable may be used. IMP has an inhibit circuit to check that the total load resistance is under 400 ohms for each channel and is powered by a clip-in rechargeable nickel-cadmium battery pack (the pack may be recharged by a small field charging unit or a mains-powered charger that can recharge up to four battery packs). The pack can supply power for up to 120 chargings.

IMP has several built-in safety measures, one of which is that to fire each channel the individual channel button must be fully depressed before the Fire button will operate. Each circuit will be de-primed if the device

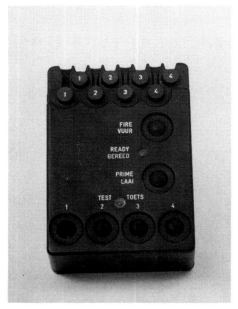

Control panel of IMP exploder

IMP exploder in carrying satchel

is not fired within approximately 20 seconds of priming. The terminals for the detonator leads are spring loaded and completely shrouded for operator safety and the device is splash-proof.

In use the detonator cable wires are inserted into the spring-loaded terminals and the appropriate channel button is pressed to illuminate a green Test light if all is well. When ready to detonate the Prime button is pressed and after five seconds or under a Ready lamp, coloured red, will flash to indicate all is ready. The appropriate channel button is then pressed with one hand while the other hand presses the Fire button. The process is then repeated for the other channels.

IMP is normally carried in a canvas pack on a belt or slung from the shoulder. The pack contains one IMP, a spare battery pack and a field charger unit which can operate off a vehicle 24-volt battery. The field charger unit is 24 mm thick, and measures 92 × 75 mm.

SPECIFICATIONS
Weight: (with battery) 0·7 kg
Length: 140 mm
Width: 95 mm
Height: 50 mm

Operating temp range: −10 to +55°C
Number of firings: 120
Battery capacity: 225 mAh

STATUS
Production. In service with the South African Defence Forces.

MANUFACTURER
Enquiries to Armscor, Private Bag X337, Pretoria 0001, South Africa.

SPAIN

M-250 and M-500 Demolition Blocks

DESCRIPTION
The M-250 and M-500 demolition blocks are charges of TNT contained in rectangular cases of shock-proof polystyrene. Each block has its corners chamfered for ease of handling and down the centre of each block is a

well with a screw plug at each end ready to take standard firing devices or a No. 8 cap. The M-250 block weighs 306 grams and the M-500 577 grams. For transport 150 M-250 blocks are packed in a wooden case that is also used to carry 75 M-500 blocks.

STATUS
Production.

MANUFACTURER
Explosivos Alaveses SA, Apartado 198, Vitoria, Spain.

Shaped Demolition Charge C.HM-1

DESCRIPTION
The shaped demolition charge C.HM-1 is contained in a steel conical casing with the steel cavity liner facing downwards towards its target. The charge may be placed over its target and held in place on three steel legs which have provision for fixing the legs in place with

clamps if required. The casing has a fixed steel handle for carrying and at the top is a well for a standard detonator or firing cap. Firing may be electrical if required.

The main charge is 3·04 kg of Composition B 50/50 with a Pentrite booster. Total weight of the complete unit with the tripod legs is 8·33 kg. For transport the charge is carried in an open frame-work wooden crate.

STATUS
Production. In service with the Spanish Army.

MANUFACTURER
Explosivos Alaveses SA, Apartado 198, Vitoria, Spain.

Concentrated Charge

DESCRIPTION
The device described as a Concentrated Charge consists of a steel cylinder containing 12 kg of grade 2 cast TNT. Each cylinder has at one end a folding steel wire carrying handle and three bayonet-type lugs which will be used to secure the charge cylinder to the correspond-

ing fittings on the base of another cylinder. In this way a series of charges can be connected to produce a pipe length of charges for use in a variety of demolition tasks. The centre of each charge contains a train of detonating material that will trigger not only the main charge but the next charge in line as well so that one electric or blasting cap can detonate a line of charges. All the fittings on the charge are steel to the extent that each charge weighing

12 kg has an extra 3 kg of steel casing and fittings to form a unit weight of 15 kg.

STATUS
Production.

MANUFACTURER
Explosivos Alaveses SA, Apartado 198, Vitoria, Spain.

UDP and UDR Satchel Charges

DESCRIPTION
The UDP and UDR satchel charges are similar differing only in the types of charge they contain. Each satchel contains a number of charges and lengths of type CIB detonating cord. Flotation bags for the charges are also provided for use when the individual charges are connected together to form a chain for the demolition of bridges or other water obstacles. The charges may be

unpacked from the satchel to be used individually or the entire contents may be detonated as a single charge.

The UDP satchel contains ten canvas bags each containing 855 grams of PG-2 plastic explosive. Combined these bags form an 8·55 kg charge and the weight of the charge, satchel and other contents is 11·3 kg.

The UDR satchel contains eight blocks of grade 2 cast TNT which combine to form a satchel charge weighing 9·736 kg. Weight of the charge, satchel and other contents is 11·1 kg.

Both types of satchel charge are normally carried in wooden boxes, each containing two complete satchels ready for use.

STATUS
Production. In service with the Spanish Army.

MANUFACTURER
Explosivos Alaveses SA, Apartado 198, Vitoria, Spain.

ERT Plastic Explosives

DESCRIPTION
ERT produces plastic explosive in several forms, one being a cold-moulded explosive that can be shaped by hand as required. This has a detonation velocity of between 7000 and 8200 metres per second and a decomposition temperature of over 200°C. It is produced in clear plastic-wrapped cartridges each weighing 100 grams or in blocks weighing 1 kg.

ERT also produces the plastic explosive in strip form based on pentrite with a binding material made from artificial cork in a plastic resin. This is manufactured with thicknesses varing between 0·5 and 10 mm. 6·5 mm is the normal thickness. The dimensions of these strips may be altered to suit customer requirements but are normally one metre long, 100 mm wide and 6·5 mm thick.

ERT also produces plastic explosive in demolition charge form packed in polyethylene containers. Each container has an explosive weight of 1·223 kg and is packed in wooden crates each holding 50 units.

STATUS
Production.

MANUFACTURER
Union Explosivos Rio Tinto (ERT) SA, P° de la Castellana 20, Madrid 1, Spain.

ERT Detonating Cord

DESCRIPTION
ERT produces three types of detonating cord. The MR-1, coloured matt brown, is used for general military demolitions. An underwater detonating cord may also be used for difficult above-water tasks, and for extreme conditions a detonating cord reinforced with extra strands of wire is produced.

SPECIFICATIONS

Type	MR-1	underwater	reinforced underwater
Colour	brown	yellow	dark red
Diameter (approx)	5·5 mm	6 mm	7 mm
Tensile strength	over 150 kg/cm²	over 150 kg/cm²	over 150 kg/cm²
Length on reel	200 m	100 m	100 m

STATUS
Production.

MANUFACTURER
Union Explosivos Rio Tinto (ERT) SA, P° de la Castellana 20, Madrid 1, Spain.

SWEDEN

Bofors Disposal Charges

DESCRIPTION
The Bofors disposal charges are the explosive component of the Bofors system for the location and disposal of unexploded ordnance. The detection component of the system is the Förster FEREX 4.021 search instrument (for details see the *Mine detection* section) which is used to detect the location of unexploded ordnance underground. Once located the disposal charge is used to detonate the device.

There are two sizes of Bofors disposal charge. The largest, the No.1 is used to destroy devices buried at depths down to about four metres under a surface layer of 100 mm of concrete and a bearing layer of 400 mm of coarse shingle. The size and number of disposal charges to be used is determined by the estimated size of the unexploded ordnance and its depth beneath ground surface. As a general guide one Charge No. 1 is used for the disposal of an object with a diameter of more than 400 mm located at a depth of between 1·5 and 3 metres. Three Charge No. 1s are used to destroy an unexploded object buried between three and four metres deep with the same number used to destroy an unexploded object with a diameter of less than 400 mm buried at between 1·5 and 3 metres. One Charge No. 2 is used to destroy unexploded ordnance buried at depths to 1·5 metres. If the detection instrument used (the detector normally used with the Bofors system is the Förster FEREX 4.021, see pages 226 and 227) indicates that the unexploded ordnance is buried more than four metres deep the earth above must be partly removed before the disposal charge is used.

Both types of disposal charge are shaped charges of the conventional beehive form held in a metal ring over the target point. Welded to the supporting ring are three steel legs with spiked feet; the legs are not adjustable and hold the charge at the optimum working distance. Firing is usually electrical but a standard No. 8 cap can be used.

SPECIFICATIONS

Model	No.1	No.2
Weight (complete charge)	22·5 kg	1·5 kg
(explosive charge)	17·5 kg	1·1 kg
(tripod)	2·6 kg	1 kg
Charge diameter	280 mm	110 mm
Charge height	470 mm	220 mm

STATUS
Production. In service with the Swedish armed forces.

MANUFACTURER
AB Bofors Ordnance Division, Box 500, S-691 80 Bofors, Sweden.

Bofors No. 2 disposal charge

UNION OF SOVIET SOCIALIST REPUBLICS

KZ Series Shaped Charges

DESCRIPTION
There are several charges in the KZ series but all are similar in appearance. On all versions the main charge is housed in a hemispherical sheet steel casing with a fuze well situated in a small domed housing at the charge top centre. The actual weight of the charge varies from version to version but is usually RDX or PETN. The tripod legs are adjustable within small limits. Detonation may be by electrical means or blasting cap.

STATUS
Production status uncertain. In service with Soviet and Warsaw Pact forces.

MANUFACTURER
Soviet state arsenals.

SPECIFICATIONS (KZ-2)
Weight: 18 kg
Weight of explosive: 10 kg
Height: 330 mm
Diameter: 210 mm
Penetration:
  (armour) 150 mm
  (reinforced concrete) 1000 mm

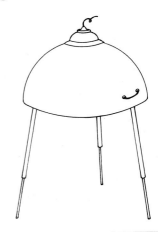

KZ series shaped charge

DSh Series Detonating Cord

DESCRIPTION
The DSh series of types of detonating cord has been in Soviet service for many years but is still likely to be encountered, not only in Soviet and Warsaw Pact use but in areas where Soviet influence has been employed. There are four types of cord in the DSh series all of which can be detonated by a standard No. 8 blasting cap. All four types are insensitive to such shocks as small arms fire but vary in their sensitivity to moisture; only the DSh 43 can be used underwater and only for periods up to ten hours. The cord is issued in 50-metre coils packed in a wooden box with each coil containing about 700 grams of explosive.

DSh 36 and DSh 40 detonating cords are virtually identical.

SPECIFICATIONS

Type	Colour	Composition	Diameter	Rate of detonation	Casing
DSh 34	red	Tetryl 71.5 73%, fulminate of mercury 28 26·5%, gelatin 0·5%	6 mm	5100 m/s	fabric
DSh 36 and DSh 40	red	Hexogen 100%	6 mm	7600 m/s	cotton fabric
DSh 39	red	Hexogen Tetryl, fulminate of mercury	6 mm	6500 m/s	double linen or jute
DSh 43	red or white	PETN 100%	6 mm	6500 m/s	cotton fabric

STATUS
Probably no longer in production but still in service with Warsaw Pact and some other armed forces.

MANUFACTURER
Soviet state arsenals.

No. 8 Blasting Caps

DESCRIPTION
While the No. 8 blasting cap is an internationally defined standard item the Soviet Union has produced six types. They can all be used as conventional blasting caps but in Soviet use they may also be converted for electrical firing by crimping an electrical fuze to the cap. The caps may also be built into MD-2 detonators which can be used to convert mines or similar charges for demolition purposes. There are several other applications of these caps.

There are various methods of issuing No. 8 caps in bulk for military purposes with the base method being cartons containing 100 caps. For service use the caps are carried in smaller containers of about ten.

SPECIFICATIONS

Model	Primer	Base	Shell	Length	Diameter
GRT 8M	fulminate of mercury	Tetryl	copper	47 mm	7 mm
GRT 8G	fulminate of mercury	Tetryl	cardboard	52 mm	7 mm
TAT 8A	TNRS lead azide	Tetryl	aluminium	47 mm	7 mm
TAT 8G	TNRS lead azide	Tetryl	cardboard	52 mm	7 mm
TAG 8A	TNRS lead azide	Hexogen	aluminium	47 mm	7 mm
TAG 8G	TNRS lead azide	Hexogen	cardboard	52 mm	7 mm

STATUS
Production. In service with the Soviet Army.

MANUFACTURER
Soviet state arsenals.

Electric Blasting Caps

DESCRIPTION
The standard Soviet electrical blasting cap is assembled as a standard item and may be found in two forms, instant or delayed action. The instant action form normally uses an iridio-platinum bridge with a resistance of one to two ohms and requiring a current of at least 0·5 amperes. There is also a version with a constant or reduced sensitivity bridge. This version has a resistance of 1·5 to 2·25 ohms and requires at least 1·25 amperes. The delayed action version has a small capsule of slow burning powder between the fuze and the blasting cap. This version usually has a small label attached for identification purposes.

Both types of cap are 50 mm long and have a diameter of 6 mm.

STATUS
Production. In service with Warsaw Pact forces.

MANUFACTURER
Soviet state arsenals.

Soviet Blasting Devices

DESCRIPTION
Outlined below are the main known types of blasting device in use with the Soviet armed forces and some Warsaw Pact forces. Not all of them are still in production and some may have passed from first-line service but are probably still used by reserve units and nations where Soviet influence has been exercised.

BM-52
A cylindrical-bodied machine with a downwards acting firing lever.

PM-1 and PM-2
Based on rather elderly German designs these two blasting machines are probably no longer in use. The PM-1 weighs 7 kg and can be used to fire up to 100 blasting caps, while the PM-2 has a capacity of only 25 caps and weighs 2·5 kg. There is a special test set for these devices.

PM-627
The PM-627 is contained in a cylindrical metal case weighing 5·5 kg. It can be used to set off 50 electrical caps and produces 150 volts.

F-10
This is a remote radio device with a 30-metre antenna and is capable of setting off three charges up to 48 metres away, and can receive radio signals from a range of up to 480 km.

K-PM-2
This blasting machine is of the dynamo condenser type with an output of 1500 volts through an external resistance of 750 ohms.

STATUS
In service with Soviet and Warsaw Pact armed forces.

MANUFACTURERS
Soviet factories and state arsenals.

UNITED KINGDOM

PE4 Plastic Explosive

DESCRIPTION
PE4 plastic explosive is an RDX-based high explosive which remains plastic at temperatures down to as low as −35°C. PE4 is described as non-toxic and unaffected by moisture. The normal bulk issue is paper-wrapped cartridges each weighing 230 grams and once issued the cartridges can be shaped by hand as required. For transport the cartridges are packed in cardboard cartons, each holding ten cartridges. These cartons are then packed four to a wooden box.

STATUS
Production. In widespread service.

MANUFACTURER
Royal Ordnance Factories.
Enquiries to Ministry of Defence, ROF Marketing, St Christopher House, Southwark Street, London SE1 0TD, England.

Sheet Explosive No. 2

DESCRIPTION
Normally referred to as SX2, this is an RDX-based explosive issued in sheet form. The sheets are flexible and can be cut with scissors or a knife to enable them to be tailored to the correct quantity and form to suit the desired effect, thus saving explosive and unwanted blast damage.

The standard sheet size for SX2 is 460 × 250 × 3 mm but sheets up to 6 mm thick can be provided. Each standard sheet weighs 620 grams and contains 88·2 ± 1% RDX grade 1A. SX2 is normally detonated by electrical means and it can be used for explosive metal forming or cutting, special demolition work and for bomb or mine disposal when cases can be cut open to reveal their contents without initiating a high order detonation of the filling.

Small quantities of SX2 can be supplied with the sheets separated by paper but for bulk packaging SX2 is packed in polythene bags inside a wooden case.

STATUS
Production. In widespread service.

MANUFACTURER
Royal Ordnance Factory, Bridgewater, Somerset, England.
Enquiries to Ministry of Defence, ROF Marketing, St Christopher House, Southwark Street, London SE1 0TD, England.

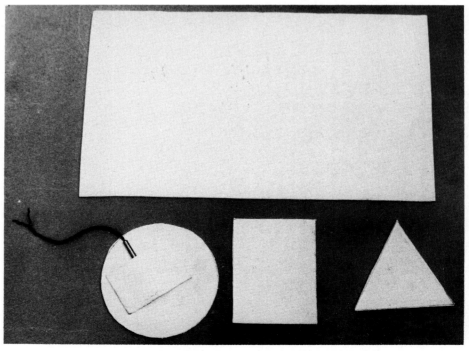

Sheet Explosive No. 2 showing some possible shapes (Royal Ordnance Factories)

Demolition Slab Charges

DESCRIPTION
Royal Ordnance Factory demolition slab charges are produced in a standard form with six explosive slabs packed into a hinged metal container. Each slab consists of 900 grams of PE4 plastic explosive and is wrapped in metal foil and contained in a plastic container with one open face. This open face allows the slab to be pressed against irregular surfaces and to assume the contours against which it is to be used. Each slab plastic container has a threaded recess at one end for an initiating device and a hole in the back for detonating cord. The metal container for the six slabs has corresponding holes for the same purposes. Hinges at the centre of the metal container allow it to be opened so that the slab faces can be pressed against a target and each half of the container can be removed to allow only three slabs to be used when required.

Individual slabs can be supplied if required.

STATUS
Production. In widespread service.

MANUFACTURER
Royal Ordnance Factories.
Enquiries to Ministry of Defence, ROF Marketing, St Christopher House, Southwark Street, London SE1 0TD, England.

ROF Charge Linear Cutting (CLC)

DESCRIPTION
ROF Charge Linear Cutting, or CLC, is an explosive charge that may be used to cut both metallic and non-metallic materials with speed and efficiency. It consists of lengths of explosive contained in a flexible covering shaped so that the cross-section resembles a miniature shaped charge. The hollow of the 'shaped charge' is positioned against the material to be cut and the length of explosive can be shaped to suit the task in hand. It can be secured in place by adhesive tape. The CLC can be cut to the required length by a sharp knife or a hacksaw, and the ends can be sealed (e.g. for underwater use) by special sealing caps and sealant. A special detonator clip can be used to attach a detonator to the cord securely at the correct angle. Normal in-service detonators such as the L2A1 or L1A1 can be used but there is a special purpose initiation system available.

The standard production length for the CLC is two metres although longer lengths may be produced for special purposes. The CLC is produced in various charge densities with the current standards being 10, 25, 40, 80, 100 and 180 grams per metre. The weights of the CLC vary from 160 grams per metre at a charge density of 10 grams per metre to 290 grams per metre at a charge density of 180 grams per metre. The detonation velocity is 6500 to 7500 metres per second.

CLC is packed and transported in pre-formed PVC tubes.

Performance Guide
The following figures provide only a general guide to CLC performance as a number of operational constraints such as temperature, CLC stand-off, target geometry, may affect the cutting ability.

Cross-sections of CLC, from left, CLC 180, 100, 80 and 40 (Royal Ordnance Factories)

Maximum Cut

CLC size (g/m)	Mild steel	Aluminium	Softwood	Hardwood
10	2 mm	3 mm	25 mm	25 mm
25	3 mm	6 mm	38 mm	50 mm
40	5 mm	10 mm	76 mm	76 mm
80	10 mm	12 mm		
100	12 mm	14 mm		
120	13 mm	16 mm		
180	15 mm	20 mm		

Material	Thickness	CLC size (g/m)
Single brick wall	115 mm	40
Double brick wall[1]	230 mm	180
Concrete[2]	50 mm	80
Concrete[2]	75 mm	120
Breeze block	75 mm	80
Blockboard	50 mm	10
Fibreglass	3 mm	10

(1) assuming no cavity between double brick walls
(2) a second cut will be needed to sever reinforcing bars in reinforced concrete

CLC charge taped to metal plate and ready to fire (Royal Ordnance Factories)

Result of firing CLC charge on metal plate (Royal Ordnance Factories)

STATUS
Production.

MANUFACTURER
Royal Ordnance Factory, Chorley.
Enquiries to Ministry of Defence, ROF Marketing, St Christopher House, Southwark Street, London SE1 0TD, England.

Charge Demolition No. 1 6-inch Mark 6

DESCRIPTION
Usually known as the '6-inch beehive', this charge has a 152·4 mm diameter shaped charge of TNT with PETN as a booster. The charge is kept at its optimum working distance by three metal legs and has a built-in primer at the top which includes a socket to enable initiation by a detonator or detonating cord.

The 6-inch beehives are packed four to a wooden box that weighs 24·3 kg complete, but an alternative packing is six charges in a cylindrical steel case.

SPECIFICATIONS
Weight: (complete) 4·5 kg
Weight of charge: 3·1 kg
Height: (overall) 330·2 mm
Charge diameter: 152·4 mm
Optimum working distance: 140 mm

STATUS
Production. In widespread service.

MANUFACTURER
Royal Ordnance Factories.
Enquiries to Ministry of Defence, ROF Marketing, St Christopher House, Southwark Street, London SE1 0TD, England.

Charge Demolition No.1 6-inch Mark 6

Charge Demolition Necklace L1A1

DESCRIPTION
Intended for the demolition of major structural units and girders the Charge Demolition Necklace L1A1 consists of a kit contained in a steel box. The box is 1.216 metres long, 304 mm wide and 150 mm high and contains five wedge-shaped hollow charges together with the links, clamps and nails required to secure the charges around steel girders and other structures. Each charge is known as a No. 14 Mark 1 'hayrick' charge which is secured in position with the shaped charge facing at the target. For really heavy structures more than one kit of five charges may be used and the charges are designed to be used side-by-side to enhance their destructive effect. Each charge has a housing at the top for the detonating device or detonator cord.

SPECIFICATIONS (No. 14 Mark 1 hayrick charge)
Weight: 9·3 kg
Weight of explosive: 5 kg
Length: 241·3 mm
Width: 134 mm
Height: 254 mm

STATUS
Production. In service with the British Army.

MANUFACTURER
Royal Ordnance Factories.
Enquiries to Ministry of Defence, ROF Marketing, St Christopher House, Southwark Street, London SE1 0TD, England.

No. 14 Mark 1 hayrick charge attached to steel girder (T J Gander)

Two No. 14 Mark 1 charges placed each side of steel girder (T J Gander)

ROF Explosive Kit Rapid Cratering

DESCRIPTION
Intended for the rapid production of craters impassible to wheeled or tracked vehicles, the Rapid Cratering Explosive Kit is a self-contained set of items packed in a pressed steel case with a hinged lid. The case is 480 mm long, 460 mm high and 400 mm wide and when complete the kit weighs 48·5 kg. Inside the box are two RDX/Wax/Aluminium charges weighing a total of 19·5 kg – these are the cratering charges. An RDX/TNT hollow charge is packed inside the box in a moulded polystyrene container and this 8·5 kg charge is used to produce the initial hole into which the cratering charges will be placed. The box also contains one further moulded polystyrene container that holds detonating cord, detonators and all the other kit accessories.

Using the kit, the hollow charge is placed in position and detonated to produce a two-metre deep hole into which the two cratering charges are placed. These are exploded using a safety fuze initiating train. The resultant crater in most soils will be from six to eight metres in diameter and two to three metres deep. Two men can create a crater in about 25 minutes using the safety fuze contained in the kit. If standard electrical demolition equipment is available this time can be reduced to about 10 minutes.

STATUS
Production. In service with the British Army.

MANUFACTURER
Royal Ordnance Factories.
Enquiries to Ministry of Defence, ROF Marketing, St Christopher House, Southwark Street, London SE1 0TD, England.

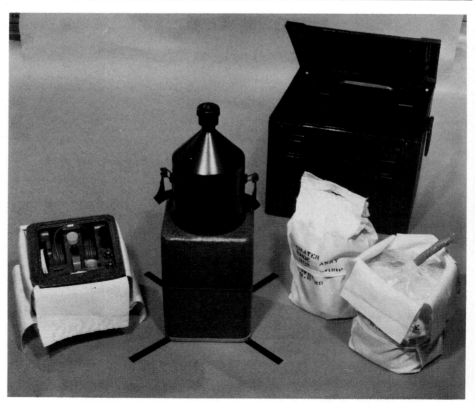

Rapid cratering explosive kit produced by Royal Ordnance Factories (Royal Ordnance Factories)

ROF Demolition Accessories

DESCRIPTION
For use with the various demolition materials and equipment produced by the Royal Ordnance Factories (and other types of equipment) the ROF produces a wide range of demolition accessories, the basic details of which are outlined below:

Safety Fuze
The ROF safety fuze is waterproof and burns at a fixed rate of two minutes for every metre. It is supplied in 7·5-metre coils and packed two coils to a round tin, along with 48 rubber sleeves which are used to seal the ends of cut fuze lengths. The tins are packed 12 to a box.

Firing Device and Flash Initiators
The firing device is used to initiate safety fuze quickly and simply. One pack contains four flash initiators in a box together with a firing device.
    The flash initiator contains an explosive cap and forms a waterproof link between a firing device and a fuze, or a fuze and a detonator. They may be packed with a firing device or individually.

Detonating Cord
ROF detonating cord is covered with a plastic coating and can be used to initiate most service explosives, directly without the need of primary intermediaries. The detonating cord is issued in 150-metre reels with two reels to a box which also contains an accessory tin containing junction clips and rubber sleeves to seal the ends of cut cord.

Demolition Couplers and Connectors
Demolition couplers may be used to make waterproof and vibration-proof connections between lengths of safety fuze and a detonator, or between a detonator and a detonating cord to quote but two examples. The connector may be used to join together two couplers when a link of safety fuze or detonating cord is required. Connectors and couplers are issued together in a small flat tin containing five couplers and two connectors.

Demolition Detonators
Demolition detonators may be of the electrical or flash type and may be used to initiate either detonating cord or service explosives directly without intermediate primers. They are issued five to a primary pack which is made from polythene to protect electrical detonators from electrostatic and radio frequency hazards. The pack is embossed with an E or an F to denote the contents. There is also a special safety pack for detonators for use in hazardous areas. This pack carries six detonators and is so arranged that should one detonator explode the other detonators will not be set off as well. Each of these safety packs contains four flash detonators and two electrical detonators.

Firing Device Demolition Pull
This device is intended primarily for use on booby traps. It has a ring at one end and a flash initiator at the other. A pull on the ring will fire the flash initiator to explode the main charge. It has a safety pin and a safety pin retainer, both operated by short lengths of cord.

Tester Ohmmeter, Safety Demolition No. 1 Mark 3
Usually known as the 'megger test set' this equipment is a commercial ohmmeter converted to meet military standards. It is used to test the continuity and resistance of electrical firing circuits. The set is normally carried and operated inside a waterproof webbing case fitted with a shoulder strap. The weight is 2·27 kg complete and the set dimensions are 190·5 mm long, 140 mm wide and 120 mm high.

Exploder Dynamo Condenser Mark 3
This ROF exploder produces 750 volts to fire an electrical demolition detonator in a firing circuit through 187·5 ohms external resistance. Working instructions are printed on the side of the exploder case which is normally carried in a waterproof webbing case with a shoulder strap. The case also contains three spare handles, three fusion jacks and 20 spare light bulbs for the instrument. Weight complete is 7·15 kg and the case measures 292 × 210 × 140 mm.

Exploder Dynamo Light Weight
Developed for use by airborne troops this exploder can fire a standard detonator in a firing circuit having a resistance of not more than two ohms. It is carried and operated in a waterproof webbing case with an adjustable shoulder strap. The case also contains a small test set that can be plugged into the output terminal of the exploder to check that it is functioning correctly. The exploder weighs 1·59 kg and the case dimensions are 190 × 102 × 76 mm. Instructions for using the exploder are printed on the case.

STATUS
All the above items are in production and in widespread service.

MANUFACTURER
Royal Ordnance Factories.
    Enquiries to Ministry of Defence, ROF Marketing, St Christopher House, Southwark Street, London SE1 0TD, England.

QED LINEX Linear Shaped Charge

DESCRIPTION
LINEX is the registered trade name for the QED Linear Cutting Charge and it uses the shaped charge principle applied to flexible lengths of explosive that can be placed over a target to be cut. The LINEX explosive content is contained within three flexible tubes of PETN in a sealed lead cover. The three tubes are so arranged that they form a rudimentary shaped charge with the hollow face being placed next to the target. Detonation is via the upper tube.

LINEX can be supplied in various weights for commercial and military uses. It may be used against metals, building materials and wood and can be used underwater.

STATUS
Production.

MANUFACTURER
QED Design and Development Limited, Borough Green, Kent TN15 8JL, England.

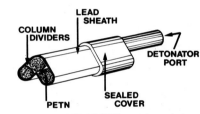

Cross-section of QED LINEX linear shaped charge

QED X1 and X1.4 Exploders

DESCRIPTION
Designed to meet exacting military requirements, the QED X1 and X1.4 are small portable exploders for electrical detonators. Both exploders can provide up to 180 volts and are powered by internal rechargeable sealed batteries that can provide power for up to 150 firings. The basic unit is the X1 which can supply power to one detonator while the X1.4 can supply power to up to four firing circuits. Both units are contained within strong plastic casings and have separated arming and firing circuits. Pressing the Arm button will prime the circuit and prove the circuit at the same time with the proving being indicated by a red lamp. Pressing the Fire button will fire a detonator through 5·15 km of E1 Mark 2 cable or 1·2 km of D10 cable. The X1.4 operates on the same principle but it has facilities for up to four firing circuits. The X1 has screw connectors for the cables while the X1.4 has spring loaded connectors in line with the relevant firing buttons. The units are splashproof and can be used in heavy rain. A belt pouch is available. The X1 is small enough to fit into a pocket. A QED battery charger for the X1.4 is available.

SPECIFICATIONS

Model	X1	X1.4
Weight	0·35 kg	0·83 kg
Length	125 mm	160 mm
Width	55 mm	120 mm
Height	45 mm	50 mm
Output voltage	up to 180 V	up to 180 V

STATUS
Production.

MANUFACTURER
QED Design and Development Limited, Borough Green, Kent TN15 8JL, England.

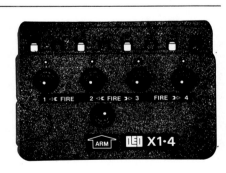

QED X1.4 exploder (top) with X1 below

UNITED STATES OF AMERICA

Atomic Demolition Munitions

DESCRIPTION
Atomic Demolition Munitions (ADM) or Charges (ADC) are used to form terrain obstacles, with a minimum of manpower, material and time, and to destroy massive structures such as bridges, dams and road networks.

The ADM is not constrained by shape or size to fit an aerodynamic case as air- or artillery-delivered nuclear weapons are. It is designed to be detonated either at ground level or below it or underwater. It is composed of a warhead and a firing device which completes the fuzing and firing circuits of the weapon through various triggering options. The 'on-call' remote firing capability consists of either a wire-triggering or radio-signal triggering option for detonation on command. The other option is a timer. The ADM can be fitted with a safety device for auto disarming on receipt of a coded signal. It may also be fitted with combinations of timers, batteries, encoders, decoders, radio or wire receivers and radio and wire transmitters. Sizes of ADM can vary from as little as one metre long and 380 mm in diameter, as in a sub-kiloton man-portable ADM which is known as a Special Atomic Demolition Munition (SADM), to 1·52 metres long and 760 mm in diameter, as in a 1 to 10 kt team-portable ADM which can be detonated by either remote control or a timer device and is known as a Medium Atomic Demolition Munition (MADM). The weight varies from 45·5 kg up to about 225 kg.

When an ADM is detonated on the surface or just below it the surrounding material is crushed, fractured and displaced. Large quantities of earth and rock are displaced mainly as fallout and a crater is formed with a parabolic cross section. Its size depends on the yield, depth of burst and surrounding material. As the depth of burial increases for a particular yield the size of crater increases until it reaches a maximum, known as the optimum depth of burial, beyond which it decreases until the burst is completely contained underground. Any depth of burial, even inches, can result in significantly enlarged craters over a surface burst. Crater dimensions can decrease by 20 per cent in hard rock over an alluvium type surrounding medium.

The crater has the best military use when the burst has occurred at the optimum burial depth. The slopes near the ground surface are almost vertical, preventing the movement of most, if not all, tracked and wheeled vehicles. The material on the crater surface is loose and difficult to negotiate thus hindering troop movements. The size of a large crater also eliminates any practical possibility of bridging.

With surface and sub-surface bursts the initial and residual radiation effects are important. Residual radiation is radiation emitted after one minute from the detonation time. It may result from neutron induced radioactivity in the surrounding medium and from fission fragments in the fallout. It affects the terrain directly surrounding the point of detonation (ground zero) and persists for several days. Decontamination is very difficult. The fallout contaminates ground zero and an area downwind of it depending on the yield, wind and burial depth. The volume of radioactive material reaches virtually zero at containment. Sub-surface bursts produce more fallout than surface bursts of the same yield. The other characteristics of nuclear explosions of this kind include:

Thermal radiation: light and heat, which may extend to great distances and depend on yield and burial depth. Maximum effects of this kind are produced by surface blasts.

Blast: at optimum burial depth close-in-air blast is reduced to between a fiftieth and a hundredth of a surface blast. Similarly the long-range air blast is decreased by 3 to 10 times. Complete containment results in no air blast.

Ground shock: burying the mine increases ground shock. The distance affected by significant ground shock depends on the medium the mine is emplaced in and the mine's yield.

STATUS
In service with the US Army and NATO as part of the theatre nuclear force. The SADM is believed to have entered service in 1964 and the MADM in 1965. A team of five to six men is used to deploy ADMs in high threat areas, although Special Forces Units may use them as well, the SADM being particularly suited for such operations.

Charge, Demolition: Block, M2 and M3

DESCRIPTION
The Charge, Demolition: Block, M2 has a US service weight of 2½ pound (1·134 kg) and is a rectangular block of 75-25 Tetrytol with a Tetryl booster pellet. At each end face there is a threaded metal well to accommodate a blasting cap and the block is wrapped in olive drab, asphalt-impregnated paper. The M2 is often used for general demolition work but it may be used for cutting or breaching purposes. The blocks are also used as assault charges when they are still packed in their transport haversack which can carry eight blocks – in this form they can be used as a satchel charge. Two of these haversacks are transported in wooden boxes weighing 25·85 kg.

The Charge, Demolition: Block M3 is the same size and shape as the M2 but it weighs 2¼ pounds (1·02 kg) and is formed of Composition C-2 or C-3. It lacks the cap well of the M2 and is wrapped in wax glazed paper with a perforation around the middle to allow the block to be broken into two halves. The M3 block is relatively plastic at normal temperatures and is more suitable for underwater use than the M2.

SPECIFICATIONS
Weight:
(M2) 1·134 kg
(M3) 1·02 kg
Length: 279 mm
Height: 51 mm
Width: 51 mm

STATUS
In service with the US Army and many other nations.

Charge, Demolition: Block, M5A1 and M112
Charge Assembly, Demolition: M37 and M183

DESCRIPTION
The M5A1 block charge is made of white Composition C-4 moulded into a rectangular block and encased in clear plastic. It has a threaded cap well in each end face and can be broken open for bulk use. It is considered particularly suitable for steel-cutting charges and may be used underwater. The M5A1 block weighs 2½ pounds/1·134 kg and is issued packed in plastic bags with 24 charges packed in a wooden box weighing 20·4 kg. The M5A1 is the main constituent for the Charge Assembly, Demolition: M37 which is a satchel charge for assault purposes. On the M37 four M5A1 blocks are placed in a single bag with two of these bags in an M85 carrying case which also contains two M15 priming assemblies. The M37 has now been largely replaced by the M183 satchel charge (see below).

The M112 block charge is half the weight (1¼ pound/0·567 kg) of the M5A1 and is used in the same manner. It is packed in clear or olive drab plastic bags in 21·77 kg wooden boxes containing 30 charges. The M112 charges may also be packed in 16 block units to form the main constituent of the Charge Assembly, Demolition: M183 that has now largely replaced the M37 as the US Army's standard satchel charge. The 16 M112 blocks are packed in two bags carried in an M85 canvas carrying case. The case also contains four priming assemblies, each made up of a RDX booster crimped to a length of detonator cord. Two packed M85 bags are transported in wooden boxes weighing 25·85 kg.

SPECIFICATIONS
Block charges

Type	M5A1	M112
Weight	1·134 kg	0·567 kg
Length	298 mm	286 mm
Width	57 mm	27 mm
Height	57 mm	27 mm

Satchel charges

Type	M37	M183
Weight of explosive	9 kg	9 kg
Length	260 mm	260 mm
Width	124 mm	124 mm
Height	324 mm	324 mm

STATUS
In service with the US Army. The M37 satchel charge has now been largely replaced by the M183.

Charge, Demolition: Block, M118

DESCRIPTION
Although officially described as a block charge, the M118 charge is four sheets of a flexible explosive known as Flex-X packed into one plastic bag. The explosive normally encountered is PETN although some forms of RDX have been used. The M118 can be cut to suit any particular demolition task and each sheet has a pressure-sensitive adhesive tape attached to one surface. Each sheet weighs 0·5 pound/0·227 kg and is suitable for underwater use. They are packed 20 charges to a 23·6 kg wooden box.

STATUS
In service with the US Army.

SPECIFICATIONS (complete M118 charge)
Weight: 0·907 kg
Length: 317·5 mm
Width: 32 mm
Height: 82·5 mm

Charge, Demolition: Roll, M186

DESCRIPTION
The M186 charge is the same as the M118 sheet charge but with the M186 the explosive is in the form of a 50-foot/15·24-metre roll on a plastic spool. The explosive strip is 76 mm wide and 6 mm thick and is protected on the spool by a strip of waxed paper. It can be cut to any length. The spool is carried in a canvas bag which also contains 15 blasting cap holders M8. The weight of a spool is 11·34 kg and three bags are contained in a wooden box weighing 52·1 kg.

STATUS
In service with the US Army.

TNT Block Demolition Charges

DESCRIPTION
These charges are standard commercial TNT block charges adopted for military use and are produced in three sizes. Using the US service notation these sizes are ¼-, ½- and 1-pound. The smallest size is little other than for training and is cylindrical. The two larger sizes are rectangular blocks. All three are wrapped in waterproof cardboard and have sheet metal end faces with a cap well at one end. They can all be used underwater.

STATUS
In service with the US Army.

SPECIFICATIONS

Size	¼-pound	½-pound	1-pound
Weight	0·11 kg	0·227 kg	0·454 kg
Length	92 mm	89 mm	178 mm
Width/diameter	38 mm	51 mm	51 mm
Height	–	51 mm	51 mm

Dynamite: Military, M1

DESCRIPTION
Military dynamite M1 is an RDX-based composite explosive and differs from commercial dynamite in that it contains no nitroglycerine. It is therefore safer to handle, store and transport. Military dynamite M1 is packaged in ½-pound/0·227 kg paraffin-coated, cylindrical paper cartridges. Compared to other military explosives dynamite is relatively inefficient but it is still eminently suitable for a large number of military demolition and construction tasks. For military use the dynamite sticks may be packed 50 sticks to a waterproof bag or 65 sticks to a carton. Both packages are further packed two to a wooden box. The individual sticks are 203 mm long and 32 mm in diameter.

STATUS
Production. In service with the US Army and many other armed forces.

Charge, Demolition: Block (40-pound) Cratering

DESCRIPTION
Intended for the rapid production of craters impassible to wheeled or tracked vehicles this cratering charge has an explosive base of approximately 13·6 kg of an ammonium nitrate-based explosive with a 4·54 kg TNT-based explosive booster. This charge is contained in a waterproof metal cylinder with two detonating cord tunnels half-way down the sides, one of which has a cap well. The charge has to be buried for full effect. The ammonium nitrate explosive has a relatively low detonating velocity but produces considerable blast and may be used to demolish buildings and fortifications if required. The explosive used is sensitive to moisture and should be dual primed to ensure detonation. The charges are packed one to a wooden box weighing 23·6 kg.

SPECIFICATIONS
Weight: 19·5 kg
Length: 610 mm
Diameter: 178 mm

STATUS
In service with the US Army.

Charge, Demolition: Shaped (15-pound) M2A3 and M2A4

DESCRIPTION
The shaped charge M2A3 contains approximately 4·3 kg of Composition B with a 50/50 Pentolite booster weighing approximately 0·9 kg. (On some early models the entire charge was Pentolite.) The cavity liner used is glass and a cylindrical fibre base can be fitted to the charge base to provide an accurate stand-off spacer. A canvas carrying handle is fitted.

On the M2A4 the booster has been replaced by a 50 gram charge of Composition A3 to reduce the charge's sensitivity to gunfire. The main charge has been increased to maintain the same weight as the main charge of the M2A3.

Both types are packed in waterproof cartons three to a wooden box that weighs 29·5 kg when transported.

STATUS
In service with the US Army.

SPECIFICATIONS
Weight: (approx) 5·2 kg
Height:
  (overall) 419 mm
  (charge) 305 mm
Diameter:
  (charge) 178 mm
  (stand-off collar) 197 mm

Charge, Demolition: Shaped (40-pound) M3 and M3A1

DESCRIPTION
The M3 shaped charge uses the conventional beehive shape placed on a metal collar and tripod to maintain the correct stand-off distance. The main charge consists of approximately 12·83 kg of Composition B with a 0·77 kg Pentolite booster. The casing for the M3 is all metal and the cavity liner is also metallic. On the M3A1 the Pentolite booster is replaced by 50 grams of Composition A3 and the main charge increased to the same weight as the M3.

Both types are packed in wooden boxes each containing one charge. Transport weight is 29·5 kg.

STATUS
In service with the US Army.

SPECIFICATIONS
Weight: (approx) 13·6 kg
Height:
  (overall) 737 mm
  (charge) 394 mm
Diameter: (max) 276 mm

US Army Demolition Kits

DESCRIPTION
The US Army specifies that units dealing with demolition should maintain set levels of demolition equipment and tools in specified quantities. These kits are sub-divided into electrical and non-electrical kits and the items mentioned below are the basic kits; the required amounts of explosive materials have to be added as and when required (these are usually employed in multiples of 20 and 50). Some other demolition accessories may also be added.

Electrical demolition kit (basic)
2 canvas carrying bags
1 10-cap capacity blasting machine
5 10-cap capacity blasting cap boxes
1 Demolition Chest (Engineer Platoon M1931)
2 Crimper, Blasting Cap: M2
1 blasting galvanometer
2 pocket knives
2 pair pliers
1 cable reel
1 cable reeling machine

Non-electrical demolition kit (basic)
2 canvas carrying bags
2 10-cap carrying boxes
2 Crimper, Blasting Cap: M2
2 pocket knives

STATUS
Both the above basic kits are in service with the US Army.

WARSAW PACT

Prepared Demolition Charges

DESCRIPTION
The prepared demolition charges described here are used throughout the Warsaw Pact armed forces but most of them originated in the Soviet Union. They all use TNT as the basic explosive charge. The three smallest sizes, a 70 gram cylinder and two blocks of 200 grams and 400 grams are wrapped in wax paper of various colours but all three have a purple dot denoting the location of the blasting cap well. Various combinations of these small charges may be used to provide concentrated charges or Bangalore torpedos. The Soviet Union employs these blocks in prepared charges contained in wooden boxes, each holding 30 400 gram blocks or 65 200 gram blocks.

There are also three larger prepared charges carried in cardboard or tin-lined wooden cases equipped with carrying handles. These are a 1 kg and a 3 kg block and a 5 kg cylinder. The 1 kg has two fuze holes, the 3 kg three and the 5 kg cylinder only one fuze hole.

STATUS
All six charges are probably still in production. In service with the Warsaw Pact armed forces.

MANUFACTURERS
Warsaw Pact state arsenals.

SPECIFICATIONS

	70 g cyl	200 g	400 g	1 kg	3 kg	5 kg cyl
Weight of block						
Length	70 mm	100 mm	100 mm	100 mm	155 mm	–
Width (diameter)	30 mm	50 mm	50 mm	60 mm	60 mm	170 mm
Height	–	25 mm	50 mm	120 mm	225 mm	182 mm

Field fortifications and related emplacements equipment

FRANCE

Matenin Trench Digger

DESCRIPTION

The Matenin trench digger was designed for the rapid excavation of trenches and defences in forward areas, and can dig straight or curved trenches or one-man foxholes.

The equipment consists of a cross country 4 × 4 chassis with a forward control cab. The trench digging equipment, mounted on the rear of the chassis, operates in the vertical position and can be swung into the horizontal position for travelling. Digging can be controlled from within the cab of the vehicle or by means of a remote control system.

The excavator itself consists of chain-driven buckets made of moulded steel with tilting bases, mounted on a boom. A conveyor belt is provided to discharge earth to the right or the left and the boom is fitted with a scraper to clean the bottom of the trench.

The power-shift hydro-mechanical transmission has six ranges, allowing for road travel, cross-country, digging and winch drive.

There are two models of the Matenin trench digger, differing in the dimensions of the trench dug. The MXD digs a trench from 0·75 to 0·85 metre wide and up to two metres deep, while the NX 7B3 digs a trench 0·6 to 0·75 metre wide to a maximum depth of two metres. Both models can dig a vertical trench on a 15 per cent side slope and have a typical output of 250 cubic metres per hour.

SPECIFICATIONS
Cab seating: 1 + 2
Configuration: 4 × 4, with locking differentials
Weight:
(NX7 B3) 14 500 kg
(MXD) 15 500 kg
Length: 7·6 m
Width: 2·5 m
Height:
(over cab) 2·8 m
(travelling) 3·6 m
Ground clearance: 0·5 m
Wheelbase: 3 m
Track: 1·98 m
Angle of approach/departure: 38°/34°
Max speed: (road) 70 km/h
Max gradient: (26°) 50%
Max side slope: 14°
Fording: 1·2 m

Matenin trench digger crossing trench

Engine: 6-cylinder water-cooled diesel developing 225 hp at 2300 rpm
Transmission: power-shift hydro-mechanical, with torque converter and 2 4-gear ranges
Steering: power-assisted
Tyres: 16.00 × 25, low pressure
Brakes: air
Winch: driven by hydraulic motor; 5000 kg capacity line pull
Electrical system: 24 V

STATUS
In production. In service with the French Army and several other armies.

MANUFACTURER
Etablissements Matenin, 34 avenue des Champs Elysées, 75008 Paris, France.

Matenin digging trench with soil being deposited to right

Trench Excavator Mk F1

DESCRIPTION

The trench excavator Mk F1 (Matenin-Batignolles) consists of a 4 × 4 cross-country chassis with a forward control cab. The trenching equipment mounted on the rear of the chassis consists of a chain of buckets 0·6 or 0·9 metre wide, which can excavate material to a maximum depth of 1·8 metres. When fitted with the 0·6 metre wide buckets, the excavated material is disposed of either side of the trench through two conveyor belts which operate each side of the trenching equipment. When fitted with the 0·9 metre wide buckets, material is deposited to the right or left of the trench via a single conveyor belt. Trenches can be excavated on slopes of up to 10 per cent.

SPECIFICATIONS
Configuration: 4 × 4
Weight: 17 000 kg
Length: 7·7 m
Width: 1·5 m
Height: 3·5 m
Engine: Alsthom 8-cylinder air-cooled diesel developing 178 bhp
Tyres: 18.00 × 24

STATUS
Production complete. In service with the French Army.

MANUFACTURER
Creusot-Loire, 15 rue Pasquier, 75008 Paris, France.

Trench Excavator Mk F1 depositing excavated material on each side of completed trench (French Army)

GERMANY, FEDERAL REPUBLIC

Schaeff HT 11A Backacter on Unimog U84/406 (Erdarbeitsgerät)

DESCRIPTION
The Erdarbeitsgerät (earthwork equipment) is provided for non-mechanised units of the Federal German forces to enable field defences to be quickly prepared. It consists of a standard commercial backacter mounted on the rear of a Daimler-Benz-Unimog cross-country vehicle, which can also be equipped with a bulldozer blade at the front. In medium soil up to 18 two-man slit trenches (1·6 m long × 0·6 m wide × 1·2 m deep) can be dug in an hour. The backacter is operated from a 30 hp hydraulic pump driven by the vehicle engine and can be speedily disconnected and removed from the vehicle. The entire assembly can be pivoted by the two-man crew through 90 degrees into its travelling position.

Details of the Unimog vehicle can be found in the *Trucks* section. The overall mobility of the vehicle is scarcely affected by the addition of the backacter. It can maintain a road speed of 74 km/h and still be transported in both the Transall transport aircraft and the CH-53G helicopter.

STATUS
377 equipments are in service with Federal German armed forces. A similar equipment mounted on the newer Unimog Model 416 is under evaluation by the US Army under the designation SEE (qv).

MANUFACTURERS
(Backacter) Schaeff.

(Unimog) Daimler Benz AG, Stuttgart-Untertürkheim, Federal Republic of Germany.

Unimog Erdarbeitsgerät in travelling order and in operation (Federal German Ministry of Defence)

UNION OF SOVIET SOCIALIST REPUBLICS

BTM Series of High-speed Ditching Machines
BTM, BTM-TMG, BTM-TMG2S, BTM-3

DESCRIPTION
The BTM trenching machine consists of the ETR-409 ditching machine mounted on the rear of the AT-T heavy tracked artillery tractor. The equipment can dig a trench 0·8 metre wide to a maximum depth of 1·5 metres at the rate of 1120 metres per hour. The BTM-TMG is a variant of the basic BTM and was designed to dig trenches in frozen ground and can dig a trench 0·6 metre wide at 100 metres per hour in frozen soil. The most recent model is the BTM-3, weighing 27 300 kg, and there is also a BTM-TMG2S model, which has a larger ditching machine.

SPECIFICATIONS

Model	BTM	BTM-TMG	BTM-TMG2S
Crew	2	2	2
Weight	26 500 kg	30 000 kg	32 000 kg
Length			
(travelling)	7·35 m	7·6 m	11·5 m
(operating)	10·85 m	–	11·5 m
Width	3·2 m	3·2 m	4·6 m
Height			
(travelling)	4·3 m	4·3 m	4·6 m
(operating)	3·5 m	–	3·2 m
Speed	35 km/h	36 km/h	36 km/h
Cruising range	500 km	400 km	400 km
Fuel capacity	810 litres	–	–
Trench crossing ability	2·1 m	2·1 m	2·1 m
Max vertical obstacle	1 m	1 m	1 m
Gradient	36°	36°	36°
Side slope	17°	17°	17°
Fording depth	0·75 m	0·75 m	0·75 m
Working capacity			
(0·8 m trench)	1120 m/h	1120 m/h (summer)	–
Depth of trench	1·5 m	–	3 m
Width of trench			
(top)	1·1 m	0·6 m	1·1 m
(bottom)	0·6 m	0·6 m	–

Rear view of BTM ditching machine, showing different method of raising and lowering ditching equipment

Model	BTM	BTM-TMG	BTM-TMG2S
Height of parapet	0·4 m	–	–

Note: automotive details are as for the basic AT-T tractor in the *Tracked prime mover* section.

STATUS
In service with members of the Warsaw Pact and other Middle Eastern and North African countries.

MANUFACTURER
Soviet state factories.

BTM ditching machine in operation

Rear view of BTM ditching machine showing soil being deposited on each side of completed trench

MDK-2 Series of Pit Digging Machines MDK-2, MDK-2M

DESCRIPTION
The MDK-2 pit digging machine is based on the chassis of the AT-T heavy tracked artillery tractor. The circular digging machine is carried horizontally on the rear of the chassis and is swung through 90 degrees into the vertical for ditching operations. The MDK-2 is used for digging weapon pits for vehicles, guns and other equipment. Depending on the soil conditions, the MDK-2 can dig a maximum of 300 cubic metres per hour. The ditch dug has a maximum depth of 4·5 metres and is 3·5 metres wide at the bottom and 4 metres wide at the top. An OTT hydraulically-operated dozer blade is mounted at the front of the vehicle. There is also a more recent MDK-2M model.

The AT-T tractor and the OTT dozer blade have separate entries in the *Tracked prime movers* and *Construction equipment* sections.

SPECIFICATIONS
(Data in square brackets relate to MDK-2M where different from MDK-2)
Crew: 2
Weight: 27 000 [28 000] kg
Length:
(travelling) 8 m
(operating) 10·23 m
Width:
(travelling) 4 [3·4] m
(operating) [4·05 m]
Height:
(travelling) 3·95 m
(operating) 3·48 m
Speed: 35 km/h
Max vertical obstacle: 1 [0·65] m
Max gradient: 36°
Side slope: [10°]
Working speed: (class 1 and 2 soil) 300 [387] m³/h
Depth of pit: 4·5 m
Width of pit:
(top) 4 m
(bottom) 3·5 m

STATUS
In service with members of the Warsaw Pact and other countries in North Africa and the Middle East. The MDK-2M is known to be in service with the East German Army.

MDK-2 in travelling position

MDK-2 in travelling position

PZM and PZM-2 Regimental Trench Digging Machines

DESCRIPTION
The PZM regimental trench digging machine is built on the basis of the T-150K wheeled tractor. The more recent PZM-2 is based on the T-155 tractor. The PZM-2 has a roller chain with digging buckets driven mechanically from the main tractor engine. A front-mounted winch is used to propel the machine when digging as the transmission must be disconnected when the excavator is in use. The winch is driven hydro-mechanically and exerts a 5000 kg pull at a rate of 60 metres per hour. The digger is raised and lowered by hand.

STATUS
Both the PZM and the PZM-2 are in service with the Soviet Army.

PZM-2 regimental trench digging machine in travelling order

UNITED KINGDOM

Light Mobile Digger

DEVELOPMENT
The Light Mobile Digger was designed in the early 1960s by the Military Engineering Experimental Establishment at Christchurch (now part of the Military Vehicles and Engineering Establishment) to meet the following requirements: excavation of a continuous slit trench 0·61 metre wide and 1·38 metres deep, with the ability to dig holes of a lesser depth, the ability to excavate rectangular holes, airportability in a C-130 Hercules aircraft, good road and cross-country performance and use by all arms at battalion level with the minimum of training. The digger rate depends on the ground conditions but on average ground a trenching speed of 4·57 to 5·49 metres a minute can be attained, equivalent to 230 to 275 cubic metres per hour.

DESCRIPTION
The Light Mobile Digger is based on a modified Thornycroft Nubian chassis. The driver is seated in the cab at the front of the hull on the right side with the engine to his immediate left. Power is transmitted to the rear axles with optional front wheel drive. The digging head is powered by an auxiliary gearbox.

The chassis has two parallel boom arms on vertical pivots approximately midway along the wheelbase. These project to the rear of the chassis and at their rear ends is a horizonal pivot on which the frame accommodating the digging head assembly is mounted. When travelling the digging head assembly is stowed between these booms, and is raised into the vertical position at the chassis rear when required for digging. The boom is locked in either position by hydraulically-operated locking pins operating between the boom arms and the chassis and situated aft of the rear road wheels.

The digging head assembly comprises the jib which carries the digging chains, and soil conveyor complete with their associated drive units. When in the vertical position, this may be raised or lowered in its mounting frame, or offset to either side. The excavated material is discharged to either side of the trench. The digging head hydraulic drive incorporates a relief valve system to prevent serious damage should an obstruction be met during excavation. When excavating, the rear springs are locked out to give additional rigidity to the machine.

Demonstration of Light Mobile Digger at Chattenden Barracks, Kent (Ministry of Defence)

Light Mobile Digger in travelling configuration (T J Gander)

Light Mobile Digger at work (T J Gander)

SPECIFICATIONS
Cab seating: 1
Configuration: 4 × 4
Weight: 9253 kg
Length:
(travelling) 6·59 m
(digging) 7·61 m
Width: 2·31 m
Height:
(travelling) 2·6 m
(ready for digging) 3·34 m
Track: 1·92 m

Wheelbase: 3·56 m
Max speed: (road) 70 km/h
Engine: Rolls-Royce B81 Mark 7D 8-cylinder petrol developing 200 bhp at 3200 rpm
Gearbox: 4 forward and 1 reverse gears, plus 2-speed transfer box
Suspension: semi-elliptical with hydraulic piston type shock absorbers
Tyres: 12.00 × 20
Brakes: air pressure/dual hydraulic
Electrical system: 24 V

STATUS
Production complete. In service with the British Army.

MANUFACTURER
Chassis: Transport Equipment (Thornycroft) Limited, Basingstoke, Hampshire.
Enquiries to Ministry of Defence, ROF Marketing, St Christopher House, Southwark Street, London SE1 0TD, England.

Light Mobile Digger Mk III

DEVELOPMENT
Now that production of the Thornycroft Nubian (4 × 4) chassis has been completed, the Royal Ordnance Factories are offering the Light Mobile Digger mounted on the rear of the new Bedford TM 4-4 (4 × 4) 8000 kg truck, already in service with the British Army.

DESCRIPTION
The unit comprises a Bedford TM 4-4 chassis which carries two parallel boom arms on vertical pivots (kingposts) positioned approximately midway along the wheelbase. These boom arms project at the back of the chassis and at their rear ends carry a horizontal pivot on which the frame accommodating the digging head assembly is mounted.

Normally the frame assembly, complete with the digging head assembly, is stowed between the boom arms and raised to the vertical position at the rear of the chassis only for digging.

The digging head assembly comprises the jib which carries the digging chains, and the spoil conveyor com-

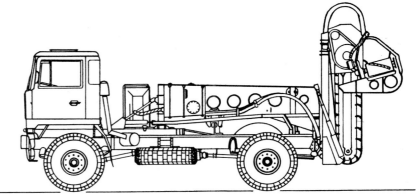

Light Mobile Digger Mk III in working configuration

plete with their associated drive units. It can be raised or lowered in its mounting frame or offset to either side of the chassis when vertical. The conveyor is able to discharge the excavated material to either side of the trench at will. The digging head hydraulic drive incorporates a relief valve system to prevent serious damage if obstructions are met in the excavation.

Power is supplied by a Bedford six-cylinder turbocharged diesel engine through a twin plate clutch and a six-speed all-synchromesh gearbox to an auxiliary gearbox. This in turn will drive mechanically the road wheels or the hydraulic pumps which transmit power to the digging chains, conveyor, forward creep motor and hydraulic actuating rams.

Only one man is required to operate the machine, and all operations are controlled from the driving cab, which tilts to facilitate servicing.

The Bedford chassis carries the two road axles on four semi-elliptical laminated springs. Four- or two-wheel drive is available in high box with four-wheel drive only in low box. Cross-axle differentials can be engaged independently by the driver on both axles. When excavating the rear springs are locked out to give additional stability to the machine.

The digging head boom arms are carried on vertical pivots which allow lateral slewing controlled by horizontal rams on the chassis sides just behind the cab and above the fuel tanks. The boom arms are locked in the central position for travelling or central digging by hydraulically operated locking pins operating between the boom arms and the chassis situated aft of the rear road wheels.

Close-up of Diggerhead (T J Gander)

VARIANTS
Diggerhead
First shown at the Aldershot BAEE in 1982, the Digger-

head is the main trench-cutting head of the Light Mobile Digger modified to be carried on the front load-carrying arms of wheeled or other loader tractors. Attached to a quick-change plate on the tractor arms, the Diggerhead can be used to dig trenches up to 1·5 metres deep. To date the Diggerhead has been tested on several types of wheeled loader and the Eager Beaver rough terrain tractor.

SPECIFICATIONS (provisional)
Weight: 10 000 kg
Length:
(travelling) 7·5 m
(operating) 8·5 m
Width: 2·5 m
Height:
(folded over conveyor) 2·8 m
(ready for digging) 3·58 m
(cab roof) 3 m
Wheelbase: 3·88 m
Max road speed: 88 km/h
Cutting chain speed: 244 m/min
Conveyor speed: 640 m/min
Digging speed: (continuous trenching)
(sandy soil) 9 m/minute
(medium soil) 6 m/minute
(clay) 2 m/minute
(chalk) 1·8 m/minute

STATUS
Production as required.

MANUFACTURER
Royal Ordnance Factories.
Enquiries to Ministry of Defence, ROF Marketing, St Christopher House, Southwark Street, London SE1 0TD, England.

UNITED STATES OF AMERICA

Small Emplacement Excavator (SEE)

DESCRIPTION
An equipment similar to the Erdarbeitsgerät of the Federal German Army is under evaluation by the US Army. Equipped with a backhoe and a dozer blade it is mounted on the Unimog 416 chassis. The Small Emplacement Excavator is of particular application to light forces such as the Rapid Deployment Force. With its speed of 62 km/h, it has better tactical mobility and survivability than current bulldozers and backhoes, and is operated by one man.

SPECIFICATIONS
Cab seating: 1 + 1
Configuration: 4 × 4
Max weight: 7258 kg
Length: 6·1 m
Width: 2·44 m
Height: 2·6 m
Ground clearance: 0·43 m
Track: 1·62 m
Wheelbase: 2·38 m
Angle of approach/departure: 30°/45°
Max speed: (road) 74 km/h
Max gradient: 60%
Side slope: 30%
Fording: 0·76 m
Engine: OM 352 4-stroke direct injection diesel developing 110 hp at 2800 rpm
Transmission: main gearing fully synchromesh, 6 forward and 2 reverse gears with cascade gearing, fully synchromesh. Total of 14 forward and 6 reverse gears
Clutch: single dry plate
Steering: hydraulic power-assisted
Turning circle diameter: 10·9 m
Suspension:
  (front) coil springs, telescopic shock absorbers
  (rear) coil springs with helper springs, telescopic shock absorbers and stabiliser
Tyres: 14.5 × 20 × 10 PR
Brakes: hydraulic dual circuit disc
Electrical system: 24 V
Batteries: 2 × 12 V, 125 Ah

Dozer
Blade width: 2·16 m
Blade height: 0·81 m
Blade drop below ground: 0·1 m

Backhoe
Bucket capacity: 176 litres
Digging depth: 4·26 m
Digging radius: 5·39 m
Loading height: 3·58 m
Loading reach: 2·01 m
Digging force: 4747 kg

STATUS
Under evaluation.

MANUFACTURER
Euclid Inc (a subsidiary of Daimler-Benz AG), 22221 St Clair Avenue, Cleveland, Ohio 4417, USA.

Small Emplacement Excavator

Small Emplacement Excavator with optional front end loading bucket fitted. Bucket has 500 litres capacity and carries 1200 kg (T J Gander)

Combat Emplacement Excavator (CEE)

DESCRIPTION
Still in the project stage, the Combat Emplacement Excavator (CEE) is intended to dig rapidly large excavations such as emplacements for self-propelled artillery and other AFVs close to front-line positions. The CEE will be mounted on a tracked chassis and will have a digging head consisting of two articulated, slewable digging chain assemblies. These can be arranged to excavate a variety of hole and trench dimensions from 0·61 to 5·5 metres wide and up to 1·83 metres deep. In use the CEE will be operated by one man and it will be able to remove up to 550 cubic metres of spoil in an hour. It will be air-transportable.

Current US Army plans call for eight CEEs in each divisional Combat Engineer Battalion.

SPECIFICATIONS (overall)
Weight: 15 100 kg
Length: 6·4 m
Width: 2·45 m
Height: 2·79 m

STATUS
Development.

Trench Digging Machines

DESCRIPTION
The United States Army uses a number of different types of trench digging machines manufactured by Barber-Greene (model 750), Parsons (model 624VL) and Unit Rig (model 4262). Gar Wood developed a lightweight (7666 kg) airportable trench digging machine in the late 1950s called the model 831 which was followed in the early 1960s by an improved version known as the model 832.

SPECIFICATIONS
(Unit Rig 4262)
Configuration: 4 × 4
Weight: 16 330 kg
Length: 8·89 m
Width: 2·44 m
Height: 3·18 m
Engine: IHC UD-691 diesel
Fuel capacity: 378·5 litres
Fuel consumption: 34 litres/h
Tyres:
  (front) 14.00 × 24
  (rear) 21.00 × 25

US Army Gar Wood 832 trench digger from rear with cutter raised (Larry Provo)

STATUS
In service with the US Army.

US Army Gar Wood 832 trench digger (Larry Provo)

Foxhole Digger Explosive Kit (EXFODA)

DESCRIPTION
Intended to rapidly produce a foxhole-sized crater on the battlefield, the Foxhole Digger Exploder Kit is a standard issue item for the US Army (the term EXFODA is a general title rather than an abbreviation). The kit is issued in a container with an end screw cap. Inside the container is a small rod, two delay fuzes, two cratering charges, string and tape. The container, which has a

carrying ring, also acts as the firing spacer for a small spaced charge fixed at one end of the container, opposite to the screw cap.

In use the container is emptied and placed on the selected site with the small rod being tied on to provide stability if required. The shaped charge is octol with an RDX booster and once fired produces a bore hole from 500 to 800 mm deep. The delay fuzes are taped to the cratering charges and lowered into the bore hole. The cratering charge is PBXN-1 with an RDX booster and once the charge is fired it leaves a small crater approxi-

mately 1 metre in diameter and 800 mm deep. The process of producing a foxhole crater takes a maximum of five minutes, and only one man carries out the operation. The kit can be carried by the operator slung from the container carrying ring.

SPECIFICATIONS (kit container packed)
Weight: 1·8 kg
Length: 300 mm
Width: 300 mm
Height: 100 mm

Overhead Foxhole Cover (OFC)

DESCRIPTION
The Overhead Foxhole Cover is now a standard issue item in the US Army and is carried and used by an individual soldier. A mylar coated polyester fabric sheet, it serves to protect a soldier using a foxhole from the

effects of the weather. It provides no other form of protection. Along each side of the cover, which is 2·34 metres long and 1·625 metres wide, are long pockets which are filled with spoil as the foxhole is excavated. The cover is then placed over the foxhole and layered

with spoil to camouflage the emplacement. The setting-up process takes five minutes.

STATUS
Production. In service with the US Army.

Parapet Foxhole Cover (PFC)

DESCRIPTION
The Parapet Foxhole Cover is a preformed fibreglass shelter resembling half of a cylinder. It is intended to provide shelter for a one- or two-man position but by itself it can protect against the weather only. If ballistic

protection is required the foxhole cover must be covered by about half a metre of spoil or earth, a process that takes approximately 15 minutes. Two of the covers can be joined together to provide shelter for a two-man foxhole. When transported the covers can nest within one another requiring less space. This cover is still under development and when complete it is expected to be issued at a rate of 40 per infantry company.

SPECIFICATIONS
Weight: 10 kg
Length: 1·524 m
Width: 0·76 m
Height: 0·457 m

STATUS
Development.

Foam Overhead Cover Support System (FOCOS)

DESCRIPTION
Also known as Tactical Fighting Emplacement Covers, the Foam Overhead Cover Support System covers are used to provide overhead shelter for tactical fighting

positions such as TOW emplacements. The covers are issued in shipping boxes containing fabric bags and the components for producing a plastic foam. The fabric bag for each cover is laid out over the emplacement to be protected and the two foam components are mixed and poured into the bag. As the foam forms inside the bag it hardens into an arch 2·44 metres in diameter and

1·524 metres long. Additional ballistic protection can then be added in the form of sandbags or spoil. Setting up one cover takes about one hour, and can be carried out by two men.

STATUS
Development.

Nuclear, biological and chemical equipment

PROTECTIVE MASKS AND CLOTHING

BULGARIA

Protective Shoulder Hood

DESCRIPTION
Although this protective hood originated in Bulgaria it is also used by some other Warsaw Pact forces. It is intended to be worn over the integral hoods of protective suits or over protective masks. As such its use is mainly confined to heavy-duty decontamination teams or personnel handling toxic agents, but it has also been issued to missile fuel handlers. The hood is a one-piece garment made from heavy rubber. It covers the head, neck and shoulders and provides protection against toxic agents, corrosive chemicals and fuels in either liquid, aerosol or vapour form.

STATUS
Probably still in limited production. In service with Bulgarian and some other Warsaw Pact armed forces.

MANUFACTURER
State arsenals.

CANADA

Gas Mask CML-BIO C3

DESCRIPTION
Developed for use by the Canadian Armed Forces, this mask provides protection against all known NBC agents. It has been evolved from a series of masks that was first introduced during the Second World War and has as its main component an injection moulded natural rubber face-piece. The face-piece is produced in three sizes, large, medium and small and is treated to remain non-tacky at temperatures as high as +53°C. The two eye-pieces are flat shatter-proof glass lens each 63·5 mm in diameter and set close to the eye so that optical equipment such as gun sights and binoculars can be used. There is an internal nose cup that is designed to allow incoming air to be passed over the interior of the eye-pieces, but expelled air is passed through an outlet valve. This outlet valve also incorporates a speech transmitter assembly. The C1 filter canister is normally sealed by a screw-type cap, when not in use, mounted on the left-hand side of the mask. The filter contains a pleated paper particulate filter and an activated impregnated charcoal bed. The mask is held in place on the head by a webbing harness, and when not in use is carried in a stout fabric bag which has pockets for accessories such as the special spectacle frames required by spectacle users.

Special versions are available for aircrew and tank crew members. A special adaptor to accommodate standard NATO filters is available.

Weight of the mask is 663 grams.

STATUS
Production. In service with the Canadian Armed Forces and some NATO and other armed forces.

MANUFACTURER
Canadian Arsenals Limited, 5 Montée des Arsenaux, Le Gardeur, Québec, Canada J5Z 2P4.

Gas Mask CML-BIO C3 (T J Gander)

Protective Coverall

DESCRIPTION
This protective coverall is a one-piece garment intended to be worn in place of normal combat clothing in conditions where NBC protection might be required. It has an attached hood and is opened up the front by a zip fastener and a Velcro front closure. Velcro is also used at the wrist and ankle openings and elastic webbing stirrups are provided on each leg to ensure that a satisfactory overlap of the trouser leg and the overboot is always maintained. The hood is designed to fit closely around the Canadian C3 mask but can be produced for other masks. Pockets are provided and the garment is produced in a number of sizes, each with a built-in suspender adjustment for height variations.

The coverall has a double layer protection. The outer shell of the garment is of lightweight 170 gram/m² 50/50 nylon/cotton combat cloth treated with a fluoro-chemical oil and water repellent finish. This finish ensures that liquid agents stay on the surface where they can be removed by field decontamination processes. The fabric is permeable to air and moisture vapour to maintain normal body heat balance. The second layer of the garment is an underlayer of open cell polyurethane foam 2·4 mm thick and containing re-activated charcoal bonded with latex. The foam layer is laminated to a knitted nylon substrate for added strength and to provide a smooth lining.

STATUS
Production. In service with the Canadian Armed Forces.

MANUFACTURERS
Outer layer: Celanese Canada Inc, Case postale 6170, succursale A, 800 boulevard Dorchester ouest, Montréal (Québec), Canada H3C 3K8.

Under layer: Uniroyal Limited, 51 Briethaupt Street, Kitchener, Ontario, Canada N2H 5G5.

Canadian protective coverall

Protective Gloves

DESCRIPTION
Specially produced for the Canadian Armed Forces, these gloves consist of duo-stretch knitted cotton coated with high molecular density butyl rubber. The gloves are olive green in colour and have gauntlet-type cuffs designed to be worn under the sleeves of protective coveralls. They are produced in a range of sizes from small to extra-large. The fingers and palm of the gloves are of curved configuration.

Extra thin unlined gloves made of dipped butyl are available for use when highly tactile operations have to be carried out under CW conditions.

STATUS
Production. In service with the Canadian Armed Forces.

MANUFACTURER
The Acton Rubber Company Limited, Case postale 300, 881 Landry, Acton Vale (Québec), Canada J0H 1A0.

Overboots

DESCRIPTION
The main protective material used in these overboots is high molecular density butyl rubber and they are intended to be worn over the normal combat boots. The individual overboot is 280 mm high and is produced, single width, in a wide range of sizes. The upper is of butyl coated duo-stretch nylon fabric while the outsole and upper reinforcing components are made of neoprene rubber. There is also an inner liner, insole cover and back strip to assist in quick donning and doffing. A cord lace ensures a close fit around the ankle with the upper intended to be worn inside protective outer garments. The sole is ribbed for traction on smooth surfaces.

STATUS
Production. In service with the Canadian Armed Forces.

MANUFACTURER
The Acton Rubber Company Limited, Case postale 300, 881 Landry, Acton Vale (Québec), Canada J0H 1A0.

Canadian NBC overboots

NBC Casualty Bag

DESCRIPTION
Manufactured from the same material as that used in the Canadian Protective Coverall, the NBC casualty bag is a container with a zip-fastener along one side and half-way across each end. Laminated plastic windows are provided at each end and the bag incorporates a metal frame to hold the bag away from the patient's face. The bag completely encloses the body and is olive green in colour. Carrying handles made from webbing material are incorporated.

The casualty bag weighs approximately 2 kg, is 2·51 metres long and 0·91 metre wide.

STATUS
Production. In service with the Canadian Armed Forces.

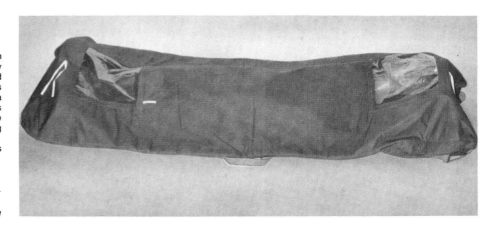

Canadian protective casualty bag

CZECHOSLOVAKIA

Protective Mask, Model M-10

DESCRIPTION
First issued during 1970, the Model M-10 mask has several advanced features, most of which are immediately noticeable. The large eye-pieces provide good visibility which is maintained by the use of an inner mask to prevent fogging. The lower part of the mask is very prominent and houses inlet valves on either side of the internally-fitted filter system. A single outlet valve at the front below the 'voicemitter' enables the wearer to communicate with relative ease. A head harness holds the mask in place.

The M-10 appears to be a close copy of the US M17 mask.

STATUS
In Czechoslovak service.

MANUFACTURER
State arsenals.

Protective Mask, Model Chema-S

DESCRIPTION
Normally issued for civilan use, the Model Chema-S uses a moulded black rubber face mask held in place by adjustable head straps. The circular eye-pieces are held in place by crimped metal rings and the prominent metal outlet valve is held in place by a non-adjustable neck strap. From the inlet valve a corrugated rubber hose connects the mask to a Chema-S-1-37(KL) filter canister. The entire equipment is normally carried in a fabric satchel.

STATUS
Held in reserve for Czechoslovak armed forces but issued for civilian use.

MANUFACTURER
State arsenals.

Protective Mask, Model Chema-S6-37

DESCRIPTION
Intended primarily for civilian use, the Model Chema-S6-37 has a face mask moulded from grey or grey-green rubber. The mask is held in place by five adjustable elastic straps which join at a point at the back of the head, and a carrying strap is fitted near the chin. A circular metal valve housing also holds the connector to the filter canister which may be fitted directly or via a hose, but in both cases the usual canister is the Chema-S1-37 which is attached via a screw fitting.

STATUS
Civilian use only.

MANUFACTURER
State arsenals.

Protective mask, model Chema-S6-37

Protective Mask, Model FATRA-38

DESCRIPTION
The Model FATRA-38 is the Czechoslovak version of the German GM-38 from which it differs mainly in having six attachment points for the head harness. It is issued for civilian use. The filter used is the Eckhardt Model EF-2. This cylindrical metal canister is 117 mm high and 98 mm in diameter.

STATUS
Probably no longer in production. Civilian use only.

MANUFACTURER
State arsenals.

Multi-purpose Protective Cape

DESCRIPTION
The Czechoslovak protective cape is a progressive development of the Soviet Model OP-1 and in many ways resembles the East German Model SBU-61. However, it does have some unique features, including three-fingered integral gloves and an inflatable waistband which can be used when crossing water obstacles and does not prevent the wearer from using his personal firearms. The cape is made from a lightweight synthetic material which is waterproof, airtight and heat resistant. As with other similar capes, the Czechoslovak design can be used either as a cape, as a coverall, or combined with one or more other capes to form small tents or shelters. It can also be used as a stretcher, and two or more capes can be combined to form a small raft for floating weapons or light supplies. Used in conjunction with overboots and a protective mask, this cape is stated to provide excellent protection against liquid agents and will partially protect against nuclear fallout particles.

STATUS
In production and service with the Czechoslovak armed forces.

MANUFACTURER
State arsenals.

FRANCE

Protective Mask, Model ANP 51 M 53

DESCRIPTION
This mask is made from thick black rubber and covers the face. It is fitted with two large circular eye-pieces and a 'voicemitter' in front of the mouth. There are several accessories that can be fitted to the mask, including special lenses for use with weapon sights or other similar optical devices. The filter canister can be either fitted directly onto the face mask or connected to it by a corrugated rubber pipe. The normal operational canister is the CF 63/67 which is circular and weighs 0·25 kg. Other similar canisters can be fitted which have less capability or are for training only, including versions for use with riot gases and carbon monoxide. If required the mask can be connected to a vehicle air system. The mask and its basic equipment are normally carried and stored in a Model 63 carrying bag; the mask alone weighs 0·4 kg. A variation of the basic mask is the Model ANP 51 M 53b which has an integral microphone.

STATUS
In production. In service with the French Army and some other French armed forces and para-military units. Some have been exported.

MANUFACTURER
Groupement Industriel des Armements Terrestres (GIAT), 10 place Georges Clémenceau, 92211 Saint-Cloud, France.

Versions of ANP 51 M 53 mask from left: with internal microphone, (ANP 51 M 53b); with large voicemitter; standard model (T J Gander)

Protective Mask Type 'Gendarmerie'

DESCRIPTION
This protective mask is intended for police and similar use and is proof against anti-riot and tear gas agents only. It consists of a one-piece clear plastic face-piece without any eye-pieces. The translucent face-piece is held in place by an easy-to-fit head harness and uses an internal fitting that entirely covers the nose and mouth to prevent internal misting. Incoming air is drawn through two filter canisters, one each side of the face-piece, and expelled through a front-mounted outlet valve that also acts as a speech transmission device. The edges of the face-piece are flexible to ensure a tight fit over the face.

The mask alone weighs 500 grams. Each of the two filter canisters weighs 130 grams so the combined weight is 760 grams.

STATUS
Pre-production.

MANUFACTURER
Groupement Industriel des Armements Terrestres (GIAT), 10 place Georges Clémenceau, 92211 Saint-Cloud, France.

Protective mask type 'Gendarmerie'

Paul Boyé NBC Protective Uniform

DESCRIPTION
With the NBC protective uniform produced by Paul Boyé, the concept of personal NBC protection for the soldier has been taken one step further from the idea of special clothing to meet the protection requirement to the adoption of a special uniform. With the Paul Boyé uniform the soldier is equipped with combat clothing that can provide a high degree of protection against the effects of chemical and biological agents and is easily decontaminated after being affected by nuclear fall-out.

The uniform consists of two outer garments, two layers of gloves and special socks. The outer garments are a jacket and trousers made of three layers of material. The outer layer is made of high density (75 g/m²) polyamide 75 taffeta that is treated with a water repellant and dyed standard NATO green with an infra-red reduction element. The centre layer is also liquid repellant to trap any aerosols or liquid that may penetrate the outer layer. It is formed from an unwoven 95 g/m² cellulose material. The inner layer is bonded to a knitted support and consists of polyurethane foam impregnated with activated charcoal.

The jacket weighs approximately 0·9 kg and the trousers 0·8 kg. An integral hood that fits round an NBC mask is provided as is a zip fastener with a velcro-fastened over-flap closure. Various reinforcement panels are provided. The trousers are held by adjustable braces and have velcro-fastened adjustment flaps at the bottom.

The gloves are in two separate layers, an outer glove and an inner glove. The outer glove is made of goatskin 0·6 to 0·8 mm thick. The inner glove has three layers of material. The outer layer is polyamide mesh with a density of 20 g/m². The middle layer is compressed polyurethane foam impregnated with activated charcoal, and the inner layer is cotton jersey. The socks have much the same make-up as the inner gloves but the foam layer is thinner to allow the socks to be worn under normal combat boots.

All the items in the NBC suit are issued in sealed envelopes.

While the NBC uniform is effective against most chemical and biological agents, it has only limited effectiveness against nuclear flash and fire. To overcome this a version of the Paul Boyé NBC uniform has been produced that has the outer garments made from a layer of 50/50 Kermel (a fire retarding fabric) and IF80. IF80 is a non-flammable fabric that retains its fire-retardent properties. Using this mixture of flame-resistant fabric the NBC uniform would have complete protection against all NBC hazards. With this fire-resistant uniform it is suggested that the outer layer should be worn separate from the inner layers which would then be supported on a removable lining held in place by velcro strips.

STATUS
Production. The NBC uniform is in service with the French Army. The fire-resistant suit is also in production.

MANUFACTURER
Paul Boyé, 53 Quai de Bosc, 34202 Sète, France.

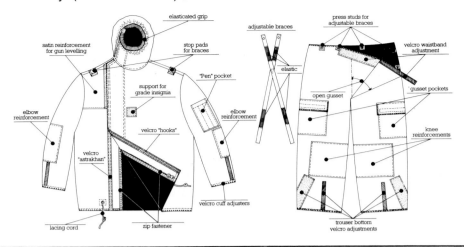

Main components of Paul Boyé NBC uniform outer garments

GERMANY, DEMOCRATIC REPUBLIC

Protective Mask, Model GM-38

DESCRIPTION
The GM-38 was first issued in 1938 and is still in use in East Germany. The face mask is made from black synthetic rubber and is held in place by an adjustable five-strap harness which is judged to be relatively comfortable to wear. At mouth level there is a cast metal housing containing the outlet and inlet valves, onto the front of which the FE-42 filter canister is screwed. The FE-42 is 108 mm in diameter and 89 mm long, and weighs about 0·45 kg. The GM-38 was originally issued in a corrugated metal cylinder but simple fabric carriers are also used.

An essentially similar model is used in Czechoslovakia as the Model FATRA-38 (qv).

STATUS
In service in East Germany and elsewhere. Probably no longer in production.

MANUFACTURER
State arsenals.

Multi-purpose Protective Cape, Model SBU-61

DESCRIPTION
This protective cape is similar to the Soviet cape-coverall OP-1 but differs in some fittings. It is normally carried in a roll on top of the standard field pack and is so arranged that it can be quickly released down the wearer's back ready for fitting. Once released it can be worn as a cape, overgarment or as a coverall, similar to the OP-1. It also has the same general versatility as the OP-1. Two can be combined to form a two-man tent about 1·8 metres long, 1·8 metres high and 1·25 metres wide. The securing items are nearly all toggle-type buttons. The cape is made from rubberised fabric and is available in grey, olive drab or dark blue and weighs about 2·5 kg. By itself it provides reasonable protection but as it is not completely airtight, even when worn as a coverall, extra protective underclothing must be worn for full protection.

STATUS
Probably no longer in production. In service with the East German forces.

MANUFACTURER
State factories.

East German motor cycle troops wearing SBU-61 capes

Protective Overboots, Model 61

DESCRIPTION
The Model 61 protective overboots are worn in conjunction with the multi-purpose cape Model SBU-61 as part of the East German protective equipment. As such they are worn over the normal field boots and are secured above the knee by straps. Further straps fasten to the wearer's belt and then tie-straps secure the overboot to the ankle. The Model 61 overboots are made from olive green rubberised cotton and are stated to provide good protection against most NBC agents.

STATUS
Probably no longer in production. In service with the East German forces.

MANUFACTURER
State factories.

Protective Overboots, Heavy

DESCRIPTION
These boots are made from heavier material than the norm and have heavy black soles. They are manufactured from rubberised fabric and can be removed without touching the possibly-contaminated sole. Normally the boots are secured in place by elastic bands but extra cords secure them to the wearer's belt. A second cord passes through loops at the ankle for a tight fit.

STATUS
Probably still in production. In service with the East German forces.

MANUFACTURER
State factories.

ISRAEL

Protective Suit

DESCRIPTION

Unlike most protective clothing, this suit is manufactured from clear polyethelene polyamid laminate. It consists of overtrousers sealed at the ankle and waist by elasticated bands and an overjacket with an integral hood. Gloves are provided as an extra. The suit material is rigorously tested for gas permeability, mechanical strength, thickness tolerances, heat seal strength and any incidental defects.

STATUS
In production.

MANUFACTURER
Chemoplast Limited, Industry Centre, POB 110, Afula, Israel.

Shalon-Chemical Industries Protective Masks

DESCRIPTION

The Israeli firm of Shalon-Chemical Industries Limited produces a range of individual NBC protective masks to suit a variety of roles. The most widely used version is the No 15A1 which is intended for general military and police use. The No 15-S-80 is a special version for armoured vehicle crews with the filter canister separate from the face mask. Other mask versions are the No 10A1 intended for children in the 4 to 12 year age range and the No 4A1 for children from 12 years upwards.

All these masks are issued with the No 80 filter-canister. On the No 15A1 the filter is mounted below the prominent 'voicemitter', and on the No 15-S-80 the filter is on the end of a flexible hose plugged directly into the armoured vehicle air system. All the masks are equipped with a leakage-proof drinking system; the wearer uses a water-bottle plugged into the mask from which the liquid is directed to the mouth by an internal tube. Also internal is an additional mouth and nose seal for extra protection. On the children's models the filter and outlet valve positions are reversed.

When not in use the masks are carried slung on the chest by a fabric strap. A special training version of the filter is available.

STATUS
In production. In service with the Israeli Defence Forces and with several foreign countries.

MANUFACTURER
Shalon-Chemical Industries Limited, 25 Nahmani Street, 65 794 Tel-Aviv, Israel.

NBC mask No 15-S-80 for tank crewmen

NBC mask No 15A1

ITALY

Sekur-Pirelli NBC Protective Clothing

DESCRIPTION
The full Sekur-Pirelli NBC protective clothing outfit consists of a jacket with an integral hood, overtrousers, gloves and overshoes. The jacket and trousers are intended to be worn over normal combat clothing with the hood worn over the M 59 or M 73 facemask. Both garments are made of a multi-layer material, the outer layer of which is impermeable to liquids. This top layer is formed on a sub-layer of glass microfibres that provide a degree of protection against nuclear flash and heat to the extent that it is largely fireproof. Then comes a six-cell layer of polyurethane foam impregnated with activated charcoal which provides a barrier against toxic gases. This foam layer is bonded to a liner of interlock knitted fabric. The combined effect of the layers is to make the garments impervious to nearly all NBC effects but at the same time some degree of permeability for body perspiration and body heat is still provided. The jacket has four pockets and a draw-string waist band. Elasticated cuffs are provided and the hood opening is lined with elasticated fabric. The suit is available in three sizes.

The overboots and gloves are mainly fabricated from butyl rubber with the overboots having nylon cloth reinforcements. The gloves are moulded to the hand shape. Both overboots and gloves are available in three sizes.

When not in use the complete outfit is carried in a light waterproof carrying case. For storage the garments are sealed in vacuum-packed plastic envelopes. Weight complete is 3 kg.

STATUS
Production.

MANUFACTURER
Sekur SpA - Pirelli Group, Via di Torrespaccata 140, 00169 Rome, Italy.

Sekur-Pirelli NBC protective clothing

Sekur-Pirelli Mod. M 59 and M 73 NBC Facemasks

DESCRIPTION
The Sekur-Pirelli Mod. M 59 NBC facemask uses a moulded rubber face-piece with two large flexible clear triplex glass eye-pieces. It has a side-mounted outlet valve and uses the Pirelli canister Mod. M 58 filter container. The M 58 uses a particulate filter and activated charcoal to produce an efficiency of more than 99·997%. Apart from the NBC version there are also

filters available for use against carbon monoxide and inorganic gases and particulates. The M 59 mask has a front-mounted speech transmitting device and the mask is available in three sizes. The connecting screw thread for the filter canister is a standard NATO item. Weight is 0·49 kg.

The M 73 facemask is a version of the M 59 with the eye-pieces replaced by circular optical interchangeable lenses. A further variation of this model is that the mask-mounted filter canister of the M 59 is replaced by a flexible tube leading to a separate filter or filter system. It is available in three sizes.

Both types of mask are normally carried in the same case, the M 66. This is a tough canvas case that carries not only the mask and filter canister but also a full range of NBC accessories and kits. Weight is 0·49 kg.

STATUS
Production. In service with the Italian armed forces and some civil defence organisations.

MANUFACTURER
Sekur SpA - Pirelli Group, Via di Torrespaccata 140, 00169 Rome, Italy.

Sekur-Pirelli Mod. M 73 NBC facemask (T J Gander)

Sekur-Pirelli Mod. M 59 NBC facemask (T J Gander)

Sekur-Pirelli NBC Facelet Mask

DESCRIPTION
Designed to be used as a precautionary measure when chemical attack is anticipated, the facelet mask can be worn for long periods. It can be carried in a pocket and is produced in one size only that can be adjusted to suit all face sizes and contours. Protection is provided by a two-layer system. The outer layer of the facelet is a water and oil-repellant fabric while the

second layer is a sub-layer of polyurethane foam impregnated with activated charcoal.

STATUS
Production.

MANUFACTURER
Sekur SpA - Pirelli Group, Via di Torrespaccata 140, 00169 Rome, Italy.

Sekur-Pirelli NBC facelet mask

Sekur-Pirelli Heavy Duty NBC Clothing

DESCRIPTION
Designed for use by personnel who have to work in a decontamination role or in hazardous conditions, the Pirelli heavy duty NBC clothing is impermeable to any NBC agents. The main garment is a one-piece coverall with a hood made of nylon cloth coated on both sides with butyl rubber. Heavy rubber boots are glued to the ends of the trouser section of the over-garment to pro-

vide a complete seal and the butyl latex gloves are sealed to the garment sleeves by a rubber 'O' ring.

Being impermeable to liquids, the outfit is also impermeable to body heat and perspiration so it cannot be worn for other than very short periods.

STATUS
Production.

MANUFACTURER
Sekur SpA - Pirelli Group, Via di Torrespaccata 140, 00169 Rome, Italy.

Sekur-Pirelli heavy duty NBC clothing

ROMANIA

Protective Mask, Diaphragm

DESCRIPTION
This protective mask is rather complex in that it is moulded to fit the wearer's face to the extent of using a rubber nose cup. The mask itself is made from natural rubber and is held in place by an intricate head harness consisting of seven straps. The diaphragm housing also contains the inlet and outlet valves and the connector for the corrugated rubber hose that joins to a filter canister. While the close moulding of the mask provides good protection against most agents, the eye-pieces have no anti-dim provision other than the usual kit and visual efficiency is low as a result. The mask is also stated to be uncomfortable to wear. Weight of the face mask alone is around 0·5 kg. The oval-shaped metal filter canister weighs about 0·9 kg and is 180 mm long and 110 mm across its widest point.

STATUS
In limited Romanian service, probably including civilian use.

MANUFACTURER
State arsenals.

TAIWAN

T62 Protective Mask

DESCRIPTION
The T62 protective mask is a locally-produced version of the American ABC-M17 mask and differs from it in few respects. It is produced with a special canvas carrying satchel which also carries a cleaning kit. The mask is stated to weigh 0·41 kg and the canister 0·265 kg.

STATUS
In production. Probably in service with Taiwan armed forces and available for export.

MANUFACTURER
Hsing Hua Company Limited, PO Box 8746 Taipei, Taiwan, Republic of China.

UNION OF SOVIET SOCIALIST REPUBLICS

Helmet-type Protective Mask, Model ShM

DESCRIPTION
The Model ShM is the standard Soviet protective mask and is also used by some other Warsaw Pact forces. As the mask completely covers the head it provides good protection against most agents but is rather uncomfortable to wear for long periods and general visibility is limited when wearing it. The helmet itself, which can be worn under a steel helmet, is made from grey or beige rubber. Crimped metal rings secure the eye-pieces to the facemask and as there is no anti-fogging interior mask, the eye-pieces can be fitted with extra internal gelatine lenses; an anti-dim set is issued with the mask. Incoming air is filtered through an MO-2 or MO-4U canister filter element that can be fitted either directly onto the mask or onto a length of fabric-reinforced corrugated rubber hose. A GP-2 carbon monoxide canister can be fitted between the mask and the standard canister and training or carbon monoxide canisters can be fitted in place of the standard canister if required. The carbon monoxide GP-2 canister may be either rectangular or cylindrical, and weighs about 0·635 kg. Incoming air is directed across the eye-pieces to reduce fogging to some extent.

Despite its general efficiency, the Model ShM is rather heavy and uncomfortable and the external filter canister and hose make it rather awkward to fit and wear. The mask is issued in a fabric carrier which also contains the filter canister, hose and the anti-dim set. The combined weight is about 2 kg.

Model ShM mask with outlet valve and hose connection to filter canister

SPECIFICATIONS
Chemical and biological filter canisters:

Model	MO-2	MO-4U
Length	195 mm	205 mm
Width	135 mm	135 mm
Depth	70 mm	68 mm
Weight (approx)	0·875 kg	0·85 kg

STATUS
In production and service with the Soviet and Warsaw Pact forces.

MANUFACTURER
Various state arsenals.

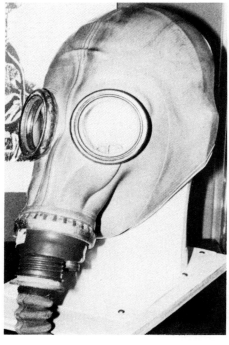

Helmet-type protective mask, Model ShM (T J Gander)

Protective Mask, Communication

DESCRIPTION
Although this mask uses the same external filter system and canister as the Model ShM it consists of a face mask only, held in place by an adjustable head harness. Thus the ears are exposed so headphones can be worn and a diaphragm 'voicemitter' in front of the mouth permits speech to be transmitted more clearly than is possible with the Model ShM. Although the deflection of incoming air across the eye-pieces is the same as that used on the Model ShM, the visual efficiency of this mask is reported to be low.

STATUS
In production and service with the Soviet and Warsaw Pact forces.

MANUFACTURER
Various state arsenals.

Head-wound Protective Mask, Model ShR

DESCRIPTION
There are two known versions of this mask which differ only in the positioning of the extra outlet valves. One is virtually identical to that used on the Model ShM and the other has an outlet valve on the right cheek, but both have the inlet valve at the level of the wearer's nose rather than at the normal mouth level which helps to prevent clogging of the air system by body liquids. The nose-level system also permits the easy supply of oxygen when necessary, but the usual anti-dim deflection of air across the eye-pieces as used in the Model ShM is not incorporated. The same hose and filter canister as on the Model ShM are used but the hose can be fitted with a T-piece to allow two canisters to be fitted to ease breathing. The Model ShR covers the whole head and it is secured in place by rubber straps.

STATUS
In production and service with the Soviet and Warsaw Pact forces.

MANUFACTURER
Various state arsenals.

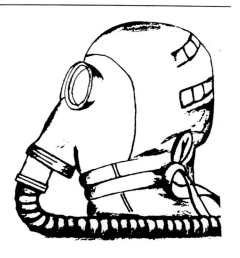

Model ShR head-wound protective mask

Civilian Protective Mask, Model GP-4U

DESCRIPTION
Designed primarily for general civilian use, the Model GP-4U uses a moulded rubber face mask which is secured to the head by three straps fitted to six points on the mask. The round glass eye-pieces are held in place by crimped aluminium rings and as there is no other method provided of keeping the eye-pieces clear when worn, an anti-dim kit is issued with the mask. A single inlet and double outlet valves are fitted and air is drawn into the mask via a corrugated rubber hose which is secured to the face mask by wire and tape. A GP-4U canister is used for filtering. When not in use the Model GP-4U is carried in a fabric carrier fitted with a shoulder strap and a waist strap. The weight of the complete equipment in its carrier is around 2·5 kg.

The filter canister used with this mask is cylindrical and weighs 0·56 kg. It is 150 mm high and 80 mm in diameter.

STATUS
In production.

MANUFACTURER
State arsenals.

Civilian Protective Mask, Model GP-5

DESCRIPTION
The Model GP-5 may be regarded as the civilian counterpart of the military Model ShM as the rubber head-covering face-piece (designated ShM-62) is almost identical to the Model ShM. Like the Model ShM, the Model GP-5 uses air deflection across the eye-piece interiors and is issued in five sizes, but with the Model GP-5 the filter canister is fitted directly onto the inlet valve. The filter canister is cylindrical and is fitted via a female connector on the face-piece. A fabric carrier contains the face-piece and canister and a set of anti-dim discs for fitting inside the glass eye-pieces. Pockets on the carrier contain a small first-aid kit and an anti-gas kit.

STATUS
In production.

MANUFACTURER
State arsenals.

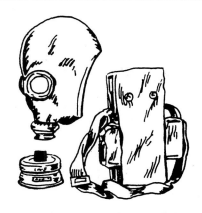

Model GP-5 civilian protective mask

Special Protective Mask, Model ShMS

DESCRIPTION
The Model ShMS has provision for fitting optically corrective lenses, either spectacle lenses or special lenses to suit binoculars or weapon sights. Normally the Model ShMS is issued with optically flat lenses which are fitted into internal or external grooves, according to the circumstances, the corrective lenses fitting into the other groove. As a measure against dimming extra gelatine lenses can be fitted inside the internal lenses. The lenses are as small as 40 mm in diameter so the mask's visual efficiency is low but, as it retains the overall protection and filter system of the Model ShM, it is effective against nearly all agents. The mask is made from grey or beige rubber and is issued in five sizes. Weight of the fabric carrier, mask, tube filter canister, hose and anti-dim set is around 2 kg.

STATUS
In production and service with the Soviet and Warsaw Pact forces.

MANUFACTURER
Various state arsenals.

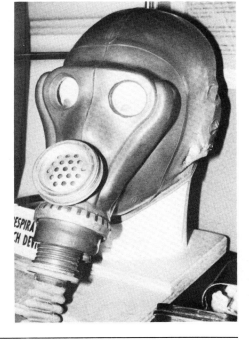

Special protective mask, Model ShMS, fitted with 'voicemitter' (T J Gander)

Protective Cape/Groundsheet

DESCRIPTION
This cape/groundsheet is normally carried in the same container/satchel as the protective mask, and it is thus issued to all Soviet troops. Two types of cape/groundsheet are in use, one of cloth-reinforced paper and the other of translucent green plastic. Both are essentially the same in shape and purpose but the cloth-paper version has reinforced hems into which canes can be inserted so the cape can be used as a shelter or small tent. The plastic cape has small black tie-wraps for the same purpose. The cloth-paper cape has a layer of cotton fabric bonded between two layers of brown paraffin-impregnated paper by water-resistant glue. When worn as a cape, both types are secured around the neck by tapes. Both types are considered expendable and weigh about 0·5 kg.

STATUS
In production. In service with the Soviet and Warsaw Pact forces.

MANUFACTURER
State arsenals.

Paper Protective Cape

DESCRIPTION
Although it has now been largely replaced by the later cloth-paper and plastic protective cape, the older paper protective cape is still in use. Normally it is carried in the same container/satchel as the wearer's protective mask, but the paper cape is intended to give only temporary protection against liquid agents and fallout particles, and is expendable. The cape is formed from two pieces of paper joined over the head and in a seam down the back. Cotton tie-wraps secure the cape in place once fitted. The cape is issued folded flat and can also be used as a groundsheet.

STATUS
No longer in production. Still used as reserve and training equipment by the Soviet and Warsaw Pact forces.

MANUFACTURER
State arsenals.

Protective Suit, Combined Arms

DESCRIPTION
This is the standard protective suit for all arms of the Soviet and Warsaw Pact forces and, although there are a few variations, the suit consists of a protective coat-overall (the OP-1), overboots and gloves.

The coat-overall OP-1 is a multi-purpose garment produced in five sizes which can be worn in several ways. With the sleeves inside the garment it can be worn as a cape or with the sleeves outside as a conventional overgarment. The lower portions may be wrapped around the legs and secured in place by straps. Apart from its protective use, the OP-1 can also be used as a raincoat, groundsheet, field shelter, flotation bag and as an emergency pannier for casualties.

The overboots are usually knee-length but hip-length versions are available. The knee-length versions are secured below the knee by tie-wraps and the hip length versions are usually secured to the wearer's belt by straps.

The gloves come in two versions: a temperate climate version with five fingers, and a cold-weather version with two fingers and a thermal lining.

All items are manufactured from rubberised fabric and provide reasonable protection against most NBC agents. However, the suit is not completely airtight and extra protective undergarments must be worn for complete protection.

The coat-coverall OP-1 weighs approximately 1·6 kg, the overboots 1 kg and the gloves 0·4 kg.

STATUS
In production. In service with the Soviet and Warsaw Pact forces.

MANUFACTURER
State arsenals.

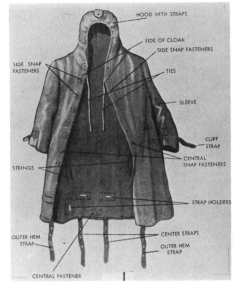

Main component parts of OP-1 protective suit

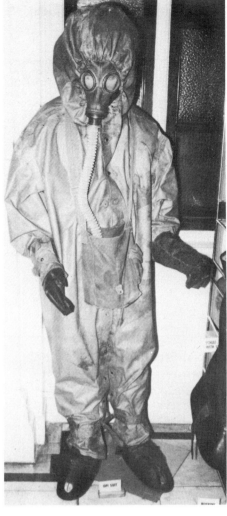

Protective suit, combined arms, shown with hood and Model ShM helmet (T J Gander)

Impregnated Coveralls, Model ZFO-58

DESCRIPTION
These coveralls are intended to protect against toxic chemical aerosols and vapours, but not against liquid agents. They can also provide partial protection against biological and radiation contamination. The coveralls are manufactured from chemically-impregnated porous cotton fabric, and are intended to be worn with underwear, socks and a hood liner impregnated with the same chemical. The suit is sealed by elastic cuffs and tie-wraps and gas flaps are provided. The coveralls can be worn either by themselves or (more normally) under protective clothing, and they are issued in three sizes.

STATUS
In production. In service with the Soviet and Warsaw Pact forces.

MANUFACTURER
State arsenals.

Heavy Protective Suit

DESCRIPTION
Designed for use by decontamination personnel and personnel handling toxic agents and munitions, this suit is produced in two basic versions: a one-piece garment and a two-piece suit. As a further variation both can have integral boots. The suits are made of cloth coated by a thick layer of rubber. They have integral hoods, sewn-in bibs, wrist, ankle and neck straps, thumb loops and belts. To complete the suits there are cloth liners and heavy gloves and boots. The suits provide excellent protection against all agents but as with other types of similar suit they are most uncomfortable to wear. Body heat build-up limits the wearing time to a maximum of two hours and in warmer climates to as little as 15 minutes.

STATUS
In production. In service with the Soviet and Warsaw Pact forces.

MANUFACTURER
State arsenals.

Lightweight Protective Suit, Rubberised, L-1

DESCRIPTION
Normally worn by Soviet and Warsaw Pact reconnaissance personnel, the L-1 protective suit consists of a jacket with fitted hood, overtrousers with integral overboots, two pairs of two-fingered gloves and a carrying satchel. It is designed so that it can be donned rapidly. The trousers have a strap at the left and a bib joins to straps fitted with elasticised sections. The trouser legs can be fitted with additional straps just below the knee and there are overboot straps at the instep. The jacket, which can be worn over or under the trouser straps (over seems to be the more likely) has an elasticated waist and another strap provides a neck seal. The jacket cuffs and the gloves have elastic sealing bands. With a face mask the L-1 suit provides complete protection against most NBC agents. The basic fabric is butyl rubber-covered cotton fabric, except the satchel, which is canvas. The L-1 protective suit weighs around 3 kg.

STATUS
In production. In service with the Soviet and Warsaw Pact forces.

MANUFACTURER
State arsenals.

L-1 rubberised lightweight protective suit

Rubberised Protective Coverall

DESCRIPTION
This coverall is for personnel involved in NBC decontamination and toxic agent handlers. It consists of a single garment with an integral jacket, hood and trousers, and it also has a sewn-in bib, wrist, neck and ankle straps, thumb loops and a belt. It is normally worn with a hood liner, heavy rubber boots and gloves and a protective mask, which provide excellent protection against all known chemical agents, but as the suit is made from cotton fabric coated with green or black synthetic rubber, it is very uncomfortable. Wearing time is limited to as little as 15 minutes in a warm climate or up to two hours in colder surroundings, which can be increased by wearing cooling-type coveralls. The suit is produced in three sizes and weighs about 3·6 kg.

STATUS
In service with the Soviet and Warsaw Pact forces.

MANUFACTURER
State arsenals.

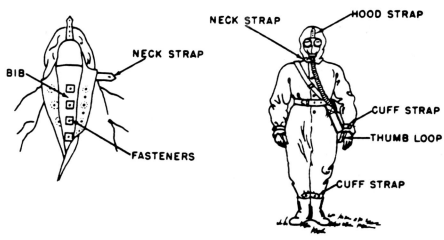

Rubberised protective coverall

Heavy Rubber Gloves

DESCRIPTION
These gloves are intended for use by decontamination teams or personnel handling toxic agents or fuels. Two types are produced, one with three fingers and one with five. Both are manufactured from heavy black synthetic

or natural rubber on a fabric backing. The three-fingered glove is moulded flat and can fit either hand; a wrist strap forms a tight seal. The five-fingered gloves are issued 'handed' and lack the sealing strap. Both types of glove are intended for use with the heavy protective suit and both weigh about 0·34 kg a pair.

STATUS
In production. In service with the Soviet and Warsaw Pact forces.

MANUFACTURER
State arsenals.

Protective Apron, Rubberised

DESCRIPTION
Intended for use by personnel involved in decontamination of weapons and heavy equipment, this apron has replaced an earlier version made of either impregnated paper or polyvinyl chloride. This version is manufac-

tured from rubberised fabric and covers the body from the chest to the knees. It is one metre long and 0·85 metre wide, and weighs about 0·4 kg.

STATUS
In production. In service with the Soviet and Warsaw Pact forces.

MANUFACTURER
State arsenals.

Cooling-type Hooded Coverall

DESCRIPTION
The limits to the length of time rubberised protective garments can be worn can be partially off-set by cooling overgarments which are designed to be worn over heavy protective clothing. The standard Soviet garment for this purpose, which is also issued to most Warsaw Pact forces, is made from cotton. It consists of a single-piece coverall with an integral hood, a five-button overlapping front opening, and securing straps or ties at the neck, wrist, ankle and mid-calf. There is a belt and a pocket for the protective mask canister. The suit is

soaked in water, and the subsequent evaporation of the water cools the suit beneath. The efficiency of the cooling process depends on humidity and temperature, but the suit is not intended for use at temperatures below +15°C.

STATUS
In production. In service with the Soviet and Warsaw Pact forces.

MANUFACTURER
State arsenals.

Cooling-type hooded coverall

UNITED KINGDOM

Respirator NBC S6

DESCRIPTION
Known to the British armed services as the respirator NBC S6 No 1 Mk 1, the S6 has several advanced features not found on many other similar items of equipment, the most noticeable of which is pneumatic sealing for a close and comfortable fit. The shaped eye-pieces provide good vision and condensation is kept at a minimum by routeing incoming air over them. Their design is such that spectacles can be worn and no special fittings are needed to use weapon sights or binoculars. Weapon handling is taken into consideration by placing the filter canister on the left side of the mask (versions are produced to suit left-handed wearers). The face mask also mounts a speech transmission

unit coupled to the outlet valve and all such fittings are made from anodised aluminium; the mouldings are natural rubber. The S6 is made in three sizes and the product has a shelf life of 25 years. It is stated that the S6 takes only 10 seconds to place into position. Normally it is carried in a chest- or shoulder-mounted haversack which weighs 0·57 kg together with a spare filter canister. The respirator itself weighs 0·83 kg. A kit containing a microphone, rubber tube and connectors can convert the S6 for AFV use in about one minute.
The Chemical Defence Establishment at Porton Down has been developing a new type of respirator based on the S6 and designated the S8. This version will be less expensive to produce and will have improved compatibility with optical instruments and gun

sights. The S8 will have less eye-piece padding and will be easier to manufacture.
A further new type of mask, the S10, is still in an early stage of development. It is expected to have a revised inlet and outlet valve arrangement and may also have a separate voicemitter that can be used directly with radio and other communications equipment.

STATUS
In production. In service with the British Armed Forces.

MANUFACTURER
The Leyland and Birmingham Rubber Company Limited, Golden Hill Lane, Leyland, Lancashire PR5 1UB, England.

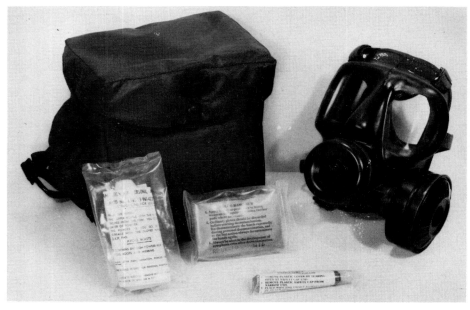

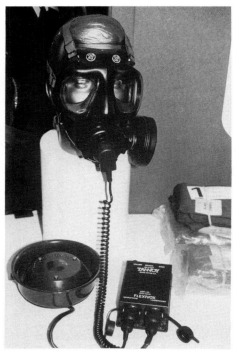

Respirator NBC S6 with satchel and cleaning/decontamination kit

Respirator NBC S6 with Tannoy loudspeaker attachment (T J Gander)

Protective Gloves NBC

DESCRIPTION
These protective gloves are in two parts, an inner light cotton liner and a black chloroprene rubber outer glove. The outer glove is impermeable to liquids and vapours, and can provide full protection for up to about six hours. The gloves are stored and issued in sealed plastic packs.

STATUS
In production and service with the British Armed Forces.

MANUFACTURER
James North and Sons Limited, PO Box 3, Hyde, Cheshire SK14 1RL, England.

NBC protective gloves

Protective NBC Suit No 1

DESCRIPTION
There are three marks of the NBC Suit No 1, all made from the same charcoal-impregnated non-woven material which is impervious to liquids but permeable to air and water vapour, making garments less uncomfortable than other comparable clothing. The material is also flame-proofed to provide a measure of protection

against nuclear flash. The charcoal-impregnated non-woven material was developed at the Chemical Defence Establishment at Porton Down in Wiltshire. All three suits, which have a shelf life of five years, are issued in sealed plastic bags. Both the Mark 2 and the Mark 3 are olive green and consist of overtrousers and a pull-over jacket. The Mark 4 uses a zip-up jacket in shades of disruptive camouflage. The No 1 Mark 2 suit is used by the Royal Navy on vessels with citadel sys-

NBC suit No 1 Mark 3 in use by RAF personnel (Ministry of Defence)

NBC suit No 1 Mark 4 (Ministry of Defence)

tems. The Mark 3 suit is the current ground forces issue but it will gradually be replaced by the Mark 4 which has completed its troop trials. All three suits can be repaired with issue repair kits that contain six self-adhesive pvc patches.

The No 1 Mark 3 suit is supplied in four sizes to fit men from 1·5 to 1·88 metres in height. The suit is a two-piece outfit which consists of a smock, with or without a hood and trousers. The smock uses two layers of material. The outer layer is modacrylic and nylon while the inner layer is of charcoal-impregnated cloth. The integral hood, when fitted, is lined and has a pull cord and cleat for adjustment and close fitting to the S6 respirator. The smock is generously cut and has a back gusset to allow freedom of movement. There is a large front flap pocket and a sleeve patch for locating detector paper. Adjustment is by Velcro with tape fastenings at the wrist and waist. The trousers are also made from two layers of material and have suspender tape fittings at the waist. There are Velcro tab fastenings at the base of the leg.

STATUS
Mark 2: in production. In service with the Royal Navy and some Commonwealth navies.

Mark 3: in production. In service with British ground forces and some European armies. 200 000 suits sold to US forces.

Mark 4: in production.

MANUFACTURERS
Bondina Limited, Greetland, Halifax, West Yorkshire HX4 8NJ, England.

The Leyland and Birmingham Rubber Company Limited, Golden Hill Lane, Leyland, Preston, Lancashire PR5 1UB, England.

J Compton, Sons & Webb Limited, Herbert Road, Newport, Gwent, Wales.

Remploy Limited, 415 Edgware Road, Cricklewood, London NW2 6LR, England.

Suit No 1 Mark 3

Protective Overboots NBC

DESCRIPTION
The standard British protective overboots come in one size only and once fitted over normal boots are adjusted with wide laces. The soles are made of chemical-resistant black butyl rubber and have a moulded tread to assist the grip when marching.

There is a special version of this overboot for use with skis which has provisions for ski-bindings.

The present service model of the NBC overboot is the Mark 3. A Mark 4 version has been developed but not yet accepted for service. The Mark 4 is produced in three sizes and is more closely tailored to follow the shape of the foot. It also has a more pronounced side tread.

STATUS
In production. In service with the British armed forces.

MANUFACTURERS
Butyl Products Limited, Radford Crescent, Billericay, Essex CM12 0DW, England.

The Leyland and Birmingham Rubber Company Limited, Golden Hill Lane, Leyland, Preston PR5 1UB, Lancashire, England.

Mk III overboots

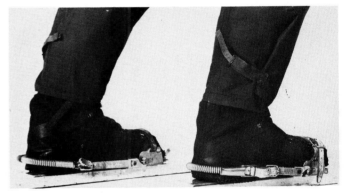
Ski March overboots

Charcoal Cloth NBC Facelet Mask

DESCRIPTION
The NBC Facelet Mask was developed by the Chemical Defence Establishment (CDE) at Porton Down, Wiltshire, to provide personnel with interim protection against surprise attack by chemical weapons including nerve agents. It entered service with the British Armed Forces during 1983.

The Facelet Mask provides oro-nasal protection and is donned as a precautionary measure when the wearer is at action stations. It has been designed to exert a minimal physiological load, with the result that it can be worn over long periods and under all operational conditions. Each mask is provided with an adjustable harness which enables one size to fit the whole service population. Other features of the Facelet Mask include its very low breathing resistance, high level of speech transmission and compatability with optical sights and other equipment. It provides a degree of protection at times

when the full face respirator is not being worn, including periods of rest and sleep. Once a chemical attack is confirmed the Facelet can be removed quickly and the full face respirator donned. It is small and robust and can be easily carried in a serviceman's kit.

The material used for the NBC Facelet Mask is activated charcoal cloth.

STATUS
Production. In service with the British Armed Forces.

MANUFACTURER
Charcoal Cloth Limited, Park Court, 1A Park Street, Maidenhead, Berkshire SL6 1SN, England.

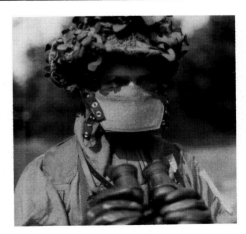
The Charcoal Cloth NBC Facelet Mask

Suit Protective NBC – Decontamination No 1 Mark 1

DESCRIPTION
This is a two-piece translucent pvc suit consisting of a smock with integral hood, and trousers. It is intended for use by personnel decontaminating equipment and areas, and is worn over the normal NBC clothing and equipment, including the S6 respirator. The suit is dis-posable and should be worn for one hour only. The suit is supplied in three sizes.

STATUS
Production. In service with the British Armed Forces.

MANUFACTURER
Remploy Limited, 415 Edgware Road, Cricklewood, London NW2 6LR, England.

Decontamination suit in use

Maximum Protection NBC Suit

DESCRIPTION
This one-piece boiler suit is made from butyl coated fabric and is designed to provide maximum protection against NBC agents during either reconnaissance or decontamination operations. It has an integral hood with a drawstring, a Velcro fly along the front and the wrists and ankles are designed to be gathered by elastic seals and tucked into NBC gloves and overboots.

STATUS
Production.

MANUFACTURER
James North and Sons Limited, PO Box 3, Hyde, Cheshire SK14 1RL, England.

Maximum protection NBC suit

NBC Poncho

DESCRIPTION
This garment is designed to provide protection over and above that available from existing NBC suits. Manufac-tured from butyl coated fabric, there is an integral hood attached to a long poncho-type garment with large loose sleeves. It is worn over the usual NBC clothing. To provide some degree of body ventilation charcoal fabric inserts are included in the groin area and in the back of the hood under the poncho. There is also an internal charcoal cloth kilt/skirt. A Velcro fly front is provided and, in addition, there is a large front access zip under the poncho. If required a number of these garments can be joined together to provide a small shelter. The garments/suits may be provided in a number of colours.

STATUS
Production.

MANUFACTURER
James North and Sons Limited, PO Box 3, Hyde, Cheshire SK14 1RL, England.

NBC poncho in sand colour scheme

NBC Casualty Bags

DESCRIPTION
There are two main types of British NBC casualty bag. The first is for use with stretchers and is intended to cover the stretcher fully with provision being made for stretcher handles. The second is for walking wounded who cannot wear a respirator and consists of a bag covering the top half of the body and secured at the waist. There are sleeves and a plastic panel in front of the face. Both casualty bags are manufactured from the normal charcoal-impregnated non-woven cloth. Velcro fasteners are fitted to the access panels of both bags.

STATUS
In production. In service with the British Armed Forces.

MANUFACTURERS
J Compton, Sons and Webb Limited, Herbert Road, Newport, Gwent, Wales.
Remploy Limited, 415 Edgware Road, Cricklewood, London NW2 6LR, England.
James North and Sons Limited, PO Box 3, Hyde, Cheshire SK14 1RL, England.

NBC casualty bag with stretcher version in background (Ministry of Defence)

Heavy-duty Respirator

DESCRIPTION
This heavy-duty respirator is for use in decontaminated areas and where severe chemical spillage is expected. The face-piece is a single heavy duty rubber moulding and the vision device is either a single one-piece hardened visor or twin circular eye-pieces. In both cases some form of demisting cream is required. The large filter canister is proof against most known chemical hazards.

STATUS
In production.

MANUFACTURER
Civil Defence Supplies, Wellingore, Lincolnshire LN5 0JF, England.

Lightweight Respirator

DESCRIPTION
Made from a one-piece heavy-duty rubber moulding, this mask has a single-piece hardened visor which is demisted by incoming filtered air directed across the interior. It is fitted with a speech diaphragm stated to give clear reception at a range of up to six metres. Only one size is manufactured but an adjustable head harness is provided. The filter canisters are standard 40 mm items and a range of different types is available from those giving full NBC protection to versions for use in industrial dust and fumes.

STATUS
In production.

MANUFACTURER
Civil Defence Supplies, Wellingore, Lincolnshire LN5 0JF, England.

Complete NBC Kit, Civilian, Heavy-duty

DESCRIPTION
This kit is intended for use by civilian and para-military authorities, including civil defence units, and can be produced to any size. The kit is stored and carried in a suitcase and consists of a heavy-duty washable and waterproof oversuit, an inner two-piece NBC protective garment, a full-face respirator with two canisters, a set of inner cotton and outer rubber gauntlets, a mask demisting pack, a pair of industrial rubber boots with steel toecaps, a roll of repair tape, decontamination powder and an instruction handbook.

The kit can be used as protection against either NBC or industrial hazards. Details of many of the above items can be found elsewhere in this section.

STATUS
In production.

MANUFACTURER
Civil Defence Supplies, Wellingore, Lincolnshire LN5 0JF, England.

Full face respirator

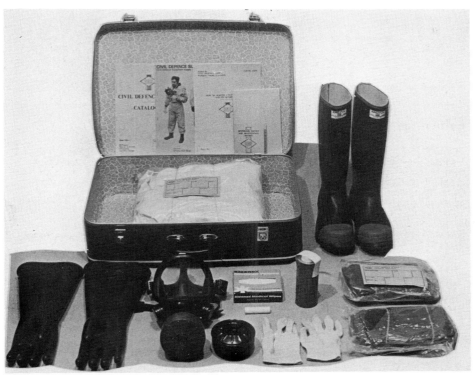

Complete individual NBC civilian kit

Lightweight Respirator

DESCRIPTION
Designed originally for civilian use this lightweight respirator has a semi-pneumatic face seal and a large soft plastic visor which is demisted by incoming filtered air. The mask has two external filter canisters (children's sizes use only one) which are produced either for full NBC protection or with particulate dust filtering only. It is produced in three adult and two children's sizes. It is carried in a soft canvas satchel.

STATUS
In production. In use with the Norwegian civil defence authorities.

SUPPLIER
Civil Defence Supplies, Wellingore, Lincolnshire LN5 0JF, England.

Complete NBC Kit, Civilian, Lightweight

DESCRIPTION
Intended primarily for civilian users as protection against NBC or industrial hazard, this kit can also be used by civil defence authorities. It consists of a complete lightweight kit of garments and equipment in a suitcase and can be produced in any appropriate size. It consists of a washable and waterproof lightweight oversuit, an inner NBC two-piece protective garment, a full-face respirator with one canister, a pair of industrial rubber boots with steel toecaps, a set of inner cotton and outer rubber garments, a mask demisting pack, decontamination powder and an instruction handbook.

Details of many of the above items can be found elsewhere in this section.

STATUS
In production.

MANUFACTURER
Civil Defence Supplies, Wellingore, Lincolnshire LN5 0JF, England.

Lightweight civilian NBC suits in different sizes

Heavy-duty Outer Suit

DESCRIPTION
This is a one-piece heavyweight oversuit that is chemical resistant and flame retardant. Manufactured from pvc-coated knitted nylon the suit has extra wear patches and double cuffs and leggings. The integral hood can be adjusted to suit a variety of respirators. It is available in large and medium sizes. Intended primarily for civilian use, it can also be used as NBC protection and by civil defence authorities, or by rescue or other such emergency squads.

A lightweight version is also produced.

STATUS
In production.

MANUFACTURER
Civil Defence Supplies, Wellingore, Lincolnshire LN5 0JF, England.

Combat suit protected against NBC agents in use

Cambridge Hood

DESCRIPTION
This decontamination hood is designed to be worn over decontamination clothing to prevent contaminants seeping through any seams or gaps in the clothing. The Cambridge Hood consists of a cape with integral arms, gloves and a clear head-piece, with sufficient space to accommodate a closed system respirator and air or oxygen cylinders. Contaminants are thus directed away from any vulnerable parts of the clothing and after use the hood can be hosed down. If the hood is seriously contaminated it can be removed using a ceiling hook or any other similar means and placed in a separate container for subsequent disposal or decontamination. The hood is made from a flame retardant material covered with an oil resistant plasticiser.

STATUS
In production.

MANUFACTURER
Civil Defence Supplies, Wellingore, Lincolnshire LN5 0JF, England.

Cambridge Hood

Two-piece Inner Protective Suit

DESCRIPTION
Manufactured from the same charcoal-impregnated material as the military Protective Suit No 1, this suit is a slightly modified version of that meant primarily for civilian use. The suit is intended for use by civil defence authorities or under a decontamination suit for industrial environments where chemical and other such hazards are present. It is produced in three adult and two children's sizes.

STATUS
In production.

MANUFACTURER
Civil Defence Supplies, Wellingore, Lincolnshire LN5 0JF, England.

UNITED STATES OF AMERICA

Mask, Chemical-biological: Field, ABC-M17 and ABC-M17A1

DESCRIPTION
This mask is the standard issue for all the US forces and has been in use since the early 1960s. The M17A1 differs from the M17 by having a self-contained drinking system and a resuscitation capability. The mask is well-designed with good vision and a voicemitter. The filter elements in the cheeks on each side are easily replaced without tools. The masks are issued in an M15 carrier with two filter elements and an M1 CB mask waterproofing bag. The M17A1 mask is carried in an M15A1 carrier which also contains an M1 water canteen cap. The mask, which is available in three sizes, is kept in place by a six-strap head harness.
The Czechoslovak Model M-10 mask design appears to be a close copy of the M17.

STATUS
In service with the US Army, Navy, Air Force and Marine Corps. Available for export.

DISTRIBUTOR
M17: Sherwood International Export Corporation, 18714 Parthenia Street, Northridge, California 91324, USA.

Mask, Chemical-biological: Field, ABC-M17

Mask, Chemical-biological: Tank, XM30

DESCRIPTION
The development of a new chemical-biological mask to replace the existing M17 and M17A1 models has been under way for some time. Two models were under development, the XM29 and the XM30. The XM29 was a one-piece mask but because of engineering difficulties with its flexible silicone lens it was passed over in favour of the XM30, a two-piece design. On the XM30 the lens is manufactured from moulded urethane. The face-piece is made from moulded elastomer with the periphery turned in to form a face seal. The lens is bonded into the face-piece. The mask uses an external filter canister developed in Canada which makes it suitable for right- and left-handed personnel. The design also has facilities for hose connections to chest-mounted filter systems, AFV or aircraft air systems, there are fittings to cater for drinking systems and mouth-to-mouth resuscitation, and there is a dual voicemitter. The mask will be manufactured in three sizes.
The design of the XM30 has been undertaken by the US Army Armament R and D Command's Chemical Systems Laboratory, Aberdeen Proving Ground. For various reasons the US Army decided not to adopt the XM30 but the mask was accepted for service by the US Air Force who ordered an initial batch of 10 000 to be delivered during 1983 and 1984.
In 1983 the Chemical Systems Laboratory produced the prototype of a new mask with a 'low risk' design incorporating the best features of many existing masks. Using this design as a basis three companies have now become involved in the development of a further design, apparently designated XM40. The programme costs are estimated at $6·7 million and it is expected that the final result will be a mask ready for production in March 1985.

STATUS
XM30 in production for the US Air Force.
XM40 under development.

Mask, Chemical-biological: Special Purpose, M9 and M9A1

DESCRIPTION
The only difference between the M9 and M9A1 is the carrier bag: the M9 uses the C15R1 and the M9A1 the M11 carrier. Other items are the M9 face-piece assembly and the M11 canister. The face masks are issued in three sizes and the filter canister can be fitted to either the left or the right. When worn the mask is held in place by a head harness. An optional extra for this mask is the winterising kit, CB mask, M1 which consists of a hood, insulating lenses, anti-snowglare lenses, a cheek pad and a plastic bag containing four spare nosecup valve discs. The kit is contained within the hood which is folded into a packet weighing approximately 0·32 kg.
The M9A1 is license-produced in South Korea as the KM9A1.

STATUS
In service with the US Army and Marine Corps.

Mask, Chemical-biological: Headwound, ABC-M18

DESCRIPTION
This head mask is intended for casualties who are unable to wear a normal protective mask and is essentially a large hood made from a permeable filter material which will allow air to pass through for breathing and allow exhaled air and moisture to be diffused. The mask is secured at the neck by a drawstring and a flexible rubber collar. There are two 203 × 76 mm plastic windows. The head-wound mask can provide protection against chemical and biological agents for at least an hour and is also effective against radioactive dust. The mask is issued folded flat in a vinyl plastic carrying bag.

STATUS
In service with the US Army.

Mask, Chemical-biological: Tank, ABC-M14A2

DESCRIPTION
This mask is designed for use by tank crewmen and can be used both inside the vehicle (connected to the vehicle's gas-particulate filter unit) or outside, using the mask system's filter canister. The face piece has a single-piece vision screen and also has a built-in microphone for connection into the vehicle's intercom. Spectacles can be worn with the mask. The mask is connected to the filter unit by an M8 hose. The filter unit is contained within the ABC-M13A1 carrier and consists of the M10A1 and the M1 canister coupling which connects the system into the vehicle filtered supply. The carrier, apart from holding the mask and other parts, also contains a personal protection kit and a mask anti-fogging kit. The mask is produced in three sizes and has an exhaust valve on the chin. A winterisation kit, the M3, consisting of an extra anti-fogging eye lens, a snow-glare lens and an insulating jacket to cover the neck and chin, is available. It can also be used with the M25A1 mask.

STATUS
In service with the US Army and Marine Corps.

Mask, Chemical-biological: Tank, M25 and ABC-M25A1

DESCRIPTION
These masks are virtually identical to the ABC-M14A2. The M25 is a modification of the M14A2 and the ABC-M25A1 is virtually the same item. In all other respects the two masks follow the same lines as the ABC-M14A2.

STATUS
In service with the US Army and Marine Corps.

Chemical Protective Outfit

DESCRIPTION
The standard American protective outfit is issued in one complete package. It consists of a protective suit, gloves, overboots and a hood and is intended to be worn with the M17 and M17A1 mask. The suit consists of a jacket and trousers, both made from charcoal-activated cloth with a nylon/cotton twill outer layer which can be either camouflaged to standard patterns or olive green. The inner layer is fire-retardant. The suit is packed in a hermatically sealed polypropylene bag which has a shelf life of five years; the pack weighs approximately 1·7 kg. The gloves, overboots and hood are all manufac-

tured from butyl rubber and the hood can be finished in a camouflage pattern if necessary. If required, the suit and other garments can be issued in one pack which also contains the M17A1 face mask. The suit is made in eight sizes from XXX-small up to XX-large.

STATUS
In production. In service with the US armed forces and some other nations.

MANUFACTURER
Winfield International Limited, Suite 6608, 350 Fifth Avenue, New York, NY 10118, USA.

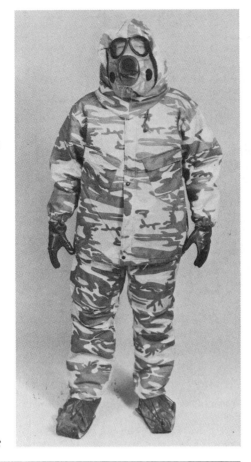

Chemical protective outfit

YUGOSLAVIA

Protective Mask

DESCRIPTION
This single-piece mask is moulded in flexible rubber and held in place by an adjustable webbing harness. There are two clear plastic eye-pieces and on the left side of the mask there is a screw housing for a filter canister. The mask may also be connected to an alternative filter system by a chin-mounted screw fitting which is normally held closed by a screw bung. The fitted canister is designated the TU-51.

This mask is used by both military and civilian personnel in Yugoslavia.

STATUS
Probably no longer in production. In service with the Yugoslav armed service and civilian organisations.

MANUFACTURER
State factories.

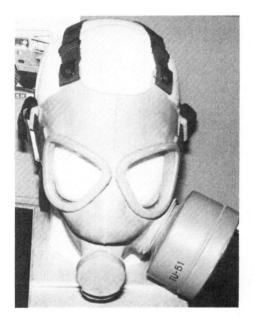

Yugoslav protective mask (T J Gander)

DECONTAMINATION KITS AND EQUIPMENT

BRAZIL

ENGESA EE-25 (4 × 4) NBC Decontamination Truck

DESCRIPTION
This vehicle has been designed and produced specifically for the NBC decontamination of troops, roads and vehicles and uses the 4 × 4 chassis of the EE-25 2500 kg truck. For details of this vehicle refer to the entry in the *Trucks* section.

The load-carrying area of the EE-25 truck has a 3000-litre capacity water tank integral with the platform, a 200-litre fuel tank for the heater, a decontaminant solution tank with a 160-litre capacity, a heater with a fuel consumption of 120 litres an hour, a decontamination solution dispenser with a normal mix of one litre of decontaminant to every 20 litres of water (graduated from zero to 30 litres an hour), a water pump with a flow of 48 litres a minute, 16 showers, two 100-mm diameter hoses, a road decontamination set and canvas covers for the shower areas.

STATUS
In production for a North African country.

MANUFACTURER
Engenheiros Espacializados SA (ENGESA), Avenida das Nacoes Unidas 22.833, Santo Amaro, 04697 Sao Paulo, Brazil.

ENGESA EE-25 (4 × 4) NBC decontamination truck

ENGESA EE-25 (4 × 4) NBC decontamination truck

CZECHOSLOVAKIA

Decontamination Apparatus, Truck-mounted, Model TZ 74

DESCRIPTION
Based on the chassis of the Tatra 148 PPR 15 truck, this equipment is a progressive development of the Soviet Model TMS-65. It follows the same general lines in that it employs a small gas turbine to spray decontaminating agents over vehicles and equipment. As with the Model TMS-65, the gas turbine is mounted on the rear of the vehicle with the operator's cabin on the right-hand side. The rest of the vehicle rear is taken up with tanks for the decontaminating liquids and fuel for the gas turbine. The gas turbine, which is designated Type M 701 c-500, can be traversed through 120 degrees, elevated 30 degrees and depressed 20 degrees. It can dispense liquids at the rate of 900 litres an hour. A fuel tank for the gas turbine holds 2000 litres. The main decontaminant tank holds 5000 litres. Fully loaded the Model TZ 74 weighs 22 000 kg and empty 14 000 kg. It has an operational crew of two. As well as being used for equipment decontamination, it can be used to create smoke screens.

STATUS
In production. In service with the Czechoslovak Army.

MANUFACTURER
Truck chassis: Tatra, Narodni Podnik, Koprinice, Czechoslovakia.

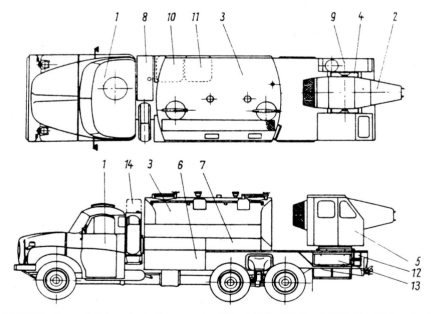

Model TZ 74 truck-mounted decontamination apparatus (1) basic Tatra 148 chassis (2) turbine (3) decontaminant tanks (4) turntable (5) operator's cabin (6) hydraulics compartment (7) water heater (8) heater fuel tank (9) smoke screen equipment (10) hydraulic fuel reservoir (11) fuel tank (12) jerrican (13) vehicle service hatch (14) camouflage net stowage

FRANCE

Chemical Decontamination Glove

DESCRIPTION
This glove is intended for personal decontamination of individual users' skin, clothing and equipment. It is a simple fingerless olive green glove made from natural fibres. One side has decontaminating powder (fuller's earth or similar) behind a fine mesh and the other is a sponge cloth. The powder is patted onto the affected surface and then wiped off with the sponge. The gloves are issued in sealed plastic bags 120 × 200 mm, and 20 mm thick. Opened and ready for use the glove measures 160 × 250 mm. Each one weighs 127 grams, ± 5 grams.

STATUS
Production probably complete. In service with the French armed forces.

MANUFACTURER
Société Industrielle de Réalisations et d'Etudes de Conditionnement (SIREC), Chemin d'en Bas, 77102 Villenroy, France.

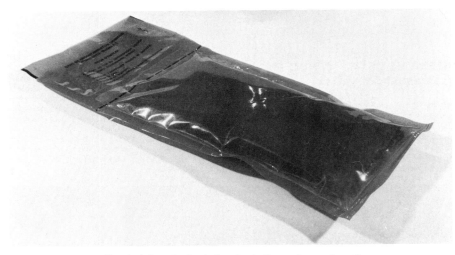

Chemical decontaminant glove in plastic envelope as issued

Decontamination Appliance, Emergency, 2·5-litre

DESCRIPTION
This apparatus is carried on vehicles for emergency decontamination of the carrier vehicle and, to a lesser extent, weapons and other equipment. Normally the apparatus is carried on a special 400 mm long rack. Once filled with a decontaminating solution, the apparatus is not brought under pressure until immediately before it is required. A commercial 'Sparklets' CO₂ bulb is used to pressurise the contents within 30 sec-

onds which enables the contents to be sprayed for up to 40 seconds approximately. The tank has a total capacity of about 2·5 litres but only 1·6 litres can be effectively used. The appliance weighs 3·5 kg and is 385 mm long with a diameter of 110 mm.

STATUS
In production.

MANUFACTURER
Groupement Industriel des Armements Terrestres (GIAT), 10 place Georges Clémenceau, 92211 Saint-Cloud, France.

2·5-litre emergency decontamination appliance

GERMANY, DEMOCRATIC REPUBLIC

Protective Kit, Medical, Model MSP-18

DESCRIPTION
The Model MSP-18 kit is issued to every soldier for self-treatment of the effects of chemical and biological warfare. It is issued in a small case 100 × 90 × 30 mm and contains several different types of medical drug administrants and an instruction sheet. One half of the case contains six squeeze-type hypodermic syringes (syrettes) for treating nerve agents, some cotton pads, and a package of six tablets for use against lung irritants. The other half of the case holds a red plastic eye dropper for flushing nerve agents from the eyes, a blue plastic syrette containing an antidote for hydrogen cyanide poisoning, a phial containing ampoules for inhaling after hydrogen cyanide poisoning, and a colour-

less syrette containing a morphine-based pain killer. The kit is said to be effective against the agents for which it is issued.

STATUS
In service.

MANUFACTURER
State factories and laboratories.

Individual Decontamination Kit Model EP-60

DESCRIPTION
The EP-60 kit is carried in a plastic bag and is used for decontaminating clothing and small items of personal equipment. The plastic bag contains three tubes, numbered 1, 2, and 3, two wooden and one metal spatulas, cotton pads and instructions. The procedure is to remove as much as possible of the contaminating agent with the spatulas and the cotton pads. If the agent is identified the contents of the appropriate tube only need be applied: tube 1 contains nerve agent decontaminant, tube 2 is for use against blister agents and tube 3 is for use against both biological and radiological agents. If the nature of the contamination is not known the ointment is applied direct from the tubes in numerical order. The ointment is removed after ten minutes using the cotton pads. Decontamination is completed by washing the area in water. Complete, the EP-60 kit weighs about 150 g.

STATUS
Probably no longer in production. In service with the East German forces.

MANUFACTURER
State factories.

Individual Decontamination Kit, Model EP-62

DESCRIPTION
The EP-62 kit is used for personal decontamination of skin, clothing, individual weapons and equipment. It is contained in a plastic or light alloy case and consists of two plastic bottles, instructions and absorbent pads. The two bottles contain ointment, one blue for use against nerve agents and the other white for use against blister agents. If the nature of any contamination is not known the blue bottle contents are used first. The agent is first removed as far as possible with the absorbent pads and the ointment is then applied thickly. It is left for ten minutes and then removed with more pads.

STATUS
Probably still in production. In service with the East German forces.

MANUFACTURER
State factories.

Large Decontamination Kit, Model GES-10

DESCRIPTION
This kit is used for decontaminating vehicles and other large equipment, and is carried as a standard item on each vehicle. The Model GES-10 is intended as 'first-aid' decontamination to make the vehicle usable until a full cleansing can be carried out by a fully-equipped decontamination unit. The kit comprises a metal tray, with two 5-litre water cans and an accessories container

which can be split into two halves which act as further trays. The kit contains two scrubbing brushes, two ring-shaped brushes, a flat short-handled brush, rags, three 50 ml bottles of Mersolat D decontaminant and three cardboard boxes each containing 0·5 kg of calcium hypochlorite. In use any large areas of contamination are wiped clean with the rags, and mud and debris are removed with a scraper. The standard decontaminant, EF1-III, is produced by mixing 0·5 kg of calcium hypochlorite in one of the cans and then pouring the solution into one or more of the trays from where it is applied with the various brushes. In a nuclear radiation environment,

one bottle of Mersolat D (a detergent) is added to a can of water and the vehicle is scrubbed. After either procedure the vehicle is dried with rags from the kit.

STATUS
Probably no longer in production in the above form. In service with the East German and some other Warsaw Pact forces.

MANUFACTURER
State factories.

Decontamination Apparatus, Backpack, Models TEG-57 and TEG-57A

DESCRIPTION
These two back-pack equipments have replaced the earlier TEG-10. They consist of two 5-litre brass tanks and the required pumping gear. Both are issued in wooden cases, and mounted on the back frame are the two tanks, a hand-operated air pump, a pressure gauge,

control valves, rubber hose, and a spray pipe with a nozzle to which a brush can be fitted. The Model TEG-57A differs from the earlier Model TEG-57 in having a redesigned frame with no base plate and an integral carrying handle (the even earlier Model TEG-10 used only a single tank). In service the decontamination solutions to be used are mixed and strained before loading the tanks. The tanks can be filled with a different solution in each, or the same solution in both: a three-way valve selects either tank or, alternatively, it can be used to dispense a mixture of the two tank contents. Both tanks are pressurised using the pumping lever to

about 6 kg/cm², and the discharge rate can be varied by fitting one of three nozzle sizes: 1·2, 0·8 and 0·6 mm, and with a 10-litre filling the spraying times are 10, 24 and 45 minutes respectively. Full, both models weigh about 22 kg and empty about 12 kg.

STATUS
It is probable that neither model remains in production. In service with the East German forces.

MANUFACTURER
State factories.

Decontamination and Deactivation Apparatus, Model EEA-61

DESCRIPTION
The Model EEA-61 is built into some East German vehicles fitted with air brakes. It is an integral part of the vehicle and consists of two 40-litre tanks, two hose lines, two spray pipes with nozzles and round

brushes, and some other fittings. Each tank is normally filled with 36 litres of decontamination solution with a different solution in each tank. Depending on the nature of the contaminant, the appropriate tank is selected and the tank is then pressurised from the vehicle's air brake system. The solution is driven through the hose system to the nozzles where the brushes assist in clearing the contaminant.

STATUS
Probably still in production. In service with the East German forces.

MANUFACTURER
State factories.

Decontamination Apparatus, Truck-mounted, Model GEW-1

DESCRIPTION
This equipment is mounted on the G-5 truck chassis and is used for decontaminating vehicles, weapons, equipment, buildings and terrain. It consists of a 4500-litre tank, a pump driven from a power take-off from the main engine, hoses, nozzles and various accessories. The pump can discharge up to 1500 litres of decontaminating solution every minute at a pressure of 8 kg/cm². Six 9·5 mm or three 42 mm hoses can be used to suit the task in hand, or two spray nozzles can be fitted to the front or rear of the vehicle to clear areas of road or terrain. One filling of the tank is enough to decontaminate 16 vehicles or a strip five metres wide and 1000 to 1500 metres long using the front-mounted nozzles. Using the nozzles mounted at the rear a strip three metres wide and 2500 metres long can be cleansed. The Model GEW-1 can be used for fire-fighting.

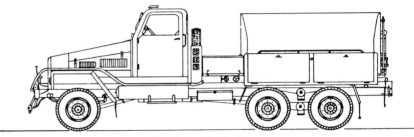

GEW-1 decontamination vehicle

STATUS
Production complete. Probably no longer in full service with the East German forces but still held in reserve.

MANUFACTURER
State factories.

Decontamination Apparatus, Truck-mounted, Model GEW-2

DESCRIPTION
The Model GEW-2 is used to dispense solid, dry decontaminants over roads and terrain. It is mounted on a G-5 truck chassis and consists mainly of a covered-hopper

body into which the decontaminating material is loaded. A hydraulically-driven spreader disc at the rear, the speed of which can be varied, dispenses the decontaminating material. The spreading width can be varied from three to six metres. The floor of the hopper is also hydraulically driven to the rear. The hopper body has a capacity of 3000 kg. The Model GEW-2 can also be used for salting or sanding roads.

STATUS
Production complete. In limited service with the East German forces.

MANUFACTURER
State factories.

Decontamination Apparatus, Truck-mounted, Model GEW-3

DESCRIPTION
The Model GEW-3 is mounted on a G-5 lorry chassis and has replaced the earlier Model GEW-1 in East German service. It is used to decontaminate vehicles, buildings, equipment and terrain and can also be used as a water or fuel carrier, for fire-fighting and as a mobile or static smoke generator. It consists of a 3100-litre tank, a diesel-engine driven pump, hoses, nozzles, fittings, valves and accessories. The tank has internal baffles, two access and filling manholes, and is corrosion-proofed internally. The diesel engine for the pump is between the cab and the tank and its exhaust pipe passes through the tank to warm the contents in winter, as does the vehicle engine exhaust pipe. The pump is at the rear of the tank and the pump and diesel engine controls are all inside the vehicle cab. Various hoses can be fitted to the equipment to suit the decontamination role and spray nozzles can be fitted to the front and rear of the vehicle for terrain or road cleansing. At the rear of the equipment there is a special fitting with five nozzles which is used to disperse smoke fumes produced by the dissemination of chlorosulphonic acid.

Model GEW-3 truck-mounted, decontamination apparatus

STATUS
Production complete. In service with the East German forces.

MANUFACTURER
State factories.

Decontamination Apparatus, Model EA-65

DESCRIPTION
This equipment is a portable decontamination system using pre-pressurised and pre-filled tanks. The tanks are carried to their point of use by specially-equipped LO 1800 A trucks which can carry 16 tanks each. The trucks are fitted with racks for the tanks, an air compressor, and a loading and unloading ramp. The corrosion-resistant steel tanks are mounted in tubular steel frames, and each has a pressure gauge, outlet hose, spray pipe, nozzle and nozzle brush. The tanks are pre-filled with an appropriate decontamination solution and pressurised on the truck to a maximum working pressure of 6 kg/cm². Tank capacity is approximately 40 litres, and the weight loaded 85 kg. The Model EA-65 cylinders can be used to decontaminate vehicles, weapons, equipment and general areas. Once empty the tanks can be collected, re-filled and re-pressurised.

STATUS
Probably still in production. In service with the East German and some other Warsaw Pact forces.

MANUFACTURER
State factories.

Decontamination Apparatus, Truck-mounted, Model MOE

DESCRIPTION
The Model MOE is not intended mainly as decontamination equipment; it was produced primarily for water-damping roadways and runways under construction. However, it can be used for decontamination, and it can also be used as a water-carrier or a water-pumping station. Mounted on the G-5 chassis, the Model MOE can be fitted with a variety of hoses and fittings but consists mainly of a 3750-litre tank, an air-cooled four-cylinder petrol engine which drives a centrifugal pump, spray booms and various other accessories. The pump can discharge 600 litres a minute which is normally passed through the extensible spray booms, but other fittings to suit particular tasks can be employed. When extended the booms cover an area 7·3 metres wide.

STATUS
Production complete. In reserve with the East German forces.

MANUFACTURER
State factories.

Decontamination Shower Apparatus, Vehicle-mounted, Model DA-2S

DESCRIPTION
The Model DA-2S replaced the earlier Model DA-2 in East German service but in its turn is being replaced by the later Model DA-66. It can be used as a normal field shower unit as well as for decontamination. It consists of two units, one, which is carried on a G-5 truck chassis, consisting of an oil-fired boiler, a heat exchanger, hoses, plumbing, pipes, pumps and controls and the other, the shower unit, which is carried on a towed trailer. The shower trailer has 12 shower heads, but on the move it also carries the associated dressing and undressing tents, canvas-covered passage-ways, duckboards, stoves and various other items. The oil-fired boiler heats the water, using a heat exchanger, to 70°C from cold in about 50 minutes. Before the water reaches the shower heads it is mixed with cold water to produce a working temperature of 35°C. The oil burner-blower and the shower pumps are driven by electric motors: the water is delivered to the shower heads at a pressure of 1·5 kg/cm². After use the shower water is collected from a single point for disposal. Tents, heated if necessary, complete the equipment.

STATUS
Production complete. Still in service with the East German forces.

MANUFACTURER
State factories.

Decontamination Shower Apparatus, Truck-mounted, Model DA-66

DESCRIPTION
The Model DA-66 is much lighter than the earlier Model DA-2S, but like it is carried in two units. One unit is carried on the chassis of an LO 1800 A truck which carries the equipment's water-heating unit and a pump. A trailer carries a compartmented tent which is divided into undressing, shower and dressing sections. This trailer has a single axle. The Model DA-66 is intended to replace the Model DA-2S.

STATUS
Production probably now complete. In service with the East German forces.

MANUFACTURER
State factories.

Decontamination Apparatus, Truck-mounted, Model EW-1
Decontamination Apparatus, Skid-mounted, Model S-4

DESCRIPTION
These two equipments are the same, but on a truck is designated Model EW-1 and on a ground skid-mount the Model S-4. They are used to decontaminate vehicles, weapons, field fortifications and equipment. Both units have two 700-litre drum tanks, a double two-piston pump, an air-cooled petrol engine, two jet pumps, hose reels and hoses, nozzles and accessories. The tanks can be filled with either decontaminants or water through their 380 mm filling apertures. The apertures are fitted with screens, and once a small quantity of liquid has been poured into the tanks it can be circulated by the piston pump to operate the jet pumps. The pump discharges through seven hoses which are stowed on two reels, three on the left reel and four on the right. The piston pump can draw from either tank separately or both together so different decontaminants can be poured into each tank. The equipment is three metres long, 1·7 metres wide, 1·5 metres high and weighs about 2100 kg.

STATUS
Production complete. In service with the East German forces and civilian defence organisations.

MANUFACTURER
State factories.

Decontamination Apparatus, Truck-mounted, Model EW-2
Decontamination Apparatus, Skid-mounted, Model S-6

DESCRIPTION
The Model EW-2 and the Model S-6 are the same equipment but the Model EW-2 is mounted on a truck and the Model S-6 on a ground skid. They differ from the earlier Models EW-1 and S-4 in several respects. The Models EW-2 and S-6 both have rectangular 700-litre tanks but each has its own air-cooled petrol engine and its own three-piston pump. There are also two jet pumps, and there are six hoses fitted to two reels. The pumps can be used either to fill the tanks or discharge the tank contents through the hoses, and each pump can draw or fill both or either of the tanks. The equipment is 2·9 metres long, 1·7 metres wide and 1·5 metres high and weighs approximately 2230 kg.

STATUS
Production complete. In service with the East German forces.

MANUFACTURER
State factories.

Decontamination Pumping Apparatus, Trailer-mounted, Model TS-8

DESCRIPTION
The Model TS-8 is a military version of a civilian fire-fighting appliance and is used for a variety of decontamination purposes. In its basic form it can be used to pump water over equipment or vehicles to remove radio-active particles, but for chemical and biological cleansing it is more often used to pump water for decontamination stations (two or more units can be connected in series if necessary). The unit consists of a pump driven by an air-cooled two-cycle engine, together with the associated hoses and fittings. The unit is carried in a box-type body on a single-axle trailer. The pumping unit, which weighs 70 kg, can deliver 800 litres a minute to a pressure head of 80 metres.

STATUS
Production complete. In service with the East German forces.

MANUFACTURER
State factories.

GERMANY, FEDERAL REPUBLIC

Kärcher HDS 1200 BK Steam-jet Decontamination Apparatus

DESCRIPTION

Alfred Kärcher GmbH has long been concerned with the production of high-pressure steam cleaning equipment and has produced the HDS 1200 BK specifically for the military role, in particular for NBC decontamination. The HDS 1200 BK can be used in a variety of forms ranging from a purely static installation to the placing of the equipment on a trailer, trolley or sledge for more mobile applications. The cleaner is powered by a petrol or diesel engine although a model known as the HDS 1200 EK can be powered by an electric motor.

In use the HDS 1200 BK takes water from either a tank, mains source or reservoir, heats it and delivers it under pressure through a pipe equipped with a nozzle or some other form of spray device. The water may be heated as high as 200°C and can both clean and decontaminate. Most chemical and biological agents will be rendered harmless at the high temperatures but for most purposes the water will not need to be more than 80°C. The equipment can be operated by one man and can clear contamination from virtually all the outer surfaces of AFVs, aircraft, vehicles and other military equipment.

Using special kits the HDS 1200 BK can be used to supply heated water to a special shower system for personnel decontamination. The shower units may be either constant flow or pulsing. The HDS 1200 can also produce steam and heated water for the cleaning and decontamination of clothing and equipment. A further fitting can be used to steam explosive out of unexploded bombs and artillery shells.

If required, the HDS 1200 BK can be used to spray decontaminants. For use with water there are three set levels of temperature; hot (80°C), steam (140°C) and saturated steam (200°C). Hot water can be supplied one minute after starting up the engine with a manual starter. The heater coil has various safeguards built in to enable it to be used with chemicals such as some of the more aggressive decontaminants, and chemicals can be fed into the water system even when the system is running. The fuel for the engine may also be drawn from a constant source.

While the HDS 1200 BK is normally used on a mobile sledge carrier, a new version known as the Decojet has been produced. This is mounted on the back of a Mercedes-Benz (4 × 4) 750 kg light vehicle. In this form the steam equipment can be carried to field units for

Kärcher Decocontain system with equipment placed in ready-fitted containers for various NBC decontamination purposes

use. Another application for the HDS 1200 BK is in the Decocontain system where a complete personnel decontamination station could be used inside a standard ISO container.

SPECIFICATIONS (HDS 1200 BK)

Weight: (without accessories) 300 kg
Weight of accessories: 70 kg
Length: 1·45 m
Width: 0·75 m
Height: 1·11 m
Pressure of jet: up to 50 bar
Pressure of steam jet: 18 bar
Pressure of saturated steam jet: 15 bar
Maximum overpressure: 62 bar

Capacity:
(high pressure stage) 1200 litres/h
(steam stage) 600 litres/h
(saturated steam stage) 240 litres/h
Fuel consumption: (high pressure) 2·4 litres/h
Fuel tank capacity: 5·6 litres
Heating coil capacity: 5·1 litres

STATUS

Production. In use with the West German armed forces and several other NATO forces.

MANUFACTURER

Alfred Kärcher GmbH & Company, Leutenbacher Strasse 30–40, D-7057 Winnenden, Federal Republic of Germany.

OWR DEKON Decontamination System

DESCRIPTION

The OWR DEKON decontamination system is a mobile system based on 6 × 6 and 8 × 8 trucks and consists of five basic components, each of which has its own carrying vehicle. The trucks used for the system are the MAN 20.280 DFAEG (6 × 6) 10 000 kg truck or the MAN 10 000 kg (8 × 8) and 7000 kg (6 × 6) high mobility tactical trucks. For details of these vehicles refer to the entries in the *Trucks* section.

The first component is the DETECT 1000, normally carried on an 8 × 8 chassis. It has three main compartments the first of which is the working area or laboratory fitted with an air-conditioned filtered over-pressure system. It contains instruments for detecting, measuring and marking NBC-contaminated areas and also has communications equipment for reporting findings. The area has space for two operators but can accommodate up to a further six persons for travelling. The second area is the decontamination lock accessible from the outside by a hinged ladder. A shower basin is installed near the ground with a direct operable shower head and drainage for contaminated liquids. This cubicle is also used as a reception area for contaminated clothing and equipment. There is access to the laboratory area. The third area, the decontamination centre, houses all necessary equipment including a 600-litre tank, the hot water plant, storage for decontaminating agents and associated accessories. A spreader and spray bar are fitted at the rear of the vehicle for area distribution of decontaminants. Warning devices such as horns and lamps may be fitted. The driver's cab has partial armour protection.

The DEKON 2000 is a decontamination disaster protection vehicle and is designed to be operated independently of the rest of the system if necessary. It can be used for personnel and equipment decontamination, area decontamination and for producing toxic-free drinking water. The equipment carried on the DEKON 2000 includes a shower lock, wide jet spray tubes, spray

DEKON 2000 system mounted on MAN 7000 kg (6 × 6) high mobility tactical truck

shower heads, water brushes with adjustable telescopic shafts, mixing injectors for liquid and powder decontaminants, a water spray device under the vehicle platform, a spreading arrangement and a foam gun, a water purifying plant, two 1500-litre drinking-water tanks, a heat-insulated special tank for the supply of 2500 litres of water, a water circulation heater, a water supply electric pump, mixing devices, an electrical control panel and 380/220 volt and 24 volt generators. All devices and equipment are carried on a flat working

area accessible by a ladder at the rear or side. Normally they are covered by a canvas tilt which can be raised when working.

The third component is the SHOWER 3000 which can supply cleansing showers for up to 3500 personnel within a 24-hour period. Personnel walk into the showers from one side and leave by ladders on the other side. The equipment consists of a water tank, electrical generator, a water circulation heater, shower cubicles with ten showers each, a water pump and switch gear.

Associated with the equipment is a collapsible 5000-litre water tank along with clothing bags, towels, decontaminating agents etc.

The fourth component is the WASH 4000, a field laundry with a capacity for processing approximately 100 to 150 kg of clothing every hour. This is enough for 150 persons. The WASH 4000 is equipped with two washing machines, one centrifuge, one rotary dryer, an electrical generator, a 3500-litre water tank, a water pump and various auxiliary appliances.

The fifth component is the MOBILE WORKSHOP 5000. This is a van containing a workshop and a supply of spares capable of maintaining the complete DEKON system in the field. It contains its own small decontamination cubicle for personnel and equipment and radio may be fitted.

STATUS
Production.

MANUFACTURERS
Odenwaldwerke Rittersbach Kern und Grosskinsky GmbH, D-6957 Elztal-Rittersbach, Federal Republic of Germany.

NBC Decontamination Truck

DESCRIPTION
The standard Bundeswehr NBC decontamination truck is a MAN 7000 kg truck which has been adapted for the role by the addition of special mounting points on the load area. The trucks may carry either decontaminating equipment for use at main centres or equipment for terrain, equipment and clothing decontamination in the field. Both equipments are low-pressure types. The field version equipment includes a 1·5 m³ tank, a continuous-flow heater and special fittings for the field decontamination role.

STATUS
Production probably complete. In service with the West Germany Army.

MANUFACTURER (decontamination equipment)
MINIMAX, Urach, Federal Republic of Germany.

MAN 7000 kg truck converted for NBC decontamination

HUNGARY

Decontamination Apparatus, Truck-mounted

DESCRIPTION
This equipment is mounted on a Csepel D-344 truck chassis and consists of a tank with a capacity of approximately 2800 litres, a heater, a pump, nozzles, hoses, fittings and various accessories. Used for decontaminating vehicles, equipment, weapons and buildings, the equipment has stowage boxes along each side for the various fittings, and the heater is just behind the cab with a smoke flue on the left-hand side.

STATUS
Production complete. In service only with the Hungarian forces.

MANUFACTURER
State factories.

ITALY

Tirrena Chemical Decontamination Equipment

DEVELOPMENT/DESCRIPTION
Most of the chemical solutions used to decontaminate vehicles and equipment after exposure to chemical warfare agents are corrosive to varying degrees. In practice this means that the decontaminants have to be mixed or otherwise prepared immediately before use or their dispenser/containers will become corroded to the point of uselessness. This has several disadvantages, not only in a time-scale, but there will be certain areas or sets of circumstances in which the water essential to produce the working solution will be either unavailable or scarce.

For these circumstances the new decontaminating equipment produced by Tirrena SpA was developed. It is a small fire extinguisher-type decontaminant dispenser designed to be carried on a vehicle for the immediate 'first aid' decontamination of the vehicle or other equipment. The Tirrena dispenser can be carried fully loaded for long periods, as it is made entirely of AISA-304 stainless steel which is proof against chemical corrosion. The equipment can be loaded at a remote point and carried in its special bracket until required. The decontaminant is propelled from the container by compressed nitrogen which is supplied with the equipment in a special loading container which weighs 300 grams and has a diameter of 40 mm. The 95 cm³ of nitrogen stored in the loading container pressurises the contents of the dispenser to a level of 15 kg/cm², and the loading container is reloadable. The dispenser itself is tested to a pressure of 50 kg/cm². The dispenser cylinder has a maximum capacity of two litres but the normal working capacity is 1·5 litres.

SPECIFICATIONS
Weight: (empty) 3·2 kg
Height: 340 mm
Diameter: 130 mm
Working pressure: 15 kg/cm²
Testing pressure: 50 kg/cm²
Contents:
   (max) 2 litres
   (working) 1·5 litres
Loading container
Weight: 0·3 kg
Diameter: 40 mm
Contents: 0·95 litre
Loading pressure: 150 kg/cm²
Testing pressure: 400 kg/cm²

STATUS
Production.

MANUFACTURER
Tirrena SpA, Via del Quirinale 22, 00187 Rome, Italy.

Tirrena stainless steel decontaminating equipment

JAPAN

Japanese NBC Systems

Chemical protection (defence) vehicle based on chassis of Type SU 60 APC
(K Ebata)

Decontamination vehicle based on 6 × 6 truck chassis (K Nogi)

NETHERLANDS

ComboPen (Autoject) Nerve Agent Antidote

DESCRIPTION
The term ComboPen is the registered trade name for a device that is often referred to as the Autoject nerve agent antidote injector. It is a personal self-administered hypodermic device that is usually issued to anyone who is likely to encounter nerve agents. The device is some 170 mm long and 20 mm in diameter with a safety cap at one end and a black cone at the other, and the body is plastic.

In use the safety cap is removed from the end and retained. Removing the cap reveals a large button against which the thumb is pressed as the black cone end is pressed against the thigh. Further pressure on the button releases a needle which can penetrate combat clothing and the skin of the thigh to introduce the atropine-based nerve agent antidote into the body. The needle is held in place for five seconds and the device can then be discarded. A small tablet inside the device safety cap is then swallowed to complete the self-treatment which is repeated after 15 minutes if the nerve agent symptoms persist. The maximum total dose is three injections. Instructions for use are printed on the body of the device.

For training an inert version with no needle or drug product is available. In place of the needle a blunt plastic button is projected and the device can be re-cocked with a special cap attachment. Various types of filling other than the nerve agent antidote can be used, and if required the ComboPen can be reloaded using a cartridge that encloses the agent and the needle.

The device is now in service with the British Armed Forces as the Autoject (ComboPen) Nerve Agent Antidote L2A1. The training device is the L3A1.

STATUS
Production. In service with the United Kingdom and other NATO armed forces.

MANUFACTURER
Duphar BV, PO Box 7006–1007 JA, Amsterdam, Netherlands.

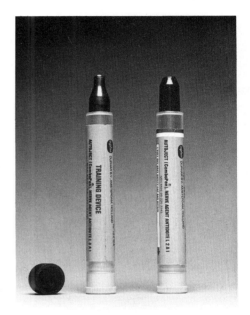

Left Autoject training device L3A1; right Autoject L2A1

POLAND

Decontamination Apparatus, Truck-mounted, Model IRS

DESCRIPTION
The Model IRS is used to decontaminate large areas of terrain, large pieces of equipment, vehicles and buildings. It can also be used as a water carrier, to provide heated water for showers or for fire fighting. The equipment is mounted on a Star-66 truck and consists of a 2500-litre tank, a pump driven by the vehicle engine, a hand pump, a heater, various hoses, pipes and nozzles, and shower equipment. The tank is fitted with internal baffles and is internally corrosion-proofed. The inlet manhole is screened and the system can be used to discharge solid or liquid decontaminants. Liquid solutions are mixed by the internal cycling of the pump which is driven by a power take-off, and when discharging the pump can deliver 600 litres a minute at a working pressure of 4 kg/cm². The tank contents are heated by a fuel-fired heater fed from the vehicle fuel tank by compressed air from the vehicle air brakes. The heater can warm 2000 litres of solution an hour to a temperature of 70°C, which is then maintained. The various accessories are stowed along the sides of the tank in cases and drums of decontaminant are stowed over the cases. The equipment consists of fourteen 10 mm hoses, each with a spray pipe, nozzle and nozzle brush. For cleansing large areas or buildings (or fire fighting) three 20-metre long hoses, 25 mm in diameter, can be fitted. The shower unit has eight heads. For terrain cleansing, fan-shaped nozzles can be fitted to the front and rear of the vehicle. The total weight of the Model IRS is 9560 kg.

IRS decontamination vehicle based on Star 66 (6 × 6) chassis

STATUS
No longer in production. In service with the Polish forces.

MANUFACTURER
State factories.

Decontamination Apparatus, Model UDU

DESCRIPTION
This equipment is carried to its place of use by a truck and placed on the ground. It is operated by two men, and is used to remove radioactive particles from clothing, tents, tarpaulins and similar equipment. The equipment has a small internal combustion engine which powers a system of beaters and a vacuum system. The contaminated clothing is fed into the equipment where it is beaten and the particles are then removed by suction to a special container for disposal. The Model UDU can process up to 120 pieces of clothing an hour. The weight of the equipment is 270 kg.

STATUS
Production complete. In service with the Polish forces.

MANUFACTURER
State factories.

UNION OF SOVIET SOCIALIST REPUBLICS

Atropine Injector

DESCRIPTION
This injector is issued to all Soviet troops and is used as a self-administered treatment for nerve agent poisoning. The injector is a squeeze-type hypodermic syringe which contains and dispenses a 1 cc dose of 0·1 per cent atropine sulphate solution from a flexible plastic capsule. The injector needle cover is removed and a piercing wire already in the needle is pushed into a membrane that seals the needle from the capsule. The wire is discarded, the needle pushed into a thigh muscle and the capsule squeezed to inject the solution. This injector is simple and relatively cheap and can be used to administer the atropine solution in about 20 to 25 seconds, but it is now likely to have been replaced by an automatic self-inject item.

STATUS
Production status uncertain. In service with the Soviet and Warsaw Pact forces.

MANUFACTURER
State factories and laboratories.

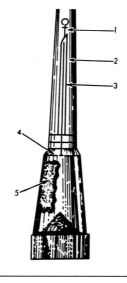

Atropine injector (1) piercing wire (2) cap (3) injector needle (4) internal seal (5) liquid antidote

Individual Decontamination Kit, IPP

DESCRIPTION
The IPP kit has now largely replaced the earlier IPP-3 kit and contains decontaminants capable of dealing with nerve agents as well as blister and biological agents. The kit is normally carried in the protective mask carrier and is contained in a plastic case. The main items inside the case are a glass phial and a plastic phial which contains a glass ampoule. Gauze pads are also included, and another small compartment contains four anti-smoke gauze-wrapped ampoules. The glass phial contains anti-nerve gas decontaminant, and the plastic phial decontaminant for use against blister gases. The plastic container holds alcohol and the glass ampoule chloramine-B powder: crushing the ampoule mixes the two, and the resultant mixture can be used once the plastic phial has been punctured with the metal point in the case lid. The gauze pads are used to apply the solution to the affected areas. Enough mixture is supplied to cover 500 square cm. In use the nerve gas decontaminant would be spread first from the glass phial, followed by the mixture from the plastic phial. The four anti-smoke ampoules can be removed quickly from the kit case by fitted drawstrings. They are crushed and placed inside the wearer's protective mask, and the resultant inhalations can overcome the effects of most irritant smoke. The ampoules contain a mixture of chloroform, ethanol, ethyl ether and ammonia water.

STATUS
In production. In service with the Soviet and Warsaw Pact forces.

MANUFACTURER
State arsenals.

Individual Decontamination Kit, IPP-3

DESCRIPTION
The Model IPP-3 is essentially the same as the later IPP kit but does not contain any nerve gas decontaminant. It has now been largely replaced by the IPP but many kits are still kept in reserve stocks. The Model IPP-3 is contained in a plastic case and is normally carried in the protective mask carrier. The case holds two plastic phials for use against blister agents, each phial containing a glass ampoule filled with chloramine-B powder. The plastic phial also contains alcohol and crushing the plastic phial mixes the powder with the alcohol. A metal spike in the case lid is used to pierce the phial and the solution can then be used with the gauze pads contained in the kit. The kit also contains four crushable anti-smoke ampoules which are the same as the ones in the IPP kit and are used in the same manner.

STATUS
No longer in production. Still in reserve and training service with the Soviet and Warsaw Pact forces.

MANUFACTURER
State arsenals.

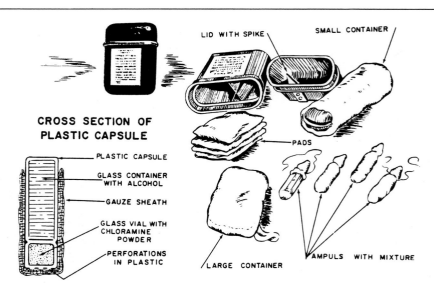

CROSS SECTION OF PLASTIC CAPSULE

PLASTIC CAPSULE
GLASS CONTAINER WITH ALCOHOL
GAUZE SHEATH
GLASS VIAL WITH CHLORAMINE POWDER
PERFORATIONS IN PLASTIC

LID WITH SPIKE
SMALL CONTAINER
PADS
LARGE CONTAINER
AMPULS WITH MIXTURE

Model IPP-3 individual decontamination kit

Decontamination Packet, Model DPS

DESCRIPTION
This packet is used for the personal decontamination of clothing once a contaminated area has been left. The packet is made from clear plastic and is issued sealed. Inside are an instruction sheet and a fabric dusting bag which is used to dust the agent-absorbing brown powder over all outside clothing and headgear. Once applied the dust is rubbed into the clothing with either the bag or rubber gloves. The dust is then shaken or brushed from the clothing before the protective headgear is removed.

STATUS
Probably still in production. In service with the Soviet and Warsaw Pact forces.

MANUFACTURER
State arsenals.

Decontamination Kit, Model PKhS

DESCRIPTION
The Model PKhS kit is for area use with personnel and clothing. It is contained in a plywood case and consists of three half-litre bottles, two large and two small packets of decontaminant, two packets containing ten gauze pads each, a mixing dish and a wooden stirrer. Two of the bottles are sealed with white wax and the other has a red wax seal. The contents of one large and one small decontaminant packet are emptied into the dish and mixed with the contents of one of the white-wax sealed bottles and the resultant solution can be freshly used as an anti-blister agent decontaminant. The contents of the red wax sealed bottle can be used direct from the bottle as a nerve agent decontaminant. Whichever solution is used is normally applied with the gauze pads. The carrying case, which is supplied with a carrying sling, is 305 mm wide, 305 mm high and 90 mm deep.

STATUS
In production. In service with the Soviet and Warsaw Pact forces.

MANUFACTURER
State arsenals.

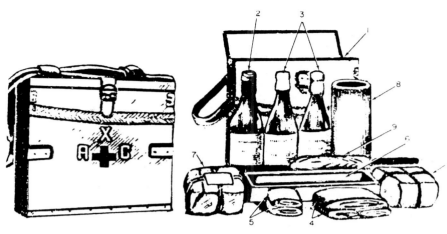

Model PKhS decontamination kit **(1)** *carrying case* **(2, 3)** *solvents* **(4, 5)** *powdered decontaminants* **(6)** *mixing dish* **(7)** *gauze pads* **(8)** *container for powdered decontaminants* **(9)** *wooden stirrer*

Personal Weapons Decontamination Kit, Model IDP

DESCRIPTION
The Model IDP kit is contained in a drab olive metal case and although primarily issued for decontaminating personal weapons, there is enough decontaminant in the kit for use on small crew-served weapons. The kit consists of five cotton swabs and two ampoules. One of the ampoules is marked with a red tip and is intended for use with blister agents. Its position in the case is marked by a 1 embossed in the case wall. The other ampoule (No 2) has a black tip and is intended for use against nerve agents. The weapon is first wiped with a swab to clear as much of the agent as possible. The appropriate ampoule is then opened and the decontaminant solution applied, after which the weapon is wiped dry and lightly oiled. Each ampoule contains 82 ml of solution. The case is 130 mm long, 80 mm wide and 40 mm deep, and the entire kit weighs 0·305 kg. Printed instructions are glued to the side of the case.

STATUS
In production. In service with the Soviet and Warsaw Pact forces.

MANUFACTURER
State arsenals.

Artillery Decontamination Kit, Model ADK

DESCRIPTION
The Model ADK kit is issued to the crews of artillery pieces and large-calibre mortars for decontaminating their weapons and is effective against both blister and nerve agents. The kit is contained in a metal case which holds four one-litre cans of decontamination solution, two smaller plastic containers, two application brushes with handle extensions, two metal scrapers, about 0·5 kg of cotton wool, a 150 mm long roll of sealing tape, and four cork gaskets. Instructions are inside the case lid and four rubber blocks keep the cans in place. Two of the four cans are embossed with the number '1' and have red lids: they are for the decontamination of blister agents and V-type nerve agents. The two black-lidded cans are embossed with the number '2' and are for use against G-type nerve agents. The scrapers are used to remove mud and dirt as the solutions, normally two, are being mixed. The first solution is made by emptying one 80-gram packet of DT-6 decontaminant powder into a red-lidded can which contains one litre of dichloro-ethane and shaking for about five to ten minutes. All possible surfaces are wiped with the cotton wool, and then the mixture is applied with the brushes supplied. The black-lidded cans contain the ready-mixed No 2 aqueous solution of 2 per cent sodium hydroxide, 5 per cent monoethanolamine and 20 per cent ammonia. Even if there are no G-type nerve agents present, the solution No 2 has to be used to remove the corrosive solution No 1 from unpainted metal surfaces. When any contaminating agent is unidentified the solutions are used in numerical order. After use the kit can be refilled with solutions and powder by an ADM-48 decontamination vehicle and the spare gaskets and tape supplied with the kit are used to re-seal the kit ready for re-use. The scrapers can also be used to loosen the solution container caps.

STATUS
In production. In service with the Soviet and Warsaw Pact forces.

ADK artillery decontamination kit

MANUFACTURER
State arsenals.

Machine Gun/Mortar Decontamination Kit, Model PM-DK

DESCRIPTION
The kit Model PM-DK follows much the same lines as the larger artillery kit model ADK and the solutions involved and their use are the same. The difference lies in the smaller sizes of the items concerned. Only two solution cans are contained in the metal case, one of the No 1 and one of the No 2. There is only one application brush which fits directly onto the solution can in use and a cleaning wire is supplied to clean the hollow handle of the brush. Each solution can contains 250 ml. Like the larger artillery kit, the Model PM-DK can be refilled and re-used and spare gaskets are supplied to re-seal the solution cans. There are two types of carrying case, both with carrying slings. One has straight sides with rounded corners and the other has curved, body-contoured sides.

STATUS
In production. In service with the Soviet and Warsaw Pact forces.

MANUFACTURER
State arsenals.

Model PM-DK machine gun/mortar decontamination kit

Decontamination Apparatus, Back-pack, Model RDP-3

DESCRIPTION
This back-pack equipment has now been largely replaced in front-line service by the later Model RDP-4V but still remains in reserve and civilian defence organisation use. It follows the same general lines as the later Model RDP-4V but differs in that the pumping handle is on the right and the nozzle is guided by the left hand. A design fault is that the pump is immersed in the corrosive decontaminating liquids in action and thus the pump life is shortened and maintenance is difficult: this fault was rectified on the later Model RDP-4V. The Model RDP-3 tank contains approximately 12 litres of decontaminant and when full weighs around 20 kg (7·2 kg empty). Pumping at a rate of 25 to 30 strokes a minute gives a discharge rate of about 0·8 litre a minute and the tank contains enough liquid to cover approximately 5·1 square metres. The Model RDP-3 is 40 mm high, 350 mm long and 180 mm wide.

STATUS
No longer in production. Probably still in reserve and training use with Soviet and Warsaw Pact forces and some civilian defence organisations.

MANUFACTURER
State arsenals.

Decontamination Apparatus, Back-pack, Model RDP-4V

DESCRIPTION
This hand-operated back-pack equipment is used to decontaminate vehicles, equipment, weapons, small buildings and small areas of ground. The back-pack is held in place by a pair of straps at the waist and shoulders. It consists mainly of a tank with a large filling aperture,, a filter screen, a clamp-on pressure cap, a piston-type air pump operated by the left hand, outlet tube and hose, and a spray pipe and nozzle to which a brush may be attached. A wrench and a small canister containing tools are fitted to the bottom of the tank. The equipment can be used to spray decontamination solution No 1 or No 2, depending on the nature of the contamination. The pump handle is normally clipped in the vertical but in use it is horizontal and operated by the left hand: a pumping rate of 25 to 30 strokes a minute gives a discharge flow of about 0·7 litre a minute. When full, the Model RDP-4V weighs approximately 17 kg and empty 8·5 kg. It is 355 mm high, 290 mm long and 190 mm wide.

STATUS
In production. In service with the Soviet and Warsaw Pact forces.

MANUFACTURER
State arsenals.

Model RDP-4V back-pack decontamination apparatus

Decontamination Kit, Model IDK-1

DESCRIPTION
The Model IDK-1 kit is normally carried in a vehicle cab and is used to decontaminate the vehicle. The kit, which is designed to be used in conjunction with a standard 20-litre jerrican, consists of a spray pipe with a nozzle and brush, a cap for the 20-litre can, a hose, an aspirator attachment and various accessories. The kit can be used in two ways: one is to mix either the decontamination solution No 1 or No 2 and strain it into the 20-litre can which is then pressurised and kept so using a hand pump, or the aspirator is used when fitted to the vehicle's air brake system.

STATUS
In production. In service with the Soviet forces.

MANUFACTURER
State arsenals.

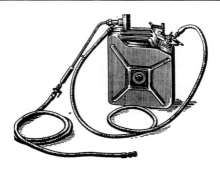

Model IDK-1 decontamination kit

Decontamination Kit, Models DK-4 and EEA-64

DESCRIPTION
These decontamination kits are essentially similar, and use the vehicle exhaust system as the pressure source. Each vehicle so equipped has provision over the exhaust for fitting a special cap with a branch valve fitted anterior to the vehicle's silencer system. To this branch valve is fitted a jet pump which uses the exhaust pressure to provide suction to power a pump. The pump drives decontaminating solution or powder from a standard 20-litre jerrican through a hose and eventually through a nozzle which may be fitted with a brush. Alternatively, the system can be driven in reverse so that the pump provides suction from the nozzle to remove radio-active fallout particles. When used like this the standard 20-litre tin can be used as the dust receptacle, but it is more usual to pass the exhaust dust through water in a specially-dug hole or channel.

The East German version of the Model DK-4 is known as the Model EEA-64. Polish versions have several designations including IZS, EZS, EZCS-34 and EZCS-54.

STATUS
In production. In service with the Soviet, East German and Polish forces.

MANUFACTURER
State arsenals and factories.

Model DK-4 decontamination kit in use

Decontamination System, Portable, Model DKV

DESCRIPTION
This portable system is used to decontaminate vehicles, and is composed of 78 cylindrical tanks carried on a specially-equipped truck and trailer. Each cylindrical tank is pre-loaded with decontamination solution No 1 or 2, and each tank can be fitted with either one or two spray pipes. The tanks are delivered to the users where they can be pressurised by either the user vehicle's air brake system or by a separate compressor. The spray pipes are usually fitted with a brush and the contents of two cylinders are usually sufficient to decontaminate a lorry; an MBT takes three cylinders. Each cylinder can take up to 30 litres. Several cylinders can be fitted to a single compressed air source, and the cylinders can be collected and refilled.

STATUS
In production. In service with the Soviet and Warsaw Pact forces.

MANUFACTURER
State arsenals.

Decontamination Apparatus, Trailer-mounted, Model DDP

DESCRIPTION
This trailer-mounted equipment follows the same general lines as the truck-mounted Model DDA-53 series, but has slightly less capacity. Otherwise the two equipments are essentially similar and the same boiler is used. However, the trailer-mounted Model DDP has only one steam chamber with a capacity of 1·4 cubic metres, even though the boiler can provide enough water for about 80 showers an hour. The equipment is mounted on a 1-AP-1 or 1-AP-5 trailer and the complete equipment weighs approximately 2050 kg.

STATUS
Probably no longer in production. In service with the Soviet and Warsaw Pact forces.

MANUFACTURER
Various state factories.

Decontamination Apparatus, Truck-mounted, Models DDA-53, DDA-53A, DDA-53B and DDA-66

DESCRIPTION
This equipment is used by decontamination units and by medical units for sterilisation, disinfecting and disinfestation. With chemical units the Model DDA-53 series is used for steam-decontamination of chemically- and biologically-contaminated clothing and small items of equipment, and the apparatus can also provide hot water for showers. Each equipment consists of a vehicle-borne system with two steam chambers, a vertical boiler (the RI-3), a fuel oil tank, a water pump, a formaldehyde tank, a 12-head shower unit and all the associated hoses and fittings. The system does not have its own water tank, so water has to be provided by another tanker vehicle or a stand tank if no natural source is available. The water boiler which produces steam or hot water contains 250 litres and is normally fired by fuel oil, although wood may be used with a loss in heating efficiency. The fuel oil tank holds 55 litres which is enough for eight to ten hours' operation. Pipes connect the boiler output to steam chambers each of which can contain 25 to 30 summer uniforms, 20 winter uniforms or 12 sheepskin jackets. Decontaminants can be added to the steam if necessary. The system can thus decontaminate up to 80 uniforms an hour in summer and up to 48 in winter. When used for showers the system is normally used in conjunction with tents which are carried on other cargo trucks, and enough water can be provided for up to 100 showers an hour in summer and 70 to 72 in winter.

DDA-53A truck-mounted, decontamination apparatus based on GAZ-63 (4 × 4) chassis

There are four models of the DDA-53 (sometimes known as the ADA). The Model DDA-53 is mounted on the GAZ-51 chassis, the Model DDA-53A on the GAZ-63 and the Model DDA-53B on a ZIL-130 chassis. The DDA-53B differs also in having the boiler and steam chambers enclosed in a metal body. The Model DDA-66 is mounted on a GAZ-66 chassis.

STATUS
Probably no longer in production. In service with the Soviet and Warsaw Pact forces.

MANUFACTURER
Various state factories.

Decontamination Apparatus, Truck-mounted, ADM-48D

DESCRIPTION
This truck-mounted equipment is used for large-scale decontamination of vehicles, weapons, equipment and ground areas. It can be mounted on either a GAZ-51 or GAZ-63 chassis, and consists of two main units. Unit No 1 on the right side is filled with the standard decontaminant solution No 1 which is an 8 per cent solution of decontaminant DT-6 in dichloroethane, effective against blister and V-type nerve agents. As this solution is corrosive all the fittings on the unit are brass. Unit No 2, on the left, is filled with decontaminant solution No 2, an aqueous solution of 2 per cent sodium hydroxide, 5 per cent monoethanolamine and 20 per cent ammonia, effective against G-type agents. Both units consist of a 500-litre tank, a hand pump, an anti-surge tank, a pipe system, a metering unit (for rapid and measured refilling of PM-DK and ADK decontamination kits), six 12-metre hoses, six nozzles and brushes, four suction hoses, spare parts and various tools. Each unit can supply up to six spray lines, and when not in use the hoses are carried in boxes by the rear tailgate. A rectangular steel tank with a 65-litre capacity fitted by the tailgate contains dichloroethane, and six RDP-4V back-pack equipments are also carried on the vehicle for remote use. The ADM-48 is one of the basic equipments used by Warsaw Pact chemical units and its employment is widespread.

STATUS
Probably no longer in production. In service with the Soviet and Warsaw Pact forces and possibly with some Middle East states.

MANUFACTURER
State arsenals.

Decontamination Apparatus, Truck-mounted, Model TMS-65

DESCRIPTION
The Model TMS-65 is intended for the rapid decontamination of vehicles and towed weapons and equipment. It is mounted on a Ural-375 chassis and the main operating component is a Model VK-1F modified gas turbine aircraft engine mounted on a turntable with the operator's cabin. A hydraulic system turns the turntable to either side of the vehicle and the operator's cabin is equipped with floodlights and a screen wiper. Fuel for the engine is contained in a 1500-litre tank between the turntable and the right rear of the cab. A tank on the left contains 1500 litres of decontaminant solution and another 4000 litres of solution are carried in a trailer towed behind the vehicle. Normally the Model TMS-65 is employed in pairs. Two equipments are placed about 50 metres apart and the engines are started. Decontamination solution is directed into the engine exhaust and so to wherever the operator directs the hot gas stream: the engine can be elevated or depressed as well as traversed. The vehicles to be decontaminated are driven between the two equipments and are cleansed in between 30 seconds to three minutes, depending on the nature and degree of contamination.

TMS-65 with turbojet covered by tarpaulin

Close-up of TMS-65 turbojet outlet showing storage tank to its rear

For nuclear cleansing, water may be used. If space allows the two Model TMS-65 equipments are driven along a static column, which is stated to be particularly effective in winter.

STATUS
In production. In service with the Soviet and Warsaw Pact forces.

MANUFACTURER
State arsenals.

Model TMS-65 truck-mounted decontamination apparatus in operational use

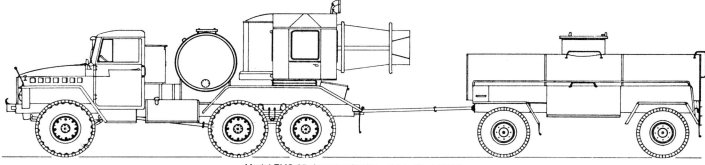

Model TMS-65 decontamination vehicle (Ural-375E)

Decontamination Apparatus, Truck-mounted, Models ARS-12D and ARS-12U

DESCRIPTION
Apart from use as decontamination equipment the Models ARS-12D and ARS-12U can be used as water carriers, for fire fighting and to provide cold showers for various purposes. The two models are basically similar but the Model ARS-12D is mounted on a ZIL-151 chassis and the Model ARS-12U on a ZIL-157. Each consists of a 2500-litre tank divided by two baffles and with a large manhole for access and filling. Also provided is a depth gauge, a self-priming pump driven from the vehicle engine, a hand pump, a piping system, hoses, nozzles and other spares and accessories. The main pump drive shaft turns at 1400 to 1600 rpm and can turn the pump to deliver 300 to 400 litres a minute. The hand pump, operated at 45 strokes a minute, can deliver 4·5 to 5·5 litres a minute. Decontaminants are mixed in the tank as water is poured in and a thorough mixture is made by internally re-cycling the solution through the pump, otherwise the vehicle motion and the filling mixing is all that is necessary. Many different decontaminants may be used but the standard solutions are numbers 1 and 2. There are several administration methods. To clear roads or terrain a wide spreading nozzle (the DN-3) can be fitted directly to the main discharge pipe and the vehicle is then driven over the affected road or terrain. A full tank can then clear a strip 500 metres long and five metres wide. For decontaminating vehicles and other equipment up to eight 18-metre hoses can be fitted, each with spray pipes, nozzles and nozzle brushes. Up to four vehicles can be cleansed at one time and there is sufficient solution in a full tank to

ARS-12U in action using DN-3 spreader nozzle

cleanse 12 MBTs, 13 APCs, 15 trucks or 45 artillery pieces. To decontaminate buildings (or for fire fighting) four 25 mm diameter hoses can be used. Racks on top of the tank hold drums of decontaminant and several RDP-4V back-pack equipments can be carried for remote use. The Model ARS-12D has been used to emit smoke screens by discharging chlorosulphonic acid.

STATUS
No longer in production. In service with the Soviet and Warsaw Pact forces, and may be in service with some Middle East states.

MANUFACTURER
State arsenals.

Decontamination Apparatus, Truck-mounted, Model ARS-14

DESCRIPTION
This equipment is a development of the earlier Model ARS-12U and it is expected that it will eventually replace the earlier models in service. The main change is the use of a ZIL-131 chassis but the full extra tank capacity this provides cannot be used because extra drums of decontaminant are carried on specially-fitted racks. However, the extra drums enable the equipment to be used over a longer period without reloading. Some changes have also been made to the piping system in that the previously fixed outlet pipes are now carried separately and fitted to the equipment by hoses. The wide-spreading DN-3 nozzle is now fitted at the vehicle front as well as the rear, and the eight hoses are wound onto only four drums instead of the former eight; these

Model ARS-14 truck-mounted decontamination apparatus

drums are at the left rear. Other changes have been made to the general 'plumbing' but an innovation is an extra rubber hose which can be fitted to the vehicle exhaust in winter to thaw out any frozen parts of the equipment. Filling pistols can also be fitted to the system for loading or reloading decontamination kits.

STATUS
In production. In service with the Soviet and East German forces.

MANUFACTURER
Various state arsenals and factories.

Decontamination Station, Models AGV-3M and AGW-3M

DESCRIPTION
The Decontamination Station Model AGV-3M is used for steam decontamination of chemically- or biologically-contaminated clothing and small pieces of equipment. It consists of four special vehicles: one Model AGV-3M truck-mounted decontamination steam and hot air generator, two Model AGV-3M truck-mounted decontamination steam chamber apparatuses and one cargo truck carrying a drying tent, a shower tent, a collapsible water tank and accessories.

The steam and hot air generating unit is mounted on a ZIL-157 or ZIL-151 chassis. It has a van-type body which contains an oil-fired heater, a 500-litre boiler with a super-heater, a petrol engine for driving the fuel oil and water pumps, a single-stage turbo-blower and a heat exchanger. The steam generated in the boiler is super-heated to between 160 and 200°C and then passed to the steam chamber vehicles. The turbo-blower supplies 350 cubic metres a minute through the heat exchanger at a pressure of 0·5 kg/cm², which is then supplied to the drying tent via a large diameter hose. The boiler also supplies hot water for the crew's shower unit. The steam chamber units are mounted on either a ZIL-130, ZIL-150 or ZIL-164 chassis. Each unit has three 2 cubic metre pressure chambers and all the pipes and other fittings. Clothing is hung inside the steam chambers which are then pressurised by the steam from the steam generator vehicle. Extra decontaminants can be added to the steam if necessary. After a period in the steam chambers the clothing is taken to the drying tent. The cargo truck used with the station is usually a ZIL-130 or a ZIL-164. The station can process between 50 and 150 uniforms an hour, depending on the type of contamination.

The decontamination station Model AGV-3M has now replaced the earlier Model AGV-2.

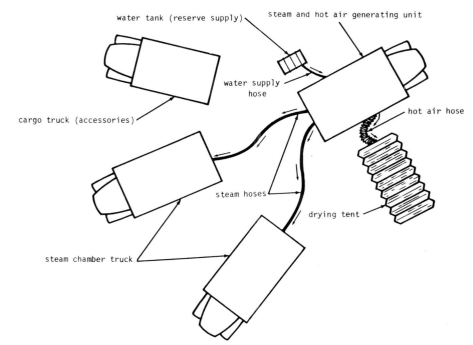

Layout of AGV-3M and AGW-3M decontamination system

In East German service the Model AGV-3M is known as the Model AGW-3M.

STATUS
Production completed. In service with the Soviet and Warsaw Pact forces. The earlier Model AGV-2 may remain in service with some civil defence organisations.

MANUFACTURER
State arsenals and factories.

Decontamination Apparatus, Clothing, Truck-mounted, Models BU-2, BU-3, BU-4 and BU-4M

DESCRIPTION
All these equipments have the same function which is to decontaminate clothing, protective clothing, small canvas shelters and similar articles by boiling, after which the items can be conventionally laundered. All the equipments are carried on either GAZ-53, GAZ-63 or LO-1800A trucks and are unloaded from the trucks by hand-operated cranes before use. The Model BU-2 has two 350-litre boilers which are heated either by a fire or by an integral steam coil. The equipment also has a collapsible water tank, or tanks, a hand pump, a hand drying press and a drying tent. Each boiler can hold 40 uniforms and up to 1000 uniforms can be processed in 24 hours. The Model BU-3 is essentially similar but has only one boiler. The Models BU-4 and BU-4M are improved versions of the Model BU-2 and differ from one another only in detail. Each equipment has two 450-litre boilers, a hand pump, one 1000- and one 1200-litre collapsible water tank, metal baskets, a hand drying press and a drying tent. The metal baskets each take ten uniforms and each boiler can accommodate four baskets. Extra decontaminants can be added to the boiling water if necessary. Normally these equipments are used in conjunction with a decontamination station Model AGV-3M.

STATUS
Production complete. In service with the Soviet and Warsaw Pact forces.

MANUFACTURER
State factories.

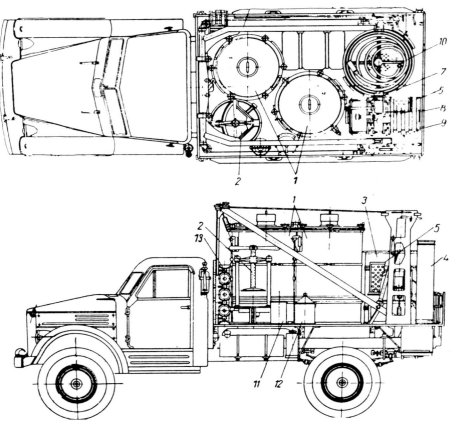

Model BU-4M truck-mounted decontamination apparatus (1) decontamination boilers (2) drying press (3) water tank (4) chimney (5) baskets (6) crane (7) storage box (8) manual water pump (9) benches (10) hose (11) bucket (12) container (13) stakes and pegs for drying tent

Dry-decontaminant Spreader, Truck-mounted, Models PDP-53 and PDM

DESCRIPTION
This spreader is usually fitted to the GAZ-51 or GAZ-63 (both of which have a payload capacity of 1500 kg) and the ZIL-150 (with a capacity of 2500 kg). The equipment is used to spread dry decontaminant over roads or terrain and it is fitted to the back of the vehicle. The spreader itself is driven by a chain, driven in turn by a sprocket fitted to the right rear wheel hub. The chain drives a rotary spreader at the bottom of a hopper which is kept topped up by two men with shovels in the rear of the truck. The actual distribution of the spreader can be varied between 0·5 to 1 kg/m² on the Model PDP-53 but on the East German Model PDM it is fixed at 0·5 kg/m².

STATUS
Production complete. In service with the Soviet and East German forces.

MANUFACTURER
State factories.

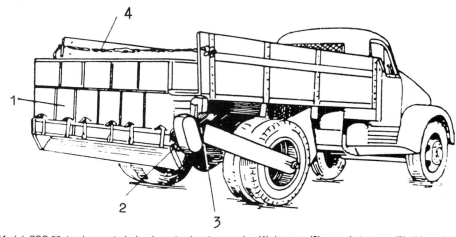

Model PDP-53 truck-mounted dry-decontaminant spreader (1) hopper (2) sprocket cover (3) drive chain cover (4) safety chain

UNITED KINGDOM

Pralidoxime Mesylate Tablets

DESCRIPTION
Pralidoxime mesylate enables personnel to survive what would be several times the lethal dose of the majority of known nerve agents. For use by troops in the field tablets are issued in one-day packs consisting of four doses to be taken every six hours. Each dose, which is packed in a separate plastic tube, consists of four large tablets, one quick-acting and the other three slow-acting.

STATUS
In service with the British Armed Forces.

Decontamination Kit, Personal No 1 Mark 1

DESCRIPTION
This decontamination kit is normally issued to all field personnel and is carried as part of their standard personal equipment. It consists of a sealed clear plastic bag containing a set of instructions and four pads charged with fuller's earth. In use the plastic bag is torn open and one pad is taken out and placed over one hand like a glove. The pad is then banged over suspected areas of skin or clothing and equipment to dispense the fuller's earth which is then rubbed over using the pad to spread the powder.

STATUS
In production. In service with the British Armed Forces.

MANUFACTURER
Leyland and Birmingham Rubber Company Limited, Leyland, Preston PR5 1UB, Lancashire, England.

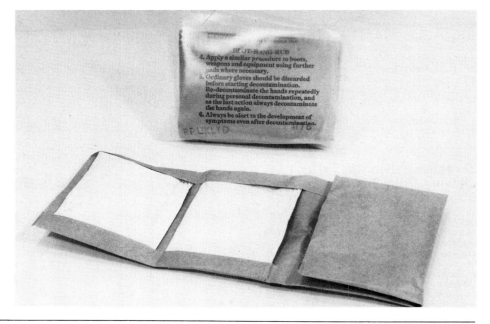

Decontamination Kit, Personal No 1 Mark 1

Decontamination Kit, Personal No 2 Mark 1

DESCRIPTION
This personal decontamination kit consists of a flat polythene dispenser containing 113 grams of fuller's earth. It is for decontaminating the user's boots and personal equipment and would normally be used in conjunction with the Decontamination Kit No 1 Mark 1.

STATUS
In production. In service with the British Armed Forces.

MANUFACTURER
Leyland and Birmingham Rubber Company Limited, Leyland, Preston PR5 1UB, Lancashire, England.

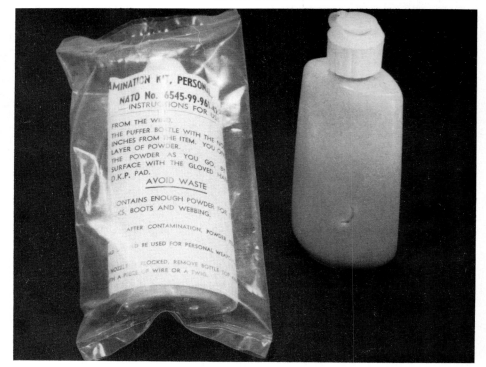

Decontamination Kit, Personal No 2 Mark 1

Decontamination Apparatus, Chemical Agent

DESCRIPTION
Intended for emergency front-line use, this kit is normally carried on vehicles and uses normal 9-litre fire extinguishers. The kit is supplied in an olive-green canvas tool roll containing two car-wash type brushes, extension pipes, fittings, a spanner, and an instruction sheet. In use the extinguisher body is charged with a water soluble decontaminant which is normally issued in sealed bags packed into tins. One tin is required for each loading of the extinguisher body. Once the fire extinguisher body has been charged it can be connected to the kit with the fittings issued and decontamination can begin.

STATUS
In production. In service with the British Armed Forces.

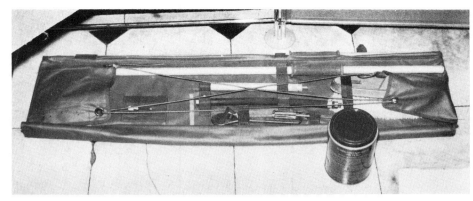

Decontamination Apparatus, Chemical Agent, tool roll, can containing decontaminant (T J Gander)

UNITED STATES OF AMERICA

Vesicant Agent Protective Ointment, M5

DESCRIPTION
This ointment is issued to all field personnel for protection against blister agents and for neutralising such agents once used. It is primarily intended for use on the skin, but can also be used for decontaminating personal weapons and equipment. The ointment is white and the main constituent is chloromide S-330. It is issued in tubes 95 mm long and 19 mm in diameter.

STATUS
In service with the US Army, Navy and Air Force.

Decontaminating and Re-impregnating Kit, Individual, ABC-M13

DESCRIPTION
The ABC-M13 kit is issued to all field personnel and is intended for the emergency decontamination of skin, clothing and equipment and it also has a limited ability to re-impregnate items of clothing. The kit is contained in a plastic bag, which itself is contained within a plastic or light alloy case, and consists of a plastic bag containing a pad filled with skin-decontaminating powder, two cloth bags filled with decontaminating and re-impregnating powder, a capsule of dye, and a cutter. The kit weighs approximately 0·318 kg and measures 476 × 730 × 105 mm.

STATUS
In service with the US Army.

Decontamination Kit, M258

DESCRIPTION
The Decontaminating Kit, M258, is intended for use by individual personnel for decontamination of skin areas, clothing, personal equipment and weapons. There are two types of M258 kit, the earlier of which is carried in a plastic container which doubles as a solution container. Inside the container are two plastic bottles and a number of tissues. The bottles are marked Solution I and Solution II and are mixed for cleansing. This type of kit can be used only once.

The newer M258 kit is contained in foil envelopes. Each envelope contains a pre-impregnated towelette, and there are enough for three separate decontaminating operations.

STATUS
Production. In service with the US forces.

Decontaminating Apparatus, Portable, DS2, 1½-quart, ABC-M11

DESCRIPTION
This equipment is carried on a rack on nearly all vehicles and is intended for the decontamination of vehicles or crew-served weapons. Normally the equipment is issued with the nitrogen pressure cartridge already filled and in place but the container has to be filled with the decontaminating agent (DS-2, a clear amber inflammable liquid which is irritating to the skin and should not be breathed; it also removes old paint and discolours new paint) before the equipment is ready for use. When used, the handle is lifted to puncture the pressure can, and a thumb lever then controls the spray. The optimum spray range is about two metres and the equipment will cover approximately 42 square metres. Full, the ABC-M11 weighs 2·8 kg. It is licence-manufactured in Israel.

STATUS
In service with the US Army, Israeli forces and some other forces.

MANUFACTURER (Licensed)
Israel: Cosmos (Israel) Advanced Fire Fighting Equipment Limited, Industrial Zone, POB 3045, Upper Tiberias, Israel.

M13 Portable Decontamination Apparatus (DAP)

DESCRIPTION
The M13 portable decontamination apparatus is a vehicle-mounted, man-portable, manually-operated unit for the decontamination of wheeled and tracked vehicles, towed artillery and crew-served weapons described as 'larger than 60 caliber', ie 0·60 inch/15 mm. Development began in 1979.

It consists of a pre-filled disposable container holding 14 litres of DS-2 decontaminating agent, an accessory container holder, a manual in-line pump, two wand sections, and a disposable brush. Weight is 'less than 60 pounds/27·2 kg'.

The M13 will replace the existing M11 apparatus in service, commencing during 1985.

STATUS
Initial production for the US Army.

DEVELOPMENT AGENCY
Chemical Research and Development Centre, Aberdeen Proving Ground, Maryland, USA.

M13 portable decontamination apparatus
(T J Gander)

Decontaminating Apparatus, Power-driven, Skid-mounted: Multi-purpose, Non-integral, 500-gallon, ABC-M12A1

DESCRIPTION

This multi-purpose equipment consists of three main components, a pump unit assembly, a tank unit assembly and personnel shower assembly (combined) and an M2 600-gallon per hour liquid fuel water heater. The ABC-M12A1 can be used for a variety of purposes including decontamination, de-icing, fire-fighting with water or foam, pumping and showering personnel or equipment. When used for decontamination the pump unit (which has two hose reels, a dc generator, a petrol engine, a fuel tank and a priming tank) can be used to pump up to 190 litres of decontaminating fluid every minute from both hoses. The decontaminant most likely to be used is STB (supertropical bleach – chlorinated lime) but other agents may be used. The tank unit has a stainless steel tank and a hopper-blender for mixing decontaminating agents, as well as a fluid agitation system. This unit also has an integral shower assembly for 25 men. The M2 water heater can provide heated water at the rate of up to 2270 litres an hour. All three components are mounted on skids and accessories are provided for inter-connection of all three units. For transport the units are contained in three crates which together weigh 1903 kg.

STATUS

In service with the US Army, Air Force and Marine Corps.

XM15 Interior Surface Decontamination Apparatus (ISDS)

DESCRIPTION

The XM15 Interior Surface Decontamination Apparatus has been under development since January 1980 and it is intended that once it is type classified it will be issued at the rate of one equipment to every vehicle, van body, shelter, etc where electrical and electronic equipment might be contained. It uses hot air for the evaporation and removal of chemical agents from interior areas and is designed not to damage electronics, optics or plastics. It consists of a small air heater unit that draws air through a filter system prior to heating it within a sealed unit. The air jets are then directed along a flexible pipe to a hand-held nozzle and so to the required surfaces.

STATUS

Advanced development.

DEVELOPMENT AGENCY

Chemical Research and Development Centre, Aberdeen Proving Ground, Maryland, USA.

XM16 Jet Exhaust Decontamination Apparatus (JEDSS)

DESCRIPTION

The XM16 Jet Exhaust Decontamination Apparatus is, in essence, an American version of the Soviet TMS-65 truck-mounted decontamination system. Currently under development, it is not expected to be type classified until the second quarter of fiscal year 1986.

The XM16 is intended to provide rapid NBC decontamination for large scale equipment such as AFVs and for maximum effect two should be used simultaneously. It has a secondary role in producing large area tactical smoke screens. The layout closely follows that of the Soviet TMS-65 in that it uses a 5-ton, 6 × 6 truck on which is mounted a J-60 jet engine on a hydraulically-operated turntable at the rear. The jet engine is controlled in azimuth and elevation by an operator seated in a sealed cab behind the engine nozzle and this cab is equipped with a collective protection system. Behind the truck driver's cabin is a divided tank for 600 gallons (2271 litres) of diesel fuel and 350 gallons (1325 litres) of water or a smoke producing liquid.

In use the XM16-carrying trucks will either be placed facing each other as contaminated vehicles are driven between the two swivelling nozzles, or two XM16-carrying trucks will be driven along a column of decontaminated vehicles.

STATUS

Advanced development.

DEVELOPMENT AGENCY

Chemical Research and Development Centre, Aberdeen Proving Ground, Maryland, USA.

MANUFACTURER

Brunswick Corporation, Defence Division, One Brunswick Plaza, Skokie, Illinois 60077, USA.

XM17 Lightweight Decontamination System

DESCRIPTION

The XM17 Lightweight Decontamination System is a self-contained portable system intended to provide water for rinsing vehicles using a high pressure spray but also to provide hot water for personnel showers. The XM17 has two main components. One, a container within an open tubular steel frame, has a two-cycle petrol engine driving a pump and a water heating unit which can produce temperatures of up to 120°C. The second component is an accessory kit which includes cleaning wands, hoses and the personnel shower hardware. Also used with the system is a self-supporting collapsible water tank holding up to 1450 gallons (5488 litres).

STATUS

Evaluation.

DEVELOPMENT AGENCY

Chemical Research and Development Centre, Aberdeen Proving Ground, Maryland, USA.

CHEMICAL AND BIOLOGICAL DETECTION AND IDENTIFICATION EQUIPMENT

CANADA

Detector Kit, Chemical Agent (C-2)

DESCRIPTION
This kit is contained in a vinyl-coated carrying case and may be used by one person after only a minimum of training. It has a variety of operational roles including determining the presence or absence of chemical agents after an attack; identifying chemical agents; collecting samples for later analysis; identifying when it is safe to unmask for long or short periods; testing for area contamination; monitoring the expected arrival of a vapour hazard; and testing for the presence of agents after decontamination operations. The kit can be used to detect and identify Tabun (GA), Sarin (GB), Soman (GD), V agent (VX), Mustard (H, HN and T), Phosgene oxime (CX), Hydrogen Cyanide (AC), Cyanogen chloride (CK) and Phosgene (CG).

The kit contains a booklet of Paper, Chemical Agent Detector, Liquid, Three-Way (see separate entry), 20 Detectors, Chemical Agent, Nerve Vapour (see separate entry), 30 plain detector tubes, 20 detector tubes with white bands for sampling, 3 bottles of chemical reagents, an air sampling pump, a container intended to hold ten detector tubes, an instruction card set, a pencil, water bottle, some anti-freeze solution, report cards and envelopes. The items are all stored in arranged compartments and pockets, and the kit is normally carried slung from a shoulder.

The kit is intended for issue down to small unit level.

SPECIFICATIONS
Weight: 1·4 kg
Length: 230 mm
Height: 148 mm
Width: 70 mm

Detector Kit, Chemical Agent (C-2)

STATUS
Production. In service with the Canadian Armed Forces.

MANUFACTURER
Anachemia Limited -LTEE, Case postale 147, Lachine (Québec), Canada H8S 4A7.

Paper, Chemical Agent Detector, Liquid, Three-Way

DESCRIPTION
This simple chemical agent detector consists of twelve sheets of 102 × 64 mm paper with adhesive backing formed into a booklet which has instructions for use on the cover. Each sheet has a paper base impregnated with a dye-stuff that will alter colour when exposed to chemical agents. G agents will produce colours varying from yellow to orange, H agents produce a red colour and V agents produce colours that vary from very dark blue-green to light blue-green.

In use a protective layer of waxed paper is removed from the adhesive backing and the sheet is then stuck onto clothing or equipment. It will not change colour if moistened by water, petrol, grease or anti-freeze but may be affected by some decontaminating fluids. In the latter case this can be recognised by the paper turning black.

STATUS
Production. In service with the Canadian Armed Forces.

Detector, Chemical Agent, Nerve Vapour

DESCRIPTION
Developed by the Canadian Armed Forces, this simple detector is intended for issue down to individual level and is intended to indicate if nerve agents are present or if it is possible to remove protective masks and clothing after a nerve agent attack. The detector is in two parts, both using clear plastic bases. On the main body is a disc of enzyme impregnated test paper, while a holder has a small sample of a chemically-impregnated test paper. In use the paper on the body is moistened. The paper on the holder is then pressed against it. If the test paper on the body changes colour to blue or green no nerve agent is present. If the test paper remains unchanged, nerve agent is present.

Each detector measures 89 × 29 × 6·5 mm and is packaged in an airtight foil wrap, together with an instruction sheet and a silica-gel air dryer pack. The individual units are packed 40 to an air tight, moisture-proof container measuring 95 × 95 × 51 mm.

STATUS
Production. In service with the Canadian Armed Forces.

Detector, Chemical Agent, Nerve Vapour

FRANCE

Chemical Detection Kit Model 1 bis

DESCRIPTION
The Model 1 bis kit is issued in two parts: the kit proper and a kit of spares. The fully equipped kit weighs 1·2 kg and is 270 mm long, 150 mm wide and 65 mm high. It consists mainly of a box containing an air pump and various tables and accessory holders. In use air is pumped through a transparent cylinder in which various sensitised papers are placed. As various agents act on the papers the colour changes can be used to identify the agents. The identification range of the kit depends on the sensitised papers used but a normal kit can detect most nerve, blood and choking agents likely to be encountered. To keep the kit fully ready for use a spares kit is issued in a metal case which weighs 7 kg complete and is 330 mm long, 200 mm wide and 205 mm high, and can keep the kit in use for ten days.
A training version of this kit is produced which uses imitation substances in place of chemical agents.

STATUS
In production. In service with the French Army.

MANUFACTURER
Groupement Industriel des Armements Terrestres (GIAT), 10 place Georges Clémenceau, 92211 Saint-Cloud, France.

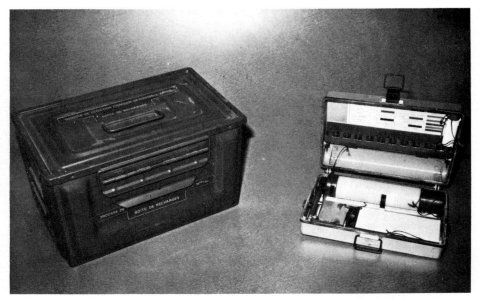

Chemical detection kit Model 1 bis

Detalac

DESCRIPTION
Detalac is used for the automatic local detection of chemical agents and operates once the surrounding air contains a concentration of 0·1 mg/m³ of organophosphorated toxics. It can operate a local or a remote alarm unit which may be either aural or connected to a lamp system. Detalac uses a hydrogen supply for the detection system and a throw-away chemical generator for the hydrogen supply. This generator has to be renewed every 24 hours. Electrical power can be supplied either by a 24-volt external battery or by a cluster of four internal cells. The Detalac detector unit is waterproof and in the operating condition weighs about 20 kg. Reaction time against toxic agents is less than two seconds.

Detalac is produced in two versions. The mle F1 is intended for use at static locations and requires a larger hydrogen supply than the mle F2, the more portable version. Both are supplied with 400 metres of cable on a spool for connection to a remote warning indicator device which has both lamp and aural signal warning devices. Also supplied with each equipment are an external power supply cable, a tool kit and accessories.

STATUS
Production.

MANUFACTURER
Groupement Industriel des Armements Terrestres (GIAT), 10 place Georges Clémencau, 92211 Saint-Cloud, France.

Detelac mle F2 (T J Gander)

Detelac mle F1 (T J Gander)

GERMANY, DEMOCRATIC REPUBLIC

Detection and Identification Set, Chemical Agent, Models CHNS and CNS-62

DESCRIPTION
This kit is intended for use by the individual soldier as a 'first-aid' detection kit, but is really meant to be used in conjunction with the PChR-54 equipment for accurate identification and detection of chemical agents. Contained in a plastic wallet 120 × 85 × 20 mm, the kit is carried by every field soldier in a uniform pocket and it contains indicator papers and several reagent ampoules, along with a colour comparison chart. The Model CHNS can detect phosgene, mustard, lewisite and hydrogen cyanide. The Model CNS-62 can detect all the above with the addition of G-type and V-type nerve agents.

STATUS
Probably no longer in production. Model CHNS now held in reserve and for civilian use, and Model CNS-62 in service with the East German forces.

MANUFACTURER
State factories.

Mobile NBC Laboratory RChLab-11

DESCRIPTION
Designed for use in rear areas, the RChLab-11 is contained within a special box body carried on a W 50 LA/A (4 × 4) truck. The laboratory is intended to be used for the analysis and identification of NBC agents and is thus equipped with benches, cupboards and drawers for the storage and use of the various types of chemical equipment and instruments necessary to the task. The body roof has partially sloping sides with inset windows to provide good lighting and the door is entered by a ladder at the right rear. A further ladder leads to the roof and a spare wheel is carried on the rear wall. The vehicle carries its own power generator and an air filtration system. It also carries a RWA-72K radiation detection and warning device with an externally-mounted sensor and an internal control unit.

STATUS
In service with the East German Army.

MANUFACTURER
State factories and laboratories.

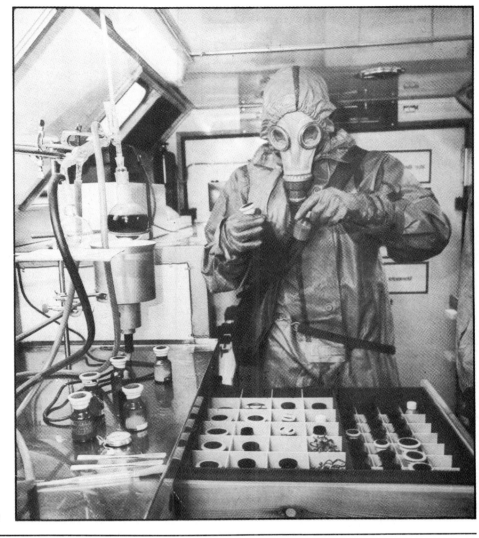

Technician working in interior of RChLab-11

GERMANY, FEDERAL REPUBLIC

Transportpanzer 1 NBC Reconnaissance Vehicle

DESCRIPTION
This NBC reconnaissance vehicle is built upon the chassis and hull of the Transportpanzer 1 armoured personnel carrier and for details of this basic vehicle refer to *Jane's Armour and Artillery 1983-84*, pages 298-302.

The NBC reconnaissance version of this vehicle is known to the West German Army as the ABC Erkundsgruppe and 140 have been ordered. The vehicle carries radiation and chemical agent detector units, sampling instruments and markers. All the detection operations are carried out from within the vehicle which is equipped with a NBC-protective ventilation system.

STATUS
Ordered for the West German Army.

MANUFACTURER
Thyssen Henschel, Postfach 102969, D-3500 Kassel, Federal Republic of Germany.

Marking Set, Contamination: Nuclear, Biological, Chemical (NBC)

DESCRIPTION
Most current indication methods for NBC use are cumbersome, heavy and awkward to use. They usually consist of some form of stakes with indicator flags that are often emplaced mechanically. For many units these mechanical methods are not possible, so some form of portable marking equipment is necessary. One form of portable equipment is the Rapp contamination marking set.

The Rapp contamination marking set is contained within a portable slung container that can be easily carried and used by one man. The container may be slung on a canvas strap over one shoulder or slung across the chest. It is a light metal frame holding three marking flag dispensers, 13 rolls of yellow marker tape, and 48 light mounting stakes and crayons.

In the simplest case, the set may be used to dispense

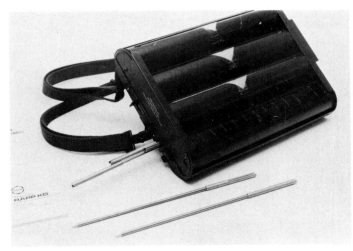

Rapp contamination marking set complete showing stake location

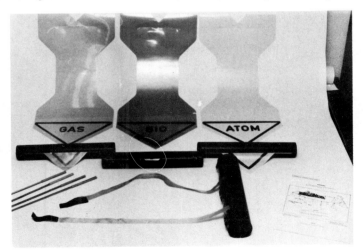

Marker flags and tapes from NBC marking set

the marker flags for attachment to existing objects such as tree branches or fence posts. The flags are simply pulled from one of the three dispensers, a white flag for nuclear contamination, a blue one for biological contamination and a yellow flag for chemical contamination. Using a crayon taken from a clip on the side of the kit container, extra information such as date and extent of contamination can be written onto the flag. The flag can then be fixed to the object by folding the head through a slot in the tail.

When stakes are required, they are removed from the container by opening latches in its side. For most purposes three stakes from the kit are required to make one pole and each stake is provided with a point at one end and a locating collar at the other. Once the first stake has been driven into the ground the others can be fitted into the sockets. The necessary flag can then be fitted onto the top of the pole by impaling it over the top. As before, extra information can be written onto the flag using the crayon from the kit.

At times it will be necessary to isolate an area by fencing it off by poles and tape. The poles are erected in the manner already described and the yellow tape can be taken from the 13 20-metre rolls carried on the kit container. The tape can also be used to form pole stabilising guys with extra stakes as the holding peg anchors. The marker flags can then be hung from the tape lengths connecting the poles.

The kit container is disposed of once used and replaced by a fresh kit. No training in using the kit is required other than a simple handbook providing general guidelines and in use the container is easy to carry and handle. It can be used even when the operators are fully covered in NBC protection clothing, and the only safety point to watch is that the sharp ends of the stakes might cut through protective clothing. The kits are issued ready for use and no form of preparation is required.

SPECIFICATIONS
Container with components
Weight: (approx) 4·5 kg

Length: 345 mm
Width: 235 mm
Height: 90 mm
Mounting stakes
Length: (each) 290 mm
Quantity: 48
Marking ribbon
Length of each roll: 20 m
Quantity: 13
Marking flags
Quantity:
(nuclear) 20 white (marked ATOM)
(biological) 20 blue (marked BIO)
(chemical) 20 yellow (marked GAS)

STATUS
Production.

MANUFACTURER
Theodor Rapp KG, Alte Hausacher Strasse 5, PO Box 1320, D-7612 Haslach iK, Federal Republic of Germany.

NETHERLANDS

Duphar 'The Button' Individual Chemical Detector

DESCRIPTION
'The Button' is a coin-sized, light, individual chemical detector and is normally carried in a gas-tight envelope. The detector consists of a small, lightweight plastic holder and contains two separated air-permeable filter papers impregnated with reagents, and an air- and liquid-tight container with a wall which can be punctured. the container is filled with a non-contaminated liquid for moistening the reagents to bring about a colour reaction.

After opening the container envelope the detector is placed in the inlet opening of the worn respirator. Air is then sucked through by inhaling 15 times. The detector is removed and the centre part is pressed inwards causing the filter papers to be pressed together. At the same time this causes the container to be pierced so moistening the reagents after which the colour reaction follows. If no nerve agent is present a blue colour appears. The transparent lid prevents unintentional activation and the whole process can be carried out with gloved hands. A drying agent is contained in the holder to prevent reagent deterioration.

A training version is available.

STATUS
Production.

MANUFACTURER
Duphar BV, PO Box 7006–1007 JA Amsterdam, Netherlands.

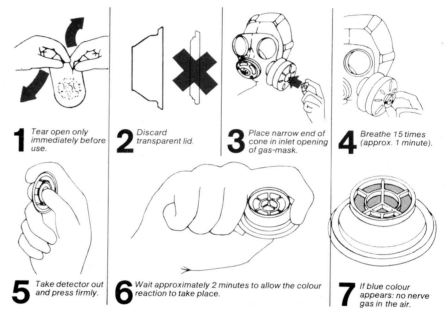

1 Tear open only immediately before use.

2 Discard transparent lid.

3 Place narrow end of cone in inlet opening of gas-mask.

4 Breathe 15 times (approx. 1 minute).

5 Take detector out and press firmly.

6 Wait approximately 2 minutes to allow the colour reaction to take place.

7 If blue colour appears: no nerve gas in the air.

Sequence of operations using 'The Button'

Duphar Water Testing Kit, Chemical Agents

DESCRIPTION
This kit is designed to determine whether water is contaminated with chemical warfare agents or other toxic substances. The equipment provides a 'go/no-go' indication showing the concentration of the toxic substance above or below a certain detection limit. These requirements are based upon a reduced daily water consumption.

The kit is carried in a hinged metal box that contains enough material for 40 nerve agent tests and 20 other agent tests, along with instructions for the user. The operating time for a trained user is 20 minutes. Some tests are combined.

The equipment will detect the following concentrations in milligrams per litre:

Sarin	0·02	Arsenics	1–2
Soman	0·02	CN	8
Tabun	0·04	ClCN	5
VX	0·02	pH	6·5–9
Mustards	2	Cl₂ consumption	5

STATUS
Production. In service with some NATO countries.

MANUFACTURER
Duphar BV, PO Box 7006–1007 JA Amsterdam, Netherlands.

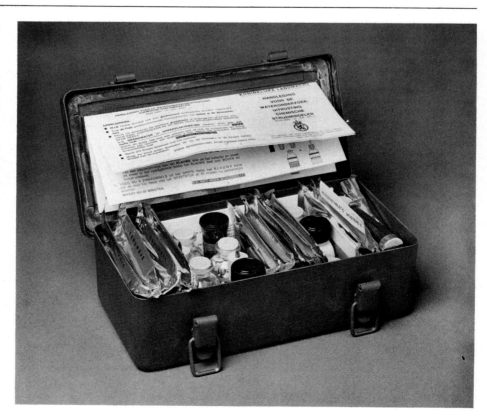

Duphar water testing kit, chemical agents

SWITZERLAND

Chemical Detection Kit CAD

DESCRIPTION
The CAD chemical detection kit has entered service with the Swiss Army and civil defence organisation. The kit is contained in a metal shoulder-slung box with dimensions of 210 × 100 × 150 mm and weighing 1·5 kg. Inside the box are a hand pump, six bottles of reagent and nerve and vesicant gas indicators; the lid interior contains instructions and colour comparison charts. The kit can detect nerve agents, including Sarin, in concentrations of 20 to 100 mg/m³ of air, and vesicants in concentrations of 2 mg/m³ of air. An operator can be trained to use the kit in about half an hour.

STATUS
In production. In service with the Swiss Army and civil defence.

MANUFACTURER
Louis Schleiffer AG, CH-8714 Feldbach, Switzerland.

UNION OF SOVIET SOCIALIST REPUBLICS

Medical-veterinary Chemical Agent Detection and Identification Kit, Model PKhR-MV

DESCRIPTION
This kit is normally used by medical units and is an enlarged version of the standard Model PKhR series kit to enable it to be used to take samples of water, food and animal fodder. The kit contains all the usual Model PKhR items with the addition of extra test-tubes, tongs, sample jars and bags, and phials. The kit can also be used to analyse water samples for chemical poisoning.

STATUS
Production probably complete. In service with Soviet medical units.

MANUFACTURER
State factories.

Chemical Agent Detection and Identification Kit, Model UPI

DESCRIPTION
This kit is a simplified version of the Model PKhR series intended for use by civilian defence agencies, and differs mainly in having no provision for taking or storing samples. It contains the usual cylindrical air pump and attachment, indicator tubes, smoke filters, rubber gloves and instruction sheet. It can detect and identify all the agents that the Model PKhR series can, although the early versions had no provision for detecting V-type agents.

STATUS
Production probably complete. In service with Soviet civil defence agencies.

MANUFACTURER
State factories.

Automatic Chemical Agent and Radiation Detector Alarm, Model GSP-1 and GSP-1M

DESCRIPTION
This equipment can be used to detect G-type nerve agents and nuclear radiation, and to provide visible and aural alarms in the presence of both. Both models, which are basically similar, provide detection and alarms only and do not determine the nature of the chemical agent or the intensity of the radiation.

The nerve agent detection system consists of a tape transport system, a reagent dropper system, an air system and a photodetector system. The tape transport system and the reagent dropper system are interconnected, and operate in 5-minute cycles separated by a 5- to 8-second cycle change, both controlled by a clockwork mechanism. At the start of each cycle reagent is dropped onto the tape which is then moved on so that the fresh drop lies under the photodetector system. An electric pump draws air into the detector system via a screening filter and over the drop on the tape. The reagent changes colour if there is any G-type nerve agent in the air and the photodetector system compares the drop colour with a reference formed from a reference beam. The reference beam is formed in different ways on the two models: on the Model GSP-1 it is derived from splitting the source beam and shining part of it onto an un-moistened part of the tape and on the Model GSM-1M the split light source is passed through a system of filters. In both cases the intensity of the two beams is compared and any change from the norm initiates the alarm systems. Air is drawn into the detector at 1·5 litres a minute and on the Model GSP-1 is then passed directly out of the system whereas on the GSM-1M it is used for interior cooling before being passed out through a grille. The detector-alarm contains enough tape and reagent to run for up to eight hours.

Electrical power comes from two rechargeable batteries, and the system is designed to operate at temperatures from −30° to +40°C.

The nuclear radiation detector system uses a halide tube detection unit. It initiates the alarm system as soon as the radiation level reaches in excess of 0·1 röntgen per hour. The alarm horn and a flashing lamp are both contained inside the case and operate both from nerve agent and radiation detection.

Without the batteries both models weigh 10 kg and with them 18 kg. The dimensions are approximately 450 × 300 × 150 mm.

STATUS
Probably no longer in production. In service with the Soviet and Warsaw Pact forces.

MANUFACTURER
State factories.

Automatic Nerve Agent Detector-alarm, Model GSP-11

DESCRIPTION
The Model GSP-11 differs mainly from the Model GSP-1 in that it can detect G-type and V-type nerve agents; the radiation detection element has been removed. The same basic tape and reagent system as that in the Model GSP-1 is retained but the reagent uses an enzyme-inhibition reaction using two reagent solutions. This enzyme-inhibition reaction is temperature-sensitive so the interior of the Model GSP-11 is maintained at between 33° and 38°C by a thermostatically-controlled heater operated by the external batteries. Otherwise the nerve agent detection and alarm systems of both detector-alarms are the same. Weights and dimensions of the Model GSP-11 are approximately the same as those of the Model GSP-1 and Model GSP-1M.

STATUS
Production probably complete. In service with the Soviet and Warsaw Pact forces.

MANUFACTURER
State factories.

Model GSP-11 automatic nerve agent detector-alarm

Field Chemical Laboratory, Model PKhL-54

DESCRIPTION
The Model PKhL-54 field laboratory can be used to detect and identify numerous chemical substances in soil, water and other materials and to analyse water and other similar substances. The equipment in the laboratory can be used for numerous chemical procedures including filtration, distillation, extractions and the like. The laboratory, which has a storage life of five years, is contained in a hinged box which is opened into three compartmented sections. The box holds 235 items including many of the items found in the Model PKhR series of kits (but in larger quantities) with the addition of numerous items of laboratory glassware and other hardware including a 50 mg chemical balance and an alcohol burner and writing materials.

The container box is 670 × 160 × 450 mm. It weighs 17·2 kg fully loaded.

STATUS
Probably still in production. In service with the Soviet forces.

MANUFACTURER
State factories and laboratories.

Biological Warfare Sampling Kit, Model KPO-1

DESCRIPTION
This sampling kit is used to obtain samples of earth, water, air, vegetation, micro-organisms and insects for analysis. It can also be used to collect unidentified chemical warfare agent specimens. The kit is carried in a case with a shoulder strap and contains, in racks, sample jars, various small sampling tools, an insect net, plastic and polyethylene bags, a soil sample separator to collect a sample of up to 15 cc, and a water sampler which can collect samples from depths to 30 metres. Atmospheric samples can be collected on gelatine filters. The kit weighs approximately 2·5 kg complete, and is about 300 mm long, 120 mm wide and 180 mm high.

STATUS
Production probably complete. In service with the Soviet forces.

MANUFACTURER
State factories.

Model KPO-1 biological warfare sampling kit (1) case (2) soil borer (3) soil sample separator (4) sample jars (5) insect net (6) cotton wool (7) gauze (8) test-tube container (9) shoulder strap (10) gelatine filters (11) polythene bags (12) forceps (13) insect net handle (14) sampling spoon (15) probe (16) knife (17) scissors

Indicator Powder and Dispenser

DESCRIPTION
This equipment consists of a flattened cylindrical dispenser with a handle at one end, a dispensing nozzle at the other and a shoulder strap. The dispenser contains an inert powder with an added indicator agent which can change colour in the presence of chemical agents. Initially the powder is pale pink but it changes to red or reddish-brown in the presence of mustard gas, reddish-brown in the presence of nitrogen mustard or G-type nerve agents, and lilac in the presence of lewisite. Depending on the amount of agent present the colour change can take place in anything from two to fifteen minutes. The container can hold from two to four kg of powder which can cover up to 40 square metres.

STATUS
Probably no longer in production. In service with the Soviet and Warsaw Pact forces.

MANUFACTURER
State factories.

Dispenser for indicator powder

UNITED KINGDOM

Chemical Agent Monitor (CAM)

DEVELOPMENT
The Chemical Agent Monitor (CAM) has been designed, developed and has undergone initial trials within three years following a Ministry of Defence contract awarded to Graseby Dynamics Limited, part of Cambridge Electronics Industries. The contract was awarded in 1980 and was based upon research work carried out at various Government research and development establishments. It is expected that final tri-service approval will be granted during 1984.

In early 1984 Bendix Corporation of Michigan, USA, took out a license agreement for the marketing and manufacture of CAM.

DESCRIPTION
CAM is a portable hand-held instrument for use by service personnel for monitoring the presence of nerve and blister agent vapour. The instrument, whose response is very specific to these agents, may be used both to indicate agent residues for decontamination and to determine whether it is safe for personnel to relax NBC safety precautions.

CAM makes use of ion mobility principles to respond selectively to agent vapours. Air, which is drawn into the unit by a pump, is ionised by a weak radioactive source. As a result of complex interchange reactions which then take place the molecules of certain species of trace vapours form ionic clusters of low mobility while others do not. The ions of these species are then further classified according to their relative mobilities. The existence of a given level of a toxic hazard is calculated by a built-in micro-computer and shown on an LCD display. The techniques employed enable specific nerve or blister agents to be monitored at very low level, whether at isolated spots or present in the general atmosphere. Discrimination is also obtained against interfering vapours likely to be found in battlefield situations.

CAM operates in real time and will recover quickly after exposure to strong concentrations of vapour but because of the sensitivity, care has to be taken not to pick up and retain agent material on the inlet probe. To prevent this happening a low cost interchangeable stand-off collar is provided. Warm-up time at an ambient temperature of +20°C is about one minute and a built-in test programme is employed to show the user that the equipment is functional and ready for use. The display panel is placed in front of the carrying handle which also contains the power supply, a single six-volt primary battery (a sealed $LiSO_2$ system). On either side of the display are the two push-button controls, on-off and nerve/blister mode. The probe is at the front of the instrument and is normally kept covered by a screw-on cap when not in use. With this cover in place the instrument can be decontaminated by normal methods. If required the instrument can be powered from an external source and the same connector can be used for fault diagnosis.

CAM may be carried in a case which also holds a spare battery, stand-off collars, accessories and a strap for hands-off carrying. If required an audible alarm for

Probe cover

Display

Battery

Battery compartment cap

CAM

Auxillary supply/test connector

General layout of Chemical Agent Monitor (CAM)

headphones can be taken off from the connector socket. For training purposes it is possible to re-programme the instrument to extend the sensitivity range to cover some riot control agents and other harmless chemical simulants.

STATUS
User trials to be completed during 1984.

MANUFACTURER
Graseby Dynamics Limited, Park Avenue, Bushey, Watford, Hertfordshire WD2 2BW, England.

SPECIFICATIONS
Weight: (hand unit) 1·5 kg
Length: (over longest dimension) 380 mm
Battery life:
(minimum) 6 h continuous
(typical) 10 h
Temperature range:
(operating) −30°C to +55°C
(storage) −55°C to +70°C
Power supply: single 6 V battery
Sensitivity: to present NATO requirements
Durability: to DEF STAN 07-55

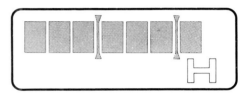
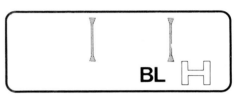

Examples of CAM display from top: nerve agent mode (G) selected, instrument in warm-up phase; nerve agent mode (G) selected with relatively low concentration indicated (two blocks visible); blister agent mode (H) selected with relatively high concentration indicated (seven blocks visible); battery low indication (BL)

NAIAD

DESCRIPTION

NAIAD stands for Nerve Agent Immobilised enzyme Alarm and Detector. It is an automatic alarm system which continually monitors the surrounding atmosphere to provide audible or visual warnings of the presence of nerve agents in either vapour or aerosol forms. The equipment consists of a sampling detector which can provide its own warning plus up to a further three remote alarm units which can be up to 500 metres away.

Its operation depends on the action of an enzyme, cholinesterase, which occurs naturally in the human body and reacts to nerve agents. Inside NAIAD a small sample of this enzyme in a plastic holder is continually irrigated by a supply of an organic ester, butyrylthiochlorine. The two substances combine by hydrolysis to form thiochlorine. Whee cholinesterase reacts to a nerve agent the resultant thiocholine shows changes in its electro-chemical reactions which are detected by a graphite measuring electrode which initiates the alarms. NAIAD can be used to detect any nerve agent, even those that are at present unknown, by using natural body chemistry. It can also be used to detect hydrogen cyanide in attack concentrations.

The mechanics of the system depends on electrical power derived from a standard 3·3 Ah Clansman battery which supplies the alarm circuits, the reagent liquid pump, the incoming air pump and the air heater. The reagent pack has the same non-stop service life as the battery: both are changed every twelve hours. The reagent pack is sealed, as is the enzyme pad holder, so there is no danger of contaminating the system by handling, and the whole system has a rapid response with a low false alarm rate. The detector is nuclear-hardened and can operate even on its side or inverted. The alarm units have flashing lights and a clearly audible alarm signal and built-in test equipment automatically tests the cable connections between the alarm and the detector.

NAIAD detector unit

NAIAD remote alarm unit

The detector is normally carried in a back-pack which also contains spare batteries and reagent packs, but it is possible to fit it into vehicles or fixed installations. A test unit suitable for use in a base workshop is available.

STATUS
In production. In service with the British Armed Forces. Ordered by two European armed forces.

MANUFACTURER
THORN EMI Simtec Limited, Sellers Wood Drive, Bulwell, Nottingham NG6 8UX, England.

SPECIFICATIONS
Detector unit:
(size) 251 × 209 × 475 mm overall
(weight) approx 12·5 kg with battery

Alarm unit:
(size) 232 × 177 × 99 mm
(weight) approx 2·5 kg with battery
Climatic range: −31°C to +52°C, 0–100% relative humidity
Minimum detectable concentration: 0·005 to 0·05 mg/m^3 dependent on agent

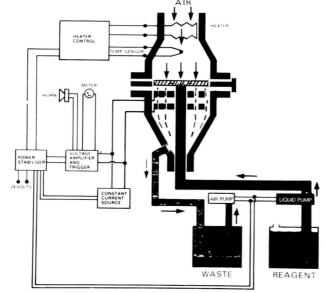

Detection process

Interior showing sealed units

Detector Paper Chemical Agent No 2 Liquid

DESCRIPTION
This detector paper is issued in booklets in a sealed clear plastic pack. Normally the paper is a neutral grey/green but exposure to liquid or aerosol chemical agents produces distinctive navy blue spots. The individual sheets of detector paper (there are 12 to a booklet) are 115 × 60 mm and have an adhesive backing to secure them to clothing, equipment or structures.

STATUS
In production. In service with the British Armed Forces.

MANUFACTURER
Dring, Limberline Road, Hilsea Industrial Estate, Portsmouth, Hampshire PO3 5JF, England.

Detector Kit Chemical Agent Residual Vapour No 1 Mk 1

DESCRIPTION
The Detector Kit No 1 Mk 1 is a personal piece of equipment normally issued to squad leaders to detect the presence of mustard or nerve agents after an attack. The kit is carried in a folding stiff canvas pack which contains instructions, reagent capsules and a small hand-pump operated sampler. In use a reagent capsule is placed in the sampler and the hand pump is actuated. If any agent is present the reagent changes colour. The kit has a shelf life of about four years imposed by the active life of the reagents employed.

STATUS
In production. In service with the British Armed Forces.

MANUFACTURER
The Leyland and Birmingham Rubber Company Limited, Golden Hill Lane, Leyland, Preston PR5 1UB, Lancashire, England.

No 1 Mk 1 detector kit

UNITED STATES OF AMERICA

Paper, Chemical Agent Detector: AN-M6A1

DESCRIPTION
This type of detector paper can be used only for detecting G-type nerve agents. The papers are issued in booklets of 25 with each paper measuring 63·5 × 101·6 mm.

Each sheet of paper is coated on one side with M5 liquid vesicant detector paint which when exposed to a liquid G-type nerve agent turns from its original olive-green colour to red or orange.

STATUS
In service with the US Army, Navy and Air Force.

Paper, Chemical Agent Detector, VGH, ABC-M8

DESCRIPTION
The ABC-M8 detector papers can detect both V- and G-type nerve agents and some blister agents. They are issued in 63·5 × 101·6 mm booklets, each containing 25 perforated papers. Directions are printed on the back of each booklet and a colour-comparison chart is on the inside cover. The ABC-M8 detector papers are included in the M18A2 and M256 detector kits.

STATUS
In service with the US Army, Air Force, Navy and Marine Corps.

Chemical Agent Detector Paper, XM9

DESCRIPTION
The Chemical Agent Detector Paper, XM9 underwent extensive testing during 1979 and may now be in service. Issued on an individual basis, the XM9 paper is a roll of adhesive-backed coated tape, 4·5 metres long and 51 mm wide. It is packed in a cardboard dispenser with a serrated edge. The serrated edge is used to cut lengths of the tape for troops to form bands around their upper arms, wrists, legs and on items of equipment. The surface is grey in colour and will display red spots when contaminated by a chemical agent providing a visual warning for the wearer to take the necessary pre-cautions. The paper may also be used as a probe or for blotting suspected surfaces.

A complete package of XM9 paper weighs approximately 140 grams.

STATUS
Uncertain. Has been through troop trial process.

Bendix BxICAD Miniature Chemical Agent Detector

DEVELOPMENT/DESCRIPTION
The Bendix Corporation's Environmental and Process Instrument's Division has completed the development of a miniature chemical agent detector, the BxICAD, which is intended to address the chemical agent threat of the 1990s. The hardware is currently undergoing laboratory and field evaluation in Europe and is scheduled for field introduction in limited quantities in mid-1984.

The BxICAD is a low-cost, miniature, limited area detector which can also be used as a personal detector badge. Based on electrochemical detection phenomenon, the BxICAD is compact and lightweight, measuring $100 \times 50 \times 15$ mm and weighing less than 230 grams.

The system consists of an electronics module and sensor module. The electronics module, consisting of the detector processor, audible alarm and warning light, is re-useable. The sensor module, which contains the battery power source and sensor cells, is disposable and designed for six months of continuous use. The sensor contains three independent interference-rejection techniques and provides an alarm response to nerve agents, mustard, lewisite, phosgene, hydrogen cyanide and cyanogen chloride. After an initial alarm the sensor will automatically reset and be capable of accepting subsequent chemical agent challenges.

A training sensor module is planned, which can be easily inserted into the BxICAD unit. Potential applications for the BxICAD include a remote monitor for fixed and mobile installations and a filter monitoring device for collective-protection equipment.

STATUS
Development complete.

BxICAD miniature chemical agent detector

MANUFACTURER
The Bendix Corporation, Environmental & Process Instruments Division, 1400 Taylor Avenue, Baltimore, Maryland 21204, USA.

XM85/XM86 Automatic Liquid Agent Detector System

DESCRIPTION
This system is under development to detect thickened nerve agents, mustard gas and lewisite down to droplets 200 microns in diameter. The system consists of two units. One is the XM85 Central Alarm Unit (CAU) which continuously monitors a network of individual XM86 Detector Units (DU). The system warns of on-target liquid chemical rain attacks by allocating each DU a unique identification code. Using this coding the XM85 CAU can identify which DU is providing an alarm. Using the known location of each DU the aerosol cloud characteristics causing the alarm can be assessed, eg course, velocity and dimensions.

STATUS
Advanced development.

DEVELOPMENT AGENCY
Chemical Research and Development Centre, Aberdeen Proving Ground, Maryland, USA.

XM85 Central Alarm Unit (CAU) (T J Gander)

XM86 Detector Unit (DU) (T J Gander)

Alarm, Chemical Agent, Automatic: Portable, M8 and M10 to M18

DESCRIPTION
This alarm system has ten variations all based on the use of two basic components, the M43 detector and the M42 alarm. Each detector unit can activate up to five alarm units. By the use of various components and associated equipment these two basic units can form the basis for the following alarm systems:

Alarm, chemical agent, automatic: portable, manpack, M8
Alarm, chemical agent, automatic: portable, fixed emplacement, M10
Alarm, chemical agent, automatic: portable, for Truck, Utility, ¼-ton, M11
Alarm, chemical agent, automatic: portable, for Truck, ¾-ton, M12 (no longer in production)

Alarm, chemical agent, automatic: portable, for Truck, 2½-ton, M13
Alarm, chemical agent, automatic: portable, for full-tracked APCs and ARVs, M14
Alarm, chemical agent, automatic: portable, for Carrier, Command and Recce, M15
Alarm, chemical agent, automatic: portable, w/power supply for Truck, Utility, 1¼-ton, M16

Alarm, chemical agent, automatic: portable, w/power supply for Truck, Utility, ¾-ton, M17 (no longer in production or service)

Alarm, chemical agent, automatic: portable, w/power supply for Truck, 2½-ton, M18

These systems differ mainly in the type of mounting used, but common to all is the M253 winterisation kit which has two special batteries and a cable assembly. This kit was not purchased by the US Army.

The M43 detector operates by passing air through an oxime solution surrounding a silver analytical electrode and a platinum reference electrode. If a chemical agent is present a reaction occurs in the solution which increases the potential between the two electrodes. Any such potential change is amplified and the alarm signal is triggered.

A new detector unit, the M43A1, is expected to enter service in 1984 and will be interchangeable with existing M43 units. The M43A1 does not have any chemical reagents in its detector system but instead uses a cell module containing 250 micro-curies of Americium 241, an alpha and gamma emitter. The M43A1 operates on the principle of molecular ion clustering. The new unit was developed at the US Army Armament R & D Command's Chemical Systems Laboratory, CB Detection and Alarms Division.

The Detector Unit, Simulator Automatic Chemical Agent Alarm, XM81, has been developed for use with the M8 system and when fitted is attached to the M43 detector unit (see page 729).

STATUS
In service with the US Army. 26 000 portable manpack M8 sets were ordered for the US Army from 1975 to 1982.

MANUFACTURERS
(M8) Bendix Corporation, Environmental and Process Instruments Division, 1400 Taylor Avenue, Baltimore, Maryland 21204, USA.
(M8A1) Brunswick Corporation, Defence Division, One Brunswick Plaza, Skokie, Illinois 60077, USA.

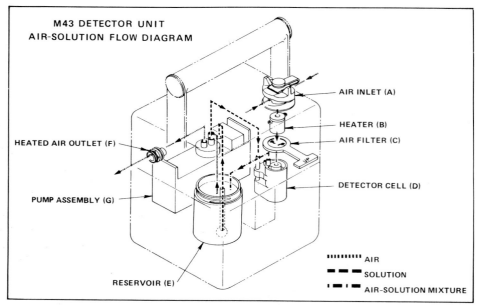

M43 detector unit air-solution flow diagram

Basic alarm, chemical agent, automatic, portable, M8. From left: M229 refill kit, BA 3517 battery, M43 detector unit (at rear), M42 alarm unit.

SPECIFICATIONS

Component	M43 Detector	M42 Alarm	M229 Refill kit	BA3517 Battery	M10 Power Supply	M228 Mounting kit	M182 Mounting kit
Length	160 mm	224 mm	330 mm	160 mm	15 mm	191 mm	191 mm
Width	196 mm	152 mm	264 mm	196 mm	163 mm	254 mm	254 mm
Height	279 mm	89 mm	229 mm	127 mm	188 mm	318 mm	203 mm
Weight	3 kg	1·7 kg	6·3 kg	3·4 kg	8·2 kg	7·3 kg	6·8 kg
Maximum distance of detector from alarm	400 m	400 m	400 m	400 m	400 m	400 m	400 m
Life on one refill (continuous use)	15 days	n/a	15 days	n/a	n/a	n/a	n/a

Detector Kit, Chemical Agent: ABC-M18A2

DESCRIPTION
The ABC-M18A2 detector kit is normally issued to specialist chemical warfare teams for the detection of a range of blister, blood and nerve agents, and can also be used to collect samples for further analysis. The kit is contained in an olive-green carrier slung from the shoulder and it holds an aspirator bulb assembly, detector paper, sampling tubes, packets of reagents and substrate solution, ABC-M8 detector paper, M7A1 detector crayon and a few other accessories. When packed the kit measures 203 × 152 × 76 mm.

STATUS
In service with the US Army, Air Force and Navy.

Detector Kit, Chemical Agent, M256

DESCRIPTION
The M256 chemical agent detector kit is gradually replacing the earlier M15A2 and M18A2 kits for most field use applications and is produced so that troops in the field can determine within ten minutes whether it is safe to remove protective masks and clothing. The kit contains 12 pocket-sized sampler-detectors, a book of M8 chemical detection paper and instruction cards, all carried in a rugged case.

Each sampler-detector contains an impregnated test spot for blister agents, a circular test spot for blood agents, a star test spot for nerve agents and a lewisite detector crayon and a few other accessories. When packed the kit measures 203 × 152 × 76 mm.

pellet and marking pad. There are eight glass ampoules, six containing reagents for testing and two in an attached chemical heater. In use the reagent ampoules are crushed by hand and preformed channels in the plastic sheet of the sampler-detector direct the flow from the ampoules to the appropriate test spot. Simple safe/

danger indicators are printed on the back of each sampler/detector and show the colour that each test spot develops if a chemical agent is present. The foil packet that encloses each sampler-detector also contains instructions printed on its outer surface.

The M256 kit measures 170 × 76 × 127 mm and weighs 0·54 kg. The kit requires about four hours training to use it with skill. A Training Kit (Simulator) for the M256 is under development.

STATUS
In production. In service with the US Army.

MANUFACTURER
Bendix Corporation, Environmental and Process Instruments Division, 1400 Taylor Avenue, Baltimore, Maryland 21204, USA.

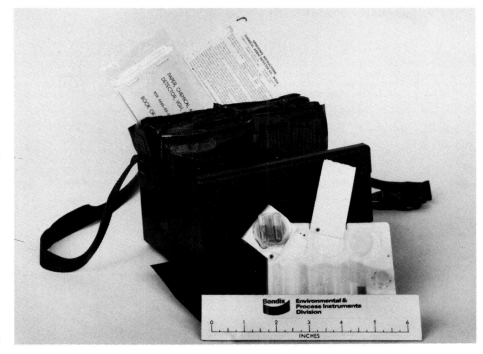

Chemical agent detector kit M256

Laboratory, Chemical, Base, M2 and M2A1

DESCRIPTION
For use in a semi-permanent or permanent structure, these two mobile laboratories are intended for the iden-

tification and evaluation of chemical agents, weapons and munitions and for testing and inspecting material. The M2A1 has the additional ability to inspect and assess nuclear warfare agents. Both types of laboratory are stored in boxes and crates and both contain general laboratory equipment including glassware, chemicals and associated equipment. In addition both have

special testing equipment and a library. The M2 is packed in 65 boxes weighing just over 10 000 kg. The M2A1 is contained in 181 crates weighing 13 620 kg.

STATUS
In service with the US Army.

Sampling and Analysing Kit, CB Agent, ABC-M19

DESCRIPTION
The contents of this kit are used by specialist personnel for detecting and identifying chemical warfare agents.

By using the kit some preliminary processing of unidentified agents is possible. The kit is carried in a storage case 356 × 432 × 178 mm which is internally compartmented to accommodate the various components. The actual components themselves are not standard but may be selected from three other kits, the M32 CB agent

sampling and analysing parts kit, the M33 CB agent analysing components refill kit, and the M34 agent sampling components refill kit.

STATUS
In service with the US Army.

Sampling Kit, CB Agent, M34

DESCRIPTION
The M34 kit can be used to sample soil, water and other items for the presence of various chemical and

biological warfare agents. The kit is issued in a fibreboard box which weighs just over 2 kg, and consists of two soil sampling kits, a phial container, and two pairs of gloves. The kit can be used for some preliminary soil testing.

STATUS
In service with the US Army, Navy and Air Force.

XM21 Remote Sensing Chemical Agent Alarm

DESCRIPTION
The XM21 is a passive remote sensing alarm system for detecting chemical agent clouds (including nerve gas) up to several kilometres away. It is a rugged, portable system that can operate unattended for up to 24 hours in all weathers.

The design is based on a Michelson interferometer that collects infra-red radiation using ambient background radiance to define a normal scene. As a chemical agent enters the XM21 field of view, the agent selectively absorbs or emits infra-red energy at specific frequencies, changing the overall scene spectrum. The change in the spectrum is detected and identified as a chemical agent by an algorithm that also rejects common battlefield interferents, thereby providing a reliable detection rate and a low probability of false alarms.

STATUS
Under advanced development.

MANUFACTURER
Honeywell Inc, Chemical Defence Centre, 13350 US Highway 19, Clearwater, Florida 33546, USA.

XM21 Remote Sensing Chemical Agent Alarm from front

XM21 Remote Sensing Chemical Agent Alarm from rear showing control panel

XM22 Automatic Chemical Agent Alarm

DESCRIPTION
The XM22 Automatic Chemical Agent Alarm is a man-portable equipment that is being developed to replace the existing M8 and M8A1 series of alarm systems. A point sampling alarm system, it is used to detect and identify all nerve agents, mustard gas and lewisite. Using a surface sampling probe with an integral heater the XM22 detects agents on the ground or other battlefield surfaces. The detector uses ion mobility spectrometry, a 'dry' system providing improved sensitivity compared with the M8/M8A1 systems.

STATUS
Advanced development.

DEVELOPMENT AGENCY
Chemical Research and Development Centre, Aberdeen Proving Ground, Maryland, USA.

Water Testing Kit, Chemical Agents, AN-M2

DESCRIPTION
The AN-M2 kit is used to test water samples in the field for the presence of various chemical warfare agents. It can be used only with unchlorinated water samples. The kit is contained in a plastic case measuring approximately 152 × 64 × 89 mm, and consists of 12 reagent containers, a metal scoop, glass containers and cleaning materials. The kits are issued to the various units in boxes of 24 kits, with each box weighing 22·7 kg.

STATUS
In service with the US Army, Navy and Air Force.

Surface Contamination Module (SCM)

DESCRIPTION
The Surface Contamination Module (SCM) is still in the development stage as a hand-held detector of chemical agents which can also provide some form of identification of the agent concerned. The SCM has two main parts, a hand-held sensor unit, which visually resembles a small video camera, and a belt-mounted discriminator unit. In use the SCM is switched on and calibrated and the hand-held sensor unit 'lens' is held close to a surface to be monitored. If an agent is present the discriminator unit will emit an audio alarm signal and a coded alphanumeric signal will appear on a readout window on the back of the sensor; this readout will identify the type or family of the agent present. The readout will also give an indication of the the strength/threat of the agent. If the surface concerned is 'safe' the discriminator unit will emit an all-clear signal. SCM is being developed by Bendix under a US Air Force contract.

STATUS
Development.

DEVELOPMENT AGENCY
Honeywell Avionics, St. Petersburg, Florida, USA.

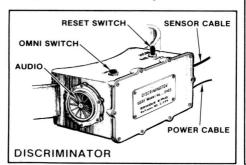

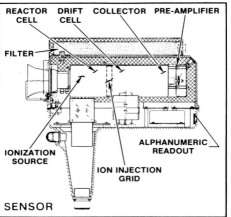

Surface Contamination Module discriminator and sensor

Alarm, G-Agent, Automatic, Fixed Installation, M5

DESCRIPTION
Designed for use in manufacturing installations and other such premises, the M5 automatic alarm operates on the continuous trace principle. Detector chemicals are fed onto a continuous paper trace which is constantly scanned for any alteration of pigment caused by the presence of G-type nerve agents. If any G-type agent is present, a photometer unit will initiate the circuits which control the alarm horn and a flashing red light. The equipment is powered by a 110-volt ac source and when installed it weighs 328·8 kg. It is two metres high, 0·66 metre wide and 0·61 metre deep. When packed the full equipment weighs 840 kg, and is contained in four packing cases, one of which contains repair parts.

STATUS
In service with the US Army in base installations and manufacturing plant.

MANUFACTURER
Leeds and Northrop, Philadelphia, Pennsylvania, USA.

WARSAW PACT

PKhR Series of Chemical Agent Detection and Identification Kits

DESCRIPTION
This series of chemical agent identification and detection kits has been under development since the late 1940s and has undergone gradual and slight changes over the years. The kits are now in service in several forms, all using the same basic operating processes, and some have been produced in East Germany as well. Some of the earlier kits are now obsolete but are still in use for training and by some of the smaller Warsaw Pact nations. The following list summarises the main types:

Soviet designation	East German designation	Comments
PKhR-50	n/app	Obsolete Used by Bulgaria
PKhR-51	n/app	Obsolete Used by Bulgaria
PKhR-54	KA-54, PChR-54	
PKhR-63	PChR-54 (improved)	
None	PChR-54U	East German version of PKhR-63
VPKhR	WPChR-64	

If the Model PKhR-54 is taken to be typical of the above series the kit is contained in a metal case fitted with waist and shoulder straps. The case lid opens forward to form a working tray. The kit box contains a hand-operated cylindrical air pump, nine or ten different types of indicator tubes (packaged in tens), a pump attachment, smoke filters, perforated plastic caps, a spatula, two sample jars, tape for marking affected areas, a torch, gloves, report forms and an instruction sheet. The kit is capable of detecting and identifying mustard, nitrogen mustard, lewisite, hydrogen cyanide, cyanogen chloride, phosgene, disphosgene, chloropicrin, adamsite, chloroacetophenone and G-type nerve agents. V-type nerve agents can also be dealt with by the addition of suitable indicator tubes. Each type of tube can normally identify and detect one type of agent but some new indicator tubes can detect up to four. The tubes are 7 mm in diameter and 110 mm long. They are packed in tens and are colour-coded as follows:

Tube marking	Agent detected
1 yellow ring	mustard
2 yellow rings	nitrogen mustard
3 yellow rings	lewisite
1 black ring	hydrogen cyanide
1 green ring	chloropicrin
2 green rings	cyanogen chloride
3 green rings	hydrogen cyanide cyanogen chloride phosgene diphosgene
1 white ring	chloroacetophenone
2 white rings	adamsite
1 red ring	G-type nerve agents
1 red ring with 1 red dot	G-type and V-type nerve agents

Each tube contains a measured quantity of reagent in a sealed ampoule. The end of the tube is broken off by inserting it in a hole on the end of the pump handle and snapping it. The ampoule is then pierced by a stiff wire contained in the pump handle and the tube placed in a socket in the head of the air pump. Hand pumping draws air through the tube and the ampoule will change colour according to the type of agent present. The pump can hold several tubes at once and the degree of agent concentration can be determined by reference to a calibrated colour scale. Fitting the air pump attachment enables sampling of soil, fabric or surfaces and a smoke filter can be used to screen smoke fumes that might

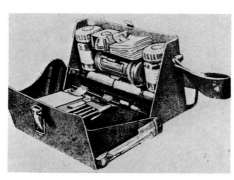

PKhR-63 chemical agent detection and identification kit

affect detection. The sample jars can be used to take samples for further laboratory analysis. The kits from the Model PKhR-54U onwards contain an indicator tube heater as an extra in place of one of the sample jars. This heater is a hollow plastic cylinder closed at both ends and filled with cotton wadding. The top has four wells to hold three indicator tubes and a heating ampoule. When the ampoule is pierced using one of the wires in the pump handle, an exothermic reaction heats the tubes, which are placed in the heater for one minute. The heater is used only when the temperature is below 15°C.

The latest and current Soviet kit is the Model VPKhR which is smaller and lighter than the previous models with a more limited detection capability. Only three types of indicator tube are now carried, but by using multi-detection tubes the kit can identify and detect mustard, phosgene, diphosgene, hydrogen cyanide, cyanogen chloride and G-type and V-type nerve agents. The sample jars have been replaced by plastic bags and a tube holder is also included. The East German Model PChR-54U kit also contains the CHNS indicator paper kit.

STATUS
Production and development continuing. Models

PKhR-50 and PKhR-51 now obsolete. The rest are in service with the Soviet and Warsaw Pact forces, with the Model VPKhR being the current version.

MANUFACTURER
State factories.

SPECIFICATIONS
Model	PKhR-54	VPKhR
Length	240 mm	205 mm
Width	100 mm	100 mm
Height	140 mm	140 mm
Weight	2·7 kg	2·3 kg

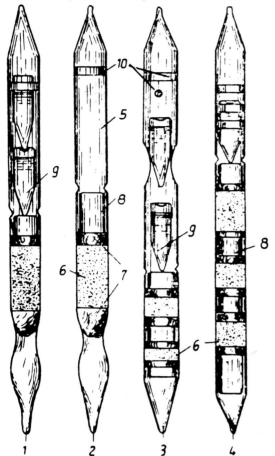

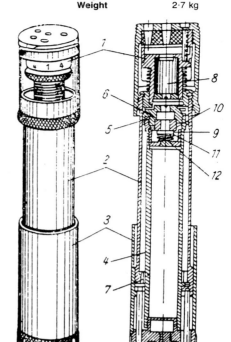

Piston-type air pump PKhR-54 (1) collector (2) pump housing (3) handle with ampoule opener (4) piston rod (5) sleeve (6) seat (7) spacer ring (8) protective cartridge (9) valve (10) valve seat (11) spring (12) spring stop

Indicator tubes (1) red ring tube (2) 1 yellow ring tube (3) 1 red ring with 1 red dot tube (4) 3 green ring tube (5) transparent glass tube (6) inert filter (7) cotton plug (8) flow-through canal (9) reagent ampoule (10) colour-code marking

Semi-automatic Chemical Agent Detection and Identification Kit, Models PPKhR and PPChR

DESCRIPTION
This kit is carried on various types of radiological and chemical reconnaissance vehicles such as the

BRDM-rkh. Basically it is a Model PKhR series kit with an electrically-driven rotary air pump in place of the cylindrical hand pump, and an electric heater replacing the indicator tube heater. Both these components are driven by the vehicle battery. The East German version is the Model PPChR which is a modified Model PChR-54U kit.

STATUS
Probably still in production. In service with the Soviet and Warsaw Pact forces.

MANUFACTURER
State factories.

Chemical and Radiological Reconnaissance Vehicles

DESCRIPTION
All the Warsaw Pact forces have vehicles devoted primarily to chemical and radiological reconnaissance. The specific vehicle in service with any particular army usually depends on the types of vehicle already in service but few of these special vehicles have any drastic modifications for their role other than the addition of lane-marking equipment to the rear. However, they nearly all carry a standard equipment kit consisting of one Model GSP-1 or GSP-1M nerve agent and radiation detector-alarm or one Model GSP-11 nerve agent

detector-alarm and a separate radiation alarm, one Model VPKhR chemical agent detection and identification kit or the equivalent, one Model PPKhR automatic chemical agent detection and identification kit, one DP-3 area survey meter, one DP-5A radiation meter, one Model KPO-1 biological warfare sampling kit, SKhT signal cartridges, RDG smoke grenades and lane flag markers and emplacers.

The vehicles involved are the UAZ-69-rkh, the UAZ-469-rkh, the BRDM-rkh, the BRDM-2-rkh and the Hungarian FUG (OT-65). The last three vehicles all have two 20-flag marker emplacers carried at the rear, but the UAZ-69-rkh may have either one 10- or 12-flag emplacer, or a flag rack from which the flags have to be emplaced manually.

STATUS
See appropriate vehicle sections. All in service with the Warsaw Pact and Soviet forces.

MANUFACTURER
See appropriate vehicle sections.

BRDM-rkh team wearing combined and protective suits and Model ShM masks, with soldier in foreground using VPKhr chemical agent detection and identification kit and soldier behind using DP-5A radiac survey meter

UAZ-469-rkh chemical and radiological reconnaissance vehicle dispensing lane flags

CHEMICAL TRAINING AND MAINTENANCE EQUIPMENT

CANADA

Chemical Simulators

DESCRIPTION
The Canadian Armed Forces are currently evaluating two new types of chemical simulator that simulate a chemical warfare attack by projecting clouds of chemical powder or liquids without using any form of mortar. The simulators are in two basic forms. One is the Groundburst Chemical Simulator (SC-300) and the other the Airburst Chemical Simulator (SC-310).

Both types of simulator can be fired from the ground or from the top of a vehicle. Each consists of a canister which acts as the projector. If required the canister may be held steady by a simple spiked holder into which the canister is clipped once the spike has been driven into the ground. The groundburst version projects a cloud of chemical powder six to ten metres into the air where the wind will carry the cloud. The airburst version projects a cloud of powder or liquid to a height of approximately 61 metres.

Both types of simulator are packed in plastic foam boxes containing 18 canisters and spike holders. The boxes measure 570 × 390 × 180 mm.

SPECIFICATIONS

Type	Groundburst	Airburst
Weight	350 g	400 g
Weight of filling	225 g	165 g
Height of canister	143 mm	143 mm
Diameter of canister	73 mm	73 mm
Height of burst	6–10 m	61 m

STATUS
Under evaluation by the Canadian Armed Forces.

MANUFACTURER
Hand Chemical Industries, 221 Nipissing Road, Milton, Ontario, Canada L3Y 1R3.

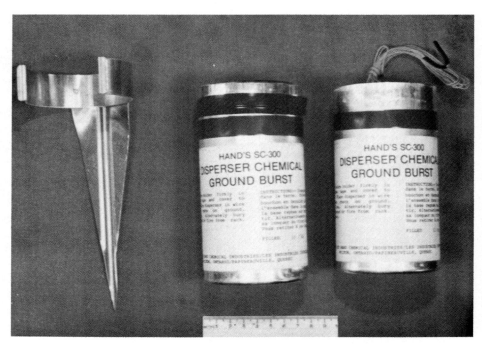

SC-300 groundburst chemical simulator with one ground spike holder

GERMANY, DEMOCRATIC REPUBLIC

WSpT Special Chemical Technology Workshop

DESCRIPTION
The WSpT special chemical technology workshop is one element in the KRCW combined radiological/chemical workshop unit (the other components being the WKCA, the WPSA and the Chemical Spares Store). The WSpT workshop is carried on a Ural-375 (6 × 6) truck which normally tows a single-axle trailer carrying a 6-6376 diesel-engined electrical generator.

The workshop is contained in a LAK 11 detachable box body unit which weighs 4305 kg when fully equipped and with a removeable canvas awning. The box body is 4·3 metres long, 2·5 metres wide and two metres high. It is mounted on a standard ISO 10-foot container bed and contains a small lathe, a generator,

heating and ventilation plant, a spark plug tester and cleaner, a compressor and welding apparatus. This equipment, along with more specialised tools and machines, is used to service and maintain chemical decontamination apparatus and in particular the ARS-12 and ARS-14 truck-mounted equipments, along with the various DD series of mass decontamination equipments. The repairs and maintenance involved is classed as either routine or medium-grade, and the WSpT can operate for periods of up to ten hours in the field with the fuels and other supplies carried.

Combat weight of the WSpT is 12 875 kg. Dimensions are 7·46 × 2·69 × 3·35 metres. It has an operating range of 570 km and can travel at speeds up to 75 km/hour.

STATUS
Production probably complete.

WSpT special chemical technology workshop

MANUFACTURER
East German state factories.

Chemical Training Kit, Model CAS-60

DESCRIPTION
This kit is used in the classroom to train chemical reconnaissance personnel and consists mainly of a number of sample bottles containing various chemical substances. Trainees can thus be taught to identify certain

substances either by smell or appearance. Included are various types of agent, decontaminants, solvents, smoke generating compounds and incendiaries. A small case containing first-aid supplies is included in the kit.

The Model CAS-60 (CAS – 'Chemische Ausbildungssatz') is contained in a wooden box measuring 750 × 600 × 900 mm.

STATUS
Probably no longer in fixed production but easily produced.

MANUFACTURER
State factories and army schools.

POLAND

Portable Gas Training Chamber

DESCRIPTION
This portable device is used for training recruits and NCOs with their chemical protection equipment. It consists of a suspended metal cover with an attached shroud which is lowered over an individual until it covers

to the knees. Inside the metal cover is a device for releasing tear gas which once scattered over the masked trainee enables him to test the efficiency and fit of his face mask. The device can be hung from a specially-erected metal or timber framework, and in the field can be suspended from a tree branch.

STATUS
Production complete. In service with the Polish forces.

MANUFACTURER
Probably state factories but could be easily improvised in the field by any unit.

UNION OF SOVIET SOCIALIST REPUBLICS

Protective Mask and Canister Leakage Tester, Model PGP

DESCRIPTION
This equipment is used to test most types of Warsaw Pact protective masks and canisters for leakage. All the components are contained in a metal box and include two rubber bulb-type air pumps, a manometer, a one-minute sand glass timer, rubber tubing and plugs, valves and various fittings. With both the masks and the canisters the units are sealed and pumped up to pressure. The pressure is measured on the simple manometer and has to be maintained for one minute without leakage; the time is determined by the sand glass timer.

STATUS
Production probably complete. In service with the Soviet and Warsaw Pact forces.

MANUFACTURER
State factories.

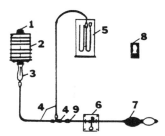

Model PGP protective mask and canister leakage tester canister testing (1) rubber plug (2) canister (3) connecting tube (4) rubber tubing (5) pressure gauge (6) wire spring clamp (7) rubber bulb (8) 1-minute sand glass timer (9) connector

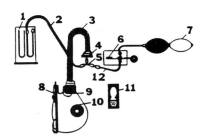

Model PGP protective mask and canister leakage tester mask testing (1) pressure gauge (2) rubber tubing (3) protective mask nose (4) connector (5) T-tube (6) wire spring clamp (7) rubber bulb (8) face-piece clamp (9) rubber plug (10) protective mask face-piece (11) 1-minute sand glass timer (12) rubber tubing

Mobile Chemical Workshop PPKhM-1M

DESCRIPTION
Based on the chassis of the GAZ-66 truck, this mobile workshop is used for field repair, maintenance, calibration and servicing of chemical and radiological equipments. The workshop is contained within a specially-equipped box body and additional tentage and equipment are carried in a towed IAPZ-738 single-axle trailer. The box body has four work spaces although more can be provided within the carried tents. Wherever possible, electrical power is taken from an external source but an AB-2T230 portable generator can supply power for lighting and the various items of test and repair equipment. A petrol heater and an air compressor are also provided.

STATUS
Production status uncertain. In service with the Soviet forces.

MANUFACTURER
State factories.

UNITED STATES OF AMERICA

Detector Unit, Simulator Automatic Chemical Agent Alarm, XM81

DEVELOPMENT
The XM81 simulator has been designed to be used with the M8 Automatic Chemical Alarm System (ACAS) and the exploratory development programme was successfully completed in December 1980. A 21-month engineering development programme was initiated in March 1981 and current plans call for the system to be type-classified in early fiscal year 1985 with a subsequent Initial Operational Capability (IOC) in fiscal year 1987.

DESCRIPTION
The XM81 system consists of a hand-held transmitter unit and four receiver modules which are fitted to the M43 detector units between the upper and lower assemblies. The transmitter can send four distinct coded radio signals to any or all four of the receiver modules which then activate the M43 detector units. The transmitter has a range of approximately one kilometre, and the frequency used is 141·925 Mhz; a frequency chosen so that it will not interfere with other electronic systems, and vice versa.

When not in use the XM81 system components are kept in a metal carrying case which contains four receivers, one transmitter unit and associated cables and spares.

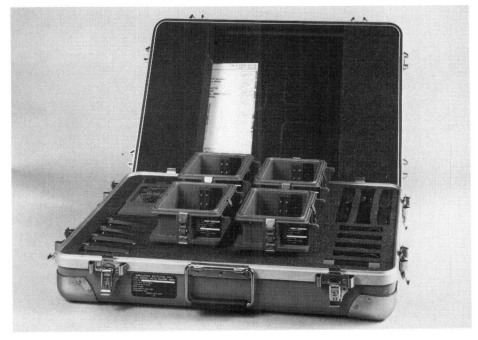

XM81 simulator set in carrying case

XM81 transmitter module

XM81 receiver module

XM81 receiver in M43 detector module

SPECIFICATIONS
Transmitter unit
Height: 184 mm
Width: 114 mm
Depth: 57 mm
Weight: 1·14 kg

Receiver module
Height: 152·4 mm

Width: 178 mm
Depth: 140 mm
Weight: 0·91 kg

System in case
Height: 241 mm
Width: 813 mm
Depth: 406 mm
Weight: 15·66 kg

System range: approx 1 km
Frequency: 141·925 Mhz

STATUS
Under development.

MANUFACTURER
Bendix Corporation, Environmental and Process Instruments Division, 1400 Taylor Avenue, Baltimore, Maryland 21204, USA.

WARSAW PACT

Protective Equipment Workbench, Model SKhM-M

DESCRIPTION
This item of equipment is a compartmented workbench specially equipped for the maintenance of protective clothing, protective masks and canisters, and breathing gear. It contains special and other tools, instruments, some spare parts and various materials for the servicing, testing and repairing of all the above.

STATUS
In service with the Soviet and Warsaw Pact forces.

MANUFACTURER
State factories.

RADIATION SURVEY METERS AND DETECTION EQUIPMENT, DOSIMETERS AND CHARGING UNITS

CANADA

Radiac Set, Remote Monitoring and Alarm, AN/FDR-502(V)

DESCRIPTION
This multi-unit equipment is intended to continuously monitor and detect gamma radiation from a mixed energy spectra, and is designed to be installed at fixed installations, although semi-fixed installations such as mobile containers and ships can accommodate the equipment. The basic unit of the equipment consists of a control group mounted in a 482 mm rack which may be connected to up to ten sensors, each of which is connected to a sensor mount and junction box. The junction box may be connected to the control group by up to two interconnecting boxes, so that the individual sensors (which are connected to their sensor mounts by a one metre long length of pipe) may be up to 3048 metres away from the control group.

Each sensor is nuclear hardened and the control group is protected against electromagnetic pulses. An indicator on the control group provides a visual display in digital form of the current dose rate. The control group also incorporates an audio-visual alarm that can be pre-set to any level between 0·1 and 100 rads per hour. The maximum reading possible is 5000 rads per hour.

The power supply for the equipment may be either 115 volts, 60 Hertz single phase, 220 volts 50 or 60 Hertz single phase or 24 volts dc from a battery.

A simulator for training purposes is available.

STATUS
Production. In service with the Canadian Armed Forces.

SPECIFICATIONS

Unit	Control group	Sensor	Sensor mount and junction box	Interconnecting box
Weight	13·6 kg	1·4 kg	8·2 kg	11·4 kg
Width	440 mm	92 mm (diameter)	400 mm	400 mm
Height	131 mm	158 mm	101 mm	101 mm
Depth	437 mm	–	464 mm	464 mm

Radiacmeter IM-5016/PD

DESCRIPTION
This is a hand-portable instrument for the measurement of low and medium-range gamma radiation of mixed energy spectra. It is of the Geiger-Müller type powered by two nine-volt mercury batteries. Radiation readings are given in röntgens per hour on two scales, the lowest from 0 to 100 mr/h and the highest from 0·1 to 10 r/h. The readings are taken from a single meter which is raised in its housing from the die-cast aluminium case. A handle below the meter is so arranged that the single operator's switch can be moved by the user's thumb. This switch has four positions; off, check, high and low. Instructions for use are printed on the body in both French and English and the instrument can be carried on a web carrying strap with a hook at each end.

There is a non-military version of this instrument known as the RD-5016.

SPECIFICATIONS
Weight: (with battery) 1·6 kg
Length: 230 mm
Height: 120 mm
Width: 120 mm

STATUS
Production. In service with the Canadian Armed Forces.

Radiacmeter IM-5016/PD

MANUFACTURER
R-Metrics Limited, 486 Wyecroft Road, Oakville, Ontario, Canada L6K 2G7.

Radiacmeter IM-108S/PD

DESCRIPTION
The Radiacmeter IM-108S/PD is a portable instrument used for the measurement of gamma radiation of mixed energy spectra. It is of the ion chamber type and is powered by a single nine-volt battery with a minimum operating life of 300 hours. Radiation readings are displayed on a single logarithmic scale of 2½ decades with range 0–500 r/hr. Calibration in Greys is also available.

The die-cast aluminium case is waterproof and the instrument operates from −50°C to +65°C. Operating instructions in both English and French are printed on the identification plate.

Operation is fully automatic with the only operator control being an on-off switch. The instrument is self-testing. When switched on the sensor is disabled while the electronics are tested for five to eight seconds. The operational condition is displayed by a meter pointer in the 'check' band and when the meter needle returns to zero the sensor is enabled and the survey begins. A

battery monitor warns of impending battery exhaustion up to several hours in advance and is continuously active while the equipment is on. Exhaustion is indicated by the needle swinging back and forth to prevent a reading.

A non-military version of this instrument is known as the RD108.

SPECIFICATIONS
Weight with batteries: 1·3 kg
Height: 120 mm
Width: 106·9 mm
Length: 171·4 mm

STATUS
Production. Previous model IM108C/PD is in service with the Canadian and US Armed Forces.

MANUFACTURER
R-Metrics Limited, 486 Wyecroft Road, Oakville, Ontario, Canada L6K 2G7.

Radiacmeter High Range IM-108S/PD

CZECHOSLOVAKIA

Tactical Dosimeter, Model DK-62

DESCRIPTION
The Model DK-62 dosimeter operates on the thermo-luminescence principle using a single-crystal phosphor glass as the energy-storing component. The dosimeter is contained in a round black plastic case 40 mm in diameter and 20 mm thick, and the energy component is 24 × 18 × 11·5 mm and weighs 30 grams. The case can be worn around the neck or in a uniform pocket with the dosimeter itself held inside the case on a piece of white plastic foam. For reading the case is opened and the dosimeter is placed inside a VDK-62 dosimeter reader, where it is heated. Heating reduces the energy level of the dosimeter to zero and the energy produced by the passage of radiation is released in the form of light which is optically matched to a colour scale to determine the level of radiation. The Model VDK-62 is powered by a 12-volt power supply and measures 200 × 150 × 120 mm.

STATUS
Production probably complete. In service with the Czechoslovak forces.

MANUFACTURER
State factories and laboratories.

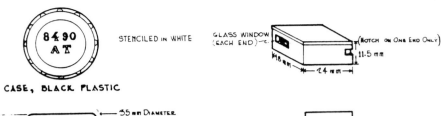

DK-62 tactical dosimeter

FRANCE

Radiation Meter Model DOK 803 and DUK 807 Collective Unit

DESCRIPTION
The basic Radiation Meter DOK 803 is an instrument contained in a lightweight rectangular moulded plastic case that can be easily carried and used in one hand. Using a Geiger-Müller tube as a detector it can detect gamma radiation. It has two indicators. One is a small lamp that flashes when radiation present is less than 0·01 r/h. At rates from 0·01 r/h up to 120 r/h the dose rate is indicated in digital form on a display panel. The only control is a single on/off switch and power is produced by two internally-housed 1·5-volt BA30 cells. These cells provide power for the instrument to be used continuously for 20 hours and intermittently for 40 hours.

The DOK 803 may be used by itself and may be carried and used in a stout fabric case with clear panels for observation of the panel and the lamp. It may also be removed from this case and used in what is described as a 'Collective Unit' which converts the DOK 803 from a portable detection unit into a monitoring and alarm unit for static use at various locations. In this arrangement the unit forms part of the DUK 807, which, apart from the DOK 803, has two radiation probes and an electronics unit into which the DOK 803 is plugged. One of the probes is a low level unit used from 10 mr/h to 120 r/h. The other is for use at higher dose rate levels from 10 r/h to 1200 r/h. These probes are plugged via cables into the side of the electronics unit as appropriate. When the DOK 803 is plugged into the electronics unit it then provides the read-out for whatever dose rate the probe in use detects.

The electronics unit may be used to provide an aural warning whenever the dose rate level reaches 10 mr/h when the low level probe is in use or 10 r/h when the high level probe is in use. The alarm may be switched off using a switch on the electronics unit. The electronics unit has its own internal battery supply and when the voltage level drops too low for continued use the lamp on the DOK 803 will flash. The DUK 807 may be powered by the mains voltage.

Each of the probe units is 150 mm high and has a diameter of 65 mm. They may be connected to the electronics unit by cables up to 50 metres long.

SPECIFICATIONS (DOK 803 only)
Weight: 450 g
Length: 160 mm
Width: 75 mm
Height: 41 mm
Power supply: 2 × 1·5 V BA30 cells

STATUS
Production. In use with the French civil defence authorities.

MANUFACTURER
SAPHYMO-STEL, Department Radiametrie, 29 avenue Carnot, 91301 Massy, France.

DUK 807 collective unit with DOK 803 inserted and showing probes

Radiation Meter Model DOK 803

Radiation Meter Model DOM 410 and Accessories

DESCRIPTION

The basic unit of this equipment is the Model DOM 410 survey meter to which other parts can be fitted to undertake a variety of tasks. The basic Model DOM 410 is a survey meter containing a Geiger-Müller counter tube. The unit is portable and waterproof and may be fitted to vehicles or fixed installations. The meter has six scales: 0 to 10, 100 and 1000 milliröntgen an hour and 0 to 10, 100 and 1000 röntgen an hour.

Power comes from two 1·5-volt type BA30 dry cells in the meter carrying handle but if required an external 110/220-volt ac supply can be connected. The 1·5-volt cells can keep the meter in use for about 16 hours. The meter weighs 2·5 kg and is 230 mm high, 100 mm wide and 190 mm deep. Issued with the meter are a carrying strap, a hermetically sealed carrying case, an extension cable for a probe, a set of instructions and a small radiation test source.

Two other units can be fitted to the basic Model DOM 410 meter: a visual alarm device and a decontamination probe which can be used to detect beta radiation. If required both devices can be fitted to the basic meter at the same time.

For training purposes the Model ROK 410 radiation simulator has been designed consisting of a transmitter, various cables and batteries, and ten receivers. The receivers are all identical to the normal Model DOM 410 meters but their interiors have been altered to pick up the variable signals emitted by the equipment's transmitter. The transmitter has a range of up to eight kilometres and can be fitted with either directional or omni-directional aerials. Operating on a frequency of between 3250 and 3400 kc/s the transmitter can emit signals that simulate radiation readings on all the receivers in range. The transmitter weighs 33 kg and each receiver weighs 2·6 kg.

STATUS

In production. In service with the French armed forces and several other overseas armed forces.

MANUFACTURER

SAPHYMO-STEL, Department Radiametrie, 29 avenue Carnot, 91301 Massy, France.

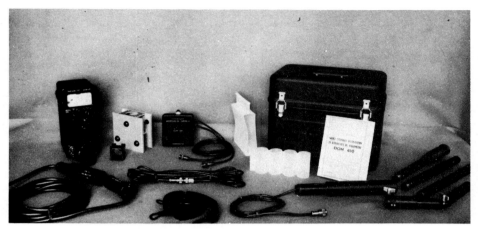

Radiation meter Model DOM 410 and accessories

Radiation Meter Model DOK 420

DESCRIPTION

Designed as a portable radiation meter, the Model DOK 420 can detect and indicate both gamma and X-ray radiation. It is a single unit with a single scale indicating from 0 to 500 röntgen an hour. The power is supplied by two 1·5-volt type BA 58 cells which can power the meter for up to 150 hours. Accuracy is stated to be ±30 per cent. The unit measures 120 × 75 × 35 mm and weighs 0·35 kg.

STATUS

In production. In service with the French armed forces.

MANUFACTURER

Groupement Industriel des Armements Terrestres (GIAT), 10 place Georges Clémenceau, 92211 Saint-Cloud, France.

DOK 420 radiation meter

Control and Alarm Radiation Meter Model RA 73

DESCRIPTION

The Model RA 73 is a small radiation meter designed to be carried on the user's belt and capable of emitting an audible alarm once a pre-set level of radiation exposure has been reached. The alarm threshold is set at the manufacturing stage and may be from 10 to 100 milliröntgen an hour. Apart from the alarm, the meter can measure from 0 to 1000 röntgen an hour on three logarithmic scales. The power comes from a single 4·5-volt battery which can supply the meter for up to 100 hours. The meter measures 165 × 75 × 50 mm and weighs 0·7 kg.

The RA 73 has been license-produced by the Swiss firm of Autophon which has produced 25 000 examples for the Swiss armed forces and a similar number for the Swiss civil defence organisations. Autophon, in conjunction with SAPHYMO-STEL, has now produced a radiation simulator for use with the RS 73 known as the SIMA-80. This is described in the Switzerland section on page 737.

STATUS

In production. In service with the Swiss armed forces and civil defence organisations.

MANUFACTURERS

SAPHYMO-STEL, Department Radiametrie, 29 avenue Carnot, 91301 Massy, France.

License production by Autophon AG, Military Products Division, Ziegelmattstrasse 1–15, CH-4500 Solothurn, Switzerland.

Control and alarm radiation meter Model RA 73

Airborne Radiation Meter/Dosimeter Model DUK-DUR 430

DESCRIPTION
Although this equipment is intended primarily for use in aircraft it can also be fitted to land vehicles and maritime craft. It consists of a single unit which can be mounted onto an instrument panel and incorporates a radiation meter capable of indicating up to 500 röntgen an hour and a dosimeter which automatically indicates the dose absorbed up to 999·9 röntgen. The unit requires a power source of 27·5 volts ac, and it measures 80 × 80 × 188 mm. The weight of the complete unit is 1·2 kg.

STATUS
In production. In service with the French Army.

MANUFACTURER
SAPHYMO-STEL, Department Radiametrie, 29 avenue Carnot, 91301 Massy, France.

Airborne radiation meter/dosimeter Model DUK-DUR 430

Vehicle-mounted Radiation Meter/Dosimeter Model DUK-DUR 440

DESCRIPTION
Designed to be mounted in vehicles, the Model DUK-DUR 440 is made up from two units. One is the main component case that contains the system electronics and mounts the two main indication panels and controls, and the other is the external sensor. The external sensor is a sealed metal case containing a Geiger-Müller counter and is connected to the electronics unit by a cable. The electronics unit is intended to be mounted under the vehicle dash-board or some similar location, with the indicators facing towards the user. One of the meters indicates the dose rate in digital form between 0·1 and 1000 r/h. The other digital meter indicates the accumulated dose between 0·1 and 1000 r. The response time is less than three seconds and the accuracy ±20% up to 999 r/h. Power is provided from a 19 to 33 volt dc source. Both units are shockproof and can withstand immersion in water to depths of up to four metres. The electronics unit may also be used to provide an aural and visual alarm when a pre-set threshold is reached.

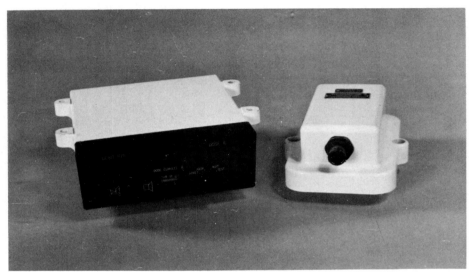

DUK-DUR 440 electronics unit (left), sensor (right)

SPECIFICATIONS

Unit	Sensor	Electronics unit
Depth	140 mm	140 mm
Height	60 mm	60 mm
Width	140 mm	70 mm

STATUS
Pre-production.

MANUFACTURER
Groupement Industriel des Armements Terrestres (GIAT), 10 places Georges Clémenceau, 92211 Saint-Cloud, France.

Individual Dosimeters and Charging Unit

DESCRIPTION
The normal individual dosimeters used by the French armed forces are the Type JER. There are seven different versions of this dosimeter with ranges of 0 to 0·2, 0 to 0·5, 0 to 5, 0 to 50, 0 to 200, 0 to 300 and 0 to 500 röntgen.

They are all conventional pen-type dosimeters, but they require a charger-reader. The normal type in French service is the Type XOP 402 which is a small unit powered by a single 1·5-volt BA30 battery which is capable of charging several hundred dosimeters. The unit measures 93 × 93 × 53 mm and weighs approximately 0·5 kg ready for use.

STATUS
In production. In service with the French armed forces.

MANUFACTURERS
Dosimeters: La Physiotechnie, 34 avenue Aristide Briand, 94110 Arcueil, France.

Charging unit: Groupement Industriel des Armements Terrestres (GIAT), 10 place Georges Clémenceau, 92211 Saint-Cloud, France.

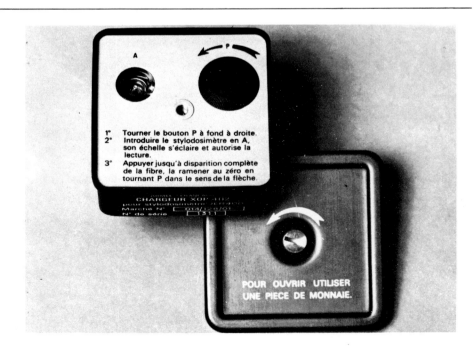

Type XOP 402 charger/reader for dosimeters

Dosimeter Model LIR 305 and Reader

DESCRIPTION
The Model LIR 305 dosimeter relies on the photo-luminescent principle. It is normally worn slung around the neck on a beaded chain in a plastic case containing the tube support and the sensitive element in a tube 6 mm long and 3·7 mm in diameter. The complete unit weighs 35 grams and measures 62 × 29 × 14 mm. The dosimeter can indicate doses of up to 1000 röntgen of gamma radiation.

The dosimeter reader UCPL Model XOR 305 is used for reading the Model LIR 305. The reader is issued in a metal carrying case 255 × 160 × 160 mm. The case also contains cables, tools for dismantling the Model LIR 305 dosimeter, spares and charging and decharging units. The reader is powered by either four 1·5-volt batteries or a 110/220-volt supply. It can give an immediate reading from a Model LIR 305 of up to 1000 röntgen. If required the dosimeter can then be recharged or left with the accumulated dose still present. Weight of the reader (with batteries) is 5·6 kg and dimensions are 255 × 160 × 160 mm.

STATUS
In production. In service with the French Air Force.

MANUFACTURERS
Dosimeter: Société de Carbonisation Entreprise et Céramique CEC, 8 place des Etats-Unis, 92120 Montrouge, France.

Reader: Groupement Industriel des Armements Terrestres (GIAT), 10 place Georges Clémenceau, 92211 Saint-Cloud, France.

Dosimeter reader Model XOR 305

GERMANY, DEMOCRATIC REPUBLIC

Radiation Meter, Model RAM-60A

DESCRIPTION
The Model RAM-60A is a highly sensitive instrument for monitoring personnel, equipment, clothing and food. It is a fully-transistorised equipment contained in a carrying case and consisting of a meter, a probe unit, headphones and several accessories. The probe contains a Geiger-Müller tube and has a shield to eliminate beta radiation from gamma radiation readings. With the shield open, beta radiation readings can be made. The meter has three ranges, ×1, ×10 and ×100, and thus the gamma radiation scales are from 0·01 to 0·4, 0·1 to 4 and 1 to 40 milliröntgen an hour. The Model RAM-60A is powered by six rechargeable nickel-cadmium batteries, and the weight of the meter and probe is about 4 kg. There is a training version in the form of the Model RAM-60A Üb in which the probe unit is inert and readings are fed into the meter electrically via an instructor's control unit.

STATUS
Production complete. In service with the East German forces but scheduled to be replaced by the Model RR-66.

MANUFACTURER
VEB Vakutronik, now VEB Robotron-Messelektronik, Dresden, German Democratic Republic.

Radiation Measuring Instrument, Model RAM-63

DESCRIPTION
The Model RAM-63 is a scintillation-type measuring instrument intended to measure both alpha and beta-gamma radiation. It is only partially transistorised and power is provided by five batteries which can be either conventional or rechargeable. The complete equipment includes the basic instrument, two scintillation heads (one for beta-gamma radiation and the other for alpha), a photo-multiplier tube, a tube stand, a carrying case and straps, connecting cables, various tools, check sources for calibration and testing, and an extra set of batteries. The meter unit weighs 3·5 kg and measures 245 × 118 × 176 mm.

In use with the Soviet Armed Forces as WPChR.

STATUS
Production probably complete. In service with the East German forces and the Soviet armed forces.

MANUFACTURER
State factories in East Germany and USSR.

Radiation measuring instrument Model RAM-63

Aerial Radiation Survey Meter, Model RAM-63L

DESCRIPTION
The Model RAM-63L is an adaptation of the Model RAM-63 for use on aircraft or helicopters, but in its airborne form it has two main components. One is an aluminium case containing the control and measuring circuitry and the other component is a highly sensitive photo-multiplier tube mounted on the outside of the aircraft or helicopter. The two units are connected by cable and both units have special shock-absorbing mountings.

STATUS
Production probably complete. In service with the East German forces.

MANUFACTURER
State factories.

Radiation Detection Meter, Model RSA-64D

DESCRIPTION
This instrument is used to detect and measure beta and gamma radiation in the field and as such its level of accuracy is reported to be of the order of ±30%. It is hand-held and has a hand generator, but it also has the facility for a jack-socket to give aural indications on a set of headphones. The Model RSA-64D has three sub-scales which can measure from 0·0025 to 50 röntgen an hour. The instrument measures 100 × 200 × 140 mm. There is a training version of this instrument, the Model RSA-64 Üb, which is identical to the Model RSA-64D except that the internal circuitry has a sensitivity factor of 1000 so that a source of 50 milliröntgen an hour will give a scale indication of 50 röntgen an hour.

STATUS
Probably no longer in production. In service with the East German forces.

MANUFACTURER
State factories.

Radiation Warning System, Models RW-64 and RW-64S

DESCRIPTION
The Model RW-64 and RW-64S are both gamma radiation warning instruments intended for use in radiological storage and handling areas. They have two main components connected by cables, the largest of which is the main instrument which has an external detection probe. The other component is an audible warning alarm, but the main instrument also has a red flashing light that operates in conjunction with the sound alarm. The operating sequence will initiate when the general radiation levels in the vicinity of the detection probe rise above one of five possible pre-set levels which vary from 0.05 to 2 röntgen an hour. The power supply is a 12-volt battery.

The RW-64 is fully contained inside a suitcase-type carrier and has a probe unit on the end of a long co-axial cable. The Model RW-64S is a version used by the East German Navy for use on ships. There is also a training version, the Model RW-64 Üb, which is externally identical to the Model RW-64. However, its circuitry has been altered so that its sensitivity is increased by a factor of 1000 to enable small radiation sources to simulate radiation alarms and initiate drills.

STATUS
Probably no longer in production. In service with the East German forces.

MANUFACTURER
State factories.

Radiation Monitoring and Survey Meter, Model RR-66

DESCRIPTION
This equipment combines the functions of both area surveying and personnel monitoring of radiation. For general area radiation survey the Model RR-66 is used as issued, but for radiation monitoring of personnel, water, food, equipment, etc, a three-section probe is used, connected to the instrument by a flexible cable.

For general survey the Model RR-66 has a scale range of from 25 milliröntgen an hour up to 250 röntgen an hour. For monitoring the range is from 0.025 to 25 milliröntgen an hour. Normally the probe head and the three-section probe handle are stowed on the side of the carrying case, and the weight of the entire equipment is approximately 3.9 kg. Headphones are supplied for optional aural indication and the instrument and extras are all contained in a carrying case suspended from the shoulder.

STATUS
In production. In service with the East German forces. In time this equipment will replace the earlier Models IH-2, RAM-60A and DP-12 in East German service.

MANUFACTURER
State factories.

Dosimeter Set, Model RDC 2

DESCRIPTION
There are two types of Model RDC 2 dosimeter set in service, one with 50 Model RDC 2 dosimeters and the other with 150. In both cases half the supplied dosimeters are of the lower range type and the other half have a higher range. Both are conventional fountain-pen type dosimeters which differ as follows:

	Range	Cap Colour	Grooves
Low range	0–10 r	yellow	one
High range	0–100 r	red	two

Both types are charged and read by the supplied charger-reader unit which can read dosimeter charges of up to 100 röntgen. The unit, which is powered by a 4.5-volt battery, has an optional scale light and is contained in an aluminium case.

STATUS
No longer in production. In service with the East German forces.

MANUFACTURER
VEB Vakutronik, now VEB Robotron-Messelektronik, Dresden, German Democratic Republic.

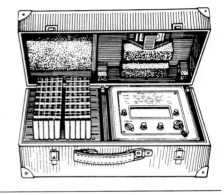

Model RDC 2 dosimeter set

Individual Dosimeter, Model RDA-64

DESCRIPTION
This type of dosimeter requires no external equipment as it relies on the ion chamber principle with a built-in electrostatic generator. The initial charge is produced by turning a knob on the instrument and re-setting the dial needle to zero. It is possible for radiation doses of up to 50 röntgen to be recorded, and the dosimeter is normally carried in a uniform pocket. Instructions are given on the back of the instrument. The Model RDA-64 measures approximately 90 × 120 × 40 mm. There is a training version in the form of the Model RDA-64 Üb in which the sensitivity is reduced by a factor of 1000 so that a scale reading of 2.5 röntgen can be produced by a 2.5 milliröntgen source. The two models are otherwise identical.

STATUS
Probably no longer in production. In service with the East German forces and some civilian organisations.

MANUFACTURER
State factories.

Dosimeter System, Model RDC-64

DESCRIPTION
This system depends on the thermoluminescence principle in which the passage of radiation through calcium fluoride powder contained in a glass tube produces an excited energy state proportional to the amount of radiation passed. The dosimeter system based on this principle consists of two components, the RDC-64D thermoluminescence dosimeter and the RDC-64A dosimeter reader. The dosimeter, which can absorb doses of from 3 to 1000 röntgen, consists of two plastic cases, one light and the other dark. Both are worn around the neck with the wearing cord fitted to the lighter half. The dark half is intended for fairly frequent readings and the light half for long-term measurements. Each half has a metal cap connected to the glass tube containing the calcium fluoride powder. For reading the glass tube is removed from the dosimeter and placed into the Model RDC-64A dosimeter reader. The tube is rotated into position and placed under a photo-electric cell. The glass tube is then heated for 20 seconds which releases the energy in the powder in the form of light and also reduces the powder to its normal energy level for re-use. The energy released in the form of light is measured by the photo-electric cell and the radiation dosage absorbed can then be read off on a scale.

This dosimeter system is expected to replace the earlier Model RDC 2 dosimeter system.

STATUS
In production. In service with the East German forces.

MANUFACTURER
State factories and laboratories.

HUNGARY

Radiation Detection Meter, Model IH-2

DESCRIPTION
The Model IH-2 is used by Hungarian and East German field units for detecting beta radiation and measuring gamma radiation. It is a small lightweight meter carried in a case suspended from the user's neck, and it operates on the conventional ion chamber principle. A beta particle window is situated on the lower side of the instrument. This equipment is used by mobile Hungarian radiological and chemical reconnaissance teams, and some have been issued to the East German forces. Total weight of the equipment is approximately 2.2 kg. It is a very simple instrument with three sub-scales measuring up to 200 röntgen an hour.

STATUS
Production complete. In service with the Hungarian forces and in partial service with the East German forces.

MANUFACTURER
State factories.

Radiation Measuring Instrument, Model IH-12

DESCRIPTION
The Model IH-12 is for low-level monitoring of personnel, weapons and other equipment as well as the monitoring of food and water supplies. It can detect and measure alpha, beta and gamma radiation on four sub-ranges, with the actual type of radiation being selected by a source selector switch – the gamma range is from 0.02 to 500 milliröntgen an hour. The complete equipment consists of the instrument proper, a probe head, an aluminium telescopic rod, a leather carrying case, control samples for calibration and checking, a screwdriver, and an instruction manual. The instrument is powered by a battery giving an operational life of over 40 hours. The probe is connected to the end of the telescopic rod by a polyethylene-covered cable and the probe head is prismatic. The complete equipment weighs approximately 2.65 kg and the case measures 105 × 180 × 210 mm.

STATUS
Production probably complete. In service with the Hungarian forces.

MANUFACTURER
State factories.

POLAND

Radiation Detection Meter, Model D-08

DESCRIPTION
The Model D-08 is an entirely conventional radiation detection meter utilising the ion chamber principle. It is battery-operated, operates over a range of from 0·1 up to 300 röntgen an hour, and weighs about 3 kg.

STATUS
Production probably complete. In limited service with the Polish forces and some Polish civil defence organisations.

MANUFACTURER
State factories.

Radiation Alarm Device, Model RIK-59

DESCRIPTION
This small alarm device is about the size of a cigarette packet and is worn in the breast pocket by medical and laboratory personnel working in potential radiation areas. The device detects beta and gamma radiation and once the radiation intensity exceeds 7·5 milliröntgen an hour the device starts to emit a buzzing tone that increases in pitch and intensity as the level rises. A neon

bulb on the side of the device glows when the device is switched on and goes out only when the alarm signal reaches a continuous state.

STATUS
Production probably complete. In limited service with the Polish forces but probably still used by various civilian organisations.

MANUFACTURER
State factories.

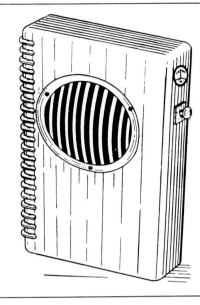

Model RIK-59 radiation alarm device

Radiation Detection Meter, Model DP-66

DESCRIPTION
The Polish Model DP-66 can be used either as an area survey meter or a low-level radiation detection meter. Normally contained in a fitted case, the equipment consists of the measuring instrument, a probe, a probe extension handle, a small earphone, internal or external power supplies, a carrying strap and instructions. The Model DP-66 can be used to measure gamma radiation at intensity levels of from 0·05 milliröntgen an hour up to 200 röntgen an hour but the general accuracy is only ±25%. The measuring instrument and probe together

weigh about 3 kg, and the equipment can operate for some 70 hours on one set of batteries.

STATUS
Production complete. In service with the Polish forces.

MANUFACTURER
State factories.

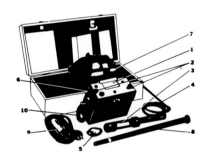

Model DP-66 radiation detection meter (1) measuring scale (2) power supply (3) probe (4) probe cable (5) miniature headphones (6) instrument case (7) extension handle for probe (8) carrying case (9) external power supply (10) carrying strap

ROMANIA

Radiation Detection Meter, Model AD-1

DESCRIPTION
This instrument is entirely Romanian-designed and produced and is used for detecting and measuring gamma radiation. It can also indicate the presence of

beta radiation. Using the ion chamber principle it can detect and measure radiation of from 0·02 to 600 röntgen an hour. The power source is two 1·5-volt cells which, when used at a temperature of about 20°C, has an operating life of about 100 hours. The instrument weighs 2·35 kg and is 240 mm long, 120 mm wide and 180 mm deep.

STATUS
Probably no longer in production. In service with the Romanian forces and possibly with Romanian civil defence organisations.

MANUFACTURER
State factories.

SWITZERLAND

SIMA-80 Radiation Simulator

DEVELOPMENT
The SIMA-80 radiation simulator has been developed by the Swiss Autophon concern in conjunction with the Swiss Gruppe für Rüstungsdienste (GRD) to provide a means of training personnel in the use of the RA 73 control and alarm radiation meter, also produced by Autophon under licence from the French firm of SAPHYMO-STEL. The first example was tested during the late 1970s and was made available for service in 1980. Seventy SIMA-80 systems were delivered during 1981 to Swiss civil defence organisations and the Swiss Army ordered 50 for delivery during 1983.

DESCRIPTION
The SIMA-80 radiation simulator uses electromagnetic radiation in place of harmful nuclear radiation sources

and is used in conjunction with a special version of the RA 73 meter. The system can be used with any number of the special RA 73 receivers which can be easily identified as they are either yellow or bright blue, not black as is the operational version. The signals from the SIMA-80 transmitter produce simulated readings on the RA 73 receiver scales up to a range of about two kilometres using the transmitter's integral aerial; for longer ranges a 6-metre antenna can be raised by one man.

The complete SIMA-80 system consists of a transmitter (the SIMA-80S), a power supply unit (the SIMA-80SG), 25 special RA 73 receiver meters known as the SIMA-80E, a long-range antenna (the SIMA-80FA), a kit of spares, spare programmes and cables. The spare programmes enable training sessions to run for either 1, 2, 4, 8, 12 or 24 hours and ten programmes are supplied

with each system. The power supply unit enables the SIMA-80 to be operated on 220-volt AC mains, a 12-volt car battery or internal rechargeable nickel-cadmium cells. If required manual settings may be introduced in place of the pre-set programmes. The entire system is contained within a sturdy metal casing with the 25 receivers in a similar-sized casing.

STATUS
In production. In service with Swiss civil defence. Ordered by the Swiss Army (50).

MANUFACTURER
Autophon AG, Military Products Division, Feldstrasse 42, Postfach 8036, Zurich 4, Switzerland.

SPECIFICATIONS
SIMA-80S transmitter
Height: 360 mm
Width: 534 mm
Depth: 348 mm
Weight: approx 26 kg
Output: max 1 watt
Range with long-range antenna: 2–5 km
Dose rate adjustable: 1–890 mR/h, 1–890 R/h

SIMA-80E receiver
Dimensions: 165 × 75 × 50 mm
Weight: 0·7 kg
Power supply: 4·5 V cell
Cell life: 24 hours

SIMA-80FA long-range antenna
Height with mast: 6 m
Weight: 8·5 kg

*SIMA-80S radiation simulator with SIMA-80E receiver·
on right. On lower left, SIMA-80SG power unit, on its left
SIMA-80S transmitter*

UNION OF SOVIET SOCIALIST REPUBLICS

Radiation Meter, Model DP-5A

DESCRIPTION
The Model DP-5A is used to monitor personnel, food and water for low levels of radiation, and has only a very limited application in area monitoring and reconnaissance. The meter is usually worn slung on the chest but the sensing elements are contained in a rod-like probe which can reach into otherwise inaccessible areas. Headphones are supplied for the aural detection of beta radiation. The meter has six separate ranges from 0·05 up to 200 milliröntgen an hour, and the power is supplied either from three 1·6-volt batteries or any external source providing between 3·5 and 12 volts dc. The meter, which is contained in a fibreglass-reinforced plastic case, weighs about 2·1 kg. The whole equipment, including the probe, carrying case, headphones, etc, weighs about 7·6 kg.

STATUS
Production complete. In service with the Soviet and Warsaw Pact forces.

MANUFACTURER
State factories.

Contamination Survey Meter, Model DP-12

DESCRIPTION
The Model DP-12 is a highly sensitive contamination meter which is primarily intended to monitor the radioactive contamination of personnel, vehicles and equipment, but can also be used in aircraft or helicopters for rapid area surveys. It consists of two main components, the control case and the probe, but a headset for the aural detection of radiation is also provided. The probe unit is connected to the control case by a flexible cable, and consists of a shaft to the end of which is secured a Geiger-Müller tube sensitive to both gamma and beta radiation – the beta radiation can be shielded by a rotating collar over the tube. The shaft itself is telescopic. When in use, the Model DP-12 is carried on the user's chest and the probe unit is held about an inch (25 mm) away from the monitored surface, and as the probe is waterproof it may also be used to monitor the contamination of fluids.

STATUS
Production probably complete. In service with the Soviet and Warsaw Pact forces.

MANUFACTURER
State factories.

Lightweight Survey Meter, Model DP-62

DESCRIPTION
This lightweight instrument is the smallest and lightest of the Warsaw Pact survey meters and is used mainly for detecting beta radiation in the range 10 to 500 milliröntgen an hour. The equipment consists of two components, the meter itself and a hand generator for power. There is no scale as the presence of beta radiation is indicated by a neon bulb flashing behind a lens on top of the instrument. A celluloid window on the bottom of the instrument allows the access of beta radiation and with this window closed by a metal shutter the indication of gamma radiation can be given. This meter has been described as 'rugged, lightweight, compact and simple to operate'.

STATUS
Probably still in production. In service with the Soviet and Warsaw Pact forces.

MANUFACTURER
State factories.

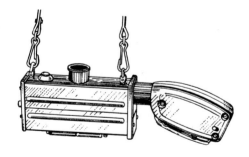

Model DP-62 lightweight survey meter showing hand-operated generator on right

Lightweight Area Survey Meter, Model DP-63A

DESCRIPTION
The Model DP-63A can detect and measure gamma and beta radiation and is widely used by all units of the Warsaw Pact forces. Using the ion chamber principle it is powered by two dry-cell batteries with a life of about 50 hours. Normally the instrument is carried in a leather carrying case (weight 0·4 kg) with a shoulder strap and the instrument has two logarithmic ranges selected by push buttons. The bottom scale measures from 0·1 to 1·5 and the other 1·5 to 50 röntgen an hour. Beta radiation is measured on the bottom scale only using a beta radiation window. Both scales can be illuminated for night use. The Model DP-63A weighs 0·8 kg and the case measures 165 × 115 × 90 mm.

STATUS
Probably still in production. In service with the Soviet and Warsaw Pact forces.

MANUFACTURER
State factories.

Individual Dosimeter Set, Model DP-23

DESCRIPTION
This dosimeter set is contained in a carrying case and consists of a charger-reader unit, 150 Model DS-50 dosimeters packed into three cases each with 50 dosimeters, and 50 Model DKP-50A dosimeters. The case also contains a torch. The Model DP-23 charger-reader unit is used to charge both models of dosimeter, but of the two models, only the Model DKP-50A can be read directly: it is issued to officers and senior NCOs. The Model DS-50 dosimeters can be read only in the charger-reader unit, ie under supervision, and are issued to the rank and file soldiers. Both models read from 0 to 50 röntgen in 2 röntgen steps and both weigh about 30 grams. The Model DS-50 is 120 mm long and 14 mm in diameter and the Model DKP-50A is 130 mm long and 13 mm in diameter. Both can operate in temperatures between −40°C and +50°C. The charger-reader unit, which is battery-powered, weighs 3·5 kg and is contained in an aluminium case. The reader function is carried out in increments of 2·5 röntgen on a meter scale.

STATUS
Production probably complete. In service with the Soviet and some Warsaw Pact forces.

MANUFACTURER
State factories.

Individual Dosimeter Sets, Models DP-21A and DP-21B

DESCRIPTION
This set consists of a charger-reader unit and a case containing 200 Model DS-50 dosimeters. Each dosimeter can be charged and read only by the charger-reader unit, and each is charged only just before issue.

The two models of this set are essentially similar, and are being phased out in favour of the later Model DP-23, but some still remain in service.

STATUS
Production complete. Held in reserve with the Soviet forces but may still be in use with some Warsaw Pact forces.

MANUFACTURER
State factories.

Chemical Dosimeter Model DP-70M and Field Colorimeter Model PK-56M

DESCRIPTION
These two equipments are used in conjunction and operate on the colorimeter principle in which any exposure to radiation of a chemical solution will cause it to change colour. This system has the advantage that

the dosimeter can be issued without prior charging or any other preparation, with each dosimeter containing a single ampoule of the detecting solution. The field colorimeter Model PK-56M is used to read off the amount of radiation absorbed by the Model DP-70M dosimeter by exposing the ampoule from the dosimeter to a beam of light and comparing it to the colour given by an unexposed ampoule. Colour differences can be compared on a scale and the equipment can be used to determine radiation doses of from 0 to 800 röntgen in 50 röntgen

steps. The Model PK-56M is issued with a carrying case and weighs about 1·5 kg.

STATUS
Probably no longer in production. In service with the Soviet and Warsaw Pact forces.

MANUFACTURER
State factories.

UNITED KINGDOM

Portable Dose Rate Meter PDRM82 Fixed Dose Rate Meter PDRM82F

DEVELOPMENT
By the late 1970s many of the radiation detection instruments in service with the various British defence agencies were becoming elderly to the extent that spare parts and batteries were no longer in production, and the number of types was too large for standardisation. For this reason a number of design projects were launched but no results were forthcoming because of various defence spending constraints, until 1982 when Plessey Controls Limited was awarded a £4 million contract to develop and supply a portable radiation dose meter in conjunction with the Ministry of Defence and the Home Office. The result is the Portable Dose Rate Meter or PDRM82. There is known to be a requirement for 80 000 of them, 79 000 for various Home Office agencies such as police, fire brigade and other such organisations and 1000 for the Royal Observer Corps as the PDRM82F.

DESCRIPTION
The PDRM82 is a small rugged instrument with only one control and a large high contrast digital display. It can measure radiation levels over a 0–3000 mGy/h range and is fully contained inside a nuclear-hardened strong plastic case. The instrument is designed to be carried and used suspended by a strap around the neck with a restraining cord holding the case at the waist. Power for the instrument comes from three standard C cells which give a service life of 400 hours. The batteries are inserted into the instrument by turning the single control knob to the Load position. This enables the knob to be

removed for battery insertion. For use the knob, which is large enough to be operated by a gloved hand, is turned to the Off position and then to the On position. Switching to On initiates a self-test sequence which covers all aspects of instrument operation and illuminating all the segments of the liquid crystal display (LCD). There are four numerical digits for the dose rate readings, an indication as to whether the dose rate is rising or falling and battery low indication which flashes when about ten hours of battery life remain. Should the self-test sequence reveal a fault the word Fail is shown on the display and the instrument is discarded. Should dose rate reading rise above the maximum indicated 3000 mGy/h the display will flash on and off. The detector used in the PDRM82 is a energy compensated Halogen quenched Geiger-Müller tube. The case is waterproof.

The PDRM82F has the detector tube outside the instrument case for use in underground locations such as Royal Observer Corps posts. The detector is in a sensor probe connected to the case by five metres of

cable. All other features of the PDRM82F are identical to the PDRM82.

A version for use on vehicles is envisaged with the indicator to be clipped under the dashboard. The same version could be used on AFVs.

SPECIFICATIONS
Weight: 560 g
Length: 175 mm
Width: 135 mm
Height: 30 mm
Operating temperature range: −10°C to +45°C

STATUS
Production. In service with the British Home Office and ordered by Norway.

MANUFACTURER
Plessey Controls Limited, Sopers Lane, Poole, Dorset BH17 7ER, England.

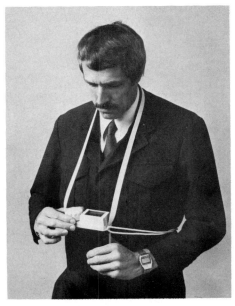

Plessey PDRM82 in use

Plessey portable dose rate meter PDRM82

Radiac Survey Meter No 2

DESCRIPTION

Intended for use by mobile nuclear survey teams, the Radiac survey meter is a self-contained device in a grey metal case. It is capable of measuring up to 300 röntgen an hour on three scales which can be selected by one of the two operating switches. The lowest scale (white) indicates from 0 to 3, the next (blue) from 0 to 30 and the highest (red) from 0 to 300 röntgen an hour. Power for the equipment comes from a single 1·5-volt U2 cell. Normally the equipment is carried in a special pvc-covered cotton haversack designed so that the meter can be read and operated without removing the equipment. For use other than within the haversack, an integral handle is provided. Normally the equipment measures only gamma radiation but by removing a panel on the base of the equipment, beta radiation can be detected and measured. Early examples of this meter used thermionic circuitry but most have now been modified to fully-transistorised circuitry. The meter weighs approximately 2·95 kg but complete with the haversack the weight is 4·03 kg. The meter is 232 mm long, 95 mm wide and 149 mm high. The meter interior is sealed and a desiccator is used to keep the contents dry.

STATUS

Production complete. In service with the British armed forces and some civilian organisations.

Radiac Survey Meter No 2

Lightweight Radiac Survey Meter

DESCRIPTION

There are six separate marks of this meter, of which the normal service marks are 3, 4 and 6. All are basically similar and are contained in identical semi-cylindrical cases carried on a shoulder strap with a cord securing the instrument around the waist. The single logarithmic scale can indicate up to 100 röntgen an hour. Power is provided by one 10·8-volt and one 1·35-volt Mallory cells. The instrument weighs just under 1·3 kg and it is 146 mm long, 127 mm wide and 95 mm deep.

STATUS

Production complete. In limited service with the British armed forces and some civilian organisations.

Fixed Survey Meter (FSM)

DESCRIPTION

As its designation implies, this survey meter is designed for use in fixed installations and in particular is intended for use in Royal Observer Corps underground monitoring posts. The equipment consists of two main components, the indicator unit and the ionisation chamber. Both are stored and carried in a stout wooden box which also contains two inter-connecting cables, two battery packs, a screwdriver and a set of screws for securing the indicator unit to a bench surface. The underground post or installation has a roof mounting for the ionisation chamber in the shape of a pipe through the roof which is enclosed at the top by a plastic dome cover held in place by a heavy metal ring. The ionisation chamber is held in place in the pipe on an aluminium telescopic rod which is capable of being withdrawn into the interior of the installation when 'shielded' readings may be taken when particularly heavy concentrations of nuclear fall-out are present; this facility increases the normal 0–500 röntgen an hour range of the equipment by a factor of ten. The indicator unit is housed in a modified 'Avometer' casing and is fitted with two operations knobs and a logarithmic scale. A battery pack, containing two 10·8-volt and one 1·35-volt Mallory cells, is positioned under a protective cover on the base.

To simulate the operation of the Fixed Survey Meter for peace-time training exercises a special Fixed Survey Meter Trainer has been produced which is visually identical to the real equipment apart from having a black body in place of the normal white. This training equipment consists of the indicator unit only which contains a clockwork mechanism driving a system that operates from the insertion of a plastic 'trace' which operates the scale needle.

STATUS

Production complete. In service with the Royal Observer Corps. Due to be replaced by the PRDM82.

Fixed Survey Meter monitor unit

Doserate Meter NIS 501

DESCRIPTION

This NIS 501 is a portable doserate meter capable of measuring both gamma and beta radiation. It can measure from 0·1 to 1000 rads an hour on a single logarithmic scale which is illuminated in low light by a Beta light source. The radiation detector is a cylindrical pressured ionisation chamber which has thin stainless steel windows to admit beta radiation when required. The instrument has two power supply batteries, the main one of which is a 2·7-volt mercury cell with an operation life of about 100 hours. The other cell is used for reference purposes and is a 1·35-volt mercury cell with a shelf life of some two years. The instrument is ready for use within three seconds of switching on. The NIS 501 is small enough to be carried in a uniform pocket but a special carrying case with a viewing window is available.

The instrument measures 160 × 108 × 54 mm and weighs 1·4 kg.

STATUS

Ready for production.

MANUFACTURER

THORN EMI Simtec Limited, Sellers Wood Drive, Bulwell, Nottinghamshire NG6 8UX, England.

NIS 501 portable doserate meter in use

Radiation Monitor

DESCRIPTION
This radiation measuring instrument is intended primarily for commercial sales and has several unusual features. One is that one of its three scales is used to give a measure of confidence in the instrument by indicating normal background radiation in the form of irregular meter pulses. The other two scales are from 0 to 100 milliröntgen per hour and from 0 to 100 röntgen an hour. Another feature is a warning lamp that stays on when the radiation level is above 10 röntgen an hour. The scale can be illuminated. A single 9-volt PP7 cell is used to provide all the power needs of the instrument and with this cell the monitor weighs 0·75 kg. The body of the instrument is manufactured from high impact polystyrene and measures 190 × 110 × 80 mm. A small carrying handle is provided.

STATUS
In production.

MANUFACTURER
Civil Service Supply, Wellingore, Lincolnshire LN5 0JF, England.

Individual Dosimeter and Charging Unit

DESCRIPTION
Operating on the ionisation chamber/quartz fibre principle, this range of individual dosimeters is manufactured to international standards and can be supplied in a range of types and materials. The standard range, which can be supplied with either brass or aluminium bodies, is 0 to 200 and 0 to 500 milliröntgen and 0 to 5, 0 to 50, 0 to 100, 0 to 200 and 0 to 500 röntgen.

Versions outside these ranges can be supplied as needed. All the above models are completely sealed and can be read directly by the user. Operationally they are sometimes carried in small clear plastic bags to prevent nuclear particles alighting on the body and give misleading readings. Normally they are worn like a fountain pen as a pocket clip is fitted to all models. Designed to operate over a wide range of climatic conditions and under all varieties of service use, these dosimeters are stated to have a calibration accuracy of ±10 per cent, and normal daily leakage is of the order of 0·25 per cent every 24 hours and should never be greater than 2 per cent over the same period. Each dosimeter is 116 mm long and has a diameter of 13·8 mm. Dosimeters with brass cases weigh 40 grams and those with aluminium weigh 32 grams.

The above dosimeters can be charged by numerous types of charger unit, but the Stephens charging unit has now been ordered by numerous armed forces and other organisations. This unit is powered by a single 1·5-volt U2 cell which provides the charging current and power for the internal light. A spare interior lamp is provided but if this also fails any convenient exterior light can be used by removing the unit base. The charging control device is actuated by a large control dial which can be operated when gloves are worn. In operation, once a dosimeter has been inserted, light pressure can be used for dosimeter reading and a slightly heavier pressure is used for the actual charging operation. The unit measures 120 × 90 × 60 mm and complete with the cell weighs 0·68 kg.

STATUS
In production. In service with the British Armed Forces and many other overseas forces and civil organisations.

MANUFACTURER
R A Stephen and Company Limited, Miles Road, Mitcham, Surrey CR4 3YP, England.

Stephen's individual dosimeter

Fisher Controls Limited Personal Dosimetry System

DEVELOPMENT
This personal dosimetry system has been developed by Fisher Controls Limited as project leader together with Marconi Electronic Devices and Salford Electrical Instruments. The system is designed to monitor the doses of gamma and neutron radiation absorbed by troops in the field at a unit level for use by unit commanders who require planning information. The system is not intended for personal reading or personal use.

DESCRIPTION
The system hardware is of two main components. One is the detector, the other the reader. The detector is a small dosimeter that resembles a wrist watch and is worn as one, although it may also be worn as a suspended locket. To detect the dose of gamma radiation the detector depends upon the action of gamma radiation on a silver activated phosphate glass which produces a property known as radiophotoluminescence. As the degree of radiation acting on the glass increases so does the degree of photoluminescence and this can be detected under the influence of ultra-violet light. Neutron radiation is detected by a wide base silicon PIN diode inside the detector. Radiation has the effect of altering the current density at a given current, thus producing alterations in voltage across the diode. Thus the detector combines two detection devices in a sealed locket which is worn by the user.

At pre-determined intervals, usually every day, the locket detectors are collected and taken to the reader. Here the lockets are opened individually and placed in a drawer on the front of the reader. This action places the detector in the correct position for reading. In two operations the detector glass is exposed to ultra-violet light and a current is passed through the terminals of the PIN diode. The resultant radiation dose absorbed can then be read once a toggle switch on the reader panel is depressed. Pressing the toggle switch produces the reading on a digital panel meter which stays on for a maximum of three seconds. In this way up to 100 detectors an hour can be read. Once the reading is complete the locket is re-sealed and returned to the user.

The reader is powered by a 24-volt vehicle battery or a portable pack. It can be carried in a special field haversack which contains both the reader and a portable battery. The combined dosimeter and reader accuracy at an 80 per cent confidence level is ±10 rads ±10%. The equipment has been designed and tested to meet military and environmental conditions as specified in BDS DEF 133.

SPECIFICATIONS
Reader
Weight: 10·25 kg
Length: 270 mm
Width: 210 mm
Height: 210 mm
Detector
Weight: 75 g
Diameter: 40 mm
Thickness: 12 mm

STATUS
Pre-production. Has been ordered by the British Army and evaluated and type classified by the US Army.

MANUFACTURER
Fisher Controls Limited, Nuclear Controls Division, Century Works, Conington Road, Lewisham, London SE13 7LN, England.

Fisher Controls Limited Personal Dosimetry System with reader in haversack and dosimeters on left

Placing dosimeter into reader

UNITED STATES OF AMERICA

AN/ADR-6(V) Aerial Radiac System (ARS)

DESCRIPTION

Developed by the US Army Electronics Research and Development Command (ERADCOM), the AN/ADR-6(V) Aerial Radiac System (ARS) is designed to be carried in any US Army helicopter and allows the rapid survey of large areas of terrain that is contaminated by radioactive material. The ARS uses sensors external to the helicopter to detect the radiation and then combines the detected radiation signal with an AN/APN-209(V) radar altimeter signal to compute the dose rate on the ground. The result is displayed on the instrument's dose rate meter and recorded on a 'hard' paper copy. The reading may also be transmitted to a ground station or another aircraft. The sensors used are of the compound scintillator type and can be used at altitudes of from zero to 3205 metres. The unit may also be used in fixed-wing aircraft and remotely-piloted vehicles (RPVs). The power required is 28 volts dc with a current requirement of 5 amps at normal operating temperatures and 7 amps below 0°C. The complete installation weighs less than 31·75 kg. The maximum aircraft dose rate measurement is from 0·04 rads/hour up to 400 rads/hour. This will indicate a ground rate measurement up to 1000 rads/hour.

STATUS

Low-rate initial production. Type-classified by the US Army.

MANUFACTURER

Development agency: US Army Electronics Research and Development Command, Combat Surveillance and Target Acquisition Laboratory, Fort Monmouth, New Jersey 07703, USA.

Prime contractor: Autonetics Strategic Systems Division, Defense Electronics Operations, Rockwell International, 3370 Miraloma Avenue, Anaheim, California 92803, USA.

Main components of AN/ADR-6(V) Aerial Radiac System (ARS)

WARSAW PACT

Area Survey Meter, Model DP-1b and Model DP-1c

DESCRIPTION

These two equipments have now largely replaced the earlier Model DP-1a and in their turn are being replaced by later models. Both models can measure gamma radiation and detect beta radiation. The gamma radiation is measured only when the beta radiation window on the bottom of the instruments is closed, and both models utilise the ion chamber principle. The main difference between the two models is that the Model DP-1b has a range of up to 400 röntgen an hour and the Model DP-1c up to 500 röntgen an hour. Each model has four scales that can be selected by a switch. The East German version of the Model DP-1b is known as the 'Röntgenmeter Type B'. The Model DP-1c can be converted for training by replacing the left-hand compartmented unit by a special unit which multiplies the sensitivity of the bottom two ranges by 3000 and the third by 1500. Range 4 is not now used.

STATUS

Production complete. Still in limited service with the Soviet and Warsaw Pact forces.

MANUFACTURER

State factories.

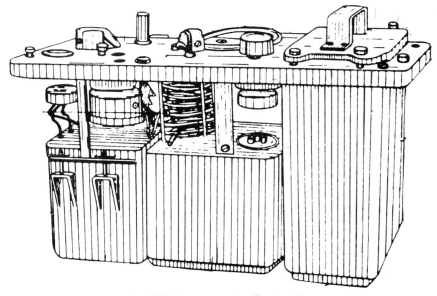

Model DP-1b survey meter without metal casing

Area Survey Meter, Model DP-2

DESCRIPTION

The Model DP-2 is used by ground survey teams for detecting gamma radiation and employs the ion chamber principle. It is normally carried in a case slung around the user's neck, and it can measure radiation levels of up to 200 röntgen an hour on three scales that are calibrated logarithmically and can be illuminated by an interior lamp if required. Batteries supply the operating power for the instrument and the hermetically-sealed aluminium case measures 240 × 170 × 130 mm. Weight is approximately 3·5 kg.

STATUS

No longer in production. Still in limited service with the Soviet and Warsaw Pact forces and civilian defence organisations.

MANUFACTURER

State factories in USSR and East Germany.

Radiation Survey Meter, Model DP-3

DESCRIPTION
This instrument is standard equipment with most Warsaw Pact radiological and chemical reconnaissance vehicles but can also be fitted to other motor vehicles, ships and even aircraft. It is normally bolted to a bulkhead or wall and power usually comes from a motor vehicle battery or a similar source. The Model DP-3 can measure gamma radiation from 0·1 up to 500 röntgen an hour on four scales selected by a single switch. Weight of the Model DP-3 is approximately 4·5 kg.

STATUS
Production probably complete. In service with the Soviet and Warsaw Pact forces.

MANUFACTURER
State factories.

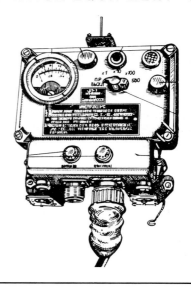

Model DP-3 radiation survey meter

YUGOSLAVIA

Dosimeter Model DL-M3 and Dosimeter Reader Model ČDL-M3

DESCRIPTION
The Model DL-M3 dosimeter works on the colorimeter principle but resembles a conventional fountain-pen dosimeter. It can detect and indicate radiation doses of from 10 to 720 röntgens. It weighs 30 grams and is 136 mm long with a diameter of 13 mm. To read the Model DL-M3 the Reader Model ČDL-M3 is used. Working in pre-set steps the dose absorbed by the dosimeter can be read off a visual scale marked on the face of the instrument. The reader weighs 0·7 kg and measures 80 × 90 × 160 mm.

STATUS
In production. In service with the Yugoslav forces.

MANUFACTURER
State factories.

Dosimeter Model DL-M3 (left) and dosimeter reader Model ČDL-M3 (right)

Miscellaneous equipment

ASSAULT BOATS AND RAIDING CRAFT

AUSTRALIA

Hercules Assault Boat

DESCRIPTION
The Hercules was originally designed by the Marine Division of Hawker de Havilland Australia as a work boat to carry 1000 kg of cargo in underdeveloped countries.

There are now three basic craft in the range, the 2803 (workboat), 2811 (runabout) and the 2831 (cabin cruiser).

The Hercules assault boat is based on the model 2803 hull, which is of all riveted aluminium alloy construction with the only welds being along the chine and around the transom. The full length keel is 203 mm wide and the floor structure is filled with 5·67 cubic metres of non-absorbent polyurethane foam flotation which will support the swamped weight of the boat, motor and crew. Over this is fitted a plywood or aluminium floor sealed at the edges to make the boat self-draining.

For even more safety the British company E P Barrus has designed, developed and fitted buoyancy collars to the craft to enable it to operate under the worst conditions. The wrap-round 305 mm diameter buoyancy collar provides two main advantages: complete stability when flooded and use as a fender when the craft is being operated alongside a larger ship. Without the flotation collars special fittings allow the Hercules to be joined back-to-back or side-to-side to serve as a heavy work boat or bridging pontoon.

SPECIFICATIONS
Weight: (approx) 210 kg
Length: (overall) 5·36 m
Beam: 1·9 m
Transom height: 0·533 m
Floor area: 5·87 m²
Max hp requirement: 50

STATUS
In production. In service with Australia (Army and Navy), New Zealand and other armed forces.

MANUFACTURER
Hawker de Havilland Australia Pty Limited, Marine Division, PO Box 30, Bankstown, New South Wales, Australia.
Agent for the United Kingdom: E P Barrus Limited, Launton Road, Bicester, Oxfordshire OX6 0UR, England.

Hercules assault boat

CZECHOSLOVAKIA

Czechoslovak Inflatable Craft

DESCRIPTION
The Czechoslovak Army uses two basic inflatable craft, small and large, for a wide variety of roles including reconnaissance and assault. The larger craft can also be used for constructing rafts to carry light vehicles and weapons across water obstacles.

SPECIFICATIONS

Model	Small	Large
Weight	65 kg	155 kg
Length	3·3 m	5·5 m
Beam	1·3 m	1·8 m
Depth	0·4 m	0·6 m
Capacity (men)	5	15–20
(cargo)	700 kg	1500 kg

STATUS
In service with the Czechoslovak armed forces.

MANUFACTURER
Czechoslovak state factories.

Fibreglass Assault Boat

DESCRIPTION
This craft was introduced into the Czechoslovak Army in the mid-1950s and is reported to be virtually unsinkable. It is made of fibreglass, has three bench seats and is propelled in the water by paddles. These boats are also used as floating supports for a footbridge.

SPECIFICATIONS
Weight: (empty) 140 kg
Length: 5 m
Beam: 1·7 m
Depth: 0·7 m
Speed: (loaded) 5 km/h
Capacity: (men) 11

STATUS
In service with the Czechoslovak Army.

MANUFACTURER
Czechoslovak state factories.

FRANCE

Bombard Commando Inflatable Craft

DESCRIPTION
The Commando range of inflatable craft has been designed for a wide range of civilian and military applications and has been adopted by many armed forces for a variety of roles including reconnaissance and assault. All craft in the range are manufactured from highly resistant black 1000 denier fabric/polyester thickly coated with neoprene and hypalon on both sides. The rear transom and floorboards are of marine plywood. Lateral and bow handles are provided for carrying, mooring and towing, and the rear transoms are fitted with drain plugs. The junction of the transom and the bottom of the craft are reinforced by strong fabric tape, as are the sides of the craft.

Commando 3
This is the smallest craft in the range and can carry five people. The manufacturer recommends that it is powered by an outboard motor rated at between 20 and 25 hp. Standard equipment includes two 1·4-metre paddles, repair kit, two carrying bags, pressure gauge,

foot bellows, two drain plugs, keel and two stringers with U-shaped alloy sections. Optional extras include cover, fuel tank support, anchor, steering wheel and launching wheels.

Commando 4
This can carry up to six people and should be powered by a 25 to 40 hp outboard motor. Standard equipment is similar to that fitted to the Commando 3 except that it has a three-element keel.

Commando 5
This can carry up to eight passengers and is powered by

an outboard motor rated at between 40 and 65 hp. Standard equipment is similar to that fitted on the Commando 4.

Commando 6
This is the largest craft in the range and can carry up to 16 people and is normally powered by an outboard motor rated at between 60 and 135 hp. Standard equipment is similar to that installed on the Commando 4, except that it has two struts at the rear.

STATUS
Production. In service with undisclosed countries.

SPECIFICATIONS

Model	C3	C4	C5	C6
Weight	60 kg	95 kg	110 kg	140 kg
Useful load	550 kg	850 kg	1300 kg	2000 kg
Length	3·6 m	4·3 m	4·7 m	6 m
Beam	1·55 m	1·7 m	2 m	2·4 m
Diameter of buoyancy tubes	0·4 m	0·45 m	0·5 m	0·55 m
Number of compartments	3	3	5	5
Inflatable volume	850 litres	1250 litres	1650 litres	2500 litres

Bombard Commando C6 inflatable craft fitted with Hotchkiss-Brandt 60 mm breech-loading mortar

Bombard Commando C6 inflatable craft fitted with Hotchkiss-Brandt 60 mm breech-loading mortar

Sillinger TRS 455 UM and TRS 500 UM Inflatable Craft

DESCRIPTION

These craft are made from Isotrope Polyamid 1680 denier fabric (made by Kleber) with a tear strength of 80 kg, rupture strength of 480 kg and an incipient strength of 25 kg. Both craft have four air compartments.

The TRS 455 UM has been designed specifically for military use and its V-shaped stem permits a high speed to be maintained even in rough weather. The TRS 500 UM is a slightly smaller and lighter craft.

The bottoms of the craft have three strakes and the floorboards are covered with an anti-slip material.

Standard equipment includes high capacity foot bellows, repair kit, two rowlocks, two oars, two carrying bags, front hood, two automatic drain holes, protective plate for motor bracket, one stainless steel front handle and five moulded handles, two life-lines either side, lateral protective rubbing strakes, windscreen of coloured altuglass, suspended seat and two interior handles.

A wide range of optional equipment is available including remote steering, trailers, rigid dismountable keel and a cover.

Both craft can also be fitted with the Italian Piaggio hydro-jet in place of the more conventional outboard motor enabling them to operate in very shallow water and making them safe for the use of divers. Two hydro-jets are available, one rated at 35 hp (weight 63 kg) and the other at 55 hp (weight 75 kg). The TRS 500 UM has a maximum speed of 38 km/h when fitted with the 35 hp hydro-jet and 50 km/h with the 55 hp waterjet and the TRS 455 UM's maximum speed is 43 km/h fitted with the 35 hp hydro-jet and 55 km/h with the 55 hp waterjet.

STATUS

In production. Known military users of Sillinger craft include Algeria, France, Greece and Syria.

Sillinger TRS 500 UM inflatable craft as used by French Navy

MANUFACTURER

TR Sillinger, 150 rue de Lyon, 75012 Paris, France.

SPECIFICATIONS

Model	TRS 500 UM	TRS 455 UM
Weight (unloaded)	130 kg	110 kg
Length (overall)	5 m	4·55 m
Beam	2 m	1·85 m
Draught (loaded)	0·5 m	0·48 m
Power (max)	70 hp	60 hp
(recommended)	40–50 hp	30–50 hp
Average speed with 50 hp engine	55/60 km/h	55 km/h
Payload	1350 kg or 10/12 men	1150 kg or 9/10 men

Sillinger TRS 630 UM Inflatable Craft

DESCRIPTION

The Sillinger TRS 630 UM is the largest mass-produced inflatable craft made in France. It is made from Isotrope Polyamid 1680 denier fabric (made by Kleber) with a tear strength of 80 kg, rupture strength of 480 kg and an incipient tear strength of 25 kg.

The TRS 630 UM has five compartments and the square shape of the bow allows it to be used as a pusher boat. On the bottom of the boat are three strakes and the floorboards are covered with anti-slip material.

Standard equipment includes two high capacity foot bellows, repair kit, carrying bags, four automatic drain holes, five towing rings, two multiple-use rings, protective plate for dual motor brackets, two document wallets, nine exterior lifting handles, eight interior handles, lifeline either side, four fuel tank supports, four paddles and reinforced outside rubbing strakes 240 mm wide. Optional equipment includes a front hood, overall cover and a steering console for the remote control of the engine.

SPECIFICATIONS

Weight: (unloaded) 240 kg
Length: 6·3 m
Beam: 2·5 m

Sillinger TRS 630 UM inflatable craft

Diameter of air chambers: 600 mm
Power:
(max) 130 hp
(recommended) 85 hp engine or 2 × 50 hp engines
Max speed: (with 115 hp engine) 55 km/h
Payload: 2200 kg or 20/22 men

STATUS

In production. A list of known users of Sillinger craft is given in the entry for the TRS 455 UM craft.

MANUFACTURER

TR Sillinger, 150 rue de Lyon, 75012 Paris, France.

Zodiac Inflatable Boats

DEVELOPMENT
The Zodiac company was founded in 1896 for the manufacture of civilian and military airships. Its first inflatable craft developed to meet a specific military requirement was completed in 1938. At present over 20 000 inflatable craft manufactured each year for both civil and military applications are exported to over 80 countries.

DESCRIPTION
The three Zodiac inflatable boats most widely used for military applications are the Mk II, Mk III and Mk V. The two smaller craft are designed primarily for commando type use while the Mk V can be used as an assault craft or for carrying cargo. A further development of this is the Light Patrol Boat 5800 for which there is a separate entry.

The Mk V is made of double-ply 840 denier nylon fabrics cemented together forming 1680 denier and heavily coated with neoprene with an interior lining to give the craft extra rigidity. The craft has five air chambers plus an inflatable keel. Standard equipment includes four marine bronze conical valves designed to release automatically any over-pressure created by lengthy exposure to the sun. Standard fittings include lifting rings, fenders, floorboards, aluminium engine mount, paddles, bellows, repair kit, self-bailers, carrying bags and life-lines. Optional equipment includes a cover, inflatable seat with back rest, fuel tank seat box, remote control steering console, launching wheels, lifting slings, collapsible 35- or 70-litre fuel tank, fuel tank support (aft or bow) and special carrying handles.

Zodiac Mk V, largest craft in Zodiac range

SPECIFICATIONS

Model	Mk II	Mk IIIGR	Mk IVGR	Mk V	Mk VI
Max load (cargo)	700 kg	1100 kg	1300 kg	1500 kg	2000 kg
(men)	6	10	12	15	–
Length (overall)	4·2 m	4·7 m	5·3 m	5·8 m	7 m
Beam	1·7 m	1·9 m	2·8 m	2·4 m	2·88 m
Max hp requirement	55	65	85	115	175

STATUS
In production. Zodiac craft are used by over 50 armed forces.

MANUFACTURER
Zodiac SA, 58 boulevard Galliéni, 92130 Issy les Moulineaux, France.

Zodiac Light Patrol Boat 5800

DESCRIPTION
The Light Patrol Boat 5800 (LPB 5800) was developed from 1973 and is based on the Zodiac Mk 5 assault boat already used by many armed forces. Mounted forward of the steering position is a 60 mm Thomson-Brandt gun mortar which can be either breech or muzzle loaded. If required a 7·62 mm light machine gun can be mounted alongside the mortar.

The LPB 5800 is powered by two outboard motors at the rear which can operate with either propellers or waterjets. The engines are started and controlled from the steering position. If required the craft can be fitted with a variety of radio installations in which case the aerial is mounted to the left of the steering position.

SPECIFICATIONS
Crew: 4
Weight: (loaded) 1750 kg
Length: 5·8 m
Beam: 2·4 m
Draught: 0·5 m
Speed: 35 km/h plus
Range: 200 km
Fuel capacity: 200 litres
Engines: 2 × 55 hp

STATUS
Development.

MANUFACTURER
Zodiac SA, 58 boulevard Galliéni, 92130 Issy les Moulineaux, France.

Zodiac Light Patrol Boat 5800 armed with Thomson-Brandt 60 mm breech/muzzle loading mortar

Zodiac Light Patrol Boat 5800 armed with Thomson-Brandt 60 mm breech/muzzle loading mortar

GERMANY, DEMOCRATIC REPUBLIC

East German Assault Boats Models FM-52 and STB-10

DESCRIPTION
The FM-52 is the older of the two East German assault boats and is powered by an SM motor-oar which consists of a powerhead unit and a drive unit. The powerhead unit contains the 15-litre fuel tank and the four-cylinder petrol engine which develops 34 hp, and the drive unit consists of a long shaft with a three-bladed propeller which extends beyond the transom like a steering oar and enables the craft to operate in very shallow water.

The FM-52 is being replaced by the much lighter STB-10 (or SB 900 as it is sometimes called) assault boat, which is constructed of a frameless monocellular compound which makes the boat almost unsinkable. The STB-10 is powered by a Wartburg HB 900 outboard motor which weighs 122 kg. Three STB-10 boats are transported nested together in a trailer towed by a Robur LO 1800A (4 × 4) truck.

STATUS
In service with the East German Army.

MANUFACTURER
East German state factories.

SPECIFICATIONS

Model	FM-52	STB-10
Weight	275 kg	180 kg
Length	n/a	7 m
Beam	n/a	1·8 m
Depth	n/a	0·65 m
Speed (empty)	25 km/h	45 km/h
(loaded)	20 km/h	35 km/h
Capacity (men)	n/a	12–15
(cargo)	n/a	1000 kg

East German Inflatable Craft

DESCRIPTION
The East German Army uses two basic inflatable craft, small and large, for a variety of roles including reconnaissance and assault. The larger craft can also be used for constructing light rafts for transporting light vehicles and weapons across water obstacles.

SPECIFICATIONS

Model	Small	Large
Weight	58 kg	150 kg
Length	3·04 m	5·5 m
Beam	1·3 m	1·8 m
Depth	—	0·6 m
Capacity (men)	5	20
(cargo)	500 kg	3000 kg

STATUS
In service with the East German armed forces.

MANUFACTURER
East German state factories.

Rescue and Security Boat RSB

DESCRIPTION
Although the RSB is described as a rescue and security boat it can also be used for a number of other tasks including snorkelling, bridge construction, obstacle- and mine-clearance, and load carrying and ferrying on inland waterways. It is intended for internal waterways running at less than three metres a second only. The RSB can be used in ice and can break ice up to 35 mm thick but it is suggested that it should not be used in floating ice more than 30 mm thick and covering 40 per cent of the water surface.

Construction is mainly from glass-reinforced polyester and many of the fittings are made from non-ferrous materials enabling it to be used for minefield clearing.

The RSB is usually powered by two East German Neptun 23 outboard motors, although a variety of other engines can be used, including the Soviet Moskva 30E. A 50-litre fuel tank gives an operational working time of between two and four hours. The maximum speed is 22 km/h and acceleration from stationary to the maximum speed takes six seconds; the reverse takes 10 seconds. With a three-man load the cruising speed is 12 km/h. On land the RSB is towed on a special single-axle trailer attached to a Ural-375D truck, with the

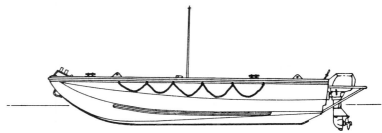

Rescue and security boat RSB

engines and other equipment carried on the truck. The time taken to prepare the RSB for the water is about 20 minutes.

SPECIFICATIONS
Length: 6·35 m
Width: 2·22 m
Height: 0·93 m
Draught:
　(with 3 persons) 360 mm
　(with 12 persons) 460 mm

Transport weight: 960 kg
Trailer weight: 360 kg
Engine power: (Neptun 23) 277 hp at 2600 rpm
Engine capacity: (Neptun 23) 346 cm^3
Fuel consumption: (Neptun 23) 9 litres/h

STATUS
In production. In service with the East German Forces.

MANUFACTURER
East German state factories.

GERMANY, FEDERAL REPUBLIC

DSB Inflatable Work Boats

DESCRIPTION
Deutsche Schlauchbootfabrik (DSB) produces a wide range of inflatable work boats to suit an equally wide range of military and civil tasks. All have inflatable keels and all have their transoms vulcanised in place on the rear. They are manufactured from high strength synthetic fabric with a synthetic rubber lining. The largest models having a five-ply thickness of material. All have wooden internal decking made up in sections and numerous extras to suit their work role.

Smallest of the DSB range is the Zephyr 405A with a load capacity of 600 kg. Next in size is the Zephyr 430 which can carry six to eight men or a load capacity of 1000 kg. Then follows the Zephyr 480 with a capacity of 1500 kg, while the Zephyr 505A is a smaller high speed craft with a capacity of 900 kg. The Zephyr 605A is similar in appearance to the Zephyr 505A but has a load capacity of 1485 kg; the Zephyr 605A is the standard West German Navy inflatable work boat. Largest of the

DSB Zephyr 480

DSB Zephyr 505A with windscreen for helmsman

DSB Zephyr 405A

DSB Zephyr 430 equipped as small fire tender

DSB S60ZM heavy duty work boat

DSB Type 5500-le with 40 hp outboard engine

standard range is the S60ZM, a heavy duty work boat with a capacity of 3500 kg.

DSB also produces a large inflatable boat known as the Type 5500-le which can carry up to ten men and is powered by a 40 hp outboard engine.

STATUS
Production.

MANUFACTURER
Deutsche Schlauchbootfabrik (DSB), Hans Scheibert GmbH & Co KG, Postfach 1169, D-3456 Eschershausen, Federal Republic of Germany.

SPECIFICATIONS

Model	Zephyr 405A	Zephyr 430	Zephyr 480	Zephyr 505A	Zephyr 605A	S60ZM
Weight	111 kg	113 kg	128 kg	133 kg	140 kg	160 kg
Capacity*	600 kg	1000 kg	1500 kg	900 kg	1485 kg	3500 kg
Length	3·85 m	4·3 m	4·8 m	4·45 m	4·63 m	6 m
Width (overall)	1·64 m	1·7 m	1·9 m	1·74 m	1·91 m	2 m
Internal width	0·84 m	0·8 m	0·9 m	0·83 m	0·95 m	0·8 m
Side wall diameter	0·4 m	0·45 m	0·5 m	0·455 m	0·48 m	0·6 m
Number of bulkheads	4	6	6	6	6	8
Max engine power	40 hp	50 hp	65 hp	50 hp	65 hp	55 hp

* carrying capacity at half depth of immersion

West German Inflatable and Assault Craft

DESCRIPTION
2–3 man inflatable boat
This inflatable boat, called the Schlauchboot 2–3 mann by the Federal German Army, is used for reconnaissance.

8–10 man inflatable boat
This inflatable boat, called the Schlauchboot 8–10 mann

by the Federal German Army, is used for a variety of roles including reconnaissance and is propelled in the water by oars.

Assault
This assault boat (Sturmboot) can carry seven fully equipped men plus the boat commander. It is powered by a 40 hp outboard motor mounted at the stern and when empty can travel at 35 km/h and when loaded at 25 km/h.

SPECIFICATIONS

Model	2–3	8–10	Assault
Weight	45 kg	140 kg	190 kg
Length	3 m	6 m	5·6 m
Beam	1·15 m	1·85 m	1·7 m
Depth	0·35 m	0·6 m	—

STATUS
In service with the West German Army.

8-man assault boat (Federal German Army)

8–10 man inflatable boat (Federal German Army)

West German assault boat (Sturmboot) fitted with outboard motor

HUNGARY

Assault Boat

DESCRIPTION
The M-48 assault boat is basically a wooden frame with an aluminium covering, with the sides and bottom of the hull reinforced with wooden battens. The craft is powered by a K4R4 motor oar weighing 130 kg with a

four-cylinder engine which develops 27 hp. In addition to being used as an assault boat it is also used for towing bridge and raft sections.

STATUS
In service with the Hungarian Army.

MANUFACTURER
Hungarian state factories.

SPECIFICATIONS
Length: 3·8 m
Beam: 1·5 m
Depth: 0·64 m
Capacity: (men) 12

ITALY

Pirelli Laros Rigid Keel Inflatable Boats

DESCRIPTION

There are three boats in the Laros rigid keel inflatable boat range, the Laros 40M, 50M and 80M. All have wooden keels and fixed wooden transoms for the outboard engine or engines. The two smaller boats use direct rudder steering but the 80M uses a small steering column-type gear. Construction is conventional and all three models can be used for sea-going missions. The normal production colour is dark grey but other colours can be produced if required. When not in use the boats may be packed into canvas valises. All three models have, as standard equipment, a non-slip decking, paddles, carrying handles, a mooring handle and ring, lifelines, a flagstaff socket, drain valves and a rubbing strake fender.

Main components of Laros range of rigid keel inflatable boats: (1) keel (2) non-slip decking (3) keel jaws (4) keel guide (5) transom (6) engine mounting plate (7) paddles (8) paddle brackets (9) valves (10) division diaphragm (11) carrying handles (12) mooring handle (13) mooring ring (14) lifelines (15) rubbing strake fender (16) socket for flagstaff (17) identification plate (18) drain valves

SPECIFICATIONS

Model	Laros 40M	Laros 50M	Laros 80M
Capacity (men)	8	10	16
Payload	1000 kg	1300 kg	2000 kg
Weight	75 kg	90 kg	175 kg
Length	4·3 m	4·7 m	6 m
Beam	1·85 m	2 m	2·4 m
Number of compartments	5	5	5
Compartment diameter	0·5 m	0·5 m	0·6 m
Max engine power	55 hp	55 hp	90 hp or 2 × 55 hp

STATUS
Production. In service with several armed forces.

MANUFACTURER
Moldip SpA – Pirelli Group, Via Milano 8, 20038 Seregno (Milano), Italy.

Pirelli Laros/Jet Inflatable Boat

DESCRIPTION

The Pirelli Laros/Jet inflatable boat is designed to make the maximum use of the waterjet propulsion system by the adaptation of the conventional inflatable boat form to accommodate a Piaggio jet drive unit at the rear. This enables the Laros boat to operate in shallow water and provides the boat with a high weight carrying capacity. The air compartments of the Laros/Jet are constructed from a Hypalon-Neoprene mixture bonded onto a special inner liner. The waterjet is mounted low on a modified transom. Two types of unit may be fitted, the Piaggio KS 150 and the KS 200. The weight of the KS 150 is 85 kg and it produces a static jet thrust of over 150 kg. Static jet thrust of the KS 200 is over 200 kg and it weighs 100 kg.

SPECIFICATIONS
Capacity: (men) 9
Payload: 1400 kg

Weight: (less motor) 120 kg
Length: 4·6 m
Beam: 2 m
Number of compartments: 5

STATUS
Production.

MANUFACTURER
Moldip SpA – Pirelli Group, Via Milano 8, 20038 Seregno (Milano), Italy.

Pirelli Laros Commando

DESCRIPTION

Intended for heavy sea-going operations, the Laros Commando is a conventional inflatable boat with four independent air compartments. The hull compartments are constructed from tough, heavy-duty nylon, coated with a mixture of Hypalon-Neoprene. Power is provided by a single outboard engine with a maximum output of 55 hp, with an engine in the 25 to 40 hp range being suggested. The boat has a non-slip internal decking, with a range of accessories including mooring and lifelines, and a canvas cover to enclose the interior when required. When not in use the Commando can be packed into three valises, one measuring 1·55 × 0·7 × 0·4 metres, the second 1·1 × 0·75 × 0·2 metres, and the third 1·7 × 0·25 × 0·2 metres.

SPECIFICATIONS
Capacity: (men) 9
Payload: 1200 kg
Weight: 100 kg

Length: (overall) 4·2 m
Beam: 2 m
Maximum engine power: 55 hp
Maximum speed: (2 men) approx 50 km/h

STATUS
Production. In service with several armed forces.

MANUFACTURER
Moldip SpA – Pirelli Group, Via Milano 8, 20038 Seregno (Milano), Italy.

Pirelli TT40 Self-inflating Boat

DESCRIPTION

Designed to be inflated from a CO_2 cylinder, the TT40 is an otherwise conventional boat powered by a medium-range outboard engine. The overall design is conventional but sturdy enough to undergo sea missions with a load of five men plus an additional 200 kg. The boat is delivered with a full range of accessories. Construction is of heavy duty nylon covered with a mixture of Hypalon-Neoprene. If no CO_2 source is available manual inflation is possible.

SPECIFICATIONS
Weight: 100 kg
Length: 4 m
Beam: 1·72 m

STATUS
Production.

MANUFACTURER
Moldip SpA – Pirelli Group, Via Milano 8, 20038 Seregno (Milano), Italy.

Tecnomatic Assault and Raiding Craft

DESCRIPTION

Tecnomatic builds two assault craft, 8 and 11·6 metres long, identical in layout and made of polyester resin reinforced with fibreglass in accordance with the Italian RINA regulations. Exposed parts of the hull are reinforced by galvanised steel plates. The craft are powered by two engines mounted at the rear of the hull. The helmsman's position is at the rear on the starboard side and if required a lightweight fully enclosed cabin can be fitted at the rear of the craft. Wooden folding bench seats are provided down either side of the hull and the bow ramp is manually operated.

Four steel hooks are provided for lifting the craft out of the water and four steel mooring bitts are fitted as standard. Standard equipment includes bilge pumps, compass, horn, navigation lights and searchlights. The electrical system includes two 12-volt batteries with a capacity of 120 amp hours with a supplementary battery of a similar capacity.

Tecnomatic also builds a Universal Sea Truck 8 or 12 metres long, powered by Castoldi marine jet engines.

SPECIFICATIONS

Model	8 m	11·6 m
Weight (empty)	2400 kg	3600 kg
(loaded)	5400 kg	7600 kg
Payload	3000 kg	4000 kg
Length	8 m	11·6 m
Beam	3·1 m	3·1 m
Draught	0·3 m	0·3 m
Engine hp	130–170	260
Max speed	33 km/h	44 km/h

STATUS
In production.

MANUFACTURER
Tecnomatic, 60100 Ancona, Zipa Molo Sud, Via Einaudi, Italy.

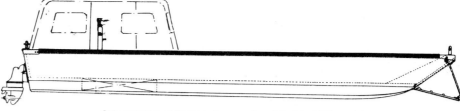

Side elevation of Tecnomatic assault craft (not to 1/76th scale)

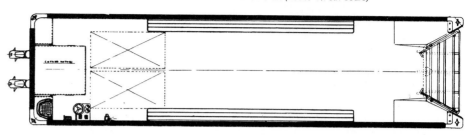

Plan of Tecnomatic assault craft (not to 1/76th scale)

Incursore 1

DESCRIPTION
The Incursore 1 is a close derivative of the well-known Dory 17 manufactured in Italy. Designed as a rapid water transport craft it can carry up to 900 kg of cargo or ten armed men. The double hull is filled with foam making the craft virtually unsinkable. Inflatable seats along each side of the hull can also be used as rollers when manhandling the craft on a beach. A variety of outboard motors can be used ranging in power from 40 hp up to a maximum of 140 hp. The maximum speed is about 23 knots with a 140 hp engine.

SPECIFICATIONS
Length: 5·2 m
Width: 2·2 m
Height: 1·1 m

Weight: (empty) 590 kg
Cargo load: 900 kg

STATUS
In production.

MANUFACTURER
Motomar Yachting, 37019 Peschiera del Garda, Piazza Marina 1, and 20159 Milano, Via Valtellina 67, Italy.

Incursore 3

DESCRIPTION
Designed along the general lines of the inflatable Gemini craft, the Incursore 3 can be used for a variety of military tasks. It can carry up to eight armed men and is usually powered by a 35 hp outboard engine. Oars are provided for silent approaches. The basic material used is neoprene which has been tested over a wide range of climatic conditions.

SPECIFICATIONS
Length: 4·5 m
Width: 2·05 m
Height: 0·55 m
Weight: 135 kg

STATUS
In production.

MANUFACTURER
Motomar Yachting, 37019 Pescheria del Garda, Piazza Marina 1, and 20159 Milano, Via Valtellina 67, Italy.

KOREA, REPUBLIC

Sam Gong Sea Eagle Inflatable Boats

DESCRIPTION
The Sam Gong Industrial Company Limited produces a four-model range of inflatable boats under the name of Sea Eagle. The three smaller boats, the Sea Eagle 3P, 7P and 15P are all fully-inflated while the largest, the Sea Eagle High Speed assault boat is of the Gemini type with wooden decking and a fixed transom.

The Sea Eagle 3P is the smallest in the range and is not intended to mount an outboard motor; provision for paddles or oars only is provided. The Sea Eagle 7P is a fully-enclosed design formed from two inflatable tubes with provision for a single 25 hp outboard motor. An anti-spray tube is fitted around the periphery. The Sea Eagle 15P has a semi-fixed transom and mounts a 25 hp engine. A total of six separate tubes make up the main sides to the boat. The Sea Eagle High Speed assault boat is entirely conventional in design and has provision on the transom for mounting a 45 hp outboard motor.

STATUS
Production.

MANUFACTURER
Sam Gong Industrial Company Limited, 136 Chung Jin-dong, Chongro-ku, Seoul, Republic of Korea.

SPECIFICATIONS

Model	3P	7P	15P	High Speed
Weight	21 kg	85 kg	145 kg	170 kg
Length	2·78 m	3·73 m	5·27 m	4·69 m
Beam	1·17 m	1·83 m	1·76 m	1·93 m
Internal width	0·57 m	0·76 m	0·82 m	0·915 m
Height	0·3 m	0·41 m	0·43 m	0·47 m
Tube diameter	n/a	0·41 m	0·47 m	0·508 m

UNION OF SOVIET SOCIALIST REPUBLICS

Soviet Inflatable Craft

DESCRIPTION
The smallest Soviet inflatable craft is the NL-5 which is essentially an improved version of the MLN (small pneumatic boat) used during the Second World War. This was replaced in the 1960s by the NL-8 which has five rather than six air compartments and can carry eight instead of five men. The NDL-10 and NDL-20 inflatable craft were also introduced in the 1960s with a carrying capacity of 1500 kg and 2500 kg respectively. The NDL-20 is also used in the PVD-20 airportable bridge, details of which will be found in the *Tactical floating bridges and ferries* section. The NDL-10 can also be used to form rafts with a capacity of 2000 kg (two boats) or 3000 kg (three boats). The NDL-10 and NDL-20 are now being replaced by the NL-15 and NL-30 inflatable craft.

STATUS
In service with the Soviet Army and other armed forces.

MANUFACTURER
Soviet state factories.

SPECIFICATIONS

Model	NL-5	NL-8	NDL-10	NL-15	NDL-20	NL-30
Weight	50 kg	55 kg	80 kg	95 kg	150 kg	200 kg
Length	3·2 m	—	5 m	—	6 m	—
Beam	1·2 m	—	1·7 m	—	2·2 m	—
Depth	0·4 m	—	0·5 m	—	0·55 m	—
Capacity (men)	5	8	15	15	27	30
(cargo)	700 kg	650 kg	1500 kg	1500 kg	2500 kg	3400 kg
Air compartments	6	5	8	—	15	—

Soviet Folding Assault Boats MSL, DSL and DL-10

DESCRIPTION
During the Second World War the Soviet Army introduced a number of folding assault boats including the MSL (small folding boat) and the DSL (assault folding boat). Both of these are made of 5 mm thick bakelised plywood with seams of rubberised fabric. The MSL is propelled by oars and is used primarily for reconnaissance. The larger DSL is used as an assault boat and can be propelled by oars or an outboard motor. The DSL can also be used to construct ferries with a 2000 kg capacity (two boats) or 3000 kg (three boats), with an improvised decking.

The post-war DL-10 folding assault boat is propelled in the water by oars, but two can be coupled stern to stern to form a full boat, or an assault boat pontoon which is normally propelled by an outboard motor.

The DL-10 can also be used to construct vehicle ferries with a capacity of 4000 kg (two full craft) or 6000 kg (three full craft). A GAZ-63 (4 × 4) truck can carry five sets of DL-10 boats and a ZIL-150 (4 × 2) truck can carry eight sets.

STATUS
In service with the Soviet Army and other armed forces.

MANUFACTURER
Soviet state factories.

SPECIFICATIONS

Model	MSL	DSL	Half DL-10	Full DL-10
Weight	65 kg	180 kg	170 kg	420 kg
Length	3·2 m	5·5 m	4·2 m	8·6 m
Beam	1·25 m	1·5 m	1·4 m	1·4 m
Depth	0·4 m	0·52 m	0·62 m	0·62 m
Capacity (men)	,4	14	15	25
(cargo)	400 kg	1500 kg	1500 kg	3000 kg

UNITED KINGDOM

Avon Inflatable Craft

DESCRIPTION
The Avon range of inflatable boats is used for both military and civil purposes for a wide variety of tasks.

The lightest crafts in the range are the M8, M9, M10 and M12 light work boats that can carry from three to seven men. The normal outboard motor is between 3 and 6 hp. The boats are all fully inflatable and are normally provided with a standard kit of combined hand/foot bellows, repair outfit, kitbag/valise, instruction manual, heavy duty rowlocks and rubbing strake, painter and life-lines and brackets for an outboard motor. A range of accessories is available as optional extras.

The WM375, WM480 and WM530 are classed as medium weight, low speed work boats carrying between 7 and 16 men. They are virtually enlarged versions of the M8 to M12 range.

The W340, W400 and W460 are medium work boats carrying from four to eight persons. This range has a rear transom capable of carrying two outboard motors, and these boats can be joined together to form light ferry rafts.

The W520, W580, W650 and W800 are heavy duty work boats and are enlarged versions of the W340, W400 and W460. The transom can accommodate two outboard motors and the three largest models have central steering consoles.

Avon W800 inflatable craft

STATUS
In production.

MANUFACTURER
Avon Inflatables Limited, Dafen, Llanelli, Dyfed SA14 8NA, Wales.

SPECIFICATIONS

Model	M8	M9	M10	M12	WM375	WM480	WM530	W340	W400	W460	W520	W580	W650	W800
Length (overall)	2·5 m	2·82 m	3·12 m	3·73 m	3·75 m	4·8 m	5·33 m	3·35 m	3·96 m	4·57 m	5·18 m	5·8 m	6·43 m	7·93 m
(inside)	1·77 m	2·08 m	2·38 m	2·86 m	2·84 m	3·73 m	4·21 m	2·26 m	2·69 m	3·27 m	3·75 m	–	–	–
Beam (overall)	1·22 m	1·37 m	1·47 m	1·68 m	1·88 m	2·23 m	2·44 m	1·47 m	1·68 m	1·88 m	2·08 m	2·37 m	2·37 m	2·92 m
(inside)	0·61 m	0·71 m	0·76 m	0·91 m	1·02 m	1·22 m	1·37 m	0·71 m	0·81 m	0·91 m	1·02 m	1·13 m	1·13 m	1·4 m
Tube diameter (bow)	0·3 m	0·33 m	0·36 m	0·38 m	0·43 m	0·51 m	0·53 m	0·34 m	0·38 m	0·42 m	0·47 m	0·54 m	0·54 m	0·67 m
(stern)	0·3 m	0·33 m	0·36 m	0·38 m	0·43 m	0·51 m	0·49 m	0·38 m	0·43 m	0·48 m	0·53 m	0·6 m	0·6 m	0·76 m
Total weight (approx)	25 kg	30 kg	36 kg	54 kg	38 kg	52 kg	70 kg	51 kg	77 kg	108 kg	140 kg	290 kg	317 kg	504 kg
Displacement (dry)	680 kg	907 kg	1182 kg	1770 kg	2045 kg	3820 kg	4770 kg	1300 kg	1763 kg	2877 kg	4045 kg	4910 kg	5730 kg	8400 kg
(swamped)	408 kg	522 kg	650 kg	930 kg	1410 kg	2100 kg	2850 kg	715 kg	1064 kg	1560 kg	2500 kg	3360 kg	3680 kg	6820 kg
Capacity (weight)	250 kg	320 kg	432 kg	567 kg	773 kg	1204 kg	1590 kg	440 kg	650 kg	950 kg	1136 kg	1300 kg	1500 kg	1800 kg
(persons)	3	4	5	7	7	12	16	4	6	8	12	16	18	27
Horse power (max)	3	4	4	6	6	paddle	paddle	25	40	55 (2 × 25)	65 (2 × 35)	2 × 70	2 × 70	2 × 85
Number of compartments	2	2	2	2	3	4	4	3	3	4	5	5	7	7
Performance (approx)	4 kts	4 kts	4 kts	4 kts	4 kts	n/a	n/a	22 kts	25 kts	30 kts	28 kts	24 kts	22 kts	22 kts
Assembly time (approx)	5 mins	7 mins	9 mins	11 mins	10 mins	15 mins	18 mins	12 mins	15 mins	30 mins	40 mins	60 mins	60 mins	60 mins

Avon Rigid Hull Inflatable Craft

DESCRIPTION
The Avon Searider 4, 5, 6, 7 and 8 is a range of craft constructed by bonding an inflatable tube to a glass fibre hull. This combines the portability and high buoyancy of an inflatable craft with the sea-going performance of V-hulled craft. The range of Seariders is produced in both military and civil forms, differing in hull lengths and corresponding performance, and load-carrying capacities. All have a water ballast system in which water ballast is taken into a forward compartment when the craft is stationary and ejected from the rear transom drain port once the craft is in motion. This makes the craft into a stable working platform once at sea. Standard equipment for the larger models includes combined hand/foot bellows, repair outfit, davit lifting points, instruction manual, life-lines, heavy duty rubbing

strakes, storage pockets, self-draining ports, stand-up steering console with steering gear, double skinning, towing bridle patches and towing point, paddles, oar/paddle retainers and grab handles.

A diesel craft is now available. This is 7·4 metres long and has the added advantage of a safer fuel for use aboard warships. It is suitable for on ship or shore operations and can be fitted with a variety of power and drive units to suit customer requirements. These craft are now in service with the US Navy and Coast Guard.

STATUS
In production. In service with the Royal Navy, US Navy and Coast Guard and numerous other forces.

MANUFACTURER
Avon Inflatables Limited, Dafen, Llanelli, Dyfed SA14 8NA, Wales.

SPECIFICATIONS

Model	SR4M	SR5M	SR6M	SR7M	SR8M
Length (overall)	4·05 m	5·43 m	6·05 m	7·16 m	8·38 m
Beam (overall)	1·8 m	2·03 m	2·34 m	2·44 m	2·84 m
(inside)	0·94 m	1·09 m	1·32 m	1·42 m	1·72 m
Tube diameter (bow)	0·38 m	0·45 m	0·47 m	0·5 m	0·55 m
(stern)	0·43 m	0·5 m	0·5 m	0·5 m	0·55 m
Total weight (approx)	160 kg	300 kg	480 kg	568 kg	820 kg
Displacement (dry)	1860 kg	2450 kg	3860 kg	2545 kg	5900 kg
(swamped)	1045 kg	1545 kg	2545 kg	–	3900 kg
Capacity (weight)	500 kg	750 kg	1125 kg	1346 kg	1800 kg
(persons)	4	10	15	18	24
Horsepower (max)	50	85	2 × 70	2 × 70	2 × 235
Number of compartments	3	5	7	7	7
Performance (approx)	30 kts	38 kts	35 kts	32 kts	45 kts

From bottom, Searider SR5M, SR6M and SR8M

Avon Gemini Inflatable Boat

DESCRIPTION

The Avon Gemini has been designed and constructed to military standards throughout, and is of conventional Gemini design. It can carry up to ten persons or 954 kg of payload, and can be powered by outboard motors of up to 50 hp. Heavy duty marine floorboards are fitted, and many other components such as the wooden keel, rubbing strake and forward jumping off board have all been built to military strength standards for hard use. Storage pockets, lifting handles and lifelines are all fitted as standard.

SPECIFICATIONS
Length: 4·72 m
Beam:
(overall) 1·9 m
(inside) 0·89 m
Weight: (approx) 144 kg
Capacity:
(men) 10
(weight) 954 kg
Horse power: (maximum) 50 hp
Performance: (approx) 23 knots
Tube diameter: 508 mm

Displacement:
(dry) 2500 kg
(swamped) 1800 kg
Assembly time: (approx) 30 mins
Number of compartments: 5

STATUS
In production. In service with several armed forces.

MANUFACTURER
Avon Inflatable Limited, Dafen, Llanelli, Dyfed SA14 8NA, Wales.

Dell Quay 5·2-metre Rigid Raiding Craft

DESCRIPTION

The Dell Quay 17-foot/5·2-metre Rigid Raider is an adaption of the standard Dory 17 hull with a completely redesigned interior featuring seating for nine armed men and a cox, and a ramp bow for easy loading and disembarking. There are a number of uses for this boat but it is particularly suited to tasks requiring high speed and load carrying, such as the transport of stores and equipment, troops, beach assault, rescue and diving work.

The boat has a cathedral hull which makes it stable both at rest and at speed. The controls are simple for ease of handling and provide instant response. It can operate in surf conditions and being foam filled is unsinkable, even when damaged. The built-in hull buoyancy will support 900 kg even when the boat is submerged.

Speeds vary according to the power of the outboard engine used and the conditions in use. The Royal Marines fit a single 140 hp Johnson which gives well over 30 knots in light conditions and over 20 knots fully loaded. Twin outboards may also be used.

The floor area provides clear stowage space in the centre and seating on inflated rollers along each side. These rollers can be detached for use as boat rollers to assist relaunching from a beach. Four heavy duty lifting points are provided, and the boats are designed to be stacked four or five high, without engines fitted.

SPECIFICATIONS
Weight: 590 kg
Length: 5·2 m
Beam: 2·2 m

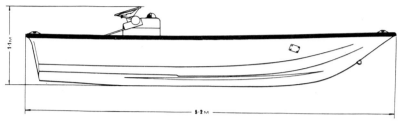

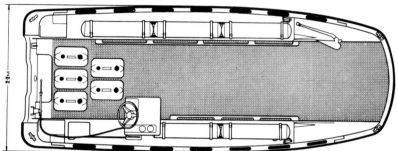

Plan and profile of Dell Quay 5·2-metre rigid raiding craft (not to 1/76 scale)

Height: 1·1 m
(3 stacked) 1·4 m
Max speed: 64 km/h
Capacity:
(men plus equipment) 10
(cargo) 900 kg
Fuel capacity: 113 litres

STATUS
Production. In service with the Royal Marines, Royal Navy, British Army and other armed forces.

MANUFACTURER
Dell Quay Marine, Clovelly Road, Southbourne, nr Emsworth, Hampshire, England.

Dunlop Gemini Inflatable Boat

DESCRIPTION

The Dunlop Gemini inflatable boat has been supplied to the Ministry of Defence (Navy) since 1953 and is available in three basic versions: assault craft, clearance diving and general purpose. A special bow fairlead and a winch are available with the clearance diving version. The craft is available in three sizes: 6-, 10-, and 15-man.

STATUS
In production. In service with many defence forces.

MANUFACTURER
Dunlop Limited, Marine Safety Products, GRG Division, Atherton Road, Hindley Green, near Wigan, Lancashire, England.

SPECIFICATIONS

Model	6-man	10-man	15-man
Weight (hull, floorboards, keel, paddles)	96·05 kg	137·4 kg	174·6 kg
Length (overall)	3·8 m	4·6 m	5·3 m
(inside)	2·38 m	3 m	3·66 m
Width	1·6 m	1·9 m	2·1 m
Tube diameter	0·46 m	0·51 m	0·51 m
Inflation pressure	0·176 kg/cm²	0·176 kg/cm²	0·176 kg/cm²
Buoyancy (dry)	1700 kg	2500 kg	3400 kg
(swamped)	1100 kg	1800 kg	2000 kg
Cockpit area	2 m²	3 m²	3·8 m²
Compartments	5	5	5
Engine hp rating	45	60	60

Dunlop Gemini inflatable boat

Dunlop Scorpio Military Inflatable Boats

DESCRIPTION

The three smallest boats in the Scorpio range of Dunlop inflatable boats intended primarily for military use are the MC6, MC8 and MC9. They are intended only for reconnaissance work and small raiding parties in sheltered waters. The two smallest boats, the MC6 and MC8, are conventional inflatable boats while the MC9 has a transom for fitting larger outboard motors.

The MC106, MC120 and MC136 are intended for use in open waters and have inflatable keels. All three have transoms.

Largest of the Dunlop Scorpio range is the Type 8007 which is a heavy duty work boat with a wooden keel. Special heavy duty materials are used in the construction. The Type 8007 can be powered by an outboard motor of up to 60 hp. If required it may be fitted with a centrally-mounted control console. This console is made mainly of GRP and adds 26·87 kg to the overall weight of the Type 8007 and when fitted the boat is then designated the Type 8007CON. The cox sits astride the console which provides cover for a battery to power an electrical starter and any other electrical equipment such as searchlights that might be carried. There is space for one other man behind the cox on the console. The Type 8007CON retains the capacity and overall dimensions of the normal Type 8007.

Standard equipment for the three smaller boats consists of rowlocks, oars, spray dodger, stowage pouch, kit bag and instruction manual. The three larger boats have as standard, floorboards, battens, inflatable keel, paddles, fitted transom, spray dodger, stowage pouch, repair kit, carrying valise and instruction manual.

STATUS
In production.

MANUFACTURER
Dunlop Limited, Marine Safety Products, GRG Division, Atherton Road, Hindley Green, Wigan, Lancashire, England.

Largest of Dunlop Scorpio range is Type 8007 (left) with Type 8007CON on right

SPECIFICATIONS

Model	MC6	MC8	MC9	MC106	MC120	MC136	8007
Length	2 m	2·5 m	2·74 m	3·2 m	3·66 m	4·12 m	5·2 m
Beam	1·32 m	1·42 m	1·42 m	1·45 m	1·68 m	1·68 m	2·1 m
Weight	15 kg	19·5 kg	24 kg	57 kg	60 kg	68 kg	174·6 kg
Tube diameter	0·33 m	0·33 m	0·33 m	0·33 m	0·46 m	0·46 m	0·5 m
Buoyancy (dry)	581 kg	726 kg	696 kg	1043 kg	1565 kg	1820 kg	n/a
(swamped)	320 kg	400 kg	407 kg	558 kg	980 kg	1090 kg	n/a
Capacity (weight)	225 kg	280 kg	280 kg	347 kg	675 kg	750 kg	1400 kg
(men)	2	3	4	4	8	8	15
Horsepower (max)	4 hp	4 hp	5 hp	15 hp	25 hp	35 hp	60 hp
Assembly time (approx)	10 mins	15 mins	20 mins	10 mins	30 mins	35 mins	n/a

Three smallest models in Dunlop Scorpio range of inflatable boats. MC6 in foreground with MC8 at right rear and MC9 on left

Manhandling Dunlop Scorpio MC8 inflatable boat

Mark IV British Army Assault Boat

DEVELOPMENT

The Mark IV assault boat was designed by the Military Engineering Experimental Establishment at Christchurch (now the Military Vehicles and Engineering Establishment) with production from 1961 by Laird of Anglesey.

The boat has been designed to transport eleven fully equipped men plus a crew of two, or a maximum load of up to about 1130 kg. The weight of the boat is such that it can be easily manhandled. In addition to its primary role as an assault boat it can be used for a variety of other purposes such as a supply craft.

Two Mark IV British Army assault boats coupled stern to stern

DESCRIPTION

The assault boat is constructed of a riveted aluminium alloy to British Specification 1470 and 1490, with a small quantity of mild steel components incorporated. It has a double bottom which forms a watertight buoyancy compartment. The boat is fitted with two steps at the bow end, beneath one of which is housed the mooring rope. Gunwales, midwales, carrying wales, and four lifting eyes are fitted externally. Provision is also made for draining the hull through the buoyancy compartment.

On the castings which secure the sides to the transom are lugs for coupling two boats together, stern to stern. A dowel and dowel hole in each transom facilitate coupling. The coupling pins are secured by chains, which are stowed in spring clips attached to the transom panel when not in use.

The gunwale has been strengthened by a light alloy extrusion enabling two or more pairs of boats, fitted with an improvised superstructure, to act as the buoyancy unit for a light vehicle ferry.

The assault boat is normally powered by an outboard motor mounted on the transom bracket. When two boats are coupled together the motor can be fitted on one bow end using the bow mounting bracket. If required, two motors can be fitted to the coupled boats, one each end. For noiseless approach operations paddles are used for which stowage clips are provided inside the boat.

| Type | Payload | Outboard motor power | | |
		10 hp	18 hp	40 hp
Single boat	272 kg	17 km/h	30 km/h	35 km/h
	1134 kg	9 km/h	10 km/h	13 km/h
Double boat	272 kg	16 km/h	18·5 km/h	22 km/h
	2268 kg	9 km/h	12 km/h	15 km/h

Mark IV British Army assault boat

SPECIFICATIONS

Weight: 190 kg
Load area: 7 m²
Length: 5·3 m
Beam: 1·8 m
Capacity: 1130 kg

STATUS

In service with the British Army and many other armed forces. Production as required.

MANUFACTURER

Laird (Anglesey) Limited, Beaumaris, Anglesey, Gwynedd LL58 8HY, Wales.

Mark V British Army Assault Boat

DESCRIPTION

Originally called Sea Jeep this is an all-aluminium assault craft designed specifically for military use and has been ordered by the British Ministry of Defence as a replacement for the Mk IV assault boat currently used by the British Army. It has been designed to carry 12 fully equipped troops or 1043 kg of stores across rivers, estuaries, lakes and coastal waters.

It is of all riveted construction using marine grade corrosion resistant aluminium alloy to British Standard Specifications NS5, NE5 and HE9WP. Any welding for fabricated parts has been carried out by the inert gas arc process.

The Mark V is virtually unsinkable and is fitted with over 0·567 cubic metre of buoyancy in watertight compartments under the rear seat and the forward step and

between the bottom and the false floor. Three heavy keel sections fitted along the bottom of the boat allow the craft to be beached at speed without fear of damage. The keels also aid directional stabilisation when under way. It is fitted with full length carrying handles, which act as grab rails when the craft is under way, and can be carried by four men and dragged by two. It has been designed to stack up to six high to facilitate economic storage and transport. As an aid to concealment the Mark V is painted with infra-red reflectant NATO green paint.

A variant of the Freezer Sea Jeep has been fitted with a waterjet propulsion unit for use in shallow waters.

STATUS

Production complete. In service with the British Army (624) and Qatar (48).

MANUFACTURER

A E Freezer and Company Limited, Mill Rithe Lane, Hayling Island, Hampshire, England.

SPECIFICATIONS

Weight: 181 kg
Capacity: 1043 kg
Length: (overall) 4·88 m
Beam: 1·68 m
Depth:
(moulded) 0·602 m
(under keels) 0·641 m
Draught:
(empty) 0·064 m
(laden) 0·245 m
Buoyancy: 0·567 m³

Freezer Sea Jeep fitted with optional waterjet propulsion unit (T J Gander)

British Army Mark V assault boat fitted with outboard motor (T J Gander)

Freezer Combat Assault Dory (CAD)

DESCRIPTION

During mid-1982 AE Freezer and Company produced the prototype of its Combat Assault Dory (CAD). The CAD is an all-aluminium craft with a trihedral hull and room for a load of 12 fully-equipped men plus the helmsman who has a control console. The prototype is equipped with a 70 hp outboard engine but the design can accommodate up to 140 hp. With the 70 hp engine trials have indicated that the CAD will achieve 27 knots loaded.

Freezer Combat Assault Dory (CAD)

Construction throughout is from 4 mm aluminium sheet. The space between the deck and the hull bottom acts as a partial buoyancy chamber and there is a towing eye welded onto the bow. All-welded construction is used throughout. Eight men can carry the CAD and the gunwales act as carrying grips. With the console unbolted the CAD can be stacked four high. When beaching the three keel splines absorb much of the shock. A non-slip deck is fitted and passengers are seated on inflatable rollers along each side. The current fuel tank holds 18·9 litres; much larger tanks will be fitted to later versions.

SPECIFICATIONS
Length: (overall) 5·41 m
Beam: 2·0955 m
Depth: 0·838 m
Draught: approx 200–210 mm

Weight: (approx) 455 kg
Payload: 12 men and equipment
Power unit: 70–140 hp outboard

STATUS
Prototype.

MANUFACTURER
A E Freezer and Company Limited, Mill Rithe Lane, Hayling Island, Hampshire, England.

RFD Inflatable Z Boats

DESCRIPTION
Z Boat Type 380
This craft is widely used for reconnaissance in coastal and sheltered waters and can carry up to six people when planing or ten when ferrying. The manufacturer recommends an outboard motor with a capacity of between 20 and 25 hp. Optional extras include stowage pockets, single point suspension sling, self boiler, flexible fuel tanks, boat cover and a sea anchor.

SPECIFICATIONS
Weight: (packed) 51 kg
Length: 3·76 m
Beam: 1·58 m
Diameter of buoyancy tubes: 0·457 m
Dimensions: (packed) 1·27 × 0·56 × 0·33 m

Z Boat Type PB16
This craft is widely used for inshore rescue duties but is also suitable for a number of military roles. It can carry up to six people when planing or 14 when ferrying. The manufacturer recommends an outboard motor with a capacity of 40 hp. Optional extras include stowage pockets, single-point suspension sling, self bailer, flexible fuel tanks, floor mattress, boat cover, sea anchor and a wooden seat.

SPECIFICATIONS
Weight: (packed) 133 kg
Length: 4·73 m
Beam: 1·88 m
Diameter of buoyancy tubes: 0·495 m
Dimensions: (packed) 1·27 × 0·69 × 0·36 m

RFD Z Boat Type 380

STATUS
In production. In service with undisclosed armed forces.

MANUFACTURER
RFD Limited, Godalming, Surrey, England.

Rotork Assault and Landing Craft

DESCRIPTION
Rotork Marine is a division of Rotork Limited and has been building Sea Trucks for both civil and military applications since 1965. The company specialises in multi-role, low-maintenance craft for use in adverse climatic and operating conditions.

Two basic types of craft are produced, each in an 8-metre and 12-metre configuration. They all feature rugged construction, unsinkability, shallow draught, high-load/high-speed performance, simple maintenance, high manoeuvrability and modular design.

The 408 and 412 hulls represent the traditional Rotork Sea Truck range in both civil and military layout. The 508 and 512 incorporate the main characteristics of the 408 and 412 with an improved hull. Greater use is made of non-corrosive materials and the flying bridge gives greater all round visibility at the same time providing better use of the valuable deck space. The 508 and 512 hull also permits the installation of heavy duty waterjet propulsion systems. The craft are propelled by a variety of systems from outboards to large inboard turbocharged diesel engines coupled to stern-drives or waterjets. The hulls of all craft are made of heavy-duty glassfibre-reinforced plastic, simplifying repair and reducing the overall weight. Listed below are some of the more important Rotork craft which have been developed specifically for military use, or have a military potential.

FAC 408 (Fast Assault Craft)
The bow ramp of the FAC 408 allows beach assault or direct launching into the water of men and equipment. Carrying capacity is 3000 kg and for amphibious work 'clipon' trailer wheels make the FAC 408 easy to tow on roads. The helmsman, fuel tanks and motors are protected by armour, and armour cladding for the welldeck can also be provided. Standard equipment includes the provision for mounting general purpose machine guns, demountable inflatable cushion seats mounted port and starboard giving straddle seating for 16 fully equipped men, grab rails, captive full load buoyancy and a rechargeable fire extinguisher. Optional equipment includes compass, deck anchor, lashing kit, and a demountable jib crane with a capacity of 500 kg.

SPECIFICATIONS (FAC 408)
Length: (overall) 7·37 m
Beam: (overall) 2·74 m
Height: (to gunwale) 1·09 m

Deck area: (overall) 15·8 m²
Width of ramp:
(at base) 1·83 m
(at gunwale) 2·28 m

Propulsion systems

Engine type	2 × 200 hp OMC outboards	2 × 140 hp OMC outboards	1 × 130 hp Volvo diesel outdrive
Speed (light)	79 km/h	66·6 km/h	7 km/h
(laden)	55·5 km/h	37 km/h	18·5 km/h
Fuel consumption (cruising)	136 litres/h	91 litres/h	25 litres/h
Weight (empty)	2090 kg	2000 kg	2300 kg
Max payload	2410 kg	2500 kg	2200 kg

Rotork FAC 408 fast assault craft

Rotork FAC 508 fast assault craft

FAC 412 (Fast Assault Craft)

The FAC 412 is capable of carrying up to 4720 kg in very shallow water, and of sprint speeds in excess of 61 km/h. It has built-in foam buoyancy which makes the craft unsinkable and if required it can be fitted with grp armour plating. The craft can be propelled by either petrol or diesel engines, depending on the operational requirement. Standard equipment includes provision for GPMG mounts, helmsman's console mounted starboard aft, demountable inflatable cushion seats mounted port and starboard giving straddle seating for 24 men, grab rails and a rechargeable fire extinguisher. Optional equipment includes navigation equipment, four-wheel trailer, deck gear, mooring line, cargo/vehicle lashing kit and demountable jib crane with a capacity of 500 kg.

FAC 508 (Fast Assault Craft)

The FAC 508 is a development of the earlier Mark 4 assault craft and was first shown in 1981. The FAC 508 has a low profile and is intended for rapid landing of troops onto a hostile shore. For this purpose it has a bow-mounted ramp and lightweight grp armour is an optional extra. The carrying capacity is 3000 kg and bulky loads can be accommodated. Fitted with twin 235 hp outboard motors the FAC 508 can reach 55 knots empty and when loaded with 20 fully equipped troops can attain 40 knots.

SPECIFICATIONS (FAC 508)
Length: 8·23 m
Beam: 3·2 m
Draft: 0·6 m
Horsepower: 2 × 235 hp
Payload: 3000 kg
Performance: (empty) 55 knots

CSB 508 (Combat Support Boat)

Details are given in the *Bridging boats* section (pages 146–147).

LSC 512 (Logistic Support Craft)

The LSC 512 has a maximum payload of over 5000 kg and can carry troops, cargo and vehicles at speed and can off-load them directly onto a beach over a winch-operated bow ramp. When used ship-to-shore the LSC can be crane-lifted on deck or davit-mounted by means of fixing points provided. Standard equipment includes a 363-litre fuel tank, provision for GPMG mounts, all-weather grp cabin mounted aft above gunwale level with canvas dropscreen giving access to the quarter-deck, helmsman's seat, observer's seat, navigation equipment, windscreen wiper, two rechargeable fire extinguishers and bilge pump. Optional equipment includes various radios, navigation equipment, cabin heating, awnings, armoured protection for helmsman, deck gear, cargo/vehicle lashing kit, demountable jib crane with a 500 kg capacity, foldaway deck seating for 32 men and a four-wheeled trailer.

The LSC 512 can be powered by the following engines: 1 × 200 hp diesel/outdrive which gives a maximum laden speed of 22·2 km/h (unladen weight 4200 kg, payload 4800 kg), 2 × 100 hp diesel/outdrive which gives a maximum laden speed of 22·2 km/h (unladen weight 4600 kg, payload 4400 kg), 2 × 130 hp diesel/outdrive which gives a maximum laden speed of 26 km/h (unladen weight 4600 kg, payload 4400 kg), 2 × 175 hp diesel/outdrive which gives a maximum laden speed of 37 km/h (unladen weight 4900 kg, payload 4100 kg), 2 × 200 hp petrol inboard/outboard which gives a maximum laden speed of 41 km/h (unladen weight 4100 kg, payload 4900 kg), 2 × 200 hp outboard motors which gives a maximum laden speed of 41 km/h (unladen weight 3700 kg, payload 5300 kg), 2 × 130 hp diesel/waterjet which gives a maximum laden speed of 20 km/h (unladen weight 4650 kg, payload 4350 kg), 2 × 175 hp diesel/waterjet which gives a maximum laden speed of 27 km/h (unladen weight 4950 kg, payload 4050 kg) and 2 × 200 hp petrol/waterjet which gives a maximum laden speed of 32 km/h (unladen weight 4150 kg, payload 4850 kg).

SPECIFICATIONS (LSC 512)
Length: (overall) 12·65 m
Beam: (overall) 3·2 m

SPECIFICATIONS (FAC 412)
Length: (overall) 11·27 m
Beam: (overall) 2·74 m
Height: (to gunwale) 1·09 m

Propulsion systems

Engine type	2 × 200 hp OMC 200 outboards	2 × 140 hp OMC 140 outboards	1 × 130 hp diesel/outdrive (Volvo AQD 40/280)
Speed (light)	63 km/h	50 km/h	48 km/h
(laden)	46 km/h	33 km/h	18·5 km/h
Fuel consumption (cruising)	136 litres/h	91 litres/h	50 litres/h
Weight (empty)	2870 kg	2780 kg	4400 kg
Max payload	4620 kg	4720 kg	3100 kg

Deck area: (overall) 30·85 m²
Width of ramp:
(at base) 1·83 m
(at gunwale) 2·28 m

Rotork FAC 412 with armoured helmsman's position

Rotork 512 logistic support craft

Height:
(overall hull) 1·487 m
(bridge) 3·525 m
(gunwale above deck) 1 m
Width:
(deck) 2·5 m
(ramp at base) 2 m
Deck area: 20·63 m²

STATUS
In production. Rotork craft are in service with more than 40 defence forces.

MANUFACTURER
Rotork Marine Limited, Lake Avenue, Hamworthy, Poole, Dorset BH15 4NY, England.

Rotork 7-metre Tube Boat TB 106

DESCRIPTION

First shown at the RNEE in 1981, the Rotork 7-metre Tube Boat TB 106 is a development of an old construction method in that the hull is formed from a number of plastic tubes to provide buoyancy and strength. The TB 106 is constructed of a number of large polythene tubes held together by steel 'spokes'. The bow section is a single polythene moulding to provide a fair entry through the water and preventing the ingress of water into the forward end of the tubes. The after end of each tube is individually sealed. The transom is constructed of heavy duty marine plywood with a galvanised steel outboard motor bracket. On the load deck the gap between the tubes is filled with foam and smaller diameter tubes. These small tubes can be used either as cable runs or as cargo lashing points. They may also be used as a basis for mounting cabin or shelter modules. The TB 106 is fitted with a bow ramp but as the boat is not designed for carrying vehicles the ramp may be used for the loading of bulky cargo. Power for the TB 106 prototype is provided by two 40 hp outboards but other power plants may be used.

The use of the tubular construction provides the TB 106 with good buoyancy and a strong structure which can withstand tough handling and repeated beaching. Polythene tubing is resistant to underwater growths and the hull requires no anti-fouling maintenance.

Rotork 7-metre Tube Boat TB 106

SPECIFICATIONS
Weight: (unladen, with motors) 1300 kg
Payload: 1000 kg
Length: (including motors) 7·26 m
Beam: 2·7 m
Overall height to gunwale: 1·02 m
Height of gunwale above deck: 0·61 m

Draught:
(laden, motor up) 0·27 m
(laden, motor down) 0·67 m
Deck area: (unobstructed) 6 m²
Max speed:
(2 × 40 hp, laden) 15 knots
(2 × 40 hp, light) over 20 knots

STATUS
Prototype.

MANUFACTURER
Rotork Marine Limited, Lake Avenue, Hamworthy, Poole, Dorset BH15 4NY, England.

Hawkins Marine Type 8057 Stackable Steel Dory

DESCRIPTION
The Hawkins Marine Type 8057 stackable steel dory is a heavy-duty 5·8-metre welded steel dory that is supplied in kit form. When complete the craft can be stacked four-high and carried four to a 6-metre ISO container or a single 4-tonne truck. All the parts are supplied fully finished and only local welding and painting is required. Only limited facilities are required for assembly and the full process takes approximately 90 man hours per dory. Up to 20 kits can be packed into one 6-metre ISO container.

Power for the Type 8057 can be supplied by a single 55 hp outboard motor or two 50 hp motors. The dory has a payload of 750 kg and can be used for a number of military and civil tasks.

SPECIFICATIONS
Weight: 925 kg
Payload: 725 kg
Length: 5·8 m
Beam: 2·25 m
Draught: 0·25 m
Max speed: 25 knots

STATUS
Production.

MANUFACTURER
Hawkins Marine Limited, Poole, Dorset, England.
Enquiries to Skelton Equipment International Limited, 103 Shaftesbury Way, Strawberry Hill, Twickenham, Middlesex, England.

Hawkins Marine Type 8057 stackable steel dory

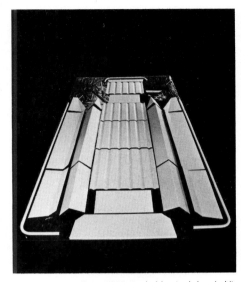

Hawkins Marine Type 8057 stackable steel dory in kit form

TaskForce Q26 Assault Craft

DESCRIPTION
The trihedral hull is constructed of glass-reinforced plastic and the hull configuration combined with the under floor box section construction of bulkheads and longitudinal beams gives additional stability. The cavities are filled with polyurethane foam for additional strength and buoyancy sufficient to support the craft fully loaded if it were filled with water. The basic model has a white hull with a blue, orange or white decking as standard and other colours are also available.

The cockpit of the Q26 is fully self-draining when the craft is under way. The long range fuel tanks are below the waterline for safety. The control console in the centre of the craft has a low profile shield, with steering, controls and instruments.

To reduce passenger fatigue the eight seats down each side of the hull are fitted with pneumatic cushioning. The seats can be quickly folded up out of the way if required.

Hoisting points enable the Q26 to be lifted aboard a mother ship when it is being used as a raiding craft. The boat can also be armed with 7·62 mm general purpose machine guns on special buffered mountings.

The Q26 assault boat can be fitted with one of three power combinations: twin or triple outboard motors, single or twin inboard engines/waterjets or single or twin inboard engines/stern drive.

SPECIFICATIONS
Length: (overall) 8 m
Beam: 2·85 m
Draught:
(stationary) 0·4 m
(at speed) 0·2 m
Speed/load performance: (with 2 × 200 Johnson/Evinrude outboard engines)
(sprint) 55 km/h
(cruising) 40 km/h
Payload: (at planing speeds) 1500 kg
Speed/load performance: (with 2.50 Sabre diesel and Castoldi 06 waterjet)
(sprint) 40 km/h
(cruising) 34 km/h
Payload: (at planing speeds) 1000 kg
Engine: Sabre 2.50 diesel
Type: 6-cylinder in-line, direct injection diesel, turbocharged and intercooled
Rating: 250 bhp at 2450 rpm
Fuel consumption:

rev/min	litres/h
1500	20·5
1750	26·8
2000	34·5
2250	45·9
2450	54·5

STATUS
Production. In service with undisclosed armed forces.

MANUFACTURER
The Boat Showrooms of London Limited, TaskForce Boats Division, 286 Kensington High Street, London W14 8PA, England.

TaskForce Q26 assault craft

Fairey Allday 13-metre Landing Craft (Trojan)

DESCRIPTION
Development of the Trojan 13-metre landing craft began in the summer of 1976 and the craft is currently under active consideration by several governments as well as being in series production for commercial use.

The Trojan has been designed as an up-to-date Landing Craft Vehicle Personnel and is built in all-welded marine grade aluminium alloy which combines light weight with great strength and minimum maintenance. The craft is built in two versions; flat bottom for minimum draught or vee bottom for rough water operations.

Several propulsion systems are available including conventional propellers protected against damage by twin skegs and mounted in half-tunnels, waterjets, stern drives or outboard motors. Power units are twin marine diesels of up to 180 shp each.

The load deck is long enough to carry two long-wheelbase Land-Rovers or a one tonne Land-Rover and a British 105 mm Light Gun. Speeds are 25 knots light, 16½ knots with 5 tonnes of cargo or 12 knots with 9 tonnes in the vee bottom version. The wheelhouse mounted at the stern is removable for transport and easy access to the engines. With a total weight of only 5700 kg the Trojan is easily transportable by road or air.

The Trojan can be used to carry light armoured vehicles such as the FV101 Scorpion. For conversion into

Fairey Allday 13-metre Trojan landing craft carrying two long-wheelbase Land-Rovers

an assault craft an extra troop carrying module can be fitted behind the wheelhouse. A field workshop version of the Trojan has been produced, and ambulance and personnel carriers are also available.

SPECIFICATIONS
Length: (overall) 12·8 m
Beam: 3·23 m
Draught: (with tunnel propellers, flat bottom) 0·76 m
Load capacity:
(vee bottom) 9000 kg
(flat bottom) 5000 kg

Ramp width: 2·28 m
Load deck length: 9 m
Power: twin diesels developing 80 to 180 shp each

STATUS
Production. Known to be used in Nigeria.

MANUFACTURER
Fairey Allday Marine Limited, Hamble, Southampton, Hampshire, England.

Watercraft Rigid Inflatable Work Craft

DESCRIPTION
There are three main models in the range of Watercraft Rigid Inflatable Work Craft, all of them capable of working in rough sea conditions and of reaching high speeds which enables them to be used as fast rescue craft. Other roles carried out by the range include diving support operations, ferry operations, police and general patrol, fishery protection and general workboat tasks.

The smallest of the range is the RI20 which has a grp-stiffened balsa sandwich construction hull. The deck is marine ply with ply longitudinal and transverse bulkheads. On the topsides grp and timber gunwales support the flotation collar which has five separate compartments. A central steering console is used.

Next in size is the RI22 which uses aluminium construction throughout. The flotation collar is made from laminated fabric and has five compartments. The steering console is to the rear.

Largest of the range is the RI28 which uses a grp and balsa sandwich hull with timber decking. Seven com-

partments are used in the flotation collar. It can carry a maximum of 22 men and crew of two.

SPECIFICATIONS

Model	RI20	RI22	RI28
Weight	n/a	1727 kg	2350 kg
Length	6 m	6·56 m	8·1 m
Beam	2·46 m	2·8 m	3 m
Draught	0·405 m	0·34 m (waterjet)	0·53 m
Fuel capacity	113·5 litres	113·5 litres	260 litres
Electrical systems	12 V	12 or 24 V	12 or 24 V

Engine variations.

Model	Engine (hp)	Speed	Endurance
RI20	1 × 60	23 knots	5 h*
	2 × 60	30 knots	3 h
	1 × 140	38 knots	3 h*
RI22	1 × 140	27 knots	7 h
	1 × 200	36 knots*	4 h*
	2 × 85	38 knots	3½ h*
RI28	1 × 215	27 knots	6 h
	1 × 300	36 knots	3½ h*
	2 × 200	48 knots	3 h*

* estimate

STATUS
Production. Used by some para-military and police forces.

MANUFACTURER
Watercraft Limited, Rescue Boat Division, Dolphin Quay, Queen Street, Emsworth, Hampshire PO10 7BJ, England.

Watercraft RI22 rigid inflatable work boat

Watercraft Assault Boats and Landing Craft

DESCRIPTION
The Defence and Commercial Division of Watercraft Limited offers a wide range of purpose built boats including 8-metre fast attack craft, combat support craft and 13·5- and 15·5-metre landing craft.

Fast Attack Craft (FAC 800)
This craft has been designed specifically for raiding and

assault roles and has a hull of glass-reinforced plastic with twin outboard motors mounted at the rear. The fuel tanks are between the engines and the steering position. If required a 7·62 mm general purpose machine gun can be mounted on either side of the craft.

SPECIFICATIONS
Length:
(overall) 8·09 m
(at waterline) 7 m
Beam: 2·64 m
Draught: (hull) 0·47 m

Combat Support Craft
This has a hull of glass-reinforced plastic with the wheelhouse, which is open at the rear, well forward. The two diesel engines mounted in the centre of the craft power two 304 mm Dowty waterjet units at the rear of the craft. There is a samson post and winch in the centre of the rear deck for towing operations.

SPECIFICATIONS
Displacement:
(empty) 3500 kg
(loaded) 5500 kg
Length:
(overall) 8·15 m
(hull) 7·7 m
Beam: 2·56 m
Draught:
(empty) 0·58 m
(loaded) 0·45 m
Freeboard:
(empty) 0·5 m
(loaded) 0·35 m
Engines: twin Sabre 180 marine diesels
Max speed:
(empty) 40 km/h
(loaded) 30 km/h

Special Logistic Landing Craft
The Special Logistic Landing Craft has been designed for both civil and military applications. The two engines

Watercraft fast attack craft

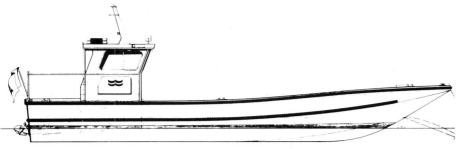

Watercraft L1550 landing craft (not to 1/76th scale)

are mounted at the stern and the fully enclosed wheel-house is forward of the engine room. The main deck is 8·3 metres long and 3·3 metres wide and the bow ramp is 2·75 metres wide. The craft can be armed with up to four 7·62 mm general purpose machine guns, mounted one on either side to the immediate rear of the wheelhouse, and one either side well forward, immediately to the rear of the bow ramp.

SPECIFICATIONS
Length:
  (excluding fenders) 13·5 m
  (water line) 11 m

Beam: 4 m
Draught: 0·5 m
Engines: twin Volvo AQD 40/208B

L1550 Landing Craft
This landing craft has been designed and constructed primarily for duties in river and estuary areas where a minimum draught is vital. The hull and deck are constructed from grp materials with the superstructure being of aluminium alloy. The trihedral hull provides a very stable working platform according to the manufacturer. The fully enclosed wheelhouse is at the rear with the machinery space below. The main deck is 9 metres long

and 3·3 metres wide and is sheathed with aluminium alloy tread plate. Alternative engines and drive units can be fitted to suit specific applications, including waterjets (as shown in the drawing) or conventional propellers.

SPECIFICATIONS
Displacement range: 15 000 to 20 000 kg
Load capacity: 5000 kg
Length:
  (overall) 15·5 m
  (water line) 14 m
Beam: (excluding fenders) 4 m
Draught: (loaded) 0·5 m
Depth: (at gunwale) 1·5 m
Engines: twin Volvo Penta TAMD 70C diesels developing 206 bhp each
Speed:
  (empty) 28 km/h
  (loaded) 22 km/h
Range: 336 km
Fuel capacity: 1500 litres

STATUS
Production as required.

MANUFACTURER
Watercraft Limited, Defence and Commercial Division, Sussex Shipyard, Shoreham-by-Sea, Sussex BN4 5RS, England.

Dowty Military Hydrojets

DESCRIPTION
The design concept for the Dowty hydrojet is based on a high mass flow of water at low pressure in order to achieve optimum propulsive efficiency at low application speeds. An axial flow type pump has been adopted, with the design based on Dowty experience and supported by comprehensive tests carried out by the National Engineering Laboratory. Additional advice has been provided by the University of Newcastle.

With an axial flow layout, the water flow is subjected to minimum change of direction and minimum obstruction is offered to the passage of hard objects. Diameter and weight is kept at a minimum. Two or more pump stages can be provided depending on performance requirements.

A typical Dowty single stage pump unit comprises an impeller rotating within a case which incorporates integrally cast fixed stator blades to remove downstream rotation of the water flow, thus avoiding a loss of energy. The drive shaft carrying the impeller is sup-

ported by bearings in the stator blade hub. The impeller blades have wide tip chords, rotating close to the case, to reduce tip losses.

The marine type intake case is arranged for bottom entry for water boats, or side entry to suit certain amphibious vehicle layouts. The case is shaped to offer the lowest possible losses, with the inlet area matched to full power flow conditions. The main drive shaft thrust bearings, located at the front of the intake case, have long rated life and run in an oil filled chamber, protected by lip type seals and an additional grease filled chamber.

Hydrojets designed to fit externally, at the rear sides of wheeled military vehicles, have short intakes, which may form part of the pump case. With this type, the main thrust bearings are located in the pump case hub.

The standard marine type tailpipe assembly (outlet duct) terminates in a reduced area outlet nozzle casting which is pivoted to swing in a horizontal plane. The reversing bucket is pivoted on the outlet nozzle and operates in a vertical plane.

For military vehicle applications, the output nozzle is

an integral part of the tailpipe casting and carries a steer and reversing bucket, pivoted to swing in a horizontal plane. Other control layouts have been developed by Dowty to suit particular requirements, including 360° rotating outlet systems which provide high thrust in any direction.

Pump cases and stator blades, impellers and shafts are made from stainless steel, thereby ensuring maximum durability. However, if requirements differ, pump cases and impellers can be made of aluminium alloy. Intakes, tailpipes, outlet nozzles and buckets are aluminium alloy castings. All fastenings are stainless steel and all joints between dissimilar metals are insulated to reduce galvanic action in seawater. Sacrificial anodes are normally incorporated.

STATUS
In production and widespread service.

MANUFACTURER
Dowty Hydraulic Units Limited, Arle Court, Cheltenham, Gloucestershire GL51 0TP, England.

Dowty two stage 300-mm diameter hydrojet unit fitted with conventional boat type steering arrangement

Dowty compact 330-mm pod type units of lightweight design for amphibious vehicles

UNITED STATES OF AMERICA

RAMO Raider Patrol Boat

DEVELOPMENT/DESCRIPTION
The Raider patrol boat has been developed as a private venture by RAMO Incorporated with the first prototype completed in December 1981 and the initial order received from the US Navy in October 1982.

It is based on the hull of a 22 ft (7-metre) Boston Whaler boat and has dual 140 hp outboard motors, four stainless steel teflon-coated propellers, two fuel and filter separators, engine controls with trim and tilt switches, engine spare parts package, engine battery disconnect switches, 6·35 kg Danferth anchor, anchor chain, 46-metre anchor line, four 6·096-metre dock lines, four fenders, one boat hook with rack, four commercial life vests, hydraulic steering, stainless steel dual

controls, compass, electrical switch panel, stainless safety rail, aluminium windscreen, 600 000 candle power spotlight, two 100 amp hour marine batteries, leaning post for operator and navigator, bow navigation lights, bilge pump forward, automatic bilge pump aft, heavy duty rub rail, heavy duty aluminium side decks, for 255 mm deck cleats, two bow lifting eyes, two stern lifting eyes and stern splashwell bulkhead with freeing port.

Armament consists of two RAMO 12·7 mm (0·50 calibre) M2 HB MGs, one fore and one aft, each mounted on RAMO stainless steel universal trolleys which are provided with armoured shields and 14 boxes, each holding 100 rounds of 12·7 mm ammunition. A 7·62 mm M60 MG can be mounted either side of the craft. A MK19 MOD3 40 mm grenade launcher can

also be mounted. The engines, firing positions and other essential parts are protected by Kelvar armour.

The Raider is launched from a heavy duty trailer with two guide banks, four roller cradles, heavy duty manual winch with wire, waterproof tail lights, heavy duty carter jack ramp wheels aft, dual metal catwalks, spare tyre, two equipment storage lockers, and a spare parts package.

STATUS
Production. Ordered by the US Navy for Special Security duties.

MANUFACTURER
RAMO Incorporated, PO Box 9449, Minneapolis, Minnesota 55440 USA, or 1101 17th Avenue South, Nashville, Tennessee 37212 USA.

SPECIFICATIONS
Weight:
(empty) 1996 kg
(loaded) 2948 kg
Length:
(overall) 6·807 m
(waterline) 6·4 m
Beam: 2·26 m

Draught:
(engines up) 0·356 m
(engines down) 0·864 m
Freeboard:
(forward) 0·94 m
(aft) 0·584 m
Max speed: (loaded) 40 knots
Fast cruising speed: 30 knots

Fuel capacity: 454 litres
Fuel consumption:
(top speed) 87 litres/h
(fast cruising speed) 60·5 litres/h
Engines: two 140 hp Johnson outboards with power trim and tilt
Steering: hydraulic
Batteries: 2 × 100 Ah

RAMO Raider patrol boats at speed

RAMO Raider showing alternative armament of two 12·7 mm (0·50 calibre) machine guns and one 7·62 mm machine gun

Three-man Inflatable Reconnaissance Boat

DESCRIPTION
The three-man inflatable reconnaissance boat is fabricated of neoprene-coated nylon cloth. The floor is a single layer mattress 102 mm deep of the same material as the flotation tube. Attached to the bottom of the mattress is a tubular keel which inflates with the mattress. The flotation tube is divided by bulkheads into floor compartments and the craft can be inflated in five minutes. It is propelled in the water by paddles and there is no provision for an outboard motor. Standard equipment includes three paddles, two oarlocks, 272 kg towing rope and a rope life-line all round the boat.

STATUS
In service with the US Army.

SPECIFICATIONS
Weight: (in pack, complete with paddles, repair kit and pump) 17 kg
Length: 2·743 m
Beam: 1·218 m
Depth: 0·355 m

16-foot Plastic Assault Boat

DESCRIPTION
The 16-foot plastic assault boat has been designed to carry a three-man engineer crew and 12 infantrymen and their weapons and equipment. It is propelled on the water by paddles or a 25 hp outboard motor mounted at the rear of the craft.
The bottom of the boat has integrally moulded plastic skids with the central one extending aft from the bow to amidships and two longitudinal stiffeners are also moulded into the floor. A total of ten carrying handles are provided. Ten of these craft can be carried inverted in the rear of a 2½-ton (6 × 6) truck or inverted on the rear of a single-axle trailer.

STATUS
In service with the US Army.

SPECIFICATIONS
Weight: 136 kg
Length: 5·006 m
Beam: 1·625 m
Depth:
(bow) 0·723 m
(stern) 0·533 m

Inflatable Assault Craft

DESCRIPTION
This inflatable assault craft (called a pneumatic assault boat by the United States Army) is fabricated from neoprene-coated nylon fabric and is divided into ten separate air-compartments. The main flotation tube is divided into six compartments and the floor consists of two 76 mm thick air mat fabric mattresses. The floor mattresses are inflated to a pressure of 0·49 kg per square centimetre, while the other compartments are inflated to a pressure of 0·21 kg per square centimetre. A 102 mm diameter spray rail is located around the periphery of the main flotation tube.
The craft is fitted with a towing bridge, two 152 mm diameter inflation/deflation pumps, a 76 mm diameter inflation/deflation pump, repair kit, eleven 1·524-metre paddles that can be broken down into 0·762-metre sections and a carrying case. An outboard motor (25 hp) can be mounted at the stern. The craft can carry 15 men and their equipment or 1530 kg of cargo.

SPECIFICATIONS
Weight: 113 kg
Length: 5·181 m
Width: 1·724 m
Depth: (bow) 0·863 m
Capacity:
(men) 15
(cargo) 1530 kg

STATUS
In service with the US Army.

Military Amphibious Reconnaissance System (MARS) Boat

DESCRIPTION
This inflatable light craft is intended to be part of the equipment used by amphibious reconnaissance units and is powered by a 35 hp outboard engine mounted on a transom at the rear. The bows and sides are formed from inflated tubes and the fuel tanks are also flexible. Two inflated tubes act as supporting cross-members. The boat can be inflated by CO_2 in about five minutes and up to 15 minutes by manual methods. Apart from reconnaissance the boat is intended to be used for diving operations and light work details. Fully loaded this boat can carry up to seven men and can operate in the open sea and along rivers and streams.

SPECIFICATIONS
Length: 4·445 m
Width: 2·083 m
Height: 0·762 m
Engine: one 35 hp outboard

STATUS
Development.

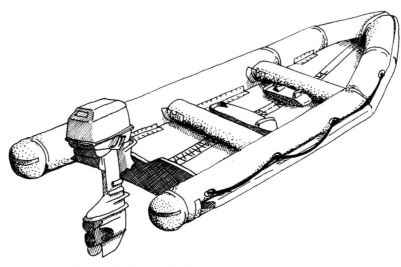

Artist's impression of Military Amphibious Reconnaissance System (MARS) boat

BARBED WIRE SYSTEMS

FRANCE

CCG Single and Double Concertina Barbed Wire

DESCRIPTION
CCG manufactures barbed wire in both single and double concertina form. The single concertina is made up of 68 twists of wire with a diameter of approximately 1·05 metres. The wire used for the coils is 3 mm in diameter and has a strength of 140 to 160 kg/mm² which is difficult to cut without special wire-cutting equipment. The barbs are between 13 and 15 mm long with each made up from two twisted wires forming four points. The rolls are delivered folded flat and about one metre high. Each roll is provided with carrying handles which can be used to pull the roll open to a length of 14 metres.

The CCG patent double concertina wire is formed of an exterior series of twists and coils similar to the single concertina wire but inside the coils is a further series of 29 elliptical coils forming a combined obstacle through which it is virtually impossible to crawl. The barbs of both coils are about 100 mm apart and are set on slight corrugations of the coiled wire to ensure they will not slip. When unfolded a coil of double concertina barbed wire is 12 to 14 metres long, but special lengths of 3·5, 7 and 21 metres can be provided. Normally the wire is supplied in a galvanised form but it can be painted in camouflage colours or as an alternative a special anti-infra-red coating may be applied.

A single coil of single or double concertina wire is sufficient to form an anti-personnel obstacle that will also provide a good barrier against vehicles. For the creation of a virtually impassible barrier, even with special equipment, two coils are laid side-by-side with a further coil on the top.

CCG double concertina barbed wire stacked in rolls of ten

Barbs of CCG barbed wire

SPECIFICATIONS

Type	Single concertina	Double concertina
Roll weight (approx)	20 kg	25 kg
Max unfolded length	14 m	14 m
Recommended unfolded length	10 m	10 m
Diameter of outside roll (packed)	1·05 m	1·05 m
Thickness of folded roll	0·16 m	0·16 m
Height of unfolded roll	0·9 m	0·9 m
Space between barbs (approx)	100 mm	100 mm
Length of barbs (approx)	13–15 mm	13–15 mm

STATUS
Production. In service with the French armed forces and security agencies. Also used in Algeria (in the 'Morice' Line) and in Angola.

MANUFACTURER
CCG Usine de Sainte-Colombe-sur-Seine, 21400 Chatillon-sur-Seine, France.

GERMANY, FEDERAL REPUBLIC

West German barbed tape with handling equipment

ISRAEL

High Tensile Reverse Twist Wire

DESCRIPTION
This form of barbed wire is manufactured from high tensile reverse twist steel wire with a diameter of 16 SWG (1·6 mm). The wire has a tensile strength of 80/120 kg/mm² making it much lighter and stronger than comparable quantities or lengths of conventional barbed wires. The reverse twist enables the wire to be stored and transported flat; it winds itself into the required coils when released from its storage coil. The wire is manufactured and stored in 500-metre coils each weighing 24 kg. For large-scale delivery the coils are bound by steel strips onto a wooden pallet, with 32 reels to a pallet.

STATUS
In production. In service with the Israeli armed forces and some other nations.

MANUFACTURER
Reshet Hamifratz Wire Works Limited, 152 Hayarkon Street, Tel-Aviv 63451, Israel.

Concertina Barbed Wire

DESCRIPTION
This concertina-type barbed wire is manufactured from high tensile steel wire 3 mm in diameter with a minimum tensile strength of 140 kg/mm². The wire is galvanised and crimped at the barbs to prevent them from slipping. The four-pronged barbs are made of 2-mm diameter soft galvanised steel wire and are spaced from 76 to 150 mm apart.

In concertina form the wire is supplied in one-metre diameter coils, each containing 70 hoops. Adjacent hoops are connected to each other with five tie clips in an alternating pattern. When pulled apart the hoops form a concertina with a continuous series of slighty curved diamond shaped openings. The steel tie clips are 1·5 mm thick and bent around two hoop wires to form a moveable joint. Each coil is provided with handles so that it can be extended to a length of between 15 and 18 metres. When packed each coil is 150 mm thick and weighs approximately 22·5 kg. Packed in units of ten, the coils tie together to form bundles 1·2 metres thick.

STATUS
Production. In service with the Israeli armed forces and some other nations.

MANUFACTURER
Reshet Hamifratz Wire Works Limited, 152 Hayarkon Street, Tel-Aviv 63451, Israel.

Barbed Tape and S-Coils

DESCRIPTION
This barbed tape is manufactured from galvanised steel strips 19 mm wide and 0·5 mm thick and is supplied in 225-mm diameter reels containing 50 metres of tape.
The S-Coils are made of barbed tape reinforced with 2·5-mm diameter high tensile galvanised steel spring. They are ideal for the rapid erection of barriers and the material can be used several times.

STATUS
Production. In service with the Israeli armed forces and some other nations.

MANUFACTURER
Reshet Hamifratz Wire Works Limited, 152 Hayarkon Street, Tel-Aviv 63451, Israel.

DTR 90 Electronic Fence

DESCRIPTION
The DTR 90 electronic fence can be used in conjunction with, or instead of, existing barbed wire or other fences and barriers. It can detect any attempt to cut the fence, deflect, climb over or crawl through it. Any such attempt using a force of between 8 and 25 kg will sound an alarm and give a visual indication of where the attempt is made. The fence can be used on virtually any structure including stone walls and fences, and even on various types of gate. It has a minimum length of six metres but a virtually unlimited maximum length and is controlled by a DTM-51 Control Unit which can control up to ten sectors of fence. The control unit may be run off either normal mains power or by a nickel-cadmium cell for up to about 20 hours. The fence is supplied in a standard height of 2·25 metres but other heights are available. Its sensitivity is fixed which gives a minimum of false alarms. The fence can operate between −35 and +65°C in a relative humidity of up to 95 per cent. Removal of any sensor post cover will initiate an alarm.

STATUS
In production. In service with the Israeli armed forces.

MANUFACTURER
Israel Aircraft Industries Limited, Ben Gurion International Airport, Israel.

DTR 90 electronic fence

UNITED KINGDOM

Sabre Tape Systems

DESCRIPTION
The Sabre Tape security fencing system was developed from late 1977 by Branglea Limited (now Pilkington Security Limited) to meet a variety of civil and military needs such as protecting airfields, command centres, POL dumps and other high risk areas.

The system basically consists of a Sabre Tape, available in a variety of corrosion-resistant colours, incorporating a fibre optic. When the tape is cut or damaged the break is automatically detected, immediately located and displayed on a visual unit.

The specially-designed Optran optical fibre is supplied by Standard Telephones and Cables Limited, the United Kingdom subsidiary of International Telephones and Telegraphs. All monitoring equipment for the system, as well as the electronic control devices, are manufactured by Pilkington Security Equipment Limited.

All fibre optics have the following inherent properties: they are not susceptible to electro-magnetic interference (EMI); they cannot be bridged or tapped; they do not allow any interference with the data or light signal being transmitted; they are not affected by climatic extremes. These characteristics all produce an extremely low false alarm rate and nuisance alarm rate when compared to other more conventional perimeter systems.

There are three basic types of Sabre Tape:

Sabre Tape FB
Unlike electric fences that can be short-circuited this barbed steel fencing contains a light-carrying optic fibre that cannot be cut without detection. Its chief advantage is that it provides both a visible deterrent in its aggressive appearance while providing the same security information as other types of fencing such as microwave, infra-red, laser and acoustic, but at a much lower cost. By combining the existing tried and tested technology of fibre optics with a simple barbed steel tape the Sabre Tape System offers the same degree of reliability

Sabre Optimesh in position on perimeter fence

as a standard communications system but with no false alarms.

Sabre Tape FP
This is an unbarbed coated steel tape swaged longitudinally to carry the fibre optic. It is used in perimeter fence construction where barbed tape is not permissible.

Sabre Collapsible Outrigger carrying Sabre Tape and Optimesh on chain link fencing

Sabre Tape SB
This is the simple Sabre Tape with no break-detecting element, yet an effective deterrent against intruders and

suitable for normal field use such as entanglements. It can be supplied in concertina form in free-standing 20-metre lengths. The barbed teeth are spaced 15 mm apart and the tape is coated with drab green 25 micron silicon polyester to provide long life in desert or coastal conditions.

Breaks can be located within the particular length of Sabre Tape, typically 500 metres but, if necessary, in less than 100 metres. For example an area 100 metres long on all four sides could be protected by four lengths of Sabre Tape, one for each side. Depending on requirements alarm equipment is to any degree of sophistication from a simple bell or light system, or a series of lights or bells, with or without mimic diagrams or charts to show the location of the break-in. In a more sophisticated Sabre Tape system a visual display unit that scans any number of fences or fence complexes, over whatever distance, provides break information in the most appropriate form. Such a visual display unit can be used in association with new or existing communication networks, and give instant state-of-security data. Systems alarm information may be carried by land line or by miniaturised radio links.

A perimeter fence system can be made up of any combination of the various Sabre Tapes depending on the level of security required. In detailing the system the length of the fence, the accuracy to which a break-in is to

be located, the position of the control post relative to the fence, the type of terrain, for example whether vulnerable to tunnelling, whether power is mains- or battery-supplied and the necessity for alternative detectors to be integrated into a complex system complete with visual display terminal should all be taken into account.

There are three basic systems: low-cost, medium-cost and high-security. A simple low-cost break-in detection with the ability to locate only one point of break-in can be based on either an optical or conductive wire coded system. The medium-cost system would have tripled strands which could locate multiple break-ins. The high-security system would have underground detector optics, radio transmission, and a visual display unit.

SPECIFICATIONS

Tape length	500 m	250 m	100 m
Total weight	30 kg	16 kg	7·5 kg
Spool diameters	1120 mm	830 mm	580 mm

Sabre Optimesh
Optimesh is a fibre optic carrying sensor designed to act as a break detection security system on perimeter fencing. The system consists of a series of looped fibre optic cables protected by pvc sleeving and formed into a mesh pattern with a series of tamperproof connectors. The mesh size is 200 mm and any attempt to cut the

mesh will result in the coded light signal being broken and an alarm signal will be generated by an electronic control unit.

Sabre Type Collapsible Outrigger
This specially designed outrigger acts as a support for Sabre Tape positioned on the top of security fences. The outrigger incorporates a shear pin supporting a fibre optic cable that passes through every outrigger on the fence. The shear pin is hollow and will break under the weight of an intruder and as it breaks it cuts through the fibre optic cable; the shear pin is in the hinge body of the outrigger. Cutting the fibre optic cable will generate an alarm. The outrigger may be set vertically for use on gates or at angles up to 45 degrees for use on fences.

The Sabre optic principle can also be applied to security grills and a loop protection system for such important items as locked valves and levers.

STATUS
Production.

MANUFACTURER
Pilkington Security Equipment Limited, Colomendy Industrial Estate, Rhyl Road, Denbigh, Clwyd LL16 5TA, Wales.

Concertina Barbed Wire

DESCRIPTION
Produced in various forms and weights, this type of barbed wire is very widely used for a great number of applications from general security to combat use on the battlefield. The steel wire, which is usually double strand, although single strand is available, can be either galvanised or coated with black bitumen. It is usually manufactured and stored in 200-metre lengths and the set and type of barb can be altered to suit any particular requirement.

STATUS
In production.

MANUFACTURER
Tinsley Wire (Sheffield) Limited, PO Box 119, Shepcote Lane, Sheffield S9 1TY, England.

Concertina barbed wire

Chain Link Fencing

DESCRIPTION
Although not a barbed wire, chain-link fencing has numerous military applications and is widely used, especially for the security of fixed premises and base areas. The chain link fencing has no physical deterrent effect but it is difficult to climb or cross and if properly erected very difficult to cut through or otherwise bypass. When topped with barbed wire, either stranded or concertina, any chain link fence becomes a difficult obstacle. The fencing can be supplied in a wide variety of

forms and can be either plastic coated or galvanised. Wire thicknesses vary from 2 to 5 mm and the usual chain mesh is 50 mm across, although a 75 mm mesh is available. Heights available vary from 0·9 metre up to 3·6 metres.

STATUS
In production and widespread use.

MANUFACTURER
Tinsley Wire (Sheffield) Limited, PO Box 119, Shepcote Lane, Sheffield S9 1TY, England.

Tinsley Wire (Sheffield) chain link fencing

UNITED STATES OF AMERICA

Barbed Tape and Barbed Tape Concertina

DEVELOPMENT

Barbed Tape/Barbed Tape Concertina provides an obstacle against personnel and vehicles and is used for protecting military establishments and other high security functions such as airfield perimeter protection, border protection, tactical entanglements and instant barriers for internal security.

Barbed Tape products were first introduced by the United States Department of Defense in 1966 and were used extensively in Viet-Nam where they demonstrated their superior qualities over concertina barbed wire. In 1969 the US Department of Defense stopped buying concertina and barbed wire and began buying only Barbed Tape Concertina and Barbed Tape. Since then it has been adopted by many armies around the world. A recent order placed by the US Defense Logistics Agency was for 400 000 coils of Bayonet Barb.

DESCRIPTION

The Barbed Tape Concertina consists of a single strand of spring steel wire and a single strand of Barbed Tape securely clenched around the line wire. Each coil is approximately 945 mm in diameter and consists of 55 4/5th continuous spiral turns connected by steel clips to form a cylindrical diamond pattern when extended to a coil length of 15·25 metres. One end is fitted with four bundling wires for securing the coil when closed and each end is fitted with two steel carrying handles. The Concertina extends to a maximum length of 15·25 metres without permanent distortion and when released can be retracted into a closed coil.

The newly introduced Double Concertina consists of two coils of Barbed Tape Concertina of different diameter linked into each other to form a highly dense barrier. The laying operation of the Double Concertina is similar to that of the single type with the coil in the coil configuration being extensible simultaneously to exactly the same length as the Barbed Tape described below. Trials under military conditions have proved that Double Concertina provides a much superior form of deterrent and barrier, delaying intruders for more than twice as long. It is also available in stainless steel.

Barbed Tape is fabricated from steel strip (0·02 inch thick nominal) with a minimum breaking strength of 226 kg and an overall width of 19 mm. The tape has an 11 mm barb at 12·7 mm intervals along each side. Fifty metres of tape are wound on a plastic reel 222 mm in diameter and 25·4 mm thick. It is finished in an electro-galvanised/hot dip coating each side and is also available in stainless steel.

The dispenser consists of two narrow arms with a swivel handle at one end and a forming head at the other. One arm is hinged for fitting the reel and the other has a spindle riveted or welded to it that fits into the core of the reel, holding it in position and acting as an axle during dispensing. The forming head incorporates two sets of rollers, in alignment initially, to facilitate insertion of the tape and can be rotated 90 degrees and locked transversely when the unit is loaded and ready for use. The offset rollers impart rotary motion to the reel carrier which produces a uniform twist to the tape as the tape is progressively drawn from the reel. The manufacturer recommends that there should be one dispenser every 195 to 200 reels depending on the number of locations in which the Barbed Tape is going to be used.

The metal, drive-type, spadeless fence posts are slotted to allow the efficient fixing of Barbed Tape and are manufactured in accordance with the US-MIL-Spec MIL-P-20636 and can be supplied painted in accordance with MIL-T-704.

An underwater protection system using stainless steel concertina is under development for safeguarding navy and marine installations.

During 1981 BATACO introduced a new sharper and more pointed barbed tape known as Bayonet Barb. The new tape has all the strength of the original barbed tape and is available in the same dimensions as Barbed Tape, Concertina.

STATUS

In production. In service with Australia, Belgium, Canada, West Germany, Hong Kong, Iran, Ireland, Korea, Libya, Spain, Thailand and the USA.

SPECIFICATIONS

Type	Barbed Tape Concertina Size 1	Barbed Tape Concertina Size 2	Double Concertina	Barbed Tape
Length	15·25 m extended	15·25 m extended	15·25 m extended	50 m per reel
Diameter	945 mm	698 mm	2 coils inner: 698 mm outer: 945 mm	n/a
Breaking load (minimum)	771 kg	771 kg	771 kg	226 kg
Weight	13·38 kg	8·39 kg	21·77 kg	2·013 kg

Barbed Tape being positioned with dispenser

Barbed Tape in position

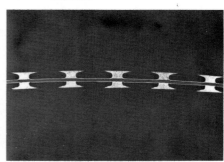

Configuration of Bayonet Barb

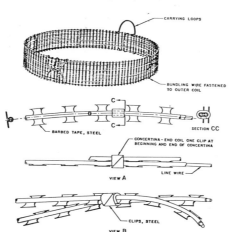

Configuration of Concertina Barbed Tape

MANUFACTURER
BATACO Industries Incorporated, PO Box 380308, Miami, Florida 33138, USA.

Double Concertina Barbed Tape protecting perimeter wall

General Purpose Barbed Tape Obstacle

DESCRIPTION

The General Purpose Barbed Tape Obstacle (GPBTO) was developed by the US Army Mobility Equipment Research and Development Command and is manufactured from stainless steel tape. It is issued in lengths which can be opened out to 20 metres, and each length consists of twin coils, each coil a helix with 33 loops and each coiled in opposition: one has a left-hand and the other a right-hand coil. The coils are interconnected with aircraft cable spacer wires and trip lines to set the coil pitch and maintain its length. The outer coil's diameter is 762 mm and the inner's 610 mm. Each barb is 60 mm long with a point length of 30 mm. Each obstacle length weighs 15·9 kg and when packed is 76 mm high with an 813 mm diameter. The packed obstacles are issued in a crate containing eight units with a total weight of 147·55 kg. A dispensing tool is included with the crate and wire ties and ground anchor posts are available.

STATUS
In production. In service with the US Army and some other armed forces.

MANUFACTURER
Man Barrier Corporation, 32 Great Hill Road, Seymour, Connecticut 06483, USA.

Section of General-Purpose Barbed Tape Obstacle

YUGOSLAVIA

Explosive Barbed Wire Obstacles

DESCRIPTION

This is a recent Yugoslav development which, compared with conventional barbed wire obstacles, uses less barbed wire, can be quickly positioned by just a few men, is more lethal and can be camouflaged if required.

The obstacle consists of barbed wire wound into tight rolls about 0·5 metre in diameter and about 0·3 to 0·35 metre thick. A 2 kg explosive charge is inserted into the hole of the roll and then tamped. Stakes about one metre long and 150 mm in diameter are driven into the ground to a depth of 300 mm and the roll of barbed wire is placed on top of the stake.

An obstacle is made up of one or more rows of prepared stakes, with rows spaced about 100 metres apart. Depending on the position being defended, these rows are positioned between 50 and 200 metres in front of the position. Each obstacle has an effective radius of 80 metres and the spaces between the obstacles are often also covered with stake type anti-personnel mines.

The obstacles can be set off by various means including a tripwire similar to that used for the anti-personnel stake mines, or command detonated from a safe distance. There are two methods of command detonation: for short distances wires pull the pins from two to four separate obstacles and for longer distances the explosives in the obstacles are connected to pull fuzes by detonating cord, with the observer initiating the detonating cord by pulling the pins from the fuzes with individual wires leading to his position.

STATUS
In service with the Yugoslav Army.

MANUFACTURER
Yugoslav state factories.

BULK FUEL STORAGE
AND DISTRIBUTION SYSTEMS

AUSTRALIA

Pumping Assembly POL 180 Litres/Minute

DEVELOPMENT
The Australian Army pump unit replaces the United States Barnes pumping assembly. The pump is utilised with the 38 mm POL system and is used in particular for filling and emptying American 1892·5-litre collapsible fabric drums.

Procurement detailing began in 1968 with the recommendation being made in 1974. Trials and testing were conducted in 1976 and as a result further modifications were made. These were completed early in 1978 and manufacture of production models began in May 1978 with completion in September 1978. The equipment specification for this item is Army (Aust) 5741.

DESCRIPTION
The pumping assembly is to be used as a general purpose fuel pumping unit. It consists of a 38 mm aluminium pump driven by a diesel engine, 50 metres of 38 mm diameter hose, two 38 mm nozzles, earthing spike and aluminium carrying case. The top of the carrying case covers the pump and engine and contains all accessories.

Pumping Assembly POL 180 litres/minute (Australian Army)

STATUS
In service with the Australian Army.

Pump Centrifugal Fuel Transfer 100 mm

DEVELOPMENT/DESCRIPTION
This pump unit was developed to replace a Volkswagen air-cooled pump/engine combination. Procurement by the Australian Army began in 1981 and was completed in 1983.

The pump is the main unit in a fuel farm reticulation circuit which has a nominal size of 100 mm. The fuel farm consists of a British collapsible fabric tank with a capacity of 45 000 litres. The pump is used as a general purpose fuel pumping unit for aircraft and ground equipment fuels. It consists of a close-coupled centrifugal pump with an engine incorporating a belt-driven vacuum pump. The pump unit delivers 45 litres per second at a 30 metre head including a six metre suction head. The inlet/outlet is 100 mm victaulic grooved. The skid is provided with two-way entry fork pockets and the attached protective frame has a removeable weatherproof cowl over the engine. The unit can be lifted from the top.

STATUS
Production complete. In service with the Australian Army.

MANUFACTURER
Regent Pumps, 1 Redwood Drive, Dingley, Victoria 3172, Australia.

Pump, centrifugal fuel transfer 100 mm

Tank and Pump Unit 4·5 m³ Capacity

DEVELOPMENT
The Australian Army tank and pump unit is based on the in-service United States two 1892·5-litre tanks and a 38 mm pump. The Australian requirement caters for fitment to a 5-ton truck. An additional Australian provision is for the use of the equipment in the static role, for example with tanks fitted on a tank stand.

The British Army uses the same type tanks (of 2273 litres each) and a 38 mm pump unit. This equipment is transportable only on a 4–5 ton truck using a common base for both tanks and pump unit (Gloster Saro demountable bulk fuel dispensing unit).

Procurement detailing began in 1970 and actual procurement was recommended in August 1975. Trials and testing were conducted during 1976 and as a result modified units were tested early in 1978. Manufacture of production models began in June 1978 and was completed by December 1978.

DESCRIPTION
The Australian equipment consists of two 2·25-cubic metre aluminium tanks and a 30 mm transfer pump. The two tanks and pump unit are to be fitted on a common base suitable for mounting on a 5-ton Army truck. The pump is driven by a diesel engine identical to the 38 mm general purpose fuel pump. Three types of pump unit are required based on functional needs:
Aviation units: the pump is fitted with a filter, separator, air eliminator, flow meter and one hose complete with nozzle and hose reel. Equipment is to be transportable on the 5-ton truck.
RAAC: pump unit is fitted with two hoses complete with nozzles and reels. Transportability requirements are as for aviation units.
RAE units: the pump is fitted with two hoses complete with nozzles and reels, and the equipment will be carried on the 5-ton truck, or two tanks can be fitted on separate tank stands. Gravity flow fills vehicles whereas the pump unit is used to fill the tanks on the stands.

The equipment meets the following specifications: Aviation Fuel Army (Aust) 5777, RAAC Fuel Transport Army (Aust) 6244 and RAE Fuel Transport Army (Aust) 6243.

STATUS
In service with the Australian Army.

Tank and pump unit 4·5 m³ capacity in static role (Australian Army)

Tank and pump unit 4·5 m³ capacity mounted on rear of 5-ton (6 × 6) truck (Australian Army)

FRANCE

ACMAT Bowser Vehicles

DESCRIPTION
ACMAT produces a range of bowser vehicle types based on the 4 × 4 4.20 SC or 6 × 6 6.40 SC chassis. The usual tank size used on the 4.20 SC is 2500 litres and the 6.40 SC uses a 4000-litre tank. In both cases the vehicle chassis used is a standard ACMAT unit with the only alteration from the usual specification being the removal of the drinking water tank. The tanks can carry all types of fuel including diesel oil and kerosene and can also be used to carry water.

Details of the vehicles can be found in the *Trucks* section.

SPECIFICATIONS
Chassis type	4 × 4	6 × 6
Length (overall)	5·706 m	6·943 m
Length of tank	2·225 m	3·33 m
Width	2·07 m	2·25 m
Height	2·14 m	2·325 m
Capacity	2500 litres	4000 litres
Tank wall thickness	3 mm	3 mm

STATUS
Production. In service.

MANUFACTURER
ACMAT, Ateliers de Construction Mecanique de l'Atlantique, Le Point de Jour, 44600 Saint-Nazaire, France.

ACMAT VLRA TPK 4.20 SC 2500-litre bowser vehicle

Trailor 5000-litre Bowser Equipment for AFVs

DESCRIPTION
The Trailor 5000-litre bowser equipment has been developed specifically for refuelling tanks and other AFVs in the field and can refuel up to four vehicles at one time. The tank used has an elliptical outline and is manufacturered from steel with a Rhomelyte interior lining. The tank has two compartments, one with a capacity of 2000 litres and the other of 3000 litres, and may be filled from either top or bottom. Each compartment has a manhole cover on top and is fitted with safety vents for internal vacuum or pressure. Access to the top of the tank is via ladders and there is a working platform covered with anti-skid and anti-spark coating. The distribution panel at the rear is under a cover which hinges upwards and locks once in place. Inside the cover is a pump driven from the vehicle gearbox power take-off and this embodies a by-pass set for an output of 20 000 litres an hour. Refuelling can be carried out with or without metering.

The full control panel contains a meter, two valves, a manifold linked to four hose reels each with a hose 20 metres long (each hose has a diameter of 30 mm and is fitted with a nozzle), a two-way valve for self-filling or bottom filling, a three-way valve, three cabinets for 80-mm diameter hoses, accessories and tools.

The complete equipment may be transported by rail or by C-160 Transall transport aircraft. Cross-country tyres are fitted and the entire equipment may be covered by a full tarpaulin camouflage cover. It is normally carried on a 6 × 6 truck chassis.

STATUS
In production. In service with the French Army.

MANUFACTURER
Trailor SA, 5 Route Nationale 10, BP 49, Coignières 78311, Maurepas Cedex, France.

Distribution panel for Trailor 5000-litre AFV bowser

Fruehauf 18 000-litre Fuel Bowser

DESCRIPTION
This fuel bowser entered service with the French Army during 1983 and uses an 18 000-litre tank mounted on the chassis of a Renault GBH 284 (6 × 4) truck chassis. The tank has three compartments of 11 000, 5000 and 2000 litres. The tank has a special interior coating that enables it to be used for the carrying of diesel fuel, petrol, kerosene and other such hydrocarbon liquids. It is fitted with a discharge pump with a capacity of 50 to 60 cubic metres an hour.

STATUS
Production. In service with the French Army.

MANUFACTURER
Fruehauf France, avenue de l'Aunette, 91130 Ris-Orange, France.

Fruehauf 18 000-litre fuel bowser mounted on Renault GBH 284 (6 × 4) truck chassis

Superflexit Helicopter Transportable Tanks

DESCRIPTION
These tanks are used for transporting fuel or drinking water and can be slung under a helicopter. They are composed of a polyamide fabric coated both sides with elastomers and are available with capacities of 500, 1000, 1500 and 2000 litres. All are provided with a single 76 mm fill/drain flange on the top.

STATUS
In production. In service with the French Army and other armed forces.

MANUFACTURER
Superflexit SA, 45 rue de Minimes, 92405 Courbevoie, France.

Superflexit helicopter transportable tank

Superflexit 20-litre Air-droppable Fuel Containers

DESCRIPTION
Superflexit produce a 20-litre flexible fuel container which can be dropped from helicopters or aircraft. These containers can be dropped from a height of 135 metres with the aircraft flying at a speed of 110 knots. The impact velocity on the ground from this height is approximately 41 to 50 metres a second. The containers may be dropped individually or in clusters of twenty, and in the latter case they can be dropped from a tilting platform.

These containers are available for use with either hydrocarbon fuels or water.

STATUS
Production. In service with the French armed forces and other nations.

MANUFACTURER
Superflexit SA, 45 rue des Minimes, 92405 Courbevoie, France.

Superflexit 20-litre air-droppable fuel container

Superflexit Flexible Storage Tanks

DESCRIPTION
Superflexit manufactures a range of flexible fuel storage tanks with capacities ranging from 500 to 300 000 litres. These are made of polyamide fabric coated with an elastomer on both sides. The tanks are provided with two elbows, relief valve and one manhole cover. Special tanks are available for the storage of water.

SPECIFICATIONS

Capacity	80 m³	300 m³
Weight (empty)	287 kg	878 kg
Volume (empty)	1·1 m³	3·1 m³
Length (empty)	9·1 m	16·9 m
(full)	8·65 m	16·5 m
Width (empty)	8·6 m	14·3 m
(full)	8·2 m	14·1 m
Height (full)	1·3 m	1·4 m

STATUS
In production. In service with the French Army and other armed forces.

MANUFACTURER
Superflexit SA, 45 rue de Minimes, 92405 Courbevoie, France.

Superflexit flexible storage tank

Kléber C70 'Commando' Portable Fuel Container

DESCRIPTION
The C70 'Commando' portable fuel container is a flexible drum container that can be towed behind a truck or carried slung from a helicopter. The main body is constructed from rayon cord and is coated with fuel resistant synthetic rubber. There is an abrasion resistant outer cover. The container is fitted with side plates with slinging shackles that can also be attached to a triangular towing bracket. A 2-inch/51-mm refuel/de-fuel port is fitted with an OPW or Guillemin coupling, and a pressure limiting coupler may be supplied. It may be used with a 1½-inch/38 mm hose but there is an adaptor for a 2-inch/51-mm hose. This container can withstand dropping from a height of over four metres.

STATUS
In production for the French Army.

MANUFACTURER
Kléber Industrie, 48 rue Jean Jaurès, 95870 Bezons, France.

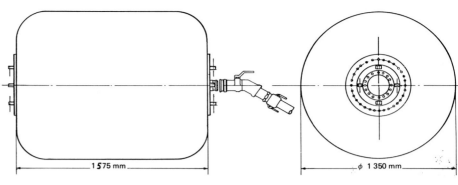

Kléber C70 'Commando' portable fuel container

SPECIFICATIONS
Weight: 125 kg
Diameter: 1·35 m
Width: 1·575 m

Capacity: 1900 litres
Working pressure: 0·35 bar
Maximum pressure: 2·1 bars

Kléber C60 Helicopter Transportable Tanks

DESCRIPTION
The Kléber C60 helicopter-portable tanks are produced in three standard sizes of 500, 1000 and 1500 litres capacity. Each tank has a fueling/de-fueling 40 or 50 mm valve which can be swivelled through 360 degrees, a 40 or 50 mm vent, a slinging ring for connection to the helicopter hoist or carriage point, lugs and adjustable harnesses, carrying handles, a bag welded onto the tank wall for carrying the various fittings, and a repair kit. The material used for the construction of the

C60 is designed to resist abrasion and weathering and is stong enough to allow the tank to be dropped from a height of one metre. The lugs and adjustable harnesses allow the tank to be carried on a truck if required. Apart from fuel the C60 can be used to carry water or other liquids.

SPECIFICATIONS

Capacity	500 litres	1000 litres	1500 litres
Dimensions (empty)	1·45 × 1·45 × 0·155 m	1·8 × 1·8 × 0·155 m	2·15 × 2·15 × 0·155 m
(filled)	1·4 × 1·4 × 0·4 m	1·75 × 1·75 × 0·5 m	2·1 × 2·1 × 0·6 m

STATUS
Production.

MANUFACTURER
Kléber Industrie, 49 rue Jean Jaurès, 95870 Bezons, France.

Kléber C40 Flexible Storage Tanks

DESCRIPTION
The Kléber C40 range of flexible storage tanks is constructed from rugged, synthetic rubber-coated fabrics and is manufactured in two grades, one for hydrocarbon fuels and the other for non-toxic liquids. Each grade is equipped with a number of standard fittings that include a stainless steel adaptor for a 50 or 80 mm hose, a bronze valve with a fire-hose type coupling and plug, an over-pressure valve for hydrocarbon grade tanks, a stack pipe with a cap for tanks holding transformer oils, a stainless steel vent pipe, a non-toxic level gauge and a repair kit.

The C40 tanks are available in a range of capacities from 3000 to 60 000 litres (see Specifications) but tanks with capacities up to 150 000 litres are available on request. Tanks for special liquids are also available.

STATUS
Production. In service with the French armed forces and some other nations.

MANUFACTURER
Kléber Industrie, 40 rue Jean Jaurès, 95870 Bezons, France.

SPECIFICATIONS

Capacity	Dimensions (empty)	Dimensions full (approx)	Volume (folded)	Weight (with fittings)
3000 litres	3·2 × 2·1 m	3·1 × 2 × 0·8 m	0·17 m³	45 kg
4000 litres	4·15 × 2·1 m	4·05 × 2 × 0·8 m	0·18 m³	52 kg
	2·8 × 2·8 m	2·7 × 2·7 × 0·95 m	0·18 m³	52 kg
5000 litres	5·1 × 2·1 m	5 × 2 × 0·8 m	0·21 m³	60 kg
	3·3 × 2·8 m	3·2 × 2·7 × 0·95 m	0·21 m³	60 kg
8000 litres	4·9 × 2·8 m	4·8 × 2·7 × 0·95 m	0·3 m³	65 kg
	3·6 × 3·5 m	3·5 × 3·4 × 1·1 m	0·3 m³	65 kg
10 000 litres	5·9 × 2·8 m	5·8 × 2·7 × 0·95 m	0·32 m³	77 kg
	4·3 × 3·5 m	4·2 × 3·4 × 1·1 m	0·32 m³	77 kg
15 000 litres	5·9 × 3·5 m	5·8 × 3·4 × 1·1 m	0·34 m³	115 kg
	4·6 × 4·2 m	4·5 × 4·1 × 1·35 m	0·34 m³	115 kg
20 000 litres	7·6 × 3·5 m	7·5 × 3·4 × 1·1 m	0·41 m³	135 kg
	5·7 × 4·2 m	5·6 × 4·1 × 1·35 m	0·41 m³	135 kg
25 000 litres	6·9 × 4·2 m	6·8 × 4·1 × 1·35 m	0·43 m³	155 kg
	6 × 4·9 m	5·9 × 4·8 × 1·45 m	0·43 m³	155 kg
30 000 litres	8·1 × 4·2 m	8 × 4·1 × 1·35 m	0·46 m³	165 kg
	6·8 × 4·9 m	6·7 × 4·8 × 1·45 m	0·46 m³	165 kg
40 000 litres	10·5 × 4·2 m	10·4 × 4·1 × 1·35 m	0·5 m³	205 kg
	8·7 × 4·9 m	8·6 × 4·8 × 1·45 m	0·5 m³	205 kg
50 000 litres	10·4 × 4·9 m	10·3 × 4·8 × 1·45 m	0·6 m³	225 kg
	8·6 × 5·6 m	8·5 × 5·5 × 1·55 m	0·6 m³	225 kg
60 000 litres	10 × 5·6 m	9·9 × 5·5 × 1·55 m	0·7 m³	250 kg
	9 × 6·3 m	8·9 × 6·2 × 1·6 m	0·7 m³	250 kg

PRONAL RSH Helicopter Transportable Tanks

DESCRIPTION
The PRONAL RSH (RSH – reservoirs souples heliportables) tanks are produced in three sizes, 500, 1000 and 1500 litres. A patented design is used in which the tank is supported in a Maltese cross-shaped skirt that immediately spreads the load of the vehicle once it is lifted from its single clip-on ring. Once in flight the skirt passes air through its panels and acts as a drogue to prevent the tank from revolving beneath the carrying helicopter. Each tank has one slinging ring, an outlet with a 2-inch/51-mm valve coupling and plug and a

symmetrical Guillemin system. The tanks may be used to carry water.

STATUS
Production. Approved for use by the French Army air arm.

MANUFACTURER
PRONAL, 139 rue des Arts, BP 25, 59051 Roubaix Cedex 1, France.

SPECIFICATIONS

Model	0·5 RSH	1·0 RSH	1·5 RSH
Capacity	500 litres	1000 litres	1500 litres
Weight (tank and fittings)	25 kg	32 kg	40 kg
Dimensions empty	1·4 × 1·4 × 0·15 m	1·8 × 1·8 × 0·15 m	2·2 × 2·2 × 0·15 m
Dimensions loaded (hanging)	1·01 × 1·01 × 1·2 m	1·4 × 1·4 × 1·55 m	1·7 × 1·7 × 1·9 m

---

PRONAL Flexible Storage and Transport Tanks

DESCRIPTION
PRONAL produces a wide range of flexible tanks for both storage and transport purposes and can produce these tanks to suit any customer requirement. For fuel storage purposes the tanks are constructed from a PVC-coated polyester with a weight of 900 grams per

square metre. Storage tanks have a 2-inch/51-mm inlet/outlet valve on one side and a centrally-located vent valve. Transport tanks are similar but have a series of lashing points along each side to allow them to be carried on almost any type of truck.

The figures provided in the Specifications table are not comprehensive as the tanks can be produced to suit almost any customer requirement. Tanks up to a capacity of 200 000 litres can be produced.

STATUS
Production. In service with the French and Swiss armed forces and some other nations.

MANUFACTURER
PRONAL, 139 rue des Arts, BP 25, 59051 Roubaix Cedex 1, France.

SPECIFICATIONS
Flexible storage tanks

Capacity	Length (empty)	Width (empty)	Height (full)	Weight	Volume (folded)
1000 litres	1·8 m	1·8 m	0·7 m	25 kg	0·13 m³
2000 litres	2·4 m	2·12 m	1·1 m	35 kg	0·16 m³
3000 litres	3·15 m	2·12 m	1·1 m	40 kg	0·2 m³
4000 litres	3·85 m	2·12 m	1·1 m	45 kg	0·23 m³
5000 litres	4·6 m	2·12 m	1·1 m	55 kg	0·26 m³
6000 litres	5·3 m	2·12 m	1·1 m	60 kg	0·29 m³
7000 litres	6 m	2·12 m	1·1 m	65 kg	0·32 m³
8000 litres	6·75 m	2·12 m	1·1 m	70 kg	0·35 m³
9000 litres	7·45 m	2·12 m	1·1 m	80 kg	0·38 m³
10 000 litres	8·2 m	2·12 m	1·1 m	85 kg	0·41 m³
11 000 litres	8·9 m	2·12 m	1·1 m	90 kg	0·44 m³
12 000 litres	9·65 m	2·12 m	1·1 m	100 kg	0·47 m³
15 000 litres	4·75 m	4·25 m	1·1 m	90 kg	0·44 m³
20 000 litres	6 m	4·25 m	1·1 m	115 kg	0·55 m³
25 000 litres	6·4 m	4·8 m	1·2 m	140 kg	0·68 m³
30 000 litres	7·25 m	4·8 m	1·25 m	155 kg	0·76 m³
40 000 litres	9 m	4·8 m	1·3 m	190 kg	0·93 m³
50 000 litres	9 m	5·8 m	1·3 m	230 kg	1·1 m³
60 000 litres	9 m	6·7 m	1·3 m	270 kg	1·33 m³
80 000 litres	9 m	8·6 m	1·3 m	330 kg	1·6 m³
100 000 litres	10·5 m	9 m	1·3 m	420 kg	2·05 m³
120 000 litres	12·4 m	9 m	1·3 m	490 kg	2·4 m³
135 000 litres	13·8 m	9 m	1·3 m	545 kg	2·65 m³

Transport tanks

Capacity	Length (empty)	Width (empty)	Height (full)	Weight	Volume (folded)
1000 litres	1·8 m	1·8 m	0·7 m	30 kg	0·15 m³
2000 litres	2·4 m	2·12 m	1·1 m	40 kg	0·2 m³
3000 litres	3·15 m	2·12 m	1·1 m	50 kg	0·25 m³
4000 litres	3·85 m	2·12 m	1·1 m	60 kg	0·3 m³
5000 litres	4·6 m	2·12 m	1·1 m	70 kg	0·35 m³
6000 litres	5·3 m	2·12 m	1·1 m	80 kg	0·4 m³
7000 litres	6 m	2·12 m	1·1 m	90 kg	0·45 m³
8000 litres	6·75 m	2·12 m	1·1 m	100 kg	0·5 m³
9000 litres	7·45 m	2·12 m	1·1 m	110 kg	0·55 m³
10 000 litres	8·2 m	2·12 m	1·1 m	120 kg	0·6 m³
11 000 litres	8·9 m	2·12 m	1·1 m	130 kg	0·65 m³
12 000 litres	9·65 m	2·12 m	1·1 m	140 kg	0·7 m³

GERMANY, DEMOCRATIC REPUBLIC

FTSB 4.0 and 25 Flexible Fuel Tanks

DESCRIPTION
Designed for use by forward units these two flexible fuel tanks are constructed from a mixture of rubber-based materials with a nylon weave outer covering. The FTSB 4.0 has a capacity of 4 cubic metres and is intended for use free-standing in open locations. The much larger FTSB 25 has a capacity of 25 cubic metres and is intended for main depot storage, usually behind some form of blast protection. The FTSB has numerous carrying and locating handles stitched into the outer surface and end-mounted valves and other hardware. The FTSB 4.0 has these components mounted on the upper surface.

STATUS
Production. In service with the East German Army.

MANUFACTURER
East German state factories.

GERMANY, FEDERAL REPUBLIC

Aluminium Storage Tank

DESCRIPTION
This storage tank has been designed for bulk storage of liquids such as oil, petrol or water. Its main advantages are its ease of transportation, short assembly time and its capability of being erected on various types of surface including concrete, earth and sand. The tank consists of 16 sections with tongue-and-groove sealing and an adjustable mast which is used as a roof support when the tank is being erected as the upper sections are assembled first and the lower sections last. The shell and supporting parts are aluminium with the bottom and roof being a fuel-resistant rubber tarpaulin.

SPECIFICATIONS
Capacity: 450 m³
Diameter: 12 m
Height:
(to eaves) 4·2 m
(filling) 4 m
(overall) 5·3 m
Weight of tank: 8300 kg
Total weight: (with transport frames) 10 780 kg

STATUS
Production. In service with Libya and the West German Army.

MANUFACTURER
Eisenwerke Kaiserslautern Göppner GmbH, Barbarossastrasse 30, D-6750 Kaiserslautern, Federal Republic of Germany.

EWK storage tank

Close-up of discharge outlet on EWK storage tank

Collapsible Tank

DESCRIPTION
A form of collapsible tank used by the West German Forces is a conventional rubber tank which can hold up to 300 cubic metres. It can be used as a storage tank or as the central point in a central refuelling system.

300-cubic metre collapsible rubber tank

ISRAEL

Portable Tank and Pump Unit

DESCRIPTION
This portable tank and pump unit consists of a pumping unit, two tanks and related items. It is designed for mounting onto a 2½- or 5-ton truck and it may be used for storage, as a mobile refuelling point, or for transporting liquid loads. The equipment is mounted onto a welded aluminium frame and the main sub-assemblies are a pump and engine assembly, two spring-loaded hose reels, a filter/separator, a meter and counter, a static reel and the associated piping. Accessories include a fire extinguisher, extra hose assemblies, a spares kit and a tool kit. Additional tanks can be towed behind the parent truck. The welded aluminium tanks incorporate lifting eyes for general lifting. There is an access panel on top of the tank which also houses the valve controls and calibrated dip-stick. RAMTA is able to supply the units to meet any specific customer requirements.

Portable tank and pump unit

SPECIFICATIONS
Capacity: 2 × 2250 litres (4500 litres/1200 US gallons)
Pumping capacity: 200 litres/minute approx
Weight:
  (empty) 685 kg
  (loaded) 3150 kg
Length: (overall) 3·665 m

Unit dimensions	Pumping Assy	Tank Unit
Length	0·7112 m	1·457 m
Width	1·6097 m	1·8288 m
Height from base	1·357 m	1·4222 m

STATUS
Production.

MANUFACTURER
RAMTA Structures and Systems – Israel Aircraft Industries Limited, POB 323, Beersheba, Israel.

ITALY

Bartoletti System

DESCRIPTION
The Bartoletti system is currently used by the Italian Army for transporting and distribution of petrol, diesel and kerosene fuels, and is in service mounted on three different chassis, the FIAT CM 52, FIAT CP 62 and the FIAT CP 70. A special model of the CP 70 is also in service fitted with a micro-filter for refuelling light aircraft and helicopters. The tanker is provided with both left and right side service points and a drum filling unit.

The left side service point contains a self-priming centrifugal pump driven by the vehicle engine, which can deliver 500 litres of fuel per minute, a 77 mm filter, intake for suction from outside, visual indicator and three operating gate valves for circuit formation. The right hand service point contains a control board with rev counter, pressure gauge, vacuum gauge, two remote controls, engine accelerator remote control, volumetric measuring unit, discharge mouth, an intake for closed cycle connection, set of gate valves, reel with hose and a 51 mm distributor nozzle. The drum filling unit has four 38 mm gate valves with rapid couplings, four rubber hoses and four distributor nozzles.

STATUS
Production. In service with the Italian Army.

MANUFACTURER
E Bartoletti, Via Leonardo da Vinci 4, 47100, Forli, Italy.

Bartoletti system on FIAT CP 70 (4 × 4) chassis (Italian Army)

SPECIFICATIONS (mounted on CP 70 chassis)
Configuration: 4 × 4
Weight:
  (empty) 7960 kg
  (loaded) 12 500 kg
Tank capacity:
  (petrol) 5800 litres
  (diesel) 5380 litres
  (kerosene) 5750 litres
Useful load: 4540 kg
Length: 6·554 m
Width: 2·5 m
Height: 2·97 m
Range: 650 km
Fuel capacity: 230 litres
Gradient: 60%

Bartoletti system on FIAT CP 70 (4 × 4) chassis
(Italian Army)

Bartoletti 4500-litre Helicopter Refuelling Vehicle

DESCRIPTION
This has been designed for the refuelling of helicopters and light aircraft and consists of a FIAT 79-F10A (4 × 2) truck fitted with a 4500-litre tank assembly. Standard equipment includes servicing equipment with 64 mm pump and fuel meter, separating filter and pipe reel with 50 mm outlet gun.

SPECIFICATIONS
Configuration: 4 × 2
Weight:
  (empty) 4050 kg
  (loaded) 7650 kg
Payload: 3600 kg
Length: 5·718 m
Height: 2·52 m
Tank:
  (greater diameter) 1·69 m
  (lesser diameter) 1·14 m
  (length including bottoms) 3·2 m
Tyres: 8.50 × 17.50 tubeless on 17.5 DC discs
Number of tyres: 6 + 1 spare

STATUS
Production.

Bartoletti 4500-litre helicopter refuelling vehicle

MANUFACTURER
E Bartoletti, Via Leonardo Da Vinci 4, 47100 Forli, Italy.

Mobile Fuel Can Filler System

DESCRIPTION
The mobile fuel can filler system is mounted on a two-wheeled trailer and can fill 600 20-litre fuel cans per hour with a gross capacity of approximately 2000 litres.

STATUS
In service with the Italian Army.

Mobile fuel can filler system deployed (Italian Army)

Mobile fuel can filler system in travelling position (Italian Army)

Mobile Fuel Transfer Station

DESCRIPTION
The trailer-mounted mobile fuel transfer station consists of two pumps which can be used together or separately, each with a capacity of approximately 300 litres per minute, complete with a by-pass filter and driven by an electric motor connected to the pump by a vee belt, one 5 kW mobile generator to supply electricity to the electric motors for the pumps, one current correction unit (5 kW, 220 volt), and a full set of attachments including metal pipes and hose for both fuel distribution and filling, and a set of cables and accessories for electrical earthing of the mobile station.

STATUS
In service with the Italian Army.

Mobile fuel transfer station in travelling position (Italian Army)

Experimental Field Pipeline System

DESCRIPTION
The experimental field pipeline system consists of one pumping station connected to the storage tank containing petrol, 2000 metres of pipeline consisting of 102 mm steel pipe, fittings (bends and take-offs), and a removable steel tank with a capacity of 80 cubic metres.

The pumping station consists of a side-mounted motor pump which can be fitted with rubber-tyred wheels to make transporting easier. The single-stage centrifugal pump can deliver 500 litres of fuel per minute, has a suction head of five metres and a delivery head of 135 metres. The flameproof pump is driven by a Porsche endothermic model 616/33 engine which develops 45·5 hp and is gravity-fed from a special tank.

The ends of the 102 mm pipe sections are grooved for the application of special Victaulic joints which consist of a shaped rubber gasket and two metal jaws, with coupling bolts. These provide rapid coupling of the elements of the pipeline, absorb expansion due to heat which the pipeline is subjected to as a result of ambient temperature, make the pipeline easier to adapt to the terrain as the special rubber gasket allows a degree of movement in the pipeline elements and compensates for axial thrust due to the pressure of the fluid circulating in the pipeline.

The special parts supplied with the system include bends, tee pieces and stub pipes whose ends are flanged or grooved as appropriate for the application of the Victaulic joints.

The valve equipment consists of standard gate valves and non-return valves inserted along the length of the pipeline to isolate sections near the pumping station and tank and to absorb hydrostatic loads when the pipeline is filled but not in use.

The temporary steel tank consists of elements that are connected by bolts, with special sealing gaskets interposed in the area of the joins. The tank may be assembled directly on the surface, which must have previously been levelled, without the need for permanent or semi-permanent structures.

A ladder is supplied with the tank to allow access to the roof. An atmospheric valve is also provided. A set of filters is connected to the tank inlet flange to filter the fuel before it is injected into the tank.

STATUS
Undergoing trials.

Portable steel tank (Italian Army)

Portable steel tank (Italian Army)

Pumping station (Italian Army)

Pipeline in position (Italian Army)

Pirelli OIL-SIL Flexible Storage Tanks

DESCRIPTION
Pirelli OIL-SIL flexible storage tanks are specifically intended for the storage of mineral and fuel oils and use an internal rubber lining. The exterior is fabric covered. They can be used laid directly on the ground and require no overhead cover. Temperature limits for use are −20 to +80°C. Each tank is supplied complete with carrying handles, a deflation device, a filling and emptying flange with a metal pipe union for a 2½-inch/63·5-mm or 4-inch/102-mm male connection and a metal gate valve with a cap. Optional items include a manhole flange, flexible hoses and fittings to suit customer requirements and a repair kit.

Other flexible tanks in the Pirelli range include HYDRO-MOBIL tanks for transporting water or liquid chemicals and HYDRO-SIL tanks for the storage of water and liquid chemicals.

SPECIFICATIONS

Capacity	Dimensions (empty)	Dimensions (full)	Weight
1500 litres	3 × 1·7 m	2·55 × 1·4 × 0·5 m	23 kg
3500 litres	3·2 × 2·4 m	2·75 × 2·1 × 0·65 m	32 kg
7500 litres	6 × 2·4 m	5·5 × 2·1 × 0·8 m	75 kg
11 500 litres	6·2 × 3·1 m	5·7 × 6·25 × 0·9 m	97 kg
20 000 litres	7·1 × 3·7 m	6·5 × 3·4 × 1 m	131 kg
38 000 litres	12·8 × 3·7 m	12 × 3·4 × 1·2 m	225 kg
50 000 litres	7·5 × 6·75 m	6·9 × 6·1 × 1·3 m	250 kg
100 000 litres	10·2 × 9·8 m	9·3 × 9·1 × 1·9 m	485 kg

STATUS
Production.

MANUFACTURER
Industrie Pirelli SpA, Azienda Accessori Industriali, Stabilimento Serbatoi Flessibili, Viale Spagna 2, 20093 Cologno Monzese (Milano), Italy.

NETHERLANDS

DAF Fuel Distribution Unit

DESCRIPTION
A recent DAF development is a containerised fuel distribution unit which can be carried on any truck with a container mounting facility, such as the DAF YA 4440 (4 × 4) truck which has been used for the trials carried out to date. The unit is mounted in a lightweight aluminium frame and consists of a 3000-litre storage tank and a motorised pumping and filtering unit (to which a dehumidifier can be added). The unit has storage space for 20 jerricans and a number of oil containers and has a closed locker for tools and other items. The storage tank and the filter unit/dehumidifier have heated sumps.

The unit is suitable for diesel fuel (F54), petrol (F46) and turbine fuel (F40), and is fully self-contained. It can be fitted to any truck with standard ISO corner fittings, and is suitable for helicopter or crane lifting. The container frame is sturdy enough to withstand limited towing directly on the container skids. In use the unit has two fuel quantity gauges and two hose reels, each with a fuel pipe 32 mm in diameter and 20 metres long. There are two alternative sizes of pistol dispenser, one with a capacity of up to 60 litres a minute and the other up to 150 litres a minute.

SPECIFICATIONS
Weight: (max gross) 4880 kg
Length: 4·25 m
Width: 2·2 m

Height:
(including skids) 1·9 m
(excluding skids) 1·82 m
Supply tank volume:
(gross) 3250 litres
(nett operational) 3000 litres
Pumping unit engine: HATZ E 780, 528 cm³ 4-stroke diesel
Pumping unit capacity: 0–300 litres/minute, max 8 bar
Electrical system: 24 V

STATUS
Prototypes on trial with the Netherlands forces.

MANUFACTURER
Military Division, DAF Trucks, Geldropsweg 303, 5645 TK Eindhoven, Netherlands.

DAF fuel distribution unit being carried on back of DAF YA 4440 (4 × 4) 4-tonne truck

DAF fuel distribution unit being carried on back of DAF YA 4440 (4 × 4) 4-tonne truck

SOUTH AFRICA

Static Storage Tanks

DESCRIPTION
Intended for the storage of fuel, oil products and water, these static storage tanks are for use in forward areas. They are made from nylon-reinforced nitrile rubber with abrasion, ozone and sunlight resistent external surfaces. Each tank is fitted with an air vent, quick connection dry-break couplings, an inspection manhole and handles for lifting when empty. Each tank is delivered packed in a wooden crate that also contains a repair kit for on-the-spot repairs. Five sizes are produced (see Specifications table).

SPECIFICATIONS

Capacity	Length*	Width*
4500 litres	3·64 m	2·64 m
13 000 litres	5·08 m	4·11 m
22 000 litres	5·38 m	5·44 m
45 000 litres	7·06 m	6·91 m
50 000 litres	7·49 m	6·91 m
* empty		

Typical SARMCOL static storage tank

STATUS
Production. In service with the South African Defence Forces.

MANUFACTURER
SARMCOL SA (Pty) Limited.

Enquiries to Armscor, Private Bag X337, Pretoria 0001, South Africa.

Transportable Fuel Tanks

DESCRIPTION
Produced in sizes up to 10 000 litres these tanks are intended to convert flat-bed or box-body trucks into fuel tankers. They are constructed from high strength and durable synthetic fibre and rubber materials. The ends of each tank are sealed with special reinforcing metal clamps with a fuelling/defuelling coupling at one end only. A simple manually operated air vent is situated at the top centre of the tank to allow the escape of air which might be present in the tank before filling. A special retaining harness is used made from high tensile nylon webbing to provide a safe and sure anchorage for the tank on standard flat-bed trucks. Each tank is delivered in a special wooden crate that contains not only the tank but all its accessories including a repair kit. When not in use the tank may be stored in the crate or rolled up.

A 10 000-litre tank laid flat will be 6·7 metres long and 2·3 metres wide.

STATUS
Production. In service with the South African Defence
Forces.

MANUFACTURER
SARMCOL SA (Pty) Limited.
  Enquiries to Armscor, Private Bag X337, Pretoria
0001, South Africa.

Transportable fuel tank on truck

2300-litre Collapsible Wheeldrum

DESCRIPTION
The 2300-litre collapsible wheeldrum is used to carry
fuels, and can be carried by aircraft, helicopter or truck
and can be para-dropped, man-handled or towed for
short distances. When empty the tanks occupy only 15
per cent of their filled volume. The wheeldrums are
manufactured from seamless nitrile rubber reinforced
by synthetic fibre. The outer surface incorporates a
nitrile/pvc rubber compound that provides a high degree
of abrasion, ozone and sunlight resistance. Each
wheeldrum is fitted with a quick connection dry-break
coupling and fittings at each end of the wheeldrum
incorporate a bearing and swivel plate with lugs for
lifting or towing.

STATUS
Production. In service with the South African Defence
Forces.

MANUFACTURER
SARMCOL SA (Pty) Limited.
  Enquiries to Armscor, Private Bag X337, Pretoria
0001, South Africa.

SARMCOL 2300-litre collapsible fuel drums

2-ton, Four-wheeled Fuel Pump

DESCRIPTION
This fuel pumping equipment is mounted on a twin-axle
trailer capable of being towed by a vehicle as light as a
Land-Rover. The trailer has a load-carrying flat base
covered by a canvas tilt and is used for the transfer of
fuels from one tanker to another or for the refuelling of
up to ten vehicles at the same time. Equipment carried
on the trailer includes a diesel engine-driven 450 litres
per minute self-priming pump, a fuel filter, flow meters,
control valves, fire extinguishers and hose reels with the
necessary couplings.

SPECIFICATIONS
Weight:
  (loaded) 3400 kg
  (empty) 1385 kg
Length: 3·32 m
Width: 2·37 m
Height: 2·66 m
Track: 1·85 m
Tyres: 9.00 × 16 × 10 ply

STATUS
Production. In service with the South African Defence
Forces.

MANUFACTURER
Enquiries to Armscor, Private Bag X337, Pretoria 0001,
South Africa.

2-ton, four-wheel fuel pump

UNION OF SOVIET SOCIALIST REPUBLICS

Fabric Reinforced Rubber Fuel Tanks

DESCRIPTION
The USSR brought this type of fuel tank into service during 1961 and since then many different types have been introduced. The first family of tanks comprise the MR-2.5, MR-4, MR-10 and MR-12. These were all orthodox reinforced rubber fuel tanks and all, except the MR-10, were used to convert flat bed trucks into mobile fuel carriers. The MR-10 was used primarily as a storage tank, not having the internal baffles fitted to the other types.

The latest family of fabric reinforced rubber fuel tanks are the MR-4, MR-6, MR-25, MR-50, MR-150 and MR-250. Only the MR-4 and MR-6 are now used for the mobile carrying of fuel and other liquids, and are fitted with metal loading brackets on all corners and diagonal partitions internally. All the tanks have an inspection manhole, filling/draining and air connections, T-pipes and air pipes. Handles are provided for folding, unfolding and handling of each, and these are situated around the periphery of each tank. The MR-150 and MR-250 have underside connectors with elbows and flexible pipes for flushing residual liquids from the tank. When folded each tank has an external pocket into which the various fittings can be stowed. When transported, each tank is carried inside a cover fitted with loading loops. For storage the tanks may be kept either folded or unfolded under cover, or under canvas outdoors.

STATUS
The original MR-2.5, MR-4, MR-10 and MR-12 are no longer in production but may be held in reserve. The later MR-4, MR-6, MR-25, MR-50, MR-150 and MR-250 are in production and Warsaw Pact service.

MANUFACTURER
State factories.

Fabric reinforced rubber fuel tanks

SPECIFICATIONS

Tank type	MR-4	MR-6	MR-25	MR-50	MR-150	MR-250
Rated capacity	4000 litres	6000 litres	25 000 litres	50 000 litres	150 000 litres	260 000 litres
Length (filled)	3·6 m	3·8 m	9 m	17·6 m	18 m	18 m
Width (filled)	2·6 m	2·5 m	3·7 m	3·7 m	7 m	10 m
Height (filled)	0·65 m	0·9 m	1 m	1 m	1·4 m	1·4 m
Weight (including cover)	125 kg	135 kg	290 kg	580 kg	1050 kg	1450 kg
Number of filling/ draining connectors	1	1	2	2	2	2
Number of air connectors	1	1	1	2	2	2

PMTP-100 Tactical Pipeline

DESCRIPTION
The PMTP-100 tactical POL pipeline is used by the pipeline regiments assigned to each Red Army front. The pipe is laid in ten-metre lengths, each with quick-connect junctions, from tractor-towed trailers which automatically lay the pipes at the rate of two to three kilometres an hour. Once connected the pipes are designed to be easily removed and replaced if damaged and the entire pipeline can be retrieved for later use. The pipeline capacity is 75 cubic metres of POL products per hour. Length of the pipeline is dependent on the number of pumping stations and pipe sections available.

STATUS
In service with Warsaw Pact forces.

MANUFACTURER
Soviet state factories.

Section of PMTP-100 tactical pipeline

UNITED KINGDOM

Demountable Bulk Fuel Dispensing Unit

DESCRIPTION
The demountable bulk fuel dispensing unit comprises two tanks, one pumping and dispensing pack, a two-tier rack and mounting beams.

The unit has been designed for mounting on the Bedford MK (4 × 4) flatbed truck but can be adapted to fit other chassis with suitable capacity. The unit can be removed from the vehicle by a fork lift truck, crane or, in an emergency, by hand.

The tanks are manufactured from AA5454 aluminium sheet and each tank has a capacity of 2100 litres. Access to the tank interior is through a 406 × 356 mm collar in the top skin. The filler cap assembly incorporates a 254 mm diameter EMCO open-fill quick-release manhole and a single pressure/vacuum vent. A dip point containing a captive dipstick is provided, and the filler cap and dip point are contained within a spillage bund. An automatic bottom loading facility fitted to each tank enables loading rates of up to 682 litres per minute and offloading rates of 455 litres per minute to be achieved. A drain plug is provided in the tank bottom skin and each tank is pressure tested to 0·703 kg/cm².

The dispensing equipment may be operated independently of the tanks if desired. The pump set is resiliently mounted inside the dispensing pack frame and is adequately protected against spillage by a firescreen and boxed-in exhaust which meets Ministry of Defence (Army) safety requirements.

A two-tier rack fitted with a drip tray and drain plug is provided. The lower tier of the rack is designed as a roller carriage which can be withdrawn from either side of the vehicle. An Alan Cobham filter/water separator with differential pressure gauge is incorporated in the design.

Two 12·192-metre 32 mm diameter smooth-bore

Demountable bulk fuel dispensing unit mounted on rear of Alvis Stalwart high mobility load carrier (Ministry of Defence)

delivery hoses terminating in automatic shut-off nozzles are stowed on a self-rewind Dean hose reel. Ten metres of 63·5 mm layflat hose are also provided. A Cross pumping off-take complete with an Avery Hardoll 63·5 mm self-sealing coupling for cross pumping to a tanker vehicle is connected to a secondary discharge outlet.

A rigid suction pipe connects at one end to the pump and at the other to bifurcated suction hoses, which connect to the two tanks via the CC41 coupling units. The suction hoses have a bore of 63·5 mm.

The whole equipment is retained on two longitudinal beams mounted on the vehicle platform. The equipment is fully bonded to the vehicle and is capable of being earthed. Two Dean bonding reels are provided each with 12·2 metres of bonding cable terminating with crocodile clip type clamps. Two fire extinguishers are mounted on the nearside and offside of the two-tier rack.

Optional equipment includes a manifold assembly box for can filling, comprising 63·5 mm Avery Hardoll hose unit type CC40, 10 metres of 38 mm bore hose to BS 3158, five-way manifold, 5 metres of 19 mm bore hose to BS 3395 (5 off) and 19 mm automatic shut-off nozzles (5 off).

The lid of the stowage box acts as holder for the cans during filling.

SPECIFICATIONS
Weight: 1798 kg
Payload: 2967 kg
Length: 3·66 m
Width: 2·44 m
Height: 1·22 m

STATUS
In production. In service with the British Army and other armed forces.

MANUFACTURER
Gloster Saro Limited, Hucclecote, Gloucestershire, England.

Demountable bulk fuel dispensing unit mounted on rear of Bedford MK (4 × 4) 4-ton truck (T J Gander)

Marston Air Portable Fuel Container (APFC)

DESCRIPTION
The Marston Air Portable Fuel Container (APFC) has a capacity of 1930 litres and has been designed to facilitate the safe movement of aviation fuels. The APFC conforms to the British Ministry of Technology Specification Number AD/S and G/1677 E and P, issue 1. Development of the system began in 1972 and first deliveries were made to the British armed forces in 1974.

The APFC can be used for carrying fuel by pressurised or non-pressurised aircraft, can be lifted and moved by helicopter, para-dropped, carried by a lorry, towed behind vehicles or manhandled on the ground. The container is sufficiently flexible to allow over 99 per cent of its capacity to be discharged and when empty the APFC can be collapsed to occupy only 12 per cent of its filled size.

The APFC is a composite seamless structure of fuel-resistant nitrile rubber reinforced by mechanically applied synthetic fibre filament windings to give maximum strength for minimum weight. The inside of the container is coated with a special barrier to protect the fuel from contamination by the rubber and ensure that the gum content is held at an acceptable level. The outside surface incorporates a nitrile/pvc rubber blend to provide maximum abrasion, weather and fuel resistance.

Standard fittings include a refuelling/defuelling valve which automatically shuts off, an air valve for inflating the container to enable it to roll when partially filled and a bleed valve to ensure maximum fuel content.

Fittings at each end of the container incorporate a bearing and swivel plate carrying lugs for attaching parachute and lifting harness, and a towing yoke. The APFC can be made suitable for carrying demineralised water with minor modification to the refuelling/defuelling valve.

There are six current marks of Marston APFCs, the Mark 3 to Mark 8. All of them use Hale Hamilton manual bleed valves apart from the Mark 7 which has a Leafield auto-bleed valve. All six marks can be towed behind a vehicle and can be lifted and underslung from a helicopter. Marks 3, 4 and 5 have a heavy duty carcass allowing them to be dropped when full by parachute or rolled from a 4-metre high platform. The Marks 6, 7 and 8 have the standard duty carcass which limits the free-fall height to 2·5 metres.

The main differences between the six marks are as follows:

Mark 3. Has a standard NATO refuel/de-fuel valve and a pressure limiting auto shut-off of 345 mb (5 lb/in²). This mark also has an aircraft-type 63·5 mm male dry-break coupling.

Mark 4. This has a standard Kamlock refuel/de-fuel valve with a 38·1 mm female dry-break coupling.

Mark 5. This mark uses a standard Avery Hardoll type CC41 refuel/de-fuel valve with an industrial type 38·1 mm male dry-break coupling.

Marston airportable container being towed by airportable Land-Rover

Marston airportable containers being used to refuel Wessex helicopters

The Marks 6 and 7 are similar to the Mark 5 apart from the fact that both use the standard-type carcass and the Mark 7 uses a Leafield auto-bleed valve.

Mark 8. This mark uses a standard Kamlock refuel/de-fuel valve with a 38·1 mm dry-break coupling.

SPECIFICATIONS
Capacity: 1930 litres
Weight:
(empty) 125 kg
(filled with fuel) 1646 kg
Width:
(overall) 1·625 m
(container) 1·549 m

Height: 1·346 m
Footprint load: 0·52 kg/cm²
Pressure:
(working) 0·345 kg/cm²
(ultimate proof) 3·103 kg/cm²
Temperature range: −26 to +70° C

STATUS
Production as required. In service with the British armed forces.

MANUFACTURER
Marston Palmer Limited, Wobaston Road, Fordhouses, Wolverhampton, West Midlands WV10 6QJ, England.

Avon Flexitanks for Fuel

DESCRIPTION
Avon Industrial Polymers produces a range of Flexitanks for static fuel storage and for use within 20 foot (6·096 metres) ISO containers. The flexible storage tanks are conventional in design and may be used with a variety of hydrocarbon fuels. The tanks for use in containers may be manufactured from neoprene, hypalon or nitrile and are supplied with a harness weighing 7·5 kg and a bulkhead set weighing 68 kg. Other details are provided below.

Flexitanks are also supplied for water storage and for details of these tanks see the entry in the *Water supplies* section.

STATUS
Production.

MANUFACTURER
Avon Industrial Polymers Limited, Bumpers Way, Bristol Road, Chippenham, Wiltshire SN14 6NF, England.

SPECIFICATIONS
Fuel storage tanks

Capacity	Dimensions (flat)	Dimensions (packed)	Weight
1000 litres	2·4 × 1·89 m	0·9 × 0·45 × 0·16 m	18 kg
2500 litres	2·4 × 3·23 m	0·9 × 0·45 × 0·23 m	29 kg
5000 litres	2·4 × 5·21 m	0·9 × 0·9 × 0·19 m	46 kg
7500 litres	3·6 × 4·78 m	1·3 × 0·9 × 0·19 m	61 kg
10 000 litres	3·6 × 6·38 m	1·3 × 0·9 × 0·22 m	80 kg
15 000 litres	4·8 × 6·88 m	1·7 × 0·9 × 0·26 m	113 kg
20 000 litres	4·8 × 8·39 m	1·7 × 0·9 × 0·31 m	134 kg
50 000 litres	6·2 × 11·75 m	1 × 1·2 × 0·7 m	296 kg
100 000 litres	7·65 × 15·24 m	1 × 1·2 × 1·05 m	481 kg

Flexitanks for use within 20 foot (6·096 m) containers

Capacity	Weight, neoprene	Weight, hypalon	Weight, nitrile
14 000 litres	85 kg	76 kg	88 kg
16 000 litres	89 kg	81 kg	92 kg
18 000 litres	95 kg	85 kg	98 kg
19 300 litres	99 kg	90 kg	102 kg
21 000 litres	102 kg	92 kg	105 kg

Dunlop Collapsible Containers

DESCRIPTION
Dunlop collapsible containers can be used to store a wide variety of liquids ranging from the usual petrol, oil and lubricants to water and chemicals for almost any purpose. The range produced is wide but all tanks are constructed from a flexible two-ply textile and polymer laminate. Both sides of the laminate are treated to ensure long life and resistance to abrasions and hard knocks. For extra strength each corner is reinforced by metal clamping bars. Joint reinforcing straps fabricated from panels of vulcanised polymer coated textiles add extra strength to the main structure and all the ports and fittings are constructed from either steel or brass. The filled tanks may be either placed on prepared surfaces or laid on earth or sand foundations. The smaller tanks may be carried on flat-bed trucks or the decks of ships. When not in use the collapsible tanks may be cleaned and rolled up for storage ready for re-use.

STATUS
In production. In service with several armed forces.

MANUFACTURER
Dunlop Limited, GRG Division, PO Box 151, Cambridge Street, Manchester M60 1PD, England.

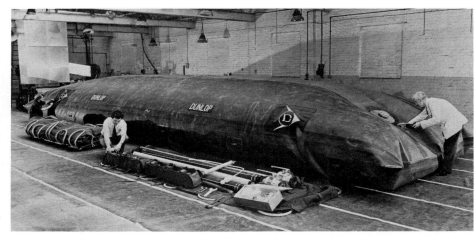

45 000-litre tank intended primarily for petroleum products undergoing final examination before delivery to British Army

SPECIFICATIONS

Tank capacity (litres)	225	1125	2250	4500	9000	11 250	22 500	45 000	90 000	135 000	225 000
Length	2·06 m	1·52 m	2·59 m	4·72 m	4·88 m	5·49 m	9·76 m	10·21 m	11·58 m	17·15 m	18·59 m
Width	0·69 m	2·06 m	2·06 m	2·06 m	3·43 m	3·43 m	3·43 m	4·8 m	7·45 m	8·92 m	11·66 m
Height (filled)	0·38 m	0·79 m	0·79 m	0·79 m	0·91 m	0·91 m	0·91 m	1·22 m	1·22 m	1·07 m	1·22 m

---

Portolite Flexible Storage Tanks

DESCRIPTION
IMI Marston Limited was the first company in Europe to develop 'pillow' tanks, which were introduced in 1958 under the name Portolite and were adopted by the British Army in 1962. Since then the tanks have been used for the transport and storage of a wide range of liquid chemicals and petroleum products. The tanks are made in a range of sizes from 220 to 136 000 litres.

Tanks of 45 000 and 136 000 litres capacity are being used extensively by the British armed forces for storing fuels. Although Portolite tanks are often employed as single storage units their prime use for military purposes is in multiples manifolded together to provide a tank farm or an airfield or shore fuelling area. The tank and its associated equipment are designed specifically for ease of packing, transport and rapid installation.

The material from which the large tanks are made consists of fuel resistant nitrile rubber reinforced with two plies of high tenacity rayon fabric. The material has a tensile strength of 1·74 kN/25 mm wide strip which is ten times the load applied to the largest tanks made.

Seams in the construction are to a patented design and consist of an interleaved joint, one edge of the material being sandwiched between each of the two plies of fabric in the material to which it is joined. All seams are fully heat cured with pressure. The external surface of the tanks has been made to achieve a very high degree of abrasion resistance. A single-ply lightweight material is also available for contents other than petroleum products in the lower capacity range.

Fitting attachments are made by bolting the components to light alloy mounting pads which are bound in

British troops rolling up Portolite tank after use

double shear to the tank material. These are fully fuel resistant joints which have endured long testing with hot fuels.

The in-service life of a tank depends on storage conditions before use and on service conditions, but with reasonable usage a minimum service life of five years can be expected. Experience has shown that this is exceeded to as much as ten years. Folded tanks can be stored for a minimum of five years, but storage life can be ensured and extended if the tanks are periodically unfolded, laid flat and refolded with folds reversed to minimise stresses in the tank fabric.

To prevent the spread of fuel in the event of damage to a tank, a containing embankment around the tank or tanks is generally considered essential. It also minimises the effect of very high winds.

Tanks of up to 22 000 litres capacity are handled by two men, for 45 000-litre tanks four men are required, and for 136 000-litre tanks eight men operating as a team are required. Folded tanks are moved on pallets. Handling consists of unfolding and laying the tank out free from creases before filling, and subsequently draining and refolding.

Large capacity tanks are provided with suction/delivery connections at each end of the tank, which includes a flame trap in the middle of the tank. After connecting suction pipes and drain lines filling can proceed at rates of up to 2000 litres per minute. During filling a calibrated dipstick is inserted in the vent pipe. Filling rates are reduced after the tank is approximately 90 per cent full. The tank can be walked on during filling and emptying.

A blunt-ended object will not penetrate the tank as the material gives with impact, but very small objects, such as small arms fire, forced into the material will puncture the tank. This type of damage should not result in the start of long tears and only minor leakage will occur. Emergency repairs for this type of damage can be made with temporary repair plugs.

STATUS
Production as required. In service with the British armed forces.

MANUFACTURER
Marston Palmer Limited, Wobaston Road, Fordhouses, Wolverhampton, West Midlands WV10 6QJ, England.

SPECIFICATIONS

Capacity (litres)	22 730	34 095	45 460	68 190	90 920	113 650	136 380
(gallons)	5000	7500	10 000	15 000	20 000	25 000	30 000
Weight (empty)	140 kg	206 kg	250 kg	360 kg	460 kg	460 kg	565 kg
Length (empty)	8·22 m	12·115 m	12·115 m	12·725 m	13·51 m	12·19 m	13·945 m
(full)	7·725 m	11·66 m	11·66 m	12·27 m	13·055 m	11·58 m	13·41 m
(folded/rolled)	2·135 m	2·135 m	2·44 m	2·59 m	4·03 m	4·03 m	4·03 m
Width (empty)	3·81 m	3·81 m	4·445 m	5·055 m	6·18 m	7·305 m	7·305 m
(full)	3·43 m	3·43 m	4·013 m	4·575 m	5·715 m	6·705 m	6·705 m
(folded/rolled)	0·38 m	0·45 m	0·5 m	0·72 m	0·8 m	0·72 m	0·8 m
Height (full)	1·065 m	1·065 m	1·22 m	1·525 m	1·525 m	1·83 m	1·83 m
(folded/rolled)	0·3 m	0·33 m	0·46 m	0·56 m	0·6 m	0·56 m	0·6 m
No of handing straps	10	10	12	12	16	20	24
Material	MM564	MM564	MM564	MM487	MM487	MM487	MM487

Two 45 000-litre Portolite tanks interconnected within retaining wall of sandbags with pumps, filters and ancillary equipment

Portolite tanks used as tank farm

UNITED STATES OF AMERICA

Uniroyal Sealdrums

DESCRIPTION
Uniroyal Sealdrums are portable, collapsible rubber containers for storing and transporting POL products, water, liquid chemicals and other fluids. They are circular drums with metal 'hubs' with the bulk of the container being constructed of elastomeric-coated rayon cord. The outer cover is neoprene with the inner lining being a nitrile material. This casing is puncture-resistant and can withstand a minimum of three successive free-fall drops from a height of 3·8 metres. Once filled the Sealdrums are non-vented and hermatically sealed. They have extremely low permeability. When empty Sealdrums collapse to about 15 per cent of their filled size.

Filled 1892·5-litre (500-gallon) Sealdrum

Collapsed 1892·5-litre (500-gallon) Sealdrum

There is a Uniroyal range of similar containers known as Sealdbins which are used for the storing and carrying of dry materials.

STATUS
Production. In service with the US Army.

MANUFACTURER
Uniroyal Inc, Engineered Systems, Mishawaka, Indiana 46544, USA.

SPECIFICATIONS

Capacity (gallons)	55	250	375	500	515
(litres)	208·2	946·25	1419·4	1892·5	1949·3
Length	0·876 m	1·524 m	1·829 m	1·575 m	2·032 m
Diameter	0·597 m	1·016 m	1·117 m	1·349 m	1·168 m
Weight (empty)	22·68 kg	113·4 kg	56·7 kg	129·3 kg	129·3 kg

Boeing-Vertol CH-47D Chinook carrying six fuel-filled 1892·5-litre (500-gallon) Sealdrums

Uniroyal Sealdtanks

DESCRIPTION
Uniroyal Sealdtanks have been in production and use for over 25 years. They are long, bag-type containers that can be used to convert ordinary cargo or closed-body trucks into fuel or other liquid containers by simply unrolling the container in the back of the truck, lashing it down, and filling the container through a valve at one end. When emptied the container can be rolled up onto a special carrying drum by hand. Sealdtanks are heavy duty rubber containers and are produced in two main widths, 2·134 metres (7 foot) and 2·235 metres (7 foot 4 inches). They can be produced in a range of lengths from 4·877 metres (16 feet) up to 12·19 metres (40 feet).

STATUS
Production.

MANUFACTURER
Uniroyal Inc, Engineered Systems, Mishawaka, Indiana 46544, USA.

SPECIFICATIONS

Length (feet)	Length (metres)	Capacity 2·134 m (litres)	Capacity 2·235 m (litres)
16	4·877	5677·5	6302
17	5·18	6094	6737
18	5·486	6491	7172·6
19	5·791	6888·7	7607·9
20	6·096	7286	8043
21	6·4	7683·5	8478·4
22	6·7	8081	8913·7
23	7·01	8478·4	9349
24	7·315	8894·75	9784·2
25	7·62	9311·1	10 257·3
26	7·925	9746·4	10 730·5
27	8·23	10 181·7	11 203·6
28	8·534	10 617	11 676·7
29	8·839	11 052	12 150
30	9·144	11 487·5	12 623
31	9·45	11 941·7	13 115
32	9·75	12 395·9	13 607
33	10·06	12 831·1	14 080·2
34	10·363	13 285·4	14 572·25
35	10·67	13 758·5	15 083·2
36	10·973	14 250·5	15 613·1
37	11·278	14 761·5	16 162
38	11·58	15 291·4	16 728·7
39	11·887	15 821·3	17 297·5
40	12·192	16 351·2	not made

Lashing down Uniroyal Sealdtank

Uniroyal Sealdtank in box-body semi-trailer

Uniroyal Static Storage Tanks

DESCRIPTION
Uniroyal produces a wide range of static storage tanks to store an equally wide range of liquids, including fuel and water (for details of the water tanks see entry in *Water supply* section). The tanks intended for fuel use are made from tough polymer-coated nylon fabric. Chafing patches at all fitting and hardware locations provide double-wall thickness and protection. Handles are moulded onto each tank to assist positioning. All the tanks are free-standing. When not in use the tanks can be stored and carried in wooden crates.

STATUS
Production.

MANUFACTURER
Uniroyal Inc, Engineered Systems, Mishawaka, Indiana 46544, USA.

SPECIFICATIONS

Capacity (gallons)	Capacity (litres)	Approximate dimensions filled		
		Width (metres)	Length (metres)	Height (metres)
250	946·3	1·88	1·88	0·305
500	1892·5	1·753	2·743	0·457
900	3406·5	2·388	2·794	0·61
1000	3785	2·388	3·073	0·61
1200	4542	3·073	2·743	0·66
1500	5677·5	2·946	3·023	0·762
2000	7570	3·353	3·353	0·813
2500	9462·5	3·581	3·734	0·813
3000	11 355	3·581	4·267	0·914
3500	13 247·5	3·581	4·724	0·914
5000	18 925	4·47	4·623	1·118
6000	22 710	4·775	4·878	1·219
10 000	37 850	6·096	6·096	1·219
15 000	56 775	7·468	7·315	1·219
20 000	75 700	6·7	8·23	1·727
25 000	94 625	6·7	10·363	1·727
50 000	189 250	6·7	19·2	1·727
100 000	378 500	18·136	18·212	1·219

Typical Uniroyal static storage tank

Forward Area Refuelling Equipment (FARE)

DESCRIPTION
The FARE is a lightweight, air transportable refuelling system intended for refuelling helicopters in forward area combat operations. As a secondary function FARE provides a means for safe rapid refuelling of all US Army aircraft ground vehicles and other equipment. FARE has been type classified as Standard A and will replace the Pumping Assembly, Flammable Liquid, Bulk Transfer, and Pump Centrifugal, Gas Driven, Base Mounted, 38 mm, 378·5 litres per minute (100 GPM).

The FARE includes a petrol engine driven centrifugal pump with a rated capacity of 378·5 litres per minute at 30·48 metres total dynamic head; a lightweight military design filter-separator with a rated capacity of 378·5 litres per minute; two closed-circuit refuelling nozzles with adapters for conventional gravity fuelling; 60·96 metres of lightweight discharge hose with 50·8 mm nominal inside diameter; 18·28 metres of suction hose with 50·8 mm nominal inside diameter; and miscellaneous fittings, valves and accessories.

The FARE is capable of dispensing fuel through two nozzles simultaneously at flow rates of up to 189·25 litres per minute through each nozzle. The maximum flow rate possible when dispensing fuel through a single nozzle is approximately 302·8 litres per minute.

Any available bulk fuel storage tank may be used to supply fuel to the FARE and it is anticipated that the standard 1892·5-litre (500-US gallon) collapsible drum will be the primary source of bulk fuel supply.

FARE being used in conjunction with standard 1892·5-litre collapsible drums to refuel Bell UH-1 Iroquois helicopter (US Army)

STATUS
In service with the US Army.

DEVELOPING AGENCY
US Army Mobility Equipment Research and Development Command, Fort Belvoir, Virginia 22060, USA.

Arctic Fuels Dispensing Equipment (AFDE)

DESCRIPTION
Arctic weather can have many severe effects on orthodox fuelling systems, from making collapsible fuel storage tanks brittle and split, to causing fuels to freeze or become slow to pump due to frozen waxes and other solids in suspension. To overcome these problems the US Army Mobility Equipment Research and Development Command (MERADCOM) began development work during 1979 on a new system of Arctic Fuels Dispensing Equipment (AFDE). If the new programme involving collapsible fuel tanks and fuel lines proves feasible after testing it is intended that an entirely new generation of fuel equipment will be produced which will be simple, lightweight, air transportable and designed for use in climatic categories 7 and 8 (between +65 and −65°F). The new equipment is expected to make extensive use of materials based on low-temperature elastomers such as polyfluorophosphazene. The pumping equipment will use gas turbine engines for easy starting and power for pumping. Two types of basic installation are envisaged: an AFDE Supply Point with collapsible tanks to store up to 120 000 gallons of fuel and a pumping capability of 600 gallons per minute and a Forward Area Refuelling Equipment made up of 500-gallon collapsible tanks and a fuel pumping capability of 200 gallons per minute.

STATUS
Development.

DEVELOPING AGENCY
US Army Mobility Equipment Research and Development Command, Fort Belvoir, Virginia 22060, USA.

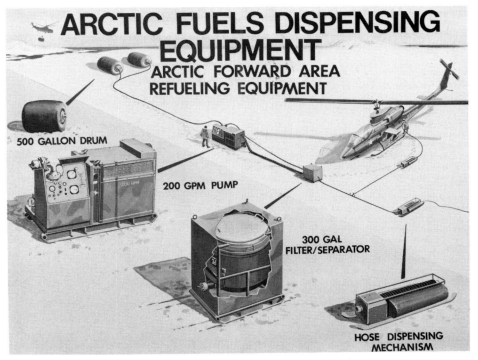

Artist's impression of arctic fuels dispensing equipment in use (US Army)

378·5/946·25 Litre Per Minute Fuelling Unit

DESCRIPTION

This unit forms the basis for a number of 'building block' systems configured according to the particular need. The equipment was adopted by the United States forces in 1966 and improved versions have since been ordered by other countries. Typical roles are:

Helicopter refuelling: three units form a system for 'hot fuelling' six helicopters simultaneously at 189 litres per minute each, for a total of 1135 litres per minute. This system includes a 7570-litre bladder-type fuel storage tank equipped with a sling set for helicopter airlift to the refuelling site.

Armour refuelling: for armour refuelling, four units in the system provide fuelling service for up to eight armoured vehicles simultaneously at 189 litres per minute each.

In this case fuel storage capacity is provided by a 37 850-litre bladder type tank.

Each pumping module contains filtration and water separation equipment, fuel/defuel manifold, a fire extinguisher and static discharge equipment. The centrifugal pump is driven by a single-cylinder air-cooled petrol engine including electric start and generator system. Filtration is in three stages, the final stage reducing particle size to 1·5 microns. A coalescer type water separator is included. The fuel manifold is arranged to deliver clean filtered fuel at 378·5 litres per minute or bulk unfiltered fuel at 946 litres per minute. By operating the appropriate manifold valves, defuelling can be accomplished without disconnecting hoses.

Each hose reel trailer has independent dry reels on which all necessary hoses are stored. All modules are mounted on wheels equipped with high flotation tyres to provide easy movement over soft or rough terrain. If required the wheels, axles and towbars can be removed

for skid mounting. Each module is equipped with lifting eyes for sling lift by helicopter, and a towbar for single or tandem towing by a vehicle. The sling set, which consists of a sling, scuff shield, and tank support strap, is used to carry the 7570-litre tank externally suspended from the helicopter cargo hook.

Each unit includes suction and delivery hoses, and 'hot fuelling', single point or gravity fuelling nozzles as required, with the necessary couplings and adapters.

STATUS

In production. In service with the United States forces and other forces.

MANUFACTURER

Air Logistics Corporation, 3600 E Foothill Blvd, Pasadena, California, USA.

British agent: Air-Log Limited, North Lane, Aldershot, Hampshire, England.

Tanker Mooring System, Multi-leg, Tactical

DEVELOPMENT

In June 1982 the US Army Mobility Equipment Research and Development Command (MERADCOM) exercised a $3·1 million option on an existing contract with Ocean Search Inc, for the purchase of two additional Military Tanker Mooring Systems. These systems are now standard items in the US Army inventory.

DESCRIPTION

The Tanker Mooring System is an air-portable system capable of handling ships as large as 25 000 deadweight tons. It is designed to unload bulk liquid fuel over undeveloped beaches from mooring points as far as 1524 metres off shore. The system is transported in a series of crates and includes buoys, boat launching and recovery equipment, a motor surf boat, underwater sur-

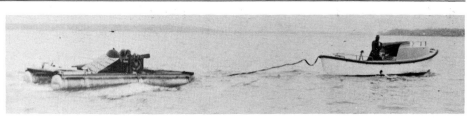

Catamaran carrying explosively embedded anchor of Tank Mooring System being towed into position

vey equipment and tanker unloading equipment. The mooring device is carried into position by a towed catamaran. Once in place the floating component is anchored in place by an explosively embedded anchor. Diving equipment is supplied in the system for the subsequent assembly of the various components. Once completed the system can carry the bulk fuel ashore where it is stored in tanks or collapsible containers

ready for distribution. A typical shore storage system is the subject of current development and is known as the Bulk Fuel Tank Assembly (BFTA) which uses a system of multiple collapsible containers connected to a distribution and pumping system.

STATUS

In service with the US Army.

Hasty Bulk Fuel Storage Reservoir, 25 000 Barrel Capacity

DESCRIPTION

This is a new item of equipment intended to provide bulk storage facilities until permanent storage can be constructed, and is expected to replace the 10 000 and 55 000 barrel steel tanks in current use. The 25 000 barrel tank can be rapidly installed by engineer troops and other troops with construction support. The system is a revetment-supported envelope-type tank constructed of a lightweight elastomer-coated nylon fabric. It is positioned within a trapezoidal cross-sectional earthen pit prepared by excavation. Empty weight of the reservoir is approximately 2812 kg. When filled to capacity it is 56·388 metres long, 28·194 metres wide and 3·962 metres deep. Continuous re-use of the reservoir is planned during wartime to the extent of the operational life of the item. It is not intended for relocation.

STATUS

In service with the US Army.

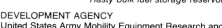

Hasty bulk fuel storage reservoir being prepared for use (US Army)

DEVELOPMENT AGENCY

United States Army Mobility Equipment Research and

Development Command, Fort Belvoir, Virginia 22060, USA.

Air Transportable Hydrant Fuelling System

DESCRIPTION

This system (Ref 113440) meets the needs of both flexible basing and the bare base concept in support of combat operations. It was originally developed in 1966 and is a standard component in the United States Air Force Grey Eagle programme.

A complete hydrant fuelling system normally consists of three identical modules, and can be air transported by C-130 aircraft. The system will fuel six aircraft simultaneously; each module is self-contained and can be used separately to fuel two aircraft.

A single module is composed of an engine/pump assembly, two 189 266-litre storage tanks, filtration and water separation equipment, and a set of suction and delivery hoses, all of which are assembled into a wheeled vehicle with a towing attachment. The undercarriage is retractable to provide vehicle stability while in use.

Air transportable hydrant fuelling module with undercarriage retracted to provide stability and storage tanks stowed on each side

Batteries and generator provide electric starting for the engine, which will operate on most fuels being pumped through the system. Flow and pressure from the pump are controlled automatically, giving 378·5 litres per minute through each hose for gravity fuelling, or 1135 litres per minute at a pressure of 3·51 kg/cm^2 through each hose for single point pressure fuelling.

The filtration and water separation equipment ensures that only pure and water-free fuel is delivered to the aircraft. Accumulated water is dumped automatically and an automatic feature can be provided to shut off fuel flow when the filter has become blocked. Valves in the fuel manifold are arranged so that fuel may be pumped back into the storage tanks where defuelling aircraft is necessary.

The storage tanks are of a lightweight flexible material, and when not in use are folded and carried on the sides of the trailer. A detachable hoist is provided for stowing the tanks.

A full set of 50·8, 76·2 and 101·6 mm suction and delivery hoses, with quick coupling fittings, provides the necessary combinations to meet any fuelling requirements. The hose set includes two gravity type fuelling nozzles and two single point pressure fuelling nozzles. When not required the hoses are stowed on top of the vehicle between the tanks.

SPECIFICATIONS
Module
Weight: 5215 kg
Length: 3·96 m
Width: 2·23 m
Height:
(in position) 2·18 m
(towing) 2·37 m

STATUS
In production. In service with the US Air Force and other countries.

Air transportable hydrant fuelling system in operation refuelling USAF F-4 Phantom aircraft

MANUFACTURER
Air Logistics Corporation, 3600 E Foothill Blvd, Pasadena, California, USA.

British agent: Air-Log Limited, North Lane, Aldershot, Hampshire, England.

Bulk Fuel Handling Unit

DESCRIPTION
The 2271 litre per minute (600 gallon per minute) Bulk Fuel Handling Unit (Ref 113755) consists of a trailer-mounted pump module designed to deliver 2271 litres per minute of non-filtered bulk fuel. The unit first entered production in 1966 with an updated model following in 1976. It may also be coupled into existing hose or metal pipeline systems to provide heavy-duty pumping capability.

The Bulk Fuel Handling System (Ref 113755-503) consists of the above pumping module plus a hose trailer with 61 metres of 152 mm diameter suction hose, 7·6 metres of 102 mm suction hose, and 61 metres of 102 mm discharge hose. Hoses are provided with quick couplings at the ends for connecting to storage tanks, pump module and to operational fuel servicing units. The pumping-module and hose trailer are equipped with identical towing attachments to permit towing the combined units by one vehicle. The engine of the unit will operate on the jet or diesel fuels being pumped.

This equipment is used in the support of fixed base and forward base fuel transfer to the smaller tanks and pumps used in direct fuel servicing of helicopters, tanks, trucks and other vehicles.

STATUS
In production. In service with undisclosed countries.

MANUFACTURER
Air Logistics Corporation, 3600 E Foothill Blvd, Pasadena, California, USA.
British agent: Air-Log Limited, North Lane, Aldershot, Hampshire, England.

Bulk fuel handling unit

Automated Pipeline System Construction Equipment

DESCRIPTION
The Automated Pipeline System Construction Equipment is a military version of existing commercial pipeline-laying equipment adapted for military use. It is intended to be used to rapidly construct high pressure fuel pipelines across country with as few construction personnel as possible.

The equipment is supplied with lengths of 101·6, 152·4 or 203 mm pipe by a tractor-towed semi-trailer. From the semi-trailer the pipes are placed into one half of a special tracked vehicle. From this vehicle half the pipes are lifted by a special vehicle-mounted crane into a hopper on the other half of the equipment. This hopper then automatically delivers the pipes into the pipe-joining mechanism that is situated to one side of the equipment, and from this the jointed pipe is laid onto the ground. Using this equipment it is intended that the pipes will be laid at the rate of 29 to 40 km a day. The equipment is fully self-propelled and apart from the pipe supply component, the personnel to handle the system will be a driver, a crane operator and two others.

STATUS
Development.

Pipeline Outfit, Petroleum (POP)

DESCRIPTION
Intended to be air-transportable, the Pipeline Outfit, Petroleum, is a simple system for laying fuel-carrying pipelines in undeveloped areas or where existing distribution methods are unusable. The system is intended to carry fuel from shore bases to forward areas. It consists of pre-packed lengths of pipe and handling equipment that can be used with a minimum of training. The main carrying vehicles will be wheeled tractors each with a side-mounted A-frame jib. The jibs will place the lengths of pipeline roughly in position and then lift them to join the previous pipe section. A following tractor carrying a pipe-joining machine will ensure that the subsequent pipe length fit is secure and leak-free. Once the join has been made the two tractors then progress to the next length.

The pipes involved will have diameters of 152·4 mm and 203 mm. The outfit is intended to deploy the pipes at the rate of 29 km a day. Once layed the pipeline system will have a capacity of 27 000 to 30 000 barrels per 20-hour day.

STATUS
Development.

Hydraulic pipe-joining press used with Pipeline Outfit, Petroleum with carrying wheeled tractor on left

Petroleum Hoseline System

DESCRIPTION
This new system is under development by the US Army Mobility Equipment Research and Development Command (MERADCOM) at Fort Belvoir, Virginia. The system is designed to deploy or recover up to 32 kilometres of 152·4-mm (6-inch) diameter petroleum hoseline a day. This hoseline has a capacity of 2271 litres a minute. Once in service the system will be used to supplement existing 102-mm diameter hoseline systems and will be deployed in corps and divisional rear areas where there is a need to move large quantities of bulk fuel where other methods are not tactically feasible.

The system consists of a skid-mounted reel assembly capable of cross-country operation from a standard 5-ton truck, the hoseline in 152·4 metre sections, and a trailer-mounted diesel engine driven pump assembly rated at 2271 litres a minute. The reel assembly has multiple reels of hose stacked one over another. Four hose sections are stored flat in each layer and are power deployed or retrieved. When retrieved the hose sections are emptied of fuel. The prime power for driving the hydraulics and air compressor comes from an on-board diesel engine. Three separate control systems are used. A guide roll system ensures hose orientation and stability and provides a signal for the reeling operation with relation to the vehicle speed.

STATUS
Prototypes to be ordered during 1984.

DEVELOPING AGENCY
United States Army Mobility Equipment Research and Development Command, Fort Belvoir, Virginia 22060, USA.

Development form of Petroleum Hoseline System

Tank, Liquid Storage, Bolted Steel

DESCRIPTION
There are four tank sizes in the Tank, Liquid Storage, Bolted Steel range. The smallest has a capacity of 21 000 gallons (79 485 litres) with the others having capacities of 42 000 gallons (158 970 litres), 126 000 gallons (476 910 litres) and 420 000 gallons (1 589 700 litres). All the four sizes are intended to be transported to their sites (by air if required) in crates containing pre-formed steel plates, bolts, gaskets, valves, gauges and various assembly items. On site they can be constructed rapidly into circular steel tanks, fully enclosed

and with a central inspection vent cover. An upper surface ladder is provided. Although intended to be for temporary use only they may be used as permanent structures if needed. They can be used for water storage as well as fuel storage.

STATUS
In service with the US Army. 21 000 gallon (97), 42 000 gallon (48), 126 000 gallon (48), 420 000 gallon (53).

SPECIFICATIONS

Capacity (gallons)	21 000	42 000	126 000	420 000
(litres)	79 485	158 970	476 910	1 589 700
Weight (empty)	4677 kg	8085 kg	13 442 kg	35 391 kg
Inside diameter	6·566 m	9·06 m	9·06 m	16·758 m
Height	2·44 m	2·438 m	7·363 m	7·379 m

WATER SUPPLIES

FRANCE

PRONAL Small Capacity Water Storage Tanks

DESCRIPTION
These small capacity tanks are manufactured from polyester fabric coated with non-toxic PVC and are resistant to ultra-violet radiation and all climatic conditions. They are produced in capacities from 20 to 500 litres and the 20 litre size is fitted with carrying handles for use when full. The larger sizes are used laid flat upon the ground. All are fitted with a 19 mm filling and emptying hose and a symmetrical coupling and plug. When not in use they can be rolled up for storage or carrying.

STATUS
Production. The 20-litre tanks are in service with the Swiss Army.

SPECIFICATIONS

Capacity	Length (empty)	Width (empty)	Height (full)	Weight (empty)	Volume (folded)
20 litres	0·62 m	0·4 m	0·14 m	1·2 kg	5 dm³
50 litres	0·75 m	0·62 m	0·17 m	1·65 kg	6·5 dm³
100 litres	1·24 m	0·6 m	0·22 m	2·45 kg	10 dm³
200 litres	1·24 m	0·95 m	0·26 m	3·4 kg	12·5 dm³
500 litres	1·7 m	1·24 m	0·39 m	5·5 kg	22 dm³

MANUFACTURER
PRONAL, 139 rue des Arts. BP 25, 59051 Roubaix Cedex 1, France.

PRONAL Flexible Open Vat Water Storage Tanks

DESCRIPTION
These open vat tanks are used for the large scale storage of water and other liquids such as decontamination fluids. They have the advantage over conventional storage tanks in that the tank may be filled and emptied very quickly and more than one user point may be employed at any one time. The tanks are placed on circular ground sheets and are filled from an over stand pipe or hose which is usually a 51-mm diameter component. The sides of the tank rise with the volume contained and if required a tarpaulin may be used to cover the contents. They are constructed of polyester fabric coated with PVC.

SPECIFICATIONS

Capacity	Diameter	Height	Weight	Volume (folded)
5000 litres	3 m	1 m	40 kg	0·45 m³
10 000 litres	4·4 m	1 m	62 kg	0·7 m³

STATUS
Production.

MANUFACTURER
PRONAL, 139 rue des Arts, BP 25, 59051 Roubaix Cedex 1, France.

PRONAL Flexible Water Storage Tanks

DESCRIPTION
PRONAL produces a wide range of flexible water storage tanks to suit specific customer requirements so examples given in the Specifications table should be regarded as typical rather than applicable to individual cases. The material used for the tanks is a PVC-coated polyester fabric with a weight of 1·1 kg per square metre. The usual fittings are 51 mm filling/discharging valves and caps which can be connected by adaptors to 51 or 76 mm hoses.

SPECIFICATIONS

Capacity	Length (empty)	Width (empty)	Height (full)	Weight (empty)	Volume (folded)
1000 litres	2·46 m	1·35 m	0·6 m	19 kg	0·09 m³
2000 litres	2·46 m	2 m	0·9 m	23 kg	0·11 m³
3000 litres	2·64 m	2·46 m	1·1 m	27 kg	0·13 m³
4000 litres	3·21 m	2·46 m	1·1 m	31 kg	0·15 m³
5000 litres	3·69 m	2·5 m	1·1 m	34 kg	0·17 m³
10 000 litres	4·12 m	3·69 m	1·1 m	50 kg	0·24 m³
15 000 litres	4·92 m	4·25 m	1·1 m	64 kg	0·31 m³
20 000 litres	5·37 m	4·92 m	1·1 m	79 kg	0·38 m³
25 000 litres	6·5 m	4·92 m	1·1 m	93 kg	0·45 m³
30 000 litres	7·62 m	4·92 m	1·1 m	107 kg	0·52 m³
35 000 litres	8·74 m	4·92 m	1·1 m	122 kg	0·59 m³

STATUS
Production. In service with the French armed forces and some other nations.

MANUFACTURER
PRONAL, 139 rue des Arts, BP 25, 59051 Roubaix Cedex 1, France.

GERMANY, DEMOCRATIC REPUBLIC

East German Water Filtering Units

DESCRIPTION
The East German armed forces use three basic forms of water filtering equipment, usually in conjunction with the MSchaK-15 well drilling equipment. The smallest unit is the WFS 1 (Wasserfilterstation 1) which is manportable. The WFS 2 is a trailer-mounted unit, while the WFS 3 is a much larger unit contained in a 6-metre long trailer towed by a Tatra 148. The two larger units contain not only water filtering and purification equipment but water sampling and analysis systems. Power for the WFS 3 is taken from a generator mounted on the truck body. The WSF 1 and 2 require external power sources. Older versions of the WFS 3 known as the WFS 3/72 may remain in service. The WSF 3/72 used an ISO 1C container body to house the filtering system in two separate compartments, one of which contained an electrical generator.

STATUS
Production.

MANUFACTURER
State factories.

ISRAEL

Aquaport Desalination Plants

DESCRIPTION
Produced in ten models with differing capacities, the Aquaport range of desalination plants can convert sea water or polluted water from inland waterways into pure distilled drinking water or water for electronic and medical purposes. The system is designed to be highly mobile and all the types of plant are carried on trailers. Each equipment is automatic and self-contained and only push-button starting is needed, but an external electrical generator is required. The whole operation takes place at low temperatures of from 30 to 50°C, and the energy requirements are from 17 to 19 kWh for every 1000 litres of water produced – in fuel terms this works out to a water-to-fuel ratio of 250:1. The standard models are produced in output capacities of 75, 100, 150, 200, 250, 300, 350, 400, 450 and 500 cubic metres per 24 hours.

STATUS
In production.

MANUFACTURER
IDE – Israel Desalination Engineering (Zarchin Process) Limited, POB 18041, Tel-Aviv, Israel.

SOUTH AFRICA

900-litre Water Tank Trailer

DESCRIPTION
Specially developed and produced to meet the stringent conditions of the South African bush this water tank trailer uses a steel frame with the frame and tank covered by a glass fibre body which acts as a measure of heat insulation and is also moulded to avoid 'snagging' on shrubs and vegetation. The 900-litre tank is filled through a top-mounted manhole and two 50 mm screw-type drain cocks are fitted in the bottom of the tank. The tank also has five 20 mm press-type taps, two at the front and three at the rear. A telescopic stabilising leg is provided under the towing eye and a spare tyre is carried in front of the tank. Over-run type brakes are fitted.

SPECIFICATIONS
Water capacity: 900 litres
Weight:
(full) 1360 kg
(empty) 450 kg
Length:
(with drawbar) 2·6 m
Height: 1·6 m
Towing eye height: 1·08 m
Track: 1·93 m
Tyres: 7.50 × 16 × 8 ply

STATUS
Production. In service with the South African Defence Forces.

MANUFACTURER
Enquiries to Armscor, Private Bag X337, Pretoria 0001, South Africa.

900-litre water tank trailer

UNION OF SOVIET SOCIALIST REPUBLICS

Mobile Water Desalination Plant OPS and POU

DESCRIPTION
These mobile water desalination plants have been produced mainly for use in desert regions and both are mounted on truck chassis. The smallest unit is the POU which is mounted on a ZIL-157 (6 × 6) truck chassis and has an output capacity of 320 litres an hour. The unit is powered by a petrol engine. The OPS has a capacity of approximately 2000 litres an hour and is carried on a KrAZ-214 (6 × 6) truck chassis. The process used with the OPS not only distills the water but also purifies it biologically. Power for the OPS is provided by a towed generator.

STATUS
Probably no longer in production. In service with the Soviet armed forces.

MANUFACTURER
Soviet state arsenals and factories.

Mobile water desalination plant OPS

LBU-200 Mobile Well Drilling Equipment

DESCRIPTION
The significance of a supply of fresh, uncontaminated water is recognised by the Soviet Army, and the LBU-200 equipment is capable of drilling for water, testing its purity and providing limited storage capacity. The equipment is mounted on three KrAZ-255B (6 × 6) trucks and three 2-PN-6M trailers. One truck is fitted with the drilling rig, while a second carries the LGR-3 laboratory. The third truck, fitted with a hydraulic loading crane, carries hose, purification equipment and other ancillaries. Components of RBD-5000 water tanks are carried on the trailers.

STATUS
Production probably complete. In service with the Soviet armed forces.

MANUFACTURER
Soviet state factories.

UNITED KINGDOM

Acro-Kool Nomad Water Filter and Cooling Trailer

DESCRIPTION
The Acro-Kool Nomad Mark III is a mobile water filter and cooling unit carried on a single-axle trailer. The filters used are Acro-Kool BF or BF3 charcoal filters activated with Super Sterasyl Candle which can remove bacteria from most water supplies. The water is passed through the filter system by an internal pump driven from the internal petrol engine which also drives the cooling unit. The petrol engine is a single-cylinder, air-cooled four stroke engine that also drives a generator for battery charging. Fuel for the engine comes from a nominal 24·6-litre tank. The main water tank has a 378·5-litre capacity and the filter/cooling system can supply 94·6 litres of treated water an hour. The fuel tank will provide the engine with an average non-stop running time of 15 hours.

The trailer unit has two jacks at the rear and a jockey wheel near the towing point. The simple control panel is on the right-hand side facing forward and at the rear are four outlet taps, three for glass-filling and one for filling larger containers. Spare filters are carried in a dust-proof box inside the unit housing.

SPECIFICATIONS (shipping dimensions)
Weight: 747 kg
Length: 2·921 m
Width: 1·7272 m
Height: 1·27 m

STATUS
Production.

MANUFACTURER
Crawley (Refrigeration) Limited, Coronation Works, Ashdon Road, Saffron Walden, Essex CB10 2NG, England.

Acro-Kool Nomad water filter and cooling trailer

Airborne Inflatable Water Tanks

DESCRIPTION
The Airborne inflatable water tanks are widely used for both civil and military applications where the ability to store water or set up an open water relay is required at short notice. The tanks are man-portable and each is packed in a valise.

The tank is deployed as follows: the tank is removed from the valise and laid on a flat surface; the ring capping the top of the tank wall, which is formed from a 350 mm diameter tube, is inflated, and floats on the water as the tank is filled supporting the wall. A webbing strap and buckle keep the filling hose in position while the tank is being filled. The tank has a cover supported on an inflatable float, which protects the contents from contamination and growth of algae. A water outlet connection is provided at the base of the wall. The tank takes a maximum of three minutes to inflate and can be used on inclines of up to 1 in 7.

SPECIFICATIONS

Capacity	22 730 litres	11 365 litres	1820 litres
Weight	77·18 kg	48·5 kg	27 kg
Dimension filled (top)	5·02 m	3 m	1·5 m
(base)	5·58 m	3·6 m	1·8 m
(height)	1·4 m	1·4 m	1·1 m
Dimensions packed	1·68 × 0·76 × 0·46 m	1 × 0·6 × 0·45 m	0·9 × 0·5 × 0·3 m

Other sizes to a maximum capacity of 113 650 litres are available to special order.

STATUS
Production. In service with the British Army.

MANUFACTURER
Airborne Industries Limited, Arterial Road, Leigh-on-Sea, Essex SS9 4EF, England.

Filled Airborne inflatable water tank

Airborne inflatable water tank being filled

Stellar NBC Decontamination Water Purification Equipment

DESCRIPTION
Stella-Meta Filters – Portals Water Treatment Limited makes equipment for precoat filtration, reverse osmosis, carbon filtration, ion exchange, chlorination and chemical dosing to remove turbid, ionic, organic, chemical, nuclear and bacterial contaminants from water supplies. Three of the available equipment sets (AB3/NBC1, 8M3/NBC4 and FSD/NBC3) have outputs of purified water from 4500 to 13 000 litres per hour from fresh water, or from 1250 to 4100 litres per hour from NBC-contaminated fresh water. A fourth unit, the NBC2/Mini-Back-Pack, can produce batches of 100 litres of purified water from fresh NBC-contaminated sources. The units are available either as 'integral' self-contained, or 'add-on' units, compatible with non-NBC Stellar water purification sets. The company has been assessed by the Ministry of Defence to quality assurance DEF STAN 05-21.

The company has produced a demonstration/pilot equipment integral water treatment unit known as the NBC5. This equipment can remove NBC contaminants from any water supply source by combining several existing Stellar components.

STATUS
Production.

MANUFACTURER
Stella-Meta Filters – Portals Water Treatment Limited, Laverstoke Mill, Whitchurch, Hampshire RG28 7NR, England.

Stella-Meta Filters – Portals Water Treatment AB3/NBC1 water purification equipment

NBC5 integral water treatment unit developed by Stella-Meta Filters for use in an NBC environment

Stellar Water Carriage Pack

DESCRIPTION

The water carriage pack has been developed by the British Ministry of Defence and replaces the older tanker unit that comprised a galvanised 700-litre storage and a Stellar filter.

The new Stellar Water Carriage Pack (WCP) has the advantage that its plastic storage tank may be transported by virtually any type of vehicle such as a two-wheeled trailer or a flatbed truck. It is also considerably cheaper than the custom-built galvanised tanker with the filter unit mounted on a trailer.

Each WCP consists of a 700-litre storage tank, filter unit, pumping set and ancillary equipment for the production of water from fresh, raw sources. The puri-

fication section comprises twin plastic Stelmet SM½ cartridge filters, a semi-rotary hand or electrically-driven pump, hoses and spares. The storage tank is manufactured from low density polythene and is supplied with attachment frame and straps, delivery hose and dispensing manifold. When empty it can be lifted by two men.

STATUS
Production.

MANUFACTURER
Stella-Meta Filters – Portals Water Treatment Limited, Laverstoke Mill, Whitchurch, Hampshire RG28 7NR, England.

Stellar water carriage pack components

Stellar water carriage pack

Stellar Mobile Water Purification Equipment

DESCRIPTION

Stellar purification sets provide clean and disinfected water from almost all water sources. The use of a diatomaceous earth precoat filter for removing suspended solids, bacteria and organisms ensures that the treated water is safe to drink. This is particularly true in respect of tropical raw water supplies which may contain chlorine-resistant organisms. Disinfection can be supplemented by injecting a small dose of chlorine in either electrolytic or gaseous form. The standard Stellar range covers six main sets: Type AB1/A, transportable

with a capacity of 2·7 cubic metres an hour, the airportable Type AB3 with a capacity of 4·5 cubic metres an hour, the transportable Type ST1 with a capacity of 6·75 cubic metres an hour, the transportable Type 8M3/A with a capacity of 8 cubic metres an hour and the trailer-mounted Type 6D and 5B with a capacity of 13·5 cubic metres an hour.

Each set comprises similar basic equipment: Stellar pressure precoat filter, Stellar Filtraider unit, Clorocel electrolytic sterilising unit, or gas chlorinator, generator to supply current to the steriliser (Clorocel type unit only), positive or centrifugal pump and a diesel or petrol engine to drive the pump and generator. The individual items can be used separately when required, for exam-

ple a filter can be connected directly to an existing water main, or the pump can be used to deliver water without the addition of chlorine. Where the raw water supply is exceptionally turbid, additional clarification before filtration can be provided. Where the supply is saline a reverse osmosis unit can be supplied.

Type AB3 airportable set
This has been developed in conjunction with the British Ministry of Defence as a lightweight airportable equipment with a maximum water-treatment capacity of 4·5 cubic metres an hour. It is capable of being dropped by parachute, and can be carried in a two-wheeled trailer.

Stellar AB3 airportable water purification equipment

Stellar 8M3/A transportable water purification set

SPECIFICATIONS
Max rated capacity: 4·5 m³/h
Size:
(filter unit) 0·94 × 0·61 × 0·47 m
(steriliser/filtraider unit) 0·57 × 0·47 × 0·66 m
(engine/pump/generator unit) 1·065 × 0·635 × 0·66 m
Weight:
(filter unit) 81 kg
(steriliser/filtraider unit) 64 kg
(engine/pump/generator unit) 146 kg

Type 8M3/A and AB1/A transportable sets
The type 8M3/A set has a similar basic design to the type AB3 but has a capacity of up to 8 cubic metres an hour. It is designed to be transported by truck or trailer but cannot be dropped by parachute. The type AB1/A is a smaller set with a rated capacity of 2·7 cubic metres an hour.

SPECIFICATIONS (8M3/A)
Max rated capacity: 8 m³/h
Size:
(filter/filtraider unit) 1·12 ×0·76 × 0·58 m
(steriliser unit) 0·445 × 0·47 × 0·66 m
(engine/pump/generator unit): 1·065 × 0·635 × 0·66 m

Weight:
(filter/filtraider unit) 78 kg
(steriliser unit) 45 kg
(engine/pump/generator unit) 146 kg

Type ST1 transportable set
This set comprises a diesel engine and pump unit, Stellar pressure precoat filter and Filtraider unit, and chlorinator unit. Each unit is mounted in a tubular frame for ease of handling and is supplied complete with suction and delivery hose assemblies. The main difference between this and other Stellar sets is that a gas chlorinator is incorporated instead of a Clorocel unit.

SPECIFICATIONS
Max rated capacity: 9 m³/h
Size:
(filter/filtraider unit) 1·12 × 0·76 × 0·58 m
(steriliser unit) 0·508 × 0·457 × 0·838 m
(engine/pump unit) 0·87 × 0·4 × 0·66 m
Weight:
(filter/filtraider unit) 78 kg
(steriliser unit) 51 kg
(engine/pump unit) 98 kg

Type 6D and 5B trailer-mounted sets
The type 6D trailer-mounted set has been developed specifically to meet the requirements of the British

armed forces. The unit is completely self-contained and is capable of delivering up to 13·5 cubic metres of water an hour. All the basic units are mounted within a four-wheel trailer chassis while the stores and accessories are kept in built-in lockers. The type 5B is similar to the type 6D but is constructed to a less stringent specification, and delivers the same amount of water.

SPECIFICATIONS (Type 6D)
Max rated capacity: 13·5 m³/h
Size:
(trailer, ready for towing) 7·07 × 2·41 × 2·78 m
Weight: (inclusive of all accessories and stores) 3860 kg

STATUS
Production. In service with many armed forces including Argentina, Australia, Canada, Ecuador, Finland, Ghana, India, Iran, Iraq, Jordan, Libya, Malawi, Malaysia, the Netherlands, New Zealand, Nigeria, Oman, Pakistan, Singapore, Sudan, Tanzania, United Arab Emirates and Zambia.

MANUFACTURER
Stella-Meta Filters – Portals Water Treatment Limited, Laverstoke Mill, Whitchurch, Hampshire RG28 7NR, England.

Stellar Type 10 Trailer-mounted Water Purification Equipment

DESCRIPTION
Stella-Meta Filters – Portals Water Treatment Limited's trailer-mounted water purification equipment Type 10 has a nominal rated capacity of 27 cubic metres of drinking water an hour, and is completely self-contained with its own diesel engine/pump/alternator set. The Type 10 comprises a filter powder pre-treatment plant, Clorocel electrolytic steriliser and a Stellar pressure filter incorporating its own automatic cleaning system.

Accessories, tools and spares are stowed within the trailer and bins are provided for storing the filter powder and common salt for the preparation of electrolytic sodium hypochlorite, an efficient sterilising agent which takes immediate effect in the water, without giving an objectionable taste. The use of common salt as a basic material for the sterilising process makes the handling and storage of corrosive chemicals such as bleaching powder or gaseous chlorine unnecessary. The salt, as a solution, is converted into the sterilising agent simply and safely using electrical power from the alternator unit.

The Type 10 set is so arranged that the pump can be used alone, the pump and filter can be used without the steriliser, or the pump and steriliser can be used without the filter, so saving filter powder and salt where filtration and/or sterilising is unnecessary, for example, for washing water.

All the equipment is mounted on a two-wheel trailer with suitable body work and fabric top and side and end screens. The side and end screens are mounted on metal frames which can be hinged to form an awning to give protection to the operator.

STATUS
Production.

Stellar Type 10 trailer-mounted water purification equipment

MANUFACTURER
Stella-Meta Filters – Portals Water Treatment Limited, Laverstoke Mill, Whitchurch, Hampshire RG28 7NR, England.

SPECIFICATIONS
Weight: 2550 kg
Length: 4·09 m
Width: 1·88 m
Height: 2·25 m

Portals Water Treatment Mobile Water Purification Equipment

DEVELOPMENT

The FSD trailer has been further refined by Portals Water Treatment to cope with nuclear, biological and chemical (NBC) contaminant removal. The treatment sequence, designed to British Ministry of Defence specifications, includes carbon filtration, specialised reverse osmosis capable of high nerve agent rejection, and ion exchange, in addition to the standard treatment processes, for the removal of ionic, organic and bacterial contaminants.

DESCRIPTION

The FSD range, which includes modular plant with an output of 0·19 cubic metres an hour and two trailer-mounted installations with outputs of 3·25 cubic metres and 6·5 cubic metres an hour, is capable of producing drinking water to World Health Organisation standard from turbid waters with a high concentration of dissolved solids. The filtration/sterilisation section may be used separately if, after tests, the operator decides that dissolved solids reduction is unnecessary. In this case the output is 13·5 cubic metres an hour. Where the water is exceptionally turbid or contaminated with iron additional clarification or iron removal equipment can be provided. The largest capacity equipment comprises raw water pump, Stellar pressure precoat filter and Filtraider unit, chemical dosing equipment, reverse osmosis unit, sterilisation unit, diesel generator and laboratory test equipment.

SPECIFICATIONS
FSD Trailer
Weight: 11 000 kg
Length:
 (including tow bar) 9·373 m
 (of van) 7·62 m
Width: 2·438 m
Height: 3·658 m

STATUS
Production. FSD water purification trailers have been sold to at least one country in Africa.

MANUFACTURER
Portals Water Treatment Limited, Permutit House, 632/652 London Road, Isleworth, Middlesex TW7 4EZ, England.

FSD trailers and prime movers awaiting despatch from Portals Water Treatment headquarters

Reverse osmosis desalination plant and control panel plus chemical mixing tanks in FSD water purification trailer

FSD water-purification trailer showing rear-mounted diesel generating set

FSD trailer and prime mover equipped for sea water desalination and water storage

Avon Flexitanks for Water

DESCRIPTION
These Avon Flexitanks follow the same general lines as those described in the Fuel Storage and Distribution section but being intended for water storage only they are generally lighter in construction. They may be used laid directly on any ground surface and connections to and from the tank may be varied to suit customer requirements.

STATUS
Production.

MANUFACTURER
Avon Industrial Polymers Limited, Bumpers Way, Bristol Road, Chippenham, Wiltshire SN14 6NF, England.

SPECIFICATIONS

Capacity	Dimensions (flat)	Dimensions (packed)	Weight
1000 litres	2·54 × 1·78 m	0·9 × 0·45 × 0·16 m	14 kg
2500 litres	2·54 × 3·05 m	0·9 × 0·45 × 0·2 m	23 kg
5000 litres	2·54 × 4·92 m	0·9 × 0·9 × 0·16 m	36 kg
7500 litres	3·81 × 4·51 m	1·3 × 0·9 × 0·16 m	51 kg
10 000 litres	3·81 × 6·02 m	1·3 × 0·9 × 0·2 m	67 kg
15 000 litres	5·08 × 6·5 m	1·7 × 0·9 × 0·25 m	97 kg
20 000 litres	5·08 × 7·92 m	1·7 × 0·9 × 0·3 m	117 kg
50 000 litres	6·22 × 11·75 m	1 × 1·2 × 0·7 m	259 kg
100 000 litres	7·65 × 15·24 m	1 × 1·2 × 1·05 m	420 kg

UNITED STATES OF AMERICA

Tactical Water Distribution System (TWDS)

DESCRIPTION
Intended for use in a Rapid Deployment Force-type situation, the Tactical Water Distribution System (TWDS) is a flexible distribution, storage and receiving system that can issue a maximum of 720 000 gallons (2 725 200 litres) of water during the course of a 20 hour working day. Using mobile tanks, collapsible containers and static inflatable tanks together with the associated hoses, pipes, pumps and other equipment, the TWDS is designed to distribute water up to 112·4 km. Working pressure is 150 to 200 psi. The basic hardware, apart from the various smaller accessories, is 152·4 mm aluminium pipe, 20 000- to 50 000-gallon (75 700- to 189 250-litre) collapsible tanks and 2271 litres per minute centrifugal, diesel-driven pumps.

The initial requirement is for 21 systems.

STATUS
First deliveries March 1984.

MANUFACTURER
Angus Fire Armour Corporation, Angier, North Carolina, USA.

Tactical Water Distribution System

Forward Area Water Point Supply System (FAWPSS)

DESCRIPTION
The Forward Area Water Point Supply System (FAWPSS) is intended to provide large volumes of drinking water to troops in remote areas where no water supplies of any type are available. Water is delivered to a central point by air, truck or any other local method and from there is distributed as required through a network of tanks, pumps and hoselines. The complete system consists of six 2271-litre collapsible water drums, one 189 litre per minute water pump assembly, three suction hose assemblies, six discharge hose assemblies, two valve assemblies, four 'Y' junctions, four dispensing nozzles, one towing and lifting yoke and the associated hoses. The complete system is air-transportable and can be set up by two men. Once in use only one man is required for operation.

STATUS
Under procurement.

Uniroyal Static Water Tanks

DESCRIPTION
Uniroyal produces a wide range of static flexible water tanks for both military and commercial purposes. The tanks produced for water and water-based products are free-standing and made from a chlorobutyl rubber-based material that is fully vulcanised and reinforced with tough nylon basket-weave fabric. These tanks can be placed at almost any location and have double-thickness panels at handling points and positions where hardware is attached. Positioning handles are provided. For transport and storage the tanks can be placed into wooden crates.

STATUS
Production.

MANUFACTURER
Uniroyal Inc, Engineered Systems, Mishawaka, Indiana 46544, USA.

SPECIFICATIONS

Capacity (gallons)	Capacity (litres)	Approximate dimensions filled			Capacity (gallons)	Capacity (litres)	Approximate dimensions filled		
		Width (metres)	Length (metres)	Height (metres)			Width (metres)	Length (metres)	Height (metres)
250	946·3	1·88	1·88	0·305	3500	13 247·5	3·581	4·724	0·914
500	1892·5	1·753	2·743	0·457	5000	18 295	4·47	4·623	1·118
900	3406·5	2·388	2·794	0·61	6000	22 710	4·775	4·878	1·219
1000	3785	2·388	3·073	0·61	10 000	37 850	6·096	6·096	1·219
1200	4542	3·073	2·743	0·66	15 000	56 775	7·468	7·315	1·219
1500	5677·5	2·946	3·023	0·762	20 000	75 700	6·7	8·23	1·727
2000	7570	3·353	3·353	0·813	25 000	94 625	6·7	10·363	1·727
2500	9462·5	3·581	3·734	0·813	50 000	189 250	6·7	19·2	1·727
3000	11 355	3·581	4·267	0·914	100 000	378 500	18·136	18·212	1·219

Typical Uniroyal static flexible water tank

Unpacking Uniroyal flexible tank

Uniroyal Collapsible Water Tanks

DESCRIPTION
The US Army uses two main types of Uniroyal collapsible water tank that are similar in form to the Uniroyal Sealdrum tanks (see separate entry in *Bulk fuel storage and distribution systems*). The two models in service are the Uniroyal Model RD105 with a 55-gallon (208-litre) capacity and the Model RD466 with a 250-gallon (946-litre) capacity. Both are cylindrical tanks constructed of water-resistant synthetic rubber-coated fabric and can be towed at slow speeds over smooth surfaces for short distances. Both can be air-lifted by helicopter.

STATUS
In service with the US Army.

MANUFACTURER
Uniroyal Inc, Engineered Systems, Mishawaka, Indiana 46544, USA.

SPECIFICATIONS

Model	RD105	RD466
Capacity (gallons)	55	250
(litres)	208	946
Length	0·876 m	1·524 m
Diameter	0·597 m	1·016 m
Weight (full)	211·4 kg	1043 kg
(empty)	22·68 kg	93 kg

Goodyear 75 700-litre Flexible Water Tanks

DEVELOPMENT/DESCRIPTION
In July 1982 the US Army Mobility Equipment Research and Development Command (MERADCOM) awarded a $1·6 million contract to the Engineered Fabrics Division of the Goodyear Aerospace Corporation for the production of flexible water tanks for use by the US Rapid Deployment Joint Task Force (RDJTF). The contract called for the delivery of 231 tanks starting in December 1982, with an option for a further 254. Delivery will be completed during fiscal year 1984.

In service the tanks are used as part of the US Army's Tactical Water Distribution System (TWDS – see separate entry). Each tank has a capacity of 20 000 gallons (75 700 litres) and is fully compatible with other US Army water distribution equipment.

STATUS
Production. In service with the US Army.

MANUFACTURER
Engineered Fabrics Division, Goodyear Aerospace Corporation, Rockmart, Georgia, USA.

Goodyear 75 700-litre flexible water tanks in position (US Army)

Collapsible Fabric Water Tanks

DESCRIPTION
Intended for static use at field hospitals, engineer units, decontamination units and similar units, these tanks are in service in three sizes (see Specifications). They are identical in construction being mainly formed from a tank manufactured from synthetic rubber-coated nylon, open at the top and supported by a system of poles or staves, and guy ropes. A ground sheet and an easily-removed cover complete the equipment. When not in use they are packed in wooden crates.

STATUS
In service with the US Army.

SPECIFICATIONS

Capacity (gallons)	500	1500	3000
(litres)	1892·5	5677·5	11 355
Diameter	1·676 m	n/a	3·429 m
Height	0·914 m	n/a	1·372 m
Weight (empty, boxed)	n/a	167·8 kg	278 kg

Water Chilling Unit

DESCRIPTION
In March 1982 the US Army Mobility Equipment Research and Development Command (MERADCOM) announced the type standardisation of a water chilling unit for use by the Rapid Deployment Joint Task Force (RDJTF). The US Army planned at that time to order 100 units with a future purchase of 530.

The water chilling unit is designed to be used with standard 400-gallon (1514-litre) water trailers and 250- or 500-gallon (946- or 1892·5-litre) collapsible water containers – the unit can be paradropped together with a water drum. The unit is intended to cool existing water supplies from local temperatures down to 20°C for con- sumption and for special equipment such as mobile darkrooms. One unit can cool 151·4 litres of water an hour or 3028 litres per day. This is capable of supporting company-size units by delivering the normal desert environment consumption of 15 litres per day per man.

STATUS
Under procurement.

Water chilling unit in use with 1514-litre water trailer

Water chilling unit ready for paradropping together with collapsible water container

Water Quality Analysis Sets

DESCRIPTION
Two water quality analysis sets developed by the US Mobility Equipment Research and Development Command to test drinking water in the field were classified as Standard A in March 1975.

The first set is designed for use by Engineer teams in tactical situations to test water supply sources and to monitor equipment performance in drinking water production. This replaces the Engineer set developed during the Second World War and affords a much more accurate means of analysis than its predecessor.

The second set has been developed for the Surgeon General; it is basically the improvised Engineer set augmented by preventive medicine teams in water quality surveillance programmes. Its additional equipment and reagents permit more extensive testing for bacteriological and chemical characteristics of sanitary significance associated with preventive medicine.

Equipment and reagents for both sets are packed in rugged watertight cases weighing less than 30 kg each.

STATUS
In service with the US Army.

DEVELOPING AGENCY
US Army Mobility Equipment Research and Development Command, Fort Belvoir, Virginia 22060, USA.

Water quality analysis set in use (US Army)

2271 Litre Per Hour Reverse Osmosis Water Purification System (ROWPU)

DESCRIPTION

This has been developed by the US Army Mobility Equipment Research and Development Command and Univox California Inc, to replace four existing water purification units. A contract was placed in January 1981 with Univox-California for 11 units. Total production orders are 455 units at a cost of $55 million.

The 2271-litre per hour reverse osmosis water purification unit is the first and smallest in a family of multipurpose units being developed for field support. When operational this system will replace the ERDLator, the 568 litre per hour distillation unit, the CW-BW decontamination kit and the mobile ion exchange unit.

The reverse osmosis (RO) system is capable of producing drinking water from polluted fresh water, sea water, and brackish water and in removing chemical and radiological contaminants from water. Reverse osmosis is the process of pressurising raw water above its osmotic pressure which forces it through a cellulose acetate or polyamide membrane fabricated into a spiral wound element. Eight elements are used in the new unit.

The development of a dry membrane represents an advancement in the state-of-the-art in reverse osmosis membrane technology. Unlike commercially available wet membranes, the dry membranes can be stored dry and are wet/dry reversible. Incoming water is pretreated with a polymer to aid filtration before final passage through the RO elements. The unit is mobile and can be air dropped to forward tactical units, or towed on a trailer. In both cases, it will supply enough water to support at least 2000 men per day.

SPECIFICATIONS
Output: 2271 litres/h
Weight:
  (on trailer) 7740 kg
  (on skid mount) 3240 kg
Feed requirement: 132·4 litres/minute at 30 psi
Length:
  (trailer) 5·842 m
  (skid mount) 2·895 m
Height:
  (trailer) 2·464 m
  (skid mount) 1·702 m
Width:
  (trailer) 2·438 m
  (skid mount) 2·108 m
Electrical power consumption: 22 kW
Generator power required: 30 kW

STATUS
In production. In service with the US Army.

DEVELOPING AGENCY
US Army Mobility Equipment Research and Development Command, Fort Belvoir, Virginia 22060, USA.

MANUFACTURER
Univox California Inc, 6551 Loisdale Court, Springfield, Virginia 22150, USA.

2271-litre per hour water purification system in use (US Army)

Univox 2271-litre per hour water purification system on trailer

Univox 2271-litre per hour water purification systems ready for delivery

Univox Reverse Osmosis Water Purification Units (ROWPUs)

DESCRIPTION

Univox California Inc produces a range of reverse osmosis water purification units (ROWPU), one of which, the 2271-litre per hour system, is covered in a separate entry but is included here to provide a complete survey of the range. All the Univox ROWPUs use the same basic system in which water contaminants are removed by pressurising untreated water through a cellulose acetate or polyamide membrane fabricated into a spiral wound element on a drum. A series of these filters completes the process. The units are highly reliable and require only relatively low power sources and are available in different outputs to meet various military and civil requirements. They may be skid-mounted for use from trailers or semi-trailers, or for paradropping and air transport, or they may be mounted on their own special trailers. If required a special pre-filtration package may be added to each model to provide full NBC treatment.

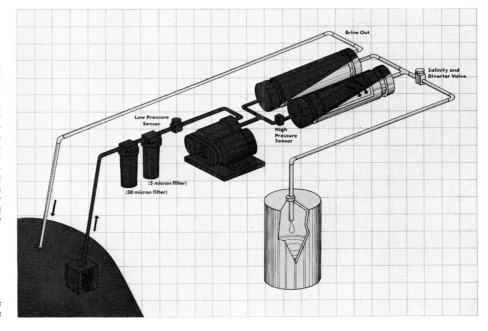

Diagrammatic representation of reverse osmosis process

SPECIFICATIONS

Model	150S	300S	600S	1000S	ROWPU 600[1]	ROWPU 1000[1]
Output	567 litres/h	1135 litres/h	2271 litres/h	3785 litres/h	2271 litres/h	3785 litres/h
Input (at 30 psi)	37·8 litres/minute	94·6 litres/minute	132·5 litres/minute	170·5 litres/minute	132·5 litres/minute	170·5 litres/minute
Weight on skid mount	2115 kg	2610 kg	2880 kg	3015 kg	3240 kg	3600 kg
Electrical power consumption	6 kW	12 kW	15 kW	19 kW	20 kW	22 kW
Primary motor supplies	7·5 hp	15 hp	20 hp	25 hp	20 hp	25 hp

[1] Includes full NBC filtration

Skid mount dimensions (all models)
Length: 2·895 m
Height: 1·702 m
Width: 2·108 m

Trailer dimensions (trailer is optional for all models)
Weight: 4500 kg
Length: 5·842 m
Height: 0·762 m
Width: 2·438 m

STATUS
Production.

MANUFACTURER
Univox California Inc, 6551 Loisdale Court, Springfield, Virginia 22150, USA.

1590-Litre Per Hour Water Purification System

DESCRIPTION
This water purification system was developed by the US Army Mobility Equipment Research and Development Centre (now Command) to meet an urgent requirement from Viet-Nam. It was type classified as Standard A late in 1972.

This is the smallest of a family of transportable water purification units developed at Fort Belvoir. The unit incorporates the same coagulation, diatomite filtration and chlorination principle as the larger equipment already in service. The main part of the system is the ERDLator, an aluminium coagulation basin that has been used in various types of US Army water purifiers for the last 20 years. Other components are a pressure diatomite filter that removes suspended solids, a chemical feeding and pumping unit for disinfection and a 3 kW generator.

The unit is used primarily to support dispersed tactical forces in the field. The US Army has found that it is more advantageous to purify local water resources than to transport water from the rear areas because of the excessive weight of the required water.

DEVELOPING AGENCY
US Army Mobility Equipment Research and Development Command, Fort Belvoir, Virginia 22060, USA.

SPECIFICATIONS (11 355 litres/h truck-mounted unit)
Weight: 8250 kg
Length: 7·1 m
Width: 2·5 m
Height: 3·3 m

Standard truck-mounted 11 355-litre per hour water purification system (US Army)

1590-litre per hour water purification system in use with generator on M274 Mule (US Army)

YUGOSLAVIA

Water Chlorination Set

DESCRIPTION
This complete set of equipment contains the means to chlorinate 250 000 litres of water. One complete set contains five self-contained packages containing calcium hypochlorite in welded glass vials, indicator tablets for chlorine, sodium thiosulphate tablets and test tubes for the determination of residual chlorine. Each package has sufficient material for the chlorination of 50 000 litres of water and is packed in a corrugated cardboard box. Five of these boxes make up a complete set which is transported in a wooden crate measuring 610 × 300 × 260 mm and weighing approximately 30 kg. Labels and instructions may be supplied in languages other than Serbo-Croat.

STATUS
Production. In service with the Yugoslav armed forces.

MANUFACTURER
Federal Directorate of Supply and Procurement (SDPR), PO Box 308, Knez Mihailova 6, Beograd, Yugoslavia.

CAMOUFLAGE EQUIPMENT AND DECOYS

FRANCE

Support Posts for Camouflage Nets

DESCRIPTION
MANURHIN support posts for camouflage nets are made of glassfibre-reinforced plastic resin and so are light, strong and have no radar echo. The system is simple, consisting of combinations of four posts each of which supports a dome with five arms that can be adjusted to any angle to support the net. Each dome arm is 400 mm long and the five are kept extended by a cord and hook. The four posts are carried one within the other and in use are connected to each other by a common locking joint. Three of the posts are 1·2 metres long and the other is 0·7 metre long. They can be joined together in any combination to support the camouflage netting and a rubber foot can be fitted to the lowest post to prevent slipping. When not in use the posts and domes can be carried in a canvas bag. The system can be used to cover almost any item of equipment or vehi-cle. For extra concealment the system can be supplied in a variety of colours.

STATUS
In production.

MANUFACTURER
Manufacture de machines du Haut-Rhin (MANURHIN), 10 rue de Soultz, 68200 Mulhouse, France.

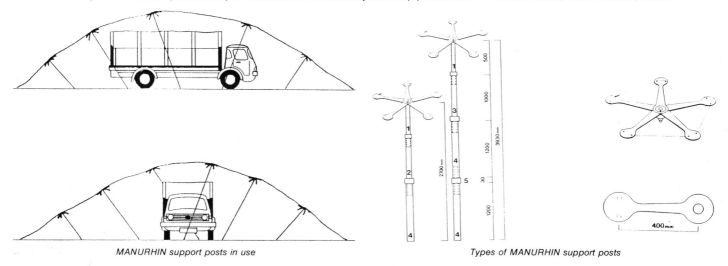

MANURHIN support posts in use   *Types of MANURHIN support posts*

ITALY

Pirelli Camouflage Nets

DESCRIPTION
Pirelli produces a range of conventional camouflage netting which is delivered in relatively small sections each measuring 4 × 4 metres or 6 × 6 metres. The net material support is made up of rubber-coated fabric with the addition of a special synthetic and vulcanised elas-tomer to which various pigments have been added. This enables the outer surface of the net to be in three or four colours according to requirements while the inner sur-face is in two shades only in a 60 : 40 ratio. The nets are not visible to infra-red or ultra-violet photographic reconnaissance and are flame resistant. If required both the support and the rubber-coated net can be provided with further support from a conventional camouflage net. Weight of the supporting net is 500 g/m² while the rubber-coated material weighs 300 g/m².

STATUS
Production. In service with the Italian armed forces.

MANUFACTURER
Moldip SpA – Pirelli Group, Via Milano 8, 20038 Seregno (Milano), Italy.

SOUTH AFRICA

Alnet Camouflage Nets

DESCRIPTION
The Alnet garnished camouflage net has been developed to meet the stringent requirements of the South African Defence Forces and has to withstand the extreme climatic conditions of South Africa. In the development stage of producing a net to meet these requirements, a technique of obtaining spectral data of the environment within a region was evolved to the extent that specific colours and disruptive patterns can be produced to resemble the local foliage.

The nets use a basic support net with a square 50 × 50 mm mesh. Low mass, high strength garnishing material is clipped onto the support net to resemble the foliage in the area in which the net is to be deployed. The garnish material is painted on both sides, one side being for winter use and the other for summer use. Joining rings on the perimeter of each net and the included joining cord and clips allow for the rapid joining separa-tion of two or more nets – the net sizes can be produced to suit. The nets are flame retardent and provide effec-tive protection in the visual and near infra-red spectra. Weight of a complete net is 350 g/m².

STATUS
Production. In service with the South African Defence Forces.

MANUFACTURER
Alnet, Moorsom Avenue, Epping 3, P.O. Box 4995, Cape Town 8000, South Africa.

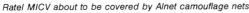

Ratel MICV about to be covered by Alnet camouflage nets

Ratel MICV covered by Alnet camouflage nets

SWEDEN

Barracuda Camouflage Systems

DEVELOPMENT/DESCRIPTION

In 1952 the Swedish net making company of Ekman and Brundin established a small development team within the company to work on camouflage net projects. In 1957 this team was separated from the company to form Barracudaverken AB, and in the same year the company received its first order for its lightweight camouflage nets from the Swedish Navy. Development work continued on a net for Army use and a standard net for use in the spring, summer and autumn was ready in 1959. In 1961 Barracuda France SA was started for the manufacture under licence of nets for the French Army and for export to other countries. Today Barracuda manufactures a wide range of nets and other camouflage systems for use by all three services.

Until the early 1960s textile nets of hemp net with a burlap garnishment were the standard equipment in most armies. Barracuda nets are significantly lighter and therefore easier to handle under field conditions, 50 square metres weighing 12·5 kg dry and 13 kg wet compared with 20 and 45 kg for textile netting of the same area.

Basic camouflage net

The frame of the net consists of synthetic fibre squares with an 85 × 85 mm mesh, with the outside edges of the net reinforced by an edge cord. If the nets are to be joined together a joining system can be provided. The finished net is built up of strips 1·7 metres wide, with the unreinforced pvc film garnishing material cemented to one side of the strips. The patches of pvc, cut in the form of symmetrical full or semi-hexagons, are sewn together to form a net of the desired shape and size.

The pattern of the Barracuda woodland camouflage net is generally built up of three different colours on each side and is designed to give good camouflage effect at short as well as long distances. Two of the colours of a standard woodland net are normally green, and their average reflection follows the so-called chlorophyll curve. The contrast of the reflection between these two colours amounts to about 25 per cent within the near-infra-red area.

The basic camouflage net can be manufactured to any size and weighs between 250 and 350 g/m², depending on the variant.

Radar scattering nets

The Barracuda radar scattering net was introduced in 1973 and, if properly deployed, substantially reduces the radar reflection of the vehicle and equipment it is covering. The material used is composed of pvc foil interlayered with special additions and the net weighs between 300 and 350 g/m². In active service an attenuation of about 10 dB is obtained against a 3 cm radar (X-band), and laboratory tests have indicated that the net will also function with the 1 cm (30 GHz), 1·5 cm (20 GHz) and 10 cm (3 GHz) wavelengths. The echo from the object plus the net then corresponds approximately to that of the surrounding terrain.

Tarpaulin cover material

This military material is intended to be used to cover vehicles, weapons and equipment. It can be made in any camouflage colour, has the desired infra-red reflection and has a completely matt surface. It weighs 690 g/m².

Umbrella camouflage

Umbrellas are used to camouflage artillery, anti-aircraft guns and missiles in vegetated terrain. Each umbrella has a top net area of one square metre and a bottom net area of five square metres. Each weighs 9 kg and has an overall height of 1·4 metres.

Pattern-printed cover material

This covering material is intended for use with vehicles, weapons and similar equipment and may be manufactured into tents and uniform items. The material has a matt finish and is flame resistant. It can be produced in virtually any colour or camouflage pattern and in weights of between 250 and 750 g/m². The normal delivery width is 1·5 metres wide.

Winter camouflage

Barracuda winter camouflage is a self-supporting garnish material which is supplied in strips 1·36 metres wide. The material is a coated synthetic fabric provided with perforations having a regular pattern. Each perforation is 12 mm in diameter and spaced at 20 mm intervals. The fabric has a weight of 350 g/m². Camouflage nets are provided by sewing together strips of the material which is finished in a shade of white.

Helmet camouflage

Barracuda helmet camouflage is provided in individual polythene bags each weighing 100 g. The helmet camouflage net is mounted on a 50 × 50 mm frame and provided with garnishing material to suit the surrounding terrain. Each net is held in place on the helmet by an elastic band and four attachment hooks, and can be used with both steel and plastic helmets.

Support poles

Barracuda support poles are made of extruded anodised aluminium with a dull dark finish. Each support comprises a telescopic pole with two removable circular supports at its top. The circular supports are mounted so that when the net is draped over them they can pivot to the angle imposed by the net. The foot of the Barracuda support pole is a combined plate/point. The point can be used on rocky ground and the plate on soft ground. The pole length can be varied from 1·5 to 2·9 metres and a catch prevents the pole from being pulled out too far. The pole weighs 0·9 kg, is 0·6 metre wide and can carry a maximum load of 40 kg.

Accessories and variations

The nets can be supplied in pvc storage bags for protection against damage during storage and transport. A repair kit is also available. The company can also design netting to suit specific military requirements, for example for use under extreme conditions of heat or cold.

Other camouflage equipment

Other camouflage systems available from Barracuda include harbour camouflage nets, helicopter camouflage nets, naval nets, aircraft decoys and camouflage paint.

Decoys

Barracuda manufactures both tank and artillery decoys. The tank decoy can be assembled by two men in about 45 minutes and weighs 45 kg. The artillery decoy weighs 75 kg and can be assembled by two men in about 20 minutes.

STATUS

In production. In service with the Canadian, French, Swedish and other armed forces.

MANUFACTURER

DIAB-Barracuda AB, Box 201, S-312 01 Laholm, Sweden.

Swedish Army truck covered with Barracuda pattern-printed cover material

Left: truck, light vehicle and 20-man tent uncamouflaged and, right, camouflaged with Barracuda nets

Tents camouflaged with Barracuda nets

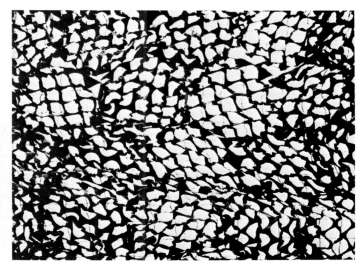

Close-up of Barracuda net

Anti-aircraft gun camouflaged under Barracuda umbrellas

Barracuda aircraft decoy

UNITED KINGDOM

Bridport Aviation Products Camouflage and Concealment Equipment

DESCRIPTION
Bridport Aviation Products has been involved in the design, development and manufacture of camouflage systems for over 35 years. Working with the British Ministry of Defence the company has developed a range of camouflage netting and associated equipment which has been proved to offer an effective camouflage at both long and short ranges.

Camouflage net
This is difficult to detect using modern reconnaissance and surveillance equipment, including infra-red sensors. It is both robust and lightweight and allows large areas of netting to be easily transported, man-handled and rigged.

Colours and patterns can be supplied for all types of terrain (vegetation, scrubland, desert and snow) and the colours on each side of the net may be varied to enable the net to be used in two different types of vegetation or climatic zones.

The nets are matt finished throughout and are suitable for use under all climatic conditions within the temperature range of $-40°$ to $+70°$ C. The colour fastness of the fabric when subjected to light, water and abrasion complies with British Ministry of Defence requirements.

The minimum size of net for a vehicle is calculated to ensure that when fitted the section of net from the top to the ground will be at an approximate angle of 45 degrees. The company recommend the following minimum net sizes: for a Land-Rover 10 × 8 m, Ferret 9 × 7·5 m, Scorpion 12·5 × 9·8 m, Saladin 15 × 12 m, 4-ton truck 17·5 × 13·5 m and Centurion 19·3 × 13 m.

Concealment nets
Concealment nets are complete, purpose-designed camouflage systems primarily used with artillery, radar equipment, self-propelled guns, aircraft and helicopters. They are used where equipment is difficult to

Harrier aircraft under Bridport Aviation Products concealment net

105 mm Light Gun camouflaged with concealment net

camouflage because of its bulk, where manpower is limited or where special counter-surveillance measures are justified in the protection of equipment with a high tactical value. Typical examples include nets which allow weapons to be fired, radar equipment to be operated and aircraft or helicopters to be refuelled and rearmed from their concealed positions. Special equipment is available for rapid camouflage of aircraft or helicopters using temporary landing sites in forward combat areas.

The base net is made of a multi-filament nylon yarn with a minimum breaking strength of 35 kg. It is of a knotted construction and can be supplied in mesh sizes of 50, 75 and 100 mm. A border cord of 226 kg breaking strength is fitted to the periphery of each net.

The net garnishing material is a polyurethane nylon fabric manufactured to Ministry of Defence specifications UK/SC/3470B and incised with a pattern of S-shaped cuts in accordance with Ministry of Defence specification UK/SC/3471, which break up the flat surface of the material and obtain the required camouflage effect. The strips, squares or triangles of garnishing material are attached to the base net with cord, ties or plastic strips. The nets can be supplied in either 60 per cent or 100 per cent coverage to suit the terrain in which the net is being used.

Ancillary equipment

Bridport Aviation Products has developed a range of equipment, including support poles, mushroom caps and ground pegs which are complementary to its range of camouflage nets. A number of support poles, clipped together and fitted with mushrooms, can be erected beneath the net thereby producing a contour which will blend with any surroundings. In addition, a quick release system may be fitted to open the net, allowing a weapon to engage its target rapidly.

STATUS
Production. In service with the British and other armed forces.

MANUFACTURER
Bridport Aviation Products, Defence Division, Bridport, Dorset, England.

Airborne Inflatable Dummy Targets

DESCRIPTION
These inflatable dummy targets have been developed to provide realistic recognition training to Forward Air Controllers (FACs) directing ground attack aircraft against AFVs and other battle formations. They are used in this role by the Royal Air Force.

At ranges of between 2000 and 3000 metres, through binoculars, they are immediately identifiable as armoured vehicles, at 900 to 1000 metres they are identifiable as to type and at a distance of less than 300 metres they are identifiable as dummies.

The targets are manufactured in synthetic rubber-coated nylon and consist of a framework of low pressure inflatable tubes which are covered to simulate the vehicle outline. Paint is used to highlight prominent features such as wheels and hatches. Support poles and guys ensure stability. Pressure relief valves are incorporated to limit the pressure to 0·07 kg/cm² during inflation or temperature increases.

Inflation is by a small battery-operated blower and can be accomplished in five to eight minutes. The support poles and guys take a further two to three minutes to position. Several outlet tubes give fast deflation and normally two people can completely deflate, pack and stow a target in ten minutes. Each target is packed in a valise for ease of handling and storage.

The current range includes a T-62 MBT, BMP-A MICV, BTR-60PB APC and a BTR-50PK. Other AFVs can be designed and the company has designed a T-72 dummy target.

STATUS
In production. In service with the Royal Air Force.

MANUFACTURER
Airborne Industries Limited, Arterial Road, Leigh-on-Sea, Essex SS9 4EF, England.

SPECIFICATIONS

Model	T-62	BMP-A	BTR-60PB	BTR-50PK
Weight	88 kg	76 kg	94 kg	69 kg
Length (inflated)	9·45 m	6·71 m	7·16 m	7·01 m
Width (inflated)	3·35 m	3·02 m	2·74 m	2·13 m
Height (inflated)	2·44 m	2·29 m	2·44 m	3·02 m
Pack size	all are approximately 1·07 × 0·6 × 0·4 m			

T-62 MBT dummy target by Airborne Industries (Ministry of Defence)

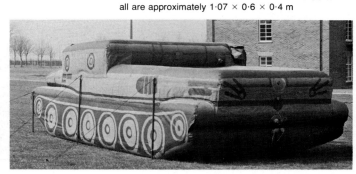

BTR-50PK dummy target by Airborne Industries (Ministry of Defence)

UNITED STATES OF AMERICA

Camouflage Paints and Pattern Painting

DESCRIPTION
Fast drying, dull, high quality alkyd paints are applied by spray gun or brush in patterns to disrupt signature characteristics of vehicles, and to reduce contrast with soil and vegetation in the background. Light green, dark green, forest green, field drab, earth yellow, earth brown, olive drab, black and white colours were provided for blends that counter visual and near infra-red surveillance and target acquisition. Solar and heat reflecting paints and easily removable white coating were also provided for special applications. By January 1977 all US Army tactical equipment was pattern painted.

As the result of a programme that began in August 1978, the US Army is now turning from alkyd paints and bringing into service a new polyurethane paint. The new finish has a much improved resistance to chemical agents which are unable to penetrate the surface. The polyurethane paint is composed of two main ingredients, a polyester and a catalyst. When combined, a surface film is formed which is resistant to the ingress of moisture in any form and thus chemical decontamination can be carried out in the field by washing the affected areas. The two components are mixed just before the paint is applied. Once applied the new paint is stated to be far more durable than the alkyd paints.

Three-colour camouflage patterns being developed by the US Army Mobility Equipment Research and Development Command (MERADCOM) will replace the four-colour pattern currently used on tactical equipment. The new brown, green and black design eliminates the tan colour formerly included in the pattern. In theory, the broad patches of colour used will break up the vehicle's silhouette making it harder to identify at a distance as well as blending better with its background at close range.

The US Army decided to adopt the new pattern as a result of discussions with Allied forces in West Germany. By standardising the camouflage used by U.S. and West German Armies, enemy forces cannot ascertain a vehicle's country of origin by its pattern. After a series of tests, the three-colour German pattern was shown to provide better protection than the four-colour American design.

To adapt the pattern to the wide variety of vehicles used by the US Army, MERADCOM has negotiated a contract for a computerised programme to create individual pattern designs. Until the programme is functional, camouflage specialists in MERADCOM's Combined Arms Support Laboratory are developing patterns for priority items by hand. This includes designs for armoured personnel carriers, self-propelled howitzers and the commercial utility cargo vehicles.

Conversion to the three-colour pattern will be in conjunction with the introduction of new chemical agent resistant coatings developed by MERADCOM's Materials, Fuels and Lubricants Laboratory. These coatings protect surfaces from absorbing chemical agents and enable soldiers to decontaminate their equipment without breaking down and dissolving the paint.

DEVELOPING AGENCY
US Army Mobility Equipment Research and Development Command, Fort Belvoir, Virginia 22060, USA.

New three-colour camouflage pattern applied to M113 armoured personnel carrier

Smoke Camouflage

DESCRIPTION
In 1975 it was stated that the United States Army would spend $45 million over a five year period in developing new smoke and aerosol screening systems. The US Army Material Command designated Edgewood Arsenal, Maryland, as the focal point for managing and implementing the programme.

Today, smoke and other aerosols are showing much promise as a means of obscuring military operations from not only visual, but also infra-red, radar and microwave detection by the enemy.

Investigation of their obscuration and effectiveness in counter-surveillance and counter target acquisition is being conducted by the United States Army Mobility Equipment Research and Development Command at Fort Belvoir, in its capacity as Army Camouflage Lead Laboratory.

Devices capable of producing an instant wall of smoke are under development to provide concealment of men and equipment when dispersal or concentration of combat units is necessary. A ground-based smoke wall has been emplaced successfully in two seconds. Rocket-launched smoke disseminations deliver in five seconds an aerial smoke screen 183 metres long and 121 metres high in the path of attacking aircraft. They are detonated at altitudes of 91, 61 and 30 metres to delay or divert attack by high speed aircraft.

Rapidly disseminated aerosols other than smoke are being studied to determine their potential for attenuating infra-red, radar and microwave sensors. In addition work is under way on miniature rocket propellant actuated, fog oil generators and coloured smoke for hide and blend applications.

Successful use of smoke screens as camouflage may also lead to their extensive employment as a decoy measure.

In addition to improved smoke projectiles for 155 mm and 105 mm artillery weapons a rapid smoke screen system for tanks and other armoured fighting vehicles is being developed. This will probably be similar to that installed on Soviet T-54/T-55 and T-62 tanks, which injects vaporised diesel oil into the exhaust system to produce a dense cloud of smoke. As an interim measure the United States Army has adopted the British smoke discharger system as fitted to the Chieftain MBT.

STATUS
Development.

DEVELOPING AGENCY
DARCOM Project Manager for Smoke/Obscurants, Aberdeen Proving Ground, Maryland 21005, USA.

Rocket-launched smoke disseminations (US Army)

"INSTANT" SMOKE FOR CAMOUFLAGE & DECEPTION

EMPLACEMENT — DETONATION — 2 SECONDS — 5.4 SECONDS

Sequence of photographs showing ground-based smoke wall in operation (US Army)

Brunswick Camouflage and Other Defensive Systems

DESCRIPTION
Camouflage Screens
Brunswick screens comprise a minimal number of parts and are manufactured from durable synthetics to withstand use and re-use in all environments. Metal fibres distributed throughout the camouflage effectively conceal military equipment from radar systems as described below. Research and development have resulted in colour pigmentations and textures which, in addition to achieving good visual and radar camouflage, provide effective concealment from spectrozal and false colour film combinations, including colour infra-red film.

Three standard colour/texture combinations are available to meet woodland, desert and snow conditions. Each screen has a different colour-texture pattern on each side for greater versatility of application. One side of the woodland screen simulates spring and summer while the reverse simulates autumn. Desert screens simulate both tan and grey desert terrain and the arctic screen provides concealment in total as well as partial snow cover with optimum reflectance in the ultra-violet necessary to preclude detection in this spectral region. Special colour/texture formulations can be

Woodland colour texture camouflage system

developed by Brunswick to meet specific environmental requirements. The screens meet United States Military Specifications MIL-C-52771 (ME) and MIL-C-52765 (ME).

Camouflage screens produced by Brunswick have been designed to scatter some of the impinging radar energy, absorb some and allow only enough to be transmitted back to the radar detector to give the military object the same general return as that of the terrain and thus prevent detection. This effect is achieved in the screens by the random dispersion of short, thin steel fibres throughout the garnishing material in combination with selected incising patterns. This combination in the woodland screen results in a proper balance of reflection, absorption, transmission and scatter to achieve the desired simulation of natural woodland surroundings.

Camouflage kits manufactured by Brunswick consist of two subsystems: a screen system and a support system. Each is packed separately in its own vinyl-coated nylon transport case. One screen system consists of a simple hexagon-shaped screen and a rhombic-shaped screen, carrying case and a repair kit. Screen edges are a uniform 4·9 metres for joining to make larger screens. Quick disconnect brackets are permanently attached to all screen edges for quick joining. The screens can be quickly disconnected by pulling a lanyard. The support system contains support poles, spikes, spreader assemblies and a carrying case.

The modular concept was designed to meet the diverse field needs encountered. The rhombic or diamond screen can be used for smaller requirements such as personnel or weapons emplacements while hexagonal nets meet the need for shielding equipment in the ¼- to ½-ton truck range, two and three module combinations provide cover for 2½-ton trucks, medium tanks and mobile artillery and regular or irregular configuration module combinations can be assembled to meet almost any installation need.

Disrupters
Disrupters are being developed to provide a quick reaction camouflage and first shot probability for mobile weapons. These disrupters will be designed to deny key signature cues and substitute cues characteristic of natural backgrounds thereby greatly reducing the probability of detection identification while not interfering with equipment and mission function.

Inflatable Trees
Brunswick has developed an inflatable tree which, when deployed, supports camouflage screens and provides effective helicopter concealment. Extending to a height of 7·9 metres the inflatable tree has three tiers of limbs to support the camouflage screens. The system can be quickly deployed and removed and has been designed primarily for helicopters which, because of their size and distinct shape, cannot be hidden in natural foliage.

Decoys
These include expansible foam decoys which provide a high level of visual fidelity. Adaptable to a wide range of military equipment, they can also be made to provide signature characteristics in response to infra-red and radar sensing systems. Expansible foam decoys compress into small shipping cubes and are quickly deployed without the use of special tools.

Inflatable Decoys
Inflatable decoys are low fidelity replications which are inflated at the deployment site and secured in position with guy wires. These can be manufactured from pre-formed, heat-sealed vinyl or polyurethane coated cloth. Fidelity can be improved by the addition of moulded foam details.

STATUS
Production. Brunswick camouflage systems are used by the US Army.

MANUFACTURER
Brunswick Corporation, Defense Division, One Brunswick Plaza, Skokie, Illinois 60076, USA.

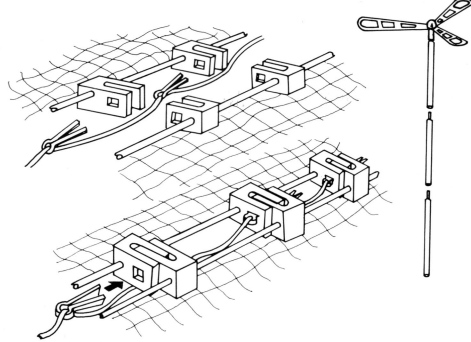

Quick connect/disconnect brackets

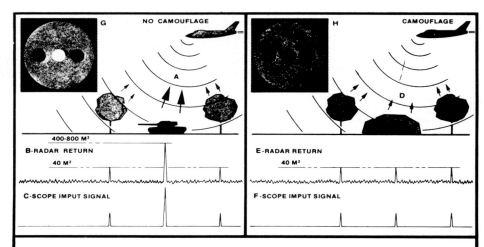

A — A representation of a tank located among trees. A reconnaissance aircraft using a side looking radar system has illuminated the area and the large dark arrows from the tank indicate a greater magnitude return while the lighter arrows from the trees indicate a return of a lesser magnitude.

B — An indication of the output of the radar system with the random noise line at the bottom indicating the inherent noise level of the electrical equipment. The spike from the trees at 40 square meters indicates the return from the trees and a much greater spike at a much greater height indicates the return from the tank at a level of 400-800 square meters.

C — In normal operation the radar observer would turn down the gain to reduce noise and therefore only the spike from

the trees and the tank would appear. It should be noted that the spike from the tank is very much greater than the spike from the trees, making the tank readily detectable.

D-E-F — In this case the tank has been camouflaged by a Brunswick screen. The return from the screen is the same magnitude as the return from the trees; i.e. approximately 40 meters. The operator, therefore, is not able to distinguish the tank installation from the trees.

G-H — Representations of a radar scope. They illustrate approximately what the operator sees in his fly-over. Note that in G the tank appears as a bright spot and in H there is no distinction from the trees.

Brunswick radar concealment net applications

Sullivan Camouflage Screening System

DESCRIPTION
The Sullivan Camouflage Screening System was designed and developed for the United States Army. It is designed to be placed over temporarily halted military vehicles, weapons and equipment, and over semi-permanent positions and installations to inhibit location and identification by target acquisition and surveillance systems. The system can also be employed to aid concealment of permanent objects, and objects in a fixed pattern of array which present an obvious target signature.

The Sullivan system consists of a basic camouflage screen, a support system, storage/transport case, repair kit and ancillary items.

The basic camouflage screen is made of two parts, one hexagonal-shaped screen and one rhombic-shaped unit interconnected by a quick release system at

Sullivan International single desert module deployed

one edge. The screen is made of synthetic support netting to which is attached specially coated synthetic fabric which has been incised to provide camouflage effective surface texture and colour patterns. It covers approximately 55 square metres with a dry weight of 15·5 kg and a packaged volume of 0·113 cubic metre. It is available in woodland, desert and snow colour-pattern-texture combinations, with each combination reversible to provide greater variety of appearance. Colour patterns and reversible combinations can be modified to provide camouflage for specific needs. For example a woodland reversible to tan/grey desert can be easily produced.

Single screens can be joined along any of their edges to form a large screen of any desired overall size and shape.

The support system (for which there is a separate entry in this section) is made of reinforced plastic spreaders and telescopic poles which raise the screen above the target in an irregular, domed configuration.

Ancillary items include strakes, ground anchors for use in soft and sandy soil and an instruction sheet.

The system is resistant to mould, rot, fungus, corrosion and colour fading. It is non-water-absorbent, and fireproof, and is not adversely affected by petrol or other POL products.

During trials the single Sullivan screen was deployed by two men over a target in less than 3·5 minutes, the minimum time to erect the multiple Sullivan screen assemblies was two screens in 3 minutes 56 seconds and four in 4 minutes 35 seconds, the minimum time to join the screens was two screens in 3 minutes 47 seconds, and four screens in 4 minutes 39 seconds (by four men), all well within requirement.

The tested woodland screens required a mean time of 0·82 second for one adjoining edge to be separated from the other, and were easily repaired within the required time limit. During trials no effects were noticed as a result of helicopter take-off and landing within 15 metres distance of the deployed nets, and visibility from beneath the screen was found to be equivalent to that available from beneath the standard burlap drape screen, as specified.

Inflatable decoys

Sullivan Industries also produces inflatable decoys which are valuable both in confusing the enemy as to field strength and in distracting enemy fire. The company has developed its inflatables from original research and development conducted for the US Air Force and Navy.

2½-ton truck under four Sullivan nets during lanyard test

Three Sullivan International modules covering M113 APC

The company can design and fabricate inflatable decoys to meet specific customer requirements using a wide variety of synthetic materials. Various degrees of broad spectrum signatures, including ultra-violet, visible, infra-red, radar etc will simulate tanks or other equipment.

STATUS
In production. In service with the US Army.

MANUFACTURER
Sullivan International, 105 Fremont Drive, Sonoma, California 94576, USA.

Sullivan Advanced Screening Support System

DESCRIPTION

This camouflage screen support system is a component of the advanced lightweight camouflage screening system designed, engineered and produced by Sullivan for the US Army.

The screening support system comprises a telescopic pole set, spreader assembly and an optional pole foot. The telescopic pole set consists of two 90 cm pole segments and one 57·5 cm pole segment of various diameters which rest or telescope together to form a 1·2 metre package and when opened extend to a height of 2·4 metres. The system may be assembled in a wide variety of ways, allowing variations of height in multiples of 15 cm, 45 cm, 77·5 cm and 90 cm, and with exten-

sions of over 4·2 metres when one or more set is assembled.

The spreader assembly consists of a cluster of three arms or spreaders, 90 cm long, a top adapter to attach the spreaders to any of the three telescopic pole diameters, and a knob to attach the spreaders to the top of the top adapter.

The optional pole foot is attached to the base of the pole assembly to prevent the support system from sinking into soft ground or snow.

All components in the system are fabricated of plastic, or glass-reinforced plastic to optimise strength and weight considerations, and for dielectric properties. Components are coated with a hard, durable material pigmented to provide a dull finish which matches the general colour scheme of the screen.

The main advantages of the Sullivan advanced

screening and support system are that it provides a more natural, irregular appearance to any camouflage screen; requires no clips or other devices to attach it to the screen; parts will not rust, corrode or deteriorate; it may be used in all terrains and environments, including soft snow; materials are all dielectric, and will not interfere with screened radar installations; and it bundles into a more compact unit for easier transportation, handling and storage.

STATUS
In production. In service with the US Army and other armed forces.

MANUFACTURER
Sullivan International, 105 Fremont Drive, Sonoma, California 94576, USA.

"Plateau Effect"

Two different pole lengths under 2·4 metres total height of current system increases regularity and may provide plateau effect which makes detection easier

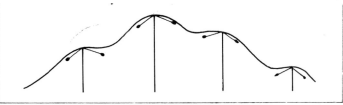

Variable Outline

Advanced Sullivan support system has over 12 different pole lengths under 2·4 metres total height, substantially increasing possibility for irregular camouflage effect profile

GENERATORS

AUSTRALIA

Rapier Fire Unit Generator Set

DESCRIPTION
This generator has been developed and produced in Australia as the power unit for the Rapier Fire Unit. One generator set is required for optical operations and a second generator is required for the Blindfire mode.

The generator set consists of a Volkswagen four cylinder, air-cooled petrol engine, flange mounted to a 16-pole, rotating field, three phase ac generator which is driven from the engine flywheel via a flexible coupling. The engine is similar to the Australian Army version of the Volkswagen VW126A industrial engine but with the addition of a 0·6 kW Bosch starter motor, a 14 volt 25 amp Bosch generator and regulator to charge the internal battery (when fitted), stellite inlet and exhaust valves, forced valve rotation and a cooling air flow thermostat.

The generator set is provided with mounting attachments which locate it, during transport, at the rear of the

Rapier launcher or Blindfire tracking radar, both of which are trailer mounted. A canvas cover is provided for use when travelling.

The electric-start version of this generator set is suitable for operation over the temperature range of −30 to +52°C. It is available with an internal battery or provision may be made for connection to the towing vehicle battery (most Australian Army Rapier units use the 1-tonne Land-Rover) to start the engine. If the −30°C starting facility is not required lighter batteries may be used. The flat top cover is fitted to the generator set when it is operating at ambient temperatures below 0°C.

The full designation of this equipment is Generator Set, Gasoline Engine, 15 kVA, 115/200 volt, 415 Hz, Three Phase Electric Start.

STATUS
Production. In service with the Australian Army.

AGENCY
Department of Defence Engineering Development Establishment, Raleigh Road, Maribyrnong, Victoria, Australia. Postal address: Private Bag No 12, PO Ascot Vale, Victoria 3032, Australia.

SPECIFICATIONS
Weight:
  (lowest starting temp, −30°C) 280 kg
  (lowest starting temp, −15°C) 274 kg
  (lowest starting temp, 0°C) 272 kg
  (internal battery not fitted) 262 kg
Length: 1·036 m
Width: 1·067 m
Height: 0·914 m
Voltage output: 115 and 200 V ac
Maximum rating: 15 kVA

Australian Army Rapier Fire Unit with top cover fitted for operation at temperatures below 0°C (Australian Army)

Australian Army Rapier Fire Unit generator set with cover removed for operation at normal ambient temperatures (Australian Army)

Generator Set 30 kVA

DESCRIPTION
Ninety-eight of these generators have been ordered for the Australian armed forces. They have been specially designed for the sub-tropical and tropical climates of Australia with all components proofed against tropical conditions and the prefabricated covers and panels have been weatherproofed. The generator is skid-mounted.

SPECIFICATIONS
Voltage output: dual, 240/415, 120/208 V
Frequency: selectable 50 or 60 Hz
Output: 30 kVA at 0·8pf
Engine: Dorman model 6DA diesel to be replaced by Deutz F51413FR diesel
Endurance: 8 h
Alternator: Dunlite dual voltage

STATUS
Production. In service with the Australian armed forces.

AGENCY
Department of Defence (Army Office), Materiel Branch, PO Box E33, Queen Victoria Terrace, Canberra ACT 2600, Australia.

Generator set 30 kVA ready for use (Australian Army)

Generator set 30 kVA with top removed (Australian Army)

Generator Set, 20 kVA, 115/200 volt, 415 Hz, Three Phase

DESCRIPTION
This generator set is designed as a lightweight portable generator for light repair facilities. It is produced in two forms, one powered by an integral hand-start petrol engine, the other by a mains-supplied induction motor. The petrol engined version can be platform mounted on a 1-ton GS trailer. Both generators use the same skid-mounted carrying frame and all components are totally enclosed allowing the sets to be used with a minimum of weather protection.

SPECIFICATIONS

Type	Petrol engine	Mains
Weight	259 kg	327 kg
Length	1·06 m	1·06 m
Width	0·84 m	0·84 m
Height	0·743 m	0·743 m

STATUS
Production. In service with the Australian armed forces.

AGENCY
Australian Army Engineering Development Establishment, Raleigh Road, Maribyrnong, Victoria, Australia. Postal address: Private Bag No 12, P O Ascot Vale, Victoria 3032, Australia.

Motor generator, 20 kVA, 115/200 volt, 415 Hz, three phase

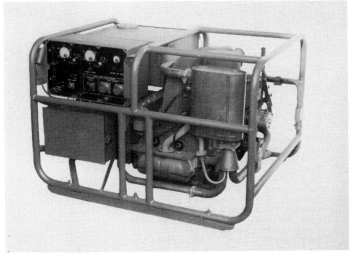

Generator set, gasoline engine, 20 kVA, 115/200 volt, 415 Hz, three phase, hand start

FRANCE

ACMAT Trailer-mounted Generator Set

DESCRIPTION
This equipment consists of a 50 kVA 220/380 volt diesel generator set mounted on a standard ACMAT RM 215S cargo trailer. The motive power is supplied by a Perkins 6.354.4 diesel engine rated at 65·5 hp at 1500 rpm. A Leroy Sommer generator is used and a 225-litre fuel tank is mounted on the skid frame of the generator. A further eight jerricans are built into the trailer giving the equipment a maximum of 30 hours operating autonomy. The unit is soundproofed down to 76 dB. If required, the unit can be removed from the trailer in 15 minutes and operated from its skid mounting.

SPECIFICATIONS
Weight: 1500 kg
Length: (overall) 2·06 m
Width: (overall) 1·1 m
Height: (overall) 1·2 m

STATUS
In production.

MANUFACTURER
ACMAT, Atéliers de Construction Mécanique de l'Atlantique, Le Point de Jour, 44600 Saint-Nazaire, France.

ACMAT trailer-mounted generator set

GERMANY, FEDERAL REPUBLIC

Knurz Enclosed Sound Proof Generating Sets

DESCRIPTION
At the behest of the West German armed forces Kirsch GmbH has developed a range of totally enclosed generating sets with a high degree of identical construction and component interchangeability. The construction provides a sound level below 70 dB. All the models are powered by proven air-cooled diesel engines with direct injection. The alternators are of asynchronous design. The dc generators are supplied with saturation control and electronic constant voltage/current regulation and a wide output voltage setting range. The ac generators are equipped with additional capacitance and an electronic two-point regulator. The two smaller generator sets can be supplied with an alternative portable tubular frame. All sets are designed to be fuelled direct from jerricans with an additional integral buffer fuel tank to maintain the fuel supply while changing jerricans.

STATUS
Production. In service with the West German Army.

MANUFACTURER
Kirsch GmbH, 231 Biewerer Strasse, D-5500 Trier, Federal Republic of Germany.

SPECIFICATIONS

Model	BG 1·9 DHA	BE 2·2 DHA	BG 3 DDA	BD 6·5 DDAE
Voltage output	28 V dc	230 V ac	28 V dc	400/230 V ac
Rated power	1·9 kW	2·2 kVA	3 kW	6·5/5 kVA
Voltage adjustment	26·6–32·2 V	–	26·6–32·2 V	–
Nominal current	68 A	9·5 A	107 A	11·7/21·7 A
Frequency	–	50 Hz	–	50 Hz
Engine model	Hatz 673 LHK	Hatz 673 LHK	KHD F1L208D	KHD F1L210D
Rated power (DIN)	3 kW	3 kW	5·25 kW	9·25 kW
Speed	3000 rpm	3000 rpm	3000 rpm	3000 rpm
Weight	115 kg	113 kg	185 kg	295 kg
Length	0·89 m	0·89 m	0·95 m	1·2 m
Width	0·5 m	0·5 m	0·46 m	0·595 m
Height	0·5 m	0·5 m	0·625 m	0·7 m

Knurz BG 1·9 DHA 1·9 kW 28 V dc generating set

Knurz BE 2·2 DHA 2·2 kW 230 V ac generating set

Knurz BD 6·5 DDAE 6·5/5 kW 430/230 V ac generating set

Knurz Petrol Engine Generating Sets

DESCRIPTION

Knurz produces a wide range of petrol-engined generating sets many of which are built to suit military requirements. The following are typical of those designed for military use.

GL 1·5 BA. This is a portable dc-generating set suitable for charging 24 volt lead-acid batteries and as a power supply for 24 volt dc equipments when a buffer battery is used. The set is powered by a four-stroke petrol engine and is fitted with an asynchronous alternator and silicon bridge rectifiers.

EG 4 BAK. This is a combined single phase ac/dc generating set. It is mounted within a portable tubular frame and is powered by a four-stroke petrol engine. It has an integral fuel tank, a three-way valve and a quick-release coupling for an external fuel supply from jerricans. The alternator is of asynchronous construction with capacitive control and subsequent silicon bridge rectification.

(D + E) 5 BSAF. This is a portable ac generating set providing both single and three-phase outputs. The set is powered by a two-stroke petrol engine fuelled via a three-way valve with a quick-release coupling for a 20-litre jerrican. It uses an asynchronous alternator with capacitor excitation. The alternator windings have been designed to take the full rated load on either three phase, single phase or any combination of the two.

SPECIFICATIONS

Model	GL 1·5 BA	EG 4 BAK	(D + E) 5 BSAF
Rated power	1·5 kW	4 kVA/1 kW	5 kVA
Nominal voltage	24 V dc	230 V ac/12 + 24 V dc	400/230 V ac
Nominal current			
(single phase dc)	62·5 A	17·4/40 A	21·7 A
(three phase)	–	–	7·2 A
Frequency	–	50 Hz/–	50 Hz
Engine	B & S 131 432	B & S 221 437	F & S Stamo 282
Number of cylinders	1	1	1
Mode of operation	4-stroke	4-stroke	2-stroke
Rated power (DIN)	2·8 kW	5·5 kW	6·2 kW
Speed	3000 rpm	3000 rpm	3000 rpm
Fuel tank capacity	2·8 litres	5·7 litres	6 litres
Weight	49 kg	103 kg	110 kg
Length	0·56 m	0·76 m	0·7 m
Width	0·37 m	0·535 m	0·44 m
Height	0·5 m	0·5 m	0·575 m

STATUS
Production. In service with several armed forces.

MANUFACTURER
Kirsch GmbH, 231 Biewerer Strasse, D-5500 Trier, Federal Republic of Germany.

Knurz (D + E) 5 BSAF petrol engine generating set

Knurz EG 4 BAK petrol engine generating set

ITALY

Astra 400 Hertz Generator Sets

DESCRIPTION

Astra Veicoli Industriali SpA produces a range of heavy-duty generator sets suitable for a number of military applications. All the sets are built onto a standard steel base-frame, and all sets have a DDA diesel engine with sufficient fuel capacity to run for eight hours.

Also fitted as standard are intake air filters, cable spools, a large radiator, an exhaust silencer and a manual control board. Electrical outputs are all three-phase and the synchronous alternator is self-regulating between plus and minus one per cent. The sets can be placed in static or towed container bodies, and in silenced surrounds for special applications. 28 to 112 dc voltage generators are available on request.

STATUS
In production.

MANUFACTURER
Astra Veicoli Industriali SpA, Via Caorsana 79, 29100 Piacenza, Italy.

SPECIFICATIONS

Model	A1000/HF	A1010/HF	A1030/HF	A2002/HF	A2000/HF	A2010/HF	A2030/HF	A2050/HF
Output	65 kVA, 115/200 V, 400 Hz	90 kVA, 115/200 V, 400 Hz	155 kVA, 115/200 V, 400 Hz	45 kVA, 115/200 V, 400 Hz	75 kVA, 115/200 V, 400 Hz	120 kVA, 115/200 V, 400 Hz	180 kVA, 115/200 V, 400 Hz	250 kVA, 115/200 V, 400 Hz
Length	2·3 m	2·6 m	3 m	2 m	2·3 m	2·6 m	3 m	3·2 m
Width	1 m	1 m	1·4 m	1 m	1 m	1 m	1·4 m	1·4 m
Height	1·4 m	1·4 m	1·85 m	1·4 m	1·4 m	1·4 m	1·85 m	1·85 m
Weight	2000 kg	3000 kg	3800 kg	1800 kg	2000 kg	3000 kg	3800 kg	4000 kg
Engine model	3/53-N50	4/53-N50	6V53-N50	2/71-N65	3/71-N70	4/71-N70	6V71-N70	8V71-N70
RPM	2400	2400	2400	2000	2000	2000	2000	2000

SOUTH AFRICA

6·5 kVA Trolley Mounted Generating Set

DESCRIPTION
Designed for workshop and similar uses this trolley-mounted generating set has a three phase and central self-excited alternator with a self regulating output of 400/230 volts, 50 Hertz, 6·5 kVA. The engine is a twin cylinder diesel which is air-cooled and uses direct injection. It has a continuous rating of 11·7 hp at 1500 rpm. The fuel tank for the main engine has a capacity of 14·5 litres which is sufficient for six hours of full load operation. The trolley on which the set is mounted has solid rubber tyres and is equipped with a steerable pull bar for towing. A running hour meter is provided, as is an outlet socket.

SPECIFICATIONS
Weight: 530 kg
Length: 1·5 m
Width: 1 m
Height: 1·022 m
Engine: two cylinder diesel, direct injection, air-cooled providing 11·7 hp continuous rating at 1500 rpm
Fuel capacity: 14·5 litres
Operating duration: 6 h
Output: 6·5 kVA, 400/230 V, 50 Hz three phase

STATUS
Production. In service with the South African Defence Forces.

MANUFACTURER
Anderson Generating Manufacturers.
   Enquiries to Armscor, Private Bag X337, Pretoria 0001, South Africa.

6·5 kVA trolley mounted generating set

7·5 kVA Trailer Mounted Generating Set

DESCRIPTION
This generating set can be towed behind any military vehicle and carries enough fuel for 24 hours of continuous operation. The generating set can be used either on the trailer or can be removed for operation on its base. For the main generator power the set is equipped with a twin-cylinder air-cooled diesel engine and the alternator is a single phase, self-exciting and self-regulating unit providing 230 volts, 7·5 kVA at 50 Hertz. The set is provided with a voltmeter and ammeter, a frequency meter, a running hour meter and three protected outlet sockets. The trailer is equipped with a dolly wheel under the towing arm and three levelling stays, one on the towing bar and two at the rear. A spare tyre is carried inside the generator housing cover. Overrun brakes are fitted to the trailer.

SPECIFICATIONS
Weight:
   (with trailer) 1250 kg
   (without trailer) 550 kg
Length:
   (with trailer) 3 m
   (without trailer) 1·38 m
Width:
   (with trailer) 2·1 m
   (without trailer) 0·93 m
Height:
   (with trailer) 1·75 m
   (without trailer) 0·86 m
Engine: two cylinder diesel, direct injection, air-cooled providing 12·3 hp continuous rating at 1500 rpm
Fuel capacity: 70 litres
Operating duration: 24 h
Output: 7·5 kVA, 230 V, 50 Hz single phase

7·5 kVA trailer mounted generating set

STATUS
Production. In service with the South African Defence Forces.

MANUFACTURER
Anderson Generating Manufacturers.
   Enquiries to Armscor, Private Bag X337, Pretoria 0001, South Africa.

150/250 kVA Mobile Generating Set

DESCRIPTION
This is a completely self-contained electrical power generating unit designed for severe continuous duty and suitable for transport by road on a purpose-built low bed trailer, or by air in a C-130 Hercules or Transall C-160 transport aircraft. The sets are normally used in pairs for installations where a reliable and uninterrupted power supply is required. In such an installation the two sets would be synchronised and run in parallel for a few minutes while exchanging the roles of stand-by and duty sets at weekly intervals. Complete servicing of the stand-by set would be possible without any interruption in the supply to the installation.

The alternator may be either a 150 kVA or a 250 kVA unit providing three phase 400/230 volts. Both units use a water cooled turbo-charged diesel with the 250 kVA unit using an extra after-cooling stage. Instrumentation includes voltmeters with a selection switch, line ammeters, a frequency meter, a zero voltmeter, a battery charge ammeter, an oil pressure meter and a water temperature gauge.

Features of the set include battery operated electric starting, semi-automatic synchronising, automatic lubricating oil make-up, and cable drums complete with cable. The 1100-litre capacity fuel tank is sufficient for the set to run for 24 hours. Protection is provided against low oil pressure, high engine temperature, overspeed, overload, over or low voltage and there is also a low fuel warning.

STATUS
Production. In service with the South African Defence Forces.

MANUFACTURER
Circon Generating Manufacturers.
   Enquiries to Armscor, Private Bag X337, Pretoria 0001, South Africa.

SPECIFICATIONS
Weight:
  (150 kVA) 11 500 kg
  (250 kVA) 12 000 kg
Length: 4·87 m
Width: 2·338 m
Height: 2·354 m
Engine:
  (150 kVA) water-cooled, turbo-charged diesel
  (250 kVA) water-cooled, turbo-charged, after-cooled
diesel
Fuel capacity: 1140 litres
Operating duration: 24 h
Output: 150 or 250 kVA, 400/230 V, three phase and
neutral

150/250 kVA mobile generating set

Portable Lead Acid Battery Charger

DESCRIPTION
Intended for the re-charging of vehicle and radio or other
equipment lead acid batteries, this portable battery
charger is carried in a square section or tubular steel
frame. It is powered by a four-stroke engine which is
started by a rope start device and sufficient fuel is carried in the tank for five hours of full load operation. A
control unit box carried on the frame contains a voltmeter, an ammeter, a circuit breaker, a rheostat and the
power output sockets. The control unit also contains the
full wave rectifier bridge and a panel on the box provides
operating instructions. The charger has a fully screened
and suppressed ignition system.

SPECIFICATIONS
Weight: 60 kg
Length: 0·6 m
Width: 0·45 m
Height: 0·5 m
Engine: four-stroke, providing 4 hp continuous rating at
2600 rpm
Fuel capacity: 4 litres
Operating duration: 5 h
Output: 960 W, 32 V dc

STATUS
Production. In service with the South African Defence
Forces.

MANUFACTURER
Anderson Generating Manufacturers.
  Enquiries to Armscor, Private Bag X337, Pretoria
0001, South Africa.

Portable battery charger

UNITED KINGDOM

5 kVA 400 Hz Lightweight Portable Generating Set

DESCRIPTION
The Air-Log 5 kVA 400 Hz generating set is ideally
suited for such uses as the power source for 400 Hz
hand tools such as drills and rock-breakers. It is man-
portable and can be carried by light vehicles and
helicopters. The continuous maximum power output of
5 kVA is available up to an equivalent altitude of 1520
metres.
  The set consists of a JLO two-stroke, air-cooled petrol
engine directly coupled to a 14-pole, three-phase alternator with self-exciting field. All the assemblies are resiliently mounted within a welded steel frame, at one
end of which are positioned the controls, instrumentation and power point unit. A stowable carrying handle is
provided at each end of the set.

STATUS
In production.

MANUFACTURER
Air-Log Limited, North Lane, Aldershot, Hampshire,
England.

*Air-Log 5 kVA 400 Hz lightweight portable
generating set*

SPECIFICATIONS
Voltage:
(output) 208 V
(regulation) ± 6%
Frequency:
(output) 400 Hz
(regulation) ± 3·5%
Power: 5 kVA at 0·8 – 1·00 pf

Sockets:
25 A: 1
16 A: 1
Earthing: spike and cable
Instruments: frequency meter and hours run meter
Engine: JLO L372 2-stroke, air-cooled with manually operated recoil starter
Fuel: 25:1 petrol/oil mixture

Fuel capacity: 9·1 litres
Fuel consumption: 4 litres/h at full load
Endurance: 2·25 h at full load
Dry weight: 106 kg
Length: 0·851 m
Width: 0·47 m
Height: 0·634 m

4·5 kVA 50 Hz Lightweight Portable Generating Set

DESCRIPTION
The Air-Log 4·5 kVA 50 Hz lightweight portable generating set can be used as a power source for mobile workshops, lighting and communications. The continuous maximum output of 4·5 kVA at 0·8 to 1·0 pf is obtainable up to an equivalent altitude of 1520 metres. The output is controlled to closer tolerances than usual in generators of this type and the set has been fully proved in extensive climatic and rough road trials.

The set consists of a welded steel framework within which all the assemblies are resiliently mounted and, except for the carrying handles and base skids, no part of the generator extends beyond this protective framework.

The power unit/alternator assembly comprises a JLO L372 two-stroke, air-cooled petrol engine directly connected to the rotating armature self-exciting alternator. The engine has an integral primary fuel tank and a secondary tank is mounted above the alternator housing. The control, instrumentation, and power point unit is contained within a protective casing at one end of the framework.

SPECIFICATIONS
Voltage:
(output) 240 V
(regulation) ± 2·5%
Frequency:
(output) 50 Hz
(regulation) ± 2·5%
Power: 4·5 kVA at 0·8 – 1·0 pf
Sockets:
25 A: 2
13 A: 2
5 A: 1
Earthing: spike and cable
Instruments: voltmeter, ammeter, frequency meter, hours run meter
Engine: JLO L372 2-stroke, air-cooled with manually operated recoil starter

Air-Log 4·5 kVA 50 Hz lightweight portable generating set

Fuel: 25:1 petrol/oil mixture
Fuel capacity: 31·81 litres
Fuel consumption: 4 litres/h (approx) at full load
Endurance: 8 h at full load
Dry weight: 152 kg
Length: 0·99 m
Width: 0·565 m
Height: 0·66 m

STATUS
Production.

MANUFACTURER
Air-Log Limited, North Lane, Aldershot, Hampshire, England.

Plessey 1·5 kW and 1·9 kVA Generating Sets

DESCRIPTION
The 1·5 kW and 1·9 kVA generating sets are both lightweight man-portable units designed to provide 28 volt dc or 240 volt 50 Hz ac respectively. Both units employ an identical single-cylinder four-stroke petrol engine and have directly coupled brushless air-cooled generators. Fuel is supplied by an integral fuel pump from a separate jerrican via a kink-proof hose and an elapsed time indicator records the number of hours run. These generators are suitable for a wide range of appli-

cations including permanent or standby sources of electrical power for battery charging, communications, field workshops and medical equipment.

Both sets can be delivered with silencing kits fitted which considerably reduce the operating noise. These are particularly useful in command post or medical post environments.

STATUS
Production.

MANUFACTURER
Plessey Aerospace Limited, Abbey Works, Titchfield, Fareham, Hampshire PO14 4QA, England.

SPECIFICATIONS

Model	1·5 kW	1·9 kVA
Weight (dry)	63 kg	81 kg
Length	0·64 m	0·712 m
Width	0·464 m	0·457 m
Height	0·541 m	0·542 m
Engine	Kohler type 181 EP single cylinder, 4-stroke, air-cooled petrol, 305 cc, 2400 rpm	
Lubrication	oil splash	oil splash
Ignition	magneto	magneto
Generator	brushless, 30 V dc at 53·5 A continuous, air-cooled	brushless, 240 V 50 Hz 1·9 kVA continuous, air-cooled

Plessey 1·5 kW generating set

Plessey 1·9 kVA generating set

Plessey 1·5 kW 28 V dc and 2 kVA 400 Hz Three-phase Engine-driven Generating Sets

DESCRIPTION
Designed primarily as a ground supply source for the Westland Lynx helicopter, these lightweight, man-portable generating sets comprise a single cylinder, 4-stroke petrol engine coupled to a generator providing dc or ac power. The sets are connected to the helicopter by an integral cable and socket assembly. They are also suitable for use with the Puma and Gazelle helicopters.

SPECIFICATIONS

Type	1·5 kW dc	2 kVA, 400 Hz
Output (nominal)	28 V dc	200 V L/L–115 V L/N 3-phase
Rating	1·5 kW continuous	2 kVA
Voltage regulation	± 1 V dc	± 3·5 V L/L steady state
Engine type	Kohler K181 EP	Kohler K181 EP
Weight (dry)	67 kg	76 kg
Dimensions	541 × 464 × 640 mm	541 × 464 × 781 mm

STATUS
Production.

MANUFACTURER
Plessey Aerospace Limited, Abbey Works, Titchfield, Fareham, Hampshire PO14 4QA, England.

Plessey 1·5 kW 28 V dc set

Plessey 2 kVA, 400 Hz set

Plessey 1·5 kW 56 V dc Engine-driven Generating Set

DESCRIPTION
This lightweight rugged generating set comprises a single cylinder, four-stroke petrol engine coupled to a brushless 56 V dc generator. The output may be used to charge a bank of batteries or directly supply equipment. Engine starting is accomplished by a rope start or by an electric motor which obtains its supply from the batteries under charge.

SPECIFICATIONS
Output: (nominal) 56 V dc
Rating: 1·5 kW continuous
Voltage adjustment range: 56 to 60 V
Current limit range: 20 to 25 A
Weight: (dry) 75 kg
Dimensions: 541 × 464 × 702 mm
Engine model: Kohler K181 EP single-cylinder 4-stroke
Engine capacity: 305 cc

STATUS
Pre-production.

MANUFACTURER
Plessey Aerospace Limited, Abbey Works, Titchfield, Fareham, Hampshire PO14 4QA, England.

Plessey 1·5 kW 56 V dc engine-driven generating set

Plessey 2 kW 120 V ac Engine-driven Generating Set

DESCRIPTION
The 2 kW 120 volt single-phase ac man-portable generating set comprises a single-cylinder four-stroke petrol engine coupled to a brushless ac generator. The unit has been designed to supply power for underwater lighting equipment under adverse environmental conditions, and incorporates a high corrosion resistant finish. The engine incorporates a mechanically-driven fuel pump which draws fuel from an integral tank to supply the side draught carburettor. The fuel tank capacity is sufficient to run the set for 1·5 hours.

STATUS
Pre-production.

MANUFACTURER
Plessey Aerospace Limited, Abbey Works, Titchfield, Fareham, Hampshire PO14 4QA, England.

Plessey 2 kW 120 V ac engine-driven generating set

SPECIFICATIONS
Output: (nominal) 120 V 280 Hz ac
Rating: 2 kW continuous
Voltage adjustment range: 105 to 125 V

Voltage regulation: ± 4 V
Length: 0·6414 m
Width: 0·4636 m
Height: 0·5461 m

Weight: (dry) 71 kg
Engine model: Kohler K181 EP single-cylinder 4-stroke
Engine capacity: 305 cc

Plessey B20 Hand-operated Generator

DESCRIPTION
This fully-sealed hand-operated generator has been designed to power portable communications equipment in remote locations under the most arduous conditions, including total water immersion, and has parachute drop capabilities. The dc output is capable of float charging a clip-on one amp hour battery and simultaneously powering communications equipment with the minimum of operator effort.

SPECIFICATIONS
Winding speed: 55 – 80 rpm
Output at standard winding speed:
   (voltage) 31·5 ± 0·5 V
   (current) 300 ± 45 mA
   (power) 8 W nominal
Weight: 2·5 kg
Height: (overall) 0·1538 m
Length: (overall) 0·2064 m
Width: (overall) 0·1413 m

STATUS
Production.

MANUFACTURER
Plessey Aerospace Limited, Abbey Works, Titchfield, Fareham, Hampshire PO14 4QA, England.

Plessey B20 hand-operated generator with clip-on battery connected

Plessey 300/500 W dc Engine-driven Generating Set

DESCRIPTION
Designed primarily to recharge batteries for communications equipment in the field, this lightweight man-portable set comprises a single cylinder, four-stroke petrol engine coupled to a brushless dc generator. An integral fuel tank provides fuel for four hours operation at normal full load. A fuel changeover cock, fuel pipe and jerrican adaptor enable fuel to be supplied from a separate source to extend the running time. Nominally rated at 300 W for full military environments, the generator has a 500 W capability under temperate climatic conditions.

SPECIFICATIONS
Weight: (dry) 23 kg
Voltage range: 24 – 36 V dc
Voltage regulation: ± 1 V
Engine: 93 cc single-cylinder 4-stroke
Length: 0·43 m
Height: 0·4 m
Width: 0·31 m

STATUS
Production.

MANUFACTURER
Plessey Aerospace Limited, Abbey Works, Titchfield, Fareham, Hampshire PO14 4QA, England.

Plessey 300/500 W dc engine-driven generating set

Plessey 6·25 kVA Engine-driven Generating Set

DESCRIPTION
The 6·25 kVA generating set is a four-man-portable unit which provides ac power for remote ground servicing of aircraft. The set comprises an air-cooled, two-cylinder, four-stroke petrol engine, a belt-driven brushless ac generator and a control box, which houses the solid state voltage regulator and protection circuits, and the panel-mounted meters and controls. The main assemblies are supported within a rigid steel carrying frame on anti-vibration mounts.

SPECIFICATIONS
Output: (nominal) 200 V L/L 400 Hz 3-phase
Rating: 6·25 kVA at 0·8 pf continuous
Engine: Weslake 2-cylinder, 4-stroke
Weight: (dry, with covers) 218 kg
Length: 1·455 m
Width: 0·635 m
Height: 0·86 m

STATUS
Production.

MANUFACTURER
Plessey Aerospace Limited, Abbey Works, Titchfield, Fareham, Hampshire PO14 4QA, England.

Plessey 6·25 kVA engine-driven generating set

Plessey 4·5 kW dc Engine-driven Generating Set

DESCRIPTION
The 4·5 kW engine-driven generating set is a self-contained power unit suited for operation where quietness is desirable. The set is enclosed by lightweight, easily removed, sound attenuating covers. Access doors are provided at the front of the enclosure for servicing. The set has been designed for vehicle mounting with, for convenience of operation on the vehicle, the meters and controls positioned at the base of the set. The control panel incorporates a remote control connector which enables the set to be operated from the vehicle cabin. Lifting eyes and fork lift guides are provided for handling.

SPECIFICATIONS
Output: (nominal) 28 V dc plus 200 V 3-phase 400 Hz
Rating: 4·5 kW total max continuous
Voltage regulation: 28 V dc ± 0·7 V
Weight: (dry) 250 kg
Engine: Petter AC2, 2-cylinder air-cooled diesel
Engine capacity: 608 cc
Length: 1·15 m
Width: 0·75 m
Height: 0·9 m

STATUS
Pre-production.

MANUFACTURER
Plessey Aerospace Limited, Abbey Works, Titchfield, Fareham, Hampshire PO14 4QA, England.

Plessey 4·5 kW engine-driven generating set

Plessey 20 kW 50 Hz Three-phase Engine-driven Generating Set

DESCRIPTION
The 20 kW engine-driven generating set is a modular, self-contained power unit suited for operation in military environments. The set is enclosed in light, easily removed, sound attenuating covers which have access doors for servicing. The set has been designed to enable two units to be mounted back-to-back on the forward section of a standard four-tonne flat-bed truck and for convenience of operation on the vehicle, the meters and controls have been positioned at the base of the set. Lifting eyes at the top corners of the unit and fork lift guides at the base provide for ease of handling.

The set comprises a lightweight, brushless, air-cooled 25 kVA generator which is toothed-belt-driven by a BLMC 2·5-litre diesel engine converted to a marine specification. The set incorporates a 90-litre fuel tank, giving a nominal eight hours operation without refuelling, and a 24-volt battery which provides power for the starting and control, and protection circuits.

SPECIFICATIONS
Output: (nominal) 415 V L/L, 240 V L/N, 50 Hz 3-phase
Rating: 25 kVA
Voltage regulation: ±1·5%
Engine: BLMC Type 25VD diesel
Acoustic level: 67 dBA at 6 m
Weight: (dry, with covers) 1187 kg
Length: 1·575 m
Width: 1·22 m
Height: 1·545 m

STATUS
Production.

MANUFACTURER
Plessey Aerospace Limited, Abbey Works, Titchfield, Fareham, Hampshire PO14 4QA, England.

Plessey 20 kW 50 Hz 3-phase engine-driven generating set

Plessey Mobile 10 kVA Generator

DESCRIPTION
The Plessey mobile 10 kVA generator provides three-phase output from an air-cooled brushless ac generator driven by a diesel engine from a belt drive. The equipment is pallet-mounted and fully enclosed in an acoustic casing for quiet operation. Automatic regulation and such features as automatic load disconnection in the event of a fault are incorporated. The equipment has a 12-gallon (45·4 litre) fuel tank giving an endurance of about eight hours and a 24-volt battery is provided for starting and control circuitry. The control panel is placed at the generator base for ease of use when the generator is placed on a truck, and the climatic range of operation is stated to be between −32 and +44°C. The weight of the complete generator is approximately 825 kg, and lashing points are provided for securing and lifting.

SPECIFICATIONS
Output: (nominal) 200 V L/L 400 Hz 3-phase
Rating: 10 kVA at 0·8 pf lag continuous
Voltage regulation: ± 2%
Engine: BLMC Type 15VD diesel
Weight: (dry with covers) 825 kg
Fuel capacity: 45·4 litres
Acoustic level: 64dBA at 6 m
Length: 1·3 m
Width: 1·14 m
Height: 1·38 m

STATUS
In production. Ordered for the British and Norwegian armies.

MANUFACTURER
Plessey Aerospace Limited, Abbey Works, Titchfield, Fareham, Hampshire PO14 4QA, England.

Plessey mobile generator mounted on Bedford MK (4 × 4) 4-tonne truck

Dale High Speed Mobile Generating Sets

DESCRIPTION
Dale Electric manufactures a range of high speed, trailer-mounted generating sets with outputs up to 40 kVA. These units are suitable for towing behind most military vehicles and provide power for mobile communication equipment.

The set comprises an air-cooled diesel engine coupled to a brushless alternator, starter batteries, fuel tank and full controls. Various Dale models can be utilised to provide the output, voltage and frequency required.

Included in the complete mobile package are a protective steel canopy, 3-tonne NATO hitch, overrun braking system, parking brake, a stabilising jack on all four corners and full road lighting.

STATUS
In production. In service with several countries.

MANUFACTURER
Dale Electric of Great Britain Limited, Electricity Buildings, Filey, North Yorkshire YO14 9PJ, England.

Trailer-mounted 27·5 kVA set powered by 6-cylinder water-cooled engine

Dale Shield Transportable Generating Sets

DESCRIPTION
These lightweight, compact units are designed for use in all conditions, in ambient temperatures from −30 to +55°C and at altitudes of up to 2440 metres. They can be quickly transported to the required location by either truck or helicopter, then positioned ready for immediate operation.

The Dale generating set, powered by an air-cooled diesel engine, is mounted on a strong, fabricated base-plate and protected by a steel weatherproof canopy. Access to the controls, cables and all necessary sections for maintenance is via hinged doors or removeable panels. Various outputs, voltages and frequencies are available to suit most power requirements.

STATUS
In production. In service with several armed forces.

MANUFACTURER
Dale Electric of Great Britain Limited, Electricity Buildings, Filey, North Yorkshire YO14 9PJ, England.

Dale Shield lightweight 40 kVA generator as used by British Army

Dale Containerised Generating Set

DESCRIPTION
Completely housed in a walk-around container, this Dale power package is designed and manufactured for easier lifting, transportation, shipping and site-to-site movement.

The self-contained unit, which requires no special foundations, is dropped into position and then connected to the load for immediate use.

The ISO container provides full protection against harsh climates and can be acoustically treated to reduce noise level.

Inside the container, the Dale diesel-powered generating set can provide an output of up to 500 kVA, with voltages and frequencies to suit the power requirements.

STATUS
Production. In service with several armed forces.

MANUFACTURER
Dale Electric of Great Britain Limited, Electricity Buildings, Filey, North Yorkshire YO14 9PJ, England.

Dale containerised generator

UNITED STATES OF AMERICA

All-Power Inc Generating Sets (Gensets)

DESCRIPTION

All-Power Inc produces a very wide range of generating sets that vary in output from 5 kW to 2500 kW. Most of the All-Power Inc sets (known as Gensets) are produced for commercial applications but nearly all the models in the range have been purchased by various agencies for military use, including a quantity for use by the US forces in the USA and overseas. More have been sold to other armed forces through commercial agencies.

Most Gensets are large heavy-duty units for static use. However, the ability of All-Power Inc to produce to precise customer requirements means that Gensets may also be placed onto trailers or semi-trailers, into containers or onto various forms of skid mounting. The choice of prime motive power is wide and is covered below but most Gensets use a revolving field, four-pole, single bearing, permanently aligned alternator with flexible steel drive discs, a high capacity cooling fan and drip-proof construction. The outboard end of the shaft is carried in a pre-lubricated anti-friction bearing, and the exciter is a brushless design (no slip ring) that requires little or no maintenance. Each machine has a solid state automatic voltage regulator, and each alternator is fully tropicalised and has anti-fungus protection. A 12- or 24-volt starting system is used on most models, and all the major models are fitted onto a heavy duty steel skid-type base.

The All-Power Gensets are provided with designations that indicate the type of prime motive power plant used, as follows:

DA Allis Chalmers, DB Mercedes-Benz, DC Cummins, DD Deutz, DE EMD, DF FIAT, DG Detroit Diesel, DH White Hercules, DK Caterpillar, DL Lister, DM Mitsubishi, DN Dorman, DO Volvo, DP Perkins, DR Rolls Royce, DT Petter, DV VM, DW Waukesha.

Typical All-Power generating set

In the Specifications table only one of these types has been given but similar tabulations could be provided for any model in the entire Genset range.

STATUS
In production. In service with the US armed forces and many other armed forces.

MANUFACTURER
All-Power Inc, 130 East Washington Street, PO Box 1189, Norristown, Pennsylvania 19404, USA.

SPECIFICATIONS (DH series – White Hercules diesel engines)

Model	AP-27DH	AP-33DH	AP-50DH	AP-60DH	AP-75DH	AP-110DH	AP-135DH
Engine model	D2000	D2300	D2300T	D3300T	D3400T	D4800T	D4800TA
Continuous standby rating (kW/kVA)							
(60 Hz)	27/33·75	33/41·25	50/62·5	60/75	75/93·75	110/137·5	135/168·75
(50 Hz)	22/27·5	27/33·75	40/50	50/62·5	62/77·5	90/112·5	110/137·5
Prime power rating (kW/kVA)							
(60 Hz)	25/31·25	30/37·5	45/56·25	54/67·5	68/85	100/125	125/156·25
(50 Hz)	20/25	25/31·25	35/43·75	44/55	55/68·75	81/101·25	102/127·5
Number of cylinders	4	4	4	6	6	6	6
Weight (dry)	824 kg	824 kg	881 kg	1031 kg	1122 kg	1613 kg	1685 kg
Length	1·676 m	1·676 m	1·742 m	2·007 m	2·083 m	2·413 m	2·413 m
Width	0·66 m	0·66 m	0·66 m	0·686 m	0·686 m	0·813 m	0·813 m
Height	1·194 m	1·194 m	1·194 m	1·448 m	1·448 m	1·524 m	1·524 m
Export weight (dry)	960 kg	960 kg	1017 kg	1190 kg	1290 kg	1804 kg	1876 kg

'Patriot' Electric Power Plants

DESCRIPTION

Developed for use with the US Army's Patriot missile system, this 150 kW turbine generator system was developed by the US Army Mobility Equipment Research and Development Command (MERADCOM) and the initial units were assembled at the Command's own shop facility and by the George Engine Company of Harvey, Louisiana. The first two service-type examples were delivered during March 1982 to Fort Bliss, Texas. Procurement plans call for 101 units by 1989.

The current generator type is the EPP 11 (the EPP 1 was a development model). The Patriot EPP 11 consists of an M811 truck chassis with two on-board fuel tanks, electric cables, cable racks, a supporting structure, and the two 150 kW turbine generators manufactured by Detroit Diesel Allison. In operation it will provide 120 and 208 volts ac at 400 Hertz to the Patriot system radar and engagement control station. A sepa-rate electrical power unit (EPU) with two 60 kW turbine generators is mounted on an M353 trailer. The EPU provides power for the Patriot system Command and Control Group and the Command Relay Group.

STATUS
Production.

AGENCY
US Army Mobility Equipment Research and Development Command, Fort Belvoir, Virginia 22060, USA.

EPP11 showing twin turbines, four cables leading to WCG and RG, and 600-gallon fuel trailer (US Army)

'Patriot' system Electric Power Unit (EPU) used for 'Patriot' Command and Control Group and Command Relay Group, consisting of two 60 kW turbine engine generators mounted on M353 trailer (US Army)

Standard US Army Mobile Generator Sets and Power Plants

The following mobile generating sets and electric power plants are standardised for US Army service:

Type	Mounted on	Outputs	End use
PU-304/MPQ-4	M103A3 or M105 Trailers	10 kW, 120/208, 120/240 V, 400 Hz	Radar Set, AN/MPQ-4
PU-332A/G	M101A1 Trailer	10 kW, 120/208 V, 60 Hz	Radio Terminal Set, AN/TRC-112
			Radar TT Set, AN/GRC-142, AN/TAQ-1A, B
PU-375B/G	M101A1 Trailer	10 kW, 120/208 V, 400 Hz	Radio Set, AN/TPS-1D
			Radar Receiving Set, AN/TKQ-1, AN/TKQ-2
PU-401/M	M200A1 Trailer	45 kW, 120/208–240/416 V, 400 Hz	Satellite Communications Terminals, AN/TSC-54, AN/MSC-46
			Weapons Monitoring Centre; Maintenance Van, Radar Processing Centre
			HAWK System
			Data Control Centre, AN/GSA-37
			AA Defence System, AN/MGS-4
			Chaparral-Vulcan System
PU-402/M	M200A1 Trailer	15 kW, 120/208–240/416 V, 60 Hz	Radar Set, AN/MPS-34
			TOE 44-235D and 44-535D
PU-405/M	M200A1 Trailer	15 kW, 120/208–240/416 V, 60 Hz	Photo Dark Room, ES-72A
			Radio Terminal Set, AN/TRC-121
			Transportable Electronic Workshop, AN/GSM-44
			Operations Controls, AN/MSQ-28, AN/TSQ-38A and B
			TOE 44-235D and 44-435D Missile System
			Flight Operations Control, AN/MSW-6
			Mobile Micro, F/EUR
			Radio Network, AN/FRC-81
PU-406/M	M200A1 Trailer	30 kW, 120/208–240/416 V, 60 Hz	Navigation Set, AN/ASN-86
			Flight Control Co-ordinating Centre, AN/TSC-61A
			Photo Dark Room, ES-38A and B
			Tactical Image Interpretation Centre, AN/TSQ-43
			Communications Systems, AN/TSC-18, AN/TSC-19
			Printing Plant, Special Warfare
			Bakery Plant, M-1945
			Computer System, Digital AN/MYK-7
			Aircraft Shop Sets, TOE 1-87G, 1-128T, 1-207G, 1-258H, 1-500G, 29-119G, 29-205F, 29-134G, 29-206G, 29-207G, 29-215G, 30-14G, 30-17G, 30-18G, 33-500G, 44-236D, 44-535G, 55-157G, 55-247G, 55-570G
PU-407/M	M200A1 Trailer	45 kW, 120/208–240/416 V, 60 Hz	Operations Controls, AN/MSQ-28B, AN/MSQ-19
			Photographic Laboratory, St. Mounted, ES-22
PU-408/M	M54 Truck	45 kW, 120/208–240/416 V, 60 Hz	HAWK and Nike-Hercules Missile Systems
PU-409A/M	M101A1 Trailer	5 kW, 120/240–120/208 V, 60 Hz	Combat Radar Surveillance Set, AN/APS-94
PU-495/G	M353 Trailer	100 kW, 120/240–240/416 V, 60 Hz	Teletype Message Centre, AN/TSC-50C
			Satellite Communications Terminal, AN/MSC-46
			Data Processing Centre, AN/MYQ-2
			Communications System, AN/TSC-48C, AN/TSC-18
PU-551/M	M200A1 Trailer	45 kW, 120/208–240/416 V, 60 Hz	Electronic Shop, Trailer-Mounted, AN/ASM-189
PU-564A/G and	M105A2 Trailer	10 kW, 120/208 V, 60 Hz	Laboratory Dark Room, AN/TFQ-7, 7A and 7B
PU-564B/G			Radio Set, AN/GLQ-2, AN/TRC-29, AN/MRC-2, 2A, 2B, 2C and 2D
			Radar Sets, AN/MPQ-10, AN/MPQ-29
			Communications Systems, AN/TSC-18, AN/TSC-19
			Sound Ranging Set, AN/TNS-50
			Direction Finder Set, AN/TRD-23
PU-614/M	M200A1 Trailer	45 kW, 120/240–240/416 V, 60 Hz	Pershing Missile System
PU-617/M	M101A1 Trailer	3 kW, 120/240–120/208 V, 60 Hz	Telephone Control Offices, AN/MTC-7A, AN/MTC-17
			Radio Terminal Set, AN/MRC-68
			Teletype Control Offices, AN/MGC-9
			Communications Switchboard, SB-675/MSC, SB-611/MRC
			Radio Beacon Set, AN/GRN-6
			Communications Patching Terminal, AN/TSC-76
PU-618/M	M103A3 Trailer	5 kW, 120/240–120/208 V, 60 Hz	Communications Patching Panel, SB-675A/M SC
			Teletype Central Offices, AN/MGC-9A
			Radio Set, AN/GRC-41, AN/TRC-110, AN/TRC-151, AN/TRC-152, AN/TRC-117
			Communications Operations Centres, AN/MSC-31 and 31A, AN/MSC-33
			Direction Finder Set, AN/TRD-4A
PU-619/M	M103A3 Trailer	10 kW, 120/240 V, 60 Hz	Teletypewriter Communications Centre, AN/MSC-29, AN/MGC-19
			Radio Relay Terminal, AN/MRC-112
			Communications Central, AN/TSC-20
			Teletype Switchboard Group, AN/TSA-15, AN/TSC-58
			Telephone Switchboard Office, Manual, AN/MTC-1 and 1A
			Radio Set, AN/GRC-26D, AN/MRG-69, 73, 102; AN/MRT-9
			Electronic Shop, AN/TSM-71, AN/TSM-55A, AN/ASM-146
			Message Centre, AN/GSQ-80 and 80A
			Teletypewriter Central, AN/MGC-9
			Radio Receiving Set, AN/MRR-8
			Radio Repeater Set, AN/MRC-54
			Telegraph-Telephone Terminal, AN/MCC-6
			Radio Repair Set, AN/MRC-103
			Multiplexer Set, AN/TCC-13
			Radio Terminal, AN/TRC-133
PU-620/M	M116A1 Trailer	5 kW, 120/240–120/208 V, 60 Hz	various applications
PU-625/G	M101A1 Trailer	3 kW, 120/240–120/208 V, 60 Hz	Repeater Set, AN/TRC-113
			Radio Terminal Set, AN/TRC-145
PU-626/G	M101A1 Trailer	3 kW, 120/240–120/208 V, 60 Hz	Radio Repeater Set, AN/TRC-109
			Radio Terminal Set, AN/TRC-108, AN/TRC-143
PU-628/G	M101A1 Trailer	3 kW, 120/240–120/208 V, 60 Hz	Telephone-Telegraph Terminals, AN/TCC-60, 65, 69, 72; AN/TCC-29
PU-629/G	M103A3 Trailer	5 kW, 120/240–120/208 V, 60 Hz	Telephone-Telegraph Terminals, AN/TCC-61 and 62; AN/TCC-23
			Terminal Equipment, AN/TSQ-84
PU-631/G	M103A3 Trailer	5 kW, 120/240–120/208 V, 60 Hz	Radio Repeater Sets, AN/TRC-111, AN/TRC-138
PU-643/M	M116A1 Trailer	5 kW, 120/240–120/208 V, 400 Hz	Landing Control Central, AN/TSQ-65
			Pershing Missile System
PU-650A/G	M200A1 Trailer	60 kW, 120/208–240/416 V, 50/60 Hz	Electrical Shop Van, Avionics, AN/ASM-189
PU-654/G	M416 Trailer	3 kW, 120-240–120/208 V, 400 Hz	Radar Set, AN/MLQ-29
PU-656/G	M103A3 Trailer	10 kW, 120/240–120/208 V, 400 Hz	Radar Surveillance Set, AN/GSS-1, AN/GSS-7
			Aircraft Control Centre, AN/TSQ-72
PU-666/G	M10⁻A1 Trailer	3 kW, 28 V dc	European Wideband Communications System (EWCS)

Type	Mounted on	Outputs	End use
PU-XM-666	M105A2 Trailer	45 kW, 120/208–240/416 V, 400 Hz	Sergeant Missile System
PU-XM-673	M105A2 Trailer	30 kW, 120/208 V, 400 Hz	Sergeant Missile System
PU-677/M	M116A1 Trailer	10 kW, 120/240–120/208 V, 60 Hz	Teletypewriter Terminal Set, AN/GRC-108
			Radio Beacon, AN/TRN-6
PU-678/M	M116A1 Trailer	10 kW, 120/240–120/208 V, 400 Hz	TOE 1-876
			Radio Set, AN/TRC-97B
			Aircraft Landing Control, AN/TSQ-71
PU-681/TLQ-15	M101A1 Trailer	10 kW, 120/240–120/208 V, 400 Hz	Counter-Measure Receiving Set, AN/TLQ-15
PU-684/GLQ-3	M101A1 Trailer	10 kW, 120/240–120/208 V, 400 Hz	Counter-Measure Receiving Set, AN/GLQ-3
PU-697/M	Dixie Van Corp (ADT P/N 200751) Trailer	750 kW, 240/416 V, 50/60 Hz	DoD Contingency Communications Systems
PU-699/M	M200A1 Trailer	60 kW, 120/208–240/416 V, 60 Hz	IWCS Communication Centre, AN/TSC-82
			Radio Set, AN/FRC-81
			Operations Centrals, AN/MSQ-19, AN/MSQ-28B
			Photo Laboratory, ES-22, AN/MSG-4
PU-700/M	M54A2 Truck	60 kW, 120/208–240/416 V, 50/60 Hz	Nike-Hercules Missile Systems
			Teletype Central Offices, AN/MGS-22, 23 and 32
PU-707/M	M200A1 Trailer	60 kW, 120/240–240/416 V, 400 Hz	Satellite Communications Terminals, AN/TSC-54, AN/MSC-46
			Weapons Monitoring Centre, Maintenance Van
			Radar Processing Centre
			HAWK Missile System
			Pershing Missile System
			Data Control Centre, AN/GSA-37
			AN/Defence System, AN/MGS-4
PU-732/M	M200A1 Trailer	15 kW, 120/240–120/208 V, 400 Hz	various applications
PU-751/M	M116A1 Trailer	5 kW, 120/240–120/208 V, 60 Hz	various applications
PU-753/M	M116A1 Trailer	10 kW, 120/240–120/208 V, 60 Hz	various applications
PU-760/M	M200A1 Trailer	30 kW, 120/240–120/208 V, 400 Hz	–
AN/MJQ-4	two M200A1 Trailers	45 kW, 120/208–240/416 V, 60 Hz	–
AN/MJQ-5	XM674 Trailer	200 kW, 120/208–240/416 V, 60 Hz	Radar Set, AN/MPQ-43
			Nike-Hercules Missile System, Mobile HIPAR
AN/MJQ-6	two M200A1 Trailers	45 kW, 120/208–240/416 V, 60 Hz	–
AN/MJQ-8	Truck or Trailer	45 kW, 120/208–240/416 V, 60 Hz	Teletype Terminals, AN/MGC-22, 23 and 32
AN/MJQ-9	M118 Trailer	15 kW, 120/208–240/416 V, 60 Hz	Communications Central, AN/MSQ-72
AN/MJQ-10	two M200A1 Trailers	30 kW, 120/208–240/416 V, 60 Hz	Base Radio Communications System, AN/TSC-26
			Radio Terminal Sets, AN/TRC-90, 90A, 90B; AN/TRC-129
			Central Telephone, PABX, AN/TTC-28
			Communications Central, AN/TSC-19
AN/MJQ-11	two XM3043W Pallets/Dolly Sets	200 kW, 120/208–240/416 V, 60 Hz	Radio Set, AN/TRC-132
AN/MJQ-12	two M200A1 Trailers	60 kW, 120/208–240/416 V, 60 Hz	Central Telephone, PABX, AN/TCC-28
			Radio Set, AN/GRC-132
AN/MJQ-14	three XM720 Dolly Sets and Pallets	60 kW, 120/208–240/416 V, 50/60 Hz	STRATCOM International Wide Band Communications System, AN/TSC-82
AN/MJQ-15	two M200A1 Trailers	15 kW, 120/240–120/208 V, 400 Hz	Tacfire
AN/MJQ-16	M103A3 Trailer	5 kW, 60 Hz	–
AN/MJQ-18	M103A3 Trailer	10 kW, 60 Hz	–

Standard US Army Static Generator Sets and Power Plants

Type	Output	Length	Width	Height	Weight	Engine power	Engine type
MEP-002A	5 kW, 60 Hz	1·286 m	0·813 m	0·94 m	422·2 kg	–	diesel
MEP-003A	10 kW, 120/240/208 V, 60 Hz	1·575 m	0·813 m	0·94 m	563 kg	20 hp	diesel
MEP-004A	15 kW, 120/208 V, 60 Hz	1·772 m	0·867 m	1·391 m	112·3 kg	36 hp	diesel
MEP-005A	30 kW, 50 and 60 Hz	2·026 m	0·864 m	1·391 m	1294 kg	55 hp	diesel
MEP-006A	60 kW, 50 and 60 Hz	2·21 m	0·864 m	0·991 m	1952·2 kg	108 hp	diesel
MEP-007A	100 kW, 120/208 V, 3-phase, 60 Hz	2·692 m	0·965 m	1·651 m	3033 kg	168 hp	diesel
MEP-009A	200 kW, 50 and 60 Hz	2·895 m	1·27 m	1·905 m	4699 kg	340 hp	diesel
MEP-011A	500 kW, 2400/4160 V, 60 Hz	5·563 m	2·235 m	2·565 m	15 603·5 kg	800 hp	diesel
MEP-014A	0·5 kW, 60 Hz	4·985 m	0·432 m	0·432 m	38·5 kg	1·5 hp	petrol
MEP-015A	1·5 kW, 120/240 V, 60 Hz	0·6953 m	0·5175 m	0·47 m	56·7 kg	3 hp	petrol
MEP-016A	3 kW, 120/240 V, 60 Hz	0·889 m	0·6033 m	0·635 m	129·3 kg	6 hp	petrol
MEP-017A	5 kW, 120/240 V, 60 Hz	1·0097 m	0·762 m	0·635 m	221·3 kg	10 hp	petrol
MEP-018A	10 kW, 60 Hz	1·448 m	0·762 m	0·711 m	385·5 kg	20 hp	petrol
MEP-019A	0·5 kW, 400 Hz	0·4985 m	0·432 m	0·432 m	38·5 kg	1·5 hp	petrol
MEP-021A	3 kW, 120/240 V, 400 Hz	0·889 m	0·6033 m	0·635 m	129·3 kg	6 hp	petrol
MEP-022A	5 kW, 120/240 V, 400 Hz	1·0097 m	0·762 m	0·635 m	221·3 kg	10 hp	petrol
MEP-023A	10 kW, 400 Hz	1·295 m	0·762 m	0·686 m	301·3 kg	20 hp	petrol
MEP-024A	0·5 kW, 28 V dc	1·4985 m	0·432 m	0·432 m	38·5 kg	1·5 hp	petrol
MEP-025A	1·5 kW, 28 V dc	0·6953 m	0·5175 m	0·47 m	56·7 kg	3 hp	petrol
MEP-026A	3 kW, 28 V dc	0·889 m	0·6033 m	0·635 m	129·3 kg	6 hp	petrol
MEP-029A	500 kW, 240/416 V, 60 Hz	5·563 m	2·235 m	2·565 m	15 603·5 kg	800 hp	diesel
MEP-103A	15 kW, 240/416 V, 60 Hz	1·772 m	0·867 m	1·391 m	112·3 kg	36 hp	diesel
MEP-104A	30 kW, 50 and 60 Hz	2·026 m	0·864 m	1·391 m	1294 kg	55 hp	diesel
MEP-105A	60 kW, 50 and 60 Hz	2·21 m	0·864 m	0·991 m	1952·2 kg	108 hp	diesel
MEP-106A	83·3 kW, 120/208 V, 3-phase, 50 Hz	2·692 m	0·965 m	1·651 m	3033 kg	168 hp	diesel
MEP-108A	200 kW, 50 and 60 Hz (precise)	2·895 m	1·27 m	1·905 m	4699 kg	340 hp	diesel
MEP-112A	10 kW, 120/240/208 V, 400 Hz	1·575 m	0·813 m	0·94 m	563 kg	20 hp	diesel
MEP-113A	15 kW, 240/416 V, 400 Hz	1·772 m	0·867 m	1·391 m	1134 kg	36 hp	diesel
MEP-114A	30 kW, 400 Hz	2·026 m	0·864 m	1·391 m	1360·7 kg	55 hp	diesel
MEP-115A	60 kW, 400 Hz	2·21 m	0·864 m	0·991 m	1859·7 kg	108 hp	diesel
MEP-116A	100 kW, 120/208 V, 3-phase, 400 Hz	2·692 m	0·965 m	1·651 m	3039 kg	168 hp	diesel
MEP-208A	750 kW, 60 Hz	12·192 m	3·15 m	3·962 m	44 450 kg	–	diesel
MEP-356A	60 kW, 115/208 V, 400 Hz	2·286 m	1·702 m	1·702 m	1270 kg	177 hp	gas turbine
MEP-404A	60 kW, 120/208–240/416 V, 400 Hz	1·524 m	0·9144 m	0·762 m	430·9 kg	90·5 hp	gas turbine
MEP-409A	750 kW, 2400/4160 V, 50/60 Hz	11·278 m	2·438 m	2·515 m	15 422 kg	1200 hp	gas turbine
MEP-412A	60 and 400 Hz	1·143 m	0·737 m	0·66 m	208·6 kg	–	gas turbine
MEP-414A	10 kW, 28 V dc	0·838 m	0·6096 m	0·5588 m	158·75 kg	28 hp	gas turbine

*MEP-208A containerised generator set which can pro-
duce 750 kW, 54 of which have been ordered or are
already in service, some with US Navy hospital units*

PORTABLE ROADWAYS

CZECHOSLOVAKIA

Truck-mounted Roadway Laying System

DESCRIPTION
This system consists of a Tatra 813 (8 × 8) cross-country truck chassis with two cassettes, each loaded with 40 linked steel plates behind the cab. The roadway is laid with the vehicle travelling in reverse. As the truck travels backwards, the trackways unfold into the horizontal, pass over rollers and are laid under each of the rear wheels. This system is used by the Czechoslovak Army to prepare exit points of bridges such as the PMP pontoon system.

STATUS
In service with the Czechoslovak Army.

MANUFACTURER
Czechoslovak state factories.

Czechoslovak truck-mounted roadway laying system on Tatra 813 (8 × 8) truck chassis showing method of operation

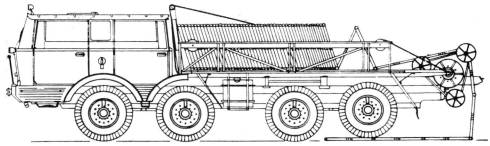

Tatra 813 (8 × 8) truck showing trackway laying method

FRANCE

ACMAT TPK 6.40 SPP Portable Roadway

DESCRIPTION
This is a plastic-based, reinforced portable roadway roller mounted on the rear of a standard 6 × 6 VLRA long-range reconnaissance vehicle chassis (refer to this entry in the *Transport equipment* section for details of the basic vehicle). The roadway roll is drum-mounted on a slewing platform on the rear of the chassis and is turned sideways for use. The roll is 60 metres long for wheeled traffic and 40 metres long for armoured vehicle use. The roadway can be laid over the front or rear of the vehicle, and can be recovered directly onto the drum, which is powered by a hydraulic winding motor. The tension of the roll during laying or recovery is controlled by a variable braking system fitted to the drum axle. Roadway laying rate is 10 metres a minute.

A lighter perforated trackway is now under development. The new track can be laid in shallow water without any flotation problems and 120 metres of trackway can be carried on each vehicle.

SPECIFICATIONS
Maximum roll length: 60 m
Weight: 12 kg/m²
Effective width: 3·33 m
Max carrying weight: 13 000 kg
Max longitudinal slope: 30%
Max side slope: 10%
Total weight of equipment: 3600 kg

6.40 SPP portable roadway in use

STATUS
In production. In service with the French Army.

MANUFACTURER
ACMAT, Ateliers de Construction Mécanique de l'Atlantique, Le Point de Jour, 44600 Saint-Nazaire, France.

6.40 SPP portable roadway ready for use (T J Gander)

GERMANY, FEDERAL REPUBLIC

Portable Roadway – Thyssen System

DESCRIPTION
The basis of this heavy portable roadway system is a hexagonal steel plate which is connected to adjoining plates by angled iron brackets. Each plate weighs 23 kg and a standard truck width can be formed by joining nine plates which form a roadway 4·2 metres wide. The roadway is constructed by hand and up to eight men can lay a metre of roadway every minute. To support a 5-tonne truck a mat of 200 plates is necessary, and for a 7-tonne truck, 288. To enable the system to be used for water crossings a method has been evolved in which a completed mat is towed across the water obstacle by a vehicle with a winch. One of the advantages of this system is that it can be assembled under cover and then dragged by winch across the ground to be covered, enabling heavy traffic to be built up rapidly in forward areas.

STATUS
In production. In service with West German forces and the Danish Army.

Thyssen portable roadway system being positioned at river crossing point (West German Army)

Close-up of Thyssen portable roadway system (West German Army)

Krupp Roll-out Matting

DESCRIPTION
Krupp roll-out matting may be used in conditions where normal road traffic would be unable to move, such as sandy ground or marshy meadowland. Under such conditions the use of this matting enables vehicles up to MLC Class 60 to cross. The roll-out matting may be laid by hand or from special laying units carried on 10-tonne trucks. The basic element of the matting is a multi-chamber aluminium alloy strip which is 250 mm wide and 57 mm deep. Each element is foam-filled and can be hinge-connected to other elements in varying widths. These widths may be as little as one metre for walkways to 16 metres for the assembly of temporary aircraft landing strips. For the rapid laying of roads from the vehicle-carried laying unit, widths of 4·6 to 5 metres are more usual. The weight per square metre of the basic elements is 33 kg. When laid from rolls, lengths may be up to 50 metres which will produce a roll diameter of 2·2 metres. If required elements may be joined together to form helicopter landing mats.

Apart from the vehicle-carried laying unit, acces-

Laying Krupp roll-out matting by hand

sories available for use with the Krupp roll-out matting include wedge-shaped panels for access ramps, safety dowels, anchors and tools.

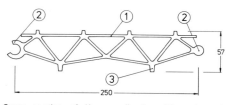

Cross section of Krupp roll-out matting element: (1) roadway surface, (2) hinge couplings, (3) spur-shaped underside

STATUS
Production.

MANUFACTURER
Krupp Industrietechnik GmbH, Franz-Schubert-Strasse 1–3, Postfach 14 19 60, D-4100 Duisburg 14 (Rheinhausen), Federal Republic of Germany.

GREECE

EBEX Class 60 Trackway

DESCRIPTION
The EBEX Class 60 Trackway uses the same components and general construction methods as the EBEX Runway Repair Decking described in the following section. The trackway is designed for both tracked and wheeled vehicles and is constructed from extruded sections made of heat-treated aluminium alloy. The trackway consists of a number of panels with a male tongue on one side and a female groove in the other. Each panel has a corrugated shape which together with additional grooves on the section faces provide an anti-slip surface. The panels are provided in 2·3- and 4·6-metre lengths which can be easily handled by one man. An end ramp panel section is supplied to enable vehicles to get onto the trackway easily.

The male and female connecting method joins panels together and for a permanent join a large bolt can be added. If the trackway is to be laid on a slope it should be anchored in place using a special chain and shackle assembly. A section handling tool can be supplied for ease of assembly and other accessories include a special towing adaptor.

To produce a standard trackway 40·4 metres long and 4·6 metres wide a full set as supplied will consist of the following; 185 4·6-metre long panels, 2 ramp panels, 4 handling tools, 4 towing adaptors, 380 locking bolts, 4 strap assemblies, 4 18-link welded chains, 24 steel guy stakes and 12 shackles.

The trackway can also be used to construct a mat to cover an area of soft ground for depot, maintenance area and other uses. A standard set can be produced to construct a mat 18·4 metres wide and 11·7 metres long. The tools and accessories supplied are the same as those used for a standard trackway set but the mat requires 185 4·6-metre panels, 54 2·3-metre panels and 8 ramp panels.

SPECIFICATIONS
Main section width:
(overall) 242 mm
(effective) 225 mm
Length:
(long panel) 4·6 m
(short panel) 2·3 m
Weight:
(long panel) 32 kg
(short panel) 16 kg
Ramp section width:
(overall) 184 mm
(effective) 152 mm
Ramp section length: (long panel) 4·6 m
Ramp section weight: (long panel) 45·4 kg
Breaking load: 1465 kg

Class 60 trackway ramp on left with long panel on right

STATUS
Production. In service with the Greek armed forces.

MANUFACTURER
EBEX SA, 2 Varnali and Dekelias Street, Nea Halkidon, Athens, Greece.

EBEX Class 60 trackway in use by M47 tank

EBEX Class 60 in use by truck

SWEDEN

Columbus Mat

DESCRIPTION
The Columbus mat was designed by Curt F Lundin and is used for a wide variety of civilian and military applications including reinforcement of soft ground to enable tracked or wheeled vehicles to cross difficult country, at river exit points, military bridge access mats and as recovery tracks for aircraft recovery after abortive take-offs and landings (100 sets have been sold to the Thai Air Force for this purpose).

The mat consists of polythene tubing held together by 15 steel cables. At the end of a 5-metre mat there are three tubes 65 mm in diameter and 15 mm thickness. The other tubes (71 in all) have an external diameter of 65 mm and are 5·8 mm thick. The cables have 171 threads and a diameter of 8 mm, and the cable ends are drawn in a loop back through the heavy end tube. Coupling links at the cable ends enable mats to be joined end-to-end to form a roadway of any length.

Laying and recovery require no special tools or equipment and the mat can be transported by truck either flat, rolled or folded.

For use by heavy vehicles at water crossings a special system called the Vehicle Mat 2 MT has been developed. The complete system consists of four mats each with 140 mm outside diameter end tubes and heavy duty cables with coupling links, two steel anchoring beams, four climbing frames, 12 chains, 10 soil anchor frames, 20 soil rod sets plus cables and other accessories. Weight of the complete equipment is

Columbus matting in use

Method of joining two sections of Columbus matting and showing polythene tube construction

5600 kg. The system was developed in close co-operation with the Swedish Army.

The basic idea is that the mats and the climbing frames, which consist of four Bailey bridge panels, are assembled on the bank on one side of the river and then winched down the far river bank by a winch on the far bank. Once in place the mats are held firmly in position by the soil anchor frames which are staked to the ground and connected to the anchoring beam by chains.

SPECIFICATIONS (Basic mat)
Width: 4·5 m (other widths available in 300 mm multiples)
Length: max 15 m (normal standard 5 m)
Weight: 20 kg/m²

STATUS
In production. In service with the armies of West Germany, Norway, Sweden, Switzerland, Thailand and the USA.

MANUFACTURER
Vårgårda Plast AB Columbus Mat Division, S-447 00 Vårgårda, Sweden.
Information and sales: Curt F Lundin, PO Box 1037, S-144 01 Rönninge 1, Sweden.

UNION OF SOVIET SOCIALIST REPUBLICS

Heavy Portable Roadway Sections

DESCRIPTION
There are three basic forms of portable heavy roadway used by the Soviet forces, two of which make use of the great timber resources of the USSR with timber girders and timber planks on timber ribs. As such there are many different forms and sizes and many are made either by local state factories or by army workshops. Although the sizes may vary, for supply purposes each section using wood planks is estimated to weigh between 160 and 220 kg less cross-pieces, and the girders are estimated to weigh between 250 and 300 kg.

Roadways using such timber sections are laid either by hand or by cranes and the rate of laying can vary between 40 and 60 metres per hour.

The third form of roadway section is manufactured from corrugated steel sheets, each weighing between 100 and 110 kg. Each section measures 2 × 1·05 × 0·08 metres, although this may vary. Roadways using these steel sheets can be assembled either by hand or by crane.

SPECIFICATIONS
(metal sections only)
Dimensions: 2 × 1·05 × 0·08 m
Wearing quality: 50 – 70 000 vehicles

Weight:
(single section) 100 – 110 kg
(section for 1 km road) 100 – 120 tonnes
Number of ZIL-164 trucks: (to transport 1 km of road) 30 – 35
Rate of laying: up to 100 m/h

STATUS
In production. In service with the Soviet and Warsaw Pact forces.

MANUFACTURER
All types: state factories. Can be assembled in army workshops.

Glued Plywood Roadway Sections – SRDP

DESCRIPTION
The lightest of the Soviet types of portable roadway is the SRDP (Sborno-Razbornoye-Dorozhnoye-Pokrytiye). The basic element of this system is a glued plywood panel 2·5 × 1 × 0·07 metres and weighing between 100 and 120 kg. Each panel is held in place by wooden inserts placed into butt-brackets at each end. The panels can be laid to form either strips or wider roadways. They are normally laid by hand with teams of 10 to 12 men, but a mechanical laying method has been developed which enables strips to be laid from amphibious PTS vehicles. This method replaces the wooden end inserts with steel cables and the panels are pre-prepared as they are loaded onto the PTS.

The panels are prepared using methods which have been especially developed to take advantage of the large timber resources of the Soviet Union. The wooden sheets that make up each panel are joined together by phenol-formaldehyde glues and are then rapidly passed to a further process which pressure coats the panels with a layer of bakelite material. The ends are covered by strips of similarly treated plywood and surface grip-

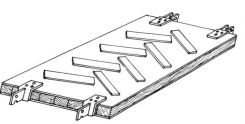
SRDP glued plywood roadway section

ping strips are added. Once manufactured the panels require no further maintenance and can be stored in the open if necessary.

SPECIFICATIONS
Panel dimensions: 2·5 × 1 × 0·7 m
Wearing quality: 40 – 50 000 vehicles
Weight:
(single panel) 100 – 120 kg
(panels for 1 km road) 80 – 100 tonnes
Number of ZIL-164 trucks: (to transport 1 km of road) 25 – 30
Rate of laying: 100 – 150 running m/h

SRDP glued plywood roadway in position

STATUS
In production. In service with the Soviet forces.

MANUFACTURER
State factories. Simplified versions may be assembled in army workshops.

UNITED KINGDOM

Laird Portable Roadways

DESCRIPTION
During the Second World War many military operations were either slowed down or halted because of the lack of sufficient and suitable equipment which could be used for rapid route repair, for example on main axis roads and river bridge entry and exit points. To meet this requirement Laird has developed the Class 30 and Class 60 Trackways. These are both portable non-skid surfaces designed for use on soft ground where conditions would become increasingly difficult with continual traffic and eventually result in the immobilisation of vehicles and mobile equipment. The Trackway can easily be taken up after use, transported elsewhere and relaid. Laird manufactures and supplies all components for these systems. The aluminium alloy (HE 30 TF) section used for the Class 30 and Class 60 Trackways was developed by the British Ministry of Defence in collaboration with the British Aluminium Company Limited, and is fabricated and marketed by Laird.

Class 30 Trackway
The Class 30 Trackway is designed for wheeled vehicles and tracked vehicles with rubber pads and entered service in 1963. Heavier vehicles can use the Trackway when ground conditions are favourable and tanks up to Class 50 may cross the Trackway at an angle provided they do not slew on the track.

The Class 30 Trackway is assembled from a number of extruded aluminium alloy planks with interlocking captive tongue-and-groove joints, forming a continuous non-skid surface 3·35 metres wide and normally 32 metres long. This standard Trackway length is reeled onto a carriage assembly mounted on the rear of a 6 × 6 or 4 × 4 truck. The British Army uses the Bedford

Class 30 Trackway being laid over rear of Bedford MK (4 × 4) 4000 kg truck (T J Gander)

RL or MK for this purpose. The spool carrying the length of track is mounted on a frame and turntable assembly which clamps to the truck platform. This arrangement permits the equipment to be stowed within the vehicle dimensions or swung through 90 degrees to the launching and recovery position. The Class 30 Trackway is launched forward over the truck cab using a quickly fitted removable roller frame launching assembly. The

track can also be launched over the rear of the truck. The preparation and launching operation can be completed in ten minutes by a three-man team. The Trackway is recovered over the rear of the vehicle and is rewound onto the spool by ratchet levers. Roller supports clamped to the rear of the truck platform support the track clear of the truck. The recovery operations can be completed in about 15 minutes by a four-man team.

SPECIFICATIONS (Class 30 trackway)
Length: 32–46 m
Width: 3·35 m
Number of planks: 140–201
Weight:
   (per metre run) 68 kg
   (carriage assembly) 760 kg
   (launching assembly) 340 kg
   (recovery equipment) 41 kg
   (total trackway and components) 3325–4280 kg
Individual plank size: 3·35 × 0·23 m

Class 60 Trackway
The heavy duty Class 60 Trackway is designed for both tracked and wheeled vehicles and entered service in 1967. Typical uses include supporting tanks on very soft ground and other areas subject to heavy traffic. The Trackway is quickly and easily assembled and the components can be transported in quantity by standard trucks. It has also been developed as an instant hard surface for repair of bomb-damaged airfield runways, for which there is a separate entry in the *Rapid runway repair equipment* section.

The Trackway is assembled from interlocking extruded aluminium alloy planks in two sizes: 4·57 × 0·23 metres and 2·28 × 0·23 metres. These dimensions enable a continuous load-carrying mat to be assembled quickly over areas of soft ground. The method of assembly is by sliding individual planks together successively and engaging a simple locking device. An access mat area 18·3 × 11·6 metres can be assembled in four hours by a team of ten men. A pre-assembled length of Class 60 Trackway 7·6 × 4·6 metres secured in a roll is easily laid and recovered by ten men. Tanks are driven onto the mat over the longitudinal lie of the planks and slewing can take place once the tracks are fully on the mat.

Two 4-ton trucks can transport components for the assembly of a trackway area measuring 18·3 × 11·6 metres. Components for assembling a roadway 15·3 metres in length and 4·6 metres in width can be loaded on one 3-ton truck as loose planks or as a single pre-assembled roll or as two pre-assembled rolls each 7·65 metres long.

SPECIFICATIONS (Class 60 applications)
Typical Class 60 mat
Length: 16·46 m
Width: 18·3 m
Area: 301 m²
Weight:
   (per m²) 34 kg
   (total) 10 300 kg

Typical Class 60 track
Length: 15·3 m
Width: 4·6 m
Weight:
   (per metre run) 156 kg
   (total) 2385 kg

Individual planks
Long plank	**Short plank**
length: 4·57 m	2·28 m
weight: 33·07 kg	16·76 kg

Class 30 Trackway being laid into position over front of Bedford MK (4 × 4) 4000 kg truck (T J Gander)

Class 30 Trackway in travelling position on Dutch Army DAF YA 616 (6 × 6) 6000 kg truck

STATUS
In production. In service with many countries including Canada, West Germany, Greece, Iraq, Japan, Netherlands, Saudi Arabia, Singapore, the United Kingdom and the USA.

MANUFACTURER
Laird (Anglesey) Limited, Beaumaris, Anglesey, Gwynedd LL58 8HY, Wales.

UNITED STATES OF AMERICA

MO-MAT Roadway System

DESCRIPTION
MO-MAT has been designed for laying over terrain such as mud, sand and snow to allow the passage of wheeled vehicles. It is also used for a variety of other roles including use as a helicopter pad.

MO-MAT is fabricated from a fibreglass-reinforced plastic called Stratoglas, which was developed by the Stratoglas Division of the Air Logistics Corporation. MO-MAT is moulded into a structural shape resembling that of a waffle with an overall thickness of 16 mm. It is also available in thicknesses of 2·2 and 3·2 mm forming a lattice cross section 16 mm thick overall and has a durable non-skid material bound to the top surface.

The standard duty MO-MAT (2·2 mm) weighs 4·9 kg/m² and the heavy duty MO-MAT (3·2 mm) 7·3 kg/m². MO-MAT is supplied in standard panels 3·709 metres wide and 14·782 metres long. Utility panels 3·709 metres wide and 6·6 metres long and sheets 3·6 metres long and 1·8 metres wide are also available. Precision holes are provided around the periphery for interconnecting panels or sheets to any desired length or width. Panels or sheets may also be attached to frames to form a variety of structures.

The MO-MAT panels reduce the ground pressure by spreading the wheel loads over a wider surface area. Excessive crowning of the roadway caused by heavy

MO-MAT roll being held ready for use by US Marine Corps bulldozer (R Young)

MO-MAT being used as helicopter pad by fully loaded CH-53 helicopter

MO-MAT rolled on pallet ready for delivery

STATUS
In production. In service with the US and other armed forces.

MANUFACTURER
Air Logistics Corporation, 3600 E Foothill Blvd, Pasadena, California, USA.
    British agent: Air-Log Limited, North Lane, Aldershot, Hampshire.

traffic can be mitigated by doubling the thickness of the roadway – laying one panel on top of the other – or increasing the width of the roadway and spreading the traffic pattern.

The sheets are supplied rolled up on a pallet for ease of transport and can be manually deployed, rerolled or assembled without the use of special tools or equipment.

Tactical Bridge Access/Egress System

DEVELOPMENT
The Tactical Bridge Access/Egress System has been developed under the aegis of the US Army Mobility Equipment Research and Development Command (MERADCOM) together with the US Army Waterways Experimental Station in Vicksburg, Mississippi. The system is designed to produce roadways for wheeled and tracked vehicles over soils and slopes normally impassible to those vehicles in order to provide access and egress from river-crossing bridges, and in particular the Ribbon Bridge. It is also intended to provide an access or egress roadway for swimming or wading vehicles to cross a water obstacle, and it should also be able to provide a general roadway for heavy traffic moving to and from the bridge point. Following a series of trials involving existing types of matting a contract for an all-new system was awarded in 1981 to Pacific Car and Foundry of Seattle, Washington, which is currently developing the system for full service acceptance.

DESCRIPTION
The system is designed to be carried on and used from existing 6 × 6 trucks already in service with US Army Ribbon Bridge and Engineer Companies. Each truck will carry a number of corrugated heat-treated steel panels which will be stacked on a stow/supply/ dispensing welded aluminium frame mounted directly on the transporter truck. The panels will be dispensed from the frame under the control of a powered three-tooth panel movement control, support and dispensing retarder sprocket. A cable and powered winch completes the system.

In use the steel panels will be stacked in concertina-fashion on the frame. To dispense the panels the truck may drive directly across the water obstacle dispensing the panels to the rear as it progresses. The connected panels unfold as they are fed outwards. An alternative is to reverse the truck towards the water obstacle dispens-ing the panels under its wheels as it moves. In this way the following number of men can lay the following track lengths.

Track length	Time	Number of men
15–20 m	15 minutes	1 Engineer Squad
100–125 m	30 minutes	10 men
250–300 m	45 minutes	1 Engineer Platoon

Once laid the system is intended to withstand 2000 to 3000 passes by military traffic, ten per cent of which will be in the MLC 70 class.

SPECIFICATIONS
Panel dimensions
Length: 4·013 m
Width: 1·295 m
Thickness: 89 mm
Weight: (stack of 35) 4536 kg

STATUS
Advanced development.

RAPID RUNWAY REPAIR EQUIPMENT/PORTABLE RUNWAYS

GREECE

EBEX Runway Repair Decking

DESCRIPTION

This runway repair decking is constructed from extruded sections of heat treated aluminium alloy and consists of panels and accessories that fit together to form a mat. The main sections have been designed to join with a male tongue at one end and a female groove at the other. Once in position the connections can be locked in place using a large bolt. The sections are supplied in two sizes, each size being man-portable. Each section is corrugated in cross-section and has an anti-skid upper surface. Ramp sections can be fitted to the sides or ends of the mat. Special tools in the form of handling picks can be supplied, along with towing adaptors. If required, securing pickets can be used.

To form a standard runway repair decking 18·4 metres wide and 11·7 metres long the following items are required: 185 long panels, 54 short panels, 8 long ramp panels, 4 handling tools, 4 towing adaptors, 480 locking devices and 40 expansion bolts. The resultant mat may be rolled for stowage if required.

The EBEX runway repair decking can be used, without anchoring, to form a forward area helicopter landing pad that can be rolled up and moved to a new location as required.

The components used for the EBEX runway repair decking are the same as those used for the EBEX Class 60 Trackway described in the previous section.

SPECIFICATIONS
Main section width:
(overall) 242 mm
(effective) 225 mm
Length:
(long panel) 4·6 m
(short panel) 2·3 m

Weight:
(long panel) 32 kg
(short panel) 16 kg
Ramp section width:
(overall) 184 mm
(effective) 152 mm
Ramp section length: (long panel) 4·6 m
Ramp section weight: (long panel) 45·4 kg
Breaking load: 1465 kg

STATUS
In production. In service with the Greek Air Force.

MANUFACTURER
EBEX SA, 2 Varnali and Dekelias Street, Nea Halkidon, Athens, Greece.

Moving rolled repair decking mat using mobile crane

Unrolling runway repair decking mat

EBEX runway repair decking in use by F-84F

EBEX runway repair decking being used as helicopter landing pad

UNITED KINGDOM

Rapid Runway Repair

DESCRIPTION

This rapid runway repair system is NATO approved and has undergone extensive trials by both the British and US Air Forces. It was accepted for service by Britain in 1970 and entered service in 1972.

It is based on the Rapid Runway Repair Mat which consists of an area of interlocking Class 60 aluminium alloy panels, a full description of which is given in the entry for Laird Portable Roadways in the *Portable roadways* section. The mat can be built to any desired size although the 22 × 16 metre mat is the accepted size for repairing of bomb craters caused by 340 to 450 kg bombs.

The mat is stowed rolled on special chocks and when required is lifted and transported on the Laird Runway Repair Mat Trolley, enabling the mat to be positioned at the crater site without additional lifting equipment. The laden trolley can be towed by a medium tractor.

Following a strike on a runway, the first task of the repair team is to locate the damage and transfer the information to a runway plan. A minimum operating strip, possibly 1500 metres long and 15 metres wide, is then plotted to establish the least amount of initial repair work necessary to restart operations.

The area around the bomb crater is first cleared of debris and fallback material is taken from inside the crater. The crater is then filled with selected stone which has been stockpiled within the perimeter of the airfield. If stone is not available crater debris can be used and pushed back into the crater.

Once the fill has been compacted the damaged area is levelled with a purpose-built screed beam and the repair mat is towed to the site on its trailer, lowered to the ground and unrolled over the levelled fill. The mat is then tensioned and fastened to the undamaged section of the runway by expanding foundation bolts which pass through the fairing panels. Special fairing panels which enable aircraft to run on to and off the repair mat are connected to each end. The final stage is to clear the area of all loose material with a motorised roller. The complete operation can take as little as 1½ hours from the time tractors start clearing debris.

To aid concealment the trackway and fairing panels are treated with pylumin, a chemical dip producing a grey/green finish. The Class 60 mat can also be used for aircraft dispersal pads and portable runways.

STATUS

In production. In service with Greece, Switzerland, Turkey, the United Kingdom and other armed forces.

MANUFACTURER

Laird (Anglesey) Limited, Beaumaris, Anglesey, Gwynedd LL58 8HY, Wales.

Rapid runway repair mat being towed on special Laird trailer

RAF Phantom passing over positioned repair mat

Rapid runway repair mat showing fairing panel on one end (Ministry of Defence)

Rapid runway repair mat being laid (Ministry of Defence)

Airfield Landing Mat

DESCRIPTION

Designed and developed by the MVEE (Christchurch) in conjunction with the British Aluminium Company Limited, the Airfield Landing Mat is usually referred to as the PSA (Prefabricated Surface Aluminium). The standard mat known as the PSA1, which weighs 15 kg/m², is suitable for most freight and passenger aircraft, and for combat aircraft with low-pressure tyres; the maximum tyre pressure is 5·62 kg/cm². The mats are made from aluminium panels and apart from their general use for aircraft landing strip assembly, can also be used for operating pads for aircraft such as the Harrier and also for rapid runway repair.

The Airfield Landing Mat uses six basic components, as follows:

Basic panel. This is 2·74 metres long with an effective width of 0·25 metre. It is light enough to be carried by one man as the PSA1 panel weighs 9·5 kg. Each panel has slots and lugs to connect it with its neighbouring panels in a brickwork pattern at an angle of 45 degrees to the line of the runway.

Double female panel. This panel is 2·7 metres long and 44·5 mm wide. It forms the centre line of the runway from which panels can be laid on both sides.

End anchor panel. This is the same as the basic panel

apart from six 25 mm picket holes which provide anchorage.

Picket. The picket is 1·2 metres long and 22 mm in diameter. It is made from galvanised steel rod and is used to anchor the end anchor panel. It has a tee-shaped head that fits flush into the panel corrugation.

Repair panel. This is a two-part basic panel with a longitudinal interlocking joint. The two halves can be held in place by nine countersunk screws.

Edge restraint device. To prevent the ripple effect that forms when aircraft land and brake on airfield surface mats, the edge restraint device is fitted to the edge of all airfield landing mats. It consists of a fabric strip filled with earth or sand, and with the fabric tied around the filling to form a sausage. The fabric is laid on a connected plywood strip 305 mm wide.

To build a runway, some site preparation is needed to ensure the area is reasonably flat and drained. In wet areas a layer of neoprene-coated nylon fabric (PSN) must be laid. The airfield landing mat can be used by unskilled labour under engineer supervision, and it is possible to lay a complete airfield runway in one or two days. Once laid the mat requires only a minimum of maintenance, but a well-laid and maintained runway can be recovered and re-used with only a minimum of panels needing replacement.

STATUS
In production. In service with the Royal Air Force and some other countries.

MANUFACTURER
Fairey Engineering Limited, PO Box 41, Crossley Road, Heaton Chapel, Stockport, Cheshire SK4 5BD, England.

Fairey airfield landing mat being used by RAF C-130 Hercules transport aircraft (Ministry of Defence)

Laying PSA1 mat (Ministry of Defence)

Fitting end anchor panel to PSA1 mat (Ministry of Defence)

Medium Girder Bridge Ski-Jump

DESCRIPTION
The Ski-Jump for the Harrier has been under development since 1974 by the Ministry of Defence in conjunction with British Aerospace. The system uses Fairey Medium Girder Bridge components which form a gentle curve when raised at one end. Apart from some special outrigger units to increase the width of the take-off runway, all the components can be taken from normal MGB stocks, but for the runway end supports special support towers and jacks can be provided. The ramp can be erected so that the end exit angle is anything between 5 and 15 degrees. With a 15-degree exit angle the ramp is 31 metres long and 6 metres high. The width with the outrigger units is 10 metres and the total weight of a 15-degree ramp is approximately 30 tons.

For land base use the Ski-Jump can be used on both prepared and unprepared surfaces. Prepared surfaces include such areas as stretches of road or motorway, taxiways, or prefabricated surfacing. On such surfaces a special mobile approach ramp can be used to connect the prepared surface with the ramp. Using such a ramp a complete Ski-Jump can be erected in under two hours.

Considerable attention is being given to the use of the Ski-Jump on container ships to enable Harriers to operate from easily converted and inexpensive sea-borne platforms. With such a configuration the ramp could be supported on standard 20-foot ISO containers and raised and lowered as required by scissors jacking systems. Other containers could be used to house fuel,

Medium Girder Bridge Ski-Jump being constructed by Royal Engineers

Completed Medium Girder Bridge Ski-Jump

British Aerospace Harrier leaving Medium Girder Bridge Ski-Jump (US Marine Corps)

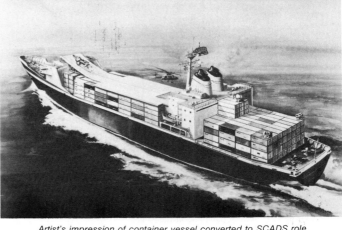

Artist's impression of container vessel converted to SCADS role

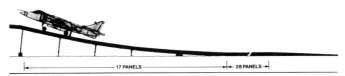

Drawing of Medium Girder Bridge Ski-Jump showing number of panels

Drawing of Medium Girder Bridge Ski-Jump showing mobile approach ramp

spares and personnel and could even be converted to form a hangar. This approach has now been formalised as the Shipborne Containerised Air Defence System (SCADS) with British Aerospace and Plessey being involved. It is envisaged that a merchant container ship or fleet support vessel could be converted to the SCADS role in 48 hours.

STATUS
Production. In service with the US Marine Corps.

MANUFACTURER
Fairey Engineering Limited, PO Box 41, Crossley Road, Heaton Chapel, Stockport, Cheshire SK4 5BD, England.

UNITED STATES OF AMERICA

Martin Marietta Aluminium Rapid Runway Repair Kit

DESCRIPTION
The Rapid Runway Repair kit (RRR) has been developed by Martin Marietta Aluminium from its AM-2 airfield matting system and is now standard equipment with the US Air Force and has been approved for use by NATO countries. Selected forward operational bases are issued with pre-positioned RRR kits, each base being provided with equipment, tools and portable airfield matting to repair three 340 kg bomb craters within four hours.

Each kit provides a patch of AM-2 matting 16·459 metres wide and 24·621 metres long, containing 35 half mats (0·61 × 1·829 m × 38 mm), 15 full mats (0·61 × 3·65 m × 38 mm) and 18 ramps each 1·829 metres long. All components have an anti-skid coating and are packed for shipment and storage in the same manner as the standard AM-2 matting.

The mats have been designed to withstand single wheel loads of up to 13 608 kg each. Half mats are contained in each pallet assembly so that the mats can be laid in a brick-type pattern. This staggered joint arrangement provides the required stability across the mat and the necessary flexibility in the direction of travel. The sides of the mat panels are constructed to interlock with a rotating motion. The end connectors are arranged with the prongs up on one end and down on the other and by properly placing the end connector on one mat over the end connector of another, a continuous layer of matting is formed. Locking couplers are then inserted into the common slot to form a bond between the plates.

There are six main steps in the repair cycle: identifying the craters for repair and establishing a temporary runway centre line, repairing the crater, delivering, stockpiling and placing the selected fill material, assembling the AM-2 matting patch, cleaning, sweeping and painting the new runway and finally placing and anchoring the ramps.

The new temporary runway may be a portion of the runway itself, a combination of the parking areas and the taxiway, or other adjacent surfaced area. The temporary runway is normally 15·24 metres wide and 1524 metres long. All material which has been blown out of the crater is pushed into the crater void and compacted with a dozer. While the crater is being refilled, a grader clears areas on the runway surface for the AM-2 matting assembly. The matting assembly is positioned to allow for a parallel pull over the crater but a sufficient distance away to allow crater repair to continue uninterrupted. When the crater is filled to the final 0·305 metre the selected fill is pushed in, compacted and levelled.

The standard patch can be assembled by 17 trained men in less than an hour, and when assembled is pulled into place over the filled crater. When the final positioning is made ramps are attached to each end to alleviate the step or contour change between the mat and the runway. Should it become practicable to rebuild the runway, the patch sections may be easily removed, dismantled and stored for future use.

STATUS
No longer in production. In service with the US Air Force.

MANUFACTURER
Martin Marietta Aluminium, 19200 South Western Avenue, Torrance, California 90509, USA.

Sales are handled by Transaero Incorporated, 80 Crossways Park Drive, Woodbury, New York 11797, USA.

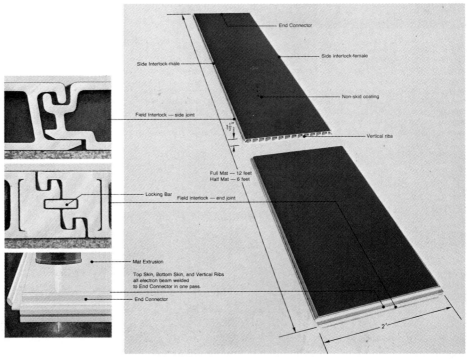

Main components of Martin Marietta aluminium rapid runway repair kit mat

SHELTERS, CONTAINERS AND VEHICLE BODIES

AUSTRALIA

Australian Army Medical Shelter

DESCRIPTION
Under contract to the Australian Army Mr R. Hines and Associates designed an air transportable medical shelter, one of many types for use in a mobile field hospital. The shelter has the same dimensions as an ISO 1C container. It is rated at 8 tonnes and can be stacked two high. The shelter has aluminium-polyurethane wall panels inserted into a structural steel frame. The integral high lift jacks enable the shelter to be dismounted from its carrying vehicle using a hydraulic system or an air line hose from the vehicle. The jacks are normally pushed into the wall housing for transportation. The double doors at both ends provide access for wide loads and the side door is used for normal entry and exit. The shelters are delivered complete apart from air conditioning, furniture and other such specialised items.

STATUS
Production.

MANUFACTURER
Olympic Hunt and Baird, 260 Musgrave Road, Coopers Plains, Brisbane, Queensland 4108, Australia.

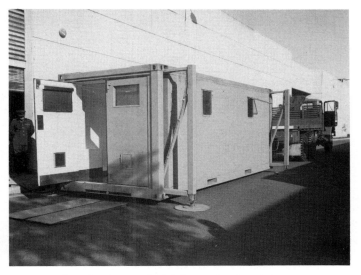

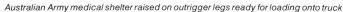
Australian Army medical shelter raised on outrigger legs ready for loading onto truck

Australian Army medical shelter emplaced ready for use

AUSTRIA

Kromag Mobile Shelters

DESCRIPTION
As an off-shoot of the Steyr-Daimler-Puch military production programme, the Austrian Kromag company has been producing a wide range of mobile shelters for military purposes. The shelters are constructed from prefabricated vacuum-compressed aluminium or steel components with the side panels filled by a plastic core. All the shelters are highly mobile and can easily be truck-mounted. Numerous variations of sizes and internal fittings and arrangements are produced.

STATUS
Production. In service with Austrian armed forces.

MANUFACTURER
Kromag Aktiengesellschaft, A-2552 Hirtenberg, Austria.

BELGIUM

Baeten Shelter Type PB 7601

DESCRIPTION
Often referred to as the Plasti-Baeten Shelter, the Type PB 7601 is made from lightweight non-metallic materials. The basic panel material consists of a 40 mm layer of non-hygroscopic pvc foam covered with a 2·5 mm skin of polyester-reinforced glass fibre. The foam has a density of 60 kg/m³. The interior floor has strong non-slip surfacing and the underside of the shelter is fitted with two longitudinal aluminium skids 4·4 metres long, 32 mm high and 180 mm wide. There is a single door 1·78 metres high and 0·8 metre wide with blocking devices incorporated. The interior sides can be fitted with up to three windows a side and there is provision for blackout screens. There is an aluminium ladder for access to the shelter when it is carried on a truck and folding handholds to gain access to the shelter roof. Lashing and lifting points are integral. Main electrical points are provided.

STATUS
In production. In service with the Belgian Army.

MANUFACTURER
nv Baeten, Autostradweg 1, B-9230 Melle, Belgium.

SPECIFICATIONS
Length:
(internal) 4·31 m
(external) 4·4 m
Width:
(internal) 2·11 m
(external) 2·2 m
Height:
(internal) 1·9 m
(external) 2 m
Weight: 940 kg
Payload: 3500 kg

Baeten Shelter Type PB 7601

Baeten Shelter Type PB 7601

FRANCE

GIAT Shelters

DESCRIPTION
The GIAT shelter consists of an all-welded steel tube frame with a welded ribbed external metal covering, polyurethane foam insulation and an internal plywood

facing. The floor of the shelter is covered with aluminium alloy anti-skid sheets.

The shelter is provided with an air-conditioning system as standard. The isothermal door (0.72×1.8 metres) has a single window with wire netting, safety glass and a blackout curtain. On either side of the shel-

ter are three fixed windows with wire netting, safety glass and blackout curtains.

The electrical system includes three different circuits: one 380-volt three-phase, one 220-volt twin-pole and one 24-volt dc which is supplied from the shelter's own batteries.

The shelter can be carried on a truck, trailer, or semi-trailer and is provided with four lifting points. The shelter is currently available fitted as a workshop, stores or machine shop.

SPECIFICATIONS (Cadre electronics workshop)
Weight:
(empty) 2000 kg
(loaded) 5000 kg
Length:
(overall) 5 m
(exterior) 4·22 m
(internal) 4·1 m
Width:
(overall) 2·24 m
(exterior) 2·12 m
(interior) 2 m
Height:
(overall) 2·11 m
(exterior) 2·08 m
(interior) 1·9 m

STATUS
Production. In service with the French Army.

MANUFACTURER
Groupement Industriel des Armements Terrestres (GIAT), 10 place Georges Clémenceau, 92211 Saint-Cloud, France.

GIAT Cadre electronics workshop shelter

Alternative form of GIAT workshop shelter

Enclosed GIAT container workshop

Air Transportable Shelters

DESCRIPTION
ERCA (Société d'Equipement Radio Câbles Aviation) manufactures four basic shelters which can be used for a wide variety of roles including use as command posts and communication centres. The first three are standard box type shelters while the fourth has extensible sides to increase its area by a factor of three.

All the containers are of a sandwich construction and the panels consist of a fire retardant rigid foam core, both faces of which are covered by aluminium sheets to offer good insulation and to form a Faraday screen room for telecommunications. All the shelters are capable of operating in a temperature range of −40 to +70°C and are fitted with shackles to enable them to be transported by helicopters.

STATUS
Production. In service with the French Army and other armed forces.

MANUFACTURER
Société d'Equipement Radio Câbles Aviation, 43 avenue Adolphe Schneider, 92140 Clamart, France.

SPECIFICATIONS

Weight (empty)	300 kg	475 kg	600 kg	2300 kg
(loaded)	1450 kg	2500 kg	4000 kg	n/a
Useful load	1150 kg	2025 kg	3400 kg	n/a
Length	2·5 m	3·5 m	4·5 m	6 m
Width	2·05 m	2·05 m	2·05 m	2·05 m travelling 6·05 m deployed
Height	2·09 m	2·09 m	2·09 m	2·2 m

Berliet GBC 8KT (6 × 6) 4000 kg truck carrying 4·5 m long ERCA shelter

AMF 80 Modular NBC Shelter

DESCRIPTION

The AMF 80 modular NBC shelter is produced by a combination of two companys, Société des Tuyaux Bonna and Sofiltra-Poelman. Being a modular system the AMF 80 can be constructed in a great variety of configurations. Six concrete modules are normally combined to form a basic unit with each of the modules having a nominal diameter of 2 metres or 2·5 metres (an optional 3·2 metres module is available). The usual module diameter is 2·5 metres and each module is 2·35 metres long. Each concrete module has a floor with two drainage channels, two 2·3-metre long wooden benches, eight 0·55-metre long detachable shelves, and two stretcher supports. The modules are connected by elastomer (neoprene) joints. Once assembled a basic unit has an entrance normally covered by a mesh door. The entrance to the shelter itself is armoured and once inside the personnel have to pass through an air-lock as the interior atmosphere is maintained slightly

over-pressure. The main shelter consists of a long 'pipe' with the ends sealed off by walls. Sanitation facilities are situated at one end. The two entrances are at both ends, one facing one way at right angles from the main shelter and the other facing in the opposite direction. The shelter is usually constructed in a trench using conventional equipment and covered with a layer of earth. If required the shelter can be moved to a new site using only conventional handling equipment.

Ventilation is provided by a mains electricity-operated twin-ventilator system with a combined output of 480 m³. The ventilators can be operated by a hand crank in the event of a breakdown. An NBC filter system uses a triple-filter arrangement to remove all harmful agents from the internal atmosphere. The ventilator system is silenced. Arrangements are provided for a power generator by one of the entrance doors

A basic AMF 80 can accommodate 60 people with 50 seated and 10 recumbent. Each basic unit can be constructed in about two days by a small construction team.

SPECIFICATIONS

Type	Model 1	Model 2
Nominal diameter	2 m	2·5 m
Internal diameter	2 m	2·5 m
External diameter	2·36 m	2·95 m
Wall thickness	0·18 m	0·225 m
Useful length	3·3 m	2·35 m
Weight per metre	3220 kg	4930 kg

STATUS

Production. In service with the French armed forces. Batch ordered for US Air Force trials in Europe.

MANUFACTURERS

Bonna, 91 rue du Faubourg Saint-Honoré, 75008 Paris, France.

Sofiltra-Poelman, 71 boulevard National, 92250 La Garenne-Colombes, France.

GERMANY, FEDERAL REPUBLIC

Dornier Mobile Shelter System

DESCRIPTION

Under contract to the Federal German armed forces, Dornier has developed two communications cabins known as the Cabin I FmB (with a maximum gross weight of 2000 kg) and the Cabin II FmB (with a maximum gross weight of 5000 kg). These cabins have been designed for transportation by truck, aircraft, helicopter, ship and rail, and can also be used for other applications such as field kitchens, medical units or workshops. All eight corners of the cabin are fitted with brackets to which hoisting and lashing equipment can be fitted.

The cabins are of a lightweight aluminium construction with the internal walls fitted with a uniform C-track system which allows a wide range of equipment to be fitted depending on the role of the cabin. The cabin is fitted with an air-conditioning system which operates under all climatic conditions.

The HF-shielding and EMP-protection are ensured by the all metal design of the cabin whereby all external corners are welded, all openings provided with special MF-seals and all supply and exit airways are fitted with honeycomb flues which are protected by special filters.

Both cabins are provided with three skids, emergency exit, roof mounting steps, 24-volt dc network, network connection box, 220/380-volt ac, connection cable to driver's cab, battery box with two 12-volt batteries, lashing equipment, access ladder, 220-volt ac network, light trap and a second battery box with two 12-volt batteries with a capacity of 100 Ah.

The C-tracks can be bolted vertically or horizontally to the internal walls depending on the type of equipment to be installed. Dornier has also developed a prefabrication unit system for use in these cabins which allows a wide range of equipment to be installed in the cabin without any modifications being made to the cabin itself.

The B suffix indicates that the cabin is used as a telecommunications cabin for the Automatic Corps Network, as an artillery centre, or for installing air defence equipment. Dornier has also developed the FmA and Standard cabins from the FmB cabins. The FmA cabin has the HF and EMP protection and the air-conditioning system removed and the rear door is provided with a window. The Standard cabin differs from the FmA cabin in that two windows are provided in each sidewall.

STATUS

In production. In service with the West German Army.

DEVELOPMENT

Dornier GmbH, Postfach 2160, 8000 Munich 66, Federal Republic of Germany.

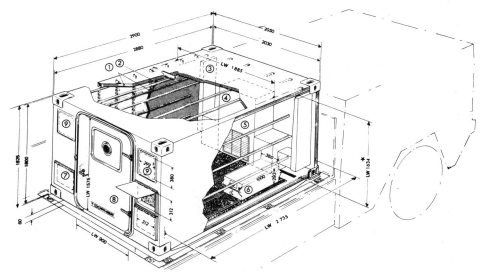

Cabin I FmB (1) insulation (2) air guidance in lateral wall (3) air duct (air-conditioning system) (4) track panelling (5) air-conditioning system (6) battery box

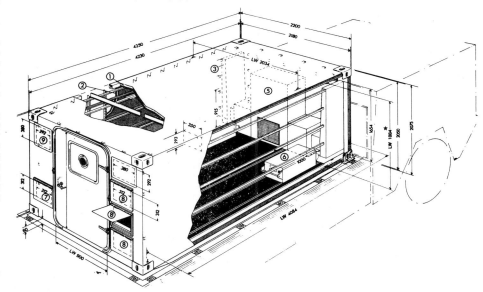

Cabin II FmB (1) insulation (2) air guidance in lateral wall (3) air duct (air conditioning system) (4) track panelling (5) air-conditioning system (6) battery box

SPECIFICATIONS

Model	Cabin I FmB	Cabin II FmB
Weight (empty)	1032 kg	1435 kg
(loaded, maximum)	2000 kg	5000 kg
Length (overall)	2·9 m	4·25 m
Width (overall)	2·05 m	2·2 m
Height (overall)	1·825 m	2·075 m

Model	Cabin I FmB	Cabin II FmB
Air conditioning system		
Heating output	2 kW	3 kW
Refrigeration output	3200 kcal/h	4500 kcal/h
Air input	900 m³/h	1000 m³/h
Power input	2·5 kW	3·9 kW

Dornier Cabin I

Dornier Cabin II

Zeppelin Shelters

DESCRIPTION
Zeppelin Metallwerke GmbH produces a wide range of containerised shelters for a wide variety of purposes ranging from mobile offices to radar cabins. The entire range is constructed from basic sandwich monocoque with the side walls, roof and floor units all having aluminium skins. The core material is polyurethane foam. Edge framing is made from heat-bonded light metal frame sections. An insulating layer is interposed between the framing sections. All external riveting is air- and water-tight, and the corner fittings are replacable. Skids are mounted lengthwise under the floor unit with each skid being approximately 60 mm high and 100 mm wide. They are riveted or bolted to the integral stiffening members of the floor unit. The shelter door is located in one end wall and mounted on the right-hand side by three heavy duty hinge units. All four corners are rounded and there is a three-point locking device fitted. The flooring is constructed from 17 mm thick marine plywood.

Various optional doors, hatches and windows can be fitted to either end and to the side walls. An air conditioning unit is available. The shelters can be lifted for transport by four heavy-duty jacks that are attached to each corner of the shelter and for some vehicle-carried shelters a special hydraulic jack is used. Most of the Zeppelin shelters are air transportable.

STATUS
Production.

MANUFACTURER
Zeppelin Metallwerke GmbH, Postfach 2540, 7990 Friedrichshafen 1, Federal Republic of Germany.

SPECIFICATIONS

Model	BW 1	BW 11	BW 111	BW 1V	N 1	N 2	N 3
Weight (empty, approx)	550 kg	900 kg	1500 kg	1400 kg	700 kg	800 kg	400 kg
(max permissible)[1]	2000 kg	4500 kg	10 000 kg	8000 kg	3000 kg	4500 kg	1150 kg
Length (over corner fittings)	2·9 m	4·25 m	6·742 m	6·058 m	3·81 m	3·81 m	2·35 m
(inside clearance)	2·78 m	4·11 m	6·595 m	5·912 m	3·69 m	3·67 m	2·23 m
Width (over corner fittings)	2·05 m	2·2 m	2·438 m	2·438 m	2·08 m	2·08 m	2·05 m
(inside clearance)	1·925 m	2·055 m	2·29 m	2·29 m	1·96 m	1·94 m	1·925 m
Height (over corner fittings)[2]	1·825 m	2·075 m	2·37 m	2·37 m	2·075 m	2·075 m	1·825 m
(inside clearance)	1·695 m	1·905 m	2·2 m	2·2 m	1·93 m	1·91 m	1·675 m

[1] load evenly distributed
[2] without skids, skid height +51 mm

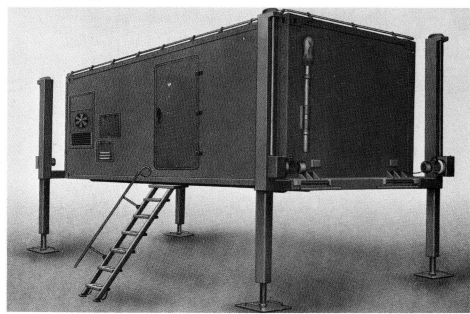

Zeppelin BW 111 10 000 kg shelter on lifting jacks

Binz Ambulance Bodies

DESCRIPTION
The West German Binz concern specialises in various forms of ambulance and other medical vehicle bodies. Apart from ambulance bodies, Binz also produces mobile medical centres, mobile operating theatres, blood transfusion unit bodies and various forms of custom-built medical purpose vehicles. Most bodies are fitted to existing commercial or military chassis such as the Unimog 404 but very extensive vehicle conversions can be produced.

STATUS
Production.

MANUFACTURER
BINZ GmbH and Co, Zollstrasse 2, Postfach 1120, D-7073 Lorch-Württ, Federal Republic of Germany.

Binz ambulance body on Unimog 404 chassis

Binz ambulance body on Unimog U 1300 L chassis

Philips Elektro-Spezial Optronics Field Workshop Trailer

DESCRIPTION
This field maintenance workshop for optronic systems was developed by the Elektro-Spezial division of Philips GmbH for the repair and field maintenance of infra-red aiming and observation equipment, image-intensifying aiming and observation systems, television aiming and surveillance systems, infra-red searchlights, thermal target locators and thermal imaging systems. The workshop is accommodated in a closed 15-tonne semi-trailer with an air-conditioned interior. The interior is divided into a darkroom and a normally-illuminated workshop. Internal fixtures are secured to the ceiling, walls and floor by standard metal profile sections from the cabin systems used by the German armed forces. Shelves, workbenches and fittings are nearly all standard components.

The workshop can carry out servicing and maintenance on the optronic equipment for the Leopard 1 and 2 MBTs, the Marder APC, the Luchs reconnaissance

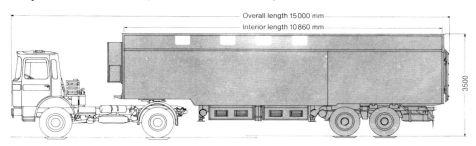
Side elevation of Philips Elektro-Spezial optronics field workshop (not to 1/76th scale)

vehicle and the Jaguar 1 (HOT) armoured missile carrier. The interior has all the workbenches, test equipment, racking, power supplies and tools necessary for all the equipments used on these vehicles, and all the equipment fitted is already type-classified by the German armed forces.

The interior length of the semi-trailer workshop is 10·86 metres and it is 3·5 metres high.

STATUS
Production. In service with the West German armed forces.

MANUFACTURER
Elektro-Spezial, Unternehmensbereich der Philips GmbH, Hans-Bredow-Strasse 20, Postfach 44 87 40, D-2800 Bremen 44, Federal Republic of Germany.

ITALY

Aermarelli Systems for Army Applications

DESCRIPTION
The Italian company of Aermarelli can design and construct underground installations for use as command posts, civil defence shelters, as well as shelters for aircraft, ships, troops, vehicles and other equipment. They can be provided with protection against conventional and/or nuclear explosions and chemical or bacteriological attack.

These shelters are made of reinforced concrete and can be provided with all or some of the following depend-

ing on the specific role of the shelter: air-conditioning system, electric power production system (with or without an auxiliary system), electric lighting, fluid distribution and treatment systems, fire extinguishing system, non-return circuits for sewage, cooling systems for refrigeration, heating system, sanitary, kitchen and laundry systems.

Defence systems against ground shocks for both conventional and nuclear blast include anti-blast valves, anti-blast doors, non-return valves for sewage systems, special equipment to avoid piping and electric wiring to be broken or damaged, screening against electromagnetic fields and low resistance earth terminal systems. To provide protection against NBC contaminated

air, all air is filtered as it enters the shelter and decontamination equipment is provided for personnel entering the shelter. The shelter can be provided with atmospheric blast monitoring equipment and optical monitoring equipment. The communications equipment would be shockproof and special aerials would be provided.

Aermarelli is also active in the fields of clean room design and construction and the provision of security systems for various types of buildings including military headquarters.

MANUFACTURER
Aermarelli SpA, 20158 Milan, Viale Vincenzo Lancetti 43, Italy.

Improved Boneschi Shelters

DESCRIPTION
The Boneschi range of shelters uses the same basic container body which is made from light alloy sheets with polyurethane fillings. The framework is of aluminium sections. The overall construction is orthodox and the shelters can be adapted to carry out a wide range of military duties. There are two optional methods of moving the Boneschi shelters, both of them incorporated into the shelter system when required. One is the 'Rolbon' system which has four hand-operated worm screws and wheels fitted to each corner of the shelter by rolling arms. The other system is the 'Uniborn' lifting system which has four hand-operated worms fitted to each corner by pivoting arms. This latter system enables the shelter to be raised and lowered onto flat-bed trucks.

One specialised form of Boneschi shelter is the 'Lifeshelter'. This is a specialised light alloy container which is insulated and enclosing a complete medical unit ready for use. Equipment in the container includes a simple stretcher-type operating table, racks for medical equipment and instruments (all included in the standard kit), oxygen and other such equipment, and lighting and air conditioning. The 'Lifeshelter' is air-transportable and is fitted with the 'Uniborn' lifting system for handling. If required, the 'Lifeshelter' can be carried slung under a helicopter.

Boneschi shelter fitted with Rolbon system

STATUS
In production. In service with the Turkish Army.

MANUFACTURER
Carrozzeria Boneschi srl, Via Delle Industrie, 20040 Cambiago (Milano), Italy.

Boneschi 'Lifeshelter' ready for loading onto C-130H Hercules

Loading Boneschi 'Lifeshelter' onto C-130H Hercules

Boneschi shelter loaded onto FIAT 6601 truck using Uniborn system

Boneschi shelter fitted out as fire-control shelter on FIAT 75 PM (4 × 4) 2000 kg truck

Piaggio Shelters

DESCRIPTION

Piaggio started building military shelters in 1964 and since then has produced shelters for both military and civil purposes. There are now five basic Piaggio shelters with a far larger number being produced for special purposes, but the overall construction remains the same.

Each cabin has eight horizontal angles all in light alloy and four vertical angles in galvanised steel or light alloy. The corner blocks may be standard ISO container type and all the wall and floor or ceiling panels are constructed from a sandwich formed from light alloy sheets 0·8 to 1·6 mm thick with a core of 50 mm thick polyurethane foam. Internal strengthening ribs are fitted and there are three underside skids. The floor has a drain plug, and the end access door is 1600 mm high and 800 mm wide. Other standard fittings are access steps, roof reinforcement in the centre and an electrical earthing point. A wide range of accessories is available and numerous fits can be produced to suit customer requirements. Piaggio has been the first manufacturer to respond to NATO's new requirements for EMP shelters (i.e. shelters protected against electromagnetic pulse from nuclear blast) and in the four year period from 1980 to 1983 Piaggio has been the sole supplier of this type of shelter to NATO and NATO affiliated nations. Piaggio EMP shelters differ from conventional shelters in that the outer skin of the cabin is fusion welded to guarantee a flawless electrical continuity.

In 1982 Piaggio was awarded the Italian Army's tender no. 00129, requiring the supply of approximately 1600 shelters over a period of a few years.

Door end of Piaggio shelter

STATUS

Production. In service with the Italian armed forces and several other nations.

MANUFACTURER

Industrie Aeronautiche e Meccaniche Rinaldo Piaggio, 16154 Genova, Via Cibrario 4, Italy.

SPECIFICATIONS

Type	NATO 1	NATO 2	NATO 3	STET 1	STET 2
Length	3·81 m	3·81 m	2·16 m	2·8 m	4·1 m
Width	2·08 m	2·08 m	2 m	2·05 m	2·3 m
Height	2·11 m	2·11 m	1·78 m	2 m	2·25 m
Weight	600 kg	650 kg	450 kg	700 kg	1500 kg
Capacity (useful load)	2400 kg	3850 kg	1000 kg	1300 kg	2500 kg

Cut-away model of Piaggio shelter fitted out as communication centre

SAI Containers

DESCRIPTION

SAI has been manufacturing containers since 1970 and now produces a wide range of specialist containers. The containers are constructed from a sandwich material made up of light aluminium alloy heat bonded to a polyurethane core. Watertight rivets and stainless steel bolts and nuts are used to hold the panels together. All panels have a special lattice of light aluminium struts to absorb stresses from internal and external loads and to provide lashing anchors for internal loads.

SAI also produces a range of air-conditioned containers for special purposes. There are three main models in this range, the smallest with a 4 kW conditioner, then a 9 kW conditioner and the largest has a 20 kW conditioner unit. These units can be used to provide refrigeration if required.

SAI air-conditioned shelter on transporter wheels

Both standard and cooled containers can be supplied with a range of accessories that includes jacks for lifting and loading, ladders, special or emergency exits and hatches, special electrical looms or lighting and radio frequency suppression. Numerous changes to suit customer requirements can be introduced.

To complete their shelters system SAI has designed and constructed a new trailer with two wheels for the transport of shelters and self-supporting platforms for radar and missile systems. The system can be towed by military tractors and has two rolling trains which can be coupled independently at either end of the shelter or platform, and both can be lifted to permit towing. If necessary the load can be further lifted to a height of 0·7 metre to permit fording or cross-country travel. The two rolling trains can be coupled together in the absence of a shelter or platform to form a compact carriage. A flexible hydraulic system allows the rear wheels to be steered to reduce the turning radius. A hydro-pneumatic suspension system is employed which permits the carriage of unevenly-distributed loads.

SPECIFICATIONS

Capacity	3000 kg	5000 kg	8000 kg
Weight	1600 kg	2700 kg	2800 kg
Length	3·25 m	4·55 m	4·55 m
Width	2·1 m	2·2 m	2·3 m

STATUS
Production. In service with the Italian Army.

MANUFACTURER
SAI Societa Aeronautica Italiana SpA, Passignano sul Trasimeno (PG), Viale Roma 25, Italy.

Swisel Shelters

DESCRIPTION
The Swisel shelter is an adaptable container-bodied shelter that is available in two basically similar models. Both models may be used either as free-standing shelters or as shelter bodies on the backs of vehicles. In both cases the shelters may be raised, either for loading or for static use, on four jacks that project 450 mm from each corner of the shelter. The jacks raise the shelter to a standard height of 1·6 metres although there is an optional height of 1·8 metres.

The shelter interiors can be fitted out to suit virtually any field requirement from command posts to medical and other such uses. All six surfaces of the shelter module are 75 mm thick and are built with inner and outer aluminium sheets riveted to extruded stiffeners. The core space is filled with a self-extinguishing pvc foam. The flooring stringer spacing is 250 mm and on other surfaces the spacing is 500 mm. Temperature insulation material is provided between all the stiffeners and the inner skin. All edges are framed for additional strength and the interior floor is provided with an electrically insulated covering. The single entry door has two unequal height 'dutch-door' sections.

Standard fittings include a door hold-open air spring, window/escape hatch with a hatch cover, built-in steps and a ladder, an exhaust fan, tie down cables and cable storage bins, four removable corner jacks and levelling pads, three towing skids, four towing hooks, four lifting lugs, an NBC installation opening with a covering hatch together with a corresponding air conditioning opening and hatch, power and cable connections, an interior electrical junction box, two built-in electrical systems (one 230-volt ac, the other 24-volt dc), a built-in telephone system, and provision for interconnection of another Type 2 shelter. Connecting shelters may be placed from 2·5 to 3·2 metres apart with the doors opening into inter-connecting tunnels.

Shelters may be stacked two high when loaded or four high when empty.

SPECIFICATIONS

Model	Type 1	Type 2
Weight (empty)	700 kg	1500 kg
(load)	1300 kg	2500 kg
(total)	2000 kg	4000 kg
Length	2·8 m	4·1 m
Width	2·05 m	2·3 m
Height	2 m	2·25 m

STATUS
Production.

MANUFACTURER
Swisel Italiana SpA, Via Rondinelli 3, 50123 Florence, Italy.

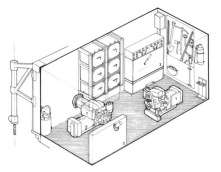

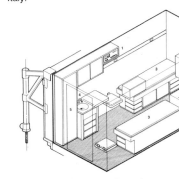

Typical internal layout of Swisel shelter used as power supply station. (1) 25 kVA generator (2) fuel tank (3) control panel (4) sink

Swisel shelter fitted out as mechanical workshop (1) vice (2) pillar drill (3) universal lathe (4) multi-purpose machine tool (5) air compressor

Swisel shelter in use as intensive care unit (1) heart monitoring equipment (2) air conditioner (3) bed (4) sink (5) gas cylinder cabinet

Oliviero Grazia Ambulance Bodies

DESCRIPTION
The Carrozzeria Oliviero Grazia company specialises in converting commercially-available vehicles into ambulances with special bodies to suit almost any application. The following illustrations show only a small part of its range and its works at Bologna convert vehicles not only for ambulances but also for armoured security vehicles, and special purpose vehicles.

MANUFACTURER
Carrozzeria Oliviero Grazia snc, Via Cimabue 10/12, 40133 Bologna, Italy.

Conversion of Alfa Romeo Saviem MM to ambulance

Conversion of FIAT Campagnola to ambulance

Land-Rover ambulance conversion

Range Rover ambulance conversion

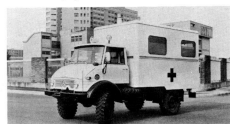

Ambulance conversion of Unimog S404

SOUTH AFRICA

Modular Operating Theatre

DESCRIPTION
This modular operating theatre is constructed from glass fibre panels supported on an aluminium framework. It has double outward-opening doors at the rear and a single door on the right-hand side. Internally it is fully equipped as an operating theatre for all types of medical operations. It has a 220-volt electrical system and a battery-operated emergency power supply. A penthouse is provided which fits to the right-hand side and rear of the module. The module is transported by means of a mobiliser wheel set.

The module is 6 metres long, 2·5 metres wide and 1·8 metres high.

STATUS
Production. In service with the Surgeon General's arm of the South African Defence Forces.

MANUFACTURER
Enquiries to Armscor, Private Bag X337, Pretoria 0001, South Africa.

Modular operating theatre with mobiliser wheel set

SWEDEN

DIAB Shelters

DESCRIPTION
The DIAB shelter can be constructed in a number of configurations and with a wide variety of fittings and extras to suit almost any application. The basic construction is made up of panels with a filling of Divinycell foamed plastic which forms a rigid core. On each side of this core a skin of fibre-glass plastic or aluminium sheeting can be bonded, depending on the application. Each surface of the shelter is formed of a single sheet of the foamed plastic and interior and exterior fittings are attached so that no thermal bridges can be formed. Internal partitions and accessories can be fitted and the door (or doors) located where necessary. Accessories such as mains electricity, air-conditioning, lighting, securing and lashing points can be fitted as required.

DIAB shelter being towed as trailer

STATUS
In production.

MANUFACTURER
DIAB-Barracuda AB, Box 201, S-31201 Laholm, Sweden.

Cross section of DIAB shelter

DIAB shelter in use as mobile office

Container for PS 70/R Radar

DESCRIPTION
This container has been designed by Hägglund and Söner to carry the Ericsson designed PS 70/R radar which is used in conjunction with the Bofors RBS-70 short range surface-to-air missile system. The container holds the mast-mounted radar and reflector, radio communications, data links to the individual RBS-70 units and a tactical control facility for the crew of five. It is normally carried on the rear of a Saab-Scania SBAT 111S (6 × 6) truck but can be deployed on its own if required.

The container consists of a framework of steel tubing covered with aluminium sheets with an insulating covering. The floor of the operator's area is electrically heated. A door is provided in the right side of the container and there is also an emergency escape hatch in the left side. If required a generator can be mounted in a soundproof area at the rear and provision has been made for the installation of an air-conditioning system.

Mounted at each corner of the cabin is a retractable ground support with a hydraulic jack, which can be operated from inside or outside the container. Mounted

on the top of the container is the hydraulically operated mast with the radar scanner mounted on top. When fully extended the scanner is 10·6 metres above the floor level of the container.

SPECIFICATIONS
Weight: 4375 kg
Length: 6·7 m
(inside) 3 m
Width:
(travelling) 2·5 m
(emplaced) 3·3 m
(inside) 2·3 m
Height:
(mast folded) 2·2 m
(inside) 1·7 m

STATUS
In production. In service with the Swedish Army and other undisclosed countries.

MANUFACTURER
AB Hägglund and Söner, Vehicle Division, S-891 01 Örnsköldsvik, Sweden.

Ericsson PS 70/R system mounted on rear of Saab-Scania SBAT 111S (6 × 6) truck

UNITED KINGDOM

CTC Adaptainer

DESCRIPTION
The CTC Adaptainer series consists of a basic container body which can be adapted internally to suit virtually any military requirement from a command post to a medical post or operating theatre. Other uses include mobile workshops, ammunition containers or accommodation. The Adaptainers are available in 10-, 20- and 40-foot lengths. All three are the same height and width and can be transported and handled as normal commercial containers. The basic framework of the Adaptainer is a steel box section of 80 × 80 mm and the walls are constructed from steel with a thickness varying between 3·5 and 5 mm.

STATUS
In production.

MANUFACTURER
CTC Container Trading Company (UK) Limited, 195 Knightsbridge, London SW7 1RQ, England.

SPECIFICATIONS

Length	10 ft/3·048 m	20 ft/6·11 m	40 ft/12·22 m
Height	2·59 m	2·59 m	2·59 m
Width	2·44 m	2·44 m	2·44 m
Internal (length)	2·88 m	5·87 m	12·04 m
(height)	2·39 m	2·2 m	2·38 m
(width)	2·34 m	2·31 m	2·34 m
(volume)	17 m³	30·7 m³	78 m³
Door opening (width)	2·26 m	2·26 m	2·31 m
(height)	2·29 m	2·26 m	2·29 m
Weight	1580 kg	1955 – 2177 kg	2950 – 3950 kg

CTC Adaptainer

Giltspur Specialist Module Containers

DESCRIPTION
Giltspur Defence Projects has realised that there is a place in the defence market for a system of pre-equipped containerised modules to enable armed forces to survive and operate in regions where no facilities exist. The system is based on standard 6- and 12-metre containers suitably modified for their particular purpose. Each container has installed all the equipment it requires to function.

Each container module is built to the dimensional requirements of ISO 668-1976 (BS 3951) and incorporates a standard handling casting at each corner. All modules can therefore be handled by ISO container equipment as well as by conventional means. Further structural members can be built into the base and front end of the modules to enable them to be handled by the British Army DROPS. Fork lift and manual handling with external legs can also be used. The main structural members and panels are reinforced as necessary for doors, apertures and special fittings appropriate to each layout. Linings and insulation are built-in. Electrical systems with full safety features are incorporated with external connections to a mains supply or self-contained generators as appropriate to the layout required. Water and other services are similarly fitted where necessary.

The Giltspur specialist module containers are available for the following roles:

Mobile hospital. Developed in co-operation with the British Army, the mobile hospital includes accommodation for operating theatres, an X-ray department, a central sterile supplies department, recovery areas and wards. Key areas may be supplied with extra protection against shrapnel.

Mobile Air Base. Designed for aircraft 1st and 2nd line support this base has each module fitted out for a different specialist role including workshops, rest areas, briefing and command rooms and communications centres. Pre-selected modules may be selected from the complete system to provide a rapid deployment 30-day support facility.

Field Cooking Module. This module has the facilities to prepare, cook and serve up to 500 meals in one session. Electrical power and a hydrocarbon fuel supply is necessary and water could be supplied from a bowser. The module has two 'eight burner' cooking units, and would normally be used by two cooks and two assistants.

Workshop Module. This module could be used as part of the Mobile Air Base but could be converted for almost any workshop role once electrical power is available. An office space inside the module can be supplied.

Field Laundry Module. This module has built-in water handling and filtering services along with a pump to draw water from a local source. Washing and drying machines are installed together with working space to process up to 200 kg dry weight in an eight-hour shift.

Field Shower Module. This module, using water from a local source and pumped using a built-in pump, can supply showers for up to six men at one time.

Command Module. This module has the basic sleeping and living needs of a senior officer in a compact personal room. There is a briefing room with space for up to six men and a radio/communications bay. Armour protection may be incorporated.

Customs Post Module. The equipment for this module may be varied as required but surveillance, communication and office facilities are incorporated.

Dental Module. To provide regular dental care in remote locations this module has a dental chair and a full complement of ancillary items. Reception and record facilities are provided by the main door and a separate bay houses the water treatment equipment necessary. Air conditioning is provided.

Opthalmic Module. The main bay of this module has a treatment couch and a full complement of ancillary items to enable minor surgery to be carried out. An air conditioner is fitted as is water treatment equipment in a separate insulated bay. There is provision for a diagnostic area and a reception and records area.

STATUS
Production.

MANUFACTURER
Giltspur Packaging Limited, Salisbury Road, Totton, Southampton, England.

Carawagon Tactical Command Post

DESCRIPTION
Built onto a standard long-wheelbase Land-Rover, the Carawagon tactical command post combines office and living space for military use. Inside the special cabin two people can work in comfort with full command facilities, including, if required, connections to mains electricity, telecommunications and standing headroom. Sleeping accommodation for one, two or three can be provided inside the vehicle, and a tent extension measuring 2·7 × 2·2 metres provides space for two more. The interior, which can be fitted as required, has an overall headroom of 1·9 metres over an area of 2·4 × 1·2 metres. The basic vehicle has a single large table folding down from the right-hand wall of the Land-Rover body to make a working surface 1·4 × 0·86 metres with a filing unit against the wall behind it. A perspex-topped chart table with storage space for maps is available as an alternative to the normal table. The basic body also includes a clipboard, a bench seat for two people to work at the table, a hanging wardrobe and a stainless steel sink. The sink has a foot-operated pump drawing water from a 20-litre portable container. A small gas cooker can be fitted to the inside of the rear door. There is roof space in the interior for two folding bunks, and other optional equipment includes air-conditioning and a refrigerator operating from a 12-volt supply; electric fans are another possibility. All windows are fitted with blackout screens. The roof can be folded for travelling

Interior of Carawagon tactical command post

Rear view of Carawagon tactical command post as delivered to British Army (Ministry of Defence)

Carawagon tactical command post as delivered to British Army (Ministry of Defence)

and a rack over the driver's cabin and windscreen can be used to carry the tent extension and camouflage netting as well as extra stores and equipment.

Although this version of the Carawagon is fitted out as a tactical command post, the basic body can also be supplied as a signals vehicle, mobile darkroom, mobile workshop or for medical or ambulance purposes.

STATUS
In production. In service with the British Army.

MANUFACTURER
Carawagon Limited, 11 Welbeck Street, London W1M 7PB, England.

CB 300 and CB 100 Series of Transportable Containers

DESCRIPTION
The CB 300 series of transportable containers was developed by Marshall of Cambridge (Engineering) from 1962 to meet a Ministry of Defence requirement for a lightweight, demountable body which would provide the best possible working conditions under extremes of temperature, would have an extended service life under minimal maintenance requirements and would have maximum utilisation by both the Army and the RAF in mobile and static roles. First production units were completed in 1964. Basic FVRDE (MVEE) Specification is 9720.

The transportable container is designed for the operational installation of specialist pneumatic, hydraulic, signals, electronic and similar equipment, for use as specialist repair modules and for use as tactical offices or command posts.

The container is constructed of aluminium alloy, is lightweight and fully insulated to provide protected working conditions for personnel and equipment under extremes of temperature, it is weather-sealed and may also be air-conditioned. The basic design concept has proven itself to be sound but whereas NBC was covered initially, now with only minor changes the container can be modified to meet EMP and RFI requirements and can be supplied in armoured or standard form. It is designed to be carried on any flat platform truck or trailer and can be operated dismounted in a static role. It is transportable by air in a Lockheed C-130 aircraft. Its modular construction allows doors, windows and access panels to be positioned to meet specific requirements. Strong points in the main framework facilitate the attachment of accessories and equipment, while heavily reinforced corners simplify the fitting of running and handling gear. Typical roles include use as a fuel injection repair shop or machine shop/automotive repair shop, when it has a wide range of installed equipment, including a combined lathe/milling machine, bench drill, battery charger and a range of specialist items and hand tools.

In addition to the CB 300 series, Marshall manufactures the CB 100 range of shelters and is also able to offer a wide variety of shelters and containers to suit individual requirements.

SPECIFICATIONS (CB 300)
Weight:
  (empty) from 925 kg depending on role
  (loaded) up to 4544 kg depending on role
Length:
  (external) 4·73 m
  (internal) 4·31 m
Width:
  (external) 2·52 m
  (internal) 2·323 m
Height:
  (external) 1·934 m
  (internal) 1·91 m

STATUS
Production. In service with the British Armed Forces and in Saudi Arabia.

MANUFACTURER
Marshall of Cambridge (Engineering) Limited, Airport Works, Cambridge CB5 8RX, England.

CB 300 series transportable container mounted on Bedford MK (4 × 4) 4-tonne general service truck

CB 300 series transportable container being dismounted from Bedford MK (4 × 4) 4-tonne truck using high-lift jacks

Interior of CB 300 fitted as machine shop/automotive repair shop

Marshall CB 100 container

Marshall of Cambridge (Engineering) Vehicle Bodies

The Vehicles Division of the Marshall Group of Companies is the largest manufacturer of military vehicle bodies in the United Kingdom. A résumé of some of the more recent bodies built for military requirements follows.

Ambulance 2/4 Stretcher Rover ¾-ton (4 × 4)
This vehicle was developed from 1963 to meet Ministry of Defence requirements for a small ambulance suitable for evacuating casualties from forward areas and full production began in 1968. The chassis (FVRDE Spec 9336) is based on the long wheelbase Land-Rover chassis modified for service use. The body (FVRDE Spec 9696) is framed and panelled in aluminium and lined with tropic proofed hardboard. The cavities between the external and internal panels of the body sides, roof, bulkhead and rear doors are packed with a resin-bonded glass fibre thermal insulating material.

A heater is connected to the engine cooling system. Fresh air is ducted to the heater and to four directionally adjustable air-flow outlet louvres, which will direct a free flow of forced air to each of the stretcher positions. The body provides accommodation for a medical attendant and two or four stretcher cases, or alternatively one or two stretcher cases and three sitting patients, or six sitting patients in addition to the driver. Stowages for spare stretchers are fitted externally on the roof.

Anti-tank 106 mm Recoilless Rifle, Land-Rover (air-portable)
Details of this model, which has been developed by Marshall specifically to meet a foreign requirement will be found in the entry for the Land-Rover (4 × 4) 508 kg Airportable light vehicle in the *Lightweight vehicles* section.

High Top Land-Rover Conversion
This is a new high top conversion of hard top or station wagon versions of the ¾-tonne Land-Rover. The height provided by the new upper body provides extra space for signals or other equipment, and extra headroom. The vehicle was developed for the Danish Army and a number are now in service.

Body General Service/Cargo Dropside 4-tonne
This was developed from 1967 for the Bedford MK (4 × 4) 4-tonne truck and entered production the following year. Its FVRDE (MVEE) Specification is 9722. The body is capable of being used as a flat platform, fitted with dropsides, suitable for use as a troop carrier, or for the carriage of a distributed load of 4 tonnes. The steel body is of welded construction, with the front bulkhead bolted to forward pillars mounted on the underframe. The hardwood floor is fitted directly to the cross-member. It is protected by steel wearing strips which cover the joints. Rotating flush-fitting lashing rings mounted directly to the cross-member are positioned to provide the most efficient securing points for lashing down bulky loads. Additional heavy duty lashing points are positioned along the main sides. The four dropsides and tailboards can be removed, and the rear and intermediate pillars unbolted to provide a flat platform. A tubular steel superstructure is fitted with a tailored tilt cover of cotton/polyester material. Secured to the underframes are two lockers and a carrier for two jerricans. Provision is made on the forward face of the front bulkhead for stowing a pickaxe head and handle, shovel and crowbar.

Body General Service/Cargo Dropside 4-tonne with hydraulic tailboard loader
This is a variant of the standard GS 4-tonne cargo body for Royal Corps of Signals for loading and unloading telephone cable drums. The loader is a commercial electro-hydraulic tailboard model with a 1-ton capacity which has been modified for service use. It is supplied in kit form which can then be fitted to the standard cargo body and transferred from one body to another using only unit REME personnel. The tailboard has a non-slip surface and can be locked in an intermediate position 600 mm above the ground where it can be used as a working platform for two men. When fitted, the loader does not affect cross-country performance. Development of this unit began during 1974 and it is now in service.

Body General Service 8-tonne
Development of this GS cargo body began during 1974 and is now in production and in service with the British Army. The body can be used as a flat platform or fitted with dropsides and a tailboard for carrying a distributed load of eight tonnes. Typical loads can be up to six standard pallets, containers up to 4.5 metres long, loose stores, and ISO containers. The body is of welded steel with a hardwood floor, both designed with a view to mass production and providing the maximum protection

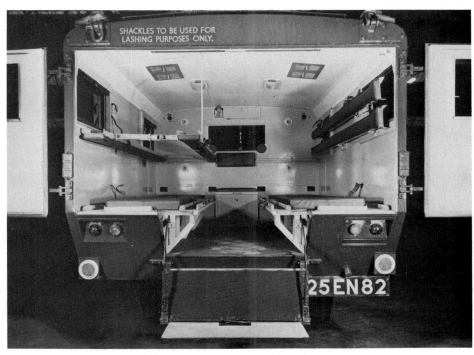

Interior view of ¾-ton Land-Rover ambulance built by Marshall of Cambridge

Foden (8 × 4) low mobility vehicle with body by Marshall of Cambridge

Bedford MK (4 × 4) 4-tonne truck with general service/cargo dropside body by Marshall of Cambridge

against corrosion. Rotating flush-fitting lashing rings are secured directly to the body underframe and, with additional heavy lashing points secured to the main-sides, are positioned to provide an efficient lashing pattern for securing all types of load. The conversion to a flat platform mode is easy and convenient. A tubular steel superstructure and tailboard cotton-polyester tilt cover is supplied. The overall length of the body is 6.637

metres and it is 2.5 metres wide. The load area is 4.53 metres long and 2.145 metres wide.

Body Cargo 16-tonne 8 × 4
This was developed from 1975 for installation on the Foden 8 × 4 low mobility range of vehicles and first production bodies were completed in 1977. Its FVRDE (MVEE) Specification is Mil 'B' V SP/B/16/1. The body is

'High top' conversion for ¾-tonne long wheelbase Land-Rover

Anti-tank 106 mm recoilless rifle, Land-Rover (airportable)

Tailboard loader fitted to MK (4 × 4) 4000 kg truck

Foden (6 × 6) medium mobility vehicle with body by Marshall of Cambridge

of the general cargo open type capable of being used as a flat platform without raves or fitted with dropsides suitable for carrying 16 000 kg of cargo. Typical loads may be up to 12 pallets, containers of ISO dimensions or loose stores.

The steel body is of all welded unit construction with the front bulkhead bolted to forward pillars mounted on to the underframe. The hardwood floor is fitted directly on top of the cross-bearers of the underframe and the floor joints are covered by steel wearing strips. The eight dropsides and tailboard can be removed and stowed in position against the front bulkhead and the rear and intermediate pillars can be removed and stowed in the appropriate lockers. Provision is made for mounting the superstructure in a high or low mode position which allows the centre supports to be removed for side loading of the body. Two rows of hooks are provided on each side for lashing the tilt in the high or low positions. The superstructure consists of 13 balehoops, four corner pillars, six vertical intermediate pillars and two longitudinal members. The balehoops, intermediate pillars and longitudinal members are stowed in the underfloor locker below the tailboard and the four corner pillars are stowed at the forward bulkhead on the stowage saddle brackets.

The waterproof canvas tilt consists of one top sheet, a front curtain and rear sheet, one rear side sheet to the left and one to the right, two centre side sheets to the left and two to the right. When in position the tilt is secured to the balehoops and longitudinals by straps. Lengths of lashing, threaded through the eyelets on the hem of the side sheets one each side, are passed below the hooks and secured to the cleats. The front and rear curtains are secured by straps. The front curtain has an opening with a roll up flap corresponding to the windows in the rear of the cab.

Secured to the underframes are four lockers, one toolbox and a carrier for two jerricans. Provision is made on the forward face of the front bulkhead for stowing a pickaxe head and handle, crowbar and shovel.

Top Hamper for Tractor and Limber FH-70
Development of this body began in 1973. It is designed to match the characteristics of the Foden 6 × 6 medium mobility chassis in the role of tractor and limber for the 155 mm FH-70 towed howitzer. The basic body is of welded and bolted construction using mild steel sections and sheet. It consists of two platform sections of underframe with hardwood board floors mounted fore and aft of the loading crane. Shackles fitted to the platform secure standard NATO ammunition pallets. A fixed bulkhead is fitted to the front end of the leading platform and detachable bulkheads are provided at the end of the platforms adjacent to the loading crane.

Tractor
A removable cabin at the front end of the forward platform provides accommodation for an eight-man gun detachment. A spare gun wheel is stowed on the roof of

SPECIFICATIONS
Tractor
Length:
 (front body interior) 3·18 m
 (rear body interior) 2·64 m
Width:
 (front body interior) 2·335 m
 (rear body interior) 2·335 m
Limber
Length:
 (front body interior) 3·18 m
 (rear body interior) 2·64 m
Width:
 (front body interior) 2·335 m
 (rear body interior) 2·64 m
Height of dropsides:
 (front) 762 mm
 (rear) 610 mm

the cabin. Stowage for a spare wheel and gun equipment is provided at the back end of the rear platform. Up to four NATO ammunition pallets may be secured to the floor lashing shackles. Dropsides and tailboard are not provided, but may be fitted if required for other roles.

Limber
Readily removable hinged dropsides are fitted to both platform sections and the rear platform is fitted with a hinged tailboard. A spare wheel is stowed on the front platform. Up to eight NATO pallets may be secured to the floor lashing shackles.

STATUS
Production as required.

MANUFACTURER
Marshall of Cambridge (Engineering) Limited, Airport Works, Cambridge CB5 8RX, England.

Body general service 8-tonne

Pilcher-Greene Ambulances

DEVELOPMENT

Since 1956 Pilcher-Greene Limited has produced a range of 4 × 4 ambulances based on the 109-inch/2·769-metre wheelbase Land-Rover. These ambulances are now used in South America, Africa, the Middle East, the Indian sub-continent and the Far East. The company recently received an order, worth £2 million, for 140 ambulances based on the Land-Rover for the Jordanian armed forces.

To date production has centred mainly on the 109-inch wheelbase Land-Rover but versions based on the Range Rover and the new Land-Rover One Ten are now in production. Pilcher-Greene offers a variety of interior layouts with various fittings to suit customer requirements. Various body types are available ranging from the basic to the fully-equipped version complete with air-conditioning and other accessories. Most body types are offered in either aluminium or aluminium and glass reinforced plastic (GRP) panels.

Series 7428

In many ways the Series 7428 is the simplest of the Pilcher-Greene Land-Rover conversions as the ambulance bodies are built directly onto the basic pick-up model. Based on the 109-inch/2·769-metre wheelbase Land-Rover the Series 7428 has two body forms, Type A and Type E. Type A is the most straightforward conversion as the complete Land-Rover cab and pick-up body are retained and the ambulance area box structure is manufactured internally and externally from moulded GRP. Type E retains the pick-up body, the doors, windscreens and sidescreens. The cab roof is custom-built and is fitted with a tropical roof (also fitted to Type A). The interior of Type E uses plastic laminates and the exterior is of GRP. Both types use fibreglass wool for insulation but only Type E has provision for full air-conditioning.

Both types offer a choice of three basic interiors although others can be fitted to suit customer requirements, and a range of specialised accessories is available.

Series 7489

The Series 7489 also uses the 109-inch/2·769-metre wheelbase Land-Rover and has two types of body, the Type J and Type P. On this series the ambulance bodies are built from the chassis upwards and have high custom-built roofs with a tropical roof added. Type J has a moulded fire retardant GRP body and Type P is constructed from light aluminium alloy sections. Type P has some refinements over Type J and was the version ordered by the Jordanian armed forces. There are five different interiors available for the Series 7489.

Series 8303

The new Land-Rover One Ten with its 110-inch/2·794-metre wheelbase and Range Rover suspension and frame, means that Pilcher-Greene has been able to offer a new ambulance body which should be suitable for military purposes. While the Series 7428 and 7489 perform as military ambulances, the new Series 8303 gives a smoother ride combined with improved cross-country capability making it suitable for use as a front-line ambulance. The longer wheelbase and larger frame allow a significant increase in internal volume, providing more space for both patients and attendants. Currently the Series 8303 is available in only one body form, the Type S, which has a body framework of mild steel, and the sides, tropical roof and the roof itself are constructed from either GRP or aluminium alloy sheet. Plastic laminates are used on the interior with a vinyl-covered aluminium alloy floor. Large double doors, common to all the Pilcher-Greene bodies, are provided for access. All five interior options for the Series 7489 are available for the Series 8303 and a typical military interior would have provision for four stretcher cases with the stretchers folding to provide seating for up to eight patients. A folding seat would be provided on the cab wall for an attendant. Numerous accessories can be included.

Range Rover ambulances

Pilcher-Greene also produces an ambulance body for the Range Rover. There are two body types, the SA and the CS. Type SA has an aluminium sheet body construction and the CS uses aluminium alloy section with fibreglass panelling. Two standard interiors are available but externally the two types are similar. The Range Rover ambulance is essentially a high-speed casualty ambulance for long-distance tasks and while it has an excellent cross-country performance, it's main function is as a road vehicle for long journeys at high speeds.

STATUS

Production.

MANUFACTURER

Pilcher-Greene Limited, Consort Way, Victoria Gardens, Burgess Hill, West Sussex RH15 8NA, England.

SPECIFICATIONS

Series	7428	7428	7489	7489	8303	Range Rover	Range Rover
Body type	A	E	J	P	S	SA	CS
Weight (approx)	1753 kg	1820 kg	1960 kg	1950 kg	1950 kg	1977 kg	1977 kg
Wheelbase	2·769 m	2·769 m	2·769 m	2·769 m	2·794 m	2·794 m	2·794 m
Length (overall)	4·445 m	4·445 m	4·801 m	4·801 m	4·786 m	4·928 m	4·928 m
(body)	1·854 m	1·981 m	2·337 m	2·337 m	2·311 m	2·159 m	2·159 m
Width (overall)	1·651 m	1·651 m	1·803 m	1·702 m	1·908 m	1·778 m	1·778 m
(body)	1·448 m	1·575 m	1·702 m	1·6 m	1·695 m	1·702 m	1·702 m
Height (overall)	2·159 m	2·337 m	2·413 m	2·337 m	2·337 m	2·159 m	2·159 m
(body)	1·321 m	1·524 m	1·524 m	1·524 m	1·536 m	1·448 m	1·448 m

Pilcher-Greene Series 7428 Type A ambulance

Pilcher-Greene Series 7489 Type P ambulance

New Pilcher-Greene Series 8303 Type S ambulance with Land-Rover One Ten chassis

Pilcher-Greene Series 7428 Type E ambulance on 109-inch/2·769-metre wheelbase Land-Rover equipped with air-conditioning

Bray Equipment Bodies

DESCRIPTION

The Bray Equipment Company, part of the CMC Group of Companies, specialises in the production of mobile workshops, lubrication units, three-in-one units and medical units for both civil and military use. These are normally built to order and are based on the chassis requested by the customer, although wherever possible British chassis are used, for example Bedford truck chassis.

The workshop unit can be either vehicle-, trailer-, skid- or container-mounted and is designed to enable operators to repair, replace parts, and test equipment and machinery. Each unit includes a comprehensive range of tools and equipment. At the 1978 British Army Equipment Exhibition the company exhibited a Bedford MJR2 (4 × 4) unit with facilities for tyre changing, lubrication equipment to provide oil, grease and air and a

workbench with a range of hand tools, welding equipment, generator and a floodlight.

The lubrication units are known as 'lubes' and are used to provide vehicles in the field with various types of oils and greases. The lightweight lube can be installed in the rear of a small vehicle such as a Land-Rover with heavier units being mounted on a Bedford 4 × 4 or 4 × 2 chassis. A typical installation on a Bedford MK (4 × 4) chassis would include high and low volume pumps designed to handle oils from 10 SAE to 140 SAE in varying temperatures with an output of up to 45 litres per minute, range of compressors giving ample pressure for lube pumps plus full airline facilities, provision for loading drums of grease without external assistance and an optional range of full servicing equipment to supplement the main lubrication capability.

Three-in-one combination units are designed to incorporate the facilities of lubrication and workshop units to allow a more general purpose application. The

unit, which can be truck- or trailer-mounted, is capable of greasing, lubricating, washing, tyre repair or changing, welding and painting. In 1978 the company delivered four trailerised (on a York chassis) multi-role units to the Jordanian Army with a further single unit being delivered to the Libyan Army for trials.

Medical units include 4 × 4 Land-Rover ambulances, trailer-mounted operating units and a mobile medical unit which includes an operating theatre, pharmacy, treatment room, X-ray area, recovery room, reception area, blood bank and other medical facilities.

STATUS

Production as required.

MANUFACTURER

Bray Equipment Sales Limited, Elm Springs, Lower Rudloe, Corsham, Wiltshire, England.

Bedford truck-mounted, multi-purpose type lube and service unit

Trailer lube service unit as supplied to Jordan

Interior view of Bray designed mobile workshop

Bedford truck-mounted lube and primary service unit

Edbro Tipper and Vehicle Bodies

DESCRIPTION

Edbro is the United Kingdom's largest manufacturer of tipper truck hoists which it produces with lift capacities from 1·5 tonnes to 65 tonnes. It is also a large producer of tipper bodies in steel and aluminium, hydraulic skip loaders and demountable tipper body systems, and scissor-lift mechanisms for airfield equipment, all of which have a military application.

A wide range of vehicle bodies in steel and aluminium – fixed as well as for tipping purposes – is available to fit virtually every type of commercial vehicle chassis in the western world. Typical is the fixed-sided steel body on a Foden LRD (8 × 4) 5·41-metre wheelbase chassis which Edbro has supplied in quantity for military purposes. Mounted on 203 × 76·2 mm steel longitudinal runners, the body's 10s gauge mild steel sides and ends have inside dimensions of 5·562 metres long, 2·337 metres wide and 0·914 metre deep. The sandwich floor has 25·4 mm thick timber between the bottom 10s gauge steel sheet and the top layer of 12s gauge mild steel. The headboard has a 1·219-metre cantilevered canopy to protect the driver's cab, and has three meshed rear-view grilles. The taildoor is swung from both top and bottom.

Rope hooks for use when a load requires to be covered are incorporated in the sides (outer), and there are chain boxes on each side and a tool box. Steel mudflaps cover the second, third and fourth axles, the latter being attached to the underside of the body. The body in this instance is raised by an Edbro 6LNC single front-ram hydraulic hoist powered from the vehicle's engine via a pump and power take-off. The power unit of the hoist is the swash-plate axial piston pump introduced by Edbro nearly 50 years ago. There is a range of six-cylinder piston pumps with outputs from 26 to 38 litres per minute at 1000 rpm, and nine-cylinder units with outputs from 59 to 95 litres per minute at 1000 rpm. The pump casing is of die-cast high-tensile aluminium. Precision ground in chromium nickel steel, the pistons are designed for a long life. Self-lubricating, under normal conditions the pump does not need an additional filter because it has a high degree of tolerance to oil contamination. Also of die-cast high-tensile aluminium, the power take-off fits standard SAE apertures, and there is a wide range of adaptor plates for other gearbox openings. More than 900 gear wheel variations are produced by Edbro to make the combined pump and power take-off suitable for any vehicle. The power take-off selector housing is identical for air, cable or rod linkage control.

Edbro tipper body fitted to Foden (8 × 4) LRD (Low Mobility) chassis

Edbro tipper bodies on Foden (8 × 4) Low Mobility chassis

Edbro tipper bodies on Foden (8 × 4) Low Mobility chassis

Normally fitted on the dashboard, the air control panel includes a power take-off switch and the hoist control lever which has positions for tip, hold and controlled lowering. An amber light shows when the power take-off gears are in mesh with the gearbox – this reduces the change of a driver leaving the power take-off in mesh after completing a tipper operation.

The cable control for the hoist also has tip, hold and controlled lowering positions. The power take-off control is in this case mounted separately. To prevent accidental engagement of the hoist controls, the operating lever is fitted with a spring loaded collar needing positive action to move from one position to another. The cables are encased in weatherproof pvc and are greased for life.

Three tipper control valves have oil flow ratings of 25, 75 and 150 litres per minutes to match different applications. Easily replaced precision engineered valve seats ensure positive control from the cab during raising and lowering of the body. Another safety feature is the tamper-proof replaceable cartridge relief valve available in six pre-set pressures. Pressure test points ease checks on the hydraulic system during routine servicing. The control valve is mounted directly on the combined ram and tank usual on most Edbro tippers.

Edbro tipping hoist configurations range from single front-end units through conventional underbody direct-thrust models to underbody link hoists. Depending on the hoist and chassis, tipping angles normally range from 45 to 50 degrees but higher angles can be catered for. Designs include both bore sealers and outside sealers.

Bore-seal hoists feature a special cup washer seal of special long-life rubber compound. The cup washer acts on the protected inside wall of the cylinders with a built-in expansion spring maintaining the effectiveness of the seal under all conditions. The cup washers are easily replaced on site. Outside-seal hoists have a seal which adjusts itself to variations in pressure, combining optimum sealing with minimum wear. These seals can be replaced with the hoist on the vehicle and can operate over a wide temperature range.

STATUS
In production. In service with the British Army.

MANUFACTURER
Edbro Limited, Lever Street, Bolton, Greater Manchester BL3 6DJ, England.

Penman Mobile Shelters and Custom-built Containers

DESCRIPTION
Penman Truck Body Systems manufactures cabins, shelters and containers for a variety of uses. The present range of lightweight, flexible equipment cabins are now built to a new and improved military specification. The materials and techniques used are fully approved for military equipment and the cabins conform to British and NATO environmental and other requirements. Standard Penman cabin designs are available corresponding to most commonly specified styles. These include NATO type II and III, S-280, S-250, and ISO 10, 20 and 30 feet.

The cabins are constructed from sandwich panels, assembled, bonded and enclosed within an aluminium framework. The panels are one-piece, aluminium-skinned polyurethane sandwich construction, reinforced with integral aluminium structural members incorporating thermal barriers. The complete panel is resin bonded under controlled conditions and conforms to widely-accepted military specifications. All the cabins have an escape hatch, wide-access personnel door, roof access steps, roof reinforcement plates, vinyl flooring and a military specification paint finish.

Many of the units that Penman supply are fitted out for

Penman Military Shelter mounted on Shelvoke SPV (4 × 4) 8000 kg truck

Interior of Penman field workshop (electrical) cabin

Double RF screened Penman cabin designed to house radar equipment

a particular role. The company has designed a range of interior layouts to suit the more common military applications, including command posts, field workshops (mechanical and electrical), and communications centres. A range of optional equipment is available including lifting and securing slings, levelling jacks, demount jack legs, a power input panel, interior power and lighting, furniture, RF screening, windows, battery and other lockers, and access ladders. Cabins can also be supplied on shock-absorbing skids and with external frames for equipment mounting.

In addition to the Field Military Cabin the company also supplies units manufactured by other techniques using sheet and composite construction. Cabins can be supplied to non-standard sizes and shapes and manufacturered in a variety of styles.

Penman are especially experienced in the design of cabins offering varying degrees of protection against radio frequency (RF), interference and other effects. Cabins are offered with an option of three levels of RF attenuation according to customer requirements. Cabin designs utilising alternative material skins, continuous joints and double isolated skins are available. Cabins can be constructed to meet a number of environmental specifications. The build standards available now include a cabin designed to withstand the full range of nuclear weapon effects including electro-magnetic pulse, thermal pulse and blast (impulse and dynamic effects). The nuclear cabin is also designed to accommodate NBC equipment, and is in service with a number of European forces.

SPECIFICATIONS (standard cabin)
Length: (overall) 4·57 m
Width: 2·44 m
Height: 2·13 m

STATUS
Production.

MANUFACTURER
A C Penman Limited, Heathhall, Dumfries DG1 3NY, Scotland.

Heywood Williams Field Shelter MEXE Mk III

DESCRIPTION
The Field Shelter MEXE Mk II (or Mexeshelter) was developed by the Military Engineering Experimental Establishment at Christchurch (now part of the Military Vehicles and Engineering Establishment), with production and marketing being undertaken by Heywood Williams Limited. The shelter provides protection against conventional attack, near miss nuclear attack and protection against chemical and bacteriological attack. Protection against the first of these two categories is given by the standard shelter with protection against chemical and bacteriological attack being provided by a kit described below.

The Mk III was originally conceived as an underground shelter for Command Posts (CPs), Observation Posts (OPs) and Regimental Aid Posts (RAPs), for use mainly by the Army in forward and rear area tactical situations, but it is now receiving consideration for the underground protection of personnel on air stations and in areas not directly related with the tactical battlefield itself. In its present configuration, it is being used on a much wider basis which includes a casualty clearing and first aid station in conjunction with triage; storage for medical supplies, including plasma, drugs, dressings; fuel, food and other combat support items, and as temporary magazines for ordnance items. In the Command Post usage it has moved into battalion and divisional use.

The Mk III consists of four components plus accessories – three metal structural members, pickets, spacers, arches, plus flexible revetting material to clad the metal structural members and which is held in place by earth backfill. All components are packaged in manportable kits and can be installed by unskilled personnel with no special tools required; all work can be accomplished with a pick and shovel. With the use of mechanical equipment such as a bull-dozer, scraper or shovel, approximately two hours are required to fully install the Mk III. In addition to the mechanical equipment, approximately 15 man-hours of troop labour are required.

The flexible revetting material used to line the walls and roof of the shelter is a pvc-coated jute fabric reinforced with wire. The pvc layer, being impermeable, provides an obstacle to chemical agent penetration, and, when this is combined with the additional barrier of 450 to 600 mm of soil over the shelter roof, it is likely that there will be no hazard in the shelter even with heavy

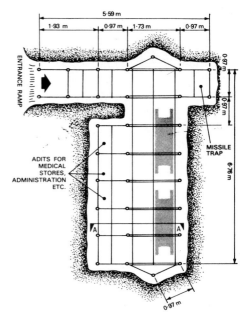

Command post MEXE Mk III modular shelter built with 18 pickets, 4 arches, 29 spacers and 4 rolls of revetting material

Regimental first-aid post built from 32 pickets, 8 arches, 55 spacers and 7 rolls of revetting material

chemical agent contamination on the ground outside. Modifications necessary to give chemical protection without the use of respirators and NBC clothing are the installation of a supply of NBC filtered air (such as the L1A1 portable NBC air filter unit) and an airlock with filtered air ventilation in the entrance tunnel of the shelter.

Driclad Limited of Sittingbourne, Kent, has developed an internal liner for the MEXE shelter to provide occupants with a safer environment in the event of a chemical attack. The liner consists of a main compartment and an air lock joined together by the patented Drilok closure. The air lock connection to the main compartment is 'handed' to enable it to be connected to either side of the main compartment. The liner is attached to the MEXE shelter's main frame by quick-action clips and can be erected by two men in 30 minutes. Further main compartments can be added to either end, again by the use of Drilok closures. Clean air is provided to the liner by a suitable air fan and filter unit (see below) which provides over-pressure to inflate the liner to its maximum size and to purge the air lock. The material used for the liner is translucent reinforced plastic. A main compartment and air lock weighs 15·875 kg and when packed in a box the dimensions are 1·097 × 0·73 × 0·73 metres.

Normalair-Garrett has produced an air filtration unit suitable for use with the MEXE shelter and its Driclad liner. The unit can provide an airflow of 50 litres per second and has a power consumption of 150 W. The power supply can be either mains or from a 24-volt source. The unit has a diameter of 400 mm and is one metre long. The weight is between 36 and 42 kg depending on the power supply requirements. Westair and one other company have developed similar units.

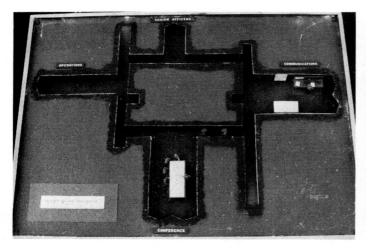

Cutaway model showing layout of MEXE shelter in use as underground command post

Interior bay of MEXE shelter showing impermeable pvc layer for protection against chemical agents

Various tests have been run to evaluate the protection provided by the Mk III in both a projected nuclear and a conventional weapon environment. In the case of a nuclear blast, the results record the protection provided against heat (thermal radiation), nuclear radiation (immediate) and nuclear fall-out. The shelter components have been designed to withstand, to a given level, the effects of a "near miss" weapons blast. The tests were undertaken by the US, the German and the British forces.

In 1974 comparative tests between the flexible-wall MEXE shelter and six United States designed rigid-wall shelters on behalf of the United States forces were carried out by Headquarters Modern Army Selected Systems Test and Evaluation and Review at Fort Hood in Texas. The result of the test indicated that the MEXE shelter proved most effective of all the structures tested and was the preferred choice of 74·6 per cent of the evaluation team who undertook the test.

STATUS
Production. In service with British, Canadian, Kuwait and Saudi Arabian armed forces. Under active evaluation by Belgium and the USA (40 sets purchased).

MANUFACTURER
Heywood Williams Limited, Military Engineering Division, Bayhall Works, Huddersfield, West Yorkshire HD1 5EJ, England.

MEXE shelter covering prior to earth backfill

Assembling MEXE shelter and showing general construction method

Barton APD Shelters

DESCRIPTION
Intended to be used buried underground the Barton APD Shelter is of modular construction designed to withstand heavy blast effects and may provide protection from NBC agents. The shelter can be supplied as a single unit or alternatively the modular design enables the shelter to be built up into underground complexes of any number of configurations. Once installed the internal construction enables the shelters to be used for a variety of purposes ranging from simple shelters to large command, control and communication complexes.

The main shelter module consists of nine octagonal main frames manufactured, as are most components, from galvanised steel. The frames are joined together by tubular distance pieces to create a main structure 3·6 metres long. On each frame a set of end covers are attached, one consisting of two outer plates and a centre plate. The other cover consists of two outer plates and a bottom plate providing an opening 1·8 metres high and 0·76 metre wide to which a conning tower is connected. Holes are provided in each end cover to take the air inlet and exhaust pipe flanges. These are normally set at opposite ends. At the air inlet end a bilge pump bracket is located together with its outlet. The main shelter is covered with pre-stressed galvanised sheets which are lap jointed and bolted to the outside of the main structure. Where joints occur in the covers, including the end covers, a rubber sealing strip is placed between mating surfaces. Fibre washers are placed under all bolt heads. Vent and exhaust pipes are connected to the end covers by a flange which is supplied complete with a sealing gasket.

Internally a bracket is supplied to house a wash basin. Hinged brackets support four bunks which are supplied with foam mattresses; each bunk is 1·8 metres long. The softwood timber floor is supported on 100 × 50 mm joists at 450 mm centres. Other items supplied for the standard interior include a hand-operated air pump, a chemical toilet and a hand-operated bilge pump.

The standard shelter has a conning tower leading to the surface bolted onto the main structure at one end. The tower is 0·76 metre wide and 3·2 metres high with an inward-opening hatch at the top. The hatch has a diameter of 450 mm and has an 8 mm armoured lid. When a number of shelter modules are combined the conning tower may be replaced by an entrance module which can serve up to four shelters in a cruciform arrangement. Bolted construction is used for the entrance module which is manufactured from 4 mm plate flanged and reinforced with 4 mm flats. It uses two ladders.

The Barton APD shelter has been tested by the British Army.

SPECIFICATIONS
Basic unit length: 3·6 m
Cross-section: 2·4 m across octagonal points
Conning tower entrance: 0·76 m²
Total weight: (including fittings) 2130 kg

Entrance module
Total weight: 2300 kg
Height: 2·75 m
Plan size: 2·75 m²

STATUS
Production.

MANUFACTURER
BC Barton and Son Limited, 1 Hainge Road, Twidale, Warley, West Midlands B69 2NJ, England.

Barton APD shelter showing entry conning tower

Barton APD shelter showing cross-section shape

UNITED STATES OF AMERICA

Gichner Shelter, Electrical Equipment S-250

DESCRIPTION
The S-250 is a T-shape, non-expansible shelter of adhesive bonded construction with seamless aluminium interior and exterior skins, extruded aluminium framework structure and a polyurethane foam core. It is used to carry communications, radar, teletype and maintenance electronic equipment and is mounted on the rear of a 1¼- or 1½-ton truck. It can be transported by a transporter/mobiliser dolly set, fixed-wing aircraft, helicopter, rail and ship.

The shelter meets military specifications MIL-S-55541 (EL) and is available with RFI integrity.

SPECIFICATIONS
Weight:
  (without RFI kit) 349 ± 9 kg
  (with RFI kit) 355 ± 9 kg
Payload: 862 kg
Interior dimensions:
  (length) 1·628 m
  (width, upper section) 1·908 m
  (width, lower section) 1·333 m
  (height, centre section) 1·79 m
  (height) 1·191 m
Exterior dimensions:
  (length) 1·953 m
  (width, upper section) 1·857 m
  (width, lower section) 2·234 m
  (height) 1·78 m

STATUS
In production. In service with the US forces and other armed forces.

MANUFACTURER
Gichner Mobile Systems, PO Box B, Dallastown, Pennsylvania 17313, USA.

Gichner shelter, electrical equipment S-250

Gichner Shelter, Electrical Equipment S-280

DESCRIPTION
The S-280 is a rigid rectangular, non-expansible shelter of adhesive bonded construction consisting of seamless aluminium interior and exterior skins, extruded aluminium framework structure and polyurethane foam core. It is used to carry communications, radar, maintenance equipment and electronic equipment, and is mounted on the rear of a standard 2½-ton truck (for example the M35). It can also be transported by a transporter/mobiliser dolly set (models M720, M832 or M840), fixed-wing aircraft, helicopter, rail or ship.

The shelter meets military specification MIL-S-55286 (EL) and is available with RFI integrity.

SPECIFICATIONS
Weight: 612 kg
Payload: 2268 kg
Interior dimensions:
  (length) 3·504 m
  (width) 2·07 m
  (height) 1·891 m
Exterior dimensions:
  (length) 3·733 m
  (width) 2·209 m
  (height) 2·117 m

STATUS
In production. In service with the US forces and other armed forces.

MANUFACTURER
Gichner Mobile Systems, PO Box B, Dallastown, Pennsylvania 17313, USA.

Gichner shelter, electrical equipment S-280

Gichner 8 × 8 × 20 ft (2·438 × 2·438 × 6·096 m) ISO Shelter/Container

DESCRIPTION
This is a rigid rectangular, non-expansible shelter/container of adhesive bonded sandwich panel consisting of seamless aluminium exterior skins, extruded aluminium framework structure and a polyurethane foam core. It has integral ISO corner fittings which meet ANSI MH 5.1 requirements. It is used as a multi-purpose electronic equipment enclosure (radar, communication, maintenance, housing, laboratory etc), with a special butting kit feature and slide-in slide-out air-conditioner unit optional. Large doors are provided for the installation and removal of equipment.

The shelter/container meets military specification MIL-M-81957 and can be transported by truck, transporter (M832 end mount or van undercarriage type), fixed wing aircraft, rail and ship (it is stackable via ISO couplers).

STATUS
In production. In service with the US forces and other armed forces.

MANUFACTURER
Gichner Mobile Systems, PO Box B, Dallastown, Pennsylvania 17313, USA.

SPECIFICATIONS
Weight: 1996 kg
Payload: 4536 kg
Interior dimensions:
  (length) 5·897 m
  (width) 2·23 m
  (height) 2·141 m
Exterior dimensions:
  (length) 6·057 m
  (width) 2·438 m
  (height, less skids) 2·438 m
  (height, with skid for van mobiliser interface) 2·514 m

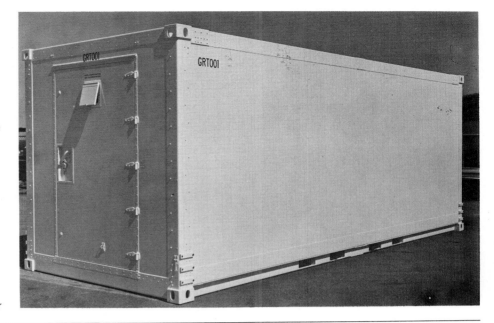

Gichner 8 × 8 × 20 ft ISO shelter/container

Gichner Modular Electronic Equipment Shelter GMS-451 Series

DESCRIPTION
The GMS-451 is a rigid rectangular modular side-to-side butting shelter and is of adhesive bonded sandwich panel construction consisting of seamless interior and exterior skins, extruded aluminium framework structure and a polyurethane foam core. It has removable side panels with GMS shear-loc design.

The shelter, which meets military specification MIL-S-55286 Modified (RFI optional) can be used for a variety of roles including communications, radar, teletype, laboratory, dormitory and hospital. It can be transported by truck, transporter, aircraft, rail or ship.

SPECIFICATIONS

Model	GMS-451	GMS-451-479	GMS-451-537	GMS-451-571
Weight (basic unit)	907 kg	1089 kg	1724 kg	1134 kg
Payload	2268 kg	2722 kg	4536 kg	2722 kg
Interior (length)	3·505 m	4·019 m	5·893 m	4·019 m
(width)	2·032 m	2·07 m	2·286 m	2·286 m
(height)	2·082 m	2·063 m	2·26 m	2·063 m
Exterior (length)	3·733 m	4·242 m	6·096 m	4·241 m
(width)	2·209 m	2·209 m	2·438 m	2·438 m
(height)	2·336 m	2·336 m	2·54 m	2·387 m

STATUS
In production. In service with the US forces and other armed forces.

MANUFACTURER
Gichner Mobile Systems, PO Box B, Dallastown, Pennsylvania 17313, USA.

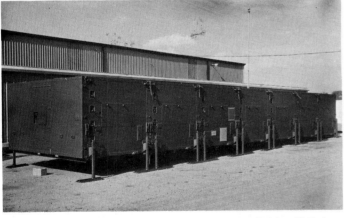

Gichner GMS-451-571 seven-shelter complex built for Melpar Division of E-Systems

Interior view of GMS-451 series shelters coupled together

Gichner Shelter, Electrical Equipment, S-514/G and S-515/G

DESCRIPTION
This expansible shelter complex (known as a 3 for 2 configuration) consists of two modules with sliding base alignment, hinged side panels, hinged roof panel and levelling jacks. It is of adhesive bonded sandwich panel construction consisting of seamless aluminium interior and exterior skins, extruded aluminium framework and polyurethane foam core. It can be used for a variety of roles including radar, maintenance, communications, weather station, dormitory, kitchen and hospital facility.

It meets military specification MIL-S-55286 (modified)

Expansible shelter complex showing hinged side panel of shelter 2 becoming roof panel of expanded area

Expansible shelter complex in position

and can be transported by 2½-ton truck (such as the M35), transporter/mobiliser dolly set (M720, M832 or M840), fixed wing aircraft, helicopter, rail or ship.

STATUS
In production. In service with the US Air Force.

MANUFACTURER
Gichner Mobile Systems, PO Box B, Dallastown, Pennsylvania 17313, USA.

SPECIFICATIONS
Weight (with sliding base jacks) 1088 kg
Payload (per module) 2268 kg

		transport mode (per module)	expansible configuration
Interior dimensions	(length)	3·502 m	3·502 m
	(width)	2·032 m	6·182 m
	(height)	2·082 m	2·082 m
Exterior dimensions	(length)	3·708 m	3·708 m
	(width)	2·21 m	6·322 m
	(height)	2·33 m	2·33 m

Gichner Transporter/Mobiliser Dolly Sets

DESCRIPTION
Tactical shelters require the use of rugged wheeled devices (end-mounted and van undercarriage type) capable of transporting the shelters via a towing vehicle over rough terrain as well as airfields and roads. This is accomplished via militarised tactical mobilisers of various capacities and types. Listed below are some of the standard units available from Gichner.

STATUS
In production. In service with the US and other armed forces.

SPECIFICATIONS

	Applicable specification	Gross load capacity	Type
M720	MIL-D-62027F(AT)	3175 kg	end-mount
M689	MIL-D-62027F(AT)	4763 kg	end-mount
M829	MIL-D-62027F(AT)	4763 kg	end-mount
M832	MIL-D-62027F(AT)	4763 kg	end-mount
M840	MIL-D-62027F(AT)	4082 kg	end-mount
VM 0503	MIL-D-62027F(AT)	3402 kg	undercarriage
VM 1003	MIL-D-62027F(AT)	4536 kg	undercarriage
VM 1503	MIL-D-62027F(AT)	6804 kg	undercarriage
VM 2003	MIL-D-62027F(AT)	9072 kg	undercarriage

MANUFACTURER
Gichner Mobile Systems, PO Box B, Dallastown, Pennsylvania 17313, USA.

Gichner shelter/container with M689 mobiliser

Gichner shelter on Gichner VM 2003 van mobilisers

Gichner Transportable Material Handling Pallet SPA-5000

DESCRIPTION
This pallet provides tactical transport/handling capability for miscellaneous accessory equipment (jacks, air-conditioners, cable reels and generators etc) used in conjunction with the transportable shelter system.

Its adhesive bonded sandwich panel constructed base consists of aluminium interior and exterior skins, extruded aluminium framework structure and foam core material.

The pallet, which meets military specification MIL-D-27925, is transportable by truck, transporter/mobiliser dolly set (M720, M832 and M689), fixed wing aircraft, helicopter, rail and ship.

SPECIFICATIONS
Weight: (with sling) 226·8 kg
Payload: 2268 kg
Payload area: (inside stanchions) 1·831 × 2·352 m
Overall exterior: (including mobiliser brackets and handles) 2·057 × 2·659 m
Standard stanchion height: 0·695 m

STATUS
In service with the US forces.

MANUFACTURER
Gichner Mobile Systems, PO Box B, Dallastown, Pennsylvania 17313, USA.

Gichner transportable material handling pallet, SPA-5000 complete with jacks and air-conditioning equipment

Gichner Levelling, Alignment and Lifting Jack Systems

DESCRIPTION
The type of jacking system depends on the basic requirements of the shelter: whether it is fixed or modular/expansible, its gross load and size, jacking height required and its purpose: levelling, truck-loading, or both. Gichner has two basic jack designs which within themselves have been modified to incorporate features which will satisfy all tactical shelter jacking requirements for all tactical military shelters. The two basic types are the fixed type and the roller base type, brief specifications for which are given here.

STATUS
Production.

MANUFACTURER
Gichner Mobile Systems, PO Box B, Dallastown, Pennsylvania 17313, USA.

SPECIFICATIONS

Reference	LWJ 2500	RBJ 2500	AWJ5000	AWJ5000-AE
Type base	fixed	roller	fixed	fixed
Lift capacity	1134 kg	1134 kg	2268 kg	2268 kg
Travel height	0·457 – 0·736 m	0·457 – 0·763 m	1·524 m	1·524 m
General application	S-280	expansible	8 ft × 8 ft × 20 ft modular	truck loading shelter
Approx weight (each)	13·6 kg	14·5 kg	40·9 kg	54·43 kg

8 × 8 × 20 ft shelter with lifting jacks in position

Gichner Transportable Material Handling Pallet SPA-1003

DESCRIPTION
This pallet provides tactical transport/handling capability for miscellaneous equipment (jacks, air-conditioners, cable reels and generators etc) used in conjunction with the transportable shelter system.

Its adhesive sandwich panel constructed base consists of aluminium interior and exterior skins, extruded aluminium framework structure and foam core material.

The pallet, which meets military specification MIL-D-27925 (modified), is transportable by truck, transporter/mobiliser dolly set (M832 or M689), fixed wing aircraft, helicopter, rail or ship.

SPECIFICATIONS
Weight: (with sling) 363 kg
Payload: 4538 kg
Payload area: (inside stanchions) 1·872 × 3·342 m
Overall exterior: (including mobiliser brackets and handles, less 463-L rails) 2·085 × 3·768 m
Standard stanchion height: 0·695 m

Gichner transportable material handling pallet SPA-1003

STATUS
In service with the US forces.

MANUFACTURER
Gichner Mobile Systems, PO Box B, Dallastown, Pennsylvania 17313, USA.

Relocatable Hospital System

DESCRIPTION
Developed in conjunction with the US armed forces, the Relocatable Hospital System has been designed for use in outlying or remote locations. It is intended for use in three basic configurations, the smallest of which is a 20-bed configuration. The addition of a single extra ward converts the unit into a 30-bed hospital and the next standard configuration is a 60-bed hospital. The entire system is based on the use of transportable shelters which can be opened out into larger units to form wards, operating theatres and laboratories. Each unit is fully equipped to carry out a certain function and the entire complex is self-sufficient apart from external supplies of water, fuels and expendable supplies. The hospital has its own power generation plant, internal water supply system and material supply centre. The separate

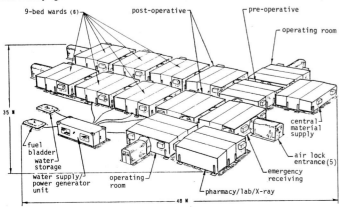

Brunswick 60-bed basic hospital

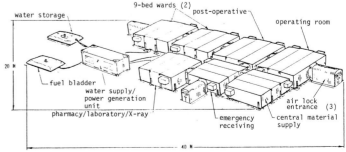

Brunswick 20-bed basic hospital

units are all inter connected and all entrances have air-locks. Each unit, when transported, is 2·4 × 2·4 × 6·1 metres but in position and opened out the shelter has a floor area of 36·5 square metres. The shelters are constructed using honeycomb cores and aluminium facings, and each contains all the necessary equipment for its role. The most common unit is a nine-bed ward which has, apart from the beds, bedside cabinets, screening curtains and chairs for nurses and orderlies. All the units have their own integral lighting and air-conditioning with power coming from a generator housed in a standard container. Fuel for the generator and water supplies are kept in collapsible tanks. The 20/30-bed hospital has a 200 kW generator and the 60-bed hospital a 400 kW generator. Both sizes of hospital use a 1900-litre water tank.

STATUS
In production. In service with the US armed forces.

MARKETING OFFICE
Brunswick Corporation, Suite 1107, 2001 Jefferson Davis Highway, Arlington, Virginia 22202, USA.

Typical Brunswick Corporation hospital system unit

Typical relocatable hospital system produced by Brunswick Corporation's Defense Division

Craig Standard and ISO Shelters

DESCRIPTION
Craig Systems is one of the largest manufacturers of mobile shelters in the USA and produces a very wide range of standard mobile shelters, shelter vans and accessories. The ISO range of shelters is produced with floors, walls and roofs of single-piece inner and outer aluminium skins with foamed-in-place polyurethane filling. Aluminium extrusions are used for structural strength and for any internal fittings. As with all Craig Systems shelters, the ISO range can be adapted for a wide range of purposes with the internal and external fittings and accessories altered accordingly.

STATUS
Production. In widespread service.

MANUFACTURER
Craig Systems, 10 Industrial Way, Amesbury, Massachusetts 01913, USA.

SPECIFICATIONS

Model	S-138	S-141	S-250	S-280	H-376	H-395	H-454	H-556	H-581	H-582	H-584	H-586	H-587
Length	2·438 m	3·404 m	1·981 m	3·505 m	3·556 m	3·607 m	6·705 m	5·944 m	1·93 m	4·674 m	2·591 m	3·861 m	3·404 m
Width	1·93 m	1·93 m	1·905 m	2·07 m	2·134 m	1·93 m	2·286 m	2·286 m	1·93 m	1·93 m	1·93 m	1·93 m	1·93 m
Height	1·867 m	1·867 m	1·625 m	1·892 m	2·007 m	1·867 m	2·184 m	2·184 m	1·93 m	2·007 m	1·93 m	1·867 m	1·93 m
Weight	454 kg	545 kg	347 kg	626·5 kg	726 kg	567·5 kg	1816 kg	1589 kg	390 kg	908 kg	463 kg	590 kg	545 kg

Craig S-250 shelter modified to accommodate ECM equipment

Craig S-141 shelter on Craig D-404B transporter

Craig Model H-835 30-foot/9·144-metre shelter

Craig S-280 shelter in use as radar shelter

Craig Model H-833 electronic equipment shelter on Craig Model D-741B transporter

Craig S-280 shelter with external air conditioner mounted on M548 tracked cargo carrier

Craig N-1080 and N-1050 Nuclear Hardened Tactical Shelters

DESCRIPTION
The Craig N-1080 nuclear hardened shelter has been developed together with Harry Diamond Laboratories and the Italian Miki SpA to house and shelter complex and expensive equipment that modern armed forces use in the front line. Such equipment includes electronics and various forms of communications equipment, and in some cases the contents of a mobile military shelter can run into millions, whatever the currency involved. To provide such equipment with protection against tactical nuclear weapon effects, the N-1080 was designed. It is a conventional shelter in appearance but the walls, floors and ceiling are Kevlar laminates and many of the fittings are Kevlar extrusions. The door has special blast-proof hinges and a Craig V-846 anti-blast valve is fitted above the door. The N-1080 has a specially strengthened air conditioning and filter unit at the front end of the shelter. The door has an emergency escape hatch, and special corner and lifting castings are provided.

The N-1080 has been tested under simulated tactical nuclear weapon detonation conditions in 'Operation Millrace' that took place at White Sands, New Mexico, in September, 1981.

The N-1080 is 3·734 metres long, 2·21 metres wide and 2·12 metres high.

The N-1050 is a smaller nuclear hardened shelter suitable for carrying on small trucks. It is 2·073 metres long, 1·994 metres wide and 1·717 metres high. Weight is 544 kg.

STATUS
Pre-production.

MANUFACTURER
Craig Systems, 10 Industrial Way, Amesbury, Massachusetts 01913, USA.

Craig N-1080 nuclear hardened shelter

Craig N-1050 nuclear hardened shelter

Craig Shelter Transporters

DESCRIPTION
There are four main types of transporter in the Craig range, the D-404, the M-832 and the D-741B and (ISO).

The Model D-404 is a lightweight transporter for up to 2721·5 kg payload. It has two dolly assemblies, front and rear. It includes front and rear axle assemblies, air-over-hydraulic brakes, mechanical parking brakes for the rear wheels, standard tyres, an airspring suspension, automotive type shock absorbers, front and rear hydraulic lifting systems, a quickly removable hinged tow bar, tail lights and stop lights. The D-404 may be used for carrying light and palletised loads.

The M-832 provides mobility for medium range payloads up to 4763 kg. The front and rear dolly assemblies are attached to the payload. Hydraulic cylinders permit lowering and raising of the shelter suspension bars and strut assemblies lock the trailer in the raised position for transport. Air-over-hydraulic brakes are provided on all four wheels of the dolly set. Tail, stop and black-out lights are mounted on the rear trailer. The M-832 is used by the US Marine Corps.

The Model D-741B transporter consists of front and rear half sections which are permanently attached to the shelter. Payload is up to 7711 kg. The front half is steerable, primarily to facilitate loading large shelters into cargo aircraft. The D-741B is in service with the US Marine Corps.

STATUS
Production. In service with the US Army, US Marine Corps and many other armed forces.

MANUFACTURER
Craig Systems, 10 Industrial Way, Amesbury, Massachusetts 01913, USA.

SPECIFICATIONS

Model	D-404	M-832	D-741B	D-741 (ISO)
Weight	802·5 kg	1664·7 kg	1927·75 kg	2565 kg
Payload (max)	2721·5 kg	4763 kg	7711 kg	7711 kg
Length	2·489 m	3·038 m	front 1·435 m	front 1·448 m
			rear 1·384 m	rear 1·422 m
Width	2·438 m	2·438 m	2·438 m	0·813 m
Height	1·245 m	1·321 m	n/a	2·337 m
Track width	2·134 m	2·134 m	2·134 m	2·134 m
Road clearance	0·3556 or	0·432 m	0·432 m	0·432 m
	0·432 m			
Shelter levelling capability	0 to 0·305 m	0 to 0·305 m	0 to 0·102 m	–
Shelter lift capability	0 to 0·432 m	0 to 0·432 m	0 to 0·143 m	0 to 0·635 m
Hydraulic lifting	standard	standard	standard	standard
Mechanical lifting	optional	no	no	no
Tyres	7.00 × 16	9.00 × 20	11.00 × 20	11.00 × 20

Craig D-404 transporter

Craig D-404 transporter

Craig Model D-741 (ISO) being used to load shelter into US Air Force C-130 Hercules transport aircraft

Craig Model M-832 transporter

Craig Transportable Air Traffic Control Shelter

DESCRIPTION
This equipment was developed for use by the US Department of Defense by Craig Systems as part of an overall Tactical Air Traffic Control System. The shelter is supplied complete with equipment pallet-mounted on levelling jacks. The shelter has tinted and heated glass panels, acoustic ceiling tiles, full lighting, cable and entry panels, shock absorbing skids, access ladders, protective screens and provision for air conditioning.

STATUS
Production. In service with the US armed forces.

MANUFACTURER
Craig Systems, 10 Industrial Way, Amesbury, Massachusetts 01913, USA.

Craig transportable air traffic control centre emplaced in the field

Craig transportable air traffic control centre

US Dual Role Cargo Pallet

DESCRIPTION
A cargo pallet designed to fit the US Army's Ribbon Bridge transporter for a dual role as a general cargo carrier has been developed by the US Army Mobility Equipment Research and Development Command (MERADCOM).

The M812 5-ton (6 × 6) transporter equipped with a hydraulic boom is used to carry, launch and retrieve complete bays of the Ribbon Bridge. When not performing its bridging mission it can launch and retrieve the specially designed 5·791 × 3·048 metre pallet loaded with up to 5 tons (US) of equipment or supplies to double as a cargo hauler.

The second capability to self-load, transport and off-load cargo was added by MERADCOM late in its Ribbon Bridge transporter development when cutbacks in military vehicles made maximum utilisation imperative. R & D pallets were procured, tested and type classified in only eight months. An initial production quantity of 120 pallets was delivered to the US Army in 1977.

STATUS
Production. In service with the US Army.

Cargo pallet in use with Ribbon Bridge transporter showing units being winched back onto truck (US Army)

OTHER EQUIPMENT

ITALY

Pirelli Protective Covers

DESCRIPTION
Pirelli produces a rubber-coated fabric which is widely used for the protection of equipment in storage and in transit. This fabric can be produced in a wide range of shapes and sizes and has a weight of between 650 and 800 grams per square metre. The fabric, usually coloured olive brown on one side and black on the other, has a minimum tensile strength of 306 kg for every 50 mm and is fire-resistant. It is also resistant to the effects of extremes of temperature and protection is provided, not only against atmospheric agents, but particularly against chemical attacks and infra-red or ultraviolet photographic observations.

One of the various articles produced using this rubber-coated fabric is a cover for use as a weather-defeating barrier on equipment in transit or in storage, but used specifically for Leopard MBTs. It is 8 metres long and 4·5 metres wide and weighs approximately 25 kg. When packed this cover occupies about 0·15 m³ and in use is lashed around the equipment to be protected.

STATUS
Production. In widespread service.

MANUFACTURER
MOLDIP SpA – Pirelli Group, Via Milano 8, 20038 Seregno (Milano), Italy.

SOUTH AFRICA

Portable Light Mast

DESCRIPTION
Intended for use in remote ares where it may be employed as a general illumination source for working areas or for security purposes, this portable light mast is a completely independent unit. It takes the power for the lamp, which is a 400 watt metal halide 30 000 lumen output colour-corrected item, from a 1·5 kW engine driven alternator mounted on the base of the mast. The weight of the alternator and engine, which are mounted in a tubular steel frame, provide a steady and secure base for the mast and extra stability can be provided by folding out outrigger arms in the base of the frame. Output of the alternator is 230/250 volts.

The mast is winch-operated and extends to a maximum of six metres. It collapses into a square-section telescopic structure. Protection for the electrical system is provided by a circuit breaker.

Weight of the complete unit is approximately 75 kg.

STATUS
Production. In service with the South African Defence Forces.

MANUFACTURER
Anderson Generating Manufacturers.
 Enquiries to Armscor, Private Bag X337, Pretoria 0001, South Africa.

Portable light mast

UNITED KINGDOM

Airflex System

DESCRIPTION
The Airflex System can produce protective covers to suit any size or shape of equipment and provides adequate protection under almost all conditions for at least ten years in warehouses, stores or open equipment parks. The system consists of a tough, flexible impermeable skin which is both airtight and waterproof, which is shaped and attached to a rigid or flexible floor. Placing the skin and attaching it to the rigid or flexible floor and partially evacuating the air inside draws the skin over and around the item to be protected. The system can involve the use of prepared containers which can be surrounded with wire cages and frames for stacking and extra protection. Airflex skins can be manufactured to almost any shape to suit any vehicle. A vehicle the size of a scout car can be covered by two men in 15 minutes and uncovered again in three minutes.

STATUS
In production. In service with several armed forces.

MANUFACTURER
Airflex Containers Limited, Brunswick Road, Cobbs Wood Industrial Estate, Ashford, Kent, England.

Airflex container covering Ferret scout car

Airflex engine containers stacked in open

Driclad Protection and Storage System

DESCRIPTION
The Driclad system is the result of applied research into the causes of corrosion and deterioration of equipment during storage and in transit. It is based on the enclosure of stores or equipment in a dry and clean atmosphere contained within a flexible plastic cover.

The Driclad system was accepted into British Army service in 1965 after extensive trials in Europe and the Far East lasting over two years. The system is now in service with many countries all over the world.

The re-usable covers are an effective barrier to water vapour in extreme conditions of climate, temperature and humidity. They also provide protection against damage by chemical gases, salt-laden air, sand, dust, fungi and insects. A system can be designed by Driclad for any shape.

The system comprises a dust- and moistureproof cover with a patented 'Drilok' closure, mechanical dehumidification or a desiccant and a humidity or metering device. Dehumidification is an essential part of the system to ensure a safe humidity level. When electrical services are available a Driclad Standard (SD) or Flame-arrested (FAD) dehumidifier is recommended. Where electrical services are not available a re-activatable desiccant system is used. Equipment protected by Driclad requires no special building or packing material.

Maintenance requirements are greatly reduced and, in some instances, maintenance procedures become redundant. At certain locations used by the British Army only two technicians are required to keep up to 80 tanks, protected by Driclad, in a state of permanent operational readiness.

Typical uses of the Driclad system include the protection and preservation of tanks, artillery, helicopters and missiles. It is also used by the Royal Navy in the laying-up of ships and the temporary shore-based protection of ships' stores. Many other items of equipment, large and small, are currently being given short-term and long-term protection against environmental attack.

STATUS
In production. In service with 39 countries.

MANUFACTURER
Driclad Limited, 152 Staplehurst Road, Sittingbourne, Kent ME10 1XE, England.

Flame-arrested dehumidifier

Driclad covers being used to protect HAWK SAMs

Drican reactivatable desiccant for use where electrical services are not readily available

Driclad covers being used for long-term protection of tanks

Drihouse military storage shelter with collapsible metal framework

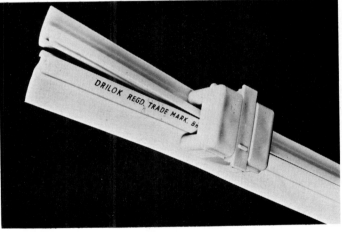

Drilok closure used with Driclad system

Armour Cases Limited Engineered Packaging

DESCRIPTION
One of the base materials used in the Armour (formerly Scotney) range of military engineered packaging is the Texikoon system. Although there are many ways in which the system can be used, the bases are three materials, Texikoon T603, T700 and T725. Using these materials the system can be tailored to suit virtually any packaging need, and Texikoon is widely used to protect military equipment ranging from aircraft to AFVs. Storage shelters are produced for a variety of purposes. Any Texikoon cover is made from one of the range of materials available, but all seams are high-frequency welded and when closed the covers provide a moisture and vapour proof seal. Examination windows and documentation pockets can be built into any cover.

The Armour range also includes glass-reinforced plastic containers for missiles, weapons and all manner of electronic equipment and spares.

STATUS
In production. In service with the British Armed Forces.

MANUFACTURER
Armour Cases Limited, Saint Ives, Huntingdon, Cambridgeshire PE17 4EY, England.

SPECIFICATIONS
Texikoon T603
Water vapour permeability: 8 g/m²/24 h (to BS3177, tropical conditions)

Texikoon T700
Water vapour permeability: 2 g/m²/24 h (to BS3177, tropical conditions)
Operating temperature: −15 to +60°C

Texikoon T725
Water vapour permeability: 5 g/m²/24 h (to BS3177, tropical conditions)
Operating temperature: −30 to +60°C

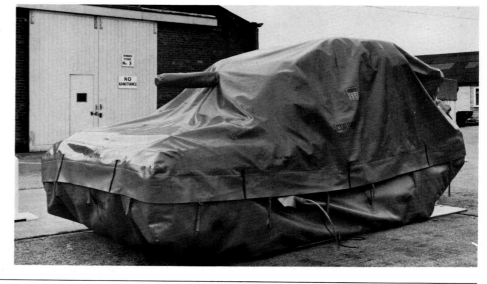

Texikoon covering Scorpion reconnaissance vehicle

Mobile Floodlighting Units

DEVELOPMENT
Henry Cooch conceived the idea of an 18-metre self-contained, trailer-mounted floodlighting unit in 1967. It was designed specifically for the construction industry, but was first used at a major railway incident. Since then it has been used for a variety of civil and military applications. The British Army placed its first order for twelve units in 1972, which were used to enable rapid runway repair work to be carried out at night. These were the standard unit modified to meet the more rigorous Service requirements. A further order for 25 units was placed in 1974 of which many are now in regular use with the Security Forces in Northern Ireland.

DESCRIPTION
The unit consists of a three-section telescopic mast of lattice construction and hot dipped galvanised for weather protection. It is erected by an automatic safety winch to a maximum height of 18·3 metres. It is mounted on a fast-tow two-wheel trailer fitted with independent suspension, overrun and parking brakes and a jockey wheel. Telescopic outriggers and jacks are fitted to provide a stable platform for the mast, which will withstand 129 km/h winds without guys. The lamp array consists of four 1500 W tungsten/halogen floodlamps powered by an air-cooled diesel generating set which is a twin-cylinder, air-cooled, hand start Lister ST2 diesel engine developing 12 bhp at 1500 rpm, close coupled to a two-bearing Brush self-exciting, self-regulating alternator. The set is 230 V, 50 Hz, single-phase, rated at 7 kW at unity power factor. The control box is weatherproof and contains 30 A high rupturing current (HRC) fuzes on each incoming line and four rotary switches, each controlling one lamp. There is also a 10 A HRC fuze in one line to each lamp. Spare fuses are carried in the box.

SPECIFICATIONS

Dimensions	Travelling	Erected
Weight	1240 kg	1240 kg
Length	8·2 m	8·9 m
Width	2·1 m	3·9 m
Height	2·9 m	18·3 m

STATUS
In production. In service with Argentina (Navy), New Zealand and the United Kingdom.

MANUFACTURER
Henry Cooch Limited, PO Box 40, Sevenoaks, Kent TN15 8LN, England.

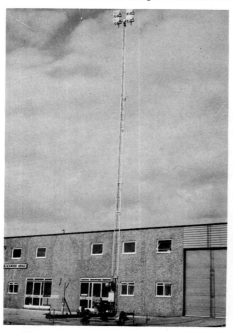

18-metre mobile floodlighting unit in position

18-metre mobile floodlighting unit in travelling order

Simplon Trailalite 25 Portable Lighting System

DESCRIPTION
The Trailalite 25 consists of a standard chassis with a diesel generator, telescopic hinged mast unit with lighting gallery, mounted on a Hi-Speed road towing trailer.

The main trailer frame is formed from rolled steel section and measures approximately 2·74 × 1·52 metres. The engine and alternator assembly sub-frame is connected through anti-vibration mountings to the main frame. The trailer has two wheels with four-ply tyres fitted to an independent torsion bar axle. The chassis has corner-mounted stabilising jacks, over-run and parking brakes, mudguards and jockey wheel.

The generator set consists of an air-cooled diesel engine rated at 6·25 bhp at 1500 rpm. This is close coupled to a 4 kVA output, single-phase, 50 cycle, 110/220 volt alternator. A pannier-type box contains the starting and running gear for the lighting array together with control panel, lamp storage and tool compartment. Two 110 volt 15 amp weatherproof supply outlets are provided, wired and mounted inside the pannier box.

The mast of telescopic sections is hinged for travelling and accommodates the lighting gallery when stowed. The mast is suitably ballasted and is positively locked when erected. The mast is extended by a hand-operated winch. The mast assembly is internally wired, allowing connection to the lighting gallery which consists of four tubular arms terminating in specially designed lanterns totally enclosing the MBFR/U lamps, and allowing universal movement to give either a circle of light, or full directional light to a given point. The lighting array consists of four 700 watt colour-corrected mercury fluorescent reflector type lamps, with a design life of 7500 hours under normal conditions. Effective floodlighting is achieved over an area 110 metres in diameter.

SPECIFICATIONS
Weight: 832 kg
Length: (overall) 3·35 m
Width: (overall) 1·53 m
Height:
(overall, mast folded) 1·7 m
(mast fully extended) 7·82 m

Other Simplon portable lighting systems include: Senior Trailalite 60 (four 1000 watt lamps, erected mast 18·3 metres high), Portatower (tripod-based system with a mast 8·32 metres high when erected), Portalite (tripod system with three 150 watt lamps, weighing 18 kg, 2·76 metres high when erected), Towerlite Mk. III (with mercury discharge lamps), and Microlite (portable unit with two 400 watt tungsten/halogen lamps and its own self-contained generator).

STATUS
Simplon portable lighting systems are in service with the British and other armed forces.

MANUFACTURER
Simplon Interline Limited.

Simplon Standard Trailalite assisting unloading of shipping in dockyard

UNITED STATES OF AMERICA

Hydraulic System Test and Repair Unit (HSTRU)

DESCRIPTON

Designed to provide the general maintenance capability required by the increasing variety of military equipment using hydraulic systems, the trailer-mounted Hydraulic System Test and Repair Unit (HSTRU) is now in production. Under a first time buy contract issued by MERADCOM to the American Development Corporation, 168 units are being built, with an option to purchase a further 200. The cost of an individual unit will be $17,500 on a total buy.

The HSTRU is easy to operate and will remove the need for specialist personnel to service the many types of system in use. The HSTRU can produce hose and tube assemblies on site, and provides a diagnostic facility for hydraulic problems that eliminate trial and error repairs.

Mounted on a ¾-ton military trailer, the test and repair equipment is sheltered by a 2438 × 1219 × 89 mm watertight enclosure. The 1362 kg unit can be towed across country or deployed by helicopter. Standard equipment includes hose cutting and skiving tools, a hose coupling assembler, a tube cutting, deburring and bending set, a multi-range pressure gauge, hydraulic system tester for temperature, flow and pressure, cleaning and flushing equipment, and various other items. The HSTRU requires 3.5 kW of 110-volt, 60 Hz supply.

STATUS
In production for the US Army.

DEVELOPMENT AGENCY
US Army Mobility Research and Development Command (MERADCOM), Fort Belvoir, Virginia 22060, USA.

MANUFACTURER
American Development Corporation, Charleston, South Carolina, USA.

Hydraulic System Test and Repair Unit (US Army)

Addenda

RECOVERY VEHICLES AND EQUIPMENT

SIBMAS (6 × 6) Armoured
Recovery Vehicle (Page 17)

SIBMAS (6 × 6) armoured recovery vehicle   SIBMAS (6 × 6) armoured recovery vehicle from front

FIAT 90 PM 16 (4 × 4) Wrecker with 5 tonne Crane

DESCRIPTION
The FIAT 90 PM 16 (4 × 4) truck chassis has been developed to mount a 5000 kg capacity FARID crane boom. The crane is mounted behind the vehicle cab on a sheet steel sub-frame connected to the chassis by brackets. Onto this sub-frame are mounted the super-structure, crane and outriggers and when the crane is in use the entire vehicle is raised onto the outriggers for overall stabilisation. The crane is a FARID model F 5 which is hydraulically operated. The maximum boom length is 5·7 metres, the maximum boom elevation 75 degrees and the traverse is a full 360 degrees. The crane has a maximum pull to the rear of 5000 kg but extra pull capacity is provided by a rear-mounted auxili-ary winch with a 4000 kg capacity. A self-recovery winch is mounted at the front and this has a capacity of 3000 kg. The four outriggers, one at each corner of the sub-frame, are hydraulically operated from a panel at the side of the vehicle; the crane controls are on a panel by the operator's seat.

Accessories include a draw bar, collapsible snatch blocks, a set of chains with hooks, a spare wheel holder and tool boxes. The deck of the sub-frame, which is covered with a non-slip steel plate, measures 3·4 metres long and 2·3 metres wide, and may be used for carrying extra equipment or cargo.

STATUS
Production. 60 ordered by Venezuela.

MANUFACTURERS
Chassis: Iveco FIAT, Direzione Mezzi Speciale, Corso G Marconi, 10/20 Turin, Italy.
Crane: FARID SpA, Corso Savona 39 bis, 10024 Moncalieri, Italy.

SPECIFICATIONS
Cab seating: 1 + 1
Configuration: 4 × 4
Weight:
(gross) 9700 kg
(curb) 8200 kg
Payload: (load hang to hook) 1500 kg
Towing capacity: 4000 kg
Length: (inc crane overhang) 7·042 m
Width: 2·476 m
Height: (cab) 2·627 m
Ground clearance: 0·47 m
Track: 1·851 m
Wheelbase: 3·7 m
Angle of approach/departure: 42°/42°
Max speed: 80 km/h
Range: 700 km
Power to weight ratio: 16·5 hp/ton

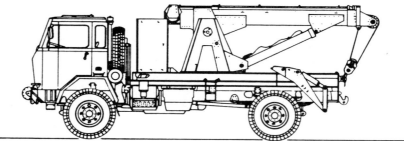

FIAT 90 PM 16 (4 × 4) wrecker with 5 tonne crane

FIAT 90 PM 16 (4 × 4) wrecker with 5 tonne crane

Max gradient: 60%
Side slope: 30%
Fording: 0·7 m
Engine: Model 8062.24 6-cylinder supercharged direct injection water-cooled diesel developing 160 hp at 3200 rpm
Gearbox: manual with 5 forward and 1 reverse gears

Clutch: single dry plate
Transfer box: 2-speed
Steering: recirculating ball with hydraulic servo
Turning radius: 7·5 m
Suspension: leaf springs (dual at rear) with hydraulic shock absorbers (telescopic)
Tyres: 12.5 R20 PR22

MINE WARFARE

Hirtenberger APM-02 Horizontal Anti-personnel Mine

DESCRIPTION
The APM-02 horizontal anti-personnel mine is of the Claymore type but is mounted on a small tripod with a pan and tilt head to enable it to be aimed in any direction. The convex face of the mine can project approximately 290 spherical steel projectiles in a 60 degree arc in such a way that ten metres from the mine there are ten or eleven effective projectiles per square metre. In a lateral dispersion range of 40 degrees at 25 metres there are four or five effective projectiles per square metre. Each projectile weighs approximately 51 grams and has a diameter of 5 mm. Each effective projectile can penetrate 20 mm of pine or 4 mm of aluminium sheet. The charge is Comp.B.

The mines are packed ten to a wooden case for transport, and the ignition devices are packed in the same case in separate containers.

SPECIFICATIONS
(all data approximate)
Weight: 1 kg
Length (mine body): 140 mm
Height (mine body): 80 mm
Width (mine body): 40 mm
Height with tripod: 280 mm
Weight of explosive charge: 0·36 kg
Fragment velocity: 1460 m/s
Number of fragments: 290
Fragment weight: 51 grams
Fragment diameter: 5 mm

STATUS
Production.

MANUFACTURER
Hirtenberger Patronen-, Zündhütchen-, und Metall-warenfabrik AG, A-2552 Hirtenberg, Austria.

Hirtenberger APM-02 horizontal anti-personnel mine

NICO Training Mine System

DESCRIPTION
The NICO training mine system is a variable form of training device that can be adapted to suit virtually any type of operational mine. In its simplest form it is a circular re-usable mine body that can be fitted with an array of triggering devices such as pressure plates, tilt rods, trip wire devices etc and when actuated produces a simulated blast effect and/or a cloud of smoke. If required the system can be incorporated into service mine bodies or the training mine body may be weighted to simulate a service mine. If required a special body simulating a service mine can be supplied.

STATUS
Production.

MANUFACTURER
NICO Pyrotechnik, Hanns-Jorgen Diederichs GmbH & Co. KG, Bei der Feuerwerkerei 4, PO Box 1227, D-2077 Trittau/Hamburg, Federal Republic of Germany.

NICO training mine (T J Gander)

TRANSPORT EQUIPMENT

CA-10 (4 × 2) Liberation 3540 kg Truck

CA-10 (4 × 2) Liberation 3540 kg trucks

Saab-Scania P 112H (4 × 4) S50 7500 kg Truck

DESCRIPTION

At the request of the Swedish Defence Materials Department (FMV) Saab-Scania has produced the prototype of a 4 × 4 truck known as the P 112H. It is built entirely of existing components produced for the Saab-Scania SBA 111 series of vehicles with the exception of the front axle and the transmission gearbox. The gearbox is a Scania G770 five-speed manual equipped with a power take-off on the right-hand side. This is allied with a two-speed transfer box with high and low gears of 1:1 and 1:1·5 respectively.

The P 112H prototype has a five-metre wheelbase but wheelbases from 3·8 metres upwards will be available. On the prototype the load-carrying area is an open steel body with drop sides and a tailgate but many other types of body can be accommodated and one vehicle is being equipped to carry and launch the Swedish Army's Ribbon Bridge System. Optional equipment being considered includes fitments related to Sweden's harsh climate and conditions and consists of a diesel fuel pre-heater, a glow spiral coil in the inlet manifold ('flame starter') and an air dryer for the braking system.

The maximum load capacity of the P 112H is 7500 kg. Pulling a single-axle trailer the towing capacity is 12 000 kg but with a double-axle trailer this can be increased to 20 000 kg. The engine is a Scania DS11 turbocharged in-line six-cylinder diesel using direct injection and providing 305 hp at 2000 rpm. The rear axle ratio is 4·8:1.

Prototype of Saab-Scania P 112H (4 × 4) S50 7500 kg truck

SPECIFICATIONS
Cab seating: 1 + 2
Configuration: 4 × 4
Weight:
(total) 16 500 kg
(front axle) 7500 kg
(rear axle) 9000 kg
Load capacity: 7500 kg

Towing capacity:
(single axle trailer) 12 000 kg
(twin axle trailer) 20 000 kg
Wheelbase:
(prototype) 5 m
(minimum) 3·8 m
Max speed: 95 km/h
Engine: Scania DS11 turbocharged 6-cylinder in-line direct injection diesel developing 305 hp at 2000 rpm

Transmission: Scania G770 5-speed manual
Transfer box: 2-speed
Tyres: 14.00 × 20

STATUS
Prototype.

MANUFACTURER
Saab-Scania AB, S-151 87 Södertälje, Sweden.

AM General HUMMER M998 Series Multi-Purpose Wheeled Vehicle Designations (Pages 449 and 450)

The M998 series 1¼ ton 4 × 4 vehicles to be produced under the production contract will consist of 15 models with the following designations:
M998 Cargo/troop carrier without winch
M1038 Cargo/troop carrier with winch
M966 TOW missile carrier, basic armour, without winch

M1036 TOW missile carrier, basic armour, with winch
M1045 TOW missile carrier, supplemental armour, without winch
M1046 TOW missile carrier, supplemental armour, with winch
M1025 Armament carrier, basic armour, without winch
M1026 Armament carrier, basic armour, with winch
M1043 Armament carrier, supplemental armour, without winch
M1044 Armament carrier, supplemental armour, with winch
M996 Mini-ambulance, 2 litter, basic armour

M997 Maxi-ambulance, 4 litter, basic armour
M1035 Soft-top ambulance, 2 litter
M1037 S-250 shelter carrier, without winch
M1042 S-250 shelter carrier, with winch
   In addition to the above, eight selected application kits will be produced as follows:
Cargo/troop carrier, soft top enclosure (2 door cab) for M998
Cargo/troop carrier, soft top enclosure (4 door cab) for M998
Cargo/troop carrier, soft top enclosure (2 door cab, troop seats) for M1038

Cargo/troop carrier, soft top enclosure (2 door cab, troop/cargo) for M1038
Cargo/troop carrier, soft top enclosure (4 door cab, cargo) for M1038
Armament carrier, basic armour with M60 7·62 mm machine gun for M1026

Armament carrier, supplemental armour with M2 ·50 calibre machine gun for M1044
Armament carrier, supplemental armour with MK19 grenade launcher for M1043
  In addition to the above production vehicles and kits a further four vehicles are being used for research and

development. These are:
RED-T with 25 mm Chain Gun
Eight-man squad carrier with M2 ·50 calibre machine gun
C4 shelter
Stinger missile team vehicle

Scottorn 125-ration Mobile Kitchen Trailer

DESCRIPTION
The Scottorn kitchen trailer is a self-contained unit housing all the equipment required to prepare and cook meals for up to 125 personnel. It is carried on an all-steel electrically welded chassis formed from rolled steel channel. It uses a 'V' shaped drawbar which is fitted with a 75 mm NATO tow eye and a solid tyred jockey wheel. The body consists of a sheet steel flooring with internal wheelboxes and a pressed steel skirt forming a shallow body allowing easy removal of stowed equipment. The trailer has a square section axle beam with roller bearing hubs and internal expanding brakes operated by an inertia system. The suspension is semi-elliptic springs with the whole unit mounted on 6.70 × 15 tyres with steel wheels. Two rear chassis props are fitted and other fittings include stop-tail lights and direction indicators, a registration number plate and other plates.

  The trailer is equipped with two cooking stands (one two container, the other three container), five six-gallon/22·71-litre cooking containers and a further five insulated containers, four frying pans, three three-gallon/11·4-litre cooking containers, a vapourising type burner and a stand end plate. All these items are held in their respective travelling positions by quick release webbing straps.

  The trailer can be towed by most light four-wheel drive vehicles of the Land-Rover type.

Scottorn 125-ration mobile kitchen trailer

STATUS
Production.

MANUFACTURER
Scottorn Trailers Limited, Chartridge, Chesham, Buckinghamshire HP5 2SH, England.

Index